CLASSICAL GUITAR MUSIC IN PRINT

Edited by

Mijndert Jape

Music-In-Print Series, Vol. 7

MUSICDATA, INC.

Philadelphia, 1989

118853

The Music-In-Print Series to date:

Vols. 1a,b. Sacred Choral Music In Print, Second Edition (1985)

Vol. 1c. Sacred Choral Music In Print, Second Edition, Arranger Index (1987)

Vol. 1s. Sacred Choral Music In Print: 1988 Supplement

Vols. 2a,b. Secular Choral Music In Print, Second Edition (1987)

Vol. 2c. Secular Choral Music In Print, Second Edition: Arranger Index (1987)

Vol. 3. Organ Music In Print, Second Edition (1984)

Vol. 4. Classical Vocal Music In Print (1976) (out of print)

Vol. 4s. Classical Vocal Music In Print: 1985 Supplement

Vol. 5. Orchestral Music In Print (1979) (out of print)

Educational Section of Orchestral Music In Print (1978)

Orchestral Music In Print: 1983 Supplement

Vol. 6. String Music In Print, Second Edition (1973) (out of print)

String Music In Print: 1984 Supplement

Vol. 7. Classical Guitar Music In Print (1989)

Music-In-Print Annual Supplement 1986

Music-In-Print Series: ISSN 0146-7883

Printed by Port City Press, Baltimore, Maryland

Musicdata, Inc.
P.O. Box 48010
Philadelphia, Pennsylvania 19144-8010

Library of Congress Cataloging-in-Publication Data

Jape, Mijndert.
  Classical guitar music in print/edited by Mijndert Jape.
    p. cm. — (Music-in-print series, ISSN 0146-7883; v. 7)
  Includes index.
  ISBN 0-88478-025-2
  1. Guitar music—Bibliography. I. Title. II. Series.
ML 128.G8J36 1989
016.78787'168'026—dc20   89-9375
                         CIP
                         MN

Contents

Preface

This bibliography found its origin in a personal need for a list of published guitar music. Before long, the scope of this list had grown much wider than I had planned initially and I decided to make it useful to others as well. So I started to extend it further and to prepare it for publication. This took many more years.

Many are those who have helped me during that time and I thank them all sincerely. My gratitude goes, first of all, to Wiel Corpeleijn, music librarian of the Provinciale Bibliotheek Centrale, Roermond (Limburg, Netherlands). I was able to take advantage of his expertise on several occasions and he answered my many questions with unfailing patience.

The Vita Nuova music store of Nijmegen (Netherlands) gave me access to its entire music stock for cataloging. The firms Albersen & Co. (The Hague, Netherlands), Bärenreiter & Neuwerk Musik- und Buchhandlung (Kassel, West Germany) – via Gerhard Littmann – and Ricordi Americana S.A. (Buenos Aires, Argentina) – via Renzo Valcarenghi – also made their music available. Publishers then did the same, or sent me complimentary copies of their editions.

I was also fortunate in receiving advice from Prof. Dr. Willem Elders, Dr. Kees Vellekoop and Gerrit Vellekoop (†).

Maestro Emilio Pujol (†) very kindly answered my questions about the Preludes, the Studies and the Technical Exercises by Francisco Tárrega.

For the list of incipits in the chapter on music by Bach, the firm VEB Breitkopf & Härtel Musikverlag (Leipzig, German Democratic Republic) obligingly allowed me to use Wolfgang Schmieder's Bach-Werke-Verzeichnis. I also thank the Free Library of Philadelphia for their assistance in this.

The former Limburgs Instituut voor Huismuziek (Limburg Institute for Amateur Music), with its director Ed Miedema (†) assisted and provided encouragement throughout the project.

The Ministerie van Welzyn, Volksgezondheid en Cultuur – formerly the Ministerie van Cultuur, Recreatie en Maatschappelijk Werk (Ministry of Culture, Recreation and Welfare) – lent its support in the form of a subsidy, given for a number of years, thereby showing its confidence in my work.

While I was still thinking of a multi-lingual edition, I was expertly assisted in the translations into French, German and English by Nicholas Burton-Page, Stephan Meijs, Ernst Rahn, Tineke de Ruijter, Josée Vigneron-Ramakers and Marc Voets.

Lucie di Ielsi and Claudia Alcover made it possible for me to correspond with Italian and Spanish publishers in their own language, which was very convenient indeed.

My special thanks go to Laura Habets, Elisabeth Heijltjes and Mirjam Janssen. During the last years before finishing this work, they assisted me in processing all the data, thereby enabling me to finish sooner.

John van der Beek, Laurent Carpentier, Wiel Corpeleijn, Jos Dukers (†), Dr. Jos Habets and Hanny Voncken were all very helpful and of great service during the final stage.

Dr. Alfons Annegarn (†) and Dr. Louis Peter Grijp studied an extract of the bibliography and provided it with useful comments.

I thank the following past and present members of the staff of Musicdata, Inc., for their assistance throughout the project: F. Mark Daugherty, Gary S. Eslinger, Stephen C. Fisher, Walter A. Frankel, Nancy K. Nardone, Thomas R. Nardone, Susan H. Simon, and Mark Resnick. I also thank Gabriel Braverman of Philadelphia for the copying of the musical incipits and examples in the Tárrega chapter; Catherine de Goederen, also of Philadelphia, for translation assistance; and Paul Rans of Leuven, Belgium, for additional translation assistance.

It is sad that six of the people intimately involved with the project will not be able to see the publication of this work. They have not been allowed to read these words of gratitude: they have had to take their leave from life on earth. I remember them with respect and deep sorrow. Among them is my friend and wife Marie-Hélène Habets. She worked very hard on this book and was involved until the very last preparations for publication. Above all she gave me immense support during the many years that I have worked on this project. That is why this book was dedicated to her. Now that she is no longer with us, I change the dedication to "In memory of Marie-Hélène, grateful for what she still means to me."

May this bibliography serve its purpose and become a safe and trusted guide in the dense forest of guitar publications.

Beek (Limburg, Netherlands)   Mijndert Jape
Easter 1988

vi

Guide to Use

THE MUSIC-IN-PRINT SERIES

The Music-In-Print series is an ongoing effort to locate and catalog all music in print throughout the world. The intention is to cover all areas of music as rapidly as resources permit, as well as to provide a mechanism for keeping the information up to date.

Since 1973, Musicdata, Inc. has solicited catalogs and listings from music publishers throughout the world. Using the information supplied by co-operating publishers, the series lists specific editions which are available from a publisher either for sale or on a rental basis in appropriate categories. The volumes in the series are basically organized by the primary performing force, instrument or instrumental family, such as Sacred Choral Music, Organ Music or String Music.

It is often difficult to define the boundaries between the various broad areas of music covered by the volumes in the series. The definition of sacred and secular choral music varies from publisher to publisher; some major choral works are no longer listed in Orchestral Music, reflecting changing editorial practice; some solo vocal music is in Orchestral Music; etc. The user is advised to consult the preface to individual volumes for greater definition of scope. Use of more than one volume may well be necessary to locate an edition or all editions of a work.

Editorial policy is to include as much information as the publisher supplies, within the limits of practicality. An important goal of the series is to try to bring together different editions of a composition under a single title.

VOLUME FORMAT

The volumes of the Music-In-Print series have two basic formats: unified or structured. Reference to the editor's preface and the table of contents will assist in determining how a given volume is organized.

The unified volumes (e.g., Organ Music, Orchestral Music) are arranged in a single alphabetical interfiling of composers' names, titles of works and cross references. The title under a composer's name serves as the focus for major information on each composition. In the absence of a composer, the title in the main alphabet becomes the focal point for this information.

The structured volumes (e.g., String Music) are arranged by an imposed framework: instrumentation, time period, type of work or other categorization. Within each section, entries are alphabetized by composer name or, in the absence of a composer, by title. Entries will be repeated in all appropriate sections. A structured volume also contains a Composer/Title Index and, in some cases, other specialized indexes. The Composer/Title Index is a single alphabetical list of composers' names, composition titles and cross references, with a reference to the section(s) of the volume in which complete edition information will be found. The running heads on each page of the catalog enable the user to quickly find the proper section.

ENTRY TYPES

Two basic types of entries appear in the Music-In-Print series: normal and collection. A normal entry describes a single piece of music. A collection consists of any two or more associated pieces.

NORMAL ENTRY CONTENT

In order to bring together all different editions of a composition under a uniform and/or structured title, many musical form titles are translated into English (so, Konzert becomes Concerto, Fantaisie becomes Fantasy, etc.).

For each title there are two types of information: a) generic information about the composition and b) specific information pertaining to the editions which are in print. Included in the generic information category are the uniform title of the composition, a structured title for the work (e.g., Concerto No. 2 In D Minor; Cantata No. 140), a thematic catalog number or opus and number designation, the larger source from which the work was taken, and remarks.

Following the generic information about the piece is the information about the individual editions. This information includes the arranger, the published title of the edition if different from the uniform title, the language of the text (for vocal works), instrumentation required for performance, the duration of the work in minutes (') and seconds (") , a difficulty rating assigned to the edition by the publisher or editor, the format of the publication, publisher, publisher's number, and price or rental information concerning the edition.

Following is an example of a typical entry under a composer:

MOZART, WOLFGANG AMADEUS (1756-1791)
   Nozze Di Figaro, Le: Overture
      [4']
      2.2.2.2. 2.2.0.0. timp,strings
      sc,parts RICORDI-IT rental   (M1)
      "Marriage of Figaro, The: Overture"
      sc,parts BREITKOPF-W f.s.   (M2)

In this entry under the composer, Wolfgang Amadeus Mozart, the title of an excerpt, "Overture", follows the original title of the complete work, "Nozze Di Figaro, Le". It is scored for 2 flutes, 2 oboes, 2 clarinets, 2 bassoons, 2 horns, 2 trumpets, timpani and strings. Duration is approximately 4 minutes. The code RICORDI-IT indicates the publisher of the first listed edition; score and parts are offered by this publisher on rental. The sequence number (M1) marks the end of the information on this edition. The English title "Marriage Of Figaro, The: Overture" is given for the next edition which is published by BREITKOPF-W; score and parts for this edition are for sale.

The full names and addresses of all publishers or U.S. agents are given in the publisher list which follows the list of editions at the end of the book.

Following is an example of an entry with a structured title:

MOZART, WOLFGANG AMADEUS (1756-1791)
   Symphony No. 25, [excerpt]
      (Gordon, Philip) 2.1.2.1.al-
      sax. ten-sax. 2.2.1.1.timp,perc,
      strings [3'] (Menuetto, [arr.])
      PRESSER sets $7.50, and up, sc
      $1.50   (M3)

Here a structured title "Symphony No. 25," requires a different form of listing. The excerpt, "Menuetto", has been arranged by Philip Gordon for 2 flutes, oboe, 2 clarinets, bassoon, alto saxophone, tenor saxophone, 2 horns, 2 trumpets, trombone, tuba, timpani, percussion and strings. Du-

ration is three minutes. The publisher, PRESSER, offers sets of parts priced at $7.50 and up. A separate score is available for $1.50.

INSTRUMENTATION

Instrumentation is given in the customary order. When a work is scored for full orchestra, the number of wind players required is indicated by two groups of numbers—four for woodwinds (flute, oboe, clarinet, bassoon) and four for brass (horn, trumpet, trombone, tuba). Other instruments are listed by name, or abbreviated name. A number placed before a named instrument indicates the number of players. A slash is used for alternate instrumentation.

The common auxiliary wind instruments are not mentioned by most publishers. For example, 2.2.3.3. for woodwinds indicates the work is scored for two flutes, but it *may* include a piccolo part which can be played by one of the flutists. Similarly, it is possible that parts for English horn, bass clarinet and contrabassoon are provided but no additional players will be required. If the publisher does specify the auxiliary instruments required, this information is given either in parentheses (the number of players is not affected) or after a plus sign (an additional player is needed).

Example:

   2(pic).2+opt ob.3(opt bass-clar).2+contrabsn.
   4.2.3.0+opt tuba.timp,2-3perc,harp,cel/pno,
   strings

This example is scored for 2 flutes and piccolo (played by one of the flutists), 2 oboes plus an optional third oboe, 3 clarinets (one may play the optional bass clarinet part), 2 bassoons plus contrabassoon (additional player required), 4 horns, 2 trumpets, 3 trombones, optional tuba, timpani, percussion (2 or 3 players), harp, celeste or piano, and strings.

The term "orch" may be substituted for a detailed listing if the publisher has not provided the instrumentation for orchestral works.

Solo instrumental parts are listed following the complete orchestration of a work.

Choral parts are given as a list of voices (e.g., SATB, TTBB, etc.). The term "cor" (and similar terms) may be substituted when the publisher has not listed the specific voices.

Solo vocal parts are given as a list of voices followed by the term "solo" or "soli." The term "solo voice(s)" is used when the publisher does not specify the voice(s). (No attempt has been made to give equivalents for scale ranges listed by publishers.)

REMARKS

The remarks are a series of codes or abbreviations giving information on the seasonal or other usage of the piece, the type of music, and the national origin and century for folk or anonymous pieces. (These codes also make it possible to retrieve, from the data base developed for the Music-In-Print series, specialized listings of music for particular seasons, types, etc.) Following this Guide to Use will be found a complete List of Abbreviations.

PRICES

Only U.S. dollar prices are given, and we can give no assurance of their accuracy. They are best used for making rough comparisons. The publishers should be consulted directly for current prices.

SEQUENCE NUMBERS

An alphanumeric number, appearing on the right margin, has been assigned to each edition represented in this catalog. These are for the purpose of easing identification and location of specific entries.

COLLECTION ENTRY CONTENT

An attempt has been made to provide the user with access to pieces contained within collections, while still keeping the work within reasonable bounds of time and space. Accordingly, the following practices have been adopted:

If the members of a collection are published separately, they are listed individually, regardless of the number of pieces involved. If the collection is only published as a whole, the members are listed only if they do not exceed six in number. For larger collections, a code is given indicating the number of pieces and whether or not the contents are listed in the publisher's catalog. For example,

CC18L indicates a collection of 18 pieces which are *listed* in the publisher's catalog
CC101U indicates a collection of 101 pieces which are *unlisted* in the publisher's catalog
CCU indicates a collection of an unknown number of pieces

Whenever the members are listed, they are also cross-referenced to the collection. For example, consider the following entry:

FIVE VOLUNTARIES, [ARR.]
  (Davies, Peter Maxwell) 3.3.2.1, 3.3.0.0.
  timp,perc,strings,cont sc,parts
  SCHOTT 10994 f.s.
  contains: Attaignant, Pierre,
    Magnificat; Clarke, Jeremiah,
    King William's March; Clarke,
    Jeremiah, Serenade; Couperin,
    Louis, Sarabande; Croft, William,
    March Tune   (F1)

Published by Schott, edition number 10994, this collection edited by Peter Maxwell Davies contains five members, which are not published separately. Under each of the members there is a cross reference saying 'see FIVE VOLUNTARIES, [ARR.]'.

Collection entries also contain many of the elements of information found in normal entries. For example, the entry shown above contains arranger, instrumentation, format of publication, publisher and publisher number.

Collections of several pieces published as a whole, but having no overall title, create another problem. In this case the complete publication information is given under the composer or title of the first piece listed, together with the comment 'contains also,' followed by titles of the other collection members.

CROSS REFERENCES

In order to provide the user with as many points of access as possible, the Music-In-Print series has been heavily cross referenced. In the unified volumes, the cross references are interfiled with the composers' names and the titles. In the structured volumes, cross references only appear in the Composer/Title Index.

Works may be located by title, with or without knowing the name of the composer. Using the first example by Mozart above, this composition may be located under either its Italian or English title in the main alphabet, as well as under the composer.

To make this possible the following cross references would exist in the main alphabet:

NOZZE DI FIGARO, LE: OVERTURE
  see Mozart, Wolfgang Amadeus

and

MARRIAGE OF FIGARO, THE: OVERTURE see
  Mozart, Wolfgang Amadeus, Nozze Di
  Figaro, Le: Overture

and in addition, the following cross reference would be found under the composer's name:

Marriage of Figaro, The: Overture
  *see Nozze Di Figaro, Le: Overture

Cross references are employed also to assist in the search for works frequently identified by popular names or subtitles, such as the "Surprise" Symphony of Haydn and the "Jupiter" Symphony of Mozart.

Numerous cross references have been made from unused and variant forms of composer names to assist the user in finding the form of name chosen for the series.

COLLECTION CROSS REFERENCES

Whenever the members of a collection are listed, they are cross referenced to the collection. In unified volumes, these are interfiled with composers' names and titles. In structured volumes, these cross references only occur in the Composer/Title Index.

Using the above example, FIVE VOLUNTARIES, [ARR.], there is a cross reference under each of the composers saying 'see FIVE VOLUNTARIES, [Arr.]'. (If a collection member lacks a composer, the cross reference will occur at the title.)

When collections are also published separately, the cross references in both directions read 'see also'. If the members are only published separately (i.e., the collection were not published as a whole) then the cross reference under the collection would read 'see' and under the members, 'see from'. Thus, 'see' and 'see also' direct the user to information concerning publication, while 'see from' provides access to the collection of which a given publication is a part.

With untitled collections, which are listed under the first composer and/or title, the cross reference 'see' under each of the other collection members directs the user to the full entry under the first member, at which point complete edition information will be found.

COMPOSER/TITLE INDEX

The Composer/Title Index is a single alphabetical listing of composer names, composition titles and cross references.

This index is used to identify the location of a specific entry in a structured volume.

The actual reference is usually under the composer name, and only under a title when a work is not attributable to a person. The reference is to the chapter and/or section of the volume which contains the entry for the music sought.

For example, in String Music, IV.1 refers the user to Chapter IV, Section 1: String Quartets. Similarly, VIII refers to Chapter VIII: Music for Eight Instruments. Reference to the table of contents and the head of each page of the volume will assist the user in finding the appropriate section containing the information sought.

Guide to Use Addendum:
Classical Guitar Music In Print

A number of special features of Classical Guitar Music In Print deserve additional discussion.

DEGREE OF DIFFICULTY

In this volume, there are ten levels or degrees of difficulty recognized. These degrees are:

1st degr.: start of single line playing (one-part music); easy two-part music

2nd degr.: two-part and easy three-part music

3rd degr.: three- (or more) part music. The first three degrees focus on easy pieces for solo guitar and ensemble pieces which are not too demanding

4th-5th degr.: beginning of the guitar concert repertoire; easy and less easy solo literature; chamber music

6th-7th degr.: medium difficult and difficult solo literature, including sonatas and sonatinas

8th-9th degr.: difficult and very difficult solo literature, including concertos for guitar and orchestra

10th degr.: the most difficult solo literature

The classification of a piece's degree of difficulty is a subjective decision and there are cases in which a piece could fit into more than one level. Furthermore, only the technical difficulties have been taken into account; artistic requirements were not considered. In determining the difficulty of a piece for ensemble playing, the guitar part was the deciding factor. Concertos for guitar and orchestra do not have an indication of the degree of difficulty, nor do the orchestral works of chapter V.

ARRANGEMENT OR ORIGINAL COMPOSITION

Music originally intended for another instrument such as the piano, violin, or harpsichord is considered an arrangement. Transcriptions of lute music and guitar music from the Renaissance and Baroque have not been considered arrangements. Folk songs are nearly always arrangements, and that is why the indication "arr" has been omitted. It is not always possible, however, to make a distinction between an arrangement of pre-existing material and an original composition. Sometimes such a piece may be listed under the composer's name rather than the folk song title.

CHAPTERS VI AND VII

These two chapters are a departure from Musicdata's usual format. Each chapter is divided into three sections. The first section contains musical incipits to identify the piece in question (in the chapter on Tárrega) or to facilitate a comparison between the original work and the guitar arrangement (in the chapter on Bach). The second section gives a uniform title and details and commentary about the music. The third section contains a list of the in-print editions of the music. The musical editions are divided into those containing only one work and those containing two or more, with each section being arranged alphabetically.

THE TARREGA INDEX

Among the Preludes, Studies, and Technical Exercises for guitar by Francisco Tárrega there is confusion about the numbering and authenticity. A comparative study was carried out to find the most authentic editions of Tárrega's works. After studying the material, a systematic order was developed, the Tárrega Index (TI). The oldest editions consulted were from the publishers Ildefonso Alier (Alier), Orfeo Tracio (OT), and Vidal, Llimona y Boceta (V.Ll.B). It is doubtful that it will ever be possible to establish a complete thematic index on the basis of original manuscripts. But since the importance of Tárrega lies in the way in which he created the fundamentals for modern guitar technique, only the Preludes, Studies, and Technical Exercises have been included. The numbering of the preludes 16 to 25, the studies, and the technical exercises is the editor's. The order of the preludes 1 to 15 comes from the editions of the above-mentioned publishers. Where musical discrepancies occur, the most authentic solutions have been selected from among the various available editions.

Some works have been considered as not by Tárrega: the "Appoggiature" and some other effects such as "Del Arrastre" and others in Mario Rodriguez Arenas — "La Escuela de la guitarra", vol. III; Karl Scheit — "Sämtliche Studien" and Meme Chacon — "Metodo y Ejercicios." The same goes for the scales in the two last-mentioned editions and others. The exercises mentioned above — as well as the scales — have not been included in this chapter because of lack of sufficient evidence of Tárrega's authorship.

INSTRUMENTATION INDEX

The Instumentation Index is a highly compartmentalized listing of the catalog's contents arranged by the instrumentation required for performance. This index broadly divides the material into studies, works for solo guitar, music for ensemble, and concertos. Within these classifications, original works are distinguished from arrangements; editions containing both original and arranged works are also distinguished.

Since the number of works for solo guitar is so great, that section is further divided into solo guitar music written prior to 1760 (pre-classical), music written between 1760 and 1850 (classical and pre-romantic), music written between 1850 and 1914 (romantic and post-romantic), and music written in the 20th century. Because the pre-1760 category is so vast, it is also divided by the composer's nationality. There are also categories for folk music as well as sonatas and sonatinas.

Music for ensemble playing is broadly divided into three parts: original works, arranged works, and editions that include arranged and original material. These sections are subdivided into works for guitar ensemble, works for guitar with other instruments, and works for guitar with voice.

The actual references and citations follow the pattern of the Composer/Title Index described in the main "Guide to Use."

SERIES INDEX

The Series Index lists the editions of a series that contain music for guitar as a solo instrument or as an ensemble instrument. The series title is listed, followed by the editor's name and the publisher. Specific volumes containing music for guitar appear under the editor-publisher information. These volumes are followed by a Musicdata citation which gives a chapter number in the catalog and a specific sequence number within that chapter where the volume can be found. The sequence number appears on the right margin for each edition represented in this catalog. By using the citation information, the user can easily find within the catalog all the volumes that make up a series.

List of Abbreviations

The following is a general list of abbreviations developed for the Music-In-Print series. Therefore, all of the abbreviations do not necessarily occur in the present volume. Also, it should be noted that terms spelled out in full in the catalog, e.g. woodwinds, tuba, Easter, Passover, folk, Swiss, do not appear in this list.

A	alto	C&W	Country & Western	Dounias	thematic catalog of the violin concertos of Giuseppe Tartini by Minous Dounias
acap	a cappella	C.Landon	numbering of the keyboard sonatas of Joseph Haydn by Christa Landon		
accomp	accompaniment			Doxol	Doxology
acord	accordion	camb	cambiata		
Adv	Advent	Can	Canadian		
Afr	African	cant	cantata		
Agnus	Agnus Dei	Carib	Caribbean	ea.	each
al-clar	alto clarinet	CC	collection	ECY	End of Church Year
al-fl	alto flute	CCU	collection, unlisted	ed	edition
al-sax	alto saxophone	CCUL	collection, partially listed	educ	educational material
Allelu	Alleluia	cel	celesta	elec	electric
AmInd	American Indian	Cen Am	Central American	Ember	Ember Days
ampl	amplified	cent	century	Eng	English
Anh.	Anhang (supplement)	cf.	compare	enl	enlarged
anti	antiphonal	Chin	Chinese	Epiph	Epiphany
app	appendix, appendices	chord	chord organ	eq voices	equal voices
arr.	arranged	Circum	Circumcision	Eur	European
Asc	Ascension	clar	clarinet	evang	evangelistic
ASD	All Saints' Day	cloth	clothbound	Eve	Evening
aud	audience	cmplt ed	complete edition		
Austral	Australian	Cnfrm	Confirmation		
		Commun	Communion		
		cong	congregation		
B	bass	Conn	Conn organ	F.	thematic catalog of the instrumental works of Antonio Vivaldi by Antonio Fanna
Bald	Baldwin organ	cont	continuo		
Bar	baritone	contrabsn	contrabassoon		
bar horn	baritone horn	copy	ed produced to order by a copy process		
bar-sax	baritone saxophone			f(f)	following
bass-clar	bass clarinet	cor	chorus	f.s.	for sale
bass-fl	bass flute	cor pts	choral parts	fac ed	facsimile edition
bass-sax	bass saxophone	cor-resp	choral response	facsim	facsimile(s)
bass-trom	bass trombone	Corpus	Corpus Christi	Fest	festivals
bass-trp	bass trumpet	cradle	cradle song	film	music from film score
bds	boards	cym	cymbals	Finn	Finnish
Belg	Belgian			fl	flute
Benton	thematic catalog of the works of Ignace Pleyel by Rita Benton			Fr	French
Bibl	Biblical				
bk	book				
Boh	Bohemian			Gd.Fri.	Good Friday
boy cor	boys' chorus			Ge.	thematic catalog of the works of Luigi Boccherini by Yves Gerard
Braz	Brazilian				
Bryan	thematic catalog of the symphonies of Johann Wanhal by Paul Bryan	D.	thematic catalog of the works of Franz Schubert by Otto Erich Deutsch		
				Gen	general
bsn	bassoon	Dan	Danish	Ger	German
BVM	Blessed Virgin Mary	db	double bass	Giegling	thematic catalog of the works of Giuseppe Torelli by Franz Giegling
BWV	Bach-Werke-Verzeichnis; thematic catalog of the works of J.S. Bach by Wolfgang Schmieder	db-tuba	double-bass tuba		
		dbl cor	double chorus		
		Ded	Dedication	girl cor	girls' chorus
		degr.	degree, 1-9 (difficulty), assigned by editor	glock	glockenspiel
BuxWV	Buxtehude-Werke-Verzeichnis; thematic catalog of the works of Dietrich Buxtehude by G. Kärstadt (Wiesbaden, 1974)			gr. I-V	grades I-V, assigned by publisher
		desc	descant		
		diag	diagram(s)	Greg	Gregorian chant
		diff	difficult	gtr	guitar
				Gulbransen	Gulbransen organ

Hamm	Hammond organ	L	listed	Paymer	thematic catalog of the
Harv	Harvest	Landon	numbering of the keyboard		works of G.B. Pergolesi
Heb	Hebrew		trios of Joseph Haydn by		by Marvin Paymer
Helm	thematic catalog of the works		H.C.R. Landon	pce, pcs	piece, pieces
	of C.P.E. Bach by	Lat	Latin	Pent	Pentecost
	Eugene Helm	liturg	liturgical	perc	percussion
Hill	thematic catalog of the	Longo	thematic catalog of the	perf mat	performance material
	works of F.L. Gassmann		sonatas of Domenico	perf sc	performance score
	by George Hill		Scarlatti by Alessandro	Perger	thematic catalog of the
Hob.	thematic catalog of the		Longo		instrumental works of
	works of Joseph Haydn	Lowery	Lowery organ		Michael Haydn by Lothar
	by Anthony van Hoboken				Perger
Holywk	Holy Week			pic	piccolo
horn	French horn	Magnif	Magnificat	pic-trp	piccolo trumpet
hpsd	harpsichord	maj	major	pipe	pipe organ
Hung	Hungarian	man	manualiter; on the manuals	pno	piano
HWC	Healey Willan Catalogue		alone	pno-cond sc	piano-conducting score
		mand	mandolin	pno red	piano reduction
		manuscript	manuscript (handwritten)	Pol	Polish
		med	medium	Polynes	Polynesian
ill	illustrated, illustrations	mel	melody	pop	popular
Ind	Indian	men cor	mens' chorus	Port	Portuguese
inst	instruments	Mex	Mexican	pos	position
intro	introduction	Mez	mezzo-soprano	PreClass	Pre-Classical
ipa	instrumental parts available	MIN	Musicdata Identification	pref	preface
ipr	instrumental parts for rent		Number	Proces	processional
Ir	Irish	min	minor	Psntd	Passiontide
Isr	Israeli	min sc	miniature score	pt, pts	part, parts
It	Italian	mix cor	mixed chorus		
		Morav	Moravian		
		Morn	Morning		
		mot	motet		
				quar	quartet
J-C	thematic catalog of the			quin	quintet
	works of G.B. Sammartini	Neth	Netherlands	Quinqua	Quinquagesima
	by Newell Jenkins and	NJ	Name of Jesus		
	Bathia Churgin	No.	number		
Jap	Japanese	Nor Am	North American		
Jew	Jewish	Norw	Norwegian	rec	recorder
jr cor	junior chorus	Nos.	numbers	Reces	recessional
Jubil	Jubilate Deo	Nunc	Nunc Dimittis	Refm	Reformation
				rent	for rent
				repr	reprint
		ob	oboe	Req	Requiem
K.	thematic catalog of the	oct	octavo	rev	revised, revision
	works of W.A. Mozart by	offer	offertory	Royal	royal occasion
	Ludwig, Ritter von	Op.	Opus	Rum	Rumanian
	Köchel; thematic catalog	Op. Posth.	Opus Posthumous	Russ	Russian
	of the works of J.J. Fux	opt	optional, ad lib	RV	Ryom-Verzeichnis; thematic
	by the same author	ora	oratorio		catalog of the works of
Kaul	thematic catalog of the	orch	orchestra		Antonio Vivaldi by Peter
	instrumental works of	org	organ		Ryom
	F.A. Rosetti by Oskar	org man	organ, manuals only		
	Kaul	orig	original		
kbd	keyboard				
Kirkpatrick	thematic catalog of the			S	soprano
	sonatas of Domenico	P., P.S.	thematic catalogs of the	s.p.	separately published
	Scarlatti by Ralph		orchestral works of	Sab	Sabbath
	Kirkpatrick		Antonio Vivaldi by Marc	sac	sacred
Kor	Korean		Pincherle	sax	saxophone
Krebs	thematic catalog of the	p(p)	page(s)	sc	score
	works of Karl Ditters	Palm	Palm Sunday	Scot	Scottish
	von Dittersdorf by Karl	pap	paperbound	sec	secular
	Krebs				

Septua	Septuagesima	trom	trombone	Wolf	thematic catalog of the symphonies of Johann Stamitz by Eugene Wolf
Sexa	Sexagesima	trp	trumpet		
show	music from musical show score	TV	music from television score	wom cor	womens' chorus
So Am	South American	TWV	Telemann-Werke-Verzeichnis; thematic catalog of the works of G.P. Telemann by Mencke and Ruhncke	WoO.	work without opus number; used in thematic catalogs of the works of Beethoven by Kinsky and Halm and of the works of J.N. Hummel by Dieter Zimmerscheid
sop-clar	soprano clarinet				
sop-sax	soprano saxophone				
Span	Spanish				
speak cor	speaking chorus				
spir	spiritual				
sr cor	senior chorus	U	unlisted	Wq.	thematic catalog of the works of C.P.E. Bach by Alfred Wotquenne
study sc	study score	UL	partially listed		
suppl	supplement	unis	unison		
Swed	Swedish	US	United States	Wurlitzer	Wurlitzer organ
SWV	Schütz-Werke-Verzeichnis; thematic catalog of the works of Heinrich Schütz by W. Bittinger (Kassel, 1960)			WV	Wagenseil-Verzeichnis; thematic catalog of the works of G.C. Wagenseil by Helga Scholz-Michelitsch
		vcl	violoncello		
		vibra	vibraphone		
		vla	viola		
T	tenor	vln	violin		
tamb	tambourine	voc pt	vocal part		
temp blks	temple blocks	voc sc	vocal score		
ten-sax	tenor saxophone	VOCG	Robert de Visée, Oeuvres Completes pour Guitare edited by Robert Strizich	Xmas	Christmas
Thanks	Thanksgiving			xylo	xylophone
Thomas	Thomas organ				
TI	Tárrega Index; thematic catalog of the Preludes, Studies, and Exercises of Francisco Tárrega by Mijndert Jape	vol(s)	volume(s)		
timp	timpani				
transl	translation	Whitsun	Whitsuntide	Z.	thematic catalog of the works of Henry Purcell by Franklin Zimmerman
treb	treble	WO	without opus number; used in thematic catalog of the works of Muzio Clementi by Alan Tyson		
Trin	Trinity				

I Music for Guitar Solo, Small Groups, and School Ensembles/Orchestras

I/IA Guitar Studies

ABLONIZ, MIGUEL (1917-   )
Studi Melodici Per Chitarra, 10
gtr (4-5th degr.) RICORDI-IT 129345
f.s.   (1)

AGUADO, DIONISIO (1784-1849)
Aguado-Brevier
(Worsching) gtr (6-8th degr.)
SCHOTT GA-55 f.s.
contains: Andante, MIN 68;
Andante, MIN 69; Andante, MIN
70; Minuet, MIN 65; Minuet, MIN
66; Minuet, MIN 67   (2)

Arpeggio Etude
gtr ESSEX f.s.   (3)

Etude Brilliante
gtr ESSEX f.s.   (4)

Etuden, 24, Und 10 Tonleiterstudien
"Etudes, 24, Et 10 Exercices De
Gammes" (Worsching) gtr (3rd
degr./6-9th degr.) SCHOTT GA-62
f.s.   (5)

Kleine Gitarrenstucke, 31, In
Fortschreitender Ordnung
(Schwarz-Reiflingen) gtr (1-3rd
degr.) HEINRICH. N-3212 f.s.   (6)

Lessons, 8
(Papas) gtr COLUMBIA 160 f.s.   (7)

2 Minuetos Y 2 Estudios
gtr FORTEA 2 f.s.   (8)

Studi, 51, Ad Uso Dei Conservatori
(Chiesa) gtr (2-9th degr.) ZERBONI
6404 $7.00   (9)

Studies, 50
"Collection De 50 Estudios" gtr (1-
3rd degr.) RICORDI-ARG BA-8438
f.s.   (10)
(Gonzalez) gtr (1-3rd degr.)
RICORDI-ENG LD-546 f.s.   (11)
"Estudios Elementales, 50" (Lara)
gtr (1-3rd degr.) RICORDI-ARG
BA-12788 f.s.   (12)

Three Studies
gtr ESSEX f.s.   (13)

ALBERT, HEINRICH (1870-1950)
Gitarre-Etuden-Werk, Vol. 1:
Elementarstufe
"Studies, 12, Vol. 1: Elementary
Grade" gtr (1-3rd degr., 2nd gtr
pt for teacher) ZIMMER. ZM-1156
f.s.   (14)

Gitarre-Etuden-Werk, Vol. 2: Obere
Elementarstufe
"Studies, 12, Vol. 2: Elementary
Grade" gtr (2-3rd degr., easy
keys in pos. I) ZIMMER. ZM-1157
f.s.   (15)

Gitarre-Etuden-Werk, Vol. 3:
Mittelstufe
"Studies, 12, Vol. 3: Moderately
Difficult" gtr (4-5th degr., easy
keys up to pos. V) ZIMMER.
ZM-1158 f.s.   (16)

Gitarre-Etuden-Werk, Vol. 4: Obere
Mittelstufe
"Studies, 12, Vol. 4: Moderately
Difficult" gtr (5-6th degr., in a
sharp key) ZIMMER. ZM-1159 f.s. (17)

Gitarre-Etuden-Werk, Vol. 5:
Oberstufe
"Studies, 12, Vol. 5: Difficult"
gtr (6-7th degr., in a flat key)
ZIMMER. ZM-1160 f.s.   (18)

Gitarre-Etuden-Werk, Vol. 6:
Reifestufe
"Studies, 12, Vol. 6: Difficult"
gtr (7th degr., concert studies)

ALBERT, HEINRICH (cont'd.)

ZIMMER. ZM-1161 f.s.   (19)

Gitarre-Solospiel-Studien, Vol. 1:
Zur Einfuhrung Fur Anfanger
[Ger] gtr (2-3rd degr., in pos. I)
ZIMMER. ZM 1348 f.s.   (20)

Gitarre-Solospiel-Studien, Vol. 2:
Weiterentwicklung Fur
Fortgeschrittene
[Ger] gtr (4-7th degr., in the
higher positions) ZIMMER. ZM-1349
f.s.   (21)

Gitarre-Solospiel-Studien, Vol. 3:
Nebenlagen, Vortrag, Solospiel
gtr (6-9th degr., contains
Introduction Et Variations Sur Un
Theme De Mozart, "Mozart-
Variationen", Op. 9 by Fernando Sor
Ausgabe) ZIMMER. ZM-1350 f.s. (22)

ALBUM DE ESTUDIOS Y PIEZAS FACILES,
PARA ALTERNAR CON EL LIBRO 1 *CCU
gtr FORTEA 1A f.s. supplement to
Metodo De Guitarra, Vol. 1   (23)

ALBUM DE ESTUDIOS Y PIEZAS FACILES,
PARA ALTERNAR CON EL LIBRO 2 *CCU
gtr FORTEA 2A f.s. supplement to
Metodo De Guitarra, Vol. 2   (24)

ALFONSO, NICOLAS
Etudes, 3
gtr (4th degr., Edition Nicolas
Alfonso, No. 100) SCHOTT-FRER
9132 f.s.   (25)

ANZAGHI, LUIGI ORESTE (1903-1963)
Chitarrista Virtuoso, Il
gtr (2-7th degr., 68 pcs) RICORDI-
IT 129461 f.s.   (26)

AUBANEL, GEORGES
Etudes Rhythmiques *CC15U
(Worschech) 1-2gtr (2nd degr.)
OUVRIERS f.s.   (27)

Gradus De La Guitare Moderne, Vol. 1
gtr (2-4th degr., 30 studies)
OUVRIERS EO-633 f.s.   (28)

BARTOLI, RENE
Etude No. 1, Tremolo
gtr ESCHIG f.s.   (29)

BEHREND, SIEGFRIED (1933-   )
Rhythmische Studien, Vol. 1
"Percussion Studies, 29" gtr
ZIMMER. 1920 f.s.   (30)

Rhythmische Studien, Vol. 2
"Percussion Studies" gtr ZIMMER.
1921 f.s.   (31)

Ubungen Von "A-Z" *CC26U
gtr (1-3rd degr.) PREISSLER JP-7041
f.s. preliminary studies to
Elementar-Etuden   (32)

BELLOW, ALEXANDER (1922-1976)
Etude In Tremolo
gtr (6th degr.) COLOMBO NY-1947
f.s.   (33)

Etudes In Scales, 2
gtr (5th degr.) COLOMBO NY-2447
f.s.   (34)

First Lessons *CC13UL
gtr (2-3rd degr.) COLOMBO NY-2446
f.s.   (35)

Studies, 10
gtr (2-3rd degr.) COLOMBO NY-2232
f.s.   (36)

BETTINELLI, BRUNO (1913-   )
12 Studi
(Chiesa) gtr (5-6th degr.) ZERBONI
8414 f.s.   (37)

BOBRI, VLADIMIR
Melodic Exercises, 8 *Op.10
gtr (1-3rd degr.) COLOMBO NY-2604
f.s.   (38)

BOCHMAN, THEO L.
Fantasia De La Guitarra, Etude De
Tremolo
gtr TEESELING VT-171 f.s.   (39)

BODA, JOHN (1922-   )
Etudes Byzantines, 4
gtr COLUMBIA 179 $2.00   (40)

BROQUA, ALFONSO (1876-1946)
Etudes Creolles, 7
(Pujol) gtr ESCHIG 1227 f.s.   (41)

BROUWER, LEO (1939-   )
Etudes Simples, Nos. 1-5
gtr ESCHIG f.s.   (42)

Etudes Simples, Nos. 6-10
gtr ESCHIG f.s.   (43)

CANO, ANTONIO (1811-1897)
Principios De Guitarra, 20 Lecciones
Muy Faciles Y Progresivas
gtr (2-3rd degr.) UNION ESP. 1002
f.s.   (44)

Study in D
gtr (6th degr.) ESSEX f.s.   (45)

Study in E
gtr (6th degr.) ESSEX f.s.   (46)

Study in G
gtr (6th degr.) ESSEX f.s.   (47)

CARCASSI, MATTEO (1792-1853)
Caprices, 6 *Op.26
"Capricen, 6" gtr (3rd degr.)
SCHOTT GA-72 f.s.   (48)
"Capricci, 6" (Azpiazu) gtr (3rd
degr.) BERBEN EB1325 f.s.   (49)
"Capricen, 6" (Dahlke) gtr (3rd
degr.) SCHOTT GA-5 f.s. contains
also: Sonatinas, "Sonatinen",
Op.1   (50)
"Capricen, 6" (Peter) gtr (3rd
degr.) HOFMEISTER 7265 f.s.   (51)
"Caprichos, 6" (Sainz de la Maza)
gtr (3rd degr.) UNION ESP. 19761
f.s.   (52)
"Leichte Capricen, 6" (Schwarz-
Reiflingen) gtr (3rd degr.)
SIKORSKI 251 $5.00   (53)

Etude De Tremolo
(Ranieri) gtr CRANZ f.s.   (54)

Etuden Fur Die Mittelstufe *Op.60
(Scheit) gtr (3-5th degr., with
preliminary studies; 12 pcs)
UNIVER. 12248 f.s.   (55)

Melodische Und Progressive Etuden, 25
*Op.60
gtr (3-7th degr.) SCHOTT GA-43 f.s.
                                       (56)
"Estudios Melodicos Progresivos,
25" gtr (3-7th degr.) UNION ESP.
EB-168 f.s.   (57)
(Chiesa) gtr (3-7th degr.) ZERBONI
8461 f.s.   (58)
"Etuden, 25" (Dobrauz) gtr (3-7th
degr.) HEINRICH. 1526 f.s.   (59)
"Estudios, 25" (Llobet) gtr (3-7th
degr.) RICORDI-ARG 10659 f.s. (60)
"Etudes, 25" (Llobet) gtr (3-7th
degr.) LEMOINE f.s.   (61)
"Studi Melodici E Progressivi"
(Margaria) gtr (3-7th degr.)
RICORDI-IT ER-2735 f.s.   (62)
"Melodische Und Progressive Etuden,
25, Vol. 1, Nos. 1-13" (Peter)
gtr (3-7th degr.) HOFMEISTER 7222
f.s.   (63)
"Melodische Und Progressive Etuden,
25, Vol. 2, Nos. 14-25" (Peter)
gtr (3-7th degr.) HOFMEISTER 7140
f.s.   (64)
"Studi Melodici E Progressivi, 25"
(Proakis) gtr (3-7th degr.)
BERBEN EB1143 $3.25   (65)
"Etuden, 25" (Ranieri) gtr (3-7th
degr.) CRANZ 1010 f.s.   (66)
"Estudios Progresivos, 25" (Sainz
de la Maza) gtr (3-7th degr.)
UNION ESP. 20151 f.s.   (67)
"Melodische Und Fortschreitende
Etuden, 25" (Schwarz-Reiflingen)
gtr (3-7th degr.) SCHOTT GA-2
f.s.   (68)
"Etudes, 25" (Stockton) gtr (3-7th
degr.) STOCKTON f.s.   (69)
"Etudes, 25" (van Puijenbroeck) gtr
(3-7th degr.) METROPOLIS f.s. (70)

Study in A
(Sensier) gtr ESSEX f.s.   (71)

CARCASSI, MATTEO (cont'd.)

Study, Op. 60, No. 3, in A
(Rosado) gtr UNION ESP. 20087 f.s.
(72)

Study, Op. 60, No. 19, in E minor
gtr (4th degr.) ESSEX f.s.   (73)

Tremolo-Etude *Op.60,No.19
(Tower) gtr TEESELING VT-177 f.s.
(74)

Tremolo Study
(Sensier) gtr ESSEX f.s.   (75)

CARULLI, FERDINANDO (1770-1841)
Carulli-Brevier, Vol. 1
(Hulsen) gtr (2-7th degr.) SCHOTT
GA-27 f.s.   (76)

Carulli-Brevier, Vol. 2
(Hulsen) gtr (2-7th degr.) SCHOTT
GA-28 f.s.   (77)

Carulli-Brevier, Vol. 3
(Hulsen) gtr (2-7th degr.) SCHOTT
GA-29 f.s.   (78)

De Tout Un Peu *Op.276
gtr (34 pieces in 6 vols.) LEMOINE
f.s.   (79)

Elementar Etuden, Vol. 4 *CC6U
(Behrend) gtr PREISSLER 7030-IV
f.s.   (80)

Methode De Guitare
"Gitarre-Schule, Vol. II:
Fortschreitende Tonstucke Und
Gelaufigkeits-Etuden, (Erganzung
Zur Gitarre-Schule" (Gotze,
Walter) [Ger] gtr (61p., repr;
1969; ed after the 5th orig ed;
1st ed, 1931; 36 pcs.-studies for
gtr) quarto PETERS 2480C f.s.
(81)

Praludien Zur Bildung Des Anschlages,
20 (from Op. 114)
(Schwarz-Reiflingen) gtr (2-3rd
degr.) HEINRICH. N-3211 f.s. (82)

Preludes, 24 (from Op. 114)
(Balesta) gtr (2-6th degr.)
RICORDI-IT ER-2476 f.s. (83)
"Preludi, 24" (Company) gtr (2-6th
degr.) ZERBONI 7073 $8.25 (84)
"Praludien, 24" (Domandl) gtr (2-
6th degr.) SIMROCK EE-3005 f.s.
(85)
"Preludi, 24" (Tonazzi) gtr (2-6th
degr.) BERBEN EB1407 $4.25 (86)

Studies, 30
"Studi, 30" (Chiesa) gtr (1-3rd
degr.) ZERBONI 6745 $8.25 (87)

Ubungen Und Spielstucke, 46
(Henze) gtr (1-4th degr.)
HOFMEISTER 7139 f.s. (88)

CASTELNUOVO-TEDESCO, MARIO (1895-1968)
Estudio Sul Nome Di Manuel Lopez
Ramos *Op.170,No.42 (from
Greeting Cards)
(Lopez Ramos) gtr (8th degr.)
BERBEN EB1187 $1.00 (89)

CAVAZZOLI, GERMANO
Study
gtr (4-5th degr.) BERBEN EB1780
$1.25 (90)

CHARPENTIER, JACQUES (1933-   )
Etude No. 1
gtr (8th degr.) LEDUC $3.75 (91)

COSTE, NAPOLEON (1806-1883)
Etudes, 25 *Op.38
"Studies, 25" gtr (5-8th degr.)
ONGAKU f.s. (92)
"Etudes De Genre" (Cottin) gtr (5-
8th degr.) COSTALL C&C-952 f.s.
(93)
"Studi, 25" (Gilardino) gtr (5-8th
degr.) BERBEN EB1371 f.s. (94)
"Etuden, 25" (Ritter) gtr (5-8th
degr.) SCHOTT GA-34 f.s. (95)
"Estudios Superiores, 25" (Rizzuti)
gtr (5-8th degr.) RICORDI-ARG
BA-11219 f.s. (96)
"Estudios, 25" (Sainz de la Maza)
gtr (5-8th degr.) UNION ESP.
18834 f.s. (97)
"Etuden, 25" (Walker, Luise) gtr
(5-8th degr.) HEINRICH. N-1525
f.s. (98)

Study in A
gtr ESSEX f.s. (99)

CZERNUSCHKA, FRITZ
Kleine Etuden, 2
gtr (3rd degr.) HEINRICH. N-1653
f.s. (100)

DAGOSTO, SYLVAIN
Etude in F
gtr (3rd degr., Collection
Longjumeau-Essonnes) TRANSAT.
1123 $1.25 (101)

Rapido, Lo, Etude
gtr (3rd degr., Collection
Longjumeau-Essonnes) TRANSAT.
1124 $1.25 (102)

DAUSEND, GERD-MICHAEL (1952-   )
Leichte Zeitgenossische Etuden
gtr (2-3rd degr.) PREISSLER 7072
f.s. (103)

DEGESE, VICENTE
Aleteo De Pajarito (Scherzo No. 1)
gtr (4-5th degr.) RICORDI-ARG
BA-12438 f.s. (104)

DEGNI, VINCENZO (1911-   )
Serenata All'antica (Study, Op. 14)
gtr (5th degr.) BERBEN EB1191 $1.00
(105)

Studio Della Chitarra Classica, Lo,
Vol. 1: Technical Exercises, 19
gtr (2-7th degr.) BERBEN EB1189
$2.75 (106)

Studio Della Chitarra Classica, Lo,
Vol. 2: Technical Exercises, 20
gtr (2-7th degr.) BERBEN EB1698
$5.25 (107)

DELAUNEY, PAUL
Feuillets, 15
(Worschech) gtr (4th degr.)
OUVRIERS EO-491 f.s. (108)

DIABELLI, ANTON (1781-1858)
Studi Facili, 30 *Op.39
"Studi" (Cimma) gtr (2-3rd degr.)
BERBEN EB1359 $2.00 (109)
"Studi Facili" (Company) gtr (2-3rd
degr., L'Arte Della Chitarra)
ZERBONI 7042 $7.00 (110)
"Sehr Leichte Ubungsstucke, 30"
(Peter) gtr (2-3rd degr.)
HOFMEISTER 7235 f.s. (111)
"Sehr Leichte Ubungsstucke, 30"
(Schwarz-Reiflingen) gtr (2-3rd
degr.) SIKORSKI 335 $5.00 (112)

Study No. 5
gtr (3-4th degr.) BERBEN EB2006
f.s. (113)

DIAZ, CLEMENTE A.
Estudio De Concierto
gtr (6th degr.) HARMONIA 2281 f.s.
(114)

DODGSON, STEPHEN (1924-   )
Studies, Vol. 1: 10 Studies (Nos. 1-
10) (composed with Quine, Hector)
gtr (5-7th degr.) RICORDI-ENG
LD-554 f.s. (115)

Studies, Vol. 2: 10 Studies (Nos. 11-
20) (composed with Quine, Hector)
gtr (7th degr.) RICORDI-ENG LD-555
f.s. (116)

DOERR, CHARLES-KIKO
Etude in B minor
gtr (7th degr.) ESCHIG 7618 f.s.
from OEUVRES DE CHARLES-KIKO
DOERR (117)

DUARTE, JOHN W. (1919-   )
Etude Diabolique *Op.49
gtr (8th degr., Collezione Di
Musiche Contemporanee) BERBEN
EB1716 $1.25 (118)

EINEM, GOTTFRIED VON (1918-   )
Studien, 3 *Op.34
(Ragossnig) gtr (8-9th degr.) BOTE
22278(1102) (119)

ELEMENTAR ETUDEN, VOL. 1 *CC25U
(Behrend) gtr PREISSLER 7030-I f.s.
contains works by: Sor (21); Coste
(2); Aguado (2) (120)

ELEMENTAR ETUDEN, VOL. 2
(Behrend) gtr (1-4th degr.) PREISSLER
7030-II. 17 pcs; contains works
by: Sor (6); Carcassi (5); Legnani
(2); Tarrega (3); Behrend (1)
contains: Tarrega, Francisco,
Prelude, TI i- 16, in D minor,
"Endecha"; Tarrega, Francisco,
Prelude, TI i- 17, in E,
"Lagrima" (121)

ELEMENTAR ETUDEN, VOL. 3 *CC1OU
(Behrend) gtr PREISSLER 7030-III f.s.
contains works by: Carulli (4); Sor
(2); Giuliani (3) (122)

ENCINAR, JOSE RAMON (1954-   )
Estudio De Alturas
gtr (8th degr.) ZERBONI 8372 f.s.
(123)

ESTUDIOS, 2
gtr (3rd degr./6th degr.) RICORDI-ARG
RF-7625 f.s.
contains: Prat, Domingo, Estudio
Original Para La Vibracion
Continua; Sor, Fernando, Etude,
Op. 29, No. 3 (124)

EYNARD, CAMILLE
Etude En Ut Majeur, Pour La
Resistance Du Barre
(Pujol) gtr (5th degr.) ESCHIG 1220
(125)

FARAILL, M.
Etude
gtr (4th degr.) LEMOINE f.s. (126)

FISCHER, FRANZ
Prelude, Orgelpunktstudie
gtr (4-5th degr.) HEINRICH. N-1629
f.s. (127)

FORTEA, DANIEL (1882-1953)
Capricho-Estudio, Op. 13
gtr (7th degr.) FORTEA BF37 f.s.
(128)

Capricho-Estudio, Op. 45
gtr (5th degr.) FORTEA BF60 f.s.
(129)

Estudio [De Arpegios] *Op.9
gtr (4th degr.) FORTEA BF33 f.s.
(130)

Estudio De Ligados *Op.26
gtr (4th degr.) FORTEA BF48 f.s.
(131)

Estudios *Op.10,No.1-2
gtr (5th degr.) FORTEA BF34 f.s.
(132)

Estudios Poeticos, Op. 25
gtr (4th degr.) FORTEA BF47 f.s.
contains: Dialogando, Op.25,No.1;
Serenata, Op.25,No.2 (133)

Murmullos (Study) Op.27
gtr (5-6th degr.) FORTEA BF49 f.s.
(134)

Preludios-Estudio, 2, Op. 4
gtr (3rd degr.) FORTEA BF28 f.s.
(135)

Preludios-Estudio, 2, Op. 5
gtr FORTEA BF29 f.s. (136)

Preludios-Estudio, 2, Op. 6 D3
gtr FORTEA BF30 f.s. (137)

Study in F *Op.36
gtr (4-5th degr.) FORTEA BF56 f.s.
(138)

FRANCERIES, MARC (1935-   )
Etudes, 6
gtr (3-5th degr.) CHOUDENS 20.461
f.s. (139)

FRANKE, J. MAX
Minuet, MIN 71
gtr (3rd degr.) HEINRICH. N-1636
f.s. contains also: Etude, MIN 72
(140)

GALL, LOUIS IGNATIUS
Bulerias De Nimega (Etude No. 33)
gtr (4th degr.) HARMONIA 1820 f.s.
contains also: Glodok (Etude No.
34); Siciliano (Etude No. 35)
(141)

GARCIA VELASCO, VENANCIO
Study No. 3
gtr (3rd degr.) UNION ESP. f.s.
(142)

Study No. 11
gtr (3rd degr.) UNION ESP. f.s.
(143)

GARZIA, PASQUALINO (1934-   )
Lezioni Sul Legato, 10
gtr (3-4th degr.) BERBEN EB1335
$1.75 (144)

GIORGIO GUTIERREZ, ARNOL DEL
Estudio Para La Practica De Los
Armonicos Octavados Compuestos
gtr (5th degr.) RICORDI-ARG
BA-11581 f.s. (145)

GITAAR-KAMERMUZIEK, VOL. 3: UIT HET
REPERTOIRE VAN HET JOEGOSLAVISCHE
DANSTHEATER
(Claessens, Anny C.H.) 1-5gtr (1-4th
degr.) sc BROEKMANS 27 f.s. arr +
orig pcs; contains works by:
Jovicic for 1 gtr (1); 9 songs and
dances; 2gtr (2); 3gtr (4); 5gtr
(2)
contains: Jovicic, Jovan, Concert-
Etude (146)

GITAAR-KAMERMUZIEK, VOL. 4: UIT HET
REPERTOIRE VAN HET JOEGOSLAVISCHE
DANSTHEATER *CC6U
(Claessens, Anny C.H.) 1-4gtr (1-4th
degr.) sc BROEKMANS 27A f.s. arr +
orig pcs; contains works by Jovicic
for: 1gtr(1); 6 songs and dances
for 2gtr (1); 3gtr (3); 4 gtr (3);
including gtr-g' (147)

GIULIANI, MAURO (1781-1829)
  Etude Spirituoso
    gtr ESSEX f.s.   (148)

  Etuden, 24 *Op.48
    "Studi, 24" (Gangi; Carfagna) gtr
    (4-7th degr.) BERBEN EB1354 $4.00
                                      (149)
    (Ritter) gtr (4-7th degr.) SCHOTT
    GA-32 f.s.   (150)
    (Scheit) gtr (4-7th degr.) UNIVER.
    13627 $4.75   (151)

  Etuden, 24, Selections *Op.48
    "Estudios Melodicos, 12
    (Seleccion)" (Sainz de la Maza)
    gtr (6-7th degr., nos. 1-12: op.
    48, nos. 8, 10, 11, 13-20, 23)
    UNION ESP. 20582 f.s.   (152)

  Etudes Progressives, 158
    gtr LEMOINE f.s.   (153)

  Fortschreitende Stucke, 18 *Op.51
    (Avila) gtr (2-4th degr.) SCHOTT
    GA-63 f.s.   (154)

  Leichte Etuden, 24 *Op.100
    (Henze) gtr (3-5th degr.)
    HOFMEISTER 7294 f.s.   (155)
    "Studien, 24" (Zuth) gtr (3-5th
    degr.) SCHOTT GA-69 f.s.   (156)

  Papillon, Le *Op.30
    "Mariposa, La" (Avila) gtr UNION
    ESP. 21842 f.s.   (157)

  Studi *CC80U
    (Chiesa) gtr (1-6th degr.) ZERBONI
    6630 $13.00   (158)

  Studies *Op.111
    "Studi" (Quattrocchi) gtr (3-5th
    degr.) BERBEN EB1333 $3.25 (159)
    "Ausgewahlte Studien, Vol. 1"
    (Zuth) gtr (3-5th degr.) SCHOTT
    GA-58 f.s.   (160)
    "Ausgewahlte Studien, Vol. 2"
    (Zuth) gtr (3-5th degr.) SCHOTT
    GA-59 f.s.   (161)

  Valse Etude
    gtr ESSEX f.s.   (162)

GIULIANI-GUGLIELMI, EMILIA
    (fl. ca. 1840)
  Preludes, 6 *Op.46
    gtr (5-7th degr.) SCHOTT GA-60 f.s.
                                      (163)

GROOT, JAAP DE
  Start On The Guitar, Vol. 1 *CC56U
    gtr (1st degr.) TEESELING VT-145
    f.s.   (164)

  Start On The Guitar, Vol. 2 *CC38U
    gtr (1st degr.) TEESELING VT-146
    f.s.   (165)

  Start On The Guitar, Vol. 3
    gtr (1st degr.) TEESELING VT-173
    f.s.   (166)

HAIDER, HANS
  Etuden, 3
    gtr (5-6th degr.) SIKORSKI 749
    $2.25   (167)

HEER, HANS DE (1927-   )
  Etude 1-3
    (Peters) gtr (3-4th degr.) HARMONIA
    1858 f.s.   (168)

  Etude 6-9
    ([Tigges]) gtr (7-8th degr.)
    TEESELING VT-68 f.s.   (169)

  Etude No. 4
    "Kwintolen Arpeggio Etude"
    (Hoogeveen) gtr (6th degr.)
    TEESELING VT-14 f.s.   (170)

  Etude No. 5
    "Tertsen Etude" (Tigges) gtr (6th
    degr.) TEESELING VT-24 f.s. (171)

  Etude No. 10
    gtr (7th degr.) TEESELING VT-109
    f.s.   (172)

HELLEMAN, JOOP
  Arpeggios, 10
    gtr (1-2nd degr.) HARMONIA 1537
    f.s.   (173)

  Hyper Studies *CC9U
    gtr (2-3rd degr.) HARMONIA 2113
    f.s.   (174)

  Melodische Etudes, 5
    gtr (3rd degr.) HARMONIA 1296 f.s.
                                      (175)

  Micro Studies *CC11U
    gtr (1-2nd degr.) HARMONIA 2064
    f.s.   (176)

HELLEMAN, JOOP (cont'd.)

  Mini Studies *CC15U
    gtr (1st degr.) HARMONIA 2045 f.s.
                                      (177)

  Snarenspel - Stringmusic, Exercises
    In Changing Positions
    gtr (2nd degr.) HARMONIA 1289 f.s.
                                      (178)

  Super Studies *CC10U
    gtr (2-3rd degr.) HARMONIA 2081
    f.s.   (179)

  Ultra Studies *CC10U
    gtr (3rd degr.) HARMONIA 2114 f.s.
                                      (180)

HELLER, STEPHEN (1813-1888)
  Estudios, 4, Para Formar El Ritmo Y
    La Expresion (from Op. 47)
    gtr (6-7th degr.) FORTEA BF85 f.s.
                                      (181)

  Etudes, 6
    (Garcia) gtr (7th degr.) LEMOINE
    f.s.   (182)

  Etudes, 10, Pour Former Au Sentiment,
    Du Rhythme Et A l'Expression
    (from Op. 47)
    (Paleologo) gtr (7-8th degr.)
    HEINRICH. N-1538 f.s.   (183)

  From Opus 47 *CC4L
    (Komter) gtr (3rd degr.) HARMONIA
    2947 f.s. contains op.47, nos.10,
    19, 23, and 3   (184)

  Heller Estudio
    (Sinopoli) gtr (6th degr.) RICORDI-
    ARG RF-7616 f.s.   (185)

HIGGINS, RALPH
  Classical Studies For Guitar
    gtr (supplement to The
    Comprehensive Guitar Method)
    BELWIN 2366 $2.50   (186)

HOEK, JAN-ANTON VAN (1936-   )
  Konzertetude, No.2
    gtr (5th degr.) MARBOT f.s.   (187)

  Polyphony And Polytonality *Op.1141
    gtr (3-4th degr., 25 modern
    studies) HARMONIA 2627 f.s.   (188)

  Praludien Und Etuden Zur
    Vervollkommnung Der Technik
    (composed with Walker, Luise)
    gtr (6-9th degr., 12 preludes, 27
    etudes) HEINRICH. 1552 f.s.   (189)

HUBSCHMANN, WERNER (1901-1969)
  Etuden, 22
    (Zimmer) gtr (3-6th degr.)
    HOFMEISTER T-4099 f.s.   (190)

  Studien, 5
    (Zimmer) gtr (4-6th degr.)
    HOFMEISTER 7297 f.s.   (191)

IPARRAGUIRRE, P.A.
  Estudios Diarios Del Mecanismo
    Tecnico
    gtr (3-10th degr.) RICORDI-ARG
    BA-11816 f.s.   (192)

JOLIVET, ANDRE (1905-1974)
  Etudes De Concert, 2
    gtr (9-10th degr.) BOOSEY-ENG 19264
    $3.75
    contains: Etude No. 1, "Etude
    Comme Un Prelude"; Etude No. 2,
    "Etude Comme Une Danse"   (193)

KLUIN, ELS
  Arpeggio Studies, 18
    gtr (1-2nd degr., in higher
    positions) HARMONIA 2224 f.s.
                                      (194)

KOMTER, JAN MAARTEN (1905-   )
  Arpeggio-Etude, A La Maniere De Sor,
    gtr (4th degr.) DONEMUS f.s. (195)

LAGOYA, ALEXANDRE
  Etudes, 6
    gtr (6-8th degr.) ESCHIG f.s. (196)

LEGNANI, LUIGI (1790-1877)
  Capricci, 6 *Op.250
    (Gotze) gtr (3-4th degr.) SCHOTT
    GA-37 f.s.   (197)
    "Pequenos Caprichos, 6" (Pomilio)
    gtr (3-4th degr.) RICORDI-ARG
    BA-11240 f.s.   (198)

  Capricci, 36 *Op.20
    (Ritter) gtr (7-8th degr.) SCHOTT
    f.s. in all major and minor keys
    contains: Capricci, 36, Vol. 1,
    Nos. 1-18; Capricci, 36, Vol.
    2, Nos. 19-36   (199)

  Capricci Scelti, 10 (from Op. 20 and
    Op. 250)
    (Storti) gtr (4-5th degr.) BERBEN
    EB1383 $3.00   (200)

LELLA, DOMENICO DI
  Impressione *Op.9
    gtr TEESELING VT-151 f.s. contains
    also: Studio Da Concierto, Op.10
                                      (201)

LISKER, ROY
  Etudes, 13
    gtr ESCHIG f.s.   (202)

LLOBET, MIGUEL (1878-1938)
  Estudio (Study in E)
    gtr (5-6th degr.) UNION ESP. 20365
    f.s.   (203)

  Estudio Capricho In D Major
    gtr (8th degr.) UNION ESP. 20366
    f.s.   (204)

MAES, JEF (1905-   )
  Etudes, 2
    gtr (3rd degr., Musica Nova)
    SCHOTT-FRER 9263 f.s.   (205)

MARGOLA, FRANCO (1908-   )
  Studi Da Concerto, 8
    (Cabassi) gtr (5-6th degr., Il
    Bucranio) ZANIBON 5076 f.s. (206)

MASALA, ROBERTO (1954-   )
  Studi, 3
    gtr (4-5th degr.) BERBEN EB1543
    f.s.   (207)

MIGNONE, FRANCISCO (1897-   )
  Etudes, 12, Vol.1
    (Barbosa-Lima) gtr COLUMBIA 186-A
    $4.00   (208)

  Etudes, 12, Vol.2
    (Barbosa-Lima) gtr COLUMBIA 186-B
    $4.50   (209)

MOLINO, FRANCESCO (1775-1847)
  Praludien, 18
    (Gotze) gtr (3-4th degr.) SCHOTT
    GA-38 f.s.   (210)

MOZZANI, LUIGI (1869-1943)
  Study
    gtr (5th degr.) BERBEN EB1107 $1.00
                                      (211)

MURTULA, GIOVANNI (1881-1964)
  Studi, 2
    gtr (6th degr.) BERBEN EB1109 $1.00
                                      (212)

  Studio, Rondo Fantasioso
    gtr (7-8th degr.) BERBEN EB1062
    $1.50   (213)

NAVARRO, ANTONIO
  Tremolo Study In A Major
    gtr (5th degr.) ESSEX f.s.   (214)

NIJENHUIS, LUC
  Barre-Etudes *CC10U
    gtr (2nd degr.) HARMONIA 1566 (215)

  Capo Tasto
    gtr (1-2nd degr.) HARMONIA 1549
                                      (216)

  In Spe
    gtr (2nd degr., 10 etudes) HARMONIA
    1585   (217)

  Legato Studies *CC10U
    gtr (2nd degr.) HARMONIA 1599 (218)

  Studies In V *CC12U
    gtr (1-2nd degr.) HARMONIA 1827
                                      (219)

NUNES, MILTON
  Luz E Saudade, Estudo Em Tremolo
    gtr (7th degr.) RICORDI-BR BR2991
                                      (220)

PAGANINI, NICCOLO (1782-1840)
  Etude
    (Behrend) gtr (4th degr.) SIRIUS
                                      (221)

PASTOR, SEGUNDO
  Estudio En Tremolo
    gtr (5th degr.) UNION ESP. 20813
                                      (222)

PATACHICH, IVAN (1922-   )
  Kis Tanulmanyok
    "Small Studies" gtr (3-4th degr.,
    13 pcs) EMB 8768 f.s.   (223)

PELEMANS, WILLEM (1901-   )
  Kleine Studies, 6
    "Petites Etudes, 6" gtr (6th degr.)
    MAURER f.s.   (224)

PONCE, MANUEL MARIA (1882-1948)
  Estudio De Tremolo
    (Segovia) gtr (8th degr.) SCHOTT
    GA131 f.s.   (225)

PRESTI, IDA (1924-1967)
  Etude Du Matin
    gtr (7th degr., concert study)
    COLUMBIA 164 $1.50   (226)

  Etudes, 6
    gtr (7-8th degr.) ESCHIG f.s. (227)

PUJOL, EMILIO (1886-1982)
Abejorro, El, Estudio
gtr (7th degr.) RICORDI-ARG BA11109
f.s.   (228)

Aquelarre
"Danse Des Sorcieres, Etude
Dynamique" gtr ESCHIG 1246 f.s.
(229)

Cancion Amatoria, Estudio
gtr (6th degr.) RICORDI-ARG
EK 324 B f.s.   (230)

Canto De Otono
"Chant d'Automne, Etude Melodique"
gtr ESCHIG 1245 f.s.   (231)

Estudios: Grado Superior *CC7U
gtr (3-7th degr.) UNION ESP. EI196
f.s.   (232)

Etude No. 1
gtr (6-7th degr.) ESCHIG 1200 f.s.
(233)

Etude No. 2
gtr (6-7th degr.) ESCHIG 1201 f.s.
(234)

Etude No. 3
gtr (6th degr.) ESCHIG 1202 f.s.
(235)

Exercises En Forme d'Etudes, Vol. 1
*CC3U
gtr (2-3rd degr.) ESCHIG 1221 f.s.
(236)

Exercises En Forme d'Etudes, Vol. 2
gtr (2-3rd degr.) ESCHIG 1243 f.s.
(237)

Libelula, La, Study
gtr (4th degr.) ESCHIG 1239 f.s.
(238)

Ondinas (Study No. 7)
gtr (8-9th degr.) RICORDI-ARG
BA-9584 f.s.   (239)

Paisaje
gtr (7-8th degr., tremolo study,
based on an unpublished motive by
Tarrega) RICORDI-ARG BA9585 f.s.
(240)

Pizzicato (Etude in C)
gtr ESCHIG 1247 f.s.   (241)

Preludes, 2
gtr (3rd degr.) ESCHIG 1233 f.s.
(242)

Triptique Campagnard
gtr (study for R.H. only on open
strings) ESCHIG 1249 f.s.   (243)

REGONDI, GIULIO (1822-1872)
Study No. 1
gtr (5-6th degr.) BERBEN EB1334
f.s.   (244)

REISER, EKKEHARD
Studien, 2
gtr (6-7th degr.) SCHOTT GA-429
f.s.   (245)

RIGACCI, MARIO
Study in B minor
gtr (8th degr.) BERBEN EB1086 f.s.
(246)

RIVIER, JEAN (1896-   )
Etude
gtr TRANSAT. $3.00   (247)

RIZZUTI, CARMELO
Tremolo Estudio
gtr (6th degr.) RICORDI-ARG
BA-12110 f.s.   (248)

SAGRERAS, JULIO S. (1879-1942)
Gitarrenunterricht Fur Anfanger, Vol.
1
[Ger] gtr (orig in Span) SYMPHON
2214 f.s.   (249)

Lessons For The Guitar, Vol. 1, The
First Lessons
"Prime Lezioni, Le" gtr (2-3rd
degr., 86 pcs) BERBEN EB1198 f.s.
(250)
"Primeras Lecciones, Las" gtr (2-
3rd degr., 86 pcs) RICORDI-ARG
BA9500 f.s.   (251)

Lessons For The Guitar, Vol. 2, The
Second Lessons
"Seconde Lezioni, Le" gtr (3-4th
degr., 44 pcs) BERBEN EB1212 f.s.
(252)
"Segundas Lecciones, Las" gtr (3-
4th degr., 44 pcs) RICORDI-ARG
BA-9529 f.s.   (253)

Lessons For The Guitar, Vol.3, The
Third Lessons
"Terceras Lecciones, Las" gtr (4-
5th degr., 38 pcs) RICORDI-ARG
BA-9557 f.s.   (254)
"Terze Lezioni, Le" gtr (4-5th
degr., 38 pcs) BERBEN EB1246 f.s.
(255)

SAGRERAS, JULIO S. (cont'd.)
Lessons For The Guitar, Vol. 4, The
Fourth Lessons
"Cuartas Lecciones, Las" gtr (5-6th
degr., 39 pcs) RICORDI-ARG
BA-9570 f.s.   (256)
"Quarte Lezioni, Le" gtr (5-6th
degr., 39 pcs) BERBEN EB1323 f.s.
(257)

Lessons For The Guitar, Vol. 5, The
Fifth Lessons
"Quintas Lecciones, Las" gtr (7-8th
degr., 48 pcs) RICORDI-ARG
BA-9573 f.s.   (258)
"Quinte Lezioni, Le" gtr (7-8th
degr., 48 pcs) BERBEN EB1447 f.s.
(259)

Lessons For The Guitar, Vol. 6, The
Sixth Lessons
"Seste Lezioni, Le" gtr (8-9th
degr., 30 pcs) BERBEN EB1528 f.s.
(260)
"Sextas Lecciones, Las" gtr (8-9th
degr., 30 pcs) RICORDI-ARG
BA-9504 f.s.   (261)

SAINZ DE LA MAZA, EDUARDO
Anoranza Lejana
"Study" gtr UNION ESP. 21192 f.s.
(262)
SAINZ DE LA MAZA, REGINO (1897-1982)
Estudio-Scherzo *Op.10
gtr (7th degr.) UNION ESP. 15647
f.s.   (263)

Study in A minor
gtr (6th degr.) UNION ESP. 15646
f.s.   (264)

SANCHEZ, BLAS
Dialogue
gtr (5th degr., Collection L'Heure
De La Guitare Classique; also
published as no. 9 in 12 Etudes
Elementaires) CHOUDENS f.s. (265)

Etudes Elementaires, 12
gtr (3-4th degr.) CHOUDENS 20.381
f.s.   (266)

Etudes Preparatoires, 12
gtr (2-3rd degr.) CHOUDENS 20.398
f.s.   (267)

Etudes Probatoires, 12
gtr (1st degr.) CHOUDENS 20.397
f.s.   (268)

Guernica 2, Etude De Concert
gtr ESCHIG f.s.   (269)

Oracion (Etude in E minor)
gtr (5th degr., Collection L'heure
De La Guitare Classique; also
published as no. 7 in 12 Etudes
Elementaires) CHOUDENS 20.223
f.s.   (270)

Variations En Forme d'Etudes, 10, Sur
Une Basse Continue
gtr (5th degr., Collection De
L'Heure De La Guitare Classique)
CHOUDENS 20.219 f.s.   (271)

SAVIO, ISAIAS (1900-1977)
Estudos, 3, Series 2
gtr (6-7th degr.) RICORDI-BR
BR-1836 f.s.   (272)

SCHAGEN, HENK VAN
Lichte Etudes, 20 *Op.31
gtr (2-3rd degr.) TEESELING VT-15
f.s.   (273)

Lopen Leren
"First Steps, The" gtr (1st degr.,
20 exercises) HARMONIA 1527 f.s.
(274)

Voor Vaardige Vingers
"For Skilled Fingers" gtr (1-2nd
degr., 6 studies in high
positions) HARMONIA 1247 f.s.
(275)

Voor Vlijtige Vingers
gtr (2nd degr., 7 etudes) HARMONIA
1275 f.s.   (276)

Zoete Invallen, 4
"Happy Thoughts, 4" gtr (3-4th
degr.) HARMONIA 1507 f.s.   (277)

SCHLICHTING, THEODOR
Bass-Studien *CC25U
gtr (2-4th degr.) VAMO EE-012 f.s.
(278)

SEGOVIA, ANDRES (1896-   )
Estudio Sin Luz
gtr (7th degr.) SCHOTT GA-179 f.s.
(279)

Estudio-Vals
gtr (also published in Andres
Segovia Album) COLUMBIA 128 f.s.
(280)

SEGOVIA, ANDRES (cont'd.)
Estudios, 3
gtr (6-7th degr., no. 3 for 2gtr)
SCHOTT GA-178 f.s.   (281)

Four Easy Lessons
gtr CEL 9 $.70   (282)

SHEARER, AARON
Tremolo Studies, 3
gtr (4-5th degr.) COLOMBO NY-2295
f.s.   (283)

SIERRA, JOSE MARIA
Etudes Superieures, 3
gtr (6-7th degr.) CHOUDENS 20.646
f.s.   (284)

SINOPOLI, ANTONIO
Preludio En Forma De Estudio
gtr (5th degr.) RICORDI-ARG BA-5197
f.s.   (285)

SOR, FERNANDO (1778-1839)
Ausgewahlte Etuden, Vol. 1:
Vorbereitende Ubungen, Kleine
Musikstucke Und Etuden *CC24L
(Dobrauz, Carl) [Ger/Eng] gtr
HEINRICH. N-1502 f.s. biogr
notes; contains: meth., lec. no.
3, 14, 16, 19, 23; op. 31, nos.
1-3, 5, 6, 9; op. 35, nos. 1-3,
14; op. 60, nos. 1-4, 6, 10, 12-
14   (286)

Ausgewahlte Etuden, Vol. 2: Kleine
Musikstucke Und Etuden *CC16L
(Dobrauz, Carl) [Ger/Eng] gtr
HEINRICH. N-1506 f.s. biogr
notes; contains: Meth.: Lec. nos.
6a, 9, 12, 21; op. 2, no. 1
(Menuet); op. 31, no. 11; op. 32,
no. 2 (Valse); op. 35, nos. 4-9;
op. 60, nos. 16, 19, 21   (287)

Ausgewahlte Etuden, Vol. 3: Kleine
Musikstucke Und Etuden *CC15L
(Dobrauz, Carl) [Ger/Eng] gtr
HEINRICH. N-1509 f.s. biogr
notes; contains: op. 23, no. 3;
op. 31, nos. 4, 7, 8, 10, 13-15;
op. 32, no. 3 (Andante
Pastorale); op. 32, no. 6
(Galop); op. 35, nos. 10, 11, 13,
16, 19   (288)

Ausgewahlte Etuden, Vol. 4: Kleine
Musikstucke Und Etuden *CC13L
(Dobrauz, Carl) [Ger/Eng] gtr
HEINRICH. N-1510 f.s. biogr
notes; contains: Meth.: Lec. nos.
17, 20, 24; op. 31, nos. 17, 20,
23; op. 32, no. 1 (Andantino);
op. 35, nos. 17, 20-22, 24; op.
60, no. 20   (289)

Ausgewahlte Etuden, Vol. 5: Etuden
*CC13L
(Dobrauz, Carl) [Ger/Eng] gtr
HEINRICH. N-1511 f.s. biogr
notes; contains: op. 6, nos. 1,
2, 4, 8; op. 29, no. 7; op. 31,
nos. 18, 19, 21, 24; op. 35, nos.
18, 23; op. 60, nos. 22, 23 (290)

Ausgewahlte Etuden, Vol. 6: Etuden
*CC11L
(Dobrauz, Carl) [Ger/Eng] gtr
HEINRICH. N-1512 f.s. biogr
notes; contains: op. 6, nos. 3,
5-7, 9-12; op. 29, no. 4; op. 31,
nos. 16, 22   (291)

Ausgewahlte Etuden, Vol. 7: Etuden
*CC10L
(Dobrauz, Carl) [Ger/Eng] gtr
HEINRICH. N-1513 f.s. biogr
notes; contains: Meth.: Lec. no.
29; op. 29, nos. 1-3, 6, 8, 9,
11, 12; op. 60, no. 25   (292)

Douze Etudes *Op.6
"Zwolf Etuden" [Ger/Fr] gtr (biogr
notes; list of Sor's studies in a
progressive order) SCHOTT GA-77
f.s.   (293)

Douze Etudes Pour Servir De Suite Aux
Douze Premieres *Op.29
"Zwolf Etuden" [Ger/Fr] gtr (biogr
notes; list of Sor's studies in a
progessive order) SCHOTT GA-78
f.s.   (294)

12 Ejercicios (from Op. 35)
(Tarrago) gtr UNION ESP. 179 f.s.
(295)

Ejercicios Y Estudios Elementales
Para Guitarra, 36, Vol. 1 *CC36L
(Bianqui Pinero, G.) gtr RICORDI-
ARG EK-249, SERIE C f.s.
contains: op. 31, nos. 1-6, 9,
11, 13-14, 18; op. 35, nos. 1-4,
9, 14, 18; op. 60, nos. 1, 2, 5-
19, 21   (296)

SOR, FERNANDO (cont'd.)

Vingt-Quatre Exercices Tres Faciles,
Op. 35, No. 23
"Harfenetude (Harp Study)" gtr
ESSEX f.s.   (347)

Vingt Quatre Lecons Progressives,
Dediees Aux Eleves Commencants
*Op.31
"Fortschreitende Studien Fur
Anfanger, 24, Vol. 1: Studies No.
1-12" [Ger/Fr] gtr (biogr notes;
list of Sor's studies in a
progressive order) SCHOTT GA-79
f.s.   (348)
"Fortschreitende Studien Fur
Anfanger, 24, Vol. 2: Studies No.
13-24" [Ger/Fr] gtr (biogr notes;
list of Sor's studies in a
progressive order) SCHOTT GA-80
f.s.   (349)
"Fortschreitende Ubungen Fur
Gitarre-Anfanger, Vol. 1: Studies
No. 1-12" (Peter, Ursula) gtr
HOFMEISTER 7210 f.s.   (350)
"Fortschreitende Ubungen Fur
Gitarre-Anfanger, Vol. 2: Studies
No. 13-24" (Peter, Ursula) gtr
HOFMEISTER 7275 f.s.   (351)

STAAK, PIETER VAN DER (1930-   )
8 Studi Sugli Armonici
gtr (5th degr.) ZERBONI 8289 f.s.
                                    (352)

STERZATI, UMBERTO (1909-1972)
Studi Divertimento, 6
gtr (3-4th degr.) BERBEN EB1094
f.s.   (353)

STINGL, ANTON (1908-   )
Lehrstucke, 30 *Op.38
gtr (1-3rd degr.) HOFMEISTER-W f.s.
                                    (354)

TARRAGO, GRACIANO
Estudio De Tremolo, Sobre Un Tema De
Alard
1-2gtr (gtr1: 6th degr.; gtr2: 4th
degr.) UNION ESP. 2257 f.s. (355)

Estudios De Cejilla, 6
gtr (7-9th degr.) UNION ESP. EI-201
f.s.   (356)

Estudios Melodicos, 25
gtr (2-5th degr.) UNION ESP. 21502
f.s.   (357)

TARREGA, FRANCISCO (1852-1909)
Estudios *see Chapter VI

ULRICH, JURGEN (1939-   )
Drei Rhapsodische Studien
gtr HANSEN-DEN f.s.   (358)

VERZIJL, HANS (1934-   )
Kennismaken, Het
gtr (1st degr., 9 studies) HARMONIA
1539 f.s.   (359)

Van Niets Tot Iets *CC25U
gtr (1st degr.) HARMONIA 1518 f.s.
                                    (360)

Van V Naar I
gtr (1-2nd degr., 30 etudes)
HARMONIA 1290 f.s.   (361)

VILLA-LOBOS, HEITOR (1887-1959)
Etudes, 12
gtr (9-10th degr.) ESCHIG 6679 f.s.
                                    (362)

VISSER, DICK (1927-   )
Anti- En Symmetria, Studie
gtr (6-7th degr.) HARMONIA 2343
f.s.   (363)

Etudes, 4
gtr (3-4th degr.) HEUWEKE. 782 f.s.
                                    (364)

Studies, 12, Vol. 1
gtr (3-5th degr., major scales)
HARMONIA 1501 f.s.   (365)

Studies, 12, Vol. 2
gtr (3-5th degr., harmonic minor
scales) HARMONIA 1502 f.s. (366)

Studies, 12, Vol. 3
gtr (3-5th degr., melodic minor
scales) HARMONIA 1503 f.s. (367)

WALKER, LUISE (1910-   )
Brasilianisch (Etude in E)
gtr (3rd degr.) HEINRICH. N-1602
f.s.   (368)

Fur Den Anfang, Vol. 1
gtr (2-3rd degr.) HEINRICH. 1606
f.s.   (369)

Fur Den Anfang, Vol. 2
gtr (2-3rd degr.) HEINRICH. 1607
f.s.   (370)

WALKER, LUISE (cont'd.)

Fur Den Anfang, Vol. 3
gtr (2-3rd degr.) HEINRICH. 1608
f.s.   (371)

Fur Den Anfang, Vol. 4
gtr (2-3rd degr.) HEINRICH. 1609
f.s.   (372)

Fur Den Anfang, Vol. 5
gtr (2-3rd degr.) HEINRICH. 1610
f.s.   (373)

Fur Den Anfang, Vol. 6
gtr (2-3rd degr.) HEINRICH. 1611
f.s.   (374)

Marsch Nach Einer Tiroler Melodie
gtr (2nd degr.) HEINRICH. N-1604
f.s. contains also: Etude
(Chromatisch)   (375)

Regenetude
gtr (7th degr.) HEINRICH. 1527 f.s.
                                    (376)

Tanzlied (Etude in C)
gtr (2nd degr.) HEINRICH. 1601 f.s.
                                    (377)

I/IA-Coll   Guitar Study Collections

CARULLI, FERDINANDO (1770-1841)
Elementar Etuden, Vol. 4 *CC6U
(Behrend) gtr PREISSLER 7030-IV
f.s.   (378)

ELEMENTAR ETUDEN, VOL. 1 *CC25U
(Behrend) gtr PREISSLER 7030-I f.s.
contains works by: Sor (21); Coste
(2); Aguado (2)   (379)

ELEMENTAR ETUDEN, VOL. 2
(Behrend) gtr (1-4th degr.) PREISSLER
7030-II f.s. 17 pcs; contains works
by: Sor (6); Carcassi (5); Legnani
(2); Tarrega (3); Behrend (1)
contains: Tarrega, Francisco,
Prelude, TI i- 16, in D minor,
"Endecha"; Tarrega, Francisco,
Prelude, TI i- 17, in E,
"Lagrima"   (380)

ELEMENTAR ETUDEN, VOL. 3 *CC10U
(Behrend) gtr PREISSLER 7030-III f.s.
contains works by: Carulli (4); Sor
(2); Giuliani (3); Aguado (1) (381)

ERSTEN ETUDEN, DIE *CC18U
(Scheit) gtr (1-2nd degr.) UNIVER.
14471 $5.00 contains works by:
Aguado (3); Carcassi (1); Carulli
(2); Coste (3); Giuliani (4); Sor
(5)   (382)

ESTUDOS PARA VIOLAO, 8 *CC8U
(Savio) gtr (4-7th degr.) RICORDI-BR
BR-2930 f.s. contains works by: Sor
(2); Coste (1); Aguado (1); Cano
(1); Giuliani (1); Carulli (1);
Carcassi (1)   (383)

KLASSZIKUS ETUDOK GITARRA *CC18U
(Puskas) gtr (3-4th degr.) EMB Z-5505
f.s. 1st-5th pos.; contains works
by: Diabelli (2); Sor (5); Carulli
(4); Carcassi (4); Giuliani (3) (384)

KONZERT-ETUDEN FUR GITARRE, VOL. 3
(Behrend) gtr (5-9th degr.) PREISSLER
7034-III f.s. 5 pcs (nos 15-19);
contains works by Mertz and Vinas
contains: Tarrega, Francisco,
Study, TI ii- 8, in A; Tarrega,
Francisco, Study, TI ii- 9, in A
minor; Tarrega, Francisco, Study,
TI ii- 19, in A   (385)

KONZERT ETUDEN, VOL. 1 *CC7U
(Behrend) gtr (5-9th degr.) PREISSLER
7034-I f.s. contains works by:
Carulli (1), Mertz (1); Coste (1);
Sor (4)   (386)

KONZERT ETUDEN, VOL. 2 *CC7U
(Behrend) gtr (5-9th degr.) PREISSLER
7034-II f.s. contains works by: Sor
(4); Mertz (1); Coste (1); Kuhnert
(1)   (387)

WYBOR ETIUD NA GITARE, VOL. 1 *CC80U
(Powrozniak, Jozef) gtr (1-3rd degr.)
POLSKIE 2532 f.s. exercises,
chords, studies   (388)

WYBOR ETIUD NA GITARE, VOL. 2 *CC60U
(Powrozniak, Jozef) gtr (4th degr.)
POLSKIE 6471 f.s. exercises,
chords, studies; contains:
Exercises TI-iii-15g-h by Francisco
Tarrega   (389)

I/IB1   Guitar Solos: Pre-Classical Music (until 1760)

ACADEMICO CALIGINOSO, L' (from Primo,
Secundo, E Terzo Libro Della
Chitarra Spagnola) CC9U
(Bellow) gtr (4th degr.) COLOMBO
NY-2401 f.s. Renaissance And
Baroque, Vol. VII   (390)

ADRIAENSSEN, EMANUEL (ca. 1550-1604)
2 Dances And 2 Fantasies
(Carlin) gtr (3-5th degr.)
MUS.SAC.PRO. LR-103 $6.00
notation: Fr tablature +
transcription for gtr
contains: Branle Double; Fantasy
No. 1; Fantasy No. 5; Grand
Ballo Du Court, Le   (391)

Fantasy No. 3
(van Puijenbroeck) gtr (3-4th
degr., g is f sharp; capotasto in
pos. III) METROPOLIS EM-4705
$2.00   (392)

ALBINONI, TOMASO (1671-1750)
Adagio in G minor
(Abloniz) gtr (E min,4-5th degr.)
BERBEN EB1287 f.s.   (393)
(Martin) gtr (4-5th degr., Guitar
Selection, No. 6) DELRIEU 1388
f.s.   (394)

Beruhmtes Adagio, Nach Einem
Themenfragment Mit Beziffertem
Generalbass (composed with
Giazotto, Remo)
(Azpiazu) gtr SYMPHON 2088 f.s.
                                    (395)

ALFONSO X, EL SABIO, KING OF CASTILE
(1221-1284)
2 Cantigas
(Garcia Velasco) gtr UNION ESP.
21935 f.s.
contains: Cantiga LX, "Entre Ave
Et Eva"; Cantiga LXV, "A Creer
Devemos"   (396)

Rosa Das Rosas, Cantiga
(Garcia Velasco) gtr UNION ESP.
21793 f.s.   (397)

ALLISON, RICHARD (ca. 1600)
Pavan
(Azpiazu, L. de) gtr (9th degr.,
Guitare, No.33) LEDUC G-33 $2.25
                                    (398)

ANONYMOUS
Altdeutsche Lautentanze, 2
(Behrend) gtr (3rd degr.) SIRIUS
f.s.
contains: Preambl, Ein; Teutscher
Tantz, Ein   (399)

Antike Tanze Und Arien *CC4U
(Behrend) gtr (2-3rd degr.)
HEINRICH. N-1622 f.s.   (400)

Aus Altitalienischen Lautenbuchern
*Suite
(Behrend) gtr (5-6th degr.,
Gitarre-Bibliothek, No.81) BOTE
GB-81 f.s.   (401)

Aus Einer Lautenhandschrift Des 16.
Jahrhunderts *CC17U
(Chilesotti; Gerwig) gtr (2-3rd
degr.) LIENAU f.s. Der Lautenist,
Vol. II; g is f sharp   (402)

Baltische Suite (from Baltisches
Lautenbuch (1740))
(de Hilster) gtr (1-2nd degr.)
TEESELING VT-52 f.s.   (403)

Barcarolle, MIN 79
(Muggia) gtr (2nd degr.) BERBEN
EB1484 $1.00   (404)

Dindandon
(Pujol) gtr ESCHIG 2001 f.s.
contains also: Tambourin Joli
                                    (405)

Fantasy, MIN 73
(Azpiazu, L. de) gtr (8th degr.,
Guitare, No.25) LEDUC G-25 f.s.
                                    (406)

ANONYMOUS (cont'd.)

Fantasy No. 7 (from Libro De Venegas
De Henestrosa)
(Tarrago) gtr (3-4th degr.) UNION
ESP. 20574 f.s.   (407)

Fantasy No. 11 (from Libro De Venegas
De Henestrosa)
(Tarrago) gtr (4th degr.) UNION
ESP. 20575 f.s.   (408)

Gagliarda Del Passo Mezzo
(Chilesotti; Ferrari) gtr (4th
degr.) BERBEN EB1120 $1.00   (409)

Greensleeves *16th cent
(Behrend) gtr (3-4th degr.,
Gitarre-Bibliothek, No.71) BOTE
GB-71 f.s.   (410)
(Elponti; Bignotto) gtr (3-4th
degr., My Repertory) ZANIBON 5432
f.s.   (411)
(Gasbarroni) gtr (3-4th degr.)
BERBEN EB1172 $1.00   (412)
(Mairants) gtr (3-4th degr.) BELWIN
f.s.   (413)
(Nobla) gtr (3-4th degr., adapted
with one variation) TRANSAT. 1234
$1.50   (414)
(Papas) 1-2gtr,opt solo voice (3-
4th degr.) sc COLUMBIA 141 f.s. (415)
(Savio) gtr (3-4th degr.) RICORDI-
BR BR-2912 f.s.   (416)
(Usher) gtr (3-4th degr.) ESSEX
f.s.   (417)

2 Piezas Para Laud Del Teatro De
Shakespeare
(Azpiazu) gtr UNION ESP. 20524 f.s.
contains: Ophelia (from Hamlet);
Sick Tune, The   (418)

4 Piezas Del S. XVIII
(Angel) gtr UNION ESP. 20086 f.s.
contains: Bourree; Courante;
Rigodon; Saraband   (419)

Prelude Et Menuet (Re Mineur) (from
Livre Pour Le Luth, Cologne) 18th
cent
(Castet) gtr (Guitare, No. 101)
LEDUC G-101 f.s. contains also:
Prelude Et Gigue (La Majeur);
Prelude Et Gigue (Do Majeur)
(420)

Sick Tune, The
(Goor) gtr (3rd degr., g is f-sharp
and g is g) METROPOLIS EM-4739
$1.50 contains also: Anonymous,
Courante, "Current"; Anonymous,
Kemp's Jig; Cutting, Francis,
Squirrel's Toy, The   (421)

Suite in G, MIN 330 (from Baltisches
Lautenbuch)
(Libbert) gtr (2-3rd degr., Das
Gitarrenwerk, Reihe A:4)
PREISSLER f.s.   (422)

Tant Que Vivray
(Castet) gtr,opt solo voice (5th
degr., Guitare, No.69) LEDUC G-69
f.s. contains also: Glose Sur
Cette Meme Chanson (gtr); Paroles
De Cette Chanson (gtr,opt solo
voice)   (423)

17 ARIEN UND TANZE (from Regensburger
Gitarrentabulatur)
(Libbert) gtr SYMPHON 2256 f.s. (424)

ASTON, HUGH (ca. 1480-ca. 1522)
Hornepype
(Galindo) gtr (7th degr.) UNION
ESP. f.s.   (425)

AUS WILLIAM BRADE'S "VISBOK"
(Gerwig) gtr (3-5th degr., Der
Lautenist, Vol. VII; g is f-sharp;
10 pces) LIENAU f.s. contains also:
Genzmer, Harald, Sonatina   (426)

BACH, CARL PHILIPP EMANUEL (1714-1788)
Siciliana
(Segovia) gtr (7th degr.) SCHOTT
GA-147 f.s.   (427)

Solfegietto
(Nunes) gtr RICORDI-BR BR-1035 f.s.
(428)

Stucke, 2
(Behrend) gtr (6-7th degr.) BOTE
GB-32 f.s. Gitarre-Bibliothek,
No.32; also published in European
Masters For The Guitar
contains: Alla Polacca; Presto
(429)

Xenophone, La
(Segovia) gtr (7th degr.) SCHOTT
146 f.s. contains also: Sybille,
La   (430)

BACH, JOHANN CHRISTIAN (1735-1782)
Minuet, MIN 80
(Zoega) gtr (6th degr.) RICORDI-BR
BR-2845 f.s.   (431)

BACH, JOHANN SEBASTIAN (1685-1750)
Menuet-Trio In G Minor *BWV 929
"Prelude" (Mazmanian) gtr (3rd
degr.) HEINRICH. 1634 f.s.
contains also: Anonymous,
Passepied   (432)

BACHELER, DANIEL (ca. 1600)
Courantes, 3 *CCU
(Castet) gtr (5-6th degr.) DELRIEU
1411 f.s. Guitarra, No. 18   (433)

Mounsieurs Almaine (from "Varietie Of
Lute Lessons" (1610))
(Azpiazu) gtr (9-10th degr.) UNION
ESP. 20051 f.s.   (434)
(Behrend) gtr (9-10th degr.,
Gitarre-Bibliothek, No.79; also
published in European Masters For
The Guitar) BOTE GB-79 f.s. (435)
(Hinojosa) gtr (9-10th degr.,
Bibliotheque De Musique Ancienne;
g is f-sharp) TRANSAT. 1211 $3.50
(436)

BAKFARK, BALINT (VALENTIN) (1507-1576)
Fantasia Seconda A Quattro Voci, For
Lute
(Cristoforetti) gtr (8th degr.)
ZERBONI 6980 $3.50   (437)

Fantasy
(Azpiazu, L. de) gtr (8th degr.,
Guitare, No.21) LEDUC G-21 f.s.
(438)

Lautenbuch Von Krakau, Das
"Cracow Lute-Book, The" (Homolya;
Benko) [Ger/Eng/Hung] gtr (8-10th
degr., Musica Per Chitarra; 12
pcs: 3 Fantasies and
Intabulations; intro; urtext ed;
G is F sharp) EMB Z-7793 f.s. (439)

Lautenbuch Von Lyon, Das - The Lyons
Lute Book, 1553
(Homolya; Benko) [Ger/Eng/Hung] gtr
(8-10th degr., "Musica Per
Chitarra", 20 pcs: 4 fantasies
and 16 intabulations; intro;
Urtext ed; g is f sharp) EMB
Z-7031 f.s.   (440)

Ricercari, 3 (Fantasy Nos. 8-10)
(Kovats) gtr (8-9th degr.) SCHOTT
GA-98 f.s.   (441)

BALLARD, ROBERT (ca. 1611)
Ballet De La Reyne Et Courante
(Castet) gtr (3-4th degr.) LEDUC
G-65 f.s. Guitare, No.65
contains: Courante; Premier
Chant; Second Chant; Troisiesme
Chant   (442)

Ballet De M. Le Daufin
(Castet) gtr (3rd degr.) LEDUC G-70
f.s. Guitare, No.70
contains: Premier Chant; Second
Chant; Troisiesme Chant   (443)

Ballets, 3, Extraits Du Premier Livre
*CC7U
(Castet) gtr (2-3rd degr.) LEDUC
G-61 f.s. Guitare, No.61   (444)

Entree-Ballet Des Insencez *CC4U
(Castet) gtr (3rd degr.) LEDUC G-67
f.s. Guitare, No.67   (445)

Pieces, 3
(Castet) gtr (4th degr.) DELRIEU
1327 f.s. Renaissance, No. 1
contains: Allemand; Ballet;
Rocantins, Les   (446)

Trois Branles
(Castet; Gousse) gtr DELRIEU f.s.
Renaissance, Vol. 4
contains: Branle De La Cornemuse;
Branle De Village; Branle Gay (447)

BARBERIS, MELCHIOR DE (ca. 1549)
Pavana E Saltarello
(Pujol) gtr (3rd degr., g is f
sharp) ESCHIG 1061 f.s.   (448)

BARBETTA PADOVANO, JULIO CESARE
(ca. 1540-1603)
Gagliarde, 10
(Muggia) gtr (4-5th degr.) ZANIBON
5324 f.s.   (449)

Pavane, 8
(Muggia) gtr (3-4th degr.) ZANIBON
5322 f.s.   (450)

BARON, ERNST GOTTLIEB (1696-1760)
Drole, Le, In F Major (from Suite In
D Major)
(Behrend) gtr (5th degr.) HEINRICH.
N-1638 f.s.   (451)

BARON, ERNST GOTTLIEB (cont'd.)

Partita in C
"Partita En Do Mayor" (Azpiazu) gtr
(3rd degr.) UNION ESP. 19880 f.s.
(452)
"Partie In C Groot" (Visser) gtr
(3rd degr.) HARMONIA 1267 f.s.
(453)

Suite in D
"Suita En Re" (Azpiazu) gtr (5-6th
degr., Guitarra, No. 6) DELRIEU
1278 f.s.   (454)
"Suite En Re Majeur" (van Eeden)
gtr (5-6th degr.) HARMONIA 1547
f.s.   (455)

BAROQUE MUSIC FOR GUITAR *CC10U
(Allison) gtr NOVELLO 12.0450.05 f.s.
contains works by: Frescobaldi (3);
Lully (2); J.S. Bach (3); Telemann,
Scarlatti and Allison   (456)

BELLMAN, CARL MICHAEL (1740-1795)
Gitarr-Solon *CC14U
(Loven) gtr (1-3rd degr.) AHLINS
841-A19 f.s.   (457)

Melodien Aus Dem Repertoire Von Carl
Michael Bellman
(Birth) gtr (2-3rd degr.) HEINRICH.
N-1189 f.s.
contains: Allegro Ma Non Troppo;
Andante; Andante Sostenuto;
Pastorale; Tempi Di Menuetto;
Tempo Di Menuetto   (458)

Opp, Amaryllis Och Andra Fredmans
Sanger Och Epistlar *CC10U
(Hansson) gtr (2-3rd degr.)
ANDERSONS 693 f.s.   (459)

BESARD, JEAN-BAPTISTE (1567-ca. 1625)
Aux Logettes De Ces Bois
(Pujol) gtr (6th degr.) ESCHIG 1063
f.s.   (460)

Branle (from Thesaurus Harmonicus)
(Tonazzi) gtr (2nd degr.) SCHOTT
GA-408 f.s. contains also: Branle
Gay   (461)

Branle Gay
(Pujol) gtr (4th degr.) ESCHIG 1052
f.s.   (462)

Dances, 8 (from Thesaurus Harmonicus)
(Seiber; Bream) gtr (6-7th degr.)
SCHOTT 10399 f.s.   (463)

Vous Me Juriez, Bergere
(Pujol) gtr (6th degr.) ESCHIG 1062
f.s.   (464)

BIANCHINI, DOMENICO (ca. 1563)
Tant Que Vivrai
(Pujol) gtr (5th degr.) ESCHIG 1069
f.s.   (465)

BLOW, JOHN (1649-1708)
Courante
(Weston) gtr ESSEX f.s.   (466)

Prelude
(Galindo) gtr (7th degr.) UNION
ESP. 20148 f.s. contains also:
Courante; Fugue   (467)

BOHM, GEORG (1661-1733)
Courante
(Klein Haneveld) gtr (4th degr.)
HARMONIA 2046 f.s. contains also:
Rigaudon   (468)

BONPORTI, FRANCESCO ANTONIO (1672-1748)
Adagio Et Gigue
(Ponce) gtr (7th degr., La
Collection L'Astree) OUVRIERS
EO-758 f.s.   (469)

BORRONO DA MILANO, PIETRO PAVOLO
Suite De La Bella Andronica
(Azpiazu, J. de; Azpiazu, L. de)
gtr (6th degr., includes Pavana;
Saltarello I-III) UNION ESP. f.s.
(470)

BOSSINENSIS, FRANCISCUS
Ricercari, 26
(Pujol) gtr ESCHIG 2013 f.s. (471)

BRAYSSING, GREGOIRE
Fantasies, 3 (from LeRoy's Quart
Livre De Tablature De Guiterre
(1553))
(Kennard) gtr (3rd degr.) SCHOTT
10545 f.s.
contains: Fantasy No. 1; Fantasy
No. 5; Fantasy No. 6   (472)

M. Gregoire Brayssing (from LeRoy's
Quart Livre De Tablature De
Guiterre) CC8U
(Bellow) gtr (3-6th degr.) COLOMBO
NY-2396 f.s. Renaissance And
Baroque, Vol. II   (473)

BRESCIANELLO, GIOVANNI ANTONIO
    (ca. 1690-1752)
    Partita No. 6
    (Chiesa) gtr (3rd degr.) ZERBONI
        8213 f.s.   (474)

    Partita No. 7
    (Chiesa) gtr (4th degr.) ZERBONI
        8284 f.s.   (475)

    Partita No. 16
    (Chiesa) gtr (3rd degr.) ZERBONI
        8282 f.s.   (476)

    Pezzi, 2
    gtr (3-4th degr.) BERBEN EB1784
        $1.25
        contains: Adagio; Capriccio (477)

    Suite in E minor
    (Teuchert) gtr (Die Sologitarre)
        SCHMIDT,H 310 f.s.   (478)

BUISSON, DU
    Pieces, 3
    (Castet) gtr (4th degr.) DELRIEU
        1328 f.s. Renaissance, No. 2
        contains: Allemand; Courante;
        Point d'Orgue   (479)

BULMAN, BARUCH (ca. 1600)
    Pavan in D minor
    (Azpiazu) gtr (8th degr.) UNION
        ESP. 20047 f.s.   (480)
    (Caceres) gtr (8th degr.) ESCHIG
        f.s.   (481)
    (Johnson) gtr (8th degr.) ANDERSONS
        AM-674 f.s.   (482)

BUXTEHUDE, DIETRICH (ca. 1637-1707)
    Suite in E minor
    (Bream) gtr (7-8th degr.) FABER
        F-0123 f.s.   (483)

    Suite No. 3
    (Azpiazu) gtr UNION ESP. 21211 f.s.
                                     (484)

BYRD, WILLIAM (1543-1623)
    Cantilena (Theme And 2 Variations)
    "Fortune And Variations" (Carfagna)
        gtr (8th degr.) BERBEN EB1103
        $1.00   (485)

    Fortune (Theme And 4 Variations)
    (Azpiazu, L. de) gtr (8-9th degr.,
        Guitare, No.10) LEDUC G-10 f.s.
                                     (486)

    Pavan in C
    (Burmanje) gtr (3rd degr.) HARMONIA
        2120 f.s.   (487)

    Pavana " The Earle Of Salisbury"
    (Galindo) gtr (7th degr.) UNION
        ESP. 20147 f.s. contains also:
        Galliard   (488)
    (Weston) gtr (7th degr.) ESSEX f.s.
                                     (489)

    Pavane Bray
    (Burmanje) gtr (6th degr.) HARMONIA
        2097 f.s.   (490)

    Two Pieces For Lute
    (Carlin) gtr (4th degr.)
        MUS.SAC.PRO. LR-101 $3.30
        notation: Fr tablature +
        transcription for gtr
        contains: Galliard; Woods So
        Wild, The   (491)

CABANILLES, JUAN BAUTISTA JOSE
    (1644-1712)
    Tiento De Falsas, 6th Tono
    (Azpiazu) gtr (6th degr., Guitarra,
        No. 17) DELRIEU 1324 f.s.   (492)

CABEZON, ANTONIO DE (1510-1566)
    Composizioni Per Chitarra, 3
    (Hinojosa) gtr (6th degr., g is f
        sharp) ZERBONI 6838 $4.75   (493)

    Diferencias Sobre El Canto Del
        Caballero
    (Garcia Velasco) gtr (6th degr.)
        UNION ESP. 20292 f.s.   (494)

    Diferencias Sobre Las Vacas, 6
    (Garcia Velasco) gtr (7th degr.)
        UNION ESP. f.s.   (495)

    Duos 1-3 Et 9 (from Obras De Musica)
    (Pujol) gtr (5th degr.) ESCHIG 2009
        f.s.   (496)

    Duviensela
    (Garcia Velasco) gtr (8th degr.)
        UNION ESP. f.s.   (497)

    Fabordon Del Quarto Tono
    (Pujol) gtr (6th degr.) ESCHIG 1072
        f.s.   (498)

    Pavana Italiana
    (Azpiazu) gtr (D min,7th degr.)
        RICORDI-ARG BA-11867 f.s.   (499)
    (Garcia Velasco) gtr (E min,7th
        degr.) UNION ESP. 20291 f.s.

CABEZON, ANTONIO DE (cont'd.)
                                     (500)
CALVI, CARLO (ca. 1646)
    Carlo Calvi (from Intavolatura Di
        Chitarra E Chitarriglia)
    (Bellow) gtr (2-3rd degr., 11 pcs;
        Renaissance And Baroque, Vol.
        III) COLOMBO NY-2397 f.s.   (501)

    Composizioni, 15 (from Intavolatura
        Di Chitarra)
    (Tonazzi) gtr (2nd degr.) ZERBONI
        7652 $4.75   (502)

CAMPION, FRANCOIS (1680-1748)
    Pieces, 20, De Son Livre De Tablature
        De Guitare
    (Baille) gtr (3-7th degr.) SALABERT
        8496 $10.00   (503)

    Prelude and Fugue
    (Azpiazu) gtr SYMPHON 2197 f.s.
                                     (504)

    Prelude and Fugue in D
    (Azpiazu, L. de) gtr (4th degr.,
        Guitare, No.23) LEDUC G-23 f.s.
                                     (505)

    Sarabande-Gigue
    (Pujol) gtr (3rd degr.) ESCHIG 1059
        f.s.   (506)

    Soiree A Versailles
    (Azpiazu) gtr (3rd degr.) SYMPHON
        347 f.s.   (507)

    Suite in B minor
    (Robert) gtr (3-4th degr., Plein
        Jeu, No.20) HEUGEL PJ-20 f.s.
                                     (508)

    Suite in D
    (de Hilster) gtr (5th degr.)
        HARMONIA 2378 f.s.   (509)

    Suite in D minor
    (Behrend) gtr (5th degr., Die
        Konzertgitarre) SIKORSKI 369
        $3.25   (510)

    Suite No. 2 in D
    (Behrend) gtr (5-6th degr.,
        Gitarre-Bibliothek, No.35) BOTE
        GB-35 f.s.   (511)

CAMPRA, ANDRE (1660-1744)
    Furlana (from L'Europe Galante)
    (Tonazzi) gtr (3rd degr.) SCHOTT
        GA-409 f.s.   (512)

CANTI MEDIOEVALI, 8 °CC8U
    (Pratesi, Minella) gtr (4th degr.)
        BERBEN EB1504 $2.50   (513)

CANZONEN UND TANZE AUS DEM XVI.
    JAHRHUNDERT
    (Scheit) gtr (3rd degr.) UNIVER.
        13071 $2.75
        contains: Canzone; Canzone; Huhner
        G'schrei; Mascherada; Tanz   (514)

CAROSO, FABRIZIO (1526-1600)
    Aria E Danza
    (Tonazzi) gtr (2nd degr.) BERBEN
        EB1090 $1.00   (515)

    Laura Soave
    (Behrend) gtr (3rd degr., Die
        Konzertgitarre; includes:
        Balletto; Gagliarda; Saltarello
        and Balletto) SIKORSKI 688 $2.75
                                     (516)

    Petites Pieces, 8
    (Castet) gtr (2nd degr., Guitare,
        No.43) LEDUC G-43 f.s.   (517)

    Pieces, 4
    (Castet) gtr (3rd degr.) LEDUC G-46
        f.s. Guitare, No.46
        contains: Alta Vittoria; Bassa
        Savella; Bellezze D'Olimpia;
        Forza D'Amore   (518)

    Selva Amorosa
    (Pujol) gtr (3rd degr., g is f
        sharp) ESCHIG 1082 f.s.   (519)

CARPENTIER, [ABBE] JOSEPH
    (fl. ca. 1775)
    Pieces, 4
    (Castet) gtr (6th degr.) DELRIEU
        1416 f.s. Renaissance, No. 5
        contains: Allemande Suisse, L';
        Ballet Hollandais; Comte De
        Provence, Le; Strasbourgeoise,
        La   (520)

    Variations Sur Les "Folies
        d'Espagne", 7
    (Castet) gtr (6th degr.,
        Renaissance, No. 6) DELRIEU 1415
        f.s.   (521)

CARVALHO, JOAO DE SOUSA (1745-1798)
    Toccata
    (Andia) gtr (Bibliotheque De
        Musique Ancienne) TRANSAT. $3.00
                                     (522)

CASTELIONO, ANTONIO
    Intabolatura De Leuto De Diversi
        Autori °CC4OU
    (Smith Brindle) [It/Eng] gtr
        (single staff) fac ed ZERBONI
        7922 f.s. contains lute works by:
        Francesco da Milano and others
                                     (523)

CHAMBONNIERES, JACQUES CHAMPION
    (ca. 1602-1672)
    Canarie
    (Galindo) gtr UNION ESP. 20149 f.s.
        contains also: Gigue; Saraband
                                     (524)

CIMAROSA, DOMENICO (1749-1801)
    Sonata
    (Prol) gtr (6th degr.) PAGANI
        CG-100 f.s.   (525)

    Sonata in D
    (Prol) gtr (6th degr.) PAGANI
        CG-123 f.s.   (526)

    Sonata, MIN 390
    (Artzt) gtr COLUMBIA 193 f.s. (527)

    Sonata No. 5
    (Caceres) gtr (Collection Oscar
        Caceres No. 7) ESCHIG   (528)

    Sonatas, 3
    (Bream) gtr (7th degr.) FABER
        F-0198 f.s.   (529)

    Sonatas, 3
    (Alfonso) gtr (7th degr., Edition
        Nicolas Alfonso, No. 15) SCHOTT-
        FRER 9172 f.s.   (530)

    Sonatas, 3, En Forma De Concierto
        Italiano
    (Azpiazu) gtr (8th degr.) RICORDI-
        ARG BA-11807 f.s.   (531)
    (Azpiazu) gtr (8th degr.) UNION
        ESP. f.s.   (532)

    Sonatas, 6
    (Pujol) gtr (6-7th degr.) ESCHIG
        1097 f.s.
        contains: Sonata No. 3; Sonata
        No. 5; Sonata No. 9; Sonata No.
        14; Sonata No. 19; Sonata No.
        23   (533)

COCQ, FRANCOIS LE
    Suite in A minor
    (van Puijenbroeck) gtr (3rd degr.)
        METROPOLIS EM-4699 $2.00   (534)

CORBETTA, FRANCESCO (FRANCISQUE
    CORBETT) (ca. 1620-1681)
    Allemande Aymee De l'Auteur
    (Leerink) gtr (6th degr.,
        Bibliotheek Van Den Gitarist, No.
        19) BROEKMANS 374 f.s.   (535)

    Allemande, Cherie De Son Altesse Le
        Duc d'York
    (Pujol) gtr (6th degr.) ESCHIG 1018
        f.s.   (536)

    Allemande Du Roy
    (Pujol) gtr (6th degr.) ESCHIG 1019
        f.s.   (537)

    Allemande Et Gigue
    (Azpiazu, L. de; Azpiazu, J. de)
        gtr (6th degr., Guitarra, No. 3)
        DELRIEU 1275 f.s.   (538)

    Allemande Sur La Mort Du Duc De
        Glocester
    (Pujol) gtr (6th degr.) ESCHIG 1020
        f.s.   (539)

    Francesco Corbetta: 16 Compositions
        Selected From "Varii Capricci Per
        La Ghitarra Spagnuola"
    (Bellow) gtr (3-4th degr.,
        Renaissance And Baroque, Vol. 5)
        COLOMBO NY-2399 f.s.   (540)

    Gavotte, Aymee Du Duc De Monmouth
    (Pujol) gtr (6th degr.) ESCHIG 1011
        f.s.   (541)

    Passacaglia
    (Pujol) gtr (6th degr.) ESCHIG 1022
        f.s.   (542)

    Prelude
    (Pujol) gtr (5th degr.) ESCHIG 1008
        f.s.   (543)

    Saraband
    (Pujol) gtr (6th degr.) ESCHIG 1023
        f.s.   (544)

    Suite in A minor
    (Kennard) gtr (5th degr.) RICORDI-
        ENG LD-531 f.s. contains also:

CORBETTA, FRANCESCO (FRANCISQUE
CORBETT) (cont'd.)

Suite in G   (545)

Suite in D (from La Guitarre Royalle,
1671)
(Kennard) gtr (4-5th degr.) SCHOTT
10541 f.s.   (546)

Tombeau De Madame d'Orleans, Le
(Pujol) gtr (7th degr.) ESCHIG 1021
f.s.   (547)

CORELLI, ARCANGELO (1653-1713)
Minuetto
(Lazarde) gtr VOGT 301 f.s.   (548)

Pieces, 6
(Alfonso) gtr (5th degr.) SCHOTT-
FRER 9305 f.s. Edition Nicolas
Alfonso, No. 25
contains: Adagio, MIN 288;
Courante, MIN 289; Largo;
Prelude, MIN 287; Saraband, MIN
281; Saraband, MIN 282   (549)

Sarabande And Minuet
(Sisley) gtr ESSEX f.s.   (550)

Sarabande E Giga
(Rossi) gtr (7-8th degr.) BERBEN
EB2103 f.s.   (551)

Sarabande E Giga
(Azpiazu) gtr SYMPHON 346 f.s.
(552)

Sonata No. 3
(Azpiazu) gtr UNION ESP. 20982 f.s.
(553)

Sonata No. 5
(Azpiazu) gtr UNION ESP. 20983 f.s.
(554)

Sonata No. 8
(Azpiazu) gtr UNION ESP. 20984 f.s.
(555)

CORREA, F.
Chant A l'Immaculee Conception
(Pujol) gtr ESCHIG 2011 f.s.   (556)

COUPERIN, FRANCOIS (LE GRAND)
(1668-1733)
Barricades Mysterieuses, Les
(Diaz) gtr (7th degr.) BROEKMANS
823 f.s.   (557)

Celebre Passacaille En Rondeau,
Huitieme Ordre, Livre 2
(Azpiazu) gtr (7th degr., Guitare,
No.71) LEDUC G-71 $3.00   (558)

Fastes, Les
(Azpiazu) gtr SYMPHON 2138 f.s.
(559)

Pieces De Clavecin
(Peters) gtr (2-4th degr., 32 pcs)
SIKORSKI 563 $6.50   (560)

Sarabanda E Gavotta
(Abloniz) gtr (3-4th degr.) BERBEN
EB-1332 f.s.   (561)

Sixieme Ordre
(Azpiazu) gtr (8th degr.) UNION
ESP. 20483 f.s.   (562)

Song Of The Devil
(Norman) gtr (4th degr.) SCHIRM.G
44819 f.s.   (563)

Sylvains, Les
(Castet) gtr (3rd degr., Guitare,
No.50) LEDUC G-50 $2.25   (564)

Tizenket Darab Gitarra *CC12U
(Vereczkey) gtr (3-5th degr.) EMB
Z-7669 f.s. Musica Per Chitarra
(565)

COUPERIN, LOUIS (ca. 1626-1661)
Chaconne, MIN 238
(Galindo) gtr (5th degr.) UNION
ESP. 20607 f.s.   (566)

Couperins, The (composed with
Couperin, Francois (le Grand))
*CC7U
(Duarte; Siirala) gtr (5-7th degr.)
BERBEN EB1844 $3.25 contains
works by: L. Couperin (2), F.
Couperin (5)   (567)

Passacaglia
(Segovia) gtr (6th degr.) SCHOTT
GA-156 f.s.   (568)

Pieces, 6
(Duarte) gtr (4-5th degr.) NOVELLO
19552 f.s.
contains: Branle De Basque;
Chaconne, MIN 239; Gigue;
Minuet; Piemontoise, La;
Saraband, MIN 240   (569)

Saraband, MIN 241
"Canon" (Galindo) gtr (5th degr.)
UNION ESP. 20606 f.s.   (570)

COUPERIN, LOUIS (cont'd.)

Tombeau Pour M. Blancrocher
(Lorimer) gtr HANSEN-US ML-007 f.s.
(571)

COURANTES, 2
(Castet) gtr (3rd degr.) LEDUC G-42
f.s. Guitare, No.42
contains: Gaultier, Ennemond,
Courante; Heart, Jean, Courante
(572)

CREMA, JOAN MARIA DA
Pass'e Mezzo E Saltarello, A La
Bolognesa
(Azpiazu, L. de) gtr (4th degr.,
Guitare, No.31) LEDUC G-31 f.s.
(573)

Recercar Undecimo Y Recercar
Tredecimo
(Azpiazu) gtr (4-5th degr.)
RICORDI-ARG BA-11866 f.s.   (574)

Ricercari, 5
(Balestra) gtr RICORDI-IT 132109
f.s.   (575)

CUTTING, FRANCIS
Almain, MIN 242
(Dirkx) gtr (5-6th degr.) HARMONIA
1595 f.s. contains also:
Galliard, MIN 244; Greensleeves
(576)

Almain, MIN 249
(Azpiazu, L. de) gtr (6th degr.)
UNION ESP. 20056 f.s.   (577)

Almain Und Jig
(Teuchert) gtr (Die Sologitarre)
SCHMIDT,H 304 f.s.   (578)

Greensleeves
(Azpiazu) gtr (5th degr.) UNION
ESP. 20055 f.s.   (579)
(van Puijenbroeck) gtr (5th degr.,
g is f sharp; capotasto in pos.
III) METROPOLIS EM-4701 f.s.
(580)

Pavan, MIN 245
(Azpiazu) gtr (8th degr.) RICORDI-
ARG BA-11871 f.s.   (581)

Pieces, 2
(Reyne) gtr (5th degr.) LEDUC G-78
f.s. Guitare, No.78
contains: Almain, MIN 246;
Galliard, MIN 247   (582)

Pieces, 5
(Jeffery) gtr (5-6th degr.) OXFORD
36.013 $1.80
contains: Almain, MIN 249;
Cutting's Comfort; Galliard,
MIN 248; Galliard, MIN 250;
Pavane Sans Pair   (583)

Walsingham
(Azpiazu) gtr (8-9th degr., E is D)
UNION ESP. 20045 f.s.   (584)
"Walsingham Variations" (Hopman)
gtr (8-9th degr.) HARMONIA 1880
f.s.   (585)

DANSES, 2
(Castet) gtr (2nd degr.) LEDUC G-34
f.s. Guitare, No.34
contains: Belleville, Courante;
Mesangeau, Rene, Allemand   (586)

DANSES, 4
(Castet) gtr (2-3rd degr.) LEDUC G-44
f.s. Guitare, No.44
contains: Ballet; Ballet; Ballet;
Bransle   (587)

DAQUIN, LOUIS-CLAUDE (1694-1772)
Coucou, Le: Rondo
(Paleologo) gtr (7th degr.)
HEINRICH. N-1539 f.s.   (588)

Guitarra, La
(Behrend) gtr (6th degr., Gitarre-
Bibliothek, No.3; also published
in European Masters For The
Guitar) BOTE GB-3 f.s.   (589)

DAZA, ESTEBAN (? - ?)
Fantasias, 4, De Pasos Largos Para
Desenvolver Las Manos
(Hinojosa) gtr (6-7th degr., g is f
sharp; Bibliotheque De Musique
Ancienne; intro. in Fr, Eng, Ger,
and Span) TRANSAT. 1204 $4.20
(590)

Fantasias A Tres, 4
(Hinojosa) gtr (4-5th degr., g is f
sharp; Bibliotheque De Musique
Ancienne) TRANSAT. 1279 $4.50
(591)

Fantasy
(Pujol) gtr (5th degr., g is f
sharp) ESCHIG 1067 f.s.   (592)

DEROSIER, NICOLAS
Chaconnes, 12
(Leerink) gtr (3rd degr.,
Bibliotheek Van Den Gitarist, No.
5) BROEKMANS 378 f.s.   (593)

DES PREZ, JOSQUIN (ca. 1440-1521)
Sanctus and Benedictus (from Missa
Pange Lingua)
(Azpiazu) gtr UNION ESP. 21308 f.s.
(594)

DOWLAND, JOHN (1562-1626)
Air
"As I Went To Walsingham" (Sensier)
gtr ESSEX f.s.   (595)

Air And Galliard
(Scheit) gtr (4-5th degr.) UNIVER.
12402 $2.75
contains: As I Went To
Walsingham; Queen Elizabeth Her
Galliard, The   (596)

Beste Aus Dem Lautenwerk, Das
(Behrend) gtr (Die Grossen Meister
Der Laute Und Gitarre, Vol. 1)
ZIMMER. 2090 f.s.   (597)

Earl Of Derby His Galliard, The
(Goor) gtr (7th degr., g is f
sharp; capotasto in pos. III)
METROPOLIS EM-4726 $1.50   (598)

Earl Of Essex His Galliard, The
(Goor) gtr (8th degr., g is f
sharp; capotasto in pos. III)
METROPOLIS EM-4727 $1.50   (599)
(Meunier) gtr (8th degr., g is f
sharp) BREITKOPF-W 6722   (600)

Fancy, A (Fantasy) (from Varietie Of
Lute-lessons, Fantasie 7, In G)
(Cristoforetti) gtr (9th degr.,
transcr. in E major) ZERBONI 6981
$3.50   (601)
(Hinojosa) gtr (9th degr., transcr
in E major; g is f sharp) SCHOTT
GA-229 f.s.   (602)
(Sainz de la Maza) gtr (9th degr.,
transcr in E major; g is f sharp)
UNION ESP. 20358 f.s.   (603)
(Sierra) gtr (9th degr., transcr in
E major; g is f sharp) CHOUDENS
20.674 f.s.   (604)
(ten Boske) gtr (9th degr., transcr
in E major; g is f sharp)
HARMONIA 2666 f.s.   (605)
(van Puijenbroeck) gtr (9th degr.,
transcr in E major; g is f sharp;
capotasto in pos. III) METROPOLIS
EM-4706 $2.00   (606)

3 Fantasias *CC3U
(Lorimer) gtr HANSEN-US ML-008 f.s.
(607)

Forlorn Hope Fancy
(Azpiazu) gtr (9th degr.) SYMPHON
420 f.s.   (608)
(Azpiazu) gtr (9th degr.) UNION
ESP. 21202 f.s.   (609)

Gaillarde Et Allemande
(Caceres) gtr ESCHIG f.s.
Collection Oscar Caceres, No. 4
contains: Captain Digorie Piper's
Galliard; Lady Hunsdon's Puffe
(610)

Gaillardes, 2
(Castet) gtr (5th degr.) LEDUC G-37
$2.25 Guitare, No.37
contains: Lady Rich Her Galliard,
The; Queen Elizabeth Her
Galliard, The   (611)

Galliard On A Galliard Of Daniel
Bacheler, A
"Galliard Of Daniel Batchelar"
(Azpiazu) gtr (7th degr.) UNION
ESP. 20044 f.s.   (612)
"Gaillarde Sur Un Theme De Daniel
Batchelar" (Castet) gtr (7th
degr., Guitare, No.38) LEDUC G-38
$2.25   (613)

Galliards, 2
(Scheit) gtr (3-4th degr.) UNIVER.
12247 $2.75
contains: Captain Digorie Piper's
Galliard; King Of Denmark His
Galliard, The   (614)

Galliards, 3
(van Gemert; Hartog) gtr (7-8th
degr.) HARMONIA 2728 f.s. g is f
sharp
contains
Earl Of Derby His
Galliard, The; Earl Of Essex
His Galliard, The; Lady Rich
Her Galliard, The   (615)

King Of Denmark His Galliard, The
"Batell Galliard" (Azpiazu) gtr (8-
9th degr.) SYMPHON 2143 f.s.
(616)
"Batell Galliard" (Castet) gtr (8-
9th degr., Guitarra, No. 15)

DOWLAND, JOHN (cont'd.)

DELRIEU 1322 f.s.   (617)
(van Gogh) gtr (8-9th degr.)
TEESELING VT-23 f.s.   (618)
(van Puijenbroeck) gtr (8-9th
degr., g is f sharp; capotasto in
pos. III) METROPOLIS EM-4700
$1.50   (619)

Lachrimae
"Lachrimae Antiquae, Pavane"
(Apiazu) gtr (8th degr.) RICORDI-
ARG BA-11868 f.s.   (620)
"Pavane Lachrimae" (Castet) gtr
(8th degr., Guitare, No.62) LEDUC
G-62 $2.25   (621)

Lachrimae Pavan Und Fantasie
(Scheit) gtr (8-9th degr., g is f
sharp) UNIVER. 14480 f.s.   (622)

Lady Hunsdon's Puffe
(Azpiazu) gtr (5th degr.) SYMPHON
2144 f.s.   (623)
(Castet) gtr (5th degr., Guitare,
No.66) LEDUC G-66 $2.25 contains
also: My Lord Willoughby's
Welcome Home   (624)
(Sensier) gtr (5th degr.) ESSEX
f.s.   (625)

Lady Rich Her Galliard, The
(Azpiazu) gtr (7th degr.) UNION
ESP. 20041 f.s.   (626)

Leichte Stucke, 4
(Scheit) gtr (2-3rd degr.) UNIVER.
13972 $2.75   (627)

Melancholy Galliard
(Goor) gtr (6th degr., g is f
sharp; capotasto in pos. III)
METROPOLIS EM-4725 f.s.   (628)
(ten Boske) gtr (6th degr., g is f
sharp) HARMONIA 2556 f.s.   (629)

Melancoly Galliard
(Scheit) gtr (5-6th degr.) UNIVER.
12472 $2.75 contains also: Lady
Hunsdon's Puffe   (630)

Mrs. Vaux's Jig
"Air And Gigue" (Scheit) gtr (3rd
degr.) UNIVER. 12669 $2.75   (631)

Pieces, 2
(Azpiazu) gtr (6-7th degr.) DELRIEU
1285 f.s. Guitarra, No. 13
contains: Dowland's Adew;
Melancholy Galliard   (632)

Pieces, 2
gtr DELRIEU 1280 f.s. Guitarra, No.
8
contains: Mr. Henry Noel His
Galliard; Sir Henry Humpton's
Funeral   (633)

Pieces, 2
gtr DELRIEU 1281 f.s. Guitarra, No.
9
contains: Mrs. Vaux's Jig; Queen
Elizabeth Her Galliard, The
(634)

Pieces, 2
(Artzt) gtr COLUMBIA 191 $1.75
contains: Can She Excuse;
Lachrimae   (635)

Pieces, 3
gtr DELRIEU 1279 f.s. Guitarra, No.
7
contains: My Lord Chamberlain His
Galliard; Piece Without A
Title, A, "Unnamed Piece, An";
Shoemaker's Wife, The   (636)

Pieces, 6
(Duarte) gtr (7-9th degr.) BERBEN
EB2015 f.s. g is f sharp
contains: Come Away; Dr. Case's
Pavan; Fancy, A; Fortune; Lady
Laiton's Almain   (637)

Pieces, 7
(Poulton) gtr (2-4th degr.) SCHOTT
GA-211 f.s.   (638)

Pieces, 8, Vol. 1
(Jeffery) gtr OXFORD 36.019 $2.70
contains: Almain, MIN 254; Dr.
Case's Pavan; Fantasy, MIN 253;
Queen Elizabeth Her Galliard,
The   (639)

Pieces, 8, Vol. 2
(Jeffery) gtr OXFORD 36.020 $1.85
contains: Fantasy, MIN 255;
Fortune, "Fortune My Foe,
Galliard"; Lachrimae; Mignarda
(640)

Piper's Pavan (from Delitiae Musicae
Of Joachim van den Hove)
"Master Piper's Pavan" (Apiazu) gtr
UNION ESP. 21212 f.s.   (641)

DOWLAND, JOHN (cont'd.)

"Pavana Pijper" (van Puijenbroeck)
gtr (4th degr., g is f sharp;
capotasto in pos. III) METROPOLIS
EM-4704 f.s.   (642)

Queen Elizabeth Her Galliard, The
(Sensier) gtr (5th degr.) ESSEX
(643)
(Teuchert) gtr (5th degr., Die
Sologitarre) SCHMIDT,H 303   (644)
(van Puijenbroeck) gtr (5th degr.,
g is f sharp; capotasto in pos.
III) METROPOLIS EM-4703 $1.50
(645)

Solowerke, Vol. 1 *CC17U
(Scheit) gtr (4-5th degr.) UNIVER.
16699 f.s.   (646)

Two Pieces
gtr COLUMBIA 191 f.s.
contains: Can She Excuse My
Wrongs; Lachrimae Pavin   (647)

DOWLAND, ROBERT (1591-1641)
Courantes, 6 (from Varietie Of Lute-
Lessons)
(van Schagen) gtr (4th degr.)
HARMONIA 1298 f.s.   (648)

Five Corantoes
(ten Boske) gtr TEESELING VT-164
f.s.   (649)

Varietie Of Lute-Lessons, Vol. 1:
Corantos *CC7U
(Duarte; Poulton) gtr BERBEN EB1591
$2.50 g is f sharp, E is D and E
is E   (650)

Varietie Of Lute-Lessons, Vol. 2:
Almaines *CC7U
(Duarte; Poulton) gtr BERBEN EB1592
$4.00 g is f sharp, E is D and E
is E   (651)

Varietie Of Lute-Lessons, Vol. 3:
Voltes *CC7U
(Duarte; Poulton) gtr BERBEN EB1693
$2.50 g is f sharp, E is D and E
is E   (652)

Varietie Of Lute-Lessons, Vol. 4:
Fantasias *CC7U
(Duarte; Poulton) gtr BERBEN EB1820
$5.25 g is f sharp, E is D and E
is E   (653)

Varietie Of Lute-Lessons, Vol. 5:
Galliards *CC7U
(Duarte; Poulton) gtr BERBEN EB1935
$4.00 g is f sharp, E is D and E
is E   (654)

Varietie Of Lute-Lessons, Vol. 6:
Pavins *CC7U
(Duarte; Poulton) gtr BERBEN EB2070
f.s. g is f sharp, E is D and E
is E   (655)

DUNCOMBE, W.
Sonatina
(Behrend) gtr (3rd degr.) HEINRICH.
N-1641 f.s.   (656)

DUOS ANCIENS, 5 *CC5U
(Pujol) gtr ESCHIG 2010 f.s.   (657)

ENCINA, JUAN DEL (1468-1529)
Ay Triste Que Vengo, Villancico
Pastoril
(Garci Velasco) gtr UNION ESP.
21791 f.s.   (658)

5 Piezas
(Garcia Velasco) gtr UNION ESP.
21934 f.s.
contains: A Tal Perdida Tan
Triste; Levanta, Pascual; Que
Es De Ti, Desconsolado;
Romerico, Tu Que Viennes;
Triste Espana Sin Ventura   (659)

EUROPAISCHE GITARREN- UND LAUTENMUSIK,
VOL. 1 *It,16-18th cent
"Italienische Meister" (Teuchert) gtr
SYMPHON 2222 f.s.   (660)

EUROPAISCHE GITARREN- UND LAUTENMUSIK,
VOL. 2 *Ger,16-18th cent
"Deutsche Meister" (Teuchert) gtr
SYMPHON 2223 f.s.   (661)

EUROPAISCHE GITARREN- UND LAUTENMUSIK,
VOL. 3 *Eng,16-18th cent
"Englische Meister" (Teuchert) gtr
SYMPHON 2224 f.s.   (662)

EUROPAISCHE GITARREN- UND LAUTENMUSIK,
VOL. 4 *Fr,16-18th cent
"Franzosische Meister" (Teuchert) gtr
SYMPHON 2225 f.s.   (663)

EUROPAISCHE GITARREN- UND LAUTENMUSIK,
VOL. 5 *Span,16-18th cent
"Spanische Meister" (Teuchert) gtr
SYMPHON 2230 f.s.   (664)

EUROPAISCHE GITARREN- UND LAUTENMUSIK,
VOL. 6 *Dutch,16-18th cent
"Hollandische Meister" (Teuchert) gtr
SYMPHON 2231 f.s.   (665)

EUROPAISCHE GITARREN- UND LAUTENMUSIK,
VOL. 7 *Polish,16-18th cent
"Polnische Meister" (Teuchert) gtr
SYMPHON 2232 f.s.   (666)

FALCKENHAGEN, ADAM (1697-1761)
Concerto
(Azpiazu, J. de; Azpiazu, L. de)
gtr (7th degr., orig. pour le
luth en si bemol) UNION ESP.
20981 f.s.   (667)

Suite in A
(Behrend) gtr ESCHIG f.s.   (668)

FANTASY NO. 4 (from Libro De Venegas De
Henestrosa)
(Tarrago) gtr (3-4th degr.) UNION
ESP. 20573 f.s.   (669)

FARNABY, GILES (ca. 1560-1640)
Pieces, 5 (from Fitzwilliam Virginal
Book)
(Duarte) gtr (5th degr.) SCHOTT
GA-220 f.s.   (670)

FERRABOSCO, ALFONSO (I) (1543-1588)
Pavan, MIN 415
(Reyne) gtr (6th degr., Guitare,
No. 90) LEDUC G-90 f.s. contains
also: Dowland, John, Earl Of
Essex Galliard, The   (671)

Pavana, 6 (from Varietie Of Lute-
Lessons)
(Azpiazu, L. de) gtr (8th degr.)
UNION ESP. 21191 f.s.   (672)

FLANDRISCHES GITARRENBUCH, VOL. 1:
FANTASIES AND SONGS *CC31U
(Giesbert) gtr (3-4th degr.) SCHOTT
GA-230 f.s.   (673)

FLANDRISCHES GITARRENBUCH, VOL. 2:
DANCES *CC53U
(Giesbert) gtr (3-4th degr.) SCHOTT
GA-236 f.s.   (674)

FRANCESCO DA MILANO
(ca. 1497?-ca. 1573?)
Fantasien, 3
(Behrend) gtr (3-4th degr.) NOETZEL
N-3172 f.s.   (675)

Fantasy
(Azpiazu, L. de) gtr (4th degr.,
Guitare, No.12) LEDUC G-12 f.s.
(676)

Pavan
"Disperata, La" (Balestra) gtr (6-
7th degr., g is f sharp) BERBEN
EB1297 f.s.   (677)

Pescatore Che Va Cantando
(Pujol) gtr (3rd degr., g is f
sharp) ESCHIG 1056 f.s.   (678)

FRANCISQUE, ANTOINE (ca. 1570-1605)
Pavane Espagnole
(Pujol) gtr ESCHIG 2012 f.s.   (679)

FRESCOBALDI, GIROLAMO (1583-1643)
Aria Con [4] Variazioni, Detta "La
Frescobalda"
"Frescobalda, La: Aria Con
Variazioni" (Azpiazu) gtr (8th
degr.) SYMPHON 2074 f.s.   (680)
"Frescobalda, La: Aria Con
Variazioni" (Carfagna) gtr (8th
degr., E minor) BERBEN EB2031
f.s.   (681)
"Aria Detta La Frescobalda"
(Castet) gtr (E min,8th degr.,
Guitare, No. 68) LEDUC G-68 $2.25
(682)
"Aria Detta La Frescobalda"
(Scheit) gtr (8th degr.) UNIVER.
16694 f.s.   (683)
"Aria Con [3] Variazioni, Detta "La
Frescobalda"" (Segovia) gtr (E
min,8th degr.) SCHOTT GA-157 f.s.
(684)

Corrente Quattro, Vol. 1
(Reyne) gtr (6-7th degr., Guitare,
No.40) LEDUC G-40 $2.25   (685)

Corrente Quattro, Vol. 2
(Reyne) gtr (6-7th degr., Guitare,
No.41) LEDUC G-41 $2.25   (686)

Galliard, MIN 256
(Galindo) gtr (6-8th degr.) UNION
ESP. 20146 f.s. contains also:
Courante; Aria Con [4]
Variazioni, Detta "La
Frescobalda", "Frescobalda, La,

FRESCOBALDI, GIROLAMO (cont'd.)

[Aria Con (4) Variazioni], A
Minor"; Corrente E Canzona   (687)

Morceaux, 5
(Segovia) gtr (6-8th degr.) SCHOTT
GA-158 f.s.
contains: Corrente, MIN 74;
Corrente, MIN 75; Corrente, MIN
76; Galliard, MIN 257;
Passacaglia   (688)

Toccata Per Spinettina Over Liuto
(Chiesa) gtr (7th degr.) ZERBONI
6763 $3.50   (689)

FROBERGER, JOHANN JAKOB (1616-1667)
Suite in A minor
(Bream) gtr (7-8th degr.) FABER
F-0227 f.s.   (690)

Tombeau Pour M. Blancrocher
(Lorimer) gtr HANSEN-US ML-009 f.s.
(691)

FUENLLANA, MIGUEL DE (fl. ca. 1560)
Contrepoints, 2, Sur Le Villancico
"Si Amore Me Han De Matar"
(Pujol) gtr (setting by Mateo
Flecha) ESCHIG 2004 f.s.   (692)

Deuxieme Fantaisie
(Pujol) gtr (3rd degr., g is f
sharp) ESCHIG 1079 f.s.   (693)

Fantasia De Redobles
(Clinton) gtr (4th degr., g is f
sharp) ESSEX f.s.   (694)

Fantasia I
(Pujol) gtr (4th degr., g is f
sharp) ESCHIG 1014 f.s.   (695)

Fantasia II
(Pujol) gtr (4th degr., g is f
sharp) ESCHIG 1015 f.s.   (696)

Fantasia III
(Pujol) gtr (6th degr., g is f
sharp) ESCHIG 1016 f.s.   (697)

Fantasia [IV]
(Tarrago) gtr (4th degr.) UNION
ESP. 19285 f.s.   (698)

Fantasy in A
(Azpiazu, L. de) gtr (4th degr.)
UNION ESP. 20660 f.s.   (699)

Fantasy in E
(Azpiazu, L. de) gtr (5th degr.)
UNION ESP. 20659 f.s.   (700)

Quatrieme Fantaisie
(Pujol) gtr (4th degr., g is f-
sharp) ESCHIG 1081 f.s.   (701)

Tiento
(Pujol) gtr (5th degr.) ESCHIG 1009
f.s.   (702)
"Tiento Del Primer Tono" (Usillos)
gtr (5th degr.) UNION ESP. f.s.
(703)

Tientos, 8: Orphenica Lyra
(Azpiazu, L. de) gtr (3-4th degr.)
UNION ESP. 20654 f.s.   (704)

Troisieme Fantaisie
(Pujol) gtr (3rd degr., g is f
sharp) ESCHIG 1080 f.s.   (705)

GAGLIARDE, 2
(Cavazzoli) gtr (4th degr.) BERBEN
EB1778 $1.25
contains: Garsi da Parma, Santino,
Galliard, MIN 309; Rore, Cipriano
de, Galliard, MIN 310   (706)

GAILLARDES, 2
(Behrend) gtr (5th degr.) HEINRICH.
N-1532 f.s.
contains: Cutting, Francis,
Galliard, MIN 251; Dowland, John,
Galliard, MIN 252   (707)

GALILEI, MICHEL ANGELO
Corrente Und Saltarello
(Teuchert) gtr (Die Sologitarre)
SCHMIDT,H 301 f.s.   (708)

Primo Libro D'Intavolatura Di Liuto,
Il (1620) *CC52U
(Chiesa, Ruggero) [Lat/Eng/Fr/Ger]
gtr ZERBONI f.s. contains pcs for
10 course lute in e; notation in
treble clef   (709)

GALILEI, VINCENZO (ca. 1520-1591)
Gagliarde, 2
gtr (4-5th degr.) BERBEN EB1774
$1.00   (710)

Passo Mezzo In Discant Y Saltarello
(Chilesotti; Sainz de la Maza) gtr
UNION ESP. 20770 f.s.   (711)

GALILEI, VINCENZO (cont'd.)

Pieces, 10
(Azpiazu) gtr (6-7th degr., Easy
Music Vol.7) SYMPHON 2091 f.s.
(712)
Saltarello, MIN 308
(Angel) gtr (5-6th degr.) UNION
ESP. 19109 f.s.   (713)
(Azpiazu) gtr (5-6th degr., 2
versions) SYMPHON 441 f.s.   (714)
(Savio) gtr (5-6th degr.) RICORDI-
BR BR-2909 f.s.   (715)
"Gagliarda" (Terzi) gtr (5-6th
degr., includes: Moderato)
RICORDI-IT 129283 f.s.   (716)

GARSI DA PARMA, SANTINO (1542-1603)
Aria Del Granduca
(Gangi) gtr (4th degr.) BERBEN
EB1166 $1.00 contains also:
Mutia, La   (717)

Pezzi, 3
(Tagliavini) gtr (5th degr.) BERBEN
EB1914 $1.00
contains: Aria Del Granduca;
Balletto; Ne Mente Per La Gola,
La   (718)

GAULTIER, DENIS (GAULTHIER)
(ca. 1603-1672)
Lautensuiten; 4 Suites
(Stingl) gtr (7-8th degr.)
HOFMEISTER-W FH-3001 f.s.   (719)

GHIZEGHEM, HAYNE VAN (ca. 1550- ?)
Amors, Amors, Trop Me Fiers De Tes
Dars
(Reyne) gtr (Guitare, No. 91) LEDUC
G-91 f.s.   (720)

GLUCK, CHRISTOPH WILLIBALD, RITTER VON
(1714-1787)
Ballet
(Segovia) gtr (also published in:
Andres Segovia Album) COLUMBIA
125 f.s.   (721)

J'ai Perdu Mon Euridice
(Weston) gtr ESSEX f.s.   (722)

GORZANIS, GIACOMO (ca. 1525-ca. 1578)
Balletto
(Behrend) gtr (5th degr., Gitarre-
Bibliothek, No.62) BOTE GB-62
f.s.   (723)

Musiche Scelte Dalle Intavolature Per
Liuto
"Musik Aus Alten Lautenbuchern"
(Tonazzi) gtr (4-7th degr., 16
pcs) HEINRICH. PE-6079 f.s. (724)

Napolitane, 15
"Neapolitanische Lieder Aus Dem 16.
Jahrhundert" (Tonazzi) [It] gtr
solo, or solo voice or 5 rec and
gtr (4th degr., orig for solo
voice and lute) sc HEINRICH.
PE-6080 f.s.   (725)

GRANATA, GIOVANNI BATTISTA
(fl. ca. 1674)
Gigue
(Pujol) gtr (4th degr.) ESCHIG 1036
f.s.   (726)

Giovanni Battista Granata: 11
Compositions (from Souavi
Concenti Di Sonate Musicali
(1659), Nuovi Souavi Concenti Di
Sonate Musicali (1684))
(Bellow) gtr (4-6th degr.,
Renaissance And Baroque, Vol. 6)
COLOMBO NY-2400 f.s.   (727)

Toccata
(Balestra) gtr (6-7th degr.) BERBEN
EB1298 $1.00   (728)

GRENERIN, HENRY
Suite No. 4 in C (from Livre De
Guitarre, Paris, 1680)
(Libbert; Schaller) gtr (5th degr.,
Das Gitarrenwerk, Series A No.
14) PREISSLER A 14 f.s. contains
also: Suite No. 6 in C minor
(Schaller)   (729)

GUERAU, FRANCISCO (fl. ca. 1694)
Canarios
(Azpiazu, L. de) gtr (6th degr.)
UNION ESP. 20591 f.s.   (730)
(Pujol) gtr (6th degr.) ESCHIG 1031
f.s.   (731)

Canarios, Danza Del Siglo XVII
(Tarrago) gtr (4th degr.) UNION
ESP. 19693 f.s.   (732)

Espanoleta
(Azpiazu, L. de) gtr (7th degr.)
UNION ESP. 20592 f.s.   (733)
(Pujol) gtr (7th degr.) ESCHIG 1027
f.s.   (734)

GUERAU, FRANCISCO (cont'd.)

Folias
(Azpiazu, L. de) gtr (6th degr.)
UNION ESP. 20593 f.s.   (735)
(Pujol) gtr (6th degr.) ESCHIG 1030
f.s.   (736)

Francisco Guerau: 5 Compositions
(from Poema Harmonico Compuesto
De Varias Cifras, Por El Temple
De La Guitarra Espanola (1694))
(Bellow) gtr (6-7th degr.) COLOMBO
NY-2403 f.s. Renaissance And
Baroque, Vol. 9
contains: Canario; Marizapalos;
Pasacalles; Sacaras; Villano
(737)

Gallardas
(Azpiazu, L. de) gtr (6th degr.)
UNION ESP. 20594 f.s.   (738)
(Pujol) gtr (6th degr.) ESCHIG 1032
f.s.   (739)

Jacaras
(Azpiazu, L. de) gtr (7th degr.)
UNION ESP. 20595 f.s.   (740)
(Pujol) gtr (7th degr.) ESCHIG 1028
f.s.   (741)

Jacaras De La Costa
(Azpiazu, L. de) gtr (7th degr.)
UNION ESP. 20596 f.s.   (742)

Marionas
(Azpiazu, L. de) gtr (6th degr.)
UNION ESP. 20597 f.s.   (743)

Marizapalos
(Azpiazu, L. de) gtr (7th degr.)
UNION ESP. 20598 f.s.   (744)
(Pujol) gtr (7th degr.) ESCHIG 1029
f.s.   (745)

Paradetas, Danza Del Siglo XVII
(Tarrago) gtr (3rd degr.) UNION
ESP. 19700 f.s.   (746)

Pavanas
(Azpiazu, L. de) gtr (6th degr.)
UNION ESP. 20599 f.s.   (747)
(Pujol) gtr (6th degr.) ESCHIG 1033
f.s.   (748)

Villano
(Azpiazu, L. de) gtr (6-7th degr.)
UNION ESP. 20600 f.s.   (749)
(Ibanez) gtr (6-7th degr.,
Collection L'Heure De La Guitare
Classique) CHOUDENS 20.524 f.s.
(750)
(Pujol) gtr (6-7th degr.) ESCHIG
1026 f.s.   (751)

HAGEN, JOACHIM BERNHARD (fl. ca. 1759)
Sonata in B minor
(van Puijenbroeck) gtr (e' is d', g
is f sharp; capotasto in pos.
III) METROPOLIS EM-14003 $2.50
(752)

HANDEL, GEORGE FRIDERIC (1685-1759)
Air (from Suite No. 10)
(Segovia) gtr (also published in:
Transcripciones Para Guitarra,
No. 1) UNION ESP. 18031 f.s.
(753)
(Weston) gtr (4th degr.) ESSEX f.s.
(754)

Allemand
(Casuscelli) gtr (7th degr.)
RICORDI-ARG BA-10819 f.s.   (755)

Aria (from Ottone)
(Abloniz) gtr (4th degr.) RICORDI-
IT RM-129653 f.s.   (756)

Aylesforder Stucke, 8
(Segovia) gtr (6-7th degr.) SCHOTT
GA-148 f.s.   (757)

Celebre Allegro
(Azpiazu) gtr UNION ESP. 21310 f.s.
(758)

Celebre Largo
(Zuccheri) gtr (5th degr.) BERBEN
EB2057 f.s.   (759)

Chaconne
(Martinez Zarate) gtr (7th degr.)
RICORDI-ARG BA-12454 f.s.   (760)

Chorale, MIN 258
(Pick) gtr (4th degr.) FORSTER f.s.
(761)

Chorale, MIN 259
(Tarrega, Fr.) gtr (4th degr.)
RICORDI-ARG BA-7925 f.s. contains
also: Tarrega, Francisco,
Prelude, TI i- 17, in E,
"Lagrima" (Lara, Roberto)   (762)

Coral Y Minueto
gtr FORTEA 242 f.s.   (763)

HANDEL, GEORGE FRIDERIC (cont'd.)

Fughetta
  (Norman) gtr (4th degr.) SCHIRM.G
  44821 f.s.   (764)

Gavotte
  (Anido) gtr (6th degr.) RICORDI-ARG
  BA-11929 f.s.   (765)

Gavotte, MIN 357 (from Ottone)
  (Weston) gtr ESSEX f.s.   (766)

Gavotte, MIN 358
  (Sensier) gtr ESSEX f.s.   (767)

Gavotte Variee (from Suite XIV)
  (Weston) gtr ESSEX f.s.   (768)

Handel-Buch, Das *CC46U
  (Schwarz-Reiflingen) gtr SIKORSKI
  374 $6.00   (769)

Harmonious Blacksmith, The (Air With
  Variations)
  "Herrero Armonioso, El: Aria Con
  [5] Variaciones" (Casuscelli) gtr
  (9th degr.) RICORDI-ARG BA-10338
  f.s.   (770)

Largo (from Xerxes)
  (Garcia Velasco) gtr UNION ESP.
  20290 f.s.   (771)

Largo, MIN 366
  (Weston) gtr ESSEX f.s.   (772)

March, MIN 368 (from Scipio)
  (Weston) gtr ESSEX f.s.   (773)

Menuetto And Variation (from Suite X)
  (Weston) gtr ESSEX f.s.   (774)

Minuet (from Suite XIV En Sol)
  (Azpiazu, L. de) gtr (6th degr.,
  Guitare, No.22) LEDUC G-22 $2.25
                                      (775)

Minuet, MIN 379 (from Berenice)
  (Weston) gtr ESSEX f.s.   (776)

Minuet, MIN 380 (from Sept Pieces)
  (Weston) gtr ESSEX f.s.   (777)

Minuet, MIN 398
  (Tarrega) gtr UNION ESP. 19031 f.s.
                                      (778)

Passacaglia, MIN 1
  (Azpiazu) gtr (8th degr.) SYMPHON
  84 f.s.   (779)

Passacaglia, MIN 260
  (Abloniz) gtr (6th degr.) BERBEN
  EB1324 $1.00   (780)

Prelude and Fugue
  (Azpiazu, L. de) gtr (8-9th degr.,
  Guitare, No.5) LEDUC G-5 $2.25
                                      (781)

Saraband, MIN 1
  (Behrend) gtr ZIMMER. f.s.   (782)

Saraband, MIN 2
  (Weston) gtr (4th degr.) ESSEX f.s.
                                      (783)

Saraband, MIN 3 (from Suite XI)
  "Sarabanda Con Variazioni"
  (Abloniz) gtr (5th degr.)
  RICORDI-IT 129654 f.s.   (784)
  (Behrend) gtr (5th degr.) ZIMMER.
  66 f.s.   (785)
  "Sarabande With Variations" (Bream)
  gtr (5th degr.) ESSEX f.s.   (786)
  (Domeniconi) gtr (5th degr.) BERBEN
  EB1159 $1.00   (787)
  (Lagoya) gtr (5th degr.) RICORDI-FR
  R-1605 f.s.   (788)
  "Zarabanda" (Pomilio) gtr (5th
  degr.) RICORDI-ARG BA-10035 f.s.
                                      (789)

Saraband, MIN 337
  gtr FORTEA 83 f.s.   (790)

Sarabande Et Gavotte
  (Azpiazu) gtr (6-7th degr.,
  Guitarra, No. 4) DELRIEU 1276
  f.s.   (791)

Skladeb, 5
  (Knobloch) gtr (4-5th degr.) CZECH
  H-4185 f.s. Kytarova Sola, No. 20
  contains: Impertinence; Minuet,
  MIN 5; Passepied; Prelude;
  Saraband, MIN 6   (792)

Time Pieces (composed with Haydn,
  [Franz] Joseph) *CC11L
  (Lawrence) gtr (3-5th degr.)
  FENTONE F-121 $4.95 works for
  musical clocks   (793)

Water Music Air
  (Weston) gtr ESSEX f.s.   (794)

HASSE, JOHANN ADOLPH (1699-1783)
  March, MIN 7 (from Artemesia)
  (Leerink) [Ger] gtr (3rd degr.,
  Bibliotheek Van Den Gitarist, No.
  65) sc BROEKMANS 373 f.s.
  contains also: Beyer, Johann
  Christian, Vergnugen, Das
  (Minuet, MIN 8) (solo voice,gtr)
                                      (795)

HASSLER, HANS LEO (1564-1612)
  Chanson
  (Castel) gtr (8th degr., Guitare,
  No.45) LEDUC G-45 f.s.   (796)

HECKEL, WOLF
  Mille Regres
  (Azpiazu) gtr UNION ESP. 21210 f.s.
                                      (797)

HEROLD, JOHANN THEODOR (1660-1720)
  Harmonia Quadripartita: Partita
  Seconda
  (Zanoskar) gtr (3-4th degr., 12
  pcs.) SCHOTT GA-100 f.s.   (798)

HINTERLEITHNER, FERDINAND IGNAZ
  (1659-1710)
  Partita in A
  (Azpiazu) gtr (5-6th degr.) UNION
  ESP. 19876 f.s.   (799)

HOLBORNE, ANTONY (? -1602)
  Larmes Des Muses Et Gaillarde, Les
  (Castel) gtr (6th degr., Guitarra,
  No. 20) DELRIEU 1413 f.s.   (800)

  Lute Pieces, 6
  (Duarte) gtr (4th degr.) BERBEN
  EB1725 $3.00 g is f sharp
  contains: Countess Of Pembroke's
  Paradise (Pavan); Fantasy, MIN
  261; Hart's Ease (Almain);
  Heigh Ho Holiday (Galliard);
  Piece Without Name; Playfellow
  (Or Wanton)   (801)

  Pavan And Galliard
  (Kadis) gtr (3rd degr.)
  MUS.SAC.PRO. LR-102 $2.40
  notation: Fr tablature +
  transcription for gtr
  contains: Mr. Southcote's
  Galliard; Pavan   (802)

  Pieces, 5
  (Jeffery) gtr (5th degr.) OXFORD
  36.010 $1.85
  contains: As It Fell On A Holy
  Eve (Courante); Countess Of
  Pembroke's Paradise, The
  (Pavan); Galliard, MIN 9; Heigh
  Ho Holiday (Courante); Night
  Watch, The (Almain)   (803)

  Praludium Und Fantasie
  (Teuchert) gtr (Die Sologitarre)
  SCHMIDT,H 314 f.s.   (804)

HOVE, JOACHIM VAN DEN (1567-1620)
  Chanson Flameng
  (van Puijenbroeck) gtr (3-4th
  degr., g is f sharp; capotasto in
  pos. III) METROPOLIS EM-4657
  $1.50   (805)

  Nederlandse Luitmuziek Uit De 17e
  Eeuw (composed with Vallet,
  Nicolas) *CC5U
  (Kwee) gtr (3-6th degr.) TEESELING
  VT-9 f.s.   (806)

  Praludien, 6 (from Praeludia
  Testudinis (1616))
  (Dirkx) gtr (5-6th degr., g is f
  sharp) HEINRICH. N-1259 f.s.
                                      (807)

  Suite
  gtr (6th degr., Edition Nicolas
  Alfonso, No. 3) SCHOTT-FRER 9122
  f.s. contains also: Bach, Johann
  Sebastian, Suite for Violoncello,
  No. 5, BWV 1001, in C minor,
  Saraband (A min)   (808)

HOWET, GREGORIO (ca. 1550-1620)
  Fantasy No. 6 (from Varietie Of Lute-
  Lessons)
  (Cristoforetti) gtr (8th degr.)
  ZERBONI 6982 $3.50   (809)
  (van Puijenbroeck) gtr (8th degr.,
  g is f sharp; capotasto in pos.
  III) METROPOLIS EM-4702 $1.50
                                      (810)

HUNT, OLIVER
  Idyll-Dance
  gtr (3-4th degr.) HEINRICH. N-1631
  f.s.   (811)

JAKOB POLAK (JACQUES POLONAIS)
  (ca. 1545-1605)
  Courante
  (Visser) gtr (4-5th degr.) HARMONIA
  1583 f.s.   (812)

  Galliard No. 1
  (Visser) gtr (8th degr.) HARMONIA
  1582 f.s. contains also: Galliard

JAKOB POLAK (JACQUES POLONAIS)
  (cont'd.)

  No. 2   (813)

JENKINS, JOHN (1592-1678)
  Arien Und Allemanden *CC10U
  (Monkemeyer) gtr/2treb inst (3rd
  degr.) sc TONGER 1216 f.s.   (814)

JEUNE, HENRI LE
  Chanson
  (Pujol) gtr (3rd degr.) ESCHIG 1093
  f.s.   (815)

JOHNSON, JOHN (1540-1594)
  Galliard, MIN 11
  gtr (4th degr.) BERBEN EB1987 $1.50
                                      (816)

JOHNSON, ROBERT [3] (ca. 1583-1633)
  Almain
  (Azpiazu) gtr (5th degr.) RICORDI-
  ARG BA-11869 f.s.   (817)

  Carman's Whistle
  (Azpiazu, L. de) gtr (8th degr.,
  Guitare, No.32) LEDUC G-32 $2.25
                                      (818)

  Noble Man, The
  (Azpiazu, L. de) gtr (5th degr.,
  Guitare, No.14) LEDUC G-14 $2.25
                                      (819)

JUDENKUNIG, HANS (ca. 1450-1526)
  Ronde Neerlandaise
  (Pujol) gtr (2nd degr., g is f
  sharp) ESCHIG 1078 f.s.   (820)

KAPSBERGER, JOHANN HIERONYMUS
  (ca. 1600-1650)
  Gagliarden, 3
  (Behrend) gtr (4-5th degr.,
  Gitarre-Bibliothek, No.66; also
  published in: European Masters
  For The Guitar) BOTE GB-66 f.s.
                                      (821)

  Toccata
  (Pujol) gtr (7th degr., g is f
  sharp) ESCHIG 1068 f.s.   (822)

KELLNER, DAVID (ca. 1670-1748)
  Fantasy in F sharp minor
  (van Puijenbroeck) gtr (7th degr.,
  e' is d', g is f sharp)
  METROPOLIS 4731 $1.50   (823)

KRIEGER, JOHANN (1651-1735)
  Bouree Et Menuet
  (Proakis) gtr (3rd degr.) BERBEN
  EB516 $1.00   (824)

KROPFGANSS, JOHANN (1708- ?)
  Partita in D
  (van Puijenbroeck) gtr (e' is d', g
  is f sharp; capotasto in pos.
  III) METROPOLIS EM-14005 $2.00
                                      (825)

KUHNAU, JOHANN (1660-1722)
  Petits Morceaux, 4
  (Segovia) gtr (5th degr.) SCHOTT
  GA-143 f.s.
  contains: Gavotte; Minuet;
  Prelude; Saraband   (826)

KUHNEL, JOHANN MICHAEL
  Suite in B minor
  (van Puijenbroeck) gtr (e' is d', g
  is f sharp; capotasto in pos.
  III) METROPOLIS EM-14002 f.s.
                                      (827)

LE ROY, ADRIEN (? -1599)
  Adrian Le Roy: 10 Compositions (from
  Premier Livre De Tablature De
  Guiterre, Et Tiers Livre De
  Tablature De Guiterre)
  (Bellow) gtr (3-4th degr.,
  Renaissance And Baroque, Vol. 1)
  COLOMBO NY-2395 f.s.   (828)

  Allemand, MIN 262
  (Pujol) gtr (2-3rd degr.) ESCHIG
  1065 f.s.   (829)

  Branle Gay
  (Pujol) gtr (2-3rd degr.) ESCHIG
  1066 f.s.   (830)

  Branles De Bourgogne, 9
  (Pujol) gtr (3rd degr.) ESCHIG 1701
  f.s.   (831)

  Danses De Cour, 4
  (Hinojosa) gtr (4th degr.) TRANSAT.
  1358 f.s. g is f sharp; opt
  capotasto in pos. III;
  Bibliotheque De Musique Ancienne
  contains: Allemand, MIN 263;
  Branle Gay; Paduane; Passemeze
                                      (832)

  Fantasy No. 1
  (Reyne) gtr (5th degr., 1551,
  Guitare, No. 93) LEDUC G-93 f.s.
                                      (833)

  Fantasy No. 2
  (Reyne) gtr (5th degr., 1551,
  Guitare, No. 94) LEDUC G-94 f.s.
                                      (834)

LE ROY, ADRIEN (cont'd.)

Gaillarde La Rocca E Il Fuso
(Pujol) gtr (3-4th degr.) ESCHIG
1089 f.s.   (835)

Pavane Et Gaillarde
(Castet) gtr (4-5th degr., Guitare,
No.51) LEDUC G-51 f.s.   (836)

Pavane "Si Ie Me Vois"
(Pujol) gtr (2nd degr.) ESCHIG 1060
f.s. contains also: Bransle De
Poictou   (837)

Pieces, 3
(Santos) gtr (Collection Turibio
Santos, No.3) ESCHIG f.s.   (838)

4 Pieces Pour Guitare (1552)
(Reyne) gtr (Guitare, No. 95) LEDUC
G-95 f.s.   (839)

Prelude Et Chanson
(Pujol) gtr (3rd degr.) ESCHIG 1075
f.s.   (840)

LECLAIR, JEAN MARIE (1697-1764)
Sarabande Und Tambourin
(Schaller) gtr BREITKOPF-W EB-6785
f.s.   (841)

**LEICHTE VERGNUGLICHE ORIGINALSTUCKE AUS
DEM 18. JAHRHUNDERT** *CC14U
(Scheit) gtr (2nd degr.) UNIVER.
13942 $3.25   (842)

LESAGE DE RICHEE, PHILIPP FRANZ
(1695- ?)
Piccolo Pezzi, 4
(Flores Mendez) gtr (4th degr.)
BERBEN EB1119 $1.00
contains: Bourree; Gavotte;
Minuet; Saraband   (843)

4 Piezas
(Galindo) gtr UNION ESP. 21565 f.s.
contains: Bourree; Gavotte;
Minuet; Saraband   (844)

LOCATELLI, PIETRO (1695-1764)
Fugue No. 18 (from Capricho Para
Violin Solo)
(Sainz de la Maza) gtr UNION ESP.
21543 f.s.   (845)

LOSY VOM LOSINTHAL, JAN ANTONIN
(1643-1721)
Ausgewahlte Leichte Stucke *CC7U
gtr (2-3rd degr.) UNIVER. 14447
$2.75 also published in: Musica
Antiqua Bohemia, No. 38   (846)

Invenciones, 3
(Azpiazu) gtr (3rd degr.) UNION
ESP. f.s.   (847)

Partita in A minor
(Scheit) gtr (4th degr., also
published in: Musica Antiqua
Bohemia, No. 38) UNIVER. 12102
$3.25   (848)

Partita in A minor, MIN 12
(Azpiazu) gtr (3-4th degr., also
published in: Musica Antiqua
Bohemia, No. 38) SYMPHON 442 f.s. (849)

Partita in A minor, MIN 13
(Proakis) gtr (also published in:
Musica Antiqua Bohemia, No. 38)
BERBEN EB515 $1.00   (850)

Partita in C
(Scheit) gtr (2nd degr., also
published in: Musica Antiqua
Bohemia, No. 38) UNIVER. 14454
$3.25   (851)

Partita in D
(Azpiazu) gtr (5th degr.) UNION
ESP. f.s.   (852)

Suite in A minor
(van Goch) gtr TEESELING VT-191
f.s.   (853)

Suite No. 1
(Urban) gtr (3rd degr., Kytarova
Sola, No. 9; also published in:
Musica Antiqua Bohemia, No. 38)
CZECH H-3631 f.s.   (854)

Suite No. 3
(Urban) gtr (3-4th degr., Kytarova
sola, no. 19; also published in:
Musica Antiqua Bohemia, No. 38)
CZECH H-4138 f.s.   (855)

LOUIS XIII, KING OF FRANCE (1601-1643)
Amaryllis
"Air Ancien (Amaryllis)" (Bertin)
gtr (4th degr.) RICORDI-ARG
BA-8819 f.s.   (856)
(Sensier) gtr (4th degr.) ESSEX
f.s.   (857)

LULLY, JEAN-BAPTISTE (LULLI)
(1632-1687)
Acht Ausgewahlte Stucke (composed
with Rameau, Jean-Philippe)
(Azpiazu) gtr SYMPHON 356 f.s.   (858)

Air No. 1
(Pujol) gtr ESCHIG 2000 f.s.
contains also: Air No. 2   (859)

Album
(Galindo) gtr UNION ESP. 20150 f.s.
contains: Air Tendre; Courante
(860)

Allemand
(Galindo) gtr UNION ESP. 20605 f.s.
contains also: Sarabande Et Gigue
(861)

Celebre Gavota
(Tarrago) gtr UNION ESP. 21530 f.s.
(862)

Gavotte
(Proakis) gtr (5th degr.) BERBEN
EB1131 $1.00   (863)

Gavotte, MIN 359
(Moore) gtr ESSEX f.s.   (864)

Minuet, MIN 264
(Behrend) gtr (2nd degr.) HEINRICH.
N-3170 f.s.   (865)

Minuet, MIN 332
(Fortea) gtr (easy) FORTEA 233
(866)

Trios, 13
(Monkemeyer) gtr/3treb inst (2-3rd
degr.) TONGER 1076 f.s.   (867)

LUTE PIECES, 2 *CC2U
(Chilesotti; Papas) gtr (3rd degr.)
COLUMBIA 138 $.75   (868)

MACE, THOMAS (1613?-1709)
Pieces, 5
(Castet) gtr (6th degr.) DELRIEU
1320 f.s. Guitarra, no. 14
contains: Allemand; Courante;
Courante Francaise; Cousin
Germain, Le; Minuet, MIN 265
(869)

Suite in D minor (from Musick's
Monument (1676))
(Azpiazu, L. de) gtr (6th degr.,
Guitare, No.48) UNION ESP. 20589
(870)

(Castet) gtr (6th degr., Guitare,
No.48) LEDUC G-48 $2.25   (871)

Suite in E minor
(Castet) gtr (6-7th degr.,
Guitarra, no. 19) DELRIEU 1412
f.s.   (872)

4 Suiten (from Musik's Monument,
London, 1676)
(Libbert) gtr SYMPHON 2274 f.s.
(873)

MAESTRI DEL '500
(Muggia) gtr (4th degr.) ZANIBON 5469
f.s.
contains: Gagliarda Del Passo E
Mezzo; Passo E Mezzo; Passo E
Mezzo; Passo E Mezzo Italiano;
Passo Mezzo Moderno; Pavan, MIN
283   (874)

MANDORBUCH 1626 *CC35U
(Back) gtr (2-3rd degr.) HANSSLER
16.013 f.s. originally for four-
and five-course mandora   (875)

MARAIS, MARIN (1656-1728)
Rondo
(Ponce) gtr (6-7th degr., La
Collection L'Astree) OUVRIERS 757
f.s.   (876)

MARCELLO, BENEDETTO (1686-1739)
Adagio (from Concerto In C Minor For
Oboe And Strings)
(Abloniz) gtr (7th degr.) BERBEN
EB1507 $1.25   (877)
(Amato) gtr (7th degr.) ZANIBON
5172   (878)

Allegro
(Orsolino) gtr (7th degr., with opt
pts for 7-stringed gt) BERBEN
EB1070 f.s.   (879)

Sonata in A
(Azpiazu) gtr (6-7th degr.) SYMPHON
2035 f.s.   (880)

MATTHESON, JOHANN (1681-1764)
Saraband
(Behrend) gtr (4th degr., Gitarre-
Bibliothek, No.39) BOTE GB-39
f.s.   (881)

MELII DA REGGIO, PIETRO PAOLO
(fl. 1614-1616)
Dimi Amore, Passeggiato Dall'autore
(Castet) gtr (8th degr., Guitare,
No.52) LEDUC G-52 f.s. contains

MELII DA REGGIO, PIETRO PAOLO (cont'd.)
also: Roncalli, Ludovico,
Passacaglia (from Suite IX
(Capricci Armonici))   (882)

Pieces, 3, [1616]
(Azpiazu, L. de) gtr (4th degr.)
LEDUC G-7 f.s. Guitare, No.7
contains: Galliard; Intrada;
Volta Alla Francese   (883)

MENUETS, 2
(Pujol) gtr (3rd degr.) ESCHIG 1057
f.s.   (884)

MILAN, LUIS (ca. 1500-ca. 1564)
Don Luis Milan
(Behrend) [Span/Eng/Ger] gtr (3-8th
degr., Alte Meister Des Lauten-
Und Gitarrespiels, Vol. 8; 6
Pavans Nos. 1-6 (No. I, II, V,
III, IV, VI In "El Maestro"), 3
Fantasies Nos. X, VIII, XVI for gtr solo;
3 Romances [Sic] ("Toda Mi Vida"
Is Villancico En Castellano [!]),
3 Villancicos for solo voice,
gtr) sc SIKORSKI 200-8 f.s.   (885)

Fantasia De L'Octavo Tono
(Pujol) gtr (4-5th degr.) ESCHIG
1055 f.s.   (886)

Fantasy, MIN 266 (from El Maestro,
No. 1)
(Sensier) gtr (3-4th degr.) ESSEX
f.s.   (887)

Fantasy, MIN 267 (from El Maestro,
No. V)
(Azpiazu, L. de) gtr (3rd degr.,
Guitare, No.79) LEDUC G-79 $2.25
(888)

Fantasy No. 1 (from El Maestro)
(Hinojosa) gtr (3-4th degr.) SCHOTT
GA-231 f.s. contains also:
Fantasy No. 11   (889)

Fantasy No. 4 (from El Maestro)
(van der Staak) gtr (4th degr.)
BROEKMANS 488 f.s. contains also:
Fantasy No. 14   (890)

Fantasy No. 16 (from El Maestro)
(Prol) gtr (6-7th degr.) PAGANI
CG-113   (891)
(Pujol) gtr (6-7th degr., E is F)
ESCHIG 1017   (892)
(Tarrago) gtr (6-7th degr.) UNION
ESP. 19694   (893)
(van Puijenbroeck) gtr (6-7th
degr., g is f sharp, capotasto in
pos. III) METROPOLIS EM-4732
$1.50   (894)

Fantasy No. 38 (from El Maestro)
(Diaz) gtr (8th degr.) BROEKMANS
822 f.s.   (895)

Maestro, El, Vol. 1: Obras Para
Vihuela Sola
(Tarrago) [Span/Fr/Eng] gtr (40
fantasias, 6 pavanas, 4 tientos)
UNION ESP. 21834-I f.s.   (896)

Maestro, El, Vol. 2: Obras Para Voz Y
Vihuela
(Tarrago) [Span/Fr/Eng] solo voice,
gtr (12 villancicos, 4 romances,
6 sonetos) UNION ESP. 21834-II
f.s.   (897)

Pavan No. 1 (from El Maestro)
(Navascues) gtr (staff notation and
tablature/5th degr.) BRUCK
BG-M1-1 f.s.   (898)
(Pujol) gtr (5th degr.) ESCHIG 1046
f.s.   (899)
(Sensier) gtr (5th degr.) ESSEX
f.s.   (900)

Pavan No. 2 (from El Maestro)
(Pujol) gtr (4th degr.) ESCHIG 1047
f.s.   (901)
(Sensier) gtr (4th degr.) ESSEX
f.s.   (902)

Pavan No. 3 (from El Maestro)
gtr (4th degr.) ESSEX f.s.   (903)
(Navascues) gtr (staff notation and
tablature/4th degr.) BRUCK
BG-M1-2 f.s.   (904)
(Pujol) gtr (4th degr.) ESCHIG 1001
f.s.   (905)

Pavan No. 4 (from El Maestro)
(Pujol) gtr (4th degr., g is f
sharp) ESCHIG 1002 f.s.   (906)
(Sensier) gtr ESSEX f.s.   (907)

Pavan No. 5 (from El Maestro)
(Pujol) gtr (4th degr.) ESCHIG 1045
f.s.   (908)

MILAN, LUIS (cont'd.)

Pavan No. 6 (from El Maestro)
(Navascues) gtr (staff notation and
tablature/4th degr.) BRUCK
BG-M1-3 f.s.   (909)
(Pujol) gtr (4th degr., g is f
sharp) ESCHIG 1003 f.s.   (910)

Pavan Nos. 1-6 (from El Maestro)
(Azpiazu) gtr (3-6th degr.)
RICORDI-ARG BA-12545   (911)
(Chiesa) gtr (3-6th degr.) ZERBONI
6597 $4.75   (912)
(Johnson) gtr (3-6th degr., with
facs) ANDERSONS 689   (913)
(Paolini) gtr (3-6th degr.)
RICORDI-IT 132074   (914)
(Prol) gtr (3-6th degr.) PAGANI
                               (915)
(Sainz de la Maza) gtr (3-6th
degr.) UNION ESP. 19767   (916)
(Scheit) gtr (3-6th degr., with
facs) UNIVER. 14458 $4.25   (917)
(Sierra) gtr (3-6th degr.) CHOUDENS
                               (918)

Pavan Nos. 5-6 (from El Maestro)
(Sensier) gtr (4th degr.) ESSEX
f.s.   (919)

Pavanas (from El Maestro, Nos. III,
VI)
(Correa) gtr (4th degr.) HEINRICH.
N-6208 f.s.   (920)

Pavanas, 6, And A Fantasia (from El
Maestro, Nos. I-VI And XVI)
(Bellow) gtr (3-7th degr.) COLOMBO
NY-2090 f.s.   (921)

Pavanen, 2
(Teuchert) gtr (Die Sologitarre)
SCHMIDT,H 309 f.s.   (922)

Pavans, 3, In D (from El Maestro,
Nos. VI, V, IV)
(Pick) gtr (4th degr., E is D)
FORSTER f.s.   (923)

Pavany, 2 (from El Maestro Nos. III,
VI)
(Urban) gtr (4th degr., Kytarova
sola, no. 7) CZECH H-3575 f.s.
                               (924)

Tientos Del Septimo Y Octavo Tono
(Pujol) gtr ESCHIG 1098 f.s. (925)

Tientos Del Tercero Y Cuarto Tono
(Pujol) gtr ESCHIG 2002 f.s. (926)

MILONI, PIETRO
Passacagli; Folia; Pavaniglia;
Gagliarda; Etc. *CC8U
(Leerink) gtr (3rd degr.) BROEKMANS
377 f.s. Bibliotheek Van Den
Gitarist, No. 6   (927)

MITTELALTERLICHE TANZE
(Behrend) gtr (1-2nd degr.) PREISSLER
JP-7024 f.s.
contains: Bayerischer Bauerntanz,
Ein; Eichstatter Hofmuhltanz;
Riedenburger Tanz; Spiel Der
Minnesanger Auf Der Rosenburg;
Tanz Auf Der Rosenburg; Tanz Im
Aicholdinger Schloss   (928)

MOLINARO, SIMONE
Pezzi, 3
(Tagliavini) gtr (5-6th degr.)
BERBEN EB1999 f.s.
contains: Ballo Detto "Il Conte
Orlando"; Galliard; Saltarello
                               (929)

Saltarello Quarto
(Reyne) gtr (5th degr., Guitare,
No. 84) LEDUC G-84 f.s. contains
also: Saltarello Sesto;
Saltarello Settimo   (930)

MORLEY, THOMAS (1557-1602)
Canzonetta I
(Reyne) gtr (6th degr.) UNION ESP.
f.s.   (931)

Canzonetta II
(Reyne) gtr (6th degr.) UNION ESP.
f.s.   (932)

5 Danses (1551)
(Castet) gtr LEDUC G-96 f.s.
Guitare, No. 96
contains: Allemand; Bransle,
MIN416; Bransle, MIN417;
Villanesque   (933)

Nancie
(Azpiazu, L. de) gtr (8-9th degr.,
Guitare, No.9) LEDUC G-9 f.s.
                               (934)

Pavan
(Azpiazu) gtr (6th degr.) UNION
ESP. 20048 f.s.   (935)
(Castet) gtr (6th degr., Guitarra,
No. 16) DELRIEU 1321 f.s.   (936)

MUDARRA, ALONSO DE (ca. 1506-1580)
Conde Claros De Doze Maneras
(Reyne) gtr (4-5th degr., Guitare,
No. 81) LEDUC G-81 f.s. contains
also: Romanesca O Guardame Las
Vegas; Fantasie Que Contrahaze La
Harpe   (937)

Fantasia De Pasos De Contado
(Clinton) gtr (3rd degr., g is f
sharp) ESSEX f.s.   (938)
(Pujol) gtr (3rd degr., g is f
sharp) ESCHIG 1012 f.s.   (939)
(Usillo) gtr (3rd degr.) UNION ESP.
f.s.   (940)

Fantasia Del Pmer Tono
(ten Boske) gtr (5th degr.)
HARMONIA 2630 f.s. contains also:
Pavan   (941)

Fantasia (Que Contrahaze La Harpa En
La Manera De Luduvico)
(Kreidler) gtr (8-9th degr.) SCHOTT
GA-441 f.s. contains also:
Neusiedler, Hans, Welscher Tantz
"Wascha Mesa" (4th degr.)   (942)

Fantasia X, Que Contrahaze La Harpa
En La Manera De Luduvico
(Diaz) gtr (8-9th degr.) ZANIBON
5179 f.s.   (943)
"Fantasia, Imitation De La Harpe A
La Maniere De Ludovico" (Ibanez)
gtr (8-9th degr.) ESCHIG 8093
f.s.   (944)
(Navascues) gtr (8-9th degr.) BRUCK
BG-M2-1 f.s.   (945)
"Fantasia, Que Contrehace La Harpa
En La Manera De Ludovico" (Prol)
gtr (8-9th degr.) PAGANI CG-101
f.s.   (946)
"Fantasia X, Que Remeda El Harpa De
Ludovico" (Tarrago) gtr (8-9th
degr.) UNION ESP. 19288 f.s.
                               (947)
(van Puijenbroeck) gtr (8-9th
degr., g is f sharp; capotasto in
pos. III) METROPOLIS EM-4690
$2.00   (948)
(Visser) gtr (8-9th degr.) HARMONIA
2146 f.s.   (949)

Fantasias, 2
(Azpiazu, L. de) gtr (6th degr.)
UNION ESP. 20664 f.s.
contains: Fantasy No. 2; Fantasy
No. 3   (950)

Fantasias, 2; 2 Tientos (from Tres
Libros De Musica En Cifra)
(Paolini) gtr RICORDI-IT 132073
f.s.   (951)

Fantasias, 4; Pavane; Romanesca (from
Tres Libros De Musica En Cifra)
(Paolini) gtr RICORDI-IT 132072
f.s.   (952)

Fantasy No. 2
(Kooyman) gtr (5-6th degr.)
HARMONIA 2280 f.s.   (953)

Fantasy No. 5
(Azpiazu L. de) gtr (6th degr.,
Guitare, No.29) LEDUC G-29 f.s.
contains also: Fantasy No. 6   (954)

Fantasy No. 7
(Azpiazu) gtr (5th degr.) UNION
ESP. 20662 f.s.   (955)

Gallarda; Tiento; Fantasia
(Azpiazu) gtr RICORDI-IT BA-12546
f.s.   (956)

Galliard
(Tarrago) gtr (5th degr.) UNION
ESP. 19287 f.s.   (957)

Keuze Uit [Selection From] Tres
Libros De Musica En Cifra *CC12U
(van Schagen) gtr (4-6th degr.)
HARMONIA 1294 f.s.   (958)

Pavan
(Balaguer) gtr (4th degr.) UNION
ESP. 20932 f.s.   (959)

Romanesca I
"O Guardame Las Vacas" (Prol) gtr
(7th degr.) PAGANI G-102 f.s.
                               (960)
"O Guardame Las Vacas" (Segovia)
gtr (7th degr.) SCHOTT GA-159
f.s.   (961)
"O Guardame Las Vacas" (Tarrago)
gtr (7th degr.) UNION ESP. 20579
f.s.   (962)
"O Guardame Las Vacas" (Usillo) gtr
(7th degr.) UNION ESP. (963)

Romanesca II
(Azpiazu) gtr (3rd degr.) UNION
ESP. 20663 f.s. contains also:
Fantasy No. 27   (964)

MUDARRA, ALONSO DE (cont'd.)

(Balestra) gtr (3rd degr.) BERBEN
EB1300 $1.00   (965)
(Pujol) gtr (3rd degr., g is f
sharp) ESCHIG 1076   (966)
(Usillo) gtr UNION ESP.   (967)

Tiento VII, VIII
(Tarrago) gtr (4-5th degr.) UNION
ESP. 20580 f.s.   (968)

Tres Libros De Musica En Cifra Para
Vihuela
(Tarrago) [Span/Fr/Eng] gtr (49 pcs
for vihuela (6 tunings), 27 pcs
for solo voice, vihuela (5
tunings), 1 pc for harp (org);
all transcr. are according to the
tablature and for gtr-e'; if
other tunings are desired, T.
recommends the use of a capotasto
in pos. II-IV) sc UNION ESP.
21652 f.s.   (969)

MUFFAT, GEORG (ca. 1645-1704)
Minuet, MIN 376
(Weston) gtr ESSEX f.s.   (970)

Passacaglia
(Azpiazu, L. de) gtr (7th degr.,
Guitare, No.6) LEDUC G-6 $2.25
                               (971)

MURCIA, SANTIAGO DE
Prelude And Allegro
(Pujol) gtr (4-5th degr.) ESCHIG
1025 f.s.   (972)
(Sainz de la Maza) gtr (4-5th
degr.) UNION ESP. 20769 f.s.
                               (973)

Suite in D
(Pujol) gtr (4th degr.) ESCHIG 1090
f.s.   (974)

Suite in D minor
(Azpiazu, J. de; Azpiazu L. de) gtr
(4-5th degr.) UNION ESP. 20834
f.s.   (975)

NARVAEZ, LUIS DE
Baxa De Contrapunto
(Tarrago) gtr (7th degr.) UNION
ESP. 20571 f.s.   (976)

Cancion Del Emperador
(Alfonso) gtr (6th degr., Edition
Nicolas Alfonso, No. 21) SCHOTT-
FRER 9265 f.s. contains also:
Weiss, Sylvius Leopold, Minuet
(not in Chiesa or Neemann)   (977)
(Azpiazu) gtr UNION ESP. 21210 f.s.
                               (978)
(Scheit) gtr (6-7th degr., suppl:
"Mille regretz" for 2-4gtr)
UNIVER. 14479 f.s. contains also:
4 Diferencias; Baxa De
Contrapunto; Fantasia   (979)

Diferencias, 7, Sobre "Guardame Las
Vacas"
(Azpiazu) gtr (6-7th degr.)
RICORDI-ARG BA-12547 f.s.   (980)
(Navascues) gtr (6-7th degr.) BRUCK
BG-N2-1 f.s.   (981)
(Prol) gtr (6-7th degr.) PAGANI
G-121 f.s.   (982)
(Tarrago) gtr (6-7th degr.) UNION
ESP. 19286 f.s.   (983)
(Yepes) gtr (6-7th degr.) ESCHIG
f.s.   (984)

Fantasia Del Primer Tono
(Pujol) gtr (3-4th degr.) ESCHIG
1041 f.s.   (985)

Fantasy No. 3
(Azpiazu, L. de) gtr (4th degr.,
Guitare, No.28) LEDUC G-28 f.s.
                               (986)

Fantasy No. 9
(Azpiazu) gtr SYMPHON 2196 f.s.
                               (987)

Seys Libros Del Delphin De Musica De
Cifra Para Taner Vihuela, Los
(Tarrago) [Span/Fr/Eng] gtr (38 pcs
for vihuela (6 tunings), 14 pcs
for solo voice, vihuela (5
tunings); all transcr are
according to the tablature and
for gtr-e'; if other tunings are
desired, T. recommends the use of
a capotasto in pos. II-IV) sc
UNION ESP. 21613 f.s.   (988)

Variations, 22, On The Romance "Conde
Claros"
"Conde Claros, 22 Diferencias"
(Pujol) gtr (7-8th degr., g is f
sharp) ESCHIG 1042 f.s.   (989)
"Variaciones, 22, Sobre Conde
Claros" (Tarrago) gtr (7-8th
degr.) UNION ESP. 19692 f.s.
                               (990)

"Variaties, 22, Over De Romance
Conde Claros" (Visser) gtr (7-8th
degr., g is f sharp) HARMONIA

NARVAEZ, LUIS DE (cont'd.)

    1269 f.s.   (991)

    Villancico No. 5 Et Fantaisie No. 14
    (Caceres) gtr (Collection Oscar
    Caceres, No.2) ESCHIG f.s.   (992)

NEGRI, CESARE (IL TROMBONE)
    (ca. 1536- ?)
    Balletti, 8 (from Le Gratie D'amore)
    (Balestra) gtr RICORDI-IT 132075
    f.s.   (993)

    Catena D'amore
    (Visser) gtr (3rd degr.) HARMONIA
    1592 f.s. contains also: Bianco
    Fiore   (994)

    Lautentanze Des XVI. Jahrhunderts
    (from Le Gratie D'amore) CC12U
    (Scheit) gtr (3rd degr.) UNIVER.
    14466 $3.75   (995)

    Nuove Inventioni Di Balli
    (Monkemeyer) gtr (3rd degr., g is f
    sharp; complete edition, 43
    balli) TONGER 1320 f.s.   (996)

NEUSIEDLER, HANS (1508-1563)
    Aus "Ein Newgeordent Kunstlich
    Lautenbuch" *CC12U
    (Gerwig) gtr (3rd degr.) LIENAU
    f.s. g is f sharp; Der Lautenist,
    Vol. 1   (997)

    Ich Klag Den Tag
    (Heyden) [Ger] gtr (Musica
    Practica, No. 17b; including the
    orig. melody for solo voice and 2
    intabulations for 4 insts;
    intabulation by Neusiedler)
    NAGELS f.s. contains also: Ich
    Klag Den Tag (intabulation by
    Gerle); Entlaubet Ist Der Walde
    (intabulation by Neusiedler)
                                     (998)

    Lautenstucke, 4
    (van Puijenbroeck) gtr (3-4th
    degr.) METROPOLIS EM-4709 $1.50 g
    is f sharp; capotasto in pos. III
    contains: Hupf Auf, Der; Juden
    Tanz, Der; Passa-Mesa; Preambel
                                     (999)

    Praambulum Und Tanz
    (Scheit) gtr (3rd degr.) UNIVER.
    12668 $2.75   (1000)

    Tanze, 3
    (Teuchert) gtr SCHMIDT,H 311 f.s.
    Die Sologitarre
    contains: Gassenhawer; Nunnen
    Tantz, Der; Welscher Tantz
                                    (1001)

NEUSIEDLER, MELCHIOR (1507-1590)
    Ausgewahlte Lautenwerke (1566-1572)
    (Klier) gtr SYMPHON 2278 f.s.
                                    (1002)

OUD-HOLLANDSCHE DANSMUZIEK UIT DEN 80-
JARIGEN OORLOG (from Luitboek Van
Thysius) CC7U
    (Leerink) gtr (3-4th degr.) BROEKMANS
    379 f.s. Bibliotheek Van Den
    Gitarist, No.4   (1003)

PACHELBEL, JOHANN (1653-1706)
    Aria
    (Azpiazu) gtr (6th degr., Guitarra,
    No. 10) DELRIEU 1282 f.s.
    contains also: Saraband; Gigue
                                    (1004)

    Suite for Lute
    (Azpiazu) gtr UNION ESP. 21309 f.s.
                                    (1005)

    Suite in D
    (Azpiazu) gtr (5-6th degr.,
    Guitarra, No. 5) DELRIEU 1277
    f.s.   (1006)

PARADIES, PIETRO DOMENICO (PARADISI)
(1707-1791)
    Toccata
    (Abloniz) gtr (8th degr.) BERBEN
    EB1326 $1.00   (1007)

PARTITA IN C
    (Scheit) gtr (3rd degr.) UNIVER.
    14424 $5.00   (1008)

PASQUINI, BERNARDO (1637-1710)
    Sonata in G minor
    (Libbert) cont (3rd degr., Das
    Gitarrenwerk, Reihe A:3) sc
    PREISSLER f.s.   (1009)

PASSEPIEDS, 2
    (Pujol) gtr (5th degr.) ESCHIG 1058
                                    (1010)

PAVAN
    (Mazmanian) gtr (3rd degr.) HEINRICH.
    N-1666 f.s. contains also:
    Passepied   (1011)

PEKIEL, BARTLOMIEJ (? -ca. 1670)
    Pieces, 4
    (Azpiazu) gtr (2-3rd degr.) LEDUC
    G-30 f.s. E is D; Guitare, No.30
    wrongly attributed to Pekiel
    contains: Allegro; Andante
    Espressivo; Andante Poco
    Deciso; Maestoso   (1012)

    Utworow Na Lutnie Lub Gitare W Stroju
    E, 40
    (Ochs) [Polish/Ger/Eng/Fr] gtr (4-
    5th degr., g is f sharp;
    biographical notes by Zygmunt M.
    Szweykowski; wrongly attributed
    to Pekiel) POLSKIE 3897 f.s.
                                    (1013)

PELLEGRINI, DOMENICO
    Domenico Pellegrini (from Armoniosi
    Concerti Sopra La Chitarra
    Spagnuola) CC14U
    (Bellow) gtr (3rd degr.) COLOMBO
    NY-2398 f.s. Renaissance And
    Baroque, Vol. IV   (1014)

PERRICHON, JULIEN (ca. 1565-1610)
    Preludes, 3
    (Castet) gtr (4th degr.,
    Renaissance, No. 7) DELRIEU 1417
    f.s.   (1015)

PHILIPS, PETER (1561-1628)
    Chromatic Pavan
    (Goor) gtr (6-7th degr., g is f
    sharp; capotasto in pos. III)
    METROPOLIS EM-4721 $1.50 contains
    also: Galliard To The Chromatic
    Pavan, The   (1016)

    Galliard
    (Azpiazu) gtr (7th degr.) UNION
    ESP. 20050 f.s.   (1017)

    Pavan
    (Azpiazu) gtr (7th degr.) UNION
    ESP. 20049 f.s.   (1018)

PICCININI, ALESSANDRO
    Toccata
    (Ferrari) gtr (4th degr.) BERBEN
    EB1377 $1.00   (1019)

PIEZAS PARA LAUD DEL SIGLO XVI, 4
    (Chilesotti; Sainz de la Maza) gtr
    (4th degr.) UNION ESP. 20771 f.s.
    contains: Biancafore; Courante, MIN
    286; Galliard, MIN 285; Prelude,
    MIN 284   (1020)

PILKINGTON, FRANCIS (ca. 1562-1638)
    Pieces, 5
    (Jeffery) gtr (4-5th degr.) OXFORD
    36.015 $1.80
    contains: Curranta For Mrs.
    Elizabeth Murcott; George
    Pilkington's Funeral, Pavan;
    Mrs. Anne Harecourt's Galliard;
    Pavane: Mr. T. Wagstaff's
    Content Of Desire; Spanish
    Pavane, The   (1021)

PISADOR, DIEGO (ca. 1508-1557)
    Fantasia Facil
    (Azpiazu, L. de) gtr (3rd degr.)
    UNION ESP. 20656 f.s.   (1022)

    Fantasy No. 1
    (Azpiazu, L. de) gtr (4-5th degr.)
    UNION ESP. 20657 f.s.   (1023)

    Pavan
    (Tarrago) gtr (2nd degr.) UNION
    ESP. 20809 f.s.   (1024)

    Villanelle: Dites Au Chevalier Que
    (Pujol) gtr (2-3rd degr., g is f
    sharp) ESCHIG 1083 f.s.   (1025)

    Villanesca
    (Azpiazu, L. de) gtr (5th degr.)
    UNION ESP. 20655 f.s.   (1026)

    Villanesca
    (Pujol) gtr (6th degr.) ESCHIG 1013
    f.s.   (1027)

PRAETORIUS, MICHAEL (1571-1621)
    Terpsichore Musarum
    (Oraison) gtr (4-5th degr.)
    TEESELING 176 f.s.
    contains: Ballet; Bourree;
    Espagnoleta; Gavotte; Saraband;
    Volta   (1028)

PRALUDIUM UND 2 MENUETTE *CCU
    (Scheit) gtr (3rd degr.) UNIVER.
    14423 $2.75   (1029)

PUES NO ME QUEREIS HABLER
    "Vous Ne Voulez Donc Pas Me Parler"
    (Pujol) gtr (romance) ESCHIG 2008
    f.s.   (1030)

PURCELL, HENRY (1658 or 59-1695)
    Album Henry Purcell *CC16U
    (Reyne) gtr LEDUC G-102 f.s.
    Guitare, No. 102   (1031)

    Almand And Minuet
    (Norman) gtr (4th degr.) COLOMBO
    NY-2000 f.s.   (1032)

    Chaconne (from Fairy Queen, The, On
    The Theme "La Folia")
    (Azpiazu) gtr (6th degr.) SYMPHON
    2065 f.s.   (1033)

    Courante, MIN 91
    (Azpiazu) gtr (7th degr.) SYMPHON
    357 f.s. contains also: Byrd,
    William, Pavan, MIN 92, "Earl Of
    Salisbury, The"   (1034)

    Gavotte, MIN 219
    (Anido) gtr (5-6th degr.) RICORDI-
    ARG BA-12480 f.s.   (1035)

    Pezzi, 3
    (Cimma) gtr (3-5th degr.) BERBEN
    EB1370 $1.00
    contains: Aria; Hornpipe; Rondo,
    MIN 268   (1036)

    Pieces, 3
    (Duarte) gtr (5th degr.) SCHOTT
    GA-216 f.s.
    contains: Air, MIN 86; Prelude,
    MIN 84; Rondo, MIN 85   (1037)

    Pieces, 3
    (Segovia) gtr (3-4th degr.)
    COLUMBIA 131 f.s. also published
    in Andres Segovia Album
    contains: Gigue, MIN 88; Minuet,
    MIN 87; New Irish Tune, A   (1038)

    Pieces, 4
    (Bream) gtr (5-6th degr.) FABER
    F-0375 f.s.
    contains: Air, MIN 81; Hornpipe
    (Minuet, MIN 83); Rondo, MIN 82
                                    (1039)

    Piezas, 4
    (Lara) gtr (3-5th degr.) RICORDI-
    ARG BA-12517 f.s.
    contains: Air, MIN 220; Gavotte,
    MIN 269; Hornpipe; Prelude, MIN
    89   (1040)

    Prelude, MIN 90
    (Anido) gtr (6-7th degr.) RICORDI-
    ARG BA-12481 f.s.   (1041)

    Preludio E Allemanda
    (Muggia) gtr (6th degr.) ZANIBON
    5121 f.s.   (1042)

    Rondeau De Abdelazar
    (Azpiazu) gtr UNION ESP. 21189 f.s.
                                    (1043)

    Suite No. 1
    (Galindo) gtr (6th degr.) UNION
    ESP. 20608 f.s.   (1044)

    Suite No. 4
    (Galindo) gtr (7th degr.) UNION
    ESP. 20609 f.s.   (1045)

QUELQUES PAGES DE GUITARE CLASSIQUE
    (Breguet) gtr (4-7th degr.) LEMOINE
    f.s. contains 24 works by:
    Chambonnieres (4), Clerambault (4),
    Seixas (4), Purcell (4)
    contains: Bach, Johann Sebastian,
    French Suite No.1, BWV812, In D
    Minor, Sarabande (E min); Bach,
    Johann Sebastian, French Suite
    No. 2, BWV813, In C Minor, Gigue
    (D min); Bach, Johann Sebastian,
    French Suite No. 2, BWV813, In C
    Minor, Minuet (D min); Bach,
    Johann Sebastian, French Suite
    No. 4, BWV815A, In E Flat, Minuet
    (G maj); Bach, Johann Sebastian,
    Minuet, BWV Anh. 120, in A minor
    (from Anna Magdalena Bach
    Notenbuchlein (1725), No.14) (D
    min); Bach, Johann Sebastian,
    Minuet, BWV Anh. 132, in D minor
    (from Anna Magdalena Bach
    Notenbuchlein (1725), No.36);
    Bach, Johann Sebastian, O
    Ewigkeit, Du Donnerwort. Chorale,
    BWV 513 (from Anna Magdalena Bach
    Notenbuchlein (1725), No.42);
    Bach, Johann Sebastian, Suite for
    Orchestra, BWV 1067, in B minor,
    Rondo   (1046)

RADOLT, WENZEL LUDWIG FREIHERR VON
(1667-1716)
    Minuet
    (Behrend) gtr (4th degr.) SIRIUS
    f.s.   (1047)

RAMEAU, JEAN-PHILIPPE (1683-1764)
Air
  (Pujol) gtr (3rd degr.) ESCHIG 1092
  f.s.   (1048)

Livri, La, Rondeau
  (Reyne) gtr (5th degr., Guitare,
  No.74) LEDUC G-74 $2.25   (1049)

Minuet
  (Anido) gtr (4th degr.) RICORDI-ARG
  BA-12483 f.s.   (1050)

Minuetti, 2
  (Segovia) gtr (5th degr.) SCHOTT
  GA-160 f.s.   (1051)

Minuetti, 6
  (Abloniz) gtr (3-5th degr.)
  RICORDI-ARG 129655 f.s.   (1052)

Minuetto, Da Platee
  (Proakis) gtr (5th degr.) BERBEN
  EB1122 $1.00   (1053)

Pieces De Clavecin
  (Duarte) gtr (5-7th degr.) BERBEN
  EB1694 $2.75
  contains: Boiteuse, La;
    Indifferente, L'; Menuet En
    Rondeau; Tambourin; Venitienne
                                 (1054)

Rappel Des Oiseaux, Le
  (Norman) gtr (6th degr.) SCHIRM.G
  44822 f.s.   (1055)
  "Llamada De Los Pajaros, La"
  (Reyne) gtr (6th degr.) UNION
  ESP. f.s.   (1056)

Sarabande Et Menuet
  (Azpiazu, L. de) gtr (3-4th degr.,
  Guitare, No.13) LEDUC G-13 $2.25
                                 (1057)

Tambourin
  (Behrend) gtr (7th degr.) BOTE
  GB-40 f.s.   (1058)
  "Gavotte, Le Tambourin" (Rodriguez
  Arenas) gtr (7th degr.) RICORDI-
  ARG RF-7579 f.s.   (1059)

Tendres Plaintes, Les *CC4U
  (Komter) gtr (5th degr.) HARMONIA
  2931 f.s.   (1060)

REUSSNER, ESAIAS (1636-1679)
Passacaglia
  (Azpiazu, L. de) gtr (5th degr.)
  UNION ESP. 20478 f.s.   (1061)

Pecas, 3
  (Sao Marcos) gtr RICORDI-BR BR-2815
  f.s.   (1062)

Sonatina
  (Behrend) gtr (3-4th degr.,
  Gitarre-Bibliothek, No.6; also
  published in: European Masters
  For The Guitar) BOTE GB-6 f.s.
                                 (1063)

Suite for Lute
  (Tarrago) gtr UNION ESP. 21513 f.s.
                                 (1064)

Suite in A minor
  (van Goch) gtr TEESELING VT-192
  f.s.   (1065)

Suite No. 1 (from Neue Lauten-
  Fruchte)
  (Behrend) gtr (5th degr., Gitarre-
  Bibliothek, No.7) BOTE GB-7 f.s.
                                 (1066)

Suite No. 5 (from Neue Lauten-
  Fruchte)
  (van Gogh) gtr (5th degr.)
  TEESELING VT-28 f.s.   (1067)

RICERCARE, PER LIUTO (from "Fronimo" Di
  Vincenzo Galilei)
  (Cristoforetti) gtr (6th degr.)
  ZERBONI 6979 f.s.   (1068)

ROBINSON, THOMAS (fl. ca. 1603)
Allemand, MIN 350
  (Sensier) gtr ESSEX f.s.   (1069)

Allemande Und Galliard (from The
  Schoole Of Musicke)
  (Scheit) gtr (3-4th degr.) UNIVER.
  12713 $2.75   (1070)

Bellvedere (from The Schoole Of
  Musicke)
  (Scheit) gtr (6th degr.) UNIVER.
  12762 f.s.   (1071)

Galliard, MIN 93
  (Sensier) gtr (4th degr.) ESSEX
  f.s.   (1072)

Pieces, 5 (from The Schoole Of
  Musicke)
  (Scheit) gtr (3-4th degr.) UNIVER.
  12761 $2.75
  contains: Bony Sweet Boy;
    Galliard, MIN 94; Lantero; Row
    Well You Marriners; Walking In

ROBINSON, THOMAS (cont'd.)
  A Country Towne   (1073)

2 Pieces
  (Castet) gtr LEDUC G-98 f.s.
  Guitare, No. 98
  contains: Row Well You Mariners;
    Toy, A   (1074)

Piezas De Laud, 4 (from The Schoole
  Of Musicke)
  (Azpiazu, L. de) gtr (4th degr.)
  UNION ESP. 20054 f.s.
  contains: Almain, MIN 95;
    Galliard, MIN 96; Gigue; Toy, A
                               (1075)

Schoole Of Musicke, The *CC17U
  (Pircher) gtr SYMPHON 2269 f.s.
                               (1076)

Spanish Pavan, The
  (Caceres) gtr (6-7th degr.,
  Collection Oscar Caceres, No.5)
  ESCHIG 8095 f.s.   (1077)

Toy, Air And Gigue (from The Schoole
  Of Musicke)
  (Scheit) gtr (3-4th degr.) UNIVER.
  12670 $2.75   (1078)

RONCALLI, LUDOVICO
Capricci Armonici: Sarabande-Gigue
  (from Suite No. 1)
  (Pujol) gtr (4th degr, 7th degr)
  ESCHIG 1038 f.s.   (1079)

Partita in D
  (Teuchert) gtr (Die Sologitarre)
  SCHMIDT,H 300 f.s.   (1080)

3 Partiten
  (Schmidt) gtr ZIMMER. 1978 f.s.
                               (1081)

Passacaglia (from Capricci Armonici,
  Suite IX)
  (Tonazzi) gtr (8th degr.) BERBEN
  EB1133 $1.00   (1082)

Preludio E Giga (from Capricci
  Armonici, Suite I)
  (Tonazzi) gtr (7th degr.) BERBEN
  EB1132 $1.00   (1083)

Preludio, Sarabande E Giga
  (Terzi) gtr RICORDI-IT 129284 f.s.
                               (1084)

Suite in B minor (from Capricci
  Armonici, No. 3)
  (Scheit) gtr (6-7th degr.) UNIVER.
  16689 f.s.   (1085)

Suite in D
  (Scheit) gtr UNIVER. 16690 f.s.
                               (1086)

Suite in D minor
  (Paolini) gtr RICORDI-IT 132111
  f.s.   (1087)

Suite in E minor (from Capricci
  Armonici, No. 2)
  (Scheit) gtr (6-7th degr.) UNIVER.
  16688 f.s.   (1088)

Suite in G
  (Scheit) gtr UNIVER. 16691 f.s.
                               (1089)

Suite No. 1 (from Capricci Armonici
  Sopra La Chitarra Spagnola)
  "Suite In G Dur" (Albert) gtr (7-
  8th degr.) ZIMMER. f.s.   (1090)
  "Sonata No. 1" (Castet) gtr (7-8th
  degr., Guitare, No.64) LEDUC G-64
  f.s.   (1091)
  "Suite E-Moll, No. 1" (Scheit) gtr
  (7-8th degr.) UNIVER. 16686 f.s.
                               (1092)

Suite No. 5 in A minor (from Capricci
  Armonici)
  (Kennard) gtr (6th degr.) SCHOTT
  10542 f.s.   (1093)

Suite No. 7 in D minor (from Capricci
  Armonici)
  (Kennard) gtr (6th degr.) SCHOTT
  10546 f.s.   (1094)

Suite No. 9 in G minor (from Capricci
  Armonici)
  (Azpiazu, L. de) gtr (8th degr.,
  Guitare, No.15) LEDUC G-15 f.s.
                               (1095)

Suiten, 9
  (Benvenuto; Briasco) gtr (6-8th
  degr., ill, introduction, facs)
  ZANIBON 5670 f.s.   (1096)
  "Capricci Armonici Sopra La
  Chitarra Spagnola" (Henze) gtr
  (6-8th degr.) HOFMEISTER T-4068
  f.s.   (1097)

Suiten Nr. 3 Und Nr. 4 (from Capricci
  Armonici Sopra La Chitarra
  Spagnola (1692))
  (Libbert) gtr (7th degr., Studio-
  Reihe Gitarre) PREISSLER 70201
  f.s.   (1098)

ROSSETER, PHILIP (ca. 1568-1623)
Galliard
  (Castet) gtr (3-4th degr., Guitare,
  No.63) LEDUC G-63 f.s. contains
  also: Anonymous, Wilson's Wilde;
  Anonymous, Petite Piece   (1099)

Galyerd Y A Pavin
  (Azpiazu) gtr (6th degr.) UNION
  ESP. 20046 f.s.   (1100)

ROTTA, ANTONIO (? -1548)
Rocca E Il Fuso, La, Chanson
  Italienne
  (Pujol) gtr (3rd degr.) ESCHIG 1070
  f.s.   (1101)

Suite Of Dances For Lute (1546)
  (Kadis) gtr (4th degr., 3 pcs;
  notation: Fr tablature +
  transcription for gtr)
  MUS.SAC.PRO. LR-104 $2.00   (1102)

ROYAL DANCES, 4 *16th cent
  (van der Staak) gtr (4th degr.)
  BROEKMANS 421 f.s.
  contains: Churfurst Augustus Tantz;
    Churfurst Moritz Tantz;
    Churfurstin Zu Sachen Tentzleyn,
    Der; Graff Johann Von Nassau
    Tantz   (1103)

RUIZ DE RIBAYAZ, LUCAS
Bailes Populares Del Siglo XVII, 6
  (San Andres) gtr (3-4th degr.)
  UNION ESP. 18868 f.s.
  contains: Canarios; Danza Del
    Hacha; Galliard; Matachin;
    Torneo; Vacas   (1104)

Dansen, 4
  (Tower) gtr (2-3rd degr.) TEESELING
  VT-17 f.s.   (1105)

Passacaglia
  (Pujol) gtr (3rd degr.) ESCHIG 1037
  f.s.   (1106)

SAINT LUC, JACQUES DE (1616- ?)
Suite in E
  (Alfonso) gtr (6-7th degr., Edition
  Nicolas Alfonso, No. 1) SCHOTT-
  FRER 9120 f.s. contains also:
  Franck, Cesar, Plaintes d'Une
  Poupee, Les   (1107)

SANTA MARIA, THOMAS DE (1510-1570)
Fabordon Y Fuga
  (Pujol) gtr (2nd degr.) ESCHIG 1091
  f.s.   (1108)

Fantasias, 8 (from Arte Del Taner
  Fantasia)
  (Azpiazu) gtr (4-5th degr.) UNION
  ESP. 20837 f.s.   (1109)

SANZ, GASPAR (1640-1710)
Airs De Danse, 5
  (Pujol) gtr (1-2nd degr.) ESCHIG
  1077 f.s.
  contains: Espanoleta; Matachin;
    Paradetas; Rujero; Saraband
                               (1110)

Anthologie Pour La Guitare Espagnole
  *CC9U
  (de Lusignan) gtr (2-4th degr.)
  LEMOINE $4.25   (1111)

Batalla, Baile Popular
  (Usillos) gtr (2nd degr.) UNION
  ESP. f.s.   (1112)

Canarios
  (Azpiazu, J. de; Azpiazu, L. de)
  gtr (4th degr.) SYMPHON 2081 f.s.
  contains also: Jacaras;
    Passacaglia   (1113)
  (Navascues) [Ger/Eng/Span] gtr
  (tablature/5-6th degr., transcr +
  arr for gtr; facs) BRUCK BG-S2-1
  f.s.   (1114)
  (Pujol) gtr (4th degr.) ESCHIG 1035
  f.s.   (1115)
  "Diferencias Escogidas Sobre El
  Canario, 15" (Santos) gtr
  (Collection Turibio Santos, No.6)
  ESCHIG f.s.   (1116)

Canarios II
  (Balestra) gtr (3rd degr.) BERBEN
  EB1329 $1.00   (1117)

Cavalleria De Napoles, La
  "Fanfare" (Navascues) [Ger/Eng/
  Span] gtr (tablature/3-4th degr.,
  transcr + arr for gtr; facs)
  BRUCK BG-S2-3 f.s.   (1118)

Chaconne
  "Danza II" (Usillos) gtr (3rd
  degr.) UNION ESP. f.s.   (1119)

Chansons Populaires Du XVIIe Siecle
  (Santos) gtr (Collection Turibio
  Santos, No.4) ESCHIG f.s.   (1120)

SANZ, GASPAR (cont'd.)

Clairons Royaux, Clairons Et
   Trompettes
   (Pujol) gtr (1-2nd degr.) ESCHIG
   1084 f.s. contains also:
   Cavalerie De Naples, La; Clairon
   Des Mousquetiers Du Roi De France
                                    (1121)
Composizioni, 10 (from Instruccion De
   Musica Sobre La Guitarra
   Espanola)
   (Balestra) gtr (3rd degr.) ZERBONI
   7609 $3.50   (1122)

Corriente
   (Sensier) gtr ESSEX f.s.   (1123)

Danzas Cervantinas
   (Sainz de la Maza) gtr (7-8th
   degr.) UNION ESP. 20236 f.s.
   contains: Canarios; Espanoleta;
   Marizapalos   (1124)

Espanoleta I
   (Tarrago) gtr (3rd degr.) UNION
   ESP. 20572 f.s. contains also:
   Espanoleta II   (1125)

Espanoleta I, Air De Danse
   (Pujol) gtr (3rd degr.) ESCHIG 1049
   f.s.   (1126)

Fantasia Original De Un Gentilhombre,
   Villanos
   (Hopman) gtr (2-4th degr.) HARMONIA
   1859 f.s. contains also: Fuga Ia
   Por Primer Tono Al Ayre Espanol;
   Espanoleta I, II; Hachas, Las;
   Cavalleria De Napoles, La;
   Canarios   (1127)

Folia
   (Scheit) gtr (3-4th degr.) UNIVER.
   14469 $3.25 contains also:
   Espanoleta; Matachin; Espanoleta;
   Preludio O Capricho; Corriente
                                    (1128)
Folias
   (Azpiazu) gtr (4-6th degr.) SYMPHON
   2119 f.s. contains also: Pavanas
                                    (1129)
   (Pujol) gtr (6th degr.) ESCHIG 1006
   f.s.   (1130)

Fuga I, Per Primer Tono Al Aire
   Espanol
   (Usillos) gtr (3rd degr.) UNION
   ESP. f.s.   (1131)

Fuga II, Al Modo De Jiga Inglesa
   (Usillos) gtr (3rd degr.) UNION
   ESP. f.s.   (1132)

Gallardas
   (Pujol) gtr (5-6th degr.) ESCHIG
   1004 f.s.   (1133)

Galliard
   (Tarrago) gtr (4th degr.) UNION
   ESP. 20576 f.s. contains also:
   Pavana En Partidas Al Aire
   Espanol   (1134)

Galliard, MIN 14
   (Usillos) gtr (2nd degr.) UNION
   ESP. f.s.   (1135)

Gaspar Sanz: 11 Compositions (from
   Instruccion De Musica Sobre La
   Guitarra Espanola; Libro Segundo
   De Cifras Sobre La Guitarra
   Espanola)
   (Bellow) gtr (2-7th degr.,
   Renaissance And Baroque, Vol.
   VIII) COLOMBO NY-2402 f.s. (1136)

Gaspar Sanz Invenit *CC7U
   (Hopman) gtr (2-3rd degr.) HARMONIA
   2333 f.s.   (1137)

Gigue (from Suite, G Minor)
   (Sensier) gtr (6th degr.) ESSEX
   f.s.   (1138)

Iacaras
   (Leerink) gtr (4th degr.,
   Bibliotheek Van Den Gitarist, No.
   10) BROEKMANS 375 f.s. contains
   also: Canarios   (1139)

Marizapalos, 5 Partidas
   (Santos) gtr (orig.: 6 partidas;
   Collection Turibio Santos, No. 5)
   ESCHIG f.s.   (1140)

Matachin, Baile Popular Del Siglo
   XVII
   (Usillos) gtr (2nd degr.) UNION
   ESP. f.s.   (1141)

Obras De Gaspar Sanz, Vol. 1
   (Tarrago) gtr (3-7th degr.) UNION
   ESP. 20926 f.s.
   contains: Espanoleta;
   Marizapalos; Matachin; Preludio

SANZ, GASPAR (cont'd.)

   O Capricho; Zarabanda   (1142)

Obras De Gaspar Sanz, Vol. 2
   (Tarrago) gtr (3-7th degr.) UNION
   ESP. 20927 f.s.
   contains: Canarios; Galliard;
   Passacaglia in D; Pavan;
   Villano   (1143)

Passacaglia
   (Pujol) gtr (4-5th degr.) ESCHIG
   1034 f.s.   (1144)
   (Tarrago) gtr (4-5th degr.) UNION
   ESP. 20704 f.s.   (1145)

Passacaglia in D
   (Azpiazu, L. de) gtr (7th degr.,
   Guitare, No.11) LEDUC G-11 f.s.
                                    (1146)
Pavan
   (Usillos) gtr (2nd degr.) UNION
   ESP. f.s.   (1147)

Pavana, Passacalle, Etc.
   (Leerink) gtr (1-4th degr.,
   Bibliotheek Van Den Gitarist, No.
   9) BROEKMANS 376 f.s.   (1148)

Pavanas
   (Pujol) gtr (4th degr.) ESCHIG 1005
   f.s.   (1149)

Pavanas
   (Scheit) gtr (4-5th degr.) UNIVER.
   14470 $3.25 contains also: Fugue;
   Canarios   (1150)

Pavanas (Suivi De Partidos Al Aire
   Espanol)
   (Castet) gtr (3-5th degr., Guitare,
   No. 85) LEDUC G-85 f.s.   (1151)

Pieces Faciles Pour Apprendre Le
   Punteado, 8
   (Azpiazu, J. de; Azpiazu, L. de)
   gtr (3rd degr.) SYMPHON 2034 f.s.
                                    (1152)
Preciosa, La
   (Sensier) gtr ESSEX f.s.   (1153)

Preludio-Fantasia (from Suite, G
   Minor)
   (Sensier) gtr (6th degr.) ESSEX
   f.s.   (1154)

Preludio O Capricho Arpeado
   (Sensier) gtr ESSEX f.s.   (1155)

Rujero
   (Navascues) [Ger/Eng/Span] gtr
   (tablature/2-3rd degr., transcr +
   arr for gtr; facs) BRUCK BG-S2-2
   f.s. contains also: Paradetas;
   Matachin; Saraband   (1156)

Sarabandes, 2 (from Suites, E Minor
   And G Minor)
   (Sensier) gtr (6th degr.) ESSEX
   f.s.   (1157)

Serenisima, La (Alemana) (from Suite,
   G Minor)
   (Sensier) gtr (6th degr.) ESSEX
   f.s.   (1158)
   (Tarrago) gtr (6th degr.) UNION
   ESP. 19282 f.s.   (1159)

Sesquialtera (from Suite, G Minor)
   "Sesquialtera II" (Sensier) gtr
   (6th degr.) ESSEX f.s.   (1160)
   (Usillos) gtr (6th degr.) UNION
   ESP. f.s.   (1161)

Sesquialtera I (from Suite, E Minor)
   (Sensier) gtr (6th degr.) ESSEX
   f.s.   (1162)

Suite Espanola
   (Yepes) gtr UNION ESP. 21354 f.s.
                                    (1163)
Suite in E minor
   (Azpiazu, J. de; Azpiazu, L. de)
   gtr (6-7th degr.) SYMPHON 2079
   f.s.   (1164)
   "Airs De Cour, 5" (Pujol) gtr (6-
   7th degr.) ESCHIG 1048 f.s.
                                    (1165)
Suite in G minor
   (Azpiazu, J. de; Azpiazu, L. de)
   gtr (6th degr.) SYMPHON 2080 f.s.
                                    (1166)
Suite No. 1 in D minor
   (Robert) gtr (2-7th degr., Plein
   Jeu, No.168) HEUGEL PJ-168 $.50
   contains also: Suite No. 2 in A
   minor   (1167)

16 Tanze
   (Moser) gtr SYMPHON 2250 f.s.
                                    (1168)
Torneo
   (Tarrago) gtr UNION ESP. 21832 f.s.
                                    (1169)

SANZ, GASPAR (cont'd.)

Torneo, Baile Popular
   (Usillos) gtr (2nd degr.) UNION
   ESP. f.s.   (1170)

Tournoi Et Bataille
   (Pujol) gtr (2nd degr.) ESCHIG 1086
   f.s.   (1171)

SCARLATTI, ALESSANDRO (1660-1725)
Minuet
   (Anido) gtr RICORDI-ARG BA-11189
   f.s.   (1172)

Minuet, MIN 381
   (Wade) gtr ESSEX f.s.   (1173)

Sento Nel Core
   (Abloniz) gtr RICORDI-IT 129349
   f.s. contains also: Caldara,
   Antonio, Selve Amiche   (1174)

SCARLATTI, DOMENICO (1685-1757)
Pieces, 5
   (Duarte) gtr (5-6th degr.) SCHOTT
   GA-228 f.s.
   contains: Sonata, Kirkpatrick 32;
   Sonata, Kirkpatrick 34; Sonata,
   Kirkpatrick 80; Sonata,
   Kirkpatrick 318; Sonata,
   Kirkpatrick 322   (1175)

Sonata, Kirkpatrick 1
   (Reyne) gtr (8th degr., Guitare,
   No.58) LEDUC G-58 $3.00 contains
   also: Sonata, Kirkpatrick 11
                                    (1176)
Sonata, Kirkpatrick 11 *Longo 352
   (Azpiazu) gtr (8th degr., Guitarra,
   No. 12) DELRIEU 1284 f.s.   (1177)
   (Prol) gtr (8th degr.) PAGANI
   CG-105 f.s.   (1178)
   (Segovia) gtr (E min,8th degr.)
   SCHOTT GA-177 f.s.   (1179)

Sonata, Kirkpatrick 32, in E minor
   (Prol) gtr (5th degr.) PAGANI
   CG-107 f.s.   (1180)

Sonata, Kirkpatrick 33
   (Sanchez Granada) gtr (9-10th
   degr.) UNION ESP. 17305 f.s.
                                    (1181)
Sonata, Kirkpatrick 54 *Longo 241
   (Andia) gtr (Bibliotheque De
   Musique Ancienne) TRANSAT. f.s.
                                    (1182)
Sonata, Kirkpatrick 64
   "Gavotta, L. 58" (Andia) gtr
   (Bibliotheque De Musique
   Ancienne) TRANSAT. $2.50   (1183)
   "Gavotta" (Proakis) gtr (5th degr.)
   BERBEN EB1123 $1.25   (1184)

Sonata, Kirkpatrick 159
   (Azpiazu) (C maj,8-9th degr.)
   SYMPHON 362 f.s. contains also:
   Scarlatti, Giuseppe, Tempo Di
   Menuetto (from Merope)   (1185)
   (Prol) gtr (C maj,9th degr.) PAGANI
   CG-122 f.s.   (1186)

Sonata, Kirkpatrick 208
   (Diaz) gtr (6th degr.) ZANIBON 5182
   f.s.   (1187)

Sonata, Kirkpatrick 209
   (Froese) gtr (A maj,5-6th degr.)
   LIENAU S-10985 f.s.   (1188)

Sonata, Kirkpatrick 322 *Longo 483
   (Abloniz) gtr (5th degr.) BERBEN
   EB1777 $1.25   (1189)
   (Prol) gtr (5th degr.) PAGANI
   CG-109 f.s.   (1190)

Sonata, Kirkpatrick 380
   (Luconi) gtr (E maj,8th degr.)
   BERBEN EB1184 $1.00   (1191)

Sonata, Kirkpatrick 391
   (Anido) gtr (G maj,7th degr., E is
   D, A is G) RICORDI-ARG BA-11380
   f.s.   (1192)
   (Sensier) gtr (G maj,7th degr., E
   is D, A is G) ESSEX f.s.   (1193)

Sonata, Kirkpatrick 428 *Longo 131
   (Andia) gtr (6-7th degr.,
   Bibliotheque De Musique Ancienne)
   TRANSAT. 1366 f.s.   (1194)

Sonata, Kirkpatrick 431 *Longo 83
   (Prol) (6th degr.) PAGANI CG-115
   f.s.   (1195)

Sonata, Kirkpatrick 440
   "Minue" (Anido) gtr (8th degr.)
   RICORDI-ARG BA-12484 f.s. (1196)

Sonata, Kirkpatrick 481
   (Segovia) (A min,8th degr.) SCHOTT
   GA-144 f.s.   (1197)

SCARLATTI, DOMENICO (cont'd.)

Sonata, Kirkpatrick 519, in F minor
(Azpiazu) (7th degr.) SYMPHON 413
f.s.   (1198)

Sonata, Kirkpatrick 544
(Caceres) (6-7th degr., Collection
Oscar Caceres, No.10) ESCHIG 8186
f.s.   (1199)

Sonata, Longo 33, Kirkpatrick 87
(Reyne) gtr (8th degr., Guitare,
No. 92) LEDUC G-92 f.s.   (1200)

Sonata, MIN 311
(Caceres) gtr (Collection Oscar
Caceres, No.8; Kirkpatrick 213?)
ESCHIG f.s.   (1201)

Sonata, MIN 312
(Caceres) gtr (Collection Oscar
Caceres, No.3; Kirkpatrick 380?)
ESCHIG f.s.   (1202)

Sonata, MIN 387
(Segovia) gtr CEL 6 $.90   (1203)

Sonata Pastorale
(Artzt) gtr COLUMBIA 192 f.s.
                                  (1204)

Sonatas, 3
(Galindo) gtr (7-8th degr.) UNION
ESP. f.s.
   contains: Sonata, Kirkpatrick 68;
   Sonata, Kirkpatrick 274;
   Sonata, Kirkpatrick 277 (1205)

Sonatas, 9, Vol. 1
(Barbosa Lima) gtr (5-8th degr.)
COLUMBIA 184A $2.50 Kirk. 391: E
is D, A is G
   contains: Sonata, Kirkpatrick 11;
   Sonata, Kirkpatrick 32; Sonata,
   Kirkpatrick 322; Sonata,
   Kirkpatrick 391; Sonata,
   Kirkpatrick 462   (1206)

Sonatas, 9, Vol. 2
(Barbosa Lima) gtr (5-8th degr.)
COLUMBIA 184B $2.50 Kirk. 380: E
is D, A is G
   contains: Sonata, Kirkpatrick
   309; Sonata, Kirkpatrick 380;
   Sonata, Kirkpatrick 431;
   Sonata, Kirkpatrick 481   (1207)

4 Sonatas, K. 391, 408, 424, 453
(Reyne) gtr (5-6th degr., Guitare,
No. 82) LEDUC G-82 f.s.   (1208)

Sonatas, Vol. 1
(Yepes) gtr (7-8th degr.) UNION
ESP. f.s. Codice Veneciano, Libro
I, No. 2, 7
   contains: Sonata, Kirkpatrick
   149; Sonata, Kirkpatrick 154
                                  (1209)

Sonatas, Vol. 2
(Yepes) gtr (7-8th degr.) UNION
ESP. f.s. Codice Veneciano, Libro
V, No. 25; Libro IX, No. 4; E is
D, A is G
   contains: Sonata, Kirkpatrick
   290; Sonata, Kirkpatrick 391
                                  (1210)

Sonatas, Vol. 3
(Yepes) gtr (7-8th degr.) UNION
ESP. f.s. Codice Veneciano, Libro
IV, No. 24; Libro VIII, No. 23
   contains: Sonata, Kirkpatrick
   259; Sonata, Kirkpatrick 380
                                  (1211)

Sonate, 2
(Diaz) gtr (6th degr.) ZANIBON 5151
f.s.
   contains: Sonata, Kirkpatrick 32,
   "Aria"; Sonata, Kirkpatrick
   431, "Allegro"   (1212)

Three Sonatas
gtr COLUMBIA 198 f.s.   (1213)

SCHENK, JOHANN (1753-1836)
Suite in A minor
(Behrend) (3-4th degr.) UNION ESP.
f.s.   (1214)

SEIXAS, (JOSE ANTONIO) CARLOS DE
(1704-1742)
Menuets, 2
(Pujol) ESCHIG 1096 f.s.   (1215)

Sonata SK 37
(Hinojosa) (Bibliotheque De Musique
Ancienne) TRANSAT. $2.75   (1216)

4 Sonatas
(Ruiz-Pipo) gtr UNION ESP. 21778
f.s.   (1217)

Sonaten, 2
(Hinojosa) (5th degr.) SCHOTT
GA-237 f.s.   (1218)

SENAILLE, JEAN BAPTISTE (1687-1730)
Sonata
(Pujol) ESCHIG 1100 f.s.   (1219)

SEVERINO, GIULIO
Fantasy
(van der Staak) (4th degr.)
BROEKMANS 810 f.s.   (1220)

SOLER, [PADRE] ANTONIO (1729-1783)
Sonata No. 1 in A
(Garcia Velasco) (6th degr.) UNION
ESP. f.s.   (1221)

Sonata No. 2
(Garcia Velasco) gtr UNION ESP.
19717 f.s.   (1222)

Sonata No. 3
(Garcia Velasco) gtr UNION ESP.
19718 f.s.   (1223)

Sonata No. 4, Bolero
(Azpiazu) (8-9th degr.) UNION ESP.
19451 f.s.   (1224)

Sonata No. 6
(Garcia Velasco) gtr UNION ESP.
21014 f.s.   (1225)

Sonata No. 8
(Azpiazu) (8th degr.) UNION ESP.
19452 f.s.   (1226)

Sonata No. 13
(Garcia Velasco) gtr UNION ESP.
19719 f.s.   (1227)

Sonata No. 14
(Garcia Velasco) gtr UNION ESP.
19720 f.s.   (1228)

Sonata No. 15
(Garcia Velasco) gtr UNION ESP.
19721 f.s.   (1229)

Sonata No. 18, En Modo Dorico
(Garcia Velasco) (5th degr.) UNION
ESP. f.s.   (1230)

Sonata No. 69
(Azpiazu) gtr UNION ESP. 20042 f.s.
                                  (1231)

Sonata No. 71
(Garcia Velasco) gtr UNION ESP.
20043 f.s.   (1232)

Sonata No. 84
(Andia) (6-7th degr., A is B;
Bibliotheque De Musique Ancienne)
TRANSAT. 1304 $2.25   (1233)

Sonata No. 87
(Andia) (8th degr., g is f sharp;
Bibliotheque De Musique Ancienne)
TRANSAT. 1296 $2.25   (1234)

SPERONTES (JOHANN SIGISMUND SCHOLZE)
(1705-1750)
Spielstucke, 22
(Monkemeyer) gtr/2treb inst (3rd
degr.) sc TONGER 1077 f.s. (1235)

STAMITZ, JOHANN WENZEL ANTON
(1717-1757)
Divertissement in D
(Azpiazu) gtr UNION ESP. 19888 f.s.
                                  (1236)

Fugue
(Norman) gtr (6th degr.) SCHIRM.G
44820 f.s.   (1237)

STRAUBE, RUDOLF
Sonata No. 1 for Lute
(Reyne) gtr (6-7th degr., Leipzig,
1746, Guitare, No. 83) LEDUC G-83
f.s.   (1238)

Sonata Para Laud
(Azpiazu, J. de; Azpiazu, L. de)
gtr (7th degr.) UNION ESP. 20833
f.s.   (1239)

SWEELINCK, JAN PIETERSZOON (1562-1621)
Lantdarabok
"Lute Pieces" (Benko) gtr (Musica
Per Chitarra) EMB 7819 f.s.
                                  (1240)

Pieces, 4
(Castet) gtr (5th degr.) LEDUC G-36
f.s. Guitare, No.36
   contains: Courante; Volte I;
   Volte II; Volte III   (1241)

Pieces, 4
(Azpiazu) gtr (5th degr.) UNION
ESP. 21214 f.s.
   contains: Courante; Volte I;
   Volte II; Volte III   (1242)

Psalm No. 5
(Leerink) gtr (6th degr., g is f
sharp; Bibliotheek Van Den
Gitarist, No. 1) BROEKMANS 381
f.s. contains also: Anonymous,
Dorische Fantasie   (1243)

SWEELINCK, JAN PIETERSZOON (cont'd.)

Psalm No. 23
(Leerink) gtr (6th degr., g is f
sharp; Bibliotheek Van Den
Gitarist, No. 2) BROEKMANS 380
f.s. contains also: Anonymous,
Phrygische Fantasie   (1244)

Voltes, 2
(Visser) gtr (5th degr.) HARMONIA
2653 f.s.   (1245)

TANZE AUS DER RENAISSANCE *CC7U
(Scheit) gtr (3rd degr.) UNIVER.
13070 $3.25   (1246)

TANZE UND WEISEN AUS DEM BAROCK *CC7U
(Scheit) gtr (2nd degr.) UNIVER.
13069 $3.25   (1247)

TELEMANN, GEORG PHILIPP (1681-1767)
Fantasy in A
(Azpiazu, L. de) gtr (8th degr.,
Guitare, No.4) LEDUC G-4 f.s.
                                  (1248)

Fantasy in B flat
(Azpiazu) gtr (8-9th degr.) UNION
ESP. 19882 f.s.   (1249)

Fantasy in D
(Azpiazu) gtr (8th degr.) UNION
ESP. 19883 f.s.   (1250)

Fantasy in E minor
(Azpiazu, L. de) gtr (8th degr.,
Guitare, No.1) LEDUC G-1 $2.25
                                  (1251)

Fantasy in F minor
(Azpiazu) gtr (8th degr.) UNION
ESP. 19881 f.s.   (1252)

Fantasy in G
(Azpiazu) gtr (8th degr.) UNION
ESP. 19884 f.s.   (1253)

Fantasy No. 7
(Azpiazu) gtr (8th degr.) ZIMMER.
ZM-1722 f.s.   (1254)

Gavotte
(Behrend) gtr (3rd degr.) ZIMMER.
EC-63 f.s.   (1255)

Passacaglia
(Azpiazu) gtr (6-7th degr.,
Guitarra, No. 11) DELRIEU 1283
f.s.   (1256)

Suita Polska
(Wilkowska-Chominska, Krystyna)
[Polish] 2gtr (single staff, incl
commentary; "Florilegium Musicae
Antiquae", Vol. 24) folio POLSKIE
6429 f.s.   (1257)

TORRE, FERNANDO DELLE
Alta Danza
(Tarrago) gtr UNION ESP. 20811 f.s.
                                  (1258)

VALDERRABANO, ENRIQUEZ DE
(fl. ca. 1550)
Diferencias Sobre "La Pavana Real"
(Usillos) gtr (4th degr.) UNION
ESP. f.s.   (1259)

Fantasy (from Silva De Sirenas)
(Sainz de la Maza) gtr UNION ESP.
18827 f.s.   (1260)

Fantasy, MIN 270
"Fantaisie Du Quatrieme Ton"
(Pujol) gtr (5-6th degr., g is f
sharp) ESCHIG 1085 f.s.   (1261)
"Fantasia XVI" (Tarrago) gtr (5-6th
degr.) UNION ESP. 20583 f.s.
                                  (1262)

Fugas, 2 (from Silva De Sirenas,
Libro I)
(Azpiazu, L. de) gtr (5th degr.)
UNION ESP. 20661 f.s.   (1263)

Guardame Las Vacas
(Pujol) gtr ESCHIG 1043 f.s. (1264)

Pavanas
(Azpiazu, L. de) gtr (6th degr.)
UNION ESP. 20658 f.s.   (1265)
(Pujol) gtr (6th degr.) ESCHIG 1044
f.s.   (1266)

Sonata No. 15
(Pujol) gtr ESCHIG 1099 f.s.
   contains also: Sonata No. 20
                                  (1267)

Soneto Lombardo, A Manera De Danza
(Hinojosa) gtr (4th degr., g is f
sharp) SCHOTT GA-407 f.s. (1268)

VALLET, NICOLAS (1583-1626)
Air Und Courante
(Teuchert) gtr (Die Sologitarre)
SCHMIDT,H 308 f.s.   (1269)

VALLET, NICOLAS (cont'd.)

Allemande Fortune Helas Pourquoi
(Visser) gtr (2-4th degr.) HARMONIA
1567 f.s. contains also: Branle;
Sarabande Espagnolle, La; Volte
(Galliard)   (1270)

Solostucke (from Second Livre De
Tablature De Luth, Le) CC3OU
(Dirkx) gtr (3-6th degr.)
HOFMEISTER-W FH-4036 f.s. g is f
sharp   (1271)

VECCHI, ORAZIO (HORATIO) (1550-1605)
Pezzi Per Liuto, 4
(Azpiazu) gtr SYMPHON 456 f.s.
contains: Aria; Galliard; Pavan;
Saltarello   (1272)

VENEGAS DE HENESTROSA, TOMAS LUIS DE
Fabordones, 2, Llano Y Glosado Del
Cuarto Tono
(Usillos) gtr (7th degr.) UNION
ESP. f.s.   (1273)

VICTORIA, TOMAS LUIS DE (ca. 1548-1611)
Motets, 2
(Pujol) gtr ESCHIG 2003 f.s.
contains: Ave Maria; Popule Meus
                                (1274)

VIRCHI, PAOLO (? -ca. 1610)
Tanze, Canzonen Und Phantasien
(Brodszky) gtr (4-5th degr.,
includes 4 Saltarelli, 7 Canzoni
Napolitane, 1 Madrigal, 2
Canzoni, 2 Fantasie) SCHOTT 6429
f.s.   (1275)
(Brodszky) gtr (4-5th degr.,
includes 4 Saltarelli, 7 Canzoni,
Napolitane, 1 Madrigal, 2
Canzoni, 2 Fantasie) EMB Z-5757
f.s.   (1276)

VISEE, ROBERT DE (ca. 1650-ca. 1775)
Allemand, MIN 351
(Battine) gtr ESSEX f.s.   (1277)

Allemand, VOCG 38
"Tombeau De Francois Corbetta, Le"
(Pujol, Emilio) gtr ESCHIG 1051
f.s.   (1278)

Beruhmte Suite In D-Moll
(Behrend, Siegfried) gtr SIKORSKI
689 f.s. Die Konzertgitarre
contains: Allemand, VOCG 62;
Bourree, VOCG 67; Courante,
VOCG 63; Gavotte, VOCG 66;
Gigue, VOCG 65; Minuet, VOCG
70; Prelude, VOCG 61; Saraband,
VOCG 64   (1279)

Darab Gitarra, 6 (6 Pieces Pour
Guitare)
(Coste, Napoleon; Vereczkey,
Laszlo) gtr EMB Z-5967 f.s.
contains: Bourree, VOCG 67;
Gavotte, VOCG 66; Minuet, VOCG
68; Minuet, VOCG 70; Minuet,
VOCG 91; Saraband, VOCG 87 (A
min)   (1280)

Easy Suite In D Minor
(Papas, Sophocles) gtr COLUMBIA 124
f.s.
contains: Bourree, VOCG 67;
Gavotte, VOCG 66; Minuet, VOCG
68, "Entrada"; Minuet, VOCG 70;
Minuet, VOCG 91 (B min)   (1281)

Gavotte, VOCG 78
(Pujol, Emilio) gtr ESCHIG 1064
f.s. contains also: Bourree, VOCG
79; Minuet, VOCG 80   (1282)

Livre De Guitarre Dedie Au Roy (1682)
*VOCG 1-50
"Gitarrenbuch" (Giesbert, Franz
Julius) 5-course gtr SCHOTT
GA-232 f.s.   (1283)

Livre De Pieces Pour La Guitarre
(1686) *VOCG 61-93
"Gitarrenstucke" (Giesbert, Franz
Julius) 5-course gtr SCHOTT
GA-233 f.s.   (1284)

Minuet, VOCG 91
(Scheit, Karl) gtr UNIVER. 14448
f.s. contains also: Saraband,
VOCG 90; Minuet, VOCG 93; Gigue,
VOCG 123   (1285)

Musica Del Re Sole
(Ferrari, Romolo) gtr BERBEN 1042
f.s. partly E IS D
contains: Allemand, VOCG 38 (A
min); Allemand, VOCG 86;
Bourree, VOCG 67; Courante,
VOCG 63; Gavotte, VOCG 66;
Gavotte, VOCG 78; Gigue, VOCG
65; Gigue, VOCG 75; Gigue, VOCG
82; Minuet, VOCG 68;
"Praeludium"; Minuet, VOCG 70;
Minuet, VOCG 84; Minuet, VOCG

VISEE, ROBERT DE (cont'd.)

91, "Trio" (B min);
Passacaglia, VOCG 92; Saraband,
VOCG 64; Saraband, VOCG 83;
Saraband, VOCG 87 (A min)
                                (1286)

Passacaglia, VOCG 92
(Behrend, Siegfried) gtr HEINRICH.
N-1621 f.s.   (1287)
(Prol, Julio) gtr PAGANI 114 f.s.
                                (1288)

Petite Suite En Re Mineur, Pt. 1
(Pujol, Emilio) gtr ESCHIG 1007
f.s.
contains: Allemand, VOCG 62;
Gigue, VOCG 65; Prelude, VOCG
61; Saraband, VOCG 64   (1289)

Petite Suite En Re Mineur, Pt. 2
(Pujol, Emilio) gtr ESCHIG 1007BIS
f.s.
contains: Bourree, VOCG 67;
Courante, VOCG 63; Gavotte,
VOCG 66; Minuet, VOCG 68;
Minuet, VOCG 70; Passacaglia,
VOCG 69   (1290)

Pieces, 6, Extraites Du Livre Publie
En 1686 Et Dedie A S.M. Louis XIV
(Coste, Napoleon) gtr LEMOINE 24117
f.s.
contains: Bourree, VOCG 67;
Gavotte, VOCG 66; Minuet, VOCG
68; Minuet, VOCG 70; Minuet,
VOCG 91; Saraband, VOCG 87 (A
min)   (1291)

Piezas, 3
(Fortea, Daniel) gtr FORTEA 278
f.s.
contains: Bourree, VOCG 67;
Gavotte, VOCG 66; Minuet, VOCG
68   (1292)

Piezas, 4
(Fortea, Daniel) gtr FORTEA 279
f.s.
contains: Gigue, VOCG 65; Gigue,
VOCG 75; Gigue, VOCG 82;
Saraband, VOCG 87 (A min)
                                (1293)

Saraband, VOCG 90
(Pujol, Emilio) gtr ESCHIG 1050
f.s. contains also: Minuet, VOCG
91; Passacaglia, VOCG 92   (1294)

Suite A-Moll
(Zanoskar, Hubert) gtr NOETZEL
N-3312 f.s.
contains: Courante, VOCG 3;
Gavotte, MIN 319 (not in VOCG);
Gavotte, VOCG 116; Gigue, MIN
321 (not in VOCG); Gigue, VOCG
75; Minuet, VOCG 76;
Passacaglia, MIN 322 (not in
VOCG); Pastorale, MIN 320 (not
in VOCG)   (1295)

Suite C-Moll
(Scheit, Karl) gtr UNIVER. 14452
f.s.
contains: Allemand, VOCG 38;
Courante, VOCG 39; Gavotte,
VOCG 42; Prelude, VOCG 37;
Saraband, VOCG 40; Saraband,
VOCG 41   (1296)

Suite D-Moll
(Scheit, Karl) gtr UNIVER. 11322
f.s.
contains: Allemand, VOCG 62;
Bourree, VOCG 67; Courante,
VOCG 63; Gavotte, VOCG 66;
Gigue, VOCG 65; Minuet, VOCG
68; Minuet, VOCG 70; Prelude,
VOCG 61; Saraband, VOCG 64
                                (1297)

Suite D-Moll (Re Mineur)
(Azpiazu, Jose de) gtr SYMPHON 345
f.s.
contains: Allemand, VOCG 62;
Bourree, VOCG 67; Courante,
VOCG 63; Gavotte, VOCG 66;
Gigue, VOCG 65; Minuet, VOCG
68; Minuet, VOCG 70; Prelude,
VOCG 61; Saraband, VOCG 64
                                (1298)

Suite E-Dur
(Scheit, Karl) gtr UNIVER. 14451
f.s.
contains: Allemand, VOCG 52;
Bourree, VOCG 60; "Villageoise,
La"; Chaconne, VOCG 57;
Courante, VOCG 53; Gavotte,
VOCG 58; Gigue, VOCG 55;
Minuet, VOCG 59; Prelude, VOCG
51; Saraband, VOCG 54;
Saraband, VOCG 56   (1299)

Suite E-Moll
(Zanoskar, Hubert) gtr NOETZEL
N-3313 f.s.
contains: Allemand, MIN 314 (not
in VOCG); Allemand, MIN 317
(not in VOCG); Allemand, MIN

VISEE, ROBERT DE (cont'd.)

318 (not in VOCG); Courante,
MIN 316 (not in VOCG);
Courante, VOCG 28; Saraband,
MIN 315 (not in VOCG);
Saraband, VOCG 115   (1300)

Suite Em La
(Alba, Luis) gtr RICORDI-BR BR-2169
f.s.
contains: Gavotte, VOCG 7; Gigue,
VOCG 82; Minuet, VOCG 84;
Prelude, VOCG 85 (A min);
Saraband, VOCG 83   (1301)

Suite En La Et Passacaille
(Azpiazu, Jose de) gtr SYMPHON 23
f.s.
contains: Allemand, VOCG 86 (A
min); Gavotte, VOCG 78 (A maj);
Gigue, VOCG 75 (A min); Gigue,
VOCG 82; Minuet, VOCG 84;
Passacaglia, VOCG 92; Prelude,
VOCG 1; Saraband, VOCG 83;
Saraband, VOCG 87 (A min)
                                (1302)

Suite En Re
(Mercado, Domingo) gtr RICORDI-ARG
BA-12447 f.s. E IS D
contains: Allemand, VOCG 62;
Bourree, VOCG 67; Danza;
Gavotte, VOCG 66; Gigue, VOCG
65; Prelude, VOCG 61; Saraband,
VOCG 64   (1303)

Suite En Re Menor
(Sainz de la Maza, Regino) gtr
UNION ESP. 18895 f.s.
contains: Allemand, VOCG 62;
Bourree, VOCG 67; Courante,
VOCG 63; Gavotte, VOCG 66;
Gigue, VOCG 65; Minuet, VOCG
68; Minuet, VOCG 70; Prelude,
VOCG 61; Saraband, VOCG 64
                                (1304)

Suite En Re Mineur
(Ragossnig, Konrad) gtr ESCHIG 7768
f.s. E IS D
contains: Allemand, VOCG 62;
Bourree, VOCG 67; Courante,
VOCG 63; Gavotte, VOCG 66;
Gigue, VOCG 65; Minuet, VOCG
68; Minuet, VOCG 70; Prelude,
VOCG 61; Saraband, VOCG 64
                                (1305)

Suite En Re Mineur
(Alfonso, Nicolas) gtr SCHOTT-FRER
9244 f.s. Edition Nicolas
Alfonso, No. 19-20
contains: Allemand, VOCG 62;
Bourree, VOCG 67; Courante,
VOCG 63; Gavotte, VOCG 66;
Gigue, VOCG 65; Minuet, MIN 313
(not in VOCG); Minuet, VOCG 68;
Prelude, VOCG 61; Saraband,
VOCG 64   (1306)

Suite En Re Mineur *VOCG 61-70
(Gousse, Claude) gtr (Renaissance,
No. 3; 2 x 9 unnumbered pcs;
introduction; without VOCG 69)
DELRIEU 1427 f.s. contains also:
Suite En Sol Mineur, VOCG 71-80
(without VOCG 77)   (1307)

Suite En Re Mineur *VOCG 61-70
(Ibanez, Pedro Jose) gtr CHOUDENS
20.558 f.s.   (1308)

Suite En Si Mineur Et 8 Pieces Du
Deuxieme Livre
(Castet; Gousse) gtr (Renaissance,
Vol. 8) DELRIEU f.s.   (1309)

Suite En Sol Majeur
(Santos, Turibio) gtr ESCHIG 8056
f.s. Collection Turibio Santos,
No. 2
contains: Allemand, VOCG 52;
Bourree, VOCG 60; Courante,
VOCG 53; Gavotte, VOCG 58;
Gigue, VOCG 55; Minuet, VOCG
59; Prelude, VOCG 51; Saraband,
VOCG 56   (1310)

Suite En Sol Mineur
(Pujol, Emilio) gtr ESCHIG 1024
f.s.
contains: Allemand, VOCG 72;
Chaconne, VOCG 77; Courante,
VOCG 73; Gigue, VOCG 75;
Minuet, VOCG 76; Prelude, VOCG
71; Saraband, VOCG 74   (1311)

Suite G-Moll
(Scheit, Karl) gtr UNIVER. 12714
f.s.
contains: Allemand, VOCG 72;
Bourree, VOCG 79; Courante,
VOCG 73; Gavotte, VOCG 78;
Gigue, VOCG 75; Minuet, VOCG
76; Minuet, VOCG 80; Prelude,
VOCG 71; Saraband, VOCG 74
                                (1312)

VISEE, ROBERT DE (cont'd.)

Suite H-Moll
(Scheit, Karl) gtr UNIVER. 14449
f.s.
contains: Allemand, VOCG 86;
Gigue, VOCG 88; Prelude, VOCG
85; Saraband, VOCG 87   (1313)

Suite In A
(Behrend, Siegfried) gtr HEINRICH.
N-1618 f.s.
contains: Gavotte, VOCG 7;
Minuet, VOCG 84; Prelude, VOCG
85 (A min); Saraband, VOCG 83
(1314)

Suite In A
(Kennard, Deric) gtr SCHOTT 10540
f.s.
contains: Allemand, VOCG 2;
Allemand, VOCG 10; Bourree,
VOCG 9; Courante, VOCG 3;
Courante, VOCG 11; Gavotte,
VOCG 7; Gavotte, VOCG 8; Gigue,
VOCG 5; Passacaglia, VOCG 6;
Prelude, VOCG 1; Saraband, VOCG
4; Saraband, VOCG 12   (1315)

Suite in D minor
(Domandl) gtr BENJ 1202 f.s. (1316)
(Paolini) gtr RICORDI-IT 137071
f.s.   (1317)

Suite In D-Moll
(Albert, Heinrich) gtr ZIMMER.
ZM-1404 f.s. E IS D
contains: Bourree, VOCG 67;
Gavotte, VOCG 66; Minuet, VOCG
68, "Praeludium"; Minuet, VOCG
70; Minuet, VOCG 91, "Trio" (B
min); Saraband, VOCG 87 (A min)
(1318)

Suite in G
(Oraison) gtr TEESELING VT-178 f.s.
(1319)

Suite In H-Moll
(Schmidt, Armin) gtr ZIMMER.
ZM-1405 f.s.
contains: Allemand, VOCG 86;
Gigue, VOCG 88; Passacaglia,
VOCG 92 (B min); Prelude, VOCG
85; Saraband, VOCG 87   (1320)

Suite In Re
(Proakis, Costa) gtr BERBEN 536
f.s. E IS D
contains: Allemand, VOCG 62;
Gigue, VOCG 65; Minuet, VOCG
70; Prelude, VOCG 61; Saraband,
VOCG 64   (1321)

Suite In Sol Minore (from Livre De
Pieces Pour La Guitarre)
(Company, Alvaro; Saldarelli,
Vincenzo) [It/Eng/Ger] gtr fac ed
ZERBONI 7659 f.s. with
transcription, version for kbd
and arr gtr; xxxiv+15p.;
introduction; l'Arte della
chitarra
contains: Allemand, VOCG 72;
Chaconne, VOCG 77; Courante,
VOCG 73; Gigue, VOCG 75;
Minuet, VOCG 76; Prelude, VOCG
71; Saraband, VOCG 74   (1322)

Suite No. 7 En Do Mayor (from Livre
De Guitare Dedie Au Roi (1682))
(Balaguer, Rafael) gtr UNION ESP.
21852 f.s.
contains: Allemand, VOCG 44;
Courante, VOCG 45; Gavotte,
VOCG 48; Giga A La Manera
Inglesa; Gigue, VOCG 47;
Minuet, VOCG 49; Prelude, VOCG
43; Saraband, VOCG 46   (1323)

VIVALDI, ANTONIO (1678-1741)
Concerto in D, MIN 388
(Byrd) gtr COLUMBIA 181 f.s. (1324)

Gigue
(Ranieri) gtr (6th degr.) CRANZ
f.s.   (1325)

WAISSEL(IUS), MATTHAUS (ca. 1540-1602)
Phantasia Und Deutscher Tanz
(Scheit) gtr (3rd degr.) UNIVER.
12712 $2.75   (1326)

WEISS, SYLVIUS LEOPOLD (1686-1750)
Air in E
(Sensier) gtr (5th degr.) ESSEX
f.s.   (1327)

Angloise
(Scheit) gtr (6th degr., Chiesa I-
from XIV, 146f.) UNIVER. 14436
$2.75   (1328)

Balletto
(Gangi) gtr (6-7th degr.,
authenticity doubtful; not in
Chiesa or Neemann) BERBEN EB1113
$1.00   (1329)

WEISS, SYLVIUS LEOPOLD (cont'd.)

Bourree, MIN 101
(Carfagna) gtr (5th degr., Neemann
- from II, 48ff.) BERBEN EB1489
$1.00   (1330)

Capriccio in D
(Azpiazu) gtr (7-8th degr., Chiesa
II-204ff.; Neemann-110ff; E is D)
UNION ESP. 19528 f.s.   (1331)
(Pick) gtr (7-8th degr., Chiesa II-
204ff.; Neemann-110ff) FORSTER
f.s.   (1332)

Chaconne in A minor
(Artzt) gtr COLUMBIA 200 f.s.
(1333)

Chaconne, MIN 102
(Azpiazu) gtr (A maj,6th degr.,
Chiesa I - from VIII, 84ff.)
SYMPHON 459 f.s.   (1334)
"Ciaccona" (Carfagna) gtr (A maj,
6th degr., Chiesa I - from VIII,
84ff.) BERBEN EB1933 $1.00 (1335)
(Sainz de la Maza) gtr (A maj,6th
degr., Chiesa I - from VIII,
84ff.) UNION ESP. 18884 f.s.
(1336)

Fantasy in C minor
(Abloniz) gtr (D min,8th degr.,
Chiesa II-168ff.; Neemann-108ff;
E is D) BERBEN EB1319 $1.00
(1337)
(Azpiazu) gtr (D min,8th degr.,
Chiesa II-168ff.; Neemann-108ff;
E is D) UNION ESP. 19530 f.s.
(1338)
(Behrend) gtr (E min,8th degr.,
Chiesa II-168ff.; Neemann-108ff;
Gitarre-Bibliothek, No.74) BOTE
GB-74 f.s.   (1339)
(Hopman) gtr (D min,8th degr.,
Chiesa II-168ff.; Neemann-108ff;
E is D) HARMONIA 2544 f.s. (1340)
(Kennard) gtr (E min,8th degr.,
Chiesa II-168ff.; Neemann-108ff)
SCHOTT GA-89 f.s.   (1341)
"Fantaisie Pour Le Luth" (Sierra)
gtr (D min,8th degr., Chiesa II-
168ff.; Neemann-108ff; E is D)
CHOUDENS 20.647 f.s.   (1342)
(Teuchert) gtr (8th degr., Chiesa
II-168ff.; Die
Sologitarre) SCHMIDT,H 302 f.s.
(1343)
(van Puijenbroeck) gtr (8th degr.,
Chiesa II-168ff.; Neemann-108ff)
METROPOLIS EM-4736 $2.00   (1344)
(Wensiecki) gtr (7-8th degr., treb
clef & tablature; transposed to e
minor; Chiesa II-168ff.; Neemann-
108ff.) HOFMEISTER-W FH-4038 f.s.
contains also: Capriccio in D
(Chiesa II-204ff.; Neemann-
104ff.); Saraband in A minor
(Chiesa- not listed; Neemann -
from IV, 81f.)   (1345)

Fantasy, MIN 103
(Wensiecki) gtr (7th degr., Chiesa
II-201ff) ZANIBON 5180 f.s.
contains also: Fugue, MIN 104
(Chiesa II-163f); Tombeau (Chiesa
II-173f); Capriccio, MIN 105
(Chiesa II-204ff; Neemann-110ff)
(1346)

Fugue No. 6
(Kennard) gtr (6th degr., Chiesa
II-163f.) SCHOTT 11082 f.s.
(1347)

Gigue in A minor
(Pujol) gtr (5th degr., not in
Chiesa or Neemann) ESCHIG 1054
f.s.   (1348)
(Sensier) gtr (5th degr., not in
Chiesa or Neemann) ESSEX f.s.
(1349)

Largo
(Goor) gtr (e' is d', g is f-sharp;
Chiesa II-156f.) METROPOLIS
EM-4724 $2.50 contains also:
Minuet, MIN 106 (Chiesa II-179);
Plainte (Chiesa II-172f.)   (1350)

2 Menuette
(Kreidler) gtr (3rd degr.) SCHOTT
GA-452 f.s.   (1351)

Minuet, MIN 77
(Scheit) gtr (D min,3-4th degr.,
Neemann - from II, 48ff.;
formerly OBV-6781-128A; E is D)
UNIVER. 14444 $2.75 contains
also: Saraband; Minuet, MIN 78
(1352)

Overture in B flat
(Kennard) gtr (A maj,8th degr.,
Chiesa II-139ff.) SCHOTT GA-97
f.s.   (1353)
(van Puijenbroeck) gtr (G maj,8th
degr., Chiesa II-139ff, g is f
sharp; capotasto in pos.
III) METROPOLIS EM-14006 $1.75
(1354)

WEISS, SYLVIUS LEOPOLD (cont'd.)

Partita No. 15
(Kennard) gtr (7-8th degr.,
includes Prelude, Toccata, Fugue;
Chiesa II-from XVIII, 14ff.)
SCHOTT GA-90 f.s.   (1355)

Passacaglia, MIN 107
(Hopman) gtr (D maj,7th degr.,
Chiesa I- from XIV, 150ff.)
HARMONIA 2681 f.s.   (1356)
(Kennard) gtr (D maj,7th degr.,
Chiesa I- from XIV, 150ff.)
SCHOTT 11083 f.s.   (1357)
(Ranalli) gtr (E maj,7th degr.,
Chiesa I- from XIV, 150ff.)
BERBEN EB2099 f.s.   (1358)
(Scheit) gtr (D maj,7th degr.,
Chiesa I- from XIV, 150ff.; with
facs) UNIVER. 14428 $3.25 (1359)

Piezas Diversas Para Laud   °CC9U
(Azpiazu) gtr UNION ESP. f.s.
Chaconne: Chiesa I- from VIII,
84ff.   (1360)

Prelude, MIN 108
(Komter) gtr (D min,4-6th degr.,
Neemann- from II, 48ff.; E is D)
HARMONIA 2258 f.s. contains also:
Courante, MIN 108; Minuet, MIN
110   (1361)

Prelude, MIN 111
(Sensier) gtr (8th degr.) ESSEX
f.s.   (1362)

Saraband in A
(Sensier) gtr (6th degr.) ESSEX
f.s.   (1363)

Six Pieces, Vol. 1
(Barbosa Lima) gtr (3 pcs) COLUMBIA
187A f.s.   (1364)

Six Pieces, Vol. 2
(Barbosa Lima) gtr (3 pcs) COLUMBIA
187B f.s.   (1365)

Sonata En Re Minore
(Azpiazu, L. de) gtr (7-8th degr.,
not in Chiesa or Neemann) UNION
ESP. 21208 f.s.   (1366)

Sonata in A minor
"Infidele, L'" (Meunier) gtr
(Chiesa II- XXV, 94ff.)
BREITKOPF-W EB-6770 f.s.   (1367)

Sonata in B minor
"London Sonata No. 16" (van
Puijenbroeck) gtr (Chiesa I- from
XVI, 163ff.; e' is d', g is f
sharp; capotasto in pos. III)
METROPOLIS EM-14010 f.s.   (1368)

Sonata in D minor
"Dresden Sonata No. 5" (Abloniz)
gtr (B min,7th degr., Neemann-
II, 48ff.; e' is d', g is f
sharp) BERBEN EB1796 $3.25 (1369)
(Azpiazu) gtr (7th degr., Neemann-
II, 48ff.; E is D) UNION ESP.
f.s.   (1370)
"Erste Sonate" (Behrend) gtr (D
min,7th degr., Neemann- II,
48ff.; Gitarre-Bibliothek, No.8;
also published in: European
Masters For The Guitar) BOTE GB-8
f.s.   (1371)
"Suite Fur Laute" (Gerrits) gtr (E
min,7th degr., Neemann- II,
48ff.) MOSELER f.s.   (1372)
"Suite Para Laud" (Sainz de la
Maza) gtr (D min,7th degr.,
Neemann- II, 48ff.; E is D) UNION
ESP. 20776 f.s.   (1373)
(Scheit) gtr (7th degr., Neemann-
II, 48ff.; E is D) UNIVER. 14426
$3.75   (1374)
(van Puijenbroeck) gtr (B min,7th
degr., Neemann- II, 48ff.; e' is
d', g is f sharp) METROPOLIS
EM-4737 $3.00   (1375)

Sonata in F sharp minor
"London Sonata No. 25" (van
Puijenbroeck) gtr (Chiesa II-
XXV, 94ff.; e' is d', g is f
sharp; capotasto in pos. III)
METROPOLIS EM-14021 f.s.   (1376)

Sonata, MIN 112
"Dresden Sonata No. 7" (van
Puijenbroeck) gtr (not in Chiesa
or Neemann; e' is d', g is f-
sharp; capotasto in pos. III)
METROPOLIS EM-14020 $3.50 (1377)

Sonata, MIN 113
"Dresden Sonata No. 12" (Goor) gtr
(Neemann III- 55ff.; e' is d', g
is f sharp) METROPOLIS EM-4728
f.s.   (1378)

WEISS, SYLVIUS LEOPOLD (cont'd.)

Sonata, MIN 114
  "London Sonata No. 4" (van
  Puijenbroeck) gtr (Chiesa I- IV,
  33ff.; e' is d', g is f sharp)
  METROPOLIS EM-4735 $3.50   (1379)

Suite in A
  (Oltremari) gtr (7-8th degr.,
  Chiesa III- XVIII, 14ff.) ZANIBON
  5253 f.s.   (1380)

Suite in A minor, MIN 361, Gigue
  (Sensier) gtr ESSEX f.s.   (1381)

Suite in A minor, MIN 362, Saraband
  (Sensier) gtr ESSEX f.s.   (1382)

Suite in D
  "Suite No. 16 In D" (Kennard) gtr
  (7th degr., Chiesa I- II, 13ff.)
  SCHOTT GA-207 f.s.   (1383)
  "London Sonata No. 2" (van
  Puijenbroeck) gtr (7th degr.,
  Chiesa I- II, 13ff.; in B major;
  e' is d', g is f sharp; capotasto
  in pos. III) METROPOLIS EM-14001
  $3.50   (1384)

Suite in D minor, MIN 349, Allemand
  (Battine) gtr ESSEX f.s.   (1385)

Suite in E minor
  (Azpiazu, L. de) gtr (7th degr.,
  Guitare, No.20; Chiesa I- V,
  44ff.) LEDUC G-20 $3.25   (1386)

Suite No. 1 in E
  (Sierra) gtr (7th degr., Neemann-
  I, 41ff.) CHOUDENS 20.690 f.s.
                              (1387)

Suite No. 4
  (Kennard) gtr (8th degr., Chiesa I-
  XV, 153ff.) SCHOTT GA 209 f.s.
                              (1388)

Suite No. 15
  (Kennard) gtr (7-8th degr., Chiesa
  II-XVIII, 14ff) SCHOTT GA-90 f.s.
                              (1389)

Toccata in D
  (Pujol) gtr (5th degr., not in
  Chiesa or Neemann) ESCHIG 1053
  f.s.   (1390)
  (Sainz de la Maza) gtr (5th degr.,
  E is D; not in Chiesa or Neemann)
  UNION ESP. 20768 f.s. contains
  also: Gigue in D minor   (1391)

Tombeau Sur La Mort De Mr. Comte
    d'Logy
  (Azpiazu) gtr (7th degr., Chiesa
  II- 193f.; Neemann- 112f.; A
  minor) RICORDI-IT 11870 f.s.
                              (1392)
  (Hopman) gtr (7th degr., Chiesa II-
  193f.; Neemann- 112f.; D minor)
  HARMONIA 2680 f.s.   (1393)
  (Meunier) gtr (7th degr., Chiesa
  II- 193f.; Neemann- 112f.; B
  minor) BREITKOPF-W 6721 f.s.
                              (1394)
  (Scheit) gtr (D min,7th degr.,
  Chiesa II- 193f.; Neemann- 112f.;
  E is D; formerly: OBV-6781-128B)
  UNIVER. 14445 $2.75   (1395)
  (van Puijenbroeck) gtr (7th degr.,
  Chiesa II- 193f.; Neemann- 112f.;
  e' is d', g is f sharp, G minor)
  METROPOLIS EM-4738 $2.00   (1396)

11 Vortragsstucke (London MS)
  (Skiera) gtr SYMPHON 2238 f.s.
                              (1397)

WYSSENBACH, RUDOLF
Pavan
  "Barroncina, La" (Azpiazu, L. de)
  gtr (6th degr., Guitare, No.8)
  LEDUC G-8 f.s.   (1398)

I/IB1-Coll Guitar Solo Collections: Pre-Classical Music (until 1760)

ALBUM: 6 BERUHMTE STUCKE
  (Azpiazu) gtr (5-9th degr.) SYMPHON
  24 f.s. edition attributes all
  pieces to Weiss; none in Chiesa or
  Neemann
  contains: Ponce, Manuel Maria,
  Suite in A minor; Telemann, Georg
  Philipp, Presto (from Der Getreue
  Music-Meister); Weiss, Sylvius
  Leopold, Air, MIN 97; Weiss,
  Sylvius Leopold, Gigue, MIN 98;
  Weiss, Sylvius Leopold, Prelude,
  MIN 99; Weiss, Sylvius Leopold,
  Saraband, MIN 100   (1399)

ALTDEUTSCHE LAUTENMUSIK *CC13U
  (Behrend) gtr (2-3rd degr.) SIKORSKI
  525 $3.75 contains works by: Anon.
  (11), Judenkunig (2)   (1400)

ALTE HAUSMUSIK
  (van Hoek) gtr (3-7th degr.)
  HEINRICH. N-1291 f.s. arr + orig
  pcs; contains works by: Bossinensis
  (1), Diomedes Cato (1), Anon. (8),
  Mikolaj Z Krakowa (1), Polak (2),
  Dlugoraj (1), Judenkunig (3),
  Neusiedler (3), Susato (1),
  Valerius (1), Attaingnant (1),
  Askue (1) Pilkington (1), Enriquez
  de Valderrabano (1), Fuenllana (1),
  Gaultier (1), Kirnberger (1), Weiss
  (1), Cimarosa (1);
  contains: Bach, Johann Sebastian,
  Partita for Keyboard Instrument,
  No. 5, BWV 829, in G, Minuet
                              (1401)

ALTE MEISTER DES 17. JAHRHUNDERTS
  (Walker, Luise) 1-2gtr (5-7th degr.)
  sc HEINRICH. N-1541 f.s. 16 arr +
  orig pcs; contains works by: Losy
  vom Losinthal (1), Handel (2),
  Visee (1), Aldrovandini (1),
  Roncalli (3), Rameau (1), For 1
  Gtr; Handel (1), Corelli (1), For 2
  Gtr
  contains: Bach, Johann Sebastian,
  Partita for Violin, No. 1, BWV
  1002, in B minor, Saraband; Bach,
  Johann Sebastian, Partita for
  Violin, No. 3, BWV 1006, in E,
  Minuet; Bach, Johann Sebastian,
  Prelude for Lute, BWV 999, in C
  minor (D min); Bach, Johann
  Sebastian, Prelude No. 22 In B
  Flat Minor (from Das
  Wohltemperierte Clavier, Book 1);
  Bach, Johann Sebastian, Suite for
  Lute, BWV 996, in E minor,
  Bourree; Visee, Robert de, Suite
  in D minor (E is D) contains:
  Prelude, VOCG 61; Allemand, VOCG
  62; Courante, VOCG 63; Saraband,
  VOCG 64; Gavotte, VOCG 66; Minuet
  I, VOCG 68; Minuet II, VOCG 70;
  Bouree, VOCG 67; Gigue, VOCG 65)
                              (1402)

ALTE MINNELIEDER *CC11L
  (Gerwig) [Ger] gtr (2-3rd degr.) sc,
  pts NAGELS EN-1109 f.s. Nagels
  Laute- und Gitarre-Archiv; contains
  works by: Anon. (2), Fabricius (1),
  Praetorius (1), Neusiedler (1),
  Isaac (1), Lechner (1), Hassler
  (1), Schaffer (1), Senfl (1), Ott
  (1), for gtr (1), treb inst, gtr
  (1), solo voice, treb inst, gtr,
  opt bass inst (9)   (1403)

ALTE SPANISCHE MEISTER *CC3L
  (Azpiazu) gtr (6-7th degr.) SYMPHON
  423 f.s. contains works by: Milan,
  Mudarra, Narvaez   (1404)

ALTE SPANISCHE MEISTER *CC33U
  (Jirmal, Jiri) gtr ARTIA 2148 f.s.
                              (1405)

ALTENGLISCHE LAUTENMUSIK *CC10L
  (Behrend) gtr (3-4th degr.) SIKORSKI
  523 $3.75 contains works by: Anon.
  (4), Purcell (1), Lee (1),
  Woodwarde (1), Clarke (1), Babell
  (1), Wormall (1)   (1406)

ALTFRANZOSISCHE LAUTENMUSIK *CC12L
  (Behrend) gtr (3rd degr./7th degr.)
  SIKORSKI 524 $3.75 contains works
  by: Anon. (6), Attaingnant (1),
  Campion (5)   (1407)

ALTITALIENISCHE LAUTENMUSIK *CC15L
  (Behrend) gtr (3rd degr.) SIKORSKI
  526 $3.75 contains works by: Anon.
  (12), Caroso (2), Negri (1) (1408)

ALTPOLNISCHE MUSIK *CC15L
  (van Hoek) gtr (4-7th degr.) ZIMMER.
  ZM-1932 f.s. arr + orig pcs;
  contains works by: Anon. (6),
  Dlugoraj (2), Polak (1),
  Strzeszkowski (1), Diomedes Cato
  (2), Bohdanowicz (1), Mikolaj Z
  Krakowa (1), Jan Z Lublina (1)
                              (1409)

ALTSPANISCHE LAUTENMUSIK *CC7L
  (Behrend) gtr (2-6th degr.) SIKORSKI
  527 $3.75 contains works by:
  Mudarra (2), Narvaez (1), Enriquez
  de Valderrabano (1), Ruiz (3)
                              (1410)

ANONYMOUS
  Nurnberger Lautenbuch: Part 1 *CCU
  (Monkemeyer, Helmut) gtr HOFMEISTER
  FH-4572 f.s. "Die Tabulatur",
  Vol. 23   (1411)

  Nurnberger Lautenbuch: Part 2 *CCU
  (Monkemeyer, Helmut) gtr HOFMEISTER
  FH-4573 f.s. "Die Tabulatur",
  Vol. 24   (1412)

  Nurnberger Lautenbuch: Part 3 *CCU
  (Monkemeyer, Helmut) gtr HOFMEISTER
  FH-4574 f.s. "Die Tabulatur",
  Vol. 25   (1413)

6 ANONYMOUS LUTE SOLOS
  (Rooley) gtr NOVELLO 12.0463.07 f.s.
                              (1414)

ANTHOLOGIE DE LA MUSIQUE ANCIENNE, VOL.
    I: POUR LE LUTH *CC18L,16-18th
    cent
  (Miteran) gtr (2-4th degr.) CHOUDENS
  20.514 f.s. Collection L'Heure De
  La Guitarre Classique; contains
  works by: Negri (1), Attaingnant
  (1), Caroso (1), Le Roy (2),
  Borrono (1), Ballard (1), Sanz (2),
  Fr. de Visee (1), R. de Visee (1),
  Corbetta (1), Gautier (1), Murcia
  (1), Weiss (1), Rameau (1), Campion
  (2)   (1415)

ANTHOLOGIE DE LA MUSIQUE ANCIENNE, VOL.
    II: POUR LA GUITARE *CC20L,16-18th
    cent
  (Miteran) gtr (2-4th degr.) CHOUDENS
  20.604 f.s. Collection L'Heure De
  La Guitarre Classique; contains
  works by: Le Roy (1), Narvaez (1),
  Barberio (1), Bianchini (1), LeCoq
  (2), Murcia (2), Grange (1),
  Corbetta (2), Derosier (3), E.
  Gaultier (2), Bittner (1), Campion
  (2), Weiss (1)   (1416)

ANTOLOGIA DE LOS VIHUELISTAS ESPANOLAS,
    VOL. 1
  (Fresno) gtr (contains works by:
  Valderrabano; Mudarra and
  Fuenllana) ALPUERTO 1117 f.s.
                              (1417)

ANTOLOGIA DE LOS VIHUELISTAS ESPANOLAS,
    VOL. 2
  (Fresno) gtr (contains works by:
  Daza; Pisador; Milan and Narvaez)
  ALPUERTO 1119 f.s.   (1418)

ANTOLOGIA DE LOS VIHUELISTAS ESPANOLAS,
    VOL. 3
  (Fresno) gtr (contains 6 pcs by
  Mudarra) ALPUERTO 1119 f.s. (1419)

ANTOLOGIA DE LOS VIHUELISTAS ESPANOLAS,
    VOL. 5
  (Fresno) gtr (contains 5 Tientos by
  Milan) ALPUERTO 1121 f.s.   (1420)

ANTOLOGIA DI CHITARRISTI DEL BAROCCO
    SPAGNOLO *CC11L
  (Tonazzi) gtr (4-5th degr.) ZERBONI
  8322 f.s. contains works by: Sanz
  (5); Santiago de Murcia (4); and
  Guerau (2)   (1421)

ANTOLOGIA DI MUSICA ANTICA, VOL. I
    *CC12L
  (Chiesa) gtr (3-7th degr.) ZERBONI
  6892 $8.25 g is f sharp; contains
  works by: Spinacino (3), Dalza (3),
  Borrono da Milano (3), Milano (3)
                              (1422)

ANTOLOGIA DI MUSICA ANTICA, VOL. II
    *CC13L
  (Chiesa) gtr (3-7th degr.) ZERBONI
  7115 $8.25 g is f sharp; contains
  works by: Capirola (2), Borrono da
  Milano (1), Dall' Aquila (1), Crema
  (3), Gorzanis (3), Barbetta (3)
                              (1423)

ANTOLOGIA DI MUSICA ANTICA, VOL. III
    *CC19L
  (Chiesa) gtr (3-7th degr.) ZERBONI
  8212 f.s. g is f sharp; contains
  works by: Holborne (2), Pilkington
  (2), Cutting (3), Johnson (3),

Dowland (9)   (1424)

ATTAIGNANT, PIERRE, [PUBLISHER]
(? -1552)
    Dixhuit Basses Dances, 1529, Part 1:
        Die Basses Dances *CC38L
    (Monkemeyer, Helmut) gtr
    (tablature) HOFMEISTER FH-4553
    f.s. contains 17 basses dances, 9
    recoupes, 9 tordions, 1 lespoir,
    1 laroque, 1 subiectum en
    musique; orig for lute in g; "Die
    Tabulatur", Vol. 4   (1425)

    Dixhuit Basses Dances, 1529, Part 2:
        Balle, Haulberroys, Branles,
        Pavanes, Sauterelles, Gaillardes
        *CC45L
    (Monkemeyer, Helmut) gtr
    (tablature) HOFMEISTER FH-4554
    f.s. contains 1 balle, 2
    haulberroys, 18 branles, 9
    pavanes, 2 sauterelles, 13
    gaillardes, 6 subjecta; orig for
    lute in g; "Die Tabulatur", Vol.
    5   (1426)

    Zwei- Und Dreistimmige Solostucke Fur
        Die Laute *CC28U
    (Bruger, Hans Dagobert) [Ger] gtr
    (4th degr.) MOSELER f.s. contains
    26 pcs for gtr (lute) and 2 pcs
    for mel inst and gtr (lute);
    incl. intro, commentary, and
    app.; g is f sharp   (1427)

AUS DEM BALTISCHEN LAUTENBUCH 1740
    *CC17L
    (Pudelko) treb inst,1-2gtr/gtr solo
    (2-3rd degr.) sc NAGELS EN-1107
    f.s. notation: treb clef; Nagels
    Laute- Und Gitarre-Archiv; contains
    works by: Anon. (16), Batchelar (1)
                                 (1428)

AUS DEM TABULATURBUCH DES CHRISTOPHORUS
    HERHOLDER (1602) *CC10U
    (Gerwig) gtr (3-4th degr.) LIENAU
    f.s. g is f sharp; Der Lautenist,
    Vol. V   (1429)

AUS TABULATUREN DES 16.-18.
    JAHRHUNDERTS *CC65U
    (Quadt) gtr (3-7th degr.) HOFMEISTER
    T-4154 $7.50 contains works by 21
    composers   (1430)

AUSGEWAHLTE STUCKE AUS EINER ANGELICA-
    UND GITARREN- TABULATUR DER 2.
    HALFTE DES 17. JAHRHUNDERTS *CC26U
    (Racke, Hans) [Ger] gtr (single
    staff/4th degr.) AKADDV f.s. incl.
    intro and commentary; "Musik Alter
    Meister", Vol. 17   (1431)

AUSGEWAHLTE WERKE AUS DER AUSSEER
    GITARRETABULATUR DES 18.
    JAHRHUNDERTS *CC57U
    (Klima, Josef) [Ger] gtr (single
    staff/4th degr.) AKADDV f.s. incl.
    intro and commentary; "Musik Alter
    Meister", Vol. 10   (1432)

BAROQUE GUITARIST, THE
    (Block) gtr (1-4th degr.) MARKS
    15219-16 $1.50 14 arr + orig pcs;
    contains works by: Telemann (1),
    Anon. (1), Purcell (1), Dowland
    (1), D. Scarlatti (2), Vivaldi (1),
    Handel (1), Rameau (1), Lully (1),
    F. Couperin (2), Corelli (2)
    contains: Bach, Johann Sebastian,
    Minuet, BWV Anh. 132, in D minor
    (from Anna Magdalena Bach
    Notenbuchlein (1725), No. 36)
                                 (1433)

BERUHMTE ARIEN, 4
    (Azpiazu) gtr (6th degr.) SYMPHON 442
    f.s.
    contains: Bach, Johann Sebastian,
    Partita for Keyboard Instrument,
    No. 6, BWV 830, in E minor, Air
    (A min); Purcell, Henry, Aria;
    Telemann, Georg Philipp, Aria;
    Zipoli, Domenico, Aria   (1434)

CAHIERS DU GUITAROLIER, LES, VOL. 2
    *16th cent
    "Danses Faciles d'Adrien Le Roy"
    (Rollin) gtr LEDUC f.s.   (1435)

CAROSO, FABRIZIO (1526-1600)
    Ballarino, Il *CC79U
    (Monkemeyer, Helmut) [Eng/Fr/Ger]
    gtr (4th degr.) set TONGER
    1374A-B f.s. g is f sharp; 2 vol.
    set; comp. ed of the "Balletti"
                                 (1436)

CHORAL UND LAUTE
    (Funck) [Ger] (3rd degr.) sc LIENAU
    1435 f.s. Das Spiel Der
    Lauteninstrumente, Series II,
    Spielbuch 12; 10 Pcs; contains
    works by: Anon., Nicolai, Neumark,
    Gastorius, Gesius [sic, i.e.-
    Hassler], Luther (2), Cruger,
    Vulpius, Forster, for solo voice,

gtr, (nos. 1-8 also transcribed for
gtr solo) arr by W. Gerwig; nos. 2,
3, 5, 6, 10 arr. by J.S. Bach
contains: Bach, Johann Sebastian,
Aus Tiefer Not Schrei Ich Zu Dir.
Chorale (from Cantata No. 38)
(gtr,solo voice); Bach, Johann
Sebastian, Befiehl Du Deine Wege.
Chorale, BWV 270 (gtr,opt solo
voice); Bach, Johann Sebastian,
Nun Ruhen Alle Walder. Chorale,
BWV 392 (gtr,solo voice); Bach,
Johann Sebastian, Wer Nur Den
Lieben Gott Lasst Walten.
Chorale, BWV 434 (gtr,opt solo
voice); Bach, Johann Sebastian,
Wie Schon Leuchtet Der
Morgenstern. Chorale, BWV 436
(gtr,opt solo voice)   (1437)

CREMA, JOAN MARIA DA
    Intavolatura Di Liuto: Libro Primo
        (1546) *CC50U
    (Ghisi, Federico) [It] gtr (single
    staff) MAURRI f.s. orig for lute
    in e; contains 15 recercari, 25
    intabulations of voc. comp., 7
    saltarelli, 3 pass' e mezzi; incl
    intro and biblio   (1438)

DA UN CODICE LAUTEN-BUCH DEL
    CINQUECENTO *CC99U
    (Chilesotti, Oscar) [It/Ger] gtr
    (single staff) quarto oblong FORNI
    f.s. orig for lute in g;
    "Bibliotheca Musica Bononiensis",
    Sezione IV, no. 32   (1439)

DALZA, JOAN AMBROSIO
    Intabulatura De Lauto (Petrucci,
        1508), Part 1: "Tastar De Corde -
        Calate" *CC13U
    (Monkemeyer, Helmut) gtr HOFMEISTER
    FH-4555 f.s. contains "Regula per
    quelli che non sanno cantare";
    orig for lute in a; It tab.; "Die
    Tabulatur", Vol. 6   (1440)

    Intabulatura De Lauto (Petrucci,
        1508), Part 2: "Padoane Alla
        Venetiana" *CCU
    (Monkemeyer, Helmut) gtr HOFMEISTER
    FH-4556 f.s. contains 5 pavanes,
    saltarelli, pivas; orig for lute
    in a; It tab.; "Die Tabulatur",
    Vol. 7   (1441)

    Intabulatura De Lauto (Petrucci,
        1508), Part 3: "Padoane Alla
        Ferrarese" *CCU
    (Monkemeyer, Helmut) gtr HOFMEISTER
    FH-4557 f.s. contains 3 pavanes,
    saltarelli, pivas; orig for lute
    in a; It tab.; "Die Tabulatur",
    Vol. 8   (1442)

DANSES, 4
    (Castet) gtr (3rd degr.) LEDUC G-49
    f.s. Guitare, No.49; contains works
    by: Anon. (2), Losy vom Losinthal
    (1), Carpentier (1)
    contains: Courante, MIN 15;
    Courante, MIN 16; Minuet, MIN 18;
    Rondo, MIN 17   (1443)

DEUTSCHE MEISTER DES EIN- UND
    ZWEISTIMMIGEN LAUTENSATZES, 16.-18.
    JAHRHUNDERT
    (Bruger) [Ger] (1-3rd degr.) MOSELER
    f.s. contains 22 arr + orig pcs; 12
    pcs by: Heckel (1), M. Neusiedler
    (1), Hainhofer (9), for gtr (1
    Line); 2 pcs by Anon., H.
    Neusiedler for gtr (2 lines); 6 pcs
    by: Anon. (2), Judenkunig (1), H.
    Neusiedler (3) for solo voice, gtr
    (2 lines)
    contains: Bach, Johann Sebastian,
    Prelude, Fugue, And Allegro For
    Lute In E Flat, BWV 998: Allegro
    (gtr) (C maj, fragment only);
    Bach, Johann Sebastian, Suite for
    Lute, BWV 996, in E minor,
    Bourree (2gtr) (partly single
    line playing); Bach, Johann
    Sebastian, Suite for Lute, BWV
    996, in E minor, Passaggio-
    Prelude (2gtr) (single line
    playing)   (1444)

DEUXIEME RECUEIL DE PIECES FACILES
    (Castet) gtr (3rd degr.) LEDUC G-77
    $3.00 Guitare, No.77; contains
    works by: Fuhrmann (1), Ballard
    (1), Anon. (2)
    contains: Ballet; Bourree, MIN 271;
    Branle; Courante, MIN 272 (1445)

DLUGORAJ, ADALBERT (WOJIECH) (ca. 1550)
    Fantazje I Wilanele *CC8U
    (Pozniak, Piotr) gtr (single staff)
    folio POLSKIE f.s. orig for lute
    in g; Wydawnictwo Dawnej Muzyki
    Polskiej (Editions De Musique
    Polonaise Ancienne) No. 23; gtr
    transcrip by Tadeusza Musialka

DLUGORAJ, ADALBERT (WOJIECH) (cont'd.)
                                 (1446)

DOWLAND, ROBERT (1591-1641)
    Six Lute Pieces (from Varietie Of
        Lute Lessons) CC6U
    (Mairants) gtr BREITKOPF-W 57.04029
    f.s.   (1447)

EARLY MUSIC FOR THE GUITAR; ORIGINAL
    PIECES FROM MEDIEVAL AND
    RENAISSANCE SOURCES *CC35L
    (Morris) gtr (3-4th degr.) SCHIRM.G
    22.48816 f.s. annotated; contains
    works by: Anon. (14), Alfonso, El
    Sabio, King Of Castile (1), Blondel
    de Nesle (1), Lassus (4), Binchois
    (3) Dandrieu (1), Landini (1),
    Machaut (5), Thibaut IV, King Of
    Navarre (1), Caccini (1), Ansunes
    (1)   (1448)

EASY 16TH CENTURY PIECES, 7 *CC7L
    (van der Staak) gtr (3rd degr.)
    BROEKMANS 506 f.s. contains works
    by: Heckel (1), Anon. (3), Pisador
    (1), Caroso (2)   (1449)

EASY MUSIC FOR GUITAR, VOL. 8 *CC10L
    (Azpiazu) gtr (3-6th degr.) SYMPHON
    2092 f.s. contains works by: Milan
    (6), Narvaez (1), Mudarra (3)
                                 (1450)

EASY MUSIC FOR GUITAR, VOL. 9 *CC10L
    (Azpiazu) gtr (3-6th degr.) SYMPHON
    2131 f.s. contains works by:
    Dowland (2), Pilkington (1), Anon.
    (4), Askue (1), Cutting (1), and 1
    pce from Ballet's [Lute Book]
                                 (1451)

ELIZABETHAN DANCES, 4
    (Rooley) gtr (4-7th degr.) OXFORD
    36.007 $2.00
    contains: Anonymous, Kemp's Jig;
    Batchelar, Mounsier's Almaine;
    Dowland, John, Piper's Pavan;
    Johnson, R., Almain   (1452)

ELIZABETHAN MELODIES, VOL. 1
    (Rodgers) gtr (3rd degr.) SCHOTT
    GA-217 f.s.   (1453)

ELIZABETHAN MELODIES, VOL. 2
    (Rodgers) gtr (3rd degr.) SCHOTT
    GA-218 f.s.   (1454)

3 ENGLISH LUTE FANTASIES
    (Rooley) gtr (contains works by:
    Holborne; Johnson and Dowland)
    NOVELLO 12.0469.06 f.s.   (1455)

EUROPAISCHE GITARREN- UND LAUTENMUSIK,
    VOL. 1 *It,16-18th cent
    "Italienische Meister" (Teuchert) gtr
    SYMPHON 2222 f.s.   (1456)

EUROPAISCHE GITARREN- UND LAUTENMUSIK,
    VOL. 2 *Ger,16-18th cent
    "Deutsche Meister" (Teuchert) gtr
    SYMPHON 2223 f.s.   (1457)

EUROPAISCHE GITARREN- UND LAUTENMUSIK,
    VOL. 3 *Eng,16-18th cent
    "Englische Meister" (Teuchert) gtr
    SYMPHON 2224 f.s.   (1458)

EUROPAISCHE GITARREN- UND LAUTENMUSIK,
    VOL. 4 *Fr,16-18th cent
    "Franzosische Meister" (Teuchert) gtr
    SYMPHON 2225 f.s.   (1459)

EUROPAISCHE GITARREN- UND LAUTENMUSIK,
    VOL. 5 *Span,16-18th cent
    "Spanische Meister" (Teuchert) gtr
    SYMPHON 2230 f.s.   (1460)

EUROPAISCHE GITARREN- UND LAUTENMUSIK,
    VOL. 6 *Dutch,16-18th cent
    "Hollandische Meister" (Teuchert) gtr
    SYMPHON 2231 f.s.   (1461)

EUROPAISCHE GITARREN- UND LAUTENMUSIK,
    VOL. 7 *Polish,16-18th cent
    "Polnische Meister" (Teuchert) gtr
    SYMPHON 2232 f.s.   (1462)

FANTASIAS *CC10L
    (Azpiazu) gtr (7-9th degr.) UNION
    ESP. 19762 f.s. contains works by:
    Venezia (1), Dowland (1), Howet
    (1), Laurencini (2), Ferrabosco
    (1), Bakfark (1), Reys (1), Le Roy
    (2)   (1463)

FANTASIAS, 4
    (Sainz de la Maza) gtr (6-8th degr.)
    UNION ESP. 18827 f.s.
    contains: Mudarra, Alonso de,
    Fantasy, MIN 273; Narvaez, Luis
    de, Fantasy, MIN 276; Santa
    Maria, Thomas de, Fantasy, MIN
    275; Valderrabano, Enriquez de,
    Fantasy, MIN 274   (1464)

FRANCESCO DA MILANO
(ca. 1497?-ca. 1573?)
Opere Complete Per Liuto, Vol. 1:
Composizioni Originali *CC104UL
(Chiesa, Ruggero) [It/Ger/Eng] gtr
(single staff) folio ZERBONI 6960
f.s. contains 60 ricercares, 41
fantasias, 1 toccata, 2 pcs for 2
lutes (gtrs); incl intro, bio
notes, commentary, 2 apps (1465)

Opere Complete Per Liuto, Vol. 2:
Intavolature Di Opere Polifoniche
Vocali *CC30L
(Chiesa, Ruggero) [It/Ger/Eng] gtr
(single staff) folio ZERBONI 7090
f.s. contains 30 intabulations
for lute; incl intro and
commentary (1466)

FROM THE BACH FAMILY *CC26L
(Norman) gtr (3-6th degr.) SCHIRM.G
2559 f.s. contains works by: W.F.
Bach (3), J.B. Bach (3), J.S. Bach
(?) (2); C.P.E. Bach (12), J.
Christoph Bach (2), J. Christian
Bach (2), W. Friedrich Ernst Bach
(1), J.M. Bach (1) (1467)

GERLE, HANS (1500-1570)
7 Lautenstucke Aus "Musica Teutsch",
1532 *CC7L
(Monkemeyer, Helmut) [Ger] gtr,kbd
(staff notation and tablature)
HOFMEISTER FH-4551 f.s. contains
6 intabulations of voc comps, 1
prelude; "Die Tabulatur", Vol. 2
(1468)

GITARREMUSIK DES BAROCK I: AUS EINEM
FRANZOSISCHEN TABULATURBUCH DES 17.
JAHRHUNDERTS
(Gerwig) gtr (3rd degr., g is f
sharp; 3 suites (15 pcs) by Anon.;
Der Lautenist, Vol. III) LIENAU
f.s. (1469)

GITARREMUSIK DES BAROCK II: AUS EINEM
FRANZOSISCHEN TABULATURBUCH DES 17.
JAHRHUNDERTS; AUS DER AUSSEER
GITARRE-TABULATUR
(Gerwig) gtr (3rd degr., g is f
sharp; 2 suites (12 pcs) and 4 pcs
by Anon. (14), Visee (2); der
lautenist, vol. iV) LIENAU f.s.
(1470)

GITARRENMUSIK DES 16.-18. JAHRHUNDERTS,
VOL. I
(Quadt) gtr (3-6th degr.) DEUTSCHER
32004 $8.50 contains 57 works by
Anon. Ca. 1700 (4), Barberis (2),
Fuenllana (2), Phalese (Ed.) (2),
Foscarini (2), Belloni (2), Granata
(6), Corbetta (3), Campion (3)
contains: Visee, Robert de, Minuet,
VOCG 91; Visee, Robert de,
Passacaglia, VOCG 92; Visee,
Robert de, Saraband, VOCG 90;
Visee, Robert de, Suite in D
(contains VOCG 25, 51-60, 70);
Visee, Robert de, Suite, MIN 115
(contains VOCG 61-69); Visee,
Robert de, Suite, MIN 116
(contains VOCG 1-9, 82) (1471)

GITARRENMUSIK DES 16.-18. JAHRHUNDERTS,
VOL. II *CC34L
(Quadt) gtr (3-6th degr.) DEUTSCHER
32023 $8.50 contains works by:
Bethune (3), Anon. (26),
Brescianello (7), Prinz Anton (1)
(1472)

GITARRENSPIEL ALTER MEISTER, ORIGINAL-
MUSIK DES 16. UND 17. JAHRHUNDERTS,
VOL.1 *CC39L
(Zanoskar) gtr (2-4th degr.) SCHOTT
4620 f.s. contains works by:
Attaingnant (5), Schele (1),
Phalese (1), Neusiedler (4), Anon.
(5), Judenkunig (6), Fugger (3),
Craus (6), Losy vom Losinthal (2),
Spinacino (1), Fuhrmann (1),
Tallard (2), Hinterleithner (1),
Weichenberger (1) (1473)

GITARRENSPIEL ALTER MEISTER, ORIGINAL-
MUSIK DES 16. UND 17. JAHRHUNDERTS,
VOL.2 *CC30L
(Zanoskar) gtr (2-4th degr.) SCHOTT
4621 f.s. contains works by: Dalza
(2), Neusiedler (5), Craus (2),
Losy vom Losinthal (12), Pipers
(1), Fuhrmann (1), Waissel (2),
Radolt (1), Tallard (2), Muffat
(1), Anon. (1) (1474)

GORZANIS, GIACOMO (ca. 1525-ca. 1578)
Libro De Intabulatura Di Liuto (1567)
*CC56U
(Tonazzi, Bruno) [It/Eng] gtr
(single staff) folio ZERBONI f.s.
orig for lute in e; incl bio
notes and biblio (1475)

GOSTENA, G.B. DELLA
Intavolatura Di Liuto (1599) *CC26U
(Gullino, Giuseppe) [It] gtr
(single staff) folio MAURRI f.s.
contains 23 fantasies, 3
intabulations of voc. comp.; orig
for lute in e; incl intro,
biblio, and app (1476)

GUITAR MUSIC OF THE 16TH, 17TH AND 18TH
CENTURIES *CC10L
(de Tourris) 1-2gtr (3-6th degr.) sc
HARGAIL HFA-28 f.s. Hargail Folk
Anthology, No.28; arr + orig pcs;
contains works by: Garsi da Parma
(1), Sanz (1), Visee (5), Roncalli
(2), Rameau (1), for gtr; Albinoni
(1) and Handel (1), for 2gtr (1477)

HISPANAE CITHARAE ARS VIVA; ANTHOLOGY
OF GUITAR MUSIC FROM OLD TABLATURES
*CC13L
(Pujol) gtr (3-8th degr.) SCHOTT
GA-176 $ is f sharp; contains
works by: Pisador (2), Enriquez de
Valderrabano (2), Milan (2),
Mudarra (3), Narvaez (4) (1478)

HOLBORNE, ANTONY (? -1602)
Cisterwerke, Die, Part 1: Werke Fur
Cister Allein *CCU
(Monkemeyer, Helmut) gtr (staff
notation and tablature)
HOFMEISTER FH-4570 f.s. "Die
Tabulatur", Vol. 21 (1479)

Cisterwerke, Die, Part 2: Werke Fur
Cister Und Ein Bassinstrument
*CCU
(Monkemeyer, Helmut) gtr (staff
notation and tablature)
HOFMEISTER FH-4571 f.s. "Die
Tabulatur", Vol. 22 (1480)

HOVE, JOACHIM VAN DEN (1567-1620)
Delitiae Musicae, 1612, Part 1:
"Praeludien Und Pavanen" *CC12L
(Monkemeyer, Helmut) gtr HOFMEISTER
FH-4562 f.s. contains 6 preludes
and 6 pavanes; orig for lute in
g; Fr tab; "Die Tabulatur", Vol.
13 (1481)

Delitiae Musicae, 1612, Part 2:
"Passamezzen Mit Ihren
Galliarden" *CC14L
(Monkemeyer, Helmut) gtr HOFMEISTER
FH-4563 f.s. contains 7
passamezes and 7 galliardes; orig
for lute in g; Fr tab; "Die
Tabulatur", Vol. 14 (1482)

Delitiae Musicae, 1612, Part 3:
"Favoritos, Galliarden,
Bergamasca, Une Jeune Fillette"
*CCUL
(Monkemeyer, Helmut) gtr HOFMEISTER
FH-4564 f.s. contains 2
favoritos, 10 galliardes, 1
bergamasca; orig for lute in g;
Fr tab; "Die Tabulatur", Vol. 15
(1483)

Delitiae Musicae, 1612, Part 4:
"Allemanden, Balletti, Branden,
Couranten, Chansons, Canarie"
*CC33L
(Monkemeyer, Helmut) gtr HOFMEISTER
FH-4565 f.s. contains 8
allemandes, 4 balletti, 4
brandes, 11 couranten, 3
chansons, 2 galliardes, 1
canarie; orig for lute in g; Fr
tab; "Die Tabulatur", Vol. 16
(1484)

HUDBA CESKYCH LOUTNOVYCH TABULATUR
"Music From Czech Lute Tablatures"
(Tichota) gtr (4-8th degr., 47 pcs
by: Anon. (16), Jacobidis (1), D.
Gaultier (2), Gallot (2), Dix (10),
Weiss (6), Jelinek (10) SUPRAPHON
5409 f.s. (1485)
"Music From Czech Lute Tablatures"
(Tichota) gtr (4-8th degr., 47 pcs
by: Anon. (16), Jacobidis (1), D.
Gaultier (2), Gallot (2), Dix (10),
Weiss (6), Jelinek (10) ARTIA 1725
f.s. (1486)

INTERNATIONAL ANTHOLOGY
(Azpiazu) [Eng] gtr (contains 30
works by ancient composers) SYMPHON
2189A f.s. (1487)
(Azpiazu) [Fr] gtr (contains 30 works
by ancient composers) SYMPHON 2189B
f.s. (1488)

ITALIAANSE LUITMUZIEK UIT DE
RENAISSANCE
(Visser) gtr (3-4th degr.) HARMONIA
1562 f.s.
contains: Barberis, Melchior De,
Pavana Et Saltarello; Crema, Joan
Maria da; Ricercar Sexto;
Gorzanis, Giacomo, Padoana Detto
"Chi Passa Per Questa Strada"
(1489)

JUDENKUNIG, HANS (ca. 1450-1526)
Schone Kunstliche Vnderweisung Auff
Der Lautten Vnd Geygen, Ain, 1523
*CC33UL
(Monkemeyer, Helmut) gtr (staff
notation and tablature)
HOFMEISTER FH-4559 f.s. 20
intabulations of voc comps, 5
preambls, 7 dances, 1 pavana;
"Die Tabulatur", Vol. 10 (1490)

KLEINE STUCKE ,3 *CC3L
(Behrend) gtr (3rd degr.) HEINRICH.
N-1623 f.s. arr + orig pcs;
contains works by: Stanley, D.
Purcell, Milano (1491)

KOSTLICHKEITEN ENGLISCHER LAUTENMUSIK
"Delight Of English Lute Music, A"
(Duarte) gtr SCHOTT GA-224 f.s.
(1492)

LAUTENMUSIK AUS DER RENAISSANCE, VOL. I
*CC78L
(Quadt) gtr (3-7th degr.) DEUTSCHER
32003 $8.50 contains works by:
Milano (3), Galilei (4), Rotta (1),
Anon. (21), Denns (6), Adriaenssen
(1), Mertel (4), Montbuisson (1),
Besard (6), Dowland (2), Kapsberger
(1), Hove (1), Aloyson (1), Romanus
(1), Diomedes Cato (1), Rudenio
(1), Ferrabosco (1), Jobin (3),
Fuhrmann (11), Perichon (1), Caroso
(1), de Moy (1), Drusina (2), M.
Neusiedler (2), Heckel (1) (1493)

LAUTENMUSIK AUS DER RENAISSANCE, VOL.
II *CC115L
(Quadt) gtr (3-7th degr.) DEUTSCHER
32022 $8.50 contains works by:
Anon. (34), Hove (15), Waissel (1),
Crema (4), Rotta (1), Adriaenssen
(2), Mertel (3), LeRoy (1), Denns
(4), Paladin (1), Bocquet (4),
Dowland (6), Besard (11), Fuhrmann
(4), Valerius (1), Mylius (1),
Caroso (5), Anerio (1), Klipstein
(1), Vallet (1), Cutting (1),
Francisque (7), Jobin (2),
Neusiedler (2) (1494)

LAUTENMUSIK DES 17. UND 18.
JAHRHUNDERTS, VOL. 1 - LUTE MUSIC
FROM THE 17TH AND 18TH CENTURY,
VOL. 1 *CC81U
(Quadt, Adalbert) gtr (3-7th degr.)
DEUTSCHER 32070 f.s. contains works
by: E. Gaultier; Gaultier le Vieux;
Du Faut; Weichenberger; Mouton;
Gelinek; Weiss; Tallard; Kuhnel;
Lauffensteiner; de Saint-Luc;
Baron; Pinell and Others (1495)

LAUTENSPIELER DES XVI. JAHRHUNDERTS
(LIUTISTI DEL CINQUECENTO)
*CC124UL
(Chilesotti, Oscar) gtr (single
staff/8th degr.) quarto oblong
FORNI f.s. repr of 1st ed., publ
Ricordi-Breitkopf & Hartel (1891);
"Bibliotheca Musica Bononiensis",
Sezione IV, No. 31; includes works
by: Newsidler, Anon., Ballet,
Gintzler, Matelart, Gorzanis, da
Milano, Galilei, Barbetta, Caroso,
Terzi, Molinaro, dalla Gostena,
Negri, Besard, Mersenne,
Gianoncelli —all for 1 gtr;
Matelart, Galilei, Besard —for 2
gtr; Caroso, Negri —for dsc inst
and gtr; Fallamero, Besard —for vce
and gtr; Terzi —for 3 gtr; Besard —
for dsc inst and 3 gtr (1496)

LEICHTE STUCKE AUS SHAKESPEARES ZEIT,
VOL. 1 *CC14L
(Scheit) gtr (2-3rd degr.) UNIVER.
13973 f.s. contains works by: Anon,
(7), Cutting (2), Robinson (3),
Dowland (2) (1497)

LEICHTE STUCKE AUS SHAKESPEARES ZEIT,
VOL. 2 *CC15L
(Scheit) gtr (2-3rd degr.) UNIVER.
16693 f.s. contains works by:
Cutting (2), Anon. (9), Whitfield
(1), Robinson (2), Dowland (2)
(1498)

LIEDER UND TANZE AUF DIE LAUTEN
(C.1540) *CC33U
(Bischof, Heinz) gtr (single staff/
4th degr.) SCHOTTS 3694 f.s. g is f
sharp, partly e is d; contains 17
intabulations of voc. comp., 1
prelude, and 15 dances; incl. intro
(1499)

LIEDER UND TANZE DER VORKLASSIK *CC30L
(Brodszky) gtr (2nd degr.) SCHOTT
5948 f.s. contains works by: Susato
(2), Anon. (12), Lully (1), Albert
(1), Schmelzer (1), Praetorius (1),
Pachelbel (1), Raison (1), Blow
(1), Campra (1), Muffat (1),
Purcell (1), Hotteterre (1),
Sperontes (1), Witthauer (1),
J.C.F. Bach (1), L. Mozart (1),

Dieupart (1)   (1500)

LOSY VOM LOSINTHAL, JAN ANTONIN
   (1643-1721)
   Pieces De Guitare *CC21L
   (Pohanka, Jaroslav) [Czech/Ger/Eng]
      gtr (single staff) folio CZECH
      f.s. contains 9 suites and 12
      pcs; commentary and biblio;
      "Musica Antiqua Bohemica", No. 38
                               (1501)

LUTE PIECES OF THE RENAISSANCE, 6
   *CC6L
   (Chilesotti; Neidle) gtr (3-5th
      degr.) COLUMBIA 142 $1.75 contains
      works by: Anon. (4), Negri (1),
      Galilei (1)   (1502)

LUTE RECERCARS *CC13UL
   (Buetens, Stanley) [Eng] gtr (staff
      notation and tablature/4th degr.)
      INST ANT JSL-1 f.s. g is f sharp; 2
      facs, 3 ill.; contains works by:
      Dalza (3), Bossinensis (6),
      Spinacino (3), Capirola (1) (1503)

MEINE ERSTEN GITARRENSTUCKE, VOL.2:
   "MEISTER DES BAROCK" *CC19L
   (Teuchert) gtr (1-3rd degr.) SYMPHON
      2200 f.s. arr + orig pcs; contains
      works by: Krieger (1), Fischer (1),
      Sperontes (1), Visee (1), Graf
      Bergen (1), Roncalli (3), Saint Luc
      (2), Losy vom Losinthal (2), Sanz
      (3), Baron (1), Corelli (1),
      Kellner (1)   (1504)

MEINE ERSTEN GITARRENSTUCKE, VOL.3:
   "MEISTER DER RENAISSANCE" *CC18L
   (Teuchert) gtr (1-3rd degr.) SYMPHON
      2201 f.s. contains works by: Ballet
      (1), Craus (1), Judenkunig (1),
      Anon. (5), Caroso (2), Phalese (2),
      Negri (1), Attaingnant (2),
      Brayssing (1), Cutting (1),
      Robinson (1)   (1505)

MILAN, LUIS (ca. 1500-ca. 1564)
   Libro De Musica De Vihuela De Mano,
      1535, Part 1: "Fantasien 1-13"
      *CC13U
   (Monkemeyer, Helmut) gtr HOFMEISTER
      FH-4566 f.s. orig for lute in g;
      "Milan" tab; "Die Tabulatur",
      Vol. 17   (1506)

   Libro De Musica De Vihuela De Mano,
      1535, Part 2: "Fantasien 14-22"
      *CC9U
   (Monkemeyer, Helmut) gtr HOFMEISTER
      FH-4567 f.s. orig for lute in g;
      "Milan" tab; "Die Tabulatur",
      Vol. 18   (1507)

   Libro De Musica De Vihuela De Mano,
      1535, Part 3: "Fantasien 23-33"
      *CC11U
   (Monkemeyer, Helmut) gtr HOFMEISTER
      FH-4568 f.s. orig for lute in g;
      "Milan" tab; "Die Tabulatur",
      Vol. 19   (1508)

   Libro De Musica De Vihuela De Mano,
      1535, Part 4: "Tientos 1-4 And
      Fantasien 34-40" *CC11U
   (Monkemeyer, Helmut) gtr HOFMEISTER
      FH-4569 f.s. orig for lute in g;
      "Milan" tab; "Die Tabulatur",
      Vol. 20   (1509)

   Maestro, El, Vol. 1: Composizioni Per
      Sola Vihuela *CC50L
   (Chiesa, Ruggero) [It] gtr (single
      staff) folio ZERBONI 6405A f.s.
      contains 40 fantasias, 6 pavanes,
      4 tientos; incl intro, bio notes,
      commentary; g is f sharp   (1510)

   Maestro, El, Vol. 2: Composizizoni
      Per Voce E Vihuela *CC22L
   (Chiesa, Ruggero) [It] gtr (single
      staff) folio ZERBONI 6405B f.s.
      contains 6 villancicos en
      castellano, 6 villancicos en
      portugues, 4 romances, and 6
      sonetos; incl commentary   (1511)

   6 Pavans And 3 Fantasias (from El
      Maestro) CC9U
   (Myers, Joan) [Eng] gtr (staff
      notation and tablature/4th degr.)
      INST ANT JV-1 f.s. orig for lute
      in g; g is f sharp; incl intro
      and commentary; "Vihuela Series"
      Vol. 1   (1512)

MOLINARO, SIMONE
   Intavolatura Di Liuto, Libro Primo
      (1599) *CC51U
   (Gullino, Giuseppe) [It] gtr
      (single staff) folio MAURRI f.s.
      contains 8 saltarelli, 1 ballo,
      11 pass' e mezzi, 11 gagliarde,
      15 fantasie, 3 intabulations of
      voc. comp., 2 canzone; incl intro
      and bio notes   (1513)

MUDARRA, ALONSO DE (ca. 1506-1580)
   Tres Libros De Musica: Ausgewahlte
      Werke *CC10L
   (Monkemeyer, Helmut) gtr HOFMEISTER
      FH-4561 f.s. contains 6
      fantasias, 1 romanesca, 1 pavana,
      1 gallarda, 1 tiento; "Die
      Tabulatur", Vol. 12   (1514)

MUSICHE DEL RINASCIMENTO *CC10L
   (Chilesotti; Balestra) gtr (3-4th
      degr.) BERBEN EB1397 f.s. contains
      works by: Anon. (8), Negri (1), de
      Barberis (1)   (1515)

MUSICHE PER CHITARRA ALLA CORTE DI
   VERSAILLES *CC15L
   (Danner) gtr (3rd degr.) ZERBONI 7783
      $6.00 orig for baroque gtr;
      contains works by: Anon. (6),
      Philidor (1), Lully (1), Couperin
      (1), Mouret (1), Marais (1),
      Senaille (1), Blamont (2), Rameau
      (1)   (1516)

MUSIK DER RENAISSANCE FUR GITARRE
   *CC25U
   (Ragossnig) gtr (4-9th degr.) SCHOTT
      GA-442 f.s. contains works by:
      Dalza (2), Capirola (2), Garsi (2),
      Mudarra (2); Le Roy (2), Besard
      (2); Neusidler; Sweelinck; Dlugorai
      (3); Bakfark; R. Johnson; Bulman;
      Cutting; Dowland (4) and Others
                               (1517)

MUSIK DER VORKLASSIK: WERKE AUS DEM 17.
   UND 18. JAHRHUNDERT
   (Brodszky; Kovats) gtr (2-3rd degr.)
      SCHOTT 5229 f.s. 30 pcs; contains
      works by: Turk (5), Anon. (5), W.A.
      Mozart (1), L. Mozart (1), Krieger
      (2), Haydn (1), Hotteterre (1),
      Barret (1), J.C.F. Bach (1), Clark
      (1), Caroubel (1), Rameau (1), W.F.
      Bach (1), Dandrieu (1), Kirchhof
      (1), Handel (2), Purcell (1), F.
      Couperin (1); same as Regi Zene
      Gitarra, EMB 2-1790
      contains: Bach, Johann Sebastian,
      Minuet, BWV Anh. 114, in G (from
      Anna Magdalena Bach Notenbuchlein
      (1725), No.4) (A maj); Bach,
      Johann Sebastian, Piece In F,
      "Aria", BWV Anh.131 (from Anna
      Magdalena Bach Notenbuchlein
      (1725), No.32) (A maj)   (1518)

MUSIK FUR LIEBHABER DES GITARRESPIELS,
   VOL. 1: AUS TABULATUREN DES 16.
   JAHRHUNDERTS *CC30L
   (Klambt) gtr (3rd degr.) NOETZEL 3123
      f.s. all works by Anon.   (1519)

MUSIK FUR LIEBHABER DES GITARRESPIELS,
   VOL. 2: AUS TABULATUREN DES 16. UND
   17. JAHRHUNDERTS *CC30L
   (Klambt) gtr (3rd degr.) NOETZEL 3124
      f.s. contains works by: Neusiedler
      (2), Anon. (15), Galilei (1),
      Ballet (1), Caroso (2), Terzi (1),
      Negri (3), Besard (4), Mersenne (1)
                               (1520)

NARVAEZ, LUIS DE
   Seys Libros Del Delphin De Musica,
      Los: Ausgewahlte Werke *CC10UL
   (Monkemeyer, Helmut) gtr HOFMEISTER
      FH-4560 f.s. contains 2
      intabulations of voc comps, 2
      fantasias, 6 diferencias (del
      hyno de nuestra senora) 0
      gloriosa domina; It tab; orig for
      vihuela in g; "Die Tabulatur",
      Vol. 11   (1521)

NEUSIEDLER, HANS (1508-1563)
   Newgeordent Kunstlich Lautenbuch, Ein
      *CC20UL
   (Monkemeyer, Helmut) [Ger] gtr,kbd
      (staff notation and tablature)
      HOFMEISTER FH-4550 f.s. contains
      9 intabulations of voc comps, 8
      dances, 3 preludes; "Die
      Tabulatur", Vol. 1   (1522)

   Newgeordent Kunstlich Lautenbuch,
      Ein: Der Ander Theil Fur Die
      Geubten Vnnd Erfarnen, 1536
      *CC9U
   (Monkemeyer, Helmut) gtr (staff
      notation and tablature)
      HOFMEISTER FH-4558 f.s. "Die
      Tabulatur", Vol. 9   (1523)

OSTPREUSSISCHES LAUTENBUCH *CCU
   (Schmidt) gtr ZIMMER. 2013 f.s.
      contains works by: de Drusina;
      Waissel; Stobaus and Albert (1524)

PEZZI, 4, DA GRANDI VIRGINALISTI
   DELL'ERA ELISABETTIANA
   (Tempestini) gtr (3-4th degr.) BERBEN
      EB1142 $1.00
      contains: Clarke, Minuet, MIN 118;
      Lawes, Saraband, MIN 117;
      Purcell, Henry, Aria; Purcell,
      Henry, Siciliana   (1525)

3 PIECES BY HOLBORNE, PERICHON, BALARD
   (Reyne) gtr (3rd degr.) LEDUC G-88
      f.s. Guitare, No. 88
      contains: Courante, MIN 411;
      Courante, MIN 412; Prelude, MIN
      410   (1526)

4 PIECES BY DOWLAND, CUTTING, MORLEY
   (Reyne) gtr (5th degr.) LEDUC G-89
      f.s. Guitare, No. 89
      contains: Galliard, MIN 413; Lady
      Clifton's Spirit; Pavan, MIN 414;
      Walsingham   (1527)

PIECES DE LA RENAISSANCE ESPAGNOLE, 4
   (Hinojosa) gtr (3-5th degr.) TRANSAT.
      1361 f.s. Bibliotheque De Musique
      Ancienne; E is D, g is f-sharp;
      5pcs
      contains: Anonymous, Fantasy
      (composed with Venegas De
      Henestrosa, Tomas Luis de);
      Anonymous, Fantasy (composed with
      Venegas De Henestrosa, Tomas Luis
      de); Cabezon, Antonio de, Chanson
      Avec Fioritures; Santa Maria,
      Cinq Variations Sur "Conde
      Claros"; Santa Maria, Hymne Sur
      "Sacris Solemniis"   (1528)

PIECES ELISABETHAINES *CC9L
   (Castet) gtr (2-3rd degr.) LEDUC G-75
      $3.00 Guitare, No.75; contains
      works by: Anon. (6), Ballet (1),
      Whitfield (1), Dowland (1)   (1529)

PIECES FROM THE FITZWILLIAM VIRGINAL
   BOOK, 13
   (Duarte) gtr (3-4th degr., contains
      works by: Bull (1), Anon. (10),
      Pearson (1), Johnson (1)) NOVELLO
      19441 f.s.   (1530)

PIECES POUR LUTH DU 16E SIECLE, 12
   (Castaldo) gtr (2-3rd degr., contains
      works by: Caroso (7), Negri (3),
      Anon. (2)) SCHOTT-FRER 9288 f.s.
                               (1531)

5 PIEZAS DEL SIGLO XVI
   (Garcia Velasco) gtr UNION ESP. 21933
      f.s.
      contains: Mudarra, Alonso de,
      Recuerde El Alma Dormida; Ribera,
      Por Unos Puertos Arriba; Salinas,
      Mi Grave Pena; Salinas, Tres
      Cortes; Vasquez, Ay, Que Non Oso
      Mirar   (1532)

POOLSE LUITMUZIEK
   (Visser) gtr (3rd degr.) HARMONIA
      1268 f.s. no. 3: g is f-sharp
      contains: Dlugoraj, Adalbert
      (Wojiech), Villanelle; Fuhrmann,
      W.A., Volta Polonica; Waissel
      (Ius), Matthaus, Dance
      Polonaise   (1533)

QUELQUES PAGES DE GUITARE CLASSIQUE
   (Breguet) gtr (4-7th degr.) LEMOINE
      f.s. contains 24 works by:
      Chambonnieres (4), Clerambault (4),
      Seixas (4), Purcell (4)
      contains: Bach, Johann Sebastian,
      French Suite No.1, BWV812, In D
      Minor, Sarabande (E min); Bach,
      Johann Sebastian, French Suite
      No. 2, BWV813, In C Minor, Gigue
      (D min); Bach, Johann Sebastian,
      French Suite No. 2, BWV813, In C
      Minor, Minuet (D min); Bach,
      Johann Sebastian, French Suite
      No. 4, BWV815A, In E Flat, Minuet
      (G maj); Bach, Johann Sebastian,
      Minuet, BWV Anh. 120, in A minor
      (from Anna Magdalena Bach
      Notenbuchlein (1725), No.14) (D
      min); Bach, Johann Sebastian,
      Minuet, BWV Anh. 132, in D minor
      (from Anna Magdalena Bach
      Notenbuchlein (1725), No.36);
      Bach, Johann Sebastian, 0
      Ewigkeit, Du Donnerwort, Chorale,
      BWV 513 (from Anna Magdalena Bach
      Notenbuchlein (1725), No.42);
      Bach, Johann Sebastian, Suite for
      Orchestra, BWV 1067, in B minor,
      Rondo   (1534)

RADINO, GIOVANNI MARIA
   Intavolatura Di Balli (1592) *CC8U
   (Gullino, Giuseppe) [It] gtr
      (single staff) folio MAURRI f.s.
      orig for lute in e   (1535)

RAMILLETE DE FLORES *CC10U
   (Rey, Juan Jose) [Span] gtr (staff
      notation and tablature/4th degr.)
      ALPUERTO 1124 f.s. contains Vihuela
      pcs by Fabricio, Anonymous, Paez,
      Mendoza, Narvaez, and Lopez (1536)

RAMILLETE DE FLORES (1530-1593)
   (Rey) gtr (Notation: tablature + treb
      clef; contains works by: Fabricio;
      Mendoza Lopez; Fr. Paez; Narvaez
      and others) ALPUERTO 1124 f.s.

REGI MAGYAR ZENE GITARRA - EARLY
HUNGARIAN MUSIC FOR GUITAR *CC11U
(Szendrey-Karper) gtr (1st degr.) EMB
8308 f.s.   (1538)

REGI ZENE GITARRA, ATIRATOK A XVII-
XVIII. SZAZAD MUZSIKAJABOL - ALTE
MUSIK FUR GITARRE, WERKE AUS DEM
17.-18. JAHRHUNDERT
(Brodsky; Kovats) gtr (2-3rd degr.)
EMB Z-1790 f.s. 29 pcs.; same as
Musik Der Vorklassik, Schott 5224,
except for no. 14, Lang, Allegro,
and no. 15, Kemeny, Andante
contains: Bach, Johann Sebastian,
Minuet, BWV Anh. 114, In G (from
Anna Magdalena Bach Notenbuchlein
(1725), No.4) (A maj); Bach,
Johann Sebastian, Piece In F,
"Aria", BWV Anh.131 (from Anna
Magdalena Bach Notenbuchlein
(1725), No.32) (A maj)   (1539)

RENAISSANCE MUSIC FOR GUITAR *CC19U
(Swanson) gtr LUDWIG $3.95 contains
works by: Byrd; Bull; Dowland;
Frescobaldi; Giles Farnaby;
Holborne; Johnson; Mikolaj Of
Kracow; H. Newsidler and others
                                     (1540)

RENAISSANCE POPULAR MUSIC
(Jeffery) gtr (5th degr.) OXFORD
36.012 $1.80
contains: Anonymous, Dargesson;
Anonymous, Packington's Pound;
Anonymous, Port, A; Anonymous,
Sick Tune, The; Dall, I Serve A
Worthy Lady; Whitfield, English
Hunt's Up, The   (1541)

SCHLICK, ARNOLT (ca. 1460-ca. 1517)
Tabulaturen Etlicher Lobgesang Und
Lidlein Vff Die Lauten, 1512
*CC15L
(Monkemeyer, Helmut) [Ger] gtr,kbd
(staff notation and tablature)
HOFMEISTER FH-4552 f.s. contains
12 intabulations of voc comps for
gtr, kbd or 2mel inst; 3
intabulations of voc comps for
gtr, kbd; "Die Tabulatur", Vol. 3
                                (1542)

SEIDEL
Zwolf Menuetten
(Quadt, Adalbert) [Ger] gtr (single
staff, orig for lute in f; intro
notation: french tab; facs) folio
BREITKOPF-L SD-163 f.s. contains
also: Baron, Ernst Gottlieb,
Fantasia   (1543)

SELECCION DE OBRAS DE LOS MAS CELEBRES
LAUDISTAS FRANCESES E ITALIANOS DE
LOS SIGLOS XVI, XVII Y XVIII
*CC17L
(Tarrago) gtr (7th degr.) UNION ESP.
2041 f.s. contains works by: Visee
(2), Besard (1), Corbetta (2),
Perla (1), Anon. (8), Roncalli (1),
Jakob Polak (1), Neusiedler (1)
                                (1544)

STUKKEN UIT DE OUD-ENGELSE
LUITLITERATUUR, 2
(Hoogeveen) gtr (7-8th degr.)
TEESELING VT-7 f.s.
contains: Bulman, Baruch, Pavan;
Johnson, Robert [3], Almain
                                (1545)

TABULATUREN FUR LAUTE, VIHUELA UND
GITARRE, IN NEUER NOTATION MIT
GEGENUBERSTELLUNG DER
ENTSPRECHENDEN ALTEN MANUSKRIPTE
(Azpiazu, J de; Azpiazu, L. de) gtr
SYMPHON 2180 f.s.   (1546)

THREE FRENCH PIECES
(Wadsworth) gtr (3-4th degr.) MSM
$2.25
contains: Chambonnieres, Jacques
Champion, Saraband; Couperin,
Francois (le Grand), Gigue;
Daquin, Louis-Claude, Aria   (1547)

VISEE, ROBERT DE (ca. 1650-ca. 1775)
Oeuvres Completes Pour Guitare
*CC105U
(Strizich, Robert W.) [Fr/Eng/Ger]
gtr (single staff) folio HEUGEL
f.s. "Le Pupitre" no. 15   (1548)

WEISS, SYLVIUS LEOPOLD (1686-1750)
Intavolatura Di Liuto *CC69U
(Chiesa, Ruggero) gtr (single
staff) ZERBONI f.s. in 2 vols:
vol. 1, no. 6652, contains 16
suites; vol. 2, no. 6731,
contains 12 suites and 41 pcs
                                (1549)

WOHLAUF MIT REICHEM SCHALLE; BICINIEN
UM 1550 *CC21L
(Monkemeyer) gtr/2treb inst (2-3rd
degr.) sc TONGER 1079 f.s. contains
works by: Schwartz (5), Anon. (11),
Voit (1), Heller (1), Fortius (1),
Stoltzer (1), Meyer (1)   (1550)

Z MUZYKI POLSKIEGO RENESANSU *CC29L
(Mazur) gtr (6-8th degr.) POLSKIE
6852 f.s. contains works by: Jakob
Polak (7), Dlugoraj (5), Anon. (6),
Diomedes Cato (11)   (1551)

ZWEISTIMMIGES GITARRENSPIEL; LEICHTE
STUCKE UND TANZE AUS DEM 16. BIS
18. JAHRHUNDERT *CC31L
(Rentmeister) gtr (1-3rd degr.)
SCHOTT 5127 f.s. contains works by:
Anon. (5), Hainhofer (1), Handel
(4), Fischer (4), Chedeville (3),
Boismortier (1), Purcell (1), Bohm
(1), Monteverdi (1), Schein (2), L.
Mozart (1), Hasse (1), Fesch (1),
Krieger (1), Telemann (2), Couperin
(1), Dittersdorf (1)   (1552)

I/IB2   Guitar Solos:
Classical and Pre-Romantic
Music (1760-1850)

AGUADO, DIONISIO (1784-1849)
Adagio, MIN 345
(Bream) gtr (4th degr.) ESSEX f.s.
                                (1553)

Allegro
gtr (4th degr.) SCHOTT GA-301 f.s.
contains also: Allegro Vivace
                                (1554)

Allegro Brillante
gtr (8th degr.) SCHOTT GA-302 f.s.
                                (1555)

Andante in A
gtr ESSEX f.s.   (1556)

Andante, MIN 353
gtr ESSEX f.s.   (1557)

Fandango Variado
gtr UNION ESP. 20474 f.s.   (1558)

Fandango Y Variaciones
(Tarrago) gtr UNION ESP. 21760 f.s.
                                (1559)

Leichte Walzer Und Etuden
gtr (2nd degr.) SCHOTT GA-303 f.s.
                                (1560)

Minuet And Waltz *Op.4,No.1
gtr ESSEX f.s.   (1561)

Minuet, MIN 354
gtr ESSEX f.s.   (1562)

2 Minuetos Y 2 Estudios
gtr FORTEA 2 f.s.   (1563)

6 Minuetos
gtr UNION ESP. 20476 f.s.   (1564)

Minuetto
gtr ESSEX f.s.   (1565)

3 Rondos Brillantes
gtr UNION ESP. 20471 f.s.   (1566)

Two Minuets
gtr (Guitare, No. 119) PAGANI G-119
f.s.   (1567)

6 Valses
gtr UNION ESP. 20473 f.s.   (1568)

Variaciones Brillantes
(Tarrago) gtr UNION ESP. 20475 f.s.
                                (1569)

ALBENIZ, MATEO (ANTONIO PEREZ DE)
(ca. 1797-1831)
Sonata in D
(Azpiazu) gtr (9th degr.) SYMPHON
365 f.s.   (1570)
(Cochran) gtr (9th degr.) COLUMBIA
211 $1.60   (1571)
(Pujol) gtr (E maj,9th degr.)
RICORDI-ARG BA-10830 f.s.   (1572)
(Sierra) gtr (9th degr.) CHOUDENS
20.512 f.s.   (1573)
(Tarrago) gtr (9th degr.) UNION
ESP. 21742 f.s.   (1574)
(Yepes) gtr (E maj,9th degr.) UNION
ESP. f.s.   (1575)

ALBRECHTSBERGER, JOHANN GEORG
(1736-1809)
Fugue
gtr (4th degr., transcribed by J.K.
Mertz) BERBEN EB1350 $1.00 (1576)

BACH, JOHANN SEBASTIAN (1685-1750)
Minuet, BWV Anh. 114, In G (from Anna
Magdalena Bach Notenbuchlein
(1725), No.4)
(Fortea) gtr (C maj,4th degr.)
FORTEA 310 f.s. contains also:
Beethoven, Ludwig van, Symphony
No. 7, Op. 92, in A, Andante

BACH, JOHANN SEBASTIAN (cont'd.)
                                (1577)

BEETHOVEN, LUDWIG VAN (1770-1827)
Album
(Llobet) gtr UNION ESP. 20380 f.s.
contains: Sonata, MIN 394; Sonata
No. 14, Allegretto; Sonata No.
23, Andante; Sonata No. 30,
Andante   (1578)

2 Andantes
gtr FORTEA 69 f.s.
contains: Sonata No. 10, Andante;
Sonata No. 15, Andante   (1579)

Bagatelles, 2
(Papas) gtr COLUMBIA 111 $1.50
                                (1580)

Beethoven For The Guitar *CC18U
(Block) gtr (2-3rd degr.) sc MARKS
15452-16 $1.50 1 pce for 2 gtr
                                (1581)

Fur Elise *Op.173
"Bagatela (Para Elisa)" gtr (5-6th
degr., arr) FORTEA 303 f.s.
                                (1582)
(Ablo niz) gtr (D min,5-6th degr.)
BERBEN EB1389 $1.00   (1583)
"Para Elisa" (Angel) gtr (5-6th
degr.) UNION ESP. 18824 f.s.
                                (1584)
(Battine) gtr (5-6th degr.) ESSEX
f.s.   (1585)
"Albumblatt "Fur Elise"" (Behrend)
gtr (A min,5-6th degr., Die
Konzertgitarre) SIKORSKI 728
$2.25   (1586)
"Para Elisa" (Herrero) gtr (5-6th
degr.) UNION ESP. 21858 f.s.
                                (1587)
(Lees) gtr (5-6th degr.) ESSEX f.s.
                                (1588)
"Pour Elise" (Martin) gtr (5-6th
degr., Guitare Selection, No. 9)
DELRIEU 1409 f.s.   (1589)
"Para Elisa" (Sinopoli) gtr (5-6th
degr.) RICORDI-ARG BA-7601 f.s.
                                (1590)
Minuet
(Segovia) gtr (also published in:
Transcripciones Para Guitarra,
No. 5) UNION ESP. 18033 f.s.
                                (1591)
Minuet, MIN 334
gtr FORTEA 214 f.s.   (1592)
Minuet, MIN 395
(Calatayud) gtr UNION ESP. 21092
f.s.   (1593)
Minuet, MIN 396
(Segovia) gtr UNION ESP. 18033 f.s.
                                (1594)
Minuet, MIN 397
(Tarrega) gtr UNION ESP. 19053 f.s.
                                (1595)
7 Minuetos
(Azpiazu) gtr UNION ESP. 21307 f.s.
                                (1596)
Romance (from Sonatina In G)
(Abloniz) gtr (4th degr.) BERBEN
EB1014 $1.00   (1597)
Romance for Violin and Orchestra
(from Op. 50)
(Abloniz) gtr (6-7th degr.) BERBEN
EB2002 f.s.   (1598)
Ruinas De Atenas, La, Marcha
(Lozano) gtr UNION ESP. 15540 f.s.
                                (1599)
Septet
(Azpiazu) gtr SYMPHON 2000 f.s.
                                (1600)
Sonata for Piano, Op. 14, No. 2, in
E,Second Movement
(Choppen) gtr (5th degr.) NOVELLO
20064 $1.95   (1601)
Sonata for Piano, Op. 27, No. 2, in C
sharp minor,First Movement (from
Op. 27, No. 2)
(Azpiazu) gtr (8th degr.) SYMPHON
492 f.s.   (1602)
"Ao Luar" (Barreiros) gtr (8th
degr.) RICORDI-BR 3018 f.s.
                                (1603)
"Claro De Luna" (Fortea) gtr (8th
degr.) FORTEA 217 f.s.   (1604)
"Claro De Luna" (Lopez Villanueva)
gtr (8th degr.) UNION ESP. 1456
f.s.   (1605)
"Erster Satz Aus Der Mondschein-
Sonate" (Ranieri) gtr (8th degr.)
CRANZ f.s.   (1606)
"Adagio De La Sonata, Op. 27, No.
2, "Claro De Luna" (Sinopoli)
gtr (8th degr.) RICORDI-ARG
BA-8033 f.s.   (1607)
"Chiaro Di Luna" (Tarrega) gtr (8th
degr.) BERBEN EB-1548 $1.25
                                (1608)
Sonata in C sharp minor, Op. 27, No.
2,Minuet
(Galindo) gtr (4th degr.) BERBEN

BEETHOVEN, LUDWIG VAN (cont'd.)

    EB1116 $1.00   (1609)

Sonata No. 2, Scherzo, MIN 335
gtr FORTEA 219 f.s.   (1610)

Sonata No. 3, Minuet
gtr FORTEA 70 f.s.   (1611)

Sonata No. 4, Op. 7, Largo
(Llobet) gtr UNION ESP. 20375 f.s.
        (1612)
(Tarrega) gtr UNION ESP. 19083 f.s.
        (1613)

Sonata No. 9, Andante
gtr FORTEA 222 f.s.   (1614)

Sonata No. 10, Andante
(Llobet) gtr UNION ESP. 20374 f.s.
        (1615)

Sonata, No.12: Marcha Funebre
gtr FORTEA 216 f.s.   (1616)

Sonata, Op. 2, No. 1, Adagio
gtr FORTEA 220 f.s.   (1617)

Sonata, Op. 2, No. 2, Scherzo
(Tarrago) gtr UNION ESP. 19030 f.s.
        (1618)

Sonata, Op. 13, Adagio
"Sonata Patetica: Adagio" gtr
  FORTEA 223 f.s.   (1619)
"Sonata Patetica: Adagio" (Lopez
  Villanueva) gtr UNION ESP. 1455
  f.s.   (1620)

Sonata, Op. 26, Andante
gtr FORTEA 221 f.s.   (1621)

Sonata, Op. 27, No. 2
"Moonlight Sonata" (Battine) gtr
ESSEX f.s.   (1622)

Tema Y Var. IV [Del] Septimino
gtr FORTEA 215 f.s.   (1623)

Valse "Le Desir"
(Azpiazu) gtr (Guitare Selection,
No. 5) DELRIEU f.s.   (1624)

BENDA, GEORG ANTON (JIRI ANTONIN)
(1722-1795)
Sonatina
(Behrend) gtr (6th degr., Gitarre-
Bibliothek, No.24) BOTE GB-24
f.s.   (1625)

Sonatinen, 2
(Segovia) gtr (7th degr.) SCHOTT
GA-155 f.s.   (1626)

BOCCHERINI, LUIGI (1743-1805)
Celebre Mineto
(Garcia Velasco) gtr UNION ESP.
20293 f.s.   (1627)

Minuet
"Beruhmtes Menuett" (Azpiazu) gtr
(5th degr.) SYMPHON 493 f.s.
        (1628)
"Minuetto" (Fortea) gtr (5th degr.)
FORTEA 24 f.s.   (1629)
"Celebre Menuet" (Martin) gtr (5th
degr., Guitare Selection, No. 10)
DELRIEU 1424 f.s.   (1630)
"Minuetto" (Savio) gtr (5th degr.)
RICORDI-BR BR-2336 f.s. (1631)
(Terzi) gtr (5th degr.) RICORDI-IT
129286 f.s.   (1632)

Minueto-Bolero (from Folia De Espana,
No. 35, Libro II)
(Azpiazu) gtr UNION ESP. 21034 f.s.
        (1633)

Minueto Espanol (from Quinteto, Op.
37)
(Azpiazu) gtr UNION ESP. 21033 f.s.
        (1634)

CARCASSI, MATTEO (1792-1853)
Allegretto
(Sensier) gtr (3rd degr.) ESSEX
f.s.   (1635)

Ausgewahlte Walzer, 20
(Schwarz-Reiflingen) gtr (2-3rd
degr.) SCHOTT GA-3 f.s. (1636)

Capriccio
(Sensier) gtr ESSEX f.s. (1637)

Capriccio Und Pastorale
(Teuchert) gtr (3-4th degr.)
SCHMIDT,H 316 f.s.   (1638)

Carcassi-Brevier *CC54U
(Schwarz-Reiflingen) gtr (2-7th
degr.) SCHOTT GA-4A-C f.s. 3
vols.   (1639)

Kleine Stucke, 24 *Op.21
(Dahlke) gtr (2-3rd degr.) SCHOTT
GA-6 f.s.   (1640)

CARCASSI, MATTEO (cont'd.)

Leichte Stucke, 12 *Op.10
gtr (3rd degr., Urtext edition)
SCHOTT GA-73 f.s.   (1641)

Leichte Variationen, 6 *Op.18
(Schmid-Kayser) gtr (3-4th degr.)
VIEWEG 1388 f.s.   (1642)

Menuets, 2
(Sanchez) gtr (3rd degr.,
Collection L'Heure De La Guitare
Classique; also published as no.
3 (p.5) and no.15 (p.12) in:
Repertoire Progressif Pour
Guitare, Vol. 1) CHOUDENS f.s.
        (1643)

Minuet
gtr ESSEX f.s.   (1644)
(Behrend) gtr (2nd degr.) HEINRICH.
N-1619 f.s.   (1645)

Minuet in G
(Rosado) gtr UNION ESP. 20088 f.s.
        (1646)

Minuet in G, MIN 333
gtr FORTEA 7 f.s.   (1647)

Rondo, MIN 383
gtr ESSEX f.s.   (1648)

Rondoletto
(Gangi) gtr (4th degr.) BERBEN
EB1259 $1.00   (1649)

Sonatinen, 3 *Op.1
(Schmid-Kayser) gtr (3-4th degr.)
VIEWEG 1377 f.s.   (1650)

Variationen Uber "Le Songe De
Rousseau" *Op.17
(Schmid-Kayser) gtr (5-6th degr.)
VIEWEG 1387 f.s.   (1651)

CARULLI, FERDINANDO (1770-1841)
Andante Grazioso
(Sensier) gtr ESSEX f.s. (1652)

6 Andanti *Op.320
(Chiesa) gtr (6th degr.) ZERBONI
8109 f.s.   (1653)

Andantino And Waltz
(Sensier) gtr ESSEX f.s. (1654)

Ballet
gtr ESSEX f.s.   (1655)

Kleine Vortragsstucke Fur Anfanger, 5
gtr (1-2nd degr.) SCHOTT GA-313
f.s.   (1656)

Moderato *Op.21,No.2
gtr (4th degr.) BERBEN EB1352 $1.00
        (1657)

Nocturne in D
(Teuchert) gtr (4-5th degr.)
SCHMIDT,H 600 f.s.   (1658)

Overture, Op. 6, No. 1
(Behrend) gtr (5-6th degr.) NOETZEL
N-3168 f.s.   (1659)

Poco Allegretto
(Sisley) gtr ESSEX f.s. (1660)

Receuil De 23 Morceaux (from Op. 276)
gtr (1-3rd degr.) LEMOINE f.s.
        (1661)

Rondo, MIN 386
gtr ESSEX f.s.   (1662)

Sehr Leichte Stucke, 18, Vol. 1
*Op.333
(Gotze) gtr (2-3rd degr., for vol.
2 see: 12 Romanzen for 2 gtr)
SCHOTT GA-67 f.s.   (1663)

Solo, Op. 76, No. 2
(Company) gtr (6th degr., L'arte
Della Chitarra) ZERBONI 7732 f.s.
        (1664)

Sonata
(Mazmanian) gtr (3-4th degr.)
HEINRICH. N-1522 f.s. contains
also: Air Varie   (1665)

Sonatine Facili, 14
(Carfagna) gtr (1-3rd degr.) BERBEN
EB1953 $3.25   (1666)

Three Easy Waltzes
(Sensier) gtr ESSEX f.s. (1667)

Variazioni Su L'Arietta Italiana "Sul
Margine D'un Rio *Op.142
(Chiesa) gtr (5-6th degr.) ZERBONI
7727 $6.00   (1668)

Variazioni Su Un Tema Di Beethoven
(Gazzelloni) gtr (6th degr.) BERBEN
EB2097 f.s.   (1669)

CARULLI, FERDINANDO (cont'd.)

Waltz And Rondo
(Sensier) gtr ESSEX f.s. (1670)

CHOPIN, FREDERIC (1810-1849)
Composiciones, 3
(Parodi) gtr RICORDI-ARG BA-11281
f.s.
  contains: Nocturne, Op. 15, No.
  2; Prelude No. 21; Waltz, Op.
  69, No. 2   (1671)

Etude No. 6
(Tarrega; Fortea) gtr FORTEA 229
f.s. contains also: Etude No. 7;
Etude No. 20   (1672)

Etude, Op. 10, No. 3, [excerpt]
"Studio Op. 10, No. 3 (Frammento)"
(Abloniz) gtr (6th degr.) BERBEN
EB1926 $1.00   (1673)
"Tristeza" (Casuscelli) gtr (6th
degr.) RICORDI-ARG BA-10360 f.s.
        (1674)
"Tristesse, Celebre" (Fortea) gtr
(6th degr.) FORTEA 45 f.s. (1675)
"So Deep Is The Night" (Medio) gtr
(6th degr.) ESSEX f.s. (1676)
"Intimite" (Ranieri) gtr (6th
degr.) CRANZ $2.00   (1677)
"Tristesse" (Sanchez Granada) gtr
(6th degr.) UNION ESP. 17480 f.s.
        (1678)
"Tristesse" (Tarrega; Fortea) gtr
(6th degr.) FORTEA 77 f.s. (1679)

Marcha Funebre
(Fortea) gtr FORTEA 43 f.s. (1680)
(Tarrega) gtr FORTEA 72 f.s. (1681)

Mazurka No. 16
(Tarrega; Fortea) gtr FORTEA 74
f.s.   (1682)

Mazurka, Op. 7, No. 1
(Diaz Loza) gtr RICORDI-ARG
BA-11912 f.s.   (1683)

Mazurka, Op. 7, No. 2
(Bignotto) gtr (3rd degr., My
Repertory) ZANIBON 5431 f.s.
        (1684)

Mazurka, Op. 23, No. 22
(Tarrega; Fortea) gtr FORTEA 232
f.s.   (1685)

Mazurka, Op. 33, No. 1
(Garcia Velasco) gtr UNION ESP.
20295 f.s.   (1686)
(Rodriguez Arenas) gtr RICORDI-ARG
RF-7578 f.s.   (1687)

Mazurka, Op. 33, No. 4
(Tarrega) gtr RICORDI-ARG BA-9311
f.s.   (1688)
(Tarrega) gtr UNION ESP. 19037 f.s.
        (1689)
(Tarrega; Fortea) gtr FORTEA 234
f.s.   (1690)

Mazurka, Op. 33, No. 22
(Tarrega; Fortea) gtr FORTEA 73
f.s.   (1691)

Mazurka, Op. 63, No. 3
(Segovia) gtr (6th degr.) SCHOTT
GA-140 f.s.   (1692)

Mazurka, Op. 64, No. 4
(Tarrega; Fortea) gtr FORTEA 233
f.s.   (1693)

Nocturne, Op. 9, No. 1
(Casuscelli) gtr RICORDI-ARG
BA-10019 f.s.   (1694)

Nocturne, Op. 9, No. 2
(Llobet) gtr UNION ESP. 20376 f.s.
        (1695)
(Nunes) gtr RICORDI-BR BR-2265 f.s.
        (1696)
(Tarrega) gtr RICORDI-ARG BA-3471
f.s.   (1697)
(Tarrega) gtr UNION ESP. 19092 f.s.
        (1698)

Nocturne, Op. 48, No. 1
(Casuscelli) gtr RICORDI-ARG
BA-11830 f.s.   (1699)

Notturno
(Rossi) gtr (8th degr.) BERBEN
EB2102 f.s.   (1700)

Notturno No. 2
gtr FORTEA 236 f.s.   (1701)

Notturno No. 9
gtr FORTEA 237 f.s.   (1702)

Prelude No. 1
(Tarrega; Fortea) gtr FORTEA 75
f.s. contains also: Prelude No.
14   (1703)

CHOPIN, FREDERIC (cont'd.)

Prelude No. 7
(Papas) gtr COLUMBIA 146 $1.00
contains also: Prelude No. 20
(1704)

(Savio) gtr RICORDI-BR BR-2667 f.s.
contains also: Prelude, No. 20;
Tristeza, Fragmento Do Estudo,
Op. 10, No. 3   (1705)

Prelude No. 15
"Gota De Agua" (Tarrega; Fortea)
gtr FORTEA 231 f.s.   (1706)

Prelude No. 20
(Sinopoli) gtr RICORDI-ARG BA-9165
f.s. contains also: Grieg, Edvard
Hagerup, Arieta, Op. 12 (from
Lyriske Stykker, Book I)   (1707)

Prelude, Op. 28, No. 4
(Terzi) gtr RICORDI-IT 129290 f.s.
(1708)

Prelude, Op. 28, No. 6
(Ranieri) gtr CRANZ $2.00 contains
also: Prelude, Op. 28, No. 7 (1709)

Prelude, Op. 28, No. 15
(Tarrega) gtr UNION ESP. 19021 f.s.
(1710)

Preludios
(Llobet) gtr UNION ESP. 20377 f.s.
contains: Prelude No. 8; Prelude
No. 9   (1711)

Preludios, 3
(Tarrega) gtr RICORDI-ARG BA-7922
f.s.
contains: Prelude, Op. 28, No. 6;
Prelude, Op. 28, No. 7;
Prelude, Op. 28, No. 20 (1712)

Preludios, 3
(Tarrega) gtr UNION ESP. 19020 f.s.
contains: Prelude, Op. 28, No. 6;
Prelude, Op. 28, No. 7;
Prelude, Op. 28, No. 20 (1713)

Preludios, 6
(Tarrega) gtr RICORDI-ARG K-16539
f.s.
contains: Prelude, Op. 28, No. 4;
Prelude, Op. 28, No. 6;
Prelude, Op. 28, No. 7;
Prelude, Op. 28, No. 11;
Prelude, Op. 28, No. 15;
Prelude, Op. 28, No. 20 (1714)

2 Preludios
gtr FORTEA 75 f.s.
contains: Prelude No. 1; Prelude
No. 14   (1715)

Two Preludes
(Weston) gtr ESSEX f.s.
contains: Prelude, Op. 28, No. 7;
Prelude, Op. 28, No. 20 (1716)

Vals Brillante *Op.18
(Casuscelli) gtr RICORDI-ARG
BA-9840 f.s.   (1717)

Waltz No. 10
(Segovia) gtr CEL 25 $.75 (1718)

Waltz, Op. 34, No. 2
(Casuscelli) gtr RICORDI-ARG
BA-12065 f.s.   (1719)
"Vals Brillante" (Tarrega; Fortea)
gtr FORTEA 235 f.s.   (1720)

Waltz, Op. 64, No. 2
(Casuscelli) gtr (7th degr.)
RICORDI-ARG BA-10063 f.s. (1721)
(Paleologo) gtr (7th degr.)
HEINRICH. N-1529 f.s.   (1722)
(Savio) gtr (7th degr.) RICORDI-BR
BR-2608 f.s.   (1723)
(Sensier) gtr (7th degr.) ESSEX
f.s.   (1724)

Waltz, Op. 69, No. 1
gtr FORTEA 76 f.s.   (1725)
(Nunes) gtr RICORDI-BR BR-858 f.s.
(1726)

Waltz, Op. 69, No. 2
(Fortea) gtr FORTEA 44 f.s. (1727)
(Garcia Velasco) gtr UNION ESP.
20294 f.s.   (1728)
(Savio) gtr RICORDI-BR BR-2338 f.s.
(1729)

Waltz, Op. 70, No. 2
(Nunes) gtr RICORDI-BR BR-2030 f.s.
(1730)

COSTE, NAPOLEON (1806-1883)
Estudio De Concierto
gtr FORTEA 12 f.s.   (1731)

Herbstblatter *Op.41
gtr (3rd degr., 12 valses) SCHOTT
GA-12 f.s.   (1732)

Melancolie
(Teuchert) gtr (3-4th degr.)
SCHMIDT,H 321 f.s.   (1733)

COSTE, NAPOLEON (cont'd.)

Originalstucke, 6 *Op.53
(Meier) gtr (4-5th degr.) SCHOTT
GA-42 f.s.   (1734)

Recreation *Op.51, CC14U
gtr (3rd degr.) SCHOTT GA-13 f.s.
(1735)

Recreation Du Guitariste *CC14U
(Cottin) gtr (1-3rd degr.) LEMOINE
f.s.   (1736)

Reverie
gtr FORTEA 11 f.s.   (1737)

Rondo, MIN 384
(Bream) gtr ESSEX f.s.   (1738)

Scherzo, MIN 385
gtr ESSEX f.s.   (1739)

9 Studien
(Scheit, Karl) gtr (from "Methode
complete pour guitare" by Sor and
Coste) UNIVER. 14468 f.s. (1740)

Tarantelle
gtr ESSEX f.s.   (1741)

Ubungs- Und Unterhaltungsstucke, 16
(Meier) gtr (2-3rd degr., for 6-
and 7-stringed gtr) SCHOTT GA-11
f.s.   (1742)

DARR, ADAM (1811-1866)
Rondino
gtr (4th degr.) BERBEN EB1873 $1.00
(1743)

DIABELLI, ANTON (1781-1858)
Andante Sostenuto
(Teuchert) gtr (3-4th degr.)
SCHMIDT,H 320 f.s.   (1744)

Fughe, 2 *Op.46
(Abloniz) gtr (5th degr.) BERBEN
EB2035 f.s.   (1745)

Leichte Altwiener Landler, 24
(Gotze) gtr (3rd degr.) SCHOTT
GA-85 f.s.   (1746)

Leichte Stucke Und Landler, Op. 89
And Op. 127
(Domandl) gtr SIMROCK 896 f.s.
(1747)

Leichte Vortragsstucke, 5 (from Op.
39)
gtr (3rd degr.) SCHOTT GA-322 f.s.
(1748)

7 Praeludien *Op.103
(Nagel; Meunier) gtr MOSELER f.s.
(1749)

Prelude in A (from Op. 103)
gtr (3rd degr.) SCHOTT GA-321 f.s.
(1750)

Rondino In C
(Sensier) gtr ESSEX f.s. (1751)

Rondinos, 4
(Schindler) gtr (4th degr.)
HEINRICH. N-1516 f.s.   (1752)

Skladby, 3 (3 Kompositionen)
(Urban) gtr (4th degr.) CZECH
H-3894 f.s. Kytarova Sola, No. 13
contains: Adagio; Allegretto;
Andante Cantabile   (1753)

Sonata, Op. 29, No. 1, in C
(Scheit) gtr (4-5th degr.) UNIVER.
14472 f.s.   (1754)

Vortragsstucke Fur Anfanger *Op.39
"Eight Little Pieces For Beginners"
(Scheit) gtr (1-2nd degr.)
UNIVER. 14464 $3.25   (1755)

Wiener Tanze, 5
(Scheit) gtr (2-3rd degr.) UNIVER.
14463 $3.25   (1756)

DUSSEK, JOHANN LADISLAUS (1760-1812)
Rondo (from Sonata For Harp In C
Minor)
(Abloniz) gtr (4th degr.) BERBEN
EB1330 $1.00   (1757)

FERANDIERE, FERNANDO
Petites Pieces, 6
(Hulsen) gtr (3rd degr.) SCHOTT
GA-71 f.s.   (1758)

FLIES, J. BERNHARD (1770- ?)
Wiegenlied "Schlafe Mein Prinzchen"
(Behrend) gtr (4th degr.,
attributed to Wolfgang Mozart)
ZIMMER. ZM-1744 f.s.   (1759)
"Cancion De Cuna" (Garcia Velasco)
gtr (4th degr., attributed to
Wolfgang Mozart) UNION ESP. 20296
f.s.   (1760)
"Berceuse" (Ranieri) gtr (4th
degr., attributed to Wolfgang
Mozart) CRANZ $2.00   (1761)

GIULIANI, MAURO (1781-1829)
Allegretto, MIN346 *Op.147,No.9
gtr (3rd degr.) ESSEX f.s. (1762)

Allegretto, MIN347 *Op.11
(Bibobi) gtr (3rd degr.) ESSEX f.s.
(1763)

Allegro E Grazioso, Op. 40, No.8, 9
gtr (2-3rd degr.) BERBEN EB1047
f.s.   (1764)

Andantino *Op.147,No.2 (from
Giulianate, Op. 148)
gtr (2nd degr.) BERBEN EB1631 $1.00
(1765)

(Behrend) gtr (5th degr., Gitarre-
Bibliothek, No.38) BOTE GB-38
f.s.   (1766)

Andantino, MIN355 *Op.147,No.2
gtr ESSEX f.s.   (1767)

Andantino, MIN356 *Op.147,No.5
gtr ESSEX f.s.   (1768)

Antologia De La Guitarra *CC20U
(Angel) gtr UNION ESP. 21158 f.s.
(1769)

Capriccio
gtr (4th degr.) SCHOTT GA-323 f.s.
contains also: Allegretto (1770)

Capriccio, Op. 100, No. 11
gtr (3rd degr.) BERBEN EB-1783
$1.00   (1771)

Caprice Fur Gitarre
(Nagel) gtr BREITKOPF-W 6743 (1772)

Choix De Mes Fleurs Cheries *Op.46
(Azpiazu) gtr ZIMMER. ZM-1305 f.s.
(1773)

Choix De Mes Fleurs Cheries (Le
Bouquet Emblematique) *Op.46,
CC10U
(Cavazzoli) gtr RICORDI-IT 132996
f.s.   (1774)

Composiciones Para Guitarra, Vol. 1
(Savio) gtr (3-7th degr., includes:
from op. 111, no. 2; Allegro;
from op. 139, no. 5; from op.
147, no. 10; op. 61; op. 46 [no.
1-5]; op. 14, no. 4; op. 71, no.
1, 2) RICORDI-ARG BA-12407 f.s.
(1775)

Composiciones Para Guitarra, Vol. 2
(Savio) gtr (3-7th degr., includes:
from op. 43, no. 10; op. 112; op.
46, [no. 7-10]; op. 14, no. 5;
op. 71, no. 3; op. 20) RICORDI-
ARG BA-12408 f.s.   (1776)

Danse Nord
gtr ESSEX f.s.   (1777)

Divertimento, Op. 37
(Nagel) gtr (4-5th degr.) SCHOTT
GA-414 f.s.   (1778)

Divertimento, Op. 40
(Nagel; Lendl) gtr (3rd degr., 12
pcs) SCHOTT GA-415 f.s. (1779)

Fughetta
(Behrend) gtr (4th degr., Gitarre-
Bibliothek, No.36; also published
in: European Masters For The
Guitar) BOTE GB-36 f.s. (1780)

Giulianate *Op.148
(Chiesa) gtr (4-7th degr., 8 pcs)
Urtext edition) ZERBONI 7761 f.s.
(1781)
(Smiroldo) gtr (4-7th degr., 8 pcs)
BERBEN EB1710 $10.50   (1782)

Grande Ouverture *Op.61
(Behrend) gtr (8th degr., Gitarre-
Bibliothek, No.82) BOTE GB-82
f.s.   (1783)
(Bream) gtr (8th degr.) FABER
F-0505 f.s.   (1784)
(Chiesa) gtr (8th degr., Urtext
edition) ZERBONI 7888 f.s. (1785)
(Stingl) gtr (8th degr.) SCHOTT
GA-432 f.s.   (1786)
(Tonazzi) gtr (8th degr.) BERBEN
EB1859 $3.25   (1787)

Grazioso
(Behrend) gtr (3rd degr.) HEINRICH.
N-1620 f.s.   (1788)

Leichte Fortschreitende Stucke, 6
*Op.139
(Avila) gtr (3rd degr.) SCHOTT
GA-76 f.s.   (1789)

Leichte Nordische Tanze, 16 *Op.147
(Avila) gtr (2nd degr.) SCHOTT
GA-70 f.s.   (1790)

Leichte Variationen Uber Ein
Osterreichisches Lied *Op.47
(Scheit) gtr (3rd degr.) UNIVER.

GIULIANI, MAURO (cont'd.)

14460 $2.75   (1791)

March, MIN 370
    gtr ESSEX f.s.   (1792)

Melancholia
    gtr ESSEX f.s.   (1793)

Minuet De La Cour
    (Sisley) gtr ESSEX f.s.   (1794)

Monferrine, 12 *Op.12
    (Chiesa) gtr (2-3rd degr.) ZERBONI
    7886 $6.00   (1795)

Oeuvres Choisies Pour Guitare *CC50U
    (Heck) gtr (3-8th degr.) HEUGEL
    LP-46 $16.00 Le Pupitre, No.46;
    illus, intro, sources; Urtext
    edition   (1796)

Papillon, Le *Op.30
    "Schmetterling, Der" (Avila) gtr
    (1-3rd degr., 32 pcs) SCHOTT
    GA-48 f.s.   (1797)
    "Schmetterling, Der" (Quattrocchi)
    gtr (1-3rd degr., 32 pcs) BERBEN
    EB1248 $2.25   (1798)

Papillon, Le (Choix d'Airs Faciles)
    gtr (1-3rd degr.) LEMOINE f.s.
                               (1799)

Polonaise, MIN 371
    (Sensier) gtr ESSEX f.s.   (1800)

Prelude in F, MIN 374
    gtr ESSEX f.s.   (1801)

Preludes, 6, Op. 83
    "Preludi, 6" (Carfagna) gtr (4-6th
    degr.) BERBEN EB2048 f.s. (1802)
    "Praludien, 6" (Domandl) gtr. (4-6th
    degr.) BENJ EE-3040 f.s.   (1803)
    "Praludien, 6" (Gotze) gtr (4-6th
    degr.) SCHOTT GA-64 f.s.   (1804)

6 Preludios
    (Sainz De La Maza) gtr UNION ESP.
    20136 f.s.   (1805)

Rondo, Op. 8, No. 2, in G
    (Tonazzi) gtr (3rd degr.) SCHOTT
    GA-410 f.s.   (1806)

Rondo, Op. 11
    (Behrend) gtr (4th degr., Gitarre-
    Bibliothek, No.4) BOTE GB-4 f.s.
                               (1807)

Rondo, Op. 17, No. 1, in A
    (Tonazzi) gtr (4th degr.) SCHOTT
    GA-411 f.s.   (1808)

Rondo Und Harfen-Etude
    (Teuchert) gtr (Die Sologitarre)
    SCHMIDT,H 307 f.s.   (1809)

Rondoletto *Op.4
    (Polasek) gtr (8th degr.) ESCHIG
    f.s.   (1810)

Rossiniana, No. 1 *Op.119
    (Chiesa) gtr (7-8th degr.) ZERBONI
    8111 f.s.   (1811)

Rossiniana, No. 2 *Op.120
    (Chiesa) gtr (7-8th degr.) ZERBONI
    8354 f.s.   (1812)

Rossiniana, No. 3 *Op.121
    (Chiesa) gtr (7-8th degr.) ZERBONI
    8355 f.s.   (1813)

Scherzo Giocoso *Op.148,No.4
    (Schindler) gtr (4th degr.) VAMO
    EE-08 f.s.   (1814)

Scozzesi, 12 *Op.33
    (Chiesa) gtr (2nd degr.) ZERBONI
    7889 $4.75   (1815)

Sostenuto
    gtr ESSEX f.s.   (1816)

Theme and Variations *Op.112
    (Heck, Thomas F.) gtr (Guitar
    Foundation of America Publ.
    Series A No.1) fac ed BELWIN
    $2.50   (1817)

Tirolesa
    gtr ESSEX f.s.   (1818)

Unterhaltungsstucke, 10 *Op.43
    (Schindler) gtr (3rd degr.)
    HEINRICH. N-1501 f.s.   (1819)

Utwory Wybrane *CC23U
    (Powrozniak, Jozef) gtr (3-6th
    degr.) POLSKIE 7734 f.s. Klasycy
    Gitary   (1820)

12 Valzer *Op.57
    (Chiesa) gtr (3rd degr.) ZERBONI
    8566 f.s.   (1821)

GIULIANI, MAURO (cont'd.)

Variations, 6: Op87
    (Nagel; Meunier) gtr (6th degr.)
    BREITKOPF-W 6699 f.s.   (1822)

Variations, Op. 2
    (Chiesa) gtr (6th degr.) ZERBONI
    7897 $6.00   (1823)

Variations, Op. 62
    (Chiesa) gtr (7th degr.) ZERBONI
    7964 $6.00   (1824)

Variations, Op. 112
    (Chiesa) gtr (7th degr.) ZERBONI
    7764 $6.00   (1825)
    "Grandi Variazioni, 6" (Muggia) gtr
    (7th degr.) ZANIBON 5325 f.s.
                               (1826)

Variazioni E Finale, 4
    (Muggia) gtr (4th degr., sul tema
    favorito napoletano "Chi T'ha
    Fatto Sta Scarpettiella") ZANIBON
    5326 f.s.   (1827)

Variazioni Su L'Aria "Schisserl Und A
    Reindl" *Op.38
    (Chiesa) gtr (6-7th degr.) ZERBONI
    7726 $4.75   (1828)

Variazioni Su Un Tema Dal Balletto
    "Die Feindlichen Vollkstame"
    *Op.7
    (Chiesa) gtr (5-6th degr.) ZERBONI
    7841 $6.00   (1829)

Variazioni Su Un Tema Di Handel
    *Op.107
    "Variationen Uber Ein Thema Von
    Handel" gtr (6-7th degr.) SIMROCK
    1201 f.s.   (1830)
    (Chiesa) gtr (6-7th degr.) ZERBONI
    7763 $6.00   (1831)
    (di Sandro) gtr (6-7th degr.)
    BERBEN EB1924 f.s.   (1832)

Variazioni Su Un Tema Originale
    *Op.20
    (Chiesa) gtr (6th degr.) ZERBONI
    8450 f.s.   (1833)

Variazioni Sul Tema Della Follia Di
    Spagna *Op.45
    "Variationen Uber "La Follia""
    (Behrend) gtr (6-7th degr.,
    Gitarre-Bibliothek, No.56) BOTE
    GB-56 f.s.   (1834)
    (Chiesa) gtr (6-7th degr.) ZERBONI
    7887 $4.75   (1835)

Variazioni Sulla Romanza Dall'Opera
    "Ruhm Und Liebe" *Op.105
    (Chiesa) gtr (7th degr.) ZERBONI
    8360 f.s.   (1836)

Variazioni Sull'Aria Favorita De "La
    Molinara" *Op.4
    (Chiesa) gtr (6th degr.) ZERBONI
    8449 f.s.   (1837)

Vivace Con Brio
    gtr ESSEX f.s.   (1838)

GOSSEC, FRANCOIS JOSEPH (1734-1829)
    Gavotte, MIN 360
    (Weston) gtr ESSEX f.s.   (1839)

    Tambourin And Gavotte
    (Lloyd) gtr (5-6th degr.) MSM $2.25
                               (1840)

HANDEL, GEORGE FRIDERIC (1685-1759)
    Time Pieces (composed with Haydn,
    [Franz] Joseph) *CC11L
    (Lawrence) gtr (3-5th degr.)
    FENTONE F-121 $4.95 works for
    musical clocks   (1841)

HAYDN, [FRANZ] JOSEPH (1732-1809)
    Allegro, MIN348
    (Weston) gtr (4-5th degr.) ESSEX
    f.s.   (1842)

    Andante, MIN 122
    (Behrend) gtr (4-5th degr.,
    Gitarre-Bibliothek, No.37; also
    published in: European Masters
    For The Guitar) BOTE GB-37 f.s.
                               (1843)

    Andante, MIN 123
    (Papas) gtr COLUMBIA 148 $1.00
                               (1844)

    Andante, MIN 338
    gtr FORTEA 243 f.s.   (1845)

    Andante, MIN 352
    (Bream) gtr ESSEX f.s.   (1846)

    Andante, MIN 399
    (Tarrega) gtr UNION ESP. 18953 f.s.
                               (1847)

    Andante Und Menuett
    (Behrend) gtr (5-6th degr., Die
    Konzertgitarre) SIKORSKI 690
    $2.75   (1848)

HAYDN, [FRANZ] JOSEPH (cont'd.)

5 Deutsche Tanze Und Coda *Hob.IX:22
    (from Ballo Tedesco Per Il
    Cembalo)
    (Scheit) gtr (3rd degr.) UNIVER.
    16695 f.s.   (1849)

Haydn-Buch, Das *CC40U
    (Schwarz-Reiflingen) gtr SIKORSKI
    481 f.s.   (1850)

Largo Anay
    gtr FORTEA 245 f.s.   (1851)

Largo Assai
    (Tarrega) gtr UNION ESP. 19032 f.s.
                               (1852)

Menuets Celebres, 2
    (Azpiazu) gtr (7th degr., Guitare,
    No.73) LEDUC G-73 $3.00   (1853)

Minuet, Hob.III: 75 (from Quartet In
    G Major)
    (Segovia) gtr (5th degr.) SCHOTT
    GA-139 f.s.   (1854)

Minuet, MIN 119
    (Segovia) gtr RICORDI-ARG BA-9594
    f.s.   (1855)

Minuet, MIN 120
    (Segovia) gtr (also published in:
    Transcripciones Para Guitarra,
    No. 6) UNION ESP. 18032 f.s.
                               (1856)

Minuet, MIN 121 (from Quartet For
    Lute, Violin, Viola And
    Violoncello)
    (Henze) gtr (3rd degr.) BERBEN
    EB1110 f.s.   (1857)

Minuet, Op. 2, No. 2
    (Abloniz) gtr RICORDI-IT 130056
    f.s.   (1858)

Minueto Del Buey
    gtr FORTEA 244 f.s.   (1859)

Minuetto, MIN 400
    (Segovia) gtr UNION ESP. 18032 f.s.
                               (1860)

Minuetto, MIN 401
    (Tarrega) gtr UNION ESP. 19054 f.s.
                               (1861)

Serenade, MIN 124 (from Quartet Op.
    3, No. 5)
    (Zuccheri) gtr (4th degr.) BERBEN
    EB2058 f.s.   (1862)

Serenade, MIN 389
    gtr COLUMBIA 202 f.s.   (1863)

HILLER, JOHANN ADAM (1728-1804)
    Lieder, 6
    (Monkemeyer) gtr,opt solo voice (3-
    4th degr.) TONGER 1283 f.s.
    contains: Abendlied Eines
    Bauermanns; Lied Hinterm Ofen
    Zu Singen; Mann Im Lehnstuhle,
    Der; Meine Wunsche; Pasteten
    Lied; Urians Reise Um Die Welt
                               (1864)

HOOK, RICHARD
    Within A Mile Of Edinboro
    (Sensier) gtr (3rd degr.) ESSEX
    f.s. contains also: Silcher,
    Friedrich, Lorelei, Die   (1865)

HORECKI, FELIKS (1799-1870)
    Utwory Wybrane
    (Powrozniak, Jozef) gtr (3-7th
    degr., Klasycy Gitary; 45 pcs for
    1 gtr; 6 pcs for 2 gtr) sc
    POLSKIE 7555 f.s.   (1866)

HUMMEL, JOHANN NEPOMUK (1778-1837)
    Allegretto (from Grand Serenade, Op.
    63)
    (Tower) gtr (5-6th degr.) TEESELING
    VT-25 f.s.   (1867)

KUFFNER, JOSEPH (1776-1856)
    24 Gitarrewerke Fur Die Unterstufe
    (Henke) gtr (1-3rd degr.) SYMPHON
    2255 f.s.   (1868)

    25 Leichte Sonatinen *Op.80, CC25U
    (Gotze) gtr (1-2nd degr.) SCHOTT
    GA-7 f.s. orig ed   (1869)

    Leichte Tanze
    (Gotze) 1-2gtr (3rd degr.) SCHOTT
    GA-84 f.s.   (1870)

LEGNANI, LUIGI (1790-1877)
    Capriccio
    gtr ESSEX f.s.   (1871)

    Capriccio in F
    (Sensier) gtr ESSEX f.s.   (1872)

    Capriccio No. 2
    gtr ESSEX f.s.   (1873)

LEGNANI, LUIGI (cont'd.)

Introduzione, Tema, Variazioni E
   Finale *Op.64
   (Chiesa) gtr (8th degr.) ZERBONI
   7765 $7.00   (1874)

Leichte Walzer
   (Gotze) gtr (2-3rd degr.) SCHOTT
   5069 f.s.   (1875)

Marionette Dance
   gtr ESSEX f.s.   (1876)

Variazioni Sul Duetto "Nel Cor Piu
   Non Mi Sento" Da "La Molinara" Di
   Paisiello *Op.16, 8-9th cent
   (Chiesa) gtr ZERBONI 8359 f.s.
                                     (1877)

MARSCHNER, HEINRICH (AUGUST)
   (1795-1861)
Bagatellen, 12 *Op.4
   (Gotze) gtr (3-4th degr.) SCHOTT
   GA-41 f.s.   (1878)

Bagatellen, Op. 4, Nos. 6, 8, 10
   (Scheit) gtr (3rd degr.) UNIVER.
   14467 f.s.   (1879)

MATIEGKA, WENZESLAUS THOMAS (1753-1830)
Andante
   (Behrend) gtr (5th degr.) NOETZEL
   N-3171 f.s.   (1880)

12 Leichte Stucke *Op.3
   "12 Pieces Faciles" (Libbert) [Ger/
   Eng] gtr (3rd degr., pref; Urtext
   ed; Studio-Reihe Gitarre)
   PREISSLER 70202 f.s.   (1881)

Minuet
   (Carfagna) gtr (4-5th degr.) BERBEN
   EB1488 $1.00   (1882)

Sechs Variationen
   (Nagel) gtr BREITKOPF-W 6724   (1883)

Zwei Konzertante Menuette
   (Teuchert) gtr SCHMIDT,H 318 f.s.
                                     (1884)

Zwolf Menuette *Op.15
   gtr BENJ 3039 f.s.   (1885)

MEISSONNIER, J. (1790- ?)
Antologia De La Guitarra, Vol. 1
   *CC26U
   (Angel) gtr (1-3rd degr.) UNION
   ESP. 20836 f.s.   (1886)

Siciliano
   (Sensier) gtr ESSEX f.s.   (1887)

Variationen Uber "Nel Cor Piu Non Mi
   Sento"
   (Ochs) gtr (2-3rd degr.,
   "Franzosische Gitarremusik Des
   19. Jahrhunderts") HOFMEISTER
   T-4150 f.s. contains also:
   Molino, Francesco, Terpsichore
                                     (1888)

MENDELSSOHN-BARTHOLDY, FELIX
   (1809-1847)
Cancion (from Songs Without Words?)
   (Anido) gtr RICORDI-ARG RF-7527
   f.s.   (1889)

Canzonetta (from String Quartet No.
   1, Op. 12, In E Flat)
   (Alfonso) gtr (8-9th degr., Edition
   Nicolas Alfonso, No. 12) SCHOTT-
   FRER 9152 f.s.   (1890)
   (Behrend) gtr (8-9th degr.,
   Gitarre-Bibliothek, No.22) BOTE
   GB-22 f.s.   (1891)
   (Sinopoli) gtr (8-9th degr.)
   RICORDI-ARG BA-7419 f.s.   (1892)
   (Tarrega) gtr (8-9th degr.) FORTEA
   253 f.s.   (1893)
   (Tarrega; Savio) gtr (8-9th degr.)
   RICORDI-ARG BA-11928 f.s.   (1894)

Fruhlingslied *Op.62,No.6 (from
   Songs Without Words)
   "Cancion De Primavera" (Sinopoli)
   gtr RICORDI-ARG BA-8417 f.s.
                                     (1895)
   "Cancion De Primavera" (Tarrega;
   Fortea) gtr FORTEA 95 f.s.   (1896)

Hilandera, La *Op.67,No.2
   (Garcia Velasco) gtr UNION ESP.
   20298 f.s.   (1897)

Marcha Nupcial
   (Fortea) gtr FORTEA 117 f.s.   (1898)

Romance, MIN 402
   (Llobet) gtr UNION ESP. 20378 f.s.
                                     (1899)

Romance, Op. 38, No. 2 (from Songs
   Without Words, Book III)
   (Tarrega; Fortea) gtr FORTEA 251
   f.s.   (1900)

MENDELSSOHN-BARTHOLDY, FELIX (cont'd.)

Romanza Senza Parole
   (Tempestini) gtr ESSEX f.s. (1901)

Romanza Sin Palabras, Op.19, No.2
   (from Songs Without Words, Book
   I)
   (Casuscelli) gtr RICORDI-ARG
   BA-11430 f.s.   (1902)

Romanza Sin Palabras, Op.19, No.3
   (from Songs Without Words, Book
   II)
   (Segovia) gtr RICORDI-ARG BA-9595
   f.s.   (1903)

Romanza Sin Palabras, Op.30, No.3
   (from Songs Without Words, Book
   II)
   (Tarrega; Fortea) gtr FORTEA 94
   f.s.   (1904)

Romanza Sin Palabras, Op. 85, No. 3
   (from Songs Without Words, Book
   VII)
   (Sinopoli) gtr RICORDI-ARG BA-9357
   f.s.   (1905)

Romanza Sin Palabras, Op. 102, No. 2
   (from Songs Without Words, Book
   VIII)
   (Casuscelli) gtr RICORDI-ARG
   BA-11831 f.s.   (1906)

Song Without Words
   "Romanza Sin Palabras" (Segovia)
   gtr (also published in:
   Transcripciones Para Guitarra,
   No. 7) UNION ESP. 18038 f.s.
                                     (1907)

Venetian Barcarolle
   (Battine) gtr ESSEX f.s.   (1908)

Venezianisches Gondellied, Op.19,
   No.6 (from Songs Without Words,
   Book I)
   "Barcarola Veneziana" (Abloniz) gtr
   RICORDI-IT 130057 f.s.   (1909)
   "Barcarola Veneziana" (Ranieri) gtr
   CRANZ $2.00   (1910)
   "Barcarola Veneziana" (Tarrega;
   Fortea) gtr FORTEA 250 f.s.
                                     (1911)

Venezianisches Gondellied, Op.30,
   No.6 (from Songs Without Words,
   Book II)
   "Gondolera Veneciana, Barcarola"
   (Robledo) gtr RICORDI-ARG RF-7173
   f.s.   (1912)
   "Gondolera Veneciana, Barcarola"
   (Rodriguez Arenas) gtr RICORDI-
   ARG BA-5094 f.s.   (1913)
   "Gondolera Veneciana, Barcarola"
   (Tarrega) gtr RICORDI-ARG BA-9764
   f.s.   (1914)

Venezianisches Gondellied, Op.62,
   No.5 (from Songs Without Words,
   Book V)
   "Gondolera Veneciana, Barcarola"
   (Casuscelli) gtr RICORDI-ARG
   BA-11431 f.s.   (1915)

MERTZ, JOHANN KASPAR (1806-1856)
Csardas
   (Ricchi) gtr (4-5th degr.) BERBEN
   EB1802 f.s.   (1916)

Fingals-Hohle *Op.13
   "Grotte Di Fingal, Le" gtr (4th
   degr.) BERBEN EB1602 $1.00 (1917)

Largo, MIN 367
   gtr ESSEX f.s.   (1918)

Lob Der Thranen
   (Sensier) gtr ESSEX f.s.   (1919)

Nocturnes, 3, Op. 4
   (Steigenberger) gtr (3rd degr.)
   NOETZEL N-3326 f.s.   (1920)

Preghiera *Op.13,No.5
   gtr (5th degr.) BERBEN EB1395 $1.00
                                     (1921)

Russisches Zigeunerlied
   (Sensier) gtr ESSEX f.s.   (1922)

Tarantella
   gtr (5th degr.) BERBEN EB1918 $1.00
                                     (1923)

MOLINO, FRANCESCO (1775-1847)
Rondo, MIN 125
   gtr (4-5th degr.) BERBEN EB2001
   f.s.   (1924)

Rondo, MIN 126 (from Op. 11)
   gtr (3rd degr.) BERBEN EB1738 $1.00
                                     (1925)

MORETTI, LUIGI
Andante (from Gran Sonata)
   (di Ponio) gtr (6th degr.) BERBEN
   EB1111 $1.00   (1926)

MOZART, WOLFGANG AMADEUS (1756-1791)
Adagio for Harmonica, K. 356
   (Behrend) gtr (6th degr., Gitarre-
   Bibliothek, No.41) BOTE GB-41
   f.s.   (1927)

Allegro
   (Anido) gtr RICORDI-ARG BA-11192
   f.s.   (1928)

Allegro, Andante, Menuetto And
   Allegro (from 12 Stucke Fur 2
   Waldhorner, K. 487)
   (Scheit) gtr (5th degr.) UNIVER.
   14461 $3.25   (1929)

Andante De La Casacion
   (Fortea) gtr FORTEA 135 f.s. (1930)

Andante, MIN 127
   (Anido) gtr RICORDI-ARG BA-11845
   f.s.   (1931)

Andante, MIN 128 (from Piano Sonata,
   K. 330)
   (Azpiazu) gtr SYMPHON 2049 f.s.
                                     (1932)

Andante, MIN 129 (from Sonata No. 3)
   (Llobet) gtr RICORDI-ARG RF-7686
   f.s.   (1933)

Larghetto And Allegro (from K. Anh.
   229)
   (Bream) gtr (7th degr.) FABER
   F-0303 f.s.   (1934)

Marcha A La Turca (Rondo)
   gtr (Transcripciones por Vicente
   Erliso, vol. 2) UNION ESP. 1016
   f.s. contains also: Schumann,
   Robert (Alexander), Volksliedchen
                                     (1935)
   (Casuscelli) gtr RICORDI-ARG
   BA-10466 f.s.   (1936)
   (Lopez Villanueva) gtr UNION ESP.
   1460 f.s.   (1937)
   (Lopez Villanueva) gtr (40 pieces)
   UNION ESP. 1460 f.s.   (1938)
   "Marcha A La Turca" (Fortea) gtr
   FORTEA 134 f.s.   (1939)

Minuet, MIN 58 (from Symphony In G
   Minor)
   (Azpiazu) gtr SYMPHON 360 f.s.
                                     (1940)

Minuet, MIN 59
   (Segovia) gtr (6th degr.) SCHOTT
   GA-117 f.s.   (1941)

Minuet, MIN 60
   (Bianqui Pinero) gtr RICORDI-ARG
   A-381 f.s.   (1942)

Minuet, MIN 61 (from Divertimento In
   D)
   (Casuscelli) gtr RICORDI-ARG
   BA-9305 f.s.   (1943)

Minuet, MIN 130 (from Don Juan)
   (Anido) gtr RICORDI-ARG BA-11575
   f.s.   (1944)
   (Calatayud) gtr UNION ESP. 19676
   f.s.   (1945)
   (Pomilio) 1-2gtr RICORDI-ARG
   BA-11237 f.s.   (1946)

Minuet, MIN 131 (from Sinfonia In E
   Flat)
   (Casuscelli) gtr RICORDI-ARG
   BA-9660 f.s.   (1947)

Minuet, MIN 377 (from Don Giovanni)
   (Weston) gtr ESSEX f.s.   (1948)

Minuet, MIN 378
   (Weston) gtr ESSEX f.s.   (1949)

Minuet, MIN 403
   (Tarrega) gtr UNION ESP. 19045 f.s.
                                     (1950)

Minuet, MIN 404 (from Eine Kleine
   Nachtmusik, K. 565)
   (Azpiazu) gtr UNION ESP. 21331 f.s.
                                     (1951)

Minuet, MIN 405 (from Cuarteto De
   Cuerda)
   (Tarrega) gtr UNION ESP. 19086 f.s.
                                     (1952)

Minueto De Don Juan
   (Fortea) gtr FORTEA 137 f.s. (1953)

Minueto Del Cuarteto En Re
   (Fortea) gtr FORTEA 138 f.s. (1954)

Mozart-Buch, Das *CC54U
   (Schwarz-Reiflingen) gtr SIKORSKI
   375 $6.00   (1955)

Mozartiana *CC20U
   (Storti) gtr (3-4th degr.) BERBEN
   EB1799 $3.25   (1956)

Serenata De Don Juan
   (Fortea) gtr FORTEA 136 f.s. (1957)

MOZART, WOLFGANG AMADEUS (cont'd.)

Sinfonia in E flat, Minuet
gtr FORTEA 99 f.s. (1958)

Sinfonia No. 1, Minuet
(Lopez Villanueva) gtr UNION ESP.
1461 f.s. (1959)

Sonata No. 2, Andante
gtr FORTEA 98 f.s. (1960)

Sonata No. 2, K. 280, Andante
(Llobet) gtr UNION ESP. 20872 f.s. (1961)

Stucke, 3
(Fischer) gtr (5th degr.) HEINRICH.
N-1630 f.s. (1962)

Themes, 4
(Papas) gtr (3-4th degr.) COLUMBIA
133 $1.50
contains: Alas I Have Lost My
Love; Allegro; Theme No. 1;
Theme No. 2 (1963)

Variaciones Sobre Un Tema De "Don
Giovanni"
(Payet) gtr UNION ESP. 21811 f.s. (1964)

Variations, 12, On "Ah, Vous Dirai-
Je, Maman" *K.265
"Tema Con Variaciones" (Casuscelli)
gtr RICORDI-ARG BA-12064 f.s. (1965)

NAVA, ANTONIO (1775-1828)
Andante (from Metodo Pubblicato Nel
1815)
gtr (3rd degr.) BERBEN EB1328 $1.00 (1966)

PAGANINI, NICCOLO (1782-1840)
Andantino
gtr ESSEX f.s. contains also:
Minuetto (1967)

Andantino In A Minor
(Sensier) gtr (3rd degr.) ESSEX
f.s. contains also: Andantino In
D Major (1968)

Arietta
(Sensier) gtr ESSEX f.s. contains
also: March (1969)

Campanella, La
(Casuscelli) gtr RICORDI-ARG
BA-8442 f.s. (1970)

Capriccio No. 9
(Abloniz) gtr (5th degr., fragment)
BERBEN EB2016 f.s. (1971)

Capriccio No. 13
(Tarrago) gtr UNION ESP. 21555 f.s. (1972)

Capriccio No. 16
(Pujol) gtr RICORDI-ARG BA-11114
f.s. (1973)
(Tarrago) gtr UNION ESP. 21556 f.s. (1974)

Capriccio No. 24
(Kluin) gtr (9th degr.) HARMONIA
2454 f.s. (1975)

Celebre Sonata
(Azpiazu) gtr (4th degr.) SYMPHON
469 (1976)
(Rossi) gtr (4th degr.) BERBEN
EB1901 $1.00 (1977)

Composizioni Inedite, 3
(Tonazzi) gtr (6th degr.) BERBEN
EB1597 $1.50
contains: Allegretto, MIN21;
Minuet, MIN 24; Minuettino No.
23 (1978)

Minuet For Dida
(Battine) gtr ESSEX f.s. (1979)

Moto Perpetuo *Op.11,No.6
(Azpiazu) 1-2gtr SYMPHON 2123 f.s. (1980)
(Fleury) 1-2gtr RICORDI-ARG
BA-11585 f.s. (1981)

Original Kompositionen, 26
"Composizioni Originali, 26"
(Quattrocchi) gtr (3-4th degr.)
BERBEN EB1958 $4.50 (1982)
(Schulz) gtr (3-4th degr.) ZIMMER.
f.s. (1983)
"Eloadasi Darabok Gitarra"
(Vereczkey) gtr (3-4th degr.) EMB
Z-6428 f.s. (1984)
"Eloadasi Darabok Gitarra"
(Vereczkey) gtr (3-4th degr.)
SCHOTT 6445 f.s. (1985)

Originalkompositionen, 6
(Scheit) gtr (2-3rd degr.) UNIVER.
14465 $3.75
contains: Allegretto, MIN 22;
Allegretto Scherzando;
Andantino, MIN 19; Andantino,
MIN 20; Minuet, MIN 23;

PAGANINI, NICCOLO (cont'd.)

Perigoldimo (1986)

Paginas Escritas Directamente Para La
Guitarra
(Angel) gtr UNION ESP. 19974 f.s.
contains: Allegretto Scherzando;
Andantino; Arieta; Perigoldino
Con Dos Variaciones; Sonatina (1987)

Piece De Salon
(Chesnakov) gtr ESSEX f.s. (1988)

Piece Intime
(Thomatos) gtr ZIMMER. ZM-1863 f.s. (1989)

5 Pieces
(Bulatoff; Behrend) gtr TRANSAT.
1420 f.s.
contains: Andantino; Deux Valses;
Ghiribizzi No. 24 And 25;
March; Sonata (1990)

Romance (from Grand Sonata A
Chittarra Sola Con
Accompagnamento Di Violino)
(Behrend) gtr (7-8th degr., for
orig version, see section: duos:
guitar and violin; Gitarre-
Bibliothek, No.5) BOTE GB-5 f.s. (1991)
(Prol) gtr (7-8th degr., for orig
version, see section: duos:
guitar and violin) PAGANI G-112
f.s. (1992)
(Rossi) gtr (7-8th degr., for orig
version, see section: duos:
guitar and violin) BERBEN EB2055
f.s. (1993)
(Scheit) gtr (7-8th degr., for orig
version, see section: duos:
guitar and violin) UNIVER. 13068
$2.75 (1994)
(Schwarz-Reiflingen) gtr (7-8th
degr., for orig version, see
section: duos: guitar and violin;
N. Paganini, Kompositionen Fur
Gitarre Und Streichinstrumente,
No. 7) ZIMMER. ZM-1192 f.s. (1995)

Romance in A minor
(Sensier) gtr ESSEX f.s. (1996)

Scherzo, Dialogo Tra Una Vecchia E
Una Giovane
"Dialog Zwischen Einer Alten Und
Einer Jungen Frau" (Behrend) gtr
(3rd degr.) ZIMMER. ZM-1715 f.s. (1997)

Sonatina
(Sensier) gtr ESSEX f.s. (1998)

Sonatina in C
(Azpiazu) gtr UNION ESP. 20024 f.s. (1999)

Sonatina, MIN 135
(Scheit) gtr (3-4th degr.) UNIVER.
14455 $2.75 (2000)

Sonatina, Op. 25
(Prat) gtr RICORDI-ARG BA-9548 f.s.
contains also: Minuet, MIN 25 (2001)

Sonatinen, 3, Fur Signora De Lucca
(Behrend) gtr (5th degr., Gitarre-
Bibliothek, No.23; also published
in: European Masters For The
Guitar) BOTE GB-23 f.s. (2002)

Theme and Variations
(Behrend) gtr (6-7th degr.,
Gitarre-Bibliothek, No.18) BOTE
GB-18 f.s. (2003)

Two Minuets
(Sensier) gtr ESSEX f.s. (2004)

PARADIS, MARIA THERESIA VON (1759-1824)
Siciliana
(Rossi) gtr (4th degr.) BERBEN
EB1893 $1.00 (2005)

REGONDI, GIULIO (1822-1872)
Reverie, Op. 19
(Chiesa) gtr (8-9th degr.) ZERBONI
8425 f.s. (2006)

SCHALE, CHRISTIAN FR. (1713-1800)
Menuette, 2
(Segovia) gtr (4th degr.) SCHOTT
GA-161 f.s. contains also:
Wenkel, Johann Fr., Musette;
Wenkel, Johann Fr., Menuette, 2 (2007)

SCHEIDLER, CHRISTIAN GOTTLIEB
(1752-1815)
Variations, 12, Sur Un Theme De
Mozart (from Don Giovanni: Finch'
Han Dal Vino)
(van Puijenbroeck) gtr (e' is d', g
is f sharp, E is D) METROPOLIS
4730 $2.00 (2008)

SCHUBERT, FRANZ (PETER) (1797-1828)
Adieu
(Tarrega; Fortea) gtr FORTEA 257
f.s. contains also: Fantasy, Op.
78, D. 894, in G, Minuet (2009)

Ecossaises *Op.18,D.145
"Escocesa" (Martinez Zarate) gtr
RICORDI-ARG BA-12455 f.s.
contains also: Pequeno Vals (2010)

Ellens Gesang III *Op.52,No.6,D.839
"Ave Maria" (Azpiazu) gtr SYMPHON
440 f.s. (2011)
"Ave Maria" (Balaguer) gtr UNION
ESP. 21769 f.s. (2012)
"Ave Maria" (Fortea) gtr FORTEA 167
f.s. (2013)
"Ave Maria" (Mercado) gtr RICORDI-
ARG BA-12607 f.s. (2014)
"Ave Maria" (Savio) gtr RICORDI-BR
BR-1810 f.s. (2015)
"Ave Maria" (Sinopoli) gtr RICORDI-
ARG BA-7913 f.s. (2016)
"Ave Maria" (Tarrega; Fortea) gtr
FORTEA 103 f.s. (2017)

Fantasy, Op. 78, D. 984, in G, Minuet
(Pomilio) gtr RICORDI-ARG BA-10036
f.s. (2018)
(Savio) gtr RICORDI-BR BR-2668 f.s. (2019)
(Sinopoli) gtr RICORDI-ARG BA-11501
f.s. (2020)

Minuet, MIN 406
(Tarrega) gtr UNION ESP. 19019 f.s. (2021)

Moment Musical
(Sensier) gtr ESSEX f.s. (2022)
(Terzi) gtr RICORDI-IT 129289 f.s. (2023)

Momento Musical
gtr FORTEA 118 f.s. (2024)

Moments Musicaux, Op. 94, No. 3,
D.780, No.3
"Momento Musical, Op. 94, No. 3"
(Azpiazu) gtr UNION ESP. 21332
f.s. (2025)
"Momento Musical, Op. 94, No. 3"
(Rodriguez Arenas) gtr RICORDI-
ARG BA-5093 f.s. (2026)
"Momento Musical, Op. 94, No. 3"
(Savio) gtr RICORDI-BR BR-152
f.s. (2027)
"Momento Musical, Op. 94, No. 3"
(Tarrega; Savio) gtr RICORDI-ARG
BA-11819 f.s. (2028)

3 Pequenos Valses
(Segovia) gtr (also published in:
Transcripciones Para Guitarra,
No. 10) UNION ESP. 18036 f.s. (2029)

Schubert-Buch, Das *CC60U
(Schwarz-Reiflingen) gtr SIKORSKI
529 $6.00 (2030)

Serenade, MIN 136
(Azpiazu) gtr (6-7th degr., Guitare
Selection, No. 3) DELRIEU 1272
f.s. (2031)
(Sanchez Granada) gtr UNION ESP.
17303 f.s. (2032)

Standchen (Serenade)
"Celebre Serenata" (Fortea) gtr
FORTEA 166 f.s. (2033)
(Medio) gtr ESSEX f.s. (2034)
"Serenata" (Rodriguez Arenas) gtr
RICORDI-ARG BA-5092 f.s. (2035)
"Serenata" (Tarrega; Fortea) gtr
FORTEA 119 f.s. (2036)

Waltz
(Worschech) gtr ESCHIG f.s.
contains also: Schumann, Robert
(Alexander), Wiegenlied, "Chant
De Berceau", Op.78,No.4 (2037)

SCHULZ, JOHANN ABRAHAM PETER
(1747-1800)
Lieder Im Volkston *CC18U
(Monkemeyer) gtr (3-4th degr.)
TONGER 1321 f.s. also for solo
voice and gtr (2038)

SCHUMANN, ROBERT (ALEXANDER)
(1810-1856)
Album (from Album Fur Die Jugend, Op.
68, and Kinderszenen, Op. 15)
(Llobet) gtr UNION ESP. 20381 f.s.
contains: Bittendes Kind,
"Suplica Del Nino"; Choral,
"Coral"; Erster Verlust,
"Premier Chagrin, Le";
Soldatenmarsch, "Marcha
Militar"; Stuckchen, "Pequena
Pieza"; Traumerei, "Reverie" (2039)

Album: Marcha, Bagatela, Siciliana,
Cancion
gtr FORTEA 120 f.s. (2040)

SCHUMANN, ROBERT (ALEXANDER) (cont'd.)

Album Per La Gioventu, 6 Pezzi, Op.
68, Nos. 1-3, 5, 16, 18 (from
Album Fur Die Jugend, Op. 68)
(Caprioglio; Ferandini) gtr (2-3rd
degr.) BERBEN EB595 $1.25
contains: Erster Verlust, "Primo
Dolore", Op.68,No.16; Melodie,
"Melodia", Op.68,No.1;
Schnitterliedchen, "Canzonetta
Del Mietitore", Op.68,No.18;
Soldatenmarsch, "Marcia Di
Soldati", Op.68,No.2;
Stuckchen, "Piccolo Pezzo",
Op.68,No.5; Trallerliedchen,
"Canzoncina", Op.68,No.3   (2041)

Albumblatt
"Feuilles Variees" (Tarrega) gtr
UNION ESP. 19042 f.s.   (2042)

Andantino, Coral
gtr FORTEA 259 f.s.   (2043)

Au Soir
gtr FORTEA 264 f.s.   (2044)
"Au Soir" (Tarrega) gtr UNION ESP.
19048 f.s.   (2045)

Ausgewahlte Stucke, 12 (from Album
Fur Die Jugend, Op. 68)
(Gotze) gtr (2-3rd degr.) SCHOTT
GA-17 f.s.   (2046)

Berceuse
(Tarrega) gtr UNION ESP. 19046 f.s.
(2047)

Bittendes Kind *Op.15,No.4 (from
Kinderscenen, Op. 15)
(Segovia) gtr (4-5th degr.) SCHOTT
GA-138 f.s. contains also:
Furchtenmachen, Op.15,No.11
(2048)

Erinnerung *Op.68,No.28
"Recuerdo Del 4 De Noviembre,
Muerte De Mendelssohn" (Robledo)
gtr RICORDI-ARG RF-7172 f.s.
(2049)

Feuilles Varias
"Hojas Varias" gtr FORTEA 263 f.s.
(2050)

Frohlicher Landmann *Op.68,No.10
(from Op. 68)
"Campesino Alegre, El" (Garcia
Velasco) gtr UNION ESP. 20300
f.s.   (2051)
"Paisano Alegre" (Sinopoli) gtr
RICORDI-ARG BA-9949 f.s. contains
also: Mendelssohn-Bartholdy,
Felix, Song Without Words,
"Fragmento De La "Romanza Sin
Palabras"", Op.85,No.6   (2052)

Fugue (from Op. 68)
(Tarrega) gtr UNION ESP. 19035 f.s.
(2053)

Fugue, MIN 340
gtr FORTEA 265 f.s.   (2054)

Fugueta
gtr FORTEA 261 f.s.   (2055)

Hoja De Album
(Anido) gtr RICORDI-ARG RF-7525
f.s.   (2056)

Jagerliedchen *Op.68,No.7 (from
Album Fur Die Jugend, Op. 68)
gtr (3rd degr.) SCHOTT GA-347 f.s.
contains also: Volksliedchen,
Op.68,No.9   (2057)

Kinderscenen *Op.15
"Escenas Infantiles" (Parodi) gtr
(13 pieces) RICORDI-ARG K-16544
f.s.   (2058)

Kindersonate *Op.118,No.1 (from Drei
Clavier-Sonaten Fur Die Jugend)
(Bream) gtr (6-7th degr.) FABER
F.0373 f.s.   (2059)

Mai, Lieber Mai *Op.68,No.13 (from
Op. 68)
"Mai, Cher Mai, Bientot Tu Seras
La..." (Azpiazu) gtr (6th degr.,
Guitare, No.72) LEDUC G-72 $2.25
(2060)
"Mayo, Buen Mayo" (Segovia) gtr
(also published in:
Transcripciones para guitarra,
no. 10) UNION ESP. 18034 f.s.
(2061)
"Mayo, Buen Mayo" (Segovia) gtr
UNION ESP. 18034 f.s.   (2062)

Marche Militaire
(Weston) gtr ESSEX f.s.   (2063)

Melodia, Labrador Alegre
gtr FORTEA 121 f.s.   (2064)

Melody (from Op. 68)
(Calatayud) gtr UNION ESP. 19676
f.s.   (2065)

SCHUMANN, ROBERT (ALEXANDER) (cont'd.)

Melody, MIN 375
gtr ESSEX f.s.   (2066)

Nocturne, Op. 23, No. 4
gtr FORTEA 122 f.s.   (2067)

Nordisches Lied *Op.68,No.41
"Cancion Del Norte" (Segovia) gtr
RICORDI-IT BA-9597 f.s. contains
also: Frohlicher Landmann,
"Alegre Labrador", Op.68,No.10
(2068)

Pezzi, 3 (from Album Fur Die Jugend,
Op. 68)
(Abloniz) gtr (4-5th degr.) BERBEN
EB1016 $1.00
contains: Erinnerung,
"Rimembranza", Op.68,No.28;
Erster Verlust, "Prima
Disillusione", Op.68,No.16;
Sicilianisch, "Siciliana",
Op.68,No.11   (2069)

5 Piezas (from Album De La Juventud,
Op. 68)
(Angel) gtr UNION ESP. 19172 f.s.
contains: Choral, "Coral"; Marcha
Militar; Melody; Pieza Breve;
Trallerliedchen, "Tarareando"
(2070)

5 Piezas (from Album De La Juventud,
Op. 68)
(Angel) gtr UNION ESP. 19289 f.s.
contains: Armes Waisenkind,
"Pobre Huerfano"; Cancion
Popular; Frohlicher Landmann,
"Campesino Alegre, El";
Jagerliedchen, "Cancion De
Caza"; Wilder Reiter,
"Caballero Del Bosque"   (2071)

Reverie-Siciliano (from Op. 68)
(Angel) gtr UNION ESP. 18979 f.s.
(2072)

Romance, MIN 137
(Segovia) gtr (also published in:
Andres Segovia Album) COLUMBIA
130 $1.75   (2073)

Romance, Op. 51
gtr FORTEA 260 f.s.   (2074)

Rundgesang *Op.68,No.22
(Xanthopoulos) gtr (5th degr.)
HEINRICH. N-1671 f.s.   (2075)

Saint Nicolas
gtr FORTEA 262 f.s.   (2076)
"Saint Nicolas" (Tarrega) gtr UNION
ESP. 19044 f.s.   (2077)

Schumann-Buch, Das *CC41U
(Schwarz-Reiflingen) gtr SIKORSKI
528 $6.00   (2078)

Siciliano, MIN 369
(Bream) gtr ESSEX f.s.   (2079)

Stucke Aus Dem "Album Fur Die Jugend,
" Op. 68 *CC16U
(Bacher) 1-2gtr (3-4th degr.) sc
NAGELS EN-1103 f.s. for 2 gtr
(12); gtr (4): Nagels Laute- Und
Gitarre-Archiv   (2080)

Sylvesterlied *Op.68,No.43
"Cancion Silvestre" (Segovia) gtr
(also published in:
Transcripciones para guitarra,
no. 9) UNION ESP. 18035 f.s.
(2081)

Traumerei (Reverie) Op.15,No.7 (from
Kinderscenen, Op. 15)
"Celebre Reverie" (Fortea) gtr
FORTEA 170 f.s.   (2082)
(Prat) gtr RICORDI-ARG BA-11709
f.s.   (2083)
(Sensier) gtr ESSEX f.s.   (2084)
(Sinopoli) gtr RICORDI-ARG BA-8079
f.s.   (2085)
(Tarrega) gtr FORTEA 123 f.s.
(2086)
"Sogno" (Zuccheri) gtr BERBEN
EB2059 f.s.   (2087)

Volksliedchen *Op.68,No.9
"Cancion Popular" (Segovia) gtr
RICORDI-IT BA-9568 f.s. contains
also: Kleine Studie, "Pequeno
Estudio", Op.68,No.14   (2088)

Von Fremden Landern Und Menschen
*Op.15,No.1
"De Paises Y Hombres Extranos"
(Anido) gtr RICORDI-ARG RF-7518
f.s.   (2089)

Wiegenlied (Berceuse) Op.78,No.4
(Tarrega) gtr RICORDI-ARG RF-7232
f.s.   (2090)

SOR, FERNANDO (1778-1839)
Adieux!, Les, Sixieme Fantaisie
*Op.21
"Abschied, Der" gtr SCHOTT GA-350
f.s.   (2091)
"Adioses, Los, Sexta Fantasia" gtr
UNION ESP. 1516 f.s.   (2092)
"Adieux, Les (La Despedida)"
(Fortea, Daniel) gtr FORTEA 178
f.s.   (2093)

Allegretto *Op.24,No.7
gtr BERBEN 1674 f.s.   (2094)

Allegro (from Grande Sonate, Op. 25)
(Segovia, Andres) gtr COLUMBIA
NY-1740 f.s.   (2095)

Andante Cantabile
gtr ESSEX f.s.   (2096)

Andante Largo *Op.5,No.5
gtr SCHOTT GA-352 f.s.   (2097)
(Fortea, Daniel) gtr FORTEA 170
f.s.   (2098)
(Llobet, Miguel) gtr UNION ESP.
21696 f.s.   (2099)
(Pujol, Emilio) gtr ESCHIG 1087
f.s.   (2100)
(Scheit, Karl) gtr UNIVER. 11960
f.s.   (2101)
(Segovia, Andres) gtr RICORDI-ARG
BA-9599 f.s.   (2102)

Andante Maestoso (Minuet, Op. 11, No.
6, in A)
(Ranieri, Silvio) gtr CRANZ 48349
f.s. contains also: Minore
(Minuet, Op. 11, No. 7)   (2103)

Andante Maestoso, Op.11, No.6
(Ranieri) gtr (published as "Minuet
en La") CRANZ f.s. contains also:
Minore, Op.11, No.7   (2104)

Andante, Op. 32, No. 5 (from Six
Petites Pieces Faciles, Op. 32)
gtr BERBEN 1979 f.s.   (2105)

Andantino *Op.2,No.3
gtr BERBEN 1322 f.s.   (2106)
(Savio, Isaias) gtr RICORDI-ARG
BA-12047 f.s.   (2107)
(Scheit, Karl) gtr UNIVER. 13941
f.s.   (2108)

Andantino, Op.2
(Fortea, Daniel) gtr FORTEA 168
f.s.   (2109)

Andantino, Op.13, No.3
(Fortea, Daniel) gtr FORTEA 169
f.s.   (2110)

Andantino, Op.31, No.5
(Sensier) gtr ESSEX f.s.   (2111)

Ausgewahlte Etuden, Vol. 1:
Vorbereitende Ubungen, Kleine
Musikstucke Und Etuden *CC24L
(Dobrauz, Carl) [Ger/Eng] gtr
HEINRICH. N-1502 f.s. biogr
notes; contains: meth., lec. no.
3, 14, 16, 19, 23; op. 31, nos.
1-3, 5, 6, 9; op. 35, nos. 1-3,
14; op. 60, nos. 1-4, 6, 10, 12-
14   (2112)

Ausgewahlte Etuden, Vol. 3: Kleine
Musikstucke Und Etuden *CC15L
(Dobrauz, Carl) [Ger/Eng] gtr
HEINRICH. N-1509 f.s. biogr
notes; contains: op. 23, no. 3;
op. 31, nos. 4, 7, 8, 10, 13-15;
op. 32, no. 3 (Andante
Pastorale); op. 32, no. 6
(Galop); op. 35, nos. 10, 11, 13,
16, 19   (2113)

Ausgewahlte Gitarre Werke,
Preliminary Vol. *CC29L
(Domandl, Willy) [Ger/Eng] gtr
(very easy) BENJ EE-589 f.s.
contains: Meth.: exerc.-6, no. 1;
op. 31, nos. 6, 17; op. 35, nos.
5, 13; op. 44, nos. 1-4, 7, 9-11,
15, 22; op. 51, nos. 1, 6; op.
57, no. 6; op. 60, nos. 1, 2, 5,
8-10, 13, 15, 17-19   (2114)

Ausgewahlte Gitarre Werke, Vol. 1
*CC22L
(Domandl, Willy) [Ger/Eng] gtr
(easy) BENJ EE-885 f.s. contains:
op. 2, no. 1 (Menuette); op. 6,
no. 1; op. 8, no. 6 (Walzer); op.
24, no. 3 (Allegretto); op. 24,
no. 7 (Allegretto); op. 31, nos.
1-3, 5, 8; op. 32, no. 6
(Galopp); op. 35, nos. 1, 3, 8;
op. 45, no. 3 (Andante); op. 47,
no. 2 (Allegretto); op. 48, no. 1
(Marsch); op. 60, nos. 6, 7, 12,
14, 16   (2115)

SOR, FERNANDO (cont'd.)

Ausgewahlte Gitarre Werke, Vol. 2
*CC20L
(Domandl, Willy) [Ger/Eng] gtr
(med) BENJ EE-886 f.s. contains:
op. 3 (Menuett); op. 6, no. 8,
no. 10 (only Maestoso); op. 8,
no. 1 (Menuett), no. 4
(Allegretto scherzoso); op. 18,
no. 1 (Walzer), no. 2 (Walzer);
op. 23, no. 2 (Allegretto), no. 5
(Menuett); op. 31, nos. 13, 21,
23; op. 32, no. 2 (Walzer); op.
35, nos. 17, 18, 20; op. 36, no.
1 (Allemande); op. 42, no. 3
(Andantino), no. 5 (Moderato);
op. 48, no. 6 (Rondo)   (2116)

Ausgewahlte Gitarre Werke, Vol. 3
(Domandl, Willy) gtr (diff) BENJ
EE-887 f.s. contains:
op. 7 (only Largo); op. 11, no.1
(Menuette), no. 3 (Menuette), no.
5 (Menuette); op. 29, nos. 1, 5,
9, 10
contains: Rondo (from Grande
Sonate, Op. 22)   (2117)

Ausgewahlte Menuette, 20
(Gotze, Walter) gtr SCHOTT GA-15
f.s. contains: op. 2, nos. 1, 4;
op. 5, nos. 1, 3; op. 8, no. 1;
op. 11, nos. 1, 3, 5-8, 10;
op. 13, no. 1; op. 23, no. 5; op. 24,
nos. 1, 5, 6; op. 36, no. 2
contains: Minuet (from Grande
Sonate, Op. 22); Minuet (from
Grande Sonate, Op. 25)   (2118)

Ausgewahlte Walzer, 20 *CC20L
(Gotze, Walter) gtr SCHOTT GA-16
f.s. contains: op. 1, no. 2; op.
2, nos. 2, 5; op. 5, no. 2; op.
8, nos. 2, 6; op. 13, no. 2; op.
17, nos. 2, 5, 6; op. 18, nos. 1,
3, 6; op. 23, no. 3; op. 32, no.
2; op. 42, nos. 2, 4; op. 45, no.
4; op. 60, no. 7   (2119)

Bolero (Altspanischer Volkstanz)
(Behrend, Siegfried) gtr (also
published in: European Masters
For The Guitar; not in op. 1-63
or works without opus number;
Gitarre-Bibliothek, No. 27) BOTE
GB-27 f.s.   (2120)

Complete Works For Guitar In
Facsimiles Of The Original
Editions, The, Vol. 1-7 *CCU
(Jeffery, Brian) [Eng] gtr TECLA
f.s. with notes and commentaries
                                (2121)

Composiciones Para Guitarra, 19
(Savio, Isaias) gtr RICORDI-ARG
BA-11618 f.s. contains: op. 1,
no. 1 (Divertissement); op. 5,
no. 5 (Andante Largo); op. 7
(Fantasia); op. 8, no. 4 (Allegro
scherzoso), op. 8, no. 5
(Marcha); op. 12 (Cuarta
Fantasia);op. 13, no. 4
(Cantabile);op. 16 (Variaciones
sobre un tema de Paisello); op.
24, no. 7 (Allegretto); op. 32,
no. 5 (Andante); op. 36, no. 1
(Allemande); op. 43, no. 3
(Andante cantabile); op. 44, no.
15 (Divertissement); op. 45, no.
5 (Andante); Le Candeur (work
without op no)
contains: Allegro Non Troppo
(From Grande Sonate, Op. 25);
Grand Solo, Op.14; Grand
Sonate, Op.22; Sonata, Op. 15,
No. 2   (2122)

Despedida, La *Op.21
gtr UNION ESP. 1515 f.s.   (2123)

Deux Themes Varies Et Douze Menuets
*Op.11
"Zwei Themen Mit Variationen Und
Zwolf Menuette" (Domandl, Willy)
gtr BENJ 1311 f.s.   (2124)

Drei Ausgewahlte Walzer (3 Valses
Choisies)
(Gotze, Walter) gtr SCHOTT GA-367
f.s.
contains: Introduction A l'Etude
De La Guitare En Vingt Cinq
Lecons Progressives, Op. 60,
No. 7; Six Petites Pieces, Op.
42, No. 2; Voyons Si C'est Ca,
6 Petites Pieces Faciles, Op.
45, No. 4   (2125)

Est-Ce Bien Ca?, Six Pieces, Op. 48:
Rondo D-Dur
gtr SCHOTT GA-363 f.s.   (2126)

Fantaisie *Op.7
"Fantasia" (Chiesa, Ruggero) gtr
ZERBONI 7890 f.s.   (2127)

SOR, FERNANDO (cont'd.)

(Pujol, Emilio) gtr ESCHIG 1095
f.s.   (2128)

Fantaisie Elegiaque *Op.59
"Fantasia Elegiaque" gtr RICORDI-
ARG RF f.s.   (2129)
"Fantasia Elegiaca" (Gascon,
Vicente) gtr RICORDI-ARG BA-12072
f.s.   (2130)

Fantaisie Elegiaque: Marche Funebre
gtr LEMOINE f.s.   (2131)

Fantasie: Largo (from Op. 7)
(Scheit, Karl) gtr UNIVER. 14434
f.s.   (2132)

Fantasie Elegiaque *Op.59
(Azpiazu) gtr SYMPHON 2135 f.s.
                                (2133)

Folies d'Espagne, Variees, Et Un
Menuet *Op.15,No.1
"Folies d'Espagne" gtr ESSEX f.s.
                                (2134)
"Folies d'Espagne, Les, Tema E
Variazioni" gtr (without Menuet)
BERBEN 1439 f.s.   (2135)
"Folias De Espana, Las,
Variationen" (Behrend, Siegfried)
gtr (without Menuet; with a coda
"mosso" (by Behrend)); Gitarre-
Bibliothek, No. 55) BOTE GB-55
f.s.   (2136)
"Folias De Espana, Las, Tema Y
Variaciones" (Fortea, Daniel) gtr
(without Menuet) FORTEA 176 f.s.
                                (2137)
"Folias De Espana" (Papas,
Sophocles) gtr COLUMBIA 100 f.s.
                                (2138)

Galop
(Sensier) gtr ESSEX f.s.   (2139)

Gran Solo *Op.14
(Aguado, Dionisio) gtr UNION ESP.
19670 f.s.   (2140)

Grand Solo *Op.14
"Gran Solo" (Aguado, Dionysio) gtr
UNION ESP. 19670 f.s.   (2141)
"Introduction Et Allegro" (Azpiazu,
Jose De) gtr SYMPHON 2013 f.s.
                                (2142)
"Grosses Solo" (Domandl, Willy) gtr
BENJ EE-1314 f.s.   (2143)
"Concierto En Re" (Fortea, Daniel)
gtr FORTEA 179 f.s.   (2144)
"Gran Solo" (Paolini, Paolo) gtr
RICORDI-IT 132090 f.s.   (2145)

Introduction Et Theme Varie *Op.20
"Introduction, Thema Und
Variationen" (Domandl, Willy) gtr
SIMROCK EE-1320 f.s.   (2146)

Introduction Et Variations Sur l'Air
"Marlbroug" *Op.28
"Variationen Uber Ein Franzosisches
Volkslied" (Behrend, Siegfried)
gtr (Gitarre-Bibliothek, No. 54)
BOTE GB-54 f.s.   (2147)
"Introduzione E Variazioni Su
L'Aria "Marlbroug"" (Chiesa,
Ruggero) gtr ZERBONI 8110 f.s.
                                (2148)
"Variations Sur Marlbrough S'en Va-
t-En Guerre" (Santos, Turibio)
gtr (Collection Turibio Santos
No. 1) ESCHIG f.s.   (2149)

Introduction Et Variations Sur l'Air
"Que Ne Suis-Je La Fougere"
*Op.26
"Introduzione E Variazioni Su
L'aria "Que Ne Suis-Je La
Fougere"" (Chiesa, Ruggero) gtr
ZERBONI 8107 f.s.   (2150)

Introduction Et Variations Sur Un
Theme De Mozart *Op.9
"Mozart-Variationen" gtr (based on
French ed., 1821) SCHOTT 361 f.s.
                                (2151)
"Variazioni Su Un Tema Del "Flauto
Magico" Di W.A. Mozart" (Abloniz,
Miguel) gtr BERBEN 2019 f.s.
                                (2152)
"Theme And Variations" (Angel,
Miguel) gtr SPAN.MUS.CTR. MA-003
f.s.   (2153)
"Variationen Uber Eine Arie Aus Der
Zauberflote Von W.A. Mozart"
(Azpiazu, Jose De) gtr (without
intro) SYMPHON 458 f.s.   (2154)
"Variationen Uber Ein Thema Von
W.A. Mozart" (Behrend, Siegfried)
gtr (Die Konzertgitarre) SIKORSKI
781 f.s.   (2155)
"Introduzione E Variazioni Su
l'Aria "O Cara Armonia" Dall'
Opera "Il Flauto Magico" Di W.A.
Mozart" (Chiesa, Ruggero) gtr
ZERBONI 8424 f.s.   (2156)
"Variationen Uber "O Cara Armonia"

SOR, FERNANDO (cont'd.)

Aus Mozarts Zauberflote"
(Domandl, Willy) gtr (based on
French ed., 1821) SIMROCK EE-1309
f.s.   (2157)
"Tema Y Variaciones Sobre Un Tema
De La "Flauta Encantada" De
Mozart" (Fortea, Daniel) gtr
FORTEA 175 f.s.   (2158)
"Variaciones Sobre Un Tema De "La
Flauta Magica" De W.A. Mozart"
(Gascon, L. Vicente) gtr (without
intro) RICORDI-ARG BA-11136 f.s.
                                (2159)
"Variations On A Theme Of Mozart"
(Ranieri, Silvio) gtr (based on
French ed., 1821; without intro)
CRANZ 48352 f.s.   (2160)
"Variaciones Sobre Un Tema De"la
Flauta Magica" De W.A. Mozart"
(Sainz De La Maza, Regino) gtr
(without intro) UNION ESP. 20826
f.s.   (2161)
"Introducao E Variacoes Sobre Um
Tema Da Opera "Flauta Magica" De
W.A. Mozart" (Savio, Isaias) gtr
RICORDI-BR BR-2726A f.s.   (2162)
"Variationen Uber Ein Thema Von
Mozart" (Scheit, Karl) gtr
UNIVER. 13628 f.s.   (2163)
"Variationen Uber Ein Thema Aus Der
Oper "Die Zauberflote") Von W.A.
Mozart" (Segovia, Andres) gtr
(without intro) SCHOTT GA-130
f.s.   (2164)
"Mozart-Variationen Uber Ein Thema
Aus Der Zauberflote (O Cara
Armonia)" (Walker, Luise) gtr
(varies from French and English
eds., 1821; without intro)
HEINRICH. N-1537 f.s.   (2165)

Kompositionen Fur Die Gitarre *CC25L
(Henze, Bruno) [Ger] gtr
HOFMEISTER-W f.s. biogr notes;
contains: op. 2, no. 1 (Menuet),
op. 2, no. 2 (Valse); op. 8, no.
1 (Menuet), op. 8, no. 2 (Valse);
op. 31, nos. 1, 2, 5, 9, 10, 13,
14; op. 32, no. 2 (Valse); op.
32, no. 3 (Andante pastorale);
op. 35, nos. 2-4, 14, 17, 18, 21,
22; op. 60, nos. 6, 7, 13, 19
                                (2166)

Larghetto *Op.35,No.3
(Bibobi) gtr ESSEX f.s.   (2167)

Meditacion
(Fortea, Daniel) gtr (not in op. 1-
63 or works without opus number)
FORTEA 172 f.s. contains also:
Romanesca   (2168)

Meditation
(Prol, Julio) gtr (not in op. 1-63
or works without opus number)
PAGANI CG-129 f.s.   (2169)

Menuets, 2
(Azpiazu, Jose De) gtr DELRIEU 1234
f.s. Guitarra
contains: Minuet, Op. 11, No. 4,
in D; Minuet, Op. 11, No. 10,
in E   (2170)

Menuets En La, 2
(Azpiazu, Lupe De) gtr LEDUC G-26
f.s. Guitare, No. 26
contains: Minuet, Op. 11, No. 6,
in A; Minuet, Op. 11, No. 8, in
A   (2171)

Menuette, 2
(Scheit, Karl) gtr UNIVER. 13629
f.s.
contains: Minuet, Op. 5, No. 3
(from Six Petites Pieces Tres
Faciles); Minuet, Op. 24, No. 1
(from Huit Petites Pieces)
                                (2172)

Menuette, 2
gtr SCHOTT GA-357 f.s.
contains: Minuet, Op. 11, No. 5,
in D; Minuet, Op. 11, No. 6, in
A   (2173)

Menuette, 2
(Teuchert, Heinz) gtr SCHMIDT,H 313
f.s. Die Sologitarre
contains: Minuet, Op. 11, No. 6,
in A; Minuet, Op. 11, No. 7, in
A   (2174)

Menuety - Menuette
(Urban, Stepan) gtr CZECH f.s.
Kytarova sola, no. 16
contains: Minuet, Op. 11, No. 6,
in A; Minuet, Op. 11, No. 7;
Minuet, Op. 11, No. 8, in A;
Minuet, Op. 11, No. 9; Minuet,
Op. 11, No. 10, in E   (2175)

Mes Ennuis, Six Bagatelles *Op.43
gtr LEMOINE f.s.   (2176)

SOR, FERNANDO (cont'd.)

Mes Ennuis, Six Bagatelles, Op. 43,
No. 3
"Andante Cantabile" gtr BERBEN 1919
f.s.   (2177)

Mes Ennuis, Six Bagatelles, Op. 43,
No. 4
"Mazurca, Moderato" (Gazzelloni,
Giuseppe) gtr BERBEN 2065 f.s.
(2178)

Mes Ennuis, Six Bagatelles, Op. 43,
No. 5
"Andante" (Teuchert, Heinz) gtr
(Die Sologitarre) SCHMIDT,H 306
f.s.   (2179)

Minuet (from Grande Sonate, Op. 22)
(Visser) gtr HARMONIA HU-1867 f.s.
(2180)

Minuet in A, MIN 364
(Bream) gtr ESSEX f.s.   (2181)

Minuet in B flat, MIN 365
gtr ESSEX f.s.   (2182)

Minuet in D, MIN 363
(Bream) gtr ESSEX f.s.   (2183)

Minuet, Op. 3, in G
(Tarrago, Graciano) gtr UNION ESP.
20610 f.s. contains also: Minuet,
Op. 11, No. 9   (2184)

Minuet, Op. 11, No. 4, in D
(Galindo, Patricio) gtr UNION ESP.
21611 f.s.   (2185)
(Llobet, Miguel) gtr UNION ESP.
21697 f.s.   (2186)

Minuet, Op. 11, No. 5, in D
(Llobet, Miguel) gtr UNION ESP.
21698 f.s.   (2187)

Minuet, Op. 11, No. 6, in A
(Galindo, Patricio) gtr UNION ESP.
21610 f.s.   (2188)
(Navascues, Santiago) gtr BRUCK
BG-S1-3 f.s.   (2189)

Minuet, Op. 23, No. 5, in G
(Tarrago, Graciano) gtr UNION ESP.
20611 f.s. contains also: Minuet,
Op. 11, No. 4, in D   (2190)

Minuet, Op. 32, No. 1 (from Six
Petites Pieces Faciles, Op. 32)
(Carfagna, Carlo) gtr BERBEN 1479
f.s.   (2191)

Minuetos, 2
(Fortea, Daniel) gtr FORTEA 155
f.s.
contains: Minuet, Op. 2, No. 1,
in G; Minuet, Op. 13, No. 1, in
A   (2192)

Minuetos, 2
(Fortea, Daniel) gtr FORTEA 158
f.s.
contains: Minuet, Op. 3, in G;
Minuet, Op. 11, No. 9, in E   (2193)

Minuetos, 3
gtr UNION ESP. 1519 f.s.
contains: Minuet, Op. 3, in G;
Minuet, Op. 11, No. 4, in D;
Minuet, Op. 11, No. 9   (2194)

Minuetos, 4
(Fortea, Daniel) gtr FORTEA 154
f.s.
contains: Minuet, Op. 2, No. 4
(from Six Divertissements);
Minuet, Op. 5, No. 1 (from Six
Petites Pieces Tres Faciles);
Minuet, Op. 5, No. 3 (from Six
Petites Pieces Tres Faciles);
Minuet, Op. 8, No. 1 (from Six
Divertissements)   (2195)

Minuetos En La, 2
(Fortea, Daniel) gtr FORTEA 160
f.s.
contains: Minuet, Op. 11, No. 6,
in A; Minuet, Op. 11, No. 8, in
A   (2196)

Minuetos En Mi, 2
(Fortea, Daniel) gtr FORTEA 161
f.s.
contains: Minuet, Op. 11, No. 10,
in E; Minuet, Op. 15, No. 1, in
E   (2197)

Minuetos En Re, 2
(Fortea, Daniel) gtr FORTEA 159
f.s.
contains: Minuet, Op. 11, No. 5,
in D; Minuet, Op. 11, No. 12,
in D (this edition in b-flat
major)   (2198)

SOR, FERNANDO (cont'd.)

Minuetos En Sol, 2
(Fortea, Daniel) gtr FORTEA 163
f.s.
contains: Minuet, Op. 11, No. 1;
Minuet, Op. 11, No. 2   (2199)

Minuetos En Sol-Re, 2
(Fortea, Daniel) gtr FORTEA 162
f.s.
contains: Minuet, Op. 11, No. 4,
in D; Minuet, Op. 23, No. 5, in
G   (2200)

Minuettos En La Mayor, 2
(Tarrago, Graciano) gtr UNION ESP.
20586 f.s.
contains: Minuet, Op. 11, No. 6,
in A; Minuet, Op. 11, No. 8, in
A   (2201)

Minuettos En Mi Mayor, 2
(Tarrago, Graciano) gtr UNION ESP.
20612 f.s.
contains: Minuet, Op. 11, No. 10,
in E; Minuet, Op. 15, No. 1, in
E   (2202)

Morceau De Concert *Op.54
gtr LEMOINE f.s.   (2203)

Opera Omnia For The Spanish Guitar,
Vol. 1 *Op.1-7
(Jape, Mijndert) [Eng/Fr/Ger/Dutch]
gtr (critical ed with commentary)
TEESELING VT-201 f.s.   (2204)

Opera Omnia For The Spanish Guitar,
Vol. 2 *Op.8-14
(Jape, Mijndert) [Eng/Fr/Ger/Dutch]
gtr (critical ed with commentary)
TEESELING VT-202 f.s.   (2205)

Opera Omnia For The Spanish Guitar,
Vol. 3 *Op.15-22
(Jape, Mijndert) [Eng/Fr/Ger/Dutch]
gtr (critical ed with commentary)
TEESELING VT-203 f.s.   (2206)

Opera Omnia For The Spanish Guitar,
Vol. 4 *Op.23-29
(Jape, Mijndert) [Eng/Fr/Ger/Dutch]
gtr (critical ed with commentary)
TEESELING VT-204 f.s.   (2207)

Opera Omnia For The Spanish Guitar,
Vol. 5 *Op.30-33
(Jape, Mijndert) [Eng/Fr/Ger/Dutch]
gtr (critical ed with commentary)
TEESELING VT-205 f.s.   (2208)

Opera Omnia For The Spanish Guitar,
Vol. 6 *Op.34-37
(Jape, Mijndert) [Eng/Fr/Ger/Dutch]
2gtr (critical ed with
commentary) TEESELING VT-206 f.s.
(2209)

Opera Omnia For The Spanish Guitar,
Vol. 7 *Op.38-42
(Jape, Mijndert) [Eng/Fr/Ger/Dutch]
2gtr (critical ed with
commentary) TEESELING VT-207 f.s.
(2210)

Opera Omnia For The Spanish Guitar,
Vol. 8 *Op.43-47
(Jape, Mijndert) [Eng/Fr/Ger/Dutch]
2gtr (critical ed with
commentary) TEESELING VT-208 f.s.
(2211)

Opera Omnia For The Spanish Guitar,
Vol. 9 *Op.48-53
(Jape, Mijndert) [Eng/Fr/Ger/Dutch]
2gtr (critical ed with
commentary) TEESELING VT-209 f.s.
(2212)

Opera Omnia For The Spanish Guitar,
Vol. 10 *Op.54-58
(Jape, Mijndert) [Eng/Fr/Ger/Dutch]
2gtr (critical ed with
commentary) TEESELING VT-210 f.s.
(2213)

Opera Omnia For The Spanish Guitar,
Vol. 11 *Op.59-62
(Jape, Mijndert) [Eng/Fr/Ger/Dutch]
2gtr (critical ed with
commentary) TEESELING VT-211 f.s.
(2214)

Opera Omnia For The Spanish Guitar,
Vol. 12 *Op.63
(Jape, Mijndert) [Eng/Fr/Ger/Dutch]
2gtr (critical ed with
commentary; also contains works
without op nos) TEESELING VT-212
f.s.   (2215)

Opus 1-20
(Noad, Frederick) gtr (facsimile
ed) HANSEN-US CGF-01 f.s.   (2216)

Pastorale, MIN 382
gtr ESSEX f.s.   (2217)

Pastorale, Op. 32, No. 3 (from Six
Petites Pieces Faciles, Op. 32)
gtr BERBEN 1688 f.s.   (2218)

SOR, FERNANDO (cont'd.)

Preludios, 4
(Fortea, Daniel) gtr FORTEA 153
f.s.
contains: Theme- Andante (Prelude
No. 1) (from Op. 11); Theme-
Andante (Prelude No. 2) (from
Op. 7); Theme- Andante Con
Moto: Var. 5 (Prelude No. 3)
(from Op. 12); Theme-Andante:
Var. 2 (Prelude No. 4) (from
Op. 11)   (2219)

Rondo (from Grande Sonate, Op. 22)
gtr SCHOTT GA-362 f.s.   (2220)
(Azpiazu, Lupe De) gtr (Guitare,
No. 24) LEDUC G-24 f.s.   (2221)
(Fortea, Daniel) gtr FORTEA 174
f.s.   (2222)
(Sainz De La Maza, Regino) gtr
UNION ESP. 20825 f.s.   (2223)
(Schneider, Simon) gtr HEINRICH.
1668 f.s.   (2224)

Septieme Fantaisie Et Variations
Brillantes Sur Deux Airs Favoris
Connus *Op.30
"Fantaisie, Sur Des Airs Favoris"
(Caceres, Oscar) gtr (Collection
Oscar Caceres No. 9) ESCHIG 8187
f.s.   (2225)
"Fantasia E Variazioni Brillanti"
(Gangi, Mario) gtr BERBEN 1209
f.s.   (2226)

Six Petites Pieces Faciles *Op.32
"Piezas Faciles, 6" gtr UNION ESP.
1517 f.s.   (2227)

Six Waltzes *Op.17
"Walzer, 6" (Domandl, Willy) gtr
SIMROCK EE-1317 f.s.   (2228)

Sixty Short Pieces, Vol. 1 *Nos.1-38
gtr COLUMBIA 170A $1.50   (2229)

Sixty Short Pieces, Vol. 2 *Nos.39-
60
gtr COLUMBIA 170B $1.75   (2230)

Sonata, Op. 22, Minuet (from Grande
Sonate, Op. 22)
(Fortea, Daniel) gtr FORTEA 156
f.s.   (2231)
"Minueto En Do Mayor" (Navascues,
Santiago) gtr BRUCK BG-S 1-2 f.s.
(2232)
(Scheit, Karl) gtr UNIVER. 14435
f.s.   (2233)
(Tarrago, Graciano) gtr UNION ESP.
20602 f.s. contains also: Sonata,
Op. 25, Minuet (from Grande
Sonate, Op. 25)   (2234)

Sonata, Op. 25, Minuet (from Grande
Sonate, Op. 25)
gtr SPAN.MUS.CTR. GE-186 f.s.
(2235)
(Fortea, Daniel) gtr FORTEA 157
f.s.   (2236)
(Navascues, Santiago) gtr BRUCK
BG-S 1-1 f.s.   (2237)
(Scheit, Karl) gtr (formerly OBV
6981.102A) UNIVER. 14442 f.s.
(2238)
"Minue" (Sinopoli, Antonio) gtr
RICORDI-ARG BA-11837 f.s.   (2239)

Theme and Variations (from Grande
Sonate, Op. 25)
gtr UNION ESP. 1518 f.s.   (2240)
(Sainz De La Maza, Regino) gtr
UNION ESP. 21533 f.s.   (2241)

Theme Varie Suive d'Un Menuet *Op.3
"Thema, Variationen Und Menuett"
(Domandl, Willy) gtr SIMROCK
EE-1303 f.s.   (2242)
"Tema Y Variaciones" (Fortea,
Daniel) gtr (without Menuet)
FORTEA 177 f.s.   (2243)

Tirana, Danza Spagnola
gtr (not in op. 1-63 or works
without opus number) BERBEN 2108
f.s.   (2244)

Trois Pieces De Societe , Op. 33, No.
1
"Piezas De Sociedad, 3, Op. 33, No.
1" gtr UNION ESP. 1520 f.s.
(2245)

Trois Pieces De Societe, Op. 33, No.
2
"Piezas De Sociedad, 3, Op33, No.
2" gtr UNION ESP. 1521 f.s.
(2246)

Trois Pieces De Societe, Op. 33, No.
3
"Piezas De Sociedad, 3, Op. 33, No.
3" gtr UNION ESP. 1522 f.s.
(2247)
"Siciliana" (Fortea, Daniel) gtr
FORTEA 171 f.s.   (2248)

SOR, FERNANDO (cont'd.)

Voyons Si C'est Ca, 6 Petites Pieces
Faciles *Op.45
"Six Petites Pieces" gtr LEMOINE
f.s.   (2249)

Voyons Si C'est Ca, 6 Petites Pieces
Faciles Nos. 2, 6
"Allegretto Und Walzer Aus Op. 45"
gtr SCHOTT GA-351 f.s.   (2250)

Voyons Si C'est Ca, 6 Petites Pieces
Faciles, Op. 45, No. 5
"Andante" gtr BERBEN 1916 f.s.
                                  (2251)

Voyons Si C'est Ca, 6 Petites Pieces
Faciles, Op. 45, No. 6
"Celebrated Valse" gtr UNION ESP.
1514 f.s.   (2252)

Waltz, Op. 32, No. 2 (from Six
Petites Pieces Faciles, Op. 32)
(Ricchi, Modesto) gtr BERBEN 1894
f.s.   (2253)

STRAUSS, JOHANN, [SR.] (1804-1849)
Valzer, 2, Op. 110 And 76
(Carfagna) gtr (6-7th degr.) BERBEN
EB1965 $4.25   (2254)

TRANSCRIPCIONES POR VICENTE ERLISO,
VOL. 2
gtr UNION ESP. 1016 f.s. arr
contains: Mozart, Wolfgang Amadeus,
Marcha Turca; Schumann, Robert
(Alexander), Volksliedchen,
Op.68,No.9   (2255)

TRANSCRIPCIONES POR VICENTE ERLISO,
VOL. V
gtr UNION ESP. 1055 f.s. arr + orig
pcs
contains: Erliso, Vincente, Minuet,
MIN 133; Erliso, Vincente,
Minuet, MIN 134; Mozart, Wolfgang
Amadeus, Fantasy, MIN 132 (2256)

WANHAL, JOHANN BAPTIST (JAN KRTITEL)
(1739-1813)
Cantabile
(Segovia) gtr (4th degr.) SCHOTT
GA-162 f.s.   (2257)

Minuette, 2
(Segovia) gtr (4th degr.) SCHOTT
GA-163 f.s.   (2258)

WEBER, CARL MARIA VON (1786-1826)
Waltz (from Der Freischutz)
(Pujol) gtr ESCHIG 2007 f.s. (2259)

WILTON, C.H.
Sonatina
(Behrend) gtr (2-3rd degr.) SIRIUS
f.s.   (2260)

ZANI DE FERRANTI, MARCO AURELIO
3 Melodies Nocturnes Et Une Etude
(Castet) gtr LEDUC G-86 f.s.
Guitare, No. 86
contains: Desir, Le; Etude No. 7;
Joie, La; Souvenir, Le (2261)

I/IB2-Coll   Guitar Solo Collections: Classical and Pre-Romantic Music (1760-1850)

ANTOLOGIA DIDATTICA PER CHITARRA, DI
AUTORI ITALIANI E STRANIERI *CC50L
(Palladino) gtr (1-2nd degr.) BERBEN
EB480 f.s. contains works by:
Aguado (12), Carcassi (4), Carulli
(14), Diabelli (2), Kuffner (8),
Sor (10)   (2262)

COMPOSICIONES FACILES, 4
(Lara) gtr (3rd degr., contains works
by: Clementi, Beethoven, Berens,
Schumann) RICORDI-ARG BA-12556 f.s.
                                  (2263)

EEUW GELEDEN, EEN: GITAARSTUKJES VAN
19E-EEUWSE KOMPONISTEN *CC12L
(van Schagen) gtr (1-2nd degr.)
HARMONIA 1273 f.s. contains works
by: Kuffner (3), Aguado (3),
Diabelli (2), Sors (2), Carcassi
(2)   (2264)

GIULIANI, MAURO (1781-1829)
Rossiniana, Op. 119-124 *CCUL
gtr fac ed BELWIN $3.00 d6:8,
Guitar Foundation of America
Publ. Series A No. 2-7   (2265)

ITALIENISCHE MEISTER DER GITARRE UM
1800 *CC10L
(Henze) gtr (4-6th degr.) HOFMEISTER
7292 $7.50 contains works by:
Carulli (2), Molino (2), Giuliani
(2), Legnani (2), Carcassi (2)
                                  (2266)

KLASSIKER DER GITARRE; STUDIEN- UND
VORTRAGSLITERATUR AUS DEM 18. UND
19. JAHRHUNDERT, VOL. 1 *CCU
(Ratz) gtr DEUTSCHER f.s.   (2267)

KLASSISCHE KOSTBARKEITEN *CC11L
(Harz) gtr (3-4th degr.) SCHOTT 6247
f.s. contains works by: Schumann
(2), Chopin (2), Schubert (1),
Beethoven (2), W.A. Mozart (1),
Boccherini (1), Haydn (1), Handel
(1)   (2268)

KLEINE SPIELSTUCKE GROSSER MEISTER
*CC5L
(Hammerschmied) gtr (1st degr.)
HEINRICH. N-1676 f.s. contains
works by: Carcassi, Kuffner,
Diabelli, Sor, Aguado   (2269)

LATWE UTWORY DAWNYCH MISTRZOW *CC41L
(Powrozniak, Jozef) gtr (1-2nd degr.)
POLSKIE 5796 f.s. Grajmy Na
Gitarze, Vol. 4; contains works by:
Sor (5), Kuffner (5), Aguado (7),
Coste (1), Carulli (10), Diabelli
(5), Giuliani (1), Carcassi (6),
Horecki (1)   (2270)

LEICHTES GITARRESPIEL, 2 VOLS. *CCU
(Gotze) gtr (2-3rd degr.) SCHOTT
5065, 5066 f.s. contains works by:
Carcassi; Carulli; Giuliani; Sor
and others   (2271)

MAGYAR ZENE GITARRA A XIX. SZADAD ELSO
FELEBOL
"Ungarische Musik Fur Gitarre Aus Der
Ersten Halfte Des 19. Jahrhunderts"
(Brodszky) [Hung] gtr (2-4th degr.,
Afterword in Hung, Ger, Eng; 59 arr
+ orig pcs; contains works by:
Jager (1), Horecki (5), Anon. (2),
Pfeifer (6), Lavotta (3), Sarkozy
(1), Svastics (2), Fay (2),
Rozsavolgyi (1), Wilt (4), Padowetz
(1), Mertz (12), Ruzitska (1),
Kossovits (2), Folksongs (16), for
gtr solo; 2 pcs. by Anon. for fl,
gtr (1) and solo voice, gtr (1)) sc
EMB Z-2985 f.s.   (2272)
"Ungarische Musik Fur Gitarre Aus Der
Ersten Halfte Des 19. Jahrhunderts"
(Brodszky) [Hung] gtr (2-4th degr.,
Afterword in Hung, Ger, Eng; 59 arr
+ orig pcs; contains works by:
Jager (1), Horecki (5), Anon. (2),
Pfeifer (6), Lavotta (3), Sarkozy
(1), Svastics (2), Fay (2),
Rozsavolgyi (1), Wilt (4), Padowetz
(1), Mertz (12), Ruzitska (1),
Kossovits (2), Folksongs (16), for
gtr solo; 2 pcs. by Anon. for fl,
gtr (1) and solo voice, gtr (1)) sc
SCHOTT 5839 f.s.   (2273)

MEINE ERSTEN GITARRENSTUCKE, VOL. 4:
MEISTER DER ROMANTIK
gtr SYMPHON 2202 f.s.   (2274)

MEINE ERSTEN GITARRENSTUCKE, VOL. I:
MEISTER DER KLASSIK *CC18L
(Teuchert) gtr (1-3rd degr.) SYMPHON
2199 f.s. arr + orig pcs; contains
works by: Carulli (7), Sor (2),
Giuliani (1), Carcassi (2), Aguado
(1), Haydn (1), Diabelli (2), Anon.
(1), W.A. Mozart (1)   (2275)

MEISTER DER ALTEREN GITARRISTIK (18.
BIS 19. JAHRHUNDERT) *CC11L
(Behrend) gtr (3-5th degr.)
HOFMEISTER 7147 f.s. contains works
by: Carulli (1), Carcassi (1),
Diabelli (3), Paganini (5),
Giuliani (1)   (2276)

MIJN EERSTE GITAARSOLI, VOL. I *CC25L
(Tower) gtr (1-3rd degr.) TEESELING
VT-8 f.s. contains works by: Sor
(4), Kuffner (8), Carulli (8),
Carcassi (4), Ferandiere (1) (2277)

MIJN EERSTE GITAARSOLI, VOL. II *CC21L
(Tower) gtr (1-3rd degr.) TEESELING
VT-16 f.s. contains works by:
Giuliani (6), Carcassi (5), Carulli
(3), Aguado (2), Sor (3), Marschner
(1), Diabelli (1)   (2278)

NOAD, FREDERICK M.
Solo Guitar Playing, A Complete
Course Of Instruction In The
Technique Of Guitar Performance
[Eng] gtr quarto COLLIER f.s.
187p., ill; repr, 1969; 1st ed,
1968; contains: Minuet from
Grande Sonate, Op. 25 by Fernando
Sor; Prelude, TI-i-17, In E

NOAD, FREDERICK M. (cont'd.)
(Lagrima) by Francisco Tarrega;
and Suite No.4 For Violoncello,
BWV 1010, In E Flat, Bourree (in
A) by Johann Sebastian Bach
                                  (2279)

PRIMO SAGGIO DEL CHITARRISTA
(Palladino) gtr (2nd degr.) BERBEN
EB473 $1.00
contains: Carcassi, Matteo,
Andante, MIN 26; Carcassi,
Matteo, Andante, MIN 27; Carulli,
Ferdinando, Theme and Variations,
MIN 138; Kuffner, Joseph,
Prelude, MIN 140; Sor, Fernando,
Theme and Variations, MIN 139
                                  (2280)

RIGHTMIRE, RICHARD W.
Wonderful Guitar, The (A Modern
Classic Guitar Method), Vol. I
[Eng] gtr quarto SMITH,WJ f.s.
32p., 1962, ill; contains:
Minuet, BWV Anh. 115 In G-Minor
(in E-Minor) by Johann Sebastian
Bach from anna magdalena bach
notenbuchlein (1725), no.5 (2281)

Wonderful Guitar, The (A Modern
Classic Guitar Method), Vol. II
[Eng] gtr quarto SMITH,WJ f.s.
32p., 1963, ill; contains:
Minuet, BWV Anh. 114 In G from
Anna Magdalena Bach Notenbuchlein
(1725), No.4; Minuet, BWV Anh.
132 In D-Minor from Anna
Magdalena Bach Notenbuchlein
(1725), No.36, by J.S. Bach; and
Minuet from Grande Sonate, Op. 22
by Fernando Sor   (2282)

RODRIGUEZ ARENAS, MARIO
Escuela De La Guitarra, La, Vol. II
[Span] gtr RICORDI-ARG BA-9531 f.s.
88p.; repr, 1966; 1st ed, 1923;
contains: Tarrega, Francisco,
Prelude, TI-i-17; Exercises, TI-
iii-15, 35; and Sor, Fernando,
Minuet, from Grande Sonate, OP.
25   (2283)

Escuela De La Guitarra, La, Vol. II
[Jap] gtr ONGAKU f.s. 88p.; repr,
1966; 1st ed, 1923; contains:
Tarrega, Francisco, Prelude, TI-
i-17; Exercises, TI-iii-15, 35;
and Sor, Fernando, Minuet, from
Grande Sonate, Op.25   (2284)

Escuela De La Guitarra, La, Vol. V
[Span] gtr RICORDI-ARG BA-9549 f.s.
55p.; repr, 1954; 1st ed, 1923;
contains: Estudios Y Preludios De
Francisco Tarrega; 28 Unnumbered
Pcs By Tarrega (22); Chopin (3);
Coste (1); Mendelssohn (1); also
contains: Tarrega, Francisco,
Preludes, TI-i-1-7, 8a, 9-11 (13
bars), 13; Studies, TI-ii-5, 6,
8, 16b, 17, 18(56bars), 19-22;
and Sor, Fernando, Introduction
Et Variations Sur Un Theme De
Mozart, Op. 9   (2285)

Escuela De La Guitarra, La, Vol. V
[Jap] gtr ONGAKU f.s. 55p.; repr,
1954; 1st ed, 1923; contains:
Estudios Y Preludios De Francisco
Tarrega; 28 Unnumbered Pcs By
Tarrega (22); Chopin (3); Coste
(1); Mendelssohn (1);also
contains: Tarrega, Francisco,
Preludes, TI-i- 2-7, 8a, 9-11,
13; Studies, TI-ii- 5, 6, 8, 16b,
17-22; and Sor, Fernando,
Introduction Et Variations Sur Un
Theme De Mozart, Op.9   (2286)

ROMANTIKUS GITARDARABOK - ROMANTIC
PIECES FOR GUITAR
(Tarrega, Fr.; Benko) gtr (4-6th
degr.) EMB Z-8327 f.s.
contains: Chopin, Frederic,
Prelude, Op. 28, No. 11; Chopin,
Frederic, Waltz, Op. 34, No. 2;
Mendelssohn-Bartholdy, Felix,
Romance, Op. 19, No. 6; Schubert,
Franz (Peter), Moment Musical,
Op.94; Schumann, Robert
(Alexander), Romance, MIN 327
                                  (2287)

SOR, FERNANDO (1778-1839)
Easy Music For Guitar, Vol. 11
(Azpiazu, Lupe De) gtr (contains
op. 2, no. 1 (Menuet); op. 24,
no. 1 (Menuet, a minor); op. 31,
nos. 1, 3, 4; op. 35, nos. 2, 8;
op. 60, nos. 5-7) SYMPHON 2176
f.s.   (2288)

Minuetos, 40
(Azpiazu, Jose De) gtr (contains
op. 1, no. 1; op. 2, no. 4; op.
3; op. 5, nos. 1, 3; op. 8, no.
1; op. 11, nos. 1-3, 5, 7, 9, 11-
12; op. 13, no. 1, 3-4; op. 15,

SOR, FERNANDO (cont'd.)

no. 1; op. 23, nos. 5-6; op. 24,
no. 1-2, 4-6, 8; op. 32, no. 1;
op. 36; nos. 1-3, 5, 8, 11, 12,
16, 18, 21, 27 are not in op. 1-
63 or works without opus number)
UNION ESP. 20683 f.s.   (2289)

Minuetos Para Guitarra, 34
(Bianqui Pinero, G.) gtr RICORDI-
ARG C-16.540 f.s. also contains:
op. 2, nos. 1, 4; op. 3; op. 5,
nos. 1, 3; op. 8, no. 1; op. 13,
nos. 1, 3; op. 15, no. 1; op. 23,
no. 5; op. 24, nos. 1, 2, 4-6, 8;
op. 36, nos. 1, 2; op. 45, no. 1;
op. 48, no. 3
contains: Deux Themes Varies Et
Douze Menuets, Op. 11, Nos. 1-
12; Minuet (from Grande Sonate,
Op. 22); Minuet (from Grande
Sonate, Op. 25)   (2290)

Obras Para Guitarra, 12, Primer Album
*CC12L
(Bianqui Pinero, G.) gtr RICORDI-
ARG BA-12488 f.s. contains: op.
1, no. 4 (Andante); op. 19, no. 1
(Marcha Religiosa); op. 19, no. 2
(Allegretto); op. 21 (La
Despedida); op. 29, no. 3; op.
42, no. 1 (Cantabile); op. 44,
no. 3 (Andantino); op. 45, no. 3
(Tema y Variaciones); op. 47, no.
32 (La Caza-Allegretto); op. 53
(El Primer Paso-Duo); op. 60, no.
19; op. 60, no. 22   (2291)

STUNDE DER GITARRE, DIE; SPIELMUSIK AUS
DER BLUTEZEIT DER GITARRE, VOL. I:
SEHR LEICHT *CC37L
(Gotze) gtr (1-3rd degr.) SCHOTT
GA-19 f.s. contains works by:
Aguado (3), Carcassi (1), Carulli
(2), Diabelli (4), Giuliani (6),
Horecki (1), Hunten (1), Kuffner
(6), Meissonier (1), Sor (9), Anon.
(3)   (2292)

STUNDE DER GITARRE, DIE; SPIELMUSIK AUS
DER BLUTEZEIT DER GITARRE, VOL. II:
LEICHT *CC28L
(Gotze) gtr (1-3rd degr.) SCHOTT
GA-20 f.s. contains works by:
Aguado (4), Borghesi (1), Call (1),
Carulli (3), Diabelli (3), Giuliani
(2), Hunten (1), Mertz (5), Paulian
(1), Sor (6), Anon. (1)   (2293)

STUNDE DER GITARRE, DIE; SPIELMUSIK AUS
DER BLUTEZEIT DER GITARRE, VOL.
III: MITTEL *CC19L
(Gotze) gtr (1-3rd degr.) SCHOTT
GA-21 f.s. contains works by:
Aguado (1), Carcassi (1), Carulli
(1), Coste (2), Giuliani (3),
Matiegka (1), Mertz (2), Molino
(1), Sor (7)   (2294)

UTWORY DAWNYCH MISTROW *CC27L
(Powrozniak, Jozef) gtr (3-4th degr.)
POLSKIE 6109 f.s. arr + orig pcs;
Grajmy Na Gitarze, Vol. VI;
contains works by: Carcassi (3),
Bobrowicz (1), Horecki (1), Padovec
(1), Sor (4), Coste (4), Molino
(1), Mertz (2), Aguado (2), Legnani
(1), Giuliani (2), Paganini (1),
Schulz (1), Seener (1), Carulli
(1), Castellucci (1)   (2295)

I/IB3 Guitar Solos:
Romantic and Post-Romantic
Music (1850-1914)

ALARD, JEAN-DELPHIN (1815-1888)
Etude, Op. 19, in A
(Rossi) gtr (8th degr.) BERBEN
EB2101 f.s.   (2296)

ALBENIZ, ISAAC (1860-1909)
Alborada
(Garcia Fortea) gtr UNION ESP.
15490 f.s.   (2297)

Angustia, Romanza Sin Palabras
(Garcia Velasco) gtr UNION ESP.
21011 f.s.   (2298)

Aragon, Fantasia *Op.181,No.6 (from
Suite Espanola)
(Azpiazu) gtr (7th degr.) SYMPHON
2114 f.s.   (2299)
(Garcia Fortea) gtr (7th degr.)
SALABERT 16268 f.s.   (2300)
(Garcia Fortea) gtr (7th degr.)

ALBENIZ, ISAAC (cont'd.)

UNION ESP. 43790 OR 1024 f.s.
(2301)

Asturias, Leyenda, Preludio *Op.181,
No.5 (from Suite Espanola)
(Abloniz) gtr (9th degr.) BERBEN
EB1222 $1.25   (2302)
(Alfonso) gtr (9th degr., Edition
Nicolas Alfonso, No. 24) SCHOTT-
FRER 9304 f.s.   (2303)
(Azpiazu) gtr (9th degr.) SYMPHON
472 f.s.   (2304)
(Beck) gtr (9th degr.) TEESELING
VT-53 f.s.   (2305)
"Asturias, Preludio. No. 1 De
"Cantos De Espana, Op. 232 [sic]"
(Garcia Fortea) gtr (9th degr.)
UNION ESP. 15487 f.s.   (2306)
(Maravilla) gtr (9th degr.) UNION
ESP. 18730 f.s.   (2307)
(Navascues) gtr (9th degr., transcr
+ orig pno pt) BRUCK BG.A1-1 f.s.
(2308)
(Papas) gtr (9th degr.) COLUMBIA
162 $1.50   (2309)
(Sainz de la Maza) gtr (9th degr.)
UNION ESP. 21626 f.s.   (2310)
(Segovia) gtr (9th degr.) COLOMBO
NY-2067 f.s.   (2311)
(Segovia) gtr (9th degr.) RICORDI-
ARG BA-9521 f.s.   (2312)
(Segovia) gtr (9th degr.) UNION
ESP. 21818 f.s.   (2313)
(Sierra) gtr (9th degr.) CHOUDENS
20.652 f.s.   (2314)
(Sinopoli) gtr (9th degr.) RICORDI-
ARG BA-9381 f.s.   (2315)

Automne, L'
(Azpiazu) gtr (6th degr.) LEDUC
$3.00   (2316)
(Sierra) gtr (6th degr.) CHOUDENS
20.689   (2317)

Bajo De La Palmera *Op.232,No.3
(from Cantos De Espana)
(Borghese) 3gtr (8th degr.) sc,pts
ZERBONI 7669 $9.50   (2318)

Barcarolle
(Garcia Fortea) gtr UNION ESP.
15675 f.s.   (2319)

Barcarolle, Op. 23
(Chacon) gtr (8th degr.) UNION ESP.
19242 f.s.   (2320)

Cadiz, Serenata *Op.181,No.4 (from
Suite Espanola)
(Azpiazu) gtr (8th degr.) SYMPHON
2111 f.s.   (2321)
(Fortea) gtr (8th degr.) FORTEA 2
f.s.   (2322)
"Cadiz, Saeta" (Garcia Fortea) gtr
(8th degr.) SALABERT 16256 f.s.
(2323)
"Cadiz, Saeta" (Garcia Fortea) gtr
(8th degr.) UNION ESP. 20336-I
f.s.   (2324)
(Llobet) gtr (8th degr.) RICORDI-
ARG BA-11817 f.s.   (2325)
(Llobet) gtr (8th degr.) UNION ESP.
19141 f.s.   (2326)
(Sinopoli) gtr (8th degr.) RICORDI-
ARG BA-7606 f.s.   (2327)
(Tarrega; rev. Llobet) gtr (8th
degr.) UNION ESP. 21683 f.s.
(2328)

Capricho Catalan (from Suite Espana,
Op.165, No.5)
(Lorimer) gtr HANSEN-US ML-010 f.s.
(2329)

Castilla, Seguidillas *Op.181,No.7
(from Suite Espanola)
(Azpiazu) gtr (8th degr.) SYMPHON
2112 f.s.   (2330)
(Sinopoli) gtr (8th degr.) RICORDI-
ARG BA-7607 f.s.   (2331)

Cataluna, Corrando *Op.181,No.2
(from Suite Espanola)
(Garcia Velasco) gtr (9th degr.)
UNION ESP. 20301 f.s.   (2332)

Cielo Sin Nobes *Op.92,No.3 (from
Piezas Caracteristicas)
(Garcia Fortea) gtr (7th degr.)
UNION ESP. 1026 f.s.   (2333)

Cordoba *Op.232,No.4 (from Cantos De
Espana)
(Angel) gtr (8-9th degr.) UNION
ESP. 18930 f.s.   (2334)
(Azpiazu) gtr (8-9th degr.) SYMPHON
2125 f.s.   (2335)
(Garcia Fortea) gtr (8-9th degr.)
SALABERT 16255 f.s.   (2336)
(Garcia Fortea) gtr (8-9th degr.)
UNION ESP. 20336-IV f.s.   (2337)
(Sinopoli) gtr (8-9th degr.)
RICORDI-ARG BA 10293 f.s.   (2338)

Danza Espanola, No. 1
(Azpiazu) gtr (A maj,7th degr.)
RICORDI-ARG BA-12264 f.s.   (2339)

ALBENIZ, ISAAC (cont'd.)

(Garcia) gtr (D maj,7th degr.)
UNION ESP. 15487 f.s.   (2340)

Danza Espanola, No. 3
(Azpiazu) gtr (6th degr.) RICORDI-
ARG BA-12266 f.s.   (2341)
(Garcia Fortea) gtr (6th degr.)
SALABERT 16257 f.s.   (2342)
(Garcia Fortea) gtr (6th degr.)
UNION ESP. 15677 f.s.   (2343)

Danza Espanola, No. 6
(Azpiazu) gtr (7th degr.) RICORDI-
ARG BA-12269 f.s.   (2344)

En La Alhambra, Capricho Morisco
(from Recuerdos De Viaje, No. 4)
(Garcia Fortea) gtr (8-9th degr.)
UNION ESP. 15488 f.s.   (2345)

En La Playa, Recuerdo (from Recuerdos
De Viaje, No. 7)
(Garcia Fortea) gtr (7th degr.)
UNION ESP. 15678 f.s.   (2346)

Gavotte
(Garcia Fortea) gtr UNION ESP. 1028
f.s.   (2347)

Gavotte, Op. 92, No. 1 (from Piezas
Caracteristicas)
(Garcia Fortea) gtr (8th degr.)
SALABERT 16265 f.s.   (2348)
(Garcia Fortea) gtr (8th degr.)
UNION ESP. 15485 f.s.   (2349)

Granada, Serenata *Op.181,No.1 (from
Suite Espanola)
gtr (A maj,9th degr.) UNION ESP.
1029 f.s.   (2350)
(Abloniz) gtr (E maj,9th degr.)
BERBEN EB1967 f.s.   (2351)
(Angel) gtr (9th degr.) UNION ESP.
18816 f.s.   (2352)
(Azpiazu) gtr (9th degr.) SYMPHON
473 f.s.   (2353)
(Fortea) gtr (9th degr.) FORTEA 1
f.s.   (2354)
(Ragossnig) gtr (9th degr.) SCHOTT
GA-434 f.s.   (2355)
(Segovia) gtr (E maj,9th degr.) CEL
4 f.s.   (2356)
(Sierra) gtr (E maj,9th degr.)
CHOUDENS 20.656 f.s.   (2357)
(Sinopoli) gtr (9th degr., version
facil) RICORDI-ARG BA-8415 f.s.
(2358)
(Tarrega) gtr (E maj,9th degr.)
RICORDI-ARG BA-9377 f.s.   (2359)
(Tarrega) gtr (E maj,9th degr.)
HEINRICH. 3309 f.s.   (2360)

Intermedia De "Pepita Jimenez"
(Azpiazu) gtr (8th degr.) SYMPHON
474 f.s.   (2361)

Malaguena *Op.165,No.3 (from Suite
Espana)
(Anido) gtr (8th degr.) RICORDI-ARG
BA11379 f.s.   (2362)
(Azpiazu) gtr (8th degr.) SYMPHON
475 f.s.   (2363)
(Balaguer) gtr (8th degr.) UNION
ESP. 20931 f.s.   (2364)
(Martin) gtr (6th degr., Guitare
Selection, No. 8) DELRIEU 1390
f.s.   (2365)

Mallorca, Barcelona *Op.202
(Abloniz) gtr (8-9th degr.) BERBEN
EB2050 f.s.   (2366)
(Azpiazu) gtr (8-9th degr.) SYMPHON
2113 f.s.   (2367)
(Garcia Fortea) gtr (8-9th degr.)
UNION ESP. 1031 f.s.   (2368)
(Maravilla) gtr (8-9th degr.) UNION
ESP. 18726 f.s.   (2369)
(Segovia) gtr (8-9th degr.) CEL 1
f.s.   (2370)
(Sierra) gtr (8-9th degr.) CHOUDENS
20.654 f.s.   (2371)
(Sinopoli) gtr (8-9th degr.)
RICORDI-ARG BA-7892 f.s.   (2372)

Minueto A Sylvia *Op.92,No.2 (from
Piezas Caracteristicas)
(Garcia Fortea) gtr (7th degr.)
SALABERT f.s.   (2373)
(Garcia Fortea) gtr (7th degr.)
UNION ESP. 15491 f.s.   (2374)

Motivos De Navarra
(Sinopoli) gtr (8-9th degr.)
RICORDI-ARG BA-11212 f.s.   (2375)

Oriental *Op.232,No.2 (from Cantos
De Espana)
(Azpiazu) gtr (8th degr.) RICORDI-
ARG BA-12032 f.s.   (2376)
(Garcia Fortea) gtr (A min,8th
degr.) SALABERT 16263 f.s.   (2377)
(Garcia Fortea) gtr (A min,8th
degr.) UNION ESP. 43789 OR 1032
f.s.   (2378)

ALBENIZ, ISAAC (cont'd.)

(Llobet) gtr (8th degr.) UNION ESP.
21333 f.s.   (2379)
(Segovia) gtr (D min,8th degr.) CEL
3 f.s.   (2380)

Pavana Capricho *Op.12
(Abloniz) gtr (8th degr.) RICORDI-
IT 130398 f.s.   (2381)
(Angel) gtr (8th degr.) UNION ESP.
1033 f.s.   (2382)
(Angel) gtr (8th degr.) UNION ESP.
18860 f.s.   (2383)
(Azpiazu) gtr (8th degr.) SYMPHON
2109 f.s.   (2384)
(Sinopoli) gtr (8th degr.) RICORDI-
ARG BA-11353 f.s.   (2385)
(Tarrega) gtr (8th degr.) UNION
ESP. 21653 f.s.   (2386)

Plegaria
(Garcia Fortea) gtr (7th degr.)
SALABERT 16267 f.s.   (2387)
(Garcia Fortea) gtr (7th degr.)
UNION ESP. 15492 f.s.   (2388)

Polo, El, Impressione (from Iberia,
Suite, No. 8)
(Abloniz) gtr (7th degr.) BERBEN
EB1139 $1.25   (2389)

Polonesa *Op.92,No.9 (from Piezas
Caracteristicas)
(Garcia Fortea) gtr (8th degr.)
UNION ESP. 15489 f.s.   (2390)

Prelude, Op. 165, No. 1 (from Suite
Espana)
(Azpiazu) gtr (7th degr.) RICORDI-
ARG BA-12270 f.s.   (2391)

Puerta De Tierra, Bolero (from
Recuerdos De Viaje, No. 5)
(Azpiazu) gtr (7th degr.) SYMPHON
2032 f.s.   (2392)
(Garcia Fortea) gtr (7th degr.)
SALABERT 16270 f.s.   (2393)
(Garcia Fortea) gtr (7th degr.)
UNION ESP. 43800 OR 1035 f.s. (2394)

Rumores De La Caleta, Malaguena (from
Recuerdos De Viaje, No. 6)
(Abloniz) gtr (7-8th degr.) BERBEN
EB1288 $1.00   (2395)
(Azpiazu) gtr (7-8th degr.) SYMPHON
476 f.s.   (2396)
(Garcia Fortea) gtr (7-8th degr.)
SALABERT 16262   (2397)
(Garcia Fortea) gtr (7-8th degr.)
UNION ESP. 43788 f.s.   (2398)
(Herrero) gtr (7-8th degr.) UNION
ESP. 21794 f.s.   (2399)
(Lozano Garcia) gtr (7-8th degr.)
UNION ESP. 18670 f.s.   (2400)
(Navascues) gtr (7-8th degr.,
includes orig. pno pt) BRUCK
BG-A1-2 f.s.   (2401)
"Malaguena" (Paleologo) gtr (7-8th
degr.) HEINRICH. 1542 f.s.   (2402)
(Sierra) gtr (7-8th degr.) CHOUDENS
20.653 f.s.   (2403)
(Sinopoli) gtr (7-8th degr.)
RICORDI-ARG BA-6769 f.s.   (2404)

Seguidillas *Op.232,No.5 (from
Cantos De Espana)
(Chacon) gtr (8-9th degr.) UNION
ESP. 19243 f.s.   (2405)
(Garcia) gtr (8-9th degr.) UNION
ESP. 15482 f.s.   (2406)

Serenade, Op. 165, No. 4 (from Suite
Espana)
(Azpiazu) gtr (9th degr.) RICORDI-
ARG BA-12271 f.s.   (2407)

Serenata Arabe
(Garcia Fortea) gtr (7th degr.)
UNION ESP. 15674 f.s.   (2408)

Sevilla, Sevillanas *Op.181,No.3
(from Suite Espanola)
(Abloniz) gtr (8-10th degr.) BERBEN
EB1438 $1.50   (2409)
(Angel) gtr (8-10th degr.) UNION
ESP. 18817   (2410)
(Azpiazu) gtr (8-10th degr.)
SYMPHON 477   (2411)
(Borghese) gtr (8-10th degr., arte
della chitarra, L') ZERBONI 7717
$6.00   (2412)
(Ragossnig) gtr (8-10th degr.)
SCHOTT GA-433   (2413)
(Sinopoli) gtr (8-10th degr.)
RICORDI-ARG BA-7608   (2414)
(Tarrega; Llobet) gtr (8-10th
degr.) RICORDI-ARG BA-12120   (2415)

Sous Le Palmier [Bajo La Palmera],
Danse Espagnole *Op.232,No.3
(from Cantos De Espana)
(Bertin) gtr (8th degr.) RICORDI-
ARG BA-8793 f.s.   (2416)
(Garcia Fortea) gtr (8th degr.)
SALABERT 16266 f.s.   (2417)

ALBENIZ, ISAAC (cont'd.)

(Garcia Fortea) gtr (8th degr.)
UNION ESP. 15676 f.s.   (2418)

Staccato
(Garcia Fortea) gtr UNION ESP. 1040
f.s.   (2419)

Tango *Op.165,No.2 (from Suite
Espana)
(Azpiazu) gtr (8-9th degr.) SYMPHON
478 f.s.   (2420)
(Garcia Velasco) gtr (D maj,8-9th
degr.) UNION ESP. 19722 f.s. (2421)
(Martin) gtr (D maj,3rd degr.,
Guitare Selection, No. 7) DELRIEU
1389 f.s.   (2422)
(Segovia) gtr (D maj,8-9th degr.)
SCHOTT GA-154 f.s.   (2423)
(Sinopoli) gtr (A maj,8-9th degr.)
RICORDI-ARG BA-7609 f.s.   (2424)

Tango Espagnol
(Azpiazu) gtr (7th degr.) LEDUC
$3.00   (2425)

Torre Bermeja, Serenata *Op.92,No.12
(from Piezas Caracteristicas)
(Azpiazu) gtr (9th degr.) SYMPHON
2033   (2426)
(Borghese) gtr (9th degr., arte
della chitarra, L') ZERBONI 7731
$6.00   (2427)
(Garcia Fortea) gtr (9th degr.)
SALABERT 16264   (2428)
(Garcia Fortea) gtr (9th degr.)
UNION ESP. 43792   (2429)
(Llobet) gtr (9th degr.) RICORDI-
ARG BA-11812   (2430)
(Llobet) gtr (9th degr.) UNION ESP.
19511   (2431)
(Lozano Garcia) gtr (9th degr.)
UNION ESP. 18912   (2432)
(Sierra) gtr (9th degr.) CHOUDENS
20.655   (2433)
(Sinopoli) gtr (9th degr.) RICORDI-
ARG BA-7916   (2434)

Zambra *Op.92,No.7 (from Piezas
Caracteristicas)
(Garcia Fortea) gtr (8th degr.)
SALABERT 16269 f.s.   (2435)
(Garcia Fortea) gtr (8th degr.)
UNION ESP. 15493 f.s.   (2436)

Zambra Granadina
(Albeniz) gtr (8th degr.) BERBEN
EB2051 f.s.   (2437)
(Azpiazu) gtr (8th degr.) SYMPHON
2115 f.s.   (2438)
(Garcia Fortea) gtr (8th degr.)
UNION ESP. 1042 f.s.   (2439)
(Segovia) gtr (8th degr.) CEL 2
f.s.   (2440)
(Sierra) gtr (8th degr.) CHOUDENS
20.660 f.s.   (2441)

Zortziko *Op.165,No.6 (from Suite
Espana)
(Azpiazu) gtr (6th degr.) SYMPHON
479 f.s.   (2442)

ANONYMOUS
Romance Anonimo
(Garcia Velasco) 2gtr (4-5th degr.)
sc UNION ESP. 20305 f.s.   (2443)
(Tarrago) 2gtr (4-5th degr.) UNION
ESP. 21531 f.s.   (2444)

Romance, MIN 141
also published in: A. Stingl,
Gitarrebuch Fur Madeleine, Vol.
2; Antologia Per Chitarra, Vol.
3; Gitarristen, Vol. 2; Guitar
Sampler; The Mel Bay Folio Of
Classic Guitar Solos, Vol. 2;
Music For Classical Guitar;
Pezzi Facili Per Chitarra, 3;
Piccola Antologia
Chitarristica; Die Solo-
Gitarre, Vol. I; 700 Years Of
Music For The Classical Guitar;
2 Guitars, Album I; Romance
d'Amour [Guitar Quartet];
Premier Cours Pour Apprendre A
Jouer De La Guitare;
Gitarrenschule, Vol. 1; The
Simplicity Tutor For Spanish
Guitar; Solo Guitar Playing;
Methode De Guitare Classique;
Materialy Do Nauki Gry Na
Gitarze; Origines Et Technique
De La Guitare
"Romance d'Amour" (Ahslund) (4-5th
degr.) REUTER f.s.   (2445)
"Burgalesa, Nach Einer
Altspanischen Melodie Aus Burgos"
(Behrend) (4-5th degr., Die
Konzertgitarre) SIKORSKI 687
$1.50   (2446)
(di Ponio) (4-5th degr.) BERBEN
EB511 $1.00   (2447)
"Romance De Amor, Theme Song"
(Gomez) (4-5th degr.)

ANONYMOUS (cont'd.)

SPAN.MUS.CTR. GE-151 f.s.   (2448)
"Romance Anonimo" (Navascues) (4-
5th degr.) BRUCK BG-A2-1 f.s.
(2449)
"Spanish Romance" (Papas) (4-5th
degr.) COLUMBIA 123 f.s.   (2450)
(Rosado) (staff notation and
tablature/4-5th degr.) UNION ESP.
19819 f.s.   (2451)
"Notturno" (Scheit) (4-5th degr.)
UNIVER. 14457 f.s.   (2452)
"Romanca d'Espagna" (Schneider) (4-
5th degr.) HEINRICH. 1669 f.s.
(2453)
"Romance De Amor" (Sensier) (4-5th
degr.) ESSEX f.s.   (2454)
"Romance De Amor" (Tower) (4-5th
degr.) TEESELING VT-51 f.s.
(2455)
(van Puijenbroeck) (4-5th degr.)
METROPOLIS EM-4570 $1.50   (2456)
"Romance De Amor Original" (Visser)
(4-5th degr.) HARMONIA 2078 f.s.
(2457)

ARCAS, JULIAN (1832-1882)
Danzas Espanolas, 2
(Azpiazu, L. de) gtr (5th degr.)
LEDUC G-16 f.s. Guitare, No.16
contains: Allegretto; Allegretto
(2458)

BIZET, GEORGES (1838-1875)
Arlesiana, La
(Llobet) gtr UNION ESP. 20382 f.s.
(2459)

Arlesien, La: Adagio
gtr FORTEA 225 f.s.   (2460)

Arlesien, La: Marcha Del Rey
gtr FORTEA 226 f.s.   (2461)

Arlesien, La: Minueto
gtr FORTEA 208 f.s.   (2462)

Celebre Minuetto (from L'Arlesienne)
(Azpiazu, L. de) gtr (7-8th degr.,
Guitare, No.18) LEDUC G-18 $3.00
(2463)

BOLZONI, GIOVANNI (1841-1919)
Beruhmtes Menuett
(Azpiazu) gtr SYMPHON 496 f.s.
(2464)
"Celebre Minueto" (Tarrega; Fortea)
gtr FORTEA 227 f.s.   (2465)

BOSCH, JACQUES
Pieces Faciles, 10, Pour l'Etude
gtr (2-3rd degr.) LEDUC f.s. (2466)

BRAHMS, JOHANNES (1833-1897)
Celebre Vals No. 15
(Fortea) gtr FORTEA 27   (2467)

Danza Hungara No. 5
(Fortea) gtr FORTEA 229   (2468)

Hungarian Dance, No. 5
"Danza Hungara No. 5" (Garcia
Velasco) gtr (6-7th degr.) UNION
ESP. 20299 f.s.   (2469)
"Danse Hongroise No. 5" (Martin)
gtr (6-7th degr., Guitare
Selection, No. 11) DELRIEU 1425
f.s.   (2470)

Hungarian Dance, No. 6
"Danse Hongroise No. 6" (Martin)
gtr (6th degr., Guitare
Selection, No. 12) DELRIEU 1426
f.s.   (2471)

Valsas
(Savio) gtr RICORDI-BR BR-1837 f.s.
contains: Waltz, Op. 39, No. 3;
Waltz, Op. 39, No. 15   (2472)

Waltz, Op. 30, No. 9, in A minor
(Tarrago) gtr UNION ESP. 20613 f.s.
contains also: Waltz, Op. 30, No.
15, in A   (2473)

Waltz, Op. 39, No. 8
(Segovia) gtr (6th degr.) SCHOTT
GA-174 f.s.   (2474)

Waltz, Op. 39, No. 15
gtr ESSEX   (2475)
(Abloniz) gtr BERBEN EB1317 $1.00
(2476)
(Bianqui Pinero) gtr RICORDI-ARG
BA-12390   (2477)
(Segovia) gtr (also published in:
Andres Segovia Album) COLUMBIA
132   (2478)
(Tarrega; Fortea) gtr FORTEA 71
(2479)

Wiegenlied *Op.49,No.4
"Cancion De Cuna" (Sinopoli) gtr
RICORDI-ARG BA-11254 f.s.   (2480)

CANO, ANTONIO (1811-1897)
Andante Grave
gtr (5th degr.) BERBEN EB1917 $1.00
(2481)

CUI, CESAR ANTONOVICH (1835-1918)
  Orientale (from Caleidoscopio, Op.
    50)
    (Rossi) gtr (4th degr.) BERBEN
    EB2032 f.s.   (2482)

DEBUSSY, CLAUDE (1862-1918)
  Clair De Lune (from Suite
    Bergamasque, No. 3)
    (Parodi) gtr (9-10th degr.)
    RICORDI-ARG BA-10272 f.s.   (2483)
    (Parodi) gtr (9-10th degr.) COLOMBO
    NY-2301 f.s.   (2484)
    "Chiaro Di Luna" (Rossi) gtr (7th
    degr.) BERBEN EB2017 f.s.   (2485)

  Compositions, 3
    (Parodi) gtr RICORDI-ARG BA-11234
    f.s.
      contains: Doctor Gradus Ad
      Parnassum (from Children's
      Corner, No. 1); Fille Aux
      Cheveux De Lin, La (from
      Preludes, Ier Livre, No. 8);
      Little Shepherd, The (from
      Children's Corner, No. 5)
                                  (2486)

  Doctor Gradus Ad Parnassum (from
    Children's Corner, No. 1)
    (Rossi) gtr (7th degr.) BERBEN
    EB2054 f.s.   (2487)

  Golliwogg's Cake-Walk (from
    Children's Corner, No. 6)
    (de Belleroche) gtr (9-10th degr.)
    DURAND 12.963 $1.75   (2488)

  Minstrels (from Preludes, Ier Livre,
    No. 12)
    (Hartman) gtr (9th degr.) DURAND
    13693 f.s.   (2489)

  Petit Negre, Le
    (Azpiazu) gtr (8th degr.) LEDUC
    22721 $3.00   (2490)

  Plus Que Lente, La, Valse
    (Rossi) gtr (6th degr.) BERBEN
    EB2033 f.s.   (2491)

  Preludes, 2
    (Bream) gtr (9th degr.) FABER
    F-0310 f.s.
      contains: Fille Aux Cheveux De
      Lin, La (from Preludes, Ier
      Livre, No. 8); Minstrels (from
      Preludes, Ier Livre, No. 12)
                                  (2492)

  Prima Arabesca
    (Parodi) gtr RICORDI-ARG BA-10271
    f.s.   (2493)

DVORAK, ANTONIN (1841-1904)
  Danza Slava *Op.72,No.2
    (Abloniz) gtr (6th degr.) BERBEN
    EB2077 f.s.   (2494)

FERRER, JOSE (1835-1916)
  Danse Des Naiades, La *Op.35
    gtr (3rd degr.) BERBEN EB1636 $1.00
                                  (2495)

FODEN, WILLIAM (1860-1947)
  Short Preludes, 6 (Chord
    Progressions)
    (Papas) gtr COLUMBIA 159 $.75
                                  (2496)

FRANCK, CESAR (1822-1890)
  Plaintes d'Une Poupee, Les
    (Alfonso) gtr (6-7th degr., orig
    pcs + arr; Edition Nicolas
    Alfonso, No. 1) SCHOTT-FRER 9120
    f.s. contains also: Saint Luc,
    Jacques de, Suite in E   (2497)

  Short Pieces, 4
    (Segovia) gtr (7th degr.) SCHOTT
    GA-118 f.s.   (2498)

GRANADOS, ENRIQUE (1867-1916)
  Anoranza (from 6 Piezas Sobre Cantos
    Populares Espanoles, No. 1)
    (Azpiazu) gtr (8th degr.) UNION
    ESP. 21079-1 f.s.   (2499)

  Aparicion
    (Azpiazu) gtr UNION ESP. 21017 f.s.
                                  (2500)

  Campana De La Tarde, La (from
    Bocetos, No. 4)
    (Garcia Velasco) gtr (6th degr.)
    UNION ESP. 21010 f.s.   (2501)
    (Pujol) gtr (6th degr.) RICORDI-ARG
    BA-10831 f.s.   (2502)

  Cancion Arabe
    (Garcia Fortea) gtr (6th degr.)
    UNION ESP. 15486 f.s.   (2503)

  Capricho Espanol *Op.39
    (Garcia Velasco) gtr (9th degr.)
    UNION ESP. 20303 f.s.   (2504)

  Cartas De Amor, Valses Intimos
    *Op.44
    (Azpiazu) gtr UNION ESP. 21028 f.s.
                                  (2505)

GRANADOS, ENRIQUE (cont'd.)

  Danza Espanola, No. 5
    "Andaluza" (Abloniz) gtr (8th
    degr.) BERBEN EB1299 $1.00 (2506)
    "Andaluza" (Fortea) gtr (8th degr.)
    FORTEA 73   (2507)
    "Andaluza" (Llobet) gtr (8th degr.)
    RICORDI-ARG BA-11809   (2508)
    "Andaluza" (Llobet) gtr (8th degr.)
    SALABERT 16279   (2509)
    "Andaluza" (Llobet) gtr (8th degr.)
    UNION ESP. 15611   (2510)
    "Andaluza" (Llobet) gtr (8th degr.)
    SPAN.MUS.CTR. GE-154   (2511)
    "Andaluza" (Sinopoli) gtr (8th
    degr.) RICORDI-ARG BA-7374 (2512)

  Danza Espanola, No. 6
    "Rondalla Aragonesa" (Angel) gtr
    (9th degr.) UNION ESP. 18928 f.s.
                                  (2513)
    "Rondalla Aragonesa" (Garcia
    Fortea) gtr (9th degr.) SALABERT
    16258 f.s.   (2514)
    "Rondalla Aragonesa" (Garcia
    Fortea) gtr (9th degr.) UNION
    ESP. 15680 f.s.   (2515)

  Danza Espanola, No. 7
    "Valenciana" (Garcia Fortea) gtr
    (8th degr.) SALABERT 16259 f.s.
                                  (2516)
    "Valenciana" (Garcia Fortea) gtr
    (8th degr.) UNION ESP. 15681 f.s.
                                  (2517)
    "Valenciana" (Llobet) gtr (8th
    degr.) UNION ESP. 21316 f.s.
                                  (2518)

  Danza Espanola, No. 10
    "Melancolica" (Fortea) gtr (9-10th
    degr.) FORTEA 74 f.s.   (2519)
    "Melancolica" (Garcia Fortea) gtr
    (A maj,9-10th degr.) SALABERT
    16260 f.s.   (2520)
    "Melancolica" (Garcia Fortea) gtr
    (A maj,9-10th degr.) UNION ESP.
    15682 f.s.   (2521)
    "Melancolica" (Llobet) gtr (G maj,
    9-10th degr.) SPAN.MUS.CTR.
    GE-248 f.s.   (2522)
    "Melancolica" (Llobet) gtr UNION
    ESP. 20383 f.s.   (2523)
    "Melancolica" (Sinopoli) gtr
    RICORDI-ARG BA-7375 f.s.   (2524)

  Danza Lenta
    (Azpiazu) gtr (7th degr.) UNION
    ESP. 21029 f.s.   (2525)

  Danzas Espanolas, Nos. 1-12
    (Azpiazu) gtr (8-9th degr.) UNION
    ESP. 19801 f.s.   (2526)

  Dedicatoria (from Cuentos De La
    Juventud, Op. 1)
    (Llobet) gtr (5th degr.)
    SPAN.MUS.CTR. GE-153 f.s. (2527)
    (Llobet) gtr (5th degr.) UNION ESP.
    20925 f.s.   (2528)

  Despertar Del Cazador, Albada (from
    Bocetos, No. 1)
    (Azpiazu) gtr (6th degr.) UNION
    ESP. 21032 f.s.   (2529)

  Ecos De La Parranda (from 6 Piezas
    Sobre Cantos Populares Espanoles,
    No. 2)
    (Azpiazu) gtr (E maj,8th degr.)
    UNION ESP. 21079-2 f.s.   (2530)
    (Garcia Fortea) gtr (A maj,8th
    degr.) SALABERT 16261 f.s. (2531)
    (Garcia Fortea) gtr (A maj,8th
    degr.) UNION ESP. 15483 f.s.
                                  (2532)

  Hada Y El Nino, El (from Bocetos, No.
    2)
    (Azpiazu) gtr (7th degr.) UNION
    ESP. 21030 f.s.   (2533)

  Intermezzo (from Goyescas)
    (Azpiazu) gtr (8-9th degr.) UNION
    ESP. 21042 f.s.   (2534)

  Marcha Oriental (from 6 Piezas Sobre
    Cantos Populares Espanoles, No.
    4)
    (Azpiazu) gtr (7-8th degr.) UNION
    ESP. 21079-4 f.s.   (2535)

  Maya De Goya, La, Tonadilla
    (Llobet) gtr (9th degr.) RICORDI-
    ARG BA-11810 f.s.   (2536)
    (Llobet) gtr (9th degr.)
    SPAN.MUS.CTR. GE-246 f.s. (2537)
    (Llobet) gtr (9th degr.) UNION ESP.
    19435 f.s.   (2538)

  Preludio (from 6 Piezas Sobre Cantos
    Populares Espanoles, Preludio)
    (Azpiazu) gtr (8th degr.) UNION
    ESP. 21079-P f.s.   (2539)

GRANADOS, ENRIQUE (cont'd.)

  Two Spanish Dances
    gtr COLUMBIA 203 f.s.   (2540)

  Vals Muy Lento (from Bocetos, No. 3)
    (Azpiazu) gtr (7th degr.) UNION
    ESP. 21031 f.s.   (2541)

  Vascongada (from 6 Piezas Sobre
    Cantos Populares Espanolas, No.
    3)
    (Azpiazu) gtr (9-10th degr.) UNION
    ESP. 21079-3 f.s.   (2542)

  Zambra (from 6 Piezas Sobre Cantos
    Populares Espanoles, No. 5)
    (Azpiazu) gtr (8th degr.) UNION
    ESP. 21079-5 f.s.   (2543)

  Zapateado (from 6 Piezas Sobre Cantos
    Populares Espanoles, No. 6)
    (Azpiazu) gtr (8th degr.) UNION
    ESP. 21079-6 f.s.   (2544)

GRIEG, EDVARD HAGERUP (1843-1907)
  Aase's Death *Op.46,No.2 (from Peer
    Gynt)
    "Muerte De Ase, La" (Bertin) gtr
    RICORDI-ARG BA-8794 f.s.   (2545)
    "Mort d'Ass, La" (Tarrega; Fortea)
    gtr FORTEA 240 f.s.   (2546)

  Anitra's Dance *Op.46,No.3 (from
    Peer Gynt)
    "Danza De Anitra" (Sagreras) gtr
    RICORDI-ARG BA-11827 f.s.   (2547)

  Ensom Vandrer (Lonely Wanderer)
    *Op.43,No.2 (from Lyriske
    Stykker, Op.43)
    "Viajero Solitario" (Sagreras) gtr
    RICORDI-ARG RF-7095 f.s.   (2548)
    "Viajero Solitario" (Tarrega;
    Fortea) gtr FORTEA 239 f.s.
                                  (2549)

  Folkvise (Folksong) *Op.38,No.2
    (from Lyriske Stykker, Book II)
    "Canto Del Campesino" (Segovia) gtr
    (also published in:
    Transcripciones Para Guitarra,
    No. 3) UNION ESP. 18037 f.s.
                                  (2550)

  Grieg-Buch, Das *CC32U
    (Schwarz-Reiflingen) gtr SIKORSKI
    579 $6.50   (2551)

  Lyric Pieces, 3 (from Lyriske
    Stykker, Op. 12)
    (Bream) gtr (7th degr.) FABER
    F-0124 f.s.
      contains: Aelfedans, "Fairy
      Dance", Op.12,No.4;
      Vaegtersang, "Watchman's Song",
      Op.12,No.3; Waltz, Op. 12, No.
      2   (2552)

  Melodia Norvega
    (Llobet) gtr UNION ESP. 20382 f.s.
                                  (2553)

  Melodie *Op.38,No.3 (from Lyriske
    Stykker, Op.38)
    "Melody" (Segovia) gtr (also
    published in: Andres Segovia
    Album) COLUMBIA 129 $1.00 (2554)

  Saraband (from Holberg's Suite)
    (Gjertsen) gtr ESSEX f.s.   (2555)

  Solveig's Song *Op.55,No.4 (from
    Peer Gynt)
    "Chanson De Solveig" (Azpiazu, L.
    de) gtr (5th degr., Guitare,
    No.19) LEDUC G-19 f.s.   (2556)

  Waltz, Op. 12, No. 2 (from Lyriske
    Stykker, Op.12)
    (Anido) gtr RICORDI-ARG BA-12085
    f.s.   (2557)

KLASSISCHE MELODIEN
    (Tucholski) 1-2gtr APOLLO 2319 f.s.
                                  (2558)

MALATS, JOACHIN (1872-1912)
  Impresiones De Espana, Danza
    (Garcia Fortea) gtr (6th degr.)
    SALABERT 16271 f.s.   (2559)
    (Garcia Fortea) gtr (6th degr.)
    UNION ESP. 15484 f.s.   (2560)

  Serenata Andaluza
    (Bertin) gtr RICORDI-ARG BA-10424
    f.s.   (2561)

  Serenata Espanola
    (Abloniz) gtr (7th degr.) BERBEN
    EB1391 $1.00   (2562)
    (Azpiazu) gtr (9th degr.) RICORDI-
    ARG BA-12198   (2563)
    (Tarrega; Sinopoli) gtr (9th degr.)
    RICORDI-ARG BA-11352   (2564)

MARIE, GABRIEL (1852-1928)
Cinquantaine, La, Aria Nello Stile
Antico
(Abloniz) gtr (4-5th degr.) BERBEN
EB1879 f.s.   (2565)

MUSSORGSKY, MODEST PETROVICH
(1839-1881)
Viejo Castillo, El (from Cuadros De
Una Exposicion)
(Balaguer) gtr UNION ESP. 20934
f.s.   (2566)

NEVIN, ETHELBERT WOODBRIDGE (1862-1901)
Narcissus
(Abloniz) gtr (4th degr.) BERBEN
EB1473 $1.00   (2567)

PADEREWSKI, IGNACE JAN (1860-1941)
Minue Celebre °Op.14,No.1
(Sinopoli) gtr RICORDI-ARG BA-11397
f.s.   (2568)

PEDRELL, CARLOS (1841-1922)
Al Atardecer En Los Jardines De
Arlaja
(Pujol) gtr (8th degr.) RICORDI-ARG
RF-7695 f.s.   (2569)

Danzas De Las Tres Princesas
Cautivas, No. 1
"Zoraida" (Pujol) gtr (8th degr.)
RICORDI-ARG BA-12045 f.s. (2570)

Danzas De Las Tres Princesas
Cautivas, No. 2
"Dona Mencia" (Pujol) gtr (8th
degr.) RICORDI-ARG RF-7693 f.s.
(2571)

Danzas De Las Tres Princesas
Cautivas, No. 3
"Betsabe" (Pujol) gtr (8th degr.)
RICORDI-ARG RF-7694 f.s.   (2572)

Impromptu
(Pujol) gtr (8-9th degr.) RICORDI-
ARG RF-7697 f.s.   (2573)

Pieces, 3, No. 1
"Lamento" (Segovia) gtr (5-7th
degr.) SCHOTT GA-119 f.s. (2574)

Pieces, 3, No. 2
"Pagina Romantica" (Segovia) gtr
(5-7th degr.) SCHOTT GA-120 f.s.
(2575)

Pieces, 3, No. 3
"Guitarreo" (Segovia) gtr (5-7th
degr.) SCHOTT GA-121 f.s. (2576)

RACHMANINOFF, SERGEY VASSILIEVICH
(1873-1943)
Prelude, Op. 3, No. 2
(Rossi) gtr (6th degr.) BERBEN
EB2034 f.s.   (2577)

REGER, MAX (1873-1916)
Gavotte (from Suite No. 2, Op. 131,
For Violoncello)
(Abloniz) gtr (6-7th degr.) BERBEN
EB1989 f.s.   (2578)

RIMSKY-KORSAKOV, NIKOLAI (1844-1908)
Chanson Hindoue (from Sadko)
(Azpiazu) gtr (7th degr., Guitare
Selection, No. 2) DELRIEU 1273
f.s.   (2579)

RUBINSTEIN, ANTON (1829-1894)
Romance, MIN 339
(Fortea) gtr FORTEA 117   (2580)
(Llobet) gtr UNION ESP. 20873 f.s.
(2581)

SAINT-SAENS, CAMILLE (1835-1921)
Cygne, Le (from Carnaval Des Animaux)
(Mornac) gtr (7th degr.) DURAND
13968 $1.50   (2582)

SCRIABIN, ALEXANDER (1872-1915)
Prelude No. 4
(Segovia) gtr CEL 8 $.60   (2583)

SHAND, ERNEST (1868-1924)
Solos, 6
(Avila) gtr (4-5th degr.) SCHOTT
GA-26 f.s.
contains: Andante; Chant Du Soir;
Gavotte Rococo; Pensieroso;
Prelude Et Impromptu; Valse
Legere   (2584)

SPANYOL TANC, 2; 2 SPANISH DANCES
(Garcia Velasco) gtr (7th degr.) EMB
Z-7020 f.s.
contains: Albeniz, Isaac, Danza
Espanola, No. 1; Granados,
Enrique, Danza Espanola, No. 6,
"Rondalla Aragonesa"   (2585)

TARREGA, FRANCISCO (1852-1909)
Adelita, Mazurka
gtr (4th degr.) ESSEX f.s.   (2586)
gtr (4th degr.) UNION ESP. 18295
f.s.   (2587)
gtr (4th degr.) RICORDI-ARG BA-7839
f.s.   (2588)

TARREGA, FRANCISCO (cont'd.)
gtr (4th degr.) SPAN.MUS.CTR.
GE-187 f.s. contains also:
Prelude, TI i- 17, in E,
"Lagrima"   (2589)
(Abloniz) gtr (4th degr.) BERBEN
EB1147 $1.00 contains also:
Prelude, TI i- 17, in E,
"Lagrima"   (2590)

Alborada, Cajita De Musica
"Music Box, The" gtr (7th degr.)
FORTEA 24 f.s.   (2591)
"Music Box, The" gtr (7th degr.)
ESSEX f.s.   (2592)
"Music Box, The" (Savio) gtr (7th
degr.) RICORDI-ARG BA-7923 f.s.
(2593)

Album, No. 1
(Tarrega, hijo) gtr (4-9th degr.)
UNION ESP. f.s. arr + orig pcs
contains: Danza Mora; Gran Jota
Da Concierto; Prelude, TI i-
17, in E, "Lagrima"; Study, TI
ii- 18, in A   (2594)

Album, No. 2
(Tarrega, hijo) gtr (4-9th degr.)
UNION ESP. f.s. arr + orig pcs
contains: Alborado, Dos
Hermanitas, Las; Pavan, MIN
142; Study, TI ii- 19, in A,
"Allegro Brillante Para
Concierto"   (2595)

Album, No. 3
(Tarrega, hijo) gtr (4-9th degr.)
UNION ESP. f.s. arr + orig pcs
contains: Danza Odalisca;
Prelude, TI i- 16, in D minor,
"En Decha"; Prelude, TI i- 18,
in D minor, "Oremus"; Study, TI
ii- 4a, in A, "Estudio En
Arpegios"; Sueno; Waltz in A   (2596)

Album, No. 4
(Tarrega, hijo) gtr (4-9th degr.)
UNION ESP. f.s. arr + orig pcs
contains: Malaguena Facil;
Paquito; Prelude, TI i- 10, in
D; Prelude, TI i- 11, in D;
Study, TI ii- 15, in A minor
(2597)

Album, No. 5
(Tarrega, hijo) gtr (4-9th degr.)
UNION ESP. f.s. arr + orig pcs
contains: Cartagenera, La;
Prelude, TI i- 25, in A,
"Preludio No. 12, Tii-12";
Study, TI ii- 1; Study, TI ii-
20, in D, "Estudio Inspirado En
Cramer"   (2598)

Album, No. 6
(Tarrega, hijo) gtr (4-9th degr.)
UNION ESP. f.s. arr + orig pcs;
includes transcr of work by P.
Albeniz (1)
contains: Pavan, MIN 143; Pepita;
Study, TI ii- 11, in E,
"Estudio Sobre Una Jiga De J.S.
Bach"   (2599)

Album, No. 7
(Tarrega, hijo) gtr (4-9th degr.)
UNION ESP. f.s. arr + orig pcs
contains: Prelude, TI i- 11, in
D, "Preludio, No.14"; Prelude,
TI i- 13, in A minor; Prelude,
TI i- 15, in C, "Preludio In C,
Ti i-15 [20 Bars]"; Study, TI
ii- 7b, in D; Tango; Waltz in D
(2600)

Album, No. 17 °CC2L
(Tarrega, hijo) gtr (4-9th degr.)
UNION ESP. f.s. arr + orig pcs;
contains transcr of works by:
Gottschalk-Tarrega; TI-Ii-25,
Chopin   (2601)

Album, No. 19 °CC2L
(Tarrega, hijo) gtr (4-9th degr.)
UNION ESP. f.s. arr + orig pcs;
contains transcr of works by
Benedictus and Grieg   (2602)

Album, No. 20 °CC2L
(Tarrega, hijo) gtr (4-9th degr.)
UNION ESP. f.s. arr + orig pcs;
contains transcr of works by
Wagner   (2603)

Album, Vol. III
(Fortea, Daniel) gtr (4-7th degr.)
FORTEA 192 f.s.
contains: Adelita, Mazurka;
Pavan; Prelude; Sueno   (2604)

Capricho Arabe, Serenata
gtr (8-9th degr.) UNION ESP. 18146
(2605)
gtr (8-9th degr.) FORTEA 189   (2606)
(Abloniz) gtr (8-9th degr.) BERBEN
EB1205 $1.00   (2607)
(Bream) gtr (8-9th degr.) ESSEX

TARREGA, FRANCISCO (cont'd.)
(2608)
(Erdmann) gtr (8-9th degr.)
HEINRICH. N-3338   (2609)
(Gascon) gtr (8-9th degr.) RICORDI-
ARG BA-12073   (2610)
(Navascues) gtr (8-9th degr.) BRUCK
BG-T1-4   (2611)
(Sinopoli) gtr (8-9th degr.,
version facilitada) RICORDI-ARG
BA-8418   (2612)

Composiciones Originales Y Estudios
Para Guitarra, Vol. I
(Bianqui Pinero) gtr (6-9th degr.)
RICORDI-ARG B-16.564 f.s. 10 pcs
contains: Study, TI ii- 9, in A
minor, "Recuerdos De La
Alhambra"   (2613)

Composiciones Originales Y Estudios
Para Guitarra, Vol. II
(Bianqui Pinero) gtr (6-9th degr.)
RICORDI-ARG B-16.565 f.s. 10 pcs
contains: Study, TI ii- 7a, in D,
"Columpio, El"; Study, TI ii-
8, in A, "Sueno"   (2614)

Composiciones Originales Y Estudios
Para Guitarra, Vol. III: 30
Preludios Originales
(Bianqui Pinero) gtr (6-9th degr.)
RICORDI-ARG C-16.563 f.s.
contains: F. Tarrega, Preludes,
TI-i-1-13, 15, 16(14 bars), 17-
24; Studies, TI-ii-4b(20 bars),
29, 30b, 32, 35, 36   (2615)

Composiciones Originales Y Estudios
Para Guitarra, Vol. III: 30
Preludios Originales
(Bianqui Pinero) gtr (6-9th degr.)
RICORDI-ARG BA-12720 f.s.
contains: F. Tarrega, Preludes,
TI-i-1-13, 15, 16(14 bars), 17-
24; Studies, TI-ii-4b(20 bars),
29, 30b, 32, 35, 36   (2616)

Composiciones Originales Y Estudios
Para Guitarra, Vol. IV
(Bianqui Pinero) gtr (6-9th degr.)
RICORDI-ARG B-16.566 f.s.
contains: Exercise, TI iii- 20,
in G; Exercise, TI iii- 24, in
E minor; Exercise, TI iii- 29;
Exercise, TI iii- 30a, in E;
Exercise, TI iii- 32; Study, TI
ii- 2a, in A; Study, TI ii- 5,
in A; Study, TI ii- 6, in D,
"Mariposa, La"; Study, TI ii-
10, in D minor; Study, TI ii-
11, in E; Study, TI ii- 12, in
E; Study, TI ii- 14, in D
minor; Study, TI ii- 15, in A
minor; Study, TI ii- 16a, in B
minor; Study, TI ii- 18, in A;
Study, TI ii- 19, in A; Study,
TI ii- 20; Study, TI ii- 22   (2617)

Composiciones Para Guitarra, 12
(Savio, Isaias) gtr (4-9th degr.)
RICORDI-ARG BA-11248 f.s. 12 pcs
contains: Prelude, TI i- 17, in
E, "Lagrima"; Study, TI ii- 8,
in A, "Sueno"; Study, TI ii- 9,
in A minor, "Recuerdos De La
Alhambra"   (2618)

Danza Mora
gtr (6th degr.) FORTEA 203   (2619)
gtr (6th degr.) ESSEX   (2620)
(Ricchi) gtr (6th degr.) BERBEN
EB1460 $1.00   (2621)
(Savio) gtr (6th degr.) RICORDI-ARG
BA-9900   (2622)

Danza Odalisca
gtr FORTEA 197 f.s.   (2623)
(Gascon) gtr RICORDI-ARG 12074 f.s.
(2624)

Guitarra Espanola: 12 Spanische
Stucke
(Helsing) gtr (4-7th degr.) MARBOT
f.s. 12 pcs
contains: Prelude, TI i- 11, in
D; Prelude, TI i- 12, in A
minor; Prelude, TI i- 13, in A
minor; Prelude, TI i- 15, in C
(20 bars); Prelude, TI i- 25,
in A; Study, TI ii- 7b, in D,
"Columpio, El"; Study, TI ii-
20, in D   (2625)

Kompositionen Fur Gitarre, Vol. I
(Schwarz-Reiflingen) gtr (4-9th
degr.) SIKORSKI 685A $7.25 19 pcs
contains: Prelude, TI i- 1, in D
minor; Prelude, TI i- 2, in A
minor; Prelude, TI i- 3, in G;
Prelude, TI i- 4, in E;
Prelude, TI i- 5, in E;
Prelude, TI i- 16, in D minor,
"Endecha"; Prelude, TI i- 18,
in D minor; Study, TI ii- 8, in
A; Study, TI ii- 9, in A minor;

TARREGA, FRANCISCO (cont'd.)

Study, TI ii- 11, in E; Study,
TI ii- 15, in A minor; Study,
TI ii- 16a, in B minor; Study,
TI ii- 19, in A   (2626)

Kompositionen Fur Gitarre, Vol. II
(Schwarz-Reiflingen) gtr (4-9th
degr.) SIKORSKI 865B $7.25 18 pcs
contains: Gran Jota De Concierto;
Prelude, TI i- 8b, in A;
Prelude, TI i- 15, in C;
Prelude, TI i- 19, in E minor;
Prelude, TI i- 23, in B minor;
Study, TI ii- 4b, in A; Study,
TI ii- 6, in D, "Mariposa, La";
Study, TI ii- 12, in E,
"Suspiro d'Amor"; Study, TI ii-
29, in A minor; Study, TI ii-
36, in A   (2627)

Maria, Gavota
gtr FORTEA 196 f.s.   (2628)
gtr RICORDI-ARG BA-9068 f.s. (2629)
gtr UNION ESP. 19036 f.s.   (2630)
(Fortea) gtr FORTEA 210 f.s. (2631)
(Sensier) gtr ESSEX f.s.   (2632)

Marieta, Mazurka
gtr (5th degr.) ESSEX f.s. (2633)
(Azpiazu, L. de) gtr (5th degr.,
Guitare, No.27) LEDUC G-27 f.s.
                            (2634)
(Gascon) gtr (5th degr.) RICORDI-
ARG BA-12075 f.s.   (2635)
(Navascues) gtr (4-5th degr.) BRUCK
BG-T1-2 f.s. contains also:
Adelita, Mazurka   (2636)

Mazurka, MIN 372
(Sensier) gtr ESSEX f.s.   (2637)

Mazurky, 2
(Urban, Stepan) gtr (3-4th degr.)
CZECH H-3641 f.s. Kytarova Sola,
No.10
contains: Mazurka; Prelude, TI i-
17, in E, "Lagrima"   (2638)

Opere Per Chitarra, Vol. I: Preludi
*CC39L
(Gangi; Carfagna) gtr (4-9th degr.)
BERBEN EB1531 $4.50 includes:
Preludes, TI-i-1-11, 13-24;
Studies, TI-ii-2b, 4b(20 bars),
16A, 29, 32, 34-36, 42;
Exercises, TI- iii- 8, 30b, 33
(14 bars); Sor, Andante-Thema,
from Fantaisie, Op. 7, [arr.];
Chopin, Prelude, Op. 28, No. 11,
[arr.]; Mendelssohn-Bartholdy,
Canzonetta In E Flat, Op. 12,
[arr.]   (2639)

Opere Per Chitarra, Vol. II: Studi
*CC34L
(Gangi; Carfagna) gtr (4-9th degr.)
BERBEN EB1532 $5.25 includes:
Prelude, TI-i-12; Studies, TI-ii-
1, 2, 3, 5, 6, 8-11, 12(41 bars)
18(48 bars), 19, 20, 22, 30, 31,
33(7 bars), 37-41; Exercises, TI-
iii-3, 20, 22-24, 29, 30a, 31, 32
                            (2640)

Opere Per Chitarra, Vol. III:
Composizioni Originali
(Gangi; Carfagna) gtr (4-9th degr.)
BERBEN EB1533 $7.75 20 pcs
contains: Gran Jota De Concierto;
Study, TI ii- 7b, in D,
"Columpio, El"   (2641)

Opere Per Chitarra, Vol. IV:
Trascrizioni
(Gangi; Carfagna) gtr (4-9th degr.)
BERBEN f.s.   (2642)

Pavan, MIN 145
(Behrend) gtr ZIMMER. f.s. (2643)
(Savio) gtr RICORDI-ARG BA-11392
f.s.   (2644)

Pavan, MIN 146
(Navascues, Santiago) gtr BRUCK
BG-T1-1 f.s. contains also:
Prelude, TI i- 17, in E,
"Lagrima"   (2645)

Pezzi Brillanti, 3
(Abloniz) gtr (5-6th degr.) BERBEN
EB1249 $1.00
contains: Mazurka; Polka; Study,
TI ii- 3, in E, "Estudio De
Velocidad"   (2646)

Prelude, TI i- 17, in E
"Lagrima" (Azpiazu) gtr (4-5th
degr.) SYMPHON 2084 f.s. contains
also: Adelita, Mazurka; Pavan,
MIN 144   (2647)
"Lagrima" (Papas) gtr (4-5th degr.)
COLUMBIA 143 $1.25 contains also:
Adelita, Mazurka   (2648)

TARREGA, FRANCISCO (cont'd.)

Rosita, Polka
gtr FORTEA 194 f.s. contains also:
Marieta, Mazurka; Mazurka in G
                            (2649)
gtr (4-5th degr., reprs of early
eds) SPAN.MUS.CTR. GE-265 f.s.
contains also: Prelude, TI i- 16,
in D minor, "Endecha"; Prelude,
TI i- 18, in D minor, "Oremus"
                            (2650)
(Gascon) gtr RICORDI-ARG BA-12076
f.s.   (2651)
(Sensier) gtr ESSEX f.s.   (2652)

Tarrega-Album, Eine Sammlung Der
Bekanntesten Original-Werke
(Walker, Luise) gtr (4-9th degr.)
HEINRICH. VH-1548 f.s. 21 pcs
contains: Prelude, TI i- 1, in D
minor; Prelude, TI i- 2, in A
minor; Prelude, TI i- 3, in G;
Prelude, TI i- 4, in E;
Prelude, TI i- 5, in E;
Prelude, TI i- 16, in D minor,
"Endecha"; Prelude, TI i- 17,
in E, "Lagrima"; Prelude, TI i-
18, in D minor, "Oremus";
Study, TI ii- 5, in A, "Estudio
En Forma De Un Minuetto";
Study, TI ii- 6, in D,
"Mariposa, La"; Study, TI ii-
8, in A, "Sueno"; Study, TI ii-
9, in A minor, "Recuerdos De La
Alhambra"   (2653)

Utwory Wybrane
(Powrozniak, Jozef) gtr (6-8th
degr.) POLSKIE 7337 f.s. 23 pcs;
Klasycy Gitary;
contains: Prelude, TI i- 1, in D
minor; Prelude, TI i- 2, in A
minor; Prelude, TI i- 6, in B
minor; Prelude, TI i- 7, in A;
Prelude, TI i- 12, in A minor;
Prelude, TI i- 16, in D minor,
"Endecha"; Prelude, TI i- 18,
in D minor, "Oremus"; Study, TI
ii- 3, in A; Study, TI ii- 4b,
in A; Study, TI ii- 5, in A;
Study, TI ii- 19, in A; Study,
TI ii- 29, in A minor   (2654)

Vyber Skladeb, Selected Compositions,
Vol. I
(Tichota, Jiri) gtr (4-9th degr.)
SUPRAPHON AP-1730 f.s. Kytarova
Sola, No.4
contains: Prelude, TI i- 16, in D
minor, "Endecha"; Prelude, TI
i- 18, in D minor, "Oremus";
Study, TI ii- 6, in D,
"Mariposa, La"; Study, TI ii-
8, in A, "Sueno"; Study, TI ii-
19, in A   (2655)

Vyber Skladeb, Selected Compositions,
Vol. II
(Tichota, Jiri) gtr (4-9th degr.)
SUPRAPHON AP f.s. 8 pcs; Kytarova
Sola, No.5; Contains Works By:
Verdi, Chopin, Schumann, J.S.
Bach, Chueca, Mendelssohn, W.A.
Mozart, Albeniz
contains: Study, TI ii- 11, in E
                            (2656)

TCHAIKOVSKY, PIOTR ILYICH (1840-1893)
Andante Cantabile
(Fortea) gtr FORTEA 236 f.s. (2657)

Chanson Triste *Op.40,No.2 (from 12
Pieces Of Moderate Difficulty)
"Cancion Triste" (Davis) gtr
RICORDI-ARG BA-11452 f.s.   (2658)
"Cancao Triste" (Savio) gtr
RICORDI-BR BR-153 f.s.   (2659)

Chant Sans Paroles *Op.2,No.3 (from
Souvenir De Hapsal)
"Cancion Sin Palabras" (Rodriguez
Arenas) gtr RICORDI-ARG BA-5084
f.s.   (2660)

In Church *Op.39,No.24 (from
Children's Album)
"Nella Chiesa Russa" (Galindo;
Abloniz) gtr (3rd degr.) BERBEN
EB1115 $1.00   (2661)

Mazurka, MIN 373
(Bream) gtr ESSEX f.s.   (2662)

Mazurka, Op. 39, No. 10 (from
Children's Album)
(Terzi) gtr RICORDI-IT 129292 f.s.
                            (2663)

None But The Lonely Heart *Op.6,No.6
"Solo El Que Sabe Amar" (Lara) gtr
RICORDI-ARG BA-12698 f.s.   (2664)

Old French Air *Op.39,No.16 (from
Children's Album)
"Antigua Cancion Francesa" (Lara)
gtr (4th degr.) RICORDI-ARG
BA-12459 f.s. contains also:

TCHAIKOVSKY, PIOTR ILYICH (cont'd.)

March Of The Wooden Soldiers,
"Marcha De Los Soldaditos De
Madera", Op.39,No.5   (2665)

Pieces, 6 (from Children's Album, Op.
39)
(Duarte) gtr (3-4th degr.) NOVELLO
19607 f.s.
contains: In Church, Op.39,No.4;
Mazurka, Op.39,No.10; Morning
Prayer, Op.39,No.1; New Doll,
The, Op.39,No.9; Old French
Air, Op.39,No.16; Russian Song,
Op.39,No.11   (2666)

Piezas, 6 (from Children's Corner,
Op. 39)
(Galindo) gtr (3-4th degr.) UNION
ESP. 20827 f.s.
contains: German Air, "Cancion
Alemana", Op.39,No.17; Mama,
"Mama, La", Op.39,No.4; March
Of The Wooden Soldiers, "Marcha
De Soldados", Op.39,No.5;
Mazurka, Op. 39, No. 10; New
Doll, The, "Muneca Nueva, La",
Op.39,No.9; Old French Air,
"Antigua Cancion Francesa",
Op.39,No.16   (2667)

Sick Doll, The *Op.39,No.6 (from
Children's Album)
"Manana De Invierno" (Lara) gtr
(4th degr.) RICORDI-ARG BA-12516
f.s. contains also: Russian Song,
"Cancion Rusa", Op.39,No.11
                            (2668)

Song Without Words
(Segovia) gtr (A min) CEL 26 $.75
                            (2669)

Tema Dal Balletto (from Swan Lake,
Op. 20)
(Putilin; Abloniz) gtr (4th degr.)
BERBEN EB1084 $1.00   (2670)

Valse Des Fleurs (from The
Nutcracker, Op. 71)
"Vals De Las Flores" (Casuscelli)
gtr RICORDI-ARG BA-11716 f.s.
                            (2671)
"Valsa Das Flores" (Nunes) gtr
RICORDI-BR BR-1036 f.s.   (2672)

TOSELLI, ENRICO (1883-1926)
Celebre Serenata *Op.6
(Azpiazu) gtr (7th degr., Guitare
Selection, No. 4) DELRIEU 1271
f.s.   (2673)

VALVERDE, JOAQUIN (1846-1910)
Clavelitos, Zambra Gitana
(Llobet) gtr (8th degr.) UNION ESP.
20384 f.s.   (2674)
(Maravilla) gtr (8th degr.) UNION
ESP. 18719 f.s.   (2675)

I/IB3-Coll   Guitar Solo Collections: Romantic and Post-Romantic Music (1850-1914)

MEINE ERSTEN GITARRENSTUCKE, VOL.4:
"MEISTER DER ROMANTIK" *CCU
(Teuchert) gtr (1-3rd degr.) SYMPHON
2202 f.s.   (2676)

6 SPANISCHE STUCKE
(Scheit) gtr (3-4th degr.) UNIVER.
16698 f.s.
contains: Tarrega, Francisco,
Prelude, TI i- 17, in E,
"Lagrima"   (2677)

SPANYOL GITARMUZSIKA – GUITAR MUSIC
FROM SPAIN
(Garcia Velasco) gtr (8-9th degr.)
EMB 7818 f.s.
contains: Albeniz, Isaac, Asturias;
Albeniz, Isaac, Cadiz; Granados,
Enrique, Danza Espanola No. 6;
Granados, Enrique, Danza Espanola
No. 10   (2678)

TARREGA, FRANCISCO (1852-1909)
Album, No. 8 *CC4L
(Tarrega, hijo) gtr (4-9th degr.)
UNION ESP. f.s. arr + orig pcs;
contains transcr of works by:
Schubert, Mendelssohn, Schumann,
Chopin   (2679)

Album, No. 10 *CC3L
(Tarrega, hijo) gtr (4-9th degr.)
UNION ESP. f.s. arr + orig pcs;
contains transcr of works by:
Arditi, Henselt-Tarrega (Study

TARREGA, FRANCISCO (cont'd.)

TI-Ii-12, "Suspiro De Amore"),
Chopin   (2680)

Album, No. 11 *CC3L
(Tarrega, hijo) gtr (4-9th degr.)
UNION ESP. f.s. arr + orig pcs;
contains transcr of works by:
Rubinstein, Chopin, Schumann
(2681)

Album, Vol. I
(Fortea, Daniel) gtr (4-7th degr.)
FORTEA 190 f.s.
contains: Prelude, TI i- 17, in
E, "Lagrima"   (2682)

Album, Vol. II: Seis [Sic] Preludios
(Fortea, Daniel) gtr (4-7th degr.)
FORTEA 191 f.s.
contains: Prelude, TI i- 1, in D
minor; Prelude, TI i- 2, in A
minor; Prelude, TI i- 3, in G;
Prelude, TI i- 4, in E;
Prelude, TI i- 5, in E;
Prelude, TI i- 7, in A;
Prelude, TI i- 16, in D minor,
"Endecha"; Prelude, TI i- 18,
in D minor, "Oremus"   (2683)

I/IB4   Guitar Solos: Music of the Twentieth Century (1914 to present)

ABLONIZ, MIGUEL (1917-   )
Blues For Rosy
gtr (4th degr.) BERBEN EB2049 f.s.
(2684)

Capriccio Flamenco, Sul Tema Popolare
"El Vito"
gtr (3rd degr.) BERBEN EB1817 $1.25
(2685)

Improvvisazione, Omaggio A Villa-
Lobos
gtr (6th degr.) RICORDI-IT
RM-129346 f.s.   (2686)

Partita in E
gtr (4th degr.) RICORDI-IT
RM-129876 f.s.   (2687)

Pequena Romanza
gtr (3-4th degr.) BERBEN EB1008
$1.00   (2688)

Pezzi Ricreativi (E Di Utilita
Tecnica), Nello Stile Polifonico,
4
gtr (4th degr.) RICORDI-IT 129648
f.s.
contains: Moderato, MIN145;
Moderato, MIN146; Moderato,
MIN147; Quasi Allegro   (2689)

Sequential
gtr (4th degr.) BERBEN EB1854 $1.00
(2690)

Tarantella Burlesca And Bossa Nova
gtr (5th degr.) BERBEN EB1770 $1.25
(2691)

ABSIL, JEAN (1893-1974)
Petit Bestiaire, Op. 151
(Alfonso, I.) gtr (5-6th degr.,
Collezione Di Musiche Per
Chitarra; 3 pcs.) BERBEN EB1711
$2.50   (2692)

Pieces, 4, Op.150
(Gilardino) gtr (8-9th degr.,
Collezione Di Musiche Per
Chitarra) BERBEN EB1871 $4.25
(2693)

Pieces, 10
(Alfonso) gtr (5th degr.) LEMOINE
$5.00   (2694)

Pieces, 12, Vol. I: Nos. 1-4 *Op.159
gtr (4-7th degr., Edition Nicolas
Alfonso, No. 109-110) SCHOTT-FRER
f.s.   (2695)

Pieces, 12, Vol II: Nos. 5-8 *Op.159
gtr (4-7th degr., Edition Nicolas
Alfonso, No. 111-112) SCHOTT-FRER
f.s.   (2696)

Pieces, 12, Vol. III: Nos. 9-12
*Op.159
gtr (4-7th degr., Edition Nicolas
Alfonso, No. 113-114) SCHOTT-FRER
f.s.   (2697)

Prelude Et Barcarolle
gtr (4th degr., Musica Nova, 1973)
SCHOTT-FRER 9279 f.s.   (2698)

ABSIL, JEAN (cont'd.)
Suite, Op. 114
gtr LEMOINE f.s.   (2699)

Sur Un Paravent Chinois, 4 Esquisses,
Op. 147
(Gilardino) gtr (9th degr.) BERBEN
EB1564 $3.50 Collezione Di
Musiche Per Chitarra
contains: Barcarolle, MIN 148;
Gigue, MIN 150; Romance, MIN
149; Scherzetto   (2700)

AGUIRRE, JULIAN (1868-1924)
Aire Criollo No. 1
(Anido) gtr (4-5th degr.) RICORDI-
ARG BA-11190 f.s.   (2701)

Aire Criollo No. 3
(Anido) gtr (5th degr.) RICORDI-ARG
BA-11191 f.s.   (2702)

Canciones No. 1, 2 y 3
(Gomez Crespo) gtr (6-7th degr.,
from op. 36, Aires Nacionales
Argentinos) RICORDI-ARG BA-7218
f.s.   (2703)

Triste No. 4
(Segovia) gtr (4th degr.) RICORDI-
ARG BA-11415 f.s.   (2704)
(Sinopoli) gtr (4th degr.) RICORDI-
ARG BA-11256 f.s.   (2705)

Tristes 1, 2 y 5
(Gomez Crespo) gtr (4-5th degr.,
from op. 17, Aires Nacionales
Argentinos) RICORDI-ARG BA-7219
f.s.   (2706)

AHSLUND, ULF-G.
Den Gula Rosen
(Ahslund) gtr (3rd degr.) REUTER
f.s.   (2707)

Hosten (Suite No. 4)
gtr (3rd degr.) REUTER f.s.   (2708)

Rytmico
(Ahslund) gtr (3rd degr.) REUTER
f.s.   (2709)

Suite No. 3
gtr (3rd degr.) REUTER f.s.   (2710)

ALFONSO, NICOLAS
Cantilene
gtr (2nd degr., Musica Nova, 1969)
SCHOTT-FRER 9222 f.s. contains
also: Rondoletto   (2711)

Ya Van Los Pastores
"Pastorale" gtr (6th degr., Edition
Nicolas Alfonso, No. 102; arr. +
orig. pcs.) SCHOTT-FRER 9168 f.s.
contains also: Foliada; Ballade
(2712)

ALTISSIMI, FRANCO
Giochi d'Acqua
gtr (4th degr.) BERBEN EB1676 $1.25
(2713)

AMBROSIUS, HERMANN (1897- ?)
Impressionen
(Gilardino) gtr (4-5th degr.)
BERBEN EB1422 $1.75 Collezione Di
Musiche Per Chitarra
contains: Exotischer Tanz;
Melancholie; Neckerei; Traum;
Ubermut   (2714)

Prelude
(Behrend) gtr (4-5th degr.) SIRIUS
f.s.   (2715)

ANGEL, MIGUEL
Cuatro Muleros, Los, Tema Y
Variaciones
gtr (8-9th degr.) SALABERT 16272
f.s.   (2716)
gtr (8-9th degr.) UNION ESP. 18705
f.s.   (2717)

Homenaje A Schoenberg, 6 Preludios,
Op. 24
gtr (6-8th degr.) UNION ESP. 20205
f.s.   (2718)

ANTIGA, JEAN
Tarraja, 24 Petites Pieces
(Azpiazu) gtr (1-3rd degr.) DELRIEU
1291 f.s.
contains: Cancion De Navidad,
"Noel Des Petits Bretons"   (2719)

ANTUNES, JORGE (1942-   )
Sighs
gtr ZIMMER. 1975 f.s.   (2720)

APIVOR, DENIS (1916-   )
Discanti, Op. 48
(Gilardino) gtr (9-10th degr.,
5pcs; Collezione Di Musiche Per
Chitarra) BERBEN EB1498 $2.25
(2721)

APIVOR, DENIS (cont'd.)
Saeta, Op. 53
(Gilardino) gtr (8th degr.,
Collezione Di Musiche Per
Chitarra) BERBEN EB1982 $2.25
(2722)

Variations for Guitar, Op. 29
gtr (8-9th degr.) SCHOTT GA-205
f.s.   (2723)

APOSTEL, HANS ERICH (1901-1972)
Musiken, 6 *Op.25
(Scheit) gtr (8-10th degr.) UNIVER.
13605 $3.25
contains: Fantasie, Die; Melodie,
Die; Rhythmus, Der; Sechsklang,
Der; Ton E, Der; Ton E, Der
(2724)

ARNELL, RICHARD (1917-   )
Pieces, 6
gtr (6-7th degr.) PEER 2047-5 $1.25
(2725)

ARNOLD, MALCOLM (1921-   )
Fantasy for Guitar, Op. 107
(Bream) gtr FABER F-0440 f.s.
(2726)

ARRIGO, GIROLAMO (1930-   )
Serenade
gtr (9-10th degr.) HEUGEL 31760
$4.25   (2727)

ASENCIO, VICENTE (1897-   )
Dipso, 3 Piezas Evangeliques, No. 1
(Gilardino) gtr (7-8th degr.,
Collezione Di Musiche Per
Chitarra) BERBEN EB1983 $1.75
(2728)

Elegy
(Alfonso) gtr (6-7th degr., Edition
Nicolas Alfonso, No. 103) SCHOTT-
FRER 9165 f.s. contains also:
Sonatina   (2729)

Suite Valenciana
(Gilardino) gtr (7-8th degr.,
Collezione Di Musiche Per
Chitarra) BERBEN EB1766 $4.50
(2730)

Tango De La Casada Infidel
(Alfonso) gtr (8th degr., Edition
Nicolas Alfonso, No. 104) SCHOTT-
FRER 9166 f.s.   (2731)

ASRIEL, ANDRE (1922-   )
Baroque In Blue: Suite
(Pauli) gtr (5th degr.) HOFMEISTER
T-4159 f.s.   (2732)

AUBANEL, GEORGES
Bergerettes
gtr (2nd degr.) OUVRIERS EO-586
f.s.   (2733)

AUBIN, TONY (1907-   )
Hidalgoyas
gtr (8-9th degr.) LEDUC f.s. (2734)

AZPIAZU, JOSE DE (1912-   )
Homenaje A Los Vihuelistas *CC7U
gtr (6-7th degr.) UNION ESP. f.s.
(2735)

Hommage A Bela Bartok
gtr (7th degr.) SYMPHON 2066 f.s.
(2736)

Joven Guitarrista, El, Vol.1: Muy
Facil
gtr (3rd degr.) UNION ESP. 20875
f.s.
contains: Caballeritos De
Azcoitia; Capri; Grinzing;
Salon De Artazcoz; Tuna, La;
Zaranz   (2737)

Joven Guitarrista, El, Vol.2: Facil
gtr (4th degr.) UNION ESP. 20876
f.s.
contains: Anguila, La; Baile En
La Aldea; Columpio, El;
Dialogando; Paseando; Riberena
(2738)

Joven Guitarrista, El, Vol.3: Menos
Facil
gtr (5th degr.) UNION ESP. 20877
f.s.
contains: Cancion Lejana;
Castellana; Clavecin De Zelaia;
Rondino; Tic-Tac Del Reloj, El;
Travesura   (2739)

Joven Guitarrista, El, Vol.4: Mediana
Dificultad
gtr (6th degr.) UNION ESP. 20878
f.s.
contains: Danza De La Muneca;
Fandango De Onate; Girasol, El;
Interludio; Tiento; Tonada   (2740)

Miniaturas Iberiques, 5
gtr (3-5th degr.) SYMPHON 2089 f.s.
(2741)

Pieces Faciles, Premier Cahier
*CC10U
gtr (3-4th degr.) LEDUC $5.00
(2742)

BACARISSE, SALVADOR (1898-1963)
  Ballade
    (Alfonso) gtr (Edition Nicolas
    Alfonso, No. 107) SCHOTT-FRER
    f.s.   (2743)

  Petite Suite
    (Alfonso) gtr (Edition Nicolas
    Alfonso, No. 108) SCHOTT-FRER
    f.s.   (2744)

BACHMANN, HELMUT
  Adagio
    gtr (5th degr.) HEINRICH. N-1649
    f.s. contains also: Minuet, MIN
    151   (2745)

  Air
    gtr (4th degr.) HEINRICH. N-1652
    f.s. contains also: Gavotte, MIN
    152   (2746)

  Altdeutscher Tanz
    gtr (3rd degr.) HEINRICH. N-1647
    f.s.   (2747)

  Andante, MIN 153
    gtr (3rd degr.) HEINRICH. N-1650
    f.s.   (2748)

  Andante, MIN 154
    gtr (3rd degr.) HEINRICH. N-1648
    f.s. contains also: Gigue   (2749)

  Andante Religioso
    gtr (4th degr.) HEINRICH. N-1651
    f.s. contains also: Gavotte, MIN
    155   (2750)

  Gavotte, MIN 156
    gtr (3rd degr.) HEINRICH. N-1660
    f.s. contains also: Widmung   (2751)

  Minuet, MIN 157
    gtr (3-4th degr.) HEINRICH. N-1643
    f.s.   (2752)

  Pastorale
    gtr (3rd degr.) HEINRICH. N-1665
    f.s.   (2753)

  Prelude
    gtr (4th degr.) HEINRICH. N-1645
    f.s.   (2754)

  Prelude in A minor
    gtr (3rd degr.) HEINRICH. N-1644
    f.s.   (2755)

  Prelude in D minor
    gtr (3rd degr.) HEINRICH. N-1642
    f.s.   (2756)

  Serenade
    gtr (3rd degr.) HEINRICH. N-1659
    f.s. contains also: Saraband   (2757)

BADINGS, HENK (1907-1987)
  Preludes, 12, Vol.1, No.1-6
    (Gilardino) gtr (8-10th degr.,
    Collezione Di Musiche Per
    Chitarra) BERBEN EB1641 $3.25
                                  (2758)

  Preludes, 12, Vol.2, No.7-12
    (Gilardino) gtr (8-10th degr.,
    Collezione Di Musiche Per
    Chitarra) BERBEN EB1642 $3.25
                                  (2759)

BAERVOETS, RAYMOND (1930-   )
  Improvisation
    (Alfonso) gtr (8th degr.)
    METROPOLIS EM-4684 $2.50   (2760)

BALADA, LEONARDO (1933-   )
  Lento With Variation
    gtr COLUMBIA 206 f.s.   (2761)

  Suite
    gtr COLUMBIA 190 f.s.   (2762)

BALLIF, CLAUDE (1924-   )
  Solfeggietto, No. 6 *Op.36
    gtr TRANSAT. f.s.   (2763)

BARBIER, RENE (AUGUSTE-ERNEST)
    (1890-1981)
  Prelude
    gtr (4th degr., Musica Nova, 1974)
    SCHOTT-FRER 9292 f.s. contains
    also: Barcarolle, Op. 119 (2764)

BARBIERI, MARIO
  Serra, La, 7 Preludi
    (Orsolino) gtr (6-7th degr.) BERBEN
    EB1125 $2.25   (2765)

BARLOW, FRED (1881-1951)
  Flute D'argent, La
    (Cotta) gtr (2nd degr.) LEMOINE
    24075 $4.25
    contains: Berceuse Pour Un Soir
    De Neige; Calme Au Village;
    Petit Source, La; Petite Fille
    Parle Au Bon Dieu, Une; Petite
    Valse-Confidence; Plainte De La
    Feuille d'Automne   (2766)

BARRIOS MANGORE, AUGUSTIN
  Catedral, La
    (Diaz) gtr (7th degr., Las Seis
    Cuerdas) ZANIBON 5311 f.s. (2767)

  Choro Da Saudade
    (Cimma) gtr (7th degr.) BERBEN
    EB1394 $1.75   (2768)

  Danza Paraguaya
    gtr (8th degr.) GUARANI f.s. (2769)
    (Diaz) gtr (8th degr., Las Seis
    Cuerdas) ZANIBON 5296 f.s. (2770)

  Medallon Antiguo, Omaggio A Pergolesi
    (Diaz) gtr (5th degr., Las Seis
    Cuerdas) ZANIBON 5315 f.s. (2771)

  Oracion
    (Diaz) gtr (5-6th degr., Las Seis
    Cuerdas) ZANIBON 5263 f.s. (2772)

BARTOK, BELA (1881-1945)
  Fur Kinder
    "For Children" (Brodzsky) gtr (3rd
    degr., 25 pcs.) EMB Z-5038 f.s.
                                  (2773)
  Gyermekeknek - Fur Kinder *CC60U
    (Szendrey-Karper) gtr (2-5th degr.)
    EMB 7495 f.s.   (2774)

  Gyermekeknek, Vol. 1, No. 1-25
    (Brodzsky) gtr (2-4th degr., for
    children) EMB Z-5790 f.s.   (2775)

  Gyermekeknek, Vol. 2, No.26-50
    (Brodzsky) gtr (2-4th degr., for
    children) EMB Z-6349 f.s.   (2776)

BARTOLI, RENE
  Aubade
    gtr ESCHIG f.s.   (2777)

  Waltz in E minor
    gtr ESCHIG f.s.   (2778)

BARTOLOZZI, BRUNO (1911-   )
  Adles
    gtr (8-9th degr.) ZERBONI 8403 f.s.
                                  (2779)
  Omaggio A Gaetano Azzolina
    gtr (8th degr.) ZERBONI 7242 $3.50
                                  (2780)
  Pezzi Per Chitarra, 3
    (Company) gtr (8-10th degr.) BRUZZI
    f.s.
    contains: Marcetta; Prelude;
    Saraband   (2781)

BARTSCH, CHARLES
  Introduction Et Danse
    (Gonzales Mohino) gtr (6th degr.)
    METROPOLIS EM-4714 $2.00   (2782)

BATTISTI D'AMARIO, BRUNO
  Preludi, 2
    gtr (6-7th degr.) ZANIBON 5346 f.s.
                                  (2783)

BAUMANN, HERBERT (1925-   )
  Fantasie, Uber "Es Geht Ein Dunkle
    Wolk Herein"
    (Behrend) gtr (7th degr., Gitarre-
    Bibliothek, No.67) BOTE GB-67
    f.s.   (2784)

  Toccata, Elegia E Danza
    (Gilardino) gtr (8th degr.,
    Collezione Di Musiche Per
    Chitarra) BERBEN EB1465 $2.25 (2785)

BAUR, JURG (1918-   )
  Fantasien, 3
    gtr (8-9th degr.) BREITKOPF-W
    EB-6441 f.s.   (2786)

BAUSEWEIN, HERBERT
  Strebsame Guitarrist, Der, Vol. 1, 14
    Leichte Spielstucke
    gtr (1-2nd degr., Suppl. 1 To Max
    Kierner, Guitar Playing Made Easy
    (Preissler) JP-7001) PREISSLER
    JP-7007   (2787)

BAUTISTA, JULIAN (1901-1961)
  Preludio Y Danza
    (Sainz de la Maza) gtr (8th degr.)
    UNION ESP. 16953 f.s.   (2788)

BECKER, GUNTHER (1924-   )
  Metathesis
    gtr (9-10th degr.) ZIMMER. 1725
    f.s.   (2789)

BEDFORD, DAVID (1937-   )
  You Asked For It, For Acoustic Guitar
    Solo
    gtr (8-9th degr.) UNIVER. 15353
    $3.25   (2790)

BEHREND, SIEGFRIED (1933-   )
  Fantasia A Sei Corde
    gtr (7th degr., Gitarre-Bibliothek,
    No.60) BOTE GB-60 f.s.   (2791)

BEHREND, SIEGFRIED (cont'd.)
  Fantasia Malaguenita
    gtr HANSEN-DEN f.s.   (2792)

  Granadina De La Rambla
    gtr HANSEN-DEN f.s.   (2793)

  Kolometrie
    mand,gtr (8th degr.) ZIMMER. 1805
    f.s. contains also: ZU-MA-GT-TON
    II (mand,gtr)   (2794)

  Monodien, 6
    gtr (graphic score) ZIMMER. 1907
    f.s.   (2795)

  Movimenti
    gtr (8-9th degr.) UNIVER. 14896
    $2.75   (2796)

  Non Te Escaparas, Capriccio Nach
    Francesco De Goya
    gtr (7th degr., Gitarre-Bibliothek,
    No.10) BOTE GB-10 f.s.   (2797)

  Pezzi Per Jim, 2
    gtr (6th degr., Gitarre-Bibliothek,
    No.49; also published in European
    Masters For The Guitar) BOTE
    GB-49 f.s.   (2798)

  Porque Fue Sensible, Capriccio Nach
    Francesco De Goya
    gtr (8-9th degr., Gitarre-
    Bibliothek, No.9) BOTE GB-9 f.s.
                                  (2799)

  Postkarten Suite *CC7U
    gtr ZIMMER. 1896 f.s.   (2800)

  Sonatine, Nach Japanischen
    Volksliedern
    gtr (3rd degr., Die Konzertgitarre)
    SIKORSKI 696 $2.75   (2801)

  Stucke, 2
    gtr (4th degr.) HEINRICH. N-1624
    f.s.   (2802)

  Suite Fur Isao Takahashi
    gtr (5th degr., Gitarre-Bibliothek,
    No.61) BOTE GB-61 f.s.   (2803)

  Suite Nach Alter Lautenmusik *CC3U
    gtr (6-7th degr.) BOTE GB-1 f.s.
    Gitarre-Bibliothek, No.1   (2804)

  Zorongo Para Murao
    gtr HANSEN-DEN f.s.   (2805)

BELASCO, LIONEL
  Juliana
    "Juliana, Valzer Venezuelano"
    (Diaz, Alirio) gtr (5-6th degr.,
    Las Seis Cuerdas) ZANIBON 5396
    f.s.   (2806)

BELASCO, M.
  Juliana
    "Juliana, Antilliaanse Wals" (Coco,
    Julian) gtr (5-6th degr.)
    BROEKMANS 737 f.s.   (2807)

BELLOW, ALEXANDER (1922-1976)
  Cavatina
    gtr (4th degr.) COLOMBO NY-2233
    f.s.   (2808)

  Diversions, 5
    gtr (7th degr.) COLOMBO NY-2019
    f.s.
    contains: Allegro; Allegro
    Moderato; Largo; Moderato,
    MIN158; Moderato, MIN159   (2809)

  Prelude And Rondo
    gtr (5th degr.) COLOMBO NY-2070
    f.s.   (2810)

  Short Pieces, 4
    gtr (3-4th degr.) COLOMBO NY-2448
    f.s.
    contains: Bolero; Etude In
    Harmonics; Etude Oriental;
    Prelude   (2811)

  Suite Miniature
    gtr (3rd degr.) COLOMBO NY-2122
    f.s.   (2812)

  Suite Provencale
    gtr (5-6th degr.) COLOMBO NY-2375
    f.s.   (2813)

BENGUEREL, XAVIER (1931-   )
  Versus
    gtr ZIMMER. ZM-1909 f.s.   (2814)

BENNETT, RICHARD RODNEY (1936-   )
  Impromptus *CC5U
    (Bream) gtr (8th degr.) UNIVER.
    14433L $3.25   (2815)

BERGMAN, ERIK (1911–   )
  Suite for Guitar, Op. 32
    gtr (8–9th degr.) FAZER 3365 f.s.
                                    (2816)
BERKELEY, [SIR] LENNOX (1903–   )
  Theme and Variations
    (Gilardino) gtr (7–8th degr.,
    Collezione Di Musiche Per
    Chitarra) BERBEN EB1643 $2.75
                                    (2817)
BETTINELLI, BRUNO (1913–   )
  Improvisation
    (Gilardino) gtr (7th degr.,
    Collezione Di Musiche Per
    Chitarra) BERBEN EB1469 $1.25
                                    (2818)
  Pezzi, 4
    (Gilardino) gtr (7th degr.) BERBEN
    EB1811 $4.00 Collezione Di
    Musiche Per Chitarra
    contains: Introduzione; Notturno;
    Ritmico; Toccata   (2819)
  Preludes, 5
    (Chiesa) gtr (3–4th degr.) ZANIBON
    5222 f.s.   (2820)
BEVEREN, ACHIEL VAN
  Suite, Op. 46
    gtr (5–6th degr.) METROPOLIS
    EM-4682 $4.00   (2821)
BIBERIAN, GILBERT E.
  Prelude and Fugue
    gtr (7th degr.) NOVELLO 19733 $2.35
                                    (2822)
BINGE, RONALD (1910–   )
  Alzbetinska Serenada
    "Elizabethan Serenade" (Sisley,
    Bartos) gtr (7th degr., Kytarova
    Sola, No.15) CZECH H-4006 f.s.
                                    (2823)
BIRTH, THOMAS (1912–   )
  Neue Gitarrenmusik *CC7U
    gtr (4th degr.) MODERN f.s. (2824)
BISCHOFF, HEINZ (1898–1963)
  Ballade
    gtr (4th degr.) BERBEN EB1834 $1.00
                                    (2825)
  Piccola Fuga
    gtr (3rd degr.) BERBEN EB1418 $1.00
                                    (2826)
BIZET, JEAN (1924–   )
  Spirale
    gtr (8th degr.) kbd pt TRANSAT.
    1161 $3.00   (2827)
  Triangles
    gtr (8–9th degr.) kbd pt TRANSAT.
    1107 $2.00   (2828)
BLYTON, CAREY (1932–   )
  Bream, The
    "Breme, La" gtr (8th degr.) ESCHIG
    ME-7900 f.s.   (2829)
  In Memoriam Django Reinhardt: 2
    Variations And A Theme For Guitar
    *Op.64a
    (Gilardino) gtr (7th degr.,
    Collezione Di Musiche Per
    Chitarra) BERBEN EB1712 $2.75
                                    (2830)
  In Memoriam Scott Fitzgerald *Op.60b
    (Gilardino) gtr (6th degr.,
    Collezione Di Musiche Per
    Chitarra) BERBEN EB1881 $1.25
                                    (2831)
  Saxe Blue *Op.65b
    (Gilardino) gtr (5–6th degr.,
    Collezione Di Musiche Per
    Chitarra) BERBEN EB2041 f.s.
                                    (2832)
BOBRI, VLADIMIR
  Very Easy Pieces, For Very, Very
    Beginners, Op.12 *CC23U
    gtr (1–3rd degr.) COLOMBO 2609 f.s.
                                    (2833)
BOCHMAN, THEO L.
  Torre Morisca, La
    gtr TEESELING VT-189 f.s.   (2834)
BODA, JOHN (1922–   )
  Introduction And Dance
    (Abril) gtr COLUMBIA 172 $1.50
                                    (2835)
BOER, JOHAN DE (1938–   )
  Grounds, 2
    gtr (3rd degr., on bass themes from
    "Dido And Aeneas" By Henry
    Purcell) TEESELING VT-34 f.s.
                                    (2836)
BOHR, HEINRICH
  Hirtentanz
    gtr (4th degr.) HEINRICH. N-1656
    f.s.   (2837)
  Klagende Lied, Das
    gtr (3rd degr.) HEINRICH. 1657 f.s.
                                    (2838)
BOIS, ROB DU (1934–   )
  Pastorale No. 4
    gtr (9th degr.) DONEMUS f.s. (2839)

BONDON, JACQUES (1927–   )
  Nocturne Nos. 1–3
    gtr ESCHIG f.s.   (2840)
  Swing No. 2
    gtr ESCHIG f.s.   (2841)
BONILLA CHAVEZ, CARLOS
  Elegia Y Danza
    (Jumez) gtr (7th degr.) ESCHIG 8211
    f.s.   (2842)
  Preludio Y Yumbo
    (Jumez) gtr (5–6th degr.) ESCHIG
    8212 f.s.   (2843)
BONNARD, ALAIN (1939–   )
  Chanson D'aube *Op.2
    (Castet) gtr (5th degr.) LEDUC
    24250 $2.75   (2844)
  Dancerie *Op.19
    (Castet) gtr (3rd degr.) LEDUC
    24249 $3.00   (2845)
BORGES, RAUL
  Prelude
    (Riera) gtr (6th degr.) SIKORSKI
    742 $2.25   (2846)
BORSODY, LASZLO
  Szin-Darabok – Color-Pieces *CC8U
    (Szendrey-Karper) gtr (4th degr.)
    EMB 7414 f.s.   (2847)
BOSCO, GILBERTO (1946–   )
  Rifrazioni
    gtr (8–9th degr.) ZERBONI 8348 f.s.
                                    (2848)
BOSMANS, ARTHUR (1908–   )
  Brasileiras, No.1
    "Ponteio" (van Puijenbroeck) gtr
    (7–8th degr.) METROPOLIS EM-14767
    $2.50   (2849)
  Brasileiras, No.2
    "Modinha" (van Puijenbroeck) gtr
    (7–8th degr.) METROPOLIS EM-14768
    $2.50   (2850)
  Brasileiras, No.3
    "Batukada" (van Puijenbroeck) gtr
    (7–8th degr.) METROPOLIS EM-14769
    $2.50   (2851)
  Brasileiras, No.4
    "Toada" (van Puijenbroeck) gtr (7–
    8th degr.) METROPOLIS EM-14770
    $2.50   (2852)
  Brasileiras, No. 5
    "Sorongo" (van Puijenbroeck) gtr
    (7–8th degr.) METROPOLIS EM-14771
    $2.50   (2853)
BOZZA, EUGENE (1905–   )
  Impressions Andalouses, 2
    gtr (7th degr.) LEDUC $4.00 (2854)
  Preludes, 3
    gtr (9–10th degr.) LEDUC $3.25
                                    (2855)
BRACALI, GIAN PAOLO (1941–   )
  Viajes
    (Ghiglia) gtr (9th degr.) ZERBONI
    7921 $11.75   (2856)
BRAUN, PEE MICHAEL
  Monophonie Fur Gitarre
    for Span gtr or ampl gtr (9th
    degr.) copy GERIG HG-593 f.s.
                                    (2857)
BREDENBEEK, HANS
  Canciones, 2
    (Noordpool) gtr (5th degr.)
    HARMONIA 2589 f.s.   (2858)
  Miniature Suite
    gtr (7th degr.) HARMONIA 2682 f.s.
                                    (2859)
  Trichordon-Dance
    gtr (6th degr.) HARMONIA 2576 f.s.
                                    (2860)
BREGUET, JACQUES
  Suite
    "Omaggio Al Liutisti Italiani" gtr
    (6th degr.) BERBEN EB1029 $1.00
                                    (2861)
BRESGEN, CESAR (1913–   )
  Malinconia *CC5U
    (Kovats) gtr (7th degr.) SCHOTT
    GA-238 f.s.   (2862)
BRIANO, GIOVANNI BATTISTA
  Fugue No. 3
    gtr (6th degr.) BERBEN EB605 $1.00
                                    (2863)
BRITTEN, [SIR] BENJAMIN (1913–1976)
  Nocturnal, After John Dowland *Op.70
    (Bream) gtr (9–10th degr.) FABER
    F0005 f.s.   (2864)

BROQUA, ALFONSO (1876–1946)
  Evocaciones Criollas, No.1
    "Ecos Del Paisage" (Pujol) gtr (4–
    9th degr.) ESCHIG 1209 f.s.
                                    (2865)
  Evocaciones Criollas, No.2
    "Vidala" (Pujol) gtr (4–9th degr.)
    ESCHIG 1210 f.s.   (2866)
  Evocaciones Criollas, No.3
    "Chacarera" (Pujol) gtr (4–9th
    degr.) ESCHIG 1211 f.s.   (2867)
  Evocaciones Criollas, No.4
    "Zamba Romantica" (Pujol) gtr (4–
    9th degr.) ESCHIG 1212 f.s.
                                    (2868)
  Evocaciones Criollas, No.5
    "Milongueos" (Llobet) gtr (4–9th
    degr.) ESCHIG 1213 f.s.   (2869)
  Evocaciones Criollas, No.6
    "Pampeana" (Pujol) gtr (4–9th
    degr.) ESCHIG 1214 f.s.   (2870)
  Evocaciones Criollas, No.7
    "Ritmos Camperos" (Llobet) gtr (4–
    9th degr.) ESCHIG 1215 f.s.
                                    (2871)
BROUWER, LEO (1939–   )
  Apuntes, 3
    "Sketches, 3" gtr (6–7th degr.)
    SCHOTT GA-426 f.s.   (2872)
  Canticum
    gtr (9th degr.) SCHOTT GA-424 f.s.
    contains: Ditirambo; Exclosion
                                    (2873)
  Danza Caracteristica, Para El
    "Quitate De La Arcera"
    gtr (8th degr.) SCHOTT GA-422 f.s.
                                    (2874)
  Elogio De La Danza *CC2U
    gtr (7–8th degr.) SCHOTT GA-425
    f.s.   (2875)
  Espiral Eterna, La
    gtr (7–8th degr.) SCHOTT GA-423
    f.s.   (2876)
  Espoiral Eterna Para Guitarra, La
    gtr SCHOTT GA-423 f.s.   (2877)
  Fugue
    gtr ESCHIG f.s.   (2878)
  Pieza Sin Titulo
    gtr ESCHIG f.s.   (2879)
  Prelude
    gtr ESCHIG f.s.   (2880)
BROWN, CHARLES
  Canzona
    gtr (3rd degr.) DELRIEU 1476 f.s.
                                    (2881)
BURGHAUSER, JARMIL (1921–   )
  Tesknice, Canti Dell'ansieta *CC5U
    (Gilardino) gtr (8–9th degr.)
    BERBEN EB1513 $4.25 Collezione Di
    Musiche Per Chitarra   (2882)
BUSCAROLI, REZIO
  Veglia Invernale, Racconto
    gtr (7th degr.) BERBEN EB1030 f.s.
                                    (2883)
CALLEJA, FRANCISCO
  Preludios, 3
    gtr (5th degr.) UNION ESP. 16629
    f.s.   (2884)
CAMERON, PEDRO BUENO
  Perspektivas
    gtr ZIMMER. 1976 f.s.   (2885)
CAMMAROTA, CARLO (1905–   )
  Acquarelli Napoletani
    (Diaz) gtr (7th degr.) ZANIBON 5262
    f.s.   (2886)
CANONICO, BENITO
  Aire De Joropo (composed with Lauro,
    Antonio)
    "Totumo De Guarenas, El" (Diaz) gtr
    (6–7th degr.) BROEKMANS 902 f.s.
                                    (2887)
CARRENO, INOCENTE
  Suite
    (Diaz) gtr (6th degr., Las Seis
    Cuerdas) ZANIBON 5487 f.s. (2888)
CASSEUS, FRANTZ GABRIEL (1921–   )
  Haitian Suite
    gtr (6th degr.) COLOMBO NY-1732
    f.s.   (2889)
  Pieces Caracteristiques, 2, Suite
    gtr COLOMBO NY-2190 f.s.   (2890)
CASTELLANOS, EVENCIO
  Evocacion
    (Diaz) gtr (6th degr./5–8th degr.,
    Las Seis Cuerdas) ZANIBON 5489
    f.s.   (2891)

CASTELLANOS, EVENCIO (cont'd.)

Homenaje
(Diaz) gtr (6th degr./5-8th degr.,
Las Seis Cuerdas) ZANIBON 5490
f.s.   (2892)

CASTELNUOVO-TEDESCO, MARIO (1895-1968)
Appunti, Preludi E Studi, Quaderno I:
Gli Intervalli *Op.210
(Chiesa) gtr ZERBONI 6725 $7.00
(2893)

Appunti, Preludi E Studi, Quaderno
II: I Ritmi, Parte I, Danze Del
600 E Del 700, No. 1-10 *Op.210
(Chiesa) gtr ZERBONI 6854 $7.00
(2894)

Appunti, Preludi E Studi, Quaderno
II: I Ritmi, Parte II, Danze
Dell' Ottocente, No. 11-16
*Op.210
(Chiesa) gtr ZERBONI 6978 $7.00
(2895)

Appunti, Preludi E Studi, Quaderno
II: I Ritmi, Parte III, Danze Del
Novecento, No. 17-22 *Op.210
(Chiesa) gtr ZERBONI 7286 $7.00
(2896)

Appunti, Preludi E Studi, Quaderno
III: Le Figurazione *Op.210
(Chiesa) gtr (Not finished as a
consequence of the early death of
the composer. Only 2 pcs. of a
series of 11 have been finished;
they are printed in Quaderno II,
Parte III, pp. 29-33) ZERBONI
f.s.   (2897)

Appunti, Preludi E Studi, Quaderno
IV: 6 Studi Seriali *Op.210
(Chiesa) gtr (Only sketches have
been left of nos. 1-3; they are
printed in Quaderno II, Parte
III, pp. 34-36) ZERBONI f.s.
(2898)

Aranci In Fiori
(Segovia) gtr RICORDI-IT 129346
f.s.   (2899)
"Naranjos En Flor" (Segovia) gtr
RICORDI-ARG BA-12544 f.s. (2900)

Aria Da Chiesa, Sul Nome Di Ruggero
Chiesa *Op.170,No.43 (from
Greeting Cards)
(Chiesa) gtr (7th degr.) BERBEN
EB1224 $1.00   (2901)

Ballatella, Sul Nome Di Christopher
Parkening *Op.170,No.34 (from
Greeting Cards)
(Tonazzi) gtr (7th degr.) BERBEN
EB661 $1.00   (2902)

Brasileira, Sul Nome Di Laurindo
Almeida *Op.170,No.44 (from
Greeting Cards)
(Almeida) gtr (8-9th degr.) BERBEN
EB1237 $1.00   (2903)

Cancion Argentina, Sul Nome Di
Ernesto Bitetti *Op.170,No.41
(from Greeting Cards)
(Bitetti) gtr (7th degr.) BERBEN
EB1185 $1.25   (2904)

Cancion Cubana, Sul Nome Di Hector
Garcia *Op.170,No.39 (from
Greeting Cards)
(Garcia) gtr (6-7th degr.) BERBEN
EB1174 $1.25   (2905)

Cancion Venezuelana, Sul Nome Di
Alirio Diaz *Op.170,Op.40
(Diaz) gtr (7th degr.) BERBEN
EB1186 f.s.   (2906)

Canto Delle Azorre, Sul Nome Di Enos
*Op.170,No.15 (from Greeting
Cards)
(Tonazzi) gtr (7th degr.) FORLIVESI
12339 f.s.   (2907)

Canzone Calabrese, Sul Nome Di Ernest
Calabria *Op.170,No.48 (from
Greeting Cards)
(Calabria) gtr (6th degr.) BERBEN
EB1230 $1.00   (2908)

Canzone Siciliana, Sul Nome Di Mario
Gangi *Op.170,No.33
(Gangi) gtr (7th degr.) BERBEN
EB1208 $1.00   (2909)

Capriccio Diabolico, Omaggio A
Paganini
(Segovia) gtr (10th degr.) RICORDI-
IT 124371 f.s.   (2910)

Caprichos De Goya, 24, Vol. 1, Nos.
1-6 *Op.195
(Gilardino) gtr (8-9th degr.,
Collezione Di Musiche Per
Chitarra) BERBEN EB1427 $5.25
(2911)

CASTELNUOVO-TEDESCO, MARIO (cont'd.)

Caprichos De Goya, 24, Vol. 2, Nos.
7-12 *Op.195
(Gilardino) gtr (8-9th degr.,
Collezione Di Musiche Per
Chitarra) BERBEN EB1428 $5.75
(2912)

Caprichos De Goya, 24, Vol. 3, Nos.
13-18 *Op.195
(Gilardino) gtr (8-9th degr.,
Collezione Di Musiche Per
Chitarra) BERBEN EB1429 $5.75
(2913)

Caprichos De Goya, 24, Vol. 4, Nos.
19-24 *Op.195
(Gilardino) gtr (8-9th degr.,
Collezione Di Musiche Per
Chitarra) BERBEN EB1430 $6.00
(2914)

Escarraman, A Suite Of Spanish Dances
From The XVIth Century (After
Cervantes) *Op.177,No.1
"Gallarda" (Ansetonius) gtr (8-9th
degr.) COLOMBO NY-1752 f.s.
(2915)
"Canario, El" (Behrend) gtr (8-9th
degr.) COLOMBO NY-1753 f.s.
(2916)
"Guarda Cuyda Dosa, La" (Behrend)
gtr (8-9th degr.) COLOMBO NY-1757
f.s.   (2917)
"Pesame Dello" (Behrend) gtr (8-9th
degr.) COLOMBO NY-1755 f.s.
(2918)
"Rey Don Alonso El Bueno, El"
(Behrend) gtr (8-9th degr.)
COLOMBO NY-1756 f.s.   (2919)
"Villano, El" (Behrend) gtr (8-9th
degr.) COLOMBO NY-1754 f.s.
(2920)

Estudio, Sul Nome Di Manuel Lopez
Ramos *Op.170,No.42 (from
Greeting Cards)
(Lopez Ramos) gtr (8th degr.)
BERBEN EB1187 $1.00   (2921)

Homage To Purcell, Fantasia Sul Nome
Di Ronald (1932-) E Henry (1659-
1695) Purcell *Op.170,No.38
(from Greeting Cards)
(Purcell) gtr (7-8th degr.) BERBEN
EB1188 $1.00   (2922)

Japanese Print, Sul Nome Di Jiro
Matsuda *Op.170,No.46 (from
Greeting Cards)
(Matsuda) gtr (7-8th degr.) BERBEN
EB1231 $1.00   (2923)

Ninna-Nanna, A Lullaby For Eugene
*Op.170,No.14 (from Greeting
Cards)
(Tonazzi) gtr (7th degr.) FORLIVESI
12338 f.s.   (2924)

Passacaglia, Omaggio A Roncalli
*Op.180
(Gilardino) gtr (8-9th degr.,
Collezione Di Musiche Per
Chitarra) BERBEN EB1452 $2.25
(2925)

Preludi Al Circeo, 3 *Op.194
(Caliendo) gtr (9th degr.) BERBEN
EB666 $1.50   (2926)

Preludi Mediterranei, 3 *Op.176
(Behrend) gtr (8-9th degr.)
FORLIVESI 12277 f.s.   (2927)

Preludio In Forma Di Habanera, Sul
Nome Di Bruno Tonazzi *Op.170,
No.7
(Tonazzi) gtr (7th degr.) FORLIVESI
12334 f.s.   (2928)

Romanza, Sul Nome Di Oscar Ghiglia
*Op.170,No.37 (from Greeting
Cards)
(Caliendo) gtr (6th degr.) BERBEN
EB664 $1.00   (2929)

Rondel, Uber Den Namen Siegfried
Behrend *Op.170,No.6 (from
Greeting Cards)
(Behrend) gtr (8th degr., Gitarre-
Bibliothek, No.26) BOTE GB-26
f.s.   (2930)

Rondo, Op. 129
(Segovia) gtr (9-10th degr.) SCHOTT
GA-168 f.s.   (2931)

Sarabande, Sul Nome Di Rey De La
Torre *Op.170,No.36 (from
Greeting Cards)
(Tonazzi) gtr (7th degr.) BERBEN
EB659 $1.00   (2932)

Suite, Op. 133
(Segovia) gtr (10th degr.) SCHOTT
GA-169 f.s.   (2933)

Tanka, Sul Nome Di Isao Takahashi
*Op.170,No.10 (from Greeting
Cards)

CASTELNUOVO-TEDESCO, MARIO (cont'd.)

(Tonazzi) gtr (6th degr.) BERBEN
EB660 $1.25   (2934)

Tarantella
(Segovia) gtr (9th degr.) RICORDI-
IT 124372 f.s.   (2935)

Tarantella Campana, Sul Nome Di
Eugene Di Novi *Op.170,No.50
(from Greeting Cards)
(Gilardino) gtr (8-9th degr.)
BERBEN EB1232 $1.00   (2936)

Tonadilla, Sur Le Nom De Andres
Segovia *Op.170,No.5 (from
Greeting Cards)
(Segovia) gtr (9th degr.) SCHOTT
GA-191 f.s.   (2937)

Variations A Travers Les Siecles
(Segovia) gtr (10th degr.) SCHOTT
GA-137 f.s.   (2938)

Variations Plaisantes, Sur Un Petit
Air Populaire, "J'ai Du Bon Tabac
(Gilardino) gtr (8-9th degr.,
Collezione Di Musiche Per
Chitarra) BERBEN EB1351 $2.75
(2939)

Volo d'Angeli, Sul Nome Di Angelo
Gilardino *Op.170,No.47 (from
Greeting Cards)
(Gilardino) gtr (6-7th degr.)
BERBEN EB1223 $1.00   (2940)

CAVAZZOLI, GERMANO
Preludi, 2
gtr (4th degr.) BERBEN EB1779 $1.25
(2941)

CERF, JACQUES (1932-)
Nuances *Op.52
gtr FRANCAIS f.s.   (2942)

Pieces Sur 6 Cordes, 5 *Op.65
gtr FRANCAIS f.s.   (2943)

Suite Enfantine *Op.47, CC17U
gtr (2-4th degr.) PAN 1707 f.s.
(2944)

CHAILLY, LUCIANO (1920-)
Invenzione, Su Quattro Note
(Gilardino) gtr (7th degr.,
Collezione Di Musiche Per
Chitarra) BERBEN EB1714 $1.75
(2945)

CHAVARRI, EDUARDO LOPEZ (1871-1970)
Piezas, 7
gtr (4-7th degr.) SCHOTT GA-101
f.s.   (2946)

CHAVEZ, CARLOS (1899-1978)
Pieces, 3
gtr BELWIN $2.00   (2947)

CHIEREGHIN, SERGIO (1933-)
Chanson Jouees, 3
(Muggia) gtr (3-4th degr.) ZANIBON
5425 f.s.   (2948)

CIURLO, ERNESTO FAUSTO
Aria
gtr (6th degr.) BERBEN EB1405 $1.00
(2949)

Barcarolle
gtr (4-5th degr.) BERBEN EB1695
$1.25   (2950)

Moerens Incedebam, Mattutino
gtr (6-7th degr.) BERBEN EB1292
$1.00   (2951)

Sotto La Pioggia
gtr (3rd degr.) BERBEN EB2028 f.s.
(2952)

COELHO SILVESTRE, LOURIVAL PINTO
Estilhacos
gtr ZIMMER. 1977 f.s.   (2953)

COMPANY, ALVARO
Seis Cuerdas, Las
gtr (10th degr.) ZERBONI 6304
$11.75   (2954)

CONSTANT, FRANZ (1910-)
Humoresque
gtr ESCHIG f.s.   (2955)

Nocturne
gtr ESCHIG f.s.   (2956)

Poem
gtr ESCHIG f.s.   (2957)

Pour La Guitare, Vol. 1 *Op.34, CC3U
gtr (5-7th degr.) METROPOLIS
EM-4691 $3.00   (2958)

Pour La Guitare, Vol. 2 *Op.36, CC3U
gtr (5-7th degr.) METROPOLIS
EM-4692 $3.00   (2959)

CORDERO, ERNESTO (1946-   )
Mapeye, Canto Di Puerto Rico
(Diaz) gtr (7th degr., Las Seis
Cuerdas) ZANIBON 5488 f.s.   (2960)

CORGHI, AZIO (1937-   )
Consonancias Y Redobles
for 1 or more gtr and opt tape
recorder (after Luys Milan's
Fantasia XVI) sc ZERBONI 7654
$7.00   (2961)

CORREGGIA, ENRICO
Trasparenze
(Gilardino) gtr (7th degr.,
Collezione Di Musiche Per
Chitarra) BERBEN EB2023 f.s.
                              (2962)

CRUZ DE CASTRO, CARLOS
Algo Para Guitarra
gtr ALPUERTO 1116 f.s.   (2963)

CZERNIK, WILLY (1904-   )
Kurzweilige Stucke, 10
gtr (2-3rd degr.) PREISSLER 7038
f.s.   (2964)

CZERNUSCHKA, FRITZ
Prelude in E minor
gtr (3rd degr.) HEINRICH. N-1654
f.s. contains also: Capriccio
                              (2965)

DAGOSTO, SYLVAIN
Petit Guitariste, Le
gtr (1st degr., Collection
Longjumeau-Essonnes) TRANSAT.
1014 $1.25   (2966)

Romance in E
gtr (3rd degr., Collection
Longjumeau-Essonnes) TRANSAT.
1039 $1.50   (2967)

DANDELOT, GEORGES (1895-1975)
Pieces, 2
gtr ESCHIG f.s.   (2968)

DE FILIPPI, AMEDEO (1900-   )
Chant Et Tarentelle
gtr (8-9th degr.) ESCHIG 7250 f.s.
                              (2969)

Gaillarde, Pavane, Et Toccata
gtr (8-9th degr.) ESCHIG 7251 f.s.
                              (2970)

Jardins De Vauxhall *CC5U
gtr (7-8th degr.) ESCHIG 7253 f.s.
                              (2971)

Preludes, 12
gtr (8-9th degr.) ESCHIG 7252 f.s.
                              (2972)

DECADT, JAN (1914-   )
Pavan
gtr (6th degr.) METROPOLIS EM-4696
$2.00   (2973)

DEFOSSEZ, RENE (1905-   )
Allegretto Et Gavotte
gtr (2nd degr., Musica Nova, 1971)
SCHOTT-FRER 9247 f.s.   (2974)

Theme Et 3 Variations
gtr (6th degr.) CBDM $5.00   (2975)

DEGNI, VINCENZO (1911-   )
Prelude
gtr RICORDI-IT 131740 f.s.   (2976)

DELAUNEY, PAUL
Petit Gitan, Le
gtr (4th degr.) TRANSAT. 918 $1.25
                              (2977)

Prelude in D
(le Blason) gtr (4th degr.)
TRANSAT. 916 $1.50   (2978)

Toccatina
gtr (3rd degr.) TRANSAT. 917 $1.25
                              (2979)

DENHOFF, MICHAEL (1955-   )
Quinterna Fur Gitarresolo
(Kappel) gtr GERIG HG-1289 f.s.
                              (2980)

DESDERI, ETTORE (1892-1974)
Serenata
gtr (8th degr.) BERBEN EB1035 $1.50
contains also: Improvviso;
Tarantella   (2981)

Toccata And Fugue
(Gilardino) gtr (8th degr.,
Collezione Di Musiche Per
Chitarra) BERBEN EB1984 $2.25
                              (2982)

DIANA, ANTOINE
Petits Morceaux Pour Les Debutants,
12
gtr ESCHIG f.s.   (2983)

DIECKMANN, CARL HEINZ
Musik Fur Gitarre Solo *CC3U
gtr (4th degr.) HOFMEISTER T-4139
$1.25   (2984)

DIGMELOFF, GERMAIN
Caprice Georgien
gtr ESCHIG f.s.   (2985)

Pieces Faciles *CC10U
gtr ESCHIG f.s.   (2986)

DJEMIL, ENYSS (1917-   )
Caprice, Complainte Et Ronde
gtr (8-9th degr.) LEDUC $3.25
                              (2987)

DODGSON, STEPHEN (1924-   )
Fantasy-Divisions
(Williams) gtr (9-10th degr.,
Collezione Di Musiche Per
Chitarra) BERBEN EB1715 $2.75
                              (2988)

Partita
(Williams) gtr (9-10th degr.)
OXFORD 36.004 $2.45   (2989)

DOERR, CHARLES-KIKO
Fantasy
gtr (3-6th degr.) ESCHIG 7617 f.s.
from OEUVRES DE CHARLES-KIKO
DOERR   (2990)

Gavotte in E
gtr (3-6th degr.) ESCHIG 7621 f.s.
from OEUVRES DE CHARLES-KIKO
DOERR   (2991)

Gavotte in E minor
gtr (3-6th degr.) ESCHIG 7615 f.s.
from OEUVRES DE CHARLES-KIKO
DOERR   (2992)

Minuet, MIN 160
gtr (3-6th degr.) ESCHIG 7616 f.s.
from OEUVRES DE CHARLES-KIKO
DOERR   (2993)

Nocturne in A minor
"Nocturne En La Mineur" gtr (3-6th
degr.) ESCHIG 7614 f.s. from
OEUVRES DE CHARLES-KIKO DOERR
                              (2994)

Petite Valse
gtr (3-6th degr.) ESCHIG 7619 f.s.
from OEUVRES DE CHARLES-KIKO
DOERR   (2995)

Quartes Et Sixtes
gtr (3-6th degr.) ESCHIG 7620 f.s.
from OEUVRES DE CHARLES-KIKO
DOERR   (2996)

DONATONI, FRANCO (1927-   )
Algo, 2 Pezzi Per Chitarra
(Chiesa) gtr (9th degr.) ZERBONI
8376 f.s.   (2997)

DORLEIJN, GILLES J.
Prelude
(de Boer) gtr (5th degr.) HARMONIA
1806 f.s.   (2998)

DRESENS, GUUS
Meringue
gtr (3rd degr.) TEESELING VT-1 f.s.
contains also: Danse; Mioche;
Songeur   (2999)

DRIGO, RICCARDO (1846-1930)
Serenade (from Les Millions
D'Arlequin)
(Garcia Velasco) gtr (8-9th degr.)
ZIMMER. ZM-1780 f.s.   (3000)

Valse Bluette (from 4 Airs De Ballet)
(Garcia Velasco) gtr (6th degr.)
ZIMMER. ZM-1781 f.s.   (3001)

DRLAC, JAN ZDENEK
Ulice
"Strassen" gtr HANSEN-DEN f.s.
                              (3002)

DROGOZ, PHILIPPE
Chocs *No.1
gtr (7-8th degr.) ESCHIG f.s. from
SUITE PERCUTANTE   (3003)

Chorale *No.4
gtr (7-8th degr.) ESCHIG f.s. from
SUITE PERCUTANTE   (3004)

Nocturne *No.5
gtr (7-8th degr.) ESCHIG f.s. from
SUITE PERCUTANTE   (3005)

Prelude *No.2
gtr (7-8th degr.) ESCHIG f.s. from
SUITE PERCUTANTE   (3006)

Rasgueado *No.6
gtr (7-8th degr.) ESCHIG f.s. from
SUITE PERCUTANTE   (3007)

Rondo *No.3
gtr (7-8th degr.) ESCHIG f.s. from
SUITE PERCUTANTE   (3008)

DUARTE, JOHN W. (1919-   )
All In A Row *Op.51
(Hartman) gtr (7th degr.,
Collezione Di Musiche Per
Chitarra) BERBEN EB1971 $2.25
                              (3009)

English Suite *Op.31
gtr (7th degr.) NOVELLO 19604 $2.35
                              (3010)

Fantasia And Fugue On "Torre Bermeja"
*Op.30
(Gilardino) gtr (8-9th degr.,
Collezione Di Musiche Per
Chitarra) BERBEN EB1717 $2.50
                              (3011)

Flight Of Fugues, A *Op.44
gtr (3rd degr., 3 pieces for 1 or 2
gtr; suppl., version for 1 gtr)
sc BROEKMANS 1015 f.s.   (3012)

For My Friends
gtr COLUMBIA 183 f.s.   (3013)

Meditation On A Ground Bass *Op.5
gtr (6th degr., Schott's Series Of
Contemporary Music For Spanish
Guitar, No. 5) SCHOTT f.s. (3014)

Miniature Suite *Op.6
gtr (4th degr., Schott's Series Of
Contemporary Music For Spanish
Guitar, No. 6) SCHOTT f.s. (3015)

Modern Miniatures, 3
gtr (4-5th degr.) SCHOTT 5725 f.s.
Schott's Series Of Contemporary
Music For Spanish Guitar, No. 12
contains: Ostinato, Op.9,No.2;
Prelude, Op. 9, No. 1;
Scherzando, Op.9,No.3   (3016)

Mutations On The "Dies Irae" *Op.58,
CC7U
(Gilardino) gtr (7th degr.) BERBEN
EB2042 f.s. Collezione Di Musiche
Per Chitarra   (3017)

Nocturne And Toccata *Op.18
gtr (8-9th degr.) BROEKMANS 936
f.s.   (3018)

Petite Suite Francaise *Op.60
(Jumez) gtr (5-6th degr.) ESCHIG
8214 f.s.   (3019)

Pieces, 2
gtr (4th degr.) COLUMBIA 153 $1.50
contains: Larghetto, Op. 4;
Prelude, Op. 3   (3020)

Prelude, Canto And Toccata *Op.38
(Gilardino) gtr (7-8th degr.,
Collezione Di Musiche Per
Chitarra) BERBEN EB1419 $3.25
                              (3021)

Prelude En Arpeges *Op.62
(Jumez) gtr (6th degr.) ESCHIG 8213
f.s.   (3022)

Simple Variations On "Las Folias"
*Op.10
gtr (4th degr.) COLUMBIA 152 $1.40
                              (3023)

Some Of Noah's Ark *Op.55
gtr (6 sketches) RICORDI-ENG LD-583
f.s.   (3024)

Suite Piemontese *Op.46
(Gilardino) gtr (7-8th degr.,
Collezione Di Musiche Per
Chitarra) BERBEN EB1514 $3.00
                              (3025)

Suo Cosa *Op.52
(Gilardino) gtr (7th degr.,
Collezione Di Musiche Per
Chitarra) BERBEN EB-2043 f.s.
                              (3026)

Variations On A Catalan Folk Song
*Op.25
"Canco Del Lladra" (Artzt) gtr (7-
8th degr.) NOVELLO 19735 $2.35
                              (3027)

EASTWOOD, THOMAS (1922-   )
Amphora
(Gilardino) gtr (8-9th degr.,
Collezione Di Musiche Per
Chitarra) BERBEN EB1566 $2.00
                              (3028)

Ballade
(Bream) gtr (9th degr.) FABER
F-0298 f.s. contains also:
Fantasy   (3029)

EKLUND, HANS (1927-   )
Pezzi, 5
(Ahslund) gtr (4-5th degr.) REUTER
f.s.
contains: Allegro; Allegro Molto;
Andante; Lento; Tempo Rubato
                              (3030)

ERLISO, VINCENTE
Minuet No. 1
gtr (arr + orig pcs;
Transcripciones Por Vicente
Erliso, Vol. 5) UNION ESP. 1055
f.s. contains also: Erliso,

ERLISO, VINCENTE (cont'd.)

Vincente, Minuet No. 2; Mozart,
Wolfgang Amadeus, Fantasy, MIN
277   (3031)

ESPLA, OSCAR (1886-1976)
Impresiones Levantinas, 6 (from
Levana)
(Azpiazu) gtr (8th degr.) UNION
ESP. 20844 f.s.   (3032)

ESTRADA, JESU
Theme Varie
gtr ESCHIG f.s.   (3033)

EYNARD, CAMILLE
Carnet De Notes
(Pujol) gtr ESCHIG 1232 f.s. (3034)

EZAKI, KENJIRO (1926-   )
Nodule Per Chitarre
gtr ZERBONI 6963 f.s.   (3035)

FABINI, EDUARDO (1883-1950)
Mozartienne
gtr (7-8th degr.) ESCHIG 1225 f.s.
                             (3036)

FALLA, MANUEL DE (1876-1946)
Chanson Du Feu Follet (from El Amor
Brujo)
(Pujol) gtr (6th degr.) ESCHIG 1236
f.s.   (3037)

Dance Of The Corregidor (from El
Sombrero De Tres Picos)
"Dances,2, No. 2" (Behrend) gtr
(8th degr.) CHESTER 1811 f.s.
                             (3038)

Dance Of The Miller (from El Sombrero
De Tres Picos)
"Dances, 2, No. 1" (Behrend) gtr
(7-8th degr.) CHESTER 1810 f.s.
                             (3039)

Omaggio, Scritto Per Le Tombeau De
Debussy
(Llobet) gtr (8th degr.) RICORDI-IT
129390 f.s.   (3040)

Recit Du Pecheur (from L'Amour
Sorcier)
(Pujol) gtr (7th degr.) ESCHIG 1237
f.s.   (3041)

Serenata Andaluza
(Garcia Velasco) gtr UNION ESP.
20302 f.s.   (3042)

FARKAS, FERENC (1905-   )
Pieces Breves, 6
(Gilardino) gtr (3-4th degr.)
BERBEN EB1515 $3.50 Collezione Di
Musiche Per Chitarra
contains: Dance Guerriere;
Grinzing; Intermezzo; Prelude;
Scene De Ballet; Tirnovo (3043)

Regi Magyar Tancok - Alte Ungarische
Tanze
(Szendrey-Karper) gtr (4th degr.)
EMB Z-6303 f.s.
contains: Chorea; Tanz Des
Fursten Von Sieben Burgen; Tanz
Des Lazar Apor, Der;
Ungarischer Tanz   (3044)

Regi Magyar Tancok - Alte Ungarische
Tanze
(Szendrey-Karper) gtr (4th degr.)
SCHOTT 6437 f.s.
contains: Chorea; Tanz Des
Fursten Von Sieben Burgen; Tanz
Des Lazar Apor, Der;
Ungarischer Tanz   (3045)

FARQUHAR, DAVID (1928-   )
Ostinato
(Gilardino) gtr (6th degr.,
Collezione Di Musiche Per
Chitarra) BERBEN EB1883 $2.25
contains also: Capriccio; Epilogo
                             (3046)

Scenes, 5
gtr (7-8th degr.) BERBEN EB1882
$3.75 Collezione Di Musiche Per
Chitarra
contains: Barcarolle; Dreaming;
Lullaby; Procession; Questions
                             (3047)

FENICIO, EDMAR
Suite in A minor
gtr (5th degr., in the old style)
RICORDI-BR BR-3011 f.s.   (3048)

FERNANDEZ, OSCAR LORENZO (1897-1948)
Old Song
gtr (4-5th degr.) PEER $.95 (3049)

Prelude
gtr (5-6th degr.) PEER $.95 (3050)

FERRARI, IVANO (1932-   )
Kuss-Tobia (Capriccio No. 1)
gtr (6-7th degr.) BERBEN EB1040
f.s.   (3051)

FERRARI, ROMOLO (1894-1959)
Danza Orientale
gtr (7th degr.) BERBEN EB1635 $1.00
                             (3052)

Grande Fugue Reale
gtr (9th degr.) ZIMMER. EC-69 f.s.
                             (3053)

FETLER, PAUL (1920-   )
Movements, 4
gtr (6th degr.) SCHOTT GA-429 f.s.
                             (3054)

Pieces, 5
gtr (7-8th degr.) SCHOTT GA-99 f.s.
contains: Adagio Quasi
Recitative; Allegretto; Allegro
Agitato; Allegro Moderato;
Andante Espressivo   (3055)

FLAMME, A. (1950-   )
Mignonne
gtr MAURER f.s.   (3056)

FLOTHUIS, MARIUS (1914-   )
Stukken, 2 *Op.22
gtr (7-8th degr.) DONEMUS f.s.
contains: Folia; Habanera   (3057)

FORTEA, DANIEL (1882-1953)
Homenaje A Sor *Op.46
gtr (8th degr.) FORTEA 318 f.s.
                             (3058)

FOX, VICTOR
Prelude
(Gilardino) gtr (7th degr.,
Collezione De Musiche Per
Chitarra) BERBEN EB1644 $2.25
contains also: Hymn; Allegro
                             (3059)

FRANCERIES, MARC (1935-   )
Pour Christiane
gtr (4-5th degr.) CHOUDENS 20.542
f.s. contains also: Comptine Pour
Sylvaine; Pour Veronique   (3060)

FRANCO, JOHAN (1908-   )
Prayers, 3
(Gilardino) gtr (6-7th degr.,
Collezione Di Musiche Per
Chitarra) BERBEN EB1499 $1.25
                             (3061)

Suite Of American Folksongs
(Gilardino) gtr (7-8th degr.,
Collezione Di Musiche Per
Chitarra) BERBEN EB1645 $2.50
                             (3062)

FRANKE, J. MAX
Bagatelle
gtr (2nd degr.) HEINRICH. N-1635
f.s. contains also: Deutscher
Tanz   (3063)

Minuet, MIN 71
gtr (3rd degr.) HEINRICH. N-1636
f.s. contains also: Etude, MIN 72
                             (3064)

FRESNO, JORGE (1937-   )
Escala Naturel
gtr (1st degr., Cuadernos De
Musica, No. 26) ALPUERTO 1170
f.s.   (3065)

Posiciones Fijas
gtr (1st degr., Cuadernos De
Musica, No. 28) ALPUERTO 1172
f.s.   (3066)

Pulsacion
gtr (1st degr., Cuadernos De
Musica, No. 27) ALPUERTO 1171
f.s.   (3067)

Sol, Si, Mi
gtr (1st degr., Cuadernos De
Musica, No. 25) ALPUERTO 1169
f.s.   (3068)

FRICKER, PETER RACINE (1920-   )
Paseo *Op.61
(Bream) gtr FABER F-0282 f.s.
                             (3069)

FRIEDEL, KURT-JOACHIM (1921-   )
Suite
gtr (7th degr.) BERBEN EB1618 $3.00
                             (3070)

FRIESSNEGG, KARL (1900-   )
Kleine Melodien Fur Den Jungen
Gitarristen, 10 *Op.21
(Walker) gtr (3rd degr.) HEINRICH.
1515 f.s.   (3071)

Kleine Suite, Op. 30
(Walker) gtr (4-5th degr.)
HEINRICH. N-1531 f.s.   (3072)

Variationen Uber Ein Thema Von Franz
Schubert (Die Forelle) *Op.15
(Walker) gtr (6-7th degr.)
HEINRICH. N-1514 f.s.   (3073)

FRITSCHE, VOLKMAR
Burlesken, 5
(Beck) gtr (4-5th degr.) TEESELING
VT-100 f.s.   (3074)

FRITSCHE, VOLKMAR (cont'd.)

Nocturne No. 1
gtr (6-7th degr.) TEESELING VT-82
f.s.   (3075)

Nocturne No. 2
gtr (6th degr.) TEESELING VT-66
f.s.   (3076)

FROBERVILLE, PH. DE
Impromptu
gtr (5th degr.) TRANSAT. 970 $1.50
                             (3077)

Prelude, Op. 33
(Ponce) gtr (6th degr.) TRANSAT.
940 $1.50   (3078)

FURSTENAU, WOLFRAM
Cadenza Amicitia
(Beck) gtr (6th degr.) TEESELING
VT-45 f.s.   (3079)

Hommage A Alberto Giacometti
(Beck) gtr (8th degr.) TEESELING
VT-44 f.s.   (3080)

Hommage A Jean Cocteau
(Beck) gtr (6th degr.) TEESELING
VT-43 f.s.   (3081)

Ommegang: Cycle
[Ger/Dutch] gtr,opt inst (8th
degr.) TEESELING VT-64 f.s.
                             (3082)

Railway-Traffic
1-5gtr (4th degr.) TEESELING VT-113
f.s.   (3083)

Reflexionen, Auf Bilder Von Max Ernst
(Beck) gtr (8th degr.) TEESELING
VT-31 f.s.
contains: Femme, Maison, Moineau;
Laicite; Monde Des Flous, Le;
Printemps, Redempteur Et
Redime; Sanctuaire   (3084)

GABUS, MONIQUE (1926-   )
Stele Pour Une Jeune Indienne
(Cadour) gtr (6-7th degr.) LEMOINE
f.s.   (3085)

GAGNEBIN, HENRI (1886-1977)
Pieces, 3
(Azpiazu) gtr (8-9th degr.) SYMPHON
354 f.s.
contains: Chanson; Gigue;
Improvisation   (3086)

GALL, LOUIS IGNATIUS
Music For Young Guitarists *Op.36,
CC24U
gtr (1-2nd degr.) TEESELING VT-48
f.s.   (3087)

Stukken, 3 *Op.19
gtr (4th degr.) TEESELING VT-2 f.s.
contains: Asiatica; Cancion;
Visit To A Museum, A   (3088)

Suite Vivat Noviomagum *Op.16
gtr (6th degr.) TEESELING VT-3 f.s.
                             (3089)

GARBER, ERICH (1916-   )
Originalkompositionen, 5
gtr (4-5th degr.) PREISSLER JP-7022
f.s.   (3090)

GARGIULO, TERENZIO (1905-1972)
Toccata
(Gangi) gtr (7th degr., Collezione
Di Musiche Per Chitarra) BERBEN
EB1524 $2.25   (3091)

GAVARONE, GERARD
Retrospective
gtr (5th degr.) CHOUDENS 20.703
f.s.   (3092)

GENERAUX, ROGER
Suite Bresilienne *CC5U
gtr ESCHIG f.s.   (3093)

GERHARD, ROBERTO (1896-1970)
Fantasy
gtr BELWIN $2.00   (3094)

GILARDINO, ANGELO
Abreuana
gtr (8th degr., Collezione Di
Musiche Per Chitarra) BERBEN
EB1565 $2.25   (3095)

Appaloosa
gtr (7th degr.) BERBEN EB1700 $3.00
Collezione Di Musiche Per
Chitarra
contains: Boot Hill; Longhorn
Ghosts; Peace-Maker 45; Riders
In The Sky, The; Saguaro (3096)

Araucaria
(Bitetti) gtr (8th degr.,
Collezione Di Musiche Per
Chitarra) BERBEN EB1646 $1.50
                             (3097)

GILARDINO, ANGELO (cont'd.)

Canzone Notturna
gtr (7th degr., Collezione Di
Musiche Per Chitarra) BERBEN
EB1353 $1.25   (3098)

Estrellas Para Estarellas, Musica
Nocturna Para La Guitarra De
Gabriel [Estarellas] *CC5U
(Estarellas) gtr (7-8th degr.)
BERBEN EB1567 $2.25 Collezione Di
Musiche Per Chittara   (3099)

Ocram, Fantasia
gtr (6-7th degr., Collezione Di
Musiche Per Chitarra) BERBEN
EB1974 $2.25   (3100)

Tenebrae Factae Sunt *CC5U
gtr (6-7th degr.) BERBEN EB2024
f.s. Collezione Di Musiche Per
Chitarra   (3101)

Trepidazioni Per Thebit
(Artzt) gtr (9th degr., Collezione
Di Musiche Per Chitarra) BERBEN
EB1884 $2.00   (3102)

GOMEZ CRESPO, JORGE
Nortena, Homenaje A Julian Aguirre
(Papas) gtr (7th degr.) COLUMBIA
185 $1.50   (3103)

GRAMBERG, JACQ
Instructieve Sonatines, 3
gtr (single line playing/1st degr.)
HARMONIA 1821 f.s.   (3104)

Petrad
gtr (4th degr.) HARMONIA 2939 f.s.
                         (3105)

GRAU, AGUSTI
Berceuse Ancienne
(Pujol) gtr (5th degr.) ESCHIG 1219
f.s.   (3106)

Corranda
(Llobet; Pujol) gtr ESCHIG 1216
f.s.   (3107)

Fable
(Pujol) gtr (9th degr.) ESCHIG 1224
f.s.   (3108)

GRAU, EDUARDO
Fuente De Nie Pastrie, La
"Fountain Of Nie Pastrie, The"
(Barbosa-Lima) gtr COLUMBIA 194
f.s.   (3109)

GREEVE, G. DE
Galante Dans
gtr MAURER f.s.   (3110)

GRILLAERT, OCT
Valdemosa
gtr MAURER f.s.   (3111)

GRIMM, FRIEDRICH KARL (1902-   )
Intermezzo D'Aragon *Op.63a
(Behrend) gtr (6th degr.) ZIMMER.
                         (3112)

Pezzi, 2 *Op.150,No.1-2
(Gilardino) gtr (6-7th degr.,
Collezione Di Musiche Per
Chitarra) BERBEN EB1523 $2.25
                         (3113)

GUDMUNDSEN-HOLMGREEN, PELLE (1932-   )
Solo Fur El-Guitar
gtr HANSEN-DEN f.s.   (3114)

GUNDHUS, LEIF
Norwegische Volksweisen
gtr NORSK f.s.   (3115)

GUNSENHEIMER, GUSTAV (1934-   )
9 Leichte Stucke
gtr VOGT 201 f.s.   (3116)

Romanische Suite
gtr VOGT 303 f.s.   (3117)

HAFNER, KURT
Leichte Originalstucke
1-2gtr SCHMIDT,H 89 f.s. (3118)

HAIDER, HANS
Skizzen, 4
gtr (5th degr.) SIKORSKI 750 $2.25
                         (3119)

HALFFTER, CRISTOBAL (1930-   )
Codex I
(Scheit) gtr (9th degr.) UNIVER.
13991 $3.25   (3120)

HALFFTER, ERNESTO (1905-   )
Danse De La Gitane
gtr ESCHIG f.s.   (3121)

Danza De La Pastora
(Azpiazu) gtr (7th degr.) ESCHIG
f.s.   (3122)

HALFFTER, ERNESTO (cont'd.)

Gigue (composed with Eschriche)
(Pujol) gtr (8th degr.) ESCHIG 1223
f.s.   (3123)

Habanera
(Azpiazu) gtr (7th degr.) ESCHIG
f.s.   (3124)

HALLNAS, HILDING (1903-   )
Partita Amabile
(Johnson) gtr (7th degr.) ANDERSONS
AM-680 f.s.   (3125)

Preludier 1-12
(Johnson) gtr (3rd degr., Musik for
Gitarr, vol. II) ANDERSONS AM-679
f.s.   (3126)

Strangaspel *CC8U
(Johnson) gtr (5th degr.) ANDERSONS
694 f.s. Musik For Gitarr (3127)

HARRIS, ALBERT (1916-   )
Homage To Unamuno
gtr COLUMBIA 189 $1.75   (3128)

Suite *CC7U
gtr COLUMBIA 196 $3.00   (3129)

Variations And Fugue On A Theme Of
Handel
gtr (8th degr.) SCHOTT GA-416 f.s.
                         (3130)

HARTIG, HEINZ FRIEDRICH (1907-1969)
Gitarresolo (Solo for Guitar)
(Behrend) gtr (7th degr.) NOVELLO
19951 $1.95   (3131)
(Behrend) gtr HANSEN-DEN f.s.
                         (3132)

Stucke Fur Gitarre, 3
(Behrend) gtr (8th degr.) BOTE f.s.
Gitarre-Bibliothek, No.12a-c
contains: Alla Danza, Op.26,No.3
(also published in European
Masters For The Guitar);
Capriccio, Op.26,No.1; Theme
and Variations, Op.26,No.2 (3133)

HASENOHRL, FRANZ (1885- ?   )
Kleine Stucke, 4
(Walker) gtr (5th degr.) HEINRICH.
1503 f.s.
contains: Barcarolle; Capriccio;
Gavotte; Kleine Serenade (3134)

Suite
(Walker) gtr HEINRICH. N-1508 f.s.
contains: Minuet; Prelude (3135)

HASHAGEN, KLAUS (1924-   )
Synchronie; 10 Graphic Parts
(Behrend) gtr ZIMMER. 2098 f.s.
                         (3136)

HAUBENSTOCK-RAMATI, ROMAN (1919-   )
Hexachord I-II
1-2gtr (8-9th degr.) UNIVER. 14478
f.s.   (3137)

HAUFRECHT, HERBERT (1909-   )
Hora
gtr (4th degr.) PEER 2098-4 f.s.
                         (3138)

Theme and Variations
gtr (6-7th degr.) COMP.FAC. f.s.
                         (3139)

Waltz
gtr (5th degr.) PEER 2097-2 f.s.
                         (3140)

HAUG, HANS (1900-1967)
Alba
(Gilardino) gtr (6th degr.,
Collezione Di Musiche Per
Chitarra) BERBEN EB1480 $1.25
                         (3141)

Prelude
(Gilardino) gtr (7th degr.,
Collezione Di Musiche Per
Chitarra) BERBEN EB1471 $1.25
                         (3142)

Prelude, Tiento Et Toccata
(Gilardino) gtr (7-8th degr.,
Collezione Di Musiche Per
Chitarra) BERBEN EB1464 $2.75
                         (3143)

HAUSWIRTH, HANS M.A. (1901-   )
Solospiel Auf Der Gitarre, Das
*CC26U
gtr (2-3rd degr.) PREISSLER JP-7027
f.s.   (3144)

HEER, HANS DE (1927-   )
3 Fuga's
gtr TEESELING VT-172 f.s. (3145)

Musing
gtr (8th degr.) TEESELING VT-108
f.s.   (3146)

Prelude No. 4
(Peters) gtr (4th degr.) TEESELING
VT-21 f.s.   (3147)

HEER, HANS DE (cont'd.)

Siciliano
gtr (6-7th degr.) HARMONIA 2725
f.s.   (3148)

HEKSTER, WALTER (1937-   )
Chain
(Gall) gtr (9th degr.) TEESELING
VT-107 f.s.   (3149)

HENZE, HANS WERNER (1926-   )
Fragmente Nach Holderlin, 3 (from
Kammermusik 1958)
(Bream) [Ger] solo voice,gtr (9th
degr.) sc SCHOTT 4886 f.s.
contains also: Tentos, 3 (gtr)
                         (3150)

Memorias De "El Cimarron"
(Brouwer) gtr (8th degr.) SCHOTT
6485 f.s.   (3151)

HERRERA, RAMON DE
Preludes, 3
gtr (3-4th degr.) LEMOINE 24058
f.s.   (3152)

HIGUET, NESTOR
Interlude
(Stecke) gtr (5th degr.) MAURER
f.s.   (3153)

HILSTER, RIES DE
Prelude No. 1, Op. 12, No. 1
gtr (5th degr.) BERBEN EB1034 f.s.
                         (3154)

HINOJOSA, JAVIER
Te Lucis Ante Terminum
"Ricercata Di Durezze E Fioriture
Sulle "Quattro Dita"" gtr (8th
degr.) ZERBONI 7776 $6.00 (3155)

HINTERMEYER, WILLY (1892-   )
Junge Gitarre-Soloist, Der, Vol. I;
Eine Sammlung Leichter,
Melodioser Solostucke *CC23U
gtr (1-3rd degr.) PREISSLER JP-7002
f.s.   (3156)

Junge Gitarre-Soloist, Der, Vol. II;
Eine Sammlung Leichter,
Melodioser Solostucke *CC25U
gtr (1-3rd degr.) PREISSLER
JP-7002-II f.s.   (3157)

HLOUSCHEK, THEODOR (1923-   )
Kompositionen *CC12U
(Peter; Zimmer) gtr (4-5th degr.)
HOFMEISTER T-4076 f.s.   (3158)

HOEK, JAN-ANTON VAN (1936-   )
Bouwstenen Van Het Polyphoon
Gitaarspel, Vol. I, Nos. 1-21
*Op.965
"Polyphonic Playing On The Guitar"
gtr (3-7th degr.) HARMONIA 1886
f.s.   (3159)

Bouwstenen Van Het Polyphoon
Gitaarspel, Vol. II, Nos. 22-37
*Op.965
"Polyphonic Playing On The Guitar"
gtr (3-7th degr.) HARMONIA 1887
f.s.   (3160)

12 Preludes
gtr TEESELING VT-215 f.s. (3161)

Suite Milanesa
(Walker) gtr (5-7th degr.)
HEINRICH. 1551 f.s. contains
also: Balladen, 2; Postlude
                         (3162)

HOLDER, DERWYN
Modern Preludes, 6
gtr COLUMBIA 155 $1.50   (3163)

HOMS, JOAQUIN (1906-   )
2 Solioquios
gtr ALPUERTO 1123 f.s.   (3164)

HUBSCHMANN, WERNER (1901-1969)
Suite
(Zimmer) gtr (6th degr.) HOFMEISTER
T-4152 f.s.   (3165)

HULSEN, ERNST (1883- ?   )
Leichte Walzer, 6 *Op.9
gtr (3-4th degr.) LEUCKART 8029
f.s.   (3166)

HUMMEL, BERTOLD (1925-   )
Metamorphosen Fur Gitarre
gtr BENJ EE-2955   (3167)

IBERT, JACQUES (1890-1962)
Ariette
gtr (5th degr.) LEDUC $1.50 (3168)

Francaise
(Azpiazu) gtr (9th degr.) LEDUC
23547 $4.00   (3169)

JANSEN, WILLY (1897-   )
Kleine Spielmusiken *CC7U
1-3gtr/gtr,2treb inst (1-2nd degr.)
sc PREISSLER JP-7009 f.s. partly
single line playing (3 gtr);
notation: 2 treb staffs (4-pt
music)   (3170)

JENTSCH, WALTER (1900-   )
Impressionen *Op.57
(Sanchez-Benimeli) gtr (7th degr.)
RIES 11.284 f.s.   (3171)

JOACHIM, OTTO (1910-   )
Stucke, 6
(Behrend) gtr (5-6th degr.)
PREISSLER 7039 f.s.   (3172)

JOVICIC, JOVAN
Balkanski Dans
(Claessens) gtr (7th degr., also
published in: Gitaar-Kamermuziek,
Vol. IV) BROEKMANS 26 f.s. (3173)

JULIA, BERNARDO
Nostalgia
(Estarellas) gtr (4th degr.,
Collezione Di Musiche Per
Chitarra) BERBEN EB1975 $1.75
(3174)

JUST, FRANZ (1937-   )
Leichte Spielstucke *CC20U
(Peter) gtr (3-4th degr.)
HOFMEISTER T-4160 f.s.   (3175)

KADOSA, PAL (1903-1983)
11 Konnyu Darab Gitarra
"Easy Pieces For Guitar" (Adrovicz)
gtr (1-2nd degr.) EMB 7912 f.s.
(3176)

KALMAR, LASZLO (1931-   )
Monologo
gtr (7th degr.) EMB Z-6332.A. f.s.
(3177)

KAPS, HANSJOACHIM
Huracan, El
gtr VOGT 401 f.s.   (3178)

KARL, SEPP (1913-   )
Junge Gitarre-Solist, Der, Vol. III;
Eine Sammlung Leichter,
Melodioser Solostucke (composed
with Witt, Fred) *CC41U
1-2gtr (2-3rd degr.) PREISSLER
JP-7002-III f.s. 36 pcs by Karl
for gtr; 5 pcs by Witt for 2 gtr
(3179)

Junge Gitarre-Solist, Der, Vol. IV;
Eine Sammlung Leichter,
Melodioser Solostucke *CC32U
gtr (3rd degr.) PREISSLER
JP-7002-IV f.s.   (3180)

Melodische Spielstucke Fur Leichtes
Lagenspiel *CC40U
gtr (2-3rd degr.) PREISSLER JP-7005
f.s.   (3181)

Strebsame Gitarrist, Der, Vol. II,
Leichte Spielstucke *CC34U
gtr (2-3rd degr.) PREISSLER
JP-7007-II f.s. suppl. 2 to Max
Kierner, Gitarre Spielen - Leicht
Gemacht   (3182)

KAUFMANN, ARMIN (1902-   )
Rhapsody, Op. 97
gtr (Collezione Di Musiche Per
Chitarra) BERBEN f.s.   (3183)

Stucke, 10
(Dobrauz) gtr (5-6th degr.)
HEINRICH. 1534 f.s.   (3184)

KEF, KEES (1894-1961)
Divertimento
gtr (8th degr.) DONEMUS f.s. (3185)

KELLY, BRYAN (1934-   )
Aubade, Toccata And Nocturne
(Duarte) gtr (6-7th degr.) NOVELLO
19367 $2.20   (3186)

KENNARD, JAN
Preludes, 2
gtr (3rd degr., Schott's Series Of
Contemporary Music For Spanish
Guitar, No. 9) SCHOTT 5724 f.s.
(3187)

KERR, HARRISON (1897-1978)
Variations On A Theme From "The Tower
Of Kel"
(Gilardino) gtr (8th degr.,
Collezione Di Musiche Per
Chitarra) BERBEN EB1647 $2.50
(3188)

KERSTERS, WILLEM (1929-   )
Nocturne, Op. 44
(van Puijenbroeck) gtr (6th degr.)
CBDM $2.00   (3189)

KODALY, ZOLTAN (1882-1967)
Bicinia *CC30U
(Vereczkey) gtr (1-2nd degr.) EMB
7713 f.s.   (3190)

KOMTER, JAN MAARTEN (1905-   )
Arpeggiata, Homenaje A Fernando Sors
gtr (3-4th degr.) HARMONIA 2708
f.s.   (3191)

Dhyanas, 6
gtr (3-4th degr.) HARMONIA 2500
f.s.
contains: Aware; Becalmed;
Beware; Serene; Storm In A
Teacup; Unaware   (3192)

Fun From The Start, Vol. II: The
Beginning Soloist On The Guitar
*CC21U
gtr (1-2nd degr.) HARMONIA 2236
f.s.   (3193)

Preludes, 2
gtr (4th degr.) DONEMUS f.s. (3194)

Preludes Faciles, 3
gtr (3rd degr.) DONEMUS f.s. (3195)

Spanish Suite
gtr (4th degr.) HARMONIA 2599 f.s.
(3196)

Suite 1945
gtr (4-5th degr.) HARMONIA 2654
f.s.   (3197)

Suite 1949
gtr (6-7th degr.) HARMONIA 2706
f.s.   (3198)

Suites, 6
gtr (3-5th degr.) DONEMUS f.s.
(3199)

KONIETZNY, HEINRICH
Permutationen
(Koch) gtr (7-8th degr., Neue Musik
Fur Klassische Gitarre; 15
Movements) ISI f.s. cmplt ed 101,
study sc 101-S   (3200)

KOPTAGEL, YUKSEL (1931-   )
Fosil Suiti
(Behrend) gtr (5th degr., Gitarre-
Bibliothek, No.42; also published
in: European Masters For The
Guitar) BOTE GB-42 f.s.   (3201)

Tamzara, Turkischer Tanz
(Behrend) gtr (6th degr., Gitarre-
Bibliothek, No.25) BOTE GB-25
f.s.   (3202)

KORN, PETER JONA (1922-   )
Arabesque *Op.61,No.1 (from Trois
Pieces Pour La Guitare)
gtr BRUCK K 1-1 f.s.   (3203)

Gigue, Op. 61, No. 3 (from Trois
Pieces Pour La Guitare)
gtr BRUCK K 1-3 f.s.   (3204)

Pavane Triste *Op.61,No.2 (from
Trois Pieces Pour La Guitare)
gtr BRUCK K 1-2 f.s.   (3205)

KOTIK, JOSEPH
Erste Vortragsstucke Fur Gitarre
gtr ARTIA f.s.   (3206)

Prvni Prednesove Skladby Pro Kytaru
*CC50U
gtr (1-3rd degr.) CZECH H-4117 f.s.
(3207)

KOVATS, BARNA (1920-   )
Minutenstucke
gtr (4-5th degr.) SCHOTT GA-413
f.s.
contains: Andantino; Leggiero,
Molto Legando; Moderato, Un
Poco Agitato; Non Troppo
Allegro; Tranquillamente
Scorrendo; Vivo, Ritmico (3208)

Mouvements, 3
gtr ESCHIG f.s.   (3209)

Petite Suite
gtr ESCHIG f.s.   (3210)

Stucke, 3
gtr (6-7th degr.) MODERN 1044 f.s.
contains: Esquisse; Estudio De
Corcheas Repetidas; Estudio
Homofonico   (3211)

Suite, Hommage A Goldoni
gtr (6-7th degr.) MODERN 1043 f.s.
(3212)

KRATOCHWIL, HEINZ (1932-   )
Triptychon *Op.68
(Scheit) gtr (8th degr.) UNIVER.
14462 $3.25   (3213)

KRENEK, ERNST (1900-   )
Suite
(Norman) gtr (8-9th degr.)
DOBLINGER 05906 f.s.   (3214)

KRIEGER, EDINO (1928-   )
Ritmata
(Santos) gtr (Collection Turibio
Santos, No. 10) ESCHIG f.s.
(3215)

KUCERA, VACLAV (1929-   )
Diario, Omaggio A Che Guevara
(Zelenka) gtr (9th degr.) PANTON
P-1375 f.s.   (3216)

LAGOYA, ALEXANDRE
Capriccio
gtr (7th degr.) RICORDI-FR R-1608
f.s.   (3217)

Reverie
gtr (6th degr.) RICORDI-FR R-1607
f.s.   (3218)

LAMPERSBERG, GERHARD (1928-   )
Stucke, 3
gtr UNIVER. rent   (3219)

LANGENBERG, JAN VAN DEN
Ballade No. 1
gtr TEESELING VT-155 f.s.   (3220)

Dance-Variations On A Dutch Song
gtr TEESELING VT-222 f.s.   (3221)

Minuet in F
gtr TEESELING VT-188 f.s.   (3222)

LARRAURI, ANTON (1932-   )
Triptico Vasco
gtr ALPUERTO 1300 f.s.   (3223)

LASALA, ANGEL (1914-   )
Preludios Americanos *CC6U
(Lopez) gtr (6-7th degr.) RICORDI-
ARG BA-11159 f.s.   (3224)

LAURO, ANTONIO (1917-   )
Angostura, Valse Venezolano
(Diaz) gtr (7th degr.) BROEKMANS
901 f.s.   (3225)

Carora, Valse Venezolano
(Diaz) gtr (6-7th degr.) BROEKMANS
904 f.s.   (3226)

Marabino, El, Valse Venezolano
(Diaz) gtr (6-7th degr.) BROEKMANS
903 f.s.   (3227)

Maria Luise, Valse Venezolano
(Diaz) gtr (7th degr.) BROEKMANS
905 f.s.   (3228)

Suite Venezolana
(Diaz) gtr (7-8th degr.) BROEKMANS
793 f.s.   (3229)

Valses Venezolanos, 4
(Diaz) gtr (7-8th degr.) BROEKMANS
794 f.s.   (3230)

Variations On A Venezolean Children's
Song
(Diaz) gtr (7th degr.) BROEKMANS
940 f.s.   (3231)

Venezuelan Waltz, Valse Criollo
(Valdes Blain, A.) gtr (7th degr.)
COLOMBO NY-2316 f.s.   (3232)

LECHTHALER, JOSEF (1891-1948)
Variationen-Suite *Op.49,No.2
(Scheit) gtr (6th degr.) UNIVER.
11321 $2.75   (3233)

LECLERCQ, NORBERT
Couleurs, 6
gtr (3rd degr.) SCHOTT-FRER 9276
f.s.
contains: Arlequin; Cyclamen;
Noir; Orange; Pourpre;
Turquoise   (3234)

LEERINK, HANS
Preludes, 4
gtr (3-4th degr., Bibliotheek Van
Den Gitarist, No. 80) BROEKMANS
371 f.s.   (3235)

LEGLEY, VICTOR (1915-   )
Pieces, 5, Op. 62
(Alfonso) gtr (8th degr.) CBDM
$3.00
contains: Allegretto Commodo;
Allegro Risoluto; Andante,
Quasi Adagio; Andantino
Grazioso; Vivace   (3236)

LELLA, DOMENICO DI
Impressione *Op.9
gtr TEESELING VT-151 f.s. contains
also: Studio Da Concierto, Op.10
(3237)

Preludi, 6
gtr (5-6th degr.) TEESELING VT-133
f.s.   (3238)

LEMELAND, AUBERT (1932-   )
    Hommage A Albert Roussel °Op.16
        (Herrera) gtr (8th degr.) BILLAUDOT
        1572 $2.50   (3239)

LERICH, PIERRE
    Chanson Et Pastorale
        gtr (6th degr.) DELRIEU 1401 f.s.
                                      (3240)

    Hommage A Villa-Lobos
        gtr (4th degr.) ESCHIG f.s. (3241)

    Pieces, 3
        gtr ESCHIG f.s.
            contains: Chateau De Sable;
            Chorinho; Toccata   (3242)

    Prelude Et Fugue, Alla Antiqua
        gtr (6th degr.) DELRIEU 1402 f.s.
                                      (3243)

    Prelude No. 3
        gtr (5th degr.) DELRIEU 1403 f.s.
                                      (3244)

    Suite Baroque
        gtr ESCHIG f.s.   (3245)

    Waltz
        gtr (3rd degr.) TRANSAT. 1073 $1.75
                                      (3246)

LETELIER VALDEZ, MIGUEL FRANCISCO
        (1939-   )
    Preludios Breves, 7
        gtr (9th degr.) RICORDI-ARG
        BA-12305 f.s.   (3247)

LEVY, MOSHE
    Twenty-Four Guitar Pieces (In All
    Keys)
        gtr (3-6th degr., for list of
        corrections ask composer: 3012
        Langenhagen 20, Kollingsmoor 20,
        Fed. Rep. of Germany)
        SPAN.MUS.CTR. GE-1125 f.s. (3248)

LIMA, CANDIDO
    Esbocos
        (Cimma) gtr (8th degr.) BERBEN
        EB1360 $1.50   (3249)

LLOBET, MIGUEL (1878-1938)
    Prelude in A
        gtr (6-7th degr.) UNION ESP. 20368
        f.s.   (3250)

    Prelude in E
        gtr (6th degr.) UNION ESP. 20369
        f.s.   (3251)

    Respuesta (Impromptu)
        gtr (9th degr.) UNION ESP. 20370
        f.s.   (3252)

    Variaciones Sobre Un Tema De Sor
        °Op.15
        gtr (9-10th degr.) UNION ESP. 20379
        f.s.   (3253)

LOPES-GRACA, FERNANDO (1906-   )
    Partita
        gtr (6th degr.) ZERBONI 7452 $6.00
                                    (3254)

    Preludio E Baileto
        (Nagy) gtr (8th degr.) ZERBONI 6815
        f.s.   (3255)

LORENTZEN, BENT (1935-   )
    Umbra
        gtr HANSEN-DEN f.s.   (3256)

LUBACH, ANDRIES A.
    Dances, 2
        gtr (4-5th degr.) HARMONIA 2441
        f.s.
            contains: Fughetta; Liza (3257)

LUENING, OTTO (1900-   )
    Fantasias I-III
        gtr (4-5th degr.) COMP.FAC. f.s.
                                    (3258)

LUMBY, HERBERT
    Preludio E Capriccio °Op.56
        (Gilardino) gtr (7-8th degr.,
        Collezione Di Musiche Per
        Chitarra) BERBEN EB1527 $2.25
                                    (3259)

LUNDIN, BENGT
    Fem Infall, Svit
        (Ahslund) gtr (5-6th degr.) REUTER
        f.s.   (3260)

LUTOSLAWSKI, WITOLD (1913-   )
    Melodii Ludowych, 9
        "Melodies Populaires, 9" (Azpiazu)
        gtr (4-5th degr.) POLSKIE 7124
        f.s.   (3261)

LUTZEMBERGER, CESARE
    Composizioni, 4
        gtr (7-8th degr.) BERBEN EB1617
        $4.25
            contains: Nocturne; Prelude in D
            minor; Prelude in G minor;
            Sonata in B minor   (3262)

MAASZ, GERHARD (1906-1984)
    Suite
        gtr (6th degr.) sc,pts HEINRICH.
        PE-6140 f.s.   (3263)

MCCABE, JOHN (1939-   )
    Canto
        (8-9th degr.) NOVELLO 19833
        $3.10   (3264)

MADERNA, BRUNO (1920-1973)
    Y Despues
        (Paolini) gtr (for 10-stringed gtr
        + transcription for 6-stringed
        gtr) RICORDI-IT 132051 f.s. (3265)

MAES, JEF (1905-   )
    Nocturne
        (van Puijenbroeck) gtr (7th degr.)
        METROPOLIS EM-4533 $1.50   (3266)

MAGHINI, RUGGERO (1913-1977)
    Umbra
        (Gilardino) gtr (8-9th degr.,
        Collezione Di Musiche Per
        Chitarra) BERBEN EB1985 $2.25
                                    (3267)

MAIRANTS, IVOR
    Drei Rhytmische Tanze Fur Gitarre
        gtr BREITKOPF-W 57.04015 f.s.
                                    (3268)

    Part Suite, 6
        gtr (3-4th degr.) FENETTE $2.25
                                    (3269)

    Sechs Bagatellen Fur Gitarre
        gtr BREITKOPF-W 57.04012 f.s.
                                    (3270)

    Sechs Progressive Stucke Fur Gitarre
        gtr BREITKOPF-W 57.04013 f.s.
                                    (3271)

    Sechs Solos Fur Gitarre
        gtr BREITKOPF-W 57.04014 f.s.
                                    (3272)

    Solos For Classic Guitar, 6
        gtr (3-5th degr.) BR.CONT.MUS.
        BC-1013 f.s.   (3273)

    Suite In Sechs Teile Fur Gitarre
        gtr BREITKOPF-W 57.04048 f.s.
                                    (3274)

    Travel-Suite
        gtr BREITKOPF-W 57.04016 f.s.
                                    (3275)

MALIPIERO, RICCARDO (1914-   )
    Aria Variata Su La Follia
        gtr (8-9th degr.) ZERBONI 8554 f.s.
                                    (3276)

MAMANGAKIS, NIKOS (1929-   )
    Penthima
        gtr (9-10th degr.) GERIG HG-908
        f.s.   (3277)

MARCO, TOMAS (1942-   )
    Albayalde
        gtr (graphic score) ZIMMER. ZM-1901
        f.s.   (3278)

    Naturaleza Muerto Con Guitarra;
        Homenaje A Pablo Picasso
        gtr ALPUERTO 1245 f.s.   (3279)

    Paisaje Grana, Homenaje A J.R.
        Jimenez
        gtr ALPUERTO 1306 f.s.   (3280)

MARGOLA, FRANCO (1908-   )
    Ballade
        (Cabassi) gtr (4-5th degr.) ZANIBON
        5255 f.s.   (3281)

    Leggenda
        (Gilardino) gtr (5th degr.,
        Collezione Di Musiche Per
        Chitarra) BERBEN EB1470 $1.25
                                    (3282)

    Nocturne
        (Cabassi) gtr (4-5th degr.) ZANIBON
        5178 f.s.   (3283)

MARGOLA, MANUEL
    Choros Brasileira
        gtr VOGT 305 f.s. contains also:
        Romanze A Tarrega   (3284)

MARTIN, FRANK (1890-1974)
    Pieces Breves, 4
        (Scheit) gtr (8th degr.) UNIVER.
        12711 $3.25
            contains: Air; Comme Une Gigue;
            Plainte; Prelude   (3285)

MARTINEZ ZARATE, JORGE
    Impromptu No. 1
        gtr (6th degr.) RICORDI-ARG
        BA-11514 f.s.   (3286)

MARTINI, MANLIO
    Piccoli Pezzi, 2
        gtr (3rd degr.) BERBEN EB1842 $1.00
                                    (3287)

MEDEK, TILO (1940-   )
    Drei Stucke Fur Gitarre
        gtr GERIG HG-1227 f.s.   (3288)

MEDIN, NINO
    Notturnino E Capriccio
        gtr (7th degr.) CARISCH 21831 f.s.
                                    (3289)

MEIER, JOST
    Reflets, 3
        (Rutscho) gtr (8-9th degr.,
        Collezione Di Musiche Per
        Chitarra) BERBEN EB1512 $2.25
                                    (3290)

MELLERS, WILFRID HOWARD (1914-   )
    Blue Epiphany, A - For J.B. Smith
        gtr FABER 0528 f.s.   (3291)

MESTRES-QUADRENY, JOSEP MARIA
        (1929-   )
    Prelude
        gtr (8-9th degr., Collezione Di
        Musiche Per Chitarra) BERBEN
        EB2044 f.s.   (3292)

MIGNOT, PIERRE
    Toccata Fantasque
        gtr (5th degr.) MAURER f.s. (3293)

MILHAUD, DARIUS (1892-1974)
    Segoviana
        gtr (9th degr.) HEUGEL 31701 $2.00
                                    (3294)

MILLER, JOHN R.
    Solo-Gitarre, Die, Vol. II °CC17U
        (Feider) gtr (1-5th degr.) PETERER
        f.s.   (3295)

MIROGLIO, FRANCIS (1924-   )
    Choreiques
        gtr (9-10th degr.) UNIVER. 13985
        $4.25
            contains: Elans; Feu; Geste
            Dansee; Voiles d'Irisations
                                    (3296)

MOMPOU, FEDERICO (1893-   )
    Barca, La
        (Sainz de la Maza) gtr UNION ESP.
        15687 f.s.   (3297)

    Cancion Y Danza No. 1
        (Mairants) gtr (9-10th degr.) UNION
        ESP. 19551 f.s.   (3298)

    Suite Compostellana
        (Segovia) gtr (8-9th degr.)
        SALABERT MC-130 $6.00   (3299)

MORANCON, GUY (1927-   )
    Petit Livre °CC5U
        gtr ESCHIG f.s.   (3300)

    Suite Latine
        gtr ESCHIG f.s.   (3301)

MORENO TORROBA, FEDERICO (1891-1982)
    Aire De La Manche °CC5U
        gtr (6-7th degr.) SCHOTT GA-235
        f.s.   (3302)

    Bolero
        (Alfonso) gtr (Madrilenas, Suite
        Para Guitarra, No.3) MUS.SUR f.s.
                                    (3303)

    Burgalesa
        (Segovia) gtr (6th degr.) SCHOTT
        GA-113 f.s.   (3304)

    Contradanza
        gtr (7th degr.) AMP 6807 f.s.
                                    (3305)

    Jota Levantina
        gtr (7th degr.) AMP 6805 f.s.
                                    (3306)

    Madronos
        gtr (8-9th degr.) AMP 9543.3 f.s.
                                    (3307)
        gtr (8-9th degr.) UNION ESP. 20477
        f.s.   (3308)

    Molinera
        gtr (6-7th degr.) AMP 6806 f.s.
                                    (3309)

    Nocturne
        (Segovia) gtr (8-9th degr.) SCHOTT
        GA-103 f.s.   (3310)

    Pieces Caracteristiques, Vol. 1
        (Segovia) gtr (7-8th degr.) SCHOTT
        GA-133 f.s.
            contains: Melodia; Oliveras;
            Preambulo   (3311)

    Pieces Caracteristiques, Vol. 2
        (Segovia) gtr (7-8th degr.) SCHOTT
        GA-134 f.s.
            contains: Albada; Mayos, Los;
            Panorama   (3312)

    Prelude
        (Segovia) gtr (6-7th degr.) SCHOTT
        GA-114 f.s.   (3313)

    Punteado Taconeo Clasico
        gtr (8th degr.) UNION ESP. 19003
        f.s.   (3314)

    Serenata Burlesca
        (Segovia) gtr (6-7th degr.) SCHOTT
        GA-115 f.s.   (3315)

MORENO TORROBA, FEDERICO (cont'd.)

Stucke, 5
gtr (7th degr.) SCHOTT GA-234 f.s.
(3316)

Suite Castellana
(Segovia) gtr (7-8th degr.) SCHOTT
GA-104 f.s.   (3317)

Suite Miniatura
gtr (6th degr.) UNION ESP.   (3318)
(Gilardino) gtr (6th degr.,
Collezione Di Musiche Per
Chitarra) BERBEN EB1423 $2.00
(3319)

MORI, AUGUSTO CESARE DE
Souvenir d'Espagne
gtr (4th degr.) BERBEN EB1661 $1.25
(3320)

MORNAC, JUAN (1897-   )
Morceaux Choisis, 15
gtr (1-2nd degr.) LEDUC $5.00
(3321)

MORTARI, VIRGILIO (1902-   )
Omaggio Ad Andres Segovia
(Tomas) gtr (7th degr.) CARISCH
21895 f.s.   (3322)

MOSSO, CARLO
Danze Nello Stile Modale, 4
(Cimma) gtr (4-5th degr.) BERBEN
EB 1426 $2.25
contains: Andantino Sereno; Con
Allegria; Moderato; Tempo Di
Sarabanda   (3323)

Forskalia
gtr (6-7th degr., Collezione Di
Musiche Per Chitarra) BERBEN
EB1812 $2.00   (3324)

MOULAERT, RAYMOND (1875-1962)
Rhapsody
gtr (7th degr., on popular Flemish
songs) CBDM $1.50   (3325)

MOURAT, JEAN-MAURICE
Melancolie
gtr (3-4th degr.) BILLAUDOT 1622
$2.00   (3326)

Palmiers, Les
gtr (3rd degr.) BILLAUDOT 1621
$1.50   (3327)

Suite Vendeenne
gtr (3rd degr.) BILLAUDOT 1941 f.s.
(3328)

Toupie, La
gtr (1st degr.) BILLAUDOT 1623
$1.50   (3329)

Valse Triste
gtr (3rd degr.) BILLAUDOT 1940 f.s.
(3330)

MRONSKI, STANISLAW
Cykle Na Gitare, 2, Cztery Utwory
(Kunce) gtr (7th degr.) POLSKIE
7789 f.s. contains also: Hommage
A Chopin   (3331)

MULLER, SIEGFRIED (1926-   )
Stucke Fur Gitarre, 5
(Peter) gtr (4-5th degr.)
HOFMEISTER 7330 f.s.
contains: Chromatik;
Improvisation; Melodie;
Prelude; Toccata   (3332)

MURTULA, GIOVANNI (1881-1964)
Carovana, Intermezzo Caratteristico
gtr (7-8th degr.) BERBEN EB1057
f.s.   (3333)

Rievocazione
(Mori, Otello) gtr (4-5th degr.)
BERBEN f.s. contains also: Bach,
Johann Sebastian, French Suite
No. 6, BWV 817, In E, Minuet,
"Piccolo Minuetto" (G maj)   (3334)

NEIJBOER, OTTO C.
Melodie En Positie *CC11U
(Peters) gtr (1-2nd degr.) HARMONIA
1897 f.s. easy pcs in various
positions   (3335)

NEUMANN, ULRIK
Guitare Melancolique
(Ahslund; Neumann) gtr (3rd degr.)
REUTER f.s.   (3336)

Leksakstaget
"Toy Train, The" (Ahslund) gtr (4-
5th degr.) REUTER f.s.   (3337)

Love Waltz (from Karleksvals)
(Ahslund) gtr (3-4th degr., with an
alternative simplified version by
Ulf G. Ahslund) REUTER f.s.
(3338)

Manresan
gtr (4th degr., with a version for
solo voice, gtr) REUTER f.s.
(3339)

NIESSEN, HANS-LUTZ (1920-1982)
Prelude and Fugue
gtr (8th degr.) HARMONIA 1848 f.s.
(3340)

NIN-CULMELL, JOAQUIN (1908-   )
Variaciones Sobre Un Tema De Milan, 6
gtr (8th degr.) UNION ESP. 18975
f.s.   (3341)

NOBRE, MARLOS (1939-   )
Momentos I
gtr ESCHIG f.s.   (3342)
(Santos) gtr (Collection Turibio
Santos, No.9) ESCHIG f.s.   (3343)

NORMAN, THEODORE (1912-   )
Mobile
gtr (7th degr.) COLOMBO NY-2238
f.s.   (3344)

OBROVSKA, JANA (1930-   )
Hommage A Bela Bartok
gtr ESCHIG f.s.   (3345)

OHANA, MAURICE (1914-   )
Si Le Jour Parait, No. 1
"Temple" (Ponce) gtr (9-10th degr.,
for 10-stringed gtr) BILLAUDOT
1610 $3.00   (3346)

Si Le Jour Parait, No. 2
"Enueg" (Ponce) gtr (9-10th degr.,
for 10-stringed gtr) BILLAUDOT
1646 $3.00   (3347)

Si Le Jour Parait, No. 3
"Maya" (Ponce) gtr (9-10th degr.,
for 10-stringed gtr) BILLAUDOT
1748 $2.75   (3348)

Si Le Jour Parait, No. 4
"20 Avril (Planh)" (Ponce) gtr (9-
10th degr., for 10-stringed gtr)
BILLAUDOT 1262 $2.50   (3349)

Si Le Jour Parait, No. 5
"Chevelure De Berenice, La" (Ponce)
gtr (9-10th degr., for 10-
stringed gtr) BILLAUDOT 1749
$2.75   (3350)

Si Le Jour Parait, No. 6
"Jeu Des Quatre Vents" (Ponce) gtr
(9-10th degr., for 10-stringed
gtr) BILLAUDOT 1754 $3.00   (3351)

Si Le Jour Parait, No. 7
"Aube" (Ponce) gtr (9-10th degr.,
for 10-stringed gtr) BILLAUDOT
1388 $2.75   (3352)

Tiento
(Yepes) gtr (9th degr., for 6- or
10-stringed gtr) BILLAUDOT 1132
$2.00   (3353)

ORBON, JULIAN (1925-   )
Preludio Y Danza
(de la Torre) gtr (7th degr.)
COLOMBO NY-2319 f.s.   (3354)

ORREGO-SALAS, JUAN A. (1919-   )
Esquinas *Op.63
(Gilardino) gtr (4-5th degr.,
Collezione Di Musiche Per
Chitarra) BERBEN EB1648 $2.75
(3355)

ORSOLINO, FEDERICO (1918-   )
Capriccio, La Cascatella
gtr (7th degr.) HEINRICH. N-1544
f.s.   (3356)

Piccole Impressioni Di Campagna
*CC3U
gtr (7th degr.) HEINRICH. N-1545
f.s.   (3357)

PALAU, MANUEL (1893-1967)
Ayer, Fantasia
(Yepes) gtr (8-9th degr.) UNION
ESP. f.s.   (3358)

Fantasy
(Balaguer) gtr UNION ESP. 21662
f.s.   (3359)

PAMMER, JOSEF
Burleske
gtr (4th degr.) HEINRICH. N-1632
f.s.   (3360)

Maria Geht Durch Bluten
gtr (4-5th degr.) HEINRICH. N-1625
f.s.   (3361)

Valse Triste
gtr (3rd degr.) HEINRICH. N-1626
f.s.   (3362)

PANIN, PETER
Neue Russische Gitarremusik, Vol. I
(composed with Slawski, Wladimir)
*CC4L
(Behrend) gtr (7-8th degr.) ZIMMER.
ZM-1854 f.s. contains works by:
Panin (3), Slawski (1)   (3363)

PAPANDOPULO, BORIS (1906-   )
Drei Jugoslavische Tanze Fur Gitarre
gtr (4th degr.) GERIG HG-1297 f.s.
(3364)

PATACHICH, IVAN (1922-   )
Gyermekdalok Gitarra, Vol. 1 -
Children's Songs For Guitar, Vol.
1 *CC5U
(Benko) gtr (6-8th degr.) EMB 8344
f.s.   (3365)

Gyermekdalok Gitarra, Vol. 2 -
Children's Songs For Guitar, Vol.
2 *CC5U
(Benko) gtr (6-8th degr.) EMB 8345
f.s.   (3366)

PAUBON, PIERRE (1910-   )
Pieces, 6
(Geoffre) gtr (2-3rd degr.)
OUVRIERS EO-656 f.s.
contains: Berceuse; Dance
Populaire; Giocoso; Obsession;
Prelude No. 1; Serenade   (3367)

PELEMANS, WILLEM (1901-   )
7 Croquis
(Alfonso) gtr MAURER f.s.   (3368)

Humoresque
(Alfonso) gtr (8-9th degr.)
METROPOLIS EM-4511, 4512 $3.00
contains also: Vlaamse Dans
(3369)

6 Romances
(Alfonso) gtr MAURER f.s.   (3370)

Speelse Wals
(Alfonso) gtr MAURER f.s.   (3371)

PELTA, MAX
Prelude Et Valse
gtr (6-7th degr., Collection
L'Heure De La Guitare Classique)
CHOUDENS 20.675 f.s.   (3372)

PERALDO BERT, NILO
Improvvisi, 2
(Gilardino) gtr (7th degr.,
Collezione Di Musiche Per
Chitarra) BERBEN EB1472 $1.75
(3373)

Omaggio A Charlie Christian *CC3U
(Gilardino) gtr (7th degr.) BERBEN
EB1718 $3.00 Collezione Di
Musiche Per Chitarra   (3374)

PERUZZI, AURELIO (1921-   )
Pezzi, 4
gtr (8-9th degr.) ZERBONI 7656
$11.75
contains: Elegia Di Croton;
Finzioni; Guernica; Recuerdos
(3375)

PETIT, PIERRE (1922-   )
Theme and Variations
gtr ESCHIG f.s.   (3376)

PETIT, RAYMOND
Nocturne
(Pujol) gtr (5th degr.) ESCHIG 1207
f.s.   (3377)

PETRASSI, GOFFREDO (1904-   )
Nunc
gtr (9-10th degr.) ZERBONI 7464
$4.75   (3378)

Suoni Notturni
(Abloniz) gtr RICORDI-IT 130354
(3379)

PEZZOLI, GIORGIO
Andante Armonioso, Tema Di Autore
Ignoto
gtr (4th degr.) BERBEN EB1076 f.s.
(3380)

PICK, RICHARD SAMUEL BURNS (1915-   )
First Repertoire For Classic Guitar
*CC22U
gtr (3-4th degr.) FORSTER f.s.
(3381)

Improvisation
(Segovia) gtr CEL 23 $.65   (3382)

Preludes, 9
gtr (3-4th degr.) FORSTER f.s.
(3383)

PIGNOCCHI, EMANUELE
Piccola Leggenda
gtr (3-4th degr.) BERBEN EB1078
f.s.   (3384)

PILSL, F.
Gitarrestucke Fur Die Jugend
(Behrend) gtr (Gitarremusik Fur Die
Jugend, Vol. 4) ZIMMER. 1963 f.s.
(3385)

Miniaturproblematicos
(Behrend) gtr (Gitarremusik Fur Die
Jugend, Vol. 5) ZIMMER. 1964 f.s.
(3386)

PIZZINI, CARLO ALBERTO (1905-   )
  Capriccio Napoletano
    (Battisti d'Amario) gtr (5th degr.)
    ZANIBON 5304 f.s.   (3387)

  Improvviso Da Concerto
    (Battisti d'Amario) gtr (6-7th
    degr.) ZANIBON 5302 f.s.   (3388)

  Suite Infantile *CC6U
    (Azpiazu) 1-2gtr (3-4th degr.) sc
    DE SANTIS 1073 f.s. for gtr (5)
    and 2 gtr (1)   (3389)

POLACZEK, DIETMAR (1942-   )
  Metamorfosen Und Fuge
    gtr UNIVER. 15644 f.s.   (3390)

PONCE, MANUEL MARIA (1882-1948)
  Canciones Populares Mexicanas, 3
    (Segovia) gtr (8th degr.) SCHOTT
    GA-111 f.s.
    contains: Allegro, MIN291;
    Allegro, MIN293; Andante, MIN
    292   (3391)

  Prelude
    (Segovia) gtr (8th degr.) SCHOTT
    GA-112 f.s.   (3392)

  Preludes, Vol. I: Nos. 1-6
    (Segovia) gtr (4-6th degr.) SCHOTT
    GA-124 f.s.   (3393)

  Preludes, Vol. II: Nos. 7-12
    (Segovia) gtr (4-6th degr.) SCHOTT
    GA-125 f.s.   (3394)

  Preludios Cortos, 6
    (Silva) gtr (3-4th degr.) PEER
    690-4 $1.50   (3395)

  Scherzino Mexicano
    (Lopez Ramos) gtr (6-7th degr.)
    PEER 1083-2 f.s.   (3396)

  Suite in A minor
    (Abloniz) gtr (8-9th degr., issued
    under the name of S.L. Weiss; 3rd
    ed, 1971 with "A Necessary
    Explanation") BERBEN EB1017 f.s.
                                         (3397)
    (Fleury) gtr (8-9th degr., issued
    under the name of S.L. Weiss)
    RICORDI-ARG BA-10981 f.s. (3398)
    (Sensier) gtr (8-9th degr., issued
    under the name of S.L. Weiss;
    Prelude, Allemande, Sarabande,
    Gavotte, Gigue from the Suite in
    A minor; all movements edited
    separately) ESSEX f.s.   (3399)

  Suite in D
    (Lopez Ramos; Vazquez) gtr (7th
    degr.) PEER 1094-15 $3.00 (3400)

  Suite In D Major: Gavotte I And II, D
    Major And D Minor (Gavotte in D)
    "Gavotta E Minuetto" (Abloniz) gtr
    (issued under the name of Antonio
    Scarlatti; 3rd ed, 1970) BERBEN
    EB1001 $1.00   (3401)
    (Bellow) gtr (C maj/C min, issued
    under the name of Antonio
    Scarlatti; contained in
    International Anthology) COLOMBO
    NY-2174 f.s.   (3402)
    (Bianqui Pinero) gtr (issued under
    the name of Antonio Scarlatti)
    RICORDI-ARG BA-12719 f.s. (3403)
    (Sensier) gtr (issued under the
    name of Antonio Scarlatti) ESSEX
    f.s.   (3404)
    (Smith) gtr (issued under the name
    of Antonio Scarlatti) COLUMBIA
    122 $.90   (3405)
    (Visser) gtr (issued under the name
    of Antonio Scarlatti) HARMONIA
    1555 f.s.   (3406)

  Theme Varie Et Finale
    (Segovia) gtr (10th degr.) SCHOTT
    GA-109 f.s.   (3407)

  Variations Sur "Folia De Espana" Et
    Fugue
    (Segovia) gtr (9th degr.) SCHOTT
    GA-135 f.s.   (3408)

  Waltz
    (Segovia) gtr (7th degr.) SCHOTT
    GA-153 f.s.   (3409)

POULENC, FRANCIS (1899-1963)
  Sarabande, Dedie A Ida Presti
    gtr (5th degr.) RICORDI-ENG L-557
    f.s.   (3410)

PRADO, JOSE-ANTONIO (ALMEIDA)
    (1943-   )
  Livre Pour Six Cordes
    "Livro Para Seis Cordas" (Santos)
    gtr (6-7th degr., 3 pcs;
    Collection Turibio Santos) ESCHIG
    8197 f.s.   (3411)

PRESTI, IDA (1924-1967)
  Danse Rythmique
    gtr (7th degr.) RICORDI-IT R-1606
    f.s.   (3412)

PROSPERI, CARLO (1921-   )
  Canto Dell'arpeggione
    (Frosali) gtr (8th degr.) ZERBONI
    7766 $7.00   (3413)

PUJOL, EMILIO (1886-1982)
  Atardecer
    gtr ESCHIG 1229 f.s.   (3414)

  Bagatelle
    gtr RICORDI-ARG BA-11006 f.s. (3415)

  Barcarolle
    gtr (5th degr.) ESCHIG 1235 f.s.
                              (3416)

  Becqueriana, Complainte
    gtr ESCHIG 1240 f.s.   (3417)

  Cancio De Cuna
    gtr ESCHIG 1203 f.s.   (3418)

  Cap I Cua
    gtr ESCHIG 1248 f.s.   (3419)

  Caprice Varie Sur Un Theme D'Aguado
    gtr ESCHIG 1242 f.s.   (3420)

  Cubana
    (Segovia) gtr CEL 11 $.75 (3421)

  Deuxieme Triquilandia *CC4U
    gtr (3rd degr.) ESCHIG 1234 f.s.
                              (3422)

  Endecha Alla Amada Ausente
    "Complainte A l'aimee Disparue" gtr
    (6th degr.) ESCHIG 1238 f.s.
                              (3423)

  Fantasia Breve Sobre El Nombre
    "Salcedo"
    gtr RICORDI-ARG BA-11110 f.s.
                              (3424)

  Festivola, Danza Catalana De Espiritu
    Popular
    gtr RICORDI-ARG BA-12046 f.s.
                              (3425)

  Homenaje A Tarrega
    gtr (7-8th degr.) SCHOTT GA-150
    f.s.   (3426)

  Impromptu
    gtr (6th degr.) ESCHIG 1206 f.s.
                              (3427)

  Manola Del Avapies, Tonadilla
    gtr RICORDI-ARG BA-11448 f.s.
                              (3428)

  Morceaux Espagnols, 3
    gtr (8-9th degr.) ESCHIG 1204 f.s.
    contains: Guajira; Tango;
    Tonadilla   (3429)

  Pequena Romanza
    gtr ESCHIG 1222 f.s.   (3430)

  Preludio Romantico
    gtr RICORDI-ARG BA-11007 f.s.
                              (3431)

  Rapsodia Valenciana
    gtr ESCHIG 1228 f.s.   (3432)

  Salve
    gtr RICORDI-ARG BA-11112 f.s.
                              (3433)

  Sequidilla
    gtr RICORDI-ARG BA-11113 f.s.
                              (3434)

  Sevilla, Evocation
    gtr (8th degr.) ESCHIG 1025 f.s.
                              (3435)

  Triquilandia, Jugando Al Escondite
    (Cache-Cache)
    gtr (4th degr.) ESCHIG 1231 f.s.
                              (3436)

  Troisieme Triquilandia *CC3U
    gtr (4th degr.) ESCHIG 1241 f.s.
                              (3437)

  Variations Sur Un Theme Obsedant
    gtr ESCHIG 1244 f.s.   (3438)

  Veneciana
    gtr ESCHIG 1230 f.s.   (3439)

  Villanesca, Danza Campesina
    gtr (8th degr.) RICORDI-ARG
    BA-12352 f.s.   (3440)

QUAGLINO, ANACLETO
  Andantino
    (Tagliavini) gtr (3-4th degr.)
    BERBEN 2063 f.s.   (3441)

RADOLE, GIUSEPPE
  Notturno
    (Tonazzi) gtr (5-6th degr.,
    Collezione Di Musiche Per
    Chitarra) BERBEN EB1649 $1.50
                              (3442)

RAMOVS, PRIMOZ (1921-   )
  Nocturnes, 2
    gtr (8-9th degr.) GERIG HG-635
    $3.75   (3443)

RATZ, MARTIN
  Kleine Serenade, Unterhaltende
    Vortragsstucke *CC11U
    gtr (2-3rd degr.) HOFMEISTER T-4161
    $5.25   (3444)

RAVEL, MAURICE (1875-1937)
  Pavane Pour Une Infante Defunte
    (Bellow) gtr (8-9th degr.) COLOMBO
    NY-2302 f.s.   (3445)
    (Gubbay; Duarte) gtr SCHOTT
    ED-10968 f.s.   (3446)

  Piece En Forme De Habanera
    (Azpiazu) gtr (8-9th degr.) LEDUC
    22722 $3.00   (3447)

READ, GARDNER (1913-   )
  Canzone Di Notte *Op.127
    gtr (8-9th degr., Collezione Di
    Musiche Per Chitarra) BERBEN
    EB1632 $2.50   (3448)

REBAY, FERDINAND (1889-1953)
  Albumblatt
    gtr (4-5th degr.) HEINRICH. N-1613
    f.s. contains also: Kleiner
    Marsch   (3449)

  Kleine Leichte Stucke, 14
    gtr (1-2nd degr.) HAWLIK 98 f.s.
                              (3450)

  Leicht Spielbare Kleinigkeiten
    *CC16L
    (Hammerschmied) gtr/gtr,pno (2-3rd
    degr.) sc,solo pt HEINRICH.
    N-1528 f.s. for gtr (15) and gtr,
    pno (1)   (3451)

  Menuette, 2
    (Hammerschmied) gtr (4th degr.)
    HEINRICH. N-1614 f.s.   (3452)

  Tanzlied
    (Hammerschmied) gtr (4th degr.)
    HEINRICH. N-1628 f.s.   (3453)

  Wiegenlied
    (Hammerschmied) gtr (3rd degr.)
    HEINRICH. N-1612 f.s. contains
    also: Melodie   (3454)

REINBOTE, HELMUT
  Leichte Stucke Fur Gitarre
    (Behrend) gtr (Gitarremusik Fur Die
    Jugend, Vol. 16) ZIMMER. 2075
    f.s.   (3455)

REISER, EKKEHARD
  Masken
    gtr (7-8th degr.) SCHOTT GA-430
    f.s.   (3456)

REYNE, GERARD (1944-   )
  Guitare
    gtr (7-8th degr., 7 new pieces)
    LEDUC $4.00   (3457)

  Homenaje A M. de Falla
    gtr (6th degr.) UNION ESP. f.s.
                              (3458)

RIERA, RODRIGO
  Merengue Venezolano
    gtr (5th degr.) SIKORSKI 741 $2.25
                              (3459)

  Preludio Criollo
    gtr (5th degr.) SIKORSKI 740 $2.75
                              (3460)

RODRIGO, JOAQUIN (1902-   )
  Bajando De La Meseta (from Por Los
    Campos De Espana, No. 2)
    (Alfonso) gtr (9th degr., Edition
    Nicolas Alfonso, No. 105) SCHOTT-
    FRER 9158 f.s.   (3461)

  Elogio De La Guitarra
    (Gilardino) gtr (9th degr.,
    Collezione Di Musiche Per
    Chitarra, 3 pcs.) BERBEN EB1568
    $7.50   (3462)

  En Los Trigales, Scene Castillane
    (from Por Los Campos De Espana)
    gtr (8-9th degr.) UNION ESP. f.s.
    contains also: Entre Olivares
                              (3463)

  Invocation Et Danse, Hommage A Manuel
    De Falla
    (Diaz) gtr (10th degr.) FRANCAIS
    755 f.s.   (3464)

  Junto Al Generalife
    (Behrend) gtr (7th degr., Gitarre-
    Bibliothek, No.20) BOTE GB-20
    f.s.   (3465)

  Pajaros De Primavera
    gtr UNION ESP. 21788 f.s. (3466)

  Pastorale
    gtr ESCHIG f.s.   (3467)

  Petites Pieces, 3
    (Sainz de la Maza) gtr (7-9th
    degr.) ESCHIG 7382 f.s.
    contains: Grazioso; Moderato; Ya

RODRIGO, JOAQUIN (cont'd.)

Se Van Los Pastores, "Bergers
S'en Vont, Les"   (3468)

Piezas Espanolas, 3
(Segovia) gtr (9th degr.) SCHOTT
GA-212 f.s.   (3469)

Piezas Faciles, 4 (from Album De
Cecilia)
(Azpiazu) gtr (5-6th degr.) UNION
ESP. 19440 f.s.   (3470)

Sarabande Lointaine
(Pujol) gtr (8-9th degr.) ESCHIG
1226 f.s.   (3471)

Tiento Antiguo
(Behrend) gtr (7-8th degr.,
Gitarre-Bibliothek, No.19; also
published in European Masters For
The Guitar) BOTE GB-19 f.s. (3472)

ROE, BETTY (1930-   )
Larcombe's Fancy
(Duarte) gtr (5-6th degr., 5 pcs.)
NOVELLO 19392 f.s.   (3473)

ROOTH, HANS
Redsleeves
gtr (4th degr.) HARMONIA 2106 f.s.
                      (3474)

ROOY, JULIO
Charlein, Antilliaanse Wals
(Coco) gtr (5th degr.) BROEKMANS
738 f.s.   (3475)

ROSETTA, GIUSEPPE
Canti Della Pianura *CC4U
(Gilardino) gtr (6th degr.) BERBEN
EB1813 $4.25 Collezione Di
Musiche Per Chitarre   (3476)

Mirage
(Estarellas) gtr (7th degr.,
Collezione Di Musiche Per
Chitarra) BERBEN EB1719 $2.50
                      (3477)

Poemi Brevi, 6
(Estarellas) gtr (7th degr.,
Collezione Di Musiche Per
Chitarra) BERBEN EB1720 $3.25
                      (3478)

Preludi Per Gilardino *CC7U
(Gilardino) gtr (8th degr.) BERBEN
EB1525 $3.50 Collezione Di
Musiche Per Chitarra   (3479)

Preludio, Barcarola E Scherzo
(Gilardino) gtr (7-8th degr.,
Collezione Di Musiche Per
Chitarra) BERBEN EB1522 $3.00
                      (3480)

Weissiana, Omaggio A S.L. Weiss
*CC4U
gtr (7-8th degr.) BERBEN EB1501
$1.75 Collezione Di Musiche Per
Chitarra   (3481)

ROSSI, ABNER
Andantino E Valzer
gtr (3-4th degr.) BERBEN EB2018
f.s.   (3482)

Contrappunto Scherzoso
gtr (5th degr.) BERBEN EB2104 f.s.
                      (3483)

Nocturne
gtr (4th degr.) BERBEN EB2056 f.s.
                      (3484)

Pensieri d'Autunno
gtr (4th degr.) BERBEN 2105 f.s.
                      (3485)

ROUSSEL, ALBERT (CHARLES PAUL)
(1869-1937)
Segovia *Op.29
gtr (7th degr.) DURAND $1.50 (3486)

RUBIN, MARCEL (1905-   )
Petite Serenade
gtr DOBLINGER 05909 f.s.   (3487)

RUCH, HANNES
Leichte Stucke, 34
gtr (1-2nd degr.) GERIG GG-160A
f.s.   (3488)

Spielmusik *CC15U
gtr (3rd degr.) HOFMEISTER-W 9504
f.s.   (3489)

RUIZ PIPO, ANTONIO
Cancion Y Danza, No.1
(Yepes) gtr (9th degr.) UNION ESP.
f.s.   (3490)

Cancion Y Danza, No.2
(Yepes) gtr UNION ESP. 21529 f.s.
                      (3491)

Canto Libre
gtr (8-9th degr.) TRANSAT. 1191
$2.25 contains also: Floreo
                      (3492)

RUIZ PIPO, ANTONIO (cont'd.)

Estancias
(Gilardino) gtr (8th degr.,
Collezione Di Musiche Per
Chitarra) BERBEN EB1420 $2.00
                      (3493)

Hommage A Antonio De Cabezon
gtr (5th degr.) ESCHIG f.s. (3494)

RUTHENFRANZ, R.
Pieces, 3
gtr (3rd degr.) METROPOLIS EM-4385
$2.50   (3495)

SACCHETTI, ARTURO
Eucalyptus
(Gilardino) gtr (8-9th degr.,
Collezione Di Musiche Per
Chitarra) BERBEN EB1721 $2.25
                      (3496)

Memorial
(Gilardino) gtr (4-5th degr.,
Collezione Di Musiche Per
Chitarra) BERBEN EB1976 $2.25
                      (3497)

SAINZ DE LA MAZA, EDUARDO
Campanas Del Alba, Tremolo
gtr (8th degr.) UNION ESP. 19923
f.s.   (3498)

Canco Del Lladre, Popular Catalana
gtr (6th degr.) UNION ESP. 20569
f.s.   (3499)

Confidencia, Preludio
gtr (7th degr.) BROEKMANS 1013 f.s.
                      (3500)

Greensleeves, Cancion Popular Inglesa
gtr (8th degr.) BROEKMANS 941 f.s.
                      (3501)

Habanera
gtr (7th degr.) UNION ESP. 18814
f.s.   (3502)

Homenaje A La Guitarra, Preludio
gtr (9th degr.) FRANCAIS 731 f.s.
                      (3503)

SALAZAR, ADOLFO (1890-1958)
Romancillo
(Llobet) gtr (5-6th degr.) ESCHIG
1217 f.s.   (3504)

SALDARELLI, VINCENZO
Per La Chitarra
gtr (7-8th degr., Collezione Di
Musiche Per Chitarra) BERBEN
EB1977 $2.75   (3505)

SAMAZEUILH, GUSTAVE (1877-1967)
Serenade
(Segovia) gtr (8-9th degr.) DURAND
$1.75   (3506)

SANCHEZ, B.
Cancion Olvidada *No.1 (from Dix
Pieces Caracteristiques)
gtr CHOUDENS f.s. contains also:
Cubana, No.2   (3507)

Complainte Funebre, Fantaisie A La
Memoire De Ida Presti (2.5.1967,
Jour De Son Enterrement)
gtr (7-8th degr.) TRANSAT. 1044
$2.00   (3508)

Criolla *No.3 (from Dix Pieces
Caracteristiques)
gtr CHOUDENS f.s.   (3509)

Danza Del Pejin *No.9 (from Dix
Pieces Caracteristiques)
gtr CHOUDENS f.s.   (3510)

Fiesta Laredana (Impromptu No. 1)
gtr (7th degr.) TRANSAT. 1025 $2.00
                      (3511)

Linares *No.10 (from Dix Pieces
Caracteristiques)
gtr CHOUDENS f.s.   (3512)

Minivalses, 4
gtr ESCHIG f.s.   (3513)

Ninfa, La
"Nymphe, La" gtr (3rd degr.,
Collection L'Heure De La Guitare
Classique; also published in
Repertoire Progressif Pour
Guitare, Vol. II) CHOUDENS f.s.
                      (3514)

Nocturne No. 1
gtr (3rd degr., Collection L'Heure
De La Guitare Classique; also
published in Repertoire
Progressif Pour Guitare, Vol. II)
CHOUDENS f.s.   (3515)

Peruviana *No.7 (from Dix Pieces
Caracteristiques)
gtr CHOUDENS f.s.   (3516)

Preambolo Y Toccata Surena
gtr (7th degr.) TRANSAT. 1101 $2.00
                      (3517)

SANCHEZ, B. (cont'd.)

Prelude in G minor *No.8 (from Dix
Pieces Caracteristiques)
gtr CHOUDENS f.s.   (3518)

Preludio Y Alborada
gtr SIKORSKI 756 $2.75   (3519)

Quimeras, No.1
"Chimeres, No. 1" gtr (4 pcs)
CHOUDENS 20.407 f.s.   (3520)

Quimeras, No.2
"Chimeres, No. 2" gtr CHOUDENS
20.423 f.s.   (3521)

Quimeras, No.3
"Chimeres, No. 3" gtr CHOUDENS
20.424 f.s.   (3522)

Ruisseau, Le
"Arroyo, El" gtr (5th degr.,
Collection L'Heure De La Guitare
Classique; also published in
Repertoire Progressif Pour
Guitare, Vol. II) CHOUDENS f.s.
                      (3523)

Serenade Villageoise
"Serenata Pueblerina" gtr (4-5th
degr., Collection L'Heure De La
Guitare Classique; also published
in Repertoire Progressif Pour
Guitare, Vol. III) CHOUDENS f.s.
                      (3524)

Serenata Canaria *No.5 (from Dix
Pieces Caracteristiques)
gtr CHOUDENS f.s.   (3525)

Tonalida Islena *No.4 (from Dix
Pieces Caracteristiques)
gtr CHOUDENS f.s.   (3526)

Vals Sombrio *No.6 (from Dix Pieces
Caracteristiques)
gtr CHOUDENS f.s.   (3527)

SANDI, LUIS (1905-   )
Fatima, Suite Galante
(Silva) gtr (4-5th degr.) PEER D-1
$1.50   (3528)

SANTORSOLA, GUIDO (1904-   )
Minuet (from Suite A Antiga, No. 2)
gtr (6th degr.) RICORDI-BR BR-2723
f.s.   (3529)

Prelude (from Suite A Antiga, No. 1)
gtr (8th degr.) RICORDI-BR BR-2372
f.s.   (3530)

Prelude No. 1
(Gilardino) gtr (6-9th degr.,
Collezione Di Musiche Per
Chitarra) BERBEN 1361 $1.75 from
PRELUDIOS, 5   (3531)

Prelude No. 2
gtr (8th degr.) RICORDI-BR BR-2795
f.s.   (3532)
(Gilardino) gtr (6-9th degr.,
Collezione Di Musiche Per
Chitarra) BERBEN 1362 $1.75 from
PRELUDIOS, 5   (3533)

Prelude No. 3
(Gilardino) gtr (6-9th degr.,
Collezione Di Musiche Per
Chitarra) BERBEN 1363 $1.25 from
PRELUDIOS, 5   (3534)

Prelude No. 4
(Gilardino) gtr (6-9th degr.,
Collezione Di Musiche Per
Chitarra) BERBEN 1364 $1.50 from
PRELUDIOS, 5   (3535)

Prelude No. 5
(Gilardino) gtr (6-9th degr.,
Collezione Di Musiche Per
Chitarra) BERBEN 1365 $1.75 from
PRELUDIOS, 5   (3536)

Tientos, 4, Sonoridades 1970
(Gilardino) gtr (8-9th degr.,
Collezione Di Musiche Per
Chitarra) BERBEN EB1477 $5.00
                      (3537)

Vals Romantico
(Gilardino) gtr (7th degr.,
Collezione Di Musiche Per
Chitarra) BERBEN EB1421 $1.75
                      (3538)

SAUGUET, HENRI (1901-   )
Preludes, 3
(Gilardino) gtr (9th degr.,
Collezione Di Musiche Per
Chitarra) BERBEN EB1516 $3.25
                      (3539)

SAVIO, ISAIAS (1900-1977)
Suite Descritiva
gtr (8-9th degr.) RICORDI-BR
BR-2981 f.s.   (3540)

SCHAGEN, HENK VAN
Kleine Solist, De - The Little
Soloist, Easy Guitar Pieces In
Various Positions *CC10U
gtr (1st degr.) HARMONIA 1274 f.s.
(3541)

Tum Tum, For Young Guitarists *CC15U
gtr (1-2nd degr.) HARMONIA 1297
f.s.
(3542)

SCHIBLER, ARMIN (1920-)
Black Guitar, The *CC9U,spir
gtr (5-6th degr.) EULENBURG ES-435
f.s.
(3543)

Every Night I Dream
gtr (4th degr.) EULENBURG f.s.
(3544)

Homme Seul, Un, Kleines Konzert
gtr (5-6th degr.) EULENBURG f.s.
(3545)

My Own Blues *CC7U
gtr (6-8th degr.) EULENBURG f.s.
(3546)

SCHINDLER, OTTO
Wiegenlied
gtr (3rd degr.) VAMO EE-017 f.s.
contains also: Lucia   (3547)

SCHNEIDER, MATTHIAS
Gingganz
gtr (Musica 3) HANSEN-DEN MUS 320
f.s.
(3548)

SCHOENBERG, ARNOLD (1874-1951)
Kleine Klavierstucke, 6 *Op.19
(Behrend) gtr (8th degr.) UNIVER.
13577 f.s.
(3549)

SCHOLZE, ARTHUR JOHANNES (1883-1945)
Kleine Solostucke *Op.257, CC3U
(Walker) gtr (6-7th degr.)
HEINRICH. 1507 f.s.
(3550)

SCHREIBER, ALFRED
Aphorismen
(Koch) gtr (7th degr.) ISI 102 f.s.
(3551)

SCHULER, ALEXANDER
Waltz
gtr (3-4th degr.) HEINRICH. N-1633
f.s.
(3552)

SCHUMANN, GERHARD (1914-)
Mikrokosmos
(Behrend) gtr (Gitarremusik Fur Die
Jugend, Vol. II) ZIMMER. 1961
f.s.
(3553)

SCHWEYDA, WILLY
Pieces, 2
(Ragossnig) gtr ESCHIG f.s. (3554)

SEGOVIA, ANDRES (1896-)
Impromptu
gtr (6th degr.) FORTEA 151 f.s.
(3555)

Prelude In Chords
gtr (3rd degr.) CEL 10 f.s. (3556)

Preludios, 3
gtr (6th degr.) FORTEA 149 f.s.
(3557)

Tonadilla
gtr (5th degr.) FORTEA 150 f.s.
(3558)

SFETSAS, KYRIACOS (1945-)
Strophes *CC4U
gtr (8-9th degr.) TRANSAT. 1268
$4.00
(3559)

SHACKELFORD, RUDOLPH OWENS (RUDY)
(1944-)
Epitaffio
(Chiesa) gtr (7th degr.) ZERBONI
8237 f.s.
(3560)

SIERRA-FORTUNY, J.M.
Introduccio
gtr (5th degr.) ESCHIG 8190 f.s.
contains also: Canco; Dansa
(3561)

SMITH BRINDLE, REGINALD (1917-)
Danza Pagana
gtr (5th degr., Schott's Series Of
Contemporary Music For Spanish
Guitar, No. 2) SCHOTT f.s. (3562)

Do Not Go Gentle...
gtr (6th degr.) ZERBONI 8021 f.s.
(3563)

Etruscan Preludes *CC4U
gtr (5-6th degr.) SCHOTT 5723 f.s.
Schott's Series Of Contemporary
Music For Spanish Guitar, No. 11
(3564)

Fuego Fatuo
gtr (6th degr., Schott's Series Of
Contemporary Music For Spanish
Guitar, No. 4) SCHOTT f.s. (3565)

Memento
(Gilardino) gtr (7th degr.,
Collezione Di Musiche Per
Chitarra) BERBEN EB1986 $2.75
(3566)

SMITH BRINDLE, REGINALD (cont'd.)

Nocturne
gtr (5th degr., Schott's Series Of
Contemporary Music For Spanish
Guitar, No. 3) SCHOTT f.s. (3567)

November Memories
gtr (6th degr.) ZERBONI 8020 f.s.
(3568)

Polifemo De Oro, Il, 4 Fragmenti
gtr (8th degr.) BRUZZI f.s. (3569)

Vita Senese
gtr (7th degr., Schott's Series Of
Contemporary Music For Spanish
Guitar) SCHOTT 5423 f.s. (3570)

SOJO, VINCENTE E.
Pieces From Venezuela, 5
(Diaz) gtr (4th degr.) BROEKMANS
837 f.s.
contains: Aguinaldo; Aire
Venezolano; Cancion; Cantico;
Galeron   (3571)

Quirpa Guatirena, Joropo
(Diaz) gtr (3rd degr.) BROEKMANS
847 f.s.
(3572)

SOLARES, ENRIQUE (1910-)
Fantasy
(Alfonso) gtr (8th degr.)
METROPOLIS EM-4679 $2.50 (3573)

Ofrenda A Fernando Sors
(Alfonso) gtr (7th degr.)
METROPOLIS EM-4351 $2.00 (3574)

Toccatina
(Alfonso) gtr (8th degr.)
METROPOLIS $2.50   (3575)

SPERLING, ERNST
Evening Song
gtr (3rd degr.) HEINRICH. N-1640
f.s.
(3576)

Preludes, 4
gtr (4th degr.) ESSEX f.s. (3577)

Silent Forests
gtr (3rd degr.) HEINRICH. N-1615
f.s.
(3578)

Slumber Song
gtr (3rd degr.) HEINRICH. N-1646
f.s.
(3579)

Springtime Waltz
gtr (3rd degr.) HEINRICH. N-1616
f.s.
(3580)

SPRONGL, NORBERT (1892-1983)
Stucke, 6
(Dobrauz) gtr (6-7th degr.)
HEINRICH. 1535 f.s.
contains: Barcarolle; Feierlicher
Tanz; Intermezzo; Minuet;
Notturno; Tanz   (3581)

SREBOTNJAK, ALOJZ F. (1931-)
2 Movimenti
(Tonazzi) gtr (6th degr.) ZERBONI
8114 f.s.
(3582)

STAAK, PIETER VAN DER (1930-)
Bolero Espanol
gtr (4th degr.) BROEKMANS 851 f.s.
(3583)

Exotic Dances, 5
gtr (2-3rd degr.) BROEKMANS 856
f.s.
contains: Armenian Dance; Dance
Of A Tribal Chief; Hungarian
Dance; Sword Dance; War Dance
(3584)

Moods From The Song Of Solomon, 3
gtr (4-5th degr.) BROEKMANS 825
f.s.
contains: Dodi Li Wa'ani Lo;
Hin'cha Jafeh Dodi; W'dodi Awar
(3585)

Pezzi, 3
gtr (4-5th degr.) BROEKMANS 808
f.s.
contains: Andante; Andantino
Quasi Allegretto; Vivo E
Burlesco   (3586)

Prelude No. 1
gtr (4th degr.) BROEKMANS 797 f.s.
(3587)

STADLMAIR, HANS (1929-)
Stucke, 5
gtr (7-8th degr.) DOBLINGER 05905
f.s.
contains: Allegro Molto; Leicht
Fliesend, Nicht Schnell; Sehr
Langsam; Sehr Langsam; Ziemlich
Rasch   (3588)

STAVINOHA-MELISEK, JAN
Suite Romantica
gtr TEESELING VT-219 f.s.   (3589)

STEFFENS, WALTER (1934-)
Fur Soto *Op.18
gtr (7-8th degr., Can be performed
simultaneously with his Op. 19,
Rose Ouest, for clar or bass
clar; Op. 20, Structure de la
Rose, for fl; and Op. 21, Grande
Rose, for ob or ob d'amore or ob
da caccia) BOTE f.s.   (3590)

STERZATI, UMBERTO (1909-1972)
Elegy
gtr (6th degr.) BERBEN EB2007 f.s.
(3591)

STEVENS, BERNARD GEORGE (1916-1983)
Ballad *Op.45
"Bramble Briar, The" (Gilardino)
gtr (8th degr., Collezione Di
Musiche Per Chitarra) BERBEN
EB1723 $3.00   (3592)

STEVENSON, RONALD (1928-)
Anger Dance
gtr (7-8th degr.) SCHOTT GA-222
f.s.
(3593)

STINGL, ANTON (1908-)
Gitarrenbuch Fur Madeleine, Vol. I
*CC21U
gtr (1-5th degr.) SCHOTT GA-420
f.s.
(3594)

Gitarrenbuch Fur Madeleine, Vol. II
*CC16U
gtr (1-5th degr.) SCHOTT GA-421
f.s.
(3595)

Improvisation, Uber Ein
Mittelalterliches Lied "Es Sass
Ein Edly Maget Schon" *Op.46
gtr (7th degr.) SCHOTT GA-427 f.s.
(3596)

Kleine Spielstucke Nach
Kinderliedern, 30 *Op.29
gtr (2-3rd degr.) HOFMEISTER T-2024
$2.50
(3597)

Leichte Stucke, 12 *Op.15c
gtr (2-3rd degr.) SCHOTT GA-86 f.s.
(3598)

Sonatine, Op. 15
gtr (3-5th degr.) HOFMEISTER T-4025
f.s.
contains: Maien Ist Kommen, Der,
Paraphrase Uber Einen Alten
Maitanz, Op.15d; Satze, 2, Zu
Einem Mahrischen Wiegenlied,
Op.15b; Sonatina, Op. 15a;
Traumbilder, Variationen Uber
Ein Wiegenlied, Op.15e   (3599)

STOCKHAUSEN, KARLHEINZ (1928-)
Spiral; Composition No. 27
for 1 soloist (gtr) with a short
wave receiver UNIVER. 14957 f.s.
(3600)

STOKER, RICHARD (1938-)
Improvisation
(Gilardino) gtr (7th degr.,
Collezione Di Musiche Per
Chitarra) BERBEN EB1569 $1.50
(3601)

STRATEGIER, HERMAN (1912-)
Short Pieces, 10
1-2gtr (2-4th degr., 8 pcs. for gtr
solo with a version for 2 gtr; 2
pcs for 2 gtr) sc HARMONIA 2344
f.s.
(3602)

STRAVINSKY, IGOR (1882-1971)
Allegro (from Les Cinq Doigts)
(Norman) gtr (4th degr.) CHESTER
1806 f.s.
(3603)

SURINACH, CARLOS (1915-)
Bolero De Los Picaros (from Suite
Espagnole)
(Lorimer) gtr (7th degr.) AMP 7403
f.s.
(3604)

SZORDIKOWSKI, BRUNO
Impromptu
gtr VOGT 304 f.s.   (3605)

Kleine Suite
gtr VOGT 306 f.s.   (3606)

TANSMAN, ALEXANDRE (1897-)
Cavatina
(Segovia) gtr (8th degr.) SCHOTT
GA-165 f.s.   (3607)

Danza Pomposa
(Segovia) gtr (6th degr.) SCHOTT
GA-206 f.s.   (3608)

Mazurka
(Segovia) gtr (8-9th degr.) SCHOTT
GA-116 f.s.   (3609)

TANSMAN, ALEXANDRE (cont'd.)

Pezzo In Modo Antico
(Gilardino) gtr (8th degr.,
Collezione Di Musiche Per
Chitarra) BERBEN EB1478 $1.75
(3610)

Pieces, 3
gtr (3-4th degr.) ESCHIG f.s.
contains: Alla Polacca; Berceuse
d'Orient; Canzonetta   (3611)

Pieces Faciles, Vol. I *CC12U
gtr ESCHIG f.s.   (3612)

Pieces Faciles, Vol. II *CC12U
gtr ESCHIG f.s.   (3613)

Suite In Modo Polonico *CC9U
gtr (6th degr.) ESCHIG f.s.   (3614)

Variations Sur Un Theme De Scriabine
gtr ESCHIG f.s.   (3615)

TARRAGO, GRACIANO
Prelude in E
gtr (6-7th degr.) UNION ESP. 2292
f.s.   (3616)

TAUBE, EVERT (1890-1976)
Nocturne
(Hansson) gtr (3rd degr.) ANDERSONS
AM-684 f.s. contains also: Sa
Skimrande Var Aldrig Havet (3617)

THOMASON, ALEXANDER (CHARLIE BYRD)
(1926-   )
Blues For Classic Guitar, 3
gtr COLUMBIA 145 $1.50   (3618)

TOMASI, HENRI (1901-1971)
Muletier Des Andes, Le
gtr ESCHIG f.s.   (3619)

TOPPER, GUIDO
Guitarist's Travelling Guide, The
*CC27U
gtr (1st degr.) BROEKMANS 850 f.s.
(3620)

Jazzy Moods, 3
gtr (2-3rd degr.) BROEKMANS 1082
f.s.
contains: Funny Face; Gay Tango;
Little Lovely   (3621)

Suite No. 1
"Animals, The" gtr (2nd degr.)
BROEKMANS 1081 f.s. contains
also: Suite No. 2, "Birds, The"
(3622)

TRUHLAR, JAN (1928-   )
Bagatelly, 3 *Op.14
(Knobloch) gtr (4th degr., Kytarova
Sola, No. 25) CZECH H-4454 f.s.
(3623)

Impromptu
(Jirmal) gtr (6th degr., Kytarova
Sola, No. 12) CZECH H-3795 f.s.
(3624)

TURINA, JOAQUIN (1882-1949)
Ensueno (from Danzas Fantasticas)
(Garcia Velasco) gtr UNION ESP.
19726 f.s.   (3625)

Fandanguillo
(Segovia) gtr (9th degr.) SCHOTT
GA-102 f.s.   (3626)

Fantasia Sevillana
""Sevillana": Fantasia" gtr (8th
degr.) COLUMBIA 158 $1.75 (3627)

Hommage A Tarrega, Garrotin-Soleares
(Segovia) gtr (8-9th degr.) SCHOTT
GA-136 f.s.   (3628)

Orgia
(Azpiazu) gtr (8-9th degr.)
RICORDI-ARG BA-11841 f.s.   (3629)
(Azpiazu) gtr (8-9th degr.) UNION
ESP. 19493 f.s.   (3630)

Rafaga
(Segovia) gtr (8th degr.) SCHOTT
GA-128 f.s.   (3631)

Sacro-Monte *Op.55,No.5
(Azpiazu) gtr (8th degr.) SALABERT
15507 $1.25   (3632)

UHL, ALFRED (1909-   )
Franzosischer Walzer
(Walker) gtr (5th degr.) HEINRICH.
1655 f.s.   (3633)

Stucke, 10, Vol. I *CC5U
(Scheit) gtr (3-5th degr.) UNIVER.
11180 $3.25   (3634)

Stucke, 10, Vol. II *CC5U
(Scheit) gtr (3-5th degr.) UNIVER.
11181 $3.25   (3635)

URBAN, STEPAN (1913-   )
Dobru Noc, Variacni Fantazie Na
Lidovou Pisen
"Good Night" gtr (6th degr.,
Kytarova Sola, No. 26) CZECH
H-4530 f.s.   (3636)

Fresken, 5
gtr ZIMMER. ZM-1831 f.s. contains
also: Bohmisch Tanze, 2   (3637)

Impromptu Nos. 1-4
gtr (7-8th degr., Kytarova Sola,
No. 11) CZECH H-3748 f.s.   (3638)

Miniatures
gtr (5-6th degr.) CZECH H-3938 f.s.
Kytarova Sola, No. 14
contains: Andante Sostenuto;
Lento; Poco Vivo, Un; Vivace
(3639)

USHER, TERRY (1909-1969)
Canzoncina *Op.6,No.1
gtr (5th degr., Schott's Series Of
Contemporary Music For Spanish
Guitar, No. 10) SCHOTT 5722 f.s.
contains also: Arabesque, Op.6,
No.2   (3640)

Impromptu, Op. 2, No. 1
gtr (4th degr., Schott's Series Of
Contemporary Music For Spanish
Guitar) SCHOTT 5348 f.s. contains
also: Minuet, Op. 2, No. 2 (3641)

VANDERMAESBRUGGE, MAX (1933-   )
Evocation *Op.32
(van Praet) gtr (6-7th degr.) CBDM
$3.00   (3642)

Miniature Variations
gtr MAURER f.s.   (3643)

Petites Pieces, 3
gtr (1-3rd degr.) SCHOTT-FRER 9239
f.s. Musica Nova, 1970
contains: Hesitation; Premier
Pas; Reveil   (3644)

Prelude
gtr (6th degr.) MAURER f.s.   (3645)

VANNETELBOSCH, P.
A Propos
gtr MAURER f.s.   (3646)

VELDEN, RENIER VAN DER (1910-   )
Improvisation
gtr (7-8th degr.) CBDM $3.00 (3647)

VEREMANS, RENAAT (1894-1969)
Petites Pieces, 3
(van Puijenbroeck) gtr (3-4th
degr.) METROPOLIS EM-4678 $2.00
(3648)

VILLA-LOBOS, HEITOR (1887-1959)
Choros, No. 1
gtr (8th degr.) ESCHIG   (3649)
(Papas) gtr (8th degr.) COLUMBIA
150 $1.50   (3650)

Preludes, 5
gtr (6-8th degr.) ESCHIG 6731-6735
f.s.   (3651)
gtr (6-8th degr.) SCHOTT GA-181-185
f.s.   (3652)

Suite Populaire Bresilienne
gtr (6th degr.) SCHOTT 186:189 f.s.
contains: Chorinho; Gavotte;
Mazurka; Schottisch; Waltz
(3653)

VINAY, VITTORIO
Thlayli
(Pincirolli) gtr (8-9th degr.)
ZERBONI 8569 f.s.   (3654)

VIOZZI, GIULIO (1912-   )
Fantasy
(Company) gtr (9th degr.) ZERBONI
6416 $4.75   (3655)

VISSER, DICK (1927-   )
Another Encore For Yepes
gtr (6th degr., cf. Anonymous,
Romance (Visser)) HARMONIA 1557
f.s.   (3656)

Expressieve Muziek
gtr (5-6th degr.) HARMONIA 1822
f.s.   (3657)

Luitspeler, De, Hommage A Frans Hals
*CC3U
gtr (3rd degr.) HARMONIA 1556 f.s.
(3658)

Suite In Rasgueado En Punteado
gtr (5-6th degr.) HARMONIA 1888
f.s.   (3659)

WAGNER-REGENY, RUDOLF (1903-1969)
Miniaturen, 5
(Henze) gtr (5-6th degr.)
HOFMEISTER T-4031 f.s.   (3660)

WALKER, LUISE (1910-   )
Brasilianisch
gtr (3rd degr.) HEINRICH. N-1602
f.s. contains also: Etude in E
(3661)

Gaucho
gtr (3rd degr.) HEINRICH. N-1605
f.s.   (3662)

Kleine Romanze
gtr (3rd degr.) HEINRICH. N-1603
f.s.   (3663)

Marsch Nach Einer Tiroler Melodie
gtr (2nd degr.) HEINRICH. N-1604
f.s. contains also: Etude
(Chromatisch)   (3664)

Miniaturen, 10 Kleine Stucke
gtr (3rd degr.) HEINRICH. N-1294
f.s.   (3665)

Tanzlied, Etude C-Dur
gtr (2-3rd degr.) HEINRICH. N-1601
f.s.   (3666)

WALTER, FRIED (1907-   )
Suite
gtr (5th degr.) ZIMMER. ZM-1735
f.s.   (3667)

WANEK, FRIEDRICH K. (1929-   )
Ten Essays
gtr SCHOTT GA-438 f.s.   (3668)

WATKINS, MICHAEL BLAKE (1948-   )
Solus For Guitar
(Bonell) gtr NOVELLO 12.0423.08
f.s.   (3669)

WEIKMANN, CHARLES
Guitar For Beginners *CC8U
gtr (1st degr.) PREISSLER 7042 f.s.
(3670)

WEISS, HARALD (1949-   )
Impressionen
gtr HANSEN-DEN 1012 f.s.   (3671)

WELLESZ, EGON (1885-1974)
Rhapsody, Op. 87
(Bayer) gtr (orig for vla)
DOBLINGER 05908 f.s.   (3672)

WENSIECKI, EDMUND
Kleine Solostucke
gtr (2-3rd degr.) HEINRICH. N-1672
f.s.
contains: Andante; Cantabile;
Capriccio; Study in E minor;
Tanz   (3673)

WERNER, JEAN-JACQUES (1935-   )
Ballades d'Antan, 5 (from Le Verseau)
gtr (3-4th degr.) OUVRIERS EO-815
f.s.
contains: Gai; Librement;
Meditatif; Narratif; Pastoral -
Tres Libre   (3674)

Trope
(Chanut) gtr (6-7th degr.,
Collection L'Heure De La Guitare
Classique) CHOUDENS 20.507 f.s.
(3675)

WILSON, THOMAS
Coplas Del Ruisenor
(Gilardino) gtr (8-9th degr.,
Collezione Di Musiche Per
Chitarra) BERBEN EB1815 $3.00
(3676)

Pieces, 3
(Gilardino) gtr (7-8th degr.)
BERBEN EB1517 $2.50 Collezione Di
Musiche Per Chitarra
contains: Allegro Molto; Lento,
Con Espressione; Moderato, Poco
Rubato   (3677)

WISSMER, PIERRE (1915-   )
Partita
(Gilardino) gtr (7-8th degr.,
Collezione Di Musiche Per
Chitarra) BERBEN EB1518 $4.75
(3678)

WOLKI, KONRAD
Stucke, 6, Op. 40
gtr (3-4th degr.) SIKORSKI 376
$2.25   (3679)

WORSCHECH, ROMAIN
Libellule, La, Divertissement Sur Les
10mes
gtr (4-5th degr.) OUVRIERS EO-657
f.s.   (3680)

Michelle Valse
gtr (1-2nd degr.) BILLAUDOT 1259
$1.00 contains also: Marie-France
Valse   (3681)

Mouvements Perpetuels
gtr ESCHIG f.s.   (3682)

Nocturne No. 9
gtr ESCHIG f.s.   (3683)

ZAGWIJN, HENRI (1878-1954)
Fandango
gtr (7-8th degr.) DONEMUS f.s.
(3684)

ZELENKA, IVAN (1941-   )
Koncertni Fantasie
gtr (6-7th degr., Kytarova Sola,
No. 18) CZECH H-4098 f.s. (3685)

ZUCCHERI, LUCIANO
Prelude No. 1
gtr (3-4th degr.) BERBEN EB1747
$1.25   (3686)

Prelude No. 2
gtr (3-4th degr.) BERBEN EB1610
$1.25   (3687)

Prelude No. 3
gtr (3-4th degr.) BERBEN EB1611
$1.25   (3688)

Prelude No. 4
gtr (3-4th degr.) BERBEN EB1748
$1.00   (3689)

Prelude No. 5
gtr (3-4th degr.) BERBEN EB1446
$1.25   (3690)

Sadness
gtr (3rd degr.) BERBEN EB1634 $1.25
(3691)

I/IB4-Coll   Guitar Solo Collections: Music of the Twentieth Century (1914 to present)

ALTE UND NEUE MUSIK ZUM SINGEN UND
SPIELEN AUF BLOCKFLOTEN, GEIGEN UND
LAUTENINSTRUMENTE *folk song
(Gerwig) [Ger] (1-3rd degr.) sc
LIENAU 1375 f.s. Das Spiel Der
Lauteninstrumente, Series II,
Spielbuch 1; contains works by:
Sperontes (4), L. Mozart (3),
Rathgeber (1), Rein (5), Rhau (2),
Langenau (1), Chemin-Petit (1): for
gtr (1), 2gtr (3), 3gtr (1), rec,
gtr (8), 2rec, gtr (2), solo voice,
gtr (3), solo voice, rec, gtr (1),
solo voice, rec, 2gtr (1), rec, vln
or vla, gtr (1); arr. + orig. pcs.;
single line playing; gtr pt partly
in bass clef
contains: Bach, Johann Sebastian,
English Suite No. 6, BWV 811, In
D Minor, Gavottes I-II (gtr,1-2A
rec); Bach, Johann Sebastian,
Minuet, BWV Anh. 118, in B flat
(from Anna Magdalena Bach
Notenbuchlein (1725), No.9) (gtr,
S rec) (C maj,single line
playing, gtr pt in bass clef)
(3692)

ANTOLOGIA PER CHITARRA *CC9L
(Abloniz) gtr (6th degr.) RICORDI-IT
129860 f.s. contains works by:
Auric; Guarnieri; Ghedini;
Malipiero; Petrassi; Poulenc;
Rodrigo; Sauguet and Surinach
(3693)

EASY PIECES, 8 *CC8L
gtr (1-2nd degr.) BROEKMANS 505 f.s.
contains works by: Forrer (2),
Topper (2), van Lier (2), van der
Staak (2)   (3694)

GUITARE D'AUJOURD'HUI (HEDENDAAGSE
GITAAR): 30 PIECES FACILES DE
COMPOSITEURS BELGES (30
GEMAKKELIJKE STUKKEN VAN BELGISCHE
COMPONISTEN) *CC28L
(Mohino) gtr (1-4th degr.) SCHOTT-
FRER 9290 f.s. contains works by:
Vandermaesbrugge (2), Legley (3),
Alfonso (2), W. Balthazar (2),
Louel (2), Luypaerts (1), Leclerc
(4), Defossez (3), Lacroix (2),
Driesen (1), Jadot (1), J.L.
Balthazar (2), Delvaux (1),
Roelstrate (3)   (3695)

KOMMT SINGT UND SPIELT: LIEDER UNSERER
ZEIT, FUR DEN ANFANGSUNTERRICHT
*folk song
(Kramer) [Ger] (1-2nd degr.) sc
HOFMEISTER T-4137 f.s. contains 30
works by: Hubschmann (1), Franz
(1), Richter (1), Mertke (1),
Dittrich (1), Bimberg (1),
Schuffenhauer (1), Stumpe (1) for 2
gtr; Groger (1), Hein (1), Richter-
Ulbrich (1), Lukowsky (2), Balzer
(1), Ahrend (1), Meyer (1),
Natschinski (1), Kochan (1),
Englert (1) for 1 gtr; Natschinski

(1), Becher (1), Eisler (1),
Naumilkat (1), Schwaen (1), Bimberg
(1), Folksongs (2), Schmidt (1) for
solo voice and gtr; partly single
line playing (2 gtr)
contains: Richter, Eva, Unsere
Tannenbaum (composed with
Ulbrich, Christel) (gtr);
Richter, Wolfgang, Weihnachtszeit
(2gtr) (single line playing)
(3696)

KUBAI GITARMUVEK - GUITAR MUSIC FROM
CUBA *CCU
gtr (7-8th degr.) EMB 7751 f.s.
contains works by: Ardevol; Brouwer
and Gramatges   (3697)

MINIATURE SLAVE, 10 *CC10L
(Storti) gtr (1-2nd degr.) BERBEN
EB1372 $1.50 contains works by:
Gnecina (2), Goldenweiser (1),
Korenewkaia (1), Solutrinskaia (1),
Anon. (1), Echpai (1), Ivanov
Kramskoi (3)   (3698)

MODERN GUITAR MUSIC *CC8L
(Quine) gtr (6-9th degr.) OXFORD
36.016 $3.10 contains works by:
Dalby, Dodgson, Forbes, Horovitz,
Josephs, Kelly, Tate, Stoker (3699)

I/IB5   Guitar Solos: Folk Music

ABLONIZ, MIGUEL (1917-   )
Incorrigible Dreamer, An, Bossa Nova
gtr (7th degr.) BERBEN EB2076 f.s.
(3700)

Moods, Jazz In Bossa Nova
(Umori) gtr (5th degr.) BERBEN
EB1988 f.s.   (3701)

ALTES RUSSISCHES LIED
(Perott) gtr (3rd degr.) HEINRICH.
N-1617 f.s.   (3702)

APONTE, PEDRO ARCILA
Bellas Noches De Maiquetia, Las,
Canzone Venezuelana
(Diaz) gtr (5th degr., Las Seis
Cuerdas) ZANIBON 5397 f.s. (3703)

AUSENTE, EL, CANZONE VENEZUELANA
(Diaz) gtr (5th degr., Las Seis
Cuerdas) ZANIBON 5312 f.s. (3704)

BEHREND, SIEGFRIED (1933-   )
Alborada
gtr (5th degr., Gitarre-Bibliothek,
No.13) BOTE GB-13 f.s.   (3705)

Danza Mora
gtr (5th degr., Gitarre-Bibliothek,
No.50; also published in European
Masters For The Guitar) BOTE
GB-50 f.s.   (3706)

Flamenco-Fantasia
gtr (5th degr., Gitarre-Bibliothek,
No.21; also published in European
Masters For The Guitar) BOTE
GB-21 f.s.   (3707)

Sevillanas
gtr (5th degr., Gitarre-Bibliothek,
No.14; also published in European
Masters For The Guitar) BOTE
GB-14 f.s.   (3708)

Spanische Tanze, 3
gtr ZIMMER. 1802 f.s.   (3709)

Trianas
gtr (5th degr., Gitarre-Bibliothek,
No.15; also published in European
Masters For The Guitar) BOTE
GB-15 f.s.   (3710)

BERTI, OSCAR
Alegres Rincones, Valse Venezolana
(Lauro) gtr (6th degr., arr) BERBEN
EB2098 f.s.   (3711)

BIELSA, VALENTIN
4 Canciones Populares Espanolas
gtr ALPUERTO 1404 f.s.
contains: Ala Orilla Del Tormes;
Reyes De La Baraja, Los;
Romance Del Conde Olinos; Tres
Hojas, Las   (3712)

BOHR, HEINRICH
Spanischer Tanz
gtr (3rd degr.) HEINRICH. N-1658
f.s.   (3713)

BROUWER, LEO (1939-   )
Airs Populaires Cubains, 2
gtr ESCHIG f.s.   (3714)

Piezas Populares Cubanas *CC2U
gtr ESCHIG f.s.   (3715)

CALZADILLA, ROMAN
Aires De Mochima, Valzer Venezolano
(Diaz) gtr (6th degr., Las Seis
Cuerdas) ZANIBON 5395 f.s. (3716)

CANCION CARORENA, MELODIA VENEZOLANA
(Diaz) gtr (6-7th degr., Las Seis
Cuerdas) ZANIBON 5493 f.s. (3717)

CANCION DE CUNA
(Sensier) gtr ESSEX f.s.   (3718)

CARLSTEDT, JAN (1926-   )
Danzas Suecas, 2
(Tomas) gtr NORDISKA 6087 f.s.
contains: Allegro; Andantino
(3719)

CERVANTES, IGNACIO (1847-1905)
Danses Cubaines, 2
(Nin-Culmell; Pujol) gtr ESCHIG
1028 f.s.   (3720)

CONDOR PASA, EL; LIEDER UND TANZE AUS
SUDAMERIKA *CCU
(Hanselmann) gtr SCHOTT 6645 f.s.
(3721)

DAGOSTO, SYLVAIN
Feria Al Prado, Sevillana
1-2gtr (5th degr., Collection
Longjumeau-Essonnes) sc TRANSAT.
1040 $1.75   (3722)

DIABLO SUELTO, EL, ANTILLIAANSE WALS
(Coco) gtr (4th degr.) BROEKMANS 739
f.s.   (3723)

FARRUCA
(Meran) gtr (4th degr.) TEESELING
VT-46 f.s.   (3724)

FERNANDEZ, HERACLIO (1851-1886)
Diablo Suelto, El, Valzer Popolare
Venezolano
(Diaz) gtr (6th degr., Las Seis
Cuerdas) ZANIBON 5242 f.s. (3725)

FILLA DEL MARXANT, LA, MELODIA POPULAR
CATALANA
(Llobet) gtr (E maj,6th degr.)
RICORDI-ARG BA-12123 f.s. (3726)
(Llobet) gtr (E maj,6th degr.)
COLUMBIA 135 $1.50   (3727)
(Sinopoli) gtr (D maj,6th degr.)
RICORDI-ARG BA-11502 f.s. (3728)

FLOR DEL CAMPO, VALZER VENEZOLANO
(Diaz) gtr (6-7th degr., Las Seis
Cuerdas) ZANIBON 5314 f.s. (3729)

FLORES NEGRAS, PASILLO ECUATORIANO
(Diaz) gtr (6-7th degr., Las Seis
Cuerdas) ZANIBON 5394 f.s. (3730)

HADJIDAKIS, MANOS
Never On Sunday
(Norman) gtr (4th degr.) COLOMBO
NY-2217 f.s.   (3731)

HINEY MA TOV
(Visser) gtr (3rd degr.) HARMONIA
1571 f.s.   (3732)

HINTERMEYER, WILLY (1892-   )
Fidele Weisen, Fur Gitarre Solo In
Leichter Spielart *CC10U
gtr (2-3rd degr.) PREISSLER 7020
f.s.   (3733)

KOCH, HANS
Musizierbuchlein, Ein, Einfuhrung In
Das Mehrstimmige Spiel Nach
Volkstanzen Und Liedern Aus Dem
Alpenraum
gtr (1-3rd degr., 29 pcs for 1 gtr;
4 pcs for rec and gtr) sc HOHLER
f.s.   (3734)

LAURO, AUGUSTIN
Venezuelan Pieces, 2
(Papas) gtr COLUMBIA 166A $1.50
contains: Pavan; Valse Criolo
(3735)

LAZARDE, ROMULO
Cancion Infantil
gtr VOGT 302 f.s. contains also:
Cancion De Cuna   (3736)

LIED UBER DIE GRENZE; FOLKLORE FREMDER
LANDER
(Cammin) gtr SCHOTT 6173 f.s. (3737)

LIEDER AUS DEUTSCHLAND
(Kammerling) 1 or more gtr (Rund Um
Die Gitarre, Vol. 3) TONGER f.s.
(3738)

LOPEZ, JOAQUIN
  Melodies Populaires Espagnoles, 4,
    Pour Les Debutants
    (Andia) gtr (1-2nd degr.) TRANSAT.
    1341 f.s.
    contains: Cantar Y Taner;
      Divertimento; Mi Tierzuca; Rio
      Mantilla   (3739)

50 MAGYAR NEPDAL
  "Ungarische Volkslieder" (Szendrey-
    Karper) gtr (1st degr.) EMB 7329
    f.s.   (3740)

MATOS RODRIGUEZ, GERARDO H.
  Cumparsita, La, Tango
    (Degese) gtr (6th degr.) RICORDI-
    ARG BA-12437 f.s.   (3741)
    (Diaz Loza) gtr (6th degr.)
    RICORDI-ARG BA-6272 f.s.   (3742)
    (Sinopoli) 2gtr (6th degr.)
    RICORDI-ARG BA-6816 f.s.   (3743)

MAZMANIAN, VROUYR
  Caprice Flamenco
    gtr (6-7th degr.) HEINRICH. N-1546
    f.s.   (3744)

MERAN, JOSE
  Hispania, 6 Very Easy Spanish Dances
    gtr (3-4th degr.) TEESELING VT-50
    f.s.   (3745)

MERENGUE, BALLO VENEZUELANO
  (Diaz) gtr (8th degr., Las Seis
    Cuerdas) ZANIBON 5494 f.s.   (3746)

MESTRE, EL, MELODIA POPULAR CATALANA
  (Llobet) gtr (7th degr.) COLUMBIA 136
    $1.50   (3747)
  (Llobet) gtr (7th degr.) RICORDI-ARG
    BA-12124 f.s.   (3748)

MILETIC, MIROSLAV (1925-   )
  Kroatiska Suite, Nach Volksweisen
    Aus Medjimurje
    gtr SCHOTT GA-437 f.s.   (3749)

MONGE, VICTOR ("SERRANITO")
  Planta Y Tacon, Zapateado
    gtr (6-7th degr.) BERBEN EB1858
    $2.75   (3750)

NEUMANN, ULRIK
  Three-Bands Bossa Nova
    (Ahslund) gtr (3rd degr.) REUTER
    f.s.   (3751)

NO SE VA LA PALOMA, CANCION POPULAR
    LEONESA
  (Garcia Velasco) gtr UNION ESP. 20823
    f.s.   (3752)

PEREZ, RAFAEL
  Carorena, Canzone Venezuelana
    (Diaz) gtr (6-7th degr., Las Seis
    Cuerdas) ZANIBON 5491 f.s.   (3753)

PONCE, MANUEL MARIA (1882-1948)
  Estrellita, Cancion Mexicana
    (Medio) gtr (6th degr.) ESSEX f.s.
                                  (3754)
    (Savio) gtr (6th degr.) RICORDI-ARG
    BA-11226 f.s.   (3755)
    (Savio) gtr (6th degr.) RICORDI-BR
    BR-636 f.s.   (3756)

PRAF, [FRAY] BENEDICTO
  Airs Russes, 3
    (Sanchez) gtr (3-4th degr.)
    CHOUDENS 20.317 f.s. Collection
    L'Heure De La Guitare Classique;
    also published in Repertoire
    Progressif Pour Guitare, Vol. II
    contains: Balalaika; Manoir, Le;
      Traineau, Le   (3757)

PUJOL, EMILIO (1886-1982)
  Tambors, Les 3, Glosa De La Cancion
    Popular Catalana
    gtr (8th degr.) RICORDI-ARG
    BA-11111 f.s.   (3758)

PUTILIN, IVAN
  Andante, Altes Volkslied
    gtr (4th degr.) HEINRICH. N-1662
    f.s.   (3759)

  Romanze, Altes Zigeunerlied
    gtr (6th degr.) HEINRICH. N-1661
    f.s.   (3760)

RAMOS, JOAQUIN
  Serenata Carorena, Cancion Venezolana
    (Diaz) gtr (6th degr., Las Seis
    Cuerdas) ZANIBON 5492 f.s.   (3761)

REBAY, FERDINAND (1889-1953)
  Russischer Tanz
    (Hammerschmied) gtr (5th degr.)
    HEINRICH. N-1627 f.s.   (3762)

SAINZ DE LA MAZA, EDUARDO
  Canco Del Lladre, Popular Catalana
    gtr UNION ESP. 20569 f.s.   (3763)

SCHNEIDER, HEINRICH
  Aragonesa, Spanischer Tanz
    gtr (4th degr.) HEINRICH. N-1670
    f.s.   (3764)

SCHOTTISCHE LIEDER UND BALLADEN °CCU
  (Buhe; Kreidler) gtr SCHOTT 6690 f.s.
                                  (3765)

SCHWERTBERGER, GERALD
  Folk Guitar: Ragtime, Blues, Country
    Music °CC18U
    gtr (2-3rd degr.) DOBLINGER 05911
    f.s.   (3766)

  Glory Hallelujah: Spirituals, Jazz,
    Blues, Beat °CC18U
    gtr (3-4th degr.) DOBLINGER 05910
    f.s.   (3767)

  Latin America: Tango, Samba, Rumba,
    Bossa-Nova
    gtr (2-3rd degr.) DOBLINGER 05912
    f.s.   (3768)

SCOTTISCH MADRILENE
  (Pujol) gtr (7th degr.) ESCHIG 1088
                                  (3769)

SONS DE CARRILHOES, TOADA
  (Abloniz) gtr (5th degr.) BERBEN
    EB1390 f.s.   (3770)

3 SPANISCHE SOLOSTUCKE
  (Kreidler) gtr SCHOTT GA-448 f.s.
                                  (3771)

TESTAMEN DE N' AMELIA, EL
  (Llobet) gtr (6th degr.) FORTEA 138
    f.s.   (3772)
  (Llobet) gtr (6th degr.) COLUMBIA 134
    $1.50   (3773)
  (Prat) gtr (6th degr.) RICORDI-ARG
    BA-9581 f.s.   (3774)
  (Teuchert; Llobet) gtr (6th degr.,
    Die Sologitarre) SCHMIDT,H 315 f.s.
                                  (3775)

TEUCHERT, HEINZ (1914-   )
  Volksweise Mit Variationen, "Ich Ging
    Durch Einen Grasgrunen Wald"
    (Teuchert) gtr (Die Sologitarre)
    SCHMIDT,H 312 f.s.   (3776)

TORRES, PEDRO MANUEL
  Gallo, El, Danza Venezolana
    (Diaz) gtr (6-7th degr., Las Seis
    Cuerdas) ZANIBON 5313 f.s.   (3777)

TROIKA, ALTRUSSISCHES TANZLIED
  (Behrend) gtr (5th degr.) SIRIUS f.s.
                                  (3778)

TRUHLAR, JAN (1928-   )
  Lidovych Pisni, 50
    "Folksongs, 50" [Czech] gtr (1-3rd
    degr.) PANTON P-521 f.s.   (3779)

TWO CATALAN FOLK SONGS
  (Sensier) gtr ESSEX f.s.   (3780)

TWO OLD ENGLISH AIRS
  (Sensier) gtr ESSEX f.s.   (3781)

TWO POLISH AIRS
  (Appleby) gtr ESSEX f.s.   (3782)

URBAN, STEPAN (1913-   )
  Deset Fantasii, Na Lidove Motivy
    "Little Phantasies, 10, On
    Folkmotives (Czech, Moravian And
    Slovak)" gtr (6-7th degr.) PANTON
    P-1101 f.s.   (3783)

VIDALITA, CANCION ARGENTINA
  "Aire De Vidalita" (Anido) gtr (7th
    degr.) BERBEN EB1019 $1.00   (3784)
  (Sinopoli) gtr (7th degr.) RICORDI-
    ARG BA-7025 f.s.   (3785)

VITO, EL
  (Azpiazu) gtr (6-7th degr.) SYMPHON
    349 f.s.   (3786)
  (Sainz de la Maza) gtr (6-7th degr.,
    nueva version) RICORDI-ARG BA-12541
    f.s.   (3787)
  (Sainz de la Maza) gtr (6-7th degr.,
    nueva version) UNION ESP. 19768
    f.s.   (3788)
  (Sensier) gtr (6-7th degr.) ESSEX
    f.s.   (3789)

WALKER, LUISE (1910-   )
  Argentinische Weise, Triste
    gtr (5th degr.) HEINRICH. N-1664
    f.s.   (3790)

WORSCHECH, ROMAIN
  Danzas De Andalucia, Style Flamenco
    (3rd degr.) BILLAUDOT 1089
    $1.00   (3791)

I/IB5-Coll   Guitar Solo Collections: Folk Music

ALPENLANDISCHE VOLKSTANZE °CC15U
  (Engel) gtr (3rd degr.) NAGELS
    EN-1098 f.s.   (3792)

ALPENLANDISCHE WEISEN, VOL. I-IV °CCU
  (Karl) gtr (3-4th degr.) PREISSLER
    7006-I-IV f.s.   (3793)

ALTRUSSISCHE VOLKSWEISEN °CC7U
  (Behrend) gtr (3-4th degr.) SIKORSKI
    674 $3.50   (3794)

ANTHOLOGIE SUR DES AIRS DU FOLKLORE
    FRANCAIS °CC27U
  (Iaconelli) gtr (1-3rd degr.)
    BILLAUDOT 1706 $2.75 La Guitare A
    Travers Les Temps   (3795)

AUTHENTIC BLUEGRASS GUITAR °CC22U
  (Flint) gtr (tablature/2-3rd degr.)
    MEL BAY f.s. +treb clef   (3796)

CANCIONES POPULARES °CC9U
  (San Andres) gtr (5th degr.) UNION
    ESP. 19151 f.s.   (3797)

CANCIONES POPULARES CATALANAS, 10
  (Llobet) gtr (5-7th degr.) UNION ESP.
    20372 f.s. 10 pcs
    contains: Nit De Nadal, La,
      "Desembre Congelat, El"   (3798)

CANCIONES POPULARES MEXICANAS, 8
  (Azpiazu) gtr SYMPHON 2193 f.s.
                                  (3799)

CATALANISCHE WEISEN, 3
  gtr (6th degr.) UNIVER. 14438 $2.75
    contains: Filla Del Marxant, La;
      Noy De La Mare, El; Testamento De
      Amalia, El   (3800)

CHANSONS BRESILIENNES, VOL. I
  (Santos) gtr (7th degr.) ESCHIG
    8271-8173 f.s. Collection Turibio
    Santos, No. 8
    contains: O Cravo E A Rosa;
      Sambalele; Sapo Cururu   (3801)

CHANSONS BRESILIENNES, VOL. II
  (Santos) gtr (7th degr.) ESCHIG
    8174-8176 f.s. Collection Turibio
    Santos, No.8
    contains: O Piao Entrou Na Roda;
      Passa Passa Gaviao; Sozinho Eu
      Nao Fico   (3802)

CHANSONS CATALANES, 2
  (Sierra) gtr (5th degr.) CHOUDENS
    20.648 f.s.
    contains: Marianneta; Pobre Mestre
                                  (3803)

CHANSONS POPULAIRES RUSSES, 7 °CCU
  (Azpiazu) gtr SYMPHON 498 f.s. (3804)

COMMUNITY SONGS, 40 °CC40U
  (Duarte) gtr (2-3rd degr.) NOVELLO
    19330 $3.30   (3805)

DANSKA OCH SVENSKA VISOR; 15 DANISH AND
    SWEDISH FOLKSONGS °CC15U
  (Scheit) 1-2gtr (1-3rd degr.) sc
    UNIVER. 14459 $4.25 2 treb staffs
                                  (3806)

DEUTSCHE VOLKSTANZE °CC11U
  (Behrend) gtr (1-2nd degr.) PREISSLER
    7026 f.s.   (3807)

EASY MUSIC, VOL. 10 °CC10L
  (Azpiazu) gtr (3-7th degr.) SYMPHON
    2175 f.s. contains 10 Folksongs
    (flamenco)   (3808)

ENGLISH FOLK SONGS, 3
  (Duarte) gtr (3-4th degr.) NOVELLO
    19520 $2.20
    contains: Blackbirds And Thrushes;
      Bushes And Briars; Greensleeves
                                  (3809)

ENGLISH FOLK SONGS, 16 °CC16U
  (Duarte) gtr (2-3rd degr.) NOVELLO
    19422 $2.25   (3810)

ERSTES LAUTENBUCH, 67 KINDERLIEDER
    °CC67U
  (Giesbert) gtr (1-2nd degr.) PFAUEN
    f.s. 2 vol ed-no.13a, b;2vols in 1-
    no.13   (3811)

ERSTES MUSIZIEREN AUF DER GITARRE -
    MUSIC-MAKING FOR GUITAR, LIEDER UND
    TANZE VERSCHIEDENER NATIONEN
    °CC24U

(Scheit) 1-2gtr (single line playing/
2nd degr.) UNIVER. 14456 $5.00
(3812)

EUROPESE VOLKSLIEDEREN, VOL. II   *CC15U
(Niessen) gtr (2-3rd degr.) HARMONIA
2638 f.s.   (3813)

FAMOUS NEGRO SPIRITUALS, 5
(Azpiazu) gtr (6-7th degr.) SYMPHON
2067 f.s.
contains: Deep River; Heav'n,
Heav'n; Nobody Knows The Trouble
I've Had; Sometimes I Feel Like A
Motherless Child; Swing Low,
Sweet Chariot   (3814)

FOLK-BLUES, 3   *CC3U
(Bronkhorst) gtr (4th degr.)
TEESELING VT-55 f.s.   (3815)

FOLKLORE DER WELT, VOLS. I-III; LIEDER
UND TANZE AUS ALLER WELT   *CC108U
(Winkelbauer) gtr (1-3rd degr.)
PREISSLER 7028-I-III f.s.   (3816)

FOLKLORISTISCHE SUITE; 12 VOLKSWEISEN
AUS ALLER WELT
(Kaps) [Ger] gtr (2nd degr.)
PREISSLER 7070 f.s.   (3817)

FOLKSONGS, 4
(Alfonso) gtr (4th degr.) SCHOTT-FRER
9167 f.s. 4 pcs; Edition Nicolas
Alfonso, No. 101
contains: Villancico Andaluz, "Noel
Andalou"   (3818)

FOLKVISOR, 30   *CC30U
(Johnson) gtr (1-3rd degr.) ANDERSONS
673 f.s. Musik For Gitarr, Vol. I
(3819)

FOUR CATALAN MELODIES
(Papas) gtr COLUMBIA 134A f.s. (3820)

GITARRENMUSI, 29 ALPENLANDISCHE LIEDER
UND TANZE   *CC29U
(Winkelbauer) gtr (2-3rd degr.)
PREISSLER 7035 f.s.   (3821)

GOD JUL, 71 VALKANDA VISOR   *CC71U
(Ahslund) gtr (1-3rd degr.) REUTER
f.s.   (3822)

HANS SPIELMANN, EIN VOLKSLIEDER-
SPIELBUCH FUR GITARRE, VOL. I: FUR
DEN ANFANGER   *CC77U
(Quadt) [Ger] gtr (1-3rd degr.)
HOFMEISTER T-4074 f.s.   (3823)

HANS SPIELMANN, EIN VOLKSLIEDER-
SPIELBUCH FUR GITARRE, VOL. II: FUR
FORTGESCHRITTENEN SPIELER   *CC48U
(Quadt) [Ger] gtr (1-3rd degr.)
HOFMEISTER T-4082 f.s.   (3824)

HOOR! DE GITARISTEN, BEKENDE LIEDJES IN
LICHTE ZETTING VOOR SOLO-GITAAR,
VOLS. I-III   *CC30U
(Peeters) gtr (1-2nd degr.) XYZ f.s.
(3825)

IRISH SONGS AND DANCES, 26   *CC26U
(Azpiazu) gtr SYMPHON 2060 f.s.
(3826)

JEUX D'ENFANTS, 25 MINIATURE FRANCESI
*CC25U
(Storti) gtr (1-2nd degr.) BERBEN
EB1606 f.s.   (3827)

LAUTENSCHLAGER, DER, VOLKSLIEDER   *CCU
(Giesbert) [Ger] gtr (3rd degr.) sc
PFAUEN f.s. 4 vols in 1-no.12; 4
vols-no.12, 1-4; vols I-II in 1-
no.12a   (3828)

LAUTENSPIELER, DER, NO. 2   *CC7U
(Funck) solo voice,gtr/gtr solo (2nd
degr.) FIDULA f.s. 6 pcs for gtr; 1
pce for solo voice and gtr   (3829)

LIEDER AUS ALLER WELT, 33 VOLKSLIEDER
AUS EUROPA UND AMERIKA   *CC33U
(Kammerling) solo voice,gtr (1-2nd
degr.) TONGER 1618 f.s. Rund Um Die
Gitarre, Vol.1; for gtr with opt
vamp-accomp (gtr II)   (3830)

MELODY OF JAPAN BY GUITARS, VOL. I
*CC12U
(Nakabayashi) [Jap] 1-4gtr (3-6th
degr.) sc SUISEISHA 402981 f.s. for
gtr (2), 2 gtr (2), 3 gtr (4), 4
gtr (4)   (3831)

MELODY OF JAPAN BY GUITARS, VOL. II
*CC17U
(Nakabayashi) [Jap] 1-4gtr (3-6th
degr.) sc SUISEISHA 402609 f.s. for
gtr (5), 2 gtr (1), 3 gtr (9), 4
gtr (2)   (3832)

MUSICA ARGENTINA, LIBRO I   *CC10U
(Pomilio) (7th degr.) RICORDI-ARG
BA-12397 f.s. contains works by:
Aguirre, Boero, Sammartino, Lopez
Buchardo, Lasala, Quaratino,
Iglesias-Villoud, Guastavino,

Pelaia, Siciliani   (3833)

MUSIZIERBUCHLEIN FUR ANFANGER   *CC20U,
folk song
(Scheit) (1-2nd degr.) UNIVER. 13487
$4.50 for 2 gtr or solo voice, gtr
or treb inst, gtr (part I) and gtr
(part II)   (3834)

NORDISCHE VOLKSWEISEN, 30, AUS
SCHWEDEN, DANEMARK, NORWEGEN UND
FINNLAND   *CC30U
(Monaci) ZIMMER. ZM-1280 f.s. (3835)

O BLACK AND UNKNOWN BARDS, 7 NEGRO
SPIRITUALS
(Witte) [Eng] gtr (3-4th degr.)
HARMONIA 2096 f.s.
contains: Virgin Mary Had A Baby
Boy, The   (3836)

OUD-VLAAMSE VOLKSLIEDEREN, 2
(van Puijenbroeck) gtr (4th degr.)
METROPOLIS EM-4658 f.s.
contains: Het Waren Twee
Koningskinderen; Ik Zag Cecilia
Komen   (3837)

PLAYFORD TUNES, 8 ENGLISH TRADITIONAL
DANCE TUNES   *CC8U
(Duarte) gtr BROEKMANS 1017 f.s.
(3838)

RUSSISCHE UND UKRAINISCHE VOLKSLIEDER
UND TANZE, 50   *CC50U
(Lebedeff) gtr (3-4th degr.) ZIMMER.
ZM-1749 f.s.   (3839)

RUSSISCHE VOLKSMUSIK   *CCU
(Tucholski) [Ger] gtr APOLLO 2211 42
pcs for solo voice, gtr; 1 pce for
gtr solo; 1 pce for 2 gtr   (3840)

RUSSISCHE VOLKSWEISEN UND TANZE   *CC11U
(Wensiecki) gtr (3-4th degr.)
PREISSLER 7032 f.s.   (3841)

SINTERKLAASLIEDSJES
(Peters) [Dutch] solo voice,gtr/gtr
solo sc HARMONIA 1861 f.s.   (3842)

SUDAMERICANA, BERUHMTE FOLKLORISTISCHE
TANZE   *CC11U, folk song
(Tucholski) [Span/Port/Ger] solo
voice,gtr/1-3gtr (3-6th degr.) sc
APOLLO 2339 f.s. contains works by:
Creutziger (1), Tucholski (1) for
solo voice, gtr; Villoldo (1),
Porschmann (1), Albeniz (1) for 3
gtr   (3843)

TANCE I PIESNI LUDOWE   *CC32U
(Powrozniak) gtr (2-3rd degr.)
POLSKIE 5864 f.s. Grajmy Na
Gitarze, Vol. I   (3844)

TANZE AUS OSTERREICH   *CC9U
(Scheit) gtr (1-2nd degr.) UNIVER.
13072 $3.25   (3845)

TONBILDUNGS-STUDIEN NACH ALTEN WEISEN -
STUDIES IN TONE FORMATION BASED ON
OLD TUNES   *CC10U
(Scheit) gtr (2nd degr.) UNIVER.
12101 $2.75   (3846)

TWEE MAAL EEN IS TWEE, EEN- EN
TWEESTEMMIGE NEDERLANDSE
VOLKSLIEDEREN   *CC20U
(Niessen) gtr (1-3rd degr.) HARMONIA
1881 f.s.   (3847)

VOLKSLIED UND TANZ; EIN TASCHENBUCH
(Gotze) gtr (2nd degr.) SCHOTT 4468
f.s.   (3848)

VOLKSLIEDER FUR GITARRE-SOLOSPIEL
*CC38U
(Teuchert) gtr (2-3rd degr.) SCHMIDT,
H 76 f.s.   (3849)

VOLKSLIEDER ZUM SINGEN UND SPIELEN
(Riehl; Weber) gtr/gtr,solo voice
SCHMIDT,H 90 f.s.   (3850)

VOLKSWEISEN AUS OSTERREICH
(Libbert) gtr (2-3rd degr.) PREISSLER
f.s. 2 suites (9 pcs); Das
Gitarrenwerk, Reihe A:11
contains: Thernberger
Hochzeitsmusik; Wiener Tanze
(3851)

VOLKSWEISEN DER WELT, VOL. I   *CC11U
(Behrend) gtr (2-3rd degr.) ZIMMER.
1399A f.s.   (3852)

VOLKSWEISEN DER WELT, VOL. II   *CC7U
(Behrend) gtr (2-3rd degr.) ZIMMER.
1399B f.s.   (3853)

VOLKSWEISEN DER WELT, VOL. III   *CC10U
(Behrend) gtr (2-3rd degr.) ZIMMER.
1754 f.s.   (3854)

WAT FRANSEN ZINGEN EN DANSEN, FRANSE
WIJSJES; 10 FRENCH TUNES   *CC10U
(van Schagen) gtr (2-3rd degr.)

HARMONIA 1245 f.s.   (3855)

ZO DOEN WIJ DAT! 24 BEKENDE MELODIETJES
VOOR JONGE GITARISTEN; 24 DUTCH
TUNES   *CC24U
(van Schagen) gtr (1st degr.)
HARMONIA 1526 f.s.   (3856)

I/IB6-Coll   Guitar Solo Collections: Miscellanea

ALBUM
(Azpiazu) gtr (4-8th degr.) SYMPHON
353 f.s. 14 arr+ orig pcs; contains
works by: Azpiazu (1), J.C. Bach
(1), C.P.E. Bach (1), Beethoven
(1), Galilei (1), Anon. (1), W.A.
Mozart (3), Vivaldi (1)
contains: Bach, Johann Sebastian,
Partita for Violin, No. 1, BWV
1002, in B minor, Saraband-
Double; Bach, Johann Sebastian,
Prelude in B sharp, BWV 934, in C
minor (A min); Bach, Johann
Sebastian, Suite for Keyboard
Instrument, BWV 824, in A,
Courante (D maj); Bach, Johann
Sebastian, Suite for Violoncello,
No. 6, BWV 1012, in D, Gavotte I-
II   (3857)

ALBUM CLASSIQUE
(Laurent) gtr (4-7th degr.) LEDUC
G-80 $6.00 10 arr pcs; Guitare,
No.80; contains works by: Exaudet
(1), Schumann (2), Lully (1),
Chopin (1), Beethoven (1), C.P.E.
Bach (1), Tchaikovsky (1)
contains: Bach, Johann Sebastian,
Prelude No. 1, BWV 846, in C
(from Das Wohltemperierte
Clavier, Book 1) (C maj); Bach,
Johann Sebastian, Suite No. 3 for
Violoncello, BWV 1009, in C,
Bourree (A maj)   (3858)

ALBUM DI MUSICHE PER CHITARRA   *CC5U
(Anido) gtr (6-7th degr.) BERBEN
EB1020 $2.50 arr + orig pcs;
contains works by: Alfonso X, El
Sabio, King Of Castile (1), Anido
(2), Rameau (1), Alcorta (1)   (3859)

ALBUM, NO. 9
(Tarrega, Francisco, hijo) gtr (4-9th
degr.) UNION ESP. f.s.
contains: Bach, Johann Sebastian,
Prelude for Lute, BWV 999, in C
minor (D min); Chopin, Frederic,
Waltz, Op. 34, No. 3, in F;
Haydn, [Franz] Joseph, Minuet,
MIN 224; Schumann, Robert
(Alexander), Romance, MIN 278
(3860)

ALBUM, NO. 12
(Tarrega, Francisco, hijo) gtr (4-9th
degr.) UNION ESP. f.s.
contains: Bach, Johann Sebastian,
Partita for Violin, No. 3, BWV
1006, in E, Gavotte En Rondeau;
Handel, George Frideric, Chorale,
MIN 225; Mendelssohn-Bartholdy,
Felix, Canzonetta   (3861)

ALBUM, NO. 13
(Tarrega, Francisco, hijo) gtr (4-9th
degr.) UNION ESP. f.s.
contains: Bach, Johann Sebastian,
Partita for Violin, No. 1, BWV
1002, in B minor, Saraband;
Chopin, Frederic, Prelude, Op.
28, No. 1, in C; Schubert, Franz
(Peter), Moment Musical;
Schumann, Robert (Alexander),
Scherzo, Op. 32, No. 1   (3862)

ALBUM, NO. 14
(Tarrega, Francisco, hijo) gtr (4-9th
degr.) UNION ESP. f.s.
contains: Beethoven, Ludwig van,
Gran Andante; Schumann, Robert
(Alexander), Waltz, MIN 279;
Tchaikovsky, Piotr Ilyich,
Mazurka, MIN 161   (3863)

ALBUM, NO. 15
(Tarrega, Francisco, hijo) gtr (4-9th
degr.) UNION ESP. f.s.
contains: Beethoven, Ludwig van,
Minueto Del Septimino; Beethoven,
Ludwig van, Teme Del Septimino;
Chopin, Frederic, Mazurka No. 16;
Schumann, Robert (Alexander),
Andantino Cantabile; Tarrega,
Francisco, Study, TI ii- 17, in A
minor, "Variacion 4 Del Septimino

De Beethoven" (16 bars)   (3864)

ALBUM, NO. 16
(Tarrega, Francisco, hijo) gtr (4-9th
degr.) UNION ESP. f.s.
contains: Tarrega, Francisco,
Study, TI ii- 24, in E minor
(3865)

ALBUM, NO. 18
(Tarrega, Francisco, hijo) gtr (4-9th
degr.) UNION ESP. f.s.
contains: Bach, Johann Sebastian,
Mass, BWV 232, In B Minor,
Crucifixus (E min); Beethoven,
Ludwig van, Andante; Mendelssohn-
Bartholdy, Felix, Romanza Sin
Palabras   (3866)

ALBUM PRIMO *CC7U
(Proakis) gtr (3-4th degr.) BERBEN
EB517 $1.50 arr; contains works by:
Schumann (3), W.A. Mozart (2),
Chopin (1), Brahms (1)   (3867)

ALBUM RICREATIVO, NO. 1 *folk song
(Ablóniz, Miguel) gtr (3-7th degr.)
BERBEN EB1140 $2.75 20 arr + orig
pcs; contains works by: Schubert
(2), Albloniz (3), Sor (1), Mertz
(1), Galilei (1), Kuhlau (1),
Cremieux (1)
contains: Bach, Johann Sebastian,
Gib Dich Zufrieden Und Sei
Stille, BWV 512 (from Anna
Magdalena Bach Notenbuchlein
(1725), No.13b) Bach,
Johann Sebastian, Komm, Susser
Tod, BWV 478 (from Schemelli's
Gesangbuch); Bach, Johann
Sebastian, Minuet, MIN 162, in A;
Bach, Johann Sebastian, Suite for
Lute, BWV 996, in E minor,
Bourree; Bach, Johann Sebastian,
Suite for Violoncello, No. 5, BWV
1011, in C minor, Saraband (A
min)   (3868)

ALBUM RICREATIVO, NO. 2 *folk song
(Ablóniz, Miguel) gtr (3-7th degr.)
BERBEN EB1280 $3.00 20 arr + orig
pcs; contains works by: Giuliani
(3), A. Scarlatti (1), Villondo
(1), Visee (2) Handel (2), Sor (3),
Thomas (1), Anon. (1)
contains: Bach, Johann Sebastian,
English Suite No. 3, BWV808, In G
Minor, Gavotte II, "Musette" (E
maj)   (3869)

ALBUM RICREATIVO, NO. 3 *folk song
(Ablóniz, Miguel) gtr (3-7th degr.)
BERBEN EB1398 $4.00 20 arr + orig
pcs; contains works by: Cervantes
(1), Schubert (2) Handel (1),
Visee (2), de Crescenzo (1), Flotow
(1), Breton Y Hernandez (1), Sor
(1), Ablóniz (2)
contains: Bach, Johann Sebastian,
Suite for Violoncello, No. 1, BWV
1007, in G, Prelude (C maj);
Bach, Johann Sebastian, Suite for
Violoncello, No. 2, BWV 1008, in
D minor, Minuet I (A min);
Tarrega, Francisco, Study, TI ii-
5, in A, "Estudio En Forma De Un
Menuetto"   (3870)

ALBUM RICREATIVO, NO. 4 *folk song
(Ablóniz, Miguel) 1-2gtr (3-7th
degr.) BERBEN EB1818 $5.75 20 arr +
orig pcs; contains works by: Visee,
Mayr, Giuliani, W.A. Mozart,
Ablóniz, Murcia, Sor, Carcassi,
Coste, Schumann, Brahms, Pergolesi,
Schubert, Molloy for 1 gtr; Ablóniz
for 2 gtr
contains: Bach, Johann Sebastian,
Partita No. 1 for Keyboard
Instrument, BWV 825, in B flat,
Gigue (A maj)   (3871)

ALBUM RICREATIVO, NO. 5 *folk song
(Ablóniz, Miguel) gtr (3-7th degr.)
BERBEN EB1810 $8.25 20 arr + orig
pcs; contains works by: Chopin, D.
Scarlatti, W.A. Mozart (1), A.
Scarlatti (1), J. Valverde (1),
Sor (1), Mendelssohn (1), Schubert
(1), Albloniz (1), Dowland (1),
Haydn (1)
contains: Bach, Johann Sebastian,
English Suite No. 3, BWV 808, In
G Minor, Gavotte I (E min); Bach,
Johann Sebastian, Liebster Herr
Jesu, BWV 484 (from Schemelli's
Gesangbuch)   (3872)

ALTE GITARRENMUSIK, VOL. 1 *CC20U
(Klambt) gtr (3rd degr.) HEINRICH.
120A f.s. contains arr + orig works
by: Carcassi (2), Diabelli (3),
Rossini (1), Carulli (1), Sor (1),
Giuliani (4), Kuffner (1), Haydn
(1), Haydn arr. Louet (1),
Eulenstein (1), Schubert (1) (3873)

ALTE GITARRENMUSIK, VOL. 2 *CC18U,folk
song
(Klambt) gtr (3rd degr.) HEINRICH.
120B f.s. contains arr + orig works
by: Hunten (2), Pelzer (1),
Eilenstein (1), Diabelli (1), Paer
(1), Beethoven (1), Mozart (1),
Horecki (1), Auber arr. Kuffner
(1), Carulli (3), Rossini arr.
Kuffner (1), Handel (1), Carcassi
(1)   (3874)

ANDRES SEGOVIA ALBUM OF GUITAR SOLOS
(Segovia) gtr COLUMBIA 171 f.s. 9 arr
+ orig pcs; contains works by:
Schumann (1), Purcell (3), Gluck
(1), Segovia (1), Brahms (1), Grieg
(1)
contains: Bach, Johann Sebastian,
Suite for Lute, BWV 996, in E
minor, Courante (A min)   (3875)

ANTOLOGIA DE OBRAS PARA GUITARRA
(Savio) gtr (4-7th degr.) RICORDI-ARG
BA-11250 f.s. 48 arr + orig pcs;
contains works by: Corbetta (1),
Visee (1), Asioli (1), Sanz (1),
Roncalli (4), Moretti (1),
Ferandiere (2), Gragnani (1),
Carulli (2), de Call (1), Matiegka
(1), Molino (1), Sor (4), Giuliani
(1), Diabelli (1), Paganini (1),
Gruber (1), Castellacci (1), Aguado
(1), Horecki (1), Legnani (2),
Carcassi (2), Hunten (1), Marschner
(1), Seegner (1), Le Dhuy (1),
Sychra (1), Donnadieu (1), Mertz
(1), Schulz (1), Coste (2), Vinas
(1), Pargas (1)
contains: Tarrega, Francisco,
Prelude, TI i- 11, in D (13
bars); Tarrega, Francisco,
Prelude, TI i- 16, in D minor (14
bars); Tarrega, Francisco,
Prelude, TI i- 18, in D minor;
Tarrega, Francisco, Study, TI ii-
14, in D minor, "Folies d'Espagne
(2a Variacion)"   (3876)

ANTOLOGIA PER CHITARRA, VOL. 1
(Anzaghi, Luigi) (1-10th degr.)
RICORDI-IT 130034 f.s. 91 arr +
orig pcs; contains works by:
Carulli (18), Giuliani (16), Sor
(11), Aguado (8) Visee (7),
Telemann (1), Molino (1), Anzaghi
(5), Schumann (1), Diabelli (1),
Buttstedt (1), Carcassi (5), Milan
(1), Stanley (1), Farrauto (1),
Paganini (4), Donnadieu (1),
Legnani (3)
contains: Bach, Johann Sebastian,
Invention No. 1 for Keyboard
Instrument, BWV 772, in C (2gtr)
(single line playing); Bach,
Johann Sebastian, Invention No. 4
for Keyboard Instrument, BWV 775,
in D minor (2gtr) (single line
playing); Bach, Johann Sebastian,
Invention No. 8 for Keyboard
Instrument, BWV 779, in F (2gtr)
(single line playing); Bach,
Johann Sebastian, Invention No.
13 for Keyboard Instrument, BWV
784, in A minor (2gtr) (single
line playing); Bach, Johann
Sebastian, Suite for Keyboard
Instrument, BWV 822, in G minor,
Minuet I (gtr) (A min)   (3877)

ANTOLOGIA PER CHITARRA, VOL. 2
(Anzaghi, Luigi) gtr (1-10th degr.)
RICORDI-IT 130035 f.s. 43arr + orig
pcs; contains works by: Carulli
(3), Coste (9), Aguado (2),
Giuliani (4), Anzaghi (1), Carcassi
(4), Legnani (2), Paganini (1), Sor
(8), Cano (3), Farrauto (2), Vinas
(1), Anon. (1)
contains: Tarrega, Francisco,
Prelude, TI i- 17, in E,
"Lagrima"   (3878)

ANTOLOGIA PER CHITARRA, VOL. 3
(Anzaghi, Luigi) gtr (1-10th degr.)
RICORDI-IT 130375 f.s. 20 arr +
orig pcs; contains works by: Anon.
(1), Le Dhuy (1), Legnani (1), Sor
(4), D. Scarlatti (1), Tarrega (9
Pcs Not In TI)
contains: Tarrega, Francisco,
Prelude, TI i- 17, in E,
"Lagrima"; Tarrega, Francisco,
Study, TI ii- 8, in A, "Reveri";
Tarrega, Francisco, Study, TI ii-
9, in A minor, "Recuerdos De La
Alhambra"   (3879)

ARMONIA, EINE SAMMLUNG POLYPHONER MUSIK
FUR GITARRE AUS VIER JAHRHUNDERTEN
(van Hoek) gtr (8-9th degr.)
HEINRICH. 1430 f.s. 18 arr + orig
pcs; contains works by: Diomedes
Cato; Blitheman; Zelechowski;
Pachelbel; Campion; Kirnberger;
Kreutzer; Carulli; Sor; Giuliani;

Carcassi; Legnani; Coste and others
contains: Bach, Johann Sebastian,
Canon Per Augmentationem In
Contrario Motu (Canon in D) (from
Die Kunst Der Fuge, No. 14, BWV
1080)   (3880)

ARTE DELLA CHITARRA, L', RACCOLTA DI
SONATE E STUDI DI AUTORI CLASSICI,
VOL. 1 *CC36U
(Muggia) gtr (2-4th degr.) ZANIBON
5337 f.s. contains works by: Sor
(6), Carulli (15), Carcassi (9),
Giuliani (6); 3 Exercises   (3881)

ARTE DELLA CHITARRA, L', RACCOLTA DI
SONATE E STUDI DI AUTORI CLASSICI,
VOL. 2 *CC44U
(Muggia) gtr (2-4th degr.) ZANIBON
5338 f.s. arr+ orig pcs; contains
works by: Paganini (2), Carulli
(9), Carcassi (6), Sanz (2), Aguado
(5), Giuliani (5), Sor (5), Anon.
(3), Roncalli (3), Caroso (4)
(3882)

AUSGEWAHLTE STUCKE ALTER UND NEUER
MEISTER FUR GITARRE, VOL. 1 *CC26U
(Behrend) gtr (3-5th degr.) HEINRICH.
1424 f.s. contains works by:
Milano (1), D. Purcell; Lully; J.S.
Bach; Radolt; Stanley; Duncombe;
Carcassi; Wilton; Reichardt;
Giuliani; Ambrosius and others
(3883)

AUSGEWAHLTE STUCKE ALTER UND NEUER
MEISTER FUR GITARRE, VOL. 2
(Behrend) gtr (3-5th degr.) HEINRICH.
1425 f.s.
contains: Aires Regionales
Espanolas; Sevillanas Popular;
Troika; Behrend, Siegfried,
Arabisches Volkslied; Paganini,
Niccolo, Etude; Visee, Robert de,
Passacaglia   (3884)

AUSGEWAHLTE STUCKE FUR GITARRE SOLO, 30
*folk song
(Teuchert) gtr (1-3rd degr.) SCHMIDT,
H 75 f.s. 30 arr + orig pcs;
contains works by: Sor (2),
Carcassi (4), Carulli (5),
Neusiedler (1), Bossinensis (1),
Losy vom Losinthal (1), Anon. (3),
Attaignant (1), Turk (1), Schumann
(1), Teuchert (2), Aguado (1),
Melii da Reggio (1), Tischer (1),
Marschner (1), Giuliani (1)
contains: Bach, Johann Sebastian,
Minuet in G, BWV Anh. 114 (from
Anna Magdalena Bach Notenbuchlein
(1725), No.4); Bach, Johann
Sebastian, Suite for Lute, BWV
996, in E minor, Bourree   (3885)

BERUHMTE OPERN MELODIEN FUR GITARRE,
VOL. 1 *CC6U
(Behrend) gtr SYMPHON 2194 f.s. arr;
contains works by: Mozart (4),
Rossini (1), Donizetti (1)   (3886)

BERUHMTE OPERN MELODIEN FUR GITARRE,
VOL. 2 *CC6U
(Behrend) gtr SYMPHON 2195 f.s.
contains works by: Lortzing (2),
Verdi (1), Bizet (2), Ponchielli
(1)   (3887)

BEST OF BREAM, THE *CC12U
gtr FABER 0525 f.s.   (3888)

BIS DEL CONCERTISTA, I, VOL. 1 *CC5U
(Tonazzi) gtr (4-8th degr.) ZERBONI
7884 $7.00 arr + orig pcs; contains
works by: Sanz, Giuliani, Paganini,
Albeniz, Tonazzi   (3889)

BIS DEL CONCERTISTA, I, VOL. 2
(Chiesa) gtr (4-8th degr.) ZERBONI
7891 $7.00 6 arr + orig pcs;
contains works by: Froberger,
Handel, M. Albeniz, Sor
contains: Bach, Johann Sebastian,
Prelude for Lute, BWV 999, in C
minor (D min); Tarrega,
Francisco, Study, TI ii- 19, in G
(3890)

BIS DEL CONCERTISTA, I, VOL. 3 *CC6U
(Tonazzi) gtr (4-8th degr.) ZERBONI
7919 $6.00 arr + orig pcs; contains
works by: Dowland, Losy vom
Losinthal, Sor, Diabelli, Coste,
Malats   (3891)

CHOIX D'ETUDES POUR GUITARE, VOL. 1:
COURS PREPARATOIRE
(Fernandez-Lavie) gtr (3-4th degr.)
ESCHIG 8058 f.s. 26 arr + orig pcs;
contains works by: Fernandez-Lavie
(4), Sor (5), Brouwer (2), Caldara
(2), Fuhrmann (1), Anon. (7),
Baumgartner (1), Fortea (1),
Purcell (1), Negri (1)
contains: Tarrega, Francisco,
Study, TI ii- 14, in D minor
(3892)

CHOIX D'ETUDES POUR GUITARE, VOL. 2,
COURS ELEMENTAIRE *CC18U
(Fernandez-Lavie) gtr (3-4th degr.)
ESCHIG 8059 f.s. arr + orig pcs.;
contains studies by: Brouwer (2),
Telemann (1), Aguado (2), Carcassi
(3), Billet (1), Cano (1), Fortea
(1), Sor (1), Garsi da Parma (2),
Anon. (1), Fuhrmann (2), Besard (1)
(3893)

CLASSIC GUITAR, THE, ALL-TIME MASTER
MELODIES
(Sisley) gtr (4-5th degr., contains
15 works by: Grieg (2), Tchaikovsky
(2), W.A. Mozart (2), Handel (1),
Chopin (2), Rubinstein (1),
Schumann (1), Borodin (1), Haydn
(1), Becucci (1), Schubert (1))
BOSTON 44390 f.s. (3894)
(Sisley) gtr (4-5th degr., contains
15 works by: Grieg (2), Tchaikovsky
(2), W.A. Mozart (2), Handel (1),
Chopin (2), Rubinstein (1),
Schumann (1), Borodin (1), Haydn
(1), Becucci (1), Schubert (1))
CHAPPELL-ENG f.s. (3895)

CLASSIC GUITAR SOLO ALBUM, VOL. 1
*CC10U
(Olcott Bickford) gtr (5-8th degr.)
PARAGON f.s. contains arranged
works by: Rimsky-Korsakov, Chopin,
Damm, Grieg, Molloy, Chaminade,
Granados, Paderewski, Mascagni,
Mozskowski (3896)

CLASSICAL ALBUM FOR GUITAR SOLO, A
(Gavall, John) gtr (1-3rd degr.)
OXFORD 36-011 $2.50 13 arr + orig
pcs; contains works by: Ginter (1),
W.A. Mozart (1), Bergen (1), Handel
(2), Weichenberger (1), Vivaldi (1)
contains: Bach, Johann Sebastian,
Ermuntre Dich, Mein Schwacher'
Geist [Chorale], BWV 454 (from
Schemelli's Gesangbuch); Bach,
Johann Sebastian, Jesus Ist Das
Schonste Licht, "Slow March", BWV
474 (from Schemelli's
Gesangbuch); Bach, Johann
Sebastian, Sonata for Violin, No.
2, BWV 1003, in A minor, Largo (C
maj); Bach, Johann Sebastian,
Suite for Violoncello, No. 6, BWV
1012, in D, Gavotte I; Bach,
Johann Sebastian, Suite for
Violoncello, No. 6, BWV 1012, in
D, Gavotte II; Bach, Johann
Sebastian, Suite for Violoncello,
No. 6, BWV 1012, in D, Saraband
(3897)

COMPOSICIONES CELEBRES, 10, VOL. 1
(Pomilio, Tomas) gtr (2-5th degr.,
arr + orig pcs; contains works by:
Sor (3), Paganini (2), Molino (1),
Giuliani (1), Carcassi (2),
Meissonnier (1)) RICORDI-ARG
BA-11241 f.s. (3898)

COMPOSICIONES CELEBRES, 10, VOL. 2
(Pomilio, Tomas) gtr (2-5th degr.,
arr + orig pcs; contains works by:
Sor (3), Paganini (2), Meissonnier
(1), Carcassi (2), Giuliani (2))
RICORDI-ARG BA-11711 f.s. (3899)

COMPOSICIONES CELEBRES, 12, VOL. 3
(Pomilio, Tomas) (2-5th degr.) sc
RICORDI-ARG BA-11997 f.s. 12 arr +
orig pcs; contains works by:
Giuliani (6), Visee (1), Carcassi
(1), Sor (1) for 1 gtr; Sor (2) for
2 gtr
contains: Tarrega, Francisco,
Study, TI ii- 5, in E, "Estudio
En Forma De Un Minuetto" (2gtr)
(3900)

COMPOSICIONES CLASICAS Y ROMANTICAS
(Pomilio, Tomas) (4-7th degr.)
RICORDI-ARG BA-12147 f.s. 13 arr
pcs; contains works by: Rameau (2),
Haydn (1), Chopin (2), Brahms (2),
Schumann (1), Grieg (1), Bach-
Gounod (1)
contains: Bach, Johann Sebastian,
Partita for Violin, No. 1, BWV
1002, in B minor, Saraband (gtr)
(A min); Bach, Johann Sebastian,
Suite for Violoncello, No. 6, BWV
1012, in D, Gavotte I-II (gtr) (E
maj); Gounod, Charles Francois,
Ave Maria (from Das
Wohltemperierte Clavier, Book 1,
Prelude No. 1) (2gtr) (G maj)
(3901)

DIVERTISSEMENT, VOL. 1 *CC7L
(Bartoli) gtr (3-4th degr.) SCHOTT-
FRER 9196 f.s. arr + orig pcs;
contains works by: Gruber,
Carcassi, Anon., Sor, Bartoli (2),
Galilei (3902)

DIVERTISSEMENT, VOL. 2
(Bartoli) gtr (3-4th degr.) SCHOTT-
FRER 9220 f.s. 7 arr + orig pcs;
contains works by: Bartoli,

Carcassi, Mertz, Sor, Aguado
contains: Tarrega, Francisco,
Prelude, TI i- 10, in D; Tarrega,
Francisco, Prelude, TI i- 11, in
D (12 bars) (3903)

EASY MUSIC, VOL. 1 *CC10L
(Azpiazu) gtr (3-7th degr.) SYMPHON
2061 f.s. arr + orig pcs; contains
works by: Anon., Krieger, Handel,
Couperin, Seixas, Telemann,
Reusner, Azpiazu, Visee, Carcassi
(3904)

EASY MUSIC, VOL. 2 *folk song
(Azpiazu) gtr (3-7th degr.) SYMPHON
2062 f.s. 10 arr pcs; contains
works by: Arbeau (1), Anon. (1),
Buttstedt (1), F. Couperin (1),
Telemann (1)
contains: Coventry Carol, The; Noel
De Gascogne; Bach, Johann
Sebastian, Suite for Lute, BWV
996, in E minor, Saraband (3905)

EASY MUSIC, VOL. 4 *folk song
(Azpiazu) gtr (3-7th degr.) SYMPHON
2064 f.s. 10 arr + orig pcs;
contains works by: D. Gaultier,
Azpiazu (2), Gastoldi, Witte, Bohm,
Telemann, Purcell
contains: Bach, Johann Sebastian,
Suite for Lute, BWV 996, in E
minor, Bourree (3906)

EASY MUSIC, VOL. 5 *CC10L
(Azpiazu) gtr (3-7th degr.) SYMPHON
2070 f.s. arr + orig pcs; contains
works by: Anon. (2), Fallamero,
Caroso, Fuhrmann, Attaignant,
Scheidt, Milano, J.C.F. Bach,
Lebegue (3907)

EASY MUSIC, VOL. 6
(Azpiazu) gtr (3-7th degr.) SYMPHON
2071 f.s. 10 arr + orig pcs;
contains works by: Anon. (3),
Lesage de Richee, Azpiazu, L.
Mozart, Milano, Haydn, Marpurg
contains: Bach, Johann Sebastian,
Minuet, BWV 113, in F (from Anna
Magdalena Bach Notenbuchlein
(1725), No.3) (A maj) (3908)

EASY PIECES, 20 *folk song
(Papas) gtr (20 arr + orig pcs;
contains works by: Flotow (1),
Gurlitt (1), Sor (1), Papas (1))
COLUMBIA 101 f.s. (3909)

EDITION NICOLAS ALFONSO, NO. 4
(Alfonso) gtr (4-9th degr.) SCHOTT-
FRER 9123 f.s.
contains: Couperin, Louis,
Saraband, MIN 163; Narvaez, Luis
de, Diferencias Sobre "Guardame
Las Vacas"; Schumann, Robert
(Alexander), Berceuse, MIN 165;
Schumann, Robert (Alexander),
Chorale, MIN 164 (3910)

EDITION NICOLAS ALFONSO, NO. 5
(Alfonso) gtr (4-9th degr.) SCHOTT-
FRER 9124 f.s.
contains: Corelli, Arcangelo,
Saraband, MIN 168; Haydn, [Franz]
Joseph, Minuet, MIN 167; Mudarra,
Alonso de, Galliard, MIN 169;
Schubert, Franz (Peter), Minuet,
MIN 166 (3911)

EDITION NICOLAS ALFONSO, NO. 6
(Alfonso) gtr (4-9th degr.) SCHOTT-
FRER 9139 f.s.
contains: Bach, Carl Philipp
Emanuel, Allegretto; Grieg,
Edvard Hagerup, Menuet De Grand
Maman; Purcell, Minuet, MIN 169
(3912)

EDITION NICOLAS ALFONSO, NO. 7
(Alfonso) gtr (4-9th degr.) SCHOTT-
FRER 9140 f.s.
contains: Bach, Carl Philipp
Emanuel, Minuet, MIN 170;
Dowland, John, Galliard, MIN 180;
Grieg, Edvard Hagerup, Chant Du
Paysan; Telemann, Georg Philipp,
Minuet, MIN 181 (3913)

EDITION NICOLAS ALFONSO, NO. 8
(Alfonso) gtr (4-9th degr.) SCHOTT-
FRER 9136 f.s.
contains: Haydn, [Franz] Joseph,
Minuet, MIN 182; Schubert, Franz
(Peter), Ecossaise; Telemann,
Georg Philipp, Bourree, MIN 183
(3914)

EDITION NICOLAS ALFONSO, NO. 9
(Alfonso) gtr (4-9th degr.) SCHOTT-
FRER 9137 f.s.
contains: Dowland, John, Galliard,
MIN 184; Handel, George Frideric,
Sarabande Variee; Mozart,
Wolfgang Amadeus, Dance Allemande
(3915)

EDITION NICOLAS ALFONSO, NO. 10
(Alfonso) gtr (4-9th degr.) SCHOTT-
FRER 9138 f.s.
contains: Bach, Wilhelm Friedemann,
Minuet, MIN 185; Grieg, Edvard
Hagerup, Melodie Populaire;
Mozart, Wolfgang Amadeus, Dance
Allemande; Purcell, Prelude, MIN
186 (3916)

ENJOY CLASSICAL AND BAROQUE GUITAR
gtr (3-9th degr.) HANSEN-US 0116A
f.s. 67 arr + orig pcs; illus;
intro; biographies, contains works
by: Sor (1), Carcassi (50), Carulli
(1), Zani de Ferranti (7), Albeniz
(2), Molitor (1), Granados (1)
contains: Sor, Fernando,
Introduction Et Variations Sur Un
Theme De Mozart, "Variations On
"The Magic Flute" By W.A.
Mozart", Op.9; Tarrega,
Francisco, Prelude, TI i- 6, in B
minor; Tarrega, Francisco,
Prelude, TI i- 8a, in A; Tarrega,
Francisco, Prelude, TI i- 9, in A
(3917)

ERLISO, VINCENTE
Transcripciones Por Vicente Erliso,
Vol. 1
gtr UNION ESP. 1011 f.s. arr + orig
pcs
contains: Prelude in C; Prelude
in C minor; Rei Mariner, El
(3918)

ERSTES GITARRENSPIEL, LIEDER UND TANZE,
SEHR LEICHT GESETZT, VOL. I
*CC55U, folk song
(Gotze) gtr (1-3rd degr.) SCHOTT 4712
f.s. arr + orig pcs; contains works
by: Kuffner (4), Gotze (10),
Carulli (1), Zelter (1), Hennes
(1), Stingl (1), Brandt (1), Anon.
(3), Bobrowitz (1), Reichardt (1),
Gehricke (1), Zilcher (1), Weiss
(1), Carcassi (1) (3919)

ERSTES GITARRENSPIEL, LIEDER UND TANZE,
SEHR LEICHT GESETZT, VOL. II
*CC34L, folk song
(Gotze) gtr (1-3rd degr.) SCHOTT 4713
f.s. arr + orig pcs; contains works
by: Sor (1), Kuffner (2), Anon.
(2), Lehmann (1), Drechsler (1),
Meissonier (3), Sartoria (1),
Carulli (1), Giuliani (1), Gotze
(2), Meyer (1), Hunten (1),
Diabelli (1), Schulz (1), Brahms
(1), W.A. Mozart (1), Carcassi (1),
Fliess (1) (3920)

ERSTES GITARRENSPIEL, LIEDER UND TANZE,
SEHR LEICHT GESETZT, VOL. III
*CC29L, folk song
(Gotze) gtr (1-3rd degr.) SCHOTT 4714
f.s. arr + orig pcs; contains works
by: Carulli (1), Bohnet (3),
Peschel (1), Carcassi (2), W.A.
Mozart (2), Giuliani (1), Anon.
(3), Sor (2), Graf (1), Diabelli
(1), Mertz (1), Nicolai (1), Kurth
(1), Coste (2); (3921)

ERSTES SPIELBUCH FUR GITARRE *CC50U
(Schwarz-Reiflingen) gtr (1-3rd
degr.) SIKORSKI 267 f.s. arr + orig
pcs; contains works by: Beethoven;
Czerny; Diabelli; Duport; Franck;
Handel; Mozart; Schumann; Schwarz-
Reiflingen; Sor; Stephenson;
Telemann and others (3922)

EUROPEAN MASTERS FOR THE GUITAR, A
SELECT LIBRARY OF 26 [SIC]
CLASSICAL AND CONTEMPORARY PIECES
(Behrend) gtr (4-8th degr.) BOTE f.s.
32 arr + orig pcs, i.e. 26
editions, see below; contains works
by: C.P.E. Bach (2), Batchelar (1),
F. Campion (1), Daquin (1),
Frescobaldi (1), Kapsberger (3),
Giuliani (1), Haydn (1), Rameau
(1), Reussner (1), Losy vom
Losinthal-Lesage de Richee (1
Suite), Weiss (1), Behrend (8),
Paganini (3), Sor (1), Rodrigo (1),
Hartig (1), Koptagel (1);
compilation of the following
separate Bote "Gitarre-Bibliothek"
Editions: 2, 3, 6, 8, 12c, 14, 15,
19, 21, 23, 27, 29, 32, 33, 36, 37,
40, 42, 49, 50, 66, 70, 72, 73, 75,
79; for individual entries see
Index III: Gitarre-Bibliothek
contains: Bach, Johann Sebastian,
Sonata for Violin, No. 1, BWV
1001, in G minor, Siciliano (A
maj); Bach, Johann Sebastian,
Suite for Violoncello, No. 1, in
G, Prelude (C maj) (3923)

EUROPEAN MASTERS FOR THE GUITAR, A
SELECT LIBRARY OF 26 [SIC]
CLASSICAL AND CONTEMPORARY PIECES
(Behrend) gtr (4-8th degr.) AMP 7223
f.s. 32 arr + orig pcs, i.e. 26

editions, see below; contains works
by: C.P.E. Bach (2), Batchelar (1),
F. Campion (1), Daquin (1),
Frescobaldi (1), Kapsberger (3),
Giuliani (1), Haydn (1), Rameau
(1), Reussner (1), Losy vom
Losinthal-Lesage de Richee (1
Suite), Weiss (1), Behrend (8),
Paganini (3), Sor (1), Rodrigo (1),
Hartig (1), Koptagel (1);
compilation of the following
separate Bote "Gitarre-Bibliothek"
Editions: 2, 3, 6, 8, 12c, 14, 15,
19, 21, 23, 27, 29, 32, 33, 36, 37,
40, 42, 49, 50, 66, 70, 72, 73, 75,
79; for individual entries see
Index III: Gitarre-Bibliothek
contains: Bach, Johann Sebastian,
Sonata for Violin, No. 1, BWV
1001, in G minor, Siciliano (A
maj); Bach, Johann Sebastian,
Suite for Violoncello, No. 1, in
G, Prelude (C maj)   (3924)

FOLK TUNES AND CLASSICS FOR SOLO GUITAR
*folk song
(Gavall) gtr (1-3rd degr.) BELWIN 644
$4.00 41 arr + orig pcs; contains
works by: purcell (3), mozart (3),
handel (1), scarlatti (1)
contains: Bach, Johann Sebastian,
An Wasserflussen Babylon
(Chorale, BWV 267); Bach, Johann
Sebastian, Nun Ruhen Alle Walder
(Chorale, BWV 392); Bach, Johann
Sebastian, Partita for Violin,
No. 1, BWV 1002, in B minor,
Saraband; Bach, Johann Sebastian,
Partita for Violin, No. 1, BWV
1002, in B minor, Saraband-
Double; Bach, Johann Sebastian,
Partita for Violin, No. 3, BWV
1006, in E, Minuet I; Bach,
Johann Sebastian, Suite for
Keyboard Instrument, BWV 820, in
F, Gigue; Bach, Johann Sebastian,
Suite for Keyboard Instrument,
BWV 823, in F minor, Gigue (E
min); Bach, Johann Sebastian,
Suite for Violoncello, No. 2, BWV
1008, in D minor, Minuet I; Bach,
Johann Sebastian, Suite for
Violoncello, No. 3, BWV 1009, in
C, Bourree I; Bach, Johann
Sebastian, Suite for Violoncello,
No. 3, BWV 1009, in C, Gigue
(3925)

FOR GUITARISTS ONLY!
gtr MMO MMO-4009 f.s.   (3926)

FOR MY FRIENDS   *folk song
(Duarte) gtr COLUMBIA 183 $2.50 11
arr + orig pcs; contains works by:
Anon. (4), Grieg (1), Duarte (2)
contains: Il Est Ne, Le Divin
Enfant   (3927)

FUR JEDEN GITARRISTEN, SONDERAUSGABE
21. INTERNATIONALER
GITARRISTENKONGRESS (TOKYO, 1962),
"IN MEMORIAM" (RICHARD JACOB
WEISGERBER 1877-1940, PROF. ROMOLO
FERRARI 1895-1958) *CC3L
(Behrend) [Ger] gtr (3-4th degr.)
ZIMMER. ZM-1742 f.s. ill; arr +
orig pcs; contains works by:
Hirota, Walter, B. Fliess
[misattributed to W.A.Mozart]
(3928)

GITAAR-KAMERMUZIEK, VOL. 3: UIT HET
REPERTOIRE VAN HET JOEGOSLAVISCHE
DANSTHEATER
(Claessens, Anny C.H.) 1-5gtr (1-4th
degr.) sc BROEKMANS 27 f.s. arr +
orig pcs; contains works by:
Jovicic for 1 gtr (1); 9 songs and
dances; 2gtr (2); 3gtr (4); 5gtr
(2)
contains: Jovicic, Jovan, Concert-
Etude   (3929)

GITAAR-SOLI, ALBUM KLASSIEKE- EN
MODERNE GITAAR-SOLI IN EENVOUDIGE
BEZETTING
(Kok) gtr (2-3rd degr.) XYZ 243 f.s.
18 arr + orig pcs; contains works
by: Carulli (3), Carcassi (3),
Czerny (3), Kok (4), Schumann (2),
Tchaikovsky (2)
contains: Bach, Johann Sebastian,
French Suite No. 1, BWV 812, In D
Minor, Minuet (A min)   (3930)

GITAARSPEELBOEK - LIVRE DE LA GUITARE
(van Puijenbroeck) gtr (2-7th degr.)
METROPOLIS EM-4722 $5.00 diatonic
and chromatic scales; 42 arr + orig
pcs; contains works by: Carcassi
(9), Carulli (6), Judenkunig (1),
Neusiedler (1), Aguado (4), Hove
(2), Adriaenssen (3), Dalza (1),
Giuliani (2), Milan (2), Dowland
(1), Lecocq (2), Weiss (1), Narvaez
(1)
contains: Bach, Johann Sebastian,
Suite for Lute, BWV 995, in G

minor, Prelude (E min, e' is d',
g is f-sharp); Bach, Johann
Sebastian, Suite for Lute, BWV
995, in G minor, Saraband (E min,
e' is d', g is f-sharp); Bach,
Johann Sebastian, Suite for Lute,
BWV 996, in E minor, Bourree (e'
is d', g is f-sharp); Tarrega,
Francisco, Exercise, TI iii- 3;
Tarrega, Francisco, Prelude, TI
i- 17, in E, "Lagrima"   (3931)

GITARMUZSIKA KEZDOKNEK - GITARRENMUSIK
FUR ANFANGER *folk song
(Vereczkey) gtr (1-2nd degr.) EMB
8110 f.s. 50 arr + orig pcs;
contains works by: Susato;
Bossinensis; Judenkunig; Narvaez;
Neusidler; Caroso; D. Gaultier;
Hove; Hotteterre; Lully; Losy;
Pachelbel; Purcell; Roncalli;
Geminiani; L. Mozart; Turk;
Boccherini; W.A. Mozart; Beethoven;
Carulli; Carcassi; Giuliani; Sor;
Diabelli; Aguado; Legnani; Molino;
Bozay; Szokolay; Karolyi; Papp and
others
contains: Bach, Johann Sebastian,
Minuet, BWV Anh. 115, in G minor
(from Anna Magdalena Bach
Notenbuchlein (1725)) (E min)
(3932)

GITARRE ALLEIN, ENTWICKLUNG DES
SOLISTISCHEN MUSIZIERENS AUS DEM
AKKORDSPIEL *CC26L
(Wolki) 1-2gtr (1-3rd degr.) sc
APOLLO 2268 f.s. contains works by:
Wolki (13), Carcassi (2), Giuliani
(2), Sor (4), Carulli (5) For Gtr;
Kuffner (5), Carulli (1) for 2 gtr;
Suppl. 2 To Wolki, Gitarre Zum Lied
(3933)

GITARRE SPEZIAL, PICKING MODERN
ARRANGEMENT, VOL. 1
(Sieber) gtr (3-4th degr.) PREISSLER
7047 f.s.
contains: Amazing Grace; Ballade
Pour Adeline; Clou, Der   (3934)

GITARRE SPEZIAL, PICKING MODERN
ARRANGEMENT, VOL. 2
(Sieber) gtr (3-4th degr.) PREISSLER
7048 f.s.
contains: Dschinghis Khan;
Kosakentanz; Moskauer Nachte;
Russische Ballade   (3935)

GITARRE SPEZIAL, PICKING MODERN
ARRANGEMENT, VOL. 3
(Sieber) gtr (3-4th degr.) PREISSLER
7049 f.s.
contains: Dolannes Melodie;
Golondrina, La; House Of The
Rising Sun   (3936)

GITARREMUSIK FUR ANFANGER, VOL. I: SEHR
LEICHT *CC10L, folk song
(Behrend) gtr (1-3rd degr.) PETERER
f.s. arr + orig pcs (?); contains
works by: Behrend (?) (9)   (3937)

GITARREMUSIK FUR ANFANGER, VOL. II:
LEICHT *CC8L, folk song
(Behrend) gtr (1-3rd degr.) PETERER
f.s. arr + orig pcs (?); contains
works by: Beethoven (1), Carulli
(1), Behrend (?) (5)   (3938)

GITARREMUSIK FUR ANFANGER, VOL. III:
MITTELSCHWER *CC7L
(Behrend) gtr (1-3rd degr.) PETERER
f.s. arr + orig pcs (?); contains
works by: Anon. (2), Behrend (?)
(5)   (3939)

GITARREMUSIK FUR ANFANGER, VOL. IV:
SCHWER *CC5L, folk song
(Behrend) gtr (1-3rd degr.) PETERER
f.s. arr + orig pcs (?); contains
works by: Sor (1), Behrend (?) (3)   (3940)

GITARRFEST *CC27L, folk song
(Ahslund) gtr (1-2nd degr.) REUTER
f.s. arr. + orig. pcs.; contains
work by: krekula (1), u.g. ahslund
(3), k. ahslund (1), sundberg (1),
kuffner (1), aguado (1)   (3941)

GITARRISTEN, VOL. II *CC4L
(Bengtsson) gtr (3-4th degr.)
NORDISKA 5545 f.s. arr + orig pcs;
contains works by: Anon. (2),
Diabelli (1), Carcassi (1); Vol. I
Out Of Print   (3942)

GITARRKLANG *folk song
(Ahslund) gtr (2-3rd degr.) REUTER
f.s. 21 arr + orig pcs; contains
works by: Ronning (1), U.G. Ahslund
(5), Taube (1), Giuliani (1), Sor
(1), Carcassi (2), Jobim (1)
contains: Tarrega, Francisco,
Study, TI ii- 27, in E minor   (3943)

GITARRLEK *CC25L, folk song
(Ahslund) gtr (1-3rd degr.) REUTER
f.s. arr + orig pcs; contains works
by: Settle (1), McCurdy (1),
Ahslund (7), Seeger (1), Aguado (2),
Seeger
(1), Giuliani (1), Hambe (1), Sor
(2), Paganini (1), Secunda (1),
Bellman (1)   (3944)

GOLDEN AGE, THE, CLASSICS FOR SOLO
GUITAR, VOL. I
(Gavall) gtr (1-4th degr.) BELWIN
1104 $4.00 40 arr + orig pcs;
contains works by: Carulli (2),
Diabelli (2), Kuffner (1), Carcassi
(2), Aguado (1), Sor (2), Melani
(1), Purcell (1), Crema (1),
Horecki (4), Giuliani (5), Handel
(1), Weiss (1); also includes:
Bach, Johann Sebastian, Wer Hat
Dich So Geschlagen. Chorale From
Johannespassion, BWV 245, No.15;
Suites For Violoncello: No. 1, BWV
1007, In G (Gigue, In G); No. 2,
BWV 1008, In D-Minor (Minuet I, In
D-Minor and Gigue, In C); No. 3,
BWV 1009, In C (Gigue, In D-Minor);
No. 4, BWV 1010, In E-Flat (Bourree
II, In E); Partitas For Violin: No.
1, BWV 1002, In B-Minor (Saraband-
Double, Saraband, Allemand-Double);
No. 3, BWV 1006, In E (Minuet,
Loure); Sonata For Violin, No. 3,
BWV 1005, In C (Adagio, Largo); and
Suites For Keyboard: BWV 820, In F-
Minor (Gigue, In F); BWV 823, In F
(Gigue, In E Minor)   (3945)

GOLDEN AGE, THE, CLASSICS FOR SOLO
GUITAR, VOL. II *CC34L
(Gavall) gtr (1-4th degr.) BELWIN
1111 $4.00 arr + orig pcs; contains
works by: Schubert (2), Carcassi
(3), Diabelli (1), Sor (2),
Meissonier (1), Attaignant (1),
Nava (1), Carulli (1), Horecki (3),
Giuliani (1), Molino (1), Aguado
(1), Kellner (1), Purcell (1),
Fuhrmann (1), Mertz (1), Sychra
(2), Paganini (1), Padovetz (1),
Milan (1), Anon. (1), Morkov (3),
Mendelssohn (1)   (3946)

GOLDENE BUCH DES GITARRISTEN, DAS (LE
LIVRE D'OR DES GUITARISTES, OP.52)
*folk song
(Coste, Napoleon; Meier) gtr (3-6th
degr.) SCHOTT GA-14 f.s. 38 arr
pcs; contains works by: Anon. (2),
Couperin (1), Du Caurroy (1), Visee
(9), W.A. Mozart (3), Exaudet (1),
Billaut (1), Haydn (4), Handel (2),
Gluck (1), Beethoven (8), Weber
(1), Donizetti (1), Schubert-Himmel
(1)
contains: Visee, Robert de,
Allemand, VOCG 86; Visee, Robert
de, Courante, VOCG 63; Visee,
Robert de, Gavotte, VOCG 78;
Visee, Robert de, Gigue, VOCG 65;
Visee, Robert de, Gigue, VOCG 75;
Visee, Robert de, Gigue, VOCG 82;
Visee, Robert de, Minuet, VOCG
84; Visee, Robert de,
Passacaglia, VOCG 92; Visee,
Robert de, Saraband, VOCG 83   (3947)

GRACE OF MINUETS, A
(Duarte) gtr (4-5th degr.) SCHOTT
11081 f.s. 7 arr pcs; contains
works by: Purcell, Handel, Fischer,
Haydn, W.A. Mozart, Gurlitt
contains: Bach, Johann Sebastian,
Partita for Keyboard Instrument,
No. 5, BWV 829, in G, Minuet   (3948)

GUITAR MASTERS, ORIGINAL GUITAR
CLASSICS SIMPLIFIED FOR BEGINNING
GUITARISTS *CC25L
(Block) gtr (1-3rd degr.) MARKS
15344-23 $2.00 arr + orig pcs;
contains works by: Aguado (2),
Carcassi (2), Carulli (2), Visee
(2), Diabelli (3), Giuliani (3),
Horecki (1), Hunten (1), Kuffner
(1), Meissonnier (1), Sor (6),
Tarrega (1)   (3949)

GUITAR SAMPLER, 5 CENTURIES OF ORIGINAL
GUITAR SOLOS
(Hoffman, John) gtr (3-4th degr.)
PRESSER 414-41100 $1.95 11 arr +
orig pcs; contains works by: Anon.
(2), Milan (1), Dowland (1), Sor
(2), Paganini (1)
contains: Bach, Johann Sebastian,
Prelude for Lute, BWV 999, in C
minor (D min); Bach, Johann
Sebastian, Suite for Lute, BWV
996, in E minor, Bourree; Sor,
Fernando, Minuet, MIN 303 (from
Grande Sonate, Op. 25); Tarrega,
Francisco, Prelude, TI i- 17, in
E, "Lagrima"   (3950)

GUITAR SONGBOOK, THE *folk song
(Noad) [Eng] (2-7th degr.) COLLIER
f.s. 72 arr + orig pcs; contains
works by: Anon. (6), Noad (1),
Gruber (1), Hopkins (1), Dun (1),
Poulton (1), Moore (1), Hume (1),
Schubert (2), Pergolesi (1), Blow
(1), Dowland (2), E. Purcell (1),
Rosseter (1), Morley (1), Martini
(1), Handel (1) for solo voice,
gtr; H. Purcell (2), Glinka (1),
Attwood (1), Gluck (1), Beethoven
(1), Schumann (1), Tchaikovsky (1),
Zipoli (1), Haydn (1), D. Scarlatti
(1) for 2 gtr; Sor (1), C.P.E. Bach
(1), Handel (2), Corelli (1),
Carcassi (1), Purcell (1), Carulli
(1), Dowland (1), Anon. (1), Mozart
(1) for gtr; with an introduction:
Complete Notes Of The Guitar, Chord
Chart, How Guitar Music Is Written,
Principal Elements Of Guitar
Technique (36p., 17 ill.)
contains: Coventry Carol, The (gtr,
solo voice); First Noel, The
(solo voice,gtr); Gruber, Franz
Xaver, Silent Night (gtr,solo
voice); Hopkins, John Henry, Jr.,
We Three Kings (gtr,solo voice)
(3951)

GUITARIANA *folk song
(Almeida) gtr (5-7th degr.) COLIN
f.s. 17 arr + orig pcs; contains
works by: Almeida (11)
contains: Bach, Johann Sebastian,
Partita for Violin, No. 1, BWV
1002, in B minor, Courante (3952)

GUTEN ABEND, GUTE NACHT *folk song
(Stancik) [Ger] gtr (3rd degr.)
PREISSLER 7036 f.s. 9 arr + orig
pcs; contains lullabies by: Brahms
(1), Schubert (1), Fliess (1),
Stancik (1), Freire (1); Appendix:
"Wie Erarbeite Ich Ein Solostuck,
Eine Kurze Stufenweise Anleitung"
contains: Still, Still, Still
(3953)

HISZPANSCY MISTRZOWIE GITARY
(Powrozniak) gtr (4-9th degr.)
POLSKIE 6432 f.s. Grajmy Na
Gitarze, Vol. XV; 16 arr + orig
pcs; contains works by: Aguado (1),
Cano (1), Broca (2), Sor (1), Bosch
(1), Arcas (3), Vinas (5);
contains: Tarrega, Francisco,
Study, TI ii- 6, in D; Tarrega,
Francisco, Study, TI ii- 8, in A
(3954)

IBERIA, 5 JAHRHUNDERTE SPANISCHER
GITARRENMUSIK, VOL. I *CC20L
(Justen, Heinz) gtr (3-8th degr.)
LEUCKART 10611 f.s. contains works
by: Milan (4), Narvaez (1), Mudarra
(1), Valderrabano (1), Fuenllana
(1), Sanz (5), Moretti (1),
Ferandiere (1), Aguado (4), Sor (1)
(3955)

IBERIA, 5 JAHRHUNDERTE SPANISCHER
GITARRENMUSIK, VOL. II
(Justen, Heinz) gtr (3-8th degr.)
LEUCKART 10630 f.s. 10 pcs;
contains works by: Vinas (1), Arcas
(1), Prudent (1), Malats (1),
Aguado (1), Bosch (2), Gomez (1)
contains: Tarrega, Francisco,
Study, TI ii- 3, in A, "Estudio
De Velocidad" (3956)

INTERNATIONAL ANTHOLOGY FOR GUITAR
(TWELFTH THROUGH EIGHTEENTH
CENTURIES)
(Bellow) gtr (3-9th degr.) COLOMBO
2174 f.s. 78 arr + orig pcs;
contains works by: Ventadour (4),
Faidit (4), Visee (17), Lesage De
Richee (2), Rameau (6), Anon. (3),
Galilei (2), Barbetta (1), Terzi
(1), A. Scarlatti (4), Vinci (1),
Galuppi (1), Leo (1), Alberti (1),
Milan (1), Fuenllana (2),
Valderrabano (1), Mudarra (3),
Soler (1), Rodriguez (1), Byrd (2),
Dowland (1), Cutting (1), Morley
(1), Batchelar (1), Pachelbel (5),
Telemann (1), Baron (7); with an
introduction and biographical notes
contains: Visee, Robert de, Suite,
VOCG 13-19; Visee, Robert de,
Suite, VOCG 51-60 (3957)

JEUX INTERDITS: MUSIQUE DU FILM
(Yepes) gtr (4-5th degr.) TRANSAT.
227 f.s.
contains: Anonymous, Romance, MIN
189; Anonymous, Saraband, MIN
190; Coste, Napoleon, Pequeno
Estudio; Rameau, Jean-Philippe,
Chanson Populaire; Visee, Robert
de, Bourree, MIN 191; Visee,
Robert de, Minuet, MIN 192 (3958)

JUNGE GITARRE-SOLOIST, DER *CC16U
(Walker) gtr (3-7th degr.) HEINRICH.
1519 f.s. contains works by:
Marschner (1), Diabelli (1), Coste

(1), Sor (3), Scholz (1),
Weichenberger (1), Giuliani (1),
Friessnegg (1), Paganini (1),
Nisters (1), Legnani (1), Rebay
(1), Winkler (2) (3959)

KITARAKIRJA-GITARRMELODIER, VOL. 1
*CC50U,folk song
(Immonen) gtr (2-4th degr.) FAZER
3366 f.s. arr + orig pcs; contains
works by: Aguado (2), Carulli (6),
Sor (5), Carcassi (2), Diabelli
(1), Paganini (2), Mertz (1),
Giuliani (1), Coste (1), Beethoven
(1), Haydn (2), W.A. Mozart (1),
Handel (1), Schumann (3), Gluck
(1), Chopin (2), Mendelssohn (1),
Brahms (1), Tchaikovsky (2), Freire
(1), Bellman (1), Merikanto (2),
Immonen (2) (3960)

KITARAKIRJA-GITARRMELODIER, VOL. 2
*folk song
(Immonen) gtr (2-4th degr.) FAZER
4155 f.s. 45 arr + orig works;
contains works by: Sor (10),
Carulli (4), Giuliani (3), Carcassi
(2), Aguado (3), Visee (2),
Paganini (1), Fortea (1), Gruber
(1), Handel (1), Beethoven (1),
W.A. Mozart (2), Schumann (2),
Fliess (1), Brahms (1), Immonen
(2), Anon. (1), Merikanto (1),
Bland (1)
contains: Bach, Johann Sebastian,
Minuet, BWV Anh. 114, in G (from
Anna Magdalena Notenbuchlein
(1725), No.4) (C maj) (3961)

KLASSIKER DER GITARRE; STUDIEN- UND
VORTRAGSLITERATUR AUS DEM 18. UND
19. JAHRHUNDERT, VOL. 2:
MITTELSTUFE — INTERMEDIATE STAGE
(Ratz) gtr (4-8th degr.) DEUTSCHER
32066 f.s. contains 91 works by:
Giuliani; Diabelli; Paganini;
Aguado; Legnani; Carcassi;
Marschner; Mertz; Coste; Tarrega;
Bosch and Cottin
contains: Tarrega, Francisco,
Prelude, TI i- 17, in E,
"Lagrima" (3962)

KLASSISCHES ALBUM, VOL. 1 *CC10U
(Nemerowski) gtr (4-6th degr.)
ZIMMER. ZM-1101 f.s. arr pcs;
contains works by: Boccherini (1),
Schubert (1), Handel (1), Beethoven
(2), Mendelssohn (2), Schumann (1),
Chopin (2) (3963)

KLASSISCHES ALBUM, VOL. 2
(Nemerowski) gtr (4-6th degr.)
ZIMMER. ZM-1102 f.s. 10 arr pcs;
contains works by: Beethoven (2),
Schumann (2), W.A. Mozart (1),
Rameau (1), Schubert (1), Chopin
(1), Weber (2)
contains: Bach, Johann Sebastian,
English Suite No. 2, BWV 867, In
A Minor, Sarabande (3964)

KLASSISCHES ALBUM, VOL. 3 *CC10U
(Nemerowski) gtr (4-6th degr.)
ZIMMER. ZM-1103 f.s. arr pcs;
contains works by: J.E. Bach (1),
Handel (1), Haydn (1), Beethoven
(2), Weber (1), Schumann (2),
Chopin (2) (3965)

KLASSZIKUSOK GITARRA *18-19th cent
"Classics For Guitar" (Brodzsky) gtr
(2-3rd degr.), 47 arr pcs; contains
works by: Hummel (4), L. Mozart
(4), Turk (4), Attwood (1), Gluck
(2), Pal (1), Spohr (1) Beethoven
(5), C.P.E. Bach (1), Haydn (3),
Clementi (1), Mozart (3), W.F.E.
Bach (1), Weber (2), Kirnberger
(1), Fasch (2), Abel (1), Czerny
(2), Wagenseil (1), Hanse (1),
Schubert (6), Hammer-Marteau (1);)
EMB Z-2848 f.s. (3966)
"Classics For Guitar" (Brodzsky) gtr
(2-3rd degr.), 47 arr pcs; contains
works by: Hummel (4), L. Mozart
(4), Turk (4), Attwood (1), Gluck
(2), Pal (1), Spohr (1) Beethoven
(5), C.P.E. Bach (1), Haydn (3),
Clementi (1), Mozart (3), W.F.E.
Bach (1), Weber (2), Kirnberger
(1), Fasch (2), Abel (1), Czerny
(2), Wagenseil (1), Hanse (1),
Schubert (6), Hammer-Marteau (1);)
SCHOTT 5228 f.s. (3967)

KLEINE WERKE GROSSER MEISTER, VOL. 1
*CC10U
(Bodenmann) gtr PETERER f.s. for 2
gtr with arr for gtr solo; single
line playing (2 gtr); degr. 1 (2
gtr), degr. 1, 2 (1 gtr); contains
works by: Franck (1), Haydn (1),
Speer (1), Krieger (1), Handel (2),
Schubert (1), Chedeville (2),
Mozart (1) (3968)

KLEINE WERKE GROSSER MEISTER, VOL. 2
*CC9U
(Bodenmann) gtr PETERER f.s. for 2
gtr with arr for gtr solo; single
line playing (2 gtr); degr. 1 (2
gtr), degr. 1, 2 (1 gtr); contains
works by: Chedeville (3), Haydn
(3), Kress (1), Schubert (1),
Mozart (1) (3969)

KLEINE WERKE GROSSER MEISTER, VOL. 3
*CC9U
(Bodenmann) gtr PETERER f.s. for 2
gtr with arr for gtr solo; single
line playing (2 gtr); degr. 1 (2
gtr), degr. 1, 2 (1 gtr); contains
works by: Rathgeber (1), Haydn (2),
Purcell (1), Praetorius (1), J.C.
Bach (1), Handel (1), Beethoven
(1), Schubert (1) (3970)

KLEINE WERKE GROSSER MEISTER, VOL. 4
*CC10U
(Bodenmann) gtr PETERER f.s. for 2
gtr with arr for gtr solo; single
line playing (2 gtr); degr. 1 (2
gtr), degr. 1, 2 (1 gtr); contains
works by: Chedeville (1), Schubert
(1), Brahms (1), Daquin (1), Schein
(1), Telemann (1), Mozart (2),
Haydn (1), Purcell (1) (3971)

KOMMT SINGT UND SPIELT: LIEDER UNSERER
ZEIT, FUR DEN ANFANGSUNTERRICHT
*folk song
(Kramer) [Ger] (1-2nd degr.) sc
HOFMEISTER T-4137 f.s. contains 30
works by: Hubschmann (1), Franz
(1), Richter (1), Mertke (1),
Dittrich (1), Bimberg (1),
Schuffenhauer (1), Stumpe (1) for 2
gtr; Groger (1), Hein (1), Richter-
Ulbrich (1), Lukowsky (2), Balzer
(1), Ahrend (1), Meyer (1),
Natschinski (1), Kochan (1),
Englert (1) for 1 gtr; Natschinski
(1), Becher (1), Eisler (1),
Naumilkat (1), Schwaen (1), Bimberg
(1), Folksongs (2), Schmidt (1) for
solo voice and gtr; partly single
line playing (2 gtr)
contains: Richter, Eva, Unsere
Tannenbaum (composed with
Ulbrich, Christel) (gtr);
Richter, Wolfgang, Weihnachtszeit
(2gtr) (single line playing)
(3972)

LAUTENIST, DER, VOL. 6
(Gerwig) gtr (g is f sharp; contains
works by: Vallet (4), Fabricus (3),
David (1), Pekiel (2) LIENAU f.s.
(3973)

LEICHTE ALTE LAUTE- UND
GITARRESTUCKLEIN, 32 *CC32U
(Schwarz-Reiflingen) gtr (2-3rd
degr.) LEUCKART 8131 f.s. arr +
orig pcs; contains works by:
Carulli (5), Sor (4), Giuliani (2),
Kuffner (1), Horecki (1), Molino
(2), Kraus (1), Bodstein (1),
Neuland (1), Gaude (1), Carcassi
(4), Anon. (3), Harder (2),
Matiegka (1), Diabelli (1) (3974)

LEICHTE UBUNGEN UND SPIELSTUCKE *CC74U
(Kovats) gtr (1-2nd degr.) SCHOTT
5930 f.s. arr + orig pcs; contains
works by: Kovats (36 studies and
exercises), Folksongs (27), Halm
(1), Orff (2), Attaignant (1),
Anon. (3), Scheidt (1), Hainhofer
(1), Luther (1), Mouton (1); Suppl.
to Technische Studien (3975)

LEICHTE VORTRAGSSTUCKE, VOL. 1 *CC26U,
folk song
(Domandl) gtr (1-3rd degr.) DOBLINGER
05903 f.s. arr + orig pcs; contains
works by: Sor (3), Kuffner (3),
Domandl (4), Giuliani (3), Carulli
(5), Diabelli (3), Aguado (1),
Mertz (1), Carcassi (1) (3976)

LEICHTE VORTRAGSSTUCKE, VOL. 2 *CC18U,
folk song
(Domandl) gtr (1-3rd degr.) DOBLINGER
05904 f.s. arr + orig pcs; contains
works by Giuliani (2), Kuffner (2),
Nava (1), Aguado (1), Mertz (1),
Diabelli (2), Carulli (3), Domandl
(3), Sor (1), de Call (1) (3977)

LEICHTESTEN SOLOSTUCKE BERUHMTER
LAUTEN- UND GITARREMEISTER, DIE
*CC27U
(Scheit) gtr (1-3rd degr.) UNIVER.
14450 $4.75 contains works by:
Judenkunig (1), H. Neusiedler (1),
M. Neusiedler (1), Adriaensen (1),
Ballet (1), Hausmann (1), Sanz (1),
Visee (1), Losy vom Losinthal (1),
Anon. (1), Carulli (6), Giuliani
(2), Diabelli (3), Carcassi (3)
(3978)

MEISTER DES GITARRENSPIELS, VOL. 1,
   LEICHTE STUCKE *CC15U
   (Schneider) gtr (2-7th degr.) NOETZEL
   N-3116 f.s. contains works by: Sor
   (3), Carulli (5), Aguado (1),
   Carcassi (2), Mertz (1), Molino
   (1), Diabelli (1), Giuliani (1)
   (3979)

MEISTER DES GITARRENSPIELS, VOL. 2,
   MITTELSCHWERE STUCKE *CC14U
   (Schneider) gtr (2-7th degr.) NOETZEL
   N-3117 f.s. contains works by:
   Diabelli (2), Carulli (2), Sor (4),
   Coste (1), Molino (1), Legnani (1),
   Giuliani (1), Carcassi (1), Tarrega
   (1)   (3980)

MEL BAY FOLIO OF CLASSIC GUITAR SOLOS,
   VOL. 1 *folk song
   (Castle) gtr (1-4th degr.) BELWIN
   $1.50 38 arr + orig pcs; contains
   works by: Castle (2), Sor (8),
   Aguado (2), Calegari (1), Anon.
   (1), Gruber (1), Rosas (1),
   Ivanovici (1), Waldteufel (1),
   Carey (1), Key (1), Reading (1),
   Delibes (1), Carulli (1), Meacham
   (1), Rameau (1), Bishop (1),
   Gautier (1), Beethoven (1),
   Giuliani (1), Dvorak (1),
   Tchaikovsky (1), Schubert (1), L.
   Mozart (1)
   contains: Bach, Johann Sebastian,
     Musette In D, BWV Anh.126 (from
     Anna Magdalena Bach Notenbuchlein
     (1725), No.22)   (3981)

MEL BAY FOLIO OF CLASSIC GUITAR SOLOS,
   VOL. 2 *folk song
   (Castle) gtr (1-4th degr.) BELWIN
   $1.50 33 arr + orig pcs; contains
   works by: Schumann (1), Diabelli
   (2), Kuffner (1), Aguado (1),
   Mozart (1), Molino (1), Paganini
   (2), Flotow (1), Beethoven (1),
   Borghesi (1), Mertz (1), Verdi (1),
   Purcell (1), Giuliani (1), Handel
   (1), Bornhardt (1), Sor (1),
   Carulli (1), Balfe (1), Visee (2),
   Castle (1)
   contains: Bach, Johann Sebastian,
     Minuet, BWV Anh. 114, in G (from
     Anna Magdalena Bach Notenbuchlein
     (1725), No.4); Bach, Johann
     Sebastian, Partita for Violin,
     No. 1, BWV 1002, in B minor,
     Saraband (A min); Hopkins, John
     Henry, Jr., We Three Kings Of
     Orient Are   (3982)

MEL BAY'S DELUXE ALBUM OF CLASSIC
   GUITAR MUSIC
   (Castle) gtr (4-9th degr.) MEL BAY
   f.s. 67 arr + orig pcs; contains
   works by: Milan (1), Palestrina
   (1), Byrd (1), Frescobaldi (1),
   Reusner (1), Visee (1), Couperin
   (1), Rameau (1), Handel (1), Lesage
   De Richee (1), Gluck (1), Haydn
   (1), Gossec (1), Mozart(2),
   Beethoven (3), Carulli (3), Molino
   (2), Sor (7), Giuliani (2),
   Diabelli (1), Paganini (2), Aguado
   (2), Weber (1), Legnani (2),
   Carcassi (3), Marschner (1),
   Schubert (1), Horenzky (1), Coste
   (1), Mertz (1), Chopin (2),
   Schumann (1), Offenbach (1), Brahms
   (2), Wienawski (1), Tchaikovsky
   (2), Massenet (1), Grieg (1),
   Scharwenka
   contains: Bach, Johann Sebastian,
     Fugue for Lute, BWV 1000, in G
     minor (A min); Bach, Johann
     Sebastian, Invention No. 1 for
     Keyboard Instrument, BWV 772, in
     C; Bach, Johann Sebastian,
     Prelude for Lute, BWV 999, in C
     minor (D min); Bach, Johann
     Sebastian, Suite for Lute, BWV
     996, in E minor, Bourree;
     Tarrega, Francisco, Prelude, TI
     i- 19, in G; Tarrega, Francisco,
     Study, TI ii- 9, in A minor,
     "Recuerdos De La Alhambra";
     Tarrega, Francisco, Study, TI ii-
     18, in A, "Scherzo De T. Damas"
     (3983)

MENUETTBUCH
   (van Hoek) gtr (3-5th degr.)
   HEINRICH. N-1345 f.s. 24 arr + orig
   pcs; contains works by: Handel (2),
   Weiss (3) Visee (1), Losy vom
   Losinthal (1), Rameau (1),
   Kirnberger (2), Krebs (1), Krieger
   (1), Marpurg (1), Haydn (1), W.A.
   Mozart (1), Schubert (1), Beethoven
   (1), Sor (1), van Hoek (3)
   contains: Bach, Johann Sebastian,
     Minuet, BWV Anh. 114, in G (from
     Anna Magdalena Bach Notenbuchlein
     (1725), No.4); Bach, Johann
     Sebastian, Partita for Lute, BWV
     1006a, in E, Minuet I-II (D maj)
     (3984)

MILLER, JOHN R.
   Solo-Gitarre, Die, Vol. II *CC17U
   (Feider) gtr (1-5th degr.) PETERER
   f.s.   (3985)

MIT DER GITARRE, UNTERHALTUNGS-ALBUM
   *CC28L,folk song
   (Grosse; Wolf) [Ger] gtr (3rd degr.)
   sc HARTH 2818 f.s. arr + orig pcs;
   contains works by: Coste (1),
   Carcassi (1), Rameau (1), Anon.
   16th Cent. (1), Yradier (1),
   Soloviev-Sedoy (1), Schubert (2),
   Smetana (1) for 1 gtr; Schumann
   (1), W.A. Mozart (1), Freire (1),
   Granados (1) for 2 gtr; W.A. Mozart
   (1), Petersen (1), Pakhmoutova (1),
   Shanty (1), Nier (1), Ostrovski
   (1), Schneider (1) for solo voice,
   gtr   (3986)

MUSIC FOR CLASSICAL GUITAR
   (Vinson) gtr (1-6th degr.) CONSOL
   f.s. 114 arr + orig pcs; Music For
   Millions Series, Vol. 59; contains
   works by: Anon. (9), Galilei (1),
   Milan (1), Morlaye (1), Narvaez
   (1), Neusiedler (2), Terzi (1),
   Besard (1), Dowland (1), Roncalli
   (1), Sanz (9), Visee (2), Aguado
   (7), Diabelli (3), Carcassi (9),
   Carulli (16), Giuliani (7), Kuffner
   (7), Kunz (2), Meignen (1), Sor
   (25), Bartok (2), Cotten (1)
   contains: Bach, Johann Sebastian,
     Suite for Lute, BWV 995, in G
     minor, Gavotte II (A min,
     fragment); Tarrega, Francisco,
     Prelude, TI i- 17, in E,
     "Lagrima"; Tarrega, Francisco,
     Prelude, TI i- 20, in A, "Adagio
     In A"   (3987)

MUSIC FOR THE CLASSICAL GUITAR, VOL. 1:
   A BOOK FOR BEGINNERS *folk song
   (Norman, Theodor) gtr (1-3rd degr.)
   SCHIRM.G 46059 f.s. 26 arr + orig
   pcs; contains works by: Anon. (1),
   Visee (1), Gruber (1), Carcassi
   (1), A. Scarlatti (1), Handel (1),
   Corelli (1), Tartini (1), Molloy
   (1), Clerambault (1), Norman (1)
   contains: Bach, Johann Sebastian,
     Minuet, BWV Anh. 115, in G minor
     (from Anna Magdalena Bach
     Notenbuchlein (1725), No.5) (D
     min)   (3988)

MUSIC FOR THE CLASSICAL GUITAR, VOL. 2:
   A BOOK FOR INTERMEDIATE PLAYERS
   *folk song
   (Norman, Theodor) gtr (3-6th degr.)
   SCHIRM.G 46819 f.s. 31 arr + orig
   pcs; contains works by: Corelli
   (2), Fesch (2), A. Scarlatti (1),
   Liszt (1), Purcell (1), Norman (6),
   Anon. (1), Laserna (1), Platti (1),
   Mendelssohn (1), Campion (1), Milan
   (1), Clementi (1), D. Scarlatti
   (1), Campagnoli (1)
   contains: Bach, Johann Sebastian,
     Minuet, BWV Anh. 132, in D minor
     (from Anna Magdalena Bach
     Notenbuchlein (1725), No.36) (A
     min)   (3989)

MUSIC FOR THE YOUNG GUITARIST *folk
   song
   (Norman, Theodor) gtr (1-3rd degr.)
   SCHIRM.G 22.47580 f.s. 50 arr pcs;
   contains works by: Norman (1),
   Dvorak (1), Haydn (1), Carey (1),
   Hill (1), Brahms (1), Lully (1),
   Schubert (1), Beethoven (1), Smith
   (1), Chopin (1), W.A. Mozart (1),
   Corelli (1), Foster (1), Kreutzer
   (1), Paganini (1), Tchaikovsky (1),
   Gruber (1), Pierpont (1), de l'Isle
   (1),
   contains: Bach, Johann Sebastian,
     Minuet No. 2, BWV 841, in G (from
     Wilhelm Friedemann Bach
     Notenbuchlein (1720), No.11);
     Bach, Johann Sebastian, Suite for
     Keyboard Instrument, BWV 822, in
     G min minor, Minuet I (A min) (3990)

MUSICA PER CHITARRA, DA ORIGINALI PER
   LIUTO E CHITARRA
   (Tonazzi) gtr (4-6th degr.) BERBEN
   G-7029 f.s.
   contains: Baron, Drole, Le;
     Carcassi, Matteo, Rondino;
     Neusiedler, Melchior, Baletto;
     Roncalli, Ludovico, Prelude, MIN
     187; Terzi, Benvenuto, Galliard,
     MIN 188   (3991)

MUSIK FUR GITARRE; NACH ORIGINALEN FUR
   LAUTE UND GITARRE AUS DEM 16.-19.
   JAHRHUNDERT *CC5U
   (Tonazzi) gtr (4-5th degr.) NOETZEL
   N-3270 f.s. contains works by:
   Roncalli, Terzi, Baron, Carcassi;
   Negri   (3992)

MUSIQUE POUR GUITARE SEULE, VOL. 1 -
   MUSIC FOR SOLO GUITAR, VOL. 1
   (Gerrits) gtr (2-6th degr.) DOBER
   DO-9 f.s. arr + orig pcs; contains
   22 works by: Besard; Neusidler;
   Dalza; van den Hove; R. Johnson;
   Baron; Stolzel; Hoffer; Weiss; D.
   Scarlatti; Chandonnet; Komter;
   Resch; Gerrits; Leblond; Gagnon and
   others
   contains: Bach, Johann Sebastian,
     Suite for Violoncello, BWV 1012,
     in D, Gavotte I-II; Bach, Johann
     Sebastian, Suite for Violoncello,
     BWV 1012, in D, Gigue   (3993)

MUSIQUE POUR GUITARE SEULE, VOL. 2 -
   MUSIC FOR SOLO GUITAR, VOL. 2 *CCU
   (Gerrits) gtr (2-6th degr.) DOBER
   D-10 f.s. arr + orig pcs   (3994)

MUSIQUE POUR GUITARE SEULE, VOL. 3 -
   MUSIC FOR SOLO GUITAR, VOL. 3
   (Chandonnet) gtr (2-6th degr.) DOBER
   DO-11 f.s. arr + orig pcs; contains
   20 works by: Paumann; LeRoy;
   Ballard; Weiss; Gerrits; C. Gagnon;
   Bruhl; A. Gagnon and others
   contains: Bach, Johann Sebastian,
     Pedal-Exercitium, BWV 598; Bach,
     Johann Sebastian, Suite for
     Keyboard Instrument, BWV 822, in
     F minor, Gavotte En Rondeau (B
     min); Bach, Johann Sebastian,
     Suite for Violoncello, BWV 1012,
     in D, Saraband; Bach, Johann
     Sebastian, Toccata for Keyboard
     Instrument, BWV 914, in E minor
     (3995)

MY FAIR LADIES *CC1OU,folk song
   (Duarte) gtr (3rd degr.) FABER F-0357
   f.s. contains arr works by: Anon.
   (6), Praetorius (1), Morley (1)
   (3996)

OBRAS CLASICAS Y ROMANTICAS, VOL. 1
   (Tarrega; Savio) gtr (4-9th degr.)
   RICORDI-ARG BA-11371 f.s. 17 arr+
   orig pcs; contains works by:
   Albeniz (1), Beethoven (1), Chopin
   (3), Haydn (1), Mendelssohn (2),
   W.A. Mozart (1), Schubert (1),
   Schumann (4)
   contains: Bach, Johann Sebastian,
     Partita for Violin, No. 1, BWV
     1002, in B minor, Bourree; Bach,
     Johann Sebastian, Sonata for
     Violin, No. 1, BWV 1001, in G
     minor, Fugue   (3997)

OBRAS CLASICAS Y ROMANTICAS, VOL. 2
   (Tarrega; Savio) gtr (4-9th degr.)
   RICORDI-ARG BA-12409 f.s. 12 arr+
   orig pcs; contains works by:
   Albeniz (1), Beethoven (2), Chopin
   (2), Gottschalk (1), Handel (2),
   Haydn (1), W.A. Mozart (1),
   Schubert (2)
   contains: Tarrega, Francisco,
     Study, TI ii- 25, in E, "Gran
     Tremolo" (ed differs greatly from
     others)   (3998)

PEZZI, 20, DEI SECOLI XVI, XVII E
   XVIII, TRATTI DALLA LETTERATURA DEL
   LIUTO, VIRGINALE E CLAVICEMBALO
   (Abloniz) gtr (3rd degr., arr + orig
   pcs; contains works by: Lully (1),
   Lebegue (1), Mattheson (1), Corelli
   (2), Telemann (2), F. Couperin (2),
   Graupner (2), Besard (2), C.P.E.
   Bach (1), Anon. (2), Dieupart (1),
   Krebs (1), Seixas (1), Handel (1),
   W.A. Mozart (1)) RICORDI-IT 130279
   f.s.   (3999)

PEZZI CELEBRI, 20
   (Farrauto) gtr (3-6th degr.) RICORDI-
   IT 129839 f.s. 20 arr pcs; contains
   works by: Donizetti (1), Anon. (4),
   Gruber (1), Paganini (1), Mayr (1),
   Schumann (1), Gluck (1), Chopin
   (1), Verdi (1), Liszt (1), Brahms
   (1), W.A. Mozart (1), Yradier (1),
   Rubinstein (1), Pergolesi (1),
   Lully (1)
   contains: Bach, Johann Sebastian,
     Minuet, BWV Anh. 132, in D minor
     (from Anna Magdalena Bach
     Notenbuchlein (1725), No.36) (A
     min)   (4000)

PEZZI FACILI, 3
   (Ricchi) gtr (4-5th degr.) BERBEN
   EB1440 f.s. arr + orig pcs
   contains: Anonymous, Due Chitarre;
     Anonymous, Romance, MIN 193;
     Tarrega, Francisco, Prelude, TI
     i- 17, in E, "Lagrima"   (4001)

PICCOLA ANTOLOGIA CHITARRISTICA *folk
   song
   (Abloniz) gtr (3-5th degr.) RICORDI-
   IT 129884 f.s. 12 arr + orig pcs;
   contains works by: Anon. (2),
   Purcell (1), Visee (1), W.A. Mozart
   (1), Gruber (1), Chopin (1)

contains: Coventry Carol, The,
"Vecchia Carola Di Coventry";
Bach, Johann Sebastian, Nicht So
Traurig, "Non Tanto Triste", BWV
489 (from Schemelli's
Gesangbuch); Gruber, Franz Xaver,
Stille Nacht, "Notte Silenziasa"
(4002)

PIECES MELODIQUES ET TRANSCRIPTIONS
*CC11U
(Worschech) gtr (2-3rd degr.)
OUVRIERS EO-490 f.s. arr + orig
pcs; contains works by: Worschech
(9), Haydn (1), Beethoven (1)
(4003)

PIERWSZE KROKI GITARZYSTY *CC130U,folk
song
(Powrozniak) gtr (1-3rd degr.)
POLSKIE 7282 f.s. arr + orig pcs;
contains works by: Anon. (12),
Neusiedler (1), Roncalli (1),
Kuhnau (1), Hove (1) Visee (3),
Besard (1), Losy vom Losinthal (2),
Seixas (1), Hotteterre (1),
Attaignant (2), Sanz (1),
Bossinensis (1), da Reggio (1), L.
Mozart (2), Hoek (1), Turk (4),
Krieger (1), Telemann (2), Stolzel
(1), Cano (2), Carulli (2),
Giuliani (2), Carcassi (3), Sor
(3), Diabelli (2), Coste (2),
Aguado (15), Mertz (1), Bellini
(1), Schubert (2), Slawska (5),
Miklaszewski, Cukierawna (1),
Rybicki (1), Leszczynska (1),
Powrozniak (2), Aleksandrow (2),
Katanski (1), Berens (1), Albert
(1), Roch (1), Mronski (1), Panin
(2), Lachowicka (1), Dastych (2),
Hoenes (1), Kepitis (2)   (4004)

POLSCY MISTRZOWIE GITARY *CC21U
(Powrozniak) gtr (3-7th degr.)
POLSKIE 4538 f.s. Grajmy Na
Gitarze, Vol.11; arr+ orig pcs;
contains works by: Horecki (9),
Bielinski (3), Salleneuve (3),
Jaworski (1), Bobrowicz (2),
Wyhowski (1), Sokolowski (2) (4005)

PRIMO REPERTORIO DEL CHITARRISTA, IL,
VOL. 1   *CC84L
(Storti) 1-2gtr (1-3rd degr.) sc
BERBEN EB1281 $6.00 contains works
by: Aguado (11), Carcassi (7),
Carulli (28), Giuliani (6), Sor
(7), Coste (5), Diabelli (6), Cano
(2) for 1 gtr; Carulli (3), Kuffner
(9) for 2 gtr   (4006)

PRIMO REPERTORIO DEL CHITARRISTA, IL,
VOL. 2
(Storti) gtr (1-5th degr.) BERBEN
EB1880 $8.25 64 pcs; contains works
by: Aguado (6), Borghesi (1);
Carcassi (10); Carulli (10); Coste
(3); Diabelli (3); Giuliani (3);
Marschner (3); Matiegka (2); Mertz
(4); Molino (1); Ressi (2); Sor
(17)
contains: Sor, Fernando, Minuet,
MIN 302 (from Grande Sonate, Op.
22); Sor, Fernando, Minuet, MIN
303 (from Grande Sonate, Op. 25)
(4007)

RACCOLTA DI MUSICHE
(Carfagna) [It/Eng] gtr (4-9th degr.)
BERBEN EB-1178 $3.25 contains 12
works by: Narvaez (1), Mudarra (1),
Visee (3), Roncalli (1), Paganini
(2), Giuliani (1), Sor (1), Gangi
(2); with an intro. and annotations
contains: Sor, Fernando, Rondo
(from Grande Sonate, Op. 22)
(4008)

REPERTOIRE PROGRESSIF, VOL. 1 *folk
song
(Sanchez, Blas) gtr (2-5th degr.)
CHOUDENS 20.339 f.s. 32 arr + orig
pcs; contains works by: Carcassi
(7), Anon. (4), Ruiz de Ribayaz
(2), Sanz (1), Carulli (1), Losy
vom Losinthal (2), Giuliani (2),
Visee (2), Campion (1), LeRoy (1),
Sor (2), Narvaez (1)
contains: Bach, Johann Sebastian,
Minuet, BWV Anh. 114, in G (from
Anna Magdalena Bach Notenbuchlein
(1725), No.4); Bach, Johann
Sebastian, Minuet, BWV Anh. 120,
in A minor (from Anna Magdalena
Bach Notenbuchlein (1725),
No.14); Bach, Johann Sebastian,
Partita for Violin, No. 1, BWV
1002, in B minor, Saraband-
Double; Bach, Johann Sebastian,
Prelude for Lute, BWV 999, in C
minor (D min)   (4009)

REPERTOIRE PROGRESSIF, VOL. 2 *CC12L
(Sanchez, Blas) gtr (2-5th degr.)
CHOUDENS 20.400 f.s. contains works
by: Sanchez (9), Praf (3)   (4010)

REPERTOIRE PROGRESSIF, VOL. 3 *CC9L,
folk song
(Sanchez, Blas) gtr (2-5th degr.)
CHOUDENS 20.418 f.s. contains works
by: Sanchez (7)   (4011)

RODRIGUEZ ARENAS, MARIO
Escuela De La Guitarra, La, Vol. IV
[Span] gtr (79p.; repr, 1967; 1st
ed, 1923; contains 27 Estudios
superiores by Cano (7); Sor (6);
Aguado (14) and 5 concert pieces
by Tarrega (3); Sor (1); Aguado
(1)) RICORDI-ARG BA-9580 f.s.
(4012)

[Jap] gtr (repr, 1967, Span ed; 1st
ed, 1923, Span ed; contains: 27
Estudios superiores by Cano (7);
Sor (6); Aguado (14); and 5
concert pieces by Tarrega (3);
Sor (1); Aguado (1)) ONGAKU f.s.
(4013)

RONNY LEE CLASSIC GUITAR BOOK, THE
(Lee, Ronny) gtr (1-3rd degr.) ALFRED
459 $2.95 38 arr+ orig pcs;
contains works by: Carcassi (9),
Carulli (8), Sor (8), Aguado (3),
Beethoven (1), Lee (2), Clarke (1),
Scarlatti (1)
contains: Bach, Johann Sebastian,
Minuet, BWV Anh. 114, in G (from
Anna Magdalena Bach Notenbuchlein
(1725), No.4); Bach, Johann
Sebastian, Minuet, BWV Anh. 132,
in D minor (from Anna Magdalena
Bach Notenbuchlein (1725), No.36)
(E min); Bach, Johann Sebastian,
Partita for Violin, No. 1, BWV
1002, in B minor, Bourree (A
min); Bach, Johann Sebastian,
Partita for Violin, No. 3, BWV
1006, in E, Gavotte En Rondeau (C
maj); Tarrega, Francisco, Study,
TI ii- 26, in C   (4014)

ROSYJSCY MISTRZOWIE GITARY *CC18L
(Powrozniak) gtr (3-6th degr.)
POLSKIE 5607 f.s. Grajmy Na
Gitarze, Vol.14; contains works by:
Sychra (3), Wysocki (4), Morkow
(3), Wietrow (2), Soloviev-Sedoy
(1), Sarenko (1), Aleksandrow
Gurilew (1)   (4015)

SAINT LUC, JACQUES DE (1616- ?)
Suite in E
(Alfonso) gtr (6-7th degr., Edition
Nicolas Alfonso, No. 1) SCHOTT-
FRER 9120 f.s. contains also:
Franck, Cesar, Plaintes d'Une
Poupee, Les   (4016)

SEHR LEICHTE BIS MITTELSCHWERE SATZE
FUR 1 UND 2 GITARREN *CC94L
(Henze, Bruno) 1-2gtr (1-3rd degr.)
sc HOFMEISTER T-4016 f.s.
Supplement to Das Gitarrespiel,
Vols. 1-3; arr + orig pcs; contains
works by: Anon. (7), Albert (1),
Waissel (1), Haussmann (2), Losy
vom Losinthal (1), Fischer (1),
Hove (1), Attaignant (1), Gastoldi
(1), Hainhofer (2), M. Neusiedler
(1), Heckel (1), Schein (1), Sor
(6), Carcassi (5), Coste (3),
Carulli (14), Giuliani (6), Henze
(10) for gtr; Kuffner (1), Sor-
Henze (10), Sor (1), Carulli (6)
for 2 gtr   (4017)

SEHR LEICHTE STUCKE FUR GITARRE, 42
*CC42L
(Schwarz-Reiflingen) gtr (1-3rd
degr.) HEINRICH. 723 f.s. arr +
orig pcs; contains works by: Anon.
(10), Hunten (1), Kuffner (3), Sor
(2), Giuliani (3), Saint Luc (2),
Mertz (5), Blum (1), Carulli (1),
Garsi da Parma (2), Nava (2), Milan
(1), Carcassi (1), Valderrabano
(1), Rore (1), Lesage de Richee
(1), Bergen (1), Playford (1),
Monteclair (1), Falckenhagen (1)
(4018)

SEVEN HUNDRED YEARS OF MUSIC FOR THE
CLASSIC GUITAR
(Valdes Blain) gtr (3-6th degr.)
HANSEN-US T-156 f.s. 22 arr + orig
pcs; contains works by: Adam de la
Hale (1), Anon. (7), Dowland (2),
A. Scarlatti (1), Giuliani (1), Sor
(2), Granados (1), Albeniz (1)
contains: Bach, Johann Sebastian,
Partita for Violin, No. 1, BWV
1002, in B minor, Saraband; Bach,
Johann Sebastian, Prelude for
Lute, BWV 999, in C minor (D
min); Bach, Johann Sebastian,
Suite for Lute, BWV 996, in E
minor, Allemand (A min); Bach,
Johann Sebastian, Suite for Lute,
BWV 996, in E minor, Bourree;
Tarrega, Francisco, Prelude, TI
i- 17, in E, "Lagrima"   (4019)

SKARBCZYK GITARZYSTY — THE GUITARIST'S
TREASURY *folk song
(Powrozniak) gtr (1-5th degr.)
POLSKIE 5047 f.s. 98 arr + orig
pcs; contains works by: Barcicki
(1), Kozar-Slobodski (1), Moniuszko
(2), Lully (1), Caroubel (1),
Rameau (1), Losy vom Losinthal (1),
Handel (1), Haydn (1), W.A. Mozart
(3), L. Mozart (1), Beethoven (2),
Clementi (1), Schubert (1),
Schumann (1), Rossini-Arr. J.
Kuffner (1), Marschner (1),
Mendelssohn-Arr. J.K. Mertz (1),
Offenbach (1), Bizet (1),
Tchaikovsky (1), Grieg (1), Verdi
(1), Noskowski (1), Rozycki (1),
Gretchaninov (1), Sor (2), Carulli
(3), Carcassi (2), Coste (2), Mertz
(2), F. Rung (1), H. Rung (1),
Hulsen (1), Tarrega (1), Urban (1),
Powrozniak (1), Emma (1), Ivanovici
(2), Waldteufel (1), Curtis (1)
contains: Bach, Johann Sebastian,
Minuet, BWV Anh. 115, in G minor
(from Anna Magdalena Bach
Notenbuchlein (1725), No.5) (A
min); Bach, Johann Sebastian,
Musette In D, BWV Anh.126 (from
Anna Magdalena Bach Notenbuchlein
(1725), No.22); Bach, Johann
Sebastian, Polonaise, BWV Anh.
119, in G minor (from Anna
Magdalena Bach Notenbuchlein
(1725), No.10) (A min)   (4020)

SOLI FUR SPANISCHE GITARRE, 10, VOL. I
*CC10L,folk song
(Ferstl) gtr (4-5th degr.) JUNNE f.s.
arr + orig pcs; contains works by:
Toselli (1), Villoldo (1),
Matallana (2), Wegmann (1), Scotto
(1), Ferstl (2)   (4021)

SOLO-GITARRE, DIE, VOL. I *CC9L,folk
song
(Feider) gtr (1-5th degr.) PETERER
f.s. arr+ orig pcs; contains works
by: Feider (3), Sor (2), Anon. (1),
Giuliani (1), Schubert (1)   (4022)

SOLO-GITARRE, DIE, VOL. III
(Feider) gtr (1-5th degr.) PETERER
f.s. 8 arr+ orig pcs; contains
works by: Feider (4), Giuliani (1),
Diabelli (1)
contains: Tarrega, Francisco,
Prelude, TI i- 16, in D minor,
"Endecha"; Tarrega, Francisco,
Prelude, TI i- 17, in E,
"Lagrima"   (4023)

SOLO-STUCKE ALTER MEISTER *CC33L,folk
song
(Gerdes) gtr (2-3rd degr.) GERIG
GG-180 f.s. arr + orig pcs;
contains works by: Kuffner (2),
Carcassi (2), Platte (1), Anon.
(4), Beethoven (1), Diabelli (2),
Giuliani (3), Weber (2), Reissiger
(1), Rossini (2), Handel (1),
Carulli (4), Wanczura (1), Sor (1),
Bellini (2), Auber (1), Arnold (1)
(4024)

SOLOBUCH FUR GITARRE, DAS
(Schwarz-Reiflingen) gtr (2-4th
degr.) SIKORSKI 268 $5.00 30 arr +
orig pcs; contains works by:
Carcassi (1), Sor (1), Stephenson
(1), Diabelli (1), Steibelt (1),
Bertini (2), Carulli (1), Handel
(2), Gluck (1), Haydn (1), W.A.
Mozart (1), Beethoven (1), Lemoine
(1), Chopin (2), Tchaikovsky (2),
Schubert (1), Schumann (3), Brahms
(1), Anon. (1), Schwarz-Reiflingen
(1)
contains: Bach, Johann Sebastian,
Fantasy for Keyboard Instrument,
BWV 919, in C minor, "Allegro
Moderato" (E min); Bach, Johann
Sebastian, Sonata for Violin, No.
2, BWV 1003, in A minor, Andante
(C maj)   (4025)

SOLOGITARRE, DIE, VOL. I
(Behrend) gtr (3-6th degr.) ZIMMER.
ZM-1721 f.s. 5 arr + orig pcs;
contains works by: Handel, W.A.
Mozart, Telemann
contains: Bach, Johann Sebastian,
Bist Du Bei Mir, BWV 508 (from
Anna Magdalena Bach Notenbuchlein
(1725), No.25) (G maj); Bach,
Johann Sebastian, Partita for
Violin, No. 1, BWV 1002, in B
minor, Saraband   (4026)

SOLOGITARRE, DIE, VOL. II *CC7L
(Behrend) gtr (3-6th degr.) ZIMMER.
ZM-1763 f.s. arr+ orig pcs;
contains works by: Lesage de
Richee, Weiss, Murcia, Reichardt,
Mendelssohn, Paganini, Tchaikovsky
(4027)

SOLOGITARRE, DIE, VOL. III °CC9L
(Behrend) gtr (3-6th degr.) ZIMMER.
ZM-1796 f.s. arr+ orig pcs;
contains works by: Legnani,
Matiegka, Giuliani, Marschner,
Wolf, Aybars, Aydintan, Takei
(4028)

SOLOGITARRE, DIE, VOL. IV °CC7L
(Behrend) gtr (3-6th degr.) ZIMMER.
ZM-1797 f.s. arr+ orig pcs;
contains works by: Fuhrmann,
Carulli, Diabelli (2), Paganini,
Giuliani, Levy
(4029)

SOLOGITARRE, DIE, VOL. V °CCU
(Behrend) gtr (3-6th degr.) ZIMMER.
ZM-1798 f.s. arr + orig pcs (4030)

SOLOS FOR THE GUITAR PLAYER °folk song
(Norman, Theodor) gtr (6-7th degr.)
SCHIRM.G f.s. 26 arr + orig pcs;
contains works by: Arensky (1),
Bacon (1), Beethoven (1), Biber
(1), Chopin (2), Giardini (1),
Gibbons (1), Handel (1), Haydn (1),
Norman (5), Paganini (3), Platti
(1), Prokofiev (1), Reger (1),
Soler (1), Schumann (1)
contains: Bach, Johann Sebastian,
Fughetta In C Minor, BWV 961 (A
min); Bach, Johann Sebastian,
Trio Sonata, BWV 1039, in G,
Andante (E min)
(4031)

SOLOS FOR THE GUITAR PLAYER °folk song
(Norman, Theodor) gtr (6-7th degr.)
CHAPPELL-ENG 22.48771 f.s. 26 arr +
orig pcs; contains works by:
Arensky (1), Bacon (1), Beethoven
(1), Biber (1), Chopin (2),
Giardini (1), Gibbons (1), Handel
(1), Haydn (1), Norman (5),
Paganini (3), Platti (1), Prokofiev
(1), Reger (1), Soler (1), Schumann
(1)
contains: Bach, Johann Sebastian,
Fughetta In C Minor, BWV 961 (A
min); Bach, Johann Sebastian,
Trio Sonata, BWV 1039, in G,
Andante (E min)
(4032)

SONNE, KOMM, EIN GITARRESPIELBUCH FUR
KINDER, 1-4. UNTERRICHTSJAHR °folk
song
(Ratz, Martin) [Ger] solo voice,gtr/
1-4gtr (single line playing/1-3rd
degr.) sc DEUTSCHER 32001 f.s. 162
arr + orig pcs; contains works by:
Schuffenhauer (2), Krug (4), Konig
(8), Ratz (22), Asriel (5), Quadt
(9), Rosenfeld (2), Haydn, Schumann
(3), Gorischk, Helmut, Wohlgemuth,
Schwaen, Schoendlinger for gtr;
Friemert (2), Buse, W.A. Mozart
(3), Beethoven, Berges,
Schuffenhauer, Hecht-Wieber for 2
gtr; Eberwein, Stephani for 3 gtr;
anon., naumilkat for 4 gtr or solo
voice(s), gtr; Skodova (2), Silcher
(2), Wendt, Friemert (2), Kern,
Krug (2), Pormova, Rodl, Hartung,
Nynkowa, Schuffenhauer, Hein,
Richter (3), W. Bender (2), Helmut,
Naumilkat for solo voice, gtr; also
contains Christmas music by:
Helmut, Schuffenhauer, Wohlgemuth
for gtr or solo voice, gtr; W.
Bender, Helmut, Naumilkat, for solo
voice, gtr
contains: Bach, Johann Sebastian,
Minuet in G minor, BWV Anh. 115
(2gtr) (A min,single line
playing); Bach, Johann Sebastian,
Piece In F, "Aria", BWV Anh.131
(2gtr) (single line playing);
Bach, Johann Sebastian, Polonaise
in G minor, BWV Anh. 119 (2gtr)
(A min,single line playing)
(4033)

SPANISCHE GITARRENMUSIK, VOL. I °CC15L
(Schwarz-Reiflingen; Weinhoppel) gtr
(4-8th degr.) LEUCKART 8714 f.s.
arr + orig pcs; contains works by:
Arcas (6), Vinas (5), Broca (2),
Sors (1), Aguado (1)
(4034)

SPANISCHE GITARRENMUSIK, VOL. II
°CC17L
(Schwarz-Reiflingen; Weinhoppel) gtr
(4-8th degr.) LEUCKART 8713 f.s.
arr + orig pcs; contains works by:
Vinas (5), Broca (5), Arcas (4),
Aguado (2), Sors (1)
(4035)

SPANISCHE GITARRENMUSIK, VOL. III
°CC15L
(Schwarz-Reiflingen; Weinhoppel) gtr
(4-8th degr.) LEUCKART 8905 f.s.
arr + orig pcs; contains works by:
Arcas (4), Vinas (4), Sancho (1),
Moretti (1), Broca (5)
(4036)

SPIELMUSIK AUS FUNF JAHRHUNDERTEN -
LEICHT BIS MITTELSCHWER
(Henze, Bruno) gtr (3-6th degr.)

HOFMEISTER T-4009 $4.50 Das
Gitarrespiel, Vol. IX; 48 arr +
orig pcs (numbered 1-30); contains
works by: Milan (1), Mudarra (1),
Fuenllana (1), Anon. (4), Molinaro
(1), Corbetta (2), Sanz (1), Losy
vom Losinthal (4), Visee (1),
Roncalli (3), Campion (1), Molitor
(1), Carulli (1), Sor (2), Giuliani
(2), Diabelli (1), Aguado (2),
Carcassi (2), Coste (1), Tarrega
(2), C. Henze (1), Ambrosius (2),
Domorowski (1), Holz (3), B. Henze
(2), Hecker (1), Stingl (1),
Schwaen (1), Dooren (1)
contains: Bach, Johann Sebastian,
Suite for Lute, BWV 996, in E
minor, Bourree
(4037)

SPIELMUSIK AUS FUNF JAHRHUNDERTEN -
MITTELSCHWER BIS SCHWER
(Henze, Bruno) gtr (5-8th degr.)
HOFMEISTER T-4010 $7.50 Das
Gitarrespiel, Vol. X; 42 arr + orig
pcs (numbered 1-32); contains works
by: Milan (1), Fuenllana (1),
Attaignant (3), Gaultier (1),
Molinaro (1), Corbetta (1), Losy
vom Losinthal (4), Joseph I (1),
Lesage de Richee (1), Campion (1),
Weichenberger (1), Bergen (1),
Lauffensteiner (1), Kropfgans (1),
Falckenhagen (1), Wyssotzki (1),
Moretti (1), Sor (1), Giuliani (1),
Aguado (2), Coste (1), Mertz (1),
Arcas (1), Tarrega (1), Rung (1),
Ambrosius (2), Henze (2), Wagner-
Regeny (1), Stingl (1), Hlouschek
(1), Behrend (1)
contains: Bach, Johann Sebastian,
Suite for Lute, BWV 995, in G
minor, Gavotte I-II (A min); Bach,
Johann Sebastian, Suite for
Lute, BWV 995, in G minor,
Saraband (A min)
(4038)

SPIELMUSIK FUR ANGEHENDE GITARRISTEN,
VOL. I °CC15L,folk song
(Behrend) gtr (1-2nd degr.) PREISSLER
JP-7023-I f.s. arr + orig pcs;
contains works by: Sor (1),
Bossinensis (1), Coste (1), H.
Neusiedler (2), Carulli (5),
Kuffner (2), Carcassi (1), Molinaro
(1)
(4039)

SPIELMUSIK FUR ANGEHENDE GITARRISTEN,
VOL. II °CC15L,folk song
(Behrend) gtr (1-2nd degr.) PREISSLER
JP-7023-II f.s. arr + orig pcs;
contains works by: Aguado (1),
Kuffner (2), H. Neusiedler (1),
Diabelli (1), Sor (2), Saint Luc
(1), Anon. (1), Coste (1), Mertz
(1), Behrend (1)
(4040)

SPIELMUSIK FUR ANGEHENDE GITARRISTEN,
VOL. III °CC16L,folk song
(Behrend) 1-3gtr (1-2nd degr.) sc
PREISSLER JP-7023-III f.s. arr +
orig pcs; contains works by: Anon.
(10), Behrend (2) for gtr (6), 2
gtr (7), 3 gtr (3); single line
playing (2 gtr, 3 gtr)
(4041)

STUDENT GUITARIST'S DELIGHT, VOL. I
°folk song
(Papas) gtr (1-2nd degr.) COLUMBIA
115A $1.00 20 arr pcs; contains
works by: Root (1), Gruber (1),
Hastings (1), Monk (1), Giardini
(1), Foster (3), Strauss (1), Verdi
(1)
(4042)

STUDENT GUITARIST'S DELIGHT, VOL. II
°folk song
(Papas) gtr (1-2nd degr.) COLUMBIA
115B $1.25 19 arr pcs; contains
works by: Dvorak (1), Schumann (1),
Beethoven (4), Chopin (2), W.A.
Mozart (1), Handel (1), Haydn (2),
Tchaikovsky (1), Brahms (1),
Fernandez (1)
(4043)

STUDIES EN STUKJES VOOR GITAAR °CC7L
(Kwist) gtr (2-3rd degr.) XYZ f.s.
arr + orig pcs; contains works by:
Kwist (4), Beethoven (1), Czibulka
(1), Carulli (1)
(4044)

SUITE IM ALTEN STIL
(Albert) gtr (4th degr.) ZIMMER. f.s.
contains: Albert, Gigue, MIN 295;
Albert, Prelude, MIN 294; Coste,
Napoleon, Rondo, MIN 297; Rameau,
Jean-Philippe, Saraband, MIN 298;
Visee, Robert de, Gavotte, MIN
296
(4045)

SUPLEMENTO AL METODO PARA GUITARRA DE
AGUADO-SINOPOLI
(Sinopoli, Antonio) gtr (4-10th
degr.) RICORDI-ARG BA-6712 f.s. 19
arr + orig pcs; contains works by:
Sinopoli (1), Sor (6), Chopin (2);
also includes: Tarrega, Francisco,

Preludes, TI-i-1 In D-Minor, 4 In
E, 5 In E, 7 In A, 8A In A, 9 In A;
Study, TI-ii-5 In A, "Estudio En
Forma De Un Minuetto"; Bach, Johann
Sebastian, Das Wohltemperierte
Clavier, Vol. I, Prelude No. 1, BWV
846, In C (In E); Suite For
Violoncello, No. 3, BWV 1009,
Courante In C (In A): Partita For
Violin, No.2, BWV 1004, Chaconne I
In D Minor (In E Minor); and Sor,
Fernando, Grande Sonata, Op. 22
(Minuet); Grande Sonata, Op. 25
(Minuet)
(4046)

TRANSCRIPCIONES PARA GUITARRA
(Segovia) gtr UNION ESP. 20235 f.s.
all pcs. also published separately
as UME 18029-38; Transcripciones
Nos. 9, 8, 1, 6, 5, 4, 2, 10, 3, 7;
10 arr pcs; contains works by:
Handel (1), Schumann (2), Grieg
(1), Beethoven (1), Haydn (1),
Mendelssohn (1), Schubert (1)
contains: Bach, Johann Sebastian,
Partita for Violin, No. 1, BWV
1002, in B minor, Saraband; Bach,
Johann Sebastian, Sonata for
Violin, No. 1, BWV 1001, in B
minor, Siciliano (A maj)
(4047)

TRANSCRIPCIONES PARA GUITARRA
(Llobet) gtr (6-7th degr.) UNION ESP.
20382 f.s.
contains: Bach, Johann Sebastian,
Partita for Violin, No. 1, BWV
1002, in B minor, Saraband;
Bizet, Georges, Arlesiana, La;
Grieg, Edvard Hagerup, Melodia
Noruega; Wagner, Richard,
Parcifal
(4048)

TRANSCRIPCIONES POR GRACIANO TARRAGO
[1]
(Tarrago) gtr (3rd degr.) UNION ESP.
1950 f.s.
contains: Cancion Catalana; Bach,
Johann Sebastian, French Suite
No. 6, BWV 817, In E, Minuet (A
maj)
(4049)

TRANSCRIPCIONES POR GRACIANO TARRAGO
[2]
(Tarrago) gtr (4th degr.) UNION ESP.
1953 f.s. arr + orig pcs
contains: Bach, Johann Sebastian,
Invention for Violin and Keyboard
Instrument, BWV Anh. 174, in B
flat, Air (D maj); Sor, Fernando,
Minuet, MIN 194; Visee, Robert
de, Minuet, MIN 195; Visee,
Robert de, Saraband, MIN 196
(4050)

TRANSCRIPCIONES POR GRACIANO TARRAGO
[3]
(Tarrago) gtr (3-4th degr.) UNION
ESP. 1955 f.s. contains works by:
W.A. Mozart, Schumann
contains: Bach, Johann Sebastian,
Suite for Lute, BWV 996, in E
minor, Bourree
(4051)

TRANSCRIPCIONES POR VICENTE ERLISO,
VOL. 3 °CC3U
gtr UNION ESP. 1030 f.s. arr + orig
pcs; contains works by: Daquin,
Erliso, Rameau
(4052)

TRANSCRIPCIONES POR VICENTE ERLISO,
VOL. 4
gtr UNION ESP. 1054 f.s. arr + orig
pcs
contains: Erliso, Vincente, Minuet,
MIN 198; Erliso, Vincente,
Minuet, MIN 199; Schumann, Robert
(Alexander), Fantasy, MIN 197
(4053)

TRANSCRIPCIONES POR VICENTE ERLISO,
VOL. 6
gtr UNION ESP. 1061 f.s. arr + orig
pcs; contains works by: Beethoven,
Erliso
contains: Bach, Johann Sebastian,
English Suite No. 3, BWV 808, In
G Minor, Gavottes I-II
(4054)

TRANSCRIPTIONS FACILES DE 12 CHEFS-
D'OEUVRE CLASSIQUE
(Mornac, Juan) gtr (2-3rd degr.)
DURAND 13969 $5.50 12 arr pcs;
contains works by: Brahms (3),
Martini (1), Schumann (3),
Mendelssohn (2), Mozart (1),
Beethoven (1)
contains: Bach, Johann Sebastian,
Minuet, BWV Anh. 114, in G (from
Anna Magdalena Bach Notenbuchlein
(1725), No.4); Bach, Johann
Sebastian, Minuet, BWV Anh. 115,
in G minor (from Anna Magdalena
Bach Notenbuchlein (1725), No.5)
(A min)
(4055)

UBEN UND SPIELEN AUF DER GITARRE, VOL.
1
(Zykan) gtr,opt gtr II WELT 1021A

f.s. 18 arr + orig pcs; contains
works by: Folksongs (11), Lyra (1),
W.A. Mozart (1), Mendelssohn (1),
Gruber (1), Anon. (1), Strauss (1),
Cerwenka (1); No. 13 With A 2nd Gtr
Pt
contains: Es Wird Scho Glei, Dumpa
(Austrian); Gruber, Franz Xaver,
Stille Nacht (A maj)   (4056)

UBEN UND SPIELEN AUF DER GITARRE, VOL.
2 *CCU
(Zykan) gtr WELT f.s. arr + orig pcs
   (4057)

UBEN UND SPIELEN AUF DER GITARRE, VOL.
3 *CCU
(Zykan) gtr WELT f.s. arr + orig pcs
   (4058)

UNTERHALTENDE MUSIK FUR SOLO-GITARRE:
LEICHTE BIS MITTELSCHWERE
GITARRESOLIS
(Gotze) gtr (1-4th degr.) PRO MUSICA
185 f.s. contains works by 28
composers (51); Folksongs (22);
Anon. ca. 1800 (15); Anon. ca. 1600
(1); 26 arr + orig pcs
contains: Sor, Fernando, Minuet,
MIN 303 (from Grande Sonate, Op.
25)   (4059)

UNTERHALTENDE MUSIK FUR SOLO-GITARRE:
LIED UND TANZ VERSCHIEDENER LANDER
*CCU
(Gotze) gtr (1-4th degr.) PRO MUSICA
185 f.s. contains works by 28
composers (51); Folksongs (22);
Anon. ca. 1800 (15); Anon. ca. 1600
(1); 15 arr + orig pcs   (4060)

UNTERHALTENDE MUSIK FUR SOLO-GITARRE:
VOLKSLIED UND TANZ IN DEUTSCHLAND
*CCU
(Gotze) gtr (1-4th degr.) PRO MUSICA
185 f.s. contains works by 28
composers (51); Folksongs (22);
Anon. ca. 1800 (15); Anon. ca. 1600
(1); 48 arr + orig pcs   (4061)

VARIETY OF GUITAR MUSIC, A *folk song
(Duarte) gtr (1-3rd degr.) FABER f.s.
34 arr + orig pcs; contains works
by: Playford (6), Anon. (7),
Dowland (3), T. Campian (1),
Bartlett (1), Aston (2), Haydn (1),
Schumann (1), Tchaikovsky (1),
Telemann (2), Handel (1)
contains: Bach, Johann Sebastian,
Musette In D, BWV Anh.126 (from
Anna Magdalena Bach Notenbuchlein
(1725), No.22) (D maj)   (4062)

VISOR PA GITARR *CC20U,folk song
(Bengtsson) gtr (3rd degr.) NORDISKA
5350 f.s. arr + orig pcs; contains
works by: Tegner (6), Westling (1),
Gullmar (1), Borje (1), Koch (2),
Soderlundh (4), Foiack (1), Norlen
(1), Taube (1)   (4063)

WETTBEWERBS-UNTERRICHTSPROGRAMM, DAS;
ARBEITSPROGRAMM FUR DEN WETTBEWERB
"JUGEND MUSIZIERT", VOL. 1:
ALTERSSTUFE IB *CCU
(Pilsl, Fritz) gtr VOGT 202 f.s.
contains works by: Bossinensis;
Carcassi and Pilsl   (4064)

WETTBEWERBS-UNTERRICHTSPROGRAMM, DAS;
ARBEITSPROGRAMM FUR DEN WETTBEWERB
"JUGEND MUSIZIERT", VOL. 2:
ALTERSSTUFE IB *CCU
(Pilsl, Fritz) gtr VOGT 203 f.s.
contains works by: Judenkunig;
Giuliani and Pilsl   (4065)

WETTBEWERBS-UNTERRICHTSPROGRAMM, DAS;
ARBEITSPROGRAMM FUR DEN WETTBEWERB
"JUGEND MUSIZIERT", VOL. 3:
ALTERSSTUFE II *CCU
(Pilsl, Fritz) gtr VOGT f.s. contains
works by: Sanz; Paganini and Pilsl
   (4066)

WIR SPIELEN GITARRE, VOL. 1 *CC31U
1-2gtr,opt treb inst (1-3rd degr.) sc
PREISSLER JP-7018I f.s. suppl. to
W. Munch and H. Bausewein, Wir
Lernen Gitarre Spielen; arr. +
orig. pcs.; single line playing;
contains 5 pcs. for 1 gtr (nos. 1-
4, 7, 24), 26 pcs. for 2 gtr, or
treb inst, gtr by Anonymous
composers and folksongs   (4067)

WIR SPIELEN GITARRE, VOL. 2 *CC50U,
folk song
1-2gtr/opt treb inst (1-3rd degr.) sc
PREISSLER JP-7018-II f.s. suppl. to
W. Munch and H. Bausewein, Wir
Lernen Gitarre Spielen; arr. +
orig. pcs.; single line playing;
contains 1 pce. for 1 gtr (no. 5),
24 pcs. for 2 gtr or treb inst,
gtr, by Bausewein (5), Foster (1),
Brahms (1), Capua (1), Fliess (1)
   (4068)

YOUNG GUITARIST, VOL. 1 *CCU
(Harris) gtr MSM f.s.   (4069)

YOUNG GUITARIST, VOL. 2 *CC16L,folk
song
(Harris) gtr (3rd degr.) MSM $2.50
contains works by: Brahms;
Schubert; Campian; Harris (4); and
others   (4070)

Z POLONEZOW POLSKICH
"Polonaises" (Powrozniak) gtr (3-5th
degr., 22 arr pcs; contains works
by: Anon. (11), Bohdanowicz (1),
Oginski (2), Stefani (1). Kurpinski
(2), Elsner (1), Lipinski (1),
Chopin (1), Moniuszko (1),
Noskowski (1)) POLSKIE 7244 f.s.
   (4071)

I/IC Guitar Solos: Sonatas and Sonatinas

ALBERT, HEINRICH (1870-1950)
Sonaten, 2
gtr (4-5th degr.) ZIMMER. f.s.
   (4072)
Sonatinen, 3
gtr (3-4th degr.) ZIMMER. f.s.
   (4073)

AUS WILLIAM BRADE'S "VISBOK"
(Gerwig) gtr (3-5th degr., Der
Lautenist, Vol. VII; g is f-sharp;
10 pces) LIENAU f.s. contains also:
Genzmer, Harald, Sonatina   (4074)

BARTA, LUBOR (1928-1972)
Sonata
gtr (8-9th degr., Kytarova Sola,
No. 24) CZECH H-4424 f.s.   (4075)

BERKELEY, [SIR] LENNOX (1903-   )
Sonatina, Op. 51
(Bream) gtr (9th degr.) CHESTER
1803 f.s.   (4076)

BURGHAUSER, JARMIL (1921-   )
Sonata in E minor
gtr (7th degr., Kytarova Sola, No.
17) CZECH H-4048 f.s.   (4077)

CALL, LEONHARD VON (ca. 1768-1815)
Sonata
(Prat) gtr RICORDI-ARG BA-12361
f.s.   (4078)

CARCASSI, MATTEO (1792-1853)
Caprices, 6 *Op.26
"Capricen, 6" (Dahlke) gtr (3rd
degr.) SCHOTT GA-5 f.s. contains
also: Sonatinas, "Sonatinen",
Op.1   (4079)

CARULLI, FERDINANDO (1770-1841)
Nice Und Fileno *Op.2, Sonata
"Ungewitter, Das" gtr, and spoken
introduction (Gitarremusik Fur
Die Jugend, Vol. 8) ZIMMER. f.s.
   (4080)

Sonata, MIN 200
(Mazmanian) gtr (3-4th degr.)
HEINRICH. N-1522 f.s. contains
also: Air Varie   (4081)

Sonaten, 3
(Ritter) gtr (3-4th degr.) SCHOTT
GA-40 f.s.   (4082)

CARY, TRISTAM (1925-   )
Sonata for Guitar
(Duarte) gtr (9th degr.) NOVELLO
f.s.   (4083)

CASTELNUOVO-TEDESCO, MARIO (1895-1968)
Sonata
"Ommagio A Boccherini" (Segovia)
gtr (9-10th degr.) SCHOTT GA-149
f.s.   (4084)

CHAVARRI, EDUARDO LOPEZ (1871-1970)
Sonata No. 2
(Robledo) gtr ESCHIG 1218 f.s.
   (4085)

DIABELLI, ANTON (1781-1858)
Sonata in A
(Bream) gtr (6-7th degr.) FABER
F-0295 f.s.   (4086)

Sonata in C
(Behrend) gtr (5th degr.) NOETZEL
N-3169 f.s.   (4087)

Sonatina
(Nagel) gtr SCHOTT GA-419 f.s.
   (4088)

(Nagel) gtr BREITKOPF-W EB-6771

DIABELLI, ANTON (cont'd.)

f.s.   (4089)

Sonatinen, 3
(Just) gtr (5-6th degr.) SCHOTT
GA-57 f.s.   (4090)

DUARTE, JOHN W. (1919-   )
Sonatina Lirica *Op.48
(Peijel) gtr (6-7th degr.,
Collezione Di Musiche Per
Chitarra) BERBEN EB1972 $2.75
   (4091)
Sonatinette *Op.35
(Artzt) gtr (6-7th degr.) NOVELLO
19720 $2.35   (4092)

FRANCO, JOHAN (1908-   )
Sonata
gtr (6-7th degr.) COMP.FAC. f.s.
   (4093)

GEELEN, MATHIEU (1933-   )
Sonatina
gtr (7th degr.) TEESELING VT-56
f.s.   (4094)

GIULIANI, MAURO (1781-1829)
Sonata Eroica *Op.150
(Avila) gtr (8-9th degr.) SCHOTT
GA-53 f.s.   (4095)
"Gran Sonata Eroica" (Chiesa) gtr
(8-9th degr., Urtext Ed.) ZERBONI
7762 $7.00   (4096)
(Gilardi) gtr (8-9th degr.) BERBEN
EB1787 $2.75   (4097)
"Sonata Heroica" (Sainz de la Maza)
gtr (8-9th degr.) UNION ESP.
20767 f.s.   (4098)

Sonata, Op. 15
"Allegro" (Alfonso) gtr (8th degr.,
Edition Nicolas Alfonso, No. 13-
14) SCHOTT-FRER 9141 f.s.   (4099)
(Azpiazu) gtr (8th degr.) SYMPHON
460 f.s.   (4100)
(Chiesa) gtr (8th degr.) ZERBONI
8426 f.s.   (4101)
"Allegro Spiritoso" (di Ponio) gtr
(8th degr.) BERBEN EB512 $1.25
   (4102)
"Sonate Brillant" (Nagel; Meunier)
gtr (8th degr.) BREITKOPF-W 6701
f.s.   (4103)
(Scheit) gtr (8th degr.) UNIVER.
11320 $3.25   (4104)

Sonatina, MIN 390
gtr (3rd degr.) LEMOINE f.s. (4105)

Sonatina, Op. 71, No. 1
(Alfonso) gtr (5th degr., Edition
Nicolas Alfonso, No. 22-23;
incorrectly labelled Op. 73)
SCHOTT-FRER 9266 f.s.   (4106)

Sonatina, Op. 71, No. 3
(Saldarelli) gtr (6th degr.)
ZERBONI 7098 $6.00   (4107)

Sonatinen, 3 *Op.71
(Albert) gtr (5-6th degr.) ZIMMER.
ZM-307 f.s.   (4108)

GOETHALS, LUCIEN (1931-   )
Sonata, Op. 22
gtr (7th degr.) CBDM f.s.   (4109)

GRAGNANI, FILIPPO (1767- ?)
Sonatina, Op. 6
(Knobloch) gtr (3-4th degr.,
Kytarova Sola, No. 23) CZECH
H-4334 f.s.   (4110)

GRAMBERG, JACQ
Instructieve Sonatines, 3
gtr (single line playing/1st degr.)
HARMONIA 1821 f.s.   (4111)

HALFFTER, RODOLFO (1900-   )
Sonata in D (from Sonatas De El
Escorial, No. 1)
(Azpiazu) gtr (8th degr.) UNION
ESP. 19436 f.s.   (4112)

HAND, COLIN (1929-   )
Sonatina, Op. 74
gtr (7th degr.) NOVELLO 20054 $2.25
   (4113)

HARRIS, ALBERT (1916-   )
Sonatina
gtr COLUMBIA 178 $2.95   (4114)

HEER, HANS DE (1927-   )
Sonata
gtr TEESELING VT-197 f.s.   (4115)
(Peters) gtr (9th degr.) TEESELING
VT-29 f.s.   (4116)

HOLDER, DERWYN
Sonatina In One Movement
gtr COLUMBIA 156 $1.50   (4117)

KOMTER, JAN MAARTEN (1905–   )
Sonate Concertante
   gtr (3–4th degr.) DONEMUS f.s.
                                (4118)

KOVATS, BARNA (1920–   )
Sonata Nova
   gtr (7–8th degr.) MODERN 1042 f.s.
                                (4119)

KUBIZEK, AUGUSTIN (1918–   )
Sonata, Op. 13a
   (Ragossnig) gtr (9th degr.)
   DÖBLINGER 05907 f.s.
                                (4120)

LAZARO, JOSE
Sonata No. 3
   gtr (8–9th degr., g is f sharp, d
   is c sharp, E is D) BERBEN EB1739
   $3.00   (4121)

MANEN, JOSE
Fantasia-Sonata *Op.22a
   (Segovia) gtr (9th degr.) SCHOTT
   GA-129 f.s.   (4122)

MATIEGKA, WENZESLAUS THOMAS (1753–1830)
Sonata, Op. 16
   (Nagel) gtr BREITKOPF-W 6759 (4123)

MEESTER, LOUIS DE (1904–   )
Sonata
   gtr (7th degr.) CBDM 71-730 $5.00
                                (4124)

MEIJER VON BREMEN, ALEXANDER
   (1930–   )
Sonatina No. 1
   (Beck) gtr (7th degr.) TEESELING
   VT-54 f.s.   (4125)

MIGOT, GEORGES (1891–1976)
Sonata
   gtr (8th degr.) TRANSAT. 997 $4.25
                                (4126)

MOLINO, FRANCESCO (1775–1847)
Sonaten, 3 *Op.6
   (Gotze) gtr (4th degr.) SCHOTT
   GA-49 f.s.   (4127)

MOLITOR, SIMON
Sonata, Op. 11
   (Henze) gtr (6–7th degr.)
   HOFMEISTER-W f.s.   (4128)

MORENO TORROBA, FEDERICO (1891–1982)
Sonatina
   gtr (9th degr.) RICORDI-ARG
   BA-10042 f.s.   (4129)
   "Sonatina In La (Primo Tempo)"
   (Ferrari) gtr (9th degr.) BERBEN
   EB1134 f.s.   (4130)
   (Segovia) gtr (9th degr., Moreno
   Torroba Album No. 7) UNION ESP.
   f.s.   (4131)
   (Segovia) gtr (9th degr., new ed.)
   COLUMBIA 168 $1.75   (4132)

MULLER, SIEGFRIED (1926–   )
Sonata
   gtr (5–6th degr.) HOFMEISTER T-4158
   $2.75   (4133)

PAGANINI, NICCOLO (1782–1840)
Sonata, MIN 201,First Movement
   (Chiesa) gtr ZERBONI 6762 $3.50
                              (4134)

PITFIELD, THOMAS BARON (1903–   )
Sonatina in A minor
   gtr BELWIN $1.25   (4135)

PONCE, MANUEL MARIA (1882–1948)
Sonata Clasica, Hommage A Fernando
   Sor
   (Segovia) gtr (8th degr.) SCHOTT
   GA-122 f.s.   (4136)

   Sonata No. 1
   "Sonata Mexicana" (Lopez Ramos) gtr
   (7th degr.) PEER 1095-15 $3.00
                            (4137)

   Sonata No. 3
   (Segovia) gtr (10th degr.) SCHOTT
   GA-110 f.s.   (4138)

   Sonata Romantica, Hommage A Franz
   Schubert Qui Aimait La Guitare
   (Segovia) gtr (9–10th degr.) SCHOTT
   GA-123 f.s.   (4139)

   Sonatina Meridional
   (Segovia) gtr (9th degr.) SCHOTT
   GA-151 f.s.   (4140)

RODRIGO, JOAQUIN (1902–   )
Sonata Giocosa
   gtr (10th degr.) CHESTER 1807 f.s.
                              (4141)

   Sonate A l'Espagnole
   gtr ESCHIG f.s.   (4142)

RODRIGUEZ ALBERT, RAFAEL (1902–   )
Sonatina En Tres Duales
   gtr ALPUERTO 1303 f.s.   (4143)

ROSETTA, GIUSEPPE
Sonatina
   (Gilardino) gtr (7–8th degr.,
   Collezione Di Musiche Per
   Chitarra) BERBEN EB1468 $3.50
                              (4144)

SANCHEZ, B.
Sonatina
   gtr ESCHIG f.s.   (4145)

SANTORSOLA, GUIDO (1904–   )
Sonata
   "Sonoridades 1969" (Carlevaro) gtr
   (9th degr., Collezione Di Musiche
   Per Chitarra) BERBEN EB1570 $5.50
                              (4146)

   Sonata No. 2
   "Hispanica, Sonoridades 1971"
   (Estarellas) gtr (9–10th degr.,
   Collezione Di Musiche Per
   Chitarra) BERBEN EB1722 $6.25
                              (4147)

SCHALLER, ERWIN (1901–   )
Sonata for Guitar
   (Libbert) gtr (5–6th degr., Das
   Gitarrenwerk) PREISSLER 7073 f.s.
                              (4148)

SCHEIDLER, CHRISTIAN GOTTLIEB
   (1752–1815)
Sonata in C
   (Scheit) gtr UNIVER. 16696 f.s.
                              (4149)

SCHOLZE, ARTHUR JOHANNES (1883–1945)
Sonata, Op. 127, in E minor
   (Walker) gtr (7–8th degr.)
   HEINRICH. N-1504 f.s.   (4150)

SMITH BRINDLE, REGINALD (1917–   )
Sonatina Fiorentina
   gtr (7th degr., Schott's Series Of
   Contemporary Music For Spanish
   Guitar, No. 8) SCHOTT f.s. (4151)

SOR, FERNANDO (1778–1839)
Grande Sonate, Op. 22
   gtr SPAN.MUS.CTR. GE-253 f.s.
                              (4152)
   (Chiesa, Ruggero) gtr ZERBONI 8282
   f.s.   (4153)
   "Grosse Sonate" (Domandl, Willy)
   gtr BENJ 1322 f.s.   (4154)

   Grande Sonate, Op. 25
   (Chiesa, Ruggero) gtr ZERBONI 8283
   f.s.   (4155)
   "Zweite Grosse Sonate" (Domandl,
   Willy) gtr SIMROCK EE-1325 f.s.
                              (4156)
   "2a Sonata" (Segovia, Andres) gtr
   RICORDI-ARG BA-9600 f.s. (4157)

   Sonata, Op. 15, No. 2, in C
   (Chiesa, Ruggero) gtr ZERBONI 8281
   f.s.   (4158)
   (Domandl, Willy) gtr SIMROCK
   EE-1315 f.s.   (4159)
   (Fortea, Daniel) gtr FORTEA 173
   f.s.   (4160)
   (Pereira Arias, Antonio) gtr
   TEESELING VT-35 f.s.   (4161)
   (Sainz De La Maza, Regino) gtr
   UNION ESP. 19760 f.s. (4162)

STOKER, RICHARD (1938–   )
Sonatina, Op. 42
   (Estarellas) gtr (7–8th degr.,
   Collezione Di Musiche Per
   Chitarra) BERBEN EB1978 $2.75
                              (4163)

TURINA, JOAQUIN (1882–1949)
Sonatina
   (Segovia) gtr (9th degr.) SCHOTT
   GA-132 f.s.   (4164)

UHL, ALFRED (1909–   )
Sonata Classica
   (Scheit) gtr (9th degr.) SCHOTT
   GA-184 f.s.   (4165)

USHER, TERRY (1909–1969)
Sonata in A, Op. 3
   gtr (6–7th degr.) ESSEX f.s. (4166)

VANDERMAESBRUGGE, MAX (1933–   )
Sonata
   (Alfonso) gtr (7–8th degr.) CBDM
   69-263 f.s.   (4167)

WAGNER-REGENY, RUDOLF (1903–1969)
Sonatina
   (Henze) gtr (6th degr.) HOFMEISTER
   T-7329 $4.00   (4168)

WEINER, STANLEY (1925–   )
Sonata, Op. 22, No. 1
   gtr ZIMMER. ZM-1914 f.s. (4169)

WERNER, JEAN-JACQUES (1935–   )
Sonatina
   gtr (7–8th degr.) TRANSAT. 900
   $2.75   (4170)

WIKMANSON, J.
Sonata in B minor
   (Nagel, Meunier) gtr BREITKOPF-W
   EB-6769 f.s.   (4171)

I/IC-Coll   Guitar Solo Collections: Sonatas and Sonatinas

SONATINY I SONATY KLASYCZNE *CC10U
(Paterek; Kowalczyk) gtr (3–6th
degr.) POLSKIE 7670 f.s. contains
works by: Gragnani (1), Carulli
(4), Molino (1), Giuliani (1),
Paganini (2), Carcassi (1)   (4172)

I/IIA1 Duets for Two Guitars

ABLONIZ, MIGUEL (1917-   )
Divertimento
2gtr (3rd degr.) sc BERBEN EB1490
$1.00   (4173)

ABSIL, JEAN (1893-1974)
Contrastes *Op.143
(Alfonso) 2gtr (7th degr.,
Collezione Di Musiche Per
Chitarra) sc BERBEN EB1526 $5.75
(4174)

Danse *Op.119,No.1
2gtr (8th degr., Edition Nicolas
Alfonso, No. 106) sc SCHOTT-FRER
9187 f.s. contains also: Musette,
Op.119,No.2; Gigue, Op.119,No.3
(4175)

Suite for 2 Guitars
2gtr sc LEMOINE $5.75   (4176)

AGUIRRE, JULIAN (1868-1924)
Triste No. 1
(Martinez Zarate) 2gtr (6th degr.)
sc RICORDI-ARG BA-11967 f.s.
(4177)

ALBENIZ, ISAAC (1860-1909)
Bajo La Palmera *Op.232,No.3 (from
Cantos De Espana)
(Llobet) 2gtr (7-8th degr.) sc
UNION ESP. 20386 f.s.   (4178)

Cadiz, Serenata *Op.181,No.4 (from
Suite Espanola)
(Tarrago) 2gtr (8th degr.) sc UNION
ESP. 19646 f.s.   (4179)

Castilla, Seguidillas *Op.181,No.7
(from Suite Espanola)
(Llobet) 2gtr (8-9th degr.) sc
UNION ESP. 20387 f.s.   (4180)

Cordoba *Op.232,No.4 (from Cantos De
Espana)
(Pujol) 2gtr (8th degr.) sc
RICORDI-ARG BA-9582 f.s.   (4181)

Cuba, Capricho *Op.181,No.8 (from
Suite Espanola)
(Tarrago) 2gtr (8th degr.) sc UNION
ESP. 19645 f.s.   (4182)

Evocacion (from Iberia, Suite, No. 1)
(Llobet) 2gtr (8th degr.) sc UNION
ESP. 20388 f.s.   (4183)

Granada *Op.181,No.1 (from Suite
Espanola)
(Tarrago) 2gtr (7-8th degr.) sc
UNION ESP. 19319 f.s.   (4184)

Mallorca, Barcarola *Op.202
(Tarrago) 2gtr (8th degr.) sc UNION
ESP. 19647 f.s.   (4185)

Oriental *Op.232,No.2 (from Cantos
De Espana)
(Cuervas; Pujol) 2gtr (8th degr.)
sc UNION ESP. 19434 f.s.   (4186)

Pavan, MIN 202
(Tarrago) 2gtr (3-4th degr.) sc
UNION ESP. 19317 f.s.   (4187)

Rumores De La Caleta, Malaguena (from
Recuerdos De Viaje, No. 6)
(Llobet) 2gtr (8th degr.) sc UNION
ESP. 20389 f.s.   (4188)
(Tarrago) 2gtr (8th degr.) sc UNION
ESP. 19318 f.s.   (4189)

Sevilla, Sevillanas *Op.181,No.3
(from Suite Espanola)
(Tarrago) 2gtr (9-10th degr.) sc
UNION ESP. 19644 f.s.   (4190)

Tango *Op.165,No.2 (from Suite
Espana)
(Tarrago) 2gtr (7th degr.) sc
SCHOTT GA-405 f.s.   (4191)

Tango Espanol
(Pujol) 2gtr (7th degr.) sc
RICORDI-ARG BA-11507 f.s.   (4192)

Torre Bermeja, Serenata *Op.92,No.12
(from Piezas Caracteristicas)
(Tarrago) 2gtr (8-9th degr.) sc
UNION ESP. 19643 f.s.   (4193)

ALBERT, HEINRICH (1870-1950)
Duo No. 1 in C
2gtr (2-3rd degr.) pts ZIMMER.
ZM-1133 f.s.   (4194)

Duo No. 2 in A minor
2gtr (3rd degr.) pts ZIMMER.
ZM-1134 f.s.   (4195)

Duo No. 3 in C
2gtr (4th degr.) pts ZIMMER.
ZM-1135 f.s.   (4196)

Duo No. 4 in G
2gtr (4th degr.) pts ZIMMER.
ZM-1136 f.s.   (4197)

Duo No. 5 in E minor
2gtr (5th degr.) pts ZIMMER.
ZM-1137 f.s.   (4198)

Duo No. 6 in D
2gtr (6th degr.) pts ZIMMER.
ZM-1138 f.s.   (4199)

Duo No. 7 in A
2gtr (7th degr.) pts ZIMMER.
ZM-1139 f.s.   (4200)

Duo No. 8 in E
2gtr (8th degr.) pts ZIMMER.
ZM-1140 f.s.   (4201)

Gitarre-Etuden-Werk, Vol. 1:
Elementarstufe
"Studies, 12, Vol. 1: Elementary
Grade" gtr (1-3rd degr.), 2nd gtr
pt for teacher) ZIMMER. ZM-1156
f.s.   (4202)

ANONYMOUS
Ah! Vous Dirai-Je Maman Et 13 Duos Du
18me Siecle
(Sanvoisin) 2gtr (single line
playing/1st degr.) sc HEUGEL
PJ-348 f.s. Plein Jeu, No.348
(4203)

Anonymous Elisabethan Duets, 2
(Duarte) 2gtr (3-4th degr., orig
for 2 lutes-g') sc BERBEN EB1875
$2.50   (4204)

Greensleeves *16th cent
(Papas) 1-2gtr,opt solo voice (3-
4th degr.) sc COLUMBIA 141 f.s.
(4205)

Lute Duets, 2 (from Jane Pickering's
Lute Book (1616))
(de Hilster) 2gtr (3-4th degr.,
orig for 2 lutes-g'; partly
single line playing) HARMONIA
2379 f.s.   (4206)

Mazurka
(Tarrega) gtr FORTEA 111 f.s.
(4207)

More Of These Anon; 10 Anonymous
Pieces (from Fitzwilliam Virginal
Book)
(Duarte) 2gtr (2-3rd degr.) sc
NOVELLO 19496 $2.55   (4208)

Muscadin (from Fitzwilliam Virginal
Book)
(van der Staak) 2gtr (2-3rd degr.)
sc BROEKMANS 828 f.s. contains
also: Watkins Ale   (4209)

Pieces Sans Titre
(Castet) 2gtr (3-4th degr.,
Guitare, No.54; partly single
line playing (gtr I); orig for 2
lutes-g') sc LEDUC G-54 $2.25
contains also: Dowland, John, My
Lord Chamberlain His Galliard
(4210)

Romance Anonimo
(Garcia Velasco) 2gtr (4-5th degr.)
sc UNION ESP. 20305 f.s.   (4211)
(Tarrago) 2gtr (4-5th degr.) UNION
ESP. 21531 f.s.   (4212)

Sonatina for 2 Guitars
(Zanoskar) 2gtr (3rd degr.) SCHOTT
GA-221 f.s.   (4213)

Tanze, 8
(Brojer) 2gtr (1-2nd degr., Die
Gitarre In Der Hausmusik, No.20)
sc HOHLER GH-20 f.s.   (4214)

To Name But None (from Elizabeth
Rogers' Virginal Book) CC7U
(Duarte) 2gtr (2-3rd degr.) sc
NOVELLO 19622 $2.35   (4215)

Variationen Uber "Greensleeves" (from
The Division Flute, 1706)
(Scheit) 2gtr (3-4th degr.) UNIVER.
16697 f.s.   (4216)

ATTAIGNANT, PIERRE, [PUBLISHER]
(? -1552)
Pavanes-Gaillardes-Basses Dances-
Branles
(Monkemeyer) 2gtr (2-3rd degr.) sc

ATTAIGNANT, PIERRE, [PUBLISHER]
(cont'd.)

TONGER 1215 f.s.   (4217)

AUBANEL, GEORGES
Chants Et Danses Populaires Francais
*CC15U
(Worschech) 2gtr,opt perc (1-3rd
degr.) sc OUVRIERS EO-531 f.s.
(4218)

Etudes Rhythmiques *CC15U
(Worschech) 1-2gtr (2nd degr.)
OUVRIERS f.s.   (4219)

AUBERT, LOUIS
Improvisation
(Lagoya) 2gtr (9th degr.) sc
RICORDI-FR R-2165 f.s.   (4220)

BACH, J.C.
Sonata in C
(Nagel; Meunier) 2gtr (orig for
vln, gtr) BREITKOPF-W EB-6772
f.s.   (4221)

BARBIER, RENE (AUGUSTE-ERNEST)
(1890-1981)
Petite Suite *Op.110
2gtr (7th degr.) pts CBDM $7.00
(4222)

Suite No. 2, Op. 115
2gtr (7-8th degr.) pts CBDM $5.00
(4223)

BARTOK, BELA (1881-1945)
Duos (from 44 Duos For 2 Violins)
CC9U
(Scheit) 2gtr (single line playing/
1-2nd degr.) sc UNIVER. 14432
f.s.   (4224)

BARTOLI, RENE
Waltz in E minor
2gtr ESCHIG f.s.   (4225)

BEETHOVEN, LUDWIG VAN (1770-1827)
Beethoven For The Guitar *CC18U
(Block) gtr (2-3rd degr.) sc MARKS
15452-16 $1.50 1 pce for 2 gtr
(4226)

Chiaro Di Luna (from Sonata For
Piano, Op. 27, No. 2, First
Movement)
(Schinina) 2gtr (3rd degr.) sc
BERBEN EB1828 $2.25   (4227)

Duo
(Schaller) 2gtr (3rd degr., 4
movements; Das Gitarrenwerk,
Series A No. 15) sc PREISSLER
A 15 f.s.   (4228)

Sonatina
(Brojer) 2gtr (4th degr., Die
Gitarre In Der Hausmusik, No.21)
HOHLER GH-21 f.s.   (4229)

Sonatina E Adagio
(Benko) 2gtr (3-4th degr., Musica
Per Chitarra; orig for mand,
hpsd) sc EMB Z-7396 f.s.   (4230)

Sonatina in G
(Behrend) 2gtr (3rd degr.) sc
SIKORSKI 666-6 $3.50   (4231)

Variacion IV
2gtr FORTEA 287 f.s.   (4232)

BEHREND, SIEGFRIED (1933-   )
Duos, 3
2gtr (4-5th degr.) sc SIKORSKI
666-29 $3.50   (4233)

Japanische Serenade
2gtr (5th degr.) sc SIKORSKI 666-28
f.s.   (4234)

Leipziger Suite
2gtr (Gitarremusik Fur Die Jugend,
Vol. 7) ZIMMER. 1966 f.s.   (4235)

Stierkampfmusik
2gtr (4th degr.) ZIMMER. 1951 f.s.
(4236)

BENGUEREL, XAVIER (1931-   )
Stella Spendens
2gtr HANSEN-DEN 1007 f.s.   (4237)

BERTOUILLE, GERARD (1898-1981)
Petite Serenade Impromptu
2gtr (6-7th degr.) sc CBDM $3.50
(4238)

BIZET, GEORGES (1838-1875)
Menuet, Deuxieme, De l'Arlesienne
(from La Jolie Fille De Perth)
(Pujol) 2gtr ESCHIG 1412 f.s.
(4239)

BLEEKER, WILLY
Serenata Espanola
2gtr TEESELING VT-190 f.s. (4240)

BOISMORTIER, JOSEPH BODIN DE
(1689-1755)
Sonata in A minor
(Brojer) 2gtr (3rd degr., Die
Gitarre In Der Hausmusik, No.2)
sc HOHLER GH-2 f.s.   (4241)

BONNARD, ALAIN (1939-   )
Ricercari, 5 *Op.37
(Castet) 2gtr (partly single line
playing/3rd degr.) sc LEDUC $4.00
(4242)

BRAHMS, JOHANNES (1833-1897)
Wiegenlied
"Cancion De Cuna" (Garcia Velasco)
2gtr UNION ESP. 19538 f.s. (4243)

BROQUA, ALFONSO (1876-1946)
Tango, El
(Pujol) 2gtr ESCHIG 1402 f.s.
(4244)

BROUWER, LEO (1939-   )
Micropiezas, Hommage A Darius Milhaud
2gtr ESCHIG f.s.   (4245)

BULL, JOHN (ca. 1562-1628)
Duchesse Of Brunswick's Toye, The
(from Fitzwilliam Virginal Book)
(van der Staak) 2gtr (4-5th degr.)
sc BROEKMANS 838 f.s. contains
also: Duke Of Brunswick's Alman,
The   (4246)

Pieces, 3
(Quine) 2gtr (5th degr.) sc OXFORD
36.017 $1.80
contains: Almain, MIN 203; Bull's
Goodnighte; Gigue, MIN 204
(4247)

BURKHART, FRANZ (1902-1978)
Toccata
2gtr (7-8th degr., Gitarre-
Kammermusik, No.14) sc,pt
DOBLINGER GKM-14 f.s.   (4248)

BYRD, WILLIAM (1543-1623)
Dances, 3
(Quine) 2gtr (3-4th degr.) sc
OXFORD 36.005 $1.55
contains: Courante, MIN 207;
Galliard, MIN 206; Pavan, MIN
205   (4249)

Kleine Stucke, 3
(Behrend) 2gtr (3rd degr.) sc
SIKORSKI 666-7 $3.50   (4250)

CABEZON, ANTONIO DE (1510-1566)
Cancion Religiosa
(Ruiz-Pipo) 2gtr UNION ESP. 21777
f.s.   (4251)

Diferencias, 2
(Hinojosa) 2gtr (6-7th degr., g is
f sharp) sc SCHOTT GA-406 f.s.
(4252)

Tiento Del Primer Tono
(Garcia Velasco) 2gtr UNION ESP.
21937 f.s.   (4253)

CALL, LEONHARD VON (ca. 1768-1815)
Duette, 6 *Op.24
(Just) 2gtr (2nd degr.) SCHOTT
GA-56 f.s.   (4254)

Romance *Op.24
(Savio) 2gtr RICORDI-ARG BA-12411
f.s.   (4255)

CAMIDGE, MICHAEL C.
Sonatina in C
(Behrend) 2gtr (3rd degr.) sc
SIKORSKI 666-8 f.s.   (4256)

CARULLI, FERDINANDO (1770-1841)
Abendmusik *Op.227
"Nocturne De Salon" (Albert) 2gtr
(Die Gitarre In Der Haus- Und
Kammermusik, No. 18) ZIMMER.
ZM-1186 f.s.   (4257)

Allegro In G
(Gangi) 2gtr (3rd degr.) sc BERBEN
EB1685 $1.25   (4258)

Duet Facile
2gtr ESSEX f.s.   (4259)

Duet Study In F
2gtr ESSEX f.s.   (4260)

Duet Study In G
2gtr ESSEX f.s.   (4261)

Duette, 3
(Behrend) 2gtr (3rd degr., nos. I
and III also published
separately: N-3173 and N-3231) sc
NOETZEL N-3356 f.s.   (4262)

Duo Concertante
gtr fac ed CHANTERL f.s.   (4263)

Duos *Op.241
(Scheit) 2gtr (3rd degr., Gitarre-
Kammermusik, No.113; set of 2

CARULLI, FERDINANDO (cont'd.)
perf sc) perf sc DOBLINGER
GKM-113 f.s.   (4264)

Duos, 2 *Op.146
(Zschiesche) 2gtr (5th degr.)
SCHOTT 6014 f.s.   (4265)

Duos, 4
(Sanchez) 2gtr (2nd degr.,
Collection L'Heure De La Guitare
Classique; orig for gtr solo; gtr
II by Sanchez) sc CHOUDENS 20.222
f.s.   (4266)

Duos, 12
(Zschiesche) 2gtr (3-4th degr.)
SCHOTT 5660 f.s.   (4267)

Kleine Duette, 6, Vol. I *Op.34,
No.1-3
(Gotze) 2gtr (3-6th degr.) sc
SCHOTT GA-65 f.s.   (4268)

Kleine Duette, 6, Vol. II *Op.34,
No.4-6
(Gotze) 2gtr (3-6th degr.) sc
SCHOTT GA-66 f.s.   (4269)

Largo Und Rondo D-Dur *Op.146
(Scheit) 2gtr (4-5th degr.,
Gitarre-Kammermusik, No.112) sc,
pt DOBLINGER GKM-112 f.s.   (4270)

Leichte Fortschreitende Stucke
*Op.120
(Munk) 2gtr (2-3rd degr.) SCHOTT
GA-87 f.s.   (4271)

Methode De Guitare
"Gitarre-Schule, Vol. III: 24
Duette Fur 2 Gitarren" (Gotze,
Walter) [Ger] gtr (43p.; repr,
1967; ed after the 5th orig ed;
1st ed, 1932; 24 pcs. for 2 gtr)
quarto,sc PETERS 2480-D f.s.
(4272)

Nocturnes *Op.90, CC3U
(Schneider) 2gtr (4-5th degr.) pts
NOETZEL 3098 f.s.   (4273)

Notturno, Op. 128, No. 1
(Behrend) 2gtr (Die Klassischen
Meisterwerke Fur 2 Gitarren)
ZIMMER. 2040 f.s.   (4274)

Notturno, Op. 128, No. 2
(Behrend) 2gtr (Die Klassischen
Meisterwerke Fur 2 Gitarren)
ZIMMER. 2041 f.s.   (4275)

Romanze, 12
(Company) 2gtr (3-4th degr., set of
2 perf sc) perf sc ZERBONI 6675
$9.50   (4276)

Romanzen, 12, Vol. II *Op.333
(Gotze) 2gtr (2-3rd degr., for
Vol.I, see Sehr Leichte Stucke,
18, Vol.I) SCHOTT GA-68 f.s.
(4277)

Study
(Usher) 2gtr ESSEX f.s.   (4278)

CASTELNUOVO-TEDESCO, MARIO (1895-1968)
Sonatina Canonica
2gtr ESCHIG f.s.   (4279)

CERF, JACQUES (1932-   )
Climat *Op.41
2gtr FRANCAIS f.s.   (4280)

Petit Ours, Le, Une Histoire Pour Les
Petits Et Les Grands Amis De La
Guitare *Op.37,No.2, CC12U
2gtr (2-5th degr.) sc PAN 1709 f.s.
(4281)

CERVANTES, IGNACIO (1847-1905)
Danse Cubaine
(Pujol) 2gtr ESCHIG 1406 f.s.
(4282)

CHAPI, R.
Serenata Morisca
(Prat) 2gtr (8th degr.) pts
RICORDI-ARG BA-9578 f.s.   (4283)

CIMAROSA, DOMENICO (1749-1801)
Sonata No. 1
(Caceres) 2gtr ESCHIG f.s.   (4284)

Sonata No. 2
(Caceres) 2gtr ESCHIG f.s.   (4285)

CLARKE, JEREMIAH (ca. 1673-1707)
King's March
(Sperling) 2gtr (3rd degr.) sc
ESSEX f.s.   (4286)

CLASSIC GUITAR DUETS
2gtr MMO MMO-4012 f.s.   (4287)

COENEN, PAUL (1908-   )
Kleine Suite *Op.61
(Behrend) 2gtr (5th degr.) sc,pt
SIKORSKI 666-30 f.s.   (4288)

CORRETTE, MICHEL (1709-1795)
Suite in A minor
2gtr (3rd degr., Die Gitarre In Der
Hausmusik, No.7) HOHLER GH-7 f.s.
(4289)

COSTE, NAPOLEON (1806-1883)
Barcarolle (from Op. 51)
2gtr (2nd degr.) sc SCHOTT GA-378
f.s. contains also: Waltz   (4290)

COUPERIN, FRANCOIS (LE GRAND)
(1668-1733)
Hat Darav Ket Gitarra *CC6U
(Vereczkey) 2gtr (6-7th degr.) sc
EMB Z-7578 f.s. Musica Per
Chitarra   (4291)

Pavan, MIN 343
2gtr FORTEA 289 f.s.   (4292)

Petits Moulins A Vent, Les
(Pujol) 2gtr ESCHIG 1117 f.s.
(4293)

CRUZ, IVO (1901-   )
Cortejo Et Danza (from Symphonie
Amadis)
(Pujol) 2gtr ESCHIG 1411 f.s.
(4294)

Pastorale *CC5U
(Pujol) 2gtr (9-10th degr.) sc
ESCHIG 1407 f.s.   (4295)

CRUZ DE CASTRO, CARLOS
Caminos
2gtr ALPUERTO 1265 f.s.   (4296)

DANSKA OCH SVENSKA VISOR; 15 DANISH AND
SWEDISH FOLKSONGS *CC15U
(Scheit) 1-2gtr (1-3rd degr.) sc
UNIVER. 14459 $4.25 2 treb staffs
(4297)

DAQUIN, LOUIS-CLAUDE (1694-1772)
Cou-Cou, Le
(Llobet) 2gtr (8-9th degr.) sc
UNION ESP. 20390 f.s.   (4298)

DEBUSSY, CLAUDE (1862-1918)
Clair De Lune
(Martinez Zarate) 2gtr COLUMBIA 175
$1.75   (4299)

DIABELLI, ANTON (1781-1858)
Andantino (from Sonatina, Op. 163,
No. 6)
(Bianqui Pinero) 2gtr RICORDI-ARG
BA-12595 f.s.   (4300)

Fugue
(Vereczkey) 2gtr (3rd degr., set of
2 perf sc) perf sc EMB Z-6844
f.s.   (4301)

DIEUPART, C.
Airs De Danse, 3
(Pujol) 2gtr ESCHIG 1119 f.s.
(4302)

DIN DON DAINE, 8 DUTCH TUNES *CC8U,
folk song
(van Schagen) 2gtr (1-2nd degr.) sc
HARMONIA 1249 f.s. partly single
line playing   (4303)

DUARTE, JOHN W. (1919-   )
Flight Of Fugues, A *Op.44
gtr (3rd degr., 3 pieces for 1 or 2
gtr; suppl., version for 1 gtr)
sc BROEKMANS 1015 f.s.   (4304)

Friendships, 6
2gtr (3-4th degr.) sc NOVELLO 19565
$2.55   (4305)

Greek Suite *Op.39
2gtr (9th degr., Collezione Di
Musiche Per Chitarra) sc BERBEN
EB1410 $6.75   (4306)

Variations On A French Nursery Song
*Op.32
2gtr (10th degr., Collezione Di
Musiche Per Chitarra) sc BERBEN
EB1442 $6.00   (4307)

10 DUETS FOR 2 GUITARS
2gtr MMO MMO 4011 f.s.   (4308)

DUETTE AUS DEM 18. JAHRHUNDERT, 2
(Behrend) 2gtr (partly single line
playing/2nd degr.) sc NOETZEL
N-3181 f.s.
contains: Kuhnau, Johann, Gavotte,
MIN 35; Mattheson, Johann,
Allegro Molto   (4309)

DURANTE, FRANCESCO (1684-1755)
Galliard
(Behrend) 2gtr (5th degr.) sc
SIKORSKI 666-10 $3.50   (4310)

EUROPESE VOLKSLIEDEREN, VOL. I *CC13U,
  folk song
  (Niessen) 2gtr (2–3rd degr.) sc
    HARMONIA 2637 f.s.   (4311)

FABIAN, GASTON
  Gitarren Duette
    2gtr HANSEN-DEN f.s.   (4312)

FALCKENHAGEN, ADAM (1697–1761)
  Duo
    (van Puijenbroeck) 2gtr (e' is d',
    g is f sharp; capotasto in pos.
    III; orig for 2 lutes–f') sc
    METROPOLIS EM–14004 $3.00 (4313)

FALLA, MANUEL DE (1876–1946)
  Dance Of The Corregidor (from The
    Three Cornered Hat)
    (Tarrago) 2gtr (9th degr.) sc
    CHESTER 1805 f.s.   (4314)

  Danse De La Frayeur (from L'Amour
    Sorcier)
    (Pujol) 2gtr ESCHIG 1416 f.s.
                                 (4315)

  Danse Espagnole No. 1 (from La Vie
    Breve)
    (Pujol) 2gtr (9th degr.) sc ESCHIG
    1401 f.s.   (4316)

  Miller's Dance, The (from The Three
    Cornered Hat)
    (Tarrago) 2gtr (8th degr.) sc
    CHESTER 1804 f.s.   (4317)

FRANCESCO DA MILANO
  (ca. 1497?–ca. 1573?)
  Fantasy
    (Kadis) 2gtr (4th degr., notation:
    Fr tablature + transcription for
    gtr) MUS.SAC.PRO. LR-201 $1.80
                                 (4318)

FRESCOBALDI, GIROLAMO (1583–1643)
  Canzona Seconda
    "Bernardina, La" (Lonardi) 2gtr/
    2lute (5th degr., if 2 gtr: g is
    f sharp; partly single line
    playing (gtr I)) sc,pts ZERBONI
    7963 $6.00   (4319)

FURSTENAU, WOLFRAM
  Psalmodia Uber Das V. Gebot Mose, In
    Memoriam Quang Duc – Vietnam
    2gtr (8th degr.) sc TEESELING FC-3
    f.s.   (4320)

  Serenata Polonia
    (Beck) 2gtr (7th degr.) sc
    TEESELING VT-47 f.s.   (4321)

GAITIS, FRIEDRICH
  Stucke, 4
    (Behrend) 2gtr (4–5th degr.)
    SIKORSKI 666-31 f.s.   (4322)

GANGI, MARIO
  Andalusa (from Suite Spagnola)
    (Garzia; Carfagna) 2gtr (8th degr.)
    sc BERBEN EB1510 $1.50   (4323)

  Fandango (from Suite Spagnola)
    2gtr (7th degr.) sc BERBEN EB1794
    $2.50   (4324)

  Sevillana (from Suite Spagnola)
    2gtr (6th degr.) sc BERBEN EB1795
    $2.50   (4325)

GASTOLDI, GIOVANNI GIACOMO
  (ca. 1556–1622)
  Duette, 8
    (Zschiesche) 2gtr (3rd degr.)
    SCHOTT GA-417 f.s.   (4326)

GATTERMAYER, HEINRICH (1923–   )
  Duo
    2gtr (4–5th degr.) sc HEINRICH.
    N-1305 f.s.   (4327)

GIBBONS, ORLANDO (1583–1625)
  Dances, 3
    (Quine) 2gtr (3rd degr.) sc OXFORD
    36.006 $1.30
    contains: Almain, MIN 299;
    Courante, MIN 300; Galliard,
    MIN 301   (4328)

GIULIANI, MAURO (1781–1829)
  Grandi Variazioni Concertanti *Op.35
    (Chiesa) 2gtr (7th degr.) sc,pts
    ZERBONI 7885 $15.25   (4329)

  Leichte Landler, 8, 2 Vols.
    2gtr (2–3rd degr.) sc SCHOTT
    GA-380, GA-381 f.s.   (4330)

  Variazioni Concertanti *Op.130
    (Chiesa) 2gtr (7th degr.) sc,pts
    ZERBONI 7965 f.s.   (4331)
    "Tema Con Variazioni Concertanti"
    (Muggia) 2gtr (7th degr.) pts
    ZANIBON 5342 f.s.   (4332)
    "Variaziones Concertantes" (Savio)
    2gtr (7th degr.) sc RICORDI-ARG
    BA-12410 f.s.   (4333)

GLUCK, CHRISTOPH WILLIBALD, RITTER VON
  (1714–1787)
  Gavotte, MIN 28
    (Carfagna) 2gtr (3rd degr.) BERBEN
    EB2003 f.s.   (4334)

  Gavotte, MIN 29 (from Iphigenie En
    Aulide)
    (Pujol) 2gtr ESCHIG 1108 f.s.
                                 (4335)

GOUNOD, CHARLES FRANCOIS (1818–1893)
  Danzas De Las Bacantas
    2gtr (4th degr.) FORTEA 290 f.s.
                                 (4336)

GRAMBERG, JACQ
  Petrad
    gtr (4th degr.) HARMONIA 2939 f.s.
                                 (4337)

GRANADOS, ENRIQUE (1867–1916)
  Danza Espanola No. 6
    "Rondalla Aragonesa" (Cuervas;
    Pujol) 2gtr (9th degr.) UNION
    ESP. 19433 f.s.   (4338)
    "Rondalla Aragonesa" (Llobet) 2gtr
    (9th degr.) sc UNION ESP. 20391
    f.s.   (4339)
    "Rondalla Aragonesa" (Tarrago) 2gtr
    (9th degr.) UNION ESP. 19316 f.s.
                                 (4340)

  Danza Espanola, No. 11
    "Arabesca" (Llobet) 2gtr (9th
    degr.) sc UNION ESP. 20392 f.s.
                                 (4341)

  Danzas Espanolas, No. 2
    "Oriental" (Leon) 2gtr (7th degr.)
    sc RICORDI-ARG BA-12692 f.s.
                                 (4342)
    "Oriental" (Pujol; Cuervas) 2gtr (D
    min,7th degr.) sc UNION ESP.
    19432 f.s.   (4343)
    "Oriental" (Tarrago) 2gtr (C min,
    7th degr.) sc UNION ESP. 19315
    f.s.   (4344)

  Intermezzo (from Goyescas)
    (Azpiazu) 2gtr (7th degr.) UNION
    ESP. 21048 f.s.   (4345)
    (Pujol) 2gtr (7th degr.) sc
    RICORDI-ARG BA-9583 f.s.   (4346)

GUERRERO, FRANCISCO (1528–1599)
  Xenias Pacatas II
    2gtr ALPUERTO 1049 f.s.   (4347)

GUITAR DUETS, TRADITIONAL SPANISH AND
  SOUTH AMERICAN SONGS *CC11U,folk
  song
  (Williams) 2gtr (3–4th degr.) sc
    SCHOTT GA-91 f.s.   (4348)

HAFNER, KURT
  Leichte Originalstucke
    1-2gtr SCHMIDT,H 89 f.s.   (4349)

HAGEN, JOACHIM BERNHARD (fl. ca. 1759)
  Duo
    (van Puijenbroeck) 2gtr (e' is d',
    g is f sharp; capotasto in pos.
    III; orig for 2 lutes–f') sc
    METROPOLIS EM-4765 $3.00 (4350)

HANDEL, GEORGE FRIDERIC (1685–1759)
  Allemand In E minor, MIN 30
    (Tarrago) 2gtr (7th degr.) sc
    SCHOTT 10581, OR GA-199 f.s.
                                 (4351)

  Chaconne In G, With 21 Variations
    (Biberian; Duarte) 2gtr (8th degr.)
    sc NOVELLO 19640 $2.55   (4352)

  Courante in C, MIN 31
    (Tarrago) 2gtr (7th degr.) sc
    SCHOTT 10587 f.s.   (4353)

  Courante in D, MIN 32
    (Tarrago) 2gtr (7th degr.) sc
    SCHOTT 10588, OR GA-201 f.s.
                                 (4354)

  Guitar Duets *CC6U
    (Gavall) 2gtr (2–3rd degr.) BELWIN
    535 $2.50 nos. 1, 3-6: single
    line playing   (4355)

  Handel's Turn *CC10U
    (Duarte) 2gtr (mainly single line
    playing/1–2nd degr.) sc NOVELLO
    19822 $2.75 The Teacher Series Of
    Guitar Publications; arr as 2nd
    yr gtr duets   (4356)

  How Beautiful Are The Feet Of Them
    (from Messiah, No. 36)
    "Que Hermosos Son Sus Pasos"
    (Martinez Zarate) 2gtr RICORDI-
    ARG BA-12671 f.s.   (4357)

  Overture, MIN 33
    (Behrend) 2gtr (4th degr., mainly
    single line playing) SIKORSKI
    666-14 f.s.   (4358)

  Passacaglia
    (Verhoef) 2gtr (4–5th degr.) sc
    HARMONIA 2184 f.s.   (4359)

HANDEL, GEORGE FRIDERIC (cont'd.)

  Sonata in C, MIN 34
    (Verhoef) 2gtr (4–5th degr.) sc
    HARMONIA 2183 f.s.   (4360)

HAUBENSTOCK-RAMATI, ROMAN (1919–   )
  Hexachord I-II
    1-2gtr (8–9th degr.) UNIVER. 14478
    f.s.   (4361)

HAYDN, [FRANZ] JOSEPH (1732–1809)
  Menuette, 22
    (Monkemeyer) 2gtr, or str inst
    (baryton, vla da gamba, vln), gtr
    (2–3rd degr., single line playing
    (gtr I)) sc TONGER 1282 f.s.
                                 (4362)

  Seeking Haydn *CC4U
    (Duarte) 2gtr (3–4th degr.) sc
    NOVELLO 19794 $2.55 The Teacher
    Series Of Guitar Publications;
    arr as 3rd yr gtr duets   (4363)

  Serenata
    2gtr FORTEA 291 f.s.   (4364)

HELLER, STEPHEN (1813–1888)
  From Opus 47 *CC4L
    (Komter) gtr (3rd degr.) HARMONIA
    2947 f.s. contains op.47, nos.10,
    19, 23, and 3   (4365)

HLOUSCHEK, THEODOR (1923–   )
  Duette *CC9U
    2gtr (partly single line playing/2-
    3rd degr.) sc PRO MUSICA 182 f.s.
                                 (4366)

  Spielstucke *CC12U
    (Peter) 2gtr (3rd degr.) sc
    HOFMEISTER T-4162 $6.00   (4367)

HOFFNER, PAUL MARX (1895–1949)
  Indianer Suite
    (Behrend) 2gtr (4th degr.) SIKORSKI
    666-36 f.s.   (4368)

HOLLFELDER, WALDRAM (1924–   )
  Kleine Tanze
    2gtr VOGT 402 f.s.   (4369)

HORECKI, FELIKS (1799–1870)
  Utwory Wybrane
    (Powrozniak, Jozef) gtr (3–7th
    degr., Klasycy Gitary; 45 pcs for
    1 gtr; 6 pcs for 2 gtr) sc
    POLSKIE 7555 f.s.   (4370)

IBERT, JACQUES (1890–1962)
  Paraboles *CC2U
    2gtr (5–6th degr.) sc LEDUC $5.00
    set of 2 perf sc   (4371)

JANSEN, WILLY (1897–   )
  Kleine Spielmusiken *CC7U
    1-3gtr/gtr,2treb inst (1–2nd degr.)
    sc PREISSLER JP-7009 f.s. partly
    single line playing (3 gtr);
    notation: 2 treb staffs (4-pt
    music)   (4372)

JENKINS, JOHN (1592–1678)
  Arien Und Allemanden *CC10U
    (Monkemeyer) gtr/2treb inst (3rd
    degr.) sc TONGER 1216 f.s. (4373)

JOHNSON, JOHN (1540–1594)
  Rogero
    (Robert) 2gtr/2gtr,vla da gamba/
    vcl/lute/hpsd/harp/2gtr,vla
    da gamba,vcl (4th degr., orig.
    for 2 lutes–g' (?); notation of
    pt-I (gtr-I, lute-g', etc.): kbd
    partitura, Plein Jeu, No.96) sc
    HEUGEL PJ-96 $.75   (4374)

JOLIVET, ANDRE (1905–1974)
  Serenade
    2gtr (10th degr.) sc HEUGEL 31700
    $7.00   (4375)

JONES, JOHN
  Sonatina in C
    (Behrend) 2gtr (3rd degr.) SIKORSKI
    666-20 $3.50   (4376)

KARL, SEPP (1913–   )
  Junge Gitarre-Solist, Der, Vol. III;
    Eine Sammlung Leichter,
    Melodioser Solostucke (composed
    with Witt, Fred) *CC41U
    1-2gtr (2–3rd degr.) PREISSLER
    JP-7002-III $. 36 pcs by Karl
    for gtr; 5 pcs by Witt for 2 gtr
                                 (4377)

  Kleine Kostbarkeiten *CC20U
    2gtr (1–3rd degr.) sc PREISSLER
    7029 f.s.   (4378)

  Leichte Gitarren-Duette, 36
    2gtr (1–2nd degr.) sc PREISSLER
    7037 f.s.   (4379)

KAUFMANN, ARMIN (1902-   )
  Suite
    (Dobrauz) 2gtr (8-9th degr.) pts
    HEINRICH. N-1530 f.s.   (4380)

KHAN, PESY
  Indisches Spielbuch *CC9U
    (Behrend) 2gtr (2-3rd degr.) sc
    PETERER 2-110-102 f.s.   (4381)

KLASSISCHE MELODIEN
  (Tucholski) 1-2gtr APOLLO 2319 f.s.
                                 (4382)

KOMTER, JAN MAARTEN (1905-   )
  Chansonatine
    2gtr (6-7th degr.) sc HARMONIA 2707
    f.s.   (4383)

  Fun From The Start, Vol. 1: Guitar
    Duets For Teacher And Pupil
    *CC20U
    2gtr (1-2nd degr.) sc HARMONIA 2235
    f.s. partly single line playing
    (gtr I)   (4384)

  Milan-Suite, On A Theme Of Don Luis
    Milan (1535)
    2gtr (5th degr.) sc HARMONIA 2353
    f.s.   (4385)

  Punteado-Suite
    2gtr (4-5th degr.) sc HARMONIA 2510
    f.s.   (4386)

  Suite in A
    2gtr (5th degr.) sc DONEMUS f.s.
                                 (4387)

KORT, WIM DE
  Fughetta's, 2 *Op.9
    2gtr (single line playing/3rd
    degr.) TEESELING VT-27 f.s.
                                 (4388)

KOUNADIS, ARGHYRIS (1924-   )
  Rebetika
    (Behrend) 2gtr (Gitarremusik Fur
    Die Jugend, Vol. 9) ZIMMER. 1968
    f.s.   (4389)

KRONSTEINER, JOSEF (1910-   )
  Partita
    (Scheit) 2gtr (mainly single line
    playing/6th degr., Gitarre-
    Kammermusik, No.30) sc DOBLINGER
    GKM-30 f.s.   (4390)

KUFFNER, JOSEPH (1776-1856)
  Duette, 12 *Op.87
    (Gotze) 2gtr (1-2nd degr.) SCHOTT
    GA-45 f.s.   (4391)

  Leichte Duette, 40
    (Gotze) 2gtr (2nd degr.) SCHOTT
    GA-83 f.s.   (4392)

  Leichte Duos (from Op. 168)
    (Gotze) 2gtr (2nd degr.) SCHOTT
    GA-384 f.s.   (4393)

  Leichte Tanze
    (Gotze) 1-2gtr (3rd degr.) SCHOTT
    GA-84 f.s.   (4394)

  Leichte Ubungstucke, 60 *Op.168
    (Gotze) 2gtr (1-2nd degr.) sc
    SCHOTT GA-9 f.s.   (4395)

  Movimientos, 3 (from Op. 168)
    (Savio) 2gtr RICORDI-ARG BA-12419
    f.s.   (4396)

KUHNAU, JOHANN (1660-1722)
  Suite in A minor
    (Allison) 2gtr (5th degr.) sc
    NOVELLO 19895 $2.55   (4397)

LABROUVE, JORGE
  Disenos
    2gtr ALPUERTO 1054 f.s.   (4398)

  Nucleos
    2gtr ALPUERTO 1056 f.s.   (4399)

  Sintesis
    2gtr ALPUERTO 1057 f.s.   (4400)

LANDLERISCHE TANZE; SUITE NACH
  VOLKSWEISEN AUS OBEROSTERREICH
  *CC5U
  (Libbert) 2gtr (3rd degr.) sc
  PREISSLER f.s. Das Gitarrenwerk,
  Reihe A:12   (4401)

LAUFFENSTEINER, WOLFF JACOB
  Sonata in A
    (Behrend) 2gtr (7th degr., orig.
    for 2 lutes-f') SIKORSKI 666-21
    f.s.   (4402)
    (Neemann) 2gtr (7th degr., orig.
    for 2 lutes-f') sc VIEWEG 1736
    f.s.   (4403)
  "Duette A-Dur" (Schaller) 2gtr (7th
    degr., orig. for 2 lutes-f';
    Gitarre-Kammermusik, No.55a) sc,
    pt DOBLINGER GKM-55A f.s.   (4404)

LAWES, WILLIAM (1602-1645)
  Suite, MIN 36
    (Bream) 2gtr (7th degr., orig. for
    2 lutes-g') sc FABER F-0125 f.s.
                                 (4405)

LECHTHALER, JOSEF (1891-1948)
  Suite, Op. 49, No. 1
    (Scheit) 2gtr (5th degr., Gitarre-
    Kammermusik, No.8) sc,pt
    DOBLINGER GKM-8 f.s.   (4406)

LECLAIR, JEAN MARIE (1697-1764)
  Sonaten, 3
    (Steigenberger) 2gtr (7th degr.)
    pts NOETZEL N-3327 f.s.   (4407)

LESUR, DANIEL (1908-   )
  Elegy
    (Lagoya) 2gtr (9-10th degr.) sc
    RICORDI-FR R-1470 f.s.   (4408)

LEVINE, M.
  Humoresque *Op.6
    (Gilardino) 2gtr (8th degr.) sc
    BERBEN EB1294 $1.50   (4409)

LULLY, JEAN-BAPTISTE (LULLI)
  (1632-1687)
  Minuet, MIN 37 (from Le Bourgeois
    Gentilhomme)
    (Martinez Zarate) 2gtr (5th degr.)
    sc RICORDI-ARG BA-12289 f.s.
                                 (4410)

MAASZ, GERHARD (1906-1984)
  Zehn Leichte Stucke
    2gtr (2-3rd degr.) sc SCHOTT GA-431
    f.s.   (4411)

MARCELLO, BENEDETTO (1686-1739)
  Adagio, MIN 38 (from Concerto In C
    Minor For Oboe And Strings)
    (Amato) 2gtr/treb inst,gtr (6th
    degr., single line playing (gtr
    I)) sc ZANIBON 5173 f.s.   (4412)

MARCO, TOMAS (1942-   )
  Duo Concertante
    2gtr ALPUERTO 1214 f.s.   (4413)

MARELLA, GIOVANNI BATTISTA
  Music For 2 Guitars
    (Colgan) 2gtr (4th degr.)
    MUS.SAC.PRO. G-201 $4.20
    contains: Gavotta Rondo; Minuet;
    Minuetto; Minuetto Con
    Variazioni   (4414)

  Suite in A
    (Scheit) 2gtr (5th degr., orig. for
    5-course guitar) sc UNIVER. 11323
    $3.25   (4415)

MASSIS, AMABLE (1893-   )
  Pieces, 2
    2gtr (9-10th degr.) sc TRANSAT. 818
    $3.25
    contains: Duo En Forme De
    Prelude; Fugato Chromatique
                                 (4416)

MATELART, JOHANNES
  Recercate Concertate, Su La Quarta
    Fantasia Di Francesco Da Milano
    (Company) 2gtr (3-4th degr., 2 full
    scores + orig fantasia; orig. for
    2 lutes-g') ZERBONI 6764 $3.50
                                 (4417)

MATOS RODRIGUEZ, GERARDO H.
  Cumparsita, La, Tango
    (Sinopoli) 2gtr (6th degr.)
    RICORDI-ARG BA-6816 f.s.   (4418)

MATTHESON, JOHANN (1681-1764)
  Air in B minor
    (Behrend) 2gtr (3rd degr.) SIKORSKI
    666-22 f.s.   (4419)

MELII DA REGGIO, PIETRO PAOLO
  (fl. 1614-1616)
  Corrente, Detta La Favorita Gonzaga
    (Castet) 2gtr (3rd degr., Guitare,
    No.53; orig for 2 lutes - g' or
    a') sc LEDUC G-53 f.s.   (4420)

MENDELSSOHN-BARTHOLDY, FELIX
  (1809-1847)
  Andante Largo, C Major
    (Behrend) 2gtr (3rd degr.) SIKORSKI
    666-23 f.s.   (4421)

  Romanza Sin Palabras No. 20
    (Llobet) 2gtr UNION ESP. 20394 f.s.
                                 (4422)

  Romanza Sin Palabras No. 25
    (Llobet) 2gtr UNION ESP. 20395 f.s.
                                 (4423)

MERCHI, GIACOMO
  Caccia
    (Castet) 2gtr (Guitare, No. 87)
    LEDUC G-87 f.s.   (4424)

MET Z'N TWEEEN, DRIEEN, VIEREN...,
  VOLKSLIEDJES VOOR 2 GITAREN, OOK
  GESCHIKT VOOR DE GROEPSLES *CC25U,
  folk song
  (de Boer) 2 or more gtr (single line
  playing/1st degr.) sc HARMONIA 2442

f.s.   (4425)

MIGOT, GEORGES (1891-1976)
  Preludes
    2gtr (8th degr.) sc TRANSAT. 1002
    $2.50
    contains: Sur Le Nom De Graciela
    Pomponio (Prelude No. 1); Sur
    Le Nom De Jorge Martinez Zarate
    (Prelude No. 2)   (4426)

  Sonata, MIN 39
    2gtr (7-8th degr.) pts TRANSAT.
    1046 $6.75   (4427)

MORE CLASSIC GUITAR DUETS WITH RODRIGO
  RIERA
  2gtr MMO MMO-4049 f.s.   (4428)

MORENO TORROBA, FEDERICO (1891-1982)
  Capriccio
    2gtr (6th degr.) sc UNION ESP. f.s.
                                 (4429)

  Prelude
    2gtr (5th degr.) UNION ESP. f.s.
    contains also: Aire Vasco   (4430)

MOZART, LEOPOLD (1719-1787)
  Kadootje Voor Wolfgang, 'N *CC7U
    (van Schagen) 2gtr (partly single
    line playing/1-2nd degr.) sc
    HARMONIA 1246 f.s.   (4431)

MOZART, WOLFGANG AMADEUS (1756-1791)
  Adagio, MIN 342
    2gtr FORTEA 292 f.s.   (4432)

  Allegro
    (Bianqui Pinero) 2gtr RICORDI-ARG
    BA-12597 f.s.   (4433)

  Duo, MIN 40 (from Waldhornduetten, K.
    487)
    (Schaller) 2gtr (4th degr.,
    Gitarre-Kammermusik, No.93) sc
    DOBLINGER GKM-93 f.s.   (4434)

  Kleine Mozart, De *CC8U
    (Helleman) 2gtr (1-2nd degr.) sc
    HARMONIA 1519 f.s. single line
    playing   (4435)

  5 Landlerischer Tanze
    (Behrend) 2gtr (Gitarremusik Fur
    Die Jugend, Vol. 13) ZIMMER. 2072
    f.s.   (4436)

  Marche Turque
    (Pujol) 2gtr ESCHIG 1114 f.s.
                                 (4437)

  Minuet, MIN 41 (from Divertimento, D
    Major)
    (Pujol) 2gtr (7th degr.) sc ESCHIG
    1105 f.s.   (4438)

  Minuet, MIN 130 (from Don Juan)
    (Pomilio) 1-2gtr RICORDI-ARG
    BA-11237 f.s.   (4439)

  Minuet, MIN 341 (from Don Juan)
    2gtr FORTEA 293 f.s.   (4440)

  3 Scherzduette
    (Behrend) 2gtr (Gitarremusik Fur
    Die Jugend, Vol. 1) ZIMMER. 1960
    f.s.   (4441)

  Sonatina in C, MIN 42
    (Brojer) 2gtr (4-5th degr., Die
    Gitarre In Der Hausmusik, No.8)
    sc HOHLER GH-8 f.s.   (4442)

  Tanze, 4
    (Theunen-Seidl) 2gtr (3rd degr.,
    Die Gitarre In Der Hausmusik,
    No.14) HOHLER GH-14 f.s.   (4443)

MUSIZIERBUCHLEIN FUR ANFANGER *CC20U,
  folk song
  (Scheit) (1-2nd degr.) UNIVER. 13487
  $4.50 for 2 gtr or solo voice, gtr
  or treb inst, gtr (part I) and gtr
  (part II)   (4444)

NARVAEZ, LUIS DE
  Diferencias Sobre "Guardame Las
    Vacas"
    (Garcia Velasco) 2gtr (orig for 1
    vihuela) UNION ESP. 21936 f.s.
                                 (4445)

NEUMULLER, WOLFGANG
  Gitarrenstuckl *CC11U
    2-3gtr (1-2nd degr.) sc PREISSLER
    7066 f.s. 1 folksong for 2 gtr;
    10 folksongs for 3 gtr   (4446)

NIJENHUIS, LUC
  Canons In II
    2gtr (1-2nd degr., partly single
    line playing) sc HARMONIA 1890
    f.s.   (4447)

NOVAK, JAN (1921-1984)
  Rosarium, 10 Divertimenti
    (Andreoli) 2gtr (4-5th degr.) sc
    ZANIBON 5300 f.s.   (4448)

PAGANINI, NICCOLO (1782-1840)
  Moto Perpetuo *Op.11,No.6
    (Azpiazu) 1-2gtr SYMPHON 2123 f.s.
                                  (4449)

    (Fleury) 1-2gtr RICORDI-ARG
    BA-11585 f.s.   (4450)

PALESTRINA, GIOVANNI PIERLUIGI DA
    (1525-1594)
  Ricercare Del Primo Tono
    (Reyne) 2gtr (4-5th degr., Gitarre,
    No.59) sc LEDUC G-59 $2.25 (4451)

PASQUINI, BERNARDO (1637-1710)
  Partita Sopra La Aria Della Folia De
    Espagna
    (Ruiz-Pipo) 2gtr UNION ESP. 21766
    f.s.   (4452)

  Sonata in D minor
    (Schaller) 2gtr (7th degr.,
    Gitarre-Kammermusik, No.18; arr
    from 2 figured basses; set of 2
    perf sc) perf sc DOBLINGER GKM-18
    f.s.   (4453)

  Toccata Sur Le Jeu De "Coucou"
    (Pujol) 2gtr (8-9th degr.) sc
    RICORDI-ARG RF-7691 f.s.   (4454)

PELEMANS, WILLEM (1901-   )
  Preludes
    (Alfonso) 2gtr MAURER f.s.   (4455)

  Sonatina
    (Alfonso) 2gtr (7-8th degr., set of
    2 perf sc) perf sc MAURER f.s.
                                  (4456)
  Suite
    (Alfonso) 2gtr (8th degr., set of 2
    perf sc) perf sc MAURER f.s.
                                  (4457)

PERGOLESI, GIOVANNI BATTISTA
    (1710-1736)
  Siciliana
    (Proakis) 2gtr (2-3rd degr.) BERBEN
    EB1192 $1.00   (4458)

PETIT, PIERRE (1922-   )
  Tarantelle
    2gtr (10th degr.) ESCHIG f.s. (4459)

  Toccata
    2gtr ESCHIG f.s.   (4460)

PFISTER, CO
  Duo Flamenco, Improvisaties Over Een
    Argentijns Volkslied
    2gtr (5th degr., capotasto in pos.
    IV) pts HARMONIA 1521 f.s. (4461)

PICCININI, ALESSANDRO
  Toccata
    (Cherici) 2gtr (5th degr.) sc
    ZERBONI 8278 f.s.   (4462)

PIECES ELIZABETHAINES, 2
  2gtr (partly single line playing/4-
    5th degr.) sc HEUGEL PJ-65 $.50
    Plein Jeu, No.65; g is f sharp;
    orig for 2 lutes-g'
    contains: Anonymous, Allemande
    Variee Sur Greensleeves; Dowland,
    John, My Lord Chamberlain His
    Galliard   (4463)

PIZZINI, CARLO ALBERTO (1905-   )
  Suite Infantile *CC6U
    (Azpiazu) 1-2gtr (3-4th degr.) sc
    DE SANTIS 1073 f.s. for gtr (5)
    and 2 gtr (1)   (4464)

PONCE, MANUEL MARIA (1882-1948)
  Pieces, 5
    (Martinez Zarate) 2gtr COLUMBIA 182
    $3.00   (4465)

POULENC, FRANCIS (1899-1963)
  Embarquement Pour Cythere
    (Pujol) 2gtr ESCHIG 1414 f.s.
                                  (4466)
  Waltz
    (Pujol) 2gtr ESCHIG 1413 f.s.
                                  (4467)

PRESTI, IDA (1924-1967)
  Danse d'Avila
    2gtr (8-9th degr.) sc RICORDI-FR
    R-1616 f.s.   (4468)

  Etude No. 1
    2gtr (9-10th degr.) sc RICORDI-FR
    R-1615 f.s.   (4469)

  Prelude No. 1
    2gtr (9-10th degr.) sc RICORDI-FR
    R-1617 f.s.   (4470)

PUJOL, EMILIO (1886-1982)
  Canaries
    2gtr ESCHIG 1415 f.s.   (4471)

  Duet (Etude)
    2gtr ESCHIG 1417 f.s. contains
    also: Tirolesa (Tyrolienne)
                                  (4472)
  Ricercare
    2gtr (3rd degr.) ESCHIG 1409 f.s.
                                  (4473)

RADOLT, WENZEL LUDWIG FREIHERR VON
    (1667-1716)
  Canon In E
    (Behrend) 2gtr (3rd degr.) SIKORSKI
    666-27 f.s.   (4474)

RAMEAU, JEAN-PHILIPPE (1683-1764)
  Tambourin, Le
    (Pujol) 2gtr (7th degr.) sc ESCHIG
    1109 f.s.   (4475)

RAVEL, MAURICE (1875-1937)
  Pavane Pour Une Infante Defunte
    (Pujol) 2gtr (8th degr.) sc ESCHIG
    1408 f.s.   (4476)

REBAY, FERDINAND (1889-1953)
  Duo's Fur 2 Gitarren, Vol. I: 12
    Kleine Stucke
    (Dobrauz) 2gtr (3-4th degr.) sc
    HEINRICH. N-1517 f.s.   (4477)

  Duo's Fur 2 Gitarren, Vol. II: 9
    Vortragsstucke
    (Dobrauz) 2gtr (3-4th degr.) sc
    HEINRICH. N-1518 f.s.   (4478)

  Duo's Fur 2 Gitarren, Vol. III: 6
    Studien Nach Beruhmten Etuden Von
    Czerny Bis Chopin
    (Dobrauz) 2gtr (3-4th degr.) sc
    HEINRICH. N-1520 f.s.   (4479)

  Duo's Fur 2 Gitarren, Vol. IV:
    Spezial-Studien
    (Dobrauz) 2gtr (3-4th degr.) sc
    HEINRICH. N-1521 f.s.   (4480)

ROBINSON, THOMAS (fl. ca. 1603)
  Duets
    (Goor) 2gtr (2-3rd degr.) sc
    METROPOLIS EM-14766 $5.00 g is f
    sharp; capotasto in pos. III;
    orig for lute-g'
    contains: Fantasy, A; Passamezzo
    Galliard; Plaine Song, A; Toy,
    A; Twenty Ways Upon The Bells
                                  (4481)
  Fantasy
    (Caceres) 2gtr (orig. for 2 lutes)
    ESCHIG f.s.   (4482)

  Plaine Song
    (Caceres) 2gtr (3rd degr., orig.
    for 2 lutes-g') ESCHIG f.s.
                                  (4483)
    (Sensier) 2gtr (3rd degr., orig.
    for 2 lutes-g') sc ESSEX f.s.
                                  (4484)

RODRIGO, JOAQUIN (1902-   )
  Fandango Del Ventorrillo
    (Pujol) 2gtr (7th degr.) sc ESCHIG
    1410 f.s.   (4485)

  Romance De Durandarte
    2gtr UNION ESP. 21285 f.s.   (4486)

  Tonadilla
    2gtr (10th degr.) sc RICORDI-FR
    R-2166 f.s.   (4487)

ROHWER, JENS (1914-   )
  Duo Fur Lauteninstrumente
    2gtr (single line playing/1st
    degr., Der Lautenspieler, No. 4)
    sc FIDULA f.s.   (4488)

RONCALLI, LUDOVICO
  Passacaglia (from Capricci Armonici)
    (Mazmanian) 2gtr (6th degr., orig
    for gtr solo) pts HEINRICH.
    N-1549 f.s.   (4489)

ROSENMULLER, JOHANN (ca. 1620-1684)
  Pavane B
    (Williams) 2gtr (6th degr.) sc
    SCHOTT GA-95 f.s.   (4490)

ROSETTA, GIUSEPPE
  Sonata
    (Abreu) 2gtr (9th degr., Collezione
    Di Musiche Per Chitarra) sc
    BERBEN EB2045 f.s.   (4491)

SANCHEZ, B.
  Etude En Forme d'Invention
    2gtr (4th degr., Collection L'Heure
    De La Guitare Classique) pts
    CHOUDENS 20.269 f.s.   (4492)

  Variations, 10, Sur "Folias De
    Espana" En Forme De Canon
    2gtr/3gtr/6-9gtr (2-4th degr.,
    Notation: 1 theme consisting of 3
    parts, 1 chord accompaniment, 5

SANCHEZ, B. (cont'd.)
    variations (single lines);
    Collection L'Heure De La Guitare
    Classique) CHOUDENS 20.318 f.s.
                                  (4493)

SANTA MARIA, THOMAS DE (1510-1570)
  Fantasias, 25 (from Arte De Taner
    Fantasia (1565))
    (Azpiazu, J. de; Azpiazu L. de)
    2gtr (4-5th degr.) sc UNION ESP.
    20835 f.s.   (4494)

SANTORSOLA, GUIDO (1904-   )
  Sonata A Duo
    2gtr (8th degr.) sc PEER 983-16
    $3.00   (4495)

  Sonata No. 2
    "Sonoridades 1969" (Abreu) 2gtr
    (9th degr., Collezione Di Musiche
    Per Chitarra) sc BERBEN EB1814
    $9.50   (4496)

  Triptico, Tres Invenciones
    2gtr (5-6th degr., Collezione Di
    Musiche Per Chitarra; mainly
    single line playing) sc BERBEN
    EB1872 f.s.   (4497)

SCARLATTI, DOMENICO (1685-1757)
  Pastorale (from Sonata No. 9,
    Kirkpatrick 9)
    (Pujol) 2gtr (8th degr.) sc ESCHIG
    EB1106 f.s.   (4498)

  Sonata in A, Kirkpatrick 322
    (Schinina) 2gtr (6th degr.) sc
    BERBEN EB1831 $3.25 contains
    also: Sonata in A, Kirkpatrick
    113   (4499)

  Sonata in E, Kirkpatrick 380
    (Schinina) 2gtr (8-9th degr.) sc
    BERBEN EB1830 $2.75 contains
    also: Sonata in E, Kirkpatrick 20
                                  (4500)
  Sonata, Kirkpatrick 20, in E
    (Libbert) 2gtr (6th degr., Studio-
    Reihe Gitarre) sc PREISSLER 70200
    f.s. contains also: Sonata,
    Kirkpatrick 54, in A minor (4501)

  Sonata, Kirkpatrick 159
    (Pujol) 2gtr (8-9th degr.) sc
    RICORDI-ARG BA-11779 f.s.   (4502)

  Sonata, Kirkpatrick 173
    (Lagoya) 2gtr (8th degr.) sc
    RICORDI-FR R-1618 f.s.   (4503)

  Sonata No. 288, Kirkpatrick 432
    (Caceres) 2gtr (Collection Oscar
    Caceres, No. 6) sc ESCHIG f.s.
                                  (4504)
  5 Sonate Per 2 Chitarre
    (Fodor; Mosoczi) 2gtr sc EMB 7665
    f.s. Musica Per Chitarra
    contains: Sonata, Kirkpatrick 54;
      Sonata, Kirkpatrick 159;
      Sonata, Kirkpatrick 278;
      Sonata, Kirkpatrick 377;
      Sonata, Kirkpatrick 380 (4505)

SCHAGEN, HENK VAN
  Samen Spelen, Vol. I *CC10U
    2gtr (1-2nd degr.) sc HARMONIA 1261
    f.s. mainly single line playing
                                  (4506)
  Samen Spelen, Vol. II *CC10U
    2gtr (1-2nd degr.) sc HARMONIA 1299
    f.s. mainly single line playing
    (gtr I)   (4507)

  Voor Het Mooie Handje, Vol. I:
    Melodie-Aanslag *CC7U
    2gtr (1-2nd degr.) sc HARMONIA 1525
    f.s. single line playing (gtr I:
    student); 1st degr. (student),
    2nd degr. (gtr II: teacher)
                                  (4508)

SCHEIDLER, CHRISTIAN GOTTLIEB
    (1752-1815)
  Duo Pour Guitarre Et Violon
    gtr,vln fac ed CHANTERL f.s. (4509)

  Sonata in D
    (Scheit) vln,gtr/2gtr (5th degr.)
    sc,pts UNIVER. 14439 f.s.   (4510)

SCHIFFELHOLZ, JOHANN PAUL (1680-1758)
  Sonata I-VI (For 2 Colascioni, 2
    Violins And Violoncello)
    (Chiesa) 2gtr (3rd degr.) sc,pts
    ZERBONI 8361-8364, 8482, 8483
    f.s.   (4511)

SCHONSTEN LIEDER FUR UNSERE JUGEND, DIE
    *CC27U
    (Reess) 2-3gtr (1-2nd degr.) sc
    PREISSLER JP-7004 f.s. Die Gitarre
    Im Gruppenspiel, Vol. 1; partly
    single line playing   (4512)

SCHONSTEN WEISEN FUR UNSERE JUGEND, DIE
  *CC25U,folk song
  (Reess) 2-3gtr (2-3rd degr.) sc
  PREISSLER JP-7004-II f.s. Die
  Gitarre Im Gruppenspiel, Vol. II;
  partly single line playing   (4513)

SCHUBERT, FRANZ (PETER) (1797-1828)
  Ave Maria
  2gtr FORTEA 297 f.s.   (4514)

  Nacht Und Traume *Op.43,No.2,D.827
  "Noche Y Ensueno" (Martinez Zarate)
  2gtr RICORDI-ARG BA-12288 f.s. (4515)

  Walsen, 9 (from Thirty-Six
  Originaltanze, Op. 9, D. 365)
  (van Schagen) 2gtr (2-3rd degr.) sc
  HARMONIA 1505 f.s.   (4516)

SCHUMANN, ROBERT (ALEXANDER)
  (1810-1856)
  Aus Dem Album Fur Die Jugend, Op. 68
  *CC14U
  (Gotze) 2gtr (2nd degr.) sc SCHOTT
  GA-18 f.s.   (4517)

  Stucke Aus Dem "Album Fur Die Jugend,
  " Op. 68 *CC16U
  (Bacher) 1-2gtr (3-4th degr.) sc
  NAGELS EN-1103 f.s. for 2 gtr
  (12); gtr (4): Nagels Laute- Und
  Gitarre-Archiv   (4518)

SEGOVIA, ANDRES (1896-   )
  Estudios, 3
  gtr (6-7th degr., no. 3 for 2gtr)
  SCHOTT GA-178 f.s.   (4519)

SHIMOYAMA, HIFUMI (1930-   )
  Dialogo, No. 1
  2gtr (8-9th degr., set of 2 perf
  sc) perf sc ZERBONI 6869 $4.75 (4520)

  Dialogo, No. 2
  2gtr (8-9th degr., set of 2 perf
  sc) perf sc ZERBONI 7235 $8.25 (4521)

SIEGL, ERWIN
  Duos, Op. 34, Vol. I
  (Schindler) 2gtr (3-4th degr.) sc
  VAMO EE-06 f.s.   (4522)

SODERLUNDH, LILLE BROR (1912-1957)
  Liten Vals
  2gtr (3-4th degr.) sc NORDISKA 2280
  f.s.   (4523)

SOLER, [PADRE] ANTONIO (1729-1783)
  Sonata in G
  (Grandio) 2gtr sc ALPUERTO 1392
  f.s.   (4524)

SOMMERFELDT, OISTEIN (1919-   )
  Three Lyric Guitar Duets
  2gtr HANSEN-DEN f.s.   (4525)

SOR, FERNANDO (1778-1839)
  Complete Works For Guitar In
  Facsimiles Of The Original
  Editions, The, Vol. 8: Guitar
  Duets, Op. 34-63 [1st Gtr Part]
  *CCU
  (Jeffery, Brian) [Eng] 2gtr TECLA
  f.s. with notes and commentaries
                              (4526)

  Complete Works For Guitar In
  Facsimiles Of The Original
  Editions, The, Vol. 9: Guitar
  Duets, Op. 34-63 [2nd Gtr Part]
  *CCU
  (Jeffery, Brian) [Eng] 2gtr TECLA
  f.s. with notes and commentaries
                              (4527)

  Deux Amis, Les, Fantaisie Pour Deux
  Guitares *Op.41
  2gtr pts LEMOINE f.s.   (4528)

  Divertissement for 2 Guitars, Op. 38
  2gtr pts LEMOINE f.s.   (4529)
  2gtr pts ZIMMER. ZM-1144 f.s.
                              (4530)
  "Divertimento From Op. 38" (Savio,
  Isaias) 2gtr (without valse) pts
  RICORDI-ARG BA-12415 f.s.   (4531)

  Divertissement Pour Deux Guitares
  *Op.62
  "Divertimiento" (Savio, Isaias) gtr
  pts RICORDI-ARG BA-12414 f.s.
                              (4532)

  Encouragement, L', Fantaisie A Deux
  Guitares *Op.34
  2gtr pts LEMOINE f.s.   (4533)
  "Aufschwung" 2gtr pts ZIMMER.
  ZM-1143 f.s.   (4534)
  "Duo Fur 2 Gitarren" (Scheit, Karl)
  2gtr (without valse; formerly OBV
  6781.175) sc,pt UNIVER. 14446
  f.s.   (4535)

  Introduction A l'Etude De La Guitare
  En Vingt Cinq Lecons Progressives
  *Op.60
  "Anfanger-Etuden Fur Gitarre, 25"
  (Schwarz-Reiflingen, Erwin) [Ger]

SOR, FERNANDO (cont'd.)
  1-2gtr SIKORSKI 271 f.s.   (4536)

  Leichte Duette Fur Anfanger
  (Gotze, Walter) 2gtr SCHOTT GA-389
  f.s.
  contains: Est-Ce Bien Ca?, Six
  Pieces, Op. 48, No. 1;
  Introduction A l'Etude De La
  Guitare En Vingt Cinq Lecons
  Progressives, Op. 60, No. 1;
  Vingt-Quatre Exercices Tres
  Faciles, Op. 35, No. 13; Vingt
  Quatre Lecons Progressives,
  Dediees Aux Eleves Commencants,
  Op. 31, No. 5; Vingt-Quatre
  Petites Pieces Progressives
  Pour La Guitare, Pour Servir De
  Lecons Aux Eleves Tout A Fait
  Commencants, Op. 44, No. 7   (4537)

  Opera Omnia For The Spanish Guitar,
  Vol. 6 *Op.34-37
  (Jape, Mijndert) [Eng/Fr/Ger/Dutch]
  2gtr (critical ed with
  commentary) TEESELING VT-206 f.s.
                              (4538)

  Opera Omnia For The Spanish Guitar,
  Vol. 7 *Op.38-42
  (Jape, Mijndert) [Eng/Fr/Ger/Dutch]
  2gtr (critical ed with
  commentary) TEESELING VT-207 f.s.
                              (4539)

  Opera Omnia For The Spanish Guitar,
  Vol. 8 *Op.43-47
  (Jape, Mijndert) [Eng/Fr/Ger/Dutch]
  2gtr (critical ed with
  commentary) TEESELING VT-208 f.s.
                              (4540)

  Opera Omnia For The Spanish Guitar,
  Vol. 9 *Op.48-53
  (Jape, Mijndert) [Eng/Fr/Ger/Dutch]
  2gtr (critical ed with
  commentary) TEESELING VT-209 f.s.
                              (4541)

  Opera Omnia For The Spanish Guitar,
  Vol. 10 *Op.54-58
  (Jape, Mijndert) [Eng/Fr/Ger/Dutch]
  2gtr (critical ed with
  commentary) TEESELING VT-210 f.s.
                              (4542)

  Opera Omnia For The Spanish Guitar,
  Vol. 11 *Op.59-62
  (Jape, Mijndert) [Eng/Fr/Ger/Dutch]
  2gtr (critical ed with
  commentary) TEESELING VT-211 f.s.
                              (4543)

  Opera Omnia For The Spanish Guitar,
  Vol. 12 *Op.63
  (Jape, Mijndert) [Eng/Fr/Ger/Dutch]
  2gtr (critical ed with
  commentary; also contains works
  without op nos) TEESELING VT-212
  f.s.   (4544)

  Premier Pas Vers Moi, Le, Petit Duo
  Pour Deux Guitares *Op.53
  "Premier Pas, Le" 2gtr pts LEMOINE
  f.s.   (4545)

  Romance *Op. Posth.
  (Scheit) vln/fl,gtr/2gtr (4-5th
  degr.) UNIVER. 16685 f.s.   (4546)

  Souvenir De Russie, Fantaisie Pour
  Deux Guitares *Op.63
  2gtr pts LEMOINE f.s.   (4547)
  (Domandl, Willy) 2gtr sc SIMROCK
  EE-1363 f.s.   (4548)
  (Savio, Isaias) 2gtr pts RICORDI-
  ARG BA-12416 f.s.   (4549)

  Study in E minor
  (Fortea) 2gtr FORTEA 284A f.s.
                              (4550)

  Trois Duos Faciles Et Progressifs
  Pour Deux Guitares *Op.55
  "Three Duos" (Domandl, Willy) 2gtr
  sc BENJ 14583 f.s.   (4551)
  "Drei Leichte Duos" (Schwarz-
  Reiflingen, Erwin) 2gtr pts
  ZIMMER. ZM-1142 f.s.   (4552)

  Vingt-Quatre Exercices Tres Faciles,
  Op. 35, No. 22
  (Fortea, Daniel) 2gtr FORTEA 164
  f.s. contains also: Vingt-Quatre
  Exercices Tres Faciles, Op. 35,
  No. 13 (gtr)   (4553)

  Vingt Quatre Lecons Progressives,
  Dediees Aux Eleves Commencants,
  Op 31., No. 5
  "Andantino" (Bianqui Pinero, G.)
  2gtr RICORDI-ARG BA-12599 f.s.
                              (4554)

STAAK, PIETER VAN DER (1930-   )
  Easy Pieces, 6
  2gtr (2-3rd degr.) sc BROEKMANS 829
  f.s.
  contains: Argentine Dance;
  Ballad; Four Variations On A
  Theme Of Guido Topper; Polish
  Dance; Song, A; Spanish
  Impression   (4555)

STAAK, PIETER VAN DER (cont'd.)
  Pocket-Music
  2gtr (7th degr.) sc BROEKMANS 744
  f.s.   (4556)

STRATEGIER, HERMAN (1912-   )
  Short Pieces, 10
  1-2gtr (2-4th degr., 8 pcs. for gtr
  solo with a version for 2 gtr; 2
  pcs for 2 gtr) sc HARMONIA 2344
  f.s.   (4557)

STRAVINSKY, IGOR (1882-1971)
  Acht Stucke
  (Norman) 2gtr CHESTER f.s. (4558)

STRAVINSKY, SOULIMA (1910-   )
  Sechs Sonatinen, Vol. 1
  (Norman) 2gtr PETERS 6590C f.s.
                              (4559)

  Sechs Sonatinen, Vol. 2
  (Norman) 2gtr PETERS 6590D f.s.
                              (4560)

SUDAMERICANA, BERUHMTE FOLKLORISTISCHE
  TANZE *CC11U,folk song
  (Tucholski) [Span/Port/Ger] solo
  voice,gtr/1-3gtr (3-6th degr.) sc
  APOLLO 2339 f.s. contains works by:
  Creutziger (1), Tucholski (1) for
  solo voice, gtr; Villoldo (1),
  Porschmann (1), Albeniz (1) for 3
  gtr   (4561)

SUSATO, TIELMAN (? -ca. 1561)
  Altflamische Tanze *CC16U
  (Zschiesche) 2gtr (3rd degr.) sc
  SCHOTT 5236 f.s.   (4562)

  Tanze, 7 (from Tanzbuch 1551)
  (Scheit) 4gtr/2gtr (single line
  playing (4 gtr); notation: 4 treb
  staffs; 1st degr. (4 gtr), 3rd-
  4th degr. (2 gtr); Gitarre-
  Kammermusik, No.100) sc DOBLINGER
  GKM-100 f.s.   (4563)

TANZE, 6 *folk song
  (Brojer) 2gtr (2-3rd degr.) sc HOHLER
  GH-16 f.s. Die Gitarre In Der
  Hausmusik, No.16
  contains: Bretonischer Tanz;
  Deutscher Tanz; Englischer Tanz;
  Marientanz; Portugiescher Tanz;
  Ungarischer Tanz   (4564)

TARRAGO, G.
  Estudios, 2, Sobre Un Tema De Alard
  2gtr sc UNION ESP. f.s.
  contains: Study No. 1 in E (6th
  degr., 3rd degr. (gtr II));
  Study No. 2 in E (4th degr.,
  3rd degr. (gtr. II))   (4565)

TARRAGO, GRACIANO
  Bolero
  2gtr (4th degr.) sc SCHOTT 10586
  f.s.   (4566)

  Estudio De Tremolo, Sobre Un Tema De
  Alard
  1-2gtr (gtr1: 6th degr.; gtr2: 4th
  degr.) UNION ESP. 2257 f.s.
                              (4567)

TARREGA, FRANCISCO (1852-1909)
  Album No. 21
  (Tarrega, Francisco, hijo) 2gtr (4-
  7th degr.) sc UNION ESP. f.s.
  contains: Gran Jota De Concierto;
  Prelude, TI i- 17, in E,
  "Lagrima",   (4568)

  Album No. 22
  (Tarrega, Francisco, hijo) 2gtr (4-
  7th degr.) sc UNION ESP. f.s.
  contains: Danza Mora; Sueno
  (Mazurka)   (4569)

  Album No. 23
  (Tarrega, Francisco, hijo) 2gtr (4-
  7th degr.) sc UNION ESP. f.s.
  contains: Alborada, Capricho;
  Study, TI ii- 18, in A   (4570)

  Danza Mora
  (Bianqui Pinero) 2gtr RICORDI-ARG
  BA-12600 f.s.   (4571)

  Gran Jota De Concierto
  "Gran Jota Aragonesa" 1-2gtr (8-9th
  degr.) RICORDI-ARG BA-7924 f.s.
                              (4572)
  (Azpiazu) 1-2gtr (8-9th degr.)
  ALIER,I [5625] NO. 21 f.s. (4573)
  (Fortea) 1-2gtr (8-9th degr.,
  without Introduccion) FORTEA 206
  f.s.   (4574)
  (Fortea) 1-2gtr (8-9th degr.)
  ALIER,I 5625 NO. 21 f.s.   (4575)

  Kompositionen Fur Gitarre, Vol. II
  (Schwarz-Reiflingen) gtr (4-9th
  degr.) SIKORSKI 865B $7.25 18 pcs
  contains: Gran Jota De Concierto;
  Prelude, TI i- 8b, in A;
  Prelude, TI i- 15, in C;

TARREGA, FRANCISCO (cont'd.)

Prelude, TI i- 19, in E minor;
Prelude, TI i- 23, in B minor;
Study, TI ii- 4b, in A; Study,
TI ii- 6, in D, "Mariposa, La";
Study, TI ii- 12, in E,
"Suspiro d'Amor"; Study, TI ii-
29, in A minor; Study, TI ii-
36, in A   (4576)

TELEMANN, GEORG PHILIPP (1681-1767)
Sonata No. 6
(Gerwig) 2gtr (single line playing/
5th degr., Spiel Zu Zweit [I];
Der Spiel Der Lauteninstrumente,
Series II, Spielbuch 9) sc LIENAU
1424 f.s.   (4577)

Sonate Im Kanon
(Scheit) 2gtr (7th degr., Gitarre-
Kammermusik, No.17) pts DOBLINGER
GKM-17 f.s.   (4578)

TSILICAS, JORGE (1930-   )
Sinegia
2gtr ALPUERTO 1215 f.s.   (4579)

URAY, ERNST LUDWIG (1906-   )
Variationen Und Fuge Uber Ein
Volkslied
(Scheit) 2gtr (6-7th degr.,
Gitarre-Kammermusik, No.21) sc,pt
DOBLINGER GKM-21 f.s.   (4580)

VILLA-LOBOS, HEITOR (1887-1959)
A Canoa Virou, Cirandinha No. 10
(Cuervas; Pujol) 2gtr (9th degr.)
sc ESCHIG 1404 f.s.   (4581)

Terezinha De Jesus
(Pujol) 2gtr ESCHIG 1405 f.s.
                              (4582)

VISSER, DICK (1927-   )
Expo
2gtr (7th degr.) sc HARMONIA 2185
f.s.   (4583)

VIVALDI, ANTONIO (1678-1741)
Andante in E minor
(Tarrago) 2gtr (4-5th degr.) sc
SCHOTT GA-202 f.s.   (4584)

Aria Del Vagante (from Juditha
Triumphans)
(Abloniz) 2gtr (4th degr.) RICORDI-
IT 129351 f.s.   (4585)

Concerto for Violin and Orchestra, RV
297, in F minor, Largo (from Le
Quattro Stagioni)
"Largo De L'Hiver" (Castet) 2gtr
(6th degr., Guitare, No.56) sc
LEDUC G-56 $2.25   (4586)

Prelude, MIN 44
(Williams) 2gtr (single line
playing/5th degr.) sc SCHOTT
GA-96 f.s. contains also:
Courante, MIN 45   (4587)

WAGNER, GERHARD D.
Impreciones Mexicanas, Vol. I: Las
Ruinas De Mitla
(Visser) 2gtr (4-5th degr.) sc
HARMONIA 1529 f.s.   (4588)

Impreciones Mexicanas, Vol. II: Lago
De Texcoco
(Visser) 2gtr (4-5th degr.) sc
HARMONIA 1532 f.s.   (4589)

Impreciones Mexicanas, Vol. III: La
Tristeza De Malintzin
(Visser) 2gtr (4-5th degr.) sc
HARMONIA 1530 f.s.   (4590)

WEBER, CARL MARIA VON (1786-1826)
Duo (from Donna Diana)
(Berger) 2gtr (3rd degr.) sc
NOETZEL N-3263 f.s.   (4591)

WEBER, REINHOLD
Miniaturen, 5
(Nagel) 2gtr (8th degr., Gitarre-
Kammermusik, No.99) sc DOBLINGER
GKM-99 f.s.   (4592)

WEISS, JOHANN ADOLF
Leichte Duette, 6
(Gotze) 2gtr (3rd degr.) SCHOTT
GA-88 f.s.   (4593)

WEISS, SYLVIUS LEOPOLD (1686-1750)
Duett Fur Gitarren
(Kreidler) 2gtr (4-5th degr., facs)
sc SCHOTT GA-454 f.s.   (4594)

WILLAERT, ADRIAN (ca. 1490-1562)
Ricercare No. 14
(Hoger) 2gtr sc BOOSEY-ENG f.s.
                              (4595)

WISSMER, PIERRE (1915-   )
Barbaresque
2gtr (8-9th degr., Collezione Di
Musiche Per Chitarra) sc BERBEN
EB1650 $2.50   (4596)

Prestilagoyana
2gtr (7-8th degr., Collezione Di
Musiche Per Chitarra) sc BERBEN
EB1651 $2.75   (4597)

WOLF, ROLAND
Viva La Guitarra
2gtr (3-4th degr.) pts PREISSLER
JP-7017 f.s.
contains: Donna Maria; Fredericos
Erzahlung; Gitano; Morgenrote
Uber Granada; Recuerdos De
Sevilla; Viva La Guitarra
                              (4598)

XANTHOPOULOS, ILIAS
Sonata
2gtr (8th degr.) pts HEINRICH.
N-1543 f.s.   (4599)

ZUCCHERI, LUCIANO
Pezzi, 6
2gtr (3rd degr.) sc BERBEN EB2078
f.s.
contains: Angolo Visivo; Ballo
Con Tina; M'ama Mammola;
Pupazzi; Ricordando Giulia;
Vicolo Delle Mimose   (4600)

I/IIA1-Coll   Duet Collections
for Two Guitars

ALBUM RICREATIVO, NO. 4 *folk song
(Abloniz, Miguel) 1-2gtr (3-7th
degr.) BERBEN EB1818 $5.75 20 arr +
orig pcs; contains works by: Visee,
Mayr, Giuliani, W.A. Mozart,
Abloniz, Murcia, Sor, Carcassi,
Coste, Schumann, Brahms, Pergolesi,
Schubert, Molloy for 1 gtr; Abloniz
for 2 gtr
contains: Bach, Johann Sebastian,
Partita No. 1 for Keyboard
Instrument, BWV 825, in B flat,
Gigue (A maj)   (4601)

3 ALTE DUOS
(Behrend) 2gtr (contains works by:
Dowland; Frescobaldi and Gabrieli)
ZIMMER. ZM-2136 f.s.   (4602)

ALTE MEISTER DES 17. JAHRHUNDERTS
(Walker, Luise) 1-2gtr (5-7th degr.)
sc HEINRICH. N-1541 f.s. 16 arr +
orig pcs; contains works by: Losy
vom Losinthal (1), Handel (2),
Visee (1), Aldrovandini (1),
Roncalli (3), Rameau (1), For 1
Gtr; Handel (1), Corelli (1), For 2
Gtr
contains: Bach, Johann Sebastian,
Partita for Violin, No. 1, BWV
1002, in B minor, Saraband; Bach,
Johann Sebastian, Partita for
Violin, No. 3, BWV 1006, in E,
Minuet; Bach, Johann Sebastian,
Prelude for Lute, BWV 999, in C
minor (D min); Bach, Johann
Sebastian, Prelude No. 22 In B
Flat Minor (from Das
Wohltemperierte Clavier, Book 1);
Bach, Johann Sebastian, Suite for
Lute, BWV 996, in E minor,
Bourree; Visee, Robert de, Suite
in D minor (E is D; contains:
Prelude, VOCG 61; Allemand, VOCG
62; Courante, VOCG 63; Saraband,
VOCG 64; Gavotte, VOCG 66; Minuet
I, VOCG 68; Minuet II, VOCG 70;
Bouree, VOCG 67; Gigue, VOCG 65)
                              (4603)

ALTE UND NEUE MUSIK ZUM SINGEN UND
SPIELEN AUF BLOCKFLOTEN, GEIGEN UND
LAUTENINSTRUMENTE   *folk song
(Gerwig) [Ger] (1-3rd degr.) sc
LIENAU 1375 f.s. Das Spiel Der
Lauteninstrumente, Series II,
Spielbuch 1; contains works by:
Sperontes (4), L. Mozart (3),
Rathgeber (1), Rein (5), Rhau (2),
Langenau (1), Chemin-Petit (1): for
gtr (1), 2gtr (3), 3gtr (1), rec,
gtr (8), 2rec, gtr (2), solo voice,
gtr (1), solo voice, rec, gtr (1),
solo voice, rec, gtr (1), rec, vln
or vla, gtr (1); arr. + orig. pcs.;
single line playing; gtr pt partly
in bass clef
contains: Bach, Johann Sebastian,
English Suite No. 6, BWV 811, In
D Minor, Gavottes I-II (gtr,1-2A

rec); Bach, Johann Sebastian,
Minuet, BWV Anh. 118, in B flat
(from Anna Magdalena Bach
Notenbuchlein (1725), No.9) (gtr,
S rec) (C maj,single line
playing, gtr pt in bass clef)
                              (4604)

ALTWIENER TANZE *CC23L
(Bacher) 2gtr (2-3rd degr.) sc NAGELS
EN-1100 f.s. Nagels Laute- Und
Gitarre-Archiv; contains works by:
W.A. Mozart (3), Haydn (5),
Schubert (15)   (4605)

ANTOLOGIA DE LOS VIHUELISTAS ESPANOLAS,
VOL. 4
(Fresno) 2gtr (contains 6 pcs by de
Cabezon) ALPUERTO 1120 f.s. (4606)

ANTOLOGIA DE LOS VIHUELISTAS ESPANOLAS,
VOL. 6
(Fresno) 2vihuelas (contains works by
Valderrabano) ALPUERTO 1122 f.s.
                              (4607)

AUS DEM BALTISCHEN LAUTENBUCH 1740
*CC17L
(Pudelko) treb inst,1-2gtr/gtr solo
(2-3rd degr.) sc NAGELS EN-1107
f.s. notation: treb clef; Nagels
Laute- Und Gitarre-Archiv; contains
works by: Anon. (16), Batchelar (1)
                              (4608)

AUS PICKERING'S LAUTENBUCH (UM 1616)
(Teuchert) 2gtr (5th degr.) SCHMIDT,H
601 f.s.
contains: Drewries Accordes;
Rossignol, La   (4609)

CAHIERS DU GUITAROLIER, LES, VOL. 1
"22 Airs Populaires En Duo" (Rollin)
2gtr (2nd degr.) LEDUC f.s. (4610)

CAHIERS DU GUITAROLIER, LES, VOL. 2
*16th cent
"Danses Faciles d'Adrien Le Roy"
(Rollin) gtr LEDUC f.s.   (4611)

10 COMPOSICIONES CELEBRES PARA
GUITARRA, VOL. III *CC9U
(Pomilio) 1-2gtr (3-4th degr.)
RICORDI-ARG BA-11997 f.s. includes
pcs by: Giuliani, De Visee,
Carcassi, Sor, and Tarrega   (4612)

DEUTSCHE MEISTER DES EIN- UND
ZWEISTIMMIGEN LAUTENSATZES, 16.-18.
JAHRHUNDERT
(Bruger) [Ger] (1-3rd degr.) MOSELER
f.s. contains 22 arr + orig pcs; 12
pcs by: Heckel (1), M. Neusiedler
(1), Hainhofer (9), for gtr (1
Line); 2 pcs by Anon., H.
Neusiedler for gtr (2 lines); 6 pcs
by: Anon. (2), Judenkunig (1), H.
Neusiedler (3) for solo voice, gtr
(2 lines)
contains: Bach, Johann Sebastian,
Prelude, Fugue, And Allegro For
Lute In E Flat, BWV 998: Allegro
(gtr) (C maj, fragment only);
Bach, Johann Sebastian, Suite for
Lute, BWV 996, in E minor,
Bourree (2gtr) (partly single
line playing); Bach, Johann
Sebastian, Suite for Lute, BWV
996, in E minor, Passaggio-
Prelude (2gtr) (single line
playing)   (4613)

DU UND ICH WIR SPIELEN GITARRE, EIN
LIEBLINGSBUCH FUR ANGEHENDE
GITARRISTEN *folk song
(Baresel) 2gtr (1st degr.) sc ZIMMER.
ZM-1782 f.s. 20 pcs.;contains works
by: Zelter (1), Zuccalmaglio (1),
Anon. (1); mainly single line
playing
contains: Morgen Kommt Der
Weihnachtsmann; O Tannenbaum
                              (4614)

DUETTE, 10, AUS DEM 16. JAHRHUNDERT
(Zschiesche) 2gtr (single line
playing/2-3rd degr., contains works
by: Othmayr (1), Gastoldi (3),
Pelletier (2), Anon. (3), Lasso
(1) sc SCHOTT 5663 f.s.   (4615)

DUETTE FUR GITARREN *CC8U
(Behrend) 2gtr (4-5th degr.) sc
HEINRICH. 3441 f.s. arr + orig pcs;
contains works by: Le Sage De
Richee; Kuhnau; Mattheson; Carulli
and Anonymous   (4616)

ELIZABETHAN DUETS, 6
(Jeffery) 2gtr (3-4th degr.) sc
OXFORD 36.014 $2.50 contains works
by: Anon. (2), Dowland (1), J.
Johnson (2), Robinson (1); orig for
2 lutes
contains: Fancy; Flat Pavane, The;
Galliard To The Flat Pavane, The;
Lesson; My Lord Chamberlain His
Galliard; Rossignol, Le   (4617)

ERSTE MUSIZIERJAHR, DAS, VOL. 1
"Leichte Duos" (Knobloch) 2gtr (1-2nd
degr.) SYMPHON 2223 f.s.   (4618)

ERSTE MUSIZIERJAHR, DAS, VOL. 2
"Duos Alter Meister" (Knobloch) 2gtr
(1-2nd degr.) SYMPHON 2234 f.s.
    (4619)

ERSTE MUSIZIERJAHR, DAS, VOL. 3
"Folklore" (Knobloch) 2gtr (1-2nd
degr.) SYMPHON 2235 f.s.   (4620)

ERSTES MUSIZIEREN AUF DER GITARRE –
MUSIC-MAKING FOR GUITAR, LIEDER UND
TANZE VERSCHIEDENER NATIONEN
*CC24U
(Scheit) 1-2gtr (single line playing/
2nd degr.) UNIVER. 14456 $5.00
    (4621)

GITAAR-KAMERMUZIEK, VOL. 2
(Claessens, Anny C.H.) 1-4gtr (1-4th
degr.) sc BROEKMANS 26A f.s. arr +
single line playing/1-4th degr.) sc
BROEKMANS 26A f.s. arr + orig pcs;
contains works by: Claessens for 1
gtr; Anon. (6), Bohm (1),
Hurlebusch (1) for 2 gtr; J.S.
Bach, Rameau, von Call for 3 gtr;
Handel for 4 gtr
contains: Bach, Johann Sebastian,
Suite for Lute, BWV 996, in E
minor, Bourree (3gtr) (single
line playing)   (4622)

GITAAR-KAMERMUZIEK, VOL. 3: UIT HET
REPERTOIRE VAN HET JOEGOSLAVISCHE
DANSTHEATER
(Claessens, Anny C.H.) 1-5gtr (1-4th
degr.) sc BROEKMANS 27 f.s. arr +
orig pcs; contains works by:
Jovicic for 1 gtr (1); 9 songs and
dances; 2gtr (2); 3gtr (4); 5gtr
(2)
contains: Jovicic, Jovan, Concert-
Etude   (4623)

GITAAR-KAMERMUZIEK, VOL. 4: UIT HET
REPERTOIRE VAN HET JOEGOSLAVISCHE
DANSTHEATER *CC6U
(Claessens, Anny C.H.) 1-4gtr (1-4th
degr.) sc BROEKMANS 27A f.s. arr +
orig pcs; contains works by Jovicic
for: 1gtr(1); 6 songs and dances
for 2gtr (1); 3gtr (3); 4 gtr (3);
including gtr-g'   (4624)

GITAARDUET, HET
(Kok) 2gtr (3-5th degr.) sc XYZ H-14
f.s. arr + orig pcs; contains works
by: Carulli, Lemoine, Schumann (2),
Kuhlau; Fliess "Wiegenlied"
misattributed to W.A. Mozart
contains: Allegretto; Allegro;
Eerste Verdriet; Etude; Vrolijke
Landman, De; Flies, J. Bernhard,
Wiegenlied   (4625)

GITAARDUETTEN
(Kok) 2gtr (partly single line
playing/3-4th degr.) sc XYZ 567
f.s. 8 arr + orig pcs; contains
works by: Carcassi (1), W.A. Mozart
(1), Carulli (2), Handel (1),
Giuliani (1), Kok (1)
contains: Bach, Johann Sebastian,
Invention No. 1 for Keyboard
Instrument, BWV 772, in C (single
line playing)   (4626)

GITARRE ALLEIN, ENTWICKLUNG DES
SOLISTISCHEN MUSIZIERENS AUS DEM
AKKORDSPIEL *CC26L
(Wolki) 1-2gtr (1-3rd degr.) sc
APOLLO 2268 f.s. contains works by:
Wolki (13), Carcassi (2), Giuliani
(2), Sor (4), Carulli (5) For Gtr;
Kuffner (5), Carulli (1) for 2 gtr;
Suppl. 2 To Wolki, Gitarre Zum Lied
    (4627)

GITARREN MUSIZIEREN, 2, VOL. 1: LEICHTE
DUETTE FUR DEN ANFANG *CC20U, folk
song
(Schwarz-Reiflingen) 2gtr (partly
single line playing/1-5th degr.) sc
SIKORSKI 530 $5.00 contains works
by: Rinck (2), Turk (3), Gebhardi
(2), Clementi (1), Weber (1), W.F.
Bach (1), F. Couperin (1), W.A.
Mozart (1), Pachelbel (1), J.S.
Bach (?) (1), Krieger (1), Dandrieu
(1)   (4628)

GITARREN MUSIZIEREN, 2, VOL. 2: DUETTE
ALTER GITARRENMEISTER *CC10U
(Schwarz-Reiflingen) 2gtr (partly
single line playing/1-5th degr.)
pts SIKORSKI 531 $5.00 contains
works by: Carulli (2), von Call
(2), Schlick (2), Suppus (1),
Diabelli (1), Sor (1), Lhoyer (1)
    (4629)

GITARREN MUSIZIEREN, 2, VOL. 3:
MITTELSCHWERE DUETTE
(Schwarz-Reiflingen) 2gtr (partly
single line playing/1-5th degr.)
pts SIKORSKI 532 $5.00 15 pcs;
contains works by: Handel (2),

Vogler (1), Zachow (1), Turk (1),
W.A. Mozart (3), Beethoven (1),
Schumann (1), Grieg (1), Schubert
(1)
contains: Bach, Johann Sebastian,
Concerto, BWV 978, in F, Largo (D
min,mainly single line playing);
Bach, Johann Sebastian, Giguetta
(from Sarabande Con Partite, BWV
990) (C maj,mainly single line
playing); Bach, Johann Sebastian,
Prelude for Keyboard Instrument,
BWV 927, in F (from Wilhelm
Friedemann Bach Notenbuchlein,
No.8) (F maj,mainly single line
playing)   (4630)

GRADED DUETS, 20
(Gavall) 2gtr (partly single line
playing/1st degr.) sc OXFORD 36.003
$3.10 20 pcs; contains works by:
Losy vom Losinthal (1); Capilupi
(1), W.A. Mozart (5), Handel (3),
Purcell (1), Stamitz (1), Weiss (1)
contains: Bach, Johann Sebastian,
Brunnquell Aller Guter, BWV 445
(from Schemelli's Gesangbuch)
(single line playing); Bach,
Johann Sebastian, Eins Ist Noth,
Ach Herr, Dies Eine, BWV 453
(from Schemelli's Gesangbuch)
(single line playing); Bach,
Johann Sebastian, Gib Dich
Zufrieden Und Sei Stille, BWV 510
(from Anna Magdalena Bach
Notenbuchlein (1725), No.12) (F
maj,single line playing); Bach,
Johann Sebastian, Jesu, Deine
Liebeswunden, BWV 471 (from
Schemelli's Gesangbuch) (single
line playing); Bach, Johann
Sebastian, O Jesulein Suss, O
Jesulein Mild, BWV 493 (from
Schemelli's Gesangbuch) (single
line playing); Bach, Johann
Sebastian, Schaffs Mit Mir, Gott,
Nach Deinem Willen, BWV 314 (from
Anna Magdalena Bach Notenbuchlein
(1725), No.35) (E maj,single line
playing); Bach, Johann Sebastian,
Und Wie Wohl Ist Mir, O Freund
Der Seelen, BWV 517 (from Anna
Magdalena Bach Notenbuchlein
(1725), No.40) (F maj,single line
playing)   (4631)

GUITAR IN ENSEMBLE, VOL. 1
(Gavall) 2gtr (1-3rd degr.) sc BELWIN
1116 f.s. arr + orig pcs; 34 pcs;
contains works by: Folksongs (19),
Kuffner (3), Sor (1), Schubert (2),
Silcher (1), Weber (1), Mozart (1),
Brahms (1), Durrner (1),
Mendelssohn (1); Eng words: 8 pcs.
(not underlaid)
contains: Bach, Johann Sebastian,
Puer Natus Est In Bethlehem.
Chorale Prelude, BWV 603 (E min);
Bach, Johann Sebastian, Sonata
for Keyboard Instrument, BWV 964,
in D minor, Andante (C maj);
Bach, Johann Sebastian, Suite for
Lute, BWV 996, in E minor,
Bourree   (4632)

GUITAR MUSIC OF THE 16TH, 17TH AND 18TH
CENTURIES *CC10L
(de Tourris) 1-2gtr (3-6th degr.) sc
HARGAIL HFA-28 f.s. Hargail Folk
Anthology, No.28; arr + orig pcs;
contains works by: Garsi da Parma
(1), Sanz (1), Visee (5), Roncalli
(2), Rameau (1), for gtr; Albinoni
(1) and Handel (1), for 2gtr (4633)

GUITAR SONGBOOK, THE *folk song
(Noad) [Eng] (2-7th degr.) COLLIER
f.s. 72 arr + orig pcs; contains
works by: Anon. (6), Noad (1),
Gruber (1), Hopkins (1), Dun (1),
Poulton (1), Moore (1), Hume (1),
Schubert (2), Pergolesi (1), Blow
(1), Dowland (2), E. Purcell (1),
Rosseter (1), Morley (1), Martini
(1), Handel (1) for solo voice,
gtr; H. Purcell (2), Glinka (1),
Attwood (1), Gluck (1), Beethoven
(1), Schumann (1), Tchaikovsky (1),
Zipoli (1), Haydn (1), D. Scarlatti
(1) for 2 gtr; Sor (1), C.P.E. Bach
(1), Handel (2), Corelli (1),
Carcassi (1), Purcell (1), Carulli
(1), Dowland (1), Anon. (1), Mozart
(1) for gtr; with an introduction:
Complete Notes Of The Guitar, Chord
Chart, How Guitar Music Is Written,
Principal Elements Of Guitar
Technique (36p., 17 ill.)
contains: Coventry Carol, The (gtr,
solo voice); First Noel, The
(solo voice,gtr); Gruber, Franz
Xaver, Silent Night (gtr,solo
voice); Hopkins, John Henry, Jr.,
We Three Kings (gtr,solo voice)
    (4634)

GUITARS, 2 *CC10U
(Gavall) 2gtr (single line playing/1-
2nd degr.) sc OXFORD 36.002 $2.85
contains works by: Weichenberger,
Bergen, Wachsmann, Fux, Albert,
Beethoven, Saint Luc, Telemann,
Weiss, Stamitz   (4635)

GUITARS, 2, A GALAXY OF DUETS *CC88U,
folk song
(Bobri; Miller) 2gtr (partly single
line playing/2-5th degr.) sc
COLLIER f.s. contains works by:
Selby (1), Th. Campian (1), Purcell
(1), Farnaby (1), Wilson (1), Milan
(1), Moniot (1), Anon. (1);
Dutertre (1), Gervaise (1), Arbeau
(1), Susato (1), Leoncavallo (1),
Soloviov-Sedoy (1), Zakharov (1),
Narimanidze (1), Saliman-Vladimirov
(1)   (4636)

GUITARS, 2, ALBUM 1
(Azpiazu) 2gtr (3-4th degr.) pts
SYMPHON 2072 f.s. 10 pcs; contains
works by: Mattheson, Gregori,
Kuhnau, Purcell, Sor, Cano,
Bononcini, Daquin, Abaco
contains: Bach, Johann Sebastian,
March, BWV Anh. 127, in E flat
(from Anna Magdalena Bach
Notenbuchlein (1725), No.23) (A
maj)   (4637)

KANONS ZUM SINGEN UND SPIELEN *CC19U,
folk song
(Treml) 2-4gtr,opt solo voices
(single line playing/1-3rd degr.)
NAGELS EN-1097 f.s. Nagels Laute-
Und Gitarre-Archiv; a
reconnaissance on the fingerboard;
contains works by: Anon. (4),
Baumann (1), Wachsmann (1),
Mandyczewski (1)   (4638)

KLEINE WERKE GROSSER MEISTER, VOL. 1
*CC10U
(Bodenmann) gtr PETERER f.s. for 2
gtr with arr for gtr solo; single
line playing (2 gtr); degr. 1 (2
gtr), degr. 1, 2 (1 gtr); contains
works by: Franck (1), Haydn (1),
Speer (1), Krieger (1), Handel (2),
Schubert (1), Chedeville (2),
Mozart (1)   (4639)

KLEINE WERKE GROSSER MEISTER, VOL. 2
*CC9U
(Bodenmann) gtr PETERER f.s. for 2
gtr with arr for gtr solo; single
line playing (2 gtr); degr. 1 (2
gtr), degr. 1, 2 (1 gtr); contains
works by: Chedeville (3), Haydn
(3), Kress (1), Schubert (1),
Mozart (1)   (4640)

KLEINE WERKE GROSSER MEISTER, VOL. 3
*CC9U
(Bodenmann) gtr PETERER f.s. for 2
gtr with arr for gtr solo; single
line playing (2 gtr); degr. 1 (2
gtr), degr. 1, 2 (1 gtr); contains
works by: Rathgeber (1), Haydn (2),
Purcell (1), Praetorius (1), J.C.
Bach (1), Handel (1), Beethoven
(1), Schubert (1)   (4641)

KLEINE WERKE GROSSER MEISTER, VOL. 4
*CC10U
(Bodenmann) gtr PETERER f.s. for 2
gtr with arr for gtr solo; single
line playing (2 gtr); degr. 1 (2
gtr), degr. 1, 2 (1 gtr); contains
works by: Chedeville (1), Schubert
(1), Brahms (1), Daquin (1), Schein
(1), Telemann (1), Mozart (2),
Haydn (1), Purcell (1)   (4642)

KLINGENDE KLEINIGKEITEN AUS ALTER UND
NEUER ZEIT *CC18U
(Krupp) 2-4gtr (single line playing/
1-2nd degr.) sc PREISSLER JP-7019
f.s. contains folksongs and
anonymous works for 2gtr (10), 3gtr
(7), 4gtr (3)   (4643)

KOMMT SINGT UND SPIELT: LIEDER UNSERER
ZEIT, FUR DEN ANFANGSUNTERRICHT
*folk song
(Kramer) [Ger] (1-2nd degr.) sc
HOFMEISTER T-4137 f.s. contains 30
works by: Hubschmann (1), Franz
(1), Richter (1), Mertke (1),
Dittrich (1), Bimberg (1),
Schuffenhauer (1), Stumpe (1) for 2
gtr; Groger (1), Hein (1), Richter-
Ulbrich (1), Lukowsky (2), Balzer
(1), Ahrend (1), Meyer (1),
Natschinski (1), Kochan (1),
Englert (1) for 1 gtr; Natschinski
(1), Becher (1), Eisler (1),
Naumilkat (1), Schwaen (1), Bimberg
(1), Folksongs (2), Schmidt (1) for
solo voice and gtr; partly single
line playing (2 gtr)
contains: Richter, Eva, Unsere

Tannenbaum (composed with
Ulbrich, Christel) (gtr);
Richter, Wolfgang, Weihnachtszeit
(2gtr) (single line playing)
(4644)

LATWE UTWORY DAWNYCH MISTRZOW *CC40U
(Powrozniak) 2gtr (1-3rd degr.) sc
POLSKIE 6108 f.s. Grajmy Na
Gitarze, Vol. 5; contains works by:
Sor (4), Kuffner (26), Carulli (8),
Weber (1), von Call (1)   (4645)

LAUTENSPIELER DES XVI. JAHRHUNDERTS
(LIUTISTI DEL CINQUECENTO)
*CC124UL
(Chilesotti, Oscar) gtr (single
staff/8th degr.) quarto oblong
FORNI f.s. repr of 1st ed., publ
Ricordi-Breitkopf & Hartel (1891);
"Bibliotheca Musica Bononiensis",
Sezione IV, No. 31; includes works
by: Newsidler, Anon., Ballet,
Gintzler, Matelart, Gorzanis, da
Milano, Galilei, Barbetta, Caroso,
Terzi, Molinaro, dalla Gostena,
Negri, Besard, Mersenne,
Gianoncelli -all for 1 gtr;
Matelart, Galilei, Besard -for 2
gtr; Caroso, Negri -for dsc inst
and gtr; Fallamero, Besard -for vce
and gtr; Terzi -for 3 gtr; Besard -
for dsc inst and 3 gtr   (4646)

LEICHTE GITARREN-DUOS, 25 *CC25U
(Kovats) 2gtr (mainly single line
playing/1-3rd degr.) sc SCHOTT 5661
f.s. contains works by: Purcell
(1), Witthauer (1), L. Mozart (6),
J.C.F. Bach (1), Krieger (3), Anon.
(5), Lasso (1), Beethoven (1),
Pachelbel (2), Dandrieu (1), F.
Couperin (2), Rameau (1)   (4647)

LEICHTE STUCKE, 4
(Brojer) 2gtr (3rd degr.) sc HOHLER
GH-4 f.s. Die Gitarre In Der
Hausmusik, No.4
contains: Coste, Napoleon,
Barcarolle; Hassler, Johann
Wilhelm, Allegro; Sor, Fernando,
Andante; Sor, Fernando, Lento
(4648)

LEICHTES ZUSAMMENSPIEL *16-18th cent
2-3gtr/rec/mel inst,vln/mel inst,gtr
(2-3rd degr.) SCHMIDT,H 93 f.s.
(4649)

LIED UND GITARRE, 40 DEUTSCHE UND
AUSLANDISCHE VOLKSLIEDER, VOL. 1
(Teuchert) (1-3rd degr.) sc,pt
SCHMIDT,H 97 f.s. 32 pcs. for solo
voice, gtr or 2gtr; 8 pcs for solo
voice, gtr; Suppl.: arr for gtr I
(single line playing) of solo voice
pt; Vol.I:18 pcs
contains: Ya Se Van Los Pastores,
"Pastores, Los" (solo voice,gtr)
(4650)

LIED UND GITARRE, 40 DEUTSCHE UND
AUSLANDISCHE VOLKSLIEDER, VOL. 2
*CCU
(Teuchert) 2gtr (1-3rd degr.) sc,pt
SCHMIDT,H 98 f.s. 32 pcs. for solo
voice, gtr or 2gtr; 8 pcs for solo
voice, gtr; Suppl.: arr for gtr I
(single line playing) of solo voice
pt; Vol. II:22 pcs, pp.49-55:
Anleitung Zur Liedbegleitung Nach
Dem Gehor   (4651)

MEISTERWERKE FUR ZWEI GITARREN *CC3U
(Behrend) 2gtr (3-5th degr.) sc
ZIMMER. ZM-1894 f.s. contains works
by: Galilei, Carulli, Weber (4652)

MELODIE SWOJKIE *CC14U,folk song
(Powrozniak) 2gtr (3-4th degr.) sc
POLSKIE 5862 f.s. Grajmy Na
Gitarze, Vol. 3; contains works by:
Anon. (4), Elsner (1), Osmanski
(1), Powiadowski (1), Wronski (1),
Oginski (1), Moniuszko (1)   (4653)

MELODY OF JAPAN BY GUITARS, VOL. I
*CC12U
(Nakabayashi) [Jap] 1-4gtr (3-6th
degr.) sc SUISEISHA 402981 f.s. for
gtr (2), 2 gtr (2), 3 gtr (4), 4
gtr (4)   (4654)

MELODY OF JAPAN BY GUITARS, VOL. II
*CC17U
(Nakabayashi) [Jap] 1-4gtr (3-6th
degr.) sc SUISEISHA 402609 f.s. for
gtr (5), 2 gtr (3), 3 gtr (9), 4
gtr (2)   (4655)

MISTRI BAROKA *CC5U
(Knobloch) 2gtr (single line playing/
2-3rd degr.) sc CZECH H-4241 f.s.
Kytarova Sola, No. 21, contains
works by: Corelli, Pachelbel,
Couperin, Daquin, and Handel (4656)

MIT DER GITARRE, UNTERHALTUNGS-ALBUM
*CC28L,folk song
(Grosse; Wolf) [Ger] gtr (3rd degr.)

sc HARTH 2818 f.s. arr + orig pcs;
contains works by: Coste (1),
Carcassi (1), Rameau (1), Anon.
16th Cent. (1), Yradier (1),
Soloviev-Sedoy (1), Schubert (2),
Smetana (1) for 1 gtr; Schumann
(1), W.A. Mozart (1), Freire (1),
Granados (1) for 2 gtr; W.A. Mozart
(1), Petersen (2), Pakhmoutova (1),
Shanty (1), Nier (1), Ostrovski
(1), Schneider (1) for solo voice,
gtr   (4657)

MUSIC FROM THE TIME OF PURCELL *CC14U
(Easley) 2gtr (partly single line
playing/2-3rd degr.) sc AMP f.s.
contains works by: Barrett (1),
Croft (1), Blow (2), D. Purcell
(2), Loeillet (2), H. Purcell (3),
Clarke (2), Eccles (1)   (4658)

MUSICA INGLESA DE SIGLO XVL
2gtr (orig for 1 lute-g'; contains
works by John Dowland and Robert
Dowland) ALPUERTO 1055 f.s. (4659)

MUSICAL VOYAGE WITH TWO GUITARS, A; 64
MELODIES AND DANCES FROM 34
COUNTRIES *CC64U
(Bobri; Miller) 2gtr CEL bds 51200
$8.95, pap 06015 $5.95   (4660)

MUSIK ITALIENISCHER MEISTER *CC4U
(Schmidt) 2gtr (2-3rd degr.) sc
ZIMMER. ZM-1908 f.s. contains works
by: Tinazoli (1), Reggio (2),
Campioni (1)   (4661)

MUSIQUE ELISABETHAINE
(Castet) 2gtr (3-5th degr.) sc LEDUC
G-76 f.s. orig for 2 lutes-g',
includes works by Anon (2) and J.
Johnson (4)
contains: Drewries Accordes; Flatt
Pavin, The; Galliard, MIN 211;
Laveches Gallyerde; Piece Sans
Titre, Une; Rossignol, Le (4662)

MUSIQUE POUR DEUX GUITARES, VOL. 1 -
MUSIC FOR TWO GUITARS, VOL. 1
(Chandonnet) 2gtr (2-6th degr.) sc,
pts DOBER DO-6 f.s. 13 arr + orig
pcs; contains works by: Haydn;
Boyce; Pachelbel; Purcell;
Praetorius; de Falla; D. Scarlatti;
A. Gabrieli; Handel and Anonymous
contains: Bach, Johann Sebastian,
Prelude No. 22 in A minor, BWV
867 (from The Well-Tempered
Clavier I) (2gtr)   (4663)

POLYPHONES SPIELHEFT *CC5U
(Bayer) 2-4gtr DOBLINGER GKM-116 f.s.
Gitarre-Kammermusik, No. 116 (4664)

POPULAIRE GITAARDUETTEN *CC10U,folk
song
(Kok) 2gtr (3rd degr.) sc XYZ H-34
f.s. contains works by: Beethoven
(1), W.A. Mozart (1), Bizet (1),
Pergolesi (1)   (4665)

PRIMO REPERTORIO DEL CHITARRISTA, IL,
VOL. 1 *CC84L
(Storti) 1-2gtr (1-3rd degr.) sc
BERBEN EB1281 $6.00 contains works
by: Aguado (11), Carcassi (7),
Carulli (28), Giuliani (6), Sor
(7), Coste (5), Diabelli (6), Cano
(2) for 1 gtr; Carulli (3), Kuffner
(9) for 2 gtr   (4666)

RUSSISCHE VOLKSMUSIK *CCU
(Tucholski) [Ger] gtr APOLLO 2211 42
pcs for solo voice, gtr; 1 pce for
gtr solo; 1 pce for 2 gtr   (4667)

SEHR LEICHTE BIS MITTELSCHWERE SATZE
FUR 1 UND 2 GITARREN *CC94L
(Henze, Bruno) 1-2gtr (1-3rd degr.)
sc HOFMEISTER T-4016 f.s.
Supplement to Das Gitarrespiel,
Vols. 1-3; arr + orig pcs; contains
works by: Anon. (7), Albert (1),
Waissel (1), Haussmann (2), Losy
vom Losinthal (1), Fischer (1),
Hove (1), Attaignant (1), Gastoldi
(1), Hainhofer (2), M. Neusiedler
(1), Heckel (1), Schein (1), Sor
(6), Carcassi (5), Coste (3),
Carulli (14), Giuliani (6), Henze
(10) for gtr; Kuffner (12), Sor-
Henze (10), Sor (1), Carulli (5)
for 2 gtr   (4668)

SONNE, KOMM, EIN GITARRESPIELBUCH FUR
KINDER, 1-4. UNTERRICHTSJAHR *folk
song
(Ratz, Martin) [Ger] solo voice,gtr/
1-4gtr (single line playing/1-3rd
degr.) sc DEUTSCHER 32001 f.s. 162
arr + orig pcs; contains works by:
Schuffenhauer (2), Krug (4), Konig
(8), Ratz (22), Asriel (5), Quadt
(9), Rosenfeld (2), Haydn, Schumann
(3), Gorischk, Helmut, Wohlgemuth,

Schwaen, Schoendlinger for gtr;
Friemert (2), Buse, W.A. Mozart
(3), Beethoven, Berges,
Schuffenhauer, Hecht-Wieber for 2
gtr; Eberwein, Stephani for 3 gtr;
anon., naumilkat for 4 gtr or solo
voice(s), gtr; Skodova (2), Silcher
(2), Wendt, Friemert (2), Kern,
Krug (2), Pormova, Rodl, Hartung,
Nynkowa, Schuffenhauer, Hein,
Richter (3), W. Bender (2), Helmut,
Naumilkat for solo voice, gtr; also
contains Christmas music by:
Helmut, Schuffenhauer, Wohlgemuth
for gtr or solo voice, gtr; W.
Bender, Helmut, Naumilkat, for solo
voice, gtr
contains: Bach, Johann Sebastian,
Minuet in G minor, BWV Anh. 115
(2gtr) (A min,single line
playing); Bach, Johann Sebastian,
Piece In F, "Aria", BWV Anh.131
(2gtr) (single line playing);
Bach, Johann Sebastian, Polonaise
in G minor, BWV Anh. 119 (2gtr)
(A min,single line playing)
(4669)

SPIEL ZU ZWEIT II
(Gerwig) 2gtr (4-6th degr.) sc LIENAU
1434 f.s. Das Spiel Der
Lauteninstrumente, Series II,
Spielbuch 11; arr + orig; g is f
sharp
contains: Francesco da Milano,
Fantasia Sexta; Gabrieli,
Giovanni, Lieto Godea Sedendo;
Hassler, Hans Leo, Canzon;
Robinson, Thomas, Fantasie, A;
Robinson, Thomas, Schoole Of
Musicke, The; Robinson, Thomas,
Toy, A   (4670)

SPIELBUCH FUR GITARREN-DUO
(Teuchert, Heinz) 2gtr (partly single
line playing/2-5th degr.) sc
SCHMIDT,H 77 f.s. 31 arr + orig
pcs; contains works by: Kuffner
(8), Fux (2), Telemann (2),
Chedeville (1), Purcell (1), L.
Mozart (1), W.A. Mozart (2),
Erlebach (1), Carulli (3),
Hotteterre (2), Radolt (1), Handel
(2), Weber (1)
contains: Bach, Johann Sebastian,
English Suite No. 3, BWV 808, In
G Minor, Musette (C maj); Bach,
Johann Sebastian, March, BWV Anh.
122, in D (from Anna Magdalena
Bach Notenbuchlein (1725), No.16)
(C maj); Bach, Johann Sebastian,
Minuet, BWV Anh. 116, in G (from
Anna Magdalena Bach Notenbuchlein
(1725), No.7) (F maj); Bach,
Johann Sebastian, Suite for
Keyboard Instrument, BWV 820, in
F, Bourree (G maj)   (4671)

SPIELHEFT KLASSIK FUR ZWEI GITARREN
(Reiser) 2gtr (1-3rd degr.) sc SCHOTT
GA-435 f.s. 13 pcs; arr; contains
works by: Praetorius; Lully;
Corelli; Chedeville; W.A. Mozart;
Weichenberger; Telemann (3); Weiss
(2); and Galilei
contains: Bach, Johann Sebastian,
Suite for Lute, BWV 996, in E
minor, Bourree (E is D)   (4672)

SPIELMUSIK FUR 2 GITARREN *CC36U
(Henze) 2gtr (2-8th degr.) pts
HOFMEISTER T-4013 f.s. Das
Gitarrespiel, Vol. 8; arr + orig
pcs (numbered 1-23); contains works
by: Galilei (1), da Milano-Matelart
(1), Lauffensteiner (1), Marella
(2), Cherubini (1), Telemann (1),
L. Mozart (1), W.A. Mozart (3),
Kuffner (8), von Call (1), Sor (2),
Carulli (1), Diabelli (1), Giuliani
(4), Henze (1), Gaitis (2),
Muhlholzl (1), Stingl (1),
Ambrosius (1), Wagner-Regeny (2)
(4673)

SPIELMUSIK FUR ANGEHENDE GITARRISTEN,
VOL. III *CC16L,folk song
(Behrend) 1-3gtr (1-2nd degr.) sc
PREISSLER JP-7023-III f.s. arr +
orig pcs; contains works by: Anon.
(10), Behrend (2) for gtr (6), 2
gtr (7), 3 gtr (3); single line
playing (2 gtr, 3 gtr)   (4674)

SUDAMERICANA, BERUHMTE FOLKLORISTISCHE
TANZE *CC11U,folk song
(Tucholski) [Span/Port/Ger] solo
voice,gtr/1-3gtr (3-6th degr.) sc
APOLLO 2339 f.s. contains works by:
Creutziger (1), Tucholski (1) for
solo voice, gtr; Villoldo (1),
Porschmann (1), Albeniz (1) for 3
gtr   (4675)

TANZBUCH DER RENAISSANCE
(Giesbert) 2-4gtr SCHOTT GA-227 f.s.
(4676)

TANZE, 10
(Brojer) 2gtr (3rd degr., Die Gitarre
In Der Hausmusik, No.19; contains
works by: Beethoven (3),
Dittersdorf (4), Haydn (3)) sc
HOHLER GH-19 f.s.   (4677)

TRANSKRYPCJE KLASYKOW
(Powrozniak) 2gtr (partly single line
playing/2-4th degr.) sc POLSKIE
2461 f.s. Grajmy Na Gitarze, Vol.
12; 17 arr + orig pcs; contains
works by: Purcell (1), Rameau (1),
Telemann (1), Handel (2); Gluck
(1), Haydn (3), W.A. Mozart (3),
Beethoven (2)
contains: Bach, Johann Sebastian,
Invention No. 13 for Keyboard
Instrument, BWV 784, in A minor
(single line playing); Bach,
Johann Sebastian, Minuet, BWV
Anh. 114, in G (from Anna
Magdalena Bach Notenbuchlein
(1725), No.4) (single line
playing); Bach, Johann Sebastian,
Minuet, BWV Anh. 116, in G (from
Anna Magdalena Bach Notenbuchlein
(1725), No.7) (single line
playing)   (4678)

UTWORY DAWNYCH MISTRZOW
(Powrozniak) 2gtr (3-4th degr.) sc
POLSKIE 1369 f.s. Grajmy Na
Gitarze, Vol. 7; 10 arr + orig pcs;
contains works by: Gluck (1), W.A.
Mozart (1), Carulli (2), Gaude (1),
von Call (1), Hoyer (1), Sor (2)
contains: Bach, Johann Sebastian,
Polonaise, BWV Anh. 119, in G
minor (from Anna Magdalena Bach
Notenbuchlein (1725), No.10)
(2gtr) (E min,single line
playing)   (4679)

WIR SPIELEN GITARRE, VOL. 1 *CC31U
1-2gtr,opt treb inst (1-3rd degr.) sc
PREISSLER JP-7018I f.s. suppl. to
W. Munch and H. Bausewein, Wir
Lernen Gitarre Spielen; arr. +
orig. pcs.; single line playing;
contains 5 pcs. for 1 gtr (nos. 1-
4, 7, 24), 26 pcs. for 2 gtr, or
treb inst, gtr by Anonymous
composers and folksongs   (4680)

WIR SPIELEN GITARRE, VOL. 2 *CC50U,
folk song
1-2gtr/opt treb inst (1-3rd degr.) sc
PREISSLER JP-7018-II f.s. suppl. to
W. Munch and H. Bausewein, Wir
Lernen Gitarre Spielen; arr. +
orig. pcs.; single line playing;
contains 1 pce. for 1 gtr (no. 5),
24 pcs. for 2 gtr or treb inst,
gtr, by Bausewein (5), Foster (1),
Brahms (1), Capua (1), Fliess (1)
(4681)

I/IIA2   Trios for Three Guitars

A STAADE MUSI *CC9U
(Hornsteiner) 3gtr (3-4th degr.) sc
PREISSLER 7074 f.s.   (4682)

ALBENIZ, ISAAC (1860-1909)
Bajo De La Palmera *Op.232,No.3
(from Cantos De Espana)
(Borghese) 3gtr (8th degr.) sc,pts
ZERBONI 7669 $9.50   (4683)

ALBERT, HEINRICH (1870-1950)
Sonatinen, 3
3gtr (3-4th degr., 3 vols.) ZIMMER.
302-304 f.s.   (4684)

ALTE LAUTENMUSIK
(Wolki) 3gtr (4th degr.) SCHOTT 6389
f.s.   (4685)

AMBROSIUS, HERMANN (1897- ?)
Eggersberger Trio
(Behrend) 3gtr (Gitarremusik Fur
Die Jugend, Vol. 10) ZIMMER. 1969
f.s.   (4686)

ASRIEL, ANDRE (1922-   )
Kanons, 5
3gtr (single line playing/2-3rd
degr.) sc,pts HOFMEISTER T-4149
$4.75   (4687)

BARAT, JACQUES
Melodie Moyenageuse
3gtr (single line playing/1-2nd
degr.) sc CHOUDENS 20.671 f.s.
(4688)

BEETHOVEN, LUDWIG VAN (1770-1827)
Minuet in G
(Pick) 3gtr (single line playing/
2nd degr.) pts FORSTER f.s.
(4689)

BEHREND, SIEGFRIED (1933-   )
Study
3gtr (single line playing/3rd
degr.) sc,pts RIES 11.106-A f.s.
(4690)

BIZET, GEORGES (1838-1875)
Minuet, MIN 280 (from L'Arlesienne)
(Pujol) 3gtr ESCHIG 1621 f.s.
(4691)

Romance (from Pecheurs De Perles,
Les)
(Mori) 3gtr (mainly single line
playing/2nd degr.) sc BERBEN
EB1942 $1.00   (4692)

BLANCHARD, CARVER WILLIAM, JR.
Country Gardens *folk song,US
3gtr (3-4th degr.) sc PREISSLER
7033 f.s.   (4693)

Prolog Und Rondo
(Behrend) 3gtr (4th degr.) sc,pts
RIES 11.287 f.s.   (4694)

BOCCHERINI, LUIGI (1743-1805)
Beruhmtes Menuett
3gtr (2-3rd degr.) sc SCHOTT GA-392
f.s.   (4695)

BRIANO, GIOVANNI BATTISTA
Fuga Terza
3gtr (single line playing/3rd
degr.) sc BERBEN EB605 $1.00
(4696)

BYRD, WILLIAM (1543-1623)
Carman's Whistle, The
(Mairants) 3gtr (2-3rd degr.) sc,
pts FENETTE $3.00   (4697)

CALL, LEONHARD VON (ca. 1768-1815)
Leichtes Trio, Op. 26
3gtr (3rd degr.) COLUMBIA 180 $1.50
(4698)
(Albert) 3gtr (3rd degr., Die
Gitarre In Der Haus- Und
Kammermusik, No. 12) ZIMMER.
ZM-1124 f.s.   (4699)
(Borghese) 3gtr (3rd degr.) sc,pts
ZERBONI 7668 $13.00   (4700)
(Gotze) 3gtr (3rd degr.) sc SCHOTT
GA-61 f.s.   (4701)

CLEMENS, JACOBUS (CLEMENS NON PAPA)
(ca. 1510-ca. 1556)
Souterlied No. 99
(Visser) 3gtr (single line playing/
2-3rd degr.) sc HARMONIA 1857
f.s.   (4702)

COUPERIN, FRANCOIS (LE GRAND)
(1668-1733)
Musette De Choisy
(Pujol) 3gtr ESCHIG 1604 f.s.
(4703)

Musette De Taverny
(Pujol) 3gtr ESCHIG 1601 f.s.
(4704)

DAVID, THOMAS CHRISTIAN (1925-   )
Canzonen, 3
(Scheit) 3gtr (single line playing/
3-4th degr., Gitarre-Kammermusik,
No.94) sc,pts DOBLINGER GKM-94
f.s.   (4705)

DEUTSCHE VOLKSTANZE *CC10U,folk song
(Wolki) 3gtr (2-3rd degr.) sc SCHOTT
5419 f.s.   (4706)

DIABELLI, ANTON (1781-1858)
Trio, Op. 62, in F
(Company) 2gtr-g', gtr-e' (5th
degr.) sc,pts ZERBONI 7896 f.s.
(4707)

FABER, JOHANN CHRISTIAN
Partita
(Scheit) 3gtr (single line playing/
1st degr., Gitarre-Kammermusik,
No.101) sc DOBLINGER GKM-101 f.s.
(4708)

FARKAS, FERENC (1905-   )
Citharoedia Strigoniensis, Sopra
Motivi Ungheresi Di Esztergom Del
XVIII Secolo
3gtr (6th degr., Collezione Di
Musiche Per Chitarra) sc BERBEN
EB1973 $2.75   (4709)

FRANCESCO DA MILANO
(ca. 1497?-ca. 1573?)
Pavan
(Behrend) 3gtr (single line
playing/2nd degr.) sc,pts RIES
11.105-G f.s.   (4710)

FRESCOBALDI, GIROLAMO (1583-1643)
Tanzstucke *CC11U
(Henze) 3gtr (single line playing/
2-3rd degr.) sc,pts ZIMMER.
ZM-1764 f.s.   (4711)

GASTOLDI, GIOVANNI GIACOMO
(ca. 1556-1622)
6 Ballets
(Duarte) 3gtr NOVELLO 12.0457.02
f.s.   (4712)

GIULIANI, MAURO (1781-1829)
Trio, Op. 71, No. 3
(Albert) 3gtr (mainly single line
playing/4th degr., Die Gitarre In
Der Haus- Und Kammermusik, No.
14) pts ZIMMER. ZM-1188 f.s.
(4713)

GRAGNANI, FILIPPO (1767- ?)
Trio, Op. 12
(Albert) 3gtr (6-7th degr., Die
Gitarre In Der Haus- Und
Kammermusik, No. 13) pts ZIMMER.
ZM-1272 f.s.   (4714)
(Behrend) 3gtr (6-7th degr.) sc,pts
RIES 11.105-C f.s.   (4715)
(Borghese) 3gtr (6-7th degr.) sc,
pts ZERBONI 7667 $14.00   (4716)

GRAMBERG, JACQ
Dances, 6
3gtr (partly single line playing/1-
3rd degr.) sc HARMONIA 2554 f.s.
contains: Dartele Eenhoorn, De;
Kanarie Dans; Langzame Wals;
Muggendans; Rumba; Spring Dans
(4717)

GREENSLEEVES TO A GROUND
(Goossens) 3gtr (2-3rd degr.) sc
HARMONIA 2143 f.s.   (4718)

GUITARRA CANTORA, LA, MELODIAS
TRADICIONALES ARGENTINAS
(Kantor) [Span] 3-4gtr/fl&3gtr
(partly single line playing/1-2nd
degr., contains 7 pcs for solo
voice or gtr, 2gtr (5); solo voice,
3gtr (1); fl or gtr, gtr or solo
voice, 2gtr (1); opt perc (2)) sc
RICORDI-ARG BA-12779 f.s.   (4719)

HANDEL, GEORGE FRIDERIC (1685-1759)
Allegro
(Verhoef) 3gtr (single line
playing/4-5th degr.) sc TEESELING
VT-38 f.s.   (4720)

Chaconne
(Behrend) 3gtr (mainly single line
playing/4th degr.) sc,pts RIES
11.105-D f.s.   (4721)

Sonata, MIN 46
(Behrend) 3gtr (5-6th degr.) sc,pts
RIES 11.105-F f.s.   (4722)

Tanze Aus Opern, 7
(Behrend) 3gtr (single line
playing/2-3rd degr.) sc,pts RIES
11.105-E f.s.   (4723)

HARTOG, CEES
Let's Take The Flip Side
3gtr (3rd degr., 2 or 3 players to
a part possible) sc HARMONIA 2611
f.s.   (4724)

HAUSWIRTH, HANS M.A. (1901-   )
Tanze Und Weisen
3gtr (3rd degr., Das Gitarren-
Gruppenspiel, Vol. III) sc
PREISSLER 7008-III f.s.   (4725)

HAYDN, [FRANZ] JOSEPH (1732-1809)
Trio, MIN 47
(Teuchert) 3gtr (3-4th degr., Der
Lautenkreis, Vol. I; for 3gtr or
vln or fl, 2gtr) sc,pts SCHMIDT,H
501 f.s.   (4726)

HINDEMITH, PAUL (1895-1963)
Rondo
(Behrend) 3gtr (4th degr.) sc
SCHOTT GA-412 f.s.   (4727)

HLOUSCHEK, THEODOR (1923-   )
Trio
(Behrend) 3gtr (5-6th degr.) sc,pts
RIES 11.283 f.s.   (4728)

HOEK, JAN-ANTON VAN (1936-   )
Trios, 3, Op. 919
3gtr (single line playing/3-4th
degr.) sc HARMONIA 2079 f.s.
contains: Burlesque, Op.919,No.3;
Fugue, Op. 919, No. 2; Pavan,
Op. 919, No. 1   (4729)

HOEKEMA, HENK
Easy Pieces, 7
3gtr (single line playing/1st
degr.) sc BROEKMANS 821 f.s.
(4730)

JANSEN, WILLY (1897-   )
  Kleine Spielmusiken *CC7U
    1-3gtr/gtr,2treb inst (1-2nd degr.)
    sc PREISSLER JP-7009 f.s. partly
    single line playing (3 gtr);
    notation: 2 treb staffs (4-pt
    music)   (4731)

KARL, SEPP (1913-   )
  Tanze Und Weisen *CC20U
    3gtr/2treb inst,gtr (single line
    playing/1-2nd degr.) sc PREISSLER
    7008-II f.s. Das Gitarren-
    Gruppenspiel, Vol. 2   (4732)

KOMTER, JAN MAARTEN (1905-   )
  Boleronda
    3gtr (3rd degr.) sc HARMONIA 2709
    f.s.   (4733)

KORT, WIM DE
  Fugas, 2, Op. 10
    3gtr (single line playing/4th
    degr.) sc TEESELING VT-26 f.s.
                                   (4734)

KUFFNER, JOSEPH (1776-1856)
  Ausgewahlte Ubungsstucke, 30 (from
    Op. 168)
    (Gotze) 3gtr (1-2nd degr.) SCHOTT
    GA-10 f.s.   (4735)

LOGAN, FREDERICK KNIGHT (1871-1928)
  Pale Moon
    (Pick) 3gtr (4-5th degr.) pts
    FORSTER f.s.   (4736)

MENGELBERG, MISJA (1935-   )
  Amaga
    gtr,bass gtr,electronic equipment,
    Hawaiian gtr (8-9th degr.) sc
    DONEMUS f.s.   (4737)

MONTEVERDI, CLAUDIO (ca. 1567-1643)
  Canzoni, 3
    (Behrend) 3gtr (single line
    playing/2-3rd degr.) sc,pts RIES
    11.105-H f.s.
      contains: Canzonetta D'amore; Chi
      Vuch Veder; Quando Sperai
                                   (4738)
  Scherzi, 3
    (Behrend) 3gtr (single line
    playing/3rd degr.) sc,pts RIES
    11.105-I f.s.
      contains: Bei Legami, I;
      Giovinetta Ritrossetta; Non
      Cosi   (4739)

MOZART, WOLFGANG AMADEUS (1756-1791)
  Adagio, MIN 212
    (Pujol) 3gtr ESCHIG 1603 f.s.
                                   (4740)
  Minuet, MIN 214 (from Symphony In C)
    3gtr (4th degr.) sc SCHOTT GA-399
    f.s.   (4741)
  Serenade, MIN 213 (from Eine Kleine
    Nachtmusik)
    (Behrend) 3gtr (6-8th degr.) sc,pts
    RIES 11.105-K f.s.   (4742)
  Wiener Sonatina
    "Sonatina Viennoise" (Pujol) 3gtr
    ESCHIG 1602 f.s.   (4743)

MULLER, SIEGFRIED (1926-   )
  Concertino
    3gtr (6th degr.) sc,pts HOFMEISTER
    T-4163 $7.50   (4744)

NEUMULLER, WOLFGANG
  Gitarrenstuck1 *CC11U
    2-3gtr (1-2nd degr.) sc PREISSLER
    7066 f.s. 1 folksong for 2 gtr;
    10 folksongs for 3 gtr   (4745)

PERGOLESI, GIOVANNI BATTISTA
    (1710-1736)
  Siciliana
    (Mori) 3gtr (3rd degr.) sc BERBEN
    EB1943 $1.00   (4746)

PROSPERI, CARLO (1921-   )
  Stelle Inerrantes
    3gtr RICORDI-IT 131897 f.s.   (4747)

SANCHEZ, B.
  Variations, 10, Sur "Folias De
    Espana" En Forme De Canon
    2gtr/3gtr/6-9gtr (2-4th degr.,
    Notation: 1 theme consisting of 3
    parts, 1 chord accompaniment, 5
    variations (single lines);
    Collection L'Heure De La Guitare
    Classique) CHOUDENS 20.318 f.s.
                                   (4748)

SCHAGEN, HENK VAN
  Fantasy
    3gtr (3-4th degr.) sc HARMONIA 1506
    f.s.   (4749)
  Zomeravondsuite
    3gtr (single line playing/1st
    degr.) sc HARMONIA 1248 f.s.
                                   (4750)

SCHONSTEN WEISEN FUR UNSERE JUGEND, DIE
    *CC25U,folk song
  (Reess) 2-3gtr (2-3rd degr.) sc
    PREISSLER JP-7004-II f.s. Die
    Gitarre Im Gruppenspiel, Vol. II;
    partly single line playing   (4751)

SCHUBERT, FRANZ (PETER) (1797-1828)
  Moment Musical *Op.94,No.3
    3gtr (3rd degr.) sc SCHOTT GA-400
    f.s. contains also: Andante (from
    Op. 42)   (4752)
  Sonatina
    (Behrend) 3gtr (single line
    playing/3-4th degr.) sc,pts RIES
    11.105-L f.s.   (4753)

SCHUMANN, GERHARD (1914-   )
  Fantasy
    (Behrend) 3gtr (5th degr.) sc,pts
    RIES 11.106-B f.s.   (4754)

SEROCKI, KAZIMIERZ (1922-1981)
  Krasnoludki
    "Zwerge, Die" 3gtr (7 easy pcs; 3
    perf sc) POLSKIE f.s.   (4755)
    "Zwerge, Die" 3gtr (7 easy pcs; 3
    perf sc) MOECK 3017 f.s.   (4756)

SMITH BRINDLE, REGINALD (1917-   )
  Music For Three Guitars
    (Borghese; Frosali; Saldarelli)
    3gtr (6-7th degr.) sc ZERBONI
    8012 f.s.   (4757)

SOR, FERNANDO (1778-1839)
  Andantino, Op. 54 [Sic]
    (Behrend, Siegfried) 3gtr (single
    line playing, arr; not in op. 1-
    63 or works without opus number)
    sc,pts RIES 11.105-O f.s.   (4758)

STREICHARDT, ANTONIUS
  Trio in E
    3gtr IMB rent   (4759)

WERDIN, EBERHARD (1911-   )
  Miniaturen, 4
    (Kammerling) 3gtr (3rd degr.,
    Gitarre-Kammermusik, No.76) sc
    DOBLINGER GKM-76 f.s.   (4760)

WIDMANN, ERASMUS (1572-1634)
  Zwei Suiten
    (Teuchert) 3-4gtr (3-4th degr.)
    SCHMIDT,H 507 f.s.   (4761)

WINKELBAUER, ALFRED
  Spanische Tanze
    gtr (3-4th degr.) sc PREISSLER 7075
    f.s.
      contains: Jota De Montes;
      Sevillana; Sevillanas;
      Tanguillo, MIN 418; Tanguillo,
      MIN 419; Zapateado   (4762)

WITT, CHRISTIAN F. (1660-1716)
  Suite
    (Teuchert) 3gtr (3-4th degr.)
    SCHMIDT,H 506 f.s.   (4763)

WOLKI, KONRAD
  Sechs Mal Drei (6 x 3)
    3gtr (mainly single line playing/1-
    2nd degr.) sc PREISSLER 7064 f.s.
      contains: Einstimmung; Entree;
      Kleine Ouverture; Nostalgie; O
      Tannenbaum; Suite in A   (4764)
  Spielstucke Fur 3 Gitarren *CC11U
    3gtr (single line playing/1-3rd
    degr.) sc SCHOTT 5128 f.s. (4765)

I/IIA2-Coll   Trio Collections
for Three Guitars

ALTE LAUTENMUSIK
  (Wolki) 3gtr (4th degr.) SCHOTT 6389
    f.s.   (4766)

ALTE POLNISCHE LAUTENMUSIK *CC16U
  (Powrozniak) 3gtr (3rd degr.) pts
    HEINRICH. 1547 f.s. contains works
    by: Anon. (6); Diomedes Cato (3);
    Dlugoraj (2); Jakob da Polak (2),
    Pekiel (1), Gallot d'Angers (2)
                                   (4767)

ALTE UND NEUE MUSIK ZUM SINGEN UND
    SPIELEN AUF BLOCKFLOTEN, GEIGEN UND
    LAUTENINSTRUMENTE *folk song
  (Gerwig) [Ger] (1-3rd degr.) sc
    LIENAU 1375 f.s. Das Spiel Der
    Lauteninstrumente, Series II,
    Spielbuch 1; contains works by:
    Sperontes (4), L. Mozart (3);
    Rathgeber (1), Rein (5), Rhau (2),
    Langenau (1), Chemin-Petit (1): for
    gtr (1), 2gtr (3), 3gtr (1), rec,
    gtr (8), 2rec, gtr (2), solo voice,
    gtr (3), solo voice, rec, gtr (1),
    solo voice, rec, 2gtr (1), rec, vln
    or vla, gtr (1); arr. + orig. pcs.;
    single line playing; gtr pt partly
    in bass clef
      contains: Bach, Johann Sebastian,
      English Suite No. 6, BWV 811, In
      D Minor, Gavottes I-II (gtr,1-2A
      rec); Bach, Johann Sebastian,
      Minuet, BWV Anh. 118, in B flat
      (from Anna Magdalena Bach
      Notenbuchlein (1725), No.9) (gtr,
      S rec) (C maj,single line
      playing, gtr pt in bass clef)
                                   (4768)

CANCIONES POPULARES MEXICANAS, 3
  (Visser) 3gtr (mainly single line
    playing/2-3rd degr.) sc HARMONIA
    2420 f.s.
      contains: Mananitas, Las; Pajarera,
      La; Valentino, La   (4769)

GITAAR-KAMERMUZIEK, VOL. 2
  (Claessens, Anny C.H.) 1-4gtr (partly
    single line playing/1-4th degr.) sc
    BROEKMANS 26A f.s. arr + orig pcs;
    contains works by: Claessens for 1
    gtr; Anon. (6), Bohm (1),
    Hurlebusch (1) for 2 gtr; J.S.
    Bach, Rameau, von Call for 3 gtr;
    Handel for 4 gtr
      contains: Bach, Johann Sebastian,
      Suite for Lute, BWV 996, in E
      minor, Bourree (3gtr) (single
      line playing)   (4770)

GITAAR-KAMERMUZIEK, VOL. 3: UIT HET
    REPERTOIRE VAN HET JOEGOSLAVISCHE
    DANSTHEATER
  (Claessens, Anny C.H.) 1-5gtr (1-4th
    degr.) sc BROEKMANS 27 f.s. arr +
    orig pcs; contains works by:
    Jovicic for 1 gtr (1); 9 songs and
    dances; 2gtr (2); 3gtr (4); 5gtr
    (2)
      contains: Jovicic, Jovan, Concert-
      Etude   (4771)

GITAAR-KAMERMUZIEK, VOL. 4: UIT HET
    REPERTOIRE VAN HET JOEGOSLAVISCHE
    DANSTHEATER *CC6U
  (Claessens, Anny C.H.) 1-4gtr (1-4th
    degr.) sc BROEKMANS 27A f.s. arr +
    orig pcs; contains works by Jovicic
    for: 1gtr(1); 6 songs and dances
    for 2gtr (1); 3gtr (4); 4 gtr (3);
    including gtr-g'   (4772)

GITARRENCHOR, DER, SCHULE DES
    GRUPPENMUSIZIERENS *folk song
  (Wolki) 3gtr (1-3rd degr., 17 arr +
    orig pcs; contains works by: Wolki
    (9), Kubik (1) for 3gtr-e' (+ opt
    2gtr-e'')) sc APOLLO 2271 f.s.
                                   (4773)

KANONS ZUM SINGEN UND SPIELEN *CC19U,
    folk song
  (Treml) 2-4gtr,opt solo voices
    (single line playing/1-3rd degr.)
    NAGELS EN-1097 f.s. Nagels Laute-
    Und Gitarre-Archiv; a
    reconnaissance on the fingerboard;
    contains works by: Anon. (4),
    Baumann (1), Wachsmann (1),
    Mandyczewski (1)   (4774)

KLINGENDE KLEINIGKEITEN AUS ALTER UND
    NEUER ZEIT *CC18U
  (Krupp) 2-4gtr (single line playing/
    1-2nd degr.) sc PREISSLER JP-7019
    f.s. contains folksongs and
    anonymous works for 2gtr (10), 3gtr
    (7), 4gtr (1)   (4775)

LAUTENCHOR II, DER *CC13U
  (Gerwig) 3-5gtr (single line playing/
    1-2nd degr.) sc LIENAU 1419-II f.s.
    Das Spiel Der Lauteninstrumente,
    Series II, Spielbuch 8; arr + orig
    pcs; contains works by: Franck (3),
    Kukuck (3), Gumpelzhaimer (3),
    Maasz (1) for 3gtr (10), 4gtr (2),
    5gtr (1)   (4776)

LAUTENSPIELER DES XVI. JAHRHUNDERTS
    (LIUTISTI DEL CINQUECENTO)
    *CC124UL
  (Chilesotti, Oscar) gtr (single
    staff/8th degr.) quarto oblong
    FORNI f.s. repr of 1st ed., publ
    Ricordi-Breitkopf & Hartel (1891);
    "Bibliotheca Musica Bononiensis",
    Sezione IV, No. 31; includes works
    by: Newsidler, Anon., Ballet,
    Gintzler, Matelart, Gorzanis, da
    Milano, Galilei, Barbetta, Caroso,
    Terzi, Molinaro, dalla Gostena,
    Negri, Besard, Mersenne,
    Gianoncelli -all for 1 gtr;
    Matelart, Galilei, Besard -for 2
    gtr; Caroso, Negri -for dsc inst
    and gtr; Fallamero, Besard -for vce

and gtr; Terzi –for 3 gtr; Besard –
for dsc inst and 3 gtr   (4777)

LEICHTE STUCKE ALTER MEISTER *CC7U
(Kammerling) 3gtr (single line
playing/1–2nd degr.) sc DOBLINGER
GKM-82 f.s. Gitarre-Kammermusik,
No.82; contains works by: Daquin
(1), Fischer (1), Anon. (2), Schein
(2), Rathgeber (1)   (4778)

LEICHTES ZUSAMMENSPIEL *16–18th cent
2–3gtr/rec/mel inst,vln/mel inst,gtr
(2–3rd degr.) SCHMIDT,H 93 f.s.   (4779)

MELODY OF JAPAN BY GUITARS, VOL. I
*CC12U
(Nakabayashi) [Jap] 1–4gtr (3–6th
degr.) sc SUISEISHA 402981 f.s. for
gtr (2), 2 gtr (2), 3 gtr (4), 4
gtr (4)   (4780)

MELODY OF JAPAN BY GUITARS, VOL. II
*CC17U
(Nakabayashi) [Jap] 1–4gtr (3–6th
degr.) sc SUISEISHA 402609 f.s. for
gtr (5), 2 gtr (1), 3 gtr (9), 4
gtr (2)   (4781)

MUSIC FOR 3 GUITARS *CC13U
(Gavall) 3gtr (single line playing/1–
2nd degr.) sc BELWIN 973 f.s.
contains works by: Byrd (2), Ives
(1), Palestrina (1), Certon (1),
Regnart (1), Corelli (2), Buxtehude
(1), Haydn (1), W.A. Mozart (1),
Schumann (1), Schubert (1)   (4782)

MUSIK DER WIENER KLASSIK *CCU
(Wolki) 3gtr (3rd degr.) SCHOTT 5129
f.s. contains works by: Gluck; L.
Mozart; Haydn; W.A. Mozart;
Beethoven and Schubert   (4783)

MUSIQUE POUR 3 ET 4 GUITARES, VOL. 1
(MUSIC FOR 3 AND 4 GUITARS, VOL. 1)
*folk song
(Gerrits) 3–4gtr (single line
playing/1–3rd degr.) sc DOBER f.s.
18 arr + orig pcs; contains works
by: Scheidt (1), Anon. (2),
Gastoldi (3), Sermisy (1), A.
Gagnon (1), Attaingnant (1), von
Call (1), Duncombe (1), Susato (2),
Dowland (1), Arbeau (1) for 3gtr;
Susato (2) for 4gtr
contains: Bach, Johann Sebastian,
English Suite No. 2, BWV 807, In
A Minor, Bouree II (3gtr) (D maj,
single line playing); Bach,
Johann Sebastian, English Suite
No. 3, BWV 808, In G Minor,
Musette (3gtr) (A maj,single line
playing); Bach, Johann Sebastian,
O Haupt Voll Blut Und Wunden.
Chorale (from Matthaus-Passion,
BWV 244, No.53) (4gtr) (single
line playing); Bach, Johann
Sebastian, Wer Hat Dich So
Geschlagen. Chorale (from
Matthaus-Passion, BWV 244, No.44)
(4gtr) (single line playing)   (4784)

MUSIQUE POUR 3 ET 4 GUITARES, VOL. 2
(MUSIC FOR 3 AND 4 GUITARS, VOL. 2)
(Gerrits) 3–4gtr (single line
playing/1–3rd degr.) sc DOBER f.s.
14 arr + orig pcs; contains works
by: Telemann (2), Haydn (1),
Praetorius (2), Scheidt (3), L.
Mozart–K. Marx (2), C.M. Gagnon
(1), for 3gtr; Scheidt (1), L.
Mozart–K. Marx (1) for 4gtr
contains: Bach, Johann Sebastian,
Ich Bitt', O Herr, Aus Herzens
Grund. Chorale (from Cantata
No.18) (3gtr)   (4785)

MUSIQUE POUR 3 ET 4 GUITARES, VOL. 3 –
MUSIC FOR 3 AND 4 GUITARS, VOL. 3
(Gerrits) 3–4gtr (1–6th degr.) sc,pts
DOBER DO-3 f.s. contains 17 works
by: Susato; Phalese; Gabriel;
Widmann; Banchieri; Molinaro;
Pratorius; Morley; Purcell and
anonymous
contains: Bach, Johann Sebastian,
Suite for Keyboard Instrument,
BWV 816, in A, Gavotte (3–4gtr)   (4786)

MUSIQUE POUR 3 ET 4 GUITARES, VOL. 4 –
MUSIC FOR 3 AND 4 GUITARS, VOL. 4
(Chandonnet) 3–4gtr (1–6th degr.) sc,
pts DOBER DO-4 f.s. contains 9
works by: Morley; Purcell;
Praetorius; A. Gabrieli, Handel and
Kuntz
contains: Bach, Johann Sebastian,
Sonata for Violin and Keyboard
Instrument, BWV 1015, in A minor,
Andante   (4787)

PIECES FROM THE TIME OF QUEEN
ELIZABETH, 4
(Knapen) 3gtr (single line playing/
3rd degr., contains works by:

Azkue, Pilkington, Anon. (2)) sc
TEESELING VT-37 f.s.   (4788)

POLYPHONES SPIELHEFT *CC5U
(Bayer) 2–4gtr DOBLINGER GKM-116 f.s.
Gitarre-Kammermusik, No. 116   (4789)

SATZE ALTER MEISTER *CC8U
(Henze) 3gtr (partly single line
playing/1–3rd degr.) sc,pts RIES
11.105–N f.s. contains works by:
Judenkunig (1), Caroso (1), Besard
(1), Anon. (5)   (4790)

SCHONSTEN LIEDER FUR UNSERE JUGEND, DIE
*CC27U
(Reess) 2–3gtr (1–2nd degr.) sc
PREISSLER JP-7004 f.s. Die Gitarre
Im Gruppenspiel, Vol. 1; partly
single line playing   (4791)

SONNE, KOMM, EIN GITARRESPIELBUCH FUR
KINDER, 1–4. UNTERRICHTSJAHR *folk
song
(Ratz, Martin) [Ger] solo voice,gtr/
1–4gtr (single line playing/1–3rd
degr.) sc DEUTSCH 32001 f.s. 162
arr + orig pcs; contains works by:
Schuffenhauer (2), Krug (4), Konig
(8), Ratz (22), Asriel (5), Quadt
(9), Rosenfeld (2), Haydn, Schumann
(3), Gorischk, Helmut, Wohlgemuth,
Schwaen, Schoendlinger for gtr;
Friemert (2), Buse, W.A. Mozart
(3), Beethoven, Berges,
Schuffenhauer, Hecht-Wieber for 2
gtr; Eberwein, Stephani for 3 gtr;
anon., naumilkat for 4 gtr or solo
voice(s), gtr; Skodova (2), Silcher
(2), Wendt, Friemert (2), Kern,
Krug (2), Pormova, Rodl, Hartung,
Nynkowa, Schuffenhauer, Hein,
Richter (3), W. Bender (2), Helmut,
Naumilkat for solo voice, gtr; also
contains Christmas music by:
Helmut, Schuffenhauer, Wohlgemuth
for gtr or solo voice, gtr; W.
Bender, Helmut, Naumilkat, for solo
voice, gtr
contains: Bach, Johann Sebastian,
Minuet in G minor, BWV Anh. 115
(2gtr) (A min,single line
playing); Bach, Johann Sebastian,
Piece In F, "Aria", BWV Anh.131
(2gtr) (single line playing);
Bach, Johann Sebastian, Polonaise
in G minor, BWV Anh. 119 (2gtr)
(A min,single line playing)   (4792)

SPIELBUCH FUR 3 GITARREN *CC15U
(Teuchert) 3gtr (partly single
line playing/1–3rd degr.) sc SCHMIDT,H
502 f.s. Der Lautenkreis, Vol.2;
contains works by: Sperontes (2),
Scheidt (1), Hausmann (1), Haydn
(1), L. Mozart (2), Monteverdi (2),
Schickhardt (1), Mattheson (1),
Hasse (1), Handel (1), Corelli (1),
W.A. Mozart (1)   (4793)

SPIELHEFT KLASSIK FUR DREI GITARREN
(Reiser) 3gtr (1–2nd degr.) sc SCHOTT
GA-436 f.s. 9 pcs; arr; contains
works by: Judenkunig (2), Dufay;
Losy; A. Scarlatti; Le Sage de
Richee; Kerll; Krieger
contains: Bach, Johann Sebastian,
Suite For Lute, BWV 996, In E
Minor, Presto (single line
playing)   (4794)

SPIELMUSIK FUR 3 GITARREN *folk song
(Henze) 3gtr (partly single line
playing/2–7th degr.) sc,pts
HOFMEISTER T-4014 $12.75 28 arr +
orig pcs (numbered 1–13); Das
Gitarrespiel, Vol. XIV; contains
works by: Molinaro (2), Telemann
(1), Fux (1), Muffat (1), von Call
(1), Gragnani (1), Diabelli (1),
Kretschmar (1), Ambrosius (1),
Stingl (1), Wagner-Regeny (1)
contains: Bach, Johann Sebastian,
English Suite No. 2, BWV 807, In
A Minor, Bouree II (3gtr) (D maj,
single line playing); Bach,
Johann Sebastian, English Suite
No. 3, BWV 808, In G Minor,
Gavotte II (3gtr) (G maj,single
line playing)   (4795)

SPIELMUSIK FUR ANGEHENDE GITARRISTEN,
VOL. III *CC16L,folk song
(Behrend) 1–3gtr (1–2nd degr.) sc
PREISSLER JP-7023-III f.s. arr +
orig pcs; contains works by: Anon.
(10), Behrend (2) for gtr (6), 2
gtr (7), 3 gtr (3); single line
playing (2 gtr, 3 gtr)   (4796)

STUCKE ALTER MEISTER, 15 *CC15U
(Teuchert) 3gtr (partly single line
playing/2–3rd degr.) sc SCHMIDT,H
503 f.s. Der Lautenkreis, Vol. III;
contains works by: Rathgeber (2),
Susato (2), Handel (2), Peuerl (2),

Salieri (1), Anon. (1), Caldara
(1), Telemann (4)   (4797)

SUDAMERICANA, BERUHMTE FOLKLORISTISCHE
TANZE *CC11U,folk song
(Tucholski) [Span/Port/Ger] solo
voice,gtr/1–3gtr (3–6th degr.) sc
APOLLO 2339 f.s. contains works by:
Creutziger (1), Tucholski (1) for
solo voice, gtr; Villoldo (1),
Porschmann (1), Albeniz (1) for 3
gtr   (4798)

SYT NU VERBLYT
(van Schagen) 3gtr (partly single
line playing/1–2nd degr.) sc
HARMONIA 1295 f.s.
contains: Anonymous, 's Ochtends
Buiten; Gumpeltzhaimer, Adam, By
Avond; Mudarra, Alonso de, Hanc
Tua Penelope; Pisador, Diego,
Pavan; Valerius, Syt Nu Verblyt;
Vecchi, Het Vogeltje   (4799)

TANZBUCH DER RENAISSANCE
(Giesbert) 2–4gtr SCHOTT GA-227 f.s.   (4800)

TANZE UND STUCKE DER BAROCKZEIT *CCU
(Wolki) 3gtr (3rd degr.) SCHOTT 5126
f.s. contains works by: Praetorius;
Scheidt; Lully; Fischer; Fux;
Erlebach; Murschhauser; Mattheson;
J.S. Bach; Handel; Grafe; C.P.E.
Bach and Nickelmann   (4801)

ULRICH, JURGEN (1939–   )
Einerseits-Andererseits, Vol. 1
2gtr (Musica 1) HANSEN-DEN MUS 101
f.s.   (4802)

Einerseits-Andererseits, Vol. 2
2gtr (Musica 2) HANSEN-DEN MUS 213
f.s.   (4803)

VOLKSTANZE, 6 *folk song
(Henze) 3gtr (single line playing/2–
3rd degr.) sc,pts RIES 11.105–M
f.s.
contains: Bammelrockchen;
Bauernhochzeit; Bohnenpott;
Dreitritt; Kegel; Walz-Quadrille   (4804)

VOLKSTANZE UND LIEDER *CC14U,folk song
(Holzfurtner) 2treb inst,gtr/3gtr
(single line playing/1–2nd degr.)
PREISSLER 7008 f.s. Das Gitarren-
Gruppenspiel, Vol. I   (4805)

I/IIA3   Quartets for Four
Guitars

ANONYMOUS
Romance D'Amour
(Ahslund) 4gtr (single line
playing/1–2nd degr.) sc REUTER
f.s.   (4806)

APOSTEL, HANS ERICH (1901–1972)
Es Waren Zwei Konigskinder
(Bayer) 4gtr (Gitarre-Kammermusik,
No. 104) DOBLINGER GKM-104 f.s.   (4807)

Hohe Des Jahres
(Bayer) 4gtr (Gitarre-Kammermusik,
No. 106) DOBLINGER GKM-106 f.s.   (4808)

BELLMAN, CARL MICHAEL (1740–1795)
Bellman For 4 Gitarrer
(Ahslund) 4gtr (mainly single line
playing/2–3rd degr.) sc REUTER
f.s.
contains: Fredmans Epistel No. 2;
Fredmans Epistel No. 71I;
Fredmans Epistel No. 71II;
Fredmans Epistel No. 78;
Vaggvisa Till Sonen Carl   (4809)

BENGUEREL, XAVIER (1931–   )
Vermelia
4gtr HANSEN-DEN f.s.   (4810)

BIBERIAN, GILBERT E.
Suite for 4 Guitars
4gtr (mainly single line playing/1–
3rd degr., 5 pcs) sc NOVELLO
19741 $2.55   (4811)

BLAKE WATKINS, MICHAEL (1948–   )
Guitar Quartet
4gtr NOVELLO f.s.   (4812)

BRUCHNER, RUDOLF
Quartettino I In C
(Witt) 4gtr (partly single line
playing/1–2nd degr.) sc PREISSLER
JP-7013 f.s.   (4813)

CARULLI, FERDINANDO (1770-1841)
Quartet, Op. 21
(Albert) 4gtr (4th degr., Die
Gitarre In Der Haus- Und
Kammermusik, No. 15) ZIMMER.
ZM-1273 f.s.   (4814)

DAVID, JOHANN NEPOMUK (1895-1977)
Volksliedsatze
(Bayer) 4gtr (single line playing/
1st degr.) sc DOBLINGER GKM-103
f.s. Gitarre-Kammermusik, No.103
contains: Es Geht Ein' Dunkle
Wolk' Herein; Ich Weiss Ein
Maidlein Hubsch Und Fein; Kume,
Kum, Geselle Min   (4815)

DOWLAND, JOHN (1562-1626)
Three Dances
(Biberian) 4gtr NOVELLO f.s.   (4816)

DUARTE, JOHN W. (1919-   )
Going Dutch
4gtr (partly single line playing/3-
4th degr.) sc BROEKMANS 868 f.s.
5 pcs
contains: Carillon, Op.36,No.4;
Dutch Dance, Op.36,No.5; March,
Op. 36, No. 3; Pastorale, Op.
36, No. 2; Windmill, Op.36,No.1
(4817)

GRAMBERG, JACQ
Dances For 4 Or More Guitars, 3
4gtr (single line playing/1st
degr.) sc HARMONIA 2079 f.s.
(4818)

Just Arrived
4gtr (1-3rd degr.) sc HARMONIA 2497
f.s.   (4819)

HEILLER, ANTON (1923-1979)
Es Liegt Ein Schloss In Osterreich
*15th cent
(Bayer) [Ger] 4gtr (single line
playing/1-2nd degr., Gitarre-
Kammermusik No. 107) sc,pts
DOBLINGER GKM-107 f.s.   (4820)

Heidi Pupeidi
(Bayer) 4gtr (Gitarre-Kammermusik,
No. 105) DOBLINGER GKM-105 f.s.
(4821)

KEINEMANN, KARL HEINZ
Sudamerikanische Tanze, Fur Den
Modernen Gitarren-Gruppen-
Unterricht
4-5gtr VOGT 103 f.s.   (4822)

LEKSANDS SKANKLAT
(Persson) 4gtr (single line playing/
2-3rd degr.) sc REUTER f.s.   (4823)

MARX, KARL (1897-1985)
Es Taget Vor Dem Walde, 6 Variationen
Uber
4gtr (mainly single line playing/2-
3rd degr., Nagels Laute- Und
Gitarre-Archiv) sc NAGELS EN-1111
f.s.   (4824)

PRAETORIUS, MICHAEL (1571-1621)
4 French Dances
(Duarte) 4gtr NOVELLO 12.0456.04
f.s.   (4825)

REISEBILDER AUS FRANKREICH, 5 *folk
song
(Kammerling) 4gtr (mainly single line
playing/2-3rd degr.) sc TONGER 1619
f.s. Rund Um Die Gitarre, Vol. II
contains: Aupres De Ma Blonde;
Derrier' Chez Mon Pere; Malbrough
s'en va-t-en Guerre; Sur Le Pont
D'Avignon; Trois Jeun's Tambours
(4826)

ROHWER, JENS (1914-   )
Heptameron, Eine Vierstimmige Suite
4gtr (single line playing) sc,pts
BREITKOPF-W CMN-7 f.s.   (4827)

SCHNEIDER, SIMON
Spielmusik, Op.126, No. 2
4gtr (single line playing/2-4th
degr.) HOFMEISTER T-4101 sc
$2.75, pts $2.00
contains: Andante; Fugue;
Gavotte; Prelude; Saraband;
Vierklange   (4828)

SCHUBERT, FRANZ (PETER) (1797-1828)
Momento Musicale
(Rossi) 4gtr (single line playing/
1-3rd degr.) sc,pts BERBEN EB1193
$1.50 contains also: Brahms,
Johannes, Valzer, Op. 39, No.15
(4829)

SOR, FERNANDO (1778-1839)
Sonata, Op. 15, No. 2, in C
"Quartett" (Albert, Heinrich) 4gtr
(Die Gitarre in der Haus- und
Kammer-Musik, No. 16) pts ZIMMER.
ZM-1274 f.s.   (4830)

STAAK, PIETER VAN DER (1930-   )
Easy Guitar Quartets, 9
4gtr (single line playing/1-3rd
degr.) sc BROEKMANS 873 f.s.
(4831)

Guitar Quartets, 7
4gtr (single line playing/1-3rd
degr.) sc BROEKMANS 842 f.s.
(4832)

SUSATO, TIELMAN (? -ca. 1561)
Pieces, 5 (from Danserye)
(van der Staak) 4gtr (single line
playing/1-2nd degr.) sc BROEKMANS
865 f.s.
contains: Gaillarde "Ghequest Bin
Ick"; Gaillarde "Mille Ducas";
Pavane "Mille Ducas"; Ronde;
Ronde "Mille Ducas"   (4833)

Tanze, 7 (from Tanzbuch 1551)
(Scheit) 4gtr/2gtr (single line
playing (4 gtr); notation: 4 treb
staffs; 1st degr. (4 gtr), 3rd-
4th degr. (2 gtr); Gitarre-
Kammermusik, No.100) sc DOBLINGER
GKM-100 f.s.   (4834)

TCHAIKOVSKY, PIOTR ILYICH (1840-1893)
Pieces, 3 (from Children's Album)
(Duarte) 4gtr (single line playing/
2-3rd degr.) sc BROEKMANS 1086
f.s.
contains: New Doll, The; Old
Wife's Tale, The; Winter
Morning, A   (4835)

TELEMANN, GEORG PHILIPP (1681-1767)
Konzert
(Teuchert) 4gtr (Der Lautenkreis,
Vol. IV; orig for 4vln) SCHMIDT,H
504 f.s.   (4836)

TITTEL, ERNST (1910-1969)
O, Du Lieber Augustin
(Bayer) 4gtr (single line playing/
1st degr., Gitarre-Kammermusik,
No.102) sc,pts DOBLINGER GKM-102
f.s.   (4837)

WESTRA, JAN
Conversation
4gtr (2-3rd degr.) sc HARMONIA 2364
f.s.   (4838)

Minutes, 5
4gtr (3-4th degr.) sc HARMONIA 2147
f.s.   (4839)

WIDMANN, ERASMUS (1572-1634)
Suite No. 1
(Riedmuller) 4-5gtr VOGT K-1002
f.s.   (4840)

Zwei Suiten
(Teuchert) 3-4gtr (3-4th degr.)
SCHMIDT,H 507 f.s.   (4841)

I/IIA3-Coll Quartet Collections for Four Guitars

ELIZABETHAN PIECES, 5
(Duarte) 4gtr (single line playing/1-
3rd degr.) sc BROEKMANS 1089 f.s.
contains: Anonymous, Shy Myze, La;
Anonymous, When Griping Griefs;
Byrd, William, Doune Cella, La;
Edwards, Courante   (4842)

GITAAR-KAMERMUZIEK, VOL. 2
(Claessens, Anny C.H.) 1-4gtr (partly
single line playing/1-4th degr.) sc
BROEKMANS 26A f.s. arr + orig pcs;
contains works by: Claessens for 1
gtr; Anon. (6), Bohm (1),
Hurlebusch (1) for 2 gtr; J.S.
Bach, Rameau, von Call for 3 gtr;
Handel for 4 gtr
contains: Bach, Johann Sebastian,
Suite for Lute, BWV 996, in E
minor, Bourree (3gtr) (single
line playing)   (4843)

GITAAR-KAMERMUZIEK, VOL. 4: UIT HET
REPERTOIRE VAN HET JOEGOSLAVISCHE
DANSTHEATER *CC6U
(Claessens, Anny C.H.) 1-4gtr (1-4th
degr.) sc BROEKMANS 27A f.s. arr +
orig pcs; contains works by Jovicic
for: 1gtr(1); 6 songs and dances
for 2gtr (1); 3gtr (3); 4 gtr (3);
including gtr-g'   (4844)

GITARRKVARTETT
(Hahn) 4gtr (mainly single line
playing/2-3rd degr.) sc REUTER f.s.
contains: Adolphson, Olle, Gatfulla

Folket, Det; Adolphson, Olle,
Mitt Eget Land; Ahslund, Ulf-G.,
Sag Du; Axelsson, C.A., Hon Gick
Pa Trottoaren; Hambe, Ostan Om
Solen-Nordan Om Jorden; Hambe,
Visa I Molom   (4845)

GUITAR ENSEMBLES *folk song
(Castle) 4gtr (mainly single line
playing/1-3rd degr.) MEL BAY f.s. 5
pcs; contains works by: Paganini,
Cui, Pleyel
contains: Bach, Johann Sebastian, 0
Haupt Voll Blut Und Wunden.
Chorale (from Matthaus-Passion,
BWV 244, Nos. 21, 23) (4gtr)
(single line playing)   (4846)

GUITARRA CANTORA, LA, MELODIAS
TRADICIONALES ARGENTINAS
(Kantor) [Span] 3-4gtr/fl&3gtr
(partly single line playing/1-2nd
degr., contains 7 pcs for solo
voice or gtr, 2gtr (5); solo voice,
3gtr (1); fl or gtr, gtr or solo
voice, 2gtr (1); opt perc (2)) sc
RICORDI-ARG BA-12779 f.s.   (4847)

KANONS ZUM SINGEN UND SPIELEN *CC19U,
folk song
(Treml) 2-4gtr,opt solo voices
(single line playing/1-3rd degr.)
NAGELS EN-1097 f.s. Nagels Laute-
Und Gitarre-Archiv; a
reconnaissance on the fingerboard;
contains works by: Anon. (4),
Baumann (1), Wachsmann (1),
Mandyczewski (1)   (4848)

KLINGENDE KLEINIGKEITEN AUS ALTER UND
NEUER ZEIT *CC18U
(Krupp) 2-4gtr (single line playing/
1-2nd degr.) sc PREISSLER JP-7019
f.s. contains folksongs and
anonymous works for 2gtr (10), 3gtr
(7), 4gtr (1)   (4849)

LAUTENCHOR I, DER *CC10U
(Gerwig) 4gtr (single line playing/
2nd degr.) sc LIENAU 1419 f.s. arr
+ orig pcs; Das Spiel Der
Lauteninstrumente, Series II,
Spielbuch 7; contains works by:
Palestrina (6); Rohwer (1); Hassler
(3)   (4850)

LAUTENCHOR II, DER *CC13U
(Gerwig) 3-5gtr (single line playing/
1-2nd degr.) sc LIENAU 1419-II f.s.
Das Spiel Der Lauteninstrumente,
Series II, Spielbuch 8; arr + orig
pcs; contains works by: Franck (3),
Kukuck (3); Gumpelzhaimer (3),
Maasz (4) for 3gtr (10), 4gtr (2),
5gtr (1)   (4851)

MELODY OF JAPAN BY GUITARS, VOL. I
*CC12U
(Nakabayashi) [Jap] 1-4gtr (3-6th
degr.) sc SUISEISHA 402981 f.s. for
gtr (2), 2 gtr (2), 3 gtr (2), 4
gtr (4)   (4852)

MELODY OF JAPAN BY GUITARS, VOL. II
*CC17U
(Nakabayashi) [Jap] 1-4gtr (3-6th
degr.) sc SUISEISHA 402609 f.s. for
gtr (5), 2 gtr (1), 3 gtr (9), 4
gtr (2)   (4853)

MUSIC FOR 4 GUITARS
(Gavall) 4gtr (single line playing/1-
2nd degr.) sc BELWIN 978 $2.50 11
pcs; contains works by: Praetorius
(1); W.A. Mozart (2); Brahms (2),
Palestrina (1), Schubert (1)
contains: Bach, Johann Sebastian,
Feste Burg Ist Unser Gott, Ein'.
Chorale, BWV 203; Bach, Johann
Sebastian, Herzlich Thut Mich
Verlangen. Chorale, "Befiel Du
Deine Wege. Chorale", BWV 270;
Bach, Johann Sebastian, Nun Lasst
Uns. Chorale, "Sprich Ja Zu
Meinen Taten", BWV 194; Bach,
Johann Sebastian, O Welt, Ich
Muss Dich Lassen. Chorale, "O
Welt, Sieh' Hier Dein Leben", BWV
393; Praetorius, Michael, Es Ist
Ein Ros' Entsprungen   (4854)

MUSIQUE POUR 3 ET 4 GUITARES, VOL. 1
(MUSIC FOR 3 AND 4 GUITARS, VOL. 1)
*folk song
(Gerrits) 3-4gtr (single line
playing/1-3rd degr.) sc DOBER f.s.
18 pcs + orig pcs; contains works
by: Scheidt (1), Anon. (2),
Gastoldi (3), Sermisy (1), A.
Gagnon (1), Attaingnant (1), von
Call (1), Duncombe (1), Susato (2),
Dowland (1), Arbeau (1) for 3gtr;
Susato (2) for 4gtr
contains: Bach, Johann Sebastian,
English Suite No. 2, BWV 807, In
A Minor, Bouree II (3gtr) (D maj,

single line playing); Bach,
Johann Sebastian, English Suite
No. 3, BWV 808, In G Minor,
Musette (3gtr) (A maj,single line
playing); Bach, Johann Sebastian,
O Haupt Voll Blut Und Wunden.
Chorale (from Matthaus-Passion,
BWV 244, No.53) (4gtr) (single
line playing); Bach, Johann
Sebastian, Wer Hat Dich So
Geschlagen. Chorale (from
Matthaus-Passion, BWV 244, No.44)
(4gtr) (single line playing)
                            (4855)

MUSIQUE POUR 3 ET 4 GUITARES, VOL. 2
(MUSIC FOR 3 AND 4 GUITARS, VOL. 2)
(Gerrits) 3-4gtr (single line
playing/1-3rd degr.) sc DOBER f.s.
14 arr + orig pcs; contains works
by: Telemann (2), Haydn (1),
Praetorius (2), Scheidt (3), L.
Mozart-K. Marx (2), C.M. Gagnon
(1), for 3gtr; Scheidt (1), L.
Mozart-K. Marx (1) for 4gtr
contains: Bach, Johann Sebastian,
Ich Bitt', O Herr, Aus Herzens
Grund. Chorale (from Cantata
No.18) (3gtr)   (4856)

MUSIQUE POUR 3 ET 4 GUITARES, VOL. 3 -
MUSIC FOR 3 AND 4 GUITARS, VOL. 3
(Gerrits) 3-4gtr (1-6th degr.) sc,pts
DOBER DO-3 f.s. contains 17 works
by: Susato; Phalese; Gabriel;
Widmann; Banchieri; Molinaro;
Pratorius; Morley; Purcell and
anonymous
contains: Bach, Johann Sebastian,
Suite for Keyboard Instrument,
BWV 816, in A, Gavotte (3-4gtr)
                            (4857)

MUSIQUE POUR 3 ET 4 GUITARES, VOL. 4 -
MUSIC FOR 3 AND 4 GUITARS, VOL. 4
(Chandonnet) 3-4gtr (1-6th degr.) sc,
pts DOBER DO-4 f.s. contains 9
works by: Morley; Purcell;
Praetorius; A. Gabrieli, Handel and
Kuntz
contains: Bach, Johann Sebastian,
Sonata for Violin and Keyboard
Instrument, BWV 1015, in A minor,
Andante   (4858)

POLYPHONES SPIELHEFT *CC5U
(Bayer) 2-4gtr DOBLINGER GKM-116 f.s.
Gitarre-Kammermusik, No. 116 (4859)

SONNE, KOMM, EIN GITARRESPIELBUCH FUR
KINDER, 1-4. UNTERRICHTSJAHR *folk
song
(Ratz, Martin) [Ger] solo voice,gtr/
1-4gtr (single line playing/1-3rd
degr.) sc DEUTSCHER 32001 f.s. 162
arr + orig pcs; contains works by:
Schuffenhauer (2), Krug (4), Konig
(8), Ratz (22), Asriel (5), Quadt
(9), Rosenfeld (2), Haydn, Schumann
(3), Gorischk, Helmut, Wohlgemuth,
Schwaen, Schoendlinger for gtr;
Friemert (2), Buse, W.A. Mozart
(3), Beethoven, Berges,
Schuffenhauer, Hecht-Wieber for 2
gtr; Eberwein, Stephani for 3 gtr;
anon., naumilkat for 4 gtr or solo
voice(s), gtr; Skodova (2), Silcher
(2), Wendt, Friemert (2), Kern,
Krug (2), Pormova, Rodl, Hartung,
Nynkowa, Schuffenhauer, Hein,
Richter (3), W. Bender (2), Helmut,
Naumilkat for solo voice, gtr; also
contains Christmas music by:
Helmut, Schuffenhauer, Wohlgemuth
for gtr or solo voice, gtr; W.
Bender, Helmut, Naumilkat, for solo
voice, gtr
contains: Bach, Johann Sebastian,
Minuet in G minor, BWV Anh. 115
(2gtr) (A min,single line
playing); Bach, Johann Sebastian,
Piece In F, "Aria", BWV Anh.131
(2gtr) (single line playing);
Bach, Johann Sebastian, Polonaise
in G minor, BWV Anh. 119 (2gtr)
(A min,single line playing)
                            (4860)

SPUNTI CLASSICI, 4
(Benizzi) 4gtr (single line playing/
1-2nd degr.) sc BERBEN EB1807 $3.75
contains: Beethoven, Ludwig van,
Minuet, MIN 215; Handel, George
Frideric, Gavotte, MIN 217;
Handel, George Frideric,
Saraband, MIN 216; Mozart,
Wolfgang Amadeus, La Caccia (4gtr)
                            (4861)

TANZBUCH DER RENAISSANCE
(Giesbert) 2-4gtr SCHOTT GA-227 f.s.
                            (4862)

I/IIA4 Quintets for Five Guitars

AIN BOER *folk song,Dutch
(Goossens) 5gtr (partly single line
playing/1-2nd degr.) sc HARMONIA
2141 f.s.   (4863)

FURSTENAU, WOLFRAM
Railway-Traffic
1-5gtr (4th degr.) TEESELING VT-113
f.s.   (4864)

KEINEMANN, KARL HEINZ
Sudamerikanische Tanze, Fur Den
Modernen Gitarren-Gruppen-
Unterricht
4-5gtr VOGT 103 f.s.   (4865)

WIDMANN, ERASMUS (1572-1634)
Suite No. 1
(Riedmuller) 4-5gtr VOGT K-1002
f.s.   (4866)

I/IIA4-Coll Quintet Collections for Five Guitars

GITAAR-KAMERMUZIEK, VOL. 3: UIT HET
REPERTOIRE VAN HET JOEGOSLAVISCHE
DANSTHEATER
(Claessens, Anny C.H.) 1-5gtr (1-4th
degr.) sc BROEKMANS 27 f.s. arr +
orig pcs; contains works by:
Jovicic for 1 gtr (1); 9 songs and
dances; 2gtr (2); 3gtr (4); 5gtr
(2)
contains: Jovicic, Jovan, Concert-
Etude   (4867)

LAUTENCHOR II, DER *CC13U
(Gerwig) 3-5gtr (single line playing/
1-2nd degr.) sc LIENAU 1419-II f.s.
Das Spiel Der Lauteninstrumente,
Series II, Spielbuch 8; arr + orig
pcs; contains works by: Franck (3),
Kukuck (3), Gumpelzhaimer (3),
Maasz (4) for 3gtr (10), 4gtr (2),
5gtr (1)   (4868)

I/IIB1 Duets for Guitar and Another Instrument

ABBOTT, ALAIN (1938-   )
Prelude No. 1
fl,gtr,opt vcl (Plein Jeu, No. 333;
notation gtr pt: kbd partitura)
sc,pts HEUGEL PJ-333 f.s.
contains also: Prelude No. 2
                            (4869)

AIRS POPULAIRES DE TCHECOSLOVAQUI
(Klapil) 1-2S rec,gtr LEDUC f.s.
                            (4870)

ALBINONI, TOMASO (1671-1750)
Sonata in A minor
(Behrend) mel inst,gtr ZIMMER. 2138
f.s.   (4871)

ANONYMOUS
Englische Tanze, 3
(Behrend) rec,gtr (5th degr.) sc,
pts ZIMMER. ZM-1361 f.s.
contains: Allegro; Allegro;
Andante, MIN 237   (4872)

Greensleeves To A Ground *folk song/
Variations
(Brojer) gtr,A rec (F maj,5-6th
degr., E is F; Die Gitarre In Der
Kammermusik, No.3) sc,pts HOHLER
GC-3 f.s.   (4873)
(Schaller) gtr,S rec (C maj,5-6th
degr., Gitarre-Kammermusik,
No.81) sc DOBLINGER GKM-81 f.s.
                            (4874)

ANONYMOUS (cont'd.)
Suite in D minor, MIN 331
(Libbert) A rec,gtr (2-3rd degr.,
Das Gitarrenwerk, Reihe A:8) sc
PREISSLER f.s.   (4875)

Suite in F
(Libbert) S rec,gtr (2-3rd degr.,
Das Gitarrenwerk, Reihe A:10) sc
PREISSLER f.s.   (4876)

Suite in G minor, MIN 329
(Libbert) A rec,gtr (3rd degr., Das
Gitarrenwerk, Reihe A:2) sc
PREISSLER f.s.   (4877)

ANTONIOU, THEODORE (1935-   )
Dialoge *Op.19
fl,gtr (9th degr.) sc,pts MODERN
f.s.   (4878)

ASRIEL, ANDRE (1922-   )
Inventionen, 5
tenor sax,bass gtr,opt perc IMB
rent   (4879)

AZPIAZU, JOSE DE (1912-   )
Sonate Basque
fl/vln,gtr (7th degr.) ZIMMER.
ZM-1268 f.s.   (4880)

BACH, J.C.
Sonata for Violin and Guitar
(Nagel; Meunier) vln,gtr BREITKOPF-
W EB-6796 f.s.   (4881)

BACH, JOHANN SEBASTIAN (1685-1750)
Sonata for Flute and Keyboard
Instrument, BWV 1035, in E
(Uhlmann) fl,gtr BREITKOPF-W
EB-6789 f.s.   (4882)

BADINGS, HENK (1907-1987)
It Is Dawning In The East,
Balladesque Variations On An Old
Dutch Love Song
org,gtr (8-9th degr.) sc,pts
DONEMUS f.s.   (4883)

BALLOU, ESTHER WILLIAMSON (1915-1973)
Dialogues
ob,gtr (7-8th degr.) sc COMP.FAC.
f.s.   (4884)

BARLOW, FRED (1881-1951)
Pavan (from Gladys)
(Cotte) fl,gtr (5th degr.) LEMOINE
$5.00   (4885)

BARON, ERNST GOTTLIEB (1696-1760)
Duetto Al Liuto E Traverso
"Duetto G-Dur" (Dirkx) fl,gtr (6-
7th degr., originally for lute-f'
and traverso) sc,pts TEESELING
VT-33 f.s.   (4886)
"Sonate" (Meunier) fl,gtr (6-7th
degr., originally for lute-f' and
traverso) sc,pts BREITKOPF-W 6720
f.s.   (4887)

Konzerte, 2
(Behrend) vln/fl,gtr,opt vla da
gamba/vcl (6th degr., originally
for lute-f' and continuo) sc,pts
ZIMMER. ZM-1904 f.s.   (4888)

Sonata A 2
(Dirkx) fl,gtr (6-7th degr.,
originally for lute-f' and
traverso) sc,pts TEESELING VT-32
f.s.   (4889)

BARRETT, JOHN
Air
(Behrend) A rec,gtr (4th degr.)
SIKORSKI 363 $2.25   (4890)

BARTOK, BELA (1881-1945)
Aus Ungarn Und Der Slowakei, Lieder
Und Tanze, Vol. I *CC16U
(Brodszky) S rec,gtr (2-3rd degr.)
sc SCHOTT 5216 f.s.   (4891)

BARTOLOZZI, BRUNO (1911-   )
Auser
ob,gtr (9th degr., 2 sc) ZERBONI
7657 f.s.   (4892)

Serenade
vln,gtr (6th degr.) PETERS f.s.
                            (4893)
vln,gtr (6th degr.) BRUZZI f.s.
                            (4894)

BAUMANN, HERBERT (1925-   )
Duetto Concertante
(Behrend) rec,gtr (7th degr.,
Gitarre-Bibliothek, No.48) sc
BOTE GB-48 f.s.   (4895)

BAUMANN, MAX GEORG (1917-   )
Duo, Op. 62
(Behrend) vcl,gtr ZIMMER. ZM-1902
f.s.   (4896)

BECKER, GUNTHER (1924-   )
  Con Buen Ayre, Duplum
    fl,gtr (9-10th degr.) sc ZIMMER.
    ZM-1401 f.s.   (4897)

BEECROFT, NORMA (1934-   )
  Pezzi Brevi, 3
    fl,gtr UNIVER. 13468 f.s.   (4898)

BEETHOVEN, LUDWIG VAN (1770-1827)
  Allegro
    (Schmidt) vla/vln,gtr (3-4th degr.,
    2 sc) ZIMMER. ZM-1848 f.s. (4899)

  Andante Mit Variationen
    (Behrend) mand,gtr (7-8th degr.)
    ZIMMER. 1808 f.s.   (4900)

  Sonata in C minor
    (Tower) vln/fl/mand,gtr TEESELING
    VT-195 f.s.   (4901)

  Sonatina, MIN 48
    (Scheit) vln/fl,gtr (5th degr.,
    Gitarre-Kammermusik, No.56) sc,
    pts DOBLINGER GKM-56 f.s.   (4902)

  Theme and Variations, MIN 218
    (Brojer) vln,gtr (Die Gitarre In
    Der Hausmusik, No.6) HOHLER GH-6
    f.s.   (4903)

BEHREND, SIEGFRIED (1933-   )
  Haiku-Suite
    (Behrend) fl,gtr (Gitarremusik Fur
    Die Jugend, Vol. 3) ZIMMER. 1962
    f.s.   (4904)

  Kolometrie
    mand,gtr (8th degr.) ZIMMER. 1805
    f.s. contains also: ZU-MA-GT-TON
    II (mand,gtr)   (4905)

  Scherzoso
    vla,gtr (4th degr.) ZIMMER. ER-68A
    f.s.   (4906)

  Solo
    gtr/cont, psalterium or dulcimer
    PREISSLER 6304 f.s.   (4907)

  Spielmusik
    mel inst,gtr (Gitarremusik Fur Die
    Jugend, Vol. 19) ZIMMER. 2078
    f.s.   (4908)

  Suite Nach Altenglischen Meistern
    A rec,gtr (4th degr.) SIKORSKI 364
    $2.25   (4909)

  Triptychon "Memento Mori Ohshima
    Norio Nostrum"
    fl,gtr ZIMMER. ZM-1852 f.s. (4910)

BENARY, PETER (1931-   )
  Fantasien, 4
    fl,gtr (5-6th degr.) sc MOSELER
    f.s.   (4911)

BENGUEREL, XAVIER (1931-   )
  Intendo A Dos
    perc,gtr ZIMMER. ZM-1851 f.s.
                                 (4912)

BISCHOFF, HEINZ (1898-1963)
  Salzburger Sonatine In F
    S rec/fl/ob/vln,gtr (3-4th degr.,
    Zeitschrift Fur Spielmusik,
    No.91) sc MOECK ZFS-91 f.s.
                                 (4913)

BLAVET, MICHEL (1700-1768)
  8 Pieces
    fl/rec,gtr (2-3rd degr.) LEDUC f.s.
                                 (4914)

BLOCH, WALDEMAR (1906-   )
  Neuberger Tanze
    vln,gtr (6th degr.) sc,pts
    DOBLINGER 05931 f.s.
    contains: Landler; March; Polka;
    Waltz; Zwiefache, Der   (4915)

  Sonata
    vln,gtr (8th degr., Gitarre-
    Kammermusik, No.16) sc,pts
    DOBLINGER GKM-16 f.s.   (4916)

BOCCHERINI, LUIGI (1743-1805)
  Introduction And Fandango
    (Bream) hpsd,gtr (8-9th degr.) sc,
    pts FABER F-0222 f.s.   (4917)

BONNARD, ALAIN (1939-   )
  Sonatine Breve
    gtr,fl (3-4th degr.) LEDUC f.s.
                                 (4918)

BORTOLAZZI, B.
  Theme and Variations, Op. 10, No. 4
    (Behrend) mand,gtr (4-5th degr.)
    ZIMMER. 1813 f.s.   (4919)

BOSKE, JIM TEN (1946-   )
  Leave Something Unexplained
    fl,gtr DONEMUS f.s.   (4920)

BOZZA, EUGENE (1905-   )
  Berceuse Et Serenade
    fl,gtr LEDUC f.s.   (4921)

  Polydiaphonie
    fl,gtr (9-10th degr.) sc,pts LEDUC
    $7.25   (4922)

  Trois Pieces
    fl,gtr LEDUC f.s.   (4923)

BRAUN, GUNTER
  Serie *CC3U
    perc,gtr (8th degr.) ZIMMER.
    ZM-1712 f.s.   (4924)

  Sonatina
    fl,gtr ZIMMER. ZM-1822 f.s. (4925)

BULL, JOHN (ca. 1562-1628)
  Pieces, 4 (from Fitzwilliam Virginal
    Book)
    (Duarte) A rec,gtr (3-4th degr.) sc
    SCHOTT 10986 f.s.
    contains: Courante, MIN 281;
    Duchess Of Brunswick's Toye,
    The; Duke Of Brunswick's Alman,
    The; Gigue, MIN 282   (4926)

BURGHAUSER, JARMIL (1921-   )
  Reflexionen
    vla,gtr ARTIA f.s.   (4927)

BURKHARD, WILLY (1900-1955)
  Serenade, Op. 71, No. 3
    fl,gtr (8-9th degr.) sc BAREN. 1935
    f.s.   (4928)

CALDARA, ANTONIO (1670-1736)
  Sonata in A minor
    (Brojer) rec/vln/ob,gtr (7th degr.,
    Die Gitarre In Der Kammermusik,
    No.18) HOHLER GC-18 f.s.   (4929)

  Sonata in E minor
    (Brojer) vln,gtr (6-7th degr., Die
    Gitarre In Der Kammermusik,
    No.17) HOHLER GC-17 f.s.   (4930)

CALL, LEONHARD VON (ca. 1768-1815)
  Variations for Flute and Guitar
    (Saldarelli) fl,gtr (6th degr.) sc
    ZERBONI 8478 f.s.   (4931)

CAMPRA, ANDRE (1660-1744)
  Menuet Vif Et Gigue
    (Kovats) ob/fl,gtr (4-7th degr., 4
    Transcriptions, no. 2) sc,pt
    ESCHIG 7918 f.s.   (4932)

CAROSO, FABRIZIO (1526-1600)
  Balletto
    (Behrend) fl,gtr (3rd degr.)
    ZIMMER. ZM-1791 f.s.   (4933)

CARULLI, FERDINANDO (1770-1841)
  Duo, Op. 37 for Piano and Guitar
    (Sicca-Fleres) pno,gtr (4th degr.)
    sc,pt ZERBONI 8120 f.s.   (4934)

  Fantasy, Op. 337 for Flute and Guitar
    *7-8th cent
    (Thomatos) fl,gtr sc,pt HEINRICH.
    1428 f.s.   (4935)

  Nocturne, Op. 190
    (Nagel; Meunier) fl,gtr (6-7th
    degr.) sc,pts BREITKOPF-W 6698
    f.s.   (4936)

  Notturno, Op. 189 (composed with
    Carulli, Gustavo)
    (Fleres) pno/hpsd,gtr (6th degr.)
    sc,pt PREISSLER 7044 f.s.   (4937)

  Serenade, Op. 109, No. 1
    (Nagel; Lendl) fl/vln,gtr (3-4th
    degr., Il Flauto Traverso, No.
    22) pts SCHOTT 6198 f.s.   (4938)

  Serenade, Op. 109, No. 6
    (Nagel; Lendl) fl/vln,gtr (3-4th
    degr., Il Flauto Traverso, No.
    23) pts SCHOTT f.s.   (4939)

  Serenaden, 5
    (Schmid-Kayser) fl/vln,gtr (4-5th
    degr.) sc VIEWEG 1572 f.s.   (4940)

  Sonata No. 1
    (Albert) pno,gtr (7th degr., Die
    Gitarre In Der Haus- Und
    Kammermusik, No. 2) sc,pts
    ZIMMER. ZM-1244 f.s.   (4941)

  Sonata No. 2
    (Albert) pno,gtr (7th degr., Die
    Gitarre In Der Haus- Und
    Kammermusik, No. 3) sc,pts
    ZIMMER. ZM-1245 f.s.   (4942)

CASTELNUOVO-TEDESCO, MARIO (1895-1968)
  Fantasy, Op. 145
    (Segovia) pno,gtr (8-9th degr.) sc,
    pts SCHOTT GA-170 f.s.   (4943)

CASTELNUOVO-TEDESCO, MARIO (cont'd.)

  Sonatina
    fl,gtr ESCHIG f.s.   (4944)

CHIEREGHIN, SERGIO (1933-   )
  Tempi, 4
    (Muggia) fl,gtr (6th degr.) sc
    ZANIBON 5327 f.s. Il Bucranio
    contains: Aria; Danza Prima;
    Danza Seconda; Prelude   (4945)

CILENSEK, JOHANN (1913-   )
  Sonata
    fl,gtr (7-8th degr.) sc BREITKOPF-L
    4440 f.s.   (4946)

COENEN, PAUL (1908-   )
  Heitere Folge Von Vogel-Liedern
    *CC7U
    (Behrend) A rec,gtr (7th degr.) sc,
    pts ZIMMER. ZM-1368 f.s.   (4947)

CONSTANT, FRANZ (1910-   )
  Musique A Deux *CC3U
    fl,gtr ESCHIG f.s.   (4948)

CORELLI, ARCANGELO (1653-1713)
  Sonata for Violin and Guitar in E
    minor, Op. 5, No. 8
    (Schaller) vln,gtr (5th degr.,
    Gitarre-Kammermusik, No.19) sc,
    pts DOBLINGER GKM-19 f.s.   (4949)

  Sonata for Violin and Guitar, Op. 5,
    No. 7, in D minor
    (Brojer) (7th degr., Gitarre-
    Kammermusik, No.46) sc,pts
    DOBLINGER GKM-46 f.s.   (4950)

CORGHI, AZIO (1937-   )
  Consonancias Y Redobles
    for 1 or more gtr and opt tape
    recorder (after Luys Milan's
    Fantasia XVI) sc ZERBONI 7654
    $7.00   (4951)

COUPERIN, FRANCOIS (LE GRAND)
    (1668-1733)
  Petits Moulins A Vent, Les
    (Kovats) ob/fl,gtr (4-7th degr., 4
    Transcriptions, no. 1) sc,pt
    ESCHIG 7919 f.s.   (4952)

DALLINGER, FRIDOLIN (1933-   )
  Sonatina for Flute and Guitar
    fl,gtr (Gitarre-Kammermusik, No.
    114) DOBLINGER GKM-114 f.s.
                                 (4953)

DAVID, JOHANN NEPOMUK (1895-1977)
  Variationen Uber Ein Eigenes Thema
    *Op.32,No.2
    rec-fl, gtr-lute-g' (notation lute
    pt: treb clef) sc BREITKOPF-L
    5783 f.s.   (4954)

DIABELLI, ANTON (1781-1858)
  Grande Sonate Brillante *Op.102
    (Behrend) pno,gtr (5-6th degr.,
    Gitarre-Bibliothek, No.28) sc,pts
    BOTE GB-28 f.s.   (4955)

  Sehr Leichte Stucke, Vol. I
    (Meier) pno,gtr (4-5th degr.)
    SCHOTT GA-22 f.s.   (4956)

  Sehr Leichte Stucke, Vol. II
    (Meier) pno,gtr (4-5th degr.)
    SCHOTT GA-23 f.s.   (4957)

  Sehr Leichte Stucke, Vol. III
    (Meier) pno,gtr (4-5th degr.)
    SCHOTT GA-24 f.s.   (4958)

  Sehr Leichte Stucke, Vol. IV
    (Meier) pno,gtr (4-5th degr.)
    SCHOTT GA-25 f.s.   (4959)

  Serenade, Op. 99
    fl,gtr SIMROCK 3069 f.s.   (4960)

  Sonatina, Op. 68
    (Albert) pno,gtr (4th degr., Die
    Gitarre In Der Haus- Und
    Kammermusik, No.1) ZIMMER.
    ZM-1187 f.s.   (4961)
    (Scheit) pno,gtr (4th degr.) sc,pts
    UNIVER. 14440 f.s.   (4962)

  Sonatina, Op. 70
    (Hauswirth) pno,gtr (3rd degr.) sc,
    pts PREISSLER JP-7011 f.s.   (4963)

  Stucke, 3
    (Nagel) fl/vln,gtr (4th degr.) sc,
    pts BREITKOPF-W 6671 f.s.
    contains: Andante Con Moto;
    March; Polonaise   (4964)

DJEMIL, ENYSS (1917-   )
  Petite Suite Medievale
    fl,gtr (3rd degr.) LEDUC f.s.
                                 (4965)

DODGSON, STEPHEN (1924-   )
  Duo Concertant
    hpsd,gtr ESCHIG f.s.   (4966)

DOHL, FRIEDHELM (1936-   )
  Pas De Deux
    vln,gtr (7-8th degr., notation: kbd
    partitura) sc,manuscript,copy
    GERIG 743 f.s.   (4967)

DUARTE, JOHN W. (1919-   )
  Danse Joyeuse *Op.42
    fl,gtr (6th degr.) sc BROEKMANS
    1010 f.s.   (4968)

  Simple Songs Without Words, 3 *Op.41
    S rec/A rec,gtr/pno (3rd degr.,
    suppl: kbd pt) sc BROEKMANS 1016
    f.s.   (4969)

  Sonatina, Op. 15
    fl,gtr (6th degr.) sc BROEKMANS 937
    f.s.   (4970)

ENCINAR, JOSE RAMON (1954-   )
  Abhava
    gtr,tape recorder (8th degr.) sc
    ZERBONI 7491 $7.00   (4971)

ERBSE, HEIMO (1924-   )
  3 Studien *Op.30
    fl,gtr DOBLINGER GKM-108 f.s.
    Gitarre-Kammermusik, No. 108
    contains: Barcarolle; Elegy;
    Scherzo   (4972)

ERDMANN, DIETRICH (1917-   )
  Episodes
    perc,gtr (6th degr.) sc GERIG
    HG-920 $5.25   (4973)

FERRITTO, JOHN E. (1937-   )
  Duos, 4 *Op.7
    S rec,gtr (6th degr.) sc COMP.FAC.
    f.s.   (4974)

FERRONATI, LODOVICO
  Sonata in C
    (Brojer) vln,gtr (5th degr., Die
    Gitarre In Der Kammermusik,
    No.14) sc,pts HOHLER GC-14 f.s.
                                    (4975)

FINK, SIEGFRIED
  Dialogue
    perc,gtr ZIMMER. ZM-1835 f.s.
                                    (4976)

FIOCCO, JOSEPH-HECTOR (1703-1741)
  Allegro
    (van Meteren) vln,gtr (3rd degr.)
    sc TEESELING VT-149 f.s.   (4977)

FISCHER, JOHANN CASPAR FERDINAND
    (ca. 1665-1746)
  Leichte Stucke, 8
    (Brojer) S rec/vln/fl/ob,gtr (2-3rd
    degr., Die Gitarre In Der
    Kammermusik, No.11) sc,pts HOHLER
    GC-11 f.s.   (4978)

  March
    (Brojer) vln/S rec/ob,gtr (3rd
    degr., Die Gitarre In Der
    Hausmusik, No.18) HOHLER GH-18
    f.s. contains also: Saraband;
    Minuet No. 1; Minuet No. 2 (4979)

FLERES, RITA MARIA
  Stucke, 5, Nach Liedern Und Tanzen
    Aus Der Renaissance
    hpsd/pno,gtr (2-3rd degr.) sc,pts
    PREISSLER 7043 f.s.
    contains: Canarios; Espanoleta;
    Funf Variationen Uber
    "Greensleeves"; Tanzlein; Vaghe
    Bellezze   (4980)

FROHLICHE TANZE AUS DEM 18. UND 19.
  JAHRHUNDERT
    (Zanoskar) S rec/treb inst,gtr (3rd
    degr.) SIKORSKI 513 $3.75   (4981)

FURSTENAU, KASPAR (1772-1819)
  Duette, 6 (from Op. 37)
    (Nagel; Lendl) fl,gtr (4th degr., 2
    sc) HEINRICH. N-1249 f.s.   (4982)

  Stucke, 12 *Op.38
    (Nagel) fl,gtr (6th degr., Il
    Flauto Traverso, No. 34) SCHOTT
    5887 f.s.   (4983)

  Suite, Op. 34
    (Behrend) fl,gtr (3rd degr.)
    ZIMMER. ZM-1367 f.s.   (4984)

  Suite, Op. 35
    (Behrend) fl,gtr ZIMMER. ZM-1803
    f.s.   (4985)
    "Original-Kompositionen, 12, Op.
    35" (Homann) fl,gtr (3-4th degr.)
    sc NAGELS NMA-31 f.s.   (4986)

  Zwolf Stucke
    (Nagel) fl,gtr BREITKOPF-W 6746
    f.s.   (4987)

FURSTENAU, WOLFRAM
  Orationen
    org,gtr (7th degr.) sc TEESELING
    FC-2 f.s.   (4988)

  Pieces Pour Une Noble Femme, 3
    vln,gtr (8th degr.) sc TEESELING
    VT-57 f.s.
    contains: Cadenza; Evolution;
    Invocation   (4989)

  Vakantiedagboek
    fl/ob/gtr TEESELING VT-221 f.s.
                                    (4990)

GALL, LOUIS IGNATIUS
  Sonatina Pirineos *Op.14
    treb inst,gtr (3-4th degr.) sc
    HARMONIA HU-1846 f.s.   (4991)

GEBAUER, MICHEL-JOSEPH (1763-1812)
  Polonaise
    (Nagel; Meunier) fl,gtr (4-5th
    degr.) sc,pt BREITKOPF-W 6696
    f.s.   (4992)

GELLI, VINCENZO (THOMATOS)
  Two Divertimenti
    (Thomatos) fl/vln,gtr COLUMBIA 174
    f.s.   (4993)

GEMINIANI, FRANCESCO (1687-1762)
  12 Pieces For Guitar And Continuo
    (from The Art Of Playing The
    Guitar (1760))
    (Barsham; Knowland) gtr,opt cont
    sc,pts OXFORD f.s.   (4994)

GERLACH, HANS CHRISTIAN
  Divertimento [Collection] *CC16U
    (Furstenau) fl/vln,gtr/vln,fl,gtr
    TEESELING VT-220 f.s.   (4995)

GIULIANI, MAURO (1781-1829)
  Divertimento
    (Thomatos) fl,gtr ZIMMER. ZM-1842
    f.s.   (4996)

  Duettino *Op.77
    (Saldarelli) fl/vln,gtr (3rd degr.)
    sc ZERBONI 8479 f.s.   (4997)

  Duettino Facile *Op.77
    (Nagel) fl/vln,gtr (3-4th degr., Il
    Flauto Traverso) pts SCHOTT
    FTR-103 f.s.   (4998)

  Gran Duetto Concertante *Op.52
    (Nagel) fl,gtr (Il Flauto Traverso,
    No. 104) SCHOTT FTR-104 f.s.
                                    (4999)

  Grosse Serenade *Op.82
    (Nagel; Meunier) fl/vln,gtr (6-7th
    degr.) sc,pt BREITKOPF-W 6672
    f.s.   (5000)

  Grosse Sonate, Op. 25
    (Albert; Schwarz-Reiflingen) vln,
    gtr (7th degr., Die Gitarre In
    Der Haus- Und Kammermusik, No. 7)
    pts ZIMMER. ZM-1116 f.s.   (5001)

  Grosse Sonate, Op. 85
    (Albert) fl/vln,gtr (6-7th degr.,
    Die Gitarre In Der Haus- Und
    Kammermusik, No. 19) pts ZIMMER.
    ZM-1189 f.s.   (5002)

  Qual Mesto Gemito
    "Quintetto Dalla "Semiramide" Di
    Rossini" (Saldarelli) fl/vln,gtr
    (6th degr.) sc ZERBONI 8480 f.s.
                                    (5003)

  Serenade, Op. 127
    (Saldarelli) fl/vln,gtr (4th degr.)
    sc ZERBONI 8481 f.s.   (5004)

  Variations, Op. 113
    (Sicca) gtr,pno (Gitarre Und
    Pianoforte, Vol. 1) ZIMMER. 2000
    f.s.   (5005)

GOEPFERT, KARL ANDREAS (1768-1818)
  Sonata, Op. 13
    (Behrend; Wojchiechowski) bsn,gtr
    (4th degr., Gitarre-Bibliothek,
    No.68) sc BOTE GB-68 f.s.   (5006)

GORZANIS, GIACOMO (ca. 1525-ca. 1578)
  Napolitane, 15
    "Neapolitanische Lieder Aus Dem 16.
    Jahrhundert" (Tonazzi) [It] gtr
    solo, or solo voice or S rec and
    gtr (4th degr., orig for solo
    voice and lute) sc HEINRICH.
    PE-6080 f.s.   (5007)

GRAGNANI, FILIPPO (1767- ?)
  Sonata, Op. 8, No. 1
    (Albert) vln,gtr (6-7th degr., Die
    Gitarre In Der Haus- Und
    Kammermusik, No. 4) pts ZIMMER.
    ZM-1046 f.s.   (5008)

  Sonata, Op. 8, No. 2
    (Albert) vln,gtr (6-7th degr., Die
    Gitarre In Der Haus- Und

GRAGNANI, FILIPPO (cont'd.)

    Kammermusik, No. 5) pts ZIMMER.
    ZM-1047 f.s.   (5009)

  Sonata, Op. 8, No. 3
    (Albert) vln,gtr (6-7th degr., Die
    Gitarre In Der Haus- Und
    Kammermusik, No. 6) pts ZIMMER.
    ZM-1048 f.s.   (5010)

GRETRY, ANDRE ERNEST MODESTE
    (1741-1813)
  Entr'acte
    (Gatti) fl,gtr (3rd degr.) sc,pt
    BERBEN EB1940 $1.75   (5011)

GRIFFITHS, JOHN (1952-   )
  Conversation Piece
    (Behrend) S rec,gtr (Gitarremusik
    Fur Die Jugend, Vol. 14) ZIMMER.
    2073 f.s.   (5012)

HANDEL, GEORGE FRIDERIC (1685-1759)
  Air Mit Variationen
    (Brojer) vln/fl/ob,gtr (2nd degr.,
    Die Gitarre In Der Hausmusik,
    No.17) HOHLER GH-17 f.s. contains
    also: Saraband, MIN 221;
    Passepied; Minuet, MIN 222 (5013)

  Alte Zupfmusik
    (Henze) 1-2mand,gtr (3-4th degr.)
    sc HOFMEISTER T-4069 $3.25 2 pcs
    for 1 mand, gtr; 1 pc for 2 mand,
    gtr
    contains: Chaconne, MIN 64;
    Courante, MIN 63; Minuet, MIN
    62   (5014)

  Leichte Stucke, 8
    (Brojer) A rec/vln/fl/ob,gtr (3rd
    degr., Die Gitarre In Der
    Kammermusik, No.21) HOHLER GC-21
    f.s.   (5015)

  Siciliana
    (Brojer) A rec/T rec/vln/ob,gtr
    (4th degr., Die Gitarre In Der
    Kammermusik, No.19) sc,pt HOHLER
    GC-19 f.s.   (5016)

  Sonata in A
    (Schaller) vln,gtr (6th degr.,
    Gitarre-Kammermusik, No.95) sc,
    pts DOBLINGER GKM-95 f.s. (5017)

  Sonata in A minor, Op. 1, No. 4
    (Scheit) A rec/fl/vln/ob,gtr (8th
    degr., Gitarre-Kammermusik, No.
    23) sc,pt DOBLINGER GKM-23 f.s.
                                    (5018)
    (Zanoskar) A rec/fl/vln/ob,gtr (8th
    degr.) sc,pts NOETZEL N-3094 f.s.
                                    (5019)

  Sonata in C
    (Zanoskar) A rec,gtr (6-7th degr.)
    sc,pts NOETZEL 3096 f.s. (5020)

  Sonata in D
    (Brojer) fl/ob/vln,gtr (6th degr.,
    Die Gitarre In Der Kammermusik,
    No. 4) sc,pt HOHLER GC-4 f.s.
                                    (5021)
    (Zanoskar) fl/ob/vln,gtr SIKORSKI
    510 f.s.   (5022)

  Sonata in D minor
    (Schaller) A rec/fl/vln/ob,gtr (9th
    degr., Gitarre-Kammermusik,
    No.24) sc,pts DOBLINGER GKM-24
    f.s.   (5023)

  Sonata in E minor, MIN 344
    fl,gtr BREITKOPF-W 6744 f.s. (5024)

  Sonata in F, Op. 1, No. 11
    (Schaller) A rec,gtr (7-8th degr.,
    Gitarre-Kammermusik, No. 9) sc,pt
    DOBLINGER GKM-9 f.s.   (5025)
    (Wensiecki) A rec,gtr sc,pts
    HOFMEISTER-W f.s.   (5026)
    (Zanoskar) A rec,gtr sc,pts
    HEINRICH. N-3097 f.s.   (5027)

  Sonata No. 2 in G minor
    (Azpiazu) A rec/fl,gtr (7th degr.)
    sc ZIMMER. ZM-1760 f.s.   (5028)
    (Zanoskar) A rec/fl,gtr (7th degr.)
    sc,pts NOETZEL N-3095 f.s. (5029)

  Suite, MIN 49
    (Brojer) treb inst,gtr (4th degr.,
    Die Gitarre In Der Hausmusik,
    No.15) sc,pt HOHLER GH-15 f.s.
                                    (5030)

HARTIG, HEINZ FRIEDRICH (1907-1969)
  Stucke, 5
    (Behrend) A rec/gtr (8-9th degr.,
    Gitarre-Bibliothek, No.30) sc,pt
    BOTE GB-30 f.s.   (5031)

HASHAGEN, KLAUS (1924-   )
  Pergiton IV
    perc,gtr (9th degr.) sc,manuscript,
    copy ZIMMER. ZM-1846 f.s.   (5032)

HASSE, JOHANN ADOLPH (1699-1783)
  Sonaten, 12, Op. 1
    (Giesbert) fl/A rec/S rec,cont,gtr/
    pno (6-7th degr.) sc PFAUEN f.s.
    Urtext; transcr for gtr and for
    pno; for A rec: capotasto in pos.
    III; for S rec: gtr tuning 1
    semitone lower, Sonata No.1,
    Pfauen No.261; Sonata No.2,
    Pfauen No.262
    contains: Sonata, Op. 1, No. 1,
    in D; Sonata, Op. 1, No. 2, in
    B minor   (5033)

HAUG, HANS (1900-1967)
  Capriccio
    fl,gtr ESCHIG f.s.   (5034)

  Fantasy
    pno,gtr (8th degr., Collezione Di
    Musiche Per Chitarra) sc BERBEN
    EB1847 $4.00   (5035)

HAUSWIRTH, HANS M.A. (1901-   )
  Sonatina No. 2
    acord/pno,gtr (4th degr.) sc,pt
    PREISSLER 7071 f.s.   (5036)

HAYDN, [FRANZ] JOSEPH (1732-1809)
  Menuette, 22
    (Monkemeyer) 2gtr, or str inst
    (baryton, vla da gamba, vln), gtr
    (2-3rd degr., single line playing
    (gtr I)) sc TONGER 1282 f.s.
                                  (5037)

HEER, HANS DE (1927-   )
  Sonatina No. 2
    fl,gtr (8-9th degr.) sc,pt DONEMUS
    f.s.   (5038)

  Sonatina No. 3
    fl,gtr sc,pts DONEMUS f.s.   (5039)

HEKSTER, WALTER (1937-   )
  Epicycle I
    fl,gtr (the works can also be
    performed separately) sc DONEMUS
    f.s. contains also: Epicycle II
    (ob,trp,bass clar,acord,perc)
                                  (5040)

HESSE, ERNST CHRISTIAN (1676-1762)
  Duo
    (Rubardt) vla da gamba/vcl,cont
    (3rd degr., transcr for gtr and
    vcl pt (cont)) sc HOFMEISTER
    V-1076 f.s.   (5041)

HEUCKEROTH VAN HESSEN, J. RICHARD
  Impression
    fl/rec/ob,gtr (3rd degr.) sc
    BROEKMANS 911 f.s.   (5042)

  Song And Dance
    fl/rec/ob,gtr (3rd degr.) sc
    BROEKMANS 912 f.s.   (5043)

HOFFNER, PAUL MARX (1895-1949)
  Sonatina
    (Behrend) A rec,gtr (5-6th degr.)
    sc,pt SIKORSKI 484 $3.75   (5044)

  Tanzstucke, 3
    (Behrend) A rec,gtr (5th degr.)
    ZIMMER. ZM-1779 f.s.   (5045)

HOMS, JOAQUIN (1906-   )
  Impromptu
    perc,gtr ALPUERTO 1052 f.s.   (5046)

HUMBLE, KEITH (1927-   )
  Arcade IV *CC4U
    perc,gtr (7-9th degr.) sc UNIVER.
    29017A f.s.   (5047)

IBERT, JACQUES (1890-1962)
  Entr'acte
    fl/vln,gtr (6th degr.) sc,pt LEDUC
    $6.00   (5048)

ISRAEL-MEYER, PIERRE (1933-   )
  Humoresque
    (Bauml) (7th degr.) sc ESCHIG 7613
    f.s.
    contains: Passacaglia (vln,gtr);
      Postlude (gtr); Prelude (gtr);
      Scherzo (vln,gtr)   (5049)

JELINEK, HANNS (1901-1969)
  Ollapotrida *Op.30
    fl,gtr (8th degr.) sc,pt MODERN 954
    f.s.   (5050)

JONG, MARINUS DE (1891-1984)
  Suite, Op. 127
    (van Puijenbroeck) fl,gtr (6-7th
    degr.) sc METROPOLIS EM-4693
    $4.00   (5051)

KAMMERLING, WERNER
  Variationen Uber 3 Alte Volkslieder,
    18
    (Kammerling) A rec,gtr (4-5th
    degr., Rund Um Die Gitarre, Vol.
    IV) sc TONGER 1620 f.s.   (5052)

KELTERBORN, RUDOLF (1931-   )
  Music for Violin and Guitar
    vln,gtr (9th degr.) sc,pt HEINRICH.
    PE-6120 f.s.   (5053)

KLEBE, GISELHER (1925-   )
  Recitativo, Aria E Duetto *Op.44
    (Behrend) A rec,gtr (8th degr.,
    Gitarre-Bibliothek, No.64) sc
    BOTE GB-64 f.s.   (5054)

KLEIN, RICHARD RUDOLF (1921-   )
  Divertimento
    A rec,gtr (3rd degr.) sc FIDULA
    f.s.   (5055)

  Partita in D
    A rec/T rec,gtr (3rd degr.) sc
    NOETZEL N-3057 f.s.   (5056)

KOCH, HANS
  Musizierbuchlein, Ein, Einfuhrung In
    Das Mehrstimmige Spiel Nach
    Volkstanzen Und Liedern Aus Dem
    Alpenraum
    gtr (1-3rd degr., 29 pcs for 1 gtr;
    4 pcs for rec and gtr) sc HOHLER
    f.s.   (5057)

KOMTER, JAN MAARTEN (1905-   )
  Andante in D
    fl/vln,gtr (3-4th degr.) sc,pt
    DONEMUS f.s.   (5058)

  Divertimento in G
    fl/vln,gtr (4th degr.) sc,pts
    DONEMUS f.s.   (5059)

  Suite in C
    treb inst,cont/gtr (4-5th degr., 2
    versions; version I: melody +
    cont; version II: melody + cont
    worked out by the composer) sc
    DONEMUS f.s.   (5060)

  Suite in D minor
    treb inst,cont/gtr (4-5th degr., 2
    versions; version I: melody +
    cont; version II: melody + cont
    worked out by the composer) sc
    DONEMUS f.s.   (5061)

KONIG, HEINZ
  Spielmusik In C
    A rec,gtr (3rd degr.) sc HOFMEISTER
    V-1482 f.s.   (5062)

KONINK, SERVAAS DE (KONING)
    (ca. 1660-ca. 1720)
  Sonata
    (Brojer) A rec/vln/ob,gtr (7th
    degr., Die Gitarre In Der
    Kammermusik, No.1) HOHLER GC-1
    f.s.   (5063)

KONT, PAUL (1920-   )
  Suite En Passant
    fl,gtr ESCHIG f.s.   (5064)

KOVATS, BARNA (1920-   )
  Sonatina
    ob/rec,gtr (7th degr.) sc,pt MODERN
    1109 f.s.   (5065)

KRENEK, ERNST (1900-   )
  Hausmusik; 7 Stucke Fur Die Sieben
    Tage Der Woche *CC7UL
    various instruments (4-5th degr.)
    sc,pts BAREN. 3478 f.s. no. 2,
    for S rec, gtr; no. 4, for vln,
    gtr; no. 7, for pno, A rec, vln,
    gtr   (5066)

KRETSCHMAR, WALTER (1902-   )
  Music in C
    (Behrend) treb inst,gtr (4th degr.)
    ZIMMER. ZM-1738 f.s.   (5067)

KROLL, GEORG (1934-   )
  Canzonabile
    B rec,gtr sc MOECK 1518 f.s. (5068)

  Re-Sonat Tibia
    gtr, shakuhachi sc,pts MOECK 5191
    f.s.   (5069)

KUFFNER, JOSEPH (1776-1856)
  Drittes Potpourri (from Tancred, Op.
    103)
    (Behrend; Henke) fl/vln,gtr ZIMMER.
    1992 f.s.   (5070)

  Serenade
    (Ochs) fl,gtr (3rd degr.) pts
    MOSELER f.s.   (5071)

  Serenade, No. 55
    (Behrend; Henke) pno,gtr (Gitarre
    Und Pianoforte, Vol. 2) ZIMMER.

KUFFNER, JOSEPH (cont'd.)

    2001 f.s.   (5072)

  Serenade, Op. 68
    (Schneider) vln,gtr (4-5th degr.)
    pts NOETZEL N-3099 f.s.   (5073)

LANGENBERG, JAN VAN DEN
  Capriccio
    fl/rec,gtr TEESELING VT-156 f.s.
                                  (5074)

LAUFFENSTEINER, WOLFF JACOB
  Sonata in A
    "Duette A-Dur" (Schaller) vla,gtr
    (7th degr., orig. for 2 lutes-f';
    Gitarre-Kammermusik, No.55c) sc,
    pt DOBLINGER GKM-55C f.s.   (5075)
    "Duette A-Dur" (Schaller) vln/fl/
    ob,gtr (7th degr., orig. for 2
    lutes-f'; Gitarre-Kammermusik,
    No. 55b) sc,pt DOBLINGER GKM-55B
    f.s.   (5076)

LEOPOLD I, HOLY ROMAN EMPEROR
    (1640-1705)
  Balletti
    (Brojer) rec/vln/ob,gtr (3rd degr.,
    Die Gitarre In Der Kammermusik,
    No.24) sc,pt HOHLER GC-24 f.s.
                                  (5077)
  Suite, Aus Einer Sammlung Von Tanzen
    (Brojer) treb inst,gtr (4th degr.,
    Die Gitarre In Der Kammermusik,
    No.5) sc,pt HOHLER GC-5 f.s.
                                  (5078)

LEUKAUF, ROBERT (1902-   )
  Altspanische Suite *CC10U
    (Walker) A rec/fl,gtr (3-4th degr.)
    sc HEINRICH. N-1550 f.s.   (5079)

LIER, WIM VAN
  Suite
    S rec,gtr (2-3rd degr.) sc
    BROEKMANS 782 f.s.   (5080)

LOCATELLI, PIETRO (1695-1764)
  Sinfonia
    (Brojer) vln,gtr (5-6th degr.,
    Gitarre-Kammermusik, No.11) sc,pt
    DOBLINGER GKM-11 f.s.   (5081)

  Sonata in D
    (Brojer) fl/vln/ob,gtr (6th degr.,
    Gitarre-Kammermusik, No.34) sc,pt
    DOBLINGER GKM-34 f.s.   (5082)

  Sonata in G
    (Brojer) fl/vln/ob,gtr (6th degr.,
    Gitarre-Kammermusik, No.47) sc,pt
    DOBLINGER GKM-47 f.s.   (5083)

  Sonata No. 2
    (Brojer) fl/vln/ob,gtr (7th degr.,
    Die Gitarre In Der Kammermusik,
    No.25) sc,pt HOHLER GC-25 f.s.
                                  (5084)

LOEILLET, JEAN-BAPTISTE (JOHN, OF
    LONDON) (1680-1730)
  Sonata in A minor, Op. 1, No. 1
    (Brojer) A rec/vln/ob,gtr (7th
    degr., Gitarre-Kammermusik,
    No.13) sc,pt DOBLINGER GKM-13
    f.s.   (5085)

  Sonata in G, Op. 1, No. 3
    (Brojer) A rec/vln/ob,gtr (6th
    degr., Gitarre-Kammermusik,
    No.63) sc,pt DOBLINGER GKM-63
    f.s.   (5086)

  Suite in E minor
    (Behrend) fl,gtr sc,pt ZIMMER.
    ZM-1817 f.s.   (5087)

LUCKY, STEPAN (1919-   )
  Duo Concertante
    vcl,gtr (8th degr.) sc PANTON 1276
    f.s.   (5088)

  Duo Concertanti
    vcl,gtr ARTIA 2195 f.s.   (5089)

MACE, THOMAS (1613?-1709)
  Prelude
    (Castet) fl/vln,gtr (4th degr.,
    Guitare, No.55) sc LEDUC G-55
    $2.25   (5090)

MADERNA, BRUNO (1920-1973)
  Aulodia Per Lothar
    ob d'amore,opt gtr ZERBONI 7000
    f.s.   (5091)

MAGANINI, QUINTO (1897-1974)
  Romanesca, La, An Ancient Italian
    Dance Air Of The 16th Century
    fl,gtr (3rd degr., also available
    in a version for clar, gtr) sc
    MUSICUS f.s.   (5092)

MAINERIO, GIORGIO
  5 Danze
    (Castellani; Paolini) 1-2rec,gtr
    RICORDI-IT 132146 f.s.   (5093)

MARCELLO, BENEDETTO (1686-1739)
Adagio, MIN 38 (from Concerto In C
Minor For Oboe And Strings)
(Amato) 2gtr/treb inst,gtr (6th
degr., single line playing (gtr
I)) sc ZANIBON 5173 f.s.   (5094)

Sonata in C, Op. 2, No. 6
(Verhoef) rec/fl,gtr (4th degr.) sc
TEESELING 39 f.s.   (5095)

Sonata in G
(Azpiazu) vla,gtr (6-7th degr.) sc
ZIMMER. ZM-1363 f.s.   (5096)

MARCO, TOMAS (1942-   )
Miriada
(Behrend) perc,gtr ZIMMER. ZM-1864
f.s.   (5097)

MARGOLA, FRANCO (1908-   )
Episodi, 4
(Cabassi) fl,gtr (5th degr., Il
Bucranio) sc,pt ZANIBON 5057 f.s.
                             (5098)

MARINI, BIAGIO (ca. 1595-1665)
Sonata
"Gardana, La" (Brojer) vln/cornet,
gtr (4th degr., Die Gitarre In
Der Kammermusik, No.29) sc,pt
HOHLER GC-29 f.s.   (5099)

MEIJER VON BREMEN, ALEXANDER
(1930-   )
Bagatellen *CC6U
(Beck) vln,gtr (7th degr.) sc
TEESELING VT-70 f.s.   (5100)

METZNER, LEONHARD
Sonata
(Brojer) vln,gtr (6th degr., Die
Gitarre In Der Kammermusik,
No.13) HOHLER GH-13 f.s.   (5101)

MIGOT, GEORGES (1891-1976)
Sonata
fl,gtr (8th degr.) sc TRANSAT. 966
$6.00   (5102)

MOLINO, FRANCESCO (1775-1847)
Nocturne No. 2, Op. 38
fl/vln,gtr BREITKOPF-W 6758 (5103)

Nocturne, Op. 37
(Henze) fl/vln,gtr (6th degr.)
ZIMMER. ZM-1723 f.s.   (5104)

MONZA, CARLO (ca. 1740-1801)
Sonate, MIN391
(Schickhaus) gtr/hpsd, dulcimer or
psalterium PREISSLER 6300 f.s.
                             (5105)

Sonate, MIN392
(Schickhaus) gtr/hpsd, dulcimer or
psalterium PREISSLER 6303 f.s.
                             (5106)

MOSCHELES, IGNAZ (1794-1870)
Grande Duo Concertante (composed with
Giuliani, Mauro)
(Behrend) pno,gtr (9-10th degr.)
sc,pt SIMROCK EE-2709 f.s. (5107)

MOZART, LEOPOLD (1719-1787)
Tanze, 6, Aus Dem Notenbuchlein Fur
Wolfgang
(Koch) rec,gtr (2-3rd degr., Die
Gitarre In Der Hausmusik, No.11)
sc,pt HOHLER GH-11 f.s.   (5108)

MOZART, WOLFGANG AMADEUS (1756-1791)
Deutsche Tanze, 6 *K.536
(Henze) mand/vln,gtr (3-4th degr.)
sc HOFMEISTER T-4098 f.s.   (5109)

Kleine Stucke, 4
(Behrend) fl,gtr ZIMMER. ZM-1903
f.s.   (5110)

Wiener Sonatine
(Brojer) vln,gtr (Die Gitarre In
Der Hausmusik, No.9) HOHLER GH-9
f.s.   (5111)

MULLER-CANT, MANFRED (1926-   )
Kinderlieder-Suite Fur Einen
Grossvater
vcl,gtr HANSSLER HE-16.101 rent
                             (5112)

MULLER-ILMENAU, WILHELM (1911-   )
Spielmusik
gtr, zither (3rd degr.) sc,pt
HOFMEISTER T-4040 f.s.
contains: Andante; Minuet in A;
Minuet in G; Rondo in E minor
                             (5113)

NIEHAUS, MANFRED (1933-   )
Suite
vln,gtr (7-8th degr.) sc,
manuscript,copy GERIG 738 f.s.
                             (5114)

NIESSEN, HANS-LUTZ (1920-1982)
Daar Gingen Twee Gespeelkens Goed,
Variaties Op Een Volkslied
"Variations On A Folk-Song" treb
inst,gtr (7th degr.) sc HARMONIA
1849 f.s.   (5115)

ORTIZ, DIEGO (ca. 1525- ?)
Recercaden, 4
A rec,gtr MOECK 2503 f.s.   (5116)

PAGANINI, NICCOLO (1782-1840)
Cantabile
(Schwarz-Reiflingen) vln,gtr (4th
degr., N. Paganini, Kompositionen
Fur Gitarre Und
Streichinstrumente, No. 8)
ZIMMER. ZM-1190 f.s.   (5117)

Centone Di Sonate; Four Sonatas
(Janetzky) vln,gtr (4-7th degr.)
sc,pt HOFMEISTER 7395 f.s. (5118)
(Schwarz-Reiflingen) vln,gtr (4-7th
degr., N. Paganini, Kompositionen
Fur Gitarre Und
Streichinstrumente, No. 3) pts
ZIMMER. ZM-1119 f.s.   (5119)

12 Duette, Vol. 1
(Bulatoff) vln,gtr (Vol.1 contains
nos.1-6) sc ZIMMER. 1987 f.s.
                             (5120)

12 Duette, Vol. 2
(Bulatoff) vln,gtr (Vol.2 contains
nos.7-12) sc ZIMMER. 1988 f.s.
                             (5121)

Grosse Sonate
(Schwarz-Reiflingen) vln,gtr solo
(8-9th degr., N. Paganini,
Kompositionen Fur Gitarre Und
Streichinstrumente, No. 1; for
eds without vln, and for gtr and
str orch, see Index) pts ZIMMER.
ZM-1037 f.s.   (5122)

Moto Perpetuo *Op.11
(Bulatoff) vln,gtr sc,pt ZIMMER.
1974 f.s.   (5123)

Sonata *Op. Posth.
(Schindler) vln,gtr (3rd degr.) pts
VAMO EE-03 f.s.   (5124)

Sonata Concertata
(Schwarz-Reiflingen) vln,gtr (8th
degr., N. Paganini, Kompositionen
Fur Gitarre Und
Streichinstrumente, No. 2) pts
ZIMMER. ZM-1049 f.s.   (5125)

Sonata, Op. 3, No. 1
(Behrend) vln,gtr (6th degr.,
Gitarre-Bibliothek, No.69) sc,pt
BOTE GB-69 f.s.   (5126)

Sonata, Op. 3, No. 5
(Behrend) vln,gtr (6th degr.,
Gitarre-Bibliothek, No.17) sc
BOTE GB-17 f.s.   (5127)

Sonata, Op. 3, No. 6
(Behrend) vln,gtr (4th degr.,
Gitarre-Bibliothek, No.59) sc,pt
BOTE GB-59 f.s.   (5128)
(Domandl) vln,gtr (4th degr.) BENJ
EE-3212 f.s.   (5129)

Sonaten, 6, Op. 2
(Schwarz-Reiflingen) vln,gtr (5th
degr., N. Paganini, Kompositionen
Fur Gitarre Und
Streichinstrumente, No. 10) pts
ZIMMER. ZM-1193 f.s.   (5130)

Sonaten, 6, Op.3
vln,gtr (4-6th degr.) RICORDI-IT
543 f.s.   (5131)
(Schwarz-Reiflingen) vln,gtr (4-6th
degr., N. Paganini, Kompositionen
Fur Gitarre Und
Streichinstrumente, No. 11) pts
ZIMMER. ZM-1194 f.s.   (5132)

Sonatine, 4
(Annessa) vln,gtr (4-5th degr.) sc,
pts PEER SM-3318 f.s.   (5133)

Tarantella
(Schwarz-Reiflingen) vln,gtr (6th
degr., N. Paganini, Kompositionen
Fur Gitarre Und
Streichinstrumente, No. 12)
ZIMMER. ZM-1195 f.s.   (5134)

Variazioni Di Bravura
(Schwarz-Reiflingen) vln,gtr/pno
(5th degr., N. Paganini,
Kompositionen Fur Gitarre Und
Streichinstrumente, No. 9) pts
ZIMMER. ZM-1197 f.s.   (5135)

PATACHICH, IVAN (1922-   )
Duo
vln/fl,gtr (7-8th degr.) sc,pt EMB
Z-7695 f.s.   (5136)

PELEMANS, WILLEM (1901-   )
Petit Duo
fl,gtr (4th degr.) sc MAURER f.s.
                             (5137)

PEPUSCH, JOHN CHRISTOPHER (1667-1752)
Beggar's Opera, The
(Wood) A rec,gtr (3rd degr., 16
pcs) sc HEINRICH. PE-6035 f.s.
                             (5138)

Sonata in D minor
(Schaller) A rec,gtr (5th degr.,
Gitarre-Kammermusik, No.10) sc,pt
DOBLINGER GKM-10 f.s.   (5139)

Sonata in G
(Brojer) A rec/vln/ob,gtr (6th
degr., Gitarre-Kammermusik,
No.12) sc,pt DOBLINGER GKM-12
f.s.   (5140)

Sonata, MIN 51
(Kovats) ob/fl,gtr (4-7th degr., 4
Transcriptions, no. 4) sc,pt
ESCHIG 7917 f.s.   (5141)

Sonaten, 3
(Giesbert) A rec/fl/vln,gtr/pno
(7th degr.) sc,pts PFAUEN 291
f.s.   (5142)

Stucke, 4 (from The Beggar's Opera)
(Brojer) rec/vln/ob,gtr (3rd degr.,
Die Gitarre In Der Kammermusik,
No.30) HOHLER GC-30 f.s.   (5143)

PERGOLESI, GIOVANNI BATTISTA
(1710-1736)
Siciliano
(Kovats) ob/fl,gtr (4-7th degr., 4
Transcriptions, no. 3) sc,pt
ESCHIG 7920 f.s.   (5144)

PIECES, 5 (from Fitzwilliam Virginal
Book) CC5U
(Duarte) A rec,gtr (3-4th degr.) sc
SCHOTT 10989 f.s. contains pcs by
Martin Peerson (1580?-1650?) and
Peter Philips (1561-1628)   (5145)

PILSS, KARL (1902-1979)
Sonatina
ob,gtr (7-8th degr., Gitarre-
Kammermusik, No.98) sc,pt
DOBLINGER GKM-98 f.s.   (5146)

PLAYFORD, JOHN (1623-1686)
Playford Tunes, 12
(Dewey; Dupre) S rec,gtr (2-3rd
degr.) sc SCHOTT 10765 f.s. (5147)

POSER, HANS (1917-1970)
Kleine Serenade
A rec,gtr (3-4th degr., Zeitschrift
Fur Spielmusik, No.279) sc MOECK
ZFS-274 f.s.   (5148)

PRAAG, HENRI C. VAN (1894-1968)
Complainte
(van der Staak) ob,gtr (4th degr.)
sc BROEKMANS 824 f.s.   (5149)

Duettino
(van der Staak) ob/fl,gtr (5th
degr.) sc BROEKMANS 826 f.s. (5150)

PRAGER, HEINRICH ALOYS (1783-1854)
Introduktion, Thema Und Variationen
*Op.21
(Nagel; Meunier) fl/vln,gtr (7th
degr.) sc,pt BREITKOPF-W 6697
f.s.   (5151)

PRIETO, CLAUDIO
Solo A Solo
fl,gtr ALPUERTO 1060 f.s.   (5152)

PROSPERI, CARLO (1921-   )
In Nocte
vln,gtr (7th degr.) sc ZERBONI 5344
f.s.   (5153)

PURCELL, DANIEL (ca. 1660-1717)
Sonata in F
(Brojer) A rec/vln/fl,gtr (6th
degr., Die Gitarre In Der
Kammermusik, No.26) sc HOHLER
GC-26 f.s.   (5154)

PURCELL, HENRY (1658 or 59-1695)
Suite
(Behrend) A rec,gtr (3rd degr.) sc
HEINRICH. N-1533 f.s.   (5155)

RATHGEBER, VALENTIN (1682-1750)
Leichte Stucke, 6
(Brojer) S rec/vln/ob/fl,gtr (2nd
degr., Die Gitarre In Der
Kammermusik, No.12) HOHLER GC-12
f.s.   (5156)

Nobilissima Musica, Von Der Edlen
Musik (from Augsburger
Tafelkonfekt) CC20U
(Zanoskar) S rec,gtr (3rd degr.)
sc,pt NOETZEL N-3110 f.s.   (5157)

REBAY, FERDINAND (1889–1953)
Leicht Spielbare Kleinigkeiten
*CC16L
(Hammerschmied) gtr/gtr,pno (2–3rd
degr.) sc,solo pt HEINRICH.
N–1528 f.s. for gtr (15) and gtr,
pno (1)   (5158)

REGT, HENDRIK DE (1950–   )
Music, Op. 21
fl,gtr (8–9th degr.) sc,pt DONEMUS
f.s.   (5159)

REICHARDT, JOHANN FRIEDRICH (1752–1814)
Sonata for Violin and Guitar in B
flat
(Schmidt) vln,gtr ZIMMER. ZM–2115
f.s.   (5160)

6 Stucke
(Schmidt) fl,gtr ZIMMER. 1959 f.s.
                            (5161)

REIN, WALTER (1893–1955)
Volkslieder Mit Variationen, 2
(Gerwig) rec,gtr (3–4th degr., Das
Spiel Der Lauteninstrumente,
Series II, Spielbuch 2) sc LIENAU
1376 f.s.   (5162)

REITER, ALBERT (1905–1970)
Sonatina
vln,gtr (7th degr., Gitarre–
Kammermusik, No.7) sc,pt
DOBLINGER GKM–7 f.s.   (5163)

REUSSNER, ESAIAS (1636–1679)
Musicalische Gesellschaftsergetzung
(Giesbert) fl/fl,gtr/pno (3rd degr.)
sc,pts PFAUEN 211 f.s.   (5164)

ROMBERG, BERNHARD (1865–1913)
Divertimento, Op. 46
vcl,gtr SIMROCK 3068 f.s.   (5165)

ROSSEAU, NORBERT (1907–1975)
Contemplatie *Op.2
perc, ampl gtr (7th degr.) sc CBDM
73–492 f.s.   (5166)

RUST, FRIEDRICH WILHELM (1739–1796)
Sonata in G
(Neemann) vln,gtr (7th degr.,
originally for vln, lute–f') sc
VIEWEG 1577 f.s.   (5167)

SAMMARTINI, GIUSEPPE
(ca. 1693–ca. 1770)
Sonata, Op. 3, No. 1, in E minor
(Giesbert) fl/vln/rec,gtr/pno (7th
degr., Urtext; transcr. for gtr
and for pno; for A rec: capotasto
in pos. III; for S rec: gtr
tuning 1 semitone lower) sc
PFAUEN 271 f.s. from SONATEN, 6,
OP. 3   (5168)

Sonata, Op. 3, No. 2, in G
(Giesbert) fl/vln/rec,gtr/pno (7th
degr., Urtext; transcr. for gtr
and for pno; for A rec: capotasto
in pos. III; for S rec: gtr
tuning 1 semitone lower) sc
PFAUEN 272 f.s. from SONATEN, 6,
OP. 3   (5169)

SANCHEZ, B.
Suite Vesperale
fl/ob,gtr (3–4th degr., Collection
L'Heure De La Guitare Classique)
sc,pts CHOUDENS 20.425 f.s.
                            (5170)

SAUX, GASTON
Serenade
A rec,hpsd/gtr (3rd degr., Plein
Jeu, No.138) sc,pts HEUGEL PJ–138
$.75   (5171)

SCHADLER, FRIEDRICH
Serenade Espagnole
(Schindler) vla/vln,gtr (4th degr.)
sc,pts VAMO EE–09 f.s.   (5172)

SCHAFER, RUDOLF (1891–1970)
Kleine Spiel– Und Ubungsstucke Fur
Den Anfang, 30 (composed with
Stetka, Franz)
1–3S rec,gtr (1st degr., contains
music for: 1rec,gtr (14); 2rec,
gtr (6); 3rec, gt (10);
spielmusik fur blockfloten und
gitarre [vol. ii]) sc DOBLINGER
04413 f.s.   (5173)

SCHAGEN, HENK VAN
Botje (Berend) Varierend
"Variations On A Dutch Nursery
Rhyme" treb inst,gtr (2nd degr.)
sc HARMONIA 1528 f.s.   (5174)

Kleine Ditirambe
A rec,gtr (3rd degr.) sc HARMONIA
1504 f.s.   (5175)

SCHALLER, ERWIN (1901–   )
Rhapsodie Und Hochzeitstanz Nach
Finnischen Volksweisen
vln,gtr BREITKOPF–W EB–6781 f.s.
                            (5176)

SCHEIDLER, CHRISTIAN GOTTLIEB
(1752–1815)
Sonata in D
(Scheit) vln,gtr/2gtr (5th degr.)
sc,pts UNIVER. 14439 f.s.   (5177)

SHERMAN, ELNA
Suite No. 1
fl/A rec,gtr/lute (6–7th degr.) sc,
pts COMP.FAC. f.s.   (5178)

SIEGL, OTTO (1896–1978)
Sonata
(Ragossnig) fl,gtr (7th degr.)
ZIMMER. ZM–1395 f.s.   (5179)

Sonatina in D minor
(Scheit) vln,gtr (6th degr.,
Gitarre–Kammermusik, No.2) sc
DOBLINGER GKM–2 f.s.   (5180)

SIMONIS, JEAN–MARIE (1931–   )
Nocturne, Op. 23
fl,gtr (7th degr.) sc CBDM f.s.
                            (5181)

SINGER, LAWRENCE (1940–   )
Musica A Due
ob,gtr (9th degr., 2 sc, Musica
Nova) ZERBONI 7019 $24.00   (5182)

SOR, FERNANDO (1778–1839)
Romance *Op. Posth.
(Scheit) vln/fl,gtr/2gtr (4–5th
degr.) UNIVER. 16685 f.s.   (5183)

Romanesca, La
(Nagel) vln,gtr SCHOTT VLB–48 f.s.
                            (5184)

Romanza, La
(Nagel) vln,gtr pts SCHOTT VLB–8
f.s.   (5185)

SOSINSKI, KAZIMIERZ
Studium Gry Akordowej Na Gitarze,
Technika Chwytow Barre, Akordy I
Ich Symbole
"Study Of Chords For Guitar, The,
The Technique Of Barre, Chords
And Their Symbols" [Polish] gtr
(xvi + 146p., ill; 1960; Intro:
Basic elements of music theory
(chords); 6 Tables: diag of the
fingerboard; 1 Table: dance–
rhythms; contains 243 Numbers, in
various keys: Chords and chord
inversions with arpeggio
formulae, Scales and scale
exercises; contains 65 studies
by: Giuliani (13), Carulli (10),
Aguado (4), Carcassi (31),
Legnani, Sor, Albert (5); 12
Duets by: Ritter, Mezzacapo,
Jarnefelt, Fibich, Boccherini,
Curtis, Nowicki, Nowikow, Zeller,
Schumann, Joteyko, Lehar for
mand, gtr (4), vln or mand, gtr
(6), vln, gtr (2); arr + 1 orig
pce (Ritter); 9 modern dances
(tango, bolero, fox–polka, samba)
by various composers for treb
inst (accord, vln, or mand), gtr;
notation of gtr pt in plectrum–
style (symbols + rhythms)) quarto
POLSKIE 6392 f.s.))   (5186)

SPERONTES (JOHANN SIGISMUND SCHOLZE)
(1705–1750)
Singende Muse An Der Pleisse *CC10U
(Tucholski) gtr,vla da gamba/vcl,
solo voice or mel inst APOLLO
2316 f.s.   (5187)

SPRONGL, NORBERT (1892–1983)
Suite
fl,gtr ESCHIG f.s.   (5188)

STINGL, ANTON (1908–   )
Stucke, Op. 34
A rec/fl,gtr (8th degr.) sc ZIMMER.
ZM–1710 f.s.
contains: Canzone; Capriccio;
Kleiner Walzer; Passacaglia;
Tanzerisches Spiel   (5189)

SULLIVAN, [SIR] ARTHUR SEYMOUR
(1842–1900)
Tunes From Gilbert And Sullivan, 10
(Duarte) S rec,gtr/pno (5–6th
degr.) sc,pts NOVELLO $1.55
                            (5190)

TAKACS, JENO (1902–   )
Dialoge *Op.77
vln,gtr (Gitarre–Kammermusik, No.
75) DOBLINGER GKM–75 f.s.   (5191)

TELEMANN, GEORG PHILIPP (1681–1767)
Air Und Bourree
(Behrend) rec,gtr (single line
playing/2–3rd degr.) sc NOETZEL
N–3175 f.s.   (5192)

TELEMANN, GEORG PHILIPP (cont'd.)

Partita in G (from Die Kleine
Kammermusik)
(Kammerling) vln/S rec/fl/ob,gtr
(4–5th degr., Gitarre–
Kammermusik, No.54) sc,pts
DOBLINGER GKM–54 f.s.   (5193)
"Partita No. 2 In G" (Rentmeister)
vln/S rec/fl/ob,gtr (4–5th degr.)
sc,pts HEINRICH. PEG–6101 f.s.
                            (5194)

Partita No. 5 in E minor
(Kammerling) vln/rec/ob,gtr (7th
degr., Gitarre–Kammermusik,
No.96) sc,pts DOBLINGER GKM–96
f.s.   (5195)

Sonata in A minor
(Behrend) fl,gtr ZIMMER. ZM–1892
f.s.   (5196)

Sonata in A minor, MIN 50
(Azpiazu) vla,gtr (7th degr., 2 sc)
ZIMMER. ZM–1362 f.s.   (5197)

Sonata in C (from Der Getreue
Musikmeister)
(Behrend) rec,gtr (6th degr.)
ZIMMER. ZM–1342 f.s.   (5198)

Sonata in F (from Der Getreue
Musikmeister)
(Behrend) A rec,gtr (7th degr.) sc
ZIMMER. ZM–1343 f.s.   (5199)
(Wensiecki) A rec,gtr (7th degr.)
sc,pts HOFMEISTER–W f.s.   (5200)

Sonaten, 2
(Behrend) A rec,gtr (7th degr.) sc,
pts SIKORSKI 356 $8.00   (5201)

TERZAKIS, DIMITRI (1938–   )
Chroniko
fl,elec gtr UNIVER. 15645 f.s.
                            (5202)

TRUHLAR, JAN (1928–   )
Sonatina Semplice *Op.18
fl,gtr (5th degr.) sc,pts ZIMMER.
ZM–1793 f.s.   (5203)

VALERIUS, ADRIANUS (1575–1625)
Gedenckklanken–ABC *CC8U
(van Schagen) treb inst,gtr (2nd
degr.) sc HARMONIA 1500 f.s.
                            (5204)

VERACINI, FRANCESCO MARIA (1690–1768)
Largo (from Sonata, Op. 2, No. 6)
(Scheit) vln/fl,gtr (7th degr., 2
sc; Gitarre–Kammermusik, No.110)
DOBLINGER GKM–110 f.s.   (5205)

Sonata No. 3
(Schaller) S rec,gtr BREITKOPF–W
EB–6783 f.s.   (5206)

VILLA–LOBOS, HEITOR (1887–1959)
Distribution De Fleurs
fl,gtr ESCHIG f.s.   (5207)

VISEE, ROBERT DE (ca. 1650–ca. 1775)
Suite in C minor
(Scheit) treb inst/fl/rec/vln,gtr
(5th degr., orig for treb inst
and cont) sc,pts UNIVER. 14453
$3.25   (5208)

VIVALDI, ANTONIO (1678–1741)
Concerto in D, MIN 328
(Fleres) hpsd/pno,gtr (7th degr.)
sc,pt PREISSLER 7045 f.s.   (5209)

Sonata in D minor
(Brojer) vln,gtr (6th degr.,
Gitarre–Kammermusik, No.45) sc,
pts DOBLINGER GKM–45 f.s.   (5210)

Sonata in G minor
(Brojer) vln,gtr (7th degr.,
Gitarre–Kammermusik, No.20) sc,
pts DOBLINGER GKM–20 f.s.   (5211)

Sonata, Op. 13a, No. 16, in G minor
(Libbert) S rec,gtr (5th degr., Das
Gitarrenwerk, Series A No. 16)
sc,pt PREISSLER A 16 f.s.   (5212)

VOLKSLIEDER UND –TANZE AUS ALLER WELT,
VOL. 1 *CC12U
(Henze) treb inst/mand/vln/fl,gtr
(3rd degr.) ZIMMER. ZM–1843 f.s.
from Germany (2), Sweden (1),
England (2) Scotland (2), France
(3), Spain (2)   (5213)

VOLKSLIEDER UND –TANZE AUS ALLER WELT,
VOL. 2 *CC11U
(Henze) treb inst/mand/vln/fl,gtr
(3rd degr.) ZIMMER. ZM–1844 f.s.
from Italy (2), Greece (2), Hungary
(1), Bulgaria (1), Poland (2),
China (2), Japan (1)   (5214)

VOLKSLIEDER UND –TANZE AUS ALLER WELT,
VOL. 3 *CC12U
(Henze) treb inst/mand/vln/fl,gtr

(3rd degr.) ZIMMER. ZM-1845 f.s.
from Haiti (1), Russia (5), Finland
(2), U.S.A. (2), Mexico (2)   (5215)

VRIES ROBBE, WILLEM DE (1902–
Danse-Arioso-Rondeau
fl,gtr (6th degr.) sc,pts DONEMUS
f.s.   (5216)

Pavane-Sarabande-Gigue
fl,gtr (7–8th degr.) sc,pts DONEMUS
f.s.   (5217)

WAGENSEIL, GEORG CHRISTOPH (1715–1777)
Divertimento
(Kammerling) pno,gtr (4th degr.,
Gitarre-Kammermusik, No.53) sc,
pts DOBLINGER GKM-53 f.s.   (5218)

WANHAL, JOHANN BAPTIST (JAN KRTITEL)
(1739–1813)
6 Variationen Uber Das Thema "Nel Cor
Piu Non Mi Sento" *Op.42
(Nagel) fl/vln,gtr (4th degr.), Il
Flauto Traverso, No. 105) pts
SCHOTT FTR-105 f.s.   (5219)

WEBER, CARL MARIA VON (1786–1826)
Divertimento, Op. 38
(Scheit) pno,gtr (5th degr.) sc,pts
UNIVER. 14441 $4.25   (5220)

WELFFENS, P.
Tafelmuziek
(van Puijenbroeck) vcl,gtr (7th
degr., 2 sc) MAURER f.s.   (5221)

WIDMANN, ERASMUS (1572–1634)
Musicalischer Tugendspiegel
(Giesbert) fl,gtr/pno (3rd degr.)
sc PFAUEN 26 f.s.   (5222)

WIJDEVELD, WOLFGANG (1910–   )
Snarenspel *Op.66
pno,gtr (8th degr.) sc,pts DONEMUS
f.s.   (5223)

WISSMER, PIERRE (1915–   )
Sonatina
fl,gtr (8th degr.) ESCHIG f.s.
                              (5224)

ZAGWIJN, HENRI (1878–1954)
Sarabande E Fandango
hpsd/pno,gtr (8–9th degr., Fandango
is arr of Fandango for solo gtr)
sc DONEMUS f.s.   (5225)

ZBINDEN, JULIEN-FRANCOIS (1917–   )
Miniatures, 4 *Op.14
(Leeb) fl,opt gtr (6th degr.) sc
GERIG ST-355 f.s.   (5226)

ZEHM, FRIEDRICH (1923–   )
Serenade
(Stingl) fl,gtr SCHOTT GA-443 f.s.
                              (5227)

ZOTTI, GIOVANNI DE
Sonata in A minor
(Brojer) vln,gtr (5–6th degr., Die
Gitarre In Der Kammermusik,
No.15) sc,pts HOHLER GC-15 f.s.
                              (5228)

I/IIB1-Coll Duet Collections for Guitar and Another Instrument

ALTE MEISTER UM 1600 *CC9U
(Brojer) S rec/vln/fl,gtr (2nd
degr.) HOHLER GC-9 f.s. Die Gitarre
In Der Kammermusik, No.9   (5229)

ALTE MEISTER UM 1700 *CC9U
(Brojer) S rec/vln/ob/fl,gtr (2nd
degr.) HOHLER GC-10 f.s. Die
Gitarre In Der Kammermusik, No.10
                              (5230)

ALTE MINNELIEDER *CC11L
(Gerwig) [Ger] gtr (2–3rd degr.) sc,
pts NAGELS EN-1109 f.s. Nagels
Laute- und Gitarre-Archiv; contains
works by: Anon. (2), Fabricius (1),
Praetorius (1), Neusiedler (1),
Isaac (1), Lechner (1), Hassler
(1), Schaffer (1), Senfl (1), Ott
(1), for gtr (1), treb inst, gtr
(1), solo voice, treb inst, gtr,
opt bass inst (9)   (5231)

ALTE SPIELMUSIK
(Kaestner; Zanoskar) S rec/T rec/treb
inst,gtr (2–3rd degr.) sc,pts
SCHOTT 4457 f.s. 24 pcs; contains
works by: Krieger (2), Anon. (9),
Kuhnau (1), Telemann (1), Purcell
(2), Daquin (1), Fischer (2),
Attaignant (1), Handel (3), L.

Mozart (1)
contains: Bach, Johann Sebastian,
Suite for Keyboard Instrument,
BWV 822, in G minor, Minuet I (S
rec/A rec,gtr)   (5232)

ALTE TANZSTUCKE (16.–18. JAHRHUNDERT),
VOL. I
(Giesbert) S rec/T rec/vln,gtr (3rd
degr., contains works by: Susato
(6), Moderne (2), Playford (7),
Reusner (3), Hotteterre (2)) sc
SCHOTT 2659 f.s.   (5233)

ALTE TANZSTUCKE (16.–18. JAHRHUNDERT),
VOL. II *CC20U
(Giesbert) A rec/vln,gtr (3rd degr.)
sc SCHOTT 2660 f.s. contains works
by: Susato (6), Playford (5),
Reusner (5), Hotteterre (4), (5234)

ALTE UND NEUE MUSIK ZUM SINGEN UND
SPIELEN AUF BLOCKFLOTEN, GEIGEN UND
LAUTENINSTRUMENTE *folk song
(Gerwig) [Ger] (1–3rd degr.) sc
LIENAU 1375 f.s. Das Spiel Der
Lauteninstrumente, Series II,
Spielbuch 1; contains works by:
Sperontes (4), L. Mozart (3),
Rathgeber (1), Rein (5), Rhau (2),
Langenau (1), Chemin-Petit (1): for
gtr (1), 2gtr (3), 3gtr (1), rec,
gtr (8), 2rec, gtr (2), solo voice,
gtr (3), solo voice, rec, gtr (1),
solo voice, rec, 2gtr (1), rec, vln
or vla, gtr (1); arr. + orig. pcs.;
single line playing; gtr pt partly
in bass clef
contains: Bach, Johann Sebastian,
English Suite No. 6, BWV 811, In
D Minor, Gavottes I–II (gtr,1–2A
rec); Bach, Johann Sebastian,
Minuet, BWV Anh. 118, in B flat
(from Anna Magdalena Bach
Notenbuchlein (1725), No.9) (gtr,
S rec) (C maj,single line
playing, gtr pt in bass clef)(5235)

ALTFRANZOSISCHE MEISTER *CC4U
(Theunen-Seidl; Muller) vln,gtr (4th
degr.) HOHLER GH-3 f.s. Die Gitarre
In Der Hausmusik, No.3; contains
works by: Dandrieu (1), Lalande
(2), Anon. (1)   (5236)

AUS ALT ENGLAND *CC20U
(Kaestner; Zanoskar) A rec,gtr (3–4th
degr.) sc,pt SCHOTT 4456 f.s.
contains works by: H. Purcell (7),
D. Purcell (1), Anon. (5), Corbett
(1), Boyce (1), Valentino (1),
Festing (1), Carey (1), Babell (1),
Lenton (1)   (5237)

AUS DEM BALTISCHEN LAUTENBUCH 1740
*CC17L
(Pudelko) treb inst,1–2gtr/gtr solo
(2–3rd degr.) sc NAGELS EN-1107
f.s. notation: treb clef; Nagels
Laute- Und Gitarre-Archiv; contains
works by: Anon. (16), Batchelar (1)
                              (5238)

BAROCKE SPIELMUSIK *17–18th cent
(Zanoskar) S rec,gtr SCHOTT 4524 f.s.
                              (5239)

BAROQUE PIECES, VOL. V
(Tada) rec,gtr (3–4th degr.) sc,pt
ONGAKU f.s. 33 pcs; vol. I–IV, for
kbd, rec; contains works by: C.P.E.
Bach (2), Corelli (2), Fischer (1),
Handel (5), Krieger (1), Kuhnau
(1), Mattheson (1), Marais (1),
Purcell (3), Rameau (3), Scarlatti
(1), Telemann (2) for S rec
contains: Bach, Johann Sebastian,
Aria, BWV 988 (G maj); Bach,
Johann Sebastian, Aria Di
Giovanni, "Willst Du Dein Herz
Mir Schenken", BWV 518; Bach,
Johann Sebastian, Auf, Auf, Die
Rechte Zeit Ist Hier, BWV 440;
Bach, Johann Sebastian, Ihr
Gestirn', Ihr Hohen Lufte, BWV
476; Bach, Johann Sebastian,
March, BWV 127, in E flat minor;
Bach, Johann Sebastian, Minuet,
BWV Anh. 120, in A minor (from
Anna Magdalena Bach Notenbuchlein
(1725), No.14); Bach, Johann
Sebastian, Minuet, BWV Anh. 132,
in D minor; Bach, Johann
Sebastian, Polonaise, BWV Anh.
119, in G minor (from Anna
Magdalena Bach Notenbuchlein
(1725), No.10); Bach, Johann
Sebastian, So Oft Ich Meine
Tobackspfeife, BWV 515a (from
Anna Magdalena Bach Notenbuchlein
(1725), No.20b) (G min)   (5240)

BAROQUE PIECES, VOL. VI
(Tada) A rec,gtr (3–4th degr.) sc,pt
ONGAKU f.s. vol. I–IV, for kbd,
rec; 24 pcs; contains works by:
C.P.E. Bach (3), Couperin (4),
Handel (7), Telemann (4 For A Rec)

contains: Bach, Johann Sebastian,
Dir, Dir, Jehova, Will Ich
Singen, BWV 299 (from Anna
Magdalena Bach Notenbuchlein
(1725), No.39b) (D maj); Bach,
Johann Sebastian, French Suite
No. 2, BWV 813, In C Minor,
Courante (A min); Bach, Johann
Sebastian, Minuet, BWV 841, in G
(from Wilhelm Friedemann Bach
Notenbuchlein, No.11) (C maj);
Bach, Johann Sebastian, Minuet,
BWV Anh. 115, in G minor (from
Anna Magdalena Bach Notenbuchlein
(1725), No.5) (A min); Bach,
Johann Sebastian, Minuet, BWV
Anh. 116, in G (from Anna
Magdalena Bach Notenbuchlein
(1725), No.7) (C maj); Bach,
Johann Sebastian, Schaff's Mit
Mir, Gott, BWV 514 (from Anna
Magdalena Bach Notenbuchlein
(1725), No.35) (G maj)   (5241)

BERUHMTE STUCKE, 3 *CC3U
(Brojer) vln/fl,gtr HOHLER GH-10 f.s.
Die Gitarre In Der Hausmusik,
No.10; contains works by:
Beethoven, Gossec, Boccherini
                              (5242)

C-MUSIK DER ENGLISCHEN KLASSIK *CCU
(Schmidt) mel inst,gtr ZIMMER. 2067
f.s. contains works by: Campbell;
Carr; Claget; Cooke and Cope (5243)

DANCES FROM SHAKESPEARE'S TIME *CC15U
(Connor) 1–2S rec,gtr/S rec,A rec,gtr
(3–4th degr.) sc CHESTER 286 f.s.
contains works by: Anon. (8),
Morley (2), Farnaby (1), Byrd (3),
Johnson (1) for: S rec, gtr (8);
for 2S rec, gtr (3); for S rec, A
rec, gtr (4)   (5244)

DANCES OF BYGONE TIMES, 6
(Duarte) A rec,gtr (2–3rd degr.) sc
BROEKMANS 945 f.s.
contains: Anonymous, Bransle Gay;
Anonymous, Courante, MIN 223;
Anonymous, Pavana In Passo E
Mezzo; Phalese, Pierre, Daunce;
Phalese, Pierre, Schiarazula
Marazula; Praetorius, Michael,
Cara Cossa Del Berdolin, La
                              (5245)

DUOS POUR FLUTE A BEC ET GUITARE
*CC32L
(Sanvoisin; Robert) S rec,A rec/T
rec,gtr (2–4th degr.) sc HEUGEL
CPJ-4 $3.75 contains works by:
Phalese (4), Susato (2), Attaignant
(2), Sermissy (1), Anon. (7),
Encina (2), Le Roy (1), Henry VIII
(1), Bull (1), Byrd (2), Robinson
(1), Dowland (1), Adam (1), Vivaldi
(1), Hotteterre (1), Rebel (1), Les
Cahiers De Plein Jeu, No.4   (5246)

EARLY RENAISSANCE DANCES, 6
(Duarte) S rec,gtr (2nd degr.) sc
BROEKMANS 946 f.s.
contains: Anonymous, Branle De La
Suitte Du Contrait Legier;
Phalese, Pierre, Ballo Anglese;
Phalese, Pierre, Cornetto;
Phalese, Pierre, Courante, MIN
226; Praetorius, Michael, Branle
Double De Poictu; Praetorius,
Michael, Passomezo La Doulce
                              (5247)

EUROPAISCHE VOLKSTANZE *CC23U
(Zanoskar) S rec,gtr (2–3rd degr.)
sc,pts SCHOTT 4504 f.s.   (5248)

FANTASIA [COLLECTION]
S rec,gtr TEESELING VT-226 f.s.
contains: Gall, Louis Ignatius,
Adagio; Gall, Louis Ignatius,
Cotillon; Gall, Louis Ignatius,
Rondo; Langenberg, Jan van den,
Pavan; Swart, Cees, Fantasy
                              (5249)

FLOTE SING, KLAMPFE KLING
(Zschiesche) rec,gtr (3rd degr.) sc
VOGGEN f.s. 50 folksongs from 11
countries; rec pt provided with
orig words   (5250)

FOLKLORE, VOL. 1 *CC13U
(Buhe) S rec,gtr (3–4th degr.) sc
HEINRICH. N-1292 f.s.   (5251)

FOLKLORE, VOL. 2 *CC21U
(Buhe) S rec,gtr (3–4th degr.) sc
HEINRICH. N-1293 f.s.   (5252)

FOLKSONGS *CC9U
(Duarte) A rec,gtr (3–4th degr.) sc
NOVELLO 19264 $2.55   (5253)

FROHLICHE TANZE AUS DEM 18. UND 19.
JAHRHUNDERT
(Zanoskar) S rec/treb inst,gtr (3rd
degr.) SIKORSKI 513 $3.75   (5254)

FROM THE BRITISH ISLES *CC8U
 (Maxwell) A rec,gtr (3-4th degr.) sc
 SCHOTT 10811 f.s.   (5255)

KAMERALNA MUZYKA GITAROWA *CC9L
 (Powrozniak) vln/fl/vcl/pno,gtr (3-
 4th degr.) sc,pt POLSKIE 1417 f.s.
 Grajmy na gitarze, vol. VIII;
 contains works by: Paganini (2),
 Carulli, Diabelli (3), Kummer, de
 Call, Weber, for vln, gtr (4); fl,
 gtr (1); vcl, gtr (1); pno, gtr (3)
                                      (5256)

KLEINE TANZE UND MARSCHE VON HAYDN BIS
 STRAUSS *CC13L
 (Heyden) S rec,gtr (1-2nd degr.) sc
 NAGELS EN-554 f.s. contains works
 by: M. Haydn (1), J. Haydn (2),
 Mozart (5), Beethoven (2), Lanner
 (1), Strauss (2)   (5257)

LAUTENSPIELER DES XVI. JAHRHUNDERTS
 (LIUTISTI DEL CINQUECENTO)
 *CC124UL
 (Chilesotti, Oscar) gtr (single
 staff/8th degr.) quarto oblong
 FORNI f.s. repr of 1st ed., publ
 Ricordi-Breitkopf & Hartel (1891);
 "Bibliotheca Musica Bononiensis",
 Sezione IV, No. 31; includes works
 by: Newsidler, Anon., Ballet,
 Gintzler, Matelart, Gorzanis, da
 Milano, Galilei, Barbetta, Caroso,
 Terzi, Molinaro, dalla Gostena,
 Negri, Besard, Mersenne,
 Gianoncelli -all for 1 gtr;
 Matelart, Galilei, Besard -for 2
 gtr; Caroso, Negri -for dsc inst
 and gtr; Fallamero, Besard -for vce
 and gtr; Terzi -for 3 gtr; Besard -
 for dsc inst and 3 gtr   (5258)

MAGYAR ZENE GITARRA A XIX. SZADAD ELSO
 FELEBOL
 "Ungarische Musik Fur Gitarre Aus Der
 Ersten Halfte Des 19. Jahrhunderts"
 (Brodszky) [Hung] gtr (2-4th degr.,
 Afterword in Hung, Ger, Eng; 59 arr
 + orig pcs; contains works by:
 Jager (1), Horecki (5), Anon. (2),
 Pfeifer (6), Lavotta (3), Sarkozy
 (1), Svastics (2), Fay (2),
 Rozsavolgyi (1), Wilt (4), Padowetz
 (1), Mertz (12), Ruzitska (1),
 Kossovits (2), Folksongs (16), for
 gtr solo; 2 pcs. by Anon. for fl,
 gtr (1) and solo voice, gtr (1)) sc
 EMB Z-2985 f.s.   (5259)
 "Ungarische Musik Fur Gitarre Aus Der
 Ersten Halfte Des 19. Jahrhunderts"
 (Brodszky) [Hung] gtr (2-4th degr.,
 Afterword in Hung, Ger, Eng; 59 arr
 + orig pcs; contains works by:
 Jager (1), Horecki (5), Anon. (2),
 Pfeifer (6), Lavotta (3), Sarkozy
 (1), Svastics (2), Fay (2),
 Rozsavolgyi (1), Wilt (4), Padowetz
 (1), Mertz (12), Ruzitska (1),
 Kossovits (2), Folksongs (16), for
 gtr solo; 2 pcs. by Anon. for fl,
 gtr (1) and solo voice, gtr (1)) sc
 SCHOTT 5839 f.s.   (5260)

MELODIES POPULAIRES POLONAISES
 (Klapil) 1-2S rec,gtr LEDUC f.s.
                                      (5261)

MUSIK AUS ITALIEN *CCU
 (Schmidt) mel inst,gtr ZIMMER.
 ZM-2066 f.s. contains works by:
 Barsanti; Bertoni; Besseghi;
 Bigaglia; Boni and Brandi   (5262)

MUZIEKBIJLAGE, NO. 53
 solo voice and gtr; treb inst and
 gtr; 2-3 solo voices (4th degr.) sc
 VER.HUIS. f.s. arr. + orig. pcs.;
 for solo voice, gtr (2), for treb
 inst, gtr (2), for 2 and 3 solo
 voices (2)
 contains: Ik Zie De Morgen Sterre;
 Zing En Blyf Tevree; Niessen,
 Hans-Lutz, Boer Had Maar Enen
 Schoen, De; Niessen, Hans-Lutz,
 Canon; Niessen, Hans-Lutz, Neem
 Het Niet Zo Precies   (5263)

NEUES SPIELBUCHLEIN *CC17L
 (Ochs) treb inst,gtr (3rd degr.) sc
 HOFMEISTER V-1330 f.s. contains
 works by: Boyce (1), W.A. Mozart
 (10), Beethoven (1); Schubert (5)
                                      (5264)

NOUVEAUX DUOS, 32 [SIC] PIECES...
 (Sanvoisin) rec,gtr (3-5th degr.) sc
 HEUGEL CPJ-19 $4.25 34 pcs
 (numbered 1-33); contains works by:
 Dandrieu (9), Attaignant (3), F.
 Couperin (2), Gardane (4), Encina
 (1), Palero (2), Morales (1), Ortiz
 (2), Anon. (5), Buxtehude (5), Bull
 (1), Farnaby (1), Munday (1),
 Dowland (1); Les Cahiers De Plein
 Jeu, No.19
 contains: Dandrieu, Jean Francois,
 Noels, 5   (5265)

PIECES FROM THE MULLINER BOOK, 10
 *CC10L
 (Duarte) A rec,gtr (3rd degr.) sc
 NOVELLO 19504 $2.75 contains works
 by: Tallis (1), Newman (2), Redford
 (1), Anon. (5), Edwards (1)   (5266)

REGI ZENE
 "Early Music" (Bantai; Kovacs; Nagy)
 fl/rec,gtr (3-4th degr., 13 pcs;
 contains works by: Milan (1), M.
 Neusiedler (2), Moy (1), Anon. (3),
 Fuhrmann (1), Dowland (3), Cutting
 (1), Bengraf (1)) sc EMB Z-7227
 f.s.   (5267)

SIMPLE FOLK
 (Duarte) A rec,gtr (1-2nd degr., easy
 settings of 12 Eng folk songs) sc
 NOVELLO 19629 $2.75   (5268)

SINTERKLAAS- EN KERSTLIEDJES
 (van der Staak) opt solo voice,S rec,
 gtr (notation: 2 treb staffs; rec
 pt is solo voice pt; 7 Holy
 Nicholas songs; 5 Christmas carols)
 sc BROEKMANS 832 f.s.   (5269)

SIX PIECES FROM THE TIME OF ELIZABETH
 (Carlin) rec,lute/gtr (4-6th degr.)
 MUS.SAC.PRO. LM-201 $3.00 contains
 works by: Richard; Munday; Giles
 Farnaby (3) and Byrd; notation for
 lute-gtr: Fr tablature + treb clef
 contains: Gigue, MIN 420; Munday's
 Joy; Nobody's Gigge; Old
 Spagnoletta; Quodlings Delight;
 Tower Hill   (5270)

SPEELMATERIAAL VOOR DE BLOKFLUIT, VOL.
 III *CC16L
 (Vellekoop) S rec,gtr (3rd degr.) sc
 XYZ f.s. contains works by: Phalese
 (4), Hotteterre (3), Schmikerer
 (1), Fux (1), de la Vigne (4),
 Naudot (2), Kress (1)   (5271)

SPIELBUCHLEIN *CC22L
 (Ochs) treb inst,gtr (3rd degr.) sc
 HOFMEISTER V-1226 f.s. contains
 works by: L. Mozart (7), Telemann
 (8), Beretgen (1), Dreyszler (1),
 Sperontes (1), Kirchoff (1), Hasse
 (1), Grafe (1), Tischer (1) (5272)

SPIELMANN AUS FLANDERN, DER
 "Old Melodies From The Netherlands
 (16th-18th Cent.), 38" (Degen;
 Schumann) 2-4treb inst (3rd degr.,
 38 pcs; nos. 3, 8, 26, 30, for 2 S
 rec, gtr (1) and S rec, gtr (3)) sc
 SCHOTT 2653 f.s.   (5273)

SPIELMUSIK FUR MELODIEINSTRUMENTE UND
 GITARRE, 16-19TH CENTURY *CC27L,
 folk song
 (Henze) (3-8th degr.) sc,pts
 HOFMEISTER T-4015 $11.25 27 arr +
 orig pcs (numbered 1-10); Das
 Gitarrespiel, Vol. XV; contains
 works by: Neusiedler (1), LeRoy
 (1), Purcell (3), F. Couperin (1),
 Handel (6), Haydn (1), W.A. Mozart
 (7), Giuliani (1), Kummer (1), for
 A rec, gtr (5), for S rec, gtr (1),
 for 2A rec, gtr (6), for vln, vcl,
 gtr (1), for 2vln, gtr (7), for
 vln, gtr (1), for fl, gtr (1), for
 S rec, A rec, gtr (5)   (5274)

SPIELMUSIK FUR MELODIEINSTRUMENTE UND
 GITARRE, 20TH CENTURY *CC10L
 (Henze) (4-7th degr.) sc,pts
 HOFMEISTER T 4017 $11.25 Das
 Gitarrespiel, Vol. XVa; contains
 works by: Gohle, Ambrosius, Pabel,
 Stingl, Naumilkat, Schuppel,
 Niessen, Hlouschek, Konig, Behrend;
 for treb inst, gtr (1), for 2 treb
 inst, gtr (1), for vln, gtr (2),
 for fl, gtr (1), for S rec, A rec,
 gtr (2), for A rec, gtr (2), for 2A
 rec, gtr (1)   (5275)

SPIELSTUCKE FUR BLOCKFLOTE UND GITARRE,
 AUS DEM 17. UND 18. JAHRHUNDERT
 *CC19L
 (Rentmeister) S rec/T rec,gtr (1-2nd
 degr.) sc SCHOTT 5132 f.s. 3rd
 degr: alternative more difficult
 gtr pt; contains works by: Daquin
 (1), Fischer (3), Haydn (7), Lully
 (1), Mattheson (1), W.A. Mozart
 (4), Sperontes (1), L. Mozart (1)
                                      (5276)

SPIELSTUCKE FUR BLOCKFLOTE UND GITARRE,
 VOL. 1 *CCU,folk song,Austrian/
 Eng/Fr/Ir/It/Russ/US
 (Koinuma) 1-4rec,gtr (3-4th degr.)
 UNIVER. 17128 f.s. contains works
 by: Bach; Scarlatti; Holborne;
 Gervaise and Haydn   (5277)

SPIELSTUCKE FUR BLOCKFLOTE UND GITARRE,
 VOL. 2 *CCU,Renaissance/Baroque
 (Koinuma) 1-3rec,gtr (3-4th degr.)

UNIVER. 17129 f.s.   (5278)

SUIT I SVENSK FOLKTON NR. 2
 (Ahslund) fl,gtr (2-3rd degr.) sc
 REUTER f.s.
 contains: Skanklat Till Spelman;
 Ahslund, E.A., Prelude; Eriksson,
 E.G., Ska Ja Val Ga Tastman
 Toretan; Eriksson, E.K., Gammal
 Jamstpolska; Sundberg, Polska i-
 De; Sundberg, Vaggvisa   (5279)

TAKE YOUR PARTNERS; 6 ENGLISH COUNTRY
 DANCES
 (Duarte) S rec,gtr (1-2nd degr.) sc
 NOVELLO 20053 $3.30
 contains: Geud Man Of Ballangigh,
 The; Goddesses; Newcastle;
 Nonesuch; Picking Up Sticks;
 Rufty Tufty   (5280)

TUNES FROM THE CECIL SHARP COLLECTION,
 7
 (Roe; Duarte) 1-2rec,gtr (2-4th
 degr., 3 pts + alternative more
 difficult gtr pt) sc,pts NOVELLO
 19498 $3.30   (5281)

VOLKSLIEDER UND -TANZE AUS ALLER WELT,
 VOL. 1 *CC12U
 (Henze) treb inst/mand/vln/fl,gtr
 (3rd degr.) ZIMMER. ZM-1843 f.s.
 from Germany (2), Sweden (1),
 England (2), Scotland (2), France
 (3), Spain (2)   (5282)

VOLKSLIEDER UND -TANZE AUS ALLER WELT,
 VOL. 2 *CC11U
 (Henze) treb inst/mand/vln/fl,gtr
 (3rd degr.) ZIMMER. ZM-1844 f.s.
 from Italy (2), Greece (2), Hungary
 (1), Bulgaria (1), Poland (2),
 China (2), Japan (1)   (5283)

VOLKSLIEDER UND -TANZE AUS ALLER WELT,
 VOL. 3 *CC12U
 (Henze) treb inst/mand/vln/fl,gtr
 (3rd degr.) ZIMMER. ZM-1845 f.s.
 from Haiti (1), Russia (5), Finland
 (2), U.S.A. (2), Mexico (2) (5284)

VON HANDEL BIS HAYDN *CC29L
 (Monkemeyer) T rec/S rec,gtr (2-4th
 degr.) sc TONGER 1078 f.s. contains
 works by: Handel (6), Kusser (2),
 Fux (2), Fux (2), Telemann (3),
 Graupner (4), Fasch (6), Stamitz
 (3), Haydn (3)   (5285)

WIR SINGEN UND SPIELEN, VOL. 1 *CCU
 (Wolki) solo voice,gtr/vln/mel inst,
 gtr APOLLO 2313 f.s.   (5286)

WIR SINGEN UND SPIELEN, VOL. 2 *CCU
 (Wolki) solo voice,gtr/mel inst,gtr
 APOLLO 2314 f.s.   (5287)

WIR SPIELEN GITARRE, VOL. 1 *CC31U
 1-2gtr,opt treb inst (1-3rd degr.) sc
 PREISSLER JP-7018I f.s. suppl. to
 W. Munch and H. Bausewein, Wir
 Lernen Gitarre Spielen; arr. +
 orig. pcs.; single line playing;
 contains 5 pcs. for 1 gtr (nos. 1-
 4, 7, 24), 26 pcs. for 2 gtr, or
 treb inst, gtr by Anonymous
 composers and folksongs   (5288)

WIR SPIELEN GITARRE, VOL. 2 *CC50U,
 folk song
 1-2gtr/opt treb inst (1-3rd degr.) sc
 PREISSLER JP-7018-II f.s. suppl. to
 W. Munch and H. Bausewein, Wir
 Lernen Gitarre Spielen; arr. +
 orig. pcs.; single line playing;
 contains 1 pce. for 1 gtr (no. 5),
 24 pcs. for 2 gtr or treb inst,
 gtr, by Bausewein (5), Foster (1),
 Brahms (1), Capua (1), Fliess (1)
                                      (5289)

YA SE VAN LOS PASTORES
 (Zschiersch) rec,gtr (3rd degr., 50
 folksongs from 11 countries; rec pt
 provided with orig words) sc
 MOSELER f.s. from FLOTE SING,
 KLAMPFE KLING   (5290)

I/IIB2 Trios for Guitar and Other Instruments

AIRS POPULAIRES DE TCHECOSLOVAQUI
 (Klapil) 1-2S rec,gtr LEDUC f.s.
                                        (5291)

ANDRIESSEN, JURRIAAN (1925-   )
 Trio No. 5
   "Sonata Da Camera" fl,vla,gtr (7th
   degr.) sc DONEMUS f.s.   (5292)

ANONYMOUS
 Trio in F, MIN 409
   (Schmidt) vln,vcl,gtr ZIMMER. 1953
   f.s.   (5293)

APOSTEL, HANS ERICH (1901-1972)
 Kleines Kammerkonzert *Op.38
   fl,vla,gtr (7-8th degr.), Gitarre-
   Kammermusik, No.62) DOBLINGER
   f.s. sc GKM-62, study sc 131
                                 (5294)

 Study, Op. 29
   (Scheit) fl,vla,gtr (5-6th degr.,
   Gitarre-Kammermusik, No.109) sc,
   pts DOBLINGER GKM-109 f.s. (5295)

AUBANEL, GEORGES
 Divertissements, 7, Sur Des Airs
   Populaires Anciens Et Modernes
   2S rec/2vln/2ob,gtr (3rd degr.) sc
   OUVRIERS EO-661 f.s.   (5296)

BADINGS, HENK (1907-1987)
 Trio No. 9
   fl,vla,gtr (7-8th degr.) sc DONEMUS
   f.s.   (5297)

BARTOK, BELA (1881-1945)
 Aus Ungarn Und Der Slowakei, Lieder
   Und Tanze, Vol. II *CC16U
   (Brodszky) S rec/A rec,gtr (2-3rd
   degr.) sc SCHOTT 5217 f.s. (5298)

BAUMANN, HERBERT (1925-   )
 Sonatine Uber Finnische Volkslieder
   ob,bsn,gtr ZIMMER. ZM-1859 f.s.
                                 (5299)

BIALAS, GUNTER (1907-   )
 Spanische Romanzen
   2treb inst/S rec,A rec,gtr (2-3rd
   degr.) sc MOECK ZFS-231 f.s. 6
   pcs; Zeitschrift Fur Spielmusik,
   No.231
   contains: Hirtentanz; Nana (5300)

BOIS, ROB DU (1934-   )
 Night Music
   fl,vla,gtr (9th degr.) sc DONEMUS
   f.s.   (5301)

 Pastorale No. 2
   rec,fl,gtr (8th degr.) sc DONEMUS
   f.s.   (5302)

BOISMORTIER, JOSEPH BODIN DE
   (1689-1755)
 Carillon
   (Sanvoisin) 2A rec/2T rec,xylo,
   (gtr, vcl pizzicato) (single line
   playing/1st degr., notation gtr
   pt: bass clef; Plein Jeu, No.80)
   sc HEUGEL PJ-80 f.s.   (5303)

BONONCINI, GIOVANNI (1670-1747)
 Trio Sonata Nos. 1-5
   (Giesbert) 2vln/2fl/2S rec,cont/
   gtr/pno (7th degr.) sc,pts PFAUEN
   31A-E f.s.   (5304)

BOOGAARD, BERNARD VAN DEN (1952-   )
 Oilles Motors
   2gtr,hpsd, (2 manuals) (8th degr.)
   sc DONEMUS f.s.   (5305)

BORRIS, SIEGFRIED (1906-   )
 Conversazione A Tre *Op.105
   rec,hpsd,gtr (6th degr.) sc,pts
   SIRIUS f.s.   (5306)

BROUWER, LEO (1939-   )
 Per Suonare A Tre
   fl,vla,gtr ESCHIG f.s.   (5307)

BUTTING, MAX (1888-1976)
 Hausmusik *Op.75
   A rec,T rec,gtr (4th degr.) sc,pt
   HOFMEISTER V-1058 $2.00   (5308)

CABEZON, ANTONIO DE (1510-1566)
 Diferencias Sobre La Gallarda
   Milanesa (1572)
   vln or descant vla da gamba or S
   rec or T rec, gtr, bass vla da
   gamba (5th degr., Plein Jeu,

CABEZON, ANTONIO DE (cont'd.)
   No.375) sc,pts HEUGEL PJ-375 f.s.
   contains also: Discante Sobre La
   Pavana Italiana (1578)   (5309)

CALL, LEONHARD VON (ca. 1768-1815)
 Notturno, Op. 85
   (Schmid-Kayser) fl/vln,vla,gtr (5th
   degr.) sc,pts VIEWEG 1769 f.s.
                                 (5310)

 Notturno, Op. 89
   (Schmid-Kayser) fl/vln,vla,gtr (5th
   degr.) sc,pts VIEWEG 1770 f.s.
                                 (5311)

 Notturno, Op. 93
   (Schmid-Kayser) fl/vln,vla,gtr (5th
   degr.) sc,pts VIEWEG 1565 f.s.
                                 (5312)

 Trio, Op. 134
   (Albert; Schwarz-Reiflingen) vln/
   fl,vla,gtr (Die Gitarre In Der
   Haus- Und Kammermusik, No. 10)
   pts ZIMMER. ZM-1045 f.s.   (5313)

CAPELLI, GIOVANNI MARIA (1648-1728)
 Trio Sonata in F
   (Brojer) 2vln,gtr (5th degr., Die
   Gitarre In Der Kammermusik,
   No.16) sc,pts HOHLER GC-16 f.s.
                                 (5314)

CARULLI, FERDINANDO (1770-1841)
 Notturno in A minor
   (Schmid-Kayser) fl,vln,gtr (5-6th
   degr.) sc,pts VIEWEG 1571 f.s.
                                 (5315)

 Notturno in C
   (Schmid-Kayser) fl,vln,gtr (6-7th
   degr.) sc,pts VIEWEG 1570 f.s.
                                 (5316)

 Trios, Vol. I *Op.9
   (Herbst) fl,vln,gtr ZIMMER. 1933A
   f.s.   (5317)

 Trios, Vol. II *Op.9
   (Herbst) fl,vln,gtr ZIMMER. 1933B
   f.s.   (5318)

 Trios, Vol. III *Op.9
   (Herbst) fl,vln,gtr ZIMMER. 1933C
   f.s.   (5319)

CECERE, C.
 Sinfonia in G
   2mand,gtr/cont (Musik Fur
   Mandoline, Vol. 20) ZIMMER.
   ZM-2022 f.s.   (5320)

CLEMENTI, ALDO (1925-   )
 Sonata
   trp,pno,gtr (9th degr., notation
   gtr pt: kbd partitura) sc ZERBONI
   6806 f.s.   (5321)

CORELLI, ARCANGELO (1653-1713)
 Sonata da Camera, Op. 2, No. 2
   (Kammerling) 2vln,gtr (6th degr.,
   Gitarre-Kammermusik, No.48) pts
   DOBLINGER GKM-48 f.s.   (5322)

 Sonata da Camera, Op. 4, No. 2
   (Libbert) A rec,T rec,gtr (4th
   degr., Das Gitarrenwerk,
   Sonderausgabe No. 2) pts
   PREISSLER f.s.   (5323)

 Sonata da Chiesa, Op. 3, No. 1
   (Azpiazu) 2vln,gtr (8-9th degr.)
   ZIMMER. ZM-1306 f.s.   (5324)

 Trio Sonata, Op. 4, No. 3
   (Schaller) 2A rec,gtr (4-5th degr.,
   Gitarre-Kammermusik, No.1) pts
   DOBLINGER GKM-1 f.s.   (5325)

 Trio Sonata, Op. 4, No. 5
   (Schaller) 2A rec,gtr (4-5th degr.,
   Gitarre-Kammermusik, No.4) pts
   DOBLINGER GKM-4 f.s.   (5326)

DAUBE, JOHANN FRIEDRICH (1730-1797)
 Trio in D minor
   (Neeman) fl/vln,pno/hpsd,gtr (7th
   degr., orig. for lute-f',
   traverso and cont) sc,pts VIEWEG
   1737 f.s.   (5327)

DAVID, JOHANN NEPOMUK (1895-1977)
 Sonata, Op. 26
   fl,vla,gtr (8th degr.) sc,pts
   BREITKOPF-W 5727 $8.00   (5328)

DELAS, JOSE LUIS DE (1928-   )
 Trio
   fl,gtr, perc (11 insts) (8th degr.)
   sc,manuscript,copy GERIG 947 f.s.
                                 (5329)

DUARTE, JOHN W. (1919-   )
 Transatlantic Dances, 4 *Op.40
   S rec,A rec,gtr/pno (3rd degr.) sc,
   pt FABER F-0329 f.s.   (5330)

FOSS, LUKAS (1922-   )
 Paradigm
   perc (1 player), conductor,
   amplified gtr (or 3 other insts)
   sc SCHOTT f.s.   (5331)

   perc (1 player), conductor,
   amplified gtr (or 3 other insts)
   sc FISCHER,C f.s.   (5332)

GABRIELI, DOMENICO (ca. 1650-1690)
 Balletto A Tre
   (Brojer) 2vln,gtr (5-6th degr., Die
   Gitarre In Der Kammermusik,
   No.28) sc,pts HOHLER GC-28 f.s.
                                 (5333)

GAL, HANS (1890-1987)
 Divertimento, Op. 68c
   2A rec,gtr (4-5th degr., Haslinger
   Blockfloten Reihe, No.24) sc
   HASLINGER HBR-24 f.s.   (5334)

GEMINIANI, FRANCESCO (1687-1762)
 Sonatas, 6 (from The Art Of Playing
   The Guitar Or Cittra)
   (Tonazzi) gtr/vln,vcl,hpsd (5-6th
   degr., orig. for gtr or cittern)
   ZERBONI sc 7553 $10.50, pts 7554
   $16.50   (5335)

GERLACH, HANS CHRISTIAN
 Divertimento [Collection] *CC16U
   (Furstenau) fl/vln,gtr/vln,fl,gtr
   TEESELING VT-220 f.s.   (5336)

GESZLER, GYORGY (1913-   )
 Trio
   fl,vcl,gtr (6-7th degr.) sc,pts EMB
   Z-3313 f.s.   (5337)

GIULIANI, MAURO (1781-1829)
 Serenade, Op. 19
   (Chiesa) vln,vcl,gtr (6-7th degr.)
   ZERBONI sc 7724 $13.00, pts 7725
   $13.00   (5338)

GRANATA, GIOVANNI BATTISTA
   (fl. ca. 1674)
 Novi Capricci Armonici (1674) *CC12U
   (Balestra) vln,vcl,gtr (5-6th
   degr.) sc BERBEN EB1296 $3.75
                                 (5339)

HANDEL, GEORGE FRIDERIC (1685-1759)
 Alte Zupfmusik
   (Henze) 1-2mand,gtr (3-4th degr.)
   sc HOFMEISTER T-4069 $3.25 2 pcs
   for 1 mand, gtr; 1 pc for 2 mand,
   gtr
   contains: Chaconne, MIN 64;
   Courante, MIN 63; Minuet, MIN
   62   (5340)

 Sonata in C minor, MIN 52
   (Brojer) 2vln/A rec,vln,gtr,opt vcl
   (8-9th degr., Gitarre-
   Kammermusik, No.26) sc,pts
   DOBLINGER GKM-26 f.s.   (5341)

HASENOHRL, FRANZ (1885- ?)
 Trio-Suite
   (Dobrauz) vln,vla,gtr (7th degr.)
   pts HEINRICH. N-1524 f.s.   (5342)

HASSE, JOHANN ADOLPH (1699-1783)
 Trio Sonata in C
   (Kammerling) fl/A rec,vln,gtr (4-
   5th degr., Gitarre-Kammermusik,
   No.77) pts DOBLINGER GKM-77 f.s.
                                 (5343)

HAYDN, [FRANZ] JOSEPH (1732-1809)
 Cassation in C, Hob.III: 6
   (Behrend) vln,vcl,gtr (7-8th degr.,
   including a cadenza by S.
   Behrend) ZIMMER. f.s.   (5344)
   (Neemann) vln,vcl,gtr (7-8th degr.)
   sc,pts VIEWEG 1716 f.s.   (5345)
   (Scheit) vln,vcl,gtr (7-8th degr.,
   Gitarre-Kammermusik, No.31) sc,
   pts DOBLINGER GKM-31 f.s.   (5346)
   (van Puijenbroeck) vln,vcl,gtr (7-
   8th degr., gtr pt: e' is d', g is
   f sharp; capotasto in pos. III)
   sc,pts METROPOLIS EM-14007 f.s.
                                 (5347)

 Divertimento, Hob.XI: 44
   (Schaller) vln,vcl,gtr (7th degr.,
   orig for baryton, vla, bass;
   Gitarre-Kammermusik, No.25) sc,
   pts DOBLINGER GKM-25 f.s.   (5348)

 Serenade (from Op. 3, No. 5)
   (Brojer) vln/rec/fl,2gtr (3rd
   degr., Die Gitarre In Der
   Hausmusik, No.5) HOHLER GH-5 f.s.
                                 (5349)

 Trio in F
   (Meunier) vln,vcl,gtr (Hob. IV:F2)
   BREITKOPF-W 6755   (5350)

 Trio In F, Hob. IV:F2
   (van Puijenbroeck) lute/gtr,vln,vcl
   (gtr pt: e' is d', g is f sharp;
   capotasto in pos. III; orig for
   lute-f') sc,pts METROPOLIS
   EM-14012 $8.00   (5351)

HAYDN, [FRANZ] JOSEPH (cont'd.)

Trio, MIN 47
(Teuchert) 3gtr (3-4th degr., Der
Lautenkreis, Vol. I; for 3gtr or
vln or fl, 2gtr) sc,pts SCHMIDT,H
501 f.s.   (5352)

HEER, HANS DE (1927-   )
Trio
fl,gtr,vla sc DONEMUS f.s.   (5353)

HEKSTER, WALTER (1937-   )
Relief No. V
fl,vla,gtr (8-9th degr.) sc DONEMUS
f.s.   (5354)

HOTTETERRE, JACQUES (MARTIN)
(ca. 1684-1762)
2 Trio Sonatas
(Hopkins) 2rec/2fl/2ob/2vln,gtr (4-
6th degr.) MUS.SAC.PRO. B-3004
$7.20   (5355)

INMITTEN DER NACHT, WEIHNACHTLICHE
SPIELMUSIK *Xmas,carol
(Bacher) S rec/A rec/T rec,gtr/2rec,
gtr (3rd degr.) sc NAGELS EN-1106
f.s. 10 pcs; Nagels Laute- Und
Gitarre-Archiv; contains works by:
Praetorius, Anon., F. Couperin
contains: Bach, Johann Sebastian,
English Suite No. 3 In G Minor,
Fifth Movement: Gavotte En
Musette, BWV 808 (gtr,T rec) (C
maj); Bach, Johann Sebastian,
English Suite No. 6 In D Minor,
Fifth Movement: Gavotte II, BWV
811 (gtr,A rec) (C maj); Bach,
Johann Sebastian, Wachet Auf!
Ruft Uns Die Stimme. Chorale,
"Gloria Sei Dir Gesungen", BWV
140,No.7 (gtr,T rec/A rec) (5356)

JANSEN, WILLY (1897-   )
Kleine Spielmusiken *CC7U
1-3gtr/gtr,2treb inst (1-2nd degr.)
sc PREISSLER JP-7009 f.s. partly
single line playing (3 gtr);
notation: 2 treb staffs (4-pt
music)   (5357)

JOHNSON, JOHN (1540-1594)
Rogero
(Robert) 2gtr/2gtr,vla da gamba/
vcl/lute/hpsd/harp,gtr/2gtr,vla
da gamba,vcl (4th degr., orig.
for 2 lutes-g' (?); notation of
pt-I (gtr-I, lute-g', etc.): kbd
partitura, Plein Jeu, No.96) sc
HEUGEL PJ-96 $.75   (5358)

KARL, SEPP (1913-   )
Tanze Und Weisen *CC20U
3gtr/2treb inst,gtr (single line
playing/1-2nd degr.) sc PREISSLER
7008-II f.s. Das Gitarren-
Gruppenspiel, Vol. 2   (5359)

KOMOROUS, RUDOLF (1931-   )
Chanson
gtr,vla, steel spirals sc UNIVER.
14793 rent   (5360)

KOMTER, JAN MAARTEN (1905-   )
Trio-Sonatine
fl,vla,gtr (3rd degr.) sc
DONEMUS f.s.   (5361)

KREUTZER, JOSEPH (1778-1832)
Trio in D, Op. 9, No. 3
(Scheit) fl/vln,vln,gtr (6th degr.,
Gitarre-Kammermusik, No.33) pts
DOBLINGER GKM-33 f.s.   (5362)

Trio, Op. 16
(Albert) fl/vln,clar/vla,gtr (7th
degr., Die Gitarre In Der Haus-
Und Kammermusik, No. 9) pts
ZIMMER. ZM-1029 f.s.   (5363)

KUFFNER, JOSEPH (1776-1856)
Notturno, Op. 110
(Schmid-Kayser) vln/fl,vla,gtr (3rd
degr.) sc,pts VIEWEG 1575 f.s.   (5364)

Serenade in A
(Schmid-Kayser) vln,vla,gtr (4th
degr.) sc,pts VIEWEG 1768 f.s.   (5365)

LEEUW, TON DE (1926-   )
Schelp
fl,vla,gtr (9th degr., performance
should be from the scores) perf
sc DONEMUS f.s.   (5366)

LEGLEY, VICTOR (1915-   )
Trio, Op. 55
fl,vla,gtr (7-8th degr.) sc,pts
CBDM $11.00   (5367)

LEGRENZI, GIOVANNI (1626-1690)
Trio Sonata in A minor
(Williams) 2gtr,vla (6th degr.) pts
SCHOTT GA-92 f.s.   (5368)

LINDE, HANS-MARTIN
Serenata A Tre
S rec/A rec/B rec,gtr,vcl/vla da
gamba (6th degr.) sc,pts SCHOTT
5536 f.s.   (5369)

LONQUICH, HEINZ MARTIN (1937-   )
Pentameron
harp,pno,gtr (9-10th degr.) sc,
manuscript,copy GERIG 731 f.s.
                                  (5370)

LOTTI, ANTONIO (1667-1740)
Sonata, MIN 54
(Behrend) fl,vcl,gtr (5th degr.,
Gitarre-Bibliothek, No.44) sc,pts
BOTE GB-44 f.s.   (5371)

LULLY, JEAN-BAPTISTE (LULLI)
(1632-1687)
Tanze, 4
(Brojer) 2vln/fl/ob,gtr,opt vcl
(3rd degr., Die Gitarre In Der
Kammermusik, No.8) HOHLER GC-8
f.s.   (5372)

LUTYENS, ELIZABETH (1906-1983)
Nocturnes, 4 *Op.30
vln,vcl,gtr (7th degr.) SCHOTT f.s.
                                  (5373)

MAASZ, GERHARD (1906-1984)
Suite
gtr,fl,vcl (6th degr.) sc,pts
HEINRICH. PE-6115 f.s.   (5374)

MAINERIO, GIORGIO
5 Danze
(Castellani; Paolini) 1-2rec,gtr
RICORDI-IT 132146 f.s.   (5375)

MAR-CHAIM, JOSEPH (1940-   )
Trio
fl/vln,gtr (8th degr.) ISRAELI f.s.
study sc 573, pts 20.573   (5376)

MATIEGKA, WENZESLAUS THOMAS (1753-1830)
Notturno, Op. 21
(Huber) fl,vla,gtr (7th degr., Die
Gitarre In Der Haus- Und
Kammermusik, No. 23) pts ZIMMER.
ZM-1299 f.s.   (5377)

Trio, Op. 26
(Albert) fl/vln,vla,gtr (6th degr.,
Die Gitarre In Der Haus- Und
Kammermusik, No. 11) pts ZIMMER.
ZM-1097 f.s.   (5378)

MENGELBERG, MISJA (1935-   )
Amaga
gtr,bass gtr,electronic equipment,
Hawaiian gtr (8-9th degr.) sc
DONEMUS f.s.   (5379)

MIYAKE, HARUNA
Musik Fur Piccoloflöten, Flöten Und
Gitarre
pic,fl,gtr ZIMMER. ZM-1777 f.s.
                                  (5380)

MOLINO, FRANCESCO (1775-1847)
Trio, Op. 45
(Albert) fl/vln,vla,gtr (Die
Gitarre In Der Haus- Und
Kammermusik, No. 8) ZIMMER.
ZM-1155 f.s.   (5381)

MOZART, WOLFGANG AMADEUS (1756-1791)
Flötenuhrstuck *K.616
(Schmidt) fl/vln,vln,gtr (4th
degr.) sc ZIMMER. ZM-1833 f.s.
                                  (5382)

Kontratanze Und Menuette
(Hoffmann; Ochs) 2S rec,gtr/A rec
(3rd degr.) sc MOECK ZFS-29 f.s.
Zeitschrift Fur Spielmusik, No.29
contains: Contratanz, MIN304;
Contratanz, MIN307; Minuet;
Minuet, MIN 305; Minuet, MIN
306   (5383)

Stucke, 4
(Schaller) A rec,T rec/2vln,gtr
(3rd degr., Die Gitarre In Der
Hausmusik, No.1) HOHLER GH-1 f.s.
                                  (5384)

MOZART-MENUETT
(Libbert) A rec,T rec,gtr (2-3rd
degr., Das Gitarrenwerk, Reihe A:1)
sc PREISSLER f.s.   (5385)

MULLER, FRIEDRICH EWALD (1934-   )
Theme and Variations
2S rec/2treb inst,opt gtr (2nd
degr., Zeitschrift Fur
Spielmusik, No.23) sc MOECK
ZFS-23 f.s.   (5386)

PAGANINI, NICCOLO (1782-1840)
Serenade
(Bulatoff; Behrend) 2vln,gtr sc,pt
ZIMMER. 1906 f.s.   (5387)

Serenade, MIN 55
(Bulatoff) 2vln,gtr (N. Paganini,
Erstausgabe Unbekannter Werke,
No. 2) ZIMMER. ZM-1906 f.s.
                                  (5388)

PAGANINI, NICCOLO (cont'd.)

Serenade, MIN 56
(Balestra) 2vln,gtr (4th degr.) sc
BERBEN EB1357 $2.00   (5389)

Terzetto
(Schwarz-Reiflingen) vln,vcl,gtr
(8th degr., N. Paganini,
Kompositionen Fur Gitarre Und
Streichinstrumente, No. 4)
ZIMMER. ZM-1030 f.s.   (5390)

Terzetto Concertante
(Schwarz-Reiflingen) vla,vcl,gtr
(8th degr., Paganini,
Kompositionen Fur Gitarre Und
Streichinstrumente, No. 5)
ZIMMER. ZM-1123. 3 f.s.   (5391)

PERONI, GIUSEPPE
Concerto A Tre
(Brojer) 2vln,gtr (5-6th degr.,
Gitarre-Kammermusik, No.5) pts
DOBLINGER GKM-5 f.s.   (5392)

PETRASSI, GOFFREDO (1904-   )
Seconda Serenata-Trio
harp,mand,gtr (7-8th degr.) ZERBONI
f.s. study sc 7524, pts 7525   (5393)

PETZ, JOHANN CHRISTOPH (PEZ)
(1664-1716)
Trio Sonata in C
(Kammerling) 2A rec,gtr,opt vcl
(5th degr., Gitarre-Kammermusik,
No.49) pts DOBLINGER GKM-49 f.s.
                                  (5394)

PEUERL, PAUL (ca. 1570-ca. 1624)
Tanze, 3
(Koch) 2rec/2vln,gtr,opt vcl/bsn
(3rd degr., Die Gitarre In Der
Kammermusik, No.20) HOHLER GC-20
f.s.   (5395)

PFISTER, HUGO (1914-1969)
Preambolo, Aria E Ballo
clar in A,db,gtr (7th degr.) sc,pts
HEINRICH. PE-1103 f.s.   (5396)

POLOLANIK, ZDENEK (1935-   )
Scherzo Contrario
gtr/xylo,clar/bass clar,vln (mainly
single line playing/6th degr., Il
Bucranio) pts ZANIBON 5126 f.s.
                                  (5397)

PRAAG, HENRI C. VAN (1894-1968)
Sonata
ob,pno,gtr (9th degr.) sc,pts
DONEMUS f.s.   (5398)

PRAETORIUS, MICHAEL (1571-1621)
Tanze *CC13U
(Bacher) treb inst/S rec/T rec,gtr,
bass inst/B rec/opt vla da gamba
(4th degr.) sc BAREN. 1031 f.s.
                                  (5399)

REALI, GIOVANNI BATTISTA
Sonata in B flat
(Brojer) 2vln,gtr,opt vcl (6th
degr., Die Gitarre In Der
Kammermusik, No.6) HOHLER GC-6
f.s.   (5400)

REGT, HENDRIK DE (1950-   )
Musica, Op. 15
fl,vla,gtr (8-9th degr.) sc DONEMUS
f.s.   (5401)

Musica, Op. 18
fl,perc,gtr (8-9th degr.) sc
DONEMUS f.s.   (5402)

Silenus En Bakchanten *Op.42
fl,ob,gtr (8th degr.) sc DONEMUS
f.s.   (5403)

RICHTER, NICO (1915-1945)
Trio
fl,vla,gtr (7th degr.) sc,pts
DONEMUS f.s.   (5404)

RODE, JACQUES-PIERRE (1744-1830)
Trio in D
(Nagytothy-Toth) vln,vla/vcl,gtr
(5th degr.) sc,pts UNION ESP.
f.s.   (5405)

ROSSI, SALOMONE (ca. 1570-ca. 1630)
Sinfonia in F
(Brojer) 2vln,gtr (5th degr., Die
Gitarre In Der Kammermusik, No.2)
sc,pts HOHLER GC-2 f.s.   (5406)

Sinfonia in G minor
(Brojer) 2vln/2rec,gtr (5-6th
degr., Die Gitarre In Der
Kammermusik, No.7) sc,pts HOHLER
GC-7 f.s.   (5407)

RUGGIERI, GIOVANNI MARIA
Sonata da Chiesa No. 1 in E minor,
Op. 3, No. 1
(Nowak; Schaller) 2vln,gtr (6-8th
degr., Gitarre-Kammermusik,
No.83) sc,pts DOBLINGER GKM-83

RUGGIERI, GIOVANNI MARIA (cont'd.)
f.s.   (5408)

Sonata da Chiesa No. 2 in B minor,
Op. 3, No. 2
(Nowak; Schaller) 2vln,gtr (6-8th
degr., Gitarre-Kammermusik,
No.84) sc,pts DOBLINGER GKM-84
f.s.   (5409)

Sonata da Chiesa No. 3 in B flat, Op.
3, No. 3
(Nowak; Schaller) 2vln,gtr (6-8th
degr., Gitarre-Kammermusik,
No.85) sc,pts DOBLINGER GKM-85
f.s.   (5410)

Sonata da Chiesa No. 4 in F, Op. 3,
No. 4
(Nowak; Schaller) 2vln,gtr (6-8th
degr., Gitarre-Kammermusik,
No.86) sc,pts DOBLINGER GKM-86
f.s.   (5411)

Sonata da Chiesa No. 5 in G minor,
Op. 3, No. 5
(Nowak; Schaller) 2vln,gtr (6-8th
degr., Gitarre-Kammermusik,
No.87) sc,pts DOBLINGER GKM-87
f.s.   (5412)

Sonata da Chiesa No. 6 in A, Op. 3,
No. 6
(Nowak; Schaller) 2vln,gtr (6-8th
degr., Gitarre-Kammermusik,
No.88) sc,pts DOBLINGER GKM-88
f.s.   (5413)

Sonata da Chiesa No. 7 in A minor,
Op. 3, No. 7
(Nowak; Schaller) 2vln,gtr (6-8th
degr., Gitarre-Kammermusik,
No.89) sc,pts DOBLINGER GKM-89
f.s.   (5414)

Sonata da Chiesa No. 8 in G, Op. 3,
No. 8
(Nowak; Schaller) 2vln,gtr (6-8th
degr., Gitarre-Kammermusik,
No.90) sc,pts DOBLINGER GKM-90
f.s.   (5415)

Sonata da Chiesa No. 9 in D minor,
Op. 3, No. 9
(Nowak; Schaller) 2vln,gtr (6-8th
degr., Gitarre-Kammermusik,
No.91) sc,pts DOBLINGER GKM-91
f.s.   (5416)

Sonata da Chiesa No. 10 in D, Op. 3,
No. 10
(Nowak; Schaller) 2vln,gtr (6-8th
degr., Gitarre-Kammermusik,
No.92) sc,pts DOBLINGER GKM-92
f.s.   (5417)

RUYNEMAN, DANIEL (1886-1963)
Reflections No. 2
fl,vla,gtr (8-9th degr.) sc DONEMUS
f.s.   (5418)

SCHAFER, RUDOLF (1891-1970)
Kleine Spiel- Und Ubungsstucke Fur
Den Anfang, 30 (composed with
Stetka, Franz)
1-3S rec,gtr (1st degr., contains
music for: 1rec, gtr (14); 2rec,
gtr (6); 3rec, gt (10),
spielmusik fur blockfloten und
gitarre [vol. i] sc DOBLINGER
04413 f.s.   (5419)

SCHALLER, ERWIN (1901-   )
Funf Miniaturen, Nach Schottischen
Volksweisen *CC5U
(Libbert) S rec,A rec,gtr (2nd
degr.) sc,pts PREISSLER f.s. Das
Gitarrenwerk, Reihe A:13   (5420)

SCHICKHARDT, JOHANN CHRISTIAN
(1670-1740)
Trio Sonata in F
(Schaller) 2A rec/vln/ob,gtr (4th
degr., Gitarre-Kammermusik,
No.15) pts DOBLINGER GKM-15 f.s.
                                       (5421)

SCHMICERER, JOHANN ABRAHAM
(fl. ca. 1680)
10 Stucke
(Hechler) S rec,A rec,gtr
(Zeitschrift Fur Spielmusik, No.
467-468) MOECK ZFS-467-468 f.s.
                                       (5422)

SCHRAMM, WERNER
Kammertrio
vln,vla,gtr (7th degr.) sc,pts
BREITKOPF-W 4060 f.s.   (5423)

SCHUBERT, FRANZ (PETER) (1797-1828)
Beliebte Walzer Und Moment Musical
(Walter) 2fl/2mel inst,gtr
(Gitarremusik Fur Die Jugend,
Vol. 6) ZIMMER. 1965 f.s.   (5424)

SKORZENY, FRITZ (1900-1965)
Trio
fl,vla,gtr (7th degr., Gitarre-
Kammermusik, No.35) pts DOBLINGER
GKM-35 f.s.   (5425)

SPERONTES (JOHANN SIGISMUND SCHOLZE)
(1705-1750)
Singende Muse An Der Pleisse *CC10U
(Tucholski) gtr,vla da gamba/vcl,
solo voice or mel inst APOLLO
2316 f.s.   (5426)

SPOHR, LUDWIG (LOUIS) (1784-1859)
Trio
(Schindler) vln,vla,gtr (5th degr.)
pts VAMO EE-010 f.s.   (5427)

SPRUNGE, DIE 4 - LES 4 SAUTS,
FRANZOSISCHE VOLKSTANZE, 1. TEIL
*CC9U
(Ochs) S rec,A rec,gtr (2-3rd degr.)
sc MOECK ZFS-212 f.s. Zeitschrift
Fur Spielmusik, No.212   (5428)

STETKA, FRANZ (1899-   )
Kleine Suite In A Minor
2S rec,gtr (2nd degr.) sc DOBLINGER
04328 f.s.   (5429)

Sonatina
S rec,vln,gtr (7th degr., Die
Gitarre In Der Hausmusik, No.12)
HOHLER GH-12 f.s.   (5430)

Tanze, Marsche Und Andere Spielstucke
S rec/A rec,gtr (1-2nd degr.) sc
DOBLINGER 04414 f.s. Spielmusik
Fur Blockfloten Und Gitarre, Vol.
II; 11 pcs for 3S rec, gtr; 1 pce
for 2S rec, A rec, gtr; 4 pcs for
S rec, A rec, gtr
contains: Kleine Weihnachtsmusik,
Eine (gtr,S rec,A rec)   (5431)

STOCKMEIER, WOLFGANG (1931-   )
Divertimento
2A rec,gtr (3-4th degr.,
Zeitschrift Fur Spielmusik,
No.361) sc MOECK ZFS-361 f.s.
                                       (5432)

TAKEMITSU, TORU (1930-   )
Ring
fl,lute, gtr-g' (8-9th degr., also
includes K. Ezaki, Moving Pulses
for 3 solo voices, perc and
Discretion, for female solo) sc
ONGAKU f.s.   (5433)

TELEMANN, GEORG PHILIPP (1681-1767)
Sonata in A minor
(Kammerling) A rec,vln,gtr (5th
degr., Gitarre-Kammermusik,
No.50) pts DOBLINGER GKM-50 f.s.
                                       (5434)

Suiten Zu 4 Stimmen, 5 *CC24U
(Monkemeyer) 2rec,gtr (2nd degr.)
sc TONGER 1251 f.s.   (5435)

Trio Sonata in C
(Schaller) S rec,vln/S rec,gtr
BREITKOPF-W EB-6789 f.s.   (5436)
(Zirnbauer) A rec,opt cont/gtr/vla
da gamba/vcl, hpsd obbligato (6th
degr.) sc,pts MOSELER f.s.   (5437)

Trio Sonata in E
(Brojer) fl,vln,gtr (7th degr., Die
Gitarre In Der Kammermusik,
No.27) sc,pts HOHLER GC-27 f.s.
                                       (5438)

Trio Sonata in E minor
(Kammerling) ob,vln,gtr (7th degr.,
Gitarre-Kammermusik, No.97) sc,
pts DOBLINGER GKM-97 f.s.   (5439)

Trio Sonata in F
(Behrend) 2A rec,gtr (4th degr.)
ZIMMER. ZM-1792 f.s.   (5440)
(Schaller) 2S rec,gtr BREITKOPF-W
EB-6790 f.s.   (5441)

ULDALL, HANS (1903-   )
Neue Musizierstucke
2S rec/2T rec,gtr (2-3rd degr.) sc,
pt SCHOTT 2662 f.s.   (5442)

VIVALDI, ANTONIO (1678-1741)
Concerto
(Behrend) 2mand/2vln,gtr (single
line playing/5th degr.) ZIMMER.
ZM-1358 f.s.   (5443)

Concerto in C
(Ochi; Behrend) 2mand/2treb inst,
gtr ZIMMER. ZM-1820 f.s.   (5444)

Trio in G minor, MIN 326
(Benko) gtr,vln,vcl (8th degr.,
orig for lute, vln, vcl) sc,pts
EMB Z-8422 f.s.   (5445)

VOLKS- UND KINDERLIEDER
(Uhl) vln,vla/2vln,gtr (1-2nd degr.)
pts HEINRICH. 1523 f.s. 26 pcs.
contains: Ihr Kinderlein Kommet; O

Du Frohliche; Gruber, Franz
Xaver, Stille Nacht   (5446)

VOLKSTANZE UND LIEDER *CC14U,folk song
(Holzfurtner) 2treb inst,gtr/3gtr
(single line playing/1-2nd degr.)
PREISSLER 7008 f.s. Das Gitarren-
Gruppenspiel, Vol. I   (5447)

WEBER, CARL MARIA VON (1786-1826)
Menuetto And Trio (from Donna Diana)
(Behrend) fl,vla/vln,gtr (4th
degr., without Trio; Gitarre-
Bibliothek, No.45) sc BOTE GB-45
f.s.   (5448)
(Berger) fl,vla/vln,gtr (4th degr.)
HEINRICH. N-3262 f.s.   (5449)
(Scheit) fl,vla/vln,gtr (4th degr.,
Gitarre-Kammermusik, No.51) sc,pt
DOBLINGER GKM-51 f.s.   (5450)

WERDIN, EBERHARD (1911-   )
Trio-Stucke
S rec,A rec,gtr (2nd degr.,
Zeitschrift Fur Spielmusik,
No.433) sc MOECK ZFS-433 f.s.
                                       (5451)

WIGGLESWORTH, FRANK (1918-   )
Serenade
fl,vla,gtr (7-8th degr.) sc,pts
AM.COMP.AL. f.s.   (5452)

WOLKI, KONRAD
Rondoletto; 11 Leichte Spielstucke
2S rec,gtr APOLLO 2299   (5453)

ZACH, JOHANN (JAN) (1699-1773)
Trio Sonata
(Hopkins) 2A rec,gtr (3-5th degr.,
including 2 gtr-pts: simple and
moderate-difficult) MUS.SAC.PRO.
B-3002 $4.20   (5454)

I/IIB2-Coll   Trio Collections for Guitar and Other Instruments

ALTE UND NEUE MUSIK ZUM SINGEN UND
SPIELEN AUF BLOCKFLOTEN, GEIGEN UND
LAUTENINSTRUMENTE *folk song
(Gerwig) [Ger] (1-3rd degr.) sc
LIENAU 1375 f.s. Das Spiel Der
Lauteninstrumente, Series II,
Spielbuch 1; contains works by:
Sperontes (4), L. Mozart (3),
Rathgeber (1), Rein (5), Rhau (2),
Langenau (1), Chemin-Petit (1): for
gtr (1), 2gtr (3), 3gtr (1), rec,
gtr (8), 2rec, gtr (2), solo voice,
gtr (3), solo voice, rec, gtr (1),
solo voice, rec, 2gtr (1), rec, vln
or vla, gtr (1); arr. + orig. pcs.;
single line playing; gtr pt partly
in bass clef
contains: Bach, Johann Sebastian,
English Suite No. 6, BWV 811, In
D Minor, Gavottes I-II (gtr,1-2A
rec); Bach, Johann Sebastian,
Minuet, BWV Anh. 118, in B flat
(from Anna Magdalena Bach
Notenbuchlein (1725), No.9) (gtr,
S rec) (C maj,single line
playing, gtr pt in bass clef)
                                       (5455)

ANONYMOUS
Allerlei Volkslieder *CC50UL
(Wolter) [Ger] 2rec and gtr; solo
voice, rec, and gtr (1-2nd degr.)
sc,pt MOECK 2030 f.s. contains 8
Christmas carols   (5456)

AUF, DU JUNGER WANDERSMANN,
WANDERLIEDER UND MARSCHE
(Heyden) [Ger] (1-2nd degr., 5 pcs.
for 2rec, solo voice, gtr by
Folksongs; 1 canon for 2 solo
voices by Reinhold Heyden; 5 pcs
for 2rec, gtr by Folksongs; 1 pce
for 2S rec, 2vln, gtr by Umlauf; 2
pcs for 2insts by Wilhelm
Twittenhof) sc NAGELS EN-544 f.s.
                                       (5457)

AUS BOHMEN UND SCHLESIEN *CC17U
(Koschinsky) 2S rec,gtr (2-3rd degr.)
sc NOETZEL 3061 f.s.   (5458)

31 BEKANNTE MELODIEN *CC31U
2S rec,gtr (4-5th degr.) UNIVER.
17126 f.s.   (5459)

DANCES FROM SHAKESPEARE'S TIME *CC15U
(Connor) 1-2S rec,gtr/S rec,A rec,gtr
(3-4th degr.) sc CHESTER 286 f.s.
contains works by: Anon. (8),
Morley (2), Farnaby (3), Byrd (3),
Johnson (1); for: S rec, gtr (8);
for 2S rec, gtr (3); for S rec, A

rec, gtr (4)   (5460)

DEUTSCHE VOLKSTANZE, 2. TEIL *CC8U
(Stave) 2S rec/S rec,A rec,gtr (3rd
degr.) sc MOECK ZFS-31 f.s.
Zeitschrift Fur Spielmusik, No.31
                                (5461)

DREISTIMMIGE SPIELSTUCKE, 16
(Heyden) S rec,A rec,gtr/vln/vla/vla
da gamba/vcl (2nd degr.) sc NAGELS
545 f.s. contains works by:
Telemann (2), L. Mozart (3), Haydn
(1), W.A. Mozart (5)
contains: Bach, Johann Sebastian,
English Suite No. 3, BWV 808, In
G Minor, Gavotte II (S rec,A rec,
gtr) (G maj); Bach, Johann
Sebastian, French Suite No. 1,
BWV 812, In D Minor, Minuet II (S
rec,A rec,gtr); Bach, Johann
Sebastian, Minuet Trio In G
Minor, BWV 929 (from Wilhelm
Friedemann Bach Notenbuchlein
(1720)) (D min); Bach, Johann
Sebastian, Partita Del Signore
Steltzeln: Bouree, BWV 929 (S
rec,A rec,gtr) (D min); Bach,
Johann Sebastian, Polonaise, BWV
Anh. 119, in G minor (from Anna
Magdalena Bach Notenbuchlein
(1725), No.10) (S rec,A rec,gtr)
                                (5462)

FROHLICH MUSIZIEREN, EIN *CC17L
(Hermann) S rec/A rec,A rec,vln/gtr/
vcl (mainly single line playing/1-
2nd degr.) sc BRATFISCH 3070 f.s.
Frankfurter Blockflotenhefte, No.
12; contains works by: Hassler (1),
Telemann (1), Fischer (1),
Rathgeber (2), Anon. (1), Quantz
(1), Gluck (2), Haydn (3), W.A.
Mozart (3), Beethoven (2)   (5463)

KLASSISCHE TANZWEISEN, VON HAYDN BIS
SCHUBERT, VOL. 1 *CC10L
(Under; Fernandez-Lavie) 2treb inst/
2S rec&A rec/S rec&A rec,gtr (1-3rd
degr.) sc,pts MOECK 2065 f.s.
contains works by: Haydn (4),
Mozart (6)   (5464)

KLASSISCHE TANZWEISEN, VON HAYDN BIS
SCHUBERT, VOL.2 *CC12L
(Under; Fernandez-Lavie) 2treb inst/
2S rec&A rec/2vln,gtr (1-3rd
degr.) sc,pts MOECK 2066 f.s.
contains works by: Beethoven (7),
Schubert (5), Weber (1)   (5465)

LEICHTES ZUSAMMENSPIEL *16-18th cent
2-3gtr/rec/mel inst,vln/mel inst,gtr
(2-3rd degr.) SCHMIDT,H 93 f.s.
                                (5466)

MEISTER DER BAROKZEIT
(Fischer; Hulsemann) 2rec,hpsd/gtr/
opt vcl (2nd degr.) sc,pts
BRATFISCH 3042 f.s. 12 pcs;
contains works by: Rosenmuller (1),
Corelli (1), Fux (1), Petz (1),
Linike (1), Heinichen (1), Handel
(2); Frankfurter
Gemeinschaftsmusiken, Vol.3
contains: Bach, Johann Sebastian,
French Suite No. 1, BWV 812, In D
Minor, Minuet II (2rec,hpsd/gtr)
(single line playing); Bach,
Johann Sebastian, Suite for
Orchestra, BWV 1066, in C,
Gavotte I (2rec,hpsd/gtr) (5467)

MELODIES POPULAIRES POLONAISES
(Klapil) 1-2S rec,gtr LEDUC f.s.
                                (5468)

NORDISCHE VOLKSMUSIK *CC8U
(Libbert) A rec,T rec,gtr (3rd degr.)
pts PREISSLER f.s. Das
Gitarrenwerk, Sonderausgabe No. 1
                                (5469)

ST. MARTINS-LIEDER
(Draths) 1-2S recs or 2 solo voices,
opt gtr SCHOTT 5944 f.s.   (5470)

SPIELMANN AUS FLANDERN, DER
"Old Melodies From The Netherlands
(16th-18th Cent.), 38" (Degen;
Schumann) 2-4treb inst (3rd degr.,
38 pcs; nos. 3, 8, 26, 30, for 2 S
rec, gtr (1) and S rec, gtr (3)) sc
SCHOTT 2653 f.s.   (5471)

SPIELMUSIK FUR MELODIEINSTRUMENTEN UND
GITARRE, 16-19TH CENTURY *CC27L,
folk song
(Henze) (3-8th degr.) sc,pts
HOFMEISTER T-4015 $11.25 27 arr +
orig pcs (numbered 1-10); Das
Gitarrespiel, Vol. XV; contains
works by: Neusiedler (1), LeRoy
(1), Purcell (3), F. Couperin (3),
Handel (6), Haydn (1), W.A. Mozart
(7), Giuliani (1), Kummer (1), for
A rec, gtr (5), for S rec, gtr (1),
for 2A rec, gtr (6), for vln, vcl,
gtr (1), for 2vln, gtr (7), for
vln, gtr (1), for fl, gtr (1), for
S rec, A rec, gtr (5)   (5472)

SPIELMUSIK FUR MELODIEINSTRUMENTE UND
GITARRE, 20TH CENTURY *CC10L
(Henze) (4-7th degr.) sc,pts
HOFMEISTER T 4017 $11.25 Das
Gitarrespiel, Vol. XVa; contains
works by: Gohle, Ambrosius, Pabel,
Stingl, Naumilkat, Schuppel,
Niessen, Hlouschek, Konig, Behrend;
for treb inst, gtr (1), for 2 treb
inst, gtr (1), for vln, gtr (2),
for fl, gtr (1), for S rec, A rec,
gtr (2), for A rec, gtr (2), for 2A
rec, gtr (1)   (5473)

SPIELMUSIK UM 1700
(Muller-Ilmenau) A rec, zither, gtr
(2-3rd degr.) sc,pt HOFMEISTER
T-4038 f.s.
contains: Abaco, Evaristo Felice
dall', Gavotte, MIN 228; Abaco,
Evaristo Felice dall', Largo,
Min227; Dandrieu, Jean Francois,
Passepied; Schickhardt, Johann
Christian, Polonaise, MIN 230;
Schickhardt, Johann Christian,
Sarabande, MIN 229; Telemann,
Georg Philipp, Gigue, MIN 231
                                (5474)

SPIELSTUCKE FUR BLOCKFLOTE UND GITARRE,
VOL. 1 *CCU,folk song,Austrian/
Eng/Fr/Ir/It/Russ/US
(Koinuma) 1-4rec,gtr (3-4th degr.)
UNIVER. 17128 f.s. contains works
by: Bach; Scarlatti; Holborne;
Gervaise and Haydn   (5475)

SPIELSTUCKE FUR BLOCKFLOTE UND GITARRE,
VOL. 2 *CCU,Renaissance/Baroque
(Koinuma) 1-3rec,gtr (3-4th degr.)
UNIVER. 17129 f.s.   (5476)

TANZE AUS DEN ALPENLANDERN *CC10U
(Kolneder) 2S rec/S rec,A rec,gtr (1-
2nd degr.) sc MOECK ZFS-149 f.s.
Zeitschrift Fur Spielmusik, No.149
                                (5477)

TANZSATZE
(Heyden) S rec,A rec,gtr (1-2nd
degr.) sc NAGELS 559 f.s. 11 pcs;
contains works by: W.A. Mozart (5),
Haydn (1), L. Mozart (2), Telemann
(1), Kuhnau (1)
contains: Bach, Johann Sebastian,
English Suite No. 2, BWV 807, In
A Minor, Bouree II (C maj) (5478)

TRIO-SONATES [COLLECTION]
2A rec,gtr UNIVER. 17127 f.s. arr +
orig pcs
contains: Carulli, Ferdinando, Trio
in G; Handel, George Frideric,
Trio Sonata in F; Petz, Johann
Christoph (Pez), Trio Sonata in D
minor; Telemann, Georg Philipp,
Trio Sonata in C; Williams,
William, Sonata in F, "In
Imitation Of Birds"   (5479)

TUNES FROM THE CECIL SHARP COLLECTION,
7
(Roe; Duarte) 1-2rec,gtr (2-4th
degr., 3 pts + alternative more
difficult gtr pt) sc,pts NOVELLO
19498 $3.30   (5480)

VOLKS- UND KINDERLIEDER
(Uhl) vln,vla/2vln,gtr (1-2nd degr.)
pts HEINRICH. 1523 f.s. 26 pcs.
contains: Ihr Kinderlein Kommet; O
Du Frohliche; Gruber, Franz
Xaver, Stille Nacht   (5481)

VOLKSMUSIK AUS OSTERREICH, VOL. I:
VOLKSMUSIK AUS KARNTEN *CC10U
(Korda; Klier) 2treb inst,gtr/acord,
opt cont (2-3rd degr.) sc DOBLINGER
07524 f.s.   (5482)

VOLKSMUSIK AUS OSTERREICH, VOL. II:
VOLKSMUSIK AUS TIROL *CC9U
(Korda; Klier) 2treb inst,gtr/acord,
opt cont (2-3rd degr.) sc DOBLINGER
07625 f.s.   (5483)

VOLKSMUSIK AUS OSTERREICH, VOL. III:
VOLKSMUSIK AUS STEIERMARK UND
BURGENLAND *CC14U
(Korda; Klier) 2treb inst,gtr/acord,
opt cont (2-3rd degr.) sc DOBLINGER
07526 f.s.   (5484)

VOLKSMUSIK AUS OSTERREICH, VOL. IV:
VOLKSMUSIK AUS VORARLBERG *CC15U
(Korda; Klier) 2treb inst,gtr/acord,
opt cont (2-3rd degr.) sc DOBLINGER
07527 f.s.   (5485)

VOLKSWEISEN UND TANZE AUS ARGENTINIEN
*CC8UL
(Gratzer) 2-3rec,perc,opt gtr (3rd
degr.) sc MOECK ZFS-328 f.s. 4 pcs
with gtr: nos. 6-8 for 2S rec or S
rec, A rec or A rec, gtr, perc; no.
5 for 2S rec, gtr; Zeitschrift Fur
Spielmusik, No.328   (5486)

I/IIB3 Quartets for Guitar and Other Instruments

BEETHOVEN, LUDWIG VAN (1770-1827)
Adagio, MIN 232
(Schmidt) fl,vln,pno,gtr ZIMMER.
ZM-1847 f.s.   (5487)

BIALAS, GUNTER (1907-   )
Rhythmische Miniaturen *CC7U
2treb inst,gtr,opt perc sc MOECK
ZFS-186 f.s. notation gtr pt:
bass clef; Zeitschrift Fur
Spielmusik, No.186   (5488)

BRESGEN, CESAR (1913-   )
Stornelli
3rec,gtr (Zeitschrift Fur
Spielmusik, No. 479-480) MOECK
ZFS-479-480 f.s.   (5489)

CHAILLY, LUCIANO (1920-   )
Recitativo E Fuga
gtr,vln,vla,vcl (7th degr., Il
Bucranio) ZANIBON f.s. sc 5024,
pts 5025   (5490)

DELDEN, LEX VAN (1919-   )
Ballet
fl,vla,bsn,gtr (7th degr.) sc
DONEMUS f.s.   (5491)

ENSEMBLE MUSIC FOR GUITARS AND
RECORDERS, VOL. I, ELEMENTARY:
TUNES OF OLD ENGLAND
(Duarte) S rec,A rec,2gtr (1-4th
degr.) sc,pts NOVELLO 19748 $3.10
The Teacher Series Of Guitar
Publications   (5492)

ENSEMBLE MUSIC FOR GUITARS AND
RECORDERS, VOL. II, INTERMEDIATE:
TUNES OF QUEEN ELIZABETH'S TIME
*CC4U
(Duarte) S rec,A rec,2gtr (1-4th
degr.) sc,pts NOVELLO 19772 $3.30
The Teacher Series Of Guitar
Publications   (5493)

ERDMANN, DIETRICH (1917-   )
Notturno
fl/A rec,3gtr (partly single line
playing/2-3rd degr.) sc,pts GERIG
484 f.s.   (5494)

FHEODOROFF, NIKOLAUS (1931-   )
Zwolftonspiele, 3
3vln,gtr (2-3rd degr., Rote Reihe,
Vol.4) UNIVER. f.s. sc 20004, pts
20-A-004   (5495)

FURSTENAU, WOLFRAM
Ch'i - Yun (Oder Das Prinzip
Intensiven Lebens In Frieden)
Nach Dem Gemalden "Schwingungen",
"Lu-Mi", "Cheng" Von Georg W.
Borsche
vln,vla,vcl,gtr (8-9th degr.) sc
TEESELING FC-4 f.s.   (5496)

FUSZ, JANOS
Quartet
vln,vla,vcl,gtr pts EMB Z-7381 f.s.
                                (5497)

GUITARRA CANTORA, LA, MELODIAS
TRADICIONALES ARGENTINAS
(Kantor) [Span] 3-4gtr/fl&3gtr
(partly single line playing/1-2nd
degr., contains 7 pcs for solo
voice or gtr, 2gtr (5); solo voice,
3gtr (1); fl or gtr, gtr or solo
voice, 2gtr (1); opt perc (2)) sc
RICORDI-ARG BA-12779 f.s.   (5498)

HASSE, JOHANN ADOLPH (1699-1783)
Concerto in G
(Wolki) vln I,vln II,cont/gtr&vcl,
opt db,mand solo (5th degr.) sc,
pts GERIG HG-299 f.s.   (5499)

HAYDN, [FRANZ] JOSEPH (1732-1809)
Quartet in D, Hob.III: 8
(Behrend) gtr,vln,vla,vcl (8th
degr., Gitarre-Bibliothek, No.16)
pts BÖTE GB-16   (5500)
(Scheit) gtr,vln,vla,vcl (8th
degr., Gitarre-Kammermusik,
No.32) sc,pts DOBLINGER GKM-32
                                (5501)
(van Puijenbroeck) gtr,vln,vla,vcl
(8th degr., gtr pt: e' is d', g
is f sharp; capotasto in pos.
III) sc,pts METROPOLIS EM-14013
$8.00   (5502)

HAYDN, [FRANZ] JOSEPH (cont'd.)

Quartet in G, Op. 5, No. 4, Hob.II: 4
(Brojer) fl/vln,vln,vla,gtr,opt vcl
(6th degr., Gitarre-Kammermusik,
No.36) sc,pts DOBLINGER GKM-36
f.s.   (5503)

HLOUSCHEK, THEODOR (1923-   )
Quartet
fl,mand,acord,gtr (3-4th degr.) sc
HOFMEISTER T-4131 f.s.   (5504)

HOTTETERRE, JEAN
Suite (from Die Landliche Hochzeit)
(Schaller) 2treb inst,gtr,bass inst
(3rd degr., Haslinger Blockfloten
Reihe, No.22) sc,pts HASLINGER
HBR-22 f.s.   (5505)

KOHAUT, KARL
Concerto in F
(Neemann) 2vln,vcl,gtr (9th degr.,
orig for lute, 2vln, vcl) sc,pts
VIEWEG 1576 f.s.   (5506)

KORDA, VIKTOR (1900-   )
Capriccio
S rec,A rec,T rec/3treb inst,gtr
(2-3rd degr., Gitarre-
Kammermusik, No.44) sc,pts
DOBLINGER GKM-44 f.s.   (5507)

KRENEK, ERNST (1900-   )
Hausmusik; 7 Stucke Fur Die Sieben
Tage Der Woche *CC7UL
various instruments (4-5th degr.)
sc,pts BAREN. 3478 f.s. no. 2,
for S rec, gtr; no. 4, for vln,
gtr; no. 7, for pno, A rec, vln,
gtr   (5508)

KUBIZEK, AUGUSTIN (1918-   )
Quartetto Da Camera *Op.24a
ob,clar in A,bsn,gtr (6th degr.,
Gitarre-Kammermusik, No.74) pts
DOBLINGER GKM-74 f.s.   (5509)

LAMPERSBERG, GERHARD (1928-   )
Quartet
fl,bass clar,gtr,vla UNIVER. rent
(5510)

LIEDER UM OSTERN *CC8L, folk song
(Schaller) [Ger] solo voice,treb
inst/vln/A rec,gtr/pno,opt vln/vla,
opt vcl (3rd degr.) sc,pts OSTER
6781.132 f.s. contains works by:
Anon. (4)   (5511)

MARTELLI, HENRI (1895-   )
Provencalische Volkstanze *CC9U
S rec,A rec,perc,gtr (3rd degr.) sc
MOECK ZFS-293 f.s. Zeitschrift
fur Spielmusik, No. 293   (5512)

MONTEVERDI, CLAUDIO (ca. 1567-1643)
Canzonette Strumentali A Tre Voci
(Omizzolo) (4th degr.) sc ZANIBON
4848 f.s. alto fl or vln (3 pcs)
and bass fl or vln (2 pcs) + vla
da braccio or vcl, vla da gamba
or vcl or bsn, lute or gtr
contains: Canzonette d'Amore; Chi
Vuol Veder d'Inverno; Fiera
Vista, La; Gual Si Puo Dir
Maggiore; Vita De l'Alma Mia
(5513)

NILOVIC, JANKO
Makedonia
2rec/S rec&A rec,tamb,gtr/hpsd (2-
3rd degr., Plein Jeu, No.224) sc,
pt HEUGEL PJ-224 f.s. contains
also: Etude Folklorique   (5514)

PAGANINI, NICCOLO (1782-1840)
Quartet
(Mangeot) vln,vla,vcl,gtr (7th
degr.) pts SCHOTT 2315 f.s.   (5515)

Quartet No. 1
(Annessa) vln,vla,vcl,gtr (4-6th
degr.) sc,pts PEER SM-3317 f.s.
(5516)

Quartet No. 7
(Schwarz-Reiflingen) vln,vla,vcl,
gtr (7th degr., N. Paganini,
Kompositionen Fur Gitarre Und
Streichinstrumente, No. 6)
ZIMMER. ZM-1191 f.s.   (5517)

PEUERL, PAUL (ca. 1570-ca. 1624)
Tanze *CC8U
(Ochs) 3rec,opt gtr (3-4th degr.)
sc MOECK ZFS-239 f.s. Zeitschrift
Fur Spielmusik, No.239   (5518)

REGT, HENDRIK DE (1950-   )
Musica, Op. 17
fl,vla,vcl,gtr (9th degr.) sc
DONEMUS f.s.   (5519)

ROSENMULLER, JOHANN (ca. 1620-1684)
Trio Sonata
(Scheit) 2vln,gtr,opt vcl (4-5th
degr., also published in
Schaller-Scheit, Lehrwerk Fur Die

ROSENMULLER, JOHANN (cont'd.)

Gitarre, Vol. 5) UNIVER. 11221
f.s.   (5520)

SANDI, CHR. D.
Quartet in G
(Sonntag) vln,vla,vcl,gtr ZIMMER.
f.s.   (5521)

SANTORSOLA, GUIDO (1904-   )
Quartet No. 2
fl,vla,vcl,gtr (8th degr.) PEER
2069-45 sc $4.50, set $6.00   (5522)

SCHAAF, PETER
Moderne Tanze, 2
S rec,perc, stabspiele, gtr sc,pts
SCHOTT B-181 f.s. Bausteine,
No.181
contains: Bossa Nova; Bounce
(5523)

SCHAFER, RUDOLF (1891-1970)
Kleine Spiel- Und Ubungsstucke Fur
Den Anfang, 30 (composed with
Stetka, Franz)
1-3S rec,gtr (1st degr., contains
music for: 1rec, gtr (14); 2rec,
gtr (6); 3rec, gtr (10),
spielmusik fur blockfloten und
gitarre [vol. i]) sc DOBLINGER
04413 f.s.   (5524)

SCHALLER, ERWIN (1901-   )
Altlothringer Hirtenmusik
2vln,S rec,gtr BREITKOPF-W EB-6780
f.s.   (5525)

SCHUBERT, FRANZ (PETER) (1797-1828)
Quartet, D. 96 for Flute, Viola,
Guitar and Violoncello
"Quartett Nach Dem Notturno, Op.
21, Von Wenzel Matiegka"
(Behrend) fl,vla,vcl,gtr (7th
degr., arr. of W. Matiegka,
Notturno, Op. 21, for fl, vla,
gtr; called Schubert's Guitar
Quartet; Gitarre-Bibliothek,
No.46) pts BOTE GB-46 f.s.   (5526)
(Kinsky) fl,vla,vcl,gtr (7th degr.,
arr. of W. Matiegka, Notturno,
Op. 21, for fl, vla, gtr; called
Schubert's Guitar Quartet; with a
foreword by Joseph Marx, about
the orig composer and the arr;
Urtext-ed) sc,pts PETERS EP-6078
f.s.   (5527)

Tanze *CC7U
(Ochs) 3treb inst,opt gtr (3rd
degr.) sc MOECK ZFS-264 f.s.
Zeitschrift Fur Spielmusik,
No.264   (5528)

STAEPS, HANS ULRICH (1909-   )
Gitter Und Ranken *CC4U
A rec,T rec, alto glock, gtr (4th
degr.) sc MOECK ZFS-376 f.s.
Zeitschrift Fur Spielmusik,
No.376   (5529)

STETKA, FRANZ (1899-   )
Tanze, Marsche Und Andere Spielstucke
S rec,A rec,gtr (1-2nd degr.) sc
DOBLINGER 04414 f.s. Spielmusik
Fur Blockfloten Und Gitarre, Vol.
II; 11 pcs for 3S rec, gtr; 1 pce
for 2S rec, A rec, gtr; 4 pcs for
S rec, A rec, gtr
contains: Kleine Weihnachtsmusik,
Eine (gtr,S rec,A rec)   (5530)

WARD-STEINMAN, DAVID (1936-   )
Quiet Dance
fl,clar,vcl,opt ampl gtr (6th
degr.) sc COMP.FAC. f.s.   (5531)

WIJDEVELD, WOLFGANG (1910-   )
Concert
vln,vla,vcl,gtr (8-9th degr.) sc
DONEMUS f.s.   (5532)

I/IIB3-Coll Quartet Collections for Guitar and Other Instruments

AUS FREMDEN LANDERN, LIEDER UND TANZE,
VOL. I
(Draths) 3rec/3treb inst,gtr,opt perc
sc SCHOTT 6090 f.s.   (5533)

AUS FREMDEN LANDERN, LIEDER UND TANZE,
VOL. II
(Draths) 3rec/3treb inst,gtr,opt perc
sc SCHOTT 6583 f.s.   (5534)

BLUES AND SPIRITUALS
(Poletzky) 3rec/2A rec&T rec/S rec&A
rec&T rec,opt gtr (1-3rd degr.) sc
MOECK ZFS-256 f.s. single line
playing or chord playing (symbols);
Zeitschrift Fur Spielmusik, No.256
contains: Amazing Grace; Go 'Way
From My Window; I'm Blue Today;
I'm Tired; They Crucified My
Lord; Two-Nineteen Blues   (5535)

DEUTSCHE TANZE AUS DER ZEIT SCHUBERTS
*CC7U
(Jode) 2S rec/S rec&A rec, A rec/T
rec,opt gtr (2-3rd degr.) sc MOECK
ZFS-84 f.s. Zeitschrift Fur
Spielmusik, No.84   (5536)

DEVIL AND THE FARMER'S WIFE, THE, AND
OTHER AMERICAN BALLADS
(Poletzky) [Eng] 3rec/2S rec&A rec,
opt gtr (3rd degr.) sc MOECK
ZFS-290 f.s. single line playing or
chord playing (symbols);
Zeitschrift Fur Spielmusik, No.290
contains: Aunt Rhody; Clementine;
Devil And The Farmer's Wife, The;
Old Dan Tucker; Swanee River;
Swing Low, Sweet Chariot   (5537)

FELSENQUELL, DER, FRANZOSISCHE
VOLKSTANZE 2. TEIL *CC15U
(Ochs) 3rec,opt gtr (3rd degr.) sc
MOECK ZFS-257 f.s. Zeitschrift Fur
Spielmusik, No.257   (5538)

SPIELSTUCKE FUR BLOCKFLOTE UND GITARRE,
VOL. 1 *CCU, folk song,Austrian/
Eng/Fr/Ir/It/Russ/US
(Koinuma) 1-4rec,gtr (3-4th degr.)
UNIVER. 17128 f.s. contains works
by: Bach; Scarlatti; Holborne;
Gervaise and Haydn   (5539)

SPIELSTUCKE FUR BLOCKFLOTE UND GITARRE,
VOL. 2 *CCU, Renaissance/Baroque
(Koinuma) 1-3rec,gtr (3-4th degr.)
UNIVER. 17129 f.s.   (5540)

I/IIB4 Quintets for Guitar and Other Instruments

BAUMANN, HERBERT (1925-   )
Memento
(Behrend) string quar,gtr (7th
degr.) ZIMMER. ZM-1369 f.s.
(5541)

BEETHOVEN, LUDWIG VAN (1770-1827)
Deutsche Tanze *CC5U
(Schaller) 4rec,opt gtr (2-3rd
degr.) sc MOECK ZFS-229 f.s.
Zeitschrift Fur Spielmusik,
No.229   (5542)

BOCCHERINI, LUIGI (1743-1805)
Quintet No. 1, Ge. 445
(Chiesa) string quar,gtr (7th
degr., Urtext ed) ZERBONI sc 7408
$9.50, pts 7409 $21.00   (5543)

Quintet No. 1 in D
(Albert; Schwarz-Reiflingen) string
quar,gtr (7th degr., Die Gitarre
In Der Haus- Und Kammermusik, No.
17) pts ZIMMER. ZM-1044 f.s.
(5544)

Quintet No. 2, Ge. 446
(Chiesa) string quar,gtr (7th
degr., Urtext ed) ZERBONI sc 7500
$9.50, pts 7501 $21.00   (5545)

BOCCHERINI, LUIGI (cont'd.)

Quintet No. 2 in C, Ge. 451
(Albert; Schwarz-Reiflingen) string
quar,gtr (7th degr., Die Gitarre
In Der Haus- Und Kammermusik, No.
20) pts ZIMMER. ZM-1153 f.s.
(5546)

Quintet No. 3, Ge. 447
(Chiesa) string quar,gtr (7th
degr., Urtext ed) ZERBONI sc 7502
$9.50, pts 7503 $21.00   (5547)

Quintet No. 3 in E minor, Ge. 452
(Albert; Schwarz-Reiflingen) string
quar,gtr (7th degr., Die Gitarre
In Der Haus- Und Kammermusik, No.
21) pts ZIMMER. ZM-1163 f.s.
(5548)

Quintet No. 4, Ge. 448
(Chiesa) string quar,gtr (7th
degr., Urtext ed) ZERBONI sc 7504
$9.50, pts 7505 $21.00   (5549)

Quintet No. 5, Ge. 449
(Chiesa) string quar,gtr (7th
degr., Urtext ed) ZERBONI sc 7506
$9.50, pts 7507 $21.00   (5550)

Quintet No. 6, Ge. 450
(Chiesa) string quar,gtr (7th
degr., Urtext ed) ZERBONI sc 7508
$9.50, pts 7509 $21.00   (5551)

Quintetti, 6, Con Chitarra, Ge. 445-
450
(Gerard) string quar,gtr (7th
degr., 6 sc) Le Pupitre, No.29)
HEUGEL LP-29 f.s.   (5552)

BOZZA, EUGENE (1905-   )
Concertino Da Camera
(Ragossnig) string quar,gtr (9th
degr.) pts TRANSAT. 1070-BIS
$6.75   (5553)

BRUCKMANN, FERDINAND
Sonatina Buffa
S rec,A rec,xylo,triangle,gtr (3rd
degr., Zeitschrift Fur
Spielmusik, No.373) sc MOECK
ZFS-373 f.s.   (5554)

CASTELNUOVO-TEDESCO, MARIO (1895-1968)
Quintet, Op. 143
string quar,gtr (9th degr.) SCHOTT
f.s. study sc 4578, pt GA-198
(5555)

DIONISI, RENATO (1910-   )
Melismi
(Oltremari) fl,clar,vla,vcl,gtr
(7th degr.) ZANIBON f.s. sc 5195,
pts 5196   (5556)

FELD, JINDRICH (1925-   )
Capriccio
(Zelenka) fl,ob,clar,bsn,gtr (6-7th
degr.) sc,pts PANTON P-460 f.s.
(5557)

FERRITTO, JOHN E. (1937-   )
Diffusione *Op.2
clar,vln,db,perc,gtr (8th degr.) sc
COMP.FAC. f.s.   (5558)

FURSTENAU, WOLFRAM
Jordaan
"Huizen, Grachten, Mensen" glock,
acord,vln,5tom-tom,gtr TEESELING
FC-6 f.s.   (5559)

Spielmusik
4treb inst,gtr (3-4th degr.) sc,pts
BREITKOPF-L 5686 f.s.   (5560)

GIULIANI, MAURO (1781-1829)
Quintet, Op. 65
(Domandl) string quar,gtr (8th
degr.) SIMROCK EE-3218 f.s.
(5561)

GUASTAVINO, CARLOS (1914-   )
Jeromita Linares
"Presencias, Las, No. 6" (Lara)
string quar,gtr RICORDI-ARG
BA-12512 f.s.   (5562)

HAYDN, [FRANZ] JOSEPH (1732-1809)
Romance in C *Hob.VIIh:3 (from
Lirenkonzert No. 3)
(Bayer) 2S rec,T rec/vln,2gtr,opt
vcl (Gitarre-Kammermusik, No.
117) sc,pts DOBLINGER GKM-117
f.s.   (5563)

KAGEL, MAURICIO (1931-   )
Sonant
[Ger/Eng/Fr] harp,db,gtr,
membranophones (2 players) (9-
10th degr.), 10 movements
(sections); a selection can be
made from the 10 movements;
explanation of symbols and
nomenclature) sc,pts PETERS 5972
f.s.   (5564)

KOCH, JOHANNES H.E. (1918-   )
Tanzerische Spielmusik
(Gerwig) (single line playing/2-4th
degr.) sc,pts LIENAU 1416 f.s. 2
folkdances for 3rec, 2gtr or
4gtr; Das Spiel Der
Lauteninstrumente, Series II,
Spielbuch 6
contains: Bulgarischer Tanz;
Tanzlied Mit Variationen (5565)

MAMANGAKIS, NIKOS (1929-   )
Trittys
cimbalom,perc,2db,gtr sc,
manuscript,copy GERIG HG-703 f.s.
(5566)

MASSEUS, JAN (1913-   )
Seven Minutes Organized Sound *Op.39
3winds,perc,gtr (7th degr.) sc
DONEMUS f.s.   (5567)

MOZART, WOLFGANG AMADEUS (1756-1791)
Contretanz "La Favorite"
(Sanvoisin) xylo,S rec/vln,A rec/
vln,db/pno/vcl/xylo/gtr,gtr/T rec
(single line playing/1st degr.,
Plein Jeu, No.347) sc,pts HEUGEL
PJ-347 f.s.   (5568)

REGT, HENDRIK DE (1950-   )
Musica, Op. 11
fl,vla,vcl,perc,gtr (8th degr.) sc
DONEMUS f.s.   (5569)

ROSENMULLER, JOHANN (ca. 1620-1684)
Studenten Music, Eine
(Gerwig) 2A rec/2treb inst,3gtr,opt
cont (single line playing/2nd
degr., Das Spiel Der
Lauteninstrumente, Series II,
Spielbuch 10; pt 5 (gtr III) in
bass clef) sc,pts LIENAU 1425
f.s.   (5570)

ROVENSTRUNCK, BERNHARD
Stucke, 5
string quar,gtr MODERN rent (5571)

SCHAT, PETER (1935-   )
First Essay On Electrocution
vln,gtr, metal perc insts (3
players) (graphic score (action
symbols)) DONEMUS   (5572)

SCHNABEL, JOSEPH (1767-1831)
Quintet
(Albert) string quar,gtr (5th
degr., Die Gitarre In Der Haus-
Und Kammermusik, No. 22) pts
ZIMMER. ZM-1275 f.s.   (5573)

SCHWARZ-SCHILLING, REINHARD (1904-   )
Kleine Kammermusik
A rec,T rec,vln,vla,gtr (3rd degr.)
MOSELER f.s.   (5574)

STAAK, PIETER VAN DER (1930-   )
Concertino No. 3
4gtr,gtr solo (4th degr.) sc
DONEMUS f.s.   (5575)

STOCKHAUSEN, KARLHEINZ (1928-   )
Solo
treb inst/gtr, with reaction (1
player and 4 assistant players)
(6 versions; composition no. 19)
UNIVER. 14789 f.s.   (5576)

TOMASI, HENRI (1901-1971)
Recuerdos De Las Baleares *CC3U
perc,ob/pic,3gtr (9th degr.) sc
LEDUC f.s.   (5577)

TORELLI, GIUSEPPE (1658-1709)
Concerto in G
(Brojer) 3vln,vcl,gtr (7th degr.,
Die Gitarre In Der Kammermusik,
No.13) HOHLER GC-13   (5578)

WERDIN, EBERHARD (1911-   )
Ungarische Suite, Nach Originalen
Csardas-Melodien
S rec,A rec,T rec,gtr,opt vcl (3rd
degr., Zeitschrift Fur
Spielmusik, No.399) sc MOECK
ZFS-399 f.s.   (5579)

I/IIB4-Coll   Quintet Collections for Guitar and Other Instruments

AUF, DU JUNGER WANDERSMANN,
WANDERLIEDER UND MARSCHE
(Heyden) [Ger] (1-2nd degr., 5 pcs.
for 2rec, solo voice, gtr by
Folksongs; 1 canon for 2 solo
voices by Reinhold Heyden; 5 pcs
for 2rec, gtr by Folksongs; 1 pce
for 2S rec, 2vln, gtr by Umlauf; 2
pcs for 2insts by Wilhelm
Twittenhof) sc NAGELS EN-544 f.s.
(5580)

SPIELSTUCKE FUR BLOCKFLOTE UND GITARRE,
VOL. 1 *CCU,folk song,Austrian/
Eng/Fr/Ir/It/Russ/US
(Koinuma) 1-4rec,gtr (3-4th degr.)
UNIVER. 17128 f.s. contains works
by: Bach; Scarlatti; Holborne;
Gervaise and Haydn   (5581)

VOLKSWEISEN UND TANZE AUS ARGENTINIEN
*CC8UL
(Gratzer) 2-3rec,perc,opt gtr (3rd
degr.) sc MOECK ZFS-328 f.s. 4 pcs
with gtr: nos. 6-8 for 2S rec or S
rec, A rec or A rec, gtr, perc; no.
5 for 2S rec, gtr; Zeitschrift Fur
Spielmusik, No.328   (5582)

I/IIB5   Music for School Ensemble/Orchestra with Guitar

BAAREN, KEES VAN (1906-1970)
Suite Voor Schoolorkest
2.0.1.0. 0.1.0.0. perc,pno,acord,
gtr,strings sc,pts DONEMUS f.s.
(5583)

CRANEN, T.
Kermis-Suite *CC3U
S rec,A rec,vln I,vln II,mand,vcl,
timp,triangle,cym,tamb,pno 4-
hands,gtr I,gtr II (1st degr.)
sc,pts HARMONIA 1293 f.s. Oranje
Reeks: School- En Jeugd-Orkest
(5584)

DIECKMANN, CARL HEINZ
Kleines Tanzchen
part 1: rec, fl, ob, acord, vln,
mand, clar; part 2: rec, ob,
acord, vln, mand, clar; part 3:
acord, gtr, vla, mandola; part 4:
bass-inst (vcl, bsn, bass-org
(acord: bass side), perc (glock,
sopr xylo, alto xylo,
metallophone, tri, small cym,
wood drum, small timp (3rd degr.,
Die Kleine Musiziergruppe) sc,pts
HOFMEISTER V-1533 f.s.   (5585)

DRESDEN, SEM (1881-1957)
Stukken, 3, Voor Schoolorkest, No. 2
soprano sax,tenor sax,perc,vln I,
vln II,vcl,opt fl,opt db,opt gtr,
pno 5 hands (1st degr.) sc,pts
DONEMUS f.s.   (5586)

Stukken, 3, Voor Schoolorkest, No. 3
clar,soprano sax,glock,perc,gtr,vln
I,vln II,vcl I,vcl II,pno 5
hands (single line playing/1st
degr.) sc,pts DONEMUS f.s. (5587)

EBENHOH, HORST (1930-   )
Bewegungsspiele
vln,vcl,gtr,xylo,perc (3rd degr.,
Das Jugend-Ensemble, No. 14) sc
DOBLINGER f.s.   (5588)

EINZUG UND REIGEN
rec (3S rec, 2A rec, T rec, B rec),
2glock, 2desc-xylo, 2 tr-xylo, t-
xylo, bass tamb, tri, cym, 6timp,
gtrs, vcl, bass instr (3-4th degr.,
Orff-Schulwerk, Jugend-Musik) sc
SCHOTT 3564 f.s.   (5589)

FEGERS, KARL (1926-   )
Suite Nach Franzosischen Volksliedern
3rec,3treb inst,gtr/bass inst,
"stabspiele" or pno (Bausteine,
No.180) sc,pts SCHOTT B-180 f.s.
(5590)

FUNK, HEINRICH (1893-   )
Thuringer Kirmes. 4 Bauerntanze Aus
Thuringen
part 1, 2: mand, acord, vln, fl,
ob, clar; part 3: mand, mandola,
acord, vln, vla, clar; part 4:
gtr, acord; part 5: bass org,
vcl, bsn (2-3rd degr.) sc,pts
HOFMEISTER V-1495 f.s. Die Kleine
Musiziergruppe; 4 pcs. for 5
groups of insts
contains: Herpfer Kirmeswalzer;
Kehraus; Kirmestanz; Thuringer
Dorfkirmes   (5591)

GATTERMAYER, HEINRICH (1923-   )
Suite Fur Spielmusikgruppen, Op. 101-
3
strings,2gtr,pno,perc (2-3rd degr.,
Sing- Und Spielmusik) UNIVER.
f.s. sc 15001, pts 15002   (5592)

GESELBRACHT, ERICH
Spieldose, Die
glock,xylo,metallophone,bass inst,
perc,gtr, treb insts (2nd degr.)
sc,pts FIDULA f.s.
contains: Bolero; Intrade; March;
Menuetto Ostinato; Serenade
(5593)

GRAETZER, GUILLERMO
Altindianische Tanze
S rec,A rec,T rec,gtr,perc,
opt bass inst (1-2nd degr.,
Bausteine, No.159) sc SCHOTT
B-159 f.s.   (5594)

Indo-Amerikanische Tanze *CC15U,folk
song
S rec,A rec,gtr,bass inst,perc,
timp, cym, tri, desc xylo, treb
xylo, treb metallophone, tamb,
drum, bass drum (1-2nd degr.) sc
SCHOTT B-143 f.s.   (5595)

GRIEND, KOOS VAN DE (1905-1950)
Stukken Voor Schoolorkest, 3
7perc,pno 4-hands,gtr,2vln,vcl,opt
db,opt glock,fl,clar,opt trom,opt
boy cor sc,pts DONEMUS f.s.
(5596)

HERRERA, RAMON DE
Minimes, 6
xylos, recs gtrs (single line
playing/1st degr., Plein Jeu,
No.293) sc HEUGEL PJ-293 f.s.
(5597)

KOCH, JOHANNES H.E. (1918-   )
Tanzerische Spielmusik
(Gerwig) (single line playing/2-4th
degr.) sc,pts LIENAU 1416 f.s. 2
folkdances for 3rec, 2gtr or
4gtr; Das Spiel Der
Lauteninstrumente, Series II,
Spielbuch 6
contains: Bulgarischer Tanz;
Tanzlied Mit Variationen (5598)

KORDA, VIKTOR (1900-   )
Festliche Suite, Fur
Spielmusikgruppen
vln,acord,vcl,bsn,gtr,perc, recs
(single line playing/1st degr.)
sc UNIVER. 15003 f.s. Sing- Und
Spielmusik
contains: Finale; Intermezzo;
Intrada   (5599)

KREBS, RUDOLF
Schwabische Baurentanze, 3
part 1, 2: mand, acord, vln, fl,
ob, clar; part 3: mand, acord,
vln, vla, clar; part 4: gtr,
acord or pno; part 5: bass org,
baryton, tuba
(2-3rd degr., Die Kleine
Musiziergruppe; 3 pcs for 5
groups of insts) sc,pts
HOFMEISTER V-1519 f.s.   (5600)

LAMPE, GUNTER (1925-   )
Tanze, 2
part 1, 2: mand, acord, vln, fl,
rec, ob, clar; part 3: mandola,
acord, vla, clar; part 4: gtr,
acord; part 5: bass org or vcl or
bsn (2-3rd degr., Die Kleine
Musiziergruppe; 2 pcs for 5
groups of insts) sc,pts
HOFMEISTER V-1493 f.s.   (5601)

MAREZ OYENS, TERA DE (1932-   )
Partita Voor David, Voor Kinderorkest
*CC12U
S rec,A rec,vln I,vln II,vln III,
vcl,bsn,vla da gamba,glock,perc,
timp,opt fl, gtr (in bass clef)
sc,pts HARMONIA 1520 f.s. for a
children's orchestra;
orchestration of the children's
opera, "Dorp Zonder Muziek"; Gele
Reeks: Kinderorkest   (5602)

MOZART, LEOPOLD (1719-1787)
Aus Leopold Mozarts Notenbuchlein Fur
Seinen Sohn Wolfgang Amadeus
(Geselbracht) glock,xylo,bass inst,
perc,gtr,metallophone, treb insts
(1-2nd degr.) sc FIDULA f.s. Das
Notenbuchlein, Vol. 1
contains: Anglaise; Burleske;
Echo-Menuett; Musette;
Polonaise, MIN 233   (5603)

MUHE, HANSGEORG
Wir Wandern Ohne Sorgen
part 1, 2: mand, acord, vln, fl,
ob, clar; part 3: mandola, acord,
vla, b-flat inst, e-flat inst
(cor e-flat); part 4: gtr, acord,
(pno), ; part 5: bass org or vcl
or bsn, baryton, trom, tuba or
other instruments (2nd degr., Die
Kleine Musiziergruppe; for 5
groups of insts) sc,pts
HOFMEISTER V-1467 f.s.   (5604)

PRAAG, HENRI C. VAN (1894-1968)
Schoolmuziek No. 1
"Music For Schools, No. 1, Version
1951" fl/rec,clar/rec,pno,8vln I,
8vln II,8vln III,4vcl,opt 2gtr,
perc (8 insts) [4'] sc,pts
DONEMUS f.s.   (5605)

Schoolmuziek No. 3
"Music For Schools No. 3, Version
1951" 2rec,perc,pno,vln I,vln II,
vln III,vcl,opt gtr,opt 3pt cor
[5'] sc,pts DONEMUS f.s.   (5606)

SCHUBERT, FRANZ (PETER) (1797-1828)
Dansmuziek Bij Kaarslicht, Walsen En
Ecossaises
(v.d. Werf) part 1: S rec, fl, ob,
mand; part 2: A rec, fl, ob, vln,
mandola; part 3: vln, gtr, mand
and-or part 3a: clar; part 4:
gtr, pno and-or part 4a: vcl, db,
bsn (1-2nd degr., Lichtblauwe
Reeks: De Muzikantenclub; 6 pcs
for 6 groups of insts; partly
single line playing (part 3)) sc
HARMONIA 1509 f.s.   (5607)

Duitse Dansen
(Beijersbergen van Henegouwen) part
1: S rec, fl, vln, ob, mand; part
2: S rec, vln, fl, ob, mand, T
rec; part 3: A rec, mandola, vln;
part 3a: gtr, acord (2nd degr.,
Rode Reeks: Een Huis Vol Muziek;
6 pcs for 4 groups of insts) sc
HARMONIA 1540 f.s.   (5608)

STAEPS, HANS ULRICH (1909-   )
Aubade Und Tanz
2S rec,2A rec,T rec,B rec,pno,gtr
(3-4th degr., Flautario, No. 4)
sc,pts DOBLINGER 12.350 f.s.
(5609)

TWITTENHOFF, WILHELM (1904-   )
Schweinehirt, Der; Musik Zu Einem
Schattenspiel
2S rec/2T rec,vln I,vln II,vln III,
vln IV,gtr,perc sc,pts VOGGEN
f.s.   (5610)

UHL, ALFRED (1909-   )
Allerlei Spielmusik
gtr,opt perc, strings or recs (S
recs, A recs) (1st degr.) sc
UNIVER. 15006 f.s. Sing- Und
Spielmusik
contains: Kinderlied; Musette-
Walzer; Schaukel; Zirkusmarsch
(5611)

USPER, FRANCESCO (? -1641)
Sinfonia in F
(Thalheimer) S rec, A rec, 2 solo
vln, vln, 2vla, vcl or 2 solo vln
or 4vla da gamba, opt gtr, db
(Instrumentalmusik In
Quellenkritischen Ausgaben, Vol.
III) sc,pts FIDULA f.s.   (5612)

VERDONK, JAN
Musette
part 1: S rec, fl, ob, mand; part
2: A rec, fl, ob, vln, mandola;
part 3: vln, gtr, mand and-or
part 3a: clar; part 4: gtr, pno
and-or part 4a: vcl, db, bsn (1-
3rd degr., Lichtblauwe Reeks: De
Muzikantenclub; 4 pcs. for 6
groups of insts; partly single
line playing (part 3)) sc
HARMONIA 1513 f.s. contains also:
Ballade; Mars; Tango   (5613)

WERDIN, EBERHARD (1911-   )
Concertino
fl,gtr,string orch (gtr and fl
parts for skillful players;
orchestral parts can also be
performed by a school orchestra)
sc,pts GERIG HG-836 f.s.   (5614)

WERDIN, EBERHARD (cont'd.)

Europaische Tanze; 7 Pieces For
Schoolensemble
vln I,vln II,vcl/db,glock/
metallophone, fl I, fl II or
recs, xylo in A, gtr(s) (2nd
degr., Bausteine, No.167) sc
SCHOTT B-167 f.s.   (5615)

Kommt, Ihr G'spielen; Folksongs For
Wind, String, Plucked, And
Percussion Instruments
(Bausteine, No.105) sc SCHOTT B-105
f.s.   (5616)

Tanze Der Volker *CC21U
treb insts (recs, vln,
metallophone), accompanying insts
(xylo, glock, metallophone,
gtrs), bass insts (vcl, bass
plucked, gtrs, timp) (1-3rd
degr.) sc SCHOTT B-148 f.s.
Bausteine, No.148   (5617)

WILIMEK, EDUARD
Spiel Mit Uns; Kleine Musikstucke Fur
Ein Konstruktives Zusammenspiel
*CC25U
2-x treb insts, gtr (1-3rd degr.)
sc VAMO EE-013 f.s. single line
playing + chord symbols ad lib.
(5618)

I/IIB5-Coll Music for School Ensemble/Orchestra with Guitar: Collections

AIRS DE COURS, 15, EN FORME DE SUITE
(Sanchez) 2-4vln,2-4fl,2clar,2trp,
trom,cym,2timp, 4 gtr-quar, bass
tamb (1-2nd degr., contains works
by: Praf (7), Encina (1),
Attaignant (1), Anon. (3), Le Roy
(1), Arbeau (1), Sanz (1);
Collection l'Heure De La Guitare
Classique) sc CHOUDENS 20.459 f.s.
(5619)

DANSMUZIEK UIT PRUIKENTIJD *CC8U
(Beijersbergen van Henegouwen) part
1, 2: S rec, fl, vln, ob, mand, A
rec; part 3: A rec, mandola, vln;
part 3a: gtr, acord (2nd degr.) sc
HARMONIA 1514 f.s. Rode Reeks: Een
Huis Vol Muziek; contains works by:
Hasse (2), Fischer (1), Lully (1),
Witt (1), Purcell (1), Krieger (2)
pcs for 4 groups of insts   (5620)

DERLIEN, MARGARETE
Flotenhannes, Der, Ein Lernbuchlein
Fur Die C"-Blockflote Und Dazu
Mancherlei Lieder Und Satze Zum
Singen Und Musizieren Mit
Verschiedenen Instrumenten
rec,vln,lute/gtr (partly single
line playing/1st degr., arr +
orig pcs; method for S rec with
ensemble playing (vln, gtr))
MOSELER f.s.   (5621)

DUBLIN TOWN, IERSE VOLKSMUZIEK
(v.d. Werf) part 1: S rec, fl, ob,
mand; part 2: A rec, fl, ob, vln,
mandola; part 3, vln, gtr, mand
and-or part 3a: clar; part 4: gtr,
pno and-or part 4a: vcl, db, bsn
(1-2nd degr., Lichtblauwe Reeks: De
Muzikantenclub; 4 pcs for 6 groups
of insts; partly single line
playing (pt 3)) sc HARMONIA 1544
f.s.   (5622)

ENGELSE VOLKSDANSEN, 2 VOLS.
(V.d. Werf) part 1: S rec, fl, ob,
mand; part 2: A rec, fl, ob, vln,
mandola; part 3: vln, gtr, mand
and-or part 3a: clar; part 4: gtr,
pno and-or part 4a: vcl, db, bsn
(1-2nd degr., Lichtblauwe Reeks: De
Muzikantenclub; 8 pcs for 6 groups
of insts.; partly single line
playing (pt 3)) sc HARMONIA
VOL. 1, 1508; VOL. 2, 1546 f.s.
(5623)

GALANTE MUZIEK, VAN COMPONISTEN UIT DE
18E EEUW *CC6L
(Verdonk) part 1: S rec, fl, ob,
mand; part 2: A rec, fl, ob, vln,
mandola; part 3: vln, gtr, mand
and-or part 3a: clar; part 4: gtr,
pno and-or part 4a: vcl, db, bsn
(1-2nd degr.) sc HARMONIA 1512 f.s.
Lichtblauwe Reeks: De
Muzikantenclub; contains works by:
Anon. (4), Telemann (2) for 6
groups of insts; partly single line

playing (part 3)   (5624)

IN EEN WEENSE MUZIEKKAMER *CC6U
  (Verdonk) 6 groups of inst: part1: S
  rec, fl, ob, mand; part 2: A rec,
  fl, ob, vln, mandola; part 3: vln,
  gtr, mand and-or part 3a clar; part
  4: gtr, pno and-or part 4a: vcl,
  db, bsn (1-3rd degr.) sc HARMONIA
  1511 f.s. arr; contains works by:
  L. Mozart (3); W.A. Mozart (2) and
  Haydn; Lichtblaue Reeks: De
  Muzikantenclub; partly single line
  playing (part 3)   (5625)

KATALANISCHE SARDANAS, 2
  (Krumscheid) 2 groups of insts (recs,
  str insts, plucked insts) or single
  insts, perc ad lib (3rd degr.,
  Zeitschrift Fur Spielmusik, No.205)
  sc MOECK ZFS-205 f.s.   (5626)

KRAKOVIAK, POOLSE DANSEN
  (v.d. Werf) part 1: S rec, fl, ob,
  mand; part 2: A rec, fl, ob, vln,
  mandola; part 3: vln, gtr, mand
  and-or part 3a: clar; part 4: gtr,
  pno and-or part 4a: vcl, db, bsn
  (1-2nd degr., Lichtblaue Reeks: De
  Muzikantenclub; 4 pcs for 6 groups
  of insts; partly single line
  playing (part 3)) sc HARMONIA 1545
  f.s.   (5627)

LIEDER AUS DEUTSCHLAND
  (Kammerling) 1 or more gtr (Rund Um
  Die Gitarre, Vol. 3) TONGER f.s. (5628)

MUSIK IM JAHRESKREIS *CC23U
  (Korda; Schnabel) (2nd degr.) sc
  OSTER 6781-2 f.s. by various
  composers, for various insts and
  voices; 9 folksongs with gtr   (5629)

MUSIQUE POUR ENSEMBLES ET MORCEAUX
  CHOISIS *CC20U
  (Fernandez Lavie) gtr PRESSES f.s.
  supplement to La Guitare Pour Tous
                                  (5630)

MUSIZIERBUCH, FUR DAS INSTRUMENTALE
  ZUSAMMENSPIEL IN SCHULE, JUGEND UND
  HAUS
  (Ochs) 1-10inst (1-3rd degr.,
  contains 102 works by 28 composers)
  sc HOFMEISTER V-1004 $6.75   (5631)
  (Ochs) 1-10inst (1-3rd degr.,
  contains 102 works by 28 composers)
  DIESTERWEG f.s. sc,cloth 5200-A,
  sc,pap 5200-B   (5632)

NEGRO-SPIRITUALS
  (v.d. Werf) part 1: S rec, fl, ob,
  mand; part 2: A rec, fl, ob, vln,
  mandola; part 3: vln, gtr, mand
  and-or part 3a: clar; part 4: gtr,
  pno and-or part 4a: vcl, db, bsn
  (1-3rd degr., Lichtblaue Reeks: De
  Muzikantenclub; partly single line
  playing (pt 3); 5 pcs for 6 groups
  of insts) sc HARMONIA 1510 f.s.
                                  (5633)

NEUE MUSIZIERBUCH, DAS, FUR
  INSTRUMENTALES ZUSAMMENSPIEL IN
  SCHULEN, MUSIZIERGRUPPEN UND IN DER
  HAUSMUSIK
  (Ochs) 2-x insts (2-3rd degr.,
  contains 61 works by 38 composers)
  sc HOFMEISTER V-1537 $11.25   (5634)
  (Ochs) 2-x insts (2-3rd degr.,
  contains 61 works by 38 composers)
  sc DIESTERWEG 3719 f.s.   (5635)

PREISSLER-SPIELHEFT, VOL. I *CC4L
  vla, vla, rec, mand, perc, etc.; part
  4: cont (gtr, pno, hpsd, vcl or
  gamba) sc,pts PREISSLER JP-6001
  f.s. pcs. for school ensembles;
  notation of part 4: bass clef +
  chord symbols; possibilities for
  performance: single line playing or
  cont; 1st degr (single line
  playing), 3rd degr (cont); contains
  works by: Lang (1), Zoll(1),
  Beckerath (1), Biebl (1)   (5636)

PREISSLER-SPIELHEFT, VOL. II *CC4L
  vla, vla, rec, mand, perc, etc.; part
  4: cont (gtr, pno, hpsd, vcl or
  gamba) sc,pts PREISSLER JP-6002
  f.s. pcs. for school ensembles;
  notation of part 4: bass clef +
  chord symbols; possibilities for
  performance: single line playing or
  cont; 1st degr (single line
  playing), 3rd degr (cont); contains
  works by: Hermann (1), Anders (1),
  Rosenstengel (1), Schlunck (1)
                                  (5637)

PREISSLER-SPIELHEFT, VOL. III *CC4L
  vla, vla, rec, mand, perc, etc.; part
  4: cont (gtr, pno, hpsd, vcl or
  gamba) sc,pts PREISSLER JP-6003
  f.s. pcs. for school ensembles;
  notation of part 4: bass clef +
  chord symbols; possibilities for
  performance: single line playing or

cont; 1st degr (single line
  playing), 3rd degr (cont); contains
  works by: Hummel (1), Lampe (1),
  Kirmsse (1), Schaper (1)   (5638)

PREISSLER-SPIELHEFT, VOL. IV *CC5L
  vla, vla, rec, mand, perc, etc.; part
  4: cont (gtr, pno, hpsd, vcl or
  gamba) sc,pts PREISSLER JP-6004
  f.s. pcs. for school ensembles;
  notation of part 4: bass clef +
  chord symbols; possibilities for
  performance: single line playing or
  cont; 1st degr (single line
  playing), 3rd degr (cont); contains
  works by: Herold (1), Frohloff (1),
  Willnecker (3)   (5639)

SPEEL EN DANS JE MEE, VOL. 1:
  HEDENDAAGSE DANSEN *CC4U
  (Beijersbergen van Henegouwen) part
  1: S rec, fl, ob, mand; part 2: S
  rec, fl, vln, ob, mand, T rec; part
  3: T rec, mandola, vln; part 3a:
  gtr, acord (2nd degr.) sc HARMONIA
  1516 f.s. Rode Reeks: Een Huis Vol
  Muziek; pcs. for 4 groups of insts
                                  (5640)

SPEEL EN DANS JE MEE, VOL. 2:
  NEDERLANDSE VOLKSDANSEN *CC8U
  (Beijersbergen Van Henegouwen) part
  1: S rec, fl, ob, mand; part 2: S
  rec, fl, vln, ob, mand, T rec; part
  3: T rec, mandola, vln; part 3a:
  gtr, acord (2nd degr.) sc HARMONIA
  1825 f.s. Rode Reeks: Een Huis Vol
  Muziek; pcs. for 4 groups of insts
                                  (5641)

SPIELBUCH FUR DIE JUGEND, VOL. I
  (Runge) recs, Orff insts sc,pts
  SCHOTT 5411 f.s.   (5642)

SPIELBUCH FUR DIE JUGEND, VOL. II
  (Runge) recs, Orff insts, gtr sc,pts
  SCHOTT 5412 f.s.   (5643)

SPIELMUSIK FUR DIE SCHULE
  (Blasl; Deutsch) desc, treb, and bass
  insts (recs, strs, acord, plucked
  insts (gtr), pno, perc (1-2nd
  degr.) sc UNIVER. 14720 f.s.
  Sonderausgabe Der Roten Reihe; 2-9
  parts; contains 106 works by 42
  medieval to Viennese classical and
  contemporary composers, folksongs;
  arr. + orig. pcs.
  contains: Ferdinand III,
  Weihnachtsmusik   (5644)

UIT MOZART'S TIJD *CC6U
  (Beijersbergen van Henegouwen) part
  1: S rec, fl, vln, ob, mand; part
  2: A rec, vln, fl, ob, mand, T rec;
  part 3: A rec, mandola, vln; part
  3a: gtr, acord (2nd degr.) sc
  HARMONIA 1517 f.s. Rode Reeks: Een
  Huis Vol Muziek; contains works by:
  W.A. Mozart (4), J. Haydn (2) pcs
  for 4 groups of insts   (5645)

VIVA LA MUSICA; CANONS (2-4 PARTS)
  (Irnich) recs, perc insts,
  Stabspiele, gtr, opt bass inst (1st
  degr., Zeitschrift Fur Spielmusik,
  No.306) sc MOECK ZFS-306 f.s.
                                  (5646)

VOLKSTANZE, 3
  (Naumilkat) 2fl,clar,acord,perc,ob,
  gtr (2nd degr.) sc,pts HOFMEISTER
  1229 f.s.   (5647)

WIR LERNEN HAUSMUSIK, FOLGE I-VIII
  *CC23U
  (Korda) (2-3rd degr.) sc OSTER
  6781-58A-H f.s. contains works by
  various composers for various insts
  and voices; 6 pcs by Folksongs (2),
  Korda (1), Strauss (1), Beethoven
  (1), Lanner (1) with gtr; arr. +
  orig. pcs.   (5648)

ZEHM, FRIEDRICH (1923-   )
  Divertimento Ritmico; 6 Moderne
  Tanzrhythmen
  strings,winds,gtr/bass gtr,perc,
  recs, Stabspiele sc,pts SCHOTT
  6164 f.s.   (5649)

I/IIC1   Duets for Guitar and Voice

ADOLPHSON, OLLE
  Trubbel *CC6U
  [Swed] solo voice,gtr (3-4th degr.)
  sc REUTER f.s.   (5650)

ANONYMOUS
  Altfranzosische Volkslieder, 4,
  Pastourelles From The 18th Cent.
  (Behrend) solo voice,gtr (6th
  degr.) sc SIKORSKI 475 $3.75
                                  (5651)

  Dindirindin, Villancico
  (Pujol) [Span] solo voice,gtr (3rd
  degr., g is f sharp; orig for
  voice and vihuela) sc ESCHIG 1301
  f.s.   (5652)

  En Avila Mis Ojos, Romance
  (Pujol) [Span] solo voice,gtr (3rd
  degr.) sc ESCHIG 1319 f.s.   (5653)

  Greensleeves *16th cent
  (Papas) 1-2gtr,opt solo voice (3-
  4th degr.) sc COLUMBIA 141 f.s.
                                  (5654)

  Italienische Canzonetten, 4, Aus Dem
  16. Jahrhundert
  (Behrend) [It/Ger/Eng] solo voice,
  gtr (4th degr.) sc SIKORSKI 673
  $3.50
  contains: Non Ardu Chiu; Orlando
  Fa Che Ti Raccordi; Siate
  Avvertiti; Vorria, Madonna
                                  (5655)

  Tant Que Vivray
  (Castet) gtr,opt solo voice (5th
  degr., Guitare, No.69) LEDUC G-69
  f.s. contains also: Glose Sur
  Cette Meme Chanson (gtr); Paroles
  De Cette Chanson (gtr,opt solo
  voice)   (5656)

APIVOR, DENIS (1916-   )
  Canciones, 6, De Federico Garcia
  Lorca *Op.8
  [Span] solo voice,gtr (7-8th degr.,
  Collezione Di Musiche Per
  Chitarra) sc BERBEN EB1640 f.s.
                                  (5657)

ASCHERO, SERGIO (1945-   )
  Canciones De Garcia Lorca *CC12U
  solo voice,gtr ALPUERTO 1042 f.s.
                                  (5658)

BEHREND, SIEGFRIED (1933-   )
  Jiddische Hochzeit, A *Suite
  solo voice,gtr HANSEN-DEN f.s.
                                  (5659)

  Suite, Nach Altpolnischen Melodien
  [Polish] solo voice,gtr (5th degr.,
  Gitarre-Bibliothek, No.65) sc
  BOTE GB-65 f.s.   (5660)

  Yo Lo Vi, Scenen Nach Francesco de
  Goya
  solo voice,gtr HANSEN-DEN f.s.
                                  (5661)

BELLINI, VINCENZO (1801-1835)
  Dolente Immagine Di Filla Mia
  (Segovia) [It] solo voice,gtr (6th
  degr.) sc SCHOTT GA-152 f.s.
                                  (5662)

BELLMAN, CARL MICHAEL (1740-1795)
  Bellmann-Brevier; Lieder Aus
  "Fredmans-Episteln", Vol. 1
  *CC10U
  (Henke) solo voice,gtr ZIMMER.
  ZM-2105 f.s.   (5663)

  Bellmann-Brevier; Lieder Aus
  "Fredmans-Episteln", Vol. 2
  *CC10U
  (Henke) solo voice,gtr ZIMMER.
  ZM-2106 f.s.   (5664)

BERMUDO, [FRAY] JUAN
  (ca. 1510-ca. 1565)
  Mir Nero De Tarpeya, Romance Viejo
  (Azpiazu) [Span] solo voice,gtr
  (4th degr.) sc UNION ESP. 19392
  f.s.   (5665)

BESARD, JEAN-BAPTISTE (1567-ca. 1625)
  Belles Deesses
  (Pujol) [Fr] solo voice,gtr (4th
  degr., g is f sharp; orig for
  voice and lute) sc ESCHIG 1307
  f.s.   (5666)

  Cruelle Departie, Chanson
  (Pujol) [Fr] solo voice,gtr (4th
  degr., g is f sharp; orig for
  voice and lute) sc ESCHIG 1308

BESARD, JEAN-BAPTISTE (cont'd.)

f.s.   (5667)

Moy, Pauvre Fille
(Pujol) [Fr] solo voice,gtr (6th
degr., g is f sharp; orig for
voice and lute) sc ESCHIG 1309
f.s.   (5668)

BLECH, LEO (1871-1958)
Liedchen, 6, (Kindern Vorzusingen)
(from Op. 22)
(Zuth) [Ger] solo voice,gtr (3-4th
degr.) sc UNIVER. 6456 $3.25
(5669)

BLUME, KARL (1883-1947)
Ausgewahlte Lieder, 12
solo voice,gtr SIMROCK 3539 f.s.
(5670)

BOESSET, ANTOINE (ca. 1585-1643)
Ennuits, Desespoirs Et Douleurs
(Castet) [Fr] solo voice,gtr (5th
degr., orig for voice and lute;
Guitare, No.47) sc LEDUC G-47
f.s.   (5671)

BORTOLAMI, GALLIANO
Rumore Di Passi, 5 Liriche
(Amato) [It/Eng] S/T solo,gtr (8th
degr.) sc ZANIBON 5099 f.s. Il
Bucranio
contains: Mi Viene Incontro Il
Mare; Non Per Me Fioriscono Le
Dalie; Orizzonte e'Svanito, L';
Se Hai Gettato Una Monetina;
Sorgeva Il Sole E Sorridevi
(5672)

BRAHMS, JOHANNES (1833-1897)
Ausgewahlte Lieder, 2 Vols.
(Domandl) [Ger] solo voice,gtr (6th
degr.) SIMROCK EE-1166, EE-1167
(5673)

BRESGEN, CESAR (1913-   )
Funf Rumanische Gesange
(Behrend) solo voice,gtr HANSEN-DEN
f.s.   (5674)

Tschechoslowakische Suite
(Behrend) solo voice,gtr HANSEN-DEN
f.s.   (5675)

BRITTEN, [SIR] BENJAMIN (1913-1976)
England
(Bream) [Eng] solo voice,gtr (7-8th
degr.) sc BOOSEY-ENG 18814 $6.00
Folksong Arrangements, Vol. VI
contains: Bonny At Morn; I Will
Give My Love An Apple; Master
Kilby; Sailor-Boy; Shooting Of
His Dear, The; Soldier And The
Sailor, The   (5676)

Songs From The Chinese *Op.58, CC6U
(Bream) [Eng] solo voice,gtr (9th
degr.) sc BOOSEY-ENG 18505 $6.00
(5677)

BROQUA, ALFONSO (1876-1946)
Chants Du Parana *CC3U
(Pujol) solo voice,gtr ESCHIG 1508
f.s.   (5678)

BUSSOTTI, SYLVANO (1931-   )
Ultima Rara, Pop Song
1 or more gtr and narrator RICORDI-
IT 131661 f.s.   (5679)

CARA, MARCHETTO (? -1525)
Io Non Compro, Frottola
(Pujol) [It] solo voice,gtr (3rd
degr., g is f sharp; orig for
voice and lute) sc ESCHIG 1317
f.s.   (5680)

CARTER, ELLIOTT COOK, JR. (1908-   )
Tell Me Where Is Fancy Bred
(Silverman) [Eng] solo voice,gtr
(5-6th degr.) sc AMP 7206 f.s.
(5681)

CASTELNUOVO-TEDESCO, MARIO (1895-1968)
Divan Of Moses-Ibn-Ezra (1055-1135),
A Cycle Of Songs *Op.207, CC19U
[Eng] solo voice,gtr (7th degr.) sc
BERBEN EB1713 $11.00 Collezione
Di Musiche Per Chitarra   (5682)

Platero Y Yo, Vol. I *Op.190, CC7U
[Span/Eng] narrator,gtr (8-9th
degr.) sc BERBEN EB1701 $8.25
Collezione Di Musiche Per
Chitarra   (5683)

Platero Y Yo, Vol. II *Op.190, CC7U
[Span/Eng] narrator,gtr (8-9th
degr.) sc BERBEN EB1702 $8.25
Collezione Di Musiche Per
Chitarra   (5684)

Platero Y Yo, Vol. III *Op.190, CC7U
[Span/Eng] narrator,gtr (8-9th
degr.) sc BERBEN EB1703 $8.25
Collezione Di Musiche Per
Chitarra   (5685)

CASTELNUOVO-TEDESCO, MARIO (cont'd.)

Platero Y Yo, Vol. IV *Op.190, CC7U
[Span/Eng] narrator,gtr (8-9th
degr.) sc BERBEN EB1704 $8.25
Collezione Di Musiche Per
Chitarra   (5686)

DAVIES, PETER MAXWELL (1934-   )
Dark Angels
gtr,solo voice BOOSEY-ENG 20296
f.s.   (5687)

DAZA, ESTEBAN (? - ?)
Enfermo Estaba Antioco, Romance
(Azpiazu) [Span] solo voice,gtr
(4th degr.) sc UNION ESP. 19387
f.s.   (5688)

DELNOOZ, HENRI (1942-   )
Oiseau De La Tour, L'
(Preemen) [Fr] solo voice,gtr (6th
degr.) sc TEESELING VT-22 f.s.
(5689)

DES PREZ, JOSQUIN (ca. 1440-1521)
Mille Regretz
(Azpiazu) [Span/Fr] solo voice,gtr
UNION ESP. 21512 f.s.   (5690)

DESDERI, ETTORE (1892-1974)
Cacce Quattrocentesche, 2
[It] solo voice,gtr (7th degr.) sc
BERBEN EB1112 f.s.   (5691)

DESSAU, PAUL (1894-1979)
Liebeslieder, 4, Nach Texten Von
Bertolt Brecht
[Ger] solo voice,gtr (6th degr.) sc
HOFMEISTER T-4056 f.s.   (5692)

Lieder, 4
[Ger] solo voice,gtr (5th degr.) sc
DEUTSCHER 9042 f.s.   (5693)

Tierverse Von Bertolt Brecht *CC5U
[Ger] solo voice, gtr + vcl or
prepared pno (2); solo voice,
gtr, pno (2); solo voice, gtr or
prepared pno (1) (7th degr.) sc
BOTE f.s.   (5694)

12 DEUTSCHE VOLKSLIEDER *CC12U
(Schaller) [Ger] solo voice,gtr (2-
3rd degr.) sc PREISSLER B 14 f.s.
Das Gitarrenwerk, Series B, No. 14
(5695)

DIMMLER, LISELOTTE
Meine Kleine Lieder
(Wolki) solo voice,gtr SCHOTT 4843
f.s.   (5696)

DOCKHORN, LOTTE
Schalk Und Scherz Zur Laute *CC15U
[Ger] solo voice,gtr (3rd degr.) sc
LEUCKART 9095 f.s.   (5697)

DOWLAND, JOHN (1562-1626)
Canzoni Elisabettiane, 2
(Rizzoli) [Eng/It] solo voice,gtr
(4th degr.) sc ZANIBON 5143 f.s.
orig. for voice and lute
contains: Can She Excuse My
Wrongs?; Now, O Now, I Needs
Must Part   (5698)

Come Again, Sweet Love
(Pujol) [Eng] solo voice,gtr (4th
degr., g is f sharp; orig. for
voice and lute) sc ESCHIG 1315
f.s.   (5699)

Lieder, 18
(Behrend) [Eng] solo voice,gtr (6-
7th degr., orig. for voice and
lute) sc SIKORSKI 558 $6.00
(5700)

Songs, 3
(Scheit) [Eng/Ger] solo voice,gtr
(4-5th degr.) sc UNIVER. 12403
$2.75 orig. for voice and lute
contains: Awake Sweet Love; Come
Again; Wilt Thou Unkind Thus
Reave Me   (5701)

Songs, 6
(Dupre) [Eng] solo voice,gtr (7th
degr.) sc SCHOTT 10328 f.s. orig
for voice and lute
contains: Come Away, Come, Sweet
Love!; Fine Knacks For Ladies;
Flow, My Tears; I Saw My Lady
Weep; In Darkness Let Me Dwell;
What If I Never Speed?   (5702)

DUARTE, JOHN W. (1919-   )
Quiet Songs, 5 *Op.37
[Eng] solo voice,gtr (7th degr.) sc
BERBEN EB1520 $3.00 Collezione Di
Musiche Per Chitarra
contains: Birds, The; Dirge In
Woods; Epitaph, An; Omar's
Lament; Silence   (5703)

DURANTE, FRANCESCO (1684-1755)
Danza Danza, Gagliarda
(Abloniz) [It] solo voice,gtr
RICORDI-IT 129883 f.s.   (5704)

ENCINA, JUAN DEL (1468-1529)
Romerico
"Rossignol" (Fernandez Lavie)
[Span] solo voice,gtr (5th degr.,
Oeuvres Anciennes Pour Chant Et
Guitare No. 3) sc ESCHIG f.s.
(5705)

"Rossignol" (Fernandez Lavie)
[Span] solo voice,gtr (5th degr.,
Oeuvres Anciennes Pour Chant Et
Guitare No. 3) sc SCHOTT GA-194
(5706)

ENRICHI, ARMINIO
Chansons, 4 *Op.58
(Amato) [Fr] S solo,gtr (7th degr.)
sc ZANIBON 4895 f.s.   (5707)

ERBSE, HEIMO (1924-   )
Nachklange *Op.33
[Ger] high solo,gtr GERIG 1082 rent
(5708)

FALLA, MANUEL DE (1876-1946)
Chansons Populaires Espagnoles, 7,
Vols. 1-7
(Llobet) [Span] solo voice,gtr (7-
9th degr.) sc ESCHIG 1501-07 f.s.
(5709)

Tus Ojillos Negros, Cancion Andaluza
(Azpiazu) solo voice,gtr UNION ESP.
18984 f.s.   (5710)

FARKAS, FERENC (1905-   )
Canzoni Dei Trovatori, 5
solo voice,gtr (5-6th degr.,
Collezione Di Musiche Per
Chitarra; in Provencal) sc BERBEN
EB1512 $2.50   (5711)

FINK, SIEGFRIED
Tangents CSB
solo voice,gtr ZIMMER. 1970 f.s.
(5712)

FLECHA, MATEO (1530-1604)
Girigonza, La, Danse Chantee
(composed with Fuenllana, Miguel
de)
(Pujol) solo voice,gtr (6th degr.,
orig for voice and vihuela) sc
ESCHIG 1034 f.s.   (5713)

FLIES, J. BERNHARD (1770- ?)
Wiegenlied "Schlafe Mein Prinzchen"
(Behrend) gtr (4th degr.,
attributed to Wolfgang Mozart)
ZIMMER. ZM-1744 f.s.   (5714)
"Cancion De Cuna" (Garcia Velasco)
gtr (4th degr., attributed to
Wolfgang Mozart) UNION ESP. 20296
f.s.   (5715)
"Berceuse" (Ranieri) gtr (4th
degr., attributed to Wolfgang
Mozart) CRANZ $2.00   (5716)

FRANCAIX, JEAN (1912-   )
Priere Du Soir
[Fr] solo voice,gtr (6-7th degr.)
sc SCHOTT 4189 f.s. contains
also: Chanson   (5717)

FRICKER, PETER RACINE (1920-   )
O Mistress Mine
[Eng] solo voice,gtr (5th degr.) sc
SCHOTT GA-210 f.s.   (5718)

FUENLLANA, MIGUEL DE (fl. ca. 1560)
Duelete De Mi, Senora
(Tarrago) solo voice,gtr (orig for
solo voice, vihuela) UNION ESP.
20029 f.s.   (5719)

FURSTENAU, WOLFRAM
Sonette
[Ger] solo voice,gtr (7-8th degr.)
sc TEESELING FC-1 f.s.   (5720)

GERHARD, ROBERTO (1896-1970)
Cantares *CC7U
(Mills) [Span] solo voice,gtr
BELWIN $4.00   (5721)

GIORDANI, TOMMASO (1730-1806)
Caro Mio Ben
(Segovia) [It] solo voice,gtr (7th
degr.) sc SCHOTT GA-175 f.s.
(5722)

GIULIANI, MAURO (1781-1829)
Lieder, 6 *Op.89
(Heck, Thomas F.) solo voice,gtr/
pno TECLA TE-004 f.s.   (5723)

6 Lieder *Op.89
(Kammerling) med solo,gtr
BREITKOPF-W EB-6793 f.s.   (5724)

GORZANIS, GIACOMO (ca. 1525-ca. 1578)
Napolitane, 15
"Neapolitanische Lieder Aus Dem 16.
Jahrhundert" (Tonazzi) [It] gtr
solo, or solo voice or S rec and
gtr (4th degr., orig for solo

GORZANIS, GIACOMO (cont'd.)
    voice and lute) sc HEINRICH.
    PE-6080 f.s.   (5725)

GRANADOS, ENRIQUE (1867-1916)
    Amor Y Odio, Tonadilla
        (Azpiazu) [Span] solo voice,gtr
        (8th degr.) sc UNION ESP. 18842
        f.s.   (5726)

    Callejeo, Tonadilla
        (Azpiazu) [Span] solo voice,gtr
        (8th degr.) sc UNION ESP. 18843
        f.s.   (5727)

    Danza Espanola No. 5, Andaluza
        (Azpiazu) [Span] solo voice,gtr
        (7th degr.) sc UNION ESP. 19235
        f.s.   (5728)

    Maja De Goya, La, Tonadilla
        (Azpiazu) [Span] solo voice,gtr
        (8th degr.) sc UNION ESP. 18849
        f.s.   (5729)

    Maja Dolorosa, La, 3 Tonadillas
        (Azpiazu) [Span] solo voice,gtr
        (8th degr.) sc UNION ESP. 18850
        f.s.   (5730)

    Majo Discreto, El, Tonadilla
        (Azpiazu) [Span] solo voice,gtr
        (7th degr.) sc UNION ESP. 18844
        f.s.   (5731)

    Majo Olvivado, El, Tonada O Cancion
        (Azpiazu) [Span] solo voice,gtr
        (7th degr.) sc UNION ESP. 18845
        f.s.   (5732)

    Majo Timido, El, Tonadilla
        (Azpiazu) [Span] solo voice,gtr
        (7th degr.) sc UNION ESP. 18846
        f.s.   (5733)

    Mirar De La Maja, El, Tonadilla
        (Azpiazu) [Span] solo voice,gtr
        (5th degr.) sc UNION ESP. 18847
        f.s.   (5734)
        (Prol) [Span] solo voice,gtr (5th
        degr.) sc PAGANI CG-131 f.s.
                                        (5735)

    Tralala, El, Y El Punteado, Tonadilla
        (Azpiazu) [Span] solo voice,gtr
        (7th degr.) sc UNION ESP. 18848
        f.s.   (5736)

GRETRY, ANDRE ERNEST MODESTE
        (1741-1813)
    Serenade
        (Behrend) [Fr] solo voice,gtr (4th
        degr.) Gitarre-Bibliothek, No.57)
        sc BOTE GB-57 f.s.   (5737)

GUERRERO, FRANCISCO (1528-1599)
    Ojos Claros, Serenos *madrigal
        (Tarrago) solo voice,gtr UNION ESP.
        20832 f.s.   (5738)

HANDEL, GEORGE FRIDERIC (1685-1759)
    No Se Emendera Jamas
        "Cantata Spagnuola A Voce Sola E
        Chitarra E Basso Continuo"
        (Azpiazu) [Span] solo voice,gtr,
        cont (6th degr.) sc,pts UNION
        ESP. 19398 f.s.   (5739)
        "Cantata Spagnuola A Voce Sola E
        Chitarra E Basso Continuo"
        (Behrend) [Span] solo voice,gtr,
        cont (6th degr.) sc,pts SIKORSKI
        575 $5.75   (5740)
        "Cantata Spagnuola A Voce Sola E
        Chitarra E Basso Continuo"
        (Sanchez Benimelli) [Span] solo
        voice,gtr,cont (6th degr.)
        ALPUERTO 1389 f.s.   (5741)
        "Cantata Spagnuola A Voce Sola E
        Chitarra E Basso Continuo"
        (Scheit) [Span] solo voice,gtr,
        cont (6th degr., Gitarre-
        Kammermusik, No.39) DOBLINGER
        GKM-39 f.s.   (5742)
        "Cantata Spagnuola A Voce Sola E
        Chitarra E Basso Continuo" (van
        der Staak) [Span] solo voice,gtr,
        cont (6th degr.) sc BROEKMANS 25
        f.s.   (5743)

HASSE, JOHANN ADOLPH (1699-1783)
    March, MIN 7 (from Artemesia)
        (Leerink) [Ger] gtr (3rd degr.,
        Bibliotheek Van Den Gitarist, No.
        65) sc BROEKMANS 373 f.s.
        contains also: Beyer, Johann
        Christian, Vergnugen, Das
        (Minuet, MIN 8) (solo voice,
        gtr)   (5744)

HAYDN, [FRANZ] JOSEPH (1732-1809)
    Lieder, 3
        (Scheit) [Ger] solo voice,gtr (4-
        5th degr.) sc DOBLINGER GKM-22
        f.s. Gitarre-Kammermusik, No.22
        contains: Landlust, Die; Sehr
        Gewohnliche Geschichte, Eine;
        Zu Spate Ankunft Der Mutter,

HAYDN, [FRANZ] JOSEPH (cont'd.)
        Die   (5745)

HENZE, HANS WERNER (1926-   )
    Fragmente Nach Holderlin, 3 (from
        Kammermusik 1958)
        (Bream) [Ger] solo voice,gtr (9th
        degr.) sc SCHOTT 4886 f.s.
        contains also: Tentos, 3 (gtr) (5746)

HILLER, JOHANN ADAM (1728-1804)
    Lieder, 6
        (Monkemeyer) gtr,opt solo voice (3-
        4th degr.) TONGER 1283 f.s.
        contains: Abendlied Eines
        Bauermanns; Lied Hinterm Ofen
        Zu Singen; Mann Im Lehnstuhle,
        Der; Meine Wunsche; Pasteten
        Lied; Urians Reise Um Die Welt
                                        (5747)

HORNUNG
    O Dream, O Dreaming
        narrator,gtr SYMPHON 2204 f.s.
                                        (5748)

HUBSCHMANN, WERNER (1901-1969)
    Alte Deutsche Spruchweisheit *CC8U
        [Ger] T solo,gtr (5-6th degr.) sc
        DEUTSCHER 9044 f.s.   (5749)

HUYGENS, CONSTANTIN
    Psaumes Et 3 Chansons, 2
        (Komter) [Lat/Fr/It] Mez solo,gtr
        (4th degr., melodie et basse
        (non-chiffree) par Constantin
        Huygens; cont realized by J.M.K;
        orig for voice and lute)
        DONEMUS f.s.   (5750)

HUZELLA, ELEK (1915-1971)
    4 Viragenek
        "Love Songs" (Mosoczi) [Hung] solo
        voice,gtr (5th degr.) sc EMB 7405
        f.s.   (5751)

JESSET, MICHAEL
    Neun Volkslieder
        solo voice,gtr CHESTER f.s.   (5752)

JEUNE, HENRI LE
    Chanson
        (Pujol) [Fr] solo voice,gtr (6th
        degr.) sc ESCHIG 1320 f.s.   (5753)

JONG, MARINUS DE (1891-1984)
    Bruegel-Liederen *CC7U
        [Dutch] Bar solo,gtr (7th degr.) sc
        CBDM 69-240 f.s.   (5754)

KNAB, ARMIN (1881-1951)
    Lautenlieder
        [Ger] solo voice,gtr (3rd degr.) sc
        MOSELER f.s.   (5755)

KOMTER, JAN MAARTEN (1905-   )
    In A Gondola
        [Eng] solo voice,gtr (4th degr.,
        Eng words by Robert Browning) sc
        DONEMUS f.s.   (5756)

KRIEGER, JOHANN PHILIPP (1649-1725)
    Lieder, 4
        (Brojer) [Ger] solo voice,gtr (4th
        degr.) sc HOHLER GC-22 f.s. Die
        Gitarre In Der Kammermusik, No.22
        contains: Du Ungluck'sel'ger
        Morgenstern; Geldheirat, Die;
        Im Dunkeln Ist Gut Munkeln;
        Kussgen In Ehren, Ein   (5757)

KUKUCK, FELICITAS (1914-   )
    Ich Hab Die Nacht Getraumet,
        Madchenlieder Nach Gedichten Aus
        Der Romantik *CC7U
        [Ger] solo voice,gtr (3rd degr.) sc
        MOSELER f.s. no. 3 also for gtr
        solo   (5758)

    Paradies, Das, Ein Tanzspiel *CC9U
        solo voice,gtr FIDULA f.s.   (5759)

KUNAD, RAINER (1936-   )
    Schattenland Strome, Conatum 37
        *CC10U
        [Ger] T solo,gtr (7th degr.) sc
        DEUTSCHER 9041 f.s. including 3
        "Ritornelli" for gtr   (5760)

    Von Der Kocherie, Ein Kulinarisches
        Loblied, Conatum 47 *CC14U
        [Ger] S solo,gtr (7-8th degr.) sc
        DEUTSCHER 9046 $4.50   (5761)

LE ROY, ADRIEN (? -1599)
    J'ai Le Rebours
        (Castet) [Fr] solo voice,gtr (5th
        degr., orig for solo voice and
        lute) sc LEDUC G-35 $2.25   (5762)
        (Pujol) [Fr] solo voice,gtr (5th
        degr., orig for solo voice and
        lute) sc ESCHIG 1311   (5763)

    Je Ne Suis Moins Aimable
        (Pujol) [Fr] solo voice,gtr (4th
        degr., orig for solo voice and
        lute) sc ESCHIG 1312 f.s.   (5764)

LE ROY, ADRIEN (cont'd.)
    Laissez La Verte Couleur, Chanson
        (Pujol) [Fr] solo voice,gtr (4th
        degr., orig for solo voice and
        lute) sc ESCHIG 1313 f.s.   (5765)

    Mes Peines Et Ennuis, Branle Gay
        (Pujol) [Fr] solo voice,gtr (4th
        degr., orig for solo voice and
        lute) sc ESCHIG 1310 f.s.   (5766)

MALIPIERO, RICCARDO (1914-   )
    Ballate, 2
        [Ger/It] solo voice,gtr (8-9th
        degr.) sc ZERBONI 6480 $14.00
                                        (5767)

MILAN, LUIS (ca. 1500-ca. 1564)
    Con Pavor Recordo El Moro, Romance
        (Azpiazu) [Span] solo voice,gtr
        (8th degr., orig. for solo voice
        and vihuela) sc UNION ESP. 19386
        f.s.   (5768)

    Don Luis Milan
        (Behrend) [Span/Eng/Ger] gtr (3-8th
        degr., Alte Meister Des Lauten-
        Und Gitarrespiels, Vol. 8; 6
        Pavans Nos. 1-6 (No. I, II, V,
        III, IV, VI In "El Maestro"), 3
        Fantasies Nos. 1-3 ("El Maestro"
        Nos. X, VIII, XVI) for gtr solo;
        3 Romances [Sic] ("Toda Mi Vida"
        Is Villancico En Castellano [!]),
        3 Villancicos for solo voice,
        gtr) sc SIKORSKI 200-8 f.s.
                                        (5769)

    Levaysme Amor d'Aquesta Terra
        (Azpiazu) [Port] solo voice,gtr
        (8th degr., orig. for solo voice
        and vihuela) sc UNION ESP. 19393
        f.s.   (5770)

    Maestro, El, Vol. 1: Obras Para
        Vihuela Sola
        (Tarrago) [Span/Fr/Eng] gtr (40
        fantasias, 6 pavanas, 4 tientos)
        UNION ESP. 21834-I f.s.   (5771)

    Maestro, El, Vol. 2: Obras Para Voz Y
        Vihuela
        (Tarrago) [Span/Fr/Eng] solo voice,
        gtr (12 villancicos, 4 romances,
        6 sonetos) UNION ESP. 21834-II
        f.s.   (5772)

    Perdida Tengo La Color
        (Tarrago) solo voice,gtr (orig for
        solo voice, vihuela) UNION ESP.
        20029 f.s.   (5773)

    Toda Mi Vida Os Ame (from El Maestro)
        "Toute Ma Vie Je Vous Ai Aimee"
        (Fernandez-Lavie) solo voice,gtr
        (6th degr., orig. for solo voice
        and vihuela; Oeuvres anciennes
        pour chant et guitare, no. 2) sc
        ESCHIG f.s.   (5774)
        "Toute Ma Vie Je Vous Ai Aimee"
        (Fernandez-Lavie) solo voice,gtr
        (6th degr., orig. for solo voice
        and vihuela; Oeuvres anciennes
        pour chant et guitare, no. 2) sc
        SCHOTT GA-193 f.s.   (5775)
        (Pujol) solo voice,gtr (6th degr.,
        orig. for solo voice and vihuela)
        sc RICORDI-ARG BA-11757 f.s.
                                        (5776)

MITTERGRADNEGGER, GUNTER (1923-   )
    Heiteres Herbarium
        [Ger] solo voice,gtr (6-7th degr.,
        Gitarre-Kammermusik, No.78) sc
        DOBLINGER GKM-78 f.s.   (5777)

MONTEVERDI, CLAUDIO (ca. 1567-1643)
    Madrigali, 3
        (Behrend) [It] solo voice,gtr (4th
        degr.) SIKORSKI 574 $3.00   (5778)

    Scherzi Musicali, Cioe Arie, Et
        Madrigali In Stile Recitativo
        (Behrend) [It/Ger] solo voice,gtr
        (5th degr.) sc SIKORSKI 672 f.s.
                                        (5779)
        (Lonardi) [It] solo voice,gtr,vla
        da gamba (5th degr.) sc ZERBONI
        8286 f.s.   (5780)

MORALES, CRISTOBAL DE (ca. 1500-1553)
    De Antequera Sale El Moro, Romance
        Viejo (composed with Fuenllana,
        Miguel de)
        (Pujol) [Span] solo voice,gtr (6th
        degr., g is f sharp; orig for
        solo voice and vihuela) sc
        RICORDI-ARG BA-11665 f.s.   (5781)
        (Tarrago) sc UNION ESP. 20029 f.s.
                                        (5782)

MORENO TORROBA, FEDERICO (1891-1982)
    Canciones Espanolas, 7
        [Span] solo voice,gtr (8th degr.)
        sc UNION ESP. f.s.   (5783)

    Marchenera, La, Petenera
        (Azpiazu) [Span] solo voice,gtr
        (8th degr.) sc UNION ESP. 18852

MORENO TORROBA, FEDERICO (cont'd.)
  f.s.   (5784)

MORETTI, FEDERICO
  Doce Canciones
    (Jeffery, Brian) solo voice,gtr
    (facsimile ed) TECLA cloth TE-010
    f.s., pap TE-011 f.s.   (5785)

MOZART, WOLFGANG AMADEUS (1756-1791)
  Berceuse, MIN 234
    (Pujol) [Fr] solo voice,gtr (3rd
    degr., actually composed by
    Bernhard Fliess) sc ESCHIG 1322
    f.s.   (5786)

  Lieder, 9
    (Behrend) solo voice,gtr (7th
    degr.) sc SIKORSKI 573 f.s.
                                   (5787)

  Serenade, MIN 235 (from Don Giovanni)
    (Castet) [Fr] solo voice,gtr (6th
    degr., Guitare, No.3) sc LEDUC
    G-3 $2.25   (5788)

MUDARRA, ALONSO DE (ca. 1506-1580)
  Claros Y Frescos Rios, Cancion
    (Tarrago) [Span] solo voice,gtr
    (5th degr., orig. for solo voice
    and vihuela) sc UNION ESP. 20830
    f.s.   (5789)

  Isabel, Perdiste La Tu Faxa
    (Azpiazu) [Span] solo voice,gtr
    (6th degr., orig for solo voice
    and vihuela) sc UNION ESP. 19394
    f.s.   (5790)
    (Tarrago) [Span] solo voice,gtr
    (6th degr., orig for solo voice
    and vihuela) UNION ESP. 20831
    f.s.   (5791)

  Tres Libros De Musica En Cifra Para
    Vihuela
    (Tarrago) [Span/Fr/Eng] gtr (49 pcs
    for vihuela (6 tunings), 27 pcs
    for solo voice, vihuela (5
    tunings), 1 pc for harp (org);
    all transcr. are according to the
    tablature and for gtr-e'; if
    other tunings are desired, T.
    recommends the use of a capotasto
    in pos. II-IV) sc UNION ESP.
    21652 f.s.   (5792)

  Triste Estaba El Rey David
    (Azpiazu) [Span] solo voice,gtr
    (4th degr., orig for solo voice
    and vihuela) UNION ESP. 19391
    f.s.   (5793)
    (Pujol) [Span] solo voice,gtr (4th
    degr., orig for solo voice and
    vihuela) ESCHIG 1302 f.s. (5794)

MUSGRAVE, THEA (1928-   )
  Five Love Songs
    high solo,gtr CHESTER f.s.   (5795)

NARVAEZ, LUIS DE
  Con Que La Lavare
    (Azpiazu) [Span] solo voice,gtr
    (4th degr., orig for solo voice
    and vihuela) sc UNION ESP. 19388
    f.s.   (5796)

  Seys Libros Del Delphin De Musica De
    Cifra Para Taner Vihuela, Los
    (Tarrago) [Span/Fr/Eng] gtr (38 pcs
    for vihuela (6 tunings), 14 pcs
    for solo voice, vihuela (5
    tunings); all transcr are
    according to the tablature and
    for gtr-e'; if other tunings are
    desired, T. recommends the use of
    a capotasto in pos. II-IV) sc
    UNION ESP. 21613 f.s.   (5797)

NEUMANN, ULRIK
  Manresan
    gtr (4th degr., with a version for
    solo voice, gtr) REUTER f.s.
                                   (5798)

NOVAK, JAN (1921-1984)
  Apicius Modulatus, Artis Coquinariae
    Praecepta Modis Numerisque
    Instructa Ad Cantum Cum Cithara
    *CC8U
    (Amato) [Lat] solo voice,gtr (7th
    degr.) sc ZANIBON 5146 f.s. Il
    Bucranio   (5799)

  Cantiones Latinae, Medii Et
    Recentioris Aevi Ad Cantum Cum
    Cithara *CC14U
    (Andreoli) [Lat] solo voice,gtr
    (5th degr.) sc ZANIBON 5259 f.s.
                                   (5800)

OBRADORS, FERNANDO
  Con Amores, La Mi Madre
    (Azpiazu) [Span] solo voice,gtr
    (7th degr.) sc UNION ESP. 19409
    f.s.   (5801)

PISADOR, DIEGO (ca. 1508-1557)
  Guarte, Guarte El Rey Don Sancho
    (Tarrago) solo voice,gtr UNION ESP.
    21620 f.s.   (5802)

  Guarte, Guarte El Rey Don Sancho,
    Romance Viejo
    (Azpiazu) [Span] solo voice,gtr
    (5th degr., orig. for solo voice
    and vihuela) sc UNION ESP. 19397
    f.s.   (5803)

  Lagrime Mesti, Villanesca
    (van der Staak) [Span] solo voice,
    gtr (4th degr., orig. for solo
    voice and vihuela) sc BROEKMANS
    817 f.s.   (5804)

  Madonna Mia Fa, Villanesca
    (Pujol) [Span] solo voice,gtr (4th
    degr., orig. for solo voice and
    vihuela; g is f sharp possible)
    sc ESCHIG 1318 f.s.   (5805)
    (van der Staak) [Span] solo voice,
    gtr (4th degr., orig. for solo
    voice and vihuela) sc BROEKMANS
    507 f.s.   (5806)

  Manana De San Juan, La, Romance Viejo
    (Azpiazu) [Span] solo voice,gtr
    (6th degr., orig. for solo voice
    and vihuela) sc UNION ESP. 19396
    f.s.   (5807)

  Quien Tu Viese Tal Poder, Villancico
    (van der Staak) [Span] solo voice,
    gtr (4th degr., orig. for solo
    voice and vihuela) sc BROEKMANS
    487 f.s.   (5808)

  Si La Noche Hace Oscura, Villancico
    (van der Staak) [Span] solo voice,
    gtr (orig. for solo voice and
    vihuela) sc BROEKMANS 489 f.s.
                                   (5809)

  Si Te Vas A Baner Juanica, Villancico
    (Pujol) [Span] solo voice,gtr (5th
    degr., orig. for solo voice and
    vihuela; g is f sharp) sc ESCHIG
    1306 f.s.   (5810)
    (Tarrago) [Span] solo voice,gtr
    (5th degr., orig. for solo voice
    and vihuela) sc UNION ESP. 20638
    f.s.   (5811)

REIN, WALTER (1893-1955)
  Vom Vielfaltigen Leben *CC12L
    [Ger] solo voice,gtr (3-5th degr.)
    sc VOGGEN MRV-396 f.s. 6 pcs for
    solo voice, gtr; 2 pcs for solo
    voice, A rec, gtr; 4 pcs for solo
    voice, rec, lute-g'   (5812)

RODRIGO, JOAQUIN (1902-   )
  Folias Canarias
    "Song From The Canary Islands"
    [Span/Eng] solo voice,gtr (8th
    degr.) sc SCHOTT 10600 f.s.
                                   (5813)

  Spanish Songs, 3
    [Span/Eng] solo voice,gtr (8th
    degr.) sc SCHOTT 10601 f.s.
    contains: Adela; De Ronda; En
    Jerez De La Frontera   (5814)

  Villancicos *Xmas,carol
    [Span/Eng] solo voice,gtr (6th
    degr.) sc SCHOTT 10705-10707 f.s.
    contains: Aire Y Donaire;
    Coplillas De Belen, "Carols Of
    Bethlehem"; Pastorcito Santo,
    "Holy Shepherd Boy"   (5815)

ROLAND, CLAUDE ROBERT (1935-   )
  Ballade De Villon *Op.37
    [Fr] Bar/T solo,gtr (7th degr.) sc
    CBDM 72-75 f.s.   (5816)

RUIZ PIPO, ANTONIO
  Cantos A La Noche
    [Span] solo voice,gtr (8-9th degr.,
    Collezione Di Musiche Per
    Chitarra) sc BERBEN EB1519 $3.25
                                   (5817)

SANCHEZ, B.
  Berceuse
    solo voice,gtr ESCHIG f.s.   (5818)

  Ingenio, Evocation
    solo voice,gtr ESCHIG f.s.   (5819)

SCARLATTI, ALESSANDRO (1660-1725)
  O Cessate Di Piagarmi
    (Fernandez-Lavie) [It] solo voice,
    gtr (5th degr., Oeuvres Anciennes
    Pour Chant Et Guitare, No. 1) sc
    ESCHIG f.s.   (5820)
    (Fernandez-Lavie) [It] solo voice,
    gtr (5th degr., Oeuvres Anciennes
    Pour Chant Et Guitare, No. 1) sc
    SCHOTT GA-192 f.s.   (5821)

  Sento Nel Core
    (Abloniz) [It] solo voice,gtr (4th
    degr.) sc RICORDI-IT RM-129352
    f.s.   (5822)

SCHUBERT, FRANZ (PETER) (1797-1828)
  Adieu
    (Coste, Napoleon) [Fr] solo voice,
    gtr (4-5th degr., Les Melodies
    Celebres De F. Schubert) sc
    COSTALL 2603 f.s.   (5823)

  Berceuse, MIN 236
    (Coste, Napoleon) [Fr] solo voice,
    gtr (4-5th degr., Les Melodies
    Celebres De F. Schubert) sc
    COSTALL 3145 f.s.   (5824)

  Des Madchens Klage
    "Plaintes De La Jeune Fille, Les"
    (Coste, Napoleon) [Fr] solo
    voice,gtr (4-5th degr., Les
    Melodies Celebres De F. Schubert)
    sc COSTALL 3350 f.s.   (5825)

  Ellens Gesang III *Op.52,No.6,D.839
    "Ave Maria" (Coste, Napoleon) [Fr]
    solo voice,gtr (4-5th degr., Les
    Melodies Celebres De F. Schubert)
    sc COSTALL 26 f.s.   (5826)

  Fischermadchen, Das (from
    Schwanengesang, D. 957, No. 10)
    "Fille Du Pecheur, La" (Coste,
    Napoleon) [Fr] solo voice,gtr (4-
    5th degr., Les Melodies Celebres
    De F. Schubert) sc COSTALL 3125
    f.s.   (5827)

  Jeune Fille Et La Mort, La
    (Coste, Napoleon) [Fr] solo voice,
    gtr (4-5th degr., Les Melodies
    Celebres De F. Schubert) sc
    COSTALL 3120 f.s.   (5828)

  Jeune Mere, La
    (Coste, Napoleon) [Fr] solo voice,
    gtr (4-5th degr., Les Melodies
    Celebres De F. Schubert) sc
    COSTALL 3383 f.s.   (5829)

  Lieder *CC12U
    (Domandl) [Ger] solo voice,gtr (4-
    6th degr.) sc RAHTER EE-3072 f.s.
                                   (5830)

  Meunier Voyageur, Le
    (Coste, Napoleon) [Fr] solo voice,
    gtr (4-5th degr., Les Melodies
    Celebres De F. Schubert) sc
    COSTALL 3370 f.s.   (5831)

  Serenade (De Shakespeare)
    (Coste, Napoleon) [Fr] solo voice,
    gtr (4-5th degr., Les Melodies
    Celebres De F. Schubert) sc
    COSTALL 3859 f.s.   (5832)

  Serenade, MIN 57
    (Coste, Napoleon) [Fr] solo voice,
    gtr (4-5th degr., Les Melodies
    Celebres De F. Schubert) sc
    COSTALL 2520 f.s.   (5833)

  Sois Toujours Mes Seuls Amours
    (Coste, Napoleon) [Fr] solo voice,
    gtr (4-5th degr., Les Melodies
    Celebres De F. Schubert) sc
    COSTALL 3349 f.s.   (5834)

  Songs *CC9U
    (Duarte) [Ger/Eng] solo voice,gtr
    (7th degr.) sc BERBEN EB1819 f.s.
                                   (5835)

SCHULZ, JOHANN ABRAHAM PETER
    (1747-1800)
  Lieder Im Volkston *CC18U
    (Monkemeyer) gtr (3-4th degr.)
    TONGER 1321 f.s. also for solo
    voice and gtr   (5836)

SCHUTZ, HEINRICH (1585-1672)
  Geistliche Gesange, 2
    (Ragossnig) [Lat] T/S solo,gtr (7th
    degr.) sc ZIMMER. ZM-1718 f.s.
                                   (5837)

SEIBER, MATYAS GYORGY (1905-1960)
  French Folk Songs, 4
    (Bream) [Fr] solo voice,gtr (9th
    degr.) sc SCHOTT 10637 f.s.
    contains: J'ai Descendu;
    Marguerite, Elle Est Malade;
    Reveillez-Vous; Rossignol, Le
                                   (5838)

SERMISY, CLAUDE DE (CLAUDIN)
    (ca. 1490-1562)
  Tant Que Vivrai, Chanson
    (Pujol) [Fr] solo voice,gtr (5th
    degr., g is f sharp; orig for
    solo voice and lute, arr. by
    Attaingnant, publisher) sc ESCHIG
    1314 f.s.   (5839)

SIBELIUS, JEAN (1865-1957)
  Komm Herbei Tod *Op.60,No.1 (from
    Twelfth Night)
    [Ger/Swed/Eng/Fr] solo voice,gtr
    (4-5th degr.) BREITKOPF-W
    DLV-5253 f.s.   (5840)

SOR, FERNANDO (1778-1839)
Seguidillas: 12 Spanish Songs
(Jeffery) solo voice,gtr (also
partly published in "6
Seguidillas Boleras", TE-003)
TECLA f.s. cloth TE-001, pap
TE-002   (5841)

SPERONTES (JOHANN SIGISMUND SCHOLZE)
(1705-1750)
Singende Muse An Der Pleisse *CC10U
(Tucholski) gtr,vla da gamba/vcl,
solo voice or mel inst APOLLO
2316 f.s.   (5842)

STAAK, PIETER VAN DER (1930-   )
Quatrains Of Omar Khayyam, 3
[Eng] solo voice,gtr (6th degr.) sc
BROEKMANS 237 f.s.
contains: Be Glad The World Will
Stand; Oh, Seek Joy; Wine Song
Of Khayyam   (5843)

TAUBE, EVERT (1890-1976)
Visor, 50, Till Luta Och Gitarr
(Hogstedt) [Swed] solo voice,gtr
(3-4th degr.) sc NORDISKA 4500
f.s.   (5844)

TAUBERT, KARL HEINZ (1921-   )
Wiegenlied
(Behrend) [Ger] solo voice,pno/gtr
(7th degr., suppl.: arr. for gtr
of the pno accomp) RIES 10349
f.s.   (5845)

THIENEMANN, H.
Aehrenlese
solo voice,gtr HUG f.s. from LIEDER
FUR GESANG UND GITARRE   (5846)

Fruhsommerblumen
solo voice,gtr HUG f.s. from LIEDER
FUR GESANG UND GITARRE   (5847)

Heimed Luegt Di Glanzig A, D'
solo voice,gtr HUG f.s. from LIEDER
FUR GESANG UND GITARRE   (5848)

In Leisen Liedern Geht Mein Tag
solo voice,gtr HUG f.s. from LIEDER
FUR GESANG UND GITARRE   (5849)

Kleines, Stilles Leuchten, Ein
solo voice,gtr HUG f.s. from LIEDER
FUR GESANG UND GITARRE   (5850)

Sunneschyn Und Rage
solo voice,gtr HUG f.s. from LIEDER
FUR GESANG UND GITARRE   (5851)

Waldmarchen
solo voice,gtr HUG f.s. from LIEDER
FUR GESANG UND GITARRE   (5852)

THOMAS, JUAN MARIA
Canciones Populares Mallorquinas, 4
(Calatayud) [Span] solo voice,gtr
(5th degr.) sc UNION ESP. 19733
f.s.
contains: Cancion De Carnaval;
Ronda Del Viejo Enamorado;
Tonada De Labrador; Vou-Veri-
Vou   (5853)

TIPPETT, [SIR] MICHAEL (1905-   )
Songs For Achilles
[Eng/Ger] solo voice,gtr (10th
degr.) sc SCHOTT 10874 f.s.
(5854)

TROMBONCINO, BARTOLOMEO
[Chants, 3]
(Pujol) solo voice,gtr (orig for
solo voice and lute) ESCHIG 1323
f.s.   (5855)

TURINA, JOAQUIN (1882-1949)
Cantares
(Azpiazu) [Span] solo voice,gtr
(8th degr.) sc UNION ESP. 18854
f.s.   (5856)

VALDERRABANO, ENRIQUEZ DE
(fl. ca. 1550)
Ay De Mi, Romance Viejo
(Azpiazu) [Span] solo voice,gtr
(7th degr., orig for solo voice
and vihuela) sc UNION ESP. 19384
f.s.   (5857)

Ya Cabalga Calainos
(Azpiazu) [Span] solo voice,gtr
(6th degr., orig for solo voice
and vihuela) sc UNION ESP. 19385
f.s.   (5858)

VALVERDE, JOAQUIN (1846-1910)
Clavelitos
(Azpiazu) [Span] solo voice,gtr
(7th degr.) sc UNION ESP. 18853
f.s.   (5859)

VANDERMAESBRUGGE, MAX (1933-   )
Chansons De Pancruche, 5 *Op.18
[Fr] Bar solo,gtr (8th degr.) sc
CBDM 75-118 f.s.   (5860)

VASQUEZ, JUAN (fl. 1500)
De Los Alamos Vengo
(Azpiazu) [Span] solo voice,gtr
(3rd degr.) sc UNION ESP. 19390
f.s.   (5861)

En La Fuente Del Rosel, Villancico
(composed with Pisador, Diego)
(Pujol) [Span] solo voice,gtr (5th
degr., orig. for voice and
vihuela; g is f sharp) sc ESCHIG
1303 f.s.   (5862)
(Tarrago) [Span] solo voice,gtr
(5th degr., orig. for voice and
vihuela) sc UNION ESP. 20638 f.s.
(5863)

Vos Me Matastes, Villancico (composed
with Fuenllana, Miguel de)
(Pujol) [Span] solo voice,gtr (3rd
degr., g is f sharp; orig for
solo voice and vihuela) sc ESCHIG
1305 f.s.   (5864)

VECCHI, ORAZIO (HORATIO) (1550-1605)
Non Vuo Pregare
(Pujol) [It] solo voice,gtr (4th
degr., g is f sharp possible;
orig for solo voice and lute) sc
ESCHIG 1316 f.s.   (5865)

VILLA-LOBOS, HEITOR (1887-1959)
Aria (Cantilena) (from Bachianas
Brasileiras, No. 5)
[Port/Eng] solo voice,gtr (8th
degr.) sc AMP f.s.   (5866)

WALTON, [SIR] WILLIAM (TURNER)
(1902-1983)
Anon. In Love; 6 Anonymous 16th- And
17th-Century Lyrics
(Bream) [Eng] solo voice,gtr (9th
degr.) sc OXFORD 63.055 $3.70
contains: Fain Would I Change
That Note; I Gave Her Cakes And
I Gave Her Ale; Lady, When I
Behold The Roses; My Love In
Her Attire; O Stay, Sweet Love
(5867)

WEBER, CARL MARIA VON (1786-1826)
Gitarrelieder *CC14U
(Schwarz-Reiflingen) [Ger] solo
voice,gtr (3-4th degr.) sc
LEUCKART 8130 f.s.   (5868)

YUN, ISANG (1917-   )
Gagok
(Behrend) solo voice,gtr BOTE
22618 (1245)   (5869)

ZANKE, HERMAN
Berglied
"Von Der Bergeshoh'" solo voice,gtr
(3rd degr.) sc VAMO EE-03 f.s.
(5870)

ZELTER, CARL FRIEDRICH (1758-1832)
Es War Ein Konig In Thule
(Libbert) [Ger] solo voice,gtr/gtr&
A rec (2-3rd degr., Das
Gitarrenwerk, Reihe B:10) sc
PREISSLER f.s. contains also: Und
In Den Schneegebirge   (5871)

ZIPP, FRIEDRICH (1914-   )
Es Steht Ein Lind Im Tiefen Tal, 6
Deutsche Balladen
[Ger] solo voice,gtr (3-4th degr.)
sc MOSELER f.s.   (5872)

I/IIC1-Coll   Duet Collections for Guitar and Voice

ALTE UND NEUE MUSIK ZUM SINGEN UND
SPIELEN AUF BLOCKFLOTEN, GEIGEN UND
LAUTENINSTRUMENTE *folk song
(Gerwig) [Ger] (1-3rd degr.) sc
LIENAU 1375 f.s. Das Spiel Der
Lauteninstrumente, Series II,
Spielbuch 1; contains works by:
Sperontes (4), L. Mozart (3),
Rathgeber (1), Rein (5), Rhau (2),
Langenau (1), Chemin-Petit (1): for
gtr (1), 2gtr (3), 3gtr (1), rec,
gtr (8), 2rec, gtr (2), solo voice,
gtr (3), solo voice, rec, gtr (1),
solo voice, rec, 2gtr (1), rec, vln
or vla, gtr (1); arr. + orig. pcs.;
single line playing; gtr pt partly
in bass clef
contains: Bach, Johann Sebastian,
English Suite No. 6, BWV 811, In
D Minor, Gavottes I-II (gtr,1-2A
rec); Bach, Johann Sebastian,
Minuet, BWV Anh. 118, in B flat
(from Anna Magdalena Bach
Notenbuchlein (1725), No.9) (gtr,
S rec) (C maj,single line
playing, gtr pt in bass clef)
(5873)

ALTITALIENISCHE ARIEN *CC5L
(Behrend) [It] solo voice,gtr (6-7th
degr.) sc SIKORSKI 671 $4.50
contains works by: Cesti, Caldara
(2), Pergolesi, A. Scarlatti (5874)

ALTJAPANISCHE GEISHALIEDER, 5
(Behrend) solo voice,gtr (4th degr.)
sc SIKORSKI 248 $3.75   (5875)

ANONYMOUS
Troika, Altrussisches Volkslied
(Behrend) [Russ/Ger] solo voice,gtr
(5th degr.) sc SIRIUS N-8901 f.s.
(5876)

ARIE ANTICHE, 5 *CC5L
(Amato) [Lat/It] solo voice,gtr (4-
5th degr.) sc ZANIBON 5058 f.s.
contains works by: Palestrina,
Peri, Vecchi (2), Anon.   (5877)

BERGERETTES; 6 PIECES FROM THE 18TH
CENTURY
(Behrend) [Fr/Ger] solo voice,gtr
(7th degr.) sc SIKORSKI 543 $3.50
(5878)

BERUHMTE RUSSISCHE LIEDER UND ROMANZEN,
15 *CC15L,folk song
(Malukoff) [Ger/Russ] solo voice,gtr
(3rd degr.) sc ZIMMER. ZM-1321 f.s.
contains works by: Batorin,
Dubuque, Steinberg, Feldmann (5879)

BERUHMTE RUSSISCHE LIEDER UND ROMANZEN,
15
(Malukoff) [Russ/Ger] solo voice,gtr
(4th degr.) sc ZIMMER. ZM-1321 f.s.
(5880)

BIMBELI, BAMBELI; 15 LAUTENLIEDER VON
DEN KINDERN UND FUR DEN KINDERN
(Roelli) solo voice,gtr (3rd degr.)
HUG GH-7783 f.s.   (5881)

BRUDER SINGER, LIEDER UNSERES VOLKES
*CC152L
(Wolki) [Ger] solo voice,gtr (2-4th
degr.) sc BAREN. 3879 f.s. contains
12 Christmas carols and 76
folksongs; contains works by: Anon.
(36), Lau (2), W.A. Mozart, Baumann
(3), Hensel (3), Bresgen (2),
Reichardt (2), Schulz (2), Luther,
Gneist, Ebeling, Marx, Vulpius (2),
Schutz, Isaac (2), Dietrich,
Kukuck, Scheidt, Silcher(2),
Albert, Nicolai (2), Zuccalmaglio,
Werlin, Walter, Cruger, Pohlenz,
Becker, Knab, Wolters   (5882)

CANCIONES ANTIGUAS, 5
(Tarrago) [Span] solo voice,gtr (7-
8th degr.) sc UNION ESP. 20029 f.s.
orig. for solo voice and vihuela;
contains works by: Anon. (2),
Morales-Fuenllana, Milan, Fuenllana
contains: Aquel Caballero, Madre;
De Antequera Sale El Moro; De Los
Alamos Vengo, Madre; Duelete De
Mi, Senora; Perdida Tengo La
Color   (5883)

CANCIONES ANTIGUAS, 6
(Tarrago) [Span] solo voice,gtr (6th
degr.) sc UNION ESP. 20638 f.s.
orig. for solo voice and vihuela;
contains works by: Milan, Vazquez-
Pisador, Anchieta, Valderrabano
Pisador (2)
contains: Agora Viniese Un Viento;
Con Amores La Mi Madre; Donde Son
Estas Serranas?; En La Fuente Del
Rosel; Porque Es, Dama, Tanto
Quereros?; Si Te Vas A Banar,
Juanica   (5884)

CANCIONES DEL SIGLO XVII, 5
(Tarrago) [Span] solo voice,gtr (7th
degr.) sc UNION ESP. 20182 f.s.
contains works by: Romero, Marin,
Anon. (2), del Vado
contains: A Quien Contare Mis
Quejas?; Al Son De Los
Arroyuelos; En Esta Larga
Ausencia; Molinillo Que Mueles
Amores; Oh, Que Bien Baila Gil!
(5885)

CANCIONES POPULARES CATALANAS, 4
(Tarrago) [Span] solo voice,gtr (5th
degr.) sc UNION ESP. 20181 f.s.
contains: Calma De La Mar, La;
Canco Del Lladre, La; Corrandes;
Lapreso De Lleida   (5886)

CANCIONES POPULARES ESPANOLAS
(Tarrago) [Span] solo voice,gtr (6-
8th degr.) sc UNION ESP. 19637 f.s.
15 pcs.
contains: Campanas De Belen; Ya Se
Van Los Pastores   (5887)

CANCIONES POPULARES ESPANOLAS, 5
(Azpiazu) [Span] solo voice,gtr (5th
degr.) sc UNION ESP. 19403 f.s.
contains: Ya Se Van Los Pastores,
"Pastores, Los"   (5888)

CHANSON D'AMOURS ELIZABETHAINES, 3
(Castet) [Fr] solo voice,gtr (7th
degr.) sc LEDUC G-17 f.s. Guitare,
No.17; orig for solo voice and
lute; contains works by: Jones,
Pilkington, Morley
contains: Et Si Je Cherche Ton
Amour?; Sous Un Cypres; Viens A
Ton Amant   (5889)

[CHANTS, 4]
(Pujol) solo voice,gtr (orig for solo
voice and lute; contains works by:
Fuenllana, Daza, Briceno, Cara)
ESCHIG 1324 f.s.   (5890)

[CHANTS, 10]
(Pujol) solo voice,gtr (arr + orig
pcs; 2 vols.; contains works by:
Anon. (5), Capitan, Marin, de los
Rios, Blas, Esteve) ESCHIG
1321A, 1321B f.s.   (5891)

CHORAL UND LAUTE
(Funck) [Ger] (3rd degr.) sc LIENAU
1435 f.s. Das Spiel Der
Lauteninstrumente, Series II,
Spielbuch 12; 10 Pcs; contains
works by: Anon., Nicolai, Neumark,
Gastorius, Gesius [sic, i.e.—
Hassler], Luther (2), Cruger,
Vulpius, Forster, for solo voice,
gtr, (nos. 1-8 also transcribed for
gtr solo) arr by W. Gerwig; nos. 2,
3, 5, 6, 10 arr. by J.S. Bach
contains: Bach, Johann Sebastian,
Aus Tiefer Not Schrei Ich Zu Dir.
Chorale (from Cantata No. 38)
(gtr,solo voice); Bach, Johann
Sebastian, Befiehl Du Deine Wege.
Chorale, BWV 270 (gtr,opt solo
voice); Bach, Johann Sebastian,
Nun Ruhen Alle Walder. Chorale,
BWV 392 (gtr,solo voice); Bach,
Johann Sebastian, Wer Nur Den
Lieben Gott Lasst Walten.
Chorale, BWV 434 (gtr,opt solo
voice); Bach, Johann Sebastian,
Wie Schon Leuchtet Der
Morgenstern. Chorale, BWV 436
(gtr,opt solo voice)   (5892)

CLASSICAL SONGS, 10
(Gavall) solo voice,gtr (4-5th degr.)
sc NOVELLO 2543 $2.75 arr + 2 pcs
orig for lute-'g'; orig words + Eng
transl; contains works by: Dowland
(2), Handel, Mozart, Liszt, Verdi,
Grieg (2)
contains: Bach, Johann Sebastian,
Bist Du Bei Mir, BWV 508 (from
Anna Magdalena Bach Notenbuchlein
(1725), No. 25) (A maj); Bach,
Johann Sebastian, Wachet Auf,
Ruft Uns Die Stimme. Chorale
(from Cantata No. 140) (C maj)
                                 (5893)

DEUTSCHE MEISTER DES EIN- UND
ZWEISTIMMIGEN LAUTENSATZES, 16.-18.
JAHRHUNDERT
(Bruger) [Ger] (1-3rd degr.) MOSELER
f.s. contains 22 arr + orig pcs; 12
pcs by: Heckel (1), M. Neusiedler
(1), Hainhofer (9), for gtr (1
Line); 2 pcs by Anon., H.
Neusiedler for gtr (2 lines); 6 pcs
by: Anon. (2), Judenkunig (1), H.
Neusiedler (3) for solo voice, gtr
(2 lines)
contains: Bach, Johann Sebastian,
Prelude, Fugue, And Allegro For
Lute In E Flat, BWV 998: Allegro
(gtr) (C maj, fragment only);
Bach, Johann Sebastian, Suite for
Lute, BWV 996, in E minor,
Bourree (2gtr) (partly single
line playing); Bach, Johann
Sebastian, Suite for Lute, BWV
996, in E minor, Passaggio-
Prelude (2gtr) (single line
playing)   (5894)

DIR ZU EIGEN; 13 LIEBESLIEDER
(Holzmeister) solo voice,gtr (1st
degr., 1 song for solo voice, gtr;
other pieces for 2 solo voices)
FIDULA f.s.   (5895)

EARLY ENGLISH LUTE SONGS AND FOLK
SONGS, VOL. I *CC24U,folk song
(Runge) [Eng] solo voice,gtr (3-4th
degr.) sc HARGAIL H-118 f.s. arr. +
orig. pcs.; contains works by:
Hume, Campion, Purcell, Anon. (6),
Niles   (5896)

EARLY ENGLISH LUTE SONGS AND FOLK
SONGS, VOL. II *CC24U, folk song
(Runge) [Eng] solo voice,gtr (3-4th
degr.) sc HARGAIL HFA-7 f.s. arr. +

orig. pcs.; contains works by:
Campion, Ford, Dowland (2), Purcell
(2), Anon., Blow, Urfey (4), Runge
(2), Wiles; Hargail Folk Anthology,
No.7   (5897)

EARLY ENGLISH LUTE SONGS AND FOLK
SONGS, VOL. III *folk song
(Runge) [Eng] solo voice,gtr (3-4th
degr.) sc HARGAIL HFA-18 f.s. arr.
+ orig. pcs.; contains 16 works by:
Anon. (2), Dowland, Pilkington,
Campion, Blow, Young; Hargail Folk
Anthology, No.18
contains: Anonymous, Agincourt
Carol, The   (5898)

EARLY ENGLISH LUTE SONGS AND FOLK
SONGS, VOL. IV *CC15L,folk song
(Runge) [Eng] solo voice,gtr (3-4th
degr.) sc HARGAIL HFA-26 f.s. arr.
+ orig. pcs.; contains works by:
Campion (2), Dowland, Playford,
Arne, Hook, Wilson; Hargail Folk
Anthology, No.26   (5899)

ENGELSE VOLKSLIEDEREN, 3
(Visser) [Eng/Dutch] solo voice,gtr
(3-4th degr.) sc HARMONIA 1263 f.s.
contains: Ash Grove, The; Drink To
Me; 0 No, John   (5900)

ENGLISH RENAISSANCE SONGS — ANGOL
RENESZANSZ DALOK *CC20U
(Benko) [Eng] gtr (6-7th degr.) sc
EMB 7799 f.s. contains works by:
Morley; Rosseter; Dowland;
Pilkington; Coprario; Hume; R.
Jones; Campian and Anonymous (5901)

ENGLISH SONGS, 3
(Choppen) [Eng] solo voice,gtr (4th
degr., contains works by: Lawes,
Humphrey, Anon.) sc SCHOTT 10871
f.s.   (5902)

ES BRENNT, LIEDER AUS DEM GHETTO *CC7U
(Behrend) [Heb] solo voice,gtr (3-4th
degr.) sc SIKORSKI 679 f.s.   (5903)

ES RITTEN DREI REITER
(Libbert) [Ger] solo voice,gtr/gtr&S
rec (2nd degr.) Das Gitarrenwerk,
Reihe B:9) sc PREISSLER f.s.
contains also: Es Wollt Ein
Leineweber Wandern   (5904)

EUROPAISCHE VOLKSLIEDER, VOL. I
(Pauli) solo voice,gtr (orig words +
Ger transl; contains 10 pcs from
France, Finland, Russia, Ukraine,
Latvia, Armenia) sc DEUTSCHER 9051
f.s.   (5905)

EUROPAISCHE VOLKSLIEDER, VOL. II
(Pauli) solo voice,gtr (orig words +
Ger transl; contains 10 pcs from
Poland, Sweden, England) sc
DEUTSCHER 9052 f.s.   (5906)

FINNISCHE VOLKSLIEDER, SUOMALAISIA
KANSANLAULUJA *CC12U
(Schaller) [Finn/Ger] solo voice,gtr
(4-5th degr.) sc NAGELS EN-1099
f.s. Nagels Laute- Und Gitarre-
Archiv   (5907)

FOLKSONGS, 10
(Kingsley) [Eng/Fr] solo voice,gtr
(3-4th degr.) sc SCHOTT GA-204 f.s.
                                 (5908)

FOLKSONGS, 10 ENGLISH FOLKSONGS
(Haring) [Eng] solo voice,gtr (7th
degr., notation: tr-clef + "cifra"
(tablature)) sc NOVELLO 19274 f.s.
                                 (5909)

FOUR CENTURIES OF SONG, FROM THE
TROUBADOUR TO THE ELIZABETHAN AGE
*CC31L
(Iadone) solo voice,gtr (4-6th degr.)
sc AMP 7401 f.s. arr + orig pcs,
for solo voice and lute (vihuela);
orig. and Eng words; contains works
by: Anon. (13), Campion (2),
Vecchi, Morales, R. Johnson,
Dowland, Jones, Isaac, Gabriel,
Bartlett, Fuenllana, Ventadour,
Guedron, Milan, Ferrabosco II,
Encina, Sermisy, Morley   (5910)

FRANSE VOLKSLIEDEREN, 3
(Visser) [Fr/Eng] solo voice,gtr (4th
degr.) sc HARMONIA 1256 f.s.
contains: Bon Secrets, Les; Fille
Matelot, La; Matinale, La   (5911)

GALEN MAN
[Swed] solo voice,gtr (5th degr.) sc
REUTER f.s. contains works by: U.G.
Ahslund (3), K. Ahslund
contains: Galen Man; Levande Barn;
Nar Bittan Hjalper Mamma; Sag Du
                                 (5912)

GITARRELIEDER FUR ALLE, VOLKSLIEDER
*CC16L,folk song
(Burkhart; Scheit) [Ger] solo voice,

gtr (2-3rd degr.) sc DOBLINGER
05924 f.s. contains works by:
Silcher, Zollner, Werner, Frohlich,
Nageli, Gluck   (5913)

GOLDEN SONGS *CC10L
(Komter) [Eng] solo voice,gtr (7-8th
degr.) sc HARMONIA 2041 f.s. orig
for solo voice and lute; contains
works by: Jones (3), Campian (2),
Dowland (5)   (5914)

GUIGNOLOT
(Grimbert) [Fr] solo voice,gtr (3rd
degr., Plein Jeu, No.298) sc HEUGEL
PJ-298 f.s.   (5915)

GUITAR SONGBOOK, THE *folk song
(Noad) [Eng] (2-7th degr.) COLLIER
f.s. 72 arr + orig pcs; contains
works by: Anon. (6), Noad (1),
Gruber (1), Hopkins (1), Dun (1),
Poulton (1), Moore (1), Hume (1),
Schubert (2), Pergolesi (1), Blow
(1), Dowland (2), E. Purcell (1),
Rosseter (1), Morley (1), Martini
(1), Handel (1) for solo voice,
gtr; H. Purcell (2), Glinka (1),
Attwood (1), Gluck (1), Beethoven
(1), Schumann (1), Tchaikovsky (1),
Zipoli (1), Haydn (1), D. Scarlatti
(1) for 2 gtr; Sor (1), C.P.E. Bach
(1), Handel (2), Corelli (1),
Carcassi (1), Purcell (1), Carulli
(1), Dowland (1), Anon. (1), Mozart
(1) for gtr; with an introduction:
Complete Notes Of The Guitar, Chord
Chart, How Guitar Music Is Written,
Principal Elements Of Guitar
Technique (36p., 17 ill.)
contains: Coventry Carol, The (gtr,
solo voice); First Noel, The
(solo voice,gtr); Gruber, Franz
Xaver, Silent Night (gtr,solo
voice); Hopkins, John Henry, Jr.,
We Three Kings (gtr,solo voice)
                                 (5916)

8 INTERNATIONALE VOLKSLIEDER *CC8U
(Schaller) solo voice,gtr (3rd degr.)
sc PREISSLER B 15 f.s. Das
Gitarrenwerk, Series B, No. 15
                                 (5917)

INTERNATIONALE VOLKSLIEDER, VOL. I
(Behrend) solo voice,gtr (7-8th
degr., orig words + Ger transl;
contains 4 pcs from Indonesia,
Ceylon, America, Israel) SIKORSKI
668A f.s.   (5918)

INTERNATIONALE VOLKSLIEDER, VOL. II
(Behrend) solo voice,gtr (7-8th
degr., orig words + Ger transl;
contains 4 pcs from Spain, Germany,
Russia, Trinidad) SIKORSKI 668B
f.s.   (5919)

INTERNATIONALE VOLKSLIEDER, VOL. III
(Behrend) solo voice,gtr (7-8th
degr., orig words + Ger transl; 5
pcs) SIKORSKI 668C f.s.   (5920)

INTERNATIONALE VOLKSLIEDER, VOL. IV
(Behrend) solo voice,gtr (7-8th
degr., orig words + Ger transl;
contains 4 pcs from Cambodia,
Israel, Congo, Philippines)
SIKORSKI 668D f.s.   (5921)

ITALIAN SONGS OF THE RENAISSANCE AND
BAROQUE PERIODS *CC16L
(Runge) [It/Eng/Fr/Ger] solo voice,
gtr (5-7th degr.) sc HARGAIL HFA-16
f.s. arr + orig pcs; contains works
by: Tromboncino, Caccini (2),
Bottegari, Peri, Kapsberger (3),
Frescobaldi, Pesenti, Tarditi,
Cesti, Anon. (3), Handel; Hargail
Folk Anthology, No.16   (5922)

JIDDISCHE LIEDER *CC4U
(Behrend) [Heb] solo voice,gtr (3-4th
degr.) sc SIKORSKI 678 f.s.   (5923)

JUGEND SINGT ZUR GITARRE, 50 [SIC]
DEUTSCHE UND AUSSERDEUTSCHE VOLKS-
UND JUGENDLIEDER *CC49L,folk song
(Wolki) [Ger/Fr] solo voice,gtr (3rd
degr.) sc MOSELER f.s. contains
works by: Baumann (7), Bendig,
Hoof, Bresgen (3), Kukuck (2),
Kraft, Lau (3), Marx, Rohwer,
Wolters, Kopp   (5924)

KLAMPFENLIED, DAS, EIN
FAHRTENLIEDERBUCH *CC76U
(Zschiesche) [Ger] solo voice,gtr
(3rd degr.) SCHOTT 4462 f.s. (5925)

KLINGENDE FAHRT, EIN LIEDERBUCH
*CC139U
(Zschiesche) [Ger] solo voice,gtr
(3rd degr.) min sc SCHOTT 4840 f.s.
                                 (5926)

KOMMT SINGT UND SPIELT: LIEDER UNSERER
ZEIT, FUR DEN ANFANGSUNTERRICHT
*folk song

(Kramer) [Ger] (1-2nd degr.) sc
HOFMEISTER T-4137 f.s. contains 30
works by: Hubschmann (1), Franz
(1), Richter (1), Mertke (1),
Dittrich (1), Bimberg (1),
Schuffenhauer (1), Stumpe (1) for 2
gtr; Groger (1), Hein (1), Richter-
Ulbrich (1), Lukowsky (2), Balzer
(1), Ahrend (1), Meyer (1),
Natschinski (1), Kochan (1),
Englert (1) for 1 gtr; Natschinski
(1), Becher (1), Eisler (1),
Naumilkat (1), Schwaen (1), Bimberg
(1), Folksongs (2), Schmidt (1) for
solo voice and gtr; partly single
line playing (2 gtr)
  contains: Richter, Eva, Unsere
  Tannenbaum (composed with
  Ulbrich, Christel) (gtr);
  Richter, Wolfgang, Weihnachtszeit
  (2gtr) (single line playing)
                                    (5927)

KUNSTLIEDER
(Henze, Bruno) [Ger] (3-7th degr.) sc
HOFMEISTER T-4012 $6.00 Das
Gitarrespiel, Vol. XII; 30 Pcs;
contains works by: Dowland (2),
Albert (2), Krieger (2), Kremberg,
Beyer (2), A. Scarlatti,
Rathgeber(2), W.A. Mozart, Weber
(2), Schubert (2), Schumann,
Brahms, Pabel (2), Stingl (4),
Hlouschek (2) for solo voice, gtr;
by W.A. Mozart for solo voice,
mando, gtr; by Ambrosius for 2 solo
voices, gtr
  contains: Bach, Johann Sebastian,
  Aria Di Giovannini, "Willst Du
  Dein Herz Mir Schenken", BWV 518
  (from Anna Magdalena Bach
  Notenbuchlein (1725), No. 37)
  (2gtr,solo voice) (C maj) (5928)

LATIN-MUSIC; FAVORITE SONGS FROM
ARGENTINA, BRESIL, CHILE, CUBA,
HAITI, HAWAII, JAMAICA, MEXICO,
SPAIN, TRINIDAD, VOL. 1 *CC15L,
folk song
(Tucholski) solo voice,gtr (3-4th
degr.) sc APOLLO 2329 f.s. arr +
orig pcs (with use of orig.
melodies); orig. words + Ger
transl.; contains works by:
Creutziger (3), Tucholski (6),
Fernandez, Yradier, Serradell
                                    (5929)

LATIN-MUSIC; FAVORITE SONGS FROM
ARGENTINA, BRESIL, CHILE, CUBA,
HAITI, HAWAII, JAMAICA, MEXICO,
SPAIN, TRINIDAD, VOL. 2 *CC15L,
folk song
(Tucholski) solo voice,gtr (3-4th
degr.) sc APOLLO 2330 f.s. arr +
orig pcs (with use of orig.
melodies); orig. words + Ger
transl.; contains works by:
Tucholski (10), Creutziger (2)
                                    (5930)

LAUTENMUSIKANT, DER *CC232U
(Gotze) solo voice,gtr (2-3rd degr.)
cmplt ed SCHOTT 4850 f.s. 3 vols.
in 1   (5931)

LAUTENMUSIKANT, DER, VOL. I *CC79U
(Gotze) solo voice,gtr (2-3rd degr.)
SCHOTT 2392 f.s.   (5932)

LAUTENMUSIKANT, DER, VOL. II *CC88U
(Gotze) solo voice,gtr (2-3rd degr.)
SCHOTT 3585 f.s.   (5933)

LAUTENMUSIKANT, DER, VOL. III *CC75U
(Gotze) solo voice,gtr (2-3rd degr.)
SCHOTT 4065 f.s.   (5934)

LAUTENSCHLAGER, DER *folk song
(Giesbert) [Ger] solo voice,gtr (3rd
degr., 4 vols.; 4 vols. in 1:
Pfauen-12; vol. 1-4: Pfauen-12, 1-
4; vol. 1-2 in 1: Pfauen-12a)
PFAUEN f.s.   (5935)

LAUTENSPIELER, DER, NO. 2 *CC7U
(Funck) solo voice,gtr/gtr solo (2nd
degr.) FIDULA f.s. 6 pcs for gtr; 1
pce for solo voice and gtr   (5936)

LAUTENSPIELER, DER, NO. 3 *CC4U
(Funck) solo voice,gtr (1-2nd degr.)
FIDULA f.s. contains 4 pcs:
Anonymous (2), and folksongs (2)
                                    (5937)

LAUTENSPIELER, DER, NO. 5 *CC4U
(Funck) solo voice,gtr (1-2nd degr.)
FIDULA f.s. contains 4pcs: Frohlich
(1), and Folksongs (3)   (5938)

LAUTENSPIELER, DER, NO. 7 *CC7U
(Funck) solo voice,gtr (1-2nd degr.)
FIDULA f.s. contains 4 pcs:
Folksongs (3), and Schulz (1)
                                    (5939)

LAUTENSPIELER, DER, NO. 8 *CC4U
(Funck) solo voice,gtr (1-2nd degr.)
FIDULA f.s. contains 4 pcs:
Folksongs (3), and Anonymous (1)

                                    (5940)
LAUTENSPIELER DES XVI. JAHRHUNDERTS
(LIUTISTI DEL CINQUECENTO)
*CC124UL
(Chilesotti, Oscar) gtr (single
staff/8th degr.) quarto oblong
FORNI f.s. repr of 1st ed., publ
Ricordi-Breitkopf & Hartel (1891);
"Bibliotheca Musica Bononiensis",
Sezione IV, No. 31; includes works
by: Newsidler, Anon., Ballet,
Gintzler, Matelart, Gorzanis, da
Milano, Galilei, Barbetta, Caroso,
Terzi, Molinaro, dalla Gostena,
Negri, Besard, Mersenne,
Gianoncelli —all for 1 gtr;
Matelart, Galilei, Besard —for 2
gtr; Caroso, Negri —for dsc inst
and gtr; Fallamero, Besard —for vce
and gtr; Terzi —for 3 gtr; Besard —
for dsc inst and 3 gtr   (5941)

LIED UND GITARRE, 40 DEUTSCHE UND
AUSLANDISCHE VOLKSLIEDER, VOL. 1
(Teuchert) (1-3rd degr.) sc,pt
SCHMIDT,H 97 f.s. 32 pcs for solo
voice, gtr or 2gtr; 8 pcs for solo
voice, gtr; Suppl.: arr for gtr I
(single line playing) of solo voice
pt; Vol.I:18 pcs
  contains: Ya Se Van Los Pastores,
  "Pastores, Los" (solo voice,gtr)
                                    (5942)

LIED UND GITARRE, 40 DEUTSCHE UND
AUSLANDISCHE VOLKSLIEDER, VOL. 2
*CCU
(Teuchert) 2gtr (1-3rd degr.) sc,pt
SCHMIDT,H 98 f.s. 32 pcs for solo
voice, gtr or 2gtr; 8 pcs for solo
voice, gtr; Suppl.: arr for gtr I
(single line playing) of solo voice
pt; Vol. II:22 pcs, pp.49-55:
Anleitungen Zur Liedbegleitung Nach
Dem Gehor   (5943)

LIED- UND GITARRENSPIEL, VOLKS- UND
TANZLIEDER, VOL. I *folk song
(Bresgen; Zanoskar) [Ger] solo voice,
gtr (3rd degr.) sc SCHOTT 5414 f.s.
30 arr + orig pcs; contains works
by: Anon. (8), Zuccalmaglio (2),
Rathgeber, Schulz (2), Albert,
Bresgen
  contains: Ihr Kinderlein Kommet;
  Still, Still, Still   (5944)

LIED- UND GITARRENSPIEL, VOLKS- UND
TANZLIEDER, VOL. II *folk song
(Bresgen; Zanoskar) [Ger] solo voice,
gtr (3rd degr.) sc SCHOTT 5415 f.s.
30 arr + orig. pcs.; contains
works by: Rathgeber, Anon. (7),
Weber (3), Zelter, Reinhardt (2),
Steuerlein, Praetorius, Telemann,
Krieger
  contains: O Tannenbaum; Bach,
  Johann Sebastian, Gib Dich
  Zufrieden, BWV 460 (from
  Schemelli's Gesangbuch); Bach,
  Johann Sebastian, Guldne Sonne,
  Die, BWV 451 (from Schemelli's
  Gesangbuch); Bach, Johann
  Sebastian, Ich Steh An Deiner
  Krippen Hier, BWV 469 (from
  Schemelli's Gesangbuch); Bach,
  Johann Sebastian, Tag Ist Hin,
  Der, BWV 447 (from Schemelli's
  Gesangbuch); Gruber, Franz Xaver,
  Stille Nacht   (5945)

LIEDER DER VOLKER, VOL. I
(Behrend) solo voice,gtr (3-6th
degr.) sc ZIMMER. ZM-1398 f.s. arr
+ orig pcs; orig words; 5 pcs;
Folksongs from Israel, Japan,
Germany, Italy
  contains: Bach, Johann Sebastian,
  Aria Di Giovannini, "Willst Du
  Dein Herz Mir Schenken", BWV 518
  (from Anna Magdalena Bach
  Notenbuchlein (1725), No. 37) (E
  maj)   (5946)

LIEDER DER VOLKER, VOL. II *CC4L
(Behrend) solo voice,gtr (3-6th
degr.) sc ZIMMER. ZM-1709 f.s. arr
+ orig pcs; orig words; Folksongs
from Turkey, Eastern Europe, Yemen,
Poland   (5947)

LIEDER DER VOLKER, VOL. III *CC4L
(Behrend) solo voice,gtr (3-6th
degr.) sc ZIMMER. ZM-1745 f.s. arr
+ orig pcs; orig words; contains
works by: Behrend, Becker;
Folksongs from Colombia (2), France
                                    (5948)

LIEDER DER VOLKER, VOL. IV *CC8L
(Behrend) solo voice,gtr (3-6th
degr.) sc ZIMMER. ZM-1784 f.s. arr
+ orig pcs; orig words; Folksongs
from Russia (4), Japan, Germany,
Yugoslavia, Israel   (5949)

LIEDER DER VOLKER, VOL. V *CC7L
(Behrend) solo voice,gtr (3-6th
degr.) sc ZIMMER. ZM-1785 f.s. arr
+ orig pcs; orig words; Folksongs
from Italy (2), Russia, Germany
(2), Japan, Eastern Europe   (5950)

LIEDER DER VOLKER, VOL. VI *CCU
(Behrend) solo voice,gtr (3-6th
degr.) sc ZIMMER. ZM-1786 f.s. arr
+ orig pcs; orig words   (5951)

LIEDER IM JAHRESKREIS *CC40L,folk song
(Karl) [Ger] solo voice,gtr (2-3rd
degr.) sc PREISSLER JP-7021 f.s.
arr + 1 orig pce; Introduction To
Accompaniment By Guitar (3p.) in
Ger; contains works by: Anon. (33),
Hensel, Demantius, Reichhardt, Karl
                                    (5952)

LIEDERSCHATZ ZUR GITARRE *CC45U
(Schmidt) solo voice,gtr SCHMIDT,H 42
f.s.   (5953)

LIEDJES ROND DE MUIDERKRING *CC9U
(Komter) [Dutch] solo voice,gtr (3rd
degr.) sc HARMONIA 2040 f.s.
contains works by: Anon., Roemer
Visser, Starter-Vredeman (2),
Starter, van der Wielen, Bredero
(2), Westerbaan   (5954)

LOSST MICH LEBEN
(Behrend) solo voice,gtr (5 Yiddish
songs) sc SIKORSKI 775 f.s. (5955)

MAGYAR ZENE GITARRA A XIX. SZADAD ELSO
FELEBOL
"Ungarische Musik Fur Gitarre Aus Der
Ersten Halfte Des 19. Jahrhunderts"
(Brodszky) [Hung] gtr (2-4th degr.)
Afterword in Hung, Ger, Eng; 59 arr
+ orig pcs; contains works by:
Jager (1), Horecki (5), Anon. (2),
Pfeifer (6), Lavotta (3), Sarkozy
(1), Svastics (2), Fay (2),
Rozsavolgyi (1), Wilt (4), Padowetz
(1), Mertz (12), Ruzitska (1),
Kossovits (2), Folksongs (16), for
gtr solo; 2 pcs. by Anon. for fl,
gtr (1) and solo voice, gtr (1)) sc
SCHOTT 5839 f.s.   (5956)
"Ungarische Musik Fur Gitarre Aus Der
Ersten Halfte Des 19. Jahrhunderts"
(Brodszky) [Hung] gtr (2-4th degr.)
Afterword in Hung, Ger, Eng; 59 arr
+ orig pcs; contains works by:
Jager (1), Horecki (5), Anon. (2),
Pfeifer (6), Lavotta (3), Sarkozy
(1), Svastics (2), Fay (2),
Rozsavolgyi (1), Wilt (4), Padowetz
(1), Mertz (12), Ruzitska (1),
Kossovits (2), Folksongs (16), for
gtr solo; 2 pcs. by Anon. for fl,
gtr (1) and solo voice, gtr (1)) sc
EMB Z-2985 f.s.   (5957)

MAITIA NUN ZIRA
"Adieu Ma Chere Vallee" (Fernandez
Lavie) solo voice,gtr (4th degr.,
Oeuvres Anciennes Pour Chant Et
Guitare, No. 4) sc SCHOTT GA-195
f.s.   (5958)
"Adieu Ma Chere Vallee" (Fernandez
Lavie) solo voice,gtr (4th degr.,
Oeuvres Anciennes Pour Chant Et
Guitare, No. 4) sc ESCHIG f.s.
                                    (5959)

MANNLEIN STEHT IM WALDE, EIN, DIE
SCHONSTEN ALTEN KINDERLIEDER
*CC38U
(Just; Muller; Quadt) [Ger] solo
voice,gtr (1-2nd degr.) sc
DEUTSCHER 32013 f.s. illus.   (5960)

MEIN ERSTES SPIELBUCH, MIT TONIKA UND
DOMINANTE *CC29U
(Holz) [Ger] solo voice,gtr (1-2nd
degr.) sc DUX f.s. 5 songs with
chord symbols only   (5961)

MIT DER GITARRE, UNTERHALTUNGS-ALBUM
*CC28L,folk song
(Grosse; Wolf) [Ger] gtr (3rd degr.)
sc HARTH 2818 f.s. arr + orig pcs;
contains works by: Coste (1),
Carcassi (1), Rameau (1), Anon.
16th Cent. (1), Yradier (1),
Soloviev-Sedoy (1), Schubert (2),
Smetana (1) for 1 gtr; Schumann
(1), W.A. Mozart (1), Freire (1),
Granados (1) for 2 gtr; W.A. Mozart
(1), Petersen (2), Pakhmoutova (1),
Shanty (1), Nier (1), Ostrovski
(1), Schneider (1) for solo voice,
gtr   (5962)

MORGEN- UND ABENDLIEDER *folk song
(Schaller, Erwin) [Ger] (3rd degr.)
sc,pts MOSELER f.s. 20 pcs;
contains works by: Bendig, Baumann
(2), Reichardt, Rohwer, Ebeling,
Weber, Bresgen for solo voice, gtr;
by Vulpius, Hensel, Ahle, Schulz,
Brahms for solo voice, A rec or vln
or vla, gtr

contains: Bach, Johann Sebastian,
Nun Ruhen Alle Walder. Chorale,
BWV 392 (gtr,solo voice) (F maj)
(5963)

MUSIK AUS WIEN; 16 DER SCHONSTEN
WIENERLIEDER
(Huber) [Ger] solo voice,gtr (4-5th
degr.) sc DOBLINGER 05924 f.s.
(5964)

MUZIEKBIJLAGE, NO. 53
solo voice and gtr; treb inst and
gtr; 2-3 solo voices (4th degr.) sc
VER.HUIS. f.s. arr. + orig. pcs.;
for solo voice, gtr (2), for treb
inst, gtr (2), for 2 and 3 solo
voices (2)
contains: Ik Zie De Morgen Sterre;
Zing En Blyf Tevree; Niessen,
Hans-Lutz, Boer Had Maar Enen
Schoen, De; Niessen, Hans-Lutz,
Canon; Niessen, Hans-Lutz, Neem
Het Niet Zo Precies   (5965)

NEDERLANDSE VOLKSLIEDEREN, 3
(Visser) [Dutch] solo voice,gtr (4th
degr.) sc HARMONIA 1257 f.s.
contains: Heer Jesus Heeft Een
Hofken; Vier Weverkens; Was Een
Maged Uitverkoren, Het   (5966)

NORDISCHE VOLKSLIEDER
(Schaller) [Ger] solo voice,gtr (3-
4th degr.) sc NAGELS EN-1110 f.s.
Nagels Laute- Und Gitarre-Archiv
contains: Am Lustigen Strand; Aus
Herzensgrund Mein Leben Lang; Es
War Ein Sommermorgen; Ich Kam Das
Morgenrot Herauf; Liebliche,
Frohliche Sommerzeit, Die; Uber
Alles Hier Auf Erden   (5967)

NUEVE CANCIONES GRANADINAS, 9 CANTOS DE
LA ALPUJARRA LLAMADOS "REMERINOS"
(Ortega Blanco) [Span] solo voice,gtr
(7th degr.) sc UNION ESP. f.s.
(5968)

OB I LACH ODER SING, VOLKSLIEDER AUS
DER DEUTSCHEN SCHWEIZ
(Leeb) [Swiss/Ger] solo voice,gtr (2-
3rd degr., 86 folksongs) sc PELIKAN
806 f.s.   (5969)

OUD-NEDERLANDSE LIEDEREN *CC8U
(Theunen-Seidl; Muller) [Dutch] solo
voice,gtr (3-4th degr.) sc MAURER
f.s.   (5970)

PIOSENKI LUDOWE I POPULARNE *CC23U
(Powrozniak) [Polish] solo voice,gtr
(3-4th degr.) sc POLSKIE 5863 f.s.
Grajmy Na Gitarze, Vol. II (5971)

PIOSENKI Z PODDASZA, NA GLOS I GITARE
*CC23L,folk song
(Powrozniak) [Polish] solo voice,gtr
(3-4th degr.) sc POLSKIE 6329 f.s.
contains works by: Schiller, Kozar-
Slobodzki, Zeller, Lewandowski,
Koschat, Katski   (5972)

PRZY GITARZE, VOL. I: UKOCHANY KRAJ,
PIESNI I TANCE POLSKIE *CC51L,folk
song
(Powrozniak) [Polish] solo voice,gtr
(3-6th degr.) sc POLSKIE f.s.
contains works by: Sygietynski (7)
(5973)

PRZY GITARZE, VOL. II: NASZE PIOSENKI
(Powrozniak) [Polish] solo voice,gtr
(3-6th degr.) sc POLSKIE   (5974)

PRZY GITARZE, VOL. III: W CICHY WIECZOR
*CC41L
(Powrozniak) [Polish] solo voice,gtr
(3-6th degr.) sc POLSKIE f.s.
contains works by: Fliess, Martini,
Schubert (5), Taubert, Moniuszko
(2), Bizet, Brahms, Rubinstein,
Tchaikovsky, Yradier, Tosti (3),
Toselli, Curtis (3), Tagliaferri,
Capua, Kotarbinski, Rutkowski,
Rozycki, Maklakiewicz, Szpilman,
Buzuk, Soloviev-Siedoy, Dunajewski,
Rodygin, Nowikow, Folksongs (7)
(5975)

RINKE RANKE ROSENSCHEIN; 77
KINDERLIEDER *folk song
(Schaller) [Ger] solo voice,gtr (1-
3rd degr.) sc BAREN. 2893 f.s. arr
+ orig pcs; contains works by:
Schmid, Schaller (4), Franck, Anon.
(3), Schulz, A. Weber, Pudelko (3),
Reichardt
contains: ABC-Krippenlied; Alle
Jahre Wieder; Drei Konige Fuhret
Die Gottliche Hand; Ihr
Kinderlein Kommet; Joseph, Lieber
Joseph Mein; Weinacht, Wie Bist
Do Schon   (5976)

RUSSISCHE VOLKSMUSIK *CCU
(Tucholski) [Ger] gtr APOLLO 2211 42
pcs for solo voice, gtr; 1 pce for
gtr solo; 1 pce for 2 gtr   (5977)

SING AND PLAY..., TO SIMPLE GUITAR
ACCOMPANIMENTS, VOL. I: SING AND
PLAY NATIONAL SONGS *CC12U
(Duarte) [Eng] solo voice,gtr (2-3rd
degr.) sc NOVELLO 19506 $3.30 The
Teacher Series Of Guitar
Publications   (5978)

SING AND PLAY..., TO SIMPLE GUITAR
ACCOMPANIMENTS, VOL. II: SING AND
PLAY NURSERY SONGS *CC18U
(Duarte) [Eng] solo voice,gtr (2-3rd
degr.) sc NOVELLO 19518 $3.30 The
Teacher Series Of Guitar
Publications   (5979)

SING AND PLAY..., TO SIMPLE GUITAR
ACCOMPANIMENTS, VOL. III: SING AND
PLAY SEA-SONGS *CC11U
(Duarte) [Eng] solo voice,gtr (2-3rd
degr.) sc NOVELLO 19508 $3.30 The
Teacher Series Of Guitar
Publications   (5980)

SING MIR, MORENA!, LIEDER ZUR GITARRE
AUS SPANIEN, SUDFRANKREICH,
LITAUEN, DALMATIEN *CC21U
(Zschiesche) [Ger] solo voice,gtr (2-
3rd degr.) sc SCHOTT 4841 f.s.
(5981)

SING NEGRO SPIRITUALS
(Duarte) [Eng] solo voice,gtr (3rd
degr.) sc SCHOTT 11076 f.s. 12
pcs.; Guitar Accompaniment - The
Easy Way, Suppl. 1; Notation of gtr
pt: tr-clef + diagrams
contains: Mary Had A Baby, Yes Lord
(5982)

SINGENDES, KLINGENDES OSTERREICH *folk
song
(Hammerschmied) [Austrian] solo
voice,gtr (2-3rd degr.) min sc
DOBLINGER 05923 f.s. 60 pcs
contains: Gruber, Franz Xaver,
Stille Nacht   (5983)

SINTERKLAASLIEDJES *CC8U
(Peters) [Dutch] solo voice,gtr/gtr
solo (1st degr.) sc HARMONIA 1861
f.s. partly capotasto in pos. III
or V   (5984)

SONGS BY ELIZABETHAN COMPOSERS, 7
(Dupre) [Eng] solo voice,gtr (6-7th
degr., orig for solo voice and
lute; contains works by: Campian
(2), Rosseter (2), Byrd, R. Johnson
(2)) sc SCHOTT 10537 f.s.   (5985)

SONNE, KOMM, EIN GITARRESPIELBUCH FUR
KINDER, 1-4. UNTERRICHTSJAHR *folk
song
(Ratz, Martin) [Ger] solo voice,gtr/
1-4gtr (single line playing/1-3rd
degr.) sc DEUTSCHER 32001 f.s. 162
arr + orig pcs; contains works by:
Schuffenhauer (2), Krug (4), Konig
(8), Ratz (22), Asriel (5), Quadt
(9), Rosenfeld (2), Haydn, Schumann
(3), Gorischk, Helmut, Wohlgemuth,
Schwaen, Schoendlinger for gtr;
Friemert (2), Buse, W.A. Mozart
(3), Beethoven, Berges,
Schuffenhauer, Hecht-Wieber for 2
gtr; Eberwein, Stephani for 3 gtr;
anon., naumilkat for 4 gtr or solo
voice(s), gtr; Skodova (2), Silcher
(2), Wendt, Friemert (2), Kern,
Krug (2), Pormova, Rodl, Hartung,
Nynkowa, Schuffenhauer, Hein,
Richter (3), W. Bender (2), Helmut,
Naumilkat for solo voice, gtr; also
contains Christmas music by:
Helmut, Schuffenhauer, Wohlgemuth
for gtr or solo voice, gtr; W.
Bender, Helmut, Naumilkat, for solo
voice, gtr
contains: Bach, Johann Sebastian,
Minuet in G minor, BWV Anh. 115
(2gtr) (A min,single line
playing); Bach, Johann Sebastian,
Piece In F, "Aria", BWV Anh.131
(2gtr) (single line playing);
Bach, Johann Sebastian, Polonaise
in G minor, BWV Anh. 119 (2gtr)
(A min,single line playing)
(5986)

SPAANSE VOLKSLIEDEREN, 3 (3 SPANISH
FOLKSONGS)
(Visser) [Span/Eng] solo voice,gtr
(3rd degr.) sc HARMONIA 1255 f.s.
contains: A La Virgen De Los
Dolores; Via Crucis; Villancico
(5987)

SPANNENLANGER HANSEL, KINDERLIEDER
*CC44U
(Vollrath) [Ger] solo voice,gtr (1-
3rd degr.) sc HOFMEISTER W-102 f.s.
arr + orig pcs   (5988)

SPIRITUALS AND FOLKSONGS *CC14U
(Buhe) [Eng] solo voice,gtr (4-5th
degr.) sc SCHOTT 4829 f.s.   (5989)

SUDAMERICANA, BERUHMTE FOLKLORISTISCHE
TANZE *CC11U,folk song
(Tucholski) [Span/Ger] solo
voice,gtr/1-3gtr (3-6th degr.) sc
APOLLO 2339 f.s. contains works by:
Creutziger (1), Tucholski (1) for
solo voice, gtr; Villoldo (1),
Porschmann (1), Albeniz (1) for 3
gtr   (5990)

THREE 17TH CENTURY AIRS
(Runge) [It/Eng] solo voice,gtr (6th
degr.) sc SCHOTT 10164 f.s.
contains works by: Caccini,
Monteverdi, Anon.
contains: Amarilli; Have You Seene
But A Whyte Lillie Grow?;
Lasciatemi Morire   (5991)

TUDOR SONGS, 6
(Shipley) [Eng] solo voice,gtr (3-4th
degr., orig. for solo voice and
lute; contains works by: Ford,
Anon., Rosseter, Dowland, Jones,
Campian) sc SCHOTT f.s.   (5992)

UKRAINISCHE VOLKSWEISEN *CC17U
(Sowiak; Stingl) [Russ/Ger] A solo,
gtr (3rd degr.) sc SCHOTT 6084 f.s.
(5993)

UND DIE LIEBE BRAUCHT EIN DACH *CC12L
(Jung; Pauli) [Ger] solo voice,gtr
(3-4th degr.) sc NEUE 285 f.s.
contains arr + orig pcs by: Asriel,
Dehler, Dessau (2), Jung, Medek
(3), Rosenfeld, Schmitz, Schneider
(2)   (5994)

VIDALITA, CHANT POPULAIRE ARGENTIN
(Fernandez-Lavie) [Span] solo voice,
gtr (6th degr., Oeuvres Anciennes
Pour Chant Et Guitare, No. 5) sc
ESCHIG f.s.   (5995)
(Fernandez-Lavie) [Span] solo voice,
gtr (6th degr., Oeuvres Anciennes
Pour Chant Et Guitare, No. 5) sc
SCHOTT GA-196 f.s.   (5996)

VILLANCICOS POPULARES, VOL. III *Xmas,
carol
(Angel) [Span] solo voice,gtr (4-6th
degr.) UNION ESP. 19269-3 f.s.
contains: Corre Al Portalico; Esta
Noche Nace El Nino; Gatatumba;
Pandereta Suena, Una   (5997)

VIVE HENRI IV, CHANSON FRANCAISE
(Fernandez-Lavie) solo voice,gtr
(Oeuvres Anciennes Pour Chant Et
Guitare, No. 6) ESCHIG f.s. (5998)
(Fernandez-Lavie) solo voice,gtr
(Oeuvres Anciennes Pour Chant Et
Guitare, No. 6) SCHOTT GA-197 f.s.
(5999)

VOLKSLIED UND LAUTE *CC30L,folk song
(Gerwig) [Ger/Fr/Dan/Swed] solo
voice,gtr (2-3rd degr.) sc LIENAU
1396 f.s. Das Spiel Der
Lauteninstrumente, Series II,
Spielbuch 3; contains works by:
Schulz, Scheidt, Zuccalmaglio,
Reichardt, Anon. (9), Fabricius,
Pohlenz   (6000)

VOLKSLIEDER *folk song
(Henze) [Ger] solo voice,gtr (1-4th
degr.) sc HOFMEISTER T-4011 $4.50
55 pcs.; Das Gitarrespiel, Vol. XI;
contains works by: Anon. (18),
Silcher, Fabricius (2),
Zuccalmaglio (2), Adam de la Hale,
Burki, Gersbach, Nicolai, Greef,
Zelter, Isaac, Nageli
contains: O Tannenbaum   (6001)

VOLKSLIEDER AUS ALLER WELT, VOL. I:
ENGLAND *CC7U
(Behrend) [Eng/Ger] solo voice,gtr
(3-7th degr.) sc BOTE f.s.   (6002)

VOLKSLIEDER AUS ALLER WELT, VOL. II:
FRANKREICH *CC8U
(Behrend) [Fr/Ger] solo voice,gtr (3-
7th degr.) sc BOTE f.s.   (6003)

VOLKSLIEDER AUS ALLER WELT, VOL. III:
SPANIEN, PORTUGAL *CC7U
(Behrend) [Span/Port/Ger] solo voice,
gtr (3-7th degr.) sc BOTE f.s.
(6004)

VOLKSLIEDER AUS ALLER WELT, VOL. IV:
ITALIEN *CC7U
(Behrend) [It/Ger] solo voice,gtr (3-
7th degr.) sc BOTE f.s.   (6005)

VOLKSLIEDER AUS ALLER WELT, VOL. V:
GRIECHENLAND *CC5U
(Behrend) [Greek/Ger] solo voice,gtr
(3-7th degr.) sc BOTE f.s.   (6006)

VOLKSLIEDER AUS ALLER WELT, VOL. VI:
TURKEI *CC7U
(Behrend) [Turkish/Ger] solo voice,
gtr (3-7th degr.) sc BOTE f.s.
(6007)

VOLKSLIEDER AUS ALLER WELT, VOL. VII:
BALKAN (UNGARN, RUMANIEN,
BULGARIEN, JUGOSLAWIEN) *CC8U
(Behrend) solo voice,gtr (3-7th
degr.) sc BOTE f.s. orig words +
Ger transl   (6008)

VOLKSLIEDER AUS ALLER WELT, VOL. VIII:
RUSSLAND *CC6U
(Behrend) [Russ/Ger] solo voice,gtr
(3-7th degr.) sc BOTE f.s.   (6009)

VOLKSLIEDER AUS ALLER WELT, VOL. IX:
POLEN, LETTLAND *CC6U
(Behrend) [Polish/Ger] solo voice,gtr
(3-7th degr.) sc BOTE f.s.   (6010)

VOLKSLIEDER AUS ALLER WELT, VOL. X:
DEUTSCHLAND *CC17U
(Behrend) [Ger] solo voice,gtr (3-7th
degr.) sc BOTE f.s.   (6011)

VOLKSLIEDER AUS ALLER WELT, VOL. XI:
AMERIKA *CC8U
(Behrend) [Eng/Ger] solo voice,gtr
(3-7th degr.) sc BOTE f.s.   (6012)

VOLKSLIEDER AUS ALLER WELT, VOL. XII:
INDONESIEN *CC6U
(Behrend) solo voice,gtr (3-7th
degr.) sc BOTE f.s. orig words +
Ger transl   (6013)

VOLKSLIEDER DES AUSLANDES, VOL. I:
SPANISCHE LIEDER *CC13U
(Schwarz-Reiflingen) [Span/Ger] solo
voice,gtr (3-7th degr.) sc LEUCKART
8710 f.s.   (6014)

VOLKSLIEDER DES AUSLANDES, VOL. II:
ITALIENISCHE LIEDER *CC21U
(Schwarz-Reiflingen) [It/Ger] solo
voice,gtr (3-7th degr.) sc LEUCKART
8711 f.s.   (6015)

VOLKSLIEDER DES AUSLANDES, VOL. III:
RUSSISCHE LIEDER *CC31U
(Schwarz-Reiflingen) [Ger] solo
voice,gtr (3-7th degr.) sc LEUCKART
8712 f.s.   (6016)

VOLKSLIEDER ZUM SINGEN UND SPIELEN
(Riehl; Weber) gtr/gtr,solo voice
SCHMIDT,H 90 f.s.   (6017)

VOLKSLIEDERBUCH ZUR GITARRE, VOL. I:
KINDERLIEDER *CC29U
(Burkhart; Scheit) [Ger] solo voice,
gtr (2-3rd degr.) sc DOBLINGER
05921 f.s.   (6018)

VOLKSLIEDERBUCH ZUR GITARRE, VOL. II:
WANDER- UND ABSCHIEDSLIEDER *CC24U
(Burkhart; Scheit) [Ger] solo voice,
gtr (2-3rd degr.) sc DOBLINGER
05922 f.s.   (6019)

VOM PUSTEWIND UND ANDEREN SACHEN, NEUE
LIEDER FUR DIE VORSCHULERZIEHUNG
*CC25L
(Jung; Pauli) [Ger] solo voice,gtr
(3rd degr.) sc NEUE 260 f.s.
children's songs; contains works
by: Nitsch (4), Klaus, Sandig,
Heinze, Hinrich (2), Richter,
Arenz, Grabs, Weitzendorf, Kettwig,
Werzlau, Rahner, Jung (2), Lesser
(3), Funk, Kolberg, Roost (2)   (6020)

WEISST DU WIEVIEL STERNLEIN STEHEN?,
VOLKS- UND KINDERLIEDER *CC35U
(Ochs) [Ger] solo voice,gtr (2nd
degr.) sc HOFMEISTER T-4080 f.s.
                                    (6021)

WIEGENLIEDER DER WELT *CCU
(Behrend) solo voice,gtr (4th degr.)
ZIMMER. 1819 f.s.   (6022)

WIR SINGEN UND SPIELEN, VOL. 1 *CCU
(Wolki) solo voice,gtr/vln/mel inst,
gtr APOLLO 2313 f.s.   (6023)

WIR SINGEN UND SPIELEN, VOL. 2 *CCU
(Wolki) solo voice,gtr/mel inst,gtr
APOLLO 2314 f.s.   (6024)

WITH VOICE AND GUITAR, VOL. I:
FOLKSONGS *CC40U
(Gavall) solo voice,gtr (3-4th degr.)
sc BELWIN $3.00 orig for solo voice
and lute; partly with original
words   (6025)

WITH VOICE AND GUITAR, VOL. II *CC19L
(Gavall) solo voice,gtr (3-4th degr.)
sc BELWIN 1118 $3.00 orig for solo
voice and lute; partly with
original words; contains works by:
Milan, Campian, Mozart (2),
Rosseter, Burns, Moore, Weber (2),
Rossini, Schubert (2), Donizetti,
Bellini, Scott, Balfe (2), Chopin
(2)   (6026)

WOHLAN DIE ZEIT IST KOMMEN, EIN VOLKS-
UND ZEITLIEDERBUCH FUR EINZEL-UND
GRUPPENGESANG *CC161U
(Peter; Muller) [Ger] solo voice,gtr
(3rd degr.) sc HOFMEISTER W-28 f.s.
contains 8 Christmas pieces   (6027)

ZUPFGEIGENHANSL, DER *CC251U
(Breuer; Scherrer) solo voice,gtr (2-
3rd degr.) min sc SCHOTT 4055 f.s.
                                    (6028)

I/IIC2   Trios for Guitar, Voice, and Another Instrument

BIALAS, GUNTER (1907-   )
Gesange, 3
[Ger] Bar solo,fl,gtr (7-8th degr.)
sc BAREN. 6128 f.s., ipa   (6029)

CLEMENT, NICOLE
Au Jardin De La Patience
solo voice,rec,gtr PRESSES f.s.
                                    (6030)

DESSAU, PAUL (1894-1979)
Tierverse Von Bertolt Brecht *CC5U
[Ger] solo voice, gtr + vcl or
prepared pno (2); solo voice,
gtr, pno (2); solo voice, gtr or
prepared pno (1) (7th degr.) sc
BOTE f.s.   (6031)

DOWLAND, JOHN (1562-1626)
Lieder, 2
(Behrend) [Eng] S solo,A rec,gtr
(5th degr., orig for solo voice
and lute-g'; Gitarre-Bibliothek,
No.43) sc,pts BOTE GB-43 f.s.
                                    (6032)

GRANADOS, ENRIQUE (1867-1916)
Currutacas Modestas, La, Tonadilla
(Azpiazu) [Span] 2solo voice,gtr
(9th degr.) sc UNION ESP. 18851
f.s.   (6033)

GUITARRA CANTORA, LA, MELODIAS
TRADICIONALES ARGENTINAS
(Kantor) [Span] 3-4gtr/fl&3gtr
(partly single line playing/1-2nd
degr., contains 7 pcs for solo
voice or gtr, 2gtr (5); solo voice,
3gtr (1); fl or gtr, gtr or solo
voice, 2gtr (1); opt perc (2)) sc
RICORDI-ARG BA-12779 f.s.   (6034)

HANDEL, GEORGE FRIDERIC (1685-1759)
Gesange, 2 (from Deutschen Arien)
(Scheit) [Ger] S solo,vln/fl,gtr,
opt vcl (5-6th degr., Gitarre-
Kammermusik, No.27) sc,pts
DOBLINGER GKM-27 f.s.   (6035)

Nel Dolce Dell'oblio *cant
(Behrend) S solo,rec/fl,gtr (4-5th
degr., Gitarre-Bibliothek, No.47)
sc,pts BOTE GB-47 f.s.   (6036)
(Schaller) S solo,A rec/fl/ob/vln,
gtr,opt vcl (4-5th degr.,
Gitarre-Kammermusik, No.28) pts
DOBLINGER GKM-28 f.s.   (6037)

KUKUCK, FELICITAS (1914-   )
Brucke, Die, Eine Kammermusik Nach
Gedichten Aus "Die Chinesische
Flote" Von Hans Bethge
(Gerwig) [Ger] solo voice,A rec,
gtr/hpsd (4th degr., Das Spiel
Der Lauteninstrumente, Series II,
Spielbuch 5) sc,pts LIENAU 1408
f.s.   (6038)

KUNSTLIEDER
(Henze, Bruno) [Ger] (3-7th degr.) sc
HOFMEISTER T-4012 $6.00 Das
Gitarrespiel, Vol. XII; 30 Pcs;
contains works by: Dowland (2),
Albert (2), Krieger (2), Kremberg,
Beyer (2), A. Scarlatti,
Rathgeber(2), W.A. Mozart, Weber
(2), Schubert (2), Schumann,
Brahms, Pabel (2), Stingl (4),
Hlouschek (2) for solo voice, gtr;
by W.A. Mozart for solo voice,
mando, gtr; by Ambrosius for 2 solo
voices, gtr
contains: Bach, Johann Sebastian,
Aria Di Giovannini, "Willst Du
Dein Herz Mir Schenken", BWV 518
(from Anna Magdalena Bach
Notenbuchlein (1725), No. 37)
(2gtr,solo voice) (C maj)   (6039)

MOZART, WOLFGANG AMADEUS (1756-1791)
Sehnsucht Nach Dem Fruhling
(Schaller) [Ger] solo voice,A rec,
gtr (3rd degr., Musik In Der
Familie, 7) sc,pts HELBLING 3092
f.s. contains also: Kinderspiel,
Das   (6040)

NEGRO SPIRITUALS *CC15U
(Harz) [Eng] solo voice,2gtr (3-4th
degr.) sc GERIG 439 f.s. gtr II in
gtr-symbols with signs for rhythm
                                    (6041)

PAESIELLO, GIOVANNI (1741-1816)
Aria Der Rosine (from Le Barbier De
Seville)
(Behrend) S solo,rec/mand,gtr (6th
degr., Gitarre-Bibliothek, No.58)
sc,pts BOTE GB-58 f.s.   (6042)

PELEMANS, WILLEM (1901-   )
Graf Van Verhaeren
[Fr/Dutch] Bar solo,vcl,gtr (6-7th
degr.) CBDM 71-458 f.s.   (6043)

REDEL, MARTIN CHRISTOPH (1947-   )
Epilog
[Ger] B/Bar solo,fl/alto fl,gtr (8-
9th degr.) sc,pts BOTE f.s.
                                    (6044)

REIN, WALTER (1893-1955)
Vom Vielfaltigen Leben *CC12L
[Ger] solo voice,gtr (3-5th degr.)
sc VOGGEN MRV-396 f.s. 6 pcs for
solo voice, gtr; 2 pcs for solo
voice, A rec, gtr; 4 pcs for solo
voice, rec, lute-g'   (6045)

SANCHEZ, BLAS
Al Pie De La Cruz Del Roque
"Au Pied De La Croix De Pierre"
solo voice,pno,gtr ESCHIG f.s.
                                    (6046)

SEIBER, MATYAS GYORGY (1905-1960)
Owl And The Pussycat, The
[Eng] solo voice,vln,gtr (8-9th
degr.) sc,pts SCHOTT 10638 f.s.
                                    (6047)

SPERONTES (JOHANN SIGISMUND SCHOLZE)
(1705-1750)
Singende Muse An Der Pleisse *CC10U
(Tucholski) gtr,vla da gamba/vcl,
solo voice or mel inst APOLLO
2316 f.s.   (6048)

TAUBERT, KARL HEINZ (1921-   )
Hausspruch
(Behrend) [Ger] solo voice,fl,pno/
gtr (6th degr., suppl.: arr for
gtr of the pno accomp) sc,pts
RIES 10282 f.s.   (6049)

VALERIUS, ADRIANUS (1575-1625)
Wenn Alle Untreu Werden
(Libbert) [Ger] A rec,gtr,solo
voice (3rd degr., Das
Gitarrenwerk, Reihe B:8, E is F)
sc PREISSLER f.s.   (6050)

WAHRE FREUNDSCHAFT SOLL NICHT WANKEN
(Libbert) [Ger] A rec,gtr,solo voice
(2nd degr., Das Gitarrenwerk, Reihe
B:4) sc PREISSLER f.s.   (6051)

WEBERN, ANTON VON (1883-1945)
Lieder, 3, Op.18
solo voice,soprano clar in E flat,
gtr (9th degr.) sc UNIVER. 8684
f.s.   (6052)

YUN, ISANG (1917-   )
Gagok
(Behrend) solo voice,perc,gtr BOTE
22488 (1226)   (6053)

I/IIC2-Coll   Trio Collections for Guitar, Voice, and Another Instrument

ALTE MINNELIEDER *CC11L
(Gerwig) [Ger] gtr (2-3rd degr.) sc,
pts NAGELS EN-1109 f.s. Nagels
Laute- und Gitarre-Archiv; contains
works by: Anon. (2), Fabricius (1),
Praetorius (1), Neusiedler (1),
Isaac (1), Lechner (1), Hassler
(1), Schaffer (1), Senfl (1), Ott
(1), for gtr (1), treb inst, gtr
(1), solo voice, treb inst, gtr,
opt bass inst (9)   (6054)

ALTE UND NEUE MUSIK ZUM SINGEN UND
SPIELEN AUF BLOCKFLOTEN, GEIGEN UND
LAUTENINSTRUMENTE *folk song
(Gerwig) [Ger] (1-3rd degr.) sc
LIENAU 1375 f.s. Das Spiel Der
Lauteninstrumente, Series II,

Spielbuch 1; contains works by:
Sperontes (4), L. Mozart (3),
Rathgeber (1), Rein (5), Rhau (2),
Langenau (1), Chemin-Petit (1): for
gtr (1), 2gtr (3), 3gtr (1), rec,
gtr (8), 2rec, gtr (2), solo voice,
gtr (3), solo voice, rec, gtr (1),
solo voice, rec, 2gtr (1), rec, vln
or vla, gtr (1); arr. + orig. pcs.;
single line playing; gtr pt partly
in bass clef
contains: Bach, Johann Sebastian,
English Suite No. 6, BWV 811, In
D Minor, Gavottes I-II (gtr,1-2A
rec); Bach, Johann Sebastian,
Minuet, BWV Anh. 118, in B flat
(from Anna Magdalena Bach
Notenbuchlein (1725), No.9) (gtr,
S rec) (C maj,single line
playing, gtr pt in bass clef)   (6055)

ANONYMOUS
All Mein Gedanken, Die Ich Hab (from
Lochamer Liederbuch) CCU
(Libbert) [Ger] S rec,gtr,solo
voice (3rd degr.) sc PREISSLER
f.s. Das Gitarrenwerk, Reihe B:3
(6056)

Allerlei Volkslieder *CC50UL
(Wolter) [Ger] 2rec,gtr; solo
voice, rec, and gtr (1-2nd degr.)
sc,pt MOECK 2030 f.s. contains 8
Christmas carols   (6057)

BUNTER HERBST *CC13L
(Derlien) [Ger] (1-2nd degr.) sc
BAREN. 1501 f.s. contains works by:
Folksongs (8), Reichardt, Anon.
(3), Baumann for solo voice, fl
(9), for solo voice, fl, gtr (4)
(6058)

ES FLOG EIN KLEINS WALDVOGELEIN
(Libbert) [Ger] S rec,gtr,solo voice
(2nd degr., Das Gitarrenwerk, Reihe
B:1) sc PREISSLER f.s.   (6059)

ES RITTEN DREI REITER
(Libbert) [Ger] solo voice,gtr/gtr&S
rec (2nd degr., Das Gitarrenwerk,
Reihe B:9) sc PREISSLER f.s.
contains also: Es Wollt Ein
Leineweber Wandern   (6060)

GUTZGAUCH, DER
(Libbert) [Ger] A rec,solo voice
(2nd degr., Das Gitarrenwerk, Reihe
B:2) sc PREISSLER f.s.   (6061)

KOMMT, IHR G'SPIELEN UND 5 WEITERE
LIEDER *CC6U
(Libbert) rec,gtr,solo voice (3-4th
degr.) sc,pts PREISSLER f.s. Das
Gitarrenwerk, Reihe B:11   (6062)

KUNSTLIEDER
(Henze, Bruno) [Ger] (3-7th degr.) sc
HOFMEISTER T-4012 $6.00 Das
Gitarrespiel, Vol. XII; 30 Pcs;
contains works by: Dowland (2),
Albert (2), Krieger (2), Kremberg,
Beyer (2), A. Scarlatti,
Rathgeber(2), W.A. Mozart, Weber
(2), Schubert (2), Schumann,
Brahms, Pabel (2), Stingl (4),
Hlouschek (2) for solo voice, gtr;
by W.A. Mozart for solo voice,
mando, gtr; by Ambrosius for 2 solo
voices, gtr
contains: Bach, Johann Sebastian,
Aria Di Giovannini, "Willst Du
Dein Herz Mir Schenken", BWV 518
(from Anna Magdalena Bach
Notenbuchlein (1725), No. 37)
(2gtr,solo voice) (C maj)   (6063)

LIEDER UM OSTERN *CC8L,folk song
(Schaller) [Ger] solo voice,treb
inst/vln/A rec,gtr/pno,opt vln/vla,
opt vcl (3rd degr.) sc,pts OSTER
6781.132 f.s. contains works by:
Anon. (4)   (6064)

MORGEN- UND ABENDLIEDER *folk song
(Schaller, Erwin) [Ger] (3rd degr.)
sc,pts MOSELER f.s. 20 pcs;
contains works by: Bendig, Baumann
(2), Reichardt, Rohwer, Ebeling,
Weber, Bresgen for solo voice, gtr;
by Vulpius, Hensel, Ahle, Schulz,
Brahms for solo voice, A rec or vln
or vla, gtr
contains: Bach, Johann Sebastian,
Nun Ruhen Alle Walder, Chorale,
BWV 392 (gtr,solo voice) (F maj)
(6065)

ST. MARTINS-LIEDER
(Draths) 1-2S recs or 2 solo voices,
opt gtr SCHOTT 5944 f.s.   (6066)

TANZLIEDER UND SPIELE FUR KINDER, 12
*CC12U
(Hoffmann) [Ger] (single line
playing/1st degr.) sc MOECK ZFS-34
f.s. for solo voice, 2rec or vln; 2
pcs. with gtr: no. 5, 7 for solo
voice, rec, (gtr colla parte),

Zeitschrift Fur Spielmusik, No.34
(6067)
VIER JAPANISCHE VOLKSLIEDER
(Libbert) solo voice,rec,gtr (2-3rd
degr.) sc,pt PREISSLER f.s. Das
Gitarrenwerk, Reihe B:12
contains: Burgruine Im Mondschein;
Gross Ist Der Mond; Kirschen
Bluhn; Momotaro, Pfirsichknabe
(6068)
ZELTER, CARL FRIEDRICH (1758-1832)
Es War Ein Konig In Thule
(Libbert) [Ger] solo voice,gtr/gtr&
A rec (2-3rd degr., Das
Gitarrenwerk, Reihe B:10) sc
PREISSLER f.s. contains also: Und
In Den Schneegebirge   (6069)

I/IIC3 Quartets for Guitar, Voice, and Other Instruments

BROQUA, ALFONSO (1876-1946)
Chants De l'Uruguay, 3
(Pujol) solo voice,fl,2gtr (9th
degr.) sc ESCHIG 1509 f.s.   (6070)

CLEMENT, NICOLE
Chanson Du Lundi, La
solo voice,rec,perc,gtr (1-2nd
degr.) PRESSES f.s.   (6071)

DUFAY, GUILLAUME (ca. 1400-1474)
Bonjour, Bon Mois
Mez solo,A rec,2gtr,opt T rec/B rec
(single line playing/1st degr.)
sc HEUGEL PJ-109 f.s. Plein Jeu,
No.109
contains: Or Vous Tremoussez,
Pasteurs   (6072)

GUITARRA CANTORA, LA, MELODIAS
TRADICIONALES ARGENTINAS
(Kantor) [Span] 3-4gtr/fl&3gtr
(partly single line playing/1-2nd
degr., contains 7 pcs for solo
voice or gtr, 2gtr (5); solo voice,
3gtr (1); fl or gtr, gtr or solo
voice, 2gtr (1); opt perc (2)) sc
RICORDI-ARG BA-12779 f.s.   (6073)

MONTEVERDI, CLAUDIO (ca. 1567-1643)
Canzonette A Tre Voci, 3
(Omizzolo) [It] solo voice,T rec/
vln,vla da gamba/bsn,lute/gtr (3-
4th degr.) sc ZANIBON 4826 f.s.
notation: treb clef; including:
"2 Madrigali", col basso
continuo, for solo voice, B rec,
vln, violone, lute, hpsd
contains: Chi Vuol Veder Un
Bosco; Fiera Vista, La; Vita De
l'Alma Mia   (6074)

SCHUBERT, FRANZ (PETER) (1797-1828)
Kantate Zur Namensfeier Des Vaters
*D.80
"Terzetto" (Scheit) [Ger] TTB soli,
gtr (6th degr., Gitarre-
Kammermusik, No.40; 2 facs of
autograph) sc,pts DOBLINGER
GKM-40 f.s.   (6075)

SEIBER, MATYAS GYORGY (1905-1960)
Medieval French Songs, 4 *Op. Posth.
[Fr] solo voice,vla d'amore/vla,vla
da gamba/vcl (7th degr.)
ZERBONI sc 5971 f.s., pts 5972
rent no. 1 without gtr
contains: A Vouz Amanz; Bergier
De Vile Champestre; Gentilz
Galans De France; Pourquoi Me
Bat   (6076)

STAHMER, KLAUS H. (1941-   )
3 Paesaggi
solo voice,perc,tape recorder,gtr
ZIMMER. 1986 f.s.   (6077)

STRAVINSKY, IGOR (1882-1971)
Russian Songs, 4
[Russ/Eng] S solo,fl,harp,gtr (9th
degr., pts available as study sc)
sc CHESTER 3831A f.s.   (6078)

TSOUYOPOULOS, GEORGES S. (1930-   )
Serenade
[It] solo voice,fl,vla,gtr (9th
degr.) MODERN rent   (6079)

I/IIC3-Coll Quartet Collections for Guitar, Voice, and Other Instruments

ALTE UND NEUE MUSIK ZUM SINGEN UND
SPIELEN AUF BLOCKFLOTEN, GEIGEN UND
LAUTENINSTRUMENTE *folk song
(Gerwig) [Ger] (1-3rd degr.) sc
LIENAU 1375 f.s. Das Spiel Der
Lauteninstrumente, Series II,
Spielbuch 1; contains works by:
Sperontes (4), L. Mozart (3),
Rathgeber (1), Rein (5), Rhau (2),
Langenau (1), Chemin-Petit (1): for
gtr (1), 2gtr (3), 3gtr (1), rec,
gtr (8), 2rec, gtr (2), solo voice,
gtr (3), solo voice, rec, gtr (1),
solo voice, rec, 2gtr (1), rec, vln
or vla, gtr (1); arr. + orig. pcs.;
single line playing; gtr pt partly
in bass clef
contains: Bach, Johann Sebastian,
English Suite No. 6, BWV 811, In
D Minor, Gavottes I-II (gtr,1-2A
rec); Bach, Johann Sebastian,
Minuet, BWV Anh. 118, in B flat
(from Anna Magdalena Bach
Notenbuchlein (1725), No.9) (gtr,
S rec) (C maj,single line
playing, gtr pt in bass clef)
(6080)
AUF, DU JUNGER WANDERSMANN,
WANDERLIEDER UND MARSCHE
(Heyden) [Ger] (1-2nd degr., 5 pcs.
for 2rec, solo voice, gtr by
Folksongs; 1 canon for 2 solo
voices by Reinhold Heyden; 5 pcs
for 2rec, gtr by Folksongs; 1 pce
for 2S rec, 2vln, gtr by Umlauf; 2
pcs for 2insts by Wilhelm
Twittenhof) sc NAGELS EN-544 f.s.
(6081)

I/IIC4 Quintets for Guitar, Voice, and Other Instruments

CAMMIN, HEINZ (1923-   )
Spirituals And Songs *CC10U
[Eng/Ger] 3solo voice,gtr,pno,opt
db sc,pts SCHOTT 6083 f.s.   (6082)

DARNAL, JEAN CLAUDE
Dites-Moi M'sieur l'Oiseau
(Ziberlin) [Fr] SMezBar soli,A rec,
gtr (3-4th degr., Plein Jeu,
No.101) sc HEUGEL PJ-101 f.s.
(6083)

FOSTER, STEPHEN COLLINS (1826-1864)
My Old Kentucky Home
(Turellier) [Eng] SATB soli,opt gtr
(4-5th degr., Plein Jeu, No.268)
sc,pts HEUGEL PJ-268 f.s.   (6084)

FRITSCHE, VOLKMAR
Improvisations, Sur "L'Anabase" De
St.-John Perse
[Fr] Mez solo,3-4perc,gtr (9th
degr.) sc TEESELING VT-81 f.s.
(6085)

I'VE BEEN TO HARLEM
(Shaw) [Eng] SATB soli,gtr (3rd
degr., Plein Jeu, No.363) sc,pts
HEUGEL PJ-363 f.s.   (6086)

KOELLREUTTER, HANS-JOACHIM (JACOBO)
(1915-   )
Haikai Des Pedro Xisto, 8
[Port/Ger] solo voice,fl,pno,perc,
ampl-gtr (8th degr.) MODERN 1207
sc f.s., pts rent   (6087)

TAKEMITSU, TORU (1930-   )
Stanza I
gtr,harp,pno/cel,vibra,female solo
(7th degr.) sc UNIVER. 15118 f.s.
(6088)

I/IIC4-Coll   Quintet Collections for Guitar, Voice, and Other Instruments

BEKANNTE VOLKSLIEDER, TEIL II °CC12U
(Wolki) [Ger] solo voice,3rec,gtr
(2nd degr.) sc MOECK ZFS-42 f.s.
Teil I, II, without gtr,
Zeitschrift Fur Spielmusik, No.42
(6089)

CHANTS DE FRANCE ET D'AILLEURS, 20
°folk song
(Sanchez) (3-5th degr.) sc CHOUDENS
20.243 f.s. 20 arr + orig pcs; orig
words; contains works by:
Despourrins, Taburot, Encina,
Anon., Attaignant, Sanchez (6) for
SATB soli, gtr (17); female solo,
male solo, fl, tamb, gtr (1); 3
solo voices (1); 5 solo voices (1)
contains: Sanchez, Blas, Toca El
Pandora, Maria (gtr,SATB)   (6090)

FLAMISCHE LIEDER UND TANZE °CC8U
(Tanner) [Dutch/Ger] solo voice,2S
rec/S rec/A rec,A rec,opt gtr
(1-3rd degr.) sc MOECK ZFS-275 f.s.
Zeitschrift Fur Spielmusik, No.275
(6091)

LIEDER UM OSTERN °CC8L,folk song
(Schaller) [Ger] solo voice,treb
inst/vln/A rec,gtr/pno,opt vln/vla,
opt vcl (3rd degr.) sc,pts OSTER
6781.132 f.s. contains works by:
Anon. (4)   (6092)

I/IIC5   Music for School Ensemble/Orchestra with Guitar and Voice

BLEUSE, MARC (1937-   )
Comptines Pour Anne, 3
[Fr] triangle,tam-tam,xylo,opt gtr,
jr cor (single line playing/1st
degr., Plein Jeu, No.166) sc
HEUGEL PJ-166 f.s.   (6093)

BRESGEN, CESAR (1913-)
Europe Curieuse, L', Eine Kuriose
Europa-Kantate Fur Kinder
S rec,A rec,trp,trp in C,perc,
2glock,metallophone,pno,gtr,vln,
vcl,jr cor (Bausteine, No.175)
sc,pts SCHOTT B-175 f.s.   (6094)

Von Mausen, Autos Und Anderen Tieren;
25 Kinderlieder Zum Singen Und
Spielen
[Ger] rec,gtr,1-2pt jr cor,
stabspiele (Bausteine, No.179) sc
SCHOTT B-179 f.s.   (6095)

BUCHTGER, FRITZ (1903-1978)
Zirkus, Der, Kantate Und
Bewegungsspiel
[Ger] vln/metallophone,fl,glock,
2xylo,triangle,cym,tamb,timp,pno,
gtr,unis jr cor [12'] sc,pts
BAREN. BE-104 f.s.   (6096)

BURTHEL, JAKOB (1926-)
Jahreswetteranzeiger "Willst Du Aufs
Wetter Im Jahr Achten"
[Ger] S rec,vln,xylo,vcl/gtr,tamb,
triangle,unis jr cor/SSA
(includes Kretzschmar, Gunther,
"Der Leopard Hat Flecken"
(without gtr)) sc HANSSLER
HE-12.309 f.s.   (6097)

CAMMIN, HEINZ (1923-)
Lied Uber Die Grenze
pno,gtr,db,unis cor sc SCHOTT 6393
f.s.   (6098)

COSSETTO, EMIL (1908-)
Chants Yougoslaves, 4 [Nos. 1-3]
[Slovene] mand/vln,vcl,gtr,SATB
(3rd degr.) sc HEUGEL PJ-283 f.s.
chant no. 4, "Moja Diridika"
(without gtr) is separate
publication; Plein Jeu, No.283
contains: Posavski Drmes;
Slavonska Poskocica; Tri Jetrve
(6099)

DERLIEN, MARGARETE
Ich Trag Mein Licht, Ein Liederspiel
Zum Laternegehen
[Ger] rec,gtr,triangle,1-dbl cor
sc,pts BAREN. 2760 f.s.   (6100)

FORTNER, WOLFGANG (1907-)
Cress Ertrinkt, Ein Schulspiel
[Ger] fl/ob,sax/clar,trp,vln,vla,
vcl,lute/gtr,pno,timp/bass drum,
perc,opt trom,SATB&speaking cor,
SABar soli [40'] SCHOTT rent
(6101)

GEESE, HEINZ (1930-)
Seefahrt Nach Rio, Die, Scenic
Cantata
(Cammin) pno/acord,bass inst,gtr,
perc,3pt jr cor,speaking voice, 2
insts in c, 2 insts in b-flat sc,
pts SCHOTT 6585 f.s.   (6102)

GRIEND, KOOS VAN DE (1905-1950)
Stukken Voor Schoolorkest, 4
1.0.1.0. 0.1.0.0. perc,pno 4-hands,
gtr,strings,opt glock,opt db,opt
boy cor sc,pts DONEMUS f.s.
(6103)

GUNSENHEIMER, GUSTAV (1934-)
Jesus Und Die Fischer; Cantata
jr cor&audience&unis cor,SA&
narrator,5rec,mel inst,3xylo,
2glock,metallophone,perc,timp,
gtr,opt vcl,db sc HANSSLER
12.524-02 f.s.   (6104)

JAUBERT, MAURICE (1900-1940)
Chanson De Tessa, La
(Ziberlin) [Fr] rec,gtr,3 eq
voices/4pt mix cor (4th degr.,
Plein Jeu, No.128) sc,pts HEUGEL
PJ-128 f.s.   (6105)

JEHN, WOLFGANG
Auferstanden Heute, Kleine
Osterkantate
[Ger] 2treb inst,xylo/gtr,2pt jr
cor (including "Christ ist
erstanden" (without gtr)) sc
HANSSLER HE-12.228 f.s.   (6106)

KERKHOFFS, GUNTER (1914-)
Zertanzten Schuhe, Die, Kinderoper
Nach Einem Marchen Der Gebruder
Grimm
[Ger] 2fl,2glock,2xylo,
2metallophone,2timp,gtr,jr cor,
solo voices sc,pts BREITKOPF-W
PB-4816 f.s.   (6107)

KLEIN, RICHARD RUDOLF (1921-)
Lasst Eure Stimm' Erklingen, Kleine
Kantate Zum Lobe Der Musik °cant
[Ger] rec,vln,opt vcl,opt gtr,opt
perc,3 eq voices/3pt mix cor sc
MOESLER f.s.   (6108)

KLEIN, WALDTRAUT
Sing- Und Maskenspiel Von Jorinde Und
Joringel, Das, Ein Spiel Fur
Kinder
[Ger] rec,opt gtr,opt vln,jr cor,
hurdy-gurdy (Barenreiter Laien-
Spiele, No.209) sc BAREN. BLS-209
f.s.   (6109)

KRAMER, GOTTHOLD
Abraham
[Ger] gtr,org,db/trom,jr cor
(includes: "Des Herrn Wort", "O
Dass Ich Tausend Zungen Hatte"
And "Der Blinde Barthimaus"
(Without Gtr)) sc HANSSLER
HE-12.510 f.s.   (6110)

KRETZSCHMAR, GUNTHER (1929-)
Blinde Bettler, Der
[Ger] gtr,opt hpsd,opt org,unis jr
cor,2 child soli sc HANSSLER
HE-12.234 f.s.   (6111)

David Und Goliath, Cantata For
Children
[Ger] children's chorus (SSA or in
3 groups: SSA+SSA+S), solo voices
(chorus I), 2rec, 2 xylo, glock,
metallophone (2 players), gtr or
hpsd, tri, drum, side drum, tamb,
cym, timp, db or vcl, pno ad lib.
sc,pts HANSSLER HE-12.231 f.s.
(6112)

Grosse Flut, Die, Kleine
Kinderkantate Von Der Arche Noach
[Ger] rec,glock,metallophone,2xylo,
gtr/kbd,opt vcl,1-3pt jr cor/SSA,
speaking voice (2nd degr.) sc,pts
HANSSLER HE-12.210 f.s.   (6113)

Ich Steh Im Bistum Fulda
[Ger] hpsd/pno,jr cor,SA soli,
rattle sc HANSSLER HE-12.311 f.s.
contains also: Es Sassen Sieben
Frosch Im See (without gtr); Hort
Die Traurige Ballade (hpsd/pno,
gtr,vcl,jr cor,SA soli)   (6114)

KRETZSCHMAR, GUNTHER (cont'd.)
Samaritaner, Der, Cantata
jr cor,S rec,A rec,glock,
metallophone,2xylo,gtr,timp,db/
vcl HANSSLER f.s. sc 12.235-02,
cor pts 12.235-05, pts
12.235-21, 22, 11, perf sc
12.235-14   (6115)

Schildburger, Die, Cantata For
Children
[Ger] fl,ob,bsn,timp,gtr,perc,pno,
strings,SSA,speaking voice sc,pts
HANSSLER HE-12.407 f.s.   (6116)

KUKUCK, FELICITAS (1914-)
Marchen Vom Dicken Fetten
Pfannekuchen, Das, Musik Zu Einem
Schattenspiel
[Ger] S rec,glock,metallophone,
xylo,bass drum,tamb,gtr,cor sc,
pts MOSELER f.s.   (6117)

Tischlein Deck Dich, Ein Lebendiges
Buhnenstuck (Ursprunglich Musik
Fur Ein Schattenspiel)
[Ger] S rec,A rec,gtr,2vln,vcl,
metallophone,perc,3 cor,7 solo
voices, precentor [30'] sc
MOSELER f.s.   (6118)

LANGHANS, HERBERT
Goldene Ei, Das, Ein Marchenspiel
[Ger] 3S rec,Orff inst,vcl,gtr,
speaking cor,female solo [25']
sc,pts MOSELER f.s.   (6119)

MARCY, ROBERT
File La Laine
(Langree; Fernandez-Lavie) [Fr] fl,
gtr,mix cor,solo voice, rec quar
or string quar (3rd degr., Plein
Jeu, No.8) sc HEUGEL PJ-8 f.s.
(6120)

MAREZ OYENS, GERRIT DE (1922-)
Als De Grote Klokke Luidt
[Dutch] perc,glock,xylo,gtr,timp,
solo voices (Gele Reeks:
Kinderorkest) sc,pts HARMONIA
2027 f.s.   (6121)

Arabine
[Dutch] (single line playing, Gele
Reeks: Kinderorkest) sc,pts
HARMONIA 2044 f.s. contains also:
Zo Gaat De Molen (without gtr);
Vinger In De Roet (perc,glock,
metallophone,xylo,gtr,timp, solo
voices); Mosselman (without gtr);
Schoon Jonkvrouw (perc,glock,
metallophone,xylo,gtr,timp, solo
voices)   (6122)

En Mijn Een Been Staat
[Dutch] perc,glock,metallophone,
xylo,gtr,timp, solo voices (1st
degr., Gele Reeks: Kinderorkest)
sc,pts HARMONIA 2029 f.s.
contains also: Geeft Wat Om De
Rommelpot (perc,glock,
metallophone,xylo,gtr,timp, solo
voices); 'T Was Nacht (without
gtr); Zige Zage Mannetje (without
gtr)   (6123)

MAREZ OYENS, TERA DE (1932-)
Kapitein Is Jarig, De, Kinderzangspel
In 2 Bedrijven
[Dutch] 2S rec,A rec,vln I,vln II,
vcl/gtr,perc,timp,xylo,glock,opt
fl,jr cor,6 solo voices (1st
degr., Kinderzangspelen; gtr in
bass clef) sc,pts HARMONIA 1896
f.s.   (6124)

Liedje Gezocht, Kinderzangspel In 10
Taferelen
[Dutch] 2rec,vln I,vln II,tamb/
triangle,vcl/gtr, voices (single
line playing, Kinderzangspelen;
gtr in bass clef) sc,pts HARMONIA
1703 f.s.   (6125)

MARX, KARL (1897-1985)
Ihr Kleinen Vogelein, Liedkantate
[Ger] S rec,ob/A rec/vln,2vln,vcl,
gtr,3 eq voices sc,pts BAREN.
3940 f.s.   (6126)

Juchhe, Der Erste Schnee, Kleine
Kantate
S rec,2vln,vcl/gtr,opt perc,2pt wom
cor/2pt jr cor sc,pts MERSEBURGER
EM-1643 f.s.   (6127)

Winter Ist Vergangen, Der,
Liedkantate
[Ger] S rec,ob/T rec,gtr,strings,
4pt mix cor (3rd degr.) sc,pts
BAREN. 3159 f.s.   (6128)

MASON, ROGER
Fete Des Ours, La
[Fr] pno,tamb,tom-tom,gtr, solo
voices (3rd degr., includes:
"Banuwa, " chanson folklorique
Liberia; Plein Jeu, No.85) sc
HEUGEL PJ-85 f.s.   (6129)

MASSEUS, JAN (1913-)
Vreemde Fluitist, De
[Dutch] gtr,perc,db,SAB (3-4th
degr., Groene Reeks: School- Of
Jeugdorkest Met Zangstemmen) sc,
pts HARMONIA 1837 f.s.   (6130)

NARDELLI, RUDOLF (1932-)
Missa In Beat
[Ger] 3gtr,perc,opt org,opt pno,3pt
jr cor&audience (Sing- Und
Spielmusik; notation gtr pt: kbd
sc + chord symbols) UNIVER. f.s.
sc 15013, pts 15014A:B   (6131)

NATY, JEAN
Au Chateau
(Fombonne) [Fr] A rec,pno/gtr,SATB
(notation gtr pt: bass clef;
Plein Jeu, No.365) sc HEUGEL
PJ-365 f.s.   (6132)

POSER, HANS (1917-1970)
Musikanten A-B-C, Das
[Ger] rec,metallophone,vcl,perc,
vln,gtr,opt acord,jr cor,
precentor (2nd degr., Mosaik, No.
100; notation: bass clef) sc
FIDULA f.s.   (6133)

PRAAG, HENRI C. VAN (1894-1968)
Schoolmuziek No. 3
"Music For Schools No. 3" 2rec,
perc,pno,vln I,vln II,vln III,
vcl,opt gtr,opt 3 cor [5'] sc,pts
DONEMUS f.s.   (6134)

SCHILLING, HANS LUDWIG (1927-)
Ich Weiss Ein Lieblich Engelspiel,
Liedkantate
[Ger] treb inst,perc,pno,plucked
insts,3pt jr cor/3pt wom cor,solo
voice BREITKOPF-W f.s. sc
PB-4750, pts OB-4750, cor pts
CHB-3626   (6135)

STRAESSER, JOEP (1934-)
Rade, En
3.2.2.1. 0.1.1.0. Orff inst,pno,
gtr,strings,3 cor [18'] sc,pts
DONEMUS f.s.   (6136)

TWITTENHOFF, WILHELM (1904-)
Lob Der Kartoffel, Liedkantate
[Ger] 3S rec,vln I/ob/clar,vln II/
clar,vln III/clar,vcl/bsn,gtr,
unis cor&3 eq voices/4pt mix cor
sc,pts BAREN. EN-1159 f.s.   (6137)

Lob Des Apfels, Liedkantate
3S rec,glock,perc,vln I,vln II/ob/
fl,vln III,vln IV/clar/vla,vcl/
bsn/opt gtr,unis cor&3 eq voices/
4pt mix cor (notation gtr pt:
bass clef) sc,pts BAREN. EN-1158
f.s.   (6138)

VIGNEAULT, GILLES
Doux Chagrin, Le
(Fombonne) [Fr] S rec,gtr,SATB (2nd
degr., Plein Jeu, No.205) sc
HEUGEL PJ-205 f.s.   (6139)

WARNER, THEODOR (1903)
Arme Schuster, Der, Ein Grosses
Singspiel, Nach Einem Marchen Der
Bruder Grimm
[Ger] 2S rec,vln,gtr,glock,perc,jr
cor (Barenreiter Laien-Spiele)
sc,pts BAREN. BLS-239 f.s. (6140)

WERDIN, EBERHARD (1911-)
Heinzelmannchen, Die, Ein
Musikalisches Stegreifspiel
[Ger] solo voices and treb insts:
glock, xylo, 2 S rec; children's
chorus, A rec, vln, vln pizz,
gtr, 2 xylo, perc (Bausteine,
No.126) sc,pts SCHOTT B-126 f.s.   (6141)

WESLEY-SMITH, MARTIN (1945-)
Wild West Show, The, Ein Buhnenstuck,
Von Kindern Zu Erfinden Und
Auszufuhren
pno,gtr,jr cor, autoharp sc UNIVER.
29001 f.s.   (6142)

ZIPP, FRIEDRICH (1914-)
Es Waren Zwei Konigskinder *CC5U
2rec,vln/gtr,perc,1-2pt jr cor/1-
2pt wom cor sc,pts PELIKAN 933
f.s.   (6143)

Frohlicher Jahrmarkt, Cantata For
Children
[Ger] rec,metallophone,vln/gtr,cym,
triangle,drums,opt pno,1-2pt jr
cor (single line playing/1st

ZIPP, FRIEDRICH (cont'd.)

degr., Bausteine, No.141) sc,pts
SCHOTT B-141 f.s.   (6144)

I/IIC5-Coll Music for School Ensemble/Orchestra with Guitar and Voice: Collections

AUX MARCHES DU PALAIS
(Turellier; Vallade) [Fr] 2fl,gtr,mix
cor (3rd degr., Plein Jeu, No.108)
sc HEUGEL PJ-108 f.s.   (6145)

EUROPAISCHE VOLKS- UND KINDERLIEDER, IN
EASY CHORAL VERSIONS WITH
INSTRUMENTS, VOL. II
(Bresgen) vln,clar/ob/trp/vla,rec,
perc,gtr,jr cor, Stabspiele (orig
words + Ger transl; vol. I without
gtr; Bausteine, No.178) SCHOTT
B-178 f.s.   (6146)

GUANTANAMERA
(Grimbert) [Span] perc,gtr,5pt mix
cor (1-3rd degr., single line
playing or chords (symbols); Plein
Jeu, No.216) sc HEUGEL PJ-216 f.s.
                                     (6147)

I WENT TO THE MARKET
(Shaw) opt gtr,male solo,SATB
(3rd degr., Plein Jeu, No.362) sc
HEUGEL PJ-362 f.s.   (6148)

KINDERCHOR, DER: MUSIK FUR
GOTTESDIENST; VOLKS- UND
KINDERLIEDSATZE *CC153U
[Ger] inst,jr cor sc HANSSLER
HE-12.901 f.s. contains works by 22
composers; 3 compositions with gtr:
nos. 100, 113, 150; also available
separately as HE12.207, HE-12.210,
HE-12.309   (6149)

MUSIK IM JAHRESKREIS
(Korda; Schnabel) [Ger] (2nd degr.)
sc OSTER 6781-2 f.s. 23 pcs;
contains works by various composers
for various insts; includes 9
folksongs with gtr
contains: Lasst Uns Das Kindelein
Wiegen   (6150)

NEDERLANDSE VOLKSLIEDEREN, 23
(Tiggers; Mul) [Dutch] gtr,S rec,vln/
fl,solo voice, side drum senza
corda (1-2nd degr.) sc TOORTS f.s.
                                     (6151)

O DENNEBOOM
(van der Linden) rec,gtr,strings
(Musica, no. 8; contains works by:
Nees, Schroyens, van der Linden) sc
DE MONTE f.s. contains also: Tel Uw
Herinneringen; Geef Wat Om De
Rommelpot   (6152)

SCHULER UND LEHRER SINGEN UND SPIELEN
(Duis) treb inst,opt xylo,jr cor&
mix cor sc SCHOTT 6089 f.s. (6153)

SINGSTUNDEN, DIE, NO. 1-36, LIEDER FUR
ALLE *CC36U
(Jode) (1-3rd degr.) MOSELER f.s. 36
"Singblatter" with various
composers from the 13th to the 20th
centuries (88), Anon. (35),
Folksongs (119); divided into three
groups ("Tageskreis",
"Jahreskreis", "Lebenskreis"), for
voices and insts; complete edition;
the "Singblatter" are also
available separately; chord
accompaniment   (6154)

SPEEL EN ZING JE MEE?, VOL. I:
VOLKSLIEDEREN OM TE SPELEN EN TE
ZINGEN *CC6U
(Beijersbergen van Henegouwen) part
1: solo voice, S rec, fl, vln, ob,
mand; part 2: S rec, vln, fl, ob,
mand, T rec; part 3: A rec,
mandola, vln; part 3a: gtr, acord
(2nd degr.) sc HARMONIA 1515 f.s.
Rode Reeks: Een Huis Vol Muziek;
orig words   (6155)

SPEEL EN ZING JE MEE?, VOL. II:
VOLKSLIEDEREN UIT BINNEN- EN
BUITENLAND *CC8U
(Beijersbergen van Henegouwen) part
1: solo voice, S rec, fl, vln, ob,
mand; part 2: S rec, vln, fl, ob,
mand, T rec; part 3: A rec,
mandola, vln; part 3a: gtr, acord
(2nd degr.) sc HARMONIA 1541 f.s.
Rode Reeks: Een Huis Vol Muziek;
orig words   (6156)

SPEEL EN ZING JE MEE?, VOL. III:
KERSTLIEDJES OM TE SPELEN EN TE
ZINGEN *CC8U
(Beijersbergen van Henegouwen) part
1: solo voice, S rec, fl, vln, ob,
mand; part 2: S rec, vln, fl, ob,
mand, T rec; part 3: A rec,
mandola, vln; part 3a: gtr, acord
(2nd degr.) sc HARMONIA 1564 f.s.
Rode Reeks: Een Huis Vol Muziek;
orig words   (6157)

SPEEL EN ZING JE MEE?, VOL. IV: NEGRO-
SPIRITUALS *CC5U
(Beijersbergen van Henegouwen) part
1: solo voice, S rec, fl, vln, ob,
mand; part 2: S rec, vln, fl, ob,
mand, T rec; part 3: A rec,
mandola, vln; part 3a: gtr, acord
(2nd degr.) sc HARMONIA 1589 f.s.
Rode Reeks: Een Huis Vol Muziek;
orig words   (6158)

SPEEL EN ZING JE MEE?, VOL. V:
VOLKSLIEDEREN OM TE SPELEN EN TE
ZINGEN *CC2U
(Beijersbergen van Henegouwen) part
1: solo voice, S rec, fl, vln, ob,
mand; part 2: S rec, vln, fl, ob,
mand, T rec; part 3: A rec,
mandola, vln; part 3a: gtr, acord;
part 4: vcl, bsn, db (2nd degr.) sc
HARMONIA 1826 f.s. Rode Reeks: Een
Huis Vol Muziek; orig words   (6159)

VOR LAUTER LIEB UND LUST, LEICHTE SATZE
ZU ALTEN LIEDERN *CC26U
(Klein) [Ger] inst,gtr, solo voices
(single line playing/1st degr.) sc,
pts MOSELER f.s. notation gtr pt:
22 pcs in bass clef with chord
symbols; 2 pcs in treb clef; 2 pcs
without gtr   (6160)

WEILL, KURT (1900-1950)
Jasager, Der, Schoolopera In 2 Acts
[Eng/Ger] 1.0.1.0.alto sax.
0.0.0.0. timp,perc,2pno,
harmonium,plucked insts,strings,
cor,MezBarTTTT soli [35'] UNIVER.
pno red 8206 f.s., pts rent   (6161)

WHAT SHALL WE DO?, CHANSONS DE MATELOTS
ANGLAIS
(Turellier; Vallade) [Eng] 2gtr,mix
cor (3rd degr., Plein Jeu, No.75)
sc HEUGEL PJ-75 f.s.   (6162)

WIE KAN DE BLAREN TELLEN
(van der Linden) rec,metallophone,
strings,gtr, solo voices (Musica,
No. 6; contains works by:
Schroyens, de Meulder, Langhans) sc
DE MONTE f.s. contains also:
Boerkens Smelten Van Vreugd En
Plezier, De; Jagerslied   (6163)

WIR LERNEN HAUSMUSIK, FOLGE I-VIII
*CC23U
(Korda) [Ger] (2-3rd degr.) sc OSTER
6781-58A-H f.s. contains works by
various composers for various insts
and voices; includes Folksongs (2),
Korda, Strauss, Beethoven, Lanner
with gtr   (6164)

I/IIIA   Concertos for Guitar

ALFONSO, JAVIER (1905-   )
    Suite En Style Ancien (After Campion)
    (Azpiazu) gtr,string orch SYMPHON
    f.s. sc 393, solo pt 395   (6165)

APIVOR, DENIS (1916-   )
    Concertino, Op. 26
    gtr,orch SCHOTT pno red,solo pt
    GA-203 f.s., pts rent   (6166)

AZPIAZU, JOSE DE (1912-   )
    Concert Baroque, In A
    gtr,string orch SYMPHON sc 2116
    f.s., solo pt 2117 f.s., pts ipa
    (6167)
    Suite Elisabethaine Sur Des Themes De
    John Dowland
    gtr,string orch SYMPHON sc 2146
    f.s., solo pt 2147 f.s., ipa
    (6168)

BAERVOETS, RAYMOND (1930-   )
    Concerto
    gtr,orch pno red,solo pt METROPOLIS
    4535 $7.50   (6169)

BALLOU, ESTHER WILLIAMSON (1915-1973)
    Concerto
    gtr,chamber orch sc,pts COMP.FAC.
    f.s.   (6170)

BARBIER, RENE (AUGUSTE-ERNEST)
    (1890-1981)
    Concerto, Op. 98
    gtr,orch pno red METROPOLIS 4589
    $8.00   (6171)

BASTON, JOHN (ca. 1700-   )
    Concerto
    (Behrend) gtr,string orch (7th
    degr., orig for fl, vln, cont;
    Gitarre-Bibliothek, No.51) sc
    BOTE GB-51 f.s.   (6172)

BAUMANN, HERBERT (1925-   )
    Concerto
    gtr,string orch SIKORSKI f.s., ipr
    sc 516-P, solo pt 516   (6173)

BEDFORD, DAVID (1937-   )
    Horse, His Name Was Hunry Fenceweaver
    Walkins, A
    gtr,chamber orch sc UNIVER. 15557
    f.s.   (6174)

BEHREND, SIEGFRIED (1933-   )
    Legnaniana
    gtr,string orch ZIMMER. f.s., ipa
    sc ZM-1352A, solo pt ZM-1352B
    (6175)

BENGUEREL, XAVIER (1931-   )
    Concerto
    gtr,orch MOECK f.s., ipr study sc
    5117, solo pt,pno red 5117B
    (6176)

BENNETT, RICHARD RODNEY (1936-   )
    Concerto
    gtr,chamber orch UNIVER. f.s. study
    sc 15406, pno red 15405   (6177)

BERKELEY, [SIR] LENNOX (1903-   )
    Concerto for Guitar and Orchestra
    gtr,orch HANSEN-DEN rent   (6178)

BLAKE WATKINS, MICHAEL (1948-   )
    Clouds And Eclipses
    gtr,string orch NOVELLO rent   (6179)

BOCCHERINI, LUIGI (1743-1805)
    Concerto in E
    (Cassado; Segovia) gtr,orch pno
    red,solo pt SCHOTT GA-223 f.s.,
    ipr   (6180)

BONDON, JACQUES (1927-   )
    Concerto De Mars
    gtr,orch pno red,solo pt ESCHIG
    f.s., ipr   (6181)

BORDHAYS, CHRISTIANE LE
    Concierto De Azul
    gtr,orch FRANCAIS f.s.   (6182)

BRANDAO, JOSE DOMINGOS (1904-   )
    Lusitano, Concerto
    gtr,orch pno red,solo pt ESCHIG
    7254 f.s., ipr   (6183)

BRESGEN, CESAR (1913-   )
    Kammerkonzert
    gtr,chamber orch pno red,solo pt
    SCHOTT GA-226 f.s., ipr   (6184)

BROUWER, LEO (1939-   )
    Concerto
    gtr,pno/orch ESCHIG rent   (6185)

CARULLI, FERDINANDO (1770-1841)
    Allegro Da Concerto
    (Porrino) gtr,chamber orch SYMPHON
    f.s., ipa sc 2139, solo pt 2140
    (6186)
    Concerto in A
    (Barison) gtr,orch (cadenza by
    Bruno Tonazzi) sc BERBEN EB1158
    $11.00   (6187)
    (Behrend) gtr,orch SYMPHON f.s. sc
    482, solo pt 483, pts 484   (6188)
    (Behrend) gtr,orch SIKORSKI f.s.,
    ipa sc 755P, solo pt 755   (6189)

CASTELNUOVO-TEDESCO, MARIO (1895-1968)
    Concerto in D, Op. 99
    (Segovia) gtr,orch SCHOTT pno red,
    solo pt GA-166 f.s., sc rent, ipa
    (6190)
    Concerto Sereno In C (Concerto in A)
    Op.160
    (Parkening) gtr,orch SCHOTT f.s.,
    ipa pno red,solo pt GA-240, sc
    137   (6191)
    Serenade, Op. 118
    gtr,chamber orch pno red,solo pt
    SCHOTT GA-167 f.s., ipr   (6192)

CERF, JACQUES (1932-   )
    Concerto Capriccioso (Concerto in A)
    gtr,orch FRANCAIS f.s.   (6193)

CHARPENTIER, JACQUES (1933-   )
    Concerto No. 2
    gtr,string orch solo pt,sc LEDUC
    $6.50, ipr   (6194)

CHAYNES, CHARLES (1925-   )
    Visions Concertantes, Concerto En 4
    Parties d'Apres 4 Toiles De
    Salvador Dali
    gtr,string orch RIDEAU f.s.   (6195)

DAVID, THOMAS CHRISTIAN (1925-   )
    Concerto
    (Scheit) gtr,chamber orch (Gitarre-
    Kammermusik, No.58) DOBLINGER
    f.s., ipa sc GKM-58, solo pt
    (6196)

FALCKENHAGEN, ADAM (1697-1761)
    Concerto in F
    (van Puijenbroeck) lute/gtr,strings
    (gtr pt: e' is d', g is f sharp,
    capotasto in pos. III) METROPOLIS
    sc EM-14016-A $6.00, solo pt
    14016-B, pno red 14016-C, pts
    14016D-I   (6197)

FASCH, JOHANN FRIEDRICH (1688-1758)
    Concerto in D minor
    lute,strings
    (Chiesa) gtr/lute,strings ZERBONI
    pno red,solo pt 7317 $16.50, sc
    7315 $11.75, pts 7316 $3.00
    (6198)
    (van Puijenbroeck) (gtr pt: e' is
    d', g is f sharp; capotasto in
    pos. III) METROPOLIS f.s. sc
    EM-14015-A, solo pt 14015-B, pno
    red 14015-C, pts 14015D-I   (6199)

FERSTL, ERICH (1934-   )
    Concertino
    gtr,string orch
    MODERN rent   (6200)
    Sol Y Sombra
    gtr,string orch MODERN rent   (6201)

GIULIANI, MAURO (1781-1829)
    Concerto in A, Op. 36
    gtr,string orch
    "Secondo Concerto" (Chiesa) ZERBONI
    sc 7422 $18.75, pts 7423 $6.00,
    pno red,solo pt 7424 $14.00
    (6202)
    "Studienkonzert" (Henze) HOFMEISTER
    f.s., ipa sc 7204, pno red 7204A
    (6203)
    Concerto No. 3 in F, Op. 70
    (Chiesa) gtr,orch (the key of the
    gtr-part: D major (gtr-e':
    capotasto in pos. III)) ZERBONI
    sc 7425 $18.75, pts 7426 rent,
    pno red,solo pt 7427 $16.50
    (6204)
    Concerto, Op. 30
    (Behrend) gtr,string orch,timp solo
    pt SIKORSKI 758 f.s., ipr   (6205)
    (Chiesa) gtr,string orch,timp
    ZERBONI sc 7838 $59.00, pno red,
    solo pt 7840 f.s., ipr   (6206)
    (Oubradous) gtr,string orch,timp
    (Collection Fernand Oubradous)
    pno red,solo pt TRANSAT. 1289
    f.s., ipr   (6207)
    (Porrino) gtr,string orch,timp
    (cadenza by Mario Gangi) SYMPHON
    f.s., ipa sc 2014, solo pt 2015
    (6208)

HARTIG, HEINZ FRIEDRICH (1907-1969)
    Concertante Suite *Op.19
    (Behrend) gtr,orch (cadenza by S.
    Behrend; Gitarre-Bibliothek,
    No.11) BOTE GB-11 rent   (6209)

HAUG, HANS (1900-1967)
    Concertino
    gtr,chamber orch BERBEN sc EB1454
    $21.50, ipa, solo pt   (6210)

HEER, HANS DE (1927-   )
    Concerto
    gtr,string orch TEESELING ipa solo
    pt VT-5, sc   (6211)

HIROTA
    Hamachidori, Japanese Song
    (Walter) gtr,string orch ZIMMER.
    rent   (6212)

HOFFMANN, JOHANN
    Concerto
    (Behrend) gtr,chamber orch ZIMMER.
    f.s.   (6213)

HOYER, ANTOINE L'
    Concerto, Op. 16
    (Nagytothy-Toth) gtr,string orch
    (7th degr.) sc,pts UNION ESP.
    f.s.   (6214)

ISHII, MAKI (1936-   )
    Japanische Suite I
    gtr,orch ZIMMER. f.s.   (6215)

KELKEL, MANFRED (1929-   )
    Zagreber Konzert *Op.19
    gtr,orch pno red,solo pt SCHOTT
    6498 f.s., ipr   (6216)

KREBS, JOHANN LUDWIG (1713-1780)
    Concerto in C for Lute and Strings
    (Chiesa) gtr,strings (orig for
    lute-f' and strings) ZERBONI pno
    red,solo pt 7275 $16.50, sc 7273,
    pts 7274 $3.00   (6217)
    Concerto in F for Lute and Strings
    "Concerto In F Per Liuto E Archi"
    (Chiesa) gtr,orch (orig for lute-
    f' and strings) ZERBONI pts 7040
    f.s., sc 6962 f.s., pno red,solo
    pt 7318 f.s.   (6218)
    "Concerto In G For Guitar And
    Strings" (Chiesa) gtr,orch (orig
    for lute-f' and strings) ZERBONI
    pno red,solo pt 7041 $16.50, pts
    7040A $3.00   (6219)
    (van Puijenbroeck) lute/gtr,strings
    (orig for lute-f' and strings;
    gtr-part: e' is d', g is f sharp;
    capotasto in pos. III) METROPOLIS
    f.s. sc EM-14008-A, solo pt
    14008-B, pno red 14008-C, pts
    14008-D-I   (6220)

MARCO, TOMAS (1942-   )
    Concerto
    "Guadiana" gtr,string orch study sc
    ALPUERTO 1199 f.s.   (6221)

MARI, PIERETTE (1929-   )
    Concerto for Guitar, Strings and
    Percussion
    gtr,string orch,perc BILLAUDOT
    f.s., ipr sc 1454, solo pt   (6222)

MORENO TORROBA, FEDERICO (1891-1982)
    Concierto De Castilla
    gtr,orch HISPAVOX f.s., ipr pno red
    1236, solo pt 1235   (6223)
    Homenaje A La Seguidilla, Concerto
    (Yepes) gtr,orch UNION ESP. f.s.
    (6224)

NOBLE
    Concertino Mexicano
    gtr,orch sc RICORDI-ARG BA-12402
    f.s.   (6225)

NOVAK, JAN (1921-1984)
    Concerto Per Euridice
    "Concentus Eurydicae" (Diaz) gtr,
    string orch (Il Bucranio) ZANIBON
    f.s. sc 5139, solo pt 5140   (6226)

PAGANINI, NICCOLO (1782-1840)
    Romance (from Grand Sonata A Chitarra
    Sola Con Accompagnamento Di
    Violino)
    (Walter) gtr,string orch ZIMMER.
    ipa sc ZM-1711, pts   (6227)

PALAU, MANUEL (1893-1967)
    Concierto Levantino
    (Yepes) gtr,orch UNION ESP. f.s.
    (6228)

PIZZINI, CARLO ALBERTO (1905-   )
    Concierto Para Tres Hermanas
    gtr,orch ZANIBON sc 5219 f.s., pts
    5220 rent, pno red,solo pt 5221
    (6229)

PONCE, MANUEL MARIA (1882-1948)
Concierto Del Sur
(Segovia) gtr,orch pno red,solo pt
PEER 2016-55 $9.00, ipr   (6230)

PORRINO, ENNIO (1910-1959)
Concerto Dell'Argentarola
gtr,orch SYMPHON sc 2056 f.s., pno
red 2020 f.s., pts rent   (6231)

PROSEV, TOMA (1931-   )
Concerto, Op. 38
gtr,orch ZIMMER. f.s.   (6232)

RODRIGO, JOAQUIN (1902-   )
Concierto De Aranjuez
gtr,orch (pno red and min sc
published by the composer; for
West Germany, pno red and solo pt
available from BOTE) solo pt
UNION ESP. f.s.   (6233)

Fantasia Para Un Gentilhombre,
Inspirada En Gaspar Sanz
gtr,orch pno red,solo pt SCHOTT
GA-208 f.s., ipr   (6234)

SANTORSOLA, GUIDO (1904-   )
Concertino
gtr,orch pno red,solo pt PEER
SMP-2233-33 $7.50, ipr   (6235)

SCHOLZ, BERND (1911-1969)
Japanisches Konzert
gtr,orch ZIMMER. rent   (6236)

SEIXAS, (JOSE ANTONIO) CARLOS DE
(1704-1742)
Concerto in A
(Pujol) gtr,strings without db sc
ESCHIG 1116 f.s.   (6237)

SMIT SIBINGA, THEO H. (1899-1958)
Concerto
gtr,orch sc,pno red,solo pt DONEMUS
f.s.   (6238)

SOR, FERNANDO (1778-1839)
Alt Spanischer Tanz Mit Variationen
(Walter) gtr,string orch ZIMMER.
f.s. sc ZM-1387A, pts ZM-1387B
(6239)

STAAK, PIETER VAN DER (1930-   )
Concertino No. 2
gtr,chamber orch pno red,solo pt
BROEKMANS 947 f.s.   (6240)

TAKACS, JENO (1902-   )
Partita, Op. 55
gtr/hpsd,orch DOBLINGER f.s. pno
red 02151, solo pt 05951   (6241)

TORELLI, GIUSEPPE (1658-1709)
Concerto in D minor
(Azpiazu) gtr,string orch SYMPHON
f.s., ipa sc 430, solo pt 431
(6242)

VILLA-LOBOS, HEITOR (1887-1959)
Concerto
gtr,chamber orch pno red,solo pt
SCHOTT GA-190 f.s., ipr   (6243)

VIVALDI, ANTONIO (1678-1741)
Concerto in A
"Lautenkonzert" (Behrend) gtr,
string orch (C maj) sc SIRIUS
f.s.   (6244)
(Pujol) gtr,vln,vla,vcl sc,pts
ESCHIG 1113 f.s.   (6245)

Concerto in C
(Azpiazu) gtr,string orch SYMPHON
f.s. sc 386, solo pt 388, pts 387
(6246)
(Nagy) gtr,string orch pno red,solo
pt EMB 5091 f.s.   (6247)
(Pujol) gtr,string orch sc ESCHIG
1115 f.s.   (6248)

Concerto in D
(Azpiazu) gtr,string orch (orig.
for desc lute and strings)
SYMPHON f.s. sc 389, solo pt 391,
pts 390   (6249)
(Behrend) gtr,string orch (orig.
for desc lute and strings)
SIKORSKI f.s. sc 378-P, solo pt,
pts 378   (6250)
(Benko) gtr,string orch (orig. for
desc lute and strings; Musica per
chitarra) EMB f.s.   (6251)
(Benko) gtr,string orch (orig. for
desc lute and strings; Musica per
chitarra) pts EULENBURG GM-252
f.s.   (6252)
(Company) gtr,string orch (orig.
for desc lute and strings)
ZERBONI sc,solo pt 7096 f.s., pts
7097 rent   (6253)
(Lancien) gtr,string orch (orig.
for desc lute and strings)
CHOUDENS f.s.   (6254)
(Mirt) gtr,string orch (orig. for
desc lute and strings) sc BERBEN
EB1053 $3.25, ipa   (6255)
(Pujol) gtr,string orch (orig. for

VIVALDI, ANTONIO (cont'd.)
desc lute and strings) sc,pts
ESCHIG 1107 f.s.   (6256)
(van Puijenbroeck) gtr,string orch
(orig. for desc lute and strings;
gtr pt: g is f sharp; capotasto
in pos. III) METROPOLIS sc
EM-14011.A, solo pt EM-14011.B,
pno red,solo pt EM-14011.C, pts
EM-14011.D-H   (6257)
(Visser) gtr,string orch (orig. for
desc lute and strings) solo pt
HARMONIA 1588 f.s., ipa   (6258)
(Yepes) gtr,string orch (orig. for
desc lute and strings) pno red,
solo pt TRANSAT. 585-BIS f.s.,
ipr   (6259)

VLAD, ROMAN (1919-   )
Ode Super "Chrysea Phorminx"
gtr,chamber orch UNIVER. rent
(6260)

WALTER, FRIED (1907-   )
Pavan
gtr,string orch sc ZIMMER. f.s.
contains also: Tarantella; Waltz
(6261)

Reflexe, Variationen Durch Die
Jahrhundert Uber Ein Thema Von
Gaspar Sanz
gtr,orch ZIMMER. f.s.   (6262)

WEISS, JOHANN ADOLF
Concerto
(Azpiazu) gtr,string orch (orig for
lute and strings) SYMPHON f.s.,
ipa sc 2159, solo pt 2160   (6263)

WUSTHOFF, KLAUS
Collagen
ZIMMER. f.s.   (6264)

I/IIIB Concertos for Two Guitars

BARBIER, RENE (AUGUSTE-ERNEST)
(1890-1981)
Concertino, Op. 116
2gtr,orch sc CBDM 72-632 f.s.
(6265)

CARULLI, FERDINANDO (1770-1841)
Concerto in A for Guitar and String
Orchestra
(Scheit) gtr,string orch,opt dbl
cor (Gitarre-Kammermusik, No. 42)
sc,pt DOBLINGER GKM-42 f.s.
(6266)

CASTELNUOVO-TEDESCO, MARIO (1895-1968)
Concerto, Op. 201
2gtr,orch (Collezione Di Musiche
Per Chitarra) BERBEN $13.50, ipr
sc EB1400, pno red,solo pt EB1890
(6267)

GAITIS, FRIEDRICH
Concertino
mand,gtr, and plucked orchestra
(mand I, mand II, mandola, gtr,
db) sc GERIG 656 f.s.   (6268)

HAYDN, [FRANZ] JOSEPH (1732-1809)
Concerto for 2 Lire Organizzate and
Orchestra, No. 2, in G
*Hob.VIIh:2
(Azpiazu) 2gtr,orch SYMPHON f.s.,
ipa sc 2167, solo pt 2173   (6269)

PETIT, PIERRE (1922-   )
Concerto
2gtr,orch FRANCAIS f.s.   (6270)

VIVALDI, ANTONIO (1678-1741)
Concerto No. 3 in G
(Azpiazu) 2mand/2gtr/2fl/vln&gtr,
string orch SYMPHON f.s., ipa sc
2023, solo pt 2024, pts 2025
(6271)
(Oubradous) 2mand/2gtr string orch,
opt hpsd (Collection Fernand
Oubradous) TRANSAT. f.s., ipr min
sc 478, pno red   (6272)

Concerto No. 23 in C for 2 Mandolins
and Strings
(Oubradous) 2gtr,string orch,opt
hpsd (Collection Fernand
Oubradous) pno red TRANSAT. f.s.
(6273)

I/IIIC Concertos for Guitar and Other Instruments

BARTOLOZZI, BRUNO (1911-   )
Memorie
orch, 3gtr concertanti sc ZERBONI
8139 f.s.   (6274)

BECKER, GUNTHER (1924-   )
Caprices Concertants
mand,gtr,perc, mandola, with
plucked orchestra sc GERIG 672
rent   (6275)

BELAUBRE, LOUIS-NOEL (1932-   )
Symphonie Concertante
gtr,hpsd/gtr,strings ESCHIG rent
(6276)

BOOGAARD, BERNARD VAN DEN (1952-   )
Concertino
harp,gtr,chamber orch DONEMUS f.s.
(6277)

CARULLI, FERDINANDO (1770-1841)
Concerto in G for Flute, Guitar and
Orchestra
(Chiesa) gtr,pno ZERBONI f.s., ipa
pno red,pt 8137, sc 8135   (6278)

FURSTENAU, WOLFRAM
Renaissance Pour Le Presence
gtr,pno,string orch TEESELING FC-7
f.s.   (6279)

HANDEL, GEORGE FRIDERIC (1685-1759)
Concerto in B flat for Lute, Harp and
Orchestra
(Azpiazu) gtr,harp,string orch
(orig for lute, harp, and orch)
SYMPHON f.s., ipa sc 2149, solo
pt 2150, solo pt 2151   (6280)

JOSEPHS, WILFRED (1927-   )
Saratoga Concerto
gtr,harp,hpsd,orch NOVELLO rent
(6281)

KONIETZNY, HEINRICH
Kammerkonzert
plucked quar (mand I, mand II,
mandola, gtr) and plucked orch
(mand I, mand II, mandola, gtr,
db) GERIG f.s. sc,copy 660, pts
(6282)

KOTONSKI, WLODZIMIERZ (1925-   )
Concerto Per Quattro
harp,gtr,hpsd,pno,perc,string orch
sc MOECK EM-50010-PWM f.s.   (6283)

TOMASI, HENRI (1901-1971)
Pastorales Provencales
2gtr,fl/pic,string orch solo pt
LEDUC 23748 f.s., ipa   (6284)

VIVALDI, ANTONIO (1678-1741)
Concerto in C
(Behrend) 2mand,2gtr/2lute, plucked
orch GERIG f.s. sc 1098, pts
(6285)

Concerto in D minor for Viola
d'Amore, Lute and Strings *RV
540
(Azpiazu) gtr,vln,string orch
SYMPHON f.s., ipa sc 2014, solo
pt 2105, solo pt 2106   (6286)
(Behrend) vla d'amore,gtr,string
orch ZIMMER. f.s. sc ZM-1320, pts
(6287)

WERDIN, EBERHARD (1911-   )
Concertino
fl,gtr,string orch (gtr and fl pts
for skillful players; orch pts
can also be performed by a school
orch) GERIG f.s. sc HG-836, pts
(6288)

II Methods

AGUADO, DIONISIO (1784-1849)
Escuela De Guitarra
"Grande Methode" gtr LEMOINE f.s. (1)
"Methode Elementaire" gtr LEMOINE f.s. (2)
"Metodo Completo De Guitarra" [Span] gtr (129p., 7 ill; new ed, repr, n.d.; 1st ed unknown) folio RICORDI-ARG BA-6231 f.s. (3)
"Methode De Guitare" (Dussart, Raymond) [Fr] gtr (140p., ill; rev and enl ed, 1969; 1 suppl (4p.); 18 ill (parts of the guitar, playing position, the hands, etc.); studies and exercises with modernised fingerings and right hand-formulae; orig text partly abridged) folio LEMOINE 24241 f.s. (4)
"Metodo Per Chitarra" (Gangi, Mario; Carfagna, Carlo) [It/Eng] gtr (115p., ill; 1968) folio BERBEN 1290 f.s. (5)
"Gitarrenschule" (Sainz de la Maza, Regino) [Ger] gtr (vi + 106p., ill; rev ed, 1963; pref, 3 app; German transl of Metodo De Guitarra) folio GERIG HG-440 f.s. (6)
"Metodo De Guitarra" (Sainz de la Maza, Regino) [Span] gtr (viii + 106p., ill; rev ed, 1943; 3 app) folio UNION ESP. 17318 f.s. (7)
"Gran Metodo Completo Para Guitarra, Con Una Recopilacion De Estudios Originales De Autores Celebres" (Sinopoli, Antonio) [Span] gtr (181p., ill; repr, 1969; 1st ed, 1947; 7 courses in 5 pts; notes; app: Observacion sobre la naturaleza o indole de la guitarra; contains: Bach, Johann Sebastian, Suite For Keyboard Instrument, BWV 821, In B Flat; Courante, [C major]; Bach Johann Sebastian, Prelude For Lute, BWV 999, In C Minor, [D minor]; Bach, Johann Sebastian, Suite For Lute, BWV 996, In E Minor, Allemande, [A minor]; Bach, Johann Sebastian, Prelude, BWV 927, In F, [G major] from Wilhelm Friedemann Bach Klavierbuchlein (1720); Bach, Johann Sebastian, Presto, BWV 970, In D Minor; Tarrega, Francisco, Prelude, TI-i-14; Tarrega, Francisco, Studies, TI-ii-2a [22 bars], 6, 14a, c, 18, 19, 20, 22, 29 [18 bars]; Tarrega, Francisco, Exercises, TI-iii-2, 14, 20, 24[12 bars], 30a, 32) folio RICORDI-ARG BA-9801 f.s. (8)

AHSLUND, ULF-G.
Gitarrskola, Spela I Grupp [Swed] gtr (1971, 60p., ill; 1st ed, 1968) quarto LIBER f.s. (9)

Gitarrskola, Spela I Grupp, Supp.2 "Teknikovningar" [Swed] gtr (16p.; n.d.; Gitarrskola, Suppl. 2; contains diatonic scales, chromatic scales, arpeggios, tremolo, intervals; includes: Tarrega, Francisco, Study, TI-ii-30, In E; Exercises, TI-iii-2a, 4, 28, 32[11 bars]) quarto LIBER f.s. (10)

Gitarrskola, Spela I Grupp, Suppl. 1 "Lararhandledning" [Swed] gtr (33p.) LIBER f.s. (11)

Gitarrskola, Spela I Grupp, Suppl. 3 "Ljudband" [Swed] gtr (45' tape recording of all melodies from Gitarrskola) LIBER f.s. (12)

AHSLUND, ULF-G. (cont'd.)
Samklang, Method For Group Tuition, Vol. 1 gtr REUTER RG-24 f.s. (13)

Samklang, Method For Group Tuition, Vol. 2 gtr REUTER RG-25 f.s. (14)

AKERMAN, SIGVARD
Gitarr- Och Lutaspelets ABC, Skola For Fingerspelning [Swed] gtr (32p., ill; 1942) quarto oblong NORDISKA 2212 f.s. (15)

ALBERT, HEINRICH (1870-1950)
Lehrgang Des Kunstlerischen Gitarrespiels, Fur Lehrzwecke Und Zum Selbstunterricht, Vol. I-A "Volkslied Zur Gitarre, Das" [Ger] gtr (1952; repr of the 2nd rev and enl ed, 1924; 1st ed, Munchen, Verlag Der Gitarrefreund, 1914; 48p., ill; Von Ersten Anfangen, Allgemeine Musiklehre und Einfuhrung In Die Harmonielehre; Die Tonarten C-, G- Und D-Dur; Volkslieder) folio LIENAU S.10189-IA f.s. (16)

Lehrgang Des Kunstlerischen Gitarrespiels, Fur Lehrzwecke Und Zum Selbstunterricht, Vol. I-B "Volkslied Zur Gitarre, Das" [Ger] gtr (1952; repr of the 2nd rev and enl ed, 1924; 1st ed, Munchen, Verlag Der Gitarrefreund, 1914; 31p.; Die Weitere Entwicklung Der Harmonielehre Und Die Ubrigen Tonarten Der Ersten Lage; Volkslieder) folio LIENAU S.10189-IB f.s. (17)

Lehrgang Des Kunstlerischen Gitarrespiels, Vol. II "Gitarrelied, Das" [Ger] gtr (52p.; repr, 1952; 1st ed, 1924; contains: Intro, Notes: Das Barrespiel, App: Die Wichtigsten Anwendungsstellen Fur Gitarre In Opern Und Orchesterwerken, barre (exercises, chords, studies), positions IV, V, VII, IX (exercises, chords, studies, pieces); includes: Bach, Johann Sebastian, Betrachte, Meine Seel from Johannes-Passion, BWV 245, NO. 31, FOR BASS SOLO AND GTR) folio LIENAU S.10189-II f.s. (18)

Lehrgang Des Kunstlerischen Gitarrespiels, Vol. III "Gitarre Als Solo-Instrument, Die" [Ger] gtr (59p.; repr, 1952; 1st ed, 1924; Intro: Die Ornamentik In Der Musik; Notes: Nagelspiel; App: Entwicklungsgeschichte Der Gitarre; contains: Legato, Secondary Positions, Harmonics, Arpeggio Formulae, Tremolo, Exercises, Studies And Solo Pieces) folio LIENAU S.10189-D f.s. (19)

Lehrgang Des Kunstlerischen Gitarrespiels, Vol. IV "Virtuose Gitarrespiels, Das" [Ger] gtr (32p.; repr, 1952; 1st ed, 1924; contains: Intro, App: Fingergymnastik, chromatic exercises and scales, scales (2, 2 and 3 octaves) + formulae, cadences, scales + formulae in thirds, sixths, sixth chords, octaves, double octaves, thirds + octaves, sixths + octaves, tenths, scales in contrary motion, chord inversions + arpeggio formulae) folio LIENAU S.10189.IV f.s. (20)

ALBERTO, A.
Kleine Gitarre- Und Lauten-Schule [Ger] gtr (63p., ill; rev ed, 1942; 1st ed unknown) oct oblong RAHTER EE-1100 f.s. (21)

ALDELAND, NILS
Elementar Improvisation, Vol. I (composed with Ahslund, Ulf-G.) "Elementary Improvisations, Vol. I: Method" [Eng] gtr (40p.) quarto SCHIRM.G 2887 f.s. (22)
"Gitarrskola" [Swed] gtr (1969)

ALDELAND, NILS (cont'd.)
REUTER f.s. (23)

Elementar Improvisation, Vol. II (composed with Ahslund, Ulf-G.) "Elementary Improvisations, Vol. II: Teacher's Handbook" [Eng] gtr (12p.) quarto SCHIRM.G 2888 f.s. (24)
"Lararhandledning" [Swed] gtr (1970) REUTER f.s. (25)

ALFONSO, NICOLAS
Guitare Theorique Et Pratique, Methode Complete, La, Vol. I [Fr/Dutch/Ger/Eng/Port/Span] gtr (47p., ill; 1960) quarto SCHOTT-FRER 9087 f.s. (26)

Guitare Theorique Et Pratique, Methode Complete, La, Vol. II [Fr/Dutch/Ger/Eng/Port/Span] gtr (59p., ill; 1960) quarto SCHOTT-FRER 9115 f.s. (27)

ALMEIDA, LAURINDO (1917-)
Guitar Tutor, An Up-To-Date Classic Guitar Method gtr (93p., ill; 3rd printing, 1957; Eng rev by Jack Duarte) quarto CRITERION f.s. (28)

AMATO, ANGELO
Prime Lezioni Di Chitarra, Le [It] gtr (19p.; 1967) quarto ZANIBON 4861 f.s. (29)

ANDREOLLI, MARIANO
Corso Preparatorio Di Chitarra [It] gtr (40p.; 1971) folio BERBEN 1579 f.s. (30)

ANDRYSZAK, ALES
Schule Der Konzertgitarre, Die: Grund- Und Mittelstufe gtr (208p.; suppl: compact-cassette with musical examples (96.8822)) HUEBER 96.8821 f.s. (31)

ANIDO, MARIA LUISA
Cuaderno Tecnico-Recreativo, Para Alumnos De Guitarra (Preparatorio) [Span] gtr (18p.; 1970) folio RICORDI-ARG BA-12895 f.s. (32)

ANZAGHI, LUIGI ORESTE (1903-1963)
Chitarra D'accompagnamento, La, Metodo Lampo Anche Per Chi Non Conosce La Musica [It] gtr (32p., ill, 1966; 1st ed, 1959; staff notation + diag) quarto oblong RICORDI-IT RM-129926 f.s. (33)

Metodo Completo Per Chitarra, Teoretico-Pratico Progressivo [It] gtr (213p., ill, 1967; 1st ed., 1956; suppl: 2 tables of the fingerboard) folio RICORDI-IT RM-129374 f.s. (34)

AUBANEL, GEORGES
Methode Elementaire De Guitare [Fr] gtr (27p., ill; rev and enl ed, 1973; 1st ed, 1962) quarto OUVRIERS EO-3253 f.s. (35)

AUBIN, CHRISTIAN
Enseignement Rationnel De La Guitare, Vol. I (composed with Chemla, Teddy) [Fr] gtr (31p., ill; 1958) folio ZURFLUH A.1040.Z f.s. (36)

Enseignement Rationnel De La Guitare, Vol. II (composed with Chemla, Teddy) [Fr] gtr (48p.; 1959) folio ZURFLUH A.1052.Z f.s. (37)

AZPIAZU, JOSE DE (1912-)
Estilo Flamenco, Metodo De Guitarra gtr (staff notation and tablature, 34p.; 1961) quarto SYMPHON 2108 f.s. (38)

Gitarrenschule, Vol. I [Ger/Fr/Span] gtr quarto SYMPHON 350 f.s. 24p.; 1954; contains: Bach, Johann Sebastian, Prelude, BWV 999, In C-Minor (in D-Minor); Minuet, BWV Anh. 114, In G (in A), Anna Magdalena Bach Notenbuchlein (1725), No.4;

CARCASSI, MATTEO (cont'd.)

　　　　　　　　　　　　　　　　　　　　(86)
"Carcassi Method For The Guitar"
(Santisteban, G.C.) gtr (196p.;
repr of the Oliver Ditson ed
(1926), n.d.) ASHLEY f.s.　　(87)
"Schule Des Kunstlerischen
Gitarrespiels; Ganzliche
Neubearbeitung Fur Den Heutigen
Gebrauch" (Schwarz-Reiflingen,
Erwin; Leipoldt, Friedrich) [Ger]
gtr (2 vols in 1 vol; 68p.; 1st
unknown; rev ed) quarto
ZIMMER. 180 f.s.　　　　　　(88)

CARULLI, FERDINANDO (1770-1841)
Methode De Guitare
"Methode De Guitare, Suivie De 44
Morceaux Progressifs Et De Six
Etudes" [Fr/Span] gtr (106p.;
app; repr, n.d., 6th orig ed; 1st
Lemoine ed unknown) folio LEMOINE
f.s.　　　　　　　　　　　　(89)
"Gitarre- Und Lautenschule, Vol. I"
(Bracony, Alberto) [Ger] gtr
(30p., ill; repr, n.d.; ed after
the 4th and 5th orig ed; 1st ed,
1912) quarto BENJ EE-51 f.s. (90)
"Gitarre- Und Lautenschule, Vol.
II" (Bracony, Alberto) [Ger] gtr
(37p., ill; repr, n.d.; ed after
the 4th and 5th orig ed; 1st ed,
1912) quarto BENJ EE-52 f.s. (91)
"Metodo Completo Para Guitarra,
Vol. 1" (Costa, J.F.) [Span] gtr
(44p.; suppl: 8 ill; 10th rev and
enl ed, 1969; ed after the 5th
orig ed; 1st ed, 1937; no further
vols published) folio RICORDI-ARG
BA-7281 f.s.　　　　　　　　(92)
"Methode De Guitare, Suivi De 44
Morceaux Progressifs Et De 6
Etudes" (Faraill Martial) [Fr/
Span] gtr (106p., ill; new rev
ed, 1955; ed after the 6th orig
ed; suppl: Figures pour la
Methode de guitare (3 ill)) folio
LEMOINE f.s.　　　　　　　　(93)
"Metodo Completo Para Guitarra,
Vol. 1" (Garay del Castillo, A.)
[Span] gtr (38p., ill; ed after
the 5th orig ed; 1966) folio
RICORDI-ARG EK-15 f.s.　　　(94)
"Gitarre-Schule, Vol. I" (Gotze,
Walter) [Ger] gtr (81p., ill; rev
and enl ed, 1930; ed after the
5th orig ed; 3 app; suppl: 5 ill;
diag of the fingerboard) quarto
PETERS 2480A f.s.　　　　　　(95)
"Gitarre-Schule, Vol. II:
Fortschreitende Tonstucke Und
Gelaufigkeits-Etuden, (Erganzung
Zur Gitarre-Schule" (Gotze,
Walter) [Ger] gtr (61p., repr;
1969; ed after the 5th orig ed;
1st ed, 1931; 36 pcs.-studies for
gtr) quarto PETERS 2480C f.s.
　　　　　　　　　　　　　　(96)
"Gitarre-Schule, Vol. III: 24
Duette Fur 2 Gitarren" (Gotze,
Walter) [Ger] gtr (43p.; repr,
1967; ed after the 5th orig ed;
1st ed, 1932; 24 pcs. for 2 gtr)
quarto,sc PETERS 2480-D f.s. (97)
"Gitarren-Schule, Vol. I" (Hulsen,
Ernst) [Ger] gtr (56p., ill; repr
of rev ed, n.d.; ed after the 4th
and 5th orig ed; 1st ed, 1927;
suppl: Ansicht Des Griffbrettes
Der Gitarre; Grifftabellen (cf.
suppl. to Carcassi, M., Gitarren-
Schule, (Ritter), Schott GA-1a-
c); also available in Eng,
(Hunt), Schott GA-50E) quarto
SCHOTT GA-50 f.s.　　　　　　(98)
"Gitarren-Schule, Vol. II: Gitarren-
Schule Fur Fortgeschrittene"
(Hulsen, Ernst) [Ger] gtr (47p.,
ill; repr of rev ed, n.d.; ed
after the 4th and 5th orig ed;
1st ed, 1927; suppl: Ansicht Des
Griffbrettes Der Gitarre;
Grifftabellen, (cf. suppl to
Carcassi, M., Gitarren-Schule,
(Ritter), Schott GA-1a-c)) quarto
SCHOTT GA-51 f.s.　　　　　　(99)
"Metodo Para Guitarra, Vol. I"
(Iparraguirre, P.A.) [Span] gtr
(31p., ill; repr of rev ed, 1970;
ed after the 5th orig ed; 1st ed
1923) quarto RICORDI-ARG BA-8074
f.s.　　　　　　　　　　　　(100)
"Metodo Para Guitarra, Vol. II"
(Iparraguirre, P.A.) [Span] gtr
(44p., ill; repr of rev ed, 1970;
ed after the 5th orig ed; 1st ed,
1923) quarto RICORDI-ARG BA-8075
f.s.　　　　　　　　　　　　(101)
"Gitaar-School" (Kok, Johan B.)
[Dutch] gtr (44p., ill; repr of
rev and enl ed, n.d.; ed after
the 4th and 5th orig ed; 1st ed
unknown; 2 app; also available in
Eng: Instruction For The Guitar;
36p.) quarto XYZ 357 f.s. (102)

CARULLI, FERDINANDO (cont'd.)

"Gitarreschule - Ecole De Guitare -
Guitar School" (Krempl, Jos)
[Ger/Fr/Eng] gtr (77p.; repr of
rev and enl ed, 1969; ed after
the 5th orig ed; 1st ed
[Guitarreschule], 1902; 2 app.)
quarto UNIVER. 276 f.s.　　(103)
"Metodo Completo Per Lo Studio
Della Chitarra" (Lenzi Mozzani,
Carmen) [It] gtr (110p.; 3 vols
in 1 vol; rev and enl ed, 1965;
ed after the 4th orig ed; suppl:
Estensione del manico o diapason;
also available separately: vol.
I, 1149; vol. II, 1150; vol. III,
1151) folio BERBEN 1152 f.s.
　　　　　　　　　　　　　　(104)
"Metodo Completo De Guitarra, Vol.
I" (Terzi, Benvenuto) [Span] gtr
(44p.; repr, 1970-71; ed after
the 5th orig ed) folio RICORDI-
ARG BA-115 f.s.　　　　　　(105)
"Metodo Completo De Guitarra, Vol.
II" (Terzi, Benvenuto) [Span] gtr
(44p.; repr, 1970-71; ed after
the 5th orig ed) folio RICORDI-
ARG BA-116 f.s.　　　　　　(106)
"Metodo Completo De Guitarra, Vol.
III" (Terzi, Benvenuto) [Span]
gtr (43p.; repr, 1970-71; ed
after the 5th orig ed) folio
RICORDI-ARG BA-12554 f.s.　(107)
"Metodo Completo Per Chitarra"
(Terzi, Benvenuto) [It/Fr] gtr (3
vols in 1 vol; 93p.; repr of rev
ed, 1969; ed after the 4th orig
ed; 1st ed, 1955; also available
separately: vol. I, ER-2471; vol.
II, ER-2472; vol. III, ER-2473)
folio RICORDI-IT ER-2474 f.s.
　　　　　　　　　　　　　　(108)

CASTAGNA, LUCIANO
Metodo Teorico-Pratico
[It] gtr (20p., ill) quarto CARISCH
1550 f.s.　　　　　　　　　　(109)

CASTET, FRANCOIS
Jeune Guitariste, Le, Premiere
Methode De Guitare
[Fr] gtr (39p., ill; 1969) folio
LEDUC f.s.　　　　　　　　　(110)

CERUTTI, L.
Methode Elementaire Pour La Guitare
[Fr] gtr (31p.; 1964; 1st ed
unknown; also available in Span)
quarto LEDUC f.s.　　　　　　(111)

CHARDOME, RAYMOND
Guitare d'Accompagnement, La, Methode
Simplifiee Pour Amateurs
gtr PRESSES f.s.　　　　　　(112)

CHIERICI, FERNANDO (1912-　　)
Invito Alla Chitarra Flamenca
(composed with Facchinetti, O.)
[It] gtr (40p.; 1970) folio BERBEN
1384 f.s.　　　　　　　　　　(113)

CORMONT, JACQUES
Methode Pour Guitare, Vol. I
"Methode Voor Gitaar" [Fr/Dutch]
gtr (24p.; 1966) folio MAURER
f.s.　　　　　　　　　　　　(114)

Methode Pour Guitare, Vol. II
"Methode Voor Gitaar" [Fr/Dutch]
gtr (28p.; 1968) folio MAURER
f.s.　　　　　　　　　　　　(115)

COTTIN, A.
Methode Complete De Guitare
[Fr] gtr (63p., ill; 1962; 1st ed
unknown) folio LEDUC f.s.　(116)

CRIMLISK, ANTHONY
Play Guitar!, Vol. I
[Eng] gtr (3 app; suppl (app 3):
chart of the gtr fingerboard;
1970) quarto BOOSEY-ENG f.s.
　　　　　　　　　　　　　　(117)
Play Guitar!, Vol. II
[Eng] gtr quarto BOOSEY-ENG f.s. 3
app; suppl (app 3): chart of the
gtr fingerboard; 41p.; 1970;
contains: Bach, Johann Sebastian,
Suite No. 6 For Violoncello, BWV
1012, In D, Gavotte　　　　(118)

CRISWICK, MARY
Guitar Tutor For Young Children
[Eng] gtr (20p.) quarto FENETTE
F-106 f.s.　　　　　　　　　(119)
gtr BREITKOPF-W 57.04056 f.s. (120)

DEDEROS, M.
Invito Alla Chitarra, Metodo Per
Chitarra Classica
[It] gtr (40p.; 1967) folio BERBEN
1201 f.s.　　　　　　　　　　(121)

DIDIER, GERARD
A La Decouverte De La Guitare
gtr quarto PRESSES f.s.　　(122)

DOMANDL, WILLY
Gitarreschule, Auch Fur Den
Selbstunterricht Geeignet
[Ger] gtr (28p., ill; 1953) oct
oblong DOBLINGER 05902 f.s. (123)

DUARTE, JOHN W. (1919-　　)
Guitar Accompaniment - The Easy Way
[Eng] gtr (31p., ill; 1965; staff
notation + diag throughout; for 2
suppl, see Sing Negro Spirituals
and Sing Christmas Carols) quarto
SCHOTT GA-215 f.s.　　　　　(124)

Young Persons' Way To The Guitar, The
[Eng] gtr (63p., ill; 1968; suppl:
For The Teacher, vi p.) quarto
NOVELLO 19628 f.s.　　　　　(125)

FABBRI, TITO
Metodo Teorico-Pratico
[It] gtr (54p., ill; 1962; 1st ed
unknown) quarto CARISCH 5670 f.s.
　　　　　　　　　　　　　　(126)

FERNANDEZ-LAVIE, FERNANDO
Ecole De Guitare, Technique Moderne,
Formation Permanente. Cours
Preparatoire-Elementaire-Moyen
[Fr] gtr (80p., ill; 1972; 3 suppl:
Conseils aux parents des jeunes
guitaristes, Plan de travail
(table), Exercices
complementaires) folio ESCHIG
f.s.　　　　　　　　　　　　(127)

Gitarrespiel Im Uberblick, Einfuhrung
In Die Spieltechnik Nach
Klassisch-Spanischer Schule
[Ger] gtr (44p., ill; 1961; app:
Kleine Musiklehre - Alphabetisch;
suppl: Studienplan Und
Grifftabelle) quarto MOECK 2049
f.s.　　　　　　　　　　　　(128)

Guitar Pour Tous, La, Methode
Progressive
gtr PRESSES f.s.　　　　　　(129)

FORTEA, DANIEL (1882-1953)
Metodo De Guitarra, Vol. I
[Span/Fr/Eng] gtr oct FORTEA 21A
f.s. 32p., ill; 18th repr, 1963;
suppl: Theory of 1st book of the
school of guitar; contains:
Tarrega, Francisco, Exercises,
TI-iii-1a, 1c, 1d　　　　　(130)

Metodo De Guitarra, Vol. II
[Span/Fr/Eng] gtr oct FORTEA 22
f.s. 32p.; 8th repr, 1958;
contains: Tarrega, Francisco,
Preludes, TI-i-8a (16 bars), 8b;
Exercises, TI-iii-3 (25 bars),
15, 22 (9 bars), 23　　　　(131)

FUNCK, EIKE
Ich Lerne Gitarre Spielen, Vol. II
"Ausfuhrliche Spielanweisung Fur
Kinder Und Jugendliche, Eine" gtr
(36p.; 1969; for vol. I, see
Gerwig, Walter) oct oblong LIENAU
1421-II f.s.　　　　　　　　(132)

GABETTI, FLORA
Guitare Mon Amie, Preparation Et
Introduction A Toutes Les
Methodes
[Fr/Dutch/Eng] gtr (40p., ill;
1966) quarto oblong SCHOTT-FRER
9183 f.s.　　　　　　　　　　(133)

GALINDO, PATRICIO
Metodo De Guitarra, Para Acompanar
Canciones Y Ritmos Populares Y
Folkloricos
[Span] gtr (staff notation and
tablature, diag, 36p.; 1959; 1st
ed, 1955) oct PENADES f.s. (134)

Quieres Aprender Musica Y Tocar La
Guitarra En 15 Lecciones?
[Span] gtr (34p.; 1949; historical
notes) folio BAYARRI f.s. (135)

GALL, LOUIS IGNATIUS
Gitaarmethode - Guitar Method -
Gitarreschule, Vol. I (composed
with Koenders, Rob)
[Dutch/Eng] gtr (24p., ill; 1968)
folio TEESELING VT-11-E f.s.
　　　　　　　　　　　　　　(136)
[Dutch/Ger] gtr (24p., ill; 1968)
folio TEESELING VT-11-D f.s.
　　　　　　　　　　　　　　(137)

Gitaarmethode - Guitar Method -
Gitarreschule, Vol. IA (composed
with Koenders, Rob)
gtr (24p.; 1972) folio TEESELING
VT-58 f.s.　　　　　　　　　(138)

GALL, LOUIS IGNATIUS (cont'd.)

Gitaarmethode - Guitar Method - Gitarreschule, Vol. II (composed with Koenders, Rob)
gtr (24p.; 1968) folio TEESELING VT-12 f.s. (139)

Gitaarmethode - Guitar Method - Gitarreschule, Vol. III (composed with Koenders, Rob)
gtr folio TEESELING VT-13 f.s. 25p.; 1969; contains: Bach, Johann Sebastian, Minuet, (Anna Magdalena Bach Notenbuchlein (1725), No.4, BWV Anh. 114, in G (140)

Voor Samenspel En Groepsles, Vol. I (composed with Lella, Domenico di)
gtr (25p.; 1973) TEESELING VT-101 f.s. (141)

Voor Samenspel En Groepsles, Vol. II (composed with Lella, Domenico di)
gtr (24p.; 1973) TEESELING VT-102 f.s. (142)

Voor Samenspel En Groepsles, Vol. III (composed with Lella, Domenico di)
gtr (21p.; 1974) TEESELING VT-103 f.s. (143)

Voor Samenspel En Groepsles, Vol. IV (composed with Lella, Domenico di)
gtr (23p.; 1974) TEESELING VT-104 f.s. (144)

Voor Samenspel En Groepsles, Vol. V (composed with Lella, Domenico di)
3gtr (1978) TEESELING VT-105 f.s. (145)

Voor Samenspel En Groepsles, Vol. VI (composed with Lella, Domenico di)
4gtr (1978) TEESELING VT-106 f.s. (146)

GANGI, MARIO
Metodo Per Chitarra, Per I Conservatori E I Licei Musicali, Vol. I
[It] gtr (58p.; repr, 1969; 1st ed, 1966; contains: 96 Right hand exercises (tirando; apoyando), Left hand exercises, Left hand and Right hand exercises, Chromatic scale, 70 Arpeggio formulae) RICORDI-IT ER-2688 f.s. (147)

Metodo Per Chitarra, Per I Conservatori E I Licei Musicali, Vol. II
[It] gtr (89p.; 1969; contains: Scales, scale-exercises, Barre, Scales and scale-exercises in thirds, sixths, octaves, tenths, Legato, Vibrato, Ornaments, Harmonics, Effects) RICORDI-IT ER-6292 f.s. (148)

GASCON, LEON VICENTE
Metodo Moderno Para Guitarra, Vol. I
[Span] gtr (ill; also available in Jap from Ongaku; 54p.; 1968; 1st ed, 1936) folio RICORDI-ARG BA-9540 f.s. (149)

Metodo Moderno Para Guitarra, Vol. II
[Span] gtr (ill; also available in Jap from Ongaku; 58p.; 1966; 1st ed, 1936?) folio RICORDI-ARG BA-9564 f.s. (150)

Metodo Moderno Para Guitarra, Vol. III
[Span] gtr (ill; also available in Jap from Ongaku; 80p.; 1964; 1st ed, 1957) folio RICORDI-ARG BA-11389 f.s. (151)

GAVALL, JOHN
Guitar Photochord Manual, No. 1: Chord Dictionary
gtr BELWIN f.s. (152)

Guitar Photochord Manual, No. 2: Beginner's Course
gtr BELWIN f.s. (153)

Learning Music Through The Guitar, Vol. I: An Introduction To Fretboard Harmony
[Eng] gtr (29p., ill; 1967) quarto BELWIN 1088 f.s. (154)

Learning Music Through The Guitar, Vol. II: Four-Part Harmony
[Eng] gtr (24p., ill; 1967) quarto BELWIN 1089 f.s. (155)

GAVALL, JOHN (cont'd.)

Learning Music Through The Guitar, Vol. III: Chord Patterns And Functions In Major Keys
[Eng] gtr (42p., ill; 1968) quarto BELWIN 1107 f.s. (156)

Learning Music Through The Guitar, Vol. IV: Minor Keys, Chromatic Chords, And Modulation
[Eng] gtr (40p., ill; 1968) quarto BELWIN 1108 f.s. (157)

Learning Music Through The Guitar, Vol. V: An Introduction To Figured Bass
[Eng] gtr quarto BELWIN BM-16 f.s. 57p.; 1972; contains: Bach, Johann Sebastian, Und Also Bald War Da Bei Dem Engel (recitative), for gtr and solo voice from Weihnachts-Oratorium, BWV 248; O Haupt Voll Blut Und Wunden. Chorale No. 21 from Matthaus-Passion, BWV 244, for 4 gtr; Schaut Hin! for 2 gtr from Weihnachts-Oratorium; Ach! Dass Nicht Die Letzte Stunde, BWV 439 (from Schemelli's Gesangbuch), for 2 gtr or 1 gtr and mel inst; Schaffs Mit Mir, Gott. Chorale, BWV 514 (from Anna Magdalena Bach Notenbuchlein (1725), No.35, in C, for 2 gtr or gtr and mel inst (158)

Play The Guitar, A Self Tutor
[Eng] gtr quarto BELWIN MM-474 f.s. 54p., ill; 9 app
contains: Coventry Carol, The (159)

Tips For Troubadours, Or How To Accompany Songs On The Guitar
[Eng] gtr (24p., ill) oct ESSEX f.s. (160)

GEBHARDT, WILHELM
Gitarrenfibel, Ein Spielbuch Vom Ersten Anfang An Fur Einzel- Und Gruppenunterricht (composed with Gebhardt, Greta)
[Ger] gtr (64p.; 1961; 1st ed, 1938) oct oblong BAREN. BA-1099 f.s. (161)

GERDES, GUSTAV
Kleine Gitarren- Und Lautenschule
[Ger] gtr (72p., ill) oct GERIG GG-183 f.s. (162)

GERRITS, PAUL
Gitarren- Und Lautenschule, Vol. I: Das Einstimmige Spiel - Guitar And Lute Method, Vol. 1: Melody Playing
[Ger/Fr/Eng] gtr quarto oblong MOSELER f.s. 36p., ill; 1967; contains: Les Anges (Noel) for 2 gtr; Bach, Johann Sebastian, Suite No. 3 for Violoncello, BWV 1009, In C, Bourree I-II; Musette In D, BWV Anh. 126 (from Anna Magdalena Bach Notenbuchlein (1725), No.22 for 2 gtr (in E); Minuet In G, BWV Anh. 114, from Anna Magdalena Bach Notenbuchlein (1725), No.4, for 2 gtr (in C); Minuet In G, BWV Anh.115 from Anna Magdalena Bach Notenbuchlein (1725), No.5 for 2 gtr (in a minor) (163)

Gitarren- Und Lautenschule, Vol. II: Ubungen Und Stucke Fur Das Mehrstimmige Spiel - Guitar And Lute Method, Vol. 2: Exercises And Pieces For Polyphonic Playing
[Ger/Fr/Eng] gtr quarto oblong MOSELER f.s. 39p.; 1968; contains: Bach, Johann Sebastian, Suite For Lute, BWV 996 In E Minor (G Is F Sharp), Bourree and Allemand (164)

Vorschule Fur Gitarre (composed with Kirsch, Dieter)
[Ger] gtr (56p., ill; 1973) oct MOSELER f.s. (165)

GERWIG, WALTER
Ich Lerne Gitarre Spielen, Vol. I "Ausfuhrliche Spielanweisung Fur Kinder, Eine" [Ger] gtr (36p., ill; 1960; for vol. II see Funck, Eike) oct oblong LIENAU 1421-I f.s. (166)

Spiel Der Lauteninstrumente, Das, Series I: Das Schulwerk, Fur Einzel- Und Gruppenunterricht, Vol. I: Die Lehre Des Einstimmigen Spiels
[Ger] gtr (36p., ill; repr, 1958; 1st ed unknown) quarto oblong LIENAU 1371-KNA f.s. (167)

GERWIG, WALTER (cont'd.)

Spiel Der Lauteninstrumente, Das, Series I: Das Schulwerk, Fur Einzel- Und Gruppenunterricht, Vol. II: Das Mehrstimmige Spiel
[Ger] gtr (35p.) quarto oblong LIENAU 1371-II f.s. (168)

Spiel Der Lauteninstrumente, Das, Series I: Das Schulwerk, Fur Einzel- Und Gruppenunterricht, Vol. III: Die Liedbegleitung, Wege Zur Improvisation
[Ger] gtr (36p.; 1955) quarto oblong LIENAU 1371-III f.s. (169)

Spiel Der Lauteninstrumente, Das, Series I: Das Schulwerk, Fur Einzel- Und Gruppenunterricht, Vol. IV: Das Generalbassspiel
[Ger] gtr quarto oblong LIENAU f.s. (170)

GIAMPIETRO, G.
Neue Schule Fur Gitarre
[Ger/Fr/It] gtr HUG f.s. (171)

GITAARLES IN GROEPSVERBAND, VOL. III "Learn The Guitar By Playing Together" [Dutch/Eng] gtr (for vol. I and II, see Gramberg, Jacq and Nijenhuis, Luc) quarto HARMONIA f.s. (172)

GOTZ, ROBERT
Spiel Auf Der Gitarre Einfach Und Gekonnt, Eine Lautenschule Fur Anfanger (Einzel- Und Gruppenunterricht)
[Ger] gtr (72p.; 1960) oct oblong VOGGEN f.s. (173)

GOTZE, WALTER
Gitarre- Und Lautenschule Der Jugend, Die, Fur Gruppen-, Einzel- Und Selbstunterricht
[Ger] gtr (64p., ill) quarto oblong SCHOTT 2397 f.s. (174)

GRAMBERG, JACQ
Gitaarles In Groepsverband, Vol. I "Learn The Guitar By Playing Together" [Dutch/Eng] gtr (33p.; 1967; for vol. II and III see Nijenhuis, Luc and Gitaarles) quarto HARMONIA 2088 f.s. (175)

GROODT, FRANS DE
Kleine Gitaar- Of Luitschool, Met Bijvoeging Van Een Keuze Plectrumgitaar-Accoorden, Ten Behoeve Van Onderwijs En Zelfstudie
[Dutch] gtr (34p., ill; 2nd rev ed, 1947; 1st ed unknown; 3 suppl: chords, fingerboard) quarto METROPOLIS 14 f.s. (176)

GUITARE EXPLIQUEE, LA, METHODE PROGRESSIVE, PART II: TECHNIQUE CLASSIQUE SUPERIEURE. 14 LESSONS
[Fr] gtr oct TRANSAT. 890 f.s. 157p. (part 1-3), ill; 1965; contains: Bach, Johann Sebastian, Suite for Lute in G minor, Saraband, BWV 995 (A min); Bach, Johann Sebastian, Suite No. 3 for Violoncello in C, Bourree I, BWV 1009 (A maj) (177)

HALL, A.D. VAN
First Exercises For Guitar, Speel- En Luisteroefeningen, Vol. I
[Eng/Dutch] gtr (15p.; 1969) oct oblong BROEKMANS 930 f.s. (178)

First Exercises For Guitar, Speel- En Luisteroefeningen, Vol. II
[Eng/Dutch] gtr (16p.; 1969) oct oblong BROEKMANS 931 f.s. (179)

First Exercises For Guitar, Speel- En Luisteroefeningen, Vol. III
[Eng/Dutch] gtr (16p.; 1969) oct oblong BROEKMANS 932 f.s. (180)

HANSSON, GUNNAR
Gitarrskola For Klassisk Gitarr "Gitarrspel, Ackompanjemang Och Solospel Efter Ackordanalys" [Swed] gtr (37p.; 1972; for other vols, see Johnson, Per-Olof) quarto ANDERSONS AM-688 f.s. (181)

HENZE, BRUNO
Gitarrespiel, Das, Vol. I, Ein Unterrichtswerk Vom Anfang Bis Zur Meisterschaft: Spielbeginn Und Studien
[Ger] gtr quarto HOFMEISTER T-4001 f.s. 28p., ill; 1950; app: Fingergymnastik; includes Giuliani, Mauro, Anschlagsubungen fur die rechte Hand; Tarrega, Francisco, and Roch, Pascual, Exercises, TI-iii-13a-f (182)

PAPAS, SOPHOCLES (cont'd.)

(A min)   (269)

PARKENING, CHRISTOPHER
Christopher Parkening Guitar Method,
The, Vol. 1
gtr (in collaboration with Jack
Marshall) ACSB $7.50   (270)

PARRAS DEL MORAL, J.
Metodo Para Guitarra, Ejercicios,
Estudios Y Escalas Diatonicas
[Span] gtr (62p.) folio UNION ESP.
EI-135 f.s.   (271)

PERSKO, CHARLES
Guitar Method, 3 Vols.
gtr BELWIN f.s.   (272)

PETER, URSULA
Anfangsunterricht Im Gitarrespiel,
Der, Vol. I
[Ger] gtr (47p.; rev and enl ed,
1962) quarto HOFMEISTER T-4070
f.s.   (273)

Anfangsunterricht Im Gitarrespiel,
Der, Vol. II
[Ger] gtr (44p.; repr, 1963) quarto
HOFMEISTER T-4094 f.s.   (274)

Anfangsunterricht Im Gitarrespiel,
Der, Vol. III
"Weg Zum Solospiel Auf Der Gitarre,
Der" [Ger] gtr (59p.; 1961)
quarto HOFMEISTER T-4106 f.s.
                                 (275)

PICK, RICHARD SAMUEL BURNS (1915-   )
Introduction To Effective
Accompaniment For Guitar
gtr FORSTER f.s.   (276)

Introduction To Guitar, Plectrum Or
Classic
[Eng] gtr (32p., ill; 1959) quarto
FORSTER M-1067 f.s.   (277)

Lessons For Classic Guitar, Vol. I:
First Lessons For Classic Guitar
[Eng] gtr (64p., ill.; repr, 1959;
1st ed, 1952) quarto FORSTER f.s.
                                 (278)

Lessons For Classic Guitar, Vol. II:
Lessons For Classic Guitar
[Eng] gtr (64p., ill.; 1955) quarto
FORSTER f.s.   (279)

PILI, SALVATORE (1933-   )
Chitarrista Moderno, Il
[It] gtr folio BERBEN 1229 f.s.
57p., ill; 2nd ed, 1974; 1st ed,
1967; contains: Suite For Lute,
BWV 996, In E-Minor, Bourree;
Minuet, BWV Anh. 114 from Anna
Magdalena Bach Notenbuchlein
(1725), No.4 (In G), for 2 gtr by
Johann Sebastian Bach   (280)

PLUMBRIDGE, W.H.
How To Play Guitar, Finger Style
[Eng] gtr (42p.) quarto DALLAS f.s.
                                 (281)

POHLERT, WERNER
Neue Gitarrenschule, Klassische Und
Moderne Spieltechnik, Anhang Fur
E-Gitarre Und E-Bass
[Ger] gtr (63p., ill; 1973; E- ,
ampl.; for plectrum-style on solo
gtr and bass) folio MULLER
2362 f.s.   (282)

POLASEK, BARBERA
Gitarre Im Gruppenunterricht °CC51U
gtr SYMPHON 2221 f.s.   (283)

POWROZNIAK, JOZEF
ABC Gitary, Czyli Jak Hania Na
Gitarze Grac Sie Nauczyla
[Polish] gtr (127p., ill; repr,
1970; 1st ed unknown) POLSKIE
5828 f.s.   (284)

Szkola Gry Na Gitarze
[Polish] gtr folio POLSKIE 2595
f.s. 86p., ill; 1957; suppl:
Tabela chwytow gitary; contains:
Minuet, from Anna Magdalena Bach
Notenbuchlein (1725), No.4, BWV
Anh. 114 (In G) by Johann
Sebastian Bach   (285)

Szkola Gry Na Gitarze, Wydanie
Zmienione Uzupelnione Dodatkiem O
Grze Na Gitarze Hawajskiej
[Polish] gtr folio POLSKIE 5748
f.s. 123p., ill; 1966; app:
[method for Hawaiian guitar];
suppl.: Tabela chwytow gitary -
akordy; contains: Minuet, from
Anna Magdalena Bach Notenbuchlein
(1725), No.4, BWV Anh. 114 (In G)
by Johann Sebastian Bach   (286)

PROL, JULIO
Sounds Of The Guitar (Spanish Guitar
Technique), A Recorded Basic
Method For Home Study
gtr (12" long play record + sc;
also available separately)
SPAN.MUS.CTR. 1077 f.s.   (287)

PUIJENBROECK, VICTOR VAN
Kunst Van Het Gitaarspel, De - Art De
Jouer De La Guitare, L'
[Dutch/Fr/Eng/Ger] gtr folio
METROPOLIS 4653 f.s. 58p., ill;
1967; contains: Exercises, TI-
iii-1a, 13a by Francisco Tarrega
                                 (288)

PUJOL, EMILIO (1886-1982)
Escuela De La Guitarra, Basada En Los
Principios De La Technica De
Tarrega
"Metodo Razionale Per Chitarra"
(Terzi) [It] gtr (2 vols in 1
vol) RICORDI-IT ER-2654 f.s.
                                 (289)

Escuela Razonada De La Guitarra, 3
Vols.
[Jap] gtr ONGAKU f.s.   (290)

Escuela Razonada De La Guitarra,
Basada En Los Principios De La
Technica De Tarrega, Vol. I
[Span/Fr] gtr (ill, historical
notes; 100p.;repr, 1961; 1st ed,
1934) folio RICORDI-ARG BA-9587
f.s.   (291)

Escuela Razonada De La Guitarra,
Basada En Los Principios De La
Technica De Tarrega, Vol. II
[Span/Fr] gtr folio RICORDI-ARG
BA-9563 f.s. ill, historical
notes; 137p.;repr, 1964; 1st ed,
1940; contains: Exercises, TI-
iii-14d, E 15, by Francisco
Tarrega   (292)

Escuela Razonada De La Guitarra,
Basada En Los Principios De La
Technica De Tarrega, Vol. III
[Span/Fr] gtr folio RICORDI-ARG
BA-10945 f.s. ill, historical
notes; 151p.; repr, 1960; 1st ed,
1954; contains: Exercises, TI-
iii-1a, 2, 5c, 6, 10, 13b, 16, 29
by Francisco Tarrega   (293)

Escuela Razonada De La Guitarra,
Basada En Los Principios De La
Technica De Tarrega, Vol. IV
[Span/Fr] gtr folio RICORDI-ARG
BA-12838 f.s. ill, historical
notes; 199p.; 1971; also contains
suppl: (33) Estudios
Complementarios (1 pce for 2
gtr); includes: Exercises, TI-
iii-1, 4 by Francisco Tarrega
                                 (294)

Escuela Razonada De La Guitarra,
Basada En Los Principios De La
Technica De Tarrega, Vol. V
[Span/Fr] gtr (ill, historical
notes) folio RICORDI-ARG f.s.
                                 (295)

PUSKAS, TIBOR
Gitariskola, Vol. I
"Gitarrenschule, Vol. I" [Hung/Ger]
gtr (61p., ill, 1970) quarto EMB
Z-5675 f.s.   (296)

QUINE, HECTOR
Introduction To The Guitar
[Eng] gtr (33p., ill; 1971) quarto
OXFORD f.s.   (297)

RANIERI, SILVIO
Method For The Guitar, Vol. I
[Fr/Eng/Ger/It] gtr (47p.; ill;
suppl: Dutch transl) folio CRANZ
813 f.s.   (298)

Method For The Guitar, Vol. II
[Fr/Eng/Ger/It] gtr (suppl: Dutch
transl) CRANZ f.s.   (299)

RICCHI, MODESTO
Chitarrista Autodidatta, Il,
Nuovissimo Metodo Facile Per
Chitarra A Numeri E A Musica,
Indispensabile Per Chi Non
Conosce La Musica, Utile Per Gli
Orchestrali
[It] gtr (30p.; chords in staff
notation and diag; 1967) oct
oblong BERBEN EB-1216 f.s.   (300)

Metodo Completo Per Lo Studio Della
Chitarra
[It] gtr (91p., ill; 4th ed, 1972;
1st ed, 1963) folio BERBEN EB-591
f.s.   (301)

RICHTER, GERD
Gitarrenfibel, Eine Neue Anleitung
Fur Das Spiel Auf Der Gitarre
[Ger] gtr (48p.; 1975) quarto
NOETZEL N-3397 f.s.   (302)

RIGHTMIRE, RICHARD W.
Manual Of Flamenco
[Eng] gtr SMITH,WJ f.s.   (303)

Wonderful Guitar, The (A Modern
Classic Guitar Method), Vol. I
[Eng] gtr quarto SMITH,WJ f.s.
32p., 1962, ill; contains:
Minuet, BWV Anh. 115 In G-Minor
(in E-Minor) by Johann Sebastian
Bach from anna magdalena bach
notenbuchlein (1725), no.5 (304)

Wonderful Guitar, The (A Modern
Classic Guitar Method), Vol. II
[Eng] gtr quarto SMITH,WJ f.s.
32p., 1963, ill; contains:
Minuet, BWV Anh. 114 In G from
Anna Magdalena Bach Notenbuchlein
(1725), No.4; Minuet, BWV Anh.
132 In D-Minor from Anna
Magdalena Bach Notenbuchlein
(1725), No.36, by J.S. Bach; and
Minuet from Grande Sonate, Op. 22
by Fernando Sor   (305)

Wonderful Guitar, The (A Modern
Classic Guitar Method), Vol. III
[Eng] gtr quarto SMITH,WJ f.s.
31p., 1963, ill; contains: March,
BWV Anh. 122 In D from Anna
Magdalena Bach Notenbuchlein
(1725), No.16; Partita No. 1 For
Keyboard Instrument, BWV 825, In
B-Flat, Minuet I (fragment);
Suite For Lute, BWV 996, In E-
Minor, Bourree, by J.S. Bach; and
Study, TI-ii-14 In D-Minor;
Prelude, TI-i-17 In E (Lagrima)
by Francisco Tarrega   (306)

RITTER, THEODOR
Gitarre-Studien, Fur Angehende Solo-
Gitarristen Und Sanger Zur
Gitarre. Ausgewahlte Leichte
Studienwerke Alter Meister
[Ger] gtr (63p.) oct oblong
HOFMEISTER-W 9966 f.s.   (307)

Lehrgang Des Modernen Gitarrespiels,
Vol. A: Das Akkordspiel
[Ger] gtr (62p.) oct oblong
HOFMEISTER-W 50A f.s.   (308)

Lehrgang Des Modernen Gitarrespiels,
Vol. B: Das Solospiel Und Die
Liedbegleitung
[Ger] gtr (48p.) oct oblong
HOFMEISTER-W 50B f.s.   (309)

Theoretisch-Praktischer Lehrgang Des
Gitarrespiels, Fur Den Einzel-,
Gruppen- Und Selbstunterricht Mit
Besonderer Berucksichtigung Des
Akkordspiels (composed with
Kramer, Erich)
[Ger] gtr (64p., ill; rev and enl
ed by Erich Kramer (1962); 1st ed
unknown) quarto HOFMEISTER 8013
f.s.   (310)

ROCH, PASCUAL
Modern Method For The Guitar, A, Vol.
1, School Of Tarrega °CCU
[Eng/Span/Fr] gtr quarto SCHIRM.G
1828 f.s. 145 p., ill; 1st ed,
1921; contains: Tarrega,
Francisco, Studies, TI-ii-32, 35,
42; Exercises, TI-iii-1a-B, 8,
13a-B, 21, 28, 30b, 33, 34, 35a-H
                                 (311)

Modern Method For The Guitar, A, Vol.
II, School Of Tarrega °CCU
[Eng/Span/Fr] gtr quarto SCHIRM.G
1829 f.s. 141p., ill; 1st ed,
1922; contains: Tarrega,
Francisco, Preludes, TI-i-8b, 14,
15, 19, 20, 23; Studies, TI-ii-4b
(20 bars), 29, 36; Exercises, TI-
iii-2a, 4, 5a-c, 6, 9-12, 15,
17a-c, 18, 19, 20a-c   (312)

Modern Method For The Guitar, A, Vol.
III, School Of Tarrega
[Eng/Span/Fr] gtr quarto SCHIRM.G
1830 f.s. 109p., ill; 1st ed,
1924; contains: Bach, Johann
Sebastian, Prelude For Keyboard,
BWV 839 In C (in E); and Tarrega,
Francisco, Prelude, TI-i-17;
Studies, TI-ii-12 and 12 (41
bars), 16b, 17, 18, 34   (313)

RODRIGUEZ ARENAS, MARIO
Escuela De La Guitarra, La, Vol. I
[Span] gtr (95p.; repr, 1966 Span
ed; 1st ed, 1923 Span ed)
RICORDI-ARG BA-9503 f.s.
[Jap] gtr (95p.; repr, 1966 Span
ed; 1st ed, 1923 Span ed) ONGAKU
f.s.   (315)

Escuela De La Guitarra, La, Vol. II
[Span] gtr RICORDI-ARG BA-9531 f.s.
88p.; repr, 1966; 1st ed, 1923;
contains: Tarrega, Francisco,

RODRIGUEZ ARENAS, MARIO (cont'd.)

Prelude, TI-i-17; Exercises, TI-iii-15, 35; and Sor, Fernando, Minuet, from Grande Sonate, OP. 25 (316)

Escuela De La Guitarra, La, Vol. II [Jap] gtr ONGAKU f.s. 88p.; repr, 1966; 1st ed, 1923; contains: Tarrega, Francisco, Prelude, TI-i-17; Exercises, TI-iii-15, 35; and Sor, Fernando, Minuet, from Grande Sonate, Op.25 (317)

Escuela De La Guitarra, La, Vol. III [Span] gtr RICORDI-ARG BA-9556 f.s. 103p.; repr, 1967; 1st ed, 1923; contains: Tarrega, Francisco, Preludes, TI-i-15, 19, 20, 22, 24; Studies, TI-ii-2a(22 bars), 9, 32, 35, 36; Exercises, TI-iii-8, 13b, 30b, 33 (318)

Escuela De La Guitarra, La, Vol. III [Jap] gtr ONGAKU f.s. 103p.; repr, 1967; 1st ed, 1923; contains: Tarrega, Francisco, Preludes, TI-i-15, 19, 20, 22, 24; Studies, TI-ii-2, 9, 32, 35, 36; Exercises, TI-iii-8, 13, 30, 33 (319)

Escuela De La Guitarra, La, Vol. IV [Jap] gtr (repr, 1967, Span ed; 1st ed, 1923, Span ed; contains: 27 Estudios superiores by Cano (7); Sor (6); Aguado (14); and 5 concert pieces by Tarrega (3); Sor (1); Aguado (1)) ONGAKU f.s. (320)

[Span] gtr (79p.; repr, 1967; 1st ed, 1923; contains 27 Estudios superiores by Cano (7); Sor (6); Aguado (14) and 5 concert pieces by Tarrega (3); Sor (1); Aguado (1)) RICORDI-ARG BA-9580 f.s. (321)

Escuela De La Guitarra, La, Vol. V [Span] gtr RICORDI-ARG BA-9549 f.s. 55p.; repr, 1954; 1st ed, 1923; contains: Estudios Y Preludios De Francisco Tarrega (22); Chopin (3); Coste (1); Mendelssohn (1); also contains: Tarrega, Francisco, Preludes, TI-i-1-7, 8a, 9-11 (13 bars), 13; Studies, TI-ii-5, 6, 8, 16b, 17, 18(56bars), 19-22; and Sor, Fernando, Introduction Et Variations Sur Un Theme De Mozart, Op. 9 (322)

Escuela De La Guitarra, La, Vol. V [Jap] gtr ONGAKU f.s. 55p.; repr, 1954; 1st ed, 1923; contains: Estudios Y Preludios De Francisco Tarrega; 28 Unnumbered Pcs By Tarrega (22); Chopin (3); Coste (1); Mendelssohn (1);also contains: Tarrega, Francisco, Preludes, TI-i- 2-7, 8a, 9-11, 13; Studies, TI-ii- 5, 6, 8, 16b, 17-22; and Sor, Fernando, Introduction Et Variations Sur Un Theme De Mozart, Op.9 (323)

Escuela De La Guitarra, Vol. VI "Technica Superior" [Span] gtr (47p.; repr, 1963; 1st ed, 1923; contains: Exercises by L.C. Hanon-Rodriguez Arenas, Exercises in thirds, sixths, octaves, by Aguado, Giuliani, Legato, barre, chords, Preludes and exercises by F. Tarrega; includes: Tarrega, Francisco, Preludes, TI-i-12, 14, 23; Tarrega, Francisco, Studies, TI-ii-4b, 29; Tarrega, Francisco, Exercises, TI-iii-2, 4, 5a-c, 6, 7a-c, 9-11, 15, 17a-c, 18, 19, 26, 27) folio RICORDI-ARG BA-9588 f.s. (324)

"Technica Superior" [Jap] gtr (repr, 1963, Span ed; 1st ed, 1923, Span ed; contains: Exercises by L.C. Hanon-Rodriguez Arenas; Exercises in thirds, sixths and octaves by Aguado, Giuliani; legato, barre, chords; Preludes and Exercises by F. Tarrega; includes: Tarrega, Francisco, Preludes, TI-i-12, 14, 23; Studies, TI-ii-4b[20 bars], 29; Exercises, TI-iii-2, 4, 5a-C, 6, 7a-C, 9-11, 15a-g, 17a-C, 18, 19, 26, 27) folio ONGAKU f.s. (325)

Escuela De La Guitarra, Vol. VII "Estudio Completo De Las Escales, Arpegios Y Ejercicios En Terceras, Sextas, Octavas Y Decimas" [Jap] gtr (repr, 1958, Span ed; 1st ed, 1923, Span ed) folio ONGAKU f.s. (326)

"Estudio Completo De Las Escales, Arpegios Y Ejercicios En

RODRIGUEZ ARENAS, MARIO (cont'd.)

Terceras, Sextas, Octavas Y Decimas" [Span] gtr (84p.; repr, 1958; 1st ed, 1923) folio RICORDI-ARG BA-11674 f.s. (327)

ROSSI, ABNER
Chitarrista Classico, Il [It] gtr (64p.; 1974) folio BERBEN 1907 f.s. (328)

SACK, GEORG CHRISTIAN
Weg Zum Kunstlerischen Gitarrespiel, Der, Vol. 1: Elemente Des Gitarrespiels "Perfection In The Art Of Playing The Guitar, Vol. 1: Fundaments Of Guitar Playing" [Ger/Eng] gtr (staff notation and tablature, 79p., ill; 1967) quarto MULLER f.s. (329)

SANCHEZ, BLAS
Methode De Guitare Classique, Premier Et Deuxieme Cycles [Fr] gtr folio CHOUDENS 20.160 f.s. 85p., ill; 1973; 2 suppl: 40 Exercises faciles pour la guitare; contains: Bach, Johann Sebastian, Toccata And Fugue, BWV 565, in D-minor (in E-minor; fragment of fugue) (330)

SAO MARCOS, MARIA LIVIA
Einfuhrung In Das Klassische Gitarrenspiel "Initiation A La Guitare Classique" [Ger/Fr] gtr (31p., ill; 1964) folio MONDIAL f.s. (331)

SAVIO, ISAIAS (1900-1977)
Escola Moderna Do Violao, Vol. II "Tecnica Do Mecanismo" [Port/Span] gtr (124p.; repr, 1967; 1st ed, 1947; contains: Scales + scale exercises and formulae, Scale exercises in thirds, sixths, tenths, Chromatic scales, Arpeggio and other right hand formulae, Broken chords along 2 and 3 octaves (major, minor, seventh, ninth, tenth and other chords), Legato, ornaments, Exercises) folio RICORDI-BR BR-2491 f.s. (332)

SCHAGEN, HENK VAN
Handleiding Voor De Gitaar [Dutch] gtr (56p., ill; 2nd rev ed) quarto HARMONIA f.s. (333)

SCHALLER, ERWIN (1901-)
Lehrwerk Fur Die Gitarre, Vol. I (composed with Scheit, Karl) [Ger] gtr (ill; first published by Hohler, 1936) quarto UNIVER. 11112 f.s. (334)
[Jap] gtr (ill, first published by Hohler, 1936, 20p.; repr, 1939, Ger ed) quarto ONGAKU f.s. (335)

Lehrwerk Fur Die Gitarre, Vol. II (composed with Scheit, Karl) [Ger] gtr (ill; first published by Hohler, 1936) quarto UNIVER. 11113 f.s. (336)
[Jap] gtr (ill; first published by Hohler, 1936, 22p.; repr, 1939, Ger ed) quarto ONGAKU f.s. (337)

Lehrwerk Fur Die Gitarre, Vol. III (composed with Scheit, Karl) [Ger] gtr (ill; first published by Hohler, 1936) quarto UNIVER. 11114 f.s. (338)
[Jap] gtr (ill; first published by Hohler, 1936, 32p.; repr, 1939, Ger ed) quarto ONGAKU f.s. (339)

Lehrwerk Fur Die Gitarre, Vol. IV (composed with Scheit, Karl) [Ger] gtr (36p.; repr, 1941; 1st ed, Hohler, 1936; contains: Legato, glissando, harmonics, Effects, Scordatura, Scales and broken chords on one string, Scales in tenths, octaves, sixths, triads, Scales in contrary motion, Scales, Broken chords along 2 and 3 octaves, Scales in sixth chords, Chord inversions with R.H. formulae) quarto UNIVER. 11218 f.s. (340)

Lehrwerk Fur Die Gitarre, Vol. V (composed with Scheit, Karl) [Ger] gtr quarto UNIVER. 11221 f.s. 31p.; repr, 1941; contains: Bach, Johann Sebastian, Aria Di Giovannini ("Willst Du Dein Herz Mir Schenken"), BWV 518, fROM ANNA MAGDALENA BACH NOTENBUCHLEIN (1725), NO.37, for solo voice and gtr (in D) (341)

SCHALLER, ERWIN (cont'd.)

Lehrwerk Fur Gitarre, Vol. IV (composed with Scheit, Karl) [Jap] gtr (repr, 1941 Ger ed, Hohler, 1936 Ger ed; contains: Legato, Glissando, Harmonics, Effects, Scordatura, Scales and Broken Chords on one string; Scales in tenths, octaves, sixths, triads, Scales in contrary motion, Scales, Broken Chords along 2 and 3 octaves, Scales in sixth chords, Chord inversions with R.H. formulae) quarto ONGAKU f.s. (342)

SCHEIT, KARL
Lehr- Und Spielbuch Fur Gitarre [Ger] gtr (76p., ill; 1st ed, 1953; repr, 20th ed, 1965; suppl: "Gitarrelehrgang von und mit Karl Scheit", nach dem "Lehr- und Spielbuch", fur Gitarre 30cm. Long play record with music and exercises from "Lehr- und Spielbuch." Performers: Karl Scheit, gtr, Melitta Heinzmann, voice and gtr, Hans Pleschberger, voice and pno. Amadeo AVRS 13057 St. Also available together with the "Lehr- und Spielbuch", ed. no. AVRS 11015) quarto OSTER 1721.13 f.s. (343)

SCHMIDT, HERMANN (1885-1950)
Neue Gitarrenschule gtr (2 vols.) SCHMIDT,H 22 f.s. (344)

SCHNEIDER, SIMON
Gitarreschule *Op.125 [Ger] gtr quarto HOFMEISTER 8014 f.s. 56p., ill; 1967; contains: Bach, Johann Sebastian, Suite For Lute, BWV 996, In E Minor, Bourree, for 2 gtr; Des Heil'gen Geistes Reiche Gnad'. Chorale, BWV 295, for 4 gtr (single line playing) (345)

SCHOLL, R.
Praktische Gitarre-Schule, Zur Selbsterlernung Nebst Zahlreichen Liedern, Soloszenen, Couplets, Duetten, usw. [Ger] gtr (118p.; rev pocket ed; 16mo) ZIMMER. SCHULE NO. 69 f.s. (346)

SCHWARZ-REIFLINGEN, ERWIN
Gitarren 1x1, Das, Die Gitarrenschule Fur Den Selbstunterricht [Ger] gtr (59p., ill; 1953) oct oblong SIKORSKI 261 f.s. (347)

Gitarren-Schule, Vol. I [Ger] gtr (85p., ill; 1953) folio SIKORSKI 170A f.s. (348)

Gitarren-Schule, Vol. II [Ger] gtr folio SIKORSKI 170B f.s. 85p., ill; 1953; contains: Bach, Johann Sebastian, Musette In D, BWV Anh. 126, Anna Magdalena Bach Notenbuchlein (1725), No.22 (349)

SERAFINI, CESARE (1928-)
Breve Guida Per Chitarra [It] gtr (23p., ill; 1973) folio BERBEN 1853 f.s. (350)

SHEARER, AARON
Classic Guitar Technique, Vol. I [Eng] gtr (vi+82p., ill; 2nd rev ed, 1963; 1st ed, 1959) quarto COLOMBO NY-1937 f.s. (351)

Classic Guitar Technique, Vol. II [Eng] gtr quarto COLOMBO NY-2325 f.s. vii+158p, ill.; 1964; contains: Tarrega, Francisco, Preludes, TI-i-10, 11 (352)

Classic Guitar Technique, Suppl. 1 "Slur, Ornament And Reach Development Exercises" [Eng] gtr (iv + 44p., ill.; 1964) quarto COLOMBO NY-2320 f.s. (353)

Classic Guitar Technique, Suppl. 2: Basic Elements Of Music Theory For The Guitar [Eng] gtr (41p.;1965) quarto COLOMBO NY-2321 f.s. (354)

Classic Guitar Technique, Suppl. 3 "Scale Pattern Studies For Guitar" [Eng] gtr (269p.; 1965; notes) quarto COLOMBO NY-2322 f.s. (355)

Classic Guitar Technique, Suppl. 4: Guitar Note Speller [Eng] gtr (To be studied in conjunction with vol. I, II; 32p.; 1959) quarto COLOMBO NY-1936 f.s. (356)

SHEER, ANITA
    Introduction To The Flamenco Guitar,
        An (composed with Berlow, Harry)
    [Eng] gtr (133p., ill; 1964) quarto
        COLOMBO NY-2296 f.s.   (357)

SING CHRISTMAS CAROLS °CC14U, Xmas,
    carol
    (Duarte) [Eng] solo voice, gtr (3rd
        degr.) sc SCHOTT GA-219 f.s. Guitar
        Accompaniment - The Easy Way,
        Suppl. 2; notation of gtr-pt: treb-
        clef + diag   (358)

SING NEGRO SPIRITUALS
    (Duarte) [Eng] solo voice, gtr (3rd
        degr.) sc SCHOTT 11076 f.s. 12
        pcs.; Guitar Accompaniment - The
        Easy Way, Suppl. 1; Notation of gtr
        pt: tr-clef + diagrams
        contains: Mary Had A Baby, Yes Lord
                                          (359)

SKIERA, EHRENHARD
    Flamenco-Gitarrenschule
        gtr SCHMIDT, H 250 f.s.   (360)

    Skiera Methode, Vol. I: Ein
        Grundlegendes Werk Zur
        Akkordbegleitung
    [Ger] gtr (32p., ill.; 1974) quarto
        APOLLO 2350 f.s.   (361)

SNYDER, JERROLD
    Comprehensive Guitar Method, The, For
        Classroom And Individual
        Instruction, Vol. A: Teacher's
        Manual (composed with Higgins,
        Ralph)
        gtr BELWIN EL-2286 f.s.   (362)

    Comprehensive Guitar Method, The, For
        Classroom And Individual
        Instruction, Vol. B: Student Book
        (composed with Higgins, Ralph)
        gtr BELWIN EL-2287 f.s.   (363)

SOR, FERNANDO (1778-1839)
    Methode Pour La Guitare
        "Metodo Completo Para Guitarra"
        (Coste, Napoleon) [Span] gtr
        (85p.; repr, n.d.; 1st ed
        unknown; 3 app; contains: Visee,
        Robert de, Minuets, VOCG 68, 70,
        91, Bourree, VOCG 67; Saraband,
        VOCG 87 (in A minor); Gavotte,
        VOCG 66) folio RICORDI-ARG
        BA-8715 f.s.   (364)
    "Sor's Method For The Spanish
        Guitar" (Merrick, Arnold) [Eng]
        gtr (48p. (text) + xlii p.
        (studies and exercises), viii
        plates) fac ed, oct DA CAPO f.s. (365)

    Methode Pour La Guitare (Escuela De
        La Guitarra)
        (Lara, Roberto; Coste, Napoleon)
        [Span] gtr folio RICORDI-ARG
        BA-12814 f.s. 146p.; 1970; rev
        and recompiled ed of the Sor-
        Coste method, fingering by R.L.;
        3 app; includes Coste, Napoleon,
        25 Etudes, Op. 38; also contains:
        Visee, Robert de, Minuets, VOCG
        68, 70, 84, 91; Bourree, VOCG 67;
        Saraband, VOCG 83, 87; Allemand,
        VOCG 86; Gavottes, VOCG 66, 78;
        Courante, VOCG 63; Gigues, VOCG
        65, 75, 82; and Passacaglia, VOCG
        92   (366)

    Methode Pour La Guitare (Escuela De
        La Guitarra)
        "Methode Complete Pour Guitare"
        [Span] gtr (rev and enl ed by N.
        Coste; date unknown; contains:
        Visee, Robert de, Minuets, VOCG
        68, 70, 91, Bourree, VOCG 67;
        Saraband, VOCG 87 (in A minor);
        Gavotte, VOCG 66) LEMOINE f.s.
                                          (367)
    "Metodo Completo Para Guitarra"
        (Coste, Napoleon; Tarrago,
        Graciano) [Span] gtr (85p.; rev
        ed, 1962; 3 app; contains: Visee,
        Robert de, Minuets, VOCG 68, 70,
        91, Bourree, VOCG 67; Saraband,
        VOCG 87 (in A minor); Gavotte,
        VOCG 66) folio UNION ESP. EI-197
        f.s.   (368)

    Methode Pour La Guitare (Methode
        Complete Pour Guitare Par
        Ferdinand Sor, Revue Et Augmentee
        De Nombreux Exemples Avec Une
        Notice Sur La Septieme Corde Par
        N. Coste)
    [Fr] gtr folio LEMOINE 15655 f.s.
        arr, 85p.; 1965; 3 app; contains:
        Visee, Robert de, Minuet, VOCG
        68; Bourree, VOCG 67; Minuet,
        VOCG 70; Saraband, VOCG 87 (in A-
        Minor); Gavotte, VOCG 66; Minuet,
        VOCG 91   (369)

STINGL, ANTON (1908-   )
    Spielbuch Fur Gitarre, 100 Leichte
        Stucke Fur Den Anfang, Vol. I
    [Ger] gtr (1939; 28p.) quarto
        oblong SCHOTT 3751 f.s.   (370)

    Spielbuch Fur Gitarre, 100 Leichte
        Stucke Fur Den Anfang, Vol. II
    [Ger] gtr (1939; 27p.) quarto
        oblong SCHOTT 3752 f.s.   (371)

STOCKTON, FRED
    Complete Classic Guitar, The, A
        Method. Complete Explanation Of
        The Right Hand
        gtr STOCKTON f.s.   (372)

STORTI, MAURO
    Lezioni Di Tecnica Elementare Per
        Chitarra, 20
    [It] gtr (20p., ill; 1966) folio
        BERBEN 1181 f.s.   (373)

SWEETLAND, ELLIOT
    Belwin Spanish Guitar Course, 4 Vols.
        gtr BELWIN f.s.   (374)

TARRAGO, GRACIANO
    Metodo Graduado Para Aprender A Tocar
        La Guitarra
        gtr UNION ESP. 203-EI f.s.   (375)

TERZI, BENVENUTO
    Chitarrista Autodidatta, Il, Metodo
        Completo Per Chitarra Classica
    [It] gtr (114p., ill; 1963; app:
        "Consiglio ai solisti", "La
        letteratura chitarristica") folio
        RICORDI-IT RM-130299 f.s.   (376)

TEUCHERT, HEINZ (1914-   )
    Gitarren-Schule, Fur Melodiespiel,
        Liedbegleitung Und Solospiel, Ein
        Anschauliches Lehr- Und
        Spielbuch, Vol. I
    [Ger] gtr (46p., ill; Suppl:
        Technische Ubungen (3p.)) quarto
        SCHMIDT, H 96 f.s.   (377)

    Gitarren-Schule, Fur Melodiespiel,
        Liedbegleitung Und Solospiel, Ein
        Anschauliches Lehr- Und
        Spielbuch, Vol. II
    [Ger] gtr quarto SCHMIDT, H 96 f.s.
        47-96p., ill; contains: Bach,
        Johann Sebastian, Minuet, BWV
        Anh. 132, from Anna Magdalena
        Bach Notenbuchlein (1725), No.36,
        In D Minor, for 2 gtr (single
        line playing); Prelude For Lute,
        BWV 999, In C Minor (in D Minor);
        and Tarrega, Francisco, Prelude,
        TI-i-17; Exercise, TI-iii-32
                                          (378)

    Klingender Gitarren-Lehrgang
        gtr (80p.; 3 30cm long play records
        are available separately) PELIKAN
        PE-970 f.s.   (379)

TOPPER, GUIDO
    Duet Approach To The Guitar, A, An
        Initial Programme For Guitar
    [Dutch/Eng/Fr] gtr (47p., ill;
        1973) folio BROEKMANS 1093 f.s.
                                          (380)

    Modern Approach To The Guitar, A,
        Based On The Principles Of Emilio
        Pujol, Vol. I
    [Eng] gtr (9p.; 1962) folio
        BROEKMANS 777 f.s.   (381)

    Modern Approach To The Guitar, A,
        Based On The Principles Of Emilio
        Pujol, Vol. II
    [Eng] gtr (9p.; 1962) folio
        BROEKMANS 778 f.s.   (382)

    Modern Approach To The Guitar, A,
        Based On The Principles Of Emilio
        Pujol, Vol. III
    [Eng] gtr (11p.; 1962) folio
        BROEKMANS 779 f.s.   (383)

    Modern Approach To The Guitar, A,
        Based On The Principles Of Emilio
        Pujol, Vol. IV
    [Eng] gtr (13p.; 1964) folio
        BROEKMANS 812 f.s.   (384)

    Modern Approach To The Guitar, A,
        Based On The Principles Of Emilio
        Pujol, Vol. V
    [Eng] gtr (13p.; 1964) folio
        BROEKMANS 814 f.s.   (385)

TREML, ROBERT
    Grundlagen Des Gitarrenspiels, Die,
        Aufbau Und Spieltechnik Aus Der
        Einstimmigkeit, Mit Vielen
        Musikbeispielen, Einzeln Oder
        Chorisch Zu Gebrauchen
    [Ger] gtr quarto NAGELS EN-1095
        f.s. 45p., ill; repr, 1954; 1st
        ed, 1938; for suppl, see
        Twittenhoff, Wilhelm; contains:
        Bach, Johann Sebastian, Sing',

TREML, ROBERT (cont'd.)
    Bet', Und Geh' Auf Gottes Wegen.
        Chorale, from Wer Nur Den Lieben
        Gott Lasst Walten, BWV 93, No. 7,
        for 4 gtr (single line playing)
                                          (386)

TWITTENHOFF, WILHELM (1904-   )
    Grundlagen Des Gitarrenspiels, Die,
        Aufbau Und Spieltechnik Aus Der
        Einstimmigkeit, Mit Vielen
        Musikbeispielen, Einzeln Oder
        Chorisch Zu Gebrauchen,
        Supplement
        "Gitarrenspielbuch Fur Den Anfang"
    [Ger] gtr (28p.; repr, 1960; 1st
        ed, 1953) quarto oblong NAGELS
        EN-1096 f.s.   (387)

URBAN, STEPAN (1913-   )
    Improvizujme Na Kytaru
    [Czech] gtr (48p.; 1964; staff
        notation + diag; app: Dixieland
        (2p.), Rytmus (3p.), Flamenco
        (6p.)) quarto PANTON f.s.   (388)

VALENCIA, JOSE DE
    Methode De Flamenco Pour La Guitare
    [Fr] gtr (32p.) folio BEUSCH 8032
        f.s.   (389)

VANDERHORST, ADRIAN (ARAI)
    Learning The Classic Guitar
    [Eng] (staff notation and
        tablature) quarto SCHIRM. G 2161
        f.s. 59p., ill; 1954
        contains: Minuet in D minor, BWV
        Anh. 132 (from Anna Magdalena
        Bach Notenbuchlein (1725),
        No.36) (2gtr) (single line
        playing)   (390)

VINSON, HARVEY
    Play Classic Guitar
    [Eng] gtr quarto AMSCO 020143 f.s.
        95p., ill; 1969; 3 app; contains:
        Bach, Johann Sebastian, Minuet,
        from Anna Magdalena Bach
        Notenbuchlein (1725), No.4, BWV
        Anh. 114, In G; Suite No. 6 For
        Violoncello, BWV 1012, In D,
        Gavotte (in C; fragment); and
        Tarrega, Francisco, Prelude, TI-
        i-17, In E "Lagrima"; in G i-20,
        in A   (391)

VRIES, F. DE
    Eerste Oefeningen In Het Gitaarspel
    [Dutch] gtr (28p.; 1960) oct oblong
        BROEKMANS 558 f.s.   (392)

WANGLER, RUDOLF
    6 Saiten-10 Finger °CCU
    [Ger] gtr BAREN. BA-6610 f.s. 84p;
        includes 2 supplemental ill.
        sheets   (393)

WINKELBAUER, ALFRED
    Lerne Gitarre, Vol. 1
        gtr WINKEL f.s.   (394)

WITTE, JACQ
    Speelboek Voor De Gitaar, Vol. I
    [Dutch] gtr (34p.) oct oblong SIJN
        f.s.   (395)

WOBERSIN, W.
    Schule Fur Bass-Gitarre (Laute), 2
        Vols In 1 Vol
        "Tutor For The Bass-Guitar (Lute)
        [Guitar-Lute]" [Ger/Eng] gtr
        quarto ZIMMER. SCHULE NO. 24 f.s.
                                          (396)
    Schule Fur Bass-Gitarre (Laute), Vol
        I
        "Tutor For The Bass-Guitar (Lute)
        [Guitar-Lute]" [Ger/Eng] gtr
        (61p., ill.) quarto ZIMMER.
        SCHULE NO. 22 f.s.   (397)

    Schule Fur Bass-Gitarre (Laute), Vol.
        II
        "Tutor For The Bass-Guitar (Lute)
        [Guitar-Lute]" [Ger/Eng] gtr
        (89p., ill) quarto ZIMMER.
        SCHULE NO. 23 f.s.   (398)

WOLKI, KONRAD
    Gitarre Zum Lied, Schule Fur Die
        Gitarre Als Begleitinstrument,
        Mit Einer Akkordlehre Und Mit
        Hinweisen Fur Das Begleiten Nach
        Dem Gehor, Vol. I (composed with
        Wolki, Gerda)
    [Ger] gtr (96p., ill; 1959) quarto
        APOLLO 2187 f.s.   (399)

    Gitarre Zum Lied, Schule Fur Die
        Gitarre Als Begleitinstrument,
        Mit Einer Akkordlehre Und Mit
        Hinweisen Fur Das Begleiten Nach
        Dem Gehor, Vol. II (composed with
        Wolki, Gerda)
    [Ger] gtr (96p., ill; 1959) quarto
        APOLLO 2188 f.s.   (400)

WOLKI, KONRAD (cont'd.)

Gitarre Zum Lied, Schule Fur Die
    Gitarre Als Begleitinstrument,
    Mit Einer Akkordlehre Und Mit
    Hinweisen Fur Das Begleiten Nach
    Dem Gehor, Supplement 1 (composed
    with Wolki, Gerda)
    "Melodisches Gitarrenspiel, Schule
    Fur Die Gitarre Als
    Soloinstrument Und Fur Das
    Zusammenspiel Mit 2 Bis 3
    Gitarren" [Ger] gtr (64p.; 1960)
    quarto APOLLO 2216 f.s.   (401)

Gitarre Zum Lied, Schule Fur Die
    Gitarre Als Begleitinstrument,
    Mit Einer Akkordlehre Und Mit
    Hinweisen Fur Das Begleiten Nach
    Dem Gehor, Supplement 2 (composed
    with Wolki, Gerda)
    "Gitarre Allein, Entwicklung Des
    Solistischen Musizierens Aus Dem
    Akkordspiel" [Ger] gtr quarto
    APOLLO f.s.   (402)

Gitarrenchor, Der, Schule Des
    Gruppenmusizierens *folk song
    [Ger] gtr (24p.; 1966; arr + orig
    pcs; contains 17 works by: Wolki
    (9), Kubik for 3 gtr-e' (+opt 2
    gtr-e'')) quarto,sc APOLLO 2771
    f.s.   (403)

Gitarrenspiel Am Anfang, Erste
    Spielanweisung Fur Kinder;
    Einfuhrung In Das Melodiespiel,
    Akkordspiel Und Beginnende
    Solospiel
    [Ger] gtr (32p., ill; 1971) quarto
    APOLLO 2317 f.s.   (404)

Gitarrenspiel Nach Dem Gehor,
    Anleitung Zur Improvisierten
    Lied- Und Tanzbegleitung
    [Ger] gtr (48p.; 1974) quarto
    APOLLO 2348 f.s.   (405)

WORSCHECH, ROMAIN
    Enseignement Pratique De La Guitare,
        Vol. I
        "Practical Guitar Teaching" [Fr/
        Eng] gtr (80p., ill; repr; 1st
        ed, 1956) folio COMBRE f.s. (406)

YEO-SIEBALD, ELSE
    Volksliederfibel Fur Den
        Gitarrenunterricht *folk song
        [Ger] gtr (32p.; 1963; arr;
        contains works by: Anon. (3),
        Mozart, Erk (2), Forster,
        Zuccalmaglio, Fink, Reichardt,
        for solo voice, gtr) sc,oct
        oblong NOETZEL N-3113 f.s. (407)

ZANOSKAR, HUBERT
    Neue Gitarren-Schule, Vol. I
        [Ger] gtr (64p.; 1969; contains
        Bach, Johann Sebastian, Gib Dich
        Zufrieden Und Sei Stille, BWV
        460, for solo voice, gtr from
        Schemelli's Gesangbuch) quarto
        SCHOTT 5665 f.s.   (408)

Neue Gitarren-Schule, Vol. I, Suppl.:
    Ubungen Und Spielstucke
    [Ger] gtr quarto SCHOTT 5667 f.s.
    46p.; 1969; contains: Bach,
    Johann Sebastian, Minuet, BWV
    Anh. 115, from Anna Magdalena
    Bach Notenbuchlein (1725), No.5,
    In G Minor, for 2 gtr; Minuet,
    BWV Anh. 116, from Anna Magdalena
    Bach Notenbuchlein (1725), No.7,
    In G, for 2 gtr; Ich Steh An
    Deiner Krippen Hier, BWV 469, in
    C minor, for solo voice and gtr
    from Schemelli's Gesangbuch (409)

Neue Gitarren-Schule, Vol. II
    [Ger] gtr quarto SCHOTT 5666 f.s.
                                  (410)
Neue Gitarren-Schule, Vol. II, SUPPL.
    [Ger] gtr quarto SCHOTT 5668 f.s.
                                  (411)
ZYKAN, OTTO M.
    Methodisches Lehrwerk Fur Die
        Gitarre, Vol. I: Grundbegriffe
        [Ger] gtr (xx+67p.; rev ed, 1960;
        1st ed, 1946) folio WELT 1142
        f.s.   (412)

Methodisches Lehrwerk Fur Die
    Gitarre, Vol. IIa, b: Die Linke
    Hand, Beherrschung Des
    Griffbrettes
    [Ger] gtr (x+148p.; suppl.: gtr-II-
    pt to 3 duets) folio WELT 1142
    f.s.   (413)

Methodisches Lehrwerk Fur Die
    Gitarre, Vol. III: die Rechte
    Hand
    [Ger] gtr folio WELT 1142 f.s.
                                  (414)

ZYKAN, OTTO M. (cont'd.)

Methodisches Lehrwerk Fur Die
    Gitarre, Vol. IV: der Vortrag
    [Ger] gtr folio WELT 1142 f.s.
                                  (415)

III Technical Studies

ABLONIZ, MIGUEL (1917-   )
Arpeggi, 50, Per La Mano Destra, La
Mano Sinistra Non Partecipa
"Arpeggios, 50, For The Right Hand,
The Left Hand Is Not Used" [It/
Eng] gtr (7p.; 5th enl ed, 1972;
1st ed, 1954; enlargement:
Arpeggio 1A-14A and 4 Exercises)
quarto BERBEN 1002 f.s.   (1)

Esercizi Essenziali Per La Mano
Sinistra
"Essential Exercises For The Left
Hand" [It/Eng] gtr (14p.; 3rd ed,
1969; enl ed of 1st (1954) and
2nd (1960) eds; enlargement: 7
Chromatic exercises for the
development of a virtuosic
technique and Study on slurs and
snaps) quarto BERBEN 1003 f.s.
                                 (2)

Imitando Il Granchio
"Crab-Fingerings" [It/Eng] gtr (2p.
text, 2p. music; 1974; contains
themes by Fernando Sor arr and
fingered) quarto BERBEN 1902 f.s.
                                 (3)

Principali Regole Tecniche
"Principal Technical Rules" [It/
Eng] gtr (2p., ill; 1970;
contains 8 photographs (with
commentary) showing wrong and
correct positions of the left and
right hand) quarto BERBEN f.s.   (4)

Riscoperta Dell'Accordatura E Dalla
Tastiera
"Tuning And Fingerboard
Rediscovered" [It/Eng] gtr (27p.;
1972; suppl: Diag of the
fingerboard; contains: About
tuning, About the fingerboard, A
fingerboard study in 9 versions)
quarto BERBEN 1677 f.s.   (5)

Scale Diatoniche, Le 24
"Diatonic Scales, The 24" [It/Eng]
gtr (9p.; 3rd ed, 1970; enl ed of
the 1st (1954) and 2nd (1960)
eds; enlargement: major and
melodic minor scales (1 octave))
quarto BERBEN 1004 f.s.   (6)

AGUADO, DIONISIO (1784-1849)
Etuden, 24, Und 10 Tonleiterstudien
Fur Gitarre
"Etudes, 24, Et 10 Exercises De
Gammes Pour Guitare" (Worsching)
gtr SCHOTT GA-62 f.s.   (7)

AHSLUND, ULF-G.
Gitarrskola, Spela I Grupp, Supp.2
"Teknikovningar" [Swed] gtr (16p.;
n.d.; Gitarrskola, Suppl. 2;
contains diatonic scales,
chromatic scales, arpeggios,
tremolo, intervals; includes:
Tarrega, Francisco, Study, TI-ii-
30, In E; Exercises, TI-iii-2a,
4, 28, 32[11 bars]) quarto LIBER
f.s.   (8)

ALBERT, HEINRICH (1870-1950)
Lehrgang Des Kunstlerischen
Gitarrespiels, Vol. II
"Gitarrelied, Das" [Ger] gtr (52p.;
repr, 1952; 1st ed, 1924;
contains: Intro, Notes: Das
Barrespiel, App: Die Wichtigsten
Anwendungsstellen Fur Gitarre In
Opern Und Orchesterwerken, barre
(exercises, chords, studies),
positions IV, V, VII, IX
(exercises, chords, studies,
pieces); includes: Bach, Johann
Sebastian, Betrachte, Meine Seel
from Johannes-Passion, BWV 245,
NO. 31, FOR BASS SOLO AND GTR)
folio LIENAU S.10189-II f.s.   (9)

ALBERT, HEINRICH (cont'd.)
Lehrgang Des Kunstlerischen
Gitarrespiels, Vol. III
"Gitarre Als Solo-Instrument, Die"
[Ger] gtr (59p.; repr, 1952; 1st
ed, 1924; Intro: Die Ornamentik
In Der Musik; Notes: Nagelspiel;
App: Entwicklungsgeschichte Der
Gitarre; contains: Legato,
Secondary Positions, Harmonics,
Arpeggio Formulae, Tremolo,
Exercises, Studies And Solo
Pieces) folio LIENAU S.10189-D
f.s.   (10)

Lehrgang Des Kunstlerischen
Gitarrespiels, Vol. IV
"Virtuose Gitarrespiels, Das" [Ger]
gtr (32p.; repr, 1952; 1st ed,
1924; contains: Intro, App:
Fingergymnastik, chromatic
exercises and scales, scales (2,
2 and 3 octaves) + formulae,
cadences, scales + formulae in
thirds, sixths, sixth chords,
octaves, double octaves, thirds +
octaves, sixths + octaves,
tenths, scales in contrary
motion, chord inversions +
arpeggio formulae) folio LIENAU
S.10189.IV f.s.   (11)

ANGEL, MIGUEL
Mecanismo Didactico Para Guitarra
[Span] gtr (85p.; folio oblong;
1955; contains: escalas,
cejillas, ejercicios, arpegios,
acordes, octavas y tremolo) UNION
ESP. 19011 f.s.   (12)

Nomenclature
"Fingerboardchart" gtr
SPAN.MUS.CTR. GE-211 f.s.   (13)

ANZAGHI, LUIGI ORESTE (1903-1963)
Esercizi Di Tecnica, 50
[It] gtr (51p.; 1958; contains:
Notes, Scale pattern exercises in
various keys and positions) folio
RICORDI-IT RM-129638 f.s.   (14)

Esercizi Di Tecnica Giornaliera, 24
[It] gtr (25p.; 1960; contains:
scales, scale exercises,
arpeggios and chords in all major
and minor keys) folio RICORDI-IT
RM-130202 f.s.   (15)

Scale Semplici, A Terze, A Seste E A
Ottave
[It] gtr (15p.; 1960) folio
RICORDI-IT RM-130036 f.s.   (16)

BAY, MEL
Deluxe Guitar Scale Book, The
[Eng] gtr (72p.; 1973; contains:
diatonic major and minor scales,
chromatic scales, whole-tone
scales) quarto MEL BAY f.s.   (17)

BECK, LEONHARD
Finger Anschlag, 5
[Ger] gtr (7p.; 1974; contains:
Exercises for the use of the d-
finger ("dedo pequeno")) oct
TEESELING VT-125 f.s.   (18)

BEHREND, SIEGFRIED (1933-   )
Tonleiterstudien
"Scale-Practice" [Ger/Eng] gtr
(14p.; 1965; contains: 24
Diatonic scales (2 and 3
octaves)) oct oblong SIKORSKI 686
f.s.   (19)

BERVOETS, GERARD
Tremolospel Op De Gitaar
[Dutch] gtr (8p.; 1974; contains:
Exercises for the development of
the tremolo-technique) folio
TEESELING VT-139 f.s.   (20)

BILDLICHE DARSTELLUNG ALLER DUR- UND
MOLL-AKKORDE
gtr (chord chart) HUG f.s.   (21)

BOBRI, VLADIMIR
Complete Study Of The Tremolo; 33
Lessons
gtr COLOMBO NY-3046 $2.50   (22)

Daily Exercises, 130 *Op.11
[Eng] gtr (19p.; 1968; contains 130
arpeggio formulae) quarto COLOMBO
NY-2605 f.s.   (23)

BOBRI, VLADIMIR (cont'd.)
130 Daily Studies For The Classic
Guitar
gtr COLOMBO NY-2605 $2.50   (24)

BORELLO, P.
Tableau d'Accords Pour La Guitare
gtr (contains: 180 pos. for over
2000 chords) LEMOINE f.s.   (25)

BOSSU, MARCEL
Accords De Guitare, d'Apres Le
Nouveau Doigte
"Gitaar Akkoorden, Volgens Nieuwe
Vingerzetting" [Dutch/Fr] gtr
(14p.; 1952; staff notation +
diag) quarto METROPOLIS 9 f.s.
                                (26)

Suite d'Accords Pour Guitare
"Akkoordenreeksen Voor Gitaar"
[Dutch/Fr] gtr (17p.; 1957; staff
notation + diag) quarto
METROPOLIS 20 f.s.   (27)

CAPONIGRO, ANDREW
Fingerboard Workbook, The, A Non-
Method For Guitar
[Eng] gtr (v + 105p., ill; 1969;
contains: Notes, Staff notation +
diag, Intro to the fingerboard
for beginners and advanced
players, Diag depict the actual
fingerboard to stimulate the
visual imagery of the guitarist,
The book may be used to
supplement any course of study
without altering the usual
approach to teaching) quarto
oblong SCHIRM.G f.s.   (28)

CASTET, FRANCOIS
Gammes, 24, De 2 Et 3 Octaves
Majeures Et Mineures (Melodiques,
Cadences Sur Differents Rythmes,
Choix d'Exercices Techniques
[Fr/Eng/Ger] gtr (16p.; 1973) folio
LEDUC 23764 f.s.   (29)

CHACON, MEME
Metodo Y Ejercicios De Francisco
Tarrega
[Span/Eng] gtr (1959; contains:
Chromatic and diatonic scales,
Exercises (triplets, arpeggios,
speed study); includes: Tarrega,
Francisco, Preludes, TI-i-6, 8a[9
bars], 8b, 9-13, 15, 19, 23[10
bars]; Tarrega, Francisco,
Studies, TI-ii-2b, 3, 29-36;
Tarrega, Francisco, Exercises,
TI-iii-1, 3, 4, 14-16, 20, 22-24,
30a, 31b, d, 33) UNION ESP. f.s.
                                (30)

CHIERICI, FERNANDO (1912-   )
Metodo Per La Ricerca Degli Accordi
Coi "Rivelatori", Metodo Pratico
Per Il Dilettante, Promemoria
Tascabile Per Il Professionista,
(100 Accordi Con "Barre" In Prima
Posizione, 1200 Accordi Coi
"Rivelatori"
[It] gtr (14p., ill; 1967;
contains: Notes, Notation in
diag, Suppl (envelope on the
innerside of the front cover): 10
"rivelatori") oct oblong BERBEN
1207 f.s.   (31)

Prontuario Di Tutti Gli Accordi Per
Chitarra, Vol. I: 2400 Posizioni
[It/Eng/Span] gtr (Staff notation +
diag;; 130p.; repr, 1971; 1st ed,
1965; contains: Chords in all
major and minor keys, in all
inversions, chromatic from C to
B) folio BERBEN 427 f.s.   (32)

Prontuario Di Tutti Gli Accordi Per
Chitarra, Vol. II: 1440 Posizioni
[It/Eng/Span] gtr (Staff notation +
diag;; 100p.; 1967; contains:
Chords in all major and minor
keys, in all inversions,
chromatic from C to B) folio
BERBEN 1195 f.s.   (33)

CHIESA, RUGGERO
Tecnica Fondamentale Della Chitarra,
Vol. I: Le Scale
[It/Eng] gtr (43p.; 1966; contains:
Scales, scales in thirds, sixths,
octaves and tenths with
preliminary exercises and Scale
exercises) quarto ZERBONI 6582
f.s.   (34)

CHIESA, RUGGERO (cont'd.)

Tecnica Fondamentale Della Chitarra,
Vol. II: Le Legature
[It/Eng] gtr (53p.; 1979; contains:
Slurs (30 exercises), slurs in
scales, etc., 32 studies by
Carulli, Carcassi, Giuliani,
Aguado, Legnani) quarto ZERBONI
8511 f.s.   (35)

DUARTE, JOHN W. (1919-   )
Foundation Studies In Classic Guitar
Technique
[Eng] gtr (70p.; 1966; contains:
Notes, Scale movements, legato,
broken chords) quarto NOVELLO
19511 f.s.   (36)

FERRARI, ROMOLO (1894-1959)
Esercizi Tecnici
[It] gtr (2p.; 1954; contains:
Chords and exercises with right
hand formulae) folio BERBEN 1069
f.s.   (37)

Tabella Degli Accordi, Per Chitarra
Classica E Jazz
[It] gtr (16p.; 1963; contains:
Notes, Staff notation + diag,
Table: Composizione e indice
degli accordi, App: Elementi di
armonia relativi agli intervalli)
folio BERBEN 1043 f.s.   (38)

FILIBERTO, ROMOLO
Guitar Technique
[Eng] gtr (40p.; 1962; notation:
treb-clef + tablature; contains:
Technical exercises, Scale
studies, Arpeggios on the
diminished chords) quarto MEL BAY
f.s.   (39)

FODEN, WILLIAM (1860-1947)
Chords [For The] Classic Guitar
[Eng] gtr (88p., ill; repr, 1961;
1st ed, 1933; staff notation +
diag and tablature; app: 5
preludes) quarto SMITH,WJ f.s.
                                   (40)

FRANCERIES, MARC (1935-   )
Gammes Et Arpeges Pour La Guitare
[Fr] gtr (53p.; 1969; app: Exercice
de recapitulation; contains:
Major and minor scales (2 and 3
octaves), Scales in thirds,
sixths, octaves, Arpeggios
(broken chords along 2 and 3
octaves)) folio CHOUDENS 20.359
f.s.   (41)

GANGI, MARIO
Metodo Per Chitarra, Per I
Conservatori E I Licei Musicali,
Vol. I
[It] gtr (58p.; repr, 1969; 1st ed,
1966; contains: 96 Right hand
exercises (tirando; apoyando),
Left hand exercises, Left hand
and Right hand exercises,
Chromatic scale, 70 Arpeggio
formulae) RICORDI-IT ER-2688 f.s.
                                   (42)

Metodo Per Chitarra, Per I
Conservatori E I Licei Musicali,
Vol. II
[It] gtr (89p.; 1969; contains:
Scales, scale-exercises, Barre,
Scales and scale-exercises in
thirds, sixths, octaves, tenths,
Legato, Vibrato, Ornaments,
Harmonics, Effects) RICORDI-IT
ER-6292 f.s.   (43)

GITAAR-KAMERMUZIEK, VOL. 2
(Claessens, Anny C.H.) 1-4gtr (partly
single line playing/1-4th degr.) sc
BROEKMANS 26A f.s. arr + orig pcs;
contains works by: Claessens for 1
gtr; Anon. (6), Bohm (1),
Hurlebusch (1) for 2 gtr; J.S.
Bach, Rameau, von Call for 3 gtr;
Handel for 4 gtr
contains: Bach, Johann Sebastian,
Suite for Lute, BWV 996, in E
minor, Bourree (3gtr) (single
line playing)   (44)

GITARRE, GRIFF- UND AKKORDTABELLE, SEHR
LEICHT
[Ger] gtr (4p.; 1970; contains: Die
Tone Der Gitarre Bis Zum 10. Bund,
Die Wichtigen Akkorde Der Gitarre)
quarto ZIMMER. GRIFF-TABELLE NO. 36
f.s.   (45)

GIULIANI, MAURO (1781-1829)
Studio Per La Chitarra *Op.1
"Studies, 120" (Bobri, Vladimir)
gtr (contains Part I) CEL 24 f.s.
                                   (46)

"Metodo Per Chitarra" (Caliendo)
[It/Fr/Eng] gtr (53p., ill; 1964;
with the orig pref and a modified
version of the commentary to the

GIULIANI, MAURO (cont'd.)
studies and exercises in Pt II
and III of the orig ed; contains
Pts I-IV) folio BERBEN 1105 f.s.
                                   (47)

"Centoventi Arpeggi Dall' Op. 1"
(Chiesa, Ruggero) gtr (contains
Pt I) ZERBONI 8090 f.s.   (48)
"Studien Fur Gitarre, Vol. I, a.
Ubungen Fur Die Rechte Hand, b.
Ubungen Fur Die Linke Hand"
(Ritter) [Ger] gtr (30p.; 1926;
pref and title in Ger and Fr;
vol. Ib with a modified version
in Ger of the commentary to the
exercises in Pt II of the orig
ed; contains Pts I and II) quarto
SCHOTT GA-30 f.s.   (49)
"Studien Fur Gitarre, Vol. II, c.
Bindungen Und Verzierungen, d.
Angewandte Vortragsstucke"
(Ritter) [Ger] gtr (23p.; 1926;
vol. IIc with a modified version
in Ger of the commentary to the
studies and exercises in Pt III
of the orig ed; contains Pts III
and IV) quarto SCHOTT GA-31 f.s.   (50)
"Ejercicios De Arpegios, Elementos
Fundamentales De La Tecnica
Guitarristica Para Guitarra"
(Savio) gtr (14p.; repr, 1970;
1st ed, 1957; contains Pt I, arr
in 12 groups) folio RICORDI-ARG
BA-11364 f.s.   (51)

GOTZE, WALTER
Tagliche Studien Zur Bildung Des
Anschlags
"Exercices Journaliers Pour Le
Developpement Du Toucher" [Ger/
Fr] gtr (5p.; n.d.; contains
Arpeggio formulae) quarto SCHOTT
GA-369 f.s.   (52)

Tonleitern Und Kadenzen, In Allen
Tonarten Und Lagen
"Gammes Et Cadences, Dans Tous Les
Tons Et Dans Toutes Les
Positions" [Ger/Fr] gtr (6p.;
n.d.; also chromatic scales)
quarto SCHOTT GA-370 f.s.   (53)

GUITAR, REMO
Guitar Chords, 4400
[Eng] gtr (160p.; 1965; diag; 9 arr
by Roy Smeck) quarto ROBBINS f.s.
                                   (54)

GUITAR DISK
gtr (a disc-chart for the notes on
the fingerboard) TEESELING 180 f.s.
                                   (55)

HEBBEL, HEINRICH
Gitarreschlussel, Der, Leichteste
Akkord-Grifftabelle Fur Gitarre
Und Laute
[Ger] gtr (9p.; n.d.; staff
notation + diag) oct oblong
ZIMMER. SCHULE NO. 192 f.s.   (56)

HEISSNER, O.
Griff-Lexikon Fur Gitarre, Mit
Anleitung Zum Selbstunterricht
[Ger] gtr (30p. + xxv (chord diag))
oct oblong GERIG 445 f.s.   (57)

HENZE, BRUNO
Gitarrespiel, Das, Vol. I, Ein
Unterrichtswerk Vom Anfang Bis
Zur Meisterschaft: Spielbeginn
Und Studien
[Ger] gtr quarto HOFMEISTER T-4001
f.s. 28p., ill; 1950; app:
Fingergymnastik; includes
Giuliani, Mauro, Anschlagsubungen
fur die rechte Hand; Tarrega,
Francisco, and Roch, Pascual,
Exercises, TI-iii-13a-f   (58)

Gitarrespiel, Das, Vol. V: Ein
Unterrichtswerk Vom Anfang Bis
Zur Meisterschaft:
Tonleiterstudien
[Ger] gtr (32p.; 1951; contains:
Diatonic scales (2, 2 and 3
octaves) + formulae, Scale
patterns, Cadences, Chromatic
scales, Scales + formulae in
thirds, sixths, octaves, tenths,
sixth chords, thirds + octaves,
sixths + octaves, double octaves,
Scales in contrary motion, Whole-
tone scales) quarto HOFMEISTER
T-4005 f.s.   (59)

Gitarrespiel, Das, Vol. VI: Ein
Unterrichtswerk Vom Anfang Bis
Zur Meisterschaft: Studien Fur
Die Linke Und Rechte Hand
[Ger] gtr (60p.; 1954; contains
Exercises, cadences, ornaments,
studies, barre, effects,
rasgueado; includes: Tarrega,
Francisco, Exercises, TI-iii-13,
for the left hand; Giuliani,

HENZE, BRUNO (cont'd.)
Mauro, Anschlagsubungen Fur Die
Rechte Hand) quarto HOFMEISTER
T-4006 f.s.   (60)

Gitarrespiel, Das, Vol. VII, Ein
Unterrichtswerk Vom Anfang Bis
Zur Meisterschaft: Die Hauptlagen
[Ger] gtr quarto HOFMEISTER T-4007
f.s. 42p.; 1954; scale and chord
studies (in pos. IV, V, VII and
IX; arr. + orig. pcs.; contains
works by: Molinaro, de Saint Luc,
Bergen, Carcassi (3), Molino, Sor
(8), Coste (2), Tarrega (2),
Friessnegg, Milan, Martino,
Corbetta, Haydn, Giuliani (2),
Sanz (2), Roncalli (3), Molitor,
Matiegka, Kellner (2), Sigismund
Weiss, Diabelli, Legnani, Cano-
Stingl, Uhl; includes: Tarrega,
Francisco, Prelude TI-i-1;
Prelude TI i-17, in E ("Lagrima")
                                   (61)
Gitarrespiel, Das, Vol. VIII, Ein
Unterrichtswerk Vom Anfang Bis
Zur Meisterschaft: Die Nebenlagen
[Ger] gtr quarto HOFMEISTER T-4008
f.s. 36p.; 1954; scale and chord
studies (in pos. I-III, VI, VIII,
X-XII); plus 15 pcs   (62)

HOLZFURTNER, FRANZ
Lagenspiel-Fibel, Volkstumliche
Einfuhrung In Das Lagenspiel Auf
Der Gitarre
[Ger] gtr (19p.; 1964; notation:
treb-clef + tablature; suppl:
Reference sliding chart
(fingerboard diag); contains
Intro to the positions) folio
PREISSLER 7012 f.s.   (63)

IPARRAGUIRRE, P.A.
Escalas, Arpegios Y Ejercicios Del
Mecanismo Tecnico
[Span] gtr folio RICORDI-ARG
BA-8076 f.s. 23p.; repr., 1966;
1st ed., 1924; contains: Tarrega,
Francisco, Studies, TI-ii-21 (in
A), 30 (19 bars, in E);
Exercises, TI-iii-14a-C, 24, 30a,
31, 32   (64)

Escalas Menores Melodicas
[Span] gtr (4p.; 1941) folio
RICORDI-ARG BA-8093 f.s.   (65)

KOK, JOH. B.
Gitaar-Accorden
[Dutch] gtr (8th degr., (n.d.),
staff notation + diagrams, 2p.)
XYZ f.s.   (66)

KOVATS, BARNA (1920-   )
Technische Studien Fur Gitarre, Vol.
I: Fingerubungen Fur Eine
Systematische Ausbildung Der
Gitarre-Spieltechnik
[Ger] gtr (31p., ill; 1966;
contains: notes, arpeggios,
chromatic scales, legato and
barre) quarto SCHOTT 5758 f.s.
                                   (67)

KYTAROVE GONIO
[Czech] gtr (circle of fifth and
fourths; notation in diag; a disc-
chart for transposing chords in all
major and minor keys in all pos.;
four-, five- and six-pt chords)
PANTON f.s.   (68)

LADRU, ANIBAL
Escuela De Mecanismo Tecnico Para
Guitarra
[Span] gtr (26p.; repr, 1966; 1st
ed, 1927; contains Diatonic
scales, chromatic scales and
exercises, scale exercises,
arpeggios, barre, exercises;
includes Tarrega, Francisco,
Preludes, TI-i-11, 16[14 bars],
17, 18, 24; Tarrega, Francisco,
Studies, TI-ii-4b, 29, 30, 33;
Tarrega, Francisco, Exercises,
TI-iii-2, 14a-c, 20a-c, 24, 25a-
d, 30a-32) folio RICORDI-ARG
BA-9523 f.s.   (69)

LAURENT, LEO
Ecole Du Jeune Guitariste, L'
"Classic Guitar Etudes" (Lee,
Ronny) [Eng] gtr (32p.; n.d.;
orig. ed [Fr] Beuscher, 1966,
1968; contains: 48 [!] Exercises
and studies: Scale studies,
chromatic scales, Intervals in
thirds, sixths, tenths and
octaves, Arpeggios, tremolo,
Chords, Modulation, Slurs, Music
theory) quarto MARKS f.s.   (70)

LELOUP, HILARION
    Escales, Acordes Y Ejercicios
    Tecnicos Para Guitarra
    [Span] gtr folio RICORDI-ARG
    BA-9565 f.s. 33p.; repr, 1964;
    1st ed, 1923; notes; contains:
    Tarrega, Francisco, Studies, TI-
    ii-28 (in A), 30 (in E), 33 (in
    E); Exercises, TI-iii-14a-C, 24,
    30a, 31, 32   (71)

LOPATEGUI, JOSE LUIS (1940-   )
    Tecnica De La Guitarra, Vol. 1
    Escalas Y Arpegios
    gtr ALPUERTO 1236 f.s.   (72)

MAIRANTS, IVOR
    Visual Aids To Chord Arpeggios
    gtr BELWIN f.s.   (73)

MARTIN, GASTON
    Etudes Elementaires Pour Guitare,
    Vol. I: Premiere Position
    [Fr] gtr (1966; 12p.; contains
    Scales, arpeggios, scale
    exercises, legato, exercises in
    various major and minor keys)
    folio DELRIEU 1371-1 f.s.   (74)

    Etudes Elementaires Pour Guitare,
    Vol. II: Etudes Des Positions Et
    Du Barre A Chaque Position
    [Fr] gtr (1966; 16p.; contains
    Exercises (scales, barre,
    arpeggios) in pos. II-IX, in
    various keys) folio DELRIEU
    1371-2 f.s.   (75)

    Etudes Elementaires Pour Guitare,
    Vol. III: Changements De
    Positions
    [Fr] gtr (1966; 8p.; contains:
    Scales, arpeggios along 1 and 2
    octaves, Scales in thirds,
    sixths, chords) folio DELRIEU
    1371-3 f.s.   (76)

MINELLA, ALDO
    Moderne Technik Der "Appoggiatura"
    Und Des Tonleiterspiels, Die
    gtr (1974) RICORDI-IT ER-2745 f.s.
                                      (77)

    Scale Diatoniche
    gtr (contains Thirds, Sixths,
    Octaves) RICORDI-IT ER-2693 f.s.
                                      (78)

MOZZANI, LUIGI (1869-1943)
    Studies For The Guitar
    "Exerzizi Di Tecnica Superiore Per
    Chitarra Classica" (Mozzani,
    Carmen Lenzi) [It] gtr (36p.,
    ill; 1967; biographical notes;
    intro; written in the USA. in
    1898; Pt I: cadences, studies in
    arpeggios and chords, cadences
    with arpeggio formulae; Part II:
    Scale exercises, diatonic scales;
    Pt III: Arpeggios, Chords,
    Exercises (barre, tremolo)) folio
    BERBEN 1213 f.s.   (79)

NORMAN, THEODORE (1912-   )
    Classical Guitar, The, A New Approach
    [Eng] gtr (48p.; 1960; contains 234
    Exercises (arpeggios, legato,
    barre, etc.)) quarto SCHIRM.G
    2360 f.s.   (80)

PAPARARO, GUGLIELMO
    Technica Degli Arpeggi Per Chitarra
    Classica, La
    [It/Eng] gtr (25p.; 1965; contains:
    280 Arpeggios: Right hand
    formulae, broken chords along 2
    octaves in various keys) folio
    BERBEN 1141 f.s.   (81)

PAPAS, SOPHOCLES
    Complete Tremolo Book For The Guitar,
    The
    gtr COLUMBIA 209 f.s.   (82)

PATT, RALPH
    Guitar Chord Dictionary
    gtr (Library of over 10, 000
    chords) BELWIN f.s.   (83)

PICK, RICHARD SAMUEL BURNS (1915-   )
    Fundamental Fingerboard Harmony For
    Guitar
    [Eng] gtr (64p.; repr, 1966; 1st
    ed, 1953; staff notation + diag;
    see also Smith, E.P., Smith's
    Theory Book For Guitarist;
    contains Arpeggios, chord
    studies, triads, seventh, ninth,
    eleventh and thirteenth chords
    patterns and exercises) quarto
    FORSTER 60037 f.s.   (84)

POMILIO, TOMAS
    Formulas Tecnicas, Para El Mecanismo
    Elemental De La Guitarra
    [Span] gtr folio RICORDI-ARG
    BA-12287 f.s. 51p.; 1964; app: 27
    pcs. by N.N. (Pomilio?) (4),

POMILIO, TOMAS (cont'd.)
    Carcassi (5), Carulli (4), Coste
    (7), Aguado (4), Damas; contains
    27 Lessons (studies, legato,
    exercises, scales, tremolo,
    harmonics); includes: Tarrega,
    Francisco, Prelude, TI-i-9 (in
    A); Exercises, TI-iii-1a, 1b, 1e,
    13b, 14g, H, 24, 30a, 32   (85)

POSUVNE TRANSPOSICNI PRAVITKO
    [Czech] gtr (circle of fifths and
    fourths; notation in diag and
    staff; a sliding-chart for
    transposing chords in all major and
    minor keys in the pos. I-IV) PANTON
    138 f.s.   (86)

PRAT, DOMINGO (1866-1944)
    Escalas Y Arpegios De Mecanismo
    Tenico Para Guitarra
    [Span] gtr folio RICORDI-ARG
    BA-9508 f.s. 15p.; repr, 1966;
    1st ed, 1910; contains Scales,
    chromatic scales, barre,
    exercises; includes: Tarrega,
    Francisco, Studies, TI-ii-30, 33;
    Exercises, TI-iii-5b, 6, 14a-c,
    24, 30a, 31, 32   (87)

    Nueva Tecnica De La Guitarra, La
    [Span] gtr (26p.; repr, 1965; 1st
    ed., 1929; contains Arpeggio
    formulae, chords) folio RICORDI-
    ARG BA-9552 f.s.   (88)

PUIJENBROECK, VICTOR VAN
    Toonladder Systeem Voor Gitaar
    "Systeme De Gammes Pour Guitare"
    [Dutch/Fr/Ger/Eng] gtr (12p.;
    1966; app: The different sounds
    (effects); contains 24 Diatonic
    scales, chords + scale and
    arpeggio formulae) folio
    METROPOLIS 4560 f.s.   (89)

REINBACH, REMO
    Meccanismo Della Chitarra, Il, Dal
    Primo Al Dodecimo Capotasto
    [It] gtr (48p.; 1963; contains 79
    Exercises in the pos. I-XII)
    quarto CARISCH 21635 f.s.   (90)

REISER, EKKEHARD
    Entwicklung Einer Technischen
    Perfektion
    gtr VOGT 100 f.s.   (91)

RODRIGUEZ ARENAS, MARIO
    Escuela De La Guitarra, Vol. VI
    "Technica Superior" [Span] gtr
    (47p.; repr, 1963; 1st ed, 1923;
    contains: Exercises by L.C.
    Hanon-Rodriguez Arenas, Exercises
    in thirds, sixths, octaves, by
    Aguado, Giuliani, Legato, barre,
    chords, Preludes and exercises by
    F. Tarrega; includes: Tarrega,
    Francisco, Preludes, TI-i-12, 14,
    23; Tarrega, Francisco, Studies,
    TI-ii-4b, 29; Tarrega, Francisco,
    Exercises, TI-iii-2, 4, 5a-c, 6,
    7a-c, 9-11, 15, 17a-c, 18, 19,
    26, 27) folio RICORDI-ARG BA-9588
    f.s.   (92)
    "Technica Superior" [Jap] gtr
    (repr, 1963, Span ed; 1st ed,
    1923, Span ed; contains:
    Exercises by L.C. Hanon-Rodriguez
    Arenas; Exercises in thirds,
    sixths and octaves by Aguado,
    Giuliani; legato, barre, chords;
    Preludes and Exercises by F.
    Tarrega; includes: Tarrega,
    Francisco, Preludes, TI-i-12, 14,
    23; Studies, TI-ii-4b[20 bars],
    29; Exercises, TI-iii-2, 4, 5a-c,
    6, 7a-C, 9-11, 15a-g, 17a-C, 18,
    19, 26, 27) folio ONGAKU f.s.
                                      (93)

    Escuela De La Guitarra, Vol. VII
    "Estudio Completo De Las Escales,
    Arpegios Y Ejercicios En
    Terceras, Sextas, Octavas Y
    Decimas" [Jap] gtr (repr, 1958,
    Span ed; 1st ed, 1923, Span ed)
    folio ONGAKU f.s.   (94)
    "Estudio Completo De Las Escales,
    Arpegios Y Ejercicios En
    Terceras, Sextas, Octavas Y
    Decimas" [Span] gtr (84p.; repr,
    1958; 1st ed, 1923) folio
    RICORDI-ARG BA-11674 f.s.   (95)

SAGRERAS, JULIO S. (1879-1942)
    Tecnica Superior De Guitarra, De
    Acuerdo Con La Moderna Escuela
    Del Maestro Tarrega
    [Span] gtr folio RICORDI-ARG
    BA-9553 f.s. 39p.; repr, 1966;
    1st ed, 1922; contains Diatonic
    scales (2 and 3 octaves) + scale
    formulae, Chromatic scales,
    Scales in thirds, sixths,
    octaves, 15 Exercises, scale

SAGRERAS, JULIO S. (cont'd.)
    exercises, studies; includes:
    Tarrega, Francisco, Studies, TI-
    ii-37 (in A), 39, 40 [10 bars in
    3-4], 41; Exercise, TI-iii-32
                                      (96)

SALVADOR, SAN
    Single String Studies For Guitar
    gtr BELWIN f.s.   (97)

SANCHEZ, BLAS
    Exercices, 40, Faciles Pour La
    Guitare, d'Apres Un Theme Mateo
    Carcassi, Vol. I: 17 Studies For
    The Right Hand
    [Fr] gtr (1975; Collection l'Heure
    de la guitare classique; 10p.,
    ill) folio CHOUDENS 20.649 f.s.   (98)

    Exercices, 40, Faciles Pour La
    Guitare, d'Apres Un Theme Mateo
    Carcassi, Vol. II: 23 Exercises
    For The Left Hand
    [Fr] gtr (1975; Collection l'Heure
    de la guitare classique; 8p.,
    ill) folio CHOUDENS 20.649 f.s.
                                      (99)

    Exercices Techniques, 20,
    Indispensables Pour La Guitare,
    Tous Degres
    [Fr] gtr (13p.; n.d.; staff
    notation + diag; contains Left
    hand exercises, 3 studies) folio
    CHOUDENS 20.436 f.s.   (100)

SAO MARCOS, MARIA LIVIA
    Erganzung Zur Gitarrentechnik
    "Complement A La Technique De La
    Guitare" [Ger/Fr] gtr (31p.;
    1964; contains: Diatonic major
    and minor scales (1, 2 and 3
    octaves), scale exercises, Major
    and minor scales in thirds,
    sixths, octaves and tenths,
    Chromatic scales and scale
    exercises, Scales with ornaments,
    Legato, Sequences) folio MONDIAL
    f.s.   (101)

SAVIO, ISAIAS (1900-1977)
    Escola Moderna Do Violao, Vol. II
    "Tecnica Do Mecanismo" [Port/Span]
    gtr (124p.; repr, 1967; 1st ed,
    1947; contains: Scales + scale
    exercises and formulae, Scale
    exercises in thirds, sixths,
    tenths, Chromatic scales,
    Arpeggio and other right hand
    formulae, Broken chords along 2
    and 3 octaves (major, minor,
    seventh, ninth, tenth and other
    chords), Legato, ornaments,
    Exercises) folio RICORDI-BR
    BR-2491 f.s.   (102)

SCHALLER, ERWIN (1901-   )
    Lehrwerk Fur Die Gitarre, Vol. IV
    (composed with Scheit, Karl)
    [Ger] gtr (36p.; repr, 1941; 1st
    ed, Hohler, 1936; contains:
    Legato, glissando, harmonics,
    Effects, Scordatura, Scales and
    broken chords on one string,
    Scales in tenths, octaves,
    sixths, triads, Scales in
    contrary motion, Scales, Broken
    chords along 2 and 3 octaves,
    Scales in sixth chords, Chord
    inversions with R.H. formulae)
    quarto UNIVER. 11218 f.s.   (103)

    Lehrwerk Fur Gitarre, Vol. IV
    (composed with Scheit, Karl)
    [Jap] gtr (repr, 1941 Ger ed,
    Hohler, 1936 Ger ed; contains:
    Legato, Glissando, Harmonics,
    Effects, Scordatura, Scales and
    Broken Chords on one string;
    Scales in tenths, octaves,
    sixths, triads, Scales in
    contrary motion, Scales, Broken
    Chords along 2 and 3 octaves,
    Scales in sixth chords, Chord
    inversions with R.H. formulae)
    quarto ONGAKU f.s.   (104)

SCHININA, LUIGI
    Accordi E Cadenze Per Chitarra
    d'Accompagnamento
    [It] gtr (24p.; 1968) folio BERBEN
    1258 f.s.   (105)

    Tutte Le Scale Per Chitarra
    [It] gtr (32p.; 1965; contains:
    Chromatic scales (2 octaves) in
    all major keys, Diatonic scales
    (2 and 3 octaves) in all keys,
    Chromatic scales in major and
    minor thirds and sixths, octaves,
    Diatonic scales in thirds,
    sixths, octaves, in all keys,
    Each scale with patterns) folio
    BERBEN 1145 f.s.   (106)

SEGOVIA, ANDRES (1896-   )
  Diatonic Major & Minor Scales
    [Eng] gtr (8p.; 1953) quarto
    COLUMBIA 127 f.s.   (107)

SHEARER, AARON
  Classic Guitar Technique, Suppl. 1
    "Slur, Ornament And Reach
    Development Exercises" [Eng] gtr
    (iv + 44p., ill.; 1964) quarto
    COLOMBO NY-2320 f.s.   (108)

  Classic Guitar Technique, Suppl. 3
    "Scale Pattern Studies For Guitar"
    [Eng] gtr (269p.; 1965; notes)
    quarto COLOMBO NY-2322 f.s. (109)

SHOLLE, EMIL
  Higher Frets On All Strings, The,
    Melodious Studies In Positions,
    Vol. 1
    [Eng] gtr (26p.; 1962; 52 pcs.; pos.
    I-III) quarto BROOK f.s.   (110)

  Higher Frets On All Strings, The,
    Melodious Studies In Positions,
    Vol. II
    [Eng] gtr (26p.; 1962; 49 pcs; I-V
    pos.) quarto BROOK f.s.   (111)

  Higher Frets On All Strings, The,
    Melodious Studies In Positions,
    Vol. III
    [Eng] gtr (26p.; 1963; 52 pcs; I-
    VII pos.) quarto BROOK f.s.   (112)

SIMONS, H.B.
  Guitar Chord Chart
    [Eng] gtr (2p., repr; 1960; 1st
    ed., 1936; notation: diag and
    text; 492 chords, chromatic from
    C to B) folio FISCHER,C 47 f.s.
                                         (113)

SOSINSKI, KAZIMIERZ
  Materialy Do Nauki Gry Na Gitarze
    "Materials For Studying The Guitar"
    [Polish] gtr (90p., ill; 2nd ed,
    1975; 1st ed, unknown; contains
    138 Studies and exercises) quarto
    POLSKIE 6835 f.s.   (114)

  Studium Gry Akordowej Na Gitarze,
    Technika Chwytow Barre, Akordy I
    Ich Symbole
    "Study Of Chords For Guitar, The,
    The Technique Of Barre, Chords
    And Their Symbols" [Polish] gtr
    (xvi + 146p., ill; 1960; Intro:
    Basic elements of music theory
    (chords); 6 Tables: diag of the
    fingerboard; 1 Table: dance-
    rhythms; contains 243 Numbers, in
    various keys: Chords and chord
    inversions with arpeggio
    formulae, Scales and scale
    exercises; contains 65 studies
    by: Giuliani (13), Carulli (10),
    Aguado (4), Carcassi (31),
    Legnani, Sor, Albert (5); 12
    Duets by: Ritter, Mezzacapo,
    Jarnefelt, Fibich, Boccherini,
    Curtis, Nowicki, Nowikow, Zeller,
    Schumann, Joteyko, Lehar for
    mand, gtr (4), vln or mand, gtr
    (6), vln, gtr (2); arr + 1 orig
    pce (Ritter); 9 modern dances
    (tango, bolero, fox-polka, samba)
    by various composers for treb
    inst (accord, vln, or mand), gtr;
    notation of gtr pt in plectrum-
    style (symbols + rhythms)) quarto
    POLSKIE 6392 f.s.   (115)

STORTI, MAURO
  Lezioni Di Tecnica Superiore Per
    Chitarra, 12
    [It] gtr (16p.; 1967; contains
    Exercises, legato, chords with
    formulae, ornaments, barre) folio
    BERBEN 1211 f.s.   (116)

TARRAGO, GRACIANO
  Escalas, Arpegios Y Armonicos Para
    Guitarra, Vol. I
    [Span] gtr (97p.; 1960; contains:
    Diatonic scales (2 and 3
    octaves), Scales in thirds,
    fourths, fifths, sixths and
    sevenths) folio UNION ESP. EI-204
    f.s.   (117)

  Escalas, Arpegios Y Armonicos Para
    Guitarra, Vol. II
    [Span] gtr (91p.; 1960; contains:
    Scales in octaves, ninths and
    tenths, Chromatic scales, Scale
    exercises with barre, Chromatic
    scales in thirds, fourths,
    fifths, sixths and octaves,
    Scales in thirds and sixths,
    Arpeggios, Harmonics, Church
    modes) folio UNION ESP. EI-205
    f.s.   (118)

TEUCHERT, HEINZ (1914-   )
  Griff-Tabellen Fur Gitarre
    [Ger] gtr (16mo; 26p., ill; n.d.;
    staff notation + diag and
    photographs; Pt I: Griff-Tabellen
    Fur Konzert-Gitarre; Part II:
    Griff-Tabellen Fur Schlag-
    Gitarre) SCHMIDT,H 74 f.s.   (119)

THOMATOS, SPIRO
  Samtliche Tonleitern Fur Gitarre
    gtr (16p.) quarto HEINRICH. N-1429
    f.s.   (120)

TIGGES, KOOS
  Diatonische Toonladders Over 2
    Octaven
    "Diatonic Tonescales Along 2
    Octaves" [Dutch/Ger/Eng] gtr
    (10p.; 1967; contains Diatonic
    scales + scale formulae: 1. With
    the use of open strings, 2. With
    fingerings to be moved upwards,
    3. With spreaded fingering, 4.
    Various fingerings) folio
    TEESELING VT-4 f.s.   (121)

TONAZZI, BRUNO
  Tecnica Dei Suoni Legati, La
    [It] gtr (4p. 1962) folio BERBEN
    537 f.s.   (122)

URBAN, STEPAN (1913-   )
  Cesta K Umelecke Hre Na Kytaru, Skola
    Vyssi Techniky
    [Czech] gtr (68p., ill; 1962;
    contains: Arpeggio formulae,
    cadences, barre, legato, Scale
    patterns, Scales in thirds,
    sixths, octaves, tenths and
    chords, Chord inversions with
    formulae, Harmonics, Effects,
    Broken chords along 2 and 3
    octaves; contains works by:
    Aguado (3), Carcassi (2),
    Giuliani (4), Paganini, Milan,
    Matiegka, Coste (2), Sor,
    Legnani, Anon. (2), Mertz;
    contains fragments of pcs by:
    Vinas, Sor (2), Albeniz, Dvorak,
    Urban (2), Burghauser, Marschner,
    Sinopoli, Turina (3), Bach (2),
    Giuliani, Carulli, Paganini,
    Granados, Llobet) quarto CZECH
    H-3407 f.s.   (123)

VERECZKEY, LASZLO
  A Gitar Hangotasa
    "Stimmen Der Gitarre, Das" [Hung/
    Ger] gtr (12p.) oct oblong EMB
    7754 f.s.   (124)

VISSER, DICK (1927-   )
  Tarrega Etcetera, Dagelijkse Studies
    "Tarrega Etcetera, Daily Studies"
    gtr (5p.; 1964; contains 21
    exercises + arpeggios formulae,
    after Tarrega-Roch; includes
    Tarrega, Francisco, Exercises,
    TI-iii-13, 13b) quarto HARMONIA
    1586 f.s.   (125)

  Technical Studies For The Guitar,
    Vol. I: Chromatic Scales
    [Dutch/Eng] gtr (1958; 7p.; 12
    scales from E-E-flat) folio
    HEUWEKE. EH-753 f.s.   (126)

  Technical Studies For The Guitar,
    Vol. II: Arpeggios
    [Dutch/Eng] gtr (1958; 4p.; The
    dominant seventh chord above C
    with inversions and arpeggio
    formulae) folio HEUWEKE. EH-754.
    f.s.   (127)

  Technical Studies For The Guitar,
    Vol. III: Interval-Systems
    [Dutch/Eng] gtr (1958; 13p.;
    Diatonic scales in thirds and
    sixths) folio HEUWEKE. EH-755
    f.s.   (128)

  Technical Studies For The Guitar,
    Vol. IV: Diatonic Scales And
    Scale-Systems
    [Dutch/Eng] gtr (1958; 7p.) folio
    HEUWEKE. EH-756 f.s.   (129)

  Technical Studies For The Guitar,
    Vol. V: Legato-Vibrato
    [Dutch/Eng] gtr (1958) folio
    HEUWEKE. EH-757 f.s.   (130)

  Technical Studies For The Guitar,
    Vol. VI: Chords a.o. Cadences;
    Broken Chords
    [Dutch/Eng] gtr (1958) folio
    HEUWEKE. EH-758 f.s.   (131)

  Technical Studies For The Guitar,
    Vol. VII: Right Hand Formulas;
    Glissando; Tremolo; Rasgueado;
    Harmonics; Pizzicato; etc.
    [Dutch/Eng] gtr (1958) folio
    HEUWEKE. EH-759 f.s.   (132)

WALKER, LUISE (1910-   )
  Tagliche Training, Das, Tonleitern
    Und Technische Studien
    [Ger] gtr quarto HEINRICH. 1505
    f.s. 34p.; 1947; Intro: contains:
    Diatonic scales (2, 2 and 3
    octaves), Scales in thirds,
    sixths, octaves, Chord
    inversions, 2x12 Exercises for
    both hands: chromatic scale,
    scale exercise, legato, barre,
    Exercises in sixths, octaves and
    chords, Effects, Harmonics;
    includes: Tarrega, Francisco,
    Study, TI-ii-38; Exercise, TI-
    iii-14f   (133)

WOLF, ROLAND
  Tremolospiel Auf Der Gitarre
    (composed with Dausend, Gerd-
    Michael)
    [Ger] gtr (13p.; rev and enl ed,
    1979; orig title: Das
    Tremolospiel Auf Der Konzert-
    Gitarre, Eine Kleine Anleitung
    Fur Den Fortgeschrittenen
    Spieler, 1966; contains Notes to
    the tremolo-play, 17 exercises, 1
    study, tremolo-formulas) folio
    PREISSLER 7016 f.s.   (134)

WYBOR ETIUD NA GITARE, VOL. 1 *CC80U
  (Powrozniak, Jozef) gtr (1-3rd degr.)
    POLSKIE 2532 f.s. exercises,
    chords, studies   (135)

WYBOR ETIUD NA GITARE, VOL. 2 *CC60U
  (Powrozniak, Jozef) gtr (4th degr.)
    POLSKIE 6471 f.s. exercises,
    chords, studies; contains:
    Exercises TI-iii-15g-h by Francisco
    Tarrega   (136)

IV Christmas Music

IV/I Guitar Solos

ALFONSO, NICOLAS
Ya Van Los Pastores
"Pastorale" gtr (6th degr., Edition
Nicolas Alfonso, No. 102; arr. +
orig. pcs) SCHOTT-FRER 9168 f.s.
contains also: Foliada; Ballade
(1)

ANTIGA, JEAN
Tarraja, 24 Petites Pieces
(Azpiazu) gtr (1-3rd degr.) DELRIEU
1291 f.s.
contains: Cancion De Navidad,
"Noel Des Petits Bretons" (2)

CANCIONES CATALANAS NAVIDENAS, 4
*Xmas,carol,Span
(Tarrago) [Span] gtr UNION ESP. 21711
f.s.
contains: Cant Dels Ocells, El;
Desembre Congelat, El; Noy De La
Mare, El; Olotina (3)

CANCIONES DE NAVIDAD, 8 *Xmas,carol,
Span
(Lara) gtr RICORDI-ARG BA-12636 f.s.
(4)

CANCIONES POPULARES CATALANAS, 10
(Llobet) gtr (5-7th degr.) UNION ESP.
20372 f.s. 10 pcs
contains: Nit De Nadal, La,
"Desembre Congelat, El" (5)

CANCIONES POPULARES GALLEGAS, 2 *Xmas,
carol,Span
(Gonzalez Martinez) gtr (4th degr.)
UNION ESP. 20778 f.s. arr
contains: Canto Del Vierzo;
Panxolina Di Nadal (6)

CANTI DI NATALE *CC8U,Xmas,carol
(Breguet) [Span/Fr/Eng/Ger] solo
voice,gtr/gtr solo (3rd degr.)
BERBEN 1126 f.s. notation: 2 treb-
staffs (accomp is gtr solo pt) (7)

CAROLS FOR GUITAR *CC18U,Xmas,carol
(Duarte) gtr (1-2nd degr.) NOVELLO
f.s. (8)

CAROLS FOR GUITAR, 6 *Xmas,carol
(Smith) gtr (1-2nd degr.) SCHOTT
11130 f.s. (9)

CATALANISCHE WEISEN, 3
gtr (6th degr.) UNIVER. 14438 $2.75
contains: Filla Del Marxant, La;
Noy De La Mare, El; Testamento De
Amalia, El (10)

CELEBRI MELODIE NATALIZIE *Xmas,carol
(Zuccheri) gtr (3rd degr.) BERBEN 705
f.s.
contains: Albero Di Natali, L';
Astro Del Ciel; Jingle Bell;
Piva, La; Tu Scendi Dalle Stelle;
Wade, John F., Adeste Fidelis (11)

CHRISTMAS CAROLS, 4 *Xmas,carol
(Bocanegra) gtr SPAN.MUS.CTR. GE-117
f.s. (12)

CHRISTMAS CAROLS, 5 *Xmas,carol
(Papas) gtr (2nd degr.) COLUMBIA 113
f.s.
contains: Away In A Manger; Good
King Wenceslas; Gruber, Franz
Xaver, Stille Nacht, "Silent
Night"; Handel, George Frideric,
Joy To The World; Wade, John F.,
Adeste Fidelis (13)

DOLCE NATALI *Xmas,carol
gtr (2-3rd degr.) ZANIBON 5428 f.s.
My repertory; orig words; arr +
orig pcs; notation: treb-clef
contains: Bignotto, Franco, Dolce
Natali; De' Liguori, S. Alfonso
Maria, Cantano Pace, Cantano
Amore; De' Liguori, S. Alfonso
Maria, Tu Scendi Dalle Stelle;
Gruber, Franz Xaver, Stille
Nacht; Wade, John F., Adeste

Fidelis (14)

EASY CHRISTMAS CAROLS, 2 *Xmas,carol
(Papas) gtr (1st degr.) COLUMBIA 163
f.s.
contains: Away In A Manger; What
Child Is This (15)

EASY MUSIC, VOL. 2 *folk song
(Azpiazu) gtr (3-7th degr.) SYMPHON
2062 f.s. 10 arr pcs; contains
works by: Arbeau (1), Anon. (1),
Buttstedt (1), F. Couperin (1),
Telemann (1)
contains: Coventry Carol, The; Noel
De Gascogne; Bach, Johann
Sebastian, Suite for Lute, BWV
996, in E minor, Saraband (16)

FOLKSONGS, 4
(Alfonso) gtr (4th degr.) SCHOTT-FRER
9167 f.s. 4 pcs; Edition Nicolas
Alfonso, No. 101
contains: Villancico Andaluz, "Noel
Andalou" (17)

FOR MY FRIENDS *folk song
(Duarte) gtr COLUMBIA 183 $2.50 11
arr + orig pcs; contains works by:
Anon. (4), Grieg (1), Duarte (2)
contains: Il Est Ne, Le Divin
Enfant (18)

FROHLICHE WEIHNACHTEN; 40 BELIEBTE
WEIHNACHTS- UND NEUJAHRSLIEDER
gtr ZIMMER. 1458 f.s. (19)

GRUBER, FRANZ XAVER (1787-1863)
Stille Nacht *Xmas,carol
(Sensier) gtr ESSEX f.s. (20)
(Tarrago) gtr UNION ESP. 1993 f.s.
(21)
"Wiegenlied" (Tarrago) gtr UNION
ESP. 2040 f.s. (22)

GUTEN ABEND, GUTE NACHT *folk song
(Stancik) [Ger] gtr (3rd degr.)
PREISSLER 7036 f.s. 9 arr + orig
pcs; contains lullabies by: Brahms
(1), Schubert (1), Fliess (1),
Stancik (1), Freire (1); Appendix:
"Wie Erarbeite Ich Ein Solostuck,
Eine Kurze Stufenweise Anleitung"
contains: Still, Still, Still (23)

KERSTLIEDEREN, EENVOUDIGE ZETTINGEN
*CC10U,Xmas,carol
(Peters) [Dutch] solo voice,gtr/gtr
solo (1-2nd degr.) HARMONIA HU-1862
f.s. notation: 2 treb-staffs
(accomp is gtr solo-pt) (24)

KERSTLIEDEREN VOOR GITAARSOLO *CC12U,
carol
(Gerits) [Dutch] gtr,opt solo voice
(1-2nd degr.) TEESELING 170 f.s.
notation: 1 treb clef (25)

KOMMT SINGT UND SPIELT: LIEDER UNSERER
ZEIT, FUR DEN ANFANGSUNTERRICHT
*folk song
(Kramer) [Ger] (1-2nd degr.) sc
HOFMEISTER T-4137 f.s. contains 30
works by: Hubschmann (1), Franz
(1), Richter (1), Mertke (1),
Dittrich (1), Bimberg (1),
Schuffenhauer (1), Stumpe (1) for 2
gtr; Groger (1), Hein (1), Richter-
Ulbrich (1), Lukowsky (2), Balzer
(1), Ahrend (1), Meyer (1),
Natschinski (1), Kochan (1),
Englert (1) for 1 gtr; Natschinski
(1), Becher (1), Eisler (1),
Naumilkat (1), Schwaen (1), Bimberg
(1), Folksongs (2), Schmidt (1) for
solo voice and gtr; partly single
line playing (2 gtr)
contains: Richter, Eva, Unsere
Tannenbaum (composed with
Ulbrich, Christel) (gtr);
Richter, Wolfgang, Weihnachtszeit
(2gtr) (single line playing) (26)

LEISE FALLT DER SCHNEE, LIEDER ZUR
WEIHNACHTSZEIT *CC27U,Xmas,carol/
folk song
(Funk) [Ger] gtr (2nd degr.)
HOFMEISTER T-4073 f.s. arr;
notation: treb-clef; contains works
by: Ebel, Schulz, Silcher, Anon.
(8), Cruger, Franck, Gruber (27)

LEISE RIESELT DER SCHNEE *CC27U,Xmas,
carol
(Funk) [Ger] gtr,opt solo voice (1-
2nd degr.) HOFMEISTER T-4073 f.s.

notation: treb-staff (28)

LET US HAVE CHRISTMAS MUSIC *CC14U,
Xmas,carol
(Davis) [Eng] gtr (1-2nd degr.)
FISCHER,C 04208 f.s. notation:
treb-staff (29)

LIEDER UM WEIHNACHT *CC18U,Xmas,carol
(Kammerling) [Ger] solo voice,gtr/gtr
solo (2-4th degr.) sc TONGER 1645
f.s. Rund Um Die Gitarre, Vol. V
(30)

MEL BAY FOLIO OF CLASSIC GUITAR SOLOS,
VOL. 2 *folk song
(Castle) gtr (1-4th degr.) BELWIN
$1.50 33 arr + orig pcs; contains
works by: Schumann (1), Diabelli
(2), Kuffner (1), Aguado (1),
Mozart (1), Molino (1), Paganini
(2), Flotow (1), Beethoven (1),
Borghesi (1), Mertz (1), Verdi (1),
Purcell (1), Giuliani (1), Handel
(1), Bornhardt (1), Sor (1),
Carulli (1), Balfe (1), Visee (2),
Castle (1)
contains: Bach, Johann Sebastian,
Minuet, BWV Anh. 114, in G (from
Anna Magdalena Bach Notenbuchlein
(1725), No.4); Bach, Johann
Sebastian, Partita for Violin,
No. 1, BWV 1002, in B minor,
Saraband (A min); Hopkins, John
Henry, Jr., We Three Kings Of
Orient Are (31)

MUSICAS PARA O NATAL *CC5U,Xmas,carol
(Savio) gtr RICORDI-BR BR-2877 f.s.
(32)

NOAD, FREDERICK M.
Playing The Guitar, A Self-
Instruction Guide To Technique
And Theory
[Eng] gtr quarto COLLIER f.s.
128p., ill; repr, 1971; 1st ed,
1963, 3 app
contains: Mananitas, "Mexican
Christmas Carol" (33)

NOELS *CC3U,Xmas,carol
(Franceries) gtr (3rd degr.) CHOUDENS
20.540 f.s. (34)

NOY DE LA MARE, EL, CANCION POPULAR
CATALAN *Xmas,carol,Span
(Abloniz) gtr (2-3rd degr.) BERBEN
1012 f.s. (35)
(Azpiazu) gtr (2-3rd degr.) SYMPHON
499 f.s. (36)
(Papas) gtr,opt gtr II (2-3rd degr.)
COLUMBIA 119 f.s. (37)
"Chico Da La Madre, El" (Prat) gtr
(2-3rd degr.) RICORDI-ARG BA-12315
f.s. (38)

O BLACK AND UNKNOWN BARDS, 7 NEGRO
SPIRITUALS
(Witte) [Eng] gtr (3-4th degr.)
HARMONIA 2096 f.s.
contains: Virgin Mary Had A Baby
Boy, The (39)

PICCOLA ANTOLOGIA CHITARRISTICA *folk
song
(Abloniz) gtr (3-5th degr.) RICORDI-
IT 129884 f.s. 12 arr + orig pcs;
contains works by: Anon. (2),
Purcell (1), Visee (1), W.A. Mozart
(1), Gruber (1), Chopin (1)
contains: Coventry Carol, The,
"Vecchia Carola Di Coventry";
Bach, Johann Sebastian, Nicht So
Traurig, "Non Tanto Triste", BWV
489 (from Schemelli's
Gesangbuch); Gruber, Franz Xaver,
Stille Nacht, "Notte Silenziasa"
(40)

PRZY CHOINCE, KOLEDY W LATWYM UKLADZIE
NA GITARE *CC25U,Xmas,carol,Polish
(Podobinski) [Polish] gtr,opt solo
voice (3rd degr.) POLSKIE f.s. arr;
notation: treb-staff (41)

RODRIGO, JOAQUIN (1902-   )
Petites Pieces, 3
(Sainz de la Maza) gtr (7-9th
degr.) ESCHIG 7382 f.s.
contains: Grazioso; Moderato; Ya
Se Van Los Pastores, "Bergers
S'en Vont, Les" (42)

SONNE, KOMM, EIN GITARRESPIELBUCH FUR
KINDER, 1-4. UNTERRICHTSJAHR *folk
song
(Ratz, Martin) [Ger] solo voice,gtr/
1-4gtr (single line playing/1-3rd

degr.) sc DEUTSCHER 32001 f.s. 162
arr + orig pcs; contains works by:
Schuffenhauer (2), Krug (4), Konig
(8), Ratz (22), Asriel (5), Quadt
(9), Rosenfeld (2), Haydn, Schumann
(3), Gorischk, Helmut, Wohlgemuth,
Schwaen, Schoendlinger for gtr;
Friemert (2), Buse, W.A. Mozart
(3), Beethoven, Berges,
Schuffenhauer, Hecht-Wieber for 2
gtr; Eberwein, Stephani for 3 gtr;
anon., naumilkat for 4 gtr or solo
voice(s), gtr; Silcher (2),
(2), Wendt, Friemert (2), Kern,
Krug (2), Pormova, Rodl, Hartung,
Nynkowa, Schuffenhauer, Hein,
Richter (3), W. Bender (2), Helmut,
Naumilkat for solo voice, gtr; also
contains Christmas music by:
Helmut, Schuffenhauer, Wohlgemuth
for gtr or solo voice, gtr; W.
Bender, Helmut, Naumilkat, for solo
voice, gtr
    contains: Bach, Johann Sebastian,
      Minuet in G minor, BWV Anh. 115
      (2gtr) (A min,single line
      playing); Bach, Johann Sebastian,
      Piece In F, "Aria", BWV Anh.131
      (2gtr) (single line playing);
      Bach, Johann Sebastian, Polonaise
      in G minor, BWV Anh. 119 (2gtr)
      (A min,single line playing)   (43)

STERNE UBER STILLEN STRASZEN, NEUE
    LIEDER ZUR WEIHNACHT *CC25U,Xmas,
    carol
  (Henze) [Ger] gtr (2nd degr.) sc
    HOFMEISTER T-4143 f.s. arr + 1 orig
    pce; contains works by: Wohlgemuth
    (5), Muller, Naumilkat, Kohler (2),
    Kochan, Werzlau, B. Henze, Meusel
    (2) for solo voice, gtr; 11 pcs.
    including a version for solo; 1
    pce. with opt 2nd solo voice   (44)

UBEN UND SPIELEN AUF DER GITARRE, VOL.
    1
  (Zykan) gtr,opt gtr II WELT 1021A
    f.s. 18 arr + orig pcs; contains
    works by: Folksongs (11), Lyra (1),
    W.A. Mozart (1), Mendelssohn (1),
    Gruber (1), Anon. (1), Strauss (1),
    Cerwenka (1); No. 13 With A 2nd Gtr
    Pt
    contains: Es Wird Scho Glei, Dumpa
      (Austrian); Gruber, Franz Xaver,
      Stille Nacht (A maj)   (45)

UNSERE WEIHNACHTSLIEDER *Xmas,carol
  (Gotze) [Ger] gtr solo,opt solo voice
    (3rd degr.) SCHOTT 4459 f.s. 43
    pcs; notation: treb-staff
    contains: Bach, Johann Sebastian,
      Lobt Gott Ihr Christen
      Allzugleich [Chorales], BWV 375
      (46)

WEIHNACHT - 8 ALTE LIEDER *Xmas,carol
  (Scharff) [Ger] 3rec, gtr or solo
    voice, 2rec, gtr or solo voice, gtr
    or gtr solo (3-4th degr.,
    Zeitschrift Fur Spielmusik, No.15)
    sc MOECK ZFS-15 f.s.   (47)

WEIHNACHTSLIEDER *Xmas,carol
  (Schindler) gtr (2-3rd degr.) VAMO
    EE-011A f.s.
    contains: Es Ist Ein Ros'
      Entsprungen; Leise Rieselt Der
      Schnee; O Du Frohliche, O Du
      Selige; O Tannenbaum; Gruber,
      Franz Xaver, Stille Nacht   (48)

WEIHNACHTSLIEDER ZUR GITARRE *CC25U,
    Xmas,carol
  (Schwarz-Reiflingen) [Ger] solo
    voice,gtr/gtr solo (2-3rd degr.) sc
    SIKORSKI 306 f.s. arr + 1 orig pce
    (49)

WEIHNACHTSZEIT - FROHLICHE ZEIT,
    ALTBEKANNTE UND NEUERE
    WEIHNACHTSLIEDER *CC28U,Xmas,carol
  (Cleff) [Ger] solo voice,gtr/gtr solo
    (2-4th degr.) sc VOGGEN f.s.
    notation for gtr solo: treb-staff;
    notation for solo voice, gtr: 2
    treb-staffs   (50)

IV/IIA1   Duets for Two Guitars

CHANSON DE NOEL *Xmas,carol
  (Azpiazu) gtr SYMPHON 2063 f.s. from
    EASY MUSIC FOR GUITAR, VOL. III
    (51)

DU UND ICH WIR SPIELEN GITARRE, EIN
    LIEBLINGSBUCH FUR ANGEHENDE
    GITARRISTEN *folk song
  (Baresel) 2gtr (1st degr.) sc ZIMMER.
    ZM-1782 f.s. 20 pcs.;contains works
    by: Zelter (1), Zuccalmaglio (1),
    Anon. (1); mainly single line
    playing
    contains: Morgen Kommt Der
      Weihnachtsmann; O Tannenbaum (52)

GERRITS, PAUL
    Gitarren- Und Lautenschule, Vol. I:
      Das Einstimmige Spiel - Guitar
      And Lute Method, Vol. 1: Melody
      Playing
    [Ger/Fr/Eng] gtr quarto oblong
      MOSELER f.s. 36p., ill; 1967;
      contains: Les Anges (Noel) for 2
      gtr; Bach, Johann Sebastian,
      Suite No. 3 for Violoncello, BWV
      1009, In C, Bourree I-II; Musette
      In D, BWV Anh. 126 (from Anna
      Magdalena Bach Notenbuchlein
      (1725), No.22 for 2 gtr (in E);
      Minuet In G, BWV Anh. 114, from
      Anna Magdalena Bach Notenbuchlein
      (1725), No.4, for 2 gtr (in C);
      Minuet In G, BWV Anh.115 from
      Anna Magdalena Bach Notenbuchlein
      (1725), No.5 for 2 gtr (in a
      minor)   (53)

    Gitarren- Und Lautenschule, Vol. II:
      Ubungen Und Stucke Fur Das
      Mehrstimmige Spiel - Guitar And
      Lute Method, Vol. 2: Exercises
      And Pieces For Polyphonic Playing
    [Ger/Fr/Eng] gtr quarto oblong
      MOSELER f.s. 39p.; 1968;
      contains: Bach, Johann Sebastian,
      Suite For Lute, BWV 996 In E
      Minor (G Is F Sharp), Bourree and
      Allemand   (54)

GRADED DUETS, 20
  (Gavall) 2gtr (partly single line
    playing/1st degr.) sc OXFORD 36.003
    $3.10 20 pcs; contains works by:
    Losy vom Losinthal (1); Capilupi
    (1), W.A. Mozart (5), Handel (3),
    Purcell (1), Stamitz (1), Weiss (1)
    contains: Bach, Johann Sebastian,
      Brunnquell Aller Guter, BWV 445
      (from Schemelli's Gesangbuch)
      (single line playing); Bach,
      Johann Sebastian, Eins Ist Noth,
      Ach Herr, Dies Eine, BWV 453
      (from Schemelli's Gesangbuch)
      (single line playing); Bach,
      Johann Sebastian, Gib Dich
      Zufrieden Und Sei Stille, BWV 510
      (from Anna Magdalena Bach
      Notenbuchlein (1725), No.12) (F
      maj,single line playing); Bach,
      Johann Sebastian, Jesu, Deine
      Liebeswunden, BWV 471 (from
      Schemelli's Gesangbuch) (single
      line playing); Bach, Johann
      Sebastian, O Jesulein Suss, O
      Jesulein Mild, BWV 493 (from
      Schemelli's Gesangbuch) (single
      line playing); Bach, Johann
      Sebastian, Schaffs Mit Mir, Gott,
      Nach Deinem Willen, BWV 314 (from
      Anna Magdalena Bach Notenbuchlein
      (1725), No.35) (E maj,single line
      playing); Bach, Johann Sebastian,
      Und Wie Wohl Ist Mir, O Freund
      Der Seelen, BWV 517 (from Anna
      Magdalena Bach Notenbuchlein
      (1725), No.40) (F maj,single line
      playing)   (55)

GRUBER, FRANZ XAVER (1787-1863)
    Stille Nacht *Xmas,carol
    "Noche De Paz" (Bianqui Pinero)
    2gtr RICORDI-ARG BA-12596 f.s.
    (56)

GUITAR IN ENSEMBLE, VOL. 1
  (Gavall) 2gtr (1-3rd degr.) sc BELWIN
    1116 f.s. arr + orig pcs; 34 pcs;
    contains works by: Folksongs (19),
    Kuffner (3), Sor (1), Schubert (2),
    Silcher (1), Weber (1), Mozart (1),
    Brahms (1), Durrner (1),
    Mendelssohn (1); Eng words: 8 pcs.
    (not underlaid)

contains: Bach, Johann Sebastian,
    Puer Natus Est In Bethlehem.
    Chorale Prelude, BWV 603 (E min);
    Bach, Johann Sebastian, Sonata
    for Keyboard Instrument, BWV 964,
    in D minor, Andante (C maj);
    Bach, Johann Sebastian, Suite for
    Lute, BWV 996, in E minor,
    Bourree   (57)

KOMMT SINGT UND SPIELT: LIEDER UNSERER
    ZEIT, FUR DEN ANFANGSUNTERRICHT
    *folk song
  (Kramer) [Ger] (1-2nd degr.) sc
    HOFMEISTER T-4137 f.s. contains 30
    works by: Hubschmann (1), Franz
    (1), Richter (1), Mertke (1),
    Dittrich (1), Bimberg (1),
    Schuffenhauer (1), Stumpe (1) for 2
    gtr; Groger (1), Hein (1), Richter-
    Ulbrich (1), Lukowsky (2), Balzer
    (1), Ahrend (1), Meyer (1),
    Natschinski (1), Kochan (1),
    Englert (1) for 1 gtr; Natschinski
    (1), Becher (1), Eisler (1),
    Naumilkat (1), Schwaen (1), Bimberg
    (1), Folksongs (2), Schmidt (1) for
    solo voice and gtr; partly single
    line playing (2 gtr)
    contains: Richter, Eva, Unsere
      Tannenbaum (composed with
      Ulbrich, Christel) (gtr);
      Richter, Wolfgang, Weihnachtszeit
      (2gtr) (single line playing) (58)

MARTINEZ ZARATE, JORGE
    Mi Primer Libro De Guitarra
    [Span] gtr (staff notation and
      tablature) folio RICORDI-ARG
      BA-11940 f.s. 43p.; repr, 1964;
      1st ed, 1961; contains: Stille
      Nacht (Noche De Paz) by Franz
      Gruber; Cancion De Navidad by
      Felix Mendelssohn-Bartholdy; and
      So Oft Ich Meine Tobackspfeife,
      BWV 515, from Anna Magdalena Bach
      Notenbuchlein (1725), No.20a
      (single line playing, 2 gtr) by
      Johann Sebastian Bach   (59)

PRAETORIUS, MICHAEL (1571-1621)
    Puer Natus In Bethlehem [Collection]
    (from Musae Sioniae)
    (Bayer) 2-4gtr DOBLINGER GKM-111
      f.s. Gitarre-Kammermusik, No. 111
      contains: In Dulci Jubilo; Puer
      Natus In Bethlehem; Vom Himmel
      Hoch   (60)

SCHALLER, ERWIN (1901-   )
    Altlothringer Hirtenmusik
    (Libbert) 2gtr (3-4th degr., Das
      Gitarrenwerk, Reihe A:9) sc
      PREISSLER f.s.   (61)

IV/IIA2   Trios For Three Guitars

BLOK, COBY
    Speelboek Voor De Gitaargroepsles,
      Vol. I
    quarto HARMONIA 2588 f.s. 39p.;
      1973
      contains: Maria Durch Ein
        Dornwald Ging (3gtr)   (62)

    Speelboek Voor De Gitaargroepsles,
      Vol. II
    (single line playing) quarto
      HARMONIA 2607 f.s. 43p.; 1974
      contains: Melchior Et Balthasar
        (3gtr)   (63)

PRAETORIUS, MICHAEL (1571-1621)
    Puer Natus In Bethlehem [Collection]
    (from Musae Sioniae)
    (Bayer) 2-4gtr DOBLINGER GKM-111
      f.s. Gitarre-Kammermusik, No. 111
      contains: In Dulci Jubilo; Puer
      Natus In Bethlehem; Vom Himmel
      Hoch   (64)

WOLKI, KONRAD
    Sechs Mal Drei (6 x 3)
    3gtr (mainly single line playing/1-
      2nd degr.) sc PREISSLER 7064 f.s.
      contains: Einstimmung; Entree;
      Kleine Ouverture; Nostalgie; O
      Tannenbaum; Suite in A   (65)

IV/IIA3   Quartets for Four Guitars

MUSIC FOR 4 GUITARS
(Gavall) 4gtr (single line playing/1-2nd degr.) sc BELWIN 978 $2.50 11 pcs; contains works by: Praetorius (1); W.A. Mozart (2); Brahms (2), Palestrina (1), Schubert (1)
contains: Bach, Johann Sebastian, Feste Burg Ist Unser Gott, Ein'. Chorale, BWV 203; Bach, Johann Sebastian, Herzlich Thut Mich Verlangen. Chorale, "Befiel Du Deine Wege. Chorale", BWV 270; Bach, Johann Sebastian, Nun Lasst Uns. Chorale, "Sprich Ja Zu Meinen Taten", BWV 194; Bach, Johann Sebastian, O Welt, Ich Muss Dich Lassen. Chorale, "O Welt, Sieh' Hier Dein Leben", BWV 393; Praetorius, Michael, Es Ist Ein Ros' Entsprungen   (66)

PRAETORIUS, MICHAEL (1571–1621)
Puer Natus In Bethlehem [Collection] (from Musae Sioniae)
(Bayer) 2-4gtr DOBLINGER GKM-111 f.s. Gitarre-Kammermusik, No. 111
contains: In Dulci Jubilo; Puer Natus In Bethlehem; Vom Himmel Hoch   (67)

SONNE, KOMM, EIN GITARRESPIELBUCH FUR KINDER, 1-4. UNTERRICHTSJAHR *folk song
(Ratz, Martin) [Ger] solo voice,gtr/1-4gtr (single line playing/1-3rd degr.) sc DEUTSCHER 32001 f.s. 162 arr + orig pcs; contains works by: Schuffenhauer (2), Krug (4), Konig (8), Ratz (22), Asriel (5), Quadt (9), Rosenfeld (2), Haydn, Schumann (3), Gorischk, Helmut, Wohlgemuth, Schwaen, Schoendlinger for gtr; Friemert (2), Buse, W.A. Mozart (3), Beethoven, Berges, Schuffenhauer, Hecht-Wieber for 2 gtr; Eberwein, Stephani for 3 gtr; anon., naumilkat for 4 gtr or solo voice(s), gtr; Skodova (2), Silcher (2), Wendt, Friemert (2), Kern, Krug (2), Pormova, Rodl, Hartung, Nynkowa, Schuffenhauer, Hein, Richter (3), W. Bender (2), Helmut, Naumilkat for solo voice, gtr; also contains Christmas music by: Helmut, Schuffenhauer, Wohlgemuth for gtr or solo voice, gtr; W. Bender, Helmut, Naumilkat, for solo voice, gtr
contains: Bach, Johann Sebastian, Minuet in G minor, BWV Anh. 115 (2gtr) (A min,single line playing); Bach, Johann Sebastian, Piece In F, "Aria", BWV Anh.131 (2gtr) (single line playing); Bach, Johann Sebastian, Polonaise in G minor, BWV Anh. 119 (2gtr) (A min,single line playing)   (68)

IV/IIB1   Duets for Guitar and Another Instrument

ALTE UND NEUE WEIHNACHTSLIEDER *Xmas, carol
(Kramer) treb inst,gtr PRO MUSICA f.s.   (69)

BRESGEN, CESAR (1913–   )
Suite Uber Altbohmische Weihnachtsweisen rec,gtr (Zeitschrift Fur Spielmusik, No. 449-450) MOECK ZFS-449-450 f.s.   (70)

FLOTE SING, KLAMPFE KLING
(Zschiesche) rec,gtr (3rd degr.) sc VOGGEN f.s. 50 folksongs from 11 countries; rec pt provided with orig words   (71)

HEILIGE NACHT, WEIHNACHTSLIEDER–ALBUM *CC51U,Xmas,carol
(Fries; Alex) [Ger] solo voice,gtr/

treb inst,gtr (2-3rd degr.) sc APOLLO 1850 f.s. arr + 2 orig pcs   (72)

INMITTEN DER NACHT, WEIHNACHTLICHE SPIELMUSIK *Xmas,carol
(Bacher) S rec/A rec/T rec,gtr/2rec, gtr (3rd degr.) sc NAGELS EN-1106 f.s. 10 pcs; Nagels Laute- Und Gitarre-Archiv; contains works by: Praetorius, Anon., F. Couperin
contains: Bach, Johann Sebastian, English Suite No. 3 In G Minor, Fifth Movement: Gavotte En Musette, BWV 808 (gtr,T rec) (C maj); Bach, Johann Sebastian, English Suite No. 6 In D Minor, Fifth Movement: Gavotte II, BWV 811 (gtr,A rec) (C maj); Bach, Johann Sebastian, Wachet Auf! Ruft Uns Die Stimme. Chorale, "Gloria Sei Dir Gesungen", BWV 140,No.7 (gtr,T rec/A rec)   (73)

NOUVEAUX DUOS, 32 [SIC] PIECES...
(Sanvoisin) rec,gtr (3-5th degr.) sc HEUGEL CPJ-19 $4.25 34 pcs (numbered 1-33); contains works by: Dandrieu (9), Attaignant (3), F. Couperin (2), Gardane (4), Encina (1), Palero (2), Morales (1), Ortiz (2), Anon. (5), Buxtehude (5), Bull (1), Farnaby (1), Munday (1), Dowland (1); Les Cahiers De Plein Jeu, No.19
contains: Dandrieu, Jean Francois, Noels, 5   (74)

SINTERKLAAS- & KERSTLIEDJES *CC12U, Xmas,carol
(van der Staak) [Dutch] S rec,gtr,opt solo voice sc BROEKMANS 832 f.s. notation: 2 treb-staffs; rec pt is solo voice pt   (75)

UNSERE WEIHNACHTSLIEDER *Xmas,carol
(Gotze) [Ger] solo voice,gtr/treb inst,gtr (2-3rd degr.) sc SCHOTT 4361 f.s. 42 pcs; also available in gtr solo ed
contains: Bach, Johann Sebastian, Lobt Gott, Ihr Christen, Allzugleich. Chorale, BWV 375   (76)

WEIHNACHTSLIEDER AUS DEUTSCHLAND UND OSTERREICH *Xmas,carol,Austrian/Ger
(Schafer-Stetka) [Ger] S rec,gtr,opt solo voice (3rd degr.) sc,pt DOBLINGER f.s. 14 pcs; notation: 2 treb-staffs; rec pt is solo voice pt
contains: Bach, Johann Sebastian, Ich Steh' An Deiner Krippen Hier, BWV 469 (from Schemelli's Gesangbuch)   (77)

YA SE VAN LOS PASTORES
(Zschiesche) rec,gtr (3rd degr., 50 folksongs from 11 countries; rec pt provided with orig words) sc MOSELER f.s. from FLOTE SING, KLAMPFE KLING   (78)

IV/IIB2   Trios for Guitar and Other Instruments

ALTE UND NEUE MUSIK ZUM SINGEN UND SPIELEN AUF BLOCKFLOTEN, GEIGEN UND LAUTENINSTRUMENTE *folk song
(Gerwig) [Ger] (1-3rd degr.) sc LIENAU 1375 f.s. Das Spiel Der Lauteninstrumente, Series II, Spielbuch 1; contains works by: Sperontes (4), L. Mozart (3), Rathgeber (5), Rein (5), Rhau (2), Langenau (1), Chemin-Petit (1): for gtr (1), 2gtr (3), 3gtr (1), rec, gtr (3), 2rec, gtr (2), solo voice, gtr (3), solo voice, rec, gtr (1), solo voice, rec, 2gtr (1), rec, vln or vla, gtr (1); arr. + orig. pcs.; single line playing; gtr pt partly in bass clef
contains: Bach, Johann Sebastian, English Suite No. 6, BWV 811, In D Minor, Gavottes I-II (gtr,1-2A rec); Bach, Johann Sebastian, Minuet, BWV Anh. 118, in B flat (from Anna Magdalena Bach Notenbuchlein (1725), No.9) (gtr, S rec) (C maj,single line playing, gtr pt in bass clef)   (79)

ANONYMOUS
Allerlei Volkslieder *CC50UL
(Wolter) [Ger] 2rec and gtr; solo voice, rec, and gtr (1-2nd degr.) sc,pt MOECK 2030 f.s. contains 8 Christmas carols   (80)

BAUMANN, HANS
Bergbauernweihnacht *CC15U,Xmas, carol
(Biebl) [Ger] for 2rec, gtr (4), 2rec, unison or 2-pt cor (partly solo voice ad lib), gtr (9), rec, solo voice, gtr (2) (1-2nd degr.) sc MOSELER f.s.   (81)

BIALAS, GUNTER (1907–   )
Spanische Romanzen
2treb inst/S rec,A rec,gtr (2-3rd degr.) sc MOECK ZFS-231 f.s. 6 pcs; Zeitschrift Fur Spielmusik, No.231
contains: Hirtentanz; Nana   (82)

CAROLS FOR PLAYING WITH GUITAR ACCOMPANIMENT *CC12U,Xmas,carol
(Duarte) S rec,A rec/treb inst,gtr (3-4th degr.) sc NOVELLO 19363 f.s. including a simple alternative gtr pt   (83)

CORELLI, ARCANGELO (1653–1713)
Pastorale (from Weihnachtsmusik) Xmas,carol
(Brojer) 2vln,gtr,opt vcl (4th degr., Die Gitarre In Der Kammermusik, No. 23) sc,pts HOHLER GC-23 f.s.   (84)

INMITTEN DER NACHT, WEIHNACHTLICHE SPIELMUSIK *Xmas,carol
(Bacher) S rec/A rec/T rec,gtr/2rec, gtr (3rd degr.) sc NAGELS EN-1106 f.s. 10 pcs; Nagels Laute- Und Gitarre-Archiv; contains works by: Praetorius, Anon., F. Couperin
contains: Bach, Johann Sebastian, English Suite No. 3 In G Minor, Fifth Movement: Gavotte En Musette, BWV 808 (gtr,T rec) (C maj); Bach, Johann Sebastian, English Suite No. 6 In D Minor, Fifth Movement: Gavotte II, BWV 811 (gtr,A rec) (C maj); Bach, Johann Sebastian, Wachet Auf! Ruft Uns Die Stimme. Chorale, "Gloria Sei Dir Gesungen", BWV 140,No.7 (gtr,T rec/A rec)   (85)

KNAB, ARMIN (1881–1951)
Pastorale Und Allegro *Xmas,carol
2A rec,gtr/lute,opt vla da gamba/vcl (4-5th degr., lute pt in Fr tablature) sc,pts BAREN. BA-1445 f.s.   (86)

O WUNDER, WAS WILL DAS BEDEUTEN, LIEDERSAMMLUNG ZUR ADVENTSZEIT *CC25U,Xmas,carol
(Draths) 1 or 2 S rec or 2 solo voices, opt gt SCHOTT 5750 f.s.   (87)

PASTORALEN ALTER MEISTER, 9 *Xmas, carol
(Ochs) 2treb inst/2vln/2rec,pno/gtr, opt vcl/vla da gamba (3rd degr., contains works by: Handel (1), Vivaldi (2), Keiser (1), Locatelli (1), Giardini (1), Corelli (1), Pez (1), Haydn (1)) sc,pts MOECK 2060 f.s.   (88)

STETKA, FRANZ (1899–   )
Tanze, Marsche Und Andere Spielstucke S rec/A rec,gtr (1-2nd degr.) sc DOBLINGER 04414 f.s. Spielmusik Fur Blockfloten Und Gitarre, Vol. II; 11 pcs for 3S rec; 1 pc for 2S rec, A rec, gtr; 4 pcs for S rec, A rec, gtr
contains: Kleine Weihnachtsmusik, Eine (gtr,S rec,A rec)   (89)

VOLKS- UND KINDERLIEDER
(Uhl) vln,vla/2vln,gtr (1-2nd degr.) pts HEINRICH. 1523 f.s. 26 pcs.
contains: Ihr Kinderlein Kommet; O Du Frohliche; Gruber, Franz Xaver, Stille Nacht   (90)

WINTERWEISSE WEIHNACHT, ALTE UND NEUE LIEDER UM DIE WEIHNACHTSZEIT *CC24U,Xmas,carol
(Kramer) [Ger] 2 solo voices or 2 treb insts or solo voice + treb inst gtr (2-3rd degr.) sc HARTH 2314 f.s. arr + orig pcs; notation of voices: 1 treb-clef + words   (91)

IV/IIB3   Quartets for Guitar and Other Instruments

ALTE WEIHNACHTSMUSIK, SPIELSTUCKE UND
LIEDER *Xmas,carol
(Schlensog) (3rd degr.) sc MOECK
ZFS-39 f.s. 12 pcs for S recs or
treb insts and solo voice(s); 2 pcs
with gtr: no.3 for solo voice, rec,
gtr; no. 5 for 3 recs, gtr;
Zeitschrift Fur Spielmusik No. 39
contains: Bach, Johann Sebastian,
Auf, Auf! Die Rechte Zeit Ist
Hier, "Adventslied", BWV 440
(from Schemelli's Gesangbuch)
(solo voice,rec,gtr) (C maj);
Bach, Johann Sebastian, Ich Steh'
An Deiner Krippe Hier, "An Der
Krippe", BWV 469 (from
Schemelli's Gesangbuch) (3rec,
gtr)   (92)

PASTORALEN ALTER MEISTER, 9 *Xmas,
carol
(Ochs) 2treb inst/2vln/2rec,pno/gtr,
opt vcl/vla da gamba (3rd degr.,
contains works by: Handel (1),
Vivaldi (2), Keiser (1), Locatelli
(1), Giardini (1), Corelli (1), Pez
(1), Haydn (1)) sc,pts MOECK 2060
f.s.   (93)

SCHALLER, ERWIN (1901-   )
Altlothringer Hirtenmusik
2vln,S rec,gtr BREITKOPF-W EB-6780
f.s.   (94)

WEIHNACHT - 8 ALTE LIEDER *Xmas,carol
(Scharff) [Ger] 3rec, gtr or solo
voice, 2rec, gtr or solo voice, gtr
or gtr solo (3-4th degr.),
Zeitschrift Fur Spielmusik, No.15)
sc MOECK ZFS-15 f.s.   (95)

IV/IIB4   Music for School Ensemble/Orchestra with Guitar

BACH, JOHANN SEBASTIAN (1685-1750)
Kleines Weihnachtsoratorium Mit
Johann Sebastian Bach
(Oberborbeck, Felix) [Ger] (single
line playing/1st degr.) sc MOECK
ZFS144 f.s. Zeitschrift Fur
Spielmusik, No. 144
contains: Bereite Dich, Zion, BWV
248,No.4 (from Weihnachts-
Oratorium) (gtr,3rec); Ehre Sei
Gott In Der Hohe. Canon, BWV
1078,No.7 (gtr,inst) (F maj);
Vom Himmel Hoch, Da Komm Ich
Her. Chorale, BWV 248,No.9
(from Weihnachts-Oratorium)
(solo voice,gtr,3rec)   (96)

HEIDSCHI BUMBEIDSCHI BUM-BUM, DIE
ALLERSCHONSTEN WEIHNACHTSLIEDER,
VOL. I: PNO ED. (WITH TEXT)
*CC28U,Xmas,carol
(Blasl) [Ger] sc UNIVER. 15902 f.s.
vols can be used separately or in
combination   (97)

HEIDSCHI BUMBEIDSCHI BUM-BUM, DIE
ALLERSCHONSTEN WEIHNACHTSLIEDER,
VOL. II: INST ED., FOR 3- OR 4-PT
ENSEMBLES *CC22U,Xmas,carol
(Blasl) [Ger] (single line playing/
1st degr.) sc UNIVER. 15903 f.s.
vols can be used separately or in
combination   (98)

HEIDSCHI BUMBEIDSCHI BUM-BUM, DIE
ALLERSCHONSTEN WEIHNACHTSLIEDER,
VOL. III: VOCAL ED *CC28U,Xmas,
carol
(Blasl) [Ger] sc UNIVER. 15904 f.s.
vols can be used separately or in
combination   (99)

HIRTENLIEDER UND TANZE AUS DEM SUDOSTEN
*CC11U,Xmas,carol
(Wunsch) S rec solo (5); S rec, A and
T rec (bowed inst, gtr), opt tamb
(2-3rd degr.) sc MOECK ZFS-223 f.s.
arr; Zeitschrift Fur Spielmusik

No.223   (100)

SPIELMUSIK FUR DIE SCHULE
(Blasl; Deutsch) desc, treb, and bass
insts (recs, strs, acord, plucked
insts (gtr), pno, perc (1-2nd
degr.) sc UNIVER. 14720 f.s.
Sonderausgabe Der Roten Reihe; 2-9
parts; contains 106 works by 42
medieval to Viennese classical and
contemporary composers, folksongs;
arr. + orig. pcs.
contains: Ferdinand III,
Weihnachtsmusik   (101)

WEIHNACHTLICHES SPIEL *CC19U,Xmas,
carol
(Runge) recs (S, A) and other treb
insts (12 pcs); recs, vln, gtr (7
pcs) (mainly single line playing/
3rd degr.) sc SCHOTT B-149 f.s.
Bausteine, no. 149 contains works
by: Buttstedt (3), Handel, Zachow
(3), Kirnberger, Walther (4),
Kaufmann (3), Gibbons, des
Milleville and two pieces from
Fridolin Sichers Tabulaturbuch
                                  (102)

IV/IIC1   Duets for Guitar and Voice

BODDECKER, PHILIPP FRIEDRICH
(1683- ?)
Natus Est Jesus, Weihnachtskonzert
*Xmas,carol
(Behrend) solo voice,gtr (arr)
ZIMMER. ZM-1899 f.s.   (103)

BRUDER SINGER, LIEDER UNSERES VOLKES
*CC152L
(Wolki) [Ger] solo voice,gtr (2-4th
degr.) sc BAREN. 3879 f.s. contains
12 Christmas carols and 76
folksongs; contains works by: Anon.
(36), Lau (2), W.A. Mozart, Baumann
(3), Hensel (3), Bresgen (2),
Reichardt (2), Schulz (2), Luther,
Gneist, Ebeling, Marx, Vulpius (2),
Schutz, Isaac (2), Dietrich,
Kukuck, Scheidt, Silcher(2),
Albert, Nicolai (2), Zuccalmaglio,
Werlin, Walter, Cruger, Pohlenz,
Becker, Knab, Wolters   (104)

CANCIONES POPULARES ESPANOLAS
(Tarrago) [Span] solo voice,gtr (6-
8th degr.) sc UNION ESP. 19637 f.s.
15 pcs.
contains: Campanas De Belen; Ya Se
Van Los Pastores   (105)

CANCIONES POPULARES ESPANOLAS, 5
(Azpiazu) [Span] solo voice,gtr (5th
degr.) sc UNION ESP. 19403 f.s.
contains: Ya Se Van Los Pastores,
"Pastores, Los"   (106)

CANTI DI NATALE *CC8U,Xmas,carol
(Breguet) [Span/Fr/Eng/Ger] solo
voice,gtr/gtr solo (3rd degr.)
BERBEN 1126 f.s. notation: 2 treb-
staffs (accomp is gtr solo pt)   (107)

CAROLS, 25, FROM THE OXFORD BOOK OF
CAROLS FOR SCHOOLS *Xmas,carol
(Stickley) [Eng] solo voice,gtr (1st
degr.) sc OXFORD f.s.   (108)

CHRISTGEBURT- UND MARIENLIEDER, VOL. I:
ALTDEUTSCHE CHRISTGEBURTLIEDER
*CC15U,Xmas,carol,14-17th cent
(Arndt) [Ger] solo voice,gtr/pno sc
PETERS 4361 f.s.   (109)

DAVON WOLL'N WIR NUN SINGEN *CC11U,
Xmas,carol
(Kothe) [Ger] solo voice,gtr (3rd
degr.) sc NOETZEL N-1112 f.s.   (110)

DEUTSCHE WEIHNACHTSWEISEN *CC7U,Xmas,
carol
(Bresgen) [Ger] 3rec, gtr (3 pcs);
solo voice, gtr (1 pce) (single
line playing/1st degr.) sc MOECK
ZFS-331 f.s. Zeitschrift Fur
Spielmusik, No. 331   (111)

EARLY ENGLISH LUTE SONGS AND FOLK
SONGS, VOL. III *folk song
(Runge) [Eng] solo voice,gtr (3-4th
degr.) sc HARGAIL HFA-18 f.s. arr.
+ orig. pcs.; contains 16 works by:
Anon. (2), Dowland, Pilkington,
Campion, Blow, Young; Hargail Folk
Anthology, No.18

contains: Anonymous, Agincourt
Carol, The   (112)

EUROPAISCHE WEIHNACHTSLIEDER *CC15U,
Xmas,carol
(Behrend) solo voice,gtr (2-3rd
degr.) SIKORSKI 488 f.s. orig
words; from 7 countries   (113)

GAVALL, JOHN
Learning Music Through The Guitar,
Vol. V: An Introduction To
Figured Bass
[Eng] gtr quarto BELWIN BM-16 f.s.
57p.; 1972; contains: Bach,
Johann Sebastian, Und Also Bald
War Da Da Bei Dem Engel
(recitative), for gtr and solo
voice from Weihnachts-Oratorium,
BWV 248; O Haupt Voll Blut Und
Wunden. Chorale No. 21 from
Matthaus-Passion, BWV 244, for 4
gtr; Schaut Hin! for 2 gtr from
Weihnachts-Oratorium; Ach! Dass
Nicht Die Letzte Stunde, BWV 439
(from Schemelli's Gesangbuch),
for 2 gtr or 1 gtr and mel inst;
Schaffs Mit Mir, Gott. Chorale,
BWV 514 (from Anna Magdalena Bach
Notenbuchlein (1725), No.35, in
C, for 2 gtr or gtr and mel inst
                                  (114)
Play The Guitar, A Self Tutor
[Eng] gtr quarto BELWIN MM-474 f.s.
54p., ill; 9 app
contains: Coventry Carol, The   (115)

GITARRE ZUM WEIHNACHTSLIED *CC27U,
Xmas,carol
(Wolki) [Ger] 1-2solo voice,gtr (1-
2nd degr.) sc APOLLO 2232 f.s. arr
                                  (116)

GUITAR SONGBOOK, THE *folk song
(Noad) [Eng] (2-7th degr.) COLLIER
f.s. 72 arr + orig pcs; contains
works by: Anon. (6), Noad (1),
Gruber (1), Hopkins (1), Dun (1),
Poulton (1), Moore (1), Hume (1),
Schubert (2), Pergolesi (1), Blow
(1), Dowland (2), E. Purcell (1),
Rosseter (1), Morley (1), Martini
(1), Handel (1) for solo voice,
gtr; H. Purcell (2), Glinka (1),
Attwood (1), Gluck (1), Beethoven
(1), Schumann (1), Tchaikovsky (1),
Zipoli (1), Haydn (1), D. Scarlatti
(1) for 2 gtr; Sor (1), C.P.E. Bach
(1), Handel (2), Corelli (1),
Carcassi (1), Purcell (1), Carulli
(1), Dowland (1), Anon. (1), Mozart
(1) for gtr; with an introduction:
Complete Notes Of The Guitar, Chord
Chart, How Guitar Music Is Written,
Principal Elements Of Guitar
Technique (36p., 17 ill.)
contains: Coventry Carol, The (gtr,
solo voice); First Noel, The
(solo voice,gtr); Gruber, Franz
Xaver, Silent Night (gtr,solo
voice); Hopkins, John Henry, Jr.,
We Three Kings (gtr,solo voice)
                                  (117)

HAUSLICHE WEIHNACHT *Xmas,carol/folk
song
(Gerwig) [Ger] solo voice,1-3gtr
(single line playing/1-3rd degr.)
sc LIENAU 1407 f.s. ;Das Spiel Der
Lauteninstrumente, Series II,
Spielbuch 4; 19pcs; contains works
by: Praetorius (3), Beutner, Anon.
(5), Braun
contains: Bach, Johann Sebastian,
Ich Steh' An Deiner Krippe Hier,
BWV 469 (from Schemelli's
Gesangbuch); Bach, Johann
Sebastian, Liebes Herz, Bedenke
Doch, BWV 482 (from Schemelli's
Gesangbuch); Bach, Johann
Sebastian, O Jesulein Suss, BWV
493 (from Schemelli's Gesangbuch)
                                  (118)

HEILIGE NACHT, WEIHNACHTSLIEDER-ALBUM
*CC51U,Xmas,carol
(Fries; Alex) [Ger] solo voice,gtr/
treb inst,gtr (2-3rd degr.) sc
APOLLO 1850 f.s. arr + 2 orig pcs
                                  (119)

JANSEN, WILLY (1897-   )
Klanglehre Zur Gitarre (Begleitspiel
auf Grund Der Harmonielehre)
[Ger] gtr SCHOTT 5845 f.s.
contains: Auf Dem Berge Da Wehet
Der Wind; Vom Himmel Hoch, Da
Komm Ich Her (Martin Luther);
Kindelein Zart, Von Guter Art
                                  (120)

KERSTLIEDEREN, EENVOUDIGE ZETTINGEN
*CC10U,Xmas,carol
(Peters) [Dutch] solo voice,gtr/gtr
solo (1-2nd degr.) HARMONIA HU-1862
f.s. notation: 2 treb-staffs
(accomp is gtr solo-pt)   (121)

KERSTLIEDEREN VOOR GITAARSOLO *CC12U,
carol
(Gerits) [Dutch] gtr,opt solo voice

(1-2nd degr.) TEESELING 170 f.s.
notation: 1 treb clef   (122)

LAUTENSPIELER, DER, NO. 1 *Xmas,carol
(Funck) [Ger] solo voice,gtr,opt fl
(1-2nd degr.) sc FIDULA f.s.
contains: Es Ist Ein Ros'
Entsprungen; I Saw Three Ships,
"Es Kommt Ein Schiff"; O
Tannenbaum   (123)

LICHTERBAUM, DER *CC20U,Xmas,carol
(Hintermeyer) [Ger] solo voice,gtr
(2-3rd degr.) sc PREISSLER JP-7003
f.s.   (124)

LIED UND GITARRE, 40 DEUTSCHE UND
AUSLANDISCHE VOLKSLIEDER, VOL. 1
(Teuchert) (1-3rd degr.) sc,pt
SCHMIDT,H 97 f.s. 32 pcs. for solo
voice, gtr or 2gtr; 8 pcs for solo
voice, gtr; Suppl.: arr for gtr I
(single line playing) of solo voice
pt; Vol.I:18 pcs
contains: Ya Se Van Los Pastores,
"Pastores, Los" (solo voice,gtr)   (125)

LIED- UND GITARRENSPIEL, VOLKS- UND
TANZLIEDER, VOL. I *folk song
(Bresgen; Zanoskar) [Ger] solo voice,
gtr (3rd degr.) sc SCHOTT 5414 f.s.
30 arr + orig pcs; contains works
by: Anon. (8), Zuccalmaglio (2),
Rathgeber, Schulz (2), Albert,
Bresgen
contains: Ihr Kinderlein Kommet;
Still, Still, Still   (126)

LIED- UND GITARRENSPIEL, VOLKS- UND
TANZLIEDER, VOL. II *folk song
(Bresgen; Zanoskar) [Ger] solo voice,
gtr (3rd degr.) sc SCHOTT 5415 f.s.
30 arr. + orig. pcs.; contains
works by: Rathgeber, Anon. (7),
Weber (3), Zelter, Reinhardt (2),
Steuerlein, Praetorius, Telemann,
Krieger
contains: O Tannenbaum; Bach,
Johann Sebastian, Gib Dich
Zufrieden, BWV 460 (from
Schemelli's Gesangbuch); Bach,
Johann Sebastian, Guldne Sonne,
Die, BWV 451 (from Schemelli's
Gesangbuch); Bach, Johann
Sebastian, Ich Steh An Deiner
Krippen Hier, BWV 469 (from
Schemelli's Gesangbuch); Bach,
Johann Sebastian, Tag Ist Hin,
Der, BWV 447 (from Schemelli's
Gesangbuch); Gruber, Franz Xaver,
Stille Nacht   (127)

LIEDER DER WEIHNACHT ZUR GITARRE
*CC21U,Xmas,carol
(Nelissen-Nicolai) [Ger] solo voice,
gtr (1-2nd degr.) sc GERIG HG-249
f.s.   (128)

LIEDER UM WEIHNACHT *CC18U,Xmas,carol
(Kammerling) [Ger] solo voice,gtr/gtr
solo (2-4th degr.) sc TONGER 1645
f.s. Rund Um Die Gitarre, Vol. V   (129)

NOELS DE PROVENCE *CC10U,Xmas,carol
(Muller; Theunen-Seidl) [Fr] solo
voice,gtr (2-3rd degr.) sc MAURER
f.s. arr   (130)

O JUBEL, O FREUD, WEIHNACHTSLIEDER ZUR
GITARRE *CC31U,Xmas,carol
(Zschiesche) solo voice,gtr (3rd
degr.) sc MOSELER f.s. orig words
(7 languages) + Ger transl; also
published by VOGGEN   (131)

O SANCTISSIMA, 10 WEIHNACHTSLIEDER AUS
ITALIEN, ENGLAND, SPANIEN UND
FRANKREICH *Xmas,carol
(Ragossnig) (4-5th degr., orig words)
sc ZIMMER. ZM-1719 f.s.   (132)

PRZY CHOINCE, KOLEDY W LATWYM UKLADZIE
NA GITARE *CC25U,Xmas,carol,Polish
(Podobinski) [Polish] gtr,opt solo
voice (3rd degr.) POLSKIE f.s. arr;
notation: treb-staff   (133)

RINKE RANKE ROSENSCHEIN; 77
KINDERLIEDER *folk song
(Schaller) [Ger] solo voice,gtr (1-
3rd degr.) sc BAREN. 2893 f.s. arr
+ orig pcs; contains works by:
Schmid, Schaller (4), Franck, Anon.
(3), Schulz, A. Weber, Pudelko (3),
Reichardt
contains: ABC-Krippenlied; Alle
Jahre Wieder; Drei Konige Fuhret
Die Gottliche Hand; Ihr
Kinderlein Kommet; Joseph, Lieber
Joseph Mein; Weinacht, Wie Bist
Do Schon   (134)

RODRIGO, JOAQUIN (1902-   )
Villancicos *Xmas,carol
[Span/Eng] solo voice,gtr (6th
degr.) sc SCHOTT 10705-10707 f.s.
contains: Aire Y Donaire;
Coplillas De Belen, "Carols Of
Bethlehem"; Pastorcito Santo,
"Holy Shepherd Boy"   (135)

SING CHRISTMAS CAROLS *CC14U,Xmas,
carol
(Duarte) [Eng] solo voice,gtr (3rd
degr.) sc SCHOTT GA-219 f.s. Guitar
Accompaniment - The Easy Way,
Suppl. 2; notation of gtr-pt: treb-
clef + diag   (136)

SING NEGRO SPIRITUALS
(Duarte) [Eng] solo voice,gtr (3rd
degr.) sc SCHOTT 11076 f.s. 12
pcs.; Guitar Accompaniment - The
Easy Way, Suppl. 1; Notation of gtr
pt: tr-clef + diagrams
contains: Mary Had A Baby, Yes Lord   (137)

SINGENDES, KLINGENDES OSTERREICH *folk
song
(Hammerschmied) [Austrian] solo
voice,gtr (2-3rd degr.) min sc
DOBLINGER 05923 f.s. 60 pcs
contains: Gruber, Franz Xaver,
Stille Nacht   (138)

SONNE, KOMM, EIN GITARRESPIELBUCH FUR
KINDER, 1-4. UNTERRICHTSJAHR *folk
song
(Ratz, Martin) [Ger] solo voice,gtr/
1-4gtr (single line playing/1-3rd
degr.) sc DEUTSCHER 32001 f.s. 162
arr + orig pcs; contains works by:
Schuffenhauer (2), Krug (4), Konig
(8), Ratz (22), Asriel (5), Quadt
(9), Rosenfeld (2), Haydn, Schumann
(3), Gorischk, Helmut, Wohlgemuth,
Schwaen, Schoendlinger for gtr;
Friemert (2), Buse, W.A. Mozart
(3), Beethoven, Berges,
Schuffenhauer, Hecht-Wieber for 2
gtr; Eberwein, Stephani for 3 gtr;
anon., naumilkat for 4 gtr or solo
voice(s), gtr; Skodova (2), Silcher
(2), Wendt, Friemert (2), Kern,
Krug (2), Pormova, Rodl, Hartung,
Nynkowa, Schuffenhauer, Hein,
Richter (3), W. Bender (2), Helmut,
Naumilkat for solo voice, gtr; also
contains Christmas music by:
Helmut, Schuffenhauer, Wohlgemuth
for gtr or solo voice, gtr; W.
Bender, Helmut, Naumilkat, for solo
voice, gtr
contains: Bach, Johann Sebastian,
Minuet in G minor, BWV Anh. 115
(2gtr) (A min,single line
playing); Bach, Johann Sebastian,
Piece In F, "Aria", BWV Anh.131
(2gtr) (single line playing);
Bach, Johann Sebastian, Polonaise
in G minor, BWV Anh. 119 (2gtr)
(A min,single line playing) (139)

SPAANSE VOLKSLIEDEREN, 3 (3 SPANISH
FOLKSONGS)
(Visser) [Span/Eng] solo voice,gtr
(3rd degr.) sc HARMONIA 1255 f.s.
contains: A La Virgen De Los
Dolores; Via Crucis; Villancico   (140)

STERNE UBER STILLEN STRASZEN, NEUE
LIEDER ZUR WEIHNACHT *CC25U,Xmas,
carol
(Henze) [Ger] gtr (2nd degr.) sc
HOFMEISTER T-4143 f.s. arr + 1 orig
pce; contains works by: Wohlgemuth
(5), Muller, Naumilkat, Kohler (2),
Kochan, Werzlau, B. Henze, Meusel
(2) for solo voice, gtr; 11 pcs.
including a version for gtr solo; 1
pce. with opt 2nd solo voice   (141)

UNSERE SCHONSTEN WEIHNACHTSLIEDER ZUR
GITARRE *Xmas,carol
(Schwarz-Reiflingen) [Ger] solo
voice,gtr (1-3rd degr.) sc ZIMMER.
Z-11878 f.s. 15 pcs
contains: Bach, Johann Sebastian,
Lobt Gott, Ihr Christen
Allzugleich [Chorales], BWV 375   (142)

UNSERE WEIHNACHTSLIEDER *Xmas,carol
(Gotze) [Ger] solo voice,gtr/treb
inst,gtr (2-3rd degr.) sc SCHOTT
4361 f.s. 42 pcs; also available in
gtr solo ed
contains: Bach, Johann Sebastian,
Lobt Gott, Ihr Christen,
Allzugleich. Chorale, BWV 375   (143)

VILLANCICOS POPULARES, VOL. I *Xmas,
carol
(Angel) [Span] solo voice,gtr (4-6th
degr.) UNION ESP. 19269-1 f.s.
contains: Barbas De San Jose, Las;
Campana Sobre Campana; Gruber,
Franz Xaver, Stille Nacht, "Noche
De Paz"; Wade, John F., Adeste

VILLANCICOS POPULARES, VOL. II *Xmas,
carol
(Angel) [Span] solo voice,gtr (4-6th
degr.) UNION ESP. 19269-2 f.s.
contains: Alla, Sota Una Penya,
"Alli, Bajo Una Pena"; Desembre
Congelat, Lo, "Helado Diciembre,
El"; Noy De La Mare, El, "Hijo De
La Virgen, El"; Sant Jose Y La
Mare De Deu, "Sand Jose Y La
Virgen"; Tres Pastorets, Els,
"Los Tres Pastorcillas"   (145)

VILLANCICOS POPULARES, VOL. III *Xmas,
carol
(Angel) [Span] solo voice,gtr (4-6th
degr.) UNION ESP. 19269-3 f.s.
contains: Corre Al Portalico; Esta
Noche Nace El Nino; Gatatumba;
Pandereta Suena, Una   (146)

VOLKSLIEDER *folk song
(Henze) [Ger] solo voice,gtr (1-4th
degr.) sc HOFMEISTER T-4011 $4.50
55 pcs.; Das Gitarrespiel, Vol. XI;
contains works by: Anon. (18),
Silcher, Fabricius (2),
Zuccalmaglio (2), Adam de la Hale,
Burki, Gersbach, Nicolai, Greef,
Zelter, Isaac, Nageli
contains: O Tannenbaum   (147)

WEIHNACHT - 8 ALTE LIEDER *Xmas,carol
(Scharff) [Ger] 3rec, gtr or solo
voice, 2rec, gtr or solo voice, gtr
or gtr solo (3-4th degr.,
Zeitschrift Fur Spielmusik, No.15)
sc MOECK ZFS-15 f.s.   (148)

WEIHNACHTS-ALBUM, SAMMLUNG DER
BELIEBTESTEN WEIHNACHTSLIEDER
*CC22U,Xmas,carol
(Ruch) [Ger] solo voice,gtr (2-3rd
degr.) sc GERIG GG-88A f.s.   (149)

11 WEIHNACHTSLIEDER *CC11U
(Schaller) [Ger] solo voice,gtr (4th
degr.) sc PREISSLER B 13 f.s. Das
Gitarrenwerk, Series B, No. 13   (150)

WEIHNACHTSLIEDER *CC29U,Xmas,carol
(Steigenberger) [Ger] solo voice,gtr
(2-3rd degr.) sc NOETZEL 1211 f.s.   (151)

WEIHNACHTSLIEDER AUS DEUTSCHLAND UND
OSTERREICH *Xmas,carol,Austrian/
Ger
(Schafer-Stetka) [Ger] S rec,gtr,opt
solo voice (3rd degr.) sc,pt
DOBLINGER f.s. 14 pcs; notation: 2
treb-staffs; rec pt is solo voice
pt
contains: Bach, Johann Sebastian,
Ich Steh' An Deiner Krippen Hier,
BWV 469 (from Schemelli's
Gesangbuch)   (152)

WEIHNACHTSLIEDER ZUR GITARRE *CC25U,
Xmas,carol
(Schwarz-Reiflingen) [Ger] solo
voice,gtr/gtr solo (2-3rd degr.) sc
SIKORSKI 306 f.s. arr + 1 orig pce   (153)

WEIHNACHTSZEIT - FROHLICHE ZEIT,
ALTBEKANNTE UND NEUERE
WEIHNACHTSLIEDER *CC28U,Xmas,carol
(Cleff) [Ger] solo voice,gtr/gtr solo
(2-4th degr.) sc VOGGEN f.s.
notation for gtr solo: treb-staff;
notation for solo voice, gtr: 2
treb-staffs   (154)

WOHLAN DIE ZEIT IST KOMMEN, EIN VOLKS-
UND ZEITLIEDERBUCH FUR EINZEL-UND
GRUPPENGESANG *CC161U,Xmas,carol
(Peter; Muller) [Ger] solo voice,gtr
(3rd degr.) sc HOFMEISTER W-28 f.s.
contains 8 Christmas pieces   (155)

ZANOSKAR, HUBERT
Neue Gitarren-Schule, Vol. I, Suppl.:
Ubungen Und Spielstucke
[Ger] gtr quarto SCHOTT 5667 f.s.
46p.; 1969; contains: Bach,
Johann Sebastian, Minuet, BWV
Anh. 115, from Anna Magdalena
Bach Notenbuchlein (1725), No.5,
In G Minor, for 2 gtr; Minuet,
BWV Anh. 116, from Anna Magdalena
Bach Notenbuchlein (1725), No.7,
In G, for 2 gtr; Ich Steh An
Deiner Krippen Hier, BWV 469, in
C minor, for solo voice and gtr
from Schemelli's Gesangbuch (156)

IV/IIC1-Coll   Duet Collections for Guitar and Voice

SONNE, KOMM, EIN GITARRESPIELBUCH FUR
   KINDER, 1-4. UNTERRICHTSJAHR *folk
   song
   (Ratz, Martin) [Ger] solo voice,gtr/
   1-4gtr (single line playing/1-3rd
   degr.) sc DEUTSCHER 32001 f.s. 162
   arr + orig pcs; contains works by:
   Schuffenhauer (2), Krug (4), Konig
   (8), Ratz (22), Asriel (5), Quadt
   (9), Rosenfeld (2), Haydn, Schumann
   (3), Gorischk, Helmut, Wohlgemuth,
   Schwaen, Schoendlinger for gtr;
   Friemert (2), Buse, W.A. Mozart
   (3), Beethoven, Berges,
   Schuffenhauer, Hecht-Wieber for 2
   gtr; Eberwein, Stephani for 3 gtr;
   anon., naumilkat for 4 gtr or solo
   voice(s), gtr; Skodova (2), Silcher
   (2), Wendt, Friemert (2), Kern,
   Krug (2), Pormova, Rodl, Hartung,
   Nynkowa, Schuffenhauer, Hein,
   Richter (3), W. Bender (2), Helmut,
   Naumilkat for solo voice, gtr; also
   contains Christmas music by:
   Helmut, Schuffenhauer, Wohlgemuth
   for gtr or solo voice, gtr; W.
   Bender, Helmut, Naumilkat, for solo
   voice, gtr
   contains: Bach, Johann Sebastian,
      Minuet in G minor, BWV Anh. 115
      (2gtr) (A min,single line
      playing); Bach, Johann Sebastian,
      Piece In F, "Aria", BWV Anh.131
      (2gtr) (single line playing);
      Bach, Johann Sebastian, Polonaise
      in G minor, BWV Anh. 119 (2gtr)
      (A min,single line playing) (157)

IV/IIC2   Trios for Guitar, Voice, and Another Instrument

ALTE WEIHNACHTSMUSIK, SPIELSTUCKE UND
   LIEDER *Xmas,carol
   (Schlensog) (3rd degr.) sc MOECK
   ZFS-39 f.s. 12 pcs for S recs or
   treb insts and solo voice(s); 2 pcs
   with gtr: no.3 for solo voice, rec,
   gtr; no. 5 for 3 recs, gtr;
   Zeitschrift Fur Spielmusik No. 39
   contains: Bach, Johann Sebastian,
   Auf, Auf! Die Rechte Zeit Ist
   Hier, "Adventslied", BWV 440
   (from Schemelli's Gesangbuch)
   (solo voice,rec,gtr) (C maj);
   Bach, Johann Sebastian, Ich Steh'
   An Deiner Krippe Hier, "An Der
   Krippe", BWV 469 (from
   Schemelli's Gesangbuch) (3rec,
   gtr)   (158)

ANONYMOUS
   Allerlei Volkslieder *CC50UL
   (Wolter) [Ger] 2rec and gtr; solo
   voice, rec, and gtr (1-2nd degr.)
   sc,pt MOECK 2030 f.s. contains 8
   Christmas carols   (159)

BACH, JOHANN SEBASTIAN (1685-1750)
   Geistliche Lieder (from Schemelli's
   Gesangbuch)
   (Schaller, Erwin) solo voice,rec,
   gtr (3-4th degr.) voc sc,pts
   HASLINGER HBR-18 f.s. Haslinger
   Blockfloten Reihe No. 18
   contains: Es Ist Vollbracht, BWV
      458; Ich Steh An Deiner Krippen
      Hier, BWV 469; Kommt, Seelen
      Dieser Tag, BWV 479; Mein Jesu,
      Was Fur Seelenweh, BWV 487; O
      Jesulein Suss, BWV 493   (160)

BAUMANN, HANS
   Bergbauernweihnacht *CC15U,Xmas,
   carol
   (Biebl) [Ger] for 2rec, gtr (4),
   2rec, unison or 2-pt cor (partly
   solo voice ad lib), gtr (9), rec,
   solo voice, gtr (2) (1-2nd degr.)
   sc MOSELER f.s.   (161)

BEHREND, SIEGFRIED (1933-   )
   Weihnachtsgeschichte *Xmas,carol
   solo voice,perc,gtr ZIMMER. ZM-1897
   f.s.   (162)

BURKHART, FRANZ (1902-1978)
   Adventlieder, 3 *Xmas,carol
   (Scheit) [Ger] solo voice,ob/S rec,
   gtr (3rd degr., Gitarre-
   Kammermusik, No. 3) sc,pts
   DOBLINGER GKM-3 f.s.   (163)

FROHLICHE WEIHNACHT, EIN
   WEIHNACHTSLIEDER-ALBUM *CC29U,
   Xmas,carol
   (Stolzenwald) [Ger] 2 solo voices,gtr
   (2-3rd degr.) sc APOLLO 2191 f.s.
                                    (164)

GITARRE ZUM WEIHNACHTSLIED *CC27U,
   Xmas,carol
   (Wolki) [Ger] 1-2solo voice,gtr (1-
   2nd degr.) sc APOLLO 2232 f.s. arr
                                    (165)

HAUSLICHE WEIHNACHT *Xmas,carol/folk
   song
   (Gerwig) [Ger] solo voice,1-3gtr
   (single line playing/1-3rd degr.)
   sc LIENAU 1407 f.s. ;Das Spiel Der
   Lauteninstrumente, Series II,
   Spielbuch 4; 19pcs; contains works
   by: Praetorius (3), Beutner, Anon.
   (5), Braun
   contains: Bach, Johann Sebastian,
      Ich Steh' An Deiner Krippe Hier,
      BWV 469 (from Schemelli's
      Gesangbuch); Bach, Johann
      Sebastian, Liebes Herz, Bedenke
      Doch, BWV 482 (from Schemelli's
      Gesangbuch); Bach, Johann
      Sebastian, O Jesulein Suss, BWV
      493 (from Schemelli's Gesangbuch)
                                    (166)

LAUTENSPIELER, DER, NO. 1 *Xmas,carol
   (Funck) [Ger] solo voice,gtr,opt fl
   (1-2nd degr.) sc FIDULA f.s.
   contains: Es Ist Ein Ros'
   Entsprungen; I Saw Three Ships,
   "Es Kommt Ein Schiff"; O
   Tannenbaum   (167)

O WUNDER, WAS WILL DAS BEDEUTEN,
   LIEDERSAMMLUNG ZUR ADVENTSZEIT
   *CC25U,Xmas,carol
   (Draths) 1 or 2 S rec or 2 solo
   voices, opt gt SCHOTT 5750 f.s.
                                    (168)

WEIHNACHTSLIEDER, 5 *Xmas,carol
   (Twittenhof) [Ger] (1-2nd degr.) sc
   BAREN. MP-37 f.s. Musica Practica,
   No. 37
   contains: Auf, Ihr Hirtenleut (gtr,
   solo voice,2rec); Lasst Uns Das
   Kindlein Wiegen (gtr,solo voice,
   2rec); Laufet, Ihr Hirten (gtr,
   solo voice,2rec); Schlaf, Mein
   Kindelein (gtr,solo voice,2rec);
   Was Soll Es Bedeuten (gtr,solo
   voice,rec)   (169)

WINTERWEISSE WEIHNACHT, ALTE UND NEUE
   LIEDER UM DIE WEIHNACHTSZEIT
   *CC24U,Xmas,carol
   (Kramer) [Ger] 2 solo voices or 2
   treb insts or solo voice + treb
   inst gtr (2-3rd degr.) sc HARTH
   2314 f.s. arr + orig pcs; notation
   of voices: 1 treb-clef + words
                                    (170)

IV/IIC3   Quartets for Guitar, Voice, and Other Instruments

BAUMANN, HANS
   Bergbauernweihnacht *CC15U,Xmas,
   carol
   (Biebl) [Ger] for 2rec, gtr (4),
   2rec, unison or 2-pt cor (partly
   solo voice ad lib), gtr (9), rec,
   solo voice, gtr (2) (1-2nd degr.)
   sc MOSELER f.s.   (171)

BLARR, OSKAR GOTTLIEB (1934-   )
   Thema Weihnachten, 3 Chansons *Xmas,
   carol
   sc,solo pt,cor pts BOSSE BE-289
   f.s., ipa
   contains: Begebenheit (speaking
   voice,pno,db, ampl-gtr);
   Botschaft, Die (solo voice,pno,
   db/perc); Wenn Das Vollkommene
   Kommt (S solo,4pt cor&cong,trp,
   tenor sax,pno,db)   (172)

DIETRICH, CHRISTOPH
   Vorspruch Zu Einem Weihnachtsspiel
   *Xmas,carol
   [Ger] 2 solo voices,gtr, precentor
   (3-4th degr.) sc VOGGEN f.s.
                                    (173)

GRUBER, FRANZ XAVER (1787-1863)
   Stille Nacht *Xmas,carol
   (Schaller) [Ger] solo voice,2rec,
   gtr (2nd degr., Musik In Der
   Familie) sc,pts HELBLING 3091
   f.s.   (174)

HAUSLICHE WEIHNACHT *Xmas,carol/folk
   song
   (Gerwig) [Ger] solo voice,1-3gtr
   (single line playing/1-3rd degr.)
   sc LIENAU 1407 f.s. ;Das Spiel Der
   Lauteninstrumente, Series II,
   Spielbuch 4; 19pcs; contains works
   by: Praetorius (3), Beutner, Anon.
   (5), Braun
   contains: Bach, Johann Sebastian,
      Ich Steh' An Deiner Krippe Hier,
      BWV 469 (from Schemelli's
      Gesangbuch); Bach, Johann
      Sebastian, Liebes Herz, Bedenke
      Doch, BWV 482 (from Schemelli's
      Gesangbuch); Bach, Johann
      Sebastian, O Jesulein Suss, BWV
      493 (from Schemelli's Gesangbuch)
                                    (175)

WEIHNACHT - 8 ALTE LIEDER *Xmas,carol
   (Scharff) [Ger] 3rec, gtr or solo
   voice, 2rec, gtr or solo voice, gtr
   or gtr solo (3-4th degr.,
   Zeitschrift Fur Spielmusik, No.15)
   sc MOECK ZFS-15 f.s.   (176)

WEIHNACHTSLIEDER, 5 *Xmas,carol
   (Twittenhof) [Ger] (1-2nd degr.) sc
   BAREN. MP-37 f.s. Musica Practica,
   No. 37
   contains: Auf, Ihr Hirtenleut (gtr,
   solo voice,2rec); Lasst Uns Das
   Kindlein Wiegen (gtr,solo voice,
   2rec); Laufet, Ihr Hirten (gtr,
   solo voice,2rec); Schlaf, Mein
   Kindelein (gtr,solo voice,2rec);
   Was Soll Es Bedeuten (gtr,solo
   voice,rec)   (177)

IV/IIC4   Quintets for Guitar, Voice, and Other Instruments

CHANTS DE FRANCE ET D'AILLEURS, 20
   *folk song
   (Sanchez) (3-5th degr.) sc CHOUDENS
   20.243 f.s. 20 arr + orig pcs; orig
   words; contains works by:
   Despourrins, Taburot, Encina,
   Anon., Attaignant, Sanchez (6) for
   SATB soli, gtr (17); female solo,
   male solo, fl, tamb, gtr (1); 3
   solo voices (1); 5 solo voices (1)
   contains: Sanchez, Blas, Toca El
      Pandora, Maria (gtr,SATB)   (178)

DEUTSCHE WEIHNACHTSWEISEN *CC7U,Xmas,
   carol
   (Bresgen) [Ger] 3rec, gtr (3 pcs);
   solo voice, gtr (1 pce) (single
   line playing/1st degr.) sc MOECK
   ZFS-331 f.s. Zeitschrift Fur
   Spielmusik, No. 331   (179)

IV/IIC4-Coll   Quintet Collections for Guitar, Voice, and Other Instruments

CHANTS DE FRANCE ET D'AILLEURS, 20
   *folk song
   (Sanchez) (3-5th degr.) sc CHOUDENS
   20.243 f.s. 20 arr + orig pcs; orig
   words; contains works by:
   Despourrins, Taburot, Encina,
   Anon., Attaignant, Sanchez (6) for
   SATB soli, gtr (17); female solo,
   male solo, fl, tamb, gtr (1); 3
   solo voices (1); 5 solo voices (1)
   contains: Sanchez, Blas, Toca El
      Pandora, Maria (gtr,SATB)   (180)

IV/IIC5 Music for School Ensemble/Orchestra with Guitar and Voice

BACH, JOHANN SEBASTIAN (1685-1750)
Kleines Weihnachtsoratorium Mit
Johann Sebastian Bach
(Oberborbeck, Felix) [Ger] (single
line playing/1st degr.) sc MOECK
ZFS144 f.s. Zeitschrift Fur
Spielmusik, No. 144
contains: Bereite Dich, Zion, BWV
248,No.4 (from Weihnachts-
Oratorium) (gtr,3rec); Ehre Sei
Gott In Der Hohe. Canon, BWV
1078,No.7 (gtr,inst) (F maj);
Vom Himmel Hoch, Da Komm Ich
Her. Chorale, BWV 248,No.9
(from Weihnachts-Oratorium)
(solo voice,gtr,3rec)   (181)

BAUMANN, HANS
Bergbauernweihnacht *CC15U,Xmas,
carol
(Biebl) [Ger] for 2rec, gtr (4),
2rec, unison or 2-pt cor (partly
solo voice ad lib), gtr (9), rec,
solo voice, gtr (2) (1-2nd degr.)
sc MOESELER f.s.   (182)

BONNAL, ERMEND
Enfant Crie En Galilee, Un *Xmas,
carol
SSSA,opt gtr sc OUVRIERS EO-801
f.s.   (183)

Princes d'Orient, 3, Noel *Xmas,
carol
SSA,opt gtr sc OUVRIERS EO-802 f.s. (184)

BRESGEN, CESAR (1913-   )
Christkindl-Kumedi, Ein Geistliches
Komodienspiel Aus Bayern *Xmas,
carol
[Ger] gtr,jr cor&mix cor, solo
voices,2A rec,T rec,ob/clar,timp,
perc,pno,3vln,vcl,db [75'] (ed
for prof soloists available)
SCHOTT 5443 sc rent, kbd pt,cor
pts,pts,pno red   (185)
[Ger] gtr,jr cor&mix cor,5 solo
voices/8 speaking voices,2A rec,T
rec,ob/clar,timp,perc,pno,3vln,
vcl,db,3trp,3trom,hpsd/harp [90']
(ed for prof soloists available)
SCHOTT 5443 sc rent, kbd pt,cor
pts,pts,pno red   (186)

CHRISTMAS TIME *CC4U,Xmas,carol
(Schutte) [Eng] 6 groups of insts: pt
1: S rec I, solo voice; pt 2: S rec
II; pt 3: vln, A rec; and-or pt 3a:
b-flat inst; pt 4: gtr; and-or pt
4a: vcl, bsn, db HARMONIA 1883 f.s.
rode reeks: Een huis vol muziek
(187)

DEUTSCH, WALTER (1923-   )
Kleine Weihnachtskantate, Nach Alten
Texten Und Weisen Aus Osterreich
*Xmas,carol
speaking voice& solo voices,cor,2S
rec/A rec/gtr/pno,2vln,opt vcl
(Sing- Und Spielmusik; free arr
of melodies and words from 1780-
1850; scenic performance also
possible) UNIVER. f.s. sc 14316,
pts 14317A-F, pt 14317G, kbd pt
14317H, cor pts 14318   (188)

ES IST EIN ROS ENTSPRUNGEN *CC12U,
Xmas,carol
(Heyden) [Ger] 1-3rec,treb inst/gtr,
gtr,2pt cor (1-2nd degr.) sc NAGELS
EN-546 f.s. arr + orig pcs; Nagels
Laute- Und Gitarre-Archiv, No. 546
(189)

FROHE BOTSCHAFT, LIEDER ZUR ADVENTS-
UND WEIHNACHTSZEIT *Xmas,carol
(Draths) 4rec/strings, solo voices,
opt gtr SCHOTT f.s. sc 5895, pts
5938   (190)

HAUS, KARL (1928-   )
Jetzt Ist Die Rechte Freudenzeit,
Short Christmas Cantata *Xmas,
carol
SAB,1-2rec,fl/ob,2vln/gtr,glock,
metallophone,triangle/cym sc
MERSEBURGER EM-1648 f.s.   (191)

HEIDSCHI BUMBEIDSCHI BUM-BUM, DIE
ALLERSCHONSTEN WEIHNACHTSLIEDER,
VOL. I: PNO ED. (WITH TEXT)
*CC28U,Xmas,carol
(Blasl) [Ger] sc UNIVER. 15902 f.s.
vols can be used separately or in
combination   (192)

HEIDSCHI BUMBEIDSCHI BUM-BUM, DIE
ALLERSCHONSTEN WEIHNACHTSLIEDER,
VOL. II: INST ED., FOR 3- OR 4-PT
ENSEMBLES *CC28U,Xmas,carol
(Blasl) [Ger] (single line playing/
1st degr.) sc UNIVER. 15903 f.s.
vols can be used separately or in
combination   (193)

HEIDSCHI BUMBEIDSCHI BUM-BUM, DIE
ALLERSCHONSTEN WEIHNACHTSLIEDER,
VOL. III: VOCAL ED *CC28U,Xmas,
carol
(Blasl) [Ger] sc UNIVER. 15904 f.s.
vols can be used separately or in
combination   (194)

HENSEL, WALTHER (1887-1956)
Susaninne, Eine Kleine
Weihnachtskantate *Xmas,carol
[Ger] 3-6pt mix cor&unis jr cor&
cong,fl,vln,vla,vcl,gtr, speaking
voices (2-3rd degr.) sc BAREN.
BA-59 f.s.   (195)

KERSTLIEDJES OM MEE TE SPELEN EN TE
ZINGEN *CC8U,Xmas,carol
(Beijersbergen van Henegouwen)
[Dutch] 4 groups of insts: pt 1:
solo voice, S rec, fl, vln, ob,
mand; pt 2: S rec, vln, fl, ob,
mand; pt 3: A rec, mandola,
vln; pt 3a: gtr, accord (1-2nd
degr.) sc HARMONIA 1564 f.s. arr;
Speel en zing je mee?, vol. III;
Rode reeks: Een huis vol muziek
(196)

KOCH, JOHANNES H.E. (1918-   )
Herr Christ, Der Einig Gotts Sohn
*Xmas,carol
solo voice&opt solo voice,2glock,
2xylo,bass inst,gtr,vcl,timp sc
HANSSLER HE-12.207 f.s.   (197)

MUSIK IM JAHRESKREIS
(Korda; Schnabel) [Ger] (2nd degr.)
sc OSTER 6781-2 f.s. 23 pcs;
contains works by various composers
for various insts; includes 9
folksongs with gtr
contains: Lasst Uns Das Kindelein
Wiegen   (198)

NEUMANN, FRIEDRICH (1915-   )
Kanonische Kantate Zur Weihnacht
*Xmas,carol
[Eng/Ger] solo voice,cor,2S rec,A
rec,vln,vcl,gtr, Stabspiele (1-
2nd degr., Sing- und Spielmusik)
UNIVER. f.s. sc 15004, cor pts
15005A, pts 15005B-C   (199)

REUSCH, FRITZ (1896-1970)
Christkindelspiel, Das, Ein
Weihnachtsspiel *Xmas,carol
[Ger] 15 solo voices,cor,2-3treb
inst,gtr/lute,opt perc [15'-20']
(Bausteine, No. 113) study sc
SCHOTT B-113 f.s.   (200)

ROESELING, KASPAR (1894-1961)
Kreisspiel Von Der Geburt Christi
*Xmas,carol
fl,ob,clar,tamb,glock,gtr/lute,vln
I,vln II,vln III,vln IV,vla,jr
cor [40'] pno red SCHOTT 3284
f.s., ipa   (201)

RYBA, JAN JAKUB SIMON (1765-1815)
Gloria, Aus Der Tschechischen
Weihnachtsmesse *Xmas,carol
(Maase) 2 female soli/2 child soli,
3pt mix cor,pno/2vln/2rec,vcl/
gtr,glock (arr) sc PELIKAN PE-940
f.s., ipa   (202)

SPITTA, HEINRICH (1902-1972)
Herbergssuche Der Maria "O Maria
Traurige", Weihnachtsmusik Um Ein
Lied Aus Der Gottschee *Xmas,
carol
SA&men cor,fl,kbd/gtr sc MOSELER
f.s.   (203)

Leichte Weihnachtskantaten, 10,
Weihnachtsmusiken Um Lieder
*Op.93,Xmas,carol
[Ger] sc MOSELER f.s.
contains: Als Ich Bei Meinen
Schafen Wacht, Um Ein Lied Aus
Oberschlesien (No. 8) (A rec/
fl,gtr/lute/vla,vcl); Ei Was
Grosses Wunder, Um Ein Lied Vom
Eichsfeld (No. 5) (2A rec,gtr/
lute/vla/vcl); Mit Gott So
Wollen Wir Lobn Und Ehrn; 3
Konig Von Saba Kommen (No. 7)
(2fl/2vln,kbd/gtr)   (204)

Weihnachtliche Liedkantate *Xmas,
carol
"Vom Himmel Hoch, Ihr Englein
Kommt" [Ger] opt solo voices,3pt
mix cor/3 eq voices,kbd/gtr,vln

SPITTA, HEINRICH (cont'd.)
I,vln II,vcl sc MOSELER f.s., ipa
(205)

STERN, ALFRED BERNARD (1901-   )
Weihnachts-Singspiel Nach Alten
Liedern, Ein *CC38U,Xmas,carol
[Ger] fl,ob,clar,gtr,lute,strings,
solo voice,2-4pt mix cor&3pt wom
cor&3pt jr cor (2nd degr.) sc,pts
NAGELS EN-1160 f.s. Nagels Laute-
Und Gitarre-Archiv, No. 1160
(206)

STERN, HERMANN (1912-1978)
Es Ist Ein Ros' Entsprungen *Xmas,
carol
[Ger] S rec,xylo,vcl/db,gtr,SA&men
cor (single line playing) sc
HANSSLER HE-8.042 f.s. contains
also: Nun Singet Und Seid Froh
(xylo/glock,A rec,vcl/db,gtr,SA&
men cor)   (207)

Gottes Sohn Ist Kommen *Xmas,carol
[Ger] A rec,vcl/db,gtr,SA&men cor
(single line playing) sc HANSSLER
HE-8.041 f.s. contains also:
Macht Hoch Die Tur, Die Tor Macht
Weit (without gtr)   (208)

WEIHNACHTSSTERN, DER, ALTE UND NEUE
LIEDER *Xmas,carol
(Langhans; Lau) solo voice/ solo
voices,2S rec,glock,xylo,
metallophone,vln/gtr,triangle,cym,
tamb,opt 2timp, Stabspiele sc
PELIKAN PE-813 f.s.   (209)

WUSTHOFF, KLAUS
Weihnachtskantate Fur Junge Leute
*Xmas,carol
[Ger] fl,2rec,gtr,elec gtr,elec
bass gtr,db,perc, solo voices, 3
4-6 pt mixed choruses pno red,
pts,sc MERSEBURGER EM-1650 f.s.
(210)

V Music for Large Groups (Other than School Ensembles/Orchestras)

V/i Ensemble and Orchestral Music with Guitar

ALCALAY, LUCIA
  Night-Club Pieces
  tenor sax,ampl gtr,elec org,perc,db
  [10'] MODERN rent   (1)

AMY, GILBERT (1936-   )
  Antiphonies Pour 2 Orchestres
  orch A: 1.2.2.1. baritone
    sax.0.0.0.0. 2perc, harp,
    strings; orch B:
    2.1.3.2.3sax.4.4.2.1. 6timp,
    2harp, cel, pno, gtr, strings
    [20'] LEMOINE f.s.   (2)

  Refrains, For Orchestra
  4.3.3.3. 4.3.3.1. timp,3perc,
    marimba,harp,cel,pno,ampl gtr,
    strings [15'] sc UNIVER. 15753
    f.s.   (3)

ANDRIESSEN, JURRIAAN (1925-   )
  Ars Antiquae Musicae; Casual Music
    For Connoisseurs And Amateurs
  fl,ob,trp,2horn,vla,perc,gtr sc
    DONEMUS f.s.   (4)

  Summer-Dances
  harp,gtr,9perc, +tuned perc [10']
    sc DONEMUS f.s.   (5)

  Symphony No. 5
    "Time Spirit, For Clarinet And
    Orchestra" 2.2.2.2. 4.0.3.1.
    perc,harp,pno,strings, pop group
    (Hamm, bass gtr, drums) [29']
    DONEMUS f.s.   (6)

ANDRIESSEN, LOUIS (1939-   )
  Hoketus
  gtr,2fl,2pno,elec pno,2bass gtr, 2
    conga dr [25'-50'] sc,cmplt ed
    DONEMUS f.s.   (7)

  Ittrospezione III
    "Concept I, Per 2 Pianisti E 3
    Gruppi Strumentali" 2pno, group
    1: clar in A, horn, tenor sax;
    group 2: 3bass trom; group 3:
    ampl gtr, db (5 strings) DONEMUS
    f.s.   (8)

  Nine Symphonies Of Beethoven, The,
    For Promenade Orchestra And Ice-
    Cream Bell
  2.2.2.2. 4.3.3.0. timp,perc,pno,
    ampl gtr,ampl bass gtr,strings sc
    DONEMUS f.s.   (9)

BANKS, DON (1923-   )
  Elizabethan Miniatures, Based On
    Music By Anonymous Elizabethan
    Composers
  fl,lute/gtr/harp,vla da gamba,
    strings SCHOTT f.s.
    contains: Almain; Carman's
      Whistle; Irish Ho-Hoane;
      Muscadin   (10)

BECKER, GUNTHER (1924-   )
  Correspondances II
  gtr,harp,hpsd,string quar [11']
    GERIG HG-729 f.s.   (11)

  Game For Nine
  fl,clar,bass clar,perc,vibra,gtr,
    vln,vla,vcl [9'] GERIG HG-501
    f.s.   (12)

BEDFORD, DAVID (1937-   )
  Ones Who Walked Away From Omelas, The
  fl,ob,clar,bsn,elec gtr,bass gtr,
    2vln,vla,vcl [25'] UNIVER. f.s.
    sc 16123, study sc 16124   (13)

  Star's End, For Rock Instruments And
    Orchestra
  3.3.3.3. 4.4.3.1. timp,gong,
    strings,ampl gtr solo,ampl bass
    gtr solo,perc solo [46'] sc
    UNIVER. 16039 f.s.   (14)

BERIO, LUCIANO (1925-   )
  Chemins II B, For Orchestra
  2.1.2.2.alto sax.tenor sax.
    2.3.2.1. vibra,3marimba,pno,elec
    org,elec gtr,6vla,4vcl,3db,vln
    solo [11'] sc UNIVER. 14948 f.s.
                                    (15)
  Chemins II C, For Bass Clarinet And
    Orchestra
  2.1.2.2.alto sax.tenor sax.
    2.3.2.1. vibra,3marimba,pno,elec
    org,elec gtr,6vla,4vcl,3db,clar
    solo [11'] sc UNIVER. 14948 f.s.
                                    (16)

BERNAL JIMENEZ, MIGUEL (1910-1956)
  Cartas De Mexico, 3
  2.2.2.2. 4.3.3.1. timp,perc,harp,
    4gtr,strings [13'] PEER rent (17)

BIALAS, GUNTER (1907-   )
  Romanzero
  3.2.2.3. 4.3.3.1. perc,harp,hpsd/
    pno,gtr,strings BAREN. BA-3693
    rent, min sc TP-109 f.s.   (18)

BIRTWISTLE, HARRISON (1934-   )
  World Is Discovered, The; 6
    Instrumental Pieces After
    Heinrich Isaac
  2fl,2ob,clar,basset horn/bass clar,
    2bsn,2horn,harp,gtr [12'] sc
    UNIVER. 12937 f.s., perf mat rent
                                    (19)

BLAKE WATKINS, MICHAEL (1948-   )
  Psallein
  2perc, 2gtr-g', 3gtr-e', basello
    [11'] NOVELLO f.s.   (20)

BOIS, ROB DU (1934-   )
  Concerto for Violin and Orchestra
  4.2.3.2.2sax. 4.3.2.1. perc,vibra,
    xylo,harp,pno/elec org,mand,2ampl
    gtr,strings,vln solo sc DONEMUS
    f.s.   (21)

  Concerto Pour Hrisanide, Le, For
    Piano And Orchestra
  2.2.1.2.tenor sax. 2.2.1.0. harp,
    acord,harmonica,mand,2ampl gtr,
    strings,pno solo sc DONEMUS f.s.
                                    (22)

BORSTLAP, DICK (1943-   )
  Echo, For Orchestra
  2.2.3.1. alto sax or tenor sax
    2.2.3.1., vibr, harp, elec org,
    ampl gtr, strings sc DONEMUS f.s.
                                    (23)

BOULEZ, PIERRE (1925-   )
  Domaines, For Clarinet And Orchestra
  1.1.0(bass clar).1.alto sax.
    1.1.4(alto trom,bass trom).0.
    marimba,harp,ampl gtr,2vln,2vla,
    2vcl,db,clar solo [29'] UNIVER.
    rent   (24)

  Eclat, For Orchestra
  gtr [8'] sc UNIVER. 14283 f.s. (25)
    alto fl,English horn,trp,trom,
    glock,tubular bells,vibra,harp,
    cel,cimbalom,2pno,mand,gtr,vla,
    vcl [8'] UNIVER. rent contains
    also: Multiples, For Orchestra
    (alto fl,basset horn,English
    horn,trp,trom,glock,tubular
    bells,vibra,harp,cel,cimbalom,
    2pno,mand,gtr,10vla,vcl) [17']
                                    (26)

BOYD, ANNE
  Voice Of The Phoenix, The
  4(2pic).3+English horn.4(bass
    clar).4. 4.3.2.1. timp,10perc,
    strings, ampl insts (harp, hpsd,
    pno, gtr), opt VCS-3 synthesizer
    [25'] sc,pts FABER rent   (27)

BURGHAUSER, JARMIL (1921-   )
  Reliefs, 7
  3.2+English horn.2+bass clar.2+
    contrabsn. 6.3.3.1. timp,4perc,
    xylo,harp,pno/cel,ampl gtr,
    strings [17'] sc ARTIA 1623 f.s.
                                    (28)

  Wege *CC8U
  timp,perc,harp,cel,ampl gtr,
    strings, ampl cimbalom study sc
    ARTIA 1668 f.s., perf mat rent
                                    (29)

BUSCHMANN, RAINER-GLEN (1928-   )
  Concerto Piccolo
  clar,gtr,db,perc,strings [14'] sc,
    pts BOSSE BE-301 f.s.   (30)

  Serenade, For Jazz Quartet And
    Chamber Orchestra
  fl,clar,tuba,perc,gtr,db,strings,
    jazz quar [10'] MODERN rent (31)

BUSSOTTI, SYLVANO (1931-   )
  Mit Einem Gewissen Sprechenden
    Ausdruck, For Chamber Orchestra
  1.1.2.1. 1.1.1.0. 4-5perc,harp,pno/
    cel,gtr,vln,vla,vcl,db [17'] sc
    MOECK 5010 f.s.   (32)

CANINO, BRUNO (1936-   )
  Cadenze, For Harpsichord And
    Instruments
  0.0.1.0. 0.1.0.0. perc,gtr,db,hpsd
    solo [10'] ZERBONI sc 5964 f.s.,
    pts 5965 rent   (33)

CERHA, FRIEDRICH (1926-   )
  Langegger Nachtmusik I, For Orchestra
  2.1+English horn.3.2.alto sax. 1+
    Wagner tuba.1+bass trp.1.1.
    5perc,harp,cel,hpsd,Hamm,mand,
    gtr,bass gtr,4vln,3vla,3vcl,db
    [12'] UNIVER. rent   (34)

CERVETTI, SERGIO (1940-   )
  Six Sequences For Dance, For Chamber
    Ensemble
  1.0.0.0. 1.0.0.0. 5perc,cel,pno,
    ampl gtr,vcl [13'] sc MOECK 5033
    f.s.   (35)

CLEMENTI, ALDO (1925-   )
  Reticolo 11
  glock,harp,cel,hpsd,harmonium,mand,
    gtr,2vln,vla,vcl ZERBONI sc 6251
    f.s., pts 6252 rent   (36)

CONYNGHAM, BARRY (1944-   )
  Water...Footsteps...Time
  harp,pno,tom-tom,ampl gtr,2orch sc
    UNIVER. 29060 f.s.   (37)

  Water-Footsteps-Times, For Four
    Instrumental Soloists And Two
    Orchestra
  each orch: 2.0.0.0. 2.2.2.1., ampl
    harp, pno, gtr, tam-tam, strings
    [19'30"] sc UNIVER. 29058 f.s.
                                    (38)

CSONIKA, PAUL (1905-   )
  Serenata, For Violoncello And
    Orchestra
  2.2.2.2. 2.2.0.0. timp,pno,acord,
    2gtr,strings,vcl solo [11'] PEER
    rent   (39)

DE GRANDIS, RENATO (1927-   )
  Antruiles
  1.0.0.0.tenor sax. 2.3.2.0. 2perc,
    marimba,vibra,xylo,harp,cel,pno,
    harmonica,ampl gtr,db BAREN.
    BA-4427 rent   (40)

DELAS, JOSE LUIS DE (1928-   )
  Eilanden, For Ten Instruments And
    Tape Recorder
  clar,perc,harp,cel,hpsd,harmonium,
    gtr,vln I,vln II,vla,electronic
    tape [13'30"] GERIG HG-633 rent
                                    (41)

ELOY, JEAN-CLAUDE (1938-   )
  Faisceaux-Diffractions, For Twenty-
    Eight Instruments
  3.2.4.0. 2.3.3.1. 2perc,xylo,vibra,
    marimba,harp,cel,Hamm,elec gtr,
    bass gtr [20'] UNIVER. rent (42)

FOREST, JEAN KURT (1909-1975)
  Indiana-Rhapsodie, For Orchestra
  3.2.2.2. 4.2.2.0. timp,perc,harp,
    pno,gtr,strings [8'] sc NEUE 210
    f.s., perf mat rent   (43)

FRENSEL WEGENER, EMMY (1901-1973)
  Rhapsody for Piano and Orchestra
  3.3.5.4.2sax. 4.4.4.1. timp,perc,
    xylo,2harp,cel,2gtr,strings,pno
    solo [8'] sc DONEMUS f.s.   (44)

FURSTENAU, WOLFRAM
  Ommegang, Cycle
  [Ger/Dutch] gtr, opt 2-x insts
    TEESELING VT-64 f.s.   (45)

GASLINI, GIORGIO (1929-   )
  Canto Della Citta Inquieta Da
    "Totale"
  pic,fl,ob,bass clar,horn,trp,timp,
    perc,pno,gtr,strings,electronic
    tape [11'] UNIVER. rent   (46)

  Totale II
  2.2.2.2. 2.2.2.0. timp,2perc,pno,
    gtr,strings, clavietta [18'] sc
    UNIVER. 14598 f.s.   (47)

GERVAISE, CLAUDE (fl. ca. 1550)
Suite Franzosischer Tanze (from
Livres de Danceries printed 1547-
1557 by Pierre Attaingnant)
(composed with Tertre, Etienne
du)
(Hindemith, Paul) 2.2.0.1. 0.1.0.0.
lute/gtr,vla I/vln,vla II/vln,vla
III,vcl I,vcl II [8']
(Concertino) sc,pts SCHOTT 4983
f.s.   (48)

GILBERT, ANTHONY (1934-   )
Serenade, Op. 3
ob,horn,gtr,vln,vla,db SCHOTT f.s.
                                  (49)

GRAAS, JOHN
Symphony No. 1
"Jazz-Symphony, For Jazz-Soloists
And Symphony Orchestra" 3.2.3.2.
4.2.3.1. timp,perc,strings, jazz-
band: alto sax, tenor sax,
baritone sax, trp, trom, gtr,
pno, perc, db [26'] MODERN rent (50)

GULDA, FRIEDRICH (1930-   )
Veiled Old Land, The
alto sax,baritone sax,horn,2trp,
bass trom,2trom,tuba,pno,db,
drums,fl solo/tenor sax solo,clar
solo/alto sax solo,trp solo,gtr
solo [16'30"] MODERN rent   (51)

HANUS, JAN (1915-   )
Staffette, Symphonic Allegro For Full
Orchestra
2(pic).2.2+bass clar.2. 4.3.3.1.
timp,3perc,xylo,pno,gtr,strings
[8'] ARTIA 2588 rent   (52)

HAUBENSTOCK-RAMATI, ROMAN (1919-   )
Symphonies De Timbres, Les
3.3.3.3. 4.3.3.0. perc,glock,bells,
vibra,harp,cel,pno,gtr,strings
[13'] study sc UNIVER. 12824 f.s.
                                  (53)

HAVELKA, SVATOPLUK (1925-   )
Ernesto Che Guevara
3.2+English horn.2+bass clar.2+
contrabsn. 4.4.3.1. 4perc,vibra,
harp,cel,pno,ampl gtr,strings
ARTIA 2589 rent   (54)

HAYDN, [FRANZ] JOSEPH (1732-1809)
Kinder-Symphonie *Hob.II:47
(Berchtolsgadener) 0.0.0.0.
0.1.0.0. 3perc,gtr,vln I,vln II,
vcl,db, nightingale, cuckoo,
quail [11'] (attributed to Haydn;
possibly by Leopold Mozart)
BREITKOPF-W f.s. sc PB-282, pts
OB-269   (55)

HEIDER, WERNER (1930-   )
American Suite, For Harpsichord And
Orchestra
2.0.1.0. 0.0.0.0. perc,ampl gtr,
strings,hpsd solo [11'] MODERN
rent   (56)

Choreographie I
0.0.1.0.2alto sax.2tenor
sax.baritone sax. 0.4.4.0. drums,
pno,gtr,db [10'] MODERN rent (57)

Essay In Jazz
3tenor sax,baritone sax,drums,gtr,
db [4'] MODERN rent   (58)

HEKSTER, WALTER (1937-   )
Epicycle I
fl,gtr (works can be performed
separately) sc DONEMUS f.s.
contains also: Epicycle II (db,
trp,bass clar,acord,perc)   (59)

HESPOS, HANS-JOACHIM (1938-   )
Einander-Bedingendes
fl/pic,clar, clar in a-flat, gtr,
tenor sax, vla [13'] BOSSE BE-509
rent   (60)

Sound
clar,clar in C,soprano sax,tenor
sax,baritone sax,horn,flugelhorn,
trp in C,trp in D,bass trp,trom/
bass trom,tuba,2perc,ampl gtr,
3db,clar in b-flat, alto trom,
cornettino piccolo in E flat
[15'] MODERN rent   (61)

HIVELY, WELLS (1902-1969)
Dance Of Chacmol ("Canek"); Music
Drama
2.2.2.2. 4.2.3.1. timp,perc,harp,
gtr,strings sc COMP.FAC. f.s.
                                  (62)

HUBER, NICOLAUS A. (1939-   )
Parusie, Annaherung Und Entfernung,
For Full Orchestra
3.3.3.3. 0.0.0.0. 2perc,harp,cel,
banjo,ampl gtr,strings,electronic
tape [11'] BAREN. 6018 rent (63)

ISTVAN, MILOSLAV (1928-   )
Dodekameron; 12 Compositions For 12
Players
3perc,ampl gtr,hpsd,pno,2vln,2vla,
2vcl [15'] study sc ARTIA 1748
f.s., perf mat rent   (64)

Studien, 6
trp,perc,hpsd,pno,gtr,2harp,8vln,
8vla [11'] ARTIA 2664 rent   (65)

JANSSEN, GUUS (1951-   )
Gieter, For Orchestra
3.3.3.3.tenor sax. 4.3.3.1. 2perc,
ampl gtr,strings sc DONEMUS f.s.
                                  (66)

KAGEL, MAURICIO (1931-   )
Acustica I: Music For Loudspeakers
electronic tape [40'] UNIVER. f.s.
contains also: Acustica II: Music
For Experimental "Sound
Generators" And Loudspeakers
(electronic tape,2-5plucked
insts, perc (traditional and
experimental)) [75']; Acustica
III: Music For Instrumentalists
(2-5 players with winds, plucked
insts, perc (traditional and
experimental)) [25']   (67)

Musi, For Plucked Orchestra
6gtr I,6gtr II,vcl, 6mand I, 6mand
II, 6mandole, 2db (4 and 5
strings) [6'] UNIVER. f.s. sc
15603, pts 15604   (68)

Musik Aus "Tremens"
elec gtr,elec bass gtr,elec bass,
Hamm,perc,2-3tape recorder [15'-
20'] sc UNIVER. 13505 rent   (69)

Schall, Der, For 5 Instrumentalists
1: cornetto, trp in C, Baroque trp,
tromba da tirarsi, various
objects; 2: Panflute,
2signalhorns, various objects; 3:
gtr-e", Stossel-lute, various
objects, string- and plucked-
stage properties; 4: 6-12org
pipes, 2panflutes, Taishokoto,
occarina, Kimuan-vln, bass
balalaika, bass mouth acord,
2brass pipes, string- and
plucked- stage-properties; 5:
"Glockenbrett", sirene, bass
drum, 2telephones, music-box,
2brass pipes, etc. [40'] sc
UNIVER. 14973 f.s.   (70)

Tactil Fur Drei
pno,plucked insts, experimental
insts [20'] UNIVER. rent   (71)

Unter Strom, For 3 Instrumentalists
Span gtr,ampl bass gtr, ampl gtr or
org-gtr, battery-fed machines
(megaphone, 3sirenes, 2buzzers,
5car-claxons), 9 other objects
(ventilators, walkie-talkies,
coffee-mill, etc.), various
stage-properties, special "sound
generator": "frame-harp" with gtr
strings, at least 6 microphones,
3 amplifiers + loudspeakers [22'-
30'] UNIVER. f.s.   (72)

KAPR, JAN (1914-   )
Symphony No. 6 for Chamber Orchestra
trp,timp,3perc,harp,hpsd,pno,ampl
gtr,strings [19'] sc ARTIA 1696
f.s., perf mat rent   (73)

KAYN, ROLAND (1933-   )
Allotropie, For Orchestra With
Multiple Articulation
5 instrumental groups without fixed
instrumentation, from which
several combinations can be made;
group 1: 2fl, ob, 4clar, 8sax
(woodwind); group 2: 7horn, 6trp,
2trom (brass); group 3: vln, vcl,
db; group 4: harp, pno, psaltery,
ampl gtr; group 5: tuned bottles,
tuned stones, xylomarimba, 3xylo,
vibra, marimba ZERBONI sc 6413
f.s., min sc 6415 f.s., pts 6414
rent   (74)

KLEBE, GISELHER (1925-   )
Herzschlage, Furcht, Bitte Und
Hoffnung, Symphonic Scene For
Beat-Band And Full Orchestra
*Op.57
0.2+English horn.3(bass clar).3.
0.3.3.3. timp,4perc,harp,pno,
strings, beat-band: perc, 3ampl
gtr [18'] BAREN. BA-6042 rent
                                  (75)

KOTONSKI, WLODZIMIERZ (1925-   )
A Battere
vla,vcl,gtr,hpsd,3perc [8'] (co-
published with POLSKIE) sc MOECK
5036 f.s., perf mat rent   (76)

KOX, HANS (1930-   )
Concerto Bandistico
4.2.4.0.2alto sax. 2.3.3.0. 6perc,
2pno,2acord,elec org,2gtr,
strings, 21little harp sc DONEMUS
f.s.   (77)

Cyclofonie IX,For Solo Percussion
Player And Orchestra
2.1.2.0.alto sax. 2.1.2.0. harp,
2pno,acord,elec org,gtr,6vln,
3vcl,3db,perc solo sc DONEMUS
f.s.   (78)

KRAUZE, ZYGMUNT (1938-   )
Voices For Ensemble
for 15 insts, which can be selected
from 25 insts, among which:
mandos, lutes, banjos, gtrs, ampl
gtrs; one inst to a pt [9'] sc
UNIVER. 15887 f.s.   (79)

KRENEK, ERNST (1900-   )
Ausgerechnet Und Verspielt:
Intermezzo I
1.1.1.0. 0.1.1.0. 2perc,harp,cel,
hpsd,2pno,harmonium,gtr,vln solo,
vla solo,vcl solo (duration:6
min) BAREN. BA-4322 rent contains
also: Ausgerechnet Und Verspielt:
Intermezzo II; Ausgerechnet Und
Verspielt: Nachspiel   (80)

Funffache Verschrankung
"Fivefold Enfoldment" 3(pic).2.2+
bass clar.3. 4.3.2.1. 7perc,harp,
cel,2pno,ampl gtr,strings [13']
BAREN. BA-6032 rent   (81)

Kleine Sinfonie *Op.58
2.0.3.2. 0.3.2.1. timp,perc,harp,
2mand,2banjo,gtr,2vln,2db [15']
UNIVER. 9650 f.s.   (82)

Perspektiven
"Perspectives" 2.2.3.2. 4.3.2.1.
timp,perc,harp,cel,pno,gtr,
strings [20'] BAREN. BA-6012 rent
                                  (83)

Quaestio Temporis *Op.170
"Question Of Time, A (Eine Frage
Der Zeit)" 1.1.1.1. 1.1.1.1.
perc,harp,cel,pno,gtr,strings
[18'] BAREN. sc BA-3560 rent, min
sc TP-110 f.s.   (84)

Ubungen Der Spaten Stunde
"Exercises Of A Late Hour" 1.0.2.1.
1.1.1.0. timp,perc,vibra,xylo,
harp,pno,gtr,strings,electronic
tape [18'] BAREN. BA-6020 rent
                                  (85)

KRUYF, TON DE (1937-   )
Quatre Pas De Deux, For Flute And
Orchestra *Op.30
0.0.0.0. 2.2.2.0. perc,2harp,cel,
hpsd,pno,mand,gtr,strings,fl solo
sc DONEMUS f.s.   (86)

KUPKOVIC, LADISLAV (1936-   )
Gesprach Mit Gott, Ein, For Orchestra
orch, kbd- and plucked-insts [25']
UNIVER. rent   (87)

Ozveny, For Orchestra
winds,brass,perc,plucked insts,
strings, kbds; orchestration free
but within the proportions of a
symphony orchestra (more strings
than winds) [11'] UNIVER. f.s.
                                  (88)

Staccato
winds,perc,plucked insts,strings,
kbds [11'] UNIVER. rent   (89)

LAMPERSBERG, GERHARD (1928-   )
Symphony
1.0.1.1. 1.1.1.0. harp,cel,gtr,vln,
vla,vcl solo [8'] UNIVER. rent
                                  (90)

LEEUW, REINBERT DE (1938-   )
Hymns And Chorals, With A Commentary
On The Music Of Erik Satie
15winds,2ampl gtr,elec org,
electronic equipment [17'-20']
DONEMUS f.s.   (91)

LEEUW, TON DE (1926-   )
Music For Organ And 12 Players
1.0.0.1. 2.2.2.0. perc,ampl gtr,
ampl bass gtr,db,org solo sc
DONEMUS f.s.   (92)

Ombres
3.3.3.2.alto sax. 2.3.2.1. timp,
perc,xylo,harp,gtr,strings [12']
sc DONEMUS f.s.   (93)

LIDHOLM, INGVAR (1921-   )
Motus Colores
2.2.3.2. 2.2.2.1. 6perc,harp,cel,
ampl gtr,strings, ampl mando
[13'] UNIVER. rent   (94)

LOMBARDI, LUCA (1945-   )
Sinfonia No. 1
2.2.2.2. 2.2.2.1. harp,pno,cel,elec
gtr,3perc,strings sc MOECK 5176
f.s.   (95)

LUDWIG, JOACHIM
Mutation, For Big Band And
Harpsichord Obbligato
1.0.2.0.5sax. 0.4.4.0. perc,vibra,
gtr,hpsd,strings [10'] MODERN
rent   (96)

LUMSDAINE, DAVID (1931-   )
Episodes, For Chamber Orchestra
2.2.2.2. 4.3.3.1. harp,elec org,
ampl gtr,strings [21'] UNIVER.
rent   (97)

LUPI, ROBERTO (1908-1971)
Studi Per Un "Homunculus"; 9 Pieces
For Orchestra
3.3.3.3. 2.2.2.1. timp,perc,xylo,
harp,cel,pno,gtr,strings CARISCH
rent   (98)

MCBRIDE, ROBERT GUYN (1911-   )
Bop Pizzicato
harp,gtr,vln I,vln II,vln III,vln
IV,vla,vcl,db,opt pno sc
COMP.FAC. ipa   (99)

MACHA, OTMAR (1922-   )
Variationen Auf Ein Thema Von Jan
Rychlik Und Uber Seinen Tod
3(pic).2+English horn.4.3. 4.3.3.1.
timp,3perc,harp,ampl bass gtr,
strings [15'] study sc ARTIA 1714
perf mat rent   (100)

MADERNA, BRUNO (1920-1973)
Amanda, For Chamber Orchestra
3perc,2harp,cel,pno,mand,gtr,6vln,
3vla,3vcl,3db [12'] ZERBONI sc
6637 f.s., pts 6638 rent   (101)

Composizione In Tre Tempi, For
Orchestra
3.3.4.3. 4.4.3.1. 7perc,harp,cel,
pno,gtr,strings [14'] pts ZERBONI
5118 rent   (102)

Concerto No. 2 for Oboe and Orchestra
0.3.4.0. 4.0.0.0. 5perc,2harp,cel,
2gtr,6vln,3vla,3vcl,3db,ob solo
[17'] ZERBONI sc 6804 f.s., pts
6805 rent, solo pt 6806, pno red
6808   (103)

MAJO, GIULIO DI (1933-   )
Passacaglia Per 7 Strumenti
fl,alto sax,horn,gtr,vibra,pno,db
SCHOTT f.s.   (104)

MARION, ROLF
Panorama Brasilia
3.2.2.2. 4.3.3.0. perc,harp,ampl
gtr,strings,opt gtr [4'30"] PEER
rent   (105)

MASQUE MUSIC
(Hirsch) 4-12inst (excerpts from
music written for masques by Lawes,
Campian, Johnson, Coperario for
full or broken consort (recs, vcl,
gt)) sc HANSEN-DEN f.s.   (106)

MAYUZUMI, TOSHIRO (1929-   )
Ectoplasme
gtr,5perc,strings, clavioline [6']
PETERS rent   (107)

Microcosmos
gtr,vibra,xylo,perc,pno,
clavioline, musical saw [13'] min
sc PETERS 6332 f.s.   (108)

MENGELBERG, MISJA (1935-   )
Met Welbeleefde Groet Van De Kameel,
For Orchestra
2.0.1.0.2alto sax.tenor sax.
2.2.2.1. timp,perc,ampl gtr, ampl
saw, ampl bore sc DONEMUS f.s.
                              (109)

Musica Per 17 Strumenti
2.0.1.1. 2.1.0.1. perc,xylo,vibra,
hpsd,gtr,2vln,vla,vcl sc DONEMUS
f.s.   (110)

MOHLER, PHILIPP (1908-1982)
Shakespeare-Suite; Dances By
Contemporaries Of William
Shakespeare
0.2.0.2. 0.0.0.0. hpsd,strings,opt
lute/gtr [24'] (Concertino) sc
SCHOTT 5309 ipa   (111)

MONTEVERDI, CLAUDIO (ca. 1567-1643)
Ballo (from Il Ballo Delle Ingrate)
(Leppard, Raymond) 2vln,2vla,vcl,
db,hpsd/2gtr [5'] FABER f.s. sc
F-0077, sc,pts F-0078, pts
F-0078A-G   (112)

NIEHAUS, MANFRED (1933-   )
Konzert, For Violin And 4 Orchestral
Groups
2.1.2.0. 1.1.2.0. timp,perc,cel,
hpsd,pno,harmonium,gtr,7vla,6vcl,
5db,vln solo [11'] GERIG HG-623
rent   (113)

NILSSON, BO (1937-   )
Frequenzen Fur 8 Spieler
pic,fl,2perc,vibra,xylo,gtr,db [4']
UNIVER. rent   (114)

PALESTER, ROMAN (1907-   )
Morte Di Don Giovanni, La: 3
Frammenti Sinfonici, For
Orchestra
3.2.4.3.sax. 3.3.3.0. timp,8perc,
harp,cel,pno,mand,gtr,strings
[15'] ZERBONI sc 6262 f.s., pts
6263 rent   (115)

PENDERECKI, KRZYSZTOF (1933-   )
Capriccio for Violin and Orchestra
4.4.5.4. 6.4.4.1. 5perc,harp,pno,
harmonium,gtr,strings,vln solo
[10'] (co-published with POLSKIE)
sc MOECK 5040 f.s.   (116)

Concerto for Violoncello and
Orchestra
3.3.3.3. 4.3.3.1. 5perc,harmonium,
bass gtr,18vln,6vcl,4db,vcl solo
[20'] (co-published with POLSKIE)
MOECK 5042 f.s.   (117)

PETRASSI, GOFFREDO (1904-   )
Concerto for Flute and Orchestra
0.0.2.2. 4.3.3.0. 5perc,harp,gtr,
8vcl,6db,fl solo [16'] ZERBONI
min sc 5739 f.s., pts 5738 rent,
pno red 5740 f.s.   (118)

POLOLANIK, ZDENEK (1935-   )
Concentus Resonabilis
tenor sax,2trp,2harp,pno,hpsd,gtr,
timp,2perc,vibra,xylo,2vln,2vla,
2vcl, Ionica [12'] sc ARTIA 1563
f.s.   (119)

Concerto Grosso
clar in E flat/fl,hpsd,gtr,strings
[15'] (Il Bucranio) ZANIBON f.s.
sc 5081, pts 5082   (120)

RICHTER, NICO (1915-1945)
Serenade (Sinfonietta No. 1 for
Chamber Orchestra)
1.0.1.0. 0.0.0.0. gtr,strings [6']
sc DONEMUS f.s.   (121)

RONNEFELD, PETER (1935-1965)
Spirale; Ballettsuite
fl,bass clar,trp in C,trom,4timp,
harp,gtr,vla,db [15'30"] MODERN
rent   (122)

RUYNEMAN, DANIEL (1886-1963)
Hieroglyphs
3fl,cel,harp,pno,2mand,2gtr,
cupbells CHESTER f.s.   (123)

SCHAT, PETER (1935-   )
Thema, For Oboe Solo, Guitars, Organ
And Wind Instruments
0.1.5.4.3sax. 3.3.0.0. Hamm,4gtr,ob
solo sc,solo pt DONEMUS f.s.
                              (124)

SCHIFRIN, LALO (BORIS) (1932-   )
Ritual Of Sound
1.1.1.1. 1.2.1.1. perc,vibra,gtr,
2db [7'] MODERN rent   (125)

SCHNEIDER, URS PETER (1939-   )
Kirchweih, No. 5, For Orchestra And
Equipment
"Umkehr, After Friedrich Weinreb"
2.2.2.2. 2.2.2.2. 2harp,2gtr,
4vln,2vla,4vcl,2db [21'30"] (can
be replaced by tape recording in
case of performance of the whole
cycle) MOECK f.s.   (126)

SCHNITTKE, ALFRED (1934-   )
Pianissimo, For Full Orchestra
1+pic.1+English horn.1+bass clar.1.
1.1.1.1. 4perc,harp,cel,hpsd,
2pno,ampl gtr,strings [9']
UNIVER. rent   (127)

SCHREKER, FRANZ (1878-1934)
Suite "Der Geburtstag Der Infantin, "
After Oscar Wilde
3.3.3.3. 4.3.3.1. perc,2harp,cel,
4gtr,4mand,strings [20'] sc
UNIVER. 7536 f.s.   (128)

SCHULLER, GUNTHER (1925-   )
Night Music
0.0.2.0.4sax. 0.4.3.0. drums,pno,
gtr,db [5'] MODERN sc f.s., pts
rent   (129)

SCHWERTSIK, KURT (1935-   )
Salotto Romano *Op.5 (from
Salonstucken)
bass clar,baritone sax,bsn,horn,
trom,tuba,gtr,vcl,db, lion's
roar, low siren [5'] MODERN rent
                              (130)

SEROCKI, KAZIMIERZ (1922-1981)
Impromptu Fantasque
6rec,3mand,3gtr,pno,perc (co-
published with POLSKIE) sc MOECK
5160 f.s., perf mat rent   (131)

Segmenti
1.1.3.1. 1.2.2.1. 4perc,harp,hpsd/
cel,pno,ampl gtr, ampl mando [7']
sc MOECK 5013 f.s.   (132)

Sinfonische Fresken, For Orchestra
4.4.4.4. 6.4.4.1. 4perc,2harp,cel,
2pno,mand,gtr,strings (co-
published with POLSKIE) sc MOECK
50007 f.s.   (133)

SHAPERO, HAROLD SAMUEL (1920-   )
On Green Mountain; Chaconne After
Monteverdi
1.0.0.0.alto sax.tenor sax.
1.1.1.0. perc,vibra,harp,pno,gtr,
db [9'] PEER rent   (134)

SMALLEY, ROGER (1943-   )
Beat Music, For Orchestra With
Amplified Instruments
3.3.4.2.alto sax. 3.4.3.1. 3perc,
ampl bass gtr,elec pno,strings,
ampl hpsd, ampl org solo, ampl
vla solo, ampl soprano sax or bsn
solo, ampl perc solo [20'-25']
sc,pts FABER rent   (135)

SMITH, WILLIAM OVERTON (1926-   )
Interplay
2.1.2.2. 2.3.1.1. timp,perc,cel,
gtr,strings,vibra solo,pno solo,
db solo,drums solo [14'] MODERN
rent   (136)

STOCKHAUSEN, KARLHEINZ (1928-   )
Aus Den Sieben Tagen; Composition No.
26
[Ger] gtr (15 compositions
(includes 1 with stage
composition) for an ensemble with
an indefinite number of players
(including gtr); duration
indefinite, performances up to
1972: each composition 4'-60')
UNIVER. 14790 f.s.   (137)
[Eng] gtr (15 compositions
(includes 1 with stage
composition) for an ensemble with
an indefinite number of players
(including gtr); duration
indefinite, performances up to
1972: each composition 4'-60')
UNIVER. 14790-E f.s.   (138)
[Fr] gtr (15 compositions (includes
1 with stage composition) for an
ensemble with an indefinite
number of players (including
gtr); duration indefinite,
performances up to 1972: each
composition 4'-60') UNIVER.
14790-F f.s.   (139)

Gruppen, For Three Orchestras
5.5.4.3.2sax. 8.6.7.1. 12perc,
2harp,cel,pno,elec gtr,strings,
kbd-glock or cel II (complete
instrumentation of the 3
orchestras) [25'] sc UNIVER.
13673 f.s.   (140)

STRADELLA, ALESSANDRO (1645-1682)
Concerto Grosso in D
(Chiesa) string orch,2vln soli,
lute/gtr solo sc ZERBONI 7642
f.s.   (141)

STRIETMAN, WILLEM (1918-   )
O Bonne Douce France (Concerto for
Harmonica and Chamber Orchestra)
1.1.1.1.sax. 1.1.1.0. perc,harp,
gtr/ampl gtr,pno/cel,strings
[31'] sc DONEMUS f.s.   (142)

SUITEN, 2, AFTER MELODIES BY FRENCH
DANCE MASTERS
(Petersen) perc,pno,strings,opt gtr
[13'30"] (Concertino) sc,pts SCHOTT
5805 f.s.   (143)

SUTER, ROBERT (1919-   )
Nocturnes, 3, For Viola And Orchestra
1.1.2.2. 4.0.0.0. 4perc,harp,cel,
cimbalom,gtr,strings,vla solo
[30'] BAREN. BA-6039 rent   (144)

TABACHNIK, MICHEL (1942-   )
Supernovae, For Chamber Orchestra And
Percussion
1.0.1.0. 0.1.1.0. 4perc,harp,cel,
hpsd,gtr,vla,vcl,2pno soli
NOVELLO f.s.   (145)

TAKEMITSU, TORU (1930-)
  Valeria
    vln,vcl,gtr,elec org,2pic [15'] sc
    UNIVER. 15116 f.s.   (146)

TERPSTRA, KOOS (1948-)
  Mimesis
    3.1.1.0.soprano sax. 1.2.3.0.
    3perc,bass gtr,6vln,2vla,2vcl,db,
    sews sc DONEMUS f.s.   (147)

TORELLI, GIUSEPPE (1658-1709)
  Concerto in A
    (Brojer) string quar,gtr,vln solo
    (Gitarre-Kammermusik, No.6) sc,
    pts DOBLINGER GKM-6 f.s.   (148)

  Concerto in D minor
    (Brojer) string quar,gtr,vln solo
    (Gitarre-Kammermusik, No. 52) sc,
    pts DOBLINGER GKM-52 f.s.   (149)

VACKAR, DALIBOR CYRIL (1906-1984)
  Charakteristikon (Concerto for
    Trombone and Orchestra)
    2.0.2.2. 0.3.3.1. perc,pno,gtr,trom
    solo [16'] ARTIA 2505 rent   (150)

VILLA-LOBOS, HEITOR (1887-1959)
  Sextuor Mystique
    fl,ob,alto sax,gtr,cel,harp sc,pts,
    study sc ESCHIG f.s.   (151)

VLIJMEN, JAN VAN (1935-)
  Interpolations
    3.3.5.3. 4.3.3.1. perc,2marimba,
    tubular bells,xylo,harp,hpsd,pno,
    2org,mand,3gtr,strings sc DONEMUS
    f.s.   (152)

  Serenata II, Per Flauto E Quattro
    Gruppi Strumentali
    0.1.4.2.tenor sax. 1.2.1.0. perc,
    marimba,xylo,vibra,harp,gtr,
    strings,fl solo DONEMUS f.s.
                                    (153)

VOGT, HANS (1911-)
  Monologe, 4 Symphonic Pieces For Full
    Orchestra
    3.3.3.3. 2.3.3.1. timp,5perc,glock,
    vibra,xylo,marimba,harp,cel,hpsd,
    pno,ampl gtr,strings BAREN. 4171
    rent   (154)

VOSTRAK, ZBYNEK (1920-)
  Schneewittchen: Suite *Op.22
    3.2.2+bass clar.2. 4.3.3.1. timp,
    3perc,harp,cel,pno,2gtr,strings
    [27'] min sc ARTIA f.s.   (155)

VRIES, KLAAS DE (1944-)
  Follia
    0.0.0.0. 5.5.5.1. 3perc,elec pno,
    elec org,ampl gtr,ampl bass gtr,
    3vln soli,2vla soli DONEMUS
    f.s.   (156)

WEBERN, ANTON VON (1883-1945)
  Funf Stucke Fur Orchester *Op.10
    1.1.2.0. 1.1.1.0. perc,glock,bells,
    xylo,harp,cel,harmonium,mand,gtr,
    vln,vla,vcl,db [6'30"] UNIVER.
    f.s. min sc 12416, min sc PH-449 (157)

WIEGOLD, PETER (1949-)
  Flowers Appear On The Earth, The
    fl,clar,perc,harp,gtr,vla,vcl [20']
    UNIVER. f.s.   (158)

ZEHM, FRIEDRICH (1923-)
  Rhythomophonie For Orchestra
    2.1.2.1. 1.2.1.0. perc,vibra,ampl
    gtr,vln I,vln II,vla/vln III,vcl,
    db sc SCHOTT 6179 f.s., ipa   (159)

ZELENKA, ISTVAN (1936-)
  Fruh-Stuck
    alto fl,bass clar,horn,trom,bass
    gtr,vla [12'] MODERN rent   (160)

ZIMMERMANN, BERND ALOIS (1918-1970)
  Cinque Capricci Di Girolamo
    Frescobaldi "La Frescobalda"
    A rec,T rec,B rec,ob d'amore,3vla
    da gamba,lute/gtr,3trp,3trom, or
    3.1.0.0. 0.3.3.0., harp, 2vln,
    vcl [15'] BAREN. BA-3367 rent   (161)

  Giostra Genovese; Five Old Dances By
    Various Masters For Small
    Orchestra
    3.3.0.3. 0.3.3.1. timp,perc,harp,
    2gtr,4db sc BAREN. BA-3572 rent (162)

  Musique Pour Les Soupers Du Roi Ubu;
    Ballet Noir En Sept Parties Et
    Une Entree
    3.3.3.sax. 4.3.3.1. timp,2perc,
    harp,cel,pno,org,mand,2gtr,4db,
    combo (clar, trp, ampl gtr, ampl
    db) [18'] (for scenic or concert
    performance) sc BAREN. BA-4180
    rent   (163)

V/ii Ensemble/Orchestral Music with Voice and Guitar

ALBINI, FELIX (1600?- ?)
  Primavera, La, For Medium Voice And
    Orchestra
    (Gentili) 2.2.0.0. 0.0.0.0. gtr,
    strings,med solo CARISCH rent   (164)

AMY, GILBERT (1936-)
  Cette Etoile Enseigne A s'Incliner
    3trom,vibra,2harp,2pno,gtr,vcl,db,
    electronic tape,7 male soli [15']
    LEMOINE f.s.   (165)

  d'Un Espace Deploye, For Soprano, 2
    Pianos And 2 Orchestral Groups
    orch 1: 4.3+English horn 5(clar in
    E flat, bsclr) 4. 6.4.4.1+db
    tuba, 5perc, pno, ampl org,
    strings; orch 2: 3perc, 2harp,
    cel, pno, ampl gt, strings, S
    solo [31'] UNIVER. rent   (166)

  Sonata Pian' E Forte, For Soprano,
    Mezzo-Soprano And Twelve Players
    fl/alto fl,English horn,bass clar,
    horn,harp,xylorimba,perc,gtr,
    mand,vla,vcl,SMez soli, pno I+
    tam-tam, pno II+crotales [25'] sc
    UNIVER. 15981 f.s.   (167)

ANDRIESSEN, LOUIS (1939-)
  Principe, Il, Quotations From "The
    Ruler" Of N. Machiavelli
    2.2.2.2. 3.0.0.1. pno,bass gtr,dbl
    cor sc DONEMUS f.s.   (168)

  Staat, De, For Solo Voices And
    Orchestra
    [Dutch] 0.0.0.0. 4.4.4.4. 2harp,
    2ampl bass gtr,2ampl gtr,2pno,
    4vla, 4 male soli [40'] sc
    DONEMUS f.s.   (169)

ANTONIOU, THEODORE (1935-)
  Epilog After Homer's Odyssey
    [Greek/Ger/Eng] ob,horn,gtr,pno,
    perc,db,Mez&speaking voice sc
    BAREN. BA-4379 ipr   (170)

  Meli *Op.17, cant
    [Greek] 1.1.0.1. 0.1.1.0. 2perc,
    gtr,vln,vla,vcl,db,med solo
    BAREN. BA-4380 rent   (171)

  Moirologhia For Jani Christou
    "Lamentation" [Greek/Lat/Eng] pno,
    fl,clar,gtr,2perc,db,Bar solo, or
    Bar solo and pno sc BAREN.
    BA-6135 f.s.   (172)

ARFKEN, ERNST (1925-)
  Gib Dich Zufrieden Und Sei Stille
    *mot
    SATB, opt db&vcl/lute/gtr sc
    HANSSLER HE-7.108 f.s.   (173)

ARRIGO, GIROLAMO (1930-)
  Occasioni, 3
    1.1.2.1. 2.1.1.1. glock,xylo,vibra,
    harp,cel,pno,mand,gtr,6vla,6vcl,
    2db,S solo [14'] min sc LEMOINE
    f.s.   (174)

BARBE, HELMUT (1927-)
  Horoskop Gefallig?
    [Ger] 1-3pt cor,clar,gtr,db,pno sc,
    cor pts BOSSE BE-109 f.s.,
    contains also: Harlem   (175)

  Ostergeschichte
    "Easter Oratorio" [Ger] 0.2.3.0.
    0.2.2.1. 2timp,perc,ampl gtr,
    strings,cor,ABar soli [34'] sc,
    cor pts HANSSLER HE10.150 f.s.,
    ipr   (176)

BARTOLOZZI, BRUNO (1911-)
  Recuerdos Del Cielo
    1.1(English horn).1.1. 0.0.0.0.
    timp,gtr,vla,vcl,db,female solo,
    opt perc [12'] ZERBONI sc 6751
    f.s., pts 6752 rent   (177)

BAUMANN, HERBERT (1925-)
  Contrasti
    cor,gtr sc SIKORSKI 662 f.s.   (178)

  Moritat Vom Eigensinnigen Eheweibe,
    Die
    (Behrend) [Ger] mix cor,B solo,gtr
    (Gitarre-Bibliothek, No. 76) sc
    BOTE GB-76 f.s.   (179)

BECKER, GUNTHER (1924-)
  Nacht- Und Traumgesange
    2.2.2.1. 2.3.3.1. 3timp,4perc,harp,
    cel,pno,ampl gtr,strings,cor
    [15'] sc GERIG HG-495 f.s.   (180)

BEDFORD, DAVID (1937-)
  Nurse's Song With Elephants
    solo voice,10gtr [18'-20'] sc
    UNIVER. 15448 f.s.   (181)

BERIO, LUCIANO (1925-)
  Passaggio, Messa In Scena
    2.0.2.2.2sax. 1.2.2.1. 5perc,harp,
    harmonium,elec gtr,vla,vcl,db,S
    solo, 1 cor in orch, 1 cor
    divided into 5 groups in
    auditorium [35'] study sc UNIVER.
    13700 f.s.   (182)

BEURLE, JURGEN (1943-)
  Objets
    1.0.2.0. 0.1.3.0. perc,harp,cel,
    pno,org,gtr,2vln,vla,2vcl,db,
    electronic tape,8 female soli&5
    male soli MOECK 5079 f.s.
    contains also: Reflexionen   (183)

BIALAS, GUNTER (1907-)
  Eichendorff-Liederbuch, Vol. 1: Das
    Zerbrochene Ringlein
    "In Einem Kuhlen Grunde" cor,2gtr
    BAREN. BA-4978 f.s.   (184)

  Eichendorff-Liederbuch, Vol. 2:
    Abschied
    "O Taler Weit" cor,2gtr BAREN.
    BA-4979 f.s.   (185)

  Eichendorff-Liederbuch, Vol. 3: Aber
    Die Zeit Geht Schnell
    "Lieb Voglein" SATBB,2gtr BAREN.
    BA-4980 f.s.   (186)

  Eichendorff-Liederbuch, Vol. 4:
    Nachtzauber
    "Horst Du Nicht Die Brunnen
    Rauschen" SATBB,S solo,2gtr
    BAREN. BA-4981 f.s.   (187)

  Eichendorff-Liederbuch, Vol. 5:
    Seliges Vergessen
    "Im Winde Facheln Die Blatter"
    SATBB,2gtr BAREN. BA-4982 f.s.
                                    (188)

  Eichendorff-Liederbuch, Vol. 6:
    Assonanzen
    "Hat Nur Lenz" cor,S solo,2gtr
    BAREN. BA-4983 f.s.   (189)

BIEBL, FRANZ (1906-)
  An Die Musik, A Hymn
    treb inst,gtr,acord/harp,eq voices/
    mix cor (Cantate E Sonate) WELT
    2569 f.s.   (190)

  Frisch Gesungen, A Hymn
    treb inst,gtr,acord/harp,eq voices/
    mix cor (Cantate E Sonate) WELT
    2568 f.s.   (191)

BLARR, OSKAR GOTTLIEB (1934-)
  Vater Unser, Der Du Bist Im Himmel;
    Melody After A Latin-American
    Calypso
    fl,kbd,db/gtr,cor&cong,SA soli
    (Chorblatt, No. 11) BOSSE BE-236
    f.s.   (192)

  Wer Wohnt Unterm Schirm Des Hochsten
    (Psalm No. 91)
    org/gtr/vibra/hpsd/db,trp,3-5 cor
    (Chorblatt, No. 26) BOSSE BE-601
    f.s.   (193)

BOEHMER, KONRAD (1941-)
  Lied Uit De Verte
    "Chanson De Lointain" 2.4.2.2.
    4.2.3.1. timp,perc,gtr,pno,vln,
    vla,vcl,db,S/Mez solo [20'] sc
    DONEMUS f.s.   (194)

BOIS, ROB DU (1934-)
  Vandaag Is Het Morgen Van Gisteren
    "Helaas Geen Sprookje" 4.2.2.2.
    1.2.1.0. perc,harp,4pno,org,ampl
    gtr,strings,2pt jr cor,S&
    narrator, brass band [63'] sc
    DONEMUS f.s.   (195)

BOOGAARD, BERNARD VAN DEN (1952-)
  De Ave Phoenice *cant
    ampl gtr,electronic equipment,8pt
    cor sc DONEMUS f.s.   (196)

BORKOVEC, PAVEL (1894-1972)
  Silentium Turbatum, Symphonic Setting
    3.2.2.2. 4.3.3.1. timp,4perc,xylo,
    harp,pno,ampl gtr,strings,A solo
    [18'] sc ARTIA 1692 ipr   (197)

BOULEZ, PIERRE (1925-)
  Marteau Sans Maitre, Le
    gtr,perc,vibra,xylorimba,vla,fl,A
    solo [34'] UNIVER. f.s. study sc
    PH-398, sc 12362   (198)

BOULEZ, PIERRE (cont'd.)

Pli Selon Pli, Portrait De Mallarme,
1
"Don" 3(alto fl).1.3.1. 4.2.3.0.
7perc,harp,cel,pno,mand,gtr,4vln,
4vla,5vcl,3db,S solo [14'30"] sc
UNIVER. 13614 f.s.   (199)

Pli Selon Pli, Portrait De Mallarme,
2
"Improvisation I: Le Vierge, Le
Vivace Et Le Bel Aujourd'hui"
2.0.1.0.2sax. 4.1.0.0. 2perc,
glock,3xylo,3vibra,3harp,cel,
mand,ampl gtr,8vla,6db,S solo,
for separate performances: harp,
vibr, glock, 4perc [6'] study sc
UNIVER. 12855 f.s.   (200)

Pli Selon Pli, Portrait De Mallarme,
4
"Improvisation III: A La Nue
Accablante Tu" 4(pic).0.0.0.
0.0.1.0. glock,tubular bells,
2xylo,3harp,cel,mand,ampl gtr,
4vcl,3db,S solo, cow-bells [19']
UNIVER. rent   (201)

Pli Selon Pli, Portrait De Mallarme,
5
"Tombeau" 3(alto fl).1.3.1.
4.2.3.0. 7perc,harp,cel,pno,mand,
gtr,4vln,4vla,5vcl,3db,S solo
[15'] study sc UNIVER. 13585 f.s.
(202)

BROWN, EARLE (1926-   )
From Here
1.1.3.1. 1.1.1.1. 2perc,harp,pno,
ampl gtr,strings,4pt mix cor [8'-
12'] sc UNIVER. 15380 f.s. (203)

BUSSOTTI, SYLVANO (1931-   )
Sette Fogli, 5
"Mobile-Stabile" gtr,pno,solo voice
(graphic sc) UNIVER. 13238-V rent
(204)

Sette Fogli, 6
"Manifesto Per Kalinowski" 1.0.0.0.
1.1.1.0. 3perc,glock,xylo,vibra,
harp,cel,pno,gtr,vln,vcl,db,opt
male solo/female solo UNIVER.
13238-VI rent   (205)

Torso
1.1.2.2. 2.1.1.1. perc,2harp,cel,
pno,gtr,2vln,3vla,4vcl,2db,SMez&
opt Bar&speaking voice sc MOECK
5017 ipr   (206)

CASTELNUOVO-TEDESCO, MARIO (1895-1968)
Romancero Gitano
(Behrend) gtr,cor (Gitarre-
Bibliothek, No. 52) sc BOTE GB-52
f.s.   (207)

CERHA, FRIEDRICH (1926-   )
Intersecazioni I For Violin And
Orchestra
4.0.3.1.3sax. 3.4.3.1. timp,10perc,
harp,cel,hpsd,pno,harmonium,mand,
gtr,strings,vln solo,SSAT [14']
UNIVER. rent   (208)

Intersecazioni II For Violin And
Orchestra
4.0.3.1. 3sax(sopranino sax,
soprano sax, alto sax) 3.4.3.1.,
timp, 10perc, harp, cel, hpsd,
pno, harmonium, mand, gtr,
strings, vln solo, 2SAT cor [15']
UNIVER. rent   (209)

DAVIES, PETER MAXWELL (1934-   )
Te Lucis Ante Terminum
[Eng] 2.1.2.0. 0.1.2.0. glock,gtr,
vcl,cor SCHOTT f.s. cor pts
10817A, sc 10817B   (210)

DENISOV, EDISON VASILIEVICH (1929-   )
Chant d'Automne For Soprano And Full
Orchestra
3.1+English horn.4.3.baritone sax.
3.4.3.1. 3perc,harp,cel,ampl gtr,
strings [15'] UNIVER. rent (211)

DES PREZ, JOSQUIN (ca. 1440-1521)
Magnificat Quarti Toni, For Chorus
And Three Groups Of Instruments
(Maderna, Bruno) 4.3.0.2. 2.3.3.0.
timp,perc,vibra,2harp,mand,2gtr,
strings,cor [9'] ZERBONI f.s.,
ipr sc 6660, pts 6661   (212)

DONATONI, FRANCO (1927-   )
Serenade for Solo Voice and Orchestra
3.0.3.0. 0.1.1.0. vibra,harp,cel,
pno,mand,gtr,vla,db,S solo [13']
ZERBONI min sc 5605 f.s., pts
5579 rent   (213)

DORATI, ANTAL (1906-   )
Madrigal Suite
0.0.0.0. 4.0.0.0. 4perc,vibra,
marimba,harp,cel,pno,gtr,vln I,
vln II,vla,vcl,db,cor [20']

DORATI, ANTAL (cont'd.)

ZERBONI sc 6313 f.s., pts 6314
rent, pno red 6315 f.s.   (214)

FRITSCH, JOHANNES GEORG (1941-   )
Akroasis
3(alto fl,pic).3(ob d'amore,English
horn).3+bass clar.2+contrabsn.
4.3.3.1. timp,6perc,harmonica,
vibra,marimba,harp,cel,pno,acord,
org,elec bass,ampl gtr,strings,
AB&narrator, barrel-org,
chromonica, music-box, jazz
group: trp, 2trom, 3sax, perc,
db, tape recorder [21'] sc,pts
FEEDBACK 7101 rent   (215)

FUSSL, KARL-HEINZ (1924-   )
Dialogue In Praise Of The Owl And The
Cuckoo
1.0.1.0. 0.0.1.0. harp,gtr,vln,db,T
solo [16'] sc UNIVER. 15180 f.s.
(216)

Drei Szenen Aus "Dybuk"
2.2.2.2. 4.3.3.1. 3timp,2perc,
glock,xylo,marimba,2-3harp,cel,2-
3gtr,strings,cor,STBarBar soli
[30'] sc UNIVER. 13567 f.s. (217)

FUX, JOHANN JOSEPH (1660-1741)
Fede Sacrilega Nella Morte Del
Precursor S. Giovanni Battista,
La *ora
(Zelzer) 0.2.0.1. 2.2.0.0. hpsd,
org,lute/gtr,strings,5pt mix cor,
SSATB soli (Collected Works,
Series IV, Vol. I) sc BAREN.
f.s., ipr   (218)

GABRIELI, ANDREA (1510-1586)
Edipo Re, Cori Per La Tragedia Di
Sofocle
(Canino, Bruno) 5.4.0.3. 4.6.3.1.
timp,perc,harp,2hpsd,org,mand,
lute/gtr,strings,cor ZERBONI 6816
ipr   (219)

GASLINI, GIORGIO (1929-   )
Totale I
3.3.3.3. 4.4.4.1. 2timp,3perc,
glock,xylo,vibra,harp,cel,pno,
strings,ST soli, jazz insts:
acord, 2elec gtr, alto sax, trp,
pno, db, drums [43'] UNIVER. rent
(220)

GIELEN, MICHAEL ANDREAS (1927-   )
Glocken Sind Auf Falscher Spur, Die
vcl,pno,perc,gtr,S&speaking voice
sc GERIG 813 rent   (221)

Tag Tritt Hervor, Ein, Pentaphony For
Piano Obbligato, Five Solo
Instruments, Five Groups Of Five
Players Each And A Speaking Role
clar,clar in A,soprano clar in E
flat,contrabass clar,9perc,harp,
cel,vln,vla,vcl,pno solo,vibra
solo,marimba solo,ampl gtr solo,
Ondes Martenot solo,harmonium
solo,SATB&speaking voice, ampl
mand [22'] sc, copy GERIG HG-505
f.s.   (222)

GOOSEN, JACQUES (1952-   )
Arno-Holz-Liederen
2.2.2.1.alto sax. 1.2.1.0. timp,
perc,vibra,harp,cel,hpsd,
harmonium,gtr,8vln,4vla,4vcl,A
solo, sopranino sax sc DONEMUS
f.s.   (223)

GUDMUNDSEN-HOLMGREEN, PELLE (1932-   )
Songs, 3
vln,vla,vcl,gtr,perc,A solo [9']
HANSEN-DEN f.s.   (224)

HANDEL, GEORGE FRIDERIC (1685-1759)
Athalia *ora
(Hiekel) [Ger/Eng] 2.2.0.2.
2.2.0.0. timp,hpsd,org,lute/gtr,
strings,4-8pt mix cor,SSSATB soli
BAREN. rent   (225)

HARTIG, HEINZ FRIEDRICH (1907-1969)
Perche *Op.28
(Behrend) cor,gtr (Gitarre-
Bibliothek, No. 31) sc BOTE GB-31
f.s.   (226)

HASHAGEN, KLAUS (1924-   )
Sechs Seemannslieder *Eng/US
"Six Sailor-Songs" [Ger] acord/kbd,
gtr,db,1-3 male soli&opt B solo
sc BOSSE BE-207 f.s., ipa (227)

HAVELKA, SVATOPLUK (1925-   )
Heptameron *cant
3.2.3.2.3sax. 3.3.3.1. timp,perc,
harp,cel,pno,gtr,strings,SATB&
speaking voice ARTIA 2315 rent (228)

HENZE, HANS WERNER (1926-   )
Kammermusik 1958
"In Lieblicher Blaue" gtr/harp,clar
solo,horn solo,bsn solo,string
quin solo,T solo SCHOTT f.s., ipa
pno red 4897, study sc 4599 (229)

HERZOG, FRANZ
Musik Zu Christian Morgensterns
"Palmstrom", Part 1 (Suite for
Chorus and Instruments)
2pno,gtr,perc,unis cor [22'] sc,
pts,cor pts BOSSE BE-102 f.s.
(230)

HESS, REIMUND (1935-   )
Cotton Fields *folk song,US
gtr,opt db,mix cor (Folklore Der
Welt) BREITKOPF-W Z-23 f.s. (231)

Cuckoo, The *folk song,Eng
"Oh, The Cuckoo, She's A Pretty
Bird" gtr,db,opt triangle,mix cor
(Folklore Der Welt) sc BREITKOPF-
W Z-24 f.s.   (232)

Glory Hallelujah "John Brown's Body"
*folk song,US
"John Brown Liegt In Seinem Kalten
Dunklen Grab" pno/acord,gtr,db,
opt tamb,mix cor (Folklore Der
Welt) sc BREITKOPF-W Z-21 f.s.
(233)

Golondrina, La *folk song,Mex
"Ich Danke Dir" pno/org,gtr,db,opt
perc,mix cor, melodica or other
treb inst (Folklore Der Welt) sc
BREITKOPF-W Z-22 f.s.   (234)

Guantanamera *folk song,So Am
pno,gtr,db,opt fl,mix cor, rattle
(Folklore Der Welt) sc BREITKOPF-
W Z-18 f.s.   (235)
pno,gtr,db,opt fl,men cor, rattle
(Folklore Der Welt) sc BREITKOPF-
W Z-34 f.s.   (236)

Hava Nagila *folk song,Isr
pno/acord,tamb,gtr,db,mix cor,Bar
solo (Folklore Der Welt) sc
BREITKOPF-W Z-19 f.s.   (237)
pno/acord,tamb,gtr,db,men cor,Bar
solo (Folklore Der Welt) sc
BREITKOPF-W Z-35 f.s.   (238)

Old Mac Donald *folk song,US
pno,gtr,db,opt perc,mix cor
(Folklore Der Welt) sc BREITKOPF-
W Z-25 f.s.   (239)

HEURICH, WINFRIED
Dein Wort Ist Nah; Neue Rhythmische
Satze Zum Gottesdienst *CC11U
kbd,gtr,opt fl,opt sax,gtr solo,1-
4pt mix cor, rhythmic group BOSSE
f.s. sc BE-812, pts BE-812-1-11
(240)

HODEIR, ANDRE (1921-   )
Anna Livia Plurabelle, For Solo
Voices And Solo Instruments
fl solo,flugelhorn solo,clar solo,
vln solo,9sax/clar solo,3trp
solo,3trom solo,2vibra solo,drums
solo,gtr solo,db solo,MezA soli,
clapping section [53'] MODERN
rent   (241)

HOFER, KARLHEINZ
Shanties From The Seven Seas *CC14U
[Eng] pno,db,gtr,men cor/mix cor,
solo voice sc,pts GERIG 913 f.s. (242)

HOLT, SIMEON TEN (1923-   )
A-.TA-LON, For Soloist And Thirty-Six
Playing And Talking
Instrumentalists
3.3.5.1. 2.3.1.0. vibra,marimba,
harp,pno,mand,gtr,3vln,3vla,3db,
Mez solo sc DONEMUS f.s.   (243)

HORST, ANTON VAN DER (1899-1965)
Alianora; Play About The Marriage Of
Reynalt Van Nassau, Duke Of
Gelre, And Alianor Of England
*Op.57
[Dutch] 1.1.1.1. 0.0.0.0. gtr,
string quin,cor,MezABar&speaking
voice [70'] min sc,pts,pno red,
set DONEMUS f.s.   (244)

HUNKINS, EUSEBIA SIMPSON (1902-   )
Appalachian Mass
org,opt gtr,unis cor FISCHER,C f.s.
(245)

JEZ, JAKOB (1928-   )
Do Fraig Amor *cant
"Bitte Um Liebe" 3plucked insts,
perc,dbl cor sc GERIG 746 f.s.
(246)

KAGEL, MAURICIO (1931-   )
Kantrimiusik (Pastorale for Solo
Voices and Instrumental Ensemble)
clar,trp in C,vln,pno,perc,
electronic tape/electronic
equipment,SMezT soli, bass tuba
in F or C, 2 gtr players (opt
insts: gtr-e", gtr-e', ukelele,

KAGEL, MAURICIO (cont'd.)

    mando, tenor banjo, etc.) [40']
    (scenic performance possible) sc
    UNIVER. 15919 f.s.   (247)

    Mare Nostrum; Entdeckung, Befriedung
    Und Konversion Des
    Mittelmeerraumes Durch Einen
    Stamm Aus Amazonien
    fl/pic,ob/English horn,gtr/mand/
    lute,harp,vcl,perc,acord,Bar&
    countertenor [60'] sc UNIVER.
    15951 f.s.   (248)

KAMINSKI, HEINRICH (1886-1946)
    Drei Gedichte Von Eichendorff, No. 1
    3gtr,6mand,6pt men cor sc UNIVER.
    7494 f.s.   (249)

KOBLER, HANS (1930-   )
    Ich Mochte Gerne Brucken Bauen
    (Gruschwitz) fl,opt gtr,4pt mix cor
    (Chorblatt, No. 41) BOSSE BE-616
    f.s.   (250)

KRENEK, ERNST (1900-   )
    Augenblick Errinert
    "Instant Remembered" [Ger/Eng/Lat]
    2(pic).0.2.0. 2.2.2.0. timp,
    4perc,glock,bells,xylo,vibra,
    harp,cel,pno,gtr,strings,
    electronic tape,S solo [15']
    BAREN. BA-6052 rent   (251)

    Nach Wie Vor Der Reihe Nach, Op. 182
    [Ger] 2.2.2.2. 4.2.2.1. 8perc,
    vibra,xylo,harp,cel,gtr,strings,
    vln solo,vcl solo,2 speaking
    voices [8'] BAREN. BA-4332 rent
                                      (252)

    Quintina Uber Die Funf Vokale
    fl,vibra,xylo,vla,2perc,
    electronic tape,S solo [10']
    BAREN. BA-4187 rent   (253)

    Sestina, Op. 161
    vln,gtr,fl,clar,trp,pno,2perc,
    glock,vibra,xylo,marimba,S solo
    [17'] BAREN. BA-3824 rent   (254)

KROL, BERNHARD (1920-   )
    Magnificat
    [Ger] trp,gtr,db,perc,org,cor&cong,
    S solo sc,pts,solo pt BOSSE
    BE-264 f.s.   (255)

    Maria Klar
    gtr,db,perc,S solo pts BOSSE BE-265
    f.s.   (256)

KUTZER, ERNST (1918-   )
    Mensch Sein In Christus; Gesange Zur
    Eucharistiefeier
    org,opt gtr,opt perc,cong,cantor,
    rhythmic group (db, bass gtr) sc
    BOSSE BE-276-ED. A f.s., ipa
                                      (257)
    org,fl,2clar,opt gtr,opt perc,cong,
    cantor, rhythmic group (db, bass
    gtr) sc BOSSE BE-276-ED. B f.s.,
    ipa   (258)

LAUTH, WOLFGANG (1931-   )
    Herr, Gib Uns Frieden (composed with
    Lehmann, Andreas)
    gtr,SATB (Chorblatt, No. 27) BOSSE
    BE-602 f.s.   (259)

LECHNER, KONRAD (1911-   )
    Cantica I
    bass clar,horn,perc,pno,gtr,vln,
    vcl,Mez solo [9'] sc GERIG HG-550
    f.s.   (260)

LEHMANN, ANDREAS (1930-   )
    Ich Rede Wenn Ich Schweigen Sollte
    gtr,db,perc,cor (Chorblatt, No. 18)
    BOSSE BE-243 f.s.   (261)

LUTYENS, ELIZABETH (1906-1983)
    Infidelio *Op.29
    [Eng] 1.0.1.1. 0.0.0.0. timp,perc,
    vibra,cel,gtr,vla,ST soli SCHOTT
    f.s.   (262)

MALIPIERO, RICCARDO (1914-   )
    In Time Of Daffodils
    1.1(English horn).1(bass clar).0.
    0.0.0.0. perc,gtr,vla,db,SBar
    soli [21'] ZERBONI min sc 6291
    f.s., pts 6292 rent, pno red 6341
    f.s.   (263)

MANNEKE, DAAN (1939-   )
    Qui Iustus Est, Iustificetur Adhuc
    *cant
    clar,trom,perc,gtr,cor sc DONEMUS
    f.s.   (264)

MIROGLIO, FRANCIS (1924-   )
    Tremplins
    1(pic).1(English horn).3.0.
    1.1.1.0. 4perc,harp,pno/cel,elec
    gtr,electronic tape [22'-26'] sc
    UNIVER. 14701 rent   (265)

MIROGLIO, FRANCIS (cont'd.)

    1(pic).1(English horn).3.0.4sax.
    1.1.1.0. 4perc,harp,elec org,pno/
    cel,elec gtr,electronic tape,4
    solo voices, 4brass insts, 4str
    insts [22'-26'] sc UNIVER. 14701
    rent   (266)

MOEVS, ROBERT WALTER (1921-   )
    Brief Mass, A
    vibra,org,gtr,db,cor pno red MARKS
    f.s.   (267)

MONTEVERDI, CLAUDIO (ca. 1567-1643)
    Concerto De Madrigali
    (Behrend) gtr,strings,cor,S solo
    (Gitarre-Bibliothek, No. 53) sc,
    cor pts BOTE GB-53 f.s.   (268)

    Orfeo: Vieni Imeneo
    (Sanvoisin) [It] S rec/vln I/vla da
    braccio,vln II/vla da braccio/
    cornetto/trp,vln III/vla da
    braccio/cornetto/trp,vla/vla da
    braccio/trom,vcl/vla da gamba/
    trom,gtr,hpsd/harp/org/lute,SSTB&
    countertenor/SSATB soli
    (notation: treb staff (gtr), pno
    sc (chitarone, lute), Plein Jeu,
    No. 143) sc HEUGEL PJ-143 f.s.,
    ipa contains also: Orfeo:
    Lasciati I Monti   (269)

    Tirsi E Clori
    (Cooper, Kenneth) [It/Eng/Ger] vcl,
    db,B solo, lute I and II or gtr I
    and II, cont (spinet or lute), S
    I solo or vln I, S II solo or vln
    II, A solo or vla I, A solo II or
    vla II (notation: treb clef (lute
    I, lute II), great staff (cont:
    spinet or lute)) set PENN STATE
    PSM-14 f.s.   (270)

    Tre Scherzi Musicali A Tre Voci
    (Sanvoisin) [It] 2vln/T rec/fl,opt
    gtr,vla da gamba/vcl,3 solo
    voices (Plein Jeu, No. 204) set
    HEUGEL PJ-204 f.s.   (271)

NEGRO-SPIRITUALS
    (v.d. Werf) part 1: S rec, fl, ob,
    mando; part 2: A rec, fl, ob, vln,
    mandola; part 3: vln, gtr, mand
    and-or part 3a: clar; part 4: gtr,
    pno and-or part 4a: vcl, db, bsn
    (1-3rd degr., Lichtblauwe Reeks: De
    Muzikantenclub); partly single line
    playing (pt 3); 5 pcs for 6 groups
    of insts) sc HARMONIA 1510 f.s.
                                      (272)

NEGRO-SPIRITUALS, VOL. 1 *CC4U
    [Eng/Ger] gtr,pno,db,mix cor/men cor
    sc,cor pts,pts SCHOTT 5926 f.s.
                                      (273)

NEGRO-SPIRITUALS, VOL. 2 *CC3U
    [Eng/Ger] gtr,pno,db,mix cor/men cor
    sc,cor pts,pts SCHOTT 5927 f.s.
                                      (274)

NICK, EDMUND (1891-1974)
    Leben In Dieser Zeit
    1.1.1.0.3sax. 0.2(flugelhorn).1.1.
    perc,harp,cel,harmonium,2pno,gtr,
    mand,banjo,strings,mix cor,2 solo
    voices&narrator, shouting cor,
    bandoneon [58'] UNIVER. f.s.
                                      (275)

NIEHAUS, MANFRED (1933-   )
    Pop & Art
    3.3.3.3. 6.3.4.0. timp,perc,2gtr,
    2bass gtr,strings,opt cor [12']
    GERIG HG-699 rent   (276)

NILSSON, BO (1937-   )
    Irrender Sohn, Ein
    timp,6perc,glock,bells,xylorimba,
    vibra,harp,cel,pno,elec gtr,alto
    fl,vla,db,A solo, elec mando [8'-
    10'] sc UNIVER. 13057 f.s.   (277)

    Madchentotenlieder
    pic,alto fl,6perc,tubular bells,
    xylorimba,vibra,cel,elec gtr,vln,
    vla,vcl,db,S solo, elec mando
    [8'] sc UNIVER. 12851 f.s.   (278)

    Und Die Zeiger Seiner Augen Wurden
    Langsam Zuruckgedreht
    1.2.3.1.soprano sax.alto sax.
    5.6.4.0. 2timp,5perc,glock,
    tubular bells,2vibra,xylorimba,
    marimba,harp,cel,pno,elec gtr,wom
    cor,SA soli, 4loudspeakers [12']
    UNIVER. rent   (279)

OBRECHT, JACOB (ca. 1430-1505)
    Missa Maria Zart
    (Crevel, Marcus van; Schat, Peter)
    0.3.2.1. 1.1.2.1. harp,gtr,5vla,
    3vcl,cor [47'] min sc DONEMUS
    f.s.   (280)

OGO, [CHORAL BROTHER]
    Weg Hinab Nach Jericho, Der
    kbd,gtr,unis cor (Liedblatt, No.
    20) BOSSE BE-273 f.s.   (281)

PIJPER, WILLEM (1894-1947)
    Romance Sans Paroles
    "C'est Le Chien De Jean De Nivelle"
    3.2.3.1. 3.3.0.0. perc,xylo,
    2harp,cel,pno,2mand,gtr,strings,
    Mez solo [5'] min sc DONEMUS f.s.
                                      (282)

RAXACH, ENRIQUE (1932-   )
    Interface (from Esoteric Garden, The)
    3.3.4.3. 4.3.3.1. 4perc,pno,2Hamm,
    ampl gtr,tape recorder,mix cor,
    ampl db sc DONEMUS f.s.   (283)

    Sine Nomine
    2.2.2.2.alto sax. 2.2.2.0. 2perc,
    harp,hpsd,Hamm/org,mand,ampl gtr,
    strings,opt pno/synthesizer,S
    solo sc DONEMUS f.s.   (284)

RAZZI, FAUSTO (1932-   )
    Helle Stimme, Die *cant
    [Ger] 0.0.2(soprano clar in E flat,
    bass clar).0.2sax. 0.2.2.0. timp,
    7perc,hpsd,gtr,cor [18'] ZERBONI
    sc 6299 f.s., pts 6301 rent, pno
    red 6300 f.s.   (285)

REDA, SIEGFRIED (1916-1968)
    Psalmus Morte Servati (Psalm No. 30)
    1.0.3.1. 0.0.2.0. timp,perc,org,
    gtr,strings,cor,Bar solo BAREN.
    BA-4189 rent   (286)

    Requiem Vel Vivorum Consolatio
    1.0.2.1. 0.0.2.0. timp,perc,gtr,
    strings,cor,SBar soli BAREN.
    BA-3513 rent   (287)

ROSENSTENGEL, ALBRECHT (1912-   )
    Polenmadchen *folk song,Polish
    "In Warschau Sind Die Madchen" gtr,
    opt tamb,4pt men cor (Folklore
    Der Welt) sc BREITKOPF-W Z-14
    f.s.   (288)

    Schlaflied Fur Juliska *folk song,
    Hung
    "Leise Kommt Die Dunkle Nacht" pno,
    gtr,perc,mix cor/eq voices
    (Folklore Der Welt) sc BREITKOPF-
    W Z-5 f.s.   (289)

    Seltene Schonheit, Eine *folk song,
    Finn
    "Liebes Madchen, Du Bist Schon"
    gtr,opt tamb,men cor (Folklore
    Der Welt) sc BREITKOPF-W Z-8 f.s.
                                      (290)

    Tanzlied Aus Israel *folk song,Isr
    "Wenn Morgens Die Sonne Erwacht"
    gtr,opt tamb,4pt men cor
    (Folklore Der Welt) cor pts
    BREITKOPF-W Z-9 f.s.   (291)

ROSSEAU, NORBERT (1907-1975)
    Stenen En Brood *cant
    gtr,perc,mix cor,STBar soli DE
    MONTE f.s.   (292)

ROVSING OLSEN, POUL (1922-   )
    A l'Inconnu *Op.48
    harp,gtr,5vln,3vla,2vcl,db,solo
    voice [7'] sc MOECK 5022 f.s.   (293)

RUTHENBERG, OTTO (1936-   )
    Slawka *CC5U,folk song,Slovak
    [Ger] pno,gtr,db,SATB sc,cor pts,
    pts MERSEBURGER EM-9301 f.s.
                                      (294)

RUYNEMAN, DANIEL (1886-1963)
    Reflexions I
    fl,gtr,vla,vibra,xylo,perc,S solo
    sc DONEMUS f.s.   (295)

SCHAT, PETER (1935-   )
    To You
    9gtr,4kbd,2elec org,Mez solo, 6tops
    [20'] sc DONEMUS f.s.   (296)

SCHILLING, HANS LUDWIG (1927-   )
    Legende Vom Weisen Und Zollner
    winds,brass,perc,cel,pno/hpsd,gtr,
    strings,cor,3 solo voices,
    recitativo solo, speaking-singing
    role pno red SCHOTT 5528 f.s.,
    ipr   (297)

    Liedstrophen, 2
    rec,hpsd/pno,gtr,perc,opt vcl,1-3pt
    cor study sc BAREN. MSP-30 f.s.
                                      (298)

    Singet Dem Herrn Ein Neues Lied
    *CC7U
    fl,vcl/db,gtr,perc,org,1-3 eq
    voices&cong,cantor, recs HANSSLER
    HE-25.004 sc f.s., ipr, cor pts
    Satze Zum Jugendgottesdienst
                                      (299)

SCHOENBERG, ARNOLD (1874-1951)
Serenade, Op. 24
clar,bass clar,mand,gtr,vln,vla,
vcl,opt Bar solo (Samtliche
Werke, Vol. XXII; 4th movement:
Sonett von Petrarcha, opt;
together with: Drei Kleine Stucke
Fur Kammerbesetzung, Pierrot
Lunaire (Op. 21), Append: Skizze)
UNIVER. f.s.   (300)

SCHONBACH, DIETER (1931-)
Canticum Psalmi Ad Laudes (Psalm No.
145)
3.0.3.0. 0.3.3.0. pno,Hamm,gtr,
3vln,3vcl,S solo [12'] PETERS
rent   (301)

Canticum Psalmi Resurrectionis (Psalm
No. 66)
2fl,trp,2vla,perc,elec gtr,S solo
[9'] study sc UNIVER. 13061 f.s.   (302)

Lyrische Gesange I
3fl,clar,vibra,cel,pno,gtr,
3vln,2vla,Mez solo [12'] PETERS
rent   (303)

SCHUBERT, FRANZ (PETER) (1797-1828)
Dorfchen, Das *D.641,No.1,Op.11,No.1
"Ich Ruhme Mir Mein Dorfchen Hier"
pno/gtr,4pt men cor BREITKOPF-W
f.s. kbd pt PS-1071, cor pts
CHB-3485   (304)

SECKINGER, KONRAD (1935-)
House Of The Rising Sun, The *folk
song,US
"There Is A House In New Orleans"
gtr,db,4pt mix cor,cantor, jingle
(Folklore Der Welt) sc BREITKOPF-
W Z-1 f.s.   (305)

SEEGER, PETER (1919-)
Schlaglichter!; 7 Songs Von Der
Unheilen Welt
[Ger] SATB&TTBB&SA/jr cor,inst,
(gts, elec org, perc) sc,cor pts
MULLER 2625 f.s., ipa   (306)

SEROCKI, KAZIMIERZ (1922-1981)
Augen Der Luft *song cycle
[Polish/Ger/Eng] 4.0.4.0. 4.3.3.1.
5perc,2harp,gtr,strings,S solo
[10'] MOECK f.s. study sc 50009,
pno red   (307)

Herz Der Nacht *song cycle
[Polish/Ger/Eng] 3.0.3.2. 2.0.0.0.
4perc,2harp,cel,pno,ampl gtr,
strings,Bar solo, ampl mando
[19'] (co-published with POLSKIE)
MOECK f.s. sc 50003, pno red
50002   (308)

STERN, HERMANN (1912-1978)
All Morgen Ist Ganz Frisch Und Neu
[Ger] xylo&glock/fl&db/gtr,SA&men
cor (Satze Zum Kirchenlied) sc
HANSSLER HE-8.054 f.s. contains
also: Steht Auf, Ihr Lieben
Kinderlein (no gtr); Tag Bricht
An Und Zeiget Sich, Der (no gtr)   (309)

Geh Aus, Mein Herz, Und Suche Freud
[Ger] vln,db/gtr,SA&men cor (Satze
Zum Kirchenlied) sc HANSSLER
HE-8.057 f.s. contains also: Wer
Wohlauf Ist Und Gesund (xylo/rec,
db/gtr,SA&men cor)   (310)

STROBL, OTTO (1927-)
Dutzend Schilieder, Ein *CC12U
gtr/acord,1-2pt men cor DOBLINGER
64260 f.s. Singheft   (311)

THOMAS, KURT (1904-1973)
Schloss In Osterreich, Das *Op.18b,
cant
pno,strings,opt fl&ob&clar&rec&
horn&trp&timp&perc&gtr,vln solo,
cor,ATB soli BREITKOPF-W rent   (312)

TITTEL, ERNST (1910-1969)
Vogelweider, Der *Op.60
2fl,vln,vla,gtr/hpsd,mix cor,ST
soli pno red,pts,cor pts
DOBLINGER 46019 f.s.   (313)

TOGNI, CAMILLO (1922-)
Helian Di Trakl
2.1.1.0. 1.1.1.1. timp,xylo,glock,
cel,pno,gtr,strings,S solo [16']
ZERBONI sc 5891 f.s., pts 5783
rent   (314)

Rondeaux Per 10
timp,glock,bells,harp,cel,hpsd,
harmonium,gtr,db,S solo [8']
ZERBONI min sc 6158 f.s., pts
6159 rent   (315)

VOGT, HANS (1911-)
Sine Nomine *cant
3.3.3.3. 3.3.3.1. timp,perc,harp,
hpsd,org,gtr,strings,cor,T solo
BAREN. AE-326 rent   (316)

WEBERN, ANTON VON (1883-1945)
Lieder, 2, Op. 19
clar,bass clar,cel,gtr,vln,cor
UNIVER. f.s. cor pts 9536, pno
red 9537
contains: Weiss Wie Lilien,
Op.19,No.1; Zieh'n Die Schafe,
Op.19,No.2   (317)

WEILL, KURT (1900-1950)
Berliner Requiem
0.0.2.2.alto sax.tenor sax.
2.2.2.0. timp,2perc,org/
harmonium,gtr,banjo,3pt men cor
[25'] pno red UNIVER. 9786 f.s.   (318)

Surabaya Johnny (from Happy End)
(Berio, Luciano) fl,clar,trp,perc,
gtr,vln,vla,vcl,db,Mez solo [5']
UNIVER. rent   (319)

WIMBERGER, GERHARD (1923-)
Songs, 4
English horn,clar,alto sax,bass
clar,horn,drums,ampl gtr,6vcl,db,
solo voice, jazz trp, jazz trb
[15'] BAREN. 6062 rent   (320)

ZAGWIJN, HENRI (1878-1954)
Kerkerballade, De
4.3.3.3. 4.3.3.1. timp,perc,2harp,
cel,2mand,gtr,strings,speaking
voice [60'] min sc,pno red
DONEMUS f.s.   (321)

ZIMMERMANN, HEINZ WERNER (1930-)
Missa Profana
2.2.2.2. 3.4.2.1. timp,perc,org,
strings,5pt mix cor,SATB soli,
jazz combo: trp, clar, trom, gtr,
pno, db, perc (all insts solo)
BAREN. BA-6014 rent   (322)

V/ii-Coll   Music for Ensemble/Orchestra with Voice and Guitar: Collections

BAUSTEINE FUR DEN GOTTESDIENST, REIHE
A: PSALMEN
HANSSLER HE-19.101 f.s.
contains: Ruppel, Paul Ernst,
Danket Dem Herrn Und Predigt
Seinen Namen (Psalm No. 105)
(gtr/kbd,bass inst,unis cor,
cantor); Ruppel, Paul Ernst, Ich
Will Dir Danken, Herr (Psalm No.
108) (gtr/kbd,bass inst,unis
cor); Schwarz, Jochen, Siehe, Es
Ist Alles Neu Geworden (Psalm No.
149) (SSATTB); Schweizer, Rolf, O
Herr, Du Unsre Unsre Zuflucht
(Psalm No. 90) (kbd/gtr,bass
inst,cor&cong)   (323)

BAUSTEINE FUR DEN GOTTESDIENST, REIHE
A: PSALMEN
HANSSLER HE-19.103 f.s.
contains: Ruppel, Paul Ernst, Ich
Hebe Meine Augen Auf Zu Dir
(Psalm No. 123) (org/cor/cong,
male solo); Ruppel, Paul Ernst,
Unser Herr Ist Gross Und Von
Grosser Kraft (Psalm Nos. 145-
147) (kbd/gtr&bass inst,unis cor,
cantor); Wehnert, Wolfram, Lobet
Den Herren, Ihr Seine Engel
(Psalm No. 103) (unis cor)   (324)

BAUSTEINE FUR DEN GOTTESDIENST, REIHE
A: PSALMEN
HANSSLER HE-19.106 f.s.
contains: Blarr, Oskar Gottlieb,
Frohlocket Mit Handen (Psalm No.
47) (tenor sax/trp,pno,db,perc,
opt gtr&vibra&org,SSATB); Ruppel,
Paul Ernst, Es Soll Nicht Durch
Heer, Sondern Durch Meinen Geist
Geschehen (db/gtr,opt 3trp&trom&
org,SSA&men cor)   (325)

BAUSTEINE FUR DEN GOTTESDIENST, REIHE
B: CHORVERSE
HANSSLER HE-19.205 f.s.
contains: Schweizer, Rolf, Komm,
Heiliger Geist (clar/fl, alto sax/
trp,trom/tenor sax,kbd/gtr,db,
cor&cong)   (326)

BAUSTEINE FUR DEN GOTTESDIENST, REIHE
B: CHORVERSE
HANSSLER HE-19.207 f.s.

contains: Ruppel, Paul Ernst, Zu
Gottes Ehre Mein Saitenspiel
(kbd/gtr,unis cor); Schweizer,
Rolf, Manchmal Kennen Wir Gottes
Willen (kbd,SSA&cong); Schweizer,
Rolf, Verleih Uns Frieden
Gnadiglich (trom/vcl/bsn,opt org,
unis cor/cor)   (327)

BAUSTEINE FUR DEN GOTTESDIENST, REIHE
C: SINGSPRUCHE UND VERSIKEL
HANSSLER HE-19.302 f.s.
contains: Planzer, Emanuel, Wende
Dich Zu Mir Und Sei Mir Gnadig
(Psalm No. 25) (pno/org,unis cor,
jazz band or gtr, db); Ruppel,
Paul Ernst, Grosste Gebot, Das
(trp,4trom,1-4pt mix cor);
Ruppel, Paul Ernst, Herr Denkt An
Uns, Der (Psalm No. 115) (1-4pt
cor,cantor); Schweizer, Rolf,
Danket Gott Und Lobet Ihn (gtr,
unis cor); Schweizer, Rolf,
Doxologie Des Vater-Unser (4inst,
4pt cor); Schweizer, Rolf, Kyrie
(hpsd/org,db,4inst,unis cor&cong)   (328)

BAUSTEINE FUR DEN GOTTESDIENST, REIHE
C: SINGSPRUCHE UND VERSIKEL
HANSSLER HE-19.303 f.s.
contains: Blarr, Oskar Gottlieb,
Gestern Ist Heute (kbd,gtr,unis
cor); Blarr, Oskar Gottlieb,
Hilf, Herr Meines Leben (gtr,db,
SATB&cong); Ruppel, Paul Ernst,
Fahret Auf Die Hohe Und Werft
Euer Netz Aus (kbd,unis cor);
Ruppel, Paul Ernst, Gelobt Sei
Der Herr Taglich (Psalm No. 68)
(4inst,unis cor)   (329)

BAUSTEINE FUR DEN GOTTESDIENST, REIHE
D: NEUE LIEDER
HANSSLER HE-19.401 f.s.
contains: Michel, Josef, Herr,
Sende Uns Botschaft (kbd,hpsd,
perc/trp,solo voice, gtrs);
Ruppel, Paul Ernst, Gott Liebt
Diese Welt (org,cor); Schweizer,
Rolf, Singet Dem Herrn Ein Neues
Lied (org/kbd,inst,4-5pt mix cor)   (330)

BAUSTEINE FUR DEN GOTTESDIENST, REIHE
D: NEUE LIEDER
HANSSLER HE-19.402 f.s.
contains: Kretzschmar, Gunther,
Gott Geht An Keinem Vorbei (2trp,
clar/trom,db,cor,speaking voice);
Michel, Josef, Herr, Ruste Uns
Von Neuem Aus (kbd/winds,unis
cor); Michel, Josef, Sieh Nicht
Deine Schwachheit An (gtr/db,
SAT); Schweizer, Rolf, Wie Lange
Noch, Herr (Psalm No. 13) (kbd,
unis cor)   (331)

BAUSTEINE FUR DEN GOTTESDIENST, REIHE
D: NEUE LIEDER
HANSSLER HE-19.406 f.s.
contains: Schweizer, Rolf, Herr Hat
Uns Das Salz Genannt, Der (org/
4trp&trom,unis cor); Schweizer,
Rolf, Herr, Mein Nachster Ruft
Mich (treb inst/fl&clar&vibra,
kbd/gtr,unis cor); Schweizer,
Rolf, Ihr Werdet Kraft Empfangen
(treb inst/fl&clar,4kbd,db,unis
cor&cong)   (332)

BAUSTEINE FUR DEN GOTTESDIENST, REIHE
D: NEUE LIEDER
HANSSLER HE-19.407 f.s.
contains: Schweizer, Rolf, Herr,
Lass Uns In Deinem Lichte (2treb
inst,4kbd,db,unis cor);
Schweizer, Rolf, Ihr Seid Das
Licht Der Welt (kbd/4inst,unis
cor); Schweizer, Rolf, Tobender
Sturm (kbd,db/gtr,cor&cong)   (333)

BAUSTEINE FUR DEN GOTTESDIENST, REIHE
D: NEUE LIEDER
HANSSLER HE-19.409 f.s.
contains: Barbe, Helmut, Kreuz Ist
Aufgerichtet, Das (kbd,unis cor);
Bossler, Kurt, Fragst Du Nach
Meiner Sunde (cor); Michel,
Josef, Wir Wissen Nicht, Was
Kommt (winds/kbd,1-2solo voice);
Trubel, Gerhard, Dein Tod
Gebietet Schweigen (kbd/gtr,unis
cor)   (334)

BAUSTEINE FUR DEN GOTTESDIENST,
SAMMELHEFTE, VOL. 1
gtr (contains: HE-19.101, HE-19.401,
and 2 other eds) HANSSLER HE-19.901
f.s.   (335)

BAUSTEINE FUR DEN GOTTESDIENST,
SAMMELHEFTE, VOL. 2
gtr (contains: HE-19.402 and 3 other
eds) HANSSLER HE-19.902 f.s.   (336)

BAUSTEINE FUR DEN GOTTESDIENST,
   SAMMELHEFTE, VOL. 3
   gtr (contains: HE-19.103, HE-19.303
   and 2 other eds) HANSSLER HE-19.903
   f.s.   (337)

BAUSTEINE FUR DEN GOTTESDIENST,
   SAMMELHEFTE, VOL. 5
   gtr (contains: HE-19.205 and 3 other
   eds) HANSSLER HE-19.905 f.s. (338)

V/iii Music for the Theater

BARBIER, RENE (AUGUSTE-ERNEST)
   (1890-1981)
   Pierres Magiques, Les, Ballet °Op.94
   2+pic.1+English horn.2.2. 4.3.3.1.
   timp,perc,harp,cel,pno,gtr,
   strings CBDM rent   (339)

BENNETT, RICHARD RODNEY (1936-   )
   Victory, Opera In 3 Acts
   [Eng] 3.2.3.3. 4.3.3.1. timp,3perc,
   harp,cel,pno,strings, on stage:
   fl, vln, vcl, mando, gtr, acord;
   cast: 24 soloists, 2 vocal
   groups, silent roles pno red
   UNIVER. 14665 f.s.   (340)

BERIO, LUCIANO (1925-   )
   Opera, Opera In 4 Acts
   2.1.2.2.2sax. 3.3.2.1. 3perc,pno,
   elec org,elec gtr,6vla,4vcl,4db,
   electronic tape,vln solo, cast:
   10 actors, S solo, T solo, B
   solo, vocal group, extras,
   children UNIVER. rent   (341)

BIRTWISTLE, HARRISON (1934-   )
   Orpheus, Opera In 3 Acts
   4.4.4.4. 4.4.6.2. 7perc,3harp,7gtr,
   3players for 3soprano sax, recs,
   etc.; cast: 12 soloists, 9
   actors, 2 speaking roles, 3
   female voices, 12-pt mix UNIVER.
   rent   (342)

BOIS, ROB DU (1934-   )
   Midas; Ballet Music For Orchestra
   4.2.2.2.alto sax.tenor sax.
   2.4.2.1. perc,harp,elec org,ampl
   gtr,strings sc DONEMUS f.s. (343)

BOYD, ANNE
   Rose Garden, The; Theatre Piece For
   Singing Actress, Double Chorus
   And Instruments
   3fl,gtr,ampl gtr,6perc,electronic
   tape,Mez solo, jazz group, 3
   mimes [70'] sc,pts FABER rent
                                  (344)

BURGHAUSER, JARMIL (1921-   )
   Diener Zweier Herren, Der; Ballet In
   Three Scenes
   2.2.2.2. 3.2.1.0. timp,perc,pno,
   strings, on stage: fl, gtr,
   mando; cast: 10 soloists, troupe
   ARTIA 2542 perf mat rent   (345)

   Tristan Und Isolde; Ballet In Ten
   Scenes
   2.2.2.2. 3.3.3.0. timp,3perc,harp,
   cel,elec pno,ampl gtr,ampl bass
   gtr,strings, cast: 11 soloists,
   extras ARTIA 2636 perf mat rent
                                  (346)

CAVALLI, (PIETRO) FRANCESCO (1602-1676)
   Calisto, La; Opera In Two Acts With A
   Prologue
   (Leppard, Raymond) strings,2hpsd,
   harp,21ute,gtr,3vcl,2db,
   chitarrone, flue org; cast: 13
   soloists, cor [180'] sc,pts FABER
   rent   (347)

   Ormindo, L'; Opera In Two Acts
   (Leppard, Raymond) strings,2hpsd,
   harp,21ute,gtr,3vcl,2cont,
   theorbo, flue org; cast: 10
   soloists [140'] sc,pts FABER rent
                                  (348)
   (Leppard, Raymond) [It/Eng/Ger]
   strings,2hpsd,harp,21ute,gtr,
   3vcl,2cont, theorbo, flue org;
   cast: 10 soloists [140'] voc sc
   FABER F-0036 f.s.   (349)

CHERUBINI, LUIGI (1760-1842)
   Ali Baba Und Die Vierzig Rauber;
   Comic Opera In Prelude And Four
   Scenes
   [Ger] 2.2.2.2. 4.4.3.1. timp,perc,
   gtr,strings, cast: 9 soloists, 1
   speaking pt, cor, ballet BAREN.
   BA-3569 rent   (350)

CIKKER, JAN (1911-   )
   Spiel Von Liebe Und Tod, Ein; Opera
   In One Act
   [Ger] 2+pic.2+English horn.2+bass
   clar.2+contrabsn. 4.3.3.1. timp,
   4perc,harp,cel,gtr,strings,
   behind stage: perc, 2pic, 2 trp
   on tape recorder; cast: 12
   soloists, 6 silent roles, cor

CIKKER, JAN (cont'd.)

   BAREN. 6021 rent   (351)

DE GRANDIS, RENATO (1927-   )
   Gloria Al Re
   "Es Lebe Der Konig; Comic Opera In
   Three Acts" [Ger] 1.1.1.1.
   4.3.3.0. timp,4perc,harp,cel,
   hpsd,pno,ampl gtr,strings, on
   stage: pic, trp or cornet, bass
   drum and cym, tuba; cast: unknown
   pno red GERIG HG-580 f.s.   (352)

FISCHER, JAN F. (1921-   )
   Krieg Mit Den Molchen, Der; Music To
   The Play Of Pavel Kohaut
   1.0.4.1. 0.3.2.1. perc,harp,cel,
   pno,acord,gtr,db ARTIA 2554 rent
                                  (353)

FORTNER, WOLFGANG (1907-   )
   In Seinem Garten Liebt Don Perlimplin
   Belisa; Opera
   [Ger] 1.2.2.2. 1.2.1.0. timp,3perc,
   harp,cel,gtr,strings, on stage:
   fl, hpsd, tape recorder; cast:
   unknown pno red SCHOTT 5266 f.s.
                                  (354)

FUSSL, KARL-HEINZ (1924-   )
   Dybuk; Opera In Three Acts And Three
   Scenes
   2.2.2.2. 4.3.3.1. 3timp,2perc,xylo,
   vibra,marimba,glock,2-3harp,cel,
   2-3gtr,strings, on stage: some
   insts of orch; cast: 9 soloists,
   some secondary roles, cor, ballet
   pno red UNIVER. 13563 f.s., perf
   mat rent   (355)

GASLINI, GIORGIO (1929-   )
   Quarto Di Vita, Un; Opera Da Strada,
   In Two Acts And Twelve Scenes
   2.2.2.2. 2.3.2.1. timp,perc,xylo,
   vibra,harp,pno,gtr,strings, cast:
   15 soloists, numerous secondary
   roles UNIVER. perf mat rent (356)

GRAF, THOMAS
   Wie Heisst Du, Josefine?; Ein
   Musikalisches Lustspiel, In Three
   Acts
   2pno/pno,gtr,db,clar,acord,perc,
   cast: 5 soloists ALKOR 121 perf
   mat rent   (357)

HANDEL, GEORGE FRIDERIC (1685-1759)
   Agrippina; A Cheerful Opera In Three
   Acts
   [Ger/It] 2.2.0.1. 0.2.0.0. timp,
   strings, cont: lute or gtr,
   theorbo or gtr, harp, hpsd; cast:
   9 soloists, extras BAREN. pts
   BA-1636 rent, pno red f.s. (358)

   Giulio Cesare
   "Julius Caesar; Opera In Three
   Acts" (Zschoch) [Ger/It] 1.2.0.1.
   4.1.0.0. strings,cont, on stage:
   ob, bsn, harp, theorbo or gtr,
   strings; cast: 8 soloists, cor,
   ballet BAREN. BA-4019 perf mat
   rent   (359)

HANUS, JAN (1915-   )
   Also Sprach Scheherazade, Opera
   [Ger] 1+pic.1+English horn.1+bass
   clar.1.alto sax. 3.2.1.1. timp,
   3perc,harp,cel,pno,ampl gtr,
   strings,tape recorder, cast: 11-
   13 soloists, cor, ballet ARTIA
   2311 perf mat rent   (360)

HAVELKA, SVATOPLUK (1925-   )
   Pyrrhos; Balletsinfonie
   3.2+English horn.2+bass clar.2+
   contrabsn. 4.4.3.1. 4perc,vibra,
   harp,cel,pno,ampl gtr ARTIA 2590
   perf mat rent   (361)

JONGEN, LEON (1885-1969)
   Venezuela; Music For The Documentary
   Film
   1(pic).1.1(soprano sax).1. 1.0.1.0.
   glock,pno,gtr,strings, perc
   (jazz) CBDM perf mat rent   (362)

KAGEL, MAURICIO (1931-   )
   Repertoire
   minimum 5 musicians and-or actors,
   ca. 100 scenic-musical actions,
   before a wind-screen;
   instrumentation: stage properties
   used as "sound generators",
   traditional plucked insts, wind
   insts; selection of actions (opt
   sequence) possible [20'-60']
   UNIVER. f.s.   (363)

   Tremens; Scenic Assembling Of An
   Experiment In One Scene
   1st group of insts: 2 actors (1 on
   stage, 1 off stage), elec gtr,
   elec bass gtr, elec db, Hamm,
   perc, tape recorders; 2nd group
   of insts: Span gtr, db (5
   strings), perc, 3 tape recorders,

KAGEL, MAURICIO (cont'd.)

4 loud speakers, 1 microphone, 3
slide projectors [45'] sc UNIVER.
13505 rent   (364)

KALAS, JULIUS (1902-1967)
Mullerin Von Granada, Die; Operetta
In Three Acts And Five Scenes
[Ger] 2.1.2.1. 3.2.2.0. timp,3perc,
harp,gtr,strings, cast: 12
soloists, 2 speaking pts, cor,
ballet ARTIA 2354 perf mat rent
                                  (365)

KASLIK, VACLAV (1917-   )
Prager Karneval; Ballet-Triptych
After Three Medieval Ballads
3.2+English horn.2.0. 4.3.3.1.
timp,5perc,harp,pno,3mand,gtr,
strings,opt cel&cimbalom,T solo,
8-19 soloists, troupe ARTIA 2549
perf mat rent   (366)

KRENEK, ERNST (1900-   )
Ausgerechnet Und Verspielt; Eine
"Spiel"-Oper *Op.179
"Computed And Confounded; A Short
Opera" 1.1.1.0. 0.1.1.0. 5perc,
harp,cel,hpsd,2pno,harmonium,gtr,
solo string trio (vln, vla, vcl),
cast: 10 soloists, 1 speaking pt,
cor (members of the public in the
casino) [80'] BAREN. BA-4322 perf
mat rent   (367)

Das Kommt Davon; Opera
"Wenn Sardakai Auf Reisen Geht;
Opera" 1(pic).1.2.1. 1.1.1.0.
timp,6perc,glock,bells,xylo,
vibra,harp,cel,2pno,ampl gtr,
strings, cast: 6 soloists, 2
silent roles, opt extras BAREN.
6038 perf mat rent   (368)

Goldene Bock, Der; Opera In Four Acts
*Op.186
"Golden Ram, The; Opera In Four
Acts" 2.2.2.2. 2.3.3.0. timp,
5perc,harp,cel,pno,ampl gtr,
strings, cast: 20 soloists, 1
silent role, 5 speaking pts, cor
BAREN. 4346 perf mat rent   (369)

Zauberspiegel, Der; Television Opera
In Fourteen Scenes
"Magic Mirror, The; Television
Opera In Fourteen Scenes"
1.1.1.1. 1.1.1.0. 4perc,glock,
xylo,vibra,harp,cel,hpsd,
cimbalom,3pno,harmonium,ampl gtr,
zither; cast: 9 soloists, 1
silent role, extras [85'] BAREN.
4169 perf mat rent   (370)

KRUYF, TON DE (1937-   )
Quauhquauhtinchan In Den Vreemde; A
Radiophonic Opera
2.2.2.2.2sax. 2.2.2.1. harp,cel,
pno,Hamm,elec gtr,strings,Mez&
speaking voice,cor, archiphone,
clavioline sc DONEMUS f.s. (371)

MILLOCKER, KARL (1842-1899)
Diana; Comic Opera In Three Acts
(Friedrich, Paul) 2.2.2.2. 4.2.3.0.
timp,2perc,harp,gtr,strings, on
stage: vln, 4horns; cast: 7
soloists, 1 speaking pt, ballet,
extras, (no cor) ALKOR 108 perf
mat rent   (372)

MONTEVERDI, CLAUDIO (ca. 1567-1643)
Incoronazione Di Poppea, L'; Opera In
Three Acts And A Prologue
(Leppard, Raymond) [It/Ger/Eng]
2trp,strings,2hpsd,harp,gtr,2vcl,
2cont, lute (doubling
chitarrone), 2org (flue and
reed); cast: 16 soloists, TB cor
[142'] sc FABER F-0037 rent (373)
(Leppard, Raymond) 2trp,strings,
2hpsd,harp,gtr,2vcl,2cont, lute
(doubling chitarrone), 2org (flue
and reed); cast: 16 soloists, TB
cor [142'] pts FABER F-0038 rent
                                  (374)
(Leppard, Raymond) [It/Eng] 2trp,
strings,2hpsd,harp,gtr,2vcl,
2cont, lute (doubling
chitarrone), 2org (flue and
reed); cast: 16 soloists, TB cor
[142'] voc sc FABER f.s.   (375)
"Kronung Der Poppea, Die; Opera In
Three Acts" (Redlich, Hans
Ferdinand) [It/Ger] 2fl,2trp,
strings, vla da gamba (2-pt
consort), cont: hpsd, bass lute
or harp or gtr, org; cast: 16
soloists, cor, extras BAREN.
BA-3845 perf mat rent   (376)

Orfeo; Favola In Musica In Five Acts
With A Prologue
"Orfeo; Opera In Five Acts"
(Leppard, Raymond) 3trp,3trom,
bass trom,alto trom,2rec,strings,

MONTEVERDI, CLAUDIO (cont'd.)

2hpsd,harp,3vcl,cont, 2cornetti
(ob, clar doubling each pt), 2org
(flue and reed), 2lutes doubling
chitarrones or gtrs; cast: 15
soloists, cor [121'] FABER perf
mat rent   (377)
"Orfeo; Favola Pastorale In Two
Parts" (Maderna, Bruno) 3.3.4.3.
4.3.3.0. timp,3perc,2harp,cel,
hpsd,org,mand,2gtr,10vln,12vla,
10vcl,6db, cast: 7 soloists, cor
ZERBONI 6634 f.s. sc 6626 f.s.,
pts 6627 rent, pno red   (378)
(Wenzinger, August) [Ger/It] 2rec,
2cornetto/2ob,3trp,5trom,strings,
cont: 3gtr, 2hpsch, 2positive
org, regal; cast: 17 soloists, cor
BAREN. sc,pts BA-2031 rent, pno
red BA-2031A f.s.   (379)

Ritorno d'Ulisse In Patria, Il; Opera
In Two Acts With A Prologue
(Leppard, Raymond) 2ob, English
horn,2bsn, alto trom,3trom,2hpsd,
harp,3lute,gtr,3vcl,2db,strings,
2org (flue and reed); cast: 19
soloists, SATB cor [190'] FABER
perf mat rent   (380)

OTTE, HANS (1926-   )
Daidalos; Ballet In Seven Scenes For
Six Players
player 6: gtr, jingles, 2tri,
2cymbales antiques, metalblock
UNIVER. perf mat rent   (381)

PALESTER, ROMAN (1907-   )
Morte Di Don Giovanni, La; Action In
Music In One Act
[It/Fr/Ger] 3.2.4.3.sax. 3.3.3.0.
timp,8perc,harp,cel,pno,mand,gtr,
strings, cast: 4 soloists, 3
speaking pts, cor [50'] sc,pts
ZERBONI 5921 rent   (382)
[Fr/Ger] 3.2.4.3.sax. 3.3.3.0.
timp,8perc,harp,cel,pno,mand,gtr,
strings, cast: 4 soloists, 3
speaking pts, cor [50'] pno red
ZERBONI 5922 f.s.   (383)

SCHELB, JOSEF (1894-1977)
Gestutzte Eros, Der; Music To The
Comedy By Herbert Tjadens
clar,gtr,pno,perc (contains among
others three ballads by Carl
Michael Bellmann) BAREN. 3142
perf mat rent   (384)

SKALKOTTAS, NIKOS (1904-1949)
Maienzauber; Stage Music To The Fairy
Drama
"Mayday Spell; Stage Music To The
Fairy Drama" 2.2.2.2. 2.1.1.1.
timp,4perc,cel,gtr,strings,S&3
speaking voices,opt cor,
chromatic harp [40'] UNIVER. f.s.
                                  (385)

SMETANA, BEDRICH (1824-1884)
Geheimnis, Das; Comic Opera In Three
Acts
[Ger] 2.2.2.2. 4.2.3.0. perc,gtr,
strings, on stage: bells and
flails; cast: 11 soloists, cor DP
2057 perf mat rent   (386)

SONZOGNO, GIULIO CESARE (1906-1976)
Leggenda Di Ognuno, La; Scenic Music
For Chorus And Orchestra
2.2.2.2. 4.3.3.1. timp,6perc,2harp,
pno,org,strings,cor, on stage:
mandos, mandola, gtr, acord
ZERBONI 3047 perf mat rent (387)

STOCKHAUSEN, KARLHEINZ (1928-   )
Aus Den Sieben Tagen; Composition No.
26
[Ger] gtr (15 compositions
(includes 1 with stage
composition) for an ensemble with
an indefinite number of players
(including gtr); duration
indefinite, performances up to
1972: each composition 4'-60')
UNIVER. 14790 f.s.   (388)
[Fr] gtr (15 compositions (includes
1 with stage composition) for an
ensemble with an indefinite
number of players (including
gtr); duration indefinite,
performances up to 1972: each
composition 4'-60') UNIVER.
14790-F f.s.   (389)
[Eng] gtr (15 compositions
(includes 1 with stage
composition) for an ensemble with
an indefinite number of players
(including gtr); duration
indefinite, performances up to
1972: each composition 4'-60')
UNIVER. 14790-E f.s.   (390)

STRAUSS, JOHANN, [JR.] (1825-1899)
Nacht In Venedig, Eine: Serenade Fur
Delaqua; Finale Of The 1st Act
(Vogg) 2+pic.2.2.2. 2.2.3.0. perc,
harp,gtr,strings,mix cor pno red
DOBLINGER 46808 f.s., perf mat
rent   (391)

SUPPE, FRANZ VON (1819-1895)
Banditenstreiche; Comic Opera In
Three Acts
(Waldenmaier, August Peter)
2.2.2.2. 4.3.3.0. timp,2-3perc,
harp,gtr,strings, cast: 12
soloists, cor, ballet ALKOR 106
rent   (392)

Schone Galathee, Die; Comic Opera In
One Act
(Waldenmaier, August Peter)
2.1.2.1. 2.2.1.0. timp,2perc,
harp,strings,opt gtr, or full
orchestra: 2.2.2.2. 4.3.3.0.,
timp, 3perc, harp, gtr, strings;
cast: 4 soloists, opt cor (off
stage) pno red ALKOR 105 f.s.
perf mat rent   (393)

VOGT, HANS (1911-   )
Athenerkomodie; Opera Giocosa In One
Act
"Metropolitans, The; Opera Giocosa
In One Act" [Ger/Eng]
1.1.1.1.alto sax. 0.1.0.0. perc,
harp,hpsd,cimbalom,gtr,string
quar,db, cast: 10 soloists, small
cor, extras ALKOR 124 perf mat
rent   (394)

VOSTRAK, ZBYNEK (1920-   )
Schneewittchen; Ballet In Four Acts
And Seven Scenes
2+pic.2.2+bass clar.2. 4.3.4.1.
timp,3perc,harp,cel,pno,2gtr,
strings, cast: 8 soloists, extras
study sc ARTIA 1485 f.s.   (395)

WEILL, KURT (1900-1950)
Aufstieg Und Fall Der Stadt
Mahagonny: Suite
(Bruckner-Ruggeberg, Wilhelm)
1.1.1.2.2sax. 2.3.2.1. timp,perc,
harmonium,pno,bass gtr,banjo,
strings, bandoneon [25'] UNIVER.
f.s.   (396)

Dreigroschenoper: Suite
(Schonherr, Max) 2.2.2.2. 4.2.2.1.
perc,harp,pno/cel,gtr,strings,opt
solo voice [15'30"] UNIVER. f.s.
                                  (397)

Kleine Dreigroschenmusik
2(pic).0.2+bass-clar.2. alto sax.
tenor sax or soprano sax.
0.2.1.0., timp, perc, pno, banjo
or gtr or bandoneon [22'] sc
UNIVER. 9712 f.s.   (398)

WIMBERGER, GERHARD (1923-   )
Lebensregeln; Katechismus Mit Musik
2.1+English horn.2+bass clar.1+
contrabsn.alto sax. 4.3.3.1.
timp,2perc,harp,cel,elec org,ampl
gtr,ampl bass gtr,vln,6vla,4vcl,
4db,tape recorder, cast: 18
soloists, 7 speaking roles, cor,
12 cor solo voices, 3 cor
speaking roles, extras BAREN.
6090 perf mat rent   (399)

ZILLIG, WINFRIED (1905-1963)
Baal; Music To The Play
gtr solo (also available on tape)
BAREN. 4152 perf mat rent   (400)

Camino Real; Music To The Play
trp,trom,perc,pno,mand,gtr,db (also
available on tape) BAREN. BA-4153
perf mat rent   (401)

Peer Gynt; Music To The Play
0.1.0.0.3sax. 0.3.1.0. perc,Hamm,
gtr,strings without vla (also
available on tape) BAREN. BA-4162
perf mat rent   (402)

ZIMMERMANN, BERND ALOIS (1918-1970)
Musique Pour Les Soupers Du Roi Ubu;
Ballet Noir En Sept Parties Et
Une Entree
3.3.3.3.sax. 4.3.3.1. timp,2perc,
harp,cel,pno,org,mand,2gtr,4db,
combo (clar, trp, ampl gtr, ampl
db) [18'] (for scenic or concert
performance) sc BAREN. BA-4180
rent   (403)

VI Thematic Index of the Preludes, Studies, and Exercises for Guitar by Francisco Tárrega
Musical Incipits

i. PRELUDIOS

Prelude, TI i- 1, in D minor

Prelude, TI i- 2, in A minor

Prelude, TI i- 3, in G

Prelude, TI i- 4, in E

Prelude, TI i- 5, in E

Prelude, TI i- 6, in B minor

Prelude, TI i- 7, in A

Prelude, TI i- 8a, in A

Prelude, TI i- 8b, in A

Prelude, TI i- 9, in A

Prelude, TI i- 10, in D

Prelude, TI i- 11, in D

Prelude, TI i- 12, in A minor

Prelude, TI i- 13, in A minor

Prelude, TI i- 14, in A minor

Prelude, TI i- 15, in C

Prelude, TI i- 16, D minor

Prelude, Tl i- 17, in E

Prelude, Tl i- 18, in D minor

Prelude, Tl i- 19, in E minor

Prelude, Tl i- 20, in A

Prelude, Tl i- 21, in D

Prelude, Tl i- 22, in E

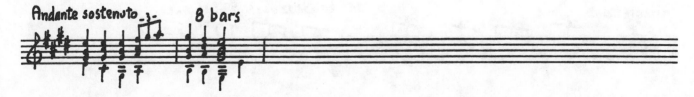

Prelude, TI i- 23, in B minor

Prelude, TI i- 24, in A minor

Prelude, TI i- 25, in A

ii. ESTUDIOS

Study, TI ii- 1, in G

Study, TI ii- 2a, in A

Study, TI ii- 2b, in A

Study, TI ii- 3, in E

Study, TI ii- 4a

Study, TI ii- 4b, in A

Study, TI ii- 5, in A

Study, TI ii- 6, in D

Study, TI ii- 7a, in G

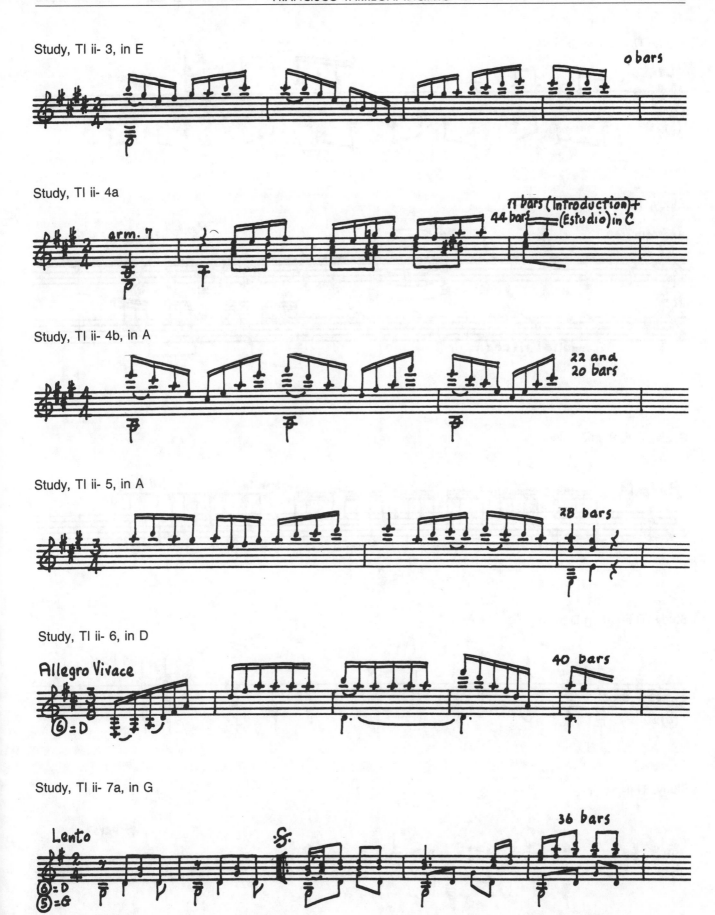

Study, TI ii- 7b, in D

Study, TI ii- 8, in A

Study, TI ii- 9, in A minor

Study, TI ii- 10, in D minor

Study, TI ii- 11, in E

Study, Tl ii- 12, in E

Study, Tl ii- 13, in E

Study, Tl ii- 14, in D minor

Study, Tl ii- 15, in A minor

Study, Tl ii- 16a, in B minor

Study, Tl ii- 16b

Study, TI ii- 17, in A minor

Study, TI ii- 18, in A

Study, TI ii- 19, in A

Study, TI ii- 20, in D

Study, TI ii- 21, in A

Study, TI ii- 22, in A

Study, TI ii- 23, in E minor

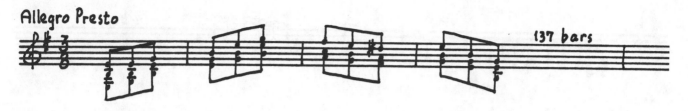

Study, TI ii- 24, in E minor

Study, TI ii- 25, in E

Study, TI ii- 26, in C

Study, TI ii- 27, in E minor

Study, TI ii- 28, in A

Study, TI ii- 29, in A minor

Study, TI ii- 30, in E

Study, TI ii- 31, in E

Study, TI ii- 32, in D

Study, TI ii- 33, in E

Study, TI ii- 34, in A

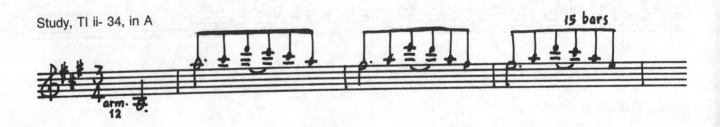

Study, TI ii- 35, in A

Study, TI ii- 36, in A

23 bars

Study, TI ii- 37, in A

32 bars

Study, TI ii- 38, in A

16 bars

Study, TI ii- 39, in A

13 bars

Study, TI ii- 40, in D

12 bars

Study, TI ii- 41, in E

36 bars

Study, TI ii- 42, in A

Lento

8 bars

iii. EJERCICIOS

Exercise, TI iii- 1

Exercise, TI iii- 2

Exercise, TI iii- 3

Exercise, TI iii- 4

Exercise, TI iii- 5

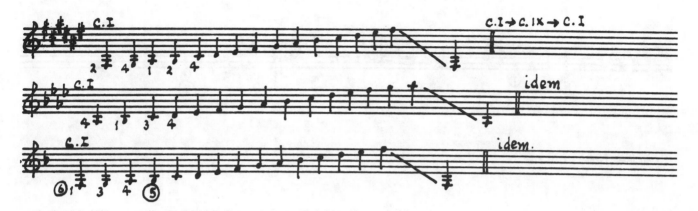

Exercise, TI iii- 6

Exercise, TI iii- 7

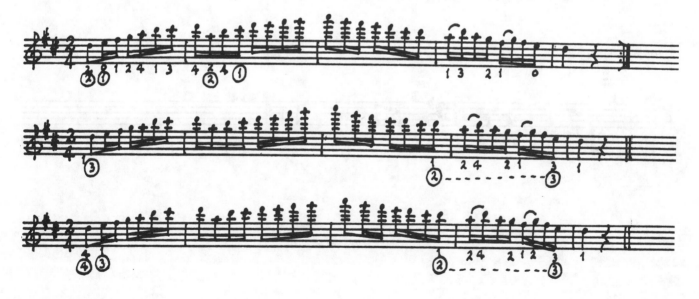

Exercise, TI iii- 8

Exercise, TI iii- 9

Exercise, TI iii- 10

Exercise, TI iii- 11

Exercise, TI iii- 12

Exercise, TI iii- 13

Arpegios y Fórmulas

Exercise, TI iii- 14

Exercise, TI iii- 15

Exercise, TI iii- 16

Exercise, TI iii- 17

Exercise, TI iii- 18

Exercise, TI iii- 19

Exercise, TI iii- 20

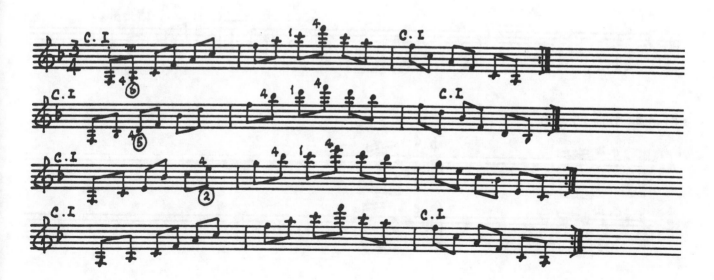

Exercise, TI iii- 21

Exercise, TI iii- 22

13 bars

Exercise, TI iii- 23

20 bars

Exercise, TI iii- 24

17 bars

Exercise, TI iii- 25

Exercise, TI iii- 26

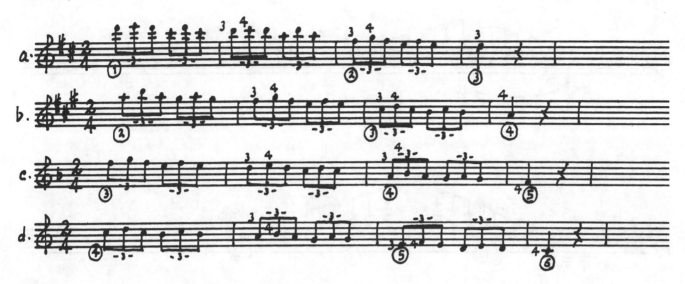

Exercise, TI iii- 27

Exercise, TI iii- 28

Exercise, TI iii- 29

Exercise, TI iii- 30a

Exercise, TI iii- 30b

Exercise, TI iii- 31

Exercise, TI iii- 32

Exercise, TI iii- 33

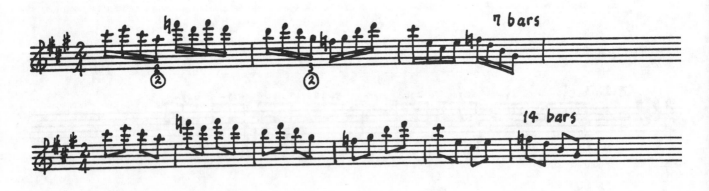

Exercise, TI iii- 34

Exercise, TI iii- 35

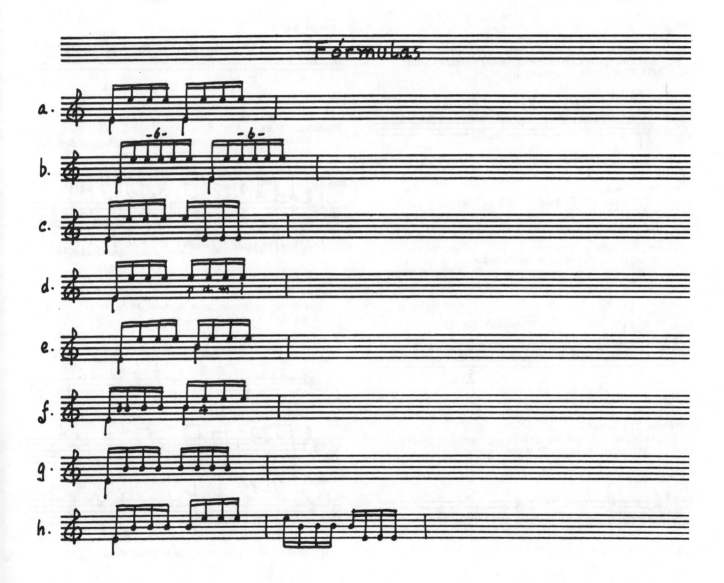

Preludes, Studies, and Exercises for Guitar by Francisco Tárrega: Details and Commentary

i. PRELUDIOS

Prelude, TI i- 1, in D minor
Preludio no. 1, D minor, 40 bars (1889) "Moderato."
Dedication: "A mi buen amigo D. Francisco Coréll, Prbo."
OT/2088 no. 31 (+ prelude 2)

Prelude, TI i- 2, in A minor
Preludio no. 2, A minor, 27 bars, without tempo indication.
Dedication: "A mi queridísimo discípalo Miguel Llobet."
OT/2088 no. 31 (+ prelude 1)

Prelude, TI i- 3, in G
Preludio no. 3, G major, 32 bars, "Allegretto."
AyT/392

Prelude, TI i- 4, in E
Preludio no. 4, Allegro, E major, 49 bars
Dedication: "A mi entrañable amigo Dr. D. Miguel Armengot."

Prelude, TI i- 5, in E
Preludio no. 5, Andante sostenuto, E major, 24 bars, (1901).
Dedication: "Al ilustre Dr. Walter Leckie."

Prelude, TI i- 6, in B minor
Preludio no. 6, without tempo indication, B minor, 26 bars, (1901). OT/1053 no. 11.
Remark at bar 1: "Ejecútese toda la obra en pizzicato."

Prelude, TI i- 7, in A
Preludio no. 7, without tempo indication, A major, 30 bars (1901). OT/1054 no. 12.

Prelude, TI i- 8a, in A
Preludio no. 8a, Allegretto, A major, 8-9 bars (Cf. bars 2-8 in TI ii- 4a). If 16 bars: notation in quavers.

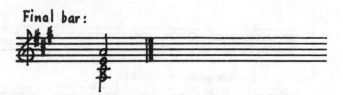

Prelude, TI i- 8b, in A
Preludio no. 8b, Andante, A major, 16 bars
(Cf. TI ii- 4a, bars 2-8)

Prelude, TI i- 9, in A
Preludio no. 9, Allegretto, A major, 16 bars

Prelude, TI i- 10, in D

Preludio no. 10, without tempo indication, D major, 8 bars.
Alier/5518 no. 15

Prelude, TI i- 11, in D

Preludio no. 11, without tempo indication, D major, 12-13 bars.
Alier/5518 no. 15

Prelude, TI i- 12, in A minor

Preludio no. 12, without tempo indication, A minor, 19-17 bars.
Alier/IA-5626 no. 22.

"Le Prélude no. 12 n'est pas original du Maître." (Emilio Pujol)

Bars 1-4 have to be repeated. If 17 bars: Bars 11/12 not repeated.

Prelude, TI i- 13, in A minor

Preludio no. 13, Andante, A minor, 8 bars

Prelude, TI i- 14, in A minor

Preludio no. 14, without tempo indication, A minor, 8 bars. Alier/5626 no. 22. Wrongly attributed to Robert Schumann in the Ildefonso Alier edition, IA/5626 no. 22 (cf. Rodriguez ed.). In reality this prelude has been composed after the Fugue in G minor for violin, BWV 1001 by J.S. Bach as a preliminary study for the complete arrangement of this fugue. Bars 1-8 from TI i- 14 are arranged from the BWV 1001: bars 79, 69/66 (combination of both), 66, 67, 90-94.

Prelude, TI i- 15, in C

Preludio no. 15, Andantino, C major, 20-21 bars

Prelude, TI i- 16, in D minor

Preludio no. 16, "Endecha," without tempo indication, D minor, 14-15 bars.
Dedication: "A Srta. Da Rosita Gonzalez de Melo."
Alier/5520 no. 17

Prelude, TI i- 17, in E

Preludio no. 17, "Lágrima," Andante, E major, 16 bars.
"C'est le Dr. Walter Leckie qui l'a baptisé "Larme" (Lágrima) en l'écoutant joué par l'auteur. La version originale était égarés. Isidro Llauradó qui habit Reus, était un passionné de la guitare qui adorait le Maître. Étant moi-même une fois dans cette ville, je fus invité par lui à visiter sa maison où abondaient les souvenirs de Tárrega. Parmi ses oeuvres pour guitare, je pus decouvrir le Prélude qu'on ne trouvait pas parmi les manuscrits de Tárrega. Isidro Llauradó eut la géenerosité de m'en faire cadeau et je l'ai apporté à la veuve de Tárrega pour qu'il puisse être ajouté à l'édition." (Emilio Pujol)

Prelude, TI i- 18, in D minor

Preludio no. 18, "Oremus," without tempo indication, 9 bars.
Alier/5520 no. 17.
"Le Prélude 'Oremus' improvisé par Tárrega chez le Chan-oine Manuel Gil pendant la prière des fidèles à l'Église, me fut offert par celui-ci à l'occasion d'un concert que j'avais donné à Teruel étant l'hôte de ce digne élève du Maître. Il est signé le 2 Décembre avant son retour à Barcelona où il décéda le 15 du même mois." (Emilio Pujol)

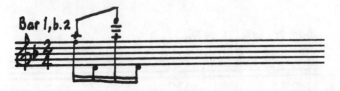

Prelude, TI i- 19, in E minor

Preludio no. 19, Andantino, E minor, 16 bars

Prelude, TI i- 20, in A

Preludio no. 20, without title, A major, 8 bars

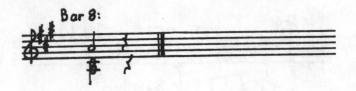

Prelude, TI i- 21, in D

Preludio no. 21, Andante sostenuto, D major, 8 bars

Prelude, TI i- 22, in E

Preludio no. 22, Andante sostenuto, E major, 8 bars

Prelude, TI i- 23, in B minor

Preludio no. 23, without title, B minor, 9-10 bars

All 10 bar versions only, use the F sharp sign at the clef.

Prelude, TI i- 24, in A minor

Preludio no. 24, without title, A minor, 8 bars

Prelude, TI i- 25, in A

Preludio no. 25, without tempo indication, A major, 8 bars

ii. ESTUDIOS

Study, TI ii- 1, in G
> Estudio no. 1; "Estudio en sol mayor," without tempo indication, 35 bars

Study, TI ii- 2a, in A
> Estudio no. 2a; "Estudio en la mayor," Allegretto, 20-22 bars.
> If 22 bars: bars 13/14 have been repeated (written out)

Study, TI ii- 2b, in A
> Estudio no. 2b; "Estudio en la mayor," (Allegretto), 16 bars
> TI ii- 2b = TI ii- 2a (bars 1-15 plus a final bar.)

Study, TI ii- 3, in E
> Estudio no. 3; "Estudio de velocidad," E major, 60 bars

Study, TI ii- 4a
> Estudio no. 4a; "Estudio en arpegios," without tempo indication (Introduction), without tempo indication (estudio), A major 11 bars (Introduction) + 44 bars (estudio) in C
> Alier/6609 no. 60
> Bars 2-8 = TI i- 8b, Bars 1-13

Study, TI ii- 4b, in A
> Estudio no. 4b; "Estudio en arpegios," without tempo indication, 20-22 bars.

Study, TI ii- 5, in A
> Estudio no. 5; "Estudio en forma de minuetto," (Tempo di minuetto) A major, 28 bars.
> Dedication: "A la Sta. Consuelo Pascual de Boldum"

Study, TI ii- 6, in D

> Estudio no. 6; "La Mariposa," Allegro vivace, D major, 40 bars.
> Dedication: "A mi querido discipulo D. Manuel Loscos."

Study, TI ii- 7a, in G
Estudio no. 7a; "El Columpio," Lento, G major, 36 bars "El Columpio fût composé par Tárrega pour le piano. Les deux versions publiées pour guitare n'ont pas été connues du Maître." (Emilio Pujol)

Study, TI ii- 7b, in D
Estudio no. 7b; "El Columpio," Lento, D major, 32 bars. Alier/6237 no. 52

Study, TI ii- 8, in A
Estudio no. 8; "Sueño," trémolo-estudio, Moderato/Allegretto, A major, 113 bars.
Dedication: "A mi querido amigo el notable aficionado Dr. D. Severino Garcia."
OT/1035 no. 5

Bar 43 has to be placed after bar 75 (as has been done in the Walker edition.)

Study, TI ii- 9, in A minor
Estudio no. 9; "Recuerdos de la Alhambra," estudio de tremolo, Andante, A minor/A major, 58 bars. "Hommage à l'eminent artiste Alfred Cottin." OT/1102 no. 13

Form: AA, BB, AA, BB, Coda

Study, TI ii- 10, in D minor
Estudio no. 10; "Estudio sobre un tema de Bach (Chacona)," without tempo indication, D minor, 17 bars. Study after Chaconne from Partita for Unaccompanied Violin, BWV 1004, in D minor.

Study, TI ii- 11, in E
Estudio no. 11; "Estudio sobre un tema de Bach (Giga)," (Tempo di Giga), E major, 49 bars. Study after the Gigue from Partita for Keyboard Instrument, BWV 825, in B flat. Alier/5755 no. 26

Study, TI ii- 12, in E

Estudio no. 12; "Estudio sobre un tema de Henselt," "Suspiro de amor," Allegretto sostenuto, E major, 41 and 43 bars. A. Henselt (1814-1889), pianist and composer. Alier/5392 no. 9

If 41 bars: bars 33 and 34 are missing.

Study, TI ii- 13, in E

Estudio no. 13; "Estudio sobre un tema de Wagner," Moderato, E major, 24 bars

Study, TI ii- 14, in D minor

Estudio no. 14; "Estudio sobre un tema de Fossa," without tempo indication, D minor, 16 bars. Francois de Fossa, composer-guitarist, end of 18th century (?).

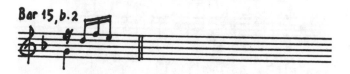

Study, TI ii- 15, in A minor

Estudio no. 15; "Estudio sobre un fragmento de Schumann," without tempo indication, A minor, 56 bars. Alier/5756 no. 27

Study, TI ii- 16a, in B minor

Estudio no. 16a; "Estudio sobre un fragmento de Mendelssohn," "de la Gruta del Fingal," without tempo indication, B minor, 47 and 48 bars. Alier/5944 no. 36

If 47 bars: a) bar 10 is missing
           b) insertion of a bar between bars 25 and 26
           c) bars 31 and 32 contracted
Bars 11-18 abbreviated in some editions.

Study, TI ii- 16b

Estudio no. 16b; 40 bars

Study, TI ii- 17, in A minor

Estudio no. 17; "Estudio sobre un fragmento del Septimino de Beethoven," Allegro, A minor, 16 and 18 bars.
If 16 bars: bars 8 and 17 (1° volta) are missing.

Study, TI ii- 18, in A

Estudio no. 18; "Estudio de Damas (Scherzo)," A major, 47 and 48 bars.
Alier/5517 no. 14
If 48 bars: bar 46 divided into 2 bars. Bars 34-37 have to be repeated.

Study, TI ii- 19, in A

Estudio no. 19; "Estudio de Alard ('Sonatina')," Allegro Moderato, A major, 87 bars
Abbreviations (repeats not written out) possible in several editions. In case of an abbreviation, the repeated bars have to be counted as well.

"L'étude d'Alard, n'est pas édité tel que Tárrega le jouait. Il y avait introduit quelques changements dans les arpèges de certains passages. Il ne ságit pas d'une version objectivement fidèle à celle de l'original pour violon, aussi bien qu'il arrive pour l'étude de Vieuxtemps."

Study, TI ii- 20, in D

Estudio no. 20; "Estudio de Cramer," without tempo indication, D major, 24 bars. Johann Baptist Cramer, born Mannheim 1771, died Kensington near London 1858; composer of piano studies. Pupil of M. Clementi.

Study, TI ii- 21, in A

Estudio no. 21; "Estudio de Parga," without tempo indication, A major, 16 bars. Juan Parga, Born El Ferrol 1843, died Málaga 1899.

Study, TI ii- 22, in A

Estudio no. 22; "Estudio de Vieuxtemps," Allegretto, A major, 64 bars. Henri Vieuxtemps, violinist-composer, born Verviers 1820, died Algiers 1881. See remarks under TI ii- 9.

Bar 1,b.1	
Bar 3,b.1	Bar 2,b.1
Bar 7,b.1	Bar 6,b.1
Bar 17,b.1	Bar 18,b.1
Bar 19,b.1	Bar 22,b.1
Bar 45,b.1	Bar 46,b.1
Bar 51,b.1	Bar 50,b.1

Study, TI ii- 23, in E minor

Estudio no. 23; "Estudio de Prudent," Allegro Presto, E minor, 137 bars.
Alier/5851 no. 31. Emile Prudent, born Paris 1817, died 1863; French composer of piano music.

Study, TI ii- 24, in E minor

Estudio no. 24; "Estudio de Thalberg," estudio de concierto (tremolo), Allegretto, E minor, 113 bars.
Alier/5390 no. 7. Sigismund Thalberg, born 1812, died 1871; concert pianist. Pupil of Joh. N. Hummel.

Study, TI ii- 25, in E

Estudio no. 25; "Estudio de Gottschalk," estudio de concierto, (Gran tremolo), Allegro moderato, E major, 96 bars. Louis Gottschalk, born New Orleans 1829, died Rio de Janeiro 1869 (studied in Paris from 1841 to 1846)

The edition by Savio differs at more than 50 places from the other editions. These differences have not been taken into consideration in the critical notes.

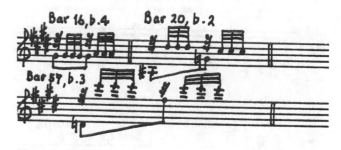

Study, TI ii- 26, in C

Estudio no. 26; without title, without tempo indication, C major, 16 bars

Study, TI ii- 27, in E minor

Estudio no. 27; without title, without tempo indication, E minor, 16 bars

Study, TI ii- 28, in A

Estudio no. 28; "Estudio de tremolo," without tempo indication, A major, 27 bars

Study, TI ii- 29, in A minor

Estudio no. 29; without title, without tempo indication, A minor, 17 bars

Study, TI ii- 30, in E

Estudio no. 30; "Estudio enterceras," Presto, E major, 24 bars

Study, TI ii- 31, in E

Estudio no. 31; without title, without tempo indication, E major, 12 bars

Study, TI ii- 32, in D
> Estudio no. 32; without title, without tempo indication, D major, 16 bars

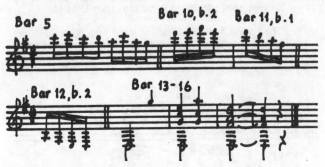

Ed.: Savio.

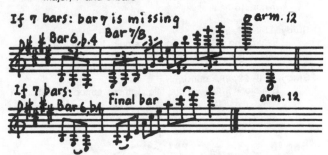

Study, TI ii- 33, in E
> Estudio no. 33; without title, without tempo indication, E major, 7 and 8 bars

Study, TI ii- 34, in A
> Estudio no. 34; without title, without tempo indication, A major, 15 bars. Identical with Finale-Coda from "Gran Jota de concierto sobre motives populares."

Study, TI ii- 35, in A
> Estudio no. 35; without title, without tempo indication, A major, 8 bars. Differences only in fingering.

Study, TI ii- 36, in A
> Estudio no. 36; without title, without tempo indication, A major, 23 bars

Study, TI ii- 37, in A
> Estudio no. 37; without title, without tempo indication, A major, 32 bars

Study, TI ii- 38, in A
> Estudio no. 38; without title, without tempo indication, A major, 16 bars

Study, TI ii- 39, in A
> Estudio no. 39; without title, without tempo indication, A major, 13 bars

Study, TI ii- 40, in D
> Estudio no. 40; without title, without tempo indication, D major, 12 bars

Study, TI ii- 41, in E
> Estudio no. 41; without title, without tempo indication, E major, 36 bars. Abbreviations (repeats) possible; in case of an abbreviation, the repeated bars have to be counted as well.

Study, TI ii- 42, in A
> Estudio no. 42; "Lento," A major, 8 bars.

iii. EJERCICIOS

Exercise, TI iii- 1
> Ejercicio no. 1, a-d; "Escala cromática en todas las cuerdas"

Exercise, TI iii- 2
> Ejercicio no. 2; "Escala cromática en cejilla"

Exercise, TI iii- 3
> Ejercicio no. 3; "Escala cromática en tresillos," 27 bars

Exercise, TI iii- 4
> Ejercicio no. 4; "Escala cromática en tresillos que recorre todo el diapasón," 22 bars

Exercise, TI iii- 5
> Ejercicio no. 5, a-c; "Escala mayor en cejilla"

Exercise, TI iii- 6
> Ejercicio no. 6; "Escala menor en cejilla"

Exercise, TI iii- 7
> Ejercicio no. 7, a-c; "Escala mayor sin cejilla"

Exercise, TI iii- 8
> Ejercicio no. 8; "Escala menor sin cejilla," 6 bars

Exercise, TI iii- 9
> Ejercicio no. 9; "Escala diatónica con arpegio sobre il acordo perfecto"

Exercise, TI iii- 10
> Ejercicio no. 10; "Escala mayor en intervalos de terceras"

Exercise, TI iii- 11
> Ejercicio no. 11; "Escala mayor en intervalos de cuartas"

Exercise, TI iii- 12

Ejercicio no. 12; "Ejercicio de familiazación del pulgar de la derecha con los otros dedos, como preparación para el estudio de los acordes, disueltos en arpegios." (Roch)

Exercise, TI iii- 13

Ejercicio no. 13, a-b; "Ejercicio de arpegios de Tárrega/Roch," 21 fórmulas.

Exercise, TI iii- 14

Ejercicio no. 14, a-h; "Ejercicio de arpegios en cejilla, F-B flat, 8 fórmulas

Exercise, TI iii- 15

Ejercicio no. 15, a-p; "Ejercicio de arpegios en cejilla," F-D flat, 16 fórmulas

Exercise, TI iii- 16

Ejercicio no. 16, a-z; "Ejercicio de arpegios sin cejilla E-C," 26 fórmulas

Exercise, TI iii- 17

Ejercicio no. 17, a-c; "Ejercicio de arpegio sobre il acordo perfecto en cejilla"

Exercise, TI iii- 18

Ejercicio no. 18; "Ejercicio de arpegio sobre il acordo perfecto sin cejilla"

Exercise, TI iii- 19

Ejercicio no. 19; "Ejercicio de arpegio sobre il acordo perfecto en intervalos simultáneos"

Exercise, TI iii- 20

Ejercicio no. 20, a, b, c, a; "Ejercicio de arpegio sobre il acordo perfecto y séptima de dóminante," F-pos. I; G-pos. III, 12 bars

Exercise, TI iii- 21

Ejercicio no. 21; "Ejercicio de arpegio sobre il acordo de séptima de dóminante," 6 bars

Exercise, TI iii- 22

Ejercicio no. 22; "Ejercicio de arpegio sobre il acordo de séptima disminuída," principio *3a cuerda*, 13 bars

Exercise, TI iii- 23

Ejercicio no. 23; "Ejercicio de arpegio sobre il acordo de séptima disminuída," principio *4a cuerda*, 20 bars

Exercise, TI iii- 24

Ejercicio no. 24; "Ejercicio de arpegio sobre il acordo de séptima disminuída," principio *5a cuerda*, 17 bars

Exercise, TI iii- 25

Ejercicio no. 25, a-d; "Ejercicio de ligado, asendente y descendente"

Exercise, TI iii- 26

Ejercicio no. 26, a-d; "Ejercicio de ligado, descendente, para la mano izquierda sola" (en una cuerda)

Exercise, TI iii- 27

Ejercicio no. 27; "Ejercicio de ligado, descendente, para la mano izquierda sola" (en todas las cuerdas)

Exercise, TI iii- 28

Ejercicio no. 28; "Ejercicio para la mano izquierda"—facilitar el pase de cualquiera de los dedos" (Roch) (facilitating the shifting of the fingers)

Exercise, TI iii- 29

Ejercicio no. 29; "Ejercicio para la mano izquierda—Arpegio de tres notas con pulsación simultánea del pulgar en la primera nota" (Pujol)

Exercise, TI iii- 30a

Ejercicio no. 30a; "Ejercicio para la mano izquierda—without further title," 9 bars

Exercise, TI iii- 30b

Ejercicio no. 30b; "Ejercicio para la mano izquierda—without further title," 5 bars

Exercise, TI iii- 31

Ejercicio no. 31; "Ejercicio para la mano izquierda—without further title," 6 bars

Exercise, TI iii- 32

Ejercicio no. 32; "Ejercicio para ambas manos," without further title, 9 bars

Exercise, TI iii- 33

Ejercicio no. 33; "Ejercicio para ambas manos" without further title, 7 and 14 bars

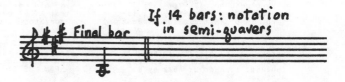

Exercise, TI iii- 34

Ejercicio no. 34; "Ejercicio para ambas manos—without further title," 4 bars

Exercise, TI iii- 35

Ejercicio no. 35, a-h; "Ejercicio para el tremolo," 8 fórmulas

Preludes, Studies, and Exercises for Guitar by Francisco Tárrega: Editions

VI Single Pieces

COMPOSICIONES CELEBRES, 12, VOL. 3
(Pomilio, Tomas) (2-5th degr.) sc
RICORDI-ARG BA-11997 f.s. 12 arr +
orig pcs; contains works by:
Giuliani (6), Visee (1), Carcassi
(1), Sor (1) for 1 gtr; Sor (2) for
2 gtr
contains: Tarrega, Francisco,
Study, TI ii- 5, in E, "Estudio
En Forma De Un Minuetto" (2gtr)
(1)

TARREGA, FRANCISCO (1852-1909)
Adelita, Mazurka
gtr (4th degr.) SPAN.MUS.CTR.
GE-187 f.s. contains also:
Prelude, TI i- 17, in E,
"Lagrima" (2)
gtr (4th degr.) RICORDI-ARG BA-7839
f.s. (3)
gtr (4th degr.) UNION ESP. 18295
f.s. (4)
gtr (4th degr.) ESSEX f.s. (5)
(Abloniz) gtr (4th degr.) BERBEN
EB1147 $1.00 contains also:
Prelude, TI i- 17, in E,
"Lagrima" (6)

Album, No. 1
(Tarrega, hijo) gtr (4-9th degr.)
UNION ESP. f.s. arr + orig pcs
contains: Danza Mora; Gran Jota
Da Concierto; Prelude, TI i-
17, in E, "Lagrima"; Study, TI
ii- 18, in A (7)

Album, No. 2
(Tarrega, hijo) gtr (4-9th degr.)
UNION ESP. f.s. arr + orig pcs
contains: Alborado; Dos
Hermanitas, Las; Pavan, MIN
142; Study, TI ii- 19, in A,
"Allegro Brillante Para
Concierto" (8)

Album, No. 3
(Tarrega, hijo) gtr (4-9th degr.)
UNION ESP. f.s. arr + orig pcs
contains: Danza Odalisca;
Prelude, TI i- 16, in D minor,
"En Decha"; Prelude, TI i- 18,
in D minor, "Oremus"; Study, TI
ii- 4a, in A, "Estudio En
Arpegios"; Sueno; Waltz in A
(9)

Album, No. 4
(Tarrega, hijo) gtr (4-9th degr.)
UNION ESP. f.s. arr + orig pcs
contains: Malaguena Facil;
Paquito; Prelude, TI i- 10, in
D; Prelude, TI i- 11, in D;
Study, TI ii- 15, in A minor
(10)

Album, No. 5
(Tarrega, hijo) gtr (4-9th degr.)
UNION ESP. f.s. arr + orig pcs
contains: Cartagenera, La;
Prelude, TI i- 25, in A,
"Preludio No. 12, Tii-12";
Study, TI ii- 1; Study, TI ii-
20, in D, "Estudio Inspirado En
Cramer" (11)

Album, No. 6
(Tarrega, hijo) gtr (4-9th degr.)
UNION ESP. f.s. arr + orig pcs;
includes transcr of work by P.
Albeniz (1)
contains: Pavan, MIN 143; Pepita;
Study, TI ii- 11, in E,
"Estudio Sobre Una Jiga De J.S.
Bach" (12)

Album, No. 7
(Tarrega, hijo) gtr (4-9th degr.)
UNION ESP. f.s. arr + orig pcs
contains: Prelude, TI i- 11, in
D, "Preludio, No.14"; Prelude,
TI i- 13, in A minor; Prelude,
TI i- 15, in C, "Preludio In C,
Ti i-15 [20 Bars]"; Study, TI
ii- 7b, in D; Tango; Waltz in D
(13)

Album, Vol. II: Seis [Sic] Preludios
(Fortea, Daniel) gtr (4-7th degr.)
FORTEA 191 f.s.
contains: Prelude, TI i- 1, in D
minor; Prelude, TI i- 2, in A
minor; Prelude, TI i- 3, in G;
Prelude, TI i- 4, in E;
Prelude, TI i- 5, in E;
Prelude, TI i- 7, in A;
Prelude, TI i- 16, in D minor,
"Endecha"; Prelude, TI i- 18,
in D minor, "Oremus" (14)

Capricho Arabe, Serenata
gtr (8-9th degr.) UNION ESP. 18146
(15)
gtr (8-9th degr.) FORTEA 189 (16)
(Abloniz) gtr (8-9th degr.) BERBEN
EB1205 $1.00 (17)
(Bream) gtr (8-9th degr.) ESSEX
(18)
(Erdmann) gtr (8-9th degr.)
HEINRICH. N-3338 (19)
(Gascon) gtr (8-9th degr.) RICORDI-
ARG BA-12073 (20)
(Navascues) gtr (8-9th degr.) BRUCK
BG-T1-4 (21)
(Sinopoli) gtr (8-9th degr.,
version facilitada) RICORDI-ARG
BA-8418 (22)

Danza Mora
(Bianqui Pinero) 2gtr RICORDI-ARG
BA-12600 f.s. (23)

Gran Jota De Concierto
"Gran Jota Aragonesa" 1-2gtr (8-9th
degr.) RICORDI-ARG BA-7924 f.s.
(24)
(Azpiazu) 1-2gtr (8-9th degr.)
ALIER,I [5625] NO. 21 f.s. (25)
(Fortea) 1-2gtr (8-9th degr.)
ALIER,I 5625 NO. 21 f.s. (26)
(Fortea) 1-2gtr (8-9th degr.,
without Introduccion) FORTEA 206
f.s. (27)

Prelude, TI i- 1, in D minor
gtr ESSEX f.s. (28)
gtr (ed after the Orfeo Tracio ed
OT-2088 no. 31) SPAN.MUS.CTR.
GE-191 f.s. contains also:
Prelude, TI i- 2, in A minor (29)
gtr UNION ESP. 19049 f.s. contains
also: Prelude, TI i- 2, in A
minor (30)

Prelude, TI i- 2, in A minor
gtr ESSEX f.s. (31)

Prelude, TI i- 4, in E
gtr ESSEX f.s. (32)

Prelude, TI i- 5, in E
gtr ESSEX f.s. (33)

Prelude, TI i- 6, in B minor
gtr ESSEX f.s. contains also:
Prelude, TI i- 7, in A (34)
gtr (a documentary reproduction of
the Orfeo Tracio ed OT 1054, nos.
11 and 12) UNION ESP. 19077 f.s.
contains also: Prelude, TI i- 7,
in A (35)

Prelude, TI i- 8a, in A
gtr ESSEX f.s. contains also:
Prelude, TI i- 9, in A (36)
gtr (a documentary reproduction of
an old ed (Orfeo Tracio ed 1104
no. 15?)) UNION ESP. 19039 f.s.
contains also: Prelude, TI i- 9,
in A (37)

Prelude, TI i- 12, in A minor
gtr (a documentary reproduction of
an ed by Antich y Tena (?))
SPAN.MUS.CTR. GE-256 f.s. (38)

Prelude, TI i- 16, in D minor
"Endecha" (Appleby, Wilfrid M.) gtr
ESSEX f.s. contains also:
Prelude, TI i- 17, in E,
"Lagrima" (39)
"Endecha" (Prol, Julio) gtr PAGANI
G-110 f.s. contains also:
Prelude, TI i- 18, in D minor,
"Oremus" (40)

Rosita, Polka
(Gascon) gtr RICORDI-ARG BA-12076
f.s. (41)
(Sensier) gtr ESSEX f.s. (42)

Study, TI ii- 1, in G
(Fortea, Daniel) gtr FORTEA 187
f.s. contains also: Study, TI ii-
5, in A (43)

Study, TI ii- 2a
(Calandra, M.T. de) gtr RICORDI-ARG
BA-11342 f.s. (44)

Study, TI ii- 3, in E
(Fortea, Daniel) gtr FORTEA 188
f.s. (45)

Study, TI ii- 5, in A
"Estudio En Forma De Minuetto" gtr
(a documentary reproduction of an
old ed (Orfeo Tracio ed 1103, no.
14?)) UNION ESP. 19038 f.s. (46)

Study, TI ii- 6, in D
"Mariposa, La" gtr UNION ESP. 19084
f.s. (47)
"Mariposa, La" (Fortea, Daniel) gtr
FORTEA 207 f.s. (48)
"Mariposa, La" (Savio, Isaias) gtr
RICORDI-ARG BA-11927 f.s. (49)
"Mariposa, La" (Sensier, Peter) gtr
ESSEX f.s. (50)

Study, TI ii- 7a, in G
"Columpio, El" (Fortea, Daniel) gtr
FORTEA 198 f.s. (51)

Study, TI ii- 8, in A
"Sueno" gtr (a documentary
reproduction of the Orfeo Tracio
ed OT 1035 no. 5) UNION ESP.
18799 f.s. (52)
"Sueno" (Fortea, Daniel) gtr FORTEA
202 f.s. (53)
"Sueno" (Savio, Isaias) gtr
RICORDI-ARG BA-11393 f.s. (54)
"Sueno - Der Traum" (Scheit, Karl)
gtr UNIVER. 16692 f.s. (55)
"Sueno" (Sensier, Peter) gtr ESSEX
f.s. (56)

Study, TI ii- 9, in A minor
"Recuerdos De La Alhambra" gtr (a
documentary reproduction of the
Orfeo Tracio ed OT-1102 no. 13)
SPAN.MUS.CTR. GE-195 f.s. (57)
"Recuerdos De La Alhambra" gtr
UNION ESP. 18347 f.s. (58)
"Recuerdos De La Alhambra" gtr
ESSEX f.s. (59)
"Recuerdos De La Alhambra"
(Abloniz, Miguel) gtr (57 bars
(bar 37 is missing)) BERBEN 1148
f.s. (60)
"Recuerdos De La Alhambra"
(Azpiazu, Jose De) gtr SYMPHON
2001 f.s. (61)
"Recuerdos De La Alhambra" (Dalmar,
Alvaro) gtr (gtr II pt arr by
Alvaro Dalmar) SPAN.MUS.CTR.
GE-223 f.s. (62)
"Recuerdos De La Alhambra"
(Erdmann, Olle) gtr NOETZEL
N-3317 f.s. (63)
"Recuerdos De La Alhambra" (Fortea,
Daniel) gtr FORTEA 195 f.s. (64)
"Recuerdos De La Alhambra"
(Navascues, Santiago) gtr BRUCK
BG-T1-3 f.s. (65)
"Vzpominky Na Alhambru :
Erinnerungen An Die Alhambra"
(Rathousky, Jiri) gtr (Kytarova
sola, no. 8; 57 bars (bar 37 is
missing)) CZECH H-3590 f.s. (66)
"Recuerdos De La Alhambra" (Rossi,
Abner) 4gtr sc,pts BERBEN 1809
f.s. (67)
"Recuerdos De La Alhambra"
(Sagreras, Julio S.) gtr (gtr II
pt arr by Julio S. Sagreras)
RICORDI-ARG BA-11530 f.s. (68)
"Recuerdos De La Alhambra" (Savio,
Isaias) gtr RICORDI-ARG BA-8873
f.s. (69)
"Recuerdos De La Alhambra" (Scheit,
Karl) gtr UNIVER. 14427 f.s. (70)
(Tower, Richard) gtr TEESELING
VT-154 f.s. (71)

Study, TI ii- 11, in E
"Estudio (Sobre Una Giga)" (Fortea,
Daniel) gtr (J.S. Bach [sic]
arreglo de F. Tarrega) FORTEA 210
f.s. (72)

Study, TI ii- 12, in E
"Henselt: Suspiro De Amor" (Fortea,
Daniel) gtr FORTEA 249 f.s. (73)

TARREGA, FRANCISCO (cont'd.)

Study, TI ii- 13, in E
  "Estudio Sobre Un Tema De Wagner"
  (Fortea, Daniel) gtr FORTEA 186
  f.s.   (74)

Study, TI ii- 16a, in B minor
  "Estudio Sobre Un Fragmento, De La
  "Gruta Del Fingal" De
  Mendelssohn" (Savio, Isaias) gtr
  (47 bars) RICORDI-ARG BA-11926
  f.s.   (75)

Study, TI ii- 18, in A
  "Scherzo De T. Damas" (Fortea,
  Daniel) gtr FORTEA 189 f.s.   (76)

Study, TI ii- 19, in A
  "Estudio Brillante, By Alard" gtr
  SPAN.MUS.CTR. GE-193 f.s.   (77)
  "Study In A Major" (Bream, Julian)
  gtr (85 bars (bar 1 is lacking;
  bars 85-86 are 1 bar) ESSEX f.s.
                                          (78)
  "Estudio De Delphin Alard" (Fortea,
  Daniel) gtr FORTEA 332 f.s.   (79)
  (Santos, Turibio) gtr ESCHIG f.s.
                                          (80)
  "Estudio Sobre La Sonatina De
  Delphin Alard" (Savio, Isaias)
  gtr RICORDI-ARG BA-11925 f.s.
                                          (81)

Study, TI ii- 23, in E minor
  "Estudio De Prudent" (Fortea,
  Daniel) gtr FORTEA 256 f.s.   (82)

Study, TI ii- 24, in E minor
  "Thalberg: Tema Y Var" (Fortea,
  Daniel) gtr FORTEA 268 f.s.   (83)

Study, TI ii- 25, in E
  "Gran Tremolo, Estudio De
  Concierto, Op. 58, Luis M.
  Gottschalk" gtr RICORDI-ARG
  BA-10157 f.s.   (84)
  "Gran Tremolo, De Gottschalk, Op.
  58" (Fortea, Daniel) gtr FORTEA
  238 f.s.   (85)

VI-Coll Tárrega Collections

ALBUM, NO. 14
  (Tarrega, Francisco, hijo) gtr (4-9th
  degr.) UNION ESP. f.s.
  contains: Beethoven, Ludwig van,
  Gran Andante; Schumann, Robert
  (Alexander), Waltz, MIN 279;
  Tchaikovsky, Piotr Ilyich,
  Mazurka, MIN 161   (86)

ALBUM, NO. 15
  (Tarrega, Francisco, hijo) gtr (4-9th
  degr.) UNION ESP. f.s.
  contains: Beethoven, Ludwig van,
  Minueto Del Septimino; Beethoven,
  Ludwig van, Teme Del Septimino;
  Chopin, Frederic, Mazurka No. 16;
  Schumann, Robert (Alexander),
  Andantino Cantabile; Tarrega,
  Francisco, Study, TI ii- 17, in A
  minor, "Variacion 4 Del Septimino
  De Beethoven" (16 bars)   (87)

ALBUM, NO. 16
  (Tarrega, Francisco, hijo) gtr (4-9th
  degr.) UNION ESP. f.s.
  contains: Tarrega, Francisco,
  Study, TI ii- 24, in E minor (88)

COMPOSICIONES ORIGINALES PARA GUITARRA,
  10
  (Bianqui Pinero) gtr (5-9th degr.)
  RICORDI-ARG C-16.529 f.s.
  contains: Prelude, TI i- 5, in E;
  Prelude, TI i- 17, in E,
  "Lagrima"; Study, TI ii- 9, in A
  minor, "Recuerdos De La
  Alhambra"; Study, TI ii- 14, in D
  minor   (89)

6 SPANISCHE STUCKE
  (Scheit) gtr (3-4th degr.) UNIVER.
  16698 f.s.
  contains: Tarrega, Francisco,
  Prelude, TI i- 17, in E,
  "Lagrima"   (90)

TARREGA, FRANCISCO (1852-1909)
  Album, No. 17 °CC2L
  (Tarrega, hijo) gtr (4-9th degr.)
  UNION ESP. f.s. arr + orig pcs;
  contains transcr of works by:
  Gottschalk-Tarrega; TI-Ii-25,
  Chopin   (91)

TARREGA, FRANCISCO (cont'd.)

Album No. 21
  (Tarrega, Francisco, hijo) 2gtr (4-
  7th degr.) sc UNION ESP. f.s.
  contains: Gran Jota De Concierto;
  Prelude, TI i- 17, in E,
  "Lagrima"   (92)

Album No. 22
  (Tarrega, Francisco, hijo) 2gtr (4-
  7th degr.) sc UNION ESP. f.s.
  contains: Danza Mora; Sueno
  (Mazurka)   (93)

Album No. 23
  (Tarrega, Francisco, hijo) 2gtr (4-
  7th degr.) sc UNION ESP. f.s.
  contains: Alborada, Capricho;
  Study, TI ii- 18, in A   (94)

Album, Vol. I
  (Fortea, Daniel) gtr (4-7th degr.)
  FORTEA 190 f.s.
  contains: Prelude, TI i- 17, in
  E, "Lagrima"   (95)

Album, Vol. II: Seis [Sic] Preludios
  (Fortea, Daniel) gtr (4-7th degr.)
  FORTEA 191 f.s.
  contains: Prelude, TI i- 1, in D
  minor; Prelude, TI i- 2, in A
  minor; Prelude, TI i- 3, in G;
  Prelude, TI i- 4, in E;
  Prelude, TI i- 5, in E;
  Prelude, TI i- 7, in A;
  Prelude, TI i- 16, in D minor,
  "Endecha"; Prelude, TI i- 18,
  in D minor, "Oremus"   (96)

Composiciones Originales Y Estudios
  Para Guitarra, Vol. I
  (Bianqui Pinero) gtr (6-9th degr.)
  RICORDI-ARG B-16.564 f.s. 10 pcs
  contains: Study, TI ii- 9, in A
  minor, "Recuerdos De La
  Alhambra"   (97)

Composiciones Originales Y Estudios
  Para Guitarra, Vol. II
  (Bianqui Pinero) gtr (6-9th degr.)
  RICORDI-ARG B-16.565 f.s. 10 pcs
  contains: Study, TI ii- 7a, in D,
  "Columpio, El"; Study, TI ii-
  8, in A, "Sueno"   (98)

Composiciones Originales Y Estudios
  Para Guitarra, Vol. III: 30
  Preludios Originales
  (Bianqui Pinero) gtr (6-9th degr.)
  RICORDI-ARG C-16.563 f.s.
  contains: F. Tarrega, Preludes,
  TI-i-1-13, 15, 16(14 bars), 17-
  24; Studies, TI-ii-4b(20 bars),
  29, 30b, 32, 35, 36   (99)

Composiciones Originales Y Estudios
  Para Guitarra, Vol. III: 30
  Preludios Originales
  (Bianqui Pinero) gtr (6-9th degr.)
  RICORDI-ARG BA-12720 f.s.
  contains: F. Tarrega, Preludes,
  TI-i-1-13, 15, 16(14 bars), 17-
  24; Studies, TI-ii-4b(20 bars),
  29, 30b, 32, 35, 36   (100)

Composiciones Originales Y Estudios
  Para Guitarra, Vol. IV
  (Bianqui Pinero) gtr (6-9th degr.)
  RICORDI-ARG B-16.566 f.s.
  contains: Exercise, TI iii- 20,
  in G; Exercise, TI iii- 24, in
  E minor; Exercise, TI iii- 29;
  Exercise, TI iii- 30a, in E;
  Exercise, TI iii- 32; Study, TI
  ii- 2a, in A; Study, TI ii- 5,
  in A; Study, TI ii- 6, in D,
  "Mariposa, La"; Study, TI ii-
  10, in D minor; Study, TI ii-
  11, in E; Study, TI ii- 12, in
  E; Study, TI ii- 14, in D
  minor; Study, TI ii- 15, in A
  minor; Study, TI ii- 16a, in B
  minor; Study, TI ii- 18, in A;
  Study, TI ii- 19, in A; Study,
  TI ii- 20; Study, TI ii- 22
                                (101)

Composiciones Para Guitarra, 12
  (Savio, Isaias) gtr (4-9th degr.)
  RICORDI-ARG BA-11248 f.s. 12 pcs
  contains: Prelude, TI i- 17, in
  E, "Lagrima"; Study, TI ii- 8,
  in A, "Sueno"; Study, TI ii- 9,
  in A minor, "Recuerdos De La
  Alhambra"   (102)

Elementos Fundamentales De La Tecnica
  Guitarristica
  (Savio, Isaias) gtr RICORDI-ARG
  BA-11343 f.s.
  contains: Exercise, TI iii- 16;
  Exercise, TI iii- 20; Exercise,
  TI iii- 24; Exercise, TI iii-
  30a; Exercise, TI iii- 32;
  Study, TI ii- 29; Study, TI ii-
  31; Study, TI ii- 36; Study,

TARREGA, FRANCISCO (cont'd.)

TIii-32 [fragment]   (103)

Estudios; 20 Studies Without Title,
  Vol. 1: Estudios 1-3
  (Fortea, Daniel) gtr FORTEA 180
  f.s.
  contains: Exercise, TI iii- 3;
  Exercise, TI iii- 22; Exercise,
  TI iii- 23   (104)

Estudios; 20 Studies Without Title,
  Vol. 2: Estudios 4-6
  (Fortea, Daniel) gtr FORTEA 181
  f.s.
  contains: Prelude, TI i- 8a, in A
  (9 bars); Prelude, TI i- 8b, in
  A; Study, TI ii- 2b, in A   (105)

Estudios; 20 Studies Without Title,
  Vol. 3: Estudios 7-10
  (Fortea, Daniel) gtr FORTEA 182
  f.s.
  contains: Exercise, TI iii- 33
  (14 bars); Prelude, TI i- 13,
  in A minor; Prelude, TI i- 15,
  in C; Study, TI ii- 32, in D
                                (106)

Estudios; 20 Studies Without Title,
  Vol. 4: Estudios 11-13
  (Fortea, Daniel) gtr FORTEA 183
  f.s.
  contains: Prelude, TI i- 12, in A
  minor; Prelude, TI i- 19, in G;
  Study, TI ii- 29, in A minor
                                (107)

Estudios; 20 Studies Without Title,
  Vol. 5: Estudios 14-17
  (Fortea, Daniel) gtr FORTEA 184
  f.s.
  contains: Prelude, TI i- 9, in A;
  Prelude, TI i- 10, in D;
  Prelude, TI i- 11, in D; Study,
  TI ii- 34, in A   (108)

Estudios; 20 Studies Without Title,
  Vol. 6: Estudios 18-20
  (Fortea, Daniel) gtr FORTEA 185
  f.s.
  contains: Prelude, TI i- 6, in B
  minor; Prelude, TI i- 14, in A
  minor; Prelude, TI i- 23, in B
  minor (10 bars)   (109)

Estudios Para Guitarra
  (Savio, Isaias) gtr RICORDI-ARG
  BA-11386 f.s.
  contains: Study, TI ii- 2a, in A;
  Study, TI ii- 4b, in A; Study,
  TI ii- 5, in A; Study, TI ii-
  6, in D; Study, TI ii- 12, in
  E; Study, TI ii- 17, in A
  minor; Study, TI ii- 19, in A;
  Study, TI ii- 26, in C; Study,
  TI ii- 27, in E minor; Study,
  TIii-16a in B minor [fragment]
                                (110)

Etuden
  (Scheit, Karl) gtr UNIVER. 14430
  f.s. 8 pcs
  contains: Prelude, TI i- 8a, in
  A; Prelude, TI i- 8b, in A;
  Prelude, TI i- 15, in C; Study,
  IIii-4b in A [fragment]; Study,
  TI ii- 2a, in A; Study, TI ii-
  5, in A; Study, TI ii- 6, in D;
  Study, TI ii- 18, in A; Study,
  TI ii- 27, in E minor   (111)

Formule Di Arpeggi
  "Esercizi Di Tarrega" gtr (Archivio
  Musicale Di Opere Rare E Inedite;
  collotype of a manuscript copy;
  13 unnumbered pcs without title;
  8 recto-numbered and -written
  sheets; contains: Prelude, TI-i-
  14; Studies, TI-ii-4b[6 bars],
  32, 35; Exercises, TIiii-1a-b,
  TI-i-8, 12, 13a, 13b, 21, 28,
  30b, 33, 34) fac ed BERBEN f.s.
                                (112)

Guitarra Espanola: 12 Spanische
  Stucke
  (Helsing) gtr (4-7th degr.) MARBOT
  f.s. 12 pcs
  contains: Prelude, TI i- 11, in
  D; Prelude, TI i- 12, in A
  minor; Prelude, TI i- 13, in A
  minor; Prelude, TI i- 15, in C
  (20 bars); Prelude, TI i- 25,
  in A; Study, TI ii- 7b, in D,
  "Columpio, El"; Study, TI ii-
  20, in D   (113)

Kompositionen Fur Gitarre, Vol. I
  (Schwarz-Reiflingen) gtr (4-9th
  degr.) SIKORSKI 685A $7.25 19 pcs
  contains: Prelude, TI i- 1, in D
  minor; Prelude, TI i- 2, in A
  minor; Prelude, TI i- 3, in G;
  Prelude, TI i- 4, in E;
  Prelude, TI i- 5, in E;
  Prelude, TI i- 16, in D minor,
  "Endecha"; Prelude, TI i- 18,
  in D minor; Study, TI ii- 8,
  in

TARREGA, FRANCISCO (cont'd.)

A; Study, TI ii- 9, in A minor;
Study, TI ii- 11, in E; Study,
TI ii- 15, in A minor; Study,
TI ii- 16a, in B minor; Study,
TI ii- 19, in A   (114)

Kompositionen Fur Gitarre, Vol. II
(Schwarz-Reiflingen) gtr (4-9th
degr.) SIKORSKI 865B $7.25 18 pcs
contains: Gran Jota De Concierto;
Prelude, TI i- 8b, in A;
Prelude, TI i- 15, in C;
Prelude, TI i- 19, in E minor;
Prelude, TI i- 23, in B minor;
Study, TI ii- 4b, in A; Study,
TI ii- 6, in D, "Mariposa, La";
Study, TI ii- 12, in E,
"Suspiro d'Amor"; Study, TI ii-
29, in A minor; Study, TI ii-
36, in A   (115)

Opere Per Chitarra, Vol. I: Preludi
*CC39L
(Gangi; Carfagna) gtr (4-9th degr.)
BERBEN EB1531 $4.50 includes:
Preludes, TI-i-1-11, 13-24;
Studies, TI-ii-2b, 4b(20 bars),
16A, 29, 32, 34-36, 42;
Exercises, TI- iii- 8, 30b, 33
(14 bars); Sor, Andante-Thema,
from Fantaisie, Op. 7, [arr.];
Chopin, Prelude, Op. 28, No. 11,
[arr.]; Mendelssohn-Bartholdy,
Canzonetta In E Flat, Op. 12,
[arr.]   (116)

Opere Per Chitarra, Vol. II: Studi
*CC34L
(Gangi; Carfagna) gtr (4-9th degr.)
BERBEN EB1532 $5.25 includes:
Prelude, TI-i-12; Studies, TI-ii-
1, 2, 3, 5, 6, 8-11, 12(41 bars)
18(48 bars), 19, 22, 30, 31,
33(7 bars), 37-41; Exercises, TI-
iii-3, 20, 22-24, 29, 30a, 31, 32
                                   (117)

Opere Per Chitarra, Vol. III:
Composizioni Originali
(Gangi; Carfagna) gtr (4-9th degr.)
BERBEN EB1533 $7.75 20 pcs
contains: Gran Jota De Concierto;
Study, TI ii- 7b, in D,
"Columpio, El"   (118)

Opere Per Chitarra, Vol. IV:
Trascrizioni
(Gangi; Carfagna) gtr (4-9th degr.)
BERBEN f.s.   (119)

Prelude, TI i- 3, in G
"Preludios Nos. 3, 4 Y 5" gtr
(No.3: a documentary reproduction
of the Antich y Tena ed no. 392)
UNION ESP. 19051 f.s. contains
also: Prelude, TI i- 4, in E (a
documentary reproduction of an
old ed (Orfeo Tracio 2094 no. 37
prel. 4?)); Prelude, TI i- 5, in
E (a documentary reproduction of
an old ed (Orfeo Tracio 2094 no.
37 prel. 5?))   (120)

Prelude, TI i- 10, in D
gtr (a documentary reproduction of
the Ildefonso Alier ed, 5518 no.
15) SPAN.MUS.CTR. GE-192 f.s.
contains also: Prelude, TI i- 11,
in D (a documentary reproduction
of the Ildefonso Alier ed, 5518
no. 15); Prelude, TI i- 6, in B
minor (a documentary reproduction
of the Orfeo Tracio ed OT-1053
no. 11)   (121)
"Preludes Nos. 10, 11 And 12" gtr
ESSEX f.s. contains also:
Prelude, TI i- 11, in D (13
bars); Prelude, TI i- 13, in A
minor   (122)

Prelude, TI i- 17, in E
"Lagrima" (Azpiazu) gtr (4-5th
degr.) SYMPHON 2084 f.s. contains
also: Adelita, Mazurka; Pavan,
MIN 144   (123)
"Lagrima" (Papas) gtr (4-5th degr.)
COLUMBIA 143 $1.25 contains also:
Adelita, Mazurka   (124)

Preludios Originales, 18 *CCU
(Savio, Isaias) gtr RICORDI-ARG
BA-11365 f.s. contains TI-i-1-7,
8a, 9-11[13 bars], 13, 16[14
bars], 17-19, 22, 24   (125)

Rosita, Polka
gtr (4-5th degr., reprs of early
eds) SPAN.MUS.CTR. GE-265 f.s.
contains also: Prelude, TI i- 16,
in D minor, "Endecha"; Prelude,
TI i- 18, in D minor, "Oremus"
                                   (126)
gtr FORTEA 194 f.s. contains also:
Marieta, Mazurka; Mazurka in G
                                   (127)

TARREGA, FRANCISCO (cont'd.)

Samtliche Praludien *CC15U
(Scheit, Karl) gtr UNIVER. 13408-Z
f.s. contains TI-i-1-7, 10, 11,
13, 16-19, 22   (128)

Samtliche Technische Studien *CC91U
(Scheit, Karl) gtr UNIVER. 14431
f.s. contains: Preludes, TI-i-9,
12[17 bars], 23; Studies, TI-ii-
3, 29-33[7 bars], 35-41;
Exercises, TI-iii-2, 5c, 6, 10,
11, 13, 13b, 14-16, 22-24, 30a,
30b, 31, 32   (129)

Tarrega-Album, Eine Sammlung Der
Bekanntesten Original-Werke
(Walker, Luise) gtr (4-9th degr.)
HEINRICH. VH-1548 f.s. 21 pcs
contains: Prelude, TI i- 1, in D
minor; Prelude, TI i- 2, in A
minor; Prelude, TI i- 3, in G;
Prelude, TI i- 4, in E;
Prelude, TI i- 5, in E;
Prelude, TI i- 16, in D minor,
"Endecha"; Prelude, TI i- 17,
in E, "Lagrima"; Prelude, TI i-
18, in D minor, "Oremus";
Study, TI ii- 5, in A, "Estudio
En Forma De Un Minuetto";
Study, TI ii- 6, in D,
"Mariposa, La"; Study, TI ii-
8, in A, "Sueno"; Study, TI ii-
9, in A minor, "Recuerdos De La
Alhambra"   (130)

Technical Studies *CCU
gtr SPAN.MUS.CTR. GE-194 f.s.
contains: Studies, TI-ii-30, 33,
35; Exercises, TI-iii-4, 14a-c,
15, 20, 24, 30a, 31, 32   (131)

Utwory Wybrane
(Powrozniak, Jozef) gtr (6-8th
degr.) POLSKIE 7337 f.s. 23 pcs;
Klasycy Gitary
contains: Prelude, TI i- 1, in D
minor; Prelude, TI i- 2, in A
minor; Prelude, TI i- 6, in B
minor; Prelude, TI i- 7, in A;
Prelude, TI i- 12, in A minor;
Prelude, TI i- 16, in D minor,
"Endecha"; Prelude, TI i- 18,
in D minor, "Oremus"; Study, TI
ii- 3, in A; Study, TI ii- 4b,
in A; Study, TI ii- 5, in A;
Study, TI ii- 19, in A; Study,
TI ii- 29, in A minor   (132)

Vyber Skladeb, Selected Compositions,
Vol. I
(Tichota, Jiri) gtr (4-9th degr.)
SUPRAPHON AP-1730 f.s. Kytarova
Sola, No.4
contains: Prelude, TI i- 16, in D
minor, "Endecha"; Prelude, TI
i- 18, in D minor, "Oremus";
Study, TI ii- 6, in D,
"Mariposa, La"; Study, TI ii-
8, in A, "Sueno"; Study, TI ii-
19, in A   (133)

Vyber Skladeb, Selected Compositions,
Vol. II
(Tichota, Jiri) gtr (4-9th degr.)
SUPRAPHON AP f.s. 8 pcs; Kytarova
Sola, No.5; Contains Works By:
Verdi, Chopin, Schumann, J.S.
Bach, Chueca, Mendelssohn, W.A.
Mozart, Albeniz
contains: Study, TI ii- 11, in E
                                   (134)

VISSER, DICK (1927-   )
Tarrega Etcetera, Dagelijkse Studies
"Tarrega Etcetera, Daily Studies"
gtr (5p.; 1964; contains 21
exercises + arpeggios formulae,
after Tarrega-Roch; includes
Tarrega, Francisco, Exercises,
TI-iii-13, 13b) quarto HARMONIA
1586 f.s.   (135)

VI-Mixed Coll   Mixed Collections: Tárrega

AGUADO, DIONISIO (1784-1849)
Escuela De Guitarra
"Gran Metodo Completo Para
Guitarra, Con Una Recopilacion De
Estudios Originales De Autores
Celebres" (Sinopoli, Antonio)
[Span] gtr (181p., ill; repr,
1969; 1st ed, 1947; 7 courses in
5 pts; notes; app: Observacion
sobre la naturaleza o indole de
la guitarra; contains: Bach,
Johann Sebastian, Suite For
Keyboard Instrument, BWV 821, In
B Flat; Courante, [C major]; Bach
Johann Sebastian, Prelude For
Lute, BWV 999, In C Minor, [D
minor]; Bach, Johann Sebastian,
Suite For Lute, BWV 996, In E
Minor: Allemande, [A minor];
Bach, Johann Sebastian, Prelude,
BWV 927, In F, [G major] from
Wilhelm Friedemann Bach
Klavierbuchlein (1720); Bach,
Johann Sebastian, Presto, BWV
970, In D Minor; Tarrega,
Francisco, Prelude, TI-i-14;
Tarrega, Francisco, Studies, TI-
ii-2a [22 bars], 6, 14a, c, 18,
19, 20, 22, 29 [18 bars];
Tarrega, Francisco, Exercises,
TI-iii-2, 14, 20, 24[12 bars],
30a, 32) folio RICORDI-ARG
BA-9801 f.s.   (136)

AHSLUND, ULF-G.
Gitarrskola, Spela I Grupp, Supp.2
"Teknikovningar" [Swed] gtr (16p.;
n.d.; Gitarrskola, Suppl. 2;
contains diatonic scales,
chromatic scales, arpeggios,
tremolo, intervals; includes:
Tarrega, Francisco, Study, TI-ii-
30, In E; Exercises, TI-iii-2a,
4, 28, 32[11 bars]) quarto LIBER
f.s.   (137)

ALBUM RICREATIVO, NO. 3 *folk song
(Abloniz, Miguel) gtr (3-7th degr.)
BERBEN EB1398 $4.00 20 arr + orig
pcs; contains works by: Cervantes
(1), Schubert (2), Handel (1),
Visee (2), de Crescenzo (1), Flotow
(1), Breton Y Hernandez (1), Sor
(1), Abloniz (2)
contains: Bach, Johann Sebastian,
Suite for Violoncello, No. 1, BWV
1007, in G, Prelude (C maj);
Bach, Johann Sebastian, Suite for
Violoncello, No. 2, BWV 1008, in
D minor, Minuet I (A min);
Tarrega, Francisco, Study, TI i-
5, in A, "Estudio En Forma De Un
Menuetto"   (138)

ANTOLOGIA DE OBRAS PARA GUITARRA
(Savio) gtr (4-7th degr.) RICORDI-ARG
BA-11250 f.s. 48 arr + orig pcs;
contains works by: Corbetta (1),
Visee (1), Asioli (1), Sanz (1),
Roncalli (4), Moretti (1),
Ferandiere (2), Gragnani (1),
Carulli (2), de Call (1), Matiegka
(1), Molino (1), Sor (4), Giuliani
(1), Diabelli (1), Paganini (1),
Gruber (1), Castellacci (1), Aguado
(1), Horecki (1), Legnani (2),
Carcassi (2), Hunten (1), Marschner
(1), Seegner (1), Le Dhuy (1),
Sychra (1), Donnadieu (1), Mertz
(1), Schulz (1), Coste (2), Vinas
(1), Pargas (1)
contains: Tarrega, Francisco,
Prelude, TI i- 11, in D (13
bars); Tarrega, Francisco,
Prelude, TI i- 16, in D minor (14
bars); Tarrega, Francisco,
Prelude, TI i- 18, in D minor;
Tarrega, Francisco, Study, TI ii-
14, in D minor, "Folies d'Espagne
(2a Variacion)"   (139)

ANTOLOGIA PER CHITARRA, VOL. 2
(Anzaghi, Luigi) gtr (1-10th degr.)
RICORDI-IT 130035 f.s. 43arr + orig
pcs; contains works by: Carulli
(3), Coste (9), Aguado (2),
Giuliani (4), Anzaghi (1), Carcassi
(4), Legnani (2), Paganini (1), Sor
(8), Cano (3), Farrauto (2), Vinas
(1), Anon. (1)
contains: Tarrega, Francisco,
Prelude, TI i- 17, in E,

"Lagrima" (140)

ANTOLOGIA PER CHITARRA, VOL. 3
(Anzaghi, Luigi) gtr (1-10th degr.)
RICORDI-IT 130375 f.s. 20 arr +
orig pcs; contains works by: Anon.
(1), Le Dhuy (1), Legnani (1), Sor
(4), D. Scarlatti (1), Tarrega (9
Pcs Not In TI)
contains: Tarrega, Francisco,
Prelude, TI i- 17, in E,
"Lagrima"; Tarrega, Francisco,
Study, TI ii- 8, in A, "Reveri";
Tarrega, Francisco, Study, TI ii-
9, in A minor, "Recuerdos De La
Alhambra" (141)

AZPIAZU, JOSE DE (1912-)
Gitarrenschule, Vol. II
[Ger/Fr/Span] gtr quarto SYMPHON
406 f.s. 32p.; 1954; contains:
Bach, Johann Sebastian, Invention
No.4, BWV 775 In D Minor for 2gtr
(single line playing); Suite For
Lute, BWV 995 In G Minor,
Saraband; and Tarrega, Francisco,
Exercise, TI-iii-3, [arr.] (142)

Gitarrenschule, Vol. III
[Ger/Fr/Span] gtr folio SYMPHON 437
f.s. 34p.; 1956; contains: Bach,
Johann Sebastian, Partita No.5
for keyboard, BWV 829, In G,
Minuet (in A); Invention No.1,
BWV 772 In C, for 2 gtr (single
line playing); Suite No.1 for
cello, BWV 1007, In G, Prelude
(in D); and Tarrega, Francisco,
Prelude, TI-i-9; Studies, TI-ii-
12, 14, 18 [48 bars, arr.] (143)

Gitarrenschule, Vol. IV *CCU
[Ger/Fr/Span] 1-2gtr folio SYMPHON
2022 f.s. 50p., facsim; 1958;
contains: Bach, Johann Sebastian,
Betrachte, Meine Seele (from
Johannes-Passion, BWV 245, No.31
lute accomp only);Partita No.1
For Violin, BWV 1002, In B-Minor,
Sarabande-Double; Toccata And
Fugue, BWV 565, In D-Minor,
[excerpt]; Prelude For Keyboard,
BWV 934, In C-Minor (in A-Minor);
Polonaise (Anna Magdalena Bach
Notenbuchlein (1725), No.28), BWV
Anh. 130, In G (in A); Suite For
Violoncello, No.6, BWV 1012, In
D, Gavotte I-I (in E); Concerto
For Harpsichord And Orchestra,
BWV 1056, In F-Minor, Largo (in
D); Invention No.2, BWV 773, In C
Minor (in E Minor), for 2gtr; and
Tarrega, Francisco, Exercise, TI-
iii-31, [arr.] (144)

Gitarrenschule, Vol. V
[Ger/Fr/Span] gtr folio SYMPHON
2174 f.s. 60p., 8 facs, tab;
1966; contains: Bach, Johann
Sebastian, Partita No.2 For
Violin, BWV 1004, In D-Minor,
Chaconne [excerpt] (in D-Minor);
Suite No.4 For Violoncello, BWV
1010, In E-Flat, Prelude (in A);
Suite No.3 For Violoncello, BWV
1009, In C, Courante (in A); and
Tarrega, Francisco, Studies, TI-
ii-3 (in A), 16a (in B-Minor), 19
(in A), 20 (in D) (145)

BIS DEL CONCERTISTA, I, VOL. 2
(Chiesa) gtr (4-8th degr.) ZERBONI
7891 $7.00 6 arr + orig pcs;
contains works by: Froberger,
Handel, M. Albeniz, Sor
contains: Bach, Johann Sebastian,
Prelude for Lute, BWV 999, in C
minor (D min); Tarrega,
Francisco, Study, TI ii- 19, in G
(146)

CHACON, MEME
Metodo Y Ejercicios De Francisco
Tarrega
[Span/Eng] gtr (1959; contains:
Chromatic and diatonic scales,
Exercises (triplets, arpeggios,
speed study); includes: Tarrega,
Francisco, Preludes, TI-i-6, 8a[9
bars], 8b, 9-13, 15, 19, 23[10
bars]; Tarrega, Francisco,
Studies, TI-ii-2b, 3, 29-36;
Tarrega, Francisco, Exercises,
TI-iii-1, 3, 4, 14-16, 20, 22-24,
30a, 31b, d, 33) UNION ESP. f.s.
(147)

**CHOIX D'ETUDES POUR GUITARE, VOL. 1:
COURS PREPARATOIRE**
(Fernandez-Lavie) gtr (3-4th degr.)
ESCHIG 8058 f.s. 26 arr + orig pcs;
contains works by: Fernandez-Lavie
(4), Sor (5), Brouwer (2), Caldara
(2), Fuhrmann (3), Anon. (7),
Baumgartner (1), Fortea (1),
Purcell (1), Negri (1)
contains: Tarrega, Francisco,
Study, TI ii- 14, in D minor

COMPOSICIONES CELEBRES, 12, VOL. 3 (148)
(Pomilio, Tomas) (2-5th degr.) sc
RICORDI-ARG BA-11997 f.s. 12 arr +
orig pcs; contains works by:
Giuliani (6), Visee (1), Carcassi
(1), Sor (1) for 1 gtr; Sor (2) for
2 gtr
contains: Tarrega, Francisco,
Study, TI ii- 5, in E, "Estudio
En Forma De Un Minuetto" (2gtr)
(149)

DIVERTISSEMENT, VOL. 2
(Bartoli) gtr (3-4th degr.) SCHOTT-
FRER 9220 f.s. 7 arr + orig pcs;
contains works by: Bartoli,
Carcassi, Mertz, Sor, Aguado
contains: Tarrega, Francisco,
Prelude, TI i- 10, in D; Tarrega,
Francisco, Prelude, TI i- 11, in
D (12 bars) (150)

ELEMENTAR ETUDEN, VOL. 2
(Behrend) gtr (1-4th degr.) PREISSLER
7030-II f.s. 17 pcs; contains works
by: Sor (6); Carcassi (5); Legnani
(2); Tarrega (3); Behrend (1)
contains: Tarrega, Francisco,
Prelude, TI i- 16, in D minor,
"Endecha"; Tarrega, Francisco,
Prelude, TI i- 17, in E,
"Lagrima" (151)

ENJOY CLASSICAL AND BAROQUE GUITAR
gtr (3-9th degr.) HANSEN-US 0116A
f.s. 67 arr + orig pcs; illus;
intro; biographies, contains works
by: Sor (1), Carcassi (50), Carulli
(1), Zani de Ferranti (7), Albeniz
(2), Molitor (1), Granados (1)
contains: Sor, Fernando,
Introduction Et Variations Sur Un
Theme De Mozart, "Variations On
"The Magic Flute" By W.A.
Mozart", Op.9; Tarrega,
Francisco, Prelude, TI i- 6, in B
minor; Tarrega, Francisco,
Prelude, TI i- 8a, in A; Tarrega,
Francisco, Prelude, TI i- 9, in A
(152)

FORTEA, DANIEL (1882-1953)
Metodo De Guitarra, Vol. I
[Span/Fr/Eng] gtr oct FORTEA 21A
f.s. 32p., ill; 18th repr, 1963;
suppl: Theory of 1st book of the
school of guitar; contains:
Tarrega, Francisco, Exercises,
TI-iii-1a, 1c, 1d (153)

Metodo De Guitarra, Vol. II
[Span/Fr/Eng] gtr oct FORTEA 22
f.s. 32p.; 8th repr, 1958;
contains: Tarrega, Francisco,
Preludes, TI-i-8a (16 bars), 8b;
Exercises, TI-iii-3 (25 bars),
15, 22 (9 bars), 23 (154)

GITAARSPEELBOEK - LIVRE DE LA GUITARE
(van Puijenbroeck) gtr (2-7th degr.)
METROPOLIS EM-4722 $5.00 diatonic
and chromatic scales; 42 arr + orig
pcs; contains works by: Carcassi
(9), Carulli (6), Judenkunig (1),
Neusiedler (1), Aguado (4), Hove
(2), Adriaenssen (3), Dalza (1),
Giuliani (1), Milan (2), Dowland
(1), Lecocq (2), Weiss (1), Narvaez
(1)
contains: Bach, Johann Sebastian,
Suite for Lute, BWV 995, in G
minor, Prelude (E min, e' is d',
g is f-sharp); Bach, Johann
Sebastian, Suite for Lute, BWV
995, in G minor, Saraband (E min,
e' is d', g is f-sharp); Bach,
Johann Sebastian, Suite for Lute,
BWV 996, in E minor, Bourree (e'
is d', g is f-sharp); Tarrega,
Francisco, Exercise, TI iii- 3;
Tarrega, Francisco, Prelude, TI
i- 17, in E, "Lagrima" (155)

GITARRKLANG *folk song
(Ahslund) gtr (2-3rd degr.) REUTER
f.s. 21 arr + orig pcs; contains
works by: Ronning (1), U.G. Ahslund
(5), Taube (1), Giuliani (1), Sor
(1), Carcassi (2), Jobim (1)
contains: Tarrega, Francisco,
Study, TI ii- 27, in E minor
(156)

**GUITAR SAMPLER, 5 CENTURIES OF ORIGINAL
GUITAR SOLOS**
(Hoffman, John) gtr (3-4th degr.)
PRESSER 414-41100 $1.95 11 arr +
orig pcs; contains works by: Anon.
(2), Milan (1), Dowland (1), Sor
(2), Paganini (1)
contains: Bach, Johann Sebastian,
Prelude for Lute, BWV 999, in C
minor (D min); Bach, Johann
Sebastian, Suite for Lute, BWV
996, in E minor, Bourree; Sor,
Fernando, Minuet, MIN 303 (from
Grande Sonate, Op. 25); Tarrega,
Francisco, Prelude, TI i- 17, in

E, "Lagrima" (157)

HENZE, BRUNO
Gitarrespiel, Das, Vol. I, Ein
Unterrichtswerk Vom Anfang Bis
Zur Meisterschaft: Spielbeginn
Und Studien
[Ger] gtr quarto HOFMEISTER T-4001
f.s. 28p., ill; 1950; app:
Fingergymnastik; includes
Giuliani, Mauro, Anschlagsubungen
fur die rechte Hand; Tarrega,
Francisco, and Roch, Pascual,
Exercises, TI-iii-13a-f (158)

Gitarrespiel, Das, Vol. VI: Ein
Unterrichtswerk Vom Anfang Bis
Zur Meisterschaft: Studien Fur
Die Linke Und Rechte Hand
[Ger] gtr (60p.; 1954; contains
Exercises, cadences, ornaments,
studies, barre, effects,
rasgueado; includes: Tarrega,
Francisco, Exercises, TI-iii-13,
for the left hand; Giuliani,
Mauro, Anschlagsubungen Fur Die
Rechte Hand) quarto HOFMEISTER
T-4006 f.s. (159)

Gitarrespiel, Das, Vol. VII, Ein
Unterrichtswerk Vom Anfang Bis
Zur Meisterschaft: Die Hauptlagen
[Ger] gtr quarto HOFMEISTER T-4007
f.s. 42p.; 1954; scale and chord
studies (in pos. IV, V, VII and
IX; arr. + orig. pcs.; contains
works by: Molinaro, de Saint Luc,
Bergen, Carcassi (3), Molino, Sor
(8), Coste (2), Tarrega (2),
Friessnegg, Milan, Martino,
Corbetta, Haydn, Giuliani (2),
Sanz (2), Roncalli (3), Molitor,
Matiegka, Kellner (2), Sigismund
Weiss, Diabelli, Legnani, Cano-
Stingl, Uhl; includes: Tarrega,
Francisco, Prelude TI-i-1;
Prelude TI i-17, in E ("Lagrima")
(160)

HISZPANSCY MISTRZOWIE GITARY
(Powrozniak) gtr (4-9th degr.)
POLSKIE 6432 f.s. Grajmy Na
Gitarze, Vol. XV; 16 arr + orig
pcs; contains works by: Aguado (1),
Cano (1), Broca (2), Sor (1), Bosch
(1), Arcas (3), Vinas (5);
contains: Tarrega, Francisco,
Study, TI ii- 6, in D; Tarrega,
Francisco, Study, TI ii- 8, in A
(161)

**IBERIA, 5 JAHRHUNDERTE SPANISCHER
GITARRENMUSIK, VOL. II**
(Justen, Heinz) gtr (3-8th degr.)
LEUCKART 10630 f.s. 10 pcs;
contains works by: Vinas (1), Arcas
(1), Prudent (1), Malats (1),
Aguado (1), Bosch (2), Gomez (1)
contains: Tarrega, Francisco,
Study, TI ii- 3, in A, "Estudio
De Velocidad" (162)

IPARRAGUIRRE, P.A.
Escalas, Arpegios Y Ejercicios Del
Mecanismo Tecnico
[Span] gtr folio RICORDI-ARG
BA-8076 f.s. 23p.; repr., 1966;
1st ed., 1924; contains: Tarrega,
Francisco, Studies, TI-ii-21 (in
A), 30 (19 bars, in E);
Exercises, TI-iii-14a-C, 24, 30a,
31, 32 (163)

JOHNSON, PER-OLOF
Gitarrskola For Klassisk Gitarr, Vol.
II: Fortsattningsskola
[Swed] gtr quarto ANDERSONS AM-682
f.s. 80p.; 1969; contains:
Preludes, TI-i-11 (in D), 17 (in
E, "Lagrima") by Francisco
Tarrega (164)

**KLASSIKER DER GITARRE; STUDIEN- UND
VORTRAGSLITERATUR AUS DEM 18. UND
19. JAHRHUNDERT, VOL. 2:
MITTELSTUFE - INTERMEDIATE STAGE**
(Ratz) gtr (4-8th degr.) DEUTSCHER
32066 f.s. contains 91 works by:
Giuliani; Diabelli; Paganini;
Aguado; Legnani; Carcassi;
Marschner; Mertz; Coste; Tarrega;
Bosch and Cottin
contains: Tarrega, Francisco,
Prelude, TI i- 17, in E,
"Lagrima" (165)

KONZERT-ETUDEN FUR GITARRE, VOL. 3
(Behrend) gtr (5-9th degr.) PREISSLER
7034-III f.s. 5 pcs (nos 15-19);
contains works by Mertz and Vinas
contains: Tarrega, Francisco,
Study, TI ii- 8, in A; Tarrega,
Francisco, Study, TI ii- 9, in A
minor; Tarrega, Francisco, Study,
TI ii- 19, in A (166)

LADRU, ANIBAL
Escuela De Mecanismo Tecnico Para
Guitarra
[Span] gtr (26p.; repr, 1966; 1st
ed, 1927; contains Diatonic
scales, chromatic scales and
exercises, scale exercises,
arpeggios, barre, exercises;
includes Tarrega, Francisco,
Preludes, TI-i-11, 16[14 bars],
17, 18, 24; Tarrega, Francisco,
Studies, TI-ii-4b, 29, 30, 33;
Tarrega, Francisco, Exercises,
TI-iii-2, 14a-c, 20a-c, 24, 25a-
d, 30a-32) folio RICORDI-ARG
BA-9523 f.s.   (167)

LELOUP, HILARION
Escales, Acordes Y Ejercicios
Tecnicos Para Guitarra
[Span] gtr folio RICORDI-ARG
BA-9565 f.s. 33p.; repr, 1964;
1st ed, 1923; notes; contains:
Tarrega, Francisco, Studies, TI-
ii-28 (in A), 30 (in E), 33 (in
E); Exercises, TI-iii-14a-c, 24,
30a, 31, 32   (168)

MEDIO, ALONSO
Clifford Essex Spanish Guitar Tutor,
The
[Eng] gtr quarto ESSEX f.s. 48p.,
ill; contains: Prelude, TI-i-17
in E (Lagrima) by Francisco
Tarrega   (169)

MEL BAY'S DELUXE ALBUM OF CLASSIC
GUITAR MUSIC
(Castle) gtr (4-9th degr.) MEL BAY
f.s. 67 arr + orig pcs; contains
works by: Milan (1), Palestrina
(1), Byrd (1), Frescobaldi (1),
Reusner (1), Visee (1), Couperin
(1), Rameau (1), Handel (1), Lesage
De Richee (1), Gluck (1), Haydn
(1), Gossec (1), Mozart(2),
Beethoven (3), Carulli (3), Molino
(2), Sor (7), Giuliani (2),
Diabelli (1), Paganini (2), Aguado
(2), Weber (1), Legnani (2),
Carcassi (3), Marschner (1),
Schubert (1), Horenzky (1), Coste
(1), Mertz (1), Chopin (2),
Schumann (1), Offenbach (1), Brahms
(2), Wienawski (1), Tchaikovsky
(2), Massenet (1), Grieg (1),
Scharwenka
contains: Bach, Johann Sebastian,
Fugue for Lute, BWV 1000, in G
minor (A min); Bach, Johann
Sebastian, Invention No. 1 for
Keyboard Instrument, BWV 772, in
C; Bach, Johann Sebastian,
Prelude for Lute, BWV 999, in C
minor (D min); Bach, Johann
Sebastian, Suite for Lute, BWV
996, in E minor, Bourree;
Tarrega, Francisco, Prelude, TI
i- 19, in G; Tarrega, Francisco,
Study, TI ii- 9, in A minor,
"Recuerdos De La Alhambra";
Tarrega, Francisco, Study, TI ii-
18, in A, "Scherzo De T. Damas"
                                (170)

MOORST, PABLO VAN
Moderne Handleiding Voor Het
Klassieke Gitaarspel, Vol. II
[Dutch] gtr quarto TOORTS f.s. ill;
1968-69; 44p.; contains: Study,
TI-ii-14 in D-Minor by Francisco
Tarrega   (171)

Moderne Handleiding Voor Het
Klassieke Gitaarspel, Vol. III
[Dutch] gtr quarto TOORTS f.s. ill;
1968-69; 46p.; contains: Study,
TI-ii-5 in A; Prelude, TI-i-14 in
A-Minor by Francisco Tarrega; and
Minuet In G, BWV Anh. 114, (from
Anna Magdalena Bach Notenbuchlein
(1725), No.4) by J.S. Bach   (172)

MOURAT, JEAN-MAURICE
Cordes, 6...Une Guitare, Methode De
Guitare A l'Usage Des Debutants
[Fr] gtr folio BILLAUDOT 1648 f.s.
72p., ill; 1973; suppl: Position
de la main droite; Position de la
main gauche; contains: Study, TI-
ii-14 by Francisco Tarrega; and
Minuet, BWV Anh. 115, From Anna
Magdalena Bach Notenbuchlein
(1725), No.5, In G (in A Minor)
for 2gtr; Minuet, BWV Anh. 114,
from Anna Magdalena Bach
Notenbuchlein (1725), No.4, In G
for 2 gtr; Suite No. 6 for
Violoncello, BWV 1012, In D,
Gavotte II by J.S. Bach   (173)

MUSIC FOR CLASSICAL GUITAR
(Vinson) gtr (1-6th degr.) CONSOL
f.s. 114 arr + orig pcs; Music For
Millions Series, Vol. 59; contains
works by: Anon. (9), Galilei (1),
Milan (1), Morlaye (1), Narvaez

(1), Neusiedler (2), Terzi (1),
Besard (1), Dowland (1), Roncalli
(1), Sanz (9), Visee (2), Aguado
(7), Diabelli (3), Carcassi (9),
Carulli (16), Giuliani (7), Kuffner
(7), Kunz (2), Meignen (1), Sor
(25), Bartok (2), Cotten (1)
contains: Bach, Johann Sebastian,
Suite for Lute, BWV 995, in G
minor, Gavotte II (A min,
fragment); Tarrega, Francisco,
Prelude, TI i- 17, in E,
"Lagrima"; Tarrega, Francisco,
Prelude, TI i- 20, in A, "Adagio
In A"   (174)

NOAD, FREDERICK M.
Solo Guitar Playing, A Complete
Course Of Instruction In The
Technique Of Guitar Performance
[Eng] gtr quarto COLLIER f.s.
187p., ill; repr, 1969; 1st ed,
1968; contains: Minuet from
Grande Sonate, Op. 25 by Fernando
Sor; Prelude, TI-i-17, In E
(Lagrima) by Francisco Tarrega;
and Suite No.4 For Violoncello,
BWV 1010, In E Flat, Bourree (in
A) by Johann Sebastian Bach (175)

OBRAS CLASICAS Y ROMANTICAS, VOL. 2
(Tarrega; Savio) gtr (4-9th degr.)
RICORDI-ARG BA-12409 f.s. 12 arr+
orig pcs; contains works by:
Albeniz (1), Beethoven (2), Chopin
(2), Gottschalk (1), Handel (2),
Haydn (1), W.A. Mozart (1),
Schubert (2)
contains: Tarrega, Francisco,
Study, TI ii- 25, in E, "Gran
Tremolo" (ed differs greatly from
others)   (176)

PEZZI FACILI, 3
(Ricchi) gtr (4-5th degr.) BERBEN
EB1440 f.s. arr + orig pcs
contains: Anonymous, Due Chitarre;
Anonymous, Romance, MIN 193;
Tarrega, Francisco, Prelude, TI
i- 17, in E, "Lagrima"   (177)

POMILIO, TOMAS
Formulas Tecnicas, Para El Mecanismo
Elemental De La Guitarra
[Span] gtr folio RICORDI-ARG
BA-12287 f.s. 51p.; 1964; app: 27
pcs. by N.N. (Pomilio?) (4),
Carcassi (5), Carulli (4), Coste
(7), Aguado (4), Damas; contains
27 Lessons (studies, legato,
exercises, scales, tremolo,
harmonics); includes: Tarrega,
Francisco, Prelude, TI-i-9 (in
A); Exercises, TI-iii-1a, 1b, 1e,
13b, 14g, H, 24, 30a, 32   (178)

PRAT, DOMINGO (1866-1944)
Escalas Y Arpegios De Mecanismo
Tenico Para Guitarra
[Span] gtr folio RICORDI-ARG
BA-9508 f.s. 15p.; repr, 1966;
1st ed, 1910; contains Scales,
chromatic scales, barre,
exercises; includes: Tarrega,
Francisco, Studies, TI-ii-30, 33;
Exercises, TI-iii-5b, 6, 14a-c,
24, 30a, 31, 32   (179)

PUIJENBROECK, VICTOR VAN
Kunst Van Het Gitaarspel, De – Art De
Jouer De La Guitare, L'
[Dutch/Fr/Eng/Ger] gtr folio
METROPOLIS 4653 f.s. 58p., ill;
1967; contains: Exercises, TI-
iii-1a, 13a by Francisco Tarrega
                                (180)

PUJOL, EMILIO (1886-1982)
Escuela Razonada De La Guitarra,
Basada En Los Principios De La
Technica De Tarrega, Vol. II
[Span/Fr] gtr folio RICORDI-ARG
BA-9563 f.s. ill, historical
notes; 137p.;repr 1964; 1st ed,
1940; contains: Exercises, TI-
iii-14d, E 15, by Francisco
Tarrega   (181)

Escuela Razonada De La Guitarra,
Basada En Los Principios De La
Technica De Tarrega, Vol. III
[Span/Fr] gtr folio RICORDI-ARG
BA-10945 f.s. ill, historical
notes; 151p.; repr, 1960; 1st ed,
1954; contains: Exercises, TI-
iii-1a, 2, 5c, 6, 10, 13b, 16, 29
by Francisco Tarrega   (182)

Escuela Razonada De La Guitarra,
Basada En Los Principios De La
Technica De Tarrega, Vol. IV
[Span/Fr] gtr folio RICORDI-ARG
BA-12838 f.s. ill, historical
notes; 199p.; 1971; also contains
suppl: (33) Estudios
Complementarios (1 pce for 2
gtr); includes: Exercises, TI-

PUJOL, EMILIO (cont'd.)
iii-1, 4 by Francisco Tarrega
                                (183)

RIGHTMIRE, RICHARD W.
Wonderful Guitar, The (A Modern
Classic Guitar Method), Vol. III
[Eng] gtr quarto SMITH,WJ f.s.
31p., 1963, ill; contains: March,
BWV Anh. 122 In D from Anna
Magdalena Bach Notenbuchlein
(1725), No.16; Partita No. 1 For
Keyboard Instrument, BWV 825, In
B-Flat, Minuet I (fragment);
Suite For Lute, BWV 996, In E-
Minor, Bourree, by J.S. Bach; and
Study, TI-ii-14 In D-Minor;
Prelude, TI-i-17 In E (Lagrima)
by Francisco Tarrega   (184)

ROCH, PASCUAL
Modern Method For The Guitar, A, Vol.
1, School Of Tarrega *CCU
[Eng/Span/Fr] gtr quarto SCHIRM.G
1828 f.s. 145 p., ill; 1st ed,
1921; contains: Tarrega,
Francisco, Studies, TI-ii-32, 35,
42; Exercises, TI-iii-1a-B, 8,
13a-B, 21, 28, 30b, 33, 34, 35a-H
                                (185)

Modern Method For The Guitar, A, Vol.
II, School Of Tarrega *CCU
[Eng/Span/Fr] gtr quarto SCHIRM.G
1829 f.s. 141p., ill; 1st ed,
1922; contains: Tarrega,
Francisco, Preludes, TI-i-8b, 14,
15, 19, 20, 23; Studies, TI-ii-4b
(20 bars), 29, 36; Exercises, TI-
iii-2a, 4, 5a-c, 6, 9-12, 15,
17a-c, 18, 19, 20a-c   (186)

Modern Method For The Guitar, A, Vol.
III, School Of Tarrega
[Eng/Span/Fr] gtr quarto SCHIRM.G
1830 f.s. 109p., ill; 1st ed,
1924; contains: Bach, Johann
Sebastian, Prelude For Keyboard,
BWV 839 In C (in E); and Tarrega,
Francisco, Prelude, TI-i-17;
Studies, TI-ii-12 and 12 (41
bars), 16b, 17, 18, 34   (187)

RODRIGUEZ ARENAS, MARIO
Escuela De La Guitarra, La, Vol. II
[Span] gtr RICORDI-ARG BA-9531 f.s.
88p.; repr, 1966; 1st ed, 1923;
contains: Tarrega, Francisco,
Prelude, TI-i-17; Exercises, TI-
iii-15, 35; and Sor, Fernando,
Minuet, from Grande Sonate, OP.
25   (188)

Escuela De La Guitarra, La, Vol. II
[Jap] gtr ONGAKU f.s. 88p.; repr,
1966; 1st ed, 1923; contains:
Tarrega, Francisco, Prelude, TI-
i-17; Exercises, TI-iii-15, 35;
and Sor, Fernando, Minuet, from
Grande Sonate, Op.25   (189)

Escuela De La Guitarra, La, Vol. III
[Span] gtr RICORDI-ARG BA-9556 f.s.
103p.; repr, 1967; 1st ed, 1923;
contains: Tarrega, Francisco,
Preludes, TI-i-15, 19, 20, 22,
24; Studies, TI-ii-2a(22 bars),
9, 32, 35, 36; Exercises, TI-iii-
8, 13b, 30b, 33   (190)

Escuela De La Guitarra, La, Vol. III
[Jap] gtr ONGAKU f.s. 103p.; repr,
1967; 1st ed, 1923; contains:
Tarrega, Francisco, Preludes, TI-
i-15, 19, 20, 22, 24; Studies,
TI-ii-2, 9, 32, 35, 36;
Exercises, TI-iii-8, 13, 30, 33
                                (191)

Escuela De La Guitarra, La, Vol. V
[Span] gtr RICORDI-ARG BA-9549 f.s.
55p.; repr, 1954; 1st ed, 1923;
contains: Estudios Y Preludios De
Francisco Tarrega (22); 28 Unnumbered
Pcs By Tarrega (22); Chopin (3);
Coste (1); Mendelssohn (1); also
contains: Tarrega, Francisco,
Preludes, TI-i-1-7, 8a, 9-11 (13
bars), 13; Studies, TI-ii-5, 6,
8, 16b, 17, 18(56bars), 19-22;
and Sor, Fernando, Introduction
Et Variations Sur Un Theme De
Mozart, Op. 9   (192)

Escuela De La Guitarra, La, Vol. V
[Jap] gtr ONGAKU f.s. 55p.; repr,
1954; 1st ed, 1923; contains:
Estudios Y Preludios De Francisco
Tarrega; 28 Unnumbered Pcs By
Tarrega (22); Chopin (3); Coste
(1); Mendelssohn (1);also
contains: Tarrega, Francisco,
Preludes, TI-i- 2-7, 8a, 9-11,
13; Studies, TI-ii- 5, 6, 8, 16b,
17-22; and Sor, Fernando,
Introduction Et Variations Sur Un
Theme De Mozart, Op.9   (193)

RODRIGUEZ ARENAS, MARIO (cont'd.)

Escuela De La Guitarra, Vol. VI
"Technica Superior" [Span] gtr
(47p.; repr, 1963; 1st ed, 1923;
contains: Exercises by L.C.
Hanon-Rodriguez Arenas, Exercises
in thirds, sixths, octaves, by
Aguado, Giuliani, Legato, barre,
chords, Preludes and exercises by
F. Tarrega; includes: Tarrega,
Francisco, Preludes, TI-i-12, 14,
23; Tarrega, Francisco, Studies,
TI-ii-4b, 29; Tarrega, Francisco,
Exercises, TI-iii-2, 4, 5a-c, 6,
7a-c, 9-11, 15, 17a-c, 18, 19,
26, 27) folio RICORDI-ARG BA-9588
f.s.   (194)
"Technica Superior" [Jap] gtr
(repr, 1963, Span ed; 1st ed,
1923, Span ed; contains:
Exercises by L.C. Hanon-Rodriguez
Arenas; Exercises in thirds,
sixths and octaves by Aguado,
Giuliani; legato, barre, chords;
Preludes and Exercises by F.
Tarrega; includes: Tarrega,
Francisco, Preludes, TI-i-12, 14,
23; Studies, TI-ii-4b[20 bars],
29; Exercises, TI-iii-2, 4, 5a-C,
6, 7a-C, 9-11, 15a-g, 17a-C, 18,
19, 26, 27) folio ONGAKU f.s.
                                  (195)

RONNY LEE CLASSIC GUITAR BOOK, THE
(Lee, Ronny) gtr (1-3rd degr.) ALFRED
459 $2.95 38 arr+ orig pcs;
contains works by: Carcassi (9),
Carulli (8), Sor (8), Aguado (3),
Beethoven (1), Lee (2), Clarke (1),
Scarlatti (1)
contains: Bach, Johann Sebastian,
Minuet, BWV Anh. 114, in G (from
Anna Magdalena Bach Notenbuchlein
(1725), No.4); Bach, Johann
Sebastian, Minuet, BWV Anh. 132,
in D minor (from Anna Magdalena
Bach Notenbuchlein (1725), No.36)
(E min); Bach, Johann Sebastian,
Partita for Violin, No. 1, BWV
1002, in B minor, Bourree (A
min); Bach, Johann Sebastian,
Partita for Violin, No. 3, BWV
1006, in E, Gavotte En Rondeau (C
maj); Tarrega, Francisco, Study,
TI ii- 26, in C   (196)

SAGRERAS, JULIO S. (1879-1942)
Tecnica Superior De Guitarra, De
Acuerdo Con La Moderna Escuela
Del Maestro Tarrega
[Span] gtr folio RICORDI-ARG
BA-9553 f.s. 39p.; repr, 1966;
1st ed, 1922; contains Diatonic
scales (2 and 3 octaves) + scale
formulae, Chromatic scales,
Scales in thirds, sixths,
octaves, 15 Exercises, scale
exercises, studies; includes:
Tarrega, Francisco, Studies, TI-
ii-37 (in A), 39, 40 [10 bars in
3-4], 41; Exercise, TI-iii-32
                                  (197)

SEVEN HUNDRED YEARS OF MUSIC FOR THE
CLASSIC GUITAR
(Valdes Blain) gtr (3-6th degr.)
HANSEN-US T-156 f.s. 22 arr + orig
pcs; contains works by: Adam de la
Hale (1), Anon. (7), Dowland (2),
A. Scarlatti (1), Giuliani (1), Sor
(2), Granados (1), Albeniz (1)
contains: Bach, Johann Sebastian,
Partita for Violin, No. 1, BWV
1002, in B minor, Saraband; Bach,
Johann Sebastian, Prelude for
Lute, BWV 999, in C minor (D
min); Bach, Johann Sebastian,
Suite for Lute, BWV 996, in E
minor, Allemand (A min); Bach,
Johann Sebastian, Suite for Lute,
BWV 996, in E minor, Bourree;
Tarrega, Francisco, Prelude, TI
i- 17, in E, "Lagrima"   (198)

SHEARER, AARON
Classic Guitar Technique, Vol. II
[Eng] gtr quarto COLOMBO NY-2325
f.s. vii+158p, ill.; 1964;
contains: Tarrega, Francisco,
Preludes, TI-i-10, 11   (199)

SOLO-GITARRE, DIE, VOL. III
(Feider) gtr (1-5th degr.) PETERER
f.s. 8 arr+ orig pcs; contains
works by: Feider (4), Giuliani (1),
Diabelli (1)
contains: Tarrega, Francisco,
Prelude, TI i- 16, in D minor,
"Endecha"; Tarrega, Francisco,
Prelude, TI i- 17, in E,
"Lagrima"   (200)

SUPLEMENTO AL METODO PARA GUITARRA DE
AGUADO-SINOPOLI
(Sinopoli, Antonio) gtr (4-10th
degr.) RICORDI-ARG BA-6712 f.s. 19
arr + orig pcs; contains works by:

Sinopoli (1), Sor (6), Chopin (2);
also includes: Tarrega, Francisco,
Preludes, TI-i-1 In D-Minor, 4 In
E, 5 In E, 7 In A, 8A In A, 9 In A;
Study, TI-ii-5 In A, "Estudio En
Forma De Un Minuetto"; Bach, Johann
Sebastian, Das Wohltemperierte
Clavier, Vol. I, Prelude No. 1, BWV
846, In C (In E); Suite For
Violoncello, No. 3, BWV 1009,
Courante In C (In A): Partita For
Violin, No.2, BWV 1004, Chaconne I
In D Minor (In E Minor); and Sor,
Fernando, Grande Sonata, Op. 22
(Minuet); Grande Sonata, Op. 25
(Minuet)   (201)

TEUCHERT, HEINZ (1914-   )
Gitarren-Schule, Fur Melodiespiel,
Liedbegleitung Und Solospiel, Ein
Anschauliches Lehr- Und
Spielbuch, Vol. II
[Ger] gtr quarto SCHMIDT,H 96 f.s.
47-96p., ill; contains: Bach,
Johann Sebastian, Minuet, BWV
Anh. 132, from Anna Magdalena
Bach Notenbuchlein (1725), No.36,
In D Minor, for 2 gtr (single
line playing); Prelude For Lute,
BWV 999, In C Minor (in D Minor);
and Tarrega, Francisco, Prelude,
TI-i-17; Exercise, TI-iii-32
                                  (202)

VINSON, HARVEY
Play Classic Guitar
[Eng] gtr quarto AMSCO 020143 f.s.
95p., ill; 1969; 3 app; contains:
Bach, Johann Sebastian, Minuet,
from Anna Magdalena Bach
Notenbuchlein (1725), No.4, BWV
Anh. 114, In G; Suite No. 6 For
Violoncello, BWV 1012, In D,
Gavotte (in C; fragment); and
Tarrega, Francisco, Prelude, TI-
i-17, In E "Lagrima"; in G i-20,
in A   (203)

WYBOR ETIUD NA GITARE, VOL. 2 *CC6OU
(Powrozniak, Jozef) gtr (4th degr.)
POLSKIE 6471 f.s. exercises,
chords, studies; contains:
Exercises TI-iii-15g-h by Francisco
Tarrega   (204)

VII Thematic Index of the Works by Johann Sebastian Bach Arranged for Guitar

Musical Incipits

i. COMPOSITIONS FOR LUTE

Suite for Lute, BWV 995, in G minor

Suite for Lute, BWV 996, in E minor

Partita for Lute, BWV 997, in C minor

Prelude, Fugue and Allegro for Lute in E flat, BWV 998

Prelude for Lute, BWV 999, in C minor

Fugue for Lute, BWV 1000, in G minor

Partita for Lute, BWV 1006a, in E

Sonata for Violin, BWV 1003, in A minor

ii. COMPOSITIONS FOR UNACCOMPANIED VIOLIN

Partita for Violin, BWV 1004, in D minor

Sonata for Violin, BWV 1005, in C

Sonata for Violin, BWV 1001, in G minor

Partita for Violin, BWV 1006, in E

Partita for Violin, BWV 1002, in B minor

iii. COMPOSITIONS FOR UNACCOMPANIED VIOLONCELLO

Suite for Violoncello, BWV 1007, in G

Suite for Violoncello, BWV 1008, in D minor

Suite for Violoncello, BWV 1009, in C

Suite for Violoncello, BWV 1010, in E flat

Suite for Violoncello, BWV 1011, in C minor

Suite for Violoncello, BWV 1012, in D

iv. COMPOSITIONS FOR UNACCOMPANIED FLUTE

Sonata for Flute, BWV 1013, in A minor

v. COMPOSITIONS FOR KEYBOARD

The Clavier-book for Wilhelm Friedemann Bach (1720)

2. Praeambulum, BWV 924, in C

4. Prelude, BWV 926, in D minor

6. Allemande, BWV 836, in G minor

8. Prelude, BWV 927, in F

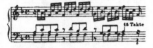

9. Prelude, BWV 930, in G minor

10. Prelude, BWV 928, in F

11. Minuet, BWV 841, in G

12. Minuet, BWV 842, in G minor

13. Minuet, BWV 843, in G

18. Prelude, BWV 855a, in E minor

27. Prelude, BWV 925, in D

31. Fugue, BWV 953, in C

47. Suite, BWV 824, in A

48. Partia di Signore Steltzeln
   + Minuet & Trio, BWV 929, in G minor

48². Air Italien

48³. Bourree

48⁵. Minuet & Trio, BWV 929

Inventions (Inventios), BWV 772-786

Sinfonias, BWV 787-801

Sinfonia 1

Sinfonia 2

Sinfonia 15

The Clavier-book for Anna Magdalena Bach (1725)

3. Minuet, BWV-Anh. 113, in F

4. Minuet, BWV-Anh. 114, in G

5. Minuet, BWV-Anh. 115, in G minor

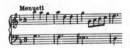

6. Rondeau, BWV-Anh. 183, in B flat (Fr. Couperin)

7. Minuet, BWV-Anh. 116, in G

8. Polonaise, BWV-Anh. 117a, in F (version 1)

8. Polonaise, BWV-Anh. 117b, in F (version 2)

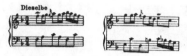

9. Minuet, BWV-Anh. 118, in B flat

10. Polonaise, BWV-Anh. 119, in G minor

12. Without title, BWV 510, in F (Choral: "Gib dich zufrieden und sei stille")

13. Choral: "Gib dich zufrieden und sei stille"
    BWV 511, in G minor
    BWV 512, in E minor

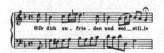

14. Minuet, BWV-Anh. 120, in A minor

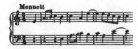

15. Minuet, BWV-Anh. 121, in C minor

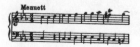

16. March, BWV-Anh. 122, in D (C.P.E. Bach)

17. Polonaise, BWV-Anh. 123, in G minor (C.P.E. Bach)

18. March, BWV-Anh. 124, in G (C.P.E. Bach)

19. Polonaise, BWV-Anh. 125, in G minor (C.P.E. Bach)

20. Aria: "So oft ich meine Tobackspfeife"
    BWV 515, in D minor
    BWV 515a, in G minor

21. Minuet fait par Mons. Böhm, in G

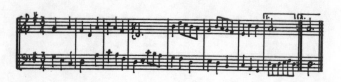

22. Musette, BWV-Anh. 126, in D

23. March, BWV-Anh. 127, in E flat

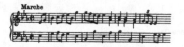

24. Polonaise, BWV-Anh. 128, in D minor

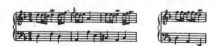

25. Aria: "Bist du bei mir" BWV 508, G.H. Stölzel (?)

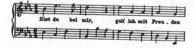

26. Aria for keyboard, BWV 988, 1, in G

27. Solo per il cembalo, BWV-Anh. 129, in E flat (C.P.E. Bach)

28. Polonaise, BWV-Anh. 130, in G

32. Without title, BWV-Anh. 131, in F

33. Aria: "Warum betrübst du dich", BWV 516

35. Choral: "Schaffs mit mir, Gott", BWV 514

36. Minuet, BWV-Anh. 132, in D minor

37. Aria di Giovannini: "Willst du dein Herz mir schenken", BWV 518

39. Choral: "Dir, dir, Jehova, will ich singen", BWV 299
    four-part setting
    for one voice and continuo

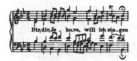

40. Choral: "Wie wohl ist mir, o Freund der Seelen", BWV 517

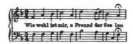

42. Choral: "O Ewigkeit, du Donnerwort", BWV 513

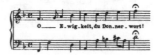

Suite for Keyboard Instrument, BWV 806, in A

Suite for Keyboard Instrument, BWV 807, in A minor

Suite for Keyboard Instrument, BWV 808, in G minor

Suite for Keyboard Instrument, BWV 810, in E minor

Sarabande

Passepied I (en Rondeau)　　　**Passepied II**

Suite for Keyboard Instrument, BWV 811, in D minor

Gavotte I　　　**Gavotte II**

Suite for Keyboard Instrument, BWV 812, in D minor

Sarabande

Menuett I

Menuett II

Suite for Keyboard Instrument, BWV 813, in C minor

Courante

Menuett

Gigue　　　**Menuett-Trio**

Suite for Keyboard Instrument, BWV 814, in B minor

Menuett

Gigue

Suite for Keyboard Instrument, BWV 815, in E flat

Suite for Keyboard Instrument, BWV 815a, in E flat

Gavotte

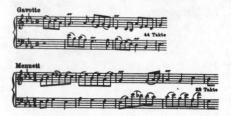

Menuett

Suite for Keyboard Instrument, BWV 816, in G

Allemande　　　**Gavotte**

Gigue

Suite for Keyboard Instrument, BWV 817, in E

Polonaise

Menuett

Suite for Keyboard Instrument, BWV 818a, in A minor

Gigue

Suite for Keyboard Instrument, BWV 820, in F

Entree

Menuett　　　**Trio**

Bourree　　　**Gigue**

Suite for Keyboard Instrument, BWV 821, in B flat

Courante   Sarabande

Suite for Keyboard Instrument, BWV 822, in G minor

Menuett I   Menuett II

Menuett (Trio)

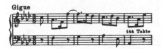

Suite for Keyboard Instrument, BWV 823, in F minor

Gigue

Partita for Keyboard Instrument, BWV 825, in B flat

Praeludium   Allemande

Courante   Sarabande

Menuett I   Menuett II

Gigue

Partita for Keyboard Instrument, BWV 829, in G

Tempo di Minuetto

Partita for Keyboard Instrument, BWV 830, in E minor

Air

Partita for Keyboard Instrument, BWV 831, in B minor

Bourrée I

Bourrée II

Partie, BWV 832, in A

Bourrée
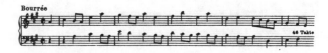

The Well Tempered Clavier, Book 1, BWV 846-869

Prelude, BWV 846, in C

Praeludium 1

Fugue, BWV 847, in C minor

Fuga 2

Prelude, BWV 853, in E flat minor

Praeludium 8

Fugue, BWV 855, in E minor

Fuga 10

Prelude, BWV 866, in B flat

Praeludium 21

Prelude, BWV 867, in B flat minor

Praeludium 22
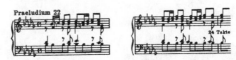

The Well Tempered Clavier, Book 2, BWV 870-893

Fugue, BWV 874, in D

Prelude and Fugue, BWV 895, in A minor

Prelude and Fugue, BWV 896, in A

Toccata, BWV 913, in D minor

Fantasia, BWV 919, in C minor

6 Little Preludes, BWV 933-938

Prelude, BWV 933, in C

Prelude, BWV 934, in C minor

Prelude, BWV 935, in D minor

Prelude, BWV 936, in D

Prelude, BWV 937, in E

Prelude, BWV 938, in E minor

5 Little Preludes, BWV 939-943

Prelude, BWV 939, in C

Prelude, BWV 940, in D minor

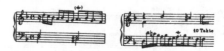

Prelude, BWV 941, in E minor

Prelude, BWV 942, in A minor

Fugues, BWV 944-962

Fughetta, BWV 961, in C minor

Sonata, BWV 964, in D minor

Presto, BWV 970, in D minor

Italian Concerto, BWV 971, in F

16 Concertos after various Masters , BWV 972-987

Concerto No. 2 for Keyboard Instrument, BWV 973, in G

Concerto No. 7 for Keyboard Instrument, BWV 978, in F

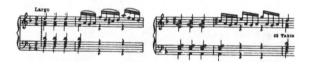

Concerto No. 15 for Keyboard Instrument, BWV 986, in G

Aria variata all maniera italiana, BWV 989, in A minor

Sarabande con Partite, BWV 990, in C

16. L'ultima Partita o Giguetta

Capriccio, sopra la lontananza del suo fratello dilettissimo, BWV 992, in B flat

vi. COMPOSITIONS FOR ORGAN

Prelude (Fantasia) and Fugue, BWV 542, in G minor

8 Little Preludes and Fugues, BWV 553-560

Prelude and Fugue, BWV 553, in C

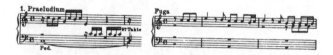

Prelude and Fugue, BWV 556, in F

Prelude and Fugue, BWV 558, in G minor

Toccata, BWV 565, in D minor

Pedal-Exercitium, BWV 598, in G minor

BGA XXXVIII, 210. — EZ Lüneburg 1700–1703.

Organ-book (for Wilhelm Friedemann Bach?), BWV 599-644

Puer natus in Bethlehem, BWV 603, in G minor

6 Chorales (Schübler), BWV 645-650

1. "Wachet auf, ruft uns die Stimme", BWV 645, in E flat

Chorale Preludes (Kirnberger Collection), BWV 690-713

"Allein Gott in der Höh' sei Ehr", Bicinium, BWV 711, in G

vii. CHAMBER MUSIC

Invention for Violin and Keyboard, BWV-Anh. 174, in B flat

Sonata for Flute and Keyboard, BWV 1031, in E flat

Sonata for Flute and Basso Continuo, BWV 1033, in C

Menuetto I

Menuetto II

Sonata for 2 Flutes and Figured Bass, BWV 1039, in G

viii. ORCHESTRAL COMPOSITIONS

7 Concertos, BWV 1052-1058

Concerto for Harpsichord, BWV 1056, in F minor

Suite for Orchestra, BWV 1066, in C

Suite for Orchestra, BWV 1067, in B minor

Suite for Orchestra, BWV 1068, in D

ix. VOCAL COMPOSITIONS

Cantata 18: "Gleich wie der Regen und Schnee"

5. Choral. Sopr., Alto, Ten., Basso; Cont. (Flauto I, II, Vla. I, II col Sopr.; Vla. III coll' Alto; Vla. IV col Ten.; Fag. coi Basso)

Ich bitt', o Herr, aus Her_zens Grund
17 Takte

Cantata 32: "Liebster Jesu, mein Verlangen"

6. Choral. Sopr., Alto, Ten., Basso; Ob.; Viol. I, II, Vla.; Cont.

Mein Gott, öff_ne mir die Pfor_ten
17 Takte

Cantata 38: "Aus tiefer Not schrei ich zu dir"

6. Choral. Sopr., Alto, Ten., Basso; Cont. (Ob. I, II, Viol. I, Tromb. I col Sopr.; Viol. II, Tromb. II coll' Alto; Vla., Tromb. III col Ten., Tromb. IV col Basso)

Ob bei uns ist der Sün_den viel, bei Gott ist viel mehr Gna_de
18 Takte

Cantata 39: "Brich dem Hungrigen dein Brot"

7. Choral. Sopr., Alto, Ten., Basso; Cont. (Flau_te I, II in 8ᵃ, Ob. I, II, Viol. I col Sopr.; Viol. II coll' Alto; Vla. col Ten.)

Se_lig sind, die aus Er_bar_men
17 Takte

Cantata 93: "Wer nur den lieben Gott lässt walten"

7. Choral. Sopr., Alto, Ten., Basso; Cont. (Ob. I, II, Viol. I col Sopr.; Viol. II coll' Alto; Vla. col Ten.)

Sing', bet' und geh' auf Got_tes We_gen,
15 Takte

Cantata 140: "Wachet auf, ruft uns die Stimme"

7. Choral. Vers 3. Sopr., Alto, Ten., Basso; Cont. (Viol. picc. in 8ᵛᵃ, Corno, Ob. I, Viol. I col Sopr.; Ob. II, Viol. II, coll' Alto; Taille e Vla. col Ten.)

Glo_ri_a sei dir ge_sun_gen
38 Takte
Glo_ri_a

Cantata 147: "Herz und Mund und Tat und Leben"

10. Choral. Sopr., Alto, Ten., Basso; Tromba, Oboi (col Viol. I.), Viol. I, II, Vla., Cont.

Je_sus blei_bet mei_ne Freu_de
71 Takte
(s. oben Nr. 6)
Takt 9

Cantata 194: "Höchsterwünschtes Freudenfest"

12. Choral. Sopr., Alto, Ten., Basso; Instru_mente wie bei Nr. 6.

Sprich Ja zu mei_nen Ta_ten
16 Takte

Cantata 212: "Mer hahn en neue Oberkeet"

1. (Instrumentalsatz.) Viol., Vla., Cont.
304
piano
67 Takte

2. Aria Duett. Sopr., Basso; Viol., Vla.; Cont.

Mer hahn en neu_e O_ber_keet an un_sern Kam_mer_herrn
24 Takte

4. Aria. Sopr.; Viol., Vla.; Cont.

Ach es schmeckt doch gar zu gut, wenn ein Paar recht freundlich tut;
30 Takte
Takt 2 u. 3
Takt 4

16. Aria. Basso; Corno, Viol., Vla.; Cont.

Es neh_me zehn_tau_send Du_ca_ten der Kam_mer_herr al_le Tag' ein
24 Takte

18. Aria. Sopr.; Corno, Viol., Vla.; Cont.

Gib, Schö_ne, viel Söh_ne von art'ger Ge_stalt
18 Takte

24. Coro. Sopr., Basso; Viol., Vla.; Cont.

Wir gehn nun wo der Tu_del_sack, der Tu_del_Tu_del_Tu_del_Tu_del_Tu_del_sack
26 Takte

Mass in B minor, BWV 232: Crucifixus

16. (Chor) Sopr. II, Alto, Ten., Basso; Flauto trav. I, II; Viol. I, II, Vla.; Cont.

Cru_ci_fi_xus
Cru_ci_fi_xus
Cru_ci_
fi_xus, Cru_ci_(fixus)
53 Takte
Basso Cru_ci_fi_xus

St. Matthew Passion, BWV 244

Four-Part Chorales, BWV 250-438

21. Choral. (Ch. 1, 2) Besetzung wie bei Nr. 3

Er kenne mich, mein Hü . ter   16 Takte

23. Choral. (Ch. 1, 2) Besetzung wie bei Nr. 16

Ich will hier bei dir ste . hen   16 Takte

44. Choral. Stromenti concordant (Ch. 1, 2)(Besetzung wie bei Nr. 3)   **53. Choral.** (Ch. 1, 2) (Besetzung wie bei Nr. 3)

Wer hat dich so ge . schla . gen   12 Takte   Be . fiehl du dei . ne We . ge   16 Takte

63. Choral. (Ch. 1, 2) Besetzung wie bei Nr. 3

O Haupt voll Blut und Wun . den   16 Takte

St. John Passion, BWV 245

15. Choral. (Besetzung wie bei Nr. 9)

Wer hat dich so ge . schla . gen   12 Takte

31. Arioso. Basso; Vla. d'amore I, II; Liuto,*) Cont., Org.

Adagio   Betrach . te, mei . ne Seel, mit ängstlichem Ver . gnü . gen   16 Takte

Viole d'am.

Liuto

Christmas Oratorio, BWV 248

4. Aria. Alto; Ob. d'amore I e Viol. I (all'unis.); Cont.

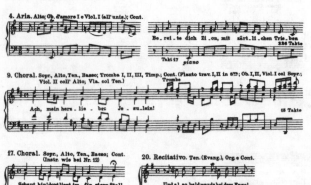

Be . rei . te dich Zi . on, mit zärt . li . chen Trie . ben   236 Takte

Takt 17 piano

9. Choral. Sopr., Alto, Ten., Basso; Tromba I, II, III, Timp.; Cont. (Flauto trav. I, II in 8va; Ob. I, II, Viol. I col Sopr.; Viol. II coll' Alto; Vla. col Ten.)

Trombe

Ach, mein herz . lie . bes Je . su . lein!   15 Takte

17. Choral. Sopr., Alto, Ten., Basso; Cont. (Instr. wie bei Nr. 12)   **20. Recitativo.** Ten. (Evang.), Org. e Cont.

Schaut hin! dort liegt im fin . stern Stall   8 Takte   Und al . so bald ward da bei dem Engel   4 Takte

---

252 Nach dem Segen
J. Crüger 1648.

Nun danket al . le Gott

267 Wolfg. Dachstein 1525.

An Was . ser flüs . sen Ba . by . lon

Ein Lämm . lein geht und trägt die Schuld

270 H. L. Hassler 1601.

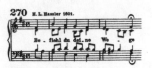

Be . fiehl du dei . ne We . ge

295 J. Herm. Schein 1627.

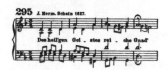

Des heil'gen Gei . stes rei . che Gnad'

302 Jos. Klug G. B. 1535.

Ein' fe . ste Burg ist un . ser Gott

375 Nic. Herman 1560 (1554).

Lobt Gott, ihr Chri . sten, all . zu . gleich

392 Georg Forster 1539.

Nun ru . hen al . le Wäl . der

393 G. Forsters Liedersammlung 1539.
Die Melodie wird Heinr. Isaak (um 1490) zugeschrieben.

O Welt, sieh' hier dein Le . ben

434 Georg Neumark 1640.

Wer nur den lie . ben   Gott läßt wal . ten

436 Philipp Nicolai 1599.

Wie schön leuch . tet der Mor . gen . stern

Sacred Songs and Arias from Schemelli's Gesangbuch, BWV 439-507

x. CANONS

Canon in seven parts, BWV 1078

xi. THE MUSICAL OFFERING

BWV 1079, Ricercares, Canons, etc., 16 movements

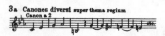

xii. THE ART OF FUGUE

BWV 1080, Contrapuncti, Canons, Fugues, 23 movements

Works by Johann Sebastian Bach Arranged for Guitar: Details and Commentary

i. COMPOSITIONS FOR LUTE

Suite for Lute, BWV 995, in G minor
Prelude/Presto - Allemand - Courante - Sarabande -
Gavotte I/II - Gigue
Transcription of Suite V for violoncello, BWV 1011.

Suite for Lute, BWV 996, in E minor
Passaggio/Presto - Allemande - Courante - Without title
(Sarabande) - Bourree - Without title (Gigue).

Partita for Lute, BWV 997, in C minor
Prelude - Fugue - Sarabande - Gigue - Double

Prelude, Fugue and Allegro for Lute in E flat, BWV 998

Prelude for Lute, BWV 999, in C minor

Fugue for Lute, BWV 1000, in G minor

Partita for Lute, BWV 1006a, in E
Prelude - Loure - Gavotte en Rondeau - Minuet I/II -
Bourree - Gigue

ii. COMPOSITIONS FOR UNACCOMPANIED VIOLIN

3 Sonatas and 3 Partitas, BWV 1001-1006

Sonata for Violin, BWV 1001, in G minor
Adagio - Fugue - Siciliano - Presto

Partita for Violin, BWV 1002, in B minor
Allemande/Double - Courante/Double - Sarabande/Double - Bourree/Double

Sonata for Violin, BWV 1003, in A minor
Grave - Fugue - Andante - Allegro

Partita for Violin, BWV 1004, in D minor
Allemande - Courante - Sarabande - Gigue - Chaconne

Sonata for Violin, BWV 1005, in C
Adagio - Fugue - Largo - Allegro assai

Partita for Violin, BWV 1006, in E
Prelude - Loure - Gavotte en Rondeau - Minuet I/II -
Bourree - Gigue

iii. COMPOSITIONS FOR UNACCOMPANIED VIOLONCELLO

6 Suites, BWV 1007-1012

Suite for Violoncello, BWV 1007, in G
Prelude - Allemande - Courante - Sarabande - Minuet I/II-
Gigue

Suite for Violoncello, BWV 1008, in D minor
Prelude - Allemande - Courante - Sarabande - Minuet I/II - Gigue

Suite for Violoncello, BWV 1009, in C
Prelude - Allemande - Courante - Sarabande - Bourree I/II - Gigue

Suite for Violoncello, BWV 1010, in E flat
Prelude - Allemande - Courante - Sarabande - Bourree I/II - Gigue

Suite for Violoncello, BWV 1011, in C minor
Prelude/without title (Presto) - Allemande - Courante - Sarabande - Gavotte
I/II - Gigue

Suite for Violoncello, BWV 1012, in D
Prelude - Allemande - Courante - Sarabande - Gavotte I/II - Gigue

iv. COMPOSITIONS FOR UNACCOMPANIED FLUTE

Sonata for Flute, BWV 1013, in A minor
Allemande - Corrente - Sarabande - Bourree anglaise

v. COMPOSITIONS FOR KEYBOARD

The Clavierbook for Wilhelm Friedemann Bach (1720) No. 1-63.
Arranged for Guitar:

2. Praeambulum 1, BWV 924, in C (JSB)
4. Prelude (Praeludium) 2, BWV 926, in D minor (JSB)
6. Allemande (1), BWV 836, in G minor (WFB & JSB)
8. Praeambulum, BWV 927, in F (JSB)
9. Praeambulum, BWV 930, in G minor (JSB)
10. Praeludium, BWV 928, in F (JSB)
11-13. Three Minuets, BWV 841-843, G/G minor/G
   11. Minuet 1 (JSB)
   12. Minuet 2 (JSB + WFB?)
   13. Minuet 3 (JSB)
14-24. Eleven Preludes from the Well Tempered Clavier, Book 1 (partly in a
   different setting). BWV 846a-851, 853, 854, 855a-857. (JSB)
   No. 18 is Praeludium 5, BWV 855a in E minor (WTC-I, no.10a).
26-28. Three Preludes, BWV 924a, 925, 932, in C, D, and C (belonging together)
   No. 27. Praeludium ex d-natural, BWV 925, in D (WFB?)
31. Fugue (3 voices), BWV 953, in C (JSB?)
47. Suite, BWV 824, in A
   Allemande - Courante - Gigue
   (G. P. Telemann)
48. Partia de Signore Steltzeln, BWV 929, in G minor
   1. Overture
   2. Air Italien
   3. Bourree
   4. Minuet
   5. Minuet-Trio
   (No. 1-4: Gottfried Heinrich Stölzel; no. 5: JSB)

Inventions, BWV 772-786
    Invention No. 1, BWV 772, in C
    Invention No. 2, BWV 773, in C minor
    Invention No. 3, BWV 774, in D
    Invention No. 4, BWV 775, in D minor
    Invention No. 5, BWV 776, in E flat
    Invention No. 6, BWV 777, in E
    Invention No. 7, BWV 778, in E minor
    Invention No. 8, BWV 779, in F
    Invention No. 9, BWV 780, in F minor
    Invention No. 10, BWV 781, in G
    Invention No. 11, BWV 782, in G minor
    Invention No. 12, BWV 783, in A
    Invention No. 13, BWV 784, in A minor
    Invention No. 14, BWV 785, in B flat
    Invention No. 15, BWV 786, in B minor

Sinfonias, BWV 787-801
    Arranged for Guitar:
    Sinfonia No. 1, BWV 787, in C
    Sinfonia No. 2, BWV 788, in C minor
    Sinfonia No. 3, BWV 801, in B minor

The Clavierbook for Anna Magdalena Bach, (1725)
    42 pieces. Nos. 4 and 5 belong together as Minuet I/II.
    Nos. 14 and 15 have been composed by the same composer. For nos. 29,
    30, and 31, see Well Tempered Clavier, Book I; French suites 1 and 2.
    Arranged for guitar:

    3. Minuet, BWV Anh. 113, in F (JSB?)
    4. Minuet, BWV Anh. 114, in G (JSB?)
    5. Minuet, BWV Anh. 115, in G minor (JSB?)
    6. Rondeau, BWV Anh. 183 (Fr. Couperin: "Les Bergeries", rondeau, Second
      Livre de Pièces de Clavecin, Paris, 1717, p. 8f)
    7. Minuet, BWV Anh. 116, in G (JSB?)
    8. Polonaise, BWV Anh. 117a, in F (version 1) (JSB?)
      Polonaise, BWV Anh. 117b, in F (version 2) (JSB?)
    9. Minuet, BWV Anh. 118, in B flat (JSB?)
   10. Polonaise, BWV Anh. 119, in G minor (JSB?)
   12. Without title, BWV 510, in F (Choral: "Gib dich zufrieden und sei stille" -
      Anonymous)
   13. Choral:: "Gib dich zufrieden und sei stille" (JSB)
      a. in G minor, BWV 511
      b. in E minor, BWV 512
   14. Minuet, BWV Anh. 120, in A minor (JSB?)
   15. Minuet, BWV Anh. 121, in C minor (JSB?)
   16. Marche, BWV Anh. 122, in D (C.P.E. Bach)
   17. Polonaise, BWV Anh. 123, in G minor (C.P.E. Bach)
   18. Marche, BWV Anh. 124, in G (C.P.E. Bach)
   19. Polonaise, BWV Anh. 125 in G minor (C.P.E. Bach)
   20. Aria: "So oft ich meine Tobackspfeife"
      a. BWV 515, in D minor (Gottfried Heinrich Bach?, 1724-1763)
      b. BWV 515a, in G minor, Bass part: JSB
      c. Poem: "Erbauliche Gedanken eines Tobackrauchers")
   21. Minuet fait par Mons. Böhm (JSB-autograph)
   22. Musette, BWV Anh. 126, in D (Anon)
   23. Marche, BWV Anh. 127, in E flat (Anon)
   24. (Polonaise), BWV Anh. 128, in D minor (Anon)
   25. Aria: "Bist du bei mir", BWV 508 (G.H. Stölzel?)
   26. Aria, BWV 988-1, in G (JSB)
   27. Solo per il cembalo, BWV Anh. 129, in E flat (C.P.E. Bach)
   28. Polonaise, BWV Anh. 130, in G (Anon)
   32. Without title, BWV Anh. 131, in F (Anon)
   33. Aria: "Warum betrübst du dich", BWV 516 (Anon)
   35. Choral: "Schaffs mit mir", BWV 514 (Anon)
   36. Minuet, BWV Anh. 132, in D minor (Anon)
   37. Aria di Giovannini: "Willst du dein Herz mir schenken", BWV 518 (Anon)
   39. Choral: "Dir, dir, Jehova, will ich singen", BWV 299 (JSB)
      a. Four part setting, autograph JSB
      b. For voice and basso continuo, autograph AMB
   40. Choral: "Wie wohl ist mir, o Freund der Seelen", BWV 517 (Anon)
   42. Choral: "O Ewigkeit, du Donnerwort", BWV 513 (JSB)

English Suites 1-6, BWV 806-811

    Suite for Keyboard Instrument, BWV 806, in A
      Prelude - Allemande - Courante I - Courante II with two Doubles (Double I/
      II) - Sarabande - Bourree I/II - Gigue

    Suite for Keyboard Instrument, BWV 807, in A minor
      Prelude - Allemande - Courante - Saraband - Bourree I/II - Gigue

    Suite for Keyboard Instrument, BWV 808, in G minor
      Prelude - Allemande - Courante - Sarabande - Gavotte I/II or Musette - Gigue

    Suite for Keyboard Instrument, BWV 810, in E minor
      Prelude - Allemande - Courante - Sarabande - Passepied I (and Rondeau)/
      Passepied II - Gigue

    Suite for Keyboard Instrument, BWV 811, in D minor
      Prelude/Allegro - Allemande - Courante - Sarabande/Double - Gavotte I/II
      - Gigue

French Suites 1-6, BWV 812-817

    Suite for Keyboard Instrument, BWV 812, in D minor
      Allemande - Courante - Sarabande - Minuet I/II - Gigue

    Suite for Keyboard Instrument, BWV 813, in C minor
      Allemande - Courante - Sarabande - Air - Minuet -
      Gigue Minuet-Trio (BWV 813a)

    Suite for Keyboard Instrument, BWV 814, in B minor
      Allemande - Courante - Sarabande - Minuet - Trio - Anglaise - Gigue

    Suite for Keyboard Instrument, BWV 815, in E flat
      Allemande – Courante – Sarabande – Gavotte – Air – Gigue

    Suite for Keyboard Instrument, BWV 815a, in E flat
      Prelude – Gavotte II – Minuet

    Suite for Keyboard Instrument, BWV 816, in G
      Allemande - Courante - Sarabande - Gavotte - Bourree - Loure - Gigue

    Suite for Keyboard Instrument, BWV 817, in E
      Allemande - Courante - Sarabande - Gavotte - Polonaise - Bourree - Minuet
      - Gigue

Suites, BWV 818-824

    Suite, BWV 818a, in A minor
      (Prelude) - Allemande - Courante - Sarabande - Minuet - Gigue

    Suite for Keyboard Instrument, BWV 820, in F (Ouverture)
      Without title (in 4/4) - Without title (in 3/4) - Entree - Minuet/Trio - Bourree
      - Gigue

    Suite for Keyboard Instrument, BWV 821, in B flat
      (Praeludium) - Allemande - Courante - Sarabande - Echo

    Suite for Keyboard Instrument, BWV 822, in G minor
      Ouverture - Aria- Gavotte en Rondeau - Without title - Minuet I/II Trio - Gigue

    Suite for Keyboard Instrument, BWV 823, in F minor (fragment)
      Prelude - Sarabande - Gigue

6 Partitas, BWV 825-830
Partita, BWV 831, in B minor
Partie, BWV 832, in A

    Partita (Suite) for Keyboard Instrument, BWV 825, in B flat
      Praeludium - Allemande - Courante - Sarabande - Minuet I/II - Gigue

    Partita (Suite) for Keyboard Instrument, BWV 829, in G
      Praeambulum - Allemande - Courante - Sarabande - Tempo di Minuetto -
      Passepied - Gigue

    Partita (Suite) for Keyboard Instrument, BWV 830, in E minor
      Toccata - Without title - Allemande - Courante - Air - Sarabande - Tempo di
      Gavotta - Gigue

    Partita for Keyboard Instrument (Overture in the French manner), BWV 831, in
      B minor
      Ouverture - Courante - Gavotte I/II - Passepied I/II - Sarabande - Bourree
      I/II - Gigue - Echo

    Partie, BWV 832, in A
      Allemande - Air pour les Trompettes - Sarabande - Bourree - Gigue

The Well Tempered Clavier, Book 1, Köthen 1722, BWV 846-869.
    24 Preludes and Fugues
    Arranged for guitar:
    Prelude, BWV 846, in C
    Fugue, BWV 847, in C minor
    Prelude, BWV 853, in E flat minor
    Fugue, BWV 855, in E minor
    Prelude, BWV 866, in B flat
    Prelude, BWV 867, in B flat minor

The Well Tempered Clavier, Book 2, finished at Leipzig 1744,
    BWV 870-893. 24 Preludes and Fugues.
    Arranged for guitar:
    Fugue, BWV 874, in D

Preludes and Fugues, Fantasias and Fugues, Toccatas, Fantasias, Preludes, BWV 894-923

    Prelude and Fugue, BWV 895, in A minor

    Prelude and Fugue, BWV 896, in A

    Toccata, BWV 913, in D minor
        First mov't (without title) - (Presto) - Adagio - Allegro

    Fantasia, BWV 919, in C minor

6 Little Preludes, BWV 933-938
    Prelude No. 1, BWV 933, in C
    Prelude No. 2, BWV 934, in C minor
    Prelude No. 3, BWV 935, in D minor
    Prelude No. 4, BWV 936, in D
    Prelude No. 5, BWV 937, in E
    Prelude No. 6, BWV 938, in E minor

5 Little Preludes, BWV 939-943
    Arranged for guitar:
    Prelude No. 1, BWV 939, in C
    Prelude No. 2, BWV 940, in D minor
    Prelude No. 3, BWV 941, in E minor
    Prelude No. 4, BWV 942, in A minor

Fugues, BWV 944-962
    Fughetta, BWV 961, in C minor

Sonatas, BWV 963-967
    Sonata, BWV 964, in D minor
        arrangement of the Sonata for Violin, BWV 1003
        Adagio - Fuga - Andante

Presto, BWV 970, in D minor

Italian Concerto, BWV 971, in F
    Without title - Andante - Presto

16 Concertos after various Masters, BWV 972-987
    Concerto No. 2 for Keyboard Instrument, BWV 973, in G
        Without title - Largo - Allegro
    Concerto No. 7 for Keyboard Instrument, BWV 978, in F
        Allegro - Largo - Allegro
    Concerto No. 15 for Keyboard Instrument, BWV 986, in G
        Without title - Adagio - Allegro

Aria variata alla maniera italiana, BWV 989, in A minor
    Aria, Variations 1-10

Sarabande con Partite, BWV 990, in C
        16 pieces numbered 1-16. Numbers 1-15 without title, no. 16:
        L'Ultima Partita o Giguetta

Capriccio, sopra la lontananza del suo fratello dilettissimo, BWV 992, in B flat
    Arioso, Adagio - (Andante) - Adagissimo - Without title - Aria di Postiglione, Adagio
    poco - Fuga all'imitazione della cornetta di postiglione

vi. COMPOSITIONS FOR ORGAN

Preludes and Fugues, BWV 531-552

    Prelude (Fantasia) and Fugue, BWV 542, in G minor

8 Little Preludes and Fugues, BWV 553-560
    Arranged for guitar:
    Prelude and Fugue, BWV 553, in C
    Prelude and Fugue, BWV 556, in F
    Prelude and Fugue, BWV 558, in G minor

Toccata, BWV 565, in D minor
    Adagio - Without title (Fuga)

Pedal-Exercitium, BWV 598, in G minor

Organ-book (For Wilhelm Friedemann Bach?), BWV 599-644
    "Orgelbüchlein"
    Puer natus in Bethlehem, BWV 603, in G minor
6 Chorales (Schübler), BWV 645-650
    Wachet auf, ruft uns die Stimme, BWV 645, in E flat

Chorale Preludes (Kirnberger Collection), BWV 690-713
    Allein Gott in der Höh' sei Ehr, Bicinium, BWV 711, in G

vii. CHAMBER MUSIC

4 Inventions by Francesco Antonio Bonporti, BWV-Anh. 173-176,
    arranged for guitar:
    Invention (No. 2) for Violin and Keyboard, BWV Anh. 174, in B flat
    Without title - Aria- Giga - Fantasia

3 Sonatas for Flute and Keyboard, BWV 1030-1032
    Sonata for Flute and Keyboard Instrument, BWV 1031, in E flat
    Allegro moderato - Siciliano - Allegro

3 Sonatas for Flute and Continuo, BWV 1033-1035
    Sonata for Flute and Continuo, BWV 1033, in C
        Andante/Presto - Allegro - Adagio - Minuet I/II
    Sonata for Flute and Keyboard Instrument, BWV 1035, in E

Sonata for 2 Flutes and Figured Bass, BWV 1039, in G
    Adagio - Allegro ma non presto - Adagio e piano - Presto

viii. ORCHESTRAL COMPOSITIONS

7 Concertos, BWV 1052-1058
    Arranged for guitar:
    Concerto for Harpsichord, BWV 1056, in F minor
    Without title - Largo - Presto

Suites for Orchestra (Overtures, Sinfonias), BWV 1066-1071
    Arranged for guitar:
    Suite for Orchestra, BWV 1066, in C
        Without title - Courante - Gavotte I alternativement/Gavotte II - Forlane -
        Minuet I alternativement/Minuet II - Bourree I alternativement/Bourree II -
        Passepied I/II.

    Suite for Orchestra, BWV 1067, in B minor (Overture)
        Without title - Lentement - Rondeau - Sarabande - Bourree I alternativement/
        Bourree II - Polonaise/Double - Minuet - Badinerie

    Suite for Orchestra, BWV 1068, in D (Overture)
        Without title/Vite - Air - Gavotte I/II - Bourree - Gigue

ix. VOCAL COMPOSITIONS

Cantatas BWV 18, 32, 38, 39, 93, 140, 147, 194, 212
    18. Gleich wie der Regen und Schnee - 5 movements
    32. Liebster Jesu, mein Verlangen - 6 movements
    38. Aus tiefer Not schrei ich zu dir - 6 movements
    39. Brich dem Hungrigen dein Brot - 7 movements

    93. Wer nur den lieben Gott lässt walten - 7 movements
    140. Wachet auf, ruft uns die Stimme - 7 movements
    147. Herz und Mund und Tat und Leben - 10 movements
    194. Höchsterwünschtes Freudenfest - 2 parts, 12 movements
    212. Mer hahn en neue Oberkeet (Bauern-kantate), cantate en burlesque - 24 movements

Mass in B minor, BWV 232: Crucifixus

St. Matthew Passion, BWV 244; 2 parts, 78 movements.
    Arranged for guitar:
    21. Erkenne mich, mein Hüter (choral)
    23. Ich will hier bei dir stehen (choral)
    44. Wer hat dich so geschlagen (choral)
    53. Befiel du deine Wege (choral)
    63. O Haupt voll Blut und Wunden (choral)

St. John Passion, BWV 245; 2 parts, 68 movements.
    (numbering after the BWV; new numbering in the NBA)
    Arranged for guitar:
    15. Wer hat dich so geschlagen (choral) NBA no. 11
    31. Betrachte meine Seel' mit ängstlichem Vergnügen (arioso) (NBA no. 19)

Christmas Oratorio, BWV 248; 6 parts, 64 movements.
    Arranged for guitar:
    Part I
    4. Aria: Bereite dich Zion, mit zärtlichen Trieben (Instrumental Prelude/Aria)
    9. Choral: Ach mein herzliebes Jesulein (with instrumental interludes: 3 trp, timp)
    Part II
    17. Choral: Schaut hin! dort liegt im finstern Stall
    20. Recitativo: Und also bald war da bei dem Engel

Four-Part Chorales, BWV 250-438
    (3 Wedding chorales: BWV 250-252; Collection J. Ph. Kirnberger/C.P.E. Bach: BWV 253-438). Arranged for guitar:
    BWV 252: Nun danket alle Gott
    BWV 267: An Wasserflüssen Babylon
    BWV 270: Befiel du deine Wege
    BWV 295: Des heil'gen Geistes reiche Gnad'
    BWV 302: Ein' feste Burg ist unser Gott
    BWV 375: Lobt Gott, ihr Christen, allzugleich
    BWV 392: Nun ruhen alle Wälder
    BWV 393: O Welt, sieh' hier dein Leben
    BWV 397: O Ewigkeit, du Donnerwort
    BWV 434: Wer nur den lieben Gott lässt walten
    BWV 436: Wie schön leuchtet der Morgenstern

Geistliche Lieder (Sacred Songs and Arias) from Schemelli's
    Gesangbuch, BWV 439-507. Arranged for guitar:
    BWV 439: Ach, dass nicht die letzte Stunde meines Lebens heute schlägt
    BWV 440: Aug, auf, die rechte Zeit ist hier
    BWV 445: Brunnquell aller Güter, Herrscher der Gemüter
    BWV 447: Der Tag ist hin, die Sonne gehet nieder
    BWV 448: Der Tag mit seinem Lichte
    BWV 451: Die goldne Sonne, voll Freud' und Wonne
    BWV 453: Eins ist Not, ach Herr, dies Eine
    BWV 454: Ermuntre dich, mein schwacher Geist
    BWV 458: Es ist vollbracht: Vergiss ja nicht dies Wort
    BWV 460: Gib dich zufrieden und sei stille
    BWV 469: Ich steh' an deiner Krippen hier
    BWV 471: Jesu, deine Liebeswunden
    BWV 474: Jesus ist das schönste Licht
    BWV 476: Ihr Gestirn', ihr hohen Lüfte
    BWV 478: Komm, süsser Tod, komm sel'ge Ruh'!
    BWV 479: Kommt, Seelen, dieser Tag muss heilig sein besungen
    BWV 482: Liebes Herz, bedenke doch
    BWV 484: Liebster Herr Jesu, wo bleibst du so lange?
    BWV 485: Liebster Immanuel, Herzog der Frommen
    BWV 487: Mein Jesu, was für Seelenweh
    BWV 489: Nicht so traurig, nicht so sehr
    BWV 493: O Jesulein süss, o Jesulein mild
    BWV 505: Vergiss mein nicht, vergiss mein nicht

x. CANONS

Canons, BWV 1072-1078 (no. 1-7)
    Canon (no. 7), in seven parts, BWV 1078

xi. THE MUSICAL OFFERING

Ricercares, Canons, etc., BWV 1079, 16 movements (numbered 1-9)
    3a. Canones diversi super thema regiam, arranged for guitar

xii. THE ART OF FUGUE

Contrapuncti, Canons, Fugues, BWV 1080, 23 movements (numbered 1-19)
    Contrapunctus 1, arranged for guitar

Works by Johann Sebastian Bach Arranged for Guitar: Editions

VII Single Pieces

BACH, JOHANN SEBASTIAN (1685-1750)
Allein Gott In Der Hoh' Sei Ehr'
  *BWV 711
  "Solamente Dios Es Todopoderoso"
  (Azpiazu, Jose de) gtr (E maj/G
  maj) UNION ESP. 21088 f.s.   (1)

Aria, BWV 508 (from Anna Magdalena
  Bach Note-Book (1725))
  "Bist Du Bei Mir" (Behrend,
  Siegfried) gtr (G maj) ZIMMER.
  ZM-E67C f.s.   (2)

2 Arias
  (Azpiazu) gtr LEDUC G-99 f.s.
  Guitare, No. 99
  contains: Bist Du Bei Mir, BWV
  508 (from Anna Magdalena Bach
  Notenbuchlein (1725), No. 25);
  Vergiss Mein Nicht, Dass Ich
  Dein Nicht, BWV 504 (from
  Schemelli's Gesangbuch)   (3)

Betrachte Meine Seel' *BWV 245,No.31
  (from Johannes-Passion)
  (Scheit, Karl) B solo,2vla d'amore,
  gtr (Gitarre-Kammermusik, No. 38)
  pts DOBLINGER GKM-38 f.s.   (4)

Canon Par Mouvement Retrograde
  (Pujol, Emilio) gtr (A min) ESCHIG
  2006 f.s.   (5)

Cantata No. 212, [excerpt], [arr.]
  "Suite Aus Der "Bauern-Kantate""
  (Behrend, Siegfried) 3gtr (single
  line playing) sc,pts RIES 11.105B
  f.s.   (6)
  "Dorfmusik Aus Der Bauernkantate"
  (Cleff, Wilhelm) rec,gtr/rec
  (single line playing) sc
  HEINRICH. 106 f.s.   (7)

Contrapunctus 1 *BWV 1080,No.1 (from
  Die Kunst Der Fuge)
  (Reyne, Gerard) 2gtr (A min,
  Guitare, No. 57) sc LEDUC G-57
  f.s.   (8)

Fughetta In C *BWV 961
  "Tweestemmige Fuga In E Mineur"
  (Verhoef, Jaap) 2gtr (E min,
  single line playing) sc HARMONIA
  2172 f.s.   (9)

Fugue, BWV 847, in C minor (from
  Wohltemperierte Clavier, Part I)
  (Pujol, Emilio) 2gtr (E min) sc
  ESCHIG 1103 f.s.   (10)

Fugue, BWV 874, in D (from
  Wohltemperierte Clavier, Part II)
  (Westra, Jan) 2gtr (5th degr.)
  HARMONIA 2365 f.s.   (11)

Fugue, BWV 953, in C (from Wilhelm
  Friedemann Bach Clavier-Buchlein
  (1720))
  (Behrend, Siegfried) 2gtr (single
  line playing) sc SIKORSKI 666-4
  f.s.   (12)

Fugue for Lute, BWV 1000, in G minor
  (Behrend, Siegfried) gtr HANSEN-DEN
  f.s.   (13)
  (Borghese, Alfonso) [It/Eng/Ger]
  gtr (A min, L'Arte Della
  Chitarra; gtr-arr + facs of orig
  lute tablature; notes (comparison
  of vln, org and lute version)
  ZERBONI 7718 f.s.   (14)
  (Navascues, Santiago) [Ger/Eng/Fr/
  Span] gtr (A min, gtr-arr +
  tablature for lute-f' and
  transcription (pno sc);
  explanations) BRUCK B-1-2 f.s.
       (15)
  (Prol, Julio) gtr (A min) PAGANI
  CG-103 f.s.   (16)
  (Puijenbroeck, Victor van) gtr (E
  min, e' is d', g is f sharp)
  METROPOLIS EM-4729 f.s.   (17)

BACH, JOHANN SEBASTIAN (cont'd.)
  (Ragossnig, Konrad) gtr (A min)
  ESCHIG 7896 f.s.   (18)
  (Scheit) gtr UNIVER. 13626 f.s.
       (19)

Invention No. 1, BWV 772, in C
  "Invenzione A Due Voci In Do"
  (Amato, Angelo) 2gtr (single line
  playing) sc ZANIBON 5021 f.s.
       (20)

Invention No. 8, BWV 779, in F
  (Pujol, Emilio) 2gtr (A maj,single
  line playing) sc ESCHIG 1102 f.s.
       (21)

Invention No. 13, BWV 784, in A minor
  "Two-Part Invention No. 8"
  (Bocanegra, Miguel) 2gtr (single
  line playing) pts SPAN.MUS.CTR.
  GE-122 f.s.   (22)
  (Gangi, Mario) 2gtr (D min,single
  line playing) sc BERBEN 1051 f.s.
       (23)

Jesus Bleibet Meine Freude. Chorale
  (from Cantata No. 147)
  "Jesus Que Ma Joie Demeure"
  (Azpiazu, Jose de) gtr (Guitare-
  Selection, No. 1) DELRIEU 1274
  f.s.   (24)
  "Jesus, Alegria De La Humanidad"
  (Calatayud, B.) gtr UNION ESP.
  20551 f.s.   (25)
  (Carfagno, Carlo) gtr BERBEN 1939
  f.s.   (26)
  "Jesus, Alegria Dos Homens" (Nunes,
  Milton) gtr (E is C) RICORDI-BR
  BR-2807 f.s.   (27)
  "Jesu, Joy Of Man's Desiring"
  (Papas, Sophocles) gtr COLUMBIA
  208 f.s.   (28)
  "Jesu, Joy Of Man's Desiring"
  (Sisley, Geoffrey) gtr ESSEX f.s.
       (29)

Komm Susser Tod *BWV 478 (from
  Schemelli's Gesangbuch)
  "Vieni, Dolce Morte" (Giordano,
  Mario) gtr (A min) RICORDI-IT 130721 f.s.
       (30)

March, BWV Anh. 124, in G (from Anna
  Magdalena Bach Notenbuchlein
  (1725))
  (Usher, Terry; Duarte, John W.)
  2gtr (single line playing) sc
  ESSEX f.s.   (31)

Mass In B Minor: Crucifixus *BWV
  232,No.16
  "Coro Crucifixus" (Tarrega,
  Francisco) gtr FORTEA 211 f.s.
       (32)

Minuet, BWV Anh. 113, in F (from Anna
  Magdalena Bach Notenbuchlein
  (1725))
  (Sobrinho, Martins) gtr RICORDI-BR
  BR-2264 f.s.   (33)

Minuet, BWV Anh. 114, in G (from Anna
  Magdalena Bach Notenbuchlein
  (1725))
  (Pujol, Emilio) 2gtr (D maj,single
  line playing) sc ESCHIG 1111 f.s.
       (34)

Minuet, BWV Anh. 115, in G minor
  (from Anna Magdalena Bach
  Notenbuchlein (1725))
  (Vallespir Peyron, F.G.) gtr (A
  min) RICORDI-ARG BA-12657 f.s.
       (35)

Minuet, BWV Anh. 120, in A minor
  (from Anna Magdalena Bach
  Notenbuchlein (1725))
  (Vallespir Peyron, F.G.) gtr
  RICORDI-ARG BA-12656 f.s.   (36)

Partita for Keyboard Instrument, BWV
  825, in B flat
  (Galindo, Patrico) gtr (D maj,
  without Courante) UNION ESP. f.s.
       (37)

Partita for Lute, BWV 997, in C minor
  "Zweite Suite" (Azpiazu, Jose de)
  gtr (D min) SYMPHON 411 f.s. (38)
  "Partita Al Liuto" (Azpiazu, Lupe
  de) gtr (A min, without Fugue)
  UNION ESP. 21203 f.s.   (39)
  "Zweite Lauten-Suite, BWV 997"
  (Behrend, Siegfried) gtr (A min)
  HANSEN-DEN f.s.   (40)
  (Company, Alvaro) [It/Eng/Ger] gtr
  (D min, L'Arte Della Chitarra;
  commentary (34p); includes
  facsims of orig tablature and ed
  of the Bach-Gesamtausgabe)
  ZERBONI 6913 f.s.   (41)
  (Puijenbroeck, Victor van) gtr (A
  min, without Fugue; e' is d', g

BACH, JOHANN SEBASTIAN (cont'd.)
  is f sharp; capotasto in pos.
  III) METROPOLIS EM-14014 f.s.
       (42)
  "Lauten-Suite Nr. II a-Moll"
  (Teuchert, Heinz) gtr SYMPHON
  2213 f.s.   (43)

Partita for Lute, BWV 997, in C
  minor, Fugue
  "Fuga De La Suite II Para Laud"
  (Azpiazu, Jose de) gtr (A min)
  UNION ESP. 21305 f.s.   (44)

Partita for Lute, BWV 997, in C
  minor, Prelude
  (Segovia, Andres) gtr (A min)
  SCHOTT GA-173 f.s.   (45)

Partita for Lute, BWV 997, in C
  minor, Saraband
  (Segovia, Andres) gtr (B min)
  SCHOTT GA-171 f.s.   (46)
  (Segovia, Andres) gtr (B min) CEL 5
  f.s.   (47)

Partita for Lute, BWV 1006a, in E
  "Lautensuite IV" (Azpiazu, Jose de)
  gtr (E maj) SYMPHON 2039 f.s.
       (48)
  "Cuarte Suite Para Laud" (Azpiazu,
  Lupe de) gtr (D maj) UNION ESP.
  21204 f.s.   (49)
  "Suite E-Dur, BWV 1006" (Scheit,
  Karl) gtr (g is f sharp; critical
  commentary) UNIVER. 14474 f.s.
       (50)
  "Lauten-Suite Nr. IV E-Dur"
  (Teuchert, Heinz) gtr SYMPHON
  2217 f.s.   (51)

Partita for Lute, BWV 1006a, in E,
  Gigue
  "Gigue De La Suite IV Para Laud"
  (Sainz de la Maza, Regio) gtr
  UNION ESP. 21476 f.s.   (52)

Partita for Lute, BWV 1006a, in E,
  Prelude
  "Preludio De La Suite IV Para Laud"
  (Sainz de la Maza, Regio) gtr
  UNION ESP. 21475 f.s.   (53)

Partita for Violin, BWV 1002, in B
  minor, Bourree
  (Llobet, Miguel) gtr UNION ESP.
  20373 f.s.   (54)
  (Tarrago, Graciano) gtr (double of
  bourree) UNION ESP. 2262 f.s.
       (55)
  (Tarrega, Francisco) gtr UNION ESP.
  19034 f.s.   (56)

Partita for Violin, BWV 1002, in B
  minor, Saraband
  gtr HEINRICH. 1541 f.s.   (57)
  (Segovia, Andres) gtr UNION ESP.
  18030 f.s.   (58)
  (Sensier, Peter) gtr ESSEX f.s.
       (59)
  (Tarrago, Graciano) gtr UNION ESP.
  2266 f.s.   (60)
  (Tarrago, Graciano) gtr (double of
  saraband) UNION ESP. 2265 f.s.
       (61)
  "Joint Solos Bach No. 3 - Saraband-
  Double" (Visser, Dick) gtr
  (includes version for 2gtr:
  Sarabande + Double played
  simultaneously) sc HARMONIA 2346
  f.s.   (62)

Partita for Violin, BWV 1004, in D
  minor
  (Azpiazu, Jose de) gtr SYMPHON 2110
  f.s.   (63)
  (Schinina, Luigi; Gangi, Mario) gtr
  (E min) BERBEN 1696 f.s.   (64)

Partita for Violin, BWV 1004, in D
  minor, Chaconne
  (Azpiazu, Lupe de) gtr UNION ESP.
  21207 f.s.   (65)
  (Behrend, Siegfried) gtr (Die
  Konzertgitarre) SIKORSKI 482 f.s.
       (66)
  (Kluin, Els) gtr HARMONIA 2724 f.s.
       (67)
  (Prol, Julio) gtr PAGANI G-124 f.s.
       (68)
  (Puijenbroeck, Victor van) gtr (B
  min, e' is d', g is f sharp;
  capotasto in pos. III) METROPOLIS
  EM-4764 f.s.   (69)
  (Segovia, Andres) gtr SCHOTT GA-141

BACH, JOHANN SEBASTIAN (cont'd.)

Suite for Keyboard Instrument, BWV
816, in G, Gavotte
(Magliano, Horacio R.) 2gtr (G maj,
partly single line playing) pts
RICORDI-ARG BA-12473 f.s. (157)
(Sainz de la Maza, Regio) gtr (A
maj) UNION ESP. 15643BIS f.s.
(158)

Suite for Keyboard Instrument, BWV
816, in G minor, Gigue
(Magliano, Horacio R.) 3gtr (G maj,
single line playing) pts RICORDI-
ARG BA-12477 f.s. (159)

Suite for Keyboard Instrument, BWV
817, in E, Polonaise
(Magliano, Horacio R.) 2gtr (single
line playing) pts RICORDI-ARG
BA-12475 f.s. (160)

Suite for Keyboard Instrument, BWV
825, in B flat, Gigue
(Bocanegra, Miguel) gtr (A maj)
SPAN.MUS.CTR. GE-201 f.s. (161)

Suite for Keyboard Instrument, BWV
825, in B flat, Minuet I-II
(Bocanegra, Miguel) gtr (C maj)
SPAN.MUS.CTR. GE-214 f.s. (162)

Suite for Keyboard Instrument, BWV
825, in B flat, Saraband
(Pujol, Emilio) gtr (D maj) ESCHIG
1010 f.s. (163)

Suite for Lute, BWV 995, in G minor
"Dritte Suite" (Azpiazu, Jose de)
gtr (A min) SYMPHON 424 f.s.
(164)
"Dritte Lauten-Suite" (Behrend,
Siegfried) gtr (A min) HANSEN-DEN
f.s. (165)
"Lautensuite No. 3" (Caceres,
Oscar) gtr (Collection Oscar
Caceres Pour Guitare, No. 1)
ESCHIG f.s. (166)
(Ghiglia, Oscar) [It/Eng/Fr/Ger]
gtr (A min, includes facsim of
autograph of complete suite)
ZERBONI SZ-7920 f.s. (167)
"Cello Suite V - Lute Suite III"
(Lorimer, Michael) gtr HANSEN-US
ML-005 f.s. (168)
"Suite III" (Prol, Julio) gtr (A
min) PAGANI CG-118 f.s. (169)
"Lautensuite (BWV 995)"
(Puijenbroeck, Victor van) gtr (E
min, app: table of ornaments; e'
is d', g is f sharp) METROPOLIS
EM-4733 f.s. (170)
(Scheit) gtr (A min, facs) UNIVER.
14475 f.s. (171)
"Lauten-Suite Nr. III a-Moll"
(Teuchert, Heinz) gtr SYMPHON
2216 f.s. (172)
"Suite Pour Le Luth (Lautensuite
Nr. III)" (Tonazzi, Bruno) gtr (A
min) ZIMMER. ZM-1746 f.s. (173)

Suite for Lute, BWV 995, in G minor,
Allemand
"Allemande De La Suite III Para
Laud" (Pereira Arias, Antonio)
gtr (A min) TEESELING VT-36 f.s.
(174)

Suite for Lute, BWV 996, in E minor
"Erste Suite" (Azpiazu, Jose de)
gtr (A min) SYMPHON 409 f.s.
(175)
"Suite En Mi Menor, Orig. Para
Laud" (Azpiazu, Lupe de) gtr
UNION ESP. 21306 f.s. (176)
"Erste Lauten-Suite, BWV 996"
(Behrend, Siegfried) gtr HANSEN-
DEN f.s. (177)
(Bream, Julian) gtr (app: table of
ornaments) FABER F-0126 f.s.
(178)
(Puijenbroeck, Victor van) gtr (e'
is d', g is f sharp) METROPOLIS
EM-4723 f.s. (179)
"Praeludio Con La Suite Of Johann
Sebastian Bach In Tablature For
Lute, The, BWV 996" (Rhodes, W.
David) gtr (includes
transcription in treb clef)
PRELUDE f.s. (180)
"Suite En Mi Mineur" (Santos,
Turibio) gtr (Collection Turibio
Santos Oeuvres Pour Guitare, No.
7) ESCHIG 8178 f.s. (181)
"Suite e-moll" (Scheit, Karl) gtr
UNIVER. 14473 f.s. (182)
"Lauten-Suite Nr. I e-Moll"
(Teuchert, Heinz) gtr SYMPHON
2212 f.s. (183)

Suite for Lute, BWV 996, in E minor,
Courante
"Courante" (Segovia, Andres) gtr (A
min, also published in Andres
Segovia Album For Guitar Solos)
COLUMBIA 126 f.s. (184)

BACH, JOHANN SEBASTIAN (cont'd.)

Suite for Lute, BWV 996, in E minor,
Passaggio-Prelude
"Praludium Und Fugato (Presto)"
(Beck, Leonhard) gtr TEESELING
VT-41 f.s. (185)
"Preludio" (Sainz de la Maza,
Regio) gtr UNION ESP. 16956 f.s.
(186)

Suite for Lute, BWV 996, in E minor,
Saraband
"Sarabanda, De La 1a. Suite Para
Laud" (Anido, Maria Luisa) gtr
RICORDI-ARG BA-11574 f.s. (187)

Suite for Orchestra, BWV 1067, in B
minor, Badinerie
"Celebre Badinerie" (Azpiazu, Jose
de) gtr (A min) UNION ESP. 21304
f.s. (188)
(Sainz de la Maza, Regio) fl/rec,
gtr sc UNION ESP. 21537 f.s.
(189)
"Badinerie" (Tower, Richard) fl,gtr
sc TEESELING VT-63 f.s. (190)

Suite for Orchestra, BWV 1067, in B
minor, Polonaise
(Sensier, Peter) gtr ESSEX f.s.
(191)

Suite for Orchestra, BWV 1067, in B
minor, Polonaise-Double
(Mazmanian, Vrouyr) gtr HEINRICH.
1667 f.s. (192)

Suite for Orchestra, BWV 1068, in D,
Air
"Celebre Aria (Lento)" (Fortea,
Daniel) gtr FORTEA 15 f.s. (193)
"Air On The G-String" (Mairants,
Ivor) gtr/2gtr BR.CONT.MUS. 1019
f.s. (194)
(Sainz de la Maza, Regio) gtr UNION
ESP. 21550 f.s. (195)

Suite for Violoncello, BWV 1007, in G
"Premiere Suite Pour Violoncelle
Seul" (Castet, Francois) gtr
(Guitare, No. 100) LEDUC G-100
f.s. (196)
(Duarte, John W.) gtr (D maj)
SCHOTT GA-213 f.s. (197)
(Dunker, James R.) gtr (D maj)
HARMONIA 2628 f.s. (198)
"Cello Suite I" (Lorimer, Michael)
gtr HANSEN-DEN ML-001 f.s. (199)

Suite for Violoncello, BWV 1007, in
G, Prelude
(Behrend, Siegfried) gtr (C maj,
Gitarre-Bibliothek, No. 2; also
published in European Masters For
The Guitar) BOTE GB-2 f.s. (200)
(Orozco, Carlos Wolf) gtr (D maj)
UNION ESP. 21051 f.s. (201)
(Pujol, Emilio) gtr (D maj) ESCHIG
1073 f.s. (202)
(Roncal, Ramon) gtr (D maj) UNION
ESP. 2059 f.s. (203)
(Sainz de la Maza, Regio) gtr UNION
ESP. 20566 f.s. (204)
(Usher, Terry; Duarte, John W.) gtr
(D maj) ESSEX f.s. (205)
(Visser, Dick) gtr (D maj) HARMONIA
1560 f.s. (206)

Suite for Violoncello, BWV 1008, in D
minor
"Cello Suite II" (Lorimer, Michael)
gtr HANSEN-US ML-002 f.s. (207)

Suite for Violoncello, BWV 1008, in D
minor, Courante
(Anido, Maria Luisa) gtr (A min)
RICORDI-ARG BA-11573 f.s. (208)

Suite for Violoncello, BWV 1009, in C
(Azpiazu, Jose de) gtr (A maj)
SYMPHON 2038 f.s. (209)
(Duarte, John W.) gtr (A maj)
SCHOTT GA-214 f.s. (210)
(Sainz de la Maza, Regio) gtr (A
maj) UNION ESP. 21480 f.s. (211)

Suite for Violoncello, BWV 1009, in
C, Bourree I-II
"Loure Aus Der Suite In C-Dur"
(Mazmanian, Vrouyr) gtr (A maj/A
min) HEINRICH. 1674 f.s. (212)
"Loure Aus Der Suite In C-Dur"
(Sinopoli, Antonio) gtr (C maj/C
min) RICORDI-ARG BA-7336 f.s.
(213)
"Loure Aus Der Suite In C-Dur"
(Tarrega, Francisco) gtr (D maj/D
min) UNION ESP. 19033 f.s. (214)
"Loure Aus Der Suite In C-Dur"
(Tarrego, Francisco) gtr (D maj/D
min) FORTEA 213 f.s. (215)

Suite for Violoncello, BWV 1009, in
C, Courante
(Angel, Miguel) gtr (A maj)
SPAN.MUS.CTR. MA-002 f.s. (216)

BACH, JOHANN SEBASTIAN (cont'd.)

Suite for Violoncello, BWV 1009, in
C, Prelude
(Tarrago, Graciano) gtr UNION ESP.
2264 f.s. (217)

Suite for Violoncello, BWV 1010, in E
flat
(Azpiazu, Jose de; Azpiazu; Lupe
de) gtr (A maj) SYMPHON 2127 f.s.
(218)
"Cello Suite IV" (Lorimer, Michael)
gtr HANSEN-US ML-004 f.s. (219)
(Tarrago, Graciano) gtr (E maj)
UNION ESP. 20687 f.s. (220)

Suite for Violoncello, BWV 1010, in E
flat, Prelude
(Llobet, Miguel) gtr (G maj)
RICORDI-ARG BA-12121 f.s. (221)
(Pujol, Emilio) gtr (G maj) ESCHIG
1040 f.s. (222)

Suite for Violoncello, BWV 1011, in C
minor
"Gitarszvit" (Brodszky, Ferenc) gtr
(E min) EMB Z-6177 f.s. (223)

Suite for Violoncello, BWV 1011, in C
minor, Gavotte I-II
(Abloniz, Miguel) gtr (B min)
RICORDI-IT 129882 f.s. (224)

Suite for Violoncello, BWV 1011, in C
minor, Saraband
(Pujol, Emilio) gtr (A min) ESCHIG
1074 f.s. (225)

Suite for Violoncello, BWV 1012, in D
(Azpiazu, Lupe de) gtr UNION ESP.
21209 f.s. (226)
"Violoncello Suite VI" (Lorimer,
Michael) gtr HANSEN-US ML-006
f.s. (227)

Suite for Violoncello, BWV 1012, in
D, Gavotte I-II
(Behrend, Siegfried) gtr (E maj,
Gitarre-Bibliothek, No. 34) BOTE
GB-34 f.s. (228)
(Bream, Julian) gtr (E maj) ESSEX
f.s. (229)
(Lagoya) gtr (E maj) RICORDI-FR
R-1604 f.s. (230)
(Pick, Richard) gtr FORSTER f.s.
(231)
(Sainz de la Maza, Regio) gtr UNION
ESP. 19759 f.s. (232)
(Savio, Isaias) gtr (E maj)
RICORDI-BR BR-2908 f.s. (233)
(Scheit, Karl) gtr UNIVER. 14437
f.s. (234)
(Segovia, Andres) gtr (E maj)
SCHOTT GA-172 f.s. (235)
(Tarrago, Graciano) gtr UNION ESP.
2267 f.s. (236)

Toccata, BWV 565, in D minor
(Azpiazu, Jose de) gtr SYMPHON 418
f.s. (237)

Toccata, BWV 913, in D minor,First
Movement
(Azpiazu, Jose) gtr (E min) SYMPHON
363 f.s. (238)

VII-Coll   Bach Collections

BACH, JOHANN SEBASTIAN (1685-1750)
Album Completo De Ana Magdalena Bach,
2 Vols. *CC2OL
(Galindo, Patricio) gtr (3-7th
degr.) UNION ESP. f.s. (239)

Album Di 10 Pezzi, Per La Formazione
Musicale E Tecnica Del
Chitarrista
(Abloniz, Miguel) gtr (4-7th degr.)
RICORDI-IT 130278 f.s.
contains: Prelude for Lute, BWV
999, in C minor (D min); Suite
for Violoncello, BWV 1007, in
G, Gigue (E maj); Suite for
Violoncello, BWV 1007, in G,
Minuet I-II (E maj/E min);
Suite for Violoncello, BWV
1010, in E flat, Bourree I-II
(A maj); Suite for Violoncello,
BWV 1010, in E flat, Courante
(A maj); Suite for Violoncello,
BWV 1012, in D, Gavotte I-II (E
maj); Suite for Violoncello,
BWV 1012, in D, Saraband (E
maj) (240)

BACH, JOHANN SEBASTIAN (cont'd.)

Album No. 1
(Fortea, Daniel) gtr (4-7th degr.)
FORTEA 68 f.s.
  contains: Partita for Violin, BWV
  1002, in B minor, Saraband;
  Prelude for Lute, BWV 999, in C
  minor (D min); Suite for Lute,
  BWV 996, in E minor, Bourree;
  Suite for Violoncello, BWV
  1009, in C, Courante (A maj)
                                    (241)

Allegretto - Allegro Non Troppo (from
Wilhelm Friedemann Bach Clavier-
Buchlein (1720))
(Verhoef, Jaap) 2gtr (single line
playing) sc HARMONIA 2174 f.s.
  contains: Prelude, BWV 927, in F
  (G maj); Prelude, BWV 939, in C
                                    (242)

Aria E Preludio
(Abloniz, Miguel) gtr BERBEN 1925
f.s.
  contains: Prelude, BWV 846, in C
  (from Wohltemperierte Clavier,
  Part I); Suite for Orchestra,
  BWV 1068, in D, Air (C maj)
                                    (243)

Ausgewahlte Stucke Fur Gitarre
(Walker, Luise; Mazmanian, Vrouyr;
Haen, O.) gtr HEINRICH. 6231 f.s.
  contains: Partita for Violin, BWV
  1002, in B minor, Saraband;
  Partita for Violin, BWV 1006,
  in E, Minuet I; Prelude, BWV
  867, in B flat minor (from Das
  Wohltemperierte Clavier, Book
  I); Prelude, BWV 929, in G
  minor (from Wilhelm Friedemann
  Bach Clavier Buchlein, 1720) (A
  min); Prelude for Lute, BWV
  999, in C minor (D min); Suite
  for Lute, BWV 996, in E minor,
  Bourree; Suite for Orchestra,
  BWV 1067, in B minor,
  Polonaise-Double; Suite for
  Violoncello, BWV 1009, in C,
  Bourree I-II (A maj/A min);
  Suite for Violoncello, BWV
  1011, in C minor, Gavotte En
  Rondeau (A min)   (244)

Bach Album *CC14L
(Papas, Sophocles) gtr (2-7th
degr.) COLUMBIA 169 f.s.   (245)

"Bach At The Beginning": 6 Pieces
From The Anna Magdalena Bach
Notenbuchlein (1725)
(Duarte, John W.) 2gtr (single line
playing/1-2nd degr.) NOVELLO
19783 f.s. The Teacher Series Of
Guitar Publications; arr. as 1st
yr gtr duets
  contains: Minuet, BWV Anh. 116,
  in G (from Anna Magdalena Bach
  Notenbuchlein (1725), No.7);
  Minuet, BWV Anh. 121, in C
  minor (from Anna Magdalena Bach
  Notenbuchlein (1725), No.15) (B
  min); Minuet in G (from Anna
  Magdalena Bach Notenbuchlein
  (1725), No.21); Musette In D,
  BWV Anh.126 (from Anna
  Magdalena Bach Notenbuchlein
  (1725), No.22); Polonaise, BWV
  Anh. 119, in G minor (from Anna
  Magdalena Bach Notenbuchlein
  (1725), No.10) (A min); So Oft
  Ich Meine Tobackspfeife, BWV
  515 (from Anna Magdalena Bach
  Notenbuchlein (1725), No.20a)
  (A min)   (246)

Bach-Buch Fur Die Gitarre *CC12L
(Gotze, Walter) gtr PRO MUSICA 82
f.s. co-published with APOLLO
2355   (247)

Bach-Buch Fur Gitarre, Das, Vol. 1
*CC43L
(Schwarz-Reiflingen, Erwin) gtr (3-
7th degr.) SIKORSKI 340 f.s.
                           (248)

Bach-Buch Fur Gitarre, Das, Vol. 2
*CC41L
(Schwarz-Reiflingen, Erwin) gtr (3-
7th degr.) SIKORSKI 480 f.s.
                           (249)

Bach For The Guitar *CC13L
(Block, Leon) gtr (2-3rd degr.)
MARKS 14893-16 f.s.   (250)

Deux Chants (from Schemelli's
Gesangbuch)
(Castet, Francois) [Ger] solo
voice,gtr sc LEDUC G-39 f.s.
Guitare, No. 39
  contains: Ach, Dass Nicht Die
  Letzte Stunde, "Derniere
  Heure", BWV 439; Tag Mit Seinem
  Lichte, Der, "Jour Et Sa
  Lumiere", BWV 448   (251)

BACH, JOHANN SEBASTIAN (cont'd.)

Drei Kleine Stucke Aus Dem
Notenbuchlein Der Anna Magdalena
Bach
(Segovia, Andres) gtr SCHOTT GA-142
f.s.
  contains: March, BWV Anh. 124, in
  G (from Anna Magdalena Bach
  Notenbuchlein (1725), No.18);
  Minuet, BWV Anh. 115, in G
  minor (from Anna Magdalena Bach
  Notenbuchlein (1725), No.5);
  Polonaise, BWV Anh. 125, in G
  minor (from Anna Magdalena Bach
  Notenbuchlein (1725), No.19) (D
  min)   (252)

Due Bourrees E Marcia
(Abloniz, Miguel) gtr RICORDI-IT
129347 f.s.
  contains: March, BWV Anh. 122, in
  D (from Anna Magdalena Bach
  Notenbuchlein (1725), No.16);
  Partita for Keyboard
  Instrument, BWV 831, in B
  minor, Bourree I-II (E min)
                           (253)

Due Preludi (from Wohltemperierte
Clavier, Part I)
(Schinina, Luigi) gtr BERBEN 1102
f.s.
  contains: Prelude, BWV 853, in E
  flat minor (E min); Prelude,
  BWV 867, in B flat minor (A
  min)   (254)

Edition Nicolas Alfonso, No. 2
(Alfonso, Nicolas) gtr (3-4th
degr.) SCHOTT-FRER 9121 f.s.
  contains: Minuet, BWV Anh. 114,
  in G (from Anna Magdalena Bach
  Notenbuchlein (1725), No.4);
  Musette, BWV Anh.126 (from Anna
  Magdalena Bach Notenbuchlein
  (1725), No.22) (D maj);
  Prelude, BWV 939, in D; Suite
  for Keyboard Instrument, BWV
  822, in G minor, Minuet-Trio (G
  maj); Suite for Lute, BWV 996,
  in E minor, Bourree; Warum
  Betrubst Du Dich, BWV 516 (from
  Anna Magdalena Bach
  Notenbuchlein (1725), No.33) (A
  min)   (255)

Edition Nicolas Alfonso, No. 16
(Alfonso, Nicolas) gtr (5th degr.)
SCHOTT-FRER 9173 f.s.
  contains: Concerto for Keyboard
  Instrument, BWV 986, in G,
  Adagio (A min); Suite for
  Keyboard Instrument, BWV 820,
  in F, Bourree (A maj); Suite
  for Keyboard Instrument, BWV
  823, in F minor, Gigue (A min)
                           (256)

Edition Nicolas Alfonso, No. 17
(Alfonso, Nicolas) gtr (6-7th
degr.) SCHOTT-FRER 9174 f.s.
  contains: Suite for Keyboard
  Instrument, BWV 820, in F,
  Minuet I (A maj); Suite for
  Keyboard Instrument, BWV 820,
  in F, Minuet II (A maj); Suite
  for Keyboard Instrument, BWV
  821, in B flat, Courante (C
  maj); Suite for Keyboard
  Instrument, BWV 821, in B flat,
  Saraband (C maj)   (257)

Edition Nicolas Alfonso, No. 18
(Alfonso, Nicolas) gtr (6th degr.)
SCHOTT-FRER 9234 f.s.
  contains: Partita for Violin, BWV
  1002, in B minor, Saraband;
  Sonata for Violin, BWV 1001, in
  G minor, Siciliano (A maj)
                           (258)

Famosissime Gavotte Di J.S. Bach, Le
(Abloniz, Miguel) gtr (5-6th degr.)
BERBEN 1855 f.s.
  contains: Partita for Violin, BWV
  1006, in E, Gavotte En Rondeau
  (C maj); Suite for Keyboard
  Instrument, BWV 816, in G,
  Gavotte (F maj); Suite for
  Violoncello, BWV 1012, in D,
  Gavotte I-II (C maj)   (259)

Five Easy Pieces For The Guitar
(Bellow, Alexander) gtr (3rd degr.)
SPAN.MUS.CTR. GE-260 f.s.
  contains: Suite for Violoncello,
  BWV 1007, in G, Minuet II (E
  min); Suite for Violoncello,
  BWV 1010, in E flat, Bourree II
  (E maj); Suite for Violoncello,
  BWV 1011, in C minor, Saraband
  (A min); Suite for Violoncello,
  BWV 1012, in D, Gavotte I-II
                           (260)

Fugue, BWV 855, in E minor (from
Wohltemperierte Clavier, Part I)
(Magliano, Horacio R.) 2gtr (single
line playing) pts RICORDI-ARG

BACH, JOHANN SEBASTIAN (cont'd.)

BA-12251 f.s.   (261)

Gavotte, De La Sonata Para Violin En
Mi Mayor
(Fortea, Daniel) gtr FORTEA 212
f.s.
  contains: Partita for Violin, BWV
  1006, in E, Gavotte En Rondeau;
  Suite for Lute, BWV 996, in E
  minor, Saraband   (262)

Geistliche Lieder (from Schemelli's
Gesangbuch)
(Schaller, Erwin) solo voice,rec,
gtr (3-4th degr.) voc sc,pts
HASLINGER HBR-18 f.s. Haslinger
Blockfloten Reihe No. 18
  contains: Es Ist Vollbracht, BWV
  458; Ich Steh An Deiner Krippen
  Hier, BWV 469; Kommt, Seelen
  Dieser Tag, BWV 479; Mein Jesu,
  Was Fur Seelenweh, BWV 487; O
  Jesulein Suss, BWV 493   (263)

Guitar Duets *CC10L
(Bellow, Alexander) 2gtr (single
line playing/3-5th degr.)
SPAN.MUS.CTR. GE-263 f.s.
  contains: Six Little Preludes,
  Nos.1-4, 6; Prelude In G Minor,
  BWV 930; Invention No.8 In F,
  BWV 779; English Suite No.3 In G
  Minor: Gavotte and Trio, BWV 808
                           (264)

Guitar Duets
(Gavall, John) 2gtr sc MILLS MUSIC
MM-480 f.s.
  contains: Concerto For
  Harpsichord And Orchestra In F
  Minor, 2nd Mov't (Arioso), BWV
  1056 (F maj); Concerto No. 2
  for Keyboard Instrument, BWV
  973, in G,Second Movement,
  Largo (E min); English Suite
  No. 6, In D-Minor, (Fifth
  Movement): Musette, BWV 811 (D
  maj); Minuet for Keyboard
  Instrument, BWV Anh. 114, in A
  (G maj); Prelude In E Minor
  (from Das Wohltemperierte
  Clavier, Book I), BWV 853;
  Sonata No. 3, BWV 1005, in C,
  First Movement, Adagio (C maj)
                           (265)

4 Inventien
(Schagen, Henk van) 2gtr (single
line playing/3-4th degr.)
HARMONIA 1262 f.s.
  contains: Invention, BWV 772, in
  C (F maj); Invention, BWV 773,
  in C minor (F min); Invention,
  BWV 774, in D (A maj);
  Invention, BWV 775, in D minor
  (A min)   (266)

Kleine Stucke *CC20L
(Bacher, Josef) 1-2gtr (1-4th
degr.) sc NAGELS EN-1101 f.s. 13
pcs for 2gtr; 7 pcs for gtr (267)

Kleine Stucke *CC16L
(Zanoskar, Hubert) 2gtr sc SCHOTT
5662 f.s.   (268)

Kleines Weihnachtsoratorium Mit
Johann Sebastian Bach
(Oberborbeck, Felix) [Ger] (single
line playing/1st degr.) sc MOECK
ZFS144 f.s. Zeitschrift Fur
Spielmusik, No. 144
  contains: Bereite Dich, Zion, BWV
  248,No.4 (from Weihnachts-
  Oratorium) (gtr,3rec); Ehre Sei
  Gott In Der Hohe. Canon, BWV
  1078,No.7 (gtr,inst) (F maj);
  Vom Himmel Hoch, Da Komm Ich
  Her. Chorale, BWV 248,No.9
  (from Weihnachts-Oratorium)
  (solo voice,gtr,3rec)   (269)

Kompositionen Fur Die Laute; Erste
Vollstandige Und Kritisch
Durchgesehene Ausgabe; Nach Altem
Quellenmaterial Fur Die Heutige
Laute Ubertragen Und
Herausgegeben
(Bruger, Hans Dagobert) [Ger] lute/
gtr MOSELER f.s. 63p.; 1 facs;
notes; app: Erlauterung der
vorkommenden Spielzeichen; repr
of 3rd ed, 1925
  contains: Fugue for Lute, BWV
  1000, in G minor; Partita for
  Lute, BWV 997, in C minor (A
  min); Partita for Lute, BWV
  1006a, in E; Prelude for Lute,
  BWV 999, in C minor; Prelude,
  Fugue And Allegro For Lute In E
  Flat, BWV 998 (C maj/D maj/E
  maj); Suite for Lute, BWV 995,
  in G minor (A min); Suite for
  Lute, BWV 996, in E minor (270)

BACH, JOHANN SEBASTIAN (cont'd.)

Lautenmusik
(Stingl, Anton) gtr (3-9th degr.)
HOFMEISTER T-4035 f.s.
contains: Fugue for Lute, BWV
1000, in G minor (A min);
Partita for Lute, BWV 997, in C
minor (D min); Partita for
Lute, BWV 1006a, in E; Prelude
for Lute, BWV 999, in C minor
(D min); Prelude, Fugue And
Allegro In E Flat, BWV 998;
Suite for Lute, BWV 995, in G
minor (A min); Suite for Lute,
BWV 996, in E minor; Suite for
Violoncello, BWV 1009, in C (A
maj) (271)

Lautenmusik
(Wensiecki, Edmund) gtr (3-9th
degr.) HOFMEISTER 4035 f.s.
notes; app: Einfuhrung in die
Lautentabulatur
contains: Fugue, BWV 1000, in G
minor (A min); Partita for
Lute, BWV 997, in C minor (D
min); Partita for Lute, BWV
1006a, in E; Prelude for Lute,
BWV 999, in C minor (D min);
Prelude, Fugue And Allegro In E
Flat, BWV 998 (D maj); Suite
for Lute, BWV 995, in G minor
(A min); Suite for Lute, BWV
996, in E minor (272)

Loure And Sarabande
(Azpiazu, Jose de) gtr SYMPHON 361
f.s.
contains: Suite for Violoncello,
BWV 1009, in C, Bourree I-II (D
maj/D min); Suite for
Violoncello, BWV 1012, in D,
Sarabande (273)

Menuett Und Gigue
(Azpiazu, Jose de) gtr SYMPHON 358
f.s.
contains: Partita for Keyboard
Instrument, BWV 825, in B flat,
Gigue (D maj); Suite for
Keyboard Instrument, BWV 814,
in B minor, Minuet (274)

Minue Y Marcha
(Lara, Roberto) gtr RICORDI-ARG
BA-12448 f.s.
contains: March, BWV Anh. 122, in
D (from Anna Magdalena Bach
Notenbuchlein (1725) No.16) (C
maj); Minuet, BWV Anh. 114, in
G (from Anna Magdalena Bach
Notenbuchlein (1725), No.5) (C
maj) (275)

Minuet, BWV Anh. 115, in G minor
(from Anna Magdalena Bach
Notenbuchlein (1725), No.5)
(Pujol, Emilio) 2gtr (single line
playing) sc ESCHIG 1110 f.s.
(276)

Opere Complete Per Liuto *CCU
(Cherici, Paolo) [It/Eng/Ger] gtr
(staff notation and tablature)
ZERBONI 8402 f.s. contains BWV
995-1000, 1006a, 198, 245; INCL.
PREF., COMMENTARY, BIBLIO,
FACSIMILES (277)

Partita for Lute, BWV 997, in C
minor, Saraband
(Bianqui Pinero, G.) gtr (A min,6-
7th degr.) RICORDI-ARG 16538 f.s.
contains also: Suite for
Violoncello, BWV 1012, in D,
Gavotte I-II; Suite for
Violoncello, BWV 1007, in G,
Prelude (D maj); Suite for
Violoncello, BWV 1009, in C,
Bourree I-II (A maj/A min);
Partita for Lute, BWV 997, in C
minor, Gigue (A min) (278)

Partita for Violin, BWV 1002, in B
minor, Bourree
(Abloniz, Miguel) gtr (A min,
Bourree-Double) RICORDI-IT 129880
f.s. contains also: Partita for
Violin, BWV 1002, in B minor,
Saraband-Double (A maj) (279)

Partita for Violin, BWV 1002, in B
minor, Saraband
(Savio, Isaias) gtr RICORDI-BR
BR-1838 f.s. contains also:
Sonata for Violin, BWV 1005, in
C, Largo (F maj) (280)
(Scheit, Karl) gtr UNIVER. 12471
f.s. contains also: Partita for
Violin, BWV 1002, in B minor,
Bourree (281)

5 Pecas
(Savio, Isaias) gtr (3-5th degr.)
RICORDI-BR BR-2335 f.s.
contains: French Suite: Courante,

BACH, JOHANN SEBASTIAN (cont'd.)

BWV 813; Minuet, BWV Anh. 114,
in G (from Anna Magdalena Bach
Notenbuchlein (1725) No.4) (A
maj); Minuet, BWV Anh. 115, in
G minor (from Anna Magdalena
Bach Notenbuchlein (1725),
No.5) (A min); Musette In D,
BWV Anh.126 (from Anna
Magdalena Bach Notenbuchlein
(1725), No.22); Suite for Lute,
BWV 996, in E minor, Bourree
(282)

26 Pieces Pour Guitare *CC26L
(Alfonso, Nicolas) gtr (3-6th
degr.) SCHOTT-FRER 9300 f.s.
(283)

20 Piezas Faciles Del Album De Ana
Magdalena Bach (from Anna
Magdalena Bach Notenbuchlein
(1725)) CC20L
(Tarrago, Graciano) 2gtr (mainly
single line playing/3-5th degr.)
sc UNION ESP. EI-213 f.s. (284)

Prelude for Lute, BWV 999, in C minor
(Abloniz, Miguel) gtr (D min)
BERBEN 1013 f.s. contains also:
Suite for Violoncello, BWV 1009,
in C, Bourree I-II (A maj) (285)
(Azpiazu, Jose de) gtr (D min)
SYMPHON 2036 f.s. contains also:
Sonata for Violin, BWV 1001, in G
minor, Fugue (A min) (286)
(Scheit, Karl) gtr (D min,3-6th
degr., including a preliminary
study for prelude) UNIVER. 11202
f.s. contains also: Suite for
Lute, BWV 995, in G minor,
Saraband (A min); Suite for Lute,
BWV 996, in E minor, Bourree
(287)
"Praludium D-Moll" (Teuchert,
Heinz) gtr (D min) SYMPHON 2211
f.s. contains also: Fugue for
Lute, BWV 1000, in G minor, "Fuge
A-Moll" (A min) (288)

Prelude, Sarabande And Gigue
(Shearer, Arton) gtr (4-5th degr.)
RICORDI-GER NY-2125 f.s.
contains: Suite for Violoncello,
BWV 1007, in G, Gigue (D maj);
Suite for Violoncello, BWV
1007, in G, Prelude (D maj);
Suite for Violoncello, BWV
1012, in D, Saraband (289)

Prelude Und Menuett
(Behrend, Siegfried) gtr SIRIUS
f.s.
contains: Minuet, BWV Anh. 114,
in G (from Anna Magdalena Bach
Notenbuchlein (1725) No.4);
Prelude, BWV 939, in C (E maj)
(290)

Preludio E Sarabanda
(Terzi, Benvenuto) gtr RICORDI-IT
129285 f.s.
contains: Prelude, BWV 846, in C
(from Das Wohltemperierte
Clavier, Book 1) (G maj); Suite
for Lute, BWV 995, in G minor,
Saraband (G min) (291)

Quattro Transcripciones
(Calleja, Francisco) gtr (5-7th
degr.) UNION ESP. 16631 f.s.
contains: Partita for Keyboard
Instrument, BWV 831, in B
minor, Bourree I; Partita for
Lute, BWV 997, in C minor,
Gigue (A min); Suite for Lute,
BWV 995, in G minor, Gavotte I
(A min); Suite for Lute, BWV
995, in G minor, Saraband (A
min) (292)

Quinze Inventions A Deux Voix, Les:
Collection l'Heure de la Guitare
Classique, Vol. I *CC8L
(Sanchez, Blas) 2gtr (single line
playing) pts CHOUDENS 20.231 f.s.
(293)

Quinze Inventions A Deux Voix, Les:
Collection l'Heure de la Guitare
Classique, Vol. II *CC7L
(Sanchez, Blas) 2gtr (single line
playing) pts CHOUDENS 20.232 f.s.
(294)

Schonsten Stucke Aus Dem
"Notenbuchlein Der Anna Magdalena
Bach" 1725, Die *CC11L
(Behrend, Siegfried) gtr (3-4th
degr.) ZIMMER. ZM-1795 f.s. (295)

Siciliana And Fugue, From Sonata No.
1 For Solo Violin
(Duarte, John W.) gtr NOVELLO 19471
f.s.
contains: Sonata for Violin, BWV
1001, in G minor, Fugue (A
min); Sonata for Violin, BWV
1001, in G minor, Siciliano (A
maj) (296)

BACH, JOHANN SEBASTIAN (cont'd.)

Sonata for Violin, BWV 1001, in G
minor, Fugue
(Alfonso, Nicolas) gtr (A min)
SCHOTT-FRER 9142 f.s. from
EDITION NICOLAS ALFONSO, NO. 11
(297)

Sonatas And Partitas, BWV 1001-1006
"Sonate E Partite, Vol. 1: BWV
1001-1003" (Mosoczi) gtr (Musica
Per Chitarra) EMB 8426 f.s. (298)
"Sonate E Partite, Vol. 2: BWV
1004-1006" (Mosoczi) gtr (Musica
Per Chitarra) EMB 8527 f.s. (299)

Sonate E Partite, Vol. 1
(Mosoczi) gtr EMB 8426 f.s. Musica
Per Chitarra
contains: Partita for Violin, BWV
1002, in B minor; Sonata for
Violin, BWV 1001, in G minor;
Sonata for Violin, BWV 1003, in
A minor (300)

Sonate E Partite, Vol. 2
(Mosoczi) gtr EMB 8527 f.s. Musica
Per Chitarra
contains: Partita for Violin, BWV
1004, in B minor; Partita for
Violin, BWV 1006, in E; Sonata
for Violin, BWV 1005, in C
(301)

Suite for Lute, BWV 996, in E minor,
Bourree
"Bourree Aus Der Lauten-Suite"
(Mazmanian, Vrouyr) gtr (A min)
HEINRICH. 1663 f.s. contains
also: Suite for Violoncello, BWV
1011, in C minor, Gavotte II,
"Gavotte En Rondeau Aus Der
Violoncello-Suite" (A min) (302)

Suite for Lute, BWV 996, in E minor,
Saraband
(Proakis, Costa) gtr BERBEN 1081
f.s. contains also: Suite for
Lute, BWV 996, Bourree (303)

Suite for Violoncello, BWV 1012, in
D, Saraband
(Johnson, Per-Olof) gtr ANDERSONS
AM-675 f.s. contains also: Suite
for Violoncello, BWV 1012, in D,
Gavotte I-II (304)
(Schaller) gtr BREITKOPF-W EB-6782
f.s. contains also: Suite for
Violoncello, BWV 1012, in D,
Gavotte I-II (305)

Trois Menuets (from Anna Magdalena
Bach Notenbuchlein (1725))
(Azpiazu, Jose de) gtr (4th degr.)
DELRIEU 1231 f.s. Guitarra, No. 1
contains: Minuet, BWV Anh. 113,
No. 3, in F (A maj); Minuet,
BWV Anh. 120, No. 14, in A
minor (D min); Minuet, BWV Anh.
121, No. 15, in C minor (D min)
(306)

Twelve Little Preludes *CC12L
(Azpiazu, Jose de; Azpiazu, Lupe
de) gtr (5-7th degr.) SYMPHON
2192 f.s. (307)

Two Cello Preludes
(Bream, Julian) gtr FABER F-0309
f.s.
contains: Suite for Violoncello,
BWV 1007, in G, Prelude; Suite
for Violoncello, BWV 1010, in E
flat, Prelude (308)

Verschiedene Stucke, Vol. 1
(Segovia, Andres) gtr (4-7th degr.)
SCHOTT GA-106 f.s.
contains: Partita for Violin, BWV
1006, in E, Minuet I-II;
Prelude for Lute, BWV 999, in C
minor (D min); Suite for Lute,
BWV 996, in E minor, Allemand
(A min) (309)

Verschiedene Stucke, Vol. 2
(Segovia, Andres) gtr (4-7th degr.)
SCHOTT GA-107 f.s.
contains: Partita for Violin, BWV
1006, in E, Gavotte En Rondeau;
Suite for Violoncello, BWV
1009, in C, Courante (A maj)
(310)

Verschiedene Stucke, Vol. 3
(Segovia, Andres) gtr (4-7th degr.)
SCHOTT GA-108 f.s.
contains: Partita for Violin, BWV
1002, in B minor, Bourree I-II;
Sonata for Violin, BWV 1003, in
A minor, Andante (C maj) (311)

Vier Leichte Stucke From The Anna
Magdalena Bach Notenbuchlein
(1725)
(Scheit, Karl) gtr UNIVER. 11958
f.s.
contains: March, BWV Anh. 122,
No. 16, in D (C maj); Minuet,

BACH, JOHANN SEBASTIAN (cont'd.)

BWV Anh. 114, No. 4, in G;
Minuet, BWV Anh. 115, No. 5, in
G minor; Musette In D, BWV
Anh.126,No.22 (C maj)   (312)

Wybrane Utwory - Pieces Choisies
*CC29L
(Powrozniak, Jozef) 1-2gtr (mainly
single line playing) POLSKIE 6847
f.s. 19 pces for gtr; 10 pces for
2gtr   (313)

Zwanzig Stucke Aus Dem Notenbuchlein
Fur Anna Magdalena Bach (from
Anna Magdalena Bach Notenbuchlein
(1725)) CC20L
(Stingl, Anton) gtr (2-5th degr.)
HOFMEISTER-W f.s.   (314)

Zwei Beruhmte Siciliane
(Azpiazu, Jose de) gtr SYMPHON 2073
f.s.
contains: Sonata for Flute and
Keyboard Instrument, BWV 1031,
in E flat, Siciliano (A min);
Sonata for Violin, BWV 1001, in
G minor, Siciliano (A maj)
                             (315)

Zwei Gitarren Musizieren, Vol. 4:
Inventionen Und Sinfonien
(Schwarz-Reiflingen, Erwin) 2gtr sc
SIKORSKI 553 f.s. contains
Inventions 1-5: BWV784, 781, 775,
772, 779; Sinfonias 6-8: BWV787,
788, 801   (316)

Zwei Kleine Praeludien
(Behrend, Siegfried) 2gtr sc
SIKORSKI 666-5 f.s. single line
playing
contains: Prelude, BWV 935, in D
minor; Prelude, BWV 937, in E
                             (317)

VII-Mixed Coll   Mixed Collections: Bach

AGUADO, DIONISIO (1784-1849)
Escuela De Guitarra
"Gran Metodo Completo Para
Guitarra, Con Una Recopilacion De
Estudios Originales De Autores
Celebres" (Sinopoli, Antonio)
[Span] gtr (181p., ill; repr,
1969; 1st ed, 1947) 7 courses in
5 pts; notes; app: Observacion
sobre la naturaleza o indole de
la guitarra; contains: Bach,
Johann Sebastian, Suite For
Keyboard Instrument, BWV 821, In
B Flat; Courante, [C major]; Bach
Johann Sebastian, Prelude For
Lute, BWV 999, In C Minor, [D
minor]; Bach, Johann Sebastian,
Suite For Lute, BWV 996, In E
Minor; Allemande, [A minor];
Bach, Johann Sebastian, Prelude,
BWV 927, In F, [G major] from
Wilhelm Friedemann Bach
Klavierbuchlein (1720); Bach,
Johann Sebastian, Presto, BWV
970, In D Minor; Tarrega,
Francisco, Prelude, TI-i-14;
Tarrega, Francisco, Studies, TI-
ii-2a [22 bars], 6, 14a, c, 18,
19, 20, 22, 29 [18 bars];
Tarrega, Francisco, Exercises,
TI-iii-2, 14, 20, 24[12 bars],
30a, 32) folio RICORDI-ARG
BA-9801 f.s.   (318)

ALBERT, HEINRICH (1870-1950)
Lehrgang Des Kunstlerischen
Gitarrespiels, Vol. II
"Gitarrelied, Das" [Ger] gtr (52p.;
repr, 1952; 1st ed, 1924)
contains: Intro, Notes: Das
Barrespiel, App: Die Wichtigsten
Anwendungsstellen Fur Gitarre In
Opern Und Orchesterwerken, barre
(exercises, chords, studies,
positions IV, V, VII, IX
(exercises, chords, studies,
pieces); includes: Bach, Johann
Sebastian, Betrachte, Meine Seel
from Johannes-Passion, BWV 245,
NO. 31, FOR BASS SOLO AND GTR)
folio LIENAU S.10189-II f.s.
                             (319)

ALBUM
(Azpiazu) gtr (4-8th degr.) SYMPHON
353 f.s. 14 arr+ orig pcs; contains
works by: Azpiazu (1), J.C. Bach
(1), C.P.E. Bach (1), Beethoven

(1), Galilei (1), Anon. (1), W.A.
Mozart (3), Vivaldi (1)
contains: Bach, Johann Sebastian,
Partita for Violin, No. 1, BWV
1002, in B minor, Saraband-
Double; Bach, Johann Sebastian,
Prelude in B sharp, BWV 934, in C
minor (A min); Bach, Johann
Sebastian, Suite for Keyboard
Instrument, BWV 824, in A,
Courante (D maj); Bach, Johann
Sebastian, Suite for Violoncello,
No. 6, BWV 1012, in D, Gavotte I-
II   (320)

ALBUM CLASSIQUE
(Laurent) gtr (4-7th degr.) LEDUC
G-80 $6.00 10 arr pcs; Guitare,
No.80; contains works by: Exaudet
(1), Schumann (2), Lully (1),
Chopin (1), Beethoven (1), C.P.E.
Bach (1), Tchaikovsky (1)
contains: Bach, Johann Sebastian,
Prelude No. 1, BWV 846, in C
(from Das Wohltemperierte
Clavier, Book 1) (C maj); Bach,
Johann Sebastian, Suite No. 3 for
Violoncello, BWV 1009, in C,
Bourree (A maj)   (321)

ALBUM, NO. 9
(Tarrega, Francisco, hijo) gtr (4-9th
degr.) UNION ESP. f.s.
contains: Bach, Johann Sebastian,
Prelude for Lute, BWV 999, in C
minor (D min); Chopin, Frederic,
Waltz, Op. 34, No. 3, in F;
Haydn, [Franz] Joseph, Minuet,
MIN 224; Schumann, Robert
(Alexander), Romance, MIN 278
                             (322)

ALBUM, NO. 12
(Tarrega, Francisco, hijo) gtr (4-9th
degr.) UNION ESP. f.s.
contains: Bach, Johann Sebastian,
Partita for Violin, No. 3, BWV
1006, in E, Gavotte En Rondeau;
Handel, George Frideric, Chorale,
MIN 225; Mendelssohn-Bartholdy,
Felix, Canzonetta   (323)

ALBUM, NO. 13
(Tarrega, Francisco, hijo) gtr (4-9th
degr.) UNION ESP. f.s.
contains: Bach, Johann Sebastian,
Partita for Violin, No. 1, BWV
1002, in B minor, Saraband;
Chopin, Frederic, Prelude, Op.
28, No. 1, in C; Schubert, Franz
(Peter), Moment Musical;
Schumann, Robert (Alexander),
Scherzo, Op. 32, No. 1   (324)

ALBUM, NO. 18
(Tarrega, Francisco, hijo) gtr (4-9th
degr.) UNION ESP. f.s.
contains: Bach, Johann Sebastian,
Mass, BWV 232, In B Minor,
Crucifixus (E min); Beethoven,
Ludwig van, Andante; Mendelssohn-
Bartholdy, Felix, Romanza Sin
Palabras   (325)

ALBUM RICREATIVO, NO. 1 *folk song
(Abloniz, Miguel) gtr (3-7th degr.)
BERBEN EB1140 $2.75 20 arr + orig
pcs; contains works by: Schubert
(2), Albloniz (3), Sor (1), Mertz
(1), Galilei (1), Kuhlau (1),
Cremieux (1)
contains: Bach, Johann Sebastian,
Gib Dich Zufrieden Und Sei
Stille, BWV 512 (from Anna
Magdalena Bach Notenbuchlein
(1725), No.13b) (A min); Bach,
Johann Sebastian, Komm, Susser
Tod, BWV 478 (from Schemelli's
Gesangbuch); Bach, Johann
Sebastian, Minuet, MIN 162, in A;
Bach, Johann Sebastian, Suite for
Lute, BWV 996, in E minor,
Bourree; Bach, Johann Sebastian,
Suite for Violoncello, No. 5, BWV
1011, in C minor, Saraband (A
min)   (326)

ALBUM RICREATIVO, NO. 2 *folk song
(Abloniz, Miguel) gtr (3-7th degr.)
BERBEN EB1280 $3.00 20 arr + orig
pcs; contains works by: Giuliani
(3), A. Scarlatti (1), Villondo
(1), Visee (2) Handel (2), Sor (3),
Thomas (1), Anon. (1)
contains: Bach, Johann Sebastian,
English Suite No. 3, BWV808, In G
Minor, Gavotte II, "Musette" (E
maj)   (327)

ALBUM RICREATIVO, NO. 3 *folk song
(Abloniz, Miguel) gtr (3-7th degr.)
BERBEN EB1398 $4.00 20 arr + orig
pcs; contains works by: Cervantes
(1), Schubert (2), Handel (1),
Visee (2), de Crescenzo (1), Flotow
(1), Breton Y Hernandez (1), Sor
(1), Abloniz (2)

contains: Bach, Johann Sebastian,
Suite for Violoncello, No. 1, BWV
1007, in G, Prelude (C maj);
Bach, Johann Sebastian, Suite for
Violoncello, No. 2, BWV 1008, in
D minor, Minuet I (A min);
Tarrega, Francisco, Study, TI ii-
5, in A, "Estudio En Forma De Un
Menuetto"   (328)

ALBUM RICREATIVO, NO. 4 *folk song
(Abloniz, Miguel) 1-2gtr (3-7th
degr.) BERBEN EB1818 $5.75 20 arr +
orig pcs; contains works by: Visee,
Mayr, Giuliani, W.A. Mozart,
Abloniz, Murcia, Sor, Carcassi,
Coste, Schumann, Brahms, Pergolesi,
Schubert, Molloy for 1 gtr; Abloniz
for 2 gtr
contains: Bach, Johann Sebastian,
Partita No. 1 for Keyboard
Instrument, BWV 825, in B flat,
Gigue (A maj)   (329)

ALBUM RICREATIVO, NO. 5 *folk song
(Abloniz, Miguel) gtr (3-7th degr.)
BERBEN EB1810 $8.25 20 arr + orig
pcs; contains works by: Chopin, D.
Scarlatti, W.A. Mozart (1), A.
Scarlatti, (1), J. Valverde (1),
Sor (1), Mendelssohn (1), Schubert
(1), Albloniz (1), Dowland (1),
Haydn (1)
contains: Bach, Johann Sebastian,
English Suite No. 3, BWV 808, In
G Minor, Gavotte I (E min); Bach,
Johann Sebastian, Liebster Herr
Jesu, BWV 484 (from Schemelli's
Gesangbuch)   (330)

ALTE HAUSMUSIK
(van Hoek) gtr (3-7th degr.)
HEINRICH. N-1291 f.s. arr + orig
pcs; contains works by: Bossinensis
(1), Diomedes Cato (1), Anon. (8),
Mikolaj Z Krakowa (1), Polak (2),
Dlugoraj (1), Judenkunig (3),
Neusiedler (3), Susato (1),
Valerius (1), Attaingnant (1),
Askue (1) Pilkington (1), Enriquez
de Valderrabano (1), Fuenllana (1),
Gaultier (1), Kirnberger (1), Weiss
(1), Cimarosa (1);
contains: Bach, Johann Sebastian,
Partita for Keyboard Instrument,
No. 5, BWV 829, in G, Minuet
                             (331)

ALTE MEISTER DES 17. JAHRHUNDERTS
(Walker, Luise) 1-2gtr (5-7th degr.)
sc HEINRICH. N-1541 f.s. 16 arr +
orig pcs; contains works by: Losy
vom Losinthal (1), Handel (2),
Visee (1), Aldrovandini (1),
Roncalli (3), Rameau (1), For 1
Gtr; Handel (1), Corelli (1), For 2
Gtr
contains: Bach, Johann Sebastian,
Partita for Violin, No. 1, BWV
1002, in B minor, Saraband; Bach,
Johann Sebastian, Partita for
Violin, No. 3, BWV 1006, in E,
Minuet; Bach, Johann Sebastian,
Prelude for Lute, BWV 999, in C
minor (D min); Bach, Johann
Sebastian, Prelude No. 22 In B
Flat Minor (from Das
Wohltemperierte Clavier, Book 1);
Bach, Johann Sebastian, Suite for
Lute, BWV 996, in E minor,
Bourree; Visee, Robert de, Suite
in D minor (E is D; contains:
Prelude, VOCG 61; Allemand, VOCG
62; Courante, VOCG 63; Saraband,
VOCG 64; Gavotte, VOCG 66; Minuet
I, VOCG 68; Minuet II, VOCG 70;
Bouree, VOCG 67; Gigue, VOCG 65)
                             (332)

ALTE SPIELMUSIK
(Kaestner; Zanoskar) S rec/T rec/treb
inst,gtr (2-3rd degr.) sc,pts
SCHOTT 4457 f.s. 24 pcs; contains
works by: Krieger (2), Anon. (9),
Kuhnau (1), Telemann (1), Purcell
(2), Daquin (1), Fischer (2),
Attaingnant (1), Handel (3), L.
Mozart (1)
contains: Bach, Johann Sebastian,
Suite for Keyboard Instrument,
BWV 822, in G minor, Minuet I (S
rec/A rec,gtr)   (333)

ALTE UND NEUE MUSIK ZUM SINGEN UND
SPIELEN AUF BLOCKFLOTEN, GEIGEN UND
LAUTENINSTRUMENTE *folk song
(Gerwig) [Ger] (1-3rd degr.) sc
LIENAU 1375 f.s. Das Spiel Der
Lauteninstrumente, Series II,
Spielbuch 1; contains works by:
Sperontes (4), L. Mozart (3),
Rathgeber (1), Rein (5), Rhau (2),
Langenau (1), Chemin-Petit (1): for
gtr (1), 2gtr (3), 3gtr (1), rec,
gtr (8), 2rec, gtr (2), solo voice,
gtr (3), solo voice, rec, gtr (1),
solo voice, rec, 2gtr (1), rec, vln
or vla, gtr (1); arr. + orig. pcs.;

single line playing; gtr pt partly
in bass clef
contains: Bach, Johann Sebastian,
English Suite No. 6, BWV 811, In
D Minor, Gavottes I-II (gtr,1-2A
rec); Bach, Johann Sebastian,
Minuet, BWV Anh. 118, in B flat
(from Anna Magdalena Bach
Notenbuchlein (1725), No.9) (gtr,
S rec) (C maj,single line
playing, gtr pt in bass clef)
(334)

ALTE WEIHNACHTSMUSIK, SPIELSTUCKE UND
LIEDER *Xmas,carol
(Schlensog) (3rd degr.) sc MOECK
ZFS-39 f.s. 12 pcs for S recs or
treb insts and solo voice(s); 2 pcs
with gtr: no.3 for solo voice, rec,
gtr; no. 5 for 3 recs, gtr;
Zeitschrift Fur Spielmusik No. 39
contains: Bach, Johann Sebastian,
Auf, Auf! Die Rechte Zeit Ist
Hier, "Adventslied", BWV 440
(from Schemelli's Gesangbuch)
(solo voice,rec,gtr) (C maj);
Bach, Johann Sebastian, Ich Steh'
An Deiner Krippe Hier, "An Der
Krippe", BWV 469 (from
Schemelli's Gesangbuch) (3rec,
gtr) (335)

ANDRES SEGOVIA ALBUM OF GUITAR SOLOS
(Segovia) gtr COLUMBIA 171 f.s. 9 arr
+ orig pcs; contains works by:
Schumann (1), Purcell (3), Gluck
(1), Segovia (1), Brahms (1), Grieg
(1)
contains: Bach, Johann Sebastian,
Suite for Lute, BWV 996, in E
minor, Courante (A min) (336)

ANTOLOGIA PER CHITARRA, VOL. 1
(Anzaghi, Luigi) (1-10th degr.)
RICORDI-IT 130034 f.s. 91 arr +
orig pcs; contains works by:
Carulli (18), Giuliani (16), Sor
(11), Aguado (8) Visee (7),
Telemann (1), Molino (1), Anzaghi
(5), Schumann (1), Diabelli (1),
Buttstedt (1), Carcassi (5), Milan
(1), Stanley (1), Farrauto (1),
Paganini (4), Donnadieu (1),
Legnani (3)
contains: Bach, Johann Sebastian,
Invention No. 1 for Keyboard
Instrument, BWV 772, in C (2gtr)
(single line playing); Bach,
Johann Sebastian, Invention No. 4
for Keyboard Instrument, BWV 775,
in D minor (2gtr) (single line
playing); Bach, Johann Sebastian,
Invention No. 8 for Keyboard
Instrument, BWV 779, in F (2gtr)
(single line playing); Bach,
Johann Sebastian, Invention No.
13 for Keyboard Instrument, BWV
784, in A minor (2gtr) (single
line playing); Bach, Johann
Sebastian, Suite for Keyboard
Instrument, BWV 822, in G minor,
Minuet I (gtr) (A min) (337)

ARMONIA, EINE SAMMLUNG POLYPHONER MUSIK
FUR GITARRE AUS VIER JAHRHUNDERTEN
(van Hoek) gtr (8-9th degr.)
HEINRICH. 1430 f.s. 18 arr + orig
pcs; contains works by: Diomedes
Cato; Blitheman; Zelechowski;
Pachelbel; Campion; Kirnberger;
Kreutzer; Carulli; Sor; Giuliani;
Carcassi; Legnani; Coste and others
contains: Bach, Johann Sebastian,
Canon Per Augmentationem In
Contrario Motu (Canon in D) (from
Die Kunst Der Fuge, No. 14, BWV
1080) (338)

AUSGEWAHLTE STUCKE FUR GITARRE SOLO, 30
*folk song
(Teuchert) gtr (1-3rd degr.) SCHMIDT,
H 75 f.s. 30 arr + orig pcs;
contains works by: Sor (2),
Carcassi (4), Carulli (5),
Neusiedler (1), Bossinensis (1),
Losy vom Losinthal (1), Anon. (3),
Attaignant (1), Turk (1), Schumann
(1), Teuchert (1), Aguado (1),
Melii da Reggio (1), Tischer (1),
Marschner (1), Giuliani (1)
contains: Bach, Johann Sebastian,
Minuet in G, BWV Anh. 114 (from
Anna Magdalena Bach Notenbuchlein
(1725), No.4); Bach, Johann
Sebastian, Suite for Lute, BWV
996, in E minor, Bourree (339)

AZPIAZU, JOSE DE (1912-   )
Gitarrenschule, Vol. I
[Ger/Fr/Span] gtr quarto SYMPHON
350 f.s. 24p.; 1954; contains:
Bach, Johann Sebastian, Prelude,
BWV 999, In C-Minor (in D-Minor);
Minuet, BWV Anh. 114, In G (in
A), Anna Magdalena Bach
Notenbuchlein (1725), No.4;
Minuet, BWV Anh. 115, In G (in A-

AZPIAZU, JOSE DE (cont'd.)
Minor), Anna Magdalena Bach
Notenbuchlein (1725), No.5 (340)

Gitarrenschule, Vol. II
[Ger/Fr/Span] gtr quarto SYMPHON
406 f.s. 32p.; 1954; contains:
Bach, Johann Sebastian, Invention
No.4, BWV 775 In D Minor for 2gtr
(single line playing); Suite For
Lute, BWV 995 In G Minor,
Saraband; and Tarrega, Francisco,
Exercise, TI-iii-3, [arr.] (341)

Gitarrenschule, Vol. III
[Ger/Fr/Span] gtr folio SYMPHON 437
f.s. 34p.; 1956; contains: Bach,
Johann Sebastian, Partita No.5
for keyboard, BWV 829, In G,
Minuet (in A); Invention No.1,
BWV 772 In C, for 2 gtr (single
line playing); Suite No.1 for
cello, BWV 1007, In G, Prelude
(in D); and Tarrega, Francisco,
Prelude, TI-i-9; Studies, TI-ii-
12, 14, 18 [48 bars, arr.] (342)

Gitarrenschule, Vol. IV *CCU
[Ger/Fr/Span] 1-2gtr folio SYMPHON
2022 f.s. 50p., facsim; 1958;
contains: Bach, Johann Sebastian,
Betrachte, Meine Seele (from
Johannes-Passion, BWV 245, No.31
lute accomp only);Partita No.1
For Violin, BWV 1002, In B-Minor,
Sarabande-Double; Toccata And
Fugue, BWV 565, In D-Minor,
[excerpt]; Prelude For Keyboard,
BWV 934, In C-Minor (in A-Minor);
Polonaise (Anna Magdalena Bach
Notenbuchlein (1725), No.28), BWV
Anh. 130, In G (in A); Suite For
Violoncello, BWV 1012, In
D, Gavotte I-I (in E); Concerto
For Harpsichord And Orchestra,
BWV 1056, In F-Minor, Largo (in
D); Invention No.2, BWV 773, In C
Minor (in E Minor), for 2gtr; and
Tarrega, Francisco, Exercise, TI-
iii-31, [arr.] (343)

Gitarrenschule, Vol. V
[Ger/Fr/Span] gtr folio SYMPHON
2174 f.s. 60p., 8 facs, tab;
1966; contains: Bach, Johann
Sebastian, Partita No.2 For
Violin, BWV 1004, In D-Minor,
Chaconne [excerpt] (in D-Minor);
Suite No.4 For Violoncello, BWV
1010, In E-Flat, Prelude (in A);
Suite No.3 For Violoncello, BWV
1009, In C, Courante (in A); and
Tarrega, Francisco, Studies, TI-
ii-3 (in A), 16a (in B-Minor), 19
(in A), 20 (in D) (344)

Premier Cours Pour Apprendre A Jouer
De La Guitare A l'Aide De Notes
Musicales Ou De Chiffres (Sans
Notes)
[Fr/Eng/Ger] gtr (staff notation
and tablature) quarto SYMPHON 468
f.s. 47p., ill; 1956; contains:
Bach, Johann Sebastian, Prelude
For Lute, BWV 999, In C-Minor (in
D-Minor); Minuet, (Anna Magdalena
Bach Notenbuchlein (1725), No.4),
BWV Anh. 114, In G (in A);
Minuet, (Anna Magdalena Bach
Notenbuchlein (1725), No.5), BWV
Anh. 115, In G (in A-Minor) (345)

BACH, JOHANN SEBASTIAN (1685-1750)
Menuet-Trio In G Minor *BWV 929
"Prelude" (Mazmanian) gtr (3rd
degr.) HEINRICH. 1634 f.s.
contains also: Anonymous,
Passepied (346)

Minuet, BWV Anh. 114, in G (from Anna
Magdalena Bach Notenbuchlein
(1725), No.4)
(Fortea) gtr (C maj,4th degr.)
FORTEA 310 f.s. contains also:
Beethoven, Ludwig van, Symphony
No. 7, Op. 92, in A, Andante
(347)

BAROQUE GUITARIST, THE
(Block) gtr (1-4th degr.) MARKS
15219-16 $1.50 14 arr + orig pcs;
contains works by: Telemann (1),
Anon. (1), Purcell (1), Dowland
(1), D. Scarlatti (2), Vivaldi (2),
Handel (1), Rameau (1), Lully (1),
F. Couperin (2), Corelli (1)
contains: Bach, Johann Sebastian,
Minuet, BWV Anh. 132, in D minor
(from Anna Magdalena Bach
Notenbuchlein (1725), No. 36)
(348)

BAROQUE PIECES, VOL. V
(Tada) rec,gtr (3-4th degr.) sc,pt
ONGAKU f.s. 33 pcs; vol. I-IV, for
kbd, rec; contains works by: C.P.E.
Bach (2), Corelli (2), Fischer (2),

Handel (5), Krieger (1), Kuhnau
(1), Mattheson (1), Marais (1),
Purcell (3), Rameau (3), Scarlatti
(1), Telemann (2) for S rec
contains: Bach, Johann Sebastian,
Aria, BWV 988 (G maj); Bach,
Johann Sebastian, Aria Di
Giovanni, "Willst Du Dein Herz
Mir Schenken", BWV 518; Bach,
Johann Sebastian, Auf, Auf, Die
Rechte Zeit Ist Hier, BWV 440;
Bach, Johann Sebastian, Ihr
Gestirn', Ihr Hohen Lufte, BWV
476; Bach, Johann Sebastian,
March, BWV 127, in E flat minor;
Bach, Johann Sebastian, Minuet,
BWV Anh. 120, in A minor (from
Anna Magdalena Bach Notenbuchlein
(1725), No.14); Bach, Johann
Sebastian, Minuet, BWV Anh. 132,
in D minor; Bach, Johann
Sebastian, Polonaise, BWV Anh.
119, in G minor (from Anna
Magdalena Bach Notenbuchlein
(1725), No.10); Bach, Johann
Sebastian, So Oft Ich Meine
Tobackspfeife, BWV 515a (from
Anna Magdalena Bach Notenbuchlein
(1725), No.20b) (G min) (349)

BAROQUE PIECES, VOL. VI
(Tada) A rec,gtr (3-4th degr.) sc,pt
ONGAKU f.s. vol. I-IV, for kbd,
rec; 24 pcs; contains works by:
C.P.E. Bach (3), Couperin (4),
Handel (7), Telemann (4 For A Rec)
contains: Bach, Johann Sebastian,
Dir, Dir, Jehova, Will Ich
Singen, BWV 299 (from Anna
Magdalena Bach Notenbuchlein
(1725), No.39b) (D maj); Bach,
Johann Sebastian, French Suite
No. 2, BWV 813, In C Minor,
Courante (A min); Bach, Johann
Sebastian, Minuet, BWV 841, in G
(from Wilhelm Friedemann Bach
Notenbuchlein, No.11) (C maj);
Bach, Johann Sebastian, Minuet,
BWV Anh. 115, in G minor (from
Anna Magdalena Bach Notenbuchlein
(1725), No.5) (A min); Bach,
Johann Sebastian, Minuet, BWV
Anh. 116, in G (from Anna
Magdalena Bach Notenbuchlein
(1725), No.7) (C maj); Bach,
Johann Sebastian, Schaff's Mit
Mir, Gott, BWV 514 (from Anna
Magdalena Bach Notenbuchlein
(1725), No.35) (G maj) (350)

BAY, MEL
New Mel Bay Classic Guitar Method,
The, Vol. II
[Eng] gtr quarto MEL BAY f.s. ill;
48p., 1971; contains: Bach,
Johann Sebastian, Suite No.6 For
Violoncello, BWV 1012, In D,
Gavotte (351)

BECK, LEONHARD
Harmonielehre Auf Der Gitarre
[Ger] gtr TEESELING VT-69 f.s.
contains: Bach, Johann Sebastian,
Nun Danket Alle Gott. Chorale,
BWV 252; and O Haupt Voll Blut
Und Wunden. Chorale N.63 from
Matthaus-Passion, BWV 244 (352)

BERUHMTE ARIEN, 4
(Azpiazu) gtr (6th degr.) SYMPHON 442
f.s.
contains: Bach, Johann Sebastian,
Partita for Keyboard Instrument,
No. 6, BWV 830, in E minor, Air
(A min); Purcell, Henry, Aria;
Telemann, Georg Philipp, Aria;
Zipoli, Domenico, Aria (353)

BIS DEL CONCERTISTA, I, VOL. 2
(Chiesa) gtr (4-8th degr.) ZERBONI
7891 $7.00 6 arr + orig pcs;
contains works by: Froberger,
Handel, M. Albeniz, Sor
contains: Bach, Johann Sebastian,
Prelude for Lute, BWV 999, in C
minor (D min); Tarrega,
Francisco, Study, TI ii- 19, in G
(354)

BRUGER, HANS DAGOBERT
Schule Des Lautenspiels, Fur Die
Gewohnliche Laute [In e'],
Basslaute, Doppelchorige Und
Theorbierte Laute, Unter
Berucksichtigung Der Regeln Und
Erfahrungen Der Beruhmtesten
Lautenmeister Des XVI. Und
Folgender Jahrhunderte Bis Zur
Gegenwart
[Ger] gtr quarto,pap,cloth MOSELER
f.s. xxx+185p., ill; repr of 2nd
rev and enl ed, 1926; 4 pts
either in 1 or 2 vols; historical
notes; numerous quotations of old
masters; app: Die Alte
Lautentabulatur; 1st ed, 1924;
contains: Bach, Johann Sebastian,

BRUGER, HANS DAGOBERT (cont'd.)

Suite For Lute, BWV 995 In E
Minor, Saraband   (355)

CHORAL UND LAUTE
(Funck) [Ger] (3rd degr.) sc LIENAU
1435 f.s. Das Spiel Der
Lauteninstrumente, Series II,
Spielbuch 12; 10 Pcs; contains
works by: Anon., Nicolai, Neumark,
Gastorius, Gesius [sic, i.e.—
Hassler], Luther (2), Cruger,
Vulpius, Forster, for solo voice,
gtr, (nos. 1–8 also transcribed for
gtr solo) arr by W. Gerwig; nos. 2,
3, 5, 6, 10 arr. by J.S. Bach
contains: Bach, Johann Sebastian,
Aus Tiefer Not Schrei Ich Zu Dir.
Chorale (from Cantata No. 38)
(gtr,solo voice); Bach, Johann
Sebastian, Befiehl Du Deine Wege.
Chorale, BWV 270 (gtr,opt solo
voice); Bach, Johann Sebastian,
Nun Ruhen Alle Walder. Chorale,
BWV 392 (gtr,solo voice); Bach,
Johann Sebastian, Wer Nur Den
Lieben Gott Lasst Walten.
Chorale, BWV 434 (gtr,opt solo
voice); Bach, Johann Sebastian,
Wie Schon Leuchtet Der
Morgenstern. Chorale, BWV 436
(gtr,opt solo voice)   (356)

CLASSICAL ALBUM FOR GUITAR SOLO, A
(Gavall, John) gtr (1–3rd degr.)
OXFORD 36–011 $2.50 13 arr + orig
pcs; contains works by: Ginter (1),
W.A. Mozart (1), Bergen (1), Handel
(2), Weichenberger (1), Vivaldi (1)
contains: Bach, Johann Sebastian,
Ermuntre Dich, Mein Schwacher'
Geist [Chorale], BWV 454 (from
Schemelli's Gesangbuch); Bach,
Johann Sebastian, Jesus Ist Das
Schonste Licht, "Slow March", BWV
474 (from Schemelli's
Gesangbuch); Bach, Johann
Sebastian, Sonata for Violin, No.
2, BWV 1003, in A minor, Largo (C
maj); Bach, Johann Sebastian,
Suite for Violoncello, No. 6, BWV
1012, in D, Gavotte I; Bach,
Johann Sebastian, Suite for
Violoncello, No. 6, BWV 1012, in
D, Gavotte II; Bach, Johann
Sebastian, Suite for Violoncello,
No. 6, BWV 1012, in D, Saraband
(357)

CLASSICAL SONGS, 10
(Gavall) solo voice,gtr (4–5th degr.)
sc NOVELLO 2543 $2.75 arr + 2 pcs
orig for lute–g'; orig words + Eng
transl; contains works by: Dowland
(2), Handel, Mozart, Liszt, Verdi,
Grieg (2)
contains: Bach, Johann Sebastian,
Bist Du Bei Mir, BWV 508 (from
Anna Magdalena Bach Notenbuchlein
(1725), No. 25) (A maj); Bach,
Johann Sebastian, Wachet Auf,
Ruft Uns Die Stimme. Chorale
(from Cantata No. 140) (C maj)
(358)

COMPOSICIONES CLASICAS Y ROMANTICAS
(Pomilio, Tomas) (4–7th degr.)
RICORDI–ARG BA–12147 f.s. 13 arr
pcs; contains works by: Rameau (2),
Haydn (1), Chopin (2), Brahms (2),
Schumann (1), Grieg (1), Bach–
Gounod (1)
contains: Bach, Johann Sebastian,
Partita for Violin, No. 1, BWV
1002, in B minor, Saraband (gtr)
(A min); Bach, Johann Sebastian,
Suite for Violoncello, No. 6, BWV
1012, in D, Gavotte I–II (gtr) (E
maj); Gounod, Charles Francois,
Ave Maria (from Das
Wohltemperierte Clavier, Book 1,
Prelude No. 1) (2gtr) (G maj)
(359)

CRIMLISK, ANTHONY
Play Guitar!, Vol. II
[Eng] gtr quarto BOOSEY–ENG f.s. 3
app; suppl (app 3): chart of the
gtr fingerboard; 41p.; 1970;
contains: Bach, Johann Sebastian,
Suite No. 6 For Violoncello, BWV
1012, In D, Gavotte   (360)

**DEUTSCHE MEISTER DES EIN– UND
ZWEISTIMMIGEN LAUTENSATZES, 16.–18.
JAHRHUNDERT**
(Bruger) [Ger] (1–3rd degr.) MOSELER
f.s. contains 22 arr + orig pcs; 12
pcs by: Heckel (1), M. Neusiedler
(1), Hainhofer (9), for gtr (1
Line); 2 pcs by Anon.; H.
Neusiedler for gtr (2 lines); 6 pcs
by: Anon. (2), Judenkunig (1), H.
Neusiedler (3) for solo voice,gtr
(2 lines)
contains: Bach, Johann Sebastian,
Prelude, Fugue, And Allegro For
Lute In E Flat, BWV 998: Allegro

(gtr) (C maj, fragment only);
Bach, Johann Sebastian, Suite for
Lute, BWV 996, in E minor,
Bourree (2gtr) (partly single
line playing); Bach, Johann
Sebastian, Suite for Lute, BWV
996, in E minor, Passaggio–
Prelude (2gtr) (single line
playing)   (361)

DREISTIMMIGE SPIELSTUCKE, 16
(Heyden) S rec,A rec,gtr/vln/vla/vla
da gamba/vcl (2nd degr.) sc NAGELS
545 f.s. contains works by:
Telemann (2), L. Mozart (3), Haydn
(1), W.A. Mozart (5)
contains: Bach, Johann Sebastian,
English Suite No. 3, BWV 808, In
G Minor, Gavotte II (S rec,A rec,
gtr) (G maj); Bach, Johann
Sebastian, French Suite No. 1,
BWV 812, In D Minor, Minuet II (S
rec,A rec,gtr); Bach, Johann
Sebastian, Minuet Trio In G
Minor, BWV 929 (from Wilhelm
Friedemann Bach Notenbuchlein
(1720)) (D min); Bach, Johann
Sebastian, Partita Del Signore
Steltzeln: Bouree, BWV 929 (S
rec,A rec,gtr) (D min); Bach,
Johann Sebastian, Polonaise, BWV
Anh. 119, in G minor (from Anna
Magdalena Bach Notenbuchlein
(1725), No.10) (S rec,A rec,gtr)
(362)

EASY MUSIC, VOL. 2 *folk song
(Azpiazu) gtr (3–7th degr.) SYMPHON
2062 f.s. 10 arr pcs; contains
works by: Arbeau (1), Anon. (1),
Buttstedt (1), F. Couperin (1),
Telemann (1)
contains: Coventry Carol, The; Noel
De Gascogne; Bach, Johann
Sebastian, Suite for Lute, BWV
996, in E minor, Saraband   (363)

EASY MUSIC, VOL. 4 *folk song
(Azpiazu) gtr (3–7th degr.) SYMPHON
2064 f.s. 10 arr + orig pcs;
contains works by: D. Gaultier,
Azpiazu (2), Gastoldi, Witte, Bohm,
Telemann, Purcell
contains: Bach, Johann Sebastian,
Suite for Lute, BWV 996, in E
minor, Bourree   (364)

EASY MUSIC, VOL. 6 *folk song
(Azpiazu) gtr (3–7th degr.) SYMPHON
2071 f.s. 10 arr + orig pcs;
contains works by: Anon. (3),
Lesage de Richee, Azpiazu, L.
Mozart, Milano, Haydn, Marpurg
contains: Bach, Johann Sebastian,
Minuet, BWV 113, in F (from Anna
Magdalena Bach Notenbuchlein
(1725), No.3) (A maj)   (365)

**EUROPEAN MASTERS FOR THE GUITAR, A
SELECT LIBRARY OF 26 [SIC]
CLASSICAL AND CONTEMPORARY PIECES**
(Behrend) gtr (4–8th degr.) BOTE f.s.
32 arr + orig pcs, i.e. 26
editions, see below; contains works
by: C.P.E. Bach (2), Batchelar (1),
F. Campion (1), Daquin (1),
Frescobaldi (1), Kapsberger (3),
Giuliani (1), Haydn (1), Rameau
(1), Reussner (1), Losy vom
Losinthal–Lesage de Richee (1
Suite), Weiss (1), Behrend (8),
Paganini (3), Sor (1), Rodrigo (1),
Hartig (1), Koptagel (1);
compilation of the following
separate Bote "Gitarre–Bibliothek"
Editions: 2, 3, 6, 8, 12c, 14, 15,
19, 21, 23, 27, 29, 32, 33, 36, 37,
40, 42, 49, 50, 66, 70, 72, 73, 75,
79; for individual entries see
Index III: Gitarre–Bibliothek
contains: Bach, Johann Sebastian,
Sonata for Violin, No. 1, BWV
1001, in G minor, Siciliano (A
maj); Bach, Johann Sebastian,
Suite for Violoncello, No. 1, in
G, Prelude (C maj)   (366)

**EUROPEAN MASTERS FOR THE GUITAR, A
SELECT LIBRARY OF 26 [SIC]
CLASSICAL AND CONTEMPORARY PIECES**
(Behrend) gtr (4–8th degr.) AMP 7223
f.s. 32 arr + orig pcs, i.e. 26
editions, see below; contains works
by: C.P.E. Bach (2), Batchelar (1),
F. Campion (1), Daquin (1),
Frescobaldi (1), Kapsberger (3),
Giuliani (1), Haydn (1), Rameau
(1), Reussner (1), Losy vom
Losinthal–Lesage de Richee (1
Suite), Weiss (1), Behrend (8),
Paganini (3), Sor (1), Rodrigo (1),
Hartig (1), Koptagel (1);
compilation of the following
separate Bote "Gitarre–Bibliothek"
Editions: 2, 3, 6, 8, 12c, 14, 15,
19, 21, 23, 27, 29, 32, 33, 36, 37,
40, 42, 49, 50, 66, 70, 72, 73, 75,

79; for individual entries see
Index III: Gitarre–Bibliothek
contains: Bach, Johann Sebastian,
Sonata for Violin, No. 1, BWV
1001, in G minor, Siciliano (A
maj); Bach, Johann Sebastian,
Suite for Violoncello, No. 1, in
G, Prelude (C maj)   (367)

FOLK TUNES AND CLASSICS FOR SOLO GUITAR
*folk song
(Gavall) gtr (1–3rd degr.) BELWIN 644
$4.00 41 arr + orig pcs; contains
works by: purcell (3), mozart (3),
handel (1), scarlatti (1)
contains: Bach, Johann Sebastian,
An Wasserflussen Babylon
(Chorale, BWV 267); Bach, Johann
Sebastian, Nun Ruhen Alle Walder
(Chorale, BWV 392); Bach, Johann
Sebastian, Partita for Violin,
No. 1, BWV 1002, in B minor,
Saraband; Bach, Johann Sebastian,
Partita for Violin, No. 1, BWV
1002, in B minor, Saraband–
Double; Bach, Johann Sebastian,
Partita for Violin, No. 3, BWV
1006, in E, Minuet I; Bach,
Johann Sebastian, Suite for
Keyboard Instrument, BWV 820, in
F, Gigue; Bach, Johann Sebastian,
Suite for Keyboard Instrument,
BWV 823, in F minor, Gigue (E
min); Bach, Johann Sebastian,
Suite for Violoncello, No. 2, BWV
1008, in D minor, Minuet I; Bach,
Johann Sebastian, Suite for
Violoncello, No. 3, BWV 1009, in
C, Bourree I; Bach, Johann
Sebastian, Suite for Violoncello,
No. 3, BWV 1009, in C, Gigue
(368)

GALL, LOUIS IGNATIUS
Gitaarmethode – Guitar Method –
Gitarreschule, Vol. III (composed
with Koenders, Rob)
gtr folio TEESELING VT–13 f.s.
25p.; 1969; contains: Bach,
Johann Sebastian, Minuet, (Anna
Magdalena Bach Notenbuchlein
(1725), No.4), BWV Anh. 114, in G
(369)

GAVALL, JOHN
Learning Music Through The Guitar,
Vol. V: An Introduction To
Figured Bass
[Eng] gtr quarto BELWIN BM–16 f.s.
57p.; 1972; contains: Bach,
Johann Sebastian, Und Also Bald
War Da Bei Dem Engel
(recitative), for gtr and solo
voice from Weihnachts–Oratorium,
BWV 248; O Haupt Voll Blut Und
Wunden. Chorale No. 21 from
Matthaus–Passion, BWV 244, for 4
gtr; Schaut Hin! for 2 gtr from
Weihnachts–Oratorium; Ach! Dass
Nicht Die Letzte Stunde, BWV 439
(from Schemelli's Gesangbuch),
for 2 gtr or 1 gtr and mel inst;
Schaffs Mit Mir, Gott. Chorale,
BWV 514 (from Anna Magdalena Bach
Notenbuchlein (1725), No.35, in
C, for 2 gtr or gtr and mel inst
(370)

GERRITS, PAUL
Gitarren– Und Lautenschule, Vol. I:
Das Einstimmige Spiel – Guitar
And Lute Method, Vol. 1: Melody
Playing
[Ger/Fr/Eng] gtr quarto oblong
MOSELER f.s. 36p., ill; 1967;
contains: Les Anges (Noel) for 2
gtr; Bach, Johann Sebastian,
Suite No. 3 for Violoncello, BWV
1009, In C, Bourree I–II; Musette
In D, BWV Anh. 126 (from Anna
Magdalena Bach Notenbuchlein
(1725), No.22 for 2 gtr (in E);
Minuet In G, BWV Anh. 114, from
Anna Magdalena Bach Notenbuchlein
(1725), No.4, for 2 gtr (in C);
Minuet In G, BWV Anh.115 from
Anna Magdalena Bach Notenbuchlein
(1725), No.5 for 2 gtr (in a
minor)   (371)

Gitarren– Und Lautenschule, Vol. II:
Ubungen Und Stucke Fur Das
Mehrstimmige Spiel – Guitar And
Lute Method, Vol. 2: Exercises
And Pieces For Polyphonic Playing
[Ger/Fr/Eng] gtr quarto oblong
MOSELER f.s. 39p.; 1968;
contains: Bach, Johann Sebastian,
Suite For Lute, BWV 996 In E
Minor (G Is F Sharp), Bourree and
Allemand   (372)

GITAAR–KAMERMUZIEK, VOL. 2
(Claessens, Anny C.H.) 1–4gtr (partly
single line playing/1–4th degr.) sc
BROEKMANS 26A f.s. arr + orig pcs;
contains works by: Claessens for 1
gtr; Anon. (6), Bohm (1),
Hurlebusch (1) for 2 gtr; J.S.

Bach, Rameau, von Call for 3 gtr;
Handel for 4 gtr
contains: Bach, Johann Sebastian,
Suite for Lute, BWV 996, in E
minor, Bourree (3gtr) (single
line playing)   (373)

GITAAR-SOLI, ALBUM KLASSIEKE- EN
MODERNE GITAAR-SOLI IN EENVOUDIGE
BEZETTING
(Kok) gtr (2-3rd degr.) XYZ 243 f.s.
18 arr + orig pcs; contains works
by: Carulli (3), Carcassi (3),
Czerny (3), Kok (4), Schumann (2),
Tchaikovsky (2)
contains: Bach, Johann Sebastian,
French Suite No. 1, BWV 812, In D
Minor, Minuet (A min)   (374)

GITAARDUETTEN
(Kok) 2gtr (partly single line
playing/3-4th degr.) sc XYZ 567
f.s. 8 arr + orig pcs; contains
works by: Carcassi (1), W.A. Mozart
(1), Carulli (2), Handel (1),
Giuliani (1), Kok (1)
contains: Bach, Johann Sebastian,
Invention No. 1 for Keyboard
Instrument, BWV 772, in C (single
line playing)   (375)

GITAARSPEELBOEK - LIVRE DE LA GUITARE
(van Puijenbroeck) gtr (2-7th degr.)
METROPOLIS EM-4722 $5.00 diatonic
and chromatic scales; 42 arr + orig
pcs; contains works by: Carcassi
(9), Carulli (6), Judenkunig (1),
Neusiedler (1), Aguado (4), Hove
(2), Adriaenssen (3), Dalza (1),
Giuliani (1), Milan (2), Dowland
(1), Lecocq (2), Weiss (1), Narvaez
(1)
contains: Bach, Johann Sebastian,
Suite for Lute, BWV 995, in G
minor, Prelude (E min, e' is d',
g is f-sharp); Bach, Johann
Sebastian, Suite for Lute, BWV
995, in G minor, Saraband (E min,
e' is d', g is f-sharp); Bach,
Johann Sebastian, Suite for Lute,
BWV 996, in E minor, Bourree (e'
is d', g is f-sharp); Tarrega,
Francisco, Exercise, TI iii-3;
Tarrega, Francisco, Prelude, TI
i- 17, in E, "Lagrima"   (376)

GITARMUZSIKA KEZDOKNEK - GITARRENMUSIK
FUR ANFANGER *folk song
(Vereczkey) gtr (1-2nd degr.) EMB
8110 f.s. 50 arr + orig pcs;
contains works by: Susato;
Bossinensis; Judenkunig; Narvaez;
Neusiedler; Caroso; D. Gaultier;
Hove; Hotteterre; Lully; Losy;
Pachelbel; Purcell; Roncalli;
Geminiani; L. Mozart; Turk;
Boccherini; W.A. Mozart; Beethoven;
Carulli; Carcassi; Giuliani; Sor;
Diabelli; Aguado; Legnani; Molino;
Bozay; Szokolay; Karolyi; Papp and
others
contains: Bach, Johann Sebastian,
Minuet, BWV Anh. 115, in G minor
(from Anna Magdalena Bach
Notenbuchlein (1725)) (E min)
                                 (377)

GITARREN MUSIZIEREN, 2, VOL. 3:
MITTELSCHWERE DUETTE
(Schwarz-Reiflingen) 2gtr (partly
single line playing/1-5th degr.)
pts SIKORSKI 532 $5.00 15 pcs;
contains works by: Handel (2),
Vogler (1), Zachow (1), Turk (1),
W.A. Mozart (3), Beethoven (1),
Schumann (1), Grieg (1), Schubert
(1)
contains: Bach, Johann Sebastian,
Concerto, BWV 978, in F, Largo (D
min,mainly single line playing);
Bach, Johann Sebastian, Giguetta
(from Sarabande Con Partite, BWV
990) (C maj,mainly single line
playing); Bach, Johann Sebastian,
Prelude for Keyboard Instrument,
BWV 927, in F (from Wilhelm
Friedemann Bach Notenbuchlein,
No.8) (F maj,mainly single line
playing)   (378)

GOLDEN AGE, THE, CLASSICS FOR SOLO
GUITAR, VOL. I
(Gavall) gtr (1-4th degr.) BELWIN
1104 $4.00 40 arr + orig pcs;
contains works by: Carulli (2),
Diabelli (2), Kuffner (1), Carcassi
(2), Aguado (1), Sor (4), Melani
(1), Purcell (2), Crema (1),
Horecki (4), Giuliani (5), Handel
(1), Weiss (1); also includes:
Bach, Johann Sebastian, Wer Hat
Dich So Geschlagen. Chorale From
Johannespassion, BWV 245, No.15;
Suites For Violoncello: No. 1, BWV
1007, In G (Gigue, In G); No. 2,
BWV 1008, In D-Minor (Minuet I, In
D-Minor and Gigue, In C); No. 3,

BWV 1009, In C (Gigue, In D-Minor);
No. 4, BWV 1010, In E-Flat (Bourree
II, In E); Partitas For Violin: No.
1, BWV 1002, In B-Minor (Saraband-
Double, Saraband, Allemand-Double);
No. 3, BWV 1006, In E (Minuet,
Loure); Sonata For Violin, No. 3,
BWV 1005, In C (Adagio, Largo); and
Suites For Keyboard: BWV 820, In F-
Minor (Gigue, In F); BWV 823, In F
(Gigue, In E Minor)   (379)

GRACE OF MINUETS, A
(Duarte) gtr (4-5th degr.) SCHOTT
11081 f.s. 7 arr pcs; contains
works by: Purcell, Handel, Fischer,
Haydn, W.A. Mozart, Gurlitt
contains: Bach, Johann Sebastian,
Partita for Keyboard Instrument,
No. 5, BWV 829, in G, Minuet
                                 (380)

GRADED DUETS, 20
(Gavall) 2gtr (partly single line
playing/1st degr.) sc OXFORD 36.003
$3.10 20 pcs; contains works by:
Losy vom Losinthal (1), Capilupi
(1), W.A. Mozart (5), Handel (3),
Purcell (1), Stamitz (1), Weiss (1)
contains: Bach, Johann Sebastian,
Brunnquell Aller Guter, BWV 445
(from Schemelli's Gesangbuch)
(single line playing); Bach,
Johann Sebastian, Eins Ist Noth,
Ach Herr, Dies Eine, BWV 453
(from Schemelli's Gesangbuch)
(single line playing); Bach,
Johann Sebastian, Gib Dich
Zufrieden Und Sei Stille, BWV 510
(from Anna Magdalena Bach
Notenbuchlein (1725), No.12) (F
maj,single line playing); Bach,
Johann Sebastian, Jesu, Deine
Liebeswunden, BWV 471 (from
Schemelli's Gesangbuch) (single
line playing); Bach, Johann
Sebastian, O Jesulein Suss, BWV
493 (from Schemelli's Gesangbuch)
(single line playing); Bach,
Johann Sebastian, Schaffs Mit Mir,
Gott, Nach Deinem Willen, BWV 314
(from Anna Magdalena Bach
Notenbuchlein (1725), No.35) (E
maj,single line playing); Bach,
Johann Sebastian, Und Wie Wohl Ist
Mir, O Freund Der Seelen, BWV 517
(from Anna Magdalena Bach
Notenbuchlein (1725), No.40) (F
maj,single line playing)   (381)

GUITAR ENSEMBLES *folk song
(Castle) 4gtr (mainly single line
playing/1-3rd degr.) MEL BAY f.s. 5
pcs; contains works by: Paganini,
Cui, Pleyel
contains: Bach, Johann Sebastian, O
Haupt Voll Blut Und Wunden.
Chorale (from Matthaus-Passion,
BWV 244, Nos. 21, 23) (4gtr)
(single line playing)   (382)

GUITAR IN ENSEMBLE, VOL. 1
(Gavall) 2gtr (1-3rd degr.) sc BELWIN
1116 f.s. arr + orig pcs; 34 pcs;
contains works by: Folksongs (19),
Kuffner (3), Sor (1), Schubert (2),
Silcher (1), Weber (1), Mozart (1),
Brahms (1), Durrner (1),
Mendelssohn (1); Eng words: 8 pcs.
(not underlaid)
contains: Bach, Johann Sebastian,
Puer Natus Est In Bethlehem.
Chorale Prelude, BWV 603 (E min);
Bach, Johann Sebastian, Sonata
for Keyboard Instrument, BWV 964,
in D minor, Andante (C maj);
Bach, Johann Sebastian, Suite for
Lute, BWV 996, in E minor,
Bourree   (383)

GUITAR SAMPLER, 5 CENTURIES OF ORIGINAL
GUITAR SOLOS
(Hoffman, John) gtr (3-4th degr.)
PRESSER 414-41100 $1.95 11 arr +
orig pcs; contains works by: Anon.
(2), Milan (1), Dowland (1), Sor
(2), Paganini (1)
contains: Bach, Johann Sebastian,
Prelude for Lute, BWV 999, in C
minor (D min); Bach, Johann
Sebastian, Suite for Lute, BWV
996, in E minor, Bourree; Sor,
Fernando, Minuet, MIN 303 (from
Grande Sonate, Op. 25); Tarrega,
Francisco, Prelude, TI i- 17, in
E, "Lagrima"   (384)

GUITARE EXPLIQUEE, LA, METHODE
PROGRESSIVE, PART II: TECHNIQUE
CLASSIQUE SUPERIEURE. 14 LESSONS
[Fr] gtr oct TRANSAT. 890 f.s. 157p.
(part 1-3); ill; 1965
contains: Bach, Johann Sebastian,
Suite for Lute in G minor,
Saraband, BWV 995 (A min); Bach,
Johann Sebastian, Suite No. 3 for

Violoncello in C, Bourree I, BWV
1009 (A maj)   (385)

GUITARIANA *folk song
(Almeida) gtr (5-7th degr.) COLIN
f.s. 17 arr + orig pcs; contains
works by: Almeida (11)
contains: Bach, Johann Sebastian,
Partita for Violin, No. 1, BWV
1002, in B minor, Courante   (386)

GUITARS, 2, ALBUM 1
(Azpiazu) 2gtr (3-4th degr.) pts
SYMPHON 2072 f.s. 10 pcs; contains
works by: Mattheson, Gregori,
Kuhnau, Purcell, Sor, Cano,
Bononcini, Daquin, Abaco
contains: Bach, Johann Sebastian,
March, BWV Anh. 127, in E flat
(from Anna Magdalena Bach
Notenbuchlein (1725), No.23) (A
maj)   (387)

HAUSLICHE WEIHNACHT *Xmas,carol/folk
song
(Gerwig) [Ger] solo voice,1-3gtr
(single line playing/1-3rd degr.)
sc LIENAU 1407 f.s. ;Das Spiel Der
Lauteninstrumente, Series II,
Spielbuch 4; 19pcs; contains works
by: Praetorius (3), Beutner, Anon.
(5), Braun
contains: Bach, Johann Sebastian,
Ich Steh' An Deiner Krippe Hier,
BWV 469 (from Schemelli's
Gesangbuch); Bach, Johann
Sebastian, Liebes Herz, Bedenke
Doch, BWV 482 (from Schemelli's
Gesangbuch); Bach, Johann
Sebastian, O Jesulein Suss, BWV
493 (from Schemelli's Gesangbuch)
                                 (388)

HENZE, BRUNO
Gitarrespiel, Das, Vol. II, Ein
Unterrichtswerk Vom Anfang Bis
Zur Meisterschaft: C-dur - a
moll; G-dur - e-moll
[Ger] gtr quarto HOFMEISTER T-4002
f.s. 29p.; 1950; contains: Bach,
Johann Sebastian, Minuet (from
Anna Magdalena Bach Notenbuchlein
(1725), No.4, BWV Anh. 114 In G
                                 (389)

Gitarrespiel, Das, Vol. III, Ein
Unterrichtswerk Vom Anfang Bis
Zur Meisterschaft: D-dur - h-moll;
A-dur - fis-moll
[Ger] gtr quarto HOFMEISTER T-4003
f.s. 39p.; 1951; contains: Bach,
Johann Sebastian, Suite For Lute,
BWV 996, In E-Minor, Bourree (in
F-Sharp Minor)   (390)

HOVE, JOACHIM VAN DEN (1567-1620)
Suite
gtr (6th degr., Edition Nicolas
Alfonso, No. 3) SCHOTT-FRER 9122
f.s. contains also: Bach, Johann
Sebastian, Suite for Violoncello,
No. 5, BWV 1001, in C minor,
Saraband (A min)   (391)

INMITTEN DER NACHT, WEIHNACHTLICHE
SPIELMUSIK *Xmas,carol
(Bacher) S rec/A rec/T rec,gtr/2rec,
gtr (3rd degr.) sc NAGELS EN-1106
f.s. 10 pcs; Nagels Laute- Und
Gitarre-Archiv; contains works by:
Praetorius, Anon., F. Couperin
contains: Bach, Johann Sebastian,
English Suite No. 3 In G Minor,
Fifth Movement: Gavotte En
Musette, BWV 808 (gtr,T rec) (C
maj); Bach, Johann Sebastian,
English Suite No. 6 In D Minor,
Fifth Movement: Gavotte II, BWV
811 (gtr,A rec) (C maj); Bach,
Johann Sebastian, Wachet Auf!
Ruft Uns Die Stimme. Chorale,
"Gloria Sei Dir Gesungen", BWV
140,No.7 (gtr,T rec/A rec)   (392)

KITARAKIRJA-GITARRMELODIER, VOL. 2
*folk song
(Immonen) gtr (2-4th degr.) FAZER
4155 f.s. 45 arr + orig works;
contains works by: Sor (10),
Carulli (4), Giuliani (3), Carcassi
(2), Aguado (3), Visee (2),
Paganini (1), Fortea (1), Gruber
(1), Handel (1), Beethoven (1),
W.A. Mozart (2), Schumann (2),
Fliess (1), Brahms (1), Immonen
(2), Anon. (1), Merikanto (1),
Bland (1)
contains: Bach, Johann Sebastian,
Minuet, BWV Anh. 114, in G (from
Anna Magdalena Notenbuchlein
(1725), No.4) (C maj)   (393)

KLASSISCHES ALBUM, VOL. 2
(Nemerowski) gtr (4-6th degr.)
ZIMMER. ZM-1102 f.s. 10 arr pcs;
contains works by: Beethoven (2),
Schumann (2), W.A. Mozart (1),
Rameau (1), Schubert (1), Chopin

(1), Weber (1)
contains: Bach, Johann Sebastian,
English Suite No. 2, BWV 867, In
A Minor, Sarabande   (394)

KUNSTLIEDER
(Henze, Bruno) [Ger] (3-7th degr.) sc
HOFMEISTER T-4012 $6.00 Das
Gitarrespiel, Vol. XII; 30 Pcs;
contains works by: Dowland (2),
Albert (2), Krieger (2), Kremberg,
Beyer (2), A. Scarlatti,
Rathgeber(2), W.A. Mozart, Weber
(2), Schubert (2), Schumann,
Brahms, Pabel (2), Stingl (4),
Hlouschek (2) for solo voice, gtr;
by W.A. Mozart for solo voice,
mando, gtr; by Ambrosius for 2 solo
voices, gtr
contains: Bach, Johann Sebastian,
Aria Di Giovannini, "Willst Du
Dein Herz Mir Schenken", BWV 518
(from Anna Magdalena Bach
Notenbuchlein (1725), No. 37)
(2gtr,solo voice) (C maj)   (395)

LIED- UND GITARRENSPIEL, VOLKS- UND
TANZLIEDER, VOL. II *folk song
(Bresgen; Zanoskar) [Ger] solo voice,
gtr (3rd degr.) sc SCHOTT 5415 f.s.
30 arr. + orig. pcs.; contains
works by: Rathgeber, Anon. (7),
Weber (3), Zelter, Reinhardt (2),
Steuerlein, Praetorius, Telemann,
Krieger
contains: O Tannenbaum; Bach,
Johann Sebastian, Gib Dich
Zufrieden, BWV 460 (from
Schemelli's Gesangbuch); Bach,
Johann Sebastian, Guldne Sonne,
Die, BWV 451 (from Schemelli's
Gesangbuch); Bach, Johann
Sebastian, Ich Steh An Deiner
Krippen Hier, BWV 469 (from
Schemelli's Gesangbuch); Bach,
Johann Sebastian, Tag Ist Hin,
Der, BWV 447 (from Schemelli's
Gesangbuch); Gruber, Franz Xaver,
Stille Nacht   (396)

LIEDER DER VOLKER, VOL. I
(Behrend) solo voice,gtr (3-6th
degr.) sc ZIMMER. ZM-1398 f.s. arr
+ orig pcs; orig words; 5 pcs;
Folksongs from Israel, Japan,
Germany, Italy
contains: Bach, Johann Sebastian,
Aria Di Giovannini, "Willst Du
Dein Herz Mir Schenken" , BWV 518
(from Anna Magdalena Bach
Notenbuchlein (1725), No. 37) (E
maj)   (397)

MAIRANTS, IVOR
Simplicity Tutor For Spanish Guitar,
The, In The Tarrega Method
[Eng] gtr (staff notation and
tablature) folio BOOSEY-ENG 17345
f.s. 27p., ill; rev ed, 1955; 1st
ed, 1954; contains: Johann
Sebastian Bach's Suite For Lute,
BWV 996, In E Minor, Bourree;
Suite For Lute, BWV 995, In G-
Minor, Saraband (in a minor, 1-2
gtr)   (398)

MARTINEZ ZARATE, JORGE
Mi Primer Libro De Guitarra
[Span] gtr (staff notation and
tablature) folio RICORDI-ARG
BA-11940 f.s. 43p.; repr, 1964;
1st ed, 1961; contains: Stille
Nacht (Noche De Paz) by Franz
Gruber; Cancion De Navidad by
Felix Mendelssohn-Bartholdy; and
So Oft Ich Meine Tobackspfeife,
BWV 515, from Anna Magdalena Bach
Notenbuchlein (1725), No.20a
(single line playing, 2 gtr) by
Johann Sebastian Bach   (399)

MEISTER DER BAROKZEIT
(Fischer; Hulsemann) 2rec,hpsd/gtr/
opt vcl (2nd degr.) sc,pts
BRATFISCH 3042 f.s. 12 pcs;
contains works by: Rosenmuller (1),
Corelli (1), Fux (1), Petz (1),
Linike (3), Heinichen (1), Handel
(2); Frankfurter
Gemeinschaftsmusiken, Vol.3
contains: Bach, Johann Sebastian,
French Suite No. 1, BWV 812, In D
Minor, Minuet II (2rec,hpsd/gtr)
(single line playing); Bach,
Johann Sebastian, Suite for
Orchestra, BWV 1066, in C,
Gavotte I (2rec,hpsd/gtr)   (400)

MEL BAY FOLIO OF CLASSIC GUITAR SOLOS,
VOL. 1 *folk song
(Castle) gtr (1-4th degr.) BELWIN
$1.50 38 arr + orig pcs; contains
works by: Castle (2), Sor (8),
Aguado (2), Calegari (1), Anon.
(1), Gruber (1), Rosas (1),
Ivanovici (1), Waldteufel (1),
Carey (1), Key (1), Reading (1),
Delibes (1), Carulli (1), Meacham
(1), Rameau (1), Bishop (1),
Gautier (1), Beethoven (1),
Giuliani (2), Dvorak (1),
Tchaikovsky (1), Schubert (1), L.
Mozart (1)
contains: Bach, Johann Sebastian,
Musette In D, BWV Anh.126 (from
Anna Magdalena Bach Notenbuchlein
(1725), No.22)   (401)

MEL BAY FOLIO OF CLASSIC GUITAR SOLOS,
VOL. 2 *folk song
(Castle) gtr (1-4th degr.) BELWIN
$1.50 33 arr + orig pcs; contains
works by: Schumann (1), Diabelli
(2), Kuffner (1), Aguado (1),
Mozart (1), Molino (1), Paganini
(2), Flotow (1), Beethoven (1),
Borghesi (1), Mertz (1), Verdi (1),
Purcell (1), Giuliani (1), Handel
(1), Bornhardt (1), Sor (1),
Carulli (1), Balfe (1), Visee (2),
Castle (1)
contains: Bach, Johann Sebastian,
Minuet, BWV Anh. 114, in G (from
Anna Magdalena Bach Notenbuchlein
(1725), No.4); Bach, Johann
Sebastian, Partita for Violin,
No. 1, BWV 1002, In b minor,
Saraband (A min); Hopkins, John
Henry, Jr., We Three Kings Of
Orient Are   (402)

MEL BAY'S DELUXE ALBUM OF CLASSIC
GUITAR MUSIC
(Castle) gtr (4-9th degr.) MEL BAY
f.s. 67 arr + orig pcs; contains
works by: Milan (1), Palestrina
(1), Byrd (1), Frescobaldi (1),
Reusner (1), Visee (1), Couperin
(1), Rameau (1), Handel (1), Lesage
De Richee (1), Gluck (1), Haydn
(1), Gossec (1), Mozart(2),
Beethoven (3), Carulli (3), Molino
(2), Sor (7), Giuliani (2),
Diabelli (2), Paganini (2), Aguado
(2), Weber (1), Legnani (2),
Carcassi (3), Marschner (1),
Schubert (1), Horenzky (1), Coste
(1), Mertz (1), Chopin (2),
Schumann (1), Offenbach (1), Brahms
(1), Wienawski (1), Tchaikovsky
(2), Massenet (1), Grieg (1),
Scharwenka
contains: Bach, Johann Sebastian,
Fugue for Lute, BWV 1000, in G
minor (A min); Bach, Johann
Sebastian, Invention No. 1 for
Keyboard Instrument, BWV 772, in
C; Bach, Johann Sebastian,
Prelude for Lute, BWV 999, in C
minor (D min); Bach, Johann
Sebastian, Suite for Lute, BWV
996, in E minor, Bourree;
Tarrega, Francisco, Prelude, TI
i- 19, in G; Tarrega, Francisco,
Study, TI ii- 9, in A minor,
"Recuerdos De La Alhambra";
Tarrega, Francisco, Study, TI ii-
18, in A, "Scherzo De T. Damas"
(403)

MENUETTBUCH
(van Hoek) gtr (3-5th degr.)
HEINRICH. N-1345 f.s. 24 arr + orig
pcs; contains works by: Handel (2),
Weiss (3) Visee (1), Losy vom
Losinthal (1), Rameau (1),
Kirnberger (2), Krebs (1), Krieger
(1), Marpurg (1), Haydn (1), W.A.
Mozart (1), Schubert (1), Beethoven
(1), Sor (1), van Hoek (3)
contains: Bach, Johann Sebastian,
Minuet, BWV Anh. 114, in G (from
Anna Magdalena Bach Notenbuchlein
(1725), No.4); Bach, Johann
Sebastian, Partita for Lute, BWV
1006a, in E, Minuet I-II (D maj)
(404)

MONKEMEYER, HELMUT
Wir Spielen Gitarre, Ein Spiel- Und
Ubungsbuch
[Ger] quarto TONGER 853 f.s. (65p.,
ill; 1959; historical notes)
contains: Schaff's Mit Mir, Gott,
BWV 514 (from Anna Magdalena
Bach Notenbuchlein (1725),
No.35) (2gtr) (C maj); Suite
for Lute, BWV 996, in E minor,
Bourree; Vergiss Mein Nicht,
BWV 505 (from Schemelli's
Gesangbuch) (2gtr)   (405)

MOORST, PABLO VAN
Moderne Handleiding Voor Het
Klassieke Gitaarspel, Vol. III
[Dutch] gtr quarto TOORTS f.s. ill;
1968-69; 46p.; contains: Study,
TI-ii-5 in A; Prelude, TI-i-14 in
A-Minor by Francisco Tarrega; and
Minuet In G, BWV Anh. 114, (from
Anna Magdalena Bach Notenbuchlein
(1725), No.4) by J.S. Bach (406)

MORGEN- UND ABENDLIEDER *folk song
(Schaller, Erwin) [Ger] (3rd degr.)
sc,pts MOSELER f.s. 20 pcs;
contains works by: Bendig, Baumann
(2), Reichardt, Rohwer, Ebeling,
Weber, Bresgen for solo voice, gtr;
by Vulpius, Hensel, Ahle, Schulz,
Brahms for solo voice, A rec or vln
or vla, gtr
contains: Bach, Johann Sebastian,
Nun Ruhen Alle Walder. Chorale,
BWV 392 (gtr,solo voice) (F maj)
(407)

MORNAC, JUAN (1897-)
Guitare Pour Tous, La, Methode
Rationelle Et Rapide De Guitare
Classique Avec De Nombreuses
Recreations
[Fr] gtr folio LEDUC 23.984 f.s.
65p., ill; 1970
contains: Minuet in G, BWV
Anh.114 (from Anna Magdalena
Bach Notenbuchlein (1725),
No.4); Sonata for Flute, BWV
1013, in A minor, Allemand (E
min); Suite No. 2 For Orchestra
In B Minor: Rondeau, BWV 1067
(A min, fragment); Suite No. 3
for Violoncello in C, Loure,
BWV 1009 (C maj)   (408)

MOURAT, JEAN-MAURICE
Cordes, 6...Une Guitare, Methode De
Guitare A l'Usage Des Debutants
[Fr] gtr folio BILLAUDOT 1648 f.s.
72p., ill; 1973; suppl: Position
de la main droite; Position de la
main gauche; contains: Study, TI-
ii-14 by Francisco Tarrega; and
Minuet, BWV Anh. 115, From Anna
Magdalena Bach Notenbuchlein
(1725), No.5, In G (in A Minor)
for 2gtr; Minuet, BWV Anh. 114,
from Anna Magdalena Bach
Notenbuchlein (1725), No.4, In G
for 2 gtr; Suite No. 6 for
Violoncello, BWV 1012, In D,
Gavotte II by J.S. Bach   (409)

MUSIC FOR 4 GUITARS
(Gavall) 4gtr (single line playing/1-
2nd degr.) sc BELWIN 978 $2.50 11
pcs; contains works by: Praetorius
(1); W.A. Mozart (2); Brahms (2),
Palestrina (1), Schubert (1)
contains: Bach, Johann Sebastian,
Feste Burg Ist Unser Gott, Ein'.
Chorale, BWV 203; Bach, Johann
Sebastian, Herzlich Thut Mich
Verlangen. Chorale, "Befiel Du
Deine Wege. Chorale", BWV 270;
Bach, Johann Sebastian, Nun Lasst
Uns. Chorale, "Sprich Ja Zu
Meinen Taten", BWV 194; Bach,
Johann Sebastian, O Welt, Ich
Muss Dich Lassen. Chorale, "O
Welt, Sieh' Hier Dein Leben", BWV
393; Praetorius, Michael, Es Ist
Ein Ros' Entsprungen   (410)

MUSIC FOR CLASSICAL GUITAR
(Vinson) gtr (1-6th degr.) CONSOL
f.s. 114 arr + orig pcs; Music For
Millions Series, Vol. 59; contains
works by: Anon. (9), Galilei (1),
Milan (1), Morlaye (1), Narvaez
(1), Neusiedler (2), Terzi (1),
Besard (1), Dowland (1), Roncalli
(1), Sanz (9), Visee (2), Aguado
(7), Diabelli (3), Carcassi (9),
Carulli (16), Giuliani (7), Kuffner
(7), Kunz (2), Meignen (1), Sor
(25), Bartok (2), Cotten (1)
contains: Bach, Johann Sebastian,
Suite for Lute, BWV 995, in G
minor, Gavotte II (A min,
fragment); Tarrega, Francisco,
Prelude, TI i- 17, in E,
"Lagrima"; Tarrega, Francisco,
Prelude, TI i- 20, in A, "Adagio
In A"   (411)

MUSIC FOR THE CLASSICAL GUITAR, VOL. 1:
A BOOK FOR BEGINNERS *folk song
(Norman, Theodor) gtr (1-3rd degr.)
SCHIRM.G 46059 f.s. 26 arr + orig
pcs; contains works by: Anon. (1),
Visee (1), Gruber (1), Carcassi
(1), A. Scarlatti (1), Handel (1),
Corelli (1), Tartini (1), Molloy
(1), Clerambault (1), Norman (1)
contains: Bach, Johann Sebastian,
Minuet, BWV Anh. 115, in G minor
(from Anna Magdalena Bach
Notenbuchlein (1725), No.5) (D
min)   (412)

MUSIC FOR THE CLASSICAL GUITAR, VOL. 2:
A BOOK FOR INTERMEDIATE PLAYERS
*folk song
(Norman, Theodor) gtr (3-6th degr.)
SCHIRM.G 46819 f.s. 31 arr + orig
pcs; contains works by: Corelli
(2), Fesch (2), A. Scarlatti (1),
Liszt (1), Purcell (1), Norman (6),
Anon. (1), Laserna (1), Platti (1),

Mendelssohn (1), Campion (2), Milan
(1), Clementi (1), D. Scarlatti
(1), Campagnoli (1)
contains: Bach, Johann Sebastian,
Minuet, BWV Anh. 132, in D minor
(from Anna Magdalena Bach
Notenbuchlein (1725), No.36) (A
min)   (413)

MUSIC FOR THE YOUNG GUITARIST *folk
song
(Norman, Theodor) gtr (1-3rd degr.)
SCHIRM.G 22.47580 f.s. 50 arr pcs;
contains works by: Norman (1),
Dvorak (1), Haydn (1), Carey (1),
Hill (1), Brahms (1), Lully (1),
Schubert (1), Beethoven (1), Smith
(1), Chopin (1), W.A. Mozart (1),
Corelli (1), Foster (1), Kreutzer
(1), Paganini (1), Tchaikovsky (1),
Gruber (1), Pierpont (1), de l'Isle
(1),
contains: Bach, Johann Sebastian,
Minuet No. 2, BWV 841, in G (from
Wilhelm Friedemann Bach
Notenbuchlein (1720), No.11);
Bach, Johann Sebastian, Suite for
Keyboard Instrument, BWV 822, in
G minor, Minuet I (A min)   (414)

MUSIK DER VORKLASSIK: WERKE AUS DEM 17.
UND 18. JAHRHUNDERT
(Brodszky; Kovats) gtr (2-3rd degr.)
SCHOTT 5229 f.s. 30 pcs; contains
works by: Turk (5), Anon. (5), W.A.
Mozart (1), L. Mozart (1), Krieger
(2), Haydn (1), Hotteterre (1),
Barret (1), J.C.F. Bach (1), Clark
(1), Caroubel (1), Rameau (1), W.F.
Bach (1), Dandrieu (1), Kirchhof
(1), Handel (2), Purcell (1), F.
Couperin (1); same as Regi Zene
Gitarra, EMB 2-1790
contains: Bach, Johann Sebastian,
Minuet, BWV Anh. 114, in G (from
Anna Magdalena Bach Notenbuchlein
(1725), No.4) (A maj); Bach,
Johann Sebastian, Piece In F,
"Aria", BWV Anh.131 (from Anna
Magdalena Bach Notenbuchlein
(1725), No.32) (A maj)   (415)

MUSIQUE POUR 3 ET 4 GUITARES, VOL. 1
(MUSIC FOR 3 AND 4 GUITARS, VOL. 1)
*folk song
(Gerrits) 3-4gtr (single line
playing/1-3rd degr.) sc DOBER f.s.
18 arr + orig pcs; contains works
by: Scheidt (1), Anon. (2),
Gastoldi (3), Sermisy (1), A.
Gagnon (1), Attaingnant (1), von
Call (1), Duncombe (1), Susato (2),
Dowland (1), Arbeau (1) for 3gtr;
Susato (2) for 4gtr
contains: Bach, Johann Sebastian,
English Suite No. 2, BWV 807, In
A Minor, Bouree II (3gtr) (D maj,
single line playing); Bach,
Johann Sebastian, English Suite
No. 3, BWV 808, In G Minor,
Musette (3gtr) (A maj, single line
playing); Bach, Johann Sebastian,
O Haupt Voll Blut Und Wunden.
Chorale (from Matthaus-Passion,
BWV 244, No.53) (4gtr) (single
line playing); Bach, Johann
Sebastian, Wer Hat Dich So
Geschlagen. Chorale (from
Matthaus-Passion, BWV 244, No.44)
(4gtr) (single line playing)
                                  (416)

MUSIQUE POUR 3 ET 4 GUITARES, VOL. 2
(MUSIC FOR 3 AND 4 GUITARS, VOL. 2)
(Gerrits) 3-4gtr (single line
playing/1-3rd degr.) sc DOBER f.s.
14 arr + orig pcs; contains works
by: Telemann (2), Haydn (1),
Praetorius (2), Scheidt (3), L.
Mozart-K. Marx (2), C.M. Gagnon
(1), for 3gtr; Scheidt (3), L.
Mozart-K. Marx (1) for 4gtr
contains: Bach, Johann Sebastian,
Ich Bitt', O Herr, Aus Herzens
Grund. Chorale (from Cantata
No.18) (3gtr)   (417)

MUSIQUE POUR 3 ET 4 GUITARES, VOL. 3 -
MUSIC FOR 3 AND 4 GUITARS, VOL. 3
(Gerrits) 3-4gtr (1-6th degr.) sc,pts
DOBER DO-3 f.s. contains 17 works
by: Susato; Phalese; Gabriel;
Widmann; Banchieri; Molinaro;
Pratorius; Morley; Purcell and
anonymous
contains: Bach, Johann Sebastian,
Suite for Keyboard Instrument,
BWV 816, in A, Gavotte (3-4gtr)
                                  (418)

MUSIQUE POUR 3 ET 4 GUITARES, VOL. 4 -
MUSIC FOR 3 AND 4 GUITARS, VOL. 4
(Chandonnet) 3-4gtr (1-6th degr.) sc,
pts DOBER DO-4 f.s. contains 9
works by: Morley; Purcell;
Praetorius; A. Gabrieli, Handel and
Kuntz
contains: Bach, Johann Sebastian,

Sonata for Violin and Keyboard
Instrument, BWV 1015, in A minor,
Andante   (419)

MUSIQUE POUR DEUX GUITARES, VOL. 1 -
MUSIC FOR TWO GUITARS, VOL. 1
(Chandonnet) 2gtr (2-6th degr.) sc,
pts DOBER DO-6 f.s. 13 arr + orig
pcs; contains works by: Haydn;
Boyce; Pachelbel; Purcell;
Praetorius; de Falla; D. Scarlatti;
A. Gabrieli; Handel and Anonymous
contains: Bach, Johann Sebastian,
Prelude No. 22 in A minor, BWV
867 (from The Well-Tempered
Clavier I) (2gtr)   (420)

MUSIQUE POUR GUITARE SEULE, VOL. 1 -
MUSIC FOR SOLO GUITAR, VOL. 1
(Gerrits) gtr (2-6th degr.) DOBER
DO-9 f.s. arr + orig pcs; contains
22 works by: Besard; Neusidler;
Dalza; van den Hove; R. Johnson;
Baron; Stolzel; Hoffer; Weiss; D.
Scarlatti; Chandonnet; Komter;
Resch; Gerrits; Leblond; Gagnon and
others
contains: Bach, Johann Sebastian,
Suite for Violoncello, BWV 1012,
in D, Gavotte I-II; Bach, Johann
Sebastian, Suite for Violoncello,
BWV 1012, in D, Gigue   (421)

MUSIQUE POUR GUITARE SEULE, VOL. 3 -
MUSIC FOR SOLO GUITAR, VOL. 3
(Chandonnet) gtr (2-6th degr.) DOBER
DO-11 f.s. arr + orig pcs; contains
20 works by: Paumann; LeRoy;
Ballard; Weiss; Gerrits; C. Gagnon;
Bruhl; A. Gagnon and others
contains: Bach, Johann Sebastian,
Pedal-Exercitium, BWV 598; Bach,
Johann Sebastian, Suite for
Keyboard Instrument, BWV 822, in
F minor, Gavotte En Rondeau (B
min); Bach, Johann Sebastian,
Suite for Violoncello, BWV 1012,
in D, Saraband; Bach, Johann
Sebastian, Toccata for Keyboard
Instrument, BWV 914, in E minor
                                  (422)

NOAD, FREDERICK M.
Solo Guitar Playing, A Complete
Course Of Instruction In The
Technique Of Guitar Performance
[Eng] gtr quarto COLLIER f.s.
187p., ill; repr, 1969; 1st ed,
1968; contains: Minuet from
Grande Sonate, Op. 25 by Fernando
Sor; Prelude, TI-i-17, In E
(Lagrima) by Francisco Tarrega;
and Suite No.4 For Violoncello,
BWV 1010, In E Flat, Bourree (in
A) by Johann Sebastian Bach (423)

OBRAS CLASICAS Y ROMANTICAS, VOL. 1
(Tarrega; Savio) gtr (4-9th degr.)
RICORDI-ARG BA-11371 f.s. 17 arr+
orig pcs; contains works by:
Albeniz (2), Beethoven (1), Chopin
(3), Haydn (1), Mendelssohn (2),
W.A. Mozart (1), Schubert (1),
Schumann (4)
contains: Bach, Johann Sebastian,
Partita for Violin, No. 1, BWV
1002, in B minor, Bourree; Bach,
Johann Sebastian, Sonata for
Violin, No. 1, BWV 1001, in G
minor, Fugue   (424)

PAPAS, SOPHOCLES
Method For The Classic Guitar
[Eng] quarto COLUMBIA 300 f.s.
61p., ill; 1963
contains: Minuet in A, BWV
Anh.114 (from Anna Magdalena
Bach Notenbuchlein (1725),
No.4) (2gtr); Piece In F
(March), BWV Anh.131 (from Anna
Magdalena Bach Notenbuchlein
(1725), No.32) (G maj); Prelude
and Fugue in G minor, BWV 542
(A min)   (425)

PEZZI CELEBRI, 20
(Farrauto) gtr (3-6th degr.) RICORDI-
IT 129839 f.s. 20 arr pcs; contains
works by: Donizetti (1), Anon. (4),
Gruber (1), Paganini (1), Mayr (1),
Schumann (1), Gluck (1), Chopin
(1), Verdi (1), Liszt (1), Brahms
(1), W.A. Mozart (1), Yradier (1),
Rubinstein (1), Pergolesi (1),
Lully (1)
contains: Bach, Johann Sebastian,
Minuet, BWV Anh. 132, in D minor
(from Anna Magdalena Bach
Notenbuchlein (1725), No.36) (A
min)   (426)

PICCOLA ANTOLOGIA CHITARRISTICA *folk
song
(Abloniz) gtr (3-5th degr.) RICORDI-
IT 129884 f.s. 12 arr + orig pcs;
contains works by: Anon. (2),
Purcell (1), Visee (1), W.A. Mozart

(1), Gruber (1), Chopin (1)
contains: Coventry Carol, The,
"Vecchia Carola Di Coventry";
Bach, Johann Sebastian, Nicht So
Traurig, "Non Tanto Triste", BWV
489 (from Schemelli's
Gesangbuch); Gruber, Franz Xaver,
Stille Nacht, "Notte Silenziasa"
                                  (427)

PILI, SALVATORE (1933-   )
Chitarrista Moderno, Il
[It] gtr folio BERBEN 1229 f.s.
57p.; ill; 2nd ed, 1974; 1st ed,
1967; contains: Suite For Lute,
BWV 996, In E-Minor, Bourree;
Minuet, BWV Anh. 114 from Anna
Magdalena Bach Notenbuchlein
(1725), No.4 (In G), for 2 gtr by
Johann Sebastian Bach   (428)

POWROZNIAK, JOZEF
Szkola Gry Na Gitarze
[Polish] gtr folio POLSKIE 2595
f.s. 86p., ill; 1957; suppl:
Tabela chwytow gitary; contains:
Minuet, from Anna Magdalena Bach
Notenbuchlein (1725), No.4, BWV
Anh. 114 (In G) by Johann
Sebastian Bach   (429)

Szkola Gry Na Gitarze, Wydanie
Zmienione Uzupelnione Dodatkiem O
Grze Na Gitarze Hawajskiej
[Polish] gtr folio POLSKIE 5748
f.s. 123p., ill; 1966; app:
[method for Hawaiian guitar];
suppl.: Tabela chwytow gitary -
akordy; contains: Minuet, from
Anna Magdalena Bach Notenbuchlein
(1725), No.4, BWV Anh. 114 (In G)
by Johann Sebastian Bach   (430)

QUELQUES PAGES DE GUITARE CLASSIQUE
(Breguet) gtr (4-7th degr.) LEMOINE
f.s. contains 24 works by:
Chambonnieres (4), Clerambault (4),
Seixas (4), Purcell (4)
contains: Bach, Johann Sebastian,
French Suite No.1, BWV812, In D
Minor, Sarabande (E min); Bach,
Johann Sebastian, French Suite
No. 2, BWV813, In C Minor, Gigue
(D min); Bach, Johann Sebastian,
French Suite No. 2, BWV813, In C
Minor, Minuet (D min); Bach,
Johann Sebastian, French Suite
No. 4, BWV815A, In E Flat, Minuet
(G maj); Bach, Johann Sebastian,
Minuet, BWV Anh. 120, in A minor
(from Anna Magdalena Bach
Notenbuchlein (1725), No.14) (D
min); Bach, Johann Sebastian,
Minuet, BWV Anh. 132, in D minor
(from Anna Magdalena Bach
Notenbuchlein (1725), No.36);
Bach, Johann Sebastian, O
Ewigkeit, Du Donnerwort. Chorale,
BWV 513 (from Anna Magdalena Bach
Notenbuchlein (1725), No.42);
Bach, Johann Sebastian, Suite for
Orchestra, BWV 1067, in B minor,
Rondo   (431)

REGI ZENE GITARRA, ATIRATOK A XVII-
XVIII. SZAZAD MUZSIKAJABOL - ALTE
MUSIK FUR GITARRE, WERKE AUS DEM
17.-18. JAHRHUNDERT
(Brodsky; Kovats) gtr (2-3rd degr.)
EMB Z-1790 f.s. 29 pcs.; same as
Musik Der Vorklassik, Schott 5224,
except for no. 14, Lang, Allegro,
and no. 15, Kemeny, Andante
contains: Bach, Johann Sebastian,
Minuet, BWV Anh. 114, in G (from
Anna Magdalena Bach Notenbuchlein
(1725), No.4) (A maj); Bach,
Johann Sebastian, Piece In F,
"Aria", BWV Anh.131 (from Anna
Magdalena Bach Notenbuchlein
(1725), No.32) (A maj)   (432)

REPERTOIRE PROGRESSIF, VOL. 1 *folk
song
(Sanchez, Blas) gtr (2-5th degr.)
CHOUDENS 20.339 f.s. 32 arr + orig
pcs; contains works by: Carcassi
(7), Anon. (4), Ruiz de Ribayaz
(2), Sanz (1), Carulli (1), Losy
vom Losinthal (2), Giuliani (2),
Visee (2), Campion (1), LeRoy (1),
Sor (2), Narvaez (1)
contains: Bach, Johann Sebastian,
Minuet, BWV Anh. 114, in G (from
Anna Magdalena Bach Notenbuchlein
(1725), No.4); Bach, Johann
Sebastian, Minuet, BWV Anh. 120,
in A minor (from Anna Magdalena
Bach Notenbuchlein (1725),
No.14); Bach, Johann Sebastian,
Partita for Violin, No. 1, BWV
1002, in B minor, Saraband-
Double; Bach, Johann Sebastian,
Prelude for Lute, BWV 999, in C
minor (D min)   (433)

RIGHTMIRE, RICHARD W.
Wonderful Guitar, The (A Modern
Classic Guitar Method), Vol. I
[Eng] gtr quarto SMITH,WJ f.s.
32p., 1962, ill; contains:
Minuet, BWV Anh. 115 In G-Minor
(in E-Minor) by Johann Sebastian
Bach from anna magdalena bach
notenbuchlein (1725), no.5 (434)

Wonderful Guitar, The (A Modern
Classic Guitar Method), Vol. II
[Eng] gtr quarto SMITH,WJ f.s.
32p., 1963, ill; contains:
Minuet, BWV Anh. 114 In G from
Anna Magdalena Bach Notenbuchlein
(1725), No.4; Minuet, BWV Anh.
132 In D-Minor from Anna
Magdalena Bach Notenbuchlein
(1725), No.36, by J.S. Bach; and
Minuet from Grande Sonate, Op. 22
by Fernando Sor (435)

Wonderful Guitar, The (A Modern
Classic Guitar Method), Vol. III
[Eng] gtr quarto SMITH,WJ f.s.
31p., 1963, ill; contains: March,
BWV Anh. 122 In D from Anna
Magdalena Bach Notenbuchlein
(1725), No.16; Partita No. 1 For
Keyboard Instrument, BWV 825, In
B-Flat, Minuet I (fragment);
Suite For Lute, BWV 996, In E-
Minor, Bourree, by J.S. Bach; and
Study, TI-ii-14 In D-Minor;
Prelude, TI-i-17 In E (Lagrima)
by Francisco Tarrega (436)

ROCH, PASCUAL
Modern Method For The Guitar, A, Vol.
III, School Of Tarrega
[Eng/Span/Fr] gtr quarto SCHIRM.G
1830 f.s. 109p., ill; 1st ed,
1924; contains: Bach, Johann
Sebastian, Prelude For Keyboard,
BWV 839 In C (in E); and Tarrega,
Francisco, Prelude, TI-i-17;
Studies, TI-ii-12 and 12 (41
bars), 16b, 17, 18, 34 (437)

RONNY LEE CLASSIC GUITAR BOOK, THE
(Lee, Ronny) gtr (1-3rd degr.) ALFRED
459 $2.95 38 arr+ orig pcs;
contains works by: Carcassi (9),
Carulli (8), Sor (8), Aguado (3),
Beethoven (1), Lee (1), Clarke (1),
Scarlatti (1)
contains: Bach, Johann Sebastian,
Minuet, BWV Anh. 114, in G (from
Anna Magdalena Bach Notenbuchlein
(1725), No.4); Bach, Johann
Sebastian, Minuet, BWV Anh. 132,
in D minor (from Anna Magdalena
Bach Notenbuchlein (1725), No.36)
(E min); Bach, Johann Sebastian,
Partita for Violin, No. 1, BWV
1002, in B minor, Bourree (A
min); Bach, Johann Sebastian,
Partita for Violin, No. 3, BWV
1006, in E, Gavotte En Rondeau (C
maj); Tarrega, Francisco, Study,
TI ii- 26, in C (438)

SANCHEZ, BLAS
Methode De Guitare Classique, Premier
Et Deuxieme Cycles
[Fr] gtr folio CHOUDENS 20.160 f.s.
85p., ill; 1973; 2 suppl: 40
Exercises faciles pour la
guitare; contains: Bach, Johann
Sebastian, Toccata And Fugue, BWV
565, in D-minor (in E-minor;
fragment of fugue) (439)

SCHALLER, ERWIN (1901-   )
Lehrwerk Fur Die Gitarre, Vol. V
(composed with Scheit, Karl)
[Ger] gtr quarto UNIVER. 11221 f.s.
31p.; repr, 1941; contains: Bach,
Johann Sebastian, Aria Di
Giovannini ("Willst Du Dein Herz
Mir Schenken"), BWV 518, fROM
ANNA MAGDALENA BACH NOTENBUCHLEIN
(1725), NO.37, for solo voice and
gtr (in D) (440)

SCHNEIDER, SIMON
Gitarreschule *Op.125
[Ger] gtr quarto HOFMEISTER 8014
f.s. 56p., ill; 1967; contains:
Bach, Johann Sebastian, Suite For
Lute, BWV 996, In E Minor,
Bourree, for 2 gtr; Des Heil'gen
Geistes Reiche Gnad'. Chorale,
BWV 295, for 4 gtr (single line
playing) (441)

SCHWARZ-REIFLINGEN, ERWIN
Gitarren-Schule, Vol. II
[Ger] gtr folio SIKORSKI 170B f.s.
85p., ill; 1953; contains: Bach,
Johann Sebastian, Musette In D,
BWV Anh. 126, Anna Magdalena Bach
Notenbuchlein (1725), No.22 (442)

SEVEN HUNDRED YEARS OF MUSIC FOR THE
CLASSIC GUITAR
(Valdes Blain) gtr (3-6th degr.)
HANSEN-US T-156 f.s. 22 arr + orig
pcs; contains works by: Adam de la
Hale (1), Anon. (7), Dowland (2),
A. Scarlatti (1), Giuliani (1), Sor
(2), Granados (1), Albeniz (1)
contains: Bach, Johann Sebastian,
Partita for Violin, No. 1, BWV
1002, in B minor, Saraband; Bach,
Johann Sebastian, Prelude for
Lute, BWV 999, in C minor (D
min); Bach, Johann Sebastian,
Suite for Lute, BWV 996, in E
minor, Allemand (A min); Bach,
Johann Sebastian, Suite for Lute,
BWV 996, in E minor, Bourree;
Tarrega, Francisco, Prelude, TI
i- 17, in E, "Lagrima" (443)

SKARBCZYK GITARZYSTY - THE GUITARIST'S
TREASURY *folk song
(Powrozniak) gtr (1-5th degr.)
POLSKIE 5047 f.s. 98 arr + orig
pcs; contains works by: Barcicki
(1), Kozar-Slobodski (1), Moniuszko
(2), Lully (1), Caroubel (1),
Rameau (1), Losy vom Losinthal (1),
Handel (1), Haydn (1), W.A. Mozart
(3), L. Mozart (1), Beethoven (2),
Clementi (1), Schubert (1),
Schumann (3), Rossini-Arr. J.
Kuffner (1), Marschner (1),
Mendelssohn-Arr. J.K. Mertz (1),
Offenbach (1), Bizet (1),
Tchaikovsky (1), Grieg (1), Verdi
(1), Noskowski (1), Rozycki (1),
Gretchaninov (1), Sor (2), Carulli
(3), Carcassi (2), Coste (2), Mertz
(2), F. Rung (1), H. Rung (1),
Hulsen (1), Tarrega (1), Urban (1),
Powrozniak (1), Emma (1), Ivanovici
(2), Waldteufel (1), Curtis (1)
contains: Bach, Johann Sebastian,
Minuet, BWV Anh. 115, in G minor
(from Anna Magdalena Bach
Notenbuchlein (1725), No.5) (A
min); Bach, Johann Sebastian,
Musette in D, BWV Anh.126 (from
Anna Magdalena Bach Notenbuchlein
(1725), No.22); Bach, Johann
Sebastian, Polonaise, BWV Anh.
119, in G minor (from Anna
Magdalena Bach Notenbuchlein
(1725), No.10) (A min) (444)

SOLOBUCH FUR GITARRE, DAS
(Schwarz-Reiflingen) gtr (2-4th
degr.) SIKORSKI 268 $5.00 30 arr +
orig pcs; contains works by:
Carcassi (1), Sor (1), Stephenson
(1), Diabelli (1), Steibelt (1),
Bertini (2), Carulli (1), Handel
(2), Gluck (2), Haydn (2), W.A.
Mozart (1), Beethoven (1), Lemoine
(1), Chopin (2), Tchaikovsky (2),
Schubert (1), Schumann (3), Brahms
(1), Anon. (1), Schwarz-Reiflingen
(1)
contains: Bach, Johann Sebastian,
Fantasy for Keyboard Instrument,
BWV 919, in C minor, "Allegro
Moderato" (E min); Bach, Johann
Sebastian, Sonata for Violin, No.
2, BWV 1003, in A minor, Andante
(C maj) (445)

SOLOGITARRE, DIE, VOL. I
(Behrend) gtr (3-6th degr.) ZIMMER.
ZM-1721 f.s. 5 arr + orig pcs;
contains works by: Handel, W.A.
Mozart, Telemann
contains: Bach, Johann Sebastian,
Bist Du Bei Mir, BWV 508 (from
Anna Magdalena Bach Notenbuchlein
(1725), No.25) (G maj); Bach,
Johann Sebastian, Partita for
Violin, No. 1, BWV 1002, in B
minor, Saraband (446)

SOLOS FOR THE GUITAR PLAYER *folk song
(Norman, Theodor) gtr (6-7th degr.)
SCHIRM.G f.s. 26 arr + orig pcs;
contains works by: Arensky (1),
Bacon (1), Beethoven (1), Biber
(1), Chopin (2), Giardini (1),
Gibbons (1), Handel (1), Haydn (1),
Norman (5), Paganini (3), Platti
(1), Prokofiev (1), Reger (1),
Soler (1), Schumann (1)
contains: Bach, Johann Sebastian,
Fughetta In C Minor, BWV 961 (A
min); Bach, Johann Sebastian,
Trio Sonata, BWV 1039, in G,
Andante (E min) (447)

SOLOS FOR THE GUITAR PLAYER *folk song
(Norman, Theodor) gtr (6-7th degr.)
CHAPPELL-ENG 22.48771 f.s. 26 arr +
orig pcs; contains works by:
Arensky (1), Bacon (1), Beethoven
(1), Biber (1), Chopin (2),
Giardini (1), Gibbons (1), Handel
(1), Haydn (1), Norman (5),
Paganini (3), Platti (1), Prokofiev

(1), Reger (1), Soler (1), Schumann
(1)
contains: Bach, Johann Sebastian,
Fughetta In C Minor, BWV 961 (A
min); Bach, Johann Sebastian,
Trio Sonata, BWV 1039, in G,
Andante (E min) (448)

SONNE, KOMM, EIN GITARRESPIELBUCH FUR
KINDER, 1-4. UNTERRICHTSJAHR *folk
song
(Ratz, Martin) [Ger] solo voice,gtr/
1-4gtr (single line playing/1-3rd
degr.) sc DEUTSCHER 32001 f.s. 162
arr + orig pcs; contains works by:
Schuffenhauer (2), Krug (4), Konig
(8), Ratz (22), Asriel (5), Quadt
(9), Rosenfeld (2), Haydn, Schumann
(3), Gorischk, Helmut, Wohlgemuth,
Schwaen, Schoendlinger for gtr;
Friemert (2), Buse, W.A. Mozart
(3), Beethoven, Berges,
Schuffenhauer, Hecht-Wieber for 2
gtr; Eberwein, Stephani for 3 gtr;
anon., naumilkat for 4 gtr or solo
voice(s), gtr; Skodova (2), Silcher
(2), Wendt, Friemert (2), Kern,
Krug (2), Pormova, Rodl, Hartung,
Nynkowa, Schuffenhauer, Hein,
Richter (3), W. Bender (2), Helmut,
Naumilkat for solo voice, gtr; also
contains Christmas music by:
Helmut, Schuffenhauer, Wohlgemuth
for gtr or solo voice, gtr; W.
Bender, Helmut, Naumilkat, for solo
voice, gtr
contains: Bach, Johann Sebastian,
Minuet in G minor, BWV Anh. 115
(2gtr) (A min,single line
playing); Bach, Johann Sebastian,
Piece In F, "Aria", BWV Anh.131
(2gtr) (single line playing);
Bach, Johann Sebastian, Polonaise
in G minor, BWV Anh. 119 (2gtr)
(A min,single line playing) (449)

SPIELBUCH FUR GITARREN-DUO
(Teuchert, Heinz) 2gtr (partly single
line playing/2-5th degr.) sc
SCHMIDT,H 77 f.s. 31 arr + orig
pcs; contains works by: Kuffner
(8), Fux (2), Telemann (2),
Chedeville (1), Purcell (1), L.
Mozart (1), W.A. Mozart (2),
Erlebach (1), Carulli (3),
Hotteterre (1), Radolt (1), Handel
(2), Weber (1)
contains: Bach, Johann Sebastian,
English Suite No. 3, BWV 808, In
G Minor, Musette (C maj); Bach,
Johann Sebastian, March, BWV Anh.
122, in D (from Anna Magdalena
Bach Notenbuchlein (1725), No.16)
(C maj); Bach, Johann Sebastian,
Minuet, BWV Anh. 116, in G (from
Anna Magdalena Bach Notenbuchlein
(1725), No.7) (F maj); Bach,
Johann Sebastian, Suite for
Keyboard Instrument, BWV 820, in
F, Bourree (G maj) (450)

SPIELHEFT KLASSIK FUR DREI GITARREN
(Reiser) 3gtr (1-2nd degr.) sc SCHOTT
GA-436 f.s. 9 pcs; arr; contains
works by: Judenkunig (2); Dufay;
Losy; A. Scarlatti; Le Sage de
Richee; Kerll; Krieger
contains: Bach, Johann Sebastian,
Suite For Lute, BWV 996, In E
Minor, Presto (single line
playing) (451)

SPIELHEFT KLASSIK FUR ZWEI GITARREN
(Reiser) 2gtr (1-3rd degr.) sc SCHOTT
GA-435 f.s. 13 pcs; arr; contains
works by: Praetorius; Lully;
Corelli; Chedeville; W.A. Mozart;
Weichenberger; Telemann (3); Weiss
(2); and Galilei
contains: Bach, Johann Sebastian,
Suite for Lute, BWV 996, in E
minor, Bourree (E is D) (452)

SPIELMUSIK AUS FUNF JAHRHUNDERTEN -
LEICHT BIS MITTELSCHWER
(Henze, Bruno) gtr (3-6th degr.)
HOFMEISTER T-4009 $4.50 Das
Gitarrespiel, Vol. IX; 48 arr +
orig pcs (numbered 1-30); contains
works by: Milan (1), Mudarra (1),
Fuenllana (1), Anon. (4), Molinaro
(1), Corbetta (1), Sanz (1), Losy
vom Losinthal (4), Visee (1),
Roncalli (3), Campion (1), Molitor
(1), Carulli (1), Sor (2), Giuliani
(2), Diabelli (1), Aguado (2),
Carcassi (2), Coste (1), Tarrega
(2), C. Henze (1), Ambrosius (2),
Domorowski (1), Holz (3), B. Henze
(2), Hecker (1), Stingl (1),
Schwaen (1), Dooren (1)
contains: Bach, Johann Sebastian,
Suite for Lute, BWV 996, in E
minor, Bourree (453)

SPIELMUSIK AUS FUNF JAHRHUNDERTEN –
    MITTELSCHWER BIS SCHWER
    (Henze, Bruno) gtr (5–8th degr.)
    HOFMEISTER T-4010 $7.50 Das
    Gitarrespiel, Vol. X; 42 arr + orig
    pcs (numbered 1–32); contains works
    by: Milan (1), Fuenllana (1),
    Attaignant (3), Gaultier (1),
    Molinaro (1), Corbetta (1), Losy
    vom Losinthal (4), Joseph I (1),
    Lesage de Richee (1), Campion (1),
    Weichenberger (1), Bergen (1),
    Lauffensteiner (1), Kropfgans (1),
    Falckenhagen (1), Wyssotzki (1),
    Moretti (1), Sor (1), Giuliani (1),
    Aguado (2), Coste (1), Mertz (1),
    Arcas (1), Tarrega (1), Rung (1),
    Ambrosius (2), Henze (2), Wagner-
    Regeny (1), Stingl (2), Hlouschek
    (1), Behrend (1)
    contains: Bach, Johann Sebastian,
        Suite for Lute, BWV 995, in G
        minor, Gavotte I–II (A min);
        Bach, Johann Sebastian, Suite for
        Lute, BWV 995, in G minor,
        Saraband (A min)   (454)

SPIELMUSIK FUR 3 GITARREN *folk song
    (Henze) 3gtr (partly single line
    playing/2–7th degr.) sc,pts
    HOFMEISTER T-4014 $12.75 28 arr +
    orig pcs (numbered 1–13); Das
    Gitarrespiel, Vol. XIV; contains
    works by: Molinaro (1), Telemann
    (1), Fux (1), Muffat (2), von Call
    (1), Gragnani (1), Diabelli (1),
    Kretschmar (1), Ambrosius (2),
    Stingl (1), Wagner-Regeny (1)
    contains: Bach, Johann Sebastian,
        English Suite No. 2, BWV 807, In
        A Minor, Bouree II (3gtr) (D maj,
        single line playing); Bach,
        Johann Sebastian, English Suite
        No. 3, BWV 808, In G Minor,
        Gavotte II (3gtr) (G maj,single
        line playing)   (455)

SUPLEMENTO AL METODO PARA GUITARRA DE
    AGUADO-SINOPOLI
    (Sinopoli, Antonio) gtr (4–10th
    degr.) RICORDI-ARG BA-6712 f.s. 19
    arr + orig pcs; contains works by:
    Sinopoli (1), Sor (6), Chopin (2);
    also includes: Tarrega, Francisco,
    Preludes, TI–i–1 In D-Minor, 4 In
    E, 5 In E, 7 In A, 8A In A, 9 In A;
    Study, TI–ii–5 In A, "Estudio En
    Forma De Un Minuetto"; Bach, Johann
    Sebastian, Das Wohltemperierte
    Clavier, Vol. I, Prelude No. 1, BWV
    846, In C (In E); Suite For
    Violoncello, No. 3, BWV 1009,
    Courante In C (In A): Partita For
    Violin, No.2, BWV 1004, Chaconne I
    In D Minor (In E Minor); and Sor,
    Fernando, Grande Sonata, Op. 22
    (Minuet); Grande Sonata, Op. 25
    (Minuet)   (456)

TANZSATZE
    (Heyden) S rec,A rec,gtr (1–2nd
    degr.) sc NAGELS 559 f.s. 11 pcs;
    contains works by: W.A. Mozart (5),
    Haydn (1), L. Mozart (2), Telemann
    (1), Kuhnau (1)
    contains: Bach, Johann Sebastian,
        English Suite No. 2, BWV 807, In
        A Minor, Bouree II (C maj)   (457)

TARREGA, FRANCISCO (1852–1909)
    Album, Vol. I
    (Fortea, Daniel) gtr (4–7th degr.)
    FORTEA 190 f.s.
        contains: Prelude, TI i– 17, in
        E, "Lagrima"   (458)

TEUCHERT, HEINZ (1914–   )
    Gitarren-Schule, Fur Melodiespiel,
    Liedbegleitung Und Solospiel, Ein
    Anschauliches Lehr- Und
    Spielbuch, Vol. II
    [Ger] gtr quarto SCHMIDT,H 96 f.s.
    47–96p., ill; contains: Bach,
    Johann Sebastian, Minuet, BWV
    Anh. 132, from Anna Magdalena
    Bach Notenbuchlein (1725), No.36,
    In D Minor, for 2 gtr (single
    line playing); Prelude For Lute,
    BWV 999, In C Minor (in D Minor);
    and Tarrega, Francisco, Prelude,
    TI–i–17; Exercise, TI–iii–32
        (459)

TRANSCRIPCIONES PARA GUITARRA
    (Segovia) gtr UNION ESP. 20235 f.s.
    all ars. also published separately
    as UME 18029–38; Transcripciones
    Nos. 9, 8, 1, 6, 5, 4, 2, 10, 3, 7;
    10 arr pcs; contains works by:
    Handel (1), Schumann (2), Grieg
    (1), Beethoven (1), Haydn (1),
    Mendelssohn (1), Schubert (1)
    contains: Bach, Johann Sebastian,
        Partita for Violin, No. 1, BWV
        1002, in B minor, Saraband; Bach,
        Johann Sebastian, Sonata for
        Violin, No. 1, BWV 1001, in B

minor, Siciliano (A maj)   (460)

TRANSCRIPCIONES PARA GUITARRA
    (Llobet) gtr (6–7th degr.) UNION ESP.
    20382 f.s.
        contains: Bach, Johann Sebastian,
        Partita for Violin, No. 1, BWV
        1002, in B minor, Saraband;
        Bizet, Georges, Arlesiana, La;
        Grieg, Edvard Hagerup, Melodia
        Noruega; Wagner, Richard,
        Parcifal   (461)

TRANSCRIPCIONES POR GRACIANO TARRAGO
    [1]
    (Tarrago) gtr (3rd degr.) UNION ESP.
    1950 f.s.
        contains: Cancion Catalana; Bach,
        Johann Sebastian, French Suite
        No. 6, BWV 817, In E, Minuet (A
        maj)   (462)

TRANSCRIPCIONES POR GRACIANO TARRAGO
    [2]
    (Tarrago) gtr (4th degr.) UNION ESP.
    1953 f.s. arr + orig pcs
        contains: Bach, Johann Sebastian,
        Invention for Violin and Keyboard
        Instrument, BWV Anh. 174, in B
        flat, Air (D maj); Sor, Fernando,
        Minuet, MIN 194; Visee, Robert
        de, Minuet, MIN 195; Visee,
        Robert de, Saraband, MIN 196
            (463)

TRANSCRIPCIONES POR GRACIANO TARRAGO
    [3]
    (Tarrago) gtr (3–4th degr.) UNION
    ESP. 1955 f.s. contains works by:
    W.A. Mozart, Schumann
        contains: Bach, Johann Sebastian,
        Suite for Lute, BWV 996, in E
        minor, Bourree   (464)

TRANSCRIPCIONES POR VICENTE ERLISO,
    VOL. 6
    gtr UNION ESP. 1061 f.s. arr + orig
    pcs; contains works by: Beethoven,
    Erliso
        contains: Bach, Johann Sebastian,
        English Suite No. 3, BWV 808, In
        G Minor, Gavottes I–II   (465)

TRANSCRIPTIONS FACILES DE 12 CHEFS-
    D'OEUVRE CLASSIQUE
    (Mornac, Juan) gtr (2–3rd degr.)
    DURAND 13969 $5.50 12 arr pcs;
    contains works by: Brahms (3),
    Martini (1), Schumann (3),
    Mendelssohn (1), Mozart (1),
    Beethoven (1)
        contains: Bach, Johann Sebastian,
        Minuet, BWV Anh. 114, in G (from
        Anna Magdalena Bach Notenbuchlein
        (1725), No.4); Bach, Johann
        Sebastian, Minuet, BWV Anh. 115,
        in G minor (from Anna Magdalena
        Bach Notenbuchlein (1725), No.5)
        (A min)   (466)

TRANSKRYPCJE KLASYKOW
    (Powrozniak) 2gtr (partly single line
    playing/2–4th degr.) sc POLSKIE
    2461 f.s. Grajmy Na Gitarze, Vol.
    12; 17 arr + orig pcs; contains
    works by: Purcell (1), Rameau (1),
    Telemann (1), Handel (2); Gluck
    (1), Haydn (3), W.A. Mozart (3),
    Beethoven (2)
        contains: Bach, Johann Sebastian,
        Invention No. 13 for Keyboard
        Instrument, BWV 784, in A minor
        (single line playing); Bach,
        Johann Sebastian, Minuet, BWV
        Anh. 114, in G (from Anna
        Magdalena Bach Notenbuchlein
        (1725), No.4) (single line
        playing); Bach, Johann Sebastian,
        Minuet, BWV Anh. 116, in G (from
        Anna Magdalena Bach Notenbuchlein
        (1725), No.7) (single line
        playing)   (467)

TREML, ROBERT
    Grundlagen Des Gitarrenspiels, Die,
    Aufbau Und Spieltechnik Aus Der
    Einstimmigkeit, Mit Vielen
    Musikbeispielen, Einzeln Oder
    Chorisch Zu Gebrauchen
    [Ger] gtr quarto NAGELS EN-1095
    f.s. 45p., ill; repr, 1954; 1st
    ed, 1938; for suppl, see
    Twittenhoff, Wilhelm; contains:
    Bach, Johann Sebastian, Sing',
    Bet', Und Geh' Auf Gottes Wegen.
    Chorale, from Wer Nur Den Lieben
    Gott Lasst Walten, BWV 93, No. 7,
    for 4 gtr (single line playing)
        (468)
UNSERE SCHONSTEN WEIHNACHTSLIEDER ZUR
    GITARRE *Xmas,carol
    (Schwarz-Reiflingen) [Ger] solo
    voice,gtr (1–3rd degr.) sc ZIMMER.
    Z-11878 f.s. 15 pcs
        contains: Bach, Johann Sebastian,
        Lobt Gott, Ihr Christen
        Allzugleich [Chorales], BWV 375

        (469)
UNSERE WEIHNACHTSLIEDER *Xmas,carol
    (Gotze) [Ger] gtr solo,opt solo voice
    (3rd degr.) SCHOTT 4459 f.s. 43
    pcs; notation: treb-staff
        contains: Bach, Johann Sebastian,
        Lobt Gott Ihr Christen
        Allzugleich [Chorales], BWV 375
            (470)
UNSERE WEIHNACHTSLIEDER *Xmas,carol
    (Gotze) [Ger] solo voice,gtr/treb
    inst,gtr (2–3rd degr.) sc SCHOTT
    4361 f.s. 42 pcs; also available in
    gtr solo ed
        contains: Bach, Johann Sebastian,
        Lobt Gott, Ihr Christen,
        Allzugleich. Chorale, BWV 375
            (471)
UTWORY DAWNYCH MISTRZOW
    (Powrozniak) 2gtr (3–4th degr.) sc
    POLSKIE 1369 f.s. Grajmy Na
    Gitarze, Vol. 7; 10 arr + orig pcs;
    contains works by: Gluck (1), W.A.
    Mozart (1), Carulli (2), Gaude (1),
    von Call (1), Hoyer (1), Sor (2)
        contains: Bach, Johann Sebastian,
        Polonaise, BWV Anh. 119, in G
        minor (from Anna Magdalena Bach
        Notenbuchlein (1725), No.10)
        (2gtr) (E min,single line
        playing)   (472)

VANDERHORST, ADRIAN (ARAI)
    Learning The Classic Guitar
    [Eng] (staff notation and
    tablature) quarto SCHIRM.G 2161
    f.s. 59p., ill; 1954
        contains: Minuet in D minor, BWV
        Anh. 132 (from Anna Magdalena
        Bach Notenbuchlein (1725),
        No.36) (2gtr) (single line
        playing)   (473)

VARIETY OF GUITAR MUSIC, A *folk song
    (Duarte) gtr (1–3rd degr.) FABER f.s.
    34 arr + orig pcs; contains works
    by: Playford (6), Anon. (7),
    Dowland (3), T. Campian (1),
    Bartlett (1), Aston (2), Haydn (1),
    Schumann (1), Tchaikovsky (1),
    Telemann (2), Handel (1)
        contains: Bach, Johann Sebastian,
        Musette In D, BWV Anh.126 (from
        Anna Magdalena Bach Notenbuchlein
        (1725), No.22) (D maj)   (474)

VINSON, HARVEY
    Play Classic Guitar
    [Eng] gtr quarto AMSCO 020143 f.s.
    95p., ill; 1969; 3 app; contains:
    Bach, Johann Sebastian, Minuet,
    from Anna Magdalena Bach
    Notenbuchlein (1725), No.4, BWV
    Anh. 114, In G; Suite No. 6 For
    Violoncello, BWV 1012, In D,
    Gavotte (in C; fragment); and
    Tarrega, Francisco, Prelude, TI–
    i–17, In E "Lagrima"; in G i–20,
    in A   (475)

WEIHNACHTSLIEDER AUS DEUTSCHLAND UND
    OSTERREICH *Xmas,carol,Austrian/
    Ger
    (Schafer-Stetka) [Ger] S rec,gtr,opt
    solo voice (3rd degr.) sc,pt
    DOBLINGER f.s. 14 pcs; notation: 2
    treb-staffs; rec pt is solo voice
    pt
        contains: Bach, Johann Sebastian,
        Ich Steh' An Deiner Krippen Hier,
        BWV 469 (from Schemelli's
        Gesangbuch)   (476)

ZANOSKAR, HUBERT
    Neue Gitarren-Schule, Vol. I
    [Ger] gtr (64p.; 1969; contains
    Bach, Johann Sebastian, Gib Dich
    Zufrieden Und Sei Stille, BWV
    460, for solo voice, gtr from
    Schemelli's Gesangbuch quarto
    SCHOTT 5665 f.s.   (477)

    Neue Gitarren-Schule, Vol. I, Suppl.:
    Ubungen Und Spielstucke
    [Ger] gtr quarto SCHOTT 5667 f.s.
    46p.; 1969; contains: Bach,
    Johann Sebastian, Minuet, BWV
    Anh. 115, from Anna Magdalena
    Bach Notenbuchlein (1725), No.5,
    In G Minor, for 2 gtr; Minuet,
    BWV Anh. 116, from Anna Magdalena
    Bach Notenbuchlein (1725), No.7,
    In G, for 2 gtr; and Ich Steh An
    Deiner Krippen Hier, BWV 469, in
    C minor, for solo voice and gtr
    from Schemelli's Gesangbuch (478)

A BATTERE see Kotonski, Wlodzimierz

A CANOA VIROU, CIRANDINHA NO. 10 see Villa-Lobos, Heitor

A GITAR HANGOTASA see Vereczkey, Laszlo

A LA DECOUVERTE DE LA GUITARE see Didier, Gerard

A LA VIRGEN DE LOS DOLORES see Spaanse Volksliederen, 3 (3 Spanish Folksongs)

A L'INCONNU see Rovsing Olsen, Poul

A PROPOS see Vannetelbosch, P.

A QUIEN CONTARE MIS QUEJAS? see Canciones Del Siglo XVII, 5

A STAADE MUSI I/IIA2

A-.TA-LON, FOR SOLOIST AND THIRTY-SIX PLAYING AND TALKING INSTRUMENTALISTS see Holt, Simeon ten

A TAL PERDIDA TAN TRISTE see Encina, Juan del

A VOUZ AMANZ see Seiber, Matyas Gyorgy

AANKOMENDE GITARIST, DE, AUDIO-VISUELE METHODE MET GRAMMOFOONPLAAT see Mohino, Gonzalez, Guitariste En Herbe, Le, Methode Audio-Visuelle Avec Disque

AASE'S DEATH see Grieg, Edvard Hagerup

ABBOTT, ALAIN (1938-   )
Prelude No. 1 I/IIB1

ABC GITARY, CZYLI JAK HANIA NA GITARZE GRAC SIE NAUCZYLA see Powrozniak, Jozef

ABC-KRIPPENLIED see Rinke Ranke Rosenschein; 77 Kinderlieder

ABEJORRO, EL, ESTUDIO see Pujol, Emilio

ABENDLIED EINES BAUERMANNS see Hiller, Johann Adam

ABENDMUSIK see Carulli, Ferdinando

ABHAVA see Encinar, Jose Ramon

ABLONIZ, MIGUEL (1917-   )
Arpeggi, 50, Per La Mano Destra, La Mano Sinistra Non Partecipa III

Arpeggios, 50, For The Right Hand, The Left Hand Is Not Used see Arpeggi, 50, Per La Mano Destra, La Mano Sinistra Non Partecipa

Blues For Rosy I/IB4

Capriccio Flamenco, Sul Tema Popolare "El Vito" I/IB4

Crab-Fingerings see Imitando Il Granchio

Diatonic Scales, The 24 see Scale Diatoniche, Le 24

Divertimento I/IIA1

Esercizi Essenziali Per La Mano Sinistra III

Essential Exercises For The Left Hand see Esercizi Essenziali Per La Mano Sinistra

Imitando Il Granchio III

Improvvisazione, Omaggio A Villa-Lobos I/IB4

Incorrigible Dreamer, An, Bossa Nova I/IB5

Moderato, MIN145 see Pezzi Ricreativi (E Di Utilita Tecnica), Nello Stile Polifonico, 4

Moderato, MIN146 see Pezzi Ricreativi (E Di Utilita Tecnica), Nello Stile Polifonico, 4

Moderato, MIN147 see Pezzi Ricreativi (E Di Utilita Tecnica), Nello Stile Polifonico, 4

ABLONIZ, MIGUEL (cont'd.)
Moods, Jazz In Bossa Nova I/IB5

Partita in E I/IB4

Pequena Romanza I/IB4

Pezzi Ricreativi (E Di Utilita Tecnica), Nello Stile Polifonico, 4 I/IB4

Principal Technical Rules see Principali Regole Tecniche

Principali Regole Tecniche III

Quasi Allegro see Pezzi Ricreativi (E Di Utilita Tecnica), Nello Stile Polifonico, 4

Riscoperta Dell'Accordatura E Dalla Tastiera III

Scale Diatoniche, Le 24 III

Sequential I/IB4

Studi Melodici Per Chitarra, 10 I/IA

Tarantella Burlesca And Bossa Nova I/IB4

Tuning And Fingerboard Rediscovered see Riscoperta Dell'Accordatura E Dalla Tastiera

ABRAHAM see Kramer, Gotthold

ABREUANA see Gilardino, Angelo

ABSCHIED, DER see Sor, Fernando, Adieux!, Les, Sixieme Fantaisie

ABSIL, JEAN (1893-1974)
Barcarolle, MIN 148 see Sur Un Paravent Chinois, 4 Esquisses, Op. 147

Contrastes I/IIA1

Danse I/IIA1

Gigue, MIN 150 see Sur Un Paravent Chinois, 4 Esquisses, Op. 147

Petit Bestiaire, Op. 151 I/IB4

Pieces, 4, Op.150 I/IB4

Pieces, 10 I/IB4

Pieces, 12, Vol. I: Nos. 1-4 I/IB4

Pieces, 12, Vol II: Nos. 5-8 I/IB4

Pieces, 12, Vol. III: Nos. 9-12 I/IB4

Prelude Et Barcarolle I/IB4

Romance, MIN 149 see Sur Un Paravent Chinois, 4 Esquisses, Op. 147

Scherzetto see Sur Un Paravent Chinois, 4 Esquisses, Op. 147

Suite for 2 Guitars I/IIA1

Suite, Op. 114 I/IB4

Sur Un Paravent Chinois, 4 Esquisses, Op. 147 I/IB4

ACADEMIC METHOD FOR CLASSICAL GUITAR see Jessic, M.

ACADEMICO CALIGINOSO, L' I/IB1

ACCOMPAGNEMENT A LA GUITARE, L', MIS A LA PORTEE DE TOUS see Laurent, Leo

ACCORDI E CADENZE PER CHITARRA D'ACCOMPAGNAMENTO see Schinina, Luigi

ACCORDS DE GUITARE, D'APRES LE NOUVEAU DOIGTE see Bossu, Marcel

ACH, DASS NICHT DIE LETZTE STUNDE see Bach, Johann Sebastian

ACHT AUSGEWAHLTE STUCKE see Lully, Jean-Baptiste (Lulli)

ACHT STUCKE see Stravinsky, Igor

ACQUARELLI NAPOLETANI see Cammarota, Carlo

ACUSTICA I: MUSIC FOR LOUDSPEAKERS see Kagel, Mauricio

ADAGIO DE LA SONATA, OP. 27, NO. 2, "CLARO DE LUNA" see Beethoven, Ludwig van, Sonata for Piano, Op.

27, No. 2, in C sharp minor, First Movement

ADAGIO ET GIGUE see Bonporti, Francesco Antonio

ADAGIO QUASI RECITATIVE see Fetler, Paul

ADELA see Rodrigo, Joaquin

ADELITA, MAZURKA see Tarrega, Francisco; Tarrega, Francisco; Tarrega, Francisco

ADIEU see Schubert, Franz (Peter); Schubert, Franz (Peter)

ADIEU MA CHERE VALLEE see Maitia Nun Zira

ADIEUX, LES (LA DESPEDIDA) see Sor, Fernando, Adieux!, Les, Sixieme Fantaisie

ADIEUX!, LES, SIXIEME FANTAISIE see Sor, Fernando

ADIOSES, LOS, SEXTA FANTASIA see Sor, Fernando, Adieux!, Les, Sixieme Fantaisie

ADLES see Bartolozzi, Bruno

ADOLPHSON, OLLE
Trubbel I/IIC1

ADRIAENSSEN, EMANUEL (ca. 1550-1604)
Branle Double see 2 Dances And 2 Fantasies

2 Dances And 2 Fantasies I/IB1

Fantasy No. 1 see 2 Dances And 2 Fantasies

Fantasy No. 3 I/IB1

Fantasy No. 5 see 2 Dances And 2 Fantasies

Grand Ballo Du Court, Le see 2 Dances And 2 Fantasies

ADRIAN LE ROY: 10 COMPOSITIONS see Le Roy, Adrien

ADVENTLIEDER, 3 see Burkhart, Franz

AEHRENLESE see Thienemann, H.

AELFEDANS see Grieg, Edvard Hagerup

AGORA VINIESE UN VIENTO see Canciones Antiguas, 6

AGRIPPINA; A CHEERFUL OPERA IN THREE ACTS see Handel, George Frideric

AGUADO, DIONISIO (1784-1849)
Adagio, MIN 345 I/IB2

Aguado-Brevier I/IA

Allegro I/IB2

Allegro Brillante I/IB2

Andante in A I/IB2

Andante, MIN 68 see Aguado-Brevier

Andante, MIN 69 see Aguado-Brevier

Andante, MIN 70 see Aguado-Brevier

Andante, MIN 353 I/IB2

Arpeggio Etude I/IA

Collection De 50 Estudios see Studies, 50

Escuela De Guitarra II, VI-Mixed Coll, VII-Mixed Coll

Estudios Elementales, 50 see Studies, 50

Etude Brilliante I/IA

Etuden, 24, Und 10 Tonleiterstudien I/IA

Etuden, 24, Und 10 Tonleiterstudien Fur Gitarre III

Etudes, 24, Et 10 Exercices De Gammes see Etuden, 24, Und 10 Tonleiterstudien

Etudes, 24, Et 10 Exercices De Gammes Pour Guitare see Etuden, 24, Und 10 Tonleiterstudien Fur Gitarre

AGUADO, DIONISIO (cont'd.)

Fandango Variado I/IB2

Fandango Y Variaciones I/IB2

Gitarrenschule see Escuela De Guitarra

Gran Metodo Completo Para Guitarra, Con Una Recopilacion De Estudios Originales De Autores Celebres see Escuela De Guitarra

Grande Methode see Escuela De Guitarra

Kleine Gitarrenstucke, 31, In Fortschreitender Ordnung I/IA

Leichte Walzer Und Etuden I/IB2

Lessons, 8 I/IA

Methode De Guitare see Escuela De Guitarra

Methode Elementaire see Escuela De Guitarra

Metodo Completo De Guitarra see Escuela De Guitarra

Metodo De Guitarra see Escuela De Guitarra

Metodo Per Chitarra see Escuela De Guitarra

Minuet And Waltz I/IB2

Minuet, MIN 65 see Aguado-Brevier

Minuet, MIN 66 see Aguado-Brevier

Minuet, MIN 67 see Aguado-Brevier

Minuet, MIN 354 I/IB2

2 Minuetos Y 2 Estudios I/IA, I/IB2

6 Minuetos I/IB2

Minuetto I/IB2

3 Rondos Brillantes I/IB2

Studi, 51, Ad Uso Dei Conservatori I/IA

Studies, 50 I/IA

Three Studies I/IA

Two Minuets I/IB2

6 Valses I/IB2

Variaciones Brillantes I/IB2

AGUADO-BREVIER see Aguado, Dionisio

AGUINALDO see Sojo, Vincente E.

AGUIRRE, JULIAN (1868-1924)
Aire Criollo No. 1 I/IB4

Aire Criollo No. 3 I/IB4

Canciones No. 1, 2 y 3 I/IB4

Triste No. 1 I/IIA1

Triste No. 4 I/IB4

Tristes 1, 2 y 5 I/IB4

AH! VOUS DIRAI-JE MAMAN ET 13 DUOS DU 18ME SIECLE see Anonymous

AHSLUND, ULF-G.
Den Gula Rosen I/IB4

Gitarrskola, Spela I Grupp II

Gitarrskola, Spela I Grupp, Supp.2 II, III, VI-Mixed Coll

Gitarrskola, Spela I Grupp, Suppl. 1 II

Gitarrskola, Spela I Grupp, Suppl. 3 II

Hosten I/IB4

Lararhandledning see Gitarrskola, Spela I Grupp, Suppl. 1

Ljudband see Gitarrskola, Spela I Grupp, Suppl. 3

Rytmico I/IB4

AHSLUND, ULF-G. (cont'd.)

Samklang, Method For Group Tuition, Vol. 1 II

Samklang, Method For Group Tuition, Vol. 2 II

Suite No. 3 I/IB4

Suite No. 4 see Hosten

Teknikovningar see Gitarrskola, Spela I Grupp, Supp.2

AIN BOER I/IIA4

AIR see Dowland, John

AIR ANCIEN (AMARYLLIS) see Louis XIII, King of France, Amaryllis

AIR AND GALLIARD see Dowland, John

AIR AND GIGUE see Dowland, John, Mrs. Vaux's Jig

AIR MIT VARIATIONEN see Handel, George Frideric

AIR ON THE G-STRING see Bach, Johann Sebastian, Suite for Orchestra, BWV 1068, in D, Air

AIR TENDRE see Lully, Jean-Baptiste (Lulli)

AIR UND BOURREE see Telemann, Georg Philipp

AIR UND COURANTE see Vallet, Nicolas

AIRE CRIOLLO NO. 1 see Aguirre, Julian

AIRE CRIOLLO NO. 3 see Aguirre, Julian

AIRE DE JOROPO see Canonico, Benito

AIRE DE LA MANCHE see Moreno Torroba, Federico

AIRE DE VIDALITA see Vidalita, Cancion Argentina

AIRE VENEZOLANO see Sojo, Vincente E.

AIRE Y DONAIRE see Rodrigo, Joaquin

AIRES DE MOCHIMA, VALZER VENEZUELANO see Calzadilla, Roman

AIRES REGIONALES ESPANOLAS see Ausgewahlte Stucke Alter Und Neuer Meister Fur Gitarre, Vol. 2

AIRS DE COUR, 5 see Sanz, Gaspar, Suite in E minor

AIRS DE COURS, 15, EN FORME DE SUITE I/IIB5-Coll

AIRS DE DANSE, 3 see Dieupart, C.

AIRS DE DANSE, 5 see Sanz, Gaspar

AIRS POPULAIRES CUBAINS, 2 see Brouwer, Leo

AIRS POPULAIRES DE TCHECOSLOVAQUI I/IIB1, I/IIB2

22 AIRS POPULAIRES EN DUO see Cahiers Du Guitarolier, Les, Vol. 1

AIRS RUSSES, 3 see Praf, [Fray] Benedicto

AKERMAN, SIGVARD
Gitarr- Och Lutaspelets ABC, Skola For Fingerspelning II

AKKOORDENREEKSEN VOOR GITAAR see Bossu, Marcel, Suite d'Accords Pour Guitare

AKROASIS see Fritsch, Johannes Georg

AL ATARDECER EN LOS JARDINES DE ARLAJA see Pedrell, Carlos

AL PIE DE LA CRUZ DEL ROQUE see Sanchez, Blas

AL SON DE LOS ARROYUELOS see Canciones Del Siglo XVII, 5

ALA ORILLA DEL TORMES see Bielsa, Valentin

ALARD, JEAN-DELPHIN (1815-1888)
Etude, Op. 19, in A I/IB3

ALAS I HAVE LOST MY LOVE see Mozart, Wolfgang Amadeus

ALBA see Haug, Hans

ALBADA see Moreno Torroba, Federico

ALBAYALDE see Marco, Tomas

ALBENIZ, ISAAC (1860-1909)
Alborada I/IB3

Angustia, Romanza Sin Palabras I/IB3

Aragon, Fantasia I/IB3

Asturias, Leyenda, Preludio I/IB3

Asturias, Preludio. No. 1 De "Cantos De Espana, Op. 232 [sic] see Asturias, Leyenda, Preludio

Automne, L' I/IB3

Bajo De La Palmera I/IB3, I/IIA2

Bajo La Palmera I/IIA1

Barcarolle I/IB3

Barcarolle, Op. 23 I/IB3

Cadiz, Saeta see Cadiz, Serenata

Cadiz, Serenata I/IB3, I/IIA1

Capricho Catalan I/IB3

Castilla, Seguidillas I/IB3, I/IIA1

Cataluna, Corrando I/IB3

Cielo Sin Nobes I/IB3

Cordoba I/IB3, I/IIA1

Cuba, Capricho I/IIA1

Danza Espanola, No. 1 I/IB3

Danza Espanola, No. 3 I/IB3

Danza Espanola, No. 6 I/IB3

En La Alhambra, Capricho Morisco I/IB3

En La Playa, Recuerdo I/IB3

Evocacion I/IIA1

Gavotte I/IB3

Gavotte, Op. 92, No. 1 I/IB3

Granada I/IIA1

Granada, Serenata I/IB3

Intermedia De "Pepita Jimenez" I/IB3

Malaguena I/IB3
see also Rumores De La Caleta, Malaguena

Mallorca, Barcarola I/IIA1

Mallorca, Barcelona I/IB3

Minueto A Sylvia I/IB3

Motivos De Navarra I/IB3

Oriental I/IB3, I/IIA1

Pavan, MIN 202 I/IIA1

Pavana Capricho I/IB3

Plegaria I/IB3

Polo, El, Impressione I/IB3

Polonesa I/IB3

Prelude, Op. 165, No. 1 I/IB3

Puerta De Tierra, Bolero I/IB3

Rumores De La Caleta, Malaguena I/IB3, I/IIA1

Seguidillas I/IB3

Serenade, Op. 165, No. 4 I/IB3

Serenata Arabe I/IB3

Sevilla, Sevillanas I/IB3, I/IIA1

Sous Le Palmier [Bajo La Palmera], Danse Espagnole I/IB3

Staccato I/IB3

Tango I/IB3, I/IIA1

ALBENIZ, ISAAC (cont'd.)

Tango Espagnol I/IB3

Tango Espanol I/IIA1

Torre Bermeja, Serenata I/IB3,
I/IIA1

Zambra I/IB3

Zambra Granadina I/IB3

Zortziko I/IB3

ALBENIZ, MATEO (ANTONIO PEREZ DE)
(ca. 1797-1831)
Sonata in D I/IB2

ALBERO DI NATALI, L' see Celebri
Melodie Natalizie

ALBERT, HEINRICH (1870-1950)
Duo No. 1 in C I/IIA1

Duo No. 2 in A minor I/IIA1

Duo No. 3 in C I/IIA1

Duo No. 4 in G I/IIA1

Duo No. 5 in E minor I/IIA1

Duo No. 6 in D I/IIA1

Duo No. 7 in A I/IIA1

Duo No. 8 in E I/IIA1

Gitarre Als Solo-Instrument, Die see
Lehrgang Des Kunstlerischen
Gitarrespiels, Vol. III

Gitarre-Etuden-Werk, Vol. 1:
Elementarstufe I/IA, I/IIA1

Gitarre-Etuden-Werk, Vol. 2: Obere
Elementarstufe I/IA

Gitarre-Etuden-Werk, Vol. 3:
Mittelstufe I/IA

Gitarre-Etuden-Werk, Vol. 4: Obere
Mittelstufe I/IA

Gitarre-Etuden-Werk, Vol. 5:
Oberstufe I/IA

Gitarre-Etuden-Werk, Vol. 6:
Reifestufe I/IA

Gitarre-Solospiel-Studien, Vol. 1:
Zur Einfuhrung Fur Anfanger I/IA

Gitarre-Solospiel-Studien, Vol. 2:
Weiterentwicklung Fur
Fortgeschrittene I/IA

Gitarre-Solospiel-Studien, Vol. 3:
Nebenlagen, Vortrag, Solospiel
I/IA

Gitarrelied, Das see Lehrgang Des
Kunstlerischen Gitarrespiels,
Vol. II

Lehrgang Des Kunstlerischen
Gitarrespiels, Fur Lehrzwecke Und
Zum Selbstunterricht, Vol. I-A
II

Lehrgang Des Kunstlerischen
Gitarrespiels, Fur Lehrzwecke Und
Zum Selbstunterricht, Vol. I-B
II

Lehrgang Des Kunstlerischen
Gitarrespiels, Vol. II II, III,
VII-Mixed Coll

Lehrgang Des Kunstlerischen
Gitarrespiels, Vol. III II, III

Lehrgang Des Kunstlerischen
Gitarrespiels, Vol. IV II, III

Sonaten, 2 I/IC

Sonatinen, 3 I/IC

Sonatinen, 3 I/IIA2

Studies, 12, Vol. 1: Elementary Grade
see Gitarre-Etuden-Werk, Vol. 1:
Elementarstufe

Studies, 12, Vol. 2: Elementary Grade
see Gitarre-Etuden-Werk, Vol. 2:
Obere Elementarstufe

Studies, 12, Vol. 3: Moderately
Difficult see Gitarre-Etuden-
Werk, Vol. 3: Mittelstufe

ALBERT, HEINRICH (cont'd.)

Studies, 12, Vol. 4: Moderately
Difficult see Gitarre-Etuden-
Werk, Vol. 4: Obere Mittelstufe

Studies, 12, Vol. 5: Difficult see
Gitarre-Etuden-Werk, Vol. 5:
Oberstufe

Studies, 12, Vol. 6: Difficult see
Gitarre-Etuden-Werk, Vol. 6:
Reifestufe

Virtuose Gitarrespiels, Das see
Lehrgang Des Kunstlerischen
Gitarrespiels, Vol. IV

Volkslied Zur Gitarre, Das see
Lehrgang Des Kunstlerischen
Gitarrespiels, Fur Lehrzwecke Und
Zum Selbstunterricht, Vol. I-A;
Lehrgang Des Kunstlerischen
Gitarrespiels, Fur Lehrzwecke Und
Zum Selbstunterricht, Vol. I-B

ALBERTO, A.
Kleine Gitarre- Und Lauten-Schule II

ALBINI, FELIX (1600?- ?)
Primavera, La, For Medium Voice And
Orchestra V/ii

ALBINONI, TOMASO (1671-1750)
Adagio in G minor I/IB1

Beruhmtes Adagio, Nach Einem
Themenfragment Mit Beziffertem
Generalbass I/IB1

Sonata in A minor I/IIB1

ALBORADA see Albeniz, Isaac; Behrend,
Siegfried

ALBORADA, CAJITA DE MUSICA see
Tarrega, Francisco

ALBORADA, CAPRICHO see Tarrega,
Francisco

ALBORADO see Tarrega, Francisco

ALBRECHTSBERGER, JOHANN GEORG
(1736-1809)
Fugue I/IB2

ALBUM: 6 BERUHMTE STUCKE I/IB1-Coll

ALBUM see Beethoven, Ludwig van

ALBUM see Lully, Jean-Baptiste (Lulli)

ALBUM see Schumann, Robert (Alexander)

ALBUM I/IB6-Coll, VII-Mixed Coll

ALBUM CLASSIQUE I/IB6-Coll,
VII-Mixed Coll

ALBUM COMPLETO DE ANA MAGDALENA BACH, 2
VOLS. see Bach, Johann Sebastian

ALBUM DE ESTUDIOS Y PIEZAS FACILES,
PARA ALTERNAR CON EL LIBRO 1 I/IA

ALBUM DE ESTUDIOS Y PIEZAS FACILES,
PARA ALTERNAR CON EL LIBRO 2 I/IA

ALBUM DI 10 PEZZI, PER LA FORMAZIONE
MUSICALE E TECNICA DEL CHITARRISTA
see Bach, Johann Sebastian

ALBUM DI MUSICHE PER CHITARRA
I/IB6-Coll

ALBUM HENRY PURCELL see Purcell, Henry

ALBUM: MARCHA, BAGATELA, SICILIANA,
CANCION see Schumann, Robert
(Alexander)

ALBUM, NO. 1 see Tarrega, Francisco

ALBUM NO. 1 see Bach, Johann Sebastian

ALBUM, NO. 2 see Tarrega, Francisco

ALBUM, NO. 3 see Tarrega, Francisco

ALBUM, NO. 4 see Tarrega, Francisco

ALBUM, NO. 5 see Tarrega, Francisco

ALBUM, NO. 6 see Tarrega, Francisco

ALBUM, NO. 7 see Tarrega, Francisco

ALBUM, NO. 8 see Tarrega, Francisco

ALBUM, NO. 9 I/IB6-Coll,
VII-Mixed Coll

ALBUM, NO. 10 see Tarrega, Francisco

ALBUM, NO. 11 see Tarrega, Francisco

ALBUM, NO. 12 I/IB6-Coll,
VII-Mixed Coll

ALBUM, NO. 13 I/IB6-Coll,
VII-Mixed Coll

ALBUM, NO. 14 I/IB6-Coll, VI-Coll

ALBUM, NO. 15 I/IB6-Coll, VI-Coll

ALBUM, NO. 16 I/IB6-Coll, VI-Coll

ALBUM, NO. 17 see Tarrega, Francisco

ALBUM, NO. 18 I/IB6-Coll,
VII-Mixed Coll

ALBUM, NO. 19 see Tarrega, Francisco

ALBUM, NO. 20 see Tarrega, Francisco

ALBUM NO. 21 see Tarrega, Francisco

ALBUM NO. 22 see Tarrega, Francisco

ALBUM NO. 23 see Tarrega, Francisco

ALBUM PER LA GIOVENTU, 6 PEZZI, OP. 68,
NOS. 1-3, 5, 16, 18 see Schumann,
Robert (Alexander)

ALBUM PRIMO I/IB6-Coll

ALBUM RICREATIVO, NO. 1 I/IB6-Coll,
VII-Mixed Coll

ALBUM RICREATIVO, NO. 2 I/IB6-Coll,
VII-Mixed Coll

ALBUM RICREATIVO, NO. 3 I/IB6-Coll,
VI-Mixed Coll, VII-Mixed Coll

ALBUM RICREATIVO, NO. 4 I/IB6-Coll,
I/IIA1-Coll, VII-Mixed Coll

ALBUM RICREATIVO, NO. 5 I/IB6-Coll,
VII-Mixed Coll

ALBUM, VOL. I see Tarrega, Francisco

ALBUM, VOL. II: SEIS [SIC] PRELUDIOS
see Tarrega, Francisco

ALBUM, VOL. III see Tarrega, Francisco

ALBUMBLATT see Rebay, Ferdinand;
Schumann, Robert (Alexander)

ALBUMBLATT "FUR ELISE" see Beethoven,
Ludwig van, Fur Elise

ALCALAY, LUCIA
Night-Club Pieces V/i

ALDELAND, NILS
Elementar Improvisation, Vol. I II

Elementar Improvisation, Vol. II II

Elementary Improvisations, Vol. I:
Method see Elementar
Improvisation, Vol. I

Elementary Improvisations, Vol. II:
Teacher's Handbook see Elementar
Improvisation, Vol. II

Gitarrskola see Elementar
Improvisation, Vol. I

Lararhandledning see Elementar
Improvisation, Vol. II

ALEGRES RINCONES, VALSE VENEZOLANA see
Berti, Oscar

ALETEO DE PAJARITO see Degese, Vicente

ALFONSO, JAVIER (1905-   )
Suite En Style Ancien (After Campion)
I/IIIA

ALFONSO, NICOLAS
Cantilene I/IB4

Etudes, 3 I/IA

Guitare Theorique Et Pratique,
Methode Complete, La, Vol. I II

Guitare Theorique Et Pratique,
Methode Complete, La, Vol. II II

Pastorale see Ya Van Los Pastores

Ya Van Los Pastores I/IB4, IV/I

ALFONSO X, EL SABIO, KING OF CASTILE
(1221-1284)
Cantiga LX see 2 Cantigas

Cantiga LXV see 2 Cantigas

ALFONSO X, EL SABIO, KING OF CASTILE
(cont'd.)

   2 Cantigas I/IB1

   Rosa Das Rosas, Cantiga I/IB1

ALGO, 2 PEZZI PER CHITARRA see
Donatoni, Franco

ALGO PARA GUITARRA see Cruz de Castro,
Carlos

ALI BABA UND DIE VIERZIG RAUBER; COMIC
OPERA IN PRELUDE AND FOUR SCENES
see Cherubini, Luigi

ALIANORA; PLAY ABOUT THE MARRIAGE OF
REYNALT VAN NASSAU, DUKE OF GELRE,
AND ALIANOR OF ENGLAND see Horst,
Anton van der

ALL IN A ROW see Duarte, John W.

ALL MEIN GEDANKEN, DIE ICH HAB see
Anonymous

ALL MORGEN IST GANZ FRISCH UND NEU see
Stern, Hermann

ALLA DANZA see Hartig, Heinz Friedrich

ALLA POLACCA see Bach, Carl Philipp
Emanuel; Tansman, Alexandre

ALLA, SOTA UNA PENYA see Villancicos
Populares, Vol. II

ALLE JAHRE WIEDER see Rinke Ranke
Rosenschein; 77 Kinderlieder

ALLEGRETTO see Gitaarduet, Het;
Carcassi, Matteo; Diabelli, Anton;
Fetler, Paul; Hummel, Johann
Nepomuk; Sor, Fernando

ALLEGRETTO see Arcas, Julian

ALLEGRETTO see Arcas, Julian

ALLEGRETTO – ALLEGRO NON TROPPO see
Bach, Johann Sebastian

ALLEGRETTO COMMODO see Legley, Victor

ALLEGRETTO ET GAVOTTE see Defossez,
Rene

ALLEGRETTO, MIN 22 see Paganini,
Niccolo

ALLEGRETTO, MIN21 see Paganini,
Niccolo

ALLEGRETTO, MIN346 see Giuliani, Mauro

ALLEGRETTO, MIN347 see Giuliani, Mauro

ALLEGRETTO SCHERZANDO see Paganini,
Niccolo

ALLEGRETTO UND WALZER AUS OP. 45 see
Sor, Fernando, Voyons Si C'est Ca,
6 Petites Pieces Faciles Nos. 2, 6

ALLEGRO see Gitaarduet, Het; Aguado,
Dionisio; Bach, Johann Sebastian,
Prelude, Fugue And Allegro For
Lute, In E: Allegro; Beethoven,
Ludwig van; Bellow, Alexander;
Carlstedt, Jan; Eklund, Hans;
Fiocco, Joseph-Hector; Giuliani,
Mauro, Sonata, Op. 15; Handel,
George Frideric; Marcello,
Benedetto; Mozart, Wolfgang
Amadeus; Pekiel, Bartlomiej; Sor,
Fernando; Stravinsky, Igor

ALLEGRO see Anonymous

ALLEGRO see Anonymous

ALLEGRO see Mozart, Wolfgang Amadeus

ALLEGRO AGITATO see Fetler, Paul

ALLEGRO, ANDANTE, MENUETTO AND ALLEGRO
see Mozart, Wolfgang Amadeus

ALLEGRO BRILLANTE see Aguado, Dionisio

ALLEGRO DA CONCERTO see Carulli,
Ferdinando

ALLEGRO E GRAZIOSO, OP. 40, NO.8, 9
see Giuliani, Mauro

ALLEGRO IN G see Carulli, Ferdinando

ALLEGRO MA NON TROPPO see Bellman,
Carl Michael

ALLEGRO, MIN291 see Ponce, Manuel
Maria

ALLEGRO, MIN293 see Ponce, Manuel
Maria

ALLEGRO, MIN348 see Haydn, [Franz]
Joseph

ALLEGRO MODERATO see Bellow,
Alexander; Fetler, Paul

ALLEGRO MOLTO see Eklund, Hans;
Stadlmair, Hans; Wilson, Thomas

ALLEGRO NON TROPPO (FROM GRANDE SONATE,
OP. 25) see Sor, Fernando

ALLEGRO RISOLUTO see Legley, Victor

ALLEGRO SPIRITOSO see Giuliani, Mauro,
Sonata, Op. 15

ALLEIN GOTT IN DER HOH' SEI EHR' see
Bach, Johann Sebastian

ALLEMANDE AYMEE DE L'AUTEUR see
Corbetta, Francesco (Francisque
Corbett)

ALLEMANDE, CHERIE DE SON ALTESSE LE DUC
D'YORK see Corbetta, Francesco
(Francisque Corbett)

ALLEMANDE DE LA SUITE III PARA LAUD
see Bach, Johann Sebastian, Suite
for Lute, BWV 995, in G minor,
Allemand

ALLEMANDE DU ROY see Corbetta,
Francesco (Francisque Corbett)

ALLEMANDE ET GIGUE see Corbetta,
Francesco (Francisque Corbett)

ALLEMANDE FORTUNE HELAS POURQUOI see
Vallet, Nicolas

ALLEMANDE SUISSE, L' see Carpentier,
[Abbe] Joseph

ALLEMANDE SUR LA MORT DU DUC DE
GLOCESTER see Corbetta, Francesco
(Francisque Corbett)

ALLEMANDE UND GALLIARD see Robinson,
Thomas

ALLERLEI SPIELMUSIK see Uhl, Alfred

ALLERLEI VOLKSLIEDER see Anonymous

ALLISON, RICHARD (ca. 1600)
   Pavan I/IB1

ALLOTROPIE, FOR ORCHESTRA WITH MULTIPLE
ARTICULATION see Kayn, Roland

ALMAIN UND JIG see Cutting, Francis

ALMAND AND MINUET see Purcell, Henry

ALMEIDA, LAURINDO (1917-   )
   Guitar Tutor, An Up-To-Date Classic
   Guitar Method II

ALPENLANDISCHE VOLKSTANZE I/IB5-Coll

ALPENLANDISCHE WEISEN, VOL. I-IV
I/IB5-Coll

ALS DE GROTE KLOKKE LUIDT see Marez
Oyens, Gerrit de

ALS ICH BEI MEINEN SCHAFEN WACHT, UM
EIN LIED AUS OBERSCHLESIEN (NO. 8)
see Spitta, Heinrich

ALSO SPRACH SCHEHERAZADE, OPERA see
Hanus, Jan

ALT SPANISCHER TANZ MIT VARIATIONEN
see Sor, Fernando

ALTA DANZA see Torre, Fernando delle

ALTA VITTORIA see Caroso, Fabrizio

ALTDEUTSCHE LAUTENMUSIK I/IB1-Coll

ALTDEUTSCHE LAUTENTANZE, 2 see
Anonymous

ALTDEUTSCHER TANZ see Bachmann, Helmut

ALTE DEUTSCHE SPRUCHWEISHEIT see
Hubschmann, Werner

3 ALTE DUOS I/IIA1-Coll

ALTE GITARRENMUSIK, VOL. 1 I/IB6-Coll

ALTE GITARRENMUSIK, VOL. 2 I/IB6-Coll

ALTE HAUSMUSIK I/IB1-Coll,
VII-Mixed Coll

ALTE LAUTENMUSIK I/IIA2, I/IIA2-Coll

ALTE MEISTER DES 17. JAHRHUNDERTS
I/IB1-Coll, I/IIA1-Coll,
VII-Mixed Coll

ALTE MEISTER UM 1600 I/IIB1-Coll

ALTE MEISTER UM 1700 I/IIB1-Coll

ALTE MINNELIEDER I/IB1-Coll,
I/IIB1-Coll, I/IIC2-Coll

ALTE POLNISCHE LAUTENMUSIK I/IIA2-Coll

ALTE SPANISCHE MEISTER I/IB1-Coll

ALTE SPANISCHE MEISTER I/IB1-Coll

ALTE SPIELMUSIK I/IIB1-Coll,
VII-Mixed Coll

ALTE TANZSTUCKE (16.-18. JAHRHUNDERT),
VOL. I I/IIB1-Coll

ALTE TANZSTUCKE (16.-18. JAHRHUNDERT),
VOL. II I/IIB1-Coll

ALTE UND NEUE MUSIK ZUM SINGEN UND
SPIELEN AUF BLOCKFLOTEN, GEIGEN UND
LAUTENINSTRUMENTE I/IB4-Coll,
I/IIA1-Coll, I/IIA2-Coll,
I/IIB1-Coll, I/IIB2-Coll,
I/IIC1-Coll, I/IIC2-Coll,
I/IIC3-Coll, IV/IIB2,
VII-Mixed Coll

ALTE UND NEUE WEIHNACHTSLIEDER IV/IIB1

ALTE WEIHNACHTSMUSIK, SPIELSTUCKE UND
LIEDER IV/IIB3, IV/IIC2,
VII-Mixed Coll

ALTE ZUPFMUSIK see Handel, George
Frideric

ALTENGLISCHE LAUTENMUSIK I/IB1-Coll

ALTES RUSSISCHES LIED I/IB5

ALTFLAMISCHE TANZE see Susato, Tielman

ALTFRANZOSISCHE LAUTENMUSIK I/IB1-Coll

ALTFRANZOSISCHE MEISTER I/IB1-Coll

ALTFRANZOSISCHE VOLKSLIEDER, 4,
PASTOURELLES FROM THE 18TH CENT.
see Anonymous

ALTINDIANISCHE TANZE see Graetzer,
Guillermo

ALTISSIMI, FRANCO
   Giochi d'Acqua I/IB4

ALTITALIENISCHE ARIEN I/IIC1-Coll

ALTITALIENISCHE LAUTENMUSIK I/IB1-Coll

ALTJAPANISCHE GEISHALIEDER, 5
I/IIC1-Coll

ALTLOTHRINGER HIRTENMUSIK see
Schaller, Erwin

ALTPOLNISCHE MUSIK I/IB1-Coll

ALTRUSSISCHE VOLKSWEISEN I/IB5-Coll

ALTSPANISCHE LAUTENMUSIK I/IB1-Coll

ALTSPANISCHE SUITE see Leukauf, Robert

ALTWIENER TANZE I/IIA1-Coll

ALZBETINSKA SERENADA see Binge, Ronald

AM LUSTIGEN STRAND see Nordische
Volkslieder

AMAGA see Mengelberg, Misja

AMANDA, FOR CHAMBER ORCHESTRA see
Maderna, Bruno

AMARILLI see Three 17th Century Airs

AMARYLLIS see Louis XIII, King of
France

AMATO, ANGELO
   Prime Lezioni Di Chitarra, Le II

AMAZING GRACE see Blues And
Spirituals; Gitarre Spezial,
Picking Modern Arrangement, Vol. 1

AMBROSIUS, HERMANN (1897- ?)
   Eggersberger Trio I/IIA2

   Exotischer Tanz see Impressionen

   Impressionen I/IB4

AMBROSIUS, HERMANN (cont'd.)

Melancholie see Impressionen

Neckerei see Impressionen

Prelude I/IB4

Traum see Impressionen

Ubermut see Impressionen

AMERICAN SUITE, FOR HARPSICHORD AND ORCHESTRA see Heider, Werner

AMOR Y ODIO, TONADILLA see Granados, Enrique

AMORS, AMORS, TROP ME FIERS DE TES DARS see Ghizeghem, Hayne van

AMPHORA see Eastwood, Thomas

AMY, GILBERT (1936-   )
Antiphonies Pour 2 Orchestres V/i

Cette Etoile Enseigne A s'Incliner V/ii

d'Un Espace Deploye, For Soprano, 2 Pianos And 2 Orchestral Groups V/ii

Refrains, For Orchestra V/i

Sonata Pian' E Forte, For Soprano, Mezzo-Soprano And Twelve Players V/ii

AN DIE MUSIK, A HYMN see Biebl, Franz

ANDALUSA see Gangi, Mario

ANDALUZA see Granados, Enrique, Danza Espanola, No. 5

ANDANTE see Sor, Fernando, Mes Ennuis, Six Bagatelles, Op. 43, No. 5; Sor, Fernando, Voyons Si C'est Ca, 6 Petites Pieces Faciles, Op. 45, No. 5

ANDANTE, ALTES VOLKSLIED see Putilin, Ivan

ANDANTE ARMONIOSO, TEMA DI AUTORE IGNOTO see Pezzoli, Giorgio

ANDANTE CANTABILE see Sor, Fernando, Mes Ennuis, Six Bagatelles, Op. 43, No. 3

ANDANTE CON MOTO see Diabelli, Anton

ANDANTE DE LA CASACION see Mozart, Wolfgang Amadeus

ANDANTE ESPRESSIVO see Fetler, Paul; Pekiel, Bartlomiej

ANDANTE GRAVE see Cano, Antonio

ANDANTE GRAZIOSO see Carulli, Ferdinando

ANDANTE LARGO see Sor, Fernando

ANDANTE LARGO, C MAJOR see Mendelssohn-Bartholdy, Felix

ANDANTE MAESTOSO see Sor, Fernando

ANDANTE MAESTOSO, OP.11, NO.6 see Sor, Fernando

ANDANTE MIT VARIATIONEN see Beethoven, Ludwig van

ANDANTE POCO DECISO see Pekiel, Bartlomiej

ANDANTE, QUASI ADAGIO see Legley, Victor

ANDANTE SOSTENUTO see Bellman, Carl Michael; Diabelli, Anton; Urban, Stepan

ANDANTE UND MENUETT see Haydn, [Franz] Joseph

2 ANDANTES see Beethoven, Ludwig van

6 ANDANTI see Carulli, Ferdinando

ANDANTINO see Bach, Johann Sebastian, Prelude, BWV 930, in F; Carlstedt, Jan; Diabelli, Anton; Giuliani, Mauro; Kovats, Barna; Paganini, Niccolo; Paganini, Niccolo; Quaglino, Anacleto; Sor, Fernando; Sor, Fernando, Vingt Quatre Lecons Progressives, Dediees Aux Eleves Commencants, Op 31., No. 5

ANDANTINO AND WALTZ see Carulli, Ferdinando

ANDANTINO, CORAL see Schumann, Robert (Alexander)

ANDANTINO E VALZER see Rossi, Abner

ANDANTINO GRAZIOSO see Legley, Victor

ANDANTINO IN A MINOR see Paganini, Niccolo

ANDANTINO, MIN 19 see Paganini, Niccolo

ANDANTINO, MIN 20 see Paganini, Niccolo

ANDANTINO, MIN355 see Giuliani, Mauro

ANDANTINO, MIN356 see Giuliani, Mauro

ANDANTINO, OP.2 see Sor, Fernando

ANDANTINO, OP.13, NO.3 see Sor, Fernando

ANDANTINO, OP.31, NO.5 see Sor, Fernando

ANDANTINO, OP. 54 [SIC] see Sor, Fernando

ANDANTINO QUASI ALLEGRETTO see Staak, Pieter van der

ANDANTINO SERENO see Mosso, Carlo

ANDREOLLI, MARIANO
Corso Preparatorio Di Chitarra II

ANDRES SEGOVIA ALBUM OF GUITAR SOLOS I/IB6-Coll, VII-Mixed Coll

ANDRIESSEN, JURRIAAN (1925-   )
Ars Antiquae Musicae; Casual Music For Connoisseurs And Amateurs V/i

Sonata Da Camera see Trio No. 5

Summer-Dances V/i

Symphony No. 5 V/i

Time Spirit, For Clarinet And Orchestra see Symphony No. 5

Trio No. 5 I/IIB2

ANDRIESSEN, LOUIS (1939-   )
Concept I, Per 2 Pianisti E 3 Gruppi Strumentali see Ittrospezione III

Hoketus V/i

Ittrospezione III V/i

Nine Symphonies Of Beethoven, The, For Promenade Orchestra And Ice-Cream Bell V/i

Principe, Il, Quotations From "The Ruler" Of N. Machiavelli V/ii

Staat, De, For Solo Voices And Orchestra V/ii

ANDRYSZAK, ALES
Schule Der Konzertgitarre, Die: Grund- Und Mittelstufe II

ANFANGER-ETUDEN FUR GITARRE, 25 see Sor, Fernando, Introduction A l'Etude De La Guitare En Vingt Cinq Lecons Progressives

ANFANGER-SCHULE FUR GITARRE see Leeb, Hermann

ANFANGSUNTERRICHT IM GITARRESPIEL, DER, VOL. I see Peter, Ursula

ANFANGSUNTERRICHT IM GITARRESPIEL, DER, VOL. II see Peter, Ursula

ANFANGSUNTERRICHT IM GITARRESPIEL, DER, VOL. III see Peter, Ursula

ANGEL, MIGUEL
Cuatro Muleros, Los, Tema Y Variaciones I/IB4

Fingerboardchart see Nomenclature

Homenaje A Schoenberg, 6 Preludios, Op. 24 I/IB4

Mecanismo Didactico Para Guitarra III

Nomenclature III

ANGER DANCE see Stevenson, Ronald

ANGLAISE see Mozart, Leopold

ANGLOISE see Weiss, Sylvius Leopold

ANGOLO VISIVO see Zuccheri, Luciano

ANGOSTURA, VALSE VENEZOLANO see Lauro, Antonio

ANGUILA, LA see Azpiazu, Jose de

ANGUSTIA, ROMANZA SIN PALABRAS see Albeniz, Isaac

ANIDO, MARIA LUISA
Cuaderno Tecnico-Recreativo, Para Alumnos De Guitarra (Preparatorio) II

ANIMALS, THE see Topper, Guido, Suite No. 1

ANITRA'S DANCE see Grieg, Edvard Hagerup

ANNA LIVIA PLURABELLE, FOR SOLO VOICES AND SOLO INSTRUMENTS see Hodeir, Andre

ANON. IN LOVE; 6 ANONYMOUS 16TH- AND 17TH-CENTURY LYRICS see Walton, [Sir] William (Turner)

ANONYMOUS
Ah! Vous Dirai-Je Maman Et 13 Duos Du 18me Siecle I/IIA1

All Mein Gedanken, Die Ich Hab I/IIC2-Coll

Allegro see Englische Tanze, 3

Allegro see Englische Tanze, 3

Allerlei Volkslieder I/IIB2-Coll, I/IIC2-Coll, IV/IIB2, IV/IIC2

Altdeutsche Lautentanze, 2 I/IB1

Altfranzosische Volkslieder, 4, Pastourelles From The 18th Cent. I/IIC1

Andante, MIN 237 see Englische Tanze, 3

Anonymous Elisabethan Duets, 2 I/IIA1

Antike Tanze Und Arien I/IB1

Aus Altitalienischen Lautenbuchern I/IB1

Aus Einer Lautenhandschrift Des 16. Jahrhunderts I/IB1

Baltische Suite I/IB1

Barcarolle, MIN 79 I/IB1

Bourree see 4 Piezas Del S. XVIII

Burgalesa, Nach Einer Altspanischen Melodie Aus Burgos see Romance, MIN 141

Courante see 4 Piezas Del S. XVIII

Dindandon I/IB1

Dindirindin, Villancico I/IIC1

En Avila Mis Ojos, Romance I/IIC1

Englische Tanze, 3 I/IIB1

Fantasy, MIN 73 I/IB1

Fantasy No. 7 I/IB1

Fantasy No. 11 I/IB1

Gagliarda Del Passo Mezzo I/IB1

Greensleeves I/IB1, I/IIA1, I/IIC1

Greensleeves To A Ground I/IIB1

Italienische Canzonetten, 4, Aus Dem 16. Jahrhundert I/IIC1

Lute Duets, 2 I/IIA1

Mazurka I/IIA1

More Of These Anon; 10 Anonymous Pieces I/IIA1

Muscadin I/IIA1

Non Ardu Chiu see Italienische Canzonetten, 4, Aus Dem 16. Jahrhundert

ANONYMOUS (cont'd.)

Notturno   see Romance, MIN 141

Nurnberger Lautenbuch: Part 1
I/IB1-Coll

Nurnberger Lautenbuch: Part 2
I/IB1-Coll

Nurnberger Lautenbuch: Part 3
I/IB1-Coll

Ophelia   see 2 Piezas Para Laud Del
Teatro De Shakespeare

Orlando Fa Che Ti Raccordi   see
Italienische Canzonetten, 4, Aus
Dem 16. Jahrhundert

Pieces Sans Titre   I/IIA1

2 Piezas Para Laud Del Teatro De
Shakespeare   I/IB1

4 Piezas Del S. XVIII   I/IB1

Preambl, Ein   see Altdeutsche
Lautentanze, 2

Prelude Et Menuet (Re Mineur)   I/IB1

Rigodon   see 4 Piezas Del S. XVIII

Romanca d'Espagna   see Romance, MIN
141

Romance Anonimo   I/IB3, I/IIA1
see also Romance, MIN 141

Romance D'Amour   I/IIA3
see also Romance, MIN 141

Romance De Amor   see Romance, MIN 141

Romance De Amor Original   see
Romance, MIN 141

Romance De Amor, Theme Song   see
Romance, MIN 141

Romance, MIN 141   I/IB3

Saraband   see 4 Piezas Del S. XVIII

Siate Avvertiti   see Italienische
Canzonetten, 4, Aus Dem 16.
Jahrhundert

Sick Tune, The   I/IB1
see also 2 Piezas Para Laud Del
Teatro De Shakespeare

Sonatina for 2 Guitars   I/IIA1

Spanish Romance   see Romance, MIN 141

Suite in D minor, MIN 331   I/IIB1

Suite in F   I/IIB1

Suite in G, MIN 330   I/IB1

Suite in G minor, MIN 329   I/IIB1

Tant Que Vivray   I/IB1, I/IIC1

Tanze, 8   I/IIA1

Teutscher Tantz, Ein   see Altdeutsche
Lautentanze, 2

To Name But None   I/IIA1

Trio in F, MIN 409   I/IIB2

Troika, Altrussisches Volkslied
I/IIC1-Coll

Variationen Uber "Greensleeves"
I/IIA1

Vorria, Madonna   see Italienische
Canzonetten, 4, Aus Dem 16.
Jahrhundert

ANONYMOUS ELISABETHAN DUETS, 2   see
Anonymous

6 ANONYMOUS LUTE SOLOS   I/IB1-Coll

ANORANZA   see Granados, Enrique

ANORANZA LEJANA   see Sainz de la Maza,
Eduardo

ANOTHER ENCORE FOR YEPES   see Visser,
Dick

ANTHOLOGIE DE LA MUSIQUE ANCIENNE, VOL.
I: POUR LE LUTH   I/IB1-Coll

ANTHOLOGIE DE LA MUSIQUE ANCIENNE, VOL.
II: POUR LA GUITARE   I/IB1-Coll

ANTHOLOGIE POUR LA GUITARE ESPAGNOLE
see Sanz, Gaspar

ANTHOLOGIE SUR DES AIRS DU FOLKLORE
FRANCAIS   I/IB5-Coll

ANTI- EN SYMMETRIA, STUDIE   see Visser,
Dick

ANTIGA, JEAN
Cancion De Navidad   see Tarraja, 24
Petites Pieces

Tarraja, 24 Petites Pieces   I/IB4,
IV/I

ANTIGUA CANCION FRANCESA   see
Tchaikovsky, Piotr Ilyich, Old
French Air

ANTIKE TANZE UND ARIEN   see Anonymous

ANTIPHONIES POUR 2 ORCHESTRES   see Amy,
Gilbert

ANTOLOGIA DE LA GUITARRA   see Giuliani,
Mauro

ANTOLOGIA DE LA GUITARRA, VOL. 1   see
Meissonnier, J.

ANTOLOGIA DE LOS VIHUELISTAS ESPANOLAS,
VOL. 1   I/IB1-Coll

ANTOLOGIA DE LOS VIHUELISTAS ESPANOLAS,
VOL. 2   I/IB1-Coll

ANTOLOGIA DE LOS VIHUELISTAS ESPANOLAS,
VOL. 3   I/IB1-Coll

ANTOLOGIA DE LOS VIHUELISTAS ESPANOLAS,
VOL. 4   I/IIA1-Coll

ANTOLOGIA DE LOS VIHUELISTAS ESPANOLAS,
VOL. 5   I/IB1-Coll

ANTOLOGIA DE LOS VIHUELISTAS ESPANOLAS,
VOL. 6   I/IIA1-Coll

ANTOLOGIA DE OBRAS PARA GUITARRA
I/IB6-Coll, VI-Mixed Coll

ANTOLOGIA DI CHITARRISTI DEL BAROCCO
SPAGNOLO   I/IB1-Coll

ANTOLOGIA DI MUSICA ANTICA, VOL. I
I/IB1-Coll

ANTOLOGIA DI MUSICA ANTICA, VOL. II
I/IB1-Coll

ANTOLOGIA DI MUSICA ANTICA, VOL. III
I/IB1-Coll

ANTOLOGIA DIDATTICA PER CHITARRA, DI
AUTORI ITALIANI E STRANIERI
I/IB2-Coll

ANTOLOGIA PER CHITARRA   I/IB4-Coll

ANTOLOGIA PER CHITARRA, VOL. 1
I/IB6-Coll, VII-Mixed Coll

ANTOLOGIA PER CHITARRA, VOL. 2
I/IB6-Coll, VI-Mixed Coll

ANTOLOGIA PER CHITARRA, VOL. 3
I/IB6-Coll, VI-Mixed Coll

ANTONIOU, THEODORE (1935-   )
Dialogue   I/IIB1

Epilog After Homer's Odyssey   V/ii

Lamentation   see Moirologhia For Jani
Christou

Meli   V/ii

Moirologhia For Jani Christou   V/ii

ANTRUILLES   see De Grandis, Renato

ANTUNES, JORGE (1942-   )
Sighs   I/IB4

ANZAGHI, LUIGI ORESTE (1903-1963)
Chitarra D'accompagnamento, La,
Metodo Lampo Anche Per Chi Non
Conosce La Musica   II

Chitarrista Virtuoso, Il   I/IA

Esercizi Di Tecnica, 50   III

Esercizi Di Tecnica Giornaliera, 24
III

Metodo Completo Per Chitarra,
Teoretico-Pratico Progressivo   II

Scale Semplici, A Terze, A Seste E A
Ottave   III

AO LUAR   see Beethoven, Ludwig van,
Sonata for Piano, Op. 27, No. 2, in
C sharp minor, First Movement

APARICION   see Granados, Enrique

APHORISMEN   see Schreiber, Alfred

APICIUS MODULATUS, ARTIS COQUINARIAE
PRAECEPTA MODIS NUMERISQUE
INSTRUCTA AD CANTUM CUM CITHARA
see Novak, Jan

APIVOR, DENIS (1916-   )
Canciones, 6, De Federico Garcia
Lorca   I/IIC1

Concertino, Op. 26   I/IIIA

Discanti, Op. 48   I/IB4

Saeta, Op. 53   I/IB4

Variations for Guitar, Op. 29   I/IB4

APONTE, PEDRO ARCILA
Bellas Noches De Maiquetia, Las,
Canzone Venezuelana   I/IB5

APOSTEL, HANS ERICH (1901-1972)
Es Waren Zwei Konigskinder   I/IIA3

Fantasie, Die   see Musiken, 6

Hohe Des Jahres   I/IIA3

Kleines Kammerkonzert   I/IIB2

Melodie, Die   see Musiken, 6

Musiken, 6   I/IB4

Rhythmus, Der   see Musiken, 6

Sechsklang, Der   see Musiken, 6

Study, Op. 29   I/IIB2

Ton E, Der   see Musiken, 6

Ton E, Der   see Musiken, 6

APPALACHIAN MASS   see Hunkins, Eusebia
Simpson

APPALOOSA   see Gilardino, Angelo

APPUNTI, PRELUDI E STUDI, QUADERNO I:
GLI INTERVALLI   see Castelnuovo-
Tedesco, Mario

APPUNTI, PRELUDI E STUDI, QUADERNO II:
I RITMI, PARTE I, DANZE DEL 600 E
DEL 700, NO. 1-10   see Castelnuovo-
Tedesco, Mario

APPUNTI, PRELUDI E STUDI, QUADERNO II:
I RITMI, PARTE II, DANZE DELL'
OTTOCENTE, NO. 11-16   see
Castelnuovo-Tedesco, Mario

APPUNTI, PRELUDI E STUDI, QUADERNO II:
I RITMI, PARTE III, DANZE DEL
NOVECENTO, NO. 17-22   see
Castelnuovo-Tedesco, Mario

APPUNTI, PRELUDI E STUDI, QUADERNO III:
LE FIGURAZIONE   see Castelnuovo-
Tedesco, Mario

APPUNTI, PRELUDI E STUDI, QUADERNO IV:
6 STUDI SERIALI   see Castelnuovo-
Tedesco, Mario

APUNTES, 3   see Brouwer, Leo

AQUEL CABALLERO, MADRE   see Canciones
Antiguas, 5

AQUELARRE   see Pujol, Emilio

ARABESCA   see Granados, Enrique, Danza
Espanola, No. 11

ARABESQUE   see Korn, Peter Jona

ARABINE   see Marez Oyens, Gerrit de

ARAGON, FANTASIA   see Albeniz, Isaac

ARAGONESA, SPANISCHER TANZ   see
Schneider, Heinrich

ARANCI IN FIORI   see Castelnuovo-
Tedesco, Mario

ARAUCARIA   see Gilardino, Angelo

ARCADE IV   see Humble, Keith

ARCAS, JULIAN (1832-1882)
Allegretto   see Danzas Espanolas, 2

Allegretto   see Danzas Espanolas, 2

AUS LEOPOLD MOZARTS NOTENBUCHLEIN FUR SEINEN SOHN WOLFGANG AMADEUS see Mozart, Leopold

AUS PICKERING'S LAUTENBUCH (UM 1616) I/IIA1-Coll

AUS TABULATUREN DES 16.-18. JAHRHUNDERTS I/IB1-Coll

AUS UNGARN UND DER SLOWAKEI, LIEDER UND TANZE, VOL. I see Bartok, Bela

AUS UNGARN UND DER SLOWAKEI, LIEDER UND TANZE, VOL. II see Bartok, Bela

AUS WILLIAM BRADE'S "VISBOK" I/IB1, I/IC

AUSENTE, EL, CANZONE VENEZUELANA I/IB5

AUSER see Bartolozzi, Bruno

AUSFUHRLICHE SPIELANWEISUNG FUR KINDER, EINE see Gerwig, Walter, Ich Lerne Gitarre Spielen, Vol. I

AUSFUHRLICHE SPIELANWEISUNG FUR KINDER UND JUGENDLICHE, EINE see Funck, Eike, Ich Lerne Gitarre Spielen, Vol. II

AUSGERECHNET UND VERSPIELT; EINE "SPIEL"-OPER see Krenek, Ernst

AUSGERECHNET UND VERSPIELT: INTERMEZZO I see Krenek, Ernst

AUSGEWAHLTE ETUDEN, VOL. 1: VORBEREITENDE UBUNGEN, KLEINE MUSIKSTUCKE UND ETUDEN see Sor, Fernando

AUSGEWAHLTE ETUDEN, VOL. 2: KLEINE MUSIKSTUCKE UND ETUDEN see Sor, Fernando

AUSGEWAHLTE ETUDEN, VOL. 3: KLEINE MUSIKSTUCKE UND ETUDEN see Sor, Fernando

AUSGEWAHLTE ETUDEN, VOL. 4: KLEINE MUSIKSTUCKE UND ETUDEN see Sor, Fernando

AUSGEWAHLTE ETUDEN, VOL. 5: ETUDEN see Sor, Fernando

AUSGEWAHLTE ETUDEN, VOL. 6: ETUDEN see Sor, Fernando

AUSGEWAHLTE ETUDEN, VOL. 7: ETUDEN see Sor, Fernando

AUSGEWAHLTE GITARRE WERKE, PRELIMINARY VOL. see Sor, Fernando

AUSGEWAHLTE GITARRE WERKE, VOL. 1 see Sor, Fernando

AUSGEWAHLTE GITARRE WERKE, VOL. 2 see Sor, Fernando

AUSGEWAHLTE GITARRE WERKE, VOL. 3 see Sor, Fernando

AUSGEWAHLTE LAUTENWERKE (1566-1572) see Neusiedler, Melchior

AUSGEWAHLTE LEICHTE STUCKE see Losy vom Losinthal, Jan Antonin

AUSGEWAHLTE LIEDER, 12 see Blume, Karl

AUSGEWAHLTE LIEDER, 2 VOLS. see Brahms, Johannes

AUSGEWAHLTE MENUETTE, 20 see Sor, Fernando

AUSGEWAHLTE STUCKE, 12 see Schumann, Robert (Alexander)

AUSGEWAHLTE STUCKE ALTER UND NEUER MEISTER FUR GITARRE, VOL. 1 I/IB6-Coll

AUSGEWAHLTE STUCKE ALTER UND NEUER MEISTER FUR GITARRE, VOL. 2 I/IB6-Coll

AUSGEWAHLTE STUCKE AUS EINER ANGELICA- UND GITARREN- TABULATUR DER 2. HALFTE DES 17. JAHRHUNDERTS I/IB1-Coll

AUSGEWAHLTE STUCKE FUR GITARRE see Bach, Johann Sebastian

AUSGEWAHLTE STUCKE FUR GITARRE SOLO, 30 I/IB6-Coll, VII-Mixed Coll

AUSGEWAHLTE STUDIEN, VOL. 1 see Giuliani, Mauro, Studies

AUSGEWAHLTE STUDIEN, VOL. 2 see Giuliani, Mauro, Studies

AUSGEWAHLTE UBUNGSSTUCKE, 30 see Kuffner, Joseph

AUSGEWAHLTE WALZER, 20 see Carcassi, Matteo

AUSGEWAHLTE WALZER, 20 see Sor, Fernando

AUSGEWAHLTE WERKE AUS DER AUSSEER GITARRETABULATUR DES 18. JAHRHUNDERTS I/IB1-Coll

AUTHENTIC BLUEGRASS GUITAR I/IB5-Coll

AUTOMNE, L' see Albeniz, Isaac

AUX LOGETTES DE CES BOIS see Besard, Jean-Baptiste

AUX MARCHES DU PALAIS I/IIC5-Coll

AVE MARIA see Schubert, Franz (Peter); Schubert, Franz (Peter), Ellens Gesang III; Victoria, Tomas Luis de

AWAKE SWEET LOVE see Dowland, John

AWARE see Komter, Jan Maarten

AWAY IN A MANGER see Christmas Carols, 5; Easy Christmas Carols, 2

AY DE MI, ROMANCE VIEJO see Valderrabano, Enriquez de

AY TRISTE QUE VENGO, VILLANCICO PASTORIL see Encina, Juan del

AYER, FANTASIA see Palau, Manuel

AYLESFORDER STUCKE, 8 see Handel, George Frideric

AZPIAZU, JOSE DE (1912-)
Anguila, La see Joven Guitarrista, El, Vol.2: Facil

Baile En La Aldea see Joven Guitarrista, El, Vol.2: Facil

Caballeritos De Azcoitia see Joven Guitarrista, El, Vol.1: Muy Facil

Cancion Lejana see Joven Guitarrista, El, Vol.3: Menos Facil

Capri see Joven Guitarrista, El, Vol.1: Muy Facil

Castellana see Joven Guitarrista, El, Vol.3: Menos Facil

Clavecin De Zelaia see Joven Guitarrista, El, Vol.3: Menos Facil

Columpio, El see Joven Guitarrista, El, Vol.2: Facil

Concert Baroque, In A I/IIIA

Danza De La Muneca see Joven Guitarrista, El, Vol.4: Mediana Dificultad

Dialogando see Joven Guitarrista, El, Vol.2: Facil

Estilo Flamenco, Metodo De Guitarra II

Fandango De Onate see Joven Guitarrista, El, Vol.4: Mediana Dificultad

Girasol, El see Joven Guitarrista, El, Vol.4: Mediana Dificultad

Gitarrenschule, Vol. I II, VII-Mixed Coll

Gitarrenschule, Vol. II II, VI-Mixed Coll, VII-Mixed Coll

Gitarrenschule, Vol. III II, VI-Mixed Coll, VII-Mixed Coll

Gitarrenschule, Vol. IV II, VI-Mixed Coll, VII-Mixed Coll

Gitarrenschule, Vol. V II, VI-Mixed Coll, VII-Mixed Coll

Grinzing see Joven Guitarrista, El, Vol.1: Muy Facil

Homenaje A Los Vihuelistas I/IB4

Hommage A Bela Bartok I/IB4

AZPIAZU, JOSE DE (cont'd.)

Interludio see Joven Guitarrista, El, Vol.4: Mediana Dificultad

Joven Guitarrista, El, Vol.1: Muy Facil I/IB4

Joven Guitarrista, El, Vol.2: Facil I/IB4

Joven Guitarrista, El, Vol.3: Menos Facil I/IB4

Joven Guitarrista, El, Vol.4: Mediana Dificultad I/IB4

Little Guitarist, The, Happy Learning; Preparatory Course II

Miniatures Iberiques, 5 I/IB4

Paseando see Joven Guitarrista, El, Vol.2: Facil

Pieces Faciles, Premier Cahier I/IB4

Premier Cours Pour Apprendre A Jouer De La Guitare A l'Aide De Notes Musicales Ou De Chiffres (Sans Notes) II, VII-Mixed Coll

Riberena see Joven Guitarrista, El, Vol.2: Facil

Rondino see Joven Guitarrista, El, Vol.3: Menos Facil

Salon De Artazcoz see Joven Guitarrista, El, Vol.1: Muy Facil

Sonate Basque I/IIB1

Suite Elisabethaine Sur Des Themes De John Dowland I/IIIA

Tic-Tac Del Reloj, El see Joven Guitarrista, El, Vol.3: Menos Facil

Tiento see Joven Guitarrista, El, Vol.4: Mediana Dificultad

Tonada see Joven Guitarrista, El, Vol.4: Mediana Dificultad

Travesura see Joven Guitarrista, El, Vol.3: Menos Facil

Tuna, La see Joven Guitarrista, El, Vol.1: Muy Facil

Zaranz see Joven Guitarrista, El, Vol.1: Muy Facil

BAAL; MUSIC TO THE PLAY see Zillig, Winfried

BAAREN, KEES VAN (1906-1970)
Suite Voor Schoolorkest I/IIB5

BACARISSE, SALVADOR (1898-1963)
Ballade I/IB4

Petite Suite I/IB4

BACH, CARL PHILIPP EMANUEL (1714-1788)
Alla Polacca see Stucke, 2

Presto see Stucke, 2

Siciliana I/IB1

Solfegietto I/IB1

Stucke, 2 I/IB1

Xenophone, La I/IB1

BACH, J.C.
Sonata for Violin and Guitar I/IIB1

Sonata in C I/IIA1

BACH, JOHANN CHRISTIAN (1735-1782)
Minuet, MIN 80 I/IB1

BACH, JOHANN SEBASTIAN (1685-1750)
Ach, Dass Nicht Die Letzte Stunde see Deux Chants

Air On The G-String see Suite for Orchestra, BWV 1068, in D, Air

Album Completo De Ana Magdalena Bach, 2 Vols. VII-Coll

Album Di 10 Pezzi, Per La Formazione Musicale E Tecnica Del Chitarrista VII-Coll

Album No. 1 VII-Coll

Allegretto - Allegro Non Troppo VII-Coll

BACH, JOHANN SEBASTIAN (cont'd.)

Allegro see Prelude, Fugue And
     Allegro For Lute, In E: Allegro

Allein Gott In Der Hoh' Sei Ehr' VII

Allemande De La Suite III Para Laud
     see Suite for Lute, BWV 995, in G
     minor, Allemand

Andantino see Prelude, BWV 930, in F

Aria, BWV 508 VII

Aria E Preludio VII-Coll

2 Arias VII

Ausgewahlte Stucke Fur Gitarre
     VII-Coll

Bach Album VII-Coll

"Bach At The Beginning": 6 Pieces
     From The Anna Magdalena Bach
     Notenbuchlein (1725) VII-Coll

Bach-Buch Fur Die Gitarre VII-Coll

Bach-Buch Fur Gitarre, Das, Vol. 1
     VII-Coll

Bach-Buch Fur Gitarre, Das, Vol. 2
     VII-Coll

Bach For The Guitar VII-Coll

Badinerie see Suite for Orchestra,
     BWV 1067, in B minor, Badinerie

Bereite Dich, Zion see Kleines
     Weihnachtsoratorium Mit Johann
     Sebastian Bach

Betrachte Meine Seel' VII

Bist Du Bei Mir see Aria, BWV 508; 2
     Arias

Bourree Aus Der Lauten-Suite see
     Suite for Lute, BWV 996, in E
     minor, Bourree

Canon Par Mouvement Retrograde VII

Cantata No. 212, [excerpt], [arr.]
     VII

Celebre Aria (Lento) see Suite for
     Orchestra, BWV 1068, in D, Air

Celebre Badinerie see Suite for
     Orchestra, BWV 1067, in B minor,
     Badinerie

Cello Suite I see Suite for
     Violoncello, BWV 1007, in G

Cello Suite II see Suite for
     Violoncello, BWV 1008, in D minor

Cello Suite IV see Suite for
     Violoncello, BWV 1010, in E flat

Cello Suite V – Lute Suite III see
     Suite for Lute, BWV 995, in G
     minor

Concerto For Harpsichord And
     Orchestra In F Minor, 2nd Mov't
     (Arioso) see Guitar Duets

Concerto for Keyboard Instrument, BWV
     986, in G, Adagio see Edition
     Nicolas Alfonso, No. 16

Concerto No. 2 for Keyboard
     Instrument, BWV 973, in G, Second
     Movement, Largo see Guitar Duets

Contrapunctus 1 VII

Coro Crucifixus see Mass In B Minor:
     Crucifixus

Courante see Suite for Lute, BWV
     996, in E minor, Courante

Cuarte Suite Para Laud see Partita
     for Lute, BWV 1006a, in E

Deux Chants VII-Coll

Dorfmusik Aus Der Bauernkantate see
     Cantata No. 212, [excerpt],
     [arr.]

Drei Kleine Stucke Aus Dem
     Notenbuchlein Der Anna Magdalena
     Bach VII-Coll

Dritte Lauten-Suite see Suite for
     Lute, BWV 995, in G minor

Dritte Suite see Suite for Lute, BWV
     995, in G minor

Due Bourrees E Marcia VII-Coll

Due Preludi VII-Coll

Edition Nicolas Alfonso, No. 2
     VII-Coll

Edition Nicolas Alfonso, No. 11 see
     Sonata for Violin, BWV 1001, in G
     minor, Fugue

Edition Nicolas Alfonso, No. 16
     VII-Coll

Edition Nicolas Alfonso, No. 17
     VII-Coll

Edition Nicolas Alfonso, No. 18
     VII-Coll

Ehre Sei Gott In Der Hohe. Canon see
     Kleines Weihnachtsoratorium Mit
     Johann Sebastian Bach

English Suite No. 6, In D-Minor,
     (Fifth Movement): Musette see
     Guitar Duets

Erste Lauten-Suite, BWV 996 see
     Suite for Lute, BWV 996, in E
     minor

Erste Suite see Suite for Lute, BWV
     996, in E minor

Es Ist Vollbracht see Geistliche
     Lieder

Famosissime Gavotte Di J.S. Bach, Le
     VII-Coll

Five Easy Pieces For The Guitar
     VII-Coll

French Suite: Courante see 5 Pecas

Fuga Dalle Composizioni Per Liuto
     see Sonata for Violin, BWV 1001,
     in G minor, Fugue

Fuga De La Suite II Para Laud see
     Partita for Lute, BWV 997, in C
     minor, Fugue

Fuga Em Sol Menor, Da 1a. Sonata Para
     Violino see Sonata for Violin,
     BWV 1001, in G minor, Fugue

Fughetta In C VII

Fugue, BWV 847, in C minor VII

Fugue, BWV 855, in E minor VII-Coll

Fugue, BWV 874, in D VII

Fugue, BWV 953, in C VII

Fugue, BWV 1000, in G minor see
     Lautenmusik

Fugue for Lute, BWV 1000, in G minor
     VII
     see also Kompositionen Fur Die
     Laute; Erste Vollstandige Und
     Kritisch Durchgesehene Ausgabe;
     Nach Altem Quellenmaterial Fur
     Die Heutige Laute Ubertragen Und
     Herausgegeben; Lautenmusik

Gavotte, De La Sonata Para Violin En
     Mi Mayor VII-Coll

Geistliche Lieder IV/IIC2, VII-Coll

Gigue De La Suite IV Para Laud see
     Partita for Lute, BWV 1006a, in
     E, Gigue

Gitarszvit see Suite for
     Violoncello, BWV 1011, in C minor

Guitar Duets VII-Coll

Guitar Duets VII-Coll

Ich Steh An Deiner Krippen Hier see
     Geistliche Lieder

4 Inventies VII-Coll

Invention, BWV 772, in C see 4
     Inventies

Invention, BWV 773, in C minor see 4
     Inventies

Invention, BWV 774, in D see 4
     Inventies

Invention, BWV 775, in D minor see 4
     Inventies

Invention No. 1, BWV 772, in C VII

Invention No. 8, BWV 779, in F VII

Invention No. 13, BWV 784, in A minor
     VII

Invenzione A Due Voci In Do see
     Invention No. 1, BWV 772, in C

Jesu, Joy Of Man's Desiring see
     Jesus Bleibet Meine Freude.
     Chorale

Jesus, Alegria De La Humanidad see
     Jesus Bleibet Meine Freude.
     Chorale

Jesus, Alegria Dos Homens see Jesus
     Bleibet Meine Freude. Chorale

Jesus Bleibet Meine Freude. Chorale
     VII

Jesus Que Ma Joie Demeure see Jesus
     Bleibet Meine Freude. Chorale

Joint Solos Bach No. 3 – Saraband-
     Double see Partita for Violin,
     BWV 1002, in B minor, Saraband

Kleine Stucke VII-Coll

Kleine Stucke VII-Coll

Kleines Weihnachtsoratorium Mit
     Johann Sebastian Bach IV/IIB4,
     IV/IIC5, VII-Coll

Komm Susser Tod VII

Kommt, Seelen Dieser Tag see
     Geistliche Lieder

Kompositionen Fur Die Laute; Erste
     Vollstandige Und Kritisch
     Durchgesehene Ausgabe; Nach Altem
     Quellenmaterial Fur Die Heutige
     Laute Ubertragen Und
     Herausgegeben VII-Coll

Lauten-Suite Nr. I e-Moll see Suite
     for Lute, BWV 996, in E minor

Lauten-Suite Nr. II a-Moll see
     Partita for Lute, BWV 997, in C
     minor

Lauten-Suite Nr. III a-Moll see
     Suite for Lute, BWV 995, in G
     minor

Lauten-Suite Nr. IV E-Dur see
     Partita for Lute, BWV 1006a, in E

Lautenmusik VII-Coll

Lautenmusik VII-Coll

Lautenpraludium see Prelude for
     Lute, BWV 999, in C minor

Lautensuite (BWV 995) see Suite for
     Lute, BWV 995, in G minor

Lautensuite IV see Partita for Lute,
     BWV 1006a, in E

Lautensuite No. 3 see Suite for
     Lute, BWV 995, in G minor

Loure And Sarabande VII-Coll

Loure Aus Der Suite In C-Dur see
     Suite for Violoncello, BWV 1009,
     in C, Bourree I-II

March, BWV Anh. 122, in D see Due
     Bourrees E Marcia; Minue Y Marcha

March, BWV Anh. 122, No. 16, in D
     see Vier Leichte Stucke From The
     Anna Magdalena Bach Notenbuchlein
     (1725)

March, BWV Anh. 124, in G VII
     see also Drei Kleine Stucke Aus Dem
     Notenbuchlein Der Anna Magdalena
     Bach

Mass In B Minor: Crucifixus VII

Mein Jesu, Was Fur Seelenweh see
     Geistliche Lieder

Menuet-Trio In G Minor I/IB1,
     VII-Mixed Coll

Menuett Und Gigue VII-Coll

BACH, JOHANN SEBASTIAN (cont'd.)

Premiere Suite Pour Violoncelle Seul
see Suite for Violoncello, BWV
1007, in G

Quattro Transcripciones VII-Coll

Quinze Inventions A Deux Voix, Les:
Collection l'Heure de la Guitare
Classique, Vol. I VII-Coll

Quinze Inventions A Deux Voix, Les:
Collection l'Heure de la Guitare
Classique, Vol. II VII-Coll

Sarabanda, De La 1a. Suite Para Laud
see Suite for Lute, BWV 996, in E
minor, Saraband

Schonsten Stucke Aus Dem
"Notenbuchlein Der Anna Magdalena
Bach" 1725, Die VII-Coll

Siciliana And Fugue, From Sonata No.
1 For Solo Violin VII-Coll

So Oft Ich Meine Tobackspfeife see
"Bach At The Beginning": 6 Pieces
From The Anna Magdalena Bach
Notenbuchlein (1725)

Solamente Dios Es Todopoderoso see
Allein Gott In Der Hoh' Sei Ehr'

Sonata see Prelude, Fugue And
Allegro For Lute, In E-Flat

Sonata for Flute and Continuo, BWV
1033, in C VII

Sonata for Flute and Keyboard
Instrument, BWV 1031, in E flat,
Siciliano VII
see also Zwei Beruhmte Siciliane

Sonata for Flute and Keyboard
Instrument, BWV 1035, in E
I/IIB1, VII

Sonata for Flute, BWV 1013, in A
minor VII

Sonata for Violin, BWV 1001, in G
minor VII
see also Sonate E Partite, Vol. 1

Sonata for Violin, BWV 1001, in G
minor, Fugue VII, VII-Coll
see also Siciliana And Fugue, From
Sonata No. 1 For Solo Violin

Sonata for Violin, BWV 1001, in G
minor, Siciliano VII
see also Edition Nicolas Alfonso,
No. 18; Siciliana And Fugue, From
Sonata No. 1 For Solo Violin;
Zwei Beruhmte Siciliane

Sonata for Violin, BWV 1003, in A
minor VII
see also Sonate E Partite, Vol. 1

Sonata for Violin, BWV 1003, in A
minor, Andante see Verschiedene
Stucke, Vol. 3

Sonata for Violin, BWV 1003, in A
minor, Fugue VII

Sonata for Violin, BWV 1005, in C
VII
see also Sonate E Partite, Vol. 2

Sonata for Violin, BWV 1005, in C,
Fugue VII

Sonata No. 3, BWV 1005, in C, First
Movement, Adagio see Guitar
Duets

Sonatas And Partitas, BWV 1001-1006
VII-Coll

Sonate E Partite, Vol. 1 VII-Coll

Sonate E Partite, Vol. 1: BWV 1001-
1003 see Sonatas And Partitas,
BWV 1001-1006

Sonate E Partite, Vol. 2 VII-Coll

Sonate E Partite, Vol. 2: BWV 1004-
1006 see Sonatas And Partitas,
BWV 1001-1006

Suite Aus Der "Bauern-Kantate" see
Cantata No. 212, [excerpt],
[arr.]

Suite, BWV 824, in A, Courante VII

Suite E-Dur, BWV 1006 see Partita
for Lute, BWV 1006a, in E

BACH, JOHANN SEBASTIAN (cont'd.)

Suite e-moll see Suite for Lute, BWV
996, in E minor

Suite En Mi Menor, Orig. Para Laud
see Suite for Lute, BWV 996, in E
minor

Suite En Mi Mineur see Suite for
Lute, BWV 996, in E minor

Suite for Keyboard Instrument, BWV
807, in A minor, Bourree I VII

Suite for Keyboard Instrument, BWV
807, in A minor, Saraband VII

Suite for Keyboard Instrument, BWV
808, in G minor VII

Suite for Keyboard Instrument, BWV
808, in G minor, Gavotte I VII

Suite for Keyboard Instrument, BWV
808, in G minor, Gavotte I-II
VII

Suite for Keyboard Instrument, BWV
810, in E minor, Passepied II
VII

Suite for Keyboard Instrument, BWV
811, in D minor, Gavotte I VII

Suite for Keyboard Instrument, BWV
812, in D minor, Saraband VII

Suite for Keyboard Instrument, BWV
814, in B minor, Gigue VII

Suite for Keyboard Instrument, BWV
814, in B minor, Minuet VII
see also Menuett Und Gigue

Suite for Keyboard Instrument, BWV
816, in G, Allemand VII

Suite for Keyboard Instrument, BWV
816, in G, Gavotte VII
see also Famosissime Gavotte Di
J.S. Bach, Le

Suite for Keyboard Instrument, BWV
816, in G minor, Gigue VII

Suite for Keyboard Instrument, BWV
817, in E, Polonaise VII

Suite for Keyboard Instrument, BWV
820, in F, Bourree see Edition
Nicolas Alfonso, No. 16

Suite for Keyboard Instrument, BWV
820, in F, Minuet I see Edition
Nicolas Alfonso, No. 17

Suite for Keyboard Instrument, BWV
820, in F, Minuet II see Edition
Nicolas Alfonso, No. 17

Suite for Keyboard Instrument, BWV
821, in B flat, Courante see
Edition Nicolas Alfonso, No. 17

Suite for Keyboard Instrument, BWV
821, in B flat, Saraband see
Edition Nicolas Alfonso, No. 17

Suite for Keyboard Instrument, BWV
822, in G minor, Minuet-Trio see
Edition Nicolas Alfonso, No. 2

Suite for Keyboard Instrument, BWV
823, in F minor, Gigue see
Edition Nicolas Alfonso, No. 16

Suite for Keyboard Instrument, BWV
825, in B flat, Gigue VII

Suite for Keyboard Instrument, BWV
825, in B flat, Minuet I-II VII

Suite for Keyboard Instrument, BWV
825, in B flat, Saraband VII

Suite for Lute, BWV 995, in G minor
VII
see also Kompositionen Fur Die
Laute; Erste Vollstandige Und
Kritisch Durchgesehene Ausgabe;
Nach Altem Quellenmaterial Fur
Die Heutige Laute Ubertragen Und
Herausgegeben; Lautenmusik;
Lautenmusik

Suite for Lute, BWV 995, in G minor,
Allemand VII

Suite for Lute, BWV 995, in G minor,
Gavotte I see Quattro
Transcripciones

Suite for Lute, BWV 995, in G minor,
Saraband see Preludio E
Sarabanda; Quattro

BACH, JOHANN SEBASTIAN (cont'd.)

Transcripciones

Suite for Lute, BWV 996, in E minor
VII
see also Kompositionen Fur Die
Laute; Erste Vollstandige Und
Kritisch Durchgesehene Ausgabe;
Nach Altem Quellenmaterial Fur
Die Heutige Laute Ubertragen Und
Herausgegeben; Lautenmusik;
Lautenmusik

Suite for Lute, BWV 996, in E minor,
Allemand see Verschiedene
Stucke, Vol. 1

Suite for Lute, BWV 996, in E minor,
Bourree VII-Coll
see also Album No. 1; Ausgewahlte
Stucke Fur Gitarre; Edition
Nicolas Alfonso, No. 2; 5 Pecas

Suite for Lute, BWV 996, in E minor,
Courante VII

Suite for Lute, BWV 996, in E minor,
Passaggio-Prelude VII

Suite for Lute, BWV 996, in E minor,
Saraband VII, VII-Coll
see also Gavotte, De La Sonata Para
Violin En Mi Mayor

Suite for Orchestra, BWV 1067, in B
minor, Badinerie VII

Suite for Orchestra, BWV 1067, in B
minor, Polonaise VII

Suite for Orchestra, BWV 1067, in B
minor, Polonaise-Double VII
see also Ausgewahlte Stucke Fur
Gitarre

Suite for Orchestra, BWV 1068, in D,
Air VII
see also Aria E Preludio

Suite for Violoncello, BWV 1007, in G
VII

Suite for Violoncello, BWV 1007, in
G, Gigue see Album Di 10 Pezzi,
Per La Formazione Musicale E
Tecnica Del Chitarrista; Prelude,
Sarabande And Gigue

Suite for Violoncello, BWV 1007, in
G, Minuet I-II see Album Di 10
Pezzi, Per La Formazione Musicale
E Tecnica Del Chitarrista

Suite for Violoncello, BWV 1007, in
G, Minuet II see Five Easy
Pieces For The Guitar

Suite for Violoncello, BWV 1007, in
G, Prelude VII
see also Prelude, Sarabande And
Gigue; Two Cello Preludes

Suite for Violoncello, BWV 1008, in D
minor VII

Suite for Violoncello, BWV 1008, in D
minor, Courante VII

Suite for Violoncello, BWV 1009, in C
VII
see also Lautenmusik

Suite for Violoncello, BWV 1009, in
C, Bourree I-II VII
see also Ausgewahlte Stucke Fur
Gitarre; Loure And Sarabande

Suite for Violoncello, BWV 1009, in
C, Courante VII
see also Album No. 1; Verschiedene
Stucke, Vol. 2

Suite for Violoncello, BWV 1009, in
C, Prelude VII

Suite for Violoncello, BWV 1010, in E
flat VII

Suite for Violoncello, BWV 1010, in E
flat, Bourree I-II see Album Di
10 Pezzi, Per La Formazione
Musicale E Tecnica Del
Chitarrista

Suite for Violoncello, BWV 1010, in E
flat, Bourree II see Five Easy
Pieces For The Guitar

Suite for Violoncello, BWV 1010, in E
flat, Courante see Album Di 10
Pezzi, Per La Formazione Musicale
E Tecnica Del Chitarrista

BACH, JOHANN SEBASTIAN (cont'd.)

Suite for Violoncello, BWV 1010, in E flat, Prelude VII
see also Two Cello Preludes

Suite for Violoncello, BWV 1011, in C minor VII

Suite for Violoncello, BWV 1011, in C minor, Gavotte En Rondeau see Ausgewahlte Stucke Fur Gitarre

Suite for Violoncello, BWV 1011, in C minor, Gavotte I-II VII

Suite for Violoncello, BWV 1011, in C minor, Saraband VII
see also Five Easy Pieces For The Guitar

Suite for Violoncello, BWV 1012, in D VII

Suite for Violoncello, BWV 1012, in D, Gavotte I-II VII
see also Album Di 10 Pezzi, Per La Formazione Musicale E Tecnica Del Chitarrista; Famosissime Gavotte Di J.S. Bach, Le; Five Easy Pieces For The Guitar

Suite for Violoncello, BWV 1012, in D, Saraband VII-Coll
see also Album Di 10 Pezzi, Per La Formazione Musicale E Tecnica Del Chitarrista; Loure And Sarabande; Prelude, Sarabande And Gigue

Suite III see Suite for Lute, BWV 995, in G minor

Suite Pour Le Luth (Lautensuite Nr. III) see Suite for Lute, BWV 995, in G minor

Tag Mit Seinem Lichte, Der see Deux Chants

Toccata, BWV 565, in D minor VII

Toccata, BWV 913, in D minor, First Movement VII

Trois Menuets VII-Coll

Tweestemmige Fuga In E Mineur see Fughetta In C

Twelve Little Preludes VII-Coll

Two Cello Preludes VII-Coll

Two-Part Invention No. 8 see Invention No. 13, BWV 784, in A minor

Vergiss Mein Nicht, Dass Ich Dein Nicht see 2 Arias

Verschiedene Stucke, Vol. 1 VII-Coll

Verschiedene Stucke, Vol. 2 VII-Coll

Verschiedene Stucke, Vol. 3 VII-Coll

Vieni, Dolce Morte see Komm Susser Tod

Vier Leichte Stucke From The Anna Magdalena Bach Notenbuchlein (1725) VII-Coll

Violin Sonata No. 2, Vol. 1: Grave And Fuga see Sonata for Violin, BWV 1003, in A minor

Violin Sonata No. 2, Vol. 2: Andante And Allegro see Sonata for Violin, BWV 1003, in A minor

Violoncello Suite VI see Suite for Violoncello, BWV 1012, in D

Vom Himmel Hoch, Da Komm Ich Her. Chorale see Kleines Weihnachtsoratorium Mit Johann Sebastian Bach

Warum Betrubst Du Dich see Edition Nicolas Alfonso, No. 2

Wybrane Utwory - Pieces Choisies VII-Coll

Zwanzig Stucke Aus Dem Notenbuchlein Fur Anna Magdalena Bach VII-Coll

Zwei Beruhmte Siciliane VII-Coll

Zwei Gitarren Musizieren, Vol. 4: Inventionen Und Sinfonien VII-Coll

BACH, JOHANN SEBASTIAN (cont'd.)

Zwei Kleine Praeludien VII-Coll

Zweite Lauten-Suite, BWV 997 see Partita for Lute, BWV 997, in C minor

Zweite Suite see Partita for Lute, BWV 997, in C minor

BACH ALBUM see Bach, Johann Sebastian

"BACH AT THE BEGINNING": 6 PIECES FROM THE ANNA MAGDALENA BACH NOTENBUCHLEIN (1725) see Bach, Johann Sebastian

BACH-BUCH FUR DIE GITARRE see Bach, Johann Sebastian

BACH-BUCH FUR GITARRE, DAS, VOL. 1 see Bach, Johann Sebastian

BACH-BUCH FUR GITARRE, DAS, VOL. 2 see Bach, Johann Sebastian

BACH FOR THE GUITAR see Bach, Johann Sebastian

BACHELER, DANIEL (ca. 1600)
Courantes, 3 I/IB1

Mounsieurs Almaine I/IB1

BACHMANN, HELMUT
Adagio I/IB4

Air I/IB4

Altdeutscher Tanz I/IB4

Andante, MIN 153 I/IB4

Andante, MIN 154 I/IB4

Andante Religioso I/IB4

Gavotte, MIN 156 I/IB4

Minuet, MIN 157 I/IB4

Pastorale I/IB4

Prelude I/IB4

Prelude in A minor I/IB4

Prelude in D minor I/IB4

Serenade I/IB4

BADINERIE see Bach, Johann Sebastian, Suite for Orchestra, BWV 1067, in B minor, Badinerie

BADINGS, HENK (1907-1987)
It Is Dawning In The East, Balladesque Variations On An Old Dutch Love Song I/IIB1

Preludes, 12, Vol.1, No.1-6 I/IB4

Preludes, 12, Vol.2, No.7-12 I/IB4

Trio No. 9 I/IIB2

BAERVOETS, RAYMOND (1930-   )
Concerto I/IIIA

Improvisation I/IB4

BAGATELA (PARA ELISA) see Beethoven, Ludwig van, Fur Elise

BAGATELLEN see Meijer Von Bremen, Alexander

BAGATELLEN, 12 see Marschner, Heinrich (August)

BAGATELLEN, OP. 4, NOS. 6, 8, 10 see Marschner, Heinrich (August)

BAGATELLES, 2 see Beethoven, Ludwig van

BAGATELLY, 3 see Truhlar, Jan

BAILE EN LA ALDEA see Azpiazu, Jose de

BAILES POPULARES DEL SIGLO XVII, 6 see Ruiz de Ribayaz, Lucas

BAJANDO DE LA MESETA see Rodrigo, Joaquin

BAJO DE LA PALMERA see Albeniz, Isaac

BAJO LA PALMERA see Albeniz, Isaac

BAKFARK, BALINT (VALENTIN) (1507-1576)
Cracow Lute-Book, The see Lautenbuch Von Krakau, Das

BAKFARK, BALINT (VALENTIN) (cont'd.)

Fantasia Seconda A Quattro Voci, For Lute I/IB1

Fantasy I/IB1

Fantasy Nos. 8-10 see Ricercari, 3

Lautenbuch Von Krakau, Das I/IB1

Lautenbuch Von Lyon, Das - The Lyons Lute Book, 1553 I/IB1

Ricercari, 3 I/IB1

BALADA, LEONARDO (1933-   )
Lento With Variation I/IB4

Suite I/IB4

BALALAIKA see Praf, [Fray] Benedicto

BALKANSKI DANS see Jovicic, Jovan

BALLAD see Staak, Pieter van der; Stevens, Bernard George

BALLADE DE VILLON see Roland, Claude Robert

BALLADE POUR ADELINE see Gitarre Spezial, Picking Modern Arrangement, Vol. 1

BALLADES D'ANTAN, 5 see Werner, Jean-Jacques

BALLARD, ROBERT (ca. 1611)
Allemand see Pieces, 3

Ballet see Pieces, 3

Ballet De La Reyne Et Courante I/IB1

Ballet De M. Le Daufin I/IB1

Ballets, 3, Extraits Du Premier Livre I/IB1

Branle De La Cornemuse see Trois Branles

Branle De Village see Trois Branles

Branle Gay see Trois Branles

Courante see Ballet De La Reyne Et Courante

Entree-Ballet Des Insencez I/IB1

Pieces, 3 I/IB1

Premier Chant see Ballet De La Reyne Et Courante; Ballet De M. Le Daufin

Rocantins, Les see Pieces, 3

Second Chant see Ballet De La Reyne Et Courante; Ballet De M. Le Daufin

Trois Branles I/IB1

Troisiesme Chant see Ballet De La Reyne Et Courante; Ballet De M. Le Daufin

BALLARINO, IL see Caroso, Fabrizio

BALLATE, 2 see Malipiero, Riccardo

BALLATELLA, SUL NOME DI CHRISTOPHER PARKENING see Castelnuovo-Tedesco, Mario

BALLET see Deuxieme Recueil De Pieces Faciles; Ballard, Robert; Carulli, Ferdinando; Delden, Lex van; Praetorius, Michael

BALLET see Gluck, Christoph Willibald, Ritter von

BALLET see Danses, 4

BALLET see Danses, 4

BALLET see Danses, 4

BALLET DE LA REYNE ET COURANTE see Ballard, Robert

BALLET DE M. LE DAUFIN see Ballard, Robert

BALLET HOLLANDAIS see Carpentier, [Abbe] Joseph

BALLETS, 3, EXTRAITS DU PREMIER LIVRE see Ballard, Robert

6 BALLETS   see Gastoldi, Giovanni
    Giacomo

BALLETTI   see Leopold I, Holy Roman
    Emperor

BALLETTI, 8   see Negri, Cesare (il
    Trombone)

BALLETTI   see Caroso, Fabrizio; Garsi
    da Parma, Santino; Weiss, Sylvius
    Leopold

BALLETTO   see Gorzanis, Giacomo

BALLETTO A TRE   see Gabrieli, Domenico

BALLIF, CLAUDE (1924-   )
    Solfeggietto, No. 6   I/IB4

BALLO   see Monteverdi, Claudio

BALLO CON TINA   see Zuccheri, Luciano

BALLO DETTO "IL CONTE ORLANDO"   see
    Molinaro, Simone

BALLOU, ESTHER WILLIAMSON (1915-1973)
    Concerto   I/IIIA

    Dialogues   I/IIB1

BALTISCHE SUITE   see Anonymous

BAMMELROCKCHEN   see Volkstanze, 6

BANDITENSTREICHE; COMIC OPERA IN THREE
    ACTS   see Suppe, Franz von

BANKS, DON (1923-   )
    Almain   see Elizabethan Miniatures,
    Based On Music By Anonymous
    Elizabethan Composers

    Carman's Whistle   see Elizabethan
    Miniatures, Based On Music By
    Anonymous Elizabethan Composers

    Elizabethan Miniatures, Based On
    Music By Anonymous Elizabethan
    Composers   V/i

    Irish Ho-Hoane   see Elizabethan
    Miniatures, Based On Music By
    Anonymous Elizabethan Composers

    Muscadin   see Elizabethan Miniatures,
    Based On Music By Anonymous
    Elizabethan Composers

BARAT, JACQUES
    Melodie Moyenageuse   I/IIA2

BARBARESQUE   see Wissmer, Pierre

BARBAS DE SAN JOSE, LAS   see
    Villancicos Populares, Vol. I

BARBE, HELMUT (1927-   )
    Easter Oratorio   see Ostergeschichte

    Horoskop Gefallig?   V/ii

    Ostergeschichte   V/ii

BARBERIS, MELCHIOR DE (ca. 1549)
    Pavana E Saltarello   I/IB1

BARBETTA PADOVANO, JULIO CESARE
    (ca. 1540-1603)
    Gagliarde, 10   I/IB1

    Pavane, 8   I/IB1

BARBIER, RENE (AUGUSTE-ERNEST)
    (1890-1981)
    Concertino, Op. 116   I/IIIB

    Concerto, Op. 98   I/IIIA

    Petite Suite   I/IIA1

    Pierres Magiques, Les, Ballet   V/iii

    Prelude   I/IB4

    Suite No. 2, Op. 115   I/IIA1

BARBIERI, MARIO
    Serra, La, 7 Preludi   I/IB4

BARCA, LA   see Mompou, Federico

BARCAROLA VENEZIANA   see Mendelssohn-
    Bartholdy, Felix, Venezianisches
    Gondellied, Op.19, No.6

BARLOW, FRED (1881-1951)
    Berceuse Pour Un Soir De Neige   see
    Flute D'argent, La

    Calme Au Village   see Flute D'argent,
    La

BARLOW, FRED (cont'd.)

    Flute D'argent, La   I/IB4

    Pavan   I/IIB1

    Petit Source, La   see Flute D'argent,
    La

    Petite Fille Parle Au Bon Dieu, Une
    see Flute D'argent, La

    Petite Valse-Confidence   see Flute
    D'argent, La

    Plainte De La Feuille d'Automne   see
    Flute D'argent, La

BAROCKE SPIELMUSIK   I/IIB1-Coll

BARON, ERNST GOTTLIEB (1696-1760)
    Drole, Le, In F Major   I/IB1

    Duetto Al Liuto E Traverso   I/IIB1

    Duetto G-Dur   see Duetto Al Liuto E
    Traverso

    Konzerte, 2   I/IIB1

    Partie In C Groot   see Partita in C

    Partita En Do Mayor   see Partita in C

    Partita in C   I/IB1

    Sonata A 2   I/IIB1

    Sonate   see Duetto Al Liuto E
    Traverso

    Suita En Re   see Suite in D

    Suite En Re Majeur   see Suite in D

    Suite in D   I/IB1

BAROQUE GUITARIST, THE   I/IB1-Coll,
    VII-Mixed Coll

BAROQUE IN BLUE: SUITE   see Asriel,
    Andre

BAROQUE MUSIC FOR GUITAR   I/IB1

BAROQUE PIECES, VOL. V   I/IIB1-Coll,
    VII-Mixed Coll

BAROQUE PIECES, VOL. VI   I/IIB1-Coll,
    VII-Mixed Coll

BARRE-ETUDES   see Nijenhuis, Luc

BARRETT, JOHN
    Air   I/IIB1

BARRICADES MYSTERIEUSES, LES   see
    Couperin, Francois (le Grand)

BARRIOS MANGORE, AUGUSTIN
    Catedral, La   I/IB4

    Choro Da Saudade   I/IB4

    Danza Paraguaya   I/IB4

    Medallon Antiguo, Omaggio A Pergolesi
    I/IB4

    Oracion   I/IB4

BARRONCINA, LA   see Wyssenbach, Rudolf,
    Pavan

BARTA, LUBOR (1928-1972)
    Sonata   I/IC

BARTOK, BELA (1881-1945)
    Aus Ungarn Und Der Slowakei, Lieder
    Und Tanze, Vol. I   I/IIB1

    Aus Ungarn Und Der Slowakei, Lieder
    Und Tanze, Vol. II   I/IIB2

    Duos   I/IIA1

    For Children   see Fur Kinder

    Fur Kinder   I/IB4

    Gyermekeknek - Fur Kinder   I/IB4

    Gyermekeknek, Vol. 1, No. 1-25   I/IB4

    Gyermekeknek, Vol. 2, No.26-50   I/IB4

BARTOLI, RENE
    Aubade   I/IB4

    Etude No. 1, Tremolo   I/IA

    Waltz in E minor   I/IB4, I/IIA1

BARTOLOZZI, BRUNO (1911-   )
    Adles   I/IB4

    Auser   I/IIB1

    Marcetta   see Pezzi Per Chitarra, 3

    Memorie   I/IIIC

    Omaggio A Gaetano Azzolina   I/IB4

    Pezzi Per Chitarra, 3   I/IB4

    Prelude   see Pezzi Per Chitarra, 3

    Recuerdos Del Cielo   V/ii

    Saraband   see Pezzi Per Chitarra, 3

    Serenade   I/IIB1

BARTOS, ANTONIN
    Skola Hry Na Kytaru, Pro Samouky I
    Pokrocile   II

BARTSCH, CHARLES
    Introduction Et Danse   I/IB4

BASS-STUDIEN   see Schlichting, Theodor

BASSA SAVELLA   see Caroso, Fabrizio

BASTON, JOHN (ca. 1700-   )
    Concerto   I/IIIA

BATALLA, BAILE POPULAR   see Sanz,
    Gaspar

BATELL GALLIARD   see Dowland, John,
    King Of Denmark His Galliard, The

BATTISTI D'AMARIO, BRUNO
    Preludi, 2   I/IB4

BATUKADA   see Bosmans, Arthur,
    Brasileiras, No.3

BAUERNHOCHZEIT   see Volkstanze, 6

BAUMANN, HANS
    Bergbauernweihnacht   IV/IIB2,
    IV/IIC2, IV/IIC3, IV/IIC5

BAUMANN, HERBERT (1925-   )
    Concerto   I/IIIA

    Contrasti   V/ii

    Duetto Concertante   I/IIB1

    Fantasie, Uber "Es Geht Ein Dunkle
    Wolk Herein"   I/IB4

    Memento   I/IIB4

    Moritat Vom Eigensinnigen Eheweibe,
    Die   V/ii

    Sonatine Uber Finnische Volkslieder
    I/IIB2

    Toccata, Elegia E Danza   I/IB4

BAUMANN, MAX GEORG (1917-   )
    Duo, Op. 62   I/IIB1

BAUR, JURG (1918-   )
    Fantasien, 3   I/IB4

BAUSEWEIN, HERBERT
    Strebsame Guitarrist, Der, Vol. 1, 14
    Leichte Spielstucke   I/IB4

BAUSTEINE FUR DEN GOTTESDIENST, REIHE
    A: PSALMEN   V/ii-Coll

BAUSTEINE FUR DEN GOTTESDIENST, REIHE
    A: PSALMEN   V/ii-Coll

BAUSTEINE FUR DEN GOTTESDIENST, REIHE
    A: PSALMEN   V/ii-Coll

BAUSTEINE FUR DEN GOTTESDIENST, REIHE
    B: CHORVERSE   V/ii-Coll

BAUSTEINE FUR DEN GOTTESDIENST, REIHE
    B: CHORVERSE   V/ii-Coll

BAUSTEINE FUR DEN GOTTESDIENST, REIHE
    C: SINGSPRUCHE UND VERSIKEL
    V/ii-Coll

BAUSTEINE FUR DEN GOTTESDIENST, REIHE
    C: SINGSPRUCHE UND VERSIKEL
    V/ii-Coll

BAUSTEINE FUR DEN GOTTESDIENST, REIHE
    D: NEUE LIEDER   V/ii-Coll

BAUSTEINE FUR DEN GOTTESDIENST, REIHE
    D: NEUE LIEDER   V/ii-Coll

BAUSTEINE FUR DEN GOTTESDIENST, REIHE
    D: NEUE LIEDER   V/ii-Coll

BAUSTEINE FUR DEN GOTTESDIENST, REIHE
    D: NEUE LIEDER V/ii-Coll

BAUSTEINE FUR DEN GOTTESDIENST, REIHE
    D: NEUE LIEDER V/ii-Coll

BAUSTEINE FUR DEN GOTTESDIENST,
    SAMMELHEFTE, VOL. 1 V/ii-Coll

BAUSTEINE FUR DEN GOTTESDIENST,
    SAMMELHEFTE, VOL. 2 V/ii-Coll

BAUSTEINE FUR DEN GOTTESDIENST,
    SAMMELHEFTE, VOL. 3 V/ii-Coll

BAUSTEINE FUR DEN GOTTESDIENST,
    SAMMELHEFTE, VOL. 5 V/ii-Coll

BAUTISTA, JULIAN (1901-1961)
    Preludio Y Danza I/IB4

BAXA DE CONTRAPUNTO see Narvaez, Luis
    de

BAY, MEL
    Deluxe Guitar Scale Book, The III

    Guitar Primer, For The Early Beginner
        II

    New Mel Bay Classic Guitar Method,
        The, Vol. I II

    New Mel Bay Classic Guitar Method,
        The, Vol. II II, VII-Mixed Coll

    New Mel Bay Classic Guitar Method,
        The, Vol. III II

BAYERISCHER BAUERNTANZ, EIN see
    Mittelalterliche Tanze

BE GLAD THE WORLD WILL STAND see
    Staak, Pieter van der

BEAT MUSIC, FOR ORCHESTRA WITH
    AMPLIFIED INSTRUMENTS see Smalley,
    Roger

BECALMED see Komter, Jan Maarten

BECK, LEONHARD
    Finger Anschlag, 5 III

    Harmonielehre Auf Der Gitarre II,
        VII-Mixed Coll

BECKER, GUNTHER (1924-   )
    Caprices Concertants I/IIIC

    Con Buen Ayre, Duplum I/IIB1

    Correspondances II V/i

    Game For Nine V/i

    Metathesis I/IB4

    Nacht- Und Traumgesange V/ii

BECQUERIANA, COMPLAINTE see Pujol,
    Emilio

BEDFORD, DAVID (1937-   )
    Horse, His Name Was Hunry Fencewaver
        Walkins, A I/IIIA

    Nurse's Song With Elephants V/ii

    Ones Who Walked Away From Omelas, The
        V/i

    Star's End, For Rock Instruments And
        Orchestra V/i

    You Asked For It, For Acoustic Guitar
        Solo I/IB4

BEECROFT, NORMA (1934-   )
    Pezzi Brevi, 3 I/IIB1

BEETHOVEN, LUDWIG VAN (1770-1827)
    Adagio De La Sonata, Op. 27, No. 2,
        "Claro De Luna" see Sonata for
        Piano, Op. 27, No. 2, in C sharp
        minor,First Movement

    Adagio, MIN 232 I/IIB3

    Album I/IB2

    Albumblatt "Fur Elise" see Fur Elise

    Allegro I/IIB1

    Andante Mit Variationen I/IIB1

    2 Andantes I/IB2

    Ao Luar see Sonata for Piano, Op.
        27, No. 2, in C sharp minor,First
        Movement

    Bagatela (Para Elisa) see Fur Elise

BEETHOVEN, LUDWIG VAN (cont'd.)

    Bagatelles, 2 I/IB2

    Beethoven For The Guitar I/IB2,
        I/IIA1

    Chiaro Di Luna I/IIA1
        see also Sonata for Piano, Op. 27,
        No. 2, in C sharp minor,First
        Movement

    Claro De Luna see Sonata for Piano,
        Op. 27, No. 2, in C sharp minor,
        First Movement

    Deutsche Tanze I/IIB4

    Duo I/IIA1

    Erster Satz Aus Der Mondschein-Sonate
        see Sonata for Piano, Op. 27, No.
        2, in C sharp minor,First
        Movement

    Fur Elise I/IB2

    Minuet I/IB2

    Minuet in G I/IIA2

    Minuet, MIN 334 I/IB2

    Minuet, MIN 395 I/IB2

    Minuet, MIN 396 I/IB2

    Minuet, MIN 397 I/IB2

    7 Minuetos I/IB2

    Moonlight Sonata see Sonata, Op. 27,
        No. 2

    Para Elisa see Fur Elise

    Pour Elise see Fur Elise

    Romance I/IB2

    Romance for Violin and Orchestra
        I/IB2

    Ruinas De Atenas, La, Marcha I/IB2

    Septet I/IB2

    Sonata for Piano, Op. 14, No. 2, in
        E,Second Movement I/IB2

    Sonata for Piano, Op. 27, No. 2, in C
        sharp minor,First Movement I/IB2

    Sonata in C minor I/IIB1

    Sonata in C sharp minor, Op. 27, No.
        2,Minuet I/IB2

    Sonata, MIN 394 see Album

    Sonata No. 2,Scherzo, MIN 335 I/IB2

    Sonata No. 3, Minuet I/IB2

    Sonata No. 4, Op. 7, Largo I/IB2

    Sonata No. 9, Andante I/IB2

    Sonata No. 10, Andante I/IB2
        see also 2 Andantes

    Sonata, No.12: Marcha Funebre I/IB2

    Sonata No. 14, Allegretto see Album

    Sonata No. 15, Andante see 2
        Andantes

    Sonata No. 23, Andante see Album

    Sonata No. 30, Andante see Album

    Sonata, Op. 2, No. 1, Adagio I/IB2

    Sonata, Op. 2, No. 2, Scherzo I/IB2

    Sonata, Op. 13, Adagio I/IB2

    Sonata, Op. 26, Andante I/IB2

    Sonata, Op. 27, No. 2 I/IB2

    Sonata Patetica: Adagio see Sonata,
        Op. 13, Adagio

    Sonatina I/IIA1

    Sonatina E Adagio I/IIA1

    Sonatina in G I/IIA1

    Sonatina, MIN 48 I/IIB1

    Tema Y Var. IV [Del] Septimino I/IB2

BEETHOVEN, LUDWIG VAN (cont'd.)

    Theme and Variations, MIN 218 I/IIB1

    Valse "Le Desir" I/IB2

    Variacion IV I/IIA1

BEETHOVEN FOR THE GUITAR see
    Beethoven, Ludwig van

BEGEBENHEIT see Blarr, Oskar Gottlieb

BEGGAR'S OPERA, THE see Pepusch, John
    Christopher

BEGLEITEN NACH DEM GEHOR, DAS,
    VOLKSTUMLICHE ANLEITUNG FUR DAS
    FREIE BEGLEITEN see Holz, Franz

BEGLEITEN NACH DEM GEHOR, DAS,
    VOLKSTUMLICHE ANLEITUNG FUR DAS
    FREIE BEGLEITEN, SUPPL 1: [THEORY
    OF ACCOMPANIMENT] see Holz, Franz

BEGLEITEN NACH DEM GEHOR, DAS,
    VOLKSTUMLICHE ANLEITUNG FUR DAS
    FREIE BEGLEITEN, SUPPL. 2:
    TONARTEN- UND AKKORDFIBEL see
    Holz, Franz

BEHREND, SIEGFRIED (1933-   )
    Alborada I/IB5

    Danza Mora I/IB5

    Duos, 3 I/IIA1

    Fantasia A Sei Corde I/IB4

    Fantasia Malaguenita I/IB4

    Flamenco-Fantasia I/IB5

    Gitarre - Mein Hobby, Zum
        Selbststudium Bis Zur
        Meisterschaft, Vol. 1 II

    Gitarre - Mein Hobby, Zum
        Selbststudium Bis Zur
        Meisterschaft, Vol. 2 II

    Gitarrenschule Fur Anfanger II

    Granadina De La Rambla I/IB4

    Haiku-Suite I/IIB1

    Japanische Serenade I/IIA1

    Jiddische Hochzeit, A I/IIC1

    Kolometrie I/IB4, I/IIB1

    Legnaniana I/IIIA

    Leipziger Suite I/IIA1

    Monodien, 6 I/IB4

    Movimenti I/IB4

    Non Te Escaparas, Capriccio Nach
        Francesco De Goya I/IB4

    Percussion Studies see Rhythmische
        Studien, Vol. 2

    Percussion Studies, 29 see
        Rhythmische Studien, Vol. 1

    Pezzi Per Jim, 2 I/IB4

    Porque Fue Sensible, Capriccio Nach
        Francesco De Goya I/IB4

    Postkarten Suite I/IB4

    Rhythmische Studien, Vol. 1 I/IA

    Rhythmische Studien, Vol. 2 I/IA

    Scale-Practice see Tonleiterstudien

    Scherzoso I/IIB1

    Sevillanas I/IB5

    Solo I/IIB1

    Sonatine, Nach Japanischen
        Volksliedern I/IB4

    Spanische Tanze, 3 I/IB5

    Spielmusik I/IIB1

    Stierkampmusik I/IIA1

    Stucke, 2 I/IB4

    Study I/IIA2

    Suite Fur Isao Takahashi I/IB4

BEHREND, SIEGFRIED (cont'd.)

Suite Nach Altenglischen Meistern
I/IIB1

Suite Nach Alter Lautenmusik I/IB4

Suite, Nach Altpolnischen Melodien
I/IIC1

Tonleiterstudien III

Trianas I/IB5

Triptychon "Memento Mori Ohshima
Norio Nostrum" I/IIB1

Ubungen Von "A-Z" I/IA

Weihnachtsgeschichte IV/IIC2

Yo Lo Vi, Scenen Nach Francesco de
Goya I/IIC1

Zorongo Para Murao I/IB4

BEI LEGAMI, I see Monteverdi, Claudio

31 BEKANNTE MELODIEN I/IIB2-Coll

BEKANNTE VOLKSLIEDER, TEIL II
I/IIC4-Coll

BELASCO, LIONEL
Juliana I/IB4

Juliana, Valzer Venezuelano see
Juliana

BELASCO, M.
Juliana I/IB4

Juliana, Antilliaanse Wals see
Juliana

BELAUBRE, LOUIS-NOEL (1932-   )
Symphonie Concertante I/IIIC

BELIEBTE WALZER UND MOMENT MUSICAL see
Schubert, Franz (Peter)

BELLAS NOCHES DE MAIQUETIA, LAS,
CANZONE VENEZUELANA see Aponte,
Pedro Arcila

BELLES DEESSES see Besard, Jean-
Baptiste

BELLEZZE D'OLIMPIA see Caroso,
Fabrizio

BELLINI, VINCENZO (1801-1835)
Dolente Immagine Di Filla Mia I/IIC1

BELLMAN, CARL MICHAEL (1740-1795)
Allegro Ma Non Troppo see Melodien
Aus Dem Repertoire Von Carl
Michael Bellman

Andante see Melodien Aus Dem
Repertoire Von Carl Michael
Bellman

Andante Sostenuto see Melodien Aus
Dem Repertoire Von Carl Michael
Bellman

Bellman For 4 Gitarrer I/IIA3

Bellmann-Brevier; Lieder Aus
"Fredmans-Episteln", Vol. 1
I/IIC1

Bellmann-Brevier; Lieder Aus
"Fredmans-Episteln", Vol. 2
I/IIC1

Fredmans Epistel No. 2 see Bellman
For 4 Gitarrer

Fredmans Epistel No. 71I see Bellman
For 4 Gitarrer

Fredmans Epistel No. 71II see
Bellman For 4 Gitarrer

Fredmans Epistel No. 78 see Bellman
For 4 Gitarrer

Gitarr-Solon I/IB1

Melodien Aus Dem Repertoire Von Carl
Michael Bellman I/IB1

Opp, Amaryllis Och Andra Fredmans
Sanger Och Epistlar I/IB1

Pastorale see Melodien Aus Dem
Repertoire Von Carl Michael
Bellman

Tempi Di Menuetto see Melodien Aus
Dem Repertoire Von Carl Michael
Bellman

BELLMAN, CARL MICHAEL (cont'd.)

Tempo Di Menuetto see Melodien Aus
Dem Repertoire Von Carl Michael
Bellman

Vaggvisa Till Sonen Carl see Bellman
For 4 Gitarrer

BELLMAN FOR 4 GITARRER see Bellman,
Carl Michael

BELLMANN-BREVIER; LIEDER AUS "FREDMANS-
EPISTELN", VOL. 1 see Bellman,
Carl Michael

BELLMANN-BREVIER; LIEDER AUS "FREDMANS-
EPISTELN", VOL. 2 see Bellman,
Carl Michael

BELLOW, ALEXANDER (1922-1976)
Allegro see Diversions, 5

Allegro Moderato see Diversions, 5

Bolero see Short Pieces, 4

Cavatina I/IB4

Diversions, 5 I/IB4

Etude In Harmonics see Short Pieces,
4

Etude In Tremolo I/IA

Etude Oriental see Short Pieces, 4

Etudes In Scales, 2 I/IA

First Lessons I/IA

Largo see Diversions, 5

Moderato, MIN158 see Diversions, 5

Moderato, MIN159 see Diversions, 5

Prelude see Short Pieces, 4

Prelude And Rondo I/IB4

Short Pieces, 4 I/IB4

Studies, 10 I/IA

Suite Miniature I/IB4

Suite Provencale I/IB4

BELLVEDERE see Robinson, Thomas

BELWIN SPANISH GUITAR COURSE, 4 VOLS.
see Sweetland, Elliot

BENARY, PETER (1931-   )
Fantasien, 4 I/IIB1

BENDA, GEORG ANTON (JIRI ANTONIN)
(1722-1795)
Sonatina I/IB2

Sonatinen, 2 I/IB2

BENGUEREL, XAVIER (1931-   )
Concerto I/IIIA

Intendo A Dos I/IIB1

Stella Spendens I/IIA1

Vermelia I/IIA3

Versus I/IB4

BENNETT, RICHARD RODNEY (1936-   )
Concerto I/IIIA

Impromptus I/IB4

Victory, Opera In 3 Acts V/iii

BERCEUSE see Flies, J. Bernhard,
Wiegenlied "Schlafe Mein Prinzchen"

BERCEUSE ANCIENNE see Grau, Agusti

BERCEUSE D'ORIENT see Tansman,
Alexandre

BERCEUSE ET SERENADE see Bozza, Eugene

BERCEUSE POUR UN SOIR DE NEIGE see
Barlow, Fred

BEREITE DICH, ZION see Bach, Johann
Sebastian

BERGBAUERNWEIHNACHT see Baumann, Hans

BERGERETTES see Aubanel, Georges

BERGERETTES; 6 PIECES FROM THE 18TH
CENTURY I/IIC1-Coll

BERGIER DE VILE CHAMPESTRE see Seiber,
Matyas Gyorgy

BERGLIED see Zanke, Herman

BERGMAN, ERIK (1911-   )
Suite for Guitar, Op. 32 I/IB4

BERIO, LUCIANO (1925-   )
Chemins II B, For Orchestra V/i

Chemins II C, For Bass Clarinet And
Orchestra V/i

Opera, Opera In 4 Acts V/iii

Passaggio, Messa In Scena V/ii

BERKELEY, [SIR] LENNOX (1903-   )
Concerto for Guitar and Orchestra
I/IIIA

Sonatina, Op. 51 I/IC

Theme and Variations I/IB4

BERLINER REQUIEM see Weill, Kurt

BERMUDO, [FRAY] JUAN
(ca. 1510-ca. 1565)
Mir Nero De Tarpeya, Romance Viejo
I/IIC1

BERNAL JIMENEZ, MIGUEL (1910-1956)
Cartas De Mexico, 3 V/i

BERNARDINA, LA see Frescobaldi,
Girolamo, Canzona Seconda

BERTHELOT, T.
Mes Premiers Pas Vers La Guitare II

BERTI, OSCAR
Alegres Rincones, Valse Venezolana
I/IB5

BERTOUILLE, GERARD (1898-1981)
Petite Serenade Impromptu I/IIA1

BERUHMTE ARIEN, 4 I/IB1-Coll,
VII-Mixed Coll

BERUHMTE OPERN MELODIEN FUR GITARRE,
VOL. 1 I/IB6-Coll

BERUHMTE OPERN MELODIEN FUR GITARRE,
VOL. 2 I/IB6-Coll

BERUHMTE RUSSISCHE LIEDER UND ROMANZEN,
15 I/IIC1-Coll

BERUHMTE STUCKE, 3 I/IIB1-Coll

BERUHMTE SUITE IN D-MOLL see Visee,
Robert de

BERUHMTES ADAGIO, NACH EINEM
THEMENFRAGMENT MIT BEZIFFERTEM
GENERALBASS see Albinoni, Tomaso

BERUHMTES MENUETT see Boccherini,
Luigi; Boccherini, Luigi, Minuet;
Bolzoni, Giovanni

BERVOETS, GERARD
Tremolospel Op De Gitaar III

BESARD, JEAN-BAPTISTE (1567-ca. 1625)
Aux Logettes De Ces Bois I/IB1

Belles Deesses I/IIC1

Branle I/IB1

Branle Gay I/IB1

Cruelle Departie, Chanson I/IIC1

Dances, 8 I/IB1

Moy, Pauvre Fille I/IIC1

Vous Me Juriez, Bergere I/IB1

BEST OF BREAM, THE I/IB6-Coll

BESTE AUS DEM LAUTENWERK, DAS see
Dowland, John

BETRACHTE MEINE SEEL' see Bach, Johann
Sebastian

BETSABE see Pedrell, Carlos, Danzas De
Las Tres Princesas Cautivas, No. 3

BETTINELLI, BRUNO (1913-   )
Improvisation I/IB4

Introduzione see Pezzi, 4

Notturno see Pezzi, 4

Pezzi, 4 I/IB4

BETTINELLI, BRUNO (cont'd.)

Preludes, 5 I/IB4

Ritmico see Pezzi, 4

12 Studi I/IA

Toccata see Pezzi, 4

BEURLE, JURGEN (1943-   )
Objets V/ii

BEVEREN, ACHIEL VAN
Suite, Op. 46 I/IB4

BEWARE see Komter, Jan Maarten

BEWEGUNGSSPIELE see Ebenhoh, Horst

BIALAS, GUNTER (1907-   )
Eichendorff-Liederbuch, Vol. 1: Das
Zerbrochene Ringlein V/ii

Eichendorff-Liederbuch, Vol. 2:
Abschied V/ii

Eichendorff-Liederbuch, Vol. 3: Aber
Die Zeit Geht Schnell V/ii

Eichendorff-Liederbuch, Vol. 4:
Nachtzauber V/ii

Eichendorff-Liederbuch, Vol. 5:
Seliges Vergessen V/ii

Eichendorff-Liederbuch, Vol. 6:
Assonanzen V/ii

Gesange, 3 I/IIC2

Hat Nur Lenz see Eichendorff-
Liederbuch, Vol. 6: Assonanzen

Hirtentanz see Spanische Romanzen

Horst Du Nicht Die Brunnen Rauschen
see Eichendorff-Liederbuch, Vol.
4: Nachtzauber

Im Winde Facheln Die Blatter see
Eichendorff-Liederbuch, Vol. 5:
Seliges Vergessen

In Einem Kuhlen Grunde see
Eichendorff-Liederbuch, Vol. 1:
Das Zerbrochene Ringlein

Lieb Voglein see Eichendorff-
Liederbuch, Vol. 3: Aber Die Zeit
Geht Schnell

Nana see Spanische Romanzen

O Taler Weit see Eichendorff-
Liederbuch, Vol. 2: Abschied

Rhythmische Miniaturen I/IIB3

Romanzero V/i

Spanische Romanzen I/IIB2, IV/IIB2

BIANCAFORE see Piezas Para Laud Del
Siglo XVI, 4

BIANCHINI, DOMENICO (ca. 1563)
Tant Que Vivrai I/IB1

BIBERIAN, GILBERT E.
Prelude and Fugue I/IB4

Suite for 4 Guitars I/IIA3

BICINIA see Kodaly, Zoltan

BIEBL, FRANZ (1906-   )
An Die Musik, A Hymn V/ii

Frisch Gesungen, A Hymn V/ii

BIELSA, VALENTIN
Ala Orilla Del Tormes see 4
Canciones Populares Espanolas

4 Canciones Populares Espanolas
I/IB5

Reyes De La Baraja, Los see 4
Canciones Populares Espanolas

Romance Del Conde Olinos see 4
Canciones Populares Espanolas

Tres Hojas, Las see 4 Canciones
Populares Espanolas

BILDLICHE DARSTELLUNG ALLER DUR- UND
MOLL-AKKORDE III

BIMBELI, BAMBELI; 15 LAUTENLIEDER VON
DEN KINDERN UND FUR DEN KINDERN
I/IIC1-Coll

BINGE, RONALD (1910-   )
Alzbetinska Serenada I/IB4

Elizabethan Serenade see Alzbetinska
Serenada

BIRDS, THE see Duarte, John W.

BIRTH, THOMAS (1912-   )
Neue Gitarrenmusik I/IB4

BIRTWISTLE, HARRISON (1934-   )
Orpheus, Opera In 3 Acts V/iii

World Is Discovered, The; 6
Instrumental Pieces After
Heinrich Isaac V/i

BIS DEL CONCERTISTA, I, VOL. 1
I/IB6-Coll

BIS DEL CONCERTISTA, I, VOL. 2
I/IB6-Coll, VI-Mixed Coll,
VII-Mixed Coll

BIS DEL CONCERTISTA, I, VOL. 3
I/IB6-Coll

BISCHOFF, HEINZ (1898-1963)
Ballade I/IB4

Piccola Fuga I/IB4

Salzburger Sonatine In F I/IIB1

BIST DU BEI MIR see Bach, Johann
Sebastian; Bach, Johann Sebastian,
Aria, BWV 508

BITTE UM LIEBE see Jez, Jakob, Do
Fraig Amor

BITTENDES KIND see Schumann, Robert
(Alexander); Schumann, Robert
(Alexander)

BIZET, GEORGES (1838-1875)
Arlesiana, La I/IB3

Arlesien, La: Adagio I/IB3

Arlesien, La: Marcha Del Rey I/IB3

Arlesien, La: Minueto I/IB3

Celebre Minuetto I/IB3

Menuet, Deuxieme, De l'Arlesienne
I/IIA1

Minuet, MIN 280 I/IIA2

Romance I/IIA2

BIZET, JEAN (1924-   )
Spirale I/IB4

Triangles I/IB4

BLACK GUITAR, THE see Schibler, Armin

BLACKBIRDS AND THRUSHES see English
Folk Songs, 3

BLAKE WATKINS, MICHAEL (1948-   )
Clouds And Éclipses I/IIIA

Guitar Quartet I/IIA3

Psallein V/i

BLANCHARD, CARVER WILLIAM, JR.
Country Gardens I/IIA2

Prolog Und Rondo I/IIA2

BLARR, OSKAR GOTTLIEB (1934-   )
Begebenheit see Thema Weihnachten, 3
Chansons

Botschaft, Die see Thema
Weihnachten, 3 Chansons

Psalm No. 91 see Wer Wohnt Unterm
Schirm Des Hochsten

Thema Weihnachten, 3 Chansons
IV/IIC3

Vater Unser, Der Du Bist Im Himmel;
Melody After A Latin-American
Calypso V/ii

Wenn Das Vollkommene Kommt see Thema
Weihnachten, 3 Chansons

Wer Wohnt Unterm Schirm Des Hochsten
V/ii

BLAVET, MICHEL (1700-1768)
8 Pieces I/IIB1

BLECH, LEO (1871-1958)
Liedchen, 6, (Kindern Vorzusingen)
I/IIC1

BLECHER, HEINZ
Spielt Auf - Singt Mit, Das Erste
Musizieren Auf Der Gitarre, Vol.
1: Einstimmiges Spiel II

Spielt Auf - Singt Mit, Das Erste
Musizieren Auf Der Gitarre, Vol.
2: Mehrstimmiges Spiel Und
Liedbegleitung II

BLEEKER, WILLY
Serenata Espanola I/IIA1

BLEUSE, MARC (1937-   )
Comptines Pour Anne, 3 I/IIC5

BLOCH, WALDEMAR (1906-   )
Landler see Neuberger Tanze

March see Neuberger Tanze

Neuberger Tanze I/IIB1

Polka see Neuberger Tanze

Sonata I/IIB1

Waltz see Neuberger Tanze

Zwiefache, Der see Neuberger Tanze

BLOK, COBY
Maria Durch Ein Dornwald Ging see
Speelboek Voor De
Gitaargroepsles, Vol. I

Melchior Et Balthasar see Speelboek
Voor De Gitaargroepsles, Vol. II

Speelboek Voor De Gitaargroepsles,
Vol. I II, IV/IIA2

Speelboek Voor De Gitaargroepsles,
Vol. II II, IV/IIA2

Speelboek Voor De Gitaargroepsles,
Vol. III II

Speelboek Voor De Gitaargroepsles,
Vol. IV II

Speelboek Voor De Gitaargroepsles,
Vol. V II

Wij Spelen Gitaar, Methode Voor
Beginners, Gebaseerd Op Het
A.M.V.-Onderwijs, Vol. I II

Wij Spelen Gitaar, Methode Voor
Beginners, Gebaseerd Op Het
A.M.V.-Onderwijs, Vol. II II

Wij Spelen Gitaar, Methode Voor
Beginners, Gebaseerd Op Het
A.M.V.-Onderwijs, Vol. III II

BLOW, JOHN (1649-1708)
Courante I/IB1

Prelude I/IB1

BLUE EPIPHANY, A - FOR J.B. SMITH see
Mellers, Wilfrid Howard

BLUES AND SPIRITUALS I/IIB3-Coll

BLUES FOR CLASSIC GUITAR, 3 see
Thomason, Alexander (Charlie Byrd)

BLUES FOR ROSY see Abloniz, Miguel

BLUME, KARL (1883-1947)
Ausgewahlte Lieder, 12 I/IIC1

BLYTON, CAREY (1932-   )
Bream, The I/IB4

Breme, La see Bream, The

In Memoriam Django Reinhardt: 2
Variations And A Theme For Guitar
I/IB4

In Memoriam Scott Fitzgerald I/IB4

Saxe Blue I/IB4

BOBRI, VLADIMIR
Complete Study Of The Tremolo; 33
Lessons III

Daily Exercises, 130 III

130 Daily Studies For The Classic
Guitar III

Melodic Exercises, 8 I/IA

BOBRI, VLADIMIR (cont'd.)

Very Easy Pieces, For Very, Very Beginners, Op.12 I/IB4

BOCCHERINI, LUIGI (1743-1805)
Beruhmtes Menuett I/IIA2
see also Minuet

Celebre Menuet see Minuet

Celebre Mineto I/IB2

Concerto in E I/IIIA

Introduction And Fandango I/IIB1

Minuet I/IB2

Minueto-Bolero I/IB2

Minueto Espanol I/IB2

Minuetto see Minuet

Quintet No. 1, Ge. 445 I/IIB4

Quintet No. 1 in D I/IIB4

Quintet No. 2, Ge. 446 I/IIB4

Quintet No. 2 in C, Ge. 451 I/IIB4

Quintet No. 3, Ge. 447 I/IIB4

Quintet No. 3 in E minor, Ge. 452 I/IIB4

Quintet No. 4, Ge. 448 I/IIB4

Quintet No. 5, Ge. 449 I/IIB4

Quintet No. 6, Ge. 450 I/IIB4

Quintetti, 6, Con Chitarra, Ge. 445-450 I/IIB4

BOCHMAN, THEO L.
Fantasia De La Guitarra, Etude De Tremolo I/IA

Torre Morisca, La I/IB4

BODA, JOHN (1922-   )
Etudes Byzantines, 4 I/IA

Introduction And Dance I/IB4

BODDECKER, PHILIPP FRIEDRICH (1683- ?)
Natus Est Jesus, Weihnachtskonzert IV/IIC1

BOEHMER, KONRAD (1941-   )
Chanson De Lointain see Lied Uit De Verte

Lied Uit De Verte V/ii

BOER, JOHAN DE (1938-   )
Grounds, 2 I/IB4

BOESSET, ANTOINE (ca. 1585-1643)
Ennuits, Desespoirs Et Douleurs I/IIC1

BOHM, GEORG (1661-1733)
Courante I/IB1

BOHNENPOTT see Volkstanze, 6

BOHR, HEINRICH
Hirtentanz I/IB4

Klagende Lied, Das I/IB4

Spanischer Tanz I/IB5

BOIS, ROB DU (1934-   )
Concerto for Violin and Orchestra V/i

Concerto Pour Hrisanide, Le, For Piano And Orchestra V/i

Helaas Geen Sprookje see Vandaag Is Het Morgen Van Gisteren

Midas; Ballet Music For Orchestra V/iii

Night Music I/IIB2

Pastorale No. 2 I/IIB2

Pastorale No. 4 I/IB4

Vandaag Is Het Morgen Van Gisteren V/ii

BOISMORTIER, JOSEPH BODIN DE (1689-1755)
Carillon I/IIB2

BOISMORTIER, JOSEPH BODIN DE (cont'd.)

Sonata in A minor I/IIA1

BOITEUSE, LA see Rameau, Jean-Philippe

BOLERO see Bellow, Alexander; Geselbracht, Erich; Moreno Torroba, Federico; Tarrago, Graciano

BOLERO (ALTSPANISCHER VOLKSTANZ) see Sor, Fernando

BOLERO DE LOS PICAROS see Surinach, Carlos

BOLERO ESPANOL see Staak, Pieter van der

BOLERONDA see Komter, Jan Maarten

BOLZONI, GIOVANNI (1841-1919)
Beruhmtes Menuett I/IB3

Celebre Minueto see Beruhmtes Menuett

BON SECRETS, LES see Franse Volksliederen, 3

BONDON, JACQUES (1927-   )
Concerto De Mars I/IIIA

Nocturne Nos. 1-3 I/IB4

Swing No. 2 I/IB4

BONILLA CHAVEZ, CARLOS
Elegia Y Danza I/IB4

Preludio Y Yumbo I/IB4

BONJOUR, BON MOIS see Dufay, Guillaume

BONNAL, ERMEND
Enfant Crie En Galilee, Un IV/IIC5

Princes d'Orient, 3, Noel IV/IIC5

BONNARD, ALAIN (1939-   )
Chanson D'aube I/IB4

Dancerie I/IB4

Ricercari, 5 I/IIA1

Sonatine Breve I/IIB1

BONNY AT MORN see Britten, [Sir] Benjamin

BONONCINI, GIOVANNI (1670-1747)
Trio Sonata Nos. 1-5 I/IIB2

BONPORTI, FRANCESCO ANTONIO (1672-1748)
Adagio Et Gigue I/IB1

BONY SWEET BOY see Robinson, Thomas

BOOGAARD, BERNARD VAN DEN (1952-   )
Concertino I/IIIC

De Ave Phoenice V/ii

Oilles Motors I/IIB2

BOOT HILL see Gilardino, Angelo

BOP PIZZICATO see McBride, Robert Guyn

BORDHAYS, CHRISTIANE LE
Concierto De Azul I/IIIA

BORELLO, P.
Tableau d'Accords Pour La Guitare III

BORGES, RAUL
Prelude I/IB4

BORKOVEC, PAVEL (1894-1972)
Silentium Turbatum, Symphonic Setting V/ii

BORRIS, SIEGFRIED (1906-   )
Conversazione A Tre I/IIB2

BORRONO DA MILANO, PIETRO PAVOLO
Suite De La Bella Andronica I/IB1

BORSODY, LASZLO
Szin-Darabok - Color-Pieces I/IB4

BORSTLAP, DICK (1943-   )
Echo, For Orchestra V/i

BORTOLAMI, GALLIANO
Mi Viene Incontro Il Mare see Rumore Di Passi, 5 Liriche

Non Per Me Fioriscono Le Dalie see Rumore Di Passi, 5 Liriche

Orizzonte e'Svanito, L' see Rumore Di Passi, 5 Liriche

BORTOLAMI, GALLIANO (cont'd.)

Rumore Di Passi, 5 Liriche I/IIC1

Se Hai Gettato Una Monetina see Rumore Di Passi, 5 Liriche

Sorgeva Il Sole E Sorridevi see Rumore Di Passi, 5 Liriche

BORTOLAZZI, B.
Theme and Variations, Op. 10, No. 4 I/IIB1

BOSCH, JACQUES
Pieces Faciles, 10, Pour l'Etude I/IB3

BOSCO, GILBERTO (1946-   )
Rifrazioni I/IB4

BOSKE, JIM TEN (1946-   )
Leave Something Unexplained I/IIB1

BOSMANS, ARTHUR (1908-   )
Batukada see Brasileiras, No.3

Brasileiras, No.1 I/IB4

Brasileiras, No.2 I/IB4

Brasileiras, No.3 I/IB4

Brasileiras, No.4 I/IB4

Brasileiras, No. 5 I/IB4

Modinha see Brasileiras, No.2

Ponteio see Brasileiras, No.1

Sorongo see Brasileiras, No. 5

Toada see Brasileiras, No.4

BOSSA NOVA see Schaaf, Peter

BOSSINENSIS, FRANCISCUS
Ricercari, 26 I/IB1

BOSSU, MARCEL
Accords De Guitare, d'Apres Le Nouveau Doigte III

Akkoordenreeksen Voor Gitaar see Suite d'Accords Pour Guitare

Gitaar Akkoorden, Volgens Nieuwe Vingerzetting see Accords De Guitare, d'Apres Le Nouveau Doigte

Suite d'Accords Pour Guitare III

BOTJE (BEREND) VARIEREND see Schagen, Henk van

BOTSCHAFT, DIE see Blarr, Oskar Gottlieb

BOULEZ, PIERRE (1925-   )
Domaines, For Clarinet And Orchestra V/i

Don see Pli Selon Pli, Portrait De Mallarme, 1

Eclat, For Orchestra V/i

Improvisation I: Le Vierge, Le Vivace Et Le Bel Aujourd'hui see Pli Selon Pli, Portrait De Mallarme, 2

Improvisation III: A La Nue Accablante Tu see Pli Selon Pli, Portrait De Mallarme, 4

Marteau Sans Maitre, Le V/ii

Pli Selon Pli, Portrait De Mallarme, 1 V/ii

Pli Selon Pli, Portrait De Mallarme, 2 V/ii

Pli Selon Pli, Portrait De Mallarme, 4 V/ii

Pli Selon Pli, Portrait De Mallarme, 5 V/ii

Tombeau see Pli Selon Pli, Portrait De Mallarme, 5

BOUNCE see Schaaf, Peter

BOUREE ET MENUET see Krieger, Johann

BOURREE AUS DER LAUTEN-SUITE see Bach, Johann Sebastian, Suite for Lute, BWV 996, in E minor, Bourree

BOURREE, MIN 271 see Deuxieme Recueil De Pieces Faciles

BOUWSTENEN VAN HET POLYPHOON
    GITAARSPEL, VOL. I, NOS. 1-21 see
    Hoek, Jan-Anton Van

BOUWSTENEN VAN HET POLYPHOON
    GITAARSPEL, VOL. II, NOS. 22-37
    see Hoek, Jan-Anton Van

BOYD, ANNE
    Rose Garden, The; Theatre Piece For
      Singing Actress, Double Chorus
      And Instruments V/iii

    Voice Of The Phoenix, The V/i

BOZZA, EUGENE (1905-   )
    Berceuse Et Serenade I/IIB1

    Concertino Da Camera I/IIB4

    Impressions Andalouses, 2 I/IB4

    Polydiaphonie I/IIB1

    Preludes, 3 I/IB4

    Trois Pieces I/IIB1

BRACALI, GIAN PAOLO (1941-   )
    Viajes I/IB4

BRAHMS, JOHANNES (1833-1897)
    Ausgewahlte Lieder, 2 Vols. I/IIC1

    Cancion De Cuna see Wiegenlied

    Celebre Vals No. 15 I/IB3

    Danse Hongroise No. 5 see Hungarian
      Dance, No. 5

    Danse Hongroise No. 6 see Hungarian
      Dance, No. 6

    Danza Hungara No. 5 I/IB3
      see also Hungarian Dance, No. 5

    Hungarian Dance, No. 5 I/IB3

    Hungarian Dance, No. 6 I/IB3

    Valsas I/IB3

    Waltz, Op. 30, No. 9, in A minor
      I/IB3

    Waltz, Op. 39, No. 3 see Valsas

    Waltz, Op. 39, No. 8 I/IB3

    Waltz, Op. 39, No. 15 I/IB3
      see also Valsas

    Wiegenlied I/IB3, I/IIA1

BRAMBILLA, GIOVANNI
    Metodo Completo Per Chitarra, Part I:
      Elementi Principali II

    Metodo Completo Per Chitarra, Part
      II: Perfezionamente II

BRAMBLE BRIAR, THE see Stevens,
    Bernard George, Ballad

BRANDAO, JOSE DOMINGOS (1904-   )
    Lusitano, Concerto I/IIIA

BRANLE see Deuxieme Recueil De Pieces
    Faciles; Besard, Jean-Baptiste

BRANLE DE BASQUE see Couperin, Louis

BRANLE DE LA CORNEMUSE see Ballard,
    Robert

BRANLE DE VILLAGE see Ballard, Robert

BRANLE DOUBLE see Adriaenssen, Emanuel

BRANLE GAY see Ballard, Robert;
    Besard, Jean-Baptiste; Le Roy,
    Adrien; Le Roy, Adrien

BRANLES DE BOURGOGNE, 9 see Le Roy,
    Adrien

BRANSLE see Danses, 4

BRANSLE, MIN416 see Morley, Thomas

BRANSLE, MIN417 see Morley, Thomas

BRANZOLI, G.
    Metodo Teorico-Pratico II

BRASILEIRA, SUL NOME DI LAURINDO
    ALMEIDA see Castelnuovo-Tedesco,
    Mario

BRASILEIRAS, NO.1 see Bosmans, Arthur

BRASILEIRAS, NO.2 see Bosmans, Arthur

BRASILEIRAS, NO.3 see Bosmans, Arthur

BRASILEIRAS, NO.4 see Bosmans, Arthur

BRASILEIRAS, NO. 5 see Bosmans, Arthur

BRASILIANISCH see Walker, Luise

BRAUN, GUNTER
    Serie I/IIB1

    Sonatina I/IIB1

BRAUN, PEE MICHAEL
    Monophonie Fur Gitarre I/IB4

BRAYSSING, GREGOIRE
    Fantasies, 3 I/IB1

    Fantasy No. 1 see Fantasies, 3

    Fantasy No. 5 see Fantasies, 3

    Fantasy No. 6 see Fantasies, 3

    M. Gregoire Brayssing I/IB1

BREAM, THE see Blyton, Carey

BREDENBEEK, HANS
    Canciones, 2 I/IB4

    Miniature Suite I/IB4

    Trichordon-Dance I/IB4

BREGUET, JACQUES
    Omaggio Al Liutisti Italiani see
      Suite

    Suite I/IB4

BREME, LA see Blyton, Carey, Bream,
    The

BRESCIANELLO, GIOVANNI ANTONIO
    (ca. 1690-1752)
    Adagio see Pezzi, 2

    Capriccio see Pezzi, 2

    Partita No. 6 I/IB1

    Partita No. 7 I/IB1

    Partita No. 16 I/IB1

    Pezzi, 2 I/IB1

    Suite in E minor I/IB1

BRESGEN, CESAR (1913-   )
    Christkindl-Kumedi, Ein Geistliches
      Komodienspiel Aus Bayern IV/IIC5

    Europe Curieuse, L', Eine Kuriose
      Europa-Kantate Fur Kinder I/IIC5

    Funf Rumanische Gesange I/IIC1

    Kammerkonzert I/IIIA

    Malinconia I/IB4

    Stornelli I/IIB3

    Suite Uber Altbohmische
      Weihnachtsweisen IV/IIB1

    Tschechoslowakische Suite I/IIC1

    Von Mausen, Autos Und Anderen Tieren;
      25 Kinderlieder Zum Singen Und
      Spielen I/IIC5

BRETONISCHER TANZ see Tanze, 6

BREVE GUIDA PER CHITARRA see Serafini,
    Cesare

BRIANO, GIOVANNI BATTISTA
    Fuga Terza I/IIA2

    Fugue No. 3 I/IB4

BRIEF MASS, A see Moevs, Robert Walter

BRINDLE, REGINALD SMITH
    see SMITH BRINDLE, REGINALD

BRITTEN, [SIR] BENJAMIN (1913-1976)
    Bonny At Morn see England

    England I/IIC1

    I Will Give My Love An Apple see
      England

    Master Kilby see England

    Nocturnal, After John Dowland I/IB4

    Sailor-Boy see England

BRITTEN, [SIR] BENJAMIN (cont'd.)
    Shooting Of His Dear, The see
      England

    Soldier And The Sailor, The see
      England

    Songs From The Chinese I/IIC1

BROJER, ROBERT
    Gitarre Im Gruppenunterricht, Die,
      Auch Fur Einzelunterricht
      Verwendbar II

BROQUA, ALFONSO (1876-1946)
    Chacarera see Evocaciones Criollas,
      No.3

    Chants De l'Uruguay, 3 I/IIC3

    Chants Du Parana I/IIC1

    Ecos Del Paisage see Evocaciones
      Criollas, No.1

    Etudes Creolles, 7 I/IA

    Evocaciones Criollas, No.1 I/IB4

    Evocaciones Criollas, No.2 I/IB4

    Evocaciones Criollas, No.3 I/IB4

    Evocaciones Criollas, No.4 I/IB4

    Evocaciones Criollas, No.5 I/IB4

    Evocaciones Criollas, No.6 I/IB4

    Evocaciones Criollas, No.7 I/IB4

    Milongueos see Evocaciones Criollas,
      No.5

    Pampeana see Evocaciones Criollas,
      No.6

    Ritmos Camperos see Evocaciones
      Criollas, No.7

    Tango, El I/IIA1

    Vidala see Evocaciones Criollas,
      No.2

    Zamba Romantica see Evocaciones
      Criollas, No.4

BROUWER, LEO (1939-   )
    Airs Populaires Cubains, 2 I/IB5

    Apuntes, 3 I/IB4

    Canticum I/IB4

    Concerto I/IIIA

    Danza Caracteristica, Para El
      "Quitate De La Arcera" I/IB4

    Ditirambo see Canticum

    Elogio De La Danza I/IB4

    Espiral Eterna, La I/IB4

    Espoiral Eterna Para Guitarra, La
      I/IB4

    Etudes Simples, Nos. 1-5 I/IA

    Etudes Simples, Nos. 6-10 I/IA

    Exclosion see Canticum

    Fugue I/IB4

    Micropiezas, Hommage A Darius Milhaud
      I/IIA1

    Per Suonare A Tre I/IIB2

    Pieza Sin Titulo I/IB4

    Piezas Populares Cubanas I/IB5

    Prelude I/IB4

    Sketches, 3 see Apuntes, 3

BROWN, CHARLES
    Canzona I/IB4

BROWN, EARLE (1926-   )
    From Here V/ii

BRUCHNER, RUDOLF
    Quartettino I In C I/IIA3

BRUCKE, DIE, EINE KAMMERMUSIK NACH
    GEDICHTEN AUS "DIE CHINESISCHE
    FLOTE" VON HANS BETHGE see Kukuck,
    Felicitas

CAMPANELLA, LA see Paganini, Niccolo

CAMPESINO ALEGRE, EL see Schumann, Robert (Alexander), Frohlicher Landmann

CAMPION, FRANCOIS (1680-1748)
Pieces, 20, De Son Livre De Tablature De Guitare I/IB1

Prelude and Fugue I/IB1

Prelude and Fugue in D I/IB1

Sarabande-Gigue I/IB1

Soiree A Versailles I/IB1

Suite in B minor I/IB1

Suite in D I/IB1

Suite in D minor I/IB1

Suite No. 2 in D I/IB1

CAMPRA, ANDRE (1660-1744)
Furlana I/IB1

Menuet Vif Et Gigue I/IIB1

CAN SHE EXCUSE see Dowland, John

CAN SHE EXCUSE MY WRONGS see Dowland, John; Dowland, John

CANARIE see Chambonnieres, Jacques Champion

CANARIES see Pujol, Emilio

CANARIO see Guerau, Francisco

CANARIO, EL see Castelnuovo-Tedesco, Mario, Escarraman, A Suite Of Spanish Dances From The XVIth Century (After Cervantes)

CANARIOS see Fleres, Rita Maria; Guerau, Francisco; Ruiz de Ribayaz, Lucas; Sanz, Gaspar; Sanz, Gaspar

CANARIOS, DANZA DEL SIGLO XVII see Guerau, Francisco

CANARIOS II see Sanz, Gaspar

CANCAO TRISTE see Tchaikovsky, Piotr Ilyich, Chanson Triste

CANCIO DE CUNA see Pujol, Emilio

CANCION see Gall, Louis Ignatius; Mendelssohn-Bartholdy, Felix; Sojo, Vincente E.

CANCION AMATORIA, ESTUDIO see Pujol, Emilio

CANCION ARABE see Granados, Enrique

CANCION ARGENTINA, SUL NOME DI ERNESTO BITETTI see Castelnuovo-Tedesco, Mario

CANCION CARORENA, MELODIA VENEZUELANA I/IB5

CANCION CATALANA see Transcripciones Por Graciano Tarrago [1]

CANCION CUBANA, SUL NOME DI HECTOR GARCIA see Castelnuovo-Tedesco, Mario

CANCION DE CARNAVAL see Thomas, Juan Maria

CANCION DE CUNA I/IB5
see also Brahms, Johannes, Wiegenlied; Flies, J. Bernhard, Wiegenlied "Schlafe Mein Prinzchen"

CANCION DE NAVIDAD see Antiga, Jean

CANCION DE PRIMAVERA see Mendelssohn-Bartholdy, Felix, Fruhlingslied

CANCION DEL EMPERADOR see Narvaez, Luis de

CANCION DEL NORTE see Schumann, Robert (Alexander), Nordisches Lied

CANCION INFANTIL see Lazarde, Romulo

CANCION LEJANA see Azpiazu, Jose de

CANCION OLVIDADA see Sanchez, B.

CANCION POPULAR see Schumann, Robert (Alexander); Schumann, Robert (Alexander), Volksliedchen

CANCION RELIGIOSA see Cabezon, Antonio de

CANCION SILVESTRE see Schumann, Robert (Alexander), Sylvesterlied

CANCION SIN PALABRAS see Tchaikovsky, Piotr Ilyich, Chant Sans Paroles

CANCION TRISTE see Tchaikovsky, Piotr Ilyich, Chanson Triste

CANCION VENEZUELANA, SUL NOME DI ALIRIO DIAZ see Castelnuovo-Tedesco, Mario

CANCION Y DANZA NO. 1 see Mompou, Federico; Ruiz Pipo, Antonio

CANCION Y DANZA, NO.2 see Ruiz Pipo, Antonio

CANCIONES, 2 see Bredenbeek, Hans

CANCIONES, 6, DE FEDERICO GARCIA LORCA see ApIvor, Denis

CANCIONES ANTIGUAS, 5 I/IIC1-Coll

CANCIONES ANTIGUAS, 6 I/IIC1-Coll

CANCIONES CATALANAS NAVIDENAS, 4 IV/I

CANCIONES DE GARCIA LORCA see Aschero, Sergio

CANCIONES DE NAVIDAD, 8 IV/I

CANCIONES DEL SIGLO XVII, 5 I/IIC1-Coll

CANCIONES ESPANOLAS, 7 see Moreno Torroba, Federico

CANCIONES NO. 1, 2 Y 3 see Aguirre, Julian

CANCIONES POPULARES I/IB5-Coll

CANCIONES POPULARES CATALANAS, 4 I/IIC1-Coll

CANCIONES POPULARES CATALANAS, 10 I/IB5-Coll, IV/I

CANCIONES POPULARES ESPANOLAS I/IIC1-Coll, IV/IIC1

CANCIONES POPULARES ESPANOLAS, 5 I/IIC1-Coll, IV/IIC1

4 CANCIONES POPULARES ESPANOLAS see Bielsa, Valentin

CANCIONES POPULARES GALLEGAS, 2 IV/I

CANCIONES POPULARES MALLORQUINAS, 4 see Thomas, Juan Maria

CANCIONES POPULARES MEXICANAS, 3 see Ponce, Manuel Maria

CANCIONES POPULARES MEXICANAS, 3 I/IIA2-Coll

CANCIONES POPULARES MEXICANAS, 8 I/IB5-Coll

CANCO DEL LLADRA see Duarte, John W., Variations On A Catalan Folk Song

CANCO DEL LLADRE, LA see Canciones Populares Catalanas, 4

CANCO DEL LLADRE, POPULAR CATALANA see Sainz de la Maza, Eduardo

CANINO, BRUNO (1936-   )
Cadenze, For Harpsichord And Instruments V/i

CANO, ANTONIO (1811-1897)
Andante Grave I/IB3

Metodo De Guitarra II

Principios De Guitarra, 20 Lecciones Muy Faciles Y Progresivas I/IA

Study in D I/IA

Study in E I/IA

Study in G I/IA

CANON see Couperin, Louis, Saraband, MIN 241

CANON IN E see Radolt, Wenzel Ludwig Freiherr von

CANON PAR MOUVEMENT RETROGRADE see Bach, Johann Sebastian

CANONICO, BENITO
Aire De Joropo I/IB4

Totumo De Guarenas, El see Aire De Joropo

CANONS IN II see Nijenhuis, Luc

CANT DELS OCELLS, EL see Canciones Catalanas Navidenas, 4

CANTABILE see Paganini, Niccolo; Wanhal, Johann Baptist (Jan Krtitel); Wensiecki, Edmund

CANTAR Y TANER see Lopez, Joaquin

CANTARES see Gerhard, Roberto; Turina, Joaquin

CANTATA SPAGNUOLA A VOCE SOLA E CHITARRA E BASSO CONTINUO see Handel, George Frideric, No Se Emendera Jamas

CANTI DELLA PIANURA see Rosetta, Giuseppe

CANTI DI NATALE IV/I

CANTI DI NATALE IV/IIC1

CANTI MEDIOEVALI, 8 I/IB1

CANTICA I see Lechner, Konrad

CANTICO see Sojo, Vincente E.

CANTICUM see Brouwer, Leo

CANTICUM PSALMI AD LAUDES see Schonbach, Dieter

CANTICUM PSALMI RESURRECTIONIS see Schonbach, Dieter

CANTIGA LX see Alfonso X, el Sabio, King of Castile

CANTIGA LXV see Alfonso X, el Sabio, King of Castile

2 CANTIGAS see Alfonso X, el Sabio, King of Castile

CANTILENA (THEME AND 2 VARIATIONS) see Byrd, William

CANTILENE see Alfonso, Nicolas

CANTIONES LATINAE, MEDII ET RECENTIORIS AEVI AD CANTUM CUM CITHARA see Novak, Jan

CANTO see McCabe, John

CANTO DE OTONO see Pujol, Emilio

CANTO DEL CAMPESINO see Grieg, Edvard Hagerup, Folkvise (Folksong)

CANTO DEL VIERZO see Canciones Populares Gallegas, 2

CANTO DELLA CITTA INQUIETA DA "TOTALE" see Gaslini, Giorgio

CANTO DELL'ARPEGGIONE see Prosperi, Carlo

CANTO DELLE AZORRE, SUL NOME DI ENOS see Castelnuovo-Tedesco, Mario

CANTO LIBRE see Ruiz Pipo, Antonio

CANTOS A LA NOCHE see Ruiz Pipo, Antonio

CANZONA see Brown, Charles

CANZONA SECONDA see Frescobaldi, Girolamo

CANZONABILE see Kroll, Georg

CANZONCINA see Usher, Terry

CANZONE see Stingl, Anton

CANZONE see Canzonen Und Tanze Aus Dem XVI. Jahrhundert

CANZONE see Canzonen Und Tanze Aus Dem XVI. Jahrhundert

CANZONE CALABRESE, SUL NOME DI ERNEST CALABRIA see Castelnuovo-Tedesco, Mario

CANZONE DI NOTTE see Read, Gardner

CANZONE NOTTURNA see Gilardino, Angelo

CANZONE SICILIANA, SUL NOME DI MARIO GANGI see Castelnuovo-Tedesco, Mario

CANZONEN, 3 see David, Thomas Christian

CANZONEN UND TANZE AUS DEM XVI. JAHRHUNDERT I/IB1

CANZONETTA see Mendelssohn-Bartholdy, Felix; Tansman, Alexandre

CANZONETTA D'AMORE see Monteverdi, Claudio

CANZONETTA I see Morley, Thomas

CANZONETTA II see Morley, Thomas

CANZONETTE A TRE VOCI, 3 see Monteverdi, Claudio

CANZONETTE D'AMORE see Monteverdi, Claudio

CANZONETTE STRUMENTALI A TRE VOCI see Monteverdi, Claudio

CANZONI, 3 see Monteverdi, Claudio

CANZONI DEI TROVATORI, 5 see Farkas, Ferenc

CANZONI ELISABETTIANE, 2 see Dowland, John

CAP I CUA see Pujol, Emilio

CAPELLI, GIOVANNI MARIA (1648-1728)
    Trio Sonata in F I/IIB2

CAPO TASTO see Nijenhuis, Luc

CAPONIGRO, ANDREW
    Fingerboard Workbook, The, A Non-Method For Guitar III

CAPRI see Azpiazu, Jose de

CAPRICCI, 6 see Carcassi, Matteo, Caprices, 6; Legnani, Luigi

CAPRICCI, 36 see Legnani, Luigi

CAPRICCI, 36, VOL. 1, NOS. 1-18 see Legnani, Luigi

CAPRICCI, 36, VOL. 2, NOS. 19-36 see Legnani, Luigi

CAPRICCI ARMONICI: SARABANDE-GIGUE see Roncalli, Ludovico

CAPRICCI ARMONICI SOPRA LA CHITARRA SPAGNOLA see Roncalli, Ludovico, Suiten, 9

CAPRICCI SCELTI, 10 see Legnani, Luigi

CAPRICCIO DIABOLICO, OMAGGIO A PAGANINI see Castelnuovo-Tedesco, Mario

CAPRICCIO FLAMENCO, SUL TEMA POPOLARE "EL VITO" see Abloniz, Miguel

CAPRICCIO, LA CASCATELLA see Orsolino, Federico

CAPRICCIO NAPOLETANO see Pizzini, Carlo Alberto

CAPRICCIO UND PASTORALE see Carcassi, Matteo

CAPRICE, COMPLAINTE ET RONDE see Djemil, Enyss

CAPRICE FLAMENCO see Mazmanian, Vrouyr

CAPRICE FUR GITARRE see Giuliani, Mauro

CAPRICE GEORGIEN see Digmeloff, Germain

CAPRICE VARIE SUR UN THEME D'AGUADO see Pujol, Emilio

CAPRICEN, 6 see Carcassi, Matteo, Caprices, 6

CAPRICES, 6 see Carcassi, Matteo

CAPRICES CONCERTANTS see Becker, Gunther

CAPRICHO ARABE, SERENATA see Tarrega, Francisco

CAPRICHO CATALAN see Albeniz, Isaac

CAPRICHO ESPANOL see Granados, Enrique

CAPRICHO-ESTUDIO, OP. 13 see Fortea, Daniel

CAPRICHO-ESTUDIO, OP. 45 see Fortea, Daniel

CAPRICHOS, 6 see Carcassi, Matteo, Caprices, 6

CAPRICHOS DE GOYA, 24, VOL. 1, NOS. 1-6 see Castelnuovo-Tedesco, Mario

CAPRICHOS DE GOYA, 24, VOL. 2, NOS. 7-12 see Castelnuovo-Tedesco, Mario

CAPRICHOS DE GOYA, 24, VOL. 3, NOS. 13-18 see Castelnuovo-Tedesco, Mario

CAPRICHOS DE GOYA, 24, VOL. 4, NOS. 19-24 see Castelnuovo-Tedesco, Mario

CAPTAIN DIGORIE PIPER'S GALLIARD see Dowland, John

CARA, MARCHETTO (? -1525)
    Io Non Compro, Frottola I/IIC1

CARCASSI, MATTEO (1792-1853)
    Allegretto I/IB2

    Ausgewahlte Walzer, 20 I/IB2

    Capricci, 6 see Caprices, 6

    Capriccio I/IB2

    Capriccio Und Pastorale I/IB2

    Capricen, 6 see Caprices, 6

    Caprices, 6 I/IA, I/IC

    Caprichos, 6 see Caprices, 6

    Carcassi-Brevier I/IB2

    Carcassi Method For The Guitar see Vollstandige Guitarre-Schule

    Classical Guitar Method see Vollstandige Guitarre-Schule

    Estudios, 25 see Melodische Und Progressive Etuden, 25

    Estudios Melodicos Progresivos, 25 see Melodische Und Progressive Etuden, 25

    Estudios Progresivos, 25 see Melodische Und Progressive Etuden, 25

    Etude De Tremolo I/IA

    Etuden, 25 see Melodische Und Progressive Etuden, 25

    Etuden Fur Die Mittelstufe I/IA

    Etudes, 25 see Melodische Und Progressive Etuden, 25; Melodische Und Progressive Etuden, 25

    Gitarren-Schule, Vol. I see Vollstandige Guitarre-Schule

    Gitarren-Schule, Vol. II see Vollstandige Guitarre-Schule

    Gitarren-Schule, Vol. III: 50 Ubungen In Fortschreitender Schwierigkeit see Vollstandige Guitarre-Schule

    Kleine Stucke, 24 I/IB2

    Leichte Capricen, 6 see Caprices, 6

    Leichte Stucke, 12 I/IB2

    Leichte Variationen, 6 I/IB2

    Melodische Und Fortschreitende Etuden, 25 see Melodische Und Progressive Etuden, 25

    Melodische Und Progressive Etuden, 25 I/IA

    Melodische Und Progressive Etuden, 25, Vol. 1, Nos. 1-13 see Melodische Und Progressive Etuden, 25

    Melodische Und Progressive Etuden, 25, Vol. 2, Nos. 14-25 see Melodische Und Progressive Etuden, 25

    Menuets, 2 I/IB2

    Metodo Completo Para Guitarra, Vol. I see Vollstandige Guitarre-Schule

    Metodo Per Chitarra, Vol. I see Vollstandige Guitarre-Schule

    Metodo Per Chitarra, Vol. II see Vollstandige Guitarre-Schule

CARCASSI, MATTEO (cont'd.)

    Minuet I/IB2

    Minuet in G I/IB2

    Minuet in G, MIN 333 I/IB2

    Rondo, MIN 383 I/IB2

    Rondoletto I/IB2

    Schule Des Kunstlerischen Gitarrespiels; Ganzliche Neubearbeitung Fur Den Heutigen Gebrauch see Vollstandige Guitarre-Schule

    Skola Igry Na Westistrinnoi Gitare (Method For Playing The 6-Stringed Guitar) see Vollstandige Guitarre-Schule

    Sonatinen, 3 I/IB2

    Studi Melodici E Progressivi see Melodische Und Progressive Etuden, 25

    Studi Melodici E Progressivi, 25 see Melodische Und Progressive Etuden, 25

    Study in A I/IA

    Study, Op. 60, No. 3, in A I/IA

    Study, Op. 60, No. 19, in E minor I/IA

    Tremolo-Etude I/IA

    Tremolo Study I/IA

    Variationen Uber "Le Songe De Rousseau" I/IB2

    Vollstandige Guitarre-Schule II

CARCASSI-BREVIER see Carcassi, Matteo

CARCASSI METHOD FOR THE GUITAR see Carcassi, Matteo, Vollstandige Guitarre-Schule

CARILLON see Boismortier, Joseph Bodin de; Duarte, John W.

CARLO CALVI see Calvi, Carlo

CARLSTEDT, JAN (1926-   )
    Allegro see Danzas Suecas, 2

    Andantino see Danzas Suecas, 2

    Danzas Suecas, 2 I/IB5

CARMAN'S WHISTLE see Banks, Don; Johnson, Robert [3]

CARMAN'S WHISTLE, THE see Byrd, William

CARNET DE NOTES see Eynard, Camille

CARO MIO BEN see Giordani, Tommaso

CAROLS, 25, FROM THE OXFORD BOOK OF CAROLS FOR SCHOOLS IV/IIC1

CAROLS FOR GUITAR IV/I

CAROLS FOR GUITAR, 6 IV/I

CAROLS FOR PLAYING WITH GUITAR ACCOMPANIMENT IV/IIB2

CARORA, VALSE VENEZOLANO see Lauro, Antonio

CARORENA, CANZONE VENEZUELANA see Perez, Rafael

CAROSO, FABRIZIO (1526-1600)
    Alta Vittoria see Pieces, 4

    Aria E Danza I/IB1

    Ballarino, Il I/IB1-Coll

    Balletto I/IIB1

    Bassa Savella see Pieces, 4

    Bellezze D'Olimpia see Pieces, 4

    Forza D'Amore see Pieces, 4

    Laura Soave I/IB1

    Petites Pieces, 8 I/IB1

    Pieces, 4 I/IB1

CASTELNUOVO-TEDESCO, MARIO (cont'd.)

Cancion Cubana, Sul Nome Di Hector
Garcia I/IB4

Cancion Venezuelana, Sul Nome Di
Alirio Diaz I/IB4

Canto Delle Azorre, Sul Nome Di Enos
I/IB4

Canzone Calabrese, Sul Nome Di Ernest
Calabria I/IB4

Canzone Siciliana, Sul Nome Di Mario
Gangi I/IB4

Capriccio Diabolico, Omaggio A
Paganini I/IB4

Caprichos De Goya, 24, Vol. 1, Nos.
1-6 I/IB4

Caprichos De Goya, 24, Vol. 2, Nos.
7-12 I/IB4

Caprichos De Goya, 24, Vol. 3, Nos.
13-18 I/IB4

Caprichos De Goya, 24, Vol. 4, Nos.
19-24 I/IB4

Concerto in A see Concerto Sereno In
C

Concerto in D, Op. 99 I/IIIA

Concerto, Op. 201 I/IIIB

Concerto Sereno In C I/IIIA

Divan Of Moses-Ibn-Ezra (1055-1135),
A Cycle Of Songs I/IIC1

Escarraman, A Suite Of Spanish Dances
From The XVIth Century (After
Cervantes) I/IB4

Estudio Sul Nome Di Manuel Lopez
Ramos I/IA, I/IB4

Fantasy, Op. 145 I/IIB1

Gallarda see Escarraman, A Suite Of
Spanish Dances From The XVIth
Century (After Cervantes)

Guarda Cuyda Dosa, La see
Escarraman, A Suite Of Spanish
Dances From The XVIth Century
(After Cervantes)

Homage To Purcell, Fantasia Sul Nome
Di Ronald (1932-) E Henry (1659-
1695) Purcell I/IB4

Japanese Print, Sul Nome Di Jiro
Matsuda I/IB4

Naranjos En Flor see Aranci In Fiori

Ninna-Nanna, A Lullaby For Eugene
I/IB4

Ommagio A Boccherini see Sonata

Passacaglia, Omaggio A Roncalli
I/IB4

Pesame Dello see Escarraman, A Suite
Of Spanish Dances From The XVIth
Century (After Cervantes)

Platero Y Yo, Vol. I I/IIC1

Platero Y Yo, Vol. II I/IIC1

Platero Y Yo, Vol. III I/IIC1

Platero Y Yo, Vol. IV I/IIC1

Preludi Al Circeo, 3 I/IB4

Preludi Mediterranei, 3 I/IB4

Preludio In Forma Di Habanera, Sul
Nome Di Bruno Tonazzi I/IB4

Quintet, Op. 143 I/IIB4

Rey Don Alonso El Bueno, El see
Escarraman, A Suite Of Spanish
Dances From The XVIth Century
(After Cervantes)

Romancero Gitano V/ii

Romanza, Sul Nome Di Oscar Ghiglia
I/IB4

Rondel, Uber Den Namen Siegfried
Behrend I/IB4

Rondo, Op. 129 I/IB4

CASTELNUOVO-TEDESCO, MARIO (cont'd.)

Sarabande, Sul Nome Di Rey De La
Torre I/IB4

Serenade, Op. 118 I/IIIA

Sonata I/IC

Sonatina I/IIB1

Sonatina Canonica I/IIA1

Suite, Op. 133 I/IB4

Tanka, Sul Nome Di Isao Takahashi
I/IB4

Tarantella I/IB4

Tarantella Campana, Sul Nome Di
Eugene Di Novi I/IB4

Tonadilla, Sur Le Nom De Andres
Segovia I/IB4

Variations A Travers Les Siecles
I/IB4

Variations Plaisantes, Sur Un Petit
Air Populaire, "J'ai Du Bon Tabac
I/IB4

Villano, El see Escarraman, A Suite
Of Spanish Dances From The XVIth
Century (After Cervantes)

Volo d'Angeli, Sul Nome Di Angelo
Gilardino I/IB4

CASTET, FRANCOIS
Gammes, 24, De 2 Et 3 Octaves
Majeures Et Mineures (Melodiques,
Cadences Sur Differents Rythmes,
Choix d'Exercices Techniques III

Jeune Guitariste, Le, Premiere
Methode De Guitare II

CASTILLA, SEGUIDILLAS see Albeniz,
Isaac

CATALANISCHE WEISEN, 3 I/IB5-Coll,
IV/I

CATALUNA, CORRANDO see Albeniz, Isaac

CATEDRAL, LA see Barrios Mangore,
Augustin

CATENA D'AMORE see Negri, Cesare (il
Trombone)

CAVALLERIA DE NAPOLES, LA see Sanz,
Gaspar

CAVALLI, (PIETRO) FRANCESCO (1602-1676)
Calisto, La; Opera In Two Acts With A
Prologue V/iii

Ormindo, L'; Opera In Two Acts V/iii

CAVATINA see Bellow, Alexander;
Tansman, Alexandre

CAVAZZOLI, GERMANO
Preludi, 2 I/IIB2

Study I/IA

CECERE, C.
Sinfonia in G I/IIB2

CELEBRATED VALSE see Sor, Fernando,
Voyons Si C'est Ca, 6 Petites
Pieces Faciles, Op. 45, No. 6

CELEBRE ALLEGRO see Handel, George
Frideric

CELEBRE ARIA (LENTO) see Bach, Johann
Sebastian, Suite for Orchestra, BWV
1068, in D, Air

CELEBRE BADINERIE see Bach, Johann
Sebastian, Suite for Orchestra, BWV
1067, in B minor, Badinerie

CELEBRE GAVOTA see Lully, Jean-
Baptiste (Lulli)

CELEBRE LARGO see Handel, George
Frideric

CELEBRE MENUET see Boccherini, Luigi,
Minuet

CELEBRE MINETO see Boccherini, Luigi

CELEBRE MINUETO see Bolzoni, Giovanni,
Beruhmtes Menuett

CELEBRE MINUETTO see Bizet, Georges

CELEBRE PASSACAILLE EN RONDEAU,
HUITIEME ORDRE, LIVRE 2 see
Couperin, Francois (le Grand)

CELEBRE REVERIE see Schumann, Robert
(Alexander), Traumerei

CELEBRE SERENATA see Schubert, Franz
(Peter), Standchen; Toselli, Enrico

CELEBRE SONATA see Paganini, Niccolo

CELEBRE VALS NO. 15 see Brahms,
Johannes

CELEBRI MELODIE NATALIZIE IV/I

CELLO SUITE I see Bach, Johann
Sebastian, Suite for Violoncello,
BWV 1007, in G

CELLO SUITE II see Bach, Johann
Sebastian, Suite for Violoncello,
BWV 1008, in D minor

CELLO SUITE IV see Bach, Johann
Sebastian, Suite for Violoncello,
BWV 1010, in E flat

CELLO SUITE V - LUTE SUITE III see
Bach, Johann Sebastian, Suite for
Lute, BWV 995, in G minor

CENTONE DI SONATE; FOUR SONATAS see
Paganini, Niccolo

CENTOVENTI ARPEGGI DALL' OP. 1 see
Giuliani, Mauro, Studio Per La
Chitarra

CERF, JACQUES (1932-   )
Climat I/IIA1

Concerto Capriccioso I/IIIA

Concerto in A see Concerto
Capriccioso

Nuances I/IB4

Petit Ours, Le, Une Histoire Pour Les
Petits Et Les Grands Amis De La
Guitare I/IIA1

Pieces Sur 6 Cordes, 5 I/IB4

Suite Enfantine I/IB4

CERHA, FRIEDRICH (1926-   )
Intersecazioni I For Violin And
Orchestra V/ii

Intersecazioni II For Violin And
Orchestra V/ii

Langegger Nachtmusik I, For Orchestra
V/i

CERUTTI, L.
Methode Elementaire Pour La Guitare
II

CERVANTES, IGNACIO (1847-1905)
Danse Cubaine I/IIA1

Danses Cubaines, 2 I/IB5

CERVETTI, SERGIO (1940-   )
Six Sequences For Dance, For Chamber
Ensemble V/i

C'EST LE CHIEN DE JEAN DE NIVELLE see
Pijper, Willem, Romance Sans
Paroles

CESTA K UMELECKE HRE NA KYTARU, SKOLA
VYSSI TECHNIKY see Urban, Stepan

CETTE ETOILE ENSEIGNE A S'INCLINER see
Amy, Gilbert

CHACARERA see Broqua, Alfonso,
Evocaciones Criollas, No.3

CHACON, MEME
Metodo Y Ejercicios De Francisco
Tarrega III, VI-Mixed Coll

CHACONNE IN G, WITH 21 VARIATIONS see
Handel, George Frideric

CHACONNES, 12 see Derosier, Nicolas

CHAIKOVSKII, PETR IL'ICH
see TCHAIKOVSKY, PIOTR ILYICH

CHAILLY, LUCIANO (1920-   )
Invenzione, Su Quattro Note I/IB4

Recitativo E Fuga I/IIB3

CHAIN see Hekster, Walter

CHAMBONNIERES, JACQUES CHAMPION
    (ca. 1602-1672)
    Canarie I/IB1

CHANSON see Gagnebin, Henri; Hassler,
    Hans Leo; Jeune, Henri le;
    Komorous, Rudolf

CHANSON D'AMOURS ELIZABETHAINES, 3
    I/IIC1-Coll

CHANSON D'AUBE see Bonnard, Alain

CHANSON DE LOINTAIN see Boehmer,
    Konrad, Lied Uit De Verte

CHANSON DE NOEL IV/IIA1

CHANSON DE SOLVEIG see Grieg, Edvard
    Hagerup, Solveig's Song

CHANSON DE TESSA, LA see Jaubert,
    Maurice

CHANSON DU FEU FOLLET see Falla,
    Manuel de

CHANSON DU LUNDI, LA see Clement,
    Nicole

CHANSON ET PASTORALE see Lerich,
    Pierre

CHANSON FLAMENG see Hove, Joachim van
    den

CHANSON HINDOUE see Rimsky-Korsakov,
    Nikolai

CHANSON JOUEES, 3 see Chiereghin,
    Sergio

CHANSON TRISTE see Tchaikovsky, Piotr
    Ilyich

CHANSONATINE see Komter, Jan Maarten

CHANSONS, 4 see Enrichi, Arminio

CHANSONS BRESILIENNES, VOL. I
    I/IB5-Coll

CHANSONS BRESILIENNES, VOL. II
    I/IB5-Coll

CHANSONS CATALANES, 2 I/IB5-Coll

CHANSONS DE PANCRUCHE, 5 see
    Vandermaesbrugge, Max

CHANSONS POPULAIRES DU XVIIE SIECLE
    see Sanz, Gaspar

CHANSONS POPULAIRES ESPAGNOLES, 7,
    VOLS. 1-7 see Falla, Manuel de

CHANSONS POPULAIRES RUSSES, 7
    I/IB5-Coll

CHANT A L'IMMACULEE CONCEPTION see
    Correa, F.

CHANT D'AUTOMNE, ETUDE MELODIQUE see
    Pujol, Emilio, Canto De Otono

CHANT D'AUTOMNE FOR SOPRANO AND FULL
    ORCHESTRA see Denisov, Edison
    Vasilievich

CHANT DU SOIR see Shand, Ernest

CHANT ET TARENTELLE see De Filippi,
    Amedeo

CHANT SANS PAROLES see Tchaikovsky,
    Piotr Ilyich

[CHANTS, 3] see Tromboncino,
    Bartolomeo

[CHANTS, 4] I/IIC1-Coll

[CHANTS, 10] I/IIC1-Coll

CHANTS DE FRANCE ET D'AILLEURS, 20
    I/IIC4-Coll, IV/IIC4, IV/IIC4-Coll

CHANTS DE L'URUGUAY, 3 see Broqua,
    Alfonso

CHANTS DU PARANA see Broqua, Alfonso

CHANTS ET DANSES POPULAIRES FRANCAIS
    see Aubanel, Georges

CHANTS YOUGOSLAVES, 4 [NOS. 1-3] see
    Cossetto, Emil

CHAPI, R.
    Serenata Morisca I/IIA1

CHARAKTERISTIKON see Vackar, Dalibor
    Cyril

CHARDOME, RAYMOND
    Guitare d'Accompagnement, La, Methode
    Simplifiee Pour Amateurs II

CHARLEIN, ANTILLIAANSE WALS see Rooy,
    Julio

CHARPENTIER, JACQUES (1933-   )
    Concerto No. 2 I/IIIA

    Etude No. 1 I/IA

CHATEAU DE SABLE see Lerich, Pierre

CHAVARRI, EDUARDO LOPEZ (1871-1970)
    Piezas, 7 I/IB4

    Sonata No. 2 I/IC

CHAVEZ, CARLOS (1899-1978)
    Pieces, 3 I/IB4

CHAYNES, CHARLES (1925-   )
    Visions Concertantes, Concerto En 4
    Parties d'Apres 4 Toiles De
    Salvador Dali I/IIIA

CHEMINS II B, FOR ORCHESTRA see Berio,
    Luciano

CHEMINS II C, FOR BASS CLARINET AND
    ORCHESTRA see Berio, Luciano

CHERUBINI, LUIGI (1760-1842)
    Ali Baba Und Die Vierzig Rauber;
    Comic Opera In Prelude And Four
    Scenes V/iii

CHEVELURE DE BERENICE, LA see Ohana,
    Maurice, Si Le Jour Parait, No. 5

CHI VUCH VEDER see Monteverdi, Claudio

CHI VUOL VEDER D'INVERNO see
    Monteverdi, Claudio

CHI VUOL VEDER UN BOSCO see
    Monteverdi, Claudio

CH'I - YUN (ODER DAS PRINZIP INTENSIVEN
    LEBENS IN FRIEDEN) NACH DEM
    GEMALDEN "SCHWINGUNGEN", "LU-MI",
    "CHENG" VON GEORG W. BORSCHE see
    Furstenau, Wolfram

CHIARO DI LUNA see Beethoven, Ludwig
    van; Beethoven, Ludwig van, Sonata
    for Piano, Op. 27, No. 2, in C
    sharp minor,First Movement;
    Debussy, Claude, Clair De Lune

CHICO DA LA MADRE, EL see Noy De La
    Mare, El, Cancion Popular Catalan

CHIEREGHIN, SERGIO (1933-   )
    Aria see Tempi, 4

    Chanson Jouees, 3 I/IB4

    Danza Prima see Tempi, 4

    Danza Seconda see Tempi, 4

    Prelude see Tempi, 4

    Tempi, 4 I/IIB1

CHIERICI, FERNANDO (1912-   )
    Invito Alla Chitarra Flamenca II

    Metodo Per La Ricerca Degli Accordi
    Coi "Rivelatori", Metodo Pratico
    Per Il Dilettante, Promemoria
    Tascabile Per Il Professionista,
    (100 Accordi Con "Barre" In Prima
    Posizione, 1200 Accordi Coi
    "Rivelatori" III

    Prontuario Di Tutti Gli Accordi Per
    Chitarra, Vol. I: 2400 Posizioni
    III

    Prontuario Di Tutti Gli Accordi Per
    Chitarra, Vol. II: 1440 Posizioni
    III

CHIESA, RUGGERO
    Tecnica Fondamentale Della Chitarra,
    Vol. I: Le Scale III

    Tecnica Fondamentale Della Chitarra,
    Vol. II: Le Legature III

CHIMERES, NO. 1 see Sanchez, B.,
    Quimeras, No.1

CHIMERES, NO. 2 see Sanchez, B.,
    Quimeras, No.2

CHIMERES, NO. 3 see Sanchez, B.,
    Quimeras, No.3

CHITARRA D'ACCOMPAGNAMENTO, LA, METODO
    LAMPO ANCHE PER CHI NON CONOSCE LA
    MUSICA see Anzaghi, Luigi Oreste

CHITARRISTA AUTODIDATTA, IL, METODO
    COMPLETO PER CHITARRA CLASSICA see
    Terzi, Benvenuto

CHITARRISTA AUTODIDATTA, IL, NUOVISSIMO
    METODO FACILE PER CHITARRA A NUMERI
    E A MUSICA, INDISPENSABILE PER CHI
    NON CONOSCE LA MUSICA, UTILE PER
    GLI ORCHESTRALI see Ricchi,
    Modesto

CHITARRISTA CLASSICO, IL see Rossi,
    Abner

CHITARRISTA MODERNO, IL see Pili,
    Salvatore

CHITARRISTA VIRTUOSO, IL see Anzaghi,
    Luigi Oreste

CHOCS see Drogoz, Philippe

CHOIX DE MES FLEURS CHERIES see
    Giuliani, Mauro

CHOIX DE MES FLEURS CHERIES (LE BOUQUET
    EMBLEMATIQUE) see Giuliani, Mauro

CHOIX D'ETUDES POUR GUITARE, VOL. 1:
    COURS PREPARATOIRE I/IB6-Coll,
    VI-Mixed Coll

CHOIX D'ETUDES POUR GUITARE, VOL. 2,
    COURS ELEMENTAIRE I/IB6-Coll

CHOPIN, FREDERIC (1810-1849)
    Composiciones, 3 I/IB2

    Etude No. 6 I/IB2

    Etude, Op. 10, No. 3, [excerpt]
    I/IB2

    Gota De Agua see Prelude No. 15

    Intimite see Etude, Op. 10, No. 3,
    [excerpt]

    Marcha Funebre I/IB2

    Mazurka No. 16 I/IB2

    Mazurka, Op. 7, No. 1 I/IB2

    Mazurka, Op. 7, No. 2 I/IB2

    Mazurka, Op. 23, No. 22 I/IB2

    Mazurka, Op. 33, No. 1 I/IB2

    Mazurka, Op. 33, No. 4 I/IB2

    Mazurka, Op. 33, No. 22 I/IB2

    Mazurka, Op. 63, No. 3 I/IB2

    Mazurka, Op. 64, No. 4 I/IB2

    Nocturne, Op. 9, No. 1 I/IB2

    Nocturne, Op. 9, No. 2 I/IB2

    Nocturne, Op. 15, No. 2 see
    Composiciones, 3

    Nocturne, Op. 48, No. 1 I/IB2

    Notturno I/IB2

    Notturno No. 2 I/IB2

    Notturno No. 9 I/IB2

    Prelude No. 1 I/IB2
    see also 2 Preludios

    Prelude No. 7 I/IB2

    Prelude No. 8 see Preludios

    Prelude No. 9 see Preludios

    Prelude No. 14 see 2 Preludios

    Prelude No. 15 I/IB2

    Prelude No. 20 I/IB2

    Prelude No. 21 see Composiciones, 3

    Prelude, Op. 28, No. 4 I/IB2
    see also Preludios, 6

    Prelude, Op. 28, No. 6 I/IB2
    see also Preludios, 3; Preludios,
    3; Preludios, 6

    Prelude, Op. 28, No. 7 see
    Preludios, 3; Preludios, 3;
    Preludios, 6; Two Preludes

    Prelude, Op. 28, No. 11 see
    Preludios, 6

CHOPIN, FREDERIC (cont'd.)

Prelude, Op. 28, No. 15 I/IB2
see also Preludios, 6

Prelude, Op. 28, No. 20 see
Preludios, 3; Preludios, 3;
Preludios, 6; Two Preludes

Preludios I/IB2

Preludios, 3 I/IB2

Preludios, 3 I/IB2

Preludios, 6 I/IB2

2 Preludios I/IB2

So Deep Is The Night see Etude, Op.
10, No. 3, [excerpt]

Studio Op. 10, No. 3 (Frammento) see
Etude, Op. 10, No. 3, [excerpt]

Tristesse see Etude, Op. 10, No. 3,
[excerpt]

Tristesse, Celebre see Etude, Op.
10, No. 3, [excerpt]

Tristeza see Etude, Op. 10, No. 3,
[excerpt]

Two Preludes I/IB2

Vals Brillante I/IB2
see also Waltz, Op. 34, No. 2

Waltz No. 10 I/IB2

Waltz, Op. 34, No. 2 I/IB2

Waltz, Op. 64, No. 2 I/IB2

Waltz, Op. 69, No. 1 I/IB2

Waltz, Op. 69, No. 2 I/IB2
see also Composiciones, 3

Waltz, Op. 70, No. 2 I/IB2

CHORAL see Schumann, Robert
(Alexander)

CHORAL UND LAUTE I/IB1-Coll,
I/IIC1-Coll, VII-Mixed Coll

CHORDS [FOR THE] CLASSIC GUITAR see
Foden, William

CHOREA see Farkas, Ferenc

CHOREIQUES see Miroglio, Francis

CHOREOGRAPHIE I see Heider, Werner

CHORINHO see Lerich, Pierre; Villa-
Lobos, Heitor

CHORO DA SAUDADE see Barrios Mangore,
Augustin

CHOROS BRASILEIRA see Margola, Manuel

CHOROS, NO. 1 see Villa-Lobos, Heitor

CHRISTGEBURT- UND MARIENLIEDER, VOL. I:
ALTDEUTSCHE CHRISTGEBURTLIEDER
IV/IIC1

CHRISTKINDELSPIEL, DAS, EIN
WEIHNACHTSPIEL see Reusch, Fritz

CHRISTKINDL-KUMEDI, EIN GEISTLICHES
KOMODIENSPIEL AUS BAYERN see
Bresgen, Cesar

CHRISTMAS CAROLS, 4 IV/I

CHRISTMAS CAROLS, 5 IV/I

CHRISTMAS TIME IV/IIC5

CHRISTOPHER PARKENING GUITAR METHOD,
THE, VOL. 1 see Parkening,
Christopher

CHROMATIC PAVAN see Philips, Peter

CHROMATIK see Muller, Siegfried

CHRONIKO see Terzakis, Dimitri

CHURFURST AUGUSTUS TANTZ see Royal
Dances, 4

CHURFURST MORITZ TANTZ see Royal
Dances, 4

CHURFURSTIN ZU SACHEN TENTZLEYN, DER
see Royal Dances, 4

CIACCONA see Weiss, Sylvius Leopold,
Chaconne, MIN 102

CIAIKOVSKI, PIETRO
see TCHAIKOVSKY, PIOTR ILYICH

CIELO SIN NOBES see Albeniz, Isaac

CIKKER, JAN (1911-   )
Spiel Von Liebe Und Tod, Ein; Opera
In One Act V/iii

CILENSEK, JOHANN (1913-   )
Sonata I/IIB1

CIMAROSA, DOMENICO (1749-1801)
Sonata I/IB1

Sonata in D I/IB1

Sonata, MIN 390 I/IB1

Sonata No. 1 I/IIA1

Sonata No. 2 I/IIA1

Sonata No. 3 see Sonatas, 6

Sonata No. 5 I/IB1
see also Sonatas, 6

Sonata No. 9 see Sonatas, 6

Sonata No. 14 see Sonatas, 6

Sonata No. 19 see Sonatas, 6

Sonata No. 23 see Sonatas, 6

Sonatas, 3 I/IB1

Sonatas, 3 I/IB1

Sonatas, 3, En Forma De Concierto
Italiano I/IB1

Sonatas, 6 I/IB1

CINQUANTAINE, LA, ARIA NELLO STILE
ANTICO see Marie, Gabriel

CINQUE CAPRICCI DI GIROLAMO FRESCOBALDI
"LA FRESCOBALDA" see Zimmermann,
Bernd Alois

CISTERWERKE, DIE, PART 1: WERKE FUR
CISTER ALLEIN see Holborne, Antony

CISTERWERKE, DIE, PART 2: WERKE FUR
CISTER UND EIN BASSINSTRUMENT see
Holborne, Antony

CITHAROEDIA STRIGONIENSIS, SOPRA MOTIVI
UNGHERESI DI ESZTERGOM DEL XVIII
SECOLO see Farkas, Ferenc

CIURLO, ERNESTO FAUSTO
Aria I/IB4

Barcarolle I/IB4

Moerens Incedebam, Mattutino I/IB4

Sotto La Pioggia I/IB4

CLAIR DE LUNE see Debussy, Claude

CLAIRONS ROYAUX, CLAIRONS ET TROMPETTES
see Sanz, Gaspar

CLARKE, JEREMIAH (ca. 1673-1707)
King's March I/IIA1

CLARO DE LUNA see Beethoven, Ludwig
van, Sonata for Piano, Op. 27, No.
2, in C sharp minor, First Movement

CLAROS Y FRESCOS RIOS, CANCION see
Mudarra, Alonso de

CLASSIC GUITAR, THE, ALL-TIME MASTER
MELODIES I/IB6-Coll

CLASSIC GUITAR, THE - TRADITIONAL AND
RELATED TECHNIQUES, A BASIC METHOD
see Buckingham, Jack

CLASSIC GUITAR DUETS I/IIA1

CLASSIC GUITAR ETUDES see Laurent,
Leo, Ecole Du Jeune Guitariste, L'

CLASSIC GUITAR SOLO ALBUM, VOL. 1
I/IB6-Coll

CLASSIC GUITAR TECHNIQUE, VOL. I see
Shearer, Aaron

CLASSIC GUITAR TECHNIQUE, VOL. II see
Shearer, Aaron

CLASSIC GUITAR TECHNIQUE, SUPPL. 1 see
Shearer, Aaron

CLASSIC GUITAR TECHNIQUE, SUPPL. 2:
BASIC ELEMENTS OF MUSIC THEORY FOR
THE GUITAR see Shearer, Aaron

CLASSIC GUITAR TECHNIQUE, SUPPL. 3 see
Shearer, Aaron

CLASSIC GUITAR TECHNIQUE, SUPPL. 4:
GUITAR NOTE SPELLER see Shearer,
Aaron

CLASSICAL ALBUM FOR GUITAR SOLO, A
I/IB6-Coll, VII-Mixed Coll

CLASSICAL GUITAR, THE, A NEW APPROACH
see Norman, Theodore

CLASSICAL GUITAR METHOD see Carcassi,
Matteo, Vollstandige Guitarre-
Schule

CLASSICAL SONGS, 10 I/IIC1-Coll,
VII-Mixed Coll

CLASSICAL STUDIES FOR GUITAR see
Higgins, Ralph

CLASSICS FOR GUITAR see Klasszikusok
Gitarra

CLAVECIN DE ZELAIA see Azpiazu, Jose
de

CLAVELITOS see Valverde, Joaquin

CLAVELITOS, ZAMBRA GITANA see
Valverde, Joaquin

CLEMENS, JACOBUS (CLEMENS NON PAPA)
(ca. 1510-ca. 1556)
Souterlied No. 99 I/IIA2

CLEMENS NON PAPA
see CLEMENS, JACOBUS

CLEMENT, JACOBUS
see CLEMENS, JACOBUS

CLEMENT, NICOLE
Au Jardin De La Patience I/IIC2

Chanson Du Lundi, La I/IIC3

CLEMENTI, ALDO (1925-   )
Reticolo 11 V/i

Sonata I/IIB2

CLEMENTINE see Devil And The Farmer's
Wife, The, And Other American
Ballads

CLIFFORD ESSEX SPANISH GUITAR TUTOR,
THE see Medio, Alonso

CLIMAT see Cerf, Jacques

CLOU, DER see Gitarre Spezial, Picking
Modern Arrangement, Vol. 1

CLOUDS AND ECLIPSES see Blake Watkins,
Michael

COCQ, FRANCOIS LE
Suite in A minor I/IB1

CODEX I see Halffter, Cristobal

COELHO SILVESTRE, LOURIVAL PINTO
Estilhacos I/IB4

COENEN, PAUL (1908-   )
Heitere Folge Von Vogel-Liedern
I/IIB1

Kleine Suite I/IIA1

COLLAGEN see Wusthoff, Klaus

COLLECTION DE 50 ESTUDIOS see Aguado,
Dionisio, Studies, 50

COLUMPIO, EL see Azpiazu, Jose de;
Tarrega, Francisco, Study, TI ii-
7a, in G

COME AGAIN see Dowland, John

COME AGAIN, SWEET LOVE see Dowland,
John

COME AWAY see Dowland, John

COME AWAY, COME, SWEET LOVE! see
Dowland, John

COMME UNE GIGUE see Martin, Frank

COMMUNITY SONGS, 40 I/IB5-Coll

COMPANY, ALVARO
Seis Cuerdas, Las I/IB4

COMPLAINTE see Praag, Henri C. van

COMPLAINTE A L'AIMEE DISPARUE see
Pujol, Emilio, Endecha Alla Amada
Ausente

COMPLAINTE FUNEBRE, FANTAISIE A LA
MEMOIRE DE IDA PRESTI (2.5.1967,
JOUR DE SON ENTERREMENT) see
Sanchez, B.

COMPLEMENT A LA TECHNIQUE DE LA GUITARE
see Sao Marcos, Maria Livia,
Erganzung Zur Gitarrentechnik

COMPLETE CLASSIC GUITAR, THE, A METHOD.
COMPLETE EXPLANATION OF THE RIGHT
HAND see Stockton, Fred

COMPLETE STUDY OF THE TREMOLO; 33
LESSONS see Bobri, Vladimir

COMPLETE TREMOLO BOOK FOR THE GUITAR,
THE see Papas, Sophocles

COMPLETE WORKS FOR GUITAR IN FACSIMILES
OF THE ORIGINAL EDITIONS, THE, VOL.
1-7 see Sor, Fernando

COMPLETE WORKS FOR GUITAR IN FACSIMILES
OF THE ORIGINAL EDITIONS, THE, VOL.
8: GUITAR DUETS, OP. 34-63 [1ST GTR
PART] see Sor, Fernando

COMPLETE WORKS FOR GUITAR IN FACSIMILES
OF THE ORIGINAL EDITIONS, THE, VOL.
9: GUITAR DUETS, OP. 34-63 [2ND GTR
PART] see Sor, Fernando

COMPOSICIONES, 3 see Chopin, Frederic

COMPOSICIONES CELEBRES, 10, VOL. 1
I/IB6-Coll

COMPOSICIONES CELEBRES, 10, VOL. 2
I/IB6-Coll

COMPOSICIONES CELEBRES, 12, VOL. 3
I/IB6-Coll, VI, VI-Mixed Coll

10 COMPOSICIONES CELEBRES PARA
GUITARRA, VOL. III I/IIA1-Coll

COMPOSICIONES CLASICAS Y ROMANTICAS
I/IB6-Coll, VII-Mixed Coll

COMPOSICIONES FACILES, 4 I/IB2-Coll

COMPOSICIONES ORIGINALES PARA GUITARRA,
10 VI-Coll

COMPOSICIONES ORIGINALES Y ESTUDIOS
PARA GUITARRA, VOL. I see Tarrega,
Francisco

COMPOSICIONES ORIGINALES Y ESTUDIOS
PARA GUITARRA, VOL. II see
Tarrega, Francisco

COMPOSICIONES ORIGINALES Y ESTUDIOS
PARA GUITARRA, VOL. III: 30
PRELUDIOS ORIGINALES see Tarrega,
Francisco

COMPOSICIONES ORIGINALES Y ESTUDIOS
PARA GUITARRA, VOL. III: 30
PRELUDIOS ORIGINALES see Tarrega,
Francisco

COMPOSICIONES ORIGINALES Y ESTUDIOS
PARA GUITARRA, VOL. IV see
Tarrega, Francisco

COMPOSICIONES PARA GUITARRA, 12 see
Tarrega, Francisco

COMPOSICIONES PARA GUITARRA, 19 see
Sor, Fernando

COMPOSICIONES PARA GUITARRA, VOL. 1
see Giuliani, Mauro

COMPOSICIONES PARA GUITARRA, VOL. 2
see Giuliani, Mauro

COMPOSITIONS, 3 see Debussy, Claude

COMPOSIZIONE IN TRE TEMPI, FOR
ORCHESTRA see Maderna, Bruno

COMPOSIZIONI, 4 see Lutzemberger,
Cesare

COMPOSIZIONI, 10 see Sanz, Gaspar

COMPOSIZIONI, 15 see Calvi, Carlo

COMPOSIZIONI INEDITE, 3 see Paganini,
Niccolo

COMPOSIZIONI ORIGINALI, 26 see
Paganini, Niccolo, Original
Kompositionen, 26

COMPOSIZIONI PER CHITARRA, 3 see
Cabezon, Antonio de

COMPREHENSIVE GUITAR METHOD, THE, FOR
CLASSROOM AND INDIVIDUAL
INSTRUCTION, VOL. A: TEACHER'S
MANUAL see Snyder, Jerrold

COMPREHENSIVE GUITAR METHOD, THE, FOR
CLASSROOM AND INDIVIDUAL
INSTRUCTION, VOL. B: STUDENT BOOK
see Snyder, Jerrold

COMPTINES POUR ANNE, 3 see Bleuse,
Marc

COMPUTED AND CONFOUNDED; A SHORT OPERA
see Krenek, Ernst, Ausgerechnet Und
Verspielt; Eine "Spiel"-Oper

COMTE DE PROVENCE, LE see Carpentier,
[Abbe] Joseph

CON ALLEGRIA see Mosso, Carlo

CON AMORES LA MI MADRE see Canciones
Antiguas, 6; Obradors, Fernando

CON BUEN AYRE, DUPLUM see Becker,
Gunther

CON PAVOR RECORDO EL MORO, ROMANCE see
Milan, Luis

CON QUE LA LAVARE see Narvaez, Luis de

CONCENTUS EURYDICAE see Novak, Jan,
Concerto Per Euridice

CONCENTUS RESONABILIS see Pololanik,
Zdenek

CONCEPT I, PER 2 PIANISTI E 3 GRUPPI
STRUMENTALI see Andriessen, Louis,
Ittrospezione III

CONCERT see Wijdeveld, Wolfgang

CONCERT BAROQUE, IN A see Azpiazu,
Jose de

CONCERTANTE SUITE see Hartig, Heinz
Friedrich

CONCERTINO DA CAMERA see Bozza, Eugene

CONCERTINO MEXICANO see Noble

CONCERTO A TRE see Peroni, Giuseppe

CONCERTO BANDISTICO see Kox, Hans

CONCERTO CAPRICCIOSO see Cerf, Jacques

CONCERTO DE MADRIGALI see Monteverdi,
Claudio

CONCERTO DE MARS see Bondon, Jacques

CONCERTO DELL'ARGENTAROLA see Porrino,
Ennio

CONCERTO FOR HARPSICHORD AND ORCHESTRA
IN F MINOR, 2ND MOV'T (ARIOSO) see
Bach, Johann Sebastian

CONCERTO IN F PER LIUTO E ARCHI see
Krebs, Johann Ludwig, Concerto in F
for Lute and Strings

CONCERTO IN G FOR GUITAR AND STRINGS
see Krebs, Johann Ludwig, Concerto
in F for Lute and Strings

CONCERTO PER EURIDICE see Novak, Jan

CONCERTO PER QUATTRO see Kotonski,
Wlodzimierz

CONCERTO PICCOLO see Buschmann,
Rainer-Glen

CONCERTO POUR HRISANIDE, LE, FOR PIANO
AND ORCHESTRA see Bois, Rob du

CONCERTO SERENO IN C see Castelnuovo-
Tedesco, Mario

CONCIERTO DE ARANJUEZ see Rodrigo,
Joaquin

CONCIERTO DE AZUL see Bordhays,
Christiane le

CONCIERTO DE CASTILLA see Moreno
Torroba, Federico

CONCIERTO DEL SUR see Ponce, Manuel
Maria

CONCIERTO EN RE see Sor, Fernando,
Grand Solo

CONCIERTO LEVANTINO see Palau, Manuel

CONCIERTO PARA TRES HERMANAS see
Pizzini, Carlo Alberto

CONDE CLAROS, 22 DIFERENCIAS see
Narvaez, Luis de, Variations, 22,
On The Romance "Conde Claros"

CONDE CLAROS DE DOZE MANERAS see
Mudarra, Alonso de

CONDOR PASA, EL; LIEDER UND TANZE AUS
SUDAMERIKA I/IB5

CONFIDENCIA, PRELUDIO see Sainz de la
Maza, Eduardo

CONSONANCIAS Y REDOBLES see Corghi,
Azio

CONSTANT, FRANZ (1910-   )
Humoresque I/IB4

Musique A Deux I/IIB1

Nocturne I/IB4

Poem I/IB4

Pour La Guitare, Vol. 1 I/IB4

Pour La Guitare, Vol. 2 I/IB4

CONTEMPLATIE see Rosseau, Norbert

CONTRADANZA see Moreno Torroba,
Federico

CONTRAPPUNTO SCHERZOSO see Rossi,
Abner

CONTRAPUNCTUS 1 see Bach, Johann
Sebastian

CONTRASTES see Absil, Jean

CONTRASTI see Baumann, Herbert

CONTRATANZ, MIN304 see Mozart,
Wolfgang Amadeus

CONTRATANZ, MIN307 see Mozart,
Wolfgang Amadeus

CONTREPOINTS, 2, SUR LE VILLANCICO "SI
AMORE ME HAN DE MATAR" see
Fuenllana, Miguel de

CONTRETANZ "LA FAVORITE" see Mozart,
Wolfgang Amadeus

CONVERSATION see Westra, Jan

CONVERSATION PIECE see Griffiths, John

CONVERSAZIONE A TRE see Borris,
Siegfried

CONYNGHAM, BARRY (1944-   )
Water...Footsteps...Time V/i

Water-Footsteps-Times, For Four
Instrumental Soloists And Two
Orchestra V/i

COPLAS DEL RUISENOR see Wilson, Thomas

COPLILLAS DE BELEN see Rodrigo,
Joaquin

CORAL Y MINUETO see Handel, George
Frideric

CORBETTA, FRANCESCO (FRANCISQUE
CORBETT) (ca. 1620-1681)
Allemande Aymee De l'Auteur I/IB1

Allemande, Cherie De Son Altesse Le
Duc d'York I/IB1

Allemande Du Roy I/IB1

Allemande Et Gigue I/IB1

Allemande Sur La Mort Du Duc De
Glocester I/IB1

Francesco Corbetta: 16 Compositions
Selected From "Varii Capricci Per
La Ghitarra Spagnuola" I/IB1

Gavotte, Aymee Du Duc De Monmouth
I/IB1

Passacaglia I/IB1

Prelude I/IB1

Saraband I/IB1

Suite in A minor I/IB1

Suite in D I/IB1

Tombeau De Madame d'Orleans, Le
I/IB1

CORDERO, ERNESTO (1946-   )
Mapeye, Canto Di Puerto Rico I/IB4

CORDES, 6...UNE GUITARE, METHODE DE
GUITARE A L'USAGE DES DEBUTANTS
see Mourat, Jean-Maurice

CORDOBA see Albeniz, Isaac; Albeniz, Isaac

CORELLI, ARCANGELO (1653-1713)
Adagio, MIN 288 see Pieces, 6

Courante, MIN 289 see Pieces, 6

Largo see Pieces, 6

Minuetto I/IB1

Pastorale IV/IIB2

Pieces, 6 I/IB1

Prelude, MIN 287 see Pieces, 6

Saraband, MIN 281 see Pieces, 6

Saraband, MIN 282 see Pieces, 6

Sarabande And Minuet I/IB1

Sarabande E Giga I/IB1

Sarabande E Giga I/IB1

Sonata da Camera, Op. 2, No. 2 I/IIB2

Sonata da Camera, Op. 4, No. 2 I/IIB2

Sonata da Chiesa, Op. 3, No. 1 I/IIB2

Sonata for Violin and Guitar in E minor, Op. 5, No. 8 I/IIB1

Sonata for Violin and Guitar, Op. 5, No. 7, in D minor I/IIB1

Sonata No. 3 I/IB1

Sonata No. 5 I/IB1

Sonata No. 8 I/IB1

Trio Sonata, Op. 4, No. 3 I/IIB2

Trio Sonata, Op. 4, No. 5 I/IIB2

CORGHI, AZIO (1937-)
Consonancias Y Redobles I/IB4, I/IIB1

CORMONT, JACQUES
Methode Pour Guitare, Vol. I II

Methode Pour Guitare, Vol. II II

Methode Voor Gitaar see Methode Pour Guitare, Vol. I; Methode Pour Guitare, Vol. II

CORO CRUCIFIXUS see Bach, Johann Sebastian, Mass In B Minor: Crucifixus

CORRANDA see Grau, Agusti

CORRANDES see Canciones Populares Catalanas, 4

CORRE AL PORTALICO see Villancicos Populares, Vol. III

CORREA, F.
Chant A l'Immaculee Conception I/IB1

CORREGGIA, ENRICO
Trasparenze I/IB4

CORRENTE, DETTA LA FAVORITA GONZAGA see Melii da Reggio, Pietro Paolo

CORRENTE QUATTRO, VOL. 1 see Frescobaldi, Girolamo

CORRENTE QUATTRO, VOL. 2 see Frescobaldi, Girolamo

CORRENTE UND SALTARELLO see Galilei, Michel Angelo

CORRESPONDANCES II see Becker, Gunther

CORRETTE, MICHEL (1709-1795)
Suite in A minor I/IIA1

CORRIENTE see Sanz, Gaspar

CORSO PREPARATORIO DI CHITARRA see Andreolli, Mariano

CORTEJO ET DANZA see Cruz, Ivo

COSSETTO, EMIL (1908-)
Chants Yougoslaves, 4 [Nos. 1-3] I/IIC5

Posavski Drmes see Chants Yougoslaves, 4 [Nos. 1-3]

COSSETTO, EMIL (cont'd.)
Slavonska Poskocica see Chants Yougoslaves, 4 [Nos. 1-3]

Tri Jetrve see Chants Yougoslaves, 4 [Nos. 1-3]

COSTE, NAPOLEON (1806-1883)
Barcarolle I/IIA1

Estudio De Concierto I/IB2

Estudios, 25 see Etudes, 25

Estudios Superiores, 25 see Etudes, 25

Etuden, 25 see Etudes, 25

Etudes, 25 I/IA

Etudes De Genre see Etudes, 25

Herbstblatter I/IB2

Melancolie I/IB2

Originalstucke, 6 I/IB2

Recreation I/IB2

Recreation Du Guitariste I/IB2

Reverie I/IB2

Rondo, MIN 384 I/IB2

Scherzo, MIN 385 I/IB2

Studi, 25 see Etudes, 25

9 Studien I/IB2

Studies, 25 see Etudes, 25

Study in A I/IA

Tarantelle I/IB2

Ubungs- Und Unterhaltungsstucke, 16 I/IB2

COTTIN, A.
Methode Complete De Guitare II

COTTON FIELDS see Hess, Reimund

COU-COU, LE see Daquin, Louis-Claude

COUCOU, LE: RONDO see Daquin, Louis-Claude

COULEURS, 6 see Leclercq, Norbert

COUNTESS OF PEMBROKE'S PARADISE see Holborne, Antony

COUNTESS OF PEMBROKE'S PARADISE, THE see Holborne, Antony

COUNTRY GARDENS see Blanchard, Carver William, Jr.

COUPERIN, FRANCOIS (LE GRAND) (1668-1733)
Barricades Mysterieuses, Les I/IB1

Celebre Passacaille En Rondeau, Huitieme Ordre, Livre 2 I/IB1

Fastes, Les I/IB1

Hat Darav Ket Gitarra I/IIA1

Musette De Choisy I/IIA2

Musette De Taverny I/IIA2

Pavan, MIN 343 I/IIA1

Petits Moulins A Vent, Les I/IIA1, I/IIB1

Pieces De Clavecin I/IB1

Sarabanda E Gavotta I/IB1

Sixieme Ordre I/IB1

Song Of The Devil I/IB1

Sylvains, Les I/IB1

Tizenket Darab Gitarra I/IB1

COUPERIN, LOUIS (ca. 1626-1661)
Branle De Basque see Pieces, 6

Canon see Saraband, MIN 241

Chaconne, MIN 238 I/IB1

Chaconne, MIN 239 see Pieces, 6

COUPERIN, LOUIS (cont'd.)
Couperins, The I/IB1

Gigue see Pieces, 6

Minuet see Pieces, 6

Passacaglia I/IB1

Pieces, 6 I/IB1

Piemontoise, La see Pieces, 6

Saraband, MIN 240 see Pieces, 6

Saraband, MIN 241 I/IB1

Tombeau Pour M. Blancrocher I/IB1

COUPERINS, THE see Couperin, Louis

COURANTE see Bach, Johann Sebastian, Suite for Lute, BWV 996, in E minor, Courante

COURANTE FRANCAISE see Mace, Thomas

COURANTE, MIN 15 see Danses, 4

COURANTE, MIN 16 see Danses, 4

COURANTE, MIN 272 see Deuxieme Recueil De Pieces Faciles

COURANTE, MIN 286 see Piezas Para Laud Del Siglo XVI, 4

COURANTE, MIN 411 see 3 Pieces By Holborne, Perichon, Balard

COURANTE, MIN 412 see 3 Pieces By Holborne, Perichon, Balard

COURANTES, 3 see Bacheler, Daniel

COURANTES, 6 see Dowland, Robert

COURANTES, 2 I/IB1

COUSIN GERMAIN, LE see Mace, Thomas

COVENTRY CAROL, THE see Easy Music, Vol. 2; Guitar Songbook, The; Piccola Antologia Chitarristica; Gavall, John

CRAB-FINGERINGS see Abloniz, Miguel, Imitando Il Granchio

CRACOW LUTE-BOOK, THE see Bakfark, Balint (Valentin), Lautenbuch Von Krakau, Das

CRANEN, T.
Kermis-Suite I/IIB5

CREMA, JOAN MARIA DA
Intavolatura Di Liuto: Libro Primo (1546) I/IB1-Coll

Pass'e Mezzo E Saltarello, A La Bolognesa I/IB1

Recercar Undecimo Y Recercar Tredecimo I/IB1

Ricercari, 5 I/IB1

CRESS ERTRINKT, EIN SCHULSPIEL see Fortner, Wolfgang

CRIMLISK, ANTHONY
Play Guitar!, Vol. I II

Play Guitar!, Vol. II II, VII-Mixed Coll

CRIOLLA see Sanchez, B.

CRISWICK, MARY
Guitar Tutor For Young Children II

7 CROQUIS see Pelemans, Willem

CRUELLE DEPARTIE, CHANSON see Besard, Jean-Baptiste

CRUZ, IVO (1901-)
Cortejo Et Danza I/IIA1

Pastorale I/IIA1

CRUZ DE CASTRO, CARLOS
Algo Para Guitarra I/IB4

Caminos I/IIA1

CSARDAS see Mertz, Johann Kaspar

CSONIKA, PAUL (1905-)
Serenata, For Violoncello And Orchestra V/i

CUADERNO TECNICO-RECREATIVO, PARA ALUMNOS DE GUITARRA (PREPARATORIO) see Anido, Maria Luisa

CUARTAS LECCIONES, LAS see Sagreras, Julio S., Lessons For The Guitar, Vol. 4, The Fourth Lessons

CUARTE SUITE PARA LAUD see Bach, Johann Sebastian, Partita for Lute, BWV 1006a, in E

CUATRO MULEROS, LOS, TEMA Y VARIACIONES see Angel, Miguel

CUBA, CAPRICHO see Albeniz, Isaac

CUBANA see Pujol, Emilio

CUCKOO, THE see Hess, Reimund

CUI, CESAR ANTONOVICH (1835-1918) Orientale I/IB3

CUMPARSITA, LA, TANGO see Matos Rodriguez, Gerardo H.

CURRANTA FOR MRS. ELIZABETH MURCOTT see Pilkington, Francis

CURRUTACAS MODESTAS, LA, TONADILLA see Granados, Enrique

CUTTING, FRANCIS
Almain, MIN 242 I/IB1

Almain, MIN 246 see Pieces, 2

Almain, MIN 249 I/IB1 see also Pieces, 5

Almain Und Jig I/IB1

Cutting's Comfort see Pieces, 5

Galliard, MIN 247 see Pieces, 2

Galliard, MIN 248 see Pieces, 5

Galliard, MIN 250 see Pieces, 5

Greensleeves I/IB1

Pavan, MIN 245 I/IB1

Pavane Sans Pair see Pieces, 5

Pieces, 2 I/IB1

Pieces, 5 I/IB1

Walsingham I/IB1

Walsingham Variations see Walsingham

CUTTING'S COMFORT see Cutting, Francis

CYCLAMEN see Leclercq, Norbert

CYCLOFONIE IX, FOR SOLO PERCUSSION PLAYER AND ORCHESTRA see Kox, Hans

CYGNE, LE see Saint-Saens, Camille

CYKLE NA GITARE, 2, CZTERY UTWORY see Mronski, Stanislaw

CZERNIK, WILLY (1904-   ) Kurzweilige Stucke, 10 I/IB4

CZERNUSCHKA, FRITZ Kleine Etuden, 2 I/IA

Prelude in E minor I/IB4

DA UN CODICE LAUTEN-BUCH DEL CINQUECENTO I/IB1-Coll

DAAR GINGEN TWEE GESPEELKENS GOED, VARIATIES OP EEN VOLKSLIED see Niessen, Hans-Lutz

DAGOSTO, SYLVAIN Etude in F I/IA

Feria Al Prado, Sevillana I/IB5

Petit Guitariste, Le I/IB4

Rapido, Lo, Etude I/IA

Romance in E I/IB4

DAIDALOS; BALLET IN SEVEN SCENES FOR SIX PLAYERS see Otte, Hans

DAILY EXERCISES, 130 see Bobri, Vladimir

130 DAILY STUDIES FOR THE CLASSIC GUITAR see Bobri, Vladimir

DALLINGER, FRIDOLIN (1933-   ) Sonatina for Flute and Guitar I/IIB1

DALZA, JOAN AMBROSIO Intabulatura De Lauto (Petrucci, 1508), Part 1: "Tastar De Corde - Calate" I/IB1-Coll

Intabulatura De Lauto (Petrucci, 1508), Part 2: "Padoane Alla Venetiana" I/IB1-Coll

Intabulatura De Lauto (Petrucci, 1508), Part 3: "Padoane Alla Ferrarese" I/IB1-Coll

DANCE GUERRIERE see Farkas, Ferenc

DANCE OF A TRIBAL CHIEF see Staak, Pieter van der

DANCE OF CHACMOL ("CANEK"); MUSIC DRAMA see Hively, Wells

DANCE OF THE CORREGIDOR see Falla, Manuel de

DANCE OF THE MILLER see Falla, Manuel de

DANCE POPULAIRE see Paubon, Pierre

DANCE-VARIATIONS ON A DUTCH SONG see Langenberg, Jan van den

DANCERIE see Bonnard, Alain

DANCES, 2 see Lubach, Andries A.

DANCES, 2, NO. 1 see Falla, Manuel de, Dance Of The Miller

DANCES, 2, NO. 2 see Falla, Manuel de, Dance Of The Corregidor

DANCES, 3 see Byrd, William

DANCES, 3 see Gibbons, Orlando

DANCES, 6 see Gramberg, Jacq

DANCES, 8 see Besard, Jean-Baptiste

2 DANCES AND 2 FANTASIES see Adriaenssen, Emanuel

DANCES FOR 4 OR MORE GUITARS, 3 see Gramberg, Jacq

DANCES FROM SHAKESPEARE'S TIME I/IIB1-Coll, I/IIB2-Coll

DANCES OF BYGONE TIMES, 6 I/IIB1-Coll

DANDELOT, GEORGES (1895-1975) Pieces, 2 I/IB4

DANIEL-LESUR see LESUR, DANIEL

DANSE see Absil, Jean

DANSE-ARIOSO-RONDEAU see Vries Robbe, Willem de

DANSE CUBAINE see Cervantes, Ignacio

DANSE D'AVILA see Presti, Ida

DANSE DE LA FRAYEUR see Falla, Manuel de

DANSE DE LA GITANE see Halffter, Ernesto

DANSE DES NAIADES, LA see Ferrer, Jose

DANSE DES SORCIERES, ETUDE DYNAMIQUE see Pujol, Emilio, Aquelarre

DANSE ESPAGNOLE NO. 1 see Falla, Manuel de

DANSE HONGROISE NO. 5 see Brahms, Johannes, Hungarian Dance, No. 5

DANSE HONGROISE NO. 6 see Brahms, Johannes, Hungarian Dance, No. 6

DANSE JOYEUSE see Duarte, John W.

DANSE NORD see Giuliani, Mauro

DANSE RYTHMIQUE see Presti, Ida

DANSEN, 4 see Ruiz de Ribayaz, Lucas

DANSES, 2 I/IB1

DANSES, 4 I/IB1

DANSES, 4 I/IB1-Coll

5 DANSES (1551) see Morley, Thomas

DANSES CUBAINES, 2 see Cervantes, Ignacio

DANSES DE COUR, 4 see Le Roy, Adrien

DANSES FACILES D'ADRIEN LE ROY see Cahiers Du Guitarolier, Les, Vol. 2

DANSKA OCH SVENSKA VISOR; 15 DANISH AND SWEDISH FOLKSONGS I/IB5-Coll, I/IIA1

DANSMUZIEK BIJ KAARSLICHT, WALSEN EN ECOSSAISES see Schubert, Franz (Peter)

DANSMUZIEK UIT PRUIKENTIJD I/IIB5-Coll

DANZA see Visee, Robert de

DANZA CARACTERISTICA, PARA EL "QUITATE DE LA ARCERA" see Brouwer, Leo

DANZA DANZA, GAGLIARDA see Durante, Francesco

DANZA DE ANITRA see Grieg, Edvard Hagerup, Anitra's Dance

DANZA DE LA MUNECA see Azpiazu, Jose de

DANZA DE LA PASTORA see Halffter, Ernesto

DANZA DEL HACHA see Ruiz de Ribayaz, Lucas

DANZA DEL PEJIN see Sanchez, B.

DANZA ESPANOLA, NO. 1 see Albeniz, Isaac

DANZA ESPANOLA, NO. 3 see Albeniz, Isaac

DANZA ESPANOLA, NO. 5 see Granados, Enrique

DANZA ESPANOLA NO. 5, ANDALUZA see Granados, Enrique

DANZA ESPANOLA, NO. 6 see Albeniz, Isaac; Granados, Enrique; Granados, Enrique

DANZA ESPANOLA, NO. 7 see Granados, Enrique

DANZA ESPANOLA, NO. 10 see Granados, Enrique

DANZA ESPANOLA, NO. 11 see Granados, Enrique

DANZA HUNGARA NO. 5 see Brahms, Johannes; Brahms, Johannes, Hungarian Dance, No. 5

DANZA II see Sanz, Gaspar, Chaconne

DANZA LENTA see Granados, Enrique

DANZA MORA see Behrend, Siegfried; Tarrega, Francisco; Tarrega, Francisco; Tarrega, Francisco; Tarrega, Francisco; Tarrega, Francisco

DANZA ODALISCA see Tarrega, Francisco; Tarrega, Francisco; Tarrega, Francisco

DANZA ORIENTALE see Ferrari, Romolo

DANZA PAGANA see Smith Brindle, Reginald

DANZA PARAGUAYA see Barrios Mangore, Augustin

DANZA POMPOSA see Tansman, Alexandre

DANZA PRIMA see Chiereghin, Sergio

DANZA SECONDA see Chiereghin, Sergio

DANZA SLAVA see Dvorak, Antonin

DANZAS CERVANTINAS see Sanz, Gaspar

DANZAS DE ANDALUCIA, STYLE FLAMENCO see Worschech, Romain

DANZAS DE LAS BACANTAS see Gounod, Charles Francois

DANZAS DE LAS TRES PRINCESAS CAUTIVAS, NO. 1 see Pedrell, Carlos

DANZAS DE LAS TRES PRINCESAS CAUTIVAS, NO. 2 see Pedrell, Carlos

DANZAS DE LAS TRES PRINCESAS CAUTIVAS, NO. 3 see Pedrell, Carlos

DANZAS ESPANOLAS, 2 see Arcas, Julian

DANZAS ESPANOLAS, NO. 2 see Granados, Enrique

DANZAS ESPANOLAS, NOS. 1-12 see Granados, Enrique

DANZAS SUECAS, 2 see Carlstedt, Jan

5 DANZE see Mainerio, Giorgio

DANZE NELLO STILE MODALE, 4 see Mosso, Carlo

DAQUIN, LOUIS-CLAUDE (1694-1772)
Cou-Cou, Le I/IIA1

Coucou, Le: Rondo I/IB1

Guitarra, La I/IB1

DARAB GITARRA, 6 (6 PIECES POUR GUITARE) see Visee, Robert de

DARK ANGELS see Davies, Peter Maxwell

DARNAL, JEAN CLAUDE
Dites-Moi M'sieur l'Oiseau I/IIC4

DARR, ADAM (1811-1866)
Rondino I/IB2

DARTELE EENHOORN, DE see Gramberg, Jacq

DAS KOMMT DAVON; OPERA see Krenek, Ernst

DAUBE, JOHANN FRIEDRICH (1730-1797)
Trio in D minor I/IIB2

DAUSEND, GERD-MICHAEL (1952-   )
Leichte Zeitgenossische Etuden I/IA

DAVID, JOHANN NEPOMUK (1895-1977)
Es Geht Ein' Dunkle Wolk' Herein see Volksliedsatze

Ich Weiss Ein Maidlein Hubsch Und Fein see Volksliedsatze

Kume, Kum, Geselle Min see Volksliedsatze

Sonata, Op. 26 I/IIB2

Variationen Uber Ein Eigenes Thema I/IIB1

Volksliedsatze I/IIA3

DAVID, THOMAS CHRISTIAN (1925-   )
Canzonen, 3 I/IIA2

Concerto I/IIIA

DAVID UND GOLIATH, CANTATA FOR CHILDREN see Kretzschmar, Gunther

DAVIES, PETER MAXWELL (1934-   )
Dark Angels I/IIC1

Te Lucis Ante Terminum V/ii

DAVON WOLL'N WIR NUN SINGEN IV/IIC1

DAZA, ESTEBAN (? - ?)
Enfermo Estaba Antioco, Romance I/IIC1

Fantasias, 4, De Pasos Largos Para Desenvolver Las Manos I/IB1

Fantasias A Tres, 4 I/IB1

Fantasy I/IB1

DE ANTEQUERA SALE EL MORO see Canciones Antiguas, 5

DE ANTEQUERA SALE EL MORO, ROMANCE VIEJO see Morales, Cristobal de

DE AVE PHOENICE see Boogaard, Bernard van den

DE FILIPPI, AMEDEO (1900-   )
Chant Et Tarentelle I/IB4

Gaillarde, Pavane, Et Toccata I/IB4

Jardins De Vauxhall I/IB4

Preludes, 12 I/IB4

DE GRANDIS, RENATO (1927-   )
Antruilles V/i

Es Lebe Der Konig; Comic Opera In Three Acts see Gloria Al Re

Gloria Al Re V/iii

DE JONG, MARINUS
see JONG, MARINUS DE

DE LOS ALAMOS VENGO see Vasquez, Juan

DE LOS ALAMOS VENGO, MADRE see Canciones Antiguas, 5

DE MORALES, CRISTOBAL
see MORALES, CRISTOBAL DE

DE PAISES Y HOMBRES EXTRANOS see Schumann, Robert (Alexander), Von Fremden Landern Und Menschen

DE RONDA see Rodrigo, Joaquin

DE TOUT UN PEU see Carulli, Ferdinando

DE VICTORIA, TOMAS LUIS
see VICTORIA, TOMAS LUIS DE

DE VISEE, ROBERT
see VISEE, ROBERT DE

DEBUSSY, CLAUDE (1862-1918)
Chiaro Di Luna see Clair De Lune

Clair De Lune I/IB3, I/IIA1

Compositions, 3 I/IB3

Doctor Gradus Ad Parnassum I/IB3
see also Compositions, 3

Fille Aux Cheveux De Lin, La see Compositions, 3; Preludes, 2

Golliwogg's Cake-Walk I/IB3

Little Shepherd, The see Compositions, 3

Minstrels I/IB3
see also Preludes, 2

Petit Negre, Le I/IB3

Plus Que Lente, La, Valse I/IB3

Preludes, 2 I/IB3

Prima Arabesca I/IB3

DECADT, JAN (1914-   )
Pavan I/IB4

DEDEROS, M.
Invito Alla Chitarra, Metodo Per Chitarra Classica II

DEDICATORIA see Granados, Enrique

DEEP RIVER see Famous Negro Spirituals, 5

DEFOSSEZ, RENE (1905-   )
Allegretto Et Gavotte I/IB4

Theme Et 3 Variations I/IB4

DEGESE, VICENTE
Aleteo De Pajarito I/IA

Scherzo No. 1 see Aleteo De Pajarito

DEGNI, VINCENZO (1911-   )
Prelude I/IB4

Serenata All'antica I/IA

Studio Della Chitarra Classica, Lo, Vol. 1: Technical Exercises, 19 I/IA

Studio Della Chitarra Classica, Lo, Vol. 2: Technical Exercises, 20 I/IA

Study, Op. 14 see Serenata All'antica

DEIN WORT IST NAH; NEUE RHYTHMISCHE SATZE ZUM GOTTESDIENST see Heurich, Winfried

DEL ENCINA, JUAN
see ENCINA, JUAN DEL

DELAS, JOSE LUIS DE (1928-   )
Eilanden, For Ten Instruments And Tape Recorder V/i

Trio I/IIB2

DELAUNEY, PAUL
Feuillets, 15 I/IA

Petit Gitan, Le I/IB4

Prelude in D I/IB4

Toccatina I/IB4

DELDEN, LEX VAN (1919-   )
Ballet I/IIB3

DELIGHT OF ENGLISH LUTE MUSIC, A see Kostlichkeiten Englischer Lautenmusik

DELITIAE MUSICAE, 1612, PART 1: "PRAELUDIEN UND PAVANEN" see Hove, Joachim van den

DELITIAE MUSICAE, 1612, PART 2: "PASSAMEZZEN MIT IHREN GALLIARDEN" see Hove, Joachim van den

DELITIAE MUSICAE, 1612, PART 3: "FAVORITOS, GALLIARDEN, BERGAMASCA, UNE JEUNE FILLETTE" see Hove, Joachim van den

DELITIAE MUSICAE, 1612, PART 4: "ALLEMANDEN, BALLETTI, BRANDEN, COURANTEN, CHANSONS, CANARIE" see Hove, Joachim van den

DELNOOZ, HENRI (1942-   )
Oiseau De La Tour, L' I/IIC1

DELUXE GUITAR SCALE BOOK, THE see Bay, Mel

DEN GULA ROSEN see Ahslund, Ulf-G.

DENHOFF, MICHAEL (1955-   )
Quinterna Fur Gitarresolo I/IB4

DENISOV, EDISON VASILIEVICH (1929-   )
Chant d'Automne For Soprano And Full Orchestra V/ii

DERLIEN, MARGARETE
Flotenhannes, Der, Ein Lernbuchlein Fur Die C"-Blockflote Und Dazu Mancherlei Lieder Und Satze Zum Singen Und Musizieren Mit Verschiedenen Instrumenten I/IIB5-Coll

Ich Trag Mein Licht, Ein Liederspiel Zum Laternegehen I/IIC5

DEROSIER, NICOLAS
Chaconnes, 12 I/IB1

DERRIER' CHEZ MON PERE see Reisebilder Aus Frankreich, 5

DES MADCHENS KLAGE see Schubert, Franz (Peter)

DES PREZ, JOSQUIN (ca. 1440-1521)
Magnificat Quarti Toni, For Chorus And Three Groups Of Instruments V/ii

Mille Regretz I/IIC1

Sanctus and Benedictus I/IB1

DESDERI, ETTORE (1892-1974)
Cacce Quattrocentesche, 2 I/IIC1

Serenata I/IB4

Toccata And Fugue I/IB4

DESEMBRE CONGELAT, EL see Canciones Catalanas Navidenas, 4

DESEMBRE CONGELAT, LO see Villancicos Populares, Vol. II

DESET FANTASII, NA LIDOVE MOTIVY see Urban, Stepan

DESIR, LE see Zani de Ferranti, Marco Aurelio

DESPEDIDA, LA see Sor, Fernando

DESPERTAR DEL CAZADOR, ALBADA see Granados, Enrique

DESPRES, JOSQUIN
see DES PREZ, JOSQUIN

DESSAU, PAUL (1894-1979)
Liebeslieder, 4, Nach Texten Von Bertolt Brecht I/IIC1

Lieder, 4 I/IIC1

Tierverse Von Bertolt Brecht I/IIC1, I/IIC2

DEUTSCH, WALTER (1923-   )
Kleine Weihnachtskantate, Nach Alten Texten Und Weisen Aus Osterreich IV/IIC5

DEUTSCHE MEISTER see Europaische Gitarren- Und Lautenmusik, Vol. 2

DEUTSCHE MEISTER DES EIN- UND ZWEISTIMMIGEN LAUTENSATZES, 16.-18. JAHRHUNDERT I/IB1-Coll,

DJEMIL, ENYSS (1917-)
Caprice, Complainte Et Ronde I/IB4

Petite Suite Medievale I/IIB1

DLUGORAJ, ADALBERT (WOJIECH) (ca. 1550)
Fantazje I Wilanele I/IB1-Coll

DO FRAIG AMOR see Jez, Jakob

DO NOT GO GENTLE... see Smith Brindle,
Reginald

DOBRU NOC, VARIACNI FANTAZIE NA LIDOVOU
PISEN see Urban, Stepan

DOCE CANCIONES see Moretti, Federico

DOCKHORN, LOTTE
Schalk Und Scherz Zur Laute I/IIC1

DR. CASE'S PAVAN see Dowland, John

DOCTOR GRADUS AD PARNASSUM see
Debussy, Claude; Debussy, Claude

DODEKAMERON; 12 COMPOSITIONS FOR 12
PLAYERS see Istvan, Miloslav

DODGSON, STEPHEN (1924-)
Duo Concertant I/IIB1

Fantasy-Divisions I/IB4

Partita I/IB4

Studies, Vol. 1: 10 Studies (Nos. 1-
10) I/IA

Studies, Vol. 2: 10 Studies (Nos. 11-
20) I/IA

DODI LI WA'ANI LO see Staak, Pieter
van der

DOERR, CHARLES-KIKO
Etude in B minor I/IA

Fantasy I/IB4

Gavotte in E I/IB4

Gavotte in E minor I/IB4

Minuet, MIN 160 I/IB4

Nocturne En La Mineur see Nocturne
in A minor

Nocturne in A minor I/IB4

Oeuvres De Charles-Kiko Doerr see
Etude in B minor; Fantasy;
Gavotte in E; Gavotte in E minor;
Minuet, MIN 160; Nocturne in A
minor; Petite Valse; Quartes Et
Sixtes

Petite Valse I/IB4

Quartes Et Sixtes I/IB4

DOHL, FRIEDHELM (1936-)
Pas De Deux I/IIB1

DOLANNES MELODIE see Gitarre Spezial,
Picking Modern Arrangement, Vol. 3

DOLCE NATALI IV/I

DOLENTE IMMAGINE DI FILLA MIA see
Bellini, Vincenzo

DOMAINES, FOR CLARINET AND ORCHESTRA
see Boulez, Pierre

DOMANDL, WILLY
Gitarreschule, Auch Fur Den
Selbstunterricht Geeignet II

DOMENICO PELLEGRINI see Pellegrini,
Domenico

DON see Boulez, Pierre, Pli Selon Pli,
Portrait De Mallarme, 1

DON LUIS MILAN see Milan, Luis

DONA MENCIA see Pedrell, Carlos,
Danzas De Las Tres Princesas
Cautivas, No. 2

DONATONI, FRANCO (1927-)
Algo, 2 Pezzi Per Chitarra I/IB4

Serenade for Solo Voice and Orchestra
V/ii

DONDE SON ESTAS SERRANAS? see
Canciones Antiguas, 6

DONNA MARIA see Wolf, Roland

DORATI, ANTAL (1906-)
Madrigal Suite V/ii

DORFCHEN, DAS see Schubert, Franz
(Peter)

DORFMUSIK AUS DER BAUERNKANTATE see
Bach, Johann Sebastian, Cantata No.
212, [excerpt], [arr.]

DORLEIJN, GILLES J.
Prelude I/IB4

DOS HERMANITAS, LAS see Tarrega,
Francisco

DOUX CHAGRIN, LE see Vigneault, Gilles

DOUZE ETUDES see Sor, Fernando

DOUZE ETUDES, OP. 6, NO. 4 see Sor,
Fernando

DOUZE ETUDES POUR SERVIR DE SUITE AUX
DOUZE PREMIERES see Sor, Fernando;
Sor, Fernando

DOUZE ETUDES POUR SERVIR DE SUITE AUX
DOUZE PREMIERES, OP. 29, NO. 1 see
Sor, Fernando

DOUZE ETUDES POUR SERVIR DE SUITE AUX
DOUZE PREMIERES, OP. 29, NO. 5 see
Sor, Fernando

DOUZE ETUDES POUR SERVIR DE SUITE AUX
DOUZE PREMIERES, OP. 29, NO. 6 see
Sor, Fernando

DOUZE ETUDES POUR SERVIR DE SUITE AUX
DOUZE PREMIERES, OP. 29, NO. 10
see Sor, Fernando

DOWLAND, JOHN (1562-1626)
Air I/IB1

Air And Galliard I/IB1

Air And Gigue see Mrs. Vaux's Jig

Almain, MIN 254 see Pieces, 8, Vol.
1

As I Went To Walsingham see Air; Air
And Galliard

Awake Sweet Love see Songs, 3

Batell Galliard see King Of Denmark
His Galliard, The

Beste Aus Dem Lautenwerk, Das I/IB1

Can She Excuse see Pieces, 2

Can She Excuse My Wrongs? see
Canzoni Elisabettiane, 2; Two
Pieces

Canzoni Elisabettiane, 2 I/IIC1

Captain Digorie Piper's Galliard see
Gaillarde Et Allemande;
Galliards, 2

Come Again see Songs, 3

Come Again, Sweet Love I/IIC1

Come Away see Pieces, 6

Come Away, Come, Sweet Love! see
Songs, 6

Dr. Case's Pavan see Pieces, 6;
Pieces, 8, Vol. 1

Dowland's Adew see Pieces, 2

Earl Of Derby His Galliard, The
I/IB1
see also Galliards, 3

Earl Of Essex His Galliard, The
I/IB1
see also Galliards, 3

Fancy, A I/IB1
see also Pieces, 6

3 Fantasias I/IB1

Fantasy see Fancy, A

Fantasy, MIN 253 see Pieces, 8, Vol.
1

Fantasy, MIN 255 see Pieces, 8, Vol.
2

Fine Knacks For Ladies see Songs, 6

Flow, My Tears see Songs, 6

DOWLAND, JOHN (cont'd.)

Forlorn Hope Fancy I/IB1

Fortune see Pieces, 6; Pieces, 8,
Vol. 2

Gaillarde Et Allemande I/IB1

Gaillarde Sur Un Theme De Daniel
Batchelar see Galliard On A
Galliard Of Daniel Bacheler, A

Gaillardes, 2 I/IB1

Galliard Of Daniel Batchelar see
Galliard On A Galliard Of Daniel
Bacheler, A

Galliard On A Galliard Of Daniel
Bacheler, A I/IB1

Galliards, 2 I/IB1

Galliards, 3 I/IB1

I Saw My Lady Weep see Songs, 6

In Darkness Let Me Dwell see Songs,
6

King Of Denmark His Galliard, The
I/IB1
see also Galliards, 2

Lachrimae I/IB1
see also Pieces, 2; Pieces, 8, Vol.
2

Lachrimae Antiquae, Pavane see
Lachrimae

Lachrimae Pavan Und Fantasie I/IB1

Lachrimae Pavin see Two Pieces

Lady Hunsdon's Puffe I/IB1
see also Gaillarde Et Allemande

Lady Laiton's Almain see Pieces, 6

Lady Rich Her Galliard, The I/IB1
see also Gaillardes, 2; Galliards,
3

Leichte Stucke, 4 I/IB1

Lieder, 2 I/IIC2

Lieder, 18 I/IIC1

Master Piper's Pavan see Piper's
Pavan

Melancholy Galliard I/IB1
see also Pieces, 2

Melancoly Galliard I/IB1

Mignarda see Pieces, 8, Vol. 2

Mr. Henry Noel His Galliard see
Pieces, 2

Mrs. Vaux's Jig I/IB1
see also Pieces, 2

My Lord Chamberlain His Galliard see
Pieces, 3

Now, O Now, I Needs Must Part see
Canzoni Elisabettiane, 2

Pavana Pijper see Piper's Pavan

Pavane Lachrimae see Lachrimae

Piece Without A Title, A see Pieces,
3

Pieces, 2 I/IB1

Pieces, 2 I/IB1

Pieces, 2 I/IB1

Pieces, 2 I/IB1

Pieces, 3 I/IB1

Pieces, 6 I/IB1

Pieces, 7 I/IB1

Pieces, 8, Vol. 1 I/IB1

Pieces, 8, Vol. 2 I/IB1

Piper's Pavan I/IB1

Queen Elizabeth Her Galliard, The
I/IB1
see also Air And Galliard;
Gaillardes, 2; Pieces, 2; Pieces,
8, Vol. 1

DOWLAND, JOHN (cont'd.)

Shoemaker's Wife, The see Pieces, 3

Sir Henry Humpton's Funeral see
    Pieces, 2

Solowerke, Vol. 1 I/IB1

Songs, 3 I/IIC1

Songs, 6 I/IIC1

Three Dances I/IIA3

Two Pieces I/IB1

What If I Never Speed? see Songs, 6

Wilt Thou Unkind Thus Reave Me see
    Songs, 3

DOWLAND, ROBERT (1591-1641)
    Courantes, 6 I/IB1

Five Corantoes I/IB1

Six Lute Pieces I/IB1-Coll

Varietie Of Lute-Lessons, Vol. 1:
    Corantos I/IB1

Varietie Of Lute-Lessons, Vol. 2:
    Almaines I/IB1

Varietie Of Lute-Lessons, Vol. 3:
    Voltes I/IB1

Varietie Of Lute-Lessons, Vol. 4:
    Fantasias I/IB1

Varietie Of Lute-Lessons, Vol. 5:
    Galliards I/IB1

Varietie Of Lute-Lessons, Vol. 6:
    Pavins I/IB1

DOWLAND'S ADEW see Dowland, John

DREAMING see Farquhar, David

DREI AUSGEWAHLTE WALZER (3 VALSES
    CHOISIES) see Sor, Fernando

DREI GEDICHTE VON EICHENDORFF, NO. 1
    see Kaminski, Heinrich

DREI JUGOSLAVISCHE TANZE FUR GITARRE
    see Papandopulo, Boris

DREI KLEINE STUCKE AUS DEM
    NOTENBUCHLEIN DER ANNA MAGDALENA
    BACH see Bach, Johann Sebastian

DREI KONIGE FUHRET DIE GOTTLICHE HAND
    see Rinke Ranke Rosenschein; 77
    Kinderlieder

DREI LEICHTE DUOS see Sor, Fernando,
    Trois Duos Faciles Et Progressifs
    Pour Deux Guitares

DREI RHAPSODISCHE STUDIEN see Ulrich,
    Jurgen

DREI RHYTMISCHE TANZE FUR GITARRE see
    Mairants, Ivor

DREI STUCKE FUR GITARRE see Medek,
    Tilo

DREI SZENEN AUS "DYBUK" see Fussl,
    Karl-Heinz

DREIGROSCHENOPER: SUITE see Weill,
    Kurt

DREISTIMMIGE SPIELSTUCKE, 16
    I/IIB2-Coll, VII-Mixed Coll

DREITRITT see Volkstanze, 6

DRESDEN, SEM (1881-1957)
    Stukken, 3, Voor Schoolorkest, No. 2
        I/IIB5

Stukken, 3, Voor Schoolorkest, No. 3
    I/IIB5

DRESDEN SONATA NO. 5 see Weiss,
    Sylvius Leopold, Sonata in D minor

DRESDEN SONATA NO. 7 see Weiss,
    Sylvius Leopold, Sonata, MIN 112

DRESDEN SONATA NO. 12 see Weiss,
    Sylvius Leopold, Sonata, MIN 113

DRESENS, GUUS
    Meringue I/IB4

DREWRIES ACCORDES see Aus Pickering's
    Lautenbuch (Um 1616); Musique
    Elisabethaine

DRIGO, RICCARDO (1846-1930)
    Serenade I/IB4

Valse Bluette I/IB4

DRINK TO ME see Engelse Volksliederen,
    3

DRITTE LAUTEN-SUITE see Bach, Johann
    Sebastian, Suite for Lute, BWV 995,
    in G minor

DRITTE SUITE see Bach, Johann
    Sebastian, Suite for Lute, BWV 995,
    in G minor

DRITTES POTPOURRI see Kuffner, Joseph

DRLAC, JAN ZDENEK
    Strassen see Ulice

Ulice I/IB4

DROGOZ, PHILIPPE
    Chocs I/IB4

Chorale I/IB4

Nocturne I/IB4

Prelude I/IB4

Rasgueado I/IB4

Rondo I/IB4

Suite Percutante see Chocs; Chorale;
    Nocturne; Prelude; Rasgueado;
    Rondo

DROLE, LE, IN F MAJOR see Baron, Ernst
    Gottlieb

DSCHINGHIS KHAN see Gitarre Spezial,
    Picking Modern Arrangement, Vol. 2

DU BOIS, ROB
    see BOIS, ROB DU

DU UND ICH WIR SPIELEN GITARRE, EIN
    LIEBLINGSBUCH FUR ANGEHENDE
    GITARRISTEN I/IIA1-Coll, IV/IIA1

DU UNGLUCK'SEL'GER MORGENSTERN see
    Krieger, Johann Philipp

DUARTE, JOHN W. (1919-   )
    All In A Row I/IB4

Birds, The see Quiet Songs, 5

Canco Del Lladra see Variations On A
    Catalan Folk Song

Carillon see Going Dutch

Danse Joyeuse I/IIB1

Dirge In Woods see Quiet Songs, 5

Dutch Dance see Going Dutch

English Suite I/IB4

Epitaph, An see Quiet Songs, 5

Etude Diabolique I/IA

Fantasia And Fugue On "Torre Bermeja"
    I/IB4

Flight Of Fugues, A I/IB4, I/IIA1

For My Friends I/IB4

Foundation Studies In Classic Guitar
    Technique III

Friendships, 6 I/IIA1

Going Dutch I/IIA3

Greek Suite I/IIA1

Guitar Accompaniment - The Easy Way
    II

Larghetto, Op. 4 see Pieces, 2

March, Op. 36, No. 3 see Going Dutch

Meditation On A Ground Bass I/IB4

Miniature Suite I/IB4

Modern Miniatures, 3 I/IB4

Mutations On The "Dies Irae" I/IB4

Nocturne And Toccata I/IB4

Omar's Lament see Quiet Songs, 5

Ostinato see Modern Miniatures, 3

DUARTE, JOHN W. (cont'd.)

Pastorale, Op. 36, No. 2 see Going
    Dutch

Petite Suite Francaise I/IB4

Pieces, 2 I/IB4

Prelude, Canto And Toccata I/IB4

Prelude En Arpeges I/IB4

Prelude, Op. 3 see Pieces, 2

Prelude, Op. 9, No. 1 see Modern
    Miniatures, 3

Quiet Songs, 5 I/IIC1

Scherzando see Modern Miniatures, 3

Silence see Quiet Songs, 5

Simple Songs Without Words, 3 I/IIB1

Simple Variations On "Las Folias"
    I/IB4

Some Of Noah's Ark I/IB4

Sonatina Lirica I/IC

Sonatina, Op. 15 I/IIB1

Sonatinette I/IC

Suite Piemontese I/IB4

Suo Cosa I/IB4

Transatlantic Dances, 4 I/IIB2

Variations On A Catalan Folk Song
    I/IB4

Variations On A French Nursery Song
    I/IIA1

Windmill see Going Dutch

Young Persons' Way To The Guitar, The
    II

DUBLIN TOWN, IERSE VOLKSMUZIEK
    I/IIB5-Coll

DUCHESS OF BRUNSWICK'S TOYE, THE see
    Bull, John

DUCHESSE OF BRUNSWICK'S TOYE, THE see
    Bull, John

DUE BOURREES E MARCIA see Bach, Johann
    Sebastian

DUE PRELUDI see Bach, Johann Sebastian

DUELETE DE MI, SENORA see Canciones
    Antiguas, 5; Fuenllana, Miguel de

DUET APPROACH TO THE GUITAR, A, AN
    INITIAL PROGRAMME FOR GUITAR see
    Topper, Guido

DUET (ETUDE) see Pujol, Emilio

DUET FACILE see Carulli, Ferdinando

DUET STUDY IN F see Carulli,
    Ferdinando

DUET STUDY IN G see Carulli,
    Ferdinando

DUETS see Robinson, Thomas

10 DUETS FOR 2 GUITARS I/IIA1

DUETT FUR GITARREN see Weiss, Sylvius
    Leopold

DUETTE see Hlouschek, Theodor

DUETTE, 3 see Carulli, Ferdinando

DUETTE, 6 see Call, Leonhard von;
    Furstenau, Kaspar

DUETTE, 8 see Gastoldi, Giovanni
    Giacomo

DUETTE, 10, AUS DEM 16. JAHRHUNDERT
    I/IIA1-Coll

DUETTE, 12 see Kuffner, Joseph

12 DUETTE, VOL. 1 see Paganini,
    Niccolo

12 DUETTE, VOL. 2 see Paganini,
    Niccolo

DUETTE A-DUR see Lauffensteiner, Wolff
    Jacob, Sonata in A

DUETTE AUS DEM 18. JAHRHUNDERT, 2
  I/IIA1

DUETTE FUR GITARREN I/IIA1-Coll

DUETTINO see Giuliani, Mauro; Praag,
  Henri C. van

DUETTINO FACILE see Giuliani, Mauro

DUETTO AL LIUTO E TRAVERSO see Baron,
  Ernst Gottlieb

DUETTO CONCERTANTE see Baumann,
  Herbert

DUETTO G-DUR see Baron, Ernst
  Gottlieb, Duetto Al Liuto E
  Traverso

DUFAY, GUILLAUME (ca. 1400-1474)
  Bonjour, Bon Mois I/IIC3

  Or Vous Tremoussez, Pasteurs see
    Bonjour, Bon Mois

DUITSE DANSEN see Schubert, Franz
  (Peter)

DUKE OF BRUNSWICK'S ALMAN, THE see
  Bull, John

D'UN ESPACE DEPLOYE, FOR SOPRANO, 2
  PIANOS AND 2 ORCHESTRAL GROUPS see
  Amy, Gilbert

DUNCOMBE, W.
  Sonatina I/IB1

DUO CONCERTANT see Dodgson, Stephen

DUO CONCERTANTE see Carulli,
  Ferdinando; Lucky, Stepan; Marco,
  Tomas

DUO CONCERTANTI see Lucky, Stepan

DUO EN FORME DE PRELUDE see Massis,
  Amable

DUO FLAMENCO, IMPROVISATIES OVER EEN
  ARGENTIJNS VOLKSLIED see Pfister,
  Co

DUO FUR 2 GITARREN see Sor, Fernando,
  Encouragement, L', Fantaisie A Deux
  Guitares

DUO FUR LAUTENINSTRUMENTE see Rohwer,
  Jens

DUO POUR GUITARRE ET VIOLON see
  Scheidler, Christian Gottlieb

DUOS see Bartok, Bela; Carulli,
  Ferdinando

DUOS, 2 see Carulli, Ferdinando

DUOS, 3 see Behrend, Siegfried

DUOS, 4 see Carulli, Ferdinando

DUOS, 4 see Ferritto, John E.

DUOS, 12 see Carulli, Ferdinando

DUOS 1-3 ET 9 see Cabezon, Antonio de

DUOS ALTER MEISTER see Erste
  Musizierjahr, Das, Vol. 2

DUOS ANCIENS, 5 I/IB1

DUO'S FUR 2 GITARREN, VOL. I: 12 KLEINE
  STUCKE see Rebay, Ferdinand

DUO'S FUR 2 GITARREN, VOL. II: 9
  VORTRAGSSTUCKE see Rebay,
  Ferdinand

DUO'S FUR 2 GITARREN, VOL. III: 6
  STUDIEN NACH BERUHMTEN ETUDEN VON
  CZERNY BIS CHOPIN see Rebay,
  Ferdinand

DUO'S FUR 2 GITARREN, VOL. IV: SPEZIAL-
  STUDIEN see Rebay, Ferdinand

DUOS, OP. 34, VOL. I see Siegl, Erwin

DUOS POUR FLUTE A BEC ET GUITARE
  I/IIB1-Coll

DURANTE, FRANCESCO (1684-1755)
  Danza Danza, Gagliarda I/IIC1

  Galliard I/IIA1

DUSIK, JAN LADISLAV
  see DUSSEK, JOHANN LADISLAUS

DUSSEK, JOHANN LADISLAUS (1760-1812)
  Rondo I/IB2

DUTCH DANCE see Duarte, John W.

DUTZEND SCHILIEDER, EIN see Strobl,
  Otto

DUVIENSELA see Cabezon, Antonio de

DVORAK, ANTONIN (1841-1904)
  Danza Slava I/IB3

DYBUK; OPERA IN THREE ACTS AND THREE
  SCENES see Fussl, Karl-Heinz

EARL OF DERBY HIS GALLIARD, THE see
  Dowland, John; Dowland, John

EARL OF ESSEX HIS GALLIARD, THE see
  Dowland, John; Dowland, John

EARLY ENGLISH LUTE SONGS AND FOLK
  SONGS, VOL. I I/IIC1-Coll

EARLY ENGLISH LUTE SONGS AND FOLK
  SONGS, VOL. II I/IIC1-Coll

EARLY ENGLISH LUTE SONGS AND FOLK
  SONGS, VOL. III I/IIC1-Coll,
  IV/IIC1

EARLY ENGLISH LUTE SONGS AND FOLK
  SONGS, VOL. IV I/IIC1-Coll

EARLY MUSIC see Regi Zene

EARLY MUSIC FOR THE GUITAR; ORIGINAL
  PIECES FROM MEDIEVAL AND
  RENAISSANCE SOURCES I/IB1-Coll

EARLY RENAISSANCE DANCES, 6
  I/IIB1-Coll

EASTER ORATORIO see Barbe, Helmut,
  Ostergeschichte

EASTWOOD, THOMAS (1922-   )
  Amphora I/IB4

  Ballade I/IB4

EASY 16TH CENTURY PIECES, 7 I/IB1-Coll

EASY CHRISTMAS CAROLS, 2 IV/I

EASY GUITAR QUARTETS, 9 see Staak,
  Pieter van der

EASY MUSIC FOR GUITAR, VOL. 8
  I/IB1-Coll

EASY MUSIC FOR GUITAR, VOL. 9
  I/IB1-Coll

EASY MUSIC FOR GUITAR, VOL. 11 see
  Sor, Fernando

EASY MUSIC FOR GUITAR, VOL. III see
  Chanson De Noel

EASY MUSIC, VOL. 1 I/IB6-Coll

EASY MUSIC, VOL. 2 I/IB6-Coll, IV/I,
  VII-Mixed Coll

EASY MUSIC, VOL. 4 I/IB6-Coll,
  VII-Mixed Coll

EASY MUSIC, VOL. 5 I/IB6-Coll

EASY MUSIC, VOL. 6 I/IB6-Coll,
  VII-Mixed Coll

EASY MUSIC, VOL. 10 I/IB5-Coll

EASY PIECES, 6 see Staak, Pieter van
  der

EASY PIECES, 7 see Hoekema, Henk

EASY PIECES, 8 I/IB4-Coll

EASY PIECES, 20 I/IB6-Coll

EASY PIECES FOR GUITAR see Kadosa,
  Pal, 11 Konnyu Darab Gitarra

EASY SUITE IN D MINOR see Visee,
  Robert de

EBENHOH, HORST (1930-   )
  Bewegungsspiele I/IIB5

ECHO, FOR ORCHESTRA see Borstlap, Dick

ECHO-MENUETT see Mozart, Leopold

ECLAT, FOR ORCHESTRA see Boulez,
  Pierre

ECOLE DE GUITARE, TECHNIQUE MODERNE,
  FORMATION PERMANENTE. COURS
  PREPARATOIRE-ELEMENTAIRE-MOYEN see
  Fernandez-Lavie, Fernando

ECOLE DU JEUNE GUITARISTE, L' see
  Laurent, Leo

ECOS DE LA PARRANDA see Granados,
  Enrique

ECOS DEL PAISAGE see Broqua, Alfonso,
  Evocaciones Criollas, No.1

ECOSSAISES see Schubert, Franz (Peter)

ECTOPLASME see Mayuzumi, Toshiro

EDIPO RE, CORI PER LA TRAGEDIA DI
  SOFOCLE see Gabrieli, Andrea

EDITION NICOLAS ALFONSO, NO. 2 see
  Bach, Johann Sebastian

EDITION NICOLAS ALFONSO, NO. 4
  I/IB6-Coll

EDITION NICOLAS ALFONSO, NO. 5
  I/IB6-Coll

EDITION NICOLAS ALFONSO, NO. 6
  I/IB6-Coll

EDITION NICOLAS ALFONSO, NO. 7
  I/IB6-Coll

EDITION NICOLAS ALFONSO, NO. 8
  I/IB6-Coll

EDITION NICOLAS ALFONSO, NO. 9
  I/IB6-Coll

EDITION NICOLAS ALFONSO, NO. 10
  I/IB6-Coll

EDITION NICOLAS ALFONSO, NO. 11 see
  Bach, Johann Sebastian

EDITION NICOLAS ALFONSO, NO. 16 see
  Bach, Johann Sebastian

EDITION NICOLAS ALFONSO, NO. 17 see
  Bach, Johann Sebastian

EDITION NICOLAS ALFONSO, NO. 18 see
  Bach, Johann Sebastian

EERSTE OEFENINGEN IN HET GITAARSPEL
  see Vries, F. de

EERSTE VERDRIET see Gitaarduet, Het

EEUW GELEDEN, EEN: GITAARSTUKJES VAN
  19E-EEUWSE KOMPONISTEN I/IB2-Coll

EGGERSBERGER TRIO see Ambrosius,
  Hermann

EHRE SEI GOTT IN DER HOHE. CANON see
  Bach, Johann Sebastian

EI WAS GROSSES WUNDER, UM EIN LIED VOM
  EICHSFELD (NO. 5) see Spitta,
  Heinrich

EICHENDORFF-LIEDERBUCH, VOL. 1: DAS
  ZERBROCHENE RINGLEIN see Bialas,
  Gunter

EICHENDORFF-LIEDERBUCH, VOL. 2:
  ABSCHIED see Bialas, Gunter

EICHENDORFF-LIEDERBUCH, VOL. 3: ABER
  DIE ZEIT GEHT SCHNELL see Bialas,
  Gunter

EICHENDORFF-LIEDERBUCH, VOL. 4:
  NACHTZAUBER see Bialas, Gunter

EICHENDORFF-LIEDERBUCH, VOL. 5: SELIGES
  VERGESSEN see Bialas, Gunter

EICHENDORFF-LIEDERBUCH, VOL. 6:
  ASSONANZEN see Bialas, Gunter

EICHSTATTER HOFMUHLTANZ see
  Mittelalterliche Tanze

EIGHT LITTLE PIECES FOR BEGINNERS see
  Diabelli, Anton, Vortragsstucke Fur
  Anfanger

EILANDEN, FOR TEN INSTRUMENTS AND TAPE
  RECORDER see Delas, Jose Luis de

EINANDER-BEDINGENDES see Hespos, Hans-
  Joachim

EINEM, GOTTFRIED VON (1918-   )
  Studien, 3 I/IA

EINERSEITS-ANDERERSEITS, VOL. 1 see
  Ulrich, Jurgen

EINERSEITS-ANDERERSEITS, VOL. 2 see
  Ulrich, Jurgen

EINFUHRUNG IN DAS KLASSISCHE
  GITARRENSPIEL see Sao Marcos,
  Maria Livia

EINLEITENDE ETUDEN – ETUDES
PREPARATOIRES see Sor, Fernando,
Introduction A l'Etude De La
Guitare En Vingt Cinq Lecons
Progressives

EINSTIMMUNG see Wolki, Konrad

EINZUG UND REIGEN I/IIB5

12 EJERCICIOS see Sor, Fernando

EJERCICIOS DE ARPEGIOS, ELEMENTOS
FUNDAMENTALES DE LA TECNICA
GUITARRISTICA PARA GUITARRA see
Giuliani, Mauro, Studio Per La
Chitarra

EJERCICIOS Y ESTUDIOS ELEMENTALES PARA
GUITARRA, 36, VOL. 1 see Sor,
Fernando

EKLUND, HANS (1927-   )
Allegro see Pezzi, 5

Allegro Molto see Pezzi, 5

Andante see Pezzi, 5

Lento see Pezzi, 5

Pezzi, 5 I/IB4

Tempo Rubato see Pezzi, 5

ELANS see Miroglio, Francis

ELEGIA DI CROTON see Peruzzi, Aurelio

ELEGIA Y DANZA see Bonilla Chavez,
Carlos

ELEMENTAR ETUDEN, VOL. 1 I/IA,
I/IA-Coll

ELEMENTAR ETUDEN, VOL. 2 I/IA,
I/IA-Coll, VI-Mixed Coll

ELEMENTAR ETUDEN, VOL. 3 I/IA,
I/IA-Coll

ELEMENTAR ETUDEN, VOL. 4 see Carulli,
Ferdinando

ELEMENTAR IMPROVISATION, VOL. I see
Aldeland, Nils

ELEMENTAR IMPROVISATION, VOL. II see
Aldeland, Nils

ELEMENTARY IMPROVISATIONS, VOL. I:
METHOD see Aldeland, Nils,
Elementar Improvisation, Vol. I

ELEMENTARY IMPROVISATIONS, VOL. II:
TEACHER'S HANDBOOK see Aldeland,
Nils, Elementar Improvisation, Vol.
II

ELEMENTOS FUNDAMENTALES DE LA TECNICA
GUITARRISTICA see Tarrega,
Francisco

ELIZABETHAN DANCES, 4 I/IB1-Coll

ELIZABETHAN DUETS, 6 I/IIA1-Coll

ELIZABETHAN MELODIES, VOL. 1
I/IB1-Coll

ELIZABETHAN MELODIES, VOL. 2
I/IB1-Coll

ELIZABETHAN MINIATURES, BASED ON MUSIC
BY ANONYMOUS ELIZABETHAN COMPOSERS
see Banks, Don

ELIZABETHAN PIECES, 5 I/IIA3-Coll

ELIZABETHAN SERENADE see Binge,
Ronald, Alzbetinska Serenada

ELLENS GESANG III see Schubert, Franz
(Peter)

ELOADASI DARABOK GITARRA see Paganini,
Niccolo, Original Kompositionen, 26

ELOGIO DE LA DANZA see Brouwer, Leo

ELOGIO DE LA GUITARRA see Rodrigo,
Joaquin

ELOY, JEAN-CLAUDE (1938-   )
Faisceaux-Diffractions, For Twenty-
Eight Instruments V/i

EMBARQUEMENT POUR CYTHERE see Poulenc,
Francis

EN AVILA MIS OJOS, ROMANCE see
Anonymous

EN ESTA LARGA AUSENCIA see Canciones
Del Siglo XVII, 5

EN JEREZ DE LA FRONTERA see Rodrigo,
Joaquin

EN LA ALHAMBRA, CAPRICHO MORISCO see
Albeniz, Isaac

EN LA FUENTE DEL ROSEL see Canciones
Antiguas, 6

EN LA FUENTE DEL ROSEL, VILLANCICO see
Vasquez, Juan

EN LA PLAYA, RECUERDO see Albeniz,
Isaac

EN LOS TRIGALES, SCENE CASTILLANE see
Rodrigo, Joaquin

EN MIJN EEN BEEN STAAT see Marez
Oyens, Gerrit de

ENCINA, JUAN DEL (1468-1529)
A Tal Perdida Tan Triste see 5
Piezas

Ay Triste Que Vengo, Villancico
Pastoril I/IB1

Levanta, Pascual see 5 Piezas

5 Piezas I/IB1

Que Es De Ti, Desconsolado see 5
Piezas

Romerico I/IIC1

Romerico, Tu Que Viennes see 5
Piezas

Rossignol see Romerico

Triste Espana Sin Ventura see 5
Piezas

ENCINAR, JOSE RAMON (1954-   )
Abhava I/IIB1

Estudio De Alturas I/IA

ENCOURAGEMENT, L', FANTAISIE A DEUX
GUITARES see Sor, Fernando

ENDECHA see Tarrega, Francisco,
Prelude, TI i- 16, in D minor

ENDECHA ALLA AMADA AUSENTE see Pujol,
Emilio

ENFANT CRIE EN GALILEE, UN see Bonnal,
Ermend

ENFERMO ESTABA ANTIOCO, ROMANCE see
Daza, Esteban

ENGELSE VOLKSDANSEN, 2 VOLS.
I/IIB5-Coll

ENGELSE VOLKSLIEDEREN, 3 I/IIC1-Coll

ENGLAND see Britten, [Sir] Benjamin

ENGLISCHE MEISTER see Europaische
Gitarren- Und Lautenmusik, Vol. 3

ENGLISCHE TANZE, 3 see Anonymous

ENGLISCHER TANZ see Tanze, 6

ENGLISH FOLK SONGS, 3 I/IB5-Coll

ENGLISH FOLK SONGS, 16 I/IB5-Coll

3 ENGLISH LUTE FANTASIES I/IB1-Coll

ENGLISH RENAISSANCE SONGS – ANGOL
RENESZANSZ DALOK I/IIC1-Coll

ENGLISH SONGS, 3 I/IIC1-Coll

ENGLISH SUITE see Duarte, John W.

ENGLISH SUITE NO. 6, IN D-MINOR, (FIFTH
MOVEMENT): MUSETTE see Bach,
Johann Sebastian

ENJOY CLASSICAL AND BAROQUE GUITAR
I/IB6-Coll, VI-Mixed Coll

ENNUITS, DESESPOIRS ET DOULEURS see
Boesset, Antoine

ENRICHI, ARMINIO
Chansons, 4 I/IIC1

ENRIQUEZ DE VALDERRABANO, ENRIQUE
see VALDERRABANO, ENRIQUEZ de

ENSEIGNEMENT PRATIQUE DE LA GUITARE,
VOL. I see Worschech, Romain

ENSEIGNEMENT RATIONNEL DE LA GUITARE,
VOL. I see Aubin, Christian

ENSEIGNEMENT RATIONNEL DE LA GUITARE,
VOL. II see Aubin, Christian

ENSEMBLE MUSIC FOR GUITARS AND
RECORDERS, VOL. I, ELEMENTARY:
TUNES OF OLD ENGLAND I/IIB3

ENSEMBLE MUSIC FOR GUITARS AND
RECORDERS, VOL. II, INTERMEDIATE:
TUNES OF QUEEN ELIZABETH'S TIME
I/IIB3

ENSOM VANDRER (LONELY WANDERER) see
Grieg, Edvard Hagerup

ENSUENO see Turina, Joaquin

ENTR'ACTE see Gretry, Andre Ernest
Modeste; Ibert, Jacques

ENTREE see Wolki, Konrad

ENTREE-BALLET DES INSENCEZ see
Ballard, Robert

ENTWICKLUNG EINER TECHNISCHEN
PERFEKTION see Reiser, Ekkehard

ENUEG see Ohana, Maurice, Si Le Jour
Parait, No. 2

EPICYCLE I see Hekster, Walter

EPILOG see Redel, Martin Christoph

EPILOG AFTER HOMER'S ODYSSEY see
Antoniou, Theodore

EPISODES see Erdmann, Dietrich

EPISODES, FOR CHAMBER ORCHESTRA see
Lumsdaine, David

EPISODI, 4 see Margola, Franco

EPITAFFIO see Shackelford, Rudolph
Owens (Rudy)

EPITAPH, AN see Duarte, John W.

ERBSE, HEIMO (1924-   )
Barcarolle see 3 Studien

Elegy see 3 Studien

Nachklange I/IIC1

Scherzo see 3 Studien

3 Studien I/IIB1

ERDMANN, DIETRICH (1917-   )
Episodes I/IIB1

Notturno I/IIB3

ERGANZUNG ZUR GITARRENTECHNIK see Sao
Marcos, Maria Livia

ERINNERUNG see Schumann, Robert
(Alexander); Schumann, Robert
(Alexander)

ERLISO, VINCENTE
Minuet No. 1 I/IB4

Prelude in C see Transcripciones Por
Vicente Erliso, Vol. 1

Prelude in C minor see
Transcripciones Por Vicente
Erliso, Vol. 1

Rei Mariner, El see Transcripciones
Por Vicente Erliso, Vol. 1

Transcripciones Por Vicente Erliso,
Vol. 1 I/IB6-Coll

ERNESTO CHE GUEVARA see Havelka,
Svatopluk

ERSTE LAUTEN-SUITE, BWV 996 see Bach,
Johann Sebastian, Suite for Lute,
BWV 996, in E minor

ERSTE LEKTIONEN FUR GITARRE see Kotik,
Joseph

ERSTE MUSIZIERJAHR, DAS, VOL. 1
I/IIA1-Coll

ERSTE MUSIZIERJAHR, DAS, VOL. 2
I/IIA1-Coll

ERSTE MUSIZIERJAHR, DAS, VOL. 3
I/IIA1-Coll

ERSTE SONATE see Weiss, Sylvius
Leopold, Sonata in D minor

ERSTE SOR, DER see Sor, Fernando

ERSTE SUITE see Bach, Johann
Sebastian, Suite for Lute, BWV 996,
in E minor

ERSTE VORTRAGSSTUCKE FUR GITARRE see
Kotik, Joseph

ERSTEN ETUDEN, DIE I/IA-Coll

ERSTER SATZ AUS DER MONDSCHEIN-SONATE
see Beethoven, Ludwig van, Sonata
for Piano, Op. 27, No. 2, in C
sharp minor, First Movement

ERSTER VERLUST see Schumann, Robert
(Alexander)

ERSTES GITARRENSPIEL, LIEDER UND TANZE,
SEHR LEICHT GESETZT, VOL. I
I/IB6-Coll

ERSTES GITARRENSPIEL, LIEDER UND TANZE,
SEHR LEICHT GESETZT, VOL. II
I/IB6-Coll

ERSTES GITARRENSPIEL, LIEDER UND TANZE,
SEHR LEICHT GESETZT, VOL. III
I/IB6-Coll

ERSTES LAUTENBUCH, 67 KINDERLIEDER
I/IB5-Coll

ERSTES MUSIZIEREN AUF DER GITARRE -
MUSIC-MAKING FOR GUITAR, LIEDER UND
TANZE VERSCHIEDENER NATIONEN
I/IB5-Coll, I/IIA1-Coll

ERSTES SPIELBUCH FUR GITARRE
I/IB6-Coll

ES BRENNT, LIEDER AUS DEM GHETTO
I/IIC1-Coll

ES FLOG EIN KLEINS WALDVOGELEIN
I/IIC2-Coll

ES GEHT EIN' DUNKLE WOLK' HEREIN see
David, Johann Nepomuk

ES IST EIN ROS ENTSPRUNGEN IV/IIC5
see also Lautenspieler, Der, No. 1;
Weihnachtslieder; Stern, Hermann

ES IST VOLLBRACHT see Bach, Johann
Sebastian

ES LEBE DER KONIG; COMIC OPERA IN THREE
ACTS see De Grandis, Renato,
Gloria Al Re

ES LIEGT EIN SCHLOSS IN OSTERREICH see
Heiller, Anton

ES RITTEN DREI REITER I/IIC1-Coll,
I/IIC2-Coll

ES STEHT EIN LIND IM TIEFEN TAL, 6
DEUTSCHE BALLADEN see Zipp,
Friedrich

ES TAGET VOR DEM WALDE, 6 VARIATIONEN
UBER see Marx, Karl

ES WAR EIN KONIG IN THULE see Zelter,
Carl Friedrich

ES WAR EIN SOMMERMORGEN see Nordische
Volkslieder

ES WAREN ZWEI KONIGSKINDER see
Apostel, Hans Erich; Zipp,
Friedrich

ES WIRD SCHO GLEI, DUMPA see Uben Und
Spielen Auf Der Gitarre, Vol. 1

ESBOCOS see Lima, Candido

ESCALA NATUREL see Fresno, Jorge

ESCALAS, ARPEGIOS Y ARMONICOS PARA
GUITARRA, VOL. I see Tarrago,
Graciano

ESCALAS, ARPEGIOS Y ARMONICOS PARA
GUITARRA, VOL. II see Tarrago,
Graciano

ESCALAS, ARPEGIOS Y EJERCICIOS DEL
MECANISMO TECNICO see
Iparraguirre, P.A.

ESCALAS MENORES MELODICAS see
Iparraguirre, P.A.

ESCALAS Y ARPEGIOS DE MECANISMO TENICO
PARA GUITARRA see Prat, Domingo

ESCALES, ACORDES Y EJERCICIOS TECNICOS
PARA GUITARRA see Leloup, Hilarion

ESCARRAMAN, A SUITE OF SPANISH DANCES
FROM THE XVITH CENTURY (AFTER
CERVANTES) see Castelnuovo-
Tedesco, Mario

ESCENAS INFANTILES see Schumann,
Robert (Alexander), Kinderscenen

ESCOCESA see Schubert, Franz (Peter),
Ecossaises

ESCOLA MODERNA DO VIOLAO, VOL. II see
Savio, Isaias

ESCUELA DE GUITARRA see Aguado,
Dionisio

ESCUELA DE LA GUITARRA, LA, VOL. I see
Rodriguez Arenas, Mario

ESCUELA DE LA GUITARRA, LA, VOL. II
see Rodriguez Arenas, Mario

ESCUELA DE LA GUITARRA, LA, VOL. II
see Rodriguez Arenas, Mario

ESCUELA DE LA GUITARRA, LA, VOL. III
see Rodriguez Arenas, Mario

ESCUELA DE LA GUITARRA, LA, VOL. III
see Rodriguez Arenas, Mario

ESCUELA DE LA GUITARRA, LA, VOL. IV
see Rodriguez Arenas, Mario

ESCUELA DE LA GUITARRA, LA, VOL. V see
Rodriguez Arenas, Mario

ESCUELA DE LA GUITARRA, LA, VOL. V see
Rodriguez Arenas, Mario

ESCUELA DE LA GUITARRA, BASADA EN LOS
PRINCIPIOS DE LA TECHNICA DE
TARREGA see Pujol, Emilio

ESCUELA DE LA GUITARRA, VOL. VI see
Rodriguez Arenas, Mario

ESCUELA DE LA GUITARRA, VOL. VII see
Rodriguez Arenas, Mario

ESCUELA DE MECANISMO TECNICO PARA
GUITARRA see Ladru, Anibal

ESCUELA RAZONADA DE LA GUITARRA, 3
VOLS. see Pujol, Emilio

ESCUELA RAZONADA DE LA GUITARRA, BASADA
EN LOS PRINCIPIOS DE LA TECHNICA DE
TARREGA, VOL. I see Pujol, Emilio

ESCUELA RAZONADA DE LA GUITARRA, BASADA
EN LOS PRINCIPIOS DE LA TECHNICA DE
TARREGA, VOL. II see Pujol, Emilio

ESCUELA RAZONADA DE LA GUITARRA, BASADA
EN LOS PRINCIPIOS DE LA TECHNICA DE
TARREGA, VOL. III see Pujol,
Emilio

ESCUELA RAZONADA DE LA GUITARRA, BASADA
EN LOS PRINCIPIOS DE LA TECHNICA DE
TARREGA, VOL. IV see Pujol, Emilio

ESCUELA RAZONADA DE LA GUITARRA, BASADA
EN LOS PRINCIPIOS DE LA TECHNICA DE
TARREGA, VOL. V see Pujol, Emilio

ESERCIZI DI TARREGA see Tarrega,
Francisco, Formule Di Arpeggi

ESERCIZI DI TECNICA, 50 see Anzaghi,
Luigi Oreste

ESERCIZI DI TECNICA GIORNALIERA, 24
see Anzaghi, Luigi Oreste

ESERCIZI ESSENZIALI PER LA MANO
SINISTRA see Abloniz, Miguel

ESERCIZI TECNICI see Ferrari, Romolo

ESPAGNOLETA see Praetorius, Michael

ESPANOLETA see Fleres, Rita Maria;
Guerau, Francisco; Sanz, Gaspar

ESPANOLETA I see Sanz, Gaspar

ESPANOLETA I, AIR DE DANSE see Sanz,
Gaspar

ESPIRAL ETERNA, LA see Brouwer, Leo

ESPLA, OSCAR (1886-1976)
Impresiones Levantinas, 6 I/IB4

ESPOIRAL ETERNA PARA GUITARRA, LA see
Brouwer, Leo

ESQUINAS see Orrego-Salas, Juan A.

ESQUISSE see Kovats, Barna

ESSAY IN JAZZ see Heider, Werner

ESSENTIAL EXERCISES FOR THE LEFT HAND
see Abloniz, Miguel, Esercizi
Essenziali Per La Mano Sinistra

EST-CE BIEN CA?, SIX PIECES, OP. 48,
NO. 1 see Sor, Fernando

EST-CE BIEN CA?, SIX PIECES, OP. 48:
RONDO D-DUR see Sor, Fernando

ESTA NOCHE NACE EL NINO see
Villancicos Populares, Vol. III

ESTANCIAS see Ruiz Pipo, Antonio

ESTILHACOS see Coelho Silvestre,
Lourival Pinto

ESTILO FLAMENCO, METODO DE GUITARRA
see Azpiazu, Jose de

ESTRADA, JESU
Theme Varie I/IB4

ESTRELLAS PARA ESTARELLAS, MUSICA
NOCTURNA PARA LA GUITARRA DE
GABRIEL [ESTARELLAS] see
Gilardino, Angelo

ESTRELLITA, CANCION MEXICANA see
Ponce, Manuel Maria

ESTUDIO see Llobet, Miguel

ESTUDIO BRILLANTE, BY ALARD see
Tarrega, Francisco, Study, TI ii-
19, in A

ESTUDIO CAPRICHO IN D MAJOR see
Llobet, Miguel

ESTUDIO COMPLETO DE LAS ESCALES,
ARPEGIOS Y EJERCICIOS EN TERCERAS,
SEXTAS, OCTAVAS Y DECIMAS see
Rodriguez Arenas, Mario, Escuela De
La Guitarra, Vol. VII

ESTUDIO DE ALTURAS see Encinar, Jose
Ramon

ESTUDIO [DE ARPEGIOS] see Fortea,
Daniel

ESTUDIO DE CONCIERTO see Coste,
Napoleon; Diaz, Clemente A.

ESTUDIO DE CORCHEAS REPETIDAS see
Kovats, Barna

ESTUDIO DE DELPHIN ALARD see Tarrega,
Francisco, Study, TI ii- 19, in A

ESTUDIO DE LIGADOS see Fortea, Daniel

ESTUDIO DE PRUDENT see Tarrega,
Francisco, Study, TI ii- 23, in E
minor

ESTUDIO DE TREMOLO see Ponce, Manuel
Maria

ESTUDIO DE TREMOLO, SOBRE UN TEMA DE
ALARD see Tarrago, Graciano

ESTUDIO EN DO see Sor, Fernando,
Etude, Op. 29, No. 5

ESTUDIO EN FORMA DE MINUETTO see
Tarrega, Francisco, Study, TI ii-
5, in A

ESTUDIO EN MI BEMOL see Sor, Fernando,
Etude, Op. 29, No. 10

ESTUDIO EN MI BEMOL MAYOR see Sor,
Fernando, Etude, Op. 29, No. 10

ESTUDIO EN SI BEMOL see Sor, Fernando,
Etude, Op. 29, No. 1

ESTUDIO EN TREMOLO see Pastor, Segundo

ESTUDIO (ETUDE), FROM OP. 35, NO. 22
see Sor, Fernando, Vingt-Quatre
Exercices Tres Faciles, Op. 35, No.
22

ESTUDIO HOMOFONICO see Kovats, Barna

ESTUDIO PARA LA PRACTICA DE LOS
ARMONICOS OCTAVADOS COMPUESTOS see
Giorgio Gutierrez, Arnol Del

ESTUDIO-SCHERZO see Sainz de la Maza,
Regino

ESTUDIO SIN LUZ see Segovia, Andres

ESTUDIO SOBRE LA SONATINA DE DELPHIN
ALARD see Tarrega, Francisco,
Study, TI ii- 19, in A

ESTUDIO SOBRE UN FRAGMENTO, DE LA
"GRUTA DEL FINGAL" DE MENDELSSOHN
see Tarrega, Francisco, Study, TI
ii- 16a, in B minor

ESTUDIO SOBRE UN TEMA DE WAGNER see
Tarrega, Francisco, Study, TI ii-
13, in E

ESTUDIO (SOBRE UNA GIGA) see Tarrega, Francisco, Study, TI ii- 11, in E

ESTUDIO SUL NOME DI MANUEL LOPEZ RAMOS see Castelnuovo-Tedesco, Mario; Castelnuovo-Tedesco, Mario

ESTUDIO-VALS see Segovia, Andres

ESTUDIOS see Fortea, Daniel

ESTUDIOS, 2 I/IA

ESTUDIOS, 2, SOBRE UN TEMA DE ALARD see Tarrago, G.

ESTUDIOS, 3 see Segovia, Andres

ESTUDIOS, 4, PARA FORMAR EL RITMO Y LA EXPRESIÓN see Heller, Stephen

ESTUDIOS, 25 see Carcassi, Matteo, Melodische Und Progressive Etuden, 25; Coste, Napoleon, Etudes, 25

ESTUDIOS, 26 see Sor, Fernando

12 ESTUDIOS see Sor, Fernando

ESTUDIOS; 20 STUDIES WITHOUT TITLE, VOL. 1: ESTUDIOS 1-3 see Tarrega, Francisco

ESTUDIOS; 20 STUDIES WITHOUT TITLE, VOL. 2: ESTUDIOS 4-6 see Tarrega, Francisco

ESTUDIOS; 20 STUDIES WITHOUT TITLE, VOL. 3: ESTUDIOS 7-10 see Tarrega, Francisco

ESTUDIOS; 20 STUDIES WITHOUT TITLE, VOL. 4: ESTUDIOS 11-13 see Tarrega, Francisco

ESTUDIOS; 20 STUDIES WITHOUT TITLE, VOL. 5: ESTUDIOS 14-17 see Tarrega, Francisco

ESTUDIOS; 20 STUDIES WITHOUT TITLE, VOL. 6: ESTUDIOS 18-20 see Tarrega, Francisco

ESTUDIOS DE CEJILLA, 6 see Tarrago, Graciano

ESTUDIOS DE GUITARRA, 30 see Sor, Fernando

ESTUDIOS DIARIOS DEL MECANISMO TECNICO see Iparraguirre, P.A.

ESTUDIOS ELEMENTALES, 50 see Aguado, Dionisio, Studies, 50

ESTUDIOS: GRADO SUPERIOR see Pujol, Emilio

ESTUDIOS MELODICOS, 12 (SELECCION) see Giuliani, Mauro, Etuden, 24, Selections

ESTUDIOS MELODICOS, 25 see Tarrago, Graciano

ESTUDIOS MELODICOS PROGRESIVOS, 25 see Carcassi, Matteo, Melodische Und Progressive Etuden, 25

12 ESTUDIOS, OP.60 see Sor, Fernando

ESTUDIOS PARA GUITARRA see Tarrega, Francisco

ESTUDIOS PARA GUITARRA, 26 see Sor, Fernando

ESTUDIOS POETICOS, OP. 25 see Fortea, Daniel

ESTUDIOS PROGRESIVOS, 25 see Carcassi, Matteo, Melodische Und Progressive Etuden, 25

12 ESTUDIOS PROGRESIVOS see Sor, Fernando

ESTUDIOS SUPERIORES, 25 see Coste, Napoleon, Etudes, 25

ESTUDOS, 3, SERIES 2 see Savio, Isaias

ESTUDOS PARA VIOLAO, 8 I/IA-Coll

ET SI JE CHERCHE TON AMOUR? see Chanson D'Amours Elizabethaines, 3

ETRUSCAN PRELUDES see Smith Brindle, Reginald

ETUDE see Gitaarduet, Het

ETUDE 1-3 see Heer, Hans De

ETUDE 6-9 see Heer, Hans De

ETUDE BRILLIANTE see Aguado, Dionisio

ETUDE DE TREMOLO see Carcassi, Matteo

ETUDE DIABOLIQUE see Duarte, John W.

ETUDE DU MATIN see Presti, Ida

ETUDE EN FORME D'INVENTION see Sanchez, B.

ETUDE EN UT MAJEUR, POUR LA RESISTANCE DU BARRE see Eynard, Camille

ETUDE IN A MAJOR see Sor, Fernando, Vingt-Quatre Exercices Tres Faciles, Op. 35, No. 20

ETUDE IN HARMONICS see Bellow, Alexander

ETUDE IN TREMOLO see Bellow, Alexander

ETUDE NO. 1, TREMOLO see Bartoli, Rene

ETUDE ORIENTAL see Bellow, Alexander

ETUDE SPIRITUOSO see Giuliani, Mauro

ETUDEN see Tarrega, Francisco

ETUDEN, 3 see Haider, Hans

ETUDEN, 22 see Hubschmann, Werner

ETUDEN, 24 see Giuliani, Mauro

ETUDEN, 24, SELECTIONS see Giuliani, Mauro

ETUDEN, 24, UND 10 TONLEITERSTUDIEN see Aguado, Dionisio

ETUDEN, 24, UND 10 TONLEITERSTUDIEN FUR GITARRE see Aguado, Dionisio

ETUDEN, 25 see Carcassi, Matteo, Melodische Und Progressive Etuden, 25; Coste, Napoleon, Etudes, 25

ETUDEN FUR DIE MITTELSTUFE see Carcassi, Matteo

ETUDEN FUR GITARRE, 14 see Sor, Fernando

ETUDES, 2 see Maes, Jef

ETUDES, 3 see Alfonso, Nicolas

ETUDES, 4 see Visser, Dick

ETUDES, 6 see Franceries, Marc; Heller, Stephen; Lagoya, Alexandre; Presti, Ida

ETUDES, 10, POUR FORMER AU SENTIMENT, DU RHYTHME ET A L'EXPRESSION see Heller, Stephen

ETUDES, 12 see Villa-Lobos, Heitor

ETUDES, 12, VOL.1 see Mignone, Francisco

ETUDES, 12, VOL.2 see Mignone, Francisco

ETUDES, 13 see Lisker, Roy

ETUDES, 24, ET 10 EXERCICES DE GAMMES see Aguado, Dionisio, Etuden, 24, Und 10 Tonleiterstudien

ETUDES, 24, ET 10 EXERCISES DE GAMMES POUR GUITARE see Aguado, Dionisio, Etuden, 24, Und 10 Tonleiterstudien Fur Gitarre

ETUDES, 25 see Carcassi, Matteo, Melodische Und Progressive Etuden, 25; Carcassi, Matteo, Melodische Und Progressive Etuden, 25; Coste, Napoleon

ETUDES, 30 see Sor, Fernando

ETUDES BYZANTINES, 4 see Boda, John

ETUDES CHOISES, 24 see Sor, Fernando

ETUDES CREOLLES, 7 see Broqua, Alfonso

ETUDES DE CONCERT, 2 see Jolivet, Andre

ETUDES DE GENRE see Coste, Napoleon, Etudes, 25

ETUDES ELEMENTAIRES, 12 see Sanchez, Blas

ETUDES ELEMENTAIRES POUR GUITARE, VOL. I: PREMIERE POSITION see Martin, Gaston

ETUDES ELEMENTAIRES POUR GUITARE, VOL. II: ETUDES DES POSITIONS ET DU BARRE A CHAQUE POSITION see Martin, Gaston

ETUDES ELEMENTAIRES POUR GUITARE, VOL. III: CHANGEMENTS DE POSITIONS see Martin, Gaston

ETUDES IN SCALES, 2 see Bellow, Alexander

ETUDES POUR LA GUITARE, 20 see Sor, Fernando

ETUDES POUR LA GUITARE, 26, VOL. 1 see Sor, Fernando

ETUDES POUR LA GUITARE, 26, VOL. 2 see Sor, Fernando

ETUDES POUR LA GUITARE, 26, VOL. 3 see Sor, Fernando

ETUDES POUR LA GUITARE, 26, VOL. 4 see Sor, Fernando

ETUDES PREPARATOIRES, 12 see Sanchez, Blas

ETUDES PROBATOIRES, 12 see Sanchez, Blas

ETUDES PROGRESSIVES, 158 see Giuliani, Mauro

ETUDES RHYTHMIQUES see Aubanel, Georges

ETUDES SIMPLES, NOS. 1-5 see Brouwer, Leo

ETUDES SIMPLES, NOS. 6-10 see Brouwer, Leo

ETUDES SUPERIEURES, 3 see Sierra, Jose Maria

EUCALYPTUS see Sacchetti, Arturo

EUROPAISCHE GITARREN- UND LAUTENMUSIK, VOL. 1 I/IB1, I/IB1-Coll

EUROPAISCHE GITARREN- UND LAUTENMUSIK, VOL. 2 I/IB1, I/IB1-Coll

EUROPAISCHE GITARREN- UND LAUTENMUSIK, VOL. 3 I/IB1, I/IB1-Coll

EUROPAISCHE GITARREN- UND LAUTENMUSIK, VOL. 4 I/IB1, I/IB1-Coll

EUROPAISCHE GITARREN- UND LAUTENMUSIK, VOL. 5 I/IB1, I/IB1-Coll

EUROPAISCHE GITARREN- UND LAUTENMUSIK, VOL. 6 I/IB1, I/IB1-Coll

EUROPAISCHE GITARREN- UND LAUTENMUSIK, VOL. 7 I/IB1, I/IB1-Coll

EUROPAISCHE TANZE; 7 PIECES FOR SCHOOLENSEMBLE see Werdin, Eberhard

EUROPAISCHE VOLKS- UND KINDERLIEDER, IN EASY CHORAL VERSIONS WITH INSTRUMENTS, VOL. II I/IIC5-Coll

EUROPAISCHE VOLKSLIEDER, VOL. I I/IIC1-Coll

EUROPAISCHE VOLKSLIEDER, VOL. II I/IIC1-Coll

EUROPAISCHE VOLKSTANZE I/IIB1-Coll

EUROPAISCHE WEIHNACHTSLIEDER IV/IIC1

EUROPE CURIEUSE, L', EINE KURIOSE EUROPA-KANTATE FUR KINDER see Bresgen, Cesar

EUROPEAN MASTERS FOR THE GUITAR, A SELECT LIBRARY OF 26 [SIC] CLASSICAL AND CONTEMPORARY PIECES I/IB6-Coll, VII-Mixed Coll

EUROPEAN MASTERS FOR THE GUITAR, A SELECT LIBRARY OF 26 [SIC] CLASSICAL AND CONTEMPORARY PIECES I/IB6-Coll, VII-Mixed Coll

EUROPESE VOLKSLIEDEREN, VOL. I I/IIA1

EUROPESE VOLKSLIEDEREN, VOL. II I/IB5-Coll

EVENING SONG see Sperling, Ernst

EVERY NIGHT I DREAM see Schibler, Armin

EVOCACION see Albeniz, Isaac; Castellanos, Evencio

EVOCACIONES CRIOLLAS, NO.1 see Broqua, Alfonso

EVOCACIONES CRIOLLAS, NO.2 see Broqua, Alfonso

EVOCACIONES CRIOLLAS, NO.3 see Broqua, Alfonso

EVOCACIONES CRIOLLAS, NO.4 see Broqua, Alfonso

EVOCACIONES CRIOLLAS, NO.5 see Broqua, Alfonso

EVOCACIONES CRIOLLAS, NO.6 see Broqua, Alfonso

EVOCACIONES CRIOLLAS, NO.7 see Broqua, Alfonso

EVOCATION see Vandermaesbrugge, Max

EVOLUTION see Furstenau, Wolfram

EXCLOSION see Brouwer, Leo

EXERCICES, 40, FACILES POUR LA GUITARE, D'APRES UN THEME MATEO CARCASSI, VOL. I: 17 STUDIES FOR THE RIGHT HAND see Sanchez, Blas

EXERCICES, 40, FACILES POUR LA GUITARE, D'APRES UN THEME MATEO CARCASSI, VOL. II: 23 EXERCISES FOR THE LEFT HAND see Sanchez, Blas

EXERCICES JOURNALIERS POUR LE DEVELOPPEMENT DU TOUCHER see Gotze, Walter, Tagliche Studien Zur Bildung Des Anschlags

EXERCICES TECHNIQUES, 20, INDISPENSABLES POUR LA GUITARE, TOUS DEGRES see Sanchez, Blas

EXERCISES EN FORME D'ETUDES, VOL. 1 see Pujol, Emilio

EXERCISES EN FORME D'ETUDES, VOL. 2 see Pujol, Emilio

EXERCISES OF A LATE HOUR see Krenek, Ernst, Ubungen Der Spaten Stunde

EXOTIC DANCES, 5 see Staak, Pieter van der

EXOTISCHER TANZ see Ambrosius, Hermann

EXPO see Visser, Dick

EXPRESSIEVE MUZIEK see Visser, Dick

EYNARD, CAMILLE
Carnet De Notes I/IB4

Etude En Ut Majeur, Pour La Resistance Du Barre I/IA

EZAKI, KENJIRO (1926-   )
Nodule Per Chitarre I/IB4

EZERCIZI DI TECNICA SUPERIORE PER CHITARRA CLASSICA see Mozzani, Luigi, Studies For The Guitar

FABBRI, TITO
Metodo Teorico-Pratico II

FABER, JOHANN CHRISTIAN
Partita I/IIA2

FABIAN, GASTON
Gitarren Duette I/IIA1

FABINI, EDUARDO (1883-1950)
Mozartienne I/IB4

FABLE see Grau, Agusti

FABORDON DEL QUARTO TONO see Cabezon, Antonio de

FABORDON Y FUGA see Santa Maria, Thomas de

FABORDONES, 2, LLANO Y GLOSADO DEL CUARTO TONO see Venegas De Henestrosa, Tomas Luis de

FAIN WOULD I CHANGE THAT NOTE see Walton, [Sir] William (Turner)

FAISCEAUX-DIFFRACTIONS, FOR TWENTY-EIGHT INSTRUMENTS see Eloy, Jean-Claude

FALCKENHAGEN, ADAM (1697-1761)
Concerto I/IB1

Concerto in F I/IIIA

Duo I/IIA1

Suite in A I/IB1

FALLA, MANUEL DE (1876-1946)
Chanson Du Feu Follet I/IB4

Chansons Populaires Espagnoles, 7, Vols. 1-7 I/IIC1

Dance Of The Corregidor I/IB4, I/IIA1

Dance Of The Miller I/IB4

Dances, 2, No. 1 see Dance Of The Miller

Dances, 2, No. 2 see Dance Of The Corregidor

Danse De La Frayeur I/IIA1

Danse Espagnole No. 1 I/IIA1

Miller's Dance, The I/IIA1

Omaggio, Scritto Per Le Tombeau De Debussy I/IB4

Recit Du Pecheur I/IB4

Serenata Andaluza I/IB4

Tus Ojillos Negros, Cancion Andaluza I/IIC1

FAMOSISSIME GAVOTTE DI J.S. BACH, LE see Bach, Johann Sebastian

FAMOUS NEGRO SPIRITUALS, 5 I/IB5-Coll

FANCY see Elizabethan Duets, 6

FANCY, A see Dowland, John; Dowland, John

FANDANGO see Gangi, Mario; Zagwijn, Henri

FANDANGO DE ONATE see Azpiazu, Jose de

FANDANGO DEL VENTORRILLO see Rodrigo, Joaquin

FANDANGO VARIADO see Aguado, Dionisio

FANDANGO Y VARIACIONES see Aguado, Dionisio

FANDANGUILLO see Turina, Joaquin

FANFARE see Sanz, Gaspar, Cavalleria De Napoles, La

FANTAISIE see Sor, Fernando

FANTAISIE DU QUATRIEME TON see Valderrabano, Enriquez de, Fantasy, MIN 270

FANTAISIE ELEGIAQUE see Sor, Fernando

FANTAISIE ELEGIAQUE: MARCHE FUNEBRE see Sor, Fernando

FANTAISIE: LARGO see Sor, Fernando

FANTAISIE POUR LE LUTH see Weiss, Sylvius Leopold, Fantasy in C minor

FANTAISIE, SUR DES AIRS FAVORIS see Sor, Fernando, Septieme Fantaisie Et Variations Brillantes Sur Deux Airs Favoris Connus

FANTASIA see Sor, Fernando, Fantaisie

FANTASIA A SEI CORDE see Behrend, Siegfried

FANTASIA AND FUGUE ON "TORRE BERMEJA" see Duarte, John W.

FANTASIA BREVE SOBRE EL NOMBRE "SALCEDO" see Pujol, Emilio

FANTASIA [COLLECTION] I/IIB1-Coll

FANTASIA DE LA GUITARRA, ETUDE DE TREMOLO see Bochman, Theo L.

FANTASIA DE L'OCTAVO TONO see Milan, Luis

FANTASIA DE PASOS DE CONTADO see Mudarra, Alonso de

FANTASIA DE REDOBLES see Fuenllana, Miguel de

FANTASIA DEL PMER TONO see Mudarra, Alonso de

FANTASIA DEL PRIMER TONO see Narvaez, Luis de

FANTASIA E VARIAZIONI BRILLANTI see Sor, Fernando, Septieme Fantaisie Et Variations Brillantes Sur Deux Airs Favoris Connus

FANTASIA ELEGIACA see Sor, Fernando, Fantaisie Elegiaque

FANTASIA ELEGIAQUE see Sor, Fernando, Fantaisie Elegiaque

FANTASIA FACIL see Pisador, Diego

FANTASIA I see Fuenllana, Miguel de

FANTASIA II see Fuenllana, Miguel de

FANTASIA III see Fuenllana, Miguel de

FANTASIA, IMITATION DE LA HARPE A LA MANIERE DE LUDOVICO see Mudarra, Alonso de, Fantasia X, Que Contrahaze La Harpa En La Manera De Luduvico

FANTASIA [IV] see Fuenllana, Miguel de

FANTASIA MALAGUENITA see Behrend, Siegfried

FANTASIA ORIGINAL DE UN GENTILHOMBRE, VILLANOS see Sanz, Gaspar

FANTASIA PARA UN GENTILHOMBRE, INSPIRADA EN GASPAR SANZ see Rodrigo, Joaquin

FANTASIA (QUE CONTRAHAZE LA HARPA EN LA MANERA DE LUDUVICO) see Mudarra, Alonso de

FANTASIA, QUE CONTREHACE LA HARPA EN LA MANERA DE LUDOVICO see Mudarra, Alonso de, Fantasia X, Que Contrahaze La Harpa En La Manera De Luduvico

FANTASIA SECONDA A QUATTRO VOCI, FOR LUTE see Bakfark, Balint (Valentin)

FANTASIA SEVILLANA see Turina, Joaquin

FANTASIA-SONATA see Manen, Jose

FANTASIA X, QUE CONTRAHAZE LA HARPA EN LA MANERA DE LUDOVICO see Mudarra, Alonso de

FANTASIA X, QUE REMEDA EL HARPA DE LUDOVICO see Mudarra, Alonso de, Fantasia X, Que Contrahaze La Harpa En La Manera De Luduvico

FANTASIA XVI see Valderrabano, Enriquez de, Fantasy, MIN 270

FANTASIAS I/IB1-Coll

FANTASIAS, 2 see Mudarra, Alonso de

FANTASIAS, 2; 2 TIENTOS see Mudarra, Alonso de

FANTASIAS, 4 I/IB1-Coll

FANTASIAS, 4, DE PASOS LARGOS PARA DESENVOLVER LAS MANOS see Daza, Esteban

FANTASIAS, 4; PAVANE; ROMANESCA see Mudarra, Alonso de

FANTASIAS, 8 see Santa Maria, Thomas de

FANTASIAS, 25 see Santa Maria, Thomas de

3 FANTASIAS see Dowland, John

FANTASIAS A TRES, 4 see Daza, Esteban

FANTASIAS I-III see Luening, Otto

FANTASIE, DIE see Apostel, Hans Erich

FANTASIE ELEGIAQUE see Sor, Fernando

FANTASIE, UBER "ES GEHT EIN DUNKLE WOLK HEREIN" see Baumann, Herbert

FANTASIEN, 3 see Baur, Jurg; Francesco da Milano

FANTASIEN, 4 see Benary, Peter

FANTASIES, 3 see Brayssing, Gregoire

FANTASY, A see Robinson, Thomas

FANTASY-DIVISIONS see Dodgson, Stephen

FANTASY NO. 4 I/IB1

FANTAZJE I WILANELE see Dlugoraj,
   Adalbert (Wojiech)

FARAILL, M.
   Etude I/IA

FARKAS, FERENC (1905-   )
   Canzoni Dei Trovatori, 5 I/IIC1

   Chorea see Regi Magyar Tancok - Alte
      Ungarische Tanze; Regi Magyar
      Tancok - Alte Ungarische Tanze

   Citharoedia Strigoniensis, Sopra
      Motivi Ungheresi Di Esztergom Del
      XVIII Secolo I/IIA2

   Dance Guerriere see Pieces Breves, 6

   Grinzing see Pieces Breves, 6

   Intermezzo see Pieces Breves, 6

   Pieces Breves, 6 I/IB4

   Prelude see Pieces Breves, 6

   Regi Magyar Tancok - Alte Ungarische
      Tanze I/IB4

   Regi Magyar Tancok - Alte Ungarische
      Tanze I/IB4

   Scene De Ballet see Pieces Breves, 6

   Tanz Des Fursten Von Sieben Burgen
      see Regi Magyar Tancok - Alte
      Ungarische Tanze; Regi Magyar
      Tancok - Alte Ungarische Tanze

   Tanz Des Lazar Apor, Der see Regi
      Magyar Tancok - Alte Ungarische
      Tanze; Regi Magyar Tancok - Alte
      Ungarische Tanze

   Tirnovo see Pieces Breves, 6

   Ungarischer Tanz see Regi Magyar
      Tancok - Alte Ungarische Tanze;
      Regi Magyar Tancok - Alte
      Ungarische Tanze

FARNABY, GILES (ca. 1560-1640)
   Pieces, 5 I/IB1

FARQUHAR, DAVID (1928-   )
   Barcarolle see Scenes, 5

   Dreaming see Scenes, 5

   Lullaby see Scenes, 5

   Ostinato I/IB4

   Procession see Scenes, 5

   Questions see Scenes, 5

   Scenes, 5 I/IB4

FARRUCA I/IB5

FASCH, JOHANN FRIEDRICH (1688-1758)
   Concerto in D minor I/IIIA

FASTES, LES see Couperin, Francois (le
   Grand)

FATIMA, SUITE GALANTE see Sandi, Luis

FEDE SACRILEGA NELLA MORTE DEL
   PRECURSOR S. GIOVANNI BATTISTA, LA
   see Fux, Johann Joseph

FEGERS, KARL (1926-   )
   Suite Nach Franzosischen Volksliedern
      I/IIB5

FEIERLICHER TANZ see Sprongl, Norbert

FELD, JINDRICH (1925-   )
   Capriccio I/IIB4

FELSENQUELL, DER, FRANZOSISCHE
   VOLKSTANZE 2. TEIL I/IIB3-Coll

FEM INFALL, SVIT see Lundin, Bengt

FEMME, MAISON, MOINEAU see Furstenau,
   Wolfram

FENICIO, EDMAR
   Suite in A minor I/IB4

FERANDIERE, FERNANDO
   Petites Pieces, 6 I/IB2

FERIA AL PRADO, SEVILLANA see Dagosto,
   Sylvain

FERNANDEZ, HERACLIO (1851-1886)
   Diablo Suelto, El, Valzer Popolare
      Venezuelano I/IB5

FERNANDEZ, OSCAR LORENZO (1897-1948)
   Old Song I/IB4

   Prelude I/IB4

FERNANDEZ-LAVIE, FERNANDO
   Ecole De Guitare, Technique Moderne,
      Formation Permanente. Cours
      Preparatoire-Elementaire-Moyen
      II

   Gitarrespiel Im Uberblick, Einfuhrung
      In Die Spieltechnik Nach
      Klassisch-Spanischer Schule II

   Guitar Pour Tous, La, Methode
      Progressive II

FERRABOSCO, ALFONSO (I) (1543-1588)
   Pavan, MIN 415 I/IB1

   Pavana, 6 I/IB1

FERRARI, IVANO (1932-   )
   Capriccio No. 1 see Kuss-Tobia

   Kuss-Tobia I/IB4

FERRARI, ROMOLO (1894-1959)
   Danza Orientale I/IB4

   Esercizi Tecnici III

   Grande Fugue Reale I/IB4

   Tabella Degli Accordi, Per Chitarra
      Classica E Jazz III

FERRER, JOSE (1835-1916)
   Danse Des Naiades, La I/IB3

FERRITTO, JOHN E. (1937-   )
   Diffusione I/IIB4

   Duos, 4 I/IIB1

FERRONATI, LODOVICO
   Sonata in C I/IIB1

FERSTL, ERICH (1934-   )
   Concertino I/IIIA

   Sol Y Sombra I/IIIA

FESTIVOLA, DANZA CATALANA DE ESPIRITU
   POPULAR see Pujol, Emilio

FESTLICHE SUITE, FUR SPIELMUSIKGRUPPEN
   see Korda, Viktor

FETE DES OURS, LA see Mason, Roger

FETLER, PAUL (1920-   )
   Adagio Quasi Recitative see Pieces,
      5

   Allegretto see Pieces, 5

   Allegro Agitato see Pieces, 5

   Allegro Moderato see Pieces, 5

   Andante Espressivo see Pieces, 5

   Movements, 4 I/IB4

   Pieces, 5 I/IB4

FEU see Miroglio, Francis

FEUILLES VARIAS see Schumann, Robert
   (Alexander)

FEUILLES VARIEES see Schumann, Robert
   (Alexander), Albumblatt

FEUILLETS, 15 see Delauney, Paul

FHEODOROFF, NIKOLAUS (1931-   )
   Zwolftonspiele, 3 I/IIB3

FIDELE WEISEN, FUR GITARRE SOLO IN
   LEICHTER SPIELART see Hintermeyer,
   Willy

FIERA VISTA, LA see Monteverdi,
   Claudio

FIESTA LAREDANA see Sanchez, B.

FILE LA LAINE see Marcy, Robert

FILIBERTO, ROMOLO
   Guitar Technique III

FILIPPI, AMADEO DE
   see DE FILIPPI, AMEDEO

FILLA DEL MARXANT, LA see Catalanische
   Weisen, 3

FILLA DEL MARXANT, LA, MELODIA POPULAR
   CATALANA I/IB5

FILLE AUX CHEVEUX DE LIN, LA see
   Debussy, Claude

FILLE DU PECHEUR, LA see Schubert,
   Franz (Peter), Fischermadchen, Das

FILLE MATELOT, LA see Franse
   Volksliederen, 3

FINALE see Korda, Viktor

FINE KNACKS FOR LADIES see Dowland,
   John

FINGALS-HOHLE see Mertz, Johann Kaspar

FINGER ANSCHLAG, 5 see Beck, Leonhard

FINGERBOARD WORKBOOK, THE, A NON-METHOD
   FOR GUITAR see Caponigro, Andrew

FINGERBOARDCHART see Angel, Miguel,
   Nomenclature

FINK, SIEGFRIED
   Dialoge I/IIB1

   Tangents CSB I/IIC1

FINNISCHE VOLKSLIEDER, SUOMALAISIA
   KANSANLAULUJA I/IIC1-Coll

FINZIONI see Peruzzi, Aurelio

FIOCCO, JOSEPH-HECTOR (1703-1741)
   Allegro I/IIB1

FIRST ESSAY ON ELECTROCUTION see
   Schat, Peter

FIRST EXERCISES FOR GUITAR, SPEEL- EN
   LUISTEROEFENINGEN, VOL. I see
   Hall, A.D. van

FIRST EXERCISES FOR GUITAR, SPEEL- EN
   LUISTEROEFENINGEN, VOL. II see
   Hall, A.D. van

FIRST EXERCISES FOR GUITAR, SPEEL- EN
   LUISTEROEFENINGEN, VOL. III see
   Hall, A.D. van

FIRST GUITAR BOOK, A PRACTICE COURSE
   FOR BEGINNERS see Irving,
   Jacquelyn

FIRST LESSONS see Bellow, Alexander

FIRST NOEL, THE see Guitar Songbook,
   The

FIRST REPERTOIRE FOR CLASSIC GUITAR
   see Pick, Richard Samuel Burns

FIRST STEPS, THE see Schagen, Henk
   van, Lopen Leren

FISCHER, FRANZ
   Prelude, Orgelpunktstudie I/IA

FISCHER, JAN F. (1921-   )
   Krieg Mit Den Molchen, Der; Music To
      The Play Of Pavel Kohaut V/iii

FISCHER, JOHANN CASPAR FERDINAND
   (ca. 1665-1746)
   Leichte Stucke, 8 I/IIB1

   March I/IIB1

FISCHERMADCHEN, DAS see Schubert,
   Franz (Peter)

FIVE CORANTOES see Dowland, Robert

FIVE EASY PIECES FOR THE GUITAR see
   Bach, Johann Sebastian

FIVE LOVE SONGS see Musgrave, Thea

FIVEFOLD ENFOLDMENT see Krenek, Ernst,
   Funffache Verschrankung

FLAMENCO-FANTASIA see Behrend,
   Siegfried

FLAMENCO-GITARREN-SCHULE see Kaps,
   Hansjoachim

FLAMENCO-GITARRENSCHULE see Skiera,
   Ehrenhard

FLAMENCO GUITAR, A COMPLETE METHOD FOR
   PLAYING FLAMENCO, PART I: [METHOD]
   see Mairants, Ivor

FLAMENCO GUITAR, A COMPLETE METHOD FOR
   PLAYING FLAMENCO, PART II: 25 SHORT
   PCS OF VARIOUS RHYTHMS see
   Mairants, Ivor

FLAMENCO GUITAR, A COMPLETE METHOD FOR PLAYING FLAMENCO, PART III: 8 PCS [SPANISH DANCES] see Mairants, Ivor

FLAMENCO GUITAR METHOD, A BASIC COURSE IN FLAMENCO GUITAR TECHNIQUE see Leventhal, Ronald

FLAMISCHE LIEDER UND TANZE I/IIC4-Coll

FLAMME, A. (1950-)
Mignonne I/IB4

FLANDRISCHES GITARRENBUCH, VOL. 1: FANTASIES AND SONGS I/IB1

FLANDRISCHES GITARRENBUCH, VOL. 2: DANCES I/IB1

FLAT PAVANE, THE see Elizabethan Duets, 6

FLATT PAVIN, THE see Musique Elisabethaine

FLECHA, MATEO (1530-1604)
Girigonza, La, Danse Chantee I/IIC1

FLERES, RITA MARIA
Canarios see Stucke, 5, Nach Liedern Und Tanzen Aus Der Renaissance

Espanoleta see Stucke, 5, Nach Liedern Und Tanzen Aus Der Renaissance

Funf Variationen Uber "Greensleeves" see Stucke, 5, Nach Liedern Und Tanzen Aus Der Renaissance

Stucke, 5, Nach Liedern Und Tanzen Aus Der Renaissance I/IIB1

Tanzlein see Stucke, 5, Nach Liedern Und Tanzen Aus Der Renaissance

Vaghe Bellezze see Stucke, 5, Nach Liedern Und Tanzen Aus Der Renaissance

FLIES, J. BERNHARD (1770- ?)
Berceuse see Wiegenlied "Schlafe Mein Prinzchen"

Cancion De Cuna see Wiegenlied "Schlafe Mein Prinzchen"

Wiegenlied "Schlafe Mein Prinzchen" I/IB2, I/IIC1

FLIGHT OF FUGUES, A see Duarte, John W.

FLOR DEL CAMPO, VALZER VENEZUELANO I/IB5

FLORES NEGRAS, PASILLO ECUATORIANO I/IB5

FLOTE SING, KLAMPFE KLING see Ya Se Van Los Pastores

FLOTE SING, KLAMPFE KLING I/IIB1-Coll, IV/IIB1

FLOTENHANNES, DER, EIN LERNBUCHLEIN FUR DIE C"-BLOCKFLOTE UND DAZU MANCHERLEI LIEDER UND SATZE ZUM SINGEN UND MUSIZIEREN MIT VERSCHIEDENEN INSTRUMENTEN see Derlien, Margarete

FLOTENUHRSTUCK see Mozart, Wolfgang Amadeus

FLOTHUIS, MARIUS (1914-)
Folia see Stukken, 2

Habanera see Stukken, 2

Stukken, 2 I/IB4

FLOW, MY TEARS see Dowland, John

FLOWERS APPEAR ON THE EARTH, THE see Wiegold, Peter

FLUTE D'ARGENT, LA see Barlow, Fred

FODEN, WILLIAM (1860-1947)
Chords [For The] Classic Guitar III

Short Preludes, 6 (Chord Progressions) I/IB3

FOLIA see Flothuis, Marius; Sanz, Gaspar

FOLIAS see Guerau, Francisco; Sanz, Gaspar

FOLIAS CANARIAS see Rodrigo, Joaquin

FOLIAS DE ESPANA see Sor, Fernando, Folies d'Espagne, Variees, Et Un Menuet

FOLIAS DE ESPANA, LAS, TEMA Y VARIACIONES see Sor, Fernando, Folies d'Espagne, Variees, Et Un Menuet

FOLIAS DE ESPANA, LAS, VARIATIONEN see Sor, Fernando, Folies d'Espagne, Variees, Et Un Menuet

FOLIES D'ESPAGNE see Sor, Fernando, Folies d'Espagne, Variees, Et Un Menuet

FOLIES D'ESPAGNE, LES, TEMA E VARIAZIONI see Sor, Fernando, Folies d'Espagne, Variees, Et Un Menuet

FOLIES D'ESPAGNE, VARIEES, ET UN MENUET see Sor, Fernando

FOLK-BLUES, 3 I/IB5-Coll

FOLK GUITAR: RAGTIME, BLUES, COUNTRY MUSIC see Schwertberger, Gerald

FOLK TUNES AND CLASSICS FOR SOLO GUITAR I/IB6-Coll, VII-Mixed Coll

FOLKLORE see Erste Musizierjahr, Das, Vol. 3

FOLKLORE DER WELT, VOLS. I-III; LIEDER UND TANZE AUS ALLER WELT I/IB5-Coll

FOLKLORE, VOL. 1 I/IIB1-Coll

FOLKLORE, VOL. 2 I/IIB1-Coll

FOLKLORISTISCHE SUITE; 12 VOLKSWEISEN AUS ALLER WELT I/IB5-Coll

FOLKSONGS, 4 I/IB5-Coll, IV/I

FOLKSONGS, 10 I/IIC1-Coll

FOLKSONGS, 50 see Truhlar, Jan, Lidovych Pisni, 50

FOLKSONGS, 10 ENGLISH FOLKSONGS I/IIC1-Coll

FOLKSONGS I/IIB1-Coll

FOLKVISE (FOLKSONG) see Grieg, Edvard Hagerup

FOLKVISOR, 30 I/IB5-Coll

FOLLIA see Vries, Klaas de

FOR CHILDREN see Bartok, Bela, Fur Kinder

FOR GUITARISTS ONLY! I/IB6-Coll

FOR MY FRIENDS I/IB6-Coll, IV/I see also Duarte, John W.

FOR SKILLED FINGERS see Schagen, Henk van, Voor Vaardige Vingers

FOREST, JEAN KURT (1909-1975)
Indiana-Rhapsodie, For Orchestra V/i

FORLORN HOPE FANCY see Dowland, John

FORMULAS TECNICAS, PARA EL MECANISMO ELEMENTAL DE LA GUITARRA see Pomilio, Tomas

FORMULE DI ARPEGGI see Tarrega, Francisco

FORSKALIA see Mosso, Carlo

FORTEA, DANIEL (1882-1953)
Capricho-Estudio, Op. 13 I/IA

Capricho-Estudio, Op. 45 I/IA

Dialogando see Estudios Poeticos, Op. 25

Estudio [De Arpegios] I/IA

Estudio De Ligados I/IA

Estudios I/IA

Estudios Poeticos, Op. 25 I/IA

Homenaje A Sor I/IB4

Metodo De Guitarra, Vol. I II, VI-Mixed Coll

Metodo De Guitarra, Vol. II II, VI-Mixed Coll

FORTEA, DANIEL (cont'd.)
Murmullos I/IA

Preludios-Estudio, 2, Op. 4 I/IA

Preludios-Estudio, 2, Op. 5 I/IA

Preludios-Estudio, 2, Op. 6 D3 I/IA

Serenata see Estudios Poeticos, Op. 25

Study see Murmullos

Study in F I/IA

FORTNER, WOLFGANG (1907-)
Cress Ertrinkt, Ein Schulspiel I/IIC5

In Seinem Garten Liebt Don Perlimplin Belisa; Opera V/iii

FORTSCHREITENDE STUCKE, 18 see Giuliani, Mauro

FORTSCHREITENDE STUDIEN FUR ANFANGER, 24, VOL. 1: STUDIES NO. 1-12 see Sor, Fernando, Vingt Quatre Lecons Progressives, Dediees Aux Eleves Commencants

FORTSCHREITENDE STUDIEN FUR ANFANGER, 24, VOL. 2: STUDIES NO. 13-24 see Sor, Fernando, Vingt Quatre Lecons Progressives, Dediees Aux Eleves Commencants

FORTSCHREITENDE UBUNGEN FUR GITARRE-ANFANGER, VOL. 1: STUDIES NO. 1-12 see Sor, Fernando, Vingt Quatre Lecons Progressives, Dediees Aux Eleves Commencants

FORTSCHREITENDE UBUNGEN FUR GITARRE-ANFANGER, VOL. 2: STUDIES NO. 13-24 see Sor, Fernando, Vingt Quatre Lecons Progressives, Dediees Aux Eleves Commencants

FORTUNE see Dowland, John

FORTUNE AND VARIATIONS see Byrd, William, Cantilena (Theme And 2 Variations)

FORTUNE (THEME AND 4 VARIATIONS) see Byrd, William

FORZA D'AMORE see Caroso, Fabrizio

FOSIL SUITI see Koptagel, Yuksel

FOSS, LUKAS (1922-)
Paradigm I/IIB2

FOSTER, STEPHEN COLLINS (1826-1864)
My Old Kentucky Home I/IIC4

FOUNDATION STUDIES IN CLASSIC GUITAR TECHNIQUE see Duarte, John W.

FOUNTAIN OF NIE PASTRIE, THE see Grau, Eduardo, Fuente De Nie Pastrie, La

FOUR CATALAN MELODIES I/IB5-Coll

FOUR CENTURIES OF SONG, FROM THE TROUBADOUR TO THE ELIZABETHAN AGE I/IIC1-Coll

FOUR EASY LESSONS see Segovia, Andres

FOUR VARIATIONS ON A THEME OF GUIDO TOPPER see Staak, Pieter van der

FOX, VICTOR
Prelude I/IB4

FRAGMENTE NACH HOLDERLIN, 3 see Henze, Hans Werner

FRANCAISE see Ibert, Jacques

FRANCAIX, JEAN (1912-)
Priere Du Soir I/IIC1

FRANCERIES, MARC (1935-)
Etudes, 6 I/IA

Gammes Et Arpeges Pour La Guitare III

Pour Christiane I/IB4

FRANCESCO CORBETTA: 16 COMPOSITIONS SELECTED FROM "VARII CAPRICCI PER LA GHITARRA SPAGNUOLA" see Corbetta, Francesco (Francisque Corbett)

FUNF VARIATIONEN UBER "GREENSLEEVES"
see Fleres, Rita Maria

FUNFFACHE VERSCHRANKUNG see Krenek,
Ernst

FUNK, HEINRICH (1893-)
Herpfer Kirmeswalzer see Thuringer
Kirmes. 4 Bauerntanze Aus
Thuringen

Kehraus see Thuringer Kirmes. 4
Bauerntanz Aus Thuringen

Kirmestanz see Thuringer Kirmes. 4
Bauerntanze Aus Thuringen

Thuringer Dorfkirmes see Thuringer
Kirmes. 4 Bauerntanze Aus
Thuringen

Thuringer Kirmes. 4 Bauerntanze Aus
Thuringen I/IIB5

FUNNY FACE see Topper, Guido

FUR DEN ANFANG, VOL. 1 see Walker,
Luise

FUR DEN ANFANG, VOL. 2 see Walker,
Luise

FUR DEN ANFANG, VOL. 3 see Walker,
Luise

FUR DEN ANFANG, VOL. 4 see Walker,
Luise

FUR DEN ANFANG, VOL. 5 see Walker,
Luise

FUR DEN ANFANG, VOL. 6 see Walker,
Luise

FUR ELISE see Beethoven, Ludwig van

FUR JEDEN GITARRISTEN, SONDERAUSGABE
21. INTERNATIONALER
GITARRISTENKONGRESS (TOKYO, 1962),
"IN MEMORIAM" (RICHARD JACOB
WEISGERBER 1877-1940, PROF. ROMOLO
FERRARI 1895-1958) I/IB6-Coll

FUR KINDER see Bartok, Bela

FUR SOTO see Steffens, Walter

FURLANA see Campra, Andre

FURSTENAU, KASPAR (1772-1819)
Duette, 6 I/IIB1

Original-Kompositionen, 12, Op. 35
see Suite, Op. 35

Stucke, 12 I/IIB1

Suite, Op. 34 I/IIB1

Suite, Op. 35 I/IIB1

Zwolf Stucke I/IIB1

FURSTENAU, WOLFRAM
Cadenza see Pieces Pour Une Noble
Femme, 3

Cadenza Amicitia I/IB4

Ch'i - Yun (Oder Das Prinzip
Intensiven Lebens In Frieden)
Nach Dem Gemalden "Schwingungen",
"Lu-Mi", "Cheng" Von Georg W.
Borsche I/IIB3

Evolution see Pieces Pour Une Noble
Femme, 3

Femme, Maison, Moineau see
Reflexionen, Auf Bilder Von Max
Ernst

Hommage A Alberto Giacometti I/IB4

Hommage A Jean Cocteau I/IB4

Huizen, Grachten, Mensen see Jordaan

Invocation see Pieces Pour Une Noble
Femme, 3

Jordaan I/IIB4

Laicite see Reflexionen, Auf Bilder
Von Max Ernst

Monde Des Flous, Le see Reflexionen,
Auf Bilder Von Max Ernst

Ommegang: Cycle I/IB4, V/i

Orationen I/IIB1

Pieces Pour Une Noble Femme, 3
I/IIB1

FURSTENAU, WOLFRAM (cont'd.)

Printemps, Redempteur Et Redime see
Reflexionen, Auf Bilder Von Max
Ernst

Psalmodia Uber Das V. Gebot Mose, In
Memoriam Quang Duc - Vietnam
I/IIA1

Railway-Traffic I/IB4, I/IIA4

Reflexionen, Auf Bilder Von Max Ernst
I/IB4

Renaissance Pour Le Presence I/IIIC

Sanctuaire see Reflexionen, Auf
Bilder Von Max Ernst

Serenata Polonia I/IIA1

Sonette I/IIC1

Spielmusik I/IIB4

Vakantiedagboek I/IIB1

FUSSL, KARL-HEINZ (1924-)
Dialogue In Praise Of The Owl And The
Cuckoo V/ii

Drei Szenen Aus "Dybuk" V/ii

Dybuk; Opera In Three Acts And Three
Scenes V/iii

FUSZ, JANOS
Quartet I/IIB3

FUX, JOHANN JOSEPH (1660-1741)
Fede Sacrilega Nella Morte Del
Precursor S. Giovanni Battista,
La V/ii

GABETTI, FLORA
Guitare Mon Amie, Preparation Et
Introduction A Toutes Les
Methodes II

GABRIEL-MARIE
see MARIE, GABRIEL

GABRIELI, ANDREA (1510-1586)
Edipo Re, Cori Per La Tragedia Di
Sofocle V/ii

GABRIELI, DOMENICO (ca. 1650-1690)
Balletto A Tre I/IIB2

GABUS, MONIQUE (1926-)
Stele Pour Une Jeune Indienne I/IB4

GAGLIARDA see Galilei, Vincenzo,
Saltarello, MIN 308

GAGLIARDA DEL PASSO E MEZZO see
Maestri Del '500

GAGLIARDA DEL PASSO MEZZO see
Anonymous

GAGLIARDE, 2 see Galilei, Vincenzo

GAGLIARDE, 2 I/IB1

GAGLIARDE, 10 see Barbetta Padovano,
Julio Cesare

GAGLIARDEN, 3 see Kapsberger, Johann
Hieronymus

GAGNEBIN, HENRI (1886-1977)
Chanson see Pieces, 3

Gigue see Pieces, 3

Improvisation see Pieces, 3

Pieces, 3 I/IB4

GAGOK see Yun, Isang

GAI see Werner, Jean-Jacques

GAILLARDE ET ALLEMANDE see Dowland,
John

GAILLARDE "GHEQUEST BIN ICK" see
Susato, Tielman

GAILLARDE LA ROCCA E IL FUSO see Le
Roy, Adrien

GAILLARDE "MILLE DUCAS" see Susato,
Tielman

GAILLARDE, PAVANE, ET TOCCATA see De
Filippi, Amedeo

GAILLARDE SUR UN THEME DE DANIEL
BATCHELAR see Dowland, John,
Galliard On A Galliard Of Daniel
Bacheler, A

GAILLARDES, 2 see Dowland, John

GAILLARDES, 2 I/IB1

GAITIS, FRIEDRICH
Concertino I/IIIB

Stucke, 4 I/IIA1

GAL, HANS (1890-1987)
Divertimento, Op. 68c I/IIB2

GALANTE DANS see Greeve, G. de

GALANTE MUZIEK, VAN COMPONISTEN UIT DE
18E EEUW I/IIB5-Coll

GALEN MAN I/IIC1-Coll
see also Galen Man

GALERON see Sojo, Vincente E.

GALILEI, MICHEL ANGELO
Corrente Und Saltarello I/IB1

Primo Libro D'Intavolatura Di Liuto,
I1 (1620) I/IB1

GALILEI, VINCENZO (ca. 1520-1591)
Gagliarda see Saltarello, MIN 308

Gagliarde, 2 I/IB1

Passo Mezzo In Discant Y Saltarello
I/IB1

Pieces, 10 I/IB1

Saltarello, MIN 308 I/IB1

GALINDO, PATRICIO
Metodo De Guitarra, Para Acompanar
Canciones Y Ritmos Populares Y
Folkloricos II

Quieres Aprender Musica Y Tocar La
Guitarra En 15 Lecciones? II

GALL, LOUIS IGNATIUS
Asiatica see Stukken, 3

Bulerias De Nimega I/IA

Cancion see Stukken, 3

Etude No. 33 see Bulerias De Nimega

Gitaarmethode - Guitar Method -
Gitarreschule, Vol. I II

Gitaarmethode - Guitar Method -
Gitarreschule, Vol. IA II

Gitaarmethode - Guitar Method -
Gitarreschule, Vol. II II

Gitaarmethode - Guitar Method -
Gitarreschule, Vol. III II,
VII-Mixed Coll

Music For Young Guitarists I/IB4

Sonatina Pirineos I/IIB1

Stukken, 3 I/IB4

Suite Vivat Noviomagum I/IB4

Visit To A Museum, A see Stukken, 3

Voor Samenspel En Groepsles, Vol. I
II

Voor Samenspel En Groepsles, Vol. II
II

Voor Samenspel En Groepsles, Vol. III
II

Voor Samenspel En Groepsles, Vol. IV
II

Voor Samenspel En Groepsles, Vol. V
II

Voor Samenspel En Groepsles, Vol. VI
II

GALLARDA see Castelnuovo-Tedesco,
Mario, Escarraman, A Suite Of
Spanish Dances From The XVIth
Century (After Cervantes)

GALLARDA; TIENTO; FANTASIA see
Mudarra, Alonso de

GALLARDAS see Guerau, Francisco; Sanz,
Gaspar

GALLIARD, MIN 211 see Musique
Elisabethaine

GALLIARD, MIN 285 see Piezas Para Laud
Del Siglo XVI, 4

GALLIARD, MIN 413 see 4 Pieces By
     Dowland, Cutting, Morley

GALLIARD OF DANIEL BATCHELAR see
     Dowland, John, Galliard On A
     Galliard Of Daniel Bacheler, A

GALLIARD ON A GALLIARD OF DANIEL
     BACHELER, A see Dowland, John

GALLIARD TO THE FLAT PAVANE, THE see
     Elizabethan Duets, 6

GALLIARDS, 2 see Dowland, John

GALLIARDS, 3 see Dowland, John

GALLO, EL, DANZA VENEZUELANA see
     Torres, Pedro Manuel

GALOP see Sor, Fernando

GALYERD Y A PAVIN see Rosseter, Philip

GAME FOR NINE see Becker, Gunther

GAMMES, 24, DE 2 ET 3 OCTAVES MAJEURES
     ET MINEURES (MELODIQUES, CADENCES
     SUR DIFFERENTS RYTHMES, CHOIX
     D'EXERCICES TECHNIQUES see Castet,
     Francois

GAMMES ET ARPEGES POUR LA GUITARE see
     Franceries, Marc

GAMMES ET CADENCES, DANS TOUS LES TONS
     ET DANS TOUTES LES POSITIONS see
     Gotze, Walter, Tonleitern Und
     Kadenzen, In Allen Tonarten Und
     Lagen

GANGI, MARIO
     Andalusa I/IIA1

     Fandango I/IIA1

     Metodo Per Chitarra, Per I
          Conservatori E I Licei Musicali,
          Vol. I II, III

     Metodo Per Chitarra, Per I
          Conservatori E I Licei Musicali,
          Vol. II II, III

     Sevillana I/IIA1

GARBER, ERICH (1916-   )
     Originalkompositionen, 5 I/IB4

GARCIA VELASCO, VENANCIO
     Study No. 3 I/IA

     Study No. 11 I/IA

GARDANA, LA see Marini, Biagio, Sonata

GARGIULO, TERENZIO (1905-1972)
     Toccata I/IB4

GARSI DA PARMA, SANTINO (1542-1603)
     Aria Del Granduca I/IB1
          see also Pezzi, 3

     Balletto see Pezzi, 3

     Ne Mente Per La Gola, La see Pezzi,
          3

     Pezzi, 3 I/IB1

GARZIA, PASQUALINO (1934-   )
     Lezioni Sul Legato, 10 I/IA

GASCON, LEON VICENTE
     Metodo Moderno Para Guitarra, Vol. I
          II

     Metodo Moderno Para Guitarra, Vol. II
          II

     Metodo Moderno Para Guitarra, Vol.
          III II

GASLINI, GIORGIO (1929-   )
     Canto Della Citta Inquieta Da
          "Totale" V/i

     Quarto Di Vita, Un; Opera Da Strada,
          In Two Acts And Twelve Scenes
          V/iii

     Totale I V/ii

     Totale II V/i

GASPAR SANZ: 11 COMPOSITIONS see Sanz,
     Gaspar

GASPAR SANZ INVENIT see Sanz, Gaspar

GASSENHAWER see Neusiedler, Hans

GASTOLDI, GIOVANNI GIACOMO
     (ca. 1556-1622)
     6 Ballets I/IIA2

     Duette, 8 I/IIA1

GATATUMBA see Villancicos Populares,
     Vol. III

GATTERMAYER, HEINRICH (1923-   )
     Duo I/IIA1

     Suite Fur Spielmusikgruppen, Op. 101-
          3 I/IIB5

GAUCHO see Walker, Luise

GAULTIER, DENIS (GAULTHIER)
     (ca. 1603-1672)
     Lautensuiten; 4 Suites I/IB1

GAVALL, JOHN
     Coventry Carol, The see Play The
          Guitar, A Self Tutor

     Guitar Photochord Manual, No. 1:
          Chord Dictionary II

     Guitar Photochord Manual, No. 2:
          Beginner's Course II

     Learning Music Through The Guitar,
          Vol. I: An Introduction To
          Fretboard Harmony II

     Learning Music Through The Guitar,
          Vol. II: Four-Part Harmony II

     Learning Music Through The Guitar,
          Vol. III: Chord Patterns And
          Functions In Major Keys II

     Learning Music Through The Guitar,
          Vol. IV: Minor Keys, Chromatic
          Chords, And Modulation II

     Learning Music Through The Guitar,
          Vol. V: An Introduction To
          Figured Bass II, IV/IIC1,
          VII-Mixed Coll

     Play The Guitar, A Self Tutor II,
          IV/IIC1

     Tips For Troubadours, Or How To
          Accompany Songs On The Guitar II

GAVARONE, GERARD
     Retrospective I/IB4

GAVOTTA see Scarlatti, Domenico,
     Sonata, Kirkpatrick 64

GAVOTTA E MINUETTO see Ponce, Manuel
     Maria, Suite In D Major: Gavotte I
     And II, D Major And D Minor

GAVOTTA, L. 58 see Scarlatti,
     Domenico, Sonata, Kirkpatrick 64

GAVOTTA RONDO see Marella, Giovanni
     Battista

GAVOTTE, AYMEE DU DUC DE MONMOUTH see
     Corbetta, Francesco (Francisque
     Corbett)

GAVOTTE, DE LA SONATA PARA VIOLIN EN MI
     MAYOR see Bach, Johann Sebastian

GAVOTTE, LE TAMBOURIN see Rameau,
     Jean-Philippe, Tambourin

GAVOTTE ROCOCO see Shand, Ernest

GAVOTTE VARIEE see Handel, George
     Frideric

GAY TANGO see Topper, Guido

GEBAUER, MICHEL-JOSEPH (1763-1812)
     Polonaise I/IIB1

GEBHARDT, WILHELM
     Gitarrenfibel, Ein Spielbuch Vom
          Ersten Anfang An Fur Einzel- Und
          Gruppenunterricht II

GEDENCKKLANKEN-ABC see Valerius,
     Adrianus

GEELEN, MATHIEU (1933-   )
     Sonatina I/IC

GEESE, HEINZ (1930-   )
     Seefahrt Nach Rio, Die, Scenic
          Cantata I/IIC5

GEH AUS, MEIN HERZ, UND SUCHE FREUD
     see Stern, Hermann

GEHEIMNIS, DAS; COMIC OPERA IN THREE
     ACTS see Smetana, Bedrich

GEISTLICHE GESANGE, 2 see Schutz,
     Heinrich

GEISTLICHE LIEDER see Bach, Johann
     Sebastian

GELDHEIRAT, DIE see Krieger, Johann
     Philipp

GELLI, VINCENZO (THOMATOS)
     Two Divertimenti I/IIB1

GEMINIANI, FRANCESCO (1687-1762)
     12 Pieces For Guitar And Continuo
          I/IIB1

     Sonatas, 6 I/IIB2

GENERAUX, ROGER
     Suite Bresilienne I/IB4

GENTILZ GALANS DE FRANCE see Seiber,
     Matyas Gyorgy

GEORGE PILKINGTON'S FUNERAL, PAVAN see
     Pilkington, Francis

GERDES, GUSTAV
     Kleine Gitarren- Und Lautenschule II

GERHARD, ROBERTO (1896-1970)
     Cantares I/IIC1

     Fantasy I/IB4

GERLACH, HANS CHRISTIAN
     Divertimento [Collection] I/IIB1,
          I/IIB2

GERLE, HANS (1500-1570)
     7 Lautenstucke Aus "Musica Teutsch",
          1532 I/IB1-Coll

GERMAN AIR see Tchaikovsky, Piotr
     Ilyich

GERRITS, PAUL
     Gitarren- Und Lautenschule, Vol. I:
          Das Einstimmige Spiel - Guitar
          And Lute Method, Vol. 1: Melody
          Playing II, IV/IIA1,
          VII-Mixed Coll

     Gitarren- Und Lautenschule, Vol. II:
          Ubungen Und Stucke Fur Das
          Mehrstimmige Spiel - Guitar And
          Lute Method, Vol. 2: Exercises
          And Pieces For Polyphonic Playing
          II, IV/IIA1, VII-Mixed Coll

     Vorschule Fur Gitarre II

GERVAISE, CLAUDE (fl. ca. 1550)
     Suite Franzosischer Tanze V/i

GERWIG, WALTER
     Ausfuhrliche Spielanweisung Fur
          Kinder, Eine see Ich Lerne
          Gitarre Spielen, Vol. I

     Ich Lerne Gitarre Spielen, Vol. I II

     Spiel Der Lauteninstrumente, Das,
          Series I: Das Schulwerk, Fur
          Einzel- Und Gruppenunterricht,
          Vol. I: Die Lehre Des
          Einstimmigen Spiels II

     Spiel Der Lauteninstrumente, Das,
          Series I: Das Schulwerk, Fur
          Einzel- Und Gruppenunterricht,
          Vol. II: Das Mehrstimmige Spiel
          II

     Spiel Der Lauteninstrumente, Das,
          Series I: Das Schulwerk, Fur
          Einzel- Und Gruppenunterricht,
          Vol. III: Die Liedbegleitung,
          Wege Zur Improvisation II

     Spiel Der Lauteninstrumente, Das,
          Series I: Das Schulwerk, Fur
          Einzel- Und Gruppenunterricht,
          Vol. IV: Das Generalbassspiel II

GESANGE, 2 see Handel, George Frideric

GESANGE, 3 see Bialas, Gunter

GESELBRACHT, ERICH
     Bolero see Spieldose, Die

     Intrade see Spieldose, Die

     March see Spieldose, Die

     Menuetto Ostinato see Spieldose, Die

     Serenade see Spieldose, Die

     Spieldose, Die I/IIB5

GESPRACH MIT GOTT, EIN, FOR ORCHESTRA
     see Kupkovic, Ladislav

GESTE DANSEE see Miroglio, Francis

GESTUTZTE EROS, DER; MUSIC TO THE
     COMEDY BY HERBERT TJADENS see
     Schelb, Josef

GESZLER, GYORGY (1913-   )
     Trio I/IIB2

GEUD MAN OF BALLANGIGH, THE see Take
     Your Partners; 6 English Country
     Dances

GHIRIBIZZI NO. 24 AND 25 see Paganini,
     Niccolo

GHIZEGHEM, HAYNE VAN (ca. 1550- ?)
     Amors, Amors, Trop Me Fiers De Tes
          Dars I/IB1

GIAMPIETRO, G.
     Neue Schule Fur Gitarre II

GIB DICH ZUFRIEDEN UND SEI STILLE see
     Arfken, Ernst

GIBBONS, ORLANDO (1583-1625)
     Almain, MIN 299 see Dances, 3

     Courante, MIN 300 see Dances, 3

     Dances, 3 I/IIA1

     Galliard, MIN 301 see Dances, 3

GIELEN, MICHAEL ANDREAS (1927-   )
     Glocken Sind Auf Falscher Spur, Die
          V/ii

     Tag Tritt Hervor, Ein, Pentaphony For
          Piano Obbligato, Five Solo
          Instruments, Five Groups Of Five
          Players Each And A Speaking Role
          V/ii

GIETER, FOR ORCHESTRA see Janssen,
     Guus

GIGA A LA MANERA INGLESA see Visee,
     Robert de

GIGUE DE LA SUITE IV PARA LAUD see
     Bach, Johann Sebastian, Partita for
     Lute, BWV 1006a, in E, Gigue

GIGUE, MIN 420 see Six Pieces From The
     Time Of Elizabeth

GILARDINO, ANGELO
     Abreuana I/IB4

     Appaloosa I/IB4

     Araucaria I/IB4

     Boot Hill see Appaloosa

     Canzone Notturna I/IB4

     Estrellas Para Estarellas, Musica
          Nocturna Para La Guitarra De
          Gabriel [Estarellas] I/IB4

     Longhorn Ghosts see Appaloosa

     Ocram, Fantasia I/IB4

     Peace-Maker 45 see Appaloosa

     Riders In The Sky, The see Appaloosa

     Saguaro see Appaloosa

     Tenebrae Factae Sunt I/IB4

     Trepidazioni Per Thebit I/IB4

GILBERT, ANTHONY (1934-   )
     Serenade, Op. 3 V/i

GINGGANZ see Schneider, Matthias

GIOCHI D'ACQUA see Altissimi, Franco

GIOCOSO see Paubon, Pierre

GIORDANI, TOMMASO (1730-1806)
     Caro Mio Ben I/IIC1

GIORGIO GUTIERREZ, ARNOL DEL
     Estudio Para La Practica De Los
          Armonicos Octavados Compuestos
          I/IA

GIOSTRA GENOVESE; FIVE OLD DANCES BY
     VARIOUS MASTERS FOR SMALL ORCHESTRA
     see Zimmermann, Bernd Alois

GIOVANNI BATTISTA GRANATA: 11
     COMPOSITIONS see Granata, Giovanni
     Battista

GIOVINETTA RITROSSETTA see Monteverdi,
     Claudio

GIRASOL, EL see Azpiazu, Jose de

GIRIGONZA, LA, DANSE CHANTEE see
     Flecha, Mateo

GITAAR-ACCORDEN see Kok, Joh. B.

GITAAR AKKOORDEN, VOLGENS NIEUWE
     VINGERZETTING see Bossu, Marcel,
     Accords De Guitare, d'Apres Le
     Nouveau Doigte

GITAAR-KAMERMUZIEK, VOL. 2
     I/IIA1-Coll, I/IIA2-Coll,
     I/IIA3-Coll, III, VII-Mixed Coll

GITAAR-KAMERMUZIEK, VOL. 3: UIT HET
     REPERTOIRE VAN HET JOEGOSLAVISCHE
     DANSTHEATER I/IA, I/IB6-Coll,
     I/IIA1-Coll, I/IIA2-Coll,
     I/IIA4-Coll

GITAAR-KAMERMUZIEK, VOL. 4: UIT HET
     REPERTOIRE VAN HET JOEGOSLAVISCHE
     DANSTHEATER I/IA, I/IIA1-Coll,
     I/IIA2-Coll, I/IIA3-Coll

GITAAR-SCHOOL see Carulli, Ferdinando,
     Methode De Guitare

GITAAR-SOLI, ALBUM KLASSIEKE- EN
     MODERNE GITAAR-SOLI IN EENVOUDIGE
     BEZETTING I/IB6-Coll,
     VII-Mixed Coll

GITAARDUET, HET I/IIA1-Coll

GITAARDUETTEN I/IIA1-Coll,
     VII-Mixed Coll

GITAARLES IN GROEPSVERBAND, VOL. I see
     Gramberg, Jacq

GITAARLES IN GROEPSVERBAND, VOL. II
     see Nijenhuis, Luc

GITAARLES IN GROEPSVERBAND, VOL. III
     II

GITAARMETHODE - GUITAR METHOD -
     GITARRESCHULE, VOL. I see Gall,
     Louis Ignatius

GITAARMETHODE - GUITAR METHOD -
     GITARRESCHULE, VOL. IA see Gall,
     Louis Ignatius

GITAARMETHODE - GUITAR METHOD -
     GITARRESCHULE, VOL. II see Gall,
     Louis Ignatius

GITAARMETHODE - GUITAR METHOD -
     GITARRESCHULE, VOL. III see Gall,
     Louis Ignatius

GITAARSPEELBOEK - LIVRE DE LA GUITARE
     I/IB6-Coll, VI-Mixed Coll,
     VII-Mixed Coll

GITANO see Wolf, Roland

GITARISKOLA, VOL. I see Kovats, Barna;
     Puskas, Tibor

GITARMUZSIKA KEZDOKNEK - GITARRENMUSIK
     FUR ANFANGER I/IB6-Coll,
     VII-Mixed Coll

GITARR- OCH LUTASPELETS ABC, SKOLA FOR
     FINGERSPELNING see Akerman,
     Sigvard

GITARR-SOLON see Bellman, Carl Michael

GITARRE ALLEIN, ENTWICKLUNG DES
     SOLISTISCHEN MUSIZIERENS AUS DEM
     AKKORDSPIEL I/IB6-Coll,
     I/IIA1-Coll
     see also Wolki, Konrad, Gitarre Zum
     Lied, Schule Fur Die Gitarre Als
     Begleitinstrument, Mit Einer
     Akkordlehre Und Mit Hinweisen Fur
     Das Begleiten Nach Dem Gehor,
     Supplement 2

GITARRE ALS SOLO-INSTRUMENT, DIE see
     Albert, Heinrich, Lehrgang Des
     Kunstlerischen Gitarrespiels, Vol.
     III

GITARRE-ETUDEN-WERK, VOL. 1:
     ELEMENTARSTUFE see Albert,
     Heinrich

GITARRE-ETUDEN-WERK, VOL. 2: OBERE
     ELEMENTARSTUFE see Albert,
     Heinrich

GITARRE-ETUDEN-WERK, VOL. 3:
     MITTELSTUFE see Albert, Heinrich

GITARRE-ETUDEN-WERK, VOL. 4: OBERE
     MITTELSTUFE see Albert, Heinrich

GITARRE-ETUDEN-WERK, VOL. 5: OBERSTUFE
     see Albert, Heinrich

GITARRE-ETUDEN-WERK, VOL. 6: REIFESTUFE
     see Albert, Heinrich

GITARRE, GRIFF- UND AKKORDTABELLE, SEHR
     LEICHT III

GITARRE IM GRUPPENUNTERRICHT see
     Polasek, Barbera

GITARRE IM GRUPPENUNTERRICHT, DIE, AUCH
     FUR EINZELUNTERRICHT VERWENDBAR
     see Brojer, Robert

GITARRE - MEIN HOBBY, ZUM SELBSTSTUDIUM
     BIS ZUR MEISTERSCHAFT, VOL. 1 see
     Behrend, Siegfried

GITARRE - MEIN HOBBY, ZUM SELBSTSTUDIUM
     BIS ZUR MEISTERSCHAFT, VOL. 2 see
     Behrend, Siegfried

GITARRE-SCHULE, VOL. I see Carulli,
     Ferdinando, Methode De Guitare

GITARRE-SCHULE, VOL. II:
     FORTSCHREITENDE TONSTUCKE UND
     GELAUFIGKEITS-ETUDEN, (ERGANZUNG
     ZUR GITARRE-SCHULE see Carulli,
     Ferdinando, Methode De Guitare

GITARRE-SCHULE, VOL. III: 24 DUETTE FUR
     2 GITARREN see Carulli,
     Ferdinando, Methode De Guitare

GITARRE-SOLOSPIEL-STUDIEN, VOL. 1: ZUR
     EINFUHRUNG FUR ANFANGER see
     Albert, Heinrich

GITARRE-SOLOSPIEL-STUDIEN, VOL. 2:
     WEITERENTWICKLUNG FUR
     FORTGESCHRITTENE see Albert,
     Heinrich

GITARRE-SOLOSPIEL-STUDIEN, VOL. 3:
     NEBENLAGEN, VORTRAG, SOLOSPIEL see
     Albert, Heinrich

GITARRE SPEZIAL, PICKING MODERN
     ARRANGEMENT, VOL. 1 I/IB6-Coll

GITARRE SPEZIAL, PICKING MODERN
     ARRANGEMENT, VOL. 2 I/IB6-Coll

GITARRE SPEZIAL, PICKING MODERN
     ARRANGEMENT, VOL. 3 I/IB6-Coll

GITARRE SPIELEN - LEICHT GEMACHT,
     VOLKSTUMLICHE GITARRESCHULE FUR DEN
     EINZEL-, GRUPPEN- ODER
     SELBSTUNTERRICHT see Kierner, Max

GITARRE-STUDIEN, FUR ANGEHENDE SOLO-
     GITARRISTEN UND SANGER ZUR GITARRE.
     AUSGEWAHLTE LEICHTE STUDIENWERKE
     ALTER MEISTER see Ritter, Theodor

GITARRE- UND LAUTENSCHULE DER JUGEND,
     DIE, FUR GRUPPEN-, EINZEL- UND
     SELBSTUNTERRICHT see Gotze, Walter

GITARRE- UND LAUTENSCHULE, VOL. I see
     Carulli, Ferdinando, Methode De
     Guitare

GITARRE- UND LAUTENSCHULE, VOL. II see
     Carulli, Ferdinando, Methode De
     Guitare

GITARRE ZUM LIED, SCHULE FUR DIE
     GITARRE ALS BEGLEITINSTRUMENT, MIT
     EINER AKKORDLEHRE UND MIT HINWEISEN
     FUR DAS BEGLEITEN NACH DEM GEHOR,
     VOL. I see Wolki, Konrad

GITARRE ZUM LIED, SCHULE FUR DIE
     GITARRE ALS BEGLEITINSTRUMENT, MIT
     EINER AKKORDLEHRE UND MIT HINWEISEN
     FUR DAS BEGLEITEN NACH DEM GEHOR,
     VOL. II see Wolki, Konrad

GITARRE ZUM LIED, SCHULE FUR DIE
     GITARRE ALS BEGLEITINSTRUMENT, MIT
     EINER AKKORDLEHRE UND MIT HINWEISEN
     FUR DAS BEGLEITEN NACH DEM GEHOR,
     SUPPLEMENT 1 see Wolki, Konrad

GITARRE ZUM LIED, SCHULE FUR DIE
     GITARRE ALS BEGLEITINSTRUMENT, MIT
     EINER AKKORDLEHRE UND MIT HINWEISEN
     FUR DAS BEGLEITEN NACH DEM GEHOR,
     SUPPLEMENT 2 see Wolki, Konrad

GITARRE ZUM WEIHNACHTSLIED IV/IIC1,
     IV/IIC2

GITARREBUCH FUR MADELEINE, VOL. I see
     Stingl, Anton

GITARREBUCH FUR MADELEINE, VOL. II see
     Stingl, Anton

GITARRELIED, DAS see Albert, Heinrich, Lehrgang Des Kunstlerischen Gitarrespiels, Vol. II

GITARRELIEDER see Weber, Carl Maria von

GITARRELIEDER FUR ALLE, VOLKSLIEDER I/IIC1-Coll

GITARREMUSIK DES BAROCK I: AUS EINEM FRANZOSISCHEN TABULATURBUCH DES 17. JAHRHUNDERTS I/IB1-Coll

GITARREMUSIK DES BAROCK II: AUS EINEM FRANZOSISCHEN TABULATURBUCH DES 17. JAHRHUNDERTS; AUS DER AUSSEER GITARRE-TABULATUR I/IB1-Coll

GITARREMUSIK FUR ANFANGER, VOL. I: SEHR LEICHT I/IB6-Coll

GITARREMUSIK FUR ANFANGER, VOL. II: LEICHT I/IB6-Coll

GITARREMUSIK FUR ANFANGER, VOL. III: MITTELSCHWER I/IB6-Coll

GITARREMUSIK FUR ANFANGER, VOL. IV: SCHWER I/IB6-Coll

GITARREN 1X1, DAS, DIE GITARRENSCHULE FUR DEN SELBSTUNTERRICHT see Schwarz-Reiflingen, Erwin

GITARREN DUETTE see Fabian, Gaston

GITARREN MUSIZIEREN, 2, VOL. 1: LEICHTE DUETTE FUR DEN ANFANG I/IIA1-Coll

GITARREN MUSIZIEREN, 2, VOL. 2: DUETTE ALTER GITARRENMEISTER I/IIA1-Coll

GITARREN MUSIZIEREN, 2, VOL. 3: MITTELSCHWERE DUETTE I/IIA1-Coll, VII-Mixed Coll

GITARREN-SCHULE, FUR MELODIESPIEL, LIEDBEGLEITUNG UND SOLOSPIEL, EIN ANSCHAULICHES LEHR- UND SPIELBUCH, VOL. I see Teuchert, Heinz

GITARREN-SCHULE, FUR MELODIESPIEL, LIEDBEGLEITUNG UND SOLOSPIEL, EIN ANSCHAULICHES LEHR- UND SPIELBUCH, VOL. II see Teuchert, Heinz

GITARREN-SCHULE, VOL. I see Carcassi, Matteo, Vollstandige Guitarre-Schule; Carulli, Ferdinando, Methode De Guitare; Schwarz-Reiflingen, Erwin

GITARREN-SCHULE, VOL. II see Carcassi, Matteo, Vollstandige Guitarre-Schule; Schwarz-Reiflingen, Erwin

GITARREN-SCHULE, VOL. II: GITARRE-SCHULE FUR FORTGESCHRITTENE see Carulli, Ferdinando, Methode De Guitare

GITARREN-SCHULE, VOL. III: 50 UBUNGEN IN FORTSCHREITENDER SCHWIERIGKEIT see Carcassi, Matteo, Vollstandige Guitarre-Schule

GITARREN- UND LAUTENSCHULE, VOL. I: DAS EINSTIMMIGE SPIEL - GUITAR AND LUTE METHOD, VOL. 1: MELODY PLAYING see Gerrits, Paul

GITARREN- UND LAUTENSCHULE, VOL. II: UBUNGEN UND STUCKE FUR DAS MEHRSTIMMIGE SPIEL - GUITAR AND LUTE METHOD, VOL. 2: EXERCISES AND PIECES FOR POLYPHONIC PLAYING see Gerrits, Paul

GITARRENBUCH see Visee, Robert de, Livre De Guitarre Dedie Au Roy (1682)

GITARRENCHOR, DER, SCHULE DES GRUPPENMUSIZIERENS I/IIA2-Coll see also Wolki, Konrad

GITARRENFIBEL, EIN SPIELBUCH VOM ERSTEN ANFANG AN FUR EINZEL- UND GRUPPENUNTERRICHT see Gebhardt, Wilhelm

GITARRENFIBEL, EINE NEUE ANLEITUNG FUR DAS SPIEL AUF DER GITARRE see Richter, Gerd

GITARRENMUSI, 29 ALPENLANDISCHE LIEDER UND TANZE I/IB5-Coll

GITARRENMUSIK DES 16.-18. JAHRHUNDERTS, VOL. I I/IB1-Coll

GITARRENMUSIK DES 16.-18. JAHRHUNDERTS, VOL. II I/IB1-Coll

GITARRENSCHULE see Aguado, Dionisio, Escuela De Guitarra; Kovats, Barna, Gitariskola, Vol. I

GITARRENSCHULE FUR ANFANGER see Behrend, Siegfried

GITARRENSCHULE, VOL. I see Azpiazu, Jose de; Puskas, Tibor, Gitariskola, Vol. I

GITARRENSCHULE, VOL. II see Azpiazu, Jose de

GITARRENSCHULE, VOL. III see Azpiazu, Jose de

GITARRENSCHULE, VOL. IV see Azpiazu, Jose de

GITARRENSCHULE, VOL. V see Azpiazu, Jose de

GITARRENSPIEL ALTER MEISTER, ORIGINAL-MUSIK DES 16. UND 17. JAHRHUNDERTS, VOL.1 I/IB1-Coll

GITARRENSPIEL ALTER MEISTER, ORIGINAL-MUSIK DES 16. UND 17. JAHRHUNDERTS, VOL.2 I/IB1-Coll

GITARRENSPIEL AM ANFANG, ERSTE SPIELANWEISUNG FUR KINDER; EINFUHRUNG IN DAS MELODIESPIEL, AKKORDSPIEL UND BEGINNENDE SOLOSPIEL see Wolki, Konrad

GITARRENSPIEL NACH DEM GEHOR, ANLEITUNG ZUR IMPROVISIERTEN LIED- UND TANZBEGLEITUNG see Wolki, Konrad

GITARRENSPIELBUCH FUR DEN ANFANG see Twittenhoff, Wilhelm, Grundlagen Des Gitarrenspiels, Die, Aufbau Und Spieltechnik Aus Der Einstimmigkeit, Mit Vielen Musikbeispielen, Einzeln Oder Chorisch Zu Gebrauchen, Supplement

GITARRENSTUCKE see Visee, Robert de, Livre De Pieces Pour La Guitarre (1686)

GITARRENSTUCKL see Neumuller, Wolfgang

GITARRENUNTERRICHT FUR ANFANGER, VOL. 1 see Sagreras, Julio S.

GITARRESCHLUSSEL, DER, LEICHTESTE AKKORD-GRIFFTABELLE FUR GITARRE UND LAUTE see Hebbel, Heinrich

GITARRESCHULE see Schneider, Simon

GITARRESCHULE, AUCH FUR DEN SELBSTUNTERRICHT GEEIGNET see Domandl, Willy

GITARRESCHULE - ECOLE DE GUITARE - GUITAR SCHOOL see Carulli, Ferdinando, Methode De Guitare

GITARRESCHULE, FUR EINZEL- ODER GRUPPEN-UNTERRICHT, VOL. 1 see Kreidler, Dieter

GITARRESCHULE, FUR EINZEL- ODER GRUPPEN-UNTERRICHT, VOL.2 see Kreidler, Dieter

GITARRESOLO see Hartig, Heinz Friedrich

GITARRESPIEL, DAS, VOL. I, EIN UNTERRICHTSWERK VOM ANFANG BIS ZUR MEISTERSCHAFT: SPIELBEGINN UND STUDIEN see Henze, Bruno

GITARRESPIEL, DAS, VOL. II, EIN UNTERRICHTSWERK VOM ANFANG BIS ZUR MEISTERSCHAFT: C-DUR - A MOLL; G-DUR - E-MOLL see Henze, Bruno

GITARRESPIEL, DAS, VOL. III, EIN UNTERRICHTSWERK VOM ANFANG BIS ZUR MEISTERSCHAFT: D-DUR - H-MOL; A-DUR - FIS-MOLL see Henze, Bruno

GITARRESPIEL, DAS, VOL. IV, EIN UNTERRICHTSWERK VOM ANFANG BIS ZUR MEISTERSCHAFT: E-DUR - CIS-MOLL; F-DUR - D-MOLL see Henze, Bruno

GITARRESPIEL, DAS, VOL. V: EIN UNTERRICHTSWERK VOM ANFANG BIS ZUR MEISTERSCHAFT: TONLEITERSTUDIEN see Henze, Bruno

GITARRESPIEL, DAS, VOL. VI: EIN UNTERRICHTSWERK VOM ANFANG BIS ZUR MEISTERSCHAFT: STUDIEN FUR DIE LINKE UND RECHTE HAND see Henze, Bruno

GITARRESPIEL, DAS, VOL. VII, EIN UNTERRICHTSWERK VOM ANFANG BIS ZUR MEISTERSCHAFT: DIE HAUPTLAGEN see Henze, Bruno

GITARRESPIEL, DAS, VOL. VIII, EIN UNTERRICHTSWERK VOM ANFANG BIS ZUR MEISTERSCHAFT: DIE NEBENLAGEN see Henze, Bruno

GITARRESPIEL IM UBERBLICK, EINFUHRUNG IN DIE SPIELTECHNIK NACH KLASSISCH-SPANISCHER SCHULE see Fernandez-Lavie, Fernando

GITARRESTUCKE FUR DIE JUGEND see Pilsl, F.

24 GITARREWERKE FUR DIE UNTERSTUFE see Kuffner, Joseph

GITARRFEST I/IB6-Coll

GITARRISTEN, VOL. II I/IB6-Coll

GITARRKLANG I/IB6-Coll, VI-Mixed Coll

GITARRKVARTETT I/IIA3-Coll

GITARRLEK I/IB6-Coll

GITARRSKOLA see Aldeland, Nils, Elementar Improvisation, Vol. I

GITARRSKOLA FOR KLASSISK GITARR see Hansson, Gunnar

GITARRSKOLA FOR KLASSISK GITARR, SUPPL.: LARAR-HANDLEDNUNG see Johnson, Per-Olof

GITARRSKOLA FOR KLASSISK GITARR, VOL. I: NYBORJARSKOLA see Johnson, Per-Olof

GITARRSKOLA FOR KLASSISK GITARR, VOL. II: FORTSATTNINGSSKOLA see Johnson, Per-Olof

GITARRSKOLA, SPELA I GRUPP see Ahslund, Ulf-G.

GITARRSKOLA, SPELA I GRUPP, SUPP.2 see Ahslund, Ulf-G.

GITARRSKOLA, SPELA I GRUPP, SUPPL. 1 see Ahslund, Ulf-G.

GITARRSKOLA, SPELA I GRUPP, SUPPL. 3 see Ahslund, Ulf-G.

GITARRSPEL, ACKOMPANJEMANG OCH SOLOSPEL EFTER ACKORDANALYS see Hansson, Gunnar, Gitarrskola For Klassisk Gitarr

GITARSZVIT see Bach, Johann Sebastian, Suite for Violoncello, BWV 1011, in C minor

GITTER UND RANKEN see Staeps, Hans Ulrich

GIULIANATE see Giuliani, Mauro

GIULIANI, MAURO (1781-1829)
Allegretto, MIN346 I/IB2

Allegretto, MIN347 I/IB2

Allegro see Sonata, Op. 15

Allegro E Grazioso, Op. 40, No.8, 9 I/IB2

Allegro Spiritoso see Sonata, Op. 15

Andantino I/IB2

Andantino, MIN355 I/IB2

Andantino, MIN356 I/IB2

Antologia De La Guitarra I/IB2

Ausgewahlte Studien, Vol. 1 see Studies

Ausgewahlte Studien, Vol. 2 see Studies

Capriccio I/IB2

Capriccio, Op. 100, No. 11 I/IB2

Caprice Fur Gitarre I/IB2

Centoventi Arpeggi Dall' Op. 1 see Studio Per La Chitarra

Choix De Mes Fleurs Cheries I/IB2

Choix De Mes Fleurs Cheries (Le Bouquet Emblematique) I/IB2

GIULIANI, MAURO (cont'd.)

Composiciones Para Guitarra, Vol. 1
  I/IB2

Composiciones Para Guitarra, Vol. 2
  I/IB2

Concerto in A, Op. 36   I/IIIA

Concerto No. 3 in F, Op. 70 I/IIIA

Concerto, Op. 30 I/IIIA

Danse Nord I/IB2

Divertimento I/IIB1

Divertimento, Op. 37 I/IB2

Divertimento, Op. 40 I/IB2

Duettino I/IIB1

Duettino Facile I/IIB1

Ejercicios De Arpegios, Elementos
  Fundamentales De La Tecnica
  Guitarristica Para Guitarra see
  Studio Per La Chitarra

Estudios Melodicos, 12 (Seleccion)
  see Etuden, 24, Selections

Etude Spirituoso I/IA

Etuden, 24 I/IA

Etuden, 24, Selections I/IA

Etudes Progressives, 158 I/IA

Fortschreitende Stucke, 18 I/IA

Fughetta I/IB2

Giulianate I/IB2

Gran Duetto Concertante I/IIB1

Gran Sonata Eroica see Sonata Eroica

Grande Ouverture I/IB2

Grandi Variazioni, 6 see Variations,
  Op. 112

Grandi Variazioni Concertanti I/IIA1

Grazioso I/IB2

Grosse Serenade I/IIB1

Grosse Sonate, Op.25 I/IIB1

Grosse Sonate, Op.85 I/IIB1

Leichte Etuden, 24 I/IA

Leichte Fortschreitende Stucke, 6
  I/IB2

Leichte Landler, 8, 2 Vols. I/IIA1

Leichte Nordische Tanze, 16 I/IB2

Leichte Variationen Uber Ein
  Osterreichisches Lied I/IB2

Lieder, 6 I/IIC1

6 Lieder I/IIC1

March, MIN 370 I/IB2

Mariposa, La see Papillon, Le

Melancholia I/IB2

Metodo Per Chitarra see Studio Per
  La Chitarra

Minuet De La Cour I/IB2

Monferrine, 12 I/IB2

Oeuvres Choisies Pour Guitare I/IB2

Papillon, Le I/IA, I/IB2

Papillon, Le (Choix d'Airs Faciles)
  I/IB2

Polonaise, MIN 371 I/IB2

Praludien, 6 see Preludes, 6, Op. 83

Prelude in F, MIN 374 I/IB2

Preludes, 6, Op. 83 I/IB2

Preludi, 6 see Preludes, 6, Op. 83

6 Preludios I/IB2

GIULIANI, MAURO (cont'd.)

Qual Mesto Gemito I/IIB1

Quintet, Op. 65 I/IIB4

Quintetto Dalla "Semiramide" Di
  Rossini see Qual Mesto Gemito

Rondo, Op. 8, No. 2, in G I/IB2

Rondo, Op. 11 I/IB2

Rondo, Op. 17, No. 1, in A I/IB2

Rondo Und Harfen-Etude I/IB2

Rondoletto I/IB2

Rossiniana, No. 1 I/IB2

Rossiniana, No. 2 I/IB2

Rossiniana, No. 3 I/IB2

Rossiniana, Op. 119-124 I/IB2-Coll

Scherzo Giocoso I/IB2

Schmetterling, Der see Papillon, Le

Scozzesi, 12 I/IB2

Secondo Concerto see Concerto in A,
  Op. 36

Serenade, Op. 19 I/IIB2

Serenade, Op. 127 I/IIB1

Sonata Eroica I/IC

Sonata Heroica see Sonata Eroica

Sonata, Op. 15 I/IC

Sonate Brillant see Sonata, Op. 15

Sonatina, MIN 390 I/IC

Sonatina, Op. 71, No. 1 I/IC

Sonatina, Op. 71, No. 3 I/IC

Sonatinen, 3 I/IC

Sostenuto I/IB2

Studi I/IA
  see also Studies

Studi, 24 see Etuden, 24

Studien, 24 see Leichte Etuden, 24

Studien Fur Gitarre, Vol. I, a.
  Ubungen Fur Die Rechte Hand, b.
  Ubungen Fur Die Linke Hand see
  Studio Per La Chitarra

Studien Fur Gitarre, Vol. II, c.
  Bindungen Und Verzierungen, d.
  Angewandte Vortragsstucke see
  Studio Per La Chitarra

Studienkonzert see Concerto in A,
  Op. 36

Studies I/IA

Studies, 120 see Studio Per La
  Chitarra

Studio Per La Chitarra III

Tema Con Variazioni Concertanti see
  Variazioni Concertanti

Theme and Variations I/IB2

Tirolesa I/IB2

Trio, Op. 71, No. 3 I/IIA2

Unterhaltungsstucke, 10 I/IB2

Utwory Wybrane I/IB2

Valse Etude I/IA

12 Valzer I/IB2

Variaciones Concertantes see
  Variazioni Concertanti

Variationen Uber Ein Thema Von Handel
  see Variazioni Su Un Tema Di
  Handel

Variationen Uber "La Follia" see
  Variazioni Sul Tema Della Follia
  Di Spagna

Variations, 6: Op87 I/IB2

GIULIANI, MAURO (cont'd.)

Variations, Op. 2 I/IB2

Variations, Op. 62 I/IB2

Variations, Op. 112 I/IB2

Variations, Op. 113 I/IIB1

Variazioni Concertanti I/IIA1

Variazioni E Finale, 4 I/IB2

Variazioni Su L'Aria "Schisserl Und A
  Reindl" I/IB2

Variazioni Su Un Tema Dal Balletto
  "Die Feindlichen Vollkstame"
  I/IB2

Variazioni Su Un Tema Di Handel
  I/IB2

Variazioni Su Un Tema Originale
  I/IB2

Variazioni Sul Tema Della Follia Di
  Spagna I/IB2

Variazioni Sulla Romanza Dall'Opera
  "Ruhm Und Liebe" I/IB2

Variazioni Sull'Aria Favorita De "La
  Molinara" I/IB2

Vivace Con Brio I/IB2

GIULIANI-GUGLIELMI, EMILIA
  (fl. ca. 1840)
  Preludes, 6 I/IA

GIULIO CESARE see Handel, George
  Frideric

GLOCKEN SIND AUF FALSCHER SPUR, DIE
  see Gielen, Michael Andreas

GLORIA AL RE see De Grandis, Renato

GLORIA, AUS DER TSCHECHISCHEN
  WEIHNACHTSMESSE see Ryba, Jan
  Jakub Simon

GLORY HALLELUJAH "JOHN BROWN'S BODY"
  see Hess, Reimund

GLORY HALLELUJAH: SPIRITUALS, JAZZ,
  BLUES, BEAT see Schwertberger,
  Gerald

GLUCK, CHRISTOPH WILLIBALD, RITTER VON
  (1714-1787)
  Ballet I/IIB1

  Gavotte, MIN 28 I/IIA1

  Gavotte, MIN 29 I/IIA1

  J'ai Perdu Mon Euridice I/IIB1

GO 'WAY FROM MY WINDOW see Blues And
  Spirituals

GOD JUL, 71 VALKANDA VISOR I/IB5-Coll

GODDESSES see Take Your Partners; 6
  English Country Dances

GOEPFERT, KARL ANDREAS (1768-1818)
  Sonata, Op. 13 I/IIB1

GOETHALS, LUCIEN (1931-   )
  Sonata, Op. 22 I/IC

GOING DUTCH see Duarte, John W.

GOLDEN AGE, THE, CLASSICS FOR SOLO
  GUITAR, VOL. I I/IB6-Coll,
  VII-Mixed Coll

GOLDEN AGE, THE, CLASSICS FOR SOLO
  GUITAR, VOL. II I/IB6-Coll

GOLDEN RAM, THE; OPERA IN FOUR ACTS
  see Krenek, Ernst, Goldene Bock,
  Der; Opera In Four Acts

GOLDEN SONGS I/IIC1-Coll

GOLDENE BOCK, DER; OPERA IN FOUR ACTS
  see Krenek, Ernst

GOLDENE BUCH DES GITARRISTEN, DAS (LE
  LIVRE D'OR DES GUITARISTES, OP.52)
  I/IB6-Coll

GOLDENE EI, DAS, EIN MARCHENSPIEL see
  Langhans, Herbert

GOLLIWOGG'S CAKE-WALK see Debussy,
  Claude

GOLONDRINA, LA see Gitarre Spezial,
  Picking Modern Arrangement, Vol. 3;
  Hess, Reimund

HANDEL, GEORGE FRIDERIC (cont'd.)

Saraband, MIN 337 I/IB1

Sarabanda Con Variazioni see Saraband, MIN 3

Sarabande Et Gavotte I/IB1

Sarabande With Variations see Saraband, MIN 3

Siciliana I/IIB1

Skladeb, 5 I/IB1

Sonata in A I/IIB1

Sonata in A minor, Op. 1, No. 4 I/IIB1

Sonata in C I/IIB1

Sonata in C, MIN 34 I/IIA1

Sonata in C minor, MIN 52 I/IIB2

Sonata in D I/IIB1

Sonata in D minor I/IIB1

Sonata in E minor, MIN 344 I/IIB1

Sonata in F, Op. 1, No. 11 I/IIB1

Sonata, MIN 46 I/IIA2

Sonata No. 2 in G minor I/IIB1

Suite, MIN 49 I/IIB1

Tanze Aus Opern, 7 I/IIA2

Time Pieces I/IB1, I/IB2

Water Music Air I/IB1

Zarabanda see Saraband, MIN 3

HANDEL-BUCH, DAS see Handel, George Frideric

HANDEL'S TURN see Handel, George Frideric

HANDLEIDING VOOR DE GITAAR see Schagen, Henk van

HANS SPIELMANN, EIN VOLKSLIEDER-SPIELBUCH FUR GITARRE, VOL. I: FUR DEN ANFANGER I/IB5-Coll

HANS SPIELMANN, EIN VOLKSLIEDER-SPIELBUCH FUR GITARRE, VOL. II: FUR FORTGESCHRITTENEN SPIELER I/IB5-Coll

HANSSON, GUNNAR
Gitarrskola For Klassisk Gitarr II

Gitarrspel, Ackompanjemang Och Solospel Efter Ackordanalys see Gitarrskola For Klassisk Gitarr

HANUS, JAN (1915-   )
Also Sprach Scheherazade, Opera V/iii

Staffette, Symphonic Allegro For Full Orchestra V/i

HAPPY THOUGHTS, 4 see Schagen, Henk van, Zoete Invallen, 4

HARFENETUDE (HARP STUDY) see Sor, Fernando, Vingt-Quatre Exercices Tres Faciles, Op. 35, No. 23

HARMONIA QUADRIPARTITA: PARTITA SECONDA see Herold, Johann Theodor

HARMONIELEHRE AUF DER GITARRE see Beck, Leonhard

HARMONIOUS BLACKSMITH, THE (AIR WITH VARIATIONS) see Handel, George Frideric

HARRIS, ALBERT (1916-   )
Homage To Unamuno I/IB4

Sonatina I/IC

Suite I/IB4

Variations And Fugue On A Theme Of Handel I/IB4

HARTIG, HEINZ FRIEDRICH (1907-1969)
Alla Danza see Stucke Fur Gitarre, 3

Capriccio see Stucke Fur Gitarre, 3

Concertante Suite I/IIIA

HARTIG, HEINZ FRIEDRICH (cont'd.)

Gitarresolo I/IB4

Perche V/ii

Solo for Guitar see Gitarresolo

Stucke, 5 I/IIB1

Stucke Fur Gitarre, 3 I/IB4

Theme and Variations see Stucke Fur Gitarre, 3

HARTOG, CEES
Let's Take The Flip Side I/IIA2

HART'S EASE see Holborne, Antony

HASENOHRL, FRANZ (1885- ?)
Barcarolle see Kleine Stucke, 4

Capriccio see Kleine Stucke, 4

Gavotte see Kleine Stucke, 4

Kleine Serenade see Kleine Stucke, 4

Kleine Stucke, 4 I/IB4

Minuet see Suite

Prelude see Suite

Suite I/IB4

Trio-Suite I/IIB2

HASHAGEN, KLAUS (1924-   )
Pergiton IV I/IIB1

Sechs Seemannslieder V/ii

Six Sailor-Songs see Sechs Seemannslieder

Synchronie; 10 Graphic Parts I/IB4

HASSE, JOHANN ADOLPH (1699-1783)
Concerto in G I/IIB3

March, MIN 7 I/IB1, I/IIC1

Sonata, Op. 1, No. 1, in D see Sonaten, 12, Op. 1

Sonata, Op. 1, No. 2, in B minor see Sonaten, 12, Op. 1

Sonaten, 12, Op. 1 I/IIB1

Trio Sonata in C I/IIB2

HASSLER, HANS LEO (1564-1612)
Chanson I/IB1

HAT DARAV KET GITARRA see Couperin, Francois (le Grand)

HAT NUR LENZ see Bialas, Gunter, Eichendorff-Liederbuch, Vol. 6: Assonanzen

HAUBENSTOCK-RAMATI, ROMAN (1919-   )
Hexachord I-II I/IB4, I/IIA1

Symphonies De Timbres, Les V/i

HAUFRECHT, HERBERT (1909-   )
Hora I/IB4

Theme and Variations I/IB4

Waltz I/IB4

HAUG, HANS (1900-1967)
Alba I/IB4

Capriccio I/IIB1

Concertino I/IIIA

Fantasy I/IIB1

Prelude I/IB4

Prelude, Tiento Et Toccata I/IB4

HAUS, KARL (1928-   )
Jetzt Ist Die Rechte Freudenzeit, Short Christmas Cantata IV/IIC5

HAUSLICHE WEIHNACHT IV/IIC1, IV/IIC2, IV/IIC3, VII-Mixed Coll

HAUSMUSIK see Butting, Max

HAUSMUSIK; 7 STUCKE FUR DIE SIEBEN TAGE DER WOCHE see Krenek, Ernst

HAUSSPRUCH see Taubert, Karl Heinz

HAUSWIRTH, HANS M.A. (1901-   )
Solospiel Auf Der Gitarre, Das I/IB4

Sonatina No. 2 I/IIB1

Tanze Und Weisen I/IIA2

HAVA NAGILA see Hess, Reimund

HAVE YOU SEENE BUT A WHYTE LILLIE GROW? see Three 17th Century Airs

HAVELKA, SVATOPLUK (1925-   )
Ernesto Che Guevara V/i

Heptameron V/ii

Pyrrhos; Balletsinfonie V/iii

HAYDN, [FRANZ] JOSEPH (1732-1809)
Allegro, MIN348 I/IB2

Andante, MIN 122 I/IB2

Andante, MIN 123 I/IB2

Andante, MIN 338 I/IB2

Andante, MIN 352 I/IB2

Andante, MIN 399 I/IB2

Andante Und Menuett I/IB2

Cassation in C, Hob.III: 6 I/IIB2

Concerto for 2 Lire Organizzate and Orchestra, No. 2, in G I/IIIB

5 Deutsche Tanze Und Coda I/IB2

Divertimento, Hob.XI: 44 I/IIB2

Haydn-Buch, Das I/IB2

Kinder-Symphonie V/i

Landlust, Die see Lieder, 3

Largo Anay I/IB2

Largo Assai I/IB2

Lieder, 3 I/IIC1

Menuets Celebres, 2 I/IB2

Menuette, 22 I/IIA1, I/IIB1

Minuet, Hob.III: 75 I/IB2

Minuet, MIN 119 I/IB2

Minuet, MIN 120 I/IB2

Minuet, MIN 121 I/IB2

Minuet, Op. 2, No. 2 I/IB2

Minueto Del Buey I/IB2

Minuetto, MIN 400 I/IB2

Minuetto, MIN 401 I/IB2

Quartet in D, Hob.III: 8 I/IIB3

Quartet in G, Op. 5, No. 4, Hob.II: 4 I/IIB3

Romance in C I/IIB4

Seeking Haydn I/IIA1

Sehr Gewohnliche Geschichte, Eine see Lieder, 3

Serenade I/IIB2

Serenade, MIN 124 I/IB2

Serenade, MIN 389 I/IB2

Serenata I/IIA1

Trio in F I/IIB2

Trio In F, Hob. IV:F2 I/IIB2

Trio, MIN 47 I/IIA2, I/IIB2

Zu Spate Ankunft Der Mutter, Die see Lieder, 3

HAYDN-BUCH, DAS see Haydn, [Franz] Joseph

HEAV'N, HEAV'N see Famous Negro Spirituals, 5

HEBBEL, HEINRICH
Gitarreschlussel, Der, Leichteste Akkord-Grifftabelle Fur Gitarre Und Laute III

HECKEL, WOLF
Mille Regres I/IB1

HEER, HANS DE (1927-   )
Concerto I/IIIA

Etude 1-3 I/IA

Etude 6-9 I/IA

Etude No. 4 I/IA

Etude No. 5 I/IA

Etude No. 10 I/IA

3 Fuga's I/IB4

Kwintolen Arpeggio Etude see Etude
No. 4

Musing I/IB4

Prelude No. 4 I/IB4

Siciliano I/IB4

Sonata I/IC

Sonatina No. 2 I/IIB1

Sonatina No. 3 I/IIB1

Tertsen Etude see Etude No. 5

Trio I/IIB2

HEER JESUS HEEFT EEN HOFKEN see
Nederlandse Volksliederen, 3

HEIDER, WERNER (1930-   )
American Suite, For Harpsichord And
Orchestra V/i

Choreographie I V/i

Essay In Jazz V/i

HEIDI PUPEIDI see Heiller, Anton

HEIDSCHI BUMBEIDSCHI BUM-BUM, DIE
ALLERSCHONSTEN WEIHNACHTSLIEDER,
VOL. I: PNO ED. (WITH TEXT)
IV/IIB4, IV/IIC5

HEIDSCHI BUMBEIDSCHI BUM-BUM, DIE
ALLERSCHONSTEN WEIHNACHTSLIEDER,
VOL. II: INST ED., FOR 3- OR 4-PT
ENSEMBLES IV/IIB4, IV/IIC5

HEIDSCHI BUMBEIDSCHI BUM-BUM, DIE
ALLERSCHONSTEN WEIHNACHTSLIEDER,
VOL. III: VOCAL ED IV/IIB4,
IV/IIC5

HEIGH HO HOLIDAY see Holborne, Antony

HEILIGE NACHT, WEIHNACHTSLIEDER-ALBUM
IV/IIB1, IV/IIC1

HEILLER, ANTON (1923-1979)
Es Liegt Ein Schloss In Osterreich
I/IIA3

Heidi Pupeidi I/IIA3

HEIMED LUEGT DI GLANZIG A, D' see
Thienemann, H.

HEINZELMANNCHEN, DIE, EIN MUSIKALISCHES
STEGREIFSPIEL see Werdin, Eberhard

HEISSNER, O.
Griff-Lexikon Fur Gitarre, Mit
Anleitung Zum Selbstunterricht
III

HEITERE FOLGE VON VOGEL-LIEDERN see
Coenen, Paul

HEITERES HERBARIUM see
Mittergradnegger, Gunter

HEKSTER, WALTER (1937-   )
Chain I/IB4

Epicycle I I/IIB1, V/i

Relief No. V I/IIB2

HELAAS GEEN SPROOKJE see Bois, Rob du,
Vandaag Is Het Morgen Van Gisteren

HELIAN DI TRAKL see Togni, Camillo

HELLE STIMME, DIE see Razzi, Fausto

HELLEMAN, JOOP
Arpeggios, 10 I/IA

Hyper Studies I/IA

Melodische Etudes, 5 I/IA

HELLEMAN, JOOP (cont'd.)
Micro Studies I/IA

Mini Studies I/IA

Snarenspel — Stringmusic, Exercises
In Changing Positions I/IA

Super Studies I/IA

Ultra Studies I/IA

HELLER, STEPHEN (1813-1888)
Estudios, 4, Para Formar El Ritmo Y
La Expresion I/IA

Etudes, 6 I/IA

Etudes, 10, Pour Former Au Sentiment,
Du Rhythme Et A l'Expression
I/IA

From Opus 47 I/IA, I/IIA1

Heller Estudio I/IA

HELLER ESTUDIO see Heller, Stephen

HENSEL, WALTHER (1887-1956)
Susaninne, Eine Kleine
Weihnachtskantate IV/IIC5

HENSELT: SUSPIRO DE AMOR see Tarrega,
Francisco, Study, TI ii- 12, in E

HENZE, BRUNO
Gitarrespiel, Das, Vol. I, Ein
Unterrichtswerk Vom Anfang Bis
Zur Meisterschaft: Spielbeginn
Und Studien II, III,
VI-Mixed Coll

Gitarrespiel, Das, Vol. II, Ein
Unterrichtswerk Vom Anfang Bis
Zur Meisterschaft: C-dur — a
moll; G-dur — e-moll II,
VII-Mixed Coll

Gitarrespiel, Das, Vol. III, Ein
Unterrichtswerk Vom Anfang Bis
Zur Meisterschaft: D-dur — h-mol;
A-dur — fis-moll II,
VII-Mixed Coll

Gitarrespiel, Das, Vol. IV, Ein
Unterrichtswerk Vom Anfang Bis
Zur Meisterschaft: E-dur — cis-
moll; F-dur — d-moll II

Gitarrespiel, Das, Vol. V: Ein
Unterrichtswerk Vom Anfang Bis
Zur Meisterschaft:
Tonleiterstudien II, III

Gitarrespiel, Das, Vol. VI: Ein
Unterrichtswerk Vom Anfang Bis
Zur Meisterschaft: Studien Fur
Die Linke Und Rechte Hand II,
III, VI-Mixed Coll

Gitarrespiel, Das, Vol. VII, Ein
Unterrichtswerk Vom Anfang Bis
Zur Meisterschaft: Die Hauptlagen
II, III, VI-Mixed Coll

Gitarrespiel, Das, Vol. VIII, Ein
Unterrichtswerk Vom Anfang Bis
Zur Meisterschaft: Die Nebenlagen
II, III

HENZE, HANS WERNER (1926-   )
Fragmente Nach Holderlin, 3 I/IB4,
I/IIC1

In Lieblicher Blaue see Kammermusik
1958

Kammermusik 1958 V/ii

Memorias De "El Cimarron" I/IB4

HEPTAMERON see Havelka, Svatopluk

HEPTAMERON, EINE VIERSTIMMIGE SUITE
see Rohwer, Jens

HERBERGSSUCHE DER MARIA "O MARIA
TRAURIGE", WEIHNACHTSMUSIK UM EIN
LIED AUS DER GOTTSCHEE see Spitta,
Heinrich

HERBSTBLATTER see Coste, Napoleon

HEROLD, JOHANN THEODOR (1660-1720)
Harmonia Quadripartita: Partita
Seconda I/IB1

HERPFER KIRMESWALZER see Funk,
Heinrich

HERR CHRIST, DER EINIG GOTTS SOHN see
Koch, Johannes H.E.

HERR, GIB UNS FRIEDEN see Lauth,
Wolfgang

HERRERA, RAMON DE
Minimes, 6 I/IIB5

Preludes, 3 I/IB4

HERRERO ARMONIOSO, EL: ARIA CON [5]
VARIACIONES see Handel, George
Frideric, Harmonious Blacksmith,
The (Air With Variations)

HERZ DER NACHT see Serocki, Kazimierz

HERZOG, FRANZ
Musik Zu Christian Morgensterns
"Palmstrom", Part 1 V/ii

Suite for Chorus and Instruments see
Musik Zu Christian Morgensterns
"Palmstrom", Part 1

HERZSCHLAGE, FURCHT, BITTE UND
HOFFNUNG, SYMPHONIC SCENE FOR BEAT-
BAND AND FULL ORCHESTRA see Klebe,
Giselher

HESITATION see Vandermaesbrugge, Max

HESPOS, HANS-JOACHIM (1938-   )
Einander-Bedingendes V/i

Sound V/i

HESS, REIMUND (1935-   )
Cotton Fields V/ii

Cuckoo, The V/ii

Glory Hallelujah "John Brown's Body"
V/ii

Golondrina, La V/ii

Guantanamera V/ii

Hava Nagila V/ii

Ich Danke Dir see Golondrina, La

John Brown Liegt In Seinem Kalten
Dunklen Grab see Glory
Hallelujah "John Brown's Body"

Oh, The Cuckoo, She's A Pretty Bird
see Cuckoo, The

Old Mac Donald V/ii

HESSE, ERNST CHRISTIAN (1676-1762)
Duo I/IIB1

HET WAREN TWEE KONINGSKINDEREN see
Oud-Vlaamse Volksliederen, 2

HEUCKEROTH VAN HESSEN, J. RICHARD
Impression I/IIB1

Song And Dance I/IIB1

HEURICH, WINFRIED
Dein Wort Ist Nah; Neue Rhythmische
Satze Zum Gottesdienst V/ii

HEXACHORD I-II see Haubenstock-Ramati,
Roman

HIDALGOYAS see Aubin, Tony

HIEROGLYPHS see Ruyneman, Daniel

HIGGINS, RALPH
Classical Studies For Guitar I/IA

Introduction To Finger-Picking Guitar
II

Introduction To Guitar Notation II

HIGHER FRETS ON ALL STRINGS, THE,
MELODIOUS STUDIES IN POSITIONS,
VOL. 1 see Sholle, Emil

HIGHER FRETS ON ALL STRINGS, THE,
MELODIOUS STUDIES IN POSITIONS,
VOL. II see Sholle, Emil

HIGHER FRETS ON ALL STRINGS, THE,
MELODIOUS STUDIES IN POSITIONS,
VOL. III see Sholle, Emil

HIGUET, NESTOR
Interlude I/IB4

HILANDERA, LA see Mendelssohn-
Bartholdy, Felix

HILLER, JOHANN ADAM (1728-1804)
Abendlied Eines Bauermanns see
Lieder, 6

Lied Hinterm Ofen Zu Singen see
Lieder, 6

HILLER, JOHANN ADAM (cont'd.)

Lieder, 6 I/IB2, I/IIC1

Mann Im Lehnstuhle, Der see Lieder, 6

Meine Wunsche see Lieder, 6

Pasteten Lied see Lieder, 6

Urians Reise Um Die Welt see Lieder, 6

HILSTER, RIES DE
Prelude No. 1, Op. 12, No. 1 I/IB4

HIN'CHA JAFEH DODI see Staak, Pieter van der

HINDEMITH, PAUL (1895-1963)
Rondo I/IIA2

HINEY MA TOV I/IB5

HINOJOSA, JAVIER
Ricercata Di Durezze E Fioriture Sulle "Quattro Dita" see Te Lucis Ante Terminum

Te Lucis Ante Terminum I/IB4

HINTERLEITHNER, FERDINAND IGNAZ (1659-1710)
Partita in A I/IB1

HINTERMEYER, WILLY (1892-   )
Fidele Weisen, Fur Gitarre Solo In Leichter Spielart I/IB5

Junge Gitarre-Soloist, Der, Vol. I; Eine Sammlung Leichter, Melodioser Solostucke I/IB4

Junge Gitarre-Soloist, Der, Vol. II; Eine Sammlung Leichter, Melodioser Solostucke I/IB4

HIROTA
Hamachidori, Japanese Song I/IIIA

HIRTENLIEDER UND TANZE AUS DEM SUDOSTEN IV/IIB4

HIRTENTANZ see Bialas, Gunter; Bohr, Heinrich

HISPANAE CITHARAE ARS VIVA; ANTHOLOGY OF GUITAR MUSIC FROM OLD TABLATURES I/IB1-Coll

HISPANIA, 6 VERY EASY SPANISH DANCES see Meran, Jose

HISPANICA, SONORIDADES 1971 see Santorsola, Guido, Sonata No. 2

HISZPANSCY MISTRZOWIE GITARY I/IB6-Coll, VI-Mixed Coll

HIVELY, WELLS (1902-1969)
Dance Of Chacmol ("Canek"); Music Drama V/i

HLOUSCHEK, THEODOR (1923-   )
Duette I/IIA1

Kompositionen I/IB4

Quartet I/IIB3

Spielstucke I/IIA1

Trio I/IIA2

HODEIR, ANDRE (1921-   )
Anna Livia Plurabelle, For Solo Voices And Solo Instruments V/ii

HOEK, JAN-ANTON VAN (1936-   )
Bouwstenen Van Het Polyphoon Gitaarspel, Vol. I, Nos. 1-21 I/IB4

Bouwstenen Van Het Polyphoon Gitaarspel, Vol. II, Nos. 22-37 I/IB4

Burlesque see Trios, 3, Op. 919

Fugue, Op. 919, No. 2 see Trios, 3, Op. 919

Konzertetude, No.2 I/IA

Pavan, Op. 919, No. 1 see Trios, 3, Op. 919

Polyphonic Playing On The Guitar see Bouwstenen Van Het Polyphoon Gitaarspel, Vol. I, Nos. 1-21; Bouwstenen Van Het Polyphoon Gitaarspel, Vol. II, Nos. 22-37

HOEK, JAN-ANTON VAN (cont'd.)

Polyphony And Polytonality I/IA

Praludien Und Etuden Zur Vervollkommnung Der Technik I/IA

12 Preludes I/IB4

Suite Milanesa I/IB4

Trios, 3, Op. 919 I/IIA2

HOEKEMA, HENK
Easy Pieces, 7 I/IIA2

HOFER, KARLHEINZ
Shanties From The Seven Seas V/ii

HOFFMANN, JOHANN
Concerto I/IIIA

HOFFNER, PAUL MARX (1895-1949)
Indianer Suite I/IIA1

Sonatina I/IIB1

Tanzstucke, 3 I/IIB1

HOHE DES JAHRES see Apostel, Hans Erich

HOJA DE ALBUM see Schumann, Robert (Alexander)

HOJAS VARIAS see Schumann, Robert (Alexander), Feuilles Varias

HOKETUS see Andriessen, Louis

HOLBORNE, ANTONY (? -1602)
As It Fell On A Holy Eve see Pieces, 5

Cisterwerke, Die, Part 1: Werke Fur Cister Allein I/IB1-Coll

Cisterwerke, Die, Part 2: Werke Fur Cister Und Ein Bassinstrument I/IB1-Coll

Countess Of Pembroke's Paradise see Lute Pieces, 6

Countess Of Pembroke's Paradise, The see Pieces, 5

Fantasy, MIN 261 see Lute Pieces, 6

Galliard, MIN 9 see Pieces, 5

Hart's Ease see Lute Pieces, 6

Heigh Ho Holiday see Lute Pieces, 6; Pieces, 5

Larmes Des Muses Et Gaillarde, Les I/IB1

Lute Pieces, 6 I/IB1

Mr. Southcote's Galliard see Pavan And Galliard

Night Watch, The see Pieces, 5

Pavan see Pavan And Galliard

Pavan And Galliard I/IB1

Piece Without Name see Lute Pieces, 6

Pieces, 5 I/IB1

Playfellow (Or Wanton) see Lute Pieces, 6

Praludium Und Fantasie I/IB1

HOLDER, DERWYN
Modern Preludes, 6 I/IB4

Sonatina In One Movement I/IC

HOLLANDISCHE MEISTER see Europaische Gitarren- Und Lautenmusik, Vol. 6

HOLLFELDER, WALDRAM (1924-   )
Kleine Tanze I/IIA1

HOLT, SIMEON TEN (1923-   )
A-.TA-LON, For Soloist And Thirty-Six Playing And Talking Instrumentalists V/ii

HOLZ, FRANZ
Begleiten Nach Dem Gehor, Das, Volkstumliche Anleitung Fur Das Freie Begleiten II

Begleiten Nach Dem Gehor, Das, Volkstumliche Anleitung Fur Das Freie Begleiten, Suppl 1: [Theory Of Accompaniment] II

HOLZ, FRANZ (cont'd.)

Begleiten Nach Dem Gehor, Das, Volkstumliche Anleitung Fur Das Freie Begleiten, Suppl. 2: Tonarten- Und Akkordfibel II

Volkstumliche Gitarrespiel, Das, Kurz-Lehrgang Fur Den Gruppen- Und Einzel- Bzw. Selbstunterricht II

Volkstumliche Gitarrespiel, Das, Kurz-Lehrgang Fur Den Gruppen- Und Einzel- Bzw. Selbstunterricht, Suppl. 1: Die Gitarre In Bild Und Ton II

Volkstumliche Gitarrespiel, Das, Kurz-Lehrgang Fur Den Gruppen- Und Einzel- Bzw. Selbstunterricht, Suppl. 2: Griffbildschema II

Volkstumliche Gitarrespiel, Das, Kurz-Lehrgang Fur Den Gruppen- Und Einzel- Bzw. Selbstunterricht, Suppl. 3: Liedertextblatt II

HOLZFURTNER, FRANZ
Lagenspiel-Fibel, Volkstumliche Einfuhrung In Das Lagenspiel Auf Der Gitarre III

HOMAGE TO PURCELL, FANTASIA SUL NOME DI RONALD (1932-) E HENRY (1659-1695) PURCELL see Castelnuovo-Tedesco, Mario

HOMAGE TO UNAMUNO see Harris, Albert

HOMENAJE see Castellanos, Evencio

HOMENAJE A LA GUITARRA, PRELUDIO see Sainz de la Maza, Eduardo

HOMENAJE A LA SEGUIDILLA, CONCERTO see Moreno Torroba, Federico

HOMENAJE A LOS VIHUELISTAS see Azpiazu, Jose de

HOMENAJE A M. DE FALLA see Reyne, Gerard

HOMENAJE A SCHOENBERG, 6 PRELUDIOS, OP. 24 see Angel, Miguel

HOMENAJE A SOR see Fortea, Daniel

HOMENAJE A TARREGA see Pujol, Emilio

HOMMAGE A ALBERT ROUSSEL see Lemeland, Aubert

HOMMAGE A ALBERTO GIACOMETTI see Fursentau, Wolfram

HOMMAGE A ANTONIO DE CABEZON see Ruiz Pipo, Antonio

HOMMAGE A BELA BARTOK see Azpiazu, Jose de; Obrovska, Jana

HOMMAGE A JEAN COCTEAU see Furstenau, Wolfram

HOMMAGE A TARREGA, GARROTIN-SOLEARES see Turina, Joaquin

HOMMAGE A VILLA-LOBOS see Lerich, Pierre

HOMME SEUL, UN, KLEINES KONZERT see Schibler, Armin

HOMS, JOAQUIN (1906-   )
Impromptu I/IIB1

2 Soliloquios I/IB4

HOOK, RICHARD
Within A Mile Of Edinboro I/IB2

HOOR! DE GITARISTEN, BEKENDE LIEDJES IN LICHTE ZETTING VOOR SOLO-GITAAR, VOLS. I-III I/IB5-Coll

HORA see Haufrecht, Herbert

HORECKI, FELIKS (1799-1870)
Utwory Wybrane I/IB2, I/IIA1

HORNEPYPE see Aston, Hugh

HORNPIPE see Purcell, Henry

HORNPIPE see Purcell, Henry

HORNPIPE see Purcell, Henry

HORNUNG
   O Dream, O Dreaming I/IIC1

HOROSKOP GEFALLIG? see Barbe, Helmut

HORSE, HIS NAME WAS HUNRY FENCEWAVER
   WALKINS, A see Bedford, David

HORST, ANTON VAN DER (1899-1965)
   Alianora; Play About The Marriage Of
      Reynalt Van Nassau, Duke Of
      Gelre, And Alianor Of England
      V/ii

HORST DU NICHT DIE BRUNNEN RAUSCHEN
   see Bialas, Gunter, Eichendorff-
   Liederbuch, Vol. 4: Nachtzauber

HOSTEN see Ahslund, Ulf-G.

HOTTETERRE, JACQUES (MARTIN)
   (ca. 1684-1762)
   2 Trio Sonatas I/IIB2

HOTTETERRE, JEAN
   Suite I/IIB3

HOUSE OF THE RISING SUN see Gitarre
   Spezial, Picking Modern
   Arrangement, Vol. 3

HOUSE OF THE RISING SUN, THE see
   Seckinger, Konrad

HOVE, JOACHIM VAN DEN (1567-1620)
   Chanson Flameng I/IB1

   Delitiae Musicae, 1612, Part 1:
      "Praeludien Und Pavanen"
      I/IB1-Coll

   Delitiae Musicae, 1612, Part 2:
      "Passamezzen Mit Ihren
      Galliarden" I/IB1-Coll

   Delitiae Musicae, 1612, Part 3:
      "Favoritos, Galliarden,
      Bergamasca, Une Jeune Fillette"
      I/IB1-Coll

   Delitiae Musicae, 1612, Part 4:
      "Allemanden, Balletti, Branden,
      Couranten, Chansons, Canarie"
      I/IB1-Coll

   Nederlandse Luitmuziek Uit De 17e
      Eeuw I/IB1

   Praludien, 6 I/IB1

   Suite I/IB1, VII-Mixed Coll

HOW BEAUTIFUL ARE THE FEET OF THEM see
   Handel, George Frideric

HOW TO PLAY GUITAR, FINGER STYLE see
   Plumbridge, W.H.

HOWET, GREGORIO (ca. 1550-1620)
   Fantasy No. 6 I/IB1

HOYER, ANTOINE L'
   Concerto, Op. 16 I/IIIA

HUBER, NICOLAUS A. (1939-   )
   Parusie, Annaherung Und Entfernung,
      For Full Orchestra V/i

HUBSCHMANN, WERNER (1901-1969)
   Alte Deutsche Spruchweisheit I/IIC1

   Etuden, 22 I/IA

   Studien, 5 I/IA

   Suite I/IB4

HUDBA CESKYCH LOUTNOVYCH TABULATUR
   I/IB1-Coll

HUHNER G'SCHREI see Canzonen Und Tanze
   Aus Dem XVI. Jahrhundert

HUIZEN, GRACHTEN, MENSEN see
   Furstenau, Wolfram, Jordaan

HULSEN, ERNST (1883- ?)
   Leichte Walzer, 6 I/IB4

HUMBLE, KEITH (1927-   )
   Arcade IV I/IIB1

HUMMEL, BERTOLD (1925-   )
   Metamorphosen Fur Gitarre I/IB4

HUMMEL, JOHANN NEPOMUK (1778-1837)
   Allegretto I/IB2

HUMORESQUE see Constant, Franz;
   Israel-Meyer, Pierre; Levine, M.;
   Pelemans, Willem

HUNGARIAN DANCE see Staak, Pieter van
   der

HUNGARIAN DANCE, NO. 5 see Brahms,
   Johannes

HUNGARIAN DANCE, NO. 6 see Brahms,
   Johannes

HUNKINS, EUSEBIA SIMPSON (1902-   )
   Appalachian Mass V/ii

HUNT, EDGAR
   Introduction To Playing The Spanish
      Guitar, An II

HUNT, OLIVER
   Idyll-Dance I/IB1

HUPF AUF, DER see Neusiedler, Hans

HURACAN, EL see Kaps, Hansjoachim

HUYGENS, CONSTANTIN
   Psaumes Et 3 Chansons, 2 I/IIC1

HUZELLA, ELEK (1915-1971)
   Love Songs see 4 Viragenek

   4 Viragenek I/IIC1

HYMNS AND CHORALS, WITH A COMMENTARY ON
   THE MUSIC OF ERIK SATIE see Leeuw,
   Reinbert de

HYPER STUDIES see Helleman, Joop

I GAVE HER CAKES AND I GAVE HER ALE
   see Walton, [Sir] William (Turner)

I SAW MY LADY WEEP see Dowland, John

I SAW THREE SHIPS see Lautenspieler,
   Der, No. 1

I WENT TO THE MARKET I/IIC5-Coll

I WILL GIVE MY LOVE AN APPLE see
   Britten, [Sir] Benjamin

IACARAS see Sanz, Gaspar

IBERIA, 5 JAHRHUNDERTE SPANISCHER
   GITARRENMUSIK, VOL. I I/IB6-Coll

IBERIA, 5 JAHRHUNDERTE SPANISCHER
   GITARRENMUSIK, VOL. II I/IB6-Coll,
   VI-Mixed Coll

IBERT, JACQUES (1890-1962)
   Ariette I/IB4

   Entr'acte I/IIB1

   Francaise I/IB4

   Paraboles I/IIA1

ICH DANKE DIR see Hess, Reimund,
   Golondrina, La

ICH HAB DIE NACHT GETRAUMET,
   MADCHENLIEDER NACH GEDICHTEN AUS
   DER ROMANTIK see Kukuck, Felicitas

ICH KAM DAS MORGENROT HERAUF see
   Nordische Volkslieder

ICH KLAG DEN TAG see Neusiedler, Hans

ICH LERNE GITARRE SPIELEN, VOL. I see
   Gerwig, Walter

ICH LERNE GITARRE SPIELEN, VOL. II see
   Funck, Eike

ICH MOCHTE GERNE BRUCKEN BAUEN see
   Kobler, Hans

ICH REDE WENN ICH SCHWEIGEN SOLLTE see
   Lehmann, Andreas

ICH RUHME MIR MEIN DORFCHEN HIER see
   Schubert, Franz (Peter), Dorfchen,
   Das

ICH STEH AN DEINER KRIPPEN HIER see
   Bach, Johann Sebastian

ICH STEH IM BISTUM FULDA see
   Kretzschmar, Gunther

ICH TRAG MEIN LICHT, EIN LIEDERSPIEL
   ZUM LATERNEGEHEN see Derlien,
   Margarete

ICH WEISS EIN LIEBLICH ENGELSPIEL,
   LIEDKANTATE see Schilling, Hans
   Ludwig

ICH WEISS EIN MAIDLEIN HUBSCH UND FEIN
   see David, Johann Nepomuk

IDYLL-DANCE see Hunt, Oliver

IHR KINDERLEIN KOMMET see Lied- Und
   Gitarrenspiel, Volks- Und
   Tanzlieder, Vol. I; Rinke Ranke
   Rosenschein; 77 Kinderlieder;

   Volks- Und Kinderlieder

IHR KLEINEN VOGELEIN, LIEDKANTATE see
   Marx, Karl

IK ZAG CECILIA KOMEN see Oud-Vlaamse
   Volksliederen, 2

IK ZIE DE MORGEN STERRE see
   Muziekbijlage, No. 53

IL EST NE, LE DIVIN ENFANT see For My
   Friends

I'M BLUE TODAY see Blues And
   Spirituals

IM DUNKELN IST GUT MUNKELN see
   Krieger, Johann Philipp

I'M TIRED see Blues And Spirituals

IM WINDE FACHELN DIE BLATTER see
   Bialas, Gunter, Eichendorff-
   Liederbuch, Vol. 5: Seliges
   Vergessen

IMITANDO IL GRANCHIO see Abloniz,
   Miguel

IMPERTINENCE see Handel, George
   Frideric

IMPRECIONES MEXICANAS, VOL. I: LAS
   RUINAS DE MITLA see Wagner,
   Gerhard D.

IMPRECIONES MEXICANAS, VOL. II: LAGO DE
   TEXCOCO see Wagner, Gerhard D.

IMPRECIONES MEXICANAS, VOL. III: LA
   TRISTEZA DE MALINTZIN see Wagner,
   Gerhard D.

IMPRESIONES DE ESPANA, DANZA see
   Malats, Joachin

IMPRESIONES LEVANTINAS, 6 see Espla,
   Oscar

IMPRESSION see Heuckeroth van Hessen,
   J. Richard

IMPRESSIONE see Lella, Domenico di

IMPRESSIONEN see Ambrosius, Hermann;
   Jentsch, Walter; Weiss, Harald

IMPRESSIONS ANDALOUSES, 2 see Bozza,
   Eugene

IMPROMPTU FANTASQUE see Serocki,
   Kazimierz

IMPROMPTUS see Bennett, Richard Rodney

IMPROVISATION I: LE VIERGE, LE VIVACE
   ET LE BEL AUJOURD'HUI see Boulez,
   Pierre, Pli Selon Pli, Portrait De
   Mallarme, 2

IMPROVISATION III: A LA NUE ACCABLANTE
   TU see Boulez, Pierre, Pli Selon
   Pli, Portrait De Mallarme, 4

IMPROVISATION, UBER EIN
   MITTELALTERLICHES LIED "ES SASS EIN
   EDLY MAGET SCHON" see Stingl,
   Anton

IMPROVISATIONS, SUR "L'ANABASE" DE ST.-
   JOHN PERSE see Fritsche, Volkmar

IMPROVIZUJME NA KYTARU see Urban,
   Stepan

IMPROWISAZIONE, OMAGGIO A VILLA-LOBOS
   see Abloniz, Miguel

IMPROVVISI, 2 see Peraldo Bert, Nilo

IMPROVVISO DA CONCERTO see Pizzini,
   Carlo Alberto

IN A GONDOLA see Komter, Jan Maarten

IN CHURCH see Tchaikovsky, Piotr
   Ilyich; Tchaikovsky, Piotr Ilyich

IN DARKNESS LET ME DWELL see Dowland,
   John

IN DULCI JUBILO see Praetorius,
   Michael

IN EEN WEENSE MUZIEKKAMER I/IIB5-Coll

IN EINEM KUHLEN GRUNDE see Bialas,
   Gunter, Eichendorff-Liederbuch,
   Vol. 1: Das Zerbrochene Ringlein

IN LEISEN LIEDERN GEHT MEIN TAG see
   Thienemann, H.

IN LIEBLICHER BLAUE   see Henze, Hans
  Werner, Kammermusik 1958

IN MEMORIAM DJANGO REINHARDT: 2
  VARIATIONS AND A THEME FOR GUITAR
  see Blyton, Carey

IN MEMORIAM SCOTT FITZGERALD   see
  Blyton, Carey

IN NOCTE   see Prosperi, Carlo

IN SEINEM GARTEN LIEBT DON PERLIMPLIN
  BELISA; OPERA   see Fortner,
  Wolfgang

IN SPE   see Nijenhuis, Luc

IN TIME OF DAFFODILS   see Malipiero,
  Riccardo

IN WARSCHAU SIND DIE MADCHEN   see
  Rosenstengel, Albrecht,
  Polenmadchen

INCORONAZIONE DI POPPEA, L'; OPERA IN
  THREE ACTS AND A PROLOGUE   see
  Monteverdi, Claudio

INCORRIGIBLE DREAMER, AN, BOSSA NOVA
  see Abloniz, Miguel

INDIANA-RHAPSODIE, FOR ORCHESTRA   see
  Forest, Jean Kurt

INDIANER SUITE   see Hoffner, Paul Marx

INDIFFERENTE, L'   see Rameau, Jean-
  Philippe

INDISCHES SPIELBUCH   see Khan, Pesy

INDO-AMERIKANISCHE TANZE   see Graetzer,
  Guillermo

INFIDELE, L'   see Weiss, Sylvius
  Leopold, Sonata in A minor

INFIDELIO   see Lutyens, Elizabeth

INGENIO, EVOCATION   see Sanchez, B.

INITIATION A LA GUITARE CLASSIQUE   see
  Sao Marcos, Maria Livia, Einfuhrung
  In Das Klassische Gitarrenspiel

INMITTEN DER NACHT, WEIHNACHTLICHE
  SPIELMUSIK   I/IIB2, IV/IIB1,
  IV/IIB2, VII-Mixed Coll

INSTANT REMEMBERED   see Krenek, Ernst,
  Augenblick Errinert

INSTRUCTIEVE SONATINES, 3   see
  Gramberg, Jacq

INTABOLATURA DE LEUTO DE DIVERSI AUTORI
  see Casteliono, Antonio

INTABULATURA DE LAUTO (PETRUCCI, 1508),
  PART 1: "TASTAR DE CORDE - CALATE"
  see Dalza, Joan Ambrosio

INTABULATURA DE LAUTO (PETRUCCI, 1508),
  PART 2: "PADOANE ALLA VENETIANA"
  see Dalza, Joan Ambrosio

INTABULATURA DE LAUTO (PETRUCCI, 1508),
  PART 3: "PADOANE ALLA FERRARESE"
  see Dalza, Joan Ambrosio

INTAVOLATURA DI BALLI (1592)   see
  Radino, Giovanni Maria

INTAVOLATURA DI LIUTO   see Weiss,
  Sylvius Leopold

INTAVOLATURA DI LIUTO (1599)   see
  Gostena, G.B. della

INTAVOLATURA DI LIUTO: LIBRO PRIMO
  (1546)   see Crema, Joan Maria da

INTAVOLATURA DI LIUTO, LIBRO PRIMO
  (1599)   see Molinaro, Simone

INTENDO A DOS   see Benguerel, Xavier

INTERFACE   see Raxach, Enrique

INTERLUDE   see Higuet, Nestor

INTERLUDIO   see Azpiazu, Jose de

INTERMEDIA DE "PEPITA JIMENEZ"   see
  Albeniz, Isaac

INTERMEZZO D'ARAGON   see Grimm,
  Friedrich Karl

INTERNATIONAL ANTHOLOGY   I/IB1-Coll

INTERNATIONAL ANTHOLOGY FOR GUITAR
  (TWELFTH THROUGH EIGHTEENTH
  CENTURIES)   I/IB6-Coll

8 INTERNATIONALE VOLKSLIEDER
  I/IIC1-Coll

INTERNATIONALE VOLKSLIEDER, VOL. I
  I/IIC1-Coll

INTERNATIONALE VOLKSLIEDER, VOL. II
  I/IIC1-Coll

INTERNATIONALE VOLKSLIEDER, VOL. III
  I/IIC1-Coll

INTERNATIONALE VOLKSLIEDER, VOL. IV
  I/IIC1-Coll

INTERPLAY   see Smith, William Overton

INTERPOLATIONS   see Vlijmen, Jan van

INTERSECAZIONI I FOR VIOLIN AND
  ORCHESTRA   see Cerha, Friedrich

INTERSECAZIONI II FOR VIOLIN AND
  ORCHESTRA   see Cerha, Friedrich

INTIMITE   see Chopin, Frederic, Etude,
  Op. 10, No. 3, [excerpt]

INTRADA   see Korda, Viktor; Melii da
  Reggio, Pietro Paolo

INTRADE   see Geselbracht, Erich

INTRODUCAO E VARIACOES SOBRE UM TEMA DA
  OPERA "FLAUTA MAGICA" DE W.A.
  MOZART   see Sor, Fernando,
  Introduction Et Variations Sur Un
  Theme De Mozart

INTRODUCCIO   see Sierra-Fortuny, J.M.

INTRODUCTION A L'ETUDE DE LA GUITARE EN
  VINGT CINQ LECONS PROGRESSIVES   see
  Sor, Fernando; Sor, Fernando; Sor,
  Fernando

INTRODUCTION A L'ETUDE DE LA GUITARE EN
  VINGT CINQ LECONS PROGRESSIVES, OP.
  60, NO. 1   see Sor, Fernando

INTRODUCTION A L'ETUDE DE LA GUITARE EN
  VINGT CINQ LECONS PROGRESSIVES, OP.
  60., NO. 2   see Sor, Fernando

INTRODUCTION A L'ETUDE DE LA GUITARE EN
  VINGT CINQ LECONS PROGRESSIVES, OP.
  60, NO. 5   see Sor, Fernando

INTRODUCTION A L'ETUDE DE LA GUITARE EN
  VINGT CINQ LECONS PROGRESSIVES, OP.
  60, NO. 7   see Sor, Fernando

INTRODUCTION AND DANCE   see Boda, John

INTRODUCTION AND FANDANGO   see
  Boccherini, Luigi

INTRODUCTION ET ALLEGRO   see Sor,
  Fernando, Grand Solo

INTRODUCTION ET DANSE   see Bartsch,
  Charles

INTRODUCTION ET THEME VARIE   see Sor,
  Fernando

INTRODUCTION ET VARIATIONS SUR L'AIR
  "MARLBROUG"   see Sor, Fernando

INTRODUCTION ET VARIATIONS SUR L'AIR
  "QUE NE SUIS-JE LA FOUGERE"   see
  Sor, Fernando

INTRODUCTION ET VARIATIONS SUR UN THEME
  DE MOZART   see Sor, Fernando

INTRODUCTION, THEMA UND VARIATIONEN
  see Sor, Fernando, Introduction Et
  Theme Varie

INTRODUCTION TO EFFECTIVE ACCOMPANIMENT
  FOR GUITAR   see Pick, Richard
  Samuel Burns

INTRODUCTION TO FINGER-PICKING GUITAR
  see Higgins, Ralph

INTRODUCTION TO GUITAR NOTATION   see
  Higgins, Ralph

INTRODUCTION TO GUITAR, PLECTRUM OR
  CLASSIC   see Pick, Richard Samuel
  Burns

INTRODUCTION TO PLAYING THE SPANISH
  GUITAR, AN   see Hunt, Edgar

INTRODUCTION TO THE FLAMENCO GUITAR, AN
  see Sheer, Anita

INTRODUCTION TO THE GUITAR   see Quine,
  Hector

INTRODUKTION, THEMA UND VARIATIONEN
  see Prager, Heinrich Aloys

INTRODUZIONE   see Bettinelli, Bruno

INTRODUZIONE E VARIAZIONI SU L'ARIA
  "MARLBROUG"   see Sor, Fernando,
  Introduction Et Variations Sur
  l'Air "Marlbroug"

INTRODUZIONE E VARIAZIONI SU L'ARIA "O
  CARA ARMONIA" DALL' OPERA "IL
  FLAUTO MAGICO" DI W.A. MOZART   see
  Sor, Fernando, Introduction Et
  Variations Sur Un Theme De Mozart

INTRODUZIONE E VARIAZIONI SU L'ARIA
  "QUE NE SUIS-JE LA FOUGERE"   see
  Sor, Fernando, Introduction Et
  Variations Sur l'Air "Que Ne Suis-
  Je La Fougere"

INTRODUZIONE, TEMA, VARIAZIONI E FINALE
  see Legnani, Luigi

INVENCIONES, 3   see Losy vom Losinthal,
  Jan Antonin

4 INVENTIES   see Bach, Johann Sebastian

INVENTIONEN, 5   see Asriel, Andre

INVENZIONE A DUE VOCI IN DO   see Bach,
  Johann Sebastian, Invention No. 1,
  BWV 772, in C

INVENZIONE, SU QUATTRO NOTE   see
  Chailly, Luciano

INVITO ALLA CHITARRA FLAMENCA   see
  Chierici, Fernando

INVITO ALLA CHITARRA, METODO PER
  CHITARRA CLASSICA   see Dederos, M.

INVOCATION   see Furstenau, Wolfram

INVOCATION ET DANSE, HOMMAGE A MANUEL
  DE FALLA   see Rodrigo, Joaquin

IO NON COMPRO, FROTTOLA   see Cara,
  Marchetto

IPARRAGUIRRE, P.A.
  Escalas, Arpegios Y Ejercicios Del
    Mecanismo Tecnico III,
    VI-Mixed Coll

  Escalas Menores Melodicas III

  Estudios Diarios Del Mecanismo
    Tecnico I/IA

  Principiante, El, (20) Lecciones
    Elementales II

IRISH HO-HOANE   see Banks, Don

IRISH SONGS AND DANCES, 26 I/IB5-Coll

IRRENDER SOHN, EIN   see Nilsson, Bo

IRVING, JACQUELYN
  First Guitar Book, A Practice Course
    For Beginners II

ISABEL, PERDISTE LA TU FAXA   see
  Mudarra, Alonso de

ISHII, MAKI (1936-   )
  Japanische Suite I I/IIIA

ISRAEL-MEYER, PIERRE (1933-   )
  Humoresque I/IIB1

  Passacaglia   see Humoresque

  Postlude   see Humoresque

  Prelude   see Humoresque

  Scherzo   see Humoresque

ISTVAN, MILOSLAV (1928-   )
  Dodekameron; 12 Compositions For 12
    Players V/i

  Studien, 6 V/i

IT IS DAWNING IN THE EAST, BALLADESQUE
  VARIATIONS ON AN OLD DUTCH LOVE
  SONG   see Badings, Henk

ITALIAANSE LUITMUZIEK UIT DE
  RENAISSANCE I/IB1-Coll

ITALIAN SONGS OF THE RENAISSANCE AND
  BAROQUE PERIODS I/IIC1-Coll

ITALIENISCHE CANZONETTEN, 4, AUS DEM
  16. JAHRHUNDERT   see Anonymous

ITALIENISCHE MEISTER   see Europaische
  Gitarren- Und Lautenmusik, Vol. 1

ITALIENISCHE MEISTER DER GITARRE UM
  1800 I/IB2-Coll

ITTROSPEZIONE III see Andriessen,
Louis

I'VE BEEN TO HARLEM I/IIC4

JACARAS see Guerau, Francisco

JACARAS DE LA COSTA see Guerau,
Francisco

JAGERLIEDCHEN see Schumann, Robert
(Alexander); Schumann, Robert
(Alexander)

JAHRESWETTERANZEIGER "WILLST DU AUFS
WETTER IM JAHR ACHTEN" see
Burthel, Jakob

J'AI DESCENDU see Seiber, Matyas
Gyorgy

J'AI LE REBOURS see Le Roy, Adrien

J'AI PERDU MON EURIDICE see Gluck,
Christoph Willibald, Ritter von

JAKOB POLAK (JACQUES POLONAIS)
(ca. 1545-1605)
Courante I/IB1

Galliard No. 1 I/IB1

JANSEN, WILLY (1897-   )
Arpeggio Semplice, Vom Einfachen
Harfenspiel Auf Der Gitarre II

Klanglehre Zur Gitarre (Begleitspiel
Auf Grund Der Harmonielehre) II,
IV/IIC1

Kleine Spielmusiken I/IB4, I/IIA1,
I/IIA2, I/IIB2

JANSSEN, GUUS (1951-   )
Gieter, For Orchestra V/i

JAPANESE PRINT, SUL NOME DI JIRO
MATSUDA see Castelnuovo-Tedesco,
Mario

JAPANISCHE SERENADE see Behrend,
Siegfried

JAPANISCHE SUITE I see Ishii, Maki

JAPANISCHES KONZERT see Scholz, Bernd

JARDINS DE VAUXHALL see De Filippi,
Amedeo

JASAGER, DER, SCHOOLOPERA IN 2 ACTS
see Weill, Kurt

JAUBERT, MAURICE (1900-1940)
Chanson De Tessa, La I/IIC5

JAZZ-SYMPHONY, FOR JAZZ-SOLOISTS AND
SYMPHONY ORCHESTRA see Graas,
John, Symphony No. 1

JAZZY MOODS, 3 see Topper, Guido

JE NE SUIS MOINS AIMABLE see Le Roy,
Adrien

JEHN, WOLFGANG
Auferstanden Heute, Kleine
Osterkantate I/IIC5

JELINEK, HANNS (1901-1969)
Ollapotrida I/IIB1

JENKINS, JOHN (1592-1678)
Arien Und Allemanden I/IB1, I/IIA1

JENTSCH, WALTER (1900-   )
Impressionen I/IB4

JEROMITA LINARES see Guastavino,
Carlos

JESSET, MICHAEL
Neun Volkslieder I/IIC1

JESSIC, M.
Academic Method For Classical Guitar
II

JESU, JOY OF MAN'S DESIRING see Bach,
Johann Sebastian, Jesus Bleibet
Meine Freude. Chorale

JESUS, ALEGRIA DE LA HUMANIDAD see
Bach, Johann Sebastian, Jesus
Bleibet Meine Freude. Chorale

JESUS, ALEGRIA DOS HOMENS see Bach,
Johann Sebastian, Jesus Bleibet
Meine Freude. Chorale

JESUS BLEIBET MEINE FREUDE. CHORALE
see Bach, Johann Sebastian

JESUS QUE MA JOIE DEMEURE see Bach,
Johann Sebastian, Jesus Bleibet
Meine Freude. Chorale

JESUS UND DIE FISCHER; CANTATA see
Gunsenheimer, Gustav

JETZT IST DIE RECHTE FREUDENZEIT, SHORT
CHRISTMAS CANTATA see Haus, Karl

JEU DES QUATRE VENTS see Ohana,
Maurice, Si Le Jour Parait, No. 6

JEUNE, HENRI LE
Chanson I/IB1, I/IIC1

JEUNE FILLE ET LA MORT, LA see
Schubert, Franz (Peter)

JEUNE GUITARISTE, LE, PREMIERE METHODE
DE GUITARE see Castet, Francois

JEUNE MERE, LA see Schubert, Franz
(Peter)

JEUX D'ENFANTS, 25 MINIATURE FRANCESI
I/IB5-Coll

JEUX INTERDITS: MUSIQUE DU FILM
I/IB6-Coll

JEZ, JAKOB (1928-   )
Bitte Um Liebe see Do Fraig Amor

Do Fraig Amor V/ii

JIDDISCHE HOCHZEIT, A see Behrend,
Siegfried

JIDDISCHE LIEDER I/IIC1-Coll

JINGLE BELL see Celebri Melodie
Natalizie

JOACHIM, OTTO (1910-   )
Stucke, 6 I/IB4

JOHN BROWN LIEGT IN SEINEM KALTEN
DUNKLEN GRAB see Hess, Reimund,
Glory Hallelujah "John Brown's
Body"

JOHNSON, JOHN (1540-1594)
Galliard, MIN 11 I/IB1

Rogero I/IIA1, I/IIB2

JOHNSON, PER-OLOF
Gitarrskola For Klassisk Gitarr,
Suppl.: Larar-Handlednung II

Gitarrskola For Klassisk Gitarr, Vol.
I: Nyborjarskola II

Gitarrskola For Klassisk Gitarr, Vol.
II: Fortsattningsskola II,
VI-Mixed Coll

JOHNSON, ROBERT [3] (ca. 1583-1633)
Almain I/IB1

Carman's Whistle I/IB1

Noble Man, The I/IB1

JOIE, LA see Zani de Ferranti, Marco
Aurelio

JOINT SOLOS BACH NO. 3 - SARABAND-
DOUBLE see Bach, Johann Sebastian,
Partita for Violin, BWV 1002, in B
minor, Saraband

JOLIVET, ANDRE (1905-1974)
Etude No. 1 see Etudes De Concert, 2

Etude No. 2 see Etudes De Concert, 2

Etudes De Concert, 2 I/IA

Serenade I/IIA1

JONES, JOHN
Sonatina in C I/IIA1

JONG, MARINUS DE (1891-1984)
Bruegel-Liederen I/IIC1

Suite, Op. 127 I/IIB1

JONGE, CHARLES DE
Methode De Guitare see Methode Voor
Gitaar

Methode Pratique Pour La Guitare see
Praktisch Leerboek Voor Gitaar,
Vol. I; Praktisch Leerboek Voor
Gitaar, Vol. II

Methode Voor Gitaar II

Praktisch Leerboek Voor Gitaar, Vol.
I II

Praktisch Leerboek Voor Gitaar, Vol.
II II

JONGEN, LEON (1885-1969)
Venezuela; Music For The Documentary
Film V/iii

JORDAAN see Furstenau, Wolfram

JOSEPH, LIEBER JOSEPH MEIN see Rinke
Ranke Rosenschein; 77 Kinderlieder

JOSEPHS, WILFRED (1927-   )
Saratoga Concerto I/IIIC

JOSQUIN
see DES PREZ, JOSQUIN

JOTA DE MONTES see Winkelbauer, Alfred

JOTA LEVANTINA see Moreno Torroba,
Federico

JOVEN GUITARRISTA, EL, VOL.1: MUY FACIL
see Azpiazu, Jose de

JOVEN GUITARRISTA, EL, VOL.2: FACIL
see Azpiazu, Jose de

JOVEN GUITARRISTA, EL, VOL.3: MENOS
FACIL see Azpiazu, Jose de

JOVEN GUITARRISTA, EL, VOL.4: MEDIANA
DIFICULTAD see Azpiazu, Jose de

JOVICIC, JOVAN
Balkanski Dans I/IB4

JUCHHE, DER ERSTE SCHNEE, KLEINE
KANTATE see Marx, Karl

JUDEN TANZ, DER see Neusiedler, Hans

JUDENKUNIG, HANS (ca. 1450-1526)
Ronde Neerlandaise I/IB1

Schone Kunstliche Vnderweisung Auff
Der Lautten Vnd Geygen, Ain, 1523
I/IB1-Coll

JUGEND SINGT ZUR GITARRE, 50 [SIC]
DEUTSCHE UND AUSSERDEUTSCHE VOLKS-
UND JUGENDLIEDER I/IIC1-Coll

JULIA, BERNARDO
Nostalgia I/IB4

JULIANA see Belasco, Lionel; Belasco,
M.

JULIANA, ANTILLIAANSE WALS see
Belasco, M., Juliana

JULIANA, VALZER VENEZUELANO see
Belasco, Lionel, Juliana

JULIUS CAESAR; OPERA IN THREE ACTS see
Handel, George Frideric, Giulio
Cesare

JUNGE GITARRE-SOLIST, DER, VOL. III;
EINE SAMMLUNG LEICHTER, MELODIOSER
SOLOSTUCKE see Karl, Sepp

JUNGE GITARRE-SOLIST, DER, VOL. IV;
EINE SAMMLUNG LEICHTER, MELODIOSER
SOLOSTUCKE see Karl, Sepp

JUNGE GITARRE-SOLOIST, DER I/IB6-Coll

JUNGE GITARRE-SOLOIST, DER, VOL. I;
EINE SAMMLUNG LEICHTER, MELODIOSER
SOLOSTUCKE see Hintermeyer, Willy

JUNGE GITARRE-SOLOIST, DER, VOL. II;
EINE SAMMLUNG LEICHTER, MELODIOSER
SOLOSTUCKE see Hintermeyer, Willy

JUNTO AL GENERALIFE see Rodrigo,
Joaquin

JUST, FRANZ (1937-   )
Leichte Spielstucke I/IB4

JUST ARRIVED see Gramberg, Jacq

KADOOTJE VOOR WOLFGANG, 'N see Mozart,
Leopold

KADOSA, PAL (1903-1983)
Easy Pieces For Guitar see 11 Konnyu
Darab Gitarra

11 Konnyu Darab Gitarra I/IB4

KAGEL, MAURICIO (1931-   )
Acustica I: Music For Loudspeakers
V/i

Kantrimiusik V/ii

Mare Nostrum; Entdeckung, Befriedung
Und Konversion Des
Mittelmeerraumes Durch Einen
Stamm Aus Amazonien V/ii

Musi, For Plucked Orchestra V/i

KAGEL, MAURICIO (cont'd.)

Musik Aus "Tremens" V/i

Pastorale for Solo Voices and
Instrumental Ensemble see
Kantrimiusik

Repertoire V/iii

Schall, Der, For 5 Instrumentalists
V/i

Sonant I/IIB4

Tactil Fur Drei V/i

Tremens; Scenic Assembling Of An
Experiment In One Scene V/iii

Unter Strom, For 3 Instrumentalists
V/i

KALAS, JULIUS (1902-1967)
Mullerin Von Granada, Die; Operetta
In Three Acts And Five Scenes
V/iii

KALMAR, LASZLO (1931-   )
Monologo I/IB4

KAMERALNA MUZYKA GITAROWA I/IIB1-Coll

KAMINSKI, HEINRICH (1886-1946)
Drei Gedichte Von Eichendorff, No. 1
V/ii

KAMMERKONZERT see Bresgen, Cesar;
Konietzny, Heinrich

KAMMERLING, WERNER
Variationen Uber 3 Alte Volkslieder,
18 I/IIB1

KAMMERMUSIK 1958 see Henze, Hans
Werner

KAMMERTRIO see Schramm, Werner

KANARIE DANS see Gramberg, Jacq

KANONISCHE KANTATE ZUR WEIHNACHT see
Neumann, Friedrich

KANONS, 5 see Asriel, Andre

KANONS ZUM SINGEN UND SPIELEN
I/IIA1-Coll, I/IIA2-Coll,
I/IIA3-Coll

KANTATE ZUR NAMENSFEIER DES VATERS see
Schubert, Franz (Peter)

KANTRIMIUSIK see Kagel, Mauricio

KAPITEIN IS JARIG, DE, KINDERZANGSPEL
IN 2 BEDRIJVEN see Marez Oyens,
Tera de

KAPR, JAN (1914-   )
Symphony No. 6 for Chamber Orchestra
V/i

KAPS, HANSJOACHIM
Flamenco-Gitarren-Schule II

Huracan, El I/IB4

KAPSBERGER, JOHANN HIERONYMUS
(ca. 1600-1650)
Gagliarden, 3 I/IB1

Toccata I/IB1

KARL, SEPP (1913-   )
Junge Gitarre-Solist, Der, Vol. III;
Eine Sammlung Leichter,
Melodioser Solostucke I/IB4,
I/IIA1

Junge Gitarre-Solist, Der, Vol. IV;
Eine Sammlung Leichter,
Melodioser Solostucke I/IB4

Kleine Kostbarkeiten I/IIA1

Leichte Gitarren-Duette, 36 I/IIA1

Melodische Spielstucke Fur Leichtes
Lagenspiel I/IB4

Strebsame Gitarrist, Der, Vol. II,
Leichte Spielstucke I/IB4

Tanze Und Weisen I/IIA2, I/IIB2

KASLIK, VACLAV (1917-   )
Prager Karneval; Ballet-Triptych
After Three Medieval Ballads
V/iii

KATALANISCHE SARDANAS, 2 I/IIB5-Coll

KAUFMANN, ARMIN (1902-   )
Rhapsody, Op. 97 I/IB4

Stucke, 10 I/IB4

Suite I/IIA1

KAYN, ROLAND (1933-   )
Allotropie, For Orchestra With
Multiple Articulation V/i

KEF, KEES (1894-1961)
Divertimento I/IB4

KEGEL see Volkstanze, 6

KEHRAUS see Funk, Heinrich

KEINEMANN, KARL HEINZ
Sudamerikanische Tanze, Fur Den
Modernen Gitarren-Gruppen-
Unterricht I/IIA3, I/IIA4

KELKEL, MANFRED (1929-   )
Zagreber Konzert I/IIIA

KELLNER, DAVID (ca. 1670-1748)
Fantasy in F sharp minor I/IB1

KELLY, BRYAN (1934-   )
Aubade, Toccata And Nocturne I/IB4

KELTERBORN, RUDOLF (1931-   )
Music for Violin and Guitar I/IIB1

KENNARD, JAN
Preludes, 2 I/IB4

KENNISMAKEN, HET see Verzijl, Hans

KERKERBALLADE, DE see Zagwijn, Henri

KERKHOFFS, GUNTER (1914-   )
Zertanzten Schuhe, Die, Kinderoper
Nach Einem Marchen Der Gebruder
Grimm I/IIC5

KERMIS-SUITE see Cranen, T.

KERR, HARRISON (1897-1978)
Variations On A Theme From "The Tower
Of Kel" I/IB4

KERSTERS, WILLEM (1929-   )
Nocturne, Op. 44 I/IB4

KERSTLIEDEREN, EENVOUDIGE ZETTINGEN
IV/I, IV/IIC1

KERSTLIEDEREN VOOR GITAARSOLO IV/I,
IV/IIC1

KERSTLIEDJES OM MEE TE SPELEN EN TE
ZINGEN IV/IIC5

KEUZE UIT [SELECTION FROM] TRES LIBROS
DE MUSICA EN CIFRA see Mudarra,
Alonso de

KHAN, PESY
Indisches Spielbuch I/IIA1

KIERNER, MAX
Gitarre Spielen - Leicht Gemacht,
Volkstumliche Gitarreschule Fur
Den Einzel-, Gruppen- Oder
Selbstunterricht II

KINDER-SYMPHONIE see Haydn, [Franz]
Joseph

KINDERCHOR, DER: MUSIK FUR
GOTTESDIENST; VOLKS- UND
KINDERLIEDSATZE I/IIC5-Coll

KINDERLIED see Uhl, Alfred

KINDERLIEDER-SUITE FUR EINEN GROSSVATER
see Muller-Cant, Manfred

KINDERSCENEN see Schumann, Robert
(Alexander)

KINDERSONATE see Schumann, Robert
(Alexander)

KING OF DENMARK HIS GALLIARD, THE see
Dowland, John; Dowland, John

KING'S MARCH see Clarke, Jeremiah

KIRCHWEIH, NO. 5, FOR ORCHESTRA AND
EQUIPMENT see Schneider, Urs Peter

KIRMESTANZ see Funk, Heinrich

KIRSCHEN BLUHN see Vier Japanische
Volkslieder

KIS TANULMANYOK see Patachich, Ivan

KITARAKIRJA-GITARRMELODIER, VOL. 1
I/IB6-Coll

KITARAKIRJA-GITARRMELODIER, VOL. 2
I/IB6-Coll, VII-Mixed Coll

KLAGENDE LIED, DAS see Bohr, Heinrich

KLAMPFENLIED, DAS, EIN
FAHRTENLIEDERBUCH I/IIC1-Coll

KLANGLEHRE ZUR GITARRE (BEGLEITSPIEL
AUF GRUND DER HARMONIELEHRE) see
Jansen, Willy

KLASSIKER DER GITARRE; STUDIEN- UND
VORTRAGSLITERATUR AUS DEM 18. UND
19. JAHRHUNDERT, VOL. 1 I/IB2-Coll

KLASSIKER DER GITARRE; STUDIEN- UND
VORTRAGSLITERATUR AUS DEM 18. UND
19. JAHRHUNDERT, VOL. 2:
MITTELSTUFE - INTERMEDIATE STAGE
I/IB6-Coll, VI-Mixed Coll

KLASSISCHE KOSTBARKEITEN I/IB2-Coll

KLASSISCHE MELODIEN I/IB3, I/IIA1

KLASSISCHE TANZWEISEN, VON HAYDN BIS
SCHUBERT, VOL. 1 I/IIB2-Coll

KLASSISCHE TANZWEISEN, VON HAYDN BIS
SCHUBERT, VOL.2 I/IIB2-Coll

KLASSISCHES ALBUM, VOL. 1 I/IB6-Coll

KLASSISCHES ALBUM, VOL. 2 I/IB6-Coll,
VII-Mixed Coll

KLASSISCHES ALBUM, VOL. 3 I/IB6-Coll

KLASSZIKUS ETUDOK GITARRA I/IA-Coll

KLASSZIKUSOK GITARRA I/IB6-Coll

KLEBE, GISELHER (1925-   )
Herzschlage, Furcht, Bitte Und
Hoffnung, Symphonic Scene For
Beat-Band And Full Orchestra V/i

Recitativo, Aria E Duetto I/IIB1

KLEIN, RICHARD RUDOLF (1921-   )
Divertimento I/IIB1

Lasst Eure Stimm' Erklingen, Kleine
Kantate Zum Lobe Der Musik
I/IIC5

Partita in D I/IIB1

KLEIN, WALDTRAUT
Sing- Und Maskenspiel Von Jorinde Und
Joringel, Das, Ein Spiel Fur
Kinder I/IIC5   -

KLEINE DITIRAMBE see Schagen, Henk van

KLEINE DREIGROSCHENMUSIK see Weill,
Kurt

KLEINE DUETTE, 6, VOL. I see Carulli,
Ferdinando

KLEINE DUETTE, 6, VOL. II see Carulli,
Ferdinando

KLEINE ETUDEN, 2 see Czernuschka,
Fritz

KLEINE GEMAKKELIJKE GIDS VOOR
GITAARBEGELEIDING see Mille, Jo,
Petit Guide Facile d'Accompagnement
A La Guitare

KLEINE GITAAR- OF LUITSCHOOL, MET
BIJVOEGING VAN EEN KEUZE
PLECTRUMGITAAR-ACCOORDEN, TEN
BEHOEVE VAN ONDERWJS EN ZELFSTUDIE
see Groodt, Frans de

KLEINE GITARRE- UND LAUTEN-SCHULE see
Alberto, A.

KLEINE GITARREN- UND LAUTENSCHULE see
Gerdes, Gustav

KLEINE GITARRENSTUCKE, 31, IN
FORTSCHREITENDER ORDNUNG see
Aguado, Dionisio

KLEINE KAMMERMUSIK see Schwarz-
Schilling, Reinhard

KLEINE KLAVIERSTUCKE, 6 see
Schoenberg, Arnold

KLEINE KOSTBARKEITEN see Karl, Sepp

KLEINE LEICHTE STUCKE, 14 see Rebay,
Ferdinand

KLEINE MELODIEN FUR DEN JUNGEN
GITARRISTEN, 10 see Friessnegg,
Karl

KLEINE MOZART, DE see Mozart, Wolfgang
Amadeus

KLEINE OUVERTURE see Wolki, Konrad

KLEINE ROMANZE see Walker, Luise

KLEINE SERENADE see Hasenohrl, Franz;
Poser, Hans

KLEINE SERENADE, UNTERHALTENDE
VORTRAGSSTUCKE see Ratz, Martin

KLEINE SINFONIE see Krenek, Ernst

KLEINE SOLIST, DE – THE LITTLE SOLOIST,
EASY GUITAR PIECES IN VARIOUS
POSITIONS see Schagen, Henk van

KLEINE SOLOSTUCKE see Scholze, Arthur
Johannes

KLEINE SOLOSTUCKE see Wensiecki,
Edmund

KLEINE SPIEL- UND UBUNGSSTUCKE FUR DEN
ANFANG, 30 see Schafer, Rudolf

KLEINE SPIELMUSIKEN see Jansen, Willy

KLEINE SPIELSTUCKE GROSSER MEISTER
I/IB2-Coll

KLEINE SPIELSTUCKE NACH KINDERLIEDERN,
30 see Stingl, Anton

KLEINE STUCKE ,3 I/IB1-Coll
see also Byrd, William

KLEINE STUCKE, 4 see Hasenohrl, Franz;
Mozart, Wolfgang Amadeus

KLEINE STUCKE, 24 see Carcassi, Matteo

KLEINE STUCKE see Bach, Johann
Sebastian

KLEINE STUCKE see Bach, Johann
Sebastian

KLEINE STUDIES, 6 see Pelemans, Willem

KLEINE SUITE see Coenen, Paul;
Szordikowski, Bruno

KLEINE SUITE IN A MINOR see Stetka,
Franz

KLEINE SUITE, OP. 30 see Friessnegg,
Karl

KLEINE TANZE see Hollfelder, Waldram

KLEINE TANZE UND MARSCHE VON HAYDN BIS
STRAUSS I/IIB1-Coll

KLEINE VORTRAGSSTUCKE FUR ANFANGER, 5
see Carulli, Ferdinando

KLEINE WEIHNACHTSKANTATE, NACH ALTEN
TEXTEN UND WEISEN AUS OSTERREICH
see Deutsch, Walter

KLEINE WEIHNACHTSMUSIK, EINE see
Stetka, Franz

KLEINE WERKE GROSSER MEISTER, VOL. 1
I/IB6-Coll, I/IIA1-Coll

KLEINE WERKE GROSSER MEISTER, VOL. 2
I/IB6-Coll, I/IIA1-Coll

KLEINE WERKE GROSSER MEISTER, VOL. 3
I/IB6-Coll, I/IIA1-Coll

KLEINE WERKE GROSSER MEISTER, VOL. 4
I/IB6-Coll, I/IIA1-Coll

KLEINER WALZER see Stingl, Anton

KLEINES KAMMERKONZERT see Apostel,
Hans Erich

KLEINES, STILLES LEUCHTEN, EIN see
Thienemann, H.

KLEINES TANZCHEN see Dieckmann, Carl
Heinz

KLEINES WEIHNACHTSORATORIUM MIT JOHANN
SEBASTIAN BACH see Bach, Johann
Sebastian

KLINGENDE FAHRT, EIN LIEDERBUCH
I/IIC1-Coll

KLINGENDE KLEINIGKEITEN AUS ALTER UND
NEUER ZEIT I/IIA1-Coll,
I/IIA2-Coll, I/IIA3-Coll

KLINGENDER GITARREN-LEHRGANG see
Teuchert, Heinz

KLUIN, ELS
Arpeggio Studies, 18 I/IA

KNAB, ARMIN (1881-1951)
Lautenlieder I/IIC1

Pastorale Und Allegro IV/IIB2

KOBLER, HANS (1930-   )
Ich Mochte Gerne Brucken Bauen V/ii

KOCH, HANS
Musizierbuchlein, Ein, Einfuhrung In
Das Mehrstimmige Spiel Nach
Volkstanzen Und Liedern Aus Dem
Alpenraum I/IB5, I/IIB1

KOCH, JOHANNES H.E. (1918-   )
Bulgarischer Tanz see Tanzerische
Spielmusik

Herr Christ, Der Einig Gotts Sohn
IV/IIC5

Tanzerische Spielmusik I/IIB4,
I/IIB5

Tanzlied Mit Variationen see
Tanzerische Spielmusik

KODALY, ZOLTAN (1882-1967)
Bicinia I/IB4

KOELLREUTTER, HANS-JOACHIM (JACOBO)
(1915-   )
Haikai Des Pedro Xisto, 8 I/IIC4

KOHAUT, KARL
Concerto in F I/IIB3

KOK, JOH. B.
Gitaar-Accorden III

Nieuwe Gitaar-School, De, Volledige,
Moderne Methode II

KOLOMETRIE see Behrend, Siegfried

KOMM HERBEI TOD see Sibelius, Jean

KOMM SUSSER TOD see Bach, Johann
Sebastian

KOMMT, IHR G'SPIELEN; FOLKSONGS FOR
WIND, STRING, PLUCKED, AND
PERCUSSION INSTRUMENTS see Werdin,
Eberhard

KOMMT, IHR G'SPIELEN UND 5 WEITERE
LIEDER I/IIC2-Coll

KOMMT, SEELEN DIESER TAG see Bach,
Johann Sebastian

KOMMT SINGT UND SPIELT: LIEDER UNSERER
ZEIT, FUR DEN ANFANGSUNTERRICHT
I/IB4-Coll, I/IB6-Coll,
I/IIA1-Coll, I/IIC1-Coll, IV/I,
IV/IIA1

KOMOROUS, RUDOLF (1931-   )
Chanson I/IIB2

KOMPOSITIONEN see Hlouschek, Theodor

KOMPOSITIONEN FUR DIE GITARRE see Sor,
Fernando

KOMPOSITIONEN FUR DIE LAUTE; ERSTE
VOLLSTANDIGE UND KRITISCH
DURCHGESEHENE AUSGABE; NACH ALTEM
QUELLENMATERIAL FUR DIE HEUTIGE
LAUTE UBERTRAGEN UND HERAUSGEGEBEN
see Bach, Johann Sebastian

KOMPOSITIONEN FUR GITARRE, VOL. I see
Tarrega, Francisco

KOMPOSITIONEN FUR GITARRE, VOL. II see
Tarrega, Francisco

KOMTER, JAN MAARTEN (1905-   )
Andante in D I/IIB1

Arpeggiata, Homenaje A Fernando Sors
I/IB4

Arpeggio-Etude, A La Maniere De Sor,
I/IA

Aware see Dhyanas, 6

Becalmed see Dhyanas, 6

Beware see Dhyanas, 6

Boleronda I/IIA2

Chansonatine I/IIA1

Dhyanas, 6 I/IB4

Divertimento in G I/IIB1

KOMTER, JAN MAARTEN (cont'd.)

Fun From The Start, Vol. 1: Guitar
Duets For Teacher And Pupil
I/IIA1

Fun From The Start, Vol. II: The
Beginning Soloist On The Guitar
I/IB4

In A Gondola I/IIC1

Milan-Suite, On A Theme Of Don Luis
Milan (1535) I/IIA1

Preludes, 2 I/IB4

Preludes Faciles, 3 I/IB4

Punteado-Suite I/IIA1

Serene see Dhyanas, 6

Sonate Concertante I/IC

Spanish Suite I/IB4

Storm In A Teacup see Dhyanas, 6

Suite 1945 I/IB4

Suite 1949 I/IB4

Suite in A I/IIA1

Suite in C I/IIB1

Suite in D minor I/IIB1

Suites, 6 I/IB4

Trio-Sonatine I/IIB2

Unaware see Dhyanas, 6

KONCERTNI FANTASIE see Zelenka, Ivan

KONIETZNY, HEINRICH
Kammerkonzert I/IIIC

Permutationen I/IB4

KONIG, HEINZ
Liedbegleitung Auf Der Gitarre,
Anleitung Zur Stilvollen
Improvisation, Satz- Und
Bearbeitungstechnik II

Spielmusik In C I/IIB1

KONINK, SERVAAS DE (KONING)
(ca. 1660-ca. 1720)
Sonata I/IIB1

11 KONNYU DARAB GITARRA see Kadosa,
Pal

KONT, PAUL (1920-   )
Suite en Passant I/IIB1

KONTRATANZE UND MENUETTE see Mozart,
Wolfgang Amadeus

KONZERT see Telemann, Georg Philipp

KONZERT, FOR VIOLIN AND 4 ORCHESTRAL
GROUPS see Niehaus, Manfred

KONZERT-ETUDEN, 4 see Sor, Fernando

KONZERT-ETUDEN FUR GITARRE, VOL. 3
I/IA-Coll, VI-Mixed Coll

KONZERT ETUDEN, VOL. 1 I/IA-Coll

KONZERT ETUDEN, VOL. 2 I/IA-Coll

KONZERTE, 2 see Baron, Ernst Gottlieb

KONZERTETUDE, NO.2 see Hoek, Jan-Anton
Van

KOPTAGEL, YUKSEL (1931-   )
Fosil Suiti I/IB4

Tamzara, Turkischer Tanz I/IB4

KORDA, VIKTOR (1900-   )
Capriccio I/IIB3

Festliche Suite, Fur
Spielmusikgruppen I/IIB5

Finale see Festliche Suite, Fur
Spielmusikgruppen

Intermezzo see Festliche Suite, Fur
Spielmusikgruppen

Intrada see Festliche Suite, Fur
Spielmusikgruppen

KORN, PETER JONA (1922-   )
Arabesque I/IB4

Gigue, Op. 61, No. 3 I/IB4

Pavane Triste I/IB4

KORT, WIM DE
Fugas, 2, Op. 10 I/IIA2

Fughetta's, 2 I/IIA1

KOSAKENTANZ see Gitarre Spezial,
Picking Modern Arrangement, Vol. 2

KOSTLICHKEITEN ENGLISCHER LAUTENMUSIK
I/IB1-Coll

KOTIK, JOSEPH
Erste Lektionen Fur Gitarre II

Erste Vortragsstucke Fur Gitarre
I/IB4

Prvni Prednesove Skladby Pro Kytaru
I/IB4

KOTONSKI, WLODZIMIERZ (1925-   )
A Battere V/i

Concerto Per Quattro I/IIIC

KOUNADIS, ARGHYRIS (1924-   )
Rebetika I/IIA1

KOVATS, BARNA (1920-   )
Andantino see Minutenstucke

Esquisse see Stucke, 3

Estudio De Corcheas Repetidas see
Stucke, 3

Estudio Homofonico see Stucke, 3

Gitariskola, Vol. I II

Gitarrenschule see Gitariskola, Vol.
I

Leggiero, Molto Legando see
Minutenstucke

Minutenstucke I/IB4

Moderato, Un Poco Agitato see
Minutenstucke

Mouvements, 3 I/IB4

Non Troppo Allegro see Minutenstucke

Petite Suite I/IB4

Sonata Nova I/IC

Sonatina I/IIB1

Stucke, 3 I/IB4

Suite, Hommage A Goldoni I/IB4

Technische Studien Fur Gitarre, Vol.
I: Fingerubungen Fur Eine
Systematische Ausbildung Der
Gitarre-Spieltechnik III

Tranquillamente Scorrendo see
Minutenstucke

Vivo, Ritmico see Minutenstucke

KOX, HANS (1930-   )
Concerto Bandistico V/i

Cyclofonie IX, For Solo Percussion
Player And Orchestra V/i

KRAKOVIAK, POOLSE DANSEN I/IIB5-Coll

KRAMER, GOTTHOLD
Abraham I/IIC5

KRASNOLUDKI see Serocki, Kazimierz

KRATOCHWIL, HEINZ (1932-   )
Triptychon I/IB4

KRAUZE, ZYGMUNT (1938-   )
Voices For Ensemble V/i

KREBS, JOHANN LUDWIG (1713-1780)
Concerto in C for Lute and Strings
I/IIIA

Concerto in F for Lute and Strings
I/IIIA

Concerto In F Per Liuto E Archi see
Concerto in F for Lute and
Strings

Concerto In G For Guitar And Strings
see Concerto in F for Lute and
Strings

KREBS, RUDOLF
Schwabische Baurentanze, 3 I/IIB5

KREIDLER, DIETER
Gitarreschule, Fur Einzel- Oder
Gruppen-Unterricht, Vol. 1 II

Gitarreschule, Fur Einzel- Oder
Gruppen-Unterricht, Vol.2 II

KREISSPIEL VON DER GEBURT CHRISTI see
Roeseling, Kaspar

KRENEK, ERNST (1900-   )
Augenblick Errinert V/ii

Ausgerechnet Und Verspielt; Eine
"Spiel"-Oper V/iii

Ausgerechnet Und Verspielt:
Intermezzo I V/i

Computed And Confounded; A Short
Opera see Ausgerechnet Und
Verspielt; Eine "Spiel"-Oper

Das Kommt Davon; Opera V/iii

Exercises Of A Late Hour see Ubungen
Der Spaten Stunde

Fivefold Enfoldment see Funffache
Verschrankung

Funffache Verschrankung V/i

Golden Ram, The; Opera In Four Acts
see Goldene Bock, Der; Opera In
Four Acts

Goldene Bock, Der; Opera In Four Acts
V/iii

Hausmusik; 7 Stucke Fur Die Sieben
Tage Der Woche I/IIB1, I/IIB3

Instant Remembered see Augenblick
Errinert

Kleine Sinfonie V/i

Magic Mirror, The; Television Opera
In Fourteen Scenes see
Zauberspiegel, Der; Television
Opera In Fourteen Scenes

Nach Wie Vor Der Reihe Nach, Op. 182
V/ii

Perspectives see Perspektiven

Perspektiven V/i

Quaestio Temporis V/i

Question Of Time, A (Eine Frage Der
Zeit) see Quaestio Temporis

Quintina Uber Die Funf Vokale V/ii

Sestina, Op. 161 V/ii

Suite I/IB4

Ubungen Der Spaten Stunde V/i

Wenn Sardakai Auf Reisen Geht; Opera
see Das Kommt Davon; Opera

Zauberspiegel, Der; Television Opera
In Fourteen Scenes V/iii

KRETSCHMAR, WALTER (1902-   )
Music in C I/IIB1

KRETZSCHMAR, GUNTHER (1929-   )
Blinde Bettler, Der I/IIC5

David Und Goliath, Cantata For
Children I/IIC5

Grosse Flut, Die, Kleine
Kinderkantate Von Der Arche Noach
I/IIC5

Ich Steh Im Bistum Fulda I/IIC5

Samaritaner, Der, Cantata I/IIC5

Schildburger, Die, Cantata For
Children I/IIC5

KREUTZER, JOSEPH (1778-1832)
Trio in D, Op. 9, No. 3 I/IIB2

Trio, Op. 16 I/IIB2

KRIEG MIT DEN MOLCHEN, DER; MUSIC TO
THE PLAY OF PAVEL KOHAUT see
Fischer, Jan F.

KRIEGER, EDINO (1928-   )
Ritmata I/IB4

KRIEGER, JOHANN (1651-1735)
Bouree Et Menuet I/IB1

KRIEGER, JOHANN PHILIPP (1649-1725)
Du Ungluck'sel'ger Morgenstern see
Lieder, 4

Geldheirat, Die see Lieder, 4

Im Dunkeln Ist Gut Munkeln see
Lieder, 4

Kussgen In Ehren, Ein see Lieder, 4

Lieder, 4 I/IIC1

KROATISCHE SUITE, NACH VOLKSWEISEN AUS
MEDJIMURJE see Miletic, Miroslav

KROL, BERNHARD (1920-   )
Magnificat V/ii

Maria Klar V/ii

KROLL, GEORG (1934-   )
Canzonabile I/IIB1

Re-Sonat Tibia I/IIB1

KRONSTEINER, JOSEF (1910-   )
Partita I/IIA1

KRONUNG DER POPPEA, DIE; OPERA IN THREE
ACTS see Monteverdi, Claudio,
Incoronazione Di Poppea, L'; Opera
In Three Acts And A Prologue

KROPFGANSS, JOHANN (1708- ?)
Partita in D I/IB1

KRUGER, M.
Neue Wege Zur Meisterschaft Auf Der
Gitarre II

KRUYF, TON DE (1937-   )
Quatre Pas De Deux, For Flute And
Orchestra V/i

Quauhquauhtinchan In Den Vreemde; A
Radiophonic Opera V/iii

KUBAI GITARMUVEK - GUITAR MUSIC FROM
CUBA I/IB4-Coll

KUBIZEK, AUGUSTIN (1918-   )
Quartetto Da Camera I/IIB3

Sonata, Op. 13a I/IC

KUCERA, VACLAV (1929-   )
Diario, Omaggio A Che Guevarra I/IB4

KUFFNER, JOSEPH (1776-1856)
Ausgewahlte Ubungsstucke, 30 I/IIA2

Drittes Potpourri I/IIB1

Duette, 12 I/IIA1

24 Gitarrewerke Fur Die Unterstufe
I/IB2

Leichte Duette, 40 I/IIA1

Leichte Duos I/IIA1

25 Leichte Sonatinen I/IB2

Leichte Tanze I/IB2, I/IIA1

Leichte Ubungstucke, 60 I/IIA1

Movimientos, 3 I/IIA1

Notturno, Op. 110 I/IIB2

Serenade I/IIB1

Serenade in A I/IIB2

Serenade, No. 55 I/IIB1

Serenade, Op. 68 I/IIB1

KUHNAU, JOHANN (1660-1722)
Gavotte see Petits Morceaux, 4

Minuet see Petits Morceaux, 4

Petits Morceaux, 4 I/IB1

Prelude see Petits Morceaux, 4

Saraband see Petits Morceaux, 4

Suite in A minor I/IIA1

KUHNEL, JOHANN MICHAEL
Suite in B minor I/IB1

KUKUCK, FELICITAS (1914-   )
Brucke, Die, Eine Kammermusik Nach
Gedichten Aus "Die Chinesische
Flote" Von Hans Bethge I/IIC2

KUKUCK, FELICITAS (cont'd.)

   Ich Hab Die Nacht Getraumet,
     Madchenlieder Nach Gedichten Aus
     Der Romantik I/IIC1

   Marchen Vom Dicken Fetten
     Pfannekuchen, Das, Musik Zu Einem
     Schattenspiel I/IIC5

   Paradies, Das, Ein Tanzspiel I/IIC1

   Spiel Mit Auf Deiner Gitarre II

   Tischlein Deck Dich, Ein Lebendiges
     Buhnenstuck (Ursprunglich Musik
     Fur Ein Schattenspiel I/IIC5

KUME, KUM, GESELLE MIN see David,
   Johann Nepomuk

KUNAD, RAINER (1936-   )
   Schattenland Strome, Conatum 37
     I/IIC1

   Von Der Kocherie, Ein Kulinarisches
     Loblied, Conatum 47 I/IIC1

KUNST VAN HET GITAARSPEL, DE - ART DE
   JOUER DE LA GUITARE, L' see
   Puijenbroeck, Victor van

KUNSTLIEDER I/IIC1-Coll, I/IIC2,
   I/IIC2-Coll, VII-Mixed Coll

KUPKOVIC, LADISLAV (1936-   )
   Gesprach Mit Gott, Ein, For Orchestra
     V/i

   Ozveny, For Orchestra V/i

   Staccato V/i

KURZGEFASSTE GITARRE-SCHULE, FUR
   LEHRERBILDUNGSANSTALTEN UND ZUM
   SELBSTUNTERRICHT GEEIGNET see
   Ortner, Jacob

KURZWEILIGE STUCKE, 10 see Czernik,
   Willy

KUSS-TOBIA see Ferrari, Ivano

KUSSGEN IN EHREN, EIN see Krieger,
   Johann Philipp

KUTZER, ERNST (1918-   )
   Mensch Sein In Christus; Gesange Zur
     Eucharistiefeier V/ii

KWINTOLEN ARPEGGIO ETUDE see Heer,
   Hans De, Etude No. 4

KYTAROVE GONIO III

LABROUVE, JORGE
   Disenos I/IIA1

   Nucleos I/IIA1

   Sintesis I/IIA1

LACHRIMAE see Dowland, John; Dowland,
   John

LACHRIMAE ANTIQUAE, PAVANE see
   Dowland, John, Lachrimae

LACHRIMAE PAVAN UND FANTASIE see
   Dowland, John

LACHRIMAE PAVIN see Dowland, John

LADRU, ANIBAL
   Escuela De Mecanismo Tecnico Para
     Guitarra III, VI-Mixed Coll

LADY CLIFTON'S SPIRIT see 4 Pieces By
   Dowland, Cutting, Morley

LADY HUNSDON'S PUFFE see Dowland,
   John; Dowland, John

LADY LAITON'S ALMAIN see Dowland, John

LADY RICH HER GALLIARD, THE see
   Dowland, John; Dowland, John

LADY, WHEN I BEHOLD THE ROSES see
   Walton, [Sir] William (Turner)

LAGENSPIEL-FIBEL, VOLKSTUMLICHE
   EINFUHRUNG IN DAS LAGENSPIEL AUF
   DER GITARRE see Holzfurtner, Franz

LAGO, MARIO
   Metodo Teorico-Pratico, Per Lo Studio
     Della Chitarra II

LAGOYA, ALEXANDRE
   Capriccio I/IB4

   Etudes, 6 I/IA

LAGOYA, ALEXANDRE (cont'd.)

   Reverie I/IB4

LAGRIMA see Tarrega, Francisco,
   Prelude, TI i- 17, in E

LAGRIME MESTI, VILLANESCA see Pisador,
   Diego

LAICITE see Furstenau, Wolfram

LAISSEZ LA VERTE COULEUR, CHANSON see
   Le Roy, Adrien

LAMENTATION see Antoniou, Theodore,
   Moirologhia For Jani Christou

LAMENTO see Pedrell, Carlos, Pieces,
   3, No. 1

LAMPE, GUNTER (1925-   )
   Tanze, 2 I/IIB5

LAMPERSBERG, GERHARD (1928-   )
   Quartet I/IIB3

   Stucke, 3 I/IB4

   Symphony V/i

LANDLER see Bloch, Waldemar

LANDLERISCHE TANZE; SUITE NACH
   VOLKSWEISEN AUS OBEROSTERREICH
   I/IIA1

5 LANDLERISCHER TANZE see Mozart,
   Wolfgang Amadeus

LANDLUST, DIE see Haydn, [Franz]
   Joseph

LANGEGGER NACHTMUSIK I, FOR ORCHESTRA
   see Cerha, Friedrich

LANGENBERG, JAN VAN DEN
   Ballade No. 1 I/IB4

   Capriccio I/IIB1

   Dance-Variations On A Dutch Song
     I/IB4

   Minuet in F I/IB4

LANGHANS, HERBERT
   Goldene Ei, Das, Ein Marchenspiel
     I/IIC5

LANGZAME WALS see Gramberg, Jacq

LANTDARABOK see Sweelinck, Jan
   Pieterszoon

LANTERO see Robinson, Thomas

LAPRESO DE LLEIDA see Canciones
   Populares Catalanas, 4

LARARHANDLEDNING see Ahslund, Ulf-G.,
   Gitarrskola, Spela I Grupp, Suppl.
   1; Aldeland, Nils, Elementar
   Improvisation, Vol. II

LARCOMBE'S FANCY see Roe, Betty

LARGHETTO see Sor, Fernando

LARGHETTO AND ALLEGRO see Mozart,
   Wolfgang Amadeus

LARGHETTO, OP. 4 see Duarte, John W.

LARGO see Bellow, Alexander; Corelli,
   Arcangelo; Handel, George Frideric;
   Veracini, Francesco Maria

LARGO ANAY see Haydn, [Franz] Joseph

LARGO ASSAI see Haydn, [Franz] Joseph

LARGO DE L'HIVER see Vivaldi, Antonio,
   Concerto for Violin and Orchestra,
   RV 297, in F minor, Largo

LARGO UND RONDO D-DUR see Carulli,
   Ferdinando

LARMES DES MUSES ET GAILLARDE, LES see
   Holborne, Antony

LARRAURI, ANTON (1932-   )
   Triptico Vasco I/IB4

LARSEN, LOUIS
   Vi Spelar Gitarr, Metodisk
     Handledning For Nyborjarstadiet,
     Vol. I II

   Vi Spelar Gitarr, Metodisk
     Handledning For Nyborjarstadiet,
     Vol. II II

LASALA, ANGEL (1914-   )
   Preludios Americanos I/IB4

LASCIATEMI MORIRE see Three 17th
   Century Airs

LASST EURE STIMM' ERKLINGEN, KLEINE
   KANTATE ZUM LOBE DER MUSIK see
   Klein, Richard Rudolf

LASST UNS DAS KINDELEIN WIEGEN see
   Musik Im Jahreskreis

LASST UNS DAS KINDLEIN WIEGEN see
   Weihnachtslieder, 5

LATIN AMERICA: TANGO, SAMBA, RUMBA,
   BOSSA-NOVA see Schwertberger,
   Gerald

LATIN-MUSIC; FAVORITE SONGS FROM
   ARGENTINA, BRESIL, CHILE, CUBA,
   HAITI, HAWAII, JAMAICA, MEXICO,
   SPAIN, TRINIDAD, VOL. 1
   I/IIC1-Coll

LATIN-MUSIC; FAVORITE SONGS FROM
   ARGENTINA, BRESIL, CHILE, CUBA,
   HAITI, HAWAII, JAMAICA, MEXICO,
   SPAIN, TRINIDAD, VOL. 2
   I/IIC1-Coll

LATWE UTWORY DAWNYCH MISTRZOW
   I/IB2-Coll

LATWE UTWORY DAWNYCH MISTRZOW
   I/IB1-Coll

LAUFET, IHR HIRTEN see
   Weihnachtslieder, 5

LAUFFENSTEINER, WOLFF JACOB
   Duette A-Dur see Sonata in A

   Sonata in A I/IIA1, I/IIB1

LAURA SOAVE see Caroso, Fabrizio

LAURENT, LEO
   Accompagnement A La Guitare, L', Mis
     A La Portee De Tous II

   Classic Guitar Etudes see Ecole Du
     Jeune Guitariste, L'

   Ecole Du Jeune Guitariste, L' III

LAURO, ANTONIO (1917-   )
   Angostura, Valse Venezolano I/IB4

   Carora, Valse Venezolano I/IB4

   Marabino, El, Valse Venezolano I/IB4

   Maria Luise, Valse Venezolano I/IB4

   Suite Venezolana I/IB4

   Valses Venezolanos, 4 I/IB4

   Variations On A Venezolean Children's
     Song I/IB4

   Venezuelan Waltz, Valse Criollo
     I/IB4

LAURO, AUGUSTIN
   Pavan see Venezuelan Pieces, 2

   Valse Criolo see Venezuelan Pieces,
     2

   Venezuelan Pieces, 2 I/IB5

LAUTEN-SUITE NR. I E-MOLL see Bach,
   Johann Sebastian, Suite for Lute,
   BWV 996, in E minor

LAUTEN-SUITE NR. II A-MOLL see Bach,
   Johann Sebastian, Partita for Lute,
   BWV 997, in C minor

LAUTEN-SUITE NR. III A-MOLL see Bach,
   Johann Sebastian, Suite for Lute,
   BWV 995, in G minor

LAUTEN-SUITE NR. IV E-DUR see Bach,
   Johann Sebastian, Partita for Lute,
   BWV 1006a, in E

LAUTENBUCH VON KRAKAU, DAS see
   Bakfark, Balint (Valentin)

LAUTENBUCH VON LYON, DAS - THE LYONS
   LUTE BOOK, 1553 see Bakfark,
   Balint (Valentin)

LAUTENCHOR I, DER I/IIA3-Coll

LAUTENCHOR II, DER I/IIA2-Coll,
   I/IIA3-Coll, I/IIA4-Coll

LAUTENIST, DER, VOL. 6 I/IB6-Coll

LAUTENKONZERT   see Vivaldi, Antonio,
  Concerto in A

LAUTENLIEDER   see Knab, Armin

LAUTENMUSIK   see Bach, Johann Sebastian

LAUTENMUSIK AUS DER RENAISSANCE, VOL. I
  I/IB1-Coll

LAUTENMUSIK AUS DER RENAISSANCE, VOL.
  II I/IB1-Coll

LAUTENMUSIK DES 17. UND 18.
  JAHRHUNDERTS, VOL. 1 - LUTE MUSIC
  FROM THE 17TH AND 18TH CENTURY,
  VOL. 1 I/IB1-Coll

LAUTENMUSIKANT, DER   I/IIC1-Coll

LAUTENMUSIKANT, DER, VOL. I
  I/IIC1-Coll

LAUTENMUSIKANT, DER, VOL. II
  I/IIC1-Coll

LAUTENMUSIKANT, DER, VOL. III
  I/IIC1-Coll

LAUTENMUSIK   see Bach, Johann Sebastian

LAUTENPRALUDIUM   see Bach, Johann
  Sebastian, Prelude for Lute, BWV
  999, in C minor

LAUTENSCHLAGER, DER   I/IIC1-Coll

LAUTENSCHLAGER, DER, VOLKSLIEDER
  I/IB5-Coll

LAUTENSPIELER, DER, NO. 1   IV/IIC1,
  IV/IIC2

LAUTENSPIELER, DER, NO. 2   I/IB5-Coll,
  I/IIC1-Coll

LAUTENSPIELER, DER, NO. 3   I/IIC1-Coll

LAUTENSPIELER, DER, NO. 5   I/IIC1-Coll

LAUTENSPIELER, DER, NO. 7   I/IIC1-Coll

LAUTENSPIELER, DER, NO. 8   I/IIC1-Coll

LAUTENSPIELER DES XVI. JAHRHUNDERTS
  (LIUTISTI DEL CINQUECENTO)
  I/IB1-Coll, I/IIA1-Coll,
  I/IIA2-Coll, I/IIB1-Coll,
  I/IIC1-Coll

LAUTENSTUCKE, 4   see Neusiedler, Hans

7 LAUTENSTUCKE AUS "MUSICA TEUTSCH",
  1532   see Gerle, Hans

LAUTENSUITE (BWV 995)   see Bach, Johann
  Sebastian, Suite for Lute, BWV 995,
  in G minor

LAUTENSUITE IV   see Bach, Johann
  Sebastian, Partita for Lute, BWV
  1006a, in E

LAUTENSUITE NO. 3   see Bach, Johann
  Sebastian, Suite for Lute, BWV 995,
  in G minor

LAUTENSUITEN; 4 SUITES   see Gaultier,
  Denis (Gaulthier)

LAUTENTANZE DES XVI. JAHRHUNDERTS   see
  Negri, Cesare (il Trombone)

LAUTH, WOLFGANG (1931-   )
  Herr, Gib Uns Frieden V/ii

LAVECHES GALLYERDE   see Musique
  Elisabethaine

LAWES, WILLIAM (1602-1645)
  Suite, MIN 36 I/IIA1

LAZARDE, ROMULO
  Cancion Infantil I/IB5

LAZARO, JOSE
  Sonata No. 3 I/IC

LE ROY, ADRIEN (? -1599)
  Adrian Le Roy: 10 Compositions I/IB1

  Allemand, MIN 262 I/IB1

  Allemand, MIN 263   see Danses De
    Cour, 4

  Branle Gay I/IB1
    see also Danses De Cour, 4

  Branles De Bourgogne, 9 I/IB1

  Danses De Cour, 4 I/IB1

  Fantasy No. 1 I/IB1

LE ROY, ADRIEN (cont'd.)

  Fantasy No. 2 I/IB1

  Gaillarde La Rocca E Il Fuso I/IB1

  J'ai Le Rebours I/IIC1

  Je Ne Suis Moins Aimable I/IIC1

  Laissez La Verte Couleur, Chanson
    I/IIC1

  Mes Peines Et Ennuis, Branle Gay
    I/IIC1

  Paduane   see Danses De Cour, 4

  Passemeze   see Danses De Cour, 4

  Pavane Et Gaillarde I/IB1

  Pavane "Si Ie Me Vois" I/IB1

  Pieces, 3 I/IB1

  4 Pieces Pour Guitare (1552) I/IB1

  Prelude Et Chanson I/IB1

LEARN THE GUITAR BY PLAYING TOGETHER
  see Gitaarles In Groepsverband,
  Vol. III; Gramberg, Jacq, Gitaarles
  In Groepsverband, Vol. I;
  Nijenhuis, Luc, Gitaarles In
  Groepsverband, Vol. II

LEARNING MUSIC THROUGH THE GUITAR, VOL.
  I: AN INTRODUCTION TO FRETBOARD
  HARMONY   see Gavall, John

LEARNING MUSIC THROUGH THE GUITAR, VOL.
  II: FOUR-PART HARMONY   see Gavall,
  John

LEARNING MUSIC THROUGH THE GUITAR, VOL.
  III: CHORD PATTERNS AND FUNCTIONS
  IN MAJOR KEYS   see Gavall, John

LEARNING MUSIC THROUGH THE GUITAR, VOL.
  IV: MINOR KEYS, CHROMATIC CHORDS,
  AND MODULATION   see Gavall, John

LEARNING MUSIC THROUGH THE GUITAR, VOL.
  V: AN INTRODUCTION TO FIGURED BASS
  see Gavall, John

LEARNING THE CLASSIC GUITAR   see
  Vanderhorst, Adrian (Arai)

LEAVE SOMETHING UNEXPLAINED   see Boske,
  Jim Ten

LEBEN IN DIESER ZEIT   see Nick, Edmund

LEBENSREGELN; KATECHISMUS MIT MUSIK
  see Wimberger, Gerhard

12 LECCIONES PROGRESIVAS   see Sor,
  Fernando

LECHNER, KONRAD (1911-   )
  Cantica I V/ii

LECHTHALER, JOSEF (1891-1948)
  Suite, Op. 49, No. 1 I/IIA1

  Variationen-Suite I/IB4

LECLAIR, JEAN MARIE (1697-1764)
  Sarabande Und Tambourin I/IB1

  Sonaten, 3 I/IIA1

LECLERCQ, NORBERT
  Arlequin   see Couleurs, 6

  Couleurs, 6 I/IB4

  Cyclamen   see Couleurs, 6

  Noir   see Couleurs, 6

  Orange   see Couleurs, 6

  Pourpre   see Couleurs, 6

  Turquoise   see Couleurs, 6

LEE, RONNY
  see LEVENTHAL, RONALD

LEEB, HERMANN
  Anfanger-Schule Fur Gitarre II

  Methode Elementaire De Guitare   see
    Anfanger-Schule Fur Gitarre

LEERINK, HANS
  Preludes, 4 I/IB4

LEEUW, REINBERT DE (1938-   )
  Hymns And Chorals, With A Commentary
    On The Music Of Erik Satie V/i

LEEUW, TON DE (1926-   )
  Music For Organ And 12 Players V/i

  Ombres V/i

  Schelp I/IIB2

LEGATO STUDIES   see Nijenhuis, Luc

LEGENDE VOM WEISEN UND ZOLLNER   see
  Schilling, Hans Ludwig

LEGGENDA   see Margola, Franco

LEGGENDA DI OGNUNO, LA; SCENIC MUSIC
  FOR CHORUS AND ORCHESTRA   see
  Sonzogno, Giulio Cesare

LEGGIERO, MOLTO LEGANDO   see Kovats,
  Barna

LEGLEY, VICTOR (1915-   )
  Allegretto Commodo   see Pieces, 5,
    Op. 62

  Allegro Risoluto   see Pieces, 5, Op.
    62

  Andante, Quasi Adagio   see Pieces, 5,
    Op. 62

  Andantino Grazioso   see Pieces, 5,
    Op. 62

  Pieces, 5, Op. 62 I/IB4

  Trio, Op. 55 I/IIB2

  Vivace   see Pieces, 5, Op. 62

LEGNANI, LUIGI (1790-1877)
  Capricci, 6 I/IA

  Capricci, 36 I/IA

  Capricci, 36, Vol. 1, Nos. 1-18   see
    Capricci, 36

  Capricci, 36, Vol. 2, Nos. 19-36   see
    Capricci, 36

  Capricci Scelti, 10 I/IA

  Capriccio I/IB2

  Capriccio in F I/IB2

  Capriccio No. 2 I/IB2

  Introduzione, Tema, Variazioni E
    Finale I/IB2

  Leichte Walzer I/IB2

  Marionette Dance I/IB2

  Pequenos Caprichos, 6   see Capricci,
    6

  Variazioni Sul Duetto "Nel Cor Piu
    Non Mi Sento" Da "La Molinara" Di
    Paisiello I/IB2

LEGNANIANA   see Behrend, Siegfried

LEGRENZI, GIOVANNI (1626-1690)
  Trio Sonata in A minor I/IIB2

LEHMANN, ANDREAS (1930-   )
  Ich Rede Wenn Ich Schweigen Sollte
    V/ii

LEHR- UND SPIELBUCH FUR GITARRE   see
  Scheit, Karl

LEHRGANG DES KUNSTLERISCHEN
  GITARRESPIELS, FUR LEHRZWECKE UND
  ZUM SELBSTUNTERRICHT, VOL. I-A   see
  Albert, Heinrich

LEHRGANG DES KUNSTLERISCHEN
  GITARRESPIELS, FUR LEHRZWECKE UND
  ZUM SELBSTUNTERRICHT, VOL. I-B   see
  Albert, Heinrich

LEHRGANG DES KUNSTLERISCHEN
  GITARRESPIELS, VOL. II   see Albert,
  Heinrich

LEHRGANG DES KUNSTLERISCHEN
  GITARRESPIELS, VOL. III   see
  Albert, Heinrich

LEHRGANG DES KUNSTLERISCHEN
  GITARRESPIELS, VOL. IV   see Albert,
  Heinrich

LEHRGANG DES MODERNEN GITARRESPIELS,
  VOL. A: DAS AKKORDSPIEL   see
  Ritter, Theodor

LEHRGANG DES MODERNEN GITARRESPIELS,
  VOL. B: DAS SOLOSPIEL UND DIE
  LIEDBEGLEITUNG   see Ritter, Theodor

LEHRSTUCKE, 30 see Stingl, Anton

LEHRWERK FUR DIE GITARRE, VOL. I see
Schaller, Erwin

LEHRWERK FUR DIE GITARRE, VOL. II see
Schaller, Erwin

LEHRWERK FUR DIE GITARRE, VOL. III see
Schaller, Erwin

LEHRWERK FUR DIE GITARRE, VOL. IV see
Schaller, Erwin

LEHRWERK FUR DIE GITARRE, VOL. V see
Schaller, Erwin

LEHRWERK FUR GITARRE, VOL. IV see
Schaller, Erwin

LEICHT FLIESEND, NICHT SCHNELL see
Stadlmair, Hans

LEICHT SPIELBARE KLEINIGKEITEN see
Rebay, Ferdinand

LEICHTE ALTE LAUTE- UND
GITARRESTUCKLEIN, 32 I/IB6-Coll

LEICHTE ALTWIENER LANDLER, 24 see
Diabelli, Anton

LEICHTE CAPRICEN, 6 see Carcassi,
Matteo, Caprices, 6

LEICHTE DUETTE, 6 see Weiss, Johann
Adolf

LEICHTE DUETTE, 40 see Kuffner, Joseph

LEICHTE DUETTE FUR ANFANGER see Sor,
Fernando

LEICHTE DUOS see Erste Musizierjahr,
Das, Vol. 1; Kuffner, Joseph

LEICHTE ETUDEN, 2 see Sor, Fernando

LEICHTE ETUDEN, 24 see Giuliani, Mauro

LEICHTE ETUDEN AUS OP. 60, 12 see Sor,
Fernando

LEICHTE FORTSCHREITENDE STUCKE see
Carulli, Ferdinando

LEICHTE FORTSCHREITENDE STUCKE, 6 see
Giuliani, Mauro

LEICHTE GITARREN-DUETTE, 36 see Karl,
Sepp

LEICHTE GITARREN-DUOS, 25 I/IIA1-Coll

LEICHTE LANDLER, 8, 2 VOLS. see
Giuliani, Mauro

LEICHTE NORDISCHE TANZE, 16 see
Giuliani, Mauro

LEICHTE ORIGINALSTUCKE see Hafner,
Kurt

25 LEICHTE SONATINEN see Kuffner,
Joseph

LEICHTE SPIELSTUCKE see Just, Franz

LEICHTE STUCKE, 4 see Dowland, John

LEICHTE STUCKE, 4 I/IIA1-Coll

LEICHTE STUCKE, 6 see Rathgeber,
Valentin

LEICHTE STUCKE, 8 see Handel, George
Frideric

LEICHTE STUCKE, 8 see Fischer, Johann
Caspar Ferdinand

LEICHTE STUCKE, 12 see Carcassi,
Matteo; Stingl, Anton

LEICHTE STUCKE, 34 see Ruch, Hannes

9 LEICHTE STUCKE see Gunsenheimer,
Gustav

12 LEICHTE STUCKE see Matiegka,
Wenzeslaus Thomas

LEICHTE STUCKE ALTER MEISTER
I/IIA2-Coll

LEICHTE STUCKE AUS SHAKESPEARES ZEIT,
VOL. 1 I/IB1-Coll

LEICHTE STUCKE AUS SHAKESPEARES ZEIT,
VOL. 2 I/IB1-Coll

LEICHTE STUCKE FUR GITARRE see
Reinbote, Helmut

LEICHTE STUCKE UND LANDLER, OP. 89 AND
OP. 127 see Diabelli, Anton

LEICHTE TANZE see Kuffner, Joseph

LEICHTE UBUNGEN FUR GITARRE, 24, VOL.
1: STUDIES NO. 1-12 see Sor,
Fernando, Vingt-Quatre Exercices
Tres Faciles

LEICHTE UBUNGEN FUR GITARRE, 24, VOL.
2: STUDIES NO. 13-24 see Sor,
Fernando, Vingt-Quatre Exercices
Tres Faciles

LEICHTE UBUNGEN UND SPIELSTUCKE
I/IB6-Coll

LEICHTE UBUNGSTUCKE, 60 see Kuffner,
Joseph

LEICHTE VARIATIONEN, 6 see Carcassi,
Matteo

LEICHTE VARIATIONEN UBER EIN
OSTERREICHISCHES LIED see
Giuliani, Mauro

LEICHTE VERGNUGLICHE ORIGINALSTUCKE AUS
DEM 18. JAHRHUNDERT I/IB1

LEICHTE VORTRAGSSTUCKE, 5 see
Diabelli, Anton

LEICHTE VORTRAGSSTUCKE, VOL. 1
I/IB6-Coll

LEICHTE VORTRAGSSTUCKE, VOL. 2
I/IB6-Coll

LEICHTE WALZER see Legnani, Luigi

LEICHTE WALZER, 6 see Hulsen, Ernst

LEICHTE WALZER UND ETUDEN see Aguado,
Dionisio

LEICHTE WEIHNACHTSKANTATEN, 10,
WEIHNACHTSMUSIKEN UM LIEDER see
Spitta, Heinrich

LEICHTE ZEITGENOSSISCHE ETUDEN see
Dausend, Gerd-Michael

LEICHTES GITARRESPIEL, 2 VOLS.
I/IB2-Coll

LEICHTES TRIO, OP. 26 see Call,
Leonhard von

LEICHTES ZUSAMMENSPIEL I/IIA1-Coll,
I/IIA2-Coll, I/IIB2-Coll

LEICHTESTEN SOLOSTUCKE BERUHMTER
LAUTEN- UND GITARREMEISTER, DIE
I/IB6-Coll

LEIPZIGER SUITE see Behrend, Siegfried

LEISE FALLT DER SCHNEE, LIEDER ZUR
WEIHNACHTSZEIT IV/I

LEISE KOMMT DIE DUNKLE NACHT see
Rosenstengel, Albrecht, Schlaflied
Fur Juliska

LEISE RIESELT DER SCHNEE IV/I
see also Weihnachtslieder

LEKSAKSTAGET see Neumann, Ulrik

LEKSANDS SKANKLAT I/IIA3

LELLA, DOMENICO DI
Impressione I/IA, I/IB4

Preludi, 6 I/IB4

LELOUP, HILARION
Escales, Acordes Y Ejercicios
Tecnicos Para Guitarra III,
VI-Mixed Coll

Metodo Elemental Para Guitarra,
Preparado Y Digitado De Acuerdo
Con La Verdadera Escuela Moderna
De Tarrega II

LEMELAND, AUBERT (1932-   )
Hommage A Albert Roussel I/IB4

LENTO see Eklund, Hans; Urban, Stepan

LENTO, CON ESPRESSIONE see Wilson,
Thomas

LENTO WITH VARIATION see Balada,
Leonardo

LEOPOLD I, HOLY ROMAN EMPEROR
(1640-1705)
Balletti I/IIB1

Suite, Aus Einer Sammlung Von Tanzen
I/IIB1

LERICH, PIERRE
Chanson Et Pastorale I/IB4

Chateau De Sable see Pieces, 3

Chorinho see Pieces, 3

Hommage A Villa-Lobos I/IB4

Pieces, 3 I/IB4

Prelude Et Fugue, Alla Antiqua I/IB4

Prelude No. 3 I/IB4

Suite Baroque I/IB4

Toccata see Pieces, 3

Waltz I/IB4

LERNE GITARRE, VOL. 1 see Winkelbauer,
Alfred

LESAGE DE RICHEE, PHILIPP FRANZ
(1695- ?)
Bourree see Piccolo Pezzi, 4; 4
Piezas

Gavotte see Piccolo Pezzi, 4; 4
Piezas

Minuet see Piccolo Pezzi, 4; 4
Piezas

Piccolo Pezzi, 4 I/IB1

4 Piezas I/IB1

Saraband see Piccolo Pezzi, 4; 4
Piezas

LESSON see Elizabethan Duets, 6

LESSONS, 8 see Aguado, Dionisio

LESSONS FOR CLASSIC GUITAR, VOL. I:
FIRST LESSONS FOR CLASSIC GUITAR
see Pick, Richard Samuel Burns

LESSONS FOR CLASSIC GUITAR, VOL. II:
LESSONS FOR CLASSIC GUITAR see
Pick, Richard Samuel Burns

LESSONS FOR THE GUITAR, VOL. 1, THE
FIRST LESSONS see Sagreras, Julio
S.

LESSONS FOR THE GUITAR, VOL. 2, THE
SECOND LESSONS see Sagreras, Julio
S.

LESSONS FOR THE GUITAR, VOL.3, THE
THIRD LESSONS see Sagreras, Julio
S.

LESSONS FOR THE GUITAR, VOL. 4, THE
FOURTH LESSONS see Sagreras, Julio
S.

LESSONS FOR THE GUITAR, VOL. 5, THE
FIFTH LESSONS see Sagreras, Julio
S.

LESSONS FOR THE GUITAR, VOL. 6, THE
SIXTH LESSONS see Sagreras, Julio
S.

LESUR, DANIEL (1908-   )
Elegy I/IIA1

LET ME TEACH YOU PLAY THE GUITAR II

LET US HAVE CHRISTMAS MUSIC IV/I

LETELIER VALDEZ, MIGUEL FRANCISCO
(1939-   )
Preludios Breves, 7 I/IB4

LET'S TAKE THE FLIP SIDE see Hartog,
Cees

LEUKAUF, ROBERT (1902-   )
Altspanische Suite I/IIB1

LEVANDE BARN see Galen Man

LEVANTA, PASCUAL see Encina, Juan del

LEVAYSME AMOR D'AQUESTA TERRA see
Milan, Luis

LEVENTHAL, RONALD (1927-   )
Flamenco Guitar Method, A Basic
Course In Flamenco Guitar
Technique II

LEVINE, M.
Humoresque I/IIA1

LEVY, MOSHE
Twenty-Four Guitar Pieces (In All
Keys) I/IB4

LOSY VOM LOSINTHAL, JAN ANTONIN
    (1643-1721)
    Ausgewahlte Leichte Stucke I/IB1

    Invenciones, 3 I/IB1

    Partita in A minor I/IB1

    Partita in A minor, MIN 12 I/IB1

    Partita in A minor, MIN 13 I/IB1

    Partita in C I/IB1

    Partita in D I/IB1

    Pieces De Guitare I/IB1-Coll

    Suite in A minor I/IB1

    Suite No. 1 I/IB1

    Suite No. 3 I/IB1

LOTTI, ANTONIO (1667-1740)
    Sonata, MIN 54 I/IIB2

LOUIS XIII, KING OF FRANCE (1601-1643)
    Air Ancien (Amaryllis) see Amaryllis

    Amaryllis I/IB1

LOURE AND SARABANDE see Bach, Johann
    Sebastian

LOURE AUS DER SUITE IN C-DUR see Bach,
    Johann Sebastian, Suite for
    Violoncello, BWV 1009, in C,
    Bourree I-II

LOVE SONGS see Huzella, Elek, 4
    Viragenek

LOVE WALTZ see Neumann, Ulrik

LUBACH, ANDRIES A.
    Dances, 2 I/IB4

    Fughetta see Dances, 2

    Liza see Dances, 2

LUCKY, STEPAN (1919-)
    Duo Concertante I/IIB1

    Duo Concertanti I/IIB1

LUDWIG, JOACHIM
    Mutation, For Big Band And
        Harpsichord Obbligato V/i

LUENING, OTTO (1900-)
    Fantasias I-III I/IB4

LUITSPELER, DE, HOMMAGE A FRANS HALS
    see Visser, Dick

LULLABY see Farquhar, David

LULLY, JEAN-BAPTISTE (LULLI)
    (1632-1687)
    Acht Ausgewahlte Stucke I/IB1

    Air No. 1 I/IB1

    Air Tendre see Album

    Album I/IB1

    Allemand I/IB1

    Celebre Gavota I/IB1

    Courante see Album

    Gavotte I/IB1

    Gavotte, MIN 359 I/IB1

    Minuet, MIN 37 I/IIA1

    Minuet, MIN 264 I/IB1

    Minuet, MIN 332 I/IB1

    Tanze, 4 I/IIB2

    Trios, 13 I/IB1

LUMBY, HERBERT
    Preludio E Capriccio I/IB4

LUMSDAINE, DAVID (1931-)
    Episodes, For Chamber Orchestra V/i

LUNDIN, BENGT
    Fem Infall, Svit I/IB4

LUPI, ROBERTO (1908-1971)
    Studi Per Un "Homunculus"; 9 Pieces
        For Orchestra V/i

LUSITANO, CONCERTO see Brandao, Jose
    Domingos

LUTE DUETS, 2 see Anonymous

LUTE PIECES see Sweelinck, Jan
    Pieterszoon, Lantdarabok

LUTE PIECES, 2 I/IB1

LUTE PIECES, 6 see Holborne, Antony

LUTE PIECES OF THE RENAISSANCE, 6
    I/IB1-Coll

LUTE RECERCARS I/IB1-Coll

LUTOSLAWSKI, WITOLD (1913-)
    Melodies Populaires, 9 see Melodii
        Ludowych, 9

    Melodii Ludowych, 9 I/IB4

LUTYENS, ELIZABETH (1906-1983)
    Infidelio V/ii

    Nocturnes, 4 I/IIB2

LUTZEMBERGER, CESARE
    Composizioni, 4 I/IB4

    Nocturne see Composizioni, 4

    Prelude in D minor see Composizioni,
        4

    Prelude in G minor see Composizioni,
        4

    Sonata in B minor see Composizioni,
        4

LUZ E SAUDADE, ESTUDO EM TREMOLO see
    Nunes, Milton

LYRIC PIECES, 3 see Grieg, Edvard
    Hagerup

LYRISCHE GESANGE I see Schonbach,
    Dieter

MAASZ, GERHARD (1906-1984)
    Suite I/IB4, I/IIB2

    Zehn Leichte Stucke I/IIA1

MCBRIDE, ROBERT GUYN (1911-)
    Bop Pizzicato V/i

MCCABE, JOHN (1939-)
    Canto I/IB4

MACE, THOMAS (1613?-1709)
    Allemand see Pieces, 5

    Courante see Pieces, 5

    Courante Francaise see Pieces, 5

    Cousin Germain, Le see Pieces, 5

    Minuet, MIN 265 see Pieces, 5

    Pieces, 5 I/IB1

    Prelude I/IIB1

    Suite in D minor I/IB1

    Suite in E minor I/IB1

    4 Suiten I/IB1

MACHA, OTMAR (1922-)
    Variationen Auf Ein Thema Von Jan
        Rychlik Und Uber Seinen Tod V/i

MADCHENTOTENLIEDER see Nilsson, Bo

MADERNA, BRUNO (1920-1973)
    Amanda, For Chamber Orchestra V/i

    Aulodia Per Lothar I/IIB1

    Composizione In Tre Tempi, For
        Orchestra V/i

    Concerto No. 2 for Oboe and Orchestra
        V/i

    Y Despues I/IB4

MADONNA MIA FA, VILLANESCA see
    Pisador, Diego

MADRIGAL SUITE see Dorati, Antal

MADRIGALI, 3 see Monteverdi, Claudio

MADRONOS see Moreno Torroba, Federico

MAES, JEF (1905-)
    Etudes, 2 I/IA

    Nocturne I/IB4

MAESTOSO see Pekiel, Bartlomiej

MAESTRI DEL '500 I/IB1

MAESTRO, EL, VOL. 1: COMPOSIZIONI PER
    SOLA VIHUELA see Milan, Luis

MAESTRO, EL, VOL. 1: OBRAS PARA VIHUELA
    SOLA see Milan, Luis

MAESTRO, EL, VOL. 2: COMPOSIZIZONI PER
    VOCE E VIHUELA see Milan, Luis

MAESTRO, EL, VOL. 2: OBRAS PARA VOZ Y
    VIHUELA see Milan, Luis

MAGANINI, QUINTO (1897-1974)
    Romanesca, La, An Ancient Italian
        Dance Air Of The 16th Century
        I/IIB1

MAGHINI, RUGGERO (1913-1977)
    Umbra I/IB4

MAGIC MIRROR, THE; TELEVISION OPERA IN
    FOURTEEN SCENES see Krenek, Ernst,
    Zauberspiegel, Der; Television
    Opera In Fourteen Scenes

MAGNIFICAT QUARTI TONI, FOR CHORUS AND
    THREE GROUPS OF INSTRUMENTS see
    Des Prez, Josquin

50 MAGYAR NEPDAL I/IB5

MAGYAR ZENE GITARRA A XIX. SZADAD ELSO
    FELEBOL I/IB2-Coll, I/IIB1-Coll,
    I/IIC1-Coll

MAI, CHER MAI, BIENTOT TU SERAS LA...
    see Schumann, Robert (Alexander),
    Mai, Lieber Mai

MAI, LIEBER MAI see Schumann, Robert
    (Alexander)

MAIEN IST KOMMEN, DER, PARAPHRASE UBER
    EINEN ALTEN MAITANZ see Stingl,
    Anton

MAIENZAUBER; STAGE MUSIC TO THE FAIRY
    DRAMA see Skalkottas, Nikos

MAINERIO, GIORGIO
    5 Danze I/IIB1, I/IIB2

MAIRANTS, IVOR
    Drei Rhytmische Tanze Fur Gitarre
        I/IB4

    Flamenco Guitar, A Complete Method
        For Playing Flamenco, Part I:
        [Method] II

    Flamenco Guitar, A Complete Method
        For Playing Flamenco, Part II: 25
        Short Pcs Of Various Rhythms II

    Flamenco Guitar, A Complete Method
        For Playing Flamenco, Part III: 8
        Pcs [Spanish Dances] II

    Part Suite, 6 I/IB4

    Sechs Bagatellen Fur Gitarre I/IB4

    Sechs Progressive Stucke Fur Gitarre
        I/IB4

    Sechs Solos Fur Gitarre I/IB4

    Simplicity Tutor For Spanish Guitar,
        The, In The Tarrega Method II,
        VII-Mixed Coll

    Solos For Classic Guitar, 6 I/IB4

    Suite In Sechs Teile Fur Gitarre
        I/IB4

    Travel-Suite I/IB4

    Visual Aids To Chord Arpeggios III

MAITIA NUN ZIRA I/IIC1-Coll

MAJA DE GOYA, LA, TONADILLA see
    Granados, Enrique

MAJA DOLOROSA, LA, 3 TONADILLAS see
    Granados, Enrique

MAJO, GIULIO DI (1933-)
    Passacaglia Per 7 Strumenti V/i

MAJO DISCRETO, EL, TONADILLA see
    Granados, Enrique

MAJO OLVIDADO, EL, TONADA O CANCION
    see Granados, Enrique

MAJO TIMIDO, EL, TONADILLA see
    Granados, Enrique

MAKEDONIA see Nilovic, Janko

MALAGUENA   see Albeniz, Isaac; Albeniz,
   Isaac, Rumores De La Caleta,
   Malaguena

MALAGUENA FACIL   see Tarrega, Francisco

MALATS, JOACHIN (1872-1912)
   Impresiones De Espana, Danza   I/IB3

   Serenata Andaluza   I/IB3

   Serenata Espanola   I/IB3

MALBROUGH S'EN VA-T-EN GUERRE   see
   Reisebilder Aus Frankreich, 5

MALINCONIA   see Bresgen, Cesar

MALIPIERO, RICCARDO (1914-   )
   Aria Variata Su La Follia   I/IB4

   Ballate, 2   I/IIC1

   In Time Of Daffodils   V/ii

MALLORCA, BARCAROLA   see Albeniz, Isaac

MALLORCA, BARCELONA   see Albeniz, Isaac

MAMA   see Tchaikovsky, Piotr Ilyich

M'AMA MAMMOLA   see Zuccheri, Luciano

MAMANGAKIS, NIKOS (1929-   )
   Penthima   I/IB4

   Trittys   I/IIB4

MANANA DE INVIERNO   see Tchaikovsky,
   Piotr Ilyich, Sick Doll, The

MANANA DE SAN JUAN, LA, ROMANCE VIEJO
   see Pisador, Diego

MANANITAS   see Noad, Frederick M.

MANANITAS, LAS   see Canciones Populares
   Mexicanas, 3

MANDORBUCH 1626   I/IB1

MANEN, JOSE
   Fantasia-Sonata   I/IC

MANIFESTO PER KALINOWSKI   see Bussotti,
   Sylvano, Sette Fogli, 6

MANN IM LEHNSTUHLE, DER   see Hiller,
   Johann Adam

MANNEKE, DAAN (1939-   )
   Qui Iustus Est, Iustificetur Adhuc
   V/ii

MANNLEIN STEHT IM WALDE, EIN, DIE
   SCHONSTEN ALTEN KINDERLIEDER
   I/IIC1-Coll

MANOIR, LE   see Praf, [Fray] Benedicto

MANOLA DEL AVAPIES, TONADILLA   see
   Pujol, Emilio

MANRESAN   see Neumann, Ulrik

MANUAL OF FLAMENCO   see Rightmire,
   Richard W.

MAPEYE, CANTO DI PUERTO RICO   see
   Cordero, Ernesto

MAR-CHAIM, JOSEPH (1940-   )
   Trio   I/IIB2

MARABINO, EL, VALSE VENEZOLANO   see
   Lauro, Antonio

MARAIS, MARIN (1656-1728)
   Rondo   I/IB1

MARCELLO, BENEDETTO (1686-1739)
   Adagio   I/IB1

   Adagio, MIN 38   I/IIA1, I/IIB1

   Allegro   I/IB1

   Sonata in A   I/IB1

   Sonata in C, Op. 2, No. 6   I/IIB1

   Sonata in G   I/IIB1

MARCETTA   see Bartolozzi, Bruno

MARCH OF THE WOODEN SOLDIERS   see
   Tchaikovsky, Piotr Ilyich

MARCHA A LA TURCA   see Mozart, Wolfgang
   Amadeus; Mozart, Wolfgang Amadeus,
   Marcha A La Turca

MARCHA FUNEBRE   see Chopin, Frederic

MARCHA MILITAR   see Schumann, Robert
   (Alexander)

MARCHA NUPCIAL   see Mendelssohn-
   Bartholdy, Felix

MARCHA ORIENTAL   see Granados, Enrique

MARCHE MILITAIRE   see Schumann, Robert
   (Alexander)

MARCHE TURQUE   see Mozart, Wolfgang
   Amadeus

MARCHEN VOM DICKEN FETTEN PFANNEKUCHEN,
   DAS, MUSIK ZU EINEM SCHATTENSPIEL
   see Kukuck, Felicitas

MARCHENERA, LA, PETENERA   see Moreno
   Torroba, Federico

MARCO, TOMAS (1942-   )
   Albayalde   I/IB4

   Concerto   I/IIIA

   Duo Concertante   I/IIA1

   Guadiana   see Concerto

   Miriada   I/IIB1

   Naturaleza Muerto Con Guitarra;
      Homenaje A Pablo Picasso   I/IB4

   Paisaje Grana, Homenaje A J.R.
      Jimenez   I/IB4

MARCY, ROBERT
   File La Laine   I/IIC5

MARE NOSTRUM; ENTDECKUNG, BEFRIEDUNG
   UND KONVERSION DES MITTELMEERRAUMES
   DURCH EINEN STAMM AUS AMAZONIEN
   see Kagel, Mauricio

MARELLA, GIOVANNI BATTISTA
   Gavotta Rondo   see Music For 2
      Guitars

   Minuet   see Music For 2 Guitars

   Minuetto   see Music For 2 Guitars

   Minuetto Con Variazioni   see Music
      For 2 Guitars

   Music For 2 Guitars   I/IIA1

   Suite in A   I/IIA1

MAREZ OYENS, GERRIT DE (1922-   )
   Als De Grote Klokke Luidt   I/IIC5

   Arabine   I/IIC5

   En Mijn Een Been Staat   I/IIC5

MAREZ OYENS, TERA DE (1932-   )
   Kapitein Is Jarig, De, Kinderzangspel
      In 2 Bedrijven   I/IIC5

   Liedje Gezocht, Kinderzangspel In 10
      Taferelen   I/IIC5

   Partita Voor David, Voor Kinderorkest
      I/IIB5

MARGOLA, FRANCO (1908-   )
   Ballade   I/IB4

   Episodi, 4   I/IIB1

   Leggenda   I/IB4

   Nocturne   I/IB4

   Studi Da Concerto, 8   I/IA

MARGOLA, MANUEL
   Choros Brasileira   I/IB4

MARGUERITE, ELLE EST MALADE   see
   Seiber, Matyas Gyorgy

MARI, PIERETTE (1929-   )
   Concerto for Guitar, Strings and
      Percussion   I/IIIA

MARIA DURCH EIN DORNWALD GING   see
   Blok, Coby

MARIA, GAVOTA   see Tarrega, Francisco

MARIA GEHT DURCH BLUTEN   see Pammer,
   Josef

MARIA KLAR   see Krol, Bernhard

MARIA LUISE, VALSE VENEZOLANO   see
   Lauro, Antonio

MARIANNETA   see Chansons Catalanes, 2

MARIE, GABRIEL (1852-1928)
   Cinquantaine, La, Aria Nello Stile
      Antico   I/IB3

MARIENTANZ   see Tanze, 6

MARIETA, MAZURKA   see Tarrega,
   Francisco

MARINI, BIAGIO (ca. 1595-1665)
   Gardana, La   see Sonata

   Sonata   I/IIB1

MARION, ROLF
   Panorama Brasilia   V/i

MARIONAS   see Guerau, Francisco

MARIONETTE DANCE   see Legnani, Luigi

MARIPOSA, LA   see Giuliani, Mauro,
   Papillon, Le; Tarrega, Francisco,
   Study, TI ii- 6, in D

MARIZAPALOS   see Guerau, Francisco;
   Guerau, Francisco; Sanz, Gaspar

MARIZAPALOS, 5 PARTIDAS   see Sanz,
   Gaspar

MARSCH NACH EINER TIROLER MELODIE   see
   Walker, Luise

MARSCHNER, HEINRICH (AUGUST)
   (1795-1861)
   Bagatellen, 12   I/IB2

   Bagatellen, Op. 4, Nos. 6, 8, 10
      I/IB2

MARTEAU SANS MAITRE, LE   see Boulez,
   Pierre

MARTELLI, HENRI (1895-   )
   Provencalische Volkstanze   I/IIB3

MARTIN, FRANK (1890-1974)
   Air   see Pieces Breves, 4

   Comme Une Gigue   see Pieces Breves, 4

   Pieces Breves, 4   I/IB4

   Plaint   see Pieces Breves, 4

   Prelude   see Pieces Breves, 4

MARTIN, GASTON
   Etudes Elementaires Pour Guitare,
      Vol. I: Premiere Position   III

   Etudes Elementaires Pour Guitare,
      Vol. II: Etudes Des Positions Et
      Du Barre A Chaque Position   III

   Etudes Elementaires Pour Guitare,
      Vol. III: Changements De
      Positions   III

MARTINEZ ZARATE, JORGE
   Impromptu No. 1   I/IB4

   Mi Primer Libro De Guitarra   II,
      IV/IIA1, VII-Mixed Coll

MARTINI, MANLIO
   Piccoli Pezzi, 2   I/IB4

MARX, KARL (1897-1985)
   Es Taget Vor Dem Walde, 6 Variationen
      Uber   I/IIA3

   Ihr Kleinen Vogelein, Liedkantate
      I/IIC5

   Juchhe, Der Erste Schnee, Kleine
      Kantate   I/IIC5

   Winter Ist Vergangen, Der,
      Liedkantate   I/IIC5

MARY HAD A BABY, YES LORD   see Sing
   Negro Spirituals

MASALA, ROBERTO (1954-   )
   Studi, 3   I/IA

MASCHERADA   see Canzonen Und Tanze Aus
   Dem XVI. Jahrhundert

MASKEN   see Reiser, Ekkehard

MASON, ROGER
   Fete Des Ours, La   I/IIC5

MASQUE MUSIC   V/i

MASS IN B MINOR: CRUCIFIXUS   see Bach,
   Johann Sebastian

MASSEUS, JAN (1913-   )
   Seven Minutes Organized Sound   I/IIB4

MASSEUS, JAN (cont'd.)

Vreemde Fluitist, De I/IIC5

MASSIS, AMABLE (1893-   )
Duo En Forme De Prelude see Pieces,
2

Fugato Chromatique see Pieces, 2

Pieces, 2 I/IIA1

MASTER KILBY see Britten, [Sir]
Benjamin

MASTER PIPER'S PAVAN see Dowland,
John, Piper's Pavan

MATACHIN see Ruiz de Ribayaz, Lucas;
Sanz, Gaspar; Sanz, Gaspar

MATACHIN, BAILE POPULAR DEL SIGLO XVII
see Sanz, Gaspar

MATELART, JOHANNES
Recercate Concertate, Su La Quarta
Fantasia Di Francesco Da Milano
I/IIA1

MATERIALS FOR STUDYING THE GUITAR see
Sosinski, Kazimierz, Materialy Do
Nauki Gry Na Gitarze

MATERIALY DO NAUKI GRY NA GITARZE see
Sosinski, Kazimierz

MATIEGKA, WENZESLAUS THOMAS (1753-1830)
Andante I/IB2

12 Leichte Stucke I/IB2

Minuet I/IB2

Notturno, Op. 21 I/IIB2

12 Pieces Faciles see 12 Leichte
Stucke

Sechs Variationen I/IB2

Sonata, Op. 16 I/IC

Trio, Op. 26 I/IIB2

Zwei Konzertante Menuette I/IB2

Zwolf Menuette I/IB2

MATINALE, LA see Franse Volksliederen,
3

MATOS RODRIGUEZ, GERARDO H.
Cumparsita, La, Tango I/IB5, I/IIA1

MATTHESON, JOHANN (1681-1764)
Air in B minor I/IIA1

Saraband I/IB1

MAXWELL DAVIES, PETER
see DAVIES, PETER MAXWELL

MAYA see Ohana, Maurice, Si Le Jour
Parait, No. 3

MAYA DE GOYA, LA, TONADILLA see
Granados, Enrique

MAYDAY SPELL; STAGE MUSIC TO THE FAIRY
DRAMA see Skalkottas, Nikos,
Maienzauber; Stage Music To The
Fairy Drama

MAYER, ALOIS
Praktische Und Leichtverstandliche
Schule Zum Selbstunterricht Fur
Die Gitarre, Op. 35 II

MAYO, BUEN MAYO see Schumann, Robert
(Alexander), Mai, Lieber Mai

MAYOS, LOS see Moreno Torroba,
Federico

MAYUZUMI, TOSHIRO (1929-   )
Ectoplasme V/i

Microcosmos V/i

MAZMANIAN, VROUYR
Caprice Flamenco I/IB5

MAZURCA, MODERATO see Sor, Fernando,
Mes Ennuis, Six Bagatelles, Op. 43,
No. 4

MAZURKY, 2 see Tarrega, Francisco

MECANISMO DIDACTICO PARA GUITARRA see
Angel, Miguel

MECCANISMO DELLA CHITARRA, IL, DAL
PRIMO AL DODECIMO CAPOTASTO see
Reinbach, Remo

MEDALLON ANTIGUO, OMAGGIO A PERGOLESI
see Barrios Mangore, Augustin

MEDEK, TILO (1940-   )
Drei Stucke Fur Gitarre I/IB4

MEDIEVAL FRENCH SONGS, 4 see Seiber,
Matyas Gyorgy

MEDIN, NINO
Notturnino E Capriccio I/IB4

MEDINA, EMILIO
Metodo De Guitarra Flamenca, Sus
Antecedentes, Su Escuela, Su
Aprendizaje II

MEDIO, ALONSO
Clifford Essex Spanish Guitar Tutor,
The II, VI-Mixed Coll

MEDITACION see Sor, Fernando

MEDITATIF see Werner, Jean-Jacques

MEDITATION ON A GROUND BASS see
Duarte, John W.

MEESTER, LOUIS DE (1904-   )
Sonata I/IC

MEIER, JOST
Reflets, 3 I/IB4

MEIJER VON BREMEN, ALEXANDER
(1930-   )
Bagatellen I/IIB1

Sonatina No. 1 I/IC

MEIN ERSTES SPIELBUCH, MIT TONIKA UND
DOMINANTE I/IIC1-Coll

MEIN JESU, WAS FUR SEELENWEH see Bach,
Johann Sebastian

MEINE ERSTEN GITARRENSTUCKE, VOL.2:
"MEISTER DES BAROCK" I/IB1-Coll

MEINE ERSTEN GITARRENSTUCKE, VOL.3:
"MEISTER DER RENAISSANCE"
I/IB1-Coll

MEINE ERSTEN GITARRENSTUCKE, VOL. 4:
MEISTER DER ROMANTIK I/IB2-Coll,
I/IB3-Coll

MEINE ERSTEN GITARRENSTUCKE, VOL. I:
MEISTER DER KLASSIK I/IB2-Coll

MEINE KLEINE LIEDER see Dimmler,
Liselotte

MEINE WUNSCHE see Hiller, Johann Adam

MEISSONNIER, J. (1790- ?)
Antologia De La Guitarra, Vol. 1
I/IB2

Siciliano I/IB2

Variationen Uber "Nel Cor Piu Non Mi
Sento" I/IB2

MEISTER DER ALTEREN GITARRISTIK (18.
BIS 19. JAHRHUNDERT) I/IB2-Coll

MEISTER DER BAROKZEIT I/IIB2-Coll,
VII-Mixed Coll

MEISTER DES GITARRENSPIELS, VOL. 1,
LEICHTE STUCKE I/IB6-Coll

MEISTER DES GITARRENSPIELS, VOL. 2,
MITTELSCHWERE STUCKE I/IB6-Coll

MEISTERWERKE FUR ZWEI GITARREN
I/IIA1-Coll

MEL BAY FOLIO OF CLASSIC GUITAR SOLOS,
VOL. 1 I/IB6-Coll, VII-Mixed Coll

MEL BAY FOLIO OF CLASSIC GUITAR SOLOS,
VOL. 2 I/IB6-Coll, IV/I,
VII-Mixed Coll

MEL BAY'S DELUXE ALBUM OF CLASSIC
GUITAR MUSIC I/IB6-Coll,
VI-Mixed Coll, VII-Mixed Coll

MELANCHOLIA see Giuliani, Mauro

MELANCHOLIE see Ambrosius, Hermann

MELANCHOLY GALLIARD see Dowland, John;
Dowland, John

MELANCOLICA see Granados, Enrique,
Danza Espanola, No. 10

MELANCOLIE see Coste, Napoleon;
Mourat, Jean-Maurice

MELANCOLY GALLIARD see Dowland, John

MELCHIOR ET BALTHASAR see Blok, Coby

MELI see Antoniou, Theodore

MELII DA REGGIO, PIETRO PAOLO
(fl. 1614-1616)
Corrente, Detta La Favorita Gonzaga
I/IIA1

Dimi Amore, Passeggiato Dall'autore
I/IB1

Galliard see Pieces, 3, [1616]

Intrada see Pieces, 3, [1616]

Pieces, 3, [1616] I/IB1

Volta Alla Francese see Pieces, 3,
[1616]

MELISMI see Dionisi, Renato

MELLERS, WILFRID HOWARD (1914-   )
Blue Epiphany, A - For J.B. Smith
I/IB4

MELODIA see Moreno Torroba, Federico

MELODIA, LABRADOR ALEGRE see Schumann,
Robert (Alexander)

MELODIA NORVEGA see Grieg, Edvard
Hagerup

MELODIC EXERCISES, 8 see Bobri,
Vladimir

MELODIE see Grieg, Edvard Hagerup;
Muller, Siegfried; Schumann, Robert
(Alexander)

MELODIE, DIE see Apostel, Hans Erich

MELODIE EN POSITIE see Neijboer, Otto
C.

MELODIE MOYENAGEUSE see Barat, Jacques

MELODIE SWOJKIE I/IIA1-Coll

MELODIEN AUS DEM REPERTOIRE VON CARL
MICHAEL BELLMAN see Bellman, Carl
Michael

3 MELODIES NOCTURNES ET UNE ETUDE see
Zani de Ferranti, Marco Aurelio

MELODIES POPULAIRES, 9 see
Lutoslawski, Witold, Melodii
Ludowych, 9

MELODIES POPULAIRES ESPAGNOLES, 4, POUR
LES DEBUTANTS see Lopez, Joaquin

MELODIES POPULAIRES POLONAISES
I/IIB1-Coll, I/IIB2-Coll

MELODII LUDOWYCH, 9 see Lutoslawski,
Witold

MELODISCHE ETUDES, 5 see Helleman,
Joop

MELODISCHE SPIELSTUCKE FUR LEICHTES
LAGENSPIEL see Karl, Sepp

MELODISCHE UND FORTSCHREITENDE ETUDEN,
25 see Carcassi, Matteo,
Melodische Und Progressive Etuden,
25

MELODISCHE UND PROGRESSIVE ETUDEN, 25
see Carcassi, Matteo

MELODISCHE UND PROGRESSIVE ETUDEN, 25,
VOL. 1, NOS. 1-13 see Carcassi,
Matteo, Melodische Und Progressive
Etuden, 25

MELODISCHE UND PROGRESSIVE ETUDEN, 25,
VOL. 2, NOS. 14-25 see Carcassi,
Matteo, Melodische Und Progressive
Etuden, 25

MELODISCHES GITARRENSPIEL, SCHULE FUR
DIE GITARRE ALS SOLOINSTRUMENT UND
FUR DAS ZUSAMMENSPIEL MIT 2 BIS 3
GITARREN see Wolki, Konrad,
Gitarre Zum Lied, Schule Fur Die
Gitarre Als Begleitinstrument, Mit
Einer Akkordlehre Und Mit Hinweisen
Fur Das Begleiten Nach Dem Gehor,
Supplement 1

MELODY see Grieg, Edvard Hagerup,
Melodie

MELODY OF JAPAN BY GUITARS, VOL. I
I/IB5-Coll, I/IIA1-Coll,
I/IIA2-Coll, I/IIA3-Coll

MELODY OF JAPAN BY GUITARS, VOL. II
I/IB5-Coll, I/IIA1-Coll,
I/IIA2-Coll, I/IIA3-Coll

MEMENTO   see Baumann, Herbert; Smith
    Brindle, Reginald

MEMORIAL   see Sacchetti, Arturo

MEMORIAS DE "EL CIMARRON"   see Henze,
    Hans Werner

MEMORIE   see Bartolozzi, Bruno

MENDELSSOHN-BARTHOLDY, FELIX
    (1809-1847)
    Andante Largo, C Major   I/IIA1

    Barcarola Veneziana   see
        Venezianisches Gondellied, Op.19,
        No.6

    Cancion   I/IB2

    Cancion De Primavera   see
        Fruhlingslied

    Canzonetta   I/IB2

    Fruhlingslied   I/IB2

    Gondolera Veneciana, Barcarola   see
        Venezianisches Gondellied, Op.30,
        No.6; Venezianisches Gondellied,
        Op.62, No.5

    Hilandera, La   I/IB2

    Marcha Nupcial   I/IB2

    Romance, MIN 402   I/IB2

    Romance, Op. 38, No. 2   I/IB2

    Romanza Senza Parole   I/IB2

    Romanza Sin Palabras   see Song
        Without Words

    Romanza Sin Palabras No. 20   I/IIA1

    Romanza Sin Palabras No. 25   I/IIA1

    Romanza Sin Palabras, Op.19, No.2
        I/IB2

    Romanza Sin Palabras, Op.19, No.3
        I/IB2

    Romanza Sin Palabras, Op.30, No.3
        I/IB2

    Romanza Sin Palabras, Op. 85, No. 3
        I/IB2

    Romanza Sin Palabras, Op. 102, No. 2
        I/IB2

    Song Without Words   I/IB2

    Venetian Barcarolle   I/IB2

    Venezianisches Gondellied, Op.19,
        No.6   I/IB2

    Venezianisches Gondellied, Op.30,
        No.6   I/IB2

    Venezianisches Gondellied, Op.62,
        No.5   I/IB2

MENGELBERG, MISJA (1935-   )
    Amaga   I/IIA2, I/IIB2

    Met Welbeleefde Groet Van De Kameel,
        For Orchestra   V/i

    Musica Per 17 Strumenti   V/i

MENSCH SEIN IN CHRISTUS; GESANGE ZUR
    EUCHARISTIEFEIER   see Kutzer, Ernst

MENUET, DEUXIEME, DE L'ARLESIENNE   see
    Bizet, Georges

MENUET EN RONDEAU   see Rameau, Jean-
    Philippe

MENUET-TRIO IN G MINOR   see Bach,
    Johann Sebastian

MENUET VIF ET GIGUE   see Campra, Andre

MENUETS, 2   I/IB1
    see also Seixas, (Jose Antonio)
    Carlos de

MENUETS, 2   see Carcassi, Matteo

MENUETS, 2   see Sor, Fernando

MENUETS CELEBRES, 2   see Haydn, [Franz]
    Joseph

MENUETS EN LA, 2   see Sor, Fernando

MENUETT UND GIGUE   see Bach, Johann
    Sebastian

MENUETTBUCH   I/IB6-Coll, VII-Mixed Coll

MENUETTE, 2   see Rebay, Ferdinand;
    Schale, Christian Fr.

MENUETTE, 2   see Sor, Fernando

MENUETTE, 2   see Sor, Fernando

MENUETTE, 2   see Sor, Fernando

MENUETTE, 22   see Haydn, [Franz] Joseph

2 MENUETTE   see Weiss, Sylvius Leopold

MENUETTO AND TRIO   see Weber, Carl
    Maria von

MENUETTO AND VARIATION   see Handel,
    George Frideric

MENUETTO OSTINATO   see Geselbracht,
    Erich

MENUETY - MENUETTE   see Sor, Fernando

MERAN, JOSE
    Hispania, 6 Very Easy Spanish Dances
        I/IB5

MERCHI, GIACOMO
    Caccia   I/IIA1

MERENGUE, BALLO VENEZUELANO   I/IB5

MERENGUE VENEZOLANO   see Riera, Rodrigo

MERINGUE   see Dresens, Guus

MERTZ, JOHANN KASPAR (1806-1856)
    Csardas   I/IB2

    Fingals-Hohle   I/IB2

    Grotte Di Fingal, Le   see Fingals-
        Hohle

    Largo, MIN 367   I/IB2

    Lob Der Thranen   I/IB2

    Nocturnes, 3, Op. 4   I/IB2

    Preghiera   I/IB2

    Russisches Zigeunerlied   I/IB2

    Tarantella   I/IB2

MES ENNUIS, SIX BAGATELLES   see Sor,
    Fernando

MES ENNUIS, SIX BAGATELLES, OP. 43, NO.
    3   see Sor, Fernando

MES ENNUIS, SIX BAGATELLES, OP. 43, NO.
    4   see Sor, Fernando

MES ENNUIS, SIX BAGATELLES, OP. 43, NO.
    5   see Sor, Fernando

MES PEINES ET ENNUIS, BRANLE GAY   see
    Le Roy, Adrien

MES PREMIERS PAS VERS LA GUITARE   see
    Berthelot, T.

MESTRE, EL, MELODIA POPULAR CATALANA
    I/IB5

MESTRES-QUADRENY, JOSEP MARIA
    (1929-   )
    Prelude   I/IB4

MET WELBELEEFDE GROET VAN DE KAMEEL,
    FOR ORCHESTRA   see Mengelberg,
    Misja

MET Z'N TWEEEN, DRIEEN, VIEREN...,
    VOLKSLIEDJES VOOR 2 GITAREN, OOK
    GESCHIKT VOOR DE GROEPSLES   I/IIA1

METAMORFOSEN UND FUGE   see Polaczek,
    Dietmar

METAMORPHOSEN FUR GITARRE   see Hummel,
    Bertold

METATHESIS   see Becker, Gunther

METHOD FOR THE CLASSIC GUITAR   see
    Papas, Sophocles

METHOD FOR THE GUITAR, VOL. I   see
    Ranieri, Silvio

METHOD FOR THE GUITAR, VOL. II   see
    Ranieri, Silvio

[METHOD], VOL. I: METHOD FOR CLASSIC
    GUITAR   see Olcott-Bickford, Vadah

[METHOD], VOL. II: ADVANCED COURSE FOR
    CLASSIC GUITAR   see Olcott-
    Bickford, Vadah

METHODE COMPLETE DE GUITARE   see
    Cottin, A.

METHODE COMPLETE POUR GUITARE   see Sor,
    Fernando, Methode Pour La Guitare
    (Escuela De La Guitarra)

METHODE DE FLAMENCO POUR LA GUITARE
    see Valencia, Jose de

METHODE DE GUITARE   see Aguado,
    Dionisio, Escuela De Guitarra;
    Carulli, Ferdinando; Jonge, Charles
    de, Methode Voor Gitaar; Miranda,
    Basilio

METHODE DE GUITARE CLASSIQUE, PREMIER
    ET DEUXIEME CYCLES   see Sanchez,
    Blas

METHODE DE GUITARE, SUIVI DE 44
    MORCEAUX PROGRESSIFS ET DE 6 ETUDES
    see Carulli, Ferdinando, Methode De
    Guitare

METHODE DE GUITARE, SUIVIE DE 44
    MORCEAUX PROGRESSIFS ET DE SIX
    ETUDES   see Carulli, Ferdinando,
    Methode De Guitare

METHODE ELEMENTAIRE   see Aguado,
    Dionisio, Escuela De Guitarra

METHODE ELEMENTAIRE DE GUITARE   see
    Aubanel, Georges; Leeb, Hermann,
    Anfanger-Schule Fur Gitarre

METHODE ELEMENTAIRE POUR LA GUITARE
    see Cerutti, L.

METHODE POUR GUITARE, VOL. I   see
    Cormont, Jacques

METHODE POUR GUITARE, VOL. II   see
    Cormont, Jacques

METHODE POUR LA GUITARE   see Sor,
    Fernando

METHODE POUR LA GUITARE (ESCUELA DE LA
    GUITARRA)   see Sor, Fernando

METHODE POUR LA GUITARE (METHODE
    COMPLETE POUR GUITARE PAR FERDINAND
    SOR, REVUE ET AUGMENTEE DE NOMBREUX
    EXEMPLES AVEC UNE NOTICE SUR LA
    SEPTIEME CORDE PAR N. COSTE)   see
    Sor, Fernando

METHODE PRATIQUE POUR LA GUITARE   see
    Jonge, Charles de, Praktisch
    Leerboek Voor Gitaar, Vol. I;
    Jonge, Charles de, Praktisch
    Leerboek Voor Gitaar, Vol. II

METHODE VOOR GITAAR   see Cormont,
    Jacques, Methode Pour Guitare, Vol.
    I; Cormont, Jacques, Methode Pour
    Guitare, Vol. II; Jonge, Charles de

METHODISCHES LEHRWERK FUR DIE GITARRE,
    VOL. I: GRUNDBEGRIFFE   see Zykan,
    Otto M.

METHODISCHES LEHRWERK FUR DIE GITARRE,
    VOL. IIA, B: DIE LINKE HAND,
    BEHERRSCHUNG DES GRIFFBRETTES   see
    Zykan, Otto M.

METHODISCHES LEHRWERK FUR DIE GITARRE,
    VOL. III: DIE RECHTE HAND   see
    Zykan, Otto M.

METHODISCHES LEHRWERK FUR DIE GITARRE,
    VOL. IV: DER VORTRAG   see Zykan,
    Otto M.

METODO COMPLETO DE GUITARRA   see
    Aguado, Dionisio, Escuela De
    Guitarra

METODO COMPLETO DE GUITARRA, VOL. I
    see Carulli, Ferdinando, Methode De
    Guitare

METODO COMPLETO DE GUITARRA, VOL. II
    see Carulli, Ferdinando, Methode De
    Guitare

METODO COMPLETO DE GUITARRA, VOL. III
    see Carulli, Ferdinando, Methode De
    Guitare

METODO COMPLETO PARA GUITARRA   see Sor,
    Fernando, Methode Pour La Guitare;
    Sor, Fernando, Methode Pour La
    Guitare (Escuela De La Guitarra)

METODO COMPLETO PARA GUITARRA, VOL. 1
    see Carulli, Ferdinando, Methode De
    Guitare

METODO COMPLETO PARA GUITARRA, VOL. I
    see Carcassi, Matteo, Vollstandige
    Guitarre-Schule

METODO COMPLETO PER CHITARRA see
    Carulli, Ferdinando, Methode De
    Guitare

METODO COMPLETO PER CHITARRA, PART I:
    ELEMENTI PRINCIPALI see Brambilla,
    Giovanni

METODO COMPLETO PER CHITARRA, PART II:
    PERFEZIONAMENTE see Brambilla,
    Giovanni

METODO COMPLETO PER CHITARRA,
    TEORETICO-PRATICO PROGRESSIVO see
    Anzaghi, Luigi Oreste

METODO COMPLETO PER LO STUDIO DELLA
    CHITARRA see Carulli, Ferdinando,
    Methode De Guitare; Ricchi, Modesto

METODO DE GUITARRA see Aguado,
    Dionisio, Escuela De Guitarra;
    Cano, Antonio

METODO DE GUITARRA FLAMENCA, SUS
    ANTECEDENTES, SU ESCUELA, SU
    APRENDIZAJE see Medina, Emilio

METODO DE GUITARRA, PARA ACOMPANAR
    CANCIONES Y RITMOS POPULARES Y
    FOLKLORICOS see Galindo, Patricio

METODO DE GUITARRA, VOL. I see Fortea,
    Daniel

METODO DE GUITARRA, VOL. II see
    Fortea, Daniel

METODO ELEMENTAL PARA GUITARRA,
    PREPARADO Y DIGITADO DE ACUERDO CON
    LA VERDADERA ESCUELA MODERNA DE
    TARREGA see Leloup, Hilarion

METODO GRADUADO PARA APRENDER A TOCAR
    LA GUITARRA see Tarrago, Graciano

METODO MODERNO PARA GUITARRA, VOL. I
    see Gascon, Leon Vicente

METODO MODERNO PARA GUITARRA, VOL. II
    see Gascon, Leon Vicente

METODO MODERNO PARA GUITARRA, VOL. III
    see Gascon, Leon Vicente

METODO MODERNO PER CHITARRA see
    Palladino, Carlo

METODO PARA GUITARRA, EJERCICIOS,
    ESTUDIOS Y ESCALAS DIATONICAS see
    Parras del Moral, J.

METODO PARA GUITARRA, VOL. I see
    Carulli, Ferdinando, Methode De
    Guitare

METODO PARA GUITARRA, VOL. II see
    Carulli, Ferdinando, Methode De
    Guitare

METODO PER CHITARRA see Aguado,
    Dionisio, Escuela De Guitarra;
    Giuliani, Mauro, Studio Per La
    Chitarra

METODO PER CHITARRA, PER I CONSERVATORI
    E I LICEI MUSICALI, VOL. I see
    Gangi, Mario

METODO PER CHITARRA, PER I CONSERVATORI
    E I LICEI MUSICALI, VOL. II see
    Gangi, Mario

METODO PER CHITARRA, VOL. I see
    Carcassi, Matteo, Vollstandige
    Guitarre-Schule

METODO PER CHITARRA, VOL. II see
    Carcassi, Matteo, Vollstandige
    Guitarre-Schule

METODO PER LA RICERCA DEGLI ACCORDI COI
    "RIVELATORI", METODO PRATICO PER IL
    DILETTANTE, PROMEMORIA TASCABILE
    PER IL PROFESSIONISTA, (100 ACCORDI
    CON "BARRE" IN PRIMA POSIZIONE,
    1200 ACCORDI COI "RIVELATORI" see
    Chierici, Fernando

METODO RAZIONALE PER CHITARRA see
    Pujol, Emilio, Escuela De La
    Guitarra, Basada En Los Principios
    De La Technica De Tarrega

METODO TEORICO-PRATICO see Branzoli,
    G.; Castagna, Luciano; Fabbri, Tito

METODO TEORICO-PRATICO, PER LO STUDIO
    DELLA CHITARRA see Lago, Mario

METODO Y EJERCICIOS DE FRANCISCO
    TARREGA see Chacon, Meme

METROPOLITANS, THE; OPERA GIOCOSA IN
    ONE ACT see Vogt, Hans,
    Athenerkomodie; Opera Giocosa In
    One Act

METZNER, LEONHARD
    Sonata I/IIB1

MEUNIER VOYAGEUR, LE see Schubert,
    Franz (Peter)

MI PRIMER LIBRO DE GUITARRA see
    Martinez Zarate, Jorge

MI TIERZUCA see Lopez, Joaquin

MI VIENE INCONTRO IL MARE see
    Bortolami, Galliano

MICHELLE VALSE see Worschech, Romain

MICRO STUDIES see Helleman, Joop

MICROCOSMOS see Mayuzumi, Toshiro

MICROPIEZAS, HOMMAGE A DARIUS MILHAUD
    see Brouwer, Leo

MIDAS; BALLET MUSIC FOR ORCHESTRA see
    Bois, Rob du

MIGNARDA see Dowland, John

MIGNONE, FRANCISCO (1897-   )
    Etudes, 12, Vol.1 I/IA

    Etudes, 12, Vol.2 I/IA

MIGNONNE see Flamme, A.

MIGNOT, PIERRE
    Toccata Fantasque I/IB4

MIGOT, GEORGES (1891-1976)
    Preludes I/IIA1

    Sonata I/IC, I/IIB1

    Sonata, MIN 39 I/IIA1

    Sur Le Nom De Graciela Pomponio see
        Preludes

    Sur Le Nom De Jorge Martinez Zarate
        see Preludes

MIJN EERSTE GITAARSOLI, VOL. I
    I/IB2-Coll

MIJN EERSTE GITAARSOLI, VOL. II
    I/IB2-Coll

MIKROKOSMOS see Schumann, Gerhard

MILAN, LUIS (ca. 1500-ca. 1564)
    Con Pavor Recordo El Moro, Romance
        I/IIC1

    Don Luis Milan I/IB1, I/IIC1

    Fantasia De L'Octavo Tono I/IB1

    Fantasy, MIN 266 I/IB1

    Fantasy, MIN 267 I/IB1

    Fantasy No. 1 I/IB1

    Fantasy No. 4 I/IB1

    Fantasy No. 16 I/IB1

    Fantasy No. 38 I/IB1

    Levaysme Amor d'Aquesta Terra I/IIC1

    Libro De Musica De Vihuela De Mano,
        1535, Part 1: "Fantasien 1-13"
        I/IB1-Coll

    Libro De Musica De Vihuela De Mano,
        1535, Part 2: "Fantasien 14-22"
        I/IB1-Coll

    Libro De Musica De Vihuela De Mano,
        1535, Part 3: "Fantasien 23-33"
        I/IB1-Coll

    Libro De Musica De Vihuela De Mano,
        1535, Part 4: "Tientos 1-4 And
        Fantasien 34-40" I/IB1-Coll

    Maestro, El, Vol. 1: Composizioni Per
        Sola Vihuela I/IB1-Coll

    Maestro, El, Vol. 1: Obras Para
        Vihuela Sola I/IB1, I/IIC1

    Maestro, El, Vol. 2: Composizizoni
        Per Voce E Vihuela I/IB1-Coll

    Maestro, El, Vol. 2: Obras Para Voz Y
        Vihuela I/IB1, I/IIC1

    Pavan No. 1 I/IB1

    Pavan No. 2 I/IB1

MILAN, LUIS (cont'd.)

    Pavan No. 3 I/IB1

    Pavan No. 4 I/IB1

    Pavan No. 5 I/IB1

    Pavan No. 6 I/IB1

    Pavan Nos. 1-6 I/IB1

    Pavan Nos. 5-6 I/IB1

    Pavanas I/IB1

    Pavanas, 6, And A Fantasia I/IB1

    Pavanen, 2 I/IB1

    Pavans, 3, In D I/IB1

    6 Pavans And 3 Fantasias I/IB1-Coll

    Pavany, 2 I/IB1

    Perdida Tengo La Color I/IIC1

    Tientos Del Septimo Y Octavo Tono
        I/IB1

    Tientos Del Tercero Y Cuarto Tono
        I/IB1

    Toda Mi Vida Os Ame I/IIC1

    Toute Ma Vie Je Vous Ai Aimee see
        Toda Mi Vida Os Ame

MILAN-SUITE, ON A THEME OF DON LUIS
    MILAN (1535) see Komter, Jan
    Maarten

MILANO, FRANCESCO DA
    see FRANCESCO DA MILANO

MILETIC, MIROSLAV (1925-   )
    Kroatische Suite, Nach Volksweisen
        Aus Medjimurje I/IB5

MILHAUD, DARIUS (1892-1974)
    Segoviana I/IB4

MILLE, JO
    Kleine Gemakkelijke Gids Voor
        Gitaarbegeleiding see Petit
        Guide Facile d'Accompagnement A
        La Guitare

    Petit Guide Facile d'Accompagnement A
        La Guitare II

MILLE REGRES see Heckel, Wolf

MILLE REGRETZ see Des Prez, Josquin

MILLER, JOHN R.
    Solo-Gitarre, Die, Vol. II I/IB4,
        I/IB6-Coll

MILLER'S DANCE, THE see Falla, Manuel
    de

MILLOCKER, KARL (1842-1899)
    Diana; Comic Opera In Three Acts
        V/iii

MILONGUEOS see Broqua, Alfonso,
    Evocaciones Criollas, No.5

MILONI, PIETRO
    Passacagli; Folia; Pavaniglia;
        Gagliarda; Etc. I/IB1

MIMESIS see Terpstra, Koos

MINELLA, ALDO
    Moderne Technik Der "Appoggiatura"
        Und Des Tonleiterspiels, Die III

    Scale Diatoniche III

MINI STUDIES see Helleman, Joop

MINIATURE SLAVE, 10 I/IB4-Coll

MINIATURE SUITE see Bredenbeek, Hans;
    Duarte, John W.

MINIATURE VARIATIONS see
    Vandermaesbrugge, Max

MINIATUREN, 4 see Werdin, Eberhard

MINIATUREN, 5 see Wagner-Regeny,
    Rudolf; Weber, Reinhold

MINIATUREN, 10 KLEINE STUCKE see
    Walker, Luise

MINIATURES see Urban, Stepan

MINIATURES, 4 see Zbinden, Julien-
    Francois

MINIATURES IBERIQUES, 5 see Azpiazu, Jose de

MINIATURPROBLEMATICOS see Pilsl, F.

MINIMES, 6 see Herrera, Ramon de

MINIVALSES, 4 see Sanchez, B.

MINSTRELS see Debussy, Claude; Debussy, Claude

MINUE see Scarlatti, Domenico, Sonata, Kirkpatrick 440; Sor, Fernando, Sonata, Op. 25, Minuet

MINUE CELEBRE see Paderewski, Ignace Jan

MINUE Y MARCHA see Bach, Johann Sebastian

MINUET AND WALTZ see Aguado, Dionisio

MINUET DE LA COUR see Giuliani, Mauro

MINUET FOR DIDA see Paganini, Niccolo

MINUET, MIN 18 see Danses, 4

MINUETO A SYLVIA see Albeniz, Isaac

MINUETO-BOLERO see Boccherini, Luigi

MINUETO DE DON JUAN see Mozart, Wolfgang Amadeus

MINUETO DEL BUEY see Haydn, [Franz] Joseph

MINUETO DEL CUARTETO EN RE see Mozart, Wolfgang Amadeus

MINUETO EN DO MAYOR see Sor, Fernando, Sonata, Op. 22, Minuet

MINUETO ESPANOL see Boccherini, Luigi

MINUETOS, 2 see Sor, Fernando

MINUETOS, 2 see Sor, Fernando

MINUETOS, 3 see Sor, Fernando

MINUETOS, 4 see Sor, Fernando

MINUETOS, 40 see Sor, Fernando

2 MINUETOS Y 2 ESTUDIOS see Aguado, Dionisio

7 MINUETOS see Beethoven, Ludwig van

MINUETOS EN LA, 2 see Sor, Fernando

MINUETOS EN MI, 2 see Sor, Fernando

MINUETOS EN RE, 2 see Sor, Fernando

MINUETOS EN SOL, 2 see Sor, Fernando

MINUETOS EN SOL-RE, 2 see Sor, Fernando

MINUETOS PARA GUITARRA, 34 see Sor, Fernando

6 MINUETOS see Aguado, Dionisio

MINUETTE, 2 see Wanhal, Johann Baptist (Jan Krtitel)

MINUETTI, 2 see Rameau, Jean-Philippe

MINUETTI, 6 see Rameau, Jean-Philippe

MINUETTINO NO. 23 see Paganini, Niccolo

MINUETTO see Aguado, Dionisio; Boccherini, Luigi, Minuet; Corelli, Arcangelo; Marella, Giovanni Battista

MINUETTO CON VARIAZIONI see Marella, Giovanni Battista

MINUETTO, DA PLATEE see Rameau, Jean-Philippe

MINUETTO, MIN 400 see Haydn, [Franz] Joseph

MINUETTO, MIN 401 see Haydn, [Franz] Joseph

MINUETTOS EN LA MAYOR, 2 see Sor, Fernando

MINUETTOS EN MI MAYOR, 2 see Sor, Fernando

MINUTENSTUCKE see Kovats, Barna

MINUTES, 5 see Westra, Jan

MIR NERO DE TARPEYA, ROMANCE VIEJO see Bermudo, [Fray] Juan

MIRAGE see Rosetta, Giuseppe

MIRANDA, BASILIO
Methode De Guitare II

MIRAR DE LA MAJA, EL, TONADILLA see Granados, Enrique

MIRIADA see Marco, Tomas

MIROGLIO, FRANCIS (1924-)
Choreiques I/IB4

Elans see Choreiques

Feu see Choreiques

Geste Dansee see Choreiques

Tremplins V/ii

Voiles d'Irisations see Choreiques

MISSA IN BEAT see Nardelli, Rudolf

MISSA MARIA ZART see Obrecht, Jacob

MISSA PROFANA see Zimmermann, Heinz Werner

MR. HENRY NOEL HIS GALLIARD see Dowland, John

MR. SOUTHCOTE'S GALLIARD see Holborne, Antony

MRS. ANNE HARECOURT'S GALLIARD see Pilkington, Francis

MRS. VAUX'S JIG see Dowland, John; Dowland, John

MISTRI BAROKA I/IIA1-Coll

MIT DER GITARRE, UNTERHALTUNGS-ALBUM I/IB6-Coll, I/IIA1-Coll, I/IIC1-Coll

MIT EINEM GEWISSEN SPRECHENDEN AUSDRUCK, FOR CHAMBER ORCHESTRA see Bussotti, Sylvano

MIT GOTT SO WOLLEN WIR LOBN UND EHRN; 3 KONIG VON SABA KOMMEN (NO. 7) see Spitta, Heinrich

MITTELALTERLICHE TANZE I/IB1

MITTELSCHWERE ETUDEN (INTERMEDIATE STUDIES) see Sor, Fernando

MITTELSCHWERE UND SCHWERE ETUDEN AUS OP. 6, 29 UND 31, 16 see Sor, Fernando

MITTERGRADNEGGER, GUNTER (1923-)
Heiteres Herbarium I/IIC1

MIYAKE, HARUNA
Musik Fur Piccoloflofen, Floten Und Gitarre I/IIB2

MOBILE see Norman, Theodore

MOBILE-STABILE see Bussotti, Sylvano, Sette Fogli, 5

MODERATO see Carulli, Ferdinando; Mosso, Carlo; Rodrigo, Joaquin

MODERATO, MIN145 see Abloniz, Miguel

MODERATO, MIN146 see Abloniz, Miguel

MODERATO, MIN147 see Abloniz, Miguel

MODERATO, MIN158 see Bellow, Alexander

MODERATO, MIN159 see Bellow, Alexander

MODERATO, POCO RUBATO see Wilson, Thomas

MODERATO, UN POCO AGITATO see Kovats, Barna

MODERN APPROACH TO THE GUITAR, A, BASED ON THE PRINCIPLES OF EMILIO PUJOL, VOL. I see Topper, Guido

MODERN APPROACH TO THE GUITAR, A, BASED ON THE PRINCIPLES OF EMILIO PUJOL, VOL. II see Topper, Guido

MODERN APPROACH TO THE GUITAR, A, BASED ON THE PRINCIPLES OF EMILIO PUJOL, VOL. III see Topper, Guido

MODERN APPROACH TO THE GUITAR, A, BASED ON THE PRINCIPLES OF EMILIO PUJOL, VOL. IV see Topper, Guido

MODERN APPROACH TO THE GUITAR, A, BASED ON THE PRINCIPLES OF EMILIO PUJOL, VOL. V see Topper, Guido

MODERN GUITAR MUSIC I/IB4-Coll

MODERN METHOD FOR THE GUITAR, A, VOL. 1, SCHOOL OF TARREGA see Roch, Pascual

MODERN METHOD FOR THE GUITAR, A, VOL. II, SCHOOL OF TARREGA see Roch, Pascual

MODERN METHOD FOR THE GUITAR, A, VOL. III, SCHOOL OF TARREGA see Roch, Pascual

MODERN MINIATURES, 3 see Duarte, John W.

MODERN PRELUDES, 6 see Holder, Derwyn

MODERNE HANDLEIDING VOOR HET KLASSIEKE GITAARSPEL, VOL. I see Moorst, Pablo van

MODERNE HANDLEIDING VOOR HET KLASSIEKE GITAARSPEL, VOL. II see Moorst, Pablo van

MODERNE HANDLEIDING VOOR HET KLASSIEKE GITAARSPEL, VOL. III see Moorst, Pablo van

MODERNE TANZE, 2 see Schaaf, Peter

MODERNE TECHNIK DER "APPOGGIATURA" UND DES TONLEITERSPIELS, DIE see Minella, Aldo

MODINHA see Bosmans, Arthur, Brasileiras, No.2

MOERENS INCEDEBAM, MATTUTINO see Ciurlo, Ernesto Fausto

MOEVS, ROBERT WALTER (1921-)
Brief Mass, A V/ii

MOHINO, GONZALEZ
Aankomende Gitarist, De, Audio-Visuele Methode Met Grammofoonplaat see Guitariste En Herbe, Le, Methode Audio-Visuelle Avec Disque

Guitariste En Herbe, Le, Methode Audio-Visuelle Avec Disque II

MOHLER, PHILIPP (1908-1982)
Shakespeare-Suite; Dances By Contemporaries Of William Shakespeare V/i

MOIROLOGHIA FOR JANI CHRISTOU see Antoniou, Theodore

MOLINARO, SIMONE
Ballo Detto "Il Conte Orlando" see Pezzi, 3

Galliard see Pezzi, 3

Intavolatura Di Liuto, Libro Primo (1599) I/IB1-Coll

Pezzi, 3 I/IB1

Saltarello see Pezzi, 3

Saltarello Quarto I/IB1

MOLINERA see Moreno Torroba, Federico

MOLINILLO QUE MUELES AMORES see Canciones Del Siglo XVII, 5

MOLINO, FRANCESCO (1775-1847)
Nocturne No. 2, Op. 38 I/IIB1

Nocturne, Op. 37 I/IIB1

Praludien, 18 I/IA

Rondo, MIN 125 I/IB2

Rondo, MIN 126 I/IB2

Sonaten, 3 I/IC

Trio, Op. 45 I/IIB2

MOLITOR, SIMON
Sonata, Op. 11 I/IC

MOMENT MUSICAL see Schubert, Franz (Peter)

MOMENTO MUSICAL see Schubert, Franz (Peter)

MOMENTO MUSICAL, OP. 94, NO. 3 see Schubert, Franz (Peter), Moments Musicaux, Op. 94, No. 3, D.780, No.3

MOMENTO MUSICALE see Schubert, Franz (Peter)

MOMENTOS I see Nobre, Marlos

MOMENTS MUSICAUX, OP. 94, NO. 3, D.780, NO.3 see Schubert, Franz (Peter)

MOMOTARO, PFIRSICHKNABE see Vier Japanische Volkslieder

MOMPOU, FEDERICO (1893-   )
Barca, La I/IB4

  Cancion Y Danza No. 1 I/IB4

  Suite Compostellana I/IB4

MONDE DES FLOUS, LE see Furstenau, Wolfram

MONFERRINE, 12 see Giuliani, Mauro

MONGE, VICTOR ("SERRANITO")
Planta Y Tacon, Zapateado I/IB5

MONKEMEYER, HELMUT
Schaff's Mit Mir, Gott see Wir Spielen Gitarre, Ein Spiel- Und Ubungsbuch

  Suite for Lute, BWV 996, in E minor, Bourree see Wir Spielen Gitarre, Ein Spiel- Und Ubungsbuch

  Vergiss Mein Nicht see Wir Spielen Gitarre, Ein Spiel- Und Ubungsbuch

  Wir Spielen Gitarre, Ein Spiel- Und Ubungsbuch II, VII-Mixed Coll

MONODIEN, 6 see Behrend, Siegfried

MONOLOGE, 4 SYMPHONIC PIECES FOR FULL ORCHESTRA see Vogt, Hans

MONOLOGO see Kalmar, Laszlo

MONOPHONIE FUR GITARRE see Braun, Pee Michael

MONTEVERDI, CLAUDIO (ca. 1567-1643)
Ballo V/i

  Bei Legami, I see Scherzi, 3

  Canzonetta D'amore see Canzoni, 3

  Canzonette A Tre Voci, 3 I/IIC3

  Canzonette d'Amore see Canzonette Strumentali A Tre Voci

  Canzonette Strumentali A Tre Voci I/IIB3

  Canzoni, 3 I/IIA2

  Chi Vuch Veder see Canzoni, 3

  Chi Vuol Veder d'Inverno see Canzonette Strumentali A Tre Voci

  Chi Vuol Veder Un Bosco see Canzonette A Tre Voci, 3

  Concerto De Madrigali V/ii

  Fiera Vista, La see Canzonette A Tre Voci, 3; Canzonette Strumentali A Tre Voci

  Giovinetta Ritrossetta see Scherzi, 3

  Gual Si Puo Dir Maggiore see Canzonette Strumentali A Tre Voci

  Incoronazione Di Poppea, L'; Opera In Three Acts And A Prologue V/iii

  Kronung Der Poppea, Die; Opera In Three Acts see Incoronazione Di Poppea, L'; Opera In Three Acts And A Prologue

  Madrigali, 3 I/IIC1

  Non Cosi see Scherzi, 3

  Orfeo; Favola In Musica In Five Acts With A Prologue V/iii

  Orfeo; Favola Pastorale In Two Parts see Orfeo; Favola In Musica In Five Acts With A Prologue

  Orfeo; Opera In Five Acts see Orfeo; Favola In Musica In Five Acts With A Prologue

  Orfeo: Vieni Imeneo V/ii

MONTEVERDI, CLAUDIO (cont'd.)
  Quando Sperai see Canzoni, 3

  Ritorno d'Ulisse In Patria, Il; Opera In Two Acts With A Prologue V/iii

  Scherzi, 3 I/IIA2

  Scherzi Musicali, Cioe Arie, Et Madrigali In Stile Recitativo I/IIC1

  Tirsi E Clori V/ii

  Tre Scherzi Musicali A Tre Voci V/ii

  Vita De l'Alma Mia see Canzonette A Tre Voci, 3; Canzonette Strumentali A Tre Voci

MONZA, CARLO (ca. 1740-1801)
Sonate, MIN391 I/IIB1

  Sonate, MIN392 I/IIB1

MOODS FROM THE SONG OF SOLOMON, 3 see Staak, Pieter van der

MOODS, JAZZ IN BOSSA NOVA see Abloniz, Miguel

MOONLIGHT SONATA see Beethoven, Ludwig van, Sonata, Op. 27, No. 2

MOORST, PABLO VAN
Groepsles Voor Gitaar II

  Moderne Handleiding Voor Het Klassieke Gitaarspel, Vol. I II

  Moderne Handleiding Voor Het Klassieke Gitaarspel, Vol. II II, VI-Mixed Coll

  Moderne Handleiding Voor Het Klassieke Gitaarspel, Vol. III II, VI-Mixed Coll, VII-Mixed Coll

MORALES, CRISTOBAL DE (ca. 1500-1553)
De Antequera Sale El Moro, Romance Viejo I/IIC1

MORANCON, GUY (1927-   )
Petit Livre I/IB4

  Suite Latine I/IB4

MORCEAU DE CONCERT see Sor, Fernando

MORCEAUX, 5 see Frescobaldi, Girolamo

MORCEAUX CHOISIS, 15 see Mornac, Juan

MORCEAUX ESPAGNOLS, 3 see Pujol, Emilio

MORE CLASSIC GUITAR DUETS WITH RODRIGO RIERA I/IIA1

MORE OF THESE ANON; 10 ANONYMOUS PIECES see Anonymous

MORENO TORROBA, FEDERICO (1891-1982)
Aire De La Manche I/IB4

  Albada see Pieces Caracteristiques, Vol. 2

  Bolero I/IB4

  Burgalesa I/IB4

  Canciones Espanolas, 7 I/IIC1

  Capriccio I/IIA1

  Concierto De Castilla I/IIIA

  Contradanza I/IB4

  Homenaje A La Seguidilla, Concerto I/IIIA

  Jota Levantina I/IB4

  Madronos I/IB4

  Marchenera, La, Petenera I/IIC1

  Mayos, Los see Pieces Caracteristiques, Vol. 2

  Melodia see Pieces Caracteristiques, Vol. 1

  Molinera I/IB4

  Nocturne I/IB4

  Oliveras see Pieces Caracteristiques, Vol. 1

MORENO TORROBA, FEDERICO (cont'd.)
  Panorama see Pieces Caracteristiques, Vol. 2

  Pieces Caracteristiques, Vol. 1 I/IB4

  Pieces Caracteristiques, Vol. 2 I/IB4

  Preambulo see Pieces Caracteristiques, Vol. 1

  Prelude I/IB4, I/IIA1

  Punteado Taconeo Clasico I/IB4

  Serenata Burlesca I/IB4

  Sonatina I/IC

  Sonatina In La (Primo Tempo) see Sonatina

  Stucke, 5 I/IB4

  Suite Castellana I/IB4

  Suite Miniatura I/IB4

MORETTI, FEDERICO
Doce Canciones I/IIC1

MORETTI, LUIGI
Andante I/IB2

MORGEN KOMMT DER WEIHNACHTSMANN see Du Und Ich Wir Spielen Gitarre, Ein Lieblingsbuch Fur Angehende Gitarristen

MORGEN- UND ABENDLIEDER I/IIC1-Coll, I/IIC2-Coll, VII-Mixed Coll

MORGENROTE UBER GRANADA see Wolf, Roland

MORI, AUGUSTO CESARE DE
Souvenir d'Espagne I/IB4

MORITAT VOM EIGENSINNIGEN EHEWEIBE, DIE see Baumann, Herbert

MORLEY, THOMAS (1557-1602)
Allemand see 5 Danses (1551)

  Bransle, MIN416 see 5 Danses (1551)

  Bransle, MIN417 see 5 Danses (1551)

  Canzonetta I I/IB1

  Canzonetta II I/IB1

  5 Danses (1551) I/IB1

  Nancie I/IB1

  Pavan I/IB1

  Villanesque see 5 Danses (1551)

MORNAC, JUAN (1897-   )
Guitare Pour Tous, La, Methode Rationelle Et Rapide De Guitare Classique Avec De Nombreuses Recreations II, VII-Mixed Coll

  Minuet in G see Guitare Pour Tous, La, Methode Rationelle Et Rapide De Guitare Classique Avec De Nombreuses Recreations

  Morceaux Choisis, 15 I/IB4

  Sonata for Flute, BWV 1013, in A minor, Allemand see Guitare Pour Tous, La, Methode Rationelle Et Rapide De Guitare Classique Avec De Nombreuses Recreations

  Suite No. 2 For Orchestra In B Minor: Rondeau see Guitare Pour Tous, La, Methode Rationelle Et Rapide De Guitare Classique Avec De Nombreuses Recreations

  Suite No. 3 for Violoncello in C, Loure see Guitare Pour Tous, La, Methode Rationelle Et Rapide De Guitare Classique Avec De Nombreuses Recreations

MORNING PRAYER see Tchaikovsky, Piotr Ilyich

MORT D'ASS, LA see Grieg, Edvard Hagerup, Aase's Death

MORTARI, VIRGILIO (1902-   )
Omaggio Ad Andres Segovia I/IB4

MORTE DI DON GIOVANNI, LA: 3 FRAMMENTI SINFONICI, FOR ORCHESTRA see Palester, Roman

MUDARRA, ALONSO DE (cont'd.)

Isabel, Perdiste La Tu Faxa I/IIC1

Keuze Uit [Selection From] Tres
    Libros De Musica En Cifra I/IB1

O Guardame Las Vacas see Romanesca I

Pavan I/IB1

Romanesca I I/IB1

Romanesca II I/IB1

Tiento VII, VIII I/IB1

Tres Libros De Musica: Ausgewahlte
    Werke I/IB1-Coll

Tres Libros De Musica En Cifra Para
    Vihuela I/IB1, I/IIC1

Triste Estaba El Rey David I/IIC1

MUERTE DE ASE, LA see Grieg, Edvard
    Hagerup, Aase's Death

MUFFAT, GEORG (ca. 1645-1704)
    Minuet, MIN 376 I/IB1

Passacaglia I/IB1

MUGGENDANS see Gramberg, Jacq

MUHE, HANSGEORG
    Wir Wandern Ohne Sorgen I/IIB5

MULETIER DES ANDES, LE see Tomasi,
    Henri

MULLER, FRIEDRICH EWALD (1934-   )
    Theme and Variations I/IIB2

MULLER, SIEGFRIED (1926-   )
    Chromatik see Stucke Fur Gitarre, 5

Concertino I/IIA2

Improvisation see Stucke Fur
    Gitarre, 5

Melodie see Stucke Fur Gitarre, 5

Prelude see Stucke Fur Gitarre, 5

Sonata I/IC

Stucke Fur Gitarre, 5 I/IB4

Toccata see Stucke Fur Gitarre, 5

MULLER-CANT, MANFRED (1926-   )
    Kinderlieder-Suite Fur Einen
    Grossvater I/IIB1

MULLER-ILMENAU, WILHELM (1911-   )
    Andante see Spielmusik

Minuet in A see Spielmusik

Minuet in G see Spielmusik

Rondo in E minor see Spielmusik

Spielmusik I/IIB1

MULLER-MEDEK, TILO
    see MEDEK, TILO

MULLERIN VON GRANADA, DIE; OPERETTA IN
    THREE ACTS AND FIVE SCENES see
    Kalas, Julius

MUNCH, WILLI
    Wir Lernen Gitarre Spielen,
    Grundschule Fur Den Einzel- Und
    Gruppenunterricht, Suppl. 1 II

Wir Lernen Gitarre Spielen,
    Grundschule Fur Den Einzel- Und
    Gruppenunterricht, Suppl. 2 II

Wir Lernen Gitarre Spielen,
    Grundschule Fur Den Einzel- Und
    Gruppenunterricht, Vol I II

Wir Lernen Gitarre Spielen,
    Grundschule Fur Den Einzel- Und
    Gruppenunterricht, Vol. II II

Wir Spielen Gitarre, Vol. I see Wir
    Lernen Gitarre Spielen,
    Grundschule Fur Den Einzel- Und
    Gruppenunterricht, Suppl. 1

Wir Spielen Gitarre, Vol. II see Wir
    Lernen Gitarre Spielen,
    Grundschule Fur Den Einzel- Und
    Gruppenunterricht, Suppl. 2

MUNDAY'S JOY see Six Pieces From The
    Time Of Elizabeth

MUNIER, CARLO
    Scuola Della Chitarra, Pratica
    d'Accompagnamento, Op. 137 II

MURCIA, SANTIAGO DE
    Prelude And Allegro I/IB1

Suite in D I/IB1

Suite in D minor I/IB1

MURMULLOS see Fortea, Daniel

MURTULA, GIOVANNI (1881-1964)
    Carovana, Intermezzo Caratteristico
    I/IB4

Rievocazione I/IB4

Studi, 2 I/IA

Studio, Rondo Fantasioso I/IA

MUSCADIN see Anonymous; Banks, Don

MUSETTE see Bach, Johann Sebastian;
    Mozart, Leopold; Verdonk, Jan

MUSETTE DE CHOISY see Couperin,
    Francois (le Grand)

MUSETTE DE TAVERNY see Couperin,
    Francois (le Grand)

MUSETTE IN D see Bach, Johann
    Sebastian

MUSETTE-WALZER see Uhl, Alfred

MUSGRAVE, THEA (1928-   )
    Five Love Songs I/IIC1

MUSI, FOR PLUCKED ORCHESTRA see Kagel,
    Mauricio

MUSIC BOX, THE see Tarrega, Francisco,
    Alborada, Cajita De Musica

MUSIC FOR 2 GUITARS see Marella,
    Giovanni Battista

MUSIC FOR 3 GUITARS I/IIA2-Coll

MUSIC FOR 4 GUITARS I/IIA3-Coll,
    IV/IIA3, VII-Mixed Coll

MUSIC FOR CLASSICAL GUITAR I/IB6-Coll,
    VI-Mixed Coll, VII-Mixed Coll

MUSIC FOR ORGAN AND 12 PLAYERS see
    Leeuw, Ton de

MUSIC FOR SCHOOLS, NO. 1, VERSION 1951
    see Praag, Henri C. van,
    Schoolmuziek No. 1

MUSIC FOR SCHOOLS NO. 3 see Praag,
    Henri C. van, Schoolmuziek No. 3

MUSIC FOR SCHOOLS NO. 3, VERSION 1951
    see Praag, Henri C. van,
    Schoolmuziek No. 3

MUSIC FOR THE CLASSICAL GUITAR, VOL. 1:
    A BOOK FOR BEGINNERS I/IB6-Coll,
    VII-Mixed Coll

MUSIC FOR THE CLASSICAL GUITAR, VOL. 2:
    A BOOK FOR INTERMEDIATE PLAYERS
    I/IB6-Coll, VII-Mixed Coll

MUSIC FOR THE YOUNG GUITARIST
    I/IB6-Coll, VII-Mixed Coll

MUSIC FOR THREE GUITARS see Smith
    Brindle, Reginald

MUSIC FOR YOUNG GUITARISTS see Gall,
    Louis Ignatius

MUSIC FROM CZECH LUTE TABLATURES see
    Hudba Ceskych Loutnovych Tabulatur

MUSIC FROM THE TIME OF PURCELL
    I/IIA1-Coll

MUSICA A DUE see Singer, Lawrence

MUSICA ARGENTINA, LIBRO I I/IB5-Coll

MUSICA DEL RE SOLE see Visee, Robert
    de

MUSICA INGLESA DE SIGLO XVL
    I/IIA1-Coll

MUSICA, OP. 11 see Regt, Hendrik de

MUSICA, OP. 15 see Regt, Hendrik de

MUSICA, OP. 17 see Regt, Hendrik de

MUSICA, OP. 18 see Regt, Hendrik de

MUSICA PER 17 STRUMENTI see
    Mengelberg, Misja

MUSICA PER CHITARRA, DA ORIGINALI PER
    LIUTO E CHITARRA I/IB6-Coll

MUSICAL VOYAGE WITH TWO GUITARS, A; 64
    MELODIES AND DANCES FROM 34
    COUNTRIES I/IIA1-Coll

MUSICALISCHE GESELLSCHAFTSERGETZUNG
    see Reussner, Esaias

MUSICALISCHER TUGENDSPIEGEL see
    Widmann, Erasmus

MUSICAS PARA O NATAL IV/I

MUSICHE DEL RINASCIMENTO I/IB1-Coll

MUSICHE PER CHITARRA ALLA CORTE DI
    VERSAILLES I/IB1-Coll

MUSICHE SCELTE DALLE INTAVOLATURE PER
    LIUTO see Gorzanis, Giacomo

MUSIK AUS ALTEN LAUTENBUCHERN see
    Gorzanis, Giacomo, Musiche Scelte
    Dalle Intavolature Per Liuto

MUSIK AUS ITALIEN I/IIB1-Coll

MUSIK AUS "TREMENS" see Kagel,
    Mauricio

MUSIK AUS WIEN; 16 DER SCHONSTEN
    WIENERLIEDER I/IIC1-Coll

MUSIK DER RENAISSANCE FUR GITARRE
    I/IB1-Coll

MUSIK DER VORKLASSIK: WERKE AUS DEM 17.
    UND 18. JAHRHUNDERT I/IB1-Coll,
    VII-Mixed Coll

MUSIK DER WIENER KLASSIK I/IIA2-Coll

MUSIK FUR GITARRE; NACH ORIGINALEN FUR
    LAUTE UND GITARRE AUS DEM 16.-19.
    JAHRHUNDERT I/IB6-Coll

MUSIK FUR GITARRE SOLO see Dieckmann,
    Carl Heinz

MUSIK FUR LIEBHABER DES GITARRESPIELS,
    VOL. 1: AUS TABULATUREN DES 16.
    JAHRHUNDERTS I/IB1-Coll

MUSIK FUR LIEBHABER DES GITARRESPIELS,
    VOL. 2: AUS TABULATUREN DES 16. UND
    17. JAHRHUNDERTS I/IB1-Coll

MUSIK FUR PICCOLOFLOTEN, FLOTEN UND
    GITARRE see Miyake, Haruna

MUSIK IM JAHRESKREIS I/IIB5-Coll

MUSIK IM JAHRESKREIS I/IIC5-Coll,
    IV/IIC5

MUSIK ITALIENISCHER MEISTER
    I/IIA1-Coll

MUSIK ZU CHRISTIAN MORGENSTERNS
    "PALMSTROM", PART 1 see Herzog,
    Franz

MUSIKANTEN A-B-C, DAS see Poser, Hans

MUSIKEN, 6 see Apostel, Hans Erich

MUSING see Heer, Hans De

MUSIQUE A DEUX see Constant, Franz

MUSIQUE ELISABETHAINE I/IIA1-Coll

MUSIQUE POUR 3 ET 4 GUITARES, VOL. 1
    (MUSIC FOR 3 AND 4 GUITARS, VOL. 1)
    I/IIA2-Coll, I/IIA3-Coll,
    VII-Mixed Coll

MUSIQUE POUR 3 ET 4 GUITARES, VOL. 2
    (MUSIC FOR 3 AND 4 GUITARS, VOL. 2)
    I/IIA2-Coll, I/IIA3-Coll,
    VII-Mixed Coll

MUSIQUE POUR 3 ET 4 GUITARES, VOL. 3 -
    MUSIC FOR 3 AND 4 GUITARS, VOL. 3
    I/IIA2-Coll, I/IIA3-Coll,
    VII-Mixed Coll

MUSIQUE POUR 3 ET 4 GUITARES, VOL. 4 -
    MUSIC FOR 3 AND 4 GUITARS, VOL. 4
    I/IIA2-Coll, I/IIA3-Coll,
    VII-Mixed Coll

MUSIQUE POUR DEUX GUITARES, VOL. 1 -
    MUSIC FOR TWO GUITARS, VOL. 1
    I/IIA1-Coll, VII-Mixed Coll

MUSIQUE POUR ENSEMBLES ET MORCEAUX
    CHOISIS I/IIB5-Coll

MUSIQUE POUR GUITARE SEULE, VOL. 1 -
  MUSIC FOR SOLO GUITAR, VOL. 1
  I/IB6-Coll, VII-Mixed Coll

MUSIQUE POUR GUITARE SEULE, VOL. 2 -
  MUSIC FOR SOLO GUITAR, VOL. 2
  I/IB6-Coll

MUSIQUE POUR GUITARE SEULE, VOL. 3 -
  MUSIC FOR SOLO GUITAR, VOL. 3
  I/IB6-Coll, VII-Mixed Coll

MUSIQUE POUR LES SOUPERS DU ROI UBU;
  BALLET NOIR EN SEPT PARTIES ET UNE
  ENTREE see Zimmermann, Bernd Alois

MUSIZIERBUCH, FUR DAS INSTRUMENTALE
  ZUSAMMENSPIEL IN SCHULE, JUGEND UND
  HAUS I/IIB5-Coll

MUSIZIERBUCHLEIN, EIN, EINFUHRUNG IN
  DAS MEHRSTIMMIGE SPIEL NACH
  VOLKSTANZEN UND LIEDERN AUS DEM
  ALPENRAUM see Koch, Hans

MUSIZIERBUCHLEIN FUR ANFANGER
  I/IB5-Coll, I/IIA1

MUSSORGSKY, MODEST PETROVICH
  (1839-1881)
  Viejo Castillo, El I/IB3

MUTATION, FOR BIG BAND AND HARPSICHORD
  OBBLIGATO see Ludwig, Joachim

MUTATIONS ON THE "DIES IRAE" see
  Duarte, John W.

MUZIEKBIJLAGE, NO. 53 I/IIB1-Coll,
  I/IIC1-Coll

MY FAIR LADIES I/IB6-Coll

MY LORD CHAMBERLAIN HIS GALLIARD see
  Elizabethan Duets, 6; Dowland, John

MY LOVE IN HER ATTIRE see Walton,
  [Sir] William (Turner)

MY OLD KENTUCKY HOME see Foster,
  Stephen Collins

MY OWN BLUES see Schibler, Armin

NACH WIE VOR DER REIHE NACH, OP. 182
  see Krenek, Ernst

NACHKLANGE see Erbse, Heimo

NACHT IN VENEDIG, EINE: SERENADE FUR
  DELAQUA; FINALE OF THE 1ST ACT see
  Strauss, Johann, [Jr.]

NACHT UND TRAUME see Schubert, Franz
  (Peter)

NACHT- UND TRAUMGESANGE see Becker,
  Gunther

NANA see Bialas, Gunter

NANCIE see Morley, Thomas

NAPOLITANE, 15 see Gorzanis, Giacomo

NAR BITTAN HJALPER MAMMA see Galen Man

NARANJOS EN FLOR see Castelnuovo-
  Tedesco, Mario, Aranci In Fiori

NARCISSUS see Nevin, Ethelbert
  Woodbridge

NARDELLI, RUDOLF (1932-   )
  Missa In Beat I/IIC5

NARRATIF see Werner, Jean-Jacques

NARVAEZ, LUIS DE
  Baxa De Contrapunto I/IB1

  Cancion Del Emperador I/IB1

  Con Que La Lavare I/IIC1

  Conde Claros, 22 Diferencias see
    Variations, 22, On The Romance
    "Conde Claros"

  Diferencias, 7, Sobre "Guardame Las
    Vacas" I/IB1

  Diferencias Sobre "Guardame Las
    Vacas" I/IIA1

  Fantasia Del Primer Tono I/IB1

  Fantasy No. 3 I/IB1

  Fantasy No. 9 I/IB1

  Seys Libros Del Delphin De Musica,
    Los: Ausgewahlte Werke
    I/IB1-Coll

NARVAEZ, LUIS DE (cont'd.)

  Seys Libros Del Delphin De Musica De
    Cifra Para Taner Vihuela, Los
    I/IB1, I/IIC1

  Variaciones, 22, Sobre Conde Claros
    see Variations, 22, On The
    Romance "Conde Claros"

  Variaties, 22, Over De Romance Conde
    Claros see Variations, 22, On
    The Romance "Conde Claros"

  Variations, 22, On The Romance "Conde
    Claros" I/IB1

  Villancico No. 5 Et Fantaisie No. 14
    I/IB1

NATURALEZA MUERTO CON GUITARRA;
  HOMENAJE A PABLO PICASSO see
  Marco, Tomas

NATUS EST JESUS, WEIHNACHTSKONZERT see
  Boddecker, Philipp Friedrich

NATY, JEAN
  Au Chateau I/IIC5

NAVA, ANTONIO (1775-1828)
  Andante I/IB2

NAVARRO, ANTONIO
  Tremolo Study In A Major I/IA

NE MENTE PER LA GOLA, LA see Garsi da
  Parma, Santino

NEAPOLITANISCHE LIEDER AUS DEM 16.
  JAHRHUNDERT see Gorzanis, Giacomo,
  Napolitane, 15

NECKEREI see Ambrosius, Hermann

NEDERLANDSE LUITMUZIEK UIT DE 17E EEUW
  see Hove, Joachim van den

NEDERLANDSE VOLKSLIEDEREN, 3
  I/IIC1-Coll

NEDERLANDSE VOLKSLIEDEREN, 23
  I/IIC5-Coll

NEGRI, CESARE (IL TROMBONE)
  (ca. 1536- ?)
  Balletti, 8 I/IB1

  Catena D'amore I/IB1

  Lautentanze Des XVI. Jahrhunderts
    I/IB1

  Nuove Inventioni Di Balli I/IB1

NEGRO-SPIRITUALS I/IIB5-Coll, I/IIC2,
  V/ii

NEGRO-SPIRITUALS, VOL. 1 V/ii

NEGRO-SPIRITUALS, VOL. 2 V/ii

NEIJBOER, OTTO C.
  Melodie En Positie I/IB4

NEL DOLCE DELL'OBLIO see Handel,
  George Frideric

NELISSEN-NICOLAI, LENI
  Zeigende Und Sprechende Gitarre-
    Schule Fur Jedermann, Vol. I II

  Zeigende Und Sprechende Gitarre-
    Schule Fur Jedermann, Vol. II II

NELLA CHIESA RUSSA see Tchaikovsky,
  Piotr Ilyich, In Church

NEUBERGER TANZE see Bloch, Waldemar

NEUE GITARREN-SCHULE, VOL. I see
  Zanoskar, Hubert

NEUE GITARREN-SCHULE, VOL. I, SUPPL.:
  UBUNGEN UND SPIELSTUCKE see
  Zanoskar, Hubert

NEUE GITARREN-SCHULE, VOL. II see
  Zanoskar, Hubert

NEUE GITARREN-SCHULE, VOL. II, SUPPL.
  see Zanoskar, Hubert

NEUE GITARRENMUSIK see Birth, Thomas

NEUE GITARRENSCHULE see Schmidt,
  Hermann

NEUE GITARRENSCHULE, KLASSISCHE UND
  MODERNE SPIELTECHNIK, ANHANG FUR E-
  GITARRE UND E-BASS see Pohlert,
  Werner

NEUE MUSIZIERBUCH, DAS, FUR
  INSTRUMENTALES ZUSAMMENSPIEL IN
  SCHULEN, MUSIZIERGRUPPEN UND IN DER

HAUSMUSIK I/IIB5-Coll

NEUE MUSIZIERSTUCKE see Uldall, Hans

NEUE RUSSISCHE GITARREMUSIK, VOL. I
  see Panin, Peter

NEUE SCHULE FUR GITARRE see
  Giampietro, G.

NEUE WEGE ZUR MEISTERSCHAFT AUF DER
  GITARRE see Kruger, M.

NEUES SPIELBUCHLEIN I/IIB1-Coll

NEUMANN, FRIEDRICH (1915-   )
  Kanonische Kantate Zur Weihnacht
    IV/IIC5

NEUMANN, ULRIK
  Guitare Melancolique I/IB4

  Leksakstaget I/IB4

  Love Waltz I/IB4

  Manresan I/IB4, I/IIC1

  Three-Bands Bossa Nova I/IB5

  Toy Train, The see Leksakstaget

NEUMULLER, WOLFGANG
  Gitarrenstuck1 I/IIA1, I/IIA2

NEUN VOLKSLIEDER see Jesset, Michael

NEUSIEDLER, HANS (1508-1563)
  Aus "Ein Newgeordent Kunstlich
    Lautenbuch" I/IB1

  Gassenhawer see Tanze, 3

  Hupf Auf, Der see Lautenstucke, 4

  Ich Klag Den Tag I/IB1

  Juden Tanz, Der see Lautenstucke, 4

  Lautenstucke, 4 I/IB1

  Newgeordent Kunstlich Lautenbuch, Ein
    I/IB1-Coll

  Newgeordent Kunstlich Lautenbuch,
    Ein: Der Ander Theil Fur Die
    Geubten Vnnd Erfarnen, 1536
    I/IB1-Coll

  Nunnen Tantz, Der see Tanze, 3

  Passa-Mesa see Lautenstucke, 4

  Praambulum Und Tanz I/IB1

  Preambel see Lautenstucke, 4

  Tanze, 3 I/IB1

  Welscher Tantz see Tanze, 3

NEUSIEDLER, MELCHIOR (1507-1590)
  Ausgewahlte Lautenwerke (1566-1572)
    I/IB1

NEVER ON SUNDAY see Hadjidakis, Manos

NEVIN, ETHELBERT WOODBRIDGE (1862-1901)
  Narcissus I/IB3

NEW DOLL, THE see Tchaikovsky, Piotr
  Ilyich

NEW IRISH TUNE, A see Purcell, Henry

NEW MEL BAY CLASSIC GUITAR METHOD, THE,
  VOL. I see Bay, Mel

NEW MEL BAY CLASSIC GUITAR METHOD, THE,
  VOL. II see Bay, Mel

NEW MEL BAY CLASSIC GUITAR METHOD, THE,
  VOL. III see Bay, Mel

NEWCASTLE see Take Your Partners; 6
  English Country Dances

NEWGEORDENT KUNSTLICH LAUTENBUCH, EIN
  see Neusiedler, Hans

NEWGEORDENT KUNSTLICH LAUTENBUCH, EIN:
  DER ANDER THEIL FUR DIE GEUBTEN
  VNND ERFARNEN, 1536 see
  Neusiedler, Hans

NEWSIDLER, HANS
  see NEUSIEDLER, HANS

NEWSIDLER, MELCHIOR
  see NEUSIEDLER, MELCHIOR

NICE UND FILENO see Carulli,
  Ferdinando

NICK, EDMUND (1891-1974)
Leben In Dieser Zeit V/ii

NIEHAUS, MANFRED (1933-   )
Konzert, For Violin And 4 Orchestral
Groups V/i

Pop & Art V/ii

Suite I/IIB1

NIESSEN, HANS-LUTZ (1920-1982)
Daar Gingen Twee Gespeelkens Goed,
Variaties Op Een Volkslied
I/IIB1

Prelude and Fugue I/IB4

Variations On A Folk-Song see Daar
Gingen Twee Gespeelkens Goed,
Variaties Op Een Volkslied

NIEUWE GITAAR-SCHOOL, DE, VOLLEDIGE,
MODERNE METHODE see Kok, Joh. B.

NIGHT-CLUB PIECES see Alcalay, Lucia

NIGHT MUSIC see Bois, Rob du;
Schuller, Gunther

NIGHT WATCH, THE see Holborne, Antony

NIJENHUIS, LUC
Barre-Etudes I/IA

Canons In II I/IIA1

Capo Tasto I/IA

Gitaarles In Groepsverband, Vol. II
II

In Spe I/IA

Learn The Guitar By Playing Together
see Gitaarles In Groepsverband,
Vol. II

Legato Studies I/IA

Studies In V I/IA

NILOVIC, JANKO
Makedonia I/IIB3

NILSSON, BO (1937-   )
Frequenzen Fur 8 Spieler V/i

Irrender Sohn, Ein V/ii

Madchentotenlieder V/ii

Und Die Zeiger Seiner Augen Wurden
Langsam Zuruckgedreht V/ii

NIN-CULMELL, JOAQUIN (1908-   )
Variaciones Sobre Un Tema De Milan, 6
I/IB4

NINE SYMPHONIES OF BEETHOVEN, THE, FOR
PROMENADE ORCHESTRA AND ICE-CREAM
BELL see Andriessen, Louis

NINFA, LA see Sanchez, B.

NINNA-NANNA, A LULLABY FOR EUGENE see
Castelnuovo-Tedesco, Mario

NIT DE NADAL, LA see Canciones
Populares Catalanas, 10

NO SE EMENDERA JAMAS see Handel,
George Frideric

NO SE VA LA PALOMA, CANCION POPULAR
LEONESA I/IB5

NOAD, FREDERICK M.
Mananitas see Playing The Guitar, A
Self-Instruction Guide To
Technique And Theory

Playing The Guitar, A Self-
Instruction Guide To Technique
And Theory II, IV/I

Solo Guitar Playing, A Complete
Course Of Instruction In The
Technique Of Guitar Performance
I/IB2-Coll, II, VI-Mixed Coll,
VII-Mixed Coll

NOBILISSIMA MUSICA, VON DER EDLEN MUSIK
see Rathgeber, Valentin

NOBLA, MARCEL
Guitare Expliquee, La, Methode
Progressive, Part I: Technique
Classique Elementaire. 18 Lessons
II

Guitare Expliquee, La, Methode
Progressive, Part III: Initiation
Au Flamenco II

NOBLE
Concertino Mexicano I/IIIA

NOBLE MAN, THE see Johnson, Robert [3]

NOBODY KNOWS THE TROUBLE I'VE HAD see
Famous Negro Spirituals, 5

NOBODY'S GIGGE see Six Pieces From The
Time Of Elizabeth

NOBRE, MARLOS (1939-   )
Momentos I I/IB4

NOCHE DE PAZ see Gruber, Franz Xaver,
Stille Nacht

NOCHE Y ENSUENO see Schubert, Franz
(Peter), Nacht Und Traume

NOCTURNAL, AFTER JOHN DOWLAND see
Britten, [Sir] Benjamin

NOCTURNE AND TOCCATA see Duarte, John
W.

NOCTURNE DE SALON see Carulli,
Ferdinando, Abendmusik

NOCTURNE EN LA MINEUR see Doerr,
Charles-Kiko, Nocturne in A minor

NOCTURNES see Carulli, Ferdinando

NOCTURNES, 2 see Ramovs, Primoz

NOCTURNES, 3, FOR VIOLA AND ORCHESTRA
see Suter, Robert

NOCTURNES, 3, OP. 4 see Mertz, Johann
Kaspar

NOCTURNES, 4 see Lutyens, Elizabeth

NODULE PER CHITARRE see Ezaki, Kenjiro

NOEL DE GASCOGNE see Easy Music, Vol.
2

NOELS IV/I

NOELS DE PROVENCE IV/IIC1

NOIR see Leclercq, Norbert

NOMENCLATURE see Angel, Miguel

NON ARDU CHIU see Anonymous

NON COSI see Monteverdi, Claudio

NON PAPA, JACOBUS CLEMENS
see CLEMENS, JACOBUS

NON PER ME FIORISCONO LE DALIE see
Bortolami, Galliano

NON TE ESCAPARAS, CAPRICCIO NACH
FRANCESCO DE GOYA see Behrend,
Siegfried

NON TROPPO ALLEGRO see Kovats, Barna

NON VUO PREGARE see Vecchi, Orazio
(Horatio)

NONE BUT THE LONELY HEART see
Tchaikovsky, Piotr Ilyich

NONESUCH see Take Your Partners; 6
English Country Dances

NORDISCHE VOLKSLIEDER I/IIC1-Coll

NORDISCHE VOLKSMUSIK I/IIB2-Coll

NORDISCHE VOLKSWEISEN, 30, AUS
SCHWEDEN, DANEMARK, NORWEGEN UND
FINNLAND I/IB5-Coll

NORDISCHES LIED see Schumann, Robert
(Alexander)

NORMAN, THEODORE (1912-   )
Classical Guitar, The, A New Approach
III

Mobile I/IB4

NORTENA, HOMENAJE A JULIAN AGUIRRE see
Gomez Crespo, Jorge

NORWEGISCHE VOLKSWEISEN see Gundhus,
Leif

NOSTALGIA see Julia, Bernardo

NOSTALGIE see Wolki, Konrad

NOTTURNINO E CAPRICCIO see Medin, Nino

NOTTURNO see Anonymous, Romance, MIN
141

NOUVEAUX DUOS, 32 [SIC] PIECES...
I/IIB1-Coll, IV/IIB1

NOVAK, JAN (1921-1984)
Apicius Modulatus, Artis Coquinariae
Praecepta Modis Numerisque
Instructa Ad Cantum Cum Cithara
I/IIC1

Cantiones Latinae, Medii Et
Recentioris Aevi Ad Cantum Cum
Cithara I/IIC1

Concentus Eurydicae see Concerto Per
Euridice

Concerto Per Euridice I/IIIA

Rosarium, 10 Divertimenti I/IIA1

NOVEMBER MEMORIES see Smith Brindle,
Reginald

NOVI CAPRICCI ARMONICI (1674) see
Granata, Giovanni Battista

NOW, O NOW, I NEEDS MUST PART see
Dowland, John

NOY DE LA MARE, EL see Canciones
Catalanas Navidenas, 4;
Catalanische Weisen, 3; Villancicos
Populares, Vol. II

NOY DE LA MARE, EL, CANCION POPULAR
CATALAN IV/I

NUANCES see Cerf, Jacques

NUCLEOS see Labrouve, Jorge

NUEVA TECNICA DE LA GUITARRA, LA see
Prat, Domingo

NUEVE CANCIONES GRANADINAS, 9 CANTOS DE
LA ALPUJARRA LLAMADOS "REMERINOS"
I/IIC1-Coll

NUEVO METODO PARA EL ARTE DE ACOMPANAR
EN LA GUITARRA, COMPUESTO CON
MUSICA Y CIFRA see Lluquet,
Guillermo

NUNC see Petrassi, Goffredo

NUNES, MILTON
Luz E Saudade, Estudo Em Tremolo
I/IA

NUNNEN TANTZ, DER see Neusiedler, Hans

NUOVE INVENTIONI DI BALLI see Negri,
Cesare (il Trombone)

NURNBERGER LAUTENBUCH: PART 1 see
Anonymous

NURNBERGER LAUTENBUCH: PART 2 see
Anonymous

NURNBERGER LAUTENBUCH: PART 3 see
Anonymous

NURSE'S SONG WITH ELEPHANTS see
Bedford, David

NYMPHE, LA see Sanchez, B., Ninfa, La

O BLACK AND UNKNOWN BARDS, 7 NEGRO
SPIRITUALS I/IB5-Coll, IV/I

O BONNE DOUCE FRANCE see Strietman,
Willem

O CESSATE DI PIAGARMI see Scarlatti,
Alessandro

O CRAVO E A ROSA see Chansons
Bresiliennes, Vol. I

O DENNEBOOM I/IIC5-Coll

O DREAM, O DREAMING see Hornung

O DU FROHLICHE see Volks- Und
Kinderlieder

O DU FROHLICHE, O DU SELIGE see
Weihnachtslieder

O, DU LIEBER AUGUSTIN see Tittel,
Ernst

O GUARDAME LAS VACAS see Mudarra,
Alonso de, Romanesca I

O JESULEIN SUSS see Bach, Johann
Sebastian

O JUBEL, O FREUD, WEIHNACHTSLIEDER ZUR
GITARRE IV/IIC1

O MISTRESS MINE see Fricker, Peter
Racine

O NO, JOHN   see Engelse Volksliederen, 3

O PIAO ENTROU NA RODA   see Chansons Bresiliennes, Vol. II

O SANCTISSIMA, 10 WEIHNACHTSLIEDER AUS ITALIEN, ENGLAND, SPANIEN UND FRANKREICH   IV/IIC1

O STAY, SWEET LOVE   see Walton, [Sir] William (Turner)

O TALER WEIT   see Bialas, Gunter, Eichendorff-Liederbuch, Vol. 2: Abschied

O TANNENBAUM   see Du Und Ich Wir Spielen Gitarre, Ein Lieblingsbuch Fur Angehende Gitarristen; Lautenspieler, Der, No. 1; Lied- Und Gitarrenspiel, Volks- Und Tanzlieder, Vol. II; Volkslieder; Weihnachtslieder; Wolki, Konrad

O WUNDER, WAS WILL DAS BEDEUTEN, LIEDERSAMMLUNG ZUR ADVENTSZEIT IV/IIB2, IV/IIC2

OB I LACH ODER SING, VOLKSLIEDER AUS DER DEUTSCHEN SCHWEIZ   I/IIC1-Coll

OBJETS   see Beurle, Jurgen

OBRADORS, FERNANDO
Con Amores, La Mi Madre   I/IIC1

OBRAS CLASICAS Y ROMANTICAS, VOL. 1 I/IB6-Coll, VII-Mixed Coll

OBRAS CLASICAS Y ROMANTICAS, VOL. 2 I/IB6-Coll, VI-Mixed Coll

OBRAS DE GASPAR SANZ, VOL. 1   see Sanz, Gaspar

OBRAS DE GASPAR SANZ, VOL. 2   see Sanz, Gaspar

OBRAS PARA GUITARRA, 12, PRIMER ALBUM see Sor, Fernando

OBRECHT, JACOB (ca. 1430-1505)
Missa Maria Zart   V/ii

OBROVSKA, JANA (1930-   )
Hommage A Bela Bartok   I/IB4

OBSESSION   see Paubon, Pierre

OCCASIONI, 3   see Arrigo, Girolamo

OCRAM, FANTASIA   see Gilardino, Angelo

ODE SUPER "CHRYSEA PHORMINX"   see Vlad, Roman

OEUVRES CHOISIES POUR GUITARE   see Giuliani, Mauro

OEUVRES COMPLETES POUR GUITARE   see Visee, Robert de

OEUVRES DE CHARLES-KIKO DOERR   see Doerr, Charles-Kiko

OFRENDA A FERNANDO SORS   see Solares, Enrique

OGO, [CHORAL BROTHER]
Weg Hinab Nach Jericho, Der   V/ii

OH, QUE BIEN BAILA GIL!   see Canciones Del Siglo XVII, 5

OH, SEEK JOY   see Staak, Pieter van der

OH, THE CUCKOO, SHE'S A PRETTY BIRD see Hess, Reimund, Cuckoo, The

OHANA, MAURICE (1914-   )
Aube   see Si Le Jour Parait, No. 7

Chevelure De Berenice, La   see Si Le Jour Parait, No. 5

Enueg   see Si Le Jour Parait, No. 2

Jeu Des Quatre Vents   see Si Le Jour Parait, No. 6

Maya   see Si Le Jour Parait, No. 3

Si Le Jour Parait, No. 1   I/IB4

Si Le Jour Parait, No. 2   I/IB4

Si Le Jour Parait, No. 3   I/IB4

Si Le Jour Parait, No. 4   I/IB4

Si Le Jour Parait, No. 5   I/IB4

Si Le Jour Parait, No. 6   I/IB4

OHANA, MAURICE (cont'd.)

Si Le Jour Parait, No. 7   I/IB4

Temple   see Si Le Jour Parait, No. 1

Tiento   I/IB4

20 Avril (Planh)   see Si Le Jour Parait, No. 4

OILLES MOTORS   see Boogaard, Bernard van den

OISEAU DE LA TOUR, L'   see Delnooz, Henri

OJOS CLAROS, SERENOS   see Guerrero, Francisco

OLCOTT-BICKFORD, VADAH
[Method], Vol. I: Method For Classic Guitar   II

[Method], Vol. II: Advanced Course For Classic Guitar   II

OLD DAN TUCKER   see Devil And The Farmer's Wife, The, And Other American Ballads

OLD FRENCH AIR   see Tchaikovsky, Piotr Ilyich; Tchaikovsky, Piotr Ilyich

OLD MAC DONALD   see Hess, Reimund

OLD MELODIES FROM THE NETHERLANDS (16TH-18TH CENT.), 38   see Spielmann Aus Flandern, Der

OLD SONG   see Fernandez, Oscar Lorenzo

OLD SPAGNOLETTA   see Six Pieces From The Time Of Elizabeth

OLD WIFE'S TALE, THE   see Tchaikovsky, Piotr Ilyich

OLF, MARK
Spanish Guitar Technique, A Recorded Basic Method For Home Study   II

OLIVERAS   see Moreno Torroba, Federico

OLLAPOTRIDA   see Jelinek, Hanns

OLOTINA   see Canciones Catalanas Navidenas, 4

OLSEN, POUL ROVSING
see ROVSING OLSEN, POUL

OMAGGIO A CHARLIE CHRISTIAN   see Peraldo Bert, Nilo

OMAGGIO A GAETANO AZZOLINA   see Bartolozzi, Bruno

OMAGGIO AD ANDRES SEGOVIA   see Mortari, Virgilio

OMAGGIO AL LIUTISTI ITALIANI   see Breguet, Jacques, Suite

OMAGGIO, SCRITTO PER LE TOMBEAU DE DEBUSSY   see Falla, Manuel de

OMAR'S LAMENT   see Duarte, John W.

OMBRES   see Leeuw, Ton de

OMMAGIO A BOCCHERINI   see Castelnuovo-Tedesco, Mario, Sonata

OMMEGANG: CYCLE   see Furstenau, Wolfram; Furstenau, Wolfram

ON GREEN MOUNTAIN; CHACONNE AFTER MONTEVERDI   see Shapero, Harold Samuel

ONDINAS   see Pujol, Emilio

ONES WHO WALKED AWAY FROM OMELAS, THE see Bedford, David

OPERA, OPERA IN 4 ACTS   see Berio, Luciano

OPERA OMNIA FOR THE SPANISH GUITAR, VOL. 1   see Sor, Fernando

OPERA OMNIA FOR THE SPANISH GUITAR, VOL. 2   see Sor, Fernando

OPERA OMNIA FOR THE SPANISH GUITAR, VOL. 3   see Sor, Fernando

OPERA OMNIA FOR THE SPANISH GUITAR, VOL. 4   see Sor, Fernando

OPERA OMNIA FOR THE SPANISH GUITAR, VOL. 5   see Sor, Fernando

OPERA OMNIA FOR THE SPANISH GUITAR, VOL. 6   see Sor, Fernando

OPERA OMNIA FOR THE SPANISH GUITAR, VOL. 7   see Sor, Fernando

OPERA OMNIA FOR THE SPANISH GUITAR, VOL. 8   see Sor, Fernando

OPERA OMNIA FOR THE SPANISH GUITAR, VOL. 9   see Sor, Fernando

OPERA OMNIA FOR THE SPANISH GUITAR, VOL. 10   see Sor, Fernando

OPERA OMNIA FOR THE SPANISH GUITAR, VOL. 11   see Sor, Fernando

OPERA OMNIA FOR THE SPANISH GUITAR, VOL. 12   see Sor, Fernando

OPERE COMPLETE PER LIUTO   see Bach, Johann Sebastian

OPERE COMPLETE PER LIUTO, VOL. 1: COMPOSIZIONI ORIGINALI   see Francesco da Milano

OPERE COMPLETE PER LIUTO, VOL. 2: INTAVOLATURE DI OPERE POLIFONICHE VOCALI   see Francesco da Milano

OPERE PER CHITARRA, VOL. I: PRELUDI see Tarrega, Francisco

OPERE PER CHITARRA, VOL. II: STUDI   see Tarrega, Francisco

OPERE PER CHITARRA, VOL. III: COMPOSIZIONI ORIGINALI   see Tarrega, Francisco

OPERE PER CHITARRA, VOL. IV: TRASCRIZIONI   see Tarrega, Francisco

OPHELIA   see Anonymous

OPP, AMARYLLIS OCH ANDRA FREDMANS SANGER OCH EPISTLAR   see Bellman, Carl Michael

OPUS 1-20   see Sor, Fernando

OR VOUS TREMOUSSEZ, PASTEURS   see Dufay, Guillaume

ORACION   see Barrios Mangore, Augustin; Sanchez, Blas

ORANGE   see Leclercq, Norbert

ORATIONEN   see Furstenau, Wolfram

ORBON, JULIAN (1925-   )
Preludio Y Danza   I/IB4

ORFEO; FAVOLA IN MUSICA IN FIVE ACTS WITH A PROLOGUE   see Monteverdi, Claudio

ORFEO; FAVOLA PASTORALE IN TWO PARTS see Monteverdi, Claudio, Orfeo; Favola In Musica In Five Acts With A Prologue

ORFEO; OPERA IN FIVE ACTS   see Monteverdi, Claudio, Orfeo; Favola In Musica In Five Acts With A Prologue

ORFEO: VIENI IMENEO   see Monteverdi, Claudio

ORGIA   see Turina, Joaquin

ORIENTAL   see Albeniz, Isaac; Granados, Enrique, Danzas Espanolas, No. 2

ORIENTALE   see Cui, Cesar Antonovich

ORIGINAL-KOMPOSITIONEN, 12, OP. 35   see Furstenau, Kaspar, Suite, Op. 35

ORIGINAL KOMPOSITIONEN, 26   see Paganini, Niccolo

ORIGINALKOMPOSITIONEN, 5   see Garber, Erich

ORIGINALKOMPOSITIONEN, 6   see Paganini, Niccolo

ORIGINALSTUCKE, 6   see Coste, Napoleon

ORIZZONTE E'SVANITO, L'   see Bortolami, Galliano

ORLANDO FA CHE TI RACCORDI   see Anonymous

ORMINDO, L'; OPERA IN TWO ACTS   see Cavalli, (Pietro) Francesco

ORPHEUS, OPERA IN 3 ACTS   see
    Birtwistle, Harrison

ORREGO-SALAS, JUAN A. (1919-   )
    Esquinas I/IB4

ORSOLINO, FEDERICO (1918-   )
    Capriccio, La Cascatella I/IB4

    Piccole Impressioni Di Campagna
        I/IB4

    Prime 48 Lezioni Di Chitarra, Le,
        Part I: Esercizi A Mani Separate
        II

    Prime 48 Lezioni Di Chitarra, Le,
        Part II: Ezercizi A Mani Unite
        II

ORTIZ, DIEGO (ca. 1525- ?)
    Recercaden, 4 I/IIB1

ORTNER, JACOB
    Kurzgefasste Gitarre-Schule, Fur
        Lehrerbildungsanstalten Und Zum
        Selbstunterricht Geeignet II

OSTERGESCHICHTE see Barbe, Helmut

OSTINATO see Duarte, John W.;
    Farquhar, David

OSTPREUSSISCHES LAUTENBUCH I/IB1-Coll

OTTE, HANS (1926-   )
    Daidalos; Ballet In Seven Scenes For
        Six Players V/iii

OUD-HOLLANDSCHE DANSMUZIEK UIT DEN 80-
    JARIGEN OORLOG I/IB1

OUD-NEDERLANDSE LIEDEREN I/IIC1-Coll

OUD-VLAAMSE VOLKSLIEDEREN, 2
    I/IB5-Coll

OWL AND THE PUSSYCAT, THE see Seiber,
    Matyas Gyorgy

OYENS, TERA DE MARZ
    see MAREZ OYENS, TERA DE

OZVENY, FOR ORCHESTRA see Kupkovic,
    Ladislav

PACHELBEL, JOHANN (1653-1706)
    Aria I/IB1

    Suite for Lute I/IB1

    Suite in D I/IB1

PADEREWSKI, IGNACE JAN (1860-1941)
    Minue Celebre I/IB3

PADUANE see Le Roy, Adrien

3 PAESAGGI see Stahmer, Klaus H.

PAESIELLO, GIOVANNI (1741-1816)
    Aria Der Rosine I/IIC2

PAGANINI, NICCOLO (1782-1840)
    Allegretto, MIN 22 see
        Originalkompositionen, 6

    Allegretto, MIN21 see Composizioni
        Inedite, 3

    Allegretto Scherzando see
        Originalkompositionen, 6; Paginas
        Escritas Directamente Para La
        Guitarra

    Andantino I/IB2
        see also Paginas Escritas
        Directamente Para La Guitarra; 5
        Pieces

    Andantino In A Minor I/IB2

    Andantino, MIN 19 see
        Recercaden, 6

    Andantino, MIN 20 see
        Originalkompositionen, 6

    Arieta see Paginas Escritas
        Directamente Para La Guitarra

    Arietta I/IB2

    Campanella, La I/IB2

    Cantabile I/IIB1

    Capriccio No. 9 I/IB2

    Capriccio No. 13 I/IB2

    Capriccio No. 16 I/IB2

    Capriccio No. 24 I/IB2

PAGANINI, NICCOLO (cont'd.)
    Celebre Sonata I/IB2

    Centone Di Sonate; Four Sonatas
        I/IIB1

    Composizioni Inedite, 3 I/IB2

    Composizioni Originali, 26 see
        Original Kompositionen, 26

    Deux Valses see 5 Pieces

    Dialog Zwischen Einer Alten Und Einer
        Jungen Frau see Scherzo, Dialogo
        Tra Una Vecchia E Una Giovane

    12 Duette, Vol. 1 I/IIB1

    12 Duette, Vol. 2 I/IIB1

    Eloadasi Darabok Gitarra see
        Original Kompositionen, 26

    Etude I/IA

    Ghiribizzi No. 24 And 25 see 5
        Pieces

    Grosse Sonate I/IIB1

    March see 5 Pieces

    Minuet For Dida I/IB2

    Minuet, MIN 23 see
        Originalkompositionen, 6

    Minuet, MIN 24 see Composizioni
        Inedite, 3

    Minuettino No. 23 see Composizioni
        Inedite, 3

    Moto Perpetuo I/IB2, I/IIA1, I/IIB1

    Original Kompositionen, 26 I/IB2

    Originalkompositionen, 6 I/IB2

    Paginas Escritas Directamente Para La
        Guitarra I/IB2

    Perigoldimo see
        Originalkompositionen, 6

    Perigoldino Con Dos Variaciones see
        Paginas Escritas Directamente
        Para La Guitarra

    Piece De Salon I/IB2

    Piece Intime I/IB2

    5 Pieces I/IB2

    Quartet I/IIB3

    Quartet No. 1 I/IIB3

    Quartet No. 7 I/IIB3

    Romance I/IB2, I/IIIA

    Romance in A minor I/IB2

    Scherzo, Dialogo Tra Una Vecchia E
        Una Giovane I/IB2

    Serenade I/IIB2

    Serenade, MIN 55 I/IIB2

    Serenade, MIN 56 I/IIB2

    Sonata I/IIB1
        see also 5 Pieces

    Sonata Concertata I/IIB1

    Sonata, MIN 201,First Movement I/IC

    Sonata, Op. 3, No. 1 I/IIB1

    Sonata, Op. 3, No. 5 I/IIB1

    Sonata, Op. 3, No. 6 I/IIB1

    Sonaten, 6, Op. 2 I/IIB1

    Sonaten, 6, Op.3 I/IIB1

    Sonatina I/IB2
        see also Paginas Escritas
        Directamente Para La Guitarra

    Sonatina in C I/IB2

    Sonatina, MIN 135 I/IB2

    Sonatina, Op. 25 I/IB2

    Sonatine, 4 I/IIB1

PAGANINI, NICCOLO (cont'd.)
    Sonatinen, 3, Fur Signora De Lucca
        I/IB2

    Tarantella I/IIB1

    Terzetto I/IIB2

    Terzetto Concertante I/IIB2

    Theme and Variations I/IB2

    Two Minuets I/IB2

    Variazioni Di Bravura I/IIB1

PAGINA ROMANTICA see Pedrell, Carlos,
    Pieces, 3, No. 2

PAGINAS ESCRITAS DIRECTAMENTE PARA LA
    GUITARRA see Paganini, Niccolo

PAISAJE see Pujol, Emilio

PAISAJE GRANA, HOMENAJE A J.R. JIMENEZ
    see Marco, Tomas

PAISANO ALEGRE see Schumann, Robert
    (Alexander), Frohlicher Landmann

PAJARERA, LA see Canciones Populares
    Mexicanas, 3

PAJAROS DE PRIMAVERA see Rodrigo,
    Joaquin

PALAU, MANUEL (1893-1967)
    Ayer, Fantasia I/IB4

    Concierto Levantino I/IIIA

    Fantasy I/IB4

PALE MOON see Logan, Frederick Knight

PALESTER, ROMAN (1907-   )
    Morte Di Don Giovanni, La: 3
        Frammenti Sinfonici, For
        Orchestra V/i

    Morte Di Don Giovanni, La; Action In
        Music In One Act V/iii

PALESTRINA, GIOVANNI PIERLUIGI DA
    (1525-1594)
    Ricercare Del Primo Tono I/IIA1

PALLADINO, CARLO
    Metodo Moderno Per Chitarra II

PALMIERS, LES see Mourat, Jean-Maurice

PAMMER, JOSEF
    Burleske I/IB4

    Maria Geht Durch Bluten I/IB4

    Valse Triste I/IB4

PAMPEANA see Broqua, Alfonso,
    Evocaciones Criollas, No.6

PANDERETA SUENA, UNA see Villancicos
    Populares, Vol. III

PANIN, PETER
    Neue Russische Gitarremusik, Vol. I
        I/IB4

PANORAMA see Moreno Torroba, Federico

PANORAMA BRASILIA see Marion, Rolf

PANXOLINA DI NADAL see Canciones
    Populares Gallegas, 2

PAPAI, GYORGY
    Gyakorlofuzet Gitarra, Vol. 1 II

    Gyakorlofuzet Gitarra, Vol. 2 II

    Ubungsheft Fur Gitarre, Vol. 1 see
        Gyakorlofuzet Gitarra, Vol. 1

    Ubungsheft Fur Gitarre, Vol. 2 see
        Gyakorlofuzet Gitarra, Vol. 2

PAPANDOPULO, BORIS (1906-   )
    Drei Jugoslavische Tanze Fur Gitarre
        I/IB4

PAPARARO, GUGLIELMO
    Technica Degli Arpeggi Per Chitarra
        Classica, La III

PAPAS, SOPHOCLES
    Complete Tremolo Book For The Guitar,
        The III

    Method For The Classic Guitar II,
        VII-Mixed Coll

    Minuet in A see Method For The
        Classic Guitar

PAPAS, SOPHOCLES (cont'd.)

Piece In F (March) see Method For The Classic Guitar

Prelude and Fugue in G minor see Method For The Classic Guitar

PAPILLON, LE see Giuliani, Mauro

PAPILLON, LE (CHOIX D'AIRS FACILES) see Giuliani, Mauro

PAQUITO see Tarrega, Francisco

PARA ELISA see Beethoven, Ludwig van, Fur Elise

PARABOLES see Ibert, Jacques

PARADETAS see Sanz, Gaspar

PARADETAS, DANZA DEL SIGLO XVII see Guerau, Francisco

PARADIES, DAS, EIN TANZSPIEL see Kukuck, Felicitas

PARADIES, PIETRO DOMENICO (PARADISI) (1707-1791)
Toccata I/IB1

PARADIGM see Foss, Lukas

PARADIS, MARIA THERESIA VON (1759-1824)
Siciliana I/IB2

PARKENING, CHRISTOPHER
Christopher Parkening Guitar Method, The, Vol. 1 II

PARRAS DEL MORAL, J.
Metodo Para Guitarra, Ejercicios, Estudios Y Escalas Diatonicas II

PART SUITE, 6 see Mairants, Ivor

PARTIE IN C GROOT see Baron, Ernst Gottlieb, Partita in C

PARTITA AL LIUTO see Bach, Johann Sebastian, Partita for Lute, BWV 997, in C minor

PARTITA AMABILE see Hallnas, Hilding

PARTITA EN DO MAYOR see Baron, Ernst Gottlieb, Partita in C

PARTITA IN C I/IB1

PARTITA NO. 2 IN G see Telemann, Georg Philipp, Partita in G

PARTITA SOPRA LA ARIA DELLA FOLIA DE ESPAGNA see Pasquini, Bernardo

PARTITA VOOR DAVID, VOOR KINDERORKEST see Marez Oyens, Tera de

3 PARTITEN see Roncalli, Ludovico

PARUSIE, ANNAHERUNG UND ENTFERNUNG, FOR FULL ORCHESTRA see Huber, Nicolaus A.

PAS DE DEUX see Dohl, Friedhelm

PASACALLES see Guerau, Francisco

PASEANDO see Azpiazu, Jose de

PASEO see Fricker, Peter Racine

PASQUINI, BERNARDO (1637-1710)
Partita Sopra La Aria Della Folia De Espagna I/IIA1

Sonata in D minor I/IIA1

Sonata in G minor I/IB1

Toccata Sur Le Jeu De "Coucou" I/IIA1

PASSA-MESA see Neusiedler, Hans

PASSA PASSA GAVIAO see Chansons Bresiliennes, Vol. II

PASSACAGLI; FOLIA; PAVANIGLIA; GAGLIARDA; ETC. see Miloni, Pietro

PASSACAGLIA, OMAGGIO A RONCALLI see Castelnuovo-Tedesco, Mario

PASSACAGLIA PER 7 STRUMENTI see Majo, Giulio di

PASSAGGIO, MESSA IN SCENA see Berio, Luciano

PASSAMEZZO GALLIARD see Robinson, Thomas

PASS'E MEZZO E SALTARELLO, A LA BOLOGNESA see Crema, Joan Maria da

PASSEMEZE see Le Roy, Adrien

PASSEPIED see Handel, George Frideric

PASSEPIEDS, 2 I/IB1

PASSO E MEZZO see Maestri Del '500

PASSO E MEZZO see Maestri Del '500

PASSO E MEZZO ITALIANO see Maestri Del '500

PASSO MEZZO IN DISCANT Y SALTARELLO see Galilei, Vincenzo

PASSO MEZZO MODERNO see Maestri Del '500

PASTETEN LIED see Hiller, Johann Adam

PASTOR, SEGUNDO
Estudio En Tremolo I/IA

PASTORAL – TRES LIBRE see Werner, Jean-Jacques

PASTORALE see Alfonso, Nicolas, Ya Van Los Pastores; Cruz, Ivo

PASTORALE UND ALLEGRO see Knab, Armin

PASTORALEN ALTER MEISTER, 9 IV/IIB2, IV/IIB3

PASTORALES PROVENCALES see Tomasi, Henri

PASTORCITO SANTO see Rodrigo, Joaquin

PATACHICH, IVAN (1922-)
Duo I/IIB1

Gyermekdalok Gitarra, Vol. 1 – Children's Songs For Guitar, Vol. 1 I/IB4

Gyermekdalok Gitarra, Vol. 2 – Children's Songs For Guitar, Vol. 2 I/IB4

Kis Tanulmanyok I/IA

Small Studies see Kis Tanulmanyok

PATT, RALPH
Guitar Chord Dictionary III

PAUBON, PIERRE (1910-)
Berceuse see Pieces, 6

Dance Populaire see Pieces, 6

Giocoso see Pieces, 6

Obsession see Pieces, 6

Pieces, 6 I/IB4

Prelude No. 1 see Pieces, 6

Serenade see Pieces, 6

PAVAN I/IB1
see also Allison, Richard

PAVAN AND GALLIARD see Holborne, Antony

PAVAN, MIN 283 see Maestri Del '500

PAVAN, MIN 414 see 4 Pieces By Dowland, Cutting, Morley

PAVANA, 6 see Ferrabosco, Alfonso (I)

PAVANA CAPRICHO see Albeniz, Isaac

PAVANA E SALTARELLO see Barberis, Melchior De

PAVANA ITALIANA see Cabezon, Antonio de

PAVANA, PASSACALLE, ETC. see Sanz, Gaspar

PAVANA PIJPER see Dowland, John, Piper's Pavan

PAVANA " THE EARLE OF SALISBURY" see Byrd, William

PAVANAS see Milan, Luis; Valderrabano, Enriquez de

PAVANAS, 6, AND A FANTASIA see Milan, Luis

PAVANAS see Guerau, Francisco

PAVANAS see Sanz, Gaspar

PAVANAS see Sanz, Gaspar

PAVANAS (SUIVI DE PARTIDOS AL AIRE ESPANOL) see Sanz, Gaspar

PAVANE, 8 see Barbetta Padovano, Julio Cesare

PAVANE B see Rosenmuller, Johann

PAVANE BRAY see Byrd, William

PAVANE ESPAGNOLE see Francisque, Antoine

PAVANE ET GAILLARDE see Le Roy, Adrien

PAVANE LACHRIMAE see Dowland, John, Lachrimae

PAVANE "MILLE DUCAS" see Susato, Tielman

PAVANE: MR. T. WAGSTAFF'S CONTENT OF DESIRE see Pilkington, Francis

PAVANE POUR UNE INFANTE DEFUNTE see Ravel, Maurice

PAVANE SANS PAIR see Cutting, Francis

PAVANE-SARABANDE-GIGUE see Vries Robbe, Willem de

PAVANE "SI IE ME VOIS" see Le Roy, Adrien

PAVANE TRISTE see Korn, Peter Jona

PAVANEN, 2 see Milan, Luis

PAVANES-GAILLARDES-BASSES DANCES-BRANLES see Attaignant, Pierre, [publisher]

PAVANS, 3, IN D see Milan, Luis

6 PAVANS AND 3 FANTASIAS see Milan, Luis

PAVANY, 2 see Milan, Luis

PEACE-MAKER 45 see Gilardino, Angelo

PECAS, 3 see Reussner, Esaias

5 PECAS see Bach, Johann Sebastian

PEDAL-EXERCITIUM IN G MINOR see Bach, Johann Sebastian

PEDRELL, CARLOS (1841-1922)
Al Atardecer En Los Jardines De Arlaja I/IB3

Betsabe see Danzas De Las Tres Princesas Cautivas, No. 3

Danzas De Las Tres Princesas Cautivas, No. 1 I/IB3

Danzas De Las Tres Princesas Cautivas, No. 2 I/IB3

Danzas De Las Tres Princesas Cautivas, No. 3 I/IB3

Dona Mencia see Danzas De Las Tres Princesas Cautivas, No. 2

Guitarreo see Pieces, 3, No. 3

Impromptu I/IB3

Lamento see Pieces, 3, No. 1

Pagina Romantica see Pieces, 3, No. 2

Pieces, 3, No. 1 I/IB3

Pieces, 3, No. 2 I/IB3

Pieces, 3, No. 3 I/IB3

Zoraida see Danzas De Las Tres Princesas Cautivas, No. 1

PEER GYNT; MUSIC TO THE PLAY see Zillig, Winfried

PEKIEL, BARTLOMIEJ (? -ca. 1670)
Allegro see Pieces, 4

Andante Espressivo see Pieces, 4

Andante Poco Deciso see Pieces, 4

Maestoso see Pieces, 4

Pieces, 4 I/IB1

PEKIEL, BARTLOMIEJ (cont'd.)

Utworow Na Lutnie Lub Gitare W Stroju E, 40 I/IB1

PELEMANS, WILLEM (1901-   )
7 Croquis I/IB4

Graf Van Verhaeren I/IIC2

Humoresque I/IB4

Kleine Studies, 6 I/IA

Petit Duo I/IIB1

Petites Etudes, 6 see Kleine Studies, 6

Preludes I/IIA1

6 Romances I/IB4

Sonatina I/IIA1

Speelse Wals I/IB4

Suite I/IIA1

PELLEGRINI, DOMENICO
Domenico Pellegrini I/IB1

PELTA, MAX
Prelude Et Valse I/IB4

PENDERECKI, KRZYSZTOF (1933-   )
Capriccio for Violin and Orchestra V/i

Concerto for Violoncello and Orchestra V/i

PENSIERI D'AUTUNNO see Rossi, Abner

PENSIEROSO see Shand, Ernest

PENTAMERON see Lonquich, Heinz Martin

PENTHIMA see Mamangakis, Nikos

PEPITA see Tarrega, Francisco

PEPUSCH, JOHN CHRISTOPHER (1667-1752)
Beggar's Opera, The I/IIB1

Sonata in D minor I/IIB1

Sonata in G I/IIB1

Sonata, MIN 51 I/IIB1

Sonaten, 3 I/IIB1

Stucke, 4 I/IIB1

PEQUENA ROMANZA see Abloniz, Miguel; Pujol, Emilio

PEQUENOS CAPRICHOS, 6 see Legnani, Luigi, Capricci, 6

3 PEQUENOS VALSES see Schubert, Franz (Peter)

PER LA CHITARRA see Saldarelli, Vincenzo

PER SUONARE A TRE see Brouwer, Leo

PERALDO BERT, NILO
Improvvisi, 2 I/IB4

Omaggio A Charlie Christian I/IB4

PERCHE see Hartig, Heinz Friedrich

PERCUSSION STUDIES see Behrend, Siegfried, Rhythmische Studien, Vol. 2

PERCUSSION STUDIES, 29 see Behrend, Siegfried, Rhythmische Studien, Vol. 1

PERDIDA TENGO LA COLOR see Canciones Antiguas, 5; Milan, Luis

PEREZ, RAFAEL
Carorena, Canzone Venezuelana I/IB5

PERFECTION IN THE ART OF PLAYING THE GUITAR, VOL. 1: FUNDAMENTS OF GUITAR PLAYING see Sack, Georg Christian, Weg Zum Kunstlerischen Gitarrespiel, Der, Vol. 1: Elemente Des Gitarrespiels

PERGITON IV see Hashagen, Klaus

PERGOLESI, GIOVANNI BATTISTA (1710-1736)
Siciliana I/IIA1, I/IIA2

Siciliano I/IIB1

PERIGOLDIMO see Paganini, Niccolo

PERIGOLDINO CON DOS VARIACIONES see Paganini, Niccolo

PERMUTATIONEN see Konietzny, Heinrich

PERONI, GIUSEPPE
Concerto A Tre I/IIB2

PERRICHON, JULIEN (ca. 1565-1610)
Preludes, 3 I/IB1

PERSKO, CHARLES
Guitar Method, 3 Vols. II

PERSPECTIVES see Krenek, Ernst, Perspektiven

PERSPEKTIVAS see Cameron, Pedro Bueno

PERSPEKTIVEN see Krenek, Ernst

PERUVIANA see Sanchez, B.

PERUZZI, AURELIO (1921-   )
Elegia Di Croton see Pezzi, 4

Finzioni see Pezzi, 4

Guernica see Pezzi, 4

Pezzi, 4 I/IB4

Recuerdos see Pezzi, 4

PESAME DELLO see Castelnuovo-Tedesco, Mario, Escarraman, A Suite Of Spanish Dances From The XVIth Century (After Cervantes)

PESCATORE CHE VA CANTANDO see Francesco da Milano

PETER, URSULA
Anfangsunterricht Im Gitarrespiel, Der, Vol. I II

Anfangsunterricht Im Gitarrespiel, Der, Vol. II II

Anfangsunterricht Im Gitarrespiel, Der, Vol. III II

Weg Zum Solospiel Auf Der Gitarre, Der see Anfangsunterricht Im Gitarrespiel, Der, Vol. III

PETIT, PIERRE (1922-   )
Concerto I/IIIB

Tarantelle I/IIA1

Theme and Variations I/IB4

Toccata I/IIA1

PETIT, RAYMOND
Nocturne I/IB4

PETIT BESTIAIRE, OP. 151 see Absil, Jean

PETIT DUO see Pelemans, Willem

PETIT GITAN, LE see Delauney, Paul

PETIT GUIDE FACILE D'ACCOMPAGNEMENT A LA GUITARE see Mille, Jo

PETIT GUITARISTE, LE see Dagosto, Sylvain

PETIT LIVRE see Morancon, Guy

PETIT NEGRE, LE see Debussy, Claude

PETIT OURS, LE, UNE HISTOIRE POUR LES PETITS ET LES GRANDS AMIS DE LA GUITARE see Cerf, Jacques

PETIT SOURCE, LA see Barlow, Fred

PETITE FILLE PARLE AU BON DIEU, UNE see Barlow, Fred

PETITE SERENADE see Rubin, Marcel

PETITE SERENADE IMPROMPTU see Bertouille, Gerard

PETITE SUITE see Bacarisse, Salvador; Barbier, Rene (Auguste-Ernest); Kovats, Barna

PETITE SUITE EN RE MINEUR, PT. 1 see Visee, Robert de

PETITE SUITE EN RE MINEUR, PT. 2 see Visee, Robert de

PETITE SUITE FRANCAISE see Duarte, John W.

PETITE SUITE MEDIEVALE see Djemil, Enyss

PETITE VALSE see Doerr, Charles-Kiko

PETITE VALSE-CONFIDENCE see Barlow, Fred

PETITES ETUDES, 6 see Pelemans, Willem, Kleine Studies, 6

PETITES PIECES, 3 see Rodrigo, Joaquin

PETITES PIECES, 3 see Vandermaesbrugge, Max

PETITES PIECES, 3 see Veremans, Renaat

PETITES PIECES, 6 see Ferandiere, Fernando

PETITES PIECES, 8 see Caroso, Fabrizio

PETITS MORCEAUX, 4 see Kuhnau, Johann

PETITS MORCEAUX POUR LES DEBUTANTS, 12 see Diana, Antoine

PETITS MOULINS A VENT, LES see Couperin, Francois (le Grand)

PETRAD see Gramberg, Jacq

PETRASSI, GOFFREDO (1904-   )
Concerto for Flute and Orchestra V/i

Nunc I/IB4

Seconda Serenata-Trio I/IIB2

Suoni Notturni I/IB4

PETZ, JOHANN CHRISTOPH (PEZ) (1664-1716)
Trio Sonata in C I/IIB2

PEUERL, PAUL (ca. 1570-ca. 1624)
Tanze, 3 I/IIB2

Tanze I/IIB3

PEZ, JOHANN CHRISTOPH
see PETZ, JOHANN CHRISTOPH

PEZZI, 2 see Grimm, Friedrich Karl

PEZZI, 2 see Brescianello, Giovanni Antonio

PEZZI, 3 see Garsi da Parma, Santino

PEZZI, 3 see Molinaro, Simone

PEZZI, 3 see Schumann, Robert (Alexander)

PEZZI, 3 see Staak, Pieter van der

PEZZI, 3 see Purcell, Henry

PEZZI, 4 see Bettinelli, Bruno

PEZZI, 4 see Peruzzi, Aurelio

PEZZI, 4, DA GRANDI VIRGINALISTI DELL'ERA ELISABETTIANA I/IB1-Coll

PEZZI, 5 see Eklund, Hans

PEZZI, 6 see Zuccheri, Luciano

PEZZI, 20, DEI SECOLI XVI, XVII E XVIII, TRATTI DALLA LETTERATURA DEL LIUTO, VIRGINALE E CLAVICEMBALO I/IB6-Coll

PEZZI BREVI, 3 see Beecroft, Norma

PEZZI BRILLANTI, 3 see Tarrega, Francisco

PEZZI CELEBRI, 20 I/IB6-Coll, VII-Mixed Coll

PEZZI FACILI, 3 I/IB6-Coll, VI-Mixed Coll

PEZZI PER CHITARRA, 3 see Bartolozzi, Bruno

PEZZI PER JIM, 2 see Behrend, Siegfried

PEZZI PER LIUTO, 4 see Vecchi, Orazio (Horatio)

PEZZI RICREATIVI (E DI UTILITA TECNICA), NELLO STILE POLIFONICO, 4 see Abloniz, Miguel

PEZZO IN MODO ANTICO see Tansman, Alexandre

PEZZOLI, GIORGIO
Andante Armonioso, Tema Di Autore
Ignoto I/IB4

PFISTER, CO
Duo Flamenco, Improvisaties Over Een
Argentijns Volkslied I/IIA1

PFISTER, HUGO (1914-1969)
Preambolo, Aria E Ballo I/IIB2

PHANTASIA UND DEUTSCHER TANZ see
Waissel(Ius), Matthaus

PHILIPS, PETER (1561-1628)
Chromatic Pavan I/IB1

Galliard I/IB1

Pavan I/IB1

PIANISSIMO, FOR FULL ORCHESTRA see
Schnittke, Alfred

PICCININI, ALESSANDRO
Toccata I/IB1, I/IIA1

PICCOLA ANTOLOGIA CHITARRISTICA
I/IB6-Coll, IV/I, VII-Mixed Coll

PICCOLA FUGA see Bischoff, Heinz

PICCOLA LEGGENDA see Pignocchi,
Emanuele

PICCOLE IMPRESSIONI DI CAMPAGNA see
Orsolino, Federico

PICCOLI PEZZI, 2 see Martini, Manlio

PICCOLO PEZZI, 4 see Lesage De Richee,
Philipp Franz

PICK, RICHARD SAMUEL BURNS (1915-   )
First Repertoire For Classic Guitar
I/IB4

Fundamental Fingerboard Harmony For
Guitar III

Improvisation I/IB4

Introduction To Effective
Accompaniment For Guitar II

Introduction To Guitar, Plectrum Or
Classic II

Lessons For Classic Guitar, Vol. I:
First Lessons For Classic Guitar
II

Lessons For Classic Guitar, Vol. II:
Lessons For Classic Guitar II

Preludes, 9 I/IB4

PICKING UP STICKS see Take Your
Partners; 6 English Country Dances

PIECE DE SALON see Paganini, Niccolo

PIECE EN FORME DE HABANERA see Ravel,
Maurice

PIECE IN F (MARCH) see Papas,
Sophocles

PIECE INTIME see Paganini, Niccolo

PIECE SANS TITRE, UNE see Musique
Elisabethaine

PIECE WITHOUT A TITLE, A see Dowland,
John

PIECE WITHOUT NAME see Holborne,
Antony

PIECES, 2 see Dowland, John

PIECES, 2 see Dowland, John

PIECES, 2 see Dowland, John

PIECES, 2 see Cutting, Francis

PIECES, 2 see Dowland, John

PIECES, 2 see Schweyda, Willy

PIECES, 2 see Massis, Amable

PIECES, 2 see Dandelot, Georges

PIECES, 2 see Duarte, John W.

PIECES, 3 see Dowland, John

PIECES, 3 see Le Roy, Adrien

PIECES, 3 see Chavez, Carlos

PIECES, 3 see Gagnebin, Henri

PIECES, 3 see Ruthenfranz, R.

PIECES, 3 see Tansman, Alexandre

PIECES, 3 see Wilson, Thomas

PIECES, 3 see Bull, John

PIECES, 3 see Tchaikovsky, Piotr
Ilyich

PIECES, 3 see Ballard, Robert

PIECES, 3 see Buisson, du

PIECES, 3 see Purcell, Henry

PIECES, 3 see Purcell, Henry

PIECES, 3, [1616] see Melii da Reggio,
Pietro Paolo

PIECES, 3 see Lerich, Pierre

PIECES, 3, NO. 1 see Pedrell, Carlos

PIECES, 3, NO. 2 see Pedrell, Carlos

PIECES, 3, NO. 3 see Pedrell, Carlos

PIECES, 4 see Pekiel, Bartlomiej

PIECES, 4 see Caroso, Fabrizio

PIECES, 4 see Carpentier, [Abbe]
Joseph

PIECES, 4 see Purcell, Henry

PIECES, 4 see Sweelinck, Jan
Pieterszoon

PIECES, 4 see Sweelinck, Jan
Pieterszoon

PIECES, 4 see Bull, John

PIECES, 4, OP.150 see Absil, Jean

PIECES, 5 see Cutting, Francis

PIECES, 5 see Farnaby, Giles

PIECES, 5 see Holborne, Antony

PIECES, 5 see Mace, Thomas

PIECES, 5 see Scarlatti, Domenico

PIECES, 5 see Fetler, Paul

PIECES, 5 see Ponce, Manuel Maria

PIECES, 5 see Susato, Tielman

PIECES, 5 I/IIB1

PIECES, 5 see Pilkington, Francis

PIECES, 5 see Robinson, Thomas

PIECES, 5, OP. 62 see Legley, Victor

PIECES, 6 see Couperin, Louis

PIECES, 6 see Dowland, John

PIECES, 6 see Tchaikovsky, Piotr
Ilyich

PIECES, 6 see Arnell, Richard

PIECES, 6 see Paubon, Pierre

PIECES, 6 see Corelli, Arcangelo

PIECES, 6, EXTRAITES DU LIVRE PUBLIE EN
1686 ET DEDIE A S.M. LOUIS XIV see
Visee, Robert de

PIECES, 7 see Dowland, John

PIECES, 8, VOL. 1 see Dowland, John

PIECES, 8, VOL. 2 see Dowland, John

PIECES, 10 see Absil, Jean; Galilei,
Vincenzo

PIECES, 12, VOL. I: NOS. 1-4 see
Absil, Jean

PIECES, 12, VOL II: NOS. 5-8 see
Absil, Jean

PIECES, 12, VOL. III: NOS. 9-12 see
Absil, Jean

PIECES, 20, DE SON LIVRE DE TABLATURE
DE GUITARE see Campion, Francois

2 PIECES see Robinson, Thomas

3 PIECES BY HOLBORNE, PERICHON, BALARD
I/IB1-Coll

4 PIECES BY DOWLAND, CUTTING, MORLEY
I/IB1-Coll

5 PIECES see Paganini, Niccolo

8 PIECES see Blavet, Michel

PIECES BREVES, 4 see Martin, Frank

PIECES BREVES, 6 see Farkas, Ferenc

PIECES CARACTERISTIQUES, 2, SUITE see
Casseus, Frantz Gabriel

PIECES CARACTERISTIQUES, VOL. 1 see
Moreno Torroba, Federico

PIECES CARACTERISTIQUES, VOL. 2 see
Moreno Torroba, Federico

PIECES DE CLAVECIN see Couperin,
Francois (le Grand)

PIECES DE CLAVECIN see Rameau, Jean-
Philippe

PIECES DE GUITARE see Losy vom
Losinthal, Jan Antonin

PIECES DE LA RENAISSANCE ESPAGNOLE, 4
I/IB1-Coll

PIECES ELISABETHAINES I/IB1-Coll

PIECES ELIZABETHAINES, 2 I/IIA1

PIECES FACILES see Digmeloff, Germain

PIECES FACILES, 10, POUR L'ETUDE see
Bosch, Jacques

12 PIECES FACILES see Matiegka,
Wenzeslaus Thomas, 12 Leichte
Stucke

PIECES FACILES POUR APPRENDRE LE
PUNTEADO, 8 see Sanz, Gaspar

PIECES FACILES, PREMIER CAHIER see
Azpiazu, Jose de

PIECES FACILES, VOL. I see Tansman,
Alexandre

PIECES FACILES, VOL. II see Tansman,
Alexandre

12 PIECES FOR GUITAR AND CONTINUO see
Geminiani, Francesco

PIECES FROM THE FITZWILLIAM VIRGINAL
BOOK, 13 I/IB1-Coll

PIECES FROM THE MULLINER BOOK, 10
I/IIB1-Coll

PIECES FROM THE TIME OF QUEEN
ELIZABETH, 4 I/IIA2-Coll

PIECES FROM VENEZUELA, 5 see Sojo,
Vincente E.

PIECES MELODIQUES ET TRANSCRIPTIONS
I/IB6-Coll

4 PIECES POUR GUITARE (1552) see Le
Roy, Adrien

26 PIECES POUR GUITARE see Bach,
Johann Sebastian

PIECES POUR LUTH DU 16E SIECLE, 12
I/IB1-Coll

PIECES POUR UNE NOBLE FEMME, 3 see
Furstenau, Wolfram

PIECES SANS TITRE see Anonymous

PIECES SUR 6 CORDES, 5 see Cerf,
Jacques

PIEMONTOISE, LA see Couperin, Louis

PIERRES MAGIQUES, LES, BALLET see
Barbier, Rene (Auguste-Ernest)

PIERWSZE KROKI GITARZYSTY I/IB6-Coll

PIEZA BREVE see Schumann, Robert
(Alexander)

PIEZA SIN TITULO see Brouwer, Leo

PIEZAS, 3 see Visee, Robert de

PIEZAS, 4 see Visee, Robert de

PIEZAS, 4 see Purcell, Henry

PIEZAS, 6 see Tchaikovsky, Piotr
Ilyich

PIEZAS, 7 see Chavarri, Eduardo Lopez

2 PIEZAS PARA LAUD DEL TEATRO DE
SHAKESPEARE see Anonymous

4 PIEZAS see Lesage De Richee, Philipp
Franz

4 PIEZAS DEL S. XVIII see Anonymous

5 PIEZAS see Encina, Juan del

5 PIEZAS see Schumann, Robert
(Alexander)

5 PIEZAS see Schumann, Robert
(Alexander)

5 PIEZAS DEL SIGLO XVI I/IB1-Coll

PIEZAS DE LAUD, 4 see Robinson, Thomas

PIEZAS DE SOCIEDAD, 3, OP. 33, NO. 1
see Sor, Fernando, Trois Pieces De
Societe , Op. 33, No. 1

PIEZAS DE SOCIEDAD, 3, OP. 33, NO. 3
see Sor, Fernando, Trois Pieces De
Societe, Op. 33, No. 3

PIEZAS DE SOCIEDAD, 3, OP33, NO. 2 see
Sor, Fernando, Trois Pieces De
Societe, Op. 33, No. 2

PIEZAS DIVERSAS PARA LAUD see Weiss,
Sylvius Leopold

PIEZAS ESPANOLAS, 3 see Rodrigo,
Joaquin

PIEZAS FACILES, 4 see Rodrigo, Joaquin

PIEZAS FACILES, 6 see Sor, Fernando,
Six Petites Pieces Faciles

20 PIEZAS FACILES DEL ALBUM DE ANA
MAGDALENA BACH see Bach, Johann
Sebastian

PIEZAS PARA LAUD DEL SIGLO XVI, 4
I/IB1

PIEZAS POPULARES CUBANAS see Brouwer,
Leo

PIGNOCCHI, EMANUELE
Piccola Leggenda I/IB4

PIJPER, WILLEM (1894-1947)
C'est Le Chien De Jean De Nivelle
see Romance Sans Paroles

Romance Sans Paroles V/ii

PILI, SALVATORE (1933-   )
Chitarrista Moderno, Il II,
VII-Mixed Coll

PILKINGTON, FRANCIS (ca. 1562-1638)
Curranta For Mrs. Elizabeth Murcott
see Pieces, 5

George Pilkington's Funeral, Pavan
see Pieces, 5

Mrs. Anne Harecourt's Galliard see
Pieces, 5

Pavane: Mr. T. Wagstaff's Content Of
Desire see Pieces, 5

Pieces, 5 I/IB1

Spanish Pavane, The see Pieces, 5

PILSL, F.
Gitarrestucke Fur Die Jugend I/IB4

Miniaturproblematicos I/IB4

PILSS, KARL (1902-1979)
Sonatina I/IIB1

PIOSENKI LUDOWE I POPULARNE
I/IIC1-Coll

PIOSENKI Z PODDASZA, NA GLOS I GITARE
I/IIC1-Coll

PIPER'S PAVAN see Dowland, John

PISADOR, DIEGO (ca. 1508-1557)
Fantasia Facil I/IB1

Fantasy No. 1 I/IB1

Guarte, Guarte El Rey Don Sancho
I/IIC1

Guarte, Guarte El Rey Don Sancho,
Romance Viejo I/IIC1

Lagrime Mesti, Villanesca I/IIC1

Madonna Mia Fa, Villanesca I/IIC1

PISADOR, DIEGO (cont'd.)
Manana De San Juan, La, Romance Viejo
I/IIC1

Pavan I/IB1

Quien Tu Viese Tal Poder, Villancico
I/IIC1

Si La Noche Hace Oscura, Villancico
I/IIC1

Si Te Vas A Baner Juanica, Villancico
I/IIC1

Villanelle: Dites Au Chevalier Que
I/IB1

Villanesca I/IB1

Villanesca I/IB1

PITFIELD, THOMAS BARON (1903-   )
Sonatina in A minor I/IC

PIVA, LA see Celebri Melodie Natalizie

PIZZICATO see Pujol, Emilio

PIZZINI, CARLO ALBERTO (1905-   )
Capriccio Napoletano I/IB4

Concierto Para Tres Hermanas I/IIIA

Improvviso Da Concerto I/IB4

Suite Infantile I/IB4, I/IIA1

PLAINE SONG see Robinson, Thomas

PLAINE SONG, A see Robinson, Thomas

PLAINTE see Martin, Frank

PLAINTE DE LA FEUILLE D'AUTOMNE see
Barlow, Fred

PLAINTES DE LA JEUNE FILLE, LES see
Schubert, Franz (Peter), Des
Madchens Klage

PLAINTES D'UNE POUPEE, LES see Franck,
Cesar

PLANTA Y TACON, ZAPATEADO see Monge,
Victor ("Serranito")

PLATERO Y YO, VOL. I see Castelnuovo-
Tedesco, Mario

PLATERO Y YO, VOL. II see Castelnuovo-
Tedesco, Mario

PLATERO Y YO, VOL. III see
Castelnuovo-Tedesco, Mario

PLATERO Y YO, VOL. IV see Castelnuovo-
Tedesco, Mario

PLAY CLASSIC GUITAR see Vinson, Harvey

PLAY GUITAR!, VOL. I see Crimlisk,
Anthony

PLAY GUITAR!, VOL. II see Crimlisk,
Anthony

PLAY THE GUITAR, A SELF TUTOR see
Gavall, John

PLAYFELLOW (OR WANTON) see Holborne,
Antony

PLAYFORD, JOHN (1623-1686)
Playford Tunes, 12 I/IIB1

PLAYFORD TUNES, 12 see Playford, John

PLAYFORD TUNES, 8 ENGLISH TRADITIONAL
DANCE TUNES I/IB5-Coll

PLAYING THE GUITAR, A SELF-INSTRUCTION
GUIDE TO TECHNIQUE AND THEORY see
Noad, Frederick M.

PLEGARIA see Albeniz, Isaac

PLI SELON PLI, PORTRAIT DE MALLARME, 1
see Boulez, Pierre

PLI SELON PLI, PORTRAIT DE MALLARME, 2
see Boulez, Pierre

PLI SELON PLI, PORTRAIT DE MALLARME, 4
see Boulez, Pierre

PLI SELON PLI, PORTRAIT DE MALLARME, 5
see Boulez, Pierre

PLUMBRIDGE, W.H.
How To Play Guitar, Finger Style II

PLUS QUE LENTE, LA, VALSE see Debussy,
Claude

POBRE MESTRE see Chansons Catalanes, 2

POCKET-MUSIC see Staak, Pieter van der

POCO ALLEGRETTO see Carulli,
Ferdinando

POCO VIVO, UN see Urban, Stepan

POEMI BREVI, 6 see Rosetta, Giuseppe

POHLERT, WERNER
Neue Gitarrenschule, Klassische Und
Moderne Spieltechnik, Anhang Fur
E-Gitarre Und E-Bass II

POINT D'ORGUE see Buisson, du

POLACZEK, DIETMAR (1942-   )
Metamorfosen Und Fuge I/IB4

POLAK, JAKOB
see JAKOB POLAK (JACQUES POLONAIS)

POLASEK, BARBERA
Gitarre Im Gruppenunterricht II

POLENMADCHEN see Rosenstengel,
Albrecht

POLIFEMO DE ORO, IL, 4 FRAGMENTI see
Smith Brindle, Reginald

POLISH DANCE see Staak, Pieter van der

POLKA see Bloch, Waldemar

POLKA see Tarrega, Francisco

POLNISCHE MEISTER see Europaische
Gitarren- Und Lautenmusik, Vol. 7

POLO, EL, IMPRESSIONE see Albeniz,
Isaac

POLOLANIK, ZDENEK (1935-   )
Concentus Resonabilis V/i

Concerto Grosso V/i

Scherzo Contrario I/IIB2

POLONAIS, JACQUES LE
see JAKOB POLAK (JACQUES POLONAIS)

POLONAISES see Z Polonezow Polskich

POLONESA see Albeniz, Isaac

POLSCY MISTRZOWIE GITARY I/IB6-Coll

POLYDIAPHONIE see Bozza, Eugene

POLYPHONES SPIELHEFT I/IIA1-Coll,
I/IIA2-Coll, I/IIA3-Coll

POLYPHONIC PLAYING ON THE GUITAR see
Hoek, Jan-Anton Van, Bouwstenen Van
Het Polyphoon Gitaarspel, Vol. I,
Nos. 1-21; Hoek, Jan-Anton Van,
Bouwstenen Van Het Polyphoon
Gitaarspel, Vol. II, Nos. 22-37

POLYPHONY AND POLYTONALITY see Hoek,
Jan-Anton Van

POMILIO, TOMAS
Formulas Tecnicas, Para El Mecanismo
Elemental De La Guitarra III,
VI-Mixed Coll

PONCE, MANUEL MARIA (1882-1948)
Allegro, MIN291 see Canciones
Populares Mexicanas, 3

Allegro, MIN293 see Canciones
Populares Mexicanas, 3

Andante, MIN 292 see Canciones
Populares Mexicanas, 3

Canciones Populares Mexicanas, 3
I/IB4

Concierto Del Sur I/IIIA

Estrellita, Cancion Mexicana I/IB5

Estudio De Tremolo I/IA

Gavotta E Minuetto see Suite In D
Major: Gavotte I And II, D Major
And D Minor

Gavotte in D see Suite In D Major:
Gavotte I And II, D Major And D
Minor

Pieces, 5 I/IIA1

Prelude I/IB4

Preludes, Vol. I: Nos. 1-6 I/IB4

PONCE, MANUEL MARIA (cont'd.)

Preludes, Vol. II: Nos. 7-12 I/IB4

Preludios Cortos, 6 I/IB4

Scherzino Mexicano I/IB4

Sonata Clasica, Hommage A Fernando Sor I/IC

Sonata Mexicana see Sonata No. 1

Sonata No. 1 I/IC

Sonata No. 3 I/IC

Sonata Romantica, Hommage A Franz Schubert Qui Aimait La Guitare I/IC

Sonatina Meridional I/IC

Suite in A minor I/IB4

Suite in D I/IB4

Suite In D Major: Gavotte I And II, D Major And D Minor I/IB4

Theme Varie Et Finale I/IB4

Variations Sur "Folia De Espana" Et Fugue I/IB4

Waltz I/IB4

PONTEIO see Bosmans, Arthur, Brasileiras, No.1

POOLSE LUITMUZIEK I/IB1-Coll

POP & ART see Niehaus, Manfred

POPULAIRE GITAARDUETTEN I/IIA1-Coll

POPULE MEUS see Victoria, Tomas Luis de

PORQUE ES, DAMA, TANTO QUEREROS? see Canciones Antiguas, 6

PORQUE FUE SENSIBLE, CAPRICCIO NACH FRANCESCO DE GOYA see Behrend, Siegfried

PORRINO, ENNIO (1910-1959)
Concerto Dell'Argentarola I/IIIA

PORTUGIESCHER TANZ see Tanze, 6

POSAVSKI DRMES see Cossetto, Emil

POSER, HANS (1917-1970)
Kleine Serenade I/IIB1

Musikanten A-B-C, Das I/IIC5

POSICIONES FIJAS see Fresno, Jorge

POSTKARTEN SUITE see Behrend, Siegfried

POSUVNE TRANSPOSICNI PRAVITKO III

POULENC, FRANCIS (1899-1963)
Embarquement Pour Cythere I/IIA1

Sarabande, Dedie A Ida Presti I/IB4

Waltz I/IIA1

POUR CHRISTIANE see Franceries, Marc

POUR ELISE see Beethoven, Ludwig van, Fur Elise

POUR LA GUITARE, VOL. 1 see Constant, Franz

POUR LA GUITARE, VOL. 2 see Constant, Franz

POURPRE see Leclercq, Norbert

POURQUOI ME BAT see Seiber, Matyas Gyorgy

POWROZNIAK, JOZEF
ABC Gitary, Czyli Jak Hania Na Gitarze Grac Sie Nauczyla II

Szkola Gry Na Gitarze II, VII-Mixed Coll

Szkola Gry Na Gitarze, Wydanie Zmienione Uzupelnione Dodatkiem O Grze Na Gitarze Hawajskiej II, VII-Mixed Coll

PRAAG, HENRI C. VAN (1894-1968)
Complainte I/IIB1

Duettino I/IIB1

PRAAG, HENRI C. VAN (cont'd.)

Music For Schools, No. 1, Version 1951 see Schoolmuziek No. 1

Music For Schools No. 3 see Schoolmuziek No. 3

Music For Schools No. 3, Version 1951 see Schoolmuziek No. 3

Schoolmuziek No. 1 I/IIB5

Schoolmuziek No. 3 I/IIB5, I/IIC5

Sonata I/IIB2

PRAAMBULUM UND TANZ see Neusiedler, Hans

PRACTICAL GUITAR TEACHING see Worschech, Romain, Enseignement Pratique De La Guitare, Vol. I

PRADO, JOSE-ANTONIO (ALMEIDA) (1943-   )
Livre Pour Six Cordes I/IB4

Livro Para Seis Cordas see Livre Pour Six Cordes

PRAELUDE IN D-MOLL see Bach, Johann Sebastian, Prelude for Lute, BWV 999, in C minor

7 PRAELUDIEN see Diabelli, Anton

PRAELUDIO CON LA SUITE OF JOHANN SEBASTIAN BACH IN TABLATURE FOR LUTE, THE, BWV 996 see Bach, Johann Sebastian, Suite for Lute, BWV 996, in E minor

PRAETORIUS, MICHAEL (1571-1621)
Ballet see Terpsichore Musarum

Bourree see Terpsichore Musarum

Espagnoleta see Terpsichore Musarum

4 French Dances I/IIA3

Gavotte see Terpsichore Musarum

In Dulci Jubilo see Puer Natus In Bethlehem [Collection]

Puer Natus In Bethlehem see Puer Natus In Bethlehem [Collection]

Puer Natus In Bethlehem [Collection] IV/IIA1, IV/IIA2, IV/IIA3

Saraband see Terpsichore Musarum

Tanze I/IIB2

Terpsichore Musarum I/IB1

Volta see Terpsichore Musarum

Vom Himmel Hoch see Puer Natus In Bethlehem [Collection]

PRAF, [FRAY] BENEDICTO
Airs Russes, 3 I/IB5

Balalaika see Airs Russes, 3

Manoir, Le see Airs Russes, 3

Traineau, Le see Airs Russes, 3

PRAGER, HEINRICH ALOYS (1783-1854)
Introduktion, Thema Und Variationen I/IIB1

PRAGER KARNEVAL; BALLET-TRIPTYCH AFTER THREE MEDIEVAL BALLADS see Kaslik, Vaclav

PRAKTISCH LEERBOEK VOOR GITAAR, VOL. I see Jonge, Charles de

PRAKTISCH LEERBOEK VOOR GITAAR, VOL. II see Jonge, Charles de

PRAKTISCHE GITARRE-SCHULE, ZUR SELBSTERLERNUNG NEBST ZAHLREICHEN LIEDERN, SOLOSZENEN, COUPLETS, DUETTEN, USW. see Scholl, R.

PRAKTISCHE UND LEICHTVERSTANDLICHE SCHULE ZUM SELBSTUNTERRICHT FUR DIE GITARRE, OP. 35 see Mayer, Alois

PRALUDIEN, 6 see Giuliani, Mauro, Preludes, 6, Op. 83; Hove, Joachim van den

PRALUDIEN, 18 see Molino, Francesco

PRALUDIEN, 24 see Carulli, Ferdinando, Preludes, 24

PRALUDIEN UND ETUDEN ZUR VERVOLLKOMMNUNG DER TECHNIK see Hoek, Jan-Anton Van

PRALUDIEN ZUR BILDUNG DES ANSCHLAGES, 20 see Carulli, Ferdinando

PRALUDIUM D-MOLL see Bach, Johann Sebastian, Prelude for Lute, BWV 999, in C minor

PRALUDIUM UND 2 MENUETTE I/IB1

PRALUDIUM UND FANTASIE see Holborne, Antony

PRALUDIUM UND FUGATO (PRESTO) see Bach, Johann Sebastian, Suite for Lute, BWV 996, in E minor, Passaggio-Prelude

PRAT, DOMINGO (1866-1944)
Escalas Y Arpegios De Mecanismo Tenico Para Guitarra III, VI-Mixed Coll

Nueva Tecnica De La Guitarra, La III

PRAYERS, 3 see Franco, Johan

PREAMBEL see Neusiedler, Hans

PREAMBL, EIN see Anonymous

PREAMBOLO, ARIA E BALLO see Pfister, Hugo

PREAMBOLO Y TOCCATA SURENA see Sanchez, B.

PREAMBULO see Moreno Torroba, Federico

PRECIOSA, LA see Sanz, Gaspar

PREGHIERA see Mertz, Johann Kaspar

PREISSLER-SPIELHEFT, VOL. I I/IIB5-Coll

PREISSLER-SPIELHEFT, VOL. II I/IIB5-Coll

PREISSLER-SPIELHEFT, VOL. III I/IIB5-Coll

PREISSLER-SPIELHEFT, VOL. IV I/IIB5-Coll

PRELUDE see Bach, Johann Sebastian, Menuet-Trio In G Minor

PRELUDE AND ALLEGRO see Murcia, Santiago de

PRELUDE AND RONDO see Bellow, Alexander

PRELUDE, CANTO AND TOCCATA see Duarte, John W.

PRELUDE EN ARPEGES see Duarte, John W.

PRELUDE ET BARCAROLLE see Absil, Jean

PRELUDE ET CHANSON see Le Roy, Adrien

PRELUDE ET FUGUE, ALLA ANTIQUA see Lerich, Pierre

PRELUDE ET IMPROMPTU see Shand, Ernest

PRELUDE ET MENUET (RE MINEUR) see Anonymous

PRELUDE ET VALSE see Pelta, Max

PRELUDE, FUGA AND ALLEGRO OF JOHANN SEBASTIAN BACH IN TABLATURE FOR LUTE, THE, BWV 998 see Bach, Johann Sebastian, Prelude, Fugue And Allegro For Lute, In E-Flat

PRELUDE - FUGUE see Bach, Johann Sebastian, Prelude, Fugue And Allegro For Lute, In E-Flat

PRELUDE, FUGUE AND ALLEGRO FOR LUTE, IN E: ALLEGRO see Bach, Johann Sebastian

PRELUDE, FUGUE AND ALLEGRO FOR LUTE, IN E-FLAT see Bach, Johann Sebastian; Bach, Johann Sebastian

PRELUDE, FUGUE AND ALLEGRO IN E FLAT see Bach, Johann Sebastian

PRELUDE IN CHORDS see Segovia, Andres

PRELUDE IN E MINOR (FROM DAS WOHLTEMPERIERTE CLAVIER, BOOK I) see Bach, Johann Sebastian

PRELUDE, MIN 284 see Piezas Para Laud Del Siglo XVI, 4

PRZY GITARZE, VOL. I: UKOCHANY KRAJ,
PIESNI I TANCE POLSKIE I/IIC1-Coll

PRZY GITARZE, VOL. II: NASZE PIOSENKI
I/IIC1-Coll

PRZY GITARZE, VOL. III: W CICHY WIECZOR
I/IIC1-Coll

PSALLEIN see Blake Watkins, Michael

PSALM NO. 5 see Sweelinck, Jan
Pieterszoon

PSALM NO. 23 see Sweelinck, Jan
Pieterszoon

PSALM NO. 30 see Reda, Siegfried,
Psalmus Morte Servati

PSALM NO. 66 see Schonbach, Dieter,
Canticum Psalmi Resurrectionis

PSALM NO. 91 see Blarr, Oskar
Gottlieb, Wer Wohnt Unterm Schirm
Des Hochsten

PSALM NO. 145 see Schonbach, Dieter,
Canticum Psalmi Ad Laudes

PSALMODIA UBER DAS V. GEBOT MOSE, IN
MEMORIAM QUANG DUC – VIETNAM see
Furstenau, Wolfram

PSALMUS MORTE SERVATI see Reda,
Siegfried

PSAUMES ET 3 CHANSONS, 2 see Huygens,
Constantin

PUER NATUS IN BETHLEHEM see
Praetorius, Michael

PUER NATUS IN BETHLEHEM [COLLECTION]
see Praetorius, Michael

PUERTA DE TIERRA, BOLERO see Albeniz,
Isaac

PUES NO ME QUEREIS HABLER I/IB1

PUIJENBROECK, VICTOR VAN
Kunst Van Het Gitaarspel, De – Art De
Jouer De La Guitare, L' II,
VI-Mixed Coll

Systeme De Gammes Pour Guitare see
Toonladder Systeem Voor Gitaar

Toonladder Systeem Voor Gitaar III

PUJOL, EMILIO (1886-1982)
Abejorro, El, Estudio I/IA

Aquelarre I/IA

Atardecer I/IB4

Bagatelle I/IB4

Barcarolle I/IB4

Becqueriana, Complainte I/IB4

Canaries I/IIA1

Cancio De Cuna I/IB4

Cancion Amatoria, Estudio I/IA

Canto De Otono I/IA

Cap I Cua I/IB4

Caprice Varie Sur Un Theme D'Aguado
I/IB4

Chant d'Automne, Etude Melodique see
Canto De Otono

Complainte A l'aimee Disparue see
Endecha Alla Amada Ausente

Cubana I/IB4

Danse Des Sorcieres, Etude Dynamique
see Aquelarre

Deuxieme Triquilandia I/IB4

Duet (Etude) I/IIA1

Endecha Alla Amada Ausente I/IB4

Escuela De La Guitarra, Basada En Los
Principios De La Technica De
Tarrega II

Escuela Razonada De La Guitarra, 3
Vols. II

Escuela Razonada De La Guitarra,
Basada En Los Principios De La
Technica De Tarrega, Vol. I II

PUJOL, EMILIO (cont'd.)

Escuela Razonada De La Guitarra,
Basada En Los Principios De La
Technica De Tarrega, Vol. II II,
VI-Mixed Coll

Escuela Razonada De La Guitarra,
Basada En Los Principios De La
Technica De Tarrega, Vol. III
II, VI-Mixed Coll

Escuela Razonada De La Guitarra,
Basada En Los Principios De La
Technica De Tarrega, Vol. IV II,
VI-Mixed Coll

Escuela Razonada De La Guitarra,
Basada En Los Principios De La
Technica De Tarrega, Vol. V II

Estudios: Grado Superior I/IA

Etude in C see Pizzicato

Etude No. 1 I/IA

Etude No. 2 I/IA

Etude No. 3 I/IA

Exercises En Forme d'Etudes, Vol. 1
I/IA

Exercises En Forme d'Etudes, Vol. 2
I/IA

Fantasia Breve Sobre El Nombre
"Salcedo" I/IB4

Festivola, Danza Catalana De Espiritu
Popular I/IB4

Guajira see Morceaux Espagnols, 3

Homenaje A Tarrega I/IB4

Impromptu I/IB4

Libelula, La, Study I/IA

Manola Del Avapies, Tonadilla I/IB4

Metodo Razionale Per Chitarra see
Escuela De La Guitarra, Basada En
Los Principios De La Technica De
Tarrega

Morceaux Espagnols, 3 I/IB4

Ondinas I/IA

Paisaje I/IA

Pequena Romanza I/IB4

Pizzicato I/IA

Preludes, 2 I/IA

Preludio Romantico I/IB4

Rapsodia Valenciana I/IB4

Ricercare I/IIA1

Salve I/IB4

Sequidilla I/IB4

Sevilla, Evocation I/IB4

Study No. 7 see Ondinas

Tambors, Les 3, Glosa De La Cancion
Popular Catalana I/IB5

Tango see Morceaux Espagnols, 3

Tonadilla see Morceaux Espagnols, 3

Triptique Campagnard I/IA

Triquilandia, Jugando Al Escondite
(Cache-Cache) I/IB4

Troisieme Triquilandia I/IB4

Variations Sur Un Theme Obsedant
I/IB4

Veneciana I/IB4

Villanesca, Danza Campesina I/IB4

PULSACION see Fresno, Jorge

PUNTEADO-SUITE see Komter, Jan Maarten

PUNTEADO TACONEO CLASICO see Moreno
Torroba, Federico

PUPAZZI see Zuccheri, Luciano

PURCELL, DANIEL (ca. 1660-1717)
Sonata in F I/IIB1

PURCELL, HENRY (1658 or 59-1695)
Air, MIN 81 see Pieces, 4

Air, MIN 86 see Pieces, 3

Air, MIN 220 see Piezas, 4

Album Henry Purcell I/IB1

Almand And Minuet I/IB1

Aria see Pezzi, 3

Chaconne I/IB1

Courante, MIN 91 I/IB1

Gavotte, MIN 219 I/IB1

Gavotte, MIN 269 see Piezas, 4

Gigue, MIN 88 see Pieces, 3

Hornpipe see Pezzi, 3

Hornpipe see Pieces, 4

Hornpipe see Piezas, 4

Minuet, MIN 87 see Pieces, 3

New Irish Tune, A see Pieces, 3

Pezzi, 3 I/IB1

Pieces, 3 I/IB1

Pieces, 3 I/IB1

Pieces, 4 I/IB1

Piezas, 4 I/IB1

Prelude, MIN 84 see Pieces, 3

Prelude, MIN 89 see Piezas, 4

Prelude, MIN 90 I/IB1

Preludio E Allemanda I/IB1

Rondeau De Abdelazar I/IB1

Rondo, MIN 82 see Pieces, 4

Rondo, MIN 85 see Pieces, 3

Rondo, MIN 268 see Pezzi, 3

Suite I/IIB1

Suite No. 1 I/IB1

Suite No. 4 I/IB1

PUSKAS, TIBOR
Gitariskola, Vol. I II

Gitarrenschule, Vol. I see
Gitariskola, Vol. I

PUTILIN, IVAN
Andante, Altes Volkslied I/IB5

Romanze, Altes Zigeunerlied I/IB5

PYRRHOS; BALLETSINFONIE see Havelka,
Svatopluk

QUAESTIO TEMPORIS see Krenek, Ernst

QUAGLINO, ANACLETO
Andantino I/IB4

QUAL MESTO GEMITO see Giuliani, Mauro

QUANDO SPERAI see Monteverdi, Claudio

QUARTE LEZIONI, LE see Sagreras, Julio
S., Lessons For The Guitar, Vol. 4,
The Fourth Lessons

QUARTES ET SIXTES see Doerr, Charles-
Kiko

QUARTETT see Sor, Fernando, Sonata,
Op. 15, No. 2, in C

QUARTETT NACH DEM NOTTURNO, OP. 21, VON
WENZEL MATIEGKA see Schubert,
Franz (Peter), Quartet, D. 96 for
Flute, Viola, Guitar and
Violoncello

QUARTETTINO I IN C see Bruchner,
Rudolf

QUARTETTO DA CAMERA see Kubizek,
Augustin

QUARTO DI VITA, UN; OPERA DA STRADA, IN
TWO ACTS AND TWELVE SCENES see
Gaslini, Giorgio

QUASI ALLEGRO see Abloniz, Miguel

QUATRAINS OF OMAR KHAYYAM, 3 see Staak, Pieter van der

QUATRE PAS DE DEUX, FOR FLUTE AND ORCHESTRA see Kruyf, Ton de

QUATRIEME FANTAISIE see Fuenllana, Miguel de

QUATTRO TRANSCRIPCIONES see Bach, Johann Sebastian

QUAUHQUAUHTINCHAN IN DEN VREEMDE; A RADIOPHONIC OPERA see Kruyf, Ton de

QUE ES DE TI, DESCONSOLADO see Encina, Juan del

QUE HERMOSOS SON SUS PASOS see Handel, George Frideric, How Beautiful Are The Feet Of Them

QUEEN ELIZABETH HER GALLIARD, THE see Dowland, John; Dowland, John; Dowland, John

QUELQUES PAGES DE GUITARE CLASSIQUE I/IB1, I/IB1-Coll, VII-Mixed Coll

QUESTION OF TIME, A (EINE FRAGE DER ZEIT) see Krenek, Ernst, Quaestio Temporis

QUESTIONS see Farquhar, David

QUI IUSTUS EST, IUSTIFICETUR ADHUC see Manneke, Daan

QUIEN TU VIESE TAL PODER, VILLANCICO see Pisador, Diego

QUIERES APRENDER MUSICA Y TOCAR LA GUITARRA EN 15 LECCIONES? see Galindo, Patricio

QUIET DANCE see Ward-Steinman, David

QUIET SONGS, 5 see Duarte, John W.

QUIMERAS, NO.1 see Sanchez, B.

QUIMERAS, NO.2 see Sanchez, B.

QUIMERAS, NO.3 see Sanchez, B.

QUINE, HECTOR
    Introduction To The Guitar II

QUINTAS LECCIONES, LAS see Sagreras, Julio S., Lessons For The Guitar, Vol. 5, The Fifth Lessons

QUINTE LEZIONI, LE see Sagreras, Julio S., Lessons For The Guitar, Vol. 5, The Fifth Lessons

QUINTERNA FUR GITARRESOLO see Denhoff, Michael

QUINTETTI, 6, CON CHITARRA, GE. 445-450 see Boccherini, Luigi

QUINTETTO DALLA "SEMIRAMIDE" DI ROSSINI see Giuliani, Mauro, Qual Mesto Gemito

QUINTINA UBER DIE FUNF VOKALE see Krenek, Ernst

QUINZE INVENTIONS A DEUX VOIX, LES: COLLECTION L'HEURE DE LA GUITARE CLASSIQUE, VOL. I see Bach, Johann Sebastian

QUINZE INVENTIONS A DEUX VOIX, LES: COLLECTION L'HEURE DE LA GUITARE CLASSIQUE, VOL. II see Bach, Johann Sebastian

QUIRPA GUATIRENA, JOROPO see Sojo, Vincente E.

QUODLINGS DELIGHT see Six Pieces From The Time Of Elizabeth

RACCOLTA DI MUSICHE I/IB6-Coll

RACHMANINOFF, SERGEY VASSILIEVICH (1873-1943)
    Prelude, Op. 3, No. 2 I/IB3

RACINE FRICKER, PETER
    see FRICKER, PETER RACINE

RADE, EN see Straesser, Joep

RADINO, GIOVANNI MARIA
    Intavolatura Di Balli (1592) I/IB1-Coll

RADOLE, GIUSEPPE
    Notturno I/IB4

RADOLT, WENZEL LUDWIG FREIHERR VON (1667-1716)
    Canon In E I/IIA1

    Minuet I/IB1

RAFAGA see Turina, Joaquin

RAILWAY-TRAFFIC see Furstenau, Wolfram

RAMEAU, JEAN-PHILIPPE (1683-1764)
    Air I/IB1

    Boiteuse, La see Pieces De Clavecin

    Gavotte, Le Tambourin see Tambourin

    Indifferente, L' see Pieces De Clavecin

    Livri, La, Rondeau I/IB1

    Llamada De Los Pajaros, La see Rappel Des Oiseaux, Le

    Menuet En Rondeau see Pieces De Clavecin

    Minuet I/IB1

    Minuetti, 2 I/IB1

    Minuetti, 6 I/IB1

    Minuetto, Da Platee I/IB1

    Pieces De Clavecin I/IB1

    Rappel Des Oiseaux, Le I/IB1

    Sarabande Et Menuet I/IB1

    Tambourin I/IB1
        see also Pieces De Clavecin

    Tambourin, Le I/IIA1

    Tendres Plaintes, Les I/IB1

    Venitienne see Pieces De Clavecin

RAMILLETE DE FLORES I/IB1-Coll

RAMILLETE DE FLORES (1530-1593) I/IB1-Coll

RAMOS, JOAQUIN
    Serenata Carorena, Cancion Venezolana I/IB5

RAMOVS, PRIMOZ (1921-   )
    Nocturnes, 2 I/IB4

RANIERI, SILVIO
    Method For The Guitar, Vol. I II

    Method For The Guitar, Vol. II II

RAPIDO, LO, ETUDE see Dagosto, Sylvain

RAPPEL DES OISEAUX, LE see Rameau, Jean-Philippe

RAPSODIA VALENCIANA see Pujol, Emilio

RASGUEADO see Drogoz, Philippe

RATHGEBER, VALENTIN (1682-1750)
    Leichte Stucke, 6 I/IIB1

    Nobilissima Musica, Von Der Edlen Musik I/IIB1

RATZ, MARTIN
    Kleine Serenade, Unterhaltende Vortragsstucke I/IB4

RAVEL, MAURICE (1875-1937)
    Pavane Pour Une Infante Defunte I/IB4, I/IIA1

    Piece En Forme De Habanera I/IB4

RAXACH, ENRIQUE (1932-   )
    Interface V/ii

    Sine Nomine V/ii

RAZZI, FAUSTO (1932-   )
    Helle Stimme, Die V/ii

RE-SONAT TIBIA see Kroll, Georg

READ, GARDNER (1913-   )
    Canzone Di Notte I/IB4

REALI, GIOVANNI BATTISTA
    Sonata in B flat I/IIB2

REBAY, FERDINAND (1889-1953)
    Albumblatt I/IB4

    Duo's Fur 2 Gitarren, Vol. I: 12 Kleine Stucke I/IIA1

    Duo's Fur 2 Gitarren, Vol. II: 9 Vortragsstucke I/IIA1

    Duo's Fur 2 Gitarren, Vol. III: 6 Studien Nach Beruhmten Etuden Von Czerny Bis Chopin I/IIA1

    Duo's Fur 2 Gitarren, Vol. IV: Spezial-Studien I/IIA1

    Kleine Leichte Stucke, 14 I/IB4

    Leicht Spielbare Kleinigkeiten I/IB4, I/IIB1

    Menuette, 2 I/IB4

    Russischer Tanz I/IB5

    Tanzlied I/IB4

    Wiegenlied I/IB4

REBETIKA see Kounadis, Arghyris

RECERCADEN, 4 see Ortiz, Diego

RECERCAR UNDECIMO Y RECERCAR TREDECIMO see Crema, Joan Maria da

RECERCATE CONCERTATE, SU LA QUARTA FANTASIA DI FRANCESCO DA MILANO see Matelart, Johannes

RECEUIL DE 23 MORCEAUX see Carulli, Ferdinando

RECIT DU PECHEUR see Falla, Manuel de

RECITATIVO, ARIA E DUETTO see Klebe, Giselher

RECITATIVO E FUGA see Chailly, Luciano

RECREATION see Coste, Napoleon

RECREATION DU GUITARISTE see Coste, Napoleon

RECUERDO DEL 4 DE NOVIEMBRE, MUERTE DE MENDELSSOHN see Schumann, Robert (Alexander), Erinnerung

RECUERDOS see Peruzzi, Aurelio

RECUERDOS DE LA ALHAMBRA see Tarrega, Francisco, Study, TI ii- 9, in A minor

RECUERDOS DE LAS BALEARES see Tomasi, Henri

RECUERDOS DE SEVILLA see Wolf, Roland

RECUERDOS DEL CIELO see Bartolozzi, Bruno

REDA, SIEGFRIED (1916-1968)
    Psalm No. 30 see Psalmus Morte Servati

    Psalmus Morte Servati V/ii

    Requiem Vel Vivorum Consolatio V/ii

REDEL, MARTIN CHRISTOPH (1947-   )
    Epilog I/IIC2

REDSLEEVES see Rooth, Hans

REFLECTIONS NO. 2 see Ruyneman, Daniel

REFLETS, 3 see Meier, Jost

REFLEXE, VARIATIONEN DURCH DIE JAHRHUNDERT UBER EIN THEMA VON GASPAR SANZ see Walter, Fried

REFLEXIONEN see Burghauser, Jarmil

REFLEXIONEN, AUF BILDER VON MAX ERNST see Furstenau, Wolfram

REFLEXIONS I see Ruyneman, Daniel

REFRAINS, FOR ORCHESTRA see Amy, Gilbert

REGENETUDE see Walker, Luise

REGER, MAX (1873-1916)
    Gavotte I/IB3

REGI MAGYAR TANCOK - ALTE UNGARISCHE TANZE see Farkas, Ferenc

REGI MAGYAR TANCOK - ALTE UNGARISCHE TANZE see Farkas, Ferenc

REGI MAGYAR ZENE GITARRA – EARLY
HUNGARIAN MUSIC FOR GUITAR
I/IB1-Coll

REGI ZENE   I/IIB1-Coll

REGI ZENE GITARRA, ATIRATOK A XVII-
XVIII. SZAZAD MUZSIKAJABOL – ALTE
MUSIK FUR GITARRE, WERKE AUS DEM
17.-18. JAHRHUNDERT I/IB1-Coll,
VII-Mixed Coll

REGONDI, GIULIO (1822–1872)
Reverie, Op. 19 I/IB2

Study No. 1 I/IA

REGT, HENDRIK DE (1950–   )
Music, Op. 21 I/IIB1

Musica, Op. 11 I/IIB4

Musica, Op. 15 I/IIB2

Musica, Op. 17 I/IIB3

Musica, Op. 18 I/IIB2

Silenus En Bakchanten I/IIB2

REI MARINER, EL see Erliso, Vincente

REICHARDT, JOHANN FRIEDRICH (1752–1814)
Sonata for Violin and Guitar in B
flat I/IIB1

6 Stucke I/IIB1

REIN, WALTER (1893–1955)
Volkslieder Mit Variationen, 2
I/IIB1

Vom Vielfaltigen Leben I/IIC1,
I/IIC2

REINBACH, REMO
Meccanismo Della Chitarra, Il, Dal
Primo Al Dodecimo Capotasto III

REINBOTE, HELMUT
Leichte Stucke Fur Gitarre I/IB4

REISEBILDER AUS FRANKREICH, 5 I/IIA3

REISER, EKKEHARD
Entwicklung Einer Technischen
Perfektion III

Masken I/IB4

Studien, 2 I/IA

REITER, ALBERT (1905–1970)
Sonatina I/IIB1

RELIEF NO. V see Hekster, Walter

RELIEFS, 7 see Burghauser, Jarmil

RENAISSANCE MUSIC FOR GUITAR
I/IB1-Coll

RENAISSANCE POPULAR MUSIC I/IB1-Coll

RENAISSANCE POUR LE PRESENCE see
Furstenau, Wolfram

REPERTOIRE see Kagel, Mauricio

REPERTOIRE PROGRESSIF, VOL. 1
I/IB6-Coll, VII-Mixed Coll

REPERTOIRE PROGRESSIF, VOL. 2
I/IB6-Coll

REPERTOIRE PROGRESSIF, VOL. 3
I/IB6-Coll

REQUIEM VEL VIVORUM CONSOLATIO see
Reda, Siegfried

RESPUESTA see Llobet, Miguel

RETICOLO 11 see Clementi, Aldo

RETROSPECTIVE see Gavarone, Gerard

REUSCH, FRITZ (1896–1970)
Christkindelspiel, Das, Ein
Weihnachtsspiel IV/IIC5

REUSSNER, ESAIAS (1636–1679)
Musicalische Gesellschaftsergetzung
I/IIB1

Passacaglia I/IB1

Pecas, 3 I/IB1

Sonatina I/IB1

Suite for Lute I/IB1

Suite in A minor I/IB1

REUSSNER, ESAIAS (cont'd.)

Suite No. 1 I/IB1

Suite No. 5 I/IB1

REVEIL see Vandermaesbrugge, Max

REVEILLEZ-VOUS see Seiber, Matyas
Gyorgy

REVERIE-SICILIANO see Schumann, Robert
(Alexander)

REY DON ALONSO EL BUENO, EL see
Castelnuovo-Tedesco, Mario,
Escarraman, A Suite Of Spanish
Dances From The XVIth Century
(After Cervantes)

REYES DE LA BARAJA, LOS see Bielsa,
Valentin

REYNE, GERARD (1944–   )
Guitare I/IB4

Homenaje A M. de Falla I/IB4

RHAPSODIE UND HOCHZEITSTANZ NACH
FINNISCHEN VOLKSWEISEN see
Schaller, Erwin

RHYTHMISCHE MINIATUREN see Bialas,
Gunter

RHYTHMISCHE STUDIEN, VOL. 1 see
Behrend, Siegfried

RHYTHMISCHE STUDIEN, VOL. 2 see
Behrend, Siegfried

RHYTHMUS, DER see Apostel, Hans Erich

RHYTHOMOPHONIE FOR ORCHESTRA see Zehm,
Friedrich

RIBERENA see Azpiazu, Jose de

RICCHI, MODESTO
Chitarrista Autodidatta, Il,
Nuovissimo Metodo Facile Per
Chitarra A Numeri E A Musica,
Indispensabile Per Chi Non
Conosce La Musica, Utile Per Gli
Orchestrali II

Metodo Completo Per Lo Studio Della
Chitarra II

RICERCARE see Pujol, Emilio

RICERCARE DEL PRIMO TONO see
Palestrina, Giovanni Pierluigi da

RICERCARE, PER LIUTO I/IB1

RICERCARI, 3 see Bakfark, Balint
(Valentin)

RICERCARI, 5 see Bonnard, Alain;
Crema, Joan Maria da

RICERCARI, 26 see Bossinensis,
Franciscus

RICERCATA DI DUREZZE E FIORITURE SULLE
"QUATTRO DITA" see Hinojosa,
Javier, Te Lucis Ante Terminum

RICHTER, GERD
Gitarrenfibel, Eine Neue Anleitung
Fur Das Spiel Auf Der Gitarre II

RICHTER, NICO (1915–1945)
Serenade V/i

Sinfonietta No. 1 for Chamber
Orchestra see Serenade

Trio I/IIB2

RICORDANDO GIULIA see Zuccheri,
Luciano

RIDERS IN THE SKY, THE see Gilardino,
Angelo

RIEDENBURGER TANZ see Mittelalterliche
Tanze

RIERA, RODRIGO
Merengue Venezolano I/IB4

Preludio Criollo I/IB4

RIEVOCAZIONE see Murtula, Giovanni

RIFRAZIONI see Bosco, Gilberto

RIGACCI, MARIO
Study in B minor I/IA

RIGHTMIRE, RICHARD W.
Manual Of Flamenco II

Wonderful Guitar, The (A Modern
Classic Guitar Method), Vol. I
I/IB2-Coll, II, VII-Mixed Coll

Wonderful Guitar, The (A Modern
Classic Guitar Method), Vol. II
I/IB2-Coll, II, VII-Mixed Coll

Wonderful Guitar, The (A Modern
Classic Guitar Method), Vol. III
II, VI-Mixed Coll, VII-Mixed Coll

RIGODON see Anonymous

RIMSKY-KORSAKOV, NIKOLAI (1844–1908)
Chanson Hindoue I/IB3

RING see Takemitsu, Toru

RINKE RANKE ROSENSCHEIN; 77
KINDERLIEDER I/IIC1-Coll, IV/IIC1

RIO MANTILLA see Lopez, Joaquin

RISCOPERTA DELL'ACCORDATURA E DALLA
TASTIERA see Abloniz, Miguel

RITMATA see Krieger, Edino

RITMICO see Bettinelli, Bruno

RITMOS CAMPEROS see Broqua, Alfonso,
Evocaciones Criollas, No.7

RITORNO D'ULISSE IN PATRIA, IL; OPERA
IN TWO ACTS WITH A PROLOGUE see
Monteverdi, Claudio

RITTER, THEODOR
Gitarre-Studien, Fur Angehende Solo-
Gitarristen Und Sanger Zur
Gitarre. Ausgewahlte Leichte
Studienwerke Alter Meister II

Lehrgang Des Modernen Gitarrespiels,
Vol. A: Das Akkordspiel II

Lehrgang Des Modernen Gitarrespiels,
Vol. B: Das Solospiel Und Die
Liedbegleitung II

Theoretisch-Praktischer Lehrgang Des
Gitarrespiels, Fur Den Einzel-,
Gruppen- Und Selbstunterricht Mit
Besonderer Berucksichtigung Des
Akkordspiels II

RITUAL OF SOUND see Schifrin, Lalo
(Boris)

RIVIER, JEAN (1896–   )
Etude I/IA

RIZZUTI, CARMELO
Tremolo Estudio I/IA

ROBINSON, THOMAS (fl. ca. 1603)
Allemand, MIN 350 I/IB1

Allemande Und Galliard I/IB1

Almain, MIN 95 see Piezas De Laud, 4

Bellvedere I/IB1

Bony Sweet Boy see Pieces, 5

Duets I/IIA1

Fantasy I/IIA1

Fantasy, A see Duets

Galliard, MIN 93 I/IB1

Galliard, MIN 94 see Pieces, 5

Galliard, MIN 96 see Piezas De Laud,
4

Gigue see Piezas De Laud, 4

Lantero see Pieces, 5

Passamezzo Galliard see Duets

Pieces, 5 I/IB1

2 Pieces I/IB1

Piezas De Laud, 4 I/IB1

Plaine Song I/IIA1

Plaine Song, A see Duets

Row Well You Mariners see 2 Pieces

Row Well You Marriners see Pieces, 5

Schoole Of Musicke, The I/IB1

ROBINSON, THOMAS (cont'd.)

Spanish Pavan, The I/IB1

Toy, A see Duets; 2 Pieces; Piezas
   De Laud, 4

Toy, Air And Gigue I/IB1

Twenty Ways Upon The Bells see Duets

Walking In A Country Towne see
   Pieces, 5

ROCANTINS, LES see Ballard, Robert

ROCCA E IL FUSO, LA, CHANSON ITALIENNE
   see Rotta, Antonio

ROCH, PASCUAL
   Modern Method For The Guitar, A, Vol.
      1, School Of Tarrega II,
      VI-Mixed Coll

   Modern Method For The Guitar, A, Vol.
      II, School Of Tarrega II,
      VI-Mixed Coll

   Modern Method For The Guitar, A, Vol.
      III, School Of Tarrega II,
      VI-Mixed Coll, VII-Mixed Coll

RODE, JACQUES-PIERRE (1744-1830)
   Trio in D I/IIB2

RODRIGO, JOAQUIN (1902-   )
   Adela see Spanish Songs, 3

   Aire Y Donaire see Villancicos

   Bajando De La Meseta I/IB4

   Concierto De Aranjuez I/IIIA

   Coplillas De Belen see Villancicos

   De Ronda see Spanish Songs, 3

   Elogio De La Guitarra I/IB4

   En Jerez De La Frontera see Spanish
      Songs, 3

   En Los Trigales, Scene Castillane
      I/IB4

   Fandango Del Ventorrillo I/IIA1

   Fantasia Para Un Gentilhombre,
      Inspirada En Gaspar Sanz I/IIIA

   Folias Canarias I/IIC1

   Grazioso see Petites Pieces, 3

   Invocation Et Danse, Hommage A Manuel
      De Falla I/IB4

   Junto Al Generalife I/IB4

   Moderato see Petites Pieces, 3

   Pajaros De Primavera I/IB4

   Pastorale I/IB4

   Pastorcito Santo see Villancicos

   Petites Pieces, 3 I/IB4, IV/I

   Piezas Espanolas, 3 I/IB4

   Piezas Faciles, 4 I/IB4

   Romance De Durandarte I/IIA1

   Sarabande Lointaine I/IB4

   Sonata Giocosa I/IC

   Sonate A l'Espagnole I/IC

   Song From The Canary Islands see
      Folias Canarias

   Spanish Songs, 3 I/IIC1

   Tiento Antiguo I/IB4

   Tonadilla I/IIA1

   Villancicos I/IIC1, IV/IIC1

   Ya Se Van Los Pastores see Petites
      Pieces, 3

RODRIGUEZ ALBERT, RAFAEL (1902-   )
   Sonatina En Tres Duales I/IC

RODRIGUEZ ARENAS, MARIO
   Escuela De La Guitarra, La, Vol. I
      II

   Escuela De La Guitarra, La, Vol. II
      I/IB2-Coll, II, VI-Mixed Coll

RODRIGUEZ ARENAS, MARIO (cont'd.)

   Escuela De La Guitarra, La, Vol. II
      I/IB2-Coll, II, VI-Mixed Coll

   Escuela De La Guitarra, La, Vol. III
      II, VI-Mixed Coll

   Escuela De La Guitarra, La, Vol. III
      II, VI-Mixed Coll

   Escuela De La Guitarra, La, Vol. IV
      I/IB6-Coll, II

   Escuela De La Guitarra, La, Vol. V
      I/IB2-Coll, II, VI-Mixed Coll

   Escuela De La Guitarra, La, Vol. V
      I/IB2-Coll, II, VI-Mixed Coll

   Escuela De La Guitarra, Vol. VI II,
      III, VI-Mixed Coll

   Escuela De La Guitarra, Vol. VII II,
      III

   Estudio Completo De Las Escales,
      Arpegios Y Ejercicios En
      Terceras, Sextas, Octavas Y
      Decimas see Escuela De La
      Guitarra, Vol. VII

   Technica Superior see Escuela De La
      Guitarra, Vol. VI

ROE, BETTY (1930-   )
   Larcombe's Fancy I/IB4

ROESELING, KASPAR (1894-1961)
   Kreisspiel Von Der Geburt Christi
      IV/IIC5

ROGERO see Johnson, John

ROHWER, JENS (1914-   )
   Duo Fur Lauteninstrumente I/IIA1

   Heptameron, Eine Vierstimmige Suite
      I/IIA3

ROLAND, CLAUDE ROBERT (1935-   )
   Ballade De Villon I/IIC1

ROMANCA D'ESPAGNA see Anonymous,
   Romance, MIN 141

ROMANCE ANONIMO see Anonymous;
   Anonymous, Romance, MIN 141

ROMANCE D'AMOUR see Anonymous;
   Anonymous, Romance, MIN 141

ROMANCE DE AMOR see Anonymous,
   Romance, MIN 141

ROMANCE DE AMOR ORIGINAL see
   Anonymous, Romance, MIN 141

ROMANCE DE AMOR, THEME SONG see
   Anonymous, Romance, MIN 141

ROMANCE DE DURANDARTE see Rodrigo,
   Joaquin

ROMANCE DEL CONDE OLINOS see Bielsa,
   Valentin

ROMANCE SANS PAROLES see Pijper,
   Willem

ROMANCERO GITANO see Castelnuovo-
   Tedesco, Mario

6 ROMANCES see Pelemans, Willem

ROMANCILLO see Salazar, Adolfo

ROMANESCA, LA see Sor, Fernando

ROMANESCA, LA, AN ANCIENT ITALIAN DANCE
   AIR OF THE 16TH CENTURY see
   Maganini, Quinto

ROMANESCA I see Mudarra, Alonso de

ROMANESCA II see Mudarra, Alonso de

ROMANISCHE SUITE see Gunsenheimer,
   Gustav

ROMANTIKUS GITARDARABOK - ROMANTIC
   PIECES FOR GUITAR I/IB2-Coll

ROMANZA, LA see Sor, Fernando

ROMANZA SENZA PAROLE see Mendelssohn-
   Bartholdy, Felix

ROMANZA SIN PALABRAS see Mendelssohn-
   Bartholdy, Felix; Song Without
   Words

ROMANZA SIN PALABRAS NO. 20 see
   Mendelssohn-Bartholdy, Felix

ROMANZA SIN PALABRAS NO. 25 see
   Mendelssohn-Bartholdy, Felix

ROMANZA SIN PALABRAS, OP.19, NO.2 see
   Mendelssohn-Bartholdy, Felix

ROMANZA SIN PALABRAS, OP.19, NO.3 see
   Mendelssohn-Bartholdy, Felix

ROMANZA SIN PALABRAS, OP.30, NO.3 see
   Mendelssohn-Bartholdy, Felix

ROMANZA SIN PALABRAS, OP. 85, NO. 3
   see Mendelssohn-Bartholdy, Felix

ROMANZA SIN PALABRAS, OP. 102, NO. 2
   see Mendelssohn-Bartholdy, Felix

ROMANZA, SUL NOME DI OSCAR GHIGLIA see
   Castelnuovo-Tedesco, Mario

ROMANZE, 12 see Carulli, Ferdinando

ROMANZE, ALTES ZIGEUNERLIED see
   Putilin, Ivan

ROMANZEN, 12, VOL. II see Carulli,
   Ferdinando

ROMANZERO see Bialas, Gunter

ROMBERG, BERNHARD (1865-1913)
   Divertimento, Op. 46 I/IIB1

ROMERICO see Encina, Juan del

ROMERICO, TU QUE VIENNES see Encina,
   Juan del

RONCALLI, LUDOVICO
   Capricci Armonici: Sarabande-Gigue
      I/IB1

   Capricci Armonici Sopra La Chitarra
      Spagnola see Suiten, 9

   Partita in D I/IB1

   3 Partiten I/IB1

   Passacaglia I/IB1, I/IIA1

   Preludio E Giga I/IB1

   Preludio, Sarabande E Giga I/IB1

   Sonata No. 1 see Suite No. 1

   Suite E-Moll, No. 1 see Suite No. 1

   Suite in B minor I/IB1

   Suite in D I/IB1

   Suite in D minor I/IB1

   Suite in E minor I/IB1

   Suite in G I/IB1

   Suite In G Dur see Suite No. 1

   Suite No. 1 I/IB1

   Suite No. 5 in A minor I/IB1

   Suite No. 7 in D minor I/IB1

   Suite No. 9 in G minor I/IB1

   Suiten, 9 I/IB1

   Suiten Nr. 3 Und Nr. 4 I/IB1

RONDA DEL VIEJO ENAMORADO see Thomas,
   Juan Maria

RONDALLA ARAGONESA see Granados,
   Enrique, Danza Espanola, No. 6;
   Granados, Enrique, Danza Espanola
   No. 6

RONDE see Susato, Tielman

RONDE "MILLE DUCAS" see Susato,
   Tielman

RONDE NEERLANDAISE see Judenkunig,
   Hans

RONDEAU DE ABDELAZAR see Purcell,
   Henry

RONDEAUX PER 10 see Togni, Camillo

RONDEL, UBER DEN NAMEN SIEGFRIED
   BEHREND see Castelnuovo-Tedesco,
   Mario

RONDINO see Azpiazu, Jose de; Darr,
   Adam

RONDINO IN C see Diabelli, Anton

RONDINOS, 4   see Diabelli, Anton

RONDO, MIN 17   see Danses, 4

RONDO UND HARFEN-ETUDE   see Giuliani, Mauro

RONDOLETTO   see Carcassi, Matteo; Giuliani, Mauro

RONDOLETTO; 11 LEICHTE SPIELSTUCKE   see Wolki, Konrad

3 RONDOS BRILLANTES   see Aguado, Dionisio

RONNEFELD, PETER (1935-1965)
Spirale; Ballettsuite V/i

RONNY LEE CLASSIC GUITAR BOOK, THE
I/IB6-Coll, VI-Mixed Coll,
VII-Mixed Coll

ROOTH, HANS
Redsleeves   I/IB4

ROOY, JULIO
Charlein, Antilliaanse Wals   I/IB4

ROSA DAS ROSAS, CANTIGA   see Alfonso X, el Sabio, King of Castile

ROSARIUM, 10 DIVERTIMENTI   see Novak, Jan

ROSE GARDEN, THE; THEATRE PIECE FOR
SINGING ACTRESS, DOUBLE CHORUS AND
INSTRUMENTS   see Boyd, Anne

ROSENMULLER, JOHANN (ca. 1620-1684)
Pavane B   I/IIA1

Studenten Music, Eine   I/IIB4

Trio Sonata   I/IIB3

ROSENSTENGEL, ALBRECHT (1912-   )
In Warschau Sind Die Madchen   see Polenmadchen

Leise Kommt Die Dunkle Nacht   see Schlaflied Fur Juliska

Liebes Madchen, Du Bist Schon   see Seltene Schonheit, Eine

Polenmadchen   V/ii

Schlaflied Fur Juliska   V/ii

Seltene Schonheit, Eine   V/ii

Tanzlied Aus Israel   V/ii

Wenn Morgens Die Sonne Erwacht   see Tanzlied Aus Israel

ROSETTA, GIUSEPPE
Canti Della Pianura   I/IB4

Mirage   I/IB4

Poemi Brevi, 6   I/IB4

Preludi Per Gilardino   I/IB4

Preludio, Barcarola E Scherzo   I/IB4

Sonata   I/IIA1

Sonatina   I/IC

Weissiana, Omaggio A S.L. Weiss
I/IB4

ROSITA, POLKA   see Tarrega, Francisco

ROSSEAU, NORBERT (1907-1975)
Contemplatie   I/IIB1

Stenen En Brood   V/ii

ROSSETER, PHILIP (ca. 1568-1623)
Galliard   I/IB1

Galyerd Y A Pavin   I/IB1

ROSSI, ABNER
Andantino E Valzer   I/IB4

Chitarrista Classico, Il   II

Contrappunto Scherzoso   I/IB4

Nocturne   I/IB4

Pensieri d'Autunno   I/IB4

ROSSI, SALOMONE (ca. 1570-ca. 1630)
Sinfonia in F   I/IIB2

Sinfonia in G minor   I/IIB2

ROSSIGNOL   see Encina, Juan del, Romerico

ROSSIGNOL, LA   see Aus Pickering's Lautenbuch (Um 1616)

ROSSIGNOL, LE   see Elizabethan Duets, 6; Musique Elisabethaine; Seiber, Matyas Gyorgy

ROSSINIANA, NO. 1   see Giuliani, Mauro

ROSSINIANA, NO. 2   see Giuliani, Mauro

ROSSINIANA, NO. 3   see Giuliani, Mauro

ROSSINIANA, OP. 119-124   see Giuliani, Mauro

ROSYJSCY MISTRZOWIE GITARY   I/IB6-Coll

ROTTA, ANTONIO (? -1548)
Rocca E Il Fuso, La, Chanson Italienne   I/IB1

Suite Of Dances For Lute (1546)
I/IB1

ROUSSEL, ALBERT (CHARLES PAUL)
(1869-1937)
Segovia   I/IB4

ROVENSTRUNCK, BERNHARD
Stucke, 5   I/IIB4

ROVSING OLSEN, POUL (1922-   )
A l'Inconnu   V/ii

ROW WELL YOU MARINERS   see Robinson, Thomas

ROW WELL YOU MARRINERS   see Robinson, Thomas

ROYAL DANCES, 4   I/IB1

RUBIN, MARCEL (1905-   )
Petite Serenade   I/IB4

RUBINSTEIN, ANTON (1829-1894)
Romance, MIN 339   I/IB3

RUCH, HANNES
Leichte Stucke, 34   I/IB4

Spielmusik   I/IB4

RUFTY TUFTY   see Take Your Partners; 6 English Country Dances

RUGGIERI, GIOVANNI MARIA
Sonata da Chiesa No. 1 in E minor, Op. 3, No. 1   I/IIB2

Sonata da Chiesa No. 2 in B minor, Op. 3, No. 2   I/IIB2

Sonata da Chiesa No. 3 in B flat, Op. 3, No. 3   I/IIB2

Sonata da Chiesa No. 4 in F, Op. 3, No. 4   I/IIB2

Sonata da Chiesa No. 5 in G minor, Op. 3, No. 5   I/IIB2

Sonata da Chiesa No. 6 in A, Op. 3, No. 6   I/IIB2

Sonata da Chiesa No. 7 in A minor, Op. 3, No. 7   I/IIB2

Sonata da Chiesa No. 8 in G, Op. 3, No. 8   I/IIB2

Sonata da Chiesa No. 9 in D minor, Op. 3, No. 9   I/IIB2

Sonata da Chiesa No. 10 in D, Op. 3, No. 10   I/IIB2

RUINAS DE ATENAS, LA, MARCHA   see Beethoven, Ludwig van

RUISSEAU, LE   see Sanchez, B.

RUIZ DE RIBAYAZ, LUCAS
Bailes Populares Del Siglo XVII, 6
I/IB1

Canarios   see Bailes Populares Del Siglo XVII, 6

Dansen, 4   I/IB1

Danza Del Hacha   see Bailes Populares Del Siglo XVII, 6

Galliard   see Bailes Populares Del Siglo XVII, 6

Matachin   see Bailes Populares Del Siglo XVII, 6

Passacaglia   I/IB1

Torneo   see Bailes Populares Del Siglo XVII, 6

RUIZ DE RIBAYAZ, LUCAS (cont'd.)

Vacas   see Bailes Populares Del Siglo XVII, 6

RUIZ PIPO, ANTONIO
Cancion Y Danza, No.1   I/IB4

Cancion Y Danza, No.2   I/IB4

Canto Libre   I/IB4

Cantos A La Noche   I/IIC1

Estancias   I/IB4

Hommage A Antonio De Cabezon   I/IB4

RUJERO   see Sanz, Gaspar; Sanz, Gaspar

RUMBA   see Gramberg, Jacq

RUMORE DI PASSI, 5 LIRICHE   see Bortolami, Galliano

RUMORES DE LA CALETA, MALAGUENA   see Albeniz, Isaac; Albeniz, Isaac

RUNDGESANG   see Schumann, Robert (Alexander)

RUSSIAN SONG   see Tchaikovsky, Piotr Ilyich

RUSSIAN SONGS, 4   see Stravinsky, Igor

RUSSISCHE BALLADE   see Gitarre Spezial, Picking Modern Arrangement, Vol. 2

RUSSISCHE UND UKRAINISCHE VOLKSLIEDER
UND TANZE, 50   I/IB5-Coll

RUSSISCHE VOLKSMUSIK   I/IB5-Coll,
I/IIA1-Coll, I/IIC1-Coll

RUSSISCHE VOLKSWEISEN UND TANZE
I/IB5-Coll

RUSSISCHER TANZ   see Rebay, Ferdinand

RUSSISCHES ZIGEUNERLIED   see Mertz, Johann Kaspar

RUST, FRIEDRICH WILHELM (1739-1796)
Sonata in G   I/IIB1

RUTHENBERG, OTTO (1936-   )
Slawka   V/ii

RUTHENFRANZ, R.
Pieces, 3   I/IB4

RUYNEMAN, DANIEL (1886-1963)
Hieroglyphs   V/i

Reflections No. 2   I/IIB2

Reflexions I   V/ii

RYBA, JAN JAKUB SIMON (1765-1815)
Gloria, Aus Der Tschechischen Weihnachtsmesse   IV/IIC5

RYTMICO   see Ahslund, Ulf-G.

SACARAS   see Guerau, Francisco

SACCHETTI, ARTURO
Eucalyptus   I/IB4

Memorial   I/IB4

SACK, GEORG CHRISTIAN
Perfection In The Art Of Playing The
Guitar, Vol. 1: Fundaments Of
Guitar Playing   see Weg Zum
Kunstlerischen Gitarrespiel, Der,
Vol. 1: Elemente Des
Gitarrespiels

Weg Zum Kunstlerischen Gitarrespiel,
Der, Vol. 1: Elemente Des
Gitarrespiels   II

SACRO-MONTE   see Turina, Joaquin

SADNESS   see Zuccheri, Luciano

SAETA, OP. 53   see ApIvor, Denis

SAG DU   see Galen Man

SAGRERAS, JULIO S. (1879-1942)
Cuartas Lecciones, Las   see Lessons
For The Guitar, Vol. 4, The
Fourth Lessons

Gitarrenunterricht Fur Anfanger, Vol.
1   I/IA

Lessons For The Guitar, Vol. 1, The
First Lessons   I/IA

Lessons For The Guitar, Vol. 2, The
Second Lessons   I/IA

SAGRERAS, JULIO S. (cont'd.)

Lessons For The Guitar, Vol.3, The Third Lessons I/IA

Lessons For The Guitar, Vol. 4, The Fourth Lessons I/IA

Lessons For The Guitar, Vol. 5, The Fifth Lessons I/IA

Lessons For The Guitar, Vol. 6, The Sixth Lessons I/IA

Prime Lezioni, Le see Lessons For The Guitar, Vol. 1, The First Lessons

Primeras Lecciones, Las see Lessons For The Guitar, Vol. 1, The First Lessons

Quarte Lezioni, Le see Lessons For The Guitar, Vol. 4, The Fourth Lessons

Quintas Lecciones, Las see Lessons For The Guitar, Vol. 5, The Fifth Lessons

Quinte Lezioni, Le see Lessons For The Guitar, Vol. 5, The Fifth Lessons

Seconde Lezioni, Le see Lessons For The Guitar, Vol. 2, The Second Lessons

Segundas Lecciones, Las see Lessons For The Guitar, Vol. 2, The Second Lessons

Seste Lezioni, Le see Lessons For The Guitar, Vol. 6, The Sixth Lessons

Sextas Lecciones, Las see Lessons For The Guitar, Vol. 6, The Sixth Lessons

Tecnica Superior De Guitarra, De Acuerdo Con La Moderna Escuela Del Maestro Tarrega III, VI-Mixed Coll

Terceras Lecciones, Las see Lessons For The Guitar, Vol.3, The Third Lessons

Terze Lezioni, Le see Lessons For The Guitar, Vol.3, The Third Lessons

SAGUARO see Gilardino, Angelo

SAILOR-BOY see Britten, [Sir] Benjamin

SAINT LUC, JACQUES DE (1616- ?)
Suite in E I/IB1, I/IB6-Coll

SAINT NICOLAS see Schumann, Robert (Alexander); Schumann, Robert (Alexander), Saint Nicolas

SAINT-SAENS, CAMILLE (1835-1921)
Cygne, Le I/IB3

SAINZ DE LA MAZA, EDUARDO
Anoranza Lejana I/IA

Campanas Del Alba, Tremolo I/IB4

Canco Del Lladre, Popular Catalana I/IB4, I/IB5

Confidencia, Preludio I/IB4

Greensleeves, Cancion Popular Inglesa I/IB4

Habanera I/IB4

Homenaje A La Guitarra, Preludio I/IB4

Study see Anoranza Lejana

SAINZ DE LA MAZA, REGINO (1897-1982)
Estudio-Scherzo I/IA

Study in A minor I/IA

6 SAITEN-10 FINGER see Wangler, Rudolf

SALAS, JUAN ORREGO
see ORREGO-SALAS, JUAN

SALAZAR, ADOLFO (1890-1958)
Romancillo I/IB4

SALDARELLI, VINCENZO
Per La Chitarra I/IB4

SALON DE ARTAZCOZ see Azpiazu, Jose de

SALOTTO ROMANO see Schwertsik, Kurt

SALTARELLO see Molinaro, Simone; Vecchi, Orazio (Horatio)

SALTARELLO QUARTO see Molinaro, Simone

SALVADOR, SAN
Single String Studies For Guitar III

SALVE see Pujol, Emilio

SALZBURGER SONATINE IN F see Bischoff, Heinz

SAMARITANER, DER, CANTATA see Kretzschmar, Gunther

SAMAZEUILH, GUSTAVE (1877-1967)
Serenade I/IB4

SAMBALELE see Chansons Bresiliennes, Vol. I

SAMEN SPELEN, VOL. I see Schagen, Henk van

SAMEN SPELEN, VOL. II see Schagen, Henk van

SAMKLANG, METHOD FOR GROUP TUITION, VOL. 1 see Ahslund, Ulf-G.

SAMKLANG, METHOD FOR GROUP TUITION, VOL. 2 see Ahslund, Ulf-G.

SAMMARTINI, GIUSEPPE
(ca. 1693-ca. 1770)
Sonata, Op. 3, No. 1, in E minor I/IIB1

Sonata, Op. 3, No. 2, in G I/IIB1

Sonaten, 6, Op. 3 see Sonata, Op. 3, No. 1, in E minor; Sonata, Op. 3, No. 2, in G

SAMTLICHE PRALUDIEN see Tarrega, Francisco

SAMTLICHE TECHNISCHE STUDIEN see Tarrega, Francisco

SAMTLICHE TONLEITERN FUR GITARRE see Thomatos, Spiro

SANCHEZ, B.
Arroyo, El see Ruisseau, Le

Berceuse I/IIC1

Cancion Olvidada I/IB4

Chimeres, No. 1 see Quimeras, No.1

Chimeres, No. 2 see Quimeras, No.2

Chimeres, No. 3 see Quimeras, No.3

Complainte Funebre, Fantaisie A La Memoire De Ida Presti (2.5.1967, Jour De Son Enterrement) I/IB4

Criolla I/IB4

Danza Del Pejin I/IB4

Etude En Forme d'Invention I/IIA1

Fiesta Laredana I/IB4

Impromptu No. 1 see Fiesta Laredana

Ingenio, Evocation I/IIC1

Linares I/IB4

Minivalses, 4 I/IB4

Ninfa, La I/IB4

Nocturne No. 1 I/IB4

Nymphe, La see Ninfa, La

Peruviana I/IB4

Preambolo Y Toccata Surena I/IB4

Prelude in G minor I/IB4

Preludio Y Alborada I/IB4

Quimeras, No.1 I/IB4

Quimeras, No.2 I/IB4

Quimeras, No.3 I/IB4

Ruisseau, Le I/IB4

Serenade Villageoise I/IB4

Serenata Canaria I/IB4

SANCHEZ, B. (cont'd.)

Serenata Pueblerina see Serenade Villageoise

Sonatina I/IC

Suite Vesperale I/IIB1

Tonalida Islena I/IB4

Vals Sombrio I/IB4

Variations, 10, Sur "Folias De Espana" En Forme De Canon I/IIA1, I/IIA2

SANCHEZ, BLAS
Al Pie De La Cruz Del Roque I/IIC2

Au Pied De La Croix De Pierre see Al Pie De La Cruz Del Roque

Dialogue I/IA

Etude in E minor see Oracion

Etudes Elementaires, 12 I/IA

Etudes Preparatoires, 12 I/IA

Etudes Probatoires, 12 I/IA

Exercices, 40, Faciles Pour La Guitare, d'Apres Un Theme Mateo Carcassi, Vol. I: 17 Studies For The Right Hand III

Exercices, 40, Faciles Pour La Guitare, d'Apres Un Theme Mateo Carcassi, Vol. II: 23 Exercises For The Left Hand III

Exercices Techniques, 20, Indispensables Pour La Guitare, Tous Degres III

Guernica 2, Etude De Concert I/IA

Methode De Guitare Classique, Premier Et Deuxieme Cycles II, VII-Mixed Coll

Oracion I/IA

Variations En Forme d'Etudes, 10, Sur Une Basse Continue I/IA

SANCTUAIRE see Furstenau, Wolfram

SANDI, CHR. D.
Quartet in G I/IIB3

SANDI, LUIS (1905-   )
Fatima, Suite Galante I/IB4

ST. MARTINS-LIEDER I/IIB2-Coll, I/IIC2-Coll

SANT JOSE Y LA MARE DE DEU see Villancicos Populares, Vol. II

SANTA MARIA, THOMAS DE (1510-1570)
Fabordon Y Fuga I/IB1

Fantasias, 8 I/IB1

Fantasias, 25 I/IIA1

SANTORSOLA, GUIDO (1904-   )
Concertino I/IIIA

Hispanica, Sonoridades 1971 see Sonata No. 2

Minuet I/IB4

Prelude I/IB4

Prelude No. 1 I/IB4

Prelude No. 2 I/IB4

Prelude No. 3 I/IB4

Prelude No. 4 I/IB4

Prelude No. 5 I/IB4

Preludios, 5 see Prelude No. 1; Prelude No. 2; Prelude No. 3; Prelude No. 4; Prelude No. 5

Quartet No. 2 I/IIB3

Sonata I/IC

Sonata A Duo I/IIA1

Sonata No. 2 I/IC, I/IIA1

Sonoridades 1969 see Sonata; Sonata No. 2

SANTORSOLA, GUIDO (cont'd.)

Tientos, 4, Sonoridades 1970 I/IB4

Triptico, Tres Invenciones I/IIA1

Vals Romantico I/IB4

SANZ, GASPAR (1640-1710)
Airs De Cour, 5 see Suite in E minor

Airs De Danse, 5 I/IB1

Anthologie Pour La Guitare Espagnole
I/IB1

Batalla, Baile Popular I/IB1

Canarios I/IB1
see also Danzas Cervantinas; Obras
De Gaspar Sanz, Vol. 2

Canarios II I/IB1

Cavalleria De Napoles, La I/IB1

Chaconne I/IB1

Chansons Populaires Du XVIIe Siecle
I/IB1

Clairons Royaux, Clairons Et
Trompettes I/IB1

Composizioni, 10 I/IB1

Corriente I/IB1

Danza II see Chaconne

Danzas Cervantinas I/IB1

Diferencias Escogidas Sobre El
Canario, 15 see Canarios

Espanoleta see Airs De Danse, 5;
Danzas Cervantinas; Obras De
Gaspar Sanz, Vol. 1

Espanoleta I I/IB1

Espanoleta I, Air De Danse I/IB1

Fanfare see Cavalleria De Napoles,
La

Fantasia Original De Un Gentilhombre,
Villanos I/IB1

Folia I/IB1

Folias I/IB1

Fuga I, Per Primer Tono Al Aire
Espanol I/IB1

Fuga II, Al Modo De Jiga Inglesa
I/IB1

Gallardas I/IB1

Galliard I/IB1
see also Obras De Gaspar Sanz, Vol.
2

Galliard, MIN 14 I/IB1

Gaspar Sanz: 11 Compositions I/IB1

Gaspar Sanz Invenit I/IB1

Gigue I/IB1

Iacaras I/IB1

Marizapalos see Danzas Cervantinas;
Obras De Gaspar Sanz, Vol. 1

Marizapalos, 5 Partidas I/IB1

Matachin see Airs De Danse, 5; Obras
De Gaspar Sanz, Vol. 1

Matachin, Baile Popular Del Siglo
XVII I/IB1

Obras De Gaspar Sanz, Vol. 1 I/IB1

Obras De Gaspar Sanz, Vol. 2 I/IB1

Paradetas see Airs De Danse, 5

Passacaglia I/IB1

Passacaglia in D I/IB1
see also Obras De Gaspar Sanz, Vol.
2

Pavan I/IB1
see also Obras De Gaspar Sanz, Vol.
2

Pavana, Passacalle, Etc. I/IB1

SANZ, GASPAR (cont'd.)

Pavanas I/IB1

Pavanas I/IB1

Pavanas (Suivi De Partidos Al Aire
Espanol) I/IB1

Pieces Faciles Pour Apprendre Le
Punteado, 8 I/IB1

Preciosa, La I/IB1

Preludio-Fantasia I/IB1

Preludio O Capricho see Obras De
Gaspar Sanz, Vol. 1

Preludio O Capricho Arpeado I/IB1

Rujero I/IB1
see also Airs De Danse, 5

Saraband see Airs De Danse, 5

Sarabandes, 2 I/IB1

Serenisima, La (Alemana) I/IB1

Sesquialtera I/IB1

Sesquialtera I I/IB1

Sesquialtera II see Sesquialtera

Suite Espanola I/IB1

Suite in E minor I/IB1

Suite in G minor I/IB1

Suite No. 1 in D minor I/IB1

16 Tanze I/IB1

Torneo I/IB1

Torneo, Baile Popular I/IB1

Tournoi Et Bataille I/IB1

Villano see Obras De Gaspar Sanz,
Vol. 2

Zarabanda see Obras De Gaspar Sanz,
Vol. 1

SAO MARCOS, MARIA LIVIA
Complement A La Technique De La
Guitare see Erganzung Zur
Gitarrentechnik

Einfuhrung In Das Klassische
Gitarrenspiel II

Erganzung Zur Gitarrentechnik III

Initiation A La Guitare Classique
see Einfuhrung In Das Klassische
Gitarrenspiel

SAPO CURURU see Chansons Bresiliennes,
Vol. I

SARABANDA CON VARIAZIONI see Handel,
George Frideric, Saraband, MIN 3

SARABANDA, DE LA 1A. SUITE PARA LAUD
see Bach, Johann Sebastian, Suite
for Lute, BWV 996, in E minor,
Saraband

SARABANDA E GAVOTTA see Couperin,
Francois (le Grand)

SARABANDE AND MINUET see Corelli,
Arcangelo

SARABANDE, DEDIE A IDA PRESTI see
Poulenc, Francis

SARABANDE E FANDANGO see Zagwijn,
Henri

SARABANDE E GIGA see Corelli,
Arcangelo

SARABANDE E GIGA see Corelli,
Arcangelo

SARABANDE ET GAVOTTE see Handel,
George Frideric

SARABANDE ET MENUET see Rameau, Jean-
Philippe

SARABANDE-GIGUE see Campion, Francois

SARABANDE LOINTAINE see Rodrigo,
Joaquin

SARABANDE, SUL NOME DI REY DE LA TORRE
see Castelnuovo-Tedesco, Mario

SARABANDE UND TAMBOURIN see Leclair,
Jean Marie

SARABANDE WITH VARIATIONS see Handel,
George Frideric, Saraband, MIN 3

SARABANDES, 2 see Sanz, Gaspar

SARATOGA CONCERTO see Josephs, Wilfred

SATZE, 2, ZU EINEM MAHRISCHEN
WIEGENLIED see Stingl, Anton

SATZE ALTER MEISTER I/IIA2-Coll

SAUGUET, HENRI (1901-   )
Preludes, 3 I/IB4

SAUX, GASTON
Serenade I/IIB1

SAVIO, ISAIAS (1900-1977)
Escola Moderna Do Violao, Vol. II
II, III

Estudos, 3, Series 2 I/IA

Suite Descritiva I/IB4

Tecnica Do Mecanismo see Escola
Moderna Do Violao, Vol. II

SAXE BLUE see Blyton, Carey

SCALE DIATONICHE see Minella, Aldo

SCALE DIATONICHE, LE 24 see Abloniz,
Miguel

SCALE PATTERN STUDIES FOR GUITAR see
Shearer, Aaron, Classic Guitar
Technique, Suppl. 3

SCALE-PRACTICE see Behrend, Siegfried,
Tonleiterstudien

SCALE SEMPLICI, A TERZE, A SESTE E A
OTTAVE see Anzaghi, Luigi Oreste

SCARLATTI, ALESSANDRO (1660-1725)
Minuet I/IB1

Minuet, MIN 381 I/IB1

O Cessate Di Piagarmi I/IIC1

Sento Nel Core I/IB1, I/IIC1

SCARLATTI, DOMENICO (1685-1757)
Gavotta see Sonata, Kirkpatrick 64

Gavotta, L. 58 see Sonata,
Kirkpatrick 64

Minue see Sonata, Kirkpatrick 440

Pastorale I/IIA1

Pieces, 5 I/IB1

Sonata in A, Kirkpatrick 322 I/IIA1

Sonata in E, Kirkpatrick 380 I/IIA1

Sonata, Kirkpatrick 1 I/IB1

Sonata, Kirkpatrick 11 I/IB1
see also Sonatas, 9, Vol. 1

Sonata, Kirkpatrick 20, in E I/IIA1

Sonata, Kirkpatrick 32 see Pieces,
5; Sonatas, 9, Vol. 1; Sonate, 2

Sonata, Kirkpatrick 32, in E minor
I/IB1

Sonata, Kirkpatrick 33 I/IB1

Sonata, Kirkpatrick 34 see Pieces, 5

Sonata, Kirkpatrick 54 I/IB1
see also 5 Sonate Per 2 Chitarre

Sonata, Kirkpatrick 64 I/IB1

Sonata, Kirkpatrick 68 see Sonatas,
3

Sonata, Kirkpatrick 80 see Pieces, 5

Sonata, Kirkpatrick 149 see Sonatas,
Vol. 1

Sonata, Kirkpatrick 154 see Sonatas,
Vol. 1

Sonata, Kirkpatrick 159 I/IB1,
I/IIA1
see also 5 Sonate Per 2 Chitarre

Sonata, Kirkpatrick 173 I/IIA1

Sonata, Kirkpatrick 208 I/IB1

SCARLATTI, DOMENICO (cont'd.)

   Sonata, Kirkpatrick 209 I/IB1

   Sonata, Kirkpatrick 259 see Sonatas,
     Vol. 3

   Sonata, Kirkpatrick 274 see Sonatas,
     3

   Sonata, Kirkpatrick 277 see Sonatas,
     3

   Sonata, Kirkpatrick 278 see 5 Sonate
     Per 2 Chitarre

   Sonata, Kirkpatrick 290 see Sonatas,
     Vol. 2

   Sonata, Kirkpatrick 309 see Sonatas,
     9, Vol. 2

   Sonata, Kirkpatrick 318 see Pieces,
     5

   Sonata, Kirkpatrick 322 I/IB1
     see also Pieces, 5; Sonatas, 9,
     Vol. 1

   Sonata, Kirkpatrick 377 see 5 Sonate
     Per 2 Chitarre

   Sonata, Kirkpatrick 380 I/IB1
     see also Sonatas, 9, Vol. 2;
     Sonatas, Vol. 3; 5 Sonate Per 2
     Chitarre

   Sonata, Kirkpatrick 391 I/IB1
     see also Sonatas, 9, Vol. 1;
     Sonatas, Vol. 2

   Sonata, Kirkpatrick 428 I/IB1

   Sonata, Kirkpatrick 431 I/IB1
     see also Sonatas, 9, Vol. 2;
     Sonate, 2

   Sonata, Kirkpatrick 440 I/IB1

   Sonata, Kirkpatrick 462 see Sonatas,
     9, Vol. 1

   Sonata, Kirkpatrick 481 I/IB1
     see also Sonatas, 9, Vol. 2

   Sonata, Kirkpatrick 519, in F minor
     I/IB1

   Sonata, Kirkpatrick 544 I/IB1

   Sonata, Longo 33, Kirkpatrick 87
     I/IB1

   Sonata, MIN 311 I/IB1

   Sonata, MIN 312 I/IB1

   Sonata, MIN 387 I/IB1

   Sonata No. 288, Kirkpatrick 432
     I/IIA1

   Sonata Pastorale I/IB1

   Sonatas, 3 I/IB1

   Sonatas, 9, Vol. 1 I/IB1

   Sonatas, 9, Vol. 2 I/IB1

   4 Sonatas, K. 391, 408, 424, 453
     I/IB1

   Sonatas, Vol. 1 I/IB1

   Sonatas, Vol. 2 I/IB1

   Sonatas, Vol. 3 I/IB1

   Sonate, 2 I/IB1

   5 Sonate Per 2 Chitarre I/IIA1

   Three Sonatas I/IB1

SCENE DE BALLET see Farkas, Ferenc

SCENES, 5 see Farquhar, David

SCHAAF, PETER
   Bossa Nova see Moderne Tanze, 2

   Bounce see Moderne Tanze, 2

   Moderne Tanze, 2 I/IIB3

SCHADLER, FRIEDRICH
   Serenade Espagnole I/IIB1

SCHAFER, RUDOLF (1891-1970)
   Kleine Spiel- Und Ubungsstucke Fur
     Den Anfang, 30 I/IIB1, I/IIB2,
     I/IIB3

SCHAFF'S MIT MIR, GOTT see Monkemeyer,
   Helmut

SCHAGEN, HENK VAN
   Botje (Berend) Varierend I/IIB1

   Fantasy I/IIA2

   First Steps, The see Lopen Leren

   For Skilled Fingers see Voor
     Vaardige Vingers

   Handleiding Voor De Gitaar II

   Happy Thoughts, 4 see Zoete
     Invallen, 4

   Kleine Ditirambe I/IIB1

   Kleine Solist, De - The Little
     Soloist, Easy Guitar Pieces In
     Various Positions I/IB4

   Lichte Etudes, 20 I/IA

   Lopen Leren I/IA

   Samen Spelen, Vol. I I/IIA1

   Samen Spelen, Vol. II I/IIA1

   Tum Tum, For Young Guitarists I/IB4

   Variations On A Dutch Nursery Rhyme
     see Botje (Berend) Varierend

   Voor Het Mooie Handje, Vol. I:
     Melodie-Aanslag I/IIA1

   Voor Vaardige Vingers I/IA

   Voor Vlijtige Vingers I/IA

   Zoete Invallen, 4 I/IA

   Zomeravondsuite I/IIA2

SCHALE, CHRISTIAN FR. (1713-1800)
   Menuette, 2 I/IIB2

SCHALK UND SCHERZ ZUR LAUTE see
   Dockhorn, Lotte

SCHALL, DER, FOR 5 INSTRUMENTALISTS
   see Kagel, Mauricio

SCHALLER, ERWIN (1901-   )
   Altlothringer Hirtenmusik I/IIB3,
     IV/IIA1, IV/IIB3

   Funf Miniaturen, Nach Schottischen
     Volksweisen I/IIB2

   Lehrwerk Fur Die Gitarre, Vol. I II

   Lehrwerk Fur Die Gitarre, Vol. II II

   Lehrwerk Fur Die Gitarre, Vol. III
     II

   Lehrwerk Fur Die Gitarre, Vol. IV
     II, III

   Lehrwerk Fur Die Gitarre, Vol. V II,
     VII-Mixed Coll

   Lehrwerk Fur Gitarre, Vol. IV II,
     III

   Rhapsodie Und Hochzeitstanz Nach
     Finnischen Volksweisen I/IIB1

   Sonata for Guitar I/IC

SCHAT, PETER (1935-   )
   First Essay On Electrocution I/IIB4

   Thema, For Oboe Solo, Guitars, Organ
     And Wind Instruments V/i

   To You V/ii

SCHATTENLAND STROME, CONATUM 37 see
   Kunad, Rainer

SCHAUKEL see Uhl, Alfred

SCHEIDLER, CHRISTIAN GOTTLIEB
   (1752-1815)
   Duo Pour Guitarre Et Violon I/IIA1

   Sonata in C I/IC

   Sonata in D I/IIA1, I/IIB1

   Variations, 12, Sur Un Theme De
     Mozart I/IB2

SCHEIT, KARL
   Lehr- Und Spielbuch Fur Gitarre II

SCHELB, JOSEF (1894-1977)
   Gestutzte Eros, Der; Music To The
     Comedy By Herbert Tjadens V/iii

SCHELP see Leeuw, Ton de

SCHENK, JOHANN (1753-1836)
   Suite in A minor I/IB1

SCHERZANDO see Duarte, John W.

3 SCHERZDUETTE see Mozart, Wolfgang
   Amadeus

SCHERZETTO see Absil, Jean

SCHERZI, 3 see Monteverdi, Claudio

SCHERZI MUSICALI, CIOE ARIE, ET
   MADRIGALI IN STILE RECITATIVO see
   Monteverdi, Claudio

SCHERZINO MEXICANO see Ponce, Manuel
   Maria

SCHERZO CONTRARIO see Pololanik,
   Zdenek

SCHERZO DE T. DAMAS see Tarrega,
   Francisco, Study, TI ii- 18, in A

SCHERZO, DIALOGO TRA UNA VECCHIA E UNA
   GIOVANE see Paganini, Niccolo

SCHERZO GIOCOSO see Giuliani, Mauro

SCHERZOSO see Behrend, Siegfried

SCHIBLER, ARMIN (1920-   )
   Black Guitar, The I/IB4

   Every Night I Dream I/IB4

   Homme Seul, Un, Kleines Konzert
     I/IB4

   My Own Blues I/IB4

SCHICKHARDT, JOHANN CHRISTIAN
   (1670-1740)
   Trio Sonata in F I/IIB2

SCHIFFELHOLZ, JOHANN PAUL (1680-1758)
   Sonata I-VI (For 2 Colascioni, 2
     Violins And Violoncello) I/IIA1

SCHIFRIN, LALO (BORIS) (1932-   )
   Ritual Of Sound V/i

SCHILDBURGER, DIE, CANTATA FOR CHILDREN
   see Kretzschmar, Gunther

SCHILLING, HANS LUDWIG (1927-   )
   Ich Weiss Ein Lieblich Engelspiel,
     Liedkantate I/IIC5

   Legende Vom Weisen Und Zollner V/ii

   Liedstrophen, 2 V/ii

   Singet Dem Herrn Ein Neues Lied V/ii

SCHINDLER, OTTO
   Wiegenlied I/IB4

SCHININA, LUIGI
   Accordi E Cadenze Per Chitarra
     d'Accompagnamento III

   Tutte Le Scale Per Chitarra III

SCHLAF, MEIN KINDELEIN see
   Weihnachtslieder, 5

SCHLAFLIED FUR JULISKA see
   Rosenstengel, Albrecht

SCHLAGLICHTER!; 7 SONGS VON DER
   UNHEILEN WELT see Seeger, Peter

SCHLICHTING, THEODOR
   Bass-Studien I/IA

SCHLICK, ARNOLT (ca. 1460-ca. 1517)
   Tabulaturen Etlicher Lobgesang Und
     Lidlein Vff Die Lauten, 1512
     I/IB1-Coll

SCHLOSS IN OSTERREICH, DAS see Thomas,
   Kurt

SCHMETTERLING, DER see Giuliani,
   Mauro, Papillon, Le

SCHMICERER, JOHANN ABRAHAM
   (fl. ca. 1680)
   10 Stucke I/IIB2

SCHMIDT, HERMANN (1885-1950)
   Neue Gitarrenschule II

SCHNABEL, JOSEPH (1767-1831)
   Quintet I/IIB4

SCHUMANN, ROBERT (ALEXANDER) (cont'd.)

Erinnerung I/IB2
see also Pezzi, 3

Erster Verlust see Album; Album Per
La Gioventu, 6 Pezzi, Op. 68,
Nos. 1-3, 5, 16, 18; Pezzi, 3

Escenas Infantiles see Kinderscenen

Feuilles Varias I/IB2

Feuilles Variees see Albumblatt

Frohlicher Landmann I/IB2
see also 5 Piezas

Fugue I/IB2

Fugue, MIN 340 I/IB2

Fugueta I/IB2

Hoja De Album I/IB2

Hojas Varias see Feuilles Varias

Jagerliedchen I/IB2
see also 5 Piezas

Kinderscenen I/IB2

Kindersonate I/IB2

Mai, Cher Mai, Bientot Tu Seras La...
see Mai, Lieber Mai

Mai, Lieber Mai I/IB2

Marcha Militar see 5 Piezas

Marche Militaire I/IB2

Mayo, Buen Mayo see Mai, Lieber Mai

Melodia, Labrador Alegre I/IB2

Melodie see Album Per La Gioventu, 6
Pezzi, Op. 68, Nos. 1-3, 5, 16,
18

Melody I/IB2
see also 5 Piezas

Melody, MIN 375 I/IB2

Nocturne, Op. 23, No. 4 I/IB2

Nordisches Lied I/IB2

Paisano Alegre see Frohlicher
Landmann

Pezzi, 3 I/IB2

Pieza Breve see 5 Piezas

5 Piezas I/IB2

5 Piezas I/IB2

Recuerdo Del 4 De Noviembre, Muerte
De Mendelssohn see Erinnerung

Reverie see Traumerei

Reverie-Siciliano I/IB2

Romance, MIN 137 I/IB2

Romance, Op. 51 I/IB2

Rundgesang I/IB2

Saint Nicolas I/IB2
see also Saint Nicolas

Schnitterliedchen see Album Per La
Gioventu, 6 Pezzi, Op. 68, Nos.
1-3, 5, 16, 18

Schumann-Buch, Das I/IB2

Sicilianisch see Pezzi, 3

Siciliano, MIN 369 I/IB2

Sogno see Traumerei

Soldatenmarsch see Album; Album Per
La Gioventu, 6 Pezzi, Op. 68,
Nos. 1-3, 5, 16, 18

Stuckchen see Album; Album Per La
Gioventu, 6 Pezzi, Op. 68, Nos.
1-3, 5, 16, 18

Stucke Aus Dem "Album Fur Die Jugend,
" Op. 68 I/IB2, I/IIA1

Sylvesterlied I/IB2

Trallerliedchen see Album Per La
Gioventu, 6 Pezzi, Op. 68, Nos.
1-3, 5, 16, 18; 5 Piezas

SCHUMANN, ROBERT (ALEXANDER) (cont'd.)

Traumerei I/IB2
see also Album

Volksliedchen I/IB2

Von Fremden Landern Und Menschen
I/IB2

Wiegenlied I/IB2

Wilder Reiter see 5 Piezas

SCHUMANN-BUCH, DAS see Schumann,
Robert (Alexander)

SCHUTZ, HEINRICH (1585-1672)
Geistliche Gesange, 2 I/IIC1

SCHWABISCHE BAURENTANZE, 3 see Krebs,
Rudolf

SCHWARZ-REIFLINGEN, ERWIN
Gitarren 1x1, Das, Die Gitarrenschule
Fur Den Selbstunterricht II

Gitarren-Schule, Vol. I II

Gitarren-Schule, Vol. II II,
VII-Mixed Coll

SCHWARZ-SCHILLING, REINHARD (1904-   )
Kleine Kammermusik I/IIB4

SCHWEINEHIRT, DER; MUSIK ZU EINEM
SCHATTENSPIEL see Twittenhoff,
Wilhelm

SCHWERTBERGER, GERALD
Folk Guitar: Ragtime, Blues, Country
Music I/IB5

Glory Hallelujah: Spirituals, Jazz,
Blues, Beat I/IB5

Latin America: Tango, Samba, Rumba,
Bossa-Nova I/IB5

SCHWERTSIK, KURT (1935-   )
Salotto Romano V/i

SCHWEYDA, WILLY
Pieces, 2 I/IB4

SCOTTISCH MADRILENE I/IB5

SCOZZESI, 12 see Giuliani, Mauro

SCRIABIN, ALEXANDER (1872-1915)
Prelude No. 4 I/IB3

SCUOLA DELLA CHITARRA, PRATICA
D'ACCOMPAGNAMENTO, OP. 137 see
Munier, Carlo

SE HAI GETTATO UNA MONETINA see
Bortolami, Galliano

SECHS BAGATELLEN FUR GITARRE see
Mairants, Ivor

SECHS MAL DREI (6 X 3) see Wolki,
Konrad

SECHS PROGRESSIVE STUCKE FUR GITARRE
see Mairants, Ivor

SECHS SEEMANNSLIEDER see Hashagen,
Klaus

SECHS SOLOS FUR GITARRE see Mairants,
Ivor

SECHS SONATINEN, VOL. 1 see
Stravinsky, Soulima

SECHS SONATINEN, VOL. 2 see
Stravinsky, Soulima

SECHS VARIATIONEN see Matiegka,
Wenzeslaus Thomas

SECHSKLANG, DER see Apostel, Hans
Erich

SECKINGER, KONRAD (1935-   )
House Of The Rising Sun, The V/ii

There Is A House In New Orleans see
House Of The Rising Sun, The

SECOND CHANT see Ballard, Robert

SECONDA SERENATA-TRIO see Petrassi,
Goffredo

SECONDE LEZIONI, LE see Sagreras,
Julio S., Lessons For The Guitar,
Vol. 2, The Second Lessons

SECONDO CONCERTO see Giuliani, Mauro,
Concerto in A, Op. 36

SEEFAHRT NACH RIO, DIE, SCENIC CANTATA
see Geese, Heinz

SEEGER, PETER (1919-   )
Schlaglichter!; 7 Songs Von Der
Unheilen Welt V/ii

SEEKING HAYDN see Haydn, [Franz]
Joseph

SEGMENTI see Serocki, Kazimierz

SEGOVIA see Roussel, Albert (Charles
Paul)

SEGOVIA, ANDRES (1896-   )
Diatonic Major & Minor Scales III

Estudio Sin Luz I/IA

Estudio-Vals I/IA

Estudios, 3 I/IA, I/IIA1

Four Easy Lessons I/IA

Impromptu I/IB4

Prelude In Chords I/IB4

Preludios, 3 I/IB4

Tonadilla I/IB4

SEGOVIANA see Milhaud, Darius

SEGUIDILLAS see Albeniz, Isaac

SEGUIDILLAS: 12 SPANISH SONGS see Sor,
Fernando

SEGUNDAS LECCIONES, LAS see Sagreras,
Julio S., Lessons For The Guitar,
Vol. 2, The Second Lessons

SEHNSUCHT NACH DEM FRUHLING see
Mozart, Wolfgang Amadeus

SEHR GEWOHNLICHE GESCHICHTE, EINE see
Haydn, [Franz] Joseph

SEHR LANGSAM see Stadlmair, Hans

SEHR LANGSAM see Stadlmair, Hans

SEHR LEICHTE BIS MITTELSCHWERE SATZE
FUR 1 UND 2 GITARREN I/IB6-Coll,
I/IIA1-Coll

SEHR LEICHTE STUCKE, 18, VOL. 1 see
Carulli, Ferdinando

SEHR LEICHTE STUCKE FUR GITARRE, 42
I/IB6-Coll

SEHR LEICHTE STUCKE, VOL. I see
Diabelli, Anton

SEHR LEICHTE STUCKE, VOL. II see
Diabelli, Anton

SEHR LEICHTE STUCKE, VOL. III see
Diabelli, Anton

SEHR LEICHTE STUCKE, VOL. IV see
Diabelli, Anton

SEHR LEICHTE UBUNGEN, 24, VOL. 1:
STUDIES NO. 1-12 see Sor,
Fernando, Vingt-Quatre Exercices
Tres Faciles

SEHR LEICHTE UBUNGEN, 24, VOL. 2:
STUDIES NO. 13-24 see Sor,
Fernando, Vingt-Quatre Exercices
Tres Faciles

SEHR LEICHTE UBUNGSSTUCKE, 30 see
Diabelli, Anton, Studi Facili, 30

SEHR LEICHTE UBUNGSTUCKE, 30 see
Diabelli, Anton, Studi Facili, 30

SEIBER, MATYAS GYORGY (1905-1960)
A Vouz Amanz see Medieval French
Songs, 4

Bergier De Vile Champestre see
Medieval French Songs, 4

French Folk Songs, 4 I/IIC1

Gentilz Galans De France see
Medieval French Songs, 4

J'ai Descendu see French Folk Songs,
4

Marguerite, Elle Est Malade see
French Folk Songs, 4

Medieval French Songs, 4 I/IIC3

Owl And The Pussycat, The I/IIC2

SEIBER, MATYAS GYORGY (cont'd.)

Pourquoi Me Bat   see Medieval French
Songs, 4

Reveillez-Vous   see French Folk
Songs, 4

Rossignol, Le   see French Folk Songs,
4

SEIDEL
Zwolf Menuetten   I/IB1-Coll

SEIS CUERDAS, LAS   see Company, Alvaro

SEIXAS, (JOSE ANTONIO) CARLOS DE
(1704-1742)
Concerto in A   I/IIIA

Menuets, 2   I/IB1

Sonata SK 37   I/IB1

4 Sonatas   I/IB1

Sonaten, 2   I/IB1

SELECCION DE OBRAS DE LOS MAS CELEBRES
LAUDISTAS FRANCESES E ITALIANOS DE
LOS SIGLOS XVI, XVII Y XVIII
I/IB1-Coll

SELTENE SCHONHEIT, EINE   see
Rosenstengel, Albrecht

SELVA AMOROSA   see Caroso, Fabrizio

SENAILLE, JEAN BAPTISTE (1687-1730)
Sonata   I/IB1

SENTO NEL CORE   see Scarlatti,
Alessandro

SEPTIEME FANTAISIE ET VARIATIONS
BRILLANTES SUR DEUX AIRS FAVORIS
CONNUS   see Sor, Fernando

SEQUENTIAL   see Abloniz, Miguel

SEQUIDILLA   see Pujol, Emilio

SERAFINI, CESARE (1928-   )
Breve Guida Per Chitarra   II

SERENADE   see Richter, Nico

SERENADE, FOR JAZZ QUARTET AND CHAMBER
ORCHESTRA   see Buschmann, Rainer-
Glen

SERENADE (DE SHAKESPEARE)   see
Schubert, Franz (Peter)

SERENADE ESPAGNOLE   see Schadler,
Friedrich

SERENADE VILLAGEOISE   see Sanchez, B.

SERENADEN, 5   see Carulli, Ferdinando

SERENATA   see Desderi, Ettore; Fortea,
Daniel; Haydn, [Franz] Joseph;
Schubert, Franz (Peter), Standchen

SERENATA, FOR VIOLONCELLO AND ORCHESTRA
see Csonika, Paul

SERENATA A TRE   see Linde, Hans-Martin

SERENATA ALL'ANTICA   see Degni,
Vincenzo

SERENATA ANDALUZA   see Falla, Manuel
de; Malats, Joachin

SERENATA ARABE   see Albeniz, Isaac

SERENATA BURLESCA   see Moreno Torroba,
Federico

SERENATA CANARIA   see Sanchez, B.

SERENATA CARORENA, CANCION VENEZOLANA
see Ramos, Joaquin

SERENATA DE DON JUAN   see Mozart,
Wolfgang Amadeus

SERENATA ESPANOLA   see Bleeker, Willy;
Malats, Joachin

SERENATA II, PER FLAUTO E QUATTRO
GRUPPI STRUMENTALI   see Vlijmen,
Jan van

SERENATA MORISCA   see Chapi, R.

SERENATA POLONIA   see Furstenau,
Wolfram

SERENATA PUEBLERINA   see Sanchez, B.,
Serenade Villageoise

SERENE   see Komter, Jan Maarten

SERENISIMA, LA (ALEMANA)   see Sanz,
Gaspar

SERIE   see Braun, Gunter

SERMISY, CLAUDE DE (CLAUDIN)
(ca. 1490-1562)
Tant Que Vivrai, Chanson   I/IIC1

SEROCKI, KAZIMIERZ (1922-1981)
Augen Der Luft   V/ii

Herz Der Nacht   V/ii

Impromptu Fantasque   V/i

Krasnoludki   I/IIA2

Segmenti   V/i

Sinfonische Fresken, For Orchestra
V/i

Zwerge, Die   see Krasnoludki

SERRA, LA, 7 PRELUDI   see Barbieri,
Mario

SERRANITO
see MONGE, VICTOR ("SERRANITO")

SESQUIALTERA   see Sanz, Gaspar

SESQUIALTERA I   see Sanz, Gaspar

SESQUIALTERA II   see Sanz, Gaspar,
Sesquialtera

SESTE LEZIONI, LE   see Sagreras, Julio
S., Lessons For The Guitar, Vol. 6,
The Sixth Lessons

SESTINA, OP. 161   see Krenek, Ernst

SETTE FOGLI, 5   see Bussotti, Sylvano

SETTE FOGLI, 6   see Bussotti, Sylvano

SEVEN HUNDRED YEARS OF MUSIC FOR THE
CLASSIC GUITAR   I/IB6-Coll,
VI-Mixed Coll, VII-Mixed Coll

SEVEN MINUTES ORGANIZED SOUND   see
Masseus, Jan

SEVERINO, GIULIO
Fantasy   I/IB1

SEVILLA, EVOCATION   see Pujol, Emilio

SEVILLA, SEVILLANAS   see Albeniz, Isaac

SEVILLANA   see Gangi, Mario;
Winkelbauer, Alfred

"SEVILLANA": FANTASIA   see Turina,
Joaquin, Fantasia Sevillana

SEVILLANAS   see Behrend, Siegfried;
Winkelbauer, Alfred

SEVILLANAS POPULAR   see Ausgewahlte
Stucke Alter Und Neuer Meister Fur
Gitarre, Vol. 2

SEXTAS LECCIONES, LAS   see Sagreras,
Julio S., Lessons For The Guitar,
Vol. 6, The Sixth Lessons

SEXTUOR MYSTIQUE   see Villa-Lobos,
Heitor

SEYS LIBROS DEL DELPHIN DE MUSICA, LOS:
AUSGEWAHLTE WERKE   see Narvaez,
Luis de

SEYS LIBROS DEL DELPHIN DE MUSICA DE
CIFRA PARA TANER VIHUELA, LOS   see
Narvaez, Luis de

SFETSAS, KYRIACOS (1945-   )
Strophes   I/IB4

SHACKELFORD, RUDOLPH OWENS (RUDY)
(1944-   )
Epitaffio   I/IB4

SHAKESPEARE-SUITE; DANCES BY
CONTEMPORARIES OF WILLIAM
SHAKESPEARE   see Mohler, Philipp

SHAND, ERNEST (1868-1924)
Andante   see Solos, 6

Chant Du Soir   see Solos, 6

Gavotte Rococo   see Solos, 6

Pensieroso   see Solos, 6

Prelude Et Impromptu   see Solos, 6

SHAND, ERNEST (cont'd.)

Solos, 6   I/IB3

Valse Legere   see Solos, 6

SHANTIES FROM THE SEVEN SEAS   see
Hofer, Karlheinz

SHAPERO, HAROLD SAMUEL (1920-   )
On Green Mountain; Chaconne After
Monteverdi   V/i

SHEARER, AARON
Classic Guitar Technique, Vol. I   II

Classic Guitar Technique, Vol. II
II, VI-Mixed Coll

Classic Guitar Technique, Suppl. 1
II, III

Classic Guitar Technique, Suppl. 2:
Basic Elements Of Music Theory
For The Guitar   II

Classic Guitar Technique, Suppl. 3
II, III

Classic Guitar Technique, Suppl. 4:
Guitar Note Speller   II

Scale Pattern Studies For Guitar   see
Classic Guitar Technique, Suppl.
3

Slur, Ornament And Reach Development
Exercises   see Classic Guitar
Technique, Suppl. 1

Tremolo Studies, 3   I/IA

SHEER, ANITA
Introduction To The Flamenco Guitar,
An   II

SHERMAN, ELNA
Suite No. 1   I/IIB1

SHIMOYAMA, HIFUMI (1930-   )
Dialogo, No. 1   I/IIA1

Dialogo, No. 2   I/IIA1

SHOEMAKER'S WIFE, THE   see Dowland,
John

SHOLLE, EMIL
Higher Frets On All Strings, The,
Melodious Studies In Positions,
Vol. 1   III

Higher Frets On All Strings, The,
Melodious Studies In Positions,
Vol. II   III

Higher Frets On All Strings, The,
Melodious Studies In Positions,
Vol. III   III

SHOOTING OF HIS DEAR, THE   see Britten,
[Sir] Benjamin

SHORT PIECES, 4   see Bellow, Alexander;
Franck, Cesar

SHORT PIECES, 10   see Strategier,
Herman

SHORT PRELUDES, 6 (CHORD PROGRESSIONS)
see Foden, William

SI LA NOCHE HACE OSCURA, VILLANCICO
see Pisador, Diego

SI LE JOUR PARAIT, NO. 1   see Ohana,
Maurice

SI LE JOUR PARAIT, NO. 2   see Ohana,
Maurice

SI LE JOUR PARAIT, NO. 3   see Ohana,
Maurice

SI LE JOUR PARAIT, NO. 4   see Ohana,
Maurice

SI LE JOUR PARAIT, NO. 5   see Ohana,
Maurice

SI LE JOUR PARAIT, NO. 6   see Ohana,
Maurice

SI LE JOUR PARAIT, NO. 7   see Ohana,
Maurice

SI TE VAS A BANAR, JUANICA   see
Canciones Antiguas, 6

SI TE VAS A BANER JUANICA, VILLANCICO
see Pisador, Diego

SIATE AVVERTITI   see Anonymous

SIBELIUS, JEAN (1865-1957)
Komm Herbei Tod I/IIC1

SICILIANA see Bach, Carl Philipp
Emanuel; Handel, George Frideric;
Paradis, Maria Theresia von;
Pergolesi, Giovanni Battista; Sor,
Fernando, Trois Pieces De Societe,
Op. 33, No. 3

SICILIANA AND FUGUE, FROM SONATA NO. 1
FOR SOLO VIOLIN see Bach, Johann
Sebastian

SICILIANISCH see Schumann, Robert
(Alexander)

SICILIANO see Heer, Hans De;
Pergolesi, Giovanni Battista

SICK DOLL, THE see Tchaikovsky, Piotr
Ilyich

SICK TUNE, THE see Anonymous;
Anonymous

SIEGL, ERWIN
Duos, Op. 34, Vol. I I/IIA1

SIEGL, OTTO (1896-1978)
Sonata I/IIB1

Sonatina in D minor I/IIB1

SIERRA, JOSE MARIA
Etudes Superieures, 3 I/IA

SIERRA-FORTUNY, J.M.
Introduccio I/IB4

SIGHS see Antunes, Jorge

SILENCE see Duarte, John W.

SILENT FORESTS see Sperling, Ernst

SILENTIUM TURBATUM, SYMPHONIC SETTING
see Borkovec, Pavel

SILENUS EN BAKCHANTEN see Regt,
Hendrik de

SIMONIS, JEAN-MARIE (1931-   )
Nocturne, Op. 23 I/IIB1

SIMONS, H.B.
Guitar Chord Chart III

SIMPLE FOLK I/IIB1-Coll

SIMPLE SONGS WITHOUT WORDS, 3 see
Duarte, John W.

SIMPLE VARIATIONS ON "LAS FOLIAS" see
Duarte, John W.

SIMPLICITY TUTOR FOR SPANISH GUITAR,
THE, IN THE TARREGA METHOD see
Mairants, Ivor

SINE NOMINE see Raxach, Enrique; Vogt,
Hans

SINEGIA see Tsilicas, Jorge

SINFONISCHE FRESKEN, FOR ORCHESTRA see
Serocki, Kazimierz

SING AND PLAY..., TO SIMPLE GUITAR
ACCOMPANIMENTS, VOL. I: SING AND
PLAY NATIONAL SONGS I/IIC1-Coll

SING AND PLAY..., TO SIMPLE GUITAR
ACCOMPANIMENTS, VOL. II: SING AND
PLAY NURSERY SONGS I/IIC1-Coll

SING AND PLAY..., TO SIMPLE GUITAR
ACCOMPANIMENTS, VOL. III: SING AND
PLAY SEA-SONGS I/IIC1-Coll

SING CHRISTMAS CAROLS II, IV/IIC1

SING MIR, MORENA!, LIEDER ZUR GITARRE
AUS SPANIEN, SUDFRANKREICH,
LITAUEN, DALMATIEN I/IIC1-Coll

SING NEGRO SPIRITUALS I/IIC1-Coll, II,
IV/IIC1

SING- UND MASKENSPIEL VON JORINDE UND
JORINGEL, DAS, EIN SPIEL FUR KINDER
see Klein, Waldtraut

SINGENDE MUSE AN DER PLEISSE see
Sperontes (Johann Sigismund
Scholze)

SINGENDES, KLINGENDES OSTERREICH
I/IIC1-Coll, IV/IIC1

SINGER, LAWRENCE (1940-   )
Musica A Due I/IIB1

SINGET DEM HERRN EIN NEUES LIED see
Schilling, Hans Ludwig

SINGLE STRING STUDIES FOR GUITAR see
Salvador, San

SINGSTUNDEN, DIE, NO. 1-36, LIEDER FUR
ALLE I/IIC5-Coll

SINOPOLI, ANTONIO
Preludio En Forma De Estudio I/IA

SINTERKLAAS- EN KERSTLIEDJES
I/IIB1-Coll

SINTERKLAAS- & KERSTLIEDJES IV/IIB1

SINTERKLAASLIEDJES I/IB5-Coll

SINTERKLAASLIEDJES I/IIC1-Coll

SINTESIS see Labrouve, Jorge

SIR HENRY HUMPTON'S FUNERAL see
Dowland, John

SIX LUTE PIECES see Dowland, Robert

SIX PETITES PIECES see Sor, Fernando,
Voyons Si C'est Ca, 6 Petites
Pieces Faciles

SIX PETITES PIECES FACILES see Sor,
Fernando

SIX PETITES PIECES, OP. 42, NO. 2 see
Sor, Fernando

SIX PIECES FROM THE TIME OF ELIZABETH
I/IIB1-Coll

SIX PIECES, VOL. 1 see Weiss, Sylvius
Leopold

SIX PIECES, VOL. 2 see Weiss, Sylvius
Leopold

SIX SAILOR-SONGS see Hashagen, Klaus,
Sechs Seemannslieder

SIX SEQUENCES FOR DANCE, FOR CHAMBER
ENSEMBLE see Cervetti, Sergio

SIX WALTZES see Sor, Fernando

SIXIEME ORDRE see Couperin, Francois
(1e Grand)

SIXTY SHORT PIECES, VOL. 1 see Sor,
Fernando

SIXTY SHORT PIECES, VOL. 2 see Sor,
Fernando

SKALKOTTAS, NIKOS (1904-1949)
Maienzauber; Stage Music To The Fairy
Drama V/iii

Mayday Spell; Stage Music To The
Fairy Drama see Maienzauber;
Stage Music To The Fairy Drama

SKANKLAT TILL SPELMAN see Suit I
Svensk Folkton Nr. 2

SKARBCZYK GITARZYSTY - THE GUITARIST'S
TREASURY I/IB6-Coll,
VII-Mixed Coll

SKETCHES, 3 see Brouwer, Leo, Apuntes,
3

SKIERA, EHRENHARD
Flamenco-Gitarrenschule II

Skiera Methode, Vol. I: Ein
Grundlegendes Werk Zur
Akkordbegleitung II

SKIERA METHODE, VOL. I: EIN
GRUNDLEGENDES WERK ZUR
AKKORDBEGLEITUNG see Skiera,
Ehrenhard

SKIZZEN, 4 see Haider, Hans

SKLADBY, 3 (3 KOMPOSITIONEN) see
Diabelli, Anton

SKLADEB, 5 see Handel, George Frideric

SKOLA HRY NA KYTARU, PRO SAMOUKY I
POKROCILE see Bartos, Antonin

SKOLA IGRY NA WESTISTRINNOI GITARE
(METHOD FOR PLAYING THE 6-STRINGED
GUITAR) see Carcassi, Matteo,
Vollstandige Guitarre-Schule

SKORZENY, FRITZ (1900-1965)
Trio I/IIB2

SLAVONSKA POSKOCICA see Cossetto, Emil

SLAWKA see Ruthenberg, Otto

SLUMBER SONG see Sperling, Ernst

SLUR, ORNAMENT AND REACH DEVELOPMENT
EXERCISES see Shearer, Aaron,
Classic Guitar Technique, Suppl. 1

SMALL STUDIES see Patachich, Ivan, Kis
Tanulmanyok

SMALLEY, ROGER (1943-   )
Beat Music, For Orchestra With
Amplified Instruments V/i

SMETANA, BEDRICH (1824-1884)
Geheimnis, Das; Comic Opera In Three
Acts V/iii

SMIT SIBINGA, THEO H. (1899-1958)
Concerto I/IIIA

SMITH, WILLIAM OVERTON (1926-   )
Interplay V/i

SMITH BRINDLE, REGINALD (1917-   )
Danza Pagana I/IB4

Do Not Go Gentle... I/IB4

Etruscan Preludes I/IB4

Fuego Fatuo I/IB4

Memento I/IB4

Music For Three Guitars I/IIA2

Nocturne I/IB4

November Memories I/IB4

Polifemo De Oro, Il, 4 Fragmenti
I/IB4

Sonatina Fiorentina I/IC

Vita Senese I/IB4

SNARENSPEL see Wijdeveld, Wolfgang

SNARENSPEL - STRINGMUSIC, EXERCISES IN
CHANGING POSITIONS see Helleman,
Joop

SNYDER, JERROLD
Comprehensive Guitar Method, The, For
Classroom And Individual
Instruction, Vol. A: Teacher's
Manual II

Comprehensive Guitar Method, The, For
Classroom And Individual
Instruction, Vol. B: Student Book
II

SO DEEP IS THE NIGHT see Chopin,
Frederic, Etude, Op. 10, No. 3,
[excerpt]

SO OFT ICH MEINE TOBACKSPFEIFE see
Bach, Johann Sebastian

SODERLUNDH, LILLE BROR (1912-1957)
Liten Vals I/IIA1

SOGNO see Schumann, Robert
(Alexander), Traumerei

SOIREE A VERSAILLES see Campion,
Francois

SOIS TOUJOURS MES SEULS AMOURS see
Schubert, Franz (Peter)

SOJO, VINCENTE E.
Aguinaldo see Pieces From Venezuela,
5

Aire Venezolano see Pieces From
Venezuela, 5

Cancion see Pieces From Venezuela, 5

Cantico see Pieces From Venezuela, 5

Galeron see Pieces From Venezuela, 5

Pieces From Venezuela, 5 I/IB4

Quirpa Guatirena, Joropo I/IB4

SOL, SI, MI see Fresno, Jorge

SOL Y SOMBRA see Ferstl, Erich

SOLAMENTE DIOS ES TODOPODEROSO see
Bach, Johann Sebastian, Allein Gott
In Der Hoh' Sei Ehr'

SOLARES, ENRIQUE (1910-   )
Fantasy I/IB4

Ofrenda A Fernando Sors I/IB4

Toccatina I/IB4

SOLDATENMARSCH see Schumann, Robert
(Alexander)

SOLDIER AND THE SAILOR, THE   see Britten, [Sir] Benjamin

SOLER, [PADRE] ANTONIO (1729-1783)
   Sonata in G   I/IIA1

   Sonata No. 1 in A   I/IB1

   Sonata No. 2   I/IB1

   Sonata No. 3   I/IB1

   Sonata No. 4, Bolero   I/IB1

   Sonata No. 6   I/IB1

   Sonata No. 8   I/IB1

   Sonata No. 13   I/IB1

   Sonata No. 14   I/IB1

   Sonata No. 15   I/IB1

   Sonata No. 18, En Modo Dorico   I/IB1

   Sonata No. 69   I/IB1

   Sonata No. 71   I/IB1

   Sonata No. 84   I/IB1

   Sonata No. 87   I/IB1

SOLFEGGIETTO, NO. 6   see Ballif, Claude

SOLFEGIETTO   see Bach, Carl Philipp Emanuel

SOLI FUR SPANISCHE GITARRE, 10, VOL. I   I/IB6-Coll

2 SOLIOQUIOS   see Homs, Joaquin

SOLO A SOLO   see Prieto, Claudio

SOLO EL QUE SABE AMAR   see Tchaikovsky, Piotr Ilyich, None But The Lonely Heart

SOLO FUR EL-GUITAR   see Gudmundsen-Holmgreen, Pelle

SOLO-GITARRE, DIE, VOL. I   I/IB6-Coll

SOLO-GITARRE, DIE, VOL. II   see Miller, John R.

SOLO-GITARRE, DIE, VOL. III   I/IB6-Coll, VI-Mixed Coll

SOLO GUITAR PLAYING, A COMPLETE COURSE OF INSTRUCTION IN THE TECHNIQUE OF GUITAR PERFORMANCE   see Noad, Frederick M.

SOLO-STUCKE ALTER MEISTER   I/IB6-Coll

SOLOBUCH FUR GITARRE, DAS   I/IB6-Coll, VII-Mixed Coll

SOLOGITARRE, DIE, VOL. I   I/IB6-Coll, VII-Mixed Coll

SOLOGITARRE, DIE, VOL. II   I/IB6-Coll

SOLOGITARRE, DIE, VOL. III   I/IB6-Coll

SOLOGITARRE, DIE, VOL. IV   I/IB6-Coll

SOLOGITARRE, DIE, VOL. V   I/IB6-Coll

SOLOS, 6   see Shand, Ernest

SOLOS FOR CLASSIC GUITAR, 6   see Mairants, Ivor

SOLOS FOR THE GUITAR PLAYER   I/IB6-Coll, VII-Mixed Coll

SOLOS FOR THE GUITAR PLAYER   I/IB6-Coll, VII-Mixed Coll

SOLOSPIEL AUF DER GITARRE, DAS   see Hauswirth, Hans M.A.

SOLOSTUCKE   see Vallet, Nicolas

SOLOWERKE, VOL. 1   see Dowland, John

SOLUS FOR GUITAR   see Watkins, Michael Blake

SOLVEIG'S SONG   see Grieg, Edvard Hagerup

SOME OF NOAH'S ARK   see Duarte, John W.

SOMETIMES I FEEL LIKE A MOTHERLESS CHILD   see Famous Negro Spirituals, 5

SOMMERFELDT, OISTEIN (1919-   )
   Three Lyric Guitar Duets   I/IIA1

SONANT   see Kagel, Mauricio

SONATA   see Bach, Johann Sebastian, Prelude, Fugue And Allegro For Lute, In E-Flat

2A SONATA   see Sor, Fernando, Grande Sonate, Op. 25

SONATA A 2   see Baron, Ernst Gottlieb

SONATA A DUO   see Santorsola, Guido

SONATA CLASICA, HOMMAGE A FERNANDO SOR   see Ponce, Manuel Maria

SONATA CLASSICA   see Uhl, Alfred

SONATA CONCERTATA   see Paganini, Niccolo

SONATA DA CAMERA   see Andriessen, Jurriaan, Trio No. 5

SONATA EN RE MINORE   see Weiss, Sylvius Leopold

SONATA EROICA   see Giuliani, Mauro

SONATA GIOCOSA   see Rodrigo, Joaquin

SONATA HEROICA   see Giuliani, Mauro, Sonata Eroica

SONATA I-VI (FOR 2 COLASCIONI, 2 VIOLINS AND VIOLONCELLO)   see Schiffelholz, Johann Paul

SONATA MEXICANA   see Ponce, Manuel Maria, Sonata No. 1

SONATA NO. 1   see Roncalli, Ludovico, Suite No. 1

SONATA NO. 4, BOLERO   see Soler, [Padre] Antonio

SONATA, NO.12: MARCHA FUNEBRE   see Beethoven, Ludwig van

SONATA NO. 14, ALLEGRETTO   see Beethoven, Ludwig van

SONATA NO. 18, EN MODO DORICO   see Soler, [Padre] Antonio

SONATA NOVA   see Kovats, Barna

SONATA, OP. 2, NO. 2, SCHERZO   see Beethoven, Ludwig van

SONATA PARA LAUD   see Straube, Rudolf

SONATA PASTORALE   see Scarlatti, Domenico

SONATA PATETICA: ADAGIO   see Beethoven, Ludwig van, Sonata, Op. 13, Adagio

SONATA PIAN' E FORTE, FOR SOPRANO, MEZZO-SOPRANO AND TWELVE PLAYERS   see Amy, Gilbert

SONATA ROMANTICA, HOMMAGE A FRANZ SCHUBERT QUI AIMAIT LA GUITARE   see Ponce, Manuel Maria

SONATA SK 37   see Seixas, (Jose Antonio) Carlos de

SONATAS, 3   see Cimarosa, Domenico; Scarlatti, Domenico

SONATAS, 3   see Cimarosa, Domenico

SONATAS, 3, EN FORMA DE CONCIERTO ITALIANO   see Cimarosa, Domenico

SONATAS, 6   see Geminiani, Francesco

SONATAS, 6   see Cimarosa, Domenico

SONATAS, 9, VOL. 1   see Scarlatti, Domenico

SONATAS, 9, VOL. 2   see Scarlatti, Domenico

4 SONATAS   see Seixas, (Jose Antonio) Carlos de

4 SONATAS, K. 391, 408, 424, 453   see Scarlatti, Domenico

SONATAS AND PARTITAS, BWV 1001-1006   see Bach, Johann Sebastian

SONATAS, VOL. 1   see Scarlatti, Domenico

SONATAS, VOL. 2   see Scarlatti, Domenico

SONATAS, VOL. 3   see Scarlatti, Domenico

SONATE   see Baron, Ernst Gottlieb, Duetto Al Liuto E Traverso

SONATE, 2   see Scarlatti, Domenico

SONATE A L'ESPAGNOLE   see Rodrigo, Joaquin

SONATE BASQUE   see Azpiazu, Jose de

SONATE BRILLANT   see Giuliani, Mauro, Sonata, Op. 15

SONATE CONCERTANTE   see Komter, Jan Maarten

SONATE E PARTITE, VOL. 1   see Bach, Johann Sebastian

SONATE E PARTITE, VOL. 1: BWV 1001-1003   see Bach, Johann Sebastian, Sonatas And Partitas, BWV 1001-1006

SONATE E PARTITE, VOL. 2   see Bach, Johann Sebastian

SONATE E PARTITE, VOL. 2: BWV 1004-1006   see Bach, Johann Sebastian, Sonatas And Partitas, BWV 1001-1006

SONATE IM KANON   see Telemann, Georg Philipp

SONATE, MIN391   see Monza, Carlo

SONATE, MIN392   see Monza, Carlo

5 SONATE PER 2 CHITARRE   see Scarlatti, Domenico

SONATEN, 2   see Albert, Heinrich; Seixas, (Jose Antonio) Carlos de

SONATEN, 2   see Telemann, Georg Philipp

SONATEN, 3   see Carulli, Ferdinando; Leclair, Jean Marie; Molino, Francesco; Pepusch, John Christopher

SONATEN, 6, OP. 2   see Paganini, Niccolo

SONATEN, 6, OP.3   see Paganini, Niccolo; Sammartini, Giuseppe

SONATEN, 12, OP. 1   see Hasse, Johann Adolph

SONATINA   see Paganini, Niccolo

SONATINA BUFFA   see Bruckmann, Ferdinand

SONATINA CANONICA   see Castelnuovo-Tedesco, Mario

SONATINA E ADAGIO   see Beethoven, Ludwig van

SONATINA EN TRES DUALES   see Rodriguez Albert, Rafael

SONATINA FIORENTINA   see Smith Brindle, Reginald

SONATINA IN LA (PRIMO TEMPO)   see Moreno Torroba, Federico, Sonatina

SONATINA IN ONE MOVEMENT   see Holder, Derwyn

SONATINA LIRICA   see Duarte, John W.

SONATINA MERIDIONAL   see Ponce, Manuel Maria

SONATINA PIRINEOS   see Gall, Louis Ignatius

SONATINA SEMPLICE   see Truhlar, Jan

SONATINA VIENNOISE   see Mozart, Wolfgang Amadeus, Wiener Sonatina

SONATINE, 4   see Paganini, Niccolo

SONATINE BREVE   see Bonnard, Alain

SONATINE FACILI, 14   see Carulli, Ferdinando

SONATINE, NACH JAPANISCHEN VOLKSLIEDERN   see Behrend, Siegfried

SONATINE, OP. 15   see Stingl, Anton

SONATINE UBER FINNISCHE VOLKSLIEDER   see Baumann, Herbert

SONATINEN, 2   see Benda, Georg Anton (Jiri Antonin)

SONATINEN, 3 see Albert, Heinrich;
  Diabelli, Anton; Giuliani, Mauro

SONATINEN, 3 see Carcassi, Matteo

SONATINEN, 3 see Albert, Heinrich

SONATINEN, 3, FUR SIGNORA DE LUCCA see
  Paganini, Niccolo

SONATINETTE see Duarte, John W.

SONATINY I SONATY KLASYCZNE I/IC-Coll

SONETO LOMBARDO, A MANERA DE DANZA see
  Valderrabano, Enriquez de

SONETTE see Furstenau, Wolfram

SONG, A see Staak, Pieter van der

SONG AND DANCE see Heuckeroth van
  Hessen, J. Richard

SONG FROM THE CANARY ISLANDS see
  Rodrigo, Joaquin, Folias Canarias

SONG OF THE DEVIL see Couperin,
  Francois (le Grand)

SONG WITHOUT WORDS see Mendelssohn-
  Bartholdy, Felix; Tchaikovsky,
  Piotr Ilyich

SONGS see Schubert, Franz (Peter)

SONGS, 3 see Dowland, John;
  Gudmundsen-Holmgreen, Pelle

SONGS, 4 see Wimberger, Gerhard

SONGS, 6 see Dowland, John

SONGS BY ELIZABETHAN COMPOSERS, 7
  I/IIC1-Coll

SONGS FOR ACHILLES see Tippett, [Sir]
  Michael

SONGS FROM THE CHINESE see Britten,
  [Sir] Benjamin

SONNE, KOMM, EIN GITARRESPIELBUCH FUR
  KINDER, 1-4. UNTERRICHTSJAHR
  I/IB6-Coll, I/IIA1-Coll,
  I/IIA2-Coll, I/IIA3-Coll,
  I/IIC1-Coll, IV/I, IV/IIA3,
  IV/IIC1, IV/IIC1-Coll,
  VII-Mixed Coll

SONORIDADES 1969 see Santorsola,
  Guido, Sonata; Santorsola, Guido,
  Sonata No. 2

SONS DE CARRILHOES, TOADA I/IB5

SONZOGNO, GIULIO CESARE (1906-1976)
  Leggenda Di Ognuno, La; Scenic Music
    For Chorus And Orchestra V/iii

SOR, FERNANDO (1778-1839)
  Abschied, Der see Adieux!, Les,
    Sixieme Fantaisie

  Adieux, Les (La Despedida) see
    Adieux!, Les, Sixieme Fantaisie

  Adieux!, Les, Sixieme Fantaisie
    I/IB2

  Adioses, Los, Sexta Fantasia see
    Adieux!, Les, Sixieme Fantaisie

  Allegretto I/IB2

  Allegretto Und Walzer Aus Op. 45 see
    Voyons Si C'est Ca, 6 Petites
    Pieces Faciles Nos. 2, 6

  Allegro I/IB2

  Allegro Non Troppo (From Grande
    Sonate, Op. 25) see
    Composiciones Para Guitarra, 19

  Alt Spanischer Tanz Mit Variationen
    I/IIIA

  Andante see Mes Ennuis, Six
    Bagatelles, Op. 43, No. 5; Voyons
    Si C'est Ca, 6 Petites Pieces
    Faciles, Op. 45, No. 5

  Andante Cantabile I/IB2
    see also Mes Ennuis, Six
    Bagatelles, Op. 43, No. 3

  Andante Largo I/IB2

  Andante Maestoso I/IB2

  Andante Maestoso, Op.11, No.6 I/IB2

  Andante, Op. 32, No. 5 I/IB2

SOR, FERNANDO (cont'd.)

  Andantino I/IB2
    see also Vingt Quatre Lecons
    Progressives, Dediees Aux Eleves
    Commencants, Op 31., No. 5

  Andantino, Op.2 I/IB2

  Andantino, Op.13, No.3 I/IB2

  Andantino, Op.31, No.5 I/IB2

  Andantino, Op. 54 [Sic] I/IIA2

  Anfanger-Etuden Fur Gitarre, 25 see
    Introduction A l'Etude De La
    Guitare En Vingt Cinq Lecons
    Progressives

  Aufschwung see Encouragement, L',
    Fantaisie A Deux Guitares

  Ausgewahlte Etuden, Vol. 1:
    Vorbereitende Ubungen, Kleine
    Musikstucke Und Etuden I/IA,
    I/IB2

  Ausgewahlte Etuden, Vol. 2: Kleine
    Musikstucke Und Etuden I/IA

  Ausgewahlte Etuden, Vol. 3: Kleine
    Musikstucke Und Etuden I/IA,
    I/IB2

  Ausgewahlte Etuden, Vol. 4: Kleine
    Musikstucke Und Etuden I/IA

  Ausgewahlte Etuden, Vol. 5: Etuden
    I/IA

  Ausgewahlte Etuden, Vol. 6: Etuden
    I/IA

  Ausgewahlte Etuden, Vol. 7: Etuden
    I/IA

  Ausgewahlte Gitarre Werke,
    Preliminary Vol. I/IB2

  Ausgewahlte Gitarre Werke, Vol. 1
    I/IB2

  Ausgewahlte Gitarre Werke, Vol. 2
    I/IB2

  Ausgewahlte Gitarre Werke, Vol. 3
    I/IB2

  Ausgewahlte Menuette, 20 I/IB2

  Ausgewahlte Walzer, 20 I/IB2

  Bolero (Altspanischer Volkstanz)
    I/IB2

  Celebrated Valse see Voyons Si C'est
    Ca, 6 Petites Pieces Faciles, Op.
    45, No. 6

  Complete Works For Guitar In
    Facsimiles Of The Original
    Editions, The, Vol. 1-7 I/IB2

  Complete Works For Guitar In
    Facsimiles Of The Original
    Editions, The, Vol. 8: Guitar
    Duets, Op. 34-63 [1st Gtr Part]
    I/IIA1

  Complete Works For Guitar In
    Facsimiles Of The Original
    Editions, The, Vol. 9: Guitar
    Duets, Op. 34-63 [2nd Gtr Part]
    I/IIA1

  Composiciones Para Guitarra, 19
    I/IB2

  Concierto En Re see Grand Solo

  Despedida, La I/IB2

  Deux Amis, Les, Fantaisie Pour Deux
    Guitares I/IIA1

  Deux Themes Varies Et Douze Menuets
    I/IB2

  Deux Themes Varies Et Douze Menuets,
    Op. 11, Nos. 1-12 see Minuetos
    Para Guitarra, 34

  Divertimento From Op. 38 see
    Divertissement for 2 Guitars, Op.
    38

  Divertimiento see Divertissement
    Pour Deux Guitares

  Divertissement for 2 Guitars, Op. 38
    I/IIA1

  Divertissement Pour Deux Guitares
    I/IIA1

SOR, FERNANDO (cont'd.)

  Douze Etudes I/IA

  Douze Etudes, Op. 6, No. 4 see
    Etudes Pour La Guitare, 26, Vol.
    2

  Douze Etudes Pour Servir De Suite Aux
    Douze Premieres I/IA
    see also Studi Per Chitarra, Vol. 2

  Douze Etudes Pour Servir De Suite Aux
    Douze Premieres, Op. 29, No. 1
    see Etudes Pour La Guitare, 26,
    Vol. 4

  Douze Etudes Pour Servir De Suite Aux
    Douze Premieres, Op. 29, No. 5
    see Etudes Pour La Guitare, 26,
    Vol. 4

  Douze Etudes Pour Servir De Suite Aux
    Douze Premieres, Op. 29, No. 6
    see Etudes Pour La Guitare, 26,
    Vol. 4

  Douze Etudes Pour Servir De Suite Aux
    Douze Premieres, Op. 29, No. 10
    see Etudes Pour La Guitare, 26,
    Vol. 4

  Drei Ausgewahlte Walzer (3 Valses
    Choisies) I/IB2

  Drei Leichte Duos see Trois Duos
    Faciles Et Progressifs Pour Deux
    Guitares

  Duo Fur 2 Gitarren see
    Encouragement, L', Fantaisie A
    Deux Guitares

  Easy Music For Guitar, Vol. 11
    I/IB2-Coll

  Einleitende Etuden - Etudes
    Preparatoires see Introduction A
    l'Etude De La Guitare En Vingt
    Cinq Lecons Progressives

  12 Ejercicios I/IA

  Ejercicios Y Estudios Elementales
    Para Guitarra, 36, Vol. 1 I/IA

  Encouragement, L', Fantaisie A Deux
    Guitares I/IIA1

  Erste Sor, Der I/IA

  Est-Ce Bien Ca?, Six Pieces, Op. 48,
    No. 1 see Leichte Duette Fur
    Anfanger

  Est-Ce Bien Ca?, Six Pieces, Op. 48:
    Rondo D-Dur I/IB2

  Estudio En Do see Etude, Op. 29, No.
    5

  Estudio En Mi Bemol see Etude, Op.
    29, No. 10

  Estudio En Mi Bemol Mayor see Etude,
    Op. 29, No. 10

  Estudio En Si Bemol see Etude, Op.
    29, No. 1

  Estudio (Etude), From Op. 35, No. 22
    see Vingt-Quatre Exercices Tres
    Faciles, Op. 35, No. 22

  Estudios, 26 I/IA

  12 Estudios I/IA

  Estudios De Guitarra, 30 I/IA

  12 Estudios, Op.60 I/IA

  Estudios Para Guitarra, 26 I/IA

  12 Estudios Progresivos I/IA

  Etude In A Major see Vingt-Quatre
    Exercices Tres Faciles, Op. 35,
    No. 20

  Etude, Op. 29, No. 1 I/IA
    see also Konzert-Etuden, 4

  Etude, Op. 29, No. 5 I/IA
    see also Konzert-Etuden, 4

  Etude, Op. 29, No. 10 I/IA

  Etude, Op. 31, No. 14 I/IA

  Etude, Op. 31, No. 17 see Leichte
    Etuden, 2

  Etude, Op. 31, No. 19 see Konzert-
    Etuden, 4

SOR, FERNANDO (cont'd.)

Etude, Op. 31, No. 20   I/IA

Etude, Op. 31, No. 24   see Konzert-
Etuden, 4

Etude, Op. 35, No. 13   see Leichte
Etuden, 2

Etuden Fur Gitarre, 14   I/IA

Etudes, 30   I/IA

Etudes Choises, 24   I/IA

Etudes Pour La Guitare, 20   I/IA

Etudes Pour La Guitare, 26, Vol. 1
I/IA

Etudes Pour La Guitare, 26, Vol. 2
I/IA

Etudes Pour La Guitare, 26, Vol. 3
I/IA

Etudes Pour La Guitare, 26, Vol. 4
I/IA

Fantaisie   I/IB2

Fantaisie Elegiaque   I/IB2

Fantaisie Elegiaque: Marche Funebre
I/IB2

Fantaisie: Largo   I/IB2

Fantaisie, Sur Des Airs Favoris   see
Septieme Fantaisie Et Variations
Brillantes Sur Deux Airs Favoris
Connus

Fantasia   see Fantaisie

Fantasia E Variazioni Brillanti   see
Septieme Fantaisie Et Variations
Brillantes Sur Deux Airs Favoris
Connus

Fantasia Elegiaca   see Fantaisie
Elegiaque

Fantasia Elegiaque   see Fantaisie
Elegiaque

Fantasie Elegiaque   I/IB2

Folias De Espana   see Folies
d'Espagne, Variees, Et Un Menuet

Folias De Espana, Las, Tema Y
Variaciones   see Folies
d'Espagne, Variees, Et Un Menuet

Folias De Espana, Las, Variationen
see Folies d'Espagne, Variees, Et
Un Menuet

Folies d'Espagne   see Folies
d'Espagne, Variees, Et Un Menuet

Folies d'Espagne, Les, Tema E
Variazioni   see Folies d'Espagne,
Variees, Et Un Menuet

Folies d'Espagne, Variees, Et Un
Menuet   I/IB2

Fortschreitende Studien Fur Anfanger,
24, Vol. 1: Studies No. 1-12   see
Vingt Quatre Lecons Progressives,
Dediees Aux Eleves Commencants

Fortschreitende Studien Fur Anfanger,
24, Vol. 2: Studies No. 13-24
see Vingt Quatre Lecons
Progressives, Dediees Aux Eleves
Commencants

Fortschreitende Ubungen Fur Gitarre-
Anfanger, Vol. 1: Studies No. 1-
12   see Vingt Quatre Lecons
Progressives, Dediees Aux Eleves
Commencants

Fortschreitende Ubungen Fur Gitarre-
Anfanger, Vol. 2: Studies No. 13-
24   see Vingt Quatre Lecons
Progressives, Dediees Aux Eleves
Commencants

Galop   I/IB2

Gran Solo   I/IB2
see also Grand Solo

Grand Solo   I/IB2
see also Composiciones Para
Guitarra, 19

Grand Sonate   see Composiciones Para
Guitarra, 19

SOR, FERNANDO (cont'd.)

Grande Sonate, Op. 22   I/IC

Grande Sonate, Op. 25   I/IC

Grosse Sonate   see Grande Sonate, Op.
22

Grosses Solo   see Grand Solo

Harfenetude (Harp Study)   see Vingt-
Quatre Exercices Tres Faciles,
Op. 35, No. 23

Introducao E Variacoes Sobre Um Tema
Da Opera "Flauta Magica" De W.A.
Mozart   see Introduction Et
Variations Sur Un Theme De Mozart

Introduction A l'Etude De La Guitare
En Vingt Cinq Lecons Progressives
I/IA, I/IIA1
see also Studi Per Chitarra, Vol. 1

Introduction A l'Etude De La Guitare
En Vingt Cinq Lecons
Progressives, Op. 60, No. 1   see
Erste Sor, Der; Leichte Duette
Fur Anfanger

Introduction A l'Etude De La Guitare
En Vingt Cinq Lecons
Progressives, Op. 60., No. 2   see
Erste Sor, Der

Introduction A l'Etude De La Guitare
En Vingt Cinq Lecons
Progressives, Op. 60, No. 5   see
Erste Sor, Der

Introduction A l'Etude De La Guitare
En Vingt Cinq Lecons
Progressives, Op. 60, No. 7   see
Drei Ausgewahlte Walzer (3 Valses
Choisies)

Introduction Et Allegro   see Grand
Solo

Introduction Et Theme Varie   I/IB2

Introduction Et Variations Sur l'Air
"Marlbroug"   I/IB2

Introduction Et Variations Sur l'Air
"Que Ne Suis-Je La Fougere"
I/IB2

Introduction Et Variations Sur Un
Theme De Mozart   I/IB2

Introduction, Thema Und Variationen
see Introduction Et Theme Varie

Introduzione E Variazioni Su L'Aria
"Marlbroug"   see Introduction Et
Variations Sur l'Air "Marlbroug"

Introduzione E Variazioni Su l'Aria
"O Cara Armonia" Dall' Opera "Il
Flauto Magico" Di W.A. Mozart
see Introduction Et Variations
Sur Un Theme De Mozart

Introduzione E Variazioni Su L'aria
"Que Ne Suis-Je La Fougere"   see
Introduction Et Variations Sur
l'Air "Que Ne Suis-Je La Fougere"

Kompositionen Fur Die Gitarre   I/IB2

Konzert-Etuden, 4   I/IA

Larghetto   I/IB2

12 Lecciones Progresivas   I/IA

Leichte Duette Fur Anfanger   I/IIA1

Leichte Etuden, 2   I/IA

Leichte Etuden Aus Op. 60, 12   I/IA

Leichte Ubungen Fur Gitarre, 24, Vol.
1: Studies No. 1-12   see Vingt-
Quatre Exercices Tres Faciles

Leichte Ubungen Fur Gitarre, 24, Vol.
2: Studies No. 13-24   see Vingt-
Quatre Exercices Tres Faciles

Mazurca, Moderato   see Mes Ennuis,
Six Bagatelles, Op. 43, No. 4

Meditacion   I/IB2

Meditation   I/IB2

Menuets, 2   I/IB2

Menuets En La, 2   I/IB2

Menuette, 2   I/IB2

SOR, FERNANDO (cont'd.)

Menuette, 2   I/IB2

Menuette, 2   I/IB2

Menuety - Menuette   I/IB2

Mes Ennuis, Six Bagatelles   I/IB2

Mes Ennuis, Six Bagatelles, Op. 43,
No. 3   I/IB2

Mes Ennuis, Six Bagatelles, Op. 43,
No. 4   I/IB2

Mes Ennuis, Six Bagatelles, Op. 43,
No. 5   I/IB2

Methode Complete Pour Guitare   see
Methode Pour La Guitare (Escuela
De La Guitarra)

Methode Pour La Guitare   II

Methode Pour La Guitare (Escuela De
La Guitarra)   II

Methode Pour La Guitare (Methode
Complete Pour Guitare Par
Ferdinand Sor, Revue Et Augmentee
De Nombreux Exemples Avec Une
Notice Sur La Septieme Corde Par
N. Coste)   II

Metodo Completo Para Guitarra   see
Methode Pour La Guitare; Methode
Pour La Guitare (Escuela De La
Guitarra)

Minue   see Sonata, Op. 25, Minuet

Minuet   I/IB2
see also Ausgewahlte Menuette, 20;
Minuetos Para Guitarra, 34

Minuet in A, MIN 364   I/IB2

Minuet in B flat, MIN 365   I/IB2

Minuet in D, MIN 363   I/IB2

Minuet, Op. 2, No. 1, in G   see
Minuetos, 2

Minuet, Op. 2, No. 4   see Minuetos, 4

Minuet, Op. 3, in G   I/IB2
see also Minuetos, 2; Minuetos, 3

Minuet, Op. 5, No. 1   see Minuetos, 4

Minuet, Op. 5, No. 3   see Menuette,
2; Minuetos, 4

Minuet, Op. 8, No. 1   see Minuetos, 4

Minuet, Op. 11, No. 1   see Minuetos
En Sol, 2

Minuet, Op. 11, No. 2   see Minuetos
En Sol, 2

Minuet, Op. 11, No. 4, in D   I/IB2
see also Menuets, 2; Minuetos, 3;
Minuetos En Sol-Re, 2

Minuet, Op. 11, No. 5, in D   I/IB2
see also Menuette, 2; Minuetos En
Re, 2

Minuet, Op. 11, No. 6, in A   I/IB2
see also Andante Maestoso; Menuets
En La, 2; Menuette, 2; Menuette,
2; Menuety - Menuette; Minuetos
En La, 2; Minuettos En La Mayor, 2

Minuet, Op. 11, No. 7   see Menuety -
Menuette

Minuet, Op. 11, No. 7, in A   see
Menuette, 2

Minuet, Op. 11, No. 8, in A   see
Menuets En La, 2; Menuety -
Menuette; Minuetos En La, 2;
Minuettos En La Mayor, 2

Minuet, Op. 11, No. 9   see Menuety -
Menuette; Minuetos, 3

Minuet, Op. 11, No. 9, in E   see
Minuetos, 2

Minuet, Op. 11, No. 10, in E   see
Menuets, 2; Menuety - Menuette;
Minuetos En Mi, 2; Minuettos En
Mi Mayor, 2

Minuet, Op. 11, No. 12, in D   see
Minuetos En Re, 2

Minuet, Op. 13, No. 1, in A   see
Minuetos, 2

SOR, FERNANDO (cont'd.)

Anfanger

Vingt-Quatre Exercices Tres Faciles, Op. 35, No. 14 see Vier Leichte Stucke Aus Op. 35

Vingt-Quatre Exercices Tres Faciles, Op. 35, No. 17 I/IA

Vingt-Quatre Exercices Tres Faciles, Op. 35, No. 19 see Etudes Pour La Guitare, 26, Vol. 2

Vingt-Quatre Exercices Tres Faciles, Op. 35, No. 20 I/IA

Vingt-Quatre Exercices Tres Faciles, Op. 35, No. 22 I/IA, I/IIA1

Vingt-Quatre Exercices Tres Faciles, Op. 35, No. 23 I/IA see also Etudes Pour La Guitare, 26, Vol. 2

Vingt-Quatre Exercices Tres Faciles, Op. 35, No. 24 see Etudes Pour La Guitare, 26, Vol. 2

Vingt-Quatre Exercises Tres Faciles see Studi Per Chitarra, Vol. 2

Vingt Quatre Lecons Progressives, Dediees Aux Eleves Commencants I/IA see also Studi Per Chitarra, Vol. 1

Vingt Quatre Lecons Progressives, Dediees Aux Eleves Commencants, Op 31., No. 5 I/IIA1 see also Leichte Duette Fur Anfanger

Vingt Quatre Lecons Progressives, Dediees Aux Eleves Commencants, Op. 31, No. 19 see Etudes Pour La Guitare, 26, Vol. 2

Vingt Quatre Lecons Progressives, Dediees Aux Eleves Commencants, Op. 31, No. 20 see Etudes Pour La Guitare, 26, Vol. 2

Vingt-Quatre Petites Pieces Progressives Pour La Guitare, Pour Servir De Lecons Aux Eleves Tout A Fait Commencants, Op. 44, No. 7 see Leichte Duette Fur Anfanger

Voyons Si C'est Ca, 6 Petites Pieces Faciles I/IB2

Voyons Si C'est Ca, 6 Petites Pieces Faciles Nos. 2, 6 I/IB2

Voyons Si C'est Ca, 6 Petites Pieces Faciles, Op. 45, No. 4 see Drei Ausgewahlte Walzer (3 Valses Choisies)

Voyons Si C'est Ca, 6 Petites Pieces Faciles, Op. 45, No. 5 I/IB2

Voyons Si C'est Ca, 6 Petites Pieces Faciles, Op. 45, No. 6 I/IB2

Waltz, Op. 32, No. 2 I/IB2

Walzer, 6 see Six Waltzes

Zwei Themen Mit Variationen Und Zwolf Menuette see Deux Themes Varies Et Douze Menuets

Zweite Grosse Sonate see Grande Sonate, Op. 25

Zwolf Etuden see Douze Etudes; Douze Etudes Pour Servir De Suite Aux Douze Premieres

SORGEVA IL SOLE E SORRIDEVI see Bortolami, Galliano

SORONGO see Bosmans, Arthur, Brasileiras, No. 5

SOR'S METHOD FOR THE SPANISH GUITAR see Sor, Fernando, Methode Pour La Guitare

SOSINSKI, KAZIMIERZ
Materials For Studying The Guitar see Materialy Do Nauki Gry Na Gitarze

Materialy Do Nauki Gry Na Gitarze III

Studium Gry Akordowej Na Gitarze, Technika Chwytow Barre, Akordy I Ich Symbole I/IIB1, III

SOSINSKI, KAZIMIERZ (cont'd.)

Study Of Chords For Guitar, The, The Technique Of Barre, Chords And Their Symbols see Studium Gry Akordowej Na Gitarze, Technika Chwytow Barre, Akordy I Ich Symbole

SOSTENUTO see Giuliani, Mauro

SOTTO LA PIOGGIA see Ciurlo, Ernesto Fausto

SOUND see Hespos, Hans-Joachim

SOUNDS OF THE GUITAR (SPANISH GUITAR TECHNIQUE), A RECORDED BASIC METHOD FOR HOME STUDY see Prol, Julio

SOUS LE PALMIER [BAJO LA PALMERA], DANSE ESPAGNOLE see Albeniz, Isaac

SOUS UN CYPRES see Chanson D'Amours Elizabethaines, 3

SOUTERLIED NO. 99 see Clemens, Jacobus (Clemens non Papa)

SOUVENIR, LE see Zani de Ferranti, Marco Aurelio

SOUVENIR DE RUSSIE, FANTAISIE POUR DEUX GUITARES see Sor, Fernando

SOUVENIR D'ESPAGNE see Mori, Augusto Cesare de

SOUZA CARVALHO, JOAO DE see CARVALHO, JOAO DE SOUSA

SOZINHO EU NAO FICO see Chansons Bresiliennes, Vol. II

SPAANSE VOLKSLIEDEREN, 3 (3 SPANISH FOLKSONGS) I/IIC1-Coll, IV/IIC1

SPANISCHE GITARRENMUSIK, VOL. I I/IB6-Coll

SPANISCHE GITARRENMUSIK, VOL. II I/IB6-Coll

SPANISCHE GITARRENMUSIK, VOL. III I/IB6-Coll

SPANISCHE MEISTER see Europaische Gitarren- Und Lautenmusik, Vol. 5

SPANISCHE ROMANZEN see Bialas, Gunter

3 SPANISCHE SOLOSTUCKE I/IB5

6 SPANISCHE STUCKE I/IB3-Coll, VI-Coll

SPANISCHE TANZE see Winkelbauer, Alfred

SPANISCHE TANZE, 3 see Behrend, Siegfried

SPANISCHER TANZ see Bohr, Heinrich

SPANISH GUITAR TECHNIQUE, A RECORDED BASIC METHOD FOR HOME STUDY see Olf, Mark

SPANISH IMPRESSION see Staak, Pieter van der

SPANISH PAVAN, THE see Robinson, Thomas

SPANISH PAVANE, THE see Pilkington, Francis

SPANISH ROMANCE see Anonymous, Romance, MIN 141

SPANISH SONGS, 3 see Rodrigo, Joaquin

SPANISH SUITE see Komter, Jan Maarten

SPANNENLANGER HANSEL, KINDERLIEDER I/IIC1-Coll

SPANYOL GITARMUZSIKA - GUITAR MUSIC FROM SPAIN I/IB3-Coll

SPANYOL TANC, 2; 2 SPANISH DANCES I/IB3

SPEEL EN DANS JE MEE, VOL. 1: HEDENDAAGSE DANSEN I/IIB5-Coll

SPEEL EN DANS JE MEE, VOL. 2: NEDERLANDSE VOLKSDANSEN I/IIB5-Coll

SPEEL EN ZING JE MEE?, VOL. I: VOLKSLIEDEREN OM TE SPELEN EN TE ZINGEN I/IIC5-Coll

SPEEL EN ZING JE MEE?, VOL. II: VOLKSLIEDEREN UIT BINNEN- EN BUITENLAND I/IIC5-Coll

SPEEL EN ZING JE MEE?, VOL. III: KERSTLIEDJES OM TE SPELEN EN TE ZINGEN I/IIC5-Coll

SPEEL EN ZING JE MEE?, VOL. IV: NEGRO-SPIRITUALS I/IIC5-Coll

SPEEL EN ZING JE MEE?, VOL. V: VOLKSLIEDEREN OM TE SPELEN EN TE ZINGEN I/IIC5-Coll

SPEELBOEK VOOR DE GITAAR, VOL. I see Witte, Jacq.

SPEELBOEK VOOR DE GITAARGROEPSLES, VOL. I see Blok, Coby

SPEELBOEK VOOR DE GITAARGROEPSLES, VOL. II see Blok, Coby

SPEELBOEK VOOR DE GITAARGROEPSLES, VOL. III see Blok, Coby

SPEELBOEK VOOR DE GITAARGROEPSLES, VOL. IV see Blok, Coby

SPEELBOEK VOOR DE GITAARGROEPSLES, VOL. V see Blok, Coby

SPEELMATERIAAL VOOR DE BLOKFLUIT, VOL. III I/IIB1-Coll

SPEELSE WALS see Pelemans, Willem

SPERLING, ERNST
Evening Song I/IB4

Preludes, 4 I/IB4

Silent Forests I/IB4

Slumber Song I/IB4

Springtime Waltz I/IB4

SPERONTES (JOHANN SIGISMUND SCHOLZE) (1705-1750)
Singende Muse An Der Pleisse I/IIB1, I/IIB2, I/IIC1, I/IIC2

Spielstucke, 22 I/IB1

SPIEL AUF DER GITARRE EINFACH UND GEKONNT, EINE LAUTENSCHULE FUR ANFANGER (EINZEL- UND GRUPPENUNTERRICHT) see Gotz, Robert

SPIEL DER LAUTENINSTRUMENTE, DAS, SERIES I: DAS SCHULWERK, FUR EINZEL- UND GRUPPENUNTERRICHT, VOL. I: DIE LEHRE DES EINSTIMMIGEN SPIELS see Gerwig, Walter

SPIEL DER LAUTENINSTRUMENTE, DAS, SERIES I: DAS SCHULWERK, FUR EINZEL- UND GRUPPENUNTERRICHT, VOL. II: DAS MEHRSTIMMIGE SPIEL see Gerwig, Walter

SPIEL DER LAUTENINSTRUMENTE, DAS, SERIES I: DAS SCHULWERK, FUR EINZEL- UND GRUPPENUNTERRICHT, VOL. III: DIE LIEDBEGLEITUNG, WEGE ZUR IMPROVISATION see Gerwig, Walter

SPIEL DER LAUTENINSTRUMENTE, DAS, SERIES I: DAS SCHULWERK, FUR EINZEL- UND GRUPPENUNTERRICHT, VOL. IV: DAS GENERALBASSSPIEL see Gerwig, Walter

SPIEL DER MINNESANGER AUF DER ROSENBURG see Mittelalterliche Tanze

SPIEL MIT AUF DEINER GITARRE see Kukuck, Felicitas

SPIEL MIT UNS; KLEINE MUSIKSTUCKE FUR EIN KONSTRUKTIVES ZUSAMMENSPIEL see Wilimek, Eduard

SPIEL VON LIEBE UND TOD, EIN; OPERA IN ONE ACT see Cikker, Jan

SPIEL ZU ZWEIT II I/IIA1-Coll

SPIELBUCH FUR 3 GITARREN I/IIA2-Coll

SPIELBUCH FUR DIE JUGEND, VOL. I I/IIB5-Coll

SPIELBUCH FUR DIE JUGEND, VOL. II I/IIB5-Coll

SPIELBUCH FUR GITARRE, 100 LEICHTE STUCKE FUR DEN ANFANG, VOL. I see Stingl, Anton

SPIELBUCH FUR GITARRE, 100 LEICHTE STUCKE FUR DEN ANFANG, VOL. II see Stingl, Anton

SPIELBUCH FUR GITARREN-DUO I/IIA1-Coll, VII-Mixed Coll

STETKA, FRANZ (cont'd.)

Sonatina I/IIB2

Tanze, Marsche Und Andere Spielstucke
I/IIB2, I/IIB3, IV/IIB2

STEVENS, BERNARD GEORGE (1916-1983)
Ballad I/IB4

Bramble Briar, The see Ballad

STEVENSON, RONALD (1928-   )
Anger Dance I/IB4

STIERKAMPMUSIK see Behrend, Siegfried

STILL, STILL, STILL see Guten Abend,
Gute Nacht; Lied- Und
Gitarrenspiel, Volks- Und
Tanzlieder, Vol. I

STILLE NACHT see Gruber, Franz Xaver

STIMMEN DER GITARRE, DAS see
Vereczkey, Laszlo, A Gitar
Hangotasa

STINGL, ANTON (1908-   )
Canzone see Stucke, Op. 34

Capriccio see Stucke, Op. 34

Gitarrebuch Fur Madeleine, Vol. I
I/IB4

Gitarrebuch Fur Madeleine, Vol. II
I/IB4

Improvisation, Uber Ein
Mittelalterliches Lied "Es Sass
Ein Edly Maget Schon" I/IB4

Kleine Spielstucke Nach
Kinderliedern, 30 I/IB4

Kleiner Walzer see Stucke, Op. 34

Lehrstucke, 30 I/IA

Leichte Stucke, 12 I/IB4

Maien Ist Kommen, Der, Paraphrase
Uber Einen Alten Maitanz see
Sonatine, Op. 15

Passacaglia see Stucke, Op. 34

Satze, 2, Zu Einem Mahrischen
Wiegenlied see Sonatine, Op. 15

Sonatina, Op. 15a see Sonatine, Op.
15

Sonatine, Op. 15 I/IB4

Spielbuch Fur Gitarre, 100 Leichte
Stucke Fur Den Anfang, Vol. I II

Spielbuch Fur Gitarre, 100 Leichte
Stucke Fur Den Anfang, Vol. II
II

Stucke, Op. 34 I/IIB1

Tanzerisches Spiel see Stucke, Op.
34

Traumbilder, Variationen Uber Ein
Wiegenlied see Sonatine, Op. 15

STOCKHAUSEN, KARLHEINZ (1928-   )
Aus Den Sieben Tagen; Composition No.
26 V/i, V/iii

Gruppen, For Three Orchestras V/i

Solo I/IIB4

Spiral; Composition No. 27 I/IB4

STOCKMEIER, WOLFGANG (1931-   )
Divertimento I/IIB2

STOCKTON, FRED
Complete Classic Guitar, The, A
Method. Complete Explanation Of
The Right Hand II

STOKER, RICHARD (1938-   )
Improvisation I/IB4

Sonatina, Op. 42 I/IC

STORM IN A TEACUP see Komter, Jan
Maarten

STORNELLI see Bresgen, Cesar

STORTI, MAURO
Lezioni Di Tecnica Elementare Per
Chitarra, 20 II

Lezioni Di Tecnica Superiore Per
Chitarra, 12 III

STRADELLA, ALESSANDRO (1645-1682)
Concerto Grosso in D V/i

STRAESSER, JOEP (1934-   )
Rade, En I/IIC5

STRANGASPEL see Hallnas, Hilding

STRASBOURGEOISE, LA see Carpentier,
[Abbe] Joseph

STRASSEN see Drlac, Jan Zdenek, Ulice

STRATEGIER, HERMAN (1912-   )
Short Pieces, 10 I/IB4, I/IIA1

STRAUBE, RUDOLF
Sonata No. 1 for Lute I/IB1

Sonata Para Laud I/IB1

STRAUSS, JOHANN, [SR.] (1804-1849)
Valzer, 2, Op. 110 And 76 I/IB2

STRAUSS, JOHANN, [JR.] (1825-1899)
Nacht In Venedig, Eine: Serenade Fur
Delaqua; Finale Of The 1st Act
V/iii

STRAVINSKY, IGOR (1882-1971)
Acht Stucke I/IIA1

Allegro I/IB4

Russian Songs, 4 I/IIC3

STRAVINSKY, SOULIMA (1910-   )
Sechs Sonatinen, Vol. 1 I/IIA1

Sechs Sonatinen, Vol. 2 I/IIA1

STREBSAME GITARRIST, DER, VOL. II,
LEICHTE SPIELSTUCKE see Karl, Sepp

STREBSAME GUITARRIST, DER, VOL. 1, 14
LEICHTE SPIELSTUCKE see Bausewein,
Herbert

STREICHARDT, ANTONIUS
Trio in E I/IIA2

STRIETMAN, WILLEM (1918-   )
Concerto for Harmonica and Chamber
Orchestra see O Bonne Douce
France

O Bonne Douce France V/i

STROBL, OTTO (1927-   )
Dutzend Schilieder, Ein V/ii

STROPHES see Sfetsas, Kyriacos

STUCKCHEN see Schumann, Robert
(Alexander)

STUCKE, 2 see Bach, Carl Philipp
Emanuel

STUCKE, 2 see Behrend, Siegfried

STUCKE, 3 see Mozart, Wolfgang Amadeus

STUCKE, 3 see Kovats, Barna

STUCKE, 3 see Lampersberg, Gerhard

STUCKE, 3 see Diabelli, Anton

STUCKE, 4 see Gaitis, Friedrich;
Mozart, Wolfgang Amadeus; Pepusch,
John Christopher

STUCKE, 5 see Hartig, Heinz Friedrich;
Moreno Torroba, Federico;
Rovenstrunck, Bernhard; Stadlmair,
Hans

STUCKE, 5, NACH LIEDERN UND TANZEN AUS
DER RENAISSANCE see Fleres, Rita
Maria

STUCKE, 6 see Joachim, Otto; Sprongl,
Norbert

STUCKE, 6, OP. 40 see Wolki, Konrad

STUCKE, 10 see Kaufmann, Armin

STUCKE, 10, VOL. I see Uhl, Alfred

STUCKE, 10, VOL. II see Uhl, Alfred

STUCKE, 12 see Furstenau, Kaspar

6 STUCKE see Reichardt, Johann
Friedrich

10 STUCKE see Schmicerer, Johann
Abraham

STUCKE ALTER MEISTER, 15 I/IIA2-Coll

STUCKE AUS DEM "ALBUM FUR DIE JUGEND, "
OP. 68 see Schumann, Robert
(Alexander)

STUCKE FUR GITARRE, 3 see Hartig,
Heinz Friedrich

STUCKE FUR GITARRE, 5 see Muller,
Siegfried

STUCKE, OP. 34 see Stingl, Anton

STUDENT GUITARIST'S DELIGHT, VOL. I
I/IB6-Coll

STUDENT GUITARIST'S DELIGHT, VOL. II
I/IB6-Coll

STUDENTEN MUSIC, EINE see Rosenmuller,
Johann

STUDI see Diabelli, Anton, Studi
Facili, 30; Giuliani, Mauro;
Giuliani, Mauro, Studies

STUDI, 2 see Murtula, Giovanni

STUDI, 3 see Masala, Roberto

STUDI, 24 see Giuliani, Mauro, Etuden,
24

STUDI, 25 see Coste, Napoleon, Etudes,
25

STUDI, 30 see Carulli, Ferdinando,
Studies, 30

STUDI, 51, AD USO DEI CONSERVATORI see
Aguado, Dionisio

12 STUDI see Bettinelli, Bruno

STUDI DA CONCERTO, 8 see Margola,
Franco

STUDI DIVERTIMENTO, 6 see Sterzati,
Umberto

STUDI FACILI see Diabelli, Anton,
Studi Facili, 30

STUDI FACILI, 30 see Diabelli, Anton

STUDI MELODICI E PROGRESSIVI see
Carcassi, Matteo, Melodische Und
Progressive Etuden, 25

STUDI MELODICI E PROGRESSIVI, 25 see
Carcassi, Matteo, Melodische Und
Progressive Etuden, 25

STUDI MELODICI PER CHITARRA, 10 see
Abloniz, Miguel

STUDI PER CHITARRA, 20 see Sor,
Fernando, Etudes Pour La Guitare,
20

STUDI PER CHITARRA, AD USO DEI
CONSERVATORI see Sor, Fernando

STUDI PER CHITARRA, VOL. 1 see Sor,
Fernando

STUDI PER CHITARRA, VOL. 2 see Sor,
Fernando

STUDI PER UN "HOMUNCULUS"; 9 PIECES FOR
ORCHESTRA see Lupi, Roberto

8 STUDI SUGLI ARMONICI see Staak,
Pieter van der

STUDIEN, 2 see Reiser, Ekkehard

STUDIEN, 3 see Einem, Gottfried von

STUDIEN, 5 see Hubschmann, Werner

STUDIEN, 6 see Istvan, Miloslav

STUDIEN, 24 see Giuliani, Mauro,
Leichte Etuden, 24

3 STUDIEN see Erbse, Heimo

9 STUDIEN see Coste, Napoleon

STUDIEN FUR GITARRE, VOL. I, A. UBUNGEN
FUR DIE RECHTE HAND, B. UBUNGEN FUR
DIE LINKE HAND see Giuliani,
Mauro, Studio Per La Chitarra

STUDIEN FUR GITARRE, VOL. II, C.
BINDUNGEN UND VERZIERUNGEN, D.
ANGEWANDTE VORTRAGSSTUCKE see
Giuliani, Mauro, Studio Per La
Chitarra

STUDIENKONZERT see Giuliani, Mauro,
Concerto in A, Op. 36

STUDIES see Giuliani, Mauro

STUDIES, 10 see Bellow, Alexander

STUDIES, 12, VOL. 1 see Visser, Dick

STUDIES, 12, VOL. 1: ELEMENTARY GRADE see Albert, Heinrich, Gitarre-Etuden-Werk, Vol. 1: Elementarstufe

STUDIES, 12, VOL. 2 see Visser, Dick

STUDIES, 12, VOL. 2: ELEMENTARY GRADE see Albert, Heinrich, Gitarre-Etuden-Werk, Vol. 2: Obere Elementarstufe

STUDIES, 12, VOL. 3 see Visser, Dick

STUDIES, 12, VOL. 3: MODERATELY DIFFICULT see Albert, Heinrich, Gitarre-Etuden-Werk, Vol. 3: Mittelstufe

STUDIES, 12, VOL. 4: MODERATELY DIFFICULT see Albert, Heinrich, Gitarre-Etuden-Werk, Vol. 4: Obere Mittelstufe

STUDIES, 12, VOL. 5: DIFFICULT see Albert, Heinrich, Gitarre-Etuden-Werk, Vol. 5: Oberstufe

STUDIES, 12, VOL. 6: DIFFICULT see Albert, Heinrich, Gitarre-Etuden-Werk, Vol. 6: Reifestufe

STUDIES, 25 see Coste, Napoleon, Etudes, 25

STUDIES, 30 see Carulli, Ferdinando

STUDIES, 50 see Aguado, Dionisio

STUDIES, 120 see Giuliani, Mauro, Studio Per La Chitarra

STUDIES EN STUKJES VOOR GITAAR I/IB6-Coll

STUDIES FOR THE GUITAR see Mozzani, Luigi

STUDIES FOR THE GUITAR, 20 see Sor, Fernando, Etudes Pour La Guitare, 20

STUDIES FOR THE GUITAR, 20 see Sor, Fernando

STUDIES IN V see Nijenhuis, Luc

STUDIES, VOL. 1: 10 STUDIES (NOS. 1-10) see Dodgson, Stephen

STUDIES, VOL. 2: 10 STUDIES (NOS. 11-20) see Dodgson, Stephen

STUDIO DELLA CHITARRA CLASSICA, LO, VOL. 1: TECHNICAL EXERCISES, 19 see Degni, Vincenzo

STUDIO DELLA CHITARRA CLASSICA, LO, VOL. 2: TECHNICAL EXERCISES, 20 see Degni, Vincenzo

STUDIO OP. 10, NO. 3 (FRAMMENTO) see Chopin, Frederic, Etude, Op. 10, No. 3, [excerpt]

STUDIO PER LA CHITARRA see Giuliani, Mauro

STUDIO, RONDO FANTASIOSO see Murtula, Giovanni

STUDIUM GRY AKORDOWEJ NA GITARZE, TECHNIKA CHWYTOW BARRE, AKORDY I ICH SYMBOLE see Sosinski, Kazimierz

STUDY see Sainz de la Maza, Eduardo, Anoranza Lejana; Sor, Fernando, Etude, Op. 29, No. 1

STUDY, IIII-4B IN A [FRAGMENT] see Tarrega, Francisco

STUDY IN A MAJOR see Tarrega, Francisco, Study, TI ii- 19, in A

STUDY IN A MINOR see Sor, Fernando, Etude, Op. 31, No. 20

STUDY IN B MINOR see Sor, Fernando, Vingt-Quatre Exercices Tres Faciles, Op. 35, No. 22

STUDY IN D see Sor, Fernando, Vingt-Quatre Exercices Tres Faciles, Op. 35, No. 17

STUDY IN G see Sor, Fernando, Etude, Op. 31, No. 14

STUDY OF CHORDS FOR GUITAR, THE, THE TECHNIQUE OF BARRE, CHORDS AND THEIR SYMBOLS see Sosinski, Kazimierz, Studium Gry Akordowej Na Gitarze, Technika Chwytow Barre, Akordy I Ich Symbole

STUDY, TI II- 9, IN A MINOR see Composiciones Originales Para Guitarra, 10

STUDY, TI II- 14, IN D MINOR see Composiciones Originales Para Guitarra, 10

STUDY, TIII-16A IN B MINOR [FRAGMENT] see Tarrega, Francisco

STUDY, TIII-32 [FRAGMENT] see Tarrega, Francisco

STUKKEN, 2 see Flothuis, Marius

STUKKEN, 3 see Gall, Louis Ignatius

STUKKEN, 3, VOOR SCHOOLORKEST, NO. 2 see Dresden, Sem

STUKKEN, 3, VOOR SCHOOLORKEST, NO. 3 see Dresden, Sem

STUKKEN UIT DE OUD-ENGELSE LUITLITERATUUR, 2 I/IB1-Coll

STUKKEN VOOR SCHOOLORKEST, 3 see Griend, Koos van de

STUNDE DER GITARRE, DIE; SPIELMUSIK AUS DER BLUTEZEIT DER GITARRE, VOL. I: SEHR LEICHT I/IB2-Coll

STUNDE DER GITARRE, DIE; SPIELMUSIK AUS DER BLUTEZEIT DER GITARRE, VOL. II: LEICHT I/IB2-Coll

STUNDE DER GITARRE, DIE; SPIELMUSIK AUS DER BLUTEZEIT DER GITARRE, VOL. III: MITTEL I/IB2-Coll

SUDAMERICANA, BERUHMTE FOLKLORISTISCHE TANZE I/IB5-Coll, I/IIA1, I/IIA1-Coll, I/IIA2-Coll, I/IIC1-Coll

SUDAMERIKANISCHE TANZE, FUR DEN MODERNEN GITARREN-GRUPPEN-UNTERRICHT see Keinemann, Karl Heinz

SUENO see Tarrega, Francisco; Tarrega, Francisco, Study, TI ii- 8, in A

SUENO - DER TRAUM see Tarrega, Francisco, Study, TI ii- 8, in A

SUENO (MAZURKA) see Tarrega, Francisco

SUENO see Tarrega, Francisco

SUIT I SVENSK FOLKTON NR. 2 I/IB1-Coll

SUITA EN RE see Baron, Ernst Gottlieb, Suite in D

SUITA POLSKA see Telemann, Georg Philipp

SUITE see Harris, Albert

SUITE see Hasenohrl, Franz

SUITE 1945 see Komter, Jan Maarten

SUITE 1949 see Komter, Jan Maarten

SUITE A-MOLL see Visee, Robert de

SUITE AUS DER "BAUERN-KANTATE" see Bach, Johann Sebastian, Cantata No. 212, [excerpt], [arr.]

SUITE, AUS EINER SAMMLUNG VON TANZEN see Leopold I, Holy Roman Emperor

SUITE BAROQUE see Lerich, Pierre

SUITE BRESILIENNE see Generaux, Roger

SUITE C-MOLL see Visee, Robert de

SUITE CASTELLANA see Moreno Torroba, Federico

SUITE COMPOSTELLANA see Mompou, Federico

SUITE D-MOLL see Visee, Robert de

SUITE D-MOLL (RE MINEUR) see Visee, Robert de

SUITE D'ACCORDS POUR GUITARE see Bossu, Marcel

SUITE DE LA BELLA ANDRONICA see Borrono da Milano, Pietro Pavolo

SUITE "DER GEBURTSTAG DER INFANTIN," AFTER OSCAR WILDE see Schreker, Franz

SUITE DESCRITIVA see Savio, Isaias

SUITE E-DUR see Visee, Robert de

SUITE E-DUR, BWV 1006 see Bach, Johann Sebastian, Partita for Lute, BWV 1006a, in E

SUITE E-MOLL see Bach, Johann Sebastian, Suite for Lute, BWV 996, in E minor; Visee, Robert de

SUITE E-MOLL, NO. 1 see Roncalli, Ludovico, Suite No. 1

SUITE ELISABETHAINE SUR DES THEMES DE JOHN DOWLAND see Azpiazu, Jose de

SUITE EM LA see Visee, Robert de

SUITE EN LA ET PASSACAILLE see Visee, Robert de

SUITE EN MI MENOR, ORIG. PARA LAUD see Bach, Johann Sebastian, Suite for Lute, BWV 996, in E minor

SUITE EN MI MINEUR see Bach, Johann Sebastian, Suite for Lute, BWV 996, in E minor

SUITE EN PASSANT see Kont, Paul

SUITE EN RE see Visee, Robert de

SUITE EN RE MAJEUR see Baron, Ernst Gottlieb, Suite in D

SUITE EN RE MENOR see Visee, Robert de

SUITE EN RE MINEUR see Visee, Robert de

SUITE EN RE MINEUR see Visee, Robert de

SUITE EN RE MINEUR see Visee, Robert de

SUITE EN RE MINEUR see Visee, Robert de

SUITE EN SI MINEUR ET 8 PIECES DU DEUXIEME LIVRE see Visee, Robert de

SUITE EN SOL MAJEUR see Visee, Robert de

SUITE EN SOL MINEUR see Visee, Robert de

SUITE EN STYLE ANCIEN (AFTER CAMPION) see Alfonso, Javier

SUITE ENFANTINE see Cerf, Jacques

SUITE ESPANOLA see Sanz, Gaspar

SUITE FRANZOSISCHER TANZE see Gervaise, Claude

SUITE FUR ISAO TAKAHASHI see Behrend, Siegfried

SUITE FUR LAUTE see Weiss, Sylvius Leopold, Sonata in D minor

SUITE FUR SPIELMUSIKGRUPPEN, OP. 101-3 see Gattermayer, Heinrich

SUITE G-MOLL see Visee, Robert de

SUITE H-MOLL see Visee, Robert de

SUITE, HOMMAGE A GOLDONI see Kovats, Barna

SUITE III see Bach, Johann Sebastian, Suite for Lute, BWV 995, in G minor

SUITE IM ALTEN STIL I/IB6-Coll

SUITE IN A see Visee, Robert de

SUITE IN A see Visee, Robert de

SUITE IN D MAJOR: GAVOTTE I AND II, D MAJOR AND D MINOR see Ponce, Manuel Maria

SUITE IN D-MOLL see Visee, Robert de

SUITE IN G DUR see Roncalli, Ludovico, Suite No. 1

SUITE IN H-MOLL see Visee, Robert de

SUITE IN MODO POLONICO see Tansman, Alexandre

SUITE IN RASGUEADO EN PUNTEADO see Visser, Dick

SUITE IN RE   see Visee, Robert de

SUITE IN SECHS TEILE FUR GITARRE   see Mairants, Ivor

SUITE IN SOL MINORE   see Visee, Robert de

SUITE INFANTILE   see Pizzini, Carlo Alberto

SUITE LATINE   see Morancon, Guy

SUITE MILANESA   see Hoek, Jan-Anton Van

SUITE MINIATURA   see Moreno Torroba, Federico

SUITE MINIATURE   see Bellow, Alexander

SUITE NACH ALTENGLISCHEN MEISTERN   see Behrend, Siegfried

SUITE NACH ALTER LAUTENMUSIK   see Behrend, Siegfried

SUITE, NACH ALTPOLNISCHEN MELODIEN   see Behrend, Siegfried

SUITE NACH FRANZOSISCHEN VOLKSLIEDERN   see Fegers, Karl

SUITE NO. 2 FOR ORCHESTRA IN B MINOR: RONDEAU   see Mornac, Juan

SUITE NO. 7 EN DO MAYOR   see Visee, Robert de

SUITE NO. 15   see Weiss, Sylvius Leopold

SUITE NO. 16 IN D   see Weiss, Sylvius Leopold, Suite in D

SUITE OF AMERICAN FOLKSONGS   see Franco, Johan

SUITE OF DANCES FOR LUTE (1546)   see Rotta, Antonio

SUITE PARA LAUD   see Weiss, Sylvius Leopold, Sonata in D minor

SUITE PERCUTANTE   see Drogoz, Philippe

SUITE PIEMONTESE   see Duarte, John W.

SUITE POPULAIRE BRESILIENNE   see Villa-Lobos, Heitor

SUITE POUR LE LUTH (LAUTENSUITE NR. III)   see Bach, Johann Sebastian, Suite for Lute, BWV 995, in G minor

SUITE PROVENCALE   see Bellow, Alexander

SUITE ROMANTICA   see Stavinoha-Melisek, Jan

SUITE UBER ALTBOHMISCHE WEIHNACHTSWEISEN   see Bresgen, Cesar

SUITE VALENCIANA   see Asencio, Vicente

SUITE VENDEENNE   see Mourat, Jean-Maurice

SUITE VENEZOLANA   see Lauro, Antonio

SUITE VESPERALE   see Sanchez, B.

SUITE VIVAT NOVIOMAGUM   see Gall, Louis Ignatius

SUITE VOOR SCHOOLORKEST   see Baaren, Kees van

SUITEN, 2, AFTER MELODIES BY FRENCH DANCE MASTERS   V/i

SUITEN, 9   see Roncalli, Ludovico

4 SUITEN   see Mace, Thomas

SUITEN NR. 3 UND NR. 4   see Roncalli, Ludovico

SUITEN ZU 4 STIMMEN, 5   see Telemann, Georg Philipp

SUITES, 6   see Komter, Jan Maarten

SULLIVAN, [SIR] ARTHUR SEYMOUR (1842-1900)
Tunes From Gilbert And Sullivan, 10 I/IIB1

SUMMER-DANCES   see Andriessen, Jurriaan

SUNNESCHYN UND RAGE   see Thienemann, H.

SUO COSA   see Duarte, John W.

SUONI NOTTURNI   see Petrassi, Goffredo

SUPER STUDIES   see Helleman, Joop

SUPERNOVAE, FOR CHAMBER ORCHESTRA AND PERCUSSION   see Tabachnik, Michel

SUPLEMENTO AL METODO PARA GUITARRA DE AGUADO-SINOPOLI   I/IB6-Coll, VI-Mixed Coll, VII-Mixed Coll

SUPPE, FRANZ VON (1819-1895)
Banditenstreiche; Comic Opera In Three Acts   V/iii

Schone Galathee, Die; Comic Opera In One Act   V/iii

SUR LE NOM DE GRACIELA POMPONIO   see Migot, Georges

SUR LE NOM DE JORGE MARTINEZ ZARATE   see Migot, Georges

SUR LE PONT D'AVIGNON   see Reisebilder Aus Frankreich, 5

SUR UN PARAVENT CHINOIS, 4 ESQUISSES, OP. 147   see Absil, Jean

SURABAYA JOHNNY   see Weill, Kurt

SURINACH, CARLOS (1915-   )
Bolero De Los Picaros   I/IB4

SUSANINNE, EINE KLEINE WEIHNACHTSKANTATE   see Hensel, Walther

SUSATO, TIELMAN (? -ca. 1561)
Altflamische Tanze   I/IIA1

Gaillarde "Ghequest Bin Ick"   see Pieces, 5

Gaillarde "Mille Ducas"   see Pieces, 5

Pavane "Mille Ducas"   see Pieces, 5

Pieces, 5   I/IIA3

Ronde   see Pieces, 5

Ronde "Mille Ducas"   see Pieces, 5

Tanze, 7   I/IIA1, I/IIA3

SUTER, ROBERT (1919-   )
Nocturnes, 3, For Viola And Orchestra V/i

SWANEE RIVER   see Devil And The Farmer's Wife, The, And Other American Ballads

SWEELINCK, JAN PIETERSZOON (1562-1621)
Courante   see Pieces, 4; Pieces, 4

Lantdarabok   I/IB1

Lute Pieces   see Lantdarabok

Pieces, 4   I/IB1

Pieces, 4   I/IB1

Psalm No. 5   I/IB1

Psalm No. 23   I/IB1

Volte I   see Pieces, 4; Pieces, 4

Volte II   see Pieces, 4; Pieces, 4

Volte III   see Pieces, 4; Pieces, 4

Voltes, 2   I/IB1

SWEETLAND, ELLIOT
Belwin Spanish Guitar Course, 4 Vols. II

SWING LOW, SWEET CHARIOT   see Devil And The Farmer's Wife, The, And Other American Ballads; Famous Negro Spirituals, 5

SWING NO. 2   see Bondon, Jacques

SWORD DANCE   see Staak, Pieter van der

SYLVAINS, LES   see Couperin, Francois (le Grand)

SYLVESTERLIED   see Schumann, Robert (Alexander)

SYMPHONIE CONCERTANTE   see Belaubre, Louis-Noel

SYMPHONIES DE TIMBRES, LES   see Haubenstock-Ramati, Roman

SYNCHRONIE; 10 GRAPHIC PARTS   see Hashagen, Klaus

SYSTEME DE GAMMES POUR GUITARE   see Puijenbroeck, Victor van, Toonladder Systeem Voor Gitaar

SYT NU VERBLYT   I/IIA2-Coll

SZIN-DARABOK - COLOR-PIECES   see Borsody, Laszlo

SZKOLA GRY NA GITARZE   see Powrozniak, Jozef

SZKOLA GRY NA GITARZE, WYDANIE ZMIENIONE UZUPELNIONE DODATKIEM O GRZE NA GITARZE HAWAJSKIEJ   see Powrozniak, Jozef

SZORDIKOWSKI, BRUNO
Impromptu   I/IB4

Kleine Suite   I/IB4

TABACHNIK, MICHEL (1942-   )
Supernovae, For Chamber Orchestra And Percussion   V/i

TABELLA DEGLI ACCORDI, PER CHITARRA CLASSICA E JAZZ   see Ferrari, Romolo

TABLEAU D'ACCORDS POUR LA GUITARE   see Borello, P.

TABULATUREN ETLICHER LOBGESANG UND LIDLEIN VFF DIE LAUTEN, 1512   see Schlick, Arnolt

TABULATUREN FUR LAUTE, VIHUELA UND GITARRE, IN NEUER NOTATION MIT GEGENUBERSTELLUNG DER ENTSPRECHENDEN ALTEN MANUSKRIPTE I/IB1-Coll

TACTIL FUR DREI   see Kagel, Mauricio

TAFELMUZIEK   see Welffens, P.

TAG MIT SEINEM LICHTE, DER   see Bach, Johann Sebastian

TAG TRITT HERVOR, EIN, PENTAPHONY FOR PIANO OBBLIGATO, FIVE SOLO INSTRUMENTS, FIVE GROUPS OF FIVE PLAYERS EACH AND A SPEAKING ROLE   see Gielen, Michael Andreas

TAGLICHE STUDIEN ZUR BILDUNG DES ANSCHLAGS   see Gotze, Walter

TAGLICHE TRAINING, DAS, TONLEITERN UND TECHNISCHE STUDIEN   see Walker, Luise

TAKACS, JENO (1902-   )
Dialoge   I/IIB1

Partita, Op. 55   I/IIIA

TAKE YOUR PARTNERS; 6 ENGLISH COUNTRY DANCES   I/IIB1-Coll

TAKEMITSU, TORU (1930-   )
Ring   I/IIB2

Stanza I   I/IIC4

Valeria   V/i

TAMBORS, LES 3, GLOSA DE LA CANCION POPULAR CATALANA   see Pujol, Emilio

TAMBOURIN   see Rameau, Jean-Philippe; Rameau, Jean-Philippe

TAMBOURIN, LE   see Rameau, Jean-Philippe

TAMBOURIN AND GAVOTTE   see Gossec, Francois Joseph

TAMZARA, TURKISCHER TANZ   see Koptagel, Yuksel

TANCE I PIESNI LUDOWE   I/IB5-Coll

TANGENTS CSB   see Fink, Siegfried

TANGO   see Albeniz, Isaac; Pujol, Emilio; Tarrega, Francisco

TANGO, EL   see Broqua, Alfonso

TANGO DE LA CASADA INFIDEL   see Asencio, Vicente

TANGO ESPAGNOL   see Albeniz, Isaac

TANGO ESPANOL   see Albeniz, Isaac

TANGUILLO, MIN 418   see Winkelbauer, Alfred

TANGUILLO, MIN 419 see Winkelbauer,
    Alfred

TANKA, SUL NOME DI ISAO TAKAHASHI see
    Castelnuovo-Tedesco, Mario

TANSMAN, ALEXANDRE (1897-   )
    Alla Polacca see Pieces, 3

    Berceuse d'Orient see Pieces, 3

    Canzonetta see Pieces, 3

    Cavatina I/IB4

    Danza Pomposa I/IB4

    Mazurka I/IB4

    Pezzo In Modo Antico I/IB4

    Pieces, 3 I/IB4

    Pieces Faciles, Vol. I I/IB4

    Pieces Faciles, Vol. II I/IB4

    Suite In Modo Polonico I/IB4

    Variations Sur Un Theme De Scriabine
        I/IB4

TANT QUE VIVRAI see Bianchini,
    Domenico

TANT QUE VIVRAI, CHANSON see Sermisy,
    Claude de (Claudin)

TANT QUE VIVRAY see Anonymous

TANZ see Canzonen Und Tanze Aus Dem
    XVI. Jahrhundert; Sprongl, Norbert;
    Wensiecki, Edmund

TANZ AUF DER ROSENBURG see
    Mittelalterliche Tanze

TANZ DES FURSTEN VON SIEBEN BURGEN see
    Farkas, Ferenc

TANZ DES LAZAR APOR, DER see Farkas,
    Ferenc

TANZ IM AICHOLDINGER SCHLOSS see
    Mittelalterliche Tanze

TANZBUCH DER RENAISSANCE I/IIA1-Coll,
    I/IIA2-Coll, I/IIA3-Coll

TANZE, 2 see Lampe, Gunter

TANZE, 3 see Neusiedler, Hans; Peuerl,
    Paul

TANZE, 4 see Lully, Jean-Baptiste
    (Lulli); Mozart, Wolfgang Amadeus

TANZE, 6 I/IIA1

TANZE, 6, AUS DEM NOTENBUCHLEIN FUR
    WOLFGANG see Mozart, Leopold

TANZE, 7 see Susato, Tielman

TANZE, 8 see Anonymous

TANZE, 10 I/IIA1-Coll

TANZE see Praetorius, Michael

TANZE see Peuerl, Paul

TANZE see Schubert, Franz (Peter)

TANZE AUS DEN ALPENLANDERN I/IIB2-Coll

TANZE AUS DER RENAISSANCE I/IB1

TANZE AUS OPERN, 7 see Handel, George
    Frideric

TANZE AUS OSTERREICH I/IB5-Coll

TANZE, CANZONEN UND PHANTASIEN see
    Virchi, Paolo

TANZE DER VOLKER see Werdin, Eberhard

TANZE, MARSCHE UND ANDERE SPIELSTUCKE
    see Stetka, Franz

TANZE UND STUCKE DER BAROCKZEIT
    I/IIA2-Coll

TANZE UND WEISEN see Hauswirth, Hans
    M.A.

TANZE UND WEISEN see Karl, Sepp

TANZE UND WEISEN AUS DEM BAROCK I/IB1

16 TANZE see Sanz, Gaspar

TANZERISCHE SPIELMUSIK see Koch,
    Johannes H.E.

TANZERISCHES SPIEL see Stingl, Anton

TANZLEIN see Fleres, Rita Maria

TANZLIED see Rebay, Ferdinand; Walker,
    Luise

TANZLIED AUS ISRAEL see Rosenstengel,
    Albrecht

TANZLIED, ETUDE C-DUR see Walker,
    Luise

TANZLIED MIT VARIATIONEN see Koch,
    Johannes H.E.

TANZLIEDER UND SPIELE FUR KINDER, 12
    I/IIC2-Coll

TANZSATZE I/IIB2-Coll, VII-Mixed Coll

TANZSTUCKE, 3 see Hoffner, Paul Marx

TANZSTUCKE see Frescobaldi, Girolamo

TARANTELLA see Castelnuovo-Tedesco,
    Mario; Mertz, Johann Kaspar;
    Paganini, Niccolo

TARANTELLA BURLESCA AND BOSSA NOVA see
    Abloniz, Miguel

TARANTELLA CAMPANA, SUL NOME DI EUGENE
    DI NOVI see Castelnuovo-Tedesco,
    Mario

TARANTELLE see Coste, Napoleon; Petit,
    Pierre

TARRAGO, G.
    Estudios, 2, Sobre Un Tema De Alard
        I/IIA1

    Study No. 1 in E see Estudios, 2,
        Sobre Un Tema De Alard

    Study No. 2 in E see Estudios, 2,
        Sobre Un Tema De Alard

TARRAGO, GRACIANO
    Bolero I/IIA1

    Escalas, Arpegios Y Armonicos Para
        Guitarra, Vol. I III

    Escalas, Arpegios Y Armonicos Para
        Guitarra, Vol. II III

    Estudio De Tremolo, Sobre Un Tema De
        Alard I/IA, I/IIA1

    Estudios De Cejilla, 6 I/IA

    Estudios Melodicos, 25 I/IA

    Metodo Graduado Para Aprender A Tocar
        La Guitarra II

    Prelude in E I/IB4

TARRAJA, 24 PETITES PIECES see Antiga,
    Jean

TARREGA, FRANCISCO (1852-1909)
    Adelita, Mazurka I/IB3, VI
        see also Album, Vol. III

    Alborada, Cajita De Musica I/IB3

    Alborada, Capricho see Album No. 23

    Alborado see Album, No. 2

    Album, No. 1 I/IB3, VI

    Album, No. 2 I/IB3, VI

    Album, No. 3 I/IB3, VI

    Album, No. 4 I/IB3, VI

    Album, No. 5 I/IB3, VI

    Album, No. 6 I/IB3, VI

    Album, No. 7 I/IB3, VI

    Album, No. 8 I/IB3-Coll

    Album, No. 10 I/IB3-Coll

    Album, No. 11 I/IB3-Coll

    Album, No. 17 I/IB3, VI-Coll

    Album, No. 19 I/IB3

    Album, No. 20 I/IB3

    Album No. 21 I/IIA1, VI-Coll

    Album No. 22 I/IIA1, VI-Coll

    Album No. 23 I/IIA1, VI-Coll

TARREGA, FRANCISCO (cont'd.)
    Album, Vol. I I/IB3-Coll, VI-Coll,
        VII-Mixed Coll

    Album, Vol. II: Seis [Sic] Preludios
        I/IB3-Coll, VI, VI-Coll

    Album, Vol. III I/IB3

    Capricho Arabe, Serenata I/IB3, VI

    Cartagenera, La see Album, No. 5

    Columpio, El see Study, TI ii- 7a,
        in G

    Composiciones Originales Y Estudios
        Para Guitarra, Vol. I I/IB3,
        VI-Coll

    Composiciones Originales Y Estudios
        Para Guitarra, Vol. II I/IB3,
        VI-Coll

    Composiciones Originales Y Estudios
        Para Guitarra, Vol. III: 30
        Preludios Originales I/IB3,
        VI-Coll

    Composiciones Originales Y Estudios
        Para Guitarra, Vol. III: 30
        Preludios Originales I/IB3,
        VI-Coll

    Composiciones Originales Y Estudios
        Para Guitarra, Vol. IV I/IB3,
        VI-Coll

    Composiciones Para Guitarra, 12
        I/IB3, VI-Coll

    Danza Mora I/IB3, I/IIA1, VI
        see also Album, No. 1; Album No. 22

    Danza Odalisca I/IB3
        see also Album, No. 3

    Dos Hermanitas, Las see Album, No. 2

    Elementos Fundamentales De La Tecnica
        Guitarristica VI-Coll

    Endecha see Prelude, TI i- 16, in D
        minor

    Esercizi Di Tarrega see Formule Di
        Arpeggi

    Estudio Brillante, By Alard see
        Study, TI ii- 19, in A

    Estudio De Delphin Alard see Study,
        TI ii- 19, in A

    Estudio De Prudent see Study, TI ii-
        23, in E minor

    Estudio En Forma De Minuetto see
        Study, TI ii- 5, in A

    Estudio Sobre La Sonatina De Delphin
        Alard see Study, TI ii- 19, in A

    Estudio Sobre Un Fragmento, De La
        "Gruta Del Fingal" De Mendelssohn
        see Study, TI ii- 16a, in B minor

    Estudio Sobre Un Tema De Wagner see
        Study, TI ii- 13, in E

    Estudio (Sobre Una Giga) see Study,
        TI ii- 11, in E

    Estudios I/IA

    Estudios; 20 Studies Without Title,
        Vol. 1: Estudios 1-3 VI-Coll

    Estudios; 20 Studies Without Title,
        Vol. 2: Estudios 4-6 VI-Coll

    Estudios; 20 Studies Without Title,
        Vol. 3: Estudios 7-10 VI-Coll

    Estudios; 20 Studies Without Title,
        Vol. 4: Estudios 11-13 VI-Coll

    Estudios; 20 Studies Without Title,
        Vol. 5: Estudios 14-17 VI-Coll

    Estudios; 20 Studies Without Title,
        Vol. 6: Estudios 18-20 VI-Coll

    Estudios Para Guitarra VI-Coll

    Etuden VI-Coll

    Exercise, TI iii- 3 see Estudios; 20
        Studies Without Title, Vol. 1:
        Estudios 1-3

    Exercise, TI iii- 16 see Elementos
        Fundamentales De La Tecnica
        Guitarristica

TARREGA, FRANCISCO (cont'd.)

Compositions, Vol. I

Study, TI ii- 7a, in D see Composiciones Originales Y Estudios Para Guitarra, Vol. II

Study, TI ii- 7a, in G VI

Study, TI ii- 7b, in D see Album, No. 7; Guitarra Espanola: 12 Spanische Stucke; Opere Per Chitarra, Vol. III: Composizioni Originali

Study, TI ii- 8, in A VI see also Composiciones Originales Y Estudios Para Guitarra, Vol. I; Composiciones Para Guitarra, 12; Kompositionen Fur Gitarre, Vol. I; Tarrega-Album, Eine Sammlung Der Bekanntesten Original-Werke; Vyber Skladeb, Selected Compositions, Vol. I

Study, TI ii- 9, in A minor VI see also Composiciones Originales Y Estudios Para Guitarra, Vol. I; Composiciones Para Guitarra, 12; Kompositionen Fur Gitarre, Vol. I; Tarrega-Album, Eine Sammlung Der Bekanntesten Original-Werke

Study, TI ii- 10, in D minor see Composiciones Originales Y Estudios Para Guitarra, Vol. IV

Study, TI ii- 11, in E VI see also Album, No. 6; Composiciones Originales Y Estudios Para Guitarra, Vol. IV; Kompositionen Fur Gitarre, Vol. I; Vyber Skladeb, Selected Compositions, Vol. II

Study, TI ii- 12, in E VI see also Composiciones Originales Y Estudios Para Guitarra, Vol. IV; Estudios Para Guitarra; Kompositionen Fur Gitarre, Vol. II

Study, TI ii- 13, in E VI

Study, TI ii- 14, in D minor see Composiciones Originales Y Estudios Para Guitarra, Vol. IV

Study, TI ii- 15, in A minor see Album, No. 4; Composiciones Originales Y Estudios Para Guitarra, Vol. IV; Kompositionen Fur Gitarre, Vol. I

Study, TI ii- 16a, in B minor VI see also Composiciones Originales Y Estudios Para Guitarra, Vol. IV; Kompositionen Fur Gitarre, Vol. I

Study, TI ii- 17, in A minor see Estudios Para Guitarra

Study, TI ii- 18, in A VI see also Album, No. 1; Album No. 23; Composiciones Originales Y Estudios Para Guitarra, Vol. IV; Etuden

Study, TI ii- 19, in A VI see also Album, No. 2; Composiciones Originales Y Estudios Para Guitarra, Vol. IV; Estudios Para Guitarra; Kompositionen Fur Gitarre, Vol. I; Utwory Wybrane; Vyber Skladeb, Selected Compositions, Vol. I

Study, TI ii- 20 see Composiciones Originales Y Estudios Para Guitarra, Vol. IV

Study, TI ii- 20, in D see Album, No. 5; Guitarra Espanola: 12 Spanische Stucke

Study, TI ii- 22 see Composiciones Originales Y Estudios Para Guitarra, Vol. IV

Study, TI ii- 23, in E minor VI

Study, TI ii- 24, in E minor VI

Study, TI ii- 25, in E VI

Study, TI ii- 26, in C see Estudios Para Guitarra

Study, TI ii- 27, in E minor see Estudios Para Guitarra; Etuden

Study, TI ii- 29 see Elementos Fundamentales De La Tecnica Guitarristica

TARREGA, FRANCISCO (cont'd.)

Study, TI ii- 29, in A minor see Estudios; 20 Studies Without Title, Vol. 4: Estudios 11-13; Kompositionen Fur Gitarre, Vol. II; Utwory Wybrane

Study, TI ii- 31 see Elementos Fundamentales De La Tecnica Guitarristica

Study, TI ii- 32, in D see Estudios; 20 Studies Without Title, Vol. 3: Estudios 7-10

Study, TI ii- 34, in A see Estudios; 20 Studies Without Title, Vol. 5: Estudios 14-17

Study, TI ii- 36 see Elementos Fundamentales De La Tecnica Guitarristica

Study, TI ii- 36, in A see Kompositionen Fur Gitarre, Vol. II

Study, TIii-16a in B minor [fragment] see Estudios Para Guitarra

Study, TIii-32 [fragment] see Elementos Fundamentales De La Tecnica Guitarristica

Sueno see Album, Vol. III; Study, TI ii- 8, in A

Sueno - Der Traum see Study, TI ii- 8, in A

Sueno (Mazurka) see Album No. 22

Sueno see Album, No. 3

Tango see Album, No. 7

Tarrega-Album, Eine Sammlung Der Bekanntesten Original-Werke I/IB3, VI-Coll

Technical Studies VI-Coll

Thalberg: Tema Y Var see Study, TI ii- 24, in E minor

Utwory Wybrane I/IB3, VI-Coll

Vyber Skladeb, Selected Compositions, Vol. I I/IB3, VI-Coll

Vyber Skladeb, Selected Compositions, Vol. II I/IB3, VI-Coll

Vzpominky Na Alhambru : Erinnerungen An Die Alhambra see Study, TI ii- 9, in A minor

Waltz in A see Album, No. 3

Waltz in D see Album, No. 7

TARREGA-ALBUM, EINE SAMMLUNG DER BEKANNTESTEN ORIGINAL-WERKE see Tarrega, Francisco

TARREGA ETCETERA, DAGELIJKSE STUDIES see Visser, Dick

TARREGA ETCETERA, DAILY STUDIES see Visser, Dick, Tarrega Etcetera, Dagelijkse Studies

TAUBE, EVERT (1890-1976) Nocturne I/IB4

Visor, 50, Till Luta Och Gitarr I/IIC1

TAUBERT, KARL HEINZ (1921-   ) Hausspruch I/IIC2

Wiegenlied I/IIC1

TCHAIKOVSKY, PIOTR ILYICH (1840-1893) Andante Cantabile I/IB3

Antigua Cancion Francesa see Old French Air

Cancao Triste see Chanson Triste

Cancion Sin Palabras see Chant Sans Paroles

Cancion Triste see Chanson Triste

Chanson Triste I/IB3

Chant Sans Paroles I/IB3

German Air see Piezas, 6

In Church I/IB3 see also Pieces, 6

TCHAIKOVSKY, PIOTR ILYICH (cont'd.)

Mama see Piezas, 6

Manana De Invierno see Sick Doll, The

March Of The Wooden Soldiers see Piezas, 6

Mazurka see Pieces, 6

Mazurka, MIN 373 I/IB3

Mazurka, Op. 39, No. 10 I/IB3 see also Piezas, 6

Morning Prayer see Pieces, 6

Nella Chiesa Russa see In Church

New Doll, The see Pieces, 3; Pieces, 6; Piezas, 6

None But The Lonely Heart I/IB3

Old French Air I/IB3 see also Pieces, 6; Piezas, 6

Old Wife's Tale, The see Pieces, 3

Pieces, 3 I/IIA3

Pieces, 6 I/IB3

Piezas, 6 I/IB3

Russian Song see Pieces, 6

Sick Doll, The I/IB3

Solo El Que Sabe Amar see None But The Lonely Heart

Song Without Words I/IB3

Tema Dal Balletto I/IB3

Vals De Las Flores see Valse Des Fleurs

Valsa Das Flores see Valse Des Fleurs

Valse Des Fleurs I/IB3

Winter Morning, A see Pieces, 3

TE LUCIS ANTE TERMINUM see Davies, Peter Maxwell; Hinojosa, Javier

TECHNICA DEGLI ARPEGGI PER CHITARRA CLASSICA, LA see Papararo, Guglielmo

TECHNICA SUPERIOR see Rodriguez Arenas, Mario, Escuela De La Guitarra, Vol. VI

TECHNICAL STUDIES see Tarrega, Francisco

TECHNICAL STUDIES FOR THE GUITAR, VOL. I: CHROMATIC SCALES see Visser, Dick

TECHNICAL STUDIES FOR THE GUITAR, VOL. II: ARPEGGIOS see Visser, Dick

TECHNICAL STUDIES FOR THE GUITAR, VOL. III: INTERVAL-SYSTEMS see Visser, Dick

TECHNICAL STUDIES FOR THE GUITAR, VOL. IV: DIATONIC SCALES AND SCALE-SYSTEMS see Visser, Dick

TECHNICAL STUDIES FOR THE GUITAR, VOL. V: LEGATO-VIBRATO see Visser, Dick

TECHNICAL STUDIES FOR THE GUITAR, VOL. VI: CHORDS A.O. CADENCES; BROKEN CHORDS see Visser, Dick

TECHNICAL STUDIES FOR THE GUITAR, VOL. VII: RIGHT HAND FORMULAS; GLISSANDO; TREMOLO; RASGUEADO; HARMONICS; PIZZICATO; ETC. see Visser, Dick

TECHNISCHE STUDIEN FUR GITARRE, VOL. I: FINGERUBUNGEN FUR EINE SYSTEMATISCHE AUSBILDUNG DER GITARRE-SPIELTECHNIK see Kovats, Barna

TECNICA DE LA GUITARRA, VOL. 1 ESCALAS Y ARPEGIOS see Lopategui, Jose Luis

TECNICA DEI SUONI LEGATI, LA see Tonazzi, Bruno

TECNICA DO MECANISMO see Savio, Isaias, Escola Moderna Do Violao, Vol. II

TIENTO VII, VIII   see Mudarra, Alonso
de

TIENTOS, 4, SONORIDADES 1970   see
Santorsola, Guido

TIENTOS, 8: ORPHENICA LYRA   see
Fuenllana, Miguel de

TIENTOS DEL SEPTIMO Y OCTAVO TONO   see
Milan, Luis

TIENTOS DEL TERCERO Y CUARTO TONO   see
Milan, Luis

TIERVERSE VON BERTOLT BRECHT   see
Dessau, Paul

TIGGES, KOOS
Diatonic Tonescales Along 2 Octaves
see Diatonische Toonladders Over
2 Octaven

Diatonische Toonladders Over 2
Octaven   III

TIME PIECES   see Handel, George
Frideric

TIME SPIRIT, FOR CLARINET AND ORCHESTRA
see Andriessen, Jurriaan, Symphony
No. 5

TIPPETT, [SIR] MICHAEL (1905-   )
Songs For Achilles   I/IIC1

TIPS FOR TROUBADOURS, OR HOW TO
ACCOMPANY SONGS ON THE GUITAR   see
Gavall, John

TIRANA, DANZA SPAGNOLA   see Sor,
Fernando

TIRNOVO   see Farkas, Ferenc

TIROLESA   see Giuliani, Mauro

TIRSI E CLORI   see Monteverdi, Claudio

TISCHLEIN DECK DICH, EIN LEBENDIGES
BUHNENSTUCK (URSPRUNGLICH MUSIK FUR
EIN SCHATTENSPIEL   see Kukuck,
Felicitas

TITTEL, ERNST (1910-1969)
O, Du Lieber Augustin   I/IIA3

Vogelweider, Der   V/ii

TIZENKET DARAB GITARRA   see Couperin,
Francois (le Grand)

TO NAME BUT NONE   see Anonymous

TO YOU   see Schat, Peter

TOADA   see Bosmans, Arthur,
Brasileiras, No.4

TOCCATA, ELEGIA E DANZA   see Baumann,
Herbert

TOCCATA FANTASQUE   see Mignot, Pierre

TOCCATA PER SPINETTINA OVER LIUTO   see
Frescobaldi, Girolamo

TOCCATA SUR LE JEU DE "COUCOU"   see
Pasquini, Bernardo

TOCCATINA   see Delauney, Paul; Solares,
Enrique

TODA MI VIDA OS AME   see Milan, Luis

TOGNI, CAMILLO (1922-   )
Helian Di Trakl   V/ii

Rondeaux Per 10   V/ii

TOMASI, HENRI (1901-1971)
Muletier Des Andes, Le   I/IB4

Pastorales Provencales   I/IIIC

Recuerdos De Las Baleares   I/IIB4

TOMBEAU   see Boulez, Pierre, Pli Selon
Pli, Portrait De Mallarme, 5

TOMBEAU DE FRANCOIS CORBETTA, LE   see
Visee, Robert de, Allemand, VOCG 38

TOMBEAU DE MADAME D'ORLEANS, LE   see
Corbetta, Francesco (Francisque
Corbett)

TOMBEAU POUR M. BLANCROCHER   see
Couperin, Louis; Froberger, Johann
Jakob

TOMBEAU SUR LA MORT DE MR. COMTE D'LOGY
see Weiss, Sylvius Leopold

TON E, DER   see Apostel, Hans Erich

TON E, DER   see Apostel, Hans Erich

TONADA   see Azpiazu, Jose de

TONADA DE LABRADOR   see Thomas, Juan
Maria

TONADILLA   see Pujol, Emilio; Rodrigo,
Joaquin; Segovia, Andres

TONADILLA, SUR LE NOM DE ANDRES SEGOVIA
see Castelnuovo-Tedesco, Mario

TONALIDA ISLENA   see Sanchez, B.

TONAZZI, BRUNO
Tecnica Dei Suoni Legati, La   III

TONBILDUNGS-STUDIEN NACH ALTEN WEISEN -
STUDIES IN TONE FORMATION BASED ON
OLD TUNES   I/IB5-Coll

TONLEITERN UND KADENZEN, IN ALLEN
TONARTEN UND LAGEN   see Gotze,
Walter

TONLEITERSTUDIEN   see Behrend,
Siegfried

TOONLADDER SYSTEEM VOOR GITAAR   see
Puijenbroeck, Victor van

TOPPER, GUIDO
Animals, The   see Suite No. 1

Duet Approach To The Guitar, A, An
Initial Programme For Guitar   II

Funny Face   see Jazzy Moods, 3

Gay Tango   see Jazzy Moods, 3

Guitarist's Travelling Guide, The
I/IB4

Jazzy Moods, 3   I/IB4

Little Lovely   see Jazzy Moods, 3

Modern Approach To The Guitar, A,
Based On The Principles Of Emilio
Pujol, Vol. I   II

Modern Approach To The Guitar, A,
Based On The Principles Of Emilio
Pujol, Vol. II   II

Modern Approach To The Guitar, A,
Based On The Principles Of Emilio
Pujol, Vol. III   II

Modern Approach To The Guitar, A,
Based On The Principles Of Emilio
Pujol, Vol. IV   II

Modern Approach To The Guitar, A,
Based On The Principles Of Emilio
Pujol, Vol. V   II

Suite No. 1   I/IB4

TORELLI, GIUSEPPE (1658-1709)
Concerto in A   V/i

Concerto in D minor   I/IIIA, V/i

Concerto in G   I/IIB4

TORNEO   see Ruiz de Ribayaz, Lucas;
Sanz, Gaspar

TORNEO, BAILE POPULAR   see Sanz, Gaspar

TORRE, FERNANDO DELLE
Alta Danza   I/IB1

TORRE BERMEJA, SERENATA   see Albeniz,
Isaac

TORRE MORISCA, LA   see Bochman, Theo L.

TORRES, PEDRO MANUEL
Gallo, El, Danza Venezuelana   I/IB5

TORSO   see Bussotti, Sylvano

TOSELLI, ENRICO (1883-1926)
Celebre Serenata   I/IB3

TOTALE I   see Gaslini, Giorgio

TOTALE II   see Gaslini, Giorgio

TOTUMO DE GUARENAS, EL   see Canonico,
Benito, Aire De Joropo

TOUPIE, LA   see Mourat, Jean-Maurice

TOURNOI ET BATAILLE   see Sanz, Gaspar

TOUTE MA VIE JE VOUS AI AIMEE   see
Milan, Luis, Toda Mi Vida Os Ame

TOWER HILL   see Six Pieces From The
Time Of Elizabeth

TOY, A   see Robinson, Thomas

TOY, AIR AND GIGUE   see Robinson,
Thomas

TOY TRAIN, THE   see Neumann, Ulrik,
Leksakstaget

TRAINEAU, LE   see Praf, [Fray]
Benedicto

TRALALA, EL, Y EL PUNTEADO, TONADILLA
see Granados, Enrique

TRALLERLIEDCHEN   see Schumann, Robert
(Alexander)

TRANQUILLAMENTE SCORRENDO   see Kovats,
Barna

TRANSATLANTIC DANCES, 4   see Duarte,
John W.

TRANSCRIPCIONES PARA GUITARRA
I/IB6-Coll, VII-Mixed Coll

TRANSCRIPCIONES PARA GUITARRA
I/IB6-Coll, VII-Mixed Coll

TRANSCRIPCIONES POR GRACIANO TARRAGO
[1]   I/IB6-Coll, VII-Mixed Coll

TRANSCRIPCIONES POR GRACIANO TARRAGO
[2]   I/IB6-Coll, VII-Mixed Coll

TRANSCRIPCIONES POR GRACIANO TARRAGO
[3]   I/IB6-Coll, VII-Mixed Coll

TRANSCRIPCIONES POR VICENTE ERLISO,
VOL. 1   see Erliso, Vincente

TRANSCRIPCIONES POR VICENTE ERLISO,
VOL. 2   I/IB2

TRANSCRIPCIONES POR VICENTE ERLISO,
VOL. 3   I/IB6-Coll

TRANSCRIPCIONES POR VICENTE ERLISO,
VOL. 4   I/IB6-Coll

TRANSCRIPCIONES POR VICENTE ERLISO,
VOL. 6   I/IB6-Coll, VII-Mixed Coll

TRANSCRIPCIONES POR VICENTE ERLISO,
VOL. V   I/IB2

TRANSCRIPTIONS FACILES DE 12 CHEFS-
D'OEUVRE CLASSIQUE   I/IB6-Coll,
VII-Mixed Coll

TRANSKRYPCJE KLASYKOW   I/IIA1-Coll,
VII-Mixed Coll

TRASPARENZE   see Correggia, Enrico

TRAUM   see Ambrosius, Hermann

TRAUMBILDER, VARIATIONEN UBER EIN
WIEGENLIED   see Stingl, Anton

TRAUMEREI   see Schumann, Robert
(Alexander); Schumann, Robert
(Alexander)

TRAVEL-SUITE   see Mairants, Ivor

TRAVESURA   see Azpiazu, Jose de

TRE SCHERZI MUSICALI A TRE VOCI   see
Monteverdi, Claudio

TREMENS; SCENIC ASSEMBLING OF AN
EXPERIMENT IN ONE SCENE   see Kagel,
Mauricio

TREML, ROBERT
Grundlagen Des Gitarrenspiels, Die,
Aufbau Und Spieltechnik Aus Der
Einstimmigkeit, Mit Vielen
Musikbeispielen, Einzeln Oder
Chorisch Zu Gebrauchen   II,
VII-Mixed Coll

TREMOLO ESTUDIO   see Rizzuti, Carmelo

TREMOLO-ETUDE   see Carcassi, Matteo

TREMOLO STUDIES, 3   see Shearer, Aaron

TREMOLO STUDY   see Carcassi, Matteo

TREMOLO STUDY IN A MAJOR   see Navarro,
Antonio

TREMOLOSPEL OP DE GITAAR   see Bervoets,
Gerard

TREMOLOSPIEL AUF DER GITARRE   see Wolf,
Roland

TREMPLINS   see Miroglio, Francis

UHL, ALFRED (cont'd.)

  Stucke, 10, Vol. II   I/IB4

  Zirkusmarsch   see Allerlei Spielmusik

UIT MOZART'S TIJD   I/IIB5-Coll

UKRAINISCHE VOLKSWEISEN   I/IIC1-Coll

ULDALL, HANS (1903-   )
  Neue Musizierstucke   I/IIB2

ULICE   see Drlac, Jan Zdenek

ULRICH, JURGEN (1939-   )
  Drei Rhapsodische Studien   I/IA

  Einerseits-Andererseits, Vol. 1
    I/IIA2-Coll

  Einerseits-Andererseits, Vol. 2
    I/IIA2-Coll

ULTIMA RARA, POP SONG   see Bussotti,
  Sylvano

ULTRA STUDIES   see Helleman, Joop

UMBRA   see Lorentzen, Bent; Maghini,
  Ruggero

UMKEHR, AFTER FRIEDRICH WEINREB   see
  Schneider, Urs Peter, Kirchweih,
  No. 5, For Orchestra And Equipment

UNAWARE   see Komter, Jan Maarten

UND DIE LIEBE BRAUCHT EIN DACH
  I/IIC1-Coll

UND DIE ZEIGER SEINER AUGEN WURDEN
  LANGSAM ZURUCKGEDREHT   see Nilsson,
  Bo

UNGARISCHE MUSIK FUR GITARRE AUS DER
  ERSTEN HALFTE DES 19. JAHRHUNDERTS
  see Magyar Zene Gitarra A XIX.
  Szadad Elso Felebol

UNGARISCHE SUITE, NACH ORIGINALEN
  CSARDAS-MELODIEN   see Werdin,
  Eberhard

UNGARISCHE VOLKSLIEDER   see 50 Magyar
  Nepdal

UNGARISCHER TANZ   see Tanze, 6; Farkas,
  Ferenc

UNGEWITTER, DAS   see Carulli,
  Ferdinando, Nice Und Fileno

UNSERE SCHONSTEN WEIHNACHTSLIEDER ZUR
  GITARRE   IV/IIC1, VII-Mixed Coll

UNSERE WEIHNACHTSLIEDER   IV/I,
  VII-Mixed Coll

UNSERE WEIHNACHTSLIEDER   IV/IIB1,
  IV/IIC1, VII-Mixed Coll

UNTER STROM, FOR 3 INSTRUMENTALISTS
  see Kagel, Mauricio

UNTERHALTENDE MUSIK FUR SOLO-GITARRE:
  LEICHTE BIS MITTELSCHWERE
  GITARRESOLIS   I/IB6-Coll

UNTERHALTENDE MUSIK FUR SOLO-GITARRE:
  LIED UND TANZ VERSCHIEDENER LANDER
  I/IB6-Coll

UNTERHALTENDE MUSIK FUR SOLO-GITARRE:
  VOLKSLIED UND TANZ IN DEUTSCHLAND
  I/IB6-Coll

UNTERHALTUNGSSTUCKE, 10   see Giuliani,
  Mauro

URAY, ERNST LUDWIG (1906-   )
  Variationen Und Fuge Uber Ein
    Volkslied   I/IIA1

URBAN, STEPAN (1913-   )
  Andante Sostenuto   see Miniatures

  Cesta K Umelecke Hre Na Kytaru, Skola
    Vyssi Techniky   III

  Deset Fantasii, Na Lidove Motivy
    I/IB5

  Dobru Noc, Variacni Fantazie Na
    Lidovou Pisen   I/IB4

  Fresken, 5   I/IB4

  Good Night   see Dobru Noc, Variacni
    Fantazie Na Lidovou Pisen

  Impromptu Nos. 1-4   I/IB4

  Improvizujme Na Kytaru   II

URBAN, STEPAN (cont'd.)

  Lento   see Miniatures

  Little Phantasies, 10, On Folkmotives
    (Czech, Moravian And Slovak)   see
    Deset Fantasii, Na Lidove Motivy

  Miniatures   I/IB4

  Poco Vivo, Un   see Miniatures

  Vivace   see Miniatures

URIANS REISE UM DIE WELT   see Hiller,
  Johann Adam

USHER, TERRY (1909-1969)
  Canzoncina   I/IB4

  Impromptu, Op. 2, No. 1   I/IB4

  Sonata in A, Op. 3   I/IC

USPER, FRANCESCO (? -1641)
  Sinfonia in F   I/IIB5

UTWOROW NA LUTNIE LUB GITARE W STROJU
  E, 40   see Pekiel, Bartlomiej

UTWORY DAWNYCH MISTROW   I/IB2-Coll

UTWORY DAWNYCH MISTRZOW   I/IIA1-Coll,
  VII-Mixed Coll

UTWORY WYBRANE   see Giuliani, Mauro

UTWORY WYBRANE   see Horecki, Feliks

UTWORY WYBRANE   see Tarrega, Francisco

VACAS   see Ruiz de Ribayaz, Lucas

VACKAR, DALIBOR CYRIL (1906-1984)
  Charakteristikon   V/i

  Concerto for Trombone and Orchestra
    see Charakteristikon

VAEGTERSANG   see Grieg, Edvard Hagerup

VAGGVISA TILL SONEN CARL   see Bellman,
  Carl Michael

VAGHE BELLEZZE   see Fleres, Rita Maria

VAKANTIEDAGBOEK   see Furstenau, Wolfram

VALDEMOSA   see Grillaert, Oct

VALDERRABANO, ENRIQUEZ DE
  (fl. ca. 1550)
  Ay De Mi, Romance Viejo   I/IIC1

  Diferencias Sobre "La Pavana Real"
    I/IB1

  Fantaisie Du Quatrieme Ton   see
    Fantasy, MIN 270

  Fantasia XVI   see Fantasy, MIN 270

  Fantasy   I/IB1

  Fantasy, MIN 270   I/IB1

  Fugas, 2   I/IB1

  Guardame Las Vacas   I/IB1

  Pavanas   I/IB1

  Sonata No. 15   I/IB1

  Soneto Lombardo, A Manera De Danza
    I/IB1

  Ya Cabalga Calainos   I/IIC1

VALENCIA, JOSE DE
  Methode De Flamenco Pour La Guitare
    II

VALENCIANA   see Granados, Enrique,
  Danza Espanola, No. 7

VALENTINO, LA   see Canciones Populares
  Mexicanas, 3

VALERIA   see Takemitsu, Toru

VALERIUS, ADRIANUS (1575-1625)
  Gedenckklanken-ABC   I/IIB1

  Wenn Alle Untreu Werden   I/IIC2

VALLET, NICOLAS (1583-1626)
  Air Und Courante   I/IB1

  Allemande Fortune Helas Pourquoi
    I/IB1

  Solostucke   I/IB1

VALS BRILLANTE   see Chopin, Frederic;
  Chopin, Frederic, Waltz, Op. 34,
  No. 2

VALS DE LAS FLORES   see Tchaikovsky,
  Piotr Ilyich, Valse Des Fleurs

VALS MUY LENTO   see Granados, Enrique

VALS ROMANTICO   see Santorsola, Guido

VALS SOMBRIO   see Sanchez, B.

VALSA DAS FLORES   see Tchaikovsky,
  Piotr Ilyich, Valse Des Fleurs

VALSAS   see Brahms, Johannes

VALSE BLUETTE   see Drigo, Riccardo

VALSE CRIOLO   see Lauro, Augustin

VALSE DES FLEURS   see Tchaikovsky,
  Piotr Ilyich

VALSE ETUDE   see Giuliani, Mauro; Sor,
  Fernando

VALSE "LE DESIR"   see Beethoven, Ludwig
  van

VALSE LEGERE   see Shand, Ernest

VALSE TRISTE   see Mourat, Jean-Maurice;
  Pammer, Josef

VALSES VENEZOLANOS, 4   see Lauro,
  Antonio

6 VALSES   see Aguado, Dionisio

VALVERDE, JOAQUIN (1846-1910)
  Clavelitos   I/IIC1

  Clavelitos, Zambra Gitana   I/IB3

VALZER, 2, OP. 110 AND 76   see Strauss,
  Johann, [Sr.]

12 VALZER   see Giuliani, Mauro

VAN DELDEN, LEX
  see DELDEN, LEX VAN

VAN DER VELDEN, RENIER
  see VELDEN, RENIER VAN DER

VAN NIETS TOT IETS   see Verzijl, Hans

VAN V NAAR I   see Verzijl, Hans

VANDAAG IS HET MORGEN VAN GISTEREN   see
  Bois, Rob du

VANDERHORST, ADRIAN (ARAI)
  Learning The Classic Guitar   II,
    VII-Mixed Coll

  Minuet in D minor, BWV Anh. 132   see
    Learning The Classic Guitar

VANDERMAESBRUGGE, MAX (1933-   )
  Chansons De Pancruche, 5   I/IIC1

  Evocation   I/IB4

  Hesitation   see Petites Pieces, 3

  Miniature Variations   I/IB4

  Petites Pieces, 3   I/IB4

  Prelude   I/IB4

  Premier Pas   see Petites Pieces, 3

  Reveil   see Petites Pieces, 3

  Sonata   I/IC

VANHAL, JOHANN BAPTIST
  see WANHAL, JOHANN BAPTIST

VANHALL, JAN KRTITEL
  see WANHAL, JOHANN BAPTIST

VANNETELBOSCH, P.
  A Propos   I/IB4

VARIACION IV   see Beethoven, Ludwig van

VARIACIONES, 22, SOBRE CONDE CLAROS
  see Narvaez, Luis de, Variations,
  22, On The Romance "Conde Claros"

VARIACIONES BRILLANTES   see Aguado,
  Dionisio

VARIACIONES CONCERTANTES   see Giuliani,
  Mauro, Variazioni Concertanti

VARIACIONES SOBRE UN TEMA DE "DON
  GIOVANNI"   see Mozart, Wolfgang
  Amadeus

VARIACIONES SOBRE UN TEMA DE "LA FLAUTA MAGICA" DE W.A. MOZART   see Sor, Fernando, Introduction Et Variations Sur Un Theme De Mozart; Sor, Fernando, Introduction Et Variations Sur Un Theme De Mozart

VARIACIONES SOBRE UN TEMA DE MILAN, 6   see Nin-Culmell, Joaquin

VARIACIONES SOBRE UN TEMA DE SOR   see Llobet, Miguel

VARIATIES, 22, OVER DE ROMANCE CONDE CLAROS   see Narvaez, Luis de, Variations, 22, On The Romance "Conde Claros"

VARIATIONEN AUF EIN THEMA VON JAN RYCHLIK UND UBER SEINEN TOD   see Macha, Otmar

VARIATIONEN-SUITE   see Lechthaler, Josef

VARIATIONEN UBER 3 ALTE VOLKSLIEDER, 18   see Kammerling, Werner

6 VARIATIONEN UBER DAS THEMA "NEL COR PIU NON MI SENTO"   see Wanhal, Johann Baptist (Jan Krtitel)

VARIATIONEN UBER EIN EIGENES THEMA   see David, Johann Nepomuk

VARIATIONEN UBER EIN FRANZOSISCHES VOLKSLIED   see Sor, Fernando, Introduction Et Variations Sur l'Air "Marlbroug"

VARIATIONEN UBER EIN THEMA AUS DER OPER "DIE ZAUBERFLOTE" VON W.A. MOZART   see Sor, Fernando, Introduction Et Variations Sur Un Theme De Mozart

VARIATIONEN UBER EIN THEMA VON FRANZ SCHUBERT (DIE FORELLE)   see Friessnegg, Karl

VARIATIONEN UBER EIN THEMA VON HANDEL   see Giuliani, Mauro, Variazioni Su Un Tema Di Handel

VARIATIONEN UBER EIN THEMA VON MOZART   see Sor, Fernando, Introduction Et Variations Sur Un Theme De Mozart

VARIATIONEN UBER EIN THEMA VON W.A. MOZART   see Sor, Fernando, Introduction Et Variations Sur Un Theme De Mozart

VARIATIONEN UBER EINE ARIE AUS DER ZAUBERFLOTE VON W.A. MOZART   see Sor, Fernando, Introduction Et Variations Sur Un Theme De Mozart

VARIATIONEN UBER "GREENSLEEVES"   see Anonymous

VARIATIONEN UBER "LA FOLLIA"   see Giuliani, Mauro, Variazioni Sul Tema Della Follia Di Spagna

VARIATIONEN UBER "LE SONGE DE ROUSSEAU"   see Carcassi, Matteo

VARIATIONEN UBER "NEL COR PIU NON MI SENTO"   see Meissonnier, J.

VARIATIONEN UBER "O CARA ARMONIA" AUS MOZARTS ZAUBERFLOTE   see Sor, Fernando, Introduction Et Variations Sur Un Theme De Mozart

VARIATIONEN UND FUGE UBER EIN VOLKSLIED   see Uray, Ernst Ludwig

VARIATIONS, 6: OP87   see Giuliani, Mauro

VARIATIONS, 10, SUR "FOLIAS DE ESPANA" EN FORME DE CANON   see Sanchez, B.

VARIATIONS, 12, ON "AH, VOUS DIRAI-JE, MAMAN"   see Mozart, Wolfgang Amadeus

VARIATIONS, 12, SUR UN THEME DE MOZART   see Scheidler, Christian Gottlieb

VARIATIONS, 22, ON THE ROMANCE "CONDE CLAROS"   see Narvaez, Luis de

VARIATIONS A TRAVERS LES SIECLES   see Castelnuovo-Tedesco, Mario

VARIATIONS AND FUGUE ON A THEME OF HANDEL   see Harris, Albert

VARIATIONS EN FORME D'ETUDES, 10, SUR UNE BASSE CONTINUE   see Sanchez, Blas

VARIATIONS ON A CATALAN FOLK SONG   see Duarte, John W.

VARIATIONS ON A DUTCH NURSERY RHYME   see Schagen, Henk van, Botje (Berend) Varierend

VARIATIONS ON A FOLK-SONG   see Niessen, Hans-Lutz, Daar Gingen Twee Gespeelkens Goed, Variaties Op Een Volkslied

VARIATIONS ON A FRENCH NURSERY SONG   see Duarte, John W.

VARIATIONS ON A THEME FROM "THE TOWER OF KEL"   see Kerr, Harrison

VARIATIONS ON A THEME OF MOZART   see Sor, Fernando, Introduction Et Variations Sur Un Theme De Mozart

VARIATIONS ON A VENEZOLEAN CHILDREN'S SONG   see Lauro, Antonio

VARIATIONS PLAISANTES, SUR UN PETIT AIR POPULAIRE, "J'AI DU BON TABAC   see Castelnuovo-Tedesco, Mario

VARIATIONS SUR "FOLIA DE ESPANA" ET FUGUE   see Ponce, Manuel Maria

VARIATIONS SUR LES "FOLIES D'ESPAGNE", 7   see Carpentier, [Abbe] Joseph

VARIATIONS SUR MARLBROUGH S'EN VA-T-EN GUERRE   see Sor, Fernando, Introduction Et Variations Sur l'Air "Marlbroug"

VARIATIONS SUR UN THEME DE SCRIABINE   see Tansman, Alexandre

VARIATIONS SUR UN THEME OBSEDANT   see Pujol, Emilio

VARIAZIONI CONCERTANTI   see Giuliani, Mauro

VARIAZIONI DI BRAVURA   see Paganini, Niccolo

VARIAZIONI E FINALE, 4   see Giuliani, Mauro

VARIAZIONI SU L'ARIA "SCHISSERL UND A REINDL"   see Giuliani, Mauro

VARIAZIONI SU L'ARIETTA ITALIANA "SUL MARGINE D'UN RIO   see Carulli, Ferdinando

VARIAZIONI SU UN TEMA DAL BALLETTO "DIE FEINDLICHEN VOLLKSTAME"   see Giuliani, Mauro

VARIAZIONI SU UN TEMA DEL "FLAUTO MAGICO" DI W.A. MOZART   see Sor, Fernando, Introduction Et Variations Sur Un Theme De Mozart

VARIAZIONI SU UN TEMA DI BEETHOVEN   see Carulli, Ferdinando

VARIAZIONI SU UN TEMA DI HANDEL   see Giuliani, Mauro

VARIAZIONI SU UN TEMA ORIGINALE   see Giuliani, Mauro

VARIAZIONI SUL DUETTO "NEL COR PIU NON MI SENTO" DA "LA MOLINARA" DI PAISIELLO   see Legnani, Luigi

VARIAZIONI SUL TEMA DELLA FOLLIA DI SPAGNA   see Giuliani, Mauro

VARIAZIONI SULLA ROMANZA DALL'OPERA "RUHM UND LIEBE"   see Giuliani, Mauro

VARIAZIONI SULL'ARIA FAVORITA DE "LA MOLINARA"   see Giuliani, Mauro

VARIETIE OF LUTE-LESSONS, VOL. 1: CORANTOS   see Dowland, Robert

VARIETIE OF LUTE-LESSONS, VOL. 2: ALMAINES   see Dowland, Robert

VARIETIE OF LUTE-LESSONS, VOL. 3: VOLTES   see Dowland, Robert

VARIETIE OF LUTE-LESSONS, VOL. 4: FANTASIAS   see Dowland, Robert

VARIETIE OF LUTE-LESSONS, VOL. 5: GALLIARDS   see Dowland, Robert

VARIETIE OF LUTE-LESSONS, VOL. 6: PAVINS   see Dowland, Robert

VARIETY OF GUITAR MUSIC, A   I/IB6-Coll, VII-Mixed Coll

VASCONGADA   see Granados, Enrique

VASQUEZ, JUAN (fl. 1500)
    De Los Alamos Vengo   I/IIC1

    En La Fuente Del Rosel, Villancico   I/IIC1

    Vos Me Matastes, Villancico   I/IIC1

VATER UNSER, DER DU BIST IM HIMMEL; MELODY AFTER A LATIN-AMERICAN CALYPSO   see Blarr, Oskar Gottlieb

VECCHI, ORAZIO (HORATIO) (1550-1605)
    Aria   see Pezzi Per Liuto, 4

    Galliard   see Pezzi Per Liuto, 4

    Non Vuo Pregare   I/IIC1

    Pavan   see Pezzi Per Liuto, 4

    Pezzi Per Liuto, 4   I/IB1

    Saltarello   see Pezzi Per Liuto, 4

VEGLIA INVERNALE, RACCONTO   see Buscaroli, Rezio

VEILED OLD LAND, THE   see Gulda, Friedrich

20 AVRIL (PLANH)   see Ohana, Maurice, Si Le Jour Parait, No. 4

VELDEN, RENIER VAN DER (1910-   )
    Improvisation   I/IB4

VENECIANA   see Pujol, Emilio

VENEGAS DE HENESTROSA, TOMAS LUIS DE
    Fabordones, 2, Llano Y Glosado Del Cuarto Tono   I/IB1

VENETIAN BARCAROLLE   see Mendelssohn-Bartholdy, Felix

VENEZIANISCHES GONDELLIED, OP.19, NO.6   see Mendelssohn-Bartholdy, Felix

VENEZIANISCHES GONDELLIED, OP.30, NO.6   see Mendelssohn-Bartholdy, Felix

VENEZIANISCHES GONDELLIED, OP.62, NO.5   see Mendelssohn-Bartholdy, Felix

VENEZUELA; MUSIC FOR THE DOCUMENTARY FILM   see Jongen, Leon

VENEZUELAN PIECES, 2   see Lauro, Augustin

VENEZUELAN WALTZ, VALSE CRIOLLO   see Lauro, Antonio

VENITIENNE   see Rameau, Jean-Philippe

VERACINI, FRANCESCO MARIA (1690-1768)
    Largo   I/IIB1

    Sonata No. 3   I/IIB1

VERDONK, JAN
    Musette   I/IIB5

VERECZKEY, LASZLO
    A Gitar Hangotasa   III

    Stimmen Der Gitarre, Das   see A Gitar Hangotasa

VEREMANS, RENAAT (1894-1969)
    Petites Pieces, 3   I/IB4

VERGISS MEIN NICHT   see Monkemeyer, Helmut

VERGISS MEIN NICHT, DASS ICH DEIN NICHT   see Bach, Johann Sebastian

VERMELIA   see Benguerel, Xavier

VERSCHIEDENE STUCKE, VOL. 1   see Bach, Johann Sebastian

VERSCHIEDENE STUCKE, VOL. 2   see Bach, Johann Sebastian

VERSCHIEDENE STUCKE, VOL. 3   see Bach, Johann Sebastian

VERSUS   see Benguerel, Xavier

VERY EASY PIECES, FOR VERY, VERY BEGINNERS, OP.12   see Bobri, Vladimir

VERZIJL, HANS (1934-   )
    Kennismaken, Het   I/IA

    Van Niets Tot Iets   I/IA

    Van V Naar I   I/IA

VI SPELAR GITARR, METODISK HANDLEDNING FOR NYBORJARSTADIET, VOL. I see Larsen, Louis

VI SPELAR GITARR, METODISK HANDLEDNING FOR NYBORJARSTADIET, VOL. II see Larsen, Louis

VIA CRUCIS see Spaanse Volksliederen, 3 (3 Spanish Folksongs)

VIAJERO SOLITARIO see Grieg, Edvard Hagerup, Ensom Vandrer (Lonely Wanderer)

VIAJES see Bracali, Gian Paolo

VICOLO DELLE MIMOSE see Zuccheri, Luciano

VICTORIA, TOMAS LUIS DE (ca. 1548-1611)
   Ave Maria see Motets, 2

   Motets, 2 I/IB1

   Popule Meus see Motets, 2

VICTORY, OPERA IN 3 ACTS see Bennett, Richard Rodney

VIDALA see Broqua, Alfonso, Evocaciones Criollas, No.2

VIDALITA, CANCION ARGENTINA I/IB5

VIDALITA, CHANT POPULAIRE ARGENTIN I/IIC1-Coll

VIEJO CASTILLO, EL see Mussorgsky, Modest Petrovich

VIENI, DOLCE MORTE see Bach, Johann Sebastian, Komm Susser Tod

VIENS A TON AMANT see Chanson D'Amours Elizabethaines, 3

VIER JAPANISCHE VOLKSLIEDER I/IIC2-Coll

VIER LEICHTE STUCKE AUS OP. 35 see Sor, Fernando

VIER LEICHTE STUCKE FROM THE ANNA MAGDALENA BACH NOTENBUCHLEIN (1725) see Bach, Johann Sebastian

VIER WEVERKENS see Nederlandse Volksliederen, 3

VIERKLANGE see Schneider, Simon

VIGNEAULT, GILLES
   Doux Chagrin, Le I/IIC5

VILLA-LOBOS, HEITOR (1887-1959)
   A Canoa Virou, Cirandinha No. 10 I/IIA1

   Aria (Cantilena) I/IIC1

   Chorinho see Suite Populaire Bresilienne

   Choros, No. 1 I/IB4

   Concerto I/IIIA

   Distribution De Fleurs I/IIB1

   Etudes, 12 I/IA

   Gavotte see Suite Populaire Bresilienne

   Mazurka see Suite Populaire Bresilienne

   Preludes, 5 I/IB4

   Schottisch see Suite Populaire Bresilienne

   Sextuor Mystique V/i

   Suite Populaire Bresilienne I/IB4

   Terezinha De Jesus I/IIA1

   Waltz see Suite Populaire Bresilienne

VILLANCICO see Spaanse Volksliederen, 3 (3 Spanish Folksongs)

VILLANCICO ANDALUZ see Folksongs, 4

VILLANCICO NO. 5 ET FANTAISIE NO. 14 see Narvaez, Luis de

VILLANCICOS see Rodrigo, Joaquin

VILLANCICOS POPULARES, VOL. I IV/IIC1

VILLANCICOS POPULARES, VOL. II IV/IIC1

VILLANCICOS POPULARES, VOL. III I/IIC1-Coll, IV/IIC1

VILLANELLE: DITES AU CHEVALIER QUE see Pisador, Diego

VILLANESCA see Pisador, Diego

VILLANESCA see Pisador, Diego

VILLANESCA, DANZA CAMPESINA see Pujol, Emilio

VILLANESQUE see Morley, Thomas

VILLANO see Guerau, Francisco; Sanz, Gaspar

VILLANO, EL see Castelnuovo-Tedesco, Mario, Escarraman, A Suite Of Spanish Dances From The XVIth Century (After Cervantes)

VILLANO see Guerau, Francisco

VINAY, VITTORIO
   Thlayli I/IB4

VINGT-QUATRE EXERCICES TRES FACILES see Sor, Fernando

VINGT-QUATRE EXERCICES TRES FACILES, OP. 35, NO. 1 see Sor, Fernando

VINGT-QUATRE EXERCICES TRES FACILES, OP. 35, NO. 2 see Sor, Fernando

VINGT-QUATRE EXERCICES TRES FACILES, OP 35, NO. 3 see Sor, Fernando

VINGT-QUATRE EXERCICES TRES FACILES, OP. 35, NO. 13 see Sor, Fernando; Sor, Fernando

VINGT-QUATRE EXERCICES TRES FACILES, OP. 35, NO. 14 see Sor, Fernando

VINGT-QUATRE EXERCICES TRES FACILES, OP. 35, NO. 17 see Sor, Fernando

VINGT-QUATRE EXERCICES TRES FACILES, OP. 35, NO. 19 see Sor, Fernando

VINGT-QUATRE EXERCICES TRES FACILES, OP. 35, NO. 20 see Sor, Fernando

VINGT-QUATRE EXERCICES TRES FACILES, OP. 35, NO. 22 see Sor, Fernando

VINGT-QUATRE EXERCICES TRES FACILES, OP. 35, NO. 23 see Sor, Fernando; Sor, Fernando

VINGT-QUATRE EXERCICES TRES FACILES, OP. 35, NO. 24 see Sor, Fernando

VINGT-QUATRE EXERCISES TRES FACILES see Sor, Fernando

VINGT QUATRE LECONS PROGRESSIVES DEDIEES AUX ELEVES COMMENCANTS see Sor, Fernando; Sor, Fernando

VINGT QUATRE LECONS PROGRESSIVES, DEDIEES AUX ELEVES COMMENCANTS, OP 31., NO. 5 see Sor, Fernando; Sor, Fernando

VINGT QUATRE LECONS PROGRESSIVES, DEDIEES AUX ELEVES COMMENCANTS, OP. 31, NO. 19 see Sor, Fernando

VINGT QUATRE LECONS PROGRESSIVES DEDIEES AUX ELEVES COMMENCANTS, OP. 31, NO. 20 see Sor, Fernando

VINGT-QUATRE PETITES PIECES PROGRESSIVES POUR LA GUITARE, POUR SERVIR DE LECONS AUX ELEVES TOUT A FAIT COMMENCANTS, OP. 44, NO. 7 see Sor, Fernando

VINSON, HARVEY
   Play Classic Guitar II, VI-Mixed Coll, VII-Mixed Coll

VIOLIN SONATA NO. 2, VOL. 1: GRAVE AND FUGA see Bach, Johann Sebastian, Sonata for Violin, BWV 1003, in A minor

VIOLIN SONATA NO. 2, VOL. 2: ANDANTE AND ALLEGRO see Bach, Johann Sebastian, Sonata for Violin, BWV 1003, in A minor

VIOLONCELLO SUITE VI see Bach, Johann Sebastian, Suite for Violoncello, BWV 1012, in D

VIOZZI, GIULIO (1912-   )
   Fantasy I/IB4

4 VIRAGENEK see Huzella, Elek

VIRCHI, PAOLO (? -ca. 1610)
   Tanze, Canzonen Und Phantasien I/IB1

VIRGIN MARY HAD A BABY BOY, THE see O Black And Unknown Bards, 7 Negro Spirituals

VIRTUOSE GITARRESPIELS, DAS see Albert, Heinrich, Lehrgang Des Kunstlerischen Gitarrespiels, Vol. IV

VISEE, ROBERT DE (ca. 1650-ca. 1775)
   Allemand, MIN 314 see Suite E-Moll

   Allemand, MIN 317 see Suite E-Moll

   Allemand, MIN 318 see Suite E-Moll

   Allemand, MIN 351 I/IB1

   Allemand, VOCG 2 see Suite In A

   Allemand, VOCG 10 see Suite In A

   Allemand, VOCG 38 I/IB1
      see also Musica Del Re Sole; Suite C-Moll

   Allemand, VOCG 44 see Suite No. 7 En Do Mayor

   Allemand, VOCG 52 see Suite E-Dur; Suite En Sol Majeur

   Allemand, VOCG 62 see Beruhmte Suite In D-Moll; Petite Suite En Re Mineur, Pt. 1; Suite D-Moll; Suite D-Moll (Re Mineur); Suite En Re; Suite En Re Menor; Suite En Re Mineur; Suite En Re Mineur; Suite In Re

   Allemand, VOCG 72 see Suite En Sol Mineur; Suite G-Moll; Suite In Sol Minore

   Allemand, VOCG 86 see Musica Del Re Sole; Suite En La Et Passacaille; Suite H-Moll; Suite In H-Moll

   Beruhmte Suite In D-Moll I/IB1

   Bourree, VOCG 9 see Suite In A

   Bourree, VOCG 60 see Suite E-Dur; Suite En Sol Majeur

   Bourree, VOCG 67 see Beruhmte Suite In D-Moll; Darab Gitarra, 6 (6 Pieces Pour Guitare); Easy Suite In D Minor; Musica Del Re Sole; Petite Suite En Re Mineur, Pt. 2; Pieces, 6, Extraites Du Livre Publie En 1686 Et Dedie A S.M. Louis XIV; Piezas, 3; Suite D-Moll; Suite D-Moll (Re Mineur); Suite En Re; Suite En Re Menor; Suite En Re Mineur; Suite En Re Mineur; Suite In D-Moll

   Bourree, VOCG 79 see Suite G-Moll

   Chaconne, VOCG 57 see Suite E-Dur

   Chaconne, VOCG 77 see Suite En Sol Mineur; Suite In Sol Minore

   Courante, MIN 316 see Suite E-Moll

   Courante, VOCG 3 see Suite A-Moll; Suite In A

   Courante, VOCG 11 see Suite In A

   Courante, VOCG 28 see Suite E-Moll

   Courante, VOCG 39 see Suite C-Moll

   Courante, VOCG 45 see Suite No. 7 En Do Mayor

   Courante, VOCG 53 see Suite E-Dur; Suite En Sol Majeur

   Courante, VOCG 63 see Beruhmte Suite In D-Moll; Musica Del Re Sole; Petite Suite En Re Mineur, Pt. 2; Suite D-Moll; Suite D-Moll (Re Mineur); Suite En Re Menor; Suite En Re Mineur; Suite En Re Mineur

   Courante, VOCG 73 see Suite En Sol Mineur; Suite G-Moll; Suite In Sol Minore

   Danza see Suite En Re

   Darab Gitarra, 6 (6 Pieces Pour Guitare) I/IB1

VISEE, ROBERT DE (cont'd.)

Easy Suite In D Minor I/IB1

Gavotte, MIN 319 see Suite A-Moll

Gavotte, VOCG 7 see Suite Em La;
Suite In A; Suite In A

Gavotte, VOCG 8 see Suite In A

Gavotte, VOCG 42 see Suite C-Moll

Gavotte, VOCG 48 see Suite No. 7 En
Do Mayor

Gavotte, VOCG 58 see Suite E-Dur;
Suite En Sol Majeur

Gavotte, VOCG 66 see Beruhmte Suite
In D-Moll; Darab Gitarra, 6 (6
Pieces Pour Guitare); Easy Suite
In D Minor; Musica Del Re Sole;
Petite Suite En Re Mineur, Pt. 2;
Pieces, 6, Extraites Du Livre
Publie En 1686 Et Dedie A S.M.
Louis XIV; Piezas, 3; Suite D-
Moll; Suite D-Moll (Re Mineur);
Suite En Re; Suite En Re Menor;
Suite En Re Mineur; Suite En Re
Mineur; Suite In D-Moll

Gavotte, VOCG 78 I/IB1
see also Musica Del Re Sole; Suite
En La Et Passacaille; Suite G-
Moll

Gavotte, VOCG 116 see Suite A-Moll

Giga A La Manera Inglesa see Suite
No. 7 En Do Mayor

Gigue, MIN 321 see Suite A-Moll

Gigue, VOCG 5 see Suite In A

Gigue, VOCG 47 see Suite No. 7 En Do
Mayor

Gigue, VOCG 55 see Suite E-Dur;
Suite En Sol Majeur

Gigue, VOCG 65 see Beruhmte Suite In
D-Moll; Musica Del Re Sole;
Petite Suite En Re Mineur, Pt. 1;
Piezas, 4; Suite D-Moll; Suite D-
Moll (Re Mineur); Suite En Re;
Suite En Re Menor; Suite En Re
Mineur; Suite En Re Mineur; Suite
In Re

Gigue, VOCG 75 see Musica Del Re
Sole; Piezas, 4; Suite A-Moll;
Suite En La Et Passacaille; Suite
En Sol Mineur; Suite G-Moll;
Suite In Sol Minore

Gigue, VOCG 82 see Musica Del Re
Sole; Piezas, 4; Suite Em La;
Suite En La Et Passacaille

Gigue, VOCG 88 see Suite H-Moll;
Suite In H-Moll

Gitarrenbuch see Livre De Guitarre
Dedie Au Roy (1682)

Gitarrenstucke see Livre De Pieces
Pour La Guitarre (1686)

Livre De Guitarre Dedie Au Roy (1682)
I/IB1

Livre De Pieces Pour La Guitarre
(1686) I/IB1

Minuet, MIN 313 see Suite En Re
Mineur

Minuet, VOCG 49 see Suite No. 7 En
Do Mayor

Minuet, VOCG 59 see Suite E-Dur;
Suite En Sol Majeur

Minuet, VOCG 68 see Darab Gitarra, 6
(6 Pieces Pour Guitare); Easy
Suite In D Minor; Musica Del Re
Sole; Petite Suite En Re Mineur,
Pt. 2; Pieces, 6, Extraites Du
Livre Publie En 1686 Et Dedie A
S.M. Louis XIV; Piezas, 3; Suite
D-Moll; Suite D-Moll (Re Mineur);
Suite En Re Menor; Suite En Re
Mineur; Suite En Re Mineur; Suite
In D-Moll

Minuet, VOCG 70 see Beruhmte Suite
In D-Moll; Darab Gitarra, 6 (6
Pieces Pour Guitare); Easy Suite
In D Minor; Musica Del Re Sole;
Petite Suite En Re Mineur, Pt. 2;
Pieces, 6, Extraites Du Livre
Publie En 1686 Et Dedie A S.M.
Louis XIV; Suite D-Moll; Suite D-
Moll (Re Mineur); Suite En

VISEE, ROBERT DE (cont'd.)

Menor; Suite En Re Mineur; Suite
In D-Moll; Suite In Re

Minuet, VOCG 76 see Suite A-Moll;
Suite En Sol Mineur; Suite G-
Moll; Suite In Sol Minore

Minuet, VOCG 80 see Suite G-Moll

Minuet, VOCG 84 see Musica Del Re
Sole; Suite Em La; Suite En La Et
Passacaille; Suite In A

Minuet, VOCG 91 I/IB1
see also Darab Gitarra, 6 (6 Pieces
Pour Guitare); Easy Suite In D
Minor; Musica Del Re Sole;
Pieces, 6, Extraites Du Livre
Publie En 1686 Et Dedie A S.M.
Louis XIV; Suite In D-Moll

Musica Del Re Sole I/IB1

Oeuvres Completes Pour Guitare
I/IB1-Coll

Passacaglia, MIN 322 see Suite A-
Moll

Passacaglia, VOCG 6 see Suite In A

Passacaglia, VOCG 69 see Petite
Suite En Re Mineur, Pt. 2

Passacaglia, VOCG 92 I/IB1
see also Musica Del Re Sole; Suite
En La Et Passacaille; Suite In H-
Moll

Pastorale, MIN 320 see Suite A-Moll

Petite Suite En Re Mineur, Pt. 1
I/IB1

Petite Suite En Re Mineur, Pt. 2
I/IB1

Pieces, 6, Extraites Du Livre Publie
En 1686 Et Dedie A S.M. Louis XIV
I/IB1

Piezas, 3 I/IB1

Piezas, 4 I/IB1

Prelude, VOCG 1 see Suite En La Et
Passacaille; Suite In A

Prelude, VOCG 37 see Suite C-Moll

Prelude, VOCG 43 see Suite No. 7 En
Do Mayor

Prelude, VOCG 51 see Suite E-Dur;
Suite En Sol Majeur

Prelude, VOCG 61 see Beruhmte Suite
In D-Moll; Petite Suite En Re
Mineur, Pt. 1; Suite D-Moll;
Suite D-Moll (Re Mineur); Suite
En Re; Suite En Re Menor; Suite
En Re Mineur; Suite En Re Mineur;
Suite In Re

Prelude, VOCG 71 see Suite En Sol
Mineur; Suite G-Moll; Suite In
Sol Minore

Prelude, VOCG 85 see Suite Em La;
Suite H-Moll; Suite In A; Suite
In H-Moll

Saraband, MIN 315 see Suite E-Moll

Saraband, VOCG 4 see Suite In A

Saraband, VOCG 12 see Suite In A

Saraband, VOCG 40 see Suite C-Moll

Saraband, VOCG 41 see Suite C-Moll

Saraband, VOCG 46 see Suite No. 7 En
Do Mayor

Saraband, VOCG 54 see Suite E-Dur

Saraband, VOCG 56 see Suite E-Dur;
Suite En Sol Majeur

Saraband, VOCG 64 see Beruhmte Suite
In D-Moll; Musica Del Re Sole;
Petite Suite En Re Mineur, Pt. 1;
Suite D-Moll; Suite D-Moll (Re
Mineur); Suite En Re; Suite En Re
Menor; Suite En Re Mineur; Suite
En Re Mineur; Suite In Re

Saraband, VOCG 74 see Suite En Sol
Mineur; Suite G-Moll; Suite In
Sol Minore

VISEE, ROBERT DE (cont'd.)

Saraband, VOCG 83 see Musica Del Re
Sole; Suite Em La; Suite En La Et
Passacaille; Suite In A

Saraband, VOCG 87 see Darab Gitarra,
6 (6 Pieces Pour Guitare); Musica
Del Re Sole; Pieces, 6, Extraites
Du Livre Publie En 1686 Et Dedie
A S.M. Louis XIV; Piezas, 4;
Suite En La Et Passacaille; Suite
H-Moll; Suite In D-Moll; Suite In
H-Moll

Saraband, VOCG 90 I/IB1

Saraband, VOCG 115 see Suite E-Moll

Suite A-Moll I/IB1

Suite C-Moll I/IB1

Suite D-Moll I/IB1

Suite D-Moll (Re Mineur) I/IB1

Suite E-Dur I/IB1

Suite E-Moll I/IB1

Suite Em La I/IB1

Suite En La Et Passacaille I/IB1

Suite En Re I/IB1

Suite En Re Menor I/IB1

Suite En Re Mineur I/IB1

Suite En Re Mineur I/IB1

Suite En Re Mineur I/IB1

Suite En Si Mineur Et 8 Pieces Du
Deuxieme Livre I/IB1

Suite En Sol Majeur I/IB1

Suite En Sol Mineur I/IB1

Suite G-Moll I/IB1

Suite H-Moll I/IB1

Suite In A I/IB1

Suite In A I/IB1

Suite in C minor I/IIB1

Suite in D minor I/IB1

Suite In D-Moll I/IB1

Suite in G I/IB1

Suite In H-Moll I/IB1

Suite In Re I/IB1

Suite In Sol Minore I/IB1

Suite No. 7 En Do Mayor I/IB1

Tombeau De Francois Corbetta, Le see
Allemand, VOCG 38

VISIONS CONCERTANTES, CONCERTO EN 4
PARTIES D'APRES 4 TOILES DE
SALVADOR DALI see Chaynes, Charles

VISIT TO A MUSEUM, A see Gall, Louis
Ignatius

VISOR, 50, TILL LUTA OCH GITARR see
Taube, Evert

VISOR PA GITARR I/IB6-Coll

VISSER, DICK (1927-   )
Another Encore For Yepes I/IB4

Anti- En Symmetria, Studie I/IA

Etudes, 4 I/IA

Expo I/IIA1

Expressieve Muziek I/IB4

Luitspeler, De, Hommage A Frans Hals
I/IB4

Studies, 12, Vol. 1 I/IA

Studies, 12, Vol. 2 I/IA

Studies, 12, Vol. 3 I/IA

Suite In Rasgueado En Punteado I/IB4

VISSER, DICK (cont'd.)

Tarrega Etcetera, Dagelijkse Studies
III, VI-Coll

Tarrega Etcetera, Daily Studies see
Tarrega Etcetera, Dagelijkse
Studies

Technical Studies For The Guitar,
Vol. I: Chromatic Scales III

Technical Studies For The Guitar,
Vol. II: Arpeggios III

Technical Studies For The Guitar,
Vol. III: Interval-Systems III

Technical Studies For The Guitar,
Vol. IV: Diatonic Scales And
Scale-Systems III

Technical Studies For The Guitar,
Vol. V: Legato-Vibrato III

Technical Studies For The Guitar,
Vol. VI: Chords a.o. Cadences;
Broken Chords III

Technical Studies For The Guitar,
Vol. VII: Right Hand Formulas;
Glissando; Tremolo; Rasgueado;
Harmonics; Pizzicato; etc. III

VISUAL AIDS TO CHORD ARPEGGIOS see
Mairants, Ivor

VITA DE L'ALMA MIA see Monteverdi,
Claudio

VITA SENESE see Smith Brindle,
Reginald

VITO, EL I/IB5

VITTORIA, LUDOVICO
see VICTORIA, TOMAS LUIS DE

VITTORIA, TOMASSO
see VICTORIA, TOMAS LUIS DE

VIVA LA GUITARRA see Wolf, Roland;
Wolf, Roland

VIVA LA MUSICA; CANONS (2-4 PARTS)
I/IIB5-Coll

VIVACE see Legley, Victor; Urban,
Stepan

VIVACE CON BRIO see Giuliani, Mauro

VIVALDI, ANTONIO (1678-1741)
Andante in E minor I/IIA1

Aria Del Vagante I/IIA1

Concerto I/IIB2

Concerto for Violin and Orchestra, RV
297, in F minor, Largo I/IIA1

Concerto in A I/IIIA

Concerto in C I/IIB2, I/IIIA, I/IIIC

Concerto in D I/IIIA

Concerto in D, MIN 328 I/IIB1

Concerto in D, MIN 388 I/IB1

Concerto in D minor for Viola
d'Amore, Lute and Strings I/IIIC

Concerto No. 3 in G I/IIIB

Concerto No. 23 in C for 2 Mandolins
and Strings I/IIIB

Gigue I/IB1

Largo De L'Hiver see Concerto for
Violin and Orchestra, RV 297, in
F minor, Largo

Lautenkonzert see Concerto in A

Prelude, MIN 44 I/IIA1

Sonata in D minor I/IIB1

Sonata in G minor I/IIB1

Sonata, Op. 13a, No. 16, in G minor
I/IIB1

Trio in G minor, MIN 326 I/IIB2

VIVE HENRI IV, CHANSON FRANCAISE
I/IIC1-Coll

VIVO E BURLESCO see Staak, Pieter van
der

VIVO, RITMICO see Kovats, Barna

VLAD, ROMAN (1919-)
Ode Super "Chrysea Phorminx" I/IIIA

VLIJMEN, JAN VAN (1935-   )
Interpolations V/i

Serenata II, Per Flauto E Quattro
Gruppi Strumentali V/i

VOGELWEIDER, DER see Tittel, Ernst

VOGT, HANS (1911-   )
Athenerkomodie; Opera Giocosa In One
Act V/iii

Metropolitans, The; Opera Giocosa In
One Act see Athenerkomodie;
Opera Giocosa In One Act

Monologe, 4 Symphonic Pieces For Full
Orchestra V/i

Sine Nomine V/ii

VOICE OF THE PHOENIX, THE see Boyd,
Anne

VOICES FOR ENSEMBLE see Krauze,
Zygmunt

VOILES D'IRISATIONS see Miroglio,
Francis

VOLKS- UND KINDERLIEDER I/IIB2,
I/IIB2-Coll, IV/IIB2

VOLKSLIED UND LAUTE I/IIC1-Coll

VOLKSLIED UND TANZ; EIN TASCHENBUCH
I/IB5-Coll

VOLKSLIED ZUR GITARRE, DAS see Albert,
Heinrich, Lehrgang Des
Kunstlerischen Gitarrespiels, Fur
Lehrzwecke Und Zum
Selbstunterricht, Vol. I-A; Albert,
Heinrich, Lehrgang Des
Kunstlerischen Gitarrespiels, Fur
Lehrzwecke Und Zum
Selbstunterricht, Vol. I-B

VOLKSLIEDCHEN see Schumann, Robert
(Alexander)

VOLKSLIEDER I/IIC1-Coll, IV/IIC1

VOLKSLIEDER AUS ALLER WELT, VOL. I:
ENGLAND I/IIC1-Coll

VOLKSLIEDER AUS ALLER WELT, VOL. II:
FRANKREICH I/IIC1-Coll

VOLKSLIEDER AUS ALLER WELT, VOL. III:
SPANIEN, PORTUGAL I/IIC1-Coll

VOLKSLIEDER AUS ALLER WELT, VOL. IV:
ITALIEN I/IIC1-Coll

VOLKSLIEDER AUS ALLER WELT, VOL. V:
GRIECHENLAND I/IIC1-Coll

VOLKSLIEDER AUS ALLER WELT, VOL. VI:
TURKEI I/IIC1-Coll

VOLKSLIEDER AUS ALLER WELT, VOL. VII:
BALKAN (UNGARN, RUMANIEN,
BULGARIEN, JUGOSLAWIEN)
I/IIC1-Coll

VOLKSLIEDER AUS ALLER WELT, VOL. VIII:
RUSSLAND I/IIC1-Coll

VOLKSLIEDER AUS ALLER WELT, VOL.IX:
POLEN, LETTLAND I/IIC1-Coll

VOLKSLIEDER AUS ALLER WELT, VOL. X:
DEUTSCHLAND I/IIC1-Coll

VOLKSLIEDER AUS ALLER WELT, VOL. XI:
AMERIKA I/IIC1-Coll

VOLKSLIEDER AUS ALLER WELT, VOL. XII:
INDONESIEN I/IIC1-Coll

VOLKSLIEDER DES AUSLANDES, VOL. I:
SPANISCHE LIEDER I/IIC1-Coll

VOLKSLIEDER DES AUSLANDES, VOL. II:
ITALIENISCHE LIEDER I/IIC1-Coll

VOLKSLIEDER DES AUSLANDES, VOL. III:
RUSSISCHE LIEDER I/IIC1-Coll

VOLKSLIEDER FUR GITARRE-SOLOSPIEL
I/IB5-Coll

VOLKSLIEDER MIT VARIATIONEN, 2 see
Rein, Walter

VOLKSLIEDER UND -TANZE AUS ALLER WELT,
VOL. 1 I/IIB1, I/IIB1-Coll

VOLKSLIEDER UND -TANZE AUS ALLER WELT,
VOL. 2 I/IIB1, I/IIB1-Coll

VOLKSLIEDER UND -TANZE AUS ALLER WELT,
VOL. 3 I/IIB1, I/IIB1-Coll

VOLKSLIEDER ZUM SINGEN UND SPIELEN
I/IB5-Coll, I/IIC1-Coll

VOLKSLIEDERBUCH ZUR GITARRE, VOL. I:
KINDERLIEDER I/IIC1-Coll

VOLKSLIEDERBUCH ZUR GITARRE, VOL. II:
WANDER- UND ABSCHIEDSLIEDER
I/IIC1-Coll

VOLKSLIEDERFIBEL FUR DEN
GITARRENUNTERRICHT see Yeo-
Siebald, Else

VOLKSLIEDSATZE see David, Johann
Nepomuk

VOLKSMUSIK AUS OSTERREICH, VOL. I:
VOLKSMUSIK AUS KARNTEN I/IIB2-Coll

VOLKSMUSIK AUS OSTERREICH, VOL. II:
VOLKSMUSIK AUS TIROL I/IIB2-Coll

VOLKSMUSIK AUS OSTERREICH, VOL. III:
VOLKSMUSIK AUS STEIERMARK UND
BURGENLAND I/IIB2-Coll

VOLKSMUSIK AUS OSTERREICH, VOL. IV:
VOLKSMUSIK AUS VORARLBERG
I/IIB2-Coll

VOLKSTANZE, 3 I/IIB5-Coll

VOLKSTANZE, 6 I/IIA2-Coll

VOLKSTANZE UND LIEDER I/IIA2-Coll,
I/IIB2

VOLKSTUMLICHE GITARRESPIEL, DAS, KURZ-
LEHRGANG FUR DEN GRUPPEN- UND
EINZEL- BZW. SELBSTUNTERRICHT see
Holz, Franz

VOLKSTUMLICHE GITARRESPIEL, DAS, KURZ-
LEHRGANG FUR DEN GRUPPEN- UND
EINZEL- BZW. SELBSTUNTERRICHT,
SUPPL. 1: DIE GITARRE IN BILD UND
TON see Holz, Franz

VOLKSTUMLICHE GITARRESPIEL, DAS, KURZ-
LEHRGANG FUR DEN GRUPPEN- UND
EINZEL- BZW. SELBSTUNTERRICHT,
SUPPL. 2: GRIFFBILDSCHEMA see
Holz, Franz

VOLKSTUMLICHE GITARRESPIEL, DAS, KURZ-
LEHRGANG FUR DEN GRUPPEN- UND
EINZEL- BZW. SELBSTUNTERRICHT,
SUPPL. 3: LIEDERTEXTBLATT see
Holz, Franz

VOLKSWEISE MIT VARIATIONEN, "ICH GING
DURCH EINEN GRASGRUNEN WALD" see
Teuchert, Heinz

VOLKSWEISEN AUS OSTERREICH I/IB5-Coll

VOLKSWEISEN DER WELT, VOL. I
I/IB5-Coll

VOLKSWEISEN DER WELT, VOL. II
I/IB5-Coll

VOLKSWEISEN DER WELT, VOL. III
I/IB5-Coll

VOLKSWEISEN UND TANZE AUS ARGENTINIEN
I/IIB2-Coll, I/IIB4-Coll

VOLLSTANDIGE GUITARRE-SCHULE see
Carcassi, Matteo

VOLO D'ANGELI, SUL NOME DI ANGELO
GILARDINO see Castelnuovo-Tedesco,
Mario

VOLTA see Praetorius, Michael

VOLTA ALLA FRANCESE see Melii da
Reggio, Pietro Paolo

VOLTE I see Sweelinck, Jan Pieterszoon

VOLTE II see Sweelinck, Jan
Pieterszoon

VOLTE III see Sweelinck, Jan
Pieterszoon

VOLTES, 2 see Sweelinck, Jan
Pieterszoon

VOM HIMMEL HOCH see Praetorius,
Michael

VOM HIMMEL HOCH, DA KOMM ICH HER.
CHORALE see Bach, Johann Sebastian

VOM HIMMEL HOCH, IHR ENGLEIN KOMMT see Spitta, Heinrich, Weihnachtliche Liedkantate

VOM PUSTEWIND UND ANDEREN SACHEN, NEUE LIEDER FUR DIE VORSCHULERZIEHUNG I/IIC1-Coll

VOM VIELFALTIGEN LEBEN see Rein, Walter

VON DER BERGESHOH' see Zanke, Herman, Berglied

VON DER KOCHERIE, EIN KULINARISCHES LOBLIED, CONATUM 47 see Kunad, Rainer

VON FREMDEN LANDERN UND MENSCHEN see Schumann, Robert (Alexander)

VON HANDEL BIS HAYDN I/IIB1-Coll

VON MAUSEN, AUTOS UND ANDEREN TIEREN; 25 KINDERLIEDER ZUM SINGEN UND SPIELEN see Bresgen, Cesar

VOOR HET MOOIE HANDJE, VOL. I: MELODIE-AANSLAG see Schagen, Henk van

VOOR SAMENSPEL EN GROEPSLES, VOL. I see Gall, Louis Ignatius

VOOR SAMENSPEL EN GROEPSLES, VOL. II see Gall, Louis Ignatius

VOOR SAMENSPEL EN GROEPSLES, VOL. III see Gall, Louis Ignatius

VOOR SAMENSPEL EN GROEPSLES, VOL. IV see Gall, Louis Ignatius

VOOR SAMENSPEL EN GROEPSLES, VOL. V see Gall, Louis Ignatius

VOOR SAMENSPEL EN GROEPSLES, VOL. VI see Gall, Louis Ignatius

VOOR VAARDIGE VINGERS see Schagen, Henk van

VOOR VLIJTIGE VINGERS see Schagen, Henk van

VOR LAUTER LIEB UND LUST, LEICHTE SATZE ZU ALTEN LIEDERN I/IIC5-Coll

VORRIA, MADONNA see Anonymous

VORSCHULE FUR GITARRE see Gerrits, Paul

VORSPRUCH ZU EINEM WEIHNACHTSSPIEL see Dietrich, Christoph

11 VORTRAGSSTUCKE (LONDON MS) see Weiss, Sylvius Leopold

VORTRAGSSTUCKE FUR ANFANGER see Diabelli, Anton

VOS ME MATASTES, VILLANCICO see Vasquez, Juan

VOSTRAK, ZBYNEK (1920-   )
Schneewittchen; Ballet In Four Acts And Seven Scenes V/iii

Schneewittchen: Suite V/i

VOU-VERI-VOU see Thomas, Juan Maria

VOUS ME JURIEZ, BERGERE see Besard, Jean-Baptiste

VOUS NE VOULEZ DONC PAS ME PARLER see Pues No Me Quereis Habler

VOYONS SI C'EST CA, 6 PETITES PIECES FACILES see Sor, Fernando

VOYONS SI C'EST CA, 6 PETITES PIECES FACILES NOS. 2, 6 see Sor, Fernando

VOYONS SI C'EST CA, 6 PETITES PIECES FACILES, OP. 45, NO. 4 see Sor, Fernando

VOYONS SI C'EST CA, 6 PETITES PIECES FACILES, OP. 45, NO. 5 see Sor, Fernando

VOYONS SI C'EST CA, 6 PETITES PIECES FACILES, OP. 45, NO. 6 see Sor, Fernando

VREEMDE FLUITIST, DE see Masseus, Jan

VRIES, F. DE
Eerste Oefeningen In Het Gitaarspel II

VRIES, KLAAS DE (1944-   )
Follia V/i

VRIES ROBBE, WILLEM DE (1902-   )
Danse-Arioso-Rondeau I/IIB1

Pavane-Sarabande-Gigue I/IIB1

VROLIJKE LANDMAN, DE see Gitaarduet, Het

VYBER SKLADEB, SELECTED COMPOSITIONS, VOL. I see Tarrega, Francisco

VYBER SKLADEB, SELECTED COMPOSITIONS, VOL. II see Tarrega, Francisco

VZPOMINKY NA ALHAMBRU : ERINNERUNGEN AN DIE ALHAMBRA see Tarrega, Francisco, Study, TI ii- 9, in A minor

WAGENSEIL, GEORG CHRISTOPH (1715-1777)
Divertimento I/IIB1

WAGNER, GERHARD D.
Impreciones Mexicanas, Vol. I: Las Ruinas De Mitla I/IIA1

Impreciones Mexicanas, Vol. II: Lago De Texcoco I/IIA1

Impreciones Mexicanas, Vol. III: La Tristeza De Malintzin I/IIA1

WAGNER-REGENY, RUDOLF (1903-1969)
Miniaturen, 5 I/IB4

Sonatina I/IC

WAHRE FREUNDSCHAFT SOLL NICHT WANKEN I/IIC2

WAISSEL(IUS), MATTHAUS (ca. 1540-1602)
Phantasia Und Deutscher Tanz I/IB1

WALDMARCHEN see Thienemann, H.

WALKER, LUISE (1910-   )
Argentinische Weise, Triste I/IB5

Brasilianisch I/IA, I/IB4

Etude in C see Tanzlied

Etude in E see Brasilianisch

Fur Den Anfang, Vol. 1 I/IA

Fur Den Anfang, Vol. 2 I/IA

Fur Den Anfang, Vol. 3 I/IA

Fur Den Anfang, Vol. 4 I/IA

Fur Den Anfang, Vol. 5 I/IA

Fur Den Anfang, Vol. 6 I/IA

Gaucho I/IB4

Kleine Romanze I/IB4

Marsch Nach Einer Tiroler Melodie I/IA, I/IB4

Miniaturen, 10 Kleine Stucke I/IB4

Regenetude I/IA

Tagliche Training, Das, Tonleitern Und Technische Studien III

Tanzlied I/IA

Tanzlied, Etude C-Dur I/IB4

WALKING IN A COUNTRY TOWNE see Robinson, Thomas

WALSEN, 9 see Schubert, Franz (Peter)

WALSINGHAM see 4 Pieces By Dowland, Cutting, Morley; Cutting, Francis

WALSINGHAM VARIATIONS see Cutting, Francis, Walsingham

WALTER, FRIED (1907-   )
Pavan I/IIIA

Reflexe, Variationen Durch Die Jahrhundert Uber Ein Thema Von Gaspar Sanz I/IIIA

Suite I/IB4

WALTON, [SIR] WILLIAM (TURNER) (1902-1983)
Anon. In Love; 6 Anonymous 16th- And 17th-Century Lyrics I/IIC1

Fain Would I Change That Note see Anon. In Love; 6 Anonymous 16th- And 17th-Century Lyrics

WALTON, [SIR] WILLIAM (TURNER) (cont'd.)

I Gave Her Cakes And I Gave Her Ale see Anon. In Love; 6 Anonymous 16th- And 17th-Century Lyrics

Lady, When I Behold The Roses see Anon. In Love; 6 Anonymous 16th- And 17th-Century Lyrics

My Love In Her Attire see Anon. In Love; 6 Anonymous 16th- And 17th-Century Lyrics

O Stay, Sweet Love see Anon. In Love; 6 Anonymous 16th- And 17th-Century Lyrics

WALTZ AND RONDO see Carulli, Ferdinando

WALZ-QUADRILLE see Volkstanze, 6

WALZER, 6 see Sor, Fernando, Six Waltzes

WANEK, FRIEDRICH K. (1929-   )
Ten Essays I/IB4

WANGLER, RUDOLF
6 Saiten-10 Finger II

WANHAL, JOHANN BAPTIST (JAN KRTITEL) (1739-1813)
Cantabile I/IB2

Minuette, 2 I/IB2

6 Variationen Uber Das Thema "Nel Cor Piu Non Mi Sento" I/IIB1

WAR DANCE see Staak, Pieter van der

WARD-STEINMAN, DAVID (1936-   )
Quiet Dance I/IIB3

WARNER, THEODOR (1903)
Arme Schuster, Der, Ein Grosses Singspiel, Nach Einem Marchen Der Bruder Grimm I/IIC5

WARUM BETRUBST DU DICH see Bach, Johann Sebastian

WAS EEN MAGED UITVERKOREN, HET see Nederlandse Volksliederen, 3

WAS SOLL ES BEDEUTEN see Weihnachtslieder, 5

WAT FRANSEN ZINGEN EN DANSEN, FRANSE WIJSJES; 10 FRENCH TUNES I/IB5-Coll

WATER...FOOTSTEPS...TIME see Conyngham, Barry

WATER-FOOTSTEPS-TIMES, FOR FOUR INSTRUMENTAL SOLOISTS AND TWO ORCHESTRA see Conyngham, Barry

WATER MUSIC AIR see Handel, George Frideric

WATKINS, MICHAEL BLAKE (1948-   )
Solus For Guitar I/IB4

W'DODI AWAR see Staak, Pieter van der

WEBER, CARL MARIA VON (1786-1826)
Divertimento, Op. 38 I/IIB1

Duo I/IIA1

Gitarrelieder I/IIC1

Menuetto And Trio I/IIB2

Waltz I/IB2

WEBER, REINHOLD
Miniaturen, 5 I/IIA1

WEBERN, ANTON VON (1883-1945)
Funf Stucke Fur Orchester V/i

Lieder, 2, Op. 19 V/ii

Lieder, 3, Op.18 I/IIC2

Weiss Wie Lilien see Lieder, 2, Op. 19

Zieh'n Die Schafe see Lieder, 2, Op. 19

WEG HINAB NACH JERICHO, DER see Ogo, [Choral Brother]

WEG ZUM KUNSTLERISCHEN GITARRESPIEL, DER, VOL. 1: ELEMENTE DES GITARRESPIELS see Sack, Georg Christian

WEG ZUM SOLOSPIEL AUF DER GITARRE, DER
   see Peter, Ursula,
   Anfangsunterricht Im Gitarrespiel,
   Der, Vol. III

WEGE see Burghauser, Jarmil

WEIHNACHT - 8 ALTE LIEDER IV/I,
   IV/IIB3, IV/IIC1, IV/IIC3

WEIHNACHTLICHE LIEDKANTATE see Spitta,
   Heinrich

WEIHNACHTLICHES SPIEL IV/IIB4

WEIHNACHTS-ALBUM, SAMMLUNG DER
   BELIEBTESTEN WEIHNACHTSLIEDER
   IV/IIC1

WEIHNACHTS-SINGSPIEL NACH ALTEN
   LIEDERN, EIN see Stern, Alfred
   Bernard

WEIHNACHTSGESCHICHTE see Behrend,
   Siegfried

WEIHNACHTSKANTATE FUR JUNGE LEUTE see
   Wusthoff, Klaus

WEIHNACHTSLIEDER, 5 IV/IIC2, IV/IIC3

11 WEIHNACHTSLIEDER IV/IIC1

WEIHNACHTSLIEDER IV/I

WEIHNACHTSLIEDER IV/IIC1

WEIHNACHTSLIEDER AUS DEUTSCHLAND UND
   OSTERREICH IV/IIB1, IV/IIC1,
   VII-Mixed Coll

WEIHNACHTSLIEDER ZUR GITARRE IV/I,
   IV/IIC1

WEIHNACHTSSTERN, DER, ALTE UND NEUE
   LIEDER IV/IIC5

WEIHNACHTSZEIT - FROHLICHE ZEIT,
   ALTBEKANNTE UND NEUERE
   WEIHNACHTSLIEDER IV/I, IV/IIC1

WEIKMANN, CHARLES
   Guitar For Beginners I/IB4

WEILL, KURT (1900-1950)
   Aufstieg Und Fall Der Stadt
     Mahagonny: Suite V/iii

   Berliner Requiem V/ii

   Dreigroschenoper: Suite V/iii

   Jasager, Der, Schoolopera In 2 Acts
     I/IIC5-Coll

   Kleine Dreigroschenmusik V/iii

   Surabaya Johnny V/ii

WEINACHT, WIE BIST DO SCHON see Rinke
   Ranke Rosenschein; 77 Kinderlieder

WEINER, STANLEY (1925-   )
   Sonata, Op. 22, No. 1 I/IC

WEISS, HARALD (1949-   )
   Impressionen I/IB4

WEISS, JOHANN ADOLF
   Concerto I/IIIA

   Leichte Duette, 6 I/IIA1

WEISS, SYLVIUS LEOPOLD (1686-1750)
   Air in E I/IB1

   Angloise I/IB1

   Balletto I/IB1

   Bourree, MIN 101 I/IB1

   Capriccio in D I/IB1

   Chaconne in A minor I/IB1

   Chaconne, MIN 102 I/IB1

   Ciaccona see Chaconne, MIN 102

   Dresden Sonata No. 5 see Sonata in D
     minor

   Dresden Sonata No. 7 see Sonata, MIN
     112

   Dresden Sonata No. 12 see Sonata,
     MIN 113

   Duett Fur Gitarren I/IIA1

   Erste Sonate see Sonata in D minor

   Fantaisie Pour Le Luth see Fantasy
     in C minor

WEISS, SYLVIUS LEOPOLD (cont'd.)
   Fantasy in C minor I/IB1

   Fantasy, MIN 103 I/IB1

   Fugue No. 6 I/IB1

   Gigue in A minor I/IB1

   Infidele, L' see Sonata in A minor

   Intavolatura Di Liuto I/IB1-Coll

   Largo I/IB1

   London Sonata No. 2 see Suite in D

   London Sonata No. 4 see Sonata, MIN
     114

   London Sonata No. 16 see Sonata in B
     minor

   London Sonata No. 25 see Sonata in F
     sharp minor

   2 Menuette I/IB1

   Minuet, MIN 77 I/IB1

   Overture in B flat I/IB1

   Partita No. 15 I/IB1

   Passacaglia, MIN 107 I/IB1

   Piezas Diversas Para Laud I/IB1

   Prelude, MIN 108 I/IB1

   Prelude, MIN 111 I/IB1

   Saraband in A I/IB1

   Six Pieces, Vol. 1 I/IB1

   Six Pieces, Vol. 2 I/IB1

   Sonata En Re Minore I/IB1

   Sonata in A minor I/IB1

   Sonata in B minor I/IB1

   Sonata in D minor I/IB1

   Sonata in F sharp minor I/IB1

   Sonata, MIN 112 I/IB1

   Sonata, MIN 113 I/IB1

   Sonata, MIN 114 I/IB1

   Suite Fur Laute see Sonata in D
     minor

   Suite in A I/IB1

   Suite in A minor, MIN 361, Gigue
     I/IB1

   Suite in A minor, MIN 362, Saraband
     I/IB1

   Suite in D I/IB1

   Suite in D minor, MIN 349, Allemand
     I/IB1

   Suite in E minor I/IB1

   Suite No. 1 in E I/IB1

   Suite No. 4 I/IB1

   Suite No. 15 I/IB1

   Suite No. 16 In D see Suite in D

   Suite Para Laud see Sonata in D
     minor

   Toccata in D I/IB1

   Tombeau Sur La Mort De Mr. Comte
     d'Logy I/IB1

   11 Vortragsstucke (London MS) I/IB1

WEISS WIE LILIEN see Webern, Anton von

WEISSIANA, OMAGGIO A S.L. WEISS see
   Rosetta, Giuseppe

WEISST DU WIEVIEL STERNLEIN STEHEN?,
   VOLKS- UND KINDERLIEDER
   I/IIC1-Coll

WELFFENS, P.
   Tafelmuziek I/IIB1

WELLESZ, EGON (1885-1974)
   Rhapsody, Op. 87 I/IB4

WELSCHER TANTZ see Neusiedler, Hans

WENN ALLE UNTREU WERDEN see Valerius,
   Adrianus

WENN DAS VOLLKOMMENE KOMMT see Blarr,
   Oskar Gottlieb

WENN MORGENS DIE SONNE ERWACHT see
   Rosenstengel, Albrecht, Tanzlied
   Aus Israel

WENN SARDAKAI AUF REISEN GEHT; OPERA
   see Krenek, Ernst, Das Kommt Davon;
   Opera

WENSIECKI, EDMUND
   Andante see Kleine Solostucke

   Cantabile see Kleine Solostucke

   Capriccio see Kleine Solostucke

   Kleine Solostucke I/IB4

   Study in E minor see Kleine
     Solostucke

   Tanz see Kleine Solostucke

WER WOHNT UNTERM SCHIRM DES HOCHSTEN
   see Blarr, Oskar Gottlieb

WERDIN, EBERHARD (1911-   )
   Concertino I/IIB5, I/IIIC

   Europaische Tanze; 7 Pieces For
     Schoolensemble I/IIB5

   Heinzelmannchen, Die, Ein
     Musikalisches Stegreifspiel
     I/IIC5

   Kommt, Ihr G'spielen; Folksongs For
     Wind, String, Plucked, And
     Percussion Instruments I/IIB5

   Miniaturen, 4 I/IIA2

   Tanze Der Volker I/IIB5

   Trio-Stucke I/IIB2

   Ungarische Suite, Nach Originalen
     Csardas-Melodien I/IIB4

WERNER, JEAN-JACQUES (1935-   )
   Ballades d'Antan, 5 I/IB4

   Gai see Ballades d'Antan, 5

   Librement see Ballades d'Antan, 5

   Meditatif see Ballades d'Antan, 5

   Narratif see Ballades d'Antan, 5

   Pastoral - Tres Libre see Ballades
     d'Antan, 5

   Sonatina I/IC

   Trope I/IB4

WESLEY-SMITH, MARTIN (1945-   )
   Wild West Show, The, Ein Buhnenstuck,
     Von Kindern Zu Erfinden Und
     Auszufuhren I/IIC5

WESTRA, JAN
   Conversation I/IIA3

   Minutes, 5 I/IIA3

WETTBEWERBS-UNTERRICHTSPROGRAMM, DAS;
   ARBEITSPROGRAMM FUR DEN WETTBEWERB
   "JUGEND MUSIZIERT", VOL. 1:
   ALTERSSTUFE IB I/IB6-Coll

WETTBEWERBS-UNTERRICHTSPROGRAMM, DAS;
   ARBEITSPROGRAMM FUR DEN WETTBEWERB
   "JUGEND MUSIZIERT", VOL. 2:
   ALTERSSTUFE IB I/IB6-Coll

WETTBEWERBS-UNTERRICHTSPROGRAMM, DAS;
   ARBEITSPROGRAMM FUR DEN WETTBEWERB
   "JUGEND MUSIZIERT", VOL. 3:
   ALTERSSTUFE II I/IB6-Coll

WHAT CHILD IS THIS see Easy Christmas
   Carols, 2

WHAT IF I NEVER SPEED? see Dowland,
   John

WHAT SHALL WE DO?, CHANSONS DE MATELOTS
   ANGLAIS I/IIC5-Coll

WIDMANN, ERASMUS (1572-1634)
   Musicalischer Tugendspiegel I/IIB1

WIDMANN, ERASMUS (cont'd.)

Suite No. 1 I/IIA3, I/IIA4

Zwei Suiten I/IIA2, I/IIA3

WIE HEISST DU, JOSEFINE?; EIN MUSIKALISCHES LUSTSPIEL, IN THREE ACTS see Graf, Thomas

WIE KAN DE BLAREN TELLEN I/IIC5-Coll

WIEGENLIED see Brahms, Johannes; Gruber, Franz Xaver, Stille Nacht; Rebay, Ferdinand; Schindler, Otto; Schumann, Robert (Alexander); Taubert, Karl Heinz

WIEGENLIED "SCHLAFE MEIN PRINZCHEN" see Flies, J. Bernhard

WIEGENLIEDER DER WELT I/IIC1-Coll

WIEGOLD, PETER (1949-   )
Flowers Appear On The Earth, The V/i

WIENER SONATINA see Mozart, Wolfgang Amadeus

WIENER SONATINE see Mozart, Wolfgang Amadeus

WIENER TANZE see Volksweisen Aus Osterreich

WIENER TANZE, 5 see Diabelli, Anton

WIGGLESWORTH, FRANK (1918-   )
Serenade I/IIB2

WIJ SPELEN GITAAR, METHODE VOOR BEGINNERS, GEBASEERD OP HET A.M.V.-ONDERWIJS, VOL. I see Blok, Coby

WIJ SPELEN GITAAR, METHODE VOOR BEGINNERS, GEBASEERD OP HET A.M.V.-ONDERWIJS, VOL. II see Blok, Coby

WIJ SPELEN GITAAR, METHODE VOOR BEGINNERS, GEBASEERD OP HET A.M.V.-ONDERWIJS, VOL. III see Blok, Coby

WIJDEVELD, WOLFGANG (1910-   )
Concert I/IIB3

Snarenspel I/IIB1

WIKMANSON, J.
Sonata in B minor I/IC

WILD WEST SHOW, THE, EIN BUHNENSTUCK, VON KINDERN ZU ERFINDEN UND AUSZUFUHREN see Wesley-Smith, Martin

WILDER REITER see Schumann, Robert (Alexander)

WILIMEK, EDUARD
Spiel Mit Uns; Kleine Musikstucke Fur Ein Konstruktives Zusammenspiel I/IIB5

WILLAERT, ADRIAN (ca. 1490-1562)
Ricercare No. 14 I/IIA1

WILSON, THOMAS
Allegro Molto see Pieces, 3

Coplas Del Ruisenor I/IB4

Lento, Con Espressione see Pieces, 3

Moderato, Poco Rubato see Pieces, 3

Pieces, 3 I/IB4

WILT THOU UNKIND THUS REAVE ME see Dowland, John

WILTON, C.H.
Sonatina I/IB2

WIMBERGER, GERHARD (1923-   )
Lebensregeln; Katechismus Mit Musik V/iii

Songs, 4 V/ii

WINDMILL see Duarte, John W.

WINE SONG OF KHAYYAM see Staak, Pieter van der

WINKELBAUER, ALFRED
Jota De Montes see Spanische Tanze

Lerne Gitarre, Vol. 1 II

Sevillana see Spanische Tanze

Sevillanas see Spanische Tanze

Spanische Tanze I/IIA2

WINKELBAUER, ALFRED (cont'd.)

Tanguillo, MIN 418 see Spanische Tanze

Tanguillo, MIN 419 see Spanische Tanze

Zapateado see Spanische Tanze

WINTER IST VERGANGEN, DER, LIEDKANTATE see Marx, Karl

WINTER MORNING, A see Tchaikovsky, Piotr Ilyich

WINTERWEISSE WEIHNACHT, ALTE UND NEUE LIEDER UM DIE WEIHNACHTSZEIT IV/IIB2, IV/IIC2

WIR LERNEN GITARRE SPIELEN, GRUNDSCHULE FUR DEN EINZEL- UND GRUPPENUNTERRICHT, SUPPL. 1 see Munch, Willi

WIR LERNEN GITARRE SPIELEN, GRUNDSCHULE FUR DEN EINZEL- UND GRUPPENUNTERRICHT, SUPPL. 2 see Munch, Willi

WIR LERNEN GITARRE SPIELEN, GRUNDSCHULE FUR DEN EINZEL- UND GRUPPENUNTERRICHT, VOL I see Munch, Willi

WIR LERNEN GITARRE SPIELEN, GRUNDSCHULE FUR DEN EINZEL- UND GRUPPENUNTERRICHT, VOL. II see Munch, Willi

WIR LERNEN HAUSMUSIK, FOLGE I-VIII I/IIC5-Coll

WIR LERNEN HAUSMUSIK, FOLGE I-VIII I/IIB5-Coll

WIR SINGEN UND SPIELEN, VOL. 1 I/IIB1-Coll, I/IIC1-Coll

WIR SINGEN UND SPIELEN, VOL. 2 I/IIB1-Coll, I/IIC1-Coll

WIR SPIELEN GITARRE, EIN SPIEL- UND UBUNGSBUCH see Monkemeyer, Helmut

WIR SPIELEN GITARRE, VOL. 1 I/IB6-Coll, I/IIA1-Coll, I/IIB1-Coll

WIR SPIELEN GITARRE, VOL. 2 I/IB6-Coll, I/IIA1-Coll, I/IIB1-Coll

WIR SPIELEN GITARRE, VOL. I see Munch, Willi, Wir Lernen Gitarre Spielen, Grundschule Fur Den Einzel- Und Gruppenunterricht, Suppl. 1

WIR SPIELEN GITARRE, VOL. II see Munch, Willi, Wir Lernen Gitarre Spielen, Grundschule Fur Den Einzel- Und Gruppenunterricht, Suppl. 2

WIR WANDERN OHNE SORGEN see Muhe, Hansgeorg

WISSMER, PIERRE (1915-   )
Barbaresque I/IIA1

Partita I/IB4

Prestilagoyana I/IIA1

Sonatina I/IIB1

WITH VOICE AND GUITAR, VOL. I: FOLKSONGS I/IIC1-Coll

WITH VOICE AND GUITAR, VOL. II I/IIC1-Coll

WITHIN A MILE OF EDINBORO see Hook, Richard

WITT, CHRISTIAN F. (1660-1716)
Suite I/IIA2

WITTE, JACQ.
Speelboek Voor De Gitaar, Vol. I II

WOBERSIN, W.
Schule Fur Bass-Gitarre (Laute), 2 Vols In 1 Vol II

Schule Fur Bass-Gitarre (Laute), Vol I II

Schule Fur Bass-Gitarre (Laute), Vol. II II

Tutor For The Bass-Guitar (Lute) [Guitar-Lute] see Schule Fur Bass-Gitarre (Laute), 2 Vols In 1 Vol; Schule Fur Bass-Gitarre (Laute), Vol I; Schule Fur Bass-

WOBERSIN, W. (cont'd.)

Gitarre (Laute), Vol. II

WOHLAN DIE ZEIT IST KOMMEN, EIN VOLKS- UND ZEITLIEDERBUCH FUR EINZEL-UND GRUPPENGESANG I/IIC1-Coll, IV/IIC1

WOHLAUF MIT REICHEM SCHALLE; BICINIEN UM 1550 I/IB1-Coll

WOLF, ROLAND
Donna Maria see Viva La Guitarra

Fredericos Erzahlung see Viva La Guitarra

Gitano see Viva La Guitarra

Morgenrote Uber Granada see Viva La Guitarra

Recuerdos De Sevilla see Viva La Guitarra

Tremolospiel Auf Der Gitarre III

Viva La Guitarra I/IIA1 see also Viva La Guitarra

WOLKI, KONRAD
Einstimmung see Sechs Mal Drei (6 x 3)

Entree see Sechs Mal Drei (6 x 3)

Gitarre Allein, Entwicklung Des Solistischen Musizierens Aus Dem Akkordspiel see Gitarre Zum Lied, Schule Fur Die Gitarre Als Begleitinstrument, Mit Einer Akkordlehre Und Mit Hinweisen Fur Das Begleiten Nach Dem Gehor, Supplement 2

Gitarre Zum Lied, Schule Fur Die Gitarre Als Begleitinstrument, Mit Einer Akkordlehre Und Mit Hinweisen Fur Das Begleiten Nach Dem Gehor, Vol. I II

Gitarre Zum Lied, Schule Fur Die Gitarre Als Begleitinstrument, Mit Einer Akkordlehre Und Mit Hinweisen Fur Das Begleiten Nach Dem Gehor, Vol. II II

Gitarre Zum Lied, Schule Fur Die Gitarre Als Begleitinstrument, Mit Einer Akkordlehre Und Mit Hinweisen Fur Das Begleiten Nach Dem Gehor, Supplement 1 II

Gitarre Zum Lied, Schule Fur Die Gitarre Als Begleitinstrument, Mit Einer Akkordlehre Und Mit Hinweisen Fur Das Begleiten Nach Dem Gehor, Supplement 2 II

Gitarrenchor, Der, Schule Des Gruppenmusizierens II

Gitarrenspiel Am Anfang, Erste Spielanweisung Fur Kinder; Einfuhrung In Das Melodiespiel, Akkordspiel Und Beginnende Solospiel II

Gitarrenspiel Nach Dem Gehor, Anleitung Zur Improvisierten Lied- Und Tanzbegleitung II

Kleine Ouverture see Sechs Mal Drei (6 x 3)

Melodisches Gitarrenspiel, Schule Fur Die Gitarre Als Soloinstrument Und Fur Das Zusammenspiel Mit 2 Bis 3 Gitarren see Gitarre Zum Lied, Schule Fur Die Gitarre Als Begleitinstrument, Mit Einer Akkordlehre Und Mit Hinweisen Fur Das Begleiten Nach Dem Gehor, Supplement 1

Nostalgie see Sechs Mal Drei (6 x 3)

O Tannenbaum see Sechs Mal Drei (6 x 3)

Rondoletto; 11 Leichte Spielstucke I/IIB2

Sechs Mal Drei (6 x 3) I/IIA2, IV/IIA2

Spielstucke Fur 3 Gitarren I/IIA2

Stucke, 6, Op. 40 I/IB4

Suite in A see Sechs Mal Drei (6 x 3)

WONDERFUL GUITAR, THE (A MODERN CLASSIC GUITAR METHOD), VOL. I see Rightmire, Richard W.

WONDERFUL GUITAR, THE (A MODERN CLASSIC
    GUITAR METHOD), VOL. II see
    Rightmire, Richard W.

WONDERFUL GUITAR, THE (A MODERN CLASSIC
    GUITAR METHOD), VOL. III see
    Rightmire, Richard W.

WOODS SO WILD, THE see Byrd, William

WORLD IS DISCOVERED, THE; 6
    INSTRUMENTAL PIECES AFTER HEINRICH
    ISAAC see Birtwistle, Harrison

WORSCHECH, ROMAIN
    Danzas De Andalucia, Style Flamenco
        I/IB5

    Enseignement Pratique De La Guitare,
        Vol. I II

    Libellule, La, Divertissement Sur Les
        10mes I/IB4

    Michelle Valse I/IB4

    Mouvements Perpetuels I/IB4

    Nocturne No. 9 I/IB4

    Practical Guitar Teaching see
        Enseignement Pratique De La
        Guitare, Vol. I

WUSTHOFF, KLAUS
    Collagen I/IIIA

    Weihnachtskantate Fur Junge Leute
        IV/IIC5

WYBOR ETIUD NA GITARE, VOL. 1
    I/IA-Coll, III

WYBOR ETIUD NA GITARE, VOL. 2
    I/IA-Coll, III, VI-Mixed Coll

WYBRANE UTWORY - PIECES CHOISIES see
    Bach, Johann Sebastian

WYSSENBACH, RUDOLF
    Barroncina, La see Pavan

    Pavan I/IB1

XANTHOPOULOS, ILIAS
    Sonata I/IIA1

XENIAS PACATAS II see Guerrero,
    Francisco

XENOPHONE, LA see Bach, Carl Philipp
    Emanuel

Y DESPUES see Maderna, Bruno

YA CABALGA CALAINOS see Valderrabano,
    Enriquez de

YA SE VAN LOS PASTORES I/IIB1-Coll,
    IV/IIB1
    see also Canciones Populares
        Espanolas; Canciones Populares
        Espanolas, 5; Lied Und Gitarre, 40
        Deutsche Und Auslandische
        Volkslieder, Vol. 1; Rodrigo,
        Joaquin

YA VAN LOS PASTORES see Alfonso,
    Nicolas

YEO-SIEBALD, ELSE
    Volksliederfibel Fur Den
        Gitarrenunterricht II

YO LO VI, SCENEN NACH FRANCESCO DE GOYA
    see Behrend, Siegfried

YOU ASKED FOR IT, FOR ACOUSTIC GUITAR
    SOLO see Bedford, David

YOUNG GUITARIST, VOL. 1 I/IB6-Coll

YOUNG GUITARIST, VOL. 2 I/IB6-Coll

YOUNG PERSONS' WAY TO THE GUITAR, THE
    see Duarte, John W.

YUN, ISANG (1917-   )
    Gagok I/IIC1, I/IIC2

Z MUZYKI POLSKIEGO RENESANSU
    I/IB1-Coll

Z POLONEZOW POLSKICH I/IB6-Coll

ZACH, JOHANN (JAN) (1699-1773)
    Trio Sonata I/IIB2

ZAGREBER KONZERT see Kelkel, Manfred

ZAGWIJN, HENRI (1878-1954)
    Fandango I/IB4

    Kerkerballade, De V/ii

ZAGWIJN, HENRI (cont'd.)

    Sarabande E Fandango I/IIB1

ZAMBA ROMANTICA see Broqua, Alfonso,
    Evocaciones Criollas, No.4

ZAMBRA see Albeniz, Isaac; Granados,
    Enrique

ZAMBRA GRANADINA see Albeniz, Isaac

ZANI DE FERRANTI, MARCO AURELIO
    Desir, Le see 3 Melodies Nocturnes
        Et Une Etude

    Etude No. 7 see 3 Melodies Nocturnes
        Et Une Etude

    Joie, La see 3 Melodies Nocturnes Et
        Une Etude

    3 Melodies Nocturnes Et Une Etude
        I/IB2

    Souvenir, Le see 3 Melodies
        Nocturnes Et Une Etude

ZANKE, HERMAN
    Berglied I/IIC1

    Von Der Bergeshoh' see Berglied

ZANOSKAR, HUBERT
    Neue Gitarren-Schule, Vol. I II,
        VII-Mixed Coll

    Neue Gitarren-Schule, Vol. I, Suppl.:
        Ubungen Und Spielstucke II,
        IV/IIC1, VII-Mixed Coll

    Neue Gitarren-Schule, Vol. II II

    Neue Gitarren-Schule, Vol. II, SUPPL.
        II

ZAPATEADO see Granados, Enrique;
    Winkelbauer, Alfred

ZARABANDA see Handel, George Frideric,
    Saraband, MIN 3; Sanz, Gaspar

ZARANZ see Azpiazu, Jose de

ZAUBERSPIEGEL, DER; TELEVISION OPERA IN
    FOURTEEN SCENES see Krenek, Ernst

ZBINDEN, JULIEN-FRANCOIS (1917-   )
    Miniatures, 4 I/IIB1

ZEHM, FRIEDRICH (1923-   )
    Divertimento Ritmico; 6 Moderne
        Tanzrhythmen I/IIB5-Coll

    Rhythomophonie For Orchestra V/i

    Serenade I/IIB1

ZEHN LEICHTE STUCKE see Maasz, Gerhard

ZEIGENDE UND SPRECHENDE GITARRE-SCHULE
    FUR JEDERMANN, VOL. I see
    Nelissen-Nicolai, Leni

ZEIGENDE UND SPRECHENDE GITARRE-SCHULE
    FUR JEDERMANN, VOL. II see
    Nelissen-Nicolai, Leni

ZELENKA, ISTVAN (1936-   )
    Fruh-Stuck V/i

ZELENKA, IVAN (1941-   )
    Koncertni Fantasie I/IB4

ZELTER, CARL FRIEDRICH (1758-1832)
    Es War Ein Konig In Thule I/IIC1,
        I/IIC2-Coll

ZERTANZTEN SCHUHE, DIE, KINDEROPER NACH
    EINEM MARCHEN DER GEBRUDER GRIMM
    see Kerkhoffs, Gunter

ZIEH'N DIE SCHAFE see Webern, Anton
    von

ZIEMLICH RASCH see Stadlmair, Hans

ZILLIG, WINFRIED (1905-1963)
    Baal; Music To The Play V/iii

    Camino Real; Music To The Play V/iii

    Peer Gynt; Music To The Play V/iii

ZIMMERMANN, BERND ALOIS (1918-1970)
    Cinque Capricci Di Girolamo
        Frescobaldi "La Frescobalda" V/i

    Giostra Genovese; Five Old Dances By
        Various Masters For Small
        Orchestra V/i

    Musique Pour Les Soupers Du Roi Ubu;
        Ballet Noir En Sept Parties Et
        Une Entree V/i, V/iii

ZIMMERMANN, HEINZ WERNER (1930-   )
    Missa Profana V/ii

ZING EN BLYF TEVREE see Muziekbijlage,
    No. 53

ZIPP, FRIEDRICH (1914-   )
    Es Steht Ein Lind Im Tiefen Tal, 6
        Deutsche Balladen I/IIC1

    Es Waren Zwei Konigskinder I/IIC5

    Frohlicher Jahrmarkt, Cantata For
        Children I/IIC5

ZIRKUS, DER, KANTATE UND BEWEGUNGSPIEL
    see Buchtger, Fritz

ZIRKUSMARSCH see Uhl, Alfred

ZO DOEN WIJ DAT! 24 BEKENDE MELODIETJES
    VOOR JONGE GITARISTEN; 24 DUTCH
    TUNES I/IB5-Coll

ZOETE INVALLEN, 4 see Schagen, Henk
    van

ZOMERAVONDSUITE see Schagen, Henk van

ZORAIDA see Pedrell, Carlos, Danzas De
    Las Tres Princesas Cautivas, No. 1

ZORONGO PARA MURAO see Behrend,
    Siegfried

ZORTZIKO see Albeniz, Isaac

ZOTTI, GIOVANNI DE
    Sonata in A minor I/IIB1

ZU SPATE ANKUNFT DER MUTTER, DIE see
    Haydn, [Franz] Joseph

ZUCCHERI, LUCIANO
    Angolo Visivo see Pezzi, 6

    Ballo Con Tina see Pezzi, 6

    M'ama Mammola see Pezzi, 6

    Pezzi, 6 I/IIA1

    Prelude No. 1 I/IB4

    Prelude No. 2 I/IB4

    Prelude No. 3 I/IB4

    Prelude No. 4 I/IB4

    Prelude No. 5 I/IB4

    Pupazzi see Pezzi, 6

    Ricordando Giulia see Pezzi, 6

    Sadness I/IB4

    Vicolo Delle Mimose see Pezzi, 6

ZUPFGEIGENHANSL, DER I/IIC1-Coll

ZWANZIG STUCKE AUS DEM NOTENBUCHLEIN
    FUR ANNA MAGDALENA BACH see Bach,
    Johann Sebastian

ZWEI BERUHMTE SICILIANE see Bach,
    Johann Sebastian

ZWEI GITARREN MUSIZIEREN, VOL. 4:
    INVENTIONEN UND SINFONIEN see
    Bach, Johann Sebastian

ZWEI KLEINE PRAELUDIEN see Bach,
    Johann Sebastian

ZWEI KONZERTANTE MENUETTE see
    Matiegka, Wenzeslaus Thomas

ZWEI SUITEN see Widmann, Erasmus

ZWEI THEMEN MIT VARIATIONEN UND ZWOLF
    MENUETTE see Sor, Fernando, Deux
    Themes Varies Et Douze Menuets

ZWEI- UND DREISTIMMIGE SOLOSTUCKE FUR
    DIE LAUTE see Attaignant, Pierre,
    [publisher]

ZWEISTIMMIGES GITARRENSPIEL; LEICHTE
    STUCKE UND TANZE AUS DEM 16. BIS
    18. JAHRHUNDERT I/IB1-Coll

ZWEITE GROSSE SONATE see Sor,
    Fernando, Grande Sonate, Op. 25

ZWEITE LAUTEN-SUITE, BWV 997 see Bach,
    Johann Sebastian, Partita for Lute,
    BWV 997, in C minor

ZWEITE SUITE see Bach, Johann
    Sebastian, Partita for Lute, BWV
    997, in C minor

ZWERGE, DIE   see Serocki, Kazimierz, Krasnoludki

ZWIEFACHE, DER   see Bloch, Waldemar

ZWOLF ETUDEN   see Sor, Fernando, Douze Etudes; Sor, Fernando, Douze Etudes Pour Servir De Suite Aux Douze Premieres

ZWOLF MENUETTE   see Matiegka, Wenzeslaus Thomas

ZWOLF MENUETTEN   see Seidel

ZWOLF STUCKE   see Furstenau, Kaspar

ZWOLFTONSPIELE, 3   see Fheodoroff, Nikolaus

ZYKAN, OTTO M.
    Methodisches Lehrwerk Fur Die Gitarre, Vol. I: Grundbegriffe II

    Methodisches Lehrwerk Fur Die Gitarre, Vol. IIa, b: Die Linke Hand, Beherrschung Des Griffbrettes II

    Methodisches Lehrwerk Fur Die Gitarre, Vol. III: die Rechte Hand II

    Methodisches Lehrwerk Fur Die Gitarre, Vol. IV: der Vortrag II

Studies

ABLONIZ, MIGUEL (1917-   )
Studi Melodici Per Chitarra, 10 I/IA

AGUADO, DIONISIO (1784-1849)
Aguado-Brevier I/IA

Arpeggio Etude I/IA

Etude Brilliante I/IA

Etuden, 24, Und 10 Tonleiterstudien
I/IA

Kleine Gitarrenstucke, 31, In
Fortschreitender Ordnung I/IA

Lessons, 8 I/IA

2 Minuetos Y 2 Estudios I/IA

Studi, 51, Ad Uso Dei Conservatori
I/IA

Studies, 50 I/IA

Three Studies I/IA

ALBERT, HEINRICH (1870-1950)
Gitarre-Etuden-Werk, Vol. 1:
Elementarstufe I/IA

Gitarre-Etuden-Werk, Vol. 2: Obere
Elementarstufe I/IA

Gitarre-Etuden-Werk, Vol. 3:
Mittelstufe I/IA

Gitarre-Etuden-Werk, Vol. 4: Obere
Mittelstufe I/IA

Gitarre-Etuden-Werk, Vol. 5:
Oberstufe I/IA

Gitarre-Etuden-Werk, Vol. 6:
Reifestufe I/IA

Gitarre-Solospiel-Studien, Vol. 1:
Zur Einfuhrung Fur Anfanger I/IA

Gitarre-Solospiel-Studien, Vol. 2:
Weiterentwicklung Fur
Fortgeschrittene I/IA

Gitarre-Solospiel-Studien, Vol. 3:
Nebenlagen, Vortrag, Solospiel
I/IA

ALBUM DE ESTUDIOS Y PIEZAS FACILES,
PARA ALTERNAR CON EL LIBRO 1 I/IA

ALBUM DE ESTUDIOS Y PIEZAS FACILES,
PARA ALTERNAR CON EL LIBRO 2 I/IA

ALFONSO, NICOLAS
Etudes, 3 I/IA

ANZAGHI, LUIGI ORESTE (1903-1963)
Chitarrista Virtuoso, Il I/IA

AUBANEL, GEORGES
Etudes Rhythmiques I/IA

Gradus De La Guitare Moderne, Vol. 1
I/IA

BARTOLI, RENE
Etude No. 1, Tremolo I/IA

BEHREND, SIEGFRIED (1933-   )
Rhythmische Studien, Vol. 1 I/IA

Rhythmische Studien, Vol. 2 I/IA

Ubungen Von "A-Z" I/IA

BELLOW, ALEXANDER (1922-1976)
Etude In Tremolo I/IA

Etudes In Scales, 2 I/IA

First Lessons I/IA

Studies, 10 I/IA

BETTINELLI, BRUNO (1913-   )
12 Studi I/IA

BOBRI, VLADIMIR
Melodic Exercises, 8 I/IA

BOCHMAN, THEO L.
Fantasia De La Guitarra, Etude De
Tremolo I/IA

BODA, JOHN (1922-   )
Etudes Byzantines, 4 I/IA

BROQUA, ALFONSO (1876-1946)
Etudes Creolles, 7 I/IA

BROUWER, LEO (1939-   )
Etudes Simples, Nos. 1-5 I/IA

Etudes Simples, Nos. 6-10 I/IA

CANO, ANTONIO (1811-1897)
Principios De Guitarra, 20 Lecciones
Muy Faciles Y Progresivas I/IA

Study in D I/IA

Study in E I/IA

Study in G I/IA

CARCASSI, MATTEO (1792-1853)
Caprices, 6 I/IA

Etude De Tremolo I/IA

Etuden Fur Die Mittelstufe I/IA

Melodische Und Progressive Etuden, 25
I/IA

Study in A I/IA

Study, Op. 60, No. 3, in A I/IA

Study, Op. 60, No. 19, in E minor
I/IA

Tremolo-Etude I/IA

Tremolo Study I/IA

CARULLI, FERDINANDO (1770-1841)
Carulli-Brevier, Vol. 1 I/IA

Carulli-Brevier, Vol. 2 I/IA

Carulli-Brevier, Vol. 3 I/IA

De Tout Un Peu I/IA

Elementar Etuden, Vol. 4 I/IA,
I/IA-Coll

Methode De Guitare I/IA

Praludien Zur Bildung Des Anschlages,
20 I/IA

Preludes, 24 I/IA

Studies, 30 I/IA

Ubungen Und Spielstucke, 46 I/IA

CASTELNUOVO-TEDESCO, MARIO (1895-1968)
Estudio Sul Nome Di Manuel Lopez
Ramos I/IA

CAVAZZOLI, GERMANO
Study I/IA

CHARPENTIER, JACQUES (1933-   )
Etude No. 1 I/IA

COSTE, NAPOLEON (1806-1883)
Etudes, 25 I/IA

Study in A I/IA

CZERNUSCHKA, FRITZ
Kleine Etuden, 2 I/IA

DAGOSTO, SYLVAIN
Etude in F I/IA

Rapido, Lo, Etude I/IA

DAUSEND, GERD-MICHAEL (1952-   )
Leichte Zeitgenossische Etuden I/IA

DEGESE, VICENTE
Aleteo De Pajarito I/IA

DEGNI, VINCENZO (1911-   )
Serenata All'antica I/IA

Studio Della Chitarra Classica, Lo,
Vol. 1: Technical Exercises, 19
I/IA

Studio Della Chitarra Classica, Lo,
Vol. 2: Technical Exercises, 20
I/IA

DELAUNEY, PAUL
Feuillets, 15 I/IA

DIABELLI, ANTON (1781-1858)
Studi Facili, 30 I/IA

Study No. 5 I/IA

DIAZ, CLEMENTE A.
Estudio De Concierto I/IA

DODGSON, STEPHEN (1924-   )
Studies, Vol. 1: 10 Studies (Nos. 1-
10) I/IA

Studies, Vol. 2: 10 Studies (Nos. 11-
20) I/IA

DOERR, CHARLES-KIKO
Etude in B minor I/IA

DUARTE, JOHN W. (1919-   )
Etude Diabolique I/IA

EINEM, GOTTFRIED VON (1918-   )
Studien, 3 I/IA

ELEMENTAR ETUDEN, VOL. 1 I/IA,
I/IA-Coll

ELEMENTAR ETUDEN, VOL. 2 I/IA,
I/IA-Coll

ELEMENTAR ETUDEN, VOL. 3 I/IA,
I/IA-Coll

ENCINAR, JOSE RAMON (1954-   )
Estudio De Alturas I/IA

ERSTEN ETUDEN, DIE I/IA-Coll

ESTUDIOS, 2 I/IA

ESTUDOS PARA VIOLAO, 8 I/IA-Coll

EYNARD, CAMILLE
Etude En Ut Majeur, Pour La
Resistance Du Barre I/IA

FARAILL, M.
Etude I/IA

FISCHER, FRANZ
Prelude, Orgelpunktstudie I/IA

FORTEA, DANIEL (1882-1953)
Capricho-Estudio, Op. 13 I/IA

Capricho-Estudio, Op. 45 I/IA

Estudio [De Arpegios] I/IA

Estudio De Ligados I/IA

Estudios I/IA

Estudios Poeticos, Op. 25 I/IA

Murmullos I/IA

Preludios-Estudio, 2, Op. 4 I/IA

Preludios-Estudio, 2, Op. 5 I/IA

Preludios-Estudio, 2, Op. 6 D3 I/IA

Study in F I/IA

FRANCERIES, MARC (1935-   )
Etudes, 6 I/IA

FRANKE, J. MAX
Minuet, MIN 71 I/IA

GALL, LOUIS IGNATIUS
Bulerias De Nimega I/IA

GARCIA VELASCO, VENANCIO
Study No. 3 I/IA

Study No. 11 I/IA

GARZIA, PASQUALINO (1934-   )
Lezioni Sul Legato, 10 I/IA

GIORGIO GUTIERREZ, ARNOL DEL
Estudio Para La Practica De Los
Armonicos Octavados Compuestos
I/IA

GITAAR-KAMERMUZIEK, VOL. 3: UIT HET
REPERTOIRE VAN HET JOEGOSLAVISCHE
DANSTHEATER I/IA

GITAAR-KAMERMUZIEK, VOL. 4: UIT HET
REPERTOIRE VAN HET JOEGOSLAVISCHE
DANSTHEATER I/IA

GIULIANI, MAURO (1781-1829)
Etude Spirituoso I/IA

Etuden, 24 I/IA

Etuden, 24, Selections I/IA

Etudes Progressives, 158 I/IA

SOR, FERNANDO (cont'd.)

Ausgewahlte Etuden, Vol. 5: Etuden I/IA

Ausgewahlte Etuden, Vol. 6: Etuden I/IA

Ausgewahlte Etuden, Vol. 7: Etuden I/IA

Douze Etudes I/IA

Douze Etudes Pour Servir De Suite Aux Douze Premieres I/IA

12 Ejercicios I/IA

Ejercicios Y Estudios Elementales Para Guitarra, 36, Vol. 1 I/IA

Erste Sor, Der I/IA

Estudios, 26 I/IA

12 Estudios I/IA

Estudios De Guitarra, 30 I/IA

12 Estudios, Op.60 I/IA

Estudios Para Guitarra, 26 I/IA

12 Estudios Progresivos I/IA

Etude, Op. 29, No. 1 I/IA

Etude, Op. 29, No. 5 I/IA

Etude, Op. 29, No. 10 I/IA

Etude, Op. 31, No. 14 I/IA

Etude, Op. 31, No. 20 I/IA

Etuden Fur Gitarre, 14 I/IA

Etudes, 30 I/IA

Etudes Choises, 24 I/IA

Etudes Pour La Guitare, 20 I/IA

Etudes Pour La Guitare, 26, Vol. 1 I/IA

Etudes Pour La Guitare, 26, Vol. 2 I/IA

Etudes Pour La Guitare, 26, Vol. 3 I/IA

Etudes Pour La Guitare, 26, Vol. 4 I/IA

Introduction A l'Etude De La Guitare En Vingt Cinq Lecons Progressives I/IA

Konzert-Etuden, 4 I/IA

12 Lecciones Progresivas I/IA

Leichte Etuden, 2 I/IA

Leichte Etuden Aus Op. 60, 12 I/IA

Mittelschwere Etuden (Intermediate Studies) I/IA

Mittelschwere Und Schwere Etuden Aus Op. 6, 29 Und 31, 16 I/IA

Studi Per Chitarra, Ad Uso Dei Conservatori I/IA

Studi Per Chitarra, Vol. 1 I/IA

Studi Per Chitarra, Vol. 2 I/IA

Studies For The Guitar, 20 I/IA

Valse Etude I/IA

Vier Leichte Stucke Aus Op. 35 I/IA

Vingt-Quatre Exercices Tres Faciles I/IA

Vingt-Quatre Exercices Tres Faciles, Op. 35, No. 13 I/IA

Vingt-Quatre Exercices Tres Faciles, Op. 35, No. 17 I/IA

Vingt-Quatre Exercices Tres Faciles, Op. 35, No. 20 I/IA

Vingt-Quatre Exercices Tres Faciles, Op. 35, No. 22 I/IA

Vingt-Quatre Exercices Tres Faciles, Op. 35, No. 23 I/IA

SOR, FERNANDO (cont'd.)

Vingt Quatre Lecons Progressives, Dediees Aux Eleves Commencants I/IA

STAAK, PIETER VAN DER (1930-   )
8 Studi Sugli Armonici I/IA

STERZATI, UMBERTO (1909-1972)
Studi Divertimento, 6 I/IA

STINGL, ANTON (1908-   )
Lehrstucke, 30 I/IA

TARRAGO, GRACIANO
Estudio De Tremolo, Sobre Un Tema De Alard I/IA

Estudios De Cejilla, 6 I/IA

Estudios Melodicos, 25 I/IA

TARREGA, FRANCISCO (1852-1909)
Elementos Fundamentales De La Tecnica Guitarristica VI-Coll

Estudios; 20 Studies Without Title, Vol. 1: Estudios 1-3 VI-Coll

Estudios; 20 Studies Without Title, Vol. 2: Estudios 4-6 VI-Coll

Estudios; 20 Studies Without Title, Vol. 3: Estudios 7-10 VI-Coll

Estudios; 20 Studies Without Title, Vol. 4: Estudios 11-13 VI-Coll

Estudios; 20 Studies Without Title, Vol. 5: Estudios 14-17 VI-Coll

Estudios; 20 Studies Without Title, Vol. 6: Estudios 18-20 VI-Coll

Estudios Para Guitarra VI-Coll

Etuden VI-Coll

Formule Di Arpeggi VI-Coll

Samtliche Technische Studien VI-Coll

Technical Studies VI-Coll

ULRICH, JURGEN (1939-   )
Drei Rhapsodische Studien I/IA

VERZIJL, HANS (1934-   )
Kennismaken, Het I/IA

Van Niets Tot Iets I/IA

Van V Naar I I/IA

VILLA-LOBOS, HEITOR (1887-1959)
Etudes, 12 I/IA

VISSER, DICK (1927-   )
Anti- En Symmetria, Studie I/IA

Etudes, 4 I/IA

Studies, 12, Vol. 1 I/IA

Studies, 12, Vol. 2 I/IA

Studies, 12, Vol. 3 I/IA

WALKER, LUISE (1910-   )
Brasilianisch I/IA

Fur Den Anfang, Vol. 1 I/IA

Fur Den Anfang, Vol. 2 I/IA

Fur Den Anfang, Vol. 3 I/IA

Fur Den Anfang, Vol. 4 I/IA

Fur Den Anfang, Vol. 5 I/IA

Fur Den Anfang, Vol. 6 I/IA

Marsch Nach Einer Tiroler Melodie I/IA

Regenetude I/IA

Tanzlied I/IA

WYBOR ETIUD NA GITARE, VOL. 1 I/IA-Coll

WYBOR ETIUD NA GITARE, VOL. 2 I/IA-Coll

Guitar Solos — Pre-Classical — Original Works — Switzerland

ACADEMICO CALIGINOSO, L' I/IB1

WYSSENBACH, RUDOLF
Pavan I/IB1

Guitar Solos — Pre-Classical — Original Works — Czechoslovakia

LOSY VOM LOSINTHAL, JAN ANTONIN (1643-1721)
Ausgewahlte Leichte Stucke I/IB1

Invenciones, 3 I/IB1

Partita in A minor I/IB1

Partita in A minor, MIN 12 I/IB1

Partita in A minor, MIN 13 I/IB1

Partita in C I/IB1

Partita in D I/IB1

Pieces De Guitare I/IB1-Coll

Suite in A minor I/IB1

Suite No. 1 I/IB1

Suite No. 3 I/IB1

Guitar Solos — Pre-Classical — Original Works — Germany

ALBUM: 6 BERUHMTE STUCKE I/IB1-Coll

ALTDEUTSCHE LAUTENMUSIK I/IB1-Coll

ANONYMOUS
Altdeutsche Lautentanze, 2 I/IB1

Baltische Suite I/IB1

Nurnberger Lautenbuch: Part 1 I/IB1-Coll

Nurnberger Lautenbuch: Part 2 I/IB1-Coll

Nurnberger Lautenbuch: Part 3 I/IB1-Coll

Prelude Et Menuet (Re Mineur) I/IB1

Suite in G, MIN 330 I/IB1

17 ARIEN UND TANZE I/IB1

AUSGEWAHLTE STUCKE AUS EINER ANGELICA- UND GITARREN- TABULATUR DER 2. HALFTE DES 17. JAHRHUNDERTS I/IB1-Coll

AUSGEWAHLTE WERKE AUS DER AUSSEER GITARRETABULATUR DES 18. JAHRHUNDERTS I/IB1-Coll

BARON, ERNST GOTTLIEB (1696-1760)
Drole, Le, In F Major I/IB1

Partita in C I/IB1

Suite in D I/IB1

BRAYSSING, GREGOIRE
Fantasies, 3 I/IB1

M. Gregoire Brayssing I/IB1

EUROPAISCHE GITARREN- UND LAUTENMUSIK,
     VOL. 2   I/IB1

FALCKENHAGEN, ADAM (1697-1761)
     Concerto   I/IB1

     Suite in A   I/IB1

GERLE, HANS (1500-1570)
     7 Lautenstucke Aus "Musica Teutsch",
     1532   I/IB1-Coll

GITARREMUSIK DES BAROCK II: AUS EINEM
     FRANZOSISCHEN TABULATURBUCH DES 17.
     JAHRHUNDERTS; AUS DER AUSSEER
     GITARRE-TABULATUR   I/IB1-Coll

HAGEN, JOACHIM BERNHARD (fl. ca. 1759)
     Sonata in B minor   I/IB1

HECKEL, WOLF
     Mille Regres   I/IB1

HEROLD, JOHANN THEODOR (1660-1720)
     Harmonia Quadripartita: Partita
     Seconda   I/IB1

HINTERLEITHNER, FERDINAND IGNAZ
     (1659-1710)
     Partita in A   I/IB1

JUDENKUNIG, HANS (ca. 1450-1526)
     Ronde Neerlandaise   I/IB1

     Schone Kunstliche Vnderweisung Auff
         Der Lautten Vnd Geygen, Ain, 1523
         I/IB1-Coll

KELLNER, DAVID (ca. 1670-1748)
     Fantasy in F sharp minor   I/IB1

KROPFGANSS, JOHANN (1708- ?)
     Partita in D   I/IB1

KUHNEL, JOHANN MICHAEL
     Suite in B minor   I/IB1

LESAGE DE RICHEE, PHILIPP FRANZ
     (1695- ?)
     Piccolo Pezzi, 4   I/IB1

     4 Piezas   I/IB1

MANDORBUCH 1626   I/IB1

NEUSIEDLER, HANS (1508-1563)
     Aus "Ein Newgeordent Kunstlich
         Lautenbuch"   I/IB1

     Ich Klag Den Tag   I/IB1

     Lautenstucke, 4   I/IB1

     Newgeordent Kunstlich Lautenbuch, Ein
         I/IB1-Coll

     Newgeordent Kunstlich Lautenbuch,
         Ein: Der Ander Theil Fur Die
         Geubten Vnnd Erfarnen, 1536
         I/IB1-Coll

     Praambulum Und Tanz   I/IB1

     Tanze, 3   I/IB1

NEUSIEDLER, MELCHIOR (1507-1590)
     Ausgewahlte Lautenwerke (1566-1572)
         I/IB1

OSTPREUSSISCHES LAUTENBUCH   I/IB1-Coll

PARTITA IN C   I/IB1

PRAETORIUS, MICHAEL (1571-1621)
     Terpsichore Musarum   I/IB1

RADOLT, WENZEL LUDWIG FREIHERR VON
     (1667-1716)
     Minuet   I/IB1

REUSSNER, ESAIAS (1636-1679)
     Passacaglia   I/IB1

     Pecas, 3   I/IB1

     Sonatina   I/IB1

     Suite for Lute   I/IB1

     Suite in A minor   I/IB1

     Suite No. 1   I/IB1

     Suite No. 5   I/IB1

ROYAL DANCES, 4   I/IB1

SCHLICK, ARNOLT (ca. 1460-ca. 1517)
     Tabulaturen Etlicher Lobgesang Und
         Lidlein Vff Die Lauten, 1512
         I/IB1-Coll

SEIDEL
     Zwolf Menuetten   I/IB1-Coll

STRAUBE, RUDOLF
     Sonata No. 1 for Lute   I/IB1

     Sonata Para Laud   I/IB1

TELEMANN, GEORG PHILIPP (1681-1767)
     Suita Polska   I/IB1

WAISSEL(IUS), MATTHAUS (ca. 1540-1602)
     Phantasia Und Deutscher Tanz   I/IB1

WEISS, SYLVIUS LEOPOLD (1686-1750)
     Air in E   I/IB1

     Angloise   I/IB1

     Balletto   I/IB1

     Bourree, MIN 101   I/IB1

     Capriccio in D   I/IB1

     Chaconne in A minor   I/IB1

     Chaconne, MIN 102   I/IB1

     Fantasy in C minor   I/IB1

     Fantasy, MIN 103   I/IB1

     Fugue No. 6   I/IB1

     Gigue in A minor   I/IB1

     Intavolatura Di Liuto   I/IB1-Coll

     Largo   I/IB1

     2 Menuette   I/IB1

     Minuet, MIN 77   I/IB1

     Overture in B flat   I/IB1

     Partita No. 15   I/IB1

     Passacaglia, MIN 107   I/IB1

     Piezas Diversas Para Laud   I/IB1

     Prelude, MIN 108   I/IB1

     Prelude, MIN 111   I/IB1

     Saraband in A   I/IB1

     Six Pieces, Vol. 1   I/IB1

     Six Pieces, Vol. 2   I/IB1

     Sonata En Re Minore   I/IB1

     Sonata in A minor   I/IB1

     Sonata in B minor   I/IB1

     Sonata in D minor   I/IB1

     Sonata in F sharp minor   I/IB1

     Sonata, MIN 112   I/IB1

     Sonata, MIN 113   I/IB1

     Sonata, MIN 114   I/IB1

     Suite in A   I/IB1

     Suite in A minor, MIN 361, Gigue
         I/IB1

     Suite in A minor, MIN 362, Saraband
         I/IB1

     Suite in D   I/IB1

     Suite in D minor, MIN 349, Allemand
         I/IB1

     Suite in E minor   I/IB1

     Suite No. 1 in E   I/IB1

     Suite No. 4   I/IB1

     Suite No. 15   I/IB1

     Toccata in D   I/IB1

     Tombeau Sur La Mort De Mr. Comte
         d'Logy   I/IB1

     11 Vortragsstucke (London MS)   I/IB1

Pre-Classical — Original Works — Spain

ALFONSO X, EL SABIO, KING OF CASTILE
     (1221-1284)
     2 Cantigas   I/IB1

     Rosa Das Rosas, Cantiga   I/IB1

ALTE SPANISCHE MEISTER   I/IB1-Coll

ALTE SPANISCHE MEISTER   I/IB1-Coll

ALTSPANISCHE LAUTENMUSIK   I/IB1-Coll

ANONYMOUS
     Fantasy No. 7   I/IB1

     Fantasy No. 11   I/IB1

     Tant Que Vivray   I/IB1

ANTOLOGIA DE LOS VIHUELISTAS ESPANOLAS,
     VOL. 1   I/IB1-Coll

ANTOLOGIA DE LOS VIHUELISTAS ESPANOLAS,
     VOL. 2   I/IB1-Coll

ANTOLOGIA DE LOS VIHUELISTAS ESPANOLAS,
     VOL. 3   I/IB1-Coll

ANTOLOGIA DE LOS VIHUELISTAS ESPANOLAS,
     VOL. 5   I/IB1-Coll

ANTOLOGIA DI CHITARRISTI DEL BAROCCO
     SPAGNOLO   I/IB1-Coll

DAZA, ESTEBAN (? - ?)
     Fantasias, 4, De Pasos Largos Para
         Desenvolver Las Manos   I/IB1

     Fantasias A Tres, 4   I/IB1

     Fantasy   I/IB1

EASY MUSIC FOR GUITAR, VOL. 8
     I/IB1-Coll

EUROPAISCHE GITARREN- UND LAUTENMUSIK,
     VOL. 5   I/IB1

FANTASIAS, 4   I/IB1-Coll

FANTASY NO. 4   I/IB1

FUENLLANA, MIGUEL DE (fl. ca. 1560)
     Contrepoints, 2, Sur Le Villancico
         "Si Amore Me Han De Matar"   I/IB1

     Deuxieme Fantaisie   I/IB1

     Fantasia De Redobles   I/IB1

     Fantasia I   I/IB1

     Fantasia II   I/IB1

     Fantasia III   I/IB1

     Fantasia [IV]   I/IB1

     Fantasy in A   I/IB1

     Fantasy in E   I/IB1

     Quatrieme Fantaisie   I/IB1

     Tiento   I/IB1

     Tientos, 8: Orphenica Lyra   I/IB1

     Troisieme Fantaisie   I/IB1

GUERAU, FRANCISCO (fl. ca. 1694)
     Canarios   I/IB1

     Canarios, Danza Del Siglo XVII   I/IB1

     Espanoleta   I/IB1

     Folias   I/IB1

     Francisco Guerau: 5 Compositions
         I/IB1

     Gallardas   I/IB1

     Jacaras   I/IB1

     Jacaras De La Costa   I/IB1

     Marionas   I/IB1

GUERAU, FRANCISCO (cont'd.)

Marizapalos I/IB1

Paradetas, Danza Del Siglo XVII
    I/IB1

Pavanas I/IB1

Villano I/IB1

HISPANAE CITHARAE ARS VIVA; ANTHOLOGY
    OF GUITAR MUSIC FROM OLD TABLATURES
    I/IB1-Coll

MILAN, LUIS (ca. 1500-ca. 1564)
    Don Luis Milan I/IB1

Fantasia De L'Octavo Tono I/IB1

Fantasy, MIN 266 I/IB1

Fantasy, MIN 267 I/IB1

Fantasy No. 1 I/IB1

Fantasy No. 4 I/IB1

Fantasy No. 16 I/IB1

Fantasy No. 38 I/IB1

Libro De Musica De Vihuela De Mano,
    1535, Part 1: "Fantasien 1-13"
    I/IB1-Coll

Libro De Musica De Vihuela De Mano,
    1535, Part 2: "Fantasien 14-22"
    I/IB1-Coll

Libro De Musica De Vihuela De Mano,
    1535, Part 3: "Fantasien 23-33"
    I/IB1-Coll

Libro De Musica De Vihuela De Mano,
    1535, Part 4: "Tientos 1-4 And
    Fantasien 34-40" I/IB1-Coll

Maestro, El, Vol. 1: Composizioni Per
    Sola Vihuela I/IB1-Coll

Maestro, El, Vol. 1: Obras Para
    Vihuela Sola I/IB1

Maestro, El, Vol. 2: Composizizoni
    Per Voce E Vihuela I/IB1-Coll

Maestro, El, Vol. 2: Obras Para Voz Y
    Vihuela I/IB1

Pavan No. 1 I/IB1

Pavan No. 2 I/IB1

Pavan No. 3 I/IB1

Pavan No. 4 I/IB1

Pavan No. 5 I/IB1

Pavan No. 6 I/IB1

Pavan Nos. 1-6 I/IB1

Pavan Nos. 5-6 I/IB1

Pavanas I/IB1

Pavanas, 6, And A Fantasia I/IB1

Pavanen, 2 I/IB1

Pavans, 3, In D I/IB1

6 Pavans And 3 Fantasias I/IB1-Coll

Pavany, 2 I/IB1

Tientos Del Septimo Y Octavo Tono
    I/IB1

Tientos Del Tercero Y Cuarto Tono
    I/IB1

MUDARRA, ALONSO DE (ca. 1506-1580)
    Conde Claros De Doze Maneras I/IB1

Fantasia De Pasos De Contado I/IB1

Fantasia Del Pmer Tono I/IB1

Fantasia (Que Contrahaze La Harpa En
    La Manera De Luduvico) I/IB1

Fantasia X, Que Contrahaze La Harpa
    En La Manera De Luduvico I/IB1

Fantasias, 2 I/IB1

Fantasias, 2; 2 Tientos I/IB1

Fantasias, 4; Pavane; Romanesca
    I/IB1

MUDARRA, ALONSO DE (cont'd.)

Fantasy No. 2 I/IB1

Fantasy No. 5 I/IB1

Fantasy No. 7 I/IB1

Gallarda; Tiento; Fantasia I/IB1

Galliard I/IB1

Keuze Uit [Selection From] Tres
    Libros De Musica En Cifra I/IB1

Pavan I/IB1

Romanesca I I/IB1

Romanesca II I/IB1

Tiento VII, VIII I/IB1

Tres Libros De Musica: Ausgewahlte
    Werke I/IB1-Coll

Tres Libros De Musica En Cifra Para
    Vihuela I/IB1

MURCIA, SANTIAGO DE
    Prelude And Allegro I/IB1

Suite in D I/IB1

Suite in D minor I/IB1

NARVAEZ, LUIS DE
    Baxa De Contrapunto I/IB1

Cancion Del Emperador I/IB1

Diferencias, 7, Sobre "Guardame Las
    Vacas" I/IB1

Fantasia Del Primer Tono I/IB1

Fantasy No. 3 I/IB1

Fantasy No. 9 I/IB1

Seys Libros Del Delphin De Musica,
    Los: Ausgewahlte Werke
    I/IB1-Coll

Seys Libros Del Delphin De Musica De
    Cifra Para Taner Vihuela, Los
    I/IB1

Variations, 22, On The Romance "Conde
    Claros" I/IB1

Villancico No. 5 Et Fantaisie No. 14
    I/IB1

5 PIEZAS DEL SIGLO XVI I/IB1-Coll

PISADOR, DIEGO (ca. 1508-1557)
    Fantasia Facil I/IB1

Fantasy No. 1 I/IB1

Pavan I/IB1

Villanelle: Dites Au Chevalier Que
    I/IB1

Villanesca I/IB1

Villanesca I/IB1

RAMILLETE DE FLORES I/IB1-Coll

RAMILLETE DE FLORES (1530-1593)
    I/IB1-Coll

RUIZ DE RIBAYAZ, LUCAS
    Bailes Populares Del Siglo XVII, 6
    I/IB1

Dansen, 4 I/IB1

Passacaglia I/IB1

SANZ, GASPAR (1640-1710)
    Airs De Danse, 5 I/IB1

Anthologie Pour La Guitare Espagnole
    I/IB1

Batalla, Baile Popular I/IB1

Canarios I/IB1

Canarios II I/IB1

Cavalleria De Napoles, La I/IB1

Chaconne I/IB1

Chansons Populaires Du XVIIe Siecle
    I/IB1

Clairons Royaux, Clairons Et
    Trompettes I/IB1

SANZ, GASPAR (cont'd.)

Composizioni, 10 I/IB1

Corriente I/IB1

Danzas Cervantinas I/IB1

Espanoleta I I/IB1

Espanoleta I, Air De Danse I/IB1

Fantasia Original De Un Gentilhombre,
    Villanos I/IB1

Folia I/IB1

Folias I/IB1

Fuga I, Per Primer Tono Al Aire
    Espanol I/IB1

Fuga II, Al Modo De Jiga Inglesa
    I/IB1

Gallardas I/IB1

Galliard I/IB1

Galliard, MIN 14 I/IB1

Gaspar Sanz: 11 Compositions I/IB1

Gaspar Sanz Invenit I/IB1

Gigue I/IB1

Iacaras I/IB1

Marizapalos, 5 Partidas I/IB1

Matachin, Baile Popular Del Siglo
    XVII I/IB1

Obras De Gaspar Sanz, Vol. 1 I/IB1

Obras De Gaspar Sanz, Vol. 2 I/IB1

Passacaglia I/IB1

Passacaglia in D I/IB1

Pavan I/IB1

Pavana, Passacalle, Etc. I/IB1

Pavanas I/IB1

Pavanas I/IB1

Pavanas (Suivi De Partidos Al Aire
    Espanol) I/IB1

Pieces Faciles Pour Apprendre Le
    Punteado, 8 I/IB1

Preciosa, La I/IB1

Preludio-Fantasia I/IB1

Preludio O Capricho Arpeado I/IB1

Rujero I/IB1

Sarabandes, 2 I/IB1

Serenisima, La (Alemana) I/IB1

Sesquialtera I/IB1

Sesquialtera I I/IB1

Suite Espanola I/IB1

Suite in E minor I/IB1

Suite in G minor I/IB1

Suite No. 1 in D minor I/IB1

16 Tanze I/IB1

Torneo I/IB1

Torneo, Baile Popular I/IB1

Tournoi Et Bataille I/IB1

VALDERRABANO, ENRIQUEZ DE
    (fl. ca. 1550)
    Diferencias Sobre "La Pavana Real"
    I/IB1

Fantasy I/IB1

Fantasy, MIN 270 I/IB1

Fugas, 2 I/IB1

Guardame Las Vacas I/IB1

Pavanas I/IB1

Sonata No. 15 I/IB1

VALDERRABANO, ENRIQUEZ DE (cont'd.)

Soneto Lombardo, A Manera De Danza
    I/IB1

Pre-Classical — Original
Works — France

ALTE MEISTER DES 17. JAHRHUNDERTS
    I/IB1-Coll

ALTFRANZOSISCHE LAUTENMUSIK I/IB1-Coll

ATTAIGNANT, PIERRE, [PUBLISHER]
    (? -1552)
    Dixhuit Basses Dances, 1529, Part 1:
        Die Basses Dances I/IB1-Coll

    Dixhuit Basses Dances, 1529, Part 2:
        Balle, Haulberroys, Branles,
        Pavanes, Sauterelles, Gaillardes
        I/IB1-Coll

    Zwei- Und Dreistimmige Solostucke Fur
        Die Laute I/IB1-Coll

BALLARD, ROBERT (ca. 1611)
    Ballet De La Reyne Et Courante I/IB1

    Ballet De M. Le Daufin I/IB1

    Ballets, 3, Extraits Du Premier Livre
        I/IB1

    Entree-Ballet Des Insencez I/IB1

    Pieces, 3 I/IB1

    Trois Branles I/IB1

BESARD, JEAN-BAPTISTE (1567-ca. 1625)
    Aux Logettes De Ces Bois I/IB1

    Branle I/IB1

    Branle Gay I/IB1

    Dances, 8 I/IB1

    Vous Me Juriez, Bergere I/IB1

BUISSON, DU
    Pieces, 3 I/IB1

CAHIERS DU GUITAROLIER, LES, VOL. 2
    I/IB1-Coll

CAMPION, FRANCOIS (1680-1748)
    Pieces, 20, De Son Livre De Tablature
        De Guitare I/IB1

    Prelude and Fugue I/IB1

    Prelude and Fugue in D I/IB1

    Sarabande-Gigue I/IB1

    Soiree A Versailles I/IB1

    Suite in B minor I/IB1

    Suite in D I/IB1

    Suite in D minor I/IB1

    Suite No. 2 in D I/IB1

CORBETTA, FRANCESCO (FRANCISQUE
    CORBETT) (ca. 1620-1681)
    Allemande Aymee De l'Auteur I/IB1

    Allemande, Cherie De Son Altesse Le
        Duc d'York I/IB1

    Allemande Du Roy I/IB1

    Allemande Et Gigue I/IB1

    Allemande Sur La Mort Du Duc De
        Glocester I/IB1

    Francesco Corbetta: 16 Compositions
        Selected From "Varii Capricci Per
        La Ghitarra Spagnuola" I/IB1

    Gavotte, Aymee Du Duc De Monmouth
        I/IB1

    Passacaglia I/IB1

    Prelude I/IB1

    Saraband I/IB1

CORBETTA, FRANCESCO (FRANCISQUE
    CORBETT) (cont'd.)

    Suite in A minor I/IB1

    Suite in D I/IB1

    Tombeau De Madame d'Orleans, Le
        I/IB1

COURANTES, 2 I/IB1

DANSES, 2 I/IB1

DANSES, 4 I/IB1

EUROPAISCHE GITARREN- UND LAUTENMUSIK,
    VOL. 4 I/IB1

FRANCISQUE, ANTOINE (ca. 1570-1605)
    Pavane Espagnole I/IB1

GAULTIER, DENIS (GAULTHIER)
    (ca. 1603-1672)
    Lautensuiten; 4 Suites I/IB1

GITARREMUSIK DES BAROCK I: AUS EINEM
    FRANZOSISCHEN TABULATURBUCH DES 17.
    JAHRHUNDERTS I/IB1-Coll

GITARREMUSIK DES BAROCK II: AUS EINEM
    FRANZOSISCHEN TABULATURBUCH DES 17.
    JAHRHUNDERTS; AUS DER AUSSEER
    GITARRE-TABULATUR I/IB1-Coll

GITARRENMUSIK DES 16.-18. JAHRHUNDERTS,
    VOL. I I/IB1-Coll

GRENERIN, HENRY
    Suite No. 4 in C I/IB1

JEUNE, HENRI LE
    Chanson I/IB1

LE ROY, ADRIEN (? -1599)
    Adrian Le Roy: 10 Compositions I/IB1

    Allemand, MIN 262 I/IB1

    Branle Gay I/IB1

    Branles De Bourgogne, 9 I/IB1

    Danses De Cour, 4 I/IB1

    Fantasy No. 1 I/IB1

    Fantasy No. 2 I/IB1

    Gaillarde La Rocca E Il Fuso I/IB1

    Pavane Et Gaillarde I/IB1

    Pavane "Si Ie Me Vois" I/IB1

    Pieces, 3 I/IB1

    4 Pieces Pour Guitare (1552) I/IB1

    Prelude Et Chanson I/IB1

LOUIS XIII, KING OF FRANCE (1601-1643)
    Amaryllis I/IB1

MUSICHE PER CHITARRA ALLA CORTE DI
    VERSAILLES I/IB1-Coll

PAVAN I/IB1

PERRICHON, JULIEN (ca. 1565-1610)
    Preludes, 3 I/IB1

VISEE, ROBERT DE (ca. 1650-ca. 1775)
    Allemand, MIN 351 I/IB1

    Allemand, VOCG 38 I/IB1

    Beruhmte Suite In D-Moll I/IB1

    Darab Gitarra, 6 (6 Pieces Pour
        Guitare) I/IB1

    Easy Suite In D Minor I/IB1

    Gavotte, VOCG 78 I/IB1

    Livre De Guitarre Dedie Au Roy (1682)
        I/IB1

    Livre De Pieces Pour La Guitarre
        (1686) I/IB1

    Minuet, VOCG 91 I/IB1

    Musica Del Re Sole I/IB1

    Oeuvres Completes Pour Guitare
        I/IB1-Coll

    Passacaglia, VOCG 92 I/IB1

    Petite Suite En Re Mineur, Pt. 1
        I/IB1

VISEE, ROBERT DE (cont'd.)

    Petite Suite En Re Mineur, Pt. 2
        I/IB1

    Pieces, 6, Extraites Du Livre Publie
        En 1686 Et Dedie A S.M. Louis XIV
        I/IB1

    Piezas, 3 I/IB1

    Piezas, 4 I/IB1

    Saraband, VOCG 90 I/IB1

    Suite A-Moll I/IB1

    Suite C-Moll I/IB1

    Suite D-Moll I/IB1

    Suite D-Moll (Re Mineur) I/IB1

    Suite E-Dur I/IB1

    Suite E-Moll I/IB1

    Suite Em La I/IB1

    Suite En La Et Passacaille I/IB1

    Suite En Re I/IB1

    Suite En Re Menor I/IB1

    Suite En Re Mineur I/IB1

    Suite En Re Mineur I/IB1

    Suite En Re Mineur I/IB1

    Suite En Re Mineur I/IB1

    Suite En Si Mineur Et 8 Pieces Du
        Deuxieme Livre I/IB1

    Suite En Sol Majeur I/IB1

    Suite En Sol Mineur I/IB1

    Suite G-Moll I/IB1

    Suite H-Moll I/IB1

    Suite In A I/IB1

    Suite In A I/IB1

    Suite in D minor I/IB1

    Suite In D-Moll I/IB1

    Suite in G I/IB1

    Suite In H-Moll I/IB1

    Suite In Re I/IB1

    Suite In Sol Minore I/IB1

    Suite No. 7 En Do Mayor I/IB1

Pre-Classical — Original
Works — Great Britain

ALLISON, RICHARD (ca. 1600)
    Pavan I/IB1

ALTENGLISCHE LAUTENMUSIK I/IB1-Coll

ANONYMOUS
    Greensleeves I/IB1

    2 Piezas Para Laud Del Teatro De
        Shakespeare I/IB1

    Sick Tune, The I/IB1

ANTOLOGIA DI MUSICA ANTICA, VOL. III
    I/IB1-Coll

BACHELER, DANIEL (ca. 1600)
    Courantes, 3 I/IB1

    Mounsieurs Almaine I/IB1

BLOW, JOHN (1649-1708)
    Courante I/IB1

BULMAN, BARUCH (ca. 1600)
    Pavan in D minor I/IB1

BYRD, WILLIAM (1543-1623)
Two Pieces For Lute I/IB1

CUTTING, FRANCIS
Almain, MIN 242 I/IB1

Almain, MIN 249 I/IB1

Almain Und Jig I/IB1

Greensleeves I/IB1

Pavan, MIN 245 I/IB1

Pieces, 2 I/IB1

Pieces, 5 I/IB1

Walsingham I/IB1

DOWLAND, JOHN (1562-1626)
Air I/IB1

Air And Galliard I/IB1

Beste Aus Dem Lautenwerk, Das I/IB1

Earl Of Derby His Galliard, The I/IB1

Earl Of Essex His Galliard, The I/IB1

Fancy, A I/IB1

3 Fantasias I/IB1

Forlorn Hope Fancy I/IB1

Gaillarde Et Allemande I/IB1

Gaillardes, 2 I/IB1

Galliard On A Galliard Of Daniel Bacheler, A I/IB1

Galliards, 2 I/IB1

Galliards, 3 I/IB1

King Of Denmark His Galliard, The I/IB1

Lachrimae I/IB1

Lachrimae Pavan Und Fantasie I/IB1

Lady Hunsdon's Puffe I/IB1

Lady Rich Her Galliard, The I/IB1

Leichte Stucke, 4 I/IB1

Melancholy Galliard I/IB1

Melancoly Galliard I/IB1

Mrs. Vaux's Jig I/IB1

Pieces, 2 I/IB1

Pieces, 2 I/IB1

Pieces, 2 I/IB1

Pieces, 2 I/IB1

Pieces, 3 I/IB1

Pieces, 6 I/IB1

Pieces, 7 I/IB1

Pieces, 8, Vol. 1 I/IB1

Pieces, 8, Vol. 2 I/IB1

Piper's Pavan I/IB1

Queen Elizabeth Her Galliard, The I/IB1

Solowerke, Vol. 1 I/IB1

Two Pieces I/IB1

DOWLAND, ROBERT (1591-1641)
Courantes, 6 I/IB1

Five Corantoes I/IB1

Six Lute Pieces I/IB1-Coll

Varietie Of Lute-Lessons, Vol. 1: Corantos I/IB1

Varietie Of Lute-Lessons, Vol. 2: Almaines I/IB1

Varietie Of Lute-Lessons, Vol. 3: Voltes I/IB1

Varietie Of Lute-Lessons, Vol. 4: Fantasias I/IB1

DOWLAND, ROBERT (cont'd.)

Varietie Of Lute-Lessons, Vol. 5: Galliards I/IB1

Varietie Of Lute-Lessons, Vol. 6: Pavins I/IB1

EASY MUSIC FOR GUITAR, VOL. 9 I/IB1-Coll

ELIZABETHAN DANCES, 4 I/IB1-Coll

ELIZABETHAN MELODIES, VOL. 1 I/IB1-Coll

ELIZABETHAN MELODIES, VOL. 2 I/IB1-Coll

3 ENGLISH LUTE FANTASIES I/IB1-Coll

EUROPAISCHE GITARREN- UND LAUTENMUSIK, VOL. 3 I/IB1

FERRABOSCO, ALFONSO (I) (1543-1588)
Pavan, MIN 415 I/IB1

Pavana, 6 I/IB1

GAILLARDES, 2 I/IB1

HOLBORNE, ANTONY (? -1602)
Cisterwerke, Die, Part 1: Werke Fur Cister Allein I/IB1-Coll

Cisterwerke, Die, Part 2: Werke Fur Cister Und Ein Bassinstrument I/IB1-Coll

Larmes Des Muses Et Gaillarde, Les I/IB1

Lute Pieces, 6 I/IB1

Pieces, 5 I/IB1

Praludium Und Fantasie I/IB1

JOHNSON, JOHN (1540-1594)
Galliard, MIN 11 I/IB1

JOHNSON, ROBERT [3] (ca. 1583-1633)
Almain I/IB1

Carman's Whistle I/IB1

Noble Man, The I/IB1

KOSTLICHKEITEN ENGLISCHER LAUTENMUSIK I/IB1-Coll

LEICHTE STUCKE AUS SHAKESPEARES ZEIT, VOL. 1 I/IB1-Coll

LEICHTE STUCKE AUS SHAKESPEARES ZEIT, VOL. 2 I/IB1-Coll

MACE, THOMAS (1613?-1709)
Pieces, 5 I/IB1

Suite in D minor I/IB1

Suite in E minor I/IB1

4 Suiten I/IB1

PHILIPS, PETER (1561-1628)
Chromatic Pavan I/IB1

Galliard I/IB1

Pavan I/IB1

PIECES ELISABETHAINES I/IB1-Coll

PILKINGTON, FRANCIS (ca. 1562-1638)
Pieces, 5 I/IB1

RENAISSANCE POPULAR MUSIC I/IB1-Coll

ROBINSON, THOMAS (fl. ca. 1603)
Allemand, MIN 350 I/IB1

Allemande Und Galliard I/IB1

Bellvedere I/IB1

Galliard, MIN 93 I/IB1

Pieces, 5 I/IB1

2 Pieces I/IB1

Piezas De Laud, 4 I/IB1

Schoole Of Musicke, The I/IB1

Spanish Pavan, The I/IB1

Toy, Air And Gigue I/IB1

ROSSETER, PHILIP (ca. 1568-1623)
Galliard I/IB1

ROSSETER, PHILIP (cont'd.)

Galyerd Y A Pavin I/IB1

STUKKEN UIT DE OUD-ENGELSE LUITLITERATUUR, 2 I/IB1-Coll

Pre-Classical — Original Works — Hungary

BAKFARK, BALINT (VALENTIN) (1507-1576)
Fantasia Seconda A Quattro Voci, For Lute I/IB1

Fantasy I/IB1

Lautenbuch Von Krakau, Das I/IB1

Lautenbuch Von Lyon, Das - The Lyons Lute Book, 1553 I/IB1

Ricercari, 3 I/IB1

REGI MAGYAR ZENE GITARRA – EARLY HUNGARIAN MUSIC FOR GUITAR I/IB1-Coll

Pre-Classical — Original Works — Italy

ALTITALIENISCHE LAUTENMUSIK I/IB1-Coll

ANONYMOUS
Aus Altitalienischen Lautenbuchern I/IB1

Aus Einer Lautenhandschrift Des 16. Jahrhunderts I/IB1

Gagliarda Del Passo Mezzo I/IB1

ANTOLOGIA DI MUSICA ANTICA, VOL. I I/IB1-Coll

ANTOLOGIA DI MUSICA ANTICA, VOL. II I/IB1-Coll

BARBERIS, MELCHIOR DE (ca. 1549)
Pavana E Saltarello I/IB1

BARBETTA PADOVANO, JULIO CESARE (ca. 1540-1603)
Gagliarde, 10 I/IB1

Pavane, 8 I/IB1

BIANCHINI, DOMENICO (ca. 1563)
Tant Que Vivrai I/IB1

BOSSINENSIS, FRANCISCUS
Ricercari, 26 I/IB1

BRESCIANELLO, GIOVANNI ANTONIO (ca. 1690-1752)
Partita No. 6 I/IB1

Partita No. 7 I/IB1

Partita No. 16 I/IB1

Pezzi, 2 I/IB1

Suite in E minor I/IB1

CALVI, CARLO (ca. 1646)
Carlo Calvi I/IB1

Composizioni, 15 I/IB1

CANZONEN UND TANZE AUS DEM XVI. JAHRHUNDERT I/IB1

CAROSO, FABRIZIO (1526-1600)
Aria E Danza I/IB1

Laura Soave I/IB1

Petites Pieces, 8 I/IB1

Pieces, 4 I/IB1

Selva Amorosa I/IB1

CASTELIONO, ANTONIO
   Intabolatura De Leuto De Diversi
     Autori   I/IB1

CREMA, JOAN MARIA DA
   Intavolatura Di Liuto: Libro Primo
     (1546)   I/IB1-Coll

   Pass'e Mezzo E Saltarello, A La
     Bolognesa   I/IB1

   Recercar Undecimo Y Recercar
     Tredecimo   I/IB1

   Ricercari, 5   I/IB1

DALZA, JOAN AMBROSIO
   Intabulatura De Lauto (Petrucci,
     1508), Part 1: "Tastar De Corde –
     Calate"   I/IB1-Coll

   Intabulatura De Lauto (Petrucci,
     1508), Part 2: "Padoane Alla
     Venetiana"   I/IB1-Coll

   Intabulatura De Lauto (Petrucci,
     1508), Part 3: "Padoane Alla
     Ferrarese"   I/IB1-Coll

EUROPAISCHE GITARREN- UND LAUTENMUSIK,
   VOL. 1   I/IB1

FRANCESCO DA MILANO
     (ca. 1497?-ca. 1573?)
   Fantasien, 3   I/IB1

   Fantasy   I/IB1

   Opere Complete Per Liuto, Vol. 1:
     Composizioni Originali
     I/IB1-Coll

   Opere Complete Per Liuto, Vol. 2:
     Intavolature Di Opere Polifoniche
     Vocali   I/IB1-Coll

   Pavan   I/IB1

   Pescatore Che Va Cantando   I/IB1

GAGLIARDE, 2   I/IB1

GALILEI, MICHEL ANGELO
   Corrente Und Saltarello   I/IB1

   Primo Libro D'Intavolatura Di Liuto,
     Il (1620)   I/IB1

GALILEI, VINCENZO (ca. 1520-1591)
   Gagliarde, 2   I/IB1

   Passo Mezzo In Discant Y Saltarello
     I/IB1

   Pieces, 10   I/IB1

   Saltarello, MIN 308   I/IB1

GARSI DA PARMA, SANTINO (1542-1603)
   Aria Del Granduca   I/IB1

   Pezzi, 3   I/IB1

GORZANIS, GIACOMO (ca. 1525-ca. 1578)
   Balletto   I/IB1

   Libro De Intabulatura Di Liuto (1567)
     I/IB1-Coll

   Musiche Scelte Dalle Intavolature Per
     Liuto   I/IB1

   Napolitane, 15   I/IB1

GOSTENA, G.B. DELLA
   Intavolatura Di Liuto (1599)
     I/IB1-Coll

GRANATA, GIOVANNI BATTISTA
     (fl. ca. 1674)
   Gigue   I/IB1

   Giovanni Battista Granata: 11
     Compositions   I/IB1

   Toccata   I/IB1

ITALIAANSE LUITMUZIEK UIT DE
   RENAISSANCE   I/IB1-Coll

KAPSBERGER, JOHANN HIERONYMUS
     (ca. 1600-1650)
   Gagliarden, 3   I/IB1

   Toccata   I/IB1

LUTE PIECES, 2   I/IB1

LUTE PIECES OF THE RENAISSANCE, 6
   I/IB1-Coll

MAESTRI DEL '500   I/IB1

MELII DA REGGIO, PIETRO PAOLO
     (fl. 1614-1616)
   Dimi Amore, Passeggiato Dall'autore
     I/IB1

   Pieces, 3, [1616]   I/IB1

MILONI, PIETRO
   Passacagli; Folia; Pavaniglia;
     Gagliarda; Etc.   I/IB1

MOLINARO, SIMONE
   Intavolatura Di Liuto, Libro Primo
     (1599)   I/IB1-Coll

   Pezzi, 3   I/IB1

   Saltarello Quarto   I/IB1

MUSICHE DEL RINASCIMENTO   I/IB1-Coll

NEGRI, CESARE (IL TROMBONE)
     (ca. 1536- ?)
   Balletti, 8   I/IB1

   Catena D'amore   I/IB1

   Lautentanze Des XVI. Jahrhunderts
     I/IB1

   Nuove Inventioni Di Balli   I/IB1

PELLEGRINI, DOMENICO
   Domenico Pellegrini   I/IB1

PICCININI, ALESSANDRO
   Toccata   I/IB1

PIECES POUR LUTH DU 16E SIECLE, 12
   I/IB1-Coll

PIEZAS PARA LAUD DEL SIGLO XVI, 4
   I/IB1

RADINO, GIOVANNI MARIA
   Intavolatura Di Balli (1592)
     I/IB1-Coll

RICERCARE, PER LIUTO   I/IB1

RONCALLI, LUDOVICO
   Capricci Armonici: Sarabande-Gigue
     I/IB1

   Partita in D   I/IB1

   3 Partiten   I/IB1

   Passacaglia   I/IB1

   Preludio E Giga   I/IB1

   Preludio, Sarabande E Giga   I/IB1

   Suite in B minor   I/IB1

   Suite in D   I/IB1

   Suite in D minor   I/IB1

   Suite in E minor   I/IB1

   Suite in G   I/IB1

   Suite No. 1   I/IB1

   Suite No. 5 in A minor   I/IB1

   Suite No. 7 in D minor   I/IB1

   Suite No. 9 in G minor   I/IB1

   Suiten, 9   I/IB1

   Suiten Nr. 3 Und Nr. 4   I/IB1

ROTTA, ANTONIO (? -1548)
   Rocca E Il Fuso, La, Chanson
     Italienne   I/IB1

   Suite Of Dances For Lute (1546)
     I/IB1

SEVERINO, GIULIO
   Fantasy   I/IB1

TANZE AUS DER RENAISSANCE   I/IB1

VECCHI, ORAZIO (HORATIO) (1550-1605)
   Pezzi Per Liuto, 4   I/IB1

VIRCHI, PAOLO (? -ca. 1610)
   Tanze, Canzonen Und Phantasien   I/IB1

Pre-Classical — Original Works — The Netherlands

ADRIAENSSEN, EMANUEL (ca. 1550-1604)
   2 Dances And 2 Fantasies   I/IB1

   Fantasy No. 3   I/IB1

COCQ, FRANCOIS LE
   Suite in A minor   I/IB1

DEROSIER, NICOLAS
   Chaconnes, 12   I/IB1

EUROPAISCHE GITARREN- UND LAUTENMUSIK,
   VOL. 6   I/IB1

FLANDRISCHES GITARRENBUCH, VOL. 1:
   FANTASIES AND SONGS   I/IB1

FLANDRISCHES GITARRENBUCH, VOL. 2:
   DANCES   I/IB1

HOVE, JOACHIM VAN DEN (1567-1620)
   Chanson Flameng   I/IB1

   Delitiae Musicae, 1612, Part 1:
     "Praeludien Und Pavanen"
     I/IB1-Coll

   Delitiae Musicae, 1612, Part 2:
     "Passamezzen Mit Ihren
     Galliarden"   I/IB1-Coll

   Delitiae Musicae, 1612, Part 3:
     "Favoritos, Galliarden,
     Bergamasca, Une Jeune Fillette"
     I/IB1-Coll

   Delitiae Musicae, 1612, Part 4:
     "Allemanden, Balletti, Branden,
     Couranten, Chansons, Canarie"
     I/IB1-Coll

   Nederlandse Luitmuziek Uit De 17e
     Eeuw   I/IB1

   Praludien, 6   I/IB1

   Suite   I/IB1

HOWET, GREGORIO (ca. 1550-1620)
   Fantasy No. 6   I/IB1

OUD-HOLLANDSCHE DANSMUZIEK UIT DEN 80-
   JARIGEN OORLOG   I/IB1

SAINT LUC, JACQUES DE (1616- ?)
   Suite in E   I/IB1

SWEELINCK, JAN PIETERSZOON (1562-1621)
   Lantdarabok   I/IB1

   Pieces, 4   I/IB1

   Pieces, 4   I/IB1

   Psalm No. 5   I/IB1

   Psalm No. 23   I/IB1

   Voltes, 2   I/IB1

VALLET, NICOLAS (1583-1626)
   Air Und Courante   I/IB1

   Allemande Fortune Helas Pourquoi
     I/IB1

   Solostucke   I/IB1

Pre-Classical — Original Works — Poland

DLUGORAJ, ADALBERT (WOJIECH) (ca. 1550)
  Fantazje I Wilanele I/IB1-Coll

EUROPAISCHE GITARREN- UND LAUTENMUSIK,
  VOL. 7 I/IB1

JAKOB POLAK (JACQUES POLONAIS)
  (ca. 1545-1605)
  Courante I/IB1

  Galliard No. 1 I/IB1

PEKIEL, BARTLOMIEJ (? -ca. 1670)
  Pieces, 4 I/IB1

  Utworow Na Lutnie Lub Gitare W Stroju
  E, 40 I/IB1

POOLSE LUITMUZIEK I/IB1-Coll

Z MUZYKI POLSKIEGO RENESANSU
  I/IB1-Coll

Pre-Classical — Original Works — Sweden

AUS WILLIAM BRADE'S "VISBOK" I/IB1

Pre-Classical — Original Works — Unknown Countries

ACADEMICO CALIGINOSO, L' I/IB1

ANONYMOUS
  Barcarolle, MIN 79 I/IB1

  Fantasy, MIN 73 I/IB1

LEICHTE VERGNUGLICHE ORIGINALSTUCKE AUS
  DEM 18. JAHRHUNDERT I/IB1

MENUETS, 2 I/IB1

PASSEPIEDS, 2 I/IB1

PRALUDIUM UND 2 MENUETTE I/IB1

TANZE UND WEISEN AUS DEM BAROCK I/IB1

Pre-Classical — Original Works — Miscellaneous

6 ANONYMOUS LUTE SOLOS I/IB1-Coll

AUS DEM BALTISCHEN LAUTENBUCH 1740
  I/IB1-Coll

AUS DEM TABULATURBUCH DES CHRISTOPHORUS
  HERHOLDER (1602) I/IB1-Coll

AUS TABULATUREN DES 16.-18.
  JAHRHUNDERTS I/IB1-Coll

DANSES, 4 I/IB1-Coll

DEUXIEME RECUEIL DE PIECES FACILES
  I/IB1-Coll

EASY 16TH CENTURY PIECES, 7 I/IB1-Coll

EUROPAISCHE GITARREN- UND LAUTENMUSIK,
  VOL. 1 I/IB1-Coll

EUROPAISCHE GITARREN- UND LAUTENMUSIK,
  VOL. 2 I/IB1-Coll

EUROPAISCHE GITARREN- UND LAUTENMUSIK,
  VOL. 3 I/IB1-Coll

EUROPAISCHE GITARREN- UND LAUTENMUSIK,
  VOL. 4 I/IB1-Coll

EUROPAISCHE GITARREN- UND LAUTENMUSIK,
  VOL. 5 I/IB1-Coll

EUROPAISCHE GITARREN- UND LAUTENMUSIK,
  VOL. 6 I/IB1-Coll

EUROPAISCHE GITARREN- UND LAUTENMUSIK,
  VOL. 7 I/IB1-Coll

FANTASIAS I/IB1-Coll

GITARRENMUSIK DES 16.-18. JAHRHUNDERTS,
  VOL. I I/IB1-Coll

GITARRENMUSIK DES 16.-18. JAHRHUNDERTS,
  VOL. II I/IB1-Coll

GITARRENSPIEL ALTER MEISTER, ORIGINAL-
  MUSIK DES 16. UND 17. JAHRHUNDERTS,
  VOL.1 I/IB1-Coll

GITARRENSPIEL ALTER MEISTER, ORIGINAL-
  MUSIK DES 16. UND 17. JAHRHUNDERTS,
  VOL.2 I/IB1-Coll

HUDBA CESKYCH LOUTNOVYCH TABULATUR
  I/IB1-Coll

LAUTENMUSIK AUS DER RENAISSANCE, VOL. I
  I/IB1-Coll

LAUTENMUSIK AUS DER RENAISSANCE, VOL.
  II I/IB1-Coll

LAUTENMUSIK DES 17. UND 18.
  JAHRHUNDERTS, VOL. 1 - LUTE MUSIC
  FROM THE 17TH AND 18TH CENTURY,
  VOL. 1 I/IB1-Coll

MEINE ERSTEN GITARRENSTUCKE, VOL.3:
  "MEISTER DER RENAISSANCE"
  I/IB1-Coll

MUSIK DER RENAISSANCE FUR GITARRE
  I/IB1-Coll

MUSIK FUR LIEBHABER DES GITARRESPIELS,
  VOL. 1: AUS TABULATUREN DES 16.
  JAHRHUNDERTS I/IB1-Coll

MUSIK FUR LIEBHABER DES GITARRESPIELS,
  VOL. 2: AUS TABULATUREN DES 16. UND
  17. JAHRHUNDERTS I/IB1-Coll

3 PIECES BY HOLBORNE, PERICHON, BALARD
  I/IB1-Coll

QUELQUES PAGES DE GUITARE CLASSIQUE
  I/IB1-Coll

REGI MAGYAR ZENE GITARRA - EARLY
  HUNGARIAN MUSIC FOR GUITAR
  I/IB1-Coll

SELECCION DE OBRAS DE LOS MAS CELEBRES
  LAUDISTAS FRANCESES E ITALIANOS DE
  LOS SIGLOS XVI, XVII Y XVIII
  I/IB1-Coll

TABULATUREN FUR LAUTE, VIHUELA UND
  GITARRE, IN NEUER NOTATION MIT
  GEGENUBERSTELLUNG DER
  ENTSPRECHENDEN ALTEN MANUSKRIPTE
  I/IB1-Coll

Pre-Classical Arrangements

ACADEMICO CALIGINOSO, L' I/IB1

ALBINONI, TOMASO (1671-1750)
  Adagio in G minor I/IB1

  Beruhmtes Adagio, Nach Einem
  Themenfragment Mit Beziffertem
  Generalbass I/IB1

ALTE MINNELIEDER I/IB1-Coll

ANONYMOUS
  Antike Tanze Und Arien I/IB1

ANONYMOUS (cont'd.)

  Dindandon I/IB1

  4 Piezas Del S. XVIII I/IB1

ASTON, HUGH (ca. 1480-ca. 1522)
  Hornepype I/IB1

BACH, CARL PHILIPP EMANUEL (1714-1788)
  Siciliana I/IB1

  Solfegietto I/IB1

  Stucke, 2 I/IB1

  Xenophone, La I/IB1

BACH, JOHANN CHRISTIAN (1735-1782)
  Minuet, MIN 80 I/IB1

BACH, JOHANN SEBASTIAN (1685-1750)
  Album Completo De Ana Magdalena Bach,
  2 Vols. VII-Coll

  Album Di 10 Pezzi, Per La Formazione
  Musicale E Tecnica Del
  Chitarrista VII-Coll

  Album No. 1 VII-Coll

  Allein Gott In Der Hoh' Sei Ehr' VII

  Aria, BWV 508 VII

  Aria E Preludio VII-Coll

  2 Arias VII

  Ausgewahlte Stucke Fur Gitarre
  VII-Coll

  Bach Album VII-Coll

  Bach-Buch Fur Die Gitarre VII-Coll

  Bach-Buch Fur Gitarre, Das, Vol. 1
  VII-Coll

  Bach-Buch Fur Gitarre, Das, Vol. 2
  VII-Coll

  Bach For The Guitar VII-Coll

  Canon Par Mouvement Retrograde VII

  Drei Kleine Stucke Aus Dem
  Notenbuchlein Der Anna Magdalena
  Bach VII-Coll

  Due Bourrees E Marcia VII-Coll

  Due Preludi VII-Coll

  Edition Nicolas Alfonso, No. 2
  VII-Coll

  Edition Nicolas Alfonso, No. 16
  VII-Coll

  Edition Nicolas Alfonso, No. 17
  VII-Coll

  Edition Nicolas Alfonso, No. 18
  VII-Coll

  Famosissime Gavotte Di J.S. Bach, Le
  VII-Coll

  Five Easy Pieces For The Guitar
  VII-Coll

  Fugue, BWV 855, in E minor VII-Coll

  Fugue for Lute, BWV 1000, in G minor
  VII

  Gavotte, De La Sonata Para Violin En
  Mi Mayor VII-Coll

  Jesus Bleibet Meine Freude. Chorale
  VII

  Kleine Stucke VII-Coll

  Komm Susser Tod VII

  Kompositionen Fur Die Laute; Erste
  Vollstandige Und Kritisch
  Durchgesehene Ausgabe; Nach Altem
  Quellenmaterial Fur Die Heutige
  Laute Ubertragen Und
  Herausgegeben VII-Coll

  Lautenmusik VII-Coll

  Lautenmusik VII-Coll

  Loure And Sarabande VII-Coll

  Mass In B Minor: Crucifixus VII

  Menuet-Trio In G Minor I/IB1

BACH, JOHANN SEBASTIAN (cont'd.)

Menuett Und Gigue VII-Coll

Minue Y Marcha VII-Coll

Minuet, BWV Anh. 113, in F VII

Minuet, BWV Anh. 115, in G minor
  VII, VII-Coll

Minuet, BWV Anh. 120, in A minor VII

Opere Complete Per Liuto VII-Coll

Partita for Keyboard Instrument, BWV
  825, in B flat VII

Partita for Lute, BWV 997, in C minor
  VII

Partita for Lute, BWV 997, in C
  minor, Fugue VII

Partita for Lute, BWV 997, in C
  minor, Prelude VII

Partita for Lute, BWV 997, in C
  minor, Saraband VII, VII-Coll

Partita for Lute, BWV 1006a, in E
  VII

Partita for Lute, BWV 1006a, in E,
  Gigue VII

Partita for Lute, BWV 1006a, in E,
  Prelude VII

Partita for Violin, BWV 1002, in B
  minor, Bourree VII, VII-Coll

Partita for Violin, BWV 1002, in B
  minor, Saraband VII, VII-Coll

Partita for Violin, BWV 1004, in D
  minor VII

Partita for Violin, BWV 1004, in D
  minor, Chaconne VII

Partita for Violin, BWV 1006, in E
  VII

Partita for Violin, BWV 1006, in E,
  Gavotte En Rondeau VII

Partita for Violin, BWV 1006, in E,
  Gigue VII

Partita for Violin, BWV 1006, in E,
  Minuet I VII

Partita for Violin, BWV 1006, in E,
  Prelude VII

Partita for Violin in B minor, BWV
  1002, Saraband-Double VII

5 Pecas VII-Coll

Pedal-Exercitium In G Minor VII

26 Pieces Pour Guitare VII-Coll

Prelude and Fugue, BWV 553, in C VII

Prelude, BWV 846, in C VII

Prelude, BWV 853, in E flat minor
  VII

Prelude, BWV 866, in B flat VII

Prelude, BWV 927, in F VII

Prelude, BWV Anh. 114, in G VII

Prelude for Lute, BWV 999, in C minor
  VII, VII-Coll

Prelude, Fugue And Allegro For Lute,
  In E: Allegro VII

Prelude, Fugue And Allegro For Lute,
  In E-Flat VII

Prelude, Sarabande And Gigue
  VII-Coll

Prelude Und Menuett VII-Coll

Preludio E Sarabanda VII-Coll

Quattro Transcripciones VII-Coll

Schonsten Stucke Aus Dem
  "Notenbuchlein Der Anna Magdalena
  Bach" 1725, Die VII-Coll

Siciliana And Fugue, From Sonata No.
  1 For Solo Violin VII-Coll

Sonata for Flute, BWV 1013, in A
  minor VII

BACH, JOHANN SEBASTIAN (cont'd.)

Sonata for Violin, BWV 1001, in G
  minor VII

Sonata for Violin, BWV 1001, in G
  minor, Fugue VII, VII-Coll

Sonata for Violin, BWV 1001, in G
  minor, Siciliano VII

Sonata for Violin, BWV 1003, in A
  minor VII

Sonata for Violin, BWV 1003, in A
  minor, Fugue VII

Sonata for Violin, BWV 1005, in C
  VII

Sonata for Violin, BWV 1005, in C,
  Fugue VII

Sonatas And Partitas, BWV 1001-1006
  VII-Coll

Sonate E Partite, Vol. 1 VII-Coll

Sonate E Partite, Vol. 2 VII-Coll

Suite, BWV 824, in A, Courante VII

Suite for Keyboard Instrument, BWV
  807, in A minor, Saraband VII

Suite for Keyboard Instrument, BWV
  808, in G minor, Gavotte I VII

Suite for Keyboard Instrument, BWV
  810, in E minor, Passepied II
  VII

Suite for Keyboard Instrument, BWV
  814, in B minor, Minuet VII

Suite for Keyboard Instrument, BWV
  816, in G, Gavotte VII

Suite for Keyboard Instrument, BWV
  825, in B flat, Gigue VII

Suite for Keyboard Instrument, BWV
  825, in B flat, Minuet I-II VII

Suite for Keyboard Instrument, BWV
  825, in B flat, Saraband VII

Suite for Lute, BWV 995, in G minor
  VII

Suite for Lute, BWV 995, in G minor,
  Allemand VII

Suite for Lute, BWV 996, in E minor
  VII

Suite for Lute, BWV 996, in E minor,
  Bourree VII-Coll

Suite for Lute, BWV 996, in E minor,
  Courante VII

Suite for Lute, BWV 996, in E minor,
  Passaggio-Prelude VII

Suite for Lute, BWV 996, in E minor,
  Saraband VII, VII-Coll

Suite for Orchestra, BWV 1067, in B
  minor, Badinerie VII

Suite for Orchestra, BWV 1067, in B
  minor, Polonaise VII

Suite for Orchestra, BWV 1067, in B
  minor, Polonaise-Double VII

Suite for Orchestra, BWV 1068, in D,
  Air VII

Suite for Violoncello, BWV 1007, in G
  VII

Suite for Violoncello, BWV 1007, in
  G, Prelude VII

Suite for Violoncello, BWV 1008, in D
  minor VII

Suite for Violoncello, BWV 1008, in D
  minor, Courante VII

Suite for Violoncello, BWV 1009, in C
  VII

Suite for Violoncello, BWV 1009, in
  C, Bourree I-II VII

Suite for Violoncello, BWV 1009, in
  C, Courante VII

Suite for Violoncello, BWV 1009, in
  C, Prelude VII

BACH, JOHANN SEBASTIAN (cont'd.)

Suite for Violoncello, BWV 1010, in E
  flat VII

Suite for Violoncello, BWV 1010, in E
  flat, Prelude VII

Suite for Violoncello, BWV 1011, in C
  minor VII

Suite for Violoncello, BWV 1011, in C
  minor, Gavotte I-II VII

Suite for Violoncello, BWV 1011, in C
  minor, Saraband VII

Suite for Violoncello, BWV 1012, in D
  VII

Suite for Violoncello, BWV 1012, in
  D, Gavotte I-II VII

Suite for Violoncello, BWV 1012, in
  D, Saraband VII-Coll

Toccata, BWV 565, in D minor VII

Toccata, BWV 913, in D minor, First
  Movement VII

Trois Menuets VII-Coll

Twelve Little Preludes VII-Coll

Two Cello Preludes VII-Coll

Verschiedene Stucke, Vol. 1 VII-Coll

Verschiedene Stucke, Vol. 2 VII-Coll

Verschiedene Stucke, Vol. 3 VII-Coll

Vier Leichte Stucke From The Anna
  Magdalena Bach Notenbuchlein
  (1725) VII-Coll

Wybrane Utwory - Pieces Choisies
  VII-Coll

Zwanzig Stucke Aus Dem Notenbuchlein
  Fur Anna Magdalena Bach VII-Coll

Zwei Beruhmte Siciliane VII-Coll

Zwei Gitarren Musizieren, Vol. 4:
  Inventionen Und Sinfonien
  VII-Coll

BAROQUE MUSIC FOR GUITAR I/IB1

BELLMAN, CARL MICHAEL (1740-1795)
  Gitarr-Solon I/IB1

  Melodien Aus Dem Repertoire Von Carl
    Michael Bellman I/IB1

  Opp, Amaryllis Och Andra Fredmans
    Sanger Och Epistlar I/IB1

BERUHMTE ARIEN, 4 I/IB1-Coll

BLOW, JOHN (1649-1708)
  Prelude I/IB1

BOHM, GEORG (1661-1733)
  Courante I/IB1

BONPORTI, FRANCESCO ANTONIO (1672-1748)
  Adagio Et Gigue I/IB1

BORRONO DA MILANO, PIETRO PAVOLO
  Suite De La Bella Andronica I/IB1

BUXTEHUDE, DIETRICH (ca. 1637-1707)
  Suite in E minor I/IB1

  Suite No. 3 I/IB1

BYRD, WILLIAM (1543-1623)
  Cantilena (Theme And 2 Variations)
    I/IB1

  Fortune (Theme And 4 Variations)
    I/IB1

  Pavan in C I/IB1

  Pavana " The Earle Of Salisbury"
    I/IB1

  Pavane Bray I/IB1

CABANILLES, JUAN BAUTISTA JOSE
  (1644-1712)
  Tiento De Falsas, 6th Tono I/IB1

CABEZON, ANTONIO DE (1510-1566)
  Composizioni Per Chitarra, 3 I/IB1

  Diferencias Sobre El Canto Del
    Caballero I/IB1

  Diferencias Sobre Las Vacas, 6 I/IB1

PARADIES, PIETRO DOMENICO (PARADISI)
    (1707-1791)
  Toccata I/IB1

PASQUINI, BERNARDO (1637-1710)
  Sonata in G minor I/IB1

PEZZI, 4, DA GRANDI VIRGINALISTI
    DELL'ERA ELISABETTIANA I/IB1-Coll

PIECES DE LA RENAISSANCE ESPAGNOLE, 4
    I/IB1-Coll

PIECES FROM THE FITZWILLIAM VIRGINAL
    BOOK, 13 I/IB1-Coll

PRAETORIUS, MICHAEL (1571-1621)
  Terpsichore Musarum I/IB1

PUES NO ME QUEREIS HABLER I/IB1

PURCELL, HENRY (1658 or 59-1695)
  Album Henry Purcell I/IB1

  Almand And Minuet I/IB1

  Chaconne I/IB1

  Courante, MIN 91 I/IB1

  Gavotte, MIN 219 I/IB1

  Pezzi, 3 I/IB1

  Pieces, 3 I/IB1

  Pieces, 3 I/IB1

  Pieces, 4 I/IB1

  Piezas, 4 I/IB1

  Prelude, MIN 90 I/IB1

  Preludio E Allemanda I/IB1

  Rondeau De Abdelazar I/IB1

  Suite No. 1 I/IB1

  Suite No. 4 I/IB1

QUELQUES PAGES DE GUITARE CLASSIQUE
    I/IB1

RAMEAU, JEAN-PHILIPPE (1683-1764)
  Air I/IB1

  Livri, La, Rondeau I/IB1

  Minuet I/IB1

  Minuetti, 2 I/IB1

  Minuetti, 6 I/IB1

  Minuetto, Da Platee I/IB1

  Pieces De Clavecin I/IB1

  Rappel Des Oiseaux, Le I/IB1

  Sarabande Et Menuet I/IB1

  Tambourin I/IB1

  Tendres Plaintes, Les I/IB1

REGI ZENE GITARRA, ATIRATOK A XVII-
    XVIII. SZAZAD MUZSIKAJABOL - ALTE
    MUSIK FUR GITARRE, WERKE AUS DEM
    17.-18. JAHRHUNDERT I/IB1-Coll

SANTA MARIA, THOMAS DE (1510-1570)
  Fabordon Y Fuga I/IB1

  Fantasias, 8 I/IB1

SCARLATTI, ALESSANDRO (1660-1725)
  Minuet I/IB1

  Minuet, MIN 381 I/IB1

  Sento Nel Core I/IB1

SCARLATTI, DOMENICO (1685-1757)
  Pieces, 5 I/IB1

  Sonata, Kirkpatrick 1 I/IB1

  Sonata, Kirkpatrick 11 I/IB1

  Sonata, Kirkpatrick 32, in E minor
    I/IB1

  Sonata, Kirkpatrick 33 I/IB1

  Sonata, Kirkpatrick 54 I/IB1

  Sonata, Kirkpatrick 64 I/IB1

  Sonata, Kirkpatrick 159 I/IB1

  Sonata, Kirkpatrick 208 I/IB1

SCARLATTI, DOMENICO (cont'd.)

  Sonata, Kirkpatrick 209 I/IB1

  Sonata, Kirkpatrick 322 I/IB1

  Sonata, Kirkpatrick 380 I/IB1

  Sonata, Kirkpatrick 391 I/IB1

  Sonata, Kirkpatrick 428 I/IB1

  Sonata, Kirkpatrick 431 I/IB1

  Sonata, Kirkpatrick 440 I/IB1

  Sonata, Kirkpatrick 481 I/IB1

  Sonata, Kirkpatrick 519, in F minor
    I/IB1

  Sonata, Kirkpatrick 544 I/IB1

  Sonata, Longo 33, Kirkpatrick 87
    I/IB1

  Sonata, MIN 311 I/IB1

  Sonata, MIN 312 I/IB1

  Sonata, MIN 387 I/IB1

  Sonata Pastorale I/IB1

  Sonatas, 3 I/IB1

  Sonatas, 9, Vol. 1 I/IB1

  Sonatas, 9, Vol. 2 I/IB1

  4 Sonatas, K. 391, 408, 424, 453
    I/IB1

  Sonatas, Vol. 1 I/IB1

  Sonatas, Vol. 2 I/IB1

  Sonatas, Vol. 3 I/IB1

  Sonate, 2 I/IB1

  Three Sonatas I/IB1

SCHENK, JOHANN (1753-1836)
  Suite in A minor I/IB1

SEIXAS, (JOSE ANTONIO) CARLOS DE
    (1704-1742)
  Menuets, 2 I/IB1

  Sonata SK 37 I/IB1

  4 Sonatas I/IB1

  Sonaten, 2 I/IB1

SENAILLE, JEAN BAPTISTE (1687-1730)
  Sonata I/IB1

SOLER, [PADRE] ANTONIO (1729-1783)
  Sonata No. 1 in A I/IB1

  Sonata No. 2 I/IB1

  Sonata No. 3 I/IB1

  Sonata No. 4, Bolero I/IB1

  Sonata No. 6 I/IB1

  Sonata No. 8 I/IB1

  Sonata No. 13 I/IB1

  Sonata No. 14 I/IB1

  Sonata No. 15 I/IB1

  Sonata No. 18, En Modo Dorico I/IB1

  Sonata No. 69 I/IB1

  Sonata No. 71 I/IB1

  Sonata No. 84 I/IB1

  Sonata No. 87 I/IB1

SPERONTES (JOHANN SIGISMUND SCHOLZE)
    (1705-1750)
  Spielstucke, 22 I/IB1

STAMITZ, JOHANN WENZEL ANTON
    (1717-1757)
  Divertissement in D I/IB1

  Fugue I/IB1

TELEMANN, GEORG PHILIPP (1681-1767)
  Fantasy in A I/IB1

  Fantasy in B flat I/IB1

  Fantasy in D I/IB1

TELEMANN, GEORG PHILIPP (cont'd.)

  Fantasy in E minor I/IB1

  Fantasy in F minor I/IB1

  Fantasy in G I/IB1

  Fantasy No. 7 I/IB1

  Gavotte I/IB1

  Passacaglia I/IB1

THREE FRENCH PIECES I/IB1-Coll

TORRE, FERNANDO DELLE
  Alta Danza I/IB1

VENEGAS DE HENESTROSA, TOMAS LUIS DE
  Fabordones, 2, Llano Y Glosado Del
    Cuarto Tono I/IB1

VICTORIA, TOMAS LUIS DE (ca. 1548-1611)
  Motets, 2 I/IB1

VIVALDI, ANTONIO (1678-1741)
  Concerto in D, MIN 388 I/IB1

  Gigue I/IB1

WOHLAUF MIT REICHEM SCHALLE; BICINIEN
    UM 1550 I/IB1-Coll

Pre-Classical — Original Works and Arrangements

ALTE HAUSMUSIK I/IB1-Coll

ALTE MEISTER DES 17. JAHRHUNDERTS
    I/IB1-Coll

ALTPOLNISCHE MUSIK I/IB1-Coll

ANTHOLOGIE DE LA MUSIQUE ANCIENNE, VOL.
    I: POUR LE LUTH I/IB1-Coll

ANTHOLOGIE DE LA MUSIQUE ANCIENNE, VOL.
    II: POUR LA GUITARE I/IB1-Coll

BAROQUE GUITARIST, THE I/IB1-Coll

DEUTSCHE MEISTER DES EIN- UND
    ZWEISTIMMIGEN LAUTENSATZES, 16.-18.
    JAHRHUNDERT I/IB1-Coll

FROM THE BACH FAMILY I/IB1-Coll

GUITAR MUSIC OF THE 16TH, 17TH AND 18TH
    CENTURIES I/IB1-Coll

INTERNATIONAL ANTHOLOGY I/IB1-Coll

KLEINE STUCKE ,3 I/IB1-Coll

MEINE ERSTEN GITARRENSTUCKE, VOL.2:
    "MEISTER DES BAROCK" I/IB1-Coll

4 PIECES BY DOWLAND, CUTTING, MORLEY
    I/IB1-Coll

RENAISSANCE MUSIC FOR GUITAR
    I/IB1-Coll

ZWEISTIMMIGES GITARRENSPIEL; LEICHTE
    STUCKE UND TANZE AUS DEM 16. BIS
    18. JAHRHUNDERT I/IB1-Coll

Classical and Pre-Romantic — Original Works

AGUADO, DIONISIO (1784-1849)
Adagio, MIN 345 I/IB2

Allegro I/IB2

Allegro Brillante I/IB2

Andante in A I/IB2

Andante, MIN 353 I/IB2

Fandango Variado I/IB2

Fandango Y Variaciones I/IB2

Leichte Walzer Und Etuden I/IB2

Minuet And Waltz I/IB2

Minuet, MIN 354 I/IB2

2 Minuetos Y 2 Estudios I/IB2

6 Minuetos I/IB2

Minuetto I/IB2

3 Rondos Brillantes I/IB2

Two Minuets I/IB2

6 Valses I/IB2

Variaciones Brillantes I/IB2

ANTOLOGIA DIDATTICA PER CHITARRA, DI
AUTORI ITALIANI E STRANIERI
I/IB2-Coll

CARCASSI, MATTEO (1792-1853)
Allegretto I/IB2

Ausgewahlte Walzer, 20 I/IB2

Capriccio I/IB2

Capriccio Und Pastorale I/IB2

Carcassi-Brevier I/IB2

Kleine Stucke, 24 I/IB2

Leichte Stucke, 12 I/IB2

Leichte Variationen, 6 I/IB2

Menuets, 2 I/IB2

Minuet I/IB2

Minuet in G I/IB2

Minuet in G, MIN 333 I/IB2

Rondo, MIN 383 I/IB2

Rondoletto I/IB2

Sonatinen, 3 I/IB2

Variationen Uber "Le Songe De
Rousseau" I/IB2

CARULLI, FERDINANDO (1770-1841)
Andante Grazioso I/IB2

6 Andanti I/IB2

Andantino And Waltz I/IB2

Ballet I/IB2

Kleine Vortragsstucke Fur Anfanger, 5
I/IB2

Moderato I/IB2

Nocturne in D I/IB2

Overture, Op. 6, No. 1 I/IB2

Poco Allegretto I/IB2

Receuil De 23 Morceaux I/IB2

Rondo, MIN 386 I/IB2

Sehr Leichte Stucke, 18, Vol. 1
I/IB2

CARULLI, FERDINANDO (cont'd.)
Solo, Op. 76, No. 2 I/IB2

Sonata I/IB2

Sonatine Facili, 14 I/IB2

Three Easy Waltzes I/IB2

Variazioni Su L'Arietta Italiana "Sul
Margine D'un Rio I/IB2

Variazioni Su Un Tema Di Beethoven
I/IB2

Waltz And Rondo I/IB2

CHOPIN, FREDERIC (1810-1849)
Prelude, Op. 28, No. 15 I/IB2

Preludios I/IB2

COSTE, NAPOLEON (1806-1883)
Estudio De Concierto I/IB2

Herbstblatter I/IB2

Melancolie I/IB2

Originalstucke, 6 I/IB2

Recreation I/IB2

Recreation Du Guitariste I/IB2

Reverie I/IB2

Rondo, MIN 384 I/IB2

Scherzo, MIN 385 I/IB2

9 Studien I/IB2

Tarantelle I/IB2

Ubungs- Und Unterhaltungsstucke, 16
I/IB2

DARR, ADAM (1811-1866)
Rondino I/IB2

DIABELLI, ANTON (1781-1858)
Andante Sostenuto I/IB2

Fughe, 2 I/IB2

Leichte Altwiener Landler, 24 I/IB2

Leichte Stucke Und Landler, Op. 89
And Op. 127 I/IB2

Leichte Vortragsstucke, 5 I/IB2

7 Praeludien I/IB2

Prelude in A I/IB2

Rondinos, 4 I/IB2

Skladby, 3 (3 Kompositionen) I/IB2

Sonata, Op. 29, No. 1, in C I/IB2

Vortragsstucke Fur Anfanger I/IB2

Wiener Tanze, 5 I/IB2

EEUW GELEDEN, EEN: GITAARSTUKJES VAN
19E-EEUWSE KOMPONISTEN I/IB2-Coll

FERANDIERE, FERNANDO
Petites Pieces, 6 I/IB2

GIULIANI, MAURO (1781-1829)
Allegretto, MIN346 I/IB2

Allegretto, MIN347 I/IB2

Allegro E Grazioso, Op. 40, No.8, 9
I/IB2

Andantino I/IB2

Andantino, MIN355 I/IB2

Andantino, MIN356 I/IB2

Antologia De La Guitarra I/IB2

Capriccio I/IB2

Capriccio, Op. 100, No. 11 I/IB2

Caprice Fur Gitarre I/IB2

Choix De Mes Fleurs Cheries I/IB2

Choix De Mes Fleurs Cheries (Le
Bouquet Emblematique) I/IB2

Composiciones Para Guitarra, Vol. 1
I/IB2

GIULIANI, MAURO (cont'd.)
Composiciones Para Guitarra, Vol. 2
I/IB2

Danse Nord I/IB2

Divertimento, Op. 37 I/IB2

Divertimento, Op. 40 I/IB2

Fughetta I/IB2

Giulianate I/IB2

Grande Ouverture I/IB2

Grazioso I/IB2

Leichte Fortschreitende Stucke, 6
I/IB2

Leichte Nordische Tanze, 16 I/IB2

Leichte Variationen Uber Ein
Osterreichisches Lied I/IB2

March, MIN 370 I/IB2

Melancholia I/IB2

Minuet De La Cour I/IB2

Monferrine, 12 I/IB2

Oeuvres Choisies Pour Guitare I/IB2

Papillon, Le I/IB2

Papillon, Le (Choix d'Airs Faciles)
I/IB2

Polonaise, MIN 371 I/IB2

Prelude in F, MIN 374 I/IB2

Preludes, 6, Op. 83 I/IB2

6 Preludios I/IB2

Rondo, Op. 8, No. 2, in G I/IB2

Rondo, Op. 11 I/IB2

Rondo, Op. 17, No. 1, in A I/IB2

Rondo Und Harfen-Etude I/IB2

Rondoletto I/IB2

Rossiniana, No. 1 I/IB2

Rossiniana, No. 2 I/IB2

Rossiniana, No. 3 I/IB2

Rossiniana, Op. 119-124 I/IB2-Coll

Scherzo Giocoso I/IB2

Scozzesi, 12 I/IB2

Sostenuto I/IB2

Theme and Variations I/IB2

Tirolesa I/IB2

Unterhaltungsstucke, 10 I/IB2

Utwory Wybrane I/IB2

12 Valzer I/IB2

Variations, 6: Op87 I/IB2

Variations, Op. 2 I/IB2

Variations, Op. 62 I/IB2

Variations, Op. 112 I/IB2

Variazioni E Finale, 4 I/IB2

Variazioni Su L'Aria "Schisserl Und A
Reindl" I/IB2

Variazioni Su Un Tema Dal Balletto
"Die Feindlichen Vollkstame"
I/IB2

Variazioni Su Un Tema Di Handel
I/IB2

Variazioni Su Un Tema Originale
I/IB2

Variazioni Sul Tema Della Follia Di
Spagna I/IB2

Variazioni Sulla Romanza Dall'Opera
"Ruhm Und Liebe" I/IB2

Variazioni Sull'Aria Favorita De "La
Molinara" I/IB2

SOR, FERNANDO (cont'd.)

Minuet, Op. 32, No. 1 I/IB2

Minuetos, 2 I/IB2

Minuetos, 2 I/IB2

Minuetos, 3 I/IB2

Minuetos, 4 I/IB2

Minuetos, 40 I/IB2-Coll

Minuetos En La, 2 I/IB2

Minuetos En Mi, 2 I/IB2

Minuetos En Re, 2 I/IB2

Minuetos En Sol, 2 I/IB2

Minuetos En Sol-Re, 2 I/IB2

Minuetos Para Guitarra, 34
    I/IB2-Coll

Minuettos En La Mayor, 2 I/IB2

Minuettos En Mi Mayor, 2 I/IB2

Morceau De Concert I/IB2

Obras Para Guitarra, 12, Primer Album
    I/IB2-Coll

Opera Omnia For The Spanish Guitar,
    Vol. 1 I/IB2

Opera Omnia For The Spanish Guitar,
    Vol. 2 I/IB2

Opera Omnia For The Spanish Guitar,
    Vol. 3 I/IB2

Opera Omnia For The Spanish Guitar,
    Vol. 4 I/IB2

Opera Omnia For The Spanish Guitar,
    Vol. 5 I/IB2

Opera Omnia For The Spanish Guitar,
    Vol. 6 I/IB2

Opera Omnia For The Spanish Guitar,
    Vol. 7 I/IB2

Opera Omnia For The Spanish Guitar,
    Vol. 8 I/IB2

Opera Omnia For The Spanish Guitar,
    Vol. 9 I/IB2

Opera Omnia For The Spanish Guitar,
    Vol. 10 I/IB2

Opera Omnia For The Spanish Guitar,
    Vol. 11 I/IB2

Opera Omnia For The Spanish Guitar,
    Vol. 12 I/IB2

Opus 1-20 I/IB2

Pastorale, MIN 382 I/IB2

Pastorale, Op. 32, No. 3 I/IB2

Preludios, 4 I/IB2

Rondo I/IB2

Septieme Fantaisie Et Variations
    Brillantes Sur Deux Airs Favoris
    Connus I/IB2

Six Petites Pieces Faciles I/IB2

Six Waltzes I/IB2

Sixty Short Pieces, Vol. 1 I/IB2

Sixty Short Pieces, Vol. 2 I/IB2

Sonata, Op. 22, Minuet I/IB2

Sonata, Op. 25, Minuet I/IB2

Theme and Variations I/IB2

Theme Varie Suive d'Un Menuet I/IB2

Tirana, Danza Spagnola I/IB2

Trois Pieces De Societe , Op. 33, No.
    1 I/IB2

Trois Pieces De Societe, Op. 33, No.
    2 I/IB2

Trois Pieces De Societe, Op. 33, No.
    3 I/IB2

Voyons Si C'est Ca, 6 Petites Pieces
    Faciles I/IB2

SOR, FERNANDO (cont'd.)

Voyons Si C'est Ca, 6 Petites Pieces
    Faciles Nos. 2, 6 I/IB2

Voyons Si C'est Ca, 6 Petites Pieces
    Faciles, Op. 45, No. 5 I/IB2

Voyons Si C'est Ca, 6 Petites Pieces
    Faciles, Op. 45, No. 6 I/IB2

Waltz, Op. 32, No. 2 I/IB2

STUNDE DER GITARRE, DIE; SPIELMUSIK AUS
    DER BLUTEZEIT DER GITARRE, VOL. I:
    SEHR LEICHT I/IB2-Coll

STUNDE DER GITARRE, DIE; SPIELMUSIK AUS
    DER BLUTEZEIT DER GITARRE, VOL. II:
    LEICHT I/IB2-Coll

STUNDE DER GITARRE, DIE; SPIELMUSIK AUS
    DER BLUTEZEIT DER GITARRE, VOL.
    III: MITTEL I/IB2-Coll

ZANI DE FERRANTI, MARCO AURELIO
    3 Melodies Nocturnes Et Une Etude
    I/IB2

Classical and Pre-Romantic — Arrangements

ALBENIZ, MATEO (ANTONIO PEREZ DE)
    (ca. 1797-1831)
    Sonata in D I/IB2

ALBRECHTSBERGER, JOHANN GEORG
    (1736-1809)
    Fugue I/IB2

BACH, JOHANN SEBASTIAN (1685-1750)
    Minuet, BWV Anh. 114, in G I/IB2

BEETHOVEN, LUDWIG VAN (1770-1827)
    Album I/IB2

2 Andantes I/IB2

Bagatelles, 2 I/IB2

Beethoven For The Guitar I/IB2

Fur Elise I/IB2

Minuet I/IB2

Minuet, MIN 334 I/IB2

Minuet, MIN 395 I/IB2

Minuet, MIN 396 I/IB2

Minuet, MIN 397 I/IB2

7 Minuetos I/IB2

Romance I/IB2

Romance for Violin and Orchestra
    I/IB2

Ruinas De Atenas, La, Marcha I/IB2

Septet I/IB2

Sonata for Piano, Op. 14, No. 2, in
    E, Second Movement I/IB2

Sonata for Piano, Op. 27, No. 2, in C
    sharp minor, First Movement I/IB2

Sonata in C sharp minor, Op. 27, No.
    2, Minuet I/IB2

Sonata No. 2, Scherzo, MIN 335 I/IB2

Sonata No. 3, Minuet I/IB2

Sonata No. 4, Op. 7, Largo I/IB2

Sonata No. 9, Andante I/IB2

Sonata No. 10, Andante I/IB2

Sonata, No. 12: Marcha Funebre I/IB2

Sonata, Op. 2, No. 1, Adagio I/IB2

Sonata, Op. 2, No. 2, Scherzo I/IB2

Sonata, Op. 13, Adagio I/IB2

Sonata, Op. 26, Andante I/IB2

BEETHOVEN, LUDWIG VAN (cont'd.)

Sonata, Op. 27, No. 2 I/IB2

Tema Y Var. IV [Del] Septimino I/IB2

Valse "Le Desir" I/IB2

BENDA, GEORG ANTON (JIRI ANTONIN)
    (1722-1795)
    Sonatina I/IB2

Sonatinen, 2 I/IB2

BOCCHERINI, LUIGI (1743-1805)
    Celebre Mineto I/IB2

Minuet I/IB2

Minueto-Bolero I/IB2

Minueto Espanol I/IB2

CHOPIN, FREDERIC (1810-1849)
    Composiciones, 3 I/IB2

Etude No. 6 I/IB2

Etude, Op. 10, No. 3, [excerpt]
    I/IB2

Marcha Funebre I/IB2

Mazurka No. 16 I/IB2

Mazurka, Op. 7, No. 1 I/IB2

Mazurka, Op. 7, No. 2 I/IB2

Mazurka, Op. 23, No. 22 I/IB2

Mazurka, Op. 33, No. 1 I/IB2

Mazurka, Op. 33, No. 4 I/IB2

Mazurka, Op. 33, No. 22 I/IB2

Mazurka, Op. 63, No. 3 I/IB2

Mazurka, Op. 64, No. 4 I/IB2

Nocturne, Op. 9, No. 1 I/IB2

Nocturne, Op. 9, No. 2 I/IB2

Nocturne, Op. 48, No. 1 I/IB2

Notturno I/IB2

Notturno No. 2 I/IB2

Notturno No. 9 I/IB2

Prelude No. 1 I/IB2

Prelude No. 7 I/IB2

Prelude No. 15 I/IB2

Prelude No. 20 I/IB2

Prelude, Op. 28, No. 4 I/IB2

Prelude, Op. 28, No. 6 I/IB2

Preludios, 3 I/IB2

Preludios, 3 I/IB2

Preludios, 6 I/IB2

2 Preludios I/IB2

Two Preludes I/IB2

Vals Brillante I/IB2

Waltz No. 10 I/IB2

Waltz, Op. 34, No. 2 I/IB2

Waltz, Op. 64, No. 2 I/IB2

Waltz, Op. 69, No. 1 I/IB2

Waltz, Op. 69, No. 2 I/IB2

Waltz, Op. 70, No. 2 I/IB2

COMPOSICIONES FACILES, 4 I/IB2-Coll

DIABELLI, ANTON (1781-1858)
    Rondino In C I/IB2

DUSSEK, JOHANN LADISLAUS (1760-1812)
    Rondo I/IB2

FLIES, J. BERNHARD (1770- ?)
    Wiegenlied "Schlafe Mein Prinzchen"
    I/IB2

GOSSEC, FRANCOIS JOSEPH (1734-1829)
    Gavotte, MIN 360 I/IB2

GOSSEC, FRANCOIS JOSEPH (cont'd.)

Tambourin And Gavotte I/IB2

HANDEL, GEORGE FRIDERIC (1685-1759)
Time Pieces I/IB2

HAYDN, [FRANZ] JOSEPH (1732-1809)
Allegro, MIN348 I/IB2

Andante, MIN 122 I/IB2

Andante, MIN 123 I/IB2

Andante, MIN 338 I/IB2

Andante, MIN 352 I/IB2

Andante, MIN 399 I/IB2

Andante Und Menuett I/IB2

5 Deutsche Tanze Und Coda I/IB2

Haydn-Buch, Das I/IB2

Largo Anay I/IB2

Largo Assai I/IB2

Menuets Celebres, 2 I/IB2

Minuet, Hob.III: 75 I/IB2

Minuet, MIN 119 I/IB2

Minuet, MIN 120 I/IB2

Minuet, MIN 121 I/IB2

Minuet, Op. 2, No. 2 I/IB2

Minueto Del Buey I/IB2

Minuetto, MIN 400 I/IB2

Minuetto, MIN 401 I/IB2

Serenade, MIN 124 I/IB2

Serenade, MIN 389 I/IB2

HILLER, JOHANN ADAM (1728-1804)
Lieder, 6 I/IB2

HOOK, RICHARD
Within A Mile Of Edinboro I/IB2

HORECKI, FELIKS (1799-1870)
Utwory Wybrane I/IB2

HUMMEL, JOHANN NEPOMUK (1778-1837)
Allegretto I/IB2

KLASSISCHE KOSTBARKEITEN I/IB2-Coll

MEISSONNIER, J. (1790- ?)
Antologia De La Guitarra, Vol. 1
I/IB2

MENDELSSOHN-BARTHOLDY, FELIX
(1809-1847)
Cancion I/IB2

Canzonetta I/IB2

Fruhlingslied I/IB2

Hilandera, La I/IB2

Marcha Nupcial I/IB2

Romance, MIN 402 I/IB2

Romance, Op. 38, No. 2 I/IB2

Romanza Senza Parole I/IB2

Romanza Sin Palabras, Op.19, No.2
I/IB2

Romanza Sin Palabras, Op.19, No.3
I/IB2

Romanza Sin Palabras, Op.30, No.3
I/IB2

Romanza Sin Palabras, Op. 85, No. 3
I/IB2

Romanza Sin Palabras, Op. 102, No. 2
I/IB2

Song Without Words I/IB2

Venetian Barcarolle I/IB2

Venezianisches Gondellied, Op.19,
No.6 I/IB2

Venezianisches Gondellied, Op.30,
No.6 I/IB2

Venezianisches Gondellied, Op.62,
No.5 I/IB2

MOZART, WOLFGANG AMADEUS (1756-1791)
Adagio for Harmonica, K. 356 I/IB2

Allegro I/IB2

Allegro, Andante, Menuetto And
Allegro I/IB2

Andante De La Casacion I/IB2

Andante, MIN 127 I/IB2

Andante, MIN 128 I/IB2

Andante, MIN 129 I/IB2

Larghetto And Allegro I/IB2

Marcha A La Turca I/IB2

Minuet, MIN 58 I/IB2

Minuet, MIN 59 I/IB2

Minuet, MIN 60 I/IB2

Minuet, MIN 61 I/IB2

Minuet, MIN 130 I/IB2

Minuet, MIN 131 I/IB2

Minuet, MIN 377 I/IB2

Minuet, MIN 378 I/IB2

Minuet, MIN 403 I/IB2

Minuet, MIN 404 I/IB2

Minuet, MIN 405 I/IB2

Minueto De Don Juan I/IB2

Minueto Del Cuarteto En Re I/IB2

Mozart-Buch, Das I/IB2

Mozartiana I/IB2

Serenata De Don Juan I/IB2

Sinfonia in E flat, Minuet I/IB2

Sinfonia No. 1, Minuet I/IB2

Sonata No. 2, Andante I/IB2

Sonata No. 2, K. 280, Andante I/IB2

Stucke, 3 I/IB2

Themes, 4 I/IB2

Variaciones Sobre Un Tema De "Don
Giovanni" I/IB2

Variations, 12, On "Ah, Vous Dirai-
Je, Maman" I/IB2

NOAD, FREDERICK M.
Solo Guitar Playing, A Complete
Course Of Instruction In The
Technique Of Guitar Performance
I/IB2-Coll

PAGANINI, NICCOLO (1782-1840)
Campanella, La I/IB2

Capriccio No. 16 I/IB2

Capriccio No. 24 I/IB2

Moto Perpetuo I/IB2

Piece De Salon I/IB2

Sonatina, Op. 25 I/IB2

PARADIS, MARIA THERESIA VON (1759-1824)
Siciliana I/IB2

RIGHTMIRE, RICHARD W.
Wonderful Guitar, The (A Modern
Classic Guitar Method), Vol. I
I/IB2-Coll

RODRIGUEZ ARENAS, MARIO
Escuela De La Guitarra, La, Vol. V
I/IB2-Coll

ROMANTIKUS GITARDARABOK - ROMANTIC
PIECES FOR GUITAR I/IB2-Coll

SCHALE, CHRISTIAN FR. (1713-1800)
Menuette, 2 I/IB2

SCHUBERT, FRANZ (PETER) (1797-1828)
Adieu I/IB2

Ecossaises I/IB2

Ellens Gesang III I/IB2

SCHUBERT, FRANZ (PETER) (cont'd.)

Fantasy, Op. 78, D. 984, in G, Minuet
I/IB2

Minuet, MIN 406 I/IB2

Moment Musical I/IB2

Momento Musical I/IB2

Moments Musicaux, Op. 94, No. 3,
D.780, No.3 I/IB2

3 Pequenos Valses I/IB2

Schubert-Buch, Das I/IB2

Serenade, MIN 136 I/IB2

Standchen I/IB2

Waltz I/IB2

SCHULZ, JOHANN ABRAHAM PETER
(1747-1800)
Lieder Im Volkston I/IB2

SCHUMANN, ROBERT (ALEXANDER)
(1810-1856)
Album I/IB2

Album: Marcha, Bagatela, Siciliana,
Cancion I/IB2

Album Per La Gioventu, 6 Pezzi, Op.
68, Nos. 1-3, 5, 16, 18 I/IB2

Albumblatt I/IB2

Andantino, Coral I/IB2

Au Soir I/IB2

Ausgewahlte Stucke, 12 I/IB2

Berceuse I/IB2

Bittendes Kind I/IB2

Erinnerung I/IB2

Feuilles Varias I/IB2

Frohlicher Landmann I/IB2

Fugue I/IB2

Fugue, MIN 340 I/IB2

Fugueta I/IB2

Hoja De Album I/IB2

Jagerliedchen I/IB2

Kinderscenen I/IB2

Kindersonate I/IB2

Mai, Lieber Mai I/IB2

Marche Militaire I/IB2

Melodia, Labrador Alegre I/IB2

Melody I/IB2

Melody, MIN 375 I/IB2

Nocturne, Op. 23, No. 4 I/IB2

Nordisches Lied I/IB2

Pezzi, 3 I/IB2

5 Piezas I/IB2

5 Piezas I/IB2

Reverie-Siciliano I/IB2

Romance, MIN 137 I/IB2

Romance, Op. 51 I/IB2

Rundgesang I/IB2

Saint Nicolas I/IB2

Schumann-Buch, Das I/IB2

Siciliano, MIN 369 I/IB2

Stucke Aus Dem "Album Fur Die Jugend,
" Op. 68 I/IB2

Sylvesterlied I/IB2

Traumerei I/IB2

Volksliedchen I/IB2

Von Fremden Landern Und Menschen
I/IB2

SCHUMANN, ROBERT (ALEXANDER) (cont'd.)

Wiegenlied I/IB2

STRAUSS, JOHANN, [SR.] (1804-1849)
Valzer, 2, Op. 110 And 76 I/IB2

TRANSCRIPCIONES POR VICENTE ERLISO,
VOL. 2 I/IB2

TRANSCRIPCIONES POR VICENTE ERLISO,
VOL. V I/IB2

WANHAL, JOHANN BAPTIST (JAN KRTITEL)
(1739-1813)
Cantabile I/IB2

Minuette, 2 I/IB2

WEBER, CARL MARIA VON (1786-1826)
Waltz I/IB2

WILTON, C.H.
Sonatina I/IB2

Classical and Pre-Romantic — Original Works and Arrangements

MAGYAR ZENE GITARRA A XIX. SZADAD ELSO
FELEBOL I/IB2-Coll

MEINE ERSTEN GITARRENSTUCKE, VOL. 4:
MEISTER DER ROMANTIK I/IB2-Coll

MEINE ERSTEN GITARRENSTUCKE, VOL. I:
MEISTER DER KLASSIK I/IB2-Coll

UTWORY DAWNYCH MISTROW I/IB2-Coll

Romantic and Post-Romantic — Original Works

ALBENIZ, ISAAC (1860-1909)
Capricho Catalan I/IB3

ALBUM, NO. 14 VI-Coll

ALBUM, NO. 15 VI-Coll

ALBUM, NO. 16 VI-Coll

ANONYMOUS
Romance Anonimo I/IB3

Romance, MIN 141 I/IB3

ARCAS, JULIAN (1832-1882)
Danzas Espanolas, 2 I/IB3

BOSCH, JACQUES
Pieces Faciles, 10, Pour l'Etude
I/IB3

CANO, ANTONIO (1811-1897)
Andante Grave I/IB3

COMPOSICIONES ORIGINALES PARA GUITARRA,
10 VI-Coll

FERRER, JOSE (1835-1916)
Danse Des Naiades, La I/IB3

FODEN, WILLIAM (1860-1947)
Short Preludes, 6 (Chord
Progressions) I/IB3

6 SPANISCHE STUCKE I/IB3-Coll, VI-Coll

TARREGA, FRANCISCO (1852-1909)
Adelita, Mazurka I/IB3, VI

Alborada, Cajita De Musica I/IB3

Album, No. 1 I/IB3, VI

Album, No. 2 I/IB3, VI

Album, No. 3 I/IB3, VI

Album, No. 4 I/IB3, VI

Album, No. 5 I/IB3, VI

Album, No. 6 I/IB3, VI

Album, No. 7 I/IB3, VI

Album, No. 8 I/IB3-Coll

Album, No. 10 I/IB3-Coll

Album, No. 11 I/IB3-Coll

Album, No. 17 I/IB3, VI-Coll

Album, No. 19 I/IB3

Album, No. 20 I/IB3

Album, Vol. I I/IB3-Coll, VI-Coll

Album, Vol. II: Seis [Sic] Preludios
I/IB3-Coll, VI, VI-Coll

Album, Vol. III I/IB3

Capricho Arabe, Serenata I/IB3, VI

Composiciones Originales Y Estudios
Para Guitarra, Vol. I I/IB3,
VI-Coll

Composiciones Originales Y Estudios
Para Guitarra, Vol. II I/IB3,
VI-Coll

Composiciones Originales Y Estudios
Para Guitarra, Vol. III: 30
Preludios Originales I/IB3,
VI-Coll

Composiciones Originales Y Estudios
Para Guitarra, Vol. III: 30
Preludios Originales I/IB3,
VI-Coll

Composiciones Originales Y Estudios
Para Guitarra, Vol. IV I/IB3,
VI-Coll

Composiciones Para Guitarra, 12
I/IB3, VI-Coll

TARREGA, FRANCISCO (cont'd.)

Danza Mora I/IB3

Danza Odalisca I/IB3

Gran Jota De Concierto VI

Guitarra Espanola: 12 Spanische
Stucke I/IB3, VI-Coll

Kompositionen Fur Gitarre, Vol. I
I/IB3, VI-Coll

Kompositionen Fur Gitarre, Vol. II
I/IB3, VI-Coll

Maria, Gavota I/IB3

Marieta, Mazurka I/IB3

Mazurka, MIN 372 I/IB3

Mazurky, 2 I/IB3

Opere Per Chitarra, Vol. I: Preludi
I/IB3, VI-Coll

Opere Per Chitarra, Vol. II: Studi
I/IB3, VI-Coll

Opere Per Chitarra, Vol. III:
Composizioni Originali I/IB3,
VI-Coll

Opere Per Chitarra, Vol. IV:
Trascrizioni I/IB3, VI-Coll

Pavan, MIN 145 I/IB3

Pavan, MIN 146 I/IB3

Pezzi Brillanti, 3 I/IB3

Prelude, TI i- 1, in D minor VI

Prelude, TI i- 2, in A minor VI

Prelude, TI i- 3, in G VI-Coll

Prelude, TI i- 4, in E VI

Prelude, TI i- 5, in E VI

Prelude, TI i- 6, in B minor VI

Prelude, TI i- 8a, in A VI

Prelude, TI i- 10, in D VI-Coll

Prelude, TI i- 12, in A minor VI

Prelude, TI i- 16, in D minor VI

Prelude, TI i- 17, in E I/IB3,
VI-Coll

Preludios Originales, 18 VI-Coll

Rosita, Polka I/IB3, VI, VI-Coll

Samtliche Praludien VI-Coll

Study, TI ii- 1, in G VI

Study, TI ii- 2a VI

Study, TI ii- 3, in E VI

Study, TI ii- 5, in A VI

Study, TI ii- 6, in D VI

Study, TI ii- 7a, in G VI

Study, TI ii- 8, in A VI

Study, TI ii- 9, in A minor VI

Study, TI ii- 11, in E VI

Study, TI ii- 12, in E VI

Study, TI ii- 13, in E VI

Study, TI ii- 16a, in B minor VI

Study, TI ii- 18, in A VI

Study, TI ii- 19, in A VI

Study, TI ii- 23, in E minor VI

Study, TI ii- 24, in E minor VI

Study, TI ii- 25, in E VI

Tarrega-Album, Eine Sammlung Der
Bekanntesten Original-Werke
I/IB3, VI-Coll

Utwory Wybrane I/IB3, VI-Coll

Vyber Skladeb, Selected Compositions,
Vol. I I/IB3, VI-Coll

TARREGA, FRANCISCO (cont'd.)

Vyber Skladeb, Selected Compositions,
    Vol. II   I/IB3, VI-Coll

VISSER, DICK (1927-   )
Tarrega Etcetera, Dagelijkse Studies
    VI-Coll

Romantic and Post-Romantic
— Arrangements

ALARD, JEAN-DELPHIN (1815-1888)
Etude, Op. 19, in A   I/IB3

ALBENIZ, ISAAC (1860-1909)
Alborada   I/IB3

Angustia, Romanza Sin Palabras   I/IB3

Aragon, Fantasia   I/IB3

Asturias, Leyenda, Preludio   I/IB3

Automne, L'   I/IB3

Bajo De La Palmera   I/IB3

Barcarolle   I/IB3

Barcarolle, Op. 23   I/IB3

Cadiz, Serenata   I/IB3

Castilla, Seguidillas   I/IB3

Cataluna, Corrando   I/IB3

Cielo Sin Nobes   I/IB3

Cordoba   I/IB3

Danza Espanola, No. 1   I/IB3

Danza Espanola, No. 3   I/IB3

Danza Espanola, No. 6   I/IB3

En La Alhambra, Capricho Morisco
    I/IB3

En La Playa, Recuerdo   I/IB3

Gavotte   I/IB3

Gavotte, Op. 92, No. 1   I/IB3

Granada, Serenata   I/IB3

Intermedia De "Pepita Jimenez"   I/IB3

Malaguena   I/IB3

Mallorca, Barcelona   I/IB3

Minueto A Sylvia   I/IB3

Motivos De Navarra   I/IB3

Oriental   I/IB3

Pavana Capricho   I/IB3

Plegaria   I/IB3

Polo, El, Impressione   I/IB3

Polonesa   I/IB3

Prelude, Op. 165, No. 1   I/IB3

Puerta De Tierra, Bolero   I/IB3

Rumores De La Caleta, Malaguena
    I/IB3

Seguidillas   I/IB3

Serenade, Op. 165, No. 4   I/IB3

Serenata Arabe   I/IB3

Sevilla, Sevillanas   I/IB3

Sous Le Palmier [Bajo La Palmera],
    Danse Espagnole   I/IB3

Staccato   I/IB3

Tango   I/IB3

Tango Espagnol   I/IB3

Torre Bermeja, Serenata   I/IB3

ALBENIZ, ISAAC (cont'd.)
Zambra   I/IB3

Zambra Granadina   I/IB3

Zortziko   I/IB3

BIZET, GEORGES (1838-1875)
Arlesiana, La   I/IB3

Arlesien, La: Adagio   I/IB3

Arlesien, La: Marcha Del Rey   I/IB3

Arlesien, La: Minueto   I/IB3

Celebre Minuetto   I/IB3

BOLZONI, GIOVANNI (1841-1919)
Beruhmtes Menuett   I/IB3

BRAHMS, JOHANNES (1833-1897)
Celebre Vals No. 15   I/IB3

Danza Hungara No. 5   I/IB3

Hungarian Dance, No. 5   I/IB3

Hungarian Dance, No. 6   I/IB3

Valsas   I/IB3

Waltz, Op. 30, No. 9, in A minor
    I/IB3

Waltz, Op. 39, No. 8   I/IB3

Waltz, Op. 39, No. 15   I/IB3

Wiegenlied   I/IB3

CUI, CESAR ANTONOVICH (1835-1918)
Orientale   I/IB3

DEBUSSY, CLAUDE (1862-1918)
Clair De Lune   I/IB3

Compositions, 3   I/IB3

Doctor Gradus Ad Parnassum   I/IB3

Golliwogg's Cake-Walk   I/IB3

Minstrels   I/IB3

Petit Negre, Le   I/IB3

Plus Que Lente, La, Valse   I/IB3

Preludes, 2   I/IB3

Prima Arabesca   I/IB3

DVORAK, ANTONIN (1841-1904)
Danza Slava   I/IB3

FRANCK, CESAR (1822-1890)
Plaintes d'Une Poupee, Les   I/IB3

Short Pieces, 4   I/IB3

GRANADOS, ENRIQUE (1867-1916)
Anoranza   I/IB3

Aparicion   I/IB3

Campana De La Tarde, La   I/IB3

Cancion Arabe   I/IB3

Capricho Espanol   I/IB3

Cartas De Amor, Valses Intimos   I/IB3

Danza Espanola, No. 5   I/IB3

Danza Espanola, No. 6   I/IB3

Danza Espanola, No. 7   I/IB3

Danza Espanola, No. 10   I/IB3

Danza Lenta   I/IB3

Danzas Espanolas, Nos. 1-12   I/IB3

Dedicatoria   I/IB3

Despertar Del Cazador, Albada   I/IB3

Ecos De La Parranda   I/IB3

Hada Y El Nino, El   I/IB3

Intermezzo   I/IB3

Marcha Oriental   I/IB3

Maya De Goya, La, Tonadilla   I/IB3

Preludio   I/IB3

Two Spanish Dances   I/IB3

GRANADOS, ENRIQUE (cont'd.)
Vals Muy Lento   I/IB3

Vascongada   I/IB3

Zambra   I/IB3

Zapateado   I/IB3

GRIEG, EDVARD HAGERUP (1843-1907)
Aase's Death   I/IB3

Anitra's Dance   I/IB3

Ensom Vandrer (Lonely Wanderer)
    I/IB3

Folkvise (Folksong)   I/IB3

Grieg-Buch, Das   I/IB3

Lyric Pieces, 3   I/IB3

Melodia Norvega   I/IB3

Melodie   I/IB3

Saraband   I/IB3

Solveig's Song   I/IB3

Waltz, Op. 12, No. 2   I/IB3

KLASSISCHE MELODIEN   I/IB3

MALATS, JOACHIN (1872-1912)
Impresiones De Espana, Danza   I/IB3

Serenata Andaluza   I/IB3

Serenata Espanola   I/IB3

MARIE, GABRIEL (1852-1928)
Cinquantaine, La, Aria Nello Stile
    Antico   I/IB3

MEINE ERSTEN GITARRENSTUCKE, VOL.4:
    "MEISTER DER ROMANTIK"   I/IB3-Coll

MUSSORGSKY, MODEST PETROVICH
    (1839-1881)
Viejo Castillo, El   I/IB3

NEVIN, ETHELBERT WOODBRIDGE (1862-1901)
Narcissus   I/IB3

PADEREWSKI, IGNACE JAN (1860-1941)
Minue Celebre   I/IB3

PEDRELL, CARLOS (1841-1922)
Al Atardecer En Los Jardines De
    Arlaja   I/IB3

Danzas De Las Tres Princesas
    Cautivas, No. 1   I/IB3

Danzas De Las Tres Princesas
    Cautivas, No. 2   I/IB3

Danzas De Las Tres Princesas
    Cautivas, No. 3   I/IB3

Impromptu   I/IB3

Pieces, 3, No. 1   I/IB3

Pieces, 3, No. 2   I/IB3

Pieces, 3, No. 3   I/IB3

RACHMANINOFF, SERGEY VASSILIEVICH
    (1873-1943)
Prelude, Op. 3, No. 2   I/IB3

REGER, MAX (1873-1916)
Gavotte   I/IB3

RIMSKY-KORSAKOV, NIKOLAI (1844-1908)
Chanson Hindoue   I/IB3

RUBINSTEIN, ANTON (1829-1894)
Romance, MIN 339   I/IB3

SAINT-SAENS, CAMILLE (1835-1921)
Cygne, Le   I/IB3

SCRIABIN, ALEXANDER (1872-1915)
Prelude No. 4   I/IB3

SHAND, ERNEST (1868-1924)
Solos, 6   I/IB3

SPANYOL GITARMUZSIKA - GUITAR MUSIC
    FROM SPAIN   I/IB3-Coll

SPANYOL TANC, 2; 2 SPANISH DANCES
    I/IB3

TCHAIKOVSKY, PIOTR ILYICH (1840-1893)
Andante Cantabile   I/IB3

Chanson Triste   I/IB3

TCHAIKOVSKY, PIOTR ILYICH (cont'd.)

Chant Sans Paroles I/IB3

In Church I/IB3

Mazurka, MIN 373 I/IB3

Mazurka, Op. 39, No. 10 I/IB3

None But The Lonely Heart I/IB3

Old French Air I/IB3

Pieces, 6 I/IB3

Piezas, 6 I/IB3

Sick Doll, The I/IB3

Song Without Words I/IB3

Tema Dal Balletto I/IB3

Valse Des Fleurs I/IB3

TOSELLI, ENRICO (1883-1926)
Celebre Serenata I/IB3

VALVERDE, JOAQUIN (1846-1910)
Clavelitos, Zambra Gitana I/IB3

Twentieth Century —
Original Works

ABLONIZ, MIGUEL (1917-   )
Blues For Rosy I/IB4

Capriccio Flamenco, Sul Tema Popolare
"El Vito" I/IB4

Improvvisazione, Omaggio A Villa-
Lobos I/IB4

Partita in E I/IB4

Pequena Romanza I/IB4

Pezzi Ricreativi (E Di Utilita
Tecnica), Nello Stile Polifonico,
4 I/IB4

Sequential I/IB4

Tarantella Burlesca And Bossa Nova
I/IB4

ABSIL, JEAN (1893-1974)
Petit Bestiaire, Op. 151 I/IB4

Pieces, 4, Op.150 I/IB4

Pieces, 10 I/IB4

Pieces, 12, Vol. I: Nos. 1-4 I/IB4

Pieces, 12, Vol II: Nos. 5-8 I/IB4

Pieces, 12, Vol. III: Nos. 9-12
I/IB4

Prelude Et Barcarolle I/IB4

Suite, Op. 114 I/IB4

Sur Un Paravent Chinois, 4 Esquisses,
Op. 147 I/IB4

AGUIRRE, JULIAN (1868-1924)
Aire Criollo No. 1 I/IB4

AHSLUND, ULF-G.
Hosten I/IB4

Suite No. 3 I/IB4

ALFONSO, NICOLAS
Cantilene I/IB4

Ya Van Los Pastores I/IB4

ALTE UND NEUE MUSIK ZUM SINGEN UND
SPIELEN AUF BLOCKFLOTEN, GEIGEN UND
LAUTENINSTRUMENTE I/IB4-Coll

ALTISSIMI, FRANCO
Giochi d'Acqua I/IB4

AMBROSIUS, HERMANN (1897- ?)
Impressionen I/IB4

Prelude I/IB4

ANGEL, MIGUEL
Cuatro Muleros, Los, Tema Y
Variaciones I/IB4

Homenaje A Schoenberg, 6 Preludios,
Op. 24 I/IB4

ANTOLOGIA PER CHITARRA I/IB4-Coll

ANTUNES, JORGE (1942-   )
Sighs I/IB4

APIVOR, DENIS (1916-   )
Discanti, Op. 48 I/IB4

Saeta, Op. 53 I/IB4

Variations for Guitar, Op. 29 I/IB4

APOSTEL, HANS ERICH (1901-1972)
Musiken, 6 I/IB4

ARNELL, RICHARD (1917-   )
Pieces, 6 I/IB4

ARNOLD, MALCOLM (1921-   )
Fantasy for Guitar, Op. 107 I/IB4

ARRIGO, GIROLAMO (1930-   )
Serenade I/IB4

ASENCIO, VICENTE (1897-   )
Dipso, 3 Piezas Evangeliques, No. 1
I/IB4

Elegy I/IB4

Suite Valenciana I/IB4

Tango De La Casada Infidel I/IB4

ASRIEL, ANDRE (1922-   )
Baroque In Blue: Suite I/IB4

AUBANEL, GEORGES
Bergerettes I/IB4

AUBIN, TONY (1907-   )
Hidalgoyas I/IB4

AZPIAZU, JOSE DE (1912-   )
Homenaje A Los Vihuelistas I/IB4

Hommage A Bela Bartok I/IB4

Joven Guitarrista, El, Vol.1: Muy
Facil I/IB4

Joven Guitarrista, El, Vol.2: Facil
I/IB4

Joven Guitarrista, El, Vol.3: Menos
Facil I/IB4

Joven Guitarrista, El, Vol.4: Mediana
Dificultad I/IB4

Miniatures Iberiques, 5 I/IB4

Pieces Faciles, Premier Cahier I/IB4

BACARISSE, SALVADOR (1898-1963)
Ballade I/IB4

Petite Suite I/IB4

BACHMANN, HELMUT
Adagio I/IB4

Air I/IB4

Altdeutscher Tanz I/IB4

Andante, MIN 153 I/IB4

Andante, MIN 154 I/IB4

Andante Religioso I/IB4

Gavotte, MIN 156 I/IB4

Minuet, MIN 157 I/IB4

Pastorale I/IB4

Prelude I/IB4

Prelude in A minor I/IB4

Prelude in D minor I/IB4

Serenade I/IB4

BADINGS, HENK (1907-1987)
Preludes, 12, Vol.1, No.1-6 I/IB4

Preludes, 12, Vol.2, No.7-12 I/IB4

BAERVOETS, RAYMOND (1930-   )
Improvisation I/IB4

BALADA, LEONARDO (1933-   )
Lento With Variation I/IB4

Suite I/IB4

BALLIF, CLAUDE (1924-   )
Solfeggietto, No. 6 I/IB4

BARBIER, RENE (AUGUSTE-ERNEST)
(1890-1981)
Prelude I/IB4

BARBIERI, MARIO
Serra, La, 7 Preludi I/IB4

BARRIOS MANGORE, AUGUSTIN
Catedral, La I/IB4

Choro Da Saudade I/IB4

Danza Paraguaya I/IB4

Medallon Antiguo, Omaggio A Pergolesi
I/IB4

Oracion I/IB4

BARTOK, BELA (1881-1945)
Gyermekeknek – Fur Kinder I/IB4

BARTOLI, RENE
Aubade I/IB4

Waltz in E minor I/IB4

BARTOLOZZI, BRUNO (1911-   )
    Adles I/IB4

    Omaggio A Gaetano Azzolina I/IB4

    Pezzi Per Chitarra, 3 I/IB4

BARTSCH, CHARLES
    Introduction Et Danse I/IB4

BATTISTI D'AMARIO, BRUNO
    Preludi, 2 I/IB4

BAUMANN, HERBERT (1925-   )
    Fantasie, Uber "Es Geht Ein Dunkle
        Wolk Herein" I/IB4

    Toccata, Elegia E Danza I/IB4

BAUR, JURG (1918-   )
    Fantasien, 3 I/IB4

BAUSEWEIN, HERBERT
    Strebsame Guitarrist, Der, Vol. 1, 14
        Leichte Spielstucke I/IB4

BAUTISTA, JULIAN (1901-1961)
    Preludio Y Danza I/IB4

BECKER, GUNTHER (1924-   )
    Metathesis I/IB4

BEDFORD, DAVID (1937-   )
    You Asked For It, For Acoustic Guitar
        Solo I/IB4

BEHREND, SIEGFRIED (1933-   )
    Fantasia A Sei Corde I/IB4

    Fantasia Malaguenita I/IB4

    Granadina De La Rambla I/IB4

    Kolometrie I/IB4

    Monodien, 6 I/IB4

    Movimenti I/IB4

    Non Te Escaparas, Capriccio Nach
        Francesco De Goya I/IB4

    Pezzi Per Jim, 2 I/IB4

    Porque Fue Sensible, Capriccio Nach
        Francesco De Goya I/IB4

    Postkarten Suite I/IB4

    Sonatine, Nach Japanischen
        Volksliedern I/IB4

    Stucke, 2 I/IB4

    Suite Fur Isao Takahashi I/IB4

    Zorongo Para Murao I/IB4

BELLOW, ALEXANDER (1922-1976)
    Cavatina I/IB4

    Diversions, 5 I/IB4

    Prelude And Rondo I/IB4

    Short Pieces, 4 I/IB4

    Suite Miniature I/IB4

    Suite Provencale I/IB4

BENGUEREL, XAVIER (1931-   )
    Versus I/IB4

BENNETT, RICHARD RODNEY (1936-   )
    Impromptus I/IB4

BERGMAN, ERIK (1911-   )
    Suite for Guitar, Op. 32 I/IB4

BERKELEY, [SIR] LENNOX (1903-   )
    Theme and Variations I/IB4

BETTINELLI, BRUNO (1913-   )
    Improvisation I/IB4

    Pezzi, 4 I/IB4

    Preludes, 5 I/IB4

BEVEREN, ACHIEL VAN
    Suite, Op. 46 I/IB4

BIBERIAN, GILBERT E.
    Prelude and Fugue I/IB4

BIRTH, THOMAS (1912-   )
    Neue Gitarrenmusik I/IB4

BISCHOFF, HEINZ (1898-1963)
    Ballade I/IB4

    Piccola Fuga I/IB4

BIZET, JEAN (1924-   )
    Spirale I/IB4

    Triangles I/IB4

BLYTON, CAREY (1932-   )
    Bream, The I/IB4

    In Memoriam Django Reinhardt: 2
        Variations And A Theme For Guitar
        I/IB4

    In Memoriam Scott Fitzgerald I/IB4

    Saxe Blue I/IB4

BOBRI, VLADIMIR
    Very Easy Pieces, For Very, Very
        Beginners, Op.12 I/IB4

BOCHMAN, THEO L.
    Torre Morisca, La I/IB4

BODA, JOHN (1922-   )
    Introduction And Dance I/IB4

BOER, JOHAN DE (1938-   )
    Grounds, 2 I/IB4

BOHR, HEINRICH
    Hirtentanz I/IB4

    Klagende Lied, Das I/IB4

BOIS, ROB DU (1934-   )
    Pastorale No. 4 I/IB4

BONDON, JACQUES (1927-   )
    Nocturne Nos. 1-3 I/IB4

    Swing No. 2 I/IB4

BONILLA CHAVEZ, CARLOS
    Elegia Y Danza I/IB4

    Preludio Y Yumbo I/IB4

BONNARD, ALAIN (1939-   )
    Chanson D'aube I/IB4

    Dancerie I/IB4

BORSODY, LASZLO
    Szin-Darabok – Color-Pieces I/IB4

BOSCO, GILBERTO (1946-   )
    Rifrazioni I/IB4

BOSMANS, ARTHUR (1908-   )
    Brasileiras, No.1 I/IB4

    Brasileiras, No.2 I/IB4

    Brasileiras, No.3 I/IB4

    Brasileiras, No.4 I/IB4

    Brasileiras, No. 5 I/IB4

BOZZA, EUGENE (1905-   )
    Impressions Andalouses, 2 I/IB4

    Preludes, 3 I/IB4

BRACALI, GIAN PAOLO (1941-   )
    Viajes I/IB4

BRAUN, PEE MICHAEL
    Monophonie Fur Gitarre I/IB4

BREDENBEEK, HANS
    Canciones, 2 I/IB4

    Miniature Suite I/IB4

    Trichordon-Dance I/IB4

BREGUET, JACQUES
    Suite I/IB4

BRESGEN, CESAR (1913-   )
    Malinconia I/IB4

BRIANO, GIOVANNI BATTISTA
    Fugue No. 3 I/IB4

BRITTEN, [SIR] BENJAMIN (1913-1976)
    Nocturnal, After John Dowland I/IB4

BROQUA, ALFONSO (1876-1946)
    Evocaciones Criollas, No.1 I/IB4

    Evocaciones Criollas, No.2 I/IB4

    Evocaciones Criollas, No.3 I/IB4

    Evocaciones Criollas, No.4 I/IB4

    Evocaciones Criollas, No.5 I/IB4

    Evocaciones Criollas, No.6 I/IB4

    Evocaciones Criollas, No.7 I/IB4

BROUWER, LEO (1939-   )
    Apuntes, 3 I/IB4

    Canticum I/IB4

    Danza Caracteristica, Para El
        "Quitate De La Arcera" I/IB4

    Elogio De La Danza I/IB4

    Espiral Eterna, La I/IB4

    Espoiral Eterna Para Guitarra, La
        I/IB4

    Fugue I/IB4

    Pieza Sin Titulo I/IB4

    Prelude I/IB4

BROWN, CHARLES
    Canzona I/IB4

BURGHAUSER, JARMIL (1921-   )
    Tesknice, Canti Dell'ansieta I/IB4

BUSCAROLI, REZIO
    Veglia Invernale, Racconto I/IB4

CALLEJA, FRANCISCO
    Preludios, 3 I/IB4

CAMERON, PEDRO BUENO
    Perspektivas I/IB4

CAMMAROTA, CARLO (1905-   )
    Acquarelli Napoletani I/IB4

CARRENO, INOCENTE
    Suite I/IB4

CASSEUS, FRANTZ GABRIEL (1921-   )
    Haitian Suite I/IB4

    Pieces Caracteristiques, 2, Suite
        I/IB4

CASTELLANOS, EVENCIO
    Evocacion I/IB4

    Homenaje I/IB4

CASTELNUOVO-TEDESCO, MARIO (1895-1968)
    Appunti, Preludi E Studi, Quaderno I:
        Gli Intervalli I/IB4

    Appunti, Preludi E Studi, Quaderno
        II: I Ritmi, Parte I, Danze Del
        600 E Del 700, No. 1-10 I/IB4

    Appunti, Preludi E Studi, Quaderno
        II: I Ritmi, Parte II, Danze
        Dell' Ottocente, No. 11-16 I/IB4

    Appunti, Preludi E Studi, Quaderno
        II: I Ritmi, Parte III, Danze Del
        Novecento, No. 17-22 I/IB4

    Appunti, Preludi E Studi, Quaderno
        III: Le Figurazione I/IB4

    Appunti, Preludi E Studi, Quaderno
        IV: 6 Studi Seriali I/IB4

    Aranci In Fiori I/IB4

    Aria Da Chiesa, Sul Nome Di Ruggero
        Chiesa I/IB4

    Ballatella, Sul Nome Di Christopher
        Parkening I/IB4

    Brasileira, Sul Nome Di Laurindo
        Almeida I/IB4

    Cancion Argentina, Sul Nome Di
        Ernesto Bitetti I/IB4

    Cancion Cubana, Sul Nome Di Hector
        Garcia I/IB4

    Cancion Venezuelana, Sul Nome Di
        Alirio Diaz I/IB4

    Canto Delle Azorre, Sul Nome Di Enos
        I/IB4

    Canzone Calabrese, Sul Nome Di Ernest
        Calabria I/IB4

    Canzone Siciliana, Sul Nome Di Mario
        Gangi I/IB4

    Capriccio Diabolico, Omaggio A
        Paganini I/IB4

    Caprichos De Goya, 24, Vol. 1, Nos.
        1-6 I/IB4

    Caprichos De Goya, 24, Vol. 2, Nos.
        7-12 I/IB4

    Caprichos De Goya, 24, Vol. 3, Nos.
        13-18 I/IB4

CASTELNUOVO-TEDESCO, MARIO (cont'd.)

Caprichos De Goya, 24, Vol. 4, Nos. 19-24 I/IB4

Escarraman, A Suite Of Spanish Dances From The XVIth Century (After Cervantes) I/IB4

Estudio, Sul Nome Di Manuel Lopez Ramos I/IB4

Homage To Purcell, Fantasia Sul Nome Di Ronald (1932-) E Henry (1659-1695) Purcell I/IB4

Japanese Print, Sul Nome Di Jiro Matsuda I/IB4

Ninna-Nanna, A Lullaby For Eugene I/IB4

Passacaglia, Omaggio A Roncalli I/IB4

Preludi Al Circeo, 3 I/IB4

Preludi Mediterranei, 3 I/IB4

Preludio In Forma Di Habanera, Sul Nome Di Bruno Tonazzi I/IB4

Romanza, Sul Nome Di Oscar Ghiglia I/IB4

Rondel, Uber Den Namen Siegfried Behrend I/IB4

Rondo, Op. 129 I/IB4

Sarabande, Sul Nome Di Rey De La Torre I/IB4

Suite, Op. 133 I/IB4

Tanka, Sul Nome Di Isao Takahashi I/IB4

Tarantella I/IB4

Tarantella Campana, Sul Nome Di Eugene Di Novi I/IB4

Tonadilla, Sur Le Nom De Andres Segovia I/IB4

Variations A Travers Les Siecles I/IB4

Variations Plaisantes, Sur Un Petit Air Populaire, "J'ai Du Bon Tabac" I/IB4

Volo d'Angeli, Sul Nome Di Angelo Gilardino I/IB4

CAVAZZOLI, GERMANO
Preludi, 2 I/IB4

CERF, JACQUES (1932-   )
Nuances I/IB4

Pieces Sur 6 Cordes, 5 I/IB4

Suite Enfantine I/IB4

CHAILLY, LUCIANO (1920-   )
Invenzione, Su Quattro Note I/IB4

CHAVARRI, EDUARDO LOPEZ (1871-1970)
Piezas, 7 I/IB4

CHAVEZ, CARLOS (1899-1978)
Pieces, 3 I/IB4

CHIEREGHIN, SERGIO (1933-   )
Chanson Jouees, 3 I/IB4

CIURLO, ERNESTO FAUSTO
Aria I/IB4

Barcarolle I/IB4

Moerens Incedebam, Mattutino I/IB4

Sotto La Pioggia I/IB4

COELHO SILVESTRE, LOURIVAL PINTO
Estilhacos I/IB4

COMPANY, ALVARO
Seis Cuerdas, Las I/IB4

CONSTANT, FRANZ (1910-   )
Humoresque I/IB4

Nocturne I/IB4

Poem I/IB4

Pour La Guitare, Vol. 1 I/IB4

Pour La Guitare, Vol. 2 I/IB4

CORDERO, ERNESTO (1946-   )
Mapeye, Canto Di Puerto Rico I/IB4

CORGHI, AZIO (1937-   )
Consonancias Y Redobles I/IB4

CORREGGIA, ENRICO
Trasparenze I/IB4

CRUZ DE CASTRO, CARLOS
Algo Para Guitarra I/IB4

CZERNIK, WILLY (1904-   )
Kurzweilige Stucke, 10 I/IB4

CZERNUSCHKA, FRITZ
Prelude in E minor I/IB4

DAGOSTO, SYLVAIN
Petit Guitariste, Le I/IB4

Romance in E I/IB4

DANDELOT, GEORGES (1895-1975)
Pieces, 2 I/IB4

DE FILIPPI, AMEDEO (1900-   )
Chant Et Tarentelle I/IB4

Gaillarde, Pavane, Et Toccata I/IB4

Jardins De Vauxhall I/IB4

Preludes, 12 I/IB4

DECADT, JAN (1914-   )
Pavan I/IB4

DEFOSSEZ, RENE (1905-   )
Allegretto Et Gavotte I/IB4

Theme Et 3 Variations I/IB4

DEGNI, VINCENZO (1911-   )
Prelude I/IB4

DELAUNEY, PAUL
Petit Gitan, Le I/IB4

Prelude in D I/IB4

Toccatina I/IB4

DENHOFF, MICHAEL (1955-   )
Quinterna Fur Gitarresolo I/IB4

DESDERI, ETTORE (1892-1974)
Serenata I/IB4

Toccata And Fugue I/IB4

DIANA, ANTOINE
Petits Morceaux Pour Les Debutants, 12 I/IB4

DIECKMANN, CARL HEINZ
Musik Fur Gitarre Solo I/IB4

DIGMELOFF, GERMAIN
Caprice Georgien I/IB4

Pieces Faciles I/IB4

DJEMIL, ENYSS (1917-   )
Caprice, Complainte Et Ronde I/IB4

DODGSON, STEPHEN (1924-   )
Fantasy-Divisions I/IB4

Partita I/IB4

DOERR, CHARLES-KIKO
Fantasy I/IB4

Gavotte in E I/IB4

Gavotte in E minor I/IB4

Minuet, MIN 160 I/IB4

Nocturne in A minor I/IB4

Petite Valse I/IB4

Quartes Et Sixtes I/IB4

DONATONI, FRANCO (1927-   )
Algo, 2 Pezzi Per Chitarra I/IB4

DORLEIJN, GILLES J.
Prelude I/IB4

DRESENS, GUUS
Meringue I/IB4

DRIGO, RICCARDO (1846-1930)
Serenade I/IB4

Valse Bluette I/IB4

DRLAC, JAN ZDENEK
Ulice I/IB4

DROGOZ, PHILIPPE
Chocs I/IB4

Chorale I/IB4

Nocturne I/IB4

Prelude I/IB4

Rasgueado I/IB4

Rondo I/IB4

DUARTE, JOHN W. (1919-   )
All In A Row I/IB4

English Suite I/IB4

Fantasia And Fugue On "Torre Bermeja" I/IB4

Flight Of Fugues, A I/IB4

For My Friends I/IB4

Meditation On A Ground Bass I/IB4

Miniature Suite I/IB4

Modern Miniatures, 3 I/IB4

Mutations On The "Dies Irae" I/IB4

Nocturne And Toccata I/IB4

Petite Suite Francaise I/IB4

Pieces, 2 I/IB4

Prelude, Canto And Toccata I/IB4

Prelude En Arpeges I/IB4

Simple Variations On "Las Folias" I/IB4

Some Of Noah's Ark I/IB4

Suite Piemontese I/IB4

Suo Cosa I/IB4

Variations On A Catalan Folk Song I/IB4

EASTWOOD, THOMAS (1922-   )
Amphora I/IB4

Ballade I/IB4

EASY PIECES, 8 I/IB4-Coll

EKLUND, HANS (1927-   )
Pezzi, 5 I/IB4

ERLISO, VINCENTE
Minuet No. 1 I/IB4

ESTRADA, JESU
Theme Varie I/IB4

EYNARD, CAMILLE
Carnet De Notes I/IB4

EZAKI, KENJIRO (1926-   )
Nodule Per Chitarre I/IB4

FABINI, EDUARDO (1883-1950)
Mozartienne I/IB4

FALLA, MANUEL DE (1876-1946)
Omaggio, Scritto Per Le Tombeau De Debussy I/IB4

FARKAS, FERENC (1905-   )
Pieces Breves, 6 I/IB4

Regi Magyar Tancok – Alte Ungarische Tanze I/IB4

Regi Magyar Tancok – Alte Ungarische Tanze I/IB4

FARQUHAR, DAVID (1928-   )
Ostinato I/IB4

Scenes, 5 I/IB4

FENICIO, EDMAR
Suite in A minor I/IB4

FERNANDEZ, OSCAR LORENZO (1897-1948)
Old Song I/IB4

Prelude I/IB4

FERRARI, IVANO (1932-   )
Kuss-Tobia I/IB4

FERRARI, ROMOLO (1894-1959)
Danza Orientale I/IB4

Grande Fugue Reale I/IB4

FETLER, PAUL (1920–   )
  Movements, 4 I/IB4

  Pieces, 5 I/IB4

FLAMME, A. (1950–   )
  Mignonne I/IB4

FLOTHUIS, MARIUS (1914–   )
  Stukken, 2 I/IB4

FORTEA, DANIEL (1882–1953)
  Homenaje A Sor I/IB4

FOX, VICTOR
  Prelude I/IB4

FRANCERIES, MARC (1935–   )
  Pour Christiane I/IB4

FRANCO, JOHAN (1908–   )
  Prayers, 3 I/IB4

FRANKE, J. MAX
  Bagatelle I/IB4

  Minuet, MIN 71 I/IB4

FRESNO, JORGE (1937–   )
  Escala Naturel I/IB4

  Posiciones Fijas I/IB4

  Pulsacion I/IB4

  Sol, Si, Mi I/IB4

FRICKER, PETER RACINE (1920–   )
  Paseo I/IB4

FRIEDEL, KURT–JOACHIM (1921–   )
  Suite I/IB4

FRIESSNEGG, KARL (1900–   )
  Kleine Melodien Fur Den Jungen
     Gitarristen, 10 I/IB4

  Kleine Suite, Op. 30 I/IB4

  Variationen Uber Ein Thema Von Franz
     Schubert (Die Forelle) I/IB4

FRITSCHE, VOLKMAR
  Burlesken, 5 I/IB4

  Nocturne No. 1 I/IB4

  Nocturne No. 2 I/IB4

FROBERVILLE, PH. DE
  Impromptu I/IB4

  Prelude, Op. 33 I/IB4

FURSTENAU, WOLFRAM
  Cadenza Amicitia I/IB4

  Hommage A Alberto Giacometti I/IB4

  Hommage A Jean Cocteau I/IB4

  Ommegang: Cycle I/IB4

  Railway–Traffic I/IB4

  Reflexionen, Auf Bilder Von Max Ernst
     I/IB4

GABUS, MONIQUE (1926–   )
  Stele Pour Une Jeune Indienne I/IB4

GAGNEBIN, HENRI (1886–1977)
  Pieces, 3 I/IB4

GALL, LOUIS IGNATIUS
  Music For Young Guitarists I/IB4

  Stukken, 3 I/IB4

  Suite Vivat Noviomagum I/IB4

GARBER, ERICH (1916–   )
  Originalkompositionen, 5 I/IB4

GARGIULO, TERENZIO (1905–1972)
  Toccata I/IB4

GAVARONE, GERARD
  Retrospective I/IB4

GENERAUX, ROGER
  Suite Bresilienne I/IB4

GERHARD, ROBERTO (1896–1970)
  Fantasy I/IB4

GILARDINO, ANGELO
  Abreuana I/IB4

  Appaloosa I/IB4

  Araucaria I/IB4

  Canzone Notturna I/IB4

GILARDINO, ANGELO (cont'd.)

  Estrellas Para Estarellas, Musica
     Nocturna Para La Guitarra De
     Gabriel [Estarellas] I/IB4

  Ocram, Fantasia I/IB4

  Tenebrae Factae Sunt I/IB4

  Trepidazioni Per Thebit I/IB4

GOMEZ CRESPO, JORGE
  Nortena, Homenaje A Julian Aguirre
     I/IB4

GRAMBERG, JACQ
  Instructieve Sonatines, 3 I/IB4

  Petrad I/IB4

GRAU, EDUARDO
  Fuente De Nie Pastrie, La I/IB4

GREEVE, G. DE
  Galante Dans I/IB4

GRILLAERT, OCT
  Valdemosa I/IB4

GRIMM, FRIEDRICH KARL (1902–   )
  Pezzi, 2 I/IB4

GUDMUNDSEN–HOLMGREEN, PELLE (1932–   )
  Solo Fur El–Guitar I/IB4

GUITARE D'AUJOURD'HUI (HEDENDAAGSE
     GITAAR): 30 PIECES FACILES DE
     COMPOSITEURS BELGES (30
     GEMAKKELIJKE STUKKEN VAN BELGISCHE
     COMPONISTEN) I/IB4–Coll

GUNDHUS, LEIF
  Norwegische Volksweisen I/IB4

GUNSENHEIMER, GUSTAV (1934–   )
  9 Leichte Stucke I/IB4

  Romanische Suite I/IB4

HAFNER, KURT
  Leichte Originalstucke I/IB4

HAIDER, HANS
  Skizzen, 4 I/IB4

HALFFTER, CRISTOBAL (1930–   )
  Codex I I/IB4

HALLNAS, HILDING (1903–   )
  Partita Amabile I/IB4

  Preludier 1–12 I/IB4

  Strangaspel I/IB4

HARRIS, ALBERT (1916–   )
  Homage To Unamuno I/IB4

  Suite I/IB4

  Variations And Fugue On A Theme Of
     Handel I/IB4

HARTIG, HEINZ FRIEDRICH (1907–1969)
  Gitarresolo I/IB4

  Stucke Fur Gitarre, 3 I/IB4

HASENOHRL, FRANZ (1885– ?   )
  Kleine Stucke, 4 I/IB4

  Suite I/IB4

HASHAGEN, KLAUS (1924–   )
  Synchronie; 10 Graphic Parts I/IB4

HAUBENSTOCK–RAMATI, ROMAN (1919–   )
  Hexachord I–II I/IB4

HAUFRECHT, HERBERT (1909–   )
  Hora I/IB4

  Theme and Variations I/IB4

  Waltz I/IB4

HAUG, HANS (1900–1967)
  Alba I/IB4

  Prelude I/IB4

  Prelude, Tiento Et Toccata I/IB4

HAUSWIRTH, HANS M.A. (1901–   )
  Solospiel Auf Der Gitarre, Das I/IB4

HEER, HANS DE (1927–   )
  3 Fuga's I/IB4

  Musing I/IB4

  Prelude No. 4 I/IB4

HEER, HANS DE (cont'd.)

  Siciliano I/IB4

HEKSTER, WALTER (1937–   )
  Chain I/IB4

HENZE, HANS WERNER (1926–   )
  Fragmente Nach Holderlin, 3 I/IB4

HERRERA, RAMON DE
  Preludes, 3 I/IB4

HILSTER, RIES DE
  Prelude No. 1, Op. 12, No. 1 I/IB4

HINOJOSA, JAVIER
  Te Lucis Ante Terminum I/IB4

HINTERMEYER, WILLY (1892–   )
  Junge Gitarre–Soloist, Der, Vol. I;
     Eine Sammlung Leichter,
     Melodioser Solostucke I/IB4

  Junge Gitarre–Soloist, Der, Vol. II;
     Eine Sammlung Leichter,
     Melodioser Solostucke I/IB4

HLOUSCHEK, THEODOR (1923–   )
  Kompositionen I/IB4

HOEK, JAN–ANTON VAN (1936–   )
  Bouwstenen Van Het Polyphoon
     Gitaarspel, Vol. I, Nos. 1–21
     I/IB4

  Bouwstenen Van Het Polyphoon
     Gitaarspel, Vol. II, Nos. 22–37
     I/IB4

  12 Preludes I/IB4

  Suite Milanesa I/IB4

HOLDER, DERWYN
  Modern Preludes, 6 I/IB4

HOMS, JOAQUIN (1906–   )
  2 Solioquios I/IB4

HUBSCHMANN, WERNER (1901–1969)
  Suite I/IB4

HULSEN, ERNST (1883– ?   )
  Leichte Walzer, 6 I/IB4

HUMMEL, BERTOLD (1925–   )
  Metamorphosen Fur Gitarre I/IB4

IBERT, JACQUES (1890–1962)
  Ariette I/IB4

  Francaise I/IB4

JANSEN, WILLY (1897–   )
  Kleine Spielmusiken I/IB4

JENTSCH, WALTER (1900–   )
  Impressionen I/IB4

JOACHIM, OTTO (1910–   )
  Stucke, 6 I/IB4

JOVICIC, JOVAN
  Balkanski Dans I/IB4

JULIA, BERNARDO
  Nostalgia I/IB4

JUST, FRANZ (1937–   )
  Leichte Spielstucke I/IB4

KALMAR, LASZLO (1931–   )
  Monologo I/IB4

KAPS, HANSJOACHIM
  Huracan, El I/IB4

KARL, SEPP (1913–   )
  Junge Gitarre–Solist, Der, Vol. III;
     Eine Sammlung Leichter,
     Melodioser Solostucke I/IB4

  Junge Gitarre–Solist, Der, Vol. IV;
     Eine Sammlung Leichter,
     Melodioser Solostucke I/IB4

  Melodische Spielstucke Fur Leichtes
     Lagenspiel I/IB4

  Strebsame Gitarrist, Der, Vol. II,
     Leichte Spielstucke I/IB4

KAUFMANN, ARMIN (1902–   )
  Rhapsody, Op. 97 I/IB4

  Stucke, 10 I/IB4

KEF, KEES (1894–1961)
  Divertimento I/IB4

KELLY, BRYAN (1934–   )
  Aubade, Toccata And Nocturne I/IB4

KENNARD, JAN
Preludes, 2 I/IB4

KERR, HARRISON (1897-1978)
Variations On A Theme From "The Tower
Of Kel" I/IB4

KERSTERS, WILLEM (1929-   )
Nocturne, Op. 44 I/IB4

KOMTER, JAN MAARTEN (1905-   )
Arpeggiata, Homenaje A Fernando Sors
I/IB4

Dhyanas, 6 I/IB4

Fun From The Start, Vol. II: The
Beginning Soloist On The Guitar
I/IB4

Preludes, 2 I/IB4

Preludes Faciles, 3 I/IB4

Spanish Suite I/IB4

Suite 1945 I/IB4

Suite 1949 I/IB4

Suites, 6 I/IB4

KONIETZNY, HEINRICH
Permutationen I/IB4

KORN, PETER JONA (1922-   )
Arabesque I/IB4

Gigue, Op. 61, No. 3 I/IB4

Pavane Triste I/IB4

KOTIK, JOSEPH
Erste Vortragsstucke Fur Gitarre
I/IB4

Prvni Prednesove Skladby Pro Kytaru
I/IB4

KOVATS, BARNA (1920-   )
Minutenstucke I/IB4

Mouvements, 3 I/IB4

Petite Suite I/IB4

Stucke, 3 I/IB4

Suite, Hommage A Goldoni I/IB4

KRATOCHWIL, HEINZ (1932-   )
Triptychon I/IB4

KRENEK, ERNST (1900-   )
Suite I/IB4

KRIEGER, EDINO (1928-   )
Ritmata I/IB4

KUBAI GITARMUVEK - GUITAR MUSIC FROM
CUBA I/IB4-Coll

KUCERA, VACLAV (1929-   )
Diario, Omaggio A Che Guevarra I/IB4

LAGOYA, ALEXANDRE
Capriccio I/IB4

Reverie I/IB4

LAMPERSBERG, GERHARD (1928-   )
Stucke, 3 I/IB4

LANGENBERG, JAN VAN DEN
Ballade No. 1 I/IB4

Dance-Variations On A Dutch Song
I/IB4

Minuet in F I/IB4

LARRAURI, ANTON (1932-   )
Triptico Vasco I/IB4

LASALA, ANGEL (1914-   )
Preludios Americanos I/IB4

LAURO, ANTONIO (1917-   )
Angostura, Valse Venezolano I/IB4

Carora, Valse Venezolano I/IB4

Marabino, El, Valse Venezolano I/IB4

Maria Luise, Valse Venezolano I/IB4

Suite Venezolana I/IB4

Valses Venezolanos, 4 I/IB4

Variations On A Venezolean Children's
Song I/IB4

Venezuelan Waltz, Valse Criollo
I/IB4

LECHTHALER, JOSEF (1891-1948)
Variationen-Suite I/IB4

LECLERCQ, NORBERT
Couleurs, 6 I/IB4

LEERINK, HANS
Preludes, 4 I/IB4

LEGLEY, VICTOR (1915-   )
Pieces, 5, Op. 62 I/IB4

LELLA, DOMENICO DI
Impressione I/IB4

Preludi, 6 I/IB4

LEMELAND, AUBERT (1932-   )
Hommage A Albert Roussel I/IB4

LERICH, PIERRE
Chanson Et Pastorale I/IB4

Hommage A Villa-Lobos I/IB4

Pieces, 3 I/IB4

Prelude Et Fugue, Alla Antiqua I/IB4

Prelude No. 3 I/IB4

Suite Baroque I/IB4

Waltz I/IB4

LETELIER VALDEZ, MIGUEL FRANCISCO
(1939-   )
Preludios Breves, 7 I/IB4

LEVY, MOSHE
Twenty-Four Guitar Pieces (In All
Keys) I/IB4

LIMA, CANDIDO
Esbocos I/IB4

LLOBET, MIGUEL (1878-1938)
Prelude in A I/IB4

Prelude in E I/IB4

Respuesta I/IB4

Variaciones Sobre Un Tema De Sor
I/IB4

LOPES-GRACA, FERNANDO (1906-   )
Partita I/IB4

Preludio E Baileto I/IB4

LORENTZEN, BENT (1935-   )
Umbra I/IB4

LUBACH, ANDRIES A.
Dances, 2 I/IB4

LUENING, OTTO (1900-   )
Fantasias I-III I/IB4

LUMBY, HERBERT
Preludio E Capriccio I/IB4

LUNDIN, BENGT
Fem Infall, Svit I/IB4

LUTOSLAWSKI, WITOLD (1913-   )
Melodii Ludowych, 9 I/IB4

LUTZEMBERGER, CESARE
Composizioni, 4 I/IB4

MAASZ, GERHARD (1906-1984)
Suite I/IB4

MCCABE, JOHN (1939-   )
Canto I/IB4

MADERNA, BRUNO (1920-1973)
Y Despues I/IB4

MAES, JEF (1905-   )
Nocturne I/IB4

MAGHINI, RUGGERO (1913-1977)
Umbra I/IB4

MAIRANTS, IVOR
Drei Rhytmische Tanze Fur Gitarre
I/IB4

Part Suite, 6 I/IB4

Sechs Bagatellen Fur Gitarre I/IB4

Sechs Progressive Stucke Fur Gitarre
I/IB4

Sechs Solos Fur Gitarre I/IB4

Solos For Classic Guitar, 6 I/IB4

Suite In Sechs Teile Fur Gitarre
I/IB4

MAIRANTS, IVOR (cont'd.)

Travel-Suite I/IB4

MALIPIERO, RICCARDO (1914-   )
Aria Variata Su La Follia I/IB4

MAMANGAKIS, NIKOS (1929-   )
Penthima I/IB4

MARCO, TOMAS (1942-   )
Albayalde I/IB4

Naturaleza Muerto Con Guitarra;
Homenaje A Pablo Picasso I/IB4

Paisaje Grana, Homenaje A J.R.
Jimenez I/IB4

MARGOLA, FRANCO (1908-   )
Ballade I/IB4

Leggenda I/IB4

Nocturne I/IB4

MARGOLA, MANUEL
Choros Brasileira I/IB4

MARTIN, FRANK (1890-1974)
Pieces Breves, 4 I/IB4

MARTINEZ ZARATE, JORGE
Impromptu No. 1 I/IB4

MARTINI, MANLIO
Piccoli Pezzi, 2 I/IB4

MEDEK, TILO (1940-   )
Drei Stucke Fur Gitarre I/IB4

MEDIN, NINO
Notturnino E Capriccio I/IB4

MEIER, JOST
Reflets, 3 I/IB4

MELLERS, WILFRID HOWARD (1914-   )
Blue Epiphany, A - For J.B. Smith
I/IB4

MESTRES-QUADRENY, JOSEP MARIA
(1929-   )
Prelude I/IB4

MIGNOT, PIERRE
Toccata Fantasque I/IB4

MILHAUD, DARIUS (1892-1974)
Segoviana I/IB4

MILLER, JOHN R.
Solo-Gitarre, Die, Vol. II I/IB4

MIROGLIO, FRANCIS (1924-   )
Choreiques I/IB4

MODERN GUITAR MUSIC I/IB4-Coll

MOMPOU, FEDERICO (1893-   )
Suite Compostellana I/IB4

MORANCON, GUY (1927-   )
Petit Livre I/IB4

Suite Latine I/IB4

MORENO TORROBA, FEDERICO (1891-1982)
Aire De La Manche I/IB4

Bolero I/IB4

Burgalesa I/IB4

Contradanza I/IB4

Jota Levantina I/IB4

Madronos I/IB4

Molinera I/IB4

Nocturne I/IB4

Pieces Caracteristiques, Vol. 1
I/IB4

Pieces Caracteristiques, Vol. 2
I/IB4

Prelude I/IB4

Punteado Taconeo Clasico I/IB4

Serenata Burlesca I/IB4

Stucke, 5 I/IB4

Suite Castellana I/IB4

Suite Miniatura I/IB4

MORI, AUGUSTO CESARE DE
    Souvenir d'Espagne I/IB4

MORNAC, JUAN (1897-   )
    Morceaux Choisis, 15 I/IB4

MORTARI, VIRGILIO (1902-   )
    Omaggio Ad Andres Segovia I/IB4

MOSSO, CARLO
    Danze Nello Stile Modale, 4 I/IB4

    Forskalia I/IB4

MOULAERT, RAYMOND (1875-1962)
    Rhapsody I/IB4

MOURAT, JEAN-MAURICE
    Melancolie I/IB4

    Palmiers, Les I/IB4

    Suite Vendeenne I/IB4

    Toupie, La I/IB4

    Valse Triste I/IB4

MRONSKI, STANISLAW
    Cykle Na Gitare, 2, Cztery Utwory
        I/IB4

MULLER, SIEGFRIED (1926-   )
    Stucke Fur Gitarre, 5 I/IB4

MURTULA, GIOVANNI (1881-1964)
    Carovana, Intermezzo Caratteristico
        I/IB4

    Rievocazione I/IB4

NEIJBOER, OTTO C.
    Melodie En Positie I/IB4

NEUMANN, ULRIK
    Love Waltz I/IB4

    Manresan I/IB4

NIESSEN, HANS-LUTZ (1920-1982)
    Prelude and Fugue I/IB4

NIN-CULMELL, JOAQUIN (1908-   )
    Variaciones Sobre Un Tema De Milan, 6
        I/IB4

NOBRE, MARLOS (1939-   )
    Momentos I I/IB4

NORMAN, THEODORE (1912-   )
    Mobile I/IB4

OBROVSKA, JANA (1930-   )
    Hommage A Bela Bartok I/IB4

OHANA, MAURICE (1914-   )
    Si Le Jour Parait, No. 1 I/IB4

    Si Le Jour Parait, No. 2 I/IB4

    Si Le Jour Parait, No. 3 I/IB4

    Si Le Jour Parait, No. 4 I/IB4

    Si Le Jour Parait, No. 5 I/IB4

    Si Le Jour Parait, No. 6 I/IB4

    Si Le Jour Parait, No. 7 I/IB4

    Tiento I/IB4

ORBON, JULIAN (1925-   )
    Preludio Y Danza I/IB4

ORREGO-SALAS, JUAN A. (1919-   )
    Esquinas I/IB4

ORSOLINO, FEDERICO (1918-   )
    Capriccio, La Cascatella I/IB4

    Piccole Impressioni Di Campagna
        I/IB4

PALAU, MANUEL (1893-1967)
    Ayer, Fantasia I/IB4

    Fantasy I/IB4

PAMMER, JOSEF
    Burleske I/IB4

    Maria Geht Durch Bluten I/IB4

    Valse Triste I/IB4

PAPANDOPULO, BORIS (1906-   )
    Drei Jugoslavische Tanze Fur Gitarre
        I/IB4

PATACHICH, IVAN (1922-   )
    Gyermekdalok Gitarra, Vol. 1 -
        Children's Songs For Guitar, Vol.
        1 I/IB4

PATACHICH, IVAN (cont'd.)

    Gyermekdalok Gitarra, Vol. 2 -
        Children's Songs For Guitar, Vol.
        2 I/IB4

PAUBON, PIERRE (1910-   )
    Pieces, 6 I/IB4

PELEMANS, WILLEM (1901-   )
    7 Croquis I/IB4

    Humoresque I/IB4

    6 Romances I/IB4

    Speelse Wals I/IB4

PELTA, MAX
    Prelude Et Valse I/IB4

PERALDO BERT, NILO
    Improvvisi, 2 I/IB4

    Omaggio A Charlie Christian I/IB4

PERUZZI, AURELIO (1921-   )
    Pezzi, 4 I/IB4

PETIT, PIERRE (1922-   )
    Theme and Variations I/IB4

PETRASSI, GOFFREDO (1904-   )
    Nunc I/IB4

    Suoni Notturni I/IB4

PEZZOLI, GIORGIO
    Andante Armonioso, Tema Di Autore
        Ignoto I/IB4

PICK, RICHARD SAMUEL BURNS (1915-   )
    First Repertoire For Classic Guitar
        I/IB4

    Improvisation I/IB4

    Preludes, 9 I/IB4

PIGNOCCHI, EMANUELE
    Piccola Leggenda I/IB4

PILSL, F.
    Gitarrestucke Fur Die Jugend I/IB4

    Miniaturproblematicos I/IB4

PIZZINI, CARLO ALBERTO (1905-   )
    Capriccio Napoletano I/IB4

    Improvviso Da Concerto I/IB4

POLACZEK, DIETMAR (1942-   )
    Metamorfosen Und Fuge I/IB4

PONCE, MANUEL MARIA (1882-1948)
    Canciones Populares Mexicanas, 3
        I/IB4

    Prelude I/IB4

    Preludes, Vol. I: Nos. 1-6 I/IB4

    Preludes, Vol. II: Nos. 7-12 I/IB4

    Preludios Cortos, 6 I/IB4

    Suite in A minor I/IB4

    Suite in D I/IB4

    Suite In D Major: Gavotte I And II, D
        Major And D Minor I/IB4

    Theme Varie Et Finale I/IB4

    Variations Sur "Folia De Espana" Et
        Fugue I/IB4

POULENC, FRANCIS (1899-1963)
    Sarabande, Dedie A Ida Presti I/IB4

PRADO, JOSE-ANTONIO (ALMEIDA)
        (1943-   )
    Livre Pour Six Cordes I/IB4

PRESTI, IDA (1924-1967)
    Danse Rythmique I/IB4

PROSPERI, CARLO (1921-   )
    Canto Dell'arpeggione I/IB4

PUJOL, EMILIO (1886-1982)
    Atardecer I/IB4

    Bagatelle I/IB4

    Barcarolle I/IB4

    Becqueriana, Complainte I/IB4

    Cancio De Cuna I/IB4

    Cap I Cua I/IB4

PUJOL, EMILIO (cont'd.)

    Caprice Varie Sur Un Theme D'Aguado
        I/IB4

    Cubana I/IB4

    Deuxieme Triquilandia I/IB4

    Endecha Alla Amada Ausente I/IB4

    Fantasia Breve Sobre El Nombre
        "Salcedo" I/IB4

    Festivola, Danza Catalana De Espiritu
        Popular I/IB4

    Homenaje A Tarrega I/IB4

    Impromptu I/IB4

    Manola Del Avapies, Tonadilla I/IB4

    Morceaux Espagnols, 3 I/IB4

    Pequena Romanza I/IB4

    Preludio Romantico I/IB4

    Rapsodia Valenciana I/IB4

    Salve I/IB4

    Sequidilla I/IB4

    Sevilla, Evocation I/IB4

    Triquilandia, Jugando Al Escondite
        (Cache-Cache) I/IB4

    Troisieme Triquilandia I/IB4

    Variations Sur Un Theme Obsedant
        I/IB4

    Veneciana I/IB4

    Villanesca, Danza Campesina I/IB4

QUAGLINO, ANACLETO
    Andantino I/IB4

RADOLE, GIUSEPPE
    Notturno I/IB4

RAMOVS, PRIMOZ (1921-   )
    Nocturnes, 2 I/IB4

RATZ, MARTIN
    Kleine Serenade, Unterhaltende
        Vortragsstucke I/IB4

READ, GARDNER (1913-   )
    Canzone Di Notte I/IB4

REBAY, FERDINAND (1889-1953)
    Albumblatt I/IB4

    Kleine Leichte Stucke, 14 I/IB4

    Leicht Spielbare Kleinigkeiten I/IB4

    Menuette, 2 I/IB4

    Tanzlied I/IB4

    Wiegenlied I/IB4

REINBOTE, HELMUT
    Leichte Stucke Fur Gitarre I/IB4

REISER, EKKEHARD
    Masken I/IB4

REYNE, GERARD (1944-   )
    Guitare I/IB4

    Homenaje A M. de Falla I/IB4

RIERA, RODRIGO
    Merengue Venezolano I/IB4

    Preludio Criollo I/IB4

RODRIGO, JOAQUIN (1902-   )
    Bajando De La Meseta I/IB4

    Elogio De La Guitarra I/IB4

    En Los Trigales, Scene Castillane
        I/IB4

    Invocation Et Danse, Hommage A Manuel
        De Falla I/IB4

    Junto Al Generalife I/IB4

    Pajaros De Primavera I/IB4

    Pastorale I/IB4

    Petites Pieces, 3 I/IB4

    Piezas Espanolas, 3 I/IB4

RODRIGO, JOAQUIN (cont'd.)

Sarabande Lointaine I/IB4

Tiento Antiguo I/IB4

ROE, BETTY (1930-   )
Larcombe's Fancy I/IB4

ROOTH, HANS
Redsleeves I/IB4

ROSETTA, GIUSEPPE
Canti Della Pianura I/IB4

Mirage I/IB4

Poemi Brevi, 6 I/IB4

Preludi Per Gilardino I/IB4

Preludio, Barcarola E Scherzo I/IB4

Weissiana, Omaggio A S.L. Weiss
   I/IB4

ROSSI, ABNER
Andantino E Valzer I/IB4

Contrappunto Scherzoso I/IB4

Nocturne I/IB4

Pensieri d'Autunno I/IB4

ROUSSEL, ALBERT (CHARLES PAUL)
   (1869-1937)
Segovia I/IB4

RUBIN, MARCEL (1905-   )
Petite Serenade I/IB4

RUCH, HANNES
Leichte Stucke, 34 I/IB4

Spielmusik I/IB4

RUIZ PIPO, ANTONIO
Cancion Y Danza, No.1 I/IB4

Cancion Y Danza, No.2 I/IB4

Canto Libre I/IB4

Estancias I/IB4

Hommage A Antonio De Cabezon I/IB4

RUTHENFRANZ, R.
Pieces, 3 I/IB4

SACCHETTI, ARTURO
Eucalyptus I/IB4

Memorial I/IB4

SAINZ DE LA MAZA, EDUARDO
Campanas Del Alba, Tremolo I/IB4

Canco Del Lladre, Popular Catalana
   I/IB4

Confidencia, Preludio I/IB4

Habanera I/IB4

Homenaje A La Guitarra, Preludio
   I/IB4

SALAZAR, ADOLFO (1890-1958)
Romancillo I/IB4

SALDARELLI, VINCENZO
Per La Chitarra I/IB4

SAMAZEUILH, GUSTAVE (1877-1967)
Serenade I/IB4

SANCHEZ, B.
Cancion Olvidada I/IB4

Complainte Funebre, Fantaisie A La
   Memoire De Ida Presti (2.5.1967,
   Jour De Son Enterrement) I/IB4

Criolla I/IB4

Danza Del Pejin I/IB4

Fiesta Laredana I/IB4

Linares I/IB4

Minivalses, 4 I/IB4

Ninfa, La I/IB4

Nocturne No. 1 I/IB4

Peruviana I/IB4

Preambolo Y Toccata Surena I/IB4

Prelude in G minor I/IB4

SANCHEZ, B. (cont'd.)

Preludio Y Alborada I/IB4

Quimeras, No.1 I/IB4

Quimeras, No.2 I/IB4

Quimeras, No.3 I/IB4

Ruisseau, Le I/IB4

Serenade Villageoise I/IB4

Serenata Canaria I/IB4

Tonalida Islena I/IB4

Vals Sombrio I/IB4

SANDI, LUIS (1905-   )
Fatima, Suite Galante I/IB4

SANTORSOLA, GUIDO (1904-   )
Minuet I/IB4

Prelude I/IB4

Prelude No. 1 I/IB4

Prelude No. 2 I/IB4

Prelude No. 3 I/IB4

Prelude No. 4 I/IB4

Prelude No. 5 I/IB4

Tientos, 4, Sonoridades 1970 I/IB4

Vals Romantico I/IB4

SAUGUET, HENRI (1901-   )
Preludes, 3 I/IB4

SAVIO, ISAIAS (1900-1977)
Suite Descritiva I/IB4

SCHAGEN, HENK VAN
Kleine Solist, De – The Little
   Soloist, Easy Guitar Pieces In
   Various Positions I/IB4

Tum Tum, For Young Guitarists I/IB4

SCHIBLER, ARMIN (1920-   )
Black Guitar, The I/IB4

Every Night I Dream I/IB4

Homme Seul, Un, Kleines Konzert
   I/IB4

My Own Blues I/IB4

SCHINDLER, OTTO
Wiegenlied I/IB4

SCHNEIDER, MATTHIAS
Gingganz I/IB4

SCHOLZE, ARTHUR JOHANNES (1883-1945)
Kleine Solostucke I/IB4

SCHREIBER, ALFRED
Aphorismen I/IB4

SCHULER, ALEXANDER
Waltz I/IB4

SCHUMANN, GERHARD (1914-   )
Mikrokosmos I/IB4

SCHWEYDA, WILLY
Pieces, 2 I/IB4

SEGOVIA, ANDRES (1896-   )
Impromptu I/IB4

Prelude In Chords I/IB4

Preludios, 3 I/IB4

Tonadilla I/IB4

SFETSAS, KYRIACOS (1945-   )
Strophes I/IB4

SHACKELFORD, RUDOLPH OWENS (RUDY)
   (1944-   )
Epitaffio I/IB4

SIERRA-FORTUNY, J.M.
Introduccio I/IB4

SMITH BRINDLE, REGINALD (1917-   )
Danza Pagana I/IB4

Do Not Go Gentle... I/IB4

Etruscan Preludes I/IB4

Fuego Fatuo I/IB4

SMITH BRINDLE, REGINALD (cont'd.)

Memento I/IB4

Nocturne I/IB4

November Memories I/IB4

Polifemo De Oro, Il, 4 Fragmenti
   I/IB4

Vita Senese I/IB4

SOLARES, ENRIQUE (1910-   )
Fantasy I/IB4

Ofrenda A Fernando Sors I/IB4

Toccatina I/IB4

SPERLING, ERNST
Evening Song I/IB4

Preludes, 4 I/IB4

Silent Forests I/IB4

Slumber Song I/IB4

Springtime Waltz I/IB4

SPRONGL, NORBERT (1892-1983)
Stucke, 6 I/IB4

SREBOTNJAK, ALOJZ F. (1931-   )
2 Movimenti I/IB4

STAAK, PIETER VAN DER (1930-   )
Bolero Espanol I/IB4

Exotic Dances, 5 I/IB4

Moods From The Song Of Solomon, 3
   I/IB4

Pezzi, 3 I/IB4

Prelude No. 1 I/IB4

STADLMAIR, HANS (1929-   )
Stucke, 5 I/IB4

STAVINOHA-MELISEK, JAN
Suite Romantica I/IB4

STEFFENS, WALTER (1934-   )
Fur Soto I/IB4

STERZATI, UMBERTO (1909-1972)
Elegy I/IB4

STEVENS, BERNARD GEORGE (1916-1983)
Ballad I/IB4

STEVENSON, RONALD (1928-   )
Anger Dance I/IB4

STINGL, ANTON (1908-   )
Gitarrebuch Fur Madeleine, Vol. I
   I/IB4

Gitarrebuch Fur Madeleine, Vol. II
   I/IB4

Improvisation, Uber Ein
   Mittelalterliches Lied "Es Sass
   Ein Edly Maget Schon" I/IB4

Kleine Spielstucke Nach
   Kinderliedern, 30 I/IB4

Leichte Stucke, 12 I/IB4

Sonatine, Op. 15 I/IB4

STOCKHAUSEN, KARLHEINZ (1928-   )
Spiral; Composition No. 27 I/IB4

STOKER, RICHARD (1938-   )
Improvisation I/IB4

STRATEGIER, HERMAN (1912-   )
Short Pieces, 10 I/IB4

SURINACH, CARLOS (1915-   )
Bolero De Los Picaros I/IB4

SZORDIKOWSKI, BRUNO
Impromptu I/IB4

Kleine Suite I/IB4

TANSMAN, ALEXANDRE (1897-   )
Cavatina I/IB4

Danza Pomposa I/IB4

Mazurka I/IB4

Pezzo In Modo Antico I/IB4

Pieces, 3 I/IB4

Pieces Faciles, Vol. I I/IB4

Twentieth Century — Arrangements

ROOY, JULIO
   Charlein, Antilliaanse Wals   I/IB4

SAINZ DE LA MAZA, EDUARDO
   Greensleeves, Cancion Popular Inglesa
   I/IB4

SCHOENBERG, ARNOLD (1874–1951)
   Kleine Klavierstucke, 6   I/IB4

SOJO, VINCENTE E.
   Pieces From Venezuela, 5   I/IB4

   Quirpa Guatirena, Joropo   I/IB4

STRAVINSKY, IGOR (1882–1971)
   Allegro   I/IB4

TAUBE, EVERT (1890–1976)
   Nocturne   I/IB4

TURINA, JOAQUIN (1882–1949)
   Ensueno   I/IB4

   Orgia   I/IB4

   Sacro–Monte   I/IB4

WELLESZ, EGON (1885–1974)
   Rhapsody, Op. 87   I/IB4

Folk Music of Spain and Latin America

APONTE, PEDRO ARCILA
   Bellas Noches De Maiquetia, Las,
   Canzone Venezuelana   I/IB5

AUSENTE, EL, CANZONE VENEZUELANA   I/IB5

BEHREND, SIEGFRIED (1933-   )
   Alborada   I/IB5

   Danza Mora   I/IB5

   Flamenco–Fantasia   I/IB5

   Sevillanas   I/IB5

   Spanische Tanze, 3   I/IB5

   Trianas   I/IB5

BERTI, OSCAR
   Alegres Rincones, Valse Venezolana
   I/IB5

BIELSA, VALENTIN
   4 Canciones Populares Espanolas
   I/IB5

BOHR, HEINRICH
   Spanischer Tanz   I/IB5

BROUWER, LEO (1939-   )
   Airs Populaires Cubains, 2   I/IB5

   Piezas Populares Cubanas   I/IB5

CALZADILLA, ROMAN
   Aires De Mochima, Valzer Venezolano
   I/IB5

CANCION CARORENA, MELODIA VENEZUELANA
   I/IB5

CANCIONES POPULARES   I/IB5–Coll

CANCIONES POPULARES CATALANAS, 10
   I/IB5–Coll

CANCIONES POPULARES MEXICANAS, 8
   I/IB5–Coll

CATALANISCHE WEISEN, 3   I/IB5–Coll

CERVANTES, IGNACIO (1847–1905)
   Danses Cubaines, 2   I/IB5

CHANSONS BRESILIENNES, VOL. I
   I/IB5–Coll

CHANSONS BRESILIENNES, VOL. II
   I/IB5–Coll

CHANSONS CATALANES, 2   I/IB5–Coll

CONDOR PASA, EL; LIEDER UND TANZE AUS
   SUDAMERIKA   I/IB5

DAGOSTO, SYLVAIN
   Feria Al Prado, Sevillana   I/IB5

DIABLO SUELTO, EL, ANTILLIAANSE WALS
   I/IB5

EASY MUSIC, VOL. 10   I/IB5–Coll

FARRUCA   I/IB5

FERNANDEZ, HERACLIO (1851–1886)
   Diablo Suelto, El, Valzer Popolare
   Venezuelano   I/IB5

FILLA DEL MARXANT, LA, MELODIA POPULAR
   CATALANA   I/IB5

FLOR DEL CAMPO, VALZER VENEZUELANO
   I/IB5

FLORES NEGRAS, PASILLO ECUATORIANO
   I/IB5

FOLKSONGS, 4   I/IB5–Coll

FOUR CATALAN MELODIES   I/IB5–Coll

LAURO, AUGUSTIN
   Venezuelan Pieces, 2   I/IB5

LAZARDE, ROMULO
   Cancion Infantil   I/IB5

LOPEZ, JOAQUIN
   Melodies Populaires Espagnoles, 4,
   Pour Les Debutants   I/IB5

MATOS RODRIGUEZ, GERARDO H.
   Cumparsita, La, Tango   I/IB5

MAZMANIAN, VROUYR
   Caprice Flamenco   I/IB5

MERAN, JOSE
   Hispania, 6 Very Easy Spanish Dances
   I/IB5

MERENGUE, BALLO VENEZUELANO   I/IB5

MESTRE, EL, MELODIA POPULAR CATALANA
   I/IB5

MONGE, VICTOR ("SERRANITO")
   Planta Y Tacon, Zapateado   I/IB5

MUSICA ARGENTINA, LIBRO I   I/IB5–Coll

NO SE VA LA PALOMA, CANCION POPULAR
   LEONESA   I/IB5

PEREZ, RAFAEL
   Carorena, Canzone Venezuelana   I/IB5

PONCE, MANUEL MARIA (1882–1948)
   Estrellita, Cancion Mexicana   I/IB5

PUJOL, EMILIO (1886–1982)
   Tambors, Les 3, Glosa De La Cancion
   Popular Catalana   I/IB5

RAMOS, JOAQUIN
   Serenata Carorena, Cancion Venezolana
   I/IB5

SAINZ DE LA MAZA, EDUARDO
   Canco Del Lladre, Popular Catalana
   I/IB5

SCHNEIDER, HEINRICH
   Aragonesa, Spanischer Tanz   I/IB5

SCHWERTBERGER, GERALD
   Latin America: Tango, Samba, Rumba,
   Bossa–Nova   I/IB5

SONS DE CARRILHOES, TOADA   I/IB5

3 SPANISCHE SOLOSTUCKE   I/IB5

SUDAMERICANA, BERUHMTE FOLKLORISTISCHE
   TANZE   I/IB5–Coll

TESTAMEN DE N' AMELIA, EL   I/IB5

TORRES, PEDRO MANUEL
   Gallo, El, Danza Venezuelana   I/IB5

TWO CATALAN FOLK SONGS   I/IB5

VIDALITA, CANCION ARGENTINA   I/IB5

VITO, EL   I/IB5

WALKER, LUISE (1910-   )
   Argentinische Weise, Triste   I/IB5

WORSCHECH, ROMAIN
   Danzas De Andalucia, Style Flamenco
   I/IB5

Folk Music of Countries and Continents Other Than Spain and Latin America

ABLONIZ, MIGUEL (1917-   )
   Incorrigible Dreamer, An, Bossa Nova
   I/IB5

   Moods, Jazz In Bossa Nova   I/IB5

ALPENLANDISCHE VOLKSTANZE   I/IB5–Coll

ALPENLANDISCHE WEISEN, VOL. I–IV
   I/IB5–Coll

ALTES RUSSISCHES LIED   I/IB5

ALTRUSSISCHE VOLKSWEISEN   I/IB5–Coll

ANTHOLOGIE SUR DES AIRS DU FOLKLORE
   FRANCAIS   I/IB5–Coll

AUTHENTIC BLUEGRASS GUITAR   I/IB5–Coll

CANCION DE CUNA   I/IB5

CARLSTEDT, JAN (1926-   )
    Danzas Suecas, 2 I/IB5

CHANSONS POPULAIRES RUSSES, 7
    I/IB5-Coll

COMMUNITY SONGS, 40 I/IB5-Coll

DANSKA OCH SVENSKA VISOR; 15 DANISH AND
    SWEDISH FOLKSONGS I/IB5-Coll

DEUTSCHE VOLKSTANZE I/IB5-Coll

ENGLISH FOLK SONGS, 3 I/IB5-Coll

ENGLISH FOLK SONGS, 16 I/IB5-Coll

ERSTES LAUTENBUCH, 67 KINDERLIEDER
    I/IB5-Coll

ERSTES MUSIZIEREN AUF DER GITARRE -
    MUSIC-MAKING FOR GUITAR, LIEDER UND
    TANZE VERSCHIEDENER NATIONEN
    I/IB5-Coll

EUROPESE VOLKSLIEDEREN, VOL. II
    I/IB5-Coll

FAMOUS NEGRO SPIRITUALS, 5 I/IB5-Coll

FOLK-BLUES, 3 I/IB5-Coll

FOLKVISOR, 30 I/IB5-Coll

GITARRENMUSI, 29 ALPENLANDISCHE LIEDER
    UND TANZE I/IB5-Coll

GOD JUL, 71 VALKANDA VISOR I/IB5-Coll

HADJIDAKIS, MANOS
    Never On Sunday I/IB5

HANS SPIELMANN, EIN VOLKSLIEDER-
    SPIELBUCH FUR GITARRE, VOL. I: FUR
    DEN ANFANGER I/IB5-Coll

HANS SPIELMANN, EIN VOLKSLIEDER-
    SPIELBUCH FUR GITARRE, VOL. II: FUR
    FORTGESCHRITTENEN SPIELER
    I/IB5-Coll

HINEY MA TOV I/IB5

HINTERMEYER, WILLY (1892-   )
    Fidele Weisen, Fur Gitarre Solo In
    Leichter Spielart I/IB5

HOOR! DE GITARISTEN, BEKENDE LIEDJES IN
    LICHTE ZETTING VOOR SOLO-GITAAR,
    VOLS. I-III I/IB5-Coll

IRISH SONGS AND DANCES, 26 I/IB5-Coll

JEUX D'ENFANTS, 25 MINIATURE FRANCESI
    I/IB5-Coll

KOCH, HANS
    Musizierbuchlein, Ein, Einfuhrung In
        Das Mehrstimmige Spiel Nach
        Volkstanzen Und Liedern Aus Dem
        Alpenraum I/IB5

LAUTENSCHLAGER, DER, VOLKSLIEDER
    I/IB5-Coll

LAUTENSPIELER, DER, NO. 2 I/IB5-Coll

LIED UBER DIE GRENZE; FOLKLORE FREMDER
    LANDER I/IB5

LIEDER AUS DEUTSCHLAND I/IB5

50 MAGYAR NEPDAL I/IB5

MELODY OF JAPAN BY GUITARS, VOL. I
    I/IB5-Coll

MELODY OF JAPAN BY GUITARS, VOL. II
    I/IB5-Coll

MILETIC, MIROSLAV (1925-   )
    Kroatische Suite, Nach Volksweisen
        Aus Medjimurje I/IB5

MUSIZIERBUCHLEIN FUR ANFANGER
    I/IB5-Coll

NEUMANN, ULRIK
    Three-Bands Bossa Nova I/IB5

NORDISCHE VOLKSWEISEN, 30, AUS
    SCHWEDEN, DANEMARK, NORWEGEN UND
    FINNLAND I/IB5-Coll

O BLACK AND UNKNOWN BARDS, 7 NEGRO
    SPIRITUALS I/IB5-Coll

OUD-VLAAMSE VOLKSLIEDEREN, 2
    I/IB5-Coll

PLAYFORD TUNES, 8 ENGLISH TRADITIONAL
    DANCE TUNES I/IB5-Coll

PRAF, [FRAY] BENEDICTO
    Airs Russes, 3 I/IB5

PUTILIN, IVAN
    Andante, Altes Volkslied I/IB5

    Romanze, Altes Zigeunerlied I/IB5

REBAY, FERDINAND (1889-1953)
    Russischer Tanz I/IB5

RUSSISCHE UND UKRAINISCHE VOLKSLIEDER
    UND TANZE, 50 I/IB5-Coll

RUSSISCHE VOLKSMUSIK I/IB5-Coll

RUSSISCHE VOLKSWEISEN UND TANZE
    I/IB5-Coll

SCHOTTISCHE LIEDER UND BALLADEN I/IB5

SCHWERTBERGER, GERALD
    Folk Guitar: Ragtime, Blues, Country
        Music I/IB5

    Glory Hallelujah: Spirituals, Jazz,
        Blues, Beat I/IB5

SCOTTISCH MADRILENE I/IB5

SINTERKLAASLIEDJES I/IB5-Coll

TANCE I PIESNI LUDOWE I/IB5-Coll

TANZE AUS OSTERREICH I/IB5-Coll

TEUCHERT, HEINZ (1914-   )
    Volksweise Mit Variationen, "Ich Ging
        Durch Einen Grasgrunen Wald"
        I/IB5

TONBILDUNGS-STUDIEN NACH ALTEN WEISEN -
    STUDIES IN TONE FORMATION BASED ON
    OLD TUNES I/IB5-Coll

TROIKA, ALTRUSSISCHES TANZLIED I/IB5

TRUHLAR, JAN (1928-   )
    Lidovych Pisni, 50 I/IB5

TWEE MAAL EEN IS TWEE, EEN- EN
    TWEESTEMMIGE NEDERLANDSE
    VOLKSLIEDEREN I/IB5-Coll

TWO OLD ENGLISH AIRS I/IB5

TWO POLISH AIRS I/IB5

URBAN, STEPAN (1913-   )
    Deset Fantasii, Na Lidove Motivy
        I/IB5

VOLKSLIED UND TANZ; EIN TASCHENBUCH
    I/IB5-Coll

VOLKSLIEDER FUR GITARRE-SOLOSPIEL
    I/IB5-Coll

VOLKSWEISEN AUS OSTERREICH I/IB5-Coll

VOLKSWEISEN DER WELT, VOL. I
    I/IB5-Coll

VOLKSWEISEN DER WELT, VOL. II
    I/IB5-Coll

VOLKSWEISEN DER WELT, VOL. III
    I/IB5-Coll

WAT FRANSEN ZINGEN EN DANSEN, FRANSE
    WIJSJES; 10 FRENCH TUNES
    I/IB5-Coll

ZO DOEN WIJ DAT! 24 BEKENDE MELODIETJES
    VOOR JONGE GITARISTEN; 24 DUTCH
    TUNES I/IB5-Coll

International Folk Music Collections

FOLKLORE DER WELT, VOLS. I-III; LIEDER
    UND TANZE AUS ALLER WELT
    I/IB5-Coll

FOLKLORISTISCHE SUITE; 12 VOLKSWEISEN
    AUS ALLER WELT I/IB5-Coll

LIEDER AUS ALLER WELT, 33 VOLKSLIEDER
    AUS EUROPA UND AMERIKA I/IB5-Coll

VOLKSLIEDER ZUM SINGEN UND SPIELEN
    I/IB5-Coll

Miscellaneous Guitar Solo Collections

ALBUM I/IB6-Coll

ALBUM CLASSIQUE I/IB6-Coll

ALBUM DI MUSICHE PER CHITARRA
    I/IB6-Coll

ALBUM, NO. 9 I/IB6-Coll

ALBUM, NO. 12 I/IB6-Coll

ALBUM, NO. 13 I/IB6-Coll

ALBUM, NO. 14 I/IB6-Coll

ALBUM, NO. 15 I/IB6-Coll

ALBUM, NO. 16 I/IB6-Coll

ALBUM, NO. 18 I/IB6-Coll

ALBUM PRIMO I/IB6-Coll

ALBUM RICREATIVO, NO. 1 I/IB6-Coll

ALBUM RICREATIVO, NO. 2 I/IB6-Coll

ALBUM RICREATIVO, NO. 3 I/IB6-Coll

ALBUM RICREATIVO, NO. 4 I/IB6-Coll

ALBUM RICREATIVO, NO. 5 I/IB6-Coll

ALFONSO, NICOLAS
    Ya Van Los Pastores IV/I

ALTE GITARRENMUSIK, VOL. 1 I/IB6-Coll

ALTE GITARRENMUSIK, VOL. 2 I/IB6-Coll

ANDRES SEGOVIA ALBUM OF GUITAR SOLOS
    I/IB6-Coll

ANTIGA, JEAN
    Tarraja, 24 Petites Pieces IV/I

ANTOLOGIA DE OBRAS PARA GUITARRA
    I/IB6-Coll

ANTOLOGIA PER CHITARRA, VOL. 1
    I/IB6-Coll

ANTOLOGIA PER CHITARRA, VOL. 2
    I/IB6-Coll

ANTOLOGIA PER CHITARRA, VOL. 3
    I/IB6-Coll

ARMONIA, EINE SAMMLUNG POLYPHONER MUSIK
    FUR GITARRE AUS VIER JAHRHUNDERTEN
    I/IB6-Coll

ARTE DELLA CHITARRA, L', RACCOLTA DI
    SONATE E STUDI DI AUTORI CLASSICI,
    VOL. 1 I/IB6-Coll

ARTE DELLA CHITARRA, L', RACCOLTA DI
    SONATE E STUDI DI AUTORI CLASSICI,
    VOL. 2 I/IB6-Coll

AUSGEWAHLTE STUCKE ALTER UND NEUER
    MEISTER FUR GITARRE, VOL. 1
    I/IB6-Coll

AUSGEWAHLTE STUCKE ALTER UND NEUER
    MEISTER FUR GITARRE, VOL. 2
    I/IB6-Coll

AUSGEWAHLTE STUCKE FUR GITARRE SOLO, 30
    I/IB6-Coll

BERUHMTE OPERN MELODIEN FUR GITARRE,
    VOL. 1 I/IB6-Coll

BERUHMTE OPERN MELODIEN FUR GITARRE,
    VOL. 2 I/IB6-Coll

BEST OF BREAM, THE I/IB6-Coll

BIS DEL CONCERTISTA, I, VOL. 1
    I/IB6-Coll

BIS DEL CONCERTISTA, I, VOL. 2
    I/IB6-Coll

BIS DEL CONCERTISTA, I, VOL. 3
    I/IB6-Coll

CANCIONES CATALANAS NAVIDENAS, 4 IV/I

CANCIONES DE NAVIDAD, 8 IV/I

CANCIONES POPULARES CATALANAS, 10 IV/I

CANCIONES POPULARES GALLEGAS, 2 IV/I

CANTI DI NATALE IV/I

CAROLS FOR GUITAR IV/I

CAROLS FOR GUITAR, 6 IV/I

CATALANISCHE WEISEN, 3 IV/I

CELEBRI MELODIE NATALIZIE IV/I

CHOIX D'ETUDES POUR GUITARE, VOL. 1:
    COURS PREPARATOIRE I/IB6-Coll

CHOIX D'ETUDES POUR GUITARE, VOL. 2,
    COURS ELEMENTAIRE I/IB6-Coll

CHRISTMAS CAROLS, 4 IV/I

CHRISTMAS CAROLS, 5 IV/I

CLASSIC GUITAR, THE, ALL-TIME MASTER
    MELODIES I/IB6-Coll

CLASSIC GUITAR SOLO ALBUM, VOL. 1
    I/IB6-Coll

CLASSICAL ALBUM FOR GUITAR SOLO, A
    I/IB6-Coll

COMPOSICIONES CELEBRES, 10, VOL. 1
    I/IB6-Coll

COMPOSICIONES CELEBRES, 10, VOL. 2
    I/IB6-Coll

COMPOSICIONES CELEBRES, 12, VOL. 3
    I/IB6-Coll

COMPOSICIONES CLASICAS Y ROMANTICAS
    I/IB6-Coll

DIVERTISSEMENT, VOL. 1 I/IB6-Coll

DIVERTISSEMENT, VOL. 2 I/IB6-Coll

DOLCE NATALI IV/I

EASY CHRISTMAS CAROLS, 2 IV/I

EASY MUSIC, VOL. 1 I/IB6-Coll

EASY MUSIC, VOL. 2 IV/I, I/IB6-Coll

EASY MUSIC, VOL. 4 I/IB6-Coll

EASY MUSIC, VOL. 5 I/IB6-Coll

EASY MUSIC, VOL. 6 I/IB6-Coll

EASY PIECES, 20 I/IB6-Coll

EDITION NICOLAS ALFONSO, NO. 4
    I/IB6-Coll

EDITION NICOLAS ALFONSO, NO. 5
    I/IB6-Coll

EDITION NICOLAS ALFONSO, NO. 6
    I/IB6-Coll

EDITION NICOLAS ALFONSO, NO. 7
    I/IB6-Coll

EDITION NICOLAS ALFONSO, NO. 8
    I/IB6-Coll

EDITION NICOLAS ALFONSO, NO. 9
    I/IB6-Coll

EDITION NICOLAS ALFONSO, NO. 10
    I/IB6-Coll

ENJOY CLASSICAL AND BAROQUE GUITAR
    I/IB6-Coll

ERLISO, VINCENTE
    Transcripciones Por Vicente Erliso,
    Vol. 1 I/IB6-Coll

ERSTES GITARRENSPIEL, LIEDER UND TANZE,
    SEHR LEICHT GESETZT, VOL. I
    I/IB6-Coll

ERSTES GITARRENSPIEL, LIEDER UND TANZE,
    SEHR LEICHT GESETZT, VOL. II
    I/IB6-Coll

ERSTES GITARRENSPIEL, LIEDER UND TANZE,
    SEHR LEICHT GESETZT, VOL. III
    I/IB6-Coll

ERSTES SPIELBUCH FUR GITARRE
    I/IB6-Coll

EUROPEAN MASTERS FOR THE GUITAR, A
    SELECT LIBRARY OF 26 [SIC]
    CLASSICAL AND CONTEMPORARY PIECES
    I/IB6-Coll

EUROPEAN MASTERS FOR THE GUITAR, A
    SELECT LIBRARY OF 26 [SIC]
    CLASSICAL AND CONTEMPORARY PIECES
    I/IB6-Coll

FOLK TUNES AND CLASSICS FOR SOLO GUITAR
    I/IB6-Coll

FOLKSONGS, 4 IV/I

FOR GUITARISTS ONLY! I/IB6-Coll

FOR MY FRIENDS IV/I, I/IB6-Coll

FROHLICHE WEIHNACHTEN; 40 BELIEBTE
    WEIHNACHTS- UND NEUJAHRSLIEDER
    IV/I

FUR JEDEN GITARRISTEN, SONDERAUSGABE
    21. INTERNATIONALER
    GITARRISTENKONGRESS (TOKYO, 1962),
    "IN MEMORIAM" (RICHARD JACOB
    WEISGERBER 1877-1940, PROF. ROMOLO
    FERRARI 1895-1958) I/IB6-Coll

GITAAR-KAMERMUZIEK, VOL. 3: UIT HET
    REPERTOIRE VAN HET JOEGOSLAVISCHE
    DANSTHEATER I/IB6-Coll

GITAAR-SOLI, ALBUM KLASSIEKE- EN
    MODERNE GITAAR-SOLI IN EENVOUDIGE
    BEZETTING I/IB6-Coll

GITAARSPEELBOEK - LIVRE DE LA GUITARE
    I/IB6-Coll

GITARMUZSIKA KEZDOKNEK - GITARRENMUSIK
    FUR ANFANGER I/IB6-Coll

GITARRE ALLEIN, ENTWICKLUNG DES
    SOLISTISCHEN MUSIZIERENS AUS DEM
    AKKORDSPIEL I/IB6-Coll

GITARRE SPEZIAL, PICKING MODERN
    ARRANGEMENT, VOL. 1 I/IB6-Coll

GITARRE SPEZIAL, PICKING MODERN
    ARRANGEMENT, VOL. 2 I/IB6-Coll

GITARRE SPEZIAL, PICKING MODERN
    ARRANGEMENT, VOL. 3 I/IB6-Coll

GITARREMUSIK FUR ANFANGER, VOL. I: SEHR
    LEICHT I/IB6-Coll

GITARREMUSIK FUR ANFANGER, VOL. II:
    LEICHT I/IB6-Coll

GITARREMUSIK FUR ANFANGER, VOL. III:
    MITTELSCHWER I/IB6-Coll

GITARREMUSIK FUR ANFANGER, VOL. IV:
    SCHWER I/IB6-Coll

GITARRFEST I/IB6-Coll

GITARRISTEN, VOL. II I/IB6-Coll

GITARRKLANG I/IB6-Coll

GITARRLEK I/IB6-Coll

GOLDEN AGE, THE, CLASSICS FOR SOLO
    GUITAR, VOL. I I/IB6-Coll

GOLDEN AGE, THE, CLASSICS FOR SOLO
    GUITAR, VOL. II I/IB6-Coll

GOLDENE BUCH DES GITARRISTEN, DAS (LE
    LIVRE D'OR DES GUITARISTES, OP.52)
    I/IB6-Coll

GRACE OF MINUETS, A I/IB6-Coll

GRUBER, FRANZ XAVER (1787-1863)
    Stille Nacht IV/I

GUITAR MASTERS, ORIGINAL GUITAR
    CLASSICS SIMPLIFIED FOR BEGINNING
    GUITARISTS I/IB6-Coll

GUITAR SAMPLER, 5 CENTURIES OF ORIGINAL
    GUITAR SOLOS I/IB6-Coll

GUITAR SONGBOOK, THE I/IB6-Coll

GUITARIANA I/IB6-Coll

GUTEN ABEND, GUTE NACHT IV/I,
    I/IB6-Coll

HISZPANSCY MISTRZOWIE GITARY
    I/IB6-Coll

IBERIA, 5 JAHRHUNDERTE SPANISCHER
    GITARRENMUSIK, VOL. I I/IB6-Coll

IBERIA, 5 JAHRHUNDERTE SPANISCHER
    GITARRENMUSIK, VOL. II I/IB6-Coll

INTERNATIONAL ANTHOLOGY FOR GUITAR
    (TWELFTH THROUGH EIGHTEENTH
    CENTURIES) I/IB6-Coll

JEUX INTERDITS: MUSIQUE DU FILM
    I/IB6-Coll

JUNGE GITARRE-SOLOIST, DER I/IB6-Coll

KERSTLIEDEREN, EENVOUDIGE ZETTINGEN
    IV/I

KERSTLIEDEREN VOOR GITAARSOLO IV/I

KITARAKIRJA-GITARRMELODIER, VOL. 1
    I/IB6-Coll

KITARAKIRJA-GITARRMELODIER, VOL. 2
    I/IB6-Coll

KLASSIKER DER GITARRE; STUDIEN- UND
    VORTRAGSLITERATUR AUS DEM 18. UND
    19. JAHRHUNDERT, VOL. 2:
    MITTELSTUFE - INTERMEDIATE STAGE
    I/IB6-Coll

KLASSISCHES ALBUM, VOL. 1 I/IB6-Coll

KLASSISCHES ALBUM, VOL. 2 I/IB6-Coll

KLASSISCHES ALBUM, VOL. 3 I/IB6-Coll

KLASSZIKUSOK GITARRA I/IB6-Coll

KLEINE WERKE GROSSER MEISTER, VOL. 1
    I/IB6-Coll

KLEINE WERKE GROSSER MEISTER, VOL. 2
    I/IB6-Coll

KLEINE WERKE GROSSER MEISTER, VOL. 3
    I/IB6-Coll

KLEINE WERKE GROSSER MEISTER, VOL. 4
    I/IB6-Coll

KOMMT SINGT UND SPIELT: LIEDER UNSERER
    ZEIT, FUR DEN ANFANGSUNTERRICHT
    IV/I, I/IB6-Coll

LAUTENIST, DER, VOL. 6 I/IB6-Coll

LEICHTE ALTE LAUTE- UND
    GITARRESTUCKLEIN, 32 I/IB6-Coll

LEICHTE UBUNGEN UND SPIELSTUCKE
    I/IB6-Coll

LEICHTE VORTRAGSSTUCKE, VOL. 1
    I/IB6-Coll

LEICHTE VORTRAGSSTUCKE, VOL. 2
    I/IB6-Coll

LEICHTESTEN SOLOSTUCKE BERUHMTER
    LAUTEN- UND GITARREMEISTER, DIE
    I/IB6-Coll

LEISE FALLT DER SCHNEE, LIEDER ZUR
    WEIHNACHTSZEIT IV/I

LEISE RIESELT DER SCHNEE IV/I

LET US HAVE CHRISTMAS MUSIC IV/I

LIEDER UM WEIHNACHT IV/I

MEISTER DES GITARRENSPIELS, VOL. 1,
    LEICHTE STUCKE I/IB6-Coll

MEISTER DES GITARRENSPIELS, VOL. 2,
    MITTELSCHWERE STUCKE I/IB6-Coll

MEL BAY FOLIO OF CLASSIC GUITAR SOLOS,
    VOL. 1 I/IB6-Coll

MEL BAY FOLIO OF CLASSIC GUITAR SOLOS,
    VOL. 2 IV/I, I/IB6-Coll

MEL BAY'S DELUXE ALBUM OF CLASSIC
    GUITAR MUSIC I/IB6-Coll

MENUETTBUCH I/IB6-Coll

MILLER, JOHN R.
    Solo-Gitarre, Die, Vol. II
    I/IB6-Coll

MIT DER GITARRE, UNTERHALTUNGS-ALBUM
    I/IB6-Coll

MUSIC FOR CLASSICAL GUITAR I/IB6-Coll

MUSIC FOR THE CLASSICAL GUITAR, VOL. 1:
    A BOOK FOR BEGINNERS I/IB6-Coll

MUSIC FOR THE CLASSICAL GUITAR, VOL. 2:
    A BOOK FOR INTERMEDIATE PLAYERS
    I/IB6-Coll

MUSIC FOR THE YOUNG GUITARIST
    I/IB6-Coll

MUSICA PER CHITARRA, DA ORIGINALI PER
    LIUTO E CHITARRA I/IB6-Coll

MUSICAS PARA O NATAL IV/I

MUSIK FUR GITARRE; NACH ORIGINALEN FUR
LAUTE UND GITARRE AUS DEM 16.-19.
JAHRHUNDERT   I/IB6-Coll

MUSIQUE POUR GUITARE SEULE, VOL. 1 -
MUSIC FOR SOLO GUITAR, VOL. 1
I/IB6-Coll

MUSIQUE POUR GUITARE SEULE, VOL. 2 -
MUSIC FOR SOLO GUITAR, VOL. 2
I/IB6-Coll

MUSIQUE POUR GUITARE SEULE, VOL. 3 -
MUSIC FOR SOLO GUITAR, VOL. 3
I/IB6-Coll

MY FAIR LADIES   I/IB6-Coll

NOAD, FREDERICK M.
    Playing The Guitar, A Self-
    Instruction Guide To Technique
    And Theory   IV/I

NOELS   IV/I

NOY DE LA MARE, EL, CANCION POPULAR
CATALAN   IV/I

O BLACK AND UNKNOWN BARDS, 7 NEGRO
SPIRITUALS   IV/I

OBRAS CLASICAS Y ROMANTICAS, VOL. 1
I/IB6-Coll

OBRAS CLASICAS Y ROMANTICAS, VOL. 2
I/IB6-Coll

PEZZI, 20, DEI SECOLI XVI, XVII E
XVIII, TRATTI DALLA LETTERATURA DEL
LIUTO, VIRGINALE E CLAVICEMBALO
I/IB6-Coll

PEZZI CELEBRI, 20   I/IB6-Coll

PEZZI FACILI, 3   I/IB6-Coll

PICCOLA ANTOLOGIA CHITARRISTICA   IV/I,
I/IB6-Coll

PIECES MELODIQUES ET TRANSCRIPTIONS
I/IB6-Coll

PIERWSZE KROKI GITARZYSTY   I/IB6-Coll

POLSCY MISTRZOWIE GITARY   I/IB6-Coll

PRIMO REPERTORIO DEL CHITARRISTA, IL,
VOL. 1   I/IB6-Coll

PRIMO REPERTORIO DEL CHITARRISTA, IL,
VOL. 2   I/IB6-Coll

PRZY CHOINCE, KOLEDY W LATWYM UKLADZIE
NA GITARE   IV/I

RACCOLTA DI MUSICHE   I/IB6-Coll

REPERTOIRE PROGRESSIF, VOL. 1
I/IB6-Coll

REPERTOIRE PROGRESSIF, VOL. 2
I/IB6-Coll

REPERTOIRE PROGRESSIF, VOL. 3
I/IB6-Coll

RODRIGO, JOAQUIN (1902-   )
    Petites Pieces, 3   IV/I

RODRIGUEZ ARENAS, MARIO
    Escuela De La Guitarra, La, Vol. IV
    I/IB6-Coll

RONNY LEE CLASSIC GUITAR BOOK, THE
I/IB6-Coll

ROSYJSCY MISTRZOWIE GITARY   I/IB6-Coll

SAINT LUC, JACQUES DE (1616- ?)
    Suite in E   I/IB6-Coll

SEHR LEICHTE BIS MITTELSCHWERE SATZE
FUR 1 UND 2 GITARREN   I/IB6-Coll

SEHR LEICHTE STUCKE FUR GITARRE, 42
I/IB6-Coll

SEVEN HUNDRED YEARS OF MUSIC FOR THE
CLASSIC GUITAR   I/IB6-Coll

SKARBCZYK GITARZYSTY - THE GUITARIST'S
TREASURY   I/IB6-Coll

SOLI FUR SPANISCHE GITARRE, 10, VOL. I
I/IB6-Coll

SOLO-GITARRE, DIE, VOL. I   I/IB6-Coll

SOLO-GITARRE, DIE, VOL. III   I/IB6-Coll

SOLO-STUCKE ALTER MEISTER   I/IB6-Coll

SOLOBUCH FUR GITARRE, DAS   I/IB6-Coll

SOLOGITARRE, DIE, VOL. I   I/IB6-Coll

SOLOGITARRE, DIE, VOL. II   I/IB6-Coll

SOLOGITARRE, DIE, VOL. III   I/IB6-Coll

SOLOGITARRE, DIE, VOL. IV   I/IB6-Coll

SOLOGITARRE, DIE, VOL. V   I/IB6-Coll

SOLOS FOR THE GUITAR PLAYER   I/IB6-Coll

SOLOS FOR THE GUITAR PLAYER   I/IB6-Coll

SONNE, KOMM, EIN GITARRESPIELBUCH FUR
KINDER, 1-4. UNTERRICHTSJAHR   IV/I,
I/IB6-Coll

SPANISCHE GITARRENMUSIK, VOL. I
I/IB6-Coll

SPANISCHE GITARRENMUSIK, VOL. II
I/IB6-Coll

SPANISCHE GITARRENMUSIK, VOL. III
I/IB6-Coll

SPIELMUSIK AUS FUNF JAHRHUNDERTEN -
LEICHT BIS MITTELSCHWER   I/IB6-Coll

SPIELMUSIK AUS FUNF JAHRHUNDERTEN -
MITTELSCHWER BIS SCHWER   I/IB6-Coll

SPIELMUSIK FUR ANGEHENDE GITARRISTEN,
VOL. I   I/IB6-Coll

SPIELMUSIK FUR ANGEHENDE GITARRISTEN,
VOL. II   I/IB6-Coll

SPIELMUSIK FUR ANGEHENDE GITARRISTEN,
VOL. III   I/IB6-Coll

STERNE UBER STILLEN STRASZEN, NEUE
LIEDER ZUR WEIHNACHT   IV/I

STUDENT GUITARIST'S DELIGHT, VOL. I
I/IB6-Coll

STUDENT GUITARIST'S DELIGHT, VOL. II
I/IB6-Coll

STUDIES EN STUKJES VOOR GITAAR
I/IB6-Coll

SUITE IM ALTEN STIL   I/IB6-Coll

SUPLEMENTO AL METODO PARA GUITARRA DE
AGUADO-SINOPOLI   I/IB6-Coll

TRANSCRIPCIONES PARA GUITARRA
I/IB6-Coll

TRANSCRIPCIONES PARA GUITARRA
I/IB6-Coll

TRANSCRIPCIONES POR GRACIANO TARRAGO
[1]   I/IB6-Coll

TRANSCRIPCIONES POR GRACIANO TARRAGO
[2]   I/IB6-Coll

TRANSCRIPCIONES POR GRACIANO TARRAGO
[3]   I/IB6-Coll

TRANSCRIPCIONES POR VICENTE ERLISO,
VOL. 3   I/IB6-Coll

TRANSCRIPCIONES POR VICENTE ERLISO,
VOL. 4   I/IB6-Coll

TRANSCRIPCIONES POR VICENTE ERLISO,
VOL. 6   I/IB6-Coll

TRANSCRIPTIONS FACILES DE 12 CHEFS-
D'OEUVRE CLASSIQUE   I/IB6-Coll

UBEN UND SPIELEN AUF DER GITARRE, VOL.
1   IV/I, I/IB6-Coll

UBEN UND SPIELEN AUF DER GITARRE, VOL.
2   I/IB6-Coll

UBEN UND SPIELEN AUF DER GITARRE, VOL.
3   I/IB6-Coll

UNSERE WEIHNACHTSLIEDER   IV/I

UNTERHALTENDE MUSIK FUR SOLO-GITARRE:
LEICHTE BIS MITTELSCHWERE
GITARRESOLIS   I/IB6-Coll

UNTERHALTENDE MUSIK FUR SOLO-GITARRE:
LIED UND TANZ VERSCHIEDENER LANDER
I/IB6-Coll

UNTERHALTENDE MUSIK FUR SOLO-GITARRE:
VOLKSLIED UND TANZ IN DEUTSCHLAND
I/IB6-Coll

VARIETY OF GUITAR MUSIC, A   I/IB6-Coll

VISOR PA GITARR   I/IB6-Coll

WEIHNACHT - 8 ALTE LIEDER   IV/I

WEIHNACHTSLIEDER   IV/I

WEIHNACHTSLIEDER ZUR GITARRE   IV/I

WEIHNACHTSZEIT - FROHLICHE ZEIT,
ALTBEKANNTE UND NEUERE
WEIHNACHTSLIEDER   IV/I

WETTBEWERBS-UNTERRICHTSPROGRAMM, DAS;
ARBEITSPROGRAMM FUR DEN WETTBEWERB
"JUGEND MUSIZIERT", VOL. 1:
ALTERSSTUFE IB   I/IB6-Coll

WETTBEWERBS-UNTERRICHTSPROGRAMM, DAS;
ARBEITSPROGRAMM FUR DEN WETTBEWERB
"JUGEND MUSIZIERT", VOL. 2:
ALTERSSTUFE IB   I/IB6-Coll

WETTBEWERBS-UNTERRICHTSPROGRAMM, DAS;
ARBEITSPROGRAMM FUR DEN WETTBEWERB
"JUGEND MUSIZIERT", VOL. 3:
ALTERSSTUFE II   I/IB6-Coll

WIR SPIELEN GITARRE, VOL. 1   I/IB6-Coll

WIR SPIELEN GITARRE, VOL. 2   I/IB6-Coll

YOUNG GUITARIST, VOL. 1   I/IB6-Coll

YOUNG GUITARIST, VOL. 2   I/IB6-Coll

Z POLONEZOW POLSKICH   I/IB6-Coll

Sonatas and Sonatinas

ALBERT, HEINRICH (1870-1950)
Sonaten, 2 I/IC

Sonatinen, 3 I/IC

AUS WILLIAM BRADE'S "VISBOK" I/IC

BARTA, LUBOR (1928-1972)
Sonata I/IC

BERKELEY, [SIR] LENNOX (1903-   )
Sonatina, Op. 51 I/IC

BURGHAUSER, JARMIL (1921-   )
Sonata in E minor I/IC

CALL, LEONHARD VON (ca. 1768-1815)
Sonata I/IC

CARCASSI, MATTEO (1792-1853)
Caprices, 6 I/IC

CARULLI, FERDINANDO (1770-1841)
Nice Und Fileno I/IC

Sonata, MIN 200 I/IC

Sonaten, 3 I/IC

CARY, TRISTAM (1925-   )
Sonata for Guitar I/IC

CASTELNUOVO-TEDESCO, MARIO (1895-1968)
Sonata I/IC

CHAVARRI, EDUARDO LOPEZ (1871-1970)
Sonata No. 2 I/IC

DIABELLI, ANTON (1781-1858)
Sonata in A I/IC

Sonata in C I/IC

Sonatina I/IC

Sonatinen, 3 I/IC

DUARTE, JOHN W. (1919-   )
Sonatina Lirica I/IC

Sonatinette I/IC

FRANCO, JOHAN (1908-   )
Sonata I/IC

GEELEN, MATHIEU (1933-   )
Sonatina I/IC

GIULIANI, MAURO (1781-1829)
Sonata Eroica I/IC

Sonata, Op. 15 I/IC

Sonatina, MIN 390 I/IC

Sonatina, Op. 71, No. 1 I/IC

Sonatina, Op. 71, No. 3 I/IC

Sonatinen, 3 I/IC

GOETHALS, LUCIEN (1931-   )
Sonata, Op. 22 I/IC

GRAGNANI, FILIPPO (1767- ?)
Sonatina, Op. 6 I/IC

GRAMBERG, JACQ
Instructieve Sonatines, 3 I/IC

HALFFTER, RODOLFO (1900-   )
Sonata in D I/IC

HAND, COLIN (1929-   )
Sonatina, Op. 74 I/IC

HARRIS, ALBERT (1916-   )
Sonatina I/IC

HEER, HANS DE (1927-   )
Sonata I/IC

HOLDER, DERWYN
Sonatina In One Movement I/IC

KOMTER, JAN MAARTEN (1905-   )
Sonate Concertante I/IC

KOVATS, BARNA (1920-   )
Sonata Nova I/IC

KUBIZEK, AUGUSTIN (1918-   )
Sonata, Op. 13a I/IC

LAZARO, JOSE
Sonata No. 3 I/IC

MANEN, JOSE
Fantasia-Sonata I/IC

MATIEGKA, WENZESLAUS THOMAS (1753-1830)
Sonata, Op. 16 I/IC

MEESTER, LOUIS DE (1904-   )
Sonata I/IC

MEIJER VON BREMEN, ALEXANDER
(1930-   )
Sonatina No. 1 I/IC

MIGOT, GEORGES (1891-1976)
Sonata I/IC

MOLINO, FRANCESCO (1775-1847)
Sonaten, 3 I/IC

MOLITOR, SIMON
Sonata, Op. 11 I/IC

MORENO TORROBA, FEDERICO (1891-1982)
Sonatina I/IC

MULLER, SIEGFRIED (1926-   )
Sonata I/IC

PAGANINI, NICCOLO (1782-1840)
Sonata, MIN 201, First Movement I/IC

PITFIELD, THOMAS BARON (1903-   )
Sonatina in A minor I/IC

PONCE, MANUEL MARIA (1882-1948)
Sonata Clasica, Hommage A Fernando
Sor I/IC

Sonata No. 1 I/IC

Sonata No. 3 I/IC

Sonata Romantica, Hommage A Franz
Schubert Qui Aimait La Guitare
I/IC

Sonatina Meridional I/IC

RODRIGO, JOAQUIN (1902-   )
Sonata Giocosa I/IC

Sonate A l'Espagnole I/IC

RODRIGUEZ ALBERT, RAFAEL (1902-   )
Sonatina En Tres Duales I/IC

ROSETTA, GIUSEPPE
Sonatina I/IC

SANCHEZ, B.
Sonatina I/IC

SANTORSOLA, GUIDO (1904-   )
Sonata I/IC

Sonata No. 2 I/IC

SCHALLER, ERWIN (1901-   )
Sonata for Guitar I/IC

SCHEIDLER, CHRISTIAN GOTTLIEB
(1752-1815)
Sonata in C I/IC

SCHOLZE, ARTHUR JOHANNES (1883-1945)
Sonata, Op. 127, in E minor I/IC

SMITH BRINDLE, REGINALD (1917-   )
Sonatina Fiorentina I/IC

SONATINY I SONATY KLASYCZNE I/IC-Coll

SOR, FERNANDO (1778-1839)
Grande Sonate, Op. 22 I/IC

Grande Sonate, Op. 25 I/IC

Sonata, Op. 15, No. 2, in C I/IC

STOKER, RICHARD (1938-   )
Sonatina, Op. 42 I/IC

TURINA, JOAQUIN (1882-1949)
Sonatina I/IC

UHL, ALFRED (1909-   )
Sonata Classica I/IC

USHER, TERRY (1909-1969)
Sonata in A, Op. 3 I/IC

VANDERMAESBRUGGE, MAX (1933-   )
Sonata I/IC

WAGNER-REGENY, RUDOLF (1903-1969)
Sonatina I/IC

WEINER, STANLEY (1925-   )
Sonata, Op. 22, No. 1 I/IC

WERNER, JEAN-JACQUES (1935-   )
Sonatina I/IC

WIKMANSON, J.
Sonata in B minor I/IC

Duets — 2 Guitars

ABLONIZ, MIGUEL (1917-   )
Divertimento I/IIA1

ABSIL, JEAN (1893-1974)
Contrastes I/IIA1

Danse I/IIA1

Suite for 2 Guitars I/IIA1

ALBERT, HEINRICH (1870-1950)
Duo No. 1 in C I/IIA1

Duo No. 2 in A minor I/IIA1

Duo No. 3 in C I/IIA1

Duo No. 4 in G I/IIA1

Duo No. 5 in E minor I/IIA1

Duo No. 6 in D I/IIA1

Duo No. 7 in A I/IIA1

Duo No. 8 in E I/IIA1

Gitarre-Etuden-Werk, Vol. 1:
Elementarstufe I/IIA1

ALBUM RICREATIVO, NO. 4 I/IIA1-Coll

3 ALTE DUOS I/IIA1-Coll

ANONYMOUS
Pieces Sans Titre I/IIA1

ANTOLOGIA DE LOS VIHUELISTAS ESPANOLAS,
VOL. 6 I/IIA1-Coll

AUBANEL, GEORGES
Chants Et Danses Populaires Francais
I/IIA1

Etudes Rhythmiques I/IIA1

AUBERT, LOUIS
Improvisation I/IIA1

AUS DEM BALTISCHEN LAUTENBUCH 1740
I/IIA1-Coll

AUS PICKERING'S LAUTENBUCH (UM 1616)
I/IIA1-Coll

BARBIER, RENE (AUGUSTE-ERNEST)
(1890-1981)
Petite Suite I/IIA1

Suite No. 2, Op. 115 I/IIA1

BARTOLI, RENE
Waltz in E minor I/IIA1

BEHREND, SIEGFRIED (1933-   )
Duos, 3 I/IIA1

Japanische Serenade I/IIA1

Leipziger Suite I/IIA1

Stierkampmusik I/IIA1

BENGUEREL, XAVIER (1931-   )
Stella Spendens I/IIA1

BERTOUILLE, GERARD (1898-1981)
Petite Serenade Impromptu I/IIA1

BLEEKER, WILLY
Serenata Espanola I/IIA1

BONNARD, ALAIN (1939-   )
Ricercari, 5 I/IIA1

BROUWER, LEO (1939-   )
Micropiezas, Hommage A Darius Milhaud
I/IIA1

BURKHART, FRANZ (1902-1978)
Toccata I/IIA1

CAHIERS DU GUITAROLIER, LES, VOL. 1
I/IIA1-Coll

CAHIERS DU GUITAROLIER, LES, VOL. 2
I/IIA1-Coll

CALL, LEONHARD VON (ca. 1768-1815)
Duette, 6 I/IIA1

Romance I/IIA1

CARULLI, FERDINANDO (1770-1841)
Abendmusik I/IIA1

Allegro In G I/IIA1

Duet Facile I/IIA1

Duet Study In F I/IIA1

Duet Study In G I/IIA1

Duette, 3 I/IIA1

Duo Concertante I/IIA1

Duos I/IIA1

Duos, 2 I/IIA1

Duos, 12 I/IIA1

Kleine Duette, 6, Vol. I I/IIA1

Kleine Duette, 6, Vol. II I/IIA1

Largo Und Rondo D-Dur I/IIA1

Leichte Fortschreitende Stucke
I/IIA1

Methode De Guitare I/IIA1

Nocturnes I/IIA1

Notturno, Op. 128, No. 1 I/IIA1

Notturno, Op. 128, No. 2 I/IIA1

Romanze, 12 I/IIA1

Romanzen, 12, Vol. II I/IIA1

Study I/IIA1

CASTELNUOVO-TEDESCO, MARIO (1895-1968)
Sonatina Canonica I/IIA1

CERF, JACQUES (1932-   )
Climat I/IIA1

Petit Ours, Le, Une Histoire Pour Les
Petits Et Les Grands Amis De La
Guitare I/IIA1

COENEN, PAUL (1908-   )
Kleine Suite I/IIA1

COSTE, NAPOLEON (1806-1883)
Barcarolle I/IIA1

CRUZ DE CASTRO, CARLOS
Caminos I/IIA1

DIABELLI, ANTON (1781-1858)
Andantino I/IIA1

Fugue I/IIA1

DIEUPART, C.
Airs De Danse, 3 I/IIA1

DUARTE, JOHN W. (1919-   )
Flight Of Fugues, A I/IIA1

Friendships, 6 I/IIA1

Greek Suite I/IIA1

Variations On A French Nursery Song
I/IIA1

DUETTE FUR GITARREN I/IIA1-Coll

ELIZABETHAN DUETS, 6 I/IIA1-Coll

FABIAN, GASTON
Gitarren Duette I/IIA1

FALCKENHAGEN, ADAM (1697-1761)
Duo I/IIA1

FRANCESCO DA MILANO
(ca. 1497?-ca. 1573?)
Fantasy I/IIA1

FRESCOBALDI, GIROLAMO (1583-1643)
Canzona Seconda I/IIA1

FURSTENAU, WOLFRAM
Psalmodia Uber Das V. Gebot Mose, In
Memoriam Quang Duc - Vietnam
I/IIA1

Serenata Polonia I/IIA1

GAITIS, FRIEDRICH
Stucke, 4 I/IIA1

GANGI, MARIO
Andalusa I/IIA1

Fandango I/IIA1

Sevillana I/IIA1

GATTERMAYER, HEINRICH (1923-   )
Duo I/IIA1

GITARRE ALLEIN, ENTWICKLUNG DES
SOLISTISCHEN MUSIZIERENS AUS DEM
AKKORDSPIEL I/IIA1-Coll

GIULIANI, MAURO (1781-1829)
Grandi Variazioni Concertanti I/IIA1

Leichte Landler, 8, 2 Vols. I/IIA1

Variazioni Concertanti I/IIA1

GRAMBERG, JACQ
Petrad I/IIA1

GUERRERO, FRANCISCO (1528-1599)
Xenias Pacatas II I/IIA1

HAFNER, KURT
Leichte Originalstucke I/IIA1

HAGEN, JOACHIM BERNHARD (fl. ca. 1759)
Duo I/IIA1

HAUBENSTOCK-RAMATI, ROMAN (1919-   )
Hexachord I-II I/IIA1

HLOUSCHEK, THEODOR (1923-   )
Duette I/IIA1

Spielstucke I/IIA1

HOFFNER, PAUL MARX (1895-1949)
Indianer Suite I/IIA1

HOLLFELDER, WALDRAM (1924-   )
Kleine Tanze I/IIA1

HORECKI, FELIKS (1799-1870)
Utwory Wybrane I/IIA1

IBERT, JACQUES (1890-1962)
Paraboles I/IIA1

JANSEN, WILLY (1897-   )
Kleine Spielmusiken I/IIA1

JOLIVET, ANDRE (1905-1974)
Serenade I/IIA1

KARL, SEPP (1913-   )
Junge Gitarre-Solist, Der, Vol. III;
Eine Sammlung Leichter,
Melodioser Solostucke I/IIA1

Kleine Kostbarkeiten I/IIA1

Leichte Gitarren-Duette, 36 I/IIA1

KAUFMANN, ARMIN (1902-   )
Suite I/IIA1

KOMTER, JAN MAARTEN (1905-   )
Chansonatine I/IIA1

Fun From The Start, Vol. 1: Guitar
Duets For Teacher And Pupil
I/IIA1

Milan-Suite, On A Theme Of Don Luis
Milan (1535) I/IIA1

Punteado-Suite I/IIA1

Suite in A I/IIA1

KORT, WIM DE
Fughetta's, 2 I/IIA1

KOUNADIS, ARGHYRIS (1924-   )
Rebetika I/IIA1

KRONSTEINER, JOSEF (1910-   )
Partita I/IIA1

KUFFNER, JOSEPH (1776-1856)
Duette, 12 I/IIA1

Leichte Duette, 40 I/IIA1

Leichte Duos I/IIA1

Leichte Tanze I/IIA1

Leichte Ubungstucke, 60 I/IIA1

Movimientos, 3 I/IIA1

LABROUVE, JORGE
Disenos I/IIA1

Nucleos I/IIA1

Sintesis I/IIA1

LATWE UTWORY DAWNYCH MISTRZOW
I/IIA1-Coll

LAUFFENSTEINER, WOLFF JACOB
Sonata in A I/IIA1

LAWES, WILLIAM (1602-1645)
Suite, MIN 36 I/IIA1

LECHTHALER, JOSEF (1891-1948)
Suite, Op. 49, No. 1 I/IIA1

LESUR, DANIEL (1908-   )
Elegy I/IIA1

MAASZ, GERHARD (1906-1984)
Zehn Leichte Stucke I/IIA1

MARCO, TOMAS (1942-   )
Duo Concertante I/IIA1

MARELLA, GIOVANNI BATTISTA
Music For 2 Guitars I/IIA1

Suite in A I/IIA1

MASSIS, AMABLE (1893-   )
Pieces, 2 I/IIA1

MATELART, JOHANNES
Recercate Concertate, Su La Quarta
Fantasia Di Francesco Da Milano
I/IIA1

MEISTERWERKE FUR ZWEI GITARREN
I/IIA1-Coll

MELII DA REGGIO, PIETRO PAOLO
(fl. 1614-1616)
Corrente, Detta La Favorita Gonzaga
I/IIA1

MERCHI, GIACOMO
Caccia I/IIA1

MIGOT, GEORGES (1891-1976)
Preludes I/IIA1

Sonata, MIN 39 I/IIA1

MORENO TORROBA, FEDERICO (1891-1982)
Capriccio I/IIA1

Prelude I/IIA1

MUSIQUE ELISABETHAINE I/IIA1-Coll

NARVAEZ, LUIS DE
Diferencias Sobre "Guardame Las
Vacas" I/IIA1

NEUMULLER, WOLFGANG
Gitarrenstuckl I/IIA1

NIJENHUIS, LUC
Canons In II I/IIA1

NOVAK, JAN (1921-1984)
Rosarium, 10 Divertimenti I/IIA1

PELEMANS, WILLEM (1901-   )
Preludes I/IIA1

Sonatina I/IIA1

Suite I/IIA1

PETIT, PIERRE (1922-   )
Tarantelle I/IIA1

Toccata I/IIA1

PICCININI, ALESSANDRO
Toccata I/IIA1

PIECES ELIZABETHAINES, 2 I/IIA1

PRESTI, IDA (1924-1967)
Danse d'Avila I/IIA1

Etude No. 1 I/IIA1

Prelude No. 1 I/IIA1

PRIMO REPERTORIO DEL CHITARRISTA, IL,
VOL. 1 I/IIA1-Coll

PUJOL, EMILIO (1886-1982)
Canaries I/IIA1

Duet (Etude) I/IIA1

Ricercare I/IIA1

REBAY, FERDINAND (1889-1953)
Duo's Fur 2 Gitarren, Vol. I: 12
Kleine Stucke I/IIA1

Duo's Fur 2 Gitarren, Vol. II: 9
Vortragsstucke I/IIA1

Duo's Fur 2 Gitarren, Vol. III: 6
Studien Nach Beruhmten Etuden Von
Czerny Bis Chopin I/IIA1

REBAY, FERDINAND (cont'd.)

Duo's Fur 2 Gitarren, Vol. IV:
Spezial-Studien I/IIA1

ROBINSON, THOMAS (fl. ca. 1603)
Duets I/IIA1

Fantasy I/IIA1

Plaine Song I/IIA1

RODRIGO, JOAQUIN (1902-   )
Fandango Del Ventorrillo I/IIA1

Romance De Durandarte I/IIA1

Tonadilla I/IIA1

ROHWER, JENS (1914-   )
Duo Fur Lauteninstrumente I/IIA1

ROSETTA, GIUSEPPE
Sonata I/IIA1

SANCHEZ, B.
Etude En Forme d'Invention I/IIA1

Variations, 10, Sur "Folias De
Espana" En Forme De Canon I/IIA1

SANTORSOLA, GUIDO (1904-   )
Sonata A Duo I/IIA1

Sonata No. 2 I/IIA1

Triptico, Tres Invenciones I/IIA1

SCHAGEN, HENK VAN
Samen Spelen, Vol. I I/IIA1

Samen Spelen, Vol. II I/IIA1

Voor Het Mooie Handje, Vol. I:
Melodie-Aanslag I/IIA1

SCHALLER, ERWIN (1901-   )
Altlothringer Hirtenmusik IV/IIA1

SCHEIDLER, CHRISTIAN GOTTLIEB
(1752-1815)
Duo Pour Guitarre Et Violon I/IIA1

SEGOVIA, ANDRES (1896-   )
Estudios, 3 I/IIA1

SHIMOYAMA, HIFUMI (1930-   )
Dialogo, No. 1 I/IIA1

Dialogo, No. 2 I/IIA1

SIEGL, ERWIN
Duos, Op. 34, Vol. I I/IIA1

SODERLUNDH, LILLE BROR (1912-1957)
Liten Vals I/IIA1

SOMMERFELDT, OISTEIN (1919-   )
Three Lyric Guitar Duets I/IIA1

SOR, FERNANDO (1778-1839)
Complete Works For Guitar In
Facsimiles Of The Original
Editions, The, Vol. 8: Guitar
Duets, Op. 34-63 [1st Gtr Part]
I/IIA1

Complete Works For Guitar In
Facsimiles Of The Original
Editions, The, Vol. 9: Guitar
Duets, Op. 34-63 [2nd Gtr Part]
I/IIA1

Deux Amis, Les, Fantaisie Pour Deux
Guitares I/IIA1

Divertissement for 2 Guitars, Op. 38
I/IIA1

Divertissement Pour Deux Guitares
I/IIA1

Encouragement, L', Fantaisie A Deux
Guitares I/IIA1

Opera Omnia For The Spanish Guitar,
Vol. 6 I/IIA1

Opera Omnia For The Spanish Guitar,
Vol. 7 I/IIA1

Opera Omnia For The Spanish Guitar,
Vol. 8 I/IIA1

Opera Omnia For The Spanish Guitar,
Vol. 9 I/IIA1

Opera Omnia For The Spanish Guitar,
Vol. 10 I/IIA1

Opera Omnia For The Spanish Guitar,
Vol. 11 I/IIA1

Opera Omnia For The Spanish Guitar,
Vol. 12 I/IIA1

SOR, FERNANDO (cont'd.)

Premier Pas Vers Moi, Le, Petit Duo
Pour Deux Guitares I/IIA1

Romance I/IIA1

Souvenir De Russie, Fantaisie Pour
Deux Guitares I/IIA1

Study in E minor I/IIA1

Trois Duos Faciles Et Progressifs
Pour Deux Guitares I/IIA1

STAAK, PIETER VAN DER (1930-   )
Easy Pieces, 6 I/IIA1

Pocket-Music I/IIA1

STRATEGIER, HERMAN (1912-   )
Short Pieces, 10 I/IIA1

TANZBUCH DER RENAISSANCE I/IIA1-Coll

TARRAGO, G.
Estudios, 2, Sobre Un Tema De Alard
I/IIA1

TARRAGO, GRACIANO
Bolero I/IIA1

Estudio De Tremolo, Sobre Un Tema De
Alard I/IIA1

TARREGA, FRANCISCO (1852-1909)
Album No. 21 I/IIA1

Album No. 22 I/IIA1

Album No. 23 I/IIA1

Danza Mora I/IIA1

TSILICAS, JORGE (1930-   )
Sinegia I/IIA1

URAY, ERNST LUDWIG (1906-   )
Variationen Und Fuge Uber Ein
Volkslied I/IIA1

VILLA-LOBOS, HEITOR (1887-1959)
Terezinha De Jesus I/IIA1

VISSER, DICK (1927-   )
Expo I/IIA1

WAGNER, GERHARD D.
Impreciones Mexicanas, Vol. I: Las
Ruinas De Mitla I/IIA1

Impreciones Mexicanas, Vol. II: Lago
De Texcoco I/IIA1

Impreciones Mexicanas, Vol. III: La
Tristeza De Malintzin I/IIA1

WEBER, CARL MARIA VON (1786-1826)
Duo I/IIA1

WEBER, REINHOLD
Miniaturen, 5 I/IIA1

WEISS, JOHANN ADOLF
Leichte Duette, 6 I/IIA1

WEISS, SYLVIUS LEOPOLD (1686-1750)
Duett Fur Gitarren I/IIA1

WISSMER, PIERRE (1915-   )
Barbaresque I/IIA1

Prestilagoyana I/IIA1

WOLF, ROLAND
Viva La Guitarra I/IIA1

XANTHOPOULOS, ILIAS
Sonata I/IIA1

ZUCCHERI, LUCIANO
Pezzi, 6 I/IIA1

Trios — 3 Guitars

A STAADE MUSI I/IIA2

ALBERT, HEINRICH (1870-1950)
    Sonatinen, 3 I/IIA2

ALTE LAUTENMUSIK I/IIA2, I/IIA2-Coll

AMBROSIUS, HERMANN (1897- ?)
    Eggersberger Trio I/IIA2

ASRIEL, ANDRE (1922-   )
    Kanons, 5 I/IIA2

BARAT, JACQUES
    Melodie Moyenageuse I/IIA2

BEHREND, SIEGFRIED (1933-   )
    Study I/IIA2

BLANCHARD, CARVER WILLIAM, JR.
    Country Gardens I/IIA2

    Prolog Und Rondo I/IIA2

BRIANO, GIOVANNI BATTISTA
    Fuga Terza I/IIA2

CALL, LEONHARD VON (ca. 1768-1815)
    Leichtes Trio, Op. 26 I/IIA2

DAVID, THOMAS CHRISTIAN (1925-   )
    Canzonen, 3 I/IIA2

DIABELLI, ANTON (1781-1858)
    Trio, Op. 62, in F I/IIA2

FARKAS, FERENC (1905-   )
    Citharoedia Strigoniensis, Sopra
        Motivi Ungheresi Di Esztergom Del
        XVIII Secolo I/IIA2

GRAGNANI, FILIPPO (1767- ?)
    Trio, Op. 12 I/IIA2

GRAMBERG, JACQ
    Dances, 6 I/IIA2

HARTOG, CEES
    Let's Take The Flip Side I/IIA2

HAUSWIRTH, HANS M.A. (1901-   )
    Tanze Und Weisen I/IIA2

HLOUSCHEK, THEODOR (1923-   )
    Trio I/IIA2

HOEK, JAN-ANTON VAN (1936-   )
    Trios, 3, Op. 919 I/IIA2

HOEKEMA, HENK
    Easy Pieces, 7 I/IIA2

JANSEN, WILLY (1897-   )
    Kleine Spielmusiken I/IIA2

KARL, SEPP (1913-   )
    Tanze Und Weisen I/IIA2

KOMTER, JAN MAARTEN (1905-   )
    Boleronda I/IIA2

KORT, WIM DE
    Fugas, 2, Op. 10 I/IIA2

MENGELBERG, MISJA (1935-   )
    Amaga I/IIA2

MULLER, SIEGFRIED (1926-   )
    Concertino I/IIA2

NEUMULLER, WOLFGANG
    Gitarrenstuckl I/IIA2

PROSPERI, CARLO (1921-   )
    Stelle Inerrantes I/IIA2

SANCHEZ, B.
    Variations, 10, Sur "Folias De
        Espana" En Forme De Canon I/IIA2

SCHAGEN, HENK VAN
    Fantasy I/IIA2

    Zomeravondsuite I/IIA2

SCHUMANN, GERHARD (1914-   )
    Fantasy I/IIA2

SEROCKI, KAZIMIERZ (1922-1981)
    Krasnoludki I/IIA2

SMITH BRINDLE, REGINALD (1917-   )
    Music For Three Guitars I/IIA2

STREICHARDT, ANTONIUS
    Trio in E I/IIA2

TANZBUCH DER RENAISSANCE I/IIA2-Coll

ULRICH, JURGEN (1939-   )
    Einerseits-Andererseits, Vol. 1
        I/IIA2-Coll

    Einerseits-Andererseits, Vol. 2
        I/IIA2-Coll

WERDIN, EBERHARD (1911-   )
    Miniaturen, 4 I/IIA2

WINKELBAUER, ALFRED
    Spanische Tanze I/IIA2

WOLKI, KONRAD
    Sechs Mal Drei (6 x 3) I/IIA2,
        IV/IIA2

    Spielstucke Fur 3 Gitarren I/IIA2

Quartets — 4 Guitars

BENGUEREL, XAVIER (1931-   )
    Vermelia I/IIA3

BIBERIAN, GILBERT E.
    Suite for 4 Guitars I/IIA3

BLAKE WATKINS, MICHAEL (1948-   )
    Guitar Quartet I/IIA3

DOWLAND, JOHN (1562-1626)
    Three Dances I/IIA3

DUARTE, JOHN W. (1919-   )
    Going Dutch I/IIA3

GRAMBERG, JACQ
    Dances For 4 Or More Guitars, 3
        I/IIA3

    Just Arrived I/IIA3

KEINEMANN, KARL HEINZ
    Sudamerikanische Tanze, Fur Den
        Modernen Gitarren-Gruppen-
        Unterricht I/IIA3

MARX, KARL (1897-1985)
    Es Taget Vor Dem Walde, 6 Variationen
        Uber I/IIA3

ROHWER, JENS (1914-   )
    Heptameron, Eine Vierstimmige Suite
        I/IIA3

SCHNEIDER, SIMON
    Spielmusik, Op.126, No. 2 I/IIA3

STAAK, PIETER VAN DER (1930-   )
    Easy Guitar Quartets, 9 I/IIA3

    Guitar Quartets, 7 I/IIA3

TANZBUCH DER RENAISSANCE I/IIA3-Coll

WESTRA, JAN
    Conversation I/IIA3

    Minutes, 5 I/IIA3

Quintets — 5 Guitars

FURSTENAU, WOLFRAM
    Railway-Traffic I/IIA4

KEINEMANN, KARL HEINZ
    Sudamerikanische Tanze, Fur Den
        Modernen Gitarren-Gruppen-
        Unterricht I/IIA4

Duets — Gtr, Flute

ABBOTT, ALAIN (1938-   )
    Prelude No. 1 I/IIB1

ANTONIOU, THEODORE (1935-   )
    Dialoge I/IIB1

AZPIAZU, JOSE DE (1912-   )
    Sonate Basque I/IIB1

BARON, ERNST GOTTLIEB (1696-1760)
    Duetto Al Liuto E Traverso I/IIB1

    Konzerte, 2 I/IIB1

    Sonata A 2 I/IIB1

BECKER, GUNTHER (1924-   )
    Con Buen Ayre, Duplum I/IIB1

BEECROFT, NORMA (1934-   )
    Pezzi Brevi, 3 I/IIB1

BEHREND, SIEGFRIED (1933-   )
    Haiku-Suite I/IIB1

    Triptychon "Memento Mori Ohshima
        Norio Nostrum" I/IIB1

BENARY, PETER (1931-   )
    Fantasien, 4 I/IIB1

BISCHOFF, HEINZ (1898-1963)
    Salzburger Sonatine In F I/IIB1

BONNARD, ALAIN (1939-   )
    Sonatine Breve I/IIB1

BOSKE, JIM TEN (1946-   )
    Leave Something Unexplained I/IIB1

BOZZA, EUGENE (1905-   )
    Berceuse Et Serenade I/IIB1

    Polydiaphonie I/IIB1

    Trois Pieces I/IIB1

BRAUN, GUNTER
    Sonatina I/IIB1

BURKHARD, WILLY (1900-1955)
    Serenade, Op. 71, No. 3 I/IIB1

CALL, LEONHARD VON (ca. 1768-1815)
    Variations for Flute and Guitar
        I/IIB1

CARULLI, FERDINANDO (1770-1841)
    Fantasy, Op. 337 for Flute and Guitar
        I/IIB1

    Nocturne, Op. 190 I/IIB1

    Serenade, Op. 109, No. 1 I/IIB1

    Serenade, Op. 109, No. 6 I/IIB1

    Serenaden, 5 I/IIB1

CASTELNUOVO-TEDESCO, MARIO (1895-1968)
    Sonatina I/IIB1

CHIEREGHIN, SERGIO (1933-   )
    Tempi, 4 I/IIB1

CILENSEK, JOHANN (1913-   )
    Sonata I/IIB1

CONSTANT, FRANZ (1910-   )
Musique A Deux I/IIB1

DALLINGER, FRIDOLIN (1933-   )
Sonatina for Flute and Guitar I/IIB1

DAVID, JOHANN NEPOMUK (1895-1977)
Variationen Uber Ein Eigenes Thema
I/IIB1

DIABELLI, ANTON (1781-1858)
Serenade, Op. 99 I/IIB1

Stucke, 3 I/IIB1

DJEMIL, ENYSS (1917-   )
Petite Suite Medievale I/IIB1

DUARTE, JOHN W. (1919-   )
Danse Joyeuse I/IIB1

Sonatina, Op. 15 I/IIB1

ERBSE, HEIMO (1924-   )
3 Studien I/IIB1

FURSTENAU, KASPAR (1772-1819)
Duette, 6 I/IIB1

Stucke, 12 I/IIB1

Suite, Op. 34 I/IIB1

Suite, Op. 35 I/IIB1

Zwolf Stucke I/IIB1

FURSTENAU, WOLFRAM
Vakantiedagboek I/IIB1

GEBAUER, MICHEL-JOSEPH (1763-1812)
Polonaise I/IIB1

GELLI, VINCENZO (THOMATOS)
Two Divertimenti I/IIB1

GERLACH, HANS CHRISTIAN
Divertimento [Collection] I/IIB1

GIULIANI, MAURO (1781-1829)
Divertimento I/IIB1

Duettino I/IIB1

Duettino Facile I/IIB1

Gran Duetto Concertante I/IIB1

Grosse Serenade I/IIB1

Grosse Sonate, Op.85 I/IIB1

Qual Mesto Gemito I/IIB1

Serenade, Op. 127 I/IIB1

HAUG, HANS (1900-1967)
Capriccio I/IIB1

HEER, HANS DE (1927-   )
Sonatina No. 2 I/IIB1

Sonatina No. 3 I/IIB1

HEKSTER, WALTER (1937-   )
Epicycle I I/IIB1

HEUCKEROTH VAN HESSEN, J. RICHARD
Impression I/IIB1

Song And Dance I/IIB1

IBERT, JACQUES (1890-1962)
Entr'acte I/IIB1

JELINEK, HANNS (1901-1969)
Ollapotrida I/IIB1

JONG, MARINUS DE (1891-1984)
Suite, Op. 127 I/IIB1

KAMERALNA MUZYKA GITAROWA I/IIB1-Coll

KOMTER, JAN MAARTEN (1905-   )
Andante in D I/IIB1

Divertimento in G I/IIB1

KONT, PAUL (1920-   )
Suite En Passant I/IIB1

KUFFNER, JOSEPH (1776-1856)
Drittes Potpourri I/IIB1

Serenade I/IIB1

LANGENBERG, JAN VAN DEN
Capriccio I/IIB1

LEUKAUF, ROBERT (1902-   )
Altspanische Suite I/IIB1

MARGOLA, FRANCO (1908-   )
Episodi, 4 I/IIB1

MIGOT, GEORGES (1891-1976)
Sonata I/IIB1

MOLINO, FRANCESCO (1775-1847)
Nocturne No. 2, Op. 38 I/IIB1

Nocturne, Op. 37 I/IIB1

PATACHICH, IVAN (1922-   )
Duo I/IIB1

PELEMANS, WILLEM (1901-   )
Petit Duo I/IIB1

PRAGER, HEINRICH ALOYS (1783-1854)
Introduktion, Thema Und Variationen
I/IIB1

PRIETO, CLAUDIO
Solo A Solo I/IIB1

REGT, HENDRIK DE (1950-   )
Music, Op. 21 I/IIB1

SANCHEZ, B.
Suite Vesperale I/IIB1

SHERMAN, ELNA
Suite No. 1 I/IIB1

SIEGL, OTTO (1896-1978)
Sonata I/IIB1

SIMONIS, JEAN-MARIE (1931-   )
Nocturne, Op. 23 I/IIB1

SOR, FERNANDO (1778-1839)
Romance I/IIB1

SPIELMUSIK FUR MELODIEINSTRUMENTE UND
GITARRE, 16-19TH CENTURY
I/IIB1-Coll

SPIELMUSIK FUR MELODIEINSTRUMENTE UND
GITARRE, 20TH CENTURY I/IIB1-Coll

SPRONGL, NORBERT (1892-1983)
Suite I/IIB1

STINGL, ANTON (1908-   )
Stucke, Op. 34 I/IIB1

TERZAKIS, DIMITRI (1938-   )
Chroniko I/IIB1

TRUHLAR, JAN (1928-   )
Sonatina Semplice I/IIB1

VILLA-LOBOS, HEITOR (1887-1959)
Distribution De Fleurs I/IIB1

VRIES ROBBE, WILLEM DE (1902-   )
Danse-Arioso-Rondeau I/IIB1

Pavane-Sarabande-Gigue I/IIB1

WISSMER, PIERRE (1915-   )
Sonatina I/IIB1

ZBINDEN, JULIEN-FRANCOIS (1917-   )
Miniatures, 4 I/IIB1

ZEHM, FRIEDRICH (1923-   )
Serenade I/IIB1

Duets — Gtr, Oboe

BALLOU, ESTHER WILLIAMSON (1915-1973)
Dialogues I/IIB1

BARTOLOZZI, BRUNO (1911-   )
Auser I/IIB1

BISCHOFF, HEINZ (1898-1963)
Salzburger Sonatine In F I/IIB1

FURSTENAU, WOLFRAM
Vakantiedagboek I/IIB1

HEUCKEROTH VAN HESSEN, J. RICHARD
Impression I/IIB1

Song And Dance I/IIB1

KOVATS, BARNA (1920-   )
Sonatina I/IIB1

MADERNA, BRUNO (1920-1973)
Aulodia Per Lothar I/IIB1

PILSS, KARL (1902-1979)
Sonatina I/IIB1

PRAAG, HENRI C. VAN (1894-1968)
Complainte I/IIB1

Duettino I/IIB1

SANCHEZ, B.
Suite Vesperale I/IIB1

SINGER, LAWRENCE (1940-   )
Musica A Due I/IIB1

Duets — Gtr, Sax

ASRIEL, ANDRE (1922-   )
Inventionen, 5 I/IIB1

Duets — Gtr, S Rec

BISCHOFF, HEINZ (1898-1963)
Salzburger Sonatine In F I/IIB1

DUARTE, JOHN W. (1919-   )
Simple Songs Without Words, 3 I/IIB1

FANTASIA [COLLECTION] I/IIB1-Coll

FERRITTO, JOHN E. (1937-   )
Duos, 4 I/IIB1

GORZANIS, GIACOMO (ca. 1525-ca. 1578)
Napolitane, 15 I/IIB1

GRIFFITHS, JOHN (1952-   )
Conversation Piece I/IIB1

KRENEK, ERNST (1900-   )
Hausmusik; 7 Stucke Fur Die Sieben
Tage Der Woche I/IIB1

LIER, WIM VAN
Suite I/IIB1

SCHAFER, RUDOLF (1891-1970)
Kleine Spiel- Und Ubungsstucke Fur
Den Anfang, 30 I/IIB1

Duets — Gtr, A Rec

BEHREND, SIEGFRIED (1933-   )
Suite Nach Altenglischen Meistern
I/IIB1

COENEN, PAUL (1908-   )
Heitere Folge Von Vogel-Liedern
I/IIB1

DUARTE, JOHN W. (1919-   )
Simple Songs Without Words, 3 I/IIB1

HARTIG, HEINZ FRIEDRICH (1907-1969)
Stucke, 5 I/IIB1

HOFFNER, PAUL MARX (1895-1949)
Sonatina I/IIB1

Tanzstucke, 3 I/IIB1

KAMMERLING, WERNER
Variationen Uber 3 Alte Volkslieder,
18 I/IIB1

KLEBE, GISELHER (1925-   )
Recitativo, Aria E Duetto I/IIB1

KLEIN, RICHARD RUDOLF (1921-   )
Divertimento I/IIB1

Partita in D I/IIB1

KONIG, HEINZ
  Spielmusik In C I/IIB1

LEUKAUF, ROBERT (1902-   )
  Altspanische Suite I/IIB1

POSER, HANS (1917-1970)
  Kleine Serenade I/IIB1

SAUX, GASTON
  Serenade I/IIB1

SCHAGEN, HENK VAN
  Kleine Ditirambe I/IIB1

SHERMAN, ELNA
  Suite No. 1 I/IIB1

SPIELMUSIK FUR MELODIEINSTRUMENTE UND
  GITARRE, 20TH CENTURY I/IIB1-Coll

STINGL, ANTON (1908-   )
  Stucke, Op. 34 I/IIB1

Duets — Gtr, T Rec

KLEIN, RICHARD RUDOLF (1921-   )
  Partita in D I/IIB1

Duets — Gtr, B Rec

KROLL, GEORG (1934-   )
  Canzonabile I/IIB1

Duets — Gtr, Rec

BAUMANN, HERBERT (1925-   )
  Duetto Concertante I/IIB1

BRESGEN, CESAR (1913-   )
  Suite Uber Altbohmische
    Weihnachtsweisen IV/IIB1

DAVID, JOHANN NEPOMUK (1895-1977)
  Variationen Uber Ein Eigenes Thema
    I/IIB1

HEUCKEROTH VAN HESSEN, J. RICHARD
  Impression I/IIB1

  Song And Dance I/IIB1

KOVATS, BARNA (1920-   )
  Sonatina I/IIB1

LANGENBERG, JAN VAN DEN
  Capriccio I/IIB1

REIN, WALTER (1893-1955)
  Volkslieder Mit Variationen, 2
    I/IIB1

Duets — Gtr, Perc

BENGUEREL, XAVIER (1931-   )
  Intendo A Dos I/IIB1

BRAUN, GUNTER
  Serie I/IIB1

ERDMANN, DIETRICH (1917-   )
  Episodes I/IIB1

FINK, SIEGFRIED
  Dialoge I/IIB1

HASHAGEN, KLAUS (1924-   )
  Pergiton IV I/IIB1

HOMS, JOAQUIN (1906-   )
  Impromptu I/IIB1

HUMBLE, KEITH (1927-   )
  Arcade IV I/IIB1

MARCO, TOMAS (1942-   )
  Miriada I/IIB1

ROSSEAU, NORBERT (1907-1975)
  Contemplatie I/IIB1

Duets — Gtr, Org

BADINGS, HENK (1907-1987)
  It Is Dawning In The East,
    Balladesque Variations On An Old
    Dutch Love Song I/IIB1

FURSTENAU, WOLFRAM
  Orationen I/IIB1

Duets — Gtr, Pno

CARULLI, FERDINANDO (1770-1841)
  Duo, Op. 37 for Piano and Guitar
    I/IIB1

  Notturno, Op. 189 I/IIB1

  Sonata No. 1 I/IIB1

  Sonata No. 2 I/IIB1

CASTELNUOVO-TEDESCO, MARIO (1895-1968)
  Fantasy, Op. 145 I/IIB1

DIABELLI, ANTON (1781-1858)
  Grande Sonate Brillante I/IIB1

  Sehr Leichte Stucke, Vol. I I/IIB1

  Sehr Leichte Stucke, Vol. II I/IIB1

  Sehr Leichte Stucke, Vol. III I/IIB1

  Sehr Leichte Stucke, Vol. IV I/IIB1

  Sonatina, Op. 68 I/IIB1

  Sonatina, Op. 70 I/IIB1

FLERES, RITA MARIA
  Stucke, 5, Nach Liedern Und Tanzen
    Aus Der Renaissance I/IIB1

GIULIANI, MAURO (1781-1829)
  Variations, Op. 113 I/IIB1

HAUG, HANS (1900-1967)
  Fantasy I/IIB1

HAUSWIRTH, HANS M.A. (1901-   )
  Sonatina No. 2 I/IIB1

KAMERALNA MUZYKA GITAROWA I/IIB1-Coll

KUFFNER, JOSEPH (1776-1856)
  Serenade, No. 55 I/IIB1

MOSCHELES, IGNAZ (1794-1870)
  Grande Duo Concertante I/IIB1

REBAY, FERDINAND (1889-1953)
  Leicht Spielbare Kleinigkeiten
    I/IIB1

WEBER, CARL MARIA VON (1786-1826)
  Divertimento, Op. 38 I/IIB1

WIJDEVELD, WOLFGANG (1910-   )
  Snarenspel I/IIB1

ZAGWIJN, HENRI (1878-1954)
  Sarabande E Fandango I/IIB1

Duets — Gtr, Acord

HAUSWIRTH, HANS M.A. (1901-   )
  Sonatina No. 2 I/IIB1

Duets — Gtr, Hpsd

CARULLI, FERDINANDO (1770-1841)
  Notturno, Op. 189 I/IIB1

DODGSON, STEPHEN (1924-   )
  Duo Concertant I/IIB1

FLERES, RITA MARIA
  Stucke, 5, Nach Liedern Und Tanzen
    Aus Der Renaissance I/IIB1

GEMINIANI, FRANCESCO (1687-1762)
  12 Pieces For Guitar And Continuo
    I/IIB1

ZAGWIJN, HENRI (1878-1954)
  Sarabande E Fandango I/IIB1

Duets — Gtr, Mandolin

BEHREND, SIEGFRIED (1933-   )
  Kolometrie I/IIB1

BORTOLAZZI, B.
  Theme and Variations, Op. 10, No. 4
    I/IIB1

Duets — Gtr, Zither

BEHREND, SIEGFRIED (1933-)
Solo I/IIB1

MONZA, CARLO (ca. 1740-1801)
Sonate, MIN391 I/IIB1

Sonate, MIN392 I/IIB1

MULLER-ILMENAU, WILHELM (1911-)
Spielmusik I/IIB1

Duets — Gtr, Vln

AZPIAZU, JOSE DE (1912-)
Sonate Basque I/IIB1

BARON, ERNST GOTTLIEB (1696-1760)
Konzerte, 2 I/IIB1

BARTOLOZZI, BRUNO (1911-)
Serenade I/IIB1

BEETHOVEN, LUDWIG VAN (1770-1827)
Sonata in C minor I/IIB1

BISCHOFF, HEINZ (1898-1963)
Salzburger Sonatine In F I/IIB1

BLOCH, WALDEMAR (1906-)
Neuberger Tanze I/IIB1

Sonata I/IIB1

CARULLI, FERDINANDO (1770-1841)
Serenade, Op. 109, No. 1 I/IIB1

Serenade, Op. 109, No. 6 I/IIB1

Serenaden, 5 I/IIB1

DIABELLI, ANTON (1781-1858)
Stucke, 3 I/IIB1

DOHL, FRIEDHELM (1936-)
Pas De Deux I/IIB1

FURSTENAU, WOLFRAM
Pieces Pour Une Noble Femme, 3
I/IIB1

GELLI, VINCENZO (THOMATOS)
Two Divertimenti I/IIB1

GERLACH, HANS CHRISTIAN
Divertimento [Collection] I/IIB1

GIULIANI, MAURO (1781-1829)
Duettino I/IIB1

Duettino Facile I/IIB1

Grosse Serenade I/IIB1

Grosse Sonate, Op.25 I/IIB1

Grosse Sonate, Op.85 I/IIB1

Qual Mesto Gemito I/IIB1

Serenade, Op. 127 I/IIB1

GRAGNANI, FILIPPO (1767- ?)
Sonata, Op. 8, No. 1 I/IIB1

Sonata, Op. 8, No. 2 I/IIB1

Sonata, Op. 8, No. 3 I/IIB1

IBERT, JACQUES (1890-1962)
Entr'acte I/IIB1

ISRAEL-MEYER, PIERRE (1933-)
Humoresque I/IIB1

KAMERALNA MUZYKA GITAROWA I/IIB1-Coll

KELTERBORN, RUDOLF (1931-)
Music for Violin and Guitar I/IIB1

KOMTER, JAN MAARTEN (1905-)
Andante in D I/IIB1

Divertimento in G I/IIB1

KRENEK, ERNST (1900-)
Hausmusik; 7 Stucke Fur Die Sieben
Tage Der Woche I/IIB1

KUFFNER, JOSEPH (1776-1856)
Drittes Potpourri I/IIB1

Serenade, Op. 68 I/IIB1

MEIJER VON BREMEN, ALEXANDER
(1930-)
Bagatellen I/IIB1

MOLINO, FRANCESCO (1775-1847)
Nocturne No. 2, Op. 38 I/IIB1

Nocturne, Op. 37 I/IIB1

NIEHAUS, MANFRED (1933-)
Suite I/IIB1

PAGANINI, NICCOLO (1782-1840)
Cantabile I/IIB1

Centone Di Sonate; Four Sonatas
I/IIB1

12 Duette, Vol. 1 I/IIB1

12 Duette, Vol. 2 I/IIB1

Grosse Sonate I/IIB1

Moto Perpetuo I/IIB1

Sonata I/IIB1

Sonata Concertata I/IIB1

Sonata, Op. 3, No. 1 I/IIB1

Sonata, Op. 3, No. 5 I/IIB1

Sonata, Op. 3, No. 6 I/IIB1

Sonaten, 6, Op. 2 I/IIB1

Sonaten, 6, Op.3 I/IIB1

Sonatine, 4 I/IIB1

Tarantella I/IIB1

Variazioni Di Bravura I/IIB1

PATACHICH, IVAN (1922-)
Duo I/IIB1

PRAGER, HEINRICH ALOYS (1783-1854)
Introduktion, Thema Und Variationen
I/IIB1

PROSPERI, CARLO (1921-)
In Nocte I/IIB1

REITER, ALBERT (1905-1970)
Sonatina I/IIB1

RUST, FRIEDRICH WILHELM (1739-1796)
Sonata in G I/IIB1

SCHADLER, FRIEDRICH
Serenade Espagnole I/IIB1

SCHEIDLER, CHRISTIAN GOTTLIEB
(1752-1815)
Sonata in D I/IIB1

SIEGL, OTTO (1896-1978)
Sonatina in D minor I/IIB1

SOR, FERNANDO (1778-1839)
Romance I/IIB1

Romanza, La I/IIB1

SPIELMUSIK FUR MELODIEINSTRUMENTE UND
GITARRE, 16-19TH CENTURY
I/IIB1-Coll

SPIELMUSIK FUR MELODIEINSTRUMENTE UND
GITARRE, 20TH CENTURY I/IIB1-Coll

TAKACS, JENO (1902-)
Dialoge I/IIB1

Duets — Gtr, Vla

BEHREND, SIEGFRIED (1933-)
Scherzoso I/IIB1

BURGHAUSER, JARMIL (1921-)
Reflexionen I/IIB1

SCHADLER, FRIEDRICH
Serenade Espagnole I/IIB1

Duets — Gtr, Vcl

BAUMANN, MAX GEORG (1917-)
Duo, Op. 62 I/IIB1

KAMERALNA MUZYKA GITAROWA I/IIB1-Coll

LUCKY, STEPAN (1919-)
Duo Concertante I/IIB1

Duo Concertanti I/IIB1

MULLER-CANT, MANFRED (1926-)
Kinderlieder-Suite Fur Einen
Grossvater I/IIB1

ROMBERG, BERNHARD (1865-1913)
Divertimento, Op. 46 I/IIB1

WELFFENS, P.
Tafelmuziek I/IIB1

Duets — Gtr, Treb Inst

ALTE UND NEUE WEIHNACHTSLIEDER IV/IIB1

AUS DEM BALTISCHEN LAUTENBUCH 1740
I/IIB1-Coll

BEHREND, SIEGFRIED (1933-)
Spielmusik I/IIB1

GALL, LOUIS IGNATIUS
Sonatina Pirineos I/IIB1

HEILIGE NACHT, WEIHNACHTSLIEDER-ALBUM
IV/IIB1

INMITTEN DER NACHT, WEIHNACHTLICHE
SPIELMUSIK IV/IIB1

KOMTER, JAN MAARTEN (1905-)
Suite in C I/IIB1

Suite in D minor I/IIB1

KRETSCHMAR, WALTER (1902-)
Music in C I/IIB1

KROLL, GEORG (1934-)
Re-Sonat Tibia I/IIB1

MUZIEKBIJLAGE, NO. 53 I/IIB1-Coll

NIESSEN, HANS-LUTZ (1920-1982)
Daar Gingen Twee Gespeelkens Goed,
Variaties Op Een Volkslied
I/IIB1

SCHAGEN, HENK VAN
Botje (Berend) Varierend I/IIB1

SINTERKLAAS- & KERSTLIEDJES IV/IIB1

SOSINSKI, KAZIMIERZ
Studium Gry Akordowej Na Gitarze,
Technika Chwytow Barre, Akordy I
Ich Symbole I/IIB1

SPIELMUSIK FUR MELODIEINSTRUMENTE UND
   GITARRE, 20TH CENTURY I/IIB1-Coll

Duets — Gtr, Elec. Tape

CORGHI, AZIO (1937-   )
   Consonancias Y Redobles I/IIB1

ENCINAR, JOSE RAMON (1954-   )
   Abhava I/IIB1

Trios — Gtr, Fl, Pic

MIYAKE, HARUNA
   Musik Fur Piccolofloten, Floten Und
      Gitarre I/IIB2

Trios — Gtr, Fl, Ob

REGT, HENDRIK DE (1950-   )
   Silenus En Bakchanten I/IIB2

Trios — Gtr, Fl, Clar

KREUTZER, JOSEPH (1778-1832)
   Trio, Op. 16 I/IIB2

Trios — Gtr, Fl, Rec

BOIS, ROB DU (1934-   )
   Pastorale No. 2 I/IIB2

Trios — Gtr, Fl, Perc

DELAS, JOSE LUIS DE (1928-   )
   Trio I/IIB2

REGT, HENDRIK DE (1950-   )
   Musica, Op. 18 I/IIB2

Trios — Gtr, Fl, Pno

DAUBE, JOHANN FRIEDRICH (1730-1797)
   Trio in D minor I/IIB2

Trios — Gtr, Fl, Hpsd

DAUBE, JOHANN FRIEDRICH (1730-1797)
   Trio in D minor I/IIB2

Trios — Gtr, Fl, Lute

TAKEMITSU, TORU (1930-   )
   Ring I/IIB2

Trios — Gtr, Fl, Vln

CARULLI, FERDINANDO (1770-1841)
   Notturno in A minor I/IIB2

   Notturno in C I/IIB2

   Trios, Vol. I I/IIB2

   Trios, Vol. II I/IIB2

   Trios, Vol. III I/IIB2

GERLACH, HANS CHRISTIAN
   Divertimento [Collection] I/IIB2

KREUTZER, JOSEPH (1778-1832)
   Trio in D, Op. 9, No. 3 I/IIB2

MAR-CHAIM, JOSEPH (1940-   )
   Trio I/IIB2

WEBER, CARL MARIA VON (1786-1826)
   Menuetto And Trio I/IIB2

Trios — Gtr, Fl, Vla

ANDRIESSEN, JURRIAAN (1925-   )
   Trio No. 5 I/IIB2

APOSTEL, HANS ERICH (1901-1972)
   Kleines Kammerkonzert I/IIB2

   Study, Op. 29 I/IIB2

BADINGS, HENK (1907-1987)
   Trio No. 9 I/IIB2

BOIS, ROB DU (1934-   )
   Night Music I/IIB2

BROUWER, LEO (1939-   )
   Per Suonare A Tre I/IIB2

CALL, LEONHARD VON (ca. 1768-1815)
   Notturno, Op. 85 I/IIB2

   Notturno, Op. 89 I/IIB2

   Notturno, Op. 93 I/IIB2

   Trio, Op. 134 I/IIB2

DAVID, JOHANN NEPOMUK (1895-1977)
   Sonata, Op. 26 I/IIB2

HEER, HANS DE (1927-   )
   Trio I/IIB2

HEKSTER, WALTER (1937-   )
   Relief No. V I/IIB2

KOMTER, JAN MAARTEN (1905-   )
   Trio-Sonatine I/IIB2

KREUTZER, JOSEPH (1778-1832)
   Trio, Op. 16 I/IIB2

KUFFNER, JOSEPH (1776-1856)
   Notturno, Op. 110 I/IIB2

LEEUW, TON DE (1926-   )
   Schelp I/IIB2

LEGLEY, VICTOR (1915-   )
   Trio, Op. 55 I/IIB2

MATIEGKA, WENZESLAUS THOMAS (1753-1830)
   Notturno, Op. 21 I/IIB2

   Trio, Op. 26 I/IIB2

MOLINO, FRANCESCO (1775-1847)
   Trio, Op. 45 I/IIB2

REGT, HENDRIK DE (1950-   )
   Musica, Op. 15 I/IIB2

RICHTER, NICO (1915-1945)
   Trio I/IIB2

RUYNEMAN, DANIEL (1886-1963)
   Reflections No. 2 I/IIB2

SKORZENY, FRITZ (1900-1965)
   Trio I/IIB2

WEBER, CARL MARIA VON (1786-1826)
   Menuetto And Trio I/IIB2

WIGGLESWORTH, FRANK (1918-   )
   Serenade I/IIB2

Trios — Gtr, Fl, Vcl

GESZLER, GYORGY (1913-   )
   Trio I/IIB2

MAASZ, GERHARD (1906-1984)
   Suite I/IIB2

Trios — Gtr, Mel Inst, Vla da Gamba

SPERONTES (JOHANN SIGISMUND SCHOLZE)
   (1705-1750)
   Singende Muse An Der Pleisse I/IIB2

Trios — Gtr, Mel Inst, Vcl

SPERONTES (JOHANN SIGISMUND SCHOLZE)
(1705-1750)
Singende Muse An Der Pleisse I/IIB2

Trios — Gtr, 2 Ob

AUBANEL, GEORGES
Divertissements, 7, Sur Des Airs
Populaires Anciens Et Modernes
I/IIB2

Trios — Gtr, Ob, Bsn

BAUMANN, HERBERT (1925-   )
Sonatine Uber Finnische Volkslieder
I/IIB2

Trios — Gtr, Ob, Pno

PRAAG, HENRI C. VAN (1894-1968)
Sonata I/IIB2

Trios — Gtr, Clar, Vln

KREUTZER, JOSEPH (1778-1832)
Trio, Op. 16 I/IIB2

POLOLANIK, ZDENEK (1935-   )
Scherzo Contrario I/IIB2

Trios — Gtr, Clar, DB

PFISTER, HUGO (1914-1969)
Preambolo, Aria E Ballo I/IIB2

Trios — Gtr, 2 S Rec

AUBANEL, GEORGES
Divertissements, 7, Sur Des Airs
Populaires Anciens Et Modernes
I/IIB2

MULLER, FRIEDRICH EWALD (1934-   )
Theme and Variations I/IIB2

O WUNDER, WAS WILL DAS BEDEUTEN,
LIEDERSAMMLUNG ZUR ADVENTSZEIT
IV/IIB2

SCHAFER, RUDOLF (1891-1970)
Kleine Spiel- Und Ubungsstucke Fur
Den Anfang, 30 I/IIB2

STETKA, FRANZ (1899-   )
Kleine Suite In A Minor I/IIB2

ULDALL, HANS (1903-   )
Neue Musizierstucke I/IIB2

WOLKI, KONRAD
Rondoletto; 11 Leichte Spielstucke
I/IIB2

Trios — Gtr, S Rec, A Rec

BIALAS, GUNTER (1907-   )
Spanische Romanzen I/IIB2

DUARTE, JOHN W. (1919-   )
Transatlantic Dances, 4 I/IIB2

SCHALLER, ERWIN (1901-   )
Funf Miniaturen, Nach Schottischen
Volksweisen I/IIB2

SPIELMUSIK FUR MELODIEINSTRUMENTE UND
GITARRE, 20TH CENTURY I/IIB2-Coll

STETKA, FRANZ (1899-   )
Tanze, Marsche Und Andere Spielstucke
IV/IIB2, I/IIB2

WERDIN, EBERHARD (1911-   )
Trio-Stucke I/IIB2

Trios — Gtr, A Rec, T Rec

BUTTING, MAX (1888-1976)
Hausmusik I/IIB2

Trios — Gtr, S Rec, Vln

STETKA, FRANZ (1899-   )
Sonatina I/IIB2

Trios — Gtr, S Rec, Vla da Gamba

LINDE, HANS-MARTIN
Serenata A Tre I/IIB2

Trios — Gtr, S Rec, Vcl

LINDE, HANS-MARTIN
Serenata A Tre I/IIB2

Trios — Gtr, 2 A Rec

GAL, HANS (1890-1987)
Divertimento, Op. 68c I/IIB2

KNAB, ARMIN (1881-1951)
Pastorale Und Allegro IV/IIB2

SPIELMUSIK FUR MELODIEINSTRUMENTE UND
GITARRE, 20TH CENTURY I/IIB2-Coll

STOCKMEIER, WOLFGANG (1931-   )
Divertimento I/IIB2

TRIO-SONATES [COLLECTION] I/IIB2-Coll

Trios — Gtr, A Rec, Vla da Gamba

LINDE, HANS-MARTIN
Serenata A Tre I/IIB2

Trios — Gtr, A Rec, Vcl

LINDE, HANS-MARTIN
Serenata A Tre I/IIB2

Trios — Gtr, 2 T Rec

ULDALL, HANS (1903–)
  Neue Musizierstucke I/IIB2

Trios — Gtr, B Rec, Vla da Gamba

LINDE, HANS–MARTIN
  Serenata A Tre I/IIB2

Trios — Gtr, B Rec, Vcl

LINDE, HANS–MARTIN
  Serenata A Tre I/IIB2

Trios — Gtr, Rec, Hpsd

BORRIS, SIEGFRIED (1906–)
  Conversazione A Tre I/IIB2

Trios — Gtr, Rec, Vln

ALTE UND NEUE MUSIK ZUM SINGEN UND
  SPIELEN AUF BLOCKFLOTEN, GEIGEN UND
  LAUTENINSTRUMENTE I/IIB2-Coll

Trios — Gtr, Rec, Vla

ALTE UND NEUE MUSIK ZUM SINGEN UND
  SPIELEN AUF BLOCKFLOTEN, GEIGEN UND
  LAUTENINSTRUMENTE I/IIB2-Coll

Trios — Gtr, Rec, Vla da Gamba

LINDE, HANS–MARTIN
  Serenata A Tre I/IIB2

Trios — Gtr, Rec, Vcl

LINDE, HANS–MARTIN
  Serenata A Tre I/IIB2

Trios — Gtr, Trp, Pno

CLEMENTI, ALDO (1925–)
  Sonata I/IIB2

Trios — Gtr, Perc, Conductor

FOSS, LUKAS (1922–)
  Paradigm I/IIB2

Trios — Gtr, Vla, Perc

KOMOROUS, RUDOLF (1931–)
  Chanson I/IIB2

Trios — Gtr, Harp, Pno

LONQUICH, HEINZ MARTIN (1937–)
  Pentameron I/IIB2

Trios — Gtr, Mand, Harp

PETRASSI, GOFFREDO (1904–)
  Seconda Serenata-Trio I/IIB2

Trios — Gtr, Vla da Gamba, Harp

JOHNSON, JOHN (1540–1594)
  Rogero I/IIB2

Trios — Gtr, Vcl, Harp

JOHNSON, JOHN (1540–1594)
  Rogero I/IIB2

Trios — 2 Gtr, Hpsd

BOOGAARD, BERNARD VAN DEN (1952–)
  Oilles Motors I/IIB2

Trios — Gtr, Vln, Hpsd

DAUBE, JOHANN FRIEDRICH (1730–1797)
  Trio in D minor I/IIB2

Trios — Gtr, Vla da Gamba, Hpsd

JOHNSON, JOHN (1540–1594)
  Rogero I/IIB2

Trios — Gtr, Vcl, Hpsd

GEMINIANI, FRANCESCO (1687-1762)
Sonatas, 6 I/IIB2

JOHNSON, JOHN (1540-1594)
Rogero I/IIB2

Trios — Gtr, Vln, Pno

DAUBE, JOHANN FRIEDRICH (1730-1797)
Trio in D minor I/IIB2

Trios — Gtr, Vla da Gamba, Lute

JOHNSON, JOHN (1540-1594)
Rogero I/IIB2

Trios — Gtr, Vcl, Lute

JOHNSON, JOHN (1540-1594)
Rogero I/IIB2

Trios — Gtr, B Gtr, Hawaiian Gtr

MENGELBERG, MISJA (1935-   )
Amaga I/IIB2

Trios — 2 Gtr, Vla da Gamba

JOHNSON, JOHN (1540-1594)
Rogero I/IIB2

Trios — 2 Gtr, Vcl

JOHNSON, JOHN (1540-1594)
Rogero I/IIB2

Trios — Gtr, 2 Vln

AUBANEL, GEORGES
Divertissements, 7, Sur Des Airs
Populaires Anciens Et Modernes
I/IIB2

KREUTZER, JOSEPH (1778-1832)
Trio in D, Op. 9, No. 3 I/IIB2

PAGANINI, NICCOLO (1782-1840)
Serenade I/IIB2

Serenade, MIN 55 I/IIB2

Serenade, MIN 56 I/IIB2

Trios — Gtr, Vln, Vla

CALL, LEONHARD VON (ca. 1768-1815)
Notturno, Op. 85 I/IIB2

Notturno, Op. 89 I/IIB2

Notturno, Op. 93 I/IIB2

Trio, Op. 134 I/IIB2

HASENOHRL, FRANZ (1885- ?)
Trio-Suite I/IIB2

KOMTER, JAN MAARTEN (1905-   )
Trio-Sonatine I/IIB2

KREUTZER, JOSEPH (1778-1832)
Trio, Op. 16 I/IIB2

KUFFNER, JOSEPH (1776-1856)
Notturno, Op. 110 I/IIB2

Serenade in A I/IIB2

MATIEGKA, WENZESLAUS THOMAS (1753-1830)
Trio, Op. 26 I/IIB2

MOLINO, FRANCESCO (1775-1847)
Trio, Op. 45 I/IIB2

SCHRAMM, WERNER
Kammertrio I/IIB2

SPOHR, LUDWIG (LOUIS) (1784-1859)
Trio I/IIB2

Trios — Gtr, Vln, Vcl

ANONYMOUS
Trio in F, MIN 409 I/IIB2

GIULIANI, MAURO (1781-1829)
Serenade, Op. 19 I/IIB2

GRANATA, GIOVANNI BATTISTA
(fl. ca. 1674)
Novi Capricci Armonici (1674) I/IIB2

HAYDN, [FRANZ] JOSEPH (1732-1809)
Trio In F, Hob. IV:F2 I/IIB2

LUTYENS, ELIZABETH (1906-1983)
Nocturnes, 4 I/IIB2

PAGANINI, NICCOLO (1782-1840)
Terzetto I/IIB2

Terzetto Concertante I/IIB2

VIVALDI, ANTONIO (1678-1741)
Trio in G minor, MIN 326 I/IIB2

Trios — Gtr, 2 Treb Inst

BIALAS, GUNTER (1907-   )
Spanische Romanzen I/IIB2

CECERE, C.
Sinfonia in G I/IIB2

JANSEN, WILLY (1897-   )
Kleine Spielmusiken I/IIB2

KARL, SEPP (1913-   )
Tanze Und Weisen I/IIB2

MULLER, FRIEDRICH EWALD (1934-   )
Theme and Variations I/IIB2

SPIELMUSIK FUR MELODIEINSTRUMENTE UND
GITARRE, 20TH CENTURY I/IIB2-Coll

Quartets — Gtr, Fl, Clar, Vla

LAMPERSBERG, GERHARD (1928-   )
Quartet I/IIB3

Quartets — Gtr, Fl, Clar, Vcl

WARD-STEINMAN, DAVID (1936-   )
Quiet Dance I/IIB3

Quartets — Gtr, Fl, Bsn, Vla

DELDEN, LEX VAN (1919-   )
    Ballet I/IIB3

MONTEVERDI, CLAUDIO (ca. 1567-1643)
    Canzonette Strumentali A Tre Voci
    I/IIB3

Quartets — Gtr, Fl, Mand, Acord

HLOUSCHEK, THEODOR (1923-   )
    Quartet I/IIB3

Quartets — 3 Gtr, Fl

ERDMANN, DIETRICH (1917-   )
    Notturno I/IIB3

Quartets — Gtr, Fl, Vla, Vcl

REGT, HENDRIK DE (1950-   )
    Musica, Op. 17 I/IIB3

SANTORSOLA, GUIDO (1904-   )
    Quartet No. 2 I/IIB3

Quartets — Gtr, Fl, Vla da Braccia, Vla da Gamba

MONTEVERDI, CLAUDIO (ca. 1567-1643)
    Canzonette Strumentali A Tre Voci
    I/IIB3

Quartets — Gtr, Ob, Clar, Bsn

KUBIZEK, AUGUSTIN (1918-   )
    Quartetto Da Camera I/IIB3

Quartets — Gtr, 3 S Rec

SCHAFER, RUDOLF (1891-1970)
    Kleine Spiel- Und Ubungsstucke Fur
    Den Anfang, 30 I/IIB3

STETKA, FRANZ (1899-   )
    Tanze, Marsche Und Andere Spielstucke
    I/IIB3

Quartets — Gtr, 2 S Rec, A Rec

STETKA, FRANZ (1899-   )
    Tanze, Marsche Und Andere Spielstucke
    I/IIB3

Quartets — Gtr, S Rec, A Rec, T Rec

KORDA, VIKTOR (1900-   )
    Capriccio I/IIB3

Quartets — Gtr, S Rec, A Rec, Perc

MARTELLI, HENRI (1895-   )
    Provencalische Volkstanze I/IIB3

NILOVIC, JANKO
    Makedonia I/IIB3

Quartets — Gtr, S Rec, Stabspiele, Perc

SCHAAF, PETER
    Moderne Tanze, 2 I/IIB3

Quartets — Gtr, A Rec, T Rec, Glock

STAEPS, HANS ULRICH (1909-   )
    Gitter Und Ranken I/IIB3

Quartets — Gtr, A Rec, Vln, Pno

KRENEK, ERNST (1900-   )
    Hausmusik; 7 Stucke Fur Die Sieben
    Tage Der Woche I/IIB3

Quartets — 3 Gtr, A Rec

ERDMANN, DIETRICH (1917-   )
    Notturno I/IIB3

Quartets — Gtr, 2 Rec, Perc

NILOVIC, JANKO
    Makedonia I/IIB3

Quartets — Gtr, 3 Vln

FHEODOROFF, NIKOLAUS (1931-   )
    Zwolftonspiele, 3 I/IIB3

Quartets — Gtr, 2 Vln, Vcl

KOHAUT, KARL
    Concerto in F I/IIB3

ROSENMULLER, JOHANN (ca. 1620-1684)
    Trio Sonata I/IIB3

Quartets — Gtr, Vln, Vla, Vcl

CHAILLY, LUCIANO (1920-   )
Recitativo E Fuga I/IIB3

FURSTENAU, WOLFRAM
Ch'i - Yun (Oder Das Prinzip
Intensiven Lebens In Frieden)
Nach Dem Gemalden "Schwingungen",
"Lu-Mi", "Cheng" Von Georg W.
Borsche I/IIB3

FUSZ, JANOS
Quartet I/IIB3

MONTEVERDI, CLAUDIO (ca. 1567-1643)
Canzonette Strumentali A Tre Voci
I/IIB3

PAGANINI, NICCOLO (1782-1840)
Quartet I/IIB3

Quartet No. 1 I/IIB3

Quartet No. 7 I/IIB3

WIJDEVELD, WOLFGANG (1910-   )
Concert I/IIB3

Quartets — Gtr, 3 Treb Inst

BRESGEN, CESAR (1913-   )
Stornelli I/IIB3

KORDA, VIKTOR (1900-   )
Capriccio I/IIB3

Quartets — Gtr, 2 Treb Inst, Perc

BIALAS, GUNTER (1907-   )
Rhythmische Miniaturen I/IIB3

Quintets — Gtr, 2 Fl, Eng H, Perc

MASSEUS, JAN (1913-   )
Seven Minutes Organized Sound I/IIB4

Quintets — Gtr, Fl, Ob, Clar, Bsn

FELD, JINDRICH (1925-   )
Capriccio I/IIB4

Quintets — Gtr, Fl, Ob, Clar, Perc

MASSEUS, JAN (1913-   )
Seven Minutes Organized Sound I/IIB4

Quintets — Gtr, Fl, Clar, Vla, Vcl

DIONISI, RENATO (1910-   )
Melismi I/IIB4

Quintets — 3 Gtr, Pic, Perc

TOMASI, HENRI (1901-1971)
Recuerdos De Las Baleares I/IIB4

Quintets — Gtr, Fl, Vla, Vcl, Perc

REGT, HENDRIK DE (1950-   )
Musica, Op. 11 I/IIB4

Quintets — 3 Gtr, Ob, Perc

TOMASI, HENRI (1901-1971)
Recuerdos De Las Baleares I/IIB4

Quintets — Gtr, 3 Clar, Perc

MASSEUS, JAN (1913-   )
Seven Minutes Organized Sound I/IIB4

Quintets — Gtr, Clar, Vln, DB, Perc

FERRITTO, JOHN E. (1937-   )
Diffusione I/IIB4

Quintets — Gtr, S Rec, A Rec, Tri, Xylo

BRUCKMANN, FERDINAND
Sonatina Buffa I/IIB4

Quintets — Gtr, A Rec, T Rec, Vln, Vla

SCHWARZ-SCHILLING, REINHARD (1904-   )
Kleine Kammermusik I/IIB4

Quintets — Gtr, A Rec, T Rec, 2 Fiddles

SCHWARZ-SCHILLING, REINHARD (1904-   )
Kleine Kammermusik I/IIB4

Quintets — 2 Gtr, 3 Rec

HAYDN, [FRANZ] JOSEPH (1732-1809)
Romance in C I/IIB4

KOCH, JOHANNES H.E. (1918-   )
Tanzerische Spielmusik I/IIB4

Quintets — Gtr, DB, Harp, 2 Perc

KAGEL, MAURICIO (1931-   )
Sonant I/IIB4

Quintets — Gtr, Vln, 3 Perc

SCHAT, PETER (1935-   )
First Essay On Electrocution I/IIB4

Quintets — Gtr, 2 DB, Cimbalom, Perc

MAMANGAKIS, NIKOS (1929-   )
Trittys I/IIB4

Quintets — Gtr, 4 Gtr

STAAK, PIETER VAN DER (1930-   )
Concertino No. 3 I/IIB4

Quintets — Gtr, 2 Vln, Vla, Vcl

BAUMANN, HERBERT (1925-   )
Memento I/IIB4

BOCCHERINI, LUIGI (1743-1805)
Quintet No. 1, Ge. 445 I/IIB4

Quintet No. 1 in D I/IIB4

Quintet No. 2, Ge. 446 I/IIB4

Quintet No. 2 in C, Ge. 451 I/IIB4

Quintet No. 3, Ge. 447 I/IIB4

Quintet No. 3 in E minor, Ge. 452
I/IIB4

Quintet No. 4, Ge. 448 I/IIB4

Quintet No. 5, Ge. 449 I/IIB4

Quintet No. 6, Ge. 450 I/IIB4

Quintetti, 6, Con Chitarra, Ge. 445-
450 I/IIB4

BOZZA, EUGENE (1905-   )
Concertino Da Camera I/IIB4

CASTELNUOVO-TEDESCO, MARIO (1895-1968)
Quintet, Op. 143 I/IIB4

GIULIANI, MAURO (1781-1829)
Quintet, Op. 65 I/IIB4

GUASTAVINO, CARLOS (1914-   )
Jeromita Linares I/IIB4

ROVENSTRUNCK, BERNHARD
Stucke, 5 I/IIB4

SCHNABEL, JOSEPH (1767-1831)
Quintet I/IIB4

Quintets — Gtr, 4 Treb Inst

FURSTENAU, WOLFRAM
Spielmusik I/IIB4

Quintets — Gtr, 4 Players

FURSTENAU, WOLFRAM
Jordaan I/IIB4

STOCKHAUSEN, KARLHEINZ (1928-   )
Solo I/IIB4

School Ens/Orch with Gtr

BAAREN, KEES VAN (1906-1970)
Suite Voor Schoolorkest I/IIB5

CRANEN, T.
Kermis-Suite I/IIB5

DIECKMANN, CARL HEINZ
Kleines Tanzchen I/IIB5

DRESDEN, SEM (1881-1957)
Stukken, 3, Voor Schoolorkest, No. 2
I/IIB5

Stukken, 3, Voor Schoolorkest, No. 3
I/IIB5

EBENHOH, HORST (1930-   )
Bewegungsspiele I/IIB5

EINZUG UND REIGEN I/IIB5

FEGERS, KARL (1926-   )
Suite Nach Franzosischen Volksliedern
I/IIB5

FUNK, HEINRICH (1893-   )
Thuringer Kirmes. 4 Bauerntanze Aus
Thuringen I/IIB5

GATTERMAYER, HEINRICH (1923-   )
Suite Fur Spielmusikgruppen, Op. 101-
3 I/IIB5

GESELBRACHT, ERICH
Spieldose, Die I/IIB5

GRAETZER, GUILLERMO
Altindianische Tanze I/IIB5

Indo-Amerikanische Tanze I/IIB5

GRIEND, KOOS VAN DE (1905-1950)
Stukken Voor Schoolorkest, 3 I/IIB5

HEIDSCHI BUMBEIDSCHI BUM-BUM, DIE
ALLERSCHONSTEN WEIHNACHTSLIEDER,
VOL. I: PNO ED. (WITH TEXT)
IV/IIB4

HEIDSCHI BUMBEIDSCHI BUM-BUM, DIE
ALLERSCHONSTEN WEIHNACHTSLIEDER,
VOL. II: INST ED., FOR 3- OR 4-PT
ENSEMBLES IV/IIB4

HEIDSCHI BUMBEIDSCHI BUM-BUM, DIE
ALLERSCHONSTEN WEIHNACHTSLIEDER,
VOL. III: VOCAL ED IV/IIB4

HERRERA, RAMON DE
Minimes, 6 I/IIB5

KOCH, JOHANNES H.E. (1918-   )
Tanzerische Spielmusik I/IIB5

KORDA, VIKTOR (1900-   )
Festliche Suite, Fur
Spielmusikgruppen I/IIB5

LAMPE, GUNTER (1925-   )
Tanze, 2 I/IIB5

MAREZ OYENS, TERA DE (1932-   )
Partita Voor David, Voor Kinderorkest
I/IIB5

MUHE, HANSGEORG
Wir Wandern Ohne Sorgen I/IIB5

PRAAG, HENRI C. VAN (1894-1968)
Schoolmuziek No. 1 I/IIB5

Schoolmuziek No. 3 I/IIB5

PREISSLER-SPIELHEFT, VOL. I
I/IIB5-Coll

PREISSLER-SPIELHEFT, VOL. II
I/IIB5-Coll

PREISSLER-SPIELHEFT, VOL. III
I/IIB5-Coll

PREISSLER-SPIELHEFT, VOL. IV
I/IIB5-Coll

SPIELBUCH FUR DIE JUGEND, VOL. I
I/IIB5-Coll

SPIELBUCH FUR DIE JUGEND, VOL. II
I/IIB5-Coll

SPIELMUSIK FUR DIE SCHULE I/IIB5-Coll,
IV/IIB4

STAEPS, HANS ULRICH (1909-   )
Aubade Und Tanz I/IIB5

TWITTENHOFF, WILHELM (1904-   )
Schweinehirt, Der; Musik Zu Einem
Schattenspiel I/IIB5

UHL, ALFRED (1909-   )
Allerlei Spielmusik I/IIB5

USPER, FRANCESCO (? -1641)
Sinfonia in F I/IIB5

VERDONK, JAN
Musette I/IIB5

VIVA LA MUSICA; CANONS (2-4 PARTS)
I/IIB5-Coll

WERDIN, EBERHARD (1911-   )
Concertino I/IIB5

Europaische Tanze; 7 Pieces For
Schoolensemble I/IIB5

Kommt, Ihr G'spielen; Folksongs For
Wind, String, Plucked, And
Percussion Instruments I/IIB5

Tanze Der Volker I/IIB5

WILIMEK, EDUARD
Spiel Mit Uns; Kleine Musikstucke Fur
Ein Konstruktives Zusammenspiel
I/IIB5

ZEHM, FRIEDRICH (1923-   )
Divertimento Ritmico; 6 Moderne
Tanzrhythmen I/IIB5-Coll

Duets — Gtr, Voice

ADOLPHSON, OLLE
Trubbel I/IIC1

ANONYMOUS
Dindirindin, Villancico I/IIC1

En Avila Mis Ojos, Romance I/IIC1

Tant Que Vivray I/IIC1

APIVOR, DENIS (1916-   )
Canciones, 6, De Federico Garcia
Lorca I/IIC1

ASCHERO, SERGIO (1945-   )
Canciones De Garcia Lorca I/IIC1

BEHREND, SIEGFRIED (1933-   )
Jiddische Hochzeit, A I/IIC1

Suite, Nach Altpolnischen Melodien
I/IIC1

Yo Lo Vi, Scenen Nach Francesco de
Goya I/IIC1

BELLMAN, CARL MICHAEL (1740-1795)
Bellmann-Brevier; Lieder Aus
"Fredmans-Episteln", Vol. 1
I/IIC1

Bellmann-Brevier; Lieder Aus
"Fredmans-Episteln", Vol. 2
I/IIC1

BESARD, JEAN-BAPTISTE (1567-ca. 1625)
Belles Deesses I/IIC1

Cruelle Departie, Chanson I/IIC1

Moy, Pauvre Fille I/IIC1

BOESSET, ANTOINE (ca. 1585-1643)
Ennuits, Desespoirs Et Douleurs
I/IIC1

BORTOLAMI, GALLIANO
Rumore Di Passi, 5 Liriche I/IIC1

BRESGEN, CESAR (1913-   )
Funf Rumanische Gesange I/IIC1

Tschechoslowakische Suite I/IIC1

BRITTEN, [SIR] BENJAMIN (1913-1976)
Songs From The Chinese I/IIC1

CANCIONES ANTIGUAS, 5 I/IIC1-Coll

CANCIONES ANTIGUAS, 6 I/IIC1-Coll

CARA, MARCHETTO (? -1525)
Io Non Compro, Frottola I/IIC1

CAROLS, 25, FROM THE OXFORD BOOK OF
CAROLS FOR SCHOOLS IV/IIC1

CARTER, ELLIOTT COOK, JR. (1908-   )
Tell Me Where Is Fancy Bred I/IIC1

CASTELNUOVO-TEDESCO, MARIO (1895-1968)
Divan Of Moses-Ibn-Ezra (1055-1135),
A Cycle Of Songs I/IIC1

Platero Y Yo, Vol. I I/IIC1

Platero Y Yo, Vol. II I/IIC1

Platero Y Yo, Vol. III I/IIC1

Platero Y Yo, Vol. IV I/IIC1

CHANSON D'AMOURS ELIZABETHAINES, 3
I/IIC1-Coll

[CHANTS, 4] I/IIC1-Coll

DAVIES, PETER MAXWELL (1934-   )
Dark Angels I/IIC1

DELNOOZ, HENRI (1942-   )
Oiseau De La Tour, L' I/IIC1

DESDERI, ETTORE (1892-1974)
Cacce Quattrocentesche, 2 I/IIC1

DESSAU, PAUL (1894-1979)
Liebeslieder, 4, Nach Texten Von
Bertolt Brecht I/IIC1

Lieder, 4 I/IIC1

Tierverse Von Bertolt Brecht I/IIC1

DEUTSCHE MEISTER DES EIN- UND
ZWEISTIMMIGEN LAUTENSATZES, 16.-18.
JAHRHUNDERT I/IIC1-Coll

DOCKHORN, LOTTE
Schalk Und Scherz Zur Laute I/IIC1

DOWLAND, JOHN (1562-1626)
Canzoni Elisabettiane, 2 I/IIC1

Come Again, Sweet Love I/IIC1

Lieder, 18 I/IIC1

Songs, 3 I/IIC1

Songs, 6 I/IIC1

DUARTE, JOHN W. (1919-   )
Quiet Songs, 5 I/IIC1

ENGLISH RENAISSANCE SONGS - ANGOL
RENESZANSZ DALOK I/IIC1-Coll

ENRICHI, ARMINIO
Chansons, 4 I/IIC1

ERBSE, HEIMO (1924-   )
Nachklange I/IIC1

FALLA, MANUEL DE (1876-1946)
Chansons Populaires Espagnoles, 7,
Vols. 1-7 I/IIC1

Tus Ojillos Negros, Cancion Andaluza
I/IIC1

FARKAS, FERENC (1905-   )
Canzoni Dei Trovatori, 5 I/IIC1

FINK, SIEGFRIED
Tangents CSB I/IIC1

FLECHA, MATEO (1530-1604)
Girigonza, La, Danse Chantee I/IIC1

FRANCAIX, JEAN (1912-   )
Priere Du Soir I/IIC1

FRICKER, PETER RACINE (1920-   )
O Mistress Mine I/IIC1

FUENLLANA, MIGUEL DE (fl. ca. 1560)
Duelete De Mi, Senora I/IIC1

FURSTENAU, WOLFRAM
Sonette I/IIC1

GALEN MAN I/IIC1-Coll

GAVALL, JOHN
Play The Guitar, A Self Tutor
IV/IIC1

GERHARD, ROBERTO (1896-1970)
Cantares I/IIC1

GIULIANI, MAURO (1781-1829)
Lieder, 6 I/IIC1

6 Lieder I/IIC1

GOLDEN SONGS I/IIC1-Coll

GORZANIS, GIACOMO (ca. 1525-ca. 1578)
Napolitane, 15 I/IIC1

HENZE, HANS WERNER (1926-   )
Fragmente Nach Holderlin, 3 I/IIC1

HUBSCHMANN, WERNER (1901-1969)
Alte Deutsche Spruchweisheit I/IIC1

HUYGENS, CONSTANTIN
Psaumes Et 3 Chansons, 2 I/IIC1

HUZELLA, ELEK (1915-1971)
4 Viragenek I/IIC1

JESSET, MICHAEL
Neun Volkslieder I/IIC1

JONG, MARINUS DE (1891-1984)
Bruegel-Liederen I/IIC1

KNAB, ARMIN (1881-1951)
Lautenlieder I/IIC1

KOMTER, JAN MAARTEN (1905-   )
In A Gondola I/IIC1

KUKUCK, FELICITAS (1914-   )
Ich Hab Die Nacht Getraumet,
Madchenlieder Nach Gedichten Aus
Der Romantik I/IIC1

Paradies, Das, Ein Tanzspiel I/IIC1

KUNAD, RAINER (1936-   )
Schattenland Strome, Conatum 37
I/IIC1

Von Der Kocherie, Ein Kulinarisches
Loblied, Conatum 47 I/IIC1

LE ROY, ADRIEN (? -1599)
J'ai Le Rebours I/IIC1

Je Ne Suis Moins Aimable I/IIC1

Laissez La Verte Couleur, Chanson
I/IIC1

Mes Peines Et Ennuis, Branle Gay
I/IIC1

MALIPIERO, RICCARDO (1914-   )
Ballate, 2 I/IIC1

MILAN, LUIS (ca. 1500-ca. 1564)
Con Pavor Recordo El Moro, Romance
I/IIC1

Don Luis Milan I/IIC1

Levaysme Amor d'Aquesta Terra I/IIC1

Maestro, El, Vol. 1: Obras Para
Vihuela Sola I/IIC1

MILAN, LUIS (cont'd.)

Maestro, El, Vol. 2: Obras Para Voz Y
Vihuela I/IIC1

Perdida Tengo La Color I/IIC1

Toda Mi Vida Os Ame I/IIC1

MITTERGRADNEGGER, GUNTER (1923-   )
Heiteres Herbarium I/IIC1

MORALES, CRISTOBAL DE (ca. 1500-1553)
De Antequera Sale El Moro, Romance
Viejo I/IIC1

MORENO TORROBA, FEDERICO (1891-1982)
Canciones Espanolas, 7 I/IIC1

Marchenera, La, Petenera I/IIC1

MORETTI, FEDERICO
Doce Canciones I/IIC1

MUDARRA, ALONSO DE (ca. 1506-1580)
Claros Y Frescos Rios, Cancion
I/IIC1

Isabel, Perdiste La Tu Faxa I/IIC1

Tres Libros De Musica En Cifra Para
Vihuela I/IIC1

Triste Estaba El Rey David I/IIC1

MUSGRAVE, THEA (1928-   )
Five Love Songs I/IIC1

NARVAEZ, LUIS DE
Con Que La Lavare I/IIC1

Seys Libros Del Delphin De Musica De
Cifra Para Taner Vihuela, Los
I/IIC1

NEUMANN, ULRIK
Manresan I/IIC1

NOVAK, JAN (1921-1984)
Apicius Modulatus, Artis Coquinariae
Praecepta Modis Numerisque
Instructa Ad Cantum Cum Cithara
I/IIC1

Cantiones Latinae, Medii Et
Recentioris Aevi Ad Cantum Cum
Cithara I/IIC1

PISADOR, DIEGO (ca. 1508-1557)
Guarte, Guarte El Rey Don Sancho
I/IIC1

Guarte, Guarte El Rey Don Sancho,
Romance Viejo I/IIC1

Lagrime Mesti, Villanesca I/IIC1

Madonna Mia Fa, Villanesca I/IIC1

Manana De San Juan, La, Romance Viejo
I/IIC1

Quien Tu Viese Tal Poder, Villancico
I/IIC1

Si La Noche Hace Oscura, Villancico
I/IIC1

Si Te Vas A Baner Juanica, Villancico
I/IIC1

REIN, WALTER (1893-1955)
Vom Vielfaltigen Leben I/IIC1

RODRIGO, JOAQUIN (1902-   )
Folias Canarias I/IIC1

Spanish Songs, 3 I/IIC1

Villancicos I/IIC1, IV/IIC1

ROLAND, CLAUDE ROBERT (1935-   )
Ballade De Villon I/IIC1

RUIZ PIPO, ANTONIO
Cantos A La Noche I/IIC1

SANCHEZ, B.
Berceuse I/IIC1

Ingenio, Evocation I/IIC1

SERMISY, CLAUDE DE (CLAUDIN)
(ca. 1490-1562)
Tant Que Vivrai, Chanson I/IIC1

SINGENDES, KLINGENDES OSTERREICH
IV/IIC1

SOR, FERNANDO (1778-1839)
Seguidillas: 12 Spanish Songs I/IIC1

STAAK, PIETER VAN DER (1930-   )
  Quatrains Of Omar Khayyam, 3 I/IIC1

THIENEMANN, H.
  Aehrenlese I/IIC1

  Fruhsommerblumen I/IIC1

  Heimed Luegt Di Glanzig A, D' I/IIC1

  In Leisen Liedern Geht Mein Tag
    I/IIC1

  Kleines, Stilles Leuchten, Ein
    I/IIC1

  Sunneschyn Und Rage I/IIC1

  Waldmarchen I/IIC1

TIPPETT, [SIR] MICHAEL (1905-   )
  Songs For Achilles I/IIC1

TROMBONCINO, BARTOLOMEO
  [Chants, 3] I/IIC1

TUDOR SONGS, 6 I/IIC1-Coll

VALDERRABANO, ENRIQUEZ DE
    (fl. ca. 1550)
  Ay De Mi, Romance Viejo I/IIC1

  Ya Cabalga Calainos I/IIC1

VANDERMAESBRUGGE, MAX (1933-   )
  Chansons De Pancruche, 5 I/IIC1

VASQUEZ, JUAN (fl. 1500)
  En La Fuente Del Rosel, Villancico
    I/IIC1

  Vos Me Matastes, Villancico I/IIC1

VECCHI, ORAZIO (HORATIO) (1550-1605)
  Non Vuo Pregare I/IIC1

VILLA-LOBOS, HEITOR (1887-1959)
  Aria (Cantilena) I/IIC1

WALTON, [SIR] WILLIAM (TURNER)
    (1902-1983)
  Anon. In Love; 6 Anonymous 16th- And
    17th-Century Lyrics I/IIC1

WEBER, CARL MARIA VON (1786-1826)
  Gitarrelieder I/IIC1

ZANKE, HERMAN
  Berglied I/IIC1

ZIPP, FRIEDRICH (1914-   )
  Es Steht Ein Lind Im Tiefen Tal, 6
    Deutsche Balladen I/IIC1

Duets — Gtr, Narrator

BUSSOTTI, SYLVANO (1931-   )
  Ultima Rara, Pop Song I/IIC1

HORNUNG
  O Dream, O Dreaming I/IIC1

Trios — Gtr, 2 Voices

KUNSTLIEDER I/IIC2-Coll

ST. MARTINS-LIEDER I/IIC2-Coll

Trios — Gtr, Voice, Fl

BIALAS, GUNTER (1907-   )
  Gesange, 3 I/IIC2

REDEL, MARTIN CHRISTOPH (1947-   )
  Epilog I/IIC2

Trios — Gtr, Voice, Ob

BURKHART, FRANZ (1902-1978)
  Adventlieder, 3 IV/IIC2

Trios — Gtr, Voice, Clar

WEBERN, ANTON VON (1883-1945)
  Lieder, 3, Op.18 I/IIC2

Trios — Gtr, Voice, A Rec

KUKUCK, FELICITAS (1914-   )
  Brucke, Die, Eine Kammermusik Nach
    Gedichten Aus "Die Chinesische
    Flote" Von Hans Bethge I/IIC2

REIN, WALTER (1893-1955)
  Vom Vielfaltigen Leben I/IIC2

Trios — Gtr, Voice, Rec

ALTE UND NEUE MUSIK ZUM SINGEN UND
  SPIELEN AUF BLOCKFLOTEN, GEIGEN UND
  LAUTENINSTRUMENTE I/IIC2-Coll

Trios — Gtr, Voice, Perc

BEHREND, SIEGFRIED (1933-   )
  Weihnachtsgeschichte IV/IIC2

YUN, ISANG (1917-   )
  Gagok I/IIC2

Trios — Gtr, Voice, Pno

DESSAU, PAUL (1894-1979)
  Tierverse Von Bertolt Brecht I/IIC2

SANCHEZ, BLAS
  Al Pie De La Cruz Del Roque I/IIC2

Trios— Gtr, Voice, Vln

SEIBER, MATYAS GYORGY (1905-1960)
  Owl And The Pussycat, The I/IIC2

Trios — Gtr, Voice, Vcl

DESSAU, PAUL (1894-1979)
  Tierverse Von Bertolt Brecht I/IIC2

PELEMANS, WILLEM (1901-   )
  Graf Van Verhaeren I/IIC2

Quartets — Gtr, 3 Voices

DIETRICH, CHRISTOPH
  Vorspruch Zu Einem Weihnachtsspiel
    IV/IIC3

SCHUBERT, FRANZ (PETER) (1797-1828)
  Kantate Zur Namensfeier Des Vaters
    I/IIC3

Quartets — Gtr, Voice, Fl, Harp

STRAVINSKY, IGOR (1882-1971)
Russian Songs, 4 I/IIC3

Quartets — 2 Gtr, Fl, Voice

BROQUA, ALFONSO (1876-1946)
Chants De l'Uruguay, 3 I/IIC3

Quartets — Gtr, Voice, Fl, Vla

TSOUYOPOULOS, GEORGES S. (1930-   )
Serenade I/IIC3

Quartets — Gtr, Voice, Bsn, Vln

MONTEVERDI, CLAUDIO (ca. 1567-1643)
Canzonette A Tre Voci, 3 I/IIC3

Quartets — Gtr, Voice, Rec, Perc

CLEMENT, NICOLE
Chanson Du Lundi, La I/IIC3

Quartets — Gtr, Voice, T Rec, Vla da Gamba

MONTEVERDI, CLAUDIO (ca. 1567-1643)
Canzonette A Tre Voci, 3 I/IIC3

Quartets — Gtr, Voice, DB, Pno

BLARR, OSKAR GOTTLIEB (1934-   )
Thema Weihnachten, 3 Chansons
IV/IIC3

Quartets — Gtr, Voice, Vln, Vla da Gamba

MONTEVERDI, CLAUDIO (ca. 1567-1643)
Canzonette A Tre Voci, 3 I/IIC3

Quartets — Gtr, Voice, Vla, Vcl

SEIBER, MATYAS GYORGY (1905-1960)
Medieval French Songs, 4 I/IIC3

Quartets — Gtr, Voice, Vla da Gamba, Vla D'amore

SEIBER, MATYAS GYORGY (1905-1960)
Medieval French Songs, 4 I/IIC3

Quartets with Elec. Tape

STAHMER, KLAUS H. (1941-   )
3 Paesaggi I/IIC3

Quintets — Gtr, 4 Voices

CHANTS DE FRANCE ET D'AILLEURS, 20
IV/IIC4

Quintets — Gtr, Voice, Fl, Perc, Pno

KOELLREUTTER, HANS-JOACHIM (JACOBO)
(1915-   )
Haikai Des Pedro Xisto, 8 I/IIC4

Quintets — Gtr, Voice, 3 Perc

FRITSCHE, VOLKMAR
Improvisations, Sur "L'Anabase" De
St.-John Perse I/IIC4

Quintets — Gtr, Voice, Vibra, Harp, Pno

TAKEMITSU, TORU (1930-   )
Stanza I I/IIC4

School Ens/Orch with Gtr, Voice

AUX MARCHES DU PALAIS I/IIC5-Coll

BLEUSE, MARC (1937-   )
Comptines Pour Anne, 3 I/IIC5

BONNAL, ERMEND
Enfant Crie En Galilee, Un IV/IIC5

Princes d'Orient, 3, Noel IV/IIC5

BRESGEN, CESAR (1913-   )
Christkindl-Kumedi, Ein Geistliches
Komodienspiel Aus Bayern IV/IIC5

Europe Curieuse, L', Eine Kuriose
Europa-Kantate Fur Kinder I/IIC5

Von Mausen, Autos Und Anderen Tieren;
25 Kinderlieder Zum Singen Und
Spielen I/IIC5

BUCHTGER, FRITZ (1903-1978)
Zirkus, Der, Kantate Und
Bewegungspiel I/IIC5

BURTHEL, JAKOB (1926-   )
Jahreswetteranzeiger "Willst Du Aufs
Wetter Im Jahr Achten" I/IIC5

CAMMIN, HEINZ (1923-   )
Lied Uber Die Grenze I/IIC5

COSSETTO, EMIL (1908-   )
Chants Yougoslaves, 4 [Nos. 1-3]
I/IIC5

DERLIEN, MARGARETE
Ich Trag Mein Licht, Ein Liederspiel
Zum Laternegehen I/IIC5

FORTNER, WOLFGANG (1907-   )
Cress Ertrinkt, Ein Schulspiel
I/IIC5

GEESE, HEINZ (1930-   )
Seefahrt Nach Rio, Die, Scenic
Cantata I/IIC5

Duets — 2 Guitars — Arranged

TARREGA, FRANCISCO (cont'd.)

Gran Jota De Concierto I/IIA1

Kompositionen Fur Gitarre, Vol. II
I/IIA1

Study, TI ii- 9, in A minor VI

TELEMANN, GEORG PHILIPP (1681-1767)
Sonata No. 6 I/IIA1

Sonate Im Kanon I/IIA1

TRANSKRYPCJE KLASYKOW I/IIA1-Coll

VILLA-LOBOS, HEITOR (1887-1959)
A Canoa Virou, Cirandinha No. 10
I/IIA1

VIVALDI, ANTONIO (1678-1741)
Andante in E minor I/IIA1

Aria Del Vagante I/IIA1

Concerto for Violin and Orchestra, RV
297, in F minor, Largo I/IIA1

Prelude, MIN 44 I/IIA1

WILLAERT, ADRIAN (ca. 1490-1562)
Ricercare No. 14 I/IIA1

Trios — 3 Guitars

ALBENIZ, ISAAC (1860-1909)
Bajo De La Palmera I/IIA2

ALTE POLNISCHE LAUTENMUSIK I/IIA2-Coll

ALTE UND NEUE MUSIK ZUM SINGEN UND
SPIELEN AUF BLOCKFLOTEN, GEIGEN UND
LAUTENINSTRUMENTE I/IIA2-Coll

BACH, JOHANN SEBASTIAN (1685-1750)
Cantata No. 212, [excerpt], [arr.]
VII

Suite for Keyboard Instrument, BWV
811, in D minor, Gavotte I VII

Suite for Keyboard Instrument, BWV
816, in G minor, Gigue VII

BEETHOVEN, LUDWIG VAN (1770-1827)
Minuet in G I/IIA2

BIZET, GEORGES (1838-1875)
Minuet, MIN 280 I/IIA2

Romance I/IIA2

BLOK, COBY
Speelboek Voor De Gitaargroepsles,
Vol. I IV/IIA2

Speelboek Voor De Gitaargroepsles,
Vol. II IV/IIA2

BOCCHERINI, LUIGI (1743-1805)
Beruhmtes Menuett I/IIA2

BYRD, WILLIAM (1543-1623)
Carman's Whistle, The I/IIA2

CANCIONES POPULARES MEXICANAS, 3
I/IIA2-Coll

CLEMENS, JACOBUS (CLEMENS NON PAPA)
(ca. 1510-ca. 1556)
Souterlied No. 99 I/IIA2

COUPERIN, FRANCOIS (LE GRAND)
(1668-1733)
Musette De Choisy I/IIA2

Musette De Taverny I/IIA2

DEUTSCHE VOLKSTANZE I/IIA2

FABER, JOHANN CHRISTIAN
Partita I/IIA2

FRANCESCO DA MILANO
(ca. 1497?-ca. 1573?)
Pavan I/IIA2

FRESCOBALDI, GIROLAMO (1583-1643)
Tanzstucke I/IIA2

GASTOLDI, GIOVANNI GIACOMO
(ca. 1556-1622)
6 Ballets I/IIA2

GITAAR-KAMERMUZIEK, VOL. 3: UIT HET
REPERTOIRE VAN HET JOEGOSLAVISCHE
DANSTHEATER I/IIA2-Coll

GITAAR-KAMERMUZIEK, VOL. 4: UIT HET
REPERTOIRE VAN HET JOEGOSLAVISCHE
DANSTHEATER I/IIA2-Coll

GIULIANI, MAURO (1781-1829)
Trio, Op. 71, No. 3 I/IIA2

GREENSLEEVES TO A GROUND I/IIA2

GUITARRA CANTORA, LA, MELODIAS
TRADICIONALES ARGENTINAS I/IIA2

HANDEL, GEORGE FRIDERIC (1685-1759)
Allegro I/IIA2

Chaconne I/IIA2

Sonata, MIN 46 I/IIA2

Tanze Aus Opern, 7 I/IIA2

HAYDN, [FRANZ] JOSEPH (1732-1809)
Trio, MIN 47 I/IIA2

HINDEMITH, PAUL (1895-1963)
Rondo I/IIA2

KANONS ZUM SINGEN UND SPIELEN
I/IIA2-Coll

KLINGENDE KLEINIGKEITEN AUS ALTER UND
NEUER ZEIT I/IIA2-Coll

KUFFNER, JOSEPH (1776-1856)
Ausgewahlte Ubungsstucke, 30 I/IIA2

LAUTENSPIELER DES XVI. JAHRHUNDERTS
(LIUTISTI DEL CINQUECENTO)
I/IIA2-Coll

LEICHTE STUCKE ALTER MEISTER
I/IIA2-Coll

LEICHTES ZUSAMMENSPIEL I/IIA2-Coll

LOGAN, FREDERICK KNIGHT (1871-1928)
Pale Moon I/IIA2

MELODY OF JAPAN BY GUITARS, VOL. I
I/IIA2-Coll

MELODY OF JAPAN BY GUITARS, VOL. II
I/IIA2-Coll

MONTEVERDI, CLAUDIO (ca. 1567-1643)
Canzoni, 3 I/IIA2

Scherzi, 3 I/IIA2

MOZART, WOLFGANG AMADEUS (1756-1791)
Adagio, MIN 212 I/IIA2

Minuet, MIN 214 I/IIA2

Serenade, MIN 213 I/IIA2

Wiener Sonatina I/IIA2

MUSIC FOR 3 GUITARS I/IIA2-Coll

MUSIK DER WIENER KLASSIK I/IIA2-Coll

MUSIQUE POUR 3 ET 4 GUITARES, VOL. 3 -
MUSIC FOR 3 AND 4 GUITARS, VOL. 3
I/IIA2-Coll

MUSIQUE POUR 3 ET 4 GUITARES, VOL. 4 -
MUSIC FOR 3 AND 4 GUITARS, VOL. 4
I/IIA2-Coll

PERGOLESI, GIOVANNI BATTISTA
(1710-1736)
Siciliana I/IIA2

PIECES FROM THE TIME OF QUEEN
ELIZABETH, 4 I/IIA2-Coll

POLYPHONES SPIELHEFT I/IIA2-Coll

PRAETORIUS, MICHAEL (1571-1621)
Puer Natus In Bethlehem [Collection]
IV/IIA2

SATZE ALTER MEISTER I/IIA2-Coll

SCHONSTEN LIEDER FUR UNSERE JUGEND, DIE
I/IIA2-Coll

SCHONSTEN WEISEN FUR UNSERE JUGEND, DIE
I/IIA2

SCHUBERT, FRANZ (PETER) (1797-1828)
Moment Musical I/IIA2

Sonatina I/IIA2

SONNE, KOMM, EIN GITARRESPIELBUCH FUR
KINDER, 1-4. UNTERRICHTSJAHR
I/IIA2-Coll

SOR, FERNANDO (1778-1839)
Andantino, Op. 54 [Sic] I/IIA2

SPIELBUCH FUR 3 GITARREN I/IIA2-Coll

SPIELHEFT KLASSIK FUR DREI GITARREN
I/IIA2-Coll

STUCKE ALTER MEISTER, 15 I/IIA2-Coll

SYT NU VERBLYT I/IIA2-Coll

TANZE UND STUCKE DER BAROCKZEIT
I/IIA2-Coll

VOLKSTANZE, 6 I/IIA2-Coll

VOLKSTANZE UND LIEDER I/IIA2-Coll

WIDMANN, ERASMUS (1572-1634)
Zwei Suiten I/IIA2

WITT, CHRISTIAN F. (1660-1716)
Suite I/IIA2

Quartets — 4 Guitars

ANONYMOUS
Romance D'Amour I/IIA3

APOSTEL, HANS ERICH (1901-1972)
Es Waren Zwei Konigskinder I/IIA3

Hohe Des Jahres I/IIA3

BELLMAN, CARL MICHAEL (1740-1795)
Bellman For 4 Gitarrer I/IIA3

BRUCHNER, RUDOLF
Quartettino I In C I/IIA3

CARULLI, FERDINANDO (1770-1841)
Quartet, Op. 21 I/IIA3

DAVID, JOHANN NEPOMUK (1895-1977)
Volksliedsatze I/IIA3

ELIZABETHAN PIECES, 5 I/IIA3-Coll

GITAAR-KAMERMUZIEK, VOL. 2 I/IIA3-Coll

GITAAR-KAMERMUZIEK, VOL. 4: UIT HET
REPERTOIRE VAN HET JOEGOSLAVISCHE
DANSTHEATER I/IIA3-Coll

GITARRKVARTETT I/IIA3-Coll

GUITAR ENSEMBLES I/IIA3-Coll

GUITARRA CANTORA, LA, MELODIAS
TRADICIONALES ARGENTINAS
I/IIA3-Coll

HEILLER, ANTON (1923-1979)
Es Liegt Ein Schloss In Osterreich
I/IIA3

Heidi Pupeidi I/IIA3

KANONS ZUM SINGEN UND SPIELEN
I/IIA3-Coll

KLINGENDE KLEINIGKEITEN AUS ALTER UND
NEUER ZEIT I/IIA3-Coll

LAUTENCHOR II, DER I/IIA3-Coll

LEKSANDS SKANKLAT I/IIA3

MELODY OF JAPAN BY GUITARS, VOL. I
I/IIA3-Coll

MELODY OF JAPAN BY GUITARS, VOL. II
I/IIA3-Coll

MUSIC FOR 4 GUITARS I/IIA3-Coll,
IV/IIA3

MUSIQUE POUR 3 ET 4 GUITARES, VOL. 1
(MUSIC FOR 3 AND 4 GUITARS, VOL. 1)
I/IIA3-Coll

MUSIQUE POUR 3 ET 4 GUITARES, VOL. 2
(MUSIC FOR 3 AND 4 GUITARS, VOL. 2)
I/IIA3-Coll

MUSIQUE POUR 3 ET 4 GUITARES, VOL. 3 -
MUSIC FOR 3 AND 4 GUITARS, VOL. 3
I/IIA3-Coll

MUSIQUE POUR 3 ET 4 GUITARES, VOL. 4 -
MUSIC FOR 3 AND 4 GUITARS, VOL. 4
I/IIA3-Coll

POLYPHONES SPIELHEFT   I/IIA3-Coll

PRAETORIUS, MICHAEL (1571-1621)
    4 French Dances I/IIA3

    Puer Natus In Bethlehem [Collection]
        IV/IIA3

REISEBILDER AUS FRANKREICH, 5 I/IIA3

SCHUBERT, FRANZ (PETER) (1797-1828)
    Momento Musicale I/IIA3

SONNE, KOMM, EIN GITARRESPIELBUCH FUR
    KINDER, 1-4. UNTERRICHTSJAHR
    IV/IIA3

SOR, FERNANDO (1778-1839)
    Sonata, Op. 15, No. 2, in C I/IIA3

SPUNTI CLASSICI, 4 I/IIA3-Coll

SUSATO, TIELMAN (? -ca. 1561)
    Pieces, 5 I/IIA3

    Tanze, 7 I/IIA3

TARREGA, FRANCISCO (1852-1909)
    Study, TI ii- 9, in A minor VI

TCHAIKOVSKY, PIOTR ILYICH (1840-1893)
    Pieces, 3 I/IIA3

TELEMANN, GEORG PHILIPP (1681-1767)
    Konzert I/IIA3

TITTEL, ERNST (1910-1969)
    O, Du Lieber Augustin I/IIA3

WIDMANN, ERASMUS (1572-1634)
    Suite No. 1 I/IIA3

    Zwei Suiten I/IIA3

Quintets — 5 Guitars

AIN BOER I/IIA4

GITAAR-KAMERMUZIEK, VOL. 3: UIT HET
    REPERTOIRE VAN HET JOEGOSLAVISCHE
    DANSTHEATER I/IIA4-Coll

LAUTENCHOR II, DER I/IIA4-Coll

WIDMANN, ERASMUS (1572-1634)
    Suite No. 1 I/IIA4

Duets — Gtr, Fl

ALTE MEISTER UM 1600 I/IIB1-Coll

ALTE MEISTER UM 1700 I/IIB1-Coll

BACH, JOHANN SEBASTIAN (1685-1750)
    Sonata for Flute and Continuo, BWV
        1033, in C VII

    Sonata for Flute and Keyboard
        Instrument, BWV 1035, in E
        I/IIB1, VII

    Suite for Orchestra, BWV 1067, in B
        minor, Badinerie VII

BARLOW, FRED (1881-1951)
    Pavan I/IIB1

BEETHOVEN, LUDWIG VAN (1770-1827)
    Sonatina, MIN 48 I/IIB1

BERUHMTE STUCKE, 3 I/IIB1-Coll

BLAVET, MICHEL (1700-1768)
    8 Pieces I/IIB1

CAMPRA, ANDRE (1660-1744)
    Menuet Vif Et Gigue I/IIB1

CAROSO, FABRIZIO (1526-1600)
    Balletto I/IIB1

COUPERIN, FRANCOIS (LE GRAND)
        (1668-1733)
    Petits Moulins A Vent, Les I/IIB1

FISCHER, JOHANN CASPAR FERDINAND
        (ca. 1665-1746)
    Leichte Stucke, 8 I/IIB1

GRETRY, ANDRE ERNEST MODESTE
        (1741-1813)
    Entr'acte I/IIB1

HANDEL, GEORGE FRIDERIC (1685-1759)
    Air Mit Variationen I/IIB1

    Leichte Stucke, 8 I/IIB1

    Sonata in A minor, Op. 1, No. 4
        I/IIB1

    Sonata in D I/IIB1

    Sonata in D minor I/IIB1

    Sonata in E minor, MIN 344 I/IIB1

    Sonata No. 2 in G minor I/IIB1

HASSE, JOHANN ADOLPH (1699-1783)
    Sonaten, 12, Op. 1 I/IIB1

LAUFFENSTEINER, WOLFF JACOB
    Sonata in A I/IIB1

LOCATELLI, PIETRO (1695-1764)
    Sonata in D I/IIB1

    Sonata in G I/IIB1

    Sonata No. 2 I/IIB1

LOEILLET, JEAN-BAPTISTE (JOHN, OF
        LONDON) (1680-1730)
    Suite in E minor I/IIB1

MACE, THOMAS (1613?-1709)
    Prelude I/IIB1

MAGANINI, QUINTO (1897-1974)
    Romanesca, La, An Ancient Italian
        Dance Air Of The 16th Century
        I/IIB1

MAGYAR ZENE GITARRA A XIX. SZADAD ELSO
    FELEBOL I/IIB1-Coll

MARCELLO, BENEDETTO (1686-1739)
    Sonata in C, Op. 2, No. 6 I/IIB1

MOZART, WOLFGANG AMADEUS (1756-1791)
    Kleine Stucke, 4 I/IIB1

PEPUSCH, JOHN CHRISTOPHER (1667-1752)
    Sonata, MIN 51 I/IIB1

    Sonaten, 3 I/IIB1

PERGOLESI, GIOVANNI BATTISTA
        (1710-1736)
    Siciliano I/IIB1

PURCELL, DANIEL (ca. 1660-1717)
    Sonata in F I/IIB1

RATHGEBER, VALENTIN (1682-1750)
    Leichte Stucke, 6 I/IIB1

REGI ZENE I/IIB1-Coll

REICHARDT, JOHANN FRIEDRICH (1752-1814)
    6 Stucke I/IIB1

REUSSNER, ESAIAS (1636-1679)
    Musicalische Gesellschaftsergetzung
        I/IIB1

SAMMARTINI, GIUSEPPE
        (ca. 1693-ca. 1770)
    Sonata, Op. 3, No. 1, in E minor
        I/IIB1

    Sonata, Op. 3, No. 2, in G I/IIB1

SUIT I SVENSK FOLKTON NR. 2
    I/IIB1-Coll

TELEMANN, GEORG PHILIPP (1681-1767)
    Partita in G I/IIB1

    Sonata in A minor I/IIB1

VERACINI, FRANCESCO MARIA (1690-1768)
    Largo I/IIB1

VISEE, ROBERT DE (ca. 1650-ca. 1775)
    Suite in C minor I/IIB1

VOLKSLIEDER UND -TANZE AUS ALLER WELT,
    VOL. 1 I/IIB1-Coll

VOLKSLIEDER UND -TANZE AUS ALLER WELT,
    VOL. 2 I/IIB1-Coll

VOLKSLIEDER UND -TANZE AUS ALLER WELT,
    VOL. 3 I/IIB1-Coll

WANHAL, JOHANN BAPTIST (JAN KRTITEL)
        (1739-1813)
    6 Variationen Uber Das Thema "Nel Cor
        Piu Non Mi Sento" I/IIB1

WIDMANN, ERASMUS (1572-1634)
    Musicalischer Tugendspiegel I/IIB1

Duets — Gtr, Ob

ALTE MEISTER UM 1600 I/IIB1-Coll

ALTE MEISTER UM 1700 I/IIB1-Coll

CALDARA, ANTONIO (1670-1736)
    Sonata in A minor I/IIB1

CAMPRA, ANDRE (1660-1744)
    Menuet Vif Et Gigue I/IIB1

COUPERIN, FRANCOIS (LE GRAND)
        (1668-1733)
    Petits Moulins A Vent, Les I/IIB1

FISCHER, JOHANN CASPAR FERDINAND
        (ca. 1665-1746)
    Leichte Stucke, 8 I/IIB1

    March I/IIB1

HANDEL, GEORGE FRIDERIC (1685-1759)
    Air Mit Variationen I/IIB1

    Leichte Stucke, 8 I/IIB1

    Siciliana I/IIB1

    Sonata in A minor, Op. 1, No. 4
        I/IIB1

    Sonata in D I/IIB1

    Sonata in D minor I/IIB1

KONINK, SERVAAS DE (KONING)
        (ca. 1660-ca. 1720)
    Sonata I/IIB1

LAUFFENSTEINER, WOLFF JACOB
    Sonata in A I/IIB1

LEOPOLD I, HOLY ROMAN EMPEROR
        (1640-1705)
    Balletti I/IIB1

LOCATELLI, PIETRO (1695-1764)
    Sonata in D I/IIB1

    Sonata in G I/IIB1

    Sonata No. 2 I/IIB1

LOEILLET, JEAN-BAPTISTE (JOHN, OF
        LONDON) (1680-1730)
    Sonata in A minor, Op. 1, No. 1
        I/IIB1

    Sonata in G, Op. 1, No. 3 I/IIB1

PEPUSCH, JOHN CHRISTOPHER (1667-1752)
    Sonata in G I/IIB1

    Sonata, MIN 51 I/IIB1

    Stucke, 4 I/IIB1

PERGOLESI, GIOVANNI BATTISTA
        (1710-1736)
    Siciliano I/IIB1

RATHGEBER, VALENTIN (1682-1750)
    Leichte Stucke, 6 I/IIB1

TELEMANN, GEORG PHILIPP (1681-1767)
    Partita in G I/IIB1

    Partita No. 5 in E minor I/IIB1

Duets — Gtr, Clar

MAGANINI, QUINTO (1897-1974)
Romanesca, La, An Ancient Italian
Dance Air Of The 16th Century
I/IIB1

Duets — Gtr, Bsn

GOEPFERT, KARL ANDREAS (1768-1818)
Sonata, Op. 13 I/IIB1

Duets — Gtr, Cornetto

MARINI, BIAGIO (ca. 1595-1665)
Sonata I/IIB1

Duets — Gtr, S Rec

AIRS POPULAIRES DE TCHECOSLOVAQUI
I/IIB1

ALTE MEISTER UM 1600 I/IIB1-Coll

ALTE MEISTER UM 1700 I/IIB1-Coll

ALTE SPIELMUSIK I/IIB1-Coll

ALTE TANZSTUCKE (16.-18. JAHRHUNDERT),
VOL. I I/IIB1-Coll

ANONYMOUS
Greensleeves To A Ground I/IIB1

Suite in F I/IIB1

BAROCKE SPIELMUSIK I/IIB1-Coll

BAROQUE PIECES, VOL. V I/IIB1-Coll

BARTOK, BELA (1881-1945)
Aus Ungarn Und Der Slowakei, Lieder
Und Tanze, Vol. I I/IIB1

DANCES FROM SHAKESPEARE'S TIME
I/IIB1-Coll

DUOS POUR FLUTE A BEC ET GUITARE
I/IIB1-Coll

EARLY RENAISSANCE DANCES, 6
I/IIB1-Coll

EUROPAISCHE VOLKSTANZE I/IIB1-Coll

FISCHER, JOHANN CASPAR FERDINAND
(ca. 1665-1746)
Leichte Stucke, 8 I/IIB1

March I/IIB1

FOLKLORE, VOL. 1 I/IIB1-Coll

FOLKLORE, VOL. 2 I/IIB1-Coll

FROHLICHE TANZE AUS DEM 18. UND 19.
JAHRHUNDERT I/IIB1-Coll

HASSE, JOHANN ADOLPH (1699-1783)
Sonaten, 12, Op. 1 I/IIB1

INMITTEN DER NACHT, WEIHNACHTLICHE
SPIELMUSIK IV/IIB1

KLEINE TANZE UND MARSCHE VON HAYDN BIS
STRAUSS I/IIB1-Coll

MELODIES POPULAIRES POLONAISES
I/IIB1-Coll

PLAYFORD, JOHN (1623-1686)
Playford Tunes, 12 I/IIB1

RATHGEBER, VALENTIN (1682-1750)
Leichte Stucke, 6 I/IIB1

Nobilissima Musica, Von Der Edlen
Musik I/IIB1

SAMMARTINI, GIUSEPPE
(ca. 1693-ca. 1770)
Sonata, Op. 3, No. 1, in E minor
I/IIB1

Sonata, Op. 3, No. 2, in G I/IIB1

SINTERKLAAS- EN KERSTLIEDJES
I/IIB1-Coll

SPEELMATERIAAL VOOR DE BLOKFLUIT, VOL.
III I/IIB1-Coll

SPIELMANN AUS FLANDERN, DER
I/IIB1-Coll

SPIELMUSIK FUR MELODIEINSTRUMENTE UND
GITARRE, 16-19TH CENTURY
I/IIB1-Coll

SPIELSTUCKE FUR BLOCKFLOTE UND GITARRE,
AUS DEM 17. UND 18. JAHRHUNDERT
I/IIB1-Coll

SULLIVAN, [SIR] ARTHUR SEYMOUR
(1842-1900)
Tunes From Gilbert And Sullivan, 10
I/IIB1

TAKE YOUR PARTNERS; 6 ENGLISH COUNTRY
DANCES I/IIB1-Coll

TELEMANN, GEORG PHILIPP (1681-1767)
Partita in G I/IIB1

VIVALDI, ANTONIO (1678-1741)
Sonata, Op. 13a, No. 16, in G minor
I/IIB1

VON HANDEL BIS HAYDN I/IIB1-Coll

Duets — Gtr, A Rec

ALTE TANZSTUCKE (16.-18. JAHRHUNDERT),
VOL. II I/IIB1-Coll

ANONYMOUS
Greensleeves To A Ground I/IIB1

Suite in D minor, MIN 331 I/IIB1

Suite in G minor, MIN 329 I/IIB1

AUS ALT ENGLAND I/IIB1-Coll

BAROQUE PIECES, VOL. VI I/IIB1-Coll

BARRETT, JOHN
Air I/IIB1

BULL, JOHN (ca. 1562-1628)
Pieces, 4 I/IIB1

DANCES OF BYGONE TIMES, 6 I/IIB1-Coll

DUOS POUR FLUTE A BEC ET GUITARE
I/IIB1-Coll

FOLKSONGS I/IIB1-Coll

FROM THE BRITISH ISLES I/IIB1-Coll

HANDEL, GEORGE FRIDERIC (1685-1759)
Leichte Stucke, 8 I/IIB1

Siciliana I/IIB1

Sonata in A minor, Op. 1, No. 4
I/IIB1

Sonata in C I/IIB1

HANDEL, GEORGE FRIDERIC (cont'd.)

Sonata in D minor I/IIB1

Sonata in F, Op. 1, No. 11 I/IIB1

Sonata No. 2 in G minor I/IIB1

HASSE, JOHANN ADOLPH (1699-1783)
Sonaten, 12, Op. 1 I/IIB1

INMITTEN DER NACHT, WEIHNACHTLICHE
SPIELMUSIK IV/IIB1

KONINK, SERVAAS DE (KONING)
(ca. 1660-ca. 1720)
Sonata I/IIB1

LOEILLET, JEAN-BAPTISTE (JOHN, OF
LONDON) (1680-1730)
Sonata in A minor, Op. 1, No. 1
I/IIB1

Sonata in G, Op. 1, No. 3 I/IIB1

ORTIZ, DIEGO (ca. 1525- ?)
Recercaden, 4 I/IIB1

PEPUSCH, JOHN CHRISTOPHER (1667-1752)
Beggar's Opera, The I/IIB1

Sonata in D minor I/IIB1

Sonata in G I/IIB1

Sonaten, 3 I/IIB1

PIECES, 5 I/IIB1

PIECES FROM THE MULLINER BOOK, 10
I/IIB1-Coll

PURCELL, DANIEL (ca. 1660-1717)
Sonata in F I/IIB1

PURCELL, HENRY (1658 or 59-1695)
Suite I/IIB1

SAMMARTINI, GIUSEPPE
(ca. 1693-ca. 1770)
Sonata, Op. 3, No. 1, in E minor
I/IIB1

Sonata, Op. 3, No. 2, in G I/IIB1

SIMPLE FOLK I/IIB1-Coll

SPIELMUSIK FUR MELODIEINSTRUMENTE UND
GITARRE, 16-19TH CENTURY
I/IIB1-Coll

TELEMANN, GEORG PHILIPP (1681-1767)
Sonata in F I/IIB1

Sonaten, 2 I/IIB1

VERACINI, FRANCESCO MARIA (1690-1768)
Sonata No. 3 I/IIB1

Duets — Gtr, T Rec

ALTE SPIELMUSIK I/IIB1-Coll

ALTE TANZSTUCKE (16.-18. JAHRHUNDERT),
VOL. I I/IIB1-Coll

DUOS POUR FLUTE A BEC ET GUITARE
I/IIB1-Coll

HANDEL, GEORGE FRIDERIC (1685-1759)
Siciliana I/IIB1

INMITTEN DER NACHT, WEIHNACHTLICHE
SPIELMUSIK IV/IIB1

SPIELSTUCKE FUR BLOCKFLOTE UND GITARRE,
AUS DEM 17. UND 18. JAHRHUNDERT
I/IIB1-Coll

VON HANDEL BIS HAYDN I/IIB1-Coll

Duets — Gtr, Rec

ANONYMOUS
  Englische Tanze, 3 I/IIB1

BACH, JOHANN SEBASTIAN (1685-1750)
  Suite for Orchestra, BWV 1067, in B
    minor, Badinerie VII

BLAVET, MICHEL (1700-1768)
  8 Pieces I/IIB1

CALDARA, ANTONIO (1670-1736)
  Sonata in A minor I/IIB1

DUOS POUR FLUTE A BEC ET GUITARE
  I/IIB1-Coll

FLOTE SING, KLAMPFE KLING IV/IIB1,
  I/IIB1-Coll

INMITTEN DER NACHT, WEIHNACHTLICHE
  SPIELMUSIK IV/IIB1

KOCH, HANS
  Musizierbuchlein, Ein, Einfuhrung In
    Das Mehrstimmige Spiel Nach
    Volkstanzen Und Liedern Aus Dem
    Alpenraum I/IIB1

LEOPOLD I, HOLY ROMAN EMPEROR
    (1640-1705)
  Balletti I/IIB1

MAINERIO, GIORGIO
  5 Danze I/IIB1

MARCELLO, BENEDETTO (1686-1739)
  Sonata in C, Op. 2, No. 6 I/IIB1

MOZART, LEOPOLD (1719-1787)
  Tanze, 6, Aus Dem Notenbuchlein Fur
    Wolfgang I/IIB1

NOUVEAUX DUOS, 32 [SIC] PIECES...
  IV/IIB1, I/IIB1-Coll

PEPUSCH, JOHN CHRISTOPHER (1667-1752)
  Stucke, 4 I/IIB1

REGI ZENE I/IIB1-Coll

SIX PIECES FROM THE TIME OF ELIZABETH
  I/IIB1-Coll

SPIELSTUCKE FUR BLOCKFLOTE UND GITARRE,
  AUS DEM 17. UND 18. JAHRHUNDERT
  I/IIB1-Coll

SPIELSTUCKE FUR BLOCKFLOTE UND GITARRE,
  VOL. 1 I/IIB1-Coll

SPIELSTUCKE FUR BLOCKFLOTE UND GITARRE,
  VOL. 2 I/IIB1-Coll

TELEMANN, GEORG PHILIPP (1681-1767)
  Air Und Bourree I/IIB1

  Partita No. 5 in E minor I/IIB1

  Sonata in C I/IIB1

TUNES FROM THE CECIL SHARP COLLECTION,
  7 I/IIB1-Coll

VISEE, ROBERT DE (ca. 1650-ca. 1775)
  Suite in C minor I/IIB1

YA SE VAN LOS PASTORES IV/IIB1,
  I/IIB1-Coll

Duets — Gtr, Hpsd

BOCCHERINI, LUIGI (1743-1805)
  Introduction And Fandango I/IIB1

VIVALDI, ANTONIO (1678-1741)
  Concerto in D, MIN 328 I/IIB1

Duets — Gtr, Pno

VIVALDI, ANTONIO (1678-1741)
  Concerto in D, MIN 328 I/IIB1

WAGENSEIL, GEORG CHRISTOPH (1715-1777)
  Divertimento I/IIB1

Duets — Gtr, Acord

SOSINSKI, KAZIMIERZ
  Studium Gry Akordowej Na Gitarze,
    Technika Chwytow Barre, Akordy I
    Ich Symbole I/IIB1

Duets — Gtr, Mando

BEETHOVEN, LUDWIG VAN (1770-1827)
  Andante Mit Variationen I/IIB1

HANDEL, GEORGE FRIDERIC (1685-1759)
  Alte Zupfmusik I/IIB1

MOZART, WOLFGANG AMADEUS (1756-1791)
  Deutsche Tanze, 6 I/IIB1

SOSINSKI, KAZIMIERZ
  Studium Gry Akordowej Na Gitarze,
    Technika Chwytow Barre, Akordy I
    Ich Symbole I/IIB1

VOLKSLIEDER UND -TANZE AUS ALLER WELT,
  VOL. 1 I/IIB1

VOLKSLIEDER UND -TANZE AUS ALLER WELT,
  VOL. 2 I/IIB1

VOLKSLIEDER UND -TANZE AUS ALLER WELT,
  VOL. 3 I/IIB1

Duets — Gtr, Vln

ALTE MEISTER UM 1600 I/IIB1-Coll

ALTE MEISTER UM 1700 I/IIB1-Coll

ALTE TANZSTUCKE (16.-18. JAHRHUNDERT),
  VOL. I I/IIB1-Coll

ALTE TANZSTUCKE (16.-18. JAHRHUNDERT),
  VOL. II I/IIB1-Coll

ALTFRANZOSISCHE MEISTER I/IIB1-Coll

BACH, J.C.
  Sonata for Violin and Guitar I/IIB1

BACH, JOHANN SEBASTIAN (1685-1750)
  Sonata for Flute and Continuo, BWV
    1033, in C VII

BEETHOVEN, LUDWIG VAN (1770-1827)
  Allegro I/IIB1

  Sonatina, MIN 48 I/IIB1

  Theme and Variations, MIN 218 I/IIB1

BERUHMTE STUCKE, 3 I/IIB1-Coll

CALDARA, ANTONIO (1670-1736)
  Sonata in A minor I/IIB1

  Sonata in E minor I/IIB1

CORELLI, ARCANGELO (1653-1713)
  Sonata for Violin and Guitar in E
    minor, Op. 5, No. 8 I/IIB1

  Sonata for Violin and Guitar, Op. 5,
    No. 7, in D minor I/IIB1

FERRONATI, LODOVICO
  Sonata in C I/IIB1

FIOCCO, JOSEPH-HECTOR (1703-1741)
  Allegro I/IIB1

FISCHER, JOHANN CASPAR FERDINAND
    (ca. 1665-1746)
  Leichte Stucke, 8 I/IIB1

  March I/IIB1

HANDEL, GEORGE FRIDERIC (1685-1759)
  Air Mit Variationen I/IIB1

  Leichte Stucke, 8 I/IIB1

  Siciliana I/IIB1

  Sonata in A I/IIB1

  Sonata in A minor, Op. 1, No. 4
    I/IIB1

  Sonata in D I/IIB1

  Sonata in D minor I/IIB1

HAYDN, [FRANZ] JOSEPH (1732-1809)
  Menuette, 22 I/IIB1

KONINK, SERVAAS DE (KONING)
    (ca. 1660-ca. 1720)
  Sonata I/IIB1

LAUFFENSTEINER, WOLFF JACOB
  Sonata in A I/IIB1

LEOPOLD I, HOLY ROMAN EMPEROR
    (1640-1705)
  Balletti I/IIB1

LOCATELLI, PIETRO (1695-1764)
  Sinfonia I/IIB1

  Sonata in D I/IIB1

  Sonata in G I/IIB1

  Sonata No. 2 I/IIB1

LOEILLET, JEAN-BAPTISTE (JOHN, OF
    LONDON) (1680-1730)
  Sonata in A minor, Op. 1, No. 1
    I/IIB1

  Sonata in G, Op. 1, No. 3 I/IIB1

MACE, THOMAS (1613?-1709)
    Prelude I/IIB1

MARINI, BIAGIO (ca. 1595-1665)
    Sonata I/IIB1

METZNER, LEONHARD
    Sonata I/IIB1

MOZART, WOLFGANG AMADEUS (1756-1791)
    Deutsche Tanze, 6 I/IIB1

    Wiener Sonatine I/IIB1

PEPUSCH, JOHN CHRISTOPHER (1667-1752)
    Sonata in G I/IIB1

    Sonaten, 3 I/IIB1

    Stucke, 4 I/IIB1

PURCELL, DANIEL (ca. 1660-1717)
    Sonata in F I/IIB1

RATHGEBER, VALENTIN (1682-1750)
    Leichte Stucke, 6 I/IIB1

REICHARDT, JOHANN FRIEDRICH (1752-1814)
    Sonata for Violin and Guitar in B
        flat I/IIB1

SAMMARTINI, GIUSEPPE
    (ca. 1693-ca. 1770)
    Sonata, Op. 3, No. 1, in E minor
        I/IIB1

    Sonata, Op. 3, No. 2, in G I/IIB1

SCHALLER, ERWIN (1901-   )
    Rhapsodie Und Hochzeitstanz Nach
        Finnischen Volksweisen I/IIB1

SOR, FERNANDO (1778-1839)
    Romanesca, La I/IIB1

SOSINSKI, KAZIMIERZ
    Studium Gry Akordowej Na Gitarze,
        Technika Chwytow Barre, Akordy I
        Ich Symbole I/IIB1

TELEMANN, GEORG PHILIPP (1681-1767)
    Partita in G I/IIB1

    Partita No. 5 in E minor I/IIB1

VERACINI, FRANCESCO MARIA (1690-1768)
    Largo I/IIB1

VISEE, ROBERT DE (ca. 1650-ca. 1775)
    Suite in C minor I/IIB1

VIVALDI, ANTONIO (1678-1741)
    Sonata in D minor I/IIB1

    Sonata in G minor I/IIB1

VOLKSLIEDER UND -TANZE AUS ALLER WELT,
    VOL. 1 I/IIB1

VOLKSLIEDER UND -TANZE AUS ALLER WELT,
    VOL. 2 I/IIB1

VOLKSLIEDER UND -TANZE AUS ALLER WELT,
    VOL. 3 I/IIB1

WANHAL, JOHANN BAPTIST (JAN KRTITEL)
    (1739-1813)
    6 Variationen Uber Das Thema "Nel Cor
        Piu Non Mi Sento" I/IIB1

WIR SINGEN UND SPIELEN, VOL. 1
    I/IIB1-Coll

WIR SINGEN UND SPIELEN, VOL. 2
    I/IIB1-Coll

ZOTTI, GIOVANNI DE
    Sonata in A minor I/IIB1

Duets — Gtr, Vla

BEETHOVEN, LUDWIG VAN (1770-1827)
    Allegro I/IIB1

LAUFFENSTEINER, WOLFF JACOB
    Sonata in A I/IIB1

MARCELLO, BENEDETTO (1686-1739)
    Sonata in G I/IIB1

TELEMANN, GEORG PHILIPP (1681-1767)
    Sonata in A minor, MIN 50 I/IIB1

Duets — Gtr, Vla da Gamba

HAYDN, [FRANZ] JOSEPH (1732-1809)
    Menuette, 22 I/IIB1

HESSE, ERNST CHRISTIAN (1676-1762)
    Duo I/IIB1

Duets — Gtr, Baryton

HAYDN, [FRANZ] JOSEPH (1732-1809)
    Menuette, 22 I/IIB1

Duets — Gtr, Vcl

HESSE, ERNST CHRISTIAN (1676-1762)
    Duo I/IIB1

Duets — Gtr, Treb Inst

ALBINONI, TOMASO (1671-1750)
    Sonata in A minor I/IIB1

ALTE MINNELIEDER I/IIB1-Coll

ALTE SPIELMUSIK I/IIB1-Coll

C-MUSIK DER ENGLISCHEN KLASSIK
    I/IIB1-Coll

FROHLICHE TANZE AUS DEM 18. UND 19.
    JAHRHUNDERT I/IIB1

HANDEL, GEORGE FRIDERIC (1685-1759)
    Suite, MIN 49 I/IIB1

LAUTENSPIELER DES XVI. JAHRHUNDERTS
    (LIUTISTI DEL CINQUECENTO)
    I/IIB1-Coll

LEOPOLD I, HOLY ROMAN EMPEROR
    (1640-1705)
    Suite, Aus Einer Sammlung Von Tanzen
        I/IIB1

MARCELLO, BENEDETTO (1686-1739)
    Adagio, MIN 38 I/IIB1

MUSIK AUS ITALIEN I/IIB1-Coll

NEUES SPIELBUCHLEIN I/IIB1-Coll

SOSINSKI, KAZIMIERZ
    Studium Gry Akordowej Na Gitarze,
        Technika Chwytow Barre, Akordy I
        Ich Symbole I/IIB1

SPERONTES (JOHANN SIGISMUND SCHOLZE)
    (1705-1750)
    Singende Muse An Der Pleisse I/IIB1

SPIELBUCHLEIN I/IIB1-Coll

UNSERE WEIHNACHTSLIEDER IV/IIB1

VALERIUS, ADRIANUS (1575-1625)
    Gedenckklanken-ABC I/IIB1

VISEE, ROBERT DE (ca. 1650-ca. 1775)
    Suite in C minor I/IIB1

VOLKSLIEDER UND -TANZE AUS ALLER WELT,
    VOL. 1 I/IIB1

VOLKSLIEDER UND -TANZE AUS ALLER WELT,
    VOL. 2 I/IIB1

VOLKSLIEDER UND -TANZE AUS ALLER WELT,
    VOL. 3 I/IIB1

WEIHNACHTSLIEDER AUS DEUTSCHLAND UND
    OSTERREICH IV/IIB1

WIR SINGEN UND SPIELEN, VOL. 1
    I/IIB1-Coll

WIR SINGEN UND SPIELEN, VOL. 2
    I/IIB1-Coll

Trios — Gtr, 2 Fl

BONONCINI, GIOVANNI (1670-1747)
    Trio Sonata Nos. 1-5 I/IIB2

HOTTETERRE, JACQUES (MARTIN)
    (ca. 1684-1762)
    2 Trio Sonatas I/IIB2

SCHUBERT, FRANZ (PETER) (1797-1828)
    Beliebte Walzer Und Moment Musical
        I/IIB2

Trios — Gtr, Fl, Ob

LULLY, JEAN-BAPTISTE (LULLI)
    (1632-1687)
    Tanze, 4 I/IIB2

Trios — 2 Gtr, Fl

HAYDN, [FRANZ] JOSEPH (1732-1809)
    Serenade I/IIB2

    Trio, MIN 47 I/IIB2

Trios — Gtr, Fl, Vln

HASSE, JOHANN ADOLPH (1699-1783)
    Trio Sonata in C I/IIB2

LULLY, JEAN-BAPTISTE (LULLI)
    (1632-1687)
    Tanze, 4 I/IIB2

MOZART, WOLFGANG AMADEUS (1756-1791)
    Flotenuhrstuck I/IIB2

TELEMANN, GEORG PHILIPP (1681-1767)
    Trio Sonata in E I/IIB2

Trios — Gtr, Fl, Vcl

LOTTI, ANTONIO (1667-1740)
  Sonata, MIN 54   I/IIB2

Trios — Gtr, 2 Ob

HOTTETERRE, JACQUES (MARTIN)
     (ca. 1684-1762)
  2 Trio Sonatas   I/IIB2

Trios — Gtr, Ob, Vln

LULLY, JEAN-BAPTISTE (LULLI)
     (1632-1687)
  Tanze, 4   I/IIB2

SCHICKHARDT, JOHANN CHRISTIAN
     (1670-1740)
  Trio Sonata in F   I/IIB2

TELEMANN, GEORG PHILIPP (1681-1767)
  Trio Sonata in E minor   I/IIB2

Trios — Gtr, 2 S Rec

AIRS POPULAIRES DE TCHECOSLOVAQUI
     I/IIB2

AUS BOHMEN UND SCHLESIEN   I/IIB2-Coll

31 BEKANNTE MELODIEN   I/IIB2-Coll

BONONCINI, GIOVANNI (1670-1747)
  Trio Sonata Nos. 1-5   I/IIB2

DANCES FROM SHAKESPEARE'S TIME
     I/IIB2-Coll

DEUTSCHE VOLKSTANZE, 2. TEIL
     I/IIB2-Coll

KLASSISCHE TANZWEISEN, VON HAYDN BIS
     SCHUBERT, VOL. 1   I/IIB2-Coll

KLASSISCHE TANZWEISEN, VON HAYDN BIS
     SCHUBERT, VOL.2   I/IIB2-Coll

MELODIES POPULAIRES POLONAISES
     I/IIB2-Coll

MOZART, WOLFGANG AMADEUS (1756-1791)
  Kontratanze Und Menuette   I/IIB2

ST. MARTINS-LIEDER   I/IIB2-Coll

SPIELMANN AUS FLANDERN, DER
     I/IIB2-Coll

TANZE AUS DEN ALPENLANDERN   I/IIB2-Coll

TELEMANN, GEORG PHILIPP (1681-1767)
  Trio Sonata in F   I/IIB2

VOLKSWEISEN UND TANZE AUS ARGENTINIEN
     I/IIB2-Coll

Trios — Gtr, S Rec, A Rec

BACH, JOHANN SEBASTIAN (1685-1750)
  Cantata No. 212, [excerpt], [arr.]
     VII

BARTOK, BELA (1881-1945)
  Aus Ungarn Und Der Slowakei, Lieder
     Und Tanze, Vol. II   I/IIB2

BIALAS, GUNTER (1907-   )
  Spanische Romanzen   IV/IIB2

CAROLS FOR PLAYING WITH GUITAR
     ACCOMPANIMENT   IV/IIB2

DANCES FROM SHAKESPEARE'S TIME
     I/IIB2-Coll

DEUTSCHE VOLKSTANZE, 2. TEIL
     I/IIB2-Coll

DREISTIMMIGE SPIELSTUCKE, 16
     I/IIB2-Coll

FROHLICH MUSIZIEREN, EIN   I/IIB2-Coll

KLASSISCHE TANZWEISEN, VON HAYDN BIS
     SCHUBERT, VOL. 1   I/IIB2-Coll

KLASSISCHE TANZWEISEN, VON HAYDN BIS
     SCHUBERT, VOL.2   I/IIB2-Coll

SCHMICERER, JOHANN ABRAHAM
     (fl. ca. 1680)
  10 Stucke   I/IIB2

SPIELMUSIK FUR MELODIEINSTRUMENTE UND
     GITARRE, 16-19TH CENTURY
     I/IIB2-Coll

SPRUNGE, DIE 4 - LES 4 SAUTS,
     FRANZOSISCHE VOLKSTANZE, 1. TEIL
     I/IIB2

TANZE AUS DEN ALPENLANDERN   I/IIB2-Coll

TANZSATZE   I/IIB2-Coll

TELEMANN, GEORG PHILIPP (1681-1767)
  Trio Sonata in C   I/IIB2

  Trio Sonata in F   I/IIB2

Trios — Gtr, S Rec, B Rec

PRAETORIUS, MICHAEL (1571-1621)
  Tanze   I/IIB2

Trios — Gtr, S Rec, Vla da Gamba

CABEZON, ANTONIO DE (1510-1566)
  Diferencias Sobre La Gallarda
     Milanesa (1572)   I/IIB2

PRAETORIUS, MICHAEL (1571-1621)
  Tanze   I/IIB2

SPERONTES (JOHANN SIGISMUND SCHOLZE)
     (1705-1750)
  Singende Muse An Der Pleisse   I/IIB2

Trios — Gtr, 2 A Rec

BOISMORTIER, JOSEPH BODIN DE
     (1689-1755)
  Carillon   I/IIB2

CORELLI, ARCANGELO (1653-1713)
  Trio Sonata, Op. 4, No. 3   I/IIB2

  Trio Sonata, Op. 4, No. 5   I/IIB2

PETZ, JOHANN CHRISTOPH (PEZ)
     (1664-1716)
  Trio Sonata in C   I/IIB2

SCHICKHARDT, JOHANN CHRISTIAN
     (1670-1740)
  Trio Sonata in F   I/IIB2

SPIELMUSIK FUR MELODIEINSTRUMENTE UND
     GITARRE, 16-19TH CENTURY
     I/IIB2-Coll

TELEMANN, GEORG PHILIPP (1681-1767)
  Trio Sonata in F   I/IIB2

ZACH, JOHANN (JAN) (1699-1773)
  Trio Sonata   I/IIB2

Trios — Gtr, A Rec, T Rec

CORELLI, ARCANGELO (1653-1713)
  Sonata da Camera, Op. 4, No. 2
     I/IIB2

FROHLICH MUSIZIEREN, EIN   I/IIB2-Coll

INMITTEN DER NACHT, WEIHNACHTLICHE
     SPIELMUSIK   IV/IIB2

MOZART, WOLFGANG AMADEUS (1756-1791)
  Stucke, 4   I/IIB2

MOZART-MENUETT   I/IIB2

NORDISCHE VOLKSMUSIK   I/IIB2-Coll

Trios — Gtr, A Rec, Hpsd

TELEMANN, GEORG PHILIPP (1681-1767)
  Trio Sonata in C   I/IIB2

Trios — Gtr, A Rec, Zither

SPIELMUSIK UM 1700   I/IIB2-Coll

Trios — Gtr, A Rec, Vln

HANDEL, GEORGE FRIDERIC (1685-1759)
Sonata in C minor, MIN 52 I/IIB2

HASSE, JOHANN ADOLPH (1699-1783)
Trio Sonata in C I/IIB2

LEICHTES ZUSAMMENSPIEL I/IIB2-Coll

TELEMANN, GEORG PHILIPP (1681-1767)
Sonata in A minor I/IIB2

Trio Sonata in C I/IIB2

Trios — Gtr, 2 T Rec

BOISMORTIER, JOSEPH BODIN DE
(1689-1755)
Carillon I/IIB2

Trios — Gtr, T Rec, B Rec

PRAETORIUS, MICHAEL (1571-1621)
Tanze I/IIB2

Trios — Gtr, T Rec, Vla da Gamba

CABEZON, ANTONIO DE (1510-1566)
Diferencias Sobre La Gallarda
Milanesa (1572) I/IIB2

PRAETORIUS, MICHAEL (1571-1621)
Tanze I/IIB2

Trios — Gtr, 2 Rec

ALTE UND NEUE MUSIK ZUM SINGEN UND
SPIELEN AUF BLOCKFLOTEN, GEIGEN UND
LAUTENINSTRUMENTE IV/IIB2

ANONYMOUS
Allerlei Volkslieder IV/IIB2,
I/IIB2-Coll

AUF, DU JUNGER WANDERSMANN,
WANDERLIEDER UND MARSCHE
I/IIB2-Coll

BAUMANN, HANS
Bergbauernweihnacht IV/IIB2

HOTTETERRE, JACQUES (MARTIN)
(ca. 1684-1762)
2 Trio Sonatas I/IIB2

INMITTEN DER NACHT, WEIHNACHTLICHE
SPIELMUSIK I/IIB2

MAINERIO, GIORGIO
5 Danze I/IIB2

MEISTER DER BAROKZEIT I/IIB2-Coll

PEUERL, PAUL (ca. 1570-ca. 1624)
Tanze, 3 I/IIB2

ROSSI, SALOMONE (ca. 1570-ca. 1630)
Sinfonia in G minor I/IIB2

SPIELSTUCKE FUR BLOCKFLOTE UND GITARRE,
VOL. 1 I/IIB2-Coll

SPIELSTUCKE FUR BLOCKFLOTE UND GITARRE,
VOL. 2 I/IIB2-Coll

TELEMANN, GEORG PHILIPP (1681-1767)
Suiten Zu 4 Stimmen, 5 I/IIB2

Trio Sonata in C I/IIB2

TUNES FROM THE CECIL SHARP COLLECTION,
7 I/IIB2-Coll

Trios — 2 Gtr, Rec

HAYDN, [FRANZ] JOSEPH (1732-1809)
Serenade I/IIB2

Trios — Gtr, 2 Mand

HANDEL, GEORGE FRIDERIC (1685-1759)
Alte Zupfmusik I/IIB2

VIVALDI, ANTONIO (1678-1741)
Concerto I/IIB2

Concerto in C I/IIB2

Trios — 2 Gtr, Vln

HAYDN, [FRANZ] JOSEPH (1732-1809)
Serenade I/IIB2

Trio, MIN 47 I/IIB2

Trios — 2 Gtr, Vla

LEGRENZI, GIOVANNI (1626-1690)
Trio Sonata in A minor I/IIB2

Trios — Gtr, 2 Vln

BONONCINI, GIOVANNI (1670-1747)
Trio Sonata Nos. 1-5 I/IIB2

CAPELLI, GIOVANNI MARIA (1648-1728)
Trio Sonata in F I/IIB2

CORELLI, ARCANGELO (1653-1713)
Pastorale IV/IIB2

Sonata da Camera, Op. 2, No. 2
I/IIB2

Sonata da Chiesa, Op. 3, No. 1
I/IIB2

GABRIELI, DOMENICO (ca. 1650-1690)
Balletto A Tre I/IIB2

HANDEL, GEORGE FRIDERIC (1685-1759)
Sonata in C minor, MIN 52 I/IIB2

HOTTETERRE, JACQUES (MARTIN)
(ca. 1684-1762)
2 Trio Sonatas I/IIB2

KLASSISCHE TANZWEISEN, VON HAYDN BIS
SCHUBERT, VOL. 1 I/IIB2-Coll

KLASSISCHE TANZWEISEN, VON HAYDN BIS
SCHUBERT, VOL.2 I/IIB2-Coll

LULLY, JEAN-BAPTISTE (LULLI)
(1632-1687)
Tanze, 4 I/IIB2

MOZART, WOLFGANG AMADEUS (1756-1791)
Flotenuhrstuck I/IIB2

Stucke, 4 I/IIB2

PERONI, GIUSEPPE
Concerto A Tre I/IIB2

PEUERL, PAUL (ca. 1570-ca. 1624)
Tanze, 3 I/IIB2

REALI, GIOVANNI BATTISTA
Sonata in B flat I/IIB2

ROSSI, SALOMONE (ca. 1570-ca. 1630)
Sinfonia in F I/IIB2

Sinfonia in G minor I/IIB2

RUGGIERI, GIOVANNI MARIA
Sonata da Chiesa No. 1 in E minor,
Op. 3, No. 1 I/IIB2

Sonata da Chiesa No. 2 in B minor,
Op. 3, No. 2 I/IIB2

Sonata da Chiesa No. 3 in B flat, Op.
3, No. 3 I/IIB2

Sonata da Chiesa No. 4 in F, Op. 3,
No. 4 I/IIB2

Sonata da Chiesa No. 5 in G minor,
Op. 3, No. 5 I/IIB2

Sonata da Chiesa No. 6 in A, Op. 3,
No. 6 I/IIB2

Sonata da Chiesa No. 7 in A minor,
Op. 3, No. 7 I/IIB2

Sonata da Chiesa No. 8 in G, Op. 3,
No. 8 I/IIB2

Sonata da Chiesa No. 9 in D minor,
Op. 3, No. 9 I/IIB2

Sonata da Chiesa No. 10 in D, Op. 3,
No. 10 I/IIB2

SPIELMUSIK FUR MELODIEINSTRUMENTE UND
GITARRE, 16-19TH CENTURY
I/IIB2-Coll

VIVALDI, ANTONIO (1678-1741)
Concerto I/IIB2

VOLKS- UND KINDERLIEDER I/IIB2-Coll,
IV/IIB2

Trios — Gtr, Vln, Vla

RODE, JACQUES-PIERRE (1744-1830)
    Trio in D I/IIB2

VOLKS- UND KINDERLIEDER   IV/IIB2,
    I/IIB2

Trios — Gtr, Vln, Vla da Gamba

CABEZON, ANTONIO DE (1510-1566)
    Diferencias Sobre La Gallarda
    Milanesa (1572) I/IIB2

Trios — Gtr, Vln, Vcl

HAYDN, [FRANZ] JOSEPH (1732-1809)
    Cassation in C, Hob.III: 6 I/IIB2

    Divertimento, Hob.XI: 44 I/IIB2

    Trio in F I/IIB2

SPIELMUSIK FUR MELODIEINSTRUMENTE UND
    GITARRE, 16-19TH CENTURY
    I/IIB2-Coll

Trios — Gtr, Vla, Vcl

RODE, JACQUES-PIERRE (1744-1830)
    Trio in D I/IIB2

Trios — Gtr, 2 Vla da Gamba

CABEZON, ANTONIO DE (1510-1566)
    Diferencias Sobre La Gallarda
    Milanesa (1572) I/IIB2

Trios — Gtr, 2 Treb Inst

BIALAS, GUNTER (1907-   )
    Spanische Romanzen   IV/IIB2

KLASSISCHE TANZWEISEN, VON HAYDN BIS
    SCHUBERT, VOL. 1 I/IIB2-Coll

KLASSISCHE TANZWEISEN, VON HAYDN BIS
    SCHUBERT, VOL.2 I/IIB2-Coll

LEICHTES ZUSAMMENSPIEL I/IIB2-Coll

PASTORALEN ALTER MEISTER, 9 IV/IIB2

PRAETORIUS, MICHAEL (1571-1621)
    Tanze I/IIB2

SCHUBERT, FRANZ (PETER) (1797-1828)
    Beliebte Walzer Und Moment Musical
    I/IIB2

VIVALDI, ANTONIO (1678-1741)
    Concerto in C I/IIB2

VOLKSMUSIK AUS OSTERREICH, VOL. I:
    VOLKSMUSIK AUS KARNTEN I/IIB2-Coll

VOLKSMUSIK AUS OSTERREICH, VOL. II:
    VOLKSMUSIK AUS TIROL I/IIB2-Coll

VOLKSMUSIK AUS OSTERREICH, VOL. III:
    VOLKSMUSIK AUS STEIERMARK UND
    BURGENLAND I/IIB2-Coll

VOLKSMUSIK AUS OSTERREICH, VOL. IV:
    VOLKSMUSIK AUS VORARLBERG
    I/IIB2-Coll

VOLKSTANZE UND LIEDER I/IIB2

Quartets — Gtr, Fl, Vln, Pno

BEETHOVEN, LUDWIG VAN (1770-1827)
    Adagio, MIN 232 I/IIB3

Quartets — 3 Gtr, Fl

GUITARRA CANTORA, LA, MELODIAS
    TRADICIONALES ARGENTINAS I/IIB3

Quartets — Gtr, Fl, 2 Vln

HASSE, JOHANN ADOLPH (1699-1783)
    Concerto in G I/IIB3

SCHALLER, ERWIN (1901-   )
    Altlothringer Hirtenmusik I/IIB3

Quartets — Gtr, Fl, Vln, Vla

HAYDN, [FRANZ] JOSEPH (1732-1809)
    Quartet in G, Op. 5, No. 4, Hob.II: 4
    I/IIB3

Quartets — Gtr, Fl, Vla, Vcl

SCHUBERT, FRANZ (PETER) (1797-1828)
    Quartet, D. 96 for Flute, Viola,
    Guitar and Violoncello I/IIB3

Quartets — Gtr, Ob, 2 Vln

HASSE, JOHANN ADOLPH (1699-1783)
    Concerto in G I/IIB3

Quartets — Gtr, 2 S Rec, A Rec

DEUTSCHE TANZE AUS DER ZEIT SCHUBERTS
    I/IIB3-Coll

DEVIL AND THE FARMER'S WIFE, THE, AND
    OTHER AMERICAN BALLADS I/IIB3-Coll

Quartets — Gtr, S Rec, 2 A Rec

DEUTSCHE TANZE AUS DER ZEIT SCHUBERTS
    I/IIB3-Coll

Quartets — Gtr, S Rec, A Rec, T Rec

BLUES AND SPIRITUALS I/IIB3-Coll

DEUTSCHE TANZE AUS DER ZEIT SCHUBERTS
    I/IIB3-Coll

Quartets — 2 Gtr, S Rec, A Rec

ENSEMBLE MUSIC FOR GUITARS AND
    RECORDERS, VOL. I, ELEMENTARY:
    TUNES OF OLD ENGLAND I/IIB3

ENSEMBLE MUSIC FOR GUITARS AND
    RECORDERS, VOL. II, INTERMEDIATE:
    TUNES OF QUEEN ELIZABETH'S TIME
    I/IIB3

Quartets — Gtr, 2 A Rec, T Rec

BLUES AND SPIRITUALS I/IIB3-Coll

Quartets — Gtr, 3 Rec

ALTE WEIHNACHTSMUSIK, SPIELSTUCKE UND
    LIEDER IV/IIB3

AUS FREMDEN LANDERN, LIEDER UND TANZE,
    VOL. I I/IIB3-Coll, I/IIB3-Coll

AUS FREMDEN LANDERN, LIEDER UND TANZE,
    VOL. II I/IIB3-Coll, I/IIB3-Coll

BLUES AND SPIRITUALS I/IIB3-Coll

DEVIL AND THE FARMER'S WIFE, THE, AND
    OTHER AMERICAN BALLADS I/IIB3-Coll

FELSENQUELL, DER, FRANZOSISCHE
    VOLKSTANZE 2. TEIL I/IIB3-Coll

PEUERL, PAUL (ca. 1570-ca. 1624)
    Tanze I/IIB3

SPIELSTUCKE FUR BLOCKFLOTE UND GITARRE,
    VOL. 1 I/IIB3-Coll

SPIELSTUCKE FUR BLOCKFLOTE UND GITARRE,
    VOL. 2 I/IIB3-Coll

WEIHNACHT - 8 ALTE LIEDER IV/IIB3

Quartets — Gtr, 2 Vln, Mand

HASSE, JOHANN ADOLPH (1699-1783)
    Concerto in G I/IIB3

Quartets — Gtr, 3 Vln

HASSE, JOHANN ADOLPH (1699-1783)
    Concerto in G I/IIB3

Quartets — Gtr, 2 Vln, Vla

HAYDN, [FRANZ] JOSEPH (1732-1809)
    Quartet in G, Op. 5, No. 4, Hob.II: 4
    I/IIB3

Quartets — Gtr, Vln, Vla, Vcl

HAYDN, [FRANZ] JOSEPH (1732-1809)
    Quartet in D, Hob.III: 8 I/IIB3

SANDI, CHR. D.
    Quartet in G I/IIB3

Quartets — Gtr, 3 Treb Inst

SCHALLER, ERWIN (1901-   )
    Altlothringer Hirtenmusik IV/IIB3

SCHUBERT, FRANZ (PETER) (1797-1828)
    Tanze I/IIB3

Quartets — Gtr, 2 Treb Inst, Bass Inst

HOTTETERRE, JEAN
    Suite I/IIB3

PASTORALEN ALTER MEISTER, 9 IV/IIB3

Quintets — Gtr, 2 S Rec, A Rec, Perc

VOLKSWEISEN UND TANZE AUS ARGENTINIEN
    I/IIB4-Coll

Quintets — Gtr, S Rec, T Rec, DB, Xylo

MOZART, WOLFGANG AMADEUS (1756-1791)
    Contretanz "La Favorite" I/IIB4

Quintets — Gtr, 2 S Rec, 2 Vln

AUF, DU JUNGER WANDERSMANN,
    WANDERLIEDER UND MARSCHE
    I/IIB4-Coll

Quintets — Gtr, S Rec, 2 A Rec, Perc

VOLKSWEISEN UND TANZE AUS ARGENTINIEN
    I/IIB4-Coll

Quintets — Gtr, S Rec, A Rec, T Rec, Vcl

WERDIN, EBERHARD (1911-   )
    Ungarische Suite, Nach Originalen
    Csardas-Melodien I/IIB4

Quintets — 3 Gtr, 2 A Rec

ROSENMULLER, JOHANN (ca. 1620-1684)
    Studenten Music, Eine I/IIB4

Quintets — Gtr, 4 Rec

BEETHOVEN, LUDWIG VAN (1770-1827)
Deutsche Tanze I/IIB4

SPIELSTUCKE FUR BLOCKFLOTE UND GITARRE,
VOL. 1 I/IIB4-Coll

Quintets — Gtr, 3 Vln, Vcl

TORELLI, GIUSEPPE (1658-1709)
Concerto in G I/IIB4

Quintets — Gtr, 2 Vln, Vcl, Xylo

MOZART, WOLFGANG AMADEUS (1756-1791)
Contretanz "La Favorite" I/IIB4

Quintets — 3 Gtr, 2 Treb Inst

ROSENMULLER, JOHANN (ca. 1620-1684)
Studenten Music, Eine I/IIB4

School Ens/Orch with Gtr

AIRS DE COURS, 15, EN FORME DE SUITE
I/IIB5-Coll

BACH, JOHANN SEBASTIAN (1685-1750)
Kleines Weihnachtsoratorium Mit
Johann Sebastian Bach VII-Coll,
IV/IIB4

DANSMUZIEK UIT PRUIKENTIJD I/IIB5-Coll

DUBLIN TOWN, IERSE VOLKSMUZIEK
I/IIB5-Coll

ENGELSE VOLKSDANSEN, 2 VOLS.
I/IIB5-Coll

GALANTE MUZIEK, VAN COMPONISTEN UIT DE
18E EEUW I/IIB5-Coll

HIRTENLIEDER UND TANZE AUS DEM SUDOSTEN
IV/IIB4

IN EEN WEENSE MUZIEKKAMER I/IIB5-Coll

KATALANISCHE SARDANAS, 2 I/IIB5-Coll

KRAKOVIAK, POOLSE DANSEN I/IIB5-Coll

KREBS, RUDOLF
Schwabische Baurentanze, 3 I/IIB5

LIEDER AUS DEUTSCHLAND I/IIB5-Coll

MOZART, LEOPOLD (1719-1787)
Aus Leopold Mozarts Notenbuchlein Fur
Seinen Sohn Wolfgang Amadeus
I/IIB5

MUSIK IM JAHRESKREIS I/IIB5-Coll

MUSIQUE POUR ENSEMBLES ET MORCEAUX
CHOISIS I/IIB5-Coll

MUSIZIERBUCH, FUR DAS INSTRUMENTALE
ZUSAMMENSPIEL IN SCHULE, JUGEND UND
HAUS I/IIB5-Coll

NEGRO-SPIRITUALS I/IIB5-Coll

NEUE MUSIZIERBUCH, DAS, FUR
INSTRUMENTALES ZUSAMMENSPIEL IN
SCHULEN, MUSIZIERGRUPPEN UND IN DER
HAUSMUSIK I/IIB5-Coll

SCHUBERT, FRANZ (PETER) (1797-1828)
Dansmuziek Bij Kaarslicht, Walsen En
Ecossaises I/IIB5

Duitse Dansen I/IIB5

SPEEL EN DANS JE MEE, VOL. 1:
HEDENDAAGSE DANSEN I/IIB5-Coll

SPEEL EN DANS JE MEE, VOL. 2:
NEDERLANDSE VOLKSDANSEN
I/IIB5-Coll

SPIELMUSIK FUR DIE SCHULE I/IIB5-Coll,
IV/IIB4

UIT MOZART'S TIJD I/IIB5-Coll

VOLKSTANZE, 3 I/IIB5-Coll

WEIHNACHTLICHES SPIEL IV/IIB4

Duets — Gtr, Voice

ALTE UND NEUE MUSIK ZUM SINGEN UND
SPIELEN AUF BLOCKFLOTEN, GEIGEN UND
LAUTENINSTRUMENTE I/IIC1-Coll

ALTITALIENISCHE ARIEN I/IIC1-Coll

ALTJAPANISCHE GEISHALIEDER, 5
I/IIC1-Coll

ANONYMOUS
Altfranzosische Volkslieder, 4,
Pastourelles From The 18th Cent.
I/IIC1

Greensleeves I/IIC1

Italienische Canzonetten, 4, Aus Dem
16. Jahrhundert I/IIC1

Troika, Altrussisches Volkslied
I/IIC1-Coll

ARIE ANTICHE, 5 I/IIC1-Coll

BACH, JOHANN SEBASTIAN (1685-1750)
Deux Chants VII-Coll

BELLINI, VINCENZO (1801-1835)
Dolente Immagine Di Filla Mia I/IIC1

BERGERETTES; 6 PIECES FROM THE 18TH
CENTURY I/IIC1-Coll

BERMUDO, [FRAY] JUAN
(ca. 1510-ca. 1565)
Mir Nero De Tarpeya, Romance Viejo
I/IIC1

BERUHMTE RUSSISCHE LIEDER UND ROMANZEN,
15 I/IIC1-Coll

BIMBELI, BAMBELI; 15 LAUTENLIEDER VON
DEN KINDERN UND FUR DEN KINDERN
I/IIC1-Coll

BLECH, LEO (1871-1958)
Liedchen, 6, (Kindern Vorzusingen)
I/IIC1

BLUME, KARL (1883-1947)
Ausgewahlte Lieder, 12 I/IIC1

BODDECKER, PHILIPP FRIEDRICH
(1683- ?)
Natus Est Jesus, Weihnachtskonzert
IV/IIC1

BRAHMS, JOHANNES (1833-1897)
Ausgewahlte Lieder, 2 Vols. I/IIC1

BRITTEN, [SIR] BENJAMIN (1913-1976)
England I/IIC1

BROQUA, ALFONSO (1876-1946)
Chants Du Parana I/IIC1

BRUDER SINGER, LIEDER UNSERES VOLKES
I/IIC1-Coll, IV/IIC1

CANCIONES DEL SIGLO XVII, 5
I/IIC1-Coll

CANCIONES POPULARES CATALANAS, 4
I/IIC1-Coll

CANCIONES POPULARES ESPANOLAS
I/IIC1-Coll, IV/IIC1

CANCIONES POPULARES ESPANOLAS, 5
I/IIC1-Coll, IV/IIC1

CANTI DI NATALE IV/IIC1

CHORAL UND LAUTE I/IIC1-Coll

CHRISTGEBURT- UND MARIENLIEDER, VOL. I:
ALTDEUTSCHE CHRISTGEBURTLIEDER
IV/IIC1

CLASSICAL SONGS, 10 I/IIC1-Coll

DAVON WOLL'N WIR NUN SINGEN IV/IIC1

DAZA, ESTEBAN (? - ?)
Enfermo Estaba Antioco, Romance
I/IIC1

DES PREZ, JOSQUIN (ca. 1440-1521)
Mille Regretz I/IIC1

12 DEUTSCHE VOLKSLIEDER I/IIC1

DEUTSCHE WEIHNACHTSWEISEN IV/IIC1

DIMMLER, LISELOTTE
Meine Kleine Lieder I/IIC1

DIR ZU EIGEN; 13 LIEBESLIEDER
I/IIC1-Coll

DURANTE, FRANCESCO (1684-1755)
Danza Danza, Gagliarda I/IIC1

EARLY ENGLISH LUTE SONGS AND FOLK
SONGS, VOL. III IV/IIC1

ENCINA, JUAN DEL (1468-1529)
Romerico I/IIC1

ENGELSE VOLKSLIEDEREN, 3 I/IIC1-Coll

ENGLISH SONGS, 3 I/IIC1-Coll

ES BRENNT, LIEDER AUS DEM GHETTO
I/IIC1-Coll

ES RITTEN DREI REITER I/IIC1-Coll

EUROPAISCHE VOLKSLIEDER, VOL. I
I/IIC1-Coll

EUROPAISCHE VOLKSLIEDER, VOL. II
I/IIC1-Coll

EUROPAISCHE WEIHNACHTSLIEDER IV/IIC1

FINNISCHE VOLKSLIEDER, SUOMALAISIA
KANSANLAULUJA I/IIC1-Coll

FLIES, J. BERNHARD (1770- ?)
Wiegenlied "Schlafe Mein Prinzchen"
I/IIC1

FOLKSONGS, 10 I/IIC1-Coll

FOLKSONGS, 10 ENGLISH FOLKSONGS
I/IIC1-Coll

FRANSE VOLKSLIEDEREN, 3 I/IIC1-Coll

GAVALL, JOHN
Learning Music Through The Guitar,
Vol. V: An Introduction To
Figured Bass IV/IIC1

GIORDANI, TOMMASO (1730-1806)
Caro Mio Ben I/IIC1

GITARRE ZUM WEIHNACHTSLIED IV/IIC1

GITARRELIEDER FUR ALLE, VOLKSLIEDER
I/IIC1-Coll

GRANADOS, ENRIQUE (1867-1916)
Amor Y Odio, Tonadilla I/IIC1

Callejeo, Tonadilla I/IIC1

Danza Espanola No. 5, Andaluza
I/IIC1

GRANADOS, ENRIQUE (cont'd.)

Maja De Goya, La, Tonadilla I/IIC1

Maja Dolorosa, La, 3 Tonadillas
I/IIC1

Majo Discreto, El, Tonadilla I/IIC1

Majo Olvivado, El, Tonada O Cancion
I/IIC1

Majo Timido, El, Tonadilla I/IIC1

Mirar De La Maja, El, Tonadilla
I/IIC1

Tralala, El, Y El Punteado, Tonadilla
I/IIC1

GRETRY, ANDRE ERNEST MODESTE
(1741-1813)
Serenade I/IIC1

GUERRERO, FRANCISCO (1528-1599)
Ojos Claros, Serenos I/IIC1

GUIGNOLOT I/IIC1-Coll

GUITAR SONGBOOK, THE IV/IIC1

HANDEL, GEORGE FRIDERIC (1685-1759)
No Se Emendera Jamas I/IIC1

HASSE, JOHANN ADOLPH (1699-1783)
March, MIN 7 I/IIC1

HAUSLICHE WEIHNACHT IV/IIC1

HAYDN, [FRANZ] JOSEPH (1732-1809)
Lieder, 3 I/IIC1

HEILIGE NACHT, WEIHNACHTSLIEDER-ALBUM
IV/IIC1

HILLER, JOHANN ADAM (1728-1804)
Lieder, 6 I/IIC1

8 INTERNATIONALE VOLKSLIEDER
I/IIC1-Coll

INTERNATIONALE VOLKSLIEDER, VOL. I
I/IIC1-Coll

INTERNATIONALE VOLKSLIEDER, VOL. II
I/IIC1-Coll

INTERNATIONALE VOLKSLIEDER, VOL. III
I/IIC1-Coll

INTERNATIONALE VOLKSLIEDER, VOL. IV
I/IIC1-Coll

JANSEN, WILLY (1897-   )
Klanglehre Zur Gitarre (Begleitspiel
Auf Grund Der Harmonielehre)
IV/IIC1

JEUNE, HENRI LE
Chanson I/IIC1

JIDDISCHE LIEDER I/IIC1-Coll

KERSTLIEDEREN, EENVOUDIGE ZETTINGEN
IV/IIC1

KERSTLIEDEREN VOOR GITAARSOLO IV/IIC1

KLAMPFENLIED, DAS, EIN
FAHRTENLIEDERBUCH I/IIC1-Coll

KLINGENDE FAHRT, EIN LIEDERBUCH
I/IIC1-Coll

KOMMT SINGT UND SPIELT: LIEDER UNSERER
ZEIT, FUR DEN ANFANGSUNTERRICHT
I/IIC1-Coll

KRIEGER, JOHANN PHILIPP (1649-1725)
Lieder, 4 I/IIC1

LAUTENMUSIKANT, DER I/IIC1-Coll

LAUTENMUSIKANT, DER, VOL. I
I/IIC1-Coll

LAUTENMUSIKANT, DER, VOL. II
I/IIC1-Coll

LAUTENMUSIKANT, DER, VOL. III
I/IIC1-Coll

LAUTENSCHLAGER, DER I/IIC1-Coll

LAUTENSPIELER, DER, NO. 1 IV/IIC1

LAUTENSPIELER, DER, NO. 2 I/IIC1-Coll

LAUTENSPIELER, DER, NO. 3 I/IIC1-Coll

LAUTENSPIELER, DER, NO. 5 I/IIC1-Coll

LAUTENSPIELER, DER, NO. 7 I/IIC1-Coll

LAUTENSPIELER, DER, NO. 8 I/IIC1-Coll

LAUTENSPIELER DES XVI. JAHRHUNDERTS
(LIUTISTI DEL CINQUECENTO)
I/IIC1-Coll

LICHTERBAUM, DER IV/IIC1

LIED UND GITARRE, 40 DEUTSCHE UND
AUSLANDISCHE VOLKSLIEDER, VOL. 1
I/IIC1-Coll, IV/IIC1

LIED UND GITARRE, 40 DEUTSCHE UND
AUSLANDISCHE VOLKSLIEDER, VOL. 2
I/IIC1-Coll

LIED- UND GITARRENSPIEL, VOLKS- UND
TANZLIEDER, VOL. I IV/IIC1

LIEDER DER WEIHNACHT ZUR GITARRE
IV/IIC1

LIEDER UM WEIHNACHT IV/IIC1

LIEDERSCHATZ ZUR GITARRE I/IIC1-Coll

LIEDJES ROND DE MUIDERKRING
I/IIC1-Coll

LOSST MICH LEBEN I/IIC1-Coll

MAGYAR ZENE GITARRA A XIX. SZADAD ELSO
FELEBOL I/IIC1-Coll

MAITIA NUN ZIRA I/IIC1-Coll

MANNLEIN STEHT IM WALDE, EIN, DIE
SCHONSTEN ALTEN KINDERLIEDER
I/IIC1-Coll

MEIN ERSTES SPIELBUCH, MIT TONIKA UND
DOMINANTE I/IIC1-Coll

MONTEVERDI, CLAUDIO (ca. 1567-1643)
Madrigali, 3 I/IIC1

Scherzi Musicali, Cioe Arie, Et
Madrigali In Stile Recitativo
I/IIC1

MORGEN- UND ABENDLIEDER I/IIC1-Coll

MOZART, WOLFGANG AMADEUS (1756-1791)
Berceuse, MIN 234 I/IIC1

Lieder, 9 I/IIC1

Serenade, MIN 235 I/IIC1

MUSIK AUS WIEN; 16 DER SCHONSTEN
WIENERLIEDER I/IIC1-Coll

MUZIEKBIJLAGE, NO. 53 I/IIC1-Coll

NEDERLANDSE VOLKSLIEDEREN, 3
I/IIC1-Coll

NOELS DE PROVENCE IV/IIC1

NORDISCHE VOLKSLIEDER I/IIC1-Coll

NUEVE CANCIONES GRANADINAS, 9 CANTOS DE
LA ALPUJARRA LLAMADOS "REMERINOS"
I/IIC1-Coll

O SANCTISSIMA, 10 WEIHNACHTSLIEDER AUS
ITALIEN, ENGLAND, SPANIEN UND
FRANKREICH IV/IIC1

OB I LACH ODER SING, VOLKSLIEDER AUS
DER DEUTSCHEN SCHWEIZ I/IIC1-Coll

OBRADORS, FERNANDO
Con Amores, La Mi Madre I/IIC1

OUD-NEDERLANDSE LIEDEREN I/IIC1-Coll

PIOSENKI LUDOWE I POPULARNE
I/IIC1-Coll

PIOSENKI Z PODDASZA, NA GLOS I GITARE
I/IIC1-Coll

PRZY CHOINCE, KOLEDY W LATWYM UKLADZIE
NA GITARE IV/IIC1

PRZY GITARZE, VOL. I: UKOCHANY KRAJ,
PIESNI I TANCE POLSKIE I/IIC1-Coll

PRZY GITARZE, VOL. II: NASZE PIOSENKI
I/IIC1-Coll

PRZY GITARZE, VOL. III: W CICHY WIECZOR
I/IIC1-Coll

RINKE RANKE ROSENSCHEIN; 77
KINDERLIEDER IV/IIC1

RUSSISCHE VOLKSMUSIK I/IIC1-Coll

SCARLATTI, ALESSANDRO (1660-1725)
O Cessate Di Piagarmi I/IIC1

Sento Nel Core I/IIC1

SCHUBERT, FRANZ (PETER) (1797-1828)
Adieu I/IIC1

Berceuse, MIN 236 I/IIC1

Des Madchens Klage I/IIC1

Ellens Gesang III I/IIC1

Fischermadchen, Das I/IIC1

Jeune Fille Et La Mort, La I/IIC1

Jeune Mere, La I/IIC1

Lieder I/IIC1

Meunier Voyageur, Le I/IIC1

Serenade (De Shakespeare) I/IIC1

Serenade, MIN 57 I/IIC1

Sois Toujours Mes Seuls Amours
I/IIC1

Songs I/IIC1

SCHULZ, JOHANN ABRAHAM PETER
(1747-1800)
Lieder Im Volkston I/IIC1

SCHUTZ, HEINRICH (1585-1672)
Geistliche Gesange, 2 I/IIC1

SEIBER, MATYAS GYORGY (1905-1960)
French Folk Songs, 4 I/IIC1

SIBELIUS, JEAN (1865-1957)
Komm Herbei Tod I/IIC1

SING AND PLAY..., TO SIMPLE GUITAR
ACCOMPANIMENTS, VOL. I: SING AND
PLAY NATIONAL SONGS I/IIC1-Coll

SING AND PLAY..., TO SIMPLE GUITAR
ACCOMPANIMENTS, VOL. II: SING AND
PLAY NURSERY SONGS I/IIC1-Coll

SING AND PLAY..., TO SIMPLE GUITAR
ACCOMPANIMENTS, VOL. III: SING AND
PLAY SEA-SONGS I/IIC1-Coll

SING CHRISTMAS CAROLS IV/IIC1

SING MIR, MORENA!, LIEDER ZUR GITARRE
AUS SPANIEN, SUDFRANKREICH,
LITAUEN, DALMATIEN I/IIC1-Coll

SING NEGRO SPIRITUALS I/IIC1-Coll,
IV/IIC1

SINGENDES, KLINGENDES OSTERREICH
I/IIC1-Coll

SINTERKLAASLIEDJES I/IIC1-Coll

SONNE, KOMM, EIN GITARRESPIELBUCH FUR
KINDER, 1-4. UNTERRICHTSJAHR
IV/IIC1

SPAANSE VOLKSLIEDEREN, 3 (3 SPANISH
FOLKSONGS) I/IIC1-Coll, IV/IIC1

SPERONTES (JOHANN SIGISMUND SCHOLZE)
(1705-1750)
Singende Muse An Der Pleisse I/IIC1

SPIRITUALS AND FOLKSONGS I/IIC1-Coll

TAUBE, EVERT (1890-1976)
Visor, 50, Till Luta Och Gitarr
I/IIC1

TAUBERT, KARL HEINZ (1921-   )
Wiegenlied I/IIC1

THOMAS, JUAN MARIA
Canciones Populares Mallorquinas, 4
I/IIC1

THREE 17TH CENTURY AIRS I/IIC1-Coll

TURINA, JOAQUIN (1882-1949)
Cantares I/IIC1

UKRAINISCHE VOLKSWEISEN I/IIC1-Coll

UNSERE SCHONSTEN WEIHNACHTSLIEDER ZUR
GITARRE IV/IIC1

UNSERE WEIHNACHTSLIEDER IV/IIC1

VALVERDE, JOAQUIN (1846-1910)
Clavelitos I/IIC1

VASQUEZ, JUAN (fl. 1500)
De Los Alamos Vengo I/IIC1

VIDALITA, CHANT POPULAIRE ARGENTIN
I/IIC1-Coll

VILLANCICOS POPULARES, VOL. I IV/IIC1

VILLANCICOS POPULARES, VOL. II   IV/IIC1

VILLANCICOS POPULARES, VOL. III
    I/IIC1-Coll, IV/IIC1

VIVE HENRI IV, CHANSON FRANCAISE
    I/IIC1-Coll

VOLKSLIED UND LAUTE I/IIC1-Coll

VOLKSLIEDER I/IIC1-Coll, IV/IIC1

VOLKSLIEDER AUS ALLER WELT, VOL. I:
    ENGLAND I/IIC1-Coll

VOLKSLIEDER AUS ALLER WELT, VOL. II:
    FRANKREICH I/IIC1-Coll

VOLKSLIEDER AUS ALLER WELT, VOL. III:
    SPANIEN, PORTUGAL I/IIC1-Coll

VOLKSLIEDER AUS ALLER WELT, VOL. IV:
    ITALIEN I/IIC1-Coll

VOLKSLIEDER AUS ALLER WELT, VOL. V:
    GRIECHENLAND I/IIC1-Coll

VOLKSLIEDER AUS ALLER WELT, VOL. VI:
    TURKEI I/IIC1-Coll

VOLKSLIEDER AUS ALLER WELT, VOL. VII:
    BALKAN (UNGARN, RUMANIEN,
    BULGARIEN, JUGOSLAWIEN)
    I/IIC1-Coll

VOLKSLIEDER AUS ALLER WELT, VOL. VIII:
    RUSSLAND I/IIC1-Coll

VOLKSLIEDER AUS ALLER WELT, VOL.IX:
    POLEN, LETTLAND I/IIC1-Coll

VOLKSLIEDER AUS ALLER WELT, VOL. X:
    DEUTSCHLAND I/IIC1-Coll

VOLKSLIEDER AUS ALLER WELT, VOL. XI:
    AMERIKA I/IIC1-Coll

VOLKSLIEDER AUS ALLER WELT, VOL. XII:
    INDONESIEN I/IIC1-Coll

VOLKSLIEDER DES AUSLANDES, VOL. I:
    SPANISCHE LIEDER I/IIC1-Coll

VOLKSLIEDER DES AUSLANDES, VOL. II:
    ITALIENISCHE LIEDER I/IIC1-Coll

VOLKSLIEDER DES AUSLANDES, VOL. III:
    RUSSISCHE LIEDER I/IIC1-Coll

VOLKSLIEDER ZUM SINGEN UND SPIELEN
    I/IIC1-Coll

VOLKSLIEDERBUCH ZUR GITARRE, VOL. I:
    KINDERLIEDER I/IIC1-Coll

VOLKSLIEDERBUCH ZUR GITARRE, VOL. II:
    WANDER- UND ABSCHIEDSLIEDER
    I/IIC1-Coll

VOM PUSTEWIND UND ANDEREN SACHEN, NEUE
    LIEDER FUR DIE VORSCHULERZIEHUNG
    I/IIC1-Coll

WEIHNACHT - 8 ALTE LIEDER IV/IIC1

WEIHNACHTS-ALBUM, SAMMLUNG DER
    BELIEBTESTEN WEIHNACHTSLIEDER
    IV/IIC1

11 WEIHNACHTSLIEDER IV/IIC1

WEIHNACHTSLIEDER IV/IIC1

WEIHNACHTSLIEDER AUS DEUTSCHLAND UND
    OSTERREICH IV/IIC1

WEIHNACHTSZEIT - FROHLICHE ZEIT,
    ALTBEKANNTE UND NEUERE
    WEIHNACHTSLIEDER IV/IIC1

WEISST DU WIEVIEL STERNLEIN STEHEN?,
    VOLKS- UND KINDERLIEDER
    I/IIC1-Coll

WIEGENLIEDER DER WELT I/IIC1-Coll

WIR SINGEN UND SPIELEN, VOL. 1
    I/IIC1-Coll

WIR SINGEN UND SPIELEN, VOL. 2
    I/IIC1-Coll

WOHLAN DIE ZEIT IST KOMMEN, EIN VOLKS-
    UND ZEITLIEDERBUCH FUR EINZEL-UND
    GRUPPENGESANG I/IIC1-Coll, IV/IIC1

YUN, ISANG (1917-   )
    Gagok I/IIC1

ZANOSKAR, HUBERT
    Neue Gitarren-Schule, Vol. I, Suppl.:
    Ubungen Und Spielstucke IV/IIC1

ZELTER, CARL FRIEDRICH (1758-1832)
    Es War Ein Konig In Thule I/IIC1

ZUPFGEIGENHANSL, DER I/IIC1-Coll

Trios — Gtr, 2 Voices

FROHLICHE WEIHNACHT, EIN
    WEIHNACHTSLIEDER-ALBUM IV/IIC2

GITARRE ZUM WEIHNACHTSLIED IV/IIC2

GRANADOS, ENRIQUE (1867-1916)
    Currutacas Modestas, La, Tonadilla
    I/IIC2

O WUNDER, WAS WILL DAS BEDEUTEN,
    LIEDERSAMMLUNG ZUR ADVENTSZEIT
    IV/IIC2

Trios — Gtr, Voice, Fl

BUNTER HERBST I/IIC2-Coll

HANDEL, GEORGE FRIDERIC (1685-1759)
    Gesange, 2 I/IIC2

    Nel Dolce Dell'oblio I/IIC2

LAUTENSPIELER, DER, NO. 1 IV/IIC2

TAUBERT, KARL HEINZ (1921-   )
    Hausspruch I/IIC2

Trios — Gtr, Voice, Ob

HANDEL, GEORGE FRIDERIC (1685-1759)
    Nel Dolce Dell'oblio I/IIC2

Trios — Gtr, Voice, A Rec

BACH, JOHANN SEBASTIAN (1685-1750)
    Geistliche Lieder IV/IIC2, VII-Coll

DOWLAND, JOHN (1562-1626)
    Lieder, 2 I/IIC2

GUTZGAUCH, DER I/IIC2-Coll

HANDEL, GEORGE FRIDERIC (1685-1759)
    Nel Dolce Dell'oblio I/IIC2

LIEDER UM OSTERN I/IIC2-Coll

MORGEN- UND ABENDLIEDER I/IIC2-Coll

MOZART, WOLFGANG AMADEUS (1756-1791)
    Sehnsucht Nach Dem Fruhling I/IIC2

VALERIUS, ADRIANUS (1575-1625)
    Wenn Alle Untreu Werden I/IIC2

WAHRE FREUNDSCHAFT SOLL NICHT WANKEN
    I/IIC2

ZELTER, CARL FRIEDRICH (1758-1832)
    Es War Ein Konig In Thule
    I/IIC2-Coll

Trios — Gtr, Voice, Rec

ALTE WEIHNACHTSMUSIK, SPIELSTUCKE UND
    LIEDER IV/IIC2

ANONYMOUS
    All Mein Gedanken, Die Ich Hab
    I/IIC2-Coll

    Allerlei Volkslieder I/IIC2-Coll,
    IV/IIC2

BAUMANN, HANS
    Bergbauernweihnacht IV/IIC2

CLEMENT, NICOLE
    Au Jardin De La Patience I/IIC2

ES FLOG EIN KLEINS WALDVOGELEIN
    I/IIC2-Coll

ES RITTEN DREI REITER I/IIC2-Coll

KOMMT, IHR G'SPIELEN UND 5 WEITERE
    LIEDER I/IIC2-Coll

PAESIELLO, GIOVANNI (1741-1816)
    Aria Der Rosine I/IIC2

TANZLIEDER UND SPIELE FUR KINDER, 12
    I/IIC2-Coll

VIER JAPANISCHE VOLKSLIEDER
    I/IIC2-Coll

WEIHNACHTSLIEDER, 5 IV/IIC2

Trios — Gtr, Voice, Mand

KUNSTLIEDER I/IIC2-Coll

PAESIELLO, GIOVANNI (1741-1816)
    Aria Der Rosine I/IIC2

Trios — 2 Gtr, Voice

GUITARRA CANTORA, LA, MELODIAS
    TRADICIONALES ARGENTINAS I/IIC2

HAUSLICHE WEIHNACHT IV/IIC2

KUNSTLIEDER I/IIC2

NEGRO SPIRITUALS I/IIC2

Trios — Gtr, Voice, Vln

HANDEL, GEORGE FRIDERIC (1685-1759)
    Gesange, 2 I/IIC2

    Nel Dolce Dell'oblio I/IIC2

LIEDER UM OSTERN I/IIC2-Coll

MORGEN- UND ABENDLIEDER I/IIC2-Coll

Trios — Gtr, Voice, Vla

MORGEN- UND ABENDLIEDER   I/IIC2-Coll

Trios — Gtr, Voice, Vla da Gamba

SPERONTES (JOHANN SIGISMUND SCHOLZE)
     (1705-1750)
     Singende Muse An Der Pleisse   I/IIC2

Trios — Gtr, Voice, Vcl

SPERONTES (JOHANN SIGISMUND SCHOLZE)
     (1705-1750)
     Singende Muse An Der Pleisse   I/IIC2

Trios — Gtr, Voice, Treb Inst

ALTE MINNELIEDER   I/IIC2-Coll
LIEDER UM OSTERN   I/IIC2-Coll

Quartets — 2 Gtr, A Rec, Voice

DUFAY, GUILLAUME (ca. 1400-1474)
     Bonjour, Bon Mois   I/IIC3

Quartets — Gtr, Voice, 2 Rec

AUF, DU JUNGER WANDERSMANN,
     WANDERLIEDER UND MARSCHE
     I/IIC3-Coll
BAUMANN, HANS
     Bergbauernweihnacht   IV/IIC3
GRUBER, FRANZ XAVER (1787-1863)
     Stille Nacht   IV/IIC3
WEIHNACHT - 8 ALTE LIEDER   IV/IIC3
WEIHNACHTSLIEDER, 5   IV/IIC3

Quartets — 2 Gtr, Rec, Voice

ALTE UND NEUE MUSIK ZUM SINGEN UND
     SPIELEN AUF BLOCKFLOTEN, GEIGEN UND
     LAUTENINSTRUMENTE   I/IIC3-Coll

Quartets — 3 Gtr, Voice

GUITARRA CANTORA, LA, MELODIAS
     TRADICIONALES ARGENTINAS   I/IIC3
HAUSLICHE WEIHNACHT   IV/IIC3

Quartets — Gtr, Voice, 2 Vla D'amore

BACH, JOHANN SEBASTIAN (1685-1750)
     Betrachte Meine Seel'   VII

Quartets — Gtr, Voice, Vln, Vla

LIEDER UM OSTERN   I/IIB3

Quintets — Gtr, 4 Voices

FOSTER, STEPHEN COLLINS (1826-1864)
     My Old Kentucky Home   I/IIC4
I'VE BEEN TO HARLEM   I/IIC4

Quintets — Gtr, 3 Voices, Rec

DARNAL, JEAN CLAUDE
     Dites-Moi M'sieur l'Oiseau   I/IIC4

Quintets — Gtr, Voice, 3 Rec

BEKANNTE VOLKSLIEDER, TEIL II
     I/IIC4-Coll
DEUTSCHE WEIHNACHTSWEISEN   IV/IIC4

Quintets — Gtr, 3 Voices, Pno

CAMMIN, HEINZ (1923-   )
     Spirituals And Songs   I/IIC4

Quintets — Gtr, Voice, 2 S Rec, A Rec

FLAMISCHE LIEDER UND TANZE   I/IIC4-Coll

Quintets — Gtr, Voice, 2 S Rec, T Rec

FLAMISCHE LIEDER UND TANZE   I/IIC4-Coll

Quintets — Gtr, Voice, S Rec, 2 A Rec

FLAMISCHE LIEDER UND TANZE   I/IIC4-Coll

Quintets — Gtr, Voice, S Rec, A Rec, T Rec

FLAMISCHE LIEDER UND TANZE   I/IIC4-Coll

Quintets — Gtr, Voice, A Rec, Vln, Vcl — Arranged

LIEDER UM OSTERN   I/IIC4-Coll

Quintets — Gtr, Voice, A Rec, Vla, Vcl — Arranged

LIEDER UM OSTERN   I/IIC4-Coll

Quintets — Gtr, Voice, 2 Vln, Vcl — Arranged

LIEDER UM OSTERN   I/IIC4-Coll

Quintets — Gtr, Voice, Vln, Vcl, Treb Inst — Arranged

LIEDER UM OSTERN   I/IIC4-Coll

Quintets — Gtr, Voice, Vla, Vcl, Treb Inst — Arranged

LIEDER UM OSTERN   I/IIC4-Coll

School Ens/Orch with Gtr, Voice — Arranged

AUX MARCHES DU PALAIS   I/IIC5-Coll

BACH, JOHANN SEBASTIAN (1685-1750)
    Kleines Weihnachtsoratorium Mit
        Johann Sebastian Bach   VII-Coll,
        IV/IIC5

BAUMANN, HANS
    Bergbauernweihnacht   IV/IIC5

CHRISTMAS TIME   IV/IIC5

DEUTSCH, WALTER (1923-   )
    Kleine Weihnachtskantate, Nach Alten
        Texten Und Weisen Aus Osterreich
        IV/IIC5

EUROPAISCHE VOLKS- UND KINDERLIEDER, IN
    EASY CHORAL VERSIONS WITH
    INSTRUMENTS, VOL. II   I/IIC5-Coll

FROHE BOTSCHAFT, LIEDER ZUR ADVENTS-
    UND WEIHNACHTSZEIT   IV/IIC5

GUANTANAMERA   I/IIC5-Coll

I WENT TO THE MARKET   I/IIC5-Coll

JAUBERT, MAURICE (1900-1940)
    Chanson De Tessa, La   I/IIC5

KERSTLIEDJES OM MEE TE SPELEN EN TE
    ZINGEN   IV/IIC5

MUSIK IM JAHRESKREIS   I/IIC5-Coll

NATY, JEAN
    Au Chateau   I/IIC5

NEDERLANDSE VOLKSLIEDEREN, 23
    I/IIC5-Coll

RYBA, JAN JAKUB SIMON (1765-1815)
    Gloria, Aus Der Tschechischen
        Weihnachtsmesse   IV/IIC5

SPEEL EN ZING JE MEE?, VOL. I:
    VOLKSLIEDEREN OM TE SPELEN EN TE
    ZINGEN   I/IIC5-Coll

SPEEL EN ZING JE MEE?, VOL. II:
    VOLKSLIEDEREN UIT BINNEN- EN
    BUITENLAND   I/IIC5-Coll

SPEEL EN ZING JE MEE?, VOL. III:
    KERSTLIEDJES OM TE SPELEN EN TE
    ZINGEN   I/IIC5-Coll

SPEEL EN ZING JE MEE?, VOL. IV: NEGRO-
    SPIRITUALS   I/IIC5-Coll

SPEEL EN ZING JE MEE?, VOL. V:
    VOLKSLIEDEREN OM TE SPELEN EN TE
    ZINGEN   I/IIC5-Coll

STERN, HERMANN (1912-1978)
    Es Ist Ein Ros' Entsprungen   IV/IIC5

    Gottes Sohn Ist Kommen   IV/IIC5

VIGNEAULT, GILLES
    Doux Chagrin, Le   I/IIC5

VOR LAUTER LIEB UND LUST, LEICHTE SATZE
    ZU ALTEN LIEDERN   I/IIC5-Coll

WHAT SHALL WE DO?, CHANSONS DE MATELOTS
    ANGLAIS   I/IIC5-Coll

WUSTHOFF, KLAUS
    Weihnachtskantate Fur Junge Leute
        IV/IIC5

Duets — 2 Gtr — Original & Arranged

3 ALTE DUOS   I/IIA1-Coll

10 COMPOSICIONES CELEBRES PARA
    GUITARRA, VOL. III   I/IIA1-Coll

DEUTSCHE MEISTER DES EIN- UND
    ZWEISTIMMIGEN LAUTENSATZES, 16.-18.
    JAHRHUNDERT   I/IIA1-Coll

GITAAR-KAMERMUZIEK, VOL. 2   I/IIA1-Coll

GITAARDUET, HET   I/IIA1-Coll

GITAARDUETTEN   I/IIA1-Coll

GUITAR IN ENSEMBLE, VOL. 1   IV/IIA1,
    I/IIA1-Coll

GUITAR SONGBOOK, THE   I/IIA1-Coll

MIT DER GITARRE, UNTERHALTUNGS-ALBUM
    I/IIA1-Coll

SEHR LEICHTE BIS MITTELSCHWERE SATZE
    FUR 1 UND 2 GITARREN   I/IIA1-Coll

SONNE, KOMM, EIN GITARRESPIELBUCH FUR
    KINDER, 1-4. UNTERRICHTSJAHR
    I/IIA1-Coll

SPIEL ZU ZWEIT II   I/IIA1-Coll

SPIELBUCH FUR GITARREN-DUO   I/IIA1-Coll

SPIELMUSIK FUR 2 GITARREN   I/IIA1-Coll

SPIELMUSIK FUR ANGEHENDE GITARRISTEN,
    VOL. III   I/IIA1-Coll

SUDAMERICANA, BERUHMTE FOLKLORISTISCHE
    TANZE   I/IIA1-Coll

UTWORY DAWNYCH MISTRZOW   I/IIA1-Coll

WIR SPIELEN GITARRE, VOL. 1
    I/IIA1-Coll

WIR SPIELEN GITARRE, VOL. 2
    I/IIA1-Coll

Trios — 3 Gtr — Original & Arranged

GITAAR-KAMERMUZIEK, VOL. 2   I/IIA2-Coll

GITARRENCHOR, DER, SCHULE DES
    GRUPPENMUSIZIERENS   I/IIA2-Coll

LAUTENCHOR II, DER   I/IIA2-Coll

MUSIQUE POUR 3 ET 4 GUITARES, VOL. 1
    (MUSIC FOR 3 AND 4 GUITARS, VOL. 1)
    I/IIA2-Coll

MUSIQUE POUR 3 ET 4 GUITARES, VOL. 2
    (MUSIC FOR 3 AND 4 GUITARS, VOL. 2)
    I/IIA2-Coll

SONNE, KOMM, EIN GITARRESPIELBUCH FUR
    KINDER, 1-4. UNTERRICHTSJAHR
    I/IIA2-Coll

SPIELMUSIK FUR 3 GITARREN   I/IIA2-Coll

SPIELMUSIK FUR ANGEHENDE GITARRISTEN,
    VOL. III   I/IIA2-Coll

SUDAMERICANA, BERUHMTE FOLKLORISTISCHE
    TANZE   I/IIA2-Coll

Quartets — 4 Gtr

LAUTENCHOR I, DER I/IIA3-Coll

SONNE, KOMM, EIN GITARRESPIELBUCH FUR
KINDER, 1-4. UNTERRICHTSJAHR
I/IIA3-Coll

Duets — Gtr, Rec

ALTE UND NEUE MUSIK ZUM SINGEN UND
SPIELEN AUF BLOCKFLOTEN, GEIGEN UND
LAUTENINSTRUMENTE I/IIB1-Coll

Duets — Gtr, Treb Inst

MUZIEKBIJLAGE, NO. 53 I/IIB1-Coll

WIR SPIELEN GITARRE, VOL. 1
I/IIB1-Coll

WIR SPIELEN GITARRE, VOL. 2
I/IIB1-Coll

Trios — Gtr, 2 Treb Inst

WINTERWEISSE WEIHNACHT, ALTE UND NEUE
LIEDER UM DIE WEIHNACHTSZEIT
IV/IIB2

School Ens/Orch with Gtr

DERLIEN, MARGARETE
Flotenhannes, Der, Ein Lernbuchlein
Fur Die C"-Blockflote Und Dazu
Mancherlei Lieder Und Satze Zum
Singen Und Musizieren Mit
Verschiedenen Instrumenten
I/IIB5-Coll

WIR LERNEN HAUSMUSIK, FOLGE I-VIII
I/IIB5-Coll

Duets — Gtr, Voice

[CHANTS, 10] I/IIC1-Coll

CLASSICAL SONGS, 10 I/IIC1-Coll

EARLY ENGLISH LUTE SONGS AND FOLK
SONGS, VOL. I I/IIC1-Coll

EARLY ENGLISH LUTE SONGS AND FOLK
SONGS, VOL. II I/IIC1-Coll

EARLY ENGLISH LUTE SONGS AND FOLK
SONGS, VOL. III I/IIC1-Coll

EARLY ENGLISH LUTE SONGS AND FOLK
SONGS, VOL. IV I/IIC1-Coll

FOUR CENTURIES OF SONG, FROM THE
TROUBADOUR TO THE ELIZABETHAN AGE
I/IIC1-Coll

GUITAR SONGBOOK, THE I/IIC1-Coll,
IV/IIC1

ITALIAN SONGS OF THE RENAISSANCE AND
BAROQUE PERIODS I/IIC1-Coll

JUGEND SINGT ZUR GITARRE, 50 [SIC]
DEUTSCHE UND AUSSERDEUTSCHE VOLKS-
UND JUGENDLIEDER I/IIC1-Coll

KUNSTLIEDER I/IIC1-Coll

LATIN-MUSIC; FAVORITE SONGS FROM
ARGENTINA, BRESIL, CHILE, CUBA,
HAITI, HAWAII, JAMAICA, MEXICO,
SPAIN, TRINIDAD, VOL. 1
I/IIC1-Coll

LATIN-MUSIC; FAVORITE SONGS FROM
ARGENTINA, BRESIL, CHILE, CUBA,
HAITI, HAWAII, JAMAICA, MEXICO,
SPAIN, TRINIDAD, VOL. 2
I/IIC1-Coll

LIED- UND GITARRENSPIEL, VOLKS- UND
TANZLIEDER, VOL. I I/IIC1-Coll,
IV/IIC1

LIED- UND GITARRENSPIEL, VOLKS- UND
TANZLIEDER, VOL. II I/IIC1-Coll,
IV/IIC1

LIEDER DER VOLKER, VOL. I I/IIC1-Coll

LIEDER DER VOLKER, VOL. II I/IIC1-Coll

LIEDER DER VOLKER, VOL. III
I/IIC1-Coll

LIEDER DER VOLKER, VOL. IV I/IIC1-Coll

LIEDER DER VOLKER, VOL. V I/IIC1-Coll

LIEDER DER VOLKER, VOL. VI I/IIC1-Coll

LIEDER IM JAHRESKREIS I/IIC1-Coll

MIT DER GITARRE, UNTERHALTUNGS-ALBUM
I/IIC1-Coll

MUZIEKBIJLAGE, NO. 53 I/IIC1-Coll

O JUBEL, O FREUD, WEIHNACHTSLIEDER ZUR
GITARRE IV/IIC1

RINKE RANKE ROSENSCHEIN; 77
KINDERLIEDER I/IIC1-Coll, IV/IIC1

SONGS BY ELIZABETHAN COMPOSERS, 7
I/IIC1-Coll

SONNE, KOMM, EIN GITARRESPIELBUCH FUR
KINDER, 1-4. UNTERRICHTSJAHR
I/IIC1-Coll, IV/IIC1-Coll

SPANNENLANGER HANSEL, KINDERLIEDER
I/IIC1-Coll

STERNE UBER STILLEN STRASZEN, NEUE
LIEDER ZUR WEIHNACHT IV/IIC1

SUDAMERICANA, BERUHMTE FOLKLORISTISCHE
TANZE I/IIC1-Coll

UND DIE LIEBE BRAUCHT EIN DACH
I/IIC1-Coll

WEIHNACHTSLIEDER ZUR GITARRE IV/IIC1

WITH VOICE AND GUITAR, VOL. I:
FOLKSONGS I/IIC1-Coll

WITH VOICE AND GUITAR, VOL. II
I/IIC1-Coll

Trios — Gtr, 2 Voices

WINTERWEISSE WEIHNACHT, ALTE UND NEUE
LIEDER UM DIE WEIHNACHTSZEIT
IV/IIC2

Trios — Gtr, Voice, Treb Inst

WINTERWEISSE WEIHNACHT, ALTE UND NEUE
LIEDER UM DIE WEIHNACHTSZEIT
IV/IIC2

Quartets — Gtr, 3 Voices

CHANTS DE FRANCE ET D'AILLEURS, 20
IV/IIC4-Coll

Quintets — Gtr, 4 Voices

CHANTS DE FRANCE ET D'AILLEURS, 20
I/IIC4-Coll

Quintets — Gtr, 2 Voices, Fl, Perc

CHANTS DE FRANCE ET D'AILLEURS, 20
I/IIC4-Coll

School Ens/Orch with Gtr, Voice

ES IST EIN ROS ENTSPRUNGEN IV/IIC5

SINGSTUNDEN, DIE, NO. 1-36, LIEDER FUR
ALLE I/IIC5-Coll

WIR LERNEN HAUSMUSIK, FOLGE I-VIII
I/IIC5-Coll

Concertos

ALFONSO, JAVIER (1905-   )
Suite En Style Ancien (After Campion)
I/IIIA

APIVOR, DENIS (1916-   )
Concertino, Op. 26   I/IIIA

AZPIAZU, JOSE DE (1912-   )
Concert Baroque, In A   I/IIIA

Suite Elisabethaine Sur Des Themes De
John Dowland   I/IIIA

BAERVOETS, RAYMOND (1930-   )
Concerto   I/IIIA

BALLOU, ESTHER WILLIAMSON (1915-1973)
Concerto   I/IIIA

BARBIER, RENE (AUGUSTE-ERNEST)
(1890-1981)
Concertino, Op. 116   I/IIIB

Concerto, Op. 98   I/IIIA

BARTOLOZZI, BRUNO (1911-   )
Memorie   I/IIIC

BASTON, JOHN (ca. 1700-   )
Concerto   I/IIIA

BAUMANN, HERBERT (1925-   )
Concerto   I/IIIA

BECKER, GUNTHER (1924-   )
Caprices Concertants   I/IIIC

BEDFORD, DAVID (1937-   )
Horse, His Name Was Hunry Fencewaver
Walkins, A   I/IIIA

BEHREND, SIEGFRIED (1933-   )
Legnaniana   I/IIIA

BELAUBRE, LOUIS-NOEL (1932-   )
Symphonie Concertante   I/IIIC

BENGUEREL, XAVIER (1931-   )
Concerto   I/IIIA

BENNETT, RICHARD RODNEY (1936-   )
Concerto   I/IIIA

BERKELEY, [SIR] LENNOX (1903-   )
Concerto for Guitar and Orchestra
I/IIIA

BLAKE WATKINS, MICHAEL (1948-   )
Clouds And Eclipses   I/IIIA

BOCCHERINI, LUIGI (1743-1805)
Concerto in E   I/IIIA

BONDON, JACQUES (1927-   )
Concerto De Mars   I/IIIA

BOOGAARD, BERNARD VAN DEN (1952-   )
Concertino   I/IIIC

BORDHAYS, CHRISTIANE LE
Concierto De Azul   I/IIIA

BRANDAO, JOSE DOMINGOS (1904-   )
Lusitano, Concerto   I/IIIA

BRESGEN, CESAR (1913-   )
Kammerkonzert   I/IIIA

BROUWER, LEO (1939-   )
Concerto   I/IIIA

CARULLI, FERDINANDO (1770-1841)
Allegro Da Concerto   I/IIIA

Concerto in A   I/IIIA

Concerto in A for Guitar and String
Orchestra   I/IIIB

Concerto in G for Flute, Guitar and
Orchestra   I/IIIC

CASTELNUOVO-TEDESCO, MARIO (1895-1968)
Concerto in D, Op. 99   I/IIIA

Concerto, Op. 201   I/IIIB

Concerto Sereno In C   I/IIIA

Serenade, Op. 118   I/IIIA

CERF, JACQUES (1932-   )
Concerto Capriccioso   I/IIIA

CHARPENTIER, JACQUES (1933-   )
Concerto No. 2   I/IIIA

CHAYNES, CHARLES (1925-   )
Visions Concertantes, Concerto En 4
Parties d'Apres 4 Toiles De
Salvador Dali   I/IIIA

DAVID, THOMAS CHRISTIAN (1925-   )
Concerto   I/IIIA

FALCKENHAGEN, ADAM (1697-1761)
Concerto in F   I/IIIA

FASCH, JOHANN FRIEDRICH (1688-1758)
Concerto in D minor   I/IIIA

FERSTL, ERICH (1934-   )
Concertino   I/IIIA

Sol Y Sombra   I/IIIA

FURSTENAU, WOLFRAM
Renaissance Pour Le Presence   I/IIIC

GAITIS, FRIEDRICH
Concertino   I/IIIB

GIULIANI, MAURO (1781-1829)
Concerto in A, Op. 36   I/IIIA

Concerto No. 3 in F, Op. 70   I/IIIA

Concerto, Op. 30   I/IIIA

HANDEL, GEORGE FRIDERIC (1685-1759)
Concerto in B flat for Lute, Harp and
Orchestra   I/IIIC

HARTIG, HEINZ FRIEDRICH (1907-1969)
Concertante Suite   I/IIIA

HAUG, HANS (1900-1967)
Concertino   I/IIIA

HAYDN, [FRANZ] JOSEPH (1732-1809)
Concerto for 2 Lire Organizzate and
Orchestra, No. 2, in G   I/IIIB

HEER, HANS DE (1927-   )
Concerto   I/IIIA

HIROTA
Hamachidori, Japanese Song   I/IIIA

HOFFMANN, JOHANN
Concerto   I/IIIA

HOYER, ANTOINE L'
Concerto, Op. 16   I/IIIA

ISHII, MAKI (1936-   )
Japanische Suite I   I/IIIA

JOSEPHS, WILFRED (1927-   )
Saratoga Concerto   I/IIIC

KELKEL, MANFRED (1929-   )
Zagreber Konzert   I/IIIA

KONIETZNY, HEINRICH
Kammerkonzert   I/IIIC

KOTONSKI, WLODZIMIERZ (1925-   )
Concerto Per Quattro   I/IIIC

KREBS, JOHANN LUDWIG (1713-1780)
Concerto in C for Lute and Strings
I/IIIA

Concerto in F for Lute and Strings
I/IIIA

MARCO, TOMAS (1942-   )
Concerto   I/IIIA

MARI, PIERETTE (1929-   )
Concerto for Guitar, Strings and
Percussion   I/IIIA

MORENO TORROBA, FEDERICO (1891-1982)
Concierto De Castilla   I/IIIA

Homenaje A La Seguidilla, Concerto
I/IIIA

NOBLE
Concertino Mexicano   I/IIIA

NOVAK, JAN (1921-1984)
Concerto Per Euridice   I/IIIA

PAGANINI, NICCOLO (1782-1840)
Romance   I/IIIA

PALAU, MANUEL (1893-1967)
Concierto Levantino   I/IIIA

PETIT, PIERRE (1922-   )
Concerto   I/IIIB

PIZZINI, CARLO ALBERTO (1905-   )
Concierto Para Tres Hermanas   I/IIIA

PONCE, MANUEL MARIA (1882-1948)
Concierto Del Sur   I/IIIA

PORRINO, ENNIO (1910-1959)
Concerto Dell'Argentarola   I/IIIA

PROSEV, TOMA (1931-   )
Concerto, Op. 38   I/IIIA

RODRIGO, JOAQUIN (1902-   )
Concierto De Aranjuez   I/IIIA

Fantasia Para Un Gentilhombre,
Inspirada En Gaspar Sanz   I/IIIA

SANTORSOLA, GUIDO (1904-   )
Concertino   I/IIIA

SCHOLZ, BERND (1911-1969)
Japanisches Konzert   I/IIIA

SEIXAS, (JOSE ANTONIO) CARLOS DE
(1704-1742)
Concerto in A   I/IIIA

SMIT SIBINGA, THEO H. (1899-1958)
Concerto   I/IIIA

SOR, FERNANDO (1778-1839)
Alt Spanischer Tanz Mit Variationen
I/IIIA

STAAK, PIETER VAN DER (1930-   )
Concertino No. 2   I/IIIA

TAKACS, JENO (1902-   )
Partita, Op. 55   I/IIIA

TOMASI, HENRI (1901-1971)
Pastorales Provencales   I/IIIC

TORELLI, GIUSEPPE (1658-1709)
Concerto in D minor   I/IIIA

VILLA-LOBOS, HEITOR (1887-1959)
Concerto   I/IIIA

VIVALDI, ANTONIO (1678-1741)
Concerto in A   I/IIIA

Concerto in C   I/IIIC, I/IIIA

Concerto in D   I/IIIA

Concerto in D minor for Viola
d'Amore, Lute and Strings   I/IIIC

Concerto No. 3 in G   I/IIIB

Concerto No. 23 in C for 2 Mandolins
and Strings   I/IIIB

VLAD, ROMAN (1919-   )
Ode Super "Chrysea Phorminx"   I/IIIA

WALTER, FRIED (1907-   )
Pavan   I/IIIA

Reflexe, Variationen Durch Die
Jahrhundert Uber Ein Thema Von
Gaspar Sanz   I/IIIA

WEISS, JOHANN ADOLF
Concerto   I/IIIA

WERDIN, EBERHARD (1911-   )
Concertino   I/IIIC

WUSTHOFF, KLAUS
Collagen   I/IIIA

Publisher Directory

The list of publishers which follows contains the code assigned for each publisher, the name and address of the publisher, and U.S. agents who distribute the publications. This is the master list for the Music-In-Print series and represents all publishers who have submitted information for inclusion in the series. Therefore, all of the publishers do not necessarily occur in the present volume.

Code	Publisher	U.S. Agent
A COEUR JOIE	Éditions A Coeur Joie Les Passerelles, BP 9151 24 avenue Joannès Masset F-69263 Lyon cédex 09 France	
A MOLL DUR	A Moll Dur Publishing House 7244 D'Evereux Court Alexandria, VA 22301	
A-R ED	A-R Editions, Inc. 315 West Gorham Street Madison, WI 53703	
ABC	ABC Music Co.	BOURNE
ABER.GRP.	The Aberbach Group 988 Madison Avenue New York, NY 10021	
ABERDEEN	Aberdeen Music, Inc. 170 N.E. 33rd Street Fort Lauderdale, FL 33334	
ABINGDON	Abingdon Press P.O. Box 801 Nashville, TN 37202	
ABRSM	Associated Board of the Royal Schools of Music 14 Bedford Square London WC1B 3JG England	PRESSER
ACADEM	Academia Music Ltd. 16-5, Hongo 3-Chome Bunkyo-ku Tokyo, 113 Japan	KALMUS,A
ACCURA	Accura Music P.O. Box 4260 Athens, OH 45701-4260	
ACORD	Edizioni Accordo	CURCI
ACSB	Antigua Casa Sherry-Brener, Ltd. of Madrid 3145 West 63rd Street Chicago, IL 60629	
ADD.PRESS	Addington Press	ROYAL
ADD.-WESLEY	Addison-Wesley Publishing Co., Inc. 2725 Sand Hill Road Menlo Park, CA 94025	
AEOLUS	Aeolus Publishing Co. 60 Park Terrace West New York, NY 10034	
AGAPE	Agape	HOPE
AHLINS	Ahlins Musikförlag Box 26072 S-100 41 Stockholm Sweden	
AHN	Ahn & Simrock Sonnenstraße 19 D-8 München Germany	

Code	Publisher	U.S. Agent
AKADDV	Akademische Druck- und Verlagsanstalt Graz Austria	
AKADEM	Akademiska Musikförlaget Sirkkalagatan 7 B 48 SF-20500 Abo 50 Finland	
ALBERSEN	Muziekhandel Albersen & Co. Groot Hertoginnelaan 182 NL-2517 EV Den Haag Netherlands	DONEMUS
ALBERT	J. Albert & Son Pty. Ltd. 139 King Street Sydney, N.S.W. Australia 2000	
ALBERT	J. Albert & Son - U.S.A. 1619 Broadway New York, NY 10019	
ALCOVE	Alcove Music	WESTERN
ALEX.HSE.	Alexandria House P.O. Box 300 Alexandria, IN 46001	
ALFRED	Alfred Publishing Co. 16380 Roscoe Blvd. P.O. Box 10003 Van Nuys, CA 91410	
ALKOR	Alkor Edition	FOR.MUS.DIST.
ALLANS	Allans Music Australia Ltd. Box 513J, G.P.O. Melbourne 3001 Australia	PRESSER
ALLOWAY	Alloway Publications P.O. Box 25 Santa Monica, CA 90406	
ALMITRA	Almitra	KENDOR
ALMO	Almo Publications	COLUMBIA PIC.
ALPEG	Alpeg	PETERS
ALPHENAAR	W. Alphenaar Kruisweg 47-49 NL-2011 LA Haarlem Netherlands	
ALPUERTO	Editorial Alpuerto Caños del Peral 7 28013 Madrid Spain	
ALSBACH	G. Alsbach & Co. P.O. Box 338 NL-1400 AH Bussum Netherlands	
ALSBACH&D	Alsbach & Doyer	
AM.COMP.ALL.	American Composers Alliance 170 West 74th Street New York, NY 10023	
AM.INST.MUS.	American Institute of Musicology	FOSTER

Code	Publisher	U.S. Agent
AM.MUS.ED.	American Music Edition 263 East Seventh Street New York, NY 10009	PRESSER (partial)
AMADEUS	Amadeus Verlag Bernhard Päuler Am Iberghang 16 CH-8405 Winterthur Switzerland	FOR.MUS.DIST
	American Musicological Society 201 South 34th Street Philadelphia, PA 19104	SCHIRM.EC
	American String Teachers Association see ASTA	
AMICI	Gli Amici della Musica da Camera Via Bocca di Leone 25 Roma Italy	
AMP	Associated Music Publishers 24 E. 22nd St. New York, NY 10010	LEONARD-US (sales) SCHIRM.G (rental)
AMPHION	Éditions Amphion 12, rue Rougement F-75009 Paris France	KERBY
AMS PRESS	AMS Press, Inc. 56 East 13th Street New York, NY 10003	
AMSCO	AMSCO Music Publishing Co.	MUSIC
AMSI	Art Masters Studios, Inc. 2710 Nicollet Avenue Minneapolis, MN 55408	
ANDEL	Edition Andel Madeliefjeslaan, 26 B-8400 Oostende Belgium	ELKAN,H
ANDERSONS	Anderssons Musikförlag Sodra Forstadsgatan 6 Box 17018 S-200 10 Malmö Sweden	
ANDRE	Johann André Musikverlag Frankfurterstraße 28 Postfach 141 D-6050 Offenbach-am-Main Germany	
ANERCA	Anerca Music 35 St. Andrew's Garden Toronto, Ontario M4W 2C9 Canada	
ANFOR	Anfor Music Publishers (Div. of Terminal Music Supply) 1619 East Third Street Brooklyn, NY 11230	MAGNA D
ANTARA	Antara Music Group P.O. Box 210 Alexandria, IN 46001	
ANTICO	Antico Edition North Harton, Lustleigh Newton Abbot Devon TQ13 9SG England	BOSTON EMC
APM	Artist Production & Management	VIERT
APNM	Association for Promotion of New Music 2002 Central Avenue Ship Bottom, NJ 08008	
APOGEE	Apogee Press	WORLD
APOLLO	Apollo-Verlag Paul Lincke Ostpreussendamm 26 D-1000 Berlin 45 Germany	

Code	Publisher	U.S. Agent
ARCADIA	Arcadia Music Publishing Co., Ltd. P.O. Box 1 Rickmansworth Herts WD3 3AZ England	
ARCO	Arco Music Publishers	WESTERN
ARGM	Editorial Argentina de Musica & Editorial Saraceno	PEER
ARION	Coleccion Arion	MEXICANAS
ARION PUB	Arion Publications, Inc. 4964 Kathleen Avenue Castro Valley, CA 94546	
ARISTA	Arista Music Co. 8370 Wilshire Blvd. Beverly Hills, CA 90211	COLUMBIA PIC.
ARNOLD	Edward Arnold Series	NOVELLO
ARS NOVA	Ars Nova Publications 121 Washington San Diego, CA 92103	ELKAN-V
ARS POLONA	Ars Polona Krakowskie Przedmieście 7 Skrytka pocztowa 1001 PL-00-950 Warszawa Poland	
ARS VIVA	Ars Viva Verlag Weihergarten D-6500 Mainz 1 Germany	EUR.AM.MUS.
ARSIS	Arsis Press 1719 Bay Street SE Washington, DC 20003	PLYMOUTH
ARTHUR	J. Arthur Music The University Music House 4290 North High Street Columbus, OH 43214	
ARTIA	Artia Prag Ve Smečkách 30 Praha 2 Czechoslovakia	FOR.MUS.DIST.
	Artist Production & Management see APM	
ARTRANSA	Artransa Music	WESTERN
ASCHERBERG	Ascherberg, Hopwood & Crew Ltd. 50 New Bond Street London W1 A 2BR England	
ASHDOWN	Edwin Ashdown Ltd.	BRODT
ASHLEY	Ashley Publications, Inc. P.O. Box 337 Hasbrouck Heights, NJ 07604	
ASPEN	Aspen Grove Music P.O. Box 977 North Hollywood, CA 91603	
ASSMANN	Hermann Assmann, Musikverlag Franz-Werfel-Straße 36 D-6000 Frankfurt 50 Germany	
	Associated Board of the Royal Schools of Music see ABRSM	
	Associated Music Publishers see AMP	
	Association for Promotion of New Music see APNM	

Code	Publisher	U.S. Agent
ASTA	American String Teachers Association	PRESSER
ATV	ATV Music Publications 6255 Sunset Boulevard Hollywood, CA 90028	CHERRY
AUGSBURG	Augsburg Publishing House 426 South Fifth Street P.O. Box 1209 Minneapolis, MN 55440	
AULOS	Aulos Music Publishers P.O. Box 54 Montgomery, NY 12549	
AUTOGR	Autographus Musicus Ardalavägen 158 S-124 32 Bandhagen Sweden	
AUTRY	Gene Autry's Publishing Companies	COLUMBIA PIC.
AVANT	Avant Music	WESTERN
BAGGE	Jacob Bagge	STIM
BANK	Annie Bank Musiek Anna Vondelstraat 13 NL-1054 GX Amsterdam Netherlands	
BANKS	Banks Music Publications 139 Holgate Road York YO2 4DF England	BRODT
BAREN.	Bärenreiter Verlag Heinrich Schütz Allee 31-37 Postfach 100329 D-3500 Kassel-Wilhelmshöhe Germany	FOR.MUS.DIST.
BARNHS	C.L. Barnhouse 110 B Avenue East Oskaloosa, IA 52577	
BARON,M	M. Baron Co. P.O. Box 149 Oyster Bay, NY 11771	
BARRY-ARG	Barry & Cia Talcahuano 860, Bajo B Buenos Aires 1013-Cap. Federal Argentina	BOOSEY
BARTA	Barta Music Company	JERONA
BASART	Les Éditions Internationales Basart	GENERAL
BASEL	Musik-Akademie der Stadt Basel Leonhardsstraße 6 CH-4051 Basel Switzerland	
BAUER	Georg Bauer Musikverlag Luisenstraße 47-49 Postfach 1467 D-7500 Karlsruhe Germany	
BAVTON	Bavariaton-Verlag München Germany	ORLANDO
	Mel Bay Publications see MEL BAY	
BEACON HILL	Beacon Hill Music	LILLENAS
BECKEN	Beckenhorst Press P.O. Box 14273 Columbus, OH 43214	

Code	Publisher	U.S. Agent
BEECHWD	Beechwood Music Corporation 1750 Vine Street Hollywood, CA 90028	WARNER
BEEK	Beekman Music, Inc.	PRESSER
BEIAARD	Beiaardschool Belgium	
BELAIEFF	M.P. Belaieff Kennedyallee 101 D-6000 Frankfurt-am-Main 70 Germany	PETERS
	Centre Belge de Documentation Musicale see CBDM	
BELLA	Bella Roma Music 1442A Walnut Street Suite 197 Berkeley, CA 94709	
BELMONT	Belmont Music Publishers P.O. Box 231 Pacific Palisades, CA 90272	
BELWIN	Belwin-Mills Publishing Corp. 15800 N.W. 48th Avenue P.O. Box 4340 Miami, FL 33014	COLUMBIA PIC. PRESSER (rental)
BENJ	Anton J. Benjamin Werderstraße 44 Postfach 2561 D-2000 Hamburg 13 Germany	PRESSER
BENNY	Claude Benny Press 1401½ State Street Emporia, KS 66801	
BENSON	John T. Benson P.O. Box 107 Nashville, TN 37202-0107	
BERANDOL	Berandol Music Ltd. 11 St. Joseph Street Toronto, Ontario M4Y 1J8 Canada	
BERBEN	Edizioni Musicali Berben Via Redipuglia 65 I-60100 Ancona Italy	PRESSER
BERGMANS	W. Bergmans	BANK
BERKLEE	Berklee Press Publications 195 Ipswich Street Boston, MA 02215	LEONARD-US
BERLIN	Irving Berlin Music Corp. 1290 Avenue of the Americas New York, NY 10019	
BERNOUILLI	Ed. Bernouilli	DONEMUS
BESSEL	Éditions Bessel & Cie	BREITKOPF-W
BEUSCH	Éditions Paul Beuscher Arpège 27, Boulevard Beaumarchais F-75004 Paris France	
BEZIGE BIJ	De Bezige Bij	DONEMUS
BIELER	Edmund Bieler Musikverlag Thürmchenswall 72 D-5000 Köln 1 Germany	
BIG BELL	Big Bells, Inc. 33 Hovey Avenue Trenton, NJ 08610	

Code	Publisher	U.S. Agent
BIG3	Big Three Music Corp.	COLUMBIA PIC.
BILLAUDOT	Éditions Billaudot 14, rue de l'Echiquier F-75010 Paris France	PRESSER
BIRCH	Robert Fairfax Birch	PRESSER
BIRNBACH	Richard Birnbach Musikverlag Aubinger Straße 9 D-8032 Lochheim bei München Germany	
BIZET	Bizet Productions and Publications	ELKAN-V
BMI	Broadcast Music, Inc. 320 West 57th Street New York, NY 10019	
	Boccaccini and Spada Editori see BSE	
BOCK	Fred Bock Music Co. P.O. Box 333 Tarzana, CA 91356	ALEX.HSE.
BODENS	Edition Ernst Fr. W. Bodensohn Dr. Rumpfweg 1 D-7570 Baden-Baden 21 Germany see also ERST	
BOEIJENGA	Boeijenga Muziekhandel Kleinzand 89 NL-8601 BG Sneek Netherlands	
BOELKE-BOM	Boelke-Bomart Music Publications Hillsdale, NY 12529	JERONA
BOETHIUS	Boethius Press Clarabricken, Clifden Co. Kilkenny Ireland	
BOHM	Anton Böhm & Sohn Postfach 110369 Lange Gasse 26 D-8900 Augsburg 11 Germany	
BOIS	Bureau De Musique Mario Bois 17 Rue Richer F-75009 Paris France	
BOMART	Bomart Music Publications	BOELKE-BOM
BONART	Bonart Publications	CAN.MUS. CENT.
BONGIOVANI	Casa Musicale Francesco Bongiovanni Via Rizzoli 28 E I-40125 Bologna Italy	
BOONIN	Joseph Boonin, Inc.	EUR.AM.MUS.
BOOSEY	Boosey & Hawkes Inc. 24 W. 57th St. New York, NY 10019 Boosey & Hawkes Rental Library 52 Cooper Square New York, NY 10003-7102	
BOOSEY-CAN	Boosey & Hawkes Ltd. 279 Yorkland Boulevard Willowdale, Ontario M2J 1S7 Canada	BOOSEY
BOOSEY-ENG	Boosey & Hawkes 295 Regent Street London W1 R 8JH England	BOOSEY

Code	Publisher	U.S. Agent
BORNEMANN	Éditions Bornemann 15 rue de Tournon F-75006 Paris France	PRESSER
BOSSE	Gustav Bosse Verlag Von der Tann Straße 38 Postfach 417 D-8400 Regensburg 1 Germany	MMB EUR.AM.MUS.
BOSTON	Boston Music Co. 9 Airport Drive Hopedale, MA 01747	
BOSTON EMC	Boston Early Music Center P.O. Box 483 Cambridge, MA 02238-0483	
BOSWORTH	Bosworth & Company, Ltd. 14-18 Heddon Street, Regent Street London W1 R 8DP England	BRODT
BOTE	Bote & Bock Hardenbergstraße 9A D-1000 Berlin 12 Germany	LEONARD-US SCHIRM.G (rental)
BOURNE	Bourne Co. 5 W. 37th Street New York, NY 10018-6232	
BOWDOIN	Bowdoin College Music Press Department of Music Bowdoin College Brunswick, ME 04011	
BOWM	Bowmaster Productions 3351 Thornwood Road Sarasota, FL 33581	
BR.CONT.MUS.	British And Continental Music Agencies Ltd.	EMI
BRADLEY	Bradley Publications 80 8th Avenue New York, NY 10011	COLUMBIA PIC.
BRANCH	Harold Branch Publishing, Inc. 95 Eads Street West Babylon, NY 11704	
BRANDEN	Branden Press, Inc. 17 Station Street P.O. Box 843 Brookline Village, MA 02147	
BRASS PRESS	The Brass Press 136 8th Avenue North Nashville, TN 37203-3798	
BRATFISCH	Musikverlag Georg Bratfisch Kressenstein Straße 12 Postfach 1105 D-8650 Kulmbach Germany	
BRAUER	Les Éditions Musicales Herman Brauer 30, rue St. Christophe B-1000 Bruxelles Belgium	
BRAUN-PER	St. A. Braun-Peretti Hahnchenpassage D-53 Bonn Germany	
BRAVE	Brave New Music	SON-KEY
BREITKOPF-L	Breitkopf & Härtel Karlstraße 10 DDR-7010 Leipzig Germany	BROUDE,A

Code	Publisher	U.S. Agent
BREITKOPF-LN	Breitkopf & Härtel	BROUDE,A FENTONE
BREITKOPF-W	Breitkopf & Härtel Walkmühlstraße 52 Postfach 1707 D-6200 Wiesbaden 1 Germany	
BRENNAN	John Brennan Music Publisher Positif Press Ltd. 130 Southfield Road Oxford OX4 1 PA England	ORGAN LIT
BRENT	Michael Brent Publications, Inc. P.O. Box 1186 Port Chester, NY 10573	CHERRY
BRENTWOOD	Brentwood Publishing Group Inc. P.O. Box 19001 Brentwood, TN 37027	
BRIDGE	Bridge Music Publishing Co. 1350 Villa Street Mountain View, CA 94042	
BRIGHT STAR	Bright Star Music Publications	WESTERN
	British and Continental Music Agencies Inc. see BR.CONT.MUS.	
	Broadcast Music, Inc. see BMI	
BROADMAN	Broadman Press 127 Ninth Avenue, North Nashville, TN 37234	
BRODT	Brodt Music Co. P.O. Box 9345 Charlotte, NC 28299-9345	
BROEKMANS	Broekmans & Van Poppel B.V. van Baerlestraat 92-94 NL-1071 BB Amsterdam Netherlands	
BROGNEAUX	Éditions Musicales Brogneaux 73, Avenue Paul Janson B-1070 Bruxelles Belgium	ELKAN,H
BROOK	Brook Publishing Co. 3602 Cedarbrook Road Cleveland Heights, OH 44118	
BROUDE,A	Alexander Broude, Inc. 575 Eighth Avenue New York, NY 10018	
BROUDE BR.	Broude Brothers Ltd. 141 White Oaks Road Williamstown, MA 01267	
	Broude Brothers Ltd.-Rental Dept. 170 Varick St. New York, NY 10013	
BROWN	Brown University Choral Series	BOOSEY
BROWN,R	Rayner Brown 2423 Panorama Terrace Los Angeles, CA 90039	
BROWN,WC	William C. Brown Co. 2460 Kerper Boulevard Dubuque, IA 52001	
BRUCK	Musikverlag M. Bruckbauer "Biblioteca de la Guitarra" Postfach 18 D-7953 Bad Schussenried Germany	
BRUCKNER	Bruckner Verlag Austria	PETERS (rental) MMB (sales)

Code	Publisher	U.S. Agent
BRUZZI	Aldo Bruzzichelli, Editore Lungarno Guicciardini 27r I-50124 Firenze Italy	MARGUN
BSE	Boccaccini and Spada Editori	PRESSER
BUBONIC	Bubonic Publishing Co. 706 Lincoln Avenue St. Paul, MN 55105	
BUDAPEST	Editio Musica Budapest (Kultura) P.O.B. 322 H-1370 Budapest Hungary see also EMB	BOOSEY PRESSER
BUDDE	Rolf Budde Musikverlag Hohenzollerndamm 54A D-1000 Berlin 33 Germany	
BUSCH	Hans Busch Musikförlag Stubbstigen 3 S-18147 Lidingö Sweden	STIM
BUSCH,E	Ernst Busch Verlag Schlossstrasse 43 D-7531 Neulingen-Bauschlott Germany	
BUTZ	Dr. J. Butz Musikverlag Postfach 3008 5205 Sankt Augustin 3 Germany	
CAILLARD	Création & Diffusion Musicale L'Ensemble Vocal Philippe Caillard 60, rue de Brément 93130 Noisy-Le-Sec France	
CAILLET	Lucien Cailliet	SOUTHERN
CAM	Camerica Music	COLUMBIA PIC.
CAMBIATA	Cambiata Press P.O. Box 1151 Conway, AR 72032	
CAMBRIA	Cambria Records & Publishing P.O. Box 374 Lomita, CA 90717	
CAMBRIDGE	Cambridge University Press The Edinburgh Building Shaftesbury Road Cambridge CB2 2RU England	
CAMPUS	Campus Publishers 713 Ellsworth Road West Ann Arbor, MI 48104	
CAN.MUS.CENT.	Canadian Music Centre 20 St. Joseph Street Toronto, Ontario M4Y 1J9 Canada	
CAN.MUS.HER.	Canadian Musical Heritage Society Patrimoine Musical Canadien 2660 Southvale Cr., Suite 111 Ottawa, Ontario K1B 4W5 Canada	
CANAAN	Canaanland Publications	WORD
CANYON	Canyon Press, Inc. P.O. Box 447 Islamorada, FL 33036	KERBY
CAPELLA	Capella Music, Inc.	BOURNE

Code	Publisher	U.S. Agent
CAPPR	Capital Press	PODIUM
CARABO	Carabo-Cone Method Foundation 1 Sherbrooke Road Scarsdale, NY 10583	
CARISCH	Carisch S.p.A. Via General Fara, 39 Casella Postale 10170 I-20124 Milano Italy	
CARLIN	Carlin Publications P.O. Box 2289 Oakhurst, CA 93644	
CARLTON	Carlton Musikverlag	BREITKOPF-W
CARUS	Carus-Verlag	FOSTER
CATHEDRAL	Cathedral Music School House, The Croft Cocking, Midhurst West Sussex GU29 0HQ England	
	Catholic Conference see U.S.CATH	
CAVATA	Cavata Music Publishers, Inc.	PRESSER
CAVELIGHT	Cavelight Music P.O. Box 85 Oxford, NJ 07863	
CBC	Cundey Bettoney Co.	FISCHER,C
CBDM	CeBeDeM Centre Belge de Documentation Musicale rue d'Arlon 75-77 B-1040 Bruxelles Belgium	ELKAN,H
CCMP	Colorado College Music Press Colorado Springs, CO 80903	
CEL	Celesta Publishing Co. P.O. Box 560603, Kendall Branch Miami, FL 33156	
	Centre Belge de Documentation Musicale see CBDM	
	Éditions du Centre Nationale de la Recherche Scientifique see CNRS	
CENTURY	Century Music Publishing Co. 263 Veterans Boulevard Carlstadt, NJ 07072	ASHLEY
CENTURY PR	Century Press Publishers 412 North Hudson Oklahoma City, OK 73102	
CESKY HUD.	Cesky Hudebni Fond Parizska 13 CS-110 00 Praha 1 Czechoslovakia	BOOSEY (rental)
CHANT	Éditions Le Chant du Monde 23, rue Royale F-75008 Paris France	
CHANTERL	Editions Chanterelle S.A. Postfach 103909 D-69 Heidelberg Germany	BAREN.
CHANTRY	Chantry Music Press, Inc. Wittenberg University P.O. Box 1101 Springfield, OH 45501	
CHAPLET	Chaplet Music Corp.	PARAGON

Code	Publisher	U.S. Agent
CHAPPELL	Chappell & Co., Inc. 810 Seventh Avenue New York, NY 10019	LEONARD-US
CHAPPELL-CAN	Chappell Music Canada Ltd 85 Scarsdale Road, Unit 101 Don Mills, Ontario M3B 2R2 Canada	LEONARD-US
CHAPPELL-ENG	Chappell & Co., Ltd. Printed Music Division 60-70 Roden Street Ilford, Essex IG1 2AQ England	LEONARD-US
CHAPPELL-FR	Chappell S.A. 25, rue d'Hauteville F-75010 Paris France	LEONARD-US
CHAR CROS	Charing Cross Music, Inc. 1619 Broadway, Suite 500 New York, NY 10019	
CHARTER	Charter Publications, Inc. P.O. Box 850 Valley Forge, PA 19482	PEPPER
CHENANGO	Chenango Valley Music Press P.O. Box 251 Hamilton, NY 13346	
CHERITH	Cherith Publishing Co.	SON-KEY
CHERRY	Cherry Lane Music Co. Box 4247 50 Old Post Rd. Greenwich, CT 06830	ALFRED
CHESTER	J. & W. Chester, Ltd. Chester Music-Edition Wilhelm Hansen 7-9 Eagle Court London EC1M 5QD England	MMB
CHILTERN	Chiltern Music	CATHEDRAL
CHOIR	Choir Publishing Co. 564 Columbus Street Salt Lake City, UT 84103	
CHORISTERS	Choristers Guild 2834 West Kingsley Road Garland, TX 75041	LORENZ
CHOUDENS	Édition Choudens 38, rue Jean Mermoz F-75008 Paris France	ELKAN-V PETERS
CHRI	Christopher Music Co. 380 South Main Place Carol Stream, IL 60187	
CHRIS	Christophorus-Verlag Herder Hermann-Herder-Straße 4 D-7800 Freiburg Breisgau Germany	
CHURCH	John Church Co.	PRESSER
CJC	Creative Jazz Composers, Inc. P.O. Box K Odenton, MD 21113	
CLARION	Clarion Call Music	SON-KEY
CLARK	Clark and Cruickshank Music Publishers	BERANDOL
CLIVIS	Clivis Publicacions C-Còrsega, 619 Baixos Barcelona 25 Spain	

Code	Publisher	U.S. Agent
CMP	CMP Library Service MENC Historical Center/SCIM Music Library/Hornbake University of Maryland College Park, MD 20742	
CNRS	Éditions du Centre National de la Recherche Scientifique 15, quai Anatole-France F-75700 Paris France	SMPF
COBURN	Coburn Press	PRESSER
CODERG	Coderg-U.C.P. sàrl 42 bis, rue Boursault F-75017 Paris France	
COLE	M.M. Cole Publishing Co. 919 North Michigan Avenue Chicago, IL 60611	
COLEMAN	Dave Coleman Music, Inc. P.O. Box 230 Montesano, WA 98563	
COLFRANC	Colfranc Music Publishing Corp.	KERBY
COLIN	Charles Colin 315 West 53rd Street New York, NY 10019	
COLOMBO	Franco Colombo Publications	COLUMBIA PIC. PRESSER (rental)
	Colorado College Music Press see CCMP	
COLUM UNIV	Columbia University Music Press 562 West 113th Street New York, NY 10025	SCHIRM.EC
COLUMBIA	Columbia Music Co.	PRESSER
COLUMBIA PIC.	Columbia Pictures Publications 15800 N.W. 48th Avenue Miami, FL 33014	
COMBRE	Consortium Musical, Marcel Combre Editeur 24, Boulevard Poissonnière F-75009 Paris France	PRESSER
COMP.FAC.	Composers Facsimile Edition	AM.COMP.AL.
COMP.LIB.	Composer's Library Editions	PRESSER
COMP-PERF	Composer/Performer Edition 2101 22nd Street Sacramento, CA 95818	
COMP.PR.	The Composers Press, Inc.	OPUS
COMPOSER'S GR	Composer's Graphics 5702 North Avenue Carmichael, CA 95608	
CONCERT	Concert Music Publishing Co. c/o Studio P-R, Inc. 16333 N.W. 54th Avenue Hialeah, FL 33014	COLUMBIA PIC.
CONCORD	Concord Music Publishing Co.	ELKAN,H
CONCORDIA	Concordia Publishing House 3558 South Jefferson Avenue St. Louis, MO 63118-3968	
CONGRESS	Congress Music Publications 100 Biscayne Boulevard Miami, FL 33132	
CONSOL	Consolidated Music Publishers, Inc. 33 West 60th Street New York, NY 10023	

Code	Publisher	U.S. Agent
CONSORT	Consort Music, Inc. (Division of Magnamusic Distributors) Sharon, CT 06069	
CONSORT PR	Consort Press P.O. Box 50413 Santa Barbara, CA 93150-0413	MAGNA D
CONSORTIUM	Consortium Musical	ELKAN-V
	Consortium Musical, Marcel Combre Editeur see COMBRE	
CONTINUO	Continuo Music Press, Inc.	PLYMOUTH
	Editorial Cooperativa Inter-Americana de Compositores see ECOAM	
COPPENRATH	Musikverlag Alfred Coppenrath Neuottinger Straße 32 D-8262 Altotting-Obb. Germany	
COR PUB	Cor Publishing Co. 67 Bell Place Massapequa, NY 11758	
CORONA	Edition Corona-Rolf Budde Hohenzollerndamm 54A D-1 Berlin 33 Germany	
CORONET	Coronet Press	PRESSER
COROZINE	Vince Corozine Music Publishing Co. 6 Gabriel Drive Peekskill, NY 10566	
COSTALL	Éditions Costallat 60 rue de la Chaussée d'Antin F-75441 Paris Cedex 09 France	PRESSER
COVENANT	Covenant Press 3200 West Foster Avenue Chicago, IL 60625	
COVENANT MUS	Covenant Music 1640 East Big Thompson Avenue Estes Park, CO 80517	
CRAMER	J.B. Cramer & Co., Ltd. 23 Garrick Street London WC2E 9AX England	BELWIN
CRANZ	Éditions Cranz 30, rue St.-Christophe B-1000 Bruxelles Belgium	PRESSER ELKAN,H
	Creative Jazz Composers see CJC	
CRES.-NETH	Uitgeverij Crescendo	DONEMUS
CRESCENDO	Crescendo Music Sales Co. P.O. Box 395 Naperville, IL 60540	FEMA
CRESPUB	Crescendo Publications, Inc. 6311 North O'Connor Road #112 Irving, TX 75039-3112	
CRITERION	Criterion Music Corp. P.O. Box 660 Lynbrook, NY 11563	
CROATICA	Croatian Music Institute	DRUS.HRVAT. SKLAD.

Code	Publisher	U.S. Agent
CRON	Edition Cron Luzern Zinggentorstraße 5 CH-6006 Luzern Switzerland	
CROWN	Crown Music Press 4119 North Pittsburgh Chicago, IL 60634	BRASS PRESS (partial)
	Cundey Bettoney Co. see CBC	
CURCI	Edizioni Curci Galleria del Corso 4 I-20122 Milano Italy	COLUMBIA PIC.
CURTIS	Curtis Music Press	KJOS
CURWEN	J. Curwen & Sons	LEONARD-US SCHIRM.G (rental)
CZECH	Czechoslovak Music Information Centre Besedni 3 CS-118 00 Praha 1 Czechoslovakia	BOOSEY (rental)
DA CAPO	Da Capo Press, Inc. 233 Spring Street New York, NY 10013	
	Samfundet til udgivelse af Dansk Musik see SAMFUNDET	
DANTALIAN	Dantalian, Inc. Eleven Pembroke Street Newton, MA 02158	
DAVIMAR	Davimar Music M. Productions 159 West 53rd Street New York, NY 10019	
DE MONTE	De Monte Music F-82240 Septfonds France	
DE SANTIS	Edizioni de Santis Viale Mazzini, 6 I-00195 Roma Italy	
DEAN	Roger Dean Publishing Co. 345 West Jackson Street, #B Macomb, IL 61455-2112	LORENZ
DEIRO	Pietro Deiro Publications 133 Seventh Avenue South New York, NY 10014	
DELRIEU	Georges Delrieu & Cie Palais Bellecour B 14, rue Trachel F-06000 Nice France	GALAXY
DENNER	Erster Bayerischer Musikverlag Joh. Dennerlein KG Beethovenstraße 7 D-8032 Lochham Germany	
DESERET	Deseret Music Publishers P.O. Box 900 Orem, UT 84057	MUSICART
DESHON	Deshon Music, Inc.	BELWIN PRESSER (rental)
DESSAIN	Éditions Dessain Belgium	

Code	Publisher	U.S. Agent
DEUTSCHER	Deutscher Verlag für Musik Postschließfach 147 Karlstraße 10 DDR-7010 Leipzig Germany	WESL (rental)
DEWOLF	DeWolfe Ltd. 80/88 Wardour Street London W1V 3LF England	DONEMUS
DIAPASON	The Diapason Press Dr. Rudolf A. Rasch Drift 21 NL-3512 BR Utrecht Netherlands	
DIESTERWEG	Verlag Moritz Diesterweg Hochstraße 31 D-6000 Frankfurt-am-Main Germany	
	Dilia Prag see DP	
DIP PROV	Diputacion Provincal de Barcelona Servicio de Bibliotecas Carmen 47 Barcelona 1 Spain	
DITSON	Oliver Ditson Co.	PRESSER
DOBER	Les Éditions Doberman-Yppan C.P. 2021 St. Nicholas, Quebec G0S 3L0 Canada	BOOSEY
DOBLINGER	Ludwig Doblinger Verlag Dorotheergasse 10 A-1011 Wien I Austria	FOR.MUS.DIST.
DOMINIS	Dominis Music Ltd. Box 11307, Station H Ottawa Ontario K2H 7V1 Canada	
DONEMUS	Donemus Foundation Paulus Potterstraat 14 NL-1071 CZ Amsterdam Netherlands	PRESSER
DOORWAY	Doorway Music 2509 Buchanan Street Nashville, TN 37208	
DORABET	Dorabet Music Co. 1326 W. Santa Ana Anaheim, CA 92802	NATIONAL
DORING	G.F. Döring Musikverlag Hasenplatz 5-6 D-7033 Herrenburg 1 Germany	
DOUBLDAY	Doubleday & Co., Inc. 501 Franklin Avenue Garden City, NY 11530	
DOUGLAS,B	Byron Douglas	COLUMBIA PIC.
DOVEHOUSE	Dovehouse Editions 32 Glen Avenue Ottawa, Ontario K1S 2Z7 Canada	
DOVER	Dover Publications, Inc. 31 East 2nd Street Mineola, NY 11501	ALFRED
DOXO	Doxology Music P.O. Box M Aiken, SC 29801	

Code	Publisher	U.S. Agent
DP	Dilia Prag	BAREN.
DRAGON	Dragon Music Co. 28908 Grayfox Street Malibu, CA 90265	
DREIK	Dreiklang-Dreimasken Bühnen- und Musikverlag D-8000 München Germany	ORLANDO
DRUS.HRVAT. SKLAD.	Društvo Hrvatskih Skladatelja Berislavićeva 9 Zagreb Yugoslavia	
DRUSTVA	Edicije Drustva Slovenskih Skladateljev Trg Francoske Revolucije 6 YU-61000 Ljubljana Yugoslavia	
DRZAVNA	Drzavna Zalozba Slovenije	DRUSTVA
DUCKWORTH	Gerald Duckworth & Co., Ltd. 43 Gloucester Crescent London, NW1 England	
DURAND	Durand & Cie 215, rue du Faubourg St.-Honore F-75008 Paris France	ELKAN-V
DUTTON	E.P. Dutton & Co., Inc. 201 Park Avenue South New York, NY 10003	
DUX	Edition Dux Arthur Turk Beethovenstraße 7 D-8032 Lochham Germany	DENNER
EAR.MUS.FAC.	Early Music Facsimiles P.O. Box 711 Columbus, OH 43216	
	East West Publications see EWP	
EASTMAN	Eastman School of Music	FISCHER,C
EBLE	Eble Music Co. P.O. Box 2570 Iowa City, IA 52244	
ECK	Van Eck & Zn.	DONEMUS
ECOAM	Editorial Cooperativa Inter-Americana de Compositores Casilla de Correa No. 540 Montevideo Uruguay	PEER
EDI-PAN	Edi-Pan	DE SANTIS
EDUTAIN	Edu-tainment Publications (Div. of the Evolve Music Group) P.O. Box 20767 New York, NY 10023	
EERSTE	De Eerste Muziekcentrale Flevolaan 41 NL-1411 KC Naarden Netherlands	
EGTVED	Edition EGTVED P.O. Box 20 DK-6040 Egtved Denmark	EUR.AM.MUS.
EHRLING	Thore Ehrling Musik AB Linnegatan 9-11 Box 5268 S-102 45 Stockholm Sweden	

Code	Publisher	U.S. Agent
EIGEN UITGAVE	Eigen Uitgave van de Componist (Composer's Own Publication)	DONEMUS
ELITE	Elite Edition	SCHAUR
ELKAN,H	Henri Elkan Music Publisher P.O. Box 279 Hastings On Hudson, NY 10706	
ELKAN&SCH	Elkan & Schildknecht Vastmannagatan 95 S-113 43 Stockholm Sweden	
ELKAN-V	Elkan-Vogel, Inc. Presser Place Bryn Mawr, PA 19010	
ELKIN	Elkin & Co., Ltd	PRESSER
EMB	Editio Musica Budapest P.O.B. 322 H-1370 Budapest Hungary see also BUDAPEST	BOOSEY PRESSER
EMEC	Editorial de Musica Española Contemporanea Ediciones Quiroga Alcalá, 70 Madrid 9 Spain	
EMERSON	Emerson Edition Windmill Farm Ampleforth York YO6 4DD England	EBLE GROVE KING,R WOODWIND
EMI	EMI Music Publishing Ltd. 138-140 Charing Cross Road London WC2H OLD England	INTER.MUS.P.
ENGELS	Musikverlag Carl Engels Nachf. Auf dem Brand 3 D-5000 Köln 50 (Rodenkirchen) Germany	
ENGSTROEM	Engstroem & Soedering Palaegade 6 DK-1261 København K Denmark	PETERS
ENOCH	Enoch & Cie 193 Boulevard Pereire F-75017 Paris France	PRESSER
ENSEMB	Ensemble Publications P.O. Box 98, Bidwell Station Buffalo, NY 14222	
ENSEMB PR	Ensemble Music Press	FISCHER,C
EPHROS	Gershon Ephros Cantorial Anthology Foundation, Inc	TRANSCON.
ERDMANN	Rudolf Erdmann, Musikverlag Adolfsallee 34 D-62 Wiesbaden Germany	
ERES	Edition Eres Horst Schubert Hauptstrasse 35 Postfach 1220 D-2804 Lilienthal/Bremen Germany	
ERICKSON	E.J. Erickson Music Co. 606 North Fourth Street P.O.Box 97 St. Peter, MN 56082	

Code	Publisher	U.S. Agent
ERIKS	Eriks Musikhandel & Förlag AB Karlavägen 40 S-114 49 Stockholm Sweden	
ERST	Erstausgaben Bodensohn see also BODENS	
ESCHIG	Éditions Max Eschig 48 rue de Rome F-75008 Paris France	LEONARD-US SCHIRM.G (rental)
	Editorial de Musica Española Contemporanea see EMEC	
	Union Musical Española see UNION ESP	
ESSEX	Clifford Essex Music	MUSIC-ENG
ESSO	Van Esso & Co.	DONEMUS
ETLING,F	Forest R. Etling see HIGHLAND	
ETOILE	Etoile Music, Inc. Publications Division Shell Lake, WI 54871	MMB
EULENBURG	Edition Eulenburg 305 Bloomfield Ave. Nutley, NJ 07110	FOR.MUS.DIST. EUR.AM. (miniature scores)
EUR.AM.MUS.	European American Music Corp. P.O. Box 850 Valley Forge, PA 19482	
EWP	East West Publications	MUSIC
EXCELSIOR	Excelsior Music Publishing Co.	PRESSER
EXPO PR	Exposition Press 325 Kings Highway Smithtown, NY 11787	
FABER	Faber Music Ltd. 3 Queen Street London WC1N 3AU England	LEONARD-US SCHIRM.G (rental)
FAIR	Fairfield Publishing, Ltd.	PRESSER
FAITH	Faith Music	LILLENAS
FALLEN LEAF	Fallen Leaf Press P.O. Box 10034-N Berkeley, CA 94709	
FAR WEST	Far West Music	WESTERN
FARRELL	The Wes Farrell Organization	LEONARD-US
FAZER	Musik Fazer Post Box 69 SF-00381 Helsinki Finland	MMB
FEEDBACK	Feedback Studio Verlag Gentner Strasse 23 D-5 Köln 1 Germany	BAREN.
FELDMAN,B	B. Feldman & Co., Ltd	EMI
FEMA	Fema Music Publications P.O. Box 395 Naperville, IL 60566	
FENETTE	Fenette Music Ltd.	BROUDE,A
FENTONE	Fentone Music Ltd. Fleming Road, Earlstrees Corby, Northants NN17 2SN England	PRESSER

Code	Publisher	U.S. Agent
FEREOL	Fereol Publications Route 8, Box 510C Gainesville, GA 30501	
FEUCHT	Feuchtinger & Gleichauf Schwarze Bärenstraße 5 D-8400 Regensburg 11 Germany	
FIDDLE	Fiddle & Bow 7 Landview Drive Dix Hills, NY 11746	HHP
FIDELIO	Fidelio Music Publishing Co. 39 Danbury Avenue Westport, CT 06880	
FIDULA	Fidula-Verlag Johannes Holzmeister Ahornweg, Postfach 250 D-5407 Boppard/Rhein Germany	HARGAIL
FILLMH	Fillmore Music House	FISCHER,C
FINE ARTS	Fine Arts Press 2712 W. 104th Terrace Leawood, KS 66206	ALEX.HSE.
FINN MUS	Finnish Music Information Center Runeberginkatu 15 A SF-00100 Helsinki 10 Finland	
FISCHER,C	Carl Fischer, Inc. 62 Cooper Square New York, NY 10003	
FISCHER, J	J. Fischer & Bro.	BELWIN PRESSER (rental)
FISHER	Fisher Music Co.	PLYMOUTH
FITZSIMONS	H.T. FitzSimons Co., Inc. 18345 Ventura Boulevard P.O. Box 333, Suite 212 Tarzana, CA 91356	ALEX.HSE.
FLAMMER	Harold Flammer, Inc.	SHAWNEE
FMA	Florilegium Musicae Antiquae	HANSSLER
FOETISCH	Foetisch Frères Rue de Bourg 6 CH-1002 Lausanne Switzerland	SCHIRM.EC
FOG	Dan Fog Musikforlag Grabrodretorv 7 DK-1154 København K Denmark	
FOLEY,CH	Charles Foley, Inc.	FISCHER,C PRESSER (rental)
FORBERG	Rob. Forberg-P. Jurgenson, Musikverlag Mirbachstraße 9 D-5300 Bonn-Bad Godesberg Germany	PETERS
FOR.MUS.DIST.	Foreign Music Distributors 305 Bloomfield Avenue Nutley, NJ 07110	
FORLIVESI	A. Forlivesi & C. Via Roma 4 50123 Firenze Italy	
FORNI	Arnaldo Forni Editore Via Gramsci 164 I-40010 Sala Bolognese Italy	
FORSTER	Forster Music Publisher, Inc. 216 South Wabash Avenue Chicago, IL 60604	

Code	Publisher	U.S. Agent
FORTEA	Biblioteca Fortea Fucar 10 Madrid 14 Spain	
FORTISSIMO	Fortissimo Musikverlag Margaretenplatz 4 A-1050 Wien Austria	
FORTRESS PR	Fortress Press 2900 Queen Lane Philadelphia, PA 19129	
FOSTER	Mark Foster Music Co. 28 East Springfield Avenue P.O. Box 4012 Champaign, IL 61820-1312	
FOUR ST	Four Star Publishing Co.	COLUMBIA PIC.
FOX,S	Sam Fox Publishing Co. 5276 Holliser Avenue Suite 251 Santa Barbara, CA 93111	PLYMOUTH (Sales) PRESSER (rental)
FRANCAIS	Éditions Françaises de Musique 115 Rue de Bac F-75007 Paris France	PRESSER
FRANCE	France Music	AMP
FRANCIS	Francis, Day & Hunter Ltd.	COLUMBIA PIC.
FRANG	Frangipani Press P.O. Box 669 Bloomington, IN 47402	ALFRED
FRANK	Frank Music Corp.	LEONARD-US
FRANTON	Franton Music 4620 Sea Isle Memphis, TN 38117	
FREDONIA	Fredonia Press 3947 Fredonia Drive Hollywood, CA 90068	SIFLER
FREEMAN	H. Freeman & Co., Ltd.	EMI
FROHLICH	Friedrich Wilhelm Fröhlich Musikverlag Ansbacher Straße 52 D-1000 Berlin 30 Germany	
FUJIHARA	Fujihara	BROUDE,A
FURST	Fürstner Ltd.	BOOSEY
GAF	G.A.F. and Associates 1626 E. Williams Street Tempe, AZ 85281	
GAITHER	Gaither Music Company	ALEX.HSE.
GALAXY	Galaxy Music Corp. 131 West 86th Street New York, NY 10024	SCHIRM.EC
GALLEON	Galleon Press 17 West 60th St. New York, NY 10023	BOSTON
GALLERIA	Galleria Press 170 N.E. 33rd Street Fort Lauderdale, FL 33334	PLYMOUTH
GALLIARD	Galliard Ltd. Queen Anne's Road Southtown, Gt. Yarmouth Norfolk England	GALAXY

Code	Publisher	U.S. Agent
GARLAND	Garland Publishing, Inc. 136 Madison Avenue New York, NY 10016	
GARZON	Éditions J. Garzon 13 rue de l'Échiquier F-75010 Paris France	
GEHRMANS	Carl Gehrmans Musikförlag Apelbergsgatan 58 Postfack 505 S-10126 Stockholm 1 Sweden	BOOSEY
GEMINI	Gemini Press Music Div. of the Pilgrim Press Box 390 Otis, MA 01253	PRESSER
GENERAL	General Music Publishing Co., Inc. 145 Palisade Street Dobbs Ferry, NY 10522	BOSTON
GENERAL WDS	General Words and Music Co.	KJOS
GENESIS	Genesis	PLYMOUTH
GENTRY	Gentry Publications	BOCK
GERIG	Musikverlage Hans Gerig Drususgasse 7-11 (Am Museum) D-5000 Köln 1 Germany	BREITKOPF-W
GIA	GIA Publications 7404 South Mason Avenue Chicago, IL 60638	
GILBERT	Gilbert Publications 4209 Manitou Way Madison, WI 53711	
GILLMAN	Gillman Publications P.O. Box 155 San Clemente, CA 92672	
GLOCKEN	Glocken Verlag Theobaldgasse 16 A-1060 Wien Austria	EUR.AM.MUS.
GLORY	Glory Sound Delaware Water Gap, PA 18327	SHAWNEE
GLOUCHESTER	Glouchester Press P.O. Box 1044 Fairmont, WV 26554	HEILMAN
GM	G & M International Music Dealers Box 2098 Northbrook, IL 60062	
GOLDEN	Golden Music Publishing Co. P.O. Box 383 Golden, CO 80402-0383	
GOODLIFE	Alex. Hse. Goodlife Publications	BELWIN
GOODMAN	Goodman Group (formerly Regent, Arc & Goodman)	WARNER
GOODWIN	Goodwin & Tabb Publishing, Ltd.	PRESSER
GORDON	Gordon Music Co. Box 2250 Canoga Park, CA 91306	
GORNSTON	David Gornston	FOX,S
GOSPEL	Gospel Publishing House 1445 Boonville Avenue Springfield, MO 65802	

Code	Publisher	U.S. Agent
GRAHL	Grahl & Nicklas Braubachstraße 24 D-6 Frankfurt-am-Main Germany	
GRANCINO	Grancino Editions 1109 Avenida del Corto Fullerton, CA 92633	
	Grancino Editions 2 Bishopswood Road London N6 4PR England	
	Grancino Editions Schirmerweg 12 D-8 München 60 Germany	
GRAS	Éditions Gras 36 rue Pape-Carpentier F-72200 La Flèche (Sarthe) France	BARON,M
GRAY	H.W. Gray Co., Inc.	BELWIN PRESSER (rental)
GREENE ST.	Greene Street Music 354 Van Duzer Street Stapleton, NY 10304	
GREENWOOD	Greenwood Press, Inc. 88 Post Road West P.O. Box 5007 Westport, CT 06881	WORLD
GREGG	Gregg International Publishers, Ltd. 1 Westmead, Farnborough Hants GU14 7RU England	
GREGGMS	Gregg Music Sources P.O. Box 868 Novato, CA 94947	
	Gregorian Institute of America see GIA	
GROEN	Muziekuitgeverij Saul B. Groen Ferdinand Bolstraat 6 NL-1072 LJ Amsterdam Netherlands	
GROSCH	Edition Grosch Phillip Grosch Bahnhofstrasse 94a D-8032 Gräfelfing Germany	THOMI
GROVEN	Eivind Grovens Institutt for Reinstemming Ekebergveien 59 N-1181 Oslo 11 Norway	
GUARANI	Ediciones Musicals Mundo Guarani Sarmiento 444 Buenos Aires Argentina	
GUILYS	Edition Guilys Case Postale 90 CH-1702 Fribourg 2 Switzerland	
HA MA R	Ha Ma R Percussion Publications, Inc. 333 Spring Road Huntington, NY 11743	BOOSEY
HAMBLEN	Stuart Hamblen Music Co. 26101 Ravenhill Road Canyon Country, CA 91351	
HAMELLE	Hamelle & Cie 175 rue Saint-Honoré F-75040 Paris Cedex 01 France	ELKAN-V

Code	Publisher	U.S. Agent
HAMPTON	Hampton Edition	MARKS
HANSEN-DEN	Wilhelm Hansen Musikforlag Gothersgade 9-11 DK-1123 København Denmark	MMB WALTON (choral)
HANSEN-ENG	Hansen, London see CHESTER	
HANSEN-GER	Edition Wilhelm Hansen Eschersheimer Landstraße 12 Postfach 2684 D-6000 Frankfurt 1 Germany	MMB
HANSEN-NY	Edition Wilhelm Hansen New York, NY	MMB
HANSEN-SWED	Edition Wilhelm Hansen Warfvinges Vag 32 Box 745 S-101 30 Stockholm Sweden	WALTON
HANSEN-US	Hansen House Publications, Inc. 1824 West Avenue Miami Beach, FL 33139-9913	
HANSSLER	Hänssler-Verlag Bismarckstraße 4 Postfach 1220 D-7303 Neuhausen-Stuttgart Germany	FOSTER
HARGAIL	Hargail Music Press P.O. Box 118 Saugerties, NY 12477	
HARMONIA	Harmonia-Uitgave P.O. Box 126 NL-1200 AC Hilversum Netherlands	FOR.MUS.DIST.
HARMS,TB	T.B. Harms	WARNER
HARMUSE	Harmuse Publications 529 Speers Road Oakville, Ontario L6K 2G4 Canada	
HARP PUB	Harp Publications 3437-2 Tice Creek Drive Walnut Creek, CA 94595	
HARRIS	Frederick Harris Music Co., Ltd. 529 Speers Road Oakville, Ontario L6K 2G4 Canada	
HARRIS,R	Ron Harris Publications 22643 Paul Revere Drive Woodland Hills, CA 91364	ALEX.HSE.
HART	F. Pitman Hart & Co., Ltd.	BRODT
HARTH	Harth Musikverlag Karl-Liebknecht-Straße 12 DDR-701 Leipzig Germany	PRO MUSICA
HASLINGER	Verlag Carl Haslinger Tuchlauben 11 A-1010 Wien Austria	FOR.MUS.DIST.
HASTINGS	Hastings Music Corp.	COLUMBIA PIC
HATCH	Earl Hatch Publications 5140 Vineland Avenue North Hollywood, CA 91601	
HATIKVAH	Hatikvah Publications	TRANSCON.

Code	Publisher	U.S. Agent	Code	Publisher	U.S. Agent
HAWK	Hawk Music Press 668 Fairmont Avenue Oakland, CA 94611		HIEBER	Musikverlag Max Hieber KG Liebfrauenstrasse 1 D-8000 München 2 Germany	FOR.MUS.DIST.
HAYMOZ	Haydn-Mozart Presse	EUR.AM.MUS.	HIGHGATE	Highgate Press	GALAXY
	Hebrew Union College Sacred Music Press see SAC.MUS.PR.		HIGHLAND	Highland/Etling Music Co. 1344 Newport Avenue Long Beach, CA 90804	
HEER	Joh. de Heer & Zn. B.V. Muziek-Uitgeverij en Groothandel Rozenlaan 113, Postbus 3089 NL-3003 AB Rotterdam Netherlands		HINRICHSEN	Hinrichsen Edition, Ltd.	PETERS
HEIDELBERGER	Heidelberger	BAREN.	HINSHAW	Hinshaw Music, Inc. P.O. Box 470 Chapel Hill, NC 27514	
HEILMAN	Heilman Music P.O. Box 1044 Fairmont, WV 26554		HINZ	Hinz Fabrik Verlag Lankwitzerstraße 17-18 D-1000 Berlin 42 Germany	
HEINRICH.	Heinrichshofen's Verlag Liebigstraße 16 Postfach 620 D-2940 Wilhelmshaven Germany	PETERS	HIRSCHS	Abr. Hirschs Forlag Box 505 S-101 26 Stockholm Sweden	GEHRMANS
HELBING	Edition Helbling Kaplanstraße 9 A-6021 Neu-Rum b. Innsbruck Austria		HISPAVOX	Ediciones Musicales Hispavox Cuesta Je Santo Domingo 11 Madrid Spain	
HELBS	Helbling Edition Pffäfikerstraße 6 CH-8604 Volketswil-Zürich Switzerland		HOA	HOA Music Publisher 756 S. Third Street Dekalb, IL 60115	
HELICON	Helicon Music Corp.	EUR.AM.MUS.	HOFFMAN,R	Raymond A. Hoffman Co. c/o Fred Bock Music Co. P.O. Box 333 Tarzana, CA 91356	ALEX.HSE.
HELIOS	Editio Helios	FOSTER			
HENKLE	Ted Henkle 5415 Reynolds Street Savannah, GA 31405		HOFMEISTER	VEB Friedrich Hofmeister, Musikverlag, Leipzig Karlstraße 10 DDR-701 Leipzig East Germany	
HENLE	G. Henle Verlag Forstenrieder Allee 122 Postfach 71 04 66 D-8000 München 71 Germany G. Henle USA, Inc. P.O. Box 1753 2446 Centerline Industrial Drive St. Louis, MO 63043		HOFMEISTER-W	Friedrich Hofmeister Musikverlag, Taunus Ubierstraße 20 D-6238 Hofheim am Taunus West Germany	
HENMAR	Henmar Press	PETERS	HOHLER	Heinrich Hohler Verlag	SCHNEIDER,H
HENN	Editions Henn 8 rue de Hesse Genève Switzerland			Hollow Hills Press see HHP	
HENREES	Henrees Music Ltd.	EMI	HOLLY-PIX	Holly-Pix Music Publishing Co.	WESTERN
HERALD	Herald Press 616 Walnut Avenue Scottdale, PA 15683		HONG KONG	Hong Kong Music Media Publishing Co., Ltd. Kai It Building, 9th Floor 58 Pak Tai Street Tokwawan, Kowloon Hong Kong	
HERITAGE	Heritage Music Press	LORENZ			
HERITAGE PUB	Heritage Music Publishing Co.	CENTURY	HONOUR	Honour Publications	WESTERN
HEUGEL	Heugel & Cie 175 rue Saint-Honoré F-75040 Paris Cedex 01 France	PRESSER	HOPE	Hope Publishing Co. 380 South Main Place Carol Stream, IL 60188	
HEUWEKE.	Edition Heuwekemeijer & Zoon Postbus 289 NL-1740 AG Schagen Netherlands	ELKAN-V	HORNPIPE	Hornpipe Music Publishing Co. 400 Commonwealth Avenue P.O. Box CY577 Boston, MA 02215	
HHP	Hollow Hills Press 7 Landview Drive Dix Hills, NY 11746				

Code	Publisher	U.S. Agent
HUEBER	Hueber-Holzmann Pädagogischer Verlag Krausstraße 30 D-8045 Ismaning, München Germany	
HUG	Hug & Co. Flughofstrasse 61 CH-Glattbrugg Switzerland	MAGNA D
HUGUENIN	Charles Huguenin & Pro-Arte Rue des Croix 30 CH-2014 Bôle Switzerland	
HUHN	W. Huhn Musikalien-Verlag Jahnstraße 9 D-5880 Lüdenshied Germany	
HULST	De Hulst Kruisdagenlaan 75 B-1040 Bruxelles Belgium	
HUNTZINGER	R.L. Huntzinger Publications	WILLIS
HURON	Huron Press P.O. Box 2121 London, Ontario N6A 4C5 Canada	
ICELAND	Islenzk Tónverkamidstöd Iceland Music Information Centre Freyjugötu 1 Box 121 IS-121 Reykjavik Iceland	ELKAN,H
IISM	Istituto Italiano per la Storia della Musica Academia Nazionale di Santa Cecilia Via Vittoria, 6 I-00187 Roma Italy	
IMB	Internationale Musikbibliothek	BAREN.
IMC	Indiana Music Center 322 South Swain P.O. Box 582 Bloomington, IN 47401	
IMPERO	Impero-Verlag Liebigstraße 16 D-2940 Wilhelmshavn Germany	PETERS PRESSER (partial)
INDEPENDENT	Independent Publications P.O. Box 162 Park Station Paterson, NJ 07513	
INDIANA	Indiana University Press Tenth & Morton Streets Bloomington, IN 47405	
INST ANT	Instrumenta Antiqua, Inc. 2530 California Street San Francisco, CA 94115	
INST.CO.	The Instrumentalist 200 Northfield Road Northfield, IL 60093-3390	
	Institute Of Stringed Instruments Guitar & Lute see ISI	
	Editorial Cooperativa Inter-Americana de Compositores see ECOAM	
INTERLOCH	Interlochen Press	CRESCENDO

Code	Publisher	U.S. Agent
INTERNAT.	International Music Co. 5 W. 37th Street New York, NY 10018	
INTER.MUS.P	International Music Publications 60-70 Roden Street Ilford, Essex IG1 2AQ England	
	Internationale Musikbibliothek see IMB	
INTERNAT.S.	International Music Service P.O. Box 66, Ansonia Station New York, NY 10023	
IONA	Iona Music Publishing Service P.O. Box 8131 San Marino, CA 91108	
IONE	Ione Press	SCHIRM.EC
IRIS	Iris Verlag Hernerstraße 64A Postfach 740 D-4350 Recklinghausen Germany	
IROQUOIS PR	Iroquois Press P.O. Box 2121 London, Ontario N6A 4C5 Canada	
	Islenzk Tónverkamidstöd see ICELAND	
ISI	Institute of Stringed Instruments, Guitar & Lute Poststraße 30 4 Düsseldorf Germany	SANDVOSS
	Aux Presses d'Isle-de-France see PRESSES	
ISR.MUS.INST.	Israel Music Institute P.O. Box 11253 Tel-Aviv 61 112 Israel	BOOSEY (rental) TRANSCON
ISR.PUB.AG.	Israel Publishers Agency 7, Arlosoroff Street Tel-Aviv Israel	
ISRAELI	Israeli Music Publications, Ltd. 25 Keren Hayesod Jerusalem 94188 Israel	PRESSER
	Istituto Italiano per la Storia della Musica see IISM	
J.B.PUB	J.B. Publications 404 Holmes Circle Memphis TN 38111	
J.C.A.	Japan Composers Association 3-7-15, Akasaka Minato-Ku Tokyo Japan	
JACKMAN	Jackman Music Corp. P.O. Box 900 Orem, UT 84057	MUSICART
JAPAN	Japan Federation of Composers Shinanomachi Building 602 33 Shinanomachi Shinjuku-Ku Tokyo Japan	

Code	Publisher	U.S. Agent	Code	Publisher	U.S. Agent
JAREN	Jaren Music Co. 9691 Brynmar Drive Villa Park, CA 92667		KAY PR	Kay Press 612 Vicennes Court Cincinnati, OH 45231	
JASE	Jasemusiikki Ky Box 136 SF-13101 Hämeenlinna 10 Finland		KELTON	Kelton Publications 1343 Amalfi Drive Pacific Palisades, CA 90272	
JAZZ ED	Jazz Education Publications P.O. Box 802 Manhattan, KS 66502		KENDALE	Kendale Company 6595 S. Dayton Street Englewood, CO 80111	
JEANNETTE	Ed. Jeannette	DONEMUS	KENDOR	Kendor Music Inc. Main & Grove Streets P.O. Box 278 Delevan, NY 14042	
JEHLE	Jehle	HANSSLER			
JENSON	Jenson Publications, Inc. 2770 S. 171st Street P.O. Box 248 New Berlin, WI 53151-0248		KENSING.	Kensington Music Service P.O. Box 471 Tenafly, NJ 07670	
JERONA	Jerona Music Corp. P.O. Box 5010 Hackensack, NJ 07606-4210		KENYON	Kenyon Publications	LEONARD-US
			KERBY	E.C. Kerby Ltd. P.O. Box 5010 Hackensack, NJ 07606-4210	
JOBERT	Editions Jean Jobert 76, rue Quincampoix F-75003 Paris France	PRESSER	KINDRED	Kindred Press	HERALD
JOHNSON	Johnson Reprint Corp. 757 3rd Avenue New York, NY 10017		KING,R	Robert King Sales, Inc. 28 Main Street, Bldg. 15 North Easton, MA 02356	
JOHNSON,P	Paul Johnson Productions P.O. Box 2001 Irving, TX 75061		KISTNER	Fr. Kistner & C.F.W. Siegel & Co. Adrian-Kiels-Straße 2 D-5000 Köln 90 Germany	CONCORDIA
JOSHUA	Joshua Corp.	GENERAL	KJOS	Neil A. Kjos Music Co. 4382 Jutland Drive Box 178270 San Diego, CA 92117-0894	
JRB	JRB Music Education Materials Distributor	PRESSER			
JUNNE	Otto Junne GmbH Sendlinger-Tor-Platz 10 D-8000 München Germany		KLIMENT	Musikverlag Johann Kliment Kolingasse 15 A-1090 Wien 9 Austria	
JUS-AUTOR	Jus-Autor Sofia, Bulgaria	BREITKOPF-W	KNEUSSLIN	Edition Kneusslin Amselstraße 43 CH-4059 Basel Switzerland	FOR.MUS.DIST.
JUSKO	Jusko Publications	WILLIS			
KAHNT	C.F. Kahnt, Musikverlag Hohenstraße 52 D-8992 Wasserburg A.B. Germany	PETERS	KNOPF	Alfred A. Knopf 201 East 50th Street New York, NY 10022	
KALMUS	Edwin F. Kalmus Miami-Dade Industrial Park P.O. Box 1007 Opa Locka, FL 33054	BELWIN (string and miniature scores)	KNUF	Frits Knuf Uitgeverij Rodeheldenstraat 13 P.O. Box 720 NL-4116 ZJ Buren Netherlands	PENDRGN
KALMUS,A	Alfred A. Kalmus Ltd. 38 Eldon Way, Paddock Wood Tonbridge, Kent TN12 6BE England	EUR.AM.MUS.	KODALY	Kodaly Center of America, Inc. 1326 Washington Street West Newton, MA 02165	SUPPORT
KAMMEN	J. & J. Kammen Music Co.	CENTURY	KON BOND	Kon. Bond van Chr. Zang- en Oratoriumverenigingen	DONEMUS
KAPLAN	Ida R. Kaplan 1308 Olivia Avenue Ann Arbor, MI 48104		KONINKLIJK	Koninklijk Nederlands Zangersverbond	DONEMUS
KARTHAUSE	Karthause Verlag Panzermacherstrasse 5 D-5860 Iserlohn Germany		KOPER	Musikverlag Karl-Heinz Köper Schneekoppenweg 12 D-3001 Isernhagen NB/Hannover Germany	
KAWAI	Kawai Gafuku	JAPAN	KRENN	Ludwig Krenn Verlag Reindorfergasse 42 A-1150 Wien 45 Austria	
KAWE	Edition KaWe Brederodestraat 90 NL-1054 VC Amsterdam 13 Netherlands	KING,R			

Code	Publisher	U.S. Agent
KROMPHOLZ	Krompholz & Co Spitalgasse 28 CH-3001 Bern Switzerland	
KRUSEMAN	Ed. Philip Kruseman	DONEMUS
KUNZEL	Edition Kunzelmann Grutstrasse 28 CH-8134 Adliswil Switzerland	FOR.MUS.DIST.
KYSAR	Michael Kysar 1250 South 211th Place Seattle, WA 98148	
LAKES	Lake State Publishers P.O. Box 1593 Grand Rapids, MI 49501	
LAMP	Latin-American Music Pub. Co. Ltd. 8 Denmark Street London England	
LAND	A. Land & Zn. Muziekuitgevers	DONEMUS
LANDES	Landesverband Evangelischer Kirchenchöre in Bayern	HANSSLER
LANG	Lang Music Publications P.O. Box 11021 Indianapolis, IN 46201	
LANSMAN	Länsmansgarden PL-7012 S-762 00 Rimbo Sweden	
	Latin-American Music Pub. Co. Ltd. see LAMP	
LAUDINELLA	Laudinella Reihe	FOSTER
LAUMANN	Laumann Verlag Alter Gartenweg 14 Postfach 1360 D-4408 Dülmen Germany	
LAUREL	Laurel Press	LORENZ
LAVENDER	Lavender Publications, Ltd. Borough Green Sevenoaks, Kent TN15 8DT England	
LAWSON	Lawson-Gould Music Publishers, Inc. 250 W. 57th St., Suite 932 New York, NY 10107	
LEA	Lea Pocket Scores P.O. Box 138, Audubon Station New York, NY 10032	EUR.AM.MUS.
LEDUC	Alphonse Leduc 175 rue Saint-Honoré F-75040 Paris Cedex 01 France	KING,R SOUTHERN PRESSER (rental)
LEEDS	Leeds Music Ltd. MCA Building 2450 Victoria Park Avenue Willowdale, Ontario M2J 4A2 Canada	MCA
LEMOINE	Henry Lemoine & Cie 17, rue Pigalle F-75009 Paris France	ELKAN-V
LENGNICK	Alfred Lengnick & Co., Ltd. Purley Oaks Studios 421a Brighton Road South Croydon CR2 6YR, Surrey England	

Code	Publisher	U.S. Agent
LEONARD-ENG	Leonard, Gould & Bolttler	LESLIE
LEONARD-US	Hal Leonard Music 8112 West Bluemound Road Milwaukee, WI 53213	
LESLIE	Leslie Music Supply P.O. Box 471 Oakville, Ontario L6J 5A8 Canada	BRODT
LEUCKART	F.E.C. Leuckart Nibelungenstraße 48 D-8000 München 19 Germany	LEONARD-US SCHIRM.G (rental)
LEXICON	Lexicon Music P.O. Box 2222 Newbury Park, CA 91320	
LIBEN	Liben Music Publications 6265 Dawes Lane Cincinnati, OH 45230	
LIBER	Svenska Utbildningsförlaget Liber AB Utbildningsförlaget, Centrallagret S-136 01 Handen Stockholm Sweden	
LICHTENAUER	W.F. Lichtenauer	DONEMUS
LIED	VEB Lied der Zeit Musikverlag Rosa-Luxemburg-Straße 41 DDR-102 Berlin East Germany	
LIENAU	Robert Lienau, Musikverlag Lankwitzerstraße 9 D-1000 Berlin 45 Germany	PETERS
LILLENAS	Lillenas Publishing Co. P.O. Box 419527 Kansas City, MO 64141	
LINDSAY	Lindsay Music 23 Hitchin Street Biggleswade, Beds SG18 8AX England	PRESSER
LINDSBORG	Lindsborg Press P.O. Box 737 State Road 9 South Alexandria, VA 46001	ALEX. HSE.
LINGUA	Lingua Press P.O. Box 3416 Iowa City, IA 52244	
LISTER	Mosie Lister	LILLENAS
LITOLFF,H	Henry Litolff's Verlag Kennedy Allee 101 Postfach 700906 D-6000 Frankfurt 70 Germany	PETERS
LITURGICAL	Liturgical Music Press St. Johns Abbey Collegeville, MN 56321	PRESSER
LLUQUET	Guillermo Lluquet Almacen General de Musica Avendida del Oeste 43 Valencia Spain	
	London Pro Musica Edition see LPME	
LONG ISLE	Long Island Music Publishers	BRANCH
LOOP	Loop Music Co.	KJOS

Code	Publisher	U.S. Agent
LORENZ	Lorenz Corporation 501 East Third Street P.O. Box 802 Dayton, OH 45401-9969	
LPME	The London Pro Musica Edition 15 Rock Street Brighton BN2 1NF England	MAGNA D
LUCKS	Luck's Music Library P.O. Box 71397 Madison Heights, MI 48071	
LUDWIG	Ludwig Music Publishing Co. 557-67 East 140th Street Cleveland, OH 44110	
LUNDEN	Edition Lundén Bromsvagen 25 S-125 30 Alvsjö Sweden	
LUNDMARK	Lundmark Publications 811 Bayliss Drive Marietta, GA 30067	SUPPORT
LUNDQUIST	Abr. Lundquist Musikförlag AB Katarina Bangata 17 S-116 25 Stockholm Sweden	
LYCHE	Harald Lyche Postboks 2171 Stromso N-3001 Drammen Norway	WALTON (partial)
LYDIAN ORCH	Lydian Orchestrations 31000 Ruth Hill Road Orange Cove, CA 93646	SHAWNEE
LYRA	Lyra Music Co. 133 West 69th Street New York, NY 10023	
MACNUTT	Richard Macnutt Ltd. Hamm Farm House Withyham, Hartfield Sussex TN7 4BJ England	
	Mac Murray Publications see MMP	
MAGNA D	Magnamusic Distributors Route 49 Sharon, CT 06069	
MALCOLM	Malcolm Music Ltd.	SHAWNEE
MANNA	Manna Music, Inc. 2111 Kenmere Avenue P.O. Box 3257 Burbank, CA 91504	
MANNHEIM	Mannheimer Musikverlag Kunigundestraße 4 D-5300 Bonn 2 Germany	
MANU. PUB	Manuscript Publications 120 Maple Street Wrightsville, PA 17368	
MAPA MUNDI	Mapa Mundi—Music Publishers 72 Brewery Road London N7 9NE England	GALAXY
MARBOT	Edition Marbot GmbH Mühlenkamp 43 D-2000 Hamburg 60 Germany	
MARCHAND	Marchand, Paap en Strooker	DONEMUS

Code	Publisher	U.S. Agent
MARGUN	Margun Music, Inc. 167 Dudley Road Newton Centre, MA 02159	
MARI	E. & O. Mari, Inc. 38-01 23rd Avenue Long Island City, NY 11105	
MARK	Mark Publications	CRESPUB
MARKS	Edward B. Marks Music Corp. 1619 Broadway New York, NY 10019	LEONARD-US (sales) PRESSER (rental)
MARSEG	Marseg, Ltd. 18 Farmstead Road Willowdale, Ontario M2L 2G2 Canada	
MARTIN	Editions Robert Martin 106, Grande rue de la Coupée F-71009 Charnay-les-Macon France	PRESSER
MASTER	Master Music	CRESPUB
MAURER	J. Maurer Avenue du Verseau 7 B-1020 Brussel Belgium	
MAURRI	Edizioni Musicali Ditta R. Maurri Via del Corso 1 (17R.) Firenze Italy	
MCA	MCA and Mills/MCA Joint Venture Editions 445 Park Avenue New York, NY 10022	LEONARD-US (sales) PRESSER (rental)
MCAFEE	McAfee Music Corp.	BELWIN
MCGIN-MARX	McGinnis & Marx Box 252, Village Station New York, NY 10014	
MDV	Mitteldeutscher Verlag Thalmannplatz 2, Postfach 295 DDR-4010 Halle — Saale Germany	PETERS
MEDIA	Media Press P.O. Box 250 Elwyn, PA 19063	
MEDICI	Medici Press 4206 Ridgewood Bellingham, WA 98226	
MEDIT	Mediterranean	GALAXY
MEL BAY	Mel Bay Publications, Inc. P.O. Box 66 Pacific, MO 63069	
MELE LOKE	Mele Loke Publishing Co. Box 7142 Honolulu, Hawaii 96821	HIGHLAND (continental U.S.A.)
MELODI	Casa Editrice Melodi S.A. Galleria Del Corso 4 Milano Italy	
MENC	Music Educators National Conference Publications Division 1902 Association Drive Reston, VA 22091	
MERCATOR	Mercator Verlag & Wohlfahrt (Gert) Verlag Köhnenstraße 5-11 Postfach 100609 D-4100 Duisberg 1 Germany	

Code	Publisher	U.S. Agent
MERCURY	Mercury Music Corp.	PRESSER
MERIDIAN	Les Nouvelles Éditions Meridian 5, rue Lincoln F-75008 Paris 8 France	
MERION	Merion Music, Inc.	PRESSER
MERRYMOUNT	Merrymount Music, Inc.	PRESSER
MERSEBURGER	Merseburger Verlag Motzstraße 13 D-3500 Kassel Germany	MMB
METRO	Metro Muziek Uilenweg 38 Postbus 70 NL-6000 AB Weert Netherlands	
METROPOLIS	Editions Metropolis Van Ertbornstraat, 5 B-2018 Antwerpen Belgium	ELKAN,H
MEULEMANS	Arthur Meulemans Fonds Charles de Costerlaan, 6 2050 Antwerpen Belgium	
MEXICANAS	Ediciones Mexicanas de Musica Avenida Juarez 18 Mexico City Mexico	PEER
MEZ KNIGA	Mezhdunarodnaya Kniga 14 Neglinnaya St. Moscow 121200 U.S.S.R.	LEONARD-US SCHIRM,G (rental)
MIDDLE	Middle Eight Music c/o Belwin-Mills Music Ltd. 250 Purley Way Croydon Surrey CR9 4QD England	BELWIN
MILLER	Miller Music Corp.	COLUMBIA PIC.
MILLS MUSIC	Mills Music Jewish Catalogue	TRANSCON. PRESSER (rental)
MINKOFF	Minkoff Reprints 8 rue Eynard CH-1211 Genève 12 Switzerland	
MIRA	Mira Music Associates 199 Mountain Road Wilton, CT 06897	
	Mitteldeutscher Verlag see MDV	
MJQ	M.J.Q. Music, Inc. 1697 Broadway #1100 New York, NY 10019	FOX,S
MMB	MMB Music, Inc. 10370 Page Industrial Boulevard St. Louis, MO 63132	
MMP	Mac Murray Publications	MUS.SAC.PRO.
MMS	Monumenta Musica Svecicae	STIM
MOBART	Mobart Music Publications	JERONA
MOD ART	Modern Art Music	SON-KEY
MODERN	Edition Modern Musikverlag Hans Wewerka Elisabethstraße 38 D-8000 München 40 Germany	

Code	Publisher	U.S. Agent
MOECK	Hermann Moeck Verlag Postfach 143 D-3100 Celle 1 Germany	EUR.AM.MUS. MAGNA D
MOLENAAR	Molenaar's Muziekcentrale Industrieweg 23 Postbus 19 NL-1520 AA Wormerveer Netherlands	GM
MONDIAL	Mondial-Verlag KG 8 rue de Hesse Genève Switzerland	
MONTEVERDI	Fondazione Claudio Monteverdi Corso Garibaldi 178 I-26100 Cremona Italy	
	Moravian Music Foundation	BELWIN BOOSEY BRODT PETERS
MOSAIC	Mosaic Music Corporation P.O. Box 175 Mohegan Lake, NY 10547	BOSTON
MOSELER	Karl Heinrich Möseler Verlag Hoffman-von-Fallersleben-Straße 8-10 Postfach 1460 D-3340 Wolfenbüttel Germany	MMB
MOSER	Verlag G. Moser Kirschweg 8 CH-4144 Arlesheim Switzerland	
MOWBRAY	Mowbray Music Publications Saint Thomas House Becket Street Oxford OX1 1SJ England	PRESSER
MSM	MSM Music Publishers	BRODT
MT.SALUS	Mt. Salus Music 709 East Leake Street Clinton, MS 39056	
MT.TAHO	Mt. Tahoma	BROUDE,A
MULLER	Willy Müller, Süddeutscher Musikverlag Marzgasse 5 D-6900 Heidelberg Germany	
MUNSTER	Van Munster Editie	DONEMUS
MURPHY	Spud Murphy Publications	WESTERN
MUS.ANT.BOH.	Musica Antiqua Bohemica	SUPRAPHON
MUS.ART	Music Art Publications P.O. Box 1744 Chula Vista, CA 92010	
MUS.PERC.	Music For Percussion, Inc. 17 West 60th Street New York, NY 10023	
MUS.RARA	Musica Rara Le Traversier Chemin de la Buire F-84170 Monteux France	FOR.MUS.DIST.
MUS.SAC.PRO	Musica Sacra et Profana P.O. Box 7248 Berkeley, CA 94707	

Code	Publisher	U.S. Agent	Code	Publisher	U.S. Agent
MUS.SUR	Musica del Sur Apartado 5219 Barcelona Spain		MYRRH	Myrrh Music	WORD
MUS.VERA	Musica Vera Graphics & Publishers 350 Richmond Terrace 4-M Staten Island, NY 10301	ARISTA	MYRTLE	Myrtle Monroe Music 2600 Tenth Street Berkeley, CA 94710	
MUS.VIVA	Musica Viva 262 King's Drive Eastbourne Sussex, BN21 2XD England		NAGELS	Nagels Verlag	FOR.MUS.DIST.
			NATIONAL	National Music Publishers P.O. Box 8279 Anaheim, CA 92802	
MUS.VIVA HIST.	Musica Viva Historica	SUPRAPHON	NEUE	Verlag Neue Musik Leipziger Straße 26 Postfach 1306 DDR-1080 Berlin Germany	BROUDE,A
MUSIA	Musia	PETERS			
MUSIC	Music Sales Corp. 5 Bellvale Road Chester, NY 10918		NEW HORIZON	New Horizon Publications	TRANSCON.
MUSIC BOX	Music Box Dancer Publications Ltd.	PRESSER	NEW MUSIC	The New Music Co., Inc. 6595 S. Dayton St. Englewood, CO 80111	SON-KEY
	Music Educators National Conference see MENC			New Music Edition see NME	
MUSIC-ENG	Music Sales Ltd. 78 Newman Street London W1 P 3LA England	MUSIC	NEW MUSIC WEST	New Music West P.O. Box 7434 Van Nuys, CA 91409	
MUSIC INFO	Muzicki Informativni Centar—ZAMP Ulica 8 Maja 37 P.O. Box 959 YU-41001 Zagreb Yugoslavia	BREITKOPF-W	NEW VALLEY	New Valley Music Press of Smith College Sage Hall 49 Northampton, MA 01063	
			NIEUWE	De Nieuwe Muziekhandel	DONEMUS
MUSIC SEV.	Music 70, Music Publishers 250 W. 57th St., Suite 932 New York, NY 10107		NIPPON	Nippon Hosu	PRESSER
			NME	New Music Edition	PRESSER
	Société d'Éditions Musicales Internationales see SEMI		NO.AM.LIT.	North American Liturgy Resources Choral Music Department 10802 North 23rd Avenue Phoenix, AZ 85029	
MUSICART	Musicart West P.O. Box 900 Orem, UT 84057		NOBILE	Nobile Verlag Aixheimer Straße 26 D-7000 Stuttgart 75 Germany	
MUSICIANS PUB	Musicians Publications P.O. Box 7160 West Trenton, NJ 08628		NOETZEL	Noetzel Musikverlag Liebigstraße 16 Postfach 620 D-2940 Wilhelmshavn Germany	PETERS
MUSICO	Musico Muziekuitgeverij	DONEMUS			
MUSICPRINT	Musicprint Corporation P.O. Box 20767 New York, NY 10023	BROUDE,A	NOMOS	Edition Nomos	BREITKOPF-W
			NOORDHOFF	P. Noordhoff	DONEMUS
MUSICUS	Edition Musicus P.O. Box 1341 Stamford, CT 06904		NORDISKA	AB Nordiska Musikförlaget Édition Wilhelm Hansen, Stockholm Nybrogatan 3 S-114 34 Stockholm Sweden	MMB (sales-rentals) WALTON (choral)
MUSIKAL.	Musikaliska Konstföreningen Aarstryck, Sweden	WALTON			
MUSIKHOJ	Musikhojskolens Forlag ApS	EUR.AM.MUS.		See also HANSEN-SWEDEN	
MUSIKINST	Verlag das Musikinstrument Klüberstraße 9 D-6000 Frankfurt-am-Main Germany		NORGE	Norsk Musikkinformasjon Toftesgatan 69 N-0552 Oslo 5 Norway	
MUSIKK	Musikk-Huset A-S P.O. Box 822 Sentrum Oslo 1 Norway		NORRUTH	Norruth Music Publishers	MMB
			NORSK	Norsk Musikforlag AS Karl Johansgaten 39 P.O. Box 1499 Vika Oslo Norway	MMB (rentals) WALTON (choral)
MUSIKWISS.	Musikwissenschaftlicher Verlag Wien Dorotheergasse 10 A-1010 Wien 1 Austria	FOR.MUS.DIST.			
			NORTHRIDGE	Northridge Music, Inc. 7317 Greenback Lane Citrus Heights, CA 95621	COLUMBIA PIC.
	Eerste Muziekcentrale see EERSTE				

Code	Publisher	U.S. Agent
NORTON	W.W. Norton & Co., Inc. 500 Fifth Avenue New York, NY 10003	
	Norwegian Music Information Center see NORGE	
NOSKE	A.A. Noske	DONEMUS
NOTERIA	Noteria S-890 30 Borensberg Sweden	STIM
NOVA	Nova Music Ltd. Goldsmid Mews 15a Farm Road Hove Sussex BN3 1FB England	SCHIRM.EC
NOVELLO	Novello & Co., Ltd. Fairfield Road Borough Green Sevenoaks, Kent TN15 8DT England	PRESSER
NOW VIEW	Now View	PLYMOUTH
NYMPHEN	Edition Nymphenburg Unterföhring, W. Germany	PETERS
OAK	Oak Publications	MUSIC
OCTAVA	Octava Music Co., Ltd.	WEINBERGER
OISEAU	Éditions de L'Oiseau-Lyre Les Remparts Boite Postale 515 MC-98015 Monaco Cedex	MAGNA D
OJEDA	Raymond J. Ojeda 98 Briar Road Kentfield, CA 94904	
OKRA	Okra Music Corp.	SEESAW
OLIVIAN	Olivian Press	ARCADIA
OLMS	G. Olms Verlag Hagentorwall 7 D-3200 Hildesheim Germany	
ONGAKU	Ongaku-No-Tomo Sha Co., Ltd. Kagurazaka 6-30, Shinjuku-ku Tokyo Japan	PRESSER
OPUS	Opus Music Publishers, Inc. 1880 Holste Road Northbrook, IL 60062	
OPUS-CZ	Opus Ceskoslavenske Hudobne Vydaratelstro Dunajska 18 CS-815 04 Bratislava Czechoslovakia	BOOSEY (rental)
OR-TAV	Or-Tav Music Publications Israel Composers League P.O. Box 3200 Tel-Aviv Israel	
ORGAN	Organ Music Co.	WESTERN
ORGAN LIT	Organ Literature Foundation 45 Norfolk Road Braintree, MA 02184	
ORGMS	Organmaster Music Series 282 Stepstone Hill Guilford, CT 06437	
ORION MUS	Orion Music Press P.O. Box 75 Berrien Springs, MI 49103	OPUS

Code	Publisher	U.S. Agent
ORLANDO	Orlando Musikverlag Kaprunerstraße 11 D-8000 München 21 Germany	
ORPHEUM	Orpheum Music 10th & Parker Berkeley, CA 94710	
OSTARA	Ostara Press, Inc.	WESTERN
OSTER	Österreichischer Bundesverlag Schwarzenberg Platz 5 A-1010 Wien Austria	
OSTIGUY	Editions Jacques Ostiguy Inc. 12790 Rue Yamaska St. Hyacinthe, Quebec Canada J2T 1B3	
OTOS	Otos Edizioni Musicali Via Marsillo Ficino, 10 I-50132 Firenze Italy	
OUVRIERES	Les Éditions Ouvrières 12, Avenue Soeur-Rosalie F-75621 Paris Cedex 13, France	GALAXY
OXFORD	Oxford University Press Walton Street Oxford OX2 6DP England	
OXFORD	Oxford University Press 200 Madison Avenue New York, NY 10016	
PAGANI	O. Pagani & Bro., Inc. c/o P. Deiro Music 289 Bleeker Street New York, NY 10014	
PAGANINI PUB	Paganiniana Publications, Inc. P.O. Box 27 Neptune City, NJ 07753	
PALLMA	Pallma Music Co.	KJOS
PAN	Editions Pan Schaffhauserstraße 280 Postfach 260 CH-8057 Zürich Switzerland	MAGNA D
PAN AM	Pan American Union	PEER
PANTON	Panton Ricni 12 CS-118 39 Praha 1 Czechoslovakia	
PARACLETE	Paraclete Press P.O. Box 1568 Hilltop Plaza, Route 6A Orleans, MA 02653	
PARAGON	Paragon Music Publishers	CENTURY
PARAGON ASS.	Paragon Associates	ALEX.HSE.
PARIS	Uitgeverij H.J. Paris	DONEMUS
PARKS	Parks Music Corp.	KJOS
PASTORALE	Pastorale Music Company 235 Sharon Drive San Antonio, TX 78216	
PASTORINI	Musikhaus Pastorini AG Kasinostraße 25 CH-5000 Aarau Switzerland	

Code	Publisher	U.S. Agent	Code	Publisher	U.S. Agent
PATERSON	Paterson's Publications, Ltd. 10-12 Baches Street London N1 6DN England	FISCHER,C	PETERS,K	Kermit Peters 1515 90th Street Omaha, NE 68124	
	Patrimoine Musical Canadien see CAN.MUS.HER.		PETERS,M	Mitchell Peters 3231 Benda Place Los Angeles, CA 90068	
PAXTON	Paxton Publications Sevenoaks, Kent, England	PRESSER	PFAUEN	Pfauen Verlag Adolfsallee 34 Postfach 471 D-6200 Wiesbaden Germany	
PEER	Peer Southern Concert music 810 Seventh Avenue New York, NY 10019	PRESSER COLUMBIA PIC.			
			PHILH	Philharmonia	EUR.AM.MUS.
PEER MUSIK	Peer Musikverlag GmbH Muhlenkamp 43 Postfach 602129 D-2000 Hamburg Germany	PRESSER	PHILIPPO	Editions Philippo	ELKAN-V
			PIEDMONT	Piedmont Music Co.	PRESSER (rental)
PEG	Pegasus Musikverlag Liebig Straße 16 Postfach 620 D-2940 Wilhelmshaven Germany	PETERS	PILES	Piles Editorial de Musica Apartado 8.012 E-46080 Valencia Spain	
PELIKAN	Musikverlag Pelikan	HUG	PILLIN	Pillin Music	WESTERN
PEMBROKE	Pembroke Music Co., Inc.	FISCHER,C	PIPER	Piper Music Co. P.O. Box 1713 Cincinnati, OH 45201	
PENADES	José Penadés En Sanz 12 Valencia Spain		PLAINSONG	Plainsong & Medieval Music Society Catherine Harbor, Hon. Sec. c/o Turner 72 Brewery Road London N7 9NE England	
PENDRGN	Pendragon Press R.R. 1, Box 159 Stuyvesant, NY 12173-9720				
PENGUIN	Penguin Books 40 West 23rd Street New York, NY 10010		PLAYER	Player Press 139-22 Caney Lane Rosedale, NY 11422	
PENN STATE	Pennsylvania State University Press 215 Wagner Building University Park, PA 16802		PLENUM	Plenum Publishing Corp. 233 Spring Street New York, NY 10013	DA CAPO
			PLESNICAR	Don Plesnicar P.O. Box 4880 Albuquerque, NM 87106	
PENOLL	Penoll Goteberg, Sweden	STIM	PLOUGH	Plough Publishing House Rifton, NY 12471	
PEPPER	J.W. Pepper And Son, Inc. P.O. Box 850 Valley Forge, PA 19482		PLUCKED ST	Plucked String P.O. Box 11125 Arlington, VA 22210	
PERMUS	Permus Publications P.O. Box 02033 Columbus, OH 43202		PLYMOUTH	Plymouth Music Co., Inc. 170 N.E. 33rd Street P.O. Box 24330 Fort Lauderdale, FL 33334	
PETERER	Edition Melodie Anton Peterer Brunnwiesenstraße 26 Postfach 260 CH-8409 Zürich Switzerland		PODIUM	Podium Music, Inc. 360 Port Washington Boulevard Port Washington, NY 11050	
PETERS	Edition Peters C.F. Peters Corp. 373 Park Avenue South New York, NY 10016		POLSKIE	Polskie Wydawnictwo Muzyczne Al. Krasinskiego 11a PL31-111 Krakow Poland	
			POLYPH MUS	Polyphone Music Co.	ARCADIA
	Edition Peters Postfach 746 DDR-7010 Leipzig East Germany		POLYPHON	Polyphon Musikverlag	BREITKOPF-W
			PORT.MUS.	Portugaliae Musicae Fundaçao Calouste Gulbenkian Avenida de Berna 45 P-1093 Lisboa Codex Portugal	
	C.F. Peters Musikverlag Postfach 700 906 D-6000 Frankfurt 70 Germany				
	Peters Edition Ltd. Bach House 10-12 Baches Street London N1 6DN England			Positif Press Ltd. see BRENNAN	
			POWER	Power and Glory Music Co. 6595 S. Dayton St. Englewood, CO 80111	SON-KEY

Code	Publisher	U.S. Agent
PRAEGER	Praeger Publications 383 Madison Avenue New York, NY 10017	
PREISSLER	Musikverlag Josef Preissler Postfach 521 Bräuhausstraße 8 D-8000 München 2 Germany	
PRELUDE	Prelude Publications 150 Wheeler Street Glouchester, MA 01930	
PRENTICE	Prentice-Hall, Inc. Englewood Cliffs, NJ 07632	
PRESSER	Theodore Presser Co. Presser Place Bryn Mawr, PA 19010	
PRESSES	Aux Presses d'Isle-de-France 12, rue de la Chaise F-75007 Paris France	
PRICE,P	Paul Price Publications 470 Kipp Street Teaneck, NJ 07666	
PRIMAVERA	Editions Primavera	GENERAL
PRINCE	Prince Publications 1125 Francisco Street San Francisco, CA 94109	
PRO ART	Pro Art Publications, Inc.	COLUMBIA PIC.
PRO MUSICA	Pro Musica Verlag Karl-Liebknecht-Straße 12 Postfach 467 DDR-7010 Leipzig Germany	
PRO MUSICA INTL	Pro Musica International 130 Bylor P.O. Box 1687 Pueblo, CO 81002	
PROCLAM	Proclamation Productions, Inc. Orange Square Port Jervis, NY 12771	
PROGRESS	Progress Press P.O. Box 12 Winnetka, IL 60093	
PROPRIUS	Proprius Musik AB Vartavagen 35 S-115 29 Stockholm Sweden	
PROSVETNI	Prosvetni Servis	DRUSTVO
PROVIDENCE	Providence Music Press 251 Weybosset St. Providence, RI 02903	
PROVINCTWN	Provincetown Bookshop Editions 246 Commercial Street Provincetown, MA 02657	
PROWSE	Keith Prowse Music Publishing Co. 138-140 Charing Cross Road London, WC2H 0LD England	
PRUETT	Pruett Publishing Co. 2928 Pearl Boulder, CO 80301-9989	
PSALTERY	Psaltery Music Publications P.O. Box 11325 Dallas, TX 75223	KENDALE

Code	Publisher	U.S. Agent
PSI	PSI Press P.O. Box 2320 Boulder, CO 80306	
PURIFOY	Purifoy Publishing P.O. Box 30157 Knoxville, TN 37930	JENSON
PUSTET	Verlag Friedrich Pustet Gutenbergstraße 8 Postfach 339 D-8400 Regensburg 11 Germany	
PYRAMINX	Pyraminx Publications	ACCURA
QUIROGA	Ediciones Quiroga Alcalá, 70 Madrid 9 Spain	PRESSER
RAHTER	D. Rahter Werderstraße 44 D-2000 Hamburg 13 Germany	PRESSER LEONARD-US
RAMSEY	Basil Ramsey Publisher of Music	BRODT
RARITIES	Rarities For Strings Publications 11300 Juniper Drive University Circle Cleveland, OH 44106	
RECITAL	Recital Publications, Ltd. P.O. Box 1697 Huntsville, TX 77340	
	Regent, Arc & Goodman see GOODMAN	
REGENT	Regent Music Corp. 488 Madison Avenue 5th Floor New York, NY 10022	WARNER
REGINA	Regina Verlag Schumannstraße 35 Postfach 6148 D-6200 Wiesbaden 1 Germany	
REGUS	Regus Publisher 10 Birchwood Lane White Bear Lake, MN 55110	
REIMERS	Edition Reimers AB Box 15030 S-16115 Bromma Sweden	PRESSER
REINHARDT	Friedrich Reinhardt Verlag Missionsstraße 36 CH-4055 Basel Switzerland	
REN	Les Editions Renaissantes	EUR.AM.MUS.
RENK	Musikverlag Renk "Varia Edition" Herzog-Heinrich-Straße 21 D-8000 München 2 Germany	
RESEARCH	Research Publications, Inc. Lunar Drive Woodbridge, CT 06525	
REUTER	Reuter & Reuter Förlags AB Box 26072 S-100 41 Stockholm Sweden	
RHODES,R	Roger Rhodes Music, Ltd. P.O. Box 1550, Radio City Station New York, NY 10101	

Code	Publisher	U.S. Agent
RICHMOND	Richmond Music Press, Inc. P.O. Box 465 P. P. Station Richmond, IN 47374	
RICHMOND ORG.	The Richmond Organization 10 Columbus Circle New York, NY 10019 see also TRO	PLYMOUTH
RICORDI-ARG	Ricordi Americana S.A. Cangallo, 1558 1037 Buenos Aires Argentina	LEONARD-US BOOSEY (rental)
RICORDI-BR	Ricordi Brasileira S.A. R. Conselheiro Nebias 773 1 S-10-12 Sao Paolo Brazil	LEONARD-US BOOSEY (rental)
RICORDI-CAN	G. Ricordi & Co. Toronto Canada	LEONARD-US BOOSEY (rental)
RICORDI-ENG	G. Ricordi & Co., Ltd. The Bury, Church Street Chesham, Bucks HP5 1JG England	LEONARD-US BOOSEY (rental)
RICORDI-FR	Société Anonyme des Éditions Ricordi 12, rue Rougemont F-75009 Paris France	LEONARD-US BOOSEY (rental)
RICORDI-GER	G. Ricordi & Co. Gewürzmühlstraße 5 D-8000 München 22 Germany	LEONARD-US BOOSEY (rental)
RICORDI-IT	G. Ricordi & Co. Via Salomone 77 I-20138 Milano Italy	LEONARD-US BOOSEY (rental)
RIDEAU	Les Éditions Rideau Rouge 24, rue de Longchamp F-75116 Paris France	ELKAN-V
RIES	Ries & Erler Charlottenbrunner Straße 42 D-1000 Berlin 33 (Grunewald) Germany	
RILEY	Dr. Maurice W. Riley Eastern Michigan University 512 Roosevelt Boulevard Ypsilanti, MI 48197	
ROBBINS	Robbins Music Corp.	COLUMBIA PIC.
ROBERTON	Roberton Publications The Windmill, Wendover Aylesbury, Bucks, HP22 6JJ England	PRESSER
ROBERTS,L	Lee Roberts Music Publications, Inc. P.O. Box 225 Katonah, NY 10536	
ROBITSCHEK	Adolf Robitschek Musikverlag Graben 14 (Bräunerstraße 2) Postfach 42 A-1011 Wien Austria	
ROCHESTER	Rochester Music Publishers, Inc. 358 Aldrich Road Fairport, NY 14450	ACCURA
RODEHEAVER	Rodeheaver Publications	WORD
ROLLAND	Rolland String Research Associates 404 E. Oregon Urbana, IL 61801	BOOSEY

Code	Publisher	U.S. Agent
RONCORP	Roncorp, Inc. P.O. Box 724 Cherry Hill, NJ 08003	
RONGWEN	Rongwen Music, Inc.	BROUDE BR.
ROSSUM	Wed. J.R. van Rossum	ZENGERINK
ROUART	Rouart-Lerolle & Cie	SCHIRM.G
ROW	R.D. Row Music Co.	FISCHER,C
ROYAL	Royal School of Church Music Addington Palace Croydon, Surrey CR9 5AD England Royal School of Church Music in America Mr. Robert Kennedy Box 369 Litchfield, CT 06759 Associated Board of the Royal Schools of Music see ABRSM	HINSHAW (partial)
ROYAL TAP.	Royal Tapestry 50 Music Square West Suite 500A Nashville, TN 37203	ALEX. HSE.
ROZSAVO.	Rozsavölgi & Co.	BUDAPEST
RUBANK	Rubank, Inc. 16215 N.W. 15th Avenue Miami, FL 33169	LEONARD-US
RUBATO	Rubato Musikverlag Hollandstraße 18 A-1020 Wien Austria	DONEMUS
RUH,E	Emil Ruh Musikverlag Zürichstraße 33 CH-8134 Adliswil - Zürich Switzerland	
RUMAN.COMP.	Uniunea Compozitorilor din R.S. România (Union of Rumanian Composers) Str. C. Escarcu No. 2 Bucureşti, Sector 1 Rumania	BAREN.
RUTGERS	Rutgers University Editions	BROUDE,A
RYDET	Rydet Music Publishers P.O. Box 477 Purchase, NY 10577	
SAC.MUS.PR.	Sacred Music Press of Hebrew Union College One West Fourth Street New York, NY 10012	TRANSCON.
SACRED	Sacred Music Press	LORENZ
SACRED SNGS	Sacred Songs, Inc.	WORD
SALABERT	Francis Salabert Éditions 22 rue Chauchat F-75009 Paris France	LEONARD-US SCHIRM.G (rental)
SAMFUNDET	Samfundet til udgivelse af Dansk Musik Valkendorfsgade 3 DK-1151 Kobenhavn Denmark	PETERS
SAN ANDREAS	San Andreas Press 3732 Laguna Avenue Palo Alto, CA 94306	
SANJO	Sanjo Music Co. P.O. Box 7000-104 Palos Verdes Peninsula, CA 90274	

Code	Publisher	U.S. Agent
SAUL AVE	Saul Avenue Publishing Co. 4172 Fox Hollow Drive Cincinnati, OH 45241-2939	
SAVGOS	Savgos Music Inc. P.O. Box 279 Elizabeth, NJ 07207	
SCARECROW	The Scarecrow Press, Inc. 52 Liberty Street P.O. Box 656 Metuchen, NJ 08840	
SCHAUM	Schaum Publications, Inc. 2018 East North Avenue Milwaukee, WI 53202	
SCHAUR	Richard Schauer, Music Publishers 67 Belsize Lane, Hampstead London NW3 5AX England	PRESSER
SCHEIDT	Altonaer Scheidt-Ausgabe	HANSS
SCHERZANDO	Muziekuitgeverij Scherzando Lovelingstraat 20-22 B-2000 Antwerpen Belgium	ELKAN,H
SCHIRM.EC	E.C. Schirmer Music Co. 138 Ipswich Street Boston, MA 02215-3534	
SCHIRM.G	G. Schirmer Rental Performance Dept. 5 Bellvale Road Chester, NY 10918	
	G. Schirmer, Inc. (Executive Offices) 24 E. 22nd St. New York, NY 10010	LEONARD-US (sales)
SCHMIDT,H	Musikverlag Hermann Schmidt Berliner Straße 26 D-6000 Frankfurt-am-Main 1 Germany	
SCHMITT	Schmitt Music Editions	COLUMBIA PIC.
SCHNEIDER,H	Musikverlag Hans Schneider Mozartstraße 6 D-8132 Tutzing Germany	
SCHOLA	Editions Musicales de la Schola Cantorum Rue du Sapin 2A CH-2114 Fleurier Switzerland	PRESSER
SCHOTT	Schott & Co. Ltd. Brunswick Road Ashford, Kent TN23 1DX England	EUR.AM.MUS.
SCHOTT-FRER	Schott Frères 30 rue Saint-Jean B-1000 Bruxelles Belgium	EUR.AM.MUS.
SCHOTT,J	Schott & Co. #301, 3-4-3 Iidabashi, Chiyoda-ku Tokyo 102 Japan	EUR.AM.MUS.
SCHOTTS	B. Schotts Söhne Weihergarten 5 Postfach 3640 D-6500 Mainz Germany	EUR.AM.MUS.
SCHUBERTH	Edward Schuberth & Co., Inc.	CENTURY
SCHUBERTH,J	J. Schuberth & Co. Rothenbaumchaussee 1 D-2000 Hamburg 13 Germany	
SCHUL	Carl L. Schultheiß Denzenbergstraße 35 D-7400 Tübingen Germany	

Code	Publisher	U.S. Agent
SCHULZ,FR	Blasmusikverlag Fritz Schulz Am Märzengraben 6 D-7800 Freiburg-Tiengen Germany	
SCHWANN	Musikverlag Schwann	PETERS
SCHWEIZER.	Schweizerischer Kirchengesangbund Markusstrasse 6 CH-2544 Bettlach Switzerland	FOSTER
SCOTT	G. Scott Music Publishing Co.	WESTERN
SCOTT MUSIC	Scott Music Publications	ALFRED
SCOTUS	Scotus Music Publications, Ltd. 28 Dalrymple Crescent Edinburgh, EH9 2NX Scotland	
SCREEN	Screen Gems Columbia Pictures	COLUMBIA PIC.
SEESAW	Seesaw Music Corp. 2067 Broadway New York, NY 10023	
SELMER	Selmer Éditions 18, rue de la Fontaine-au-Roi F-75011 Paris France	
SEMI	Société d'Editions Musicales Internationales	PRESSER
SENART	Ed. Maurice Senart 22 rue Chauchat F-75009 Paris France	SCHIRM.G
SERENUS	Serenus Corp. 145 Palisade Street Dobbs Ferry, NY 10522	
SERVANT	Servant Publications P.O. Box 8617 840 Airport Boulevard Ann Arbor, MI 48107	
SESAC	Sesac, Inc. 10 Columbus Circle New York, NY 10019	
SHALL-U-MO	Shall-U-Mo Publications P.O. Box 2824 Rochester, NY 14626	
SHAPIRO	Shapiro, Bernstein & Co., Inc. 10 East 53 Street New York, NY 10022	PLYMOUTH
SHATTINGER	Shattinger Music Co. 1810 S. Broadway St. Louis, MO 63104	
SHAWNEE	Shawnee Press, Inc. 1 Waring Drive Delaware Water Gap, PA 18327	
SHEPPARD	John Sheppard Music Press	EUR.AM.MUS.
	Antigua Casa Sherry-Brener, Ltd. see ACSB	
SIDEMTON	Sidemton Verlag	BREITKOPF-W
SIFLER	Paul J. Sifler 3947 Fredonia Drive Hollywood, CA 90068	
SIGHT & SOUND	Sight & Sound International 3200 South 166th Street Box 27 New Berlin, WI 53151	

Code	Publisher	U.S. Agent
SIJN	D. van Sijn & Zonen Banorstraat 1 Rotterdam Netherlands	
SIKORSKI	Hans Sikorski Verlag Johnsallee 23 Postfach 132001 D-2000 Hamburg 13 Germany	LEONARD-US SCHIRM.G (rental)
SIMROCK	Nicholas Simrock Lyra House 37 Belsize Lane London NW3 England	PRESSER
SINGSPIR	Singspiration Music The Zondervan Corp. 1415 Lake Drive S.E. Grand Rapids, MI 49506	
SIRIUS	Sirius-Verlag	PETERS
SKAND.	Skandinavisk Musikforlag Gothersgade 9-11 DK-1123 København K. Denmark	MMB
SLATKINE	Slatkine Reprints 5 rue des Chaudronniers Case 765 CH-1211 Genève 3 Switzerland	
SLOV.AKA.	Slovenska Akademija Znanosti in Umetnosti Trg Francoske Revolucije 6 Ljubljana Yugoslavia	DRUSTVO
SLOV.HUD. FOND.	Slovenský Hudobný Fond Fucikova 29 CS-801 00 Bratislava Czechoslovakia	BOOSEY (rental)
SLOV.MAT.	Slovenska Matica	DRUSTVO
SMITH PUB	Smith Publications-Sonic Art Editions 2617 Gwynndale Avenue Baltimore, MD 21207	
SMPF	SMPF, Inc. 16 E. 34th St., 7th Floor New York, NY 10016	
SOC.FR.MUS.	Société Française de Music	TRANSAT.
SOC.PUB.AM.	Society for the Publication of American Music	PRESSER
	Société d'Éditions Musicales Internationales see SEMI	
	Society of Finnish Composers see SUOMEN	
SOLAR	The Solar Studio 178 Cowles Road Woodbury, CT 06798	
SOLID	Solid Foundation Music	SON-KEY
SOMERSET	Somerset Press	HOPE
SON-KEY	Son-Key, Inc. P.O. Box 31757 Aurora, CO 80041	
SONANTE	Sonante Publications P.O. Box 74, Station F Toronto, Ontario M4Y 2L4 Canada	

Code	Publisher	U.S. Agent
SONOS	Sonos Music Resources, Inc. P.O. Box 1510 Orem, UT 84057	
SONSHINE	Sonshine Productions	LORENZ
SONZOGNO	Casa Musicale Sonzogno Via Bigli 11 I-20121 Milano Italy	PRESSER (rental)
SOUTHERN	Southern Music Co. 1100 Broadway P.O. Box 329 San Antonio, TX 78292	
SOUTHRN PUB	Southern Music Publishing Co., Inc.	PRESSER
SOUTHWEST	Southwest Music Publications Box 4552 Santa Fe, NM 87501	
SPAN.MUS.CTR.	Spanish Music Center, Inc. 9302 95th Avenue New York, NY 11416-1511	
SPIRE	Spire Editions	FISCHER,C WORLD
SPRATT	Spratt Music Publishers 17 West 60th Street, 8th Fl. New York, NY 10023	PLYMOUTH
ST.GREG.	St. Gregory Publishing Co. 64 Pineheath Road High Kelling, Holt Norfolk, NR25 6RH England	ROYAL
ST. MARTIN	St. Martin Music Co., Inc.	ROYAL
STAFF	Staff Music Publishing Co., Inc. 170 N.E. 33rd St. Ft. Lauderdale, FL 33334	PLYMOUTH
STAINER	Stainer & Bell Ltd. 82 High Road East Finchley London N2 9PW England	GALAXY
STAMON	Nick Stamon Press 4280 Middlesex Drive San Diego, CA 92116	
STAMPS	Stamps-Baxter Music Publications Box 4007 Dallas, TX 75208	SINGSPIR
STANDARD	Standard Music Publishing, Inc.	
STANGLAND	Thomas C. Stangland Co. P.O. Box 19263 Portland, OR 97219	
STEIN	Edition Steingräber Auf der Reiswiese 9 D-6050 Offenbach/M. Germany	
STIM	STIMs Informationcentral för Svensk Musik Sandhamnsgatan 79 Box 27327 S-102 54 Stockholm Sweden	
STOCKHAUS	Stockhausen-Verlag Kettenberg 15 D-5067 Kürten Germany	
	Stockhausen-Verlag, U.S. 2832 Maple Lane Fairfax, VA 22030	

Code	Publisher	U.S. Agent
STOCKTON	Fred Stockton P.O. Box 814 Grass Valley, CA 95945	
STUD	Studio 224	STUDIO
STUDIO	Studio P/R, Inc.	COLUMBIA PIC.
STYRIA	Verlag Styria Schönaugasse 64 Postfach 435 A-8011 Graz Austria	
SUECIA	Edition Suecia	STIM
SUISEISHA	Suiseisha Editions	ONGAKU
SUMMIT	Summit Music Ltd. 38 North Row London W1 R 1DH England	
SUMMY	Summy-Birchard Co. P.O. Box 2072 Princeton, NJ 08540	
SUOMEN	Suomen Säveltäjät ry (Society of Finnish Composers) Runeberginkatu 15 A SF-00100 Helsinki 10 Finland	
SUPPORT	Support Services 79 South Street P.O. Box 478 Natick, MA 01760	
SUPRAPHON	Supraphon Pulackeho 1 CS-112 99 Praha Czechoslovakia	FOR.MUS.DIST.
	Svenska Utbildningsförlaget Liber AB see LIBER	
SWAN	Swan & Co. P.O. Box 1 Rickmansworth, Herts WD3 3AZ England	ARCADIA
SWAND	Swand Publications 120 North Longcross Road Linthicum Heights, MD 21090	
	Swedish Music Information Center see STIM	
SYMPHON	Symphonia Verlag	BELWIN
TAUNUS	Taunus	HOFMEIS-TER-W
TECLA	Tecla Editions Preacher's Court, Charterhouse London EC1M 6AS England	
TEESELING	Muziekuitgeverij van Teeseling Buurmansweg 29B NL-6525 RV Nijmegen Netherlands	
TEMPLETN	Templeton Publishing Co., Inc.	SHAWNEE
TEMPO	Tempo Music Publications 2712 W. 104th Terrace Leawood, KS 66206	ALEX. HSE.
TEN TIMES	Ten Times A Day P.O. Box 230 Deer Park, L.I., NY 11729	

Code	Publisher	U.S. Agent
TENUTO	Tenuto Publications see also TRI-TEN	PRESSER
TETRA	Tetra Music Corp.	PLYMOUTH WESL (rental)
TFS	Things For Strings Publishing Co. P.O. Box 9263 Alexandria, VA 22304	
THOMAS	Thomas House Publications P.O. Box 1423 San Carlos, CA 94070	ANTARA
THOMI	E. Thomi-Berg Musikverlag Bahnhofstraße 94A D-8032 Gräfelfing Germany	
THOMP.	Thompson Music House P.O. Box 12463 Nashville, TN 37212	
THOMP.G	Gordon V. Thompson, Ltd. 29 Birch Avenue Toronto, Ontario M4V 1E2 Canada	WALTON (choral)
TIEROLFF	Tierolff Muziek Centrale Markt 90-92 NL-4700 AA Roosendaal Netherlands	ELKAN,H
TISCHER	Tischer und Jagenberg Musikverlag Nibelungenstraße 48 D-8000 München 19 Germany	
TOA	Toa Editions	ONGAKU
TONGER	P.J. Tonger, Musikverlag Auf dem Brand 3 Postfach 501865 D-5000 Köln-Rodenkirchen 50 Germany	
TONOS	Editions Tonos Ahastraße 7 D-6100 Darmstadt Germany	SEESAW
TOORTS	Muziekuitgeverij De Toorts Nijverheidsweg 1 Postbus 576 NL-2003 RN Haarlem Netherlands	
TRANSAT.	Éditions Musicales Transatlantiques 50, rue Joseph-de-Maistre F-75018 Paris France	PRESSER
TRANSCON.	Transcontinental Music Publications 838 Fifth Avenue New York, NY 10021	
TREKEL	Joachim-Trekel-Verlag Postfach 620428 D-2000 Hamburg 62 Germany	
TRI-TEN	Tritone Press and Tenuto Publications P.O. Box 5081, Southern Station Hattiesburg, MS 39401	PRESSER
TRIGON	Trigon Music Inc.	LORENZ
TRINITY	Trinity House Publishing	CRESPUB
TRIUNE	Triune Music, Inc. Box 23088 Nashville, TN 37202	LORENZ

Code	Publisher	U.S. Agent
TRN	TRN Music Publishers 111 Torreon Loop P.O. Box 1076 Ruidoso, NM 88345	
TRO	Tro Songways Service, Inc. 10 Columbus Circle New York, NY 10019 see also RICHMOND ORG.	PLYMOUTH
TROY	Troy State University Library Troy, AL 36081	
TUSKEGEE	Tuskegee Institute Music Press	KJOS
U.S.CATH	United States Catholic Conference Publications Office 1312 Massachusetts Avenue N.W. Washington, D.C. 20005	
UBER,D	David Uber Music Department Trenton State College Trenton, NJ 08625	
UFATON	Ufaton-Verlag	ORLANDO
UNICORN	Unicorn Music Company, Inc. 9 Airport Drive Hopedale, MA 01747	BOSTON
UNION ESP.	Union Musical Española Carrera de San Jeronimo 26 Madrid Spain	LEONARD-US SCHIRM.G (rental)
UNISONG	Unisong Publishers	PRESSER
UNITED ART	United Artists Group	COLUMBIA PIC. PRESSER (rental)
UNITED MUS.	United Music Publishers Ltd. 42 Rivington Street London EC2A 3BN England	ELKAN-V
UNIV. ALA	University of Alabama Press Drawer 2877 University, AL 35486	
UNIV.CAL	University of California Press 2120 Berkeley Way Berkeley, CA 94720	
UNIV.CH	University of Chicago Press 5801 South Ellis Avenue Chicago, IL 60637	
UNIV.CR.	University College - Cardiff Press P.O. Box 78 Cardiff CF1 1XL, Wales United Kingdom	
UNIV.EVAN	University of Evansville Press P.O. Box 329 Evansville, IN 47702	
UNIV.IOWA	University of Iowa Press Iowa City, IA 52242	
UNIV.MIAMI	University of Miami Music Publications P.O. Box 8163 Coral Gables, FL 33124	PLYMOUTH
UNIV.MICRO	University Microfilms 300 North Zeeb Road Ann Arbor, MI 48106	
UNIV.MINN	University of Minnesota Press 2037 University Avenue S.E. Minneapolis, MN 55455	

Code	Publisher	U.S. Agent
UNIV.MUS.ED.	University Music Editions P.O. Box 192-Ft. George Station New York, NY 10040	
UNIV.NC	University of North Carolina Press P.O. Box 2288 Chapel Hill, NC 27514	
UNIV.OTAGO	University of Otago Press P.O. Box 56 Dunedin New Zealand	
UNIV.TEXAS	University of Texas Press P.O. Box 7819 Austin TX 78712	
UNIV.UTAH	University of Utah Press Salt Lake City, UT 84112	
UNIV.WASH	University of Washington Press Seattle, WA 98105	
UNIVER.	Universal Edition Bösendorfer Straße 12 Postfach 130 A-1015 Wien Austria	EUR.AM.MUS.
	Universal Edition (London) Ltd. 2/3 Fareham Street, Dean Street London W1V 4DU England	EUR.AM.MUS.
UNIVERSE	Universe Publishers 733 East 840 North Circle Orem, UT 84057	PRESSER
UP WITH	Up With People 3103 North Campbell Avenue Tucson, AZ 85719	LORENZ
VALANDO	Valando Music, Inc.	PLYMOUTH
VAMO	Musikverlag Vamö Leebgasse 52-25 Wien 10 Austria	
VAN NESS	Van Ness Press, Inc.	BROADMAN
VANDEN-RUP	Vandenhoeck & Ruprecht Theaterstrasse 13 Postfach 3753 D-3400 Göttingen Germany	
VANDERSALL	Vandersall Editions	EUR.AM.MUS.
VANGUARD	Vanguard Music Corp. 1595 Broadway, Room 313 New York, NY 10019	PLYMOUTH
VER.HUIS.	Vereniging voor Huismuziek Utrechtsestraat 77 Postbus 350 NL-3041 CT IJsselstein Netherlands	
VER.NED.MUS.	Vereniging voor Nederlandse Muziek- geschiedenis Drift 21 NL-3512 BR Utrecht Netherlands	
VEST-NORSK	Vest-Norsk Musikkforslag Nye Sandviksvei 7 N-5000 Bergen Norway	
VIERT	Viertmann Verlag Lübecker Straße 2 D-5000 Köln 1 Germany	

Code	Publisher	U.S. Agent
VIEWEG	Chr. Friedrich Vieweg, Musikverlag Nibelungenstraße 48 D-8000 München 19 Germany	AMP
VIKING	Viking Press, Inc. 625 Madison Avenue New York, NY 10022	
VIOLA	Viola World Publications 14 Fenwood Road Huntington Station, NY 11746	
VOGGEN	Voggenreiter Verlag Viktoriastraße 25 D-5300 Bonn Germany	
VOGT	Musikverlag Vogt & Fritz Friedrich-Stein-Straße 10 D-8720 Schweinfurt Germany	
VOLK	Arno Volk Verlag	BREITKOPF-W
VOLKWEIN	Volkwein Brothers, Inc.	COLUMBIA PIC.
WADSWORTH	Wadsworth Publishing Co. 10 Davis Street Belmont, CA 94002	
WAGENAAR	J.A.H. Wagenaar Oude Gracht 109 NL-3511 AG Utrecht Netherlands	ELKAN,H
WAI-TE-ATA	Wai-te-ata Press Dept. of Music Victoria Univ. of Wellington Wellington, New Zealand	CAN.MUS. CENT.
WALKER	Walker Publications P.O. Box 61 Arnold, MD 21012	
WALTON	Walton Music Corp. c/o Ashare 3 Cris Court East Brunswick, NJ 08816	HINSHAW
WARNER	Warner Brothers Publications, Inc. 265 Secaucus Road Secaucus, NJ 07094	JENSON (choral & orchestral)
WATERLOO	Waterloo Music Co. Ltd. 3 Regina Street North Waterloo, Ontario N2J 4A5 Canada	
WEHMAN BR.	Wehman Brothers, Inc. Ridgedale Avenue Morris County Mall Cedar Knolls, NJ 07927	
WEINBERGER	Josef Weinberger Ltd. 12-14 Mortimer Street London W1 N 7RD England Josef Weinberger Neulerchenfelderstraße 3-7 A-1010 Wien Austria	BOOSEY MARKS NORTHRIDGE (partial)
WEINTRAUB	Weintraub Music Co.	MUSIC
WELT	Welt Musik Josef Hochmuth Verlage Hegergasse 21 A-1030 Wien Austria	
WESL	Wesleyan Music Press P.O. Box 1072 Fort George Station New York, NY 10040	

Code	Publisher	U.S. Agent
WESSMAN	Wessmans Musikforlag S-620 30 Slite Sweden	STIM
WESTEND	Westend	PETERS
WESTERN	Western International Music, Inc. 3707 65th Avenue Greeley, CO 80634	
WESTMINSTER	The Westminster Press 925 Chestnut Street Philadelphia, PA 19107	
WESTWOOD	Westwood Press, Inc. 3759 Willow Road Schiller Park, IL 60176	WORLD
WHITE HARV.	White Harvest Music Publications P.O. Box 1144 Independence, MO 64051	
WIDE WORLD	Wide World Music, Inc. Box B Delaware Water Gap, PA 18327	
WIEN BOH.	Wiener Boheme Verlag GmbH Sonnenstraße 19 D-8000 München 2 Germany	
WIENER	Wiener Urtext Edition	EUR.AM.MUS.
WILDER	Wilder	MARGUN
WILHELM.	Wilhelmiana Musikverlag Edition Wilhelm Hansen, Frankfurt Eschersheimer Landstraße 12 D-6000 Frankfurt-am-Main Germany	MMB
	Williams School of Church Music see WSCM	
WILLIAMSN	Williamson Music, Inc.	LEONARD-US
WILLIS	Willis Music Co. 7380 Industrial Highway Florence, KY 41042	BOSTON
WILLSHIRE	Willshire Press Music Foundation, Inc.	WESTERN
WILSHORN	Wilshorn	HOPE
WILSON	Wilson Editions 13 Bank Square Wilmslow SK9 1AN England	
WIMBLEDN	Wimbledon Music Inc. 1888 Century Park East Suite 10 Century City, CA 90067	
WIND MUS	Wind Music, Inc. 153 Highland Parkway Rochester, NY 14620	KALMUS,A
WINGERT	Wingert-Jones Music, Inc. 2026 Broadway P.O. Box 1878 Kansas City, MO 64141	
WOITSCHACH	Paul Woitschach Radio-Musikverlag Grosse Friedberger Strasse 23-27 D-6000 Frankfurt Germany	
WOLF	Wolf-Mills Music	WESTERN
WOLLENWEBER	Verlag Walter Wollenweber Schiffmannstrasse 4 Postfach 1165 D-8032 Grafelfing vor München Germany	KUNZEL

Code	Publisher	U.S. Agent
WOODBURY	Woodbury Music Co. 33 Grassy Hill Road P.O. Box 447 Woodbury, CT 06798	
WOODWARD	Ralph Woodward, Jr. 1033 East 300 South Salt Lake City, UT 84102	
WOODWIND	Woodwind Editions P.O. Box 457, Station K Toronto, Ontario Canada M4P 2G9	
WORD	Word, Incorporated P.O. Box 1790 Waco, TX 76703	
WORD GOD	The Word of God Music	SERVANT
WORLD	World Library Publications, Inc. 3815 Willow Road P.O. Box 2701 Schiller Park, IL 60176	
WORLDWIDE	Worldwide Music Services P.O. Box 995, Ansonia Station New York, NY 10023	RICHMOND ORG.
WSCM	Williams School of Church Music The Bourne Harpenden England	
WYE	WYE Music Publications	EMERSON
WYNN	Wynn/Music Publications P.O. Box 739 Orinda, CA 94563	
XYZ	Muziekuitgeverij XYZ P.O. Box 338 NL-1400 AH Bussum Netherlands	
YAHRES	Yahres Publications 1315 Vance Avenue Coraopolis, PA 15108	
YBARRA	Ybarra Music P.O. Box 665 Lemon Grove, CA 92045	
YORKE	Yorke Editions 31 Thornhill Square London N1 1BR England	GALAXY

Code	Publisher	U.S. Agent
YOUNG WORLD	Young World Publications 10485 Glennon Drive Lakewood, CO 80226	
	Yugoslavian Music Information Center see MUSIC INFO	
ZALO	Zalo Publications & Services P.O. Box 913 Bloomington, IN 47402	FRANG
ZANIBON	G. Zanibon Edition Piazza dei Signori, 44 I-35100 Padova Italy	
ZEN-ON	Zen-On Music Co., Ltd. 3-14 Higashi Gokencho Shinjuku-ku Tokyo 162 Japan	EUR.AM.MUS MAGNA D
ZENEM.	Zenemukiado Vallalat	BOOSEY GENERAL
ZENGERINK	Herman Zengerink, Urlusstraat 24 NL-3533 SN Utrecht Netherlands	
ZERBONI	Edizioni Suvini Zerboni Via Quintiliano 40 I-20138 Milano Italy	
ZIMMER.	Wilhelm Zimmermann, Musikverlag Gaugrafenstraße 19-23 Postfach 940183 D-6000 Frankfurt-am-Main Germany	
ZIMMER.PUBS.	Oscar Zimmerman Publications 4671 State Park Highway Interlochen, MI 49643-9527	
	The Zondervan Corp. see SINGSPIR	
ZURFLUH	Éditions Zurfluh 73, Boulevard Raspail F-75006 Paris France	

Advertisements

Index to Advertisers

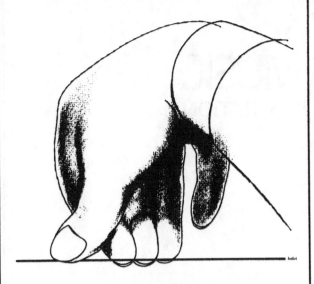

YOUR SINGLE SOURCE FOR THE PRINTED NOTE

SERVICE BY PROFESSIONALS FOR PROFESSIONALS

SERVING MUSICIANS WORLD-WIDE FOR OVER TEN YEARS

P.O. Box 5010 - HACKENSACK NEW JERSEY 07606   (201) 488-0550

WRITING ABOUT MUSIC

A Style Sheet from
the Editors of *19th-Century Music*
D. KERN HOLOMAN

How do you spell Rachmaninov? Where do you place the hyphen in Hofmannsthal if it breaks across two lines? Is it *premiere* or *première*? The answers and much more can be found in this new, essential resource for authors, students, editors, concert producers — anyone who deals with music in print. An expanded version of the style sheet for the well-known journal *19th-Century Music*, this small volume covers some of the thorniest issues of musical discourse: how to go about describing musical works and procedures in prose, the rules for citations in notes and bibliography, and proper preparation of such materials as musical examples, tables, and illustrations. One section discusses program notes, another explains the requirements of submitting manuscripts written on a word-processor. An appendix lists common problem words.

$7.50 per copy
University of California Press
2120 Berkeley Way
Berkeley, California 94720

For Visa or Mastercard charge orders,
use our Toll Free Number: 800-822-6657

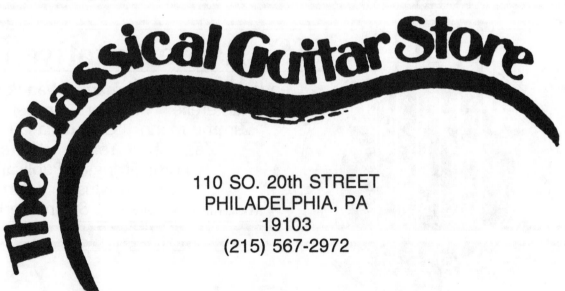

442

Revista de Música Latino Americana

Latin American Music Review

Editor: Gerard H. Béhague, University of Texas at Austin

LAMR is devoted exclusively to Latin America's diverse oral and written musical traditions. The journal features scholarly work from many countries and explores the music of many cultural groups including Puerto Ricans, Mexican Americans, Cubans and Portuguese in the United States. This journal enhances the understanding of the music-making process as one of our most highly structured expressive behaviors.

In addition to noteworthy articles, *LAMR* makes a significant contribution to the musicological community with its Book and Record Review section. Communications and Announcements informs readers of key performances and organizational activities.

Recent and Forthcoming Articles:

"Local" and "Foreign": The Popular Music Culture of Kingston, Jamaica, before Ska, Rock Steady, and Reggae by Robert Witmer.

Steelband Music in Trinidad and Tobago: The Creation of a People's Muisic by William R. Aho.

Leo Brouwer: A Portrait of the Artist in Socialist Cuba by Paul Century.

Sensemayá: A Chant for Killing a Snake by Charles K. Hoag.

Dislates en la obra, Teresa Carreño *de Marta Milinowski* by Mario Milanca Guzmán.

Rates (one year): Individual/$15; Institution/$25
Foreign add $2.50/subscription for postage
Individual single copy rate/$8
Inst. single copy rate/$13
Foreign add $1.50/copy for postage

University of Texas Press Journals, Box 7819, Austin, Texas 78713